Louisa Pansegrouw

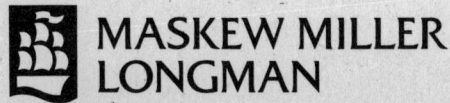

Maskew Miller Longman (Pty) Ltd
Howard Drive, Pinelands, Cape Town

Offices in Johannesburg, Durban, Port Elizabeth, Kimberley,
King William's Town, Pietersburg, Bloemfontein, Nelspruit and Mafikeng,
and representatives throughout southern Africa.

© Maskew Miller Longman (Pty) Ltd 1994

All rights reserved. No part of this publication may be reproduced,
stored in a retrieval system, or transmitted in any form or by any
means, electronic, mechanical, photocopying, recording, or
otherwise, without the prior written permission of the copyright holder.

First published 1994
Third impression 1997

ISBN 0 636 01957 8

Cover design by Chris Davis
Edited by Julie-Anne Justus
Set in 8/9 Helvetica-Narrow by Peter Newman
Printed by Creda Press, Eliot Avenue, Eppindust II, Cape Town
R6804

**Key to abbreviations**

| | | | | | |
|---|---|---|---|---|---|
| F | – | French | M | – | Maori |
| G | – | German | Sc | – | Scottish |
| I | – | Italian | Sp | – | Spanish |
| J | – | Japanese | Y | – | Yiddish |

# A

**a** una (I)
**aa** lava
**aal** al(e), currant, eel(worm), malt, mulberry, nematode, roundworm
**aardvark** ant-bear, ant-eater, edentate
**Aaron's brother** Moses
**Aaron's rod** mullein, plant
**Aaron's sister** Miriam
**ab** hati
**aba** abaya, dress, garb, garment, gown, habiliment, robe, vestment
**abac** nomogram, nomograph
**abaca** fibre, hemp, linaga, lupis, manila
**aback** backwards, behind, short
**abacus** apollon, calculator, counting-frame, cupboard, device, s(h)wanpan, soroban, suanpan
**Abadan's land** Iran
**abaft** aback, abaff, aft(er), astern, behind, rearward
**abaft the beam** large
**abalone** asseir, ear, haliotis, mollusc, mother-of-pearl, nacre, ormer, perlemoen, sea-ear, shell, u(h)llo
**abalone shell money** u(h)llo
**abandon** abdicate, abjure, cease, dash, desert, desolate, despair, discard, ditch, drop, evacuate, for(e)go, forsake, impetuosity, jettison, jilt, leave, maroon, quit, rashness, recklessness, relinquish, renege, renounce, resign, scrap, sink, surrender, unrestraint, vacate, waive, wantonness, wildness, withdraw, yield
**abandoned** adrift, corrupt, depraved, derelict, deserted, desolate, desperate, discarded, dissolute, flagrant, forlorn, forsaken, left, neglected, outcast, project, rejected, relinquished, shunned, solitary, uncontrolled, uninhibited, unoccupied, vacant, wanton, wicked, wild
**abandoned infant** castaway, foundling, outcast, pariah, waif
**abandoned property** derelict
**abandonee** underwriter
**abandon evil ways** amend, reform
**abandonment** abatement, apostasy, burial, dereliction, desertion, discontinuation, dropping, forsaking, jilting, leaving, neglect, relinquishment, renunciation, resignation, sacrifice, scrapping, surrender, waiver
**abandonment of restraint** let go, let up

**abandon on an island** maroon
**abase** asperse, belittle, debase, deflate, degrade, demean, demote, depress, devalue, discredit, disgrace, dishonour, disparage, humble, humiliate, lower, malign, mortify, reduce, sink, vitiate
**abasement** degeneration, degradation, depression, devaluation, disgrace, down(fall), humbleness, humility, ignominy, infamy, meanness, meekness, prostration, shame, vitiation
**abash** addle, affront, agitate, awe, bewilder, browbeat, chagrin, confound, confuse, cow, dampen, dash, demean, demoralise, disappoint, discomfit, disconcert, disturb, embarrass, fault, fluster, humble, humiliate, mortify, perplex, shame, upset
**abash by confident demeanour** outface
**abashed** addled, affronted, agitated, annoyed, ashamed, astounded, awed, bewildered, confounded, confused, crushed, daunted, deflated, dejected, demoralised, discomfited, discomposed, disheartened, dismayed, displeased, disturbed, embarrassed, flurried, flustered, humbled, mortified, nonplussed, perturbed, rattled, scared, shamed, shamefaced, troubled, upset, vexed, worried
**abashed by consciousness of guilt** ashamed, embarrassed, mortified
**abashment** awe, bewilderment, chagrin, compunction, confusion, discomfiture, disconcertment, humiliation, ignominy, mortification, self-consciousness, shame, shyness, vexation
**abate** allay, alleviate, allow, assuage, attenuate, bate, calm, cease, comfort, contract, cool, curtail, cut, dampen, decline, decrease, deduct, diminish, disburden, discount, drop, dwindle, ease, ebb, fade, lessen, lower, mitigate, moderate, pacify, quell, quiet, rebate, recede, reduce, relent, relieve, remit, retire, shrink, sink, slacken, slow, soothe, subside, subtract, wane, weaken
**abatement** allowance, attenuation, break, cessation, curtailment, decline, decrease, deduction, discount, easing, extenuation, gusset, interval, lessening, let-up, lull, mitigation, pause, prostration, rebate, recess, relieving, subtraction
**abatement of disease** lysis
**abating** allaying, assuaging, contracting, cooling, curtailing, dampening, declining, decreasing, diminishing, dropping, dwindling, easing, lessening, lowering, moderating, quietening, reducing, relating, shrinking, slackening, subsiding, tempering, waning
**abatis** abattis, barricade, fortification, obstacle
**abatjour (F)** sky-light
**abattoir** slaughterhouse
**abaxial** dorsal
**abb** wool, yarn
**abba** bishop, father
**abbacy** office, jurisdiction, tenure
**abbé** abbot, celibate, clergyman, cleric, curate, divine, ecclesiastic, friar, minister, monastic, monk, padre, parson, pastor, priest, prior
**abbess** amma, vicaress
**abbey** abadia, abbaye, cenoby, cloister, convent, friary, monastery, nunnery, priory, seminary
**abbey superior** abbé, abbot
**abbot** abbas, abbé, bishop, brother, canon, cleric, ecclesiarch, ecclesiastic, friar, general, head, officer, pope, prelate, priest, prior, superior
**abbotcy** abbotship
**abbot in France** abbé, monk
**abbot of misrule** bishop
**abbot's home** abbacy, abbey
**abbreviate** abridge, abstract, bobtail, clip, compress, condense, contract, curtail, cut, digest, elide, lessen, précis, prune, reduce, shorten, shrink, summarise, trim, truncate
**abbreviation** abridgment, abstract(ion), clipping, compendium, compression, condensation, contraction, curtailment, digest, epitome, précis, reduction, résumé, retrenchment, shortening, summary, synopsis
**ABC** alphabet, basics
**abderite** fool, scoffer, simpleton
**abdicate** abandon, cede, demit, disavow, disclaim, for(e)go, quit, relinquish, renounce, repudiate,

resign, retire, surrender, vacate, waive, yield
**abdication** abandonment, abnegation, disclamation, disowning, renunciation, repudiation, resignation, resigning, surrender
**abdomen** belly, boep, bowels, breadbasket, guts, insides, maw, midriff, paunch, potbelly, stomach, tummy, venter, waist, wame (Sc)
**abdomen segment in lepidopteran** (in)tegument
**abdominal** gastric, intestinal, splanchnic, stomachal, stomachic, ventral, ventricular, visceral
**abdominal dropsy** ascites
**abdominal infection** peritonitis
**abdominal organ maintaining condition of blood** spleen
**abduct** abduce, appropriate, arrogate, capture, commandeer, hijack, kidnap, lure, press, ravish, seduce, seize, shanghai, skyjack, snatch, steal, take, usurp
**abduct aircraft** hijack, skyjack
**abduct a person** kidnap
**abduction** apagoge, arrogation, capture, commandeering, expropriation, hijacking, kidnapping, rapture, robbery, seizure, theft
**abductor** crook, hijacker, kidnapper, rapist, robber, skyjacker, thief
**abductor of Helen** Paris
**abeam** abreast
**abecedarian** alphabetical, beginner, learner, novice, tyro
**abed** asleep, resting, retired, sick, sleeping
**'a' before a vowel sound** an
**abele** pine, poplar
**Abel's assassin** Cain
**Abel's brother** Cain, Seth
**aberrant** abnormal, anomalous, atypical, bizarre, capricious, changeable, chaotic, clammy, corrupt, debased, departing, depraved, desultory, deviant, deviate, different, digressing, divergent, erratic, erroneous, exceptional, fitful, fortuitous, freak, inconsistent, irregular, mistaken, odd, perverse, queer, roving, shifting, straying, twisted, unexpected, unforeseen, unnatural, unpredictable, unreliable, unstable, unusual, variable, vitiated, wandering, wayward, wild
**aberration** abnormality, anomaly, breach, craziness, defect, delusion, dementia, deviation, divergence, eccentricity, freak, hallucination, illusion, insanity, irregularity, lapse,

lunacy, madness, malformation, malfunction, malpractice, mania, monster, nonconformity, oddity, peculiarity, psychopathy, quirk, straying, unorthodoxy, wandering
**abet** advocate, aid, allow, assist, back, befriend, boost, comfort, connive, countenance, egg (on), encourage, espouse, favour, foment, goad, help, incite, instigate, promote, prompt, provoke, sanction, second, spur, succour, support, sustain, uphold, urge
**abettor** accessory, accomplish, aide, ally, arouser, assistant, associate, attendant, auxiliary, colleague, comrade, confederate, demagogue, disciple, encourager, exciter, helper, inciter, inspirer, participant, partner, patron, promoter, provoker, spurrier, supporter, sustainer, underwriter, urger
**abeyance** break, cease, deferment, delay, disuse, dormancy, inaction, intermission, interruption, latency, lull, pause, quiescence, recess, reserve, suspense, suspension
**abhor** abominate, condemn, despise, detest, disapprove, disdain, dislike, execrate, hate, irk, loathe, resent, scorn, shun, spurn
**abhorrence** abominating, abomination, animosity, antipathy, aversion, contempt, detestation, disdain, disgust, dislike, distaste, enmity, execration, hate, hatred, horror, loathing, odium, repugnance, revulsion, scorn
**abhorrent** abominable, atrocious, disgusting, displeasing, heinous, hideous, horrible, loathsome, noisome, offensive, repugnant, repulsive, revolting, sickening
**abide** accept, allow, attend, await, bear, brook, continue, dwell, endure, last, live, persevere, persist, remain, reside, second, sojourn, stand, stay, stomach, suffer, support, tarry, tolerate, wait
**abide by** acknowledge, adhere, discharge, fulfil, hold, obey, observe
**abiding effect of grief** scar
**abiding place** dwelling, seat
**abies** evergreens, firs
**ability** able, ableness, adeptness, aptitude, bent, bias, calibre, capability, capacity, cleverness, competence, competency, competent, deftness, dexterity, disposition, endowment, energy, expertise, facility, faculty, flair, force, forte, genius, gift, knack, know-how,

might, potency, potentiality, power, proficiency, qualification, skilfulness, skill, strength, talent, touch, turn, verve
**ability for particular activity** faculty, skill
**ability to affect someone's character** bias, influence, motivate, persuade, prompt, sway
**ability to bear hardship** endurance
**ability to do or act** potency, power
**ability to do things well** capability, competence, efficacy, efficiency
**ability to endure** tolerance
**ability to endure prolonged physical strain** endurance, resilience, stamina
**ability to enter** access
**ability to express oneself fluently in speech** eloquence, oracy, volubility
**ability to guide** leadership
**ability to last** durability, endurance
**ability to make money** Midas touch
**ability to read and write** literacy
**ability to recall past events** anamnesis, recollection
**ability to recuperate quickly** resilience
**ability to sail well** sea-legs
**ability to stretch** elasticity
**ability to sustain life** sustenance, vitality
**ability to throw** arm
**ability to walk on deck of rolling ship** sea-legs
**abject** base, contemptible, corrupt, debased, debasing, degenerate, degraded, degrading, deplorable, despicable, discreditable, disgraceful, disheartening, dishonourable, faithless, forlorn, grovelling, hopeless, humiliating, ignoble, inglorious, low, mean, miserable, outcast, pathetic, pitiable, servile, slavish, sordid, submissive, vile, worthless, wretched
**abject flatterer** crawler, sycophant, toady
**abjectly afraid** coward, craven
**abjectness** baseness, degradation, hopelessness, meanness, pitifulness, wretchedness
**abjure** abandon, abdicate, abnegate, cede, claim, deny, disavow, discard, disdain, disown, for(e)go, forsake, opinion, quit, recant, reject, relinquish, renege, renounce, repudiate, resign, revoke, surrender, swear, vacate, waive, withdraw, yield
**ablation** -ectomy, erosion
**ablaze** aglow, alight, angry, aroused, blazing, brilliant, burning, enthusiastic, excited, exhilarated,

fervent, fiery, flaming, flashing, frenzied, furious, glaring, gleaming, glowing, ignited, illuminated, impassioned, incensed, lighted, luminous, passionate, radiant, raging, sparkling, stimulated
**able** accomplished, adept, adequate, adroit, apt, brilliant, can, capable, clever, competent, deft, dext(e)rous, effective, efficient, experienced, expert, facile, finished, fit(ted), gifted, ingenious, intelligent, masterly, polished, power(ful), practised, proficient, qualified, revealing, skilful, skilled, strong, superior, talented
**able to absorb** absorbent
**able to be calmed down** pacifiable
**able to be comforted** pacifiable
**able to be corrected** amenable, corrigible, rectifiable
**able to be exchanged for money** commutable, exchangeable
**able to be explained** explicable
**able to be grasped by the mind** cogitable
**able to be heard** audible, loud
**able to be influenced** amenable
**able to be melted** fusible
**able to be obtained** accessible
**able to be read** legible
**able to be sold** marketable
**able to bounce back** resilient
**able to buy** affordable
**able to cause serious damage** dangerous, deadly, harmful
**able to co-exist** compatibility, compatible
**able to contain much** ample, capacious, voluminous
**able to discharge debts** liquid, solvent, sound
**able to discriminate** astute, selective
**able to endure hardship** hardy, tough
**able to express oneself clearly** articulate, eloquent
**able to fly** volant
**able to function** functional, operational
**able to laugh** risible
**able to learn** educable
**able to live both on land and in water** amphibious
**able to meet financial obligations** liquid, solvent, sound
**able to move quickly** agile, nimble
**able to pay** liquid, solvent, sound
**able to read and write** literate
**able to receive instructions** reachable
**able to resist** resistant, resistive, strong
**able to retain** retentive
**able to speak a language with ease** fluent
**able to speak two languages** bilingual
**able to stretch** tensile
**able to supply one's own needs** independent, self-sufficient, self-supporting, self-sustaining
**able to write** literate
**a blue stocking** bas bleu (F)
**a blunder** bêtise, faux pas
**ablution** baptise, bath, lotion, wash, wudu
**ably** capably, cleverly
**abnegate** abdicate, abjure, concede, decline, deny, disclaim, forbear, for(e)go, refuse, reject, relinquish, renounce, resign, sacrifice, submit, surrender, yield
**abnormal** aberrant, anomalous, curious, deviant, extraordinary, heretical, irregular, monstrous, odd, peculiar, queer, roving, strange, uncommon, unnatural, unusual, weird
**abnormal absence of menstruation** amenorrhoea
**abnormal anxiety about one's health** hypochondria, psychosomatic
**abnormal attraction to corpses** necrophilia
**abnormal change** lesion
**abnormal craving for alcoholic liquid** dipsomania
**abnormal desire** craving, fetish, mania, rapacity
**abnormal difficulty in reading and spelling** dyslexia
**abnormal enlargement of the liver** hepatomegaly
**abnormal fear** phobia
**abnormal fear of being in an enclosed space** claustrophobia
**abnormal growth** cancer, tumour
**abnormal growth of tissues** dysplasia
**abnormal hardening of body tissue** sclerosis
**abnormal hardness of the skin** callosity, call(o)us
**abnormality** aberration, anomaly, bizarreness, deformity, deviation, eccentricity, exception, flaw, freak, irregularity, monstrosity, oddity, peculiarity, singularity, strangeness, unnaturalness, unusualness, weirdness
**abnormal lack of energy** lethargy
**abnormal lack of saliva** xerostomia
**abnormal loss of strength** asthenia, debility
**abnormally active** hyperactive
**abnormally anxious** neurotic
**abnormally fast heartbeat** tachycardia
**abnormally fat** obese
**abnormally high blood pressure** hypertension
**abnormally high body temperature** fever
**abnormally large** colossal, gigantic, huge, immense, monstrous, titanic
**abnormally low acidity** hypoacidity
**abnormally low blood pressure** hypotension
**abnormally prolonged spell without rain** drought
**abnormally rapid** abrupt, prompt, sudden, swift
**abnormally rapid breathing** tachypnoea
**abnormally rapid heart action** tachycardia
**abnormally self-absorbed** autistic
**abnormally shaped red blood cell** poikilocyte
**abnormal mass of tissue** cancer, cyst, growth, sarcoma, tumour, wart
**abnormal prefix** dys-
**abnormal red colouration, as in hair** erythrism
**abnormal self-love** narcissism
**abnormal swelling** tumour
**abnormal thing** freak, monster
**abnormal urge to steal** kleptomania
**aboard** abreast, alongside, beside, in, inside, on, onto, within
**aboard ship** afloat, asea
**abode** cabin, castle, chalet, chateau, cottage, domicil(e), dwelling, habitat, habitation, haunt, hearth, home, house, mansion, palace, quarters, residence, residency, sojourn, villa
**abode for the elderly** rest-home
**abode of Adam and Eve** Eden, Paradise
**abode of ancient Irish harp** Tara
**abode of dead** aalu, aaru, Abaddon, amenti, aralu, cemetery, Hades, Heaven, hell, Orcus, shades, Sheol, xibalba
**abode of delight** Elysium
**abode of devils** Dys, Hades, hell
**abode of evil power** abyss
**abode of evil spirits** pandemonium
**abode of fauna** habitat
**abode of first parents** Eden, Paradise
**abode of free love** agapemone
**abode of giants** Utgard
**abode of God** heaven
**abode of gods** Asgard, Meru, Olympus
**abode of Norse gods** Asgard
**abode of souls** limbo
**abode of the blessed dead** Elysium
**abode of the blissful** Arcadia, Avalon, Dixie, Eden, heaven, paradise
**abode of the damned** Dys, Hades, hell, purgatory
**abode of the Grecian gods** Olympus

**abode of the spirits of the dead** Dys, Hades
**abolish** annihilate, annul, cancel, destroy, eliminate, eradicate, erase, extinguish, extirpate, invalidate, nullify, obliterate, rescind, suppress, suspend, void, withdraw
**abolition** abrogation, annihilation, annulment, cancellation, demolition, destruction, dissolvement, elimination, eradication, extirpation, nullification, obliteration, remission, repeal, suppression, termination, vitiation, withdrawal
**abolitionist** destroyer, garrison, revolutionist
**aboma** boa, bom, constrictor, serpent
**A-bomb target** Hiroshima, Nagasaki
**abominable** abhorrent, accursed, atrocious, base, contemptible, defective, deplorable, despicable, detestable, disgusting, execrable, faulty, foul, hateful, heinous, hideous, horrible, horrid, infamous, inferior, loathsome, obnoxious, obscene, odious, offensive, poor, repellent, repugnant, repulsive, revolting, sorry, terrible, vile
**abominable snowman** yeti
**aboriginal** autochthonal, autochthonous, domestic, earliest, elementary, endemic, first, indigenous, natal, native, original, primal, primary, primeval, primitive, pristine
**Aboriginal ceremonial gathering and dance festival** corroboree
**Aboriginal heavy wooden war club or throwing stick** waddy
**Aboriginal hooded stick for launching spears or darts** wo(o)mera
**Aboriginal hut** gunyah, mia-mia, wurley
**Aboriginal inhabitant of northern Japan** Ainu
**Aboriginal initiation ceremoy for boys** bora
**Aboriginal legendary monster haunting swamps and water holes** bunyip
**Aboriginal name for Ayers Rock** Uluru
**Aboriginal person** bama
**Aboriginal rite** bora
**Aboriginal sacred charm or amulet** bullroarer, churinga
**Aboriginal shelter or hut** gunyah, mia mia, wurley
**Aboriginal term for freshwater crayfish** yabbie
**Aboriginal throwing stick** wo(o)mera
**Aboriginal weapon** wo(o)mera
**Aboriginal witch doctor** boyla

**Aboriginal woman or wife** lubra
**aborigine of Sri Lanka** Vedda(h)
**abort** arrest, cease, check, end, fail, frustrate, halt, miscarry, nullify, obstruct, preclude, quell, stop, terminate, thwart
**abortion** aborticide, blemish, defeat, deformity, failure, feticide, frustration, misadventure, misbirth, miscarriage, misconception, monster, monstrosity, mutant, non-success, oddity, termination
**abortive** barren, empty, forlorn, fruitless, futile, hollow, impotent, ineffectual, nugatory, pointless, premature, profitless, rudimentary, sterile, unavailing, unproductive, unprofitable, unsuccessful, useless, vain, valueless, worthless
**abortive branch** thorn, twig
**abound** clutter, exuberate, flood, flourish, flow, increase, infest, jam, luxuriate, multiply, overflow, pack, plentiful, plentiful, pour, prevail, proliferate, rich, stream, swarm, swell, teem
**abounding in certain fuel** peaty
**abounding in flowers** flowery
**abounding in small stars** stellular
**abounding in thorns** thorny
**abounding with axioms** sententious
**abounding with frogs** froggy
**about** adjacent, almost, anent, approximately, around, beside, circa, close, concerning, de, near, nearby, nearly, of, on, over, present, re, regarding, respecting, round, surrounding, through, touching
**about as to dates** circa
**about law** forensic
**about or near that place** thereabout
**about that** concerning, regarding, thereof
**about that amount** thereby
**about this** concerning, hereof, regarding
**about to arrive** due
**about to come** forthcoming
**about to die** moribund
**about to happen** future, imminent
**about to occur** impend
**about town** local
**about-turn** volte-face
**above** aloft, atop, before, beyond, epi-, first, higher, on, over, overhead, said, sooner, superior, supra, sur-, surpassing, up, written
**above all** chiefly, especially, mainly, mostly, peculiarly, predominantly, primarily
**above and beyond** over
**above and in contact with** on, upon

**above and touching** on, onto, upon
**above a whisper** aloud
**above board** honest, reliable, trustworthy
**above foot** ankle
**above general level** apart
**above in rank** over, senior
**above line in fraction** numerator
**above oneself** presumptuous
**above one's head** abstruse, incomprehensible, obscure
**above par** choice, excellent, exceptional, first-rate, outstanding, perfect, prime, select, superior, superlative
**above reproach** faultless, flawless, immaculate, incorrupt
**above resentment** generous, magnanimous
**above suspicion** blameless, exact, faultless, honest, honourable, impeccable, incorruptible, just, pure, sinless, virtuous
**above the audible limit** supersonic
**above the axis** epaxial
**above the ear** epiotic
**above the equator** northern hemisphere
**above valuation** inestimable, invaluable
**above zero** plus
**abracadabra** gibberish, spell
**abrade** buff, chafe, corrode, erase, erode, excoriate, gnaw, grate, grind, pumice, rasp, rub, scour, scrape, smooth, wear
**abrading tool** file, grater, pumice, rasp, scourer
**Abraham's birthplace** Ur
**Abraham's nephew** Lot
**abrasion** corrosion, damage, depreciation, detrition, erosion, excoriation, fraying, fret(ting), friction, grating, grinding, irritation, resistance, rub(bing), scouring, scrape, scraping, shining, use, wear
**abrasive** biting, chafing, emery, grating, pumice, rough, sandpaper, scourer, scouring, scraping, sharp, unpleasant
**abrasive agent** emery
**abrasive material** bort, emery, pumice
**abrasive polisher** sandpaper
**abrasive stone** emery
**abreast of** alongside, au courant (F), au fait (F), beside, informed, knowledgeable, parallel, well-informed
**abret** bread, wafer
**abridge** abbreviate, abstract, brief, compress, concentrate, concise, condense, contract, curtail, cut,

decrease, deprive, digest, diminish, dispossess, elide, encapsulate, epitomise, lessen, précis, reduce, retrench, shorten, summarise, trim, truncate
**abridged and classified** digested
**abridgement** abbreviation, bind, brief, compendium, contracting, curtailment, decrease, digest, diminishment, epitome, loss, outline, précis, reducing, reduction, résumé, shortage, sketch, squeeze, survey, synopsis
**abroad** afar, broadly, continental, expansively, outside, overseas, prevalent, widely
**abrogate** annul, cancel, liberate, nullify, quash, repeal, rescind, revoke, suspend, void, withdraw
**abrupt** bluff, blunt, boorish, brief, brisk, broken, brusque, craggy, curt, direct, disconnected, discontinuous, gruff, hasty, hurried, impolite, irregular, jerky, precipitate, precipitous, quick, rapid, rough, rude, sharp, sheer, short, snappy, spasmodic, steep, sudden, surly, surprising, swift, terse, unceremonious, uncivil, uneven, unexpected, unforeseen, ungracious, vertical
**abrupt explosive sound** plop, bang
**abrupt heavy sound of impact** clonk, thud
**abrupt in manner** brusque, curt, gruff, impolite
**abruptly** bluntly, briskly, brusquely, curtly, directly, gruffly, impolitely, precipitously, roughly, rudely, sharply, sheerly, shortly, steeply, suddenly, tersely, uncivilly, ungraciously
**abrupt movement** start
**Absalom's adviser** A(c)hitophel
**Absalom's cousin** Amasa
**abscess** agnail, blister, boil, canker, carbuncle, cyst, fester, furuncle, gumboil, lesion, papula, papule, pimple, pock, pustule, sore, swelling, ulcer, ulceration, whitlow
**abscisic acid** dormin
**abscond** abandon, AWOL, bolt, decamp, desert, disappear, eloign, elope, elude, escape, flee, fly, levant, retreat, withdraw
**absconding to Gretna Green** eloping
**abscond with another** elope
**absence** defect, deficiency, lack, need, nonappearance, nonattendance, want
**absence from duty** liberty
**absence from one's country** exile

**absence of an organ** agenesia, agenesis
**absence of any sound** silence, soundlessness, stillness
**absence of appetite** anorexia, asitia
**absence of bias** detachment
**absence of blood poison** asepsis
**absence of ceremony** familiarity
**absence of complexity** simplicity
**absence of culture** barbarism
**absence of difficulty** ease, facility
**absence of disturbance** peace, quiet
**absence of familiarity** distance
**absence of feeling** apathy, coldness, indifference, insensate, numb, numbness, unconscious
**absence of fever** apyrexia, apyrexy
**absence of form** entropy
**absence of government** anarchy
**absence of government control** anarchy, lawlessness
**absence of inhibitions** animality
**absence of knowledge** ignorance, nescience
**absence of light** black, dark, darkness
**absence of marriage** agamy
**absence of menstruation** amenorrhoea
**absence of mind** abstraction
**absence of motion** inertia, rest, stationary
**absence of movement** firmness, immobility, inactivity, inertia, passivity, rest, stability, stasis, stationary
**absence of nails** anonychia
**absence of noise** silence
**absence of order** anarchy, ataxia, chaos, confusion, disarray, disorder, perplexity
**absence of pain** analgesia, anodynia
**absence of pigmentation** achrom(i)a
**absence of prejudice** disinterest, impartiality, tolerance, toleration
**absence of reserve** candour, extroverted, frankness, openness, spontaneity
**absence of restraint** freedom, liberty
**absence of secretion of milk** agalactia
**absence of sensation** anaesthesia
**absence of sepsis** asepsis
**absence of skin pigmentation** alphosis, albinism
**absence of skull** acrania
**absence of sweating** anhidrosis
**absence of tail** anury
**absence of taste** ageusia
**absence of the sense of smell** anosmia
**absence of truth** falsehood
**absence of war** peace

**absence without leave** abscond, AWOL, lam, truancy
**absent** absorbed, away, AWOL, deficient, desert, elsewhere, gone, lacking, lost, missing, musing, nonresident, off, out
**absentee** backslider, deserter, exile, fugitive, malingerer, quitter, renegade, runaway, skulker, slacker, truant
**absent in mind** abstract
**absently** absent-mindedly, abstractedly, distractedly, dreamily, heedlessly, inattentively, obliviously, unconsciously, unthinkingly, vaguely
**absent-minded** absorbed, abstracted, bemused, cogitative, distracted, distrait, dreaming, dreamy, faraway, forgetful, inadvertent, inattentive, mused, musing, preoccupied, rapt, unaware, unthinking, withdrawn
**absent oneself** abscond, depart, leave, retire
**absinth** absinthe, wormwood
**absolute** arbitrary, autocratic, categorical, certain, complete, decided, definite, despotic, dictatorial, downright, entire, exact, full, genuine, ideal, implicit, indubitable, out-and-out, outright, perfect, positive, precise, pure, sheer, sure, thorough, total, unadulterated, unconditional, unequivocal, unlimited, unmixed, unqualified, unquestionable, unrestricted, utter, whole
**absolute adjective** adnoun
**absolute blessedness** nirvana
**absolute government** autocracy
**absolute government by one person** autocracy, despotism, dictatorship, monarchy
**absolute likeness** identical
**absolutely** autocratically, categorically, certainly, clearly, completely, decidedly, decisively, definitely, entirely, exactly, fully, perfectly, positively, purely, sheerly, supremely, surely, thoroughly, totally, unconditionally, unreservedly, utterly, wholly
**absolutely clean** immaculate, impeccable, spotless, unsullied
**absolutely fascinating** enthralling, riveting
**absolutely necessary** essential, vital
**absolutely sure** cocksure, convinced, dead certain, positive
**absolutely true** correct
**absolute monarch** despot
**absolute nonsense** absurdity, drivel, tommy-rot, trash, tripe

**absolute property in land** allod, al(l)odium, freehold
**absolute rubbish** balderdash, dre(c)k, hogwash, trash
**absolute rule** autarchy
**absolute ruler** autocrat, despot, dictator, monarch, tyrant
**absolute sovereign** autocrat
**absolute sovereignty** autarchy, autocracy, autonomy
**absolute superlative** elative
**absolution** acquittal, amnesty, avenging, clearance, condonation, discharge, dismissing, disregarding, exculpating, excuse, exoneration, forgiveness, grace, ignoring, immunity, indemnity, liberation, liberty, pardon, pardoning, release, remission, reprieve, reprieving, respite, vindication
**absolve** acquit, assoil, clear, deliver, discharge, dispense, emancipate, exculpate, excuse, exempt, exonerate, forgive, free, justify, liberate, loose, pardon, ransom, redeem, release, remit, vindicate
**absolve in law** vested
**absolve sin** expiate, shrive
**absolvitor** acquittal
**absorb** amalgamate, appropriate, assimilate, consume, devour, digest, engorge, engross, engulf, enthrall, exhaust, fascinate, fathom, grasp, grip, hold, imbibe, immerse, interest, inundate, involve, monopolise, occupy, osmosis, overcome, preoccupy, receive, retain, sponge, submerge, swallow, swamp, understand
**absorb again** resorb
**absorbed** bemused, distracted, distrait, employed, engaged, engrossed, immersed, involved, meditating, oblivious, obsessed, pensive, rapt, reflective, thoughtful
**absorbed in thought** dreamy, musing
**absorbent article** blotter, sponge, swab
**absorbent material** blotter, mop, sand, sponge, swab
**absorbent pad** swab
**absorbent substance** blotter, sponge, towel
**absorb great amount of moisture** saturate
**absorbing** entrancing, fascinating, interesting
**absorb into something else** merge
**absorb into the system** assimilate
**absorb liquid colour** dye
**abstain** abnegate, avoid, cease, curb, curtail, decline, deny, desist, discontinue, eschew, fast, forbear, for(e)go, quit, refrain, refuse, reject, renounce, shun, spurn, stop, suppress, teetotal, withhold
**abstainer** ascetic, hydropot, nephalist, nondrinker, prohibitionist, puritan, teetotaller, waterdrinker
**abstain from** abandon, abjure, avoid, eschew, for(e)go, refrain, relinquish, resist, shun
**abstain from food** fast
**abstain from using** spare, save
**abstaining from alcoholic drink** teetotal
**abstemious** abstaining, abstinent, ascetic, austere, careful, chary, continent, economical, forbearing, frugal, habitually, meagre, moderate, provident, prudent, puritanical, puritanlike, saving, sober, solemn, sparing, temperate
**abstinence from alcoholic drink** teetotal, temperance
**abstinence from speech** silence, Trappism
**abstract** abbreviate, abridgement, abstruse, academic, apart, brief, compendium, complex, complicated, compression, conceptual, condensation, condense, deep, difficult, digest, dissociate, distill(ation), divert, epitome, epitomise, esoteric, essence, general, generalised, gist, hypothetical, impractical, indefinite, intellectual, isolate(d), nonrepresentational, notional, outline, philosophical, précis, profound, recapitulation, résumé, separate, special, substance, subtle, summary, synopsis, theoretical, unphotographic, unpractical, unrealistic, unrelated
**abstract being** ens, entia, entity, esse
**abstracted** absent, absent-minded, distrait, dreamy, faraway, inattentive, pensive, preoccupied, remote, withdrawn
**abstracted in mind** absent-minded
**abstract idea** concept
**abstract sculpture** stabile
**abstruse** abstract, acromatic, cabalistic, dark, deep, dim, enigmatic, esoteric, hidden, insolvable, mystic, mystical, nebulous, obscure, occult, profound, puzzling, recondite, supermundane, uncomprehensible, unknowable, vague
**abstruseness** abstractness, abstrusity, complexness, darkness, deepness, dimness, esotericism, inexplicability, inscrutability, mysteriousness, mysticity, obscureness, obscurity, occultness, profoundness, profundity, vagueness
**absurd** asinine, childish, comic, doubtful, extravagant, fantastic, fatuous, foolish, illogical, imaginary, inane, incongruous, inept, irrational, laughable, ludicrous, meaningless, nonsense, preposterous, questionable, ridiculous, senseless, silly, unbelievable, unreasonable, unthinkable
**absurd action** antic
**absurd behaviour** foolishness, silliness
**absurd failure** fiasco
**absurdity** amphigory, childishness, craziness, folly, foolishness, idiocy, illogic, incongruity, irrationality, joke, ludicrousness, meaninglessness, nonsense, ridiculousness, senselessness, silliness, stupidity
**absurdly futile proceedings** farce
**absurd posture** antic
**absurd pretence** charade
**absurd statement but may be true** paradox
**absurd story** canard, furphy
**abundance** affluence, ampleness, amplitude, bounty, copiousness, excess, fortune, heaps, lots, many, mass, much, plenitude, plenteousness, plenty, plethora, profusion, quantity, riches, richness, surplus, wealth
**abundant** abounding, ample, bountiful, copious, exuberant, filled, full, galore, generous, lavish, many, multiple, overflowing, plentiful, profuse, rank, rich, rife, several, teeming, well-supplied
**abundantly productive** prolific
**abundant means** riches
**abundant supply** affluence, granary, mine, plenty, stock, store
**abundant supply of money** affluence, wealth
**abuse** asperse, berate, betray, betrayal, blame, calumniation, condemnation, deceive, defamation, defame, denounce, denunciation, desecrate, desecration, disparage(ment), harm, hurt, ill-treat, ill-use, injure, invective, lampoon, malign, maltreat, misapply, misappropriate, misemploy, misemployment, mistreat, mistreatment, misuse, offence, offensive, profane, prostitute, reproach, revile, satirise, scold, scorn, seduction, slander, subversion, subvert, upbraid,

vilification, vilify, vituperate, vituperation
**abuse of authority** coup d'état
**abuse scornfully** insult
**abuse verbally** revile
**abusive** approbrious, brutal, censorious, cruel, defamatory, derogatory, destructive, disparaging, harmful, hurtful, injurious, insulting, libellous, maligning, offensive, reproachful, reviling, rough, rude, scathing, scolding, slanderous, traducing, upbraiding, vilifying, vituperative
**abusive allegation** mud, slur
**abusive oratory** invective
**abusive remarks** mud
**abusive speech** diatribe, tirade
**abut** adjoin, bear, bolster, border, connect, impinge, join, juxtapose, prop, reach, support, touch, upbear, uphold
**abutment of arch** alette
**abysmal** bottomless, dreadful, endless, extreme, immeasurable, unfathomable, vast
**abyss** abysm, bottomless, cab(b)alism, cavity, chasm, cleft, crevice, depth, gorge, hole, kab(b)alism, mysticity, pit, profoundness, ravine, shaft, void
**abyssal** abysmal, bottomless, plutonic
**abyss below** Hades, Tartarus
**acacia** mimosa, shrub, tree, wattle
**academic** campus, college, collegiate, impractical, literary, scholarly, scholastic, theoretical, unpractical
**academic attainment** degree
**academic cap** mortarboard
**academic conference** colloquium, seminar
**academic degree** doctorate
**academic garment** gown, toga
**academic gown** toga
**academic qualification** certificate, degree, matric
**academic rank** agrégé (F)
**academic senior** don
**academic's long leave** sabbatical
**academic term** semester
**academic theme** thesis
**academic year division** quarter, semester, term
**Academy Award** Oscar
**acaleph** jellyfish, medusa(n), medusoid, sea-nettle
**acarid** acarus, chigger, mite, tick
**acarus** acarid, chigger, insect, mite, tick
**acaudal** anourous, tailless
**accede** acknowledge, acquiesce, admit, agree, allow, approve, assent, comply, concede, consent, grant, let,
opinion, permit, proposal, request, yield
**accelerate** advance, antedate, augment, compact, compel, compress, concentrate, drive, expedite, facilitate, flourish, force, forward, grow, hasten, hurry, hurtle, hustle, impel, incite, promote, prosper, push, quicken, reduce, rush, skim, speed, spur, stimulate, succeed, thrive, urge, zoom
**acceleration racer** dragster
**accelerator** throttle
**accent** articulation, attack, brogue, burr, conspicuousness, diacritic, drawl, dwell, emphasis, emphasise, modulation, pitch, prominence, stress, tone, voice
**accented strongly** sforzando, sforzato
**accented syllable** arsis
**accent over vowel** breve, diacritic
**accent symbol** breve
**accentuate** accent, deepen, emphasise, feature, headline, highlight, intensify, present, promote, punctuate, repeat, spotlight, star, strengthen stress, underline, underscore
**accept** acknowledge, acquire, admit, adopt, assume, avow, believe, buy, concede, confirm, consent, gain, get, perceive, receive, recognise, secure, take, understand, value, yield
**acceptable** adequate, admissible, adoptable, agreeable, assumable, believable, fair, gratifying, moderate, obtainable, passable, pleasant, pleasing, receivable, recognisable, satisfactory, so-so, sufferable, tolerable, welcome
**acceptable person** persona grata (L)
**acceptance** accepting, acquisition, affirmation, approval, assent, credence, receipt, recipience, recognition, satisfaction
**acceptance of fate** equanimity
**acceptance of inheritance** cerniture
**acceptance of order** allotment
**acceptance of things as they are** realism
**accept as authoritative** receive, submit
**accept as likely** presume, suppose
**accept as one's own** adopt, nostrificate
**accept as true** accredit, admit, agree, believe, credit
**accept as truth** believe
**accept as valid** admit
**accept at random** draw
**accept bets** book
**accept delivery of** receive
**accept eagerly** leap
**accepted level** par
**accepted phrase** idiom
**accepted standard** norm
**accept formally** adopt
**accept inheritance** adiate
**acceptor** drawee
**accept readily** swallow
**accept tacitly** acquiesce
**accept the chance** gamble, risk, venture
**accept truth of statement** believe
**accept without question** abide
**access** accost, adit, admission, admittance, approach, attack, course, door, enter(ing), entrance, entrée, entry, gateway, key, onset, outburst, paroxysm, passage(way), path, portal, reception, road, spasm, use, way
**accessible** achievable, affable, approachable, attainable, available, conversable, cordial, exposed, friendly, handy, informal, liable, near(by), obtainable, open, possible, reachable, ready, subject, susceptible, vulnerable, wide-open
**accession** access, accretion, accord, acknowledg(e)ment, acquiescence, acquisition, addition, advance, advancement, agreement, approval, assent, assumption, attack, attainment, augmentation, consent, distention, elevation, enlargement, enter, growth, inaugural, increase, initiation, installation, investiture, purchase, reaching, submission, succession, yielding
**access of disease** attack
**accessory** abettor, accomplice, addition, adjunct, adornment, aid, appendage, appurtenance, assistant, associate, attachment, colleague, decoration, extension, extra, helper, partner, subsidiary, supplement, trim, trimming
**accessory fruit** false fruit, pseudocarp
**access to a mine** adit
**accident** affliction, attribute, blunder, calamity, casualty, chance, collapse, crash, disaster, fluke, fortuity, happening, hazard, misadventure, mischance, mischief, misfortune, mishap, mistake, slip, tragedy, unintentional
**accidental** casual, chance, fortuitous, inadvertent, random, serendipitous, unforeseen, unintentional
**accidentally listened to** overheard
**accidentally splashed** spilled, spilt
**accidental piece of misconduct** slip
**accidental piercing of pneumatic tyre** puncture
**accident in car racing** shunt

**accident wrecking vehicles** crash, prang, smash
**accidie** acedia, apathy, indifference
**accipitrine** accipitral, rapacious
**acclaim** acclamation, accolade, announce, applaud, applause, approval, approve, celebrate, cheer(ing), clap, commend, compliment, congratulate, crown, éclat, encore, eulogise, eulogy, exalt(ation), extol, hail, honour, ovation, plaudit, praise, salute, toast, welcome
**acclamation** acclaim, adulation, applause, cheering, ovation, shouting, tribute
**acclimatise** accustom, adapt, adjust, attune, conform, familiarise, habituate, harden, salt, season
**acclivity** ascent, cant, climb, elevation, eminence, gradient, hill(side), incline, ramp, rise, slant, submergence, talus, upgrade, upward
**accolade** acclaim, acclamation, applause, approval, award, cheering, commendation, compliment, congratulation, credit, deference, espousal, eulogium, eulogy, exaltation, flattery, homage, honour, kudos, paean, panegyric, plaudit, praise, recognition, recommendation, regard, respect, reverence, testimonial, tribute
**accommodate** abet, adapt, adjust, aid, assist, conform, contain, entertain, harmonise, help, house, oblige, provide, reconcile, serve, suit, supply
**accommodate a borrower** lend
**accommodated horses** stabled
**accommodation** agreement, compromise, housing, lodging, quarters, settlement
**accommodation at a wharf** wharfage
**accommodation for driver and car** motel
**accommodation for horses** paddock, stable, stabling
**accommodation in hired rooms** lodging
**accompanied by bloodshed** bloody, sanguinary
**accompanied vocal solo** aria
**accompanies a gentleman** lady
**accompany** affiliate, ally, associate, attend, attendant, chaperon, co-exist, combine, conduct, convoy, direct, escort, follow, guard, join, pilot, squire, supplement, support, usher, with
**accompany for protection** convoy, usher, bodyguard

**accompany ship** consort
**accomplice** abettor, accessory, ally, associate, cohort, collaborator, colleague, companion, confederate, consociate, conspirator, conspirer, contributor, deputy, partner
**accomplish** achieve, attain, clinch, complete, conclude, consummate, discharge, do, effect(uate), engineer, execute, expedite, finish, fulfil(l), manage, negotiate, obtain, perfect, perform, produce, realise, seal, succeed, talent, terminate
**accomplished** achieved, adept, adroit, apt, attained, closed, completed, cultivated, cultured, did, done, educated, elegant, ended, erudite, executed, expert, finished, fulfilled, gifted, graceful, literary, masterly, performed, proficient, refined, skilful, suave, talented
**accomplished fact** fait accompli (F)
**accomplishment** achievement, acquirement, blow, completion, conclusion, coup, deed, exploit, feat, fulfilment, move, perfection, performance, success, termination
**accomplish one's purpose** succeed
**accord** accommodate, accordance, adapt, adjust, admit, agree, agreement, amity, assent, attune, bestow, coincidence, communion, concede, concord, concur, conformity, endow, fit, grant, harmonise, harmony, match, peace, permit, resemblance, resemble, suit, sympathy, unanimity, unison
**accordance** accord, agreement, bestowal, compatibility, concert, concord, conformity, congruity, endowment, granting, harmony, similarity, union, unison
**accordance with the law** lawful, legality, legitimate
**according** agreeing, allotting, answering, assigning, awarding, bestowing, chiming, committing, conforming, congruent, corresponding, decreeing, donating, giving, granting, harmonising, imparting, lavishing, matching, presenting, rendering, squaring, suiting
**accordingly** consequently, correspondingly, ergo, hence, properly, so, suitable, suitably, therefore, thus
**according to** à la, accordingly, after, aux (F), correspondingly, per
**according to art** secundum artem (L)
**according to a system** systematic
**according to fact** factual, true

**according to Hoyle** correct
**according to law** legally, secundum legem (L)
**according to nature** natural, secundum naturam (L)
**according to order of occurrence** chronological
**according to rule** secundum regulam (L)
**according to strict etiquette** de rigueur (F)
**according to the hypothesis** ex hypothesi
**according to the law** de jure, lawfully, legal(ly), legitimately, rightfully
**according to value** ad valorem
**accordion** concertina, harmonica, harmonium, organ, squashbox
**accost** address, affront, annoy, approach, assail, attack, bore, catch, grab, greet(ing), hail, harass, invade, lure, meet, pursue, receive, salutation, salute, solicit, storm, suggest, sway, waylay, welcome
**accouchement** childbirth, obstetrics
**accoucheur** obstetrician
**account** advantage, answer, assess, benefit, bill, book, chronicle, consequence, consider, consideration, count, credit, deem, distinction, elucidate, estimate, estimation, explain, exposition, history, importance, journal, judge, ledger, motive, narration, narrative, profit, reason, recital, reckon, record, regard, reply, report, repute, score, statement, story, tale, value, view, worth
**accountable** amenable, answerable, bound, explainable, explicable, liable, obliged, responsible, subject, understandable
**accountancy** bookkeeping
**accountancy book** ledger, journal
**accountant** actuary, agent, auditor, bookkeeper, cashier, computer, controller, examiner, recorder, registrar, treasurer
**account book** ledger, journal
**account entry** credit, debit, item
**account for** clarify, destroy, elucidate, explain, illuminate, incapacitate, justify, kill, rationalise, reckoning, vindicate
**accounting notation** debit, credit
**account in words** description, narration, report
**account of events** narrative
**account received** invoice, liability
**account rendered** bill
**accounts check** audit
**accounts examiner** accountant, auditor

**accoutre** adorn, apparel, appoint, arm, attire, caparison, clothe, dress, equip, furnish, garb, gear, gird, invest, ornament, provide, rig, supply, trap

**accoutrements** accessories, adornment, apparatus, appurtenances, attire, baggage, clothes, dress, equipment, furnishings, garb, gear, harness, instruments, kit, outfit, rigging, stuff, supplies, tack(le), tools, trappings, trimmings

**accredit** accept, accuse, ascribe, associate, attribute, authorise, certify, commission, connect, count, credit, depute, empower, endorse, entrust, esteem, gain, guarantee, impute, license, place, recognise, relate, repute, sanction, send, vouch

**accrue** accumulate, advance, amass, augment, collect, ensue, expand, gain, gather, grow, increase, inure, result, save, swell, wax, yield

**accumulate** accrue, agglomerate, aggregate, amass, assemble, collect, congregate, enlarge, expand, extend, gather, hoard, mass, pile, reserve, store, swell

**accumulated snow on high mountain ranges** firn, névé

**accumulated wealth** affluence, fortune, opulence, riches, treasure

**accumulate goods** stockpile

**accumulate riches** accrue, amass, hoard

**accumulating** accruing, amassing, collecting, gathering, growing, hoarding, increasing, stockpiling, storing

**accumulating prize in lottery** jackpot

**accumulation of force** charge

**accumulation of gas on surface** adsorption

**accumulation of serous fluid** ascites, oedema

**accumulation of trifles** flotsam

**accuracy** authenticity, conformity, correctness, exactness, fact, fidelity, flawlessness, justness, perfection, preciseness, precision, rectitude, rightness, truth, validity, veracity

**accuracy of adjustment** tram

**accurate** careful, correct, exact, precise, spot-on, true, unerring

**accurate instrument** micrometer

**accurately expressed** precise, touché

**accurate time measurement** chronometry

**accursed** annoying, bad, baneful, bedeviled, bewitched, condemned, cursed, damned, despicable, detestable, doomed, execrable, fey, hateful, heinous, hopeless, luckless, malevolent, miserable, noxious, odious, profane, ravaged, ruined, unconsecrated, undone, unhallowed, unhappy, wretched

**accursed thing** anathema, nuisance, pestilence, plague, trouble

**accusable** impeachable

**accusal** accusation, incrimination, indictment

**accusation** accusal, allegation, attribution, charge, citation, complaint, condemnation, denunciation, indictment, recrimination

**accuse** arraign, assail, attack, blame, censure, charge, cite, denounce, discredit, impeach, implicate, impugn, impute, incriminate, inculpate, indict, involve, rebuke, recriminate, reprove, revile, tax

**accuse a public officer** impeach

**accused** blamed, censured, charged, defendant, imputed, incriminated, indicted, plaintiff, recriminated, taxed

**accused person** defendant

**accuse formally** arraign

**accuse formally by legal process** charge, cite, indict

**accuse of high crime before competent tribunal** impeach

**accuser** betrayer, denouncer, denunciator, discloser, imputer, informant, informer, sneak, talebearer, telltale

**accustom** acclimate, acclimatise, acquaint, adapt, attune, domesticate, drill, enure, exercise, familiarise, habituate, inure, naturalise, season, toughen, train, use, wont

**accustomed** addicted, characteristic, confirmed, customary, established, everyday, familiar, frequent, general, habitual, inured, seasoned, usual, wonted

**accustom infant to food other than milk** wean

**accustom to** habituate

**accustom to a new climate** acclimatise

**ace** adept, aviator, champion, excellent, expert, genius, hero, jot, masterly, one, pip, playing card, star, superb, top, topnotcher, unit, virtuoso, winner

**acentric** off-centre

**ace of clubs** basto

**acerb** acid, bitter, sour, tart

**acerbic** acid, acrid, astringent, biting, bitter, burning, caustic, harsh, incisive, mordant, piquant, pungent, severe, sharp, sour, tart, trenchant

**acescent** sourish

**acetic acid** acetate, ester, vinegar

**acetic acid salt** acetate

**acetone derivative** acetol

**acetum** vinegar

**acetylene** ethine, hydrocarbon

**ache** agony, hurt, pain, soreness, suffer

**a cheap shop** bon marché (F)

**ache for** melancholy, yearn

**ache in the bones** arthritis, gout, rheumatism

**ache or pain in one's back** backache, lumbago

**achieve** accomplish, acquire, attain, complete, dispatch, do, earn, effect, execute, expedite, finish, gain, get, manage, obtain, perform, reach, realise, succeed, win

**achieve harmony** agree

**achievement** accomplishment, attainment, consummation, deed, feat, realisation

**achieve orientation** adjust

**achieve success** arrive, score

**Achilles' adviser** Nestor

**Achilles' companion** Patroclus

**Achilles' father** Peleus

**Achilles' friend** Patroclus

**Achilles' heel** downfall, imperfection, nemesis, vulnerability, weakness

**Achilles' horse** Xanthus

**Achilles' mother** Thetis

**Achilles' slayer** Paris

**Achilles' sore spot** heel

**Achilles' weakness** heel

**aching** hurting, pain, painful, paining, smarting, suffering, throbbing, twinging

**achromic** achromous, colourless

**acicula** needle-shaped, spine

**acid** acrid, amino, biting, bitter, caustic, keen, sarcastic, sardonic, sour, tart, ulmic, vinegary

**acid base indicator** litmus

**acid basis of aspirin** salicylic

**acid berry** gooseberry

**acid beverage** sour

**acid boiled sweet** pear-drop

**acid causing gout** uric

**acid chemical** amide

**acid compound** thiamid

**acid condiment** vinegar

**acid counteractive** alkali, antacid

**acid etching** mordant

**acid found in apples and other fruit** malic

**acid found in citrus fruits** citric

**acid found in living cells** ribonucleic

**acid found in sour milk** lactic

**acid found in tea** tannic

**acid found in unripe apples and other fruit** malic
**acid found in vinegar** acetic
**acid found in vitamin C** ascorbic
**acid from wood sorrel** oxalic
**acid highly dangerous and corrosive** sulphuric, hydrochloric
**acidic** sour
**acid in temper** acerb(ic)
**acidity** acerbity, acridness, causticity, mordancy, pungency, sharpness, trenchancy
**acid-leaved herb used in salads** sorrel
**acid liquid** vinegar
**acid neutraliser** alkali, antacid
**acid of fruits** malic
**acid-resistant iron alloy** duriron
**acid substance from grape juice** tartar
**acid taste** sour
**acid-tasting** bitter
**acid test paper** litmus
**acid used in baking powder** tartaric
**acid used in bleaching** oxalic
**acid used in disinfectant soap** carbolic
**acid used in tanning and clarifying wine and beer** tannin
**acid used to dissolve platinum and gold** aqua regia (L), nitrohydrochloric
**ack-ack** fla(c)k
**ack-ack gun** Bofors
**acknowledge** admit, allow, appreciate, attribute, avow, concede, confess, correspond, declare, grant, own, receive, recognise, reward, thank
**acknowledge an offence** apologise, confess
**acknowledge applause** bow, curts(e)y
**acknowledge frankly** avow
**acknowledge greeting** bow, nod, wave
**acknowledgement** abidance, accedence, admission, affirmation, assent, avowal, certification, concurrence, consent, declaration, endorsement, recognition
**acknowledgement of an offence** apology, confession
**acknowledgement of merit** acclaim, accolade, honour, salute
**acknowledgement of payment** receipt
**acknowledge openly** avow
**acknowledge publicly** acclaim
**acknowledging one's fault** mea culpa (L)
**acme** apex, apogee, best, cap, climax, crest, crown, culmination, extreme, head, peak, perfection, pinnacle, pitch, point, prime, spire, summit, supremacy, tip, tiptop, top, utmost, vertex, zenith

**acolyte** assistant, follower, helper, learner, novice, server
**acomia** baldness
**a common benefit** commune bonum (L)
**aconite** aconitum, bikh, extract, monkshood, napellus, remedy, wolfsbane
**acorn bearer** oak
**acorn cup** vallonia, valonia
**acorn or goose** barnacle
**acorns and the like** masts
**acorn-shaped** balanoid
**acorn tree** oak
**acoustic** hearing, phonic, sound
**acoustic bass guitar** gittarone
**acoustical system** sonar
**acoustic vase** echea
**acquaint** advise, apprise, aware, certify, convey, impart, inform, instruct, know, notify, possess, resolve, teach, tell, verse
**acquaintance** associate, awareness, companion, familiarity, friend
**acquaintance by correspondence** pen friend, pen pal
**acquainted** familiar, informed, versed
**acquainted with** know
**acquiesce** accede, accept, agree, allow, approve, comply, concur, submit, yield
**acquiesce in** accept
**acquiescence** abidance, acceptance, accordance, agreement, approval, assent, capitulation, compliance, concession, concurrence, conformity, consent, cringing, obedience, prostration, servility, submission, surrender, willingness, yielding
**acquiescent** acceding, accepting, agreeable, agreeing, amenable, approving, assenting, bowing, compliant, conceding, conforming, consenting, docile, gentle, meek, passive, servile, submissive, submitting, timid, willing, yielding
**acquire** achieve, appropriate, assume, attain, buy, earn, gain, get, grasp, obtain, procure, purchase, reap, receive, secure, win
**acquire beforehand** pre-empt
**acquire by labour** attain, earn, reap
**acquire by seizure** pre-empt
**acquire complete knowledge of** master
**acquired immunity against poison** mithridatism
**acquire initial incisors** teethe
**acquire knowledge** learn, study
**acquire with difficulty** eke

**acquisition** accession, achievement, acquirement, addition, appropriation, attainment, buy(ing), capture, find, gain(ing), getting, gift, learning, obtaining, obtainment, possession, procurement, property, purchase, pursuit, securing, seizure, takeover
**acquisitive** avaricious, avid, covetous, grasping, greedy, materialistic, mercenary, possessive, predacious, predatory, rapacious, ravenous, selfish
**acquit** absolve, amnesty, assoil, clear, discharge, dismiss, dispense, exculpate, excuse, exonerate, forgive, free, fulfil, justify, liberate, manumit, pardon, parole, release, remit, reprieve, warrant
**acquittal** absolution, absolving, absolvitor, acquittance, balancing, clearance, clearing, compliance, deliverance, discharge, dismissal, exculpation, exoneration, forgiveness, forgiving, freedom, fulfilment, remission, satisfaction, warranting
**acreage** acres, estate, land, lot
**acreage for planting** farm
**acrid** acerb(ic), acid, acidulous, acrimonious, astringent, belligerent, biting, bitter, caustic, harsh, ironic, irritating, mocking, moody, mordant, pungent, sarcastic, sardonic, sour, stinging, subacid, tart, vinegary, vitriolic
**acrid-tasting** bitter, pungent
**acrimonious** abusive, acrid, angry, astringent, austere, bitter, caustic, censorious, cutting, irascible, keen, malicious, moody, mordant, morose, petulant, pungent, rancorous, rough, sarcastic, sardonic, satiric, severe, sharp, sour, stern, stringent, tart, testy, trenchant, unkind
**acrimony** acridness, austerity, causticity, irony, malignity, mordancy, pique, rancor, rudeness, scorn, sourness, spite, tartness
**acrobat** artist, balancer, equilibrist, gymnast, rope-dancer, rope-walker, somersaulter, tumbler
**acrobatic turn** somersault
**acrobat of India** nat
**acrobat's garment** fleshings, leotard, maillot, tights
**acrobat's net** trampoline
**acrobat's spring** trampoline
**acrobat's swing** trapeze
**acrogen** cryptogam
**acrolith** caryatic, statue
**acromegaly** giantism
**acrophobia** altophobia

**acropolis** cadmea, citadel, fort, height, hill, larissa, refuge
**across** à travers (F), aslant, astride, athwart, beyond, by, confronting, cross(ways), crosswise, facing, fronting, into, on, opposite, over, past, thwart, transverse(ly), upon
**across sea** abroad, overseas
**across the grain** athwart
**across the land** overland
**acrostic** enigma, poem, puzzle
**acrylic** synthetic
**act** accomplishment, achievement, action, behave, blow, conduct, decree, deed, dissemble, do(ing), edict, emote, enactment, fake, feat, feign, function, imitate, impersonate, law, measure, mine, operate, operation, ordinance, perform(ance), play, pose, pretend, proceeding, represent, routine, sham, statute, turn, work
**act according to rules** abide, conform
**act against** oppose, resist
**act as agent** represent
**act as a magnet** attract
**act as chairman** preside
**act as deputy** deputise
**act as go-between** intercede, mediate
**act as host** entertain
**act as interpreter** interpret, translate
**act as judge** adjudicate
**act as magnet** attract
**act as master of ceremonies** emcee
**act as mediator** intercede
**act as pal to** befriend
**act as proxy** represent
**act as reporter of event** cover, journalist
**act as secret agent** spy
**act as umpire** arbitrate
**act as wanton** rig
**act awkwardly** hocker
**act badly** ham
**act before** anticipate
**act blunderingly** bull
**act cautiously** pussyfoot
**act contrary to** infringe, oppose
**act correctly** behave
**act cruelly to** abuse, torture
**act deceitfully** double, be as a snake in the grass
**act dishonestly** cheat, feign, finagle, fudge
**act dispiritedly** mope, pout
**act downheartedly** mope
**act dreamily** maunder
**acted on by the wind** aeolian
**acted through agent** medium
**act emotionally** emote
**act evasively** avoid, shuffle, shun

**act for** deputise, do, mediate, replace, serve, substitute
**act frivolously** fribble, frivol, trifle
**act hesitatingly** falter, hesitate, waver
**act histrionically** emote
**act idly** laze, loiter
**act in accordance** abide, comply
**act in agreement** coact, concur, conform
**act in answer** reply, respond
**act in calculation** logistic
**act indecisively** dither
**act independently** sever
**act in feeble way** potter
**acting against** adverse
**acting a part** performing, playing
**acting award** Artes, Oscar
**acting by choice** voluntary
**acting by means of air** pneumatic
**acting by turn** altern(ate)
**acting from its own energy** automatous, spontaneous
**acting group** cast, company, society, troupe
**acting independently** autonomous
**acting like a tyrant** despotic, tyranny
**acting monarch** regent
**acting oddly** haywire
**acting profession** stage
**acting rapidly** drastic
**acting severely** drastic
**acting spontaneously** automatous
**acting through the skin** endermic
**acting to increase the flow of urine** diuretic
**acting without delay** instantaneous, prompt
**acting without due consideration** ill-considered, rash
**actinide** actinon
**act in law** re(s)
**act in official occupation** officiate
**actinometry** optics
**actinotherapy** radiotherapy
**act in play** characterise, emote, perform
**act in religious ceremony** rite
**act in response** react
**act in retaliation** reprisal
**act in retribution** nemesis
**act in ridiculous manner** caper
**action** -ing, act, activity, affair, battle, behaviour, conduct, conflict, deed, doing, encounter, energetic, energy, engagement, gesture, lawsuit, mechanism, meeting, movement, moving, operation, performance, performing, proceeding, process, suit, work, working
**actionable** accusable, litigated, suable
**action based on prejudice** bias, discrimination, hypercriticism

**action between horse and rider** appui
**action of dissent** object, protest, remonstrate
**action of drama** epitasis
**action offending public opinion** scandal
**action of ill-will** malice
**action of law** judicial, process
**action of observing** observation, perceive, perception
**action of reeling silk from cocoons** filature
**action of wind** aeolation
**action painting** tachism(e)
**action suffix** -ence, -ent
**action to recover goods** replevin, repossess
**action towards** behaviour, treatment
**action with an element of chance** chance-medley
**action word** verb
**activate** actuate, animate, arouse, energise, impel, incite, liven, prompt, rouse, start, stimulate, stir
**active** acting, agile, alert, alive, animated, assiduous, deedy, eager, earnest, effectual, energetic, enterprising, fervent, hard-working, indefatigable, moving, nimble, occupied, operative, practical, productive, quick, smart, spirited, sprightly, spry, untiring, vigorous, vivacious, working
**active at night** nocturnal
**active consciousness** alertness, attention, concentration
**active ill will** malice
**active ingredient in cannabis** tetrahydrocannabinol (THC)
**active involvement** participation
**active kindness** beneficent, benevolent
**actively courageous** valiant
**active male principle of universe** Yang
**active opposition** antagonism, contradiction
**active person** doer
**active place** hive, ant-hill
**active power** energy, force
**active process** operation, action
**active supporter** fan, protagonist
**active volcano** Asama, Azuma, Etna, Heimaey, Helka, Katmai, Lassen, Mauna Loa, McKinley, Paricutin, Stromboli, Surtsey, Taal, Vesuvius
**activity** action, ado, agility, animation, assiduity, briskness, bustle, celerity, commotion, deed, diligence, effort, energy, exercise, exertion, fever, flurry, frenzy, function, fuss, hustle, industry, labour, liveliness, motion, movement, nimbleness, ploy,

promptness, quickness, rapidity, robustness, rush, stir, storm, tumult, turmoil, venture, vigour, vim, vividness, work
**act jointly** co-operate
**act like** simulate
**act misleadingly** prevaricate
**act nervously** jitter
**act of acquiring knowledge** cognition
**act of aid** help, assistance
**act of anointing** (in)junction
**act of applause** cheer, clap, encore, plaudit
**act of approval** euge
**act of begging** cadge
**act of beginning quarrel** aggression, provoke
**act of being mocked by faith** irony
**act of bending the knees** genuflection
**act of binding** ligation
**act of boasting** jactation, jactitation
**act of bravery** boldness, bravado
**act of breaking links** dissociation
**act of bringing forth young** breeding, childbirth, parturition
**act of building** erection
**act of burning** arson, incinerate
**act of calling forth** elicitation
**act of carrying** bearing, portage
**act of carrying on** continuance, perseverance
**act of chasing** pursuit
**act of cheating** cog, deceiving, delude, fraud, hoodwink, swindle
**act of choking a person** strangulation
**act of choosing** choice, option, selection
**act of civility** bow, courtesy, curtsy, devoir
**act of collusion** conspiracy
**act of coming in** entrance
**act of coming in again** re-entrance
**act of concealing** camouflage, disguise, hide, secretion
**act of conning** navigation
**act of cultivating** planting, tillage
**act of cutting** severance
**act of declaring innocent in a court** acquittal
**act of declining** refusal
**act of defacing** disfigurement
**act of deferring** procrastination
**act of demonstrating** manifestation
**act of disclosing** revelation
**act of discourtesy** rebuff, slight, snub
**act of distributing cards** deal
**act of distributing cards in wrong way** cheat, misdeal
**act of dodging** evasion
**act of drinking in company** compotation
**act of drying** dehydration

**act of endearment** caress, cuddle, embrace, kiss, pat
**act of engraving** celature, xylography
**act of enlisting** enrolment
**act of escaping** getaway, runaway
**act of evening up** alignment
**act of filling** impletion
**act of flying** flight
**act of following** pursuit
**act of forcing oneself in** intrusion
**act of gaining possession** acquisition
**act of getting** acquisition
**act of giving out** issuance
**act of giving up employment** resignation
**act of going out** exit
**act of good will** favour
**act of greasing** lubrication
**act of greeting** salute, wave
**act of healing** cure
**act of hearing** audience
**act of help** service
**act of helping** assistance
**act of holding** clutch, grip, retention
**act of imploring** beg, obsecration
**act of incorporation** charter
**act of installing in office** investiture
**act of interment** burial
**act of keeping** retention
**act of killing a god** deicide
**act of killing one's wife** uxoricide
**act of kindness** benefit, caress
**act of knowing** cognition
**act of labour** diligence
**act of leasing** rental
**act of leaving** exit
**act of lending** loan
**act of listening** auscultation
**act of loan sharking** usury
**act of looting** despoliation
**act of lowering** depression
**act of making better** amelioration
**act of making clear** elucidation
**act of making regular** standardisation
**act of making sterile** castration, sterilisation
**act of marine robbery** piracy
**act of mercy** lenience, lenity
**act of migrating** trek
**act of mortification** penance
**act of moving forward** advancement
**act of neglect** omission
**act of nourishing** nutrition
**act of omission** elision
**act of planting trees** afforestation
**act of politeness** civility
**act of prayer** devotion
**act of punishing** beating, caning, rebuking, reprimanding, scolding, whipping
**act of quitting** exit
**act of reading** perusal

**act of refilling** replenishment
**act of repentance** penance
**act of reposing** reposal
**act of retaliation** avenge, reprisal, revenge
**act of retiring** retreat
**act of retribution** vengeance
**act of revending** resale
**act of revenge** reprisal
**act of robbery** depredation
**act of savagery** atrocity, barbarism
**act of seeing** sight, stare, vision
**act of selling** sale, vend
**act of selling ecclesiastical preferment** indulgence, simony
**act of settling** colonisation
**act of shaming** abashment
**act of shunning** avoidance
**act of shutting** closure
**act of slowing down** inhibiting, retardation
**act of soliciting votes** canvass
**act of speaking** speech
**act of spilling** spilth
**act of splitting into pieces** fission
**act of spying** espionage
**act of stealing** theft
**act of steering** steerage
**act of stupidity** bêtise
**act of summing** addition
**act of supplying** issuance
**act of surgery** operation
**act of swearing** oath
**act of swimming** natation
**act of taking away** removal
**act of taking leave** adieu, farewell, greeting
**act of taking part** participation
**act of taking unawares** surprisal
**act of tasting** gustation
**act of testing** experimentation
**act of theft** larceny
**act of travelling** peregrination
**act of treachery** betrayal, shenanigan
**act of turning** rotation
**act of turning on an axis** rotation
**act of twisting** torsion
**act of understanding** comprehension
**act of violence** rage, rape
**act of voiding** nullification
**act of washing** ablution, lavation
**act of wearing away** erosion
**act of withdrawing** disengagement, retirement, retreat, secession
**act of wooing** courtship
**act of worship** devotion, exercise, homage
**act of writing one's name** signature
**act on** affect, alter, comply, follow, heed, influence, modify, obey, react, sway, transform
**acton** jacket, jerkin

**act on each other** influence, interact
**actor** affector, agent, artist, comedian, creator, deceiver, doer, executor, extra, fabricator, ham, hero, histrio, impersonator, leading man, masquerader, mime, mummer, participant, performer, personator, play-actor, player, pretender, protagonist, stage player, Thespian, trouper
**actor engaged for crowd scene** extra
**actor in comedy** comedian
**actor in crowd scene** extra
**actor in traditional mime** mummer
**actor in tragedy** tragedian, tragedienne
**actor's aide** dresser, prompt, teleprompter
**actor's assistant** director, dresser, stand-in
**actor's cue** prompt
**actor's entrance** stage door, wings
**actor's exit** stage door
**actor's group** cast, company, troupe
**actor's hint** cue
**actors in a play** cast
**actor's part** function, lines, role
**actors perform on it** stage
**actor's prompt** cue
**actor's realm** stage
**actor's remark to audience** aside
**actor's role** lines, part
**actor's signal to speak** cue
**actor's speech** aside
**actor's union in UK** Equity
**actor's valet** dresser
**actor's whisper** aside
**act out of sorts** mope
**act peculiarly** wander
**act playfully** banter, dally
**act precipitately** rush
**act quickly** gird
**act rashly** rack
**act reciprocally** alternate
**actress aspiring to fame** starlet
**actress in tragedy** tragedienne
**act restlessly** fidget
**act servilely** fawn
**act smart** be snazzy
**act sportively** daff
**act suddenly** flash
**act sullenly** mope, pout, sulk
**act together** agree, co-act, co-operate, concert, concord, concur
**act toward** treat
**act treacherously** betray
**actual** absolute, authentic, certain, decided, palpable, positive, real, substantial, sure, tangible, true, veritable
**actual being** esse
**actual copy** ectypal
**actual existence** esse

**actual facts** truth
**actuality** animation, authenticity, being, certainty, concreteness, continuance, continuation, endurance, entity, existence, fact, force, genuineness, life, living, realism, reality, substance, survival, truth, truthfulness, validity, verity
**actually** absolutely, categorically, certainly, de facto, definitely, effectively, essentially, factually, genuinely, indeed, indisputably, literally, lively, physically, positively, presently, realism, reality, really, substantially, tangibly, truly, undeniable, veritably, very
**actually existing** real
**actuary** accountant, computer
**actuated by great hatred** malignant
**act up** malfunction, misbehave
**act upon** affect, handle, touch
**act up to** even
**act vigorously** twig
**act violently** rage, rant, rape, rave, row
**act wildly** rave
**act with bias** err, preconception, prejudice
**act with dispatch** abduct, hurry, hustle
**act with energy** hustle, move, stir
**act with exaggeration** amplify, hyperbole, magnify, overact, overstate
**act with mimic gestures** mime
**act without words** gesture, mime
**act with violence** rage, rant, rape, rave, row
**acuity** astuteness, edge, keenness, sharpness, wit
**acumen** acuteness, astuteness, cleverness, discernment, discrimination, esprit, flair, ingenuity, insight, intelligence, judg(e)ment, keenness, knowledge, penetration, perception, perspicacity, quickness, resourcefulness, sagaciousness, sagacity, sagacity, shrewdness, smartness, understanding, wisdom
**a cut above** distinguished, outshine, reliable, trustworthy
**acute** astute, bright, clever, crucial, discerning, distressing, extreme, fierce, ingenious, intelligent, intense, keen, nimble, penetrating, perceptive, perspicacious, piercing, poignant, pointed, severe, sharp, sharpened, shrewd, sudden, touching, violent
**acute contagious disease** smallpox
**acute difficulty** encumbrance, incumbrance, strait
**acute fear of experiencing or witnessing bodily pain** aglophobia

**acute headache** migraine
**acute inflammation of the skin, caused by streptococcus** erysipelas
**acute inflammation of the brain and spinal cord** encephalomyelitis
**acute in taking notice** observant, perceptive
**acutely** artfully, cleverly, critically, discriminatingly, distressfully, incisively, ingeniously, intensely, keenly, painfully, penetratingly, perceptively, piquantly, poignantly, pointedly, severely, sharply, shrewdly, smartly
**acutely painful** excruciating
**acutely perceptive** perspicacious
**acute mortification** chagrin, vexation
**acuteness** cleverness, discernment, discrimination, incisiveness, intuitiveness, keenness, perception, perceptiveness, perspicaciousness, perspicacity, pointedness, sharpness, smartness, subtleness, subtlety
**acuteness of mind** acumen, astuteness, intelligence
**acuteness of tone** pitch
**acute pain** agony
**acute painful viral inflammation of nerve ganglia** shingles
**acute pain in side of body** stitch
**acute perception** perspicacity
**acute physical pain** agony, anguish
**acute sense of smell** hyperosmia
**acute vexation** chagrin, mortification
**acute viral disease** dengue, influenza
**adage** aphorism, apo(ph)thegm, axiom, byword, dictum, maxim, motto, precept, proverb, saw, saying
**adagio** largo, moderato, slow, slowly
**Adam and Eve's home** Eden, paradise
**adamant** adamantine, callous, determined, firm, fixed, hard, immovable, impenetrable, inexorable, inflexible, insistent, intransigent, merciless, obdurate, relentless, resolute, rigid, set, stiff, stony, stubborn, tough, unbending, unbreakable, uncompromising, unmerciful, unrelenting, unshakable, unyielding
**adamantine** firm, flinty, hard, immovable, rigid, rock-hard, unbreakable, unyielding
**Adam's ale** water
**Adam's apple** larynx
**Adam's consort** Eve
**Adam's grandson** Enos
**Adam's home** Eden, paradise
**Adam's mate** Eve
**Adam's needle** yucca

**Adam's rib** Eve
**Adam was the first** human, man
**adapt** acclimatise, accommodate, adjust, alter, apply, attune, change, comply, conform, convert, fashion, fit, habituate, make, match, moderate, modify, prepare, qualify, reconcile, remodel, shape, suit, tailor
**adaptable** accommodate, adjustable, alterable, amenable, applicable, changeable, compliable, compliant, conformable, convertible, easy-going, flexible, malleable, matchable, modifiable, plastic, pliant, qualifiable, resilient, suitable, variable, versatile
**adaptation** adjustment, alteration, change, conversion, habituation, refitting, remodelling, shift, version
**adapted for tearing teeth** laniary
**adapted for two eyes** binocular
**adapted for walking** gressorial
**adapt for acting** dramatise
**adapt for stage** dramatise
**adapt ingeniously** contrive
**adapt to shape** fit
**adapt to the metric system of measurement** metricate
**add** affix, amplify, annex, append, attach, augment, combine, connect, enhance, enlarge, increase, join, plus, subjoin, sum, supplement, tot, unite
**add as ingredient** admix
**add at the end** annex, append, subjoin
**add beauty to** adorn, decorate
**add condiments** flavour, season
**added building** annex(e)
**added clause** parenthesis, rider
**added from without** extraneous
**added on** additional
**added security on bolt** lock-nut
**added to** complemented, increased, more
**addendum** addition, adjunct, affix, annex(e), annexure, appendage, appendix, attachment, augmentation, extension, postscript, supplement
**adder** asp, reptile, serpent, snake, viper, whorl
**adder's-tongue** dogtooth violet
**add herbs** flavour, season
**addict** adherent, buff, dependant, devotee, dope-fiend, enthusiast, fan, fanatic, fiend, follower, freak, habituate, habitue, hophead, incline, junkie, mainliner, predispose, roker, tripper, user, zealot
**addicted to alcoholic drink** bibulous
**addicted to drinking** intemperate
**addicted to petty thefts** light-fingered

**addicted to wine** vinous
**addiction** craving, dependence, depending, dipsomania, enslavement, habit, indulgence, obsession, subjugation
**addiction to wine** vinosity
**addictive drug** amphetamine, barbiturate, cocain(e), crack, heroin, marijuana, morphine, opium, PCP, tranquilliser
**addition** accession, accessory, addendum, adding, additive, adjunct, alternation, annexation, annex(e), appendage, appendix, attachment, augmentation, codicil, counting, enlargement, extension, extra, gain, inclusion, increase, increasing, increment, joining, raise, reckoning, summing-up, supplement, totalling, totting-up
**additional** added, additamentary, additory, annexed, appended, attached, augmented, extra, fresh, further, increased, more, new, other, raised, spare, supplemental, supplementary
**additional allowance** bonus, grant
**additional amount** more
**additional breathing sound** rale
**additional but subordinate** collateral
**additional charge** surcharge
**additional clause to a contract** rider
**additional equipment** accessory
**additional expense** oncost, overhead
**additional expenses** extra costs
**additional helping** seconds
**additional matter at end of book** addendum
**additional name** agnomen, alias, endearment, nickname, pseudonym
**additional one** another, other
**additional portion** rasher
**additional publication** reissue
**additional sail** drabler
**additional tax** surtax, supertax
**additional tyre used in emergency** spare
**addition of syllable** paragoge
**addition sign** plus
**addition to amend** rider
**addition to bill** rider
**addition to book** addendum, postscript
**addition to building** annex(e), el
**addition to document** annex(e), clause, rider
**addition to will** codicil
**additive** accumulative, added, addendum, adjunct, also, augend, augment, chain, component, constituent, cumulative, eke, involving, more, other, pact, summative, too

**addle** abash, confused, curdle, decay, demoralise, discomfit, discompose, disconcert, discountenance, disorient, embarrass, empty, fluster, idle, mildew, mire, mortify, muddle, nonplus, putrefy, rot, shame, spoil, turn, unsound, upset, vain
**addled egg** wind-egg
**add lustre to** adorn, gild
**add notes of explanation to** annotate, inscription
**add on** affix, annex(e), append, attach
**add pepper to** flavour, season
**address** abode, accost, bearing, cleverness, direct, discourse, domicile, dwelling, greet, habitation, house, lecture, location, lodging, manner, oration, residence, sermon, speech, talk
**address a court of law** plead, request
**address an audience** orate
**address court of law as advocate** plead
**address given in public** speech
**address God** beseech, pray
**address in rude language** abuse, snub
**address of greeting** salutation, salutatory, welcome
**address of respect to a man** lord, sir
**address to king** sire
**address unknown** missing, moved
**add salt or pepper to** flavour, season
**add spices to** flavour, season
**add spirits to** lace
**add sugar to** sweeten
**add sugar to fermenting wine** chaptalise
**add the finishing touches** complete
**add to** advance, append, augment, eke, enlarge, increase, lace, supplement
**adduce** advance, allege, allude, assign, attribute, blame, cite, illustrate, implicate, imply, incriminate, introduce, maintain, offer, present, produce, propagate, propose
**add up** amount, compute, count, imply, indicate, reckon, signify, sum, tot, total
**adenoids** growth, swelling
**adept** able, accomplished, adroit, deft, dexterous, expert, masterful, proficient, skilful, skilled, versed
**adeptly** adroitly, expertly, skilfully
**adequacy** capability, competence, fairness, sufficiency, suitability, tolerability
**adequate** able, acceptable, capable, commensurate, competent, enough, equal, fair, fit, passable, presentable, requisite, respectable, satisfactory,

serviceable, sufficient, suitable, tolerable
**adequately happy** content, pleased
**adequate resources** sufficiency
**adhere** attach, cement, cleave, cling, fasten, fix, glue, hold, maintain, obey, observe, stay, stick, support, unite
**adhere closely** cleave, follow
**adherence** accuracy, adhesion, allegiance, attachment, cementation, closeness, correspondence, devotion, exactness, fidelity, loyalty, obedience, precision, respect, stickiness, tenaciousness, viscosity
**adherent** abettor, acolyte, adhering, admirer, advocate, ally, assistant, attendant, champion, clinging, companion, confederate, confidant, devotee, disciple, fan, follower, gummy, hanger-on, ideologue, mucilaginous, parasite, partisan, partner, patron, pupil, rooter, sectary, sticking, supporter, sycophant, tenacious, upholder, vassal, viscid, viscous, votary
**adhere to** abide, cling, stay, stick
**adhering to convention** etiquette, formal, protocol
**adhesion** attachment
**adhesive** adhering, attaching, cement, clinging, cohesive, epoxy, glue(y), glutinous, gum(my), holding, mortar, paste, plaster, smeary, solder, sticking, sticky, tacky, tenacious, viscid
**adhesive design** sticker
**adhesive gum** mucilage
**adhesive label** sticker
**adhesiveness** stickiness, tenacity
**adhesive paste** glue, gum
**adhesive salve** plaster
**adhesive stamp** seal
**adhesive sticker** label
**adhesive substance** paste
**adieu** arrivederci (I), au revoir (F), auf Wiedersehen (G), bon voyage, bye, cheers, ciao (I), congé, farewell, gluckliche Reise (G), goodbye, parting, sayonara, vale (L), totsiens, valediction, valedictory
**adipose** fat, fatty, greasy, obese, oily, oleaginous, suety
**adipose tissue** fat
**adjacent** abutting, adjoining, bordering, close, contiguous, near, nearby, neighbouring
**adjacent to** beside
**adjacent to boundary** march
**adjective** epithet
**adjective ending** -al, -ene, -ent, -ese, -ial, -ian, -ile, -ine, -ish, -ite, -ive, -ous

**adjective indicating choice** optative
**adjective suffix** -al, -ene, -ent, -ese, -ial, -ian, -ile, -ine, -ish, -ite, -ive, -ous
**adjective used as noun** adnoun
**adjoin** abut, add, affix, approach, approximate, combine, connect, contact, contiguous, couple, interconnect, join, juxtapose, link, meet, overlap, scrape, touch, unite, verge
**adjoining** abutting, adjacent, bordering, connected, connecting, contiguous, joined, joining, neighbouring, next (door), verging
**adjourn** defer, delay, discontinue, interrupt, postpone, recess, stay, suspend
**adjudge** adjudicate, allot, award, decide, decree, deem, pronounce
**adjudged unfit for use** condemned, discarded, incompetent, rejected, sentenced
**adjudication** adjudg(e)ment, arbitration, decision, decreeing, determination, finding, judg(e)ment, ordainment, pronouncement, ruling, settlement, verdict
**adjudicator** arbiter, arbitrator, judge, referee, umpire
**adjunct** accessory, addendum, addition, appendix, appurtenance, attachment, auxiliary, complement, incidental, supplement
**adjunct to bed** mattress
**adjure** entreat
**adjust** accommodate, adapt, align, alter, amend, arrange, attune, change, fit, fix, rectify, regulate, repair, reset, set, suit
**adjustable nut turner** shifting spanner
**adjust a clock** set
**adjust again** reset
**adjust a piano** tune
**adjust camera to get sharp picture** focus
**adjusted for grinding** molar
**adjusted to pitch** tuned
**adjust evenly** align
**adjust for use** adapt
**adjust lens** focus
**adjustment** adaptation, adaptedness, agreement, alignment, alteration, arrangement, arranging, balancing, conformity, fit(ment), fitting, fixing, focus, focus(s)ing, measurement, modification, ordering, reconcilement, rectification, redress, regulation, remodelling, repair, setting, settlement, tune-up, tuning
**adjust sound** tune
**adjust the pitch** tune
**adjust to** acclimatise, adapt, habituate

**adjutant** aide, ally, helper, officer
**adjutant bird** argala, hurgila, marabou, stork
**ad lib** extemporise, freely, impromptu, improvise, liberally, offhand
**adminicle** aid, support
**administer** apply, conduct, contribute, control, direct, dispense, distribute, dose, execute, govern, job, manage, oversee, rule, superintend, supervise, supply
**administer corporal punishment** beat, cane, spank, whip
**administering medicine** dosing
**administer medicine** dose
**administer punishment** beat, cane, spank, whip
**administers bankrupt property** bailiff, receiver
**administer tranquilliser** sedate
**administration** administering, board, conduct, control, direction, directors, execution, executive, government, leadership, management, ministry, overseeing, performance, provision, regime, running, superintendence, supervision
**administration of justice** judicature, jurisdiction
**administrative citadel of South Africa** Pretoria
**administrative department** secretariat
**administrative district** county
**administrative region in France** Aquitaine
**administrative staff** secretariat
**administrative unit** agency, block, bureau, circle, district
**administrator** boss, director, executive, head, manager, supervisor
**administrator of funds** trustee
**administrator of justice** justiciary
**admirable** capable, commendable, desirable, enviable, esteemed, estimable, excellent, extraordinary, fine, laudable, meritorious, noble, praiseworthy, rare, respectable, super, superb, unique, unusual, valuable, worthy
**admirable appearance** attractive, beautiful, handsome, pretty
**admirably** à merveille (F)
**admire** adore, applaud, appreciate, approve, commend, enjoy, esteem, extol, honour, idolise, laud, like, love, praise, prize, respect, revere, value, venerate
**admired by many people** acclaimed, popular
**admire excessively** adore, adulate, dote

**admire grudgingly** covet, envy
**admire oneself** airs, boast, boastful, conceited, coxcomb, egotist, exhibitionist, peacock, plume, pop, preen, prideful, stuck-up, swank, vain
**admirer** adherent, adorer, beau, boyfriend, devotee, enthusiast, fan, follower, idolater, lover, partisan, suitor, supporter, sweetheart, votary, wooer, worshipper
**admire to excess** adulate
**admissible** acceptable, admirable, admitted, allowed, commendable, creditable, deserving, desirable, enviable, estimable, laudable, meritorious, perfect, praiseworthy, useful, worthy
**admission** acceptance, access, admittance, affirmation, agreement, allowance, assent, concession, concurrence, confession, consent, enlistment, enrolment, entrance, entrée, entry, inclusion, introduction, permit, reception, receptivity, revelation, welcome
**admission gate** turnstile
**admit** accept, acclaim, acknowledge, affirm, ain, allow, assent, attest, authenticate, avow, certify, concede, concur, confess, depose, employ, endorse, import, initiate, introduce, own, permit, receive, shelter, swear, testify, truthful, welcome
**admit as true** grant
**admit formally to office** inaugurate
**admit frankly** avow
**admit reluctantly** confess
**admit willingly** welcome
**admittance** access, admitting, allowing, entrance, entry, passage, reception
**admitted fact** datum
**admittedly** indeed
**admit that something is true** concede
**admit the existence of** acknowledge
**admitting that** although, however
**admit to be true** affirm, concede, own
**admit to Christian church by baptism** baptise, christen
**admit to citizenship** naturalise
**admit to hospital** hospitalise
**admit to the Christian ministry** ordain
**admit with rights** initiate
**admonish** advise, apprise, caution, censure, notify, rebuke, reprove, scold, warn
**admonish earnestly** exhort, reprimand
**admonishing** accusing, advising, blaming, cautioning, censuring, charging, chiding, condemning, counselling, criticising, disapproving, enjoining, recommending, reprehending, reproaching, reproving, suggesting, taxing, upbraiding, urging
**ado** activity, bother, bustle, commotion, disturbance, fanfare, flurry, flutter, fuss, hassle, hub-hub, hustle, motion, noise, rout, scurry, stir, to-do, travail, tumult, turmoil, upset
**adolescence** boyhood, boyishness, childishness, girlhood, girlishness, heyday, immaturity, juvenescence, juvenility, minority, nonage, pre-adulthood, puberty, pubescence, puerility, pupilage, teenage, teens, transition, wardship, youth, youthfulness
**adolescent** immature, juvenile, minor, stripling, teen(ager), young(ster), youth(ful)
**adolescent years** teens
**adopt** accept, acquire, affect, appropriate, approve, arrogate, assume, back, choose, co-opt, confirm, discriminate, elect, embrace, endorse, espouse, follow, foster, maintain, nominate, opt, propose, reserve, select, support, sustain, take, tend, will
**adopted child** foster-child
**adopted father of Ali** Mohammed
**adopted food regimen** diet
**adopted son of Mohammed** Ali
**adopt from abroad** acquire, borrow
**adoption** acceptance, acquirement, adopting, affectation, approbation, appropriation, arrogation, assumption, backing, choice, embracing, endorsement, espousal, fosterage, fostering, ratification, sanction, support, sustainment
**adorable** attractive, charming, cuddly, cute, darling, lovable, precious
**adoration** admiration, ardour, cult, deference, devotion, esteem, exaltation, fondness, honour, incense, love, loyalty, passion, prayer, respect, worship
**adore** admire, affect, appreciate, cherish, dote, endear, enjoy, esteem, exalt, extol, hallow, honour, idolise, like, love, praise, regard, relish, respect, revere, treasure, value, venerate, worship
**adored woman** goddess
**adorer** admirer, devotee, idolater, idoliser, lover, votary, worshipper
**adoring** loving
**adoring praise** glory
**adorn** array, beautify, bedeck, begem, burnish, carve, deck, decorate, dress, embellish, emboss, embroider, engrave, enhance, enrich, festoon, garnish, gild, glamourise, grace, ornament, paint, prettify, primp, stud, titivate, trim
**adorn anew** redecorate
**adorned with nacre** pearled
**adorned with sparkling ornaments** spangled
**adornment** array, bauble, beautification, bouquet, brilliance, decoration, embellishment, enrichment, fanciness, flashiness, garniture, gaudiness, illumination, ornament, posy, splendour, tinsel, trimming, trinket
**adorn too formally** overdress
**adorn with figures** emblazon, engrave
**adorn with jewels** begem
**ad patres (L)** dead
**adrenal insufficiency** Addison's disease
**Adriatic city** Trieste, Venice
**Adriatic island** Eso, Lagosta, Lastovo, Lido
**Adriatic peninsula** Istria
**Adriatic port** Fiume, Trieste
**Adriatic winter wind** bora
**adrift** afloat, aimless, amiss, astray, drifting, unmoored, wrong
**adroit** able, adept, apt, clever, competent, cunning, deft, dext(e)rous, efficient, expert, ingenious, masterly, neat, nimble, perfect, ready, resourceful, skilful, slick, versatile, wizard
**adroitness** adeptness, agility, ambidexterity, aptitude, aptness, art(istry), briskness, cleverness, craft(smanship), deftness, dexterity, expertise, facility, faculty, felicity, finesse, ingenuity, knack, knowledge, legerdemain, liveliness, mastery, method, neatness, profession, proficiency, quickness, rapidity, readiness, shrewdness, skill, sleight, talent, trade, virtuosity, wittiness
**adspeak** blurb
**adulate** flatter, over-praise
**adulator** flatterer
**adult** gentleman, grown-up, lady, man, mature, ripe(ned), twenty-one-year-old, woman
**adult caterpillar** moth
**adult cygnet** swan
**adulterate** attenuate, corrupt, debase, deteriorate, devalue, dilute, vitiate, weaken
**adulterer** co-respondent, debauchee, deceiver, flirt, gigolo, libertine, philanderer
**adulterine** illegal, illegitimate, spurious
**adult female** woman

**adult female cat** queen
**adult form of insect** imago
**adult gosling** goose
**adult heifer** cow
**adulthood** experience, fullness, majority, manhood, maturity, perfection, ripeness, wisdom
**adult leveret** hare
**adult male** man
**adult male deer** stag
**adult male sheep** ram
**adult tapeworm** scolex
**adumbrate** betoken, forebode, foreshadow, harbinger, herald, portend, predict, spell
**adust** gloomy, melancholy, parched, scorched, sunburnt
**advance** adduce, advancement, allege, appreciate, augment, dignify, elevate, flourish, forward, further, gain, grow, hasten, improve, increase, lend, offer, procedure, procession, proffer, profound, progress, promote, propose, quicken, rise, strengthen, thrive, update, way
**advanced course of study** honours, masters, seminar
**advanced in age** old, seniority
**advanced in years** aged, elderly, old
**advanced university student** post-graduate
**advance guard** van, vanguard
**advancement** furtherance, headway, improvement, progress, promotion, step
**advance money** forward, lend
**advance notice** forecast, forewarn, indication, prediction, prophesy, warning
**advance of money** imprest
**advance party** vanguard
**advance payment** ante, stake
**advance showing of forthcoming film** preview
**advance slowly** crawl
**advancing** onward, progression
**advancing by degrees** edging, gradual
**advancing the course of** furthering, promoting, supporting
**advancing to maturity** adolescent
**advancing years** age
**advantage** ascendancy, asset, avail, behalf, benefit, dividend, expediency, favourable, gain, opportunity, pre-eminence, prerogative, privilege, profit, return, service, superiority, use, usefulness, utility, value, vantage
**advantageous** beneficial, convenient, expedient, helpful, lucrative, opportune, profitable, propitious, salutary, serviceable, useful, valuable
**advent** access(ion), advance, appearance, approach, arrival, avenue, coming, debut, development, emergence, entrance, event, introduction, nearing, occurrence, onset, passage, presence, road, visitation, way
**adventitious** accessory, accidental, alien, casual, chance, extrinsic, foreign, fortuitous, incidental, random, supervenient
**adventitious lung sound** cough, rale
**adventure** enterprise, escapade, experience, quest, undertaking, venture
**adventurer** daredevil, fortune-hunter, hero(ine), swashbuckler, traveller, venturer, wanderer
**adventurer in irregular warfare** filibuster, mercenary, privateer
**adventurism** recklessness
**adventurous** audacious, bold, brave, courageous, dangerous, daredevil, dareful, daring, gallant, headlong, headstrong, heroic, impetuous, intrepid, reckless, risky, venturesome
**adventurous courage** bravado, daring
**adventurous trip** excursion, odyssey
**adverb** degree, manner, modification, so
**adverb ending** -ly
**adverb of time** when
**adversary** antagonist, assailant, attacker, contestant, debater, devil, disputant, enemy, foe, opponent, opposer, rival
**adversary of man** devil, satan
**adverse** against, alien, antagonistic, conflicting, confronting, contra(ry), detrimental, disadvantageous, facing, hostile, inexpedient, inimical, inopportune, negative, opposed, opposing, opposite, reluctant, repugnant, unfavourable, unfortunate, unfriendly
**adverse critical reaction** boo, catcall, hiss, hoot, jeer
**adverse criticism** censure, chide, upbraid
**adverse in tendency** inimical
**adverse reaction** backlash
**adversity** affliction, disaster, ill-fortune, misery, misfortune, mishap, sorrow
**advertise** advise, announce, apprise, declare, display, inform, market, notify, proclaim, promote, publicise, push, show, tout, vaunt
**advertisement** ad(vert), affiche (F), allude, announcement, bill, circular, cite, commercial, display, hint, invoke, mention, notice, placard, plug, promotion, publicity, refer, spot, teaser
**advertising handbill** dodger
**advertising jingle** slogan
**advertising letter** circular
**advertising phrase** caption, punchline, slogan
**advertising sheet** copy-instruction, handbill
**advertising sign** poster, sticker
**advice** admonition, caution, counsel, guidance, hint, information, intelligence, news, notice, notification, opinion, recommendation, suggestion, warning
**advice-boat** aviso (Sp), coast-guard
**advice on problems** assistance, guidance, support
**advisable** appropriate, apt, expedient, fitting, judicious, politic, prudent, recommended, sensible, sound, wise
**advise** admonish, caution, caution, coax, confer, consult, counsel, discuss, dissuade, encourage, guide, inform, instruct, notify, persuade, recommend, suggest, teach, tutor, warn
**advise against** argue, caution, confute, deflect, deject, deter, disaffect, disenchant, dishearten, disillusion, dissuade, expostulate, intimidate, restrain, stagger, warn
**advise of** acquaint, communicate, enlighten, inform, relate
**adviser** arbiter, arbitrator, coach, confidant, consultant, counsellor, director, expert, guide, instructor, meddler, mentor, persuader, pilot, professional, prompter, referee, resource, sage, teacher, tutor, umpire, urger
**adviser in court of law** attorney
**adviser of Achilles** Nestor
**adviser with no personal interest in the case** amicus curiae
**advise strongly** impel, urge
**advise with** consider, consult, deliberate, discuss, negotiate, weigh
**advocacy of women's political rights** feminism
**advocate** advise, attorney, barrister, counsel, counsellor, defend, defender, encourage, espouser, exponent, lawyer, promoter, propounder, recommend, solicitor, support, supporter, urge
**advocate in the higher law courts** barrister
**advocate of abolition of war** pacifist
**advocate of education** education(al)ist

**advocate pressingly** impel, urge
**advocate total liquor prohibition** pussyfoot
**advocating abstinence** teetotal
**adytum** abbey, basilica, chapel, den, mosque, sanctum, shrine, tabernacle, tomb
**Aeëtes' daughter** Medea
**Aeëtes' kingdom** Colchis
**Aegean island** Crete, Delos, Kárpathos, Lésvos, Limnos, Mikonos, Nio, Psara, Samos, Samothráki, Tenos
**aeger** excuse, ill, sick
**aegis** advocacy, aid, approval, armour, assistance, auspices, bulwark, care, championship, convoy, cover, defence, egis, escort, favour, guard, guidance, help, palladium, patronage, protection, responsibility, safeguard, sanction, screen, security, shelter, shield, sponsorship, support, surety, umbrella
**Aeneas's admirer** Dido
**aeon** age, century, days, eternity, generation, lifetime, longevity, period, time, years
**aerate** aerify, air, carbonate, expose, freshen, inflate, oxygenate, oxygenise, ventilate
**aerated water** soda
**aerial** antenna, ethereal, flying, gaseous, high, rod, telecommunication, wire
**aerial manoeuvre** glide, loop, roll, spin
**aerial object with tail of light** comet
**aerie** eyrie, house, nest
**aeriform fluid** aerosol, gas
**aeriform mixture** gas
**aerodrome** airfield, airport
**aeronaut** aviator, balloonist, pilot
**aeroplane** aereo (I), aero, aircraft, avion (F), biplane, Concorde, fighter, Flugzeug (G), giro, gyro, helicopter, jet, jumbo, MiG, monoplane, seaplane, spad, Stuka, triplane
**aeroplane climbing turn** chandelle
**aeroplane cockpit** cabin, flight deck
**aeroplane control** joystick
**aeroplane-detecting device** radar
**aeroplane formation** echelon
**aeroplane jaunt** flip
**aeroplane landing field** aerodrome, airstrip
**aeroplane manoeuvre** bank, dive, glide, loop, roll, spin
**aeroplane marker** pylon
**aeroplane operator** aviator, pilot
**aeroplane part** aileron, cowling, fin, flap, fuselage, galley, hatch, nose, prop, rudder, tail, wing
**aeroplane pilot** aviator

**aeroplane runway** strip, tarmac
**aeroplane shelter** hangar
**aeroplane stabiliser** fin
**aeroplane throttle** gun
**aeroplane transport** carrier
**aeroplane width** wingspread
**aeroplane without pilot** drone
**aeroplane with single wings** monoplane
**aeroplane with two sets of wings** biplane
**aeroplane wood** balsa
**Aesopian tale** fable
**Aesop's story** fable
**aesthete** adept, aesthetician, authority, connoisseur, epicurian, expert, maven, mavin, savant
**aesthetic** artistic, arty, attractive, beautiful, charming, classic, comely, elegant, exquisite, lovely, pure, stupendous, tasteful, well-arranged
**aesthetically pleasing** beautiful
**aesthetic creation** art
**afar** abroad, afield, away, beyond, distant, yonder
**affability** affection, civility, cordiality, courteousness, courtesy, elegance, gallantry, graciousness, happiness, heartiness, kindliness, love, polish, politeness, tenderness, urbanity, warmth
**affability to inferiors** condescension
**affable** amiable, amicable, approachable, benign, casual, cordial, courteous, easy, friendly, genial, kindly, mild, obliging, pleasant, polite, social
**affably carefree** debonair
**affair** activity, amour, business, circumstance, concern, debacle, do, episode, event, happening, incident, interest, intrigue, issue, liaison, love, matter, occasion, occurrence, operation, proceeding, project, pursuit, question, reception, relationship, responsibility, romance, subject, transaction, undertaking
**affair of honour** duel
**affair of the heart** affaire de coeur (F), amour, love affair
**affairs of chance** lottery, raffle
**affect** accomplish, act, alter, assume, change, feign, impress, influence, modify, overcome, prefer, pretend, profess, sway, transform
**affectation** affectedness, characteristic, fake, foppery, idiosyncrasy, insincerity, pose, pretence, pretension, quirk
**affect by witchcraft** bewitch, charm, enchant
**affect deeply** impress, penetrate, touch

**affected** assumed, false, feigned, phony, pretended, pretentious, unnatural
**affected by** allergic
**affected by alcohol** beery, drunk, inebriated, intoxicated, stupefied, tipsy
**affected by a sense of guilt** contrite, penitent, remorseful
**affected by disorder of the bile** bilious
**affected by emotion rather than reason** emotional, sentimental
**affected by tides** tidal
**affected by vehement emotion** passionate
**affected dandy** fop
**affectedly artistic** arty
**affectedly bashful** coy, demure
**affectedly coy** bashful, demure
**affectedly dainty** quaint, twee
**affectedly demure** bashful, coy
**affectedly modest** demure
**affectedly playful** arch, frisky, jolly, roguish, sportive
**affectedly proper** prim
**affectedly quaint** dainty, twee
**affectedly stylish** genteel, suave
**affected piety** cant
**affected smile** grimace, smirk
**affected with concussion** concussed
**affected with itch** scabious
**affected with scurvy** scorbutic
**affect harshly** rasp
**affecting** altering, assuming, changing, concerning, contriving, feigning, imitating, influencing, interesting, involving, modifying, moving, pathetic, pitiable, pitiful, poignant, pretending, regarding, sad(dening), shamming, simulating, swaying, touching, transforming
**affecting an individual** personal
**affecting great refinement** superfine
**affecting many** epidemic, plague, ubiquitous, universal
**affecting many in the community** epidemic
**affecting the hip** sciatic
**affection** adoration, attachment, bias, care, desire, devotion, emotion, endearment, esteem, feeling, fondness, friendliness, friendship, heart, inclination, infatuation, kindness, liking, love, partiality, passion, regard, sentiment, solicitude, tendency, tenderness, warmth
**affectionate** amiable, amorous, attached, cajoling, caressive, caring, coaxing, cordial, cuddlesome, devoted, doting, fervent, fond, friendly, kind, loving, nice,

responsive, sweet, tender, warm, warm-hearted, winning
**affectionate gesture** embrace, hug, kiss, pat, smile
**affectionate peck** kiss
**affectionate regard** fondness
**affectionate utterance** endearment
**affectionate word** angel, bokkie, darling, dearest, duckie, endearment, moppet, pet, poppet, precious, skat, sweetheart
**affect mutually** interact
**affect supernaturally** inspire
**affect with extreme folly** beguile, infatuate
**affect with feeling of dread** awe
**affect with pity** touch
**affect with strong disgust** repel, revolt
**afferent** centripetal
**affiance** betroth, engage, espouse, marry, pledge
**affidavit** affirmation, attestation, avowal, deposition, evidence, oath, pledge, statement, submission, testimony, voucher, witness
**affinity** affection, agreement, alliance, analogy, attraction, beau, conformity, connection, correlation, flame, homogeneity, homology, inamorata, inamorato, inclination, kinship, leaning, likeness, lover, proclivity, propensity, rapport, suitor, sweetheart, symmetry, sympathy
**affirm** advance, assert, asseverate, assure, attest, aver, avow, certify, challenge, claim, declare, defy, depose, endorse, express, maintain, posit, proclaim, profess, ratify, remark, represent, request, say, speak, stake, state, submit, swear, testify, urge, voice, vow
**affirmative** agreeing, approving, ay(e), confirming, consenting, favourable, positive, yes
**affirmative answer** all right, ay(e), yes
**affirmative response to invitation** acceptance
**affirmative vote** ay(e), yea, yes
**affirming the truth of** attesting
**affirm truth of** attest, testify, vouch, warrant
**affirm with solemnity** asseverate
**affix** add(endum), addition, adjoin, adjunct, ally, anchor, annex, append(age), appendix, attach(ment), augmentation, bind, bolt, brand, chain, combine, connect, fasten, fix, glue, grip, impress, join, label, link, lock, nail, paste, pin, postscript, prefix, seal, secure, staple, suffix, supplement, tab, tack, tag, tie, unite

**affix asterisk** star
**affix name** sign
**affix postage** stamp
**affix signature** sign
**affix symbol** seal
**afflation** afflatus, aspiration, inspiration
**afflatus** afflation, aspiration, fire, genius, inspiration, revelation, theopneusty
**afflict** ail, beset, burden, distress, grieve, harass, hurt, oppress, pain, plague, trouble, try, wound
**afflicted by nightmares** hagridden
**afflict forcibly** beat, pummel, smite, strike
**afflicting** burdening, distressing, grieving, harassing, hurting, oppressing, painful, paining, plaguing, troubling, trying, wounding
**affliction** adversity, cross, curse, depression, disease, distress, grief, misery, ordeal, plague, trial, woe
**afflict with ennui** smitten
**affluence** abundance, bounty, cornucopia, fortune, fullness, money, opulence, plenitude, plenty, profusion, property, prosperity, resources, riches, richness, superfluity, surfeit, wealth
**affluent** abounding, abundant, copious, plenteous, plentiful, rich, teeming, tributary, wealthy
**afford** bear, chance, furnish, offer, produce, provide, render, stand, supply, support, sustain, yield
**afford aid** assist, help, support
**afford enjoyment** entertain, please
**affording aid** assisting, helpful, supportive
**affording grounds for legal action** actionable
**affording legal redress** actionable
**affording passage for ships** navigable
**afford pleasure** delight, please
**affray** battle, brawl, contest, disturbance, fight, mêlée, quarrel, tumult, uprising
**affront** abuse, contumely, degradation, discountenance, disgrace, disrespect, impertinence, indignity, injury, insult, offence, offend, outrage, scorn, shame, slight
**Afghan money** abbassi, afghani, amania
**Afghan mountains** Hindukush
**Afghan prince** ameer, amir, emir
**Afghan rug** blanket, cover, coverlet
**Afghan ruler** ameer, amir, emir
**Afghan title** khan
**Afghan tribe** Safi, Ulus
**afire** ablaze, aglow, alight, blazing, burning, excited, fiery, flaming

**aflame** ablaze, afire, alight, blazing, burning, fiery, flaming, flaring, ignited, lighted, lit
**afoot** about, afloat, astir, begun, brewing, circulating, current, happening, occurring, started
**aforesaid** above-mentioned, aforementioned, antecedent, ditto, earlier, former, preceding, previous, prior, same
**aforesaid thing** ditto
**aforetime** formerly
**afraid** alarmed, anxious, apprehensive, cowardly, disquieted, distrustful, faint-hearted, fearful, frightened, hesitant, intimidated, nervous, penitent, reluctant, remorseful, scared, shocked, sorry, suspicious, tense, tentative, terrified, timid, timorous, tremulous, uneasy, unhappy
**afresh** again, anew, bis, encore, freshly, newly, over
**Africa, India and South America when still joined** Gondwana(land)
**African abode** kraal
**African adjutant bird** marabou
**African anteater** aardvark, pangolin
**African antelope** addax, blesbok, bongo, duiker, eland, gazelle, gemsbok, gnu, grysbok, impala, klipspringer, kudu, lechwe, nyala, oribi, oryx, sitatunga, suni, topi
**African ape** chimp(anzee), gorilla
**African bird** ostrich, t(o)uraco
**African blood-sucking fly** tsetse
**African camp** boma, laager
**African cat** cheetah, leopard, lion
**African charm** greegree, grigri, gris-gris
**African civet** genet, meerkat
**African clawed toad** xenopus
**African cloth measure** jacktan
**African country** Angola, Burkina Faso, Ethiopia, Kenya, Lesotho, Libya, Malawi, Morocco, Mozambique, Namibia, South Africa, Swaziland, Tanzania, Zambia, Zimbabwe
**African cuckoo** t(o)uraco
**African currency** akey, cent, kwacha, kwanza, lilangeni, metical, pesa, pula, rand, shilling
**African desert** Erg, Gobi, Kalahari, Namib, Sahara
**African disease carrier** mosquito, tsetse-fly
**African dry hot wind** berg wind, sirocco
**African equine** quagga, zebra
**African expedition** safari, trek
**African eye worm** loa
**African fly** kivu, tsetse
**African fox** fennec

**African gazelle** admi, ariel, cora, dama, korin, mhorr, mohr
**African grass** millet
**African grassland** veld(t)
**African hartebeest** tora
**African hemp** ife, sisal
**African hornbill** tock
**African hunting expedition** safari
**African javelin** assegai
**African knife** panga
**African lake** Chad, Kariba, Malawi, Nyasa, St Lucia, Tana, Tanganyika, Turkana, Victoria
**African language** Afrikaans, Nguni, Pedi, Sesotho, Setswana, Swahili, Tsonga, Xhosa, Zulu
**African lemur** galago
**African lizard** gecko, skink
**African lynx** caracal
**African mammal** camel, dassie, elephant, hippo(potamus), hyena, jackal, okapi, rhino(ceros), warthog
**African millet beer** pombe
**African monkey** blue, colobus, grivet, hussar, mona, velvet
**African mud house** tembe
**African plant** aloe
**African reed instrument** gora
**African republic** Algeria, Angola, Benin, Botswana, Burundi, Cameroon, Chad, Congo, Djibouti, Egypt, Equatorial Guinea, Gabon, Gambia, Ghana, Guinea, Guinea-Bissau, Ivory Coast, Kenya, Liberia, Madagascar, Malawi, Mauritania, Mozambique, Niger, Nigeria, Rwanda, Sao Tomé and Príncipe, Senegal, Sierra Leone, Somalia, South Africa, Sudan, Tanzania, Togo, Tunisia, Uganda, Zaïre, Zambia, Zimbabwe
**African river** Blue Nile, Calueque, Limpopo, Niger, Nile, Orange, Vaal, White Nile, Zambezi
**African ruminant** okapi
**African seaport** Beira, Cape Town, Dakar, Dar es Salaam, Durban, Mombasa, Port Elizabeth, Tunis, Walvis Bay
**African skunk** mongoose, polecat, zoril(la), zorille
**African spear** assegai
**African state** Algeria, Angola, Botswana, Cameroon, Chad, Congo, Egypt, Ethiopia, Gabon, Ghana, Guinea, Kenya, Lesotho, Liberia, Libya, Mali, Mauritania, Mozambique, Namibia, Niger, Nigeria, South Africa, Sudan, Tanzania, Zaïre, Zambia, Zimbabwe
**African stork** marabou
**African tableland** Kar(r)oo

**African talisman** greegree, grigri, gris-gris
**African title** sidi
**African tool-like machete** panga
**African tree** baobab, cola, shea
**African tribe** Hutu, Kikuyu, Maasai, Mashona, Matabele, Sotho, Swazi, Tswana, Xhosa, Zulu
**African tribesman's skin apron** beshu
**African village** boma, kraal, stat
**African water antelope** kob
**African wildcat** serval
**African wind** berg wind, sirocco, south-easter, suid-ooster
**African wood** avodire, ebony, embuia, pine, stinkwood, tamboti, yellow-wood
**Africa orchid** disa
**Afrikaans author** Breytenbach, Eitemal, Leroux, MER, Murray, Nortje, Rabie, Schoeman, Sita, Van den Bergh, Van Wyk Louw, Venter
**Afrikaans bloke** ou
**Afrikaans-speaking South African** Afrikaner
**Afrikaans uncle** oom
**aft** aback, abaft, astern, behind, near, rear, rearward, stern, sternwards, tailend
**after** back, behind, dessert, following, later, rear, subsequently
**after a fashion** moderately, somehow
**after all** anyway, eventually, however, nevertheless, ultimately
**after all others** hindmost, last
**after awhile** anon, later, shortly, soon
**after charges** net
**after corner of a sail** clew
**after cost** net(t), profit
**after dark** night
**after darkness, light** post tenebras lux (L)
**after death** post obitum (L), post-mortem
**after deductions** net, nett, profit
**after-dinner candy** mint
**after-effects caused by excess of alcohol** hangover
**after expenses** net, nett, profit
**aftermath** after-effects, afterclap, consequences, development, effect, end, issue, repercussion, results, rowen, upshot, wake
**after me the deluge** après moi le déluge (F)
**after midday** afternoon
**aftermost corner of stay sail** clew
**afternoon meal** tea
**afternoon nap** siesta
**afternoon performance in theatre** matinée
**afternoon reception** tea

**afternoon rest** siesta
**afternoon show** matinée
**afternoon snack** tea
**afternoon social** tea
**after one's own heart** desirable, pleasing
**after-part of a ship** stern
**after-part of a ship's keel** skag, skeg
**after school** extramural
**after-song** epode
**after the deed is done** ex post facto
**after the due time** late
**after the expected time** late
**after the manner of man** humanly
**after this** afterwards, hereafter, hereupon
**afterwards** after(ward), eft, later, next, posteriorly, subsequently, thereafter, ultimately
**aft of the stern of a vessel** astern
**again** additionally, afresh, also, also, anew, besides, bis, conversely, da capo (I), de novo (L), ditto, encore, further, furthermore, however, iterum (L), more, moreover, often, over, re-, recurrently, repeat, repeatedly, yet
**again and again** frequently, habitually, often, recurrently, repeatedly
**again in German** über, wieder
**again put into another language** retranslate
**against** across, anti-, beside, cata-, contra-, counter, facing, fronting, into, naes, opposing, para-, resisting, to, upon, versus
**against the current** upstream
**against the law** delinquent, illegal, illicit
**against the law of nations** contra jus gentium (L)
**against the officers of a disciplined body** mutiny
**against the world** contra mundum (L)
**against which it is useless to struggle** ineluctable
**agalloch** aloeswood, eaglewood
**agamic** asexual
**agamogony** schizogony
**agape** aghast, ajar, amazed, astonished, astounded, awestruck, shock, dismayed, dumbfounded, entranced, extended, gaping, open, open-mouthed, oscitant, overwhelmed, revealed, surprised, thunderstruck, unclosed, uncovered, unfastened, unfurled, unlocked, unsealed, wonderstruck, yawning
**Agape** charity, Christian, love(-feast)
**agaric** mushroom
**agate used in making small cameos** onyx
**agave** aloe, amhole, datil, maguey, mescal, pite

**agave fibre** istle, pita, sisal
**agave plant** sisal, ti
**age** (a)eon, century, chiliad, cycle, date, decade, duration, epoch, era, generation, life, lifetime, mature, millenium, period, ripen, season, span, time, year
**aged** advanced, ancient, anile, antiquated, antique, decrepit, deteriorated, elderly, gray, grey(headed), hoary, mature, mellow, old(en), ripe, seasoned, senescent, senile, time-worn, venerable
**aged rustic** gaffer
**agee** ajar, ajee, askew, awry, crooked
**age group** generation, peer
**ageing** declining, deteriorating, maturing, mellowing, ripening, senescent
**ageless** abiding, classic, deathless, enduring, eternal, immortal, lasting, timeless, undying
**agency** action, activity, bureau, business, company, concern, corporation, department, dispatch, enactment, execution, firm, influence, institution, means, medium, office, organisation, performance, potency, practice
**agency of vengeance** nemesis
**agency producing torsion** torque
**agenda** agendum, calendar, diary, docket, list, plan, program, programme, roster, schedule, timetable
**agenesis** impotence, sterility
**agent** actor, advocate, agency, broker, cause, channel, commissioner, consignee, delegate, deputy, doer, emissary, envoy, executor, factor, force, functionary, go-between, instrument, intermediary, means, middleman, mover, negotiator, operative, operator, performer, power, promoter, proxy, representation, rep(resentative), spy, substitute, worker
**agent of relief** mitigator
**agent provocateur** agitator
**agent that buys and sells shares in companies** stockbroker
**agent that causes disease** pathogen
**agent that causes vomiting** emetic
**agent that increases the flow of urine** diuretic
**agent that induces insomnia** agrypnotic
**agent used in treating hides** tannin
**age of sweetness** sixteen
**age of the moon** epact
**age of the universe** (a)eon

**age of universe** (a)eon
**ager** seasoner
**aggrandise** advance, amass, amplify, augment, dignify, enlarge, escalate, increase, intensify, magnify, multiply, promote, supplement, upgrade, worship
**aggravate** anger, deepen, embitter, envenom, exacerbate, heighten, incense, increase, intensify, irk, irritate, nettle, raise, rankle, vex, worsen
**aggravation** exaggeration, exasperation, increase, inflaming, irksomeness, irritation, worsening
**aggregate** accumulate, added, amass, assemblage, assemble, collective, combined, complete, corporate, gross, sum, total
**aggregate fruit** etaerio
**aggregate of votes** poll
**aggregation of bubbles** froth
**aggregation of people** crowd, mass, mob, tribe
**aggressive** assaulting, assertive, attacking, bellicose, belligerent, bold, combative, contentious, destructive, determined, dynamic, energetic, exuberant, feisty, forceful, hostile, insistent, invasive, litigious, militant, offensive, peremptory, pugnacious, pushing, quarrelsome, touchy, truculent, vigorous, warlike, warmongering, zealous
**aggressive behaviour** aggro
**aggressive conceit** arrogance
**aggressive driver** road-hog
**aggressively assertive** adamant, arrogant
**aggressively haughty** arrogant
**aggressively male** macho
**aggressiveness** belligerence, destructiveness, offensiveness, pugnaciousness, quarrelsomeness
**aggressive newcomer** upstart
**aggrieve** afflict, agonise, annoy, disquiet, distress, grieve, hurt, pain, sadden, sting, torment, torture, upset, vex, worry, wound
**aghast** afraid, amazed, appalled, astonished, astounded, horrified, shocked, startled, stunned
**agile** brisk, fleet, light, limber, lissom(e), lively, nimble, quick, sprightly, spry, supple
**agile girl** yanker
**agility** activity, activity, acumen, alacrity, alertness, briskness, co-ordination, dext(e)rousness, discernment, fleetness, litheness, nimbleness, quickness, smartness, spryness, wit

**agiotage** stock-jobbing
**agitate** controvert, debate, discuss, dispute, disturb, excite, ferment, fluster, jar, move, perturb, rouse, ruffle, stir, toss, upset, worry
**agitatedly** agitato
**agitates cream in churn** dasher
**agitate with fear** alarm
**agitate with spoon** stir
**agitation** alarm, arousal, churning, commotion, confusion, debate, discussion, dispute, disquiet, disturbance, emotion, excitation, excitement, fever, shake, stir, tossing, tumult, turbulence, turmoil, uneasiness, upheaval
**agitator** adversary, antagonist, assailant, avenger, beater, challenger, demagogue, demonstrator, firebrand, inciter, instigator, mutineer, opponent, opposer, provoker, rabble-rouser, radical, rebel, revolutionary, ringleader, rival, ruffian, stirrer, traitor, troublemaker, wrecker
**agley** aglee, askew, awry
**aglitter** glittering, sparkling
**aglow** flushed, glow, luminescent, luminous, shining, shiny
**agnail** hangnail
**agname** agnomen, alias, epithet, nickname, pseudonym
**agnate** akin, allied, related
**Agni's twin** Indra
**agnomen** agname, nickname
**agnostic** cynic, disbeliever, doubter, ignorant, nescient, non-believer, sceptic, unbeliever
**ago** past, since
**agog** avid, curious, eager, excited, expectant, impatient, keen
**agonise** disturb, fret, hurt, martyr, pain, strain, strive, suffer, toil, torture, wrestle, writhe
**agonistic** combative, competitive, polemical, strained
**agony** anguish, bliss, conflict, convulsion, distress, ecstasy, fight, hurt, misery, pain, pangs, paroxysm, rapture, struggle, suffering, torment, tribulation
**agouti** rodent
**agrarian** agrestic, agricultural, agronomic, agronomical, bucolic, country, feral, field, geoponic, georgic, landed, nonurban, pastoral, pedological, pr(a)edial, real, rural, rustic, uncultivated, undomesticated, untamed, wild
**Agra's monument** Taj Mahal
**agree** accede, accord, acknowledge, acquiesce, admit, admit, allow,

assent, coincide, combine, comply, compromise, concede, concur, conform, consent, correspond, fit, grant, harmonise, match, permit, settle, suit, tally, unite, yield
**agreeable** acceptable, amenable, amiable, amicable, appealing, appropriate, apt, attractive, complying, congenial, consenting, consistent, cordial, delectable, delicious, delightful, elegant, enjoyable, fitting, friendly, genial, gentle, good, graceful, gracious, gratifying, lekker, likeable, nice, palatable, pleasant, pleasing, pleasurable, proper, responsive, satisfying, seemly, soothing, suitable, sympathetic, tasty, well-disposed, willing, yielding
**agreeable compliance** assent
**agreeable odour** aroma, fragrance
**agreeable situation** pleasure
**agreeable smell** aroma, fragrance
**agreeable to eat** appetising, delicious, palatable, tasty
**agreeable word** ay(e), yes
**agreeably** acceptably, delightfully, enjoyably, gratifyingly, nicely, pleasantly, pleasingly, pleasurably, satisfyingly
**agreeably pungent** piquant
**agreed** acceded, acquiesced, admitted, allowed, assented, complied, conceded, concurred, consented, d'accord (F), engaged, granted, permitted, settled, tallied
**agreed ceasefire** truce
**agree in** accept
**agreeing** acceding, according, acquiescing, admitting, allowing, answering, assenting, chiming, coinciding, complying, conceding, concurring, conforming, consenting, corresponding, engaging, fitting, granting, harmonising, matching, permitting, settling, squaring, suiting, tallying
**agreeing in every detail** identical
**agree in opinion** concur
**agree in silence** acquiesce
**agreement** accord(ance), analogy, arrangement, assent, bargain, compact, compatibility, compliance, concord(ance), concordat, consensus, contract, covenant, deal, engagement, fitment, harmony, OK, okay, oneness, pact, promise, settlement, similarity, transaction, treaty, unanimity, understanding, uniformity, union, word
**agreement between states at war** compact, entente, treaty

**agreement in a design** concert
**agreement in opinion** consensus
**agreement made** concordat
**agree to** arrange, assent, validate
**agree to do something** undertake
**agree to marry** affiance, betroth, engage, espouse
**agree to receive** accept
**agree to the truth of** acknowledge, admit, concede
**agree upon** set
**agree with** accord, grant, side, suit
**agrestic** country, nonurban, rural, rustic, uncouth, unpolished
**agricultural establishment** farm
**agricultural holding** farm
**agricultural implement** harrow, hoe, mower, plough, reaper
**agricultural tool** disk, hoe, mattock, plough
**agricultural worker** farmer, labourer, peasant
**agriculture** agronomy, cropping, cultivation, culture, farming, gardening, geoponics, husbandry, hydroponics, pasturage, pedology, tillage, viticulture
**agriculturist** farmer, gardener
**agronomy** agriculture, cultivation, farming, husbandry
**aground** abandoned, ashore, beached, deserted, foundered, foundering, grounded, shipwrecked, stranded, stuck, wrecked
**agressive and discourteous** truculent
**ague** chill, cold, fever, rigor, shakes, shivering, trembling
**ague tree** sassafras
**ahead** advanced, along, before, forward, leading, on, onward(s), superior, winning
**ahead of** before, beyond, outranking, outstripping
**ahead of the times** advanced, avant-garde
**ahead of time** avant-garde, beforehand, beforetime, early, fast
**aid** abet, aide, assist, assistance, assistant, befriend, benefit, charity, encourage(ment), facilitate, favour, help(er), patronage, promote, relief, relieve, second, servant, serve, service, spell, subsidise, subsidy, succour, support(er), sustain, urge
**aid criminal act** abet
**aide** adjutant, assistant, helper, servant, supporter
**aide-de-camp** army officer, captain, commander, ensign, general, lieutenant, marshal
**aid given to starving people** famine relief

**aid illegally** abet
**aiding in crime** abetting
**aiding one's memory** mnemonic
**aiding sight** optical
**aiding the memory** mnemonic
**aid in solving** clue
**aid in wrongdoing** abet
**aid of painter** brush, easel, mahlstick, maulstick, palette
**aid to coiffure** curlers, gel, hairpin, mousse, rollers
**aid to detection** clue
**aid to remembering** memorandum, mnemonic
**aid to ships** radar, sonar
**aigret** egret, plume
**ail** afflict, bother, distress, distress, hurt, ill, indisposition, oppress, sicken, sick(ness), suffer, trouble, unwell, worry
**ailing** ill, indisposed, sick, unwell
**ailment** affliction, attack, bug, complaint, condition, defect, disability, disease, disorder, disquiet, ferment, handicap, ill(ness), impairment, indisposition, infection, infirmity, malady, malaise, sickness, sustentation, trouble, unrest, upset, weakness
**ailment of horses** colic, papies
**aim** aspiration, aspire, direct, direction, dream, end, goal, intend, intent(ion), meaning, object(ive), point, position, proclivity, purport, purpose, sight(ing), significance, strive, try
**aim at** aspire, bid, desire, dream, drive, essay, intend, point, pursue
**aim at high things** aspire, strive
**aim directly** pointblank
**aimed at peace** irenic(al)
**aim high** aspire
**aiming aid** sight
**aiming at** to
**aimless** adrift, awry, casual, chaotic, confused, dishevelled, displaced, haphazard, incoherent, irregular, meaningless, orderless, purposeless, unarranged, uncertain, untidy, useless
**aimless chatter** natter
**aimless person** drifter
**aimless verbose talk** waffle
**aimless wanderer** drifter, meanderer, roamer, vagabond
**air** aer, aero-, appearance, aspect, atmosphere, attitude, aura, bearing, breath, breeze, broadcast, carriage, circulation, conduct, demeanour, display, draught, expose, impression, look, manner, melody, mien, mood, proclaim, publication,

reveal, sky, tune, utter, ventilate, ventilation, voice, waft, wind
**air apparatus** fan, ventilator
**air ball** bubble
**air base in Greenland** Thule
**airborne** aerobatic, alar, ascending, bounce, flying, springed, winged
**airborne microbe** aerobe
**airbrushing** spraypainting
**air component** argon, carbon, nitrogen, oxygen
**air cooler** fan
**aircraft** aeroplane, airliner, balloon, biplane, glider, helicopter, jet, monoplane, plane
**aircraft body** fuselage
**aircraft-carrier** flattop, wasp
**aircraft control through systems** fly-by-wire
**aircraft flap** aileron
**aircraft flight record** log
**aircraft location device** radar
**aircraftman** erk
**aircraft shed** hangar
**aircraft shelter** hangar
**aircraft station** aerodrome, airport, airstrip
**aircraft steadier** stabiliser
**aircraft terminal** airport
**aircraft wing fin** aerofoil
**aircraft wing flap** aileron
**aircraft with no engine** glider
**aircraft with two sets of wings** biplane
**air current** breeze, draught, thermal, wind
**air-driven** pneumatic
**air drop** jump, parachute
**Airedale dog** terrier
**airfield** aerodrome, airport, airstrip
**air-filled cavity** sinus
**air-filled liquid film** bubble
**air force** flight, group, pressure, squadron, troops, wing
**air force unit** squadron
**air freshener** deodorant
**airgun** toy
**airgun ammunition** pellet
**air hero** ace
**air-hole** vent
**air in brisk motion** gust, hurricane, tornado, wind
**airing** aerating, aeration, circulating, circulation, communicating, declaring, disclosing, display(ing), disseminating, dissemination, divulging, drying, excursion, exhibiting, exposing, exposure, expression, freshening, jaunt, outing, proclaiming, promenade, publicity, revealing, stroll, telling, utterance, uttering, vent(ilating), ventilation, venting, voicing, walk

**air inlet** intake
**air in motion** breeze, current, draught, gust, wind
**air in narrow inlet** ria
**airless** breathless, close, heavy, muggy, oppressive, stale, stuffy, sultry, unventilated
**airless space** vacuum, void
**air letter** aerogram
**air-like fluid** gas
**airline** Air France, British Airways, Comair, Delta, ELAL, Iberia, Lufthansa, Luxavia, SAA, Sabena
**airline association** IATA
**airline employee** hostess, pilot, steward(ess)
**airman** pilot, flier, aviator
**airman's ejecting apparatus** parachute
**air-mixed** aerated
**air movement** draught
**air obscured by fog** murk
**air- or serum-filled bulge** blister
**air out** ventilate
**air-passage** duct, flue, vent
**air-passage from throat to lungs** trachea, windpipe
**air pirate** hijacker
**air plant** floppers
**airport** airfield, aerodrome, DF Malan, Gatwick, Heathrow, Jan Smuts, Lod, Orly
**airport controller's device** radar
**airport exit to aircraft** gate
**airport marker** pylon
**airport runway** tarmac
**airport south of Paris** Orly
**air pressure meter** barometer
**air race marker** pylon
**air-raid alarm** siren
**air-raid shelter** bunker
**air-raid signal** alert, siren
**air-raid warning** siren
**airship** blimp, dirigible, zeppelin
**air spirit** Ariel, sylph
**air sportsman** skydiver
**air stewardess** hostess
**airtight** firm, flawless, foolproof, hermetic, impregnable, invulnerable, sound, unassailable, watertight
**air transport in fairy tales** magic carpet
**air vehicle** balloon, glider, kite, plane
**air voyage** flight, hop
**airy** breezy, fanciful, light, nonchalant, spacious
**aisle** alley, ambulatory, cloister, corridor, gangway, lane, passage, passageway, path, walkway, way
**aisle between seats** gangway,
**ait** eyot, holm(e), isle(t)
**ajar** agape, extended, gaping, open, revealed, unclosed, uncovered,

unfastened, unfurled, unlocked, unsealed, yawning
**ajee** agee, ajar, awry, crooked
**ajonjoli** sesame
**akin** affiliated, alike, allied, analogous, cognate, comparable, congenial, connected, consonant, corresponding, like, parallel, related, similar
**akin by blood** related
**akin to** related
**akin to guanaco** llama
**akin to vibrato** tremolo
**alack** alas
**alacrity** alertness, animation, avidity, briskness, celerity, cheerfulness, eagerness, ebullience, gaiety, glee, go, haste, liveliness, mirth, promptitude, promptness, quickness, speed, vigour, vim, vivacity, zeal
**Aladdin's lamp sprite** genie
**Aladdin's possession** lamp
**Aladdin's spirit** genie, jinni
**à la mode** chic, craze, fashionable, in, rage, smart, stylish
**alar** pteric, winged, winglike
**alarm** agitate, alarm-bell, alert, anxiety, appal, apprehension, arouse, bell, consternation, danger, daunt, dismay, distress, fear, fright(en), horror, nervousness, panic, scare, shock, signal, siren, startle, terrify, terror(ise), tocsin, trepidation, unease, uneasiness, unnerve, warn(ing)
**alarm bell** klaxon, tocsin
**alarm clock** rouser
**alarmed agitation** trepidation
**alarmist** panicmonger, scaremonger
**alarm signal** siren, tocsin
**alarm sound** siren
**alarm system** bug
**alarm whistle** siren
**alas!** ach, alack, dear, och, well, welladay
**Alaskan bay** Prudhoe
**Alaskan bear** Kodiak
**Alaskan-Canadian highway** Alcan
**Alaskan cape** Nome
**Alaskan district** Sitka
**Alaskan garment** parka
**Alaskan glacier** Muir
**Alaskan Indian** Aleut, Sitka
**Alaskan island** Adak, Atka, Attu, Kodiak, Pribilof, Prince of Wales
**Alaskan islands** Aleutians
**Alaskan mountain pass** Chilkoot
**Alaskan native** Aleut
**Alaskan peninsula** Seward, Unga
**Alaskan sable** raccoon, skunk
**Alaskan state flower** forget-me-not
**Alaskan state tree** sitka, spruce

**alate** winged
**albacore** tuna, tunny
**Albanian currency** grosh, lek, qint, qintary
**Albanian dialect** Cham, Gheg, Gheghish, Tosk
**Albanian money** lek, qindar, qintar
**Albanian ruler** mpret
**Albanian soldier** palikar
**albatross** sea bird
**albeit** although, nevertheless, nonetheless, notwithstanding, though, whereas, while
**album** photo collection, record, scrapbook
**albumin glue** glair
**albuminous substance in blood just after digestion** pabulin
**Alcazar of the Moorish kings at Granada** Alhambra
**alchemist's furnace** athanor, solutary
**alchemist's stone** elixir
**alcheringa** alchera
**alcohol** booze, ethanol, intoxicant, liquor
**alcohol base** booze, cocktail, cognac, ethyl, highball, martini, mead, sherry
**alcohol-burning furnace** etna
**alcoholic** boozer, drunkard, inebriant, inebriate, intoxicant, sot, spirituous, swillpot, tippler, toper
**alcoholic apple drink** cider
**alcoholic beverage** ale, beer, booze, brandy, cocktail, cognac, gin, highball, martini, mead, posset, rum, scotch, sherry, whisky, wine
**alcoholic drink** cocktail, flip, highball, julep, libation, martini, sling, sour, stinger, toddy
**alcoholic drink as appetiser** aperitif
**alcoholic drink made from honey** mead
**alcoholic drink taken before meals** aperitif
**alcoholic preparation** liqueur
**alcoholic tot** dram
**alcoholism** dipsomania
**alcohol radical** amyl, ethyl
**alcohol standard** proof
**alcove** apse, ark, bay, booth, cave, cavity, cell, conservatory, corner, cove, covert, cubbyhole, cubicle, grotto, haven, indentation, niche, nook, recess, sanctuary, shelter
**alcove with a raised bench seat** exedra
**aldehyde used in perfume** citral
**ale** beer, brew
**alec** fool
**alee** shelterward
**ale house** pub
**ale keg** beer barrel

**alembicated** over-refined, precious
**ale mug** stein, toby
**alert** active, agile, alarm, attentive, awake, aware, brisk, careful, caution, cautious, circumspect, forewarn, heedful, inform, intelligent, lively, nimble, notify, observant, perceptive, prepared, prompt, quick, ready, signal, siren, spirited, vigilant, wariness, warn(ing), wary, watchful, wide-awake
**alert watchman** Argus
**Aleutian island** Adak, Atka, Attu
**ale vinegar** alegar
**Alexander's horse** Bucephalus
**Alexander's successors** Diadochi
**alexia** word-blindness
**alfalfa** fodder, lucerne
**Alfonso's queen** Ena
**alfresco diner** picnicker
**algae** thallophyte
**algarroba** carob
**algebraic computer language** ALGOL
**algebraic rule** theorem
**algebraic symbol** exponent
**Algerian cavalryman in the French army** spahi
**Algerian commune** setif
**Algerian currency** dinar
**Algerian dry measure** tarri
**Algerian governor** dey
**Algerian grass** esparto
**Algerian hill** tell
**Algerian holy man** marabout
**Algerian infantryman in the French army** Zouave
**Algerian monastery** ribat
**Algerian money** dinar
**Algerian native quarters** casbah, kasbah
**Algerian plateau** Ahaggar
**Algerian port** Oran
**Algerian ruler** bey, dey
**Algerian seaport** Bone, Oran
**Algerian ship** xebec, zebeck
**Algerian terrorists** OAS
**Algerian weight** rotl
**Algeria's former name** Numidia
**algolagnist** sadist
**algology** botany
**alias** anonym, formerly, pen-name, previously, pseudonym
**Ali Baba's pass words** open sesame
**alibi** apology, argument, defence, excuse, explanation, justification, plea, pretext, proof, reason, story, vindication, witness
**alible** nourishing, nutritious, nutritive
**alien** adverse, different, differing, exotic, foreign(er), hostile, immigrant, inappropriate, incompatible, opposed, outlandish, outsider, remote, repugnant, strange(r), Uitlander, unallied, unconnected, unfamiliar
**alienate** abandon, abjure, antagonise, disaffect, discharge, disclaim, disinherit, dismiss, disown, ditch, divert, divorce, estrange, renounce, revoke, separate, transfer, waive, wean, withdraw
**alienation** diversion, divorce, estrangement, indifference, rupture, transfer, withdrawal
**alien before Boer War** Uitlander
**alien in Mexico** gringo
**alien raider** invader, stranger
**alight** ablaze, aglow, blazing, bright, brilliant, burning, descend, disembark, dismount, fall, fiery, flaming, flaring, ignited, illuminated, land, light(ed), lit, lodge, perch, radiant, settle, settle, shining
**align** adjust, aline, arrange, array, assemble, calibrate, catalogue, class(ify), collect, collinate, conduct, control, deploy, dispose, even, gather, group, manage, marshal, muster, neaten, order, organise, orient, parallel, range, rank, rectify, regulate, straighten, systematise, tabulate, tidy
**align oneself** ally, associate, enlist, federate, join, league, membership, subscribe
**alike** equal, equivalent, identical, same, similar, similarly, uniform
**alike word** synonym
**aliment** alimentation, alimony, allowance, cheer, comestibles, eatables, fare, flesh, food, forage, keep, livelihood, living, meat, nourishment, nurture, nutriment, pabulum, pasturage, pasture, provender, provisions, rations, subsistence, support, sustenance, sustenation, upkeep, viands, victuals, vittles
**alimentary canal** gut
**alimentation** food, maintenance, nourishment, nutriment, support, sustenance
**alimony** aliment, allowance, maintenance, means, support, sustenance, sustenation
**a little** slightly
**alive** active, alert, animate, aswarm, breathing, existing, functioning, lively, living, swarming
**alive to** aware
**alive with** abundant, crammed, crowded, rich, stuffed, swarming, teeming
**alkali** soda

**alkaline carbonate** trona
**alkaline cleanser** lye
**alkaline compound** soda
**alkaline mineral** trona
**alkaline solution** lye
**alkaline substance** antacid, lime
**alkaline washing solution** lye
**alkaloid drug used to relieve asthma** ephedrine
**alkaloid in bean** eserin
**alkaloid in tea and coffee** caffein(e)
**alkaloid in tea plant** theine
**alkaloid poison** curare
**alkane** paraffin
**all** alle (G), altogether, any, aw (Sc), both, complete, completely, each, entire, entirely, every(body), everyone, everything, ganz (G), omnis (L), throughout, todo (Sp), total, toto (L), tout (F), tutto (I), whole, wholly
**all along** throughout
**all at once** abruptly, instantaneously, suddenly
**all at the same time** en bloc (F), simultaneously
**allay** alleviate, appease, assuage, blunt, calm, check, compose, diminish, ease, lessen, lull, mitigate, moderate, mollify, pacify, quell, quiet, reduce, relieve, repress, silence, smooth, soften, soothe, still, suppress, temper, tranquillise
**all but** almost, nearly, nigh
**all correct** OK, okay
**all ears** hark, hear, listen
**allegation** accusation, affirmation, assertion, attribution, charge, claim, complaint, declaration, impeachment, imputation, incrimination, indictment, plea, profession, prosecution, recrimination, statement, summons, testimony
**allege** adduce, advance, affirm, ask, assert, asseverate, attest, aver, avow, charge, cite, claim, collect, consider, contend, declare, demand, exact, hold, insist, maintain, need, offer, plead, present, profess, reckon, repute, require, state, submit, suggest, swear, take
**allege confidently** affirm
**alleged** affirmed, asserted, claimed, declared, described, designated, doubtful, dubious, inferred, ostensible, presumed, professed, purported, reputed, said, so-called, stated, supposed, suspect, suspicious
**alleged electric force** elod
**alleged force** od, odyl(e)

**allegiance** constancy, faith, faithfulness, fealty, fidelity, loyalty, patriotism, staunchness, steadfastness, trustiness, truth(fulness)
**allegorical story** parable
**allegory** analogy, apologue, comparison, emblem, fable, fantasy, fiction, illustration, metaphor, myth, parable, simile, story, symbolic, tale
**allegory told to point out a moral** parable
**all-embracing view** panoramic
**allergic to labour** workshy
**alleviate** abate, allay, appease, assuage, console, diminish, ease, lessen, lighten, mitigate, moderate, modify, mollify, palliate, relax, relieve, remedy, remit, smother
**alleviate disease without curing it** palliate
**alleviate distress of mind** anodyne
**alleviate pain** anaesthetise, relieve
**alleviation** amelioration, assuagement, calming, deadening, easing, mitigation, moderation, mollification, palliation, remission, sedation, softening
**alleviation of distress** relief
**alley** aisle, areaway, backstreet, byway, lane, passage, passageway, pathway, road, street, walk
**alley back** slum
**alleyway** alley, backstreet, byway, corridor, footway, lane, mall, passage, passageway, pathway, promenade, road, walk(way)
**all go out** exeunt omnes (L)
**all hail** health, welcome
**alliance** affiliation, assembly, association, bloc, business, coalition, combination, compact, concern, confederation, connection, contract, council, enterprise, faction, federation, guild, league, marriage, pact, parity, partnership, relationship, settlement, syndicate, treaty, union
**alliance between countries** axis, bloc, union
**allied** associated, related
**allied by nature** akin, related
**allied to** next
**allied to camel** llama, oont
**allied to elk** moose
**allied to stoat and ferret** weasel
**alligator** cayman
**alligator or avocado** pear
**alligator pear** aguacate, avocado
**all-important** crucial, essential, magnanimous, vital
**all in** collapsed, exhausted, fatigued, pooped, spent, tired, weary

**all-in-all** altogether, finally, lastly, ultimately
**all inclusive** all-in, comprehensive
**all in one piece** intact
**allium** chive, garlic, leek, onion, shallot
**all knowing** omniscient
**all leave the stage** exeunt omnes (L)
**all-male party** stag
**all muscle** wiry
**allocate** allot, apportion, appropriate, assign, budget, designate, devote, disperse, distribute, earmark, intend, issue, mete, ration, specify
**allocate again** relocate
**all of two** both
**all of us** everybody, we
**allogamy** cross-fertilisation
**allot** allocate, appoint, apportion, assign, bestow, design, designate, dispense, distribute, divide, earmark, give, grant, intend, mete, partition, provide, render, share
**allot afresh** reapportion
**allotment** allocation, allowance, apportionment, appropriation, bequeath, bestow, budget, dispensation, division, dole, donation, farm, grant, land, lot, measure, meed, part, partition, percentage, portion, quota, ration, share, stint, will
**allotted part** cut, portion, quota, ration, share
**allotted place** berth, position, post
**allotted portion** cut, quota, ration, scantling, share
**all-out** complete, determined, exhaustive, full, full-scale, intensive, limit, maximum, optimum, powerful, resolute, thorough, thoroughgoing, total, undivided, unlimited, unrestrained, utmost, vigorous, wholesale
**all over** around, ended, everywhere, finished, omnipresent, ubiquitous
**all over the place** eclectic
**allow** abet, abide, accord, acknowledge, admit, afford, allocate, allot, apportion, approve, assign, authorise, cede, concede, confess, empower, enable, endow, endure, entitle, furnish, grant, let, permit, provide, relinquish, sanction, suffer, supply, tolerate, yield
**allowable** admissible, confessable, endurable, grantable, permissible, sanctionable, sufferable, tolerable
**allowable deviation** leeway
**allowable divergence** lenience, tolerance
**allowable room for movement** leeway
**allowable variation** tolerance

**allowance** acknowledg(e)ment, admission, allotment, authorisation, concession, deduction, discount, grant, leave, licence, permission, permit, ration, rebate, sanction, stipend
**allowance for changes** margin
**allowance for contingency** margin
**allowance for depreciation** agio
**allowance for service** pension, bonus
**allowance for weight** scalage, tare, tret
**allowance of fodder** feed
**allowed deduction** rebate
**allow for** consider, foresee, include
**allow free use of** lease, lend
**allow in** admit
**allowing entry** open
**allowing that** although, if
**allow no choice of action** compel
**allow no peace of mind** irritate, pester, worry
**allow temporary use of** lend
**allow to** let, may
**allow to enter** admit
**allow to flow** pour
**allow too much light, as on film** overexpose
**allow to rest briefly** repose, spell
**allow water to run off** drain
**alloy** adulterate, amalgam(ate), blend, brew, coalesce, combination, combine, composite, composition, compound, concoction, conglomerate, cross, debase, diminish, fuse, fusion, impair, incorporate, intermingle, intermix, join, marry, medley, merge, mingle, mix(ture), mokum, oroide, pewter, steel, stir, synthesis, unify, union, unite, unity
**alloy caster** brassfounder
**alloy for domestic utensils** pewter
**alloy in jewelry** oroide
**alloy like silver** albata
**alloy of copper and tin** bronze
**alloy of copper and zinc** brass, pinchbeck, ormolu
**alloy of domestic utensils** pewter
**alloy of gold and silver** asem, egyp
**alloy of iron** steel
**alloy of lead and tin** terne, calin
**alloy of nickel and silver** alfenide
**alloy of nickel and steel** invar
**alloy of tin** pewter
**alloy of tin and lead** pewter
**alloy of tin and zinc** oroide
**alloy of zinc** spelter
**alloy of zinc and copper** ormolu, pinchbeck
**alloy used for repair** solder
**alloy used in dentistry** amalgam
**alloy used in kitchenware** pewter

**all people** everybody, we
**all possible** every
**all-powerful** omnipotent
**all right** acceptable, adequate, admissible, allowable, approvable, fair, fine, healthy, OK, okay, passable, permissible, safe, satisfactory, secure, sound, standard, unharmed, unimpaired, uninjured, unobjectionable, well, whole
**all set** arranged, completed, ready
**allspice** pimento
**all taken separately** each, individually
**all that makes a thing what it is** essence, gist
**all that matters** everything
**all the go** à la mode, chic, fashionable, modern, modish, stylish, vogue
**all the more so, with even greater reason** a fortiori
**all the people** everyone
**all there** sane
**all the same** anyhow, anyway, immaterial, nevertheless, nonetheless, notwithstanding, quand même (F), regardless
**all the time** always, ceaselessly, constantly, continuously, ever, incessantly, perpetually, throughout
**all the words contained in a language** vocabulary
**all things being equal** draw, equilibrium, equivalent, ideally, tie
**all things considered** altogether
**all thumbs** awkward, butter-fingered, clumsy, inept, maladroit
**all time** eternity, ever, infinite, perpetual
**all together** collectively, en masse, inclusive, tutti
**all two** both
**allude** advert, affirm, assert, communicate, connote, convey, declare, denote, express, hint, imply, import, indicate, infer, insinuate, intend, intimate, involve, mean, mention, refer, represent, signify, spell, suggest
**allude to** mention, refer
**allure** attract, beguile, bewitch, charm, decoy, enchant, enravish, entice, entrance, fascinate, glamour, hypnotise, incite, intrigue, inveigle, mesmerise, persuade, seduce, tantalise, tempt
**alluring** appealing, attractive, beautiful, bewitching, captivating, charming, dazzling, delightful, desirable, elegant, enchanting, entrancing, fascinating, glamorous, glittering, glossy, hypnotic, inviting, irresistible, lovely, magnetic, pleasant, provocative, seductive, smart, specious, tempting, warm
**alluring beauty** glamour
**alluring charm** glamour
**alluring quality** charm
**alluring woman** flirt, houri, Mata Hari, siren, temptress, vamp
**allusion** citation, glance, hint, inference, innuendo, intimation, mention, quotation, reference, suggestion
**alluvial** chalky, clayey, flinty, gravelly, lithic, loamy, pebbly, rocky, stony, territorial
**alluvial clay** adobe
**alluvial deposit** alluvium, cone, delta, drift, fan, geest, mud, placer, silt
**alluvial fan** delta
**alluvial matter** geest
**alluvial river mouth** delta
**all wet** wrong
**all wool** genuine, pure, real
**all wool and a yard wide** constant, genuine, real, sincere, true(-hearted)
**all Xtians** Christendom
**ally** abettor, accessory, accomplice, assistant, associate, bedfellow, collaborator, colleague, combine, confederate, consort, coworker, friend, helper, helpmate, join, leaguer, partner, side-kick, supporter, unify, unite
**alma mater** college, school, university
**almanac** annals, annual, calendar, chronology, clock, ephemeris, register, registry, timekeeper, timer, yearbook
**almandine** garnet, spinel
**almond** amygdala, essence, flavour, nut
**almond confection** marzipan
**almond emulsion** orgeat
**almond flavoured liqueur** ratafia
**almond paste** marzipan
**almond-shaped** amygdaloid
**almond syrup** orgeat
**almoner** accountant, banker, bookkeeper, bursar, consignee, croupier, pawnee, pledgee, purser, receiver, stakeholder, treasurer, trustee
**almonry** bank, bursary, safe, safe-deposit, strong-box, strongroom, treasure-chest, treasury, wallet
**almost** about, anear, approaching, approximately, barely, brink, hardly, incompletely, just, most, near(ing), nearly, nigh, partially, practically, scarcely, slightly, somewhat, toward, verge, virtually, well-nigh, within
**almost accurate** approximate

**almost an island** peninsula
**almost but not really** quasi-
**almost exact** approximate
**almost invisible** star-lit
**almost kin** nearly related
**almost leafless** subnude
**almost not** barely, hardly, scarcely
**almost premature nobleman** earl
**almost transparent** diaphanous
**almost unbelievable** fabulous
**almost without motion** still
**alms** aid, baksheesh, bounty, charity, consideration, deed, dole, favour, goodness, kindness, mercy, relief, sympathy
**alms box** arca, reliquary
**alms dispenser** almoner
**alms house** almonry, asylum, retreat, sanctuary, shelter
**alms man** beggar, pauper
**alnus** alder, birch, tree
**aloe** agave, maguey, pita, tambac
**aloe derivative** aloin
**aloe extract** orcin
**aloe product** aloin
**aloe's wood** agalloch, eaglewood
**aloft** above, ascend, atop, elevate, heavenward, overhead, overlook, overtop, skyward, soar, surmount, up, upward(s)
**alone** apart, desolate, exclusively, friendless, homeless, isolated, kinless, lonely, lonesome, one, only, orphaned, recluse, secluded, separate, single, singular, sole, solitary, solo, solus, unaccompanied, unaided, uninvited, unique, unpopular, unvisited, unwanted
**alone on stage** soliloquy, solo
**along** adjoin, beside, by, connect, contiguous, during, extend, longwise, on(ward), over, scrape, skim, tandem, via, with
**along a line** linear
**alongside** abeam, abreast, along, approximately, aside, beside, broadside, by, close, laterally, near(about), parallel, sidelong, with
**alongside each other and facing in the same direction** abreast
**along the way** en route
**along with** also, and, cum
**aloof** apart, away, chilly, cold, cool, detached, disinterested, distant, forbidding, formal, formal, frosty, haughty, inaccessible, incurious, indifferent, insular, isolated, off(ish), proud, remote, removed, reserved, separately, stand-offish, supercilious, unapproachable, unconcerned, unforthcoming, unfriendly, uninterested, unresponsive, unresponsive, unsocial, unsympathetic
**alopecia** acomia, baldheaded, baldheadedness, baldness, bareness, nudity, tonsure
**alopecoid** foxlike, vulpine
**aloud** accented, audibly, clearly, dictate, distinct(ly), fluent, loudly, noisily, oral, shout, sonant, speak, tonal, vocal
**alow** below, under
**alpaca** fibre, llama, paco, textile, wool
**alpaca like** guanaco
**alpaca relative** llama
**alpargata** espadrille
**alpestrine** subalpine
**alpha and omega** everything
**alphabet** ABC
**alphabet character** letter, rune
**alphabet component** letter
**alphabetical list** index
**alphabetical list of particles** catalogue
**alphabetic character** letter, rune
**alphabetic symbol** letter
**alphabet list** index, catalogue
**alphabet of runes** fithorc, futharc, futhark, futhork
**alphabet register** index
**alphabet unit** letter
**alphabet used for Indian languages** Devanagari
**alphabet used for Russian and Bulgarian** Cyrillic
**alphabet used for Sanskrit** Devanagari, Nagari
**Alpine cry** yodel
**Alpine dog** Saint Bernard
**alpine dress** dirndl
**Alpine flower** edelweiss
**Alpine goat** ibex
**Alpine hut** chalet
**Alpine instrument** alpenhorn, cowbell
**Alpine mountain** Blanc, Eiger
**Alpine mountain goat** ibex
**Alpine or rock plant** saxifrage
**Alpine pass** Cenis, col, Simplon
**Alpine peasant dress** dirndl
**Alpine plant** edelweiss
**Alpine primrose** auricula
**Alpine province** Tyrol
**Alpine river** Rhone
**Alpine shepherd** senn
**Alpine shoes** snowshoes
**Alpine singing** yodelling
**Alpine snow field** firn, névé
**Alpine wind** bora, foehn, föhn
**already** before, earlier, heretofore, now, previously
**Alsace** Elsass (G)
**also** additionally, and, besides, conjointly, ditto, eke, further(more), including, likewise, moreover, plus, too, withal, yet
**also known as** alias
**also-ran** loser, nonentity
**altar** adytum, ara (L), church, mound, penetralia, platform, reliquary, sanctuary, shrine, temple
**altar area of church** apse
**altar boy** acolyte
**altar canopy** ciborium
**altar carpet** pedale
**altar cloth** coster, dossal
**altar hanging** dossal, palla
**altarpiece** ancona, reredos
**altarpiece painting of three panels** triptych
**altar screen** reredos
**altar shelf** gradin(e), retable
**altar side curtain** riddel
**altar slab** mensa
**altar top** fronta, mensa
**altar vessel** chalice, monstrance, paten, pyx
**alter** adapt, adjust, amend, censor, change, convert, correct, differ, diversify, emend, modify, mutate, permute, rectify, reform, remodel, revise, shift, tamper, transfigure, transform, transmute, treat, vary
**alter a sound track** dub
**alter a suit** bushel
**alter by adding colours** variegate
**altercate** argue, bicker, brawl, clash, collide, conflict, debate, differ, disagree, dispute, feud, fight, nag, object, quarrel, remonstrate, spar, spat, squabble, tiff, wrangle
**altercation** affray, argument, brawl, broil, controversy, difference, dispute, divergence, duel, logomachy, mêlée, row, scene, scuffle, sparring, squabble, strife, tumult, variance, wrangle
**alter colour of** dye
**alter course** avert, deflect, deviate, digress, divert, err, swerve, turn, veer
**alter ego** friend, plenipotentiary
**alter fabric colour** dye
**alter in detail** amend
**altering frequently** changeable
**alternate** alter, change, correlative, corresponding, deputy, instead, interchange, intersperse, locum, oscillate, other, periodic, proxy, repeat, reserve, rotate, rotating, serialise, stand-in, substitute, successive, understudy
**alternately** about, or, reciprocally
**alternative** another, choice, continuity, course, either, fluctuate, instead, interact, option, or, other, preference, recourse, recurrence,

**alternative form of gene** allele, allelomorph
**alternatively** instead, or, otherwise
**alternative route** detour
**alternative word** either, else, or
**alter radically** revolutionise, transform
**alter the case** confute, contrary, traverse, weaken
**althorn** mellophone, saxhorn
**although** albeit, notwithstanding, though, while
**altimeter** alimetry, barograph, height-finder, hypsometer
**altitude** apex, ceiling, elevation, eminence, height, loftiness, peak, pitch, stature, summit, tallness
**altitude limit** ceiling
**altitude meter** altimeter, orometer
**altogether** absolutely, all, bodily, chiefly, completely, entirely, extremely, fully, generally, greatly, in toto (L), integrally, mainly, mostly, nude, perfectly, quite, thoroughly, throughout, totally, unconditionally, utterly, virtually, whole, wholly
**alto or tenor violin** viola
**altophobia** acrophobia
**altruism** benevolence, benignity, bounty, charitableness, charity, generosity, kind-heartedness, kindness, largess, liberality, munificence, open-hearted, patronage, philanthropy, self-denial, selflessness, unselfishness
**altruist** alms-giver, benefactor, Christian, contributor, donor, generous, hospitable, humanitarian, patron, philanthropist, Samaritan, selfless, unselfish
**altruistic** beneficient, bountiful, charitable, detached, disinterested, generous, heroic, heroical, honest, humane, humanitarian, impartial, impersonal, just, kind, liberal, loyal, modest, neutral, noble, patriotic, philanthropic, selfless, uninvolved
**alula** calypter, lobe, wing
**alum** astringent, styptic
**aluminium alloy** dural
**aluminium discoverer** Davy, Wohler
**aluminium ore** bauxite
**aluminium oxide** alumina
**aluminium silicate as blue as crystalline mineral** kyanite
**aluminium sulphate** alum
**aluminium wrapping** tinfoil
**alumnus** apostle, chela, convert, debutant, disciple, follower, graduate, learner, novice, pupil, scholar, student, trainee

**alum rock** alunite
**alveary** beehive
**alveolate** honeycombed, pitted
**always** algates, ay, aye (Sc), consistently, constantly, continually, eternally, ever(lasting), evermore, forever, in perpetuum (L), perpetually, regularly, repeatedly, sempre (I), unceasingly, uninterruptedly
**always faithful** semper fidelis (L)
**always passing** day, hour, minute, month, second, year
**always ready** semper paratus (L)
**always the same** invariable, unchangeable
**ama** chalice, diver, vessel
**am able to** can
**amah** nanny, wet-nurse
**amain** energetically, force, haste, vehemently, violently
**Amalekite king** Agag
**amalgamate** alloy, blend, coalesce, combine, fuse, incorporate, integrate, merge, mix, pool, unify, unite
**amalgamation** alliance, amalgam, coalescence, coalition, combination, composite, fusing, integration, joining, merger, mingling, mixture, unification, union
**Amalthea** goat
**Amalthea's horn** cornucopia
**a man of honour** galant homme (F)
**amanuensis** accountant, archivist, clerk, copier, copyist, notary, protonotary, receptionist, recorder, registrar, scribe, scrivener, secretary, stenographer, transcriber, transcriptionist, typist
**amaranth** cockscomb
**amaranthine** unfading
**a marriage of convenience** mariage de convenance (F)
**amass** accumulate, acquire, aggregate, assemble, bunch, centre, cluster, collect, compile, consolidate, converge, convoke, cram, crowd, cultivate, fill, focus, garner, gather, group, heap, hoard, huddle, mass, meet, muster, pack, pile, shepherd, store, swarm, throng, troop, unite
**amasser** hoarder
**amass secretly** hoard
**amateur** beginner, bungler, commoner, dabbler, dilettante, greenhorn, ham, lay(man), learner, neophyte, nonprofessional, novice, tiro, tyro, unprofessional, unskilful
**amateurish** cliché, flawed, imperfect, inefficient, inferior, insipid, mediocre, meretricious, poor, second-rate, superficial, trashy, trite, unperfected, unpolished, unprofessional, unskilled, untrained
**amateur radio operator** ham
**amateur speleologist** spelunker
**amatol** explosive
**amatory** amorous, devoted, erotic, fervent, fond, lovers, lovesick, passionate, rapturous, romantic, sentimental, tender
**amaze** alarm, astonish, astound, awe, bewilder, confound, dazzle, dumbfound, flabbergast, impress, perplex, shock, stagger, startle, stun, surprise, wonder
**amazed** aghast, alarmed, astonished, astounded, bewildered, dazed, flabbergasted, shocked, staggered, startled, stunned, stupefied, surprised
**amazement** admiration, astonishment, awe, confusion, confusion, marvel, miracle, perplexity, prodigy, stupefaction, surprise, wonder
**amazing** astonishing, astounding, fabulous, incredible, marvelous, miraculous, preternatural, prodigious, remarkable, spectacular, staggering, stunning, stupefying, stupendous, surprising, unbelievable, unexpected, unprecedented, wonderful
**amazing event** miracle
**amazingly** astonishingly, astoundingly, awesomely, awfully, dauntingly, fearfully, formidably, horribly, imposingly, impressively, majestically, mirabile dictu (L), shockingly, solemnly, staggeringly, surprisingly, terribly, wondrously
**amazing occurrence** miracle
**amazing sight** spectacle
**Amazon** athlete, emasculator, fury, giantess, scold, soldier, tartar, termagant, virago, vixen, warrior, woman, Xanthippe
**Amazon estuary** Para
**Amazon fish** candir, piranha
**Amazon mat** yappa
**Amazon mouth** Para
**Amazon port** Manaus
**Amazon queen** Hippolyta, Antiope
**Amazon rain forest** Selva, Silvas
**ambari** ambary, fibre, hemp
**ambary hemp** ambari, nalita
**ambassador** announcer, apostle, attaché, commissioner, consul(ate), courier, delegate, deputy, dignitary, diplomat, emissary, envoy, legate, minister, negotiator, nuncio, official, plenipotentiary, representative, spokesperson

**ambassador's case** portfolio
**ambassador's deputy** chargé d'affaires
**ambassador's office** embassy
**ambassador's residence** embassy
**ambassador to minor country** chargé d'affaires
**ambassador with full powers** envoy, plenipotentiary
**amber coloured** resinous
**amber fish** medregal, runner
**ambidexterity** skill
**ambience** atmosphere, aura, cast, character, circumference, climate, colour, complexion, enclosure, environment, feeling, flavour, halo, medium, milieu, mood, scene, setting, spirit, surroundings
**ambient** background, circulating, circumfused, edge, embracing, encircling, enclosing, encompassing, enfolding, environment, fence, investing, moving, scene, setting, surrounding, wall, whirling
**ambiguity** abstruseness, cloudy, darkness, deceptiveness, doubt, doubtful(ness), dubiety, dubious(ness), enigma, foggy, haziness, hazy, indefiniteness, indistinctness, irony, misty, obscurity, pun, puzzle, richness, tergiversation, uncertainty, unclearness, vagueness
**ambiguous** ambivalent, cryptic, delphic, doubtful, dubious, duplicitous, enigmatic, equivocal, figurative, indistinct, obscure, oracular, paradoxical, problematic, vague
**ambiguous wording** amphibology
**ambit** boundary, bounds, circle, circuit, circumference, compass, confines, edge, environs, extent, gyre, limits, orbit, outline, perimeter, precincts, scope, spiral, surround, tour
**ambition** aim, aspiration, avidity, belief, desire, destination, dream, drive, eagerness, energy, enterprise, enthusiasm, expectation, force, goal, hope, hoping, hunger, intention, longing, need, objective, raison d'être (F), scheme, striving, ventureness, want, wish, yearning, zeal
**ambitious** arduous, aspiring, assertive, avid, bold, challenging, demanding, desirous, difficult, driving, eager, elaborate, energetic, enterprising, enthusiastic, exacting, formidable, go-ahead, hard, hopeful, impressive, industrious, intent, keen, ostentatious, pretentious, purposeful, pushy, severe, showy, strenuous, striving, zealous
**ambitious soldier** marine
**ambivalence** acrostic, ambiguity, anagram, calembour (F), caprice, conflict, confusion, doubt, enigma, equivocation, hesitancy, indecision, instability, irony, irresolution, paradox, paragram, prevarication, pun, uncertainty, unintelligibility, unmeaningness, untruth, witticism, word-play
**amble** canter, crawl, dawdle, hobble, jaunt, limp, meander, mosey, move, pace, plod, rack, ramble, saunter, shamble, shuffle, stagger, stroll, totter, trail, trudge, walk, wander
**ambler** saunterer, stroller
**ambling horse** padnag
**ambo** desk, pulpit
**amboina pine** galagala
**ambrosia** ambrose, amrita, caviar, delicacy, honey, kingweed, nectar, relish, savouriness, wormseed
**ambrosial** aromatic, delectable, delicious, divine, Elysian, exalted, glorious, gustable, honeyed, nectarous, odorous, olent, perfumed, redolent, rosy, sugary, supernal, sweet, tasteful, tasty, toothsome
**ambrosia plant** ragweed
**ambry** aumbry, chest, closet, niche, pantry, storeroom
**ambulance** casualty, clinic, hospital
**ambulance officer** paramedic
**ambulate** amble, foot, gad, gallivant, hike, meander, move, pace, perambulate, promenade, ramble, range, roam, rove, saunter, step, straggle, traipse, travel, traverse, tread, walk
**ambulatory** drive, itinerant, meandering, migratory, mobile, nomadic, path, pavement, pedestrian, rambling, run, strolling, vagrant, walk(ing), walkway
**ambush** ambuscade, attack, blind, bushwhack, catch, concealment, cover, decoy, ensnare, entrap, hiding(-place), lure, lurk(ing), manoeuvre, net, pitfall, retreat, screen, shelter, trap, waylay, web
**ameliorate** advance, alleviate, amend, assuage, better, cure, ease, elevate, fix, improve, lessen, meliorate, mend, mitigate, promote, raise, rectify, reform, relieve, remedy, repair
**amelioration** advancement, alleviation, amend(ment), better(ment), conversion, cure, elevation, improvement, mitigation, rectification, remedy, restoration, revival, transfiguration, uplift
**amen** approval, assent, assuredly, concurrence, endorsement, honestly, indeed, literally, truthfully, verily, welcome, yes
**amenable** accountable, acquiescent, agreeable, answerable, believing, bound, chargeable, credulous, dutiful, ethical, infatuated, liable, manageable, obedient, obligation, obligatory, obliged, persuadable, reasonable, repentant, responsible, responsive, simple, submissive, superstitious, tractable
**amend** alter, ameliorate, change, correct, (e)mend, enhance, fix, improve, modify, rectify, redress, reform, revise
**amend a manuscript** revise
**amend copy for publication** edit
**amendment** addendum, addition, adjunct, adjustment, alteration, amelioration, attachment, change, clarification, correction, difference, improvement, mending, modification, recasting, reform, remedy, repair(ing), revising, revision, substitution, transformation
**amendment to document** rider
**amend proofs** edit
**amends** apology, compensation, conciliation, consideration, damages, expiration, indemnification, redress, reparation, requital, retribution, satisfaction
**amend text** edit
**amenity** affability, agreeability, appealing, attractive, bright, chivalry, civility, comity, courtesy, facility, feature, friendly, geniality, gentleness, goodness, gracefulness, joy, lovely, mildness, nice, pleasant(ness), pleasurableness, softness, suavity, sunny, tranquil
**ament** catkin, cattail, chat, dotage, idiot, imbecile, iulus, jul, lunatic, madman, moron, nucament, psychopath, raceme, senile
**amerce** fine, punish
**American** Yank(ee)
**American aeronautical inventor** Orville Wright, Wilbur Wright
**American aloe** agave, maguey
**American ant-eater** ant-bear
**American antelope** prongbuck, pronghorn
**American apple** crab
**American aroid plant** jack-in-the-pulpit
**American artist** O'Keefe
**American aviation pioneer** Orville Wright, Wilbur Wright

**American aviator** Lindbergh
**American award for literature, journalism and music** Pulitzer
**American balsam** tolu
**American bear** grizzly, Kodiak, musquaw
**American bird** towhee
**American buffalo** bison
**American burrowing rodent** gopher
**American canal** Erie, Panama
**American card game** euchre
**American cartoon film producer** Walt Disney
**American cataract** Niagara
**American cattle farm** ranch
**American chameleon** anole, anoli
**American coin** cent, dime
**American cuckoo** ani
**American currency** dollar
**American custard apple** soursop
**American custom** yankeeism
**American deer** moose, wapiti
**American dogwood** osier
**American duck** redhead
**American dustbin** trashcan
**American elk** moose, wapiti
**American elm** ulmus
**American emblem** eagle
**American essayist** Emerson
**American evangelist** Graham, McPherson
**American farmer** rancher
**American feline** cougar, ocelot, puma
**American finch** junco, tanager, towhee
**American flag** The Stars and Stripes
**American flower** frangipani
**American fox-like wild dog** zorro
**American fries** hashbrown
**American gamboge tree** wax-tree
**American game** baseball, football, keno, poker
**American girl** gal
**American grape** catawba, niagara
**American gregarious wild pig** peccary
**American grey fox** urocyon
**American ground-squirrel** chipmunk
**American hat** stetson
**American heavyweight boxer** Joe Louis, Mohammed Ali
**American humorist** Ade
**American illicit whiskey** hooch
**American Indian** Apache, Cherokee, Cheyenne, Cree, Huron, Inca, Otoe, Redskin, Ree, Sac, Seneca, Sioux, Taos, Ute
**American Indian ancestral spirit** kachina
**American Indian baby or young child** papoose
**American Indian dwelling** hogan, hut, lodge, te(e)pee, tent, wigwam
**American Indian family symbol** totem

**American Indian home** te(e)pee
**American Indian hut** wi(c)kiup, wigwam
**American Indian hut of logs** hogan
**American Indian medicine man** powwow
**American Indian peace pipe** calumet
**American Indian shoe or slipper** moccasin, pac
**American Indian smoking mixture** kinnikinick
**American Indian soft shoe** moccasin
**American Indian's pole** totem
**American Indian tent** te(e)pee, tipi, wigwam
**American Indian tribe** Osage, Sioux
**American Indian village** pueblo, rancheria
**American Indian warrior** brave
**American Indian woman or wife** squaw
**American intelligence agency** CIA
**American inventor** Edison
**American isthmus** Panama
**American jazz trumpeter** Louis Armstrong
**American larch** tamarack
**American leopard-like feline** ocelot
**American lizard** iguana
**American loricate reptile** alligator
**American machine-gun inventor** Gale
**American marsh robin** towhee
**American marsupial** opossum
**American mealie** corn
**American money** cent, dime, dollar, nickel, quarter
**American national emblem** eagle
**American negation** nope
**American Negro singer** Paul Robeson
**American nighthawk** pisk
**American nocturnal mammal** rac(c)oon
**American parrot** macaw
**American patriot** Paul Revere
**American petrol** gas
**American philosopher** Emerson, Paine
**American pine** longleaf
**American pistol** derringer
**American plated mammal** armadillo
**American poet** Auden, Creeley, Dickinson, Lowell, Plath, Poe, Stevens, Whitman
**American politician** Democrat, Republican, Senator
**American president's retreat** Camp David
**American prickly pear** tuna
**American Red Indian** Apache
**American reindeer** caribou
**American river fish** gar
**American sailor** gob

**American sardine** shadine
**American snake** copperhead, hognose, moccasin, racer, rattler, rattlesnake
**American snowy owl** wapacut
**American soldier** GI
**American songbird** bobolink, chat, chewink, finch, reedbird, ricebird, vireo
**American sport** baseball
**American state prison** penitentiary
**American statesman** senator
**American stock-farm** ranch
**American tiger** jaguar
**American tomato sauce** ketchup
**American tortoise** terrapin
**American tree** elm, wahoo
**American university** Harvard, Princeton, UCLA, Yale
**American vulture** buzzard, condor, gallinazo
**American warbler** ovenbird
**American waterfall** Niagara
**American whiskey** rye
**American wild ox** bison
**American wild sheep** bighorn
**American women's college** Bennington
**America's cotton state** Alabama
**amethyst** corundum, gem, onegite, purple, stone
**amiability** affability, beauty, benignancy, benignity, cheerfulness, chivalry, complaisance, courtesy, delightfulness, douceur, elegance, friendship, gallantry, geniality, gracious, kind(li)ness, lovable, niceness, pleasantness, pleasingness, polite, suaveness, sweetness, urbanity
**amiable** affable, agreeable, amicable, attractive, benign, charming, clever, engaging, friendly, genial, gentle, good, gracious, heavenly sweet, kind(ly), likeable, lovable, loving, mellow, nice, obliging, pleasant, pleasing, smooth, sociable, sweet, tender, warm, winsome
**amicable** accessible, agreeable, amiable, benevolent, benign, charming, companionable, complaisant, congenial, cordial, friendly, harmonious, inclined, kindhearted, kindly, peaceable, pleasant, sociable, submissive
**amice** cap(e), hood, linen, scarf, vestment
**amid** amidst, among(st), between, betwixt, during, in, intercurrent, interposed, intervenient, intervening, median, mid(dle), midst, sandwiched, with

**amidst** among(st), between, in
**amino acid** diamide, lysine, ornithine, protein, triamine, valine
**amir** emir
**amiss** astray, awry, bad(ly), confused, distressing, erroneous, false(ly), faulty, imperfectly, improper(ly), incorrect(ly), inexact, injustice, mistakenly, off, poorly, unsuitable, unsuitably, untrue, wrong(ly)
**amity** accord, agreeable, agreement, concord, conviviality, cordiality, devoted, friendly, friendship, goodwill, harmonious, harmony, loyal, peace, sociability, staunch, sympathy, true, understanding, unity
**amma** abbess, mother, vicaress
**ammonia** hartshorn, refrigerant
**ammonia compound** amide, amine
**ammoniac plant** oshac
**Ammonite king** Hanun, Uzziah
**ammonium carbonate** sal volatile
**ammonium chloride** sal ammoniac
**ammunition** ammo, armaments, bullets, cartridges, explosives, munitions
**ammunition case** bandolier
**ammunition chest** caisson
**ammunition for blowgun** dart
**ammunition holder** gun, tray
**ammunition storehouse** arsenal, magazine
**ammunition wagon** caisson
**amnesia** absence, absent-minded, aphasia, blackout, blank, forgetful(ness), fugue, lapse, oblivion, paramnesia
**amnesty** absolution, absolve, acquit, assoil, clemency, excusal, excuse, exemption, exonerate, forbearance, forgive(ness), immunity, impunity, indemnity, justify, oblivion, overlook, pardon, remission, remit(ting), reprieve
**amnion** caul, membrane, sac
**am not** ain't
**amoeba** animalcule, germ, gnat, grub, maggot, mite, mouse, protozoan, protozoon, shrimp, tick, virus
**amok** amuck, crazed, crazy, frenzied, frenzy, mad, violent
**among** amid(st), amongst, between, betwixt, in, inter, mid(st), mutually, parenthetically, sandwiched
**among or between themselves** inter se (L)
**amongst other things** inter alia (L)
**among the living** inter vivos (L)
**Amorite king** Og, Sihon
**amorous** adoring, affectionate, amatory, ardent, aroused, attached, benevolent, caring, compassionate, desirous, devoted, doting, enamoured, erotic, fond, gentle, hot, humane, indulgent, kind, libidinous, lovesick, loving, lustful, merciful, passionate, pitiful, romantic, sensual, sentimental, tender, warm
**amorous advance** attention
**amorous gazer** ogler
**amorous look** leer, ogle
**amorous man** Casanova, rake
**amorous song** serenade
**amorphous** anomalous, bitty, chaotic, characterless, confused, deficient, fluid, formless, imperfect, incomplete, liquid, nebulous, orderless, scant, scrappy, shapeless, structureless, superficial, uncompleted, uncrystallised, unformed, unorganised, vague
**amorphous brittle mass** gum
**amount** bulk, extent, import, lot, magnitude, mass, measure, number, quantity, quota, result, sum, sup(ply), tot(al), volume
**amount account is in the red** overdraft
**amount assessed** ratal
**amount expended** expenditure
**amount gained** profit
**amount lost** loss
**amount lost by waste** decrement
**amount lost needlessly** wastage
**amount of** some
**amount of business done** turnover
**amount of deviation** error
**amount of drugs** dosage
**amount of explosive needed for one explosion** charge
**amount offered** bid
**amount of force** intensity
**amount of increase** increment
**amount of liquid dropped** spillage
**amount of medicine** dosage, dose
**amount of money** fund, sum
**amount of money owed** debt
**amount of money taken in business** turnover
**amount of paper** ream
**amount of shortfall** deficit
**amount of tons** tonnage
**amount of volts** voltage
**amount of water present in the soil** chresard
**amount of work** load, stint
**amount on which rates are assessed** ratal
**amount owing** debt
**amount paid** payment
**amount produced** output
**amount sold** sales
**amount taken in** intake
**amount to** aggregate, become, equal, grow, mean, total
**amour** adultery, affair, affaire de coeur (F), amourette (F), entanglement, flirtation, fornication, intrigue, liaison, love, passion, romance, triangle
**amp** ampere
**ampere** amp
**ampere unit** volt, watt
**ampersand** &-sign, also, and, plus
**amphibian** axolotl, eft, frog, newt, olm, reptile, salamander, snake, tadpole, toad
**amphibious carnivore** mink
**amphibious marine mammal** seal
**amphibious nocturnal opossum** yapok
**amphibious quadruped rodent** beaver
**amphibole mineral** uralite
**amphitheatre** arena, centre, cirque, forum, stadium, stage
**amphitheatre in Rome** Colosseum
**amphora** cadus, jug, urn
**ample** abundant, boundless, bounteous, bountiful, broad, bulky, capacious, considerable, copious, enough, enow, exhausted, extensive, free, full, galore, generous, great, impressive, infinite, large, lavish, liberal, many, massive, multiple, numerous, overflowing, plenteous, plentiful, plenty, profuse, rich, roomy, several, spacious, substantial, umpteen, unrestricted, unsparing, vast
**ampleness** bigness, bountifulness, broadness, capaciousness, copiousness, expansiveness, extensiveness, fullness, generousness, greatness, largeness, lavishness, liberalness, plenitude, plenteousness, plentifulness, profuseness, richness, roominess
**amplification** accession, addendum, adding, addition, adjoining, adjunct, affixing, aggravation, annex(e), appendix, attachment, augmentation, boosting, concentration, doubling, elaboration, enlargement, enrichment, exaggeration, expansion, extension, gain, inclusion, increase, increment, redoubling, stretching, trebling
**amplifier** microphone, mike
**amplify** accumulate, add, augment, boost, deepen, develop, dilate, distend, double, elaborate, elongate, enlarge, escalate, expand, extend, greaten, increase, intensify, magnify, multiply, pad, prolong, strengthen, stretch, supplement, swell, thicken, widen
**amplifying device** laser, maser

**amplitude** abundance, ampleness, bigness, boundlessness, capacity, coverage, distance, expanse, extensiveness, extent, exuberance, greatness, immensity, largeness, magnitude, mass, quantity, radius, reach, scope, size, spaciousness, sphere, spread, sweep, vastness
**ampoule** phial, receptacle, socket, vial
**amputate** capitate, cleave, disengage, disjoin, dismember, dissever, dock, excise, prune, remove, separate, sever, subtract, truncate
**amputation by oblique cut** loxotomy
**amuck** amok, berserk, crazedly, ferociously, frenzied, maniacally, violently
**amulet** abrasax, abraxas, charm, fetish, gem, mascot, periapt, phylactery, safeguard, scarab, scroll, talisman, token, triskelion, wishbone
**amuse** absorb, beguile, charm, cheer, delight, divert, enliven, entertain, exhilarate, gladden, gratify, humour, interest, please, recreate, regale, rejoice, solace, tickle, titillate
**amuse by sleight of hand** juggle
**amusement** antic, avocation, celebration, cheer, dalliance, delight, diversion, enjoyment, entertainment, escapade, frolic, fun, game, hilarity, hobby, interest, jaunt, joke, joviality, lark, laughter, merriment, pastime, play, pleasure, prank, recreation, romp, sport
**amusement centre** arcade
**amuse oneself** leisure, play, relax, sport
**amusing** charming, cheering, clownish, comic(al), delightful, diverting, droll, enjoyable, entertaining, funny, humorous, laughable, lively, merry, pleasant, pleasing, ridiculous, risible, tickling, witty
**amusing drawing** cartoon
**amusing incident** joke, lark
**amusingly absurd** ludicrous
**amusingly simple** naive
**amusing person** comic
**amusing play** comedy, farce
**amusing send-up** spoof
**amusing story** joke, yarn
**amygdala** alkond, tonsil
**amyl** alcohol, amydon, isoamyl, pentyl, starch
**amylase** diastase
**amylum** starch
**an** a, any, each, one, some, un (F), une (F)
**ana** bits, events, miscellany, omniana, sayings
**Anabaptist sect** Amish

**anabasis** expedition, march
**anachronism** antedate, antique, archaism, discord, error, incongruity, misdate, mislocation, mistiming, prolepsis, untimeliness
**anaconda** aboma, boa, camoudie, sucuri, sucury
**anacoustic** soundless
**an additional charge** extra
**anadem** chaplet, coronet, crown, diadem, garland, wreath
**anaemia** chlorosis, pallidness, wanness
**anaemic** ashen, bloodless, delicate, exhausted, feeble, frail, impotent, ineffective, intolerance, lifeless, low, mealy, pale, pallid, vigourless, wan, weak
**anaesthesia** analgesia, deadness, dullness, insensibility, insensitivity, numbness
**anaesthetic** anodyne, chloroform, ether, gas, narcotic, opiate, painkiller, sedative
**anagram** acrostic, brain-teaser, crossword, cryptogram, enigma, logogriph, monogram, problem, puzzle, rebus, riddle, shuffling, teaser
**analects** ana, morsels
**analeptic** cordial, invigorator, restorative, stimulant, tonic
**analgesia** catalepsy, coma, hypnosis, narcosis, numbness, painless, paralysis, stupor, trance
**analgesic** alleviate, anaesthetic, anodyne, antipyrin, assuasive, calmative, pain-killing, pain-relieving, painkiller, phenalgin, sedative
**anal intercourse committed by a man** buggery, sodomy
**analogous** agreeing, akin, alike, appearance, associated, comparable, equivalent, fashion, form, homologous, identical, kin(dred), like, matching, related, (re)semblance, seeming, similar, similitude
**analogy** accordance, affinity, agreement, analogue, compare, comparison, conformity, correlation homology, equivalence, likeness, mutuality, parallelism, parity, relation, resemblance, similarity, similitude
**analogy prefix** anal-
**an alternative** another
**analyse** anatomise, assay, assess, clarify, class(ify), codify, consider, critique, decompose, diagnose, dissect, dissolve, divide, estimate, evaluate, examine, group, interpret, investigate, judge, reduce, resolve, review, scrutinise, separate, sift, solve, study, test
**analyse grammatically** parse
**analyse ore** assay
**analyse verse** scan
**analysis** abstract, anatomisation, anatomy, assay, breakdown, dissection, dissolution, enquiry, epitome, estimation, evaluation, examination, inquiry, interpretation, investigation, opinion, separation, study, summary, synopsis, test
**analyst** assayer, estimator, examiner, explorer, inquirer, investigator, prober, psychiatrist, reviewer, valuator
**analytic** deductive, holomorphic, inductive, logical, rational(istic), regular, subtle
**ananas** pineapple, pinguin
**anarchist** anarch, Bolshevik, insurgent, mutineer, nihilist, radical, rebel, renegade, revolutionary, revolutionist, terrorist, traitor, tyrannicide
**anarchy** apostasy, chaos, confusion, disarray, disorder, lawlessness, mayhem, misrule, mobocracy, mutiny, pandemonium, powerless, rebellion, revolt, revolution, riot, subversion, terrorism, tumult, turmoil
**anasarca** dropsy
**anathema** accursed, antipathy, aversion, ban(ishment), bête noire (F), censure, condemnation, curse, denunciation, execration, imprecation, malediction, malevolence, oath, proscription, swear, taboo, threat
**anathematise** banish, blasphemy, censure, comminate, curse, denounce, doom, excommunicate, execrate, imprecate, swear
**Anatolian goat** angora
**anatomical tube** artery, channel, duct, vein
**anatomiser** prosector
**anatomy** analysis, biology, bones, botany, dissection, examination, inquiry, investigation, research, scrutiny, skeleton, study, topology
**anatomy of horse** hippotomy
**anatomy of tissue** histology
**anaxial** asymmetrical
**ancestor** ascendant, elder, for(e)bear, forefather, forerunner, genitor, grandfather, grandmother, model, parent, patriarch, precursor, predecessor, procreator, progenitor, prototype, root, sire
**ancestor worship** necrolatry, sciotheism

**ancestral** accustomed, conventional, customary, established, folk, forefatherly, historic, old, oral, traditional, unwritten, usual
**ancestral descent** lineage
**ancestral line** pedigree
**ancestral windfall** inheritance
**ancestry** ancestors, antecedents, background, birth, blood, breeding, derivation, descent, etymology, extraction, family, forefathers, genealogy, heredity, kindred, kinship, line(age), nobility, nurture, origin, parentage, pedigree, race, raising, rearing, relations, reproduction, source, stock, strain, training, upbringing
**anchor** abide, affix, attach, berth, cockbill, connect, defence, drug, dwell, fasten, fix, foundation, hook, kedge, moor(ing), safeguard, security, settle, support, tackle, tie, warp
**anchorage** harbour, port
**anchor chain of ship** cable
**anchored float** buoy
**anchor hoist** capstan, cat
**anchoring rope** guy
**anchor in place** cockbill
**anchorman** announcer, newscaster
**anchor part** fluke
**anchor ring** tore, torus
**anchor tackle** cat
**anchovy** bocon, herring, nehu, sardine, sprat
**anchovy sauce** alec
**ancient** aged, antediluvian, antiquated, antique, archaic, atavistic, bygone, earliest, early, elderly, eolithic, obsolescent, obsolete, old(-fashioned), olden, outmoded, primal, primeval, primigenial, primitive, primordial, pristine, quaint, remote, superannuated, timeworn, unmodern
**ancient Aegean people** Samian
**ancient Alexandrian writer** Origen
**ancient Algerian city** Hippo
**ancient alloy** asem
**ancient alphabet character** rune
**ancient arena fighter** gladiator
**ancient armed galley** aesc
**ancient Aryan** Mede
**ancient Aryan language** Sanskrit
**ancient ascetic people** Essene
**ancient Asia Minor city** Ephesus
**ancient Asia Minor region** Ionia
**ancient Asian weight** mina
**ancient Asiatic country** Elam, Eolis, Medea
**ancient Assyrian city** Arbela
**ancient Athenian market-place** agora

**ancient Babylonian city** Ur
**ancient biblical city** Tyre, Ur
**ancient British and Irish alphabet** og(h)am
**ancient British tribe** Iceni
**ancient Briton** Celt, Pict, Saxon
**ancient capital of Assyria** Nineveh
**ancient capital of Burma** Ava
**ancient capital of Cambodia** Angkor
**ancient catapult** ballista
**ancient Celtic alphabet and script** og(h)am
**ancient Celtic priest** druid
**ancient cemetery** necropolis
**ancient chariot with four horses abreast** quadriga
**ancient charm** abrasax, abraxas
**ancient city** Nineveh, Tyre, Ur, Zimbabwe
**ancient city in Greece** Argos, Calydon, Corinth, Sparta
**ancient city of Sumer** Ur
**ancient classical temple** naos
**ancient copper coin** aes
**ancient country in Greece** Achaia, Doris
**ancient country of the Dead Sea** Moab
**ancient customs and beliefs** folklore
**ancient dagger** skain, skean, skene
**ancient descent** ancestry
**ancient document** papyrus
**ancient drink** morat
**ancient Egyptian city** No, Thebes
**ancient Egyptian descendant** Copt
**ancient Egyptian instrument** sistra
**ancient Egyptian king** Pharaoh, Rameses, Tutankhamun
**ancient Egyptian kingdom** Sennar
**ancient Egyptian paper** papyrus
**ancient Egyptian picture writing** hieroglyphics
**ancient Egyptian ruler** pharaoh
**ancient Egyptian scrolls** papyri
**ancient Egyptian title** soter
**ancient Egyptian tomb** mastaba
**ancient English dance** morris
**ancient European** Avar
**ancient fabulist** Aesop
**ancient firearm** dag
**ancient flute** tibia
**ancient France** Gaul
**ancient French coin** sou
**ancient Gaelic capital** Erin, Tara
**ancient Gaelic kingdom** Dalriada
**ancient galley** bireme
**ancient game** cottabus, mora
**ancient garment** chlamys, toga
**ancient Gaulish priest** Druid
**ancient Germanic carved alphabetical script** runes
**ancient gold alloy** asem

**ancient gold coin** rial
**ancient Greece** Hellas, Ionia
**ancient Greek** Corinthian, Hellene, Ionian
**ancient Greek city** Argos, Corinth, Elis, Sparta, Thebes
**ancient Greek coin** epton, obol(e), stater
**ancient Greek colonnade** stoa
**ancient Greek colony** Ionia
**ancient Greek contest** agon
**ancient Greek country** Aerolia, Eli, Epirus
**ancient Greek dagger** parazonium
**ancient Greek dialect** Aeolic, Doric, Eolic, Ionic
**ancient Greek drinking party** symposium
**ancient Greek female statue** kore
**ancient Greek flute** hemiope
**ancient Greek headband** taenia
**ancient Greek invader** Dorian
**ancient Greek jar** amphora
**ancient Greek kingdom** Attica
**ancient Greek lyre** cithara, kithara
**ancient Greek male statue** kouros
**ancient Greek merchant vessel** holcad
**ancient Greek musical instrument** lyre
**ancient Greek music hall** odeum
**ancient Greek orator** Rhetor
**ancient Greek podium** bema
**ancient Greek portico** stoa
**ancient Greek province** Acarnania
**ancient Greek silver coin** obol
**ancient Greek teaching that good was pleasure and evil was pain** Epicureanism
**ancient Greek theatre** odeum
**ancient Greek tribal area** Deme
**ancient Greek warship** galley
**ancient guitar** lute
**ancient harp** lyre, sambuca
**ancient headdress** mitre
**ancient Hebrew ascetic** Essene
**ancient Hebrew liquid measure** bath, ephah
**ancient Hebrew musical instrument** shofar, timbrel
**ancient Hebrew ram's horn** shofar
**ancient Hebrew unit of liquid** bath
**ancient Hindu scriptures** Atharva, Rig, Sama, Veda, Yajur
**ancient Hispania** Iberia
**ancient implement of war** celt, onager
**ancient infantryman** fusilier
**ancient invaders** Normans, Vikings
**ancient Iranian** Mede
**ancient Irish capital** Tara
**ancient Irish clan** Sept
**ancient Irish harp** clairschach
**ancient Irish seat** tar
**ancient Irish soldier** gallowglass

ancient Italian  Etruscan
ancient Italian city  Pompeii
ancient Italian nation  Etruria
ancient Italian people  Sabines
ancient Jerusalem  Zion
ancient Jewish ascetic  Essene
ancient Jewish cabbalistic book  Zohar
ancient Jewish coin  zuz
ancient Jewish high court and council  Sanhedrim, Sanhedrin
ancient Jewish measure  omar
ancient juror  dicast
ancient kingdom  Assyria, Elam
ancient kingdom of western Asia Minor  Lydia
ancient kings of Peru  Inca
ancient knife  skean
ancient Laconian capital  Sparta
ancient language  Gaelic, Latin, Pali, Sanskrit
ancient large lute  orpharion
ancient Latin grammar  donat
ancient length measure  cubit
anciently  high, old
ancient lyre  asor, cithara
ancient manuscript  codex
ancient measure  ell, league
ancient Mexican  Aztec
ancient Middle Eastern script using wedge-shaped characters  cuneiform
ancient military engine for throwing rocks  onager
ancient monetary unit  talent
ancient money  mina
ancient musical instrument  asor, cithara, rota
ancient name for Ecuador  Quito
ancient name for Malta  Melita
ancient name for North Africa  Libya
ancient name for Paris  Lutetia
ancient necklace  torque
ancient Norse minstrel  scald, skald
ancient ointment  nard
ancient order of priests  Druid
ancient Palestinian language  Aramaic
ancient Palestinian region  Samaria
ancient people of Albania  Illyrian
ancient people of Britain  Iceni, Picts, Silures
ancient people of Peru  Inca
ancient persecutor of Christians  Nero
ancient Persian  Mede
ancient Persian coin  daric
ancient Persian priest  magus
ancient Persian ruler  satrap
ancient Peruvian  Inca
ancient pillarlike monument  stela
ancient pistol  dag
ancient place  Eretria

ancient plant  alisma, cycad, duckweed, frogbit, nuphar, pickerelweed, pondweed, sugamo, tawkee
ancient playing card  tarot
ancient porcelain  murra
ancient priest  Druid
ancient region of Jordan  Moab
ancient remnant  relic
ancient Roman assembly  comitia
ancient Roman bathing-pond  piscina
ancient Roman calendar  ides
ancient Roman citadel  Arx
ancient Roman coin  as, sesterce
ancient Roman garment  stola, toga
ancient Roman general  Agrippa
ancient Roman household deity  lar
ancient Roman magistrate  aedile, praetor, quaestor
ancient Roman noble  patrician
ancient Roman port  Ostia
ancient Roman silver coin  denarius, sesterce, sestertius
ancient Roman sock  udo
ancient Roman unit of weight  as
ancient Roman vessel for holding vinegar  acetabulum
ancient Roman veteran  vexillary
ancient Roman wall  spina
ancient royal family  Plantaganet
ancient ruined city of Asia Minor  Troy
ancient Scandinavian  Norse
ancient Scandinavian poet  scald, skald
ancient Scot  Pict
ancient Semite  Phoenician
ancient Semitic god  Baal
ancient sepulchral mound  barrow, tumulus
ancient shield  ecu
ancient ship  galleon
ancient sign  rune
ancient silk fabric  samite
ancient South American culture  Aztec, Chimu, Inca, Maya, Toltec
ancient Spanish city  Numantia
ancient spice  stacte
ancient stone implement  eolith
ancient stone marker  stele
ancient storyteller  Aesop
ancient stringed instrument  asor, lute, lyre, nebel, rebec
ancient Syria  Aram
ancient times  antiquity
ancient tongue  Gaelic, Latin
ancient tool  artefact, artifact, (n)eolith
ancient torture instrument  rack, cross
ancient trading vessel  nef
ancient tree  olive
ancient Troy  Ilion, Ilium, Troas
ancient Turkey and Greece  Thrace

ancient two-handled narrow-necked jar  amphora
ancient vehicle  chariot
ancient war machine  catapult, onager
ancient warship  galleon, trireme
ancient war wagon  chariot
ancient weapon  ballista, catapult, celt, onager
ancient weight  as, m(i)na, talent
ancient wicked city  Sodom
ancient wine pitcher  olpe
ancient wine vessel  ama
ancient writer  Aeschylus, Aesop, Aristophanes, Catullus, Cicero, Euripides, Herodotus, Hesiod, Horace, Juvenal, Lucretius, Ovid, Plautus, Sophocles, Tacitus, Thucydides, Virgil
ancient writing implement  feather, style
ancillary  accessory, additional, auxillary, extra, subordinate, subservient, subsidiary, supplementary
ancillary item  accessory
ancillary rocket motor  booster
ancon  console, corbel, elbow
and  also, ampersand, et (F), et (L), furthermore, including, moreover, plus, too, und (G), with
and also  act etiam (L)
Andean animal  llama
Andean bird  condor
Andean cold region  puna
Andean grass  ichu
Andean mountain  Sorata
Andean republic  Peru
Andean rodent  abrocome
Andean ruminant  alpaca, llama, vicuña
Andean shrub  coca
and elsewhere  et alibi (L)
andiron  (fire)dog, hessian
and not  neither, nor
and not either  nor
and others  et al (L), et alia (L), et alii (L)
and please promenade here  esplanade
androgyne  epicene, eunuch
androgynous  bisexual, effeminate, hermaphrodite
android  automaton, robot
and so  thus
and so be it  amen
and so forth  et cetera
and that is all  amen, only
and the following  et sequens (L)
and the rest  et cetera
Andy Capp's wife  Flo
and yet it does move  eppur si muove (I)
a neat leg looks chic  elegant

**anecdote** ana, apologue, brief, fable, illustration, joke, memoir, myth, narrative, relation, reminiscence, sketch, story, tale, yarn
**anemology** aerometer, aneroid, barogram, barograph, barometer, baroscope
**anent** about, alongside, concerning, re
**aneurin** thiamine
**anew** afresh, again, de novo (L), fresh(ly), just, lately, latterly, newly, over, recently
**angel** archangel, backer, beloved, benefactor, cherub, darling, dearest, helper, jewel, patron, saint, seraph, spirit, supporter, treasure, well-wisher
**angelfish** scalare, sea-angel
**angelic** adorable, beatific, beautiful, celestial, chaste, cherubic, delicate, desirable, divine, ethical, godly, good, heavenly, holy, just, lovable, lovely, pious, pure, righteous, saintly, seraphic, sinless, sweet, virtuous
**angelic child** cherub
**angelic messenger** Gabriel
**angelic ring** halo
**angel of bottomless pit** Apollyon
**angel of death** Azrael, Sammael
**angel of highest rank** archangel
**angel of light** cherub
**angel of mercy** nurse
**angel of Tobit** Raphael
**angel of worship** Dulia
**angel's headwear** halo
**angel's instrument** harp
**angel's light** halo
**angel with the horn** Gabriel
**anger** affront, aggravate, animosity, annoy(ance), antagonise, antagonism, bile, bitterness, bother, chafe, choler, dander, displease, displeasure, enrage, exasperate, exasperation, excite, frustrate, fury, gall, hate, incense, indignation, infuriate, ira (Sp), ire, irk, irritability, irritate, irritation, madden, needle, nettle, offend, outrage, passion, pique, provoke, rage, rancour, rankle, resentment, rile, rouse, ruffle, spleen, temper, vex(ation), wrath
**angina** prunella, spasm
**angle** angularity, approach, aspect, attitude, bend, cast, corner, crevice, crook, crotch, cusp, edge, elbow, ensnare, feature, fish, focus, hook, idea, intersection, knee, niche, nook, outlook, perspective, point, position, recess, scheme, sentiment, side, slant, standpoint, theory, trawl, view(point), worm
**angled** cast, fished, slanting
**angled golf fairway** dogleg

**angled pipe** elbow, ell
**angle for** contrive, hunt, invite, scheme, seek, solicit
**angle formed by vaults** groin
**angle iron** brace
**angle of bevel** fleam, fleem
**angle of branch and trunk** axil
**angle of building** corner
**angle of club head** lie
**angle of eyelids** canthus
**angle of hat brim** break
**angle of hipbone** hook
**angle of leaf and stem** axil
**angle of rafter** heel
**angle of stem** axil
**angler** fisherman, rod, wormer
**angler's basket** creel
**angler's haul** catch
**angler's hope** bite
**angler's pole** rod, gaff
**angler's prey** fish
**angler's throw** cast
**angler throwing in line** castor
**angle worm** ess, earthworm
**angling** casting, fishing
**Anglo-** English
**Anglo-Indian nurse** amah
**Anglo-Saxon aristocrat** thane
**Anglo-Saxon assembly** gemot(e)
**Anglo-Saxon god** Tiu
**Anglo-Saxon king** Ine
**Anglo-Saxon labourer** Esne
**Anglo-Saxon letter** edh, eth, thorn
**Anglo-Saxon minstrel** scop
**Anglo-Saxon parliament** Witenagemot
**Anglo-Saxon prince** atheling
**Anglo-Saxon slave** Esne
**Angolan** Luandan
**Angolan currency** kwanza
**Angolan exclave** Esne
**Angolan kingdom** Bakonga
**Angolan language** Kimbundu
**Angolan native** Chokwe, Songo
**Angolan party** MPLA, Unita
**Angolan plateau** bie
**Angolan port** Luanda, Lobito
**Angolan tribe** Kikongo
**Angolan waterfall** Ruacana
**angora** mohair
**angora fabric** camlet, mohair
**angrily** acrimoniously, exasperatedly, furiously, heatedly, hotly, indignantly, irascibly, irately, irritably, madly, passionately, resentfully, wrathfully
**angrily combative** fierce
**angry** aggravated, annoyed, antagonised, awkward, bitter, cross, displeased, enraged, exasperated, fuming, furious, heated, hot, incensed, indignant, inflamed, infuriated, irate, ireful, irritated, mad, outraged, passionate, raging,

resentful, stroppy, surly, tempered, touchy, uptight, wrathful, wroth
**angry crowd** mob
**angry demonstration of mob** riot, tumult
**angry dispute** quarrel
**angry look** glare, glower, scowl
**angry mob** horde
**angry murmur** growl
**angry outburst** tantrum
**angry reaction** rise
**angry sound** snort
**angry speech** tirade
**anguilliform** eel-shaped
**anguilloid** eel-like
**anguish** adversity, affliction, agonise, agony, anxiety, depression, desolation, despair, desperation, discomfort, distress, endurance, fret, gloom, grief, heartache, malaise, melancholy, misery, pain, pang, sadness, sorrow, strain, sufferance, suffering, throes, torment, torture, travail, woe, worry
**anguished bark** yelp
**angular** awkward, bony, gaunt, lank(y), lean, rawboned, scrawny, skinny, stiff, unbending
**angular crookedness** zaggery
**angular distance from equator** latitude
**angular inset of material** gusset
**anil** indigo
**anile** childish, feeble, imbecile, old(-womanish)
**anility** age, eccentric, folly, fool(ish), illogical, ridiculous, silly, years
**animadversion** castigation, censure, check, criticism, derogation, disapproval, imputation, invective, rebuke, reprimand, reproach, reproof, scolding, stricture
**animal** barbarian, beast(ly), bestial, bodily, brute, brutish, carnal, creature, cur, fleshly, gross, hound, inhuman, instinctive, mammal, monster, physical, pig(gish), savage, sensual, swine, unspiritual, wild
**animal abode** menagerie, zoo
**animal anatomy** zootomy
**animal behaviour** animality, savagery
**animal behavioural study** ethology
**animal body** soma
**animal bristle** seta
**animal coat** fur, hair, pelage, pelt, wool
**animal colour** roan
**animal corpse** carcass
**animal cry** bleat, howl
**animal disease** anthrax, biliary, distemper, mange, parvovirus, rabies, rinderpest
**animal doctor** vet(erinarian)
**animal eating everything** omnivore

**animal enclosure** cage, corral, kraal, pen, stable
**animal farm** ranch, stud
**animal fat** adeps, adipose, ester, grease, lard, suet, tallow, wax
**animal feed** feed
**animal feeding on plants** herbivore
**animal flesh as food** meat
**animal foot** claw, paw
**animal form in art** theriomorph
**animal found in desert regions** camel
**animal hair** coat, fur, pelt, wool
**animal hide** pelt
**animal home** game reserve, park, zoo
**animal kept at home** pet
**animal lacking pigment** albino
**animal leash** tether
**animal life of area** fauna
**animal-like** theroid
**animal like elk** moose
**animal like mouse** shrew
**animal lover** zoophile, vegan
**animal mother** dam
**animal neck hair** mane
**animal noise** bark, growl, roar, snort, yelp
**animal of mixed parentage** brak, hybrid, mongrel, mule
**animal of myth** basilisk, Cerberus, cockatrice, dragon, hydra, lighting bird, Minotaur, naga, sphinx, unicorn
**animal of the Andes** llama
**animal of the Bible** behemoth, leviathan, reem
**animal of the cat family** cheetah, civet, cougar, feline, leopard, lion, lynx, puma, tiger, wildcat
**animal of the frog order** batrachian
**animal park** menagerie, zoo
**animal pelt** coat, fur, hair, wool
**animal physiology** zoonomist, zoonomy
**animal-plant life** biota
**animal pouch** sac
**animal related to giraffe** okapi
**animal retreat** den, lair, nest
**animals** fauna
**animal's backbone** chine, spine
**animal's bedding material** grass, leaves, straw
**animals, birds, plants** wildlife
**animal's den** lair
**animal's female parent** dam
**animal's foot** paw
**animal's foot as food** trotter
**animal's footprint** spoor, track
**animal's hand** claw, paw
**animal's heart, liver and tongue** offal
**animal shed** cote
**animal's hind part** rump
**animal similar to llama** alpaca
**animals kept for profit** livestock

**animal skin** fur, hair, hide, pelt, wool
**animal's lungs** lights
**animal's male parent** sire
**animal's nail** claw
**animal's natural home** habitat
**animal's neck hair** mane
**animal's nose and jaws** snout
**animals of region** fauna
**animal sound** bark, grown, roar, snort, yelp
**animal's side** flank
**animal's skin disease** mange
**animal's spine** backbone, chine
**animal's stomach** craw, maw
**animal's track** run, slot, spoor
**animal's trunk** snout
**animal stuffer** taxidermist
**animal subphylum** Vertebrata
**animal's unguis** hoof
**animal's untanned skin** rawhide
**animal's victim** prey
**animal that carries its young in pouch** marsupial
**animal that chews the cud** ruminant
**animal that consumes termites** aardvark, aardwolf, ant-eater
**animal that eats insects** insectivore
**animal that feeds on grass and plants** herbivore
**animal that grunts** pig
**animal that lives on another one** parasite
**animal that never forgets** elephant
**animal that preys on others** predator
**animal trail** run, slot, spoor, track
**animal trainer** tamer
**animal with hard shell** crustacean
**animal with motley coat** piebald, pinto
**animal without colouring pigment** albino
**animal without feet** apod
**animal with padded not hoofed digits** tylopod
**animal with pouch** kangaroo
**animal with quills** porcupine
**animal with two feet** biped
**animal worship** theriolatry, zoolatry
**animate** activate, alive, arouse, boost, encourage, energise, enliven, excite, exhilarate, fire, goad, heat, impel, incite, inspire, inspirit, instigate, invigorate, kindle, liven, move, provoke, quicken, rekindle, revive, rouse, stimulate, urge, vigorous, vitalise, vivify, whet
**animated** active, alive, ardent, dynamic, ebullient, enlivened, excited, gay, happy, impassioned, invigorated, lifelike, lively, pleased, reanimated, revived, vivacious, vivified, zealous
**animated being** creature

**animated film** cartoon
**animate person** being
**animating principle** anima, soul, spirit
**animating spirit** genius
**animation** action, activity, blitheness, bounce, briskness, buoyancy, bustle, dynamism, élan, elation, energy, entrain (F), excitement, exertion, fervour, force, gaiety, go, happiness, hustle, labour, lampoon, life, live(li)ness, motion, movement, panache, passion, pep, spirit, stir, verve, vigour, vim, virtuosity, vitality, vivacity, work, zip
**animato** animé (F)
**an immediate involuntary response** reflex
**animosity** alienation, allergy, anger, animus, antagonism, antipathy, aversion, bitterness, disgust, dislike, dissatisfaction, enmity, hate, hatred, hostility, loathing, malevolence, malice, malignity, rancour, repugnance, resentment, spite, unfriendly
**animus** animosity, hostility
**an incident** occurrence
**an insolent menace** bravado
**aniseed** anise
**aniseed plant** anise
**aniseed spirit** Anis(ette), ouzo, Pernod
**anise plant** anet, cumin, dill
**anisette** cordial
**ankle-bone** astragal(us), talus, tarsal, tarsus
**ankle-high work shoe** brogan
**ankle joint** coot
**ankle-length robe** gown, talar
**annals** accounts, archives, chronicles, history, journals, memorials, records, registers
**annatto** roucou
**anneal** fuse, mercerise, strengthen, temper, toughen, vulcanise
**annealing oven** leer, lehr
**annelid** earthworm, leech, lugworm, ragworm
**annex** acquire, add(ition), adjoin, affix, annexe, append(age), appropriate, attach, connect, conquer, fasten, incorporate, join, link, occupy, prompt, seize, sequester, unite, usurp, wing
**annexe to house** extension
**annihilate** abolish, annul, break, crush, discreate, dissolve, eliminate, eradicate, erase, exterminate, extirpate, humble, invalidate, obliterate, rescind, retract, rout, smash, trounce, undo
**announce** advertise, augur, broadcast, declare, disclose, divulge, foretell,

herald, intimate, introduce, portend, present, proclaim, promulgate, publicise, publish, report, state
**announce by advertisement** bill
**announce court judg(e)ment** decree
**announced beforehand** bade
**announce loudly** blare, blast
**announcement** advertisement, broadcast, bulletin, communiqué, declaration, disclosure, intimation, notice, proclamation, publication, report, statement
**announce officially** proclaim
**announcer** broadcaster, crier, harbinger, herald, messenger, newscaster, proclaimer, reporter, trumpeter
**announce receipt of** acknowledge
**announcer of important news** herald
**announce with enthusiasm** acclaim
**annoy** aggravate, anger, antagonise, badger, bedevil, bother, bug, cross, displease, disquiet, disturb, enrage, exasperate, gall, harass, harm, harry, hector, irk, irritate, madden, molest, nag, nark, needle, nettle, offend, peeve, pester, pique, plague, provoke, rile, ruffle, tease, torment, trouble, try, vex, worry
**annoyance** affliction, aggravation, anger, bind, bore, bother, chagrin, displeasure, disturbance, dudgeon, exasperation, fash, harassment, headache, irritant, irritation, nuisance, offence, ordeal, pain, peeve, pest, plague, provocation, tease, tribulation, trouble, vexation
**annoyance at failure** frustration
**annoyed** angry, displeased, irate, peeved, riled
**annoying** aggravating, angering, boring, bothersome, displeasing, disturbing, enraging, exasperating, galling, harassing, hateful, intolerable, irksome, irritating, maddening, odious, offensive, pesky, pestering, provoking, rankling, riling, teasing, tiresome, tormenting, troublesome, troubling, unpleasant, vexatious, vexing, worrisome, worrying
**annoying conduct** mischief
**annoying insect** gnat, muggie, pest
**annoying person** pest
**annoy in hostile way** molest
**annoy persistently** pester
**annoy pettily** nettle, tease
**annoy playfully** tantalise, tease
**annoys a speaker** heckler
**annual** almanac, annals, anniversary, flower, perennial, yearbook, yearlong, yearly

**annual bean** urd
**annual celebration** anniversary
**annual comic parade of students** rag
**annual feast of Jews** Passover
**annual gala** festival
**annual grass** tef
**annual horse-race at Epsom** Derby, Oaks
**annual horse-race in Durban** July
**annually** yearlong, yearly
**annual plant** flax, herb
**annual plant with fragrant leaves** mignonette
**annual potherb** spinach
**annual produce** crop
**annual receipts** income
**annual rent** canon
**annuity scheme** tontine
**annul** abolish, abrogate, annihilate, avoid, cancel, countermand, destroy, disannul, discontinue, dissolve, elide, eliminate, exterminate, extirpate, invalid(ate), liquidate, negate, nullify, obliterate, overrule, quash, recall, recant, repeal, repudiate, rescind, retract, reverse, revert, revoke, scrub, undo, vacate, void, withdraw
**annularly** ringwise
**annulment** abolishment, abolition, cancellation, divorcement, extinguishment, invalidation, nullification, repeal, rescindment, reversal, undoing, voiding, withdrawal
**annum** year
**anoint** anele, apply, appoint, bless, call, consecrate, dedicate, destine, devote, elect, embrocate, enthrone, invest, lubricate, moisten, nominate, oil, ordain, paint, place, sanctify, smear
**anointing oil** chris(o)m
**anomaly** abnorm(al)ity, deviation, difference, disparity, freak, idiosyncrasy, inaptitude, inharmony, irregularity, peculiarity
**anon** afterward, anonymous, betimes, directly, early, forthright, forthwith, hereupon, immediately, instantly, later, now, presently, promptly, readily, shortly, soon, straightaway, thereupon
**anonymous** anonymal, cryptonymous, incognito, innominate, nameless, pseudonymous, unacknowledged, uncredited, undesignated, unidentified, unknown, unnamed, unsigned
**anorak** parka, wind-cheater

**another** additional, alternative, different, diverse, extra, other, surplus
**another cricket score** run
**another drink** refill
**another exactly similar** alter idem (L)
**another name for broccoli** calabrese
**another story** different, variant
**another time** again, anew, later
**another word for per** by, the, through
**anserine** goose-like, silly, stupid
**answer** account, acknowledge, acknowledg(e)ment, agree, balance, comeback, conform, correlate, defence, excuse, explanation, fulfil, meet, outcome, plea(d), react(ion), rebuttal, refute, rejoinder, reply, resolution, resolve, respond, response, retaliate, retaliation, retort, riposte, solution, solve, suffice, suit, vindication
**answerable** accordant, accountable, agreeable, amenable, chargeable, confutable, disprovable, explainable, liable, obliged, refutable, repudiable, (re)solvable, responsible, returnable, subject, suitable
**answerable for consequences** liable
**answer affirmatively** accept, nod
**answer a purpose** serve
**answer a thrust** parry
**answer back** argue, contradict, disagree, dispute, rebut, retaliate, retort, riposte
**answer challenge** accept
**answer for** recompense, rectify, redeem, repay, vouch
**answering** acknowledging, explaining, responding, responsive
**answering its purpose** effectual, efficacious
**answering to one's highest conception** ideal
**answer in kind** respond, retort
**answer invitation affirmatively** accept
**answer negatively** decline, reject
**answer sharply** retort
**answer the purpose** do, serve
**answer to** agree, correspond, match, meet
**answer to problem** solution
**ant** emmet, hymenopter(on), insect, kelep, pismire, suffix, termite, vermin
**antagonise** annoy, counteract, evoke, irrate
**antagonism** animosity, aversion, conflict, friction, opponency, opposition, rancour, resentment
**antagonism between different races** racialism
**antagonist** adversary, competitor, contender, contestant, disputant,

enemy, foe, opponent, opposer, rival, vier
**antagonistic** a(d)verse, antipathetic, belligerent, conflicting, contentious, hostile, ill-disposed, incompatible, inimical, opposed, unfriendly
**Antarctic** antipodal, frigid
**Antarctic bird** penguin, skua
**Antarctic hero** Scott
**Antarctic penguin** Adelie
**Antarctic sea** Ross, Weddell
**Antarctic volcano** Erebus
**ant-bear** aardvark
**ant bird** ant thrush, bush shrike
**ant cow** aphid
**ante** before, bet, chance, gamble, hazard, pay, peril, pledge, price, produce, risk, speculation, stake, venture, wager
**ant-eater** aardvark, aardwolf, ant-bear, edentate
**antecede** antedate, anticipate, outrank, precede, predate, prior(ity)
**antecedent** above, aforesaid, announcer, anterior, earlier, foregoing, forerunner, forerunning, former, herald, messenger, precedent, preceding, precursor, predecessor, preliminary, prevenient, previous, prior
**antecedent period** past
**antechamber** vestibule
**antedate** accelerate, antecede, anticipate, forego, forestall, hasten, head, herald, hurry, intercept, introduce, lead, misdate, postdate, precede, preface, prevent, rush, speed, usher
**ant egg** pupa
**antelope** addax, b(e)isa, blackbuck, blesbok, bontebok, buck, eland, fawn, gai, gazelle, gemsbok, gerenuk, gnu, hind, impala, kop, kudu, n(a)gor, nilgai, nyala, oribi, oryx, saiga, springbok, stag, suni, sus, tora, waterbuck, yak
**antenna** aerial, feeler, filament, horn, nipper, palp(us), signal, tentacle, whisker, wire
**antenna socket** torulus
**anterior** aforesaid, antecedent, earlier, foregoing, forerunning, former, forward, pre-existent, precedent, preceding, preliminary
**anteroom in hotel** foyer
**anthem** antiphon, canticle, chant, chorale, chorus, hymn, motet, offertory, paean, psalm, responsory
**anthology** album, ana, citations, collection, compendium, compilation, digest, extracts, florilegium, garland,

miscellany, selection, spicilegium, treasury
**anthracite** coal, coke, culm, fuel
**anthracite refuse** culm
**anthropography** ethnography
**anthropoid animal** ape
**anthropoid ape** chimpanzee, orang(utan)
**anthropophagous** cannibal, human-eating
**anthropophagy** cannibalism
**anti-** against, counteracting, preventing
**anti-aircraft fire** ack-ack, flak
**anti-aircraft guns** ack-ack
**antibody catalyst** antigen
**antibody production stimulant** isoantigen
**antibody that causes agglutination** agglutinin
**antic** adventure, caper, clown, device, escapade, fantastic, feat, fling, frisk, frolic, fun, gambol, game, grotesque, jape, joke, juggle, lark, mischief, play, prank, revel, rollic, romp, silliness, spree, stunt, trick
**anticipate** antedate, apprehend, await, consider, contemplate, envisage, envision, expect, forecast, foreknow, foresee, forestall, foretaste, foretell, hope, intercept, intuit, nullify, obviate, precipitate, preclude, predict, prevent, prophesy
**anticipate with fear** dread
**anticipation** apprehension, awaiting, expectancy, expectation, foresight, foretaste, forethought, hope, premonition, presentiment
**anti-clockwise** counter-clockwise, widdershins, withershins
**antics** larks, pranks, sport, tomfoolery, tricks
**antidote** antipyretic, antitoxin, counterpoison, curative, cure, drug, emetic, healing, laxative, medicament, medicine, nullifier, panacea, purgative, recovery, remedy, serum, specific, theriac, treatment
**antidote to poison** mithridate
**anti-friction alloy** babbitt
**anti-glare shield** sun visor
**anti-Jewish purge** pogrom
**Antilles island** Cuba
**antinovel** anti-roman (F)
**antipasto** entrée, hors d'oeuvre
**antipathy** abhorrence, allergy, animosity, antagonism, aversion, clash, detestation, disagreement, disgust, disinclination, dislike, distaste, enmity, hate, hatred, hostility, ill-will, incompatibility, loathing, opposition, rancour,

repugnance, repulsion, resentment, unfriendliness
**antipodean soldier** Anzac
**antipodean to heel** toe
**antipyretic medicine obtained from coal-tar** phenacetin
**antiquated** abandoned, age-old, aged, ancient, antique, archaic, archaistic, atavistic, bygone, crumbling, dated, dead, decayed, decrepit, démodé (F), disused, done, elderly, extinct, grey, hoary, moth-eaten, musty, obsolete, old(-fashioned), oldest, oldish, out(dated), outmoded, passé, past, primitive, quaint, ragged, rejected, remote, senescent, shabby, stale, superannuated, timeworn, unfashionable, unmodern, unoriginal, venerable
**antique** aged, ancient, antediluvian, antiquarian, antiquated, archaic, bygone, curio, démodé (F), elderly, heirloom, obsolescent, obsolete, old(-fashioned), relic, superannuated
**antique china** Rockingham
**antique red** canna
**antirrhinum** snapdragon
**antiseptic** clean(ser), disinfectant, germ-free, germicide, hygienic, iodine, medicated, pure, purifier, sanitary, sanitised, sterile, uncontaminated, unpolluted
**antiseptic lotion** iodine
**antiseptic oil** retinol
**antisocial** alienated, anarchic, antagonistic, asocial, belligerent, closed, conflicting, cynical, disorderly, disruptive, hostile, introverted, manhating, misanthropic, opposed, rebellious, reserved, retiring, revolutionary, unacceptable, unapproachable, uncommunicative, unfriendly, unpatriotic, unsociable, withdrawn
**antisocial character** psychopathic personality
**antisocial person** hermit, loner, recluse
**anti-tank rocket launcher** bazooka
**antithesis** antipodes, background, complement, contradiction, contrariety, contrary, contrast, converse, denial, disavowal, disclaimer, foil, inverse, negation, obverse, opposite, opposition, pole, reverse, setting
**antithesis of health** illth
**antitoxin** abirritant, analgesic, antibiotic, antibody, antidote, antigen, antiserum, antivenin, counterpoison, inoculation, sera, sero, serum, theriac, vaccination, vaccine

**antitoxin fluid** serum
**antitoxin lymphs** sera
**anti-viral fluid** vaccine
**anti-viral protein** interferon
**antler** dag, horn, spike
**antlered** spiky
**antlered animal** antelope, buck, caribou, deer, moose, stag, wapiti
**antler parts** prong, tine
**antler's furry skin** velvet
**antler's spike** tine
**ant nest** formicary
**antonym of bad** good
**antonym of better** worse
**antonym of good** bad
**antonym of worse** better, good
**ant queen** gyne
**antrum** cavern
**ant slavery** dulosis
**anurous** acaudal, tailless
**Anvers** Antwerp
**anvil** bench, bickern, block, hob, incus, post, rostrum, stake, stand, stilthy, teest
**anvil of the ear** incus
**anvil's projection** beak, horn
**anxiety** angst, apprehension, care, concern, disquiet, distress, fear, foreboding, fretfulness, nervousness, solicitude, tension, trepidation, trouble, uneasiness, uneasy, worry
**anxious** afraid, anguished, apprehensive, ardent, avid, careful, concerned, desirous, disquieted, distressed, disturbed, eager, fearful, fretful, greedy, impatient, intent, keen, nervous, restless, solicitous, taught, tense, tormented, tortured, troubled, uneasy, watchful, worried
**anxious concern** solicitude
**anxious to learn** curious
**any** a, all, an, anybody, anyone, either, every, indefinite, indiscriminate, one, onie (Sc), ony (Sc), singular, some(body), someone, somewhat, unlimited, unmeasured, whatever, whichever
**any animal group** species
**any arbitrary order** ukase
**any aromatic plant** herb
**anybody** anyone, someone
**anybody's guess** doubtful, gamble, uncertainty
**any bovine animal** neat
**any edible substance** esculent
**any false god** Baal
**any flat expanse** area
**any gluey substance** agglutinant
**any gnawing animal** rodent
**any illegal drug** dope

**any indictable offense** misdemeanour, crime
**any kind of business** affair
**any large military force** legion
**any large prize** jackpot
**any legislative assembly** parliament, senate
**any of five tendons at back of human knee** hamstring
**any of hairs on eyelid** eyelash
**any of several** a, an, one
**any of several stars** deneb
**any of various postures in yoga** asana
**any one** a, an
**anyone** anybody, whoever
**anyone at all** whoever
**any one of enumerated things** item
**any one side** facet
**any opponent engaged in conflict** belligerent
**any oxygen compound** oxide
**any person** (any)one
**any place of learning** academy
**any plane of aeroplane** aerofoil
**any poison** toxin
**any quantity** batch
**any science or theory** -ology
**any small candle** taper
**any small matter** affair
**any snug retreat** nest, haven
**any soft uniform mass** pulp
**any sound** noise
**any substance that fixes dyes** mordant
**any temporary erection** booth, shack
**any theory denying duality of matter and mind** monism
**anything at all** aught
**anything cheap and showy** Brummagem
**anything delicious** ambrosia
**anything destructive** bane
**anything gigantic** colossus, titan
**anything man-made** artefact, artifact
**anything of value** asset
**anything round** ball, circle
**anything set up to frighten birds from crops** scarecrow
**anything short-lived** ephemera
**anything strictly true** fact
**anything that acts as a spur** goad
**anything that commemorates monument**, obelisk
**anything that hampers** fetter, shackle
**anything that protects** aegis, guard, shield
**anything true** fact
**anything unpaid** arrears, debt
**anything valuable** asset
**anything very large of its kind** leviathan

**anything which** whatever
**any wall painting other than true fresco** secco
**Anzac Day month** April
**aorta** artery
**aoudad** Barbary sheep
**apace** expeditiously, fast, hastily, promptly, quick(ly), rapidly, readily, speedily, swiftly
**Apache baby** pap(p)oose
**apart** afar, alone, aloof, aside, asunder, away, disjointly, distant, distinct, divorced, excluded, exclusively, independently, individually, isolated, privately, secretly, separate(d), separately, singly
**apart from** besides, beyond, excluding
**apart from anything else** per se
**apartment** accommodation, chamber(s), flat, lodging, maisonette, penthouse, quarters, room(s), suite, tenement, unit
**apartment flat** unit
**apartment for females** harem, seraglio, serail, zenana
**apartment room** flat
**apathetic** cold, emotionless, indifferent, insensible, lackadaisical, listless, pococurante, stoic(al), torpid, unemotional, uninterested, unresponsive
**apathy** accidie, acedia, coldness, coolness, disinterest, dispassion, frigidity, impassivity, incuriousness, indifference, inertness, insensibility, insentience, languor, listlessness, numbness, passiveness, spiritlessness, stoicism, tepidity, torpor, unconcern, unfeelingness
**apatite** ijolite, moroxite, phosphorite
**ape** act, affect, anthropoid, copy, counterfeit, dupe, duplicate, echo, emulate, follow, fool, imitate, imitator, mime, mimic, mirror, mock, monkey, parody, parrot, portray, pose, pretend, primate, resemble, simian
**ape-like** apish, simian
**aper** mimic
**ape resembling man** anthropoid
**aperient** laxative
**aperitif** appetiser, cocktail, drink, sherry, snack, wine
**aperture** airhole, breach, break, channel, cleft, crack, crevice, duct, eye(let), gap, gate, groove, gulf, (key)hole, leak, loophole, mouth, opening, oriel, orifice, outlet, passage, perforation, pigeonhole, pore, rent, rima, rupture, slit, slot, space, split, stoma, vent
**aperture in door** hatch

**aperture in ship's side** porthole
**aperture in vending machine** slot
**apery** mimicry
**apex** acme, aerie, apogee, border, boundary, brim, brink, cap, climax, crest, crown, culmination, depth, edge, excess, extreme, extremity, eyrie, head, height, limit, loft, maximum, nadir, peak, pinnacle, point, pole, ridge, spire, summit, supremacy, termination, tip, top, ultimate, uttermost, verge, vertex, zenith
**apex elbow** ancon
**aphis** aphid, greenfly, plant-louse
**aphorism** adage, apophthegm, axiom, byword, cliché, dictum, epigram, fundamental, gnome, maxim, motto, pithy, platitude, postulate, precept, principle, proverb, rule, saw, saying, statement, truism, witticism
**aphorism in Hindu literature** Sutra
**Aphrodite** Antheia, Cypris, Cytherea, Mylitta, Pandemos, Urania, Venus
**apiaceous plant** anise, celery, nondo, parsley
**apiarist** bee-keeper
**apiary inhabitant** bee
**apiary owner** apiarist, bee-keeper
**apices** acmes, apexes, apogees, borders, boundaries, bounds, brims, brinks, climaxes, crests, crowns, depths, edges, ends, excesses, extremes, extremities, heads, heights, limits, peaks, pinnacles, poles, ridges, summits, terminations, tops, ultimates, zeniths
**apiculture** bee-keeping, bee-rearing
**apiece** distributively, each, individually, respectively, separately, seriatim, severally
**aping wisdom** sapient
**a pleasant journey** bon voyage (F)
**aplomb** assurance, balance, calmness, collectedness, composure, confidence, coolness, equanimity, erectness, poise, rationality, sang-froid, self-assurance, self-confidence, self-possession, self-restraint, stability, verticality
**apocryphal** counterfeit, untruth
**apodal** footless
**apodal member** eel
**apogee** acme, apex, border, bound(ary), climax, crest, crown, culmination, distance, edge, end, extremity, frontier, head, heights, highlight, limit, loft, margin, peak, pinnacle, point, ridge, rim, spire, summit, terminal, tip, top, ultimate, verge, vertex, zenith
**Apollo's instrument** bow, lute

**Apollo's oracle** Delos
**Apollo's symbol** arrow
**Apollo's twin sister** Artemis
**apologetic** confessing, contrite, defensive, justificatory, palliative, penitent, penitential, regret(ful), remorseful, repentant, rueful, sorry, vindicative
**apologise humbly** grovel
**apology** acknowledg(e)ment, amend, confession, defence, excuse, explanation, extenuation, justification, mitigation, penance, penitence, plea, regrets, reparation, repentance, substitute, travesty, vindication
**apostasy** error, heresy, impiety, schism, unorthodoxy
**apostate** abjurer, backslider, defector, deserter, disloyal, dissenter, heathen, heretic(al), perfidious, rebel, recidivist, recreant, renegade, renouncer, repudiator, schismatic, sectarian, separatist, traitor, turncoat, unfaithful, unorthodox, untrue
**apostle** adherent, admirer, backer, believer, convert, devotee, disciple, evangelist, fan(cier), follower, habitué, learner, messenger, missionary, partisan, pioneer, preacher, proponent, proselyte, pupil, student, supporter, votary, worshipper
**apostle of Jesus** Andrew, Bartholomew, James, John, Judas Iscariot, Matthew, Matthias, Paul, Peter, Philip, Simon, Thaddaeus, Thomas
**apostle's letter** epistle
**apostle's office** apostolate
**apothecary's weight** drachm
**appal** alarm, astound, awe, daunt, disconcert, discourage, disgust, dishearten, dismay, frighten, harrow, horrify, intimidate, outrage, petrify, revolt, scare, shock, startle, terrify, unnerve
**apparatus** appliance, equipment, fixture, instrument, machine(ry), network, paraphernalia, structure, tackle, tool, utensil
**apparatus for cooking** stove
**apparatus for defence** armature
**apparatus for distilling** still
**apparatus for measuring velocity of projectiles** chronoscope
**apparatus for producing electrical energy** generator
**apparatus for pulping paper** macerator

**apparatus for putting out fire** extinguisher
**apparatus for separating cream from milk** separator
**apparatus for shaking and mixing** agitator
**apparatus for taking photographs** camera
**apparatus for weaving** loom
**apparel** accoutre(ment), adorn, array, attire, clothes, clothing, costume, dress, equip(ment), garb, garment, gear, guise, habiliment, ornament, outfit, raiment, rig, robe, vestment, vesture
**apparent** clear, conspicuous, detectable, discernible, evident, manifest, obvious, ostensible, overt, patent, perceptible, plain, seeming, unmistakable, unquestionable, visible
**apparent contradiction** paradox
**apparently** allegedly, blatantly, clearly, distinctly, evidently, likely, noticeably, openly, perceivably, plainly, probably, publicly, seemingly, strikingly, visibly
**apparent only** seeming
**apparition** appearance, chimera, eidolon, fata morgana (I), ghost, illusion, manifestation, phantom, presence, revenant, shape, spectre, spirit, spook, vision, visitant, visitation, wraith
**appeal** adjure, allure, application, attract(ion), beauty, entreat(y), petition, plea(d), refer, request, solicitation, suit, supplicate, supplication
**appeal a case** reopen
**appeal earnestly** beseech, plead
**appealing** cute, pretty, suppliant
**appealingly** attractively, beautifully
**appeal to for confirmation** protest
**appeal to personal interests** argumentum ad hominem (L)
**appear** act, arise, arrive, attend, dawn, develop, emerge, enter, issue, look, loom, materialise, occur, perform, play, rise, seem, surface, uprise
**appearance** advent, air, arrival, aspect, attitude, bearing, cast, character, coming, countenance, debut, demeanour, emergence, exhibition, expression, face, figure, form, front, guise, image, impression, introduction, look, manner, mien, presence, pretence, publication, rise, seeming, semblance, show, upcropping, visage
**appearance of unburnished gold** mat(t)
**appearance on the scene** arrival

**appear dimly** loom, peer
**appear for** act, attorney, negotiate, represent, substitute
**appear from** emerge
**appear in disguise** masquerade
**appear indistinctly** loom
**appearing successively** serial
**appear in play** act
**appear in summer** aestival
**appear likely** seem
**appear listless** moon
**appear melancholy** mope
**appear on stage** act, enter
**appear partially** peer
**appear suddenly** flash
**appear to be** seem
**appear vaguely** loom
**appease** abate, accommodate, adjust, allay, alleviate, arbitrate, assuage, calm, comfort, compose, compromise, concede, conciliate, ease, hush, lessen, lull, mediate, mitigate, mollify, pacificate, pacify, palliate, placate, quell, quench, quiet, relieve, satisfy, silence, soften, soothe, still, submit, surrender, tranquillise, yield
**appease hunger** stay
**appeasement** abatement, adjustment, alleviation, blunting, calumet, concession, contentment, lessening, mollification, pacification, palliation, placation, reconcilement, silencing, surrender, yielding
**appeaser** pacificator
**appeasing** placatory, propitiatory
**appellation** address, alias, anonym, by-word, definition, denomination, description, designation, epithet, honorific, identification, label, name, nom de guerre (F), nomenclature, pseudonym, style, tag, term, title
**append** add, adjoin, affix, annex, attach, (sub)join
**appendage** accessory, addition, adjunct, attachment, auxiliary, extremity, feeler, supplement, tail, tentacle
**appendage at base of leaf** stipule
**appendage of crustacean** endite
**appendage to a will** codicil
**appendix** addendum, addition, adjunct, annex(e), appendage, attachment, codicil, epilogue, extension, extra, postscript, suffix, supplement
**appendix in law** codicil
**appertain** apply, belong, fit, pertain, refer, relate, suit
**appetiser** allurement, apéritif, attraction, bait, bite, bonne bouche (F), canapé, cocktail, dainty, delicacy, drink, enticement, foretaste, hors d'oeuvre, invitation, lure, morsel, relish, teaser, temptation, titbit, whet
**appetising** appealing, delicious, inviting, mouthwatering, palatable, piquant, savoury, scrumptious, succulent, tantalising, tasty, tempting
**appetite** appetence, craving, demand, desire, gusto, hankering, hunger, inclination, liking, longing, passion, relish, stomach, taste, thirst, zeal, zest
**appetite comes with eating** l'appétit vient en mangeant (F)
**applaud** acclaim, approbation, approve, bravo, cheer, clap, commend, congratulate, encore, felicitate, hail, honour, praise, rejoice, welcome
**applaud publicly** acclaim
**applaud with hands** clap
**applause** acclaim, acclamation, accolade, approbation, approval, bravo, cheering, cheers, commendation, congratulations, éclat, encore, hand-clapping, laudation, laurels, outcry, ovation, praise, salvo, sanction, tribute, whistling
**apple** crab, esopus, fruit, pippin, pome, russet, spy, tree, winesap
**apple acid** malic
**apple brandy** calvados
**apple centre** core
**apple dessert** fritter, (pan)dowdy, pie, strudel
**apple drink** cider, cyder
**apple grown from seed** pippin
**apple liquor** applejack
**apple of one's eye** favourite, pet, precious
**apple pip** seed
**apple-pulp liqueur** calvados
**apple region** Elgin
**apples crushed by grinding** pomace
**apple seed** pip, pit
**appliance** adjunct, apparatus, application, appurtenance, device, expedient, gadget, implement, instrument, tool, use
**appliance for raising water** pump
**appliance on which a sick person can be carried** stretcher
**appliance to aid hearing** acousticon
**applicable** apposite, appropriate, apt, befitting, fit(ting), germane, legitimate, pertinent, proper, relevant, suitable, suited, useful, valid
**applicant** aspirant, candidate, claimant, competitor, contestant, enquirer, inquirer, interviewee, petitioner, postulant, solicitor, suitor, suppli(c)ant
**application** appeal, appliance, applying, appositeness, assiduity, claim, diligence, exercise, germaneness, industry, perseverance, persistence, pertinence, petition, practice, relevance, request, term, use, utilisation, utility, value
**application for head** hair-cream
**application for help** recourse
**application for the skin** poultice
**application of force** pressure
**application to a judge** motion
**application to a purpose** use
**apply** address, adhibit, administer, allot, anoint, appeal, appertain, appropriate, ask, assign, claim, credit, dedicate, devote, direct, effect, employ, engage, entreat, execute, exercise, exert, impinge, implement, persevere, pertain, practice, refer, relate, solicit, suit, treat, use, utilise
**apply asphalt** pave
**apply colour** dye, paint
**apply effort** endeavour, strive, work
**apply for redress** sue
**apply friction** massage, rub
**apply habitually** addict
**apply heat** warm
**apply improperly** abuse
**apply levy** tax
**apply logic to** rationalise, reason
**apply medicine** dose
**apply oil** anoint
**apply process to** treat
**apply remedies to** treat
**apply stimulant to** stimulate
**apply therapy** treat
**apply thickly** smear
**apply to** consult, contact
**apply to wrong purpose** abuse, misuse
**apply warmth to** foment, heat
**apply with a brush** paint
**apply wrongly** misuse
**appoint** accoutre, allot, assign, commission, constitute, designate, destine, detail, determine, elect, engage, equip, establish, furnish, name, nominate, ordain, outfit, prescribe, rig, select, supply
**appoint as agent** depute, deputise, name
**appoint as deputy** delegate, depute
**appoint as heir** entail
**appoint ceremonially to the Christian ministry** ordain
**appointed body of people** committee
**appointed by votes** elective

**appointed for a lawsuit** ad litem (L)
**appointed lot of person** fate
**appointed meeting** rendezvous, tryst
**appointed time** date, day, hour
**appointed to arrive** due
**appointing as agent** deputing
**appointment** agreement, allotment, arrangement, assignation, assignment, choice, date, delegation, deputation, designation, engagement, installation, interview, meeting, nomination, ordainment, place, position, rendezvous, sinecure, station, tryst
**appointment book** diary
**appointment to meet** rendezvous
**appoint to an office** name, nominate
**apportion** allocate, allot, appropriate, assign, bisect, cut, deal, dispense, disperse, distribute, divide, dole, dose, halve, lot, measure, mete, partition, portion, prorate, ration, share, split, zone
**apposite** adapted, appertaining, applicable, appropriate, apropos, apt, befitting, convenient, felicitous, fit(ting), germane, meet, opportune, pertinent, proper, relative, relevant, suitable, suited, timely
**appositeness** applicableness, appropriateness, aptness, pertinence, properness, suitableness
**appraisal** analysis, appreciation, ascertainment, assay, assessment, balancing, comment(ary), conviction, criticism, critique, deduction, determination, diagnosis, elucidation, estimate, estimation, evaluation, finding, judg(e)ment, notice, opinion, pricing, rating, review, survey, valuation, view
**appraise** appreciate, ascertain, assay, assess, calculate, count, determine, estimate, evaluate, gauge, inspect, measure, price, rate, review, treasure, valuate, value, vet
**appreciable amount** considerable
**appreciate** acclaim, acknowledge, admire, adore, applaud, cherish, enhance, enjoy, esteem, gain, grow, honour, inflate, know, laud, like, love, perceive, praise, prize, recognise, relish, respect, revere, savour, treasure, value
**appreciation** acclamation, acknowledg(e)ment, appraisal, awareness, enjoyment, gratitude, obligation, praise, regard, respect, review, sensitivity, thankfulness
**apprehend** anticipate, arrest, catch, crouch, distrust, dread, fear, feel, funk, grasp, imagine, immure,
imprison, nab, perceive, seize, sense, suspect
**apprehend by legal authority** arrest
**apprehend clearly** comprehend, realise
**apprehendor** captor
**apprehend through senses** feel, hear, smell, taste, touch
**apprehension** anxiety, belief, care, concern, custody, detainment, detention, distrust, dread, fear, feeling, grasp, idea, insight, intellect, intuition, ken, knowledge, mind, mistrust, opinion, presage, qualm, reason, restraint, sense, suspicion, thought, uncertainty, understanding, view, worry
**apprehensive** acute, afraid, alarmed, anxious, astute, aware, concerned, distressed, fearful, fidgety, foreboding, intelligent, mistrustful, nervous, perceptive, qualmish, queasy, sagacious, sapient, sensible, sensitive, solicitous, suspicious, thoughtful, uneasy, worried
**apprehensive with fear** quail
**apprentice** beginner, learner, neophyte, newcomer, novice, probationer, pupil, recruit, starter, student, tiro, trainee, tyro
**apprise** acquaint, advise, give, inform, notify, tell
**appriser** informant
**approach** access, accost, adit, advance, advent, application, approximate, arrival, attack, attitude, avenue, begin, close, come, commence, conduct, converge, doorway, draw, entrance, form, greet, introduce, manner, means, meet, mention, method, mote, motion, near, passage, procedure, proposal, proposition, proximity, reach, resemble, road, rout, style, technique, threshold, undertake, verge, way, wise
**approaching** advancing, approximating, coming, meeting, nearing, reaching, resembling
**approaching day** tomorrow
**approaching from the front** oncoming
**approach nearer together** converge
**approach stealthily** stalk
**approach to house** doorstep
**approbation** acclaim, applause, approval, compliment, congratulation, laudation, praise, ratification, sanction
**appropriate** adopt, allocate, applicable, apportion, apt, assign, becoming, befitting, congruous, correct, expedient, felicitous, fit(ting),
germane, individual, meet, opportune, pay, pertinent, pre-empt, proper, relevant, right, seasonable, seemly, spot-on, suitable, suited, timely, well-chosen, well-suited
**appropriate without authority** usurp
**appropriation of funds** embezzlement
**approval** acceptance, acclaim, acquiescence, admiration, agreement, applause, appreciation, approbation, assent, authorisation, blessing, commendation, compliance, confirmation, consent, countenance, endorsement, esteem, favour, imprimatur, leave, licence, liking, mandate, permission, praise, regard, respect, sanction
**approval by clapping** applause
**approve** accept, acclaim, accord, admire, advocate, allow, applaud, appreciate, authorise, bless, commend, concede, confirm, countenance, endorse, esteem, favour, like, mandate, OK, okay, pass, permit, praise, prize, ratify, recommend, respect, sanction, second, uphold, validate, value
**approved moral behaviour** ethical
**approve of** endorse, like
**approve officially** endorse
**approving** accepting, acclaiming, admiring, advocating, allowing, applauding, appreciating, authorising, blessing, confirming, countenancing, endorsing, esteeming, favouring, liking, mandating, passing, permitting, praising, ratifying, recommending, respecting, uncritical, upholding
**approximate** adjacent, adjoining, analogous, approach, approaching, bordering, close, coming, comparative, contiguous, copy, equal, estimated, figure, imitate, imminent, impending, inexact, juxtapositional, like, loose, near(by), nearly, reckon, related, relative, resemble, rough, similar, simulate, touch(ing)
**approximate calculation** estimation
**approximate judgement of amounts** estimate
**approximately** about, almost, around, circa (L), comparably, estimatingly, generally, grosso modo (I), hardly, loosely, nearly, relatively, roughly, scarcely, similarly, virtually
**appurtenance** accessory, addendum, addition, attachment, bonus, complement, extension, extra, supernumerary, supplement
**apricot disease** blight

**apricots dried with sugar and salt** mebos
**a priori** conjectural, deduced, deductive, inferential, speculative, theoretical
**apron** pinafore, pinny
**apron-like part of woman's dress** tablier
**apron top** bib
**apropos** appertaining, applicable, apposite, appropriate, apt(ly), becoming, befitting, belonging, congruous, felicitous, fit(ting), germane, opportune(ly), pat, pertinent(ly), proper, purpose, re(garding), relevant, right, seasonably, suitable, suitably, timely
**apse** apsis, arch, dome, recess, vault
**apsidal end of church** chevet
**apsis** apse
**apt** accurate, adroit, agile, applicable, apposite, appropriate, apropos, clever, correct, dext(e)rous, disposed, due, fair, felicitous, fit(ting), germane, gifted, given, inclined, intellectual, intelligent, liable, likely, meet, neat, pat, pertinent, prepared, prone, proper, quick, ready, relevant, sagacious, skilful, skilled, subject, suitable, suited, talented, timely
**apt at learning** capable, teachable
**apteral** apterous, wingless
**apteryx** kiwi
**aptitude** ability, bent, capability, capacity, cleverness, competency, craftsmanship, cunning, efficiency, expedience, fitness, flair, inclination, mastery, proneness, propensity, skill, talent, tendency, versatility
**aptly** suitably
**aptness** applicableness, appositeness, astuteness, cleverness, correctness, expertness, fitness, germaneness, liableness, likeliness, promptness, proneness, properness, quickness, readiness, skilfulness, smartness
**apt to bite** snappy
**apt to change** fluid
**apt to intrude** intrusive
**apt to shake** shaky
**apt to take offence** huffy, touchy
**aqua** water
**aqualung** scuba
**aquarium fish** guppy, orfe, rasbora
**aquatic animal** beaver, fish, newt, otter, polyp, seal
**aquatic arachnid** water spider
**aquatic beaver-like rodent** coypu
**aquatic bird** coot, dabchick, dipper, diver, duck, flamingo, goose, grebe, gull, penguin, smew, swan, tern
**aquatic blood-sucking worm** leech
**aquatic creature** sea-horse
**aquatic grass** reed
**aquatic mammal** anemone, cetacean, eel, newt, otter, polyp, seal, sirenian, sponge, whale
**aquatic mollusc** bivalve
**aquatic nocturnal marsupial** opossum
**aquatic plant** alisma, duckweed, frogbit, pickerelweed, tawkee, waterlily
**aquatic vertebrate** fish
**aquatic worm** cadew, tubifex
**aqueduct** conduit
**aqueous** adulterated, boggy, damp, dewy, diluted, feeble, humid, insipid, moist, soggy, steam, tasteless, waterish, watery, wet
**aqueous precipitation** dew
**Aquilegia genus** columbine
**Aïr** Asben
**ara** macaw, parrot
**Arab** Moor, Saracen, Semite
**Arab country** Algeria, Egypt, Iraq, Jordan, Kuwait, Lebanon, Libya, Morocco, Oman, Tunisia, Yemen
**Arabian boat** dhow
**Arabian camel** dromedary
**Arabian chief** sheikh
**Arabian chieftain** emeer, emir
**Arabian cloak** aba(ya), abba
**Arabian cloth** aba
**Arabian demon** afreet, afrit
**Arabian desert wind** simoom, simoon
**Arabian export** oil
**Arabian fabulous bird** roc
**Arabian faith** Islam
**Arabian garment** aba(ya), abba, burnous, caftan, hai(c)k
**Arabian gazelle** ariel
**Arabian Gulf** Aden, Oman
**Arabian Gulf state** Oman
**Arabian headband cord** agal
**Arabian headdress** kaffiyeh, keffiyeh
**Arabian holy city** Mecca
**Arabian holy scripture** Koran
**Arabian hooded cloak** burnous, (d)jellaba
**Arabian in design** arabesque
**Arabian judge** cadi
**Arabian kingdom** Iraq, Jordan, Yemen
**Arabian language** Arabic
**Arabian leather** mocha
**Arabian Moslem** Sunnite, Wahabi
**Arabian name** Ali
**Arabian night bird** roc
**Arabian nomad** Saracen
**Arabian open market-place** souk
**Arabian outer wrapper for head and body** hai(c)k
**Arabian peninsula** Aden, Sinai
**Arabian pilgrim** hadji, hajji
**Arabian port** Aden
**Arabian prince** caliph, emir, sharif, shereef, sherif
**Arabian reception** diffa
**Arabian river bed** wadi
**Arabian robe** aba(ya), abba
**Arabian ruler** schaik, sheik(h)
**Arabian sailboat** dhow, saic
**Arabian shrub** kat
**Arabian skull-cap** chechia
**Arabian sprite** genie
**Arabian sultanate** Oman
**Arabian tambourine** daira, taar
**Arabian veil** yashmak
**Arabian vessel** dhow
**Arabian wind** simoom, simoon
**Arabian wrap** hai(c)k
**Arabic numeral** digit
**arable** cultivable, farmable, fecund, fertile, fruitful, ploughable, productive, prolific, tillable
**Arab of the Crusades** Saracen
**Arab or Muslim** Saracen
**Arab petrol organisation** OPEC
**Arab quarter of city** casbah, kasbah
**araceous plant** arum, cabbage, lily, taro
**arachnid** acarus, mite, scorpion, spider, tick
**arachnid net** web
**Arafat's organisation** PLO
**Aram** Syria
**araroba** zebrawood
**arbiter** adjudicator, arbitrator, authority, autocrat, determiner, dictator, go-between, intercessor, intermediary, judge, linesman, mediator, moderator, negotiator, peacemaker, referee, umpire
**arbitrary** absolute, autocratic, capricious, chance, despotic, dictatorial, discretionary, dogmatic, domineering, fanciful, fascistic, high-handed, imperious, inconsistent, instinctive, magisterial, overbearing, random, tyrannical, uncertain, unreasonable, unreasoned, unrestrained, wilful
**arbitrary decree** fiat
**arbitrary disposal** will
**arbitrary supposition** fancy
**arbitrate** adjudge, adjudicate, decide, determine, intercede, interpose, judge, mediate, negotiate, reconcile, referee, sentence, settle, umpire
**arbitration** adjudicate, conciliation, decision, determination, function, intermediation, intervention, judg(e)ment, negotiation, peacemaking, settlement
**arbitrator** adjudicator, arbiter, intermediary, judge, mediator,

moderator, negotiator, peacemaker, referee, umpire
**arboreal ant-eater** tamandua
**arboreal mammal** lemur, opossum, raccoon
**arboreal marsupial** opossum
**arboreal peak** treetop
**arboreal rodent** squirrel
**arborescent** arboreous
**arbour** alcove, asylum, axle, bower, grotto, hermitage, lattice, mew, pavilion, pergola, recess, refuge, sanctuary, spindle
**arc** arcade, arch, bend, bow, crescent, curvature, curve, epicycloid, flexure, half-circle, half-moon, horseshoe, lamp, lunula, orbit, ovule, parabola, quadrant, sector, semi-circle, spotlight
**arcade** cloister, colonnade, gallery, loggia, mall, passageway, peristyle, porch, portico, precinct
**arcade over an aisle** triforium
**arcane** abstruse, baffling, concealed, cryptic, curious, dark, deep, enigmatic, esoteric, furtive, hidden, inexplicable, inscrutable, mysterious, mystic, obscure, occult, recondite, secret, strange, uncanny, unknown, weird
**arcanum** alembic, arcana, cab(b)ala, conundrum, elixir, enigma, mystery, nostrum, panacea, secret
**arc formed in sky** rainbow
**arc from zenith to horizon** azimuth
**arch** accomplished, arc, archway, artful, bend, bow, bridge, camber, chief, concave, consummate, convexity, cunning, cupola, curvature, curve, dome, expert, extend, finished, first, foremost, greatest, highest, leading, main, major, master, mischievous, playful, pre-eminent, primary, principal, provocative, rainbow, roguish, semicircle, sly, span, top, vault, waggish
**archaeological excavation** dig
**archaeological object** artefact, artifact
**archaic** ancient, antediluvian, antiquated, antique, bygone, obsolescent, obsolete, old(-fashioned), out-of-date, outdated, outmoded, passé, prehistoric, primitive, quaint, superannuated, underdeveloped, unevolved
**archaic article** ye
**archaic length** ell
**archaic preposition** unto
**archaic pronoun** thine, thy, ye
**archangel** Gabriel

**archbishop** hierarch
**arched** cambered, concave, embowed, forniciform, vaulted
**arched gallery** arcade
**arched part of foot** instep
**arched passageway** arcade
**arched recess** apse
**arched roof** apse, vault
**arched work in building** arcuate
**archer** bowman, toxophilite
**archer's missile** arrow
**archery range** butts, green
**archery score** hit
**archery unit** end
**archetype** classic, conception, exemplar, form, idea(l), model, mould, original, paradigm, paragon, pattern, precursor, predecessor, protoplast, (proto)type, standard
**arch-fiend** devil
**Archimedes' cry of discovery** eureka
**archipelago of Guinea-Bissau** Bijagos
**architect of St Paul's, London** Wren
**architect's drawing** plan
**architectural column** pilaster
**architectural design** spandrel
**architecturally grand** palatial
**architectural moulding** echinus
**architectural ornament** corbeil, dentil
**architectural pier** anta
**architectural screen** spier
**architectural style** Byzantine, Doric, Rococo
**archly** artfully, chiefly, consummately, cunningly, firstly, frolicsomely, knowingly, mainly, pertly, playfully, primarily, principally, saucily, slily, slyly
**archly demure** coy
**archly reticent** coy
**arch of human foot** instep
**arch of sky** cope
**archon** magistrate, ruler
**arch over** bridge
**arch slightly** camber
**arctic** cold(ness), far-northern, freeze, freezing, frigid, frost-bound, frosty, frozen, gelid, glacial, hyperborean, iciness, icy, polar
**Arctic** northern
**Arctic bear** polar
**Arctic bird** auk, fulmar
**Arctic citizen** Icelander
**Arctic delphinoid cetacean** narwhal
**Arctic dog** husky, Samoyed
**Arctic duck** eider
**Arctic dweller** Eskimo
**Arctic exploration base** Etah
**Arctic fish** cap(e)lin
**Arctic footwear** snowshoe
**Arctic goose** brent
**Arctic grouse** ptarmigan

**Arctic gulf** Ob
**Arctic gull** skua
**Arctic hooded jacket** anorak, parka
**Arctic island** Banks, Greenland
**Arctic mammal** narwhal, walrus
**Arctic marten** sable
**Arctic native** Eskimo
**Arctic nomad** Lapp
**Arctic Ocean island** Greenland
**Arctic plain** tundra
**Arctic rodent** lemming
**Arctic sandpiper** knot
**Arctic sea** Barents, Kara
**Arctic state** Alaska
**Arctic transportation** sled, umiak
**Arctic treeless plain** tundra
**Arctic vessel** iceboat
**Arctic whale** narwhal
**arctiid moth** ermine
**arcuate** arched
**ardent** amorous, ardour, avid, burning, dedicated, devoted, drive, eager, earnest, energy, enthusiasm, enthusiastic, fervent, fervid, fever, fierce, fiery, flashing, flushed, force(ful), heat, impassioned, intense, keen, lusty, passion(ate), punch, rethe, sensation, soulful, spirit(ed), vehement, verve, vigour, vivacity, warm, zealous
**ardent admirer** adorer, fan
**ardent affection** adoration, love
**ardent desire** yen
**ardent desire for distinction** ambition
**ardent desire for drink** thirst, dipsomania
**ardent eagerness** enthusiasm
**ardent fan** devotee
**ardent love** passion
**ardently** hotly
**ardently desirous** avid
**ardently loyal** devoted
**ardently persistent** strenuous
**ardently serious** earnest
**ardent partisan** devotee, fan
**ardent person** enthusiast
**ardent spirit** brandy, rum, whisky
**ardent supporter** aficionado, fan
**ardour** affection, dash, devotion, eagerness, ecstasy, élan, emotion, enthusiasm, fervency, fervour, flame, gusto, heat, impulse, love, passion, sentiment, spirit, vehemence, vigour, vivacity, zeal
**arduous** backbreaking, burdensome, difficult, exhausting, fatiguing, formidable, gruelling, hard, harsh, heavy, herculean, high, laborious, onerous, painful, punishing, rigorous, severe, steep, strenuous, taxing, tiring, tough, troublesome, trying, uphill

**arduous journey** trek
**arduous work** toil
**area** arena, compass, district, domain, expanse, extend, extent, locality, neighbourhood, plot, range, realm, region, scope, section, site, space, sphere, stretch, territory, tract, zone
**area of human activity** field
**area of land** tract
**area of scrub vegetation** scrubland, kar(r)oo
**area of shifting sand dunes** erg
**area of 100 square metres** hectare
**area of swift currents** rapids, cascade
**area of water sown with mines** minefield
**area outside a city** suburb, country
**area planted with shrubs** shrubbery
**area preserved for development** green belt
**area under authority of bishop or archbishop** see, diocese
**area under one rule** domain, rule, kingdom
**area where animals are displayed for auction** arena
**area with trees** forest, wood
**areca nut** betel nut
**are indebted** owe
**arena** amphitheatre, area, battlefield, battleground, bowl, coliseum, colosseum, domain, field, field, ground, hippodrome, park, ring, scene, sector, sphere, stadium, stage, venue
**arenaceous** gritty, sabulous, sandlike, sandy, sabulose
**arenite** sandstone
**are not** aren't
**argent** silvery, silvery-white
**argentine** silvery
**Argentinian cheese** goya, tafi
**Argentinian cowboy** gaucho
**Argentinian currency** argentino, centavo, peso
**Argentinian dance** cuando, gaucho, tango
**Argentinian dictator** Perón
**Argentinian estuary** Laplata
**Argentinian lake** Cardiel, Fagnano, Musters, Viedma
**Argentinian plain** chaco, llano, pampa
**Argentinian port** Rosario
**Argentinian region** Chaco, Patagonia
**Argentinian volcano** Lanin, Peteroa, Tupungato
**Argentinian waterfall** Grande, Iguazu
**Argos king** Diomedes
**argot** cant, dialect, idiom, jargon, language, nomenclature, parlance, patois, patter, slang, speech, tongue, usage, vernacular, vocabulary, words
**argue** bicker, contend, contest, controvert, debate, discuss, dispute, drive, hold, indicate, maintain, persuade, plead, quarrel, reason, remonstrate, row, show, spar, wrangle
**argue a case** plead
**argue against** remonstrate
**argue for** advocate
**argue for and against** moot
**argue formally** debate
**argue in court** plead
**argue insistently** stickle
**argue peevishly** wrangle
**argue with zeal** altercate
**arguing** altercating, asserting, bickering, claiming, contending, controverting, debating, demonstrating, disagreeing, discussing, disputing, evincing, exhibiting, expostulating, feuding, fighting, holding, implying, indicating, maintaining, pleading, quarrelling, questioning, reasoning, remonstrating, showing, squabbling, suggesting, wrangling
**argument** abstract, altercation, clash, contention, controversy, debate, disagreement, discussion, dispute, fight, précis, quarrel, reason(ing), row, scrap, statement, summary, theme, thesis, topic
**argument against** con
**argumentative** belligerent, cantankerous, combative, contentious, contrary, controversial, cranky, doubtful, dubious, humoured, irascible, irritable, opinionated, perverse, petulant, polemic(al), quarrelsome, wranglesome
**argumentatively** belligerently, contentiously, contrarily, controversially, disputatiously, doubtfully, dubiously
**argument in favour of** pro
**aria** air, carillon, carol, cavatina, chanson (F), melodic, melody, refrain, sennet, solo, song, strain, theme, tune
**arid** barren, boring, desert, dreary, dry, dull, flat, jejune, lifeless, moistureless, parched, sterile, tedious, uninspired, vapid, waterless
**aridity** aridness, barrenness, deficiency, dryness, ennui, evaporation, fatigue, fruitlessness, infertility, monotony, poverty, sterility, torridity, uselessness, weariness
**arid region** desert, Gobi, Mojave, Namib, Sahara
**arid tableland of South Africa** Kar(r)oo
**arid waste** desert
**Aries** ram
**arise** appear, ascend, awake, begin, climb, commence, emanate, emerge, get up, mount, originate, rise, scale, soar, start, tower
**arise from** emanate, ensue, issue, proceed, result
**arising from error** erroneous
**aristocracy** elite, gentility, gentry, meritocracy, nobility, noblesse, oligarchy, patrician, patriciate, peerage
**aristocrat** grandee, lady, lord, noble, patrician, peer(ess)
**aristocratic** affected, blue-blooded, courteous, delicate, disdainful, elegant, elite, fine, genteel, gentlemanly, graceful, haughty, highborn, kingly, lordly, noble, patrician, pedigreed, princely, royal, thoroughbred, titled, unnatural, upper-class
**Aristotle's school** lyceum
**arithmetical operation** addition, division, multiplication, subtraction
**arithmetical working** calculation
**arithmetic mean** average
**arithmetic term** add, divide, minus, multiply, plus, subtract
**ark** box, chest, coffer, craft, flatboat, raft
**ark builder** Noah
**ark's landing place** Ararat
**ark's resting place** Ararat
**arm** appendage, bough, brace, branch, channel, cove, creek, division, equip, estuary, fortify, furnish, gun, insignia, limb, matériel, offshoot, prepare, sleeve, strengthen, tentacle, weapon
**armada** argosy, armament, fleet, flotilla, navy, squadron, warships
**armadillo** apar, mulita, poyou, tatou
**armature** rotor
**armband** armlet, bangle, bracelet, brassard
**arm bandage** sling
**arm bone** ulna, humerus, radius
**arm covering** sleeve
**armchair** fauteuil
**armed band** cohort, commando, impi
**armed conflict** battle, war
**armed conflict between nations** war
**armed fight** battle
**armed fleet** armada, navy
**armed foe** enemy
**armed force** army, battalion, garrison, platoon, troop
**armed guard** sentry, sentinel

**armed Indian tribesmen** lashkar
**armed police** gens d'armes (F), gendarme
**armed robber** outlaw
**armed robbery** hold-up
**armed ship** battleship, man-of-war
**armed ships** navy
**armed to the teeth** powerful
**armed uprising** revolt
**armful of corn tied after reaping** sheaf
**armhole** scye
**armistice** truce, peace, ceasefire
**arm jewellery** bracelet
**arm joint** elbow, wrist, shoulder
**arm muscle** biceps, flexor, triceps
**arm of a windmill** sail
**arm of crane** gib
**arm of octopus** tentacle
**arm of sea** firth, frith
**arm of shirt** sleeve
**arm of the Mediterranean** Adriatic, Tyrrhenian
**arm of the sea** inlet, firth, frith, strait
**armorial bearings** heraldry
**arm or leg** limb
**armour** bard, covering, defence, mail, plate, plating, protection, rampart, safeguard, sheathing, shelter, weapon
**armour chain** mail
**armoured animal** armadillo, pangolin
**armoured shoe** sabaton
**armoured skirt** tace, tasse, tasset
**armoured South American animal** armadillo, pangolin
**armoured vehicle** tank, casspir, hippo, buffel
**armour for arm** vambrace, cannon
**armour for body** byrnie, chausses, cuirass, culet, lorica, placate, surcoat, tace, tasse
**armour for elbow** roundel
**armour for face** visor, beaver, mask
**armour for foot** sabaton, solleret
**armour for hand** gauntlet
**armour for head** helmet, helm, armet
**armour for hips** culet, tasse, tasset
**armour for horse** bard, barde, chamfrain, chamfron, chanfron, crinet
**armour for knee** poleyn
**armour for leg** giambeaux, greave, jambeaux
**armour for leg below knee** greave
**armour for lower body** culet
**armour for neck** aventail, buffe, gorget
**armour for shin** greave
**armour for shoulder** ailette, epaulière, pauldron, rerebrace
**armour for thigh** cuish, cuisse, taslet, tasse(t), tuille
**armour for throat** gorget

**armour jacket** acton, aketoun, haqueton
**armour part** tasset
**armour to cover the trunk** corselet
**armoury** arsenal, auditorium, coliseum, colosseum, depot, entrêpot, magazine, matchment, repository, stock, stockpile, storehouse, warehouse
**arm part** ares, elbow, hand, wrist
**armpit** ala, axilla, oxter
**arms** weapons
**arm's length** reach
**arms retailer** gunsmith
**arms storehouse** armoury, arsenal, depot, magazine
**army assistant** aide
**army camp** base
**army canteen** mess
**army cap** beret
**army chaplain** padre
**army chief** general
**army cloth** khaki
**army colour** khaki
**army conflict** warfare
**army conscription** call up, draft
**army detachment** unit, squad
**army division** corps
**army engineer** sapper
**army exercise** drill
**army follower** sutler
**army group** battalion, platoon, regiment, squad
**army jacket** tunic
**army leave** furlough
**army meal** mess
**army member** soldier
**army officer** captain, colonel, general, lieutenant, major
**army officer's belt and strap supporting it** Sam Browne
**army 'pineapple'** grenade
**army preacher** chaplain
**army rank** brigadier, captain, colonel, corporal, general, lieutenant, major, private, sergeant
**army recruit** roofie, rookie
**army servant** orderly
**army shoe** boot
**army student** cadet
**army trumpet** bugle
**army uniform** tunic
**army unit** brigade, company, legion, platoon, regiment
**army vehicle** buffel, hippo, jeep, lorry, rooikat, tank
**arnica** liniment
**aroid** arad, arum, calla
**aroid plant** arum (lily), calla
**aroma** air, bouquet, fragrance, hint, odour, perfume, redolence, savour, scent, smell, suggestion

**aromatic** balmy, fragrant, perfumed, pungent, redolent, scented, spicy
**aromatic Asian resin** myrrh
**aromatic ball** pomander
**aromatic balsam** nard, tolu
**aromatic berry** allspice
**aromatic beverage** tea
**aromatic bushy plant** feverfew
**aromatic condiment** spice
**aromatic creeping plant** camomile
**aromatic culinary plant** herb
**aromatic flavouring** spice
**aromatic gum resin** myrrh
**aromatic herb** anise, basil, calamint, caraway, chervil, marjoram, mint, oregano, parsley, pennyroyal, rosemary, sage, spearmint, tansy, tarragon, thyme
**aromatic herb for flavouring beer** acorus
**aromatic hydrocarbon** arene
**aromatic Indian plant** nard
**aromatic ointment** nard
**aromatic plant** albahaca, angelica, anise, basil, calamint, caraway, cum(m)in, dittany, lavender, mint, nard, oregano, parsley, sage, spikenard, tansy, thyme
**aromatic resin** copaiba, mastic, myrrh
**aromatic seasoning** spice
**aromatic shrub** lavender, rosemary, sage, tarragon, thyme
**aromatic spice** allspice, aniseed, caraway, cardamom, cinnamon, cloves, coriander, cumin, curry, dill, garlic, ginger, mace, mustard, nutmeg, paprika, pepper
**aromatic substance** balm
**aromatic tree gum** balsam
**aromatic wood** cedar
**around** about, approximately, circum, encircling, enclosing, environing, near, nearby, peri-, roughly, surrounding
**around here** locally
**around the clock** ceaselessly, constantly, endlessly, incessantly, nonstop
**around the corner** close (by), locally
**around town** locally
**arousal** stimulation
**arouse** agitate, animate, arise, awaken, enliven, evoke, excite, foment, foster, goad, incite, inflame, inspire, instigate, kindle, move, provoke, quicken, rouse, sharpen, spark, spur, stimulate, stir, wake, warm, whet
**arouse affection** endear
**arouse again** rekindle
**arouse horror in** horrify, shock, repel
**arouse interest** attract, intrigue

**arouse to danger** alarm
**arousing contempt** pitiful
**arousing desire** erotic
**arousing pity** pitiful
**arousing sexual desire** erogenous
**arraign** accuse, asperse, assail, attack, blame, censure, charge, cite, criticise, defame, denounce, frame, impeach, implicate, impugn, inculpate, indict, involve, libel, litigate, reprove, revile, sue, summon, tax incriminate, try
**arraignment** denouncement, impeachment, indictment
**arrange** adapt, adjust, array, classify, collocate, concoct, contrive, deploy, devise, dispose, distribute, group, order, organise, place, plan, prepare, rank, set, settle, sort, systemise
**arrange according to subject matter** classify
**arrange and inspect working** superintend
**arrange a table for eating a meal** lay
**arrange at intervals** space
**arrange beforehand** plan
**arrange by conference** negotiate
**arrange cleverly** manipulate
**arrange compactly** stow
**arrange correctly** straighten
**arrange data in a form that is usable by a computer** format
**arranged earlier** preset
**arranged in steps** echelon
**arranged in the order in which things occurred** chronological
**arranged in threes** ternate
**arrange feathers** preen
**arrange forces** deploy
**arrange for exhibition** stage
**arrange in a comfortable position** settle
**arrange in battle formation** deploy
**arrange in due order** marshal
**arrange in folds** drape
**arrange in layers** laminate, tier
**arrange in line** align
**arrange in order** file
**arrange in sequence** collate
**arrange in tabular form** tabulate
**arrange in thin layers** laminate
**arrange in two** pair
**arrangement** adaptation, adjustment, agreement, alignment, array, assortment, classification, codification, collection, design, display, disposal, disposition, form, formulation, frame, index, instrumentation, line-up, method, mixture, orchestration, order, organisation, plan, policy, preparation, provision, ranging, rank, scheme, score, series, settlement, set(up), structure, system, version
**arrangement of interwoven parts** web
**arrangement of lenses to help defective sight** spectacle, focus
**arrangement of printed pages** make-up, proofs
**arrangement of sails** rigs
**arrangement of steps for climbing over fence** stile
**arrangement of troops** echelon
**arrangement of windows in a building** fenestration
**arrangement of words** phraseology
**arrange methodically** tabulate
**arrange military forces** deploy
**arrange numbers** permutate
**arrange side by side** appose
**arrant** complete, confirmed, disgraceful, extreme, flagrant, gross, improper, infamous, nefarious, outright, scandalous, shameless, thorough, total, unmitigated
**arras** tapestry
**array** accoutre, adorn, align, allotment, apparel, arrange(ment), assemble, assortment, attire, bedeck, clothe(s), collection, decorate, demonstration, display, dispose, dress, equip, exhibit(ion), exposition, finery, formation, garments, group, line-up, marshal, muster, order, ornament, parade, place, range, rank, regalia, robes, show(ing), supply, trim
**arrest** apprehend, apprehension, attract, capture, catch, check, custody, delay, detain, detention, deter(rent), engage, hindrance, hold, imprisonment, nab, nail, obstruction, occupy, rape, restraint, rivet, stay(ing), take, withhold
**arrest of development** abortion
**arris** ridge, edge
**arrival** advent, appearance, arrive, arriving, attainment, caller, comer, coming, entrance, entrant, occurrence, reaching, visitant, visitor
**arrival at** attainment, due
**arrival at puberty** pubescence
**arrive** alight, appear, approach, attain, be(fall), come, confront, deplane, detrain, disembark, dismount, dock, emerge, enter, exist, gain, land, moor, near, occur, present, prosper, reach, return, succeed, visit
**arrive at** accomplish, achieve, appoint, arrange, attain, complete, conclude, decide, define, determine, discover, earn, establish, fix, fulfil, gain, garner, get, grasp, guess, invent, land, limit, name, reach, realise, resolve, secure, set, settle, specify, win
**arrive at a settlement** agree
**arrived at as a final result** ultimate
**arrive uninvited** gatecrash
**arrogance** bluster, conceit, contemptuousness, disdain, effrontery, haughtiness, hauteur, insolence, loftiness, lordliness, overbearing, pompousness, pretension, pride, self-importance, superciliousness, swagger, uppishness
**arrogant** assuming, blustering, chic, conceited, contemptuous, disdainful, egotistical, haughty, imperious, insolent, lordly, overbearing, pompous, presumptuous, proud, scornful, supercilious, swaggering
**arrogant assertion** dogma
**arrogant bearing** pride
**arrogant bluster** bravado
**arrogant declaration of opinion** dogma
**arrogantly scornful** supercilious
**arrogant person** upstart
**arrogate** appropriate, assume, demand, presume, usurp
**arrow** barb, bolt, dart, director, flight, harpoon, indicator, javelin, marker, missile, needle, pointer, quarrel, reed, sagitta (L), shaft, straight
**arrow body** stele, stem, shaft
**arrow case** quiver
**arrow launcher** bow
**arrow notch** nock
**arrow poison** curare, curari, inee, upas
**arsenal** armoury, caisson, entrepôt, magazine, stockpile, storehouse, supply-base
**arsenal item** rifle, gun, armoury
**arsenical pyrites** mispickel
**arsonist** firebug, incendiary, pyromaniac
**art** adroitness, aptitude, ars (L), artfulness, artwork, astuteness, cleverness, craftiness, craft(manship), cunning, deceit, deception, dexterity, drawing, duplicity, expertise, facility, finesse, flair, guile, ingenuity, intellect, knack, knowledge, mastery, method, painting, profession, science, sculpture, shrewdness, skill, slyness, strategy, subtlety, trade, trickery, visuals, wile
**art and literature intended to shock** Dada(ism)
**art and science of agriculture** geoponics, geopony
**art and science of good eating and drinking** gastronomy

**art category** genre
**artefact** artifact, creation, handiwork, masterpiece, neolith, product, production
**Artemis's twin** Apollo
**artery** adit, aorta, aqueduct, autobahn (G), avenue, blood vessel, canal, capillary, channel, conduit, duct, freeway, highroad, highway, route, throughway, toll road, turnpike, vein
**art for improving memory** mnemonic
**art form** dance, drawing, etching, painting, sculpture
**art frame** easel
**artful** cunning, wily, adept, clever, designing, adroit, crafty, foxy, masterly, tricky, sly, deceitful, dext(e)rous, ingenious, intriguing, politic, resourceful, sharp, shrewd, skilful, smart, subtle, astute, canny, inventive, proficient
**artfulness** adeptness, adroitness, cleverness, craftiness, cunningness, deceitfulness, dext(e)rousness, finesse, ingeniousness, resourcefulness, sharpness, shrewdness, skilfulness, slyness, smartness, subtleness
**artful person** dodger
**artful show** grimace
**art gallery** salon
**art gallery in Venice** Accademia
**arthropod** crustacean, insect, spider
**Arthurian knight** Lancelot, Galahad
**Arthurian magician** Merlin
**Arthurian princess** Isolde, Iseult, Yseult
**Arthurian wizard** Merlin
**Arthur's court** Camelot
**Arthur's sword** Excalibur
**article** an, causerie, chronicle, commodity, composition, detail, essay, feature, gadget, it, item, object, one, opinion, paper, particular, piece, portion, provision, report, section, single, something, source, story, substance, the, theme, thing, treatise, treaty, unit, ye
**article determiner** the
**article in document** clause
**article in newspaper** item
**article of belief** credo, creed, tenet
**article of cloth** linen
**article of clothing** garment
**article of commerce** staple
**article of dress** garment
**article of faith** tenet
**article of food** meat, provisions, viand
**article of furniture** bed, cabinet, chair, settee, sofa, table
**article of luggage** bag, case, suitcase
**article of merchandise** ware

**article of trade** commodity
**article of value** curio, antique
**article of virtue** curio
**article on a list** item
**articles collectively** ware, compendium
**article used in household** appliance, container, device, gadget, kettle, pan, pot, receptacle, utensil, vessel
**article valued as collector's item** collectable, curio
**articulate** articulative, breathe, clarify, eloquent, elucidate, express(ive), fluent, glib, intelligible, jointed, pronounce, say, slick, speaking, talkative, unify, utter, voice
**articulate confusedly** splutter
**articulated joint** hinge
**artifice** adroitness, art, blow, cleverness, complot, contrivance, coup, craft, craftiness, cunning, deceit, device, dodge, falsehood, feint, finesse, foxiness, guile, hoax, ingenuity, intrigue, invention, manoeuvre, plan, plot, ruse, scheme, skill, slyness, stratagem, strategy, trick(ery), wile
**artifice in war** stratagem
**artificer** craftsman, Daedalus
**artificial** affected, assumed, bogus, camouflaged, counterfeit, deceiving, deceptive, ersatz, fake, false, feigned, forced, illegitimate, imitation, man-made, manufactured, mock, paste, phoney, plastic, rayon, sham, simulated, specious, substitute, synthetic, ungenuine, unnatural, unreal
**artificial bait** lure
**artificial bust** falsies
**artificial butter** oleo
**artificial channel** canal
**artificial channel for water** aqueduct
**artificial conduit water** drain
**artificial elevation** tee
**artificial fishing fly** nymph
**artificial gem** paste, rhinestone
**artificial glossiness** varnish
**artificial grain** malt
**artificial hair** wig
**artificial harbour** mole, port
**artificial heart regulator** pacemaker
**artificial hill** mound
**artificial island supporting buildings** crannog
**artificial ivory** ivoride
**artificial lake** dam, reservoir, vlei
**artificial language** Esperanto, Ido, Ro, Volapuk, Fanakalo, Fanagalo
**artificial light** bulb, candle, lamp
**artificial lighting of buildings** floodlighting
**artificial lure** decoy

**artificially induced sleep** hypnosis
**artificial oyster bed** layer, stew
**artificial pool** cushion
**artificial rearing of fish** pisciculture
**artificial silk** dacron, nylon, orlon, rayon
**artificial style of writing** euphuism
**artificial sweetening agent** cyclamate, saccharin
**artificial tanning unit** sun lamp
**artificial teeth** dentures
**artificial textile fabric** dacron, orlon, nylon, rayon
**artificial water channel with gate** sluice
**artificial watercourse** canal
**artificial waterway** aqueduct, canal, sluice
**artificial yarn** nylon, rayon
**artillery** ballistae, baton, battery, cannon, firearms, gun, jingals, mortars, ordnance, sling, weapon
**artillery and military supplies** ordnance
**artillery fire** cannonade
**artillery gun** ack-ack, bazooka, Big Bertha, bombard, howitzer, long tom, mortar, pom-pom, swivel, trench-mortar
**artilleryman** artillerist, bombardier, cannoneer, fusileer, fusilier, gunner
**artillery piece** cannon, gun
**artillery salute** salvo
**artillery unit** battery
**artillery weapon** cannon, gun, mortar, tank
**artisan** artificer, craftsman, electrician, fitter, joiner, mechanic, plumber, technician, tradesman
**art is long, life short** ars longa, vita brevis (L)
**artist** actor, actress, artificer, artisan, artiste, contriver, craftsperson, designer, mechanic, painter, poet, sculptor, technician, workman
**artiste** actor, actress, performer, player, soloist
**artistic** adept, aesthetic, apt, arty, attractive, beautiful, brilliant, choice, clever, creative, cultivated, cultured, decorative, elegant, excellent, expert, exquisite, graceful, handsome, harmonious, imaginative, lovely, magnificent, masterly, refined, sensitive, stylish
**artistic ability** artistry, knack, talent
**artistic composition** study
**artistic dance** ballet
**artistic elegance** chic
**artistic literary works** classics
**artistic skill** artistry
**artist of great reputation** master

**artist's canvas support** easel
**artist's crayon** pastel
**artist's equipment** brush, easel, paint, palette
**artist's model** sitter
**artist's paint board** palette
**artist's shirt** smock
**artist's stand** easel, taboret, tabouret
**artist's studio** atelier
**artist's tripod** easel
**artist's wooden support** easel
**artist's work** oeuvre
**artist's workroom** atelier, studio
**artless** au naturel (F), awkward, blundering, candid, childlike, clownish, clumsy, coarse, credulous, direct, explicit, frank, gauche, genuine, graceless, green, guileless, honest, humble, inadept, inept, ingenuous, innocent, jejune, lumbering, naïve, oafish, open, pure, rude, simple, sincere, straightforward, true, unadorned, uncoordinated, uncouth, unfeigned, ungifted, ungraceful, unrefined, unskilled, unsophisticated, untrained
**artless young woman** ingénue
**art lover** dilettante
**art movement** Dada, Dadaism, expressionism, impressionism, modernism, post-modernism, Pre-Raphaelism
**art of a poet** poetry
**art of beautiful handwriting** calligraphy, penmanship
**art of carving or engraving upon gemstones** glyptography
**art of clipping shrubs into ornamental shapes** topiary
**art of controlling** management
**art of cultivating** horticulture
**art of cutting hair** tonsure
**art of developing the memory** mnemotechny
**art of discourse** rhetoric
**art of drawing ground plans** ichnography
**art of effective speaking** rhetoric
**art of engraving on copper or brass** chalcography
**art of expressive speaking** elocution
**art of fishing** halieutics
**art of flying aircraft** aviation
**art of fortune telling from the hand** palmistry
**art of garden cultivation** horticulture
**art of government** politics
**art of growing plants without soil** hydroponics
**art of healing** medicine, physic
**art of horsemanship** manege
**art of hunting** venery

**art of incised carving** intaglio
**art of judging character from facial features** physiognomy
**art of knotting cord** macramé
**art of making clocks** horology
**art of making pottery** ceramics
**art of making statues** sculpture
**art of measuring time** horology
**art of moving** logistics
**art of painting on walls** mural
**art of preaching** homiletics
**art of prediction by the stars** astrology
**art of preparing medicines** pharmacology, pharmacy
**art of preserving health** hygiene
**art of public speaking** elocution, oratory
**art of reckoning by figures** arithmetic
**art of refining metals** metallurgy
**art of rhythmical movement to music** ballet, dancing, eurhythmics
**art of ringing bells musically** campanology
**art of shading in drawing** sciagraphy, skiagraphy
**art of singing psalms** psalmody
**art of speech** oratory, rhetoric
**art of supplying troops** logistics
**art of telling fortunes** palmistry, divination
**art of theatrical production** dramaturgy
**art of training horses and riders** manege
**art of using fireworks** pyrotechnics
**art of war** strategy
**art of wax-modelling** ceroplastics
**art of weaving in cane** basketry
**art of writing commentaries** glossography
**art of writing well** calligraphy, penmanship
**arts award** Artes
**arts festival** eisteddfod
**art stand** easel
**arty** affected, conceited, creative, pretentious
**arum** aroid, calla, cuckoo-pint
**arum flower** aroid, calla, lily
**arum lily** aroid, calla
**as** because, being, like, seeing, since, ut (L), when, while
**as above** ut supra (L)
**as a common thing** often, commonly
**as against** to
**as a group** bodily, corporately, together
**as a matter of fact** actual, really, truly, truthfully, veritably
**as a matter of form** pro forma
**as a memorial** pro memoria (L)
**as an act of favour** ex gratia
**as an act of grace** ex gratia

**as an alternative** instead, or
**as a pauper** in forma pauperis (L)
**as a person** personally
**as a result** accordingly, again, because, certainly, consequence, consequently, inevitably, therefore, thus
**as a result of that** owing, thereby
**as a rule** chiefly, commonly, customarily, generally, largely, mainly, normally, often, ordinarily, universally, usually
**as a substitute** instead
**as a whole** altogether, en bloc (F)
**as bachelor** garçon (F)
**as before** ditto, sicut ante (L)
**as below** ut infra (L)
**Asben** Aïr
**asbestos plaster** mackite
**ascend** arise, aspire, bounce, clamber, climb, crest, escalade, escalate, leap, levitate, mount, rise, scale, shin, slope, soar, spring, surmount, tower, uprise, up(wards)
**ascendancy** dominance, domination, hegemony, ascendant, reign, rule, superiority, popularity, importance
**ascending** climbing, leaping, mounting, rising, scaling, soaring, towering, uprising
**ascending axis** stem
**ascending in thought or expression** climatic
**ascent** augmentation, climb(ing), elevation, escalading, gradient, hill, incline, increase, mounting, ramp, rise, scaling, scrambling, slope, soaring, steepness, tilt, upgrade
**ascertain** certify, conclude, confirm, decide, define, detect, determinate, determine, discern, discover, establish, fix, grasp, identify, learn, resolve, see, settle, uncover, understand, unearth, verify
**ascertain amount of** estimate, evaluate
**ascertain extent** measure
**ascertain mass** weigh
**ascertain precisely** determine
**ascertain quality** plumb
**ascertain the bearings of** orient
**ascertain the capacity of** admeasure
**ascertain the duration of** time
**ascertain the quality of coins** shroff
**ascertain the volume of** measure
**ascetic** abstainer, anchoress, anchorite, austere, bleak, celibate, chaste, classic, cloistered, eremite, essence, flagellant, forbidding, hermit, intolerant, monastic, monk, narrow-minded, penitent, plain, prudish, puritan, recluse, secluded, severe, simple, solitary, Spartan,

stern, stoic, strait-laced, strict,
unadorned, withdrawn, yogi
**ascetic Hebrew** Essene
**asceticism** abstemiousness,
abstinence, celibacy, continence,
monasticism, penance, puritanism,
scourging, self-control, self-denial,
self-discipline, self-mortification,
self-restraint, self-torment
**as compared with** than
**ascorbic acid** vitamin C
**ascribe** account, accredit, accuse,
assign, associate, attribute, blame,
charge, couple, credit, deem,
esteem, hold, impute, refer, relate,
repute
**ascribed to the occult** supernatural
**asdic** sonar
**as different as possible from** opposite
**as early as this** already
**asexual** agamic, agamous
**asexual reproduction** monogenesis,
monogeny
**as far as** to, unto
**as far as one can go** limit
**as good as** almost, close, nearly,
practically
**as good as can be** ideal, perfect
**ash** cinder, coal, ember, lava, residue,
slag, waste
**ashamed** abashed, blushing,
confused, distressed, embarrassed,
guilty, humbled, humiliated,
mortified, shamefaced, shy
**ashen** ashy, blanched, bleached,
bloodless, cadaverous, colourless,
deathlike, dim, dreadful, dull, faded,
faint, feeble, frightful, ghastly,
ghostly, grey, grim, grisly, gruesome,
hideous, hoary, horrible, hueless,
leaden, livid, loathsome, pale, pallid,
pasty, repellent, sallow, shocking,
sickly, smoky, terrifying, wan, waxen
**ash holder** ashtray, urn
**ash or elm** tree
**ashram** hermitage, monastery, recluse
**ash solution** lye
**ash tree in Norse mythology** Igdrasil,
Yg(g)drasil
**ash-tree whose roots and branches
join heaven and earth and hell**
Yg(g)drasil, Igdrasil
**Asian** Chinese, East, Hun, Indian,
Japanese, Korean, Mogolian, Orient,
Sere, Tartar, Thai
**Asian animal** panda, orang-utan
**Asian bean** ad(z)uki, dal, lablab, mung,
soy(a), urd
**Asian bird** mina, minivet, myna(h)
**Asian bovid** thar
**Asian bovine** yak, zebu
**Asian cat-like creature** linsang

**Asian cereal grass** ragge, raggy, ragi
**Asian civet** binturong, rasse, zibet
**Asian climbing pepper** betel
**Asian coast wind** monsoon
**Asian cosmetic powder** kohl
**Asian country** Afghanistan, Arabia,
Bangladesh, Burma, China, India,
Iran, Iraq, Japan, Korea, Mongolia,
Nepal, Pakistan, Russia, Sri Lanka,
Syria, Thailand, Tibet, Vietnam
**Asian desert** Gobi
**Asian domestic cattle** zobo
**Asian edible root** taro
**Asian empire** Japan, Mongolia
**Asian evergreen shrub** camellia
**Asian fibre plant** ramie
**Asian flower** aspidistra, lotus
**Asian gazelle** ahu, cora
**Asian grain** rice
**Asian head-dress** turban
**Asian hemp** pua
**Asian herbaceous plant** hemp
**Asian hunting dog** Afghan
**Asian hurricane** typhoon
**Asian invaders who ruled Egypt**
Hyksos
**Asian kingdom** Anam, Jordan, Nepal
**Asian lake** Aral, Balkhash, Baykal,
Caspian, Urmia
**Asian language** Chinese, Hindi,
Korean, Japanese, Nepali, Russian
**Asian language group** Indic
**Asian lemur** loris
**Asian leopard** panther
**Asian lily** lotus
**Asian mammal** tahr
**Asian mink** kolinsky
**Asian mongrel** pi(e)-dog, pye-dog
**Asian monkey** langur
**Asian narcotic** betel-nut, bhang,
hash(ish), jang, ke(e)f, kif, opium
**Asian noble's title** khan
**Asian ox** yak
**Asian palm** nipa
**Asian peninsula** Arabia, Korea
**Asian plant** eddo, taro
**Asian port of Turkey** Anatolia
**Asian prehensile-tailed civet** binturong
**Asian priest** shaman
**Asian region** Bengal
**Asian rice dish** pilaff, pilau, pilaw
**Asian river** Yangtze
**Asian rolled tea** cha
**Asian ruler** ameer, amir, emir
**Asian sea** Aral
**Asian sea-mammal** dugong
**Asian shrub** ti
**Asian snake** cobra, krait, katuka,
python
**Asian starling** mina, myna(h)
**Asian taxi** rickshaw
**Asian tea** cha

**Asian tree** sen, ti
**Asian ungulate** tapir
**Asian wild ass** kulan, onager
**Asian wild dog** jackal
**Asian wild goat** tahr
**Asian wild ox** gaur
**Asian wild sheep** argal(i)
**Asia or America** continent
**Asiatic** Oriental
**aside** abreast, albeit, alone, alongside,
apart, away, beside, despite,
digression, excursus, laterally, off,
privately, separately, sidewise,
soliloquy, still, tangent, withal, yet
**aside from** apart, besides, excluding
**as if** like, seemingly, supposedly,
though
**as in a mirror** veluti in speculum (L)
**asinine** absurd, careless, dull(-witted),
empty-headed, fatuous, foolish,
heedless, idiotic, ill-advised,
incautious, indiscreet, inexpressive,
muddled, obstinate, ridiculous, silly,
stupid, thoughtless, unintelligent,
unwary, unwise, unwitty, witless
**as is said to be the case** allegedly
**as it happens** actually
**as it seems** apparently, that
**as it seems at first** prima facie (L)
**as it should be** comme il faut (F)
**as it was literally** stet
**ask** appeal, apply, beg, beseech,
claim, clamour, consult, crave,
demand, enquire, entreat, implore,
inquire, interrogate, invite, order,
petition, plead, pray, press, query,
question, request, require, seek,
solicit, sue, summon, supplicate
**ask advice from** consult
**askance** awry, distrustfully, dubiously,
indirectly, obliquely, sceptical,
sideways
**ask earnestly** beg, beseech, entreat,
implore, pray
**ask earnestly for** beseech, entreat,
solicit
**askew** amiss, askance, aslant, astray,
asymmetric, atilt, awry, cockeyed,
crooked, defective, deformed,
distorted, erroneously, faulty,
inaccurately, lopsided, oblique,
off-centre, scornfully, sideways,
slanted, squint, tilting, twisted,
unbalanced, uneven, warped,
wrong, wry
**ask for** actuate, indent, induce, inspire,
order, provoke, request
**ask for alms** beg
**ask for charity** beg
**ask forcibly** demand
**ask for contribution** solicit
**ask forgiveness** apologise

**ask for politely** request
**ask for with authority** demand
**asking** inquiring, petitioning, solicitation
**asking to be supplied with** ordering
**ask in marriage** propose, woo
**ask question** inquire, enquire
**ask the cost** price
**ask to attend** invite
**ask to come** call, invite
**ask too much** overcharge
**ask to pay** dun
**aslant** askew, aslope, atilt, cockeyed, crossways, crosswise, diagonally, oblique(ly), sideways, slantingly, slantwise
**asleep** abed, catnapping, comatose, dormant, dozing, idle, inactive, inert, latent, lifeless, napping, numbed, reposing, resting, sleeping, slumbering, snoozing, unconscious
**as long as** as, because, for, provided, since, so, while
**as many as need be** enough, sufficient
**as matter of fact** actually
**as might be expected** naturally
**as much again** alterum tantum (L)
**as much as is wanted** ad libitum
**as much as one likes** agog, galore
**as much as possible** limit, maximum, utmost
**as much as required** enough
**as much as you like** quantum libet (L)
**as of now** already, onwards, yet
**as often as** toties quoties (L)
**as one** jointly, together, united
**as one man** concordantly, unanimously
**asp** adder, serpent, snake, viper
**aspect** air, appearance, attitude, attribute, character, condition, countenance, demeanour, direction, exposure, facet, feature, guise, look, mien, nature, outlook, phase, prospect, scene, side, sight, standpoint, surface, trait, view, viewpoint, visage
**aspect of phase** facet
**aspen** poplar, quaking, tremulous
**aspen tree** poplar
**asperity** acrimony, adversity, animosity, austerity, bleakness, crabbedness, hardship, malignity, mordancy, moroseness, roughness, ruggedness, scorn, severity
**as per menu** à la carte
**asperse** slander, calumniate, defame
**aspersion** censure, defamation, detraction, discredit, obloquy, reproach, slur, vituperation
**asphalt** tar
**aspherical vault** cupola
**aspirant** applicant, candidate, claimant, claimer, competitor, contender, contestant, entrant, nominee, player, pretender, runner, striver
**aspiration** afflation, afflatus, aim, ambition, breathing, craving, desire, destination, dream, eagerness, endeavour, force, goal, hope, ideal, inhalation, inspiration, intent, longing, objection, objective, sigh, target, want, wish, yearning
**aspire** aim, covet, crave, desire, dream, hanker, hope, hunger, intend, long, need, plan, pretend, purpose, pursue, reach, seek, strive, want, wish, yearn
**aspiring** ambitious, aiming, craving, desiring, desirous, dreaming, eager, enthusiastic, fervid, hankering, hopeful, hungry, longing, optimistic, pursuing, sanguine, seeking, spirited, wishful, wishing, yearning
**as regards** about, concerning, re, regarding
**as required** adequately
**ass** blockhead, blunderer, burro, dolt, domkop, donkey, dope, dunce, fool, hinny, idiot, jackass, jennet, jenny, moke, mule, neddy, nincompoop, ninny, nitwit, numskull, onager, quadruped, silly, simpleton, stupid, twit
**assail** abuse, accost, aggress, asperse, assault, attack, berate, beset, besiege, bombard, capture, charge, criticise, encroach, foray, grapple, hurt, impugn, invade, malign, maltreat, maul, overrun, pelt, ravage, savage, storm, wound
**assailant** abuser, accoster, accuser, aggressor, antagonist, assaulter, attacker, challenger, enemy, foe, opponent, vilifier
**assail by words** impugn
**assailing** assaulting, attacking, battering, castigating, casting, combating, condemning, denouncing, encroaching, engaging, hurling, infringing, invading, meeting, occupying, pelting, peppering, raiding, showering, slinging, striking, violating
**assail vigorously with questions** harass, ply
**assail with missiles** pelt
**assail with requests** besiege
**Assam silkworm** eri(a)
**assassin** butcher, executioner, hitman, homicide, killer, manslayer, matricide, murderer, slaughterer, slayer, sniper, strangler, thug, triggerman
**assassinate** blight, despatch, destroy, eliminate, kill, murder, slay
**assault** aggression, assail, attack, beset, charge, combat, invade, invasion, offensive, onset, onslaught, raid, storm, threat(en)
**assault on a fortress** storm
**assay** analyse, appraise, assess, attempt, check, estimate, evaluate, examine, experiment, explore, gauge, inspect, investigate, investigation, judge, nibble, probe, procedure, proof, prove, rank, rate, reckon, relish, research, sample, savour, search, sip, strive, study, taste, test, trial, try, undertake, value, venture, weigh
**assayed** analysed, appraised, assessed, checked, estimated, examined, experimented, gauged, judged, nibbled, proved, ranked, rated, reckoned, relished, sampled, savoured, sipped, tested, tried, valued, weighed
**assaying vessel** cupel
**assegai** javelin, lance, spear
**assemblage** accumulation, assembly, association, band, body, bunch, circle, collection, company, conclave, congregation, convention, coterie, crew, crowd, cumulation, ensemble, flock, gang, gathering, group, horde, host, league, lot, mass, meeting, mob, multitude, number, pack, party, set, swarm, throng, troop, troupe, union
**assemble** amass, build, call, collect, congregate, convene, convoke, flock, gather, ingather, manufacture, marshal, meet, rally
**assembled company** troop
**assemble the crew** muster
**assembling body** session
**assembly** assemblage, company, conclave, congress, convention, convocation, council, gathering, legislature, meeting, parliament, throng
**assembly for buying and selling** market
**assembly for company heads** board-meeting
**assembly for dancing** ball
**assembly of Bhutan** Tsongdu
**assembly of delegates** congress, diet
**assembly of hearers** audience
**assembly of people** crowd, gathering, meeting, rally, throng
**assembly of visitors** levee
**assembly of witches** coven
**assembly pack** kit

**assent** accede, accedence, accept, acceptance, acquiesce, agree(ment), allow, approval, comply, concur, confirm, consent, grant, permission, sanction, submit, yield
**assenting word** ay(e), yes
**assent to** approve, grant
**assent to wish of** gratify
**assent with head** incline, nod
**assert** advance, affirm, allege, asseverate, attest, aver, avouch, avow, claim, contend, declare, defend, emphasise, insist, maintain, predicate, press, proclaim, profess, promote, pronounce, protest, publish, say, state, stress, swear, uphold, vindicate, voice
**assert as fact** posit
**assert as true** maintain, predicate
**assert confidently** aver
**assert earnestly** protest
**assert emphatically** insist
**assert formally** protest
**asserting one's authority** officious
**assertion** affirmation, allegation, announcement, averment, avowal, declaration, dictum, expression, guarantee, pledge, predication, proclamation, promise, representation, statement
**assertion of a fact** claim
**assertion without proof** allegation
**assertive** active, aggressive, arbitrary, arrogant, ascendant, brash, bumptious, categorical, certain, cocksure, combative, commanding, decided, dictatorial, doctrinaire, dogmatic(al), dominant, downright, emphatic, firm, forcible, forward, imperious, leading, militant, obdurate, outspoken, peremptory, pushing, ruling, self-assured, self-confident, supreme, vehement
**assertive manliness** machismo
**assert positively** affirm, insist
**assert without proof** allege
**asses do it** bray
**assess** appraise, assize, cess, compute, consider, demand, determine, estimate, evaluate, evaluate, fix, gauge, impose, investigate, judge, lay, levy, rate, review, tax, toll, value, weigh
**assess again** reappraise
**assessment** appraisal, appreciation, charge, computation, duty, estimate, estimation, evaluation, exactation, examination, fee, impost, investigation, levy, rate, rating, review, surcharge, tariff, tax(ation), toll, valuation, value

**assessment of worth** appraisal, valuation
**assessor** adviser, arbiter, auditor, authority, cessor, connoisseur, critic, estimator, evaluator, expert, judge, levier, lister, rater, stentor, tasker, taxator
**assess pupil's work** mark
**assess the worth of** evaluate
**asset** advantage, aid, benefit, boon, capital, estate, means, property, resource, service, wealth
**asseverate** affirm, allege, articulate, assert, aver, avow, claim, communicate, contend, couch, declare, express, hold, insist, maintain, phrase, profess, pronounce, put, say, speak, state, tell, utter, voice, word
**assiduous** applied, attentive, constant, continuous, diligent, industrious, persistent, persisting, studious, tireless
**assign** adduce, allocate, allot, appoint, apportion, attribute, delegate, designate, detail, distribute, fix, measure, pinpoint, refer, specify, transfer
**assignation** appointment, assignment, date, duty, job, meeting, rendezvous, task, tryst
**assign by judicial sentence** award
**assign by measure** mete
**assigned service** duty
**assign for a job** appoint
**assign in due shares** admeasure
**assignment** adduction, allocation, assertion, commission, designation, duty, errand, job, lesson, naming, obligation, offer, part, post, responsibility, share, stint, task, time
**assignment of a cause** (a)etiology
**assign numbers to pages** paginate
**assign time to** date
**assign to** class, refer
**assign to a class** categorise, classify
**assign to a place** allocate
**assign to a post** station
**assign to office** appoint
**assimilate** absorb, accommodate, accustom, adapt, adjust, appropriate, convert, digest, imbibe, incorporate, ingest, learn, mingle, transform
**assimilate mentally** comprehend, digest, learn
**assimilation** absorption, accommodation, adaptation, adjustment, combining, constructive, conversion, digestion, levelling, merging, mingling, mixing, transformation

**ass in lion's skin** betrayer, deceiver, humbug
**assist** abet, aid, avail, back, befriend, benefit, boost, co-operate, collaborate, expedite, facilitate, further, help, lend-a-hand, promote, reinforce, second, serve, speed, succour, support, sustain
**assistance** abetment, aid, benefit, charity, co-operation, collaboration, complicity, furtherance, help, succour, support
**assistant** abettor, accessory, accomplice, adjutant, aide, ally, ancillary, associate, auxiliary, backer, co-operator, coadjutor, collaborator, colleague, confederate, helper, helpmate, partner, right-hand, second, subordinate, subsidiary, supporter
**assistant bishop** suffragan
**assistant chairman** croupier
**assistant in library** librarian
**assistant to a parish priest** curate
**assistant to bishop** coadjutor, verger
**assistant to clergyman** curate
**assistant to curate** vicar
**assistant to Sherlock Holmes** Watson
**assistant who inserts the banderillas during bullfight** banderillero
**assist driver by indicating correct route** navigate
**assist illegally** abet
**assist in a crime** abet
**assist offender** abet
**assist with school discipline** monitor, prefect
**associate** acquaintance, affiliate, ally, co-worker, colleague, combine, companion, compeer, comrade, connect, consort, couple, fellow, follower, friend, herd, join, league, link, mate, mix, pair, partner, peer, relate, unite, yoke
**associated meaning** connotation
**associated surroundings** context
**associated with blind readers** braille
**associate with** accompany, befriend, mingle, mix, socialise
**association** alliance, band, blend, bond, clique, club, co-operative, combination, companionship, company, concomitance, confederacy, (con)federation, connection, consortium, corporation, correlation, fellowship, firm, fraternity, friendship, group, identification, league, mixture, organisation, pairing, partnership, relation, society, syndicate, tie, union
**association for star's followers** fan club

**association of businesspeople** Chamber of Commerce
**association of clubs** league, union
**assoil** acquit, release
**assonant** similar
**assort** allot, arrange, assemble, associate, bracket, catalogue, categorise, class(ify), dispose, divide, file, gather, grade, group, index, list, marshal, number, order, organise, range, rank, rate, segregate, select, separate, sort, systematise, tabulate, type
**assorted** arranged, arrayed, different, diverse, diversified, graded, grouped, manifold, miscellaneous, mixed, motley, omnifarious, selected, sorted, sundry, varied, variegated, various
**assortment** diversity, medley, mélange, miscellany, mixture, selection, variety
**ass's bray** heehaw
**assuage** abate, allay, alleviate, appease, blunt, calm, comfort, cool, dampen, diminish, disburden, ease, lessen, lighten, mitigate, moderate, modify, modulate, pacify, palliate, placate, qualify, quiet, regulate, relax, relieve, repress, satisfy, slacken, slake, soothe, still, subdue, temper
**assuaging pain** anodyne, alleviating
**as suggested by** apropos
**assume** accept, acquire, adopt, affect, affect, appropriate, arrogate, believe, commandeer, counterfeit, deduce, embrace, expect, feign, imagine, infer, postulate, presume, presuppose, pretend, seize, simulate, suppose, surmise, suspect, think, understand, undertake, usurp
**assume an attitude** air, pose
**assume a pleased expression** smile
**assume a position** pose
**assume a reverent posture** kneel
**assume a role** act
**assume as a theory** hypothesise, suppose
**assume as fact** accept, posit
**assume a striking attitude** pose
**assume beforehand** prejudice, presuppose
**assumed** accepted, affected, believed, bogus, counterfeit, expected, fake, false, fancied, feigned, fictitious, hypothetical, imagined, imitated, imitation, impersonated, made-up, mimicked, posited, presumed, presupposed, pretended, pseudonymous, sham(med), shouldered, simulated, spurious, supposed, surmised, suspected, thought
**assumed appearance** guise, pretence, semblance
**assumed attitude** pose
**assumed character** part, role
**assumed manner** affectation, air
**assumed mannerism** air, pose
**assumed manner of speech** affectation
**assumed name** alias, anonym, nickname, nom de plume, penname, pseudonym, so(u)briquet
**assumed role** character, persona
**assume false appearance** masquerade
**assume ownership of** adopt
**assume praying position** kneel
**assume the equality** equate
**assume wrongly** misapprehend, misconceive, mistake, usurp
**assumption** acceptance, accepting, arrogance, assuming, belief, conjecture, effrontery, fancy, guess, hypothesis, postulate, premise, presumption, presupposition, superciliousness, supposition, surmise, theory
**assurance** arrogance, asseveration, averment, avowal, bravery, certainty, confidence, declaration, deposition, firmness, impertinence, oath, pledge, self-reliance, trust, warranty
**assurance of quality** guarantee, warrant
**assurance that no offence was intended** apology, pardon
**assure** affirm, attest, clinch, confirm, convince, encourage, ensure, guarantee, pledge, promise, reassure, secure, swear, vouch, vow
**assured** assertive, bold, clinched, confident, confirmed, dependable, ensured, guaranteed, irrefutable, poised, positive, self-possessed
**assuredly** boldly, certainly, certes, clearly, confidently, definitely, doubtless, expectantly, positively, precisely, surely, truly, undoubtedly, unquestionably
**assure dowry to** endow
**Assyrian god** Asur
**Assyrian goddess of love and fertility** Ishtar
**Assyrian war god** Asur
**asteraceous plant** daisy
**asterisk** punctuation, star
**astern** aft, backwards, behind
**aster plant** daisy, oxeye, tansy
**as the case may be** depending, perhaps
**as the circumstances suggest** accordingly
**asthenia** debility
**asthenic** weak
**asthmatic** chesty, short-winded, wheezy
**asthmatic breathing** wheeze
**astir** acting, active, awaken, bustling, busy, functioning, live(ly), moving, operative, working
**as to** re
**astonish** amaze, astound, bewilder, confound, daze, dum(b)found, flabbergast, shock, stagger, startle, stun, stupefy, surprise
**astonish greatly** astound
**astonishing thing** surprise
**astound** amaze, ambush, astonish, awe, bewilder, catch, daze, dum(b)found, electrify, impress, jolt, overwhelm, shock, stagger, startle, stun, surprise, trap
**astounded** aghast
**astraddle** astride
**astragalus** talus
**astral** starry
**astral body** star
**astray** abroad, adrift, afield, amiss, befooled, confused, disconcerted, faulty, incorrect, inexact, lost, misled, off, seduced, stray(ing), wandering, wrong
**astride** astraddle, spanning, straggling
**astringent** abusive, acerb, acute, astrictive, austere, bitter, constrictive, constringent, contracting, derisive, harsh, ironic(al), mordant, rough, sardonic, satirical, scornful, severe, sharp, snide, spiteful, stern, styptic, vicious, virulent
**astringent gum** kino
**astringent salt** alum
**astrologer** astroalchemist, astromancer, horoscoper, magus, seer, soothsayer
**astrologer's prediction** horoscope
**astrological signs** zodiac
**astronaut** aeronaut, aviator, cosmonaut, spaceman
**astronaut's craft** rocket, spaceship
**astronaut's path** orbit
**astronomer** astrographer, astrophotographer, cosmogonist, cosmographer, cosmologist, star-gazer, uranologist
**astronomical arc** azimuth
**astronomical instrument** orrery, telescope
**astronomical phenomenon** nebula, black hole

**astute** adroit, artful, bright, canny, crafty, cunning, discriminating, eagle-eyed, foxy, intelligent, keen, penetrating, polite, quick, sagacious, sharp, shrewd, sly, wily
**astute military man** tactician
**astuteness** adroitness, artfulness, brightness, canniness, cleverness, craftiness, cunningness, keenness, knowingness, perceptiveness, sagaciousness, sharpness, shrewdness, slyness, subtleness, wiliness
**asunder** apart, away, disjoint, distant, disunited, faraway, remote, removed, rent, separated, severed, split
**Aswan construction** dam
**Aswan or Hoover** dam
**as well** also, and, besides, preferably, too
**as well as** also, and, include, including
**as written** sic, stet
**as yet** already, hitherto, nevertheless, notwithstanding, now
**asylum** harbour, haven, hospital, institute, madhouse, refuge, retreat, sanctuary, sanitarium, shelter
**asymmetrical** lopsided, misproportioned
**asymmetry** bumpiness, crookedness, disparity, disproportion, imbalance, inequality, insufficiency, irregularity, lopsidedness, patchiness, raggedness, unevenness, roughness
**as you now have in your possession** uti possidetis (L)
**at** about, beside, by, chez (F), during, in, near, on, to(wards)
**at a bargain price** à bon marché (F)
**at a disadvantage** cornered, disabled, handicapped, vulnerable
**at a distance** afar, aloof, apart, away, beyond, off, yon
**at a great distance** afar, far
**at a leap** per saltum (L)
**at all** any, ava (Scot), ever
**at all costs** regardless
**at all events** anyhow, anyway, irrespective, regardless, so
**at all times** always, eternity, ever, generally, infinitely
**at a loss** bewildered, blank, confounded, confused, dum(b)founded, hamstrung, helpless, mystified, perplexed, puzzled, unprofitably
**at a lower level** below
**at a moderate tempo** andante
**at an advantage** ahead
**at an angle** agee, ajee, askew, aslant, aslope, diagonal, oblique, slant

**at anchor** astay
**at an end** completion, done, finished, over, terminated
**at an intermediate point** between
**at any place** anywhere
**at any price** anyhow, à tout prix (F), coûte que coûte (F), regardless
**at any rate** anyhow, anyway, leastway
**at any time** ever, whenever, random
**at a quick pace** apace, rapid, swift
**ataraxia** impassiveness, indifference, stoicism
**at a short distance** close, near
**at a slant** aslant, obliquely, sideways, slantingly, slantwise
**at a slow tempo** andante
**at a standstill** immobile
**at a time earlier than expected** already
**at a venture** alla ventura (I)
**at bay** caught, cornered, frozen, impotent, motionless, powerless, trapped, trapped
**at best** ideally
**at boat's centre** amidships
**at bottom** au fond (F)
**at ease** comfortable, comfy, idle, inactive, relaxed
**atelier** factory, garret, loft, mansard, mill, plant, shop, studio, workroom, workshop
**atelier item** easel
**at end** terminal
**at equal distances** equidistant
**at fault** answerable, culpable, erroneous, guilty, responsible
**at first** erst, initially
**at first sight** apparently, ostensibly, prima facie
**at fixed intervals** cyclic, intermittent, periodic, recurrent
**at frequent intervals** haud longis intervallis (L)
**at full gallop** tantivy
**at full length** flat, in extenso (L), prostrate
**at full speed** amain
**at great cost** dearly
**at hand** accessible, adjacent, attainable, available, by, close, forthcoming, handy, imminent, near(by), neighbouring
**at heart** basically, innately, really, truly
**atheism** disbelief, godlessness, heathenism, hereticism, infidelity, irreligion, paganism, unbelief
**atheist** agnostic, disbeliever, doubter, heathen, heretic, nonbeliever, pagan, sceptic, unbeliever
**Athenian market place** Agora
**Athenian philosopher** Socrates
**Athens' ancient foe** Sparta
**Athens' harbour** Piraeus

**Athens is there** Greece
**at high temperature** hot
**athlete** acrobat, competitor, contender, contestant, gymnast, miler, player, runner, sportsperson, sprinter
**athlete's crown** laurel
**athlete's outfit** tracksuit
**athlete's prize** medal
**athlete's race to win** run
**athlete's shoes** spikes
**athlete's spear** javelin
**athletic** active, brawny, lusty, muscular, robust, sporty, sturdy, vigorous
**athletic contest consisting of ten different events** decathlon
**athletic disc** discus
**athletic event** shot put
**athletic games** Olympics, sports
**athletic group** team
**athletic pastime** sport
**at home** available, chez (F), comfortable, composed, experienced, habituated, in, indoors, knowing, knowledgeable, present, relaxed, skilled, undisturbed
**at home in** knowledgeable, proficient, skilled
**athwart** across, against, askant, aslant, awry, crisscross, crossways, crosswise, obliquely, over, perversely, transversely, versus, wrongly
**atilt** askew, inclined, slanted, slanting
**at intervals** between, cyclic, intermittent, periodically
**at issue** controversial, unsettled
**atlantes** telamones
**Atlantic fish** cod, flounder, halibut, sole, whiting
**Atlantic islands** Azores
**Atlantic or Indian** ocean
**at large** abroad, escaped, free, generally, loose, mainly, truant, unconfined, unrestrained
**atlas page** map
**at last** amen, eureka, eventually, finally, ultimately
**at least** leastwise
**at leisure** available, free, idle, loafing, unengaged
**at length** completely, endlessly, eventually, finally, fully, interminably, thoroughly
**at liberty** free, uncaged, unconstrained, unoccupied, unrestricted
**at loggerheads** bickering, estranged, feuding, opposed, quarrelling, squabbling
**at long last** finally

**at loose ends** confused, drifting, uncertain, unsettled, wavering
**at low ebb** decreased, depleted, lessened
**atmosphere** aerospace, aerosphere, air, ambience, aura, character, element, environment, feeling, firmament, heaven, milieu, mood, setting, sky, spirit, stratosphere, surroundings
**atmosphere of a place** ambiance, ambience
**atmospheric conditions** climate, weather
**atmospheric connecting line** isobar
**atmospheric current** air-flow
**atmospheric disturbance** fog, storm
**atmospheric fog mass** cloud, stratus
**atmospheric layer** ozone
**atmospheric optical illusion** mirage
**atmospheric pollution** miasma, smog
**atmospheric pressure line** isobar
**atmospheric travelling body** meteor
**at my own risk** meo periculo (L)
**at no future time** nevermore
**at no place** nowhere
**at no set date** sine die (L)
**at no time** never
**at odds** against, antagonistic, clashing, conflicting, contradictory, disagreeing, divergent, diverging, inconsistent, loggerheads, opposed, out, quarrelling, unharmonious, unwilling
**atom** bit, dot, dyad, electron, fragment, indivisible, ion, iota, isotope, jot, mite, molecule, monad, morsel, mote, particle, proton, scintilla, triad, whit
**atom bomb particle** proton
**atom constituent** electron, nucleus, proton
**atomic** inappreciable, microbic, minute, molecular, nuclear, puny, tiny, wee
**atomic bomb** nuke
**atomic fall-out** radiation
**atomic mass unit** dalton
**atomised spray** mist
**atom part** ion
**atom with same atomic number** isotope
**atomy** skeleton
**at once** amain, anon, directly, forthwith, immediately, instanter, instantly, now, promptly, pronto, simultaneously, straightaway, together
**atone** agree, amend, answer, appease, compensate, deplore, indemnify, recompense, refund, regret, reimburse, relent, repay, repent, restore, reward, rue, satisfy, sorrow

**atone for** expiate, redeem
**atonement** amends, compensation, damages, expiation, indemnity, penalty, penance, recompense, redemption, redress, remuneration, repair, reparation, restitution, reward, satisfaction
**atonement for injury** recompense
**atonement for sin** penance
**at one's disposal** available
**at one's elbow** nearby, handy, near, side
**at one's wit's end** baffled, bewildered, stumped
**at one time** once, previously, formerly, concurrently, hitherto
**atonic** unaccented
**atop** on, above, overhead, upon
**at pleasure** ad arbitrium (L), à plaisir (F), à volonté (F), ad libitum
**at point of death** fey, in extremis (L), moribund
**at premium** costly, expensive, rare, scarce, valuable
**at present** current, now, nowadays, today
**at proper time** duly
**at random** accidentally, adventitiously, aimlessly, arbitrarily, blindly, casually, fortuitously, haphazardly, irregularly, randomly, unsystematically
**at rest** asleep, still
**at right angles to** perpendicular
**atrium** auricle, cavity, chamber, court, hall, passage
**atrium of heart** auricle
**atrocious** abominable, bad, barbarous, brutal, cruel, detestable, devilish, flagrant, grievous, heinous, hellish, inhuman, merciless, monstrous, outrageous, tasteless, terrible, wicked
**atrocity** crime, cruelty, disgrace, enormity, evilness, ferocity, harm, heinousness, horridness, inhumanity, injury, malignity, murderousness, offence, outrage, savagery, scandal, wickedness
**atrophy** consumption, decay, decline, degenerate, degeneration, emaciate, emaciation, enervate, enervation, enfeeble, exhaust, marasmus, molder, rust, sap, shrink, starve, stultify, tabes, wasting, weaken, wither, withering
**at sea** adrift, afloat, astray, baffled, bewildered, confused, insecure, launched, lost, mystified, perplexed, puzzled, upset
**at sea some distance from shore** offshore

**at short intervals** often
**at some future time** tomorrow
**at some past time** once
**at speed** briskly, hastily, rapidly
**at stake** concerned, gambled, implicated, invested, involved, risked
**at sunset or nightfall** acronyc(h)al
**attach** accompany, add, adhere, affix, annex, append, ascribe, assign, attribute, bind, cement, connect, couple, fit, join, pin, secure, stick, subjoin, unite
**attach boat** dock, moor
**attached to** on
**attached to a noun** adnominal
**attachment** accessory, addition, adhesion, adjunct, affection, affinity, appendage, appurtenance, bond, clamp, cohesion, connection, connector, coupling, devotedness, devotion, esteem, extra, fastening, friendship, holder, joint, junction, link, nexus, ornament, subjunction, supplement, tie
**attach oneself to** espouse, marry
**attach wallpaper to a wall** hang
**attack** abuse, aggression, assail, assault, beset, charge, criticise, encounter, foray, impugn, invasion, offence, offensive, onset, onslaught, oppugn, paroxysm, raid, rush, threaten, vilification
**attack and rob** mug
**attack as false** impugn
**attack at speed** charge
**attack bitterly** excoriate
**attack brutally** savage
**attack by enemy planes** air raid
**attacker** aggressor, assailant, enemy, invader, militant, molester, murderer, opponent, raider, revolter
**attacker of Odin** Fenrir, Fenris (Wolf)
**attack from all sides** beset
**attack in return** retaliate
**attack of epilepsy** fit, grand-mal, petit-mal
**attack of gout affecting the knee** gonagra
**attack of paralysis** stroke
**attack on fortified place** siege
**attack on the attacker** counter-offensive
**attack slyly** snipe
**attack verbally** abuse, belabour
**attack violently** bash, inveigh, storm
**attack warning** alert
**attack with artillery** bombard
**attack with severe criticism** scathe
**attain** accomplish, achieve, acquire, arrive, complete, earn, effect, gain, get, obtain, procure, reach, realise, secure, win

**attain an object** arrive
**attain by effort** achieve
**attainment of goal** success
**attainment of hopes** fruition
**attain success** win
**attar** oil, otto
**attempt** aim, assail, assault, attack, bid, effort, endeavour, enterprise, essay, exertion, experiment, onslaught, pass, push, seek, storm, strive, struggle, tackle, test, thrust, trial, try, undertake, undertaking, venture
**attempting** endeavouring, essaying, experimenting, seeking, striving, tackling, trying, undertaking, venturing
**attempt to arouse public opinion** agitate, canvass, incite, recruit
**attempt to catch** pursuit
**attend** accompany, appear, consider, escort, frequent, haunt, heed, hoc age (L), listen, mind, note, observe, serve, tend, visit
**attendance** aid, appearance, assemblage, assistance, attending, audience, care, crowd, gate, help, house, ministration, monitoring, presence, service, supervision, tendance, turnout
**attendant** escort, accessory, accompanier, accompaniment, accompanying, aid(e), assistant, auxiliary, butler, chaperon, companion, comrade, concomitant, consequence, consequent, flunky, follower, footman, frequenter, guard, lackey, maid, page, servant, steward, usher(ette), waiter
**attendant in charge of building** caretaker
**attendant on a lord** thane
**attendant on a priest** acolyte
**attendant on a ship's passengers** steward
**attendant on travellers** courier
**attendant to huntsman** g(r)illie
**attendant to magician** famulus
**attending** at, listening, present, with
**attend to** mind
**attend to an itch** scratch
**attention** alertness, attending, awareness, care, concentration, concern, consideration, contemplation, deference, deliberation, devotion, ear, heed, mind(fulness), notice, observation, respect, suit, treatment, watchfulness
**attention to safety** caution
**attentive** alert, alive, assiduous, awake, careful, civil, concentrating, deferential, heedful, mindful, obliging, observant, regardful, respectful, studious, watchful
**attentive consideration** ear
**attentively** alertly, carefully, closely, heedfully, intently, mindfully, observantly, studiously, watchfully
**attentiveness** heedfulness, mindfulness
**attentive regard** eye
**attentive to detail** punctilious
**attentive to small points of conscience** scrupulous
**attenuate** airy, decrease, delicate, dilute, diminish, extend, flimsy, frail, gaunt, impair, infirm, lank, lean, lessen, rarefy, reduce, scraggy, slender, slim, tapering, thin, weak, weaken
**attenuated** angular, bony, cadaverous, curtailed, diminished, emaciated, gaunt, haggard, lank, lean, meagre, minimised, pinched, pruned, rawboned, reduced, scraggy, scrawny, skinny, spare, thin, wasted, weaker
**attest** affirm, assert, certify, confirm, corroborate, declare, display, warrant, witness
**attestation of the truth** oath
**attested copy** vidimus
**attester** verifier
**attest to** allege, certify, endorse, evidence, guarantee, insure, plead, testify, warrant, witness
**at that place** there, yonder
**at that point** then, there
**at that time** then
**at the age of consent** marriageable
**at the back** abaft, astern, rear, retral
**at the back of** behind
**at the bar of the conscience** in foro conscientiae (L)
**at the beginning** in principio (L), initial
**at the centre** centric
**at the double** immediately, quickly, without delay
**at the drop of a hat** instantly, promptly
**at the end** extreme, final, finale
**at the end of one's rope** desperate, disconsolate, frantic, tether, worried, wretched
**at the front** anterior
**at the head of the class** first
**at the helm** directing, steering
**at the hub** focal
**at the last minute** behindhand, late, slowly
**at the mercy of the waves** awash
**at the mercy of the wind and waves** adrift
**at the moment** immediately, now
**at the moment of death** in articulo mortis (L)
**at the outset** first
**at the point of death** in extremis (L), moribund
**at the present time** currently, now, nowadays
**at the ready** geared, poised, prepared, waiting
**at the rear** aft, astern
**at the rear of** behind
**at the same rate or pace** pari passu (L)
**at the same time** however, meanwhile, nevertheless, nonetheless, simultaneous, simultaneously, still, yet
**at the side of** accompany, beside, by
**at the stern** aft
**at the summit** apical, atop
**at the tail** caudal
**at the time of** upon
**at the time that** as, when
**at the top** aloft, apical, atop
**at the upper surface of** on
**at the wheel** driving, steering
**at this moment** now
**at this place** here, herewith, now
**at this point** here
**at this time** hoc tempore (L), now, today
**at this very time** instantly
**attic** chaste, classic, clever, cockloft, cultured, delicate, dormer, early, elegant, garret, loft, mansard, nice, refined, witty
**Attic** Greek
**attic salt** wit
**at times** occasionally, sometimes
**at tip of foot** toenail
**attire** accoutre, accoutrement, apparel, array, clothes, clothing, costume, deck, dress, ensemble, garb, garment, guise, habiliment, habit, livery, outfit, raiment, regalia, rig, style, uniform, vest(ment), wardrobe
**attired** accoutred, armed, arrayed, attired, changed, clad, covered, decked, donned, draped, dressed, endowed, equipped, furnished, garbed, prepared, provided, rigged, robed, stocked, supplied
**attitude** affections, air, animus, appearance, approach, aspect, bearing, behaviour, bias, carapace, deportment, disposition, expression, figure, form, idea, impression, inclination, manner, mien, mood, opinion, orientation, outlook, personality, pose, position, posture, prejudice, prepossession, shape, spirit, stance, temperament, thought, view

**attitude of body** pose
**attorney in an ecclesiastical court** proctor
**attorney in India** muktar
**attract** allure, appeal, bewitch, captivate, charm, decoy, draw, engage, entice, fascinate, incline, invite, lure, magnetise
**attracting attention** conspicuous
**attraction** allure, allurement, appeal, charm, draw, entertainment, enticement, exhibition, fascination, feature, gravity, interest, inveiglement, lure, magnetism, pull, seduction, show, temptation, tendency, traction, witchery
**attraction at Niagara** falls
**attract irresistibly** fascinate
**attractive** alluring, appealing, beautiful, becoming, charming, comely, cute, dainty, delightful, elegant, enchanting, endearing, engaging, enticing, fair, fascinating, handsome, inviting, lovely, picturesque, pleasant, pleasing, pretty, seductive, striking, stunning, tempting, winsome
**attractive as a child** cute
**attractive in dainty way** pretty
**attractively slim** slender, svelte
**attractively unusual** exotic
**attractiveness** agreeableness, charm, engagingness, fairness, gorgeousness, handsomeness, loveliness, pleasingness, prettiness
**attractive to look at** beautiful, pretty, sightly
**attribute** apply, ascribe, aspect, assign, characteristic, credit, facet, feature, idiosyncrasy, impute, point, property, quality, quirk, trait, virtue
**attrition** abatement, abrasion, chafing, corrosion, debilitation, decrease, ebbing, eroding, erosion, friction, gnawing, lessening, nagging, pestering, shrinking, weakening
**attune** acclimatise, accord, accustom, adapt, assimilate, fit, harmonise, measure, proportion, reconcile, regulate
**at variance** antagonistic, divergent, inconsistent
**at whatever place** wherever
**at whatever time** whenever
**at what place?** where
**at what time?** when
**at which** whereat
**at will** ad lib, ad libitum (L), ad arbitrium (L), à plaisir (F), à volonté (F)
**at work** active, busy
**atypical horse** ewe-neck
**aubergine** bringal, brinjal, egg-plant

**auburn** reddish-brown
**auburn-haired person** redhead
**au courant (F)** au fait (F), aware, well-informed
**auction** barter, sale, sell, trade, vend, vendue
**auction bid** offer
**auction call** bid
**auctioneer's hammer** gavel, mallet
**auction item** lot
**auction room** mart
**auction word** sold
**audacious** adventurous, bold, brave, brazen, courageous, daredevil, daring, dauntless, fearless, impudent, intrepid, pert, rash, reckless, risky, rude, shameless, spirited, unabashed, undaunted, venturesome
**audacity** boldness, bravery, courage, daring, defiance, fearlessness, grit, guts, nerve, pertness, pluck, rashness, temerity
**audible** clear, detectable, discernible, distinct, hearable, heard, loud, perceivable, perceptible
**audible exhalation** sigh
**audible kind of dancing** tap
**audibly** aloud, clearly, discernibly, distinctly
**audience** assemblage, assembly, attendants, attenders, auditory, congregation, crowd, devotees, ear, fans, floor, gallery, gathering, hearing, listeners, public, reception, spectators, tribunal, viewers
**audio deck** tape recorder
**audio organ** drum, ear
**audit** balancing, check, examine, inspect, inspection, investigation, review, verification
**auditory organ** ear
**au fait (F)** (ac)knowledgeable, acquainted, clued-up, conversant, instructed, posted, well-informed
**au fond (F)** basically
**auger** borer
**augment** accumulate, add, amass, amplify, boost, complement, deepen, enhance, enlarge, expand, extend, heighten, increase, inflate, magnify, multiply, protract, raise, supplement, swell, thicken, widen
**augur** auspex, bode, diviner, foresee, herald, oracle, portend, portent, predict, promise, prophet, seer, soothsayer
**augury** clairvoyance, divination, forewarning, fortune-telling, geomancy, harbinger, omen, prediction, presage, prognostication, prophecy, sign

**august** ambitious, dignified, distinguished, elevated, eminent, exalted, formal, glorious, grand, grave, great, haughty, high, honourable, imperial, imposing, impressive, kingly, large, lofty, lordly, magnificent, majestic, noble, opulent, pompous, prestigious, princely, regal, solemn, stately, sumptuous, superb
**auk** razorbill
**au naturel (F)** nude
**aunt** tia (Sp)
**aunt's child** cousin
**aura** air, ambience, aroma, atmosphere, character, charisma, effluence, emanation, environment, feeling, halo, mood, nimbus, odour, personality, prestige, quality, scent, sensation, spirit, suggestion
**aural** auricular, heard, otic
**aural inflammation** otitis
**aural jewel** earring
**aural membrane** ear-drum
**aural organ** ear
**aureate** gilded, golden(-coloured), resplendent
**aureola** aureole, halo
**aureole** aureola, corona, effulgence, halo, luminescence, luminosity, lustre, nimbus, phosphorescence, radiance
**au revoir (F)** arrivederci (I), ciao (I)
**auric** golden
**auricle** atrium, ear, pinna
**auricle part** earlobe
**auricula plant** primrose
**auriferous mineral** quartz
**auspice** augury, foreboding, omen, portent, sign, warning
**auspices** advocacy, aegis, authority, backing, control, countenance, guidance, patronage, protection, sponsorship
**auspicious** clear, cloudless, encouraging, favourable, fortunate, halcyon, opportune, propitious, prosperous, seasonable, successful
**Aussie islander** Tasmanian
**austere** ascetic, bitter, bleak, chaste, cold, forbidding, formal, grave, hard, harsh, plain, rigorous, rough, serious, severe, simple, sober, spartan, stern, stiff, strict, stringent, subdued, uncompromising
**austere person** puritan
**austere religion** asceticism
**austerity** chastity, coldness, economy, formality, harshness, inflexibility, rigidity, rigour, self-denial, seriousness, severity, solemnity, sternness, strictness

**austerity of manner** frost
**Australia and New Zealand** antipodes
**Australian** Anzac, Aussie
**Australian Aboriginal club** nulla-nulla
**Australian Aboriginal initiation rite** bora
**Australian Aboriginal musical instrument** didgeridoo
**Australian Aboriginal painter** Namatjira
**Australian Aboriginal's hut** gunya(h), humpy, mia mia, wurley, wurlie
**Australian Aboriginal's war club** waddy
**Australian Aboriginal weapon** leangle
**Australian Aboriginal woman** gin, lubra
**Australian Aboriginal youth after initiation** kipper
**Australian Aborigine** Aboriginal
**Australian acacia** myall
**Australian animal** kangaroo, koala, wallaby, wombat
**Australian anteater** echidna
**Australian arboreal marsupial** koala
**Australian aromatic evergreen** eucalypt(us)
**Australian artist** Drysdale, Nolan
**Australian author** Clarke, White
**Australian banded anteater** numbat
**Australian beach** Manly, Bondi
**Australian bear** koala
**Australian beefwood** belah, belar
**Australian bird** brolga, budgerigar, cooee, cooey, currawong, drongo, emu, galah, koel, kookaburra, lorikeet, lyrebird
**Australian bird-like ostrich** emu
**Australian blanket** wagga
**Australian boomerang** kylie
**Australian bottle tree** baobab
**Australian bullroarer** churinga
**Australian burrowing, egg-laying mammal** echidna
**Australian burrowing, furry marsupial** wombat
**Australian bush** mulga
**Australian bush bread** damper
**Australian bush hut** humpy
**Australian cactus** pigface
**Australian canvas shoe** plimsoll
**Australian cape** Howe
**Australian carpet-shark** wobbegong
**Australian city of churches** Adelaide
**Australian clover-like plant** nardoo
**Australian cockatoo** arara, galah, lookout
**Australian coin** cent, dollar
**Australian cuckoo** koel
**Australian dabchick** grebe

**Australian desert** Arunta, Gibson, Great Sandy, Great Victoria, Simpson, Sturt, Tanami
**Australian dessert** Pavlova
**Australian drink** beer
**Australian duck-billed aquatic mammal** platypus
**Australian edible lungfish** barramundi
**Australian edible white wood-boring grub** bardie
**Australian egg-laying mammal with broad bill and webbed feet** platypus
**Australian explorer** Wentworth
**Australian fenced-in area** paddock
**Australian fern** nardoo
**Australian fish** lungfish, mado, morwong, mulloway, snook, sweet-lips, teraglin
**Australian flightless bird** cassowary, emu
**Australian fodder tree** kurrajong
**Australian food-fish** flathead, trumpet
**Australian form of ophthalmia** sandyblight
**Australian gem** opal
**Australian gum tree** eucalyptus
**Australian harbour** Brisbane, Darwin, Fremantle, Macquare, Melbourne, Newcastle, Sydney
**Australian hardwood** jarrah
**Australian honey-eater** blue-eye, tui, wattlebird
**Australian honey possum** tait
**Australian horserace** Melbourne Cup
**Australian hut** mia mia
**Australian immigrant** jackaroo
**Australian insect** laap, lerp, witchetty
**Australian inventor of machine gun** Owen
**Australian island** Cato, Coringa, Koolan, Melville, Rottnest, Tasmania
**Australian island state** Tasmania
**Australian lake** Barlee, Colac, Cowan, Everard, Eyre, Lefroy, Nabberoo, Torrens
**Australian longicorn beetle's grub** witchetty
**Australian lotus bird** jacana
**Australian marsupial** bandicoot, cuscus, dasyure, euro, kangaroo, koala, numbat, phalanger, quokka, tait, wallaby, wombat
**Australian monitor lizard** goanna
**Australian monotreme** platypus
**Australian moth** atlas
**Australian mountain range** Darling, Flinders
**Australian musical camp** corroboree
**Australian native bear** koala
**Australian native drum** ubar

**Australian native trumpet** didgeridoo, didjeridoo
**Australian opossum** phalanger
**Australian ostrich** emu
**Australian owl** boobook
**Australian pack-horse** packer
**Australian painter** Nolan
**Australian parakeet** rosella
**Australian parrot** lorikeet, lory, rosella
**Australian peninsula** Eyre
**Australian pheasant-like bird** lyrebird
**Australian pigeon** wonga-wonga
**Australian pine** beefwood
**Australian pink and grey cockatoo** galah
**Australian pioneer** Flynn
**Australian plains turkey** bustard
**Australian prima donna** Melba
**Australian primary industry** dairying
**Australian protea** hakea
**Australian radio pioneer** Fisk
**Australian ratite** emu
**Australian rat-like marsupial** bandicoot
**Australian raucous kingfisher** kookaburra
**Australian remote country areas** backblocks, outback
**Australian sea-bream** tarwhine
**Australian seafood** gemfish
**Australian sheepdog** kelpie
**Australian sheep-farmer** squatter
**Australian sheep or cattle farmer** pastoralist
**Australian shellfish** pipi
**Australian shrub with narcotic leaves** pituri
**Australian small, brightly coloured parrot** lorikeet
**Australian small farmer** cocky
**Australian small flying phalanger** glider
**Australian snake** taipan
**Australian's name for Englishman** pom
**Australian soldier** Anzac, Digger, Swaddy
**Australian spear-thrower** woomera
**Australian springs town** Alice
**Australian state** New South Wales, Northern Territory, Queensland, South Australia, Tasmania, Victoria, Western Australia
**Australian strait** Torres
**Australian tall myrtaceous tree** lilly-pilly
**Australian tree** belah, belar, billa, bunksia, gum, kari, karri, mallee, mulga, penda, tuart, waddywood
**Australian tree yielding tough bast fibre** currajong, kurrajong
**Australian tulip** waratah

Australian venomous snake  taipan
Australian vine vegetable  choko
Australian war-club  waddy
Australian waterfall  Coomera, Tully, Wallaman, Wentworth
Australian waterhole  billabong
Australian weapon  nulla-nulla
Australian wild dog  dingo, warragal, warrigal
Australian wild horse  brumby
Australian woman  lubra
Australian young street rowdy  hooligan, larrikin
Australia's highest mountain  Kosciusko
Austrian amphibian  olm
Austrian annexation  Anschluss
Austrian Celtic kingdom  Noricum
Austrian composer  Strauss
Austrian currency  ducat, groschen, gulden, krone, schilling
Austrian dance  lândler
Austrian emperor  kaiser
Austrian lake  Almsee, Bodensee, Constance, Fertoto, Neusiedler, Traunsee
Austrian leather shorts with braces  lederhosen
Austrian monetary unit and coin  schilling
Austrian pass  Arlberg, Brenner, Loibl, Plocken, Semmering
Austrian philosopher  Steiner
Austrian province  Burgenland, Carinthia, Salzburg, Skarnten, Steiermark, Styria, Tirol, Tyrol, Vienna, Vorarlburg
Austrian psychiatrist  Freud
Austrian waterfall  Gastein, Golling, Krimml
Austro-German river  Isar
authentic  accurate, actual, authoritative, certain, dependable, factual, genuine, honest, legitimate, original, pure, real, reliable, true, valid
authenticate  accredit, affirm, assure, attest, aver, guarantee, insure, justify, seal, sustain, validate, verify, vouch
author  architect, autore (I), composer, fabricator, inventor, maker, mover, originator, planner, playwright, producer, writer
authorisation  permission
authorise  accredit, allow, approve, commission, confirm, delegate, empower, enable, entitle, establish, legalise, license, permit, sanction, support, warrant
authorise again  re-enact
authorised agent  proxy

authorise use of  license
authorising letter  breve, brief
authoritarian  absolutist, austere, autocrat, despot(ic), dictator, dogmatic, domineering, harsh, severe, strict, tyrannical, tyrant, unyielding
authoritative  accurate, assertive, authentic, authoritarian, autocratic, commanding, conclusive, definitive, dogmatic, impressive, masterly, official, peremptory, positive, unquestioned, veritable
authoritative answer  oracle
authoritative command  fiat, order
authoritative decision  say-so
authoritative decree  arret, edict
authoritative demand  summons
authoritative legal decision  ruling
authoritative order  edict, fiat, injunction
authoritative permission  licence
authoritative permit  licence
authoritative prohibition  interdict, veto
authoritative requirement  mandate
authority  arbiter, ascendancy, authorisation, charge, command, control, domination, influence, jurisdiction, justification, liberty, permission, permit, power, rule, ruling, say-so, statute, supremacy, sway, testimony
authority over vassal state  protectorate
authority to act for another  mandate
author of Abbot, The  Scott
author of Abe Lincoln in Illinois  Sherwood
author of Adam Bede  Eliot
author of Adventures of Huckleberry Finn, The  Twain
author of Adventures of Tom Sawyer, The  Twain
author of Alchemist, The  Jonson
author of Alice's Adventures in Wonderland  Carroll
author of All for Love  Dryden
author of All Quiet on the Western Front  Remarque
author of All's Well that Ends Well  Shakespeare
author of Ambassadors, The  James
author of Amelia  Fielding
author of American Dream, The  Mailer
author of And Quiet Flows the Don  Sholokhov
author of Androcles and the Lion  Shaw
author of Angel Pavement  Priestley
author of Anna Karenina  Tolstoy
author of Antony and Cleopatra  Shakespeare
author of Any Woman's Blues  Jong

author of Armies of the Night, The  Mailer
author of Arms and the Man  Shaw
author of As the Crow Flies  Archer
author of As You Like It  Shakespeare
author of Babbitt  Lewis
author of Back to Methuselah  Shaw
author of Ballad of Reading Gaol, The  Wilde
author of Barchester Towers  Trollope
author of Barrack-Room Ballads  Kipling
author of Barren Ground  Glasgow
author of Bekkersdal Marathon, A  Bosman
author of Beyond Human Power  Bjørnson
author of Biographia Literaria  Coleridge
author of Bleak House  Dickens
author of Bostonians, The  James
author of Brideshead Revisited  Waugh
author of Brokenclaw  Gardner
author of Butterfield Eight  O'Hara
author of Cakes and Ale  Maugham
author of Camille  Dumas
author of Candida  Shaw
author of Canterbury Tales  Chaucer
author of Captain's Daughter  Pushkin
author of Cask of Jerepigo, A  Bosman
author of Castle of Otranto, The  Walpole
author of Cherry Orchard, The  Chekhov
author of Chico the Small One  Webster
author of Christabel  Coleridge
author of City of Dreadful Night, The  Thomson
author of Clarissa Harlowe  Richardson
author of Clayhanger  Bennett
author of Cold Stone Jug  Bosman
author of Comedy of Errors, The  Shakespeare
author of Coriolanus  Shakespeare
author of Country Wife, The  Wycherley
author of Crime and Punishment  Dostoevski, Dostoevsky
author of Crisis, The  Churchill
author of Cymbeline  Shakespeare
author of Dance with the Devil  Douglas
author of Darkness at Noon  Koestler
author of David Copperfield  Dickens
author of Day of the Scorpion, The  Scott
author of Dead End  Kingsley
author of Dead Souls  Gogol

author of **Death of an Expert Witness** James
author of **Deceiver, The** Forsyth
author of **Description of New England** Smith
author of **Desire under the Elms** O'Neill
author of **Devil's Disciple, The** Shaw
author of **Divine Comedy, The** Dante
author of **Division of the Spoils, A** Scott
author of **Doll's House, A** Ibsen
author of **Dombey and Son** Dickens
author of **Don Flows Home to the Sea, The** Sholokhov
author of **Don Juan** Byron
author of **Don Quixote** Cervantes
author of **Downfall** Zola
author of **Dr Faustus** Marlowe
author of **Drums along the Mohawk** Edmonds
author of **East End** Steinbeck
author of **Elephant Song** Smith
author of **Emma** Austen
author of **Enemy of the People, An** Ibsen
author of **Erewhon** Butler
author of **Ethan Frome** Wharton
author of **Eugenie Grandet** Balzac
author of **Evelina** Burney
author of **Exclusive** Archer
author of **Faerie Queene, The** Spencer
author of **Faithful Shepherdess** Fletcher
author of **Far from the Madding Crowd** Hardy
author of **Farewell to Arms, A** Hemingway
author of **Father Goriot** Balzac
author of **Fathers and Sons** Turgenev
author of **Faust** Goethe
author of **Financier, The** Dreiser
author of **For Whom the Bell Tolls** Hemingway
author of **Forsyte Saga, The** Galsworthy
author of **Fortitude** Walpole
author of **Fortress, The** Walpole
author of **Fortunes of Richard Mahony, The** Richardson
author of **Fourth Protocol, The** Forsyth
author of **Framley Parsonage** Trollope
author of **Frankenstein** Shelley
author of **Ghosts** Ibsen
author of **Giants in the Earth** Rölvaag
author of **Gillyvors, The** Cookson
author of **Glass Menagerie, The** Williams
author of **Gold Coast** De Mille
author of **Golden Bowl, The** James
author of **Gone with the Wind** Mitchell

author of **Good Companions, The** Priestley
author of **Good Earth, The** Buck
author of **Grand Hotel** Baum
author of **Grandmothers** Westcott
author of **Grapes of Wrath, The** Steinbeck
author of **Great Circle** Llewellyn
author of **Great Expectations** Dickens
author of **Great Gatsby, The** Fitzgerald
author of **Green Bay Tree, The** Bromfield
author of **Green Mansions** Hudson
author of **Growth of the Soil** Hamsun
author of **Guy Mannering** Scott
author of **Hamlet** Shakespeare
author of **Handful of Dust, A** Waugh
author of **Handley Cross** Surtees
author of **Hard Times** Dickens
author of **Heart of Midlothian, The** Scott
author of **Heartbreak House** Shaw
author of **Heaven's My Destination** Wilder
author of **Hedda Gabler** Ibsen
author of **Henry Esmond** Thackeray
author of **Henry V** Shakespeare
author of **Herries Chronicle, The** Walpole
author of **History of the English-Speaking Peoples** Churchill
author of **House of Mirth, The** Wharton
author of **House of the Seven Gables, The** Hawthorne
author of **How Green Was My Valley** Llewellyn
author of **Hypatia** Kingsley
author of **Idylls of the King** Tennyson
author of **If Winter Comes** Hutchinson
author of **Iliad** Homer
author of **Importance of being Earnest, The** Wilde
author of **Ivanhoe** Scott
author of **Jane Eyre** Brontë
author of **Jerusalem Delivered** Tasso
author of **Jewel in the Crown, The** Scott
author of **Jewels of the Madonna** Wolf-Ferrari
author of **John Brown's Body** Benét
author of **Joseph Andrews** Fielding
author of **Jude the Obscure** Hardy
author of **Judith Paris** Walpole
author of **Julius Ceasar** Shakespeare
author of **Jump and Other Stories** Gordimer
author of **Jungle Books, The** Kipling
author of **Jungle, The** Sinclair
author of **Just So Stories** Kipling
author of **Kane and Abel** Archer

author of **Kenilworth** Scott
author of **Kidnapped** Stevenson
author of **Kim** Kipling
author of **King John** Shakespeare
author of **King Lear** Shakespeare
author of **King Solomon's Mines** Haggard
author of **Kreutzer Sonata, The** Tolstoy
author of **Kubla Kahn** Coleridge
author of **Laburnum Grove** Priestley
author of **Lady Chatterley's Lover** Lawrence
author of **Lady of the Lake, The** Scott
author of **Lady of the Last Minstrel, The** Scott
author of **Lady Windermere's Fan** Wilde
author of **Late George Apley, The** Marquand
author of **La Temtation de Saint Antoine** Flaubert
author of **Les Miserables** Hugo
author of **Life with Father** Day
author of **Light in August** Faulkner
author of **Liliom** Molnár
author of **Little Demon** Sologub
author of **Little Dorrit** Dickens
author of **Little Minister, The** Barrie
author of **Little Women** Alcott
author of **Look Homeward, Angel** Wolfe
author of **Looking Backward** Bellamy
author of **Lord Jim** Conrad
author of **Lorna Doone** Blackmore
author of **Lost Horizon** Hilton
author of **Lost Lady, A** Cather
author of **Love's Labour's Lost** Shakespeare
author of **Macbeth** Shakespeare
author of **Madame Bovary** Flaubert
author of **Magic Mountain, The** Mann
author of **Magic Pudding, The** Lindsay
author of **Main Street** Lewis
author of **Major Barbara** Shaw
author of **Man and Superman** Shaw
author of **Mansfield Park** Austen
author of **Marlborough** Churchill
author of **Martin Chuzzlewit** Dickens
author of **Master Builder, The** Ibsen
author of **Master of Ballantrae, The** Stevenson
author of **Mayor of Casterbridge, The** Hardy
author of **Measure for Measure** Shakespeare
author of **Men at Arms** Waugh
author of **Merchant of Venice, The** Shakespeare
author of **Merry Wives of Windsor, The** Shakespeare
author of **Micah Clarke** Doyle

author of *Middlemarch* Eliot
author of *Midsummer Night's Dream, A* Shakespeare
author of *Mill on the Floss, The* Eliot
author of *Moby Dick* Melville
author of *Moll Flanders* Defoe
author of *Moon and Sixpence, The* Maugham
author of *Moonstone, The* Collins
author of *Mourning becomes Electra* O'Neill
author of *Mrs Dalloway* Woolf
author of *Mrs Warren's Profession* Shaw
author of *Much Ado about Nothing* Shakespeare
author of *Mulberry Forest, The* Matthee
author of *My Antonia* Cather
author of *My Cousin Rachel* Du Maurier
author of *My Son's Story* Gordimer
author of *Mysteries of Udolpho* Radcliffe
author of *Naked and the Dead, The* Mailer
author of *Nana* Zola
author of *Native Son* Wright
author of *Nest of Gentlefolk* Turgenev
author of *Newcomes, The* Thackeray
author of *Nicholas Nickleby* Dickens
author of *Night over Water* Follett
author of *Night's Lodging* Gorky
author of *Nightmare Abbey* Peacock
author of *No Name* Collins
author of *Novel, The* Michener
author of *Odyssey* Homer
author of *Of Human Bondage* Maugham
author of *Of Mice and Men* Steinbeck
author of *Of Time and the River* Wolfe
author of *Officers and Gentlemen* Waugh
author of *Old and the Young* Pirandello
author of *Old Curiosity Shop* Dickens
author of *Old Maid* Wharton
author of *Old Man And The Sea, The* Hemingway
author of *Old Mortality* Scott
author of *Old Wives' Tale, The* Bennett
author of *Oliver Twist* Dickens
author of *Orlando Furioso* Ariosto
author of *Othello* Shakespeare
author of *Our Mutual Friend* Dickens
author of *Our Town* Wilder
author of *Pamela* Richardson
author of *Passage to India, A* Forster
author of *Peasants, The* Reymont
author of *Peer Gynt* Ibsen
author of *Pendennis* Thackeray

author of *Penguin Island* France
author of *Peregrine Pickle* Smollett
author of *Pericles* Shakespeare
author of *Peter Ibbetson* Du Maurier
author of *Peter Pan* Barrie
author of *Pickwick Papers* Dickens
author of *Picture of Dorian Gray, The* Wilde
author of *Pilgrim's Progress* Bunyan
author of *Playboy of the Western World* Synge
author of *plays* playwright, dramatist
author of *Point Counter Point* Huxley
author of *Portrait of a Lady, The* James
author of *Pride and Prejudice* Austen
author of *Prisoner of Zenda, The* Hope
author of *Prophecy of Famine, The* Churchill
author of *Purple Land That England Lost, The* Hudson
author of *Pygmalion* Shaw
author of *Quality Street* Barrie
author of *Quentin Durward* Scott
author of *Quiet flows the Don, And* Sholokov
author of *Quo Vadis?* Sienkiewicz
author of *Rainbow, The* Lawrence
author of *Rape of the Lock* Pope
author of *Rascal Money* Garber
author of *Rasselas* Johnson
author of *Raven, The* Poe
author of *Rebecca* Du Maurier
author of *Red Rover, The* Cooper
author of *Redgauntlet* Scott
author of *Relic, The* Anthony
author of *Remember* Bradford
author of *Remembrance of Things Past* Proust
author of *Return of the Native, The* Hardy
author of *Revolt of the Angels* France
author of *Rich Jew of Malta, The* Marlowe
author of *Richard Carvel* Churchill
author of *Richard II* Shakespeare
author of *Richard III* Shakespeare
author of *Riders to the Sea* Synge
author of *Rime of the Ancient Mariner, The* Coleridge
author of *Ring and the Book, The* Browning
author of *Rise of Silas Lapham, The* Howells
author of *Rivals, The* Sheridan
author of *Rob Roy* Scott
author of *Robinson Crusoe* Defoe
author of *Roderick Random* Smollett
author of *Rogue Herries* Walpole
author of *Romany Rye* Borrow
author of *Rome Haul* Edmonds

author of *Romeo and Juliet* Shakespeare
author of *Romola* Eliot
author of *Rosciad, The* Churchill
author of *Rudin* Turgenev
author of *Salammbô* Flaubert
author of *Sappho* Daudet
author of *Scarlet Letter, The* Hawthorne
author of *School for Scandal, The* Sheridan
author of *Scoop* Waugh
author of *Sea of Grass* Richter
author of *Sea Wolf* London
author of *Seagull, The* Chek(h)ov
author of *Second World War, The* Churchill
author of *Secret Pilgrim, The* Le Carré
author of *Sense and Sensibility* Austen
author of *Sentimental Tommy* Barrie
author of *Seven Pillars of Wisdom, The* Lawrence
author of *She* Haggard
author of *Sheltered Life, The* Glasgow
author of *Shirley* Brontë
author of *Show Boat* Ferber
author of *Silas Marner* Eliot
author of *Silent Don* Sholokhov
author of *Smoke* Turgenev
author of *So Red the Rose* Young
author of *Song of Bernadette, The* Werfel
author of *Song of Hiawatha, The* Longfellow
author of *Sons and Lovers* Lawrence
author of *Sound and the Fury, The* Faulkner
author of *South Wind* Douglas
author of *Sport of Nature, A* Gordimer
author of *Spy, The* Cooper
author of *Spycatcher* Wright
author of *St Joan* Shaw
author of *Stalk and Company* Kipling
author of *State Fair* Stong
author of *Staying On* Scott
author of *Steppenwolf* Hesse
author of *Story of a Bad Boy, The* Aldrich
author of *Story of an African Farm, The* Schreiner
author of *Street Scene* Rice
author of *Study in Scarlet, A* Doyle
author of *Sun Also Rises, The* Hemingway
author of *Susanna's Secret* Wolf-Ferrari
author of *Swiss Family Robinson, The* Wyss
author of *Tale of Two Cities, A* Dickens

author of *Tamburlaine the Great* Marlowe
author of *Taming of the Shrew, The* Shakespeare
author of *Taming of the Shrew, The* Shakespeare
author of *Tanglewood Tales* Hawthorne
author of *Taras Bulba* Gogol
author of *Taste of Death, A* James
author of *Tempest, The* Shakespeare
author of *Tess of the d'Urbervilles* Hardy
author of *Thaddeus of Warsaw* Porter
author of *This Above All* Knight
author of *Three Musketeers, The* Dumas
author of *Three Sisters, The* Chekhov
author of *Time Machine, The* Wells
author of *Time of Your Life, The* Saroyan
author of *Timon of Athens* Shakespeare
author of *Titus Andronicus* Shakespeare
author of *To The Lighthouse* Woolf
author of *Tobacco Road* Caldwell
author of *Tom Jones* Fielding
author of *Tono-Bungay* Wells
author of *Towers of Silence, The* Scott
author of *Treasure Island* Stevenson
author of *Trilby* Du Maurier
author of *Troilus and Cressida* Shakespeare
author of *Trois contes* Flaubert
author of *Truth and Justice* Tammsaare
author of *Twelfth Night* Shakespeare
author of *Two Gentlemen of Verona, The* Shakespeare
author of *Typee* Melville
author of *Ulysses* Joyce
author of *Uncle Tom's Cabin* Stowe
author of *Uncle Vanya* Chekhov
author of *Unconditional Surrender* Waugh
author of *Vanity Fair* Thackeray
author of *Varieties of Religious Experience, The* James
author of *Vicar of Wakefield, The* Goldsmith
author of *Vile Bodies* Waugh
author of *Virginians, The* Thackeray
author of *Wandering Jew, The* Sue
author of *War and Peace* Tolstoy
author of *Washington Square* James
author of *Waverley* Scott
author of *Way of All Flesh, The* Butler
author of *Way of the World, The* Congreve

author of *Wealth of Nations, The* Smith
author of *Well of Loneliness, The* Hall
author of *Westward Ho* Kingsley
author of *What Every Woman Knows* Barrie
author of *What Price Glory* Anderson
author of *When We Were Very Young* Milne
author of *Why Are We In Vietnam?* Mailer
author of *Wickford Point* Marquand
author of *Wild Duck, The* Ibsen
author of *Will to Believe, The* James
author of *William Tell* Schiller
author of *Winesburg, Ohio* Anderson
author of *Wings of the Dove, The* James
author of *Winnie the Pooh* Milne
author of *Winter's Tale, The* Shakespeare
author of *Winterset* Anderson
author of *Wizard of Oz, The* Baum
author of *Woman in White, The* Collins
author of *Women in Love* Lawrence
author of *World Crisis, The* Churchill
author of *World's Illusion* Wassermann
author of *Wuthering Heights* Brontë
author of *Yearling, The* Rawlings
author of *You Can't go Home Again* Wolfe
author of *You Never Can Tell* Shaw
author's assumed name nom de plume, pseudonym
author's copy of his work manuscript
author's greatest work magnum opus
author's name byline
author's pen-name nom de plume, pseudonym
author's perquisite royalty
author unknown anon, anonymous
auto car
auto auction car mart
autobiography memoirs
autochthon aborigine, native
autocracy absolutism, dictatorship, tyranny
autocrat absolutist, despot, dictator, monarch, ruler, tyrant
autocratic absolute, all-powerful, arbitrary, authoritarian, cruel, despotic, dictatorial, disciplinarian, doctrinaire, domineering, full, harsh, high-handed, imperious, inhuman, monocratic, omnipotent, oppressive, overbearing, overweening, peremptory, rigid, severe, sovereign, strict, supreme, tyrannical, unbounded, unconditional, unjust, unlimited, unqualified, unquestionable, unrestrained, unrestricted
auto fuel gas, petrol
autogamy self-fertilisation
autograph inscribe, manual, name, sign, signature
auto hangar garage
automated machine robot
automatic automated, habitual, inevitable, instinctive, involuntary, mechanical, natural, routine, self-acting, self-moving, unavoidable, unconscious, uncontrollable, unwilled
automatic betting machine tote
automatic pistol repeater
automation android, computer, instrument, machine, robot
automaton android, marionette, pawn, puppet, robot
automobile auto(car), car, coupé, hatchback, jalopy, jeep, limousine, lorry, motor, motor-car, roadster, saloon, sedan, tjorrie, truck, van
automobile need fuel, gas, oil, petrol
automobile operator driver
automobile transportation bus, cab, car, lorry, minibus, taxi, truck, van
automotive fuel diesel, petrol
automotive vehicle motor
autonomous allodial, autonomic, free, independent, noncolonial, self-governing, sovereign, uncoerced, unfettered, unrestricted
autonomy freedom, independence, liberation, sovereignty
autopsy dissection, necropsy, post-mortem
autumnal hedgerow fruit haw
autumn flower aster
auxiliary accessory, additional, aide, ally, ancillary, assistant, assisting, associate, confederate, emergency, secondary, subordinate, subsidiary, substitute, supporting
auxiliary business activity sideline
auxiliary part adjunct
auxiliary verb do, does, have, may, might, shall, will
avail advantage, aid, benefit, help, profit, purpose, service, success, use(fulness)
availability accessibility, appropriateness, closeness, convenience, fitness, handiness, nearness, proximity, service(ability), suitability, usefulness, utility, vicinity
available accessible, advantageous, applicable, appropriate, convenient, efficacious, fit, obtainable, ready, suitable, usable, vacant, valid
available as unit married

**available in insufficient quantity** scarce
**available money** cash
**available to callers** at home
**avail oneself** exploit, use
**avail oneself of** use
**avail oneself of** utilise
**avalanche** barrage, blizzard, bouleversement (F), calamity, cascade, debacle, deluge, disaster, earthslide, flood, inundation, landslide, Niagara, snowslide, torrent, upheaval
**avarice** avidity, covetousness, cupidity, desire, esurience, greed, greed, greediness, mammon, meanness, miserliness, monopoly, niggardliness, parsimony, penury, possessiveness, rapacity, stinginess, venality
**avaricious** acquiring, acquisitive, close, covetous, grasping, greedy, hoarding, mean, mercenary, miserly, penurious, possessive, predacious, rapacious, ravenous, sordid, stingy, venal
**avaricious money lender** usurer
**avaricious person** miser
**avast** cease, stop
**avatar** incarnation, manifestation
**avaunt** depart, go
**ave** farewell, hail, recitation, salutation, welcome
**avenaceous grass** oats
**avenge** punish, repay, requite, retaliate, revenge, reward, vindicate, wreak
**avenger of blood** Goel
**avenging deity** Alastor
**avenue** access, alley, approach, boulevard, channel, course, drive(way), entrance, road, route, thoroughfare, way
**aver** affirm, allege, assert, attest, avouch, avow, claim, declare, endorse, enunciate, express, formulate, insist, maintain, proclaim, profess, pronounce, protest, state, submit, swear, testify, vow, witness
**average** common, equate, everyday, fair, general, indifferent, intermediate, mean, medial, median, mediocre, mediocrity, medium, middle, middling, midpoint, moderate, norm(al), ordinary, par, passable, proportion, regular, retaliate, rule, run(-of-the-mill), satisfactory, so-so, standard, tolerable, typical, undistinguished, unexceptional, unremarkable, usual
**average level** norm
**average level of achievement** norm

**average standard** norm
**average tidal height** sea level
**averse** antipathetic, backward, disinclined, hostile, indisposed, lo(a)th, opposed, reluctant, unfavourable, unwilling
**averseness** loathness
**averse to exertion** indolent, lazy
**averse to rapid changes** conservative
**averse to work** idle, indolent, lazy, slack, slothful
**aversion** abomination, antipathy, despite, disgust, disinclination, dislike, distaste, enmity, hate, hatred, loathing, obstinate, odium, opposition, regret, repugnance, unwillingness
**aversion to food** apositia, sitophobia
**aversion to work** ergophobia
**avert** astray, avoid, ba(u)lk, bar, bypass, check, circumvent, deflect, depart, deviate, digress, diverge, dodge, elude, err, escape, evade, forestall, frustrate, hinder, impede, obstruct, parry, preclude, prevent, repel, restrain, shirk, shun, sidestep, thwart, turn, vary, veer
**avert in advance** forestall
**avian** birdlike
**avian creature** bird
**aviary** birdcage, birdhouse, vivarium
**aviate** control, fly, manoeuvre, operate, pilot
**aviation** aerodynamics, aeronautics, flight, flying
**aviator** ace, aeronaut, airman, airplaner, airwoman, aviatrix, flier, pilot
**aviculturist** birdman
**avid** agog, anxious, ardent, breathless, covetous, craving, dedicated, desirous, devoted, eager, earnest, effusive, enthusiastic, fanatic(al), fervent, grasping, greedy, hungry, impatient, insatiable, intense, keen, passionate, rapacious, ravenous, thirsty, vivacious, voracious, zealous
**avidity** alacrity, appetite, ardour, avarice, covetousness, craving, cupidity, desire, diligence, eagerness, enthusiasm, feeling, fervour, fire, greed, greediness, heat, impatience, intensity, keenness, longing, lust, passion, rapacity, selfishness, spirit, thirst, vehemence, warmth, zeal, zest
**avidly** ardently, devotedly, eagerly, enthusiastically, fanatically, fervently, intensely, keenly, passionately, zealously
**avifauna** ornis
**avis** bird

**aviso** advice, intelligence
**avocation** employment, hobby, occupation, pastime, profession, pursuit, recreation, secondary, sideline
**avoid** abstain, avert, ba(u)lk, bypass, circumvent, detour, dodge, duck, elude, escape, eschew, evade, funk, miss, parry, prevent, procrastinate, refrain, shirk, shun, sidestep, skirt
**avoidance** dodging, eluding, escape, evasion, prevention, procrastination, shirking, shunning
**avoidance of obscenity** decency
**avoidance of rashness** caution
**avoid artfully** evade
**avoid by trickery** dodge
**avoid capture** elude
**avoid compliance with** elude
**avoid doing one's duty** scrimshank, shirk
**avoid excess** ne nimium (L)
**avoiding** centrifugal, divergent
**avoiding excess** moderate, temperate
**avoiding extremes** conservative, moderate
**avoiding light** lucifugous
**avoiding the issue** elusory
**avoiding waste** economical
**avoid paying** bilk
**avoid slyly** elude
**avow** acknowledge, admit, assert, aver, confess, declare, profess, recognise, state
**await** abide, anticipate, attend, bide, expect, pend, tarry, wait
**await best opportunity** bide
**await judgement** pend
**await the consequences** abide
**awake** activate, alert, alive, animate, (a)rouse, astir, attentive, aware, conscious, excite, fan, heedful, inspire, kindle, observant, provoke, spur, stimulate, vigilant, wakeful, watchful
**awake and on the alert** vigilant
**awake from sleep** arouse
**awaken** activate, alert, animate, (a)rouse, enliven, stimulate, vivify, wake
**awakening** animation, arousal, awareness, consciousness, invigoration, quickening, renewal, rousing, stimulating, vivifying
**award** accolade, accord, adjudication, allot, apportion, assign, bestow(al), confer(ment), decision, decoration, decree, endow, gift, give, grant, honour, medal, order, present(ation), prize, render, trophy, verdict
**award a penalty against** penalise
**award at gymkhana** rosette

**award for bravery** citation, medal
**award for excellence in American journalism, literature and music** Pulitzer prize
**award for valour** medal
**award-winning film set in India** Gandhi
**aware** acquainted, alert, apprised, au courant (F), awake, cautious, cognisant, cognizant, conscious, conversant, enlightened, informed, intelligent, knowing, knowledgeable, mindful, observant, regardful, sensible, sentient, sophisticated, wary
**awareness** acquaintance, alertness, appreciation, cautiousness, consciousness, consideration, discovery, insight, intuition, knowledge, observance, realisation, recognition, regard, sensibility, sentience, watchfulness
**aware of** know, onto
**aware of one's surroundings** conscious
**awash** flooded, water-covered
**away** abroad, abscond, absent(ee), afield, apart, aside, elsewhere, gone, incessantly, off, out, relentless, remote, repeatedly, truant, unavailable
**away from** ab-, apart, beyond, off, out
**away from home** afield, out
**away from the coast** inland
**away from the mouth** aboral
**away from the wind** lee
**away to the rear** astern
**awe** admiration, adoration, amaze(ment), apprehension, astonish(ment), daunt, dread, exaltation, fear, fright(en), inspire, intimidate, respect, reverence, solemnise, terror, veneration, wonder(ment)

**awed by theatre** stage-struck
**awesome** alarming, amazing, awful, daunting, dreadful, eerie, fearful, fearsome, horrible, imposing, inspiring, magnificent, perturbing, solemn, stunning, stupefying, terrifying, wondrous
**awful** alarming, awe(some), bad, beastly, dire, distressing, dread(ful), dreary, ghastly, gruesome, harrowing, horrible, horrid, horrific, miserable, nasty, shocking, solemn, terrible, tremendous, ugly, vrot
**awfulness** dismalness, dreariness, ghastliness, gruesomeness, horribleness, nastiness, rottenness, vileness, wretchedness
**awful smell** stench
**awhile** briefly
**awkward** angry, artless, bungling, clownish, clumsy, coarse, constrained, cumbersome, delicate, difficult, embarrassed, embarrassing, fiddly, gauche, gawky, graceless, inconvenient, inelegant, inept, inexpert, irritable, maladroit, obstinate, perplexing, prickly, rough, rude, sticky, stiff, stroppy, stubborn, touchy, troublesome, trying, unco-operative, uncomfortable, unfortunate, ungainly, ungraceful, unpolished, unrefined, unskilled, untoward, unwieldy, wooden
**awkward and tactless** gauche
**awkward fellow** clown, club, galoot, jay, looby, oaf, slough
**awkward girl** hoit
**awkward in company** shy
**awkward lout** oaf
**awkwardly large** bulky
**awkwardness** clumsiness, coarseness, delicacy, difficulty, gawkiness, irritability, oafishness, rudeness, stubbornness, ungainliness, unskilfulness
**awkward person** cuss
**awkward predicament** scrape
**awkward situation** contretemps, quagmire
**awkward youth** hobbledehoy
**awn** arrowhead, barb, chaff, javelin, missile
**awning** canopy, shade
**AWOL person** truant
**awry** aglee, ajee, amiss, around, askance, askant, askew, aslope, distorted, erroneously, haywire, oblique, perversely, slanting, tilted, wrong
**axe** ax, cancel, chop(per), cleave(r), cut, discontinue, dismiss, eliminate, fell, fire, hack, hatchet, hew, maul, remove, sack, sever, split, trim, withdraw
**axe handle** helve
**axe-like tool** adze
**axe to grind** grievance
**axial cylinder in stem or root of vascular plant** stele
**axilla** armpit, axil
**axing** chopping
**axiom** adage, aphorism, basic, dictum, gnome, maxim, postulate, principle, truism
**axis** alliance, axle, bloc, coalition, compact, entente, pivot, shaft, spindle, stem
**axle** asse (l), axis, pin, pivot, rod, shaft, spindle
**aye** affirmative, always, continually, (for)ever, immutably, unchangingly, unendingly, yea, yes
**Azores harbour** Horta
**Azores island** Fayal, Pico
**azure** blue, cerulean, cobalt, sky-blue, ultramarine

# B

**baa** bleat
**baaing** bleating
**babble** balderdash, ballyhoo, blab, blabber, blather, burble, cackle, chat, chatter, chitchat, clamour, commotion, drivel, fuss, gab, gabble, gibber, gibberish, gossip, gurgle, hubbub, jabber, jargon, jaw, mumble, murmur, mutter, natter, noise, nonsense, prate, prattle, racket, rhubarb, twaddle
**babbling in a nonexistent tongue** glossolalia
**babe** baby, child, infant, ingénue, innocent, suckling, tot
**babe in the woods** dupe, gull, simpleton, sucker
**babies joined at birth** Siamese twins
**baby** babe, bairn, bambino (I), child, coddle, coward, dwarf, indulge, infant, little, mite, neonate, newborn, nurs(e)ling, pamper, small, tiny, tot
**baby ailment** colic, croup
**baby apron** bib
**baby bear** cub
**baby bed** cot, cradle, crib
**baby belch** burp

**baby bird** chick
**baby birds do it** peep
**baby biscuit** rusk
**baby bottle has it** teat
**baby bottle's nipple** teat
**'baby-bringing' bird** stork
**baby carriage** bassinet, go-cart, perambulator, pram, push chair, stroller
**baby cat** kitten
**baby chin cloth** bib
**baby clothes** layette
**baby diaper** napkin, nappy
**baby dummy** comforter, pacifier
**baby food** pabulum, pap
**baby garment** barrow, crawler, creeper, diaper, napkin, nappy
**baby goat** kid
**baby grand** piano
**baby hat** bonnet
**babyhood** infancy
**babyish** childish, immature, infantile, puerile, silly
**babykilling** infanticide
**Babylonia** Chaldea
**Babylonian abode of the dead** Aralu
**Babylonian city** Ur
**Babylonian cycle of 3 600 years** saros
**Babylonian goddess** Aya
**Babylonian king** Nebuchadnezzar
**Babylonian sea-god** Anu
**Babylonian sky-god** Anu
**Babylonian temple-tower** ziggurat
**baby minder** sitter
**baby napkin** bib, diaper, nappy
**baby or young animal that is being suckled** nurs(e)ling
**baby outfit** layette
**baby pacifier** dummy
**baby plaything** rattle
**baby powder** talc
**baby robin** nestling
**baby room** nursery
**baby sheep** lamb
**baby-sitter** nanny, nurse(maid)
**baby sock** bootee
**baby stomach pain** colic
**baby swan** cygnet
**baby tender** sitter
**baby toy** rattle
**baby transport** go-cart, pram, pushcart, stroller
**baby walk** toddle
**baby wardrobe** layette
**bacchanal** carouser, debauch, debauchee, drunkard, orgy, revel, reveller
**bacchanalia** orgy
**bacchante cry** evoe
**bachelor** celibate, single, unmarried
**bachelor girl** spinster
**bachelor party** stag

**bachelor's men-only celebration** stag-party
**back** abet, advocate, aid, assist, countenance, dorsal, dos (F), end, endorse, favour, fro, from, hind, posterior, rear, retire, retreat, retro-, reverse, sanction, stern, support, sustain, underwrite, withdraw
**back ailment** lumbago, notalgia
**back and fill** zigzag
**back and forth** fickle, tentative, uncertain, undecided, vacillating
**back before the judge** re-trial
**backbone** basis, character, chine, determination, firmness, foundation, hardihood, mainstay, mettle, pluck, resolve, spine, vertebrae
**backbreaking** arduous, exhausting, gruelling, hard, Herculean, laborious, toilsome, wearying
**back call** revoke
**backcloths on stage** scenery
**back-country** outback
**back debt** arrear
**back door** postern
**back down** abandon, accede, back-pedal, concede, renege, retreat, submit, surrender, withdraw, yield
**backdrop** background, context, décor, location, perspective, scene(ry), set(ting), site, surrounding
**backed** abetted, advocated, assisted, backtracked, championed, countenanced, encouraged, endorsed, favoured, financed, regressed, retreated, sanctioned, seconded, sponsored, subsidised, withdrew
**backed a faction** sided
**back end** rear
**backer** adherent, advocate, ally, angel, benefactor, champion, patron, promoter, punter, second, sponsor, subscriber, supporter, underwriter, well-wisher
**back flow** ebb, recede
**back garden** yard
**back gate** postern
**background** breeding, class, education, environment, experience, history, milieu, tradition, upbringing
**backhanded** ambiguous, double-edged, dubious, equivocal, ironic, oblique, sarcastic, sardonic, two-edged
**backing** advocacy, aid, assistance, encouragement, endorsement, funds, help, patronage, sanction, support
**backing singers** chorus
**back kitchen** scullery

**back lane** alley
**backless couch** divan
**backless sandals** slip-ons, slipslops
**backless seat** stool
**backless slipper** mule, scuff
**back of** abaft
**back of animal** dorsum
**back of anything** rear
**back of boat** aft
**back off** discontinue, forbear, refrain, relent, stop
**back of foot** heel
**back of head** inion, occiput
**back of lower leg** calf
**back of neck** nape, nucha, scruff
**back of ship** aft, stern
**back of skull** occiput
**back of the thorax in insects** notum
**back out** abandon, cancel, recant, reneg(u)e, resign, retreat, withdraw
**back-pack** haversack, rucksack
**back pain** lumbago, notalgia
**back part** rear, stern
**back part of saddle that slopes upwards** cantle
**back part of ship** stern
**back part of the head or skull** occiput
**back payment** arrear
**backseat rider** pillion
**back section** rear
**backside** bottom, buttocks
**backslide** degenerate, deteriorate, deterioration, fail, lapse, recede, recidivate, recidivism, regress(ion), relapse, retrograde, retrogress, reversion, revert, sin, slide, slip, trip, weaken, worsen
**backslider** apostate, heretic, recidivist, regressor, relapser, renegade, sinner, turncoat
**backsliding** apostasy, defaulting, defection, desertion, lapse, relapse
**back street** alley, byway, lane
**back talk** backchat, insolence, sass
**back to back** dos-à-dos
**back to front** retrorse
**back tooth** molar
**back up** aid, assist, bolster, buttress, champion, confirm, corroborate, endorse, reinforce, reverse, second, substantiate, support, testify
**backveld** platteland
**back wall of a firing trench in warfare** parados
**backward** back, bashful, behind(hand), dull, hesitant, hesitating, immature, late, rearward, reluctant, retarded, retro-, shy, slow, stupid, subnormal, underdeveloped, undeveloped, unwilling, wavering
**backward and forward** completely, thoroughly, undecided, wavering

**backward bend** retortion
**backward movement** regression
**backwards** astern, confused, crablike, rearward, retrocessively
**backward view** retrospect
**backwater channel that forms a pool** billabong
**bacon cut** rasher
**bacon edge** rind
**bacon fat** lard
**bacon provider** pig
**bacon slice** rasher
**bacteria-free** asepsis, aseptic
**bacterial disease of salmon and trout** furunculosis
**bacteriology** pathology
**bacterium** bacillus, bug, germ, micro-organism, microbe, pathogen, virus
**bacterium inhabiting putrid matter** saprophile
**bad** adverse, awful, blemished, criminal, damaging, decayed, defective, deficient, deleterious, disagreeable, disobedient, distressing, dys-, evil, faulty, harmful, harmful, harsh, ill, immoral, imperfect, inadequate, inauspicious, incorrect, inferior, injurious, lousy, mal-, mischievous, mouldy, mouldy, naughty, off, off, poor, rancid, reprehensible, rotten, serious, severe, sinful, spoilt, substandard, unfavourable, unfortunate, unpleasant, unsatisfactory, useless, vile, vrot, wicked, worthless
**bad address** sty
**bad appetite** dysorexia
**bad art** kitsch
**bad behaviour** misbehaviour, misconduct
**bad blood** anger, animosity, antipathy, feud
**bad breath** halitosis, miasma
**bad choice of words or pronunciation** cacology
**bad coal** smut
**bad deed** sin
**bad dream** nightmare
**bad egg** rotter
**bad fairy** gremlin, imp
**bad faith** betrayal, disloyalty, perfidy
**bad feeling** anger, antagonism, dislike, distrust, enmity, hostility, upset
**badge** device, emblem, insignia, rosette, stamp, token
**badge in V-shape on sleeve of uniform** chevron
**badge of honour** medal
**badge of mourning** crêpe
**badge of office** insignia

**badger** annoy, bait, bedevil, brock, bully, chevy, chiv(v)y, disquiet, goad, harass, harry, hassle, heckle, hound, importune, irritate, nag, pester, plague, ride, ruffle, taunt, tease, torment, vex
**badgerlike mammal** ratel
**Badger State** Wisconsin
**bad golf swing** hook, slice
**bad government** misrule
**bad habit** vice
**bad hand at cards** bust
**bad handwriting** cacography, scrawl
**bad handwriting or spelling** cacography
**badinage** banter, derision, drollery, jocularity, joking, mock(ery), quiddity, raillery, repartee, ridicule, taunt, tease, teasing, waggery, wordplay
**bad laws** dysnomy
**bad luck** adversity, ambsace, amesace, hoodoo, mischance, misfortune
**bad-luck bringer** Jonah
**bad luck of sailor** Jonah, Jonas
**badly** carelessly, defectively, improperly, inadequately, incorrectly, mal-, poorly, unfavourably
**badly adjusted person** misfit
**badly affected** afflicted
**badly behaved** naughty
**badly damaged ship** wreck
**badly disorganised** haywire
**badly dressed person** dowd, scarecrow
**badly illuminated** dim, indistinct, obscure
**badly made garment** dreck
**badly matched** ill-assorted, incompatible
**badly shaped** distorted, misshapen
**badly timed** inopportune
**badly upset** distress
**badly ventilated** muggy, stifling, stuffy
**bad manners** discourtesy, disrespect, impoliteness, incivility, insolence, rudeness, unmannerliness
**bad name** caconym
**bad penny** blackguard, knave, rascal, rogue, scoundrel, undesirable
**bad pronunciation** cacology
**bad quarter of an hour** mauvais quart d'heure (F)
**bad reaction** allergy
**bad reputation** opprobrium
**bad smell** odour, stench
**bad spelling** cacography
**bad taste** crudity, immodesty, impropriety, indelicacy, rudeness
**bad taste in art** kitsch
**bad-tempered** brusque, cantankerous, captious, choleric, churlish, contrary, crabby, cross, crotchety, crusty, difficult, disagreeable, dyspeptic, fiery, grumpy, ill-natured, irascible, irritable, nasty, peevish, quarrelsome, rude, stroppy, testy, unfriendly, unpleasant
**bad-tempered old woman** harridan
**bad-tempered person** crank, cross-patch, curmudgeon
**bad-tempered woman** shrew
**bad turn** disservice
**bad versifier** poetaster
**bad writing** cacography
**baffle** amaze, astound, bamboozle, bemuse, bewilder, confound, confuse, daze, defeat, disconcert, dumbfound, flabbergast, flummox, foil, frustrate, hinder, mystify, perplex, puzzle, stump, stun, thwart, upset
**baffling** bewildering, elusive, elusory, thwarting
**baffling matter** mystery
**baffling question** poser
**bag** acquire, appropriate, balloon, bundle, capture, carrier, case, catch, collection, commandeer, container, corner, gain, get, grab, grip, handbag, haversack, hold-all, holder, net, obtain, pack(et), pouch, purse, receptacle, reserve, reticule, rucksack, sack, satchel, shoulder-bag, suitcase, trap, trophy
**bag and baggage** altogether, completely, entirely, fully, quite, totally, wholly
**bagatelle** bauble, brummagem, counterfeit, fake, gaud, imitation, ornament, sham, simulation, toy, trifle, trinket
**bag containing fodder, hung around horse's neck** nosebag
**bag floating in air** balloon
**bag for carrying apparel** portmanteau, suitcase, trunk
**bag forming the chief digestive organ** stomach
**baggage** belongings, equipment, luggage, suitcase(s), trunk(s), valise(s)
**baggage carrier** porter, redcap
**baggy** droopy, floppy, limp, loose, oversize, sagging, seated, slack
**baggy breeches** knickerbocker
**baggy part of fishing-net** bunt
**baggy trousers as worn in Pakistan** shalwar
**Baghdad native** Iraqi
**bag-like membrane** sac
**bag-like structure** cyst
**bag-like structure in plant** sac
**bag of letters** mail

**bagpipe** drone
**bagpipe music** pibroch
**bagpipe player** piper
**bagpipe sound** skirl
**bag-shaped net towed along the bottom of the sea** trawling
**bag with two compartments** Gladstone
**Bahama island** Abaco, Cat, Exuma, Inagua, Watlings
**Bahama Islands capital** Nassau
**Bahama Islands group** Bimini
**Bahrain island** Sitka
**Bahrain island capital** Manameh
**bail** bond, dip, guarantee, guaranty, ladle, pledge, recognisance, scoop, security, spoon, surety, warranty
**bailey of castle** ward
**bailiff** land-steward, reeve
**bailing vessel** pail, scoop
**bail out** abandon, aid, assist, escape, finance, help, quit, relieve, rescue, retreat, withdraw
**Baird's invention** television, TV
**bairn** babe, baby, boy, child, girl, infant, kid, lad, lightie, stripling, teenager, tot, youngster, youth
**bait** allure, attraction, bribe, enticement, harass, inducement, irk, irritate, lure, needle, snare, tantalise, tease, tempt(ation), torment
**bait for fishing** fly, lure
**bake** barbecue, broil, cook, frizzle, fry, griddle, grill, harden, parch, roast, sauté, scald, scorch, singe, toast
**baked** arid, desiccated, dry, parched, scorched
**baked clay** tile
**baked clay block** brick
**baked clay pot** olla
**baked dish (with crust)** pie
**baked dough** bread
**baked egg dessert** custard
**baked loaf** bread
**baked spiced apples in flaky pastry** apfelstrudel
**bake in oven** roast
**baker's dozen** thirteen
**baker's implement** peel
**baker's kneading-trough** hutch
**baker's output** bread, cake, loaf, pie
**baker's shovel** peel
**bakery item** biscuits, bread, bun, cake, roll
**bakery need** oven
**bakery purchase** biscuits, cake, pie, tart
**baking chamber** oven
**baking cube** yeast cake
**baking fat** shortening
**baking receptacle** oven
**baking soda** saleratus

**baking space** oven
**balance** assay, compare, composure, counteract, counterbalance, equaliser, equality, equate, equilibrate, equilibration, equilibrium, equipoise, estimate, level, match, neutralise, offset, poise, proportion, residue, rest, scale, self-control, square, stabilise(r), stability, steady, surplus, symmetry, weigh
**balanced** disinterested, equitable, evenhanded, impartial, just, unbiased
**balance disorder** vertigo
**balanced mind** equilibrium
**balance due** arrears
**balance of arrangement between sides** symmetry
**balance of ship's cargo** trim
**balance out** offset
**balancer** haltere
**balance sheet** account, ledger, report, statement
**balance weight** rider
**balance which remains due** arrears
**balance with unequal arms** steelyard
**balancing pole** poy
**balancing weight** ballast
**balcony** deck, gallery, portico, terrace, upstairs, veranda(h)
**balcony railing** parapet
**balcony with windows** gazebo
**bald** arrant, baldheaded, baldpated, barren, blatant, clipped, cropped, depilated, direct, downright, exposed, flagrant, forthright, glabella, glabrous, hairless, manifest, meagre, naked, notorious, obvious, open, outright, overt, plain, severe, shaven, simple, smooth, stark, straight(forward), tonsured, treeless, unadorned, uncovered, undisguised
**balderdash** absurdity, babble, blather, blather, bombast, bunkum, claptrap, drivel, flummery, folly, foolishness, fudge, gabble, gibberish, hogwash, humbug, inanity, jabber, jargon, jest, moonshine, nonsense, prattle, rant, rigmarole, rot, rot, rubbish, silliness, stuff, stupidity, trash, tripe, trumpery, twaddle
**baldheaded man** pilgarlic
**baldmoney** meu, plant, spignel
**baldness** acomia, alopecia, austerity, baldheadedness, barrenness, hairless, nakedness, simplicity
**baldric** shoulder belt
**bale** bail, bundle, destruction, dip, evil, misery, pain, scoop, spoon, woe
**Balearic island** Ibiza
**baleen** whalebone

**baleful** adverse, bad, baneful, calamitous, cataclysmic, damaging, dangerous, deadly, deathly, deleterious, destructive, fatal, harmful, injurious, lethal, malefic, malevolent, malignant, noxious, pernicious, poisonous, venomous
**bale of straw** pallet
**bale out** emerge, jump, leap
**baling machine** baler
**balk** baulk, check, defeat, demur, evade, jib, refuse, resist, shirk, shun
**Balkan republic** Albania
**Balkan state** Albania, Bulgaria, Greece
**balk as a horse** reast, reest
**ball** ammunition, dance, drop, globe, missile, orb, pellet, projectile, sphere, spheroid
**ballad** barcarole, carol, chant, chanty, ditty, fado, hymn, lay, noel, serenade, shanty, song
**ball-and-socket joint** enarthrosis
**ballast** balance, compensate, counterbalance, counterweight, equilibrate, equilibrium, filling, offset, packing, poise, sandbag, stability, stabilise(r), steadfastness, steadiness, weight
**ballerina** ballet dancer, dancer, danseur (F), danseuse (F)
**ballerina's skirt** tutu
**ballet** dance, masque
**ballet by Tchaikovsky** *Swan Lake*
**ballet dance for two** pas de deux
**ballet dancer** danseur (F), danseuse (F)
**ballet dancer's skirt** tutu
**ballet dancer's spin on point of toes** pirouette
**ballet dress** tutu
**ballet enthusiast** balletomane
**ballet movement** battement, brise, cabriole, développé, entrechat, flicflac, frappe, glissade, jeté, pas, pirouette, plié
**ballet performer** ballerina
**ballet posture** arabesque
**ballet-practice bar** barre
**ballet sequence for two** pas de deux
**ballet shoes** points
**ballet skirt** tutu
**ballet step** pas
**ballet term** arabesque, bouree, coup, pas
**ballet turn** fouette, pirouette
**ballet wear** leotard, tights
**ball from spinner** off-break
**ball game** baseball, basketball, billiards, bowls, cricket, croquet, fives, golf, hockey, lacrosse, netball, ninepins, polo, rounders, rugby, soccer, squash, tennis, volleyball

**ball hit low** liner
**ballista** catapult
**ball of mince meat** frikkadel, rissole
**ball of string** clue
**ball of the thumb** thenar
**ball of yarn** clew
**balloon ballast** sandbag
**balloon filler** air
**balloon mooring line** dragline
**balloon sail** spinnaker
**balloon's weight** ballast
**ballot** choice, choose, decide, elect(ion), franchise, opt, poll(ing), referendum, vote, voting
**ballot caster** voter
**ballpoint pen** Bic, Biro, Parker
**ballroom athlete** dancer, waltzer
**ballroom dance** cha-cha, Charleston, foxtrot, Lambeth Walk, mazurka, minuet, palais-glide, Paul Jones, polka, polonaise, quickstep, rumba, samba, tango, waltz
**ballroom event** dance
**ball-shaped** spherical
**ball-shaped fungus** puff-ball
**ball-striker** bat, cue
**ball supporter** tee
**ball that pitches immediately under bat** yorker
**ball used in tenpin** bowling
**ballyhoo** advertising, commotion, fuss, noise
**balm** anodyne, balsam, comfort, consolation, cream, curative, embrocation, lotion, nard, ointment, salve, solace, unguent
**balmy** calm, clement, fair, mild, pleasant, soft, temperate
**balneal container** bath, tub
**baloney** boloney, humbug, nonsense
**balsam** balm, nard, tolu
**Baltic gulf** Riga
**Baltic island** Dago, Faro, O(e)sel, Ossel, Riga
**Baltic seaport** Danzig, Gdansk, Kiel, Liepaja, Memel, Reval, Riga, Tallinn
**balustrade** balusters, ban(n)isters, barrier, fence, guardrail, handrail, paling, rail(ing)
**Bambi is one** deer
**bamboo cane** whangee
**bamboo-like grass** reed
**bamboo pole fighting** kendo
**bamboo shoot** achar
**bamboo stalk** reed
**bamboo stem** cane
**bamboo swordsmanship** kendo
**bamboozle** baffle, cheat, confound, deceive, defraud, delude, hoax, hoodwink, mystify, perplex, puzzle, stump, swindle, trick

**ban** banish, bar, boycott, censorship, condemnation, curse, debar, denunciation, disallow, disapproval, edict, embargo, exile, exclude, forbid, interdict(ion), ostracise, outlaw(ry), prevent, proclamation, prohibit(ion), proscribe, proscription, restrict(ion), stop(page), suppress(ion), taboo, veto
**banal** asinine, bland, boring, clichéd, commonplace, corny, empty, everyday, fatuous, flat, hackneyed, humdrum, insipid, mundane, ordinary, pedestrian, platitudinous, simple, stale, stereotyped, stock, threadbare, tired, trite, trivial, unimaginative, unoriginal, vapid
**banality** adage, axiom, cliché, commonplace, inanity, jejunity, platitude, triteness, triviality, truism, vapidity
**banal remark** platitude
**banana bunch** hand, stem
**band** assembly, association, belt, bend, body, chain, combo, company, confederate, fetter, gang, group, horde, host, identity, manacle, mark, orchestra, party, sash, set, shackle, society, sodality, stripe, tag, unite
**bandage** band, binding, blindfold, compress, compressor, cover, doctor, dressing, gauze, ligate, ligature, lint, plaster, strip, stupe, swathe
**bandanna** handkerchief
**band around horse's stomach** girth
**banded** allied, barred, leagued, pooled, striated, striped, stripy, united
**banded anteater** numbat
**band for holding stockings up** garter
**band for the carpus** wristlet
**bandicoot** badger
**band instrument** cornet, guitar, saxophone, trumpet
**bandit** brigand, crook, desperado, freebooter, gangster, gunman, hijacker, marauder, outlaw, pirate, robber, thief
**band leader** conductor
**bandlike structure** taenia
**band of acrobats** troupe
**band of colour** stripe
**band of flowers** wreath
**band of leather** belt, strap
**band of musicians** orchestra
**band of robbers** gang
**band of twisted twigs** withe, withy
**band of warriors** cohort, impi
**band together** affiliate, ally, annex, combine, unite

**bandy** barter, bow-legged, crooked, curved, exchange, interchange, pass, shuffle
**bandy limb** bow leg
**bandy words** argue, spar
**bane** bale, burden, curse, death, despair, evil, grief, misery, nuisance, pain, pest, plague, poison, ruin(ation), scourge, taint, torment, tragedy, trial, trouble, venom, virus, woe
**bang** bump, burst, clang, clash, crash, report, shot, slam
**bang door loudly** slam
**bang into** hit
**Bangkok native** Thai
**Bangladeshi money** taka
**bangle** bracelet, circlet, jewellery, ornament, wristlet
**bang shut** slam
**banish** ban, (de)bar, deport, discard, dislodge, dismiss, dispel, disregard, eject, eliminate, eradicate, evict, exclude, excommunicate, exile, expatriate, expel, ignore, isolate, ostracise, oust, outlaw, proscribe, relegate, remove, segregate, transport
**banished person** exile, outlaw
**banish from country** exile
**banishment** deportation, exile, expulsion, proscription
**banish to place of exile** relegate
**banister part** pier, spindle, upright
**banisters** balustrade, bannisters, barrier, balusters, fence, guardrail, handrail, paling, rail(ing)
**banjo player** strummer
**bank** acclivity, array, border, bound, deposit(ory), dike, embank, fund, heap, hill, knoll, mass, mound, pile, reserve, ridge, rim, shore, terrace, tier, train
**bank balance** credit, debit
**bank cashier** teller
**bank credit** loan, security
**bank customer** depositor
**banked cash** credit
**bank employee** teller
**banker or money-changer in the East** shroff
**banking game** baccarat, faro
**banking system** giro
**bank loan** overdraft
**bank note** bill
**bank official** teller
**bank of snow** drift
**bank on** assume, credit, trust
**bank payment** interest
**bankroll** finance
**bankrupt** broke, depleted, destitute, insolvent, penniless, ruined

**bankruptcy** debasement, deficiency, destitution, disaster, downfall, failure, inadequacy, indebtedness, insolvency, lack, liquidation, neediness, poverty, ruin, scantiness, scarcity
**bank statement minus** debit
**bank teller** cashier
**bank transaction** loan
**banner** banderole, bannerol, burgee, colours, eagle, ensign, flag, gonfalon, insignia, labarum, oriflamme, pennant, pennon, standard, streamer, vexillum
**banning** prohibiting
**banning vote** veto
**banquet** dine, dinner, feast, meal, repast, revel, treat
**banter** badinage, chaff, chaffing, deride, derision, jeer, jesting, joking, kidding, mock(ery), ribbing, ridicule, tease
**baobab fruit** monkeybread
**bap** breadroll, loaf
**baptise** admit, anoint, asperse, call, christen, cleanse, consecrate, dedicate, dub, immerse, initiate, lustrate, purify, recruit, sprinkle, submerge
**baptise with oil** anoint
**baptism** christening, dedication, immersion, introduction, purification, sprinkling
**baptismal bowl** font
**baptismal font** laver
**baptismal name** forename
**baptismal vessel** font
**baptismal water** laver
**baptism font** laver, piscina
**bar** advocates, attorneys, ban, barricade, barrier, barristers, batten, bench, bistro, block, cantina, check, chunk, counsel, counter, court(room), cross-piece, deterrent, dive, dock, eliminate, except, exclude, grating, handrail, hindrance, impede, impediment, ingot, inn, lawyers, lounge, lump, nightclub, nugget, obstacle, obstruct(ion), paling, pole, prevent, prohibit, pub, public-house, rail(ing), reef, restrain, ridge, rod, saloon, sandbank, save, secure, shaft, shebeen, shoal, slab, stanchion, stick, stop, tavern, tribunal, veto, wedge
**barb** bristle, point, prickle, prong, snag, spike
**Barbados cherry** acerola
**barbarian** animal, barbaric, barbarous, beast, bigot, boor, brutal, brute, coarse, crude, destroyer, feral, ferocious, harsh, hooligan, Hun, inhuman, lout, lowbrow, primitive, ruffian, savage, uncivilised, uncouth, uncultivated, vandal, vulgar
**barbaric** barbarous, cruel, gruff, inelegant, inhuman, loutish, primitive, rough, rude, rugged, rustic, savage, uncivilised, uncourtly, uncouth, unmannered, vulgar, wild
**barbaric wrecker** vandal
**barbarity** abomination, atrocity, barbarism, brutality, carnage, crime, cruelty, enormity, evil, ferity, fiendishness, fierceness, harshness, heartlessness, horror, massacre, murderousness, outrage, pitilessness, relentlessness, ruthlessness, sadism, savagery, severity, viciousness, villainy
**barbarous** barbarian, brutal, coarse, cruel, monstrous, rough, rude, savage, uncivilised
**Barbary sheep** aoudad
**barbate** bearded
**barbecue** braai(vleis)
**barbecue grille** grid(iron)
**barbecue rod** spit
**barbed fishing spear** gaff
**barbed spear** harpoon
**barber** tonsor
**barber's call** next
**barber service** haircut
**barber's itch** sycosis
**barber's speciality** shave
**bar between wheels** axle
**barb of a feather** harl, herl
**bar call** last round
**bard** minstrel, poet, troubadour
**bardic king** Lear
**bardic play** Hamlet, Macbeth, Othello, Romeo and Juliet
**Bard of Avon** Shakespeare
**Bard's river** Avon
**bare** alone, bald, barren, denuded, disclose, empty, evident, expose(d), glaring, mere, naked, nude, obvious, open, palpable, scant, scanty, sheer, simple, stark, stripped, unadorned, unclothed, uncovered, undisguised, undressed, unprotected, unsheltered, unshielded
**bare-breasted** topless
**barefaced** audacious, blatant, bold, brazen, clear, crying, dreadful, egregious, enormous, flagrant, flaunting, glaring, immodest, impudent, infamous, insolent, naked, notorious, open, ostentatious, scandalous, unconcealed
**barefoot** shoeless, unshod
**bare hill** tor
**barely** almost, hardly, just, only, scantly, scarcely, slightly, sparingly
**barely enough** scanty
**barely noticeable** imperceptible
**barely sufficient** scant
**bare rocky hill** tor
**bare sandy tract** dune
**bare skin** buff
**bar for balancing** beam
**bar for hanging pictures** rail
**bar for lifting** lever
**bargain** accord, agreement, arrangement, buy, chaffer, compact, contract, covenant, dicker, haggle, negotiate, pact, pledge, promise, sale, sell, snip, stipulate, stipulation, trade, transact(ion), transfer, treaty
**bargain event** sale
**bargain for** anticipate, expect, imagine, foresee, contemplate
**bargain on** assume
**bargain place or time** sale
**bar game** darts
**barge** flatboat, freighter, houseboat, lighter, raft, scow, tanker
**barge in** infringe, interrupt, intrude
**barge into** hit, push, shove
**bar in a boat for rower's feet** stretcher
**barium oxide** baryta
**barium sulphate** blanc fixe (F)
**bark** abrade, arf, bay, bellow, casing, cortex, covering, crust, cry, flay, growl, howl, husk, peel, rind, roar, rub, scrape, sheathing, shout, skin, snarl, strip, woof, yap, yelp, yip
**bark beetle** borer
**bark fibre** bass, olona, tapa, terap
**bark fussily** yap
**barking sound** woof
**bark in pain** yelp
**barklike** corticate
**bark of an animal** bay
**bark sharply** yelp, yip
**bark shrilly or snappishly** yap
**bark up the wrong tree** blunder, err
**bark used in tanning** leach
**bar legally** estop
**barley bristle** awn
**barley drink** orgeat
**barley steeped in water** malt
**barman** bartender, tapster
**barn** cowbarn, cowshed, mews, stables, stalls
**barnyard boss** rooster
**barnyard clucker** hen
**bar of balance** beam
**bar of cast metal** ingot
**bar of ladder** rung
**bar of tobacco** cavendish
**barometer** weather-glass
**barometric line** isobar
**bar on cricket stumps** bail

**barony** manor
**baroque** bizarre, elaborate, flamboyant, overdecorated
**baroque composer** Handel
**baroque music** sonata
**bar patron** drinker
**barrage** assault, attack, avalanche, battery, blitz, bombardment, broadside, burst, cannonade, dam, deluge, drumfire, embankment, fire, flood, fusillade, gunfire, hail, inundation, landslide, mass, onset, onslaught, profusion, rain, salvo, shelling, shower, storm, stream, superabundance, torrent, volley, weir
**barrage of criticism** flak
**barred receptacle for fodder** crib
**barrel** butt, cask, container, cylinder, hogshead, keg, rundlet, tub, tun, vat, vessel, water-butt
**barrel cork** bung
**barrel maker** cooper
**barrel making** coopery
**barrel part** hoop, side, stave
**barrel slat** stave
**barrel stopper** bung
**barrel strip** hoop
**barren** arid, bare, bleak, boring, childless, desert, desolate, dry, dull, empty, flat, fruitless, impotent, infecund, infertile, pointless, profitless, stale, stark, sterile, unbearing, unfruitful, uninformative, uninspiring, uninteresting, unproductive, unprolific, unrewarding, unsuggestive, useless, vapid, waste(land), wilderness
**barren animal** geld, yeld (Sc)
**barren hill** fell
**barren land** desert, usar
**barren locality** gall
**barrenness** aridity, aridness, bareness, childlessness, defeat, depletion, dryness, emptiness, failure, futility, imbecility, inefficacy, infecundity, infertility, poverty, scarcity, simpleness, sterility, stupidity, unfruitfulness, unproductiveness
**barren region** desert
**barren state** desolation
**barricade** bar, barrier, block, blockade, bulwark, defend, fence, obstruct(ion), palisade, rampart
**barrier** bar, barricade, blockade, boundary, drawback, fence, rampart
**barrier against attack** shelter
**barrier built across river** barrage, dam
**barrier made of rails** balustrade, paling, railing
**barrier of shrubs** hedge
**Barrier Reef island** Heron
**barrier to be surmounted** hurdle

**barrier to hold back a flow of waters** dam, weir
**barrier to surmount** hurdle
**barrister** advocate, attorney, counsel, counsellor, jurist, lawyer, legist, solicitor
**barrow** grave-mound, handcart, tumulus, wheelbarrow
**bar seat** stool
**barter** bargain, bargaining, commerce, commute, deal, exchange, haggle, higgle, interchange, interplay, merchandise, negotiate, produce, sell, staple, swap, swop, trade, traffic, transaction, transfer, truck
**Bartlett fruit** pear
**bar to slacken thread** easer
**bar to stretch** spreader
**bar to transmit force** lever
**bar used for raising** lever
**base** abject, basis, bed, bottom, cheap, contemptible, cornerstone, corrupt(ed), counterfeit, degraded, degrading, despicable, element, establish, fake, foot, found(ation), goal, ground(work), ignoble, impure, ingredient, low(ly), mean(-spirited), notorious, pedestal, plebeian, poor, principle, rest, scandalous, shameful, sordid, stand, station, substructure, understructure, unrefined, venal, vulgar, worthless
**base admixture** alloy
**baseball bowler** pitcher
**baseball club** bat
**baseball field** diamond
**baseball glove** mitt
**baseball group** nine
**baseball hat** cap
**baseball inning** frame
**baseball sack** base
**baseball score** run
**baseball team** nine
**based on emotion rather than on reason** ad hominem (L)
**based on practical experience** empiric
**based on speculation** theoretical
**based on the number eight** octonary
**based on the number three** ternary
**based on truth** factual, reliable, trustworthy, valid, veracious
**base fellow** carl(e) (Sc), scullion
**base for a statue** plinth
**base-frame of car** chassis
**baseless** unconfirmed, unfactual, unfounded, unjustified, unsound, unsupported
**basement** bunker, cellar, cellarage, crypt, dungeon, vault
**base metal** iron
**baseness** degradation, depravation, infamy, meanness, turpitude

**base of a column** patten, pedestal, plinth
**base of decimal system** ten
**base of felled tree** stump
**base of martini** vermouth
**base of sauce** roux
**base of statue** pedestal, plinth
**base of vase** pedestal
**base of wood spirit** methyl
**base person** degenerate
**base supporting a vase** plinth
**bash** attempt, break, crack, crash, crush, hit, slosh, smash, stab, strike
**bashful** abashed, ashamed, confused, constrained, coy, demure, diffident, embarrassed, modest, nervous, reserved, self-effacing, sheepish, shy, timid, unconfident
**bashful fellow** sheep
**bashfulness** diffidence, hesitation, shyness, timidity
**basic** alkaline, basal, base, central, core, crucial, elemental, elementary, essential, foundational, fundamental, important, indispensable, ingredient, inherent, intrinsic, key, necessary, primary, prime, radical(ly), root, rudimentary, staple, underlying, vital
**basically** au fond (F), essentially, firstly, fundamentally, inherently, intrinsically, mostly, primary, principally, substantially
**basic fact** essential
**basic factor in vitamin B** biotin
**basic facts of a matter** nitty-gritty
**basic food** bread
**basic idea** keynote
**basic life substance** protein
**basic nature** essence
**basic part** element
**basic rule** fundamental
**basics** ABC, bedrock, core, essentials, facts, fundamentals, necessaries, nitty-gritty, practicalities, prerequisites, principles, rudiments
**basic theme** topos
**basic unit of electric current** ampere
**basilica** canopy, church, temple
**basilica of Vatican City** St Peter's
**basilisk** cockatrice
**basin** bay, bed, bowl, cavity, container, cove, crater, depression, dip, dish, hollow, indentation, pan, pond, pool, receptacle, sink, tub, vessel
**basin for holy water** stoop, stoup
**basin in China** Tarim
**basin used at Roman Catholic mass** piscina
**basis** base, bottom, cornerstone, elementary, foundation, ground, principle, touchstone
**basis for ointment** lanolin

**basis of argument**   premise
**basis of aspirin**   salicylic acid
**basis of cheese**   casein
**basis of fruit jellies**   pectin
**basis of metric system**   ten
**basis of perfume**   musk
**basis of proteins**   amino acid
**bask**   delight, laze, luxuriate, revel, sunbathe, wallow
**basket**   bassinet, beacon, box, breadbasket, bucket, canister, case, clothes-basket, container, courge, crate, creel, cresset, dosser, flasket, frail, gabion, hamper, holder, pannier, punnet, receptacle, rusky, scuttle, skippet, vessel, wickerwork
**basketball player**   cager, hoopster
**basketball position**   centre
**basketball team**   five
**basket bottom**   slath
**basket carried on back**   pannier
**basket for crumbs**   voider
**basket for eels**   buck, courge
**basket for figs**   cabas, frail, tap, tapnet
**basket for fish**   cawl, crail, cran, creel, wicker
**basket for fruit**   cala, calathos, molly
**basketry**   rattan, upset
**basketry grass**   esoarto, otate
**basketry rod**   osier, slath
**basket to carry load on shoulder**   pannier
**basket-weaving material**   raffia
**basketwork**   slath(e), slew, slewing, stake, stroke, tee, wale
**basketwork packing-case**   hamper
**basketwork willow**   osier
**Basque ball-game**   pelota
**Basque cap**   beret
**bas-relief**   cameo, carving, relievo, rilievo (I), sculpture
**bass**   bast, deep, fish, grave, liber, low, low-toned, perch, resonant, trout
**bass brass instrument**   tuba
**basset or whippet**   hound
**bass horn**   tuba
**bassinet**   crib
**bass instrument like large violin**   cello, contrabass, double-bass
**bass oboe**   heckelphone
**bass saxhorn**   tuba
**bass singer**   basso
**bass violin**   cello, contrabass, double-bass
**bastard**   bliksem, cad, counterfeit, donder, false, fatherless, illegitimate, imperfect, impure, irregular, misbegotten, sham, spurious
**baste**   cook, cudgel, moisten, sew, stitch, tack, thrash
**basterhartbees**   sassaby

**bastion**   bulwark, citadel, fortress, rampart, stronghold
**bat**   clayslap, club, cudgel, fledermaus, hit, racket, racquet, reremouse, smack, stick, strike, stroke, wallop, wink
**bat-and-ball game**   cricket
**bat around**   confer, debate, discuss, drift, meander, prowl, roam, wander
**batch**   bunch, collection, group, lot, quantity
**batch of conscripts**   intake
**batch of twelve**   dozen
**bate**   abate, moderate, restrain, temper
**bat for striking a shuttlecock**   battledore
**bath**   shower, soap, spa, sponge, tub, wash
**bath crystals**   salts
**bathe**   cleanse, dip, immerse, moisten, rinse, soak, steep, swim, wash, wet
**bathe with hot lotions**   foment
**bathe with liquid**   steep
**bathing beach**   seaside
**bathing costume**   bather, bikini, cossie, swimsuit, trunks
**bathing venue**   lido, piscine
**bathing vessel**   tub
**bathing wear**   swimsuit
**bathos**   mush, sentimentality, soppiness
**bath robe**   dressing-gown
**bathroom finisher**   tiler
**bathroom item**   soap, towel
**bathroom slate**   tile
**bathroom water-store**   cistern
**bath sponge**   loofah
**batman**   servant
**baton**   club, mace, rod, truncheon, wand
**bat one's eyes**   blink, nictitate, wink
**baton race**   relay
**battalion**   army, brigade, contingent, impi, regiment, squadron
**batten**   bar, cloy, devour, fatten, feast, fix, flourish, gain, gorge, gormandise, grow, hook, increase, latch, lock, overdo, overeat, overfeed, profit, prosper, secure, thrive, tighten, wax
**batter**   assault, bash, beat, break, buffet, demolish, destroy, lash, pound, pummel, ruin, smash, wound
**batter cake**   crumpet, waffle
**battered**   beaten, crushed, damaged, squashed
**battering**   bludgeoning
**battery fluid**   acid
**battery inventor**   Volta
**battery-operated torch**   flashlight
**battery part**   cell
**battery terminal**   anode, cathode, pole
**battery unit**   cell

**bat the breeze**   brag, chat, exaggerate, gossip
**batting ability**   stickwork
**batting period or turn**   innings
**battle**   action, agitate, argue, attack, brawl, campaign, clamour, clash, combat, conflict, contend, contest, controversy, crusade, debate, disagreement, dispute, encounter, engagement, feud, fight, fray, hostilities, quarrel, row, skirmish, strife, strive, struggle, war(fare)
**battle-axe**   gisarme
**battle-axe with two cutting edges**   twibil
**battle cry**   catchword, cheer, motto, shout, slogan, watchword, yell
**battlefield**   arena, battleground, front
**battle fleet**   armada, squadron, troops
**battle formation**   column, deployment, herse, line, portcullis
**battle ground**   terrain
**battlement**   balustrade, bastion, circumvallation, citadel, fortification, fortress, garrison, palisade, parapet, rampart, stronghold, wall
**battle of Napoleon**   Acre, Jena, Ulm, Waterloo
**battleship**   destroyer, gunboat, minesweeper, warship
**battle trick**   gambit, maneuver, manoeuvre, stratagem
**batty**   barmy, bats, bonkers, cracked, crackers, crazy, dotty, eccentric, insane, loony, mad, nuts, nutty, odd, peculiar, potty, touched
**bat wildly**   slog
**bauble**   bagatelle, bead, bric-a-brac, clinquant, frippery, gewgaw, gimcrack, knick-knack, ornament, pendant, plaything, tinsel, toy, trash, trifle, trinket, trumpery
**Baudouin's kingdom**   Belgium
**Bavarian city**   Munich
**Bavarian community**   Passau
**bawdy**   blue, carnality, coarse, crude, filthy, gross, immodest, impurity, indecent, indelicate, lewd, lewdness, lustful, obscene, pornographic, prurience, prurient, ribald, rude, vulgar, wantonness
**bawdy house**   brothel
**bawl**   bellow, cry, howl, roar, shout, wail, weep, yell
**bawl out**   chastise, reprimand, scold
**bay**   alcove, arch, arm, bark, bawl, bell, bellow, bight, booth, carrel, chestnut, compartment, cove, cry, cubicle, cul-de-sac, dam, division, fiord, fjord, gulf, gull, holler, howl, inlet, laurel, niche, nook, opening, oriel, platform, pother, recess, reddish-brown, roan,

roar, sinus, stall, ululate, voe (Sc), wail
**bay and white in patches** skewbald
**bay at the moon** howl
**bayberry oil** myrica
**bay-coloured horse** roan
**bay in Chile** Carranza, Darwin, Eyre, Otway, Stokes, Tablas, Tongoy
**bay in China** Hangchow, Laichow
**bay in Crete** Kanca, Kisamo, Mesara, Suda
**bay in Dominican Republic** Calderas, Escocesa, Isabela, Neiba, Ocoa, Rincon, Samana, Yuma
**bay in eastern Cape** Algoa
**bay in Fiji** MBya, Natewa, Ngaloa, Savusavu
**bay in Florida** Biscayne, Waccasassa
**bay in France** Arachon, Biscay
**bay in Greenland** Baffin, Disko, Melville
**bay in Guam** Agat, Ajayan, Cetti, Umatac, Ylig
**bay in Hawaii** Halawa, Kawaihae, Kiholo, Maunalua, Pohue
**bay in Iceland** Faxa, Huna
**bay in Ireland** Bantry, Blacksod, Clew, Dingle, Donegal, Dundalk, Galway, Killala, Mal, Sligo, Tralee
**bay in Japan** Ariake, Atsumi, Mutsu, Otaru, Sendai, Suruga, Toyama, Uchiura, Wakasa
**bay in New Guinea** Collingwood, Goodenough, Oro
**bay in New York** Jamaica, Moriches, Peconic
**bay in New Zealand** Awarua, Cloudy, Golden, Hawke, Lyall, Ohua, Pegasus, Rangaunu
**bay in Portugal** Setubal
**bay in Prince Edward Island** Egmont, Orwell, Rolla
**bay in Puerto Rico** Aquadilla, Boqueron, Rincon, Sucia
**bay in Scotland** Scapa Flow
**bay in South Africa** Algoa, False, Mossel, Table
**bay in South Korea** Kanghwa
**bay in Wales** Cardigan, Swansea, Tremadoc
**baylike inlet** cove
**bay of stag** bell
**bayonet plant** datil
**Bayou descendant** Creole
**Bayou State** Mississippi
**Bay State** Massachusetts
**baytree** laurel
**bay window** mirador, oriel
**bazaar** carnival, exchange, fair, fête, marketplace, mart
**bazaar-like function** fête
**be** abide, am, are, been, breathe, endure, exist, is, last, live, was

**beach** brink, coast, edge, foreshore, margin, sands, seacoast, (sea)shore, seaside, shingle, strand
**beach area** seaside
**beach cabin** cabana
**beachcomber** drifter, loafer, scavenger, tramp, vagabond
**beached** abandoned, aground, ashore, discarded, forlorn, grounded, rejected, scorned, shipwrecked, shunned, wrecked
**beach grass** marram
**beach house** cabana
**beach in Hawaii** Waikiki
**beach pebbles** shingle
**beach resort** lido, seaside
**beach-sand mineral** rutile
**beach shelter** cabana, umbrella
**beach shop** kiosk
**beach surface** sand
**beach waves** surf
**beacon** bonfire, flare, lighthouse, lightship, pharos, seamark, signal, watchtower
**beaded moisture** dew, drizzle, fog
**bead of moisture** droplet
**beadroll** rosary
**beads** choker, necklace, pendant, rosary
**beadsman** pensioner
**beads used as money** peag
**bead with moisture** bedew
**beak** bill, bow, headland, mandible, neb, nib, nose, nozzle, pecker, point, proboscis, projection, promontory, prow, ram, rostrum, snout, snout, stem
**beaker** chalice, cup, draught, drink, flagon, goblet, jug, mug, pot, potion, tankard, trophy
**beaklike** rhamphoid, rostral
**beak of hawk** clap
**beak or bill** neb
**beam** bar, emit, girder, gleam, glimmer, glitter, laugh, prop, radiate, radiation, radiant, rafter, ray, shine, smile, spar, suggestion, timber
**beam across door or window** lintel, transom
**beam anchor** wall
**beam-compass** trammel
**beaming** beamy, brilliant, irradiant, lambent, radiant, resplendent
**beam in roof** rafter
**beam of light** gleam, ray
**beam outward** radiate
**beam over door** lintel
**beam pleasantly** smile
**beam support** template, templet
**beam that serves as a support** accouplement

**beam that supports railway track** sleeper
**beam used as a support** prop
**beam used in a floor** joist
**bean** broad, castor, goa, haricot, legume, lima, mung, pinto, soy(a), sugar
**bean curd** tofu
**beanlike plant** vetch
**beano** party
**bean's eye** hilum
**beanstalk giant** ogre
**bean tree** carob
**bear** abide, admit, advertise, affect, afford, broadcast, brook, carry, cherish, concern, conduct, confirm, demonstrate, drive, endure, force, guide, harbour, maintain, operate, panda, prove, push, relate, render, show, stand, suffer, support, sustain, take, teddy, tend, thole (Sc), tolerate, transmit, transport, undergo, uphold, yield
**bearable** admissible, endurable, passable, tolerable
**bear a burden** endure, hardship
**bear aloft** elevate, lift
**bear burden** shoulder
**bear cat** panda
**bear constellation** Ursa
**beard** brave, bristles, confront, corner, defy, goatee, stubble, trap, whiskers
**bearded** barbate, braved, bushy, challenged, confronted, dared, disregarded, flouted, hairy, scorned, shaggy, stubbly, unshaven
**bearded ruminant** goat
**bearded seal** makluk
**bearded vulture** lammergeyer
**beard in chaff** awn
**beardless Himalayan wild goat** tahr
**beard like goat's** goatee
**beard of grain** arista, awn
**bear down** approach, attack, burden, compress, encumber, near, oppress, push, strain
**bear down on** burden, compel, encumber, strain
**beard shape** goatee
**bearer** agent, carrier, conveyer, conveyor, messenger, porter, runner, servant
**bearer of aniseed** anise
**bearer of tidings** herald, messenger
**bear false witness** perjure
**bear fruit** fructify
**bear heavily on** press
**bearing** air(s), aspect, attitude, behaviour, carriage, conduct, connection, demeanour, dependency, deportment, manner,

pertinence, posture, relation, relevance
**bearing a likeness to** resembling
**bearing ill-will** malicious
**bearing no load** unladen
**bearing no name** anonymous, untitled
**bearing of person** mien
**bearing only one leaf** unifoil
**bearing on the matter** relevance
**bearing the title** titular
**bearing trials without murmuring** patient
**bearing tubers** tuberose
**bearing weapons** armed
**bear in mind** consider, heed, note, remember
**bear-like** ursine
**bear-like animal of China** panda
**bear-like walk** plantigrade
**bear on** affect, belong, concern, involve, refer, regard
**bear out** confirm, corroborate, demonstrate, endorse, justify, prove, substantiate, support, testify, uphold, vindicate
**bear puppy** whelp
**bear's ear** auricula
**bearskin** busby
**Bear State** Arkansas
**bear up** endure, persevere, suffer, withstand
**bear upon** affect, appertain
**bear with** endure, forbear, suffer, tolerate, wait
**bear witness** attest, avow, confirm, deponent, depose, prove, testify
**beast** animal, barbarian, brute, bully, creature, critter, devil, fiend, monster, pig, quadruped, rogue, ruffian, sadist, savage, swine
**beastly** awful, bad, barbarous, bestial, brutal, brute, cruel, degraded, dreadful, inhuman, nasty, sadistic, savage, unpleasant, vile
**beastly noise** snarl
**beast of burden** ass, camel, donkey, llama, mule, onager, ox, yak
**beast of prey** cheetah, hyena, jackal, leopard, lion, tiger, vampire, vulture, wolf
**beat** bang, bash, baste, batter, better, bliksem, blow, break, bruise, buffet, cane, checkmate, conquer, defeat, donder, drub, exceed, excel, flog, flutter, forge, hit, knock, lam(baste), lash, outdo, outstrip, overcome, overpower, palpitate, pelt, pound, pulsate, pulsation, pulse, punch, quake, quiver, race, scoop, shake, strap, stress, strike, stroke, subdue, surpass, swipe, tan, thrash, throb,

thump, tremble, vanquish, vibrate, whack, wham, whip, win
**beat and bruise** maul
**beat a retreat** skedaddle, withdraw
**beat around the bush** equivocate, prevaricate, shuffle, waffle
**beat a tattoo** drum
**beat by cleverness** outwit
**beat down** bate, batter, crush, defeat, haggle, quell, squelch
**beat down upon** hail
**beaten** conquered, crushed, defeated, drained, emasculated, exhausted, faint, feeble, licked, mixed, overpowered, overthrown, pounded, stirred, thwarted, vanquished, weak, whipped
**beaten eggs cooked in melted butter** omelette
**beaten path** track, trail
**beaten track** groove, rut
**beat forcefully** whack
**beat hard** hammer
**beat heavily** pound, whack
**beat hollow** defeat, outdo, overcome, thrash
**beatific** angelic, blissful, divine, exalted, heavenly, rapt, serene
**beatified girl** beata
**beat incessantly** pelt
**beat in fight** drub
**beating** battering, conquest, defeat, hiding, overpowering, palpitation, pelting, pounding, pulsation, repulse, ruin, spanking, thrash(ing), throb(bing), whacking
**beating of heart** pulse
**beating with a stick** bastinado
**beat in music** tempo
**beat it** go, scram, voetsak
**be at its height** climax, peak
**beatitude** ecstasy, bliss, felicity, happiness, saintliness
**beat it up** revel
**beat lightly** whisk
**beat of a tune** rhythm
**beat of drum** rattan, tuck
**beat out grain from corn** thrash, thresh
**beat out of shape** batter
**beat rapidly** palpitate
**beat severely** batter, flay, lambaste, thrash, trounce, whop
**beat severely with stick** thrash
**beat soundly** belabour, drub, thrash, thump, wallop
**be attentive** heed, mind, serve
**beat the drum** blare
**beat thin** malleata
**beat up** abuse, assault, attack, bash, batter, bliksem, bludgeon, clobber, donder, hit, mistreat, pound, strike, thrash

**beat with a stick** baste, thrash
**beat with a whip** flog
**beat with the fists** pummel
**beau** admirer, boyfriend, cavalier, dandy, escort, fiancé, flame, fop, inamorato, nob, popinjay, swain, sweetheart
**beau geste (F)** favour
**beautiful** admirable, alluring, attractive, bonny, charming, comely, excellent, exquisite, fine, gorgeous, handsome, lovely, pleasing, pretty, scenic, seemly, stupendous
**beautiful damsel** belle
**beautiful flower** lily, orchid, rose
**beautiful garden** Eden
**beautiful girl** belle
**beautiful handwriting considered as an art** calligraphy, chirography
**beautiful lady** belle
**beautiful locality** Xanadu
**beautiful male** Apollo
**beautiful nymph** houri
**beautiful white bird** egret, swan
**beautiful woman** belle, nymph, siren, Venus
**beautiful young man** Adonis
**beautiful young woman of Muslim paradise** houri
**beautiful youth loved by Aphrodite** Adonis
**beautify** adorn, decorate, enhance, garnish, gild, grace, improve
**beauty** allure, attraction, attractiveness, belle, bloom, charm(er), comeliness, cracker, elegance, excellence, fairness, glamour, goodlooker, grace(fulness), handsomeness, loveliness, lovely, magnificence, pleasure, pulchritude, seemliness, stunner, symmetry, Venus
**beauty of movement** grace
**beauty parlour** salon
**beauty spot** mole
**beauty treatment** cosmetics, facial, manicure, massage, rub, surgery
**beauty treatment for face** facial
**beaver away** persevere, persist
**beaver eater** wolverene, wolverine
**beaver skin** plew, plu(e)
**Beaver State** Oregon
**be aware of** behold, know, perceive
**bebeeru** greenheart, tree
**be behind** lag
**be bent** flex
**be beside oneself** rage
**be better than** excel
**be binding on** oblige
**be born again** reincarnate
**be borne along** ride
**be bound by gratitude** obliged
**be bound to repay** owe

**be buoyant** float
**became Paul** Saul
**be careful** beware, cave
**be carried by** ride
**because** as, for, inasmuch, since, therefore, through, whereas
**because of** through
**be cautious** beware, on guard, wary
**be certain of** believe, know
**be characteristic of** appertain
**be charmed by** enamoured
**beck** brook, burn, course, current, drift, flow, gesture, greeting, nod, rill, river, rivulet, run, salute, sign, signal, stream(let), torrent, watercourse
**beckon** signal, motion, gesture, summon, call
**beckon for a lift** hitch(hike), thumb
**be cleverer than** outsmart, outwit
**be clothed in** wear
**becloud** adumbrate, bedim, befog, bewilder, cloud, confuse, darken, dim, grey, muddle, mystify, obscure, overcast, pale, perplex, puzzle, shade, shadow, shield, shroud
**become** -en, befit, change, embellish, fit, flatter, grace, happen, harmonise, suit
**become accustomed** acclimate, acclimatise
**become active** stir
**become actively involved** participate
**become actual fact** materialise
**become airborne** fly, take off
**become a member of** enter
**become ashen** pale
**become attached** cling
**become aware** perceive, sense
**become aware of** learn, observe, realise, sense
**become aware of in advance** foresee
**become a Yank** Americanise
**become better** ameliorate, improve
**become bigger** grow
**become black by burning** char
**become blacker** darken
**become blurred** dim, mist
**become bone** harden, ossify, stiffen
**become bored** tire, yawn
**become boring** pall
**become bucolic** rusticate
**become citizen** take the oath of allegiance
**become cognisant of** know
**become complicated** ramify
**become confused** addle
**become conscious** awake
**become conscious of** observe
**become crooked** warp
**become dark** darken, darkle
**become different** alter
**become dim** darken, darkle

**become dry and shrivelled** wither
**become dull** hebetude
**become effaced** disappear, evanesce
**become enclosed by a thick membrane** encyst
**become encrusted with sugar** candy
**become entangled** caught, embroiled, ensnared, involved
**become enthusiastic** warm to the subject
**become excited** inflame
**become exhausted** tire
**become extinct** die, fail, perish
**become famous** arrive
**become faster** accelerando
**become fatigued** tire
**become feeble** flag
**become firm** set
**become firmer** gel
**become further apart** diverge
**become fused** accrete
**become fuzzy** blur
**become gloomy** darken
**become gradually smaller** dwindle, shrink
**become greater** augment
**become hard** indurate
**become hardened** set
**become hardened to** enure, inure
**become hazy** blur
**become hot and dry** parch
**become husky-sounding** hoarsen
**become ill** ail, sicken
**become ill again after recovery** relapse
**become impaired by use** wear
**become indistinct** blur, dim, fade
**become inflexible** ossify
**become informed** learn
**become inharmonious** sour
**become intolerant** impatient
**become involved** enter
**become irritated** chafe
**become known** emerge
**become larger** extend
**become less** abate, decrease, diminish
**become less dense** rarefy
**become less extreme** moderate
**become less heavy** lighten
**become less intense** abate
**become less savage** relent, soften
**become less severe** abate, relent
**become less strong** abate
**become less vehement** moderate
**become liable to** incur
**become liquid (by heat)** melt
**become longer** lengthen
**become mature** age, ripen
**become mellow** age, ripen
**become monarch** accede
**become morally corrupt** putrefy
**become more amenable** relent

**become more complicated** thicken
**become more profound** deepen
**become narrow** taper
**become neat** neaten
**become obsolete** disappear, vanish
**become older** age
**become one** unite
**become overcast** cloud, overcloud
**become pale and weak** etiolate, wan
**become pallid** blanch, pale
**become part of** merge
**become perverted** warp
**become pregnant** conceive
**become productive** fructify
**become purulent** fester
**become ragged** fray, tatter
**become ragged at edge** fray
**become realistic** sober
**become red in the face** blush, flush
**become rigid** set
**become rigid with cold** freeze
**become rotten** decay
**become seasoned to** acclimatise
**become semi-solid** gel
**become semi-solid by cooling** congeal
**become senile** dement
**become septic** fester, suppurate
**become shallow** shoal
**become slender** reduce, thin
**becomes less severe** abate
**become smaller** contract, dwindle, shrink
**become smaller in breadth** narrow
**become soft by soaking** macerate
**become solid** gel, harden, set
**become stable** settle
**become straight** unbend
**become stronger** strengthen
**become submerged in water** sink
**become swollen** intumesce
**become tan** burn
**become taut** tense
**become tightly fixed** fastened
**become tired** weary
**become twisted** warp
**become uninteresting** pall
**become unsteady** waver
**become unwell** ail
**become used to again** reaccustom
**become vague** blur
**become vapid** pall
**become visible** appear, emerge, surface
**become void** lapse
**become wan** pale
**become weak** attenuate
**become weary** tire
**become wet and dirty** draggle
**become white** bleach
**become withered** shriver
**become worse** deteriorate

**become wrinkled up** pursed
**become young again** rejuvenate
**becoming** appropriate, apt, attractive, comely, congenial, correct, enhancing, fitting, flattering, graceful, neat, pretty, proper, right, seemly, suitable, worthy
**becoming bigger** growing
**becoming obsolete** obsolescent
**becoming old** getting on
**becoming rotten** putrescent
**becoming slower** lentando
**becoming smaller** diminishing
**becoming young** juvenescent
**be compliant** amenable, obey
**be composed** consist
**be concealed** lurk
**be conceited** overweening
**be concerned** care
**be connected with** belong
**be conscious of** feel
**be conscious of perceiving** apperceive
**be considerate of** consult
**be consistent** cohere
**be contiguous to** adjoin
**be contrary to** contradict
**be contrite** repent, rue
**be convenient** suit
**be conveyed** ride
**be convinced of** believe
**be courageous** dare
**bed** base, bedstead, berth, border, bottom, bunk, channel, cot, couch, cradle, crib, deposit, divan, doss, embed, establish, fix, found(ation), furniture, garden, gite, ground(work), implant, insert, layer, lode, matrix, mattress, pad, pallet, patch, plant, plot, sack, seam, settle, stratus, substratum, vein, watercourse
**bedaub** bedim, besmear, blur, coat, cover, daub, dirty, overlay, patch, plaster, smear, smudge, soil, spread, stain, sully
**bedazzle** amaze, bewilder, confuse, daze, disconcert, dum(b)found, stagger, stun, stupefy
**bed board** slat
**bed canopy** tester
**bedclothes** linen
**bed cover** blanket, duvet, eiderdown, quilt, sheet, spread
**bed cushion** mattress, pillow
**bedding** linen
**bedding material** ticking
**bed down** lie, retire, sleep
**be deceived by** bite, line, swallow
**bedeck** adorn, array, decorate, embellish, festoon, ornament, trim
**be deficient in** lack, want
**be depressed and listless** mope

**be deprived of** lose
**bedevil** annoy, beset, bewitch, chaff, confound, confuse, distress, frustrate, harass, harrow, hex, irritate, muddle, possess, seduce, tease, torment, vex
**be devoted to** adhere
**bed for baby** cot
**bed headrest** pillow
**bedight** adorn, array, attire, beautify, bedeck, clothe, deck, decorate, dress, embellish, festoon, grace, ornament
**bed in cheap boarding-house** doss
**be discontented** grumble
**be discordant** clash
**be disloyal** betray
**be displayed** spread
**be displeased** resent
**be disposed** incline
**bedlam** chaos, commotion, confusion, hubbub, madhouse, mayhem, mêlée, riot, tumult, uproar
**bed linen** bedcover, (pillow-)case, sheet
**bed of coal** seam
**bed of flowers** garden
**bed of hare** form
**bed of twigs** nest
**be dogmatic** pontificate
**Bedouin** Arab, gipsy, gypsy, nomad, wanderer
**Bedouin tribe** Absi, Harb
**bed quilt** duvet, eiderdown
**bed rail** slat
**be dressed in** wear
**bedridden** ailing, confined, encouched, handicapped, homebound, ill, incapacitated, invalided, shut-in
**bedroom** boudoir, dormitory
**bed's canopy** tester
**bed sheets** linen
**bedspread** coverlet
**bed support** slat
**bed-time drink** cocoa, nightcap
**be due** mature
**be dull** mope
**bed wetting** enuresis
**bee** apis, buzzer, drone, honeymaker, insect, worker
**be eager** ambitious
**beech or birch** tree
**bee-collected juice** nectar
**be economical** save, scrape, spare
**be ecstatic** rave
**beef** boeuf (F)
**beef animal** cow, ox
**beef cut** entrecote, fillet, roast, rump, sirloin, steak, T-bone, topside
**beef emporium** steakhouse
**beef fat** suet
**be effuse** gush

**bee food** honey
**beef stew made with beer** carbonade
**beefy** brawny, bulky, fat, heavy, hulking, muscular, obese, podgy, rotund, stalwart, stocky, sturdy
**beehive** apiary, beehouse
**Beehive State** Utah
**bee house** apiary, hive
**bee-keeper** apiarist, apiculturist
**bee-keeping** apiculture
**Beelzebub** devil, Satan
**be emphatic** insist
**be engaged in a trade** work
**be engaged in learning** study
**be enough** suffice
**bee party** social
**bee product** honey, wax
**beer** ale, beer, bock, brew, lager, liquor, malt, porter, stout
**beer-bellied** paunchy
**beer belly** boep
**beer cask** butt, tun
**beer cellar** Bierkeller
**beer counter** bar
**be erect** stand
**beer factory** brewery
**beer flavour** hops
**beer garden** brasserie
**beer ingredient** barley, hops, malt
**beer-like drink** ale
**beer made from malt and hops** ale
**beer maker** brewer
**beer-mat** coaster
**beer-mug** schooner, stein, tankard, toby, toby-jug
**beer saloon** brasserie
**beer's cousin** ale
**beer's foam** head
**beer unit** pint
**beer vessel** mug, schooner, tankard, toby(-jug)
**bee's home** apiary, hive
**bee sound** buzz, drone, hum
**bee's pollen brush** scopa
**bee's produce** wax, honey
**bee's sound** buzz, drone, hum
**beestings** colostrum
**bee structure** hive
**beet** chard
**Beethoven's birthplace** Bonn
**beetle** dor, dung, elater, overhang, scarab, weevil
**beetle harmful to grain** weevil
**beetle-like insect** cockroach
**beetle's larva** grub
**beetle's wing-case** shard
**beetle talisman** scarab
**be faint with heat** swelter
**be faithful to** honour
**befall** arise, become, betide, chance, emanate, ensue, eventuate, follow,

hap(pen), intervene, occur, prove, result, supervene
**be familiar with** know
**be fearless** dare
**be firm** insist
**befit** accord, apt, become, beseem, consent, due, meet, right, seem, suit
**befitting** ad rem (L), appropriate, apropos, apt, becoming, comme il faut (F), decent, fitting, seemly, suitable
**befitting a prostitute** meretricious
**be fixed** adhere
**be fond of** care, cherish, like, love
**befool** cod, delude, dupe
**be foolishly fond of** dote
**be forced to give way** succumb
**before** afore, ago, ahead, already, ante-, anterior, avant, beforehand, earlier, ere, first, foremost, formerly, forwards, headmost, hitherto, pre-, previously, prior, sooner, until
**before a judge** coram judice (L)
**before all others** first
**before any** first
**before birth** antenatal, prenatal
**before daybreak** ante lucem (L)
**before dinner** anteprandial
**before Easter** Lent
**before expected time** earlier
**before giving birth** antenatal, prenatal
**beforehand** already, before, earlier, preliminarily, previously, sooner
**before in time** pre-
**before Lesotho** Basutoland
**before long** anon, betimes, presently, shortly, soon
**before marriage** née
**before midnight** today
**before noon** antemeridian
**before now** already, beforehand, ere, heretofore, hitherto
**before others in time** first
**before set time** early
**before that time** theretofore
**before the day** ante diem (L)
**before the expected time** early
**before the flood** antediluvian
**before the hour of** to
**before the time** until
**before the war** ante bellum (L), pre-war
**before this** ci-devant (F), erenow, former(ly)
**before this time** heretofore
**before time** early
**before tomorrow** today
**before VAT** GST
**before written records** prehistoric
**be fortunate** succeed
**be fretful** repine
**be friends** associate, fraternise
**be frugal** economise, save, scrimp, stint

**be frugal towards** stint
**be fruitful** teem
**befuddle** perplex
**be fully aware of** realise
**be furious** fume, rage, rave
**beg** adjure, ask, beseech, cadge, crave, demand, desire, entreat, implore, importune, panhandle, petition, plead, pray, request, require, scrounge, seek, solicit, sue, supplicate
**beg, borrow or steal** scrounge
**beg earnestly for** implore
**beget** can, engender, evolve, father, generate, occasion, procreate, produce, sire
**beg for** crave
**beggar** almsman, bergie, borrower, cadger, down-and-out, hobo, idler, impoverished, leech, loafer, mendicant, outcast, parasite, pauper, rogue, scoundrel, scrounger, sponger, supplicant, tramp, vagrant, wanderer
**beggar's louse** stickseed
**beggar's speech** cant
**beggar's wench** doxy
**begging** beseeching, cadging, craving, desiring, entreating, imploring, importuning, petitioning, pleading, praying, requesting, soliciting, supplicating
**begging a free ride** hitch
**begging letter** screeve
**begging the chief point or the question** petitio principii
**beg humbly** supplicate
**be giddy** swim
**begin** activate, appear, arise, become, commence, create, dawn, debut, embark, existence, inaugurate, initiate, institute, open, originate, recommence, start, undertake
**begin again** recommence, renew, reopen, repeat, restart, resume, revert
**begin again after interruption** resume
**begin an attack** aggress
**begin anew** change, improve, reform
**begin a quarrel** aggress
**begin constructive action** take steps
**begin journey** start
**beginner** abecedarian, amateur, apprentice, bungler, cub, debutant(e), experimenter, fledg(e)ling, freshman, greenhorn, initiate, learner, neophyte, newcomer, novice, probationer, pupil, recruit, rookie, scholar, starter, student, tenderfoot, tiro, trainee, tyro
**beginning** birth, cause, commencement, embryo, first,

foundation, germ, inauguration, inception, initiation, new, novice, onset, opening, origin, preliminary, seed, source, start, wellspring
**beginning of** onset
**beginning of an era** epoch
**beginning to develop** nascent
**begin to fight** engage
**begin to give way** waver
**begin to grow** burgeon, sprout
**begin to grow light** dawn
**begin to grow rapidly** burgeon
**begin to move** go, stir
**begin with same letter or sound** alliterate
**be given** receive
**be gloomy** mope
**beg of God** pray
**beg pardon** apologise
**be grateful for** appreciate
**be greater than** exceed, surpass
**begrudge** avoid, covet, crave, desire, dislike, envy, grudge, protest, refuse, regret, resent, shirk
**begrudger** resenter
**beg the question** avoid, dodge, duck, evade, hedge, quibble, shun, sidestep
**be guided by** heed
**beguile** allure, amuse, attract, bewitch, cajole, captivate, charm, cheat, cheer, coax, dazzle, deceive, decoy, delude, divert, dupe, enchant, enliven, enslave, ensnare, entertain, enthral, entice, entrance, fascinate, flatter, hoax, infatuate, inveigle, lure, mislead, occupy, please, recreate, regale, seduce, solace, spellbind, tempt, wheedle
**behalf** account, advantage, interest, side, support
**be half asleep** doze, snooze
**be harmonious** accord, agree
**behave** act, adjust, comply, conform, function, mind, obey, operate, perform, respond, run, work
**behave according to rule** adhere
**behave appropriately** act the part, strike the right note
**behave arrogantly** swagger
**behave badly** misbehave
**behave in domineering way** swagger
**behave like an ecdysiast** strip
**behave meanly** sneak
**behave reciprocally** interact
**behave servilely** fawn, toady
**behave theatrically** emote
**behave toward** treat, use
**behave violently** rage, rampage
**behaviour** attitude, bearing, conduct, control, demeanour, deportment, ethics, manner, upbringing

**behaviour towards** treatment
**behead** decapitate, decollate, execute, guillotine, hang
**beheaded queen** Anne Boleyn, Catherine Howard, Marie Antoinette
**be helpful** avail
**be hesitant** wobble
**behest** bidding, command, decree, desire, dictate, instruction, request, wish
**behind** abaft, aft, after(wards), arrear, astern, beyond, bottom, buttocks, colophon, concealment, following, hidden, late, next, overdue, posterior, postern, rear(ward), reverse, seat, slow, stern, subsequently, supporter, supporting, tail
**behind closed doors** confidentially, intimately, privately, secretly
**behind driver** back seat
**behind in place** after
**behind one's back** covertly, deceitfully, falsely, insidiously, secretly, sneakily, surreptitiously, treacherously, venomously
**behind schedule** overdue
**behind the scenes** backstage
**behind the ship** abaft
**behind the times** antiquated, archaic, dated, obsolete, old-fashioned, outdated, outmoded, passé
**behind time** behindhand, belated, late, slow
**be histrionic** emote
**behold** attend, consider, descry, discern, discover, distinguish, espy, examine, eye, heed, inspect, lo, look, note, notice, observe, peruse, presto, regard, scan, scrutinise, see, survey, view, watch
**beholden** accountable, amenable, answerable, appreciative, bound, chargeable, grateful, gratified, indebted, liable, obligated, obliged, owing, responsible, thankful
**behold the lamb of God** ecce agnus Dei (L)
**behold the man** ecce homo (L)
**behold the proof** ecce signum (L)
**be horizontal** level, lie, prone, recumbent
**be hostile to** abhor, hate
**be idle** loaf, loiter
**beige** buff, cream, ecru, fawn, neutral, oatmeal, sand, tan
**beige colour** ecru
**be ill** ail
**be important** matter
**be inaccurate** err
**be in action** operate
**be inactive** idle

**be in a fit** tiff
**be in agony** agonise
**be in anguish** agonise
**be in a rage** fulminate, fume
**be in a reverie** (day)dream, muse
**be in a trance** muse
**be inattentive to** ignore
**be in charge** officiate
**be in charge of** administer, inspect, manage, supervise
**be inclined** tend
**be inclined to believe** suspect
**be in concord** agree
**be in conflict** collide
**be in contact** adjoin
**be incorrect** err
**be in debt** owe
**be indecisive** dither
**be indisposed** ail
**be in error** mistake
**be infatuated with** dote
**be in favour of** advocate
**be infested with** abound
**be in force** prevail, stand
**be informed** hear, know
**be infuriated** bristle
**being** actuality, core, creature, esse, essence, existence, existing, human, nature, occurring, person, psyche, reality, soul, spirit
**being aglow** molten
**being alive** living
**being alone** solitude
**being a member** membership
**being anonymous** anonymity
**being away from** absent
**being beyond** ulterior
**being beyond the powers of nature** supernatural
**being beyond the world** ultramundane
**being born** nascent
**being carried across** transit
**being compared** comparison
**being confident** trusting
**being cross and peevish** petulant
**being defeated** losing
**being deprived of** losing
**being disliked** disfavour
**being dormant** torpor
**being everywhere** ubiquity
**being expelled from one's country** exile
**being famous** celebrity
**being far off** distance
**being forgotten** oblivion
**being free from captivity** liberty
**being from outer space** alien
**being furious** raging
**being gay** gaiety, mirth
**being generally ill spoken of** obloquy
**being generally liked** popularity
**being happy** felicity

**being hostile** opposition
**being hot** heat
**being in agreement** concordant, consentient
**being in definite place** ubiety
**being in heaven** bliss
**being in suspension** abeyant
**being in the place in question** present
**being lazy** idling
**being listless** moping
**being married to several wives at a time** polygamous
**being morbidly anxious about one's health** hypochondriac, valetudinarian, valetudinary
**being neutral** apolitical, voting-wise
**being nothing more than** mere
**being only in part** partial
**being on pension** retired, retirement
**being opaque** opacity
**being orthodox** orthodoxy
**being poor** poverty
**being present** presence
**being pulled behind** towed
**be in great fear** dread
**be in great plenty** abound
**being reborn** renascent
**being sent on some service** mission
**being sober** sobriety
**being solitary** solitude
**being strong** power, strength
**being subject to death** mortal, mortality
**being testate** testacy
**being that is human in form only** anthropoid
**being the apex** apical
**being the highest amount** maximal
**being too proud of oneself** conceited
**being under age** minority, nonage
**being worn away** corrosion
**being worthy of honour** dignity
**be in harmony** attuned
**be in harmony with** fit
**be in high spirits** rollick
**be in love** enamoured
**be in majority** outnumber
**be in one's prime** flourish
**be in possession of** own
**be in readiness for** await
**be in store for** await
**be insufficient** fail
**be in the red** owe
**be in the running** rampage
**be intrinsic** inhere
**be in tune** accord
**be in unison** agree, blend, harmonise
**be in want of** need
**Beirut citizen** Lebanese
**be jammed with** abound
**be jealous of** envy, begrudge
**be kept secret** confidential

**belabour** attack, batter, beat, castigate, criticise, flay, flog, lambast(e), thrash, whip
**belated** delayed, late, overdue, slow, tardy, unpunctual
**belch** burp, discharge, disgorge, eject, emit, empty, eructate, erupt, erupt, expel, explode, gush, hiccough, hiccup, regurgitate, spew, spout, vent, vomit
**beleaguer** assail, besiege, blockade, bombard, bound, encircle, enclose, environ, fence, siege, surround
**beleaguering of a town** siege
**be level with** equal, match, parallel
**belfry** bell-tower
**belfry flier** bat
**Belgian dialect** Walloon
**Belgian dog** schipperke
**Belgian lowland** polder
**Belgian marble** rance
**Belgian money** Franc
**Belgian port** Antwerp, Ostend
**Belgian province** Antwerp, Brabant, Flanders, Hainaut, Liege, Limburg, Namur
**Belgian rifle** FN
**Belgian river port** Liege
**Belgian seaport** Brabant, Hainault, Limburg, Ostend
**Belgium river port** Liege
**Belgrade soccer team** Red Star
**Belial** Satan
**belie** confute, contradict, deceive, mislead, negate, repudiate
**belief** acceptance, admission, assent, assurance, conclusion, confidence, conviction, credence, credit, credo, creed, doctrine, dogma, faith, feeling, ideology, impression, judg(e)ment, notion, opinion, persuasion, reliance, religion, tenet, theism, theory, trust, view
**belief in a perfect future or society** millenarianism
**belief in freedom** libertarianism
**belief in God based on reason** deism
**belief in God's existence** theism
**belief in pleasure as the proper aim** hedonism
**belief in religious doctrines** faith
**belief in the existence of a god** deism
**belief in the superiority of a particular race** racism
**beliefs concerning the devil** Satanology
**beliefs** credences, credos, creeds, doctrines, dogmas, faiths, feelings, ideologies, impressions, judg(e)ments, notions, opinions, persuasions, tenets, theories, trusts, views

**belief that all beings and things have a living soul** animism
**belief that everything is predetermined** fatalism
**belief that no God exists** atheism
**belief that one is a god** theomania
**belief that there is only one God** monotheism
**belief without proof** faith
**believable** acceptable, authentic, authoritative, conceivable, credible, imaginable, likely, plausible, possible, probable, reliable, trustworthy
**believe** accept, acknowledge, apprehend, assert, assume, conjecture, consider, credit, deem, hold, imagine, judge, maintain, postulate, regard, suppose, think, trust, understand
**believed report** credit
**believe guilty** suspect
**believe gulliby** swallow
**believe in** trust
**believe in Jesus** Christianity
**'believe it or not' man** Ripley
**believer** adherent, convert, devotee, disciple, follower, proselyte, supporter, theist, upholder, zealot
**believer in all religions** omnist
**believer in freedom of thought and will** libertarian
**believer in God** theist, deist
**believer in Islam** Muslim
**believe to be** deem
**believe without proof** suspect
**believing in the religion of Christ** Christian
**believing in the supernatural** fey
**be lightly asleep** drowse
**belittle** abase, bedwarf, calumniate, caricature, contemn, curtail, decry, defame, degrade, demean, deprecate, deride, devalue, discount, discredit, disdain, disparage, disprove, dwarf, flout, humiliate, jeer, lessen, mock, narrow, revile, scoff, scorn, slur, spurn, twit, underestimate, underrate, undervalue
**belittlement** deflation, depreciation, derogation, detraction, disparagement
**bell** buzzer, carillon, chime, gong, peal, ringing, signal, tintinnabulum, tolling
**belladonna** dwale
**bellboy** page, porter
**bell clapper** tongue
**belle** charmer, queen, star
**belles-lettres** literature
**bell-hop** page

**belligerence** aggressiveness, pugnaciousness
**belligerent** aggressive, antagonistic, bellicose, combative, contending, fighting, hostile, martial, militant, pugilistic, pugnacious, quarrelsome, unfriendly, unpeaceful, warlike, wrestling
**Bellini opera** I Puritani, Il Pirata, La Sonnambula, Norma
**bell-like flower** lily
**bellow** aroar, bawl, blare, bray, exclaim, holler, howl, low, moo, reverberate, roar, scream, screech, shout, shriek, squall, thunder, ululate, vociferate, whoop, yap, yell, yelp
**bellower** roarer
**bell room** belfry
**bell-shaped glass** cloche, cup
**bell-shaped hat** cloche
**bell signalling prayer** angelus
**bell sound** chime, knell, peal, toll
**bell's position when set** sally
**bell's tongue** clapper
**bell-tower** belfry, campanile, steeple
**bell used to sound alarm** tocsin
**bellwether** leader
**belly** abdomen, appetite, billow, boep, breadbasket, distend, gluttony, gut, inside, paunch, side, spread, stomach, swell, tummy, under wame (Sc), vitals
**bellyache** colic, crab, gripe
**bellyband** belt, girdle, sash
**bellybutton** navel
**belly dance** danse du ventre (F)
**be located** lie
**belonging** acceptance, attachment, fellowship, inclusion, kinship, loyalty
**belonging by birthright** native
**belongings** accoutrements, accessories, appurtenances, baggage, chattels, effects, furniture, goods, kit, movables, paraphernalia, possessions, property, things
**belonging to** of
**belonging to a club** member, membership
**belonging to a college** collegiate
**belonging to a former age** ancient
**belonging to a group** corporate
**belonging to all people** our
**belonging to a man** his
**belonging to an earlier period** old
**belonging to animal order which have no teeth** edentate
**belonging to citizens** civil
**belonging to her** hers
**belonging to him** his
**belonging to insect order** isopteran
**belonging to it** its

**belonging to kings** regius
**belonging to Lent** Quadragesimal
**belonging to man** human
**belonging to me** mine, my
**belonging to neighbourhoods** vicinal
**belonging to or appearing in summer** (a)estival
**belonging to same side of body** ipsilateral
**belonging to same time** contemporary
**belonging to summer** (a)estival
**belonging to that thing** its
**belonging to the afternoon** postmeridian
**belonging to the air** aerial
**belonging to the appreciation of the beautiful** aesthetic
**belonging to the back** dorsal
**belonging to the Church** ecclesiastic(al)
**belonging to the depths of the ocean** abyssal
**belonging to the diaphragm** phrenic
**belonging to thee** thine
**belonging to the earliest geological period** Archaean
**belonging to the house** domestic
**belonging to the individual** peculiar
**belonging to the lady** hers
**belonging to them** theirs
**belonging to the night** nocturnal
**belonging to the present time** current
**belonging to the same age** contemporary
**belonging to the side** lateral
**belonging to this world** mundane
**belonging to times long past** ancient
**belonging to us** our(s)
**belonging to you** your(s)
**belong to higher class than** outclass
**belong to sign of Ram** Arian
**be lost in thought** cogitate, muse
**beloved** admired, adored, cherished, darling, dear(est), endeared, esteemed, favourite, loved, lover, pet, precious, revered, sweetheart, treasured, valued
**beloved of Amadis** Oriana
**beloved of Gretchen** Faust
**beloved of Hermia** Lysander
**beloved of Leander** Hero
**beloved one** dear
**beloved person** darling
**below** beneath, downstairs, down(ward), lesser, low(er), neath, nether(ward), subjacent, submerged, subordinate, unbefitting, under(ground), underlying, underneath, unfit, unsuited, unworthy
**below actual value of thing** nominal
**below average standard** under par

**below par** faulty, imperfect, inadequate, inferior, lacking, lesser, substandard, unacceptable, unfit, unhealthy, unsuitable
**below standard** poor, unsatisfactory
**below the belt** cowardly, dirty, foul, unfair, unjust
**below the head** neck
**below the surface of the sea** submarine
**below the threshold of conscious awareness** subliminal
**belt** band, cinch, cincture, district, girdle, girth, region, sash, strap, stretch, strip, surround, waistband, zone
**belt fastener** buckle
**belt for sword** baldric
**belt location** waist
**belt material** leather
**beluga roe** caviar
**belvedere on Spanish house** mirador
**be made quiescent** lull
**be mannerly** behave
**be mistaken** err
**bemoan** bay, bewail, console comfort, cry, deplore, grieve, groan, howl, lament, moan, mourn, regret, rue, sob, solace, soothe, sorrow, squall, wail, whimper
**be more durable** out-wear
**be more important** outweight
**be more than** exceed, outnumber
**be most noticeable** predominate
**be motionless** stagnate, stationary, stiffen
**bemuse** addle, amaze, astonish, astound, befuddle, bemuddle, benumb, bewilder, confuse, discomfit, discompose, disconcert, muddle, muddy, numb, overwhelm, perplex, puzzle, shock, stun, stupefy, surprise, upset
**bemused** absent-minded, befuddled, bewildered, confused, dazed, distracted, engrossed, fuzzy, glaiket (Sc), glaikit (Sc), muddled, perplexed, stunned, stupefied, thoughtful, tipsy
**bench** court(room), forum, judge, judiciary, pew, seat, settee, stool, tribunal
**bench in church** pew
**bench mark** criterion, norm, standard
**bench with back and arms** settee, settle
**bend** acquiesce, agree, angle, bias, bow, curts(e)y, curvature, curve, deviate, dispose, diverge, flex, incline, influence, loop, mo(u)ld, persuade, S, stoop, subdue, submit, swerve, turn(ing), twist, yield

**bend backward** retort
**bend down** stoop
**bend downward** deflex, droop, sag
**bend easily** pliable
**bend forward** bow, stoop
**bending around** circumflex
**bending head in salutation** bow
**bending in and out** sinuous
**bending of knees in ballet** plié
**bend low** bow
**bend of arm** elbow
**bend of the knee** ham
**bend out of shape** distort, turn, twist, warp, wrench, writhe
**bend over** stoop
**bend the genua** kneel
**bend the head** bow, nod
**bend the knee in worship** genuflect
**beneath** below, down, sub-, unbefitting, under, underneath
**beneath one's dignity** infra dignitatem (L), unbecoming, undignified
**beneath the moon** sublunary
**Benedictine's title** dom
**benediction** anointing, beatitude, benison, blessing, consecration, grace, invocation, orison, prayer, thanks
**benefactor** contributor, donor, friend, giver, helper, patron, sponsor, supporter
**benefice** abbacy, bishopric, deanery, pastorate, primacy, rectorate, revenue, sinecure, vicarage
**beneficent care of God** providence
**beneficial** advantageous, auspicious, benign, contributive, favourable, good, helpful, profitable, salutary, therapeutic, useful, valuable, wholesome
**beneficiary** heir, inheritor, receiver, recipient, successor
**benefit** advancement, advantage, aid, asset, assist, avail, behalf, better, blessing, boon, efficacy, enhance, further, gain, get, help, improve, interest, profit, promote, sake, serve, service, use(fulness)
**benefit gained from the job** perk
**benefit obtained** profit
**benefit or profit** advantage
**benefit spiritually** edify
**Benelux country** Belgium, Luxembourg, The Netherlands
**be nervously hesitant** dither
**benevolence** altruism, benignity, charity, compassion, generosity, goodness, goodwill, humanity, kindliness, kindness, sympathy
**benevolent** altruistic, benign, bounteous, caring, charitable, compassionate, considerate,

generous, good-will, gracious, humane, kind(hearted), kindly, liberal, obliging, philanthrophic, tender, unselfish, well-disposed
**benevolent person** Samaritan
**be next to** adjoin
**Bengal beast** tiger
**Bengal bison** gaur
**Bengal boat** batel, baulea(h)
**Bengal cat** tiger
**Bengal gentleman** baboo, babu
**Bengal hemp** sunn
**Bengal ox-cart** hackery
**Bengal tree** bel, bola
**benighted** crude, ignorant, uncivilised, unenlightened
**benightedness** blindness, ignorance, illiteracy, illiterateness, unenlightenment, unintelligence
**benign** affable, agreeable, amiable, beneficial, benevolent, charming, cordial, curable, fatherly, favourable, friendly, genial, gentle, good(-humoured), gracious, harmless, indulgent, kind(ly), liberal, limited, lovable, mild, obliging, paternal, pleasing, propitious, refreshing, restorative, salutary, sociable, sympathetic, tender, urbane, warm, wholesome, winsome
**benignly drunk** mellow
**benign tumour of striated muscle** rhabdomyoma
**Benin** Dahomey
**benison** benediction, blessing, consecration, dedication, grace, invocation, thanksgiving
**be nosy** pry
**bent** ability, angled, aslant, bias, bowed, circled, coiled, contorted, crooked, curved, deflected, determined, disposition, facility, flexed, hunched, inclination, leaning, partially, penchant, predilection, propensity, resolved, spiralled, talent, tendency, twisted
**bent downwards** nutant
**bent like bow** arcuate
**bent on** determined, disposed, fixed, inclined, insistent, resolved
**be obedient** obey
**be obligated** owe
**be obliged** appreciate
**be obsequious** fawn
**be obvious** seem
**be occupied in thought** meditate
**be of assistance** avail, help
**be of concern** matter
**be off!** scat
**be off colour** ail
**be off guard** nap, napping
**be of importance** matter

**be of one mind** agree
**be of opinion** ween
**be of the opinion** believe, consider, deem, feel, guess, judge, suppose, think
**be of the same mind** agree
**be of use to** avail, do, satisfy, serve, suffice, suit
**be of value** avail
**be omen of** bode
**be on fire** burn
**be on guard** beware
**be on one's feet** stand
**be on one's guard** beware
**be on the mend** recuperate
**be on the point of boiling** simmer
**be on top of** surmount
**be on your guard** gardez (F)
**be opposite to** subtend
**be oppressed with heat** swelter
**be overcome** succumb
**be packed with** abound
**be parsimonious** skimp
**be partial to** favour
**be part of** belong, appertain
**be permanently present** indwell
**be pertinent** appertain
**be pleased with** approve
**be plentiful** abound
**be prepared for** await
**be present** attend
**be present at** appear, attend, witness
**be prodigal with** squander
**be prolific** teem
**be proof against** resist
**be prostrate** lie
**be proud of** boast, brag
**be pushy** obtrude
**bequeath** allot, bestow, cede, commit, communicate, consign, demise, devise, donate, dower, endow, entail, entrust, give, impart, reward, transfer, transmit, will
**bequeath income to** endow
**bequest** ancestry, bestowal, estate, gift, heritage, history, inheritance, legacy, patrimony, settlement, trust, will
**be quiet!** hush, sh
**berate** belittle, castigate, chastise, chide, criticise, curse, defame, denounce, execrate, harangue, lambast, lambaste, lampoon, lash, rate, rebuke, reprimand, reproach, revile, scold, slate, upbraid, vilify, vituperate
**Berber** Hamite, Har(r)atin, Kabyl(e), Moor, Mozabite, Riff, Shilluh, Taureg
**Berber dialect of Algeria** Senhaja, Zenata
**Berber of Algeria** Kabyl(e), Shawia, Tuareg

**be ready for** await
**bereave** deprive, dispossess, rob, strip
**bereaved husband** widower
**bereaved noblewoman** dowager
**bereaved spouse** widow, widower
**bereaved woman** Niobe, widow
**bereavement** affliction, death, loss, tribulation
**bereft** abandoned, comfortless, dejected, denuded, depressing, deprived, derelict, deserted, desolate, despondent, destitute, devoid, disadvantaged, dismal, downcast, empty, forfairn, forlorn, forsaken, gloomy, isolated, lacking, lonely, lorn, lost, melancholy, minus, miserable, needy, neglected, orb(ate), poor, quit, robbed, solitary, stripped, unoccupied, vacant, wanting, wretched
**be relevant** appertain
**be reluctant** begrudge
**be repeated** recur
**be repelled by** hate
**be resolute** continue, hold, insist, persist
**be responsible for** perpetrate
**beret** cap, tam
**be ridiculously incompetent** footle
**be riotously festive** revel
**Berkshire racecourse** Ascot, Royal Ascot
**Berkshire school** Eton
**Bermuda arrowroot** ararao, araru
**Bermuda vegetable** onion
**berserk** crazy, enraged, frantic, insane, mad, manic, violent, wild
**berth** bed, billet, bunk, cot, dock, hammock, harbour, jetty, mole, moorage, mooring, pallet, pier, port, quay, shelter, wharf
**be ruled by** obey
**be same colour as** match
**be seated** sit
**beseech** adjure, appeal, ask, beg, bid, crave, entreat, implore, importune, obtest, petition, plead, pray, solicit, sue, supplicate
**be self-evident** appear, seem
**be sequel to** continue
**beset** afflict, annoy, array, assail, attack, badger, bedevil, beleaguer, besiege, decorate, embarrass, embellish, enclose, environ, harass, hassle, perplex, pester, plague, stud, surround
**be shaken in resolution** waver
**be short of** lack, want
**be sickly** ail
**be sick of** hate

**beside** abreast, along, alongside, at, by, near(by), neighbouring, overlooking, para-
**beside oneself** angry, apoplectic, berserk, crazed, delirious, demented, deranged, desperate, distracted, distraught, frantic, fraught, frenzied, hysterical, insane, mad, raging, unbalanced, uncontrollable, unhinged
**besides** also, au reste (F), barring, else, except(ing), further(more), moreover, otherwise, save, too, without, yet
**beside that** thereby
**beside the point** immaterial, incidental, irrelevant, pointless, unimportant
**besiege** annoy, assail, assault, badger, bedevil, beleaguer, beset, blockade, bother, environ, harass, pester, plague
**be silent** tacit
**be situated** lie
**be skilled in** know
**be slow** dawdle
**be slow to depart** linger
**be smarter than** outwit
**besmirch** begrime, besmear, blemish, blot(ch), contaminate, corrupt, debase, defame, defile, desecrate, dirty, dot, dull, fleck, foul, mar, mark, oxidate, pollute, profane, smear, smudge, soil, spatter, speckle, splodge, spot, stain, sully, taint, tarnish
**be sold for** fetch
**be sorry** repent
**be sorry for** condole, grieve, lament, pity, sympathise
**be sorry for sins** repent
**be sparing** stint
**bespeak** augur, betoken, book, charter, denote, designate, engage, hire, indicate, lease, prearrange, reserve, secure, show, suggest
**best** ace, advantageous, apt, attractive, choice, conquer, cream, defeat, élite, excellent, finest, first(-class), first-rate, foremost, greatest, highest, optimal, optimum, outstanding, perfect, superior, superlative, supreme, top(notch), unequalled, unsurpassed, utmost
**best achievement** record
**best clothes** finery
**best compromise between opposing tendencies** optimum
**best for the job** ideal
**bestial** barbaric, barbarous, beastlike, beastly, inhuman, low, savage, vile
**bestiality** zoophilia
**bestial person** yahoo

**be still** rest
**best man** hero
**best of a group** élite
**bestow** allot, apply, assign, award, bequeath, cede, confer, dispense, divide, donate, expend, give, grant, pass, spend, use, utilise, vouchsafe
**bestowal** addition, adjudication, award, benefaction, bequest, boon, conferment, contribution, decision, decree, donation, fund, gift, grant, income, largess, legacy, presentation, property, revenue, subscription
**bestowal of praise** accolade
**bestow approval** nod, smile
**bestow as due** award, reward
**bestow excessive love on** dote
**bestow upon** endow, give
**best part** climax, cream, highlight, prime
**best position to watch circus** ringside seat
**bestride** bestraddle, command, cross, dominate, mount, overshadow, overstride, overtop, span, straddle, survey, traverse
**be stripped of** forfeit
**best wishes** compliments, greetings, regards
**be subject to** hinge
**be successful in** win
**be suitable to** befit
**be sullen** sulk
**be superior in rank** outrank
**be superior to** excel, outshine
**be supine** lie
**be sure of** know
**be suspended** hang
**be suspended freely** float
**be suspicious of** doubt
**bet** ante, chance, gamble, hazard, plunge, risk, speculation, stake, venture, wager
**betake** move
**be taught** learn
**be tedious** bore
**betel leaf** pan
**betel palm** areca, pinang
**be tenant of** occupy
**bête noire (F)** abomination, anathema, aversion, bane, bogey
**be terror-stricken** panic
**be thankful for** appreciate
**be the cause of** underlie
**be the name for** denote
**be the property of** belong
**be the right size** fit
**be the sign of** denote
**betide** bechance, befall, ensue, happen, occur, supervene
**betimes** early

**bet money** gamble
**betoken** adumbrate, augur, bespeak, declare, forebode, foreshadow, harbinger, herald, portend, predict, spell
**be told of** hear
**bet on horses** punt
**bet on the winners of two races** double
**be too clever for** outwit
**bet placed at any time up to the day before the race** antepost
**be transformed into** become
**betray** abandon, blab, deceive, delude, desert, disappoint, disclose, discover, display, divulge, double-cross, dupe, evince, exhibit, expose, fool, forsake, imply, indicate, jilt, manifest, mislead, reveal, show, tell, trick, uncover, unmask, vent
**betrayal** corruption, deception, disclosing, disclosure, disloyalty, double-cross, double-dealing, duplicity, falseness, mutiny, perfidy, revealing, revelation, sedition, sell-out, slip, telling, treachery, treason, trickery
**betrayal crime** treason
**betrayal of a cause by intellectuals** trahison des clercs
**betrayal of country** treason
**betrayal of trust** treachery
**betray and cheat** double-cross
**betray confidence** blab
**betrayer** conspirator, deceiver, traitor
**betrayer of Jesus** Judas
**betray for money** sell
**betray secret** split
**betray to the police** rumble
**betroth** affiance, agree, bind, commit, contract, covenant, engage, espouse, pledge, plight, promise
**betrothal** agreement, compact, covenant, engagement, espousal, pact, plighting, understanding, vow
**betrothed man** fiancé
**betrothed woman** fiancée
**be troublesome** bother
**be true to** honour
**better** advance, ameliorate, amend, beat, bettor, bigger, correct, enhance, exceed, finer, fitter, forward, further, gambler, greater, healthier, improve, improving, larger, longer, mend, nicer, outdo, outstrip, overtake, peachier, player, preferable, progressing, promote, promote, punter, raise, recovered, recovering, reform, restored, stronger, superior, surpass, surpassing, top, wagerer, worthier
**better half** spouse

**better position** advantage
**better prepared** readier
**betting advisor** tipster
**betting broker** bookie, bookmaker
**betting chances** odds
**betting facility** tote
**betting guide** odds
**betting odds** evens, price
**betting pool** exacta, perfecta, trifecta
**betting price** evens, odds
**bettor's concern** odds
**between** amid, amidst, among, betwixt, concerning, inter-, involving, linking, mid, separating
**between all religious faiths** interdenominational
**between child and adulthood** adolescence
**between fore and aft** amidships
**between maxi and mini** midi
**between midday and evening** afternoon
**between ourselves** confidentially, entre nous, inter nos (L), intimately, privately
**between people** interpersonal
**between pews** aisle
**between primary and university stages** secondary
**between rampart and ditch** relais
**between stars** interstellar
**between sunrise and sunset** day(light), daytime
**between the lines** latent, secret
**between three parties** trilaterally
**between two** à deux (F)
**between two qualities** media
**between us** confidentially
**between you and me and the bedpost** confidentially, intimately, privately
**betwixt** amid, between
**betwixt and between** midway
**be uncertain** flounder, hesitate
**be uncomfortably hot** swelter
**be undecided** doubt, pend
**be under obligation to pay** owe
**be unduly concerned** worry
**be uneasy** fidget, worry
**be unspecific** generalise
**be unsteady** topple
**be unsuccessful** fail
**be unwell** ail
**be upset** capsize
**be useful** avail
**be useful to** serve, subserve
**bevel** bias, cant, chamfer, diagonal, oblique, ream, slant, slope
**bevel edge or corner** chamfer
**bevel out** ream
**beverage** ale, beer, brew, broth, cider, cocktail, cocoa, drink, juice, liquid,
liquor, potage (F), potation, potion, refreshment, soda, soup, tea, wine
**beverage bottle** carafe
**beverage brew vessel** teapot
**beverage cooler** ice
**beverage flavoured with juniper** gin
**beverage from molasses** rum
**beverage herb** camomile, maté, tea
**beverage of the gods** ambrosia, nectar
**beverage tube** straw
**beverage vessel** teapot
**be very angry** fume
**be very good** excel
**be very hot** swelter
**be victorious** win
**bewail** bemoan, cry, deplore, grieve, lament, moan, mourn, regret, repent, rue, sob, wail, weep, whimper
**bewail the dead** keen
**beware of the dog** cave canem (L)
**be weak-minded** doat, dote
**be well** ave (L)
**bewilder** amaze, astonish, astound, baffle, befuddle, bemuse, confound, confuse, daze, dazzle, defeat, distract, flabbergast, flummox, fog, gravel, muddle, mystify, nonplus, obfuscate, perplex, puzzle, stagger, stump, stun, stupefy
**bewildered state** daze
**bewitch** allure, becharm, captivate, captivate, charm, curse, enchant, enrapture, entice, entrance, fascinate, hex, hypnotise, intrigue, inveigle, mesmerise, seduce, tempt
**bewitching look** evil eye
**bewitching woman** siren
**be without** lack, miss, need, want
**be worsted** lose
**be worth** cost, price, valued
**be worthy of** deserve, merit
**be wrong** err
**beyond** above, across, ayont (Sc), hereafter, later, over, past, yonder
**beyond a shadow of doubt** assuredly, certainly, positively, undoubtedly
**beyond belief** far-fetched, impossible, inconceivable, incredible, unbelievable
**beyond comfort** inconsolable
**beyond compare** excellent, incomparable, matchless, peerless, supreme, unmatched, unparalleled, unrivalled, unsurpassed
**beyond dispute** certain, incontestable, incontrovertible
**beyond doubt** certain, incontestable, indisputable
**beyond due limit** ultra
**beyond earth atmosphere** outer space
**beyond help** kaput
**beyond hope** despaired, hopeless, irredeemable
**beyond human hearing** ultrasonic
**beyond human knowledge** transcendent
**beyond limits** out
**beyond measure** boundless, excessive, immeasurable, infinite, limitless, needless, vast
**beyond morality** amoral
**beyond one's grasp** enigmatic, incomprehensible, obscure
**beyond one's means** costly, dear, expensive, extravagant, overpriced
**beyond price** incalculable, inestimable, invaluable, precious, priceless, treasured
**beyond question** certain, doubtless, incontestable, irrefutable, undeniably, undoubtedly
**beyond recovery** hopeless, irrecoverable
**beyond repair** hopeless, irreparable
**beyond reproach** perfect
**beyond restraint** ape
**beyond salvation** irredeemable
**beyond the bounds of a country** abroad
**beyond the bounds of possibility** hopeless, impossible, impracticable
**beyond the moon** supralunar, translunar
**beyond the mountains** tra(ns)montane, ultramontane
**beyond the pale** bizarre, improper, indiscreet, injudicious, unacceptable, unsuitable, unusual, weird
**beyond the range of ordinary knowledge** occult
**beyond the regular duties** extracurricular
**beyond the sea** abroad, overseas, transmarine
**beyond the senses** extrasensory
**beyond the usual** special
**beyond this world** transmundane
**beyond time** ago, past
**beyond valuation** priceless
**beyond what is apparent** ulterior
**beyond what is seen** metaphysical, ulterior
**beyond words** indescribable, ineffable, unutterable
**bey's jurisdiction** beylic
**bhang** hasheesh, hashish, hemp
**Bharat** India
**Bhutan pine** kail
**bi-** couple, double, dual, two
**bias** bent, bevel, diagonal(ly), dispose, favouritism, feeling, inclination, influence, leaning, narrow-mindedness, obliquely,

one-sidedness, partiality, predilection, predispose, prejudice, proclivity, proneness, propensity, skew, slant, sway, tendency, tilt, turn, unfairness, warp
**biased** angled, bigoted, blinkered, discriminative, distorted, jaundiced, loaded, one-sided, partial, predisposed, prejudiced, slanted, swayed, twisted, unfair, unreceptive, warped, weighted
**biased person** bigot
**bib** drink, serviette, tipple
**bibber** drinker, tippler
**Bible** Scriptures
**Bible city** Babel, Bethlehem, Ekron, Gaza, Hebron, Jerusalem, Nain, Nineveh, Sidon, Sodom
**Bible giant** Anak, Emim, Goliath
**Bible hawker** colporteur
**Bible hunter** Nimrod
**Bible interpreter** exegete
**Bible kingdom** Edom, Israel, Judah, Moab, Samaria, Sheba
**Bible land** Nod
**Bible outcast** leper
**Bible poem** psalm
**Bible priest** Aaron, Annas, Eli
**Bible put in hotel rooms** Gideon
**Bible queen** Esther, Jezebel, Sheba, Vashti
**Bible seller** colporteur
**Bible shepherd** Abel, David
**Bible town** Bethel, Cana, Endor, Nazareth
**Bible verse** text
**Bible version** Douay
**Bible vessel** ark
**Biblical allegory** parable
**Biblical angel** Gabriel, Michael, Raphael
**Biblical area** Judaea
**Biblical boat** ark
**Biblical boat builder** Noah
**Biblical character** Daniel, Eli, Esau
**Biblical city** Arba, Babel, Bethlehem, Dan, Ekron, Gath, Gaza, Hebron, Jerusalem, Nain, Nineveh, Nob, Sidon, Sodom, Ur, Zoar
**Biblical coin** mite, shekel
**Biblical country** Canaan, Edom, Elam, Moab, Ophir, Seba, Sheba
**Biblical dancer** Salome
**Biblical disciple** Andrew, Bartholomew, James, John, Judas Iskariot, Matthew, Peter (Simon), Philip, Simon, Thaddaeus, Thomas
**Biblical garden** Eden
**Biblical high priest** Eli
**Biblical hill** Zion
**Biblical hunter** Nimrod

**Biblical king** Agag, Ahab, Amon, Asa, David, Herod, Nadab, Og, Omri, Saul, Solomon
**Biblical language** Aramaic, Hebrew
**Biblical letter** epistle
**Biblical measure** ell
**Biblical monster** leviathan
**Biblical mountain** Ararat, Gilead, Hermon, Horeb, Nebo, Sinai, Tabor
**Biblical outcast** leper
**Biblical passage** text
**Biblical patriarch** Abraham, Isaac, Israel, Jacob, Methuselah, Noah
**Biblical poem** psalm
**Biblical pool** Siloam
**Biblical priest** Eli
**Biblical pronoun** thy, thine
**Biblical prophet** Amos, Elias, Elisha, Hosea, Isaiah, Jeremiah
**Biblical punishment** stoning
**Biblical queen** Esther, Jezebel, Sheba, Vashti
**Biblical region** Gilead
**Biblical river** Arnon, Jordan, Kishon, Nile, Pishon
**Biblical sailor** Noah
**Biblical sea** Galilee
**Biblical shepherd** Abel, David
**Biblical slave** Hagar
**biblical strong man** Samson
**biblical study** bibliology
**Biblical tower** Babel
**Biblical verse** text
**Biblical vessel** ark
**Biblical weed** tare
**Biblical well** ain, esek
**Biblical wise man** Solomon
**Biblical witch's home** Endor
**Biblical you** thou
**bib-like detachable shirt front** dick(e)y
**bicameral parliament of Iceland** Althing
**biceps** muscle
**bicker** altercate, argue, argument, brawl, conflict, disagree, discord, dispute, fight, flutter, hasten, jangle, move, patter, quarrel, quiver, row, scrap, shake, spar, spat, squabble, strife, tremble, vacillate, variance, vibrate, wrangle
**bicuspid tooth** premolar
**bicycle** two-wheeler
**bicycle made for two** tandem
**bicycle rider** cyclist
**bicycle seat** saddle
**bid** adjure, advance, advance, amount, announcement, ask, attempt, auction, call, charge, command, desire, dictate, direct, effort, endeavour, enjoin, extend, go, greet, instruct, invite, motion, offer, order, pay, price, proclaim, proffer,

proposal, propose, request, require, say, solicit, submission, submit, suggest, suggestion, sum(mon), tell, tender, try, venture, wish
**bid against** oppose
**bidding** asking, behest, call, calling, charge, charging, command(ing), demand, desiring, dictating, directing, enjoining, greeting, instructing, invitation, inviting, offering, order(ing), proffering, proposing, request, requiring, saying, soliciting, submitting, summoning, summons, telling, tendering, warning, wish(ing)
**bidding farewell** valediction
**bide** abide, await, continue, dwell, endure, face, linger, live, remain, sojourn, stay, suffer, tarry, tolerate, wait
**bide one's time** wait
**bide time** wait
**bid farewell to** speed
**bid for job** apply
**bid for twelve tricks** slam
**bid higher than** outbid
**biennial** two-yearly
**big** big-hearted, bulky, capacious, colossal, consequential, enormous, extensive, filled, generous, gigantic, great, huge, immense, important, inflated, large, massive, overflowing, pregnant, productive, swelling, swollen, teeming, tremendous
**big American battle** Alamo
**big and strong** hefty
**big ape** gorilla
**big artiodactyl** hippo(potamus)
**big band** orchestra
**big beaked bird** becard, hornbill
**big boat** ship, vessel
**big brown animal** bear
**big cask** tun
**big cat** cheetah, leopard, lion, lioness
**big-city cowboy** dude
**big clumsy person** jumbo
**big crowd disturbance** riot
**big dog** Alsatian, Doberman(n)
**big enough** ample, spacious
**big fuss** ado, to-do
**bigger than normal** overgrown
**biggest** largest
**biggest land animal** elephant
**biggest mammal** whale
**biggest plant** tree
**biggest whale** blue
**big guns** artillery
**bigheaded** conceited
**big house** mansion
**bight** arm, bay, bayou, bend, cove, creek, curve, entrance, firth, gulf, ingress, inlet, passage, slough

**big inferno of 1666** Fire of London
**big lie** whopper
**big marble** taw
**big market** emporium
**big mistake** howler
**big name** celebrity
**bigness** size
**big one** lulu
**bigot** addict, barbarian, boor, devotee, enthusiast, extremist, fanatic, ignoramus, illiterate, lowbrow, maniac, militant, persecutor, sectarian, zealot
**bigoted** biased, dogmatic, intolerant, obstinate, sectarian, warped
**big person** jumbo
**big pithy vegetable** marrow, pumpkin
**big plant** tree
**big shop** emporium
**big shot** celebrity, dignitary, personage
**big smile** grin
**big speech** oration
**big spoon** ladle
**big stitch** tack
**big stream** river
**big surprise** bombshell
**big swallow** gulp
**big talk** brag
**big timer** mogul
**big toe** hallux
**big-top show** circus
**big tree** sequoia
**big vase** urn
**big water bird** swan
**bijou** jewel, trinket
**bike footrest** pedal
**bike rider** cyclist
**bikini part** bra
**bilharzia worm** schistosome
**bilk** cheat, default, defraud, dodge, elude, evade, neglect, swindle
**bill** account, act, advertisement, beak, charge, invoice, notice, program(me), proposal, statement
**billabong** waterhole
**billet-doux** love letter
**billfold** wallet
**bill for a meal** tab
**billiard cloth** baize
**billiard hall** poolroom
**billiard rebound** carom
**billiard rod** cue
**billiard shot** cannon, carom, massé, stroke
**billiard stick** bridge, cue, rest
**billiard stroke** carom, kiss, massé, scratch, shot
**billiard term** balk, english, pool, spot
**bill in a restaurant** check
**billionth** nano
**billion trillion trillion** octillion
**billion years** (a)eon

**bill of exchange** draft, lettre de change (F)
**bill of fare** menu
**bill of rate** menu
**bill of rights** Magna Carta
**bill payer** drawee
**bill's addition** rider
**bills for viewers?** eyewitness accounts
**bill with prices** invoice
**bin** midden, receptacle
**binary** double, dual, twofold
**binary classification** dichotomy
**binary compound of oxygen** oxide
**bind** apprentice, attach, bandage, bond, border, chafe, compel, confine, constrain, detain, dilemma, edge, fasten, force, glue, hamper, hinder, hitch, knot, lash, necessitate, obligate, oblige, paste, plight, predicament, require, restrain, restrict, rope, secure, squeeze, stick, strap, tie, wrap
**bind as an apprentice** article
**bind by contract** engage, obligate
**bind by incantations** enchant
**bind during surgery** ligate
**binder** envelope, fastener, file, folder, portfolio
**binding** attaching, bandaging, compelling, compulsory, confining, constraining, dressing, fastener, fastening, forcing, gluing, hindering, indissoluble, irrevocable, lashing, mandatory, obligatory, obliging, pasting, securing, sticking, tying, unalterable, wrapping
**binding agreement** contract, obligation
**binding fabric** tape
**binding for ever** indissoluble
**binding machine** baler
**binding medicine** astringent
**binding promise** obligation, pledge
**bind morally to do a service** oblige
**bind oneself** promise, vow
**bind the mouth** gag
**bind tightly** frap
**bind together** cement, knot, tie
**bind up** bandage, lash, swathe
**bind with bandages** swathe
**bind with promise to marry** betroth
**bine** shoot, stem
**binge** bat, bout, festivity, fling, jag, orgy, rip, spree
**bingo-like game** lotto
**binocular part** lens
**biography** account, adventures, career, confessions, curriculum vitae, essay, filmography, fortunes, history, journal, life, memoir(s), narrative, profile, psychobiography, recollections, record, sketch, story
**biography of saints** hagiography

**biological factor** gene
**biologically defective** dysgenic
**biotechnology** ergonomics
**biotic** organic
**bipolar nerve cell** diaxon(e)
**birch-like tree** alder
**bird** avis (L), barbet, bittern, bokmakierie, cock, coot, crow, cuckoo, daw, dipper, diver, dove, eagle, egret, emu, finch, fowl, gannet, goose, grebe, guinea-fowl, hadeda, hamerkop, hawk, hen, hoopoe, huia, ibis, jackdaw, kingfisher, kite, kiwi, lark, lourie, loon, lorikeet, macaw, mossie, oiseau (F), osprey, ostrich, ousel, owl, partridge, pelican, penguin, pigeon, pipit, plover, rhea, robin, rook, secretary, shrike, sunbird, swallow, skua, snipe, sparrow, starling, swallow, swan, teal, tern, thrush, toco, tomtit, weaver, wren
**bird allied to the lark** bunting
**bird beak** neb
**birdcage** aviary
**birdcage rest** perch
**bird call** chirp
**bird courtship** lek
**bird deterrent** scarecrow
**bird dog** retriever, setter
**bird enclosure** aviary, cage
**bird food** grain, millet, seed
**bird having a glossy black plumage** drongo, raven
**bird having tuft of feathers** crested
**birdhouse** aviary, birdcage
**bird killed for plumage** heron
**bird laid in another's nest** cuckoo
**birdlike** avian
**bird like a snipe** woodcock
**birdman** aviculturist, ornithologist
**bird of brilliant plumage** barbet, jacamar, minivet, oriole, tanager, tody
**bird of enormous size and strength in Arabian legend** roc
**bird of falcon family** buzzard
**bird of grouse family** ptarmigan
**bird of legend** lightning bird, roc, simurg(h)
**bird of myth** phoenix
**bird of omen** waybird
**bird-of-paradise flower** strelitzia
**bird of passage** nomad, pariah, rover, vagabond, wanderer
**bird of peace** dove
**bird of prey** eagle, elanet, erne, falcon, glede, goshawk, hawk, kite, osprey, owl, raptor, raptorial, stooper, vulture
**bird of prey's claw** talon
**bird of prey's nest** eyrie
**bird of the duck family** goose

**bird of the falcon family** kite
**bird of the swallow family** martin
**bird resembling kingfisher** jacamar
**bird's abode** nest
**bird sanctuary** aviary
**bird's beak** bill, neb
**bird's bed** nest
**bird's bill** beak, neb
**bird's breeding place** nest
**bird's claw** talon
**birds collectively** avifauna
**bird's crop** craw
**bird's egg collector** oologist
**bird's-eye view** panorama
**bird's feathers** plumage
**bird's hind toe** hallux
**bird's home** nest
**bird's identifying tag** legband
**bird's migration route** flyway
**bird's nail** claw
**birds of a feather** colleagues, cronies, friends, gang, group
**bird's sanctuary** nest
**bird's second stomach for grinding food** gizzard
**bird's shrill cry** chirp, squawk
**bird's sound** chirp, coo, tweet, twitter, warble
**bird's stomach** craw, crop, gizzard, maw
**bird that carried Sinbad** roc
**bird that lays eggs in another's nest** cuckoo
**bird that swims** natatory
**bird too young to leave nest** nestling
**bird used in falconry** t(i)ercel
**bird watcher** ornithologist
**bird-watching** ornithology
**bird with brilliant plumage** peacock
**bird with distinctive cry** stonechat
**bird with pink, scarlet and black plumage** flamingo
**bird with pouched bill** pelican
**bird with showy tail** peacock
**birl** burl, spin, twirl
**birth** ancestry, beginning, descent, lineage, nativity, origin, parentage, parturition, rise
**birth and genealogy of the gods** theogony
**birthday celebration** party
**birthmark** blemish, discolouration, disfigurement, mole, naevus, patch, spiloma
**birthmark in form of sharply-defined red mark** naevus
**birthplace** beginning, cradle, fount, heritage, home, homestead, household, origin, provenance, roots, source, spring
**birthplace of Abraham** Ur
**birthplace of Alexander** Pella

**birthplace of Apollo** Delos
**birthplace of Aristotle** Stagira
**birthplace of Beethoven** Bonn
**birthplace of Diana** Delos
**birthplace of Mohammed** Mecca
**birthplace of Napoleon** Corsica
**birthplace of Orpheus** Pieria
**birthplace of Roosevelt** Boston
**birthplace of Saint Francis** Assisi
**birthplace of Saint Paul** Tarsus
**birthplace of the Muses** Pieria
**birthplace of Zeus** Ida
**birth rate** natality
**birthright seller** Esau
**biscuit** cookie, cracker, cracknel, pretzel
**biscuit of wheaten flour baked crisp** cracknel, pretzel
**bisect** halve
**bisexual** androgynous
**bishop** eparch, pontiff, prelate, primate
**bishop in chess** alfin, alphin
**bishop in relation to his archbishop** suffragan
**bishop of Rome** Pope
**bishopric** archdiocese, diocese, episcopacy, episcopate, office, pontificate, prelacy, primacy, see, territory
**bishop's backless folding chair** faldstool
**bishop's cap** miter, zucchetto
**bishop's cape** mozzetta
**bishops collectively** episcopate
**bishop's diocese** bishopric
**bishop's district** diocese
**bishop's garment** alb, chimar, chimer(e), cope, gremial, rochet
**bishop's move** diagonal
**bishop's office** episcopate, lawn, see
**bishop's pinafore** gremial
**bishop's robe** alb, chimar, chimer(e), cope, gremial, rochet, simar
**bishop's staff** crosier
**bishop's tenure** episcopate
**bishop's territory** see, bishopric
**bishop's throne in basilica** tribune
**bishop's title** abba
**bishop's view?** see
**bison** buffalo, wisent
**bissextile** leap-year
**bistort** Easterledges, snakeroot, snakeweed
**bistro** café
**bit** atom, bridle, drill, fragment, grain, iota, jot, morsel, part, particle, piece, rein, restrainer, scintilla, scrap, speck, whit
**bit by bit** gradually, piecemeal, slowly
**bite** burn, champ, cheat, chew, corrode, crunch, crush, deceive, defraud, dupe, erode, food, gnaw, gull, kick, masticate, morsel, mouthful, munch, nibble, nip, pierce, pinch, punch, pungency, refreshment, rend, smart, snack, sting, taste, tear, tingle, trick, wound
**bite gently** nibble
**bite like a rodent** gnaw
**bite one's lips** forbear, refrain, repress
**bite persistently** gnaw
**bite playfully** nip
**bite the dust** die, expire, fail, lose, perish
**bite with beak** peck
**biting** caustic, chewing, clamping, crunching, crushing, cutting, gnawing, gripping, holding, nibbling, nipping, piercing, pinching, pungent, rending, seizing, snapping, tearing, wounding
**biting fly** gnat, tsetse
**biting humour** sarcasm
**biting insect** gnat, mosquito
**bitingly cold** nippy
**bitingly ironic** sarcastic
**biting midge** sandfly
**biting part of a tool** bit
**biting remark** barb
**biting structures** teeth
**biting to the taste** acrid
**biting wit** sarcasm
**bit of butter** pat
**bit of golf turf** divot
**bit of property** asset
**bit of seafood** cockle, mussel
**bit of snow** flake
**bit played by actor** part, role
**bits and pieces** odds and ends, scrap
**bits of coarse yarn** thrum
**bitter** acerbic, acid, acrid, acrimonious, biting, caustic, cruel, cutting, distasteful, distressing, embittered, fierce, freezing, grievous, harsh, heartbreaking, hostile, intense, mean, merciless, painful, picro, piercing, poignant, raw, resentful, ruthless, sarcastic, sardonic, savage, scornful, severe, sneering, sore, sour, stinging, sullen, tart, unpleasant, unsweetened, vinegary
**bitter and hot** acrid
**bitter apple** colocynth, crab
**bitter aromatic gum resin** galbanum
**bitter aromatic plant** elecampane
**bitter bark** niepa, niota
**bitter bark of a South American tree** angostura
**bitter bit** smallpox
**bitter brush** bistort, snakeroot, snakeweed
**bitter clover** yellowtop
**bitter crystalline substance used medicinally** salicin(e)

**bitter crystalline substance from poplar bark** salicin(e)
**bitter dark cherry** morella
**bitter drug** aloe, quassia
**bitter drug obtained from cinchona bark** quinine
**bitter feeling** hatred
**bitter feelings** resentment
**bitter fluid secreted by liver** bile
**bitter grief** woe
**bitter harangue** diatribe, invective, philippic, screed, tirade
**bitter hatred** rancour
**bitter herb** aloe, rue, wormwood
**bitter ill will** rancour
**bitter infusion** rue
**bitter in temper** acrimonious
**bitter invective** philippic
**bitter ironic remark** sarcasm
**bitter-juiced herb** aloe
**bitter-juiced plant** aloe
**bitter liver secretion** bile
**bitterly** acidly, acridly, astringently, hostilely, morosely, rancorously, resentfully, sharply, sorely, sourly, sullenly, tartly
**bitterly cold** arctic, freezing, frozen, ice-cold, wintry
**bitterly in words** inveigh
**bitterly ironic** sardonic
**bitterly irritating to the feelings** acrid
**bitterly mocking** cynical, sardonic
**bitterly pungent** acrid
**bitterly scornful** sardonic
**bitterness** acerbity, acrimony, anger, animosity, aridness, causticity, edginess, gall, grudge, indignation, irascibility, malice, pungency, rancour, remorse, resentment, tartness, touchiness, venom
**bitterness of feelings** acrimony
**bitterness of taste** acerbity
**bitterness of temper** acrimony
**bitter plant** aloe
**bitter quarrel** feud
**bitter regret** remorse
**bitter remark** sarcasm
**bitter resin** asaf(o)etida
**bitter resin with an unpleasant onion-like smell** asaf(o)etida
**bitter substance secreted by liver** bile
**bitter succulent** aloe
**bitter vetch** ers
**bitter water** Marah
**bit thick** excessive, far-fetched, unfair, unjust, unreasonable
**bitumen** asphalt, pitch, resin, tar
**bitumen surface** tar
**bituminous drug** mummy
**bituminous pitch** asphalt
**bituminous substance** tar

**bivalve** clam, hinge, mollusc, mussel, oyster, pandora, pecten, scallop, two
**bivalve mollusc** clam, mussel, oyster, scallop
**bivouac** camp, encampment
**bizarre** antic, curious, eccentric, extraordinary, extravagant, fantastic, freakish, grotesque, kinky, odd, outlandish, outré, peculiar, queer, strange, unusual, weird
**bizarre costume** get-up
**bizarre person** weirdo
**bizarre posture** antic
**blab** inform, reveal, tell
**black** atrocious, calamitous, dark, depressing, devilish, diabolic, dingy, dirty, disastrous, dismal, doleful, dusky, ebon(y), evil, fiendish, forbidding, funereal, hopeless, horrible, infernal, inhuman, inky, jet, monstrous, mournful, nefarious, negro (Sp), noir (F), raven, sable, sad, sinful, soiled, sombre, sooty, stained, sullen, swart, swarthy, treacherous, wicked
**black alloy** copper, niello
**black and blue** livid
**black and blue area** bruise
**black and gold fur in heraldry** pean
**black-and-white bamboo eater** bear, panda
**black-and-white bear** panda
**black-and-white bird** crow, magpie
**black-and-yellow bird** oriole
**black art** alchemy, magic, necromancy, voodoo
**blackberry bush** bramble
**black bird** ani, crow, daw, drongo, raven, rook, starling
**blackboard** slate
**blackboard cleaner** eraser
**blackboard marker** chalk
**blackboard material** slate
**blackboard stand** easel
**blackbuck** sasin
**black bun** currant bun
**black care** atra cura (L)
**black cuckoo bird** ani
**black diamonds** coal
**blacken** befoul, calumniate, char, cloud, darken, decry, defile, denigrate, dishonour, malign, slander, smear, smirch, smudge, soil, stain, stigmatise, sully, taint, tarnish, traduce, vilify
**blacken by fire** char
**blacken the name of** impeach, incriminate, slur, stain, stigmatise
**blackest black** jet
**black European crow** rook
**black eye** mouse, shiner
**black-eyed Susan** coneflower, oxeye

**black fish** swart, tautog
**black fluid of cuttlefish** sepia
**black gang** stokers
**black garden pest** thrips, woodworm
**black garnet** melanite
**black gem** jet, melanite, onyx, rutile
**black glass** vitrite
**black gold** oil
**blackguard** devil, rake, rascal, rogue, scamp, scoundrel, villain
**black hawk tree** sloe
**black hole** dungeon, pit
**black Indian tea** souchong
**blackjack** cosh
**blackleg** scab, strikebreaker
**black leopard** panther
**black letter** gothic
**black magic** diabolism, jinx, necromancy, sorcery, theurgy, voodoo(ism), witchcraft, wizardry
**blackmail** bleed, blood-sucking, bribe, chantage, coerce, compel, demand, exaction, extort(ion), force, intimidate, intimidation, milk, pay-off, protection, ransom, squeeze, threaten
**black marble** lucullite
**black mark** demerit, stain
**black market** illegal
**black market dealer** racketeer
**black marketeer** profiteer, spiv
**black measles** apoplexy
**black mineral** coal
**black mulberry-tree** sycamine
**blackness** badness, darkness, dismalness, dolefulness, duskiness, gloom, holelessness, iniquitousness, inkiness, lugubriousness, nefariousness, nigritude, ominousness, sadness, sombreness, swarthiness, wickedness
**black ore of titanium** ilmenite
**blackout** censor(ship), collapse, coma, conceal(ment), cover(-up), darken, eclipse, extinguish, faint, gag, oblivion, secrecy, shade, suppress(ion), swoon, unconsciousness, withhold
**black people of south-eastern Nigeria** Ibo
**black pigment** abaiser, melanin, soot, tar
**black pigment of eye** melanin
**black plague** bubonic
**black porous residue** charcoal
**black rock** basalt, galena, galenite
**Black Sea peninsula** Crimea
**Black Sea port** Odessa
**black sheep** apostate, disgrace, idler, ne'er-do-well, outcast, pariah,

prodigal, recreant, renegade, reprobate, strayer, wanderer, wastrel
**Blackshirt** fascist
**blacksmith** farrier, shoer, striker
**blacksmith's tool** anvil, swage
**blacksmith's workshop** forge, smithery, smithy
**blacksmith who shoes horses** farrier
**blacksnake** racer
**black stone** onyx
**black substance formed by the burning of coal** soot
**black suit** clubs, spades
**black sweet** licorice, liquorice
**black tea** darr, pekoe, souchong
**black tea with large leaves** souchong
**blackthorn fruit** sloe
**blackthorn tree** sloe
**black, unglazed pottery** basaltware
**black vulture** urubu
**black wood** ebony
**bladder** bag, bleb, blister, bursa, cyst, pocket, pouch, receptacle, sac, saccula, saccule, theca, vescia
**bladder drug** diuretic
**bladder tube** ureter
**blade** sword, oar
**bladed weapon** sword
**blade of an oar** paddle
**blade of a paddle-wheel** paddle
**blade of a plough** share
**blade of plant** leaf
**blade of screw** vane
**blade of seeding-machine or cultivator** share
**blade of windmill** vane
**blade on helicopter** rotor
**blame** accuse, condemn, condemnation, criticise, culpability, disapproval, fault, guilt, misdeed, onus, reprehend, reprehension, reproach, reproof, reprove, stricture, wrong
**blame bearer** scapegoat
**blameless** clean, faultless, guiltless, innocent, irreproachable, perfect, stainless, unblemished, upright, virtuous
**blamelessly** cleanly, faultlessly, guiltlessly, innocently, irreproachably, perfectly, uprightly, virtuously
**blamelessness** cleanness, faultlessness, guiltlessness, innocence, perfectness, uprightness, virtuousness
**blame someone for an action** reproach
**blameworthiness** culpability, dishonourableness, evilness, feloniousness, illegitimateness, illicitness, improperness,

reprehensibleness, unfairness, unjustness, unlawfulness, wickedness
**blameworthy** blameful, condemnable, disreputable, flagitious, ignoble, immoral, inexcusable, nefarious, reprehensible, unjustifiable, wicked
**blanc fixe** barium sulphate
**blanch** bleach, decolour, dim, etiolate, fade, gray, pale, whiten
**bland** affable, agreeable, amiable, balmy, benign, calmative, complaisant, composed, courteous, dull, gentle, insipid, lenitive, mild, non-irritating, open, ordinary, smooth, soft, soothing, soulless, suave, uninteresting, urbane
**blank** amazed, astonished, astounded, complete, confused, dum(b)founded, emptiness, empty, entire, nonplussed, simple, unadorned, unadulterated, undistinguished, unmarked, unmitigated, unmixed, unqualified, utter, vacancy, vacant, virginal, void
**blank book for photographs or stamps** album
**blanket** carpet, cloak, cloud, coat(ing), conceal, cover(ing), coverlet, envelope, film, hide, layer, mantle, mask, obscure, rug, sheet, wrapper, wrapping
**blanket cloak** poncho, serape
**blanket made of pelts** kaross
**blank leaf at beginning or end of book** flyleaf
**blank space round a printed page** margin
**blank window** orb
**blare** announce, bang, blast, boom, clang, herald, honk, hoot, howl, peal, proclaim, promote, promulgate, resonate, resound, ring, scream, shout, shriek, trumpet, wail, whine
**blare of trumpet** fanfare, tantara
**blasé** bored, carefree, careless, cool, full, heedless, indifferent, listless, lukewarm, neutral, nonchalant, overfed, replete, satiated, satisfied, spoiled, surfeited, tired, unamazed, unastonished, uninteresed, unmoved, weary
**blasphemous** godless, impious, irreligious, irreverent, profane, sacrilegious
**blasphemy** cursing, impiousness, irreverence, profanity, sacrilege, swearing
**blast** annihilate, blare, bleat, blow, burst, clang, destroy, detonate, detonation, discharge, dynamite, explode, explosion, gale, gust,

outbreak, outburst, report, roar, rush, scream, shriek, split, storm, toot, wind
**blast furnace** smelter
**blasting substance** gelignate
**blast of wind** gust
**blatant** boisterous, cheap, clamant, crude, egregious, flagrant, gaudy, glaring, manifest, noisy, notorious, obtrusive, shameless
**blatant falsehood** downright lie
**blatant lie** untruth
**blaze** brightness, burn, fire, flame, glow, inferno, outburst, pyre
**blaze fighter** fireman
**blaze inhibitor** firebreak
**blazer** jacket
**blaze unsteadily** flare
**blazing** afire, aflame, burning
**bleach** blanch, blench, decolourise, dim, discolour, dull, etiolate, fade, lighten, pale, whiten(er)
**bleaching gas** ozone
**bleaching ingredient** chloride, hypo
**bleak** austere, awful, bad, bare, barren, cheerless, chilly, cold, depressing, desolate, dismal, dreary, exposed, gaunt, gloomy, grim, hopeless, joyless, miserable, open, raw, sombre, unpromising, windswept, windy
**bleat** baa
**bleeder** haemophiliac
**bleeding from womb** metrorrhage, metrorrhagia
**bleed profusely** haemorrhage
**blemish** blot, damage, deface, defect, disfigurement, flaw, impair, mar, mark, scar, spot, stain, sully, taint, tarnish
**blemish of character** fault
**blend** alloy, amalgam(ate), coalesce, combination, combine, complement, composite, compound, concoction, fit, fuse, fusion, harmonise, inosculate, intermix, interweave, join, levigate, merge, mingle, mix(ture), scramble, suit, synthesis, tone, union, unite
**blend by melting** fuse
**blender** merger, mixer
**blend gradually** merge
**blending rum** demerara
**blenny** eelpout
**bless** anoint, consecrate, dedicate, endow, exalt, hallow, magnify, ordain, praise, provide, sanctify
**blessed** adored, anointed, beatified, endowed, favoured, fortunate, joyful, joyous, lucky, sacred
**blessing** advantage, approbation, approval, authority, backing,

benediction, benefit, benison, boon, commendation, concurrence, consecration, dedication, favour, gain, gift, glorifying, godsend, grace, guarding, help, invocation, kindness, permission, praising, sanction, service, support, thanks(giving), windfall

**Bligh's ship** Bounty

**blight** affliction, annihilate, bane, blast, canker, crush, curse, dash, decay, destroy, die, disappoint, disease, eyesore, frustrate, fungus, illness, infestation, injure, mar, mildew, misfortune, nullify, pest, plague, rot, ruin, scourge, shrivel, sickness, sore, spoil, taint, torment, ulcer, wither, woe, wreck

**Blighty** England

**blind** awning, benighted, blinker, closed, concealed, cover, dark, decoy, dim, headlong, heedless, ignorant, irrational, pretence, pretext, purblind, rash, shade, sightless, stone-blind, stratagem, thoughtless, uncritical, undiscerning, unenlightened, unreasoning

**blind alley** cul-de-sac, impasse, obstacle, walled

**blind drunk** blotto, legless

**blind end of first part of large intestine** caecum

**blind fear** panic

**blind fish** pinkfish

**blind god** Hoth(r)

**blind hawk** seel

**blinding goddess** Ate

**blinding light** glare

**blind intestinal pouch** caecum

**blindness** ablepsia, carelessness, cecity, ignorance, inattentiveness, neglectfulness, rashness, sightlessness, thoughtlessness

**blind sac** caecum

**blind spot** scotoma

**blind street** cul-de-sac, dead end

**blind the eyes** hoodwink, seal

**blink** avoid, beam, blench, condone, descry, disregard, espy, evade, flicker, flutter, glimmer, glimpse, ignore, neglect, nic(ti)tate, overlook, quiver, shimmer, shine, sight, snub, sparkle, spot, squint, tremble, twinkle, wince, wink

**blinker** indicator

**blinker for horse** winker

**blink one's eye** wink

**bliss** blessedness, blissfulness, blitheness, cheer, delight, ecstasy, enjoyment, euphoria, felicity, gladness, glee, happiness, heaven, joy, jubilation, nirvana, paradise, pleasure, rapture, Utopia

**blissful** delighted, ecstatic, elated, enchanted, enraptured, euphoric, happy, joyful, rapturous

**blissful place** Eden, Paradise

**blissful state** felicity, nirvana, rapture

**blister** abscess, batter, beat, blain, bleb, blob, boil, bulge, canker, carbuncle, cyst, disgrace, furuncle, irritation, papule, pimple, prominence, protrusion, punish, pustule, sore, spank, swelling, thrash, ulcer, vesicle, welt, whip

**blistering** blackening, broiling, burning, charring, cruel, excoriating, execrable, hot, infernal, intense, lambasting, lashing, parching, roasting, sarcastic, savage, scathing, scorching, searing, shrivelling, singeing, strenuous, vicious, virulent, withering

**blisterlike swelling** cyst

**blister on skin** blain

**blithe** beaming, breezy, buoyant, carefree, casual, cheerful, cheery, cool, ecstatic, elated, exultant, frolicking, gay, genial, gleeful, happy, hearty, heedless, jocund, jolly, jovial, joyful, joyous, laughing, lively, merry, perky, pleased, radiant, rollicking, smiling, sparkling, sunny, unconcerned, vital

**blitz** attack, onslaught

**blob** bead, blemish, blot(ch), bubble, dirty, dollop, dolt, dot, drop(let), dullard, glob(ule), mark, oval, pill, simpleton, smirch, smudge, smutch, spot

**block** arrest, blockade, blockage, check, clog, close, congest, cube, deter, dolt, evade, form, hinder, hindrance, impede, impediment, jam, mass, obstacle, obstruct, obstruction, parry, pulley, shape, stop, tackle

**blockade** barricade, barrier, beleaguer(ment), besiege(ment), blockage, closure, encircle, hindrance, hurdle, impediment, obstacle, obstruction, restriction, siege, stop(page), surround

**blockage** ban, bar(rier), check, congestion, embargo, hindrance, impediment, interdict, jam, obstacle, obstruction, prohibition, restraint, restriction, snag, stop(page)

**blockhead** bonehead, dolt, dullard, dunce, fool, idiot, ignoramus, numskull, oaf, pampoen, sap

**block of compressed coal dust** briquette

**block of soap** bar

**block out** chart, plan, sketch

**blockshaped** rectangular

**blocks of lava** aa

**block up** dam, obstruct

**bloke** chap, fellow, guy, man, ou

**blond** blonde, fair

**blonde** blond, fair(-headed), fair-skinned, light-coloured, whitish, yellow

**blood** ancestry, Blut (G), descent, extraction, family, gore, lifeblood, lineage, passion, source, spirit, temper(ament)

**blood ailment** anaemia, haemophilia

**blood bath** bloodshed, butchery, carnage, decimation, massacre

**blood carrier** artery, capillary, vein, vessel

**blood clot** thrombosis, thrombus

**blood clot factor** platelet

**blood deficiency condition** anaemia

**blood factor** Rh

**blood feud** vendetta

**blood fluid** plasma, serum

**blood giver** donor

**blood horse** thoroughbred

**blood injection** transfusion

**bloodless** anaemic, apathetic, ashen, colourless, deathly, drained, drawn, dull, emaciated, faint, feeble, gaunt, grim, insipid, languid, lifeless, listless, pale, pallid, passionless, pasty, sallow, sickly, spiritless, torpid, unemotional, unfeeling, wan

**bloodlessness** anaemia, colourlessness, delicateness, feebleness, greyness, languidness, lividness, pallidness, sickliness, wanness, weakness, whiteness

**blood-letting** phlebotomy

**bloodlike fluid** ichor

**bloodline** pedigree

**blood of the gods** ichor

**blood part** fibrin, serum, platelet

**blood particle** platelet

**blood poisoning** pyaemia, septicaemia, toxaemia

**blood-red** sanguine

**blood relation** kin, sib

**blood relationship** kin, kindred, kinship, relation

**blood relative** kin, kinsman, relation, sib, tribesman

**bloodshed** butchery, carnage, gore, killing, massacre, slaughter, slaying

**blood shed from wound** gore

**bloodstained** bloody, ensanguined, gory

**bloodsucker** leech, vampire

**bloodsucking animal** leech

**bloodsucking bat** vampire

**bloodsucking fly** gnat, tsetse
**bloodsucking insect** bedbug, flea, louse, mosquito
**bloodsucking parasite** flea, tick
**bloodsucking worm** leech
**bloodthirsty** barbaric, barbarous, brutal, cruel, ferocious, inhuman, murderous, ruthless, slaughterous, vicious, warlike
**blood vessel** aorta, artery, capillary, vein
**bloody** barbarous, bloodstained, cruel, ensanguined, ferocious, gory, murderous, sanguinary, savage
**bloom** blossom, effloresce, floret, flourish, flower, flush, freshness, gloss, glow, lustre, soundness, strength, vigour
**blooming late** serotinal, serotine, serotinous
**bloom on antique bronze** patina
**blossom** bloom, bud, burgeon, develop, floret, flourish, flower, grow
**blot** bespatter, blemish, blotch, blotting, darken, destroy, disfigure, disgrace, dishonour, eclipse, efface, eliminate, erase, erasure, expunge, mark, obliterate, obliteration, obscure, smear, spot, stain, sully, taint
**blotch** blob, blot, eruption, mark, patch, pimple, pustule, smear, smirch, smudge, smutch, splash, spot, stain
**blotch on a surface** mottle
**blotch on the skin** freckle, tache
**blot out** abolish, cancel, darken, delete, destroy, eclipse, efface, erase, expunge, obliterate, obscure, shadow
**blot out of existence** annihilate
**blouse** shirt, top
**blouse under a pinafore dress** guimpe
**blouse worn by Malay women** kerbaya
**blow** breathe, buffet, exhale, fling, hit, pant, puff, punch, rush, strike, uppercut, whirl
**blow a horn** hoot, toot
**blow air through nose** snore, snort
**blowdart poison** curare
**blower** telephone
**blow gently** waft
**blow grain free of chaff** winnow
**blowgun missile** dart
**blow hot and cold** fluctuate, vacillate, waver
**blowing from land towards sea** offshore
**blowing from sea towards land** onshore
**blowing in sudden blast** gusting
**blowing sound heard in auscultation** souffle
**blown up photograph** enlargement

**blow off steam** holler, revel, roister, scream, yell
**blow one's top** explode
**blow one's trumpet** boast, brag, swagger, vaunt
**blow out** burst, erupt, explode, extinguish, shatter, smother, squash
**blow-out** binge, blast, burst, detonation, eruption, escape, explosion, feast, fuse, leak, party, puncture, rupture, spree
**blow over** cease, conclude, disappear, dissipate, end, finish, pass, subside, terminate, vanish
**blowpipe analysis** pyrology
**blowpipe missile** dart
**blow the lid off** expose, publish, release, reveal
**blow up** amplify, blast, bloat, bomb, burst, detonate, dilate, distend, enlarge(ment), erupt, exaggerate, expand, explode, fulminate, ignite, magnify, protuberate, rage, swell, tumefy
**blow up a photograph** enlarge
**blow upon** fan, winnow
**blow up with explosives** blast
**blow with a fist** punch
**blow with the open hand** slap
**blowy** windy
**blowzy** blowsy, coarse-looking, florid, frowzy, red-faced, rubicund, ruddy, slatternly, sloppy, tousled, uncombed, unkempt, untidy
**blubber** bawl, bewail, bulk, corpulent, cry, fat, flesh, foam, keen, lament, lard, mewl, obesity, overweight, paunch, snivel, sob, swollen, wail, weep, whimper, whine, whinge
**bludgeon** bat(on), club, cosh, cudgel, stick, truncheon
**bludgeoning** battering
**blue** azure, crestfallen, dejected, depressed, despondent, dispirited, doleful, gloomy, glum, indecent, irreverent, lascivious, lewd, licentious, melancholy, morose, obscene, puritanical, ribald, righteous, rigorous, risqué, sad, sapphire, sky-blue, suggestive, unbending, unhappy
**blue area on map** sea
**blueback salmon** nerka, sauqui, sockeye
**bluebill** broadbill, duck, scaup
**blue blood** aristocrat
**blue-blooded** noble
**Blue Bull country** Northern Transvaal
**blue Canadian cheese** ermite
**blue colour** azure, cerulean, cyan, indigo, sapphire, ultramarine
**blue colouring in plants** anthocyanine

**blue dye** anil, cyanine, indigo, woad
**blue earthenware** Delft
**blue-eyed boy** favourite
**blue falcon** peregrine
**blue garment** mazarine
**blue gem** lazurite, sapphire, sodalite, turquoise
**blue glass** smalt
**blue grass** poa
**Blue Grass state** Kentucky
**blue-green colour** turquoise
**blue-green pigment** bice, leucocyan
**Blue Grotto site** Capri
**blue gum** eucalyptus
**blue jeans** dungarees
**blue jeans material** denim
**blue limestone rich in fossils** lias
**blueness of skin** cyanosis
**blue Pacific shark** mako
**blue pigment** bice, ceruleum, cyanin, marennin, smalt
**blue precious stone** sapphire
**blueprint** design, draft, layout, outline, pattern, plan, project, prototype, scheme, sketch
**blueprint holder** drawing board
**blue shade** cobalt
**blue sky** azure, cerulean, firmament
**blue stocking** bas bleu (F)
**blue-veined cheese** Blaauwkrantz, Stilton
**bluey** swag
**bluff** blunt, cliff, crude, deceit, deceive, delude, direct, fake, feign, frank, fraud, headland, hearty, hill, honest, lie, mislead, open, pretend, rough
**bluish-black element** iodine
**bluish-grey colour** pewter
**bluish-purple** mauve
**bluish-red** magenta
**bluish-white metal** zinc
**bluish-white metallic element** cadmium
**blunder** bêtise, bloomer, botch, bungle, err, error, faux pas, gaffe, goof, indiscretion, mistake, slip
**blunt** abrupt, bluff, brusque, curt, deaden, dim-witted, discourteous, dull(-witted), gruff, harsh, impolite, numb, obtuse, outspoken, rough, rounded, rude, short, stark, thick, uncivil, uncourteous
**blunt-edged fencing sword** foil
**bluntly self-assertive** brash
**blunt refusal** rebuff
**blunt sword** schlager
**blur** befog, blot, confuse, confusion, fog, obscure, smear, smudge
**blurb** adspeak, ad(vert), advertisement, announcement, bill, brief, circular, commendation, commercial, copy, description,

display, hype, notice, placard, plug, poster, promotion, publicity, puff, rave, recommendation, spiel, write-up
**blur by heat** hazy
**blurred** blurry, confused, dim, faint, foggy, fuzzy, hazy, ill-defined, inconspicuous, indistinct, misty, nebulous, smudged, smudgy, unclear, vague
**blurred impression in printing** mackle
**blurred mark** smudge
**blurred vision** bleary
**blurry** misty
**blurt excitedly** splutter
**blurt out** babble, blab, blat, cry, disclose, ejaculate
**blush** colour, crimson, flush, glow, hue, mantle, redden, rosiness, tint
**blusher** rouge
**blushing** erubescent, red, reddening
**bluster** boast, bombast, brag, bragging, bravado, bulldoze, bully, crowing, domineer, hector, rant, roar, storm, strut, swagger, swell, vaunt
**blustering patriot** jingo
**blustery** bad, boisterous, breezy, dirty, disagreeable, foggy, foul, gusty, murky, rainy, rough, squally, stormy, turbulent, wet, wild, windswept, windy
**Blyton character** Noddy
**boa** aboma, anaconda, bom, constrictor, reptile, serpent, snake
**Boadicea's tribe** Iceni
**boa or rattler** reptile, snake
**boar** peccary
**board** accommodate, advisers, batten, beam, cabinet, committee, council, directors, embark, enter, feed, food, lath, lodge, lumber, meals, panel, plank, provisions, rations, salt, sheet, strip, table, tighten, timber, trustees, wood
**board above window** pelmet
**board a plane** enplane
**board a railway coach** entrain
**board a ship** embark
**boarder** lodger, resident, roomer
**board game** backgammon, checkers, chess, draughts, halma, ludo, snakes and ladders
**boarding for horses** livery
**board of directors** directorate
**board public transport** embus
**board rider** surfer, boardsailer
**board's presiding officer** chairperson
**board used in seance** ouija
**board which controls the navy** Admiralty
**boar's tusk** razor

**boast** brag(gadocio), bragging, bravado, crow, exaggerate, exalt, favourite, glorify, parade, praise, pride, self-praise, swagger, triumph, vainglory, vaunt
**boast about** vaunt
**boaster** blow, braggadocio, braggart, cracker, egotist, gascon, jingoist, prater, ruffler, windbag
**boastful** arrogant, blustering, bragging, cocky, conceited, crowing, egotistical, magniloquent, overproud, pompous, pretentious, puffed-up, rodomontade, swaggering, swollen, swollen-headed, vainglorious, vaunting
**boastful behaviour** bravado
**boastful language** magniloquence, rodomontade
**boastful person** egotist
**boastful poltroon** braggart, scaramouch
**boastful talk** bluff, rant, rodomontade
**boasting** aggrandizing, blustering, bragging, crowing, egotistical, exaggerating, exulting, flaunting, jactation, possessing, preening, puffing, strutting, swaggering, vaunting
**boast in triumph** crow
**boast of** blazon
**boat** canoe, catamaran, craft, gondola, ketch, motorboat, sailboat, ship, skiff, steamer, vessel, whaler, yacht
**boat blade** oar
**boat body** hull
**boat bottom** keel
**boat channel marker** buoy
**boat dock** marina
**boater material** straw
**boat frame** hull
**boat hoist** davit
**boating blade** oar
**boating carnival** regatta
**boat like Noah's** ark
**boat moved with foot power** pedalo
**boat on warship** launch, dinghy
**boat on which entertainments are given** show-boat
**boat overturn** capsize
**boat paddle** oar
**boat part** aft, bow, deck, helm, hull, keel, prow, rib, stern, tiller
**boat powered by motor** dory, drifter, gig, hydrofoil, hydroplane, trawler, vedette
**boat powered by sail** catamaran, coble, dhow, dinghy, felucca, gig, hoy, junk, lugger, pinnace, sampan, skiff, sloop
**boat propeller** oar, screw, wheel
**boat race** regatta

**boat-shaped** cymbiform, navicular, scaphoid
**boat-shaped ornamental plate** nef
**boat's helmsman** cox
**boat song** barcarole
**boat's rear** stern
**boat stabiliser** ballast
**boatswain** bo's'n, bo'sun, bosun
**boatswain of a Lascar crew** serang
**boat with twin hulls** catamaran
**bob** bending, bow, caper, curtsy, dance, drift, flit, float, flutter, gambol, glide, hop, inclination, jerk, jolt, jump, leap, nod, obeisance, oscillate, prance, quiver, rebound, rock, sail, shake, shilling, skip, slide, stir, toss, twitch, wave, weave, wobble
**bobbin** braid, cylinder, ratchet, reel, spool
**bobbin pin** spindle
**bobby** constable, cop, peeler
**bob down** duck
**bob head** nod
**bob head in agreement** nod
**bobolink** reedbird, ricebird
**bob one's head** nid-nod
**bob or scut** tail
**bob up** appear, (a)rise, arrive, emerge, materialise, surface
**bobwhite** colin
**bode** augur, forbode, foretell, omen, prophesy, threaten
**bodice bouquet** corsage
**bodice frill** jabot
**bodice of dress** corsage
**bodily** bestial, brutish, carnal, collectively, concrete, corporeal, earthly, en masse, fleshly, gross, incarnate, material, mortal, physical, real, sensual, somatic, substantial, tangible, true, voluptuous, wholly, worldly
**bodily and mental powers** faculty
**bodily discomfort** malaise
**bodily disposition** habitude
**bodily form** figure
**bodily infirmity** invalidity
**bodily manipulation** massage
**bodily sac** cyst
**bodily secretion** sweat, bile
**bodily shape** figure
**bodily structure and development** physique
**bodily suffering** pain
**bodily tissue** flesh
**bodily work** labour
**boding** auguring, betokening, foreboding, foreshadowing, heralding, implying, indicating, portending, predicting, presaging, promising, threatening
**bodkin** awl, eyeleteer, needle, pin

**body** association, band, bulk, cadaver, clique, collection, company, corporation, corpse, density, group, matter, set, society, substance, thickness
**body cavity** atrium, sinus
**body cells** tissue
**body covering** skin
**body duct** vas
**body framework** skeleton
**body in solar system** comet, moon, planet, satellite, sun
**body joint** hip
**body manipulation** massage, rub
**body member** limb
**body nearly a sphere in shape** spheroid
**body of aircraft** fuselage
**body of an arrow** shaft, stele
**body of armed Indian tribesmen** lashkar
**body of associates** fellowship
**body of attendants accompanying important people** retinue
**body of bishops** episcopacy
**body of black warriors** impi
**body of books accepted as genuine** canon
**body of burning gas** flame
**body of church** nave
**body of delegates** delegation
**body of deputies** legation
**body of dismantled ship** hulk
**body of electors** electorate
**body of employees** personnel
**body of epic poetry** epos
**body of experts** panel
**body of flowing water** river
**body of followers** sect
**body of human being embalmed for burial** mummy
**body of instrumental performers** orchestra
**body of investigators** committee
**body of Jewish law** Talmud, Torah
**body of Jewish law in Mishnah** Halachah
**body of judges** bench
**body of laws** code
**body of lawyers** bar
**body of laymen** laity
**body of members** membership
**body of men** posse
**body of Muslim scholars** ulema
**body of myths** mythology
**body of nobles** aristocracy
**body of persons associated in some enterprise** syndicate
**body of poetry** epos
**body of professors of a university** professoriate
**body of retainers** retinue

**body of salt water** sea
**body of servicemen** unit
**body of ship** hull
**body of ships** fleet
**body of soldiers** army, battalion, company, militia, platoon, regiment, squad, troop
**body of students** class
**body of supporters** backing
**body of three dimensions** solid
**body of traditions relating to Mohammed** Hadith
**body of troops** corps, force
**body of voters** electorate
**body of voters who elect a representative** constituency
**body of water** dam, lagoon, lake, ocean, pond, pool, sea
**body of workers** staff
**body of Zulu warriors** impi
**body organ** ear, eye, gland, heart, kidney, liver, lung, spleen, tongue
**body organs** viscera
**body part** arm, foot, hip, leg, organ
**body-plated animal** armadillo
**body powder** talc(um)
**body preserved after death** mummy
**body proportions** build
**body pump** heart
**body revolving around a planet** satellite
**body rubber** masseur, masseuse
**body science** anatomy
**body search** frisk
**body servant** maid, valet
**body that attracts** magnet
**body trunk** torso
**Boer uncle** oom
**boffin** expert, pundit, scientist
**bog** fen, marsh(land), mire, morass, muskeg, quag(mire), sink, slough, sog, swamp, wetlands
**bog down** delay, deluge, halt, hinder, impede, overwhelm, retard, sink, stall, stick
**bogeyman** ogre, tokoloshe
**bog fuel** peat
**boggle** gape, gawk, marvel, stare, wonder
**boggy area** mire
**boggy hollow** slack
**boggy land** fen, moor
**boggy marsh** morass, quag, quagmire
**boggy place** quag
**bogle** bugbear, hobgoblin, phantom, scarecrow, spectre
**bog marsh** mire
**bog product** moss, peat
**bogus** artificial, counterfeit, dummy, fake, false, forged, fraudulent, imitation, phoney, sham, snide, spurious, unauthentic

**Bohemian dance** redowa
**boil** abscess, agitate, blain, blister, brew, bubble, carbuncle, churn, cook, effervesce, erupt, explode, fizz, foam, froth, fulminate, fume, furuncle, gumboil, gurgle, inflammation, papule, parboil, percolate, pimple, pustule, rage, rant, rave, roar, seethe, simmer, sizzle, smoulder, steam, stew, storm, tumour, ulcer, wallop
**boil and partly cook** parboil
**boil down** abridge, abstract, concentrate, condense, decrease, denote, designate, digest, distil(l), reduce, shorten, signify, summarise
**boiled down** condensed
**boiled rice** canin, kanin
**boiled sweet on stick** lollipop
**boiled sweet with sharp taste** acid drop
**boil gently** simmer
**boiling** angry, blistering, ebullient, enraged, fuming, incensed, indignant, infuriated, roasting, scorching
**boiling mad** raging
**boiling process** ebullition
**boil on eyelid** sty(e)
**boil partly** parboil
**boil slowly** simmer, stew
**boils water** kettle
**boil very briefly** blanch
**boil with rage** seethe
**boisterous** clamorous, noisy, randy, roaring, rough, stormy, tempestuous, tumultuous, turbulent, unrestrained, uproarious, wild
**boisterous activity** hurly-burly
**boisterous cry** outcry, roar
**boisterous gale** snorter
**boisterous knockabout comedy** slapstick
**boisterous laugh** guffaw
**boisterously** bouncily, clamorously, impetuously, loudly, noisily, riotously, rowdily, rumbustiously, unrestrainedly, uproariously, vociferously, wildly
**boisterously jovial** rollicking
**boisterously merry** hilarious
**boisterous play** horseplay
**boke** belch, boak, bock, burp, retch, vomit
**bold** abrupt, adventurous, audacious, brash, brassy, brave, brazen, bright, colourful, conspicuous, courageous, daring, dauntless, defiant, direct, doughty, enterprising, evident, eye-catching, fearless, flashy, forward, foursquare, gallant, heroic, immodest, impudent, insolent,

intrepid, lively, loud, obvious, presumptuous, prominent, pushing, resolute, rude, saucy, spirited, stout, striking, strong, undaunted, valiant, valorous, vivid
**bold and free** mod
**bold and speedy** audax et celer (L)
**bold colour** red
**bold exploit** adventure
**bold feat** exploit
**bold fellow** hearty
**bold girl** hoiden, hoyden
**boldly** adventurously, audaciously, brightly, conspicuously, courageously, daringly, fearlessly, gallantly, heroically, intrepidly, loudly, prominently, strongly, vividly
**boldness** adventurousness, audacity, braveness, bravery, brightness, courage(ousness), fearlessness, gallantness, heroicness, liveliness, loudness, nerve, resoluteness, spiritedness, stalwartness, temerity, valiantness, valour, vividness
**boldness of cheek** nerve
**bold undertaking** adventure, enterprise
**bole** trunk
**bolero** dance, jacket, music
**Bolivian currency** centavo, peso, tomin
**Bolivian money** peso
**Bolivian volcano** Ollague
**bollard** mooring-post
**Bologna sausage** baloney, boloney, polony
**bolognese pasta** spaghetti
**boloney** baloney, humbug, nonsense
**Bolshevik** Red
**bolster** aid, assist, brace, buttress, confirm, corroborate, cushion, harden, mainstay, maintain, pillow, prop, reinforce, shore, stay, strengthen, support, sustain, truss, uphold
**bolt** arrow, blurt, dart, depart, fasten(er), investigate, latch, pin, purify, rivet, screen, screw, stopper, stud
**bolt fastener** nut, toggle
**bolt from the blue** blow
**bolt of a door** snib
**bolt tightener** spanner
**bolt together** rivet
**bombard** abuse, assail, assault, attack, batter, blitz, bomb, destroy, fusillade, lash, pelt, raid, revile, shell, storm. charge, strafe, strike, torpedo
**bombardment with artillery** stonk
**bombastic** bloated, declamatory, euphuistic, flowery, fustian, grandiloquent, grandiose, high-flown, inflated, magniloquent, pompous, rhetorical, sonorous, turgid, verbose, windy, wordy
**bombastic behaviour** grandeur
**bombastic speechmaking** bunkum
**bomber** warplane
**bomb fragments** shrapnel
**bomb heavily** saturate
**bomb hole** crater
**bombinate** hum
**bombproof chamber** casemate, shelter
**bombs, guns, etc.** ammo, ammunition
**bomb shards** shrapnel
**bomb splinters** shrapnel
**bomb thrower** terrorist
**bomb thrown by hand** grenade
**bona fide** actual, authentic, genuine, honest, lawful, legal, legitimate, real, true, valid
**bona fides** sincerity
**bond** affinity, affliation, agreement, association, attachment, band, bind(ing), bondage, captivity, cement, chains, compact, connect(ion), constraint, contract, covenant, fasten(ing), fetters, fuse, glue, gum, knot, ligament, ligature, link, mortgage, nexus, obligation, pact, paste, pledge, promise, relation, restriction, seal, security, shackle, tie, transaction, union, unite, word
**bondage** captivity, confinement, control, enslavement, enthralment, imprisonment, incarceration, indenture, oppression, peonage, prison, restraint, serfdom, servitude, slavery, subjection, subjugation, subservience, thralldom, vassalage, yoke
**bond or union** liaison
**bondsman** slave
**bone** clavicle, femur, fillet, os(so) (I), osteo-, patella, rib, spine, ulna, vertebra
**bone at end of spine** coccyx, sacrum
**bone at finger joint** knuckle
**bone behind ear** mastoid
**bone-break** fracture
**bone cavity** anthrum, sinus
**bone centre** marrow
**bone covering** periosteum
**bone disease** rickets
**bone doctor** osteopath
**boned steak cut off sirloin** entrecôte
**bone in foot** tarsus
**bone in forearm** radius, ulna
**bone in the ankle** talus, tarsus
**bone in the ear** anvil, incus
**bone in the skull** vomer
**boneless meat salted and dried in strips** biltong
**boneless piece of meat** fillet
**bone manipulator** osteopath
**bone marrow** medulla
**bone of forearm** radius, ulna
**bone of leg** femur, tibia
**bone of the head** cranium, skull
**bone of the heel** calcaneum
**bone of the rump** aitchbone
**bone of the upper arm** humerus
**bone of the wrist** carpal
**bone on outer side of lower leg** fibula
**bone photo** roentgenogram, röntgenogram, X-ray
**bone-scraper** xyster
**bones enclosing the brain** cranium, skull
**bone-setter** orthopaedist, osteopath
**bones forming hips** pelvis
**bones in ear** stapes
**bones of an animal** skeleton
**bones of the foot** metatarsi
**bone structure** skeleton
**bone tissue** marrow, medulla
**bone turquoise** odontolite
**bonfire** beacon, beam, blaze, fire, flame, flare, lighthouse, sign, signal, watchtower
**bonnet of car** hood
**bonny** beautiful, comely, fine, good, handsome, lively, merry
**bonus** benefit, bounty, dividend, extra, gift, honorarium, premium, reward
**bon vivant (F)** gourmand
**bony** angular, attenuated, cadaverous, emaciated, gaunt, haggard, indurated, lank(y), lean, meagre, osseous, rangy, sclerous, scraggy, skinny, slender, thin, wiry
**bony arch of cheek** yoke-bone, zygoma
**bony case of head** cranium, skull
**bony cavity at base of human trunk** pelvis
**bony enlargement** spavin
**bony fish** carp, shad, teleost
**bony framework** skeleton
**bony framework of head** skull, cranium
**bony outgrowth** antler
**bony-plated burrowing mammal** armadillo
**booby trap** ambush, pitfall
**boodle** buddle, caboodle, crowd, graft, loot, noodle, plunder, swag
**book** edition, engage, record, reserve, schedule, tome, volume
**bookbinder's workshop** bindery
**bookbinding** bibliopegy
**bookbinding stamp** block, fillet
**book collector** bibliophile
**book containing the service of the Mass** missal

**book containing various literary compositions** anthology, miscellany
**book cover** binding, case, jacket
**book custodian** librarian
**book edge** tranche
**book extract** excerpt
**book for child** primer, reader
**book for photographs** album
**book for studying** textbook
**book in advance** reserve
**booking** bespeaking, billing, chartering, engaging, organising, reservation, reserving, scheduling
**book introduction** foreword, preface, prelude, proem, prologue
**bookkeeper** accountant
**bookkeeping** accountancy
**bookkeeping book** ledger
**bookkeeping entry** credit, debit, item
**bookkeeping term** post
**book leaf** page
**book-length story** novel
**booklet giving performance proceedings** programme
**booklet on some special subject** monograph
**book list** bibliography
**booklouse** psocid
**book-lover** bibliophile
**bookmaker** bookie, printer
**bookmaker's enclosure** ring
**book name** title
**book of accounts** ledger
**book of daily prayers** breviary
**book of extracts** anthology
**book of fiction** novel
**book of hymns** hymnal
**book of Icelandic poems** Edda
**book of Jewish Law** Mishnah, Talmud, Torah
**book of many factual topics** encyclopaedia
**book of maps** atlas
**book of New Testament** Acts, Colossians, Corinthians, Ephesians, Galatians, Hebrews, James, John, Jude, Luke, Mark, Matthew, Peter, Philemon, Philippians, Revelation, Romans, Thessalonians, Timothy, Titus
**book of Old Testament** Amos, Chronicles, Daniel, Deuteronomy, Ecclesiastes, Esther, Exodus, Ezekiel, Ezra, Genesis, Habakkuk, Haggai, Hosea, Isaiah, Jeremiah, Job, Joel, Jonah, Joshua, Judges, Kings, Lamentations, Leviticus, Malachi, Micah, Nahum, Nehemiah, Numbers, Obadiah, Proverbs, Psalms, Ruth, Samuel, Solomon, Zacharia, Zephaniah

**book of Pentateuch** Deuteronomy, Exodus, Genesis, Leviticus, Numbers
**book of personal comments** diary
**book of prayers** missal
**book of priest** breviary
**book of psalms** psalter
**book of Revelations** Apocalypse
**book of the Apocrypha** Esdras
**book of the gospel** John, Luke, Mark, Matthew
**Book of Tobit** Apocrypha
**book of words** dictionary, thesaurus
**book of words of an opera** libretto
**book page** folio
**book part** appendix, chapter, index, leaf, page, preface, section
**book pedlar** colporteur
**book presenting a specialised vocabulary** thesaurus
**book producer** printer, publisher
**book published every year** annual
**book rack** shelf
**book recited at Seder** Haggadah
**book salesman** colporteur
**book section** chapter
**bookseller** bibliopolist
**bookselling** bibliopoly
**book sheet** page
**book's introduction** foreword, preface, proem, prologue
**books of Moses** Pentateuch
**book used by priest** breviary
**book used in church** Bible, hymnal, hymnbook
**book user** reader
**boom** advance, bang, blast, burst, crash, crash, develop, expand, expansion, explode, flourish, gain, grow(th), increase, prosper, reverberate, roar, rumble, spurt, succeed, swell, thunder, upsurge
**boomerang** backfire, kiley, kylie, rebound, recoil, return, reverse, ricochet
**booming** aroar, orotund
**boon** advantage, asset, benefaction, benefit, benevolence, blessing, donation, favour, gift, godsend, grant, gratification, gratuity, jolly, jovial, kindness, merry, present, windfall
**boor** barbarian, brute, cad, churl, clod, farmer, gawk, looby, lout, oaf, peasant, rustic, swain
**boorish** asinine, bovine, brutish, clownish, coarse, crabbed, crass, crude, dense, doltish, foul-mouthed, gruff, harsh, ill-tempered, impolite, indecent, insensitive, lewd, loutish, morose, oafish, obscene, obtuse, rough, rude, smutty, stupid, sullen, surly, tactless, tasteless, uncivil, uncouth, uncultivated, ungentlemanly, unmannerly, unrefined, vulgar
**boorish person** clown
**boost** advocate, aid, animate, assistance, commend, elevate, encourage, enlargement, expansion, facilitate, heave, help, hoist, improvement, inspire, lift, magnification, praise, promote, promotion, raise, recommend(ation), sanction, shove, support, thrust, upgrade
**booster** supercharger
**boot** drive, eject, kick, knock, oust, sack, shove
**boot front** toe
**booth** bay, closet, coop, counter, covering, cubby, cubicle, enclosure, kiosk, outhouse, protection, shack, shed, shelter, stall, stand, table, tent, wigwam
**Booth's church** Salvation Army
**bootlick** grovel, toady
**boot out** bounce
**boots for fishing** waders
**booty** haul, loot, pillage, plunder, prey
**booze** alcohol, drink, grog
**bop** hit, jive, strike
**borax** tincal
**Bordeaux wine** claret
**border** abut, adjoin, append, approach, borderline, boundary, bound(s), brim, brink, circumference, confine, connect, demarcation, edge, edging, flank, frame, fringe, frontier, hem, join, limit(s), line, margin, nearing, outpost, perimeter, periphery, rim, selvage, side, skirt, surround, trim(ming), valance, verge
**border around a shield** orle
**border for a picture** frame, mat
**bordering on the sea** maritime
**borderline** ambivalent, doubtful, edge, indecisive, indefinite, inexact, marginal, unclassifiable
**borderline case** dilemma, predicament, trouble
**border of cloth** hem
**border of land near sea** coast
**border of surface** margin
**border on** abut, adjoin, approach, approximate, connect, contact, echo, impinge, join, march, match, resemble, touch
**bore** annoy(ance), bind, bother, breadth, bug, burrow, calibre, countermine, diameter, drag, drill, dullard, dullness, eager, eagre, excavate, exhaust, fatigue, gouge, headache, hole, hollow, irk, irritate, irritation, jade, mine, nuisance,

**bore a hole**                94                **bound**

penetrate, perforate, pest(er), pierce, puncture, sap, sink, stomached, tedium, tire(some), trepan, trial, trouble, tunnel, undermine, vex(ation), wave, weary, worry
**bore a hole**   drill
**boreal**   arctic, cold, frosty, glacial, icy, northerly, northern, wintry
**Boreal area**   north
**bored by excess**   blasé
**boredom**   apathy, disinterest, dispassion, dreariness, dullness, ennui, impassivity, lethargy, listlessness, monotony, repetition, schedule, sluggishness, tedium, unconcern
**bored with pleasure**   blasé
**borer**   auger, shipworm
**boric acid salt**   borate
**boring**   bothering, dead, dreary, drilling, dry, dull, exhausting, flat, humdrum, insipid, mining, monotonous, piercing, prosaic, routine, sinking, stale, tedious, tiresome, tiring, troubling, unexciting, uninteresting, unvaried, wearisome
**boring aid**   bit
**boring and wordy**   verbose
**boring implement**   auger, awl, bit, brace, broach, drill, gimlet, trepan
**boringly routine**   mundane
**boring piece of tool**   bit
**boring routine**   tedium
**boring task**   fag
**boring tool**   auger, awl, bit, brace, broach, drill, gimlet, trepan
**born**   delivered, innate, intuitive, natural, née
**born after the death of the father**   posthumous
**born again**   renascent
**born, as a woman's maiden name**   née
**born dead**   stillborn
**Bornean sultanate**   Brunei
**borne by oaks**   acorn
**born fool**   mooncalf
**born in a particular place**   native
**born of parents married to each other**   legitimate
**born of the same mother**   uterine
**born out of wedlock**   illegitimate
**born under the sign of the Ram**   Arian
**born with no or partial brain**   anencephalic
**borough of London**   Chelsea, Clapham, Highbury, Kensington, Lambeth, Limehouse, Westminster
**borough of New York City**   Bronx, Brooklyn, Manhattan, Queens, Staten Island
**borrow**   acquire, adopt, appropriate, cadge, copy, filch, imitate, lend,

obtain, pilfer, pirate, scrounge, simulate, take, use, usurp
**boscage**   boskage, forest, grove, shaw, thicket, woods
**bosh**   folly, humbug, nonsense, rubbish, tosh
**bo'sun**   boatswain
**bosom**   affection, breast, bust, chest, close, confidential, heart, intimate
**bosom friend**   chum, pal
**bosom of one's family**   hearth
**boss**   administrator, captain, chaperone, chief, command, control, director, employer, executive, famous, foreman, gaffer, governor, head(man), hirer, knob, leader, manager, master, nub, overseer, owner, point, protuberance, stud, superintendent, supervise, supervisor, supremo, tip
**boss around**   browbeat, bulldoze, bully, dominate, domineer, oppress, order, overbear, tyrannise
**boss on a shield**   umbo
**bossy**   arrogant, despotic, dictatorial, domineering, tyrannical
**botanical sucker**   sobole
**botany**   algology
**botch**   blunder, bungle, butcher, cobble, fail, failure, fumble, goof, hash, mar, mend, spoil
**botfly**   maggot
**both**   alike, equally
**bother**   ado, ail, annoy, baffle, bewilder, bore, burden, chafe, confuse, disturb, fret, fuss, harass, hector, hinder, irk, irritate, mock, molest, nag, nuisance, perturb, pester, plague, provoke, taunt, tease, to-do, torment, trouble, tweak, vex(ation), worry
**bothersome person**   nuisance
**both handed**   ambidextrous
**Botswana currency**   pula
**Botswana desert**   Kalahari
**Botswana lake**   Dow, Ngami
**Botswana saltpan**   Makgadikgadi
**Botswana swamp**   Chobe, Okavango
**bottle**   carafe, enclose, flagon, flask, jar, vessel, vial
**bottlebrush-like shrub**   banksia
**bottle cap remover**   opener
**bottle containing two quarts of wine or spirits**   magnum
**bottle for oil**   cruet, flask
**bottle for vinegar**   cruet
**bottle nipple**   teat
**bottlenosed dolphin**   porpoise
**bottle of leather**   olpe
**bottles box**   crate
**bottle size**   Jeroboam, magnum, pint, quart

**bottle stopper**   cork
**bottle top**   cap
**bottle up**   check, conceal, contain, curb, enclose, hide, impede, inhibit, quell, restrain, restrict, suppress, trap
**bottom**   base, basic, basis, bottomless, buttocks, elementary, essence, essentials, extremity, floor, foot, foundation, fundamental, ground, inferior, last, lowest, nadir, pedestal, principle, prop, seat, stay, substratum, support, underpart, underside, understructure
**bottom edge of skirt**   hem
**bottomless**   abysmal, boundless, deep, fathomless, infinite, unlimited
**bottomless chasm**   abyss
**bottomless pit**   Abaddon
**bottom line**   minimum
**bottom of an animal's foot**   pad
**bottom of a ship**   bilge
**bottom of a statue**   base
**bottom of boat**   keel
**bottom of foot**   sole
**bottom of shaft in which water collects**   sump
**bottom of ship**   keel
**bottom of ship's hull**   bilge
**bottom of the sea**   bed
**bottom of wall**   dado
**bottom surface**   floor
**boudoir**   bedroom, chamber, closet, retreat, sanctum
**boudoir item**   bed
**boudoir linen**   bedclothes
**bough**   arm, branch, corsage, department, division, limb, offshoot, prong, ramification, section, sector, shoot, spray, sprig
**bought or sold second-hand**   used
**boulder**   greywether, rock, sarsen, stone
**boulder clay**   till
**boulevard**   avenue, circle, concourse, drive, parkway, roadway, strip, terrace, thoroughfare
**bounce**   bob, bound, caper, dap, energy, gambol, hurdle, jump, leap, lunge, prance, rebound, recoil, resile, resilience, romp, snap, vault, vitality, vivacity
**bounce a stone over water**   skim
**bounce back**   rebound, recoil, resile
**bouncer**   bumper
**bouncing movement**   bob
**bound**   adjoin, advance, ambit, bandaged, base, bob, border, bounce, boundary, caper, case, certain, chained, committed, compelled, confine, constrained, costive, curvet, dance, destined, doomed, fastened, fated, fixed, forced, frisk, frolic, gambol, held,

**hop**, hurdle, jump, leap, liable, limit, lope, lunge, obliged, pounce, prance, rebound, required, restrained, restricted, secured, skip, spring, sure, tied, vault
**boundary** barrier, border(line), bounds, brink, confines, edge, extremity, fringe, frontier, limit, march, margin, pale, perimeter, precinct, rim
**boundary line of region** edge
**boundary of a circle** circumference
**boundary score in cricket** four, six
**bound by a vow** votary
**bounder** blackyard, cad, churl, cur, dastard, knave, miscreant, rascal, rogue, rotter, scoundrel, swine, villain, wretch
**bound in gratitude** beholden
**boundless** constant, countless, endless, eternal, everlasting, extensive, immense, infinite, limitless, measureless, permanent, unbounded, undetermined, unending, unlimited, unrestricted, untold, vast
**bounds** borders, boundaries, confines, edge, limitation, limits, outskirts, scope
**bound to happen** inevitable
**bound to loose** on a hiding to nothing
**bounteous** liberal
**bountiful** abrim, abundant, altruistic, ample, beneficent, charitable, copious, exuberant, fat, free, generous, giving, good, kind, lavish, liberal, munificent, open-handed, plenteous, plentiful, princely, prolific, rich, teeming, unstinting
**bounty** aid, almsgiving, assistance, beneficence, benevolence, bestowal, bonus, charity, contribution, donation, generosity, gift, grace, grant, gratuity, help, honorarium, kindness, largess(e), liberality, loot, munificence, offering, rebate, relief, reward, subsidy, subvention, succour, tip, tribute
**bouquet** admiration, air, aroma, atmosphere, aura, batch, boutonnière, breath, bunch, bundle, character, clump, cluster, collection, commendation, complexion, compliment, congratulations, corsage, courtesy, emanation, essence, eulogy, favour, fragrance, heap, lot, mass, nose(gay), odour, parcel, perfume, pile, posy, quantity, redolence, savour, scent, sheaf, smell, spirit, spray, stack, trace, trail, tuft
**bouquet holder** vase

**bout** battle, contest, course, encounter, engagement, fit, match, spell, struggle, turn
**bout of excessive indulgence** binge
**bout of pleasure** fling
**bovid mammal** goat
**bovine** asinine, awkward, boorish, calf, clumsy, coarse, cow(like), dense, dim, doltish, dull(-witted), gross, heavy, hulking, insensitive, obtuse, ox, ponderous, retarded, sluggish, stolid, stupid, unrefined, unresponsive, unwieldy
**bovine animal** anoa, bison, bull, cow, neat, ox, steer, yak, zebu
**bovine cry** moo
**bovine hide** calfskin
**bovine mamma** udder
**bovine mammals** cattle
**bovine's foot** hoof
**bovine with long horns and long shaggy hair** yak
**bow** arc, arch(er), arcuation, bend, camber, convexity, crossbow, curvature, curve, depress, inflect, longbow, nod, parabola, prow, rainbow, sling, stoop, subdue, submit, swerve, trimming, turn, twist, vault, warp, weapon, yield
**bow and arrow user** archer
**bow and scrape** bootlick, court, grovel, kowtow
**bowdlerise** censor, expurgate
**bow down** curts(e)y, kneel
**bow down before** idolise, kowtow, submit
**bowed stringed instrument** cello
**bowels** belly, entrails, gut(s), innards, inside(s), interior, intestines, inwards, penetralia, stomach, viscera, vitals
**bower** abode, alcove, anchor, arbour, ark, asylum, boudoir, cable, cottage, dwelling, greenhouse, grot(to), haven, knave, mew, pavilion, pergola, recess, refuge, retreat, sanctuary, shack, shanty, shelter, surround
**bowfin** amia, morgay, mudfish
**bowl** basin, dish, hurl, revolve, rotate, vase, vessel, whirl
**bowled** out
**bow-legged** bandy
**bowler hat** billycock
**bowl game** championship, play-off, tournament
**bowlike curve** arc(h)
**bowl in cricket** googly, swerve, yorker
**bowling alley** lane
**bowling game** ninepin, tenpin
**bowling green** rink
**bowling lane** alley

**bowling pin** ninepin, skittle
**bowling score** spare, strike
**bowling spell** over
**bowling target** pin
**bowling term** gutter, spare, split, strike
**bowling unit** alley
**bowl of volcano** crater
**bowl over** amaze, astonish, astound, dum(b)found, fell, flabbergast, floor, stagger, startle, stun, surprise, topple, unbalance
**bowman** archer
**bowman's sport** archery
**bow missile** arrow
**bow of ship** head, prow, stern
**bow out** abandon, resign, retire, withdraw
**bow's partner** arrow, quiver
**bow sport** archery
**bow the head** nod
**bow to** adore, submit
**bow wood** yew
**box** carton, case, container, crate, enclose, fight, hit, package, spar, strike, trap
**boxer** fighter, heavyweight, lightweight, middleweight, prizefighter, pugilist, sparrer
**boxer's attendant** second
**boxer's grappling hold** clinch
**boxer's weight** bantam, feather, fly, heavy, light, middle, welter
**boxer who leads with his left** southpaw
**box for alms** arca
**box for baking porcelain** saggar, sagger
**box for bottles** crate
**box for holding tea** canister
**box for keeping cigars moist** humidor
**box for shipping** container, crate, encase
**box holding ship's compass** binnacle
**box in** cage, confine, enclose, trap
**boxing attendant** second
**boxing blow** jab, punch, upper-cut
**boxing code** Queensbury rules
**boxing contest** bout, match
**boxing division** bantam, feather, fly, heavy, light, middle, welter
**boxing match** bout, fight
**boxing ring** arena
**boxing victory** KO, TKO
**boxing-weight with upper limit of 51 kg** flyweight
**boxing-weight with upper limit of 54 kg** bantamweight
**boxing-weight with upper limit of 57 kg** featherweight
**boxing weight with upper limit of 60 kg** lightweight

**boxing-weight with upper limit of 67 kg** welterweight
**boxing-weight with upper limit of 75 kg** middleweight
**boxing win** knockout
**box in theatre** loge
**box lightly** spar
**boxlike pen for rabbits** hutch
**box of cutlery** canteen
**box-shaped, 13-stringed Japanese instrument** koto
**box used for sacred utensils** cist
**boy** assistant, lad, lightie, servant, son, stripling, youngster, youth
**boy attendant** page
**boycott** avoid, ban, bar, blackball, blacklist, cold-shoulder, disallow, embargo, exclude, ignore, interdiction, ostracise, outlaw, prohibit(ion), proscribe, refuse, reject, shun, spurn, stayway
**boyfriend** admirer, beau, escort, follower, lover, suitor, swain, sweetheart
**boy in blue** sailor
**boy's brimless hat** cap
**Boy Scout rally** jamboree
**boy servant** page
**braaivleis** barbecue
**brace** bandage, bind, bolster, buckle, clamp, clasp, clincher, couple, coupling, cramp, cure, dyad, fastener, fortify, hasp, invigorate, pair, prop, reinforce(ment), secure, squeeze, stay, steady, steel, stimulate, strap, strengthen, strut, support, tighten, truss, two(some), vice
**brace and bit** drill
**braced framework** trestle
**bracelet** armband, armlet, bangle
**bracer** stimulant
**brachial part** forearm
**bracing** brisk, crisp, exhilarating, fortifying, invigorating, refreshing, restorative, reviviscent, roborant, salubrious, stimulating, strengthening, tonic
**bracing air** ozone
**bracket** affix, buttress, cantilever, category, clasp, classification, clip, console, couple, coupling, genus, grouping, harness, order, parenthesis, pinion, prop, staple, subdivision, support
**bracket supporting the weight of a wooden arched roof** hammerbeam
**bracket to hold door** hinge
**brad** nail
**brag** bluff, bluster, boast, bombast, braggadocio, crow, enhance, exaggerate, overstate, prate, puff,
rodomontade, roister, self-praise, swagger, vapour, vaunt
**braggadocio** boaster, braggart, bravado, snorter, windbag
**braggart** bigmouth, blowhard, bluffer, blusterer, boaster, brag(gadocio), bragger, coxcomb, fop, gascon, ruffler, skite, snorter, strutter, swaggerer, windbag, windgat
**braid** coil, curl, embroider, entwine, frill, interlace, interweave, intwine, knot, lace, loop, plait, pleat, ravel, thread, trim, twill, twist, weave
**braid of hair** plait
**brain** acuity, acumen, alertness, aptitude, encephalon, genius, highbrow, intellect(ual), intelligence, mentality, mind, prodigy, reason, sagacity, savvy, wisdom
**brain box** cranium, skull
**brain-canal passage** iter
**brainchild** creation
**brain disability** mental handicap
**brain doctor** neuro-surgeon
**brain fever** encephalitis, meningitis, phrenitis
**brain groove** sulcus
**braininess** aptitude, brainpower, intellect, intelligence, mentality, sagacity, wisdom
**brain matter** alba
**brain membrane** tela
**brain membrane infection** meningitis
**brain nerve layers** alvei
**brain photo** scan
**brains** capacity, intellect, intelligence, mind, reason, sagacity, sense, shrewdness, wit
**brainstorm** confusion, idea
**brain surgery** lobotomy
**brain tumour** encephaloma, glioma
**brainwash** indoctrinate
**brainwave** idea, thought
**brainy** bright, brilliant, clever, intelligent, smart
**brake part** drum, lining, shoe
**bramble** blackberry-bush
**bramblelike shrub** caper
**bramble plant** briar, furze, gorse, thorn
**Bram Stoker's batman** Dracula
**bran** semels
**branch** arm, bough, department, divide, limb, member, offshoot, part, portion, subdivision, tributary
**branched appendage** horn
**branches of the windpipe** bronchi
**branch formation** deliquescence
**branch growing from main stem** offshoot
**branching widely** divaricate, forked
**branch of a tree** bough
**branch of government** executive
**branch of horn** antler
**branch of Islam** Sunni
**branch of knowledge** science
**branch of learning** art
**branch of linguistics** semantics
**branch of mathematics** algebra
**branch of medicine concerned with the ear** otology
**branch of medicine concerned with epidemics** epidemiology
**branch of medicine dealing with childbirth** obstetrics
**branch of metaphysics dealing with the nature of being** ontology
**branch of meteorology concerned with rainfall** ombrology
**branch of philosophy dealing with the nature of being** ontology
**branch of physics relating to humidity** hygrology
**branch of science** bionics
**branch of the Rhine** Ijssel, Lek, Maas
**branch of the sea** arm
**branch of tree** limb, offshoot
**branch of zoology dealing with birds** ornithology
**branch of Zulu tribe** Matabele
**branch out** broaden, develop, diversify, enlarge, expand, extend, increase, multiply, proliferate, ramify, vary
**branch that strikes root** stolon
**brand** dishonour, label, make, mark, sear, stigma, taint, trademark, tradename, variety
**brandish** display, disport, exhibit, flap, flourish, jerk, parade, raise, shake, strut, swagger, swing, vaunt, wag, wave, wield
**brandy** cognac, eau de vie
**brandy and egg liqueur** advocaat
**brandy and soda** peg
**brandy from grape pomace** marc
**brash** audacious, cheeky, cocky, impudent, impulsive, rash, reckless, rude
**brass** trombone
**brass and tortoiseshell inlay** boul(l)e
**brassard** armband, armlet
**brass constituent** zinc
**brass instrument** bugle, cornet, (sax)horn, saxophone, trombone, trumpet, tuba
**brass instrument like small trumpet** bugle
**brass section player** cornettist
**brassy** blatant, brazen, grating, harsh, jangling, noisy, obtrusive, pert, raucous, saucy, showy
**brat** baby, child, descendant, gamin, imp, infant, issue, juvenile, kid,

lightie, minor, offspring, progeny,
  toddler, tot, urchin, waif, youngster
**bravado** bluster, boasting, bombast,
  brag(gadocio), swaggering
**brave** audacious, bold(-spirit),
  challenge, chivalrous, confident,
  courageous, dare(devil), daring,
  dashing, dauntless, defy, face,
  fearless, gallant, game, hard,
  hero(ic), impetuous, indomitable,
  intrepid, manly, plucky, splendid,
  unafraid, undaunted, valiant,
  valorous, venturesome, virile, warrior
**brave act** deed
**brave conduct** heroism
**brave knight** preux chevalier (F)
**bravely** boldly, courageously, daringly,
  fearlessly, gallantly, heroically,
  intrepidly, pluckily, resolutely,
  valiantly
**brave man** hero
**bravery** audacity, boldness, chivalry,
  courage, daring, dauntlessness,
  élan, fearlessness, gallantry,
  heroism, intrepidity, ostentation,
  pluck, prowess, splendour, tenacity,
  valour, virility, willpower
**bravery award** medal
**brave's wife** squaw
**bravo** assassin, desperado, olé, ruffian
**brawl** affray, altercation, argue,
  argument, bicker, clamour,
  commotion, disagree(ment),
  disorder, dispute, disturbance, fight,
  fracas, fray, mêlée, quarrel, row,
  rumpus, scrap, shemozzle, shindy,
  squabble, tumult, wrangle
**brawler** breaker, fighter, scrambler,
  scrapper, squabbler
**brawn** force, heftiness, meat, might,
  muscle, muscularity, physique,
  power, sinew, strength, vitality
**brawny** able, athletic, beefy, burly,
  hard, hefty, husky, mighty, muscled,
  muscular, potent, robust, rugged,
  sinewy, solid, stalwart, staunch,
  strapping, strong, sturdy, thewy,
  tough, wiry
**bray of donkey** hee-haw
**brazen** audacious, barefaced, blatant,
  bold, brash, brass(y), coppery,
  daring, defiant, flagrant, forward,
  golden, impudent, indecent, insolent,
  loud-mouthed, metallic, metalline,
  outspoken, shameless, unashamed,
  unseemly
**brazen act** effrontery
**brazen impudence** effrontery
**brazen woman** hussy
**Brazil forest** camass, glade
**Brazilian ant** tucandera
**Brazilian armadillo** tat(o)u

**Brazilian city** Belem, Belo Horizonte,
  Brasilia, Campos, Curitiba, Manaus,
  Porto Alegre, Recife, Rio de Janeiro,
  Salvador, Sao Paulo
**Brazilian dance** bossa nova, carioca,
  maxixe, samba
**Brazilian drink** assai
**Brazilian duck** muscovy
**Brazilian estuary** Para
**Brazilian game bird** guan
**Brazilian grassland** campo
**Brazilian island** Cardoso, Comprida,
  Maraca, Mexiana
**Brazilian lake** Aima, Feia, Mirim
**Brazilian monkey** sai
**Brazilian palm** carnauba
**Brazilian parrot** ara
**Brazilian port** Bahia, Belem, Natal,
  Para, Pelotas, Rio, Salvador, Santos
**Brazilian product** coffee, nuts, rubber
**Brazilian rubber** caucho
**Brazilian snake** jararaca
**Brazilian soccer star** Bebeto, Müller,
  Pele, Romario, Socrates
**Brazilian state** Ceara
**Brazilian tree** anda, apa, arariba,
  brauna, dali, gomavel, guarabu,
  icaca, ucuuba, wallaba
**Brazilian waterfall** Glass, Iguassu,
  Iguazu
**Brazilian wood** embuia, kingwood
**Brazil's discoverer** Cabral
**breach** alienation, break, chasm,
  contravention, crack, difference,
  disaffection, disagreement, dispute,
  disruption, dissension, dissociation,
  division, estrangement, fissure,
  fracture, gap, infringement, lapse,
  offence, opening, parting, quarrel,
  rift, rupture, schism, separation,
  severance, split, transgression,
  trespass, violation
**breach, as of a law** violation
**breach of etiquette** solecism
**breach of faith** betrayal, disloyalty,
  faithlessness, falseness, perfidy,
  treachery, treason
**breach of friendship** quarrel
**breach of normal procedure**
  irregularity
**breach of oath** perjury
**breach of peace by fighting in public**
  affray
**breach of the rules of grammar**
  solecism
**breach of trust** fraud, swindle
**bread** aliment, breid (Sc), bun, cereal,
  diet, fare, funds, ilk, loaf, nutriment,
  pone, roll, sustenance, viands
**bread and butter** income, livelihood
**bread baked in a pot** potbrood
**bread basket** stomach

**bread boiled and flavoured** panada
**bread browner** toaster
**bread consecrated in the Eucharist**
  host
**bread dipped in liquid** sop
**bread edge** crust
**bread end** heel
**bread factory** bakery
**bread from heaven** manna
**bread grain** corn, rye, wheat
**bread griller** toaster
**bread ingredient** flour, yeast
**bread leavener** yeast
**bread made from entire grain**
  wholewheat
**breadmaker** baker
**bread mould** rhizopus
**bread or whisky** rye
**bread part** crust, slice
**bread portion** crumb, loaf, slice
**bread-raising agent** mos, yeast
**bread roll** bagel, bap, bun, mosbolletjie
**bread slicer** knife
**bread snack** sandwich
**bread spread** butter, jam, margarine,
  oleomargarine
**breadth** broadness, capacity, content,
  diameter, latitude, measure,
  opening, radius, section, space,
  stretch, sweep, vastness, volume,
  wideness, width
**breadth of ship** beam
**bread variety** corn, mieliebread,
  mosbolletjie, potbrood, raisin,
  roosterkoek, rye, sourdough,
  (whole)wheat
**breadwinner** earner, provider,
  supporter, worker
**break** abbreviate, bankrupt, beat,
  breach, burst, bust, caesura, chasm,
  crack, curtail, degrade, demote,
  destroy, disclose, discontinuation,
  disrupt, divulge, escape, exceed,
  fissure, fracture, gap, hiatus, hurt,
  impair, injure, interrupt, lacerate,
  lacuna, negate, open, pause,
  reneg(u)e, rent, respite, rift, rip, ruin,
  rupture, schism, separate,
  severance, shatter, smash, snap,
  splinter, split, stoppage, surpass,
  suspension, tame, tear, unfold,
  violate, weaken, wound
**breakable** beatable, brittle, capable,
  delicate, divisible, escapable, flimsy,
  fragile, frail, frangible, partible,
  separable, tearable, violable
**break abruptly** snap
**breakage** fracture, interruption
**break a hole in** stave
**break a law** infringe
**break apart** disrupt, shatter
**break a promise** reneg(u)e, revoke

**break away** decamp, depart, detach, escape, flee, fly, quit, revolt, secede, separate, split
**breakaway** apostate, dissenting, heretical, rebel, renegade, schismatic, seceding
**break away from** sever
**breakbone fever** dengue
**break codes** bug, eavesdrop, espionage, wiretapping
**break connection** disconnect
**break contact** part
**break continuity** interrupt
**break cover** emerge
**breakdown** analysis, categorisation, classification, collapse, deterioration, disintegration, disorder, disruption, dissect(ion), division, fail(ure), interruption, mishap, power, separate, stop, stoppage
**break down** collapse, decompose, demolish, fail, suppress
**breaker** billow, mug, ridge, ripple, roller, surge, swell, tide, wave
**breaker of images** iconoclast
**breakfast cereal** cornflakes, muesli, oats
**breakfast dish** bacon, cereal, eggs, porridge, toast
**breakfast favourite** egg
**breakfast food** bacon, cereal, egg, ham, porridge
**breakfast rasher** bacon
**breakfast roll** bun
**breakfast TV show** GMSA
**break forcibly** split
**break for MPs** prorogation, recess
**break free** escape
**break from control** bolt
**break in** burgle, encroach, enter, habituate, impinge, initiate, interfere, interject, interpose, interrupt, intervene, intrude, invade, invation, train
**break-in** burglary, house-breaking, intrusion, larceny, robbery, theft
**break in between** interrupt
**break in continuity** gap, hiatus
**break in friendly relation** rift
**breaking and entering** burglary, robbery
**breaking down of tissues** hystolysis
**breaking loose from restraint** escapade
**breaking ocean waves** surf
**breaking off** schism
**breaking of faith** betrayal
**breaking of rules** aberration
**breaking sea swell** surf
**breaking up** scattering
**break in journey** stop off, stopover

**break in pieces** shatter, shiver, smash, splinter
**break in sequence** hiatus
**break into** begin, burgle, commence, raid
**break into pieces** shatter, smash
**break into small fragments** crumble, shatter
**break into sudden flame** flash
**break in upon** interrupt
**break loose** escape, flee
**break moral law** sin
**break of day** dawn
**break off** adjourn, alienate, cease, detach, disconnect, discontinue, disengage, divide, end, finish, halt, interrupt, part, pause, separate, sever, snap, splinter, stop, suspend, terminate
**break off suddenly** snap
**break off temporarily** adjourn
**break one's promise** betray
**break one's word** reneg(u)e
**break out** abscond, appear, arise, begin, bolt, burst, commence, emerge, erupt, escape, flee, happen, occur, start
**break out suddenly** erupt
**break rules** aberration
**break sharply** snap
**break someone's heart** abandon, desert, disappoint, disillusion, forsake, jilt
**break suddenly** pop, snap
**break the calm of** disturb
**break the continuity of** interrupt
**break the ice** begin
**break the law** contravene
**break through** achieve, emerge, pass, penetrate, progress, succeed
**breakthrough** advance, development, discovery, find(ing), gain, headway, improvement, invention, leap, progress, step
**break to pieces** smash
**break up** adjourn, blast, demolish, destroy, destruction, disband, dismantle, disperse, disrupt, dissolve, divide, divorce, finish, harrow, part, rake, separate, sever, split, stop, suspend, terminate
**break-up** breakdown, collapse, crack-up, crumbling, disintegration, dispersal, dissolution, divorce, finish, parting, rift, separation, split(ting), termination
**break-up of friendship** quarrel
**breakwater** dock, groyne, jetty, mole, pier, quay, wharf
**break with** betray, disavow, disclaim, ditch, drop, jilt, reject, renounce, repudiate, separate

**break without warning** snap
**breast** bosom, breest (Sc), breist (Sc), bust, chest, dug, mamma, pap, torso
**breastbone** rib, sternal, sternum
**breast feathers from the eider** eiderdown
**breast-feed** suckle
**breastplate** plastron
**breastplate stone** jasper
**breastshaped** mastoid
**breath** air, animation, break, exhalation, gasp, gulp, inhalation, odour, vapour, whisper
**breathe** gasp, gulp, imbue, impart, inject, murmur, puff, respire, say, sigh, wheeze, whisper
**breathe asthmatically** wheeze
**breathe audibly through nose** sniff
**breathe hard** pant, puff
**breathe heavily** heave, pant, sigh
**breathe in** inhale, sniff(le), snivel, snuff(le), whiff
**breathe laboriously** gasp, pant
**breathe loudly while sleeping** snore
**breathe new life into** reanimate, refresh, reinvigorate, rejuvenate, restore, resuscitate
**breathe noisily in sleep** puff, snore
**breathe one's last** die
**breathe out** exhale, expire
**breathe quickly** gasp, pant
**breathe with difficulty** wheeze
**breathe with effort** gasp
**breathing** agitated, gasping, hasty, panting, rale, respiration, stridor, voiceless
**breathing apparatus** scuba
**breathing hole made in ice by a seal** agloo, aglu
**breathing organ** gill, lung
**breathing pipe** snorkel
**breathing pore** stoma
**breathing problem** dyspnoea
**breathing space** breather, freedom, leisure
**breathing upon** afflatus
**breathless** amazed, astounded, awestruck, becalmed, calm, dead, exhausted, flabbergasted, gasping, inanimate, lifeless, motionless, panting, still, wheezing
**breath of wind** breeze
**breathtaking** awesome, stunning
**breech** buttocks, rump
**breech-loading musket** agterlaaier
**breed** bear, beget, conceive, create, cultivate, develop, educate, engender, family, father, generate, grow, ilk, instruct, kind, line, mother, occasion, originate, pedigree, procreate, produce, propagate, race,

raise, reach, rear, rise, school, sort, species, stock, strain, train
**breeding** ancestry, begetting, civility, conduct, courtesy, cultivating, cultivation, culture, engendering, fostering, gentility, hatching, lineage, manners, multiplying, nourishing, nurture, polish, procreating, raising, rearing, refinement, reproduction, training, upbringing, urbanity
**breeding and care of bees** apiculture
**breeding and rearing birds** aviculture
**breeding and training hawks** falconry
**breeding farm** stud
**breeding horse** stud
**breeding-horse infection** dourine
**breeding place** nest, nidus, stud
**breeding stable** stud
**breed of animals** strain
**breed of bird dog** setter
**breed of black-faced sheep** Suffolk
**breed of cat** Burmese, Manx, Persian, Siamese
**breed of cattle** Afrikaner, Angus, Ayrshire, Devon, Drakensberger, Jersey, shorthorn, Zebu
**breed of dairy cattle** Ayrshire, Friesian, Guernsey, Jersey, shorthorn
**breed of dog** Airedale, Alsatian, basset, beagle, collie, corgi, Dalmatian, Great Dane, greyhound, Labrador, Newfoundland, Pomeranian, pug, Rhodesian ridgeback, setter, spaniel, terrier
**breed of domestic fowl** Ancona, Dorking, Leghorn, Orpington, Wyandotte
**breed of horse** Arab, Bare, Lippizaner, thoroughbred
**breed of long-woolled sheep** Wensleydale
**breed of pony** Exmoor, Shetland
**breed of sheep** Cheviot, merino
**breed of small Chinese dog** Pekinese
**breed of small dogs** Pomeranian
**breed of terrier** Airedale
**breed of Welsh terrier** Sealyham
**breed of white dairy cattle** Ayrshire
**breed with each other** interbreed
**breeze** air, blow, breath, draught, puff, whiff, wind, zephyr
**breezy** airy, animated, blowy, blusterous, buoyant, casual, debonair, fresh, gusty, lighthearted, lively, windy
**brer** brother
**brevity** briefness, compactness, conciseness, curtness, succinctness, terseness
**brew** ale, beverage, blend, boil, broth, concoct(ion), contrive, cook,

develop, devise, distillation, drink, excite, ferment(ation), foment, gather, gruel, hatch, impend, infuse, infusion, liquor, mix(ture), plan, plot, potion, preparation, prepare, project, scheme, seethe, soak, steep, stew
**brewed drink** ale, beer, tea
**brewer's driver** drayman
**brewer's fermenting vat** keel, tun
**brewer's grain** barley, corn, malt, rye
**brewer's product** beer
**brewer's refuse** draff
**brewer's tub** keeve
**brewer's vat** keel, tun
**brewer's yeast** barm, leaven
**brewery refuse** draff
**brewing** malting, plotting
**brewing ingredient** malt, yeast
**briar flower** rose
**bribable** corruptible, venal
**bribe** allurement, back-hander, corrupt, enticement, graft, grease, incentive, inducement, kickback, lure, pay-off, refresher, reward, sop, square, suborn, sweetener
**bribery** corruption, graft, greasing, inducement, lubrication, palm-greasing, protection
**bribe to commit crime** suborn
**bric-à-brac** antiques, baubles, curiosities, knick-knacks, ornaments, trinkets
**brick barrier** wall
**brick carrier** hod
**bricklayer** mason
**bricklayer's tool** trowel
**brick or stone structure reinforcing a wall** buttress
**brick oven** furnace, kiln
**brick structure** wall
**brickwork in wooden frame** nogging
**brickyard oven** kiln
**bridal** connubial, hymeneal, marital, marriage(able), matrimonial, nuptial, spousal, wedding
**bridal attendant** bridesmaid, groom, page
**bridal attire** wedding dress
**bridal confetti** rice
**bridal headgear** veil
**bridal holiday** honeymoon
**bridal linen** trousseau
**bridal money** dowry, lobola
**bridal path** aisle
**bridal veil material** tulle, net
**bridal walkway** aisle
**bridal wear** veil, wedding gown
**bridal wreath** spiraea
**bridegroom's gift to the bride** han(d)sel
**bride or groom** newlywed
**brides are carried over this** threshold

**bride's bottom drawer** trousseau
**bride's clothes** trousseau
**bride's gift to husband** dowry
**bride's partner** groom
**bride's path** aisle
**bride's portion** dowry
**bride's spouse** groom
**bride's walkway** aisle
**bridge** arch, attach, band, bind, bond, causeway, connect(ion), couple, cross(ing), fill, flyover, join, link, overpass, pontoon, span, tie, traverse, unite, viaduct
**bridge bid** slam
**bridge bidding system** Acol
**bridge builder** engineer
**bridge declaration** pass
**bridge fee** toll
**bridge framework** trestle
**bridge hand** tenace, yarborough
**bridge in London** Albert, Chelsea, Putney, Tower, Waterloo
**bridge in Venice** Rialto
**bridge match** rubber
**bridge of violin** chevalet, cheville, magas
**bridge over gorge** trestle
**bridge over highway** overpass
**bridgeplayer's aim** game, leg, rubber
**bridge span** arch
**bridge suit** trumps
**bridge support** pier, span
**bridge tax** toll
**bridge term** slam
**bridge that carries one road over another** fly-over
**bridle** bristle, check, control, curb, govern, restraint
**bridle part** bit, snaffle
**bridle strap** rein
**brief** abbreviate, abrupt, abstract, compact, concise, condensed, curt, ephemeral, fleeting, laconic, outline, pithy, scant, short, succinct, summarise, summary, synopsis, temporary, terse, transient, transitory
**brief account** sketch
**brief account of book** blurb
**brief and concise** terse
**brief and unsympathetic treatment** short shrift
**brief application of sponge** dab
**brief bathing suit** bikini
**brief biography of deceased person** obituary
**brief burlesque** skit
**brief but comprehensive in expression** concise
**brief calm** lull
**brief communication** message
**brief fall of rain** shower
**brief flash of light** glint

**brief general survey** synopsis
**brief indication** gleam
**brief inspection** look-see
**brief in speech** abrupt
**brief interruption for a drink** tea break
**brief introduction** proem
**brief letter** note
**brief look** glance, glimpse, peep
**brief love affair** fling
**brief lull** respite
**briefly** abruptly, briskly, casually, concisely, fleetingly, hastily, in short, momentarily
**briefly expressed** concise, succinct, terse
**brief minor military engagement** skirmish
**brief nasty experience** mauvais quart d'heure (F)
**brief news dispatch by radio** flash
**brief news item** flash
**brief note** memo
**brief outline** aperçu (F), summary
**brief pause for rest** breather
**brief period of calm** lull
**brief quotation** snip
**brief record** note
**brief rest** pause
**brief shorts** monokini
**brief sleep** catnap, nap
**brief song** canticle
**brief statement of a principle** aphorism
**brief stringlike bikini** tanga
**brief summary** epitome, précis
**brief swim** dip
**brief swimsuit** bikini
**brief turbulent storm** gust, squall
**brief written message** memorandum, note
**brigand** abductor, bandit, burglar, cheat, criminal, crook, depredator, desperado, forager, fraud, freebooter, gangster, gunman, highjacker, highwayman, hoodlum, looter, mafioso, marauder, outlaw, pirate, plunderer, racketeer, raider, ransacker, robber, rogue, ruffian, skollie, skolly, smuggler, stealer, thief, thug, tough, tsotsi
**bright** animated, beaming, blazing, brilliant, clear, cloudless, coruscating, discerning, effulgent, encouraging, flaming, flashing, genial, gleaming, glistening, glistering, glittering, glorious, glossy, glowing, golden, happy, illustrious, inspiring, inspiriting, intelligent, irradiant, lambent, light, limpid, lively, lucent, lucid, luminous, lustrous, pellucid, promising, radiant, radiating, refulgent, resplendent, scintillating, shimmering, shining, shiny, sparkling, splendid, sunny, translucent, transparent, twinkling, unclouded, vivid
**bright and fresh in appearance** smart
**bright and shiny** sheeny
**bright as sunlight** sunny
**bright colour** orange, red, scarlet
**bright-coloured** gay
**bright-coloured thick-lipped rock-haunting fish** wrasse
**bright conspicuous object** oriflamme
**bright constellation** Orion
**brighten up** freshen, refurbish
**brightest star** Sirius
**brightest star in constellation** Alpha
**brightest star in the constellation Aquila** Altair
**brightest star in the heavens** Sirius
**brightest star in the Pleiades** Alcyone
**bright flame of fire** blaze
**bright flower** aster
**bright glow** glare
**bright golden auburn** Titian
**bright-green precious stone** emerald
**bright light used as signal** flare
**bright loose-fitting Hawaiian dress** muu-muu
**brightly coloured bird** oriole
**brightly coloured fish** opah
**brightly coloured handkerchief** bandanna
**brightly plumed bird** kingfisher
**bright neckerchief** bandanna
**brightness** acuteness, astuteness, brilliance, cheerfulness, clearness, cleverness, cloudlessness, gayness, gladness, goodness, intenseness, inventiveness, keenness, light, lucidness, lustre, radiance, rosiness, sharpness, sheen, vividness
**bright orange-red** nacarat (F)
**bright purplish red** magenta
**bright red** cherry, crimson, scarlet
**bright red colouring** cochineal
**bright spot on solar halo** parhelion
**bright spot or streak on sun** facula
**bright star** sun
**bright star in Lyra** Vega
**bright star in northern hemisphere** Vega
**bright thought** idea
**bright toga worn in Ghana** kente
**bright unsteady flame** flare
**bright witty thought** epigram, mot
**bright yellow-orange flower** marigold
**brilliance** aptitude, braininess, brightness, cleverness, dazzle, distinction, éclat, effulgence, élan, excellence, genius, glamour, gleam, glitter, glory, gloss, grandeur, greatness, intelligence, intensity, inventiveness, light, lustre, magnificence, radiance, sheen, sparkle, splendour, talent, virtuosity, vividness
**brilliant** ablaze, accomplished, acute, brainy, bright, celebrated, clever, dazzling, eminent, expert, famous, fantastic, gifted, glittering, glossy, intellectual, intense, luminous, lustrous, outstanding, quick, radiant, refulgent, scintillating, shining, sparkling, splendid, superb, talented, vivid
**brilliant Asiatic horned pheasant** tragopan
**brilliant assembly** galaxy
**brilliant colour** scarlet
**brilliant crimson dye** magenta
**brilliant discovery** eureka
**brilliant display** bravura, éclat
**brilliant feat** exploit
**brilliant in colour** vivid
**brilliantly** acutely, astutely, brightly, cleverly, dazzlingly, discerningly, eminently, exceptionally, expertly, famously, glitteringly, gloriously, glossily, intellectually, intensely, luminously, magnificently, outstandingly, radiantly, resplendently, scintillatingly, splendidly, superbly, vividly
**brilliant person** genius
**brilliant red** scarlet
**brilliant show** pageant
**brilliant stroke** coup
**brilliant success** éclat
**brim** edge, lip, rim
**brimless cap** beret, fez, tam(-o-shanter), toque
**brimless Scottish woollen cap** glengarry
**brim over** fill
**brimstone** sulphur
**brindled cat** tabby
**brine as seasoning** salt
**brined cucumber** pickle
**bring** accompany, attract, bear, carry, cause, conduce, conduct, convey, create, deduce, deliver, draw, engender, escort, fetch, force, guide, induce, introduce, lead, procure, produce, prompt, provoke, take, transfer, transport, usher
**bring about** accomplish, achieve, beget, cause, create, do, effect, engineer, fulfil, generate, incur, induce, manage, manipulate, manoeuvre, occasion, originate, procure, produce, provoke, realise
**bring about by an effort** achieve
**bring about desired result** negotiate
**bring about trouble** brew

**bring back** fetch, replace, restore, retrieve, return
**bring back to an original state** restore
**bring back to life** revive
**bring by force** drag
**bring charges against** accuse, delate, sue
**bring cheer** gladden
**bring close** approximate
**bring discredit on** disparage
**bring disorder to** disrupt
**bring down** abase, break, debase, degrade, depreciate, drop, fell, floor, humble, level, lower, overthrow, overturn, reduce, ruin, shoot, topple, undermine, upset
**bringer of bad luck** jinx
**bring for discussion** moot
**bring forth** afford, bear, breed, engender, furnish, generate, hatch, produce, provide, supply, yield
**bring forward** advance, produce
**bring forward as an argument** allege
**bring forward as a proof** adduce
**bring from abroad** import
**bring good fortune** soncy, sonsie, sonsy
**bring in** accrue, bear, fetch, gross, import, introduce, net, profit, realise, return, yield
**bring in as income** earn
**bring in from foreign country** import
**bringing shame upon** disgracing
**bringing to mind** recalling
**bringing up** nurture
**bring in new ideas** innovate
**bring into accord** attune
**bring into active operation** exert
**bring into a row** aline, align
**bring into being** create, induce, make
**bring into conflict** engage
**bring into confusion** embroil
**bring into contact** apply
**bring into conversation** mention
**bring into desired form** shape
**bring into disfavour** degrade, discredit
**bring into disorder** disarrange, jumble, muddle
**bring into disrepute** discredit
**bring into existence** create, generate, originate
**bring into favour** engrace
**bring into harmony** agree, attune, tune, tune-up
**bring into harmony with law** legalise
**bring into line** align
**bring into musical accord** attune
**bring into mutual relation** correlate
**bring into peril** endanger
**bring into play** apply
**bring into smaller place** comprehend, compress

**bring into the open** disclose, divulge, reveal, unveil
**bring into use** exert
**bring legal proceedings against** prosecute
**bring low** abase, humiliate, mortify
**bring lower** reduce
**bring off** accomplish, achieve, discharge, execute, fulfil, perform, rescue, succeed, win
**bring on** accelerate, advance, cause, coach, conduct, expedite, generate, incur, induce, inspire, occasion, precipitate, prompt, provoke
**bring one closer** endear
**bring on oneself** incur
**bring out** accomplish, achieve, cause, create, educe, elicit, emphasise, enhance, express, highlight, introduce, issue, print, publish, utter
**bring peace to** pacify
**bring round** convince
**bring shame upon** disgrace
**bring to a close** end, stop, terminate
**bring to an end** conclude, expunge, finish, terminate
**bring to a standstill** arrest, immobilise, stop
**bring to a successful conclusion** achieve
**bring to bay** corner
**bring to bear** enforce, exert
**bring to completion** finish, perform
**bring to court** prosecute, arraign
**bring to equilibrium** balance
**bring together** accumulate, assemble, compile, unify, unite
**bring together again** reunite
**bring together by degrees** accumulate
**bring to higher position** elevate
**bring to one's knees** conquer, subjugate, vanquish
**bring to life** animate
**bring to life again** revive
**bring to light** disclose, discover, expose, reveal, show, unearth, unmask, unveil
**bring to mind** recall, remember, remind
**bring to order** rally
**bring to pass** contrive, manage
**bring to standstill** halt, stall, stop
**bring to successful issue** achieve
**bring to terms** arbitrate, bargain, intervene, mediate, negotiate
**bring to the knowledge of** apprise
**bring to the notice of the public** publicise
**bring under bondage** subjugate
**bring under cultivation** reclaim
**bring up** advance, breed, broach, develop, educate, form, foster, introduce, mention, nurture,

propose, raise, rear, regurgitate, submit, support, teach, train, vomit
**bring upon oneself** incur
**brink** apogee, border, boundary, brim, crisis, crossroads, edge, eve, extremity, fringe, frontier, juncture, limit, lip, margin, moment, nearness, perimeter, point, rim, verge
**briny** ocean, saline, salty, sea
**brio** animation, audacity, boldness, bravura, brilliance, dash, display, élan, energy, exhibitionism, flair, liveliness, ostentation, panache, spirit, style, verve, vigour, virtuosity, vivacity
**Brisbane cricket ground** Gabba
**brisk** active, acute, agile, airy, alert, animated, ardent, beneficial, bubbly, crisp, energetic, enlivened, fresh, jaunty, lively, quick, rejuvenating, sharp, snappy, spry, stimulating, tonic, vigorous, vitalised, vivacious
**brisk energy** pep
**briskly** actively, agilely, alertly, allegro, busily, energetically, firmly, nimbly, promptly, quickly, readily, smartly, speedily, vigorously, vivace, vivaciously
**briskness** activeness, alacrity, alertness, liveliness, nimbleness, quickness, speediness, vigorousness
**brisk pace** canter, jope, trot
**brisk, steady pace** trot
**bristle** awn, barb, brush, chaeta, hair, prickle, seta, spin, stiffen, whisker
**bristlelike part** chaeta, seta
**bristle on grass** awn
**bristles on cat's face** whisker
**bristly** barbed, bushy, coarse, comate, comose, disordered, hairy, hispid, pointed, prickled, prickly, rough, shaggy, sharp, spined, spinous, spiny, stubbly, stubby, tangled, thorny, uncut, unshorn
**bristly growth** stubble
**bristly mammal** pig
**Bristol Channel island** Lundy
**Britain** Albion
**Britain personified** Britannia
**British art gallery** Tate
**British baby carriage** pram
**British bar** pub, local
**British bronze coin** penny
**British colony in the West Indies** Turks and Caicos Islands
**British composer** Arne, Britten, Elgar, Sullivan
**British conservative** Tory
**British dole cheque** giro
**British explorer** Fiennes, Scott
**British folk dance** hornpipe
**British government** Whitehall

**British gun** Bren, Sten
**British hereditary title** baron(et), duke, prince(ss)
**British holiday resort** Skegnett
**British Honduras** Belize
**British honour** OM
**British island** Man, Sheppey, Wight
**British island group** Bermuda
**British island stronghold** Malta
**British Isles inhabitant** Cockney, Englishman, Irishman, Scot, Welshman
**British legislature** parliament
**British machine gun** Bren
**British Mediterranean port** Gibraltar
**British military cop** Redcap
**British money** sterling
**British naval hero** Nelson
**British nobleman** baron, count, duke, earl, lord, peer, viscount
**British nobleman ranking between earl and baron** viscount
**British peer** earl
**British racecourse** Aintree
**British river fish** chub
**British royal castle** Windsor
**British royal house** Tudor, Windsor, York
**British royal stables** mews
**British rule in India** Raj
**British sailor** limey
**British sculptor** Epstein
**British socialist** Fabian
**British soldier** redcoat, tommy
**British sovereignty in India** Raj
**British spa** Bath, Margate
**British special tax** cess
**British statesman** Churchill
**British symbol** John Bull, lion
**British system of weights** avoirdupois
**British tavern** pub
**British territorial division** shire
**British university** Cambridge, London, Oxford
**Briton** Brython, Celt, English(person), Limey, Scot
**Brittany** Bretagne
**brittle** breakable, brilliant, crisp(y), crumbling, crumbly, curt, delicate, difficult, doomed, edgy, feeble, fragile, frail, frangible, friable, infirm, irritable, mortal, nervous, nervy, perishable, powdery, rickety, shattery, shivery, short, tense, weak
**brittle candy** toffee
**brittle cookie** snap
**brittle fragment** shard
**brittle metal** antimony
**broad** ample, big, bold, clear, coarse, diffuse, extensive, free, full, general, gross, important, indecent, indelicate, large, liberal, obvious, open(-minded), plain, rough, spacious, tolerant, unrestrained, vast, vulgar, wide
**broad Australian English** Strine
**broad band** bar, fess(e), stripe
**broad-bladed instrument** spatula
**broad-brimmed hat** sombrero, stetson
**broad-brimmed hat worn by the ancient Greeks** petasos, petasus
**broad-brimmed straw hat for woman** bloomer
**broadcast** advertise, blurb, circulate, cultivate, herald, relay, scatter, send, show, sow(n), strew, telecast, televise, transmit
**broadcast anew** relay
**broadcaster** columnist, commentator, contributor, correspondent, hack, journalist, newspaperperson, pressperson, reporter, sower, stringer
**broadcast programme** transmission
**broadcast receiver** radio
**broadcast the match** commentate
**broadcast through a transmitting station** relay
**broad curved convex-edged sword** falchion
**broad edgeless blade** spatula
**broaden** augment, develop, dilate, distend, enlarge, expand, extend, increase, open, spread, stretch, supplement, swell, widen
**broadest part of a ship's bottom** bilge
**broad flat kitchen knife** spatula
**broad flat river valley** strath (Sc)
**broad heavy knife** machete, panga
**broad heraldic band** fess(e)
**broad Irish accent** brogue
**broad Japanese sash** obi
**broadly inclusive** admissive, beneficent, benign, charitable, dispassionate, fair, frank, free, general, generous, good(-hearted), impartial, impersonal, just, kind, latitudinarian, magnanimous, open, philanthropic, responsive, sympathetic, tolerant, unbiased, unbigoted, understanding, unprejudiced, wise
**broad-minded** beneficent, benign, catholic, charitable, dispassionate, fair, flexible, frank, free, generous, good(-hearted), impartial, impersonal, indulgent, just, kind, latitudinarian, liberal, magnanimous, open(-minded), permissive, philanthropic, responsive, sympathetic, tolerant, unbiased, unbigoted, understanding, unprejudiced, wise
**broad neck scarf** ascot, shawl
**broad piece of cloth** sheet
**broad pronunciation** drawl
**broad ribbon** sash
**broad sash** obi
**broad shallow vessel** pan
**broadside** assailment, assault, attack, bill, bombardment, cannonade, criticism, onslaught, placard, poster, salvo, volley
**broad smile** grin
**broad spade** shovel
**broad street** avenue
**broad strip** swath
**broad thoroughfare** avenue, boulevard, highway
**broad tie** cravat
**broad upper part of external ear** pinna
**broad view** generalisation
**Broadway smash** hit
**brochette** skewer, spit
**brochure** booklet, bulletin, chapbook, circular, essay, folder, leaflet, monograph, pamphlet, tract(ate), treatise
**brock** badger
**brogue** accent, brogan, sandal, shoe
**brogues, for instance** shoes
**broil** brawl, contention, disturbance, grill, quarrel, tumult
**broke** battered, breached, cracked, crashed, destroyed, dispirited, disregarded, erupted, exceeded, fractured, fragmented, impaired, infringed, occurred, outdid, parted, shattered, smashed, snapped, split, subdued, surpassed, topped, tore, transgressed, undermined, violated, weakened
**broken** burst, cracked, crashed, crippled, crushed, defeated, demolished, destroyed, disconnected, discontinuous, disturbed, erratic, fractured, fragmentary, fragmented, humbled, incomplete, inoperative, intermittent, interrupted, oppressed, ruptured, separated, severed, shattered, spasmodic, subdued, weak
**broken bone support** splint
**broken down** decrepit, kaput
**broken fragment** shard
**broken glass to remelt** calx
**brokenhearted** crestfallen, dejected, desolate, despising, despondent, devasted, disappointed, grief-stricken, heartbroken, inconsolable, miserable, mournful, prostrated, stricken, unhappy, wretched
**broken home** single-parent home
**broken limb support** splint
**broken marriage** divorce
**broken-off piece** cantle

**broken piece of earthenware**
  (pot)shard, (pot)sherd
**broken twigs** hedge-cuttings, thrash
**broker** agent, consignee, merchant,
  middleman, pawnbroker, stockbroker
**broker's fee** agio, commission
**brolly** gamp, sunshade, umbrella
**brolly fabric** gloria
**bronchial mucus** phlegm
**bronco** broncho, mustang, pony
**bronco-busting contest** rodeo
**bronco show** rodeo
**bronze coating** patina
**bronze coin** cent, ore, pice, sen
**bronze constituent** copper
**brooch** clasp, jewellery, ornament, pin
**brood** agonise, birth, breed, chicks,
  children, clutch, cover, family, gloom,
  hatch, incubate, issue, lineage, litter,
  meditate, mope, morbid, muse,
  offspring, ponder, progeny,
  rehearse, ruminate, set, sit, stock,
  young
**brooding** agonising, fretting,
  meditating, moping, musing,
  repining, ruminating
**brooding structure** nest
**brood of chickens** clutch
**brood of partridges** covey
**brood of pheasants** nide, nye, eye
**brood of young eels** eel-fare
**brood sullenly** sulk
**broody** angry, crabbed, cross, crusty,
  curt, dismal, doleful, downcast,
  frowning, gloomy, glum, ill-tempered,
  irritable, lugubrious, melancholy,
  miserable, moody, morose,
  offended, pensive, petulant, sad,
  saturnine, sulky, sullen,
  temperamental, testy, touchy
**brook** beck, burn, gill, rill, rivulet,
  runnel, stream, streamlet,
  watercourse
**broom** besom, brush
**broom of twigs** besom
**broth** bouillon, consommé, soup, stock
**brothel** bagnio, bawdy-house, bordel,
  bordello, cathouse, lupanar
**brother** associate, bra, brer, broer,
  bruder (G), chum, cleric, fra, fratello
  (I), frater (L), hermano (Sp), kin,
  kinsman, monk, regular, relation,
  relative, religious, sibling
**brotherhood** alliance, association,
  cameraderie, clan, clique,
  community, companionship,
  comradeship, coterie, fellowship,
  fraternity, friendliness, guild, kinship,
  league, society, union
**brother-in-law of Hobab** Moses
**brother-in-law of Moses** Hobab
**brother-in-law of Napoleon** Murat

**brotherly** affectionate, altruistic,
  amicable, cordial, fraternal, kind
**brotherly love** humanity
**brother of Aaron** Moses
**brother of Abel** Cain, Seth
**brother of Abihu** Nadab
**brother of Abimelech** Jotham
**brother of Abiram** Dathan
**brother of Abishai** Joab, Asahel
**brother of Abner** Kish
**brother of Abraham** Haran, Nahor
**brother of Acarnan** Amphterus
**brother of Acrisius** Proetus
**brother of Adonijah** Absolom,
  Ammon, Chileab
**brother of Adrastus** Mecisteus
**brother of Aegaeon** Cottus, Gyges
**brother of Agamemnon** Menelaus
**brother of Agave** Polydorus
**brother of Agenor** Belus
**brother of Andrew** Peter
**brother of Apollo** Artemis
**brother of Armoni** Mephibosheth
**brother of Cain** Abel, Seth
**brother of Caleb** Othni
**brother of Dathan** Abiram
**brother of David** Eliab, Ozem
**brother of Dinah** Levi, Simeon
**brother of Eleazar** Abihu, Ithamar,
  Nadab
**brother of Eliab** David
**brother of Esau** Jacob
**brother of father** uncle
**brother of Gad** Asher
**brother of Gilead** Hammoleketh
**brother of Goliath** Lahmi
**brother of Ham** Japhet, Shem
**brother of Hammoleketh** Gilead
**brother of Haran** Abraham
**brother of Herodias** Agrippa
**brother of Hophni** Phinehas
**brother of husband** brother-in-law, levir
**brother of Iscah** Lot
**brother of Isis** Osiris
**brother of Jacob** Esau
**brother of Japhet** Ham, Shem
**brother of John** James
**brother of Jonathan** Johanan
**brother of Joseph** Benjamin
**brother of Lahmi** Goliath
**brother of Lot** Iscah
**brother of Mamre** Aner, Eschol
**brother of Mephibosheth** Armoni
**brother of Miriam** Moses
**brother of Mishma** Mibsam
**brother of Moses** Aaron
**brother of Nahor** Abraham, Haran
**brother of Nemuel** Abiram, Dathan
**brother of Nestor** Alastor
**brother of Nethaneel** David
**brother of Odin** Ve
**brother of Othni** Caleb

**brother of Ozem** David
**brother of Peter** Andrew
**brother of Pharez** Zarah
**brother of Phinehas** Hophni
**brother of Pluto** Jupiter, Neptune,
  Poseidon, Zeus
**brother of Pollux** Castor
**brother of Poseidon** Hades, Zeus
**brother of Raddai** David
**brother of Rebekah** Laban
**brother of Remus** Romulus
**brother of Romulus** Remus
**brother of Salome** Herod
**brother of Seraiah** Baruch, Othniel
**brother of Seth** Abel, Cain
**brother of Shammah** David
**brother of Shem** Ham, Japhet
**brother of Shimma** David
**brother of Tyr** Thor
**brother of Zeus** Aides, Hades, Pluto,
  Poseidon
**brother or sister** sibling
**brother's daughter** niece
**brother's son** nephew
**brought into life** born
**brought on by too much noise**
  earache, headache
**brought to ruin** undone
**brought up** bred, reared
**brow** air, appearance, aspect, bearing,
  boundary, brim, brink, crest, edge,
  eyebrow, forehead, front, hill-top,
  margin, mien, periphery, rim,
  summit, verge
**brown** bay, mocha, sandalwood, tan,
  taupe, tawny, umber, walnut
**brown and bitter** beer
**brown cane** malacca
**brown coal with woody texture** lignite
**brown colour** tan
**brown earth** umber
**brown earth pigment** sienna
**browned bread** crouton, toast
**browned off** dejected, discontented,
  discouraged, resentful, unhappy
**brown gem** agate, andradite, jasper,
  sardonyx, tiger's-eye, tigereye
**brown gull** skua
**brown horse** bay, chestnut, roan, sorrel
**brown hyena** strandwolf
**brownie** kobold, nis(se), nix, sprite
**brown in the sun** tan
**brownish** sepia
**brownish colour** dun, russet, sepia, tan
**brownish glass with copper crystals**
  avanturine, aventurin(e), sunstone
**brownish grey** dun, taupe
**brownish orange** sorrel
**brownish pigment** sepia, sienna
**brownish purple** puce
**brownish-yellow pigment** ochre,
  sienna

**brownish-yellow variety of quartz** citrine
**brown moth** eggar, egger
**brown off** anger, ire, peeve
**brown paper** manila
**brown photo shade** sepia
**brown pigment** bistre, melanin, mummy, sepia, umber
**brown sauce** roux
**brown scales that cover the stems and leaves of young ferns** ramentum
**brown seaweed** kelp
**brown shade** tan
**brown study** absorption, abstraction, meditation, reverie
**brown sugar** demerara
**bruise** abuse, blacken, blemish, contuse, contusion, crush, damage, deface, discolour(ation), injure, injury, insult, mar(k), offend, pound, swelling, wound
**bruit** clamour, report, rumour, spread
**brume** fog, mist, vapour
**brumous** foggy, wintry
**brush** battle, besom, broom, burnish, bushes, clash, clean, collision, conflict, confrontation, contact, contest, copse, encounter, engagement, fight, flick, fracas, graze, incident, kiss, polish, rub, scrap(e), scrub, shine, shrubs, skirmish, stroke, sweep(er), thicket, touch, tussle, undergrowth, underwood
**brush aside** belittle, dismiss, disregard, flout, ignore, override, pooh-pooh
**brushed leather** suede
**brush off** cold-shoulder, cut, discourage, dismiss(al), disown, disregard, ignore, rebuff, refuse, reject(ion), repudiate, repulse, scorn, slight, snub, spurn
**brush-tailed phalanger** tuan, warmbenger
**brush turkey** Talegalla, vulturn
**brush up** cram, improve, refresh, relearn, revise, study, swot
**brush up on** review, study
**brush wolf** coyote
**brusque** abrupt, blunt, curt, discourteous, gruff, hasty, impolite, offhand, sharp, tart, unmannerly
**brutal** animal, barbarian, barbaric, barbarous, beastly, bestial, brusque, brute, coarse, crude, cruel, gross, harsh, inhuman, irrational, pitiless, rough, rude, ruthless, sadistic, savage, sensual, unfeeling, unthinking
**brutal fellow** beast, clubfist

**brutal hoodlum** thug
**brutality** abomination, acerbity, acrimony, asperity, atrocity, austerity, barbarity, bestiality, bitterness, callousness, crime, cruelty, depravity, enormity, evil, ferocity, hardness, harshness, horror, ill-temper, inhumanity, outrage, rapacity, rigour, sadism, savagery, severity, spite, venom, villainy, wildness
**brutally** barbarously, brutishly, callously, heartlessly, inhumanly, meanly, savagely, violently
**brutally sensual** bestial
**brutal person** beast, sadist, turk
**brutal ruffian** thug
**brute** animal, barbarian, beast, brutish, carnal, cruel, savage, yahoo
**brutish person** animal, beast, yahoo
**bubble** bead, bleb, boil, brittleness, drop, fizz, foam, froth, globule, insubstantial, levity, radiate, seethe, spheroid
**bubble on painted surface** bleb, blister
**bubbling** burbling, effervescent, fizzling, foaming
**bubbling over** ebullition
**bubbly-jock** turkey-cock
**bubbly wine** champagne
**bubonic plague carrier** rat
**buccaneer** adventurer, corsair, freebooter, pirate, privateer, rapparee, robber, sea rover, sea-dog, viking
**Bucharest is there** Romania
**buck** antelope, beau, blesbok, boastful, bontebok, bound, chamois, dandy, deer, dollar, eland, fop, frisk, gemsbok, impala, jerk, jump, kudu, leap, male, philander, rabbit, ram, reindeer, sable, stag, vault, vigour
**bucket** barrel, basin, can, cask, container, holder, pail, pan, pitcher, pot, scuttle, tin, vessel
**bucket wheel** lifter
**buckle** bend, bulge, catch, clasp, clip, close, collapse, crumple, fasten, fastener, fold, hook, secure, twist, warp
**buckle down** attend, begin, concentrate, prepare, start
**buckle up** brighten, encourage, fasten your seat belt, gird, girt, hearten, rally
**buck or doe** deer, rabbit
**buck up** brighten, cheer, encourage, hasten, hearten, hurry, improve, rally, stimulate
**buck with twisted horns** eland, kudu
**bucolic** agrarian, agricultural, country, idyllic, pastoral, rural, rustic, simple
**bucolic lover** swain

**bucolic poem** eclogue
**bud** bloom, blossom, buddy, develop, foliage, open, scion, shoot, sprout, swelling, tendril
**Budapest is the capital** Hungary
**Buddhism of Tibet** lamaism
**Buddhist deity** dev(a)
**Buddhist fate** karma
**Buddhist monk** lama, Talapoin
**Buddhist novice** goyin
**Buddhist perfect state** nirvana
**Buddhist priest in Tibet** lama
**Buddhist sacred book** Dhammapada
**Buddhist shrine** stupa, tope
**Buddhist state of bliss** nirvana
**Buddhist state of enlightenment** satori
**Buddhist teaching** Zen
**Buddhist temple** pagoda
**Buddhist temple gateway** toran(a)
**Buddhist title** mahatma
**Buddhist truth** dharma
**budding actress** starlet
**budding doctor** intern
**buddy** bra, broer, brother, chum, companion, crony, friend, mate, pal
**budge** change, dislodge, move, propel, push, remove, roll, shift, slide, stir, sway, yield
**budget** allocate, allocation, allotment, allowance, plan, ration
**budlike outgrowth** gemma
**bud on potato** eye
**buff** nude, polish, rub
**buffalo** arna, bison, caribou, gnu, ox, wisent
**buff-coloured fabric** nankeen, nankin(g)
**buffed leather** suede
**buffer zone** cordon sanitaire (F)
**buffet** bang, batter, box, café, cafeteria, clobber, cupboard, rasp, shove, sideboard, wallop
**buffet meal** smorgasbord
**buff fabric** nankeen, nankin(g)
**buffoon** antic, clown, comedian, comic, droll, fool, harlequin, jester, joker, oaf
**buffoon in motley dress** scaramouch
**bug** annoy, bother, eavesdrop, germ, insect, virus, wiretap
**buggy** cart
**bugle call** reveille, tantara
**build** assemble, augment, base, begin, body, constitute, construct, create, develop, edify, elevate, enlarge, erect, escalate, establish, extend, fabricate, figure, form(ulate), found, frame, improve, inaugurate, increase, initiate, institute, intensify, make, manner, manufacture, mould, originate, physique, raise, shape, size, strengthen, structure

**build a nest** nidificate, nidify
**build a picture of** deduce, reconstruct
**builder** author, beginner, benefactor, constructor, contractor, designer, establisher, father, founder, framer, generator, initiator, inventor, maker, mason, organiser, originator
**builder in stone** (stone)mason
**builder's quote** tender
**builder's tool** hod, trowel
**builder's unit** square
**building** construction, edifice, erection, high-rise, low-rise, skyscraper, structure
**building addition** annex(e), ell, wing
**building block** ashlar, brick
**building caretaker** janitor
**building complex to house soldiers** barrack
**building design** architecture
**building devoted to worship** cathedral, chapel, church, mosque, synagogue, temple
**building division** apartment, room, suite
**building extension** annex(e), ell, wing
**building facade** frontage
**building for arms** armoury, arsenal
**building for Christian worship** cathedral, church
**building for exhibits** museum
**building for grain** barn, elevator, silo
**building for horses** stable
**building for manufacture of goods** factory
**building for militia** armoury
**building for musical performances** concert hall, odean, odeum, theatre
**building for soldiers** barrack
**building for stage shows** theatre
**building for storing goods** warehouse
**building for storing tools** shed
**building for worship** cathedral, chapel, church, mosque, temple
**building front** facade
**building game** Lego, Meccano
**building in Babel** tower
**building in which dead bodies may be kept for a time** mortuary
**building location** site
**building lot** plot, site
**building material** brick, cement, concrete, mortar, steel, stone
**building of cars, bridges, etc.** engineering
**building offering accommodation** hotel, inn
**building remains** ruin
**building rock** sandstone
**building site** lot, plot
**building span** arch
**building's picturesque remains** ruins

**building spike** nail
**building step** stair
**building structure** shed
**building to store grain** barn, elevator, silo
**building toy** Lego
**building up** assembly
**building where books are kept** library
**building where old people are cared for** home
**building where things are manufactured** factory
**building wing** ell
**building with gambling tables** casino
**building with tiers of seats round open arena** amphitheatre
**building wood** timber
**building worker** bricklayer
**build nest(s)** nidificate, nidify
**build up** accrue, accumulate, advertise, amass, amplify, assemble, augment, boost, develop, enhance, expand, extend, fortify, heighten, improve, increase, intensify, plug, promote, publicise, reinforce, strengthen
**build up surface level** aggrade
**build-up unfinished work** backlog
**built-in bed** bunk
**built-out window** bay, oriel
**built-up area** conurbation, urban
**built-up region** suburb
**bulb** corm
**bulblike stem** corm
**bulbous plant** amaryllis, dahlia, freesia, galtonia, lily, sparaxis
**bulbous plant with pungent taste** garlic
**bulbous root** cullion
**bulbous spring flower** tulip
**bulbous vegetable** beet, swede
**bulb's shield** lampshade
**bulb vegetable** beet(root), carrot, onion, radish
**Bulgarian assembly** Sobranje, Sobranye
**Bulgarian cape** Emine, Kuratan, Sabla
**Bulgarian dialect** Slavonic
**Bulgarian money** lev
**Bulgarian mountain range** Balkan, Rhodope
**bulge** acceleration, augmentation, balloon, belly, bloat, boost, bump, convexity, dilate, enlarge, hump, increase, lump, mass, node, nodule, overhang, projection, protrude, protrusion, rise, swell(ing), tumefaction, tumefy
**bulging** bulbous, dilating, distending, enlarging, expanding, projecting, protruding, sagging, swelling
**bulging out** protuberant

**bulging outwards** convex
**bulging part of a barrel** bilge
**bulk** body, corpulence, enlarge, expand, extent, grow, hugeness, immensity, largeness, magnitude, majority, mass, matter, most, size, substance, vastness
**bulk sales** wholesale
**bulky** big, cumbersome, great, hefty, large, massive, stalwart, unwieldy
**bulky body** corpulent
**bull** angus, bovine, cattle, ox, Taurus, toro (Sp)
**bull after castration** bullock
**bull at archery** gold
**bullet** ammunition, dumdum, missile, pellet, projectile, shot, slug, tracer
**bullet of irregular shape** slug
**bullet-proof screens** protection
**bullet's bounce** ricochet
**bullet size** calibre
**bullfight** corrida (Sp)
**bullfight cheer** olé
**bullfighter** matador, picador, toreador, torero
**bullfighter on horse** toreador
**bullfighter on foot** torero
**bullfighter's cheer** olé
**bullfight land** Spain
**bullfight opera** *Carmen*
**bullion bar** ingot
**bull-like** taurine
**bullock** ox, steer, stot
**bullock's heart** custard apple
**bullring** arena
**bullring cheer** olé
**bull's eye** target
**bully** badger, bluster, boast, brag, browbeat(er), bulldoze, bulldozing, chivvy, coerce(r), coercing, constraining, despot, domineer(ing), dragoon, forcing, goad, harass(ing), harry, hector(ing), hound, importune, importuning, intimidate, intimidating, intimidator, menacing, nag(ging), oppress, overawe, overbear, persecute, pester(ing), plague, rant(ing), roar, ruffian, storm, swagger, swell, threaten(ing), thug, torment(ing), tormentor, tyrannise, tyrannising, vaunt(ing)
**bullying** fear, intimidation, menaces, nagging, pressure, terror, threat
**bulwark** abutment, barricade, barrier, bastion, buffer, buttress, citadel, defence, dike, embankment, fortification, levee, mainstay, outwork, palisade, rampart, ravelin, redoubt, wall
**bum** beachcomber, beggar, bergie, buttocks, derelict, drifter, drunkard, false, hobo, idler, loafer, misleading,

**bumble insect** bee
**bump** bang, blow, bounce, budge, clash, collide, collision, crash, dislodge, displace, hit, hump, impact, jar, jerk, jolt, jostle, knock, knot, lump, move, protuberance, rap, rattle, remove, shake, shift, shock, smack, smash, strike, swelling, thud, thump
**bumper** abundant, attachment, bouncer, bouncy, bountiful, buffet, enormous, excellent, exceptional, generous, great, hearty, large, massive, prodigal
**bumper crop** plenty
**bumper in cricket** bouncer
**bump into** encounter, meet
**bumpkin** boor, clown, greenhorn, hawbuck, lubber, oaf, peasant, rustic, yokel
**bump off** assassinate, dispatch, eliminate, kill, liquidate, murder, remove, top
**bump roughly** jostle
**bumptious** arrogant, brash, cocky, conceited, egotistic, impudent, pushy, showy
**bumpy** uneven
**bun** cake, roll
**bunch** bundle, cluster, collection, group, lot, mass, protuberance
**bunched hand** fist
**bunch of flowers** bouquet, nosegay, posy
**bunch of grain** sheaf, sheave
**bunch of grass** tuft
**bunch up** crowd, herd, huddle
**bunch up to leap** crouch
**bundle** bale, bunch, pack(age), packet, parcel, sheaf, sheave, truss, wad
**bundle of blankets** shiralee
**bundle of cut cereal grass** sheaf, sheave
**bundle off** abscond, decamp, depart, hustle, scamper, scurry
**bundle of firewood** cord
**bundle of grain** sheaf
**bundle of hay** bale
**bundle of iron rods** faggot
**bundle of sticks** faggot
**bundle of straw** sheaf
**bundle of things packed** package, parcel
**bundle of twigs** faggot
**bundle of undressed hides** kip
**bundle of wheat** sheaf
**bundle of wool** bale
**bun fight** tea party
**bung** bankrupt, block, choke, close, close, cork, cover, fill, pack, plug,
seal, shut, spigot, spile, stop(per), stopple, stuff, tampion, tap, throw
**bungle** blunder, botch, butcher, mar, miff, miscalculate, misjudge, mismanage, ruin
**bungled piece of work** botch
**bungled work** botch
**bungler** dolt, dotard, fool, halfwit, idiot, imbecile, moron, prat, schlemiel
**bunk** bed, berth, couch
**bunking of school** truancy
**bunk in ship** berth
**bunkum** balderdash, baloney, bombast, claptrap, drivel, gibberish, humbug, junk, nonsense, piffle, rant, rubbish, (tommy)rot, twaddle, verbiage, wind
**bunny** rabbit
**bunny covering** fur
**bunny feature** ear, tail
**buoy** beacon, dan, elate, elevate, float, guide, hearten, marker, signal, support, sustain, uplift
**buoyancy** elation, glee, joy, ruff
**buoyant** afloat, animated, bouncy, bracing, carefree, cheerful, debonair, floatable, floaty, gay, glad, gleeful, happy, jaunty, jovial, joyful, light, lively, refreshing, resilient, stimulating, vivacious, weightless
**buoyant motion** lilt
**buoy at end of harpoon line** drogue
**buoy up** boost, cheer, encourage, hearten, lift, raise, reassure, support, sustain
**burbot** birdbolt, cod, dogfish, eelpout, morgay
**burden** charge, cross, difficulty, drift, duty, encumbrance, essence, grievance, hindrance, impediment, load, misery, millstone, obligation, onus, oppress, oppression, point, refrain, responsibility, strain, substance, trial, weight, worry, yoke
**burden of proof** onus
**burden of Santa Claus** sack, toys
**burdensome** annoying, arduous, boring, crushing, cumbersome, cumbrous, difficult, disagreeable, exasperating, exhausting, fatiguing, grievous, hard, harsh, heavy, intolerable, irksome, laborious, massive, onerous, oppressive, painful, ponderous, punishing, rigorous, severe, steep, strenuous, taxing, tedious, tiresome, tiring, tough, troublesome, unwelcome, vexatious, wearisome
**burdensome charge** tax
**burdensome possession** elephant
**burden with debts** encumber
**bureau** agency, branch, cabinet, chest, counter, cupboard, department, desk, division, dresser, locker, office, portfolio, section, service, sideboard, wardrobe, writing-desk
**bureaucracy** administration, government, ministry, officialdom
**bureaux** agencies, branches, departments, desks, divisions, offices, services
**burgeon** bloom, blossom, blow, bud, develop, flourish, flower, grow, increase, open, prosper, shoot, sprout, succeed, thrive
**burgher** citizen
**burglar** cracksman, criminal, felon, forager, gangster, housebreaker, looter, mugger, picklock, pilferer, pillager, Raffles, raider, ransacker, robber, stealer, thief, yegg
**burglar's haul** swag
**burglar's tool** bar, jemmy, jimmy, picklock
**burgle** cheat, defraud, despoil, dispossess, gyp, invade, loot, pillage, plunder, raid, ransack, rifle, rob, sack, strip, swindle
**burial** entombment, exequies, funeral, inhumation, interment, obsequies, sepulture
**burial case** casket, coffin, sarcophagus
**burial ceremony** funeral
**burial chamber** cist, crypt, tomb, vault
**burial garment** shroud
**burial ground** campo santo (I), cemetery, grave(yard), necropolis
**burial hymn** dirge, elegy, requiem
**burial mound** barrow
**burial pile** pyre
**burial place** barrow, crypt, grave(yard), tomb
**burial place of Aaron** Hor
**burial sheet** shroud
**burial urn** ossuary
**burial vault** catacomb, crypt, sepulchre, tomb
**buried treasure** trove
**burlap fibre** hemp, jute
**burlap material** hessian, jute
**burlesque dancer** stripper
**burly** bulky, hefty, robust, stocky, stout, strong
**Burmese bandit** dacoit
**Burmese curved knife** dhar
**Burmese dagger** dah, dout, dow
**Burmese deer** thameng, thamin
**Burmese devil** nat
**Burmese division** Irrawaddy, Magwe, Mandalay, Pegu
**Burmese garment** tamein
**Burmese girl** mina
**Burmese gulf** Martaban

**Burmese language**  Mon, Pegu, Wa
**Burmese money**  kyat, pya
**Burmese plateau**  Shan
**Burmese port**  Akyab, Bassein, Henzada, Moulmein, Yangon
**Burmese robber**  dacoit
**Burmese seaport**  Rangoon
**Burmese three-stringed violin**  turr
**Burmese title**  u
**Burmese town**  Rangoon
**burn**  bite, blaze, brand, brook, brown, char, consume, corrode, cremate, desire, expend, flame, flare, flash, flicker, fume, glow, hurt, ignite, incinerate, kindle, light, parch, rivulet, scald, scorch, sear, seethe, shrivel, simmer, singe, smart, smoulder, sting, tan, tingle, toast, yearn
**burn brightly**  flame, flare
**burner that removes old paint**  blowlamp
**burn in**  brand
**burning**  afire, ardent, blazing, burning, charring, eager, earnest, fervent, fiery, flaming, flaring, flashing, frantic, gleaming, glowing, hot, igniting, illuminated, incinerating, intense, kindling, lighting, parching, passionate, scorching, singeing, smoking, toasting, vehement, withering, zealous
**burning crime**  arson
**burning fever**  ague
**burning fuel**  coal, gas
**burning gas**  flame
**burning glass**  sunglass
**burning of a body**  cremation
**burning particle**  spark
**burning piece of wood**  firebrand
**burning sensation**  sting
**burning torch**  flambeau
**burn lightly**  singe
**burn slightly**  char, scorch, singe
**burn slowly**  smoulder
**burn superficially**  singe
**burnt coal**  cinder
**burn the midnight oil**  lucubrate, study, swot
**burn the surface**  scorch, sear, singe
**burnt material**  ash
**burn to ashes**  cremate, incinerate
**burnt remains**  ash
**burnt sugar**  caramel
**burnt wood**  ash
**burn unsteadily**  flicker
**burn up**  cremate, incinerate
**burn up refuse**  cinerate
**burn up the road**  drive, fly, race, speed
**burn with hot liquid**  scald
**burn without flame**  smoulder
**burn with steam**  scald

**burp**  belch
**burr**  whetstone
**burro**  ass, donkey
**burrow**  delve, den, dig, dwelling, excavate, excavation, hide, hole, lair, lurk, mine, pierce, retreat, shelter, tunnel
**burrower**  mole
**burrow in earth**  mine
**burrowing American rodent**  gopher
**burrowing animal**  aardvark, ant, badger, gopher, marmot, mole, ratel, warthog
**burrowing beetle**  borer
**burrowing insect**  ant, borer, termite
**burrowing marsupial**  wombat
**burrowing night animal**  badger
**burrowing rodent**  gopher, hamster, marmot, rabbit
**burseraceous Philippine tree**  pili(nut)
**burst**  break, bust, dehisce, detonate, discharge, emerge, erupt, explode, explosion, fulminate, outpouring, pop, rend, rupture, rush, shatter, spurt
**burst forth**  appear, emerge, erupt
**burst in**  implode
**burst into anger**  flare
**burst into flames**  ignite
**burst into flower**  bloom, effloresce
**burst of anger**  fuff (Sc)
**burst of fireworks**  salvo
**burst of laughter**  guffaw
**burst of passion**  gust
**burst of rain**  gust
**burst of speed**  sprint
**burst of temper**  tantrum
**burst open**  dehisce, pop
**burst out**  erupt
**burst out angrily**  flare
**burst seam**  rip
**burst sound**  pop
**burst violently**  explode
**Burundi currency**  franc
**Burundi deity**  Imana
**Burundi lake**  Rugwero, Tshohoha
**Burundi language**  Kirundi, Swahili
**Burundi pygmy people**  Batwa
**Burundi tribe**  Bahutu, Batutsi, Batwa, Hutu, Tutsi
**bury**  cache, commit, conceal, cover, deposit, engulf, entomb, forget, hide, immerge, inearth, inhume, inter, obliterate, obscure, plunge, secrete, sepulchre, shroud, sink, submerge
**bury in earth**  inter
**burying of dead body**  burial, funeral
**bus**  coach, double-decker
**bus employee**  conductor
**bus garage**  depot
**bush**  forest, shrub, tod, wood(land)
**bushel part**  peck

**Bushman tongue**  San
**bush tale**  yarn
**bush telegraph**  rumour
**bushwalker**  hiker
**bush whose buds are used for sauce**  caper
**bush with prickly leaves**  holly
**bushy and frizzy hairstyle**  Afro
**bushy clump**  tod
**bushy herb**  basil, lavender, tarragon
**bushy sapindaceous shrub**  aalii
**bushy strong-scented perennial plant**  feverfew
**bushy-tailed carnivore**  raccoon
**bushy-tailed monkey**  marmoset
**bushy-tailed rodent**  squirrel
**business**  affair, calling, commerce, company, concern, corporation, duty, employment, enterprise, firm, function, matter, métier, occupation, profession, trade, vocation
**business agreement**  contract, deal, sale
**business alliance**  syndicate
**business chief**  manager
**business connection**  contact
**business decline**  slump
**business degree**  MBA
**business emblem**  trademark
**business finding employment for others**  agency
**business firm**  company, partnership, CC
**business location**  premises
**business man of great wealth and power**  baron, tycoon
**businessman who looks after actor**  manager
**business mogul**  tycoon
**business of exchanging currencies**  agiotage
**business of fishing**  fishery
**business operation**  affair
**business organisation**  company, partnership, CC
**business profit**  net
**business relationship**  account
**business reverse**  loss
**business room**  office
**business to be transacted at a meeting**  agenda
**business transaction**  deal, sale
**business trip**  errand
**business union**  cartel, syndicate
**bus on rails**  tram
**bus passenger**  rider
**bus station**  depot
**bust**  arrest, bosom, break, breast, burst, chest, crash, fall, ruin, rupture, torso
**bust cover**  bra(ssière)
**bus terminal**  depot, terminus

**bustle** action, activity, ado, agitate, arouse, bestir, commotion, compel, dart, disturbance, employment, engagement, excite(ment), flurry, framework, fuss, hurry, hustle, movement, occupation, pad, push, rouse, rush, scramble, scurry, skirt, stir, to-do, tumult
**bustle about** dash, flutter, fuss, rush, scuttle
**bustle with** swarm, teem
**bustling activity** ado
**bus token** fare
**bust-up** brawl, disruption, disturbance, quarrel, separation
**busy** absorbed, active, assiduous, brisk, concentrating, diligent, diverted, employed, energetic, engaged, eventful, fussy, hardworking, industrious, meddlesome, nimble, occupied, officious, prying, stirring, unresting, working
**busy and confused** excited, hectic
**busy as a bee** active, diligent
**busy farm vehicle** tractor
**busy ghoul** graverobber
**busy insect** ant, bee
**busy oneself unduly** meddle
**but** aber (G), except(ion), however, just, nevertheless, objection, only, save, sed (L), still, unless, yet
**butch and masculine** macho
**butcher** botch, bungle, kill, killer, murder(er), slaughter(er), thug
**butchered** assassinated, botched, carved, cleaned, cut, destroyed, dressed, exterminated, jointed, killed, massacred, mutilated, prepared, ruined, slain, slaughtered, slew, spoilt, wrecked
**butcher's axe** pole-axe
**butcher's chopper** cleaver
**butcher's cleaver** chopper
**butcher's hook** gambrel
**butcher's inventory** meats
**butcher's knife** cleaver
**butcher's pin** skewer
**butcher's slaughterhouse** shambles
**butcher's tool** cleaver, pole-axe
**butchery** carnage, killing, massacre, slaughter
**Butch's partner** Sundance
**but nevertheless** yet
**but now** erstwhile
**butt** barrel, cask, charge, dig, dupe, end, extremity, fag-end, gull, handle, jab, nudge, poke, prod, push, ram, scapegoat, shaft, stab, stooge, tail, tip, victim
**butt against** ram
**butter cask** firkin, tub

**butterfish** blenny, gunnel
**butterflies and moths** Lepidoptera
**butterfly catching rig** net
**butterfly expert** lepidopterist
**butterfly larva** caterpillar
**butterfly's kin** moth
**butter knife** spreader
**buttermaker** creamery
**butter-making machine** churn
**butter portion** pat
**butter substitute** margarine, oleomargarin(e)
**butter tree** shea
**butter up** blarney, cajole, coax, flatter, soft-soap, wheedle
**butter vat** churn
**butt holder** ashtray
**butt in** interfere, interpose, interrupt, intervene, intrude, kibitz, meddle
**butting animal** goat
**buttocks** backside, behind, bottom, coit, derrière, hindquarters, posterior, quoit, rear, rump(s), seat
**button** stud
**buttonhole bloom** carnation
**button part** shank
**buy** acquire, bribe, get, hire, obtain, procure, purchase
**buy and sell** trade
**buy back** redeem
**buyer** agent, applicant, chapman, client, consumer, customer, dependant, emptor, habitué, patient, patron, prospect, protégé(e), purchaser, regular, shopper, user, vendee
**buyer of Joseph** Potiphar
**buyer of useless horses for slaughter** knacker
**buyer's concern** cost, quality
**buy from overseas** import
**buying and selling** barter, commerce
**buying or selling of ecclesiastical preferment** simony
**buy off** bribe
**buy or sell** deal
**buys and sells paintings** art dealer
**buy shares** invest
**buy the drinks** treat
**buzz** drone, hiss, murmur, ring, sibilation, whirr, whisper
**buzzing insect** bee, dor
**by** along, aside, at, away, beside, beyond, close, handy, near, over, past, per, through, via
**by absence of contrary evidence** ex silentio (L)
**by accident** inadvertently, unwittingly
**by all means** absolutely, assuredly, certainly, definitely, positively, surely
**by all odds** definitely, undoubtedly, unequivocally, unquestionably

**by a long shot** easily, indubitably, never, no way, undoubtedly, unquestionably
**by and by** anon, eventually, hereafter, later, presently, soon, subsequently
**by and large** usually
**by an immense distance** toto caelo (L)
**by a nose** barely, just, narrowly, only
**by any chance** ever
**by a person unknown** anonymous
**by a small amount** fractionally
**by assertion** allegedly
**by a stated time** already
**by birth** congenital, née
**by chance** accidentally, casually, par hasard (F), peradventure, perchance, randomly, unintentionally, unwittingly
**by choice** preferably, rather, sooner
**by considerable amount** greatly
**by constancy and courage** constantia et virtute (L)
**by degrees** gradual
**by divine law** jure divino (L)
**by fair means** honestly
**by far** clearly, decidedly, easily, inimitably, obviously, plainly, visibly
**by fits and starts** erratically, intermittently, irregularly, spasmodically, sporadically
**by foot** afoot
**by force** amain
**by force and arms** vi et armis (L)
**by God's grace** Dei gratia (L)
**bygone** ancient, antiquated, antique, archaic, buried, by, dated, dead, démodé, departed, erstwhile, extinct, forgotten, former, gone, heirloom, immemorial, lapsed, late, lost, musty, obliterated, obsolete, of yore, old(-time), olden, omitted, one-time, outworn, passé, past, previous, primeval, primitive, pristine, relic, remote, sometime, unremembered
**bygone days** yore
**bygone times** history, past
**by good right** à bon droit (F)
**by half** considerably, excessively
**by halves** imperfectly, scrappily, skimpily
**by hand** manual, manually
**by heart** parrot-fashion, pat, word for word
**by hook or by crook** somehow, someway
**by human law** jure humano (L)
**by implication** indirectly, implicite (L)
**by itself** alone, apart, per se
**by its very nature** per se
**bylaw** regulation, ruling
**by leave of** pace

**by means of** per, through, using, utilising, via, whereby
**by means of the ear** auricularly
**by means of the hand** ch(e)iro-
**by mistake** accidentally, inadvertently, involuntarily
**by mouth** oral, orally
**by my fault** mea culpa (L)
**by my own wish** meo voto (L)
**by nature** basically, essentially, fundamentally, inherently, innately, naturally, radically
**by night** nocturnal
**by no amount** none
**by no means** hardly, nohow
**by now** already
**by oneself** alone, aloof, apart, deserted, isolated, lone
**bypass** avert, avoid, circumvent, detour, dodge, ignore, neglect
**by preference** preferably, rather, sooner,
**by-product** offshoot
**byre** barn, cowshed, stable
**by reason of** because, for
**by right** de jure
**by rights** equitably, honestly, justly, properly
**by sixes** senary
**by small amount** gradual
**by stages** gradually
**bystander** spectator, watcher, witness
**by the bill of fare** à la carte
**by the fact itself** ipso facto
**by the grace of God** Dei gratia (L)
**by the law itself** ipso jure
**by the means of** per
**by the people** popularly
**by the side of** alongside, beside, near
**by the skin of one's teeth** barely, hardly, just, narrowly, scarcely
**by the way** accidentally, apropos, casually, en passant, incidentally
**by the year** annually
**by this time** already, now, yet
**by turns** alternately, consecutively, reciprocally, successively
**by-verb** proverb
**by virtue of being** qua
**by virtue of one's office** ex officio
**by voice** vocally
**byway** lane, sidestreet
**by way of** along, over, through, via
**by way of example** exempli gratia (L)
**by way of the mind** telepathic
**by word of mouth** oral(ly), spoken, verbally

# C

**cab** hack, hansom, minicab, taxi(cab)
**cabal** alliance, association, band, clique, combination, complot, concoct, connivance, conspiracy, conspire, crew, faction, gang, intrigue, junta, junto, league, plan, plot, ring, scheme, sect, web
**cabaret show** revue
**cabbage** cole(wort), kale
**cabbage dish** (cole)slaw, sauerkraut
**cabbagelike plant** cole, kale
**cabbagelike vegetable** kohlrabi
**cabbage salad** cole(slaw)
**cabbage variety** kale
**cabbage with a turnip-shaped stem** kohlrabi
**cabbage with wrinkled leaves** savoy
**cab counter** taximeter
**cabin** confine, cottage, enclose, hut, shack, shanty, shed
**cabin attendant** hostess, steward(ess)
**cabinet timber** embuia, mahogany, oak, stinkwood, tambotie, teak, walnut, yellow-wood
**cable** cablegram, chain, channel, conduit, cord(age), filament, flex, hawser, line, main, message, news, pipe, rope, send, strand, string, telegram, telegraph, telex, thread, transmit, wire
**cable bearer** pylon
**cable car** telfer, telpher
**cable support** pylon
**cable TV** closed-circuit television
**cableway** funicular
**cacao powder** broma
**cacao seed drink** cocoa
**cache** bury, collection, conceal, crypt, garner, hide, hiding place, hoard, loot, repository, save, savings, secrete, stash, store, treasure, vault
**cachet** capsule, distinction, prestige, stamp
**cactus** ocotillo, saguaro, sahuaro, ti
**cactus fruit** prickly pear, sabra, tuna
**cactus-like** cactoid
**cactus-like tree** ocotillo
**cactus plantation** nopalry
**cad** assistant, boor, bounder, churl, cur, dastard, heel, knave, rascal, rogue, rotter, scamp, scoundrel
**cadaver** corpse, remains
**cadaverous** ashen, bloodless, corpselike, deathly, emaciated, pale
**caddis worm** caseworm, piper, strawworm
**cadence** accent, articulation, beat, inflection, intonation, jingle, lilt, measure, modulation, movement, ornament, pulsation, rhythm, sound, swing, tempo, tone, voice
**cadent** descending, falling, lilting
**cadet** midshipman, trainee
**cadge** beg, mooch, mutch, scrounge, sponge
**cadger** beggar, hawker, mendicant, moocher, parasite, rogue, scrounger, sponger, supplicant, tramp, vagrant
**cadmium yellow** nasturtium
**cadre** core, diagram, draft, framework, inner circle, key group, nucleus, outline, plan, shell, skeleton, sketch
**Caesar** Nero
**Caesar's betrayer** Brutus
**Caesar's colleague** Crassus, Pompey
**Caesar's river of decision** Rubicon
**café** bistro, cafeteria, restaurant, tearoom
**caffeine in tea** theine
**cage** confine, coop, immure, impound, imprison, pen, pound, restrain
**cage bird** budgerigar, budgie, canary, cockatiel, mew, parrot
**cage for animals** pen
**cage for fowls** coop
**cage for hawks** mew
**cage for poultry** coop
**cagey** alert, cagy, careful, careful, cautious, chary, circumspect, crafty, discreet, guarded, keen, noncommittal, secretive, shrewd, uncommunicative, wary, wily
**Cain killed him** Abel
**Cain's brother** Abel
**Cain's crime** fratricide
**Cain's land** Nod
**Cain's son** Enoch

**Cain's victim**  Abel
**Cairo is there**  Egypt
**Cairo scholar**  egyptologist
**cajole**  beguile, blarney, coax, entice, flatter, humour, inveigle, lure, mislead, palaver, pamper, seduce, tempt, wheedle
**cajoler**  inveigler
**cajoling talk**  beguiling, blarney, coaxing, decoying, enticing, flattering, inveigling, luring, misleading, seducing, tempting, wheedling
**Cajun**  Acadian
**cake**  bake, bar, block, bun, cement, coagulate, congeal, encrust, gateau, harden, loaf, slab, solidify
**cake decoration**  icing
**caked tobacco**  cavendish
**cake froster**  decorator, icer
**cake icing**  topping
**cake mix**  batter
**cake of choux pastry filled with cream and iced**  éclair
**cake of soap**  bar
**cakes and ale**  merry-making, prosperity
**cake's layer**  tier
**cakes produced at one baking**  batch
**cake sugar**  castor, icing
**cake to eat with wine**  madeira
**cake topping**  icing
**calabrese**  broccoli
**calamitous**  adverse, catastrophic, dire, disastrous, harmful, tragic, unlucky, woeful
**calamitous to a high degree**  dire
**calamity**  adversity, affliction, agony, cataclysm, catastrophe, desolation, disaster, distress, downfall, hardship, harm, hurt, infelicity, mischance, misfortune, mishap, reverse, ruin(ation), scourge, torture, tragedy, trial, trouble, woe
**calcaneus**  calcaneum, heel bone
**calcareous deposit**  tufa
**calcareous earth**  limestone
**calcite variety**  alabaster
**calcium carbonate**  chalk
**calcium oxide**  lime, quicklime
**calcium sulphate**  gypsum, plaster
**calculate**  ascertain, compute, count, deliberate, determine, estimate, figure, reckon, suit, weigh, weigh
**calculate roughly**  estimate
**calculating device**  abacus
**calculating frame**  abacus
**calculating frame with balls**  abacus
**calculation**  answer, anticipation, care, caution, circumspection, computation, count, deliberation, discretion, estimate, estimation, expectation, expediency, extrapolation, forecast, foresight, forethought, judg(e)ment, product, prudence, reckoning, result

**Calcutta atrocity**  Black Hole
**Calcutta nun**  Teresa
**Caledonian**  Scot, Scotsman
**calendar**  agenda, almanac, annals, chronogram, chronology, daybook, ephemeris, log, menology, programme, record, schedule
**calendar division**  day, month, year
**calf's cry**  bleat
**calf's flesh**  veal
**calfskin**  kip
**calf's meat**  veal
**calf's mother**  cow
**calf without mother**  dogey, dogie
**calibration**  assessment, calculation, estimation, evaluation, measurement, mensuration, scale, survey, valuation
**calibre**  ability, bore, diameter, endowment, faculty, gauge, gifts, importance, measure, strength, talent
**Californian beach**  Malibu
**Californian lake**  Tahoe
**Californian redwood**  sequoia
**California's motto**  Eureka
**California state flower**  poppy
**California state tree**  redwood
**caliph**  imam, imaum
**calk on rugby boot**  cleat
**call**  announce, arouse, assemble, awaken, christen, claim, consider, convene, convoke, cry, demand, designate, invitation, invite, label, name, need, nominate, outcry, page, proclaim, rouse, shout, summon(s), telephone, visit, voice, waken
**calla**  aroid, arum (lily)
**call a halt**  stop
**call back**  renege, retrieve, revoke
**callboy**  page
**call by ghost**  visitation
**call down**  chide, entreat, invoke, rebuke, reprimand, supplicate
**called**  named, yclept
**called out by public crier**  oyez
**caller**  company, guest, visitant, visitor
**call for**  collect, demand, dictate, entail, fetch, involve, necessitate, need, occasion, require, suggest, summon, uplift, want
**call for aid**  appeal
**call for alms**  beg
**call for a taxi**  hail
**call for help**  appeal, SOS
**call for repetition**  encore
**call forth**  arouse, awake, evoke
**call girl**  concubine, courtesan, harlot, mistress, paramour, prostitute
**call in**  consult, invoke

**calling**  call, craft, employment, forte, invitation, job, line, métier, mission, occupation, pursuit, summons, trade, vocation
**calling attention**  ahem, hey, ho, ps(s)t
**calling for much effort**  demanding, exacting
**calling for notice**  crying
**calling together**  convocation
**calling up the dead**  necromancy
**calling urgently**  clamant
**call in question**  challenge, dispute, impugn, oppugn, query
**call into existence**  arouse
**call into question**  assail, attack, impeach, impugn
**call it a day**  end, finish, quit
**call it off**  cancel
**call loudly**  cry, holler, shout, yell
**call names**  insult
**call of a hen**  chuck
**call off**  abandon, abort, cancel, desist, discontinue, drop, end, withdraw
**call of public crier**  oyes, oyez
**call on**  ask, bid, entreat, invite, invoke, request, summon, supplicate, visit
**call on again**  revisit
**call on beeper**  page
**call on pager**  bleep
**call on the telephone**  ring
**callous**  cold, cruel, dull, hard, hard-hearted, hardened, harsh, heartless, impassive, impervious, indifferent, indurate(d), insensible, insensitive, inured, inveterate, leathery, obdurate, obtuse, pitiless, revengeful, severe, strong, tough, uncaring, unfeeling, unimpressible, unmerciful, unsusceptible, unsympathetic
**callously**  coldly, hardheartedly, heartlessly, indifferently, insensitively, obdurately, soullessly, uncaringly, unfeelingly
**call out**  cry, evoke
**callow**  fresh, green, guileless, immature, inexperienced, innocent, juvenile, naïve, new, raw, tender, unfledged, unsophisticated, untried, young
**calls on firms with new products**  agent, rep, representative, salesperson
**call the idea of**  suggest
**call the shots**  administer, dispose, dominate, domineer, quarterback, regulate
**call the tune**  command, dictate, govern, lead, rule
**call to account**  blame, rebuke, reprimand, reprove

**call to appear before judge**
  summon(s)
**call to arms** alarm
**call together** assemble, summon
**call to mind** bethink, remember
**call to phone** bleep
**call up** beseech, evoke, phone
**call up memories** evoke, remind,
  reminisce
**call upon** appeal, beseech, visit, woo
**call upon for help** invoke
**call up spirit** evoke, invoke
**call used in hailing** ahoy, halloo
**call when tossing coin** head, tail
**calm** allay, assuage, calmness,
  collected, composed, composure,
  cool, lull, mild, mollify, motionless,
  nerveless, pacify, peaceful(ness),
  placid, quiet, repose, restful, sedate,
  serene, serenity, smooth(ness),
  soothe, still(ness), tranquil(lise),
  tranquillity, undisturbed, unruffled,
  windless
**calm and casual** nonchalant
**calm and composed** sedate
**calm and peaceful** halcyon
**calm and self-controlled** collected
**calm and tranquil** peaceful
**calm and unruffled** placid
**calm brightness** serene
**calm down** ensober, mollify
**calming** hushing, mollifying, placating,
  quietening, relaxing, sedative,
  settling, soothing
**calming drug** sedative, tranquilliser
**calm interval** lull
**calmly** coolly, easily, motionless,
  serenely
**calmly content** complacent
**calmness** composure, coolness,
  harmony, peacefulness, placidity,
  poise, repose, rest, self-control,
  self-possession, sereneness,
  serenity, stillness, tranquillity
**calmness in danger** sang-froid
**calmness of mind** composure
**calmness of mind or temper**
  equanimity
**calm pastoral composition** idyll
**calm self-control** calmness,
  composure, sang-froid
**calm with drugs** sedate, tranquillise
**calumniate** abuse, asperse, attaint,
  belie, berate, decry, defame, deflate,
  disparage, insinuate, insult, libel,
  mortify, revile, scandalise, slander,
  slur, smear, smirch, soil, spot, stain,
  sully, traduce, vilify
**calyx leaf division** sepal
**calyx part** sepal
**camaraderie** accord, brotherhood,
  cohesion, communion,
  companionship, comradeship,
  concordance, familiarity, fellowship,
  friendliness, harmony, intimacy,
  kindliness, kinship, sociability,
  solidarity, soundness, stability,
  unanimity, unity
**Cambria** Wales
**Cambrian** Welsh, Welshman
**cambric grass** ramee, ramie
**came about** arose
**came across** met
**came first** won
**came from source** emanated
**camel** caisson, dromedary, oont
**camel-driver** cameleer
**cameleer** camel-driver
**camel-footed** tylopod
**camel hair fabric** aba, camlet,
  cashmere
**camel hair garment** aba
**camellia** japonica
**camel-like animal** alpaca, llama
**camelopard** giraffe
**cameo cutting tool** spade
**cameo stone** onyx
**camera angle** shot
**camera component** lens, shutter
**camera glass** lens
**camera lens for long shots** telephoto
**camera moving platform** dolly
**camera opening** aperture
**camera part** lens, shutter
**camera shield** lens hood
**camera stand** tripod
**camisole** underbodice
**camouflage** blind, cloak,
  conceal(ment), cover(ing), deceive,
  deception, disguise, façade, falsify,
  front, garble, guise, hide, mask,
  masquerade, mimicry, muffle,
  obscure, pretence, ruse, screen,
  subterfuge, trickery, veil
**camp** barracks, base, bivouac,
  cantonment, clique, crowd,
  encamp(ment), faction, group,
  laager, lodge, party, section, side,
  station
**campaigner** advocate, backer,
  champion, counsellor, defender,
  electioneer, promoter, proposer,
  speaker, spokesman, supporter,
  upholder
**campaign for** advocate
**campanile** bell tower
**camp bed** cot, stretcher
**camp boundary** perimeter
**camper's home** tent
**camper's shelter** tent
**camper's water flask** canteen
**camp fire girl** artisan
**camp follower selling provisions**
  sutler
**camphorated tincture of opium**
  paregoric
**camphor obtained from oil of**
  **peppermint** menthol
**camping ground** site
**camping pot** billy
**camping stove** primus
**camping vehicle** trailer
**camp of wagons** laager
**camp shelter** tent
**can** container, preserve, tin
**Canaanite deity** Baal
**Canada goose** honker, outarde
**Canada/US waterfall** Niagara
**Canadian** Canuck, Ontarian
**Canadian bay** Georgian, Hudson,
  James, Ungava
**Canadian boatman** voyageur
**Canadian bog** muskeg
**Canadian cheese** Oka
**Canadian city** Banff, Calgary,
  Edmonton, Fredericton, Halifax,
  Montréal, Québec, Regina, St
  John's, Toronto, Vancouver,
  Victoria, Winnipeg
**Canadian emblem** maple-leaf
**Canadian Eskimo** Innuit, Inuit
**Canadian gannet** margot
**Canadian Indian settlement** Rancherie
**Canadian island** Anticosti, Baffin,
  Banks, Bylot, Devon, Prince Edward,
  Read, Sable, Vancouver, Victoria
**Canadian jay** whisky-jack
**Canadian lake** Abitibi, Cree, Garry,
  Louise, Nipigon, Okanagan, Slave,
  Winnipeg
**Canadian lynx** lucivee, pishu
**Canadian national park** Jasper, Yoho
**Canadian peninsula** Boothia, Gaspe,
  Melville, Ungava
**Canadian policeman** mountie
**Canadian porcupine** urson
**Canadian port** Vancouver
**Canadian province** Alberta, Manitoba,
  New Brunswick, Newfoundland,
  Nova Scotia, Ontario, Québec,
  Saskatchewan, Winnipeg
**Canadian provincial capital**
  Edmonton, Fredericton, Halifax,
  Québec, Regina, St John's, Toronto,
  Victoria, Winnipeg
**Canadian rodent** lemming
**Canadian salmon** ouananiche
**Canadian squaw** mahala
**Canadian stocking cap** tuque
**Canadian strait** Cabot, Dease,
  Georgia, Hecate
**Canadian territory** Yukon
**Canadian trapper** voyageur
**Canadian tree** maple
**Canadian university** Dalhouse, McGill

**Canadian waterfall** Della, Panther, Takakkaw
**canal** aqueduct, channel, conduit, duct, foss(e), furrow, groove, gutter, main, moat, passage, route, strait, Suez, tube, waterway
**canal between North and Baltic seas** Kiel
**canal boat** barge
**canal connecting Atlantic and Pacific oceans** Panama
**canal from mouth to anus** alimentary
**canal from mouth to stomach** gullet, oesophagus
**canal in Canada** Welland
**canal in Egypt** Suez
**canal in Germany** Kiel, Ludwig, Weser
**canal in Hungary** Cid, Sarviz
**canal in Netherlands** Drentsch, Juliana, Oranje
**canal in New York** Erie, Gowanus
**canal in Pakistan** Nara, Rohri
**canal in Romania** Bega
**canal-lined city** Amsterdam, Venice
**canal lock** chamber, coffer
**canal vessel** barge
**canapé** appetiser, sofa
**canard** buzz, gossip, hearsay, news, report, rumour, story, talk, tidings, whisper, word
**canary food** seed
**Canary Island island** Gomera, Palma
**Canary Island volcano** Tenequia
**canary wine** malmsey
**canary yellow** meline
**can be beaten** vincible
**can be ploughed** arable
**can be taken for granted** assumable
**cancel** abolish, abort, abrogate, absolve, annul, avoid, cease, delete, disannul, discharge, efface, eliminate, eradicate, erase, expunge, invalidate, negate, nullify, obliterate, offset, quash, recant, remit, rescind, revoke, undo, veto, void
**cancel a bequest** adeem
**cancel a marriage** annul
**cancel correction** stet
**cancelled** abolished, annulled, deleted, eliminated, erased, oblirated, off, quashed, repudiated
**cancelling stamp** killer
**cancel marriage** annul, divorce
**cancel out** negate
**cancer causer** carcinogen
**cancerous growth** carcinoma
**cancerous tumour** carcinoma, malignant
**cancer-producing substance** carcinogen

**candelabrum** candleholder, candlestick, lamp-holder
**candid** aboveboard, clear, direct, fair, forthright, foursquare, frank, free, guileless, heart-to-heart, honest, impartial, just, open, outspoken, plain, sincere, straightforward, unadulterated, unbiased, unprejudiced, up-front, white
**candidate** applicant, apprentice, aspirant, challenger, claimant, competitor, contender, contestant, entrant, learner, nominee, novice, probationer, rival, runner, seeker, suitor
**candidate for a position** applicant, nominee
**candidate for a post** applicant, nominee
**candidate for ordination** ordinand
**candidate on trial** probationer
**candid behaviour** candour
**candid discussion** straight-talking
**candidness** bluntness, candour, fairness, frankness, freeness, impartialness, justness, openness, plainness, truthfulness
**candied fruit** conserve, succades
**candle** bougie, cierge, dip, flame, flare, luminary, taper, torch, wax, wick
**candle burner** wick
**candle cord** wick
**candle grease** tallow
**candleholder** candelabrum, candlestick, chandelier, girandola, pricket, randole, sconce
**candle-holder** abettor
**candle lighter** spill
**candlemaker** chandler
**candle material** tallow, wax, wick
**candlestick with a handle** sconce
**candle string** wick
**candle warehouse** chandlery
**candle wax** tallow
**candle wick** snast(e)
**candlewood** pine
**can do** doable
**candour** artlessness, bluffness, bluntness, boldness, candidness, fairness, frankness, freeness, honesty, impartiality, impartialness, justness, objectivity, openness, plain-speaking, sincerity, straightforwardness, truth
**candy** confection, preserve, sweetmeat, sweets
**candy flavouring** anise, carob, chocolate, grenadine, licorice, orris, peppermint, sarsaparilla, sassafras, vanilla
**candy on stick** lollipop, sucker
**cane** rattan, reed, stick

**cane by-product** bagasse
**cane in wind instrument** reed
**cane product** sugar
**cane sound** swish
**cane sugar** sucrose
**canine** animal, bitch, cur, dog, eyetooth, fisc, fox, hound, mongrel, pet, pup(py), tike, tyke, wolf
**canine comment** bark
**canine control** dog chain
**canine creature** dog
**canine disease** rabies
**canine ligament** lytta
**canine mammal** dog
**canine tooth** cuspid, eyetooth
**canine variety** fox, hy(a)ena, jackal, wolf
**can material** tin
**cannabis** bhang, boom, cannabin, dagga, dope, ganja, grass, gunja, hashish, hemp(wort), marihuana, marijuana, pot
**cannabis cigarette** reefer, zol
**cannabis smoker** roker
**canned** tinned
**canned fish** middlecut, pilchards, salmon, sardine, tuna
**cannery** canning factory
**cannibalism** anthropophagy
**cannibalistic** anthropophagical, bestial, bloodthirsty, fiendish, flesh-eating, man-eating, ogreish
**cannibalistic giant** ogre
**canning factory** cannery
**cannon** gun, mortar, ordinance
**cannon firing stick** linstock
**cannot be appeased** implacable
**cannot be chosen** ineligible
**cannot be persuaded by entreaty** inexorable
**canny** acute, cautious, judicious, prudent, sagacious, shrewd, wise
**canny herb** sage
**canoe** ama, bidarka, bider, bongo, dugout, kaiak, kayak, kolek, piragua, pirogue, proa, waapa, waka
**canoe adjunct** paddle
**canoe for instance** boat
**canoe of Eskimo** bidar(ka), bidarkee, kayak, umiak
**canoe of Hawaii** waapa
**canoe of New Zealand** waka
**canoe propeller** oar, paddle
**canon** belief, code, command, concept, confession, convention, conviction, credo, creed, criterion, custom, decree, doctrine, dogma, edict, ethics, etiquette, exemplar, instruction, law, mandate, manners, maxim, measure, norm, opinion, order, precept, principles, regulation,

rule(s), standard, statute, system, teaching, test
**canonical dress** alp, cope
**canonical law of Islam** sharia, sheria
**canonical nineth hour** nones
**canonised person** saint
**canon law** jus canonicum
**canon's stipend** prebend
**canopy** awning, baldachin(o), baldaquin, cope, cover(ing), shade, sunshade, tarpaulin, tester, tilt
**canopy for a window frame** pelmet
**canopy of altar** baldachin(o), baldaquin
**canopy over four-poster bed** tester
**canopy supported by four pillars over the high altar** ciborium
**cant** act, argot, bevel, distortion, exaggeration, falsehood, humbug, hypocrisy, incline, insincerity, jargon, medicalese, mummery, pretence, rise, sanctimoniousness, slope, terminology, tilt, untruth
**cantankerous** bad-tempered, bilious, brusque, captious, contentious, contrary, crabby, cranky, crotchety, difficult, disagreeable, grouchy, grumpy, ill-humoured, iracund, irascible, irritable, obnoxious, peevish, perverse, quarrelsome, surly, testy, unfriendly
**canter** amble, gait, gallop, go, jog, lope, ride, run, saunter, trot
**Canterbury gallop** canter
**cant of thieves** argot, slang
**Cantonese** Chinese, dialect, inhabitant, native
**canvas** burlap, denim, drill, duck, sailcloth, sails, tarp(aulin), ticking
**canvas carrier** easel
**canvas cover** tarp(aulin)
**canvas covering** tent
**canvas hanging bed** hammock
**canvas home** tent
**canvas on ship** sail
**canvas piece** tarpaulin
**canvas rain cover** tarpaulin
**canvas roof** awning
**canvass** agitate, analyse, campaign, discuss, dispute, electioneer, examination, examine, inspect, investigate, investigation, poll, scan, scrutinise, scrutiny, seek, sift, solicit, study, survey, tally, ventilate
**canvas shelter** awning, tent
**canvas shoe** plimsoll, sandshoe, sneaker, tackie, takkie
**canvas sun-shelter** awning
**caoutchouc** rubber
**cap** beret, fez, headdress, headgear, headwear, kepi, lid, tam(-o'-shanter)
**capable** able, accomplished, adapted, admitting, allowing, competent, efficient, fitted, gifted, intelligent, qualified, skilful, susceptible
**capable of being corrected** corrigible
**capable of being cut** scissile
**capable of being dissoluble** disconnected, disintegrated, loosened
**capable of being dissolved** soluble
**capable of being hammered into shape** malleable
**capable of being kept up** maintainable
**capable of being made to fit** adaptable
**capable of being melted** dissolvable
**capable of being overcome** surmountable
**capable of being pierced** penetrable
**capable of being ploughed** arable
**capable of being read** legible
**capable of being retained** tenable
**capable of being solved** soluble
**capable of being stretched** tensile
**capable of being treated** treatable
**capable of being used** available
**capable of being weighed** ponderable
**capable of destroying bacteria** antibiotic, bacteriolytic
**capable of enduring** durable, lasting, strong, tough, wiry
**capable of exerting great force** powerful, strong
**capable of extension** elastic
**capable of feeling** sentient
**capable of grasping** prehensile
**capable of inheriting** inheritable
**capable of joining** agglutinative
**capable of life** viable
**capable of living together harmoniously** compatible
**capable of making mistakes** fallible
**capable of movement** mobile, motile
**capable of moving backwards** reversible
**capable of rational conduct** responsible
**capable of solution** soluble
**capable of splitting** fissile
**capable of thinking** cogitative
**capacitate** allow, authorise, empower, enable, endow, endue, equip, qualify, sanction, supply, warrant
**capacity** ability, ableness, acumen, ampleness, amplitude, aptitude, aptness, calibre, capability, competence, competency, dimensions, discernment, faculty, function, gift, leaning, magnitude, measure, office, position, potential, power, propensity, province, range, readiness, relation, room, sagacity, scope, skilfulness, skill, space, talent, tonnage, volume, wit
**capacity for damage** destructiveness
**capacity for work** energy, vitality
**capacity of merchant ship in mass** tonnage
**capacity of tasting** gustation
**capacity to feel pain** algesia
**capacity to last** endurance
**capacity to remember** retention
**capacity to withstand** resistance
**capacity unit in electricity** farad
**cape** cloak, foreland, head(land), ness, peninsula, point, promontory
**Cape apple town** Elgin
**cape at tip of Denmark** Skaw
**Cape doctor** southeaster
**Cape elephant reserve** Addo
**Cape gooseberry** strawberry, tomato
**cape in China** Olwanpi
**cape in Costa Rica** Blanco, Elena, Velas
**cape in Crete** Buza, Liano, Salome, Sidheros, Spatha, Stavros
**cape in Cuba** Cruz, Lucrecia, Maisi
**cape in Cyprus** Andreas, Gata, Greco, Zevgari
**cape in Dominican Republic** Cabron, Falso, Isabela, Macoris
**cape in Ecuador** Pasado, Puntilla, Rosa
**cape in Egypt** Banas
**cape in French Guiana** Orange
**cape in Greece** Arkitas, Drepanon, Grambysa, Krios, Malea, Matapan, Sideros, Spada, Tainaron
**cape in Greenland** Bismarck, Farewell, Jaal, Lowenorn, Walker
**cape in Haiti** Foux
**cape in Iran** Halileh
**cape in Ireland** Clear
**cape in Italy** Circeo, Colonne, Falcone, Licosa, Passero, Sanvito, Testa, Teulada, Vaticano
**cape in Ivory Coast** Palmas
**cape in Japan** Erimo, Esan, Mino, Muroto, Nojima, Noma, Shakotan, Shiriya, Soya, Todoga, Toi
**cape in Massachusetts** Ann, Cod
**cape in New Zealand** Egmont, Farewell, Palliser
**cape in North Carolina** Hatteras
**cape in Norway** Nordkapp, Nordkyn
**cape in Nova Scotia** Sable
**cape in Pakistan** Fasta, Jaddi, Jiwani
**cape in Portugal** Espichel, Mondego, Roca
**cape in Senegal** Verde
**cape in Sicily** Boeo, Faro, Passaro
**cape in South Africa** Agulhas
**cape in Spain** Ajo, Dartuch, Gata, Moras, Nao, Ortegal, Palos, Sacratif, Tortosa
**cape in Tunisia** Blanc, Bon

**cape in Turkey** Bafra, Hinzir, Ince, Karatas, Kerempe
**Cape mission station** Elim
**Cape orchard area** Ceres
**caper** antic, bounce, bound, cavort, condiment, dance, dido, escapade, fling, frisk, frolic, fun, gambol, hop, jape, jest, jump, lark, leap, potherb, prance, prank, romp, shenanigan, shrub, skip, somersault, sport, spring, stunt, trick
**caper excitedly** cavort
**Cape rock hyrax** dassie
**caper shrub** cleome
**caper without advancing** capriole
**Cape Town theatre** Baxter, Nico Malan
**Cape Verde island** Fogo, Sal
**cape worn by Pope** fanon, orale
**capful of wind** breeze
**capital** assets, chief, essential, excellent, fatal, first, first-rate, important, investment, metropolis, primary, principal, resources, seat, stock, wealth, worth
**capital before Tokyo** Kioto
**capital gain** interest, profit
**capital invested** amount, sum
**capitalist** magnate, nabob
**capital item** asset
**capital letter** cap, majuscule, uncial
**capital of Aargau** Aarau
**capital of Acre** Rio Branco
**capital of Afghanistan** Kabul
**capital of Aland Islands** Mariehamn, Ahvenanmaa
**capital of Alaska** Juneau
**capital of Albania** Tirana, Tiranë
**capital of Alberta, Canada** Edmonton
**capital of Algeria** Algiers
**capital of ancient Syria** Antakiya, Antakya, Antioch
**capital of Angola** Luanda
**capital of Antigua and Barbuda** St John's
**capital of Argentina** Buenos Aires
**capital of Armenia** Yerevan
**capital of Australia** Canberra
**capital of Austria** Vienna, Wien
**capital of Aveyron** Rodez
**capital of Bahamas** Nassau
**capital of Bahrain** Manama
**capital of Bali** Denpasar
**capital of Bangladesh** Dhaka
**capital of Barbados** Bridgetown
**capital of Bavaria** Munich
**capital of Belgium** Brussels, Bruxelles
**capital of Belize** Belmopan
**capital of Benin** Porto Nova
**capital of Bermuda** Hamilton
**capital of Bhutan** Thimbu, Thimphu
**capital of Bolivia** La Paz, Sucre
**capital of Botswana** Gaborone

**capital of Brazil** Brasilia
**capital of British Honduras** Belize
**capital of Brunei** Bandar Seri Begawan
**capital of Bulgaria** Sofia
**capital of Burkina-Faso** Ouagadougou
**capital of Burundi** Bujumbura
**capital of Cambodia** Phnom Penh
**capital of Cameroon** Yaoundé
**capital of Canada** Ottawa
**capital of Canary Islands** Santa Cruz
**capital of Cape Province** Cape Town
**capital of Cape Verde** Praia
**capital of Cayman Islands** George Town
**capital of Chad** Ndjamena
**capital of Chile** Santiago
**capital of China** Beijing (Peking)
**capital of Colombia** Bogotá
**capital of Comoros** Moroni
**capital of Congo** Brazzaville
**capital of Corsica** Ajaccio
**capital of Costa Rica** San José
**capital of Crete** Canea, Khaniá
**capital of Cuba** Havana
**capital of Cyprus** Nicosia
**capital of Czechoslovakia** Prague
**capital of Denmark** Copenhagen
**capital of Djibouti** Djibouti
**capital of Dominica** Roseau
**capital of Dominican Republic** Santo Domingo
**capital of Ecuador** Quito
**capital of Egypt** Cairo
**capital of El Salvador** San Salvador
**capital of England** London
**capital of Equatorial Guinea** Malabo
**capital of Ethiopia** Addis Ababa
**capital of Falkland Islands** Stanley
**capital of Fiji** Suva
**capital of Finland** Helsingfors, Helsinki
**capital of France** Paris
**capital of French Guiana** Cayenne
**capital of French Polynesia** Papeete
**capital of Gabon** Libreville
**capital of Germany** Berlin, Bonn
**capital of Ghana** Accra
**capital of Great Britain** London
**capital of Greece** Athens
**capital of Greenland** Godhaven, Nuuk
**capital of Grenada** St George's
**capital of Guadeloupe** Basse-Terre
**capital of Guam** Agana
**capital of Guatemala** Guatemala City
**capital of Guinea** Conakry
**capital of Guinea-Bissau** Bissau
**capital of Guyana** Georgetown
**capital of Haiti** Port-au-Prince
**capital of Hawaii** Honolulu
**capital of Honduras** Tegucigalpa
**capital of Hong Kong** Victoria
**capital of Hungary** Budapest
**capital of Iceland** Reykjavik

**capital of India** Delhi
**capital of Indonesia** Jakarta
**capital of Iran** Tehran
**capital of Iraq** Baghdad
**capital of Ireland** Dublin
**capital of Isle of Man** Douglas
**capital of Israel** Jerusalem
**capital of Italy** Rome
**capital of Ivory Coast** Abidjan
**capital of Jamaica** Kingston
**capital of Japan** Tokyo
**capital of Jordan** Amman
**capital of Kashmir** Jammu, Muzaffarabad, Srinagar
**capital of Kenya** Nairobi
**capital of Kiribati** Tarawa
**capital of Kuwait** Kuwait City
**capital of Laos** Vientiane
**capital of Latvia** Riga
**capital of Lebanon** Beirut
**capital of Lesotho** Maseru
**capital of Liberia** Monrovia
**capital of Libya** Tripoli
**capital of Liechtenstein** Vaduz
**capital of Lithuania** Vilnius
**capital of Luxembourg** Luxembourg
**capital of Madagascar** Antananarivo
**capital of Malawi** Lilongwe
**capital of Malaysia** Kuala Lumpur
**capital of Mali** Bamako
**capital of Malta** Valletta
**capital of Martinique** Fort-de-France
**capital of Massachusetts** Boston
**capital of Mauritania** Nouakchott
**capital of Mauritius** Port Louis
**capital of Melbourne** Victoria
**capital of Mexico** Mexico City
**capital of Moldavia** Kishinev
**capital of Monaco** Monaco-Ville
**capital of Mongolia** Ulan Bator
**capital of Montserrat** Plymouth
**capital of Morocco** Rabat
**capital of Mozambique** Maputo
**capital of Myanmar** Yangon
**capital of Namibia** Windhoek
**capital of Natal** Pietermaritzburg
**capital of Nauru** Yaren
**capital of Nepal** Katmandu
**capital of Netherlands** Amsterdam, The Hague
**capital of Netherlands Antilles** Willemstad
**capital of New Caledonia** Nouméa
**capital of New Jersey** Trenton
**capital of New Zealand** Wellington
**capital of Nicaragua** Managua
**capital of Niger** Niamey
**capital of Nigeria** Lagos
**capital of Northern Ireland** Belfast
**capital of Northern Territory, Australia** Darwin
**capital of North Korea** Pyongyang

**capital of Norway** Oslo
**capital of Oman** Masqat, Muscat
**capital of Ontario** Toronto
**capital of Orange Free State** Bloemfontein
**capital of Oregon** Salem
**capital of Orkney Islands** Kirkwall
**capital of Pakistan** Islamabad
**capital of Panama** Panama City
**capital of Papua New Guinea** Port Moresby
**capital of Paraguay** Asunción
**capital of Peru** Lima
**capital of Philippines** Quezon City
**capital of Poland** Warsaw
**capital of Portugal** Lisbon
**capital of Prince Edward Island** Charlottetown
**capital of Puerto Rico** San Juan
**capital of Qatar** Doha
**capital of Queensland** Brisbane
**capital of Republic of Maldives** Malé
**capital of Réunion** Saint-Denis
**capital of Rhode Island** Providence
**capital of Rhone department** lyon
**capital of Romania** Bucharest
**capital of Rwanda** Kigali
**capital of Samoa** Apia
**capital of Sardinia** Cagliari
**capital of Saudi Arabia** Jidda, Riyadh
**capital of Senegal** Dakar
**capital of Seychelles** Victoria
**capital of Sicily** Palermo
**capital of Sierra Leone** Freetown
**capital of Singapore** Singapore
**capital of Solomon Islands** Honiara
**capital of Somalia** Mogadiscio
**capital of South Africa** Cape Town, Pretoria
**capital of South Australia** Adelaide
**capital of South Korea** Seoul
**capital of Soviet Union** Moscow
**capital of Spain** Madrid
**capital of Sri Lanka** Colombo
**capital of St Helena** Jamestown
**capital of St Kitts-Nevis** Basseterre
**capital of St Lucia** Castries
**capital of Sudan** Khartoum
**capital of Surinam** Paramaribo
**capital of Swaziland** Mbabane
**capital of Sweden** Stockholm
**capital of Switzerland** Bern
**capital of Syria** Damascus
**capital of Tahiti** Papeete
**capital of Taiwan** Taipeh, Taipei
**capital of Tanzania** Dodoma
**capital of Tasmania** Hobart
**capital of Tennessee** Nashville
**capital of Texas** Austin
**capital of Thailand** Bangkok
**capital of The Gambia** Banjul
**capital of Tibet** Lhasa
**capital of Togo** Lomé
**capital of Tonga** Nuku'alofa
**capital of Trinidad and Tobago** Port-of-Spain
**capital of Tunisia** Tunis
**capital of Turkey** Ankara
**capital of Turks and Caicos Islands** Grand Turk
**capital of Tuvalu** Funafuti
**capital of Uganda** Kampala
**capital of Ukraine** Kiev
**capital of United Arab Emirates** Abu Dhabi
**capital of United Kingdom** London
**capital of United States of America** Washington DC
**capital of Uruguay** Montevideo
**capital of Venezuela** Caracas
**capital of Vermont** Montpelier
**capital of Victoria** Melbourne
**capital of Vietnam** Hanoi
**capital of Wales** Cardiff
**capital of West Bengal** Calcutta
**capital of Western Australia** Perth
**capital of Western Samoa** Apia
**capital of West Germany** Bonn
**capital of Yemen Republic** San'a, Aden
**capital of Yugoslavia** Belgrade
**capital of Zaire** Kinshasa
**capital of Zambia** Lusaka
**capital of Zimbabwe** Harare
**capital punishment** death, execution, scaffold
**capital ship** battleship
**capitulate** relent, submit, surrender, yield
**caplike crest on a bird's head** calotte
**cap like fez** tarboosh, tarbouche, tarbush
**cap of container** lid, top
**cap on end of walking stick** fer(r)ule
**Capri cavern** blue grotto
**caprice** absurdity, caper, craze, eccentricity, erraticism, fad, fancy, fantasy, fickleness, flightiness, freak, humour, impulse, lark, oddity, prank, quirk, spree, vagary, whim
**capricious** abnormal, arbitrary, bizarre, changeable, eccentric, erratic, fanciful, fickle, idiosyncratic, inconsistent, inconstant, irregular, odd, peculiar, personal, protean, strange, subjective, uncertain, unpredictable, unreasonable, unsettled, unsteady, variable, volatile, wavering, weird, wild, wilful
**capricious action** freak, whimsy
**capricious fit of ill-temper** tantrum
**caprid** capridae, goat
**caprine animal** goat
**capsicum** paprika, pepper
**capsicum pod** chili
**capsize** invert, keel over, overset, overthrow, overturn, spill, tip, upend, upset, upturn
**cap's peak** visor
**captain** boss, chief, chieftain, command(er), direct, foreman, governor, headman, lead(er), master, officer, pilot, principal, shipmate, skipper, steer
**captaincy** leadership
**captain of industry** capitalist, financier, industrialist, magnate
**caption** banner, device, head(ing), headline, imprint, inscribe, inscription, label, legend, motto, name, rubric, style, title
**captious objection** cavil
**captious reasoner** sophist
**captivate** allure, attract, bewitch, charm, dazzle, delight, enamour, enchant, endear, enrapture, enthral(l), entrance, fascinate, hypnotise, infatuate, inflame, intrigue, lure, mesmerise, regale, seduce, tantalise, transport, win
**captivating** alluring, attracting, beguiling, bewitching, charming, dazzling, enchanting, enslaving, enthralling, fascinating, glamorous, infatuating, luring, seducing
**captive** caged, confined, convict, detainee, ensnared, hostage, imprisoned, incarcerated, internee, prisoner, restricted, slave, subjugated
**captive as a pawn** hostage
**captivity** bondage, constraint, imprisonment, restraint, servitude, slavery, subjection
**capture** apprehend, apprehension, arrest, bag(ging), catch, gain, grab, imprison, loot, nab, net, overmaster, overpower, pillage, seize, seizure, snagging, snare, snatch, take, trap, wrest
**capture again** retake
**capture by assault** storm
**capture fish** hook, land, net
**capture interest of** attract, charm, fascinate
**capture the mind** hypnotise
**cap with broad circular flat top** Tam-o'-shanter, tammy
**cap with tassel** fez
**car** auto(mobile), carriage, coach, limousine, motorcar, sedan, tjorrie, vehicle
**carafe** bottle, jar
**car and driver for hire** taxi
**carapace** turtle's back
**caravan** trailer
**caravan animal** camel

**caravan for instance** trailer
**caravan-like vehicle** camper
**caravan nomad** gypsy
**caravanserai** inn, khan
**caraway-flavoured liqueur** kümmel
**carbamide** urea
**carbamidine** guanidine
**carbine** rifle
**car body** chassis
**carbolic acid** phenol
**carbon and iron alloy** steel
**carbonate** aerate
**carbonated drink** soda, lemonade
**carbonated water** soda
**carbon diamond** bo(a)rt, bortz
**carbon dust** soot
**carbon formation** carbonisation
**carbonised vapour** smoke
**carbonised vegetable matter** peat
**carbon particles** soot
**carbora** koala
**Carborundum** abrasive, emery
**car capacity** seater
**carcass** body, bones, cadaver, corpse, framework, skeleton
**carcinoma** blight, cancer, canker, corruption, evil, growth, malignancy, neoplasm, pestilence, rot, tumour
**car competition** Grand Prix, rally
**car crash** accident, prang
**car cylinder disk** piston
**card above the nine** honour
**car damaged beyond repair** write-off
**cardboard box** carton
**cardboard container** box, carton
**card from a sweetheart** Valentine
**card game** baccarat, beggar-my-neighbour, bezique, blackjack, brag, bridge, canasta, cas(s)ino, crib(bage), écarté, euchre, fan-tan, faro, gin, hearts, loo, matrimony, monte, nap, ombre, pam, patience, pinochle, piquet, poker, pontoon, quadrille, rouge-et-noir, rummy, skat, snap, solitaire, solo, tarot, trente-et-quarante, twenty-one, vingt-et-un, war, whist
**card game for one** patience, solitaire
**card-game for three** ombre
**card game for two** écarté, piquet
**card game like poker** brag
**card game of patience** solitaire
**cardiac insert** pacer
**cardiac organ** heart
**cardialgia** heartburn
**Cardiff's country** Wales
**cardigan or turtleneck** sweater
**cardinal number** one, two, three, etc.
**cardinal point opposite the north** south
**cardinal point opposite the west** east

**cardinal's hat** beretta, biretta
**cardinal's skullcap** zucchetto
**cardinal's title** Eminence
**cardinal under Henry VIII** Wolsey
**cardiomegaly** megalocardia
**card play** finesse
**card predicting** cartomancy
**car driver** chauffeur, motorist
**car driver's strap** seat belt
**card sequence** run, straight
**card series** coronet
**cards left after deal** talon
**cards receiving during game** hand
**cards remaining after the deal** talon
**card suit** clubs, diamonds, hearts, spades
**card that will not take a trick** loser
**card to record scores** scorecard
**card with three spots** trey
**card with two spots** deuce
**care** attention, burden, carefulness, caution, charge, circumspection, concern, heed, like, protection, regard, responsibility, solicitude, supervision,, trouble, vigilance, watchfulness, worry
**care deeply** adore, love
**careen** lilt, lurch
**career** calling, course, craft, dart, dash, employment, hurry, hustle, job, lifework, livelihood, living, movement, occupation, onrush, profession, progress, pursuit, run, rush, scramble, scud, scuttle, spank, speed, sprint, trade, vocation, work
**care for** appreciate, attend, consider, desire, enjoy, fancy, foster, keep, like, love, mind, nurse, prefer, protect, tend, treasure, want
**care for the future** foresight
**carefree** amenable, blithe, buoyant, calm, casual, cheerful, debonair, easy, easy-going, flexible, gay, happy, happy-go-lucky, jaunty, joyful, lenient, liberal, light-hearted, lively, merry, mirthful, moderate, placid, relaxed, sprightly, sunny, uncritical, vivacious
**careful** alert, anxious, attentive, awake, aware, canny, cautious, chary, circumspect, concerned, considerate, discreet, exact, fearful, finicky, guarded, heedful, judicious, meticulous, painstaking, politic, prudent, scrupulous, tactful, vigilant, wakeful, wary, watchful
**careful and deliberate** studied
**careful examination** perusal
**careful in observance** precise
**carefully considered** measured
**carefully considered observation** animadversion

**carefully groomed** soigné(e)
**careful management** husbandry
**carefulness in use of money** parsimony
**careful notice** heed
**careful thought** consideration
**careful to avoid doing wrong** scrupulous
**careful to avoid undesired consequences** prudent
**careful use of resources** economy
**careful watch** vigilance
**care in spending** economy
**careless** absent-minded, blasé, calm, casual, cool, debonair, forgetful, heedless, inaccurate, inadvertent, inattentive, inconsiderate, indifferent, indiscreet, insouciant, irresponsible, languid, lax, negligent, nonchalant, reckless, remiss, slack, slapdash, thoughtless, unconsidered, unmindful, unthinking, untidy, unwary
**careless and untidy** slovenly
**careless in dress** raffish
**carelessly** absent-mindedly, forgetfully, hastily, heedlessly, inaccurately, incautiously, indiscreetly, irresponsibly, lackadaisically, neglectfully, negligently, perfunctorily, remissly, sloppily, thoughtlessly, unconcernedly, unthinkingly
**careless mistake** blunder, boner
**careless of duty** remiss
**careless pedestrian** jaywalker
**careless preacher** martext
**careless writing** scrawl
**care of feet** pedicure
**care of hands** manicure
**care of horses at inn** ostler
**cares for** tends
**cares for sick** doctor, nurse
**caress** bestow, brush, cuddle, embrace, endearment, favour, fondle, fondling, hug, kiss, massage, nestle, pamper, pat, pet, stroke, stroking, touch
**caress with the lips** kiss
**care taken beforehand** precaution
**caretaker** concierge, custodian, guard, janitor, keeper, porter, steward, superintendent, warden, watchman
**caretaker of building** janitor, superintendent
**careworn** distressed, drawn, exhausted, haggard, jaded, pinched, run-down, toil-worn, troubled
**car exhibition** motor show
**car frame** chassis
**car fuel** gas, petrol
**car gear** drive, first, high, low, reverse, second

**cargo** burden, consignment, freight, goods, lading, load, shipment, ware
**cargo boat** freighter
**cargo overboard** jetsam
**cargo ship** freighter
**cargo stabiliser** ballast
**car horn** hooter
**car house** garage
**Caribbean dance** limbo
**Caribbean island** Barbados, Cuba, Dominica, Grenada, Guadeloupe, Haiti, Jamaica, Martinique, Montserrat, Nassau, Saba, Tobago, Trinidad
**Caribbean island group** Antilles, Caicos, Cayman, Leeward, Turks, Windward
**Caribbean island republic** Dominican, Haiti
**caribou** deer, reindeer
**caricature** burlesque, cartoon, exaggerate, exaggeration, lampoon, parody, satire, satirise, travesty
**caricaturist** cartoonist
**caring** compassionate, humane, merciful, sympathetic, tender
**car journey** drive
**carlin** pug
**car meeting** rally
**carmine** red
**carnage** bloodbath, bloodshed, butchery, cataclysm, decimation, devastation, havoc, holocaust, massacre, murder, slaughter
**carnal** animal(istic), bestial, bodily, brutish, coarse, concupiscent, corporeal, earthly, erotic, fleshly, human, impure, lecherous, lewd, libidinous, lubricious, lustful, mundane, natural, prodigal, profane, salacious, secular, sensual, sexual, temporal, voluptuous, worldly
**carnal weakness** flesh
**carnation** clove pink
**carnival** fair, feast, festival, festivity, fête, fiesta, gala, merrymaking, pageant, procession, revel(ry), sideshow, spectacle
**carnival feature** clown, sideshow
**carnivore** aardwolf, animal, bear, canine, cat, cerval, cheetah, civet, cougar, dog, ferret, fox, genet, hy(a)ena, jackal, jaguar, leopard, lion(ess), lynx, meateater, meerkat, mongoose, ocelot, otter, panda, polecat, predator, puma, ratel, seal, tiger, tigress, weasel, wolf
**carnivore's jaws** maw
**carnivorous** flesh-eating
**carnivorous animal** bear, cheetah, crocodile, dog, hy(a)ena, leopard, lion, lioness, sarcophile, tiger

**carnivorous cat** lion, lynx, margay
**carnivorous doglike mammal** hy(a)ena
**carnivorous feline** lion, tiger
**carnivorous mammal** hy(a)ena, leopard, lion, tiger, weasel, wolf
**carnivorous quadruped** bear, cheetah, dog, hy(a)ena, jackal, leopard, lion(ess)
**carob** algarroba, locust tree, pod, Saint John's bread, tree
**car of airship** nacelle
**carol** noel, song
**Caroline islands group** Palau, Pelew
**car or bus** vehicle
**carousal** bacchanal, binge, debauch, fling, jollification, merrymaking, orgy, potation, revel, romp, spree, wassail
**carouse** booze, compotation, debauch, dissipate, feast, fling, imbibe, quaff, revel, roister, spree, wanton, wassail
**carousel** merry-go-round
**carouser** partygoer, reveller
**carp** animadvert, belittle, blame, cavil, censure, complain, criticise, decry, deprecate, discredit, faultfind, hypercriticise, impugn, nag, quibble, rebuke, reproach, reprove, wrangle
**carpal joint** knee
**car part** bonnet, boot, door, gearbox, handle, hood, piston, tyre, wheel
**carpenter's boring tool** auger
**carpenter's machine** planer, shaper, lathe
**carpenter's pin** nail
**carpenter's tool** adze, auger, chisel, hammer, lathe, level, mallet, plane, saw
**carpenter's tool for smoothing wood** plane
**carpentry by-product** sawdust
**carpentry joint** mortice, mortise
**carpet** rug
**carpet covering** drugget
**carpet fibre** istle, ixtle
**carpet from Afghanistan** herat(i)
**carpet from India** agra
**carpet from the Caucasus** baku, kuba
**carpet place** floor, wall
**carpet shark** wobbegong
**carpet thread base** warp
**carpet town** Axminster
**carpet with long pile** afghan
**carpet with thick pile** moquette
**carplike fish** chub, dace, ide, roach, roud, rud(d)
**carport** garage
**carpus** wrist
**car repairer** mechanic, panelbeater
**carriage** administration, air, barouche, bearing, brougham, cabriolet, carrying, cart, chaise, chariot, clarence, coach, conduct, conveyance, demeanour, deportment, dogcart, execution, hansom, management, manner, mien, phaeton, posture, surrey, transport(ation), vehicle, wag(g)on
**carriage and horses with attendants** equipage
**carriage-driver** coachman
**carriage for the sick** ambulance
**carriage of India** ekka
**carriage of Java** sado(o)
**Carribean country** Haiti
**car ride** drive, lift, tour
**carried away** distrait, ecstatic, engrossed, rapt
**carried on the wing** airborne
**carried smoothly through** slick
**carried weight** tare
**carrier** bearer, conveyance, mailman, messenger, newsboy, porter, postman, runner, transporter
**carrier bird** pigeon
**carrier of bad luck** Jonah
**carries blood from heart** artery
**carries water** drain, vessel, waterpipe
**carrion-eating bird** vulture
**carrion-feeding carnivore** hy(a)ena
**Carroll's heroine** Alice
**carrot eater** hare, rabbit
**carrotlike plant** caraway, chervil, dill, parsnip
**carroty** orange-red
**carry** accomplish, bear, borne, bring, conduct, convey, drive, freight, gain, hump, lead, support, take, tote, transfer, transmit, transport
**carry as load** bear, freight, tote
**carry away** abduct, capture, kidnap, remove, transport
**carry away with delight** entrance
**carry blood from heart** arteries
**carry by boat across river** ferry
**carry by wagon** cart
**carry forward** extend
**carry from one place to another** transport
**carrying cargo** laden
**carrying case** étui
**carrying-chair** sedan
**carrying charge** cartage
**carrying in womb** gestation
**carrying load basket** pannier
**carrying no stress** atonic, unaccented
**carrying out** doing, implementation, performing, pursuance
**carrying out the death sentence** executing
**carrying weapons** armed
**carry into effect** do, perform
**carry in womb** gestate
**carry off** abduct, kidnap

**carry off as booty** loot, rifle
**carry off illegally** kidnap
**carry on** administer, continue, do, endure, exercise, last, lead, maintain, manage, misbehave, operate, persevere, persist, proceed(ing), run, storm, wage
**carry-on case** grip
**carry on flirtation** philander
**carry on rivalry** compete, vie
**carry on strategic movement** operate
**carry on the body** wear
**carry on underhand plot** intrigue, conspire
**carry on war** wage
**carry onward** continue
**carry out** accomplish, achieve, act, apply, conduct, discharge, do, execute, fulfil, implement, obey, perform, perpetrate, realise, undertake
**carry out again** redo, reenact
**carry out command** obey
**carry out duties** serve
**carry over** postpone, remainder, tide
**carry the torch for** admire, love, pine
**carry too far** overdo
**carry upward** escalate
**carry visibly** bear
**carry weight** bias, count, impel, incline, influence, matter, motivate, persuade
**carry with effort** lug
**car salesman** dealer
**car seat cover** tonneau
**car shelter** carport, garage
**car's ignition system part** coil
**car silencer** muffler
**car's luggage compartment** boot
**car's starter switch** ignition
**cart** barrow, bear, bring, buckwagon, buggy, carriage, carry, convey, convoy, deliver, dray, ferry, fetch, handcart, haul, lug, ossewa, portage, pushcart, transfer, transmit, transport, trolley, truck, wag(g)on
**carte blanche** authority, passe-partout, permit, power, sanction
**cart for supermarket food** trolley
**Carthaginian** Punic
**cartilage** gristle
**cartilage at root of tongue** epiglottis
**cartilage between vertebrae** disc
**cartilage under dog's tongue** lytta
**cartilaginous fish** dogfish, elasmobranch, ray, shark, skate
**cartographer draws it** map
**cartography** map-making, mapping
**carton** box, case, packet
**cartoon** animation, caricature, comic, drawing, lampoon, parody, pasquinade, portrayal, representation, satire, sketch, strip, take-off
**cartoon artist** animator
**cartoon creator** Disney
**cartoonist** caricaturist
**cartridge chamber in gun** magazine
**car under balloon** basket, gondola
**carve** chip, chisel, cut, divide, engrave, etch, fashion, form, grave, hack, hew, incise, indent, make, mould, sculpt, sculpture, slice
**carve a figure** sculpt
**carved** chiselled, clear-cut
**carved brooch** cameo
**carved clan emblem** totem
**carved form** statuary, statue
**carved gem** cameo
**carved groove** glyph
**carved image** bust, idol, relief, statue
**carved Japanese toggle** netsuke
**carved portrait** icon
**carved projection at the intersection of ceiling ribs** boss
**carved stone** menhir
**carved stone as supporting bracket** corbel
**carved toggle** netsuke (J)
**carve in relief** emboss
**carve in wood or stone** sculpt
**carving** chipping, chiselling, cutting, dividing, engraving, etching, forming, hacking, hewing, moulding, sculpting, sculpture, sculpturing, slashing, slicing, whittling
**carving in bas-relief** anaglyph
**carving in intaglio** diaglyph
**carving on stone** lithoglyph
**carving tool** burin, chisel
**car window blower** demister
**car with all seats enclosed** saloon
**car with fold-down hood** convertible
**car with folding hood** convertible, landaulet
**car with metal roof** hard-top
**cascade** avalanche, cataract, deluge, downpour, falls, flood, Niagara, slide, Victoria, waterfall
**case** action, box, chest, circumstance, condition, container, contingency, étui, example, frame, framework, illustration, instance, lawsuit, occurrence, patient, plight, pod, position, predicament, process, situation
**case containing a set of cutlery** canteen
**case containing the charge for a gun** cartridge
**case expressing object of verb** accusative
**case expressing subject of verb** nominative
**case for banknotes** wallet
**case for carrying drawings** portfolio
**case for carrying goods** crate
**case for holding arrows** quiver
**case for holding tea** canister
**case for shipping** crate
**case for ship's compass** binnacle
**case-law** precedent
**case of drawers** cabinet, dresser
**case of larva** indusium
**case on necklace** locket
**case with relics of a saint** shrine
**cash** banknotes, coin(age), currency, dough, exchange, money, redeem
**cash advance** loan
**cash and carry** self-service
**cash box** register, till
**cash corrupter** bribe
**cash down payment** lump-sum
**cashew nut** acajou
**cashew oil** cardol
**cashier** accountant, banker, bursar, purser, teller, treasurer
**cash in** redeem
**cash raffle** lottery
**cash refund** rebate
**cash register** till
**casino** gaming house
**casino card game** baccarat, blackjack, faro, poker, twenty-one
**casino employee** dealer
**casino game** baccarat, blackjack, faro, poker, roulette, twenty-one
**casino worker** croupier
**cask** barrel, butt, firkin, keg, tub, tun, vat
**cask binder** hoop iron
**cask component** stave
**cask for herrings** cade
**caskmaker** cooper
**Caspian, for instance** sea
**casque** helmet, morion
**cassava** manioc, marioca, tapioca
**cassava grains** tapioca
**casserole** stew, saucepan, skillet, terrine
**casserole of chicken in red wine** coq au vin (F)
**casserole of partly-roasted game** salmi(s)
**casserole of white meat in creamy sauce** blanquette
**cassette** tape
**cassette of movie** video
**cassette ribbon** tape
**cassia** senna
**cassia bark** cinnamon
**cassia leaves** senna
**cassia pods** senna
**cast** actors, add, allot, appoint, apportion, arrange, assign, bestow, calculate, computation, compute, confer, conjecture, consider,

contrive, defeat, demeanour, deposit, devise, direct, disband, discard, dismiss, eject, emit, fling, forecast, foretell, fortune, found, guess, hue, hurl, inclination, kind, lose, lot, mo(u)ld, pitch, plan, ponder, propel, puke, put, reckon, reject, scheme, shed, slough, tendency, throw, tint, toss, vomit
**cast a ballot** vote
**cast about** grope, look, ransack, search, seek
**cast a brief look at** glimpse, peek, peep, peer
**cast a flood of light** refulgent
**cast amorous glances** leer, ogle
**cast an eye** glance
**cast aside** abandon, discard, dismiss, postpone, reject
**cast a spell upon** enchant
**cast aspersions** slur
**castaway** outcast, shipwrecked, wreck
**cast away** throw
**cast ballot** vote
**cast doubt** impeach
**cast down** abase, condemn, crush, deject, depress, desolate, discourage, dishearten, dispirit, sadden
**cast drops over** spatter
**caster wheel** roller
**cast eyes over something** inspect, survey
**cast feathers** mew, moult
**cast glances** leer, ogle
**castigate** beat, blame, cane, censure, chasten, chastise, correct, criticise, discipline, flail, flay, flog, lace, lash, pummel, punish, rebuke, reprimand, scold, scourge, smite, spank, thrash, trounce, upbraid, whip
**casting mould** die, matrix
**casting of lots** sortition
**cast into shade** overshadow
**castle** chateau, citadel, fortress, palace, rook, stronghold
**castle defence** battlement, moat
**castle ditch** moat
**castle in France** château
**castle in Scotland** Balmoral
**castle in the air** daydream, pipedream
**castle tower** turret
**castle trench** moat
**cast loose** detach, disengage, free, loosen, undo, unfasten
**cast metal bar** ingot
**cast of characters** company, personae, players, troupe
**cast off** abandoned, discard, remove, shed, slough
**cast-offs** debris, flotsam, refuse
**Castor and Pollux** Gemini

**cast out** abort, banish, eject, evict, exorcise, expel, seclude
**castrate** asexualise, debilitate, emasculate, expurgate, geld, impoverish, neuter, purge, spay, unman, weaken
**castrated animal** gelding, neuter, seg(g), spay
**castrated bovine** steer, ox
**castrated bull** bullock, ox, steer, stot
**castrated chicken** capon
**castrated cock** capon
**castrated deer** havier
**castrated horse** gelding
**castrated male pig** hog
**castrated man** eunuch, spado
**castrated ram** hamel, wether
**castrate horse** geld
**castrato** eunuch
**cast someone into the shade** better, exceed, excel, outdo, outplay, overshadow, surpass, transcend
**cast spell** bewitch, enchant
**casual** accidental, blasé, blithe, chance, contingent, cursory, easy, facile, fortuitous, heedless, indifferent, informal, irregular, loose, nonchalant, occasional, offhand, random, relaxed, unconcerned, unexpected, unforeseen, unpremeditated
**casual affair** fling, interlude
**casual and confident** calm
**casual comment** remark
**casual event** happening
**casual labourer** handyman, odd-jobber
**casually** accidentally, casually, contingently, fortuitously, indifferently, informally, irregularly, nonchalantly, occasionally, prefunctorily, randomly, relaxedly, unconcernedly, unexpectedly, unintentionally
**casual manner** careless, offhand, unconcerned, unceremonious, uninterested
**casual meal** snack
**casual mention** passing reference
**casualness** fortuitousness, informality, perfunctoriness, randomness, unconcernedness, unexpectedness
**casual photograph** snapshot
**casual reference** allusion, mention
**casual remark** allusion, obiter dictum
**casual report** fable
**casual shoe resembling a moccasin** loafer
**casual shoes** sandals, sneakers, tackies
**casual top** T-shirt
**cat** feline, kitten, kitty, manx, mog(gy), puss(ycat), tabby, tom

**cataclysm** blow, calamity, catastrophe, collapse, convulsion, debacle, deluge, devastation, disaster, misadventure, torrent, tragedy, upheaval
**cataleptic state** trance
**catalogue** arrange, classify, codify, directory, docket, enumeration, file, group, index, inventory, itemise, list, record, register, roll, roster, schedule, tabulate
**catalogue of names** list, roll
**catamaran** boat, raft, yacht
**catapult** ballista, heave, hurl, onager, pitch, plunge, shanghai, sling(shot), toss
**cataract** cascade, chute, deluge, falls, flood, fountain, outpouring, shower, torrent, waterfall
**catarrh** rheum
**catarrhal inflammation of the mucous membrane in the nose** coryza
**catastrophe** calamity, cataclysm, conclusion, disaster, end, mischance, misfortune, mishap
**cat-boat having centreboard** una
**cat breed** Burmese, Manx, Siamese
**catcall** meow
**catch** apprehend, apprehension, arrest, captivate, capture, clasp, clutch, cop, detect, detent, ensnare, entangle, entrap, fastening, favourite, grab, grasp, grip, hasp, latch, nab, nail, net, nip, ratchet, represent, rub, secure, seize, seizure, snag, snare, snatch, stratagem, strike, surprise, take, trap, understand, win, wrestling
**catch-all word** et al, et alii, etc(etera)
**catch a thief** nab
**catch at proper time** nick
**catch attention** flag, hail
**catch breath** gasp, pant
**catch eels** sniggle
**catcher** fielder
**catch fish** gill net, hang, jab, jig
**catch fish with a net** trawl
**catch fish with hands** grabble, guddle, handfast
**catch glimpse of** espy, see
**catch herring** tack
**catch in a game of tag** tig
**catch in a snare** entrap
**catch in a trap** ensnare
**catch in door** latch, sneck, snick
**catching** captivating, charming, contagious, infectious, snaggy, winsome
**catching device** net, trap
**catch meaning of** twig, understand
**catch of fish** haul
**catch of game** bag

catch of gunlock  sear, sere
catch on  comprehend, grasp, see
catch one's breath  chink, gasp, rest
catchpenny  spurious, superficial, trivial
catch-phrase  cry, slogan
catch sight  descry, espy, find, glance,
    glimpse, recognise, see, spot, spy
catch suddenly  grab, nab, snatch
catch the attention  arrest
catch the breath  gasp
catch the eye  attract
catch the scent  smell, sniff
catch to fasten hatch  dogbolt
catch unawares  snare, trap
catch up  overtake
catch up with  approach, overtake
catchword  cue, indication, maxim,
    phrase, shibboleth, slogan
catchy phrase  punch line, slogan
catchy song  ditty
categorical  absolute, direct, downright,
    emphatic, explicit, express, positive,
    unconditional, unequivocal,
    unqualified
categorical statement  dictate, diktat
categorise  arrange, assort, class,
    classify, divide, grade, group, list,
    order, rank, sort
category  arrangement, assortment,
    class(ification), compilation,
    denomination, department, division,
    genre, genus, grouping, heading,
    kind, order, section, sort, species,
    sphere, subdivision, type, variety
category of art  genre
cater  furnish, outfit, provision, purvey,
    supply, victual
cater for  accommodate
caterpillar  larva
caterpillar that produces silk  silkworm
cater to low tastes  pander
catfish  barbel, wolffish
cat good at catching mice  mouser
catgut  whipcord
catgut for surgeon  suture
cat-headed Egyptian goddess  Bast
cathedral  minster
cathedral administrator  dean
cathedral city  Canterbury, Cape Town,
    Cologne, Ely, Frankfurt,
    Grahamstown, Guildford, Köln,
    Rheims, Rome, Paris, Winchester,
    York
cathedral clergyman  dean
cathedral in Paris  Notre Dame
cathode opposite  anode
Catholic anthem  motet
Catholic clergyman  priest
catholic in views  eclectic
Catholic's chain of beads  rosary
Catholic service  mass
catlike  feline

catlike mammal  civet
catlike predator  genet
catmint  catnip, nepeta
catnip  catmint, nepeta
cat noise  meow, mew, miaow, purr
cat of America  cougar, jaguar, puma
cat or twins  Siamese
cat's chances of survival  nine lives
cat's cry  meow, mew, miaow
cat's foot  paw
cat-sized primate of Madagascar
    aye-aye, squirrel-like lemur
cat's nails  claws
cat's-paw  dupe
cat's prey  mouse, rat
cat's screaming  caterwaul
cat's sound  purr
cat's toenail  claw
cattish  feline
cattle  beef, bovines, cows, kyloe (Sc),
    livestock, neat, oxen, stock
cattle assemblage  drove, herd
cattle breed  Aberdeen-Angus,
    Africander, Afrikan(d)er, Alderney,
    Angus, Ayrshire, Bonsmara,
    Brahman, Devon, Dexter,
    Drakensberger, Durham, Friesian,
    Galloway, Guernsey, Hereford,
    Highland, Holstein, Jersey,
    short-horn, Simmenthaler, Zebu
cattle-breeding establishment  ranch
cattle charge  stampede
cattle cry  low, moo
cattle dealer  drover
cattle disease  anthrax, murrain,
    rinderpest
cattle drover  overlander
cattle dung  mis, muck
cattle enclosure  corral, kraal, run
cattle farm  ranch
cattle fodder  hay, lucerne
cattle fold  corral, kraal, run
cattle in a stable  manger
cattle land  camp, pasture, range
cattle lane  cowpath
cattleman  rancher
cattle minder  cowherd
cattle pen  corral
cattle plague  anthrax, murrain,
    rinderpest
cattle prison  pound
cattle ranch  farm
cattle roundup  rodeo
cattle shed  helm, lair
cattle shelter  kraal
cattle station  ranch
cattle stealing  rustling
cattle tender  herder
cattle thief  rustler
cattle trough  crib, manger
cat variety  Burmese, Manx, margay,
    ocelot, Persian, Siamese

cat with no tail  Manx
caudal appendage  tail
caudal region  tail
caudal segment  urosome
caught by surprise  unprepared,
    unready
caught in the act  red-handed
caught napping  unawares,
    unprepared, unready
caught sight of  spied, spotted
caulking fibre  oakum
causal science  (a)etiology
cause  agent, aim, basis, case, create,
    creator, determinant, determine,
    effect, end, explanation, ground,
    ideal, incentive, inducement, issue,
    justification, make, motive, mover,
    object, occasion, origin, parent,
    principle, provocation, purpose,
    reason, source, topic
cause anger  rankle
cause colic  gripe, wind
caused by doctors  iatrogenic
caused by earthquakes  seismic
caused by gout  arthritis
caused by lack of thought
    thoughtlessness
caused by lice  pedicular
caused by rain  pluvial
cause death of  kill
cause discontent  embitter, stir
cause distress  straiten, upset
cause dull continuous pain  ache
cause emotion  agitate, excite, irritate
cause engine to run quickly  rev
cause fear  misgive
cause for action  suit
cause grief to  grieve
cause havoc  wreak
cause injury to  damnify, hurt
cause lingering anger  rankle
cause mental distress  annoy
cause of a disease  (a)etiology
cause of anxiety  bugbear
cause of bad luck  hoodoo, jinx
cause of disease  bacteria, germ, virus
cause of disgrace  ignominy, shame
cause of dissatisfaction  affliction,
    complaint, oppression
cause of distress  tribulation
cause of grief  dole, loss
cause of happiness  felicity
cause of infection  bacteria, germ, virus
cause of itch  irritant
cause of legal action  gravamen
cause of ruin  bane
cause of surf  tide
cause of the Titanic's sinking  iceberg
cause of trouble  bane, matter
cause of war  casus belli (L)
cause pain to  afflict, hurt
cause panic  alarm

**cause person to change beliefs** convert
**cause sharp pain** sting
**cause slight anger to** annoy
**cause slimming** diet
**cause someone to become anxious** upset
**cause someone to feel self-conscious** embarrass
**cause suppuration** fester
**cause to accept** inure
**cause to adhere** glue, paste, stick
**cause to agree** accord
**cause to approach** attract
**cause to believe** persuade
**cause to be loved** endear
**cause to bow** bend
**cause to break with** estrange
**cause to cease for a time** suspend
**cause to come** bring
**cause to contract** constrict
**cause to develop gradually** evolve
**cause to disclose** elicit
**cause to exist** effect, engender
**cause to fester** rankle
**cause to flow** pour
**cause to function** actuate
**cause to go** send
**cause to go wrong** mislead
**cause to lose confidence** dishearten
**cause to love** endear
**cause to occur by turns** alternate
**cause to remember** remind
**cause to revolve** trundle, turn
**cause to sink** settle
**cause to suffer agony** agonise
**cause to suffer for an offence** punish
**cause wonder** amaze
**causing** beginning, compelling, creating, effecting, engendering, generating, inciting, inducing, motivating, occasioning, precipitating, producing, provoking
**causing abortion** abortifacient
**causing addiction** habit-forming
**causing annoyance** irksome, irritating, troublesome
**causing argument** controversial
**causing a sharp stinging pain** smart
**causing a split** divisive
**causing awe** breathtaking
**causing cancer** carcinogenic
**causing curiosity** interesting, intriguing
**causing darkness** tenebrific
**causing death** fatal, lethal
**causing displeasure** offensive
**causing dissension** divisive
**causing excitement** breathtaking
**causing fatal injury** deadly, lethal
**causing great pain and sorrow** heart-rending

**causing great public excitement** sensational
**causing grief** grievous
**causing horror** grisly, macabre
**causing insensibility** anaesthetic
**causing laughter** comical, hilarious, humorous, ludicrous
**causing motion** motive
**causing overthrow** subversion
**causing pain** cruel, painful
**causing rancour** embittering
**causing reversion** repulsive
**causing separation** divisive
**causing sleep** hypnotic, narcotic, soporific
**causing strain** tensive
**causing sweating** sudorific
**causing sympathy** poignant
**causing trouble** onerous
**causing tumours** oncogenic, oncongenous
**causing vexation** irksome
**causing vomiting** emetic
**caustic** acid, acrid, astringent, biting, bitter, burning, corroding, corrosive, keen, mordant, sarcastic, soda, tart
**caustic agent** escharotic
**caustically witty** dry
**caustic poison** phenol
**caustic solution** alkali, lye
**caustic substance** lye, phenol
**caution** admonish, admonition, care, circumspection, concern, counsel, discretion, forewarn, heed(fulness), injunction, prudence, thought, vigilance, wariness, warn(ing), watchfulness
**cautionary traffic light** amber
**caution firmly** admonish
**caution to avoid damage or loss** care
**cautious** alert, careful, chary, circumspect, discreet, guarded, heedful, judicious, prudent, tentative, vigilant, wary
**cautious about giving information** cagey, secretive
**cautious in attitude** careful, reserved
**cavalcade** array, column, company, cortege, file, line, list, march, parade, procession, queue, rank, retinue, row, string, train, troop
**cavalry** dragoons, horse, horseman, hussars, lancers, squadron, troopers
**cavalry fabric** twill
**cavalry flag** guidon
**cavalryman** dragoon, hussar, lancer, trooper, u(h)lan
**cavalryman of Algeria** spahee, spahi
**cavalryman of India** sowar, suwar
**cavalry soldier** hussar, lancer, sabre, trooper
**cavalry spear** lance

**cavalry sword** sabre
**cavalry unit** commando, troop
**cavalry weapon** lance
**cave** cavern, cavity, den, grotto, hollow
**caveat** admonition, alarm, allowance, caution, condition, exception, forewarning, limitation, modification, requirement, reservation, stipulation, warning
**cave dweller** caveman, troglodyte
**cave-dwelling salamander** olm
**cave in** collapse, fall, give way, slip, subside, yield
**cave inhabitant** troglodyte
**cave of David** Adullan
**caver** pot-holer, spel(a)eologist, spelunker
**cavern** antrum, cave, cavity, den, grotto
**cave science** spel(a)eology
**cave searcher** pot-holer, spel(a)eologist, spelunker
**caviar** beluga, caviare, condiment, ikra, roe, savouriness
**caviar fish** beluga, shad, sterlet, sturgeon
**cavil** belittle, carp, censure, complain, criticise, decry, demur, deprecate, hassle, hypercriticise, impugn, nag, nitpick, object(ion), quibble, rebuke, reproach, subtlety
**cavity** abyss, antrum, aperture, cave, cavern, chamber, crater, crevasse, depression, dip, fissure, follicle, fossa, hole, hollow, lumen, mine, mouth, opening, orifice, pit, sac, scoop, shaft, sinus, space, tunnel, vacuole, void
**cavity behind mouth and nose** pharynx
**cavity containing blood** haematocele
**cavity in jawbone** antrum
**cavity in road** pothole
**cavity in solid body** hole
**cavity in throat containing vocal cords** larynx
**cavity of human body** belly, stomach
**cavity of the cheek** antrum
**cavity of the ear** antrum
**cavity of the middle ear** tympanum
**cavity wall** septum
**cavort** bounce, bound, caper, caracole, frisk, frolic, gambol, hop, play, prance, romp, skip, toyi-toyi, whirl
**cay** key
**cayman** alligator, caiman, crocodilian
**cease** abstain, avast, conclude, desist, discontinue, end, finish, halt, pause, quit, rest, stay, stop, terminate
**cease abruptly** abort
**ceasefire** truce
**cease from action** rest
**cease from activity** hibernate

**ceaseless** incessant
**cease opposing** surrender, yield
**cease to be** vanish
**cease to be visible** disappear
**cease to blame** forgive
**cease to exist** die, vanish
**cease to flow** stagnate
**cease to function** break down
**cease to live** die
**cease to reside at** leave, move
**cease to resist** submit
**cease to sleep** waken
**cease to stand** fall, lie, sit
**cease work** quit, rest, retire
**cease working to enforce demands** strike
**cecity** blindness
**cedar** conifer, deodar
**cedarbird** waxbill
**cedar of India** deodar
**cede** grant, relinquish, resign, surrender, transfer, yield
**ceding** allowing, conceding, donating, forsaking, giving, granting, releasing, renouncing, resigning, surrendering, transferring, yielding
**ceiling fan made of palm leaf** punka(h)
**ceiling of dome** cupola
**ceiling of room** dome
**Celebes ox** anoa
**celebrate** acclaim, advertise, announce, applaud, cheer, commemorate, exalt, extol, herald, honour, laud, observe, praise, proclaim, venerate, worship
**celebrated** distinguished, eminent, fabled, famed, famous, historical, honoured, illustrious, legendary, lustrous, notable, prominent, renowned, well-known
**celebrated for his** *Divina Commedia* Dante
**celebrated renown** fame
**celebrate extravagantly and publicly** maffick
**celebrate in song** cant, chant, sing song, warble
**celebration** anniversary, ball, carnival, carousal, ceremonial, ceremony, dance, event, extravaganza, feast, festival, festivity, fête, gala, jollification, jubilee, merrymaking, observance, occasion, party, procedure, spree
**celebration of last day of year** Hogmanay
**celebrity** dignitary, distinction, fame, famous, glory, hero, honour, lion, luminary, magnate, name, notable, personage, personality, popular, prominence, renown, star(dom), superstar

**celerity** acceleration, alacrity, animation, dispatch, expedition, go, haste, precipitance, promptness, quickness, rapidity, speed, swiftness, velocity, vigour, vim, vivacity
**celery** smallage
**celerylike plant** chicory, endive, fennel, udo
**celeste** sky-blue
**celestial** angelic, divine, Elysian, empyreal, empyrean, eternal, ethereal, hallowed, heavenly, paradisal, saintly, seraphic, sky, stellar
**celestial abode** heaven
**celestial bear** Ursa
**celestial being** angel, cherub, seraph
**celestial body** comet, moon, planet, satellite, star, sun
**celestial light** star
**celestial phenomenon** blackhole, nebula
**celestial region** sky
**celestial secrets** arcana caelestia (L)
**celestial sphere** orb, planet
**cell** cavity, chamber, cubicle, cyto-, dungeon, enclave, group, unit
**cella** naos
**cellar** base, basement, bunker, cellarage, crypt, dungeon, prison, storage, underground, vault
**cell formed by union of two gametes** zygote
**cell-like** cytoid
**cell of honeycomb** alveolus
**cello spike** endpin
**cellular compartment** loculus
**cellular framework** stroma
**cellular lava** scoria
**celluloid** xylonite
**cellulose fabric** rayon
**cell under ground** dungeon
**cell-window rod** bar
**cell without a nucleus** akaryote
**Celt** Breton, Cornish, Erse, Gael, Gaul, Manx, Welsh
**Celtic** Erse, Gael, Irish, Scots
**Celtic chief god** Dagda
**Celtic group** clan
**Celtic harp** clarsach
**Celtic language** Erse, Gaelic, Irish, Welsh
**Celtic language group** Gadhelic, Goid(h)elic
**Celtic minstrel** bard
**Celtic poet** bard
**Celtic priest** Druid
**Celtic sword** saex
**cement** cohere, combine, concrete, glue, join, mortar, paste, plaster, sealant

**cement again** reset
**cemetery** churchyard, graveyard, necropolis
**cemetery marker** tombstone
**cemetery tree** cypress, yew
**cemetery worker** grave-digger
**cenotaph** mausoleum, memorial, monument, pyramid, statue, tomb, tombstone
**censer** cauldron, incenser, scent, thurible, vessel
**censor** amend, blue-pencil, bowdlerise, cut, edit, excise, expurgate
**censure** blame, blaming, condemn(ation), criticise, criticism, disapprobation, disapproval, rebuke, reprehend, reprehension, reprimand, reproach, reprobation, reproof, reprove, scold, slate, stricture
**censure sarcastically** taunt
**censure severely** excoriate
**census** count, demography, enumeration, headcount, poll, statistics, tabulation, tally
**centipede** golach, myriapod, veri
**cento** medley
**central** basic, chief, dominant, essential, focal, inner(most), interior, key, main, median, middle, primary, principal
**Central African lake** Tanganyika, Victoria
**central African waterway** Uele River
**Central American dug-out boat** pitpan
**Central American republic** Bahamas, Costa Rica, Cuba, Dominican, El Salvador, Haiti, Jamaica, Nicaragua, Panama
**Central American tribe** Maya
**Central Asian** Uzbek
**Central Asian title** khan
**Central Asian wild ass** chigetai, dziggetai
**central boss on a shield** umbo
**central character** hero, protagonist
**central column** axis
**central court of Roman house** atrium
**central European cheese** Tilsit
**central European river** Elbe
**central heating fuel** oil
**central idea** theme
**central Italian region** Tuscany, Umbria
**central line** diameter
**central line of rotation** axis
**central part** cadre, core, heart, pith
**central part of atom** nucleus
**central part of root** stele
**central part of wheel** hub
**central pillar of a winding staircase** newel
**central pin** pivot

**central point** focus, omphalos, pivot
**central point of earthquake** epicentre
**central processing unit of computer** CPU, mainframe
**central shaft** axis
**central stairpost** newel
**central theme** keynote, leitmotif, leitmotiv
**central unit of an atom** nucleus
**central US river system** Platte
**central US state** Colorado, Oklahoma
**centre** axis, converge, core, crux, focalise, focus, fulcrum, heart, hub, kernel, marrow, middle, midst, nave(l), nucleus, omphalos, pivot, unite
**centre for trade** market
**centre of amphitheatre** arena
**centre of apple** core
**centre of attention** cynosure, limelight, target
**centre of attraction** focal
**centre of commerce** emporium
**centre of eruption** volcano
**centre of porcelain industry** Limoges
**centre of target** bull's-eye
**centre of wheel** hub
**centre ornament for dinner table** epergne
**centrepiece** cynosure, epergne, focus, highlight, hub
**centre-piece for a table** epergne
**centre remover** corer
**centrifugal** avoiding, divergent, efferent, radiating, repellent, unassembled
**centripetal** afferent
**century** era, period, siècle (F)
**century plant** aloe, pita
**cephalalgia** headache
**cephalic skin** scalp
**cephalic support** headrest
**cephalopod** octopus
**cephalopod mollusc** cuttle(fish)
**ceramic piece** tile
**ceramic resembling agate or marble** agateware
**ceramics** china, crocks, earthenware, ironstone, mosaics, porcelain, pottery, stoneware, tiles
**ceramic square** tile
**ceramics oven** kiln
**ceramic worker** potter
**cerate** balm, ointment, salve
**ceratoid** horny
**cereal** barley, buckwheat, corn, farina, grain, maize, mealie, millet, oats, porridge, rice, rye, sago, semolina, spelt, tapioca, wheat
**cereal bristle** awn
**cereal chaff** bran
**cereal coating** bran

**cereal crop** barley, buckwheat, corn, farina, grain, maize, mealie, millet, oats, porridge, rice, rice, rye, sago, semolina, spelt, tapioca, wheat
**cereal disease** blight, ergot, mildew, rust, smut
**cereal fodder** lucerne, sorg(h)o
**cereal food** bran, couscous, mealiemeal, oats, polenta, porridge
**cereal grain** barley, bran, corn, farina, flour, mealie, oat, rice, wheat
**cereal grass** lucerne, millet, oats, raggee, raggy, ragi, rice, rye, sorghum, wheat
**cereal holder** cob, ear, mealie
**cereal husks** bran
**cereal plant** barley, corn, maize, millet, rye, wheat
**cereal seed** corn, grain, kernel, mealie
**cereal seed bearer** ear, mealie
**cereal spike** cob, ear, mealie
**cerebral** brain, intellectual, mental
**cerebrate** ponder, think
**cerebrum** brain
**ceremonial** ceremony, formal, liturgical, ritual, solemnity, stately
**ceremonial act** rite
**ceremonial dress** robe
**ceremonial finery** regalia
**ceremonial form** ritual
**ceremonial of court** etiquette
**ceremonial pole** mace
**ceremonial practice** ritual
**ceremonial procession** pageant, parade
**ceremonial seat** throne
**ceremonial speech** oration
**ceremonial splendour** pomp
**ceremonial staff** mace, sceptre
**ceremonial style** pomp
**ceremonies at burial** funeral
**ceremony** celebration, formality, function, observance, pomp, rite, ritual, service
**ceremony used in conferring knighthood** accolade
**cerise** cherry-red
**certain** absolute, assured, confident, convinced, definite, determinate, determined, fixed, incontestable, incontrovertible, indisputable, indubitable, infallible, irrefutable, obvious, particular, positive, reliable, settled, special, stated, sure, undeniable, undoubted, unfailing, unquestionable
**certain attitude** pose
**certain bee** apian, drone, queen, worker
**certain freshwater algae** frog-spawn
**certain fuel** peat
**certain gesture** sign

**certainly** à coup sûr (F), assuredly, certainly, conclusively, confidently, convincedly, decidedly, definitely, fixedly, indeed, indubitably, inevitably, plainly, positively, surely, undeniably, undoubtedly, unmistakably, validly
**certainly not** never
**certain military operation** siege
**certain office machine** computer, copier, facsimile, fax, typewriter
**certain picture holder** locket
**certain quantity of** some
**certain spread** margarine, oleo-margarine
**certain to succeed** infallible
**certain turtle** snapper
**certainty** assurance, confidence, conviction, faith, inevitability, positiveness, sureness, trust, validity
**certain type of insect causing malaria** mosquito
**certain type of ship** boat, craft, ferry, galleon, liner, steamer, tanker, trawler, vessel, yacht
**certain weasel** ermine
**certificate** accredit, acknowledg(e)ment, certify, confirm, credential, diploma, document, licence, license, sanction, statement, support, testimonial, validate, voucher, warrant
**certificate giving permission** licence
**certificate in lieu of cash** check, cheque, scrip
**certificate of character** reference, testimonial
**certificate of conduct** testimonial
**certificate of holding shares** scrip
**certify** assure, attest, authorise, corroborate, declare, vouch
**certify a will** probate
**certify validity of** attest
**cerumen** earwax
**cervical muscle** scalenus
**cervical ornament** choker, necklet
**cervix** neck
**cess** rate, tax
**cessation** abatement, break, ceasefire, close, closing, completion, conclusion, culmination, delay, dénouement, discontinuance, discontinuation, end(ing), finale, finish, gap, halt, hesitation, holiday, interlude, intermission, interval, let-up, lull, pause, recess, relaxation, relief, respite, rest, stay, stoppage, wait
**cessation from hostilities** armistice, ceasefire, discontinuance
**cessation of breathing** apnoea
**cessionary** assignee, grantee

**cetacean mammal** dolphin, whale
**cha** tea
**chabouk** Eastern whip
**Chad currency** franc
**Chad lake** Chad
**Chad plateau** Ennedi
**Chad's French name** Tchad
**chafe** abrade, anger, annoy, boil, fume, gall, incense, inflame, irritate, offend, provoke, rage, rasp, rub, scrape, scratch, seethe, vex, worry
**chafed-skin bubble** blister
**chaff** banter, dregs, joking, refuse, rubbish, teasing, trash, waste
**chaffer** bargain, haggle
**chaff of grain** bran
**chagrin** abash, affront, agonise, anguish, annoy(ance), awkwardness, bashfulness, brood, confound, confusion, dampen, dash, disappoint, discomfort, discompose, disconnect, discourage, distress, embarrass(ment), fluster, fret, goad, grieve, harass, humiliation, irritate, mortification, mortify, provoke, ruffle, shame, vexation
**chain** fasten, links, lock, manacle, secure, shackle
**chain armour** mail
**chain loop** link
**chainmail** armour
**chain of anchor** cable
**chain of command** apparatus, hierarchy
**chain of flowers** festoon
**chain of mountains** sierra
**chain of rocks or coral** reef
**chain part** link, ring
**chair** administer, armchair, bench, couch, fauteuil, lead, official, preside, rocker, seat, sofa, stool, wheelchair
**chair-back timber strip** splat
**chair carried by two men** sedan
**chair for one with problem** hotseat
**chair in which criminals are electrocuted** electric
**chairman** administrator, chief, director, executive, facilitator, governor, leader, manager, principal, speaker
**chairman's hammer** gavel, mallet
**chair of state for sovereign** throne
**chair part** arm, back, cushion, rung, splat, wing
**chair rest** arm
**chairs provided** seating
**chair with no back** stool
**chaise** shay
**chalcedony** agate, jasper, onyx
**chalice** communion cup
**chalk pencil** crayon
**chalk up** accumulate, achieve, attain, gain, record, register, score, tally, win

**chalk up to** accredit, ascribe, attribute, charge, impute
**challenge** affront, brave, claim, confront, contest, dare, defiance, defy, demand, dispute, dissent, face, invitation, invite, negation, question, summons, tackle, test, threat, trial, ultimatum
**challenge as false** impugn
**challenge for the ball** tackle
**challenging** braving, claiming, daring, defiant, defying, demanding, disputing, investigating, provoking, questioning, requiring, stimulating, summoning, taxing, trying
**chalybite** siderite
**chamber** apartment, assembly, bedroom, cavity, closet, compartment, council, cubicle, enclosure, hall, harbour, haven, hollow, room, shelter
**chamber of plant's ovary** locule
**chamber of the heart** atrium, ventricle
**chamber pot** jerry, po, potty
**chamfer** bevel, channel, flute, groove
**chamois** antelope, aoudad, cloth, gems, izard, leather, shammy, skin
**champagne bottle** magnum
**champagne rating** brut, sec
**champ at the bit** chafe, fidget, fret, squirm
**champion** ace, advocate, avenger, champ, conqueror, defend, hero, leader, maintainer, paladin, protector, subjugator, support, veteran, victor, vindicator, warrior, winner
**champion of rights** ombudsman
**chance** accident(al), casual, danger, fate, fortuitous, fortune, happen, hazard, luck, occur, opportunity, peril, possibility, random, risk
**chance breeze** fluke
**chance it** risk, gamble
**chancellor's official residence** chancellery
**chancel of church** bema, bima(h)
**chance on** encounter, find, meet
**chances** odds
**chances of success** odds
**chancing** risking
**chancy** alarming, breakneck, dangerous, exposed, hazardous, insecure, menacing, nasty, perilous, risky, threatening, treacherous, ugly, uncertain, unsafe
**chancy game** gambling, lottery
**chandelier** light fitting
**change** adept, alter(ation), alternate, amend, bandy, barter, commute, convert, diversify, exchange, fluctuate, flux, interchange,

modification, modify, modulate, mutate, mutation, novelty, permute, replace, reverse, shift, shuffle, substitute, swap, swerve, switch, trade, transfigure, transform(ation), transition, transmutation, turn, variation, variegate, variety, vary
**changeability** compliancy, flexibility, malleability, pliancy, resilience, versatility
**changeable** alterable, capricious, convertible, displaceable, erratic, fickle, fitful, inconstant, irregular, mercurial, mobile, mutable, protean, reformable, removable, shifting, substitutable, transformable, transmittable, uncertain, unreliable, unstable, vacillating, variable, volatile
**changeable in mood** moody, temperamental
**changeableness** caprice, levity, vibration
**change about** alter, chop, yaw
**change and growth** diversification
**change appearance** disguise, obvert, transfigure
**change back** revert
**change character of** denature
**change colour** blush, burn, crimson, discolour, dye, flame, turn
**change colour of fabric** dye
**change completely** reverse, revolutionise
**change copy** revise
**change course** cant, deviate, dodge, drift, gybe, jibe, sag, sheer, shift, slew, stray, swerve, veer, wear, yaw
**change course in sailing** tack
**change course suddenly** dodge, veer
**change direction** angle, break, cant, chop, cut, detour, haul, knee, shift, swerve, turn, veer
**change direction during action** swerve
**change dwelling** flit, move
**change feathers** moult
**change for another use** adapt
**change for better** amend, help, improve
**change form** develop, transmute
**change for worse** bedevil, deteriorate
**change from larva to adult** metamorphose
**change from liquid to vapour** evaporate
**change from solid to liquid** melt
**change front** tergiversate
**change genetically** mutate
**change in course** sheer
**change in direction** jog, knee, snapback, step

**change in lake level** seiche
**change in the body indicating its state of health** symptom
**change into** become
**change into stone** lapidify, petrify
**change iron into steel** acierate
**change key of music** modulate
**changeless** consistent, constant, firm, fixed, immutable, invariable, stable, static, steadfast, steady, unvaried, unvarying, unwavering
**changeling** child, dolt, dunce, elf, fool, idiot, imbecile, oaf, renegade, substitute, traitor, turncoat
**change made** modification
**change music** muta
**change of character** metamorphosis
**change of direction** veer
**change of heart** conversion
**change of mind** caprice, tergiversation
**change of mood** vary
**change of place** motion
**change of sea level** eustacy
**change of vowel in related words** ablaut
**change of word** anagram
**change one's abode** flit, move, trek
**change one's dwelling** move
**change one's mind** tergiversate, turn, withdraw
**change one's principles** tergiversate
**change one's tune** reconsider
**change or adapt** modify
**change over** transfer
**change place** move, relocate
**change places** move, switch
**change position** ambulate, move, shift, veer
**change promoter** catalyst
**change radically** revolutionise
**change residence** move, trek
**change shape** creep, deform, draw
**change sides** apostatise
**changes in tissues caused by disease** histopathology
**change stolen money** launder
**change thermostat** reset
**change the time** reset, set
**change to opposite** reverse
**change to proposed motion** amendment
**change to suit** adapt
**changing** altering, alternate, bartering, converting, displacing, diversifying, exchanging, flexible, fluctuating, interchanging, moderating, modifying, mutating, reforming, remodelling, removing, reorganising, replacing, restyling, shifting, substituting, swapping, trading, transforming, transmitting, varying, veering

**changing booth** cubicle
**changing lizard** chameleon
**changing position** ambulatory, moving
**changing room** cubicle
**channel** avenue, canal, chute, conduct, conduit, duct, guide, gutter, main, passage, transmit
**channel at side of street** gutter
**channel-cleaning device** dredge
**channel for conveying liquids** conduit
**channel for conveying water** aqueduct
**channel for rainwater** drain, gutter
**channel in Chile** Ancho, Cheap, Cockburn, Moraleda
**channel in China** Bashi
**channel in Hawaii** Aua, Kaiwi, Pailolo
**channel in Mauritius** Quoin
**channel in the body** meatus
**Channel Island off Cherbourg Peninsula** Alderney
**Channel Islands** Alderney, Great Sark, Guernsey, Herm, Jersey, Jethou, Lihou, Little Sark
**channel of communication** medium
**channel of water connecting two larger areas** strait
**channel on TV** station
**channel or pipe** conduit
**chant** berceuse, canticle, carol, chorus, croon, descant, dirge, hymn, intonation, intone, melody, monody, psalm, recitation, recite, serenade, sing, song, tune, utter
**chanter** intoner
**chanticleer** cock, rooster
**chant of lamentation for the dead** dirge
**chaos** anarchy, bedlam, confusion, disarray, disorder, havoc, mess, muddle, pandemonium, tumult, turmoil, uproar
**chaotic** anarchic, confused, disorganised, riotous, uncontrolled
**chap** bloke, character, cove, fellow, guy, individual, lad, man, oke, ou, person, sort, type
**chapeau** hat
**chapel in Vatican** Sistine
**chaperon** accompany, attend, attendant, cap, chaperone, companion, custodian, duenna, escort, governess, guard(ian), hat, housemother, matron(ise), nursemaid, oversee, protector, protectress, safeguard, turban, tutelar(y), tutor(ess), watch
**chaperonage** accompaniment
**chaplain** padre
**chaplain in army** padre
**chaplet** anadem, beads, coronal, garland, loop, necklace, rosary, wreath

**chapman** pedlar
**chapter** clause, division, episode, part, period, section, stage, topic
**chapter of the Koran** sura(h)
**char** blacken, blister, burn, cleaner, cremate, fire, incinerate, oxidise, roast, scald, scorch, sear, singe, toast, torrefy
**character** characteristic, constitution, disposition, feature, figure, individuality, letter, mark, nature, personality, quality, reputation, symbol, trait
**character analysis** psychograph
**character blot** slur
**character flaw** defect, failing, fault, foible, penchant, weakness
**character in Italian comedy** Arlecchino, harlequin, Pantaloon, Scaramouch
**characterise** depict, describe, picture, portray, represent, term
**characterised by deep snoring** stertorous
**characterised by friendliness** amiable, amicable
**characterised by masses of ice** glacial
**characterised by order** methodical
**characteristic** attribute, distinctive, distinguishing, feature, nature, normal, peculiarity, property, singular, trait, typical
**characteristic air** mien
**characteristically** distinctively, distinguishingly, individually, peculiarly, representatively, singularly, specially, specifically, symbolically, typically
**characteristic cry of bird** call
**characteristic feature of thing** essence
**characteristic of old age** senescent, senile, senility
**characteristic of particular language** idiomatic
**characteristic of young people** youthful
**characteristic sign of disease** symptom
**characteristic spirit of community** ethos
**characteristic taste** savour
**characteristic vocal sound of cow** low, moo
**character of alphabet** letter, rune, hieroglyph, sign
**character of sound** tone
**character representing a word** logo(gram)
**characters in play** cast, dramatis personae
**character sketch** vignette

**character stain** blot, stigma
**charcoal** carbon
**charcoal-burner** collier
**chard** beet
**charge** accusation, accuse, allegation, allege, amount, arraign, ascribe, assault, attack, betray, bid, blame, burden, care, command, commission, concern, cost, debt, direction, duty, encumbrance, enjoin, exhort, expense, fee, freight, impeach, imputation, impute, incriminate, incrimination, inculpate, indict(ment), instruct(ion), involve, liability, load, mandate, office, onset, order, payment, precept, price, rate, require, rush, sortie, tax, trust, urge
**charge a person with an offence** accuse
**charge atoms** ionise
**charged** accused, arraigned, blamed, commanded, electric, enjoined, exhorted, impeached, indicted, instructed, involved, ordered, required
**charged atom or particle** ion
**charged with** accountable
**charge for transportation** fare
**charge for transporting mail** postage
**charge for using ferry** ferriage
**charge for using road** toll
**charge on money exchange** agio
**charge on oath** adjure
**charge per unit** rate
**charger** dish, horse, mount, platter, steed, trooper
**charge to an account** debit
**charge to excess** supercharge
**charge too high a price** overcharge
**charge with an offence** accuse, indict
**charge with bubbles** aerate
**charge with carbon dioxide** aerate, carbonate
**charge with crime** accuse, incriminate
**charge with electricity** electrify
**charge with fault** accuse
**charge with gas** aerate
**charge with wrongdoing** accuse
**charging low prices** cheap, sale
**chariot with four wheels** quadriga
**chariot with two horses** biga
**chariot with two wheels** essed
**charisma** allure, appeal, attraction, aura, charm, enchantment, fascination, grace, it, magnetism, power, talent
**charitable** beneficent, benevolent, benign(ant), bountiful, broad-minded, considerate, generous, kindly
**charitable Biblical woman** Dorcas
**charitable distribution** dole

**charitable donation** alms
**charitable gift** alms, donation, pittance
**charitable one** donor
**charity** aid, alms(giving), altruism, benefaction, bounty, compassion, courtesy, donation, favour, generosity, gift, kindness, leniency, liberality, oblation, offering, philanthropy, sympathy, tolerance, understanding, unselfishness
**charity bazaar** fête
**charity event** benefit
**charlady** cleaner
**charlatan** affecter, allurer, beguiler, cheat, deceiver, defrauder, empiric, fake(r), humbug, hypocrite, impostor, pharisee, pretender, quack(salver), sciolist, swindler
**Charles Lamb's pen name** Elia
**charley horse** cramp
**charm** allure(ment), amulet, appeal, attract(ion), attractiveness, bauble, beguile, bewitch(ment), cajole, captivate, charisma, delight, enamour, enchant, endear, enrapture, entice, entrance, fascinate, fascination, fetish, grace, greegree, grigri, jewellery, juju, lure, magic, mascot, mesmerise, obeah, obi, ornament, please, spell, subdue, talisman, trinket, win
**charmer** astrologer, beauty, belle, Circe, clairvoyant, cracker, Don Juan, enchanter, enchantress, fortuneteller, hex, palmist, seducer, seductress, siren, soothsayer, sorcerer, sorceress, stunner, temptress, Valentino, vamp, Venus, witch
**charming** adorable, amiable, delicate, delightful, endearing, engaging, entrancing, eyesome, graceful, idyllic, lovely, lovesome, picturesque, pleasing, sweet, winning, winsome, wizard
**charming hairdresser** Delilah
**charmingly correct** chic
**charming rural scene** idyll
**charm irresistibly** fascinate
**charnel house** interment, morgue, mortuary, ossuary
**Charon's ferry fee across Styx** obol
**charred candlewick** snuff
**charred remains** ashes, cinders
**charred wood** charcoal
**chart** blueprint, course, diagram, draw, graph, guide, itinerary, list, log, map, outline, plan, plot, record, represent, scheme, sketch, table, tabulate, tabulation
**charter** agreement, concession, constitute, constitution, contract, designate, engage, franchise, guaranty, hire, lease, license, permit, privilege, rent, warranty
**charter a bus** rent
**chart showing differences** graph
**charwoman** char, cleaner, domestic, housekeeper, maid(servant), servant
**chary** accurate, alert, attentive, aware, bashful, cagey, careful, cautious, choosy, circumspect, conscientious, discreet, fastidious, guarded, heedful, judicious, mindful, painstaking, precise, prudent, shy, sparing, tentative, thrifty, vigilant, wary, watchful
**chase** course, drive, emboss, engrave, expel, follow, hound, hunt, pursue, pursuit, quest, suit, track, trail
**chase after** pursue
**chase women** philander
**chasing game** tag
**chasm** abyss, breach, break, canyon, cavity, cleft, crater, crevasse, depth, fissure, gap, gorge, gulf, hiatus, pit, ravine, void
**chasm in earth or rock** rift
**chaste** austere, celibate, decent, elegant, immaculate, incorrupt, innocent, modest, moral, neat, pure, quiet, refined, restrained, simple, unaffected, undefiled, vestal, virgin, virtuous, wholesome
**chasten** afflict, castigate, correct, cow, discipline, humble, punish, repress, subdue, tame
**chastise** beat, berate, birch, castigate, correct, cudgel, curry, discipline, punish, slap, smack, spank, strap, thrash, thresh, whip
**chastise severely** castigate
**chat** chatter, converse, gossip, natter, talk, tête-à-tête, word
**chateau** castle
**chattels** accessories, appointments, assets, belongings, capital, dunnage, effects, equipment, estate, fittings, furnishings, furniture, gear, goods, holdings, impedimenta, means, movables, paraphernalia, possessions, property, resources, riches, things, trappings, wealth
**chatter** abracadabra, babble, blab, blather, cackle, chat, drivel, gab(ble), garrulity, gibber, gossip, jabber, jargon, mumble, mutter, natter, palaver, patter, prate, prattle, talk, tattle, twaddle, yak
**chatterbox** gasbag
**chatterer** gossip, magpie
**chatter idly** gabble, natter, prattle
**chatter in childish way** prattle

**chattering bird** chatterer, cotinga, magpie, mynah
**chattering talk** patter
**chatter noisily** cackle
**chatter rapidly** jabber
**chatty** conversational, familiar, friendly, informal, newsy, talkative
**chatty person** conversationalist
**chauffeur** driver
**cheap** bargain, base, common, contemptible, cut-price, despicable, economical, inexpensive, inferior, keen, low, low-priced, lowly, mean, paltry, poor, reduced, sale, scurvy, second-rate, shoddy, showy, sordid, tatty, tawdry, vulgar, worthless
**cheap and showy** flash, tawdry
**cheap café** hash house
**cheap cigar** stogie, stogy
**cheap entertainment** honky-tonk
**cheaper version of book** paperback
**cheapest passage** steerage
**cheapest sailing accommodation** steerage
**cheap hotel** hostel
**cheap inferior wine** plonk, rotgut, vaaljapie
**cheaply** bon marché (F)
**cheaply attractive** flashy
**cheaply melodramatic** transpontine
**cheap ornamentation** tinsel
**cheap shop** bon marché (F)
**cheap showy finery** tawdry
**cheap trifle** gimcrack
**cheap wine** plonk, rotgut, vaaljapie
**cheat** bilk, catch, charlatan, cheater, chicanery, chisel, con, cozen, deceit, deceive, deception, defraud, delude, diddle, dupe, entrap, fake, fool, fraud, gudgeon, gyp, hoodwink, impostor, imposture, inveigle, knave, mislead, phony, pitfall, rogue, sharper, swindle(r), trap, trick(ster), twister, victimise, welsh, wile
**cheat by flattery** cajole
**cheater** chiseller, cozener
**cheating spouse** adulterer
**cheat on** betray, cuckold, deceive
**cheat on bet** welch, welsh
**cheat out of money** swindle
**check** arrest, bar, bridle, chain, compare, confirm, constraint, control, curb, curtail, damper, delay, examination, examine, halt, hinder, hindrance, hobble, impede, impediment, inhibit, inspect, inspection, investigate, investigation, limit(ation), measure, monitor, note, obstacle, obstruct(ion), pause, probe, rebuff, rein, repress(ion), research, restrain(t), restriction, retard, scrutinise, scrutiny, stem, stop(page), stub, study, test, thwart, tick(et), verify, vet
**check accounts** audit
**check accuracy of text** edit
**checked development** aborting
**checked fabric** tattersall
**checkered material** gingham
**checkered woollen cloth** plaid, tartan
**checkerwork inlay** mosaic
**check growth** stunt
**checkmate game** chess
**check out** examine, investigate, test
**check text** edit
**check thoroughly** inspect, vet
**check to progress** setback
**check up on** overlook, oversee, regulate, supervise
**check wheel** sprag
**cheek** arrogance, audacity, boldness, brass, brazenness, chop, defiance, disrespect, effrontery, gall, gill, impertinence, impudence, insolence, jowl, leer, nerve, sass(iness), sauce, saucy, temerity
**cheekbone** malar, zygoma
**cheek cosmetic** rouge
**cheek-puffing illness** mumps
**cheeky** abrupt, abusive, audacious, bad-mannered, blunt, bold, brash, brusque, churlish, contemptuous, coquettish, curt, discourteous, disrespectful, forward, ill-bred, impertinent, impolite, impudent, insolent, insulting, irreverent, misbehaved, offhand, pert, rash, reckless, rude, sassy, saucy, temerarious, uncivil
**cheeky garden bird** mina, munah, myna(h), piet-my-vrou, robin
**cheeky smile** grin
**cheep** chirp
**cheer** acclaim, applaud, brighten, cheerfulness, clap, comfort, elate, encourage(ment), exhilarate, food, gaiety, gladden, gladness, hail, hearten, hooray, hurrah, hurray, incite, inspirit, joy, merriment, mirth, provisions, shout, solace, uplift, warm
**cheer for matador** olé
**cheerful** blithe, bright, cheering, cheery, contented, gay, gladdening, gleeful, happy, hearty, jolly, jovial, joyful, joyous, lively, merry, pleasant, riant, spirited, sprightly, sunny
**cheerful and self-confident** jaunty
**cheerful ardour** alacrity
**cheerful enthusiasm** ebullience
**cheerful manner** debonair
**cheerfulness** cheer, delight, felicity, gaiety, gayness, geniality, gladness, glee, happiness, joyfulness, joyousness, mirth, pleasure, sunshine
**cheerful play** frolic
**cheerful readiness** alacrity
**cheerful song** lilt, lyric, melody
**cheerful sprite** pixie
**cheering** applause, auspicious, comforting, encouraging, exciting, good, happy, pleasant, reassuring, revitalising
**cheering shout** rah
**cheer in trouble** solace
**cheerio** adieu, cheers, ciao (I), farewell, goodbye, hello
**cheerleader** yell-guide
**cheerless** abandoned, austere, barren, bleak, cold, dark, dejected, depressed, depressing, deserted, despondent, dismal, dispirited, downcast, drab, drear(y), dull, forlorn, gloomy, grim, heartbroken, lamenting, lightless, miserable, murky, sad, sombre, woeful
**cheer up** animate, brighten, comfort, encourage, enhearten, enliven, gladden, hearten, invigorate, quicken, solace
**cheery greeting** hello
**cheese** Amsterdam, Blamey, blue, Brie, Camembert, Carré, casein, Cheddar, Cheshire, curd, Derby, Dorset Blue, Dunlop, Edam, Emment(h)al, feta, Gloucester, Gorgonzola, Gouda, Gruyère, Herrgardsost, Killarney, mozzarella, Parmesan, ricotta, Roquefort, sweetmilk
**cheese dish** fondue, rarebit
**cheese-flavoured white sauce** mornay
**cheese sauce** fondue
**cheese with red rind** Edam
**cheesy** caseous, cheese-like
**chef** cook
**chef's garment** apron
**chef's method** recipe
**chemical** soda
**chemical action of the sun's rays** actinism
**chemical attraction** affinity
**chemical compound** enol, ester, ether
**chemical compound exploding readily** fulminate
**chemical element that looks like tin** cadmium
**chemically inactive** inert
**chemical radical** amyl
**chemical routine of living** metabolism
**chemical salt** sal
**chemical suffix** -ene
**chemical test** assay
**chemical vessel** aludel, retort
**chemical weapon** napalm

**chemise** sark
**chemistry of fermentation** zymology
**chemistry of living things** biochemistry
**chemistry room** lab(oratory)
**chemist's heater** etna
**chemist's workroom** lab(oratory)
**cheque** draft, order
**cheque counterfoil** stub
**chequered woollen cloth** plaid, tartan
**cherish** admire, appreciate, comfort, cultivate, encourage, entertain, esteem, foster, harbour, love, nourish, nurse, nurture, prize, shelter, support, sustain, tender, treasure, value
**cherished** nourished, nursed, nurtured, prized, sheltered, supported, sustained, treasured
**cherished possession** keepsake, momento, souvenir
**cherish grievance** nurse
**cheroot** cigar
**cheroot as made in Manila** Manila
**cherry brandy** Kirsch
**cherry colour** cerise
**cherry-red** cerise
**cherub** angel, baby, child, infant, seraph
**cherubic** adorable, angelic, innocent, lovable, seraphic, sweet
**cherubim** angels
**chess castle** rook
**chess deadlock** stalemate
**chess defeat** checkmate
**chess draw** stalemate
**chess move** castle, check, cook, fianchetto, fork, gambit, key, neck, ploy
**chess opening** debut, gambit, pirc, Ruy Lopez
**chesspiece** bishop, castle, king, knight, man, pawn, queen, rook
**chessplayer of highest class** grandmaster
**chess ploy** gambit
**chess sacrifice** gambit
**chess victory** checkmate
**chest** ark, bin, bosom, box, breast, bunker, bureau, bust, cabinet, case, casket, coffer, crate, cupboard, dresser, front, fund, kit, locker, safe, store, strongbox, thorax, treasury, trunk
**chest bone** rib, sternum
**chesterfield** sofa
**Chester Gould's detective** Dick Tracy
**chest for valuables** coffer, safe
**chest in which coins are tested for weight** pyx
**chest noise** rale, wheeze
**chestnut and grey** roan

**chest of drawers** chiffonier, commode, dresser, highboy, lowboy, tallboy
**chest of tools** kit
**chest sound** rale, wheeze
**chesty** asthmatic
**chevron** stripe
**chevrotain of Malaya** napu
**chew** cogitate, crunch, damage, deliberate, gnaw, grind, masticate, mumble, munch, nibble, rend, ruminate
**chew and swallow** eat
**chewed by ruminant** cud
**chewer** masticator, biter
**chewing gum from sapodilla** chicle
**chewing leaf and nut** betel
**chewing structure** jaw
**chewing tobacco** chaw, plug, quid
**chewing tooth** molar
**chew noisily** chomp, crunch, munch
**chew one's cud** cogitate
**chew the cud** ruminate
**chew through** gnaw
**chew with crushing sound** crunch
**chewy confection** caramel, taffy, toffee
**chic** à la mode, charm, culture, elegance, elegant, fashion(able), flair, grace, mod(ern), modish, neatness, panache, posh, smart, spruce, style, stylish, suave, trendy, trim, vogue
**chicanery** artfulness, deceit, deception, dishonesty, fraud, guile, hocus-pocus, rascality, treachery, trickery
**Chicano** Mexican
**chicken** fowl
**chicken breed** bantam, leghorn, wyandotte
**chicken cage** coop
**chicken cooked in wine** coq au vin (F)
**chicken farmer** poulterer
**chicken feed** cheap, negligible, peanuts, trivial
**chicken house** coop, pen
**chicken in white sauce** fricassee
**chicken minced and rolled in bacon, then fried** kromesky
**chicken pen** coop
**chickenpox** varicella
**chickens do it** peep
**chickpea** garbanzo
**chick sound** peep
**chico** greasewood
**chicory crown** endive
**chide** admonish, berate, blame, castigate, censure, check, criticise, denounce, forewarn, lecture, rag, rate, rebuke, reprehend, reprimand, reproach, reprove, scold, upbraid
**chiding** admonishing, blaming, censuring, checking, criticising,

lecturing, rebuking, reproaching, reproving, scolding, upbraiding
**chief** ag(h)a, arch, boss, cardinal, chieftain, commander, dean, director, doyen, essential, first, foreman, foremost, grand, great, head(man), leader, leading, main, manager, necessary, potentate, prime, principal, ruler, superior, supervisor, supreme, titan
**chief admiral of Turkish fleet** capitan
**chief angel** archangel
**chief Babylonian god** Adad, Bel, Ea, Hea
**chief Babylonian priest** En
**chief bishop** archbishop
**chief bishop or archbishop** primate
**chief boy in a school** captain, prefect
**chief Caribbean port** Colon
**chief city** capital, metropolis
**chief current** mainstream
**chief disciple** Peter
**chief evil jinni in Islamic mythology** Eblis
**chief executive** president
**chief female character** heroine
**chief female singer in opera** prima donna
**chief gods of Norse mythology** Aesir
**chief ground of complaint** gravamen
**chief herald of Scotland** Lyon
**chief herdsman of Saul** Doeg
**chief idea in a work of art** motive, theme
**chief in importance** principal
**chief in size or extent** main
**chief language of Ghana** Twi
**chief law officer** attorney-general
**chief leader of the Irish Republic** Taoiseach
**chiefly** eminently, especially, mainly, mostly, particularly, principally
**chief magistrate** reeve, syndic
**chief magistrate in a Spanish town** alca(l)de
**chief magistrate of Venice and Genoa** doge
**chief meal of the day** dinner
**chief monk** abbot
**chief Norse god** Odin
**chief nun** abbess, mother
**chief of evil spirits** Satan
**chief officer** mayor
**chief of some American Indian tribes** sachem
**chief of state** president
**chief place of Moslem pilgrimage** Mecca
**chief port of Mozambique** Maputo
**chief port of Syria** Latakia
**chief priest** hierarch

**chief protein constituent of egg yolk** vitellin
**chief report** main news
**chief Roman goddess** Juno
**chief singer** cantor
**chief singer in a synagogue** chazan, cantor, haz(z)an
**chief source of aluminium** bauxite
**chief stress** brunt
**chief support** mainstay
**chief supporter** cheerleader
**chieftain** ameer, captain, chief, commander, emir, head, leader, paramount, potentate, suzerain
**chief town** capital
**child** adolescent, babe, baby, chit, imp, infant, juvenile, kid, kind (G), bairn (Sc), kleintjie, lightie, lighty, offspring, scion, son, tike, tot, tyke, youngling, youngster, youth
**child bereaved of parents** orphan
**childbirth** accouchement (F), child-bearing, confinement, delivery, labour
**child during earliest period of life** infant
**child from spouse's former marriage** stepchild
**childhood** adolescence, babyhood, boyhood, girlhood, immaturity, infancy, juniority, juvenility, minority, nonage, puberty, puerility, pupilage, schooldays, teens, youth
**childhood disease** chickenpox, diphtheria, gastro-enteritis, measles, mumps, poliomyelitis, rickets, rubella, scarlatina, scarlet fever, thrush
**childhood home of Jesus** Nazareth
**childish** adolescent, anile, asinine, callow, childlike, childly, foolish, idiotic, imbecilic, immature, inexperienced, inexpert, infantile, jejune, juvenile, naïve, puerile, simple, sophomoric, undeveloped, unripe, unwise, witless, young
**childish fit of temper** tantrum
**childish goodbye** tata
**childish handwriting** scrawl
**childishly self-willed** wayward
**childishness** adolescence, boyishness, flippancy, frivolity, gaiety, girlishness, immaturity, jest, pettiness, puerility, shallowness, triviality, youthfulness
**childish walk** crawl, toddle
**child killer** infanticide
**child killing** infanticide
**child learning to walk** toddler
**childless woman** nullipara
**childlike** artless, babyish, candid, childly, credulous, docile, genuine, guileless, honest, infantile, ingenuous, innocent, meek, naïve, puerile, simple, sincere, submissive, unworldly
**child medicine** paediatrics
**child molester** nonce, paedophile
**child of nature** ingenue
**child of the devil** imp, shrew
**child of tsar** tsarevna
**children** babies, brats, descendants, infants, issues, juveniles, kids, lighties, line, minors, offspring, progenies, scions, strain, toddlers, tots, youngsters
**children like to fly this** kite
**children's card game** snap
**children's comic hero** Batman, Spiderman, Superman
**child's ailment** croup
**child's apron** overall, pinafore
**child's bear** teddy
**child's bed** cot, crib
**child's book** reader
**child's cot** crib
**child's cradle with hood** bassinet
**child's dress shield** bib
**child's flavoured drink** milk shake
**child's game** draughts, hide-and-seek, hopscotch, leapfrog, ludo, monopoly, scrabble, skop-die-blik, stingers, tag
**child's goodbye** tata
**child's illness** chickenpox, croup, diphtheria, gastro-enteritis, measles, mumps, poliomyelitis, rickets, rubella, scarlatina, scarlet fever, thrush
**child's magazine** comic(book)
**child's minder** nanny, nursemaid
**child's nanny** minder, nursemaid
**child's outfit** sunsuit
**child's overall** romper, smock
**child's party** treat
**child's peeping game** peekabo(o)
**child's pet** cat, dog, hamster
**child's picture paper** comic(book)
**child's play** easy
**child's playground game** jacks
**child's plaything** rattle, teddybear
**child's primary class** kindergarten
**child's puppet** doll
**child's pyjamas** nightie, sleepers
**child's room** nursery
**child's sleep-giver** sandman
**child's toy** rattle, teddybear
**child support** alimony, allowance
**child's vehicle** bicycle, scooter, tricycle
**child's wagon** go-cart
**child who is absent from scool without leave** truant, vagabond
**child without parents** orphan
**Chile saltpetre** soda nitre
**chill** ague, bleak, chilly, cold(ness), cool, deject, depress, freeze, frigidity, shivering, unfriendly
**chill and damp** clammy
**chilled beverage** iced tea
**chilled to the bone** freezing, frozen, shivering
**chill food** refrigerate
**chillingly cold** nippy
**chilli tortilla** enchilada
**chills and fever** ague
**chilly** algid, blowy, breezy, cold, cool, draughty, fresh, hostile, invigorating, nippy, parky, sharp, unfriendly, unwelcoming
**chime** bell, boom, dong, jingle, peal, ring, strike, tinkle
**chime in** blend, complement, enhance, harmonise, interrupt
**chime in with** accord, agree, assent
**chime with** harmonise
**chimney** cleft, duct, flue, lum (Sc), passage, stack
**chimney builder** steeplejack
**chimney carbon** soot
**chimney channel** flue
**chimney cleaner** sweep
**chimney compartment** flue
**chimney corner** fireplace, fireside, hearth
**chimney deposit** dust, soot
**chimney dirt** soot
**chimney hood** cowl
**chimney passage** flue
**chimney recess** inglenook
**chimney smoke duct** flue
**chimney top** cowl
**chimney vent** flue
**chimpanzee** ape, bonobo, nchega
**china** ceramics, crockery, earthenware, porcelain, pottery, stoneware, tableware, terracotta
**China** Cathay
**china clay** kaolin
**china figure** figurine
**China's continent** Asia
**chinaware** Noritake, Royal Doulton, Spode
**chine** arête, backbone, ridge
**Chinese** Cathay, Miao, oriental, Seres, Seric, Sin(a)ic, Sino-
**Chinese abacus** suapan, swanpan
**Chinese antelope** dzeren, goral, tserin
**Chinese arch** pailou
**Chinese aromatic root** ginseng
**Chinese bamboo stick** whangee
**Chinese basis of conduct** Tao
**Chinese berry** udo
**Chinese beverage** tea
**Chinese black tea** oolong
**Chinese boat** bark, junk, sampan
**Chinese bronze coin** li

**Chinese Buddha** Fo(h)
**Chinese Buddhist paradise** Chingtu
**Chinese Buddhist priest** bonze
**Chinese building** pagoda
**Chinese cape** Olwanpi
**Chinese card game** loo, lu
**Chinese channel** Bashi
**Chinese characters in Japan** mana
**Chinese chess** siangki
**Chinese civet** rasse
**Chinese cloth** moxa
**Chinese coin with hole** cash
**Chinese cooking pan** wok
**Chinese currency** cash, li, pu, sycee, tiao, yuan
**Chinese curtain** bamboo
**Chinese deer** Père David
**Chinese desert** Alashan, Gobi, Ordos, Shamo
**Chinese dialect** Cantonese, Hakka, Wu
**Chinese dish** bow-tie, chop suey, chow mein, foo yung, fried rice, Peking duck, spring roll, stir fry
**Chinese division** Miao
**Chinese dog** chow, peke, Pekingese, shihtzu
**Chinese dry lake** Lopnor
**Chinese duck eggs** pidan
**Chinese dynasty** Chin, Chou, Han, Manchu, Ming, Shang, Sung, Tang, Wu, Yuan
**Chinese eddo** taro
**Chinese factory** hong
**Chinese feudal state** Wei
**Chinese fish** trepang
**Chinese flat-bottomed sailing vessel** junk
**Chinese flute** tche
**Chinese food** rice
**Chinese for God** Shangti
**Chinese form of karate** kung fu
**Chinese fruit** lichee, li(t)chi, lychee
**Chinese game** mah-jong(g)
**Chinese god** Ghos, Joss, Kuant, Shen
**Chinese gooseberry** kiwi-berry
**Chinese grass** ramee, ramie
**Chinese green tea** hyson
**Chinese group islands** Crushan, Miaotao, Phengu, Tachen
**Chinese guild** ming, tang, tong
**Chinese gulf** Chihly, Liaotung, Pohai, Tonkin
**Chinese herb** ginseng
**Chinese Himalayan region** Tibet
**Chinese hired hand** coolie
**Chinese idol** Joss
**Chinese island** Amoy, Chusan, Macau, Matso, Namki, Pratas, Quemoy, Taiwan, Tungsha
**Chinese jigsaw** tangram
**Chinese labourer** coolie

**Chinese lake** Chao, Ebinor, Kapanor, Lopnor, Namtso, Oling, Poyang, Tai, Tellinor, Tungting
**Chinese language** Cantonese, Mandarin
**Chinese language spoken in Hong Kong** Cantonese
**Chinese leader** Chiang Kai-shek, Mao Tse Tung, Mao ze Dong
**Chinese luck symbol** bat
**Chinese measure** li
**Chinese measure of distance** li
**Chinese money** fen, jiao, yuan
**Chinese monkey** douc
**Chinese musical instrument** kin, samison
**Chinese mythical animal** dragon
**Chinese nurse** amah
**Chinese oil** tung
**Chinese ounce** tael
**Chinese pagoda** taa
**Chinese pan** wok
**Chinese peninsula** Leicho, Liaotung, Luichow
**Chinese philosopher** Confucius, Lao-Tzu
**Chinese philosophy** Confucianism, Taoism
**Chinese pick-me-up** ginseng
**Chinese pillory** cang(ue)
**Chinese plant** bamboo, ramee, ramie
**Chinese porcelain** Celadon, Ju, Ko, Ming, Nankeen
**Chinese port** Amoy, Dairen, Shanghai
**Chinese pottery** ceramics, china, chun, earthenware, kuan, ming, porcelain, stoneware, ting, yishing
**Chinese province** Fukien, Honan, Hupen, Kansu, Mongolia, Nationalist China, Republic of China, Shansi, Tibet, Tsinghai
**Chinese provincial governor** mandarin
**Chinese puzzle** tangram
**Chinese rebel** Taiping, Taiwan
**Chinese religion** Buddhism, Confucianism, Ju, Shinto, Taoism
**Chinese religious concept** Tao
**Chinese remedy** senso
**Chinese resident of Tibet** Amban
**Chinese rice spirit** samshoo
**Chinese river boat** sampan
**Chinese ruler** Wang, Yao(u), Yau
**Chinese sauce** soy
**Chinese sea** Echina, Schina, Yellow
**Chinese seaport** Shanghai
**Chinese secret society** Tong
**Chinese ship** junk
**Chinese shop** toko
**Chinese silk** pongee, shantung
**Chinese skiff** sampan
**Chinese sky deity** Tien
**Chinese square** Tianamien

**Chinese staple food** rice
**Chinese strait** Hanian, Taiwan
**Chinese stringed instrument** kin, samison
**Chinese tea** bohea, cha, hyson, oolong
**Chinese temple** joss-house, pagoda
**Chinese thinker** Tao
**Chinese tile game** mah-jong(g)
**Chinese tonic root** ginseng
**Chinese treaty port** Amoy, Wenchow
**Chinese tree** lichee, li(t)chi, lychee
**Chinese umbrella** tee
**Chinese unit of distance** li
**Chinese unit of length** li
**Chinese unit of value** tael
**Chinese unit of weight** li
**Chinese vehicle** rickshaw
**Chinese water chestnut** ling
**Chinese white-and-black mammal** panda
**Chinese writing symbol** ideogram, ideograph
**chin growth** beard
**chin-guard of helmet** beaver
**chin hair** beard
**chink** aperture, cleft, crack, cranny, crevice, cut, fissure, opening, rift
**chink in wall** cranny
**Chinook pony** cayuse
**chin-piece of nun's headdress** barb
**chin whiskers** beard, goatee
**chionodoxa** glory-of-the-snow
**chip** bit, cantle, chisel, chunk, collop, corner, crumb(le), dent, flake, flaw, fragment, gash, gobbet, hew, mar, morsel, nick, notch, paring, piece, scrap, scratch, shard, shaving, sliver, snick, snip(pet), spall, splinter, wafer, whittle
**chip broken from stone carving** spall
**chip in** contribute, donate, interject, interrupt, participate, pay, subscribe
**chip of the old block** image, replica
**chips of rock** spalls
**chip's partner** dip
**Chiquita's fruit** banana
**chirography** calligraphy, handwriting
**chirology** finger-speech
**chiromancy** palmistry
**chiropodist** podiatrist
**chirp** cheep, chirl, chirr(up), peep, pipe, sing, speak, trill, tweet, twitter, warble, whistle
**chirp of small bird** tweet
**chisel** bilk, carve, chase, cheat, chip, chop, cut, divide, engrave, etch, fashion, figure, form, furrow, groove, hack, hew, incise, inscribe, model, mould, saw, sculpt(ure), shape, slash, slice, swindle, whittle
**chisel-edged tooth** incisor
**chisel for cutting bricks** bolster

**chisel with concave blade** gouge
**chit** bill, docket, girl, note, shoot, voucher, youngster
**chital** axis
**chit-chat** gossip, chat
**chit for payment of goods** receipt
**chivalrous** bold, brave, courageous, courtly, gallant, heroic, honourable, mannerly, polite
**chivalrous person** Arthur, Galahad, paladin
**chivalry** audacity, boldness, bravery, courage, courteousness, courtesy, courtliness, daring, decency, dedication, devotion, dexterity, dignity, emprise, fairness, fearlessness, gallantry, generosity, gentlemanliness, graciousness, heroism, honour, intrepidity, knightliness, loyalty, manliness, nobility, pluck, politeness, reliability, reliableness, resoluteness, spirit, stout-heartedness, tenacity, valiancy, valour, virility, virtue, virtuousness
**chivy** badger, chase, flight, harass, manoeuvre, nag, pursue, pursuit, race, run, scamper, tease, torment
**chock** sprag
**chocolate bun** doughnut, éclair
**chocolate drink** cocoa
**chocolate-egg festival** Easter
**chocolate nut** cacao
**chocolate source** cacao
**chocolate substitute** carob
**chocolate tree** cacao
**chocolate-type beverage** cocoa
**choice** acceptance, alternate, alternative, best, choosing, costly, cream, dainty, decision, desire, dilemma, discrimination, elect(ion), élite, espousal, exalted, excellent, exclusive, exquisite, fine, hand-picked, inclination, nice, nomination, opting, option, pick, precious, preference, prime, prize, rare, say, select(ion), special, superior, superlative, surrogate, uncommon, unique, unusual, valuable, variety, vote, wish
**choice collection of passages from literature** anthology
**choice cut of beef** porterhouse, rump, silverside, steak, T-bone
**choice for position** appointment
**choice group** élite
**choice morsel** tidbit, titbit
**choice of words** phraseology
**choice part** élite, lead
**choice word?** either
**choir** chorale
**choirboy's collar** eton

**choir leader** cantor, precentor
**choir member** alto, bass, soprano, tenor
**choir singer** chorister
**choir voice** alto, bass, tenor, soprano
**choke** asphyxiate, bar, clog, close, gag, obstruct, smother, strangle, suppress, throttle
**choke by stopping breathing** suffocate
**choker** neckwear
**choler** anger, bile, biliousness, distemper, fury, irascibility, ire, irritation, rage, spleen, temper, wrath
**choose** adopt, assign, cull, decide, designate, desire, determine, elect, fancy, favour, judge, opt, pick, prefer, select, take, want, will, winnow, wish
**choose above another** prefer
**choose by ballot** elect, vote
**choose for office** elect, vote
**choosy** discriminating, exacting, faddy, finicky, fussy, particular, selective
**chop** axe, barter, break, burst, carve, chip, chisel, cleave, crack, cut, dice, divide, engrave, exchange, fashion, fell, form, fracture, gash, hack, hew, hew, incise, jowl, kick, lacerate, lop, mangle, mince, mouth, mutilate, nick, notch, penetrate, pierce, saw, score, sculpt(ure), sever, shape, slash, slice, slit, snap, splinter, split, swap, swipe, trade, truncate, whittle, wound
**chop and change** alter, fluctuate, vacillate, vary
**chop finely** dice, mince, process
**chop into small squares** dice
**chop off** lop
**chopped food** hash
**chopped fried bread** crouton
**chopped into small pieces** finecut, process
**chopped mixture** hash
**chopper** ax(e), block, butcher, dicer, helicopter, hewer
**chopper for trimming slates** sax
**chopper landing place** helipad, heliport
**chopping** axing
**chopping block** hacklog
**chopping machine** processor
**chopping tool** adze, ax(e), hatchet, panga
**chop roughly** hack
**chop up** cube, dice, divide, fragment, hash, mince, slice
**chop very small** dice, mince, process
**chop with an axe** hew

**choral** accordant, choric, concert, concordant, harmonious, operatic, psalmic, singing, symphonic, vocal
**chorale** cantata, choir, doxology, hymn, melody, motet, psalm
**choral group** choir
**choral music** anthem, cantata, hymn, motet
**choral work** cantata
**chore** burden, drudgery, duty, errand, fag, job, labour, nuisance, obligation, responsibility, routine, stint, task, trouble, turn, work
**chore for messenger** errand
**chores around the home** homework, housework
**chorister** singer
**chortle** cackle, chuckle, crow, guffaw
**chorus** accord, burden, call, character, choir, choristers, concert, dancers, ensemble, harmony, refrain, response, shout, singers, strain, vocalists
**chorus girl** chorine, coryphee
**chosen by election** elective
**chosen few** élite
**choux pastry cake** éclair
**chowder shellfish** clam
**Christ** Jesus
**christen** anoint, baptise, call, dedicate, designate, entitle, hallow, inaugurate, initiate, name, ritual, sanctify, sprinkle
**christen again** rename
**Christian** believer, essene, gentile, Xn, Xtian
**Christian banner** labarum
**Christian body** Church
**Christian but not Catholic** Protestant
**Christian child martyr** Agnes
**Christian countries** Christendom
**Christian emblem** IHS
**Christian festival** Christmas, Easter
**Christian hermit or recluse** eremite
**Christian holiday** Ascension, Christmas, Easter, Xmas
**Christian love** agape, charity
**Christian missionary** apostle, disciple, evangelist
**Christian name** forename
**Christian recluse** eremite, hermit
**Christian revelation** gospel
**Christian sabbath** Sunday
**Christian sacrament** Eucharist
**Christian scriptures** Bible
**Christian song** hymn
**Christian symbol** cross, fish
**Christmas (carol)** Noel
**Christmas decoration** holly, mistletoe
**Christmas fuel** yulelog
**Christmas hymn** carol

**Christmas ornament** star, tinsel, tree, wreath
**Christmas season** yule(tide)
**Christmas show** pantomime
**Christmas song** carol, Noel
**chromatic print** coloured photograph
**chromatic shade** colour
**chronic** confirmed, continual, continuing, continuous, habitual, inveterate, perpetual, unending
**chronic complainer** crab, Job
**chronic debility of body or mind** cachexia, cachexy
**chronic disease of liver** cirrhosis
**chronic drunkard** dronkie, dronklap, sot, toper
**chronic inability to take decisions** ab(o)ulia
**chronic inflammation of the hair follicles** sycosis
**chronicle** account, annals, diary, enter, history, journal, narrate, narrative, recount, register, relate, report, story, tell
**chronological error** anachronism
**chronometer** time-keeper
**chubby** buxom, chunky, corpulent, dumpy, fat, flabby, obese, overweight, paunchy, plump, podgy, portly, pudgy, rotund, round, stout, (s)tubby
**chubby chap** podge
**chubby doll with wings and curl** kewpie
**chucker-out** bouncer, ejector
**chuckle** cackle, chirp, chortle, crow, giggle, guffaw, jocundity, jollity, laugh, merriment, purr, snicker, snigger, titter
**chuckle gleefully** chortle
**chuckle-head** clod, dolt, domkop, fool, stupid
**chuck out** eject
**chum** amigo, associate, buddy, chommie, classmate, colleague, companion, comrade, confidant, crony, familiar, friend, helper, helpmate, intimate, mate, pal, partner, playmate, teammate
**chummy** buddy-buddy, familliar, friendly, intimate, pally
**chunk** lump, wedge
**chunk of cast metal** ingot
**chunky** short, thick
**chunter** complain, grumble, mutter
**church** abbey, basilica, cathedral, chapel, denomination, edifice, kirk (Sc), minster, organisation, sanctuary, sect, temple
**church anthem** motet, psalm
**church assembly** synod
**church attendant** verger

**church-bell ringer** sexton
**church bell tower** belfry
**church bench** pew
**church benefice without duties** sinecure
**church Bible stand** lectern
**church building without double colonnade and apse** basilica
**church caretaker** sexton, verger
**church cellar** crypt
**church chanter** gospeller
**church cloakroom** vestry
**church council** synod
**church decree** canon
**church desk** lectern
**church dignitary** (arch)bishop, canon, cardinal, dean, pope, prelate
**church district** parish
**church faction** cult
**church gallery** loft
**church gangway** aisle
**churchgoer** communicant, worshipper
**church helper** elder
**church instrument** organ
**church law** canon
**church lay official** deacon, elder
**church living** benefice
**churchman** bishop, cleric, dean, dominee, predikant, priest, reverend
**church minister** dominee, pastor, predikant, priest, reverend, vicar
**Church of England official** verger
**Church of England service** evensong, matins
**church office** benefice
**church officer** cleric, deacon, elder, minister, priest, sacrist, verger
**church officer attending priest** acolyte
**church official** beadle, cardinal, deacon, dean, dominee, elder, minister, pastor, pope, predikant, priest, reverend, sexton, verger
**church of monastery** minster
**church part** aisle, altar, nave, pew
**church passage** aisle, walkway
**church plate** paten, patin(e)
**church podium** pulpit
**church portico** parvis(e)
**church procedure** rite
**church projection** apse
**church property** glebe
**church province** diocese
**church reader** anagnost, lector
**church reading desk** lectern
**church recess** apse
**church seat** bench, pew
**church section** apse, chancel, choir, nave, transept, vestry
**church senior** elder
**church service** evensong, mass, matins, vespers

**church singers** choir
**church song** hymn, psalm
**church song book** hymnal, psalmbook
**church spire** steeple, tower
**church steeple** spire, tower
**church storeroom** sacristy
**church table** altar
**church tax** tithe
**church tower** belfry, steeple
**church tower with spire** steeple
**church tribunal** Inquisition, rosa
**church usher** beadle
**church vault** crypt
**church washbowl** lavabo
**church wing** transept
**churchwoman** nun, priest
**churchy** ecclesiastical
**churchyard tree** cypress, yew
**churl** boor, clown, lout, miser, niggard, oaf, peasant, rustic
**churlish** boorish, crabbed, disagreeable, ill-mannered, impolite, loutish, morose, rude, sullen, surly, uncivil, unmannerly, vulgar
**churlishness** grimness, ill-nature, melancholy, moodiness, peevishness, pettishness, sulkiness, sullenness
**churn** agitate, beat(er), blender, cream, disturb, eggbeater, heave, jiggler, mixer, rotate, shake, stir, vessel, vibrator, whisk
**chute release device** ripcord
**CIA man** spy
**ciao** goodbye, hello
**cicatrice** cicatrix, mark, scab, scar
**cicatrise** heal
**cicatrix** cicatrice, mark, scab, scar
**cider fruit** apple
**cider made from small, sweet apples** scrumpy
**cigar** cheroot, Havana, Manila, panatella, stog(e)y
**cigar case** humidor
**cigar city** Havana, Manila
**cigarette** butt, cubeb, durry, fag, gasper
**cigarette-end** fag, filter, stompie, stub
**cigarette flavour** menthol
**cigarette remains** ash
**cigarette user** smoker
**cigar residue** ash
**cigar-seller** tobacconist
**cigar storage** humidor
**cigar with both ends open** cheroot
**ciliary hair** eyelash
**cilice** haircloth
**cilium** eyelash, flagellum
**cincture** belt, girdle
**cinder** ash, clinker, coal, ember, fleck, slag
**cinders** dust, embers, remains, remnants, residue, smut

**cinema** bioscope, movie house, movie
**cinema attendant** usher(ette)
**cinema award** Oscar
**cinema doorman** commissionaire
**cinema film giving the news** newsreel
**cinema food** popcorn
**cinema presentation** film, movie
**cinema worker** projectionist, usher(ette)
**Cinzano drink** vermouth
**cipher** acrostic, anagram, character, code, compute, count, cryptograph, device, digit, figure, integer, logo, monogram, nil, nobody, nonentity, notation, nothing, nought, nullity, number, numeral, obscurity, sign, symbol, zero
**circinate** ring-shaped
**circle** area, ball, bound(s), cabal, circuit, circumference, company, coterie, cycle, encircle, encompass, faction, fraternity, include, orb(it), perimeter, periphery, province, region, revolve, ring, round, set, society, sphere, surround
**circle around the moon** halo
**circle in space** orbit
**circle of altitude** almucantar
**circle of coloured light** halo
**circle of intense light** spotlight
**circle of persons** coterie
**circle of prehistoric or upright stones** cromlech
**circle of wagons** laager
**circle part** arc, sector, segment, semicircle, slice
**circle segment** arc, section, sector, semicircle, slice
**circlet** bracelet, fillet, hoop, ring
**circlet for head** chaplet
**circuit** area, beat, boundary, circle, circumference, compass, course, district, edge, journey, lap, loop, orbit, perambulation, perimeter, periphery, pilgrimage, province, range, region, revolution, rim, round, route, space, stroll, track, tract, trip, verge, walk
**circuit breaker** fuse
**circuit court** eyre
**circuit of racecourse** lap
**circuit of track** lap
**circuitous journey** meander
**circular** advert(isement), arched, bent, booklet, circuitous, curved, cyclic, discoid, globular, handbill, perimetric, poster, release, rotund, round, spherical, statement
**circular area** henge
**circular band** fillet, gyre, hoop, ring
**circular carving in relief** tondo
**circular current** whirlpool

**circular describing company** brochure, prospectus
**circular direction** (anti-)clockwise, round
**circular eddy of water** whirlpool
**circular edge** rim
**circular figure as religious symbol of universe** mandala
**circular frilled collar** ruff
**circular head ornament** circlet, coronet, crown
**circular metal band** hoop
**circular opening in centre of iris of eye** pupil
**circular painting** tondo
**circular panorama** cyclorama
**circular pile of hay** (hay)stack, rick
**circular reef enclosing lagoon** atoll
**circular saw** edger
**circular turn** loop
**circular vault forming roof** dome
**circulate** diffuse, distribute, issue, propagate, spread
**circulation** circling, currency, distribution, flowing, motion, promulgation, spreading, transmission, vogue
**circumference** bound, brink, circuit, edge, fringe, outline, perimeter, periphery, verge
**circumspect** accurate, acute, alert, artful, astute, attentive, canny, careful, cautious, chary, clever, conscientious, deliberate, discreet, fastidious, heedful, judicious, knowing, observant, precise, prudent, sagacious, scrupulous, shrewd, subtle, thoughtful, thrifty, wary, wise
**circumstance** condition, event, occurrence, pageantry, phenomenon
**circumvent** avert, avoid, bypass, decline, dodge, duck, edge, elude, escape, evade, overtake, pass, prevent, round, shirk, shun, sidestep, skirt
**circus comic** clown, harlequin
**circus entertainer** acrobat, clown, trapezist
**circus feature** ring, trick
**circus funnyman** clown
**circus performer** artiste, clown
**circus person's long leg?** stilt
**circus pioneer** Barnum
**circus pole** stilt
**circus shelter** tent
**circus swing** trapeze
**circus tumbler** acrobat
**cirrostratus** cloud
**cisco** lake herring, whitefish
**cistern** basin, reservoir, sink, tank, vat
**cistern valve** ballcock

**citadel in Granada** Alhambra
**citadel in Moscow** Kremlin
**cite** adduce, advance, allege, allude, assemble, attest, call, commend, denote, display, document, enjoin, enumerate, excerpt, extract, manifest, mention, name, number, praise, present, quote, recall, recollect, remember, remind, revive, specify, summon, tell
**cite as instance** name
**cite as obstacle** oppose
**cite as proof** adduce
**citification** urbanisation
**citify** urbanise
**citing as proof** adducing
**citizen** burgher, civilian, denizen, dweller, house-holder, indigene, inhabitant, national, native, oppidan, resident, subject, taxpayer, villager, voter
**citizen force** militia
**citizen of Apia** Samoan
**citizen of Jaffa** Israeli
**citizen of La Paz** Bolivian
**citizen of Manila** Filipino, Tagalog
**citizen of Maseru** Basotho
**citizen of Milan** Italian
**citizen of Moscow** Muscovite
**citizen of Sacramento** Californian
**citizen of Seoul** Korean
**citizen of Stockholm** Swede
**citizen of Tel Aviv** Israeli
**citizen of the world** cosmopolite
**citizen of United States** American
**citizen of Warsaw** Pole
**citizenship** nationality
**citizen soldiers** militia
**citole** cither(n), cittern
**citron wood** sandarac(h)
**citrus disease** scale
**citrus fruit** citron, clementine, cumquat, grapefruit, kumquat, lemon, lime, mandarin, naartjie, navel, orange, ortanique, pomela, satsuma, shaddock, tangelo, tangerine, ugli, valencia
**citrus hybrid** ugli
**citrus paste** lemon cheese
**citrus vitamin** C
**cittern** cithern, citole
**city** burg, megalopolis, metropolis, municipality
**city air problem** pollution, smog
**city and port in Denmark** A(a)rhus
**city destroyed by Vesuvius** Pompeii
**city division** borough, ward
**city dweller** urbanite
**city head** mayor
**city in Abyssinia** Harar, Gondar
**city in Afghanistan** Kabul, Kandahar

**city in Alaska** Anchorage, Juneau, Nome, Sitka
**city in Albania** Durazzo, Scutari
**city in Algeria** Algiers, Annaba, Bone, Constantine, Oran
**city in America** Denver, Detroit, Houston, Kansas, Miami, New York, Washington
**city in ancient Egypt** Thebes
**city in ancient Greece** Elis, Sparta
**city in Angola** Luanda
**city in Argentina** Buenos Aires, Cordoba, La Plata, Rosario
**city in Arizona** Tucson, Yuma
**city in Armenia** Erevan
**city in Australia** Adelaide, Brisbane, Darwin, Melbourne, Perth, Sydney
**city in Austria** Admont, Andau, Ebensee, Graz, Horn, Innsbruck, Salzburg, Vienna, Wien
**city in Bangladesh** Dacca, Dhaka
**city in Belgium** Antwerpen, Bruges, Brugge, Brussels, Doorwik, G(h)ent, Liege, Ypres
**city in Bolivia** La Paz, Orubo, Potosi
**city in Botswana** Gaborone
**city in Brazil** Belem, Brasilia, Manaus, Recife, Rio de Janeiro, Salvador, Santerim, Sao Paulo
**city in Bulgaria** Plovdiv, Sofia, Varna
**city in Burma** Mandalay, Rangoon
**city in California** Los Angeles, Oakland, Pasadena, Sacramento, San Francisco
**city in Cambodia** Phnom Penh
**city in Cameroon** Douala, Yaounda
**city in Canada** Banff, Calgary, Edmonton, Montréal, Oshawa, Ottawa, Québec, Toronto, Vancouver, Winnipeg
**city in Canary Islands** Las Palmas
**city in Catalonia** Barcelona
**city in Chad** Bokoro
**city in Chile** Concepción, Santiago, Valparaiso
**city in China** Amoy, Beijing, Nanchang, Nanking, Ningpo, Pautou, Shanghai, Sian
**city in Colombia** Barranquilla, Bogota, Cali, Medellin
**city in Congo** Brazzaville
**city in Costa Rica** Cartago, San José
**city in Crete** Knossos
**city in Cuba** Bayamo, Camaguey, Havana, Santiago
**city in Czechoslovakia** Brno, Pilsen, Plzen, Prague
**city in Denmark** A(a)rhus, Copenhagen
**city in Dominican Republic** Moca, Santo Domingo
**city in Ecuador** Guayaquil, Quito, Rio Bamba

**city in Egypt** Alexandria, Asyut, Cairo, Port Said, Sais, Suez, Tanta, Thebes
**city in England** Bath, Birmingham, Cambridge, Dover, Ely, Epsom, Exeter, Leeds, Liverpool, London, Manchester, Peterborough, Preston, Salisbury, Sheffield
**city in Ethiopia** Addis Ababa, Asmara
**city in Europe** Brno, Essen, Lyons, Milan
**city in Finland** Helsinki, Oulu, Tampere
**city in Florida** Miami
**city in France** Aix, Amiens, Angers, Arles, Avignon, Ay, Besancon, Bordeaux, Bourges, Caen, Cambrai, Chartres, Douai, Limoges, Lyons, Marseille, Nancy, Nantes, Nice, Nimes, Orleans, Paris, Poitiers, Reims, Rennes, Rouen, Sens, Toulouse
**city in Gabon** Libreville
**city in Gelderland** Ede
**city in Georgia** Macon
**city in Germany** Augsburg, Berlin, Bonn, Cologne, Dresden, Düsseldorf, Ems, Essen, Frankfurt, Hamburg, Jena, Leipzig, München, Nuremberg, Potsdam, Ulm, Weimar, Wuppertal
**city in Ghana** Accra, Kumasi
**city in Greece** Arta, Athens, Corinth, Patras, Salonika, Thebes, Thessaloniki
**city in Guatemala** Coban, Guatemala City
**city in Guinea** Conakry
**city in Hawaii** Hilo, Honolulu
**city in Holland** Amsterdam, Ede
**city in Hong Kong** Kowloon, Victoria
**city in Hungary** Buda, Budapest, Debrecen, Eger, Pécs, Szeged
**city in India** Agartala, Agra, Ahmadabad, Allahabad, Assam, Bombay, Calcutta, Delhi, Goa, Golconda, Kanpur, Madras, Warangal
**city in Indonesia** Bogor, Djakarta, Malang, Medan
**city in Iowa** Ames
**city in Iran** Abadan, Esfahan, Shiraz, Tabriz, Tehran
**city in Iraq** Baghdad, Mosul
**city in Ireland** Belfast, Dublin, Ulster
**city in Israel** Acre, Jerusalem, Nazareth, Tel Aviv
**city in Italy** Aquila, Assisi, Asti, Bologna, Faenza, Florence, Genoa, Milan, Naples, Parma, Pisa, Ravenna, Rome, Salerno, Trieste, Turin, Venice, Verona
**city in Ivory Coast** Abidjan, Bouaké
**city in Jamaica** Kingston

**city in Japan** Amagasaki, Fukuoka, Hiroshima, Kyoto, Matsuyama, Nagasaki, Nagoya, Nara, Osaka
**city in Jordan** Amman
**city in Kenya** Mombasa, Nairobi
**city in Laos** Vientiane
**city in Lebanon** Beirut
**city in Libya** Bengasi, Benghazi, Tripoli
**city in Lombardy** Milan(o)
**city in Madagascar** Antananarivo, Tananarive
**city in Maine** Lewiston
**city in Mexico** Celaya, Guadalajara, Mexico City, Monterrey, Saltilo, Tampico, Torreon
**city in Morocco** Casablanca, Fès, Fez, Marrakech, Marrakesh
**city in Mozambique** Beira, Maputo
**city in Netherlands** Amsterdam, Arnhem, Rotterdam
**city in Nevada** Las Vegas, Reno
**city in New Zealand** Auckland
**city in Nicaragua** Managua
**city in Nigeria** Abeokuta, Ede, Ibadan, Kano, Lagos
**city in northern Iraq** Erbil
**city in northern Italy** Verona
**city in North Korea** Kaesong, Kaesygn, Sinuiju
**city in Norway** Oslo
**city in Oklahoma** Tulsa
**city in Pakistan** Hyderabad, Karachi, Lahore, Rawalpindi
**city in Peru** Lima, Piura, Trujillo
**city in Philippines** Davao, Manila
**city in Poland** Cracow, Krakow, Lodz, Poznan, Warsaw
**city in Portugal** Braga, Lisbon, Oporto
**city in Puerto Rico** San Juan
**city in Punjab** Amritsar
**city in Queensland** Ipswich
**city in Rhode Island** Cranston, Newport
**city in Romania** Bucharest, Iasi
**city in Saudi Arabia** Riyadh
**city in Scotland** Aberdeen, Ayr, Dundee, Glasgow
**city in Senegal** Dakar
**city in Siberia** Alma-Ata, Omsk
**city in South Africa** Bloemfontein, Cape Town, Durban, East London, Germiston, Grahamstown, Johannesburg, Pietermaritzburg, Port Elizabeth, Pretoria
**city in southern Italy** Naples
**city in South Korea** Pusan, Seoul, Taegu
**city in south-west England** Bath
**city in Spain** Avila, Barcelona, Cadiz, Cordoba, Granada, Irun, Lerida, Madrid, Reus, Seville, Toledo, Valencia

**city in Sri Lanka** Colombo
**city in Sudan** Khartoum
**city in Sweden** Falun, Göteborg, Malmo, Orebro, Stockholm
**city in Switzerland** Basel, Geneva, Zurich
**city in Syria** Damascus, Aleppo
**city in Taiwan** Gaoxiong, Taichung, Tainan, Taipei
**city in Tanzania** Dar es Salaam
**city in Tennessee** Memphis
**city in Texas** Dallas, Waco
**city in Thailand** Ayutthaya, Bangkok
**city in Tunisia** Tunis
**city in Turkey** Adana, Ankara, Antioch, Istanbul, Izmir, Tarsus
**city in Uganda** Entebbe, Kampala
**city in Ukraine** Dnepropetrovsk, Kiev
**city in United Kingdom** Birmingham, Glasgow, Liverpool, London, Manchester, Sheffield
**city in Uruguay** Montevideo
**city in USA** Boston, Chicago, Dallas, Detroit, Los Angeles, Miami, New York, Orlando, San Francisco, Washington DC
**city in USSR** Baku, Barnaul, Ki(y)ev, Leningrad, Lvov, Minsk, Moscow, Moskva, Odessa, Omsk, Riga, Tashkent
**city in Veneto** Verona
**city in Venezuela** Caracas, Maracaibo
**city in Vietnam** Hanoi, Saigon
**city in Wales** Cardiff, Neath, Pontypool, Rhondda, Swansea, Wrexham
**city in West India famous for its mosque** Ahmadabad, Ahmedabad
**city in West Yorkshire** Leeds
**city in Yugoslavia** Belgrade, Ljubljana, Skopje, Zagreb
**city in Zaïre** Kananga, Kinshasa, Kisangani
**city in Zambia** Kitwe, Lusaka, Ndola
**city in Zimbabwe** Harare
**city newspaper** daily
**city of bells** Bruges
**city of churches** Brooklyn
**city of conferences** Geneva
**city of David** Jerusalem
**city of dead** necropolis
**city of hundred towers** Pavia
**city of leaning tower** Pisa
**city of lights** Paris
**city of Port Jackson** Sydney
**city of seven hills** Rome
**city of Sumer** Ur
**city of Taj Mahal** Agra
**city of witches** Salem
**city on Dnieper** Smolensk, Kiev
**city on the Mediterranean** Gaza
**city outskirts** perimeter, suburbs

**city road** street
**city roadway** street, thoroughfare
**city's water supply** reservoir
**city thoroughfare** street
**city train** el
**city zone** conurbation
**civic** communal, community, local, municipal, public, urban
**civic leader** mayor
**civic officer** mayor
**civil** civilised, courteous, courtly, deferential, gracious, polite, refined, respectful, urbane, well-bred, well-mannered
**civil code** law
**civil disturbance** riot
**civil engineering instrument** oedometer
**civil force** police
**civilian dress** civ(v)ies, mufti
**civilian during a war** non-combatant
**civilian life** Civvy Street
**civilian quarters for troops** billet
**civilise** cultivate, educate, enlighten, humanise, improve, perfect, polish, refine, sophisticate, tame
**civilised** advanced, cultured, educated, enlightened, humane, polite, refined, sophisticated, tolerant, urbane
**civility** affability, amenity, amiability, attention, breeding, code, conduct, convention, courteousness, courtesy, cultivation, culture, customs, decorum, elegance, etiquette, gallantry, gentility, graciousness, manners, polish, politeness, propriety, protocol, refinement, rules, tact, urbanity, usage
**civil officer administering law** magistrate
**civil service** bureaucracy
**civil uprising** riot
**civil wrong** tort
**civvies** mufti
**clad** apparelled, arrayed, attired, clothed, covered, decked, draped, dressed, endowed, enwrapped, equipped, garbed, invested, rigged, robed, swathed
**claim** allege, ask, assert, challenge, declare, demand, maintain, profess, request, require(ment), right, title
**claim against property** lien
**claim amount** loss
**claimant** applicant, aspirant, claimer, complainant, contestant, disputant, heir, inheritor, litigant, party, petitioner, plaintiff, postulant, pretender, suitor, suppli(c)ant
**claim as a right** demand

**claim as one's own** arrogate
**claim damages** sue
**claim to be true** purport
**claim without proof** allege
**clairvoyant** clear-sighted, extrasensory, fey, foreseeing, otherworldly, percipient, prescient, psychic, sagacious, sapient, seer, telepathic, telepathist
**clairvoyant one** seer
**clam** mollusc
**clamant** burning, crying, dire, imperative, importunate, insistent, instant, loud, noisy, pressing, shouting, strident, urgent, vehement, vociferous
**clamber** ascend, climb, mount, rise, scale, soar, top
**clamber by gripping with hands and knees** swarm
**clammy** close, damp, dank, dewy, dripping, drizzly, glutinous, humid, miry, misty, moist, muddy, muggy, rainy, sodden, soggy, steamy, sticky, sultry, vaporous, viscose, viscous, wet, wettish
**clamorous** blatant, boisterous, bouncy, demanding, dogged, earnest, exigent, impetuous, importunate, insistent, loud, noisy, open-mouthed, persistent, pressing, riotous, rollicking, rowdy, rumbustious, strident, turbulent, unrestrained, unruly, uproarious, urgent, vehement, vociferous, wild
**clamorous biblical tower** Babel
**clamour** agitation, blair, commotion, din, hubbub, hullabaloo, noise, outcry, rumpus, uproar
**clamp for waving hair** curler
**clan** alliance, ancestors, band, breed, brotherhood, clique, community, confederation, coterie, crowd, descendants, faction, family, fellowship, fraternity, genealogy, genus, group, horde, ilk, nation, sept, set, society, tribe
**clandestine** collusive, concealed, confidential, conspiratory, covert, crafty, feline, foxy, furtive, hidden, illegal, masked, mysterious, private, secret, shrouded, silent, sly, sneaky, stealthy, undercover, underhand(ed), unlawful
**clandestine meeting** tryst
**clan emblem** totem
**clang** bang, blare, blast, blow, burst, clang, clap, crash, detonation, din, dissonance, honk, jangle, peal, pop, roar, scream, shot, smash, thud, wail
**clanging noise** clangour
**clan member** tribesman

**clannish** allied, aloof, aristocratic, bigoted, choice, cliquish, closed, cultural, elegant, exclusive, family, fashionable, illiberal, insular, intolerant, limited, narrow, parochial, prejudiced, private, related, restricted, sectarian, select, selective, selfish, snobbish, tribal, unfriendly
**clap** acclaim, applaud, applause, bang, cheer, crack, hit, slap, smack, strike, whack
**claptrap** baloney, blague, blah, bunkum, drivel, eyewash, garbage, hokum, humbug, inanity, nonsense, rot, rubbish, trash, trickery, tripe, twaddle
**claret colour** maroon, red
**claret wine** Médoc
**clarified butter** ghee
**clarify** decipher, define, demonstrate, describe, disclose, elucidate, exhibit, explain, expose, interpret, reveal, simplify, specify, uncover, unfold, unmask, unveil
**clarify a decision** settle
**clarify by melting** render
**clarinet need** reed
**clarity** cleanness, clearness, comprehensibility, definition, exactness, explicitness, intelligibility, legibility, lucidity, obviousness, precision, purity, simplicity, transparency, understandability
**clash** clang, clank, clap, clatter, collide, conflict, contradiction, crash, disagree(ment), joust, opposition, struggle
**clashing instrument** cymbal
**clashing of opposed principles** conflict
**clashing sounds** cacophony, discord
**clasp** attack, brooch, catch, clip, clutch, embrace, enfold, fastener, fastening, grasp, grip, handshake, hasp, hold, hook, hug, pin, seize
**clasp in the arms** embrace
**class** arrange, caste, category, classification, contemporary, division, elegance, excellence, form, genera, genre, genus, grade, group, head, ilk, kind, lesson, number, order, race, rank, rate, sect, sort, species, status, study, subdivision, system, type
**class-conscious person** snob
**class domination** hegemony
**classic** abiding, ageless, archetypal, best, deathless, definitive, enduring, exemplar, exemplary, finest, first-rate, ideal, immortal, lasting, master(ly), masterpiece, model, standard, undying
**classical art of riding** haute école (F)
**classical ballet position** arabesque
**classical dance** ballet
**classical dancer** ballerina
**classical language** Latin, Greek
**classical music composition** concerto
**classical studies** humanities
**classic Japanese drama** no(h)
**classic study** art
**classification** allocation, analysis, arrangement, assortment, branch, category, class, code, codification, collection, division, file, grade, group(ing), identification, index, order, range, rank, rate, rating, relation, section, system, taxonomy, variety
**classification in biology** taxonomy
**classification of diseases** nosography, nosology
**classify** allocate, allot, arrange, assign, assort, catalogue, categorise, class, distribute, file, grade, graduate, group, index, label, list, name, number, organise, range, sort, systematise, tabulate, tag, ticket, type
**class of animals** species
**class of industrial workers** proletariat
**class of people** caste, sect, tribe
**class of spiders** Arachnida
**class of things** category
**class period** session
**classroom fool** dunce
**classy** elegant, stylish, superior
**clatter** clack, confusion, din, loudness, noise, racket, rattle, rattling
**clause** addition, codicil, condition, detail, division, exemption, provision, proviso, rider, section, sentence, specification, stipulation, supplement, term
**clavicembalo** harpsichord
**clavicle** collarbone
**claviform** club-shaped
**claw** dig, foot, lacerate, maul, nail, nipper, paw, pincher, scrape, talon, tentacle, unguis
**claw of a bird** talon
**claw of lobster** pincer
**clay and silt mixture** loess
**clay bed** gault
**clay deposit** marl
**clayey soil** loam
**clayey soil used as fertiliser** marl
**clay mixture** cob, slip
**clay oven** tandoor
**clay pigeon** gyropigeon, skeet, target
**clay pigeon shooting** skeet
**clay pot** crock
**clay rock like slate but softer** shale
**clay used by potters** argil
**clean** altogether, chaste, clarified, cleanse, clear, complete(ly), decontaminate, dirtless, entire(ly), flawless, fully, immaculate, innocent, legible, light, mop, moral, neat, neatly, perfect(ly), pure, purified, purify, readable, rinse, scour, scrub, spotless, sweep, unadulterated, unblemished, uncontaminated, undefiled, unsoiled, unstained, unsullied, whole, wholly, wipe
**clean a candlewick** snuff
**clean and arrange feathers** preen
**clean by rubbing** scour, wipe
**clean by washing** edulcorate
**clean by wiping** absterge
**clean dry** wipe
**clean feathers like a bird** preen
**clean floors** brush, mop, vacuum clean
**cleaning agent** detergent, lye
**cleaning aid** brush, mop, vacuum cleaner
**cleaning cloth** duster
**cleaning implement** broom, brush, mop, vacuum cleaner
**cleaning spirit** turpentine, turps
**cleaning substance** ammonia, detergent, lye
**cleaning woman** char, servant
**cleanliness** hygiene, sanitation
**clean-living** sinless
**cleanse** absolve, bathe, clarify, clean, decontaminate, deterge, disinfect, distil, elutriate, exonerate, filter, flush, fumigate, immerse, lather, launder, lave, moisten, mop, purge, purify, refine, rinse, rub, sanctify, scour, scrub, shampoo, shower, soak, sponge, sterilise, swap, sweep, wash, wet, wipe
**cleanse completely** sterilise
**cleanse of infection** disinfect
**cleanser** detergent, disinfectant, purifier, scourer, soap, solvent
**cleanse with liquid** wash
**clean-shaven** beardless, hairless
**cleansing agent** detergent, soap
**cleansing compound** borax
**cleansing process** bath, rinse, shower, wash
**clean the board** erase
**clean up** furbish, mop, sanitise, tidy, wash
**clean vigorously** scour
**clean with a broom** sweep
**clean with a cloth** wipe
**clean with liquid** wash
**clear** acquit, apparent, assured, boundless, bright, calm, clean, cloudless, comprehensible, conspicuous, definite, distinct,

**clearance sale** close out, close-down
**clear and calm** serene
**clear and transparent** hyaloid
**clear and unmistakable** plain
**clear a riverbed** dredge
**clear as crystal** evident, obvious
**clear, as profit** net
**clear away** dispel, obviate, remove, rid
**clear blue** azure
**clear-cut** carved, chiselled
**clear enough to read** legible, readable
**clear from criticism** vindicate
**clearing** absolving, acquitting, brightening, clarifying, erasing, evacuation, excusing, jumping, justifying, leaping, lightening, missing, purifying, refining, vaulting, vindicating, wiping
**clearing of woodland** sartage
**clearing one's conscience** purgation
**clear land by hoeing** skoffel, weed
**clearly** completely, definitely, distinctly, evidently, obviously, plainly, surely
**clearly articulated** coherent
**clearly expressed** perspicuous
**clearly expressive** articulate
**clearly noticeable** marked
**clearly perceptible** obvious
**clearly revealed** manifest
**clearly visible** conspicuous
**clear meat soup** consommé
**clear meat soup with vegetables** julienne
**clearness** clarity, simplicity
**clear of all charges** acquit, free, net(t)
**clear off!** scram
**clear of suspicion** vindicate
**clear open space in forest** glade
**clear out** abscond, decamp, depart, empty, withdraw
**clear profit** net(t)
**clear shrill sound** shriek, whistle
**clear sky** azure, ether
**clear soup** consommé
**clear the throat noisily** hawk
**clear thinking** clearheadedness, wisdom

**clear up** answer, brighten, clarify, elucidate, explain, order, rearrange, resolve, solve, sort, tidy, unravel
**cleave** abscind, adhere, affix, agree, attach, bind, bisect, bond, branch, break, burst, cement, chop, clasp, cling, coalesce, cohere, crack, cut, disunite, divide, gash, hack, halve, hew, hold, open, part(ition), remain, rend, rive, rupture, separate, sever, slash, slice, split, stick, sunder, support, sustain, tear
**cleave to** adhere
**cleft** break, chasm, cleavage, crack, cranny, crevice, cut, disjointed, divergence, divided, fissure, fractured, gap, gash, gully, hiatus, notch, opening, ravine, rent, rift, slit, space, split
**clefted hoof** cloven
**cleft in glacier** crevasse
**cleft in rock** rift
**cleft into three parts** trifid
**cleg** horse-fly
**clemency** alleviation, compassion, consideration, easing, humanity, kindness, lenience, leniency, lenity, mercifulness, mercy, mildness, palliation, patience, pity, pleasantness, tenderness
**clement** balmy, benign, bright, calm, charitable, clear, cloudless, compassionate, easy, fair, forbearing, forgiving, gentle, good, humane, kind, lenient, light, low, lucid, merciful, mild, moderate, muted, placid, pleasant, quiet, serene, slight, smooth, soft, soft-hearted, soothing, sunny, sympathetic, temperate, tender, tolerant, tranquil, unclouded, understanding, untroubled
**Clementine's abode** cavern
**clench** gnash, grate, grind, grit
**clenched hand** fist
**Cleopatra's killer** asp
**clergyman** bishop, canon, chaplain, cleric, curate, deacon, dominee, minister, padre, parson, pastor, priest, rabbi, rector, reverend, vicar
**clergyman in charge of a diocese** bishop
**clergyman in the lowest stage of ordination** deacon
**clergyman's house** manse, vicarage
**clergyman's official income** stipend
**clergyman's residence** manse, vicarage
**clergyman's salary** stipend
**clergyman who directs choral services** precentor

**clergyman with administrative responsibility** archdeacon
**cleric** abbé, churchman, clergyman, clerical, deacon, dean, dominee, ecclesiastic, minister, padre, parson, pastor, priest, rabbi, vicar
**clerical** ministerial, pastoral, priestly
**clerical cap** berretta, biretta
**clerical collar** choker
**clerical dignitary** canon
**clerical dress** alb
**clerical duties** secretarial
**clerical robe** alb
**clerical worker** typist
**cleric in minor orders** abbé
**clerk** accountant, acolyte, actuary, amanuensis, assistant, attendant, clergyman, filer, intellectual, lector, notary, penman, recorder, scribe, scrivener, stenograph, typist
**clerk in bank** teller
**clerk in store** cashier, saleslady, salesman
**clever** able, adept, adroit, apt, astute, brainy, bright, cute, expert, genius, gifted, habile, handy, ingenious, intelligent, nimble, quick, quick-witted, ready, skilful, slick, smart, subtle, talented
**clever and judicious** shrewd
**clever answer** rejoinder
**cleverest** ablest, brainiest, brightest, keenest, quickest, smartest, wittiest
**clever humour** wit
**clever little fish** dab
**cleverly bowled ball** yorker
**cleverly done** ably, neat
**cleverly executed** slick
**cleverly humorous** witty
**cleverly stylish** chic
**cleverness** ability, acuteness, artifice, astuteness, brightness, canniness, competence, craftiness, cunning, cuteness, dexterity, efficiency, genius, ingenuity, intelligence, mastery, nous, originality, quickness, sagacity, shrewdness, wit
**clever remark** nifty
**clever response** repartee
**clever retort** repartee, witticism
**clever saying** epigram, mot, quibble, quip, quirk
**cliché** banality, commonplace, maxim, platitude, prosaism, stereotype, truism
**click beetle** skipjack, snapping beetle
**client** buyer, customer, dependant, patron, shopper, subject
**clientele** customers
**climate** air, atmosphere, attitude, aura, ethos, humidity, ideology, influence, locale, milieu, mood, norms, rainfall,

**climb** region, spirit, temper, temperature, undertone, weather, zone
**climatic conditions** weather
**climax** acme, crisis, peak, pinnacle, ultimate
**climb** ascend, ascent, clamber, mount, rise, scale, surmount
**climb a cliff** scale
**climb down** descend, dismount, retract, retreat
**climber's aid** ice-axe
**climber's support** foothold, oaring, topping,
**climbing aid** ladder, steps
**climbing appliance** ladder
**climbing creeper** ivy
**climbing device** ladder, steps
**climbing evergreen** ivy
**climbing fish** anabas
**climbing palm** rattan
**climbing plant** bine, briony, bryony, clematis, coralita, creeper, ivy, liana, moonseed, pea, philodendron, vetch, vine
**climbing plant organ** tendril
**climbing plant's stem** bine
**climbing rose** rambler
**climbing shrub** smilax
**climbing vine** ivy
**climb into an aircraft** board, enplane
**climb to the top** scale
**climb up** ascend, ascent
**climb up on** clamber, mount
**climb with some difficulty** clamber
**clinch** adhere, agree, arrange, assure, bargain, buttress, catch, clasp, cleave, cling, close, clutch, confirm, contract, covenant, cradle, embrace, enfold, engage, establish, fix, fortify, grab, grapple, grasp, grip, hold, negotiate, pledge, reinforce, rivet, settle, snatch, squeeze, stick, stipulate, strengthen
**cling** adhere, clasp, embrace, fasten, grasp, grip, hug, stick
**clinging** adhering, clasping, clutching, embracing, grasping, hugging, sticking, tenacious
**clinging fish** remora
**clinging plant** ivy
**clinging sea mollusc** limpet
**clinging seed-vessel** bur(r)
**clinging vine** ivy
**cling to** adhere, hold, hug
**cling together** cohere
**clinical** analytic, business-like, cold, detached, disinterested, dispassionate, impersonal, objective, scientific, unemotional
**clinker** slag
**clinquant** glittering

**clip** abstract, buckle, clamp, compress, condense, contract, coupler, crop, curtail, excerpt, fastener, fleece, grip, hasp, pare, piece, prune, reduce, shave, shear, shorten, snip, trim
**clip by bits** snip
**clip off** shear
**clip off branches** prune
**clipper** shearer
**clippers** shears
**clipping** attaching, cropping, cutting, fastening, fixing, paring, pinning, pruning, shearing, snipping, trimming
**clipping machine** stapler
**clip that is removed from hand grenade** pin
**clip wool off** shear
**clique** band, bloc, cabal, Camorra, caucus, circle, clan, club, coterie, crowd, faction, group, junta, order, party, ring, sect, set, team
**Clive Rice's game** cricket
**cloaca** cesspool, privy, sewer
**cloak** aba, cape, capote, ceil, coat, conceal, cover(ing), disguise, dolman, domino, garment, hide, manta, manteau, mantle, mask, obscure, poncho, pretext, robe, screen, shroud, wrap
**cloak of animal skins** kaross
**cloak of Hercules** lioncloth
**cloak with hood** capote
**clobber** clothing, defeat, equipment, hit, thrash
**clock a horse's speed** time
**clocked** timed, measured
**clockface** dial
**clock part** chime, dial, hand, pallet, pendulum
**clock regulator** pendulum
**clock sound** tick
**clocktower** horologion, horologium
**clockwork model of planetary system** orrery
**clod** bear, boor, churl, dirt, divot, dolt, dust, earth, field, gawk, grass, land, lout, lubber, mould, oaf, sod, soil, sward, terrain, turf, yahoo, yokel
**clod breaker** harrow
**clog** block, congest, drag, hamper, hinder, impede, jam, sabot
**clog made from a single piece of wood** sabot
**cloister** convent, nunnery
**cloistress** nun
**Clootie** The Devil
**close** adjacent, adjoining, attached, bar, block, cease, choke, clog, closed, coalesce, compact, complete, conclude, condensed, confidential, confined, constant, cork, dear, dense, devoted, enclose, end, fill, finish, grapple, immediate, intense, intent, intimate, join, lock, muggy, near(by), neighbouring, obstruct, oppressive, parsimonious, penurious, plug, precise, reserved, reticent, scarce, seal, secretive, secure, shut, silent, stingy, stop, strict, taciturn, terminate, thick, unite
**close analogy** parity
**close and open eyes** blink, nictitate, wink
**close and open one eye quickly** wink
**close and open the eyes** blink, nictitate, wink
**close at hand** near, nearby, proximity
**close beforehand** preclude
**close by** around, at, beside, near, nigh
**close cluster** fascicle, fasciculus
**close comrade** buddy, friend
**closed** concluded, fastened, locked, restricted, sealed, settled, shut, terminated
**closed area** mare clausum
**closed at one end** blind, cul-de-sac
**closed car** coupé, sedan
**closed circuit** loop
**closed curve** circle, ellipse
**closed four-wheeled horse-drawn carriage** clarence
**closed hand** fist
**closed off** insulated
**close door loudly** slam
**close down** cease, discontinue, dispatch, eliminate, exterminate, halt, shut
**close examination** canvass, scrutiny, surveillance
**close eye momentarily** blink
**close firmly** seal, shut
**close-fitting cap** coif, skull-cap
**close-fitting coat** reefer
**close-fitting cover for blade or weapon** scabbard, sheath
**close-fitting necklace** choker
**close-fitting one-piece garment** leotard
**close-fitting tartan trousers** trews
**close-fitting trousers** trews
**close-fitting undergarment** corset
**close friend** chum, crony, mate, pal, partner
**close group** cluster
**close hermetically** seal
**close imitation** echo
**close in on** approach, encircle, engrid, envelop, near, surround
**close in position** nearby
**close investigation** scrutiny, surveillance
**close kinship** propinquity
**closely** attentively, intently
**closely acquainted** familiar, intimate

**closely acquainted with** au fait (F), conversant, familiar
**closely confined** pent
**closely fitting** snug
**closely related** affined, connected, near
**closely shut up** pent, pent-up
**closely woven cotton fabric** percale
**closeness** nearness, propinquity
**closeness of substance** density
**close observation** surveillance
**close of day** dusk, eve, evening, sunset
**close of drama** finale
**close one eye** wink
**close out** decrease, discount, liquidate, lower, reduce, withdraw
**close-packed** dense
**close quarters** nearby, proximity
**close relationship** affiance, belonging, intimacy
**close row of bushes** hedge
**close securely** seal
**close shave** near thing
**closest** nearest
**closest to the rear** aftermost
**close tightly** clench, seal
**closet need** hanger
**close to** about, akin, almost, beside, by, near
**close to tears** weepy
**close to the barrier** borderline
**close to the side** alongside
**close up** seal
**close up again** reseal
**close up to** against
**close watch** surveillance
**close with a bang** slam
**closing** shutting
**closing part** finale
**closing part of a musical composition** finale
**closing the eyelids** seeling
**closure** articulation, barricade, barrier, blockade, blockage, bolt(ing), bulwark, cessation, completion, conclusion, connection, cork(ing), cover, dam, dike, end, faucet, impediment, joiner, latch(ing), levee, lid, lock(ing), obstruction, obturation, occlusion, padlock(ing), plug(ging), securing, spigot, stoppage, stopper, stopping, tap, termination, top, union, valve, windup
**clot** block, cake, clog, clump, coagulate, coagulation, condense, congeal, curd(le), deepen, gel, glob, jell(y), knot, lump, mass, precipitate, set, solidify, stupe, thicken
**cloth** drapery, fabric, goods, material, rag, textile
**cloth around corpse** shroud
**cloth badge** motif

**cloth bag** sack
**cloth colourant** dye
**cloth covering backs and arms of chairs** antimacassar
**cloth doll** golliwog, ragdoll
**clothe** apparel, attire, cover, dress, garb, rig, swathe
**clothed** arrayed, attired, clad, covered, decked, draped, dressed, endowed, enwrapped, equipped, garbed, habited, invested, rigged, robed, swathed
**cloth edge** hem
**cloth edging** list
**clothes** attire, clothing, costume, dress, garb, garments, habit, outfit, raiment, togs, vestments
**clothes collection** wardrobe
**clothes drier** airer
**clothes horse** airer
**clothes maker** seamstress, tailor
**clothes prepared for new-borne child** layette
**clothes protector** apron
**clothes tag** label
**cloth fold** pleat, tuck
**cloth for drying** towel
**cloth for straining liquids** filter
**cloth for wiping away sweat** sudarium
**cloth for wiping face** facecloth, sudarium
**cloth fragment** rag, scrap, tatter
**cloth from bark** tapa
**cloth hat** bonnet
**clothing** array, attire, clothes, costume, covering, draping, dress, endowing, ensemble, garb, garments, gear, habits, outfit, raiment, regalia, rigging, togs, vestment, vesture, wardrobe
**clothing business** couture, fashion, rag-trade
**clothing item** garment
**clothing oneself in garments of opposite sex** transvestism
**clothing repair section** patch
**clothing stiffener** starch
**clothing tag** label
**clothing to fit** suit
**cloth insert** gusset
**cloth junction** seam
**cloth machine** gig
**cloth measure** ell, metre, yard
**cloth merchant** draper
**cloth of flax** linen
**cloth pile** nap
**cloth put under a child's chin** bib
**cloth scrap** rag
**cloth spread over a coffin** pall
**cloth spread over a Muslim tomb** chad(d)ar, chador, chuddah, chuddar
**cloth surface** nap

**cloth waterproofed with oil** oilskin
**cloth worn by peasants** russet
**cloth worn round hips as sole garment** loincloth
**cloth worn round waste** sash
**cloth woven from flax** linen
**clot of blood in a living vessel** thrombus
**clotted blood** gore, scab
**clotted portion of blood** cruor
**clotting in a vessel during life** thrombosis
**clotting of blood** congeal
**cloud** becloud, bedim, cirrus, crowd, fog, haze, mist, nimbus, obscure, (over)shadow, shade, vapour
**clouded** darkened, dimmed, eclipsed, filmy, obscured, overcast, (over)shadowed, shaded, veiled
**cloud formation** cumulus, nimbus, stratus
**cloud nine** elevation, euphoria, nirvana
**cloud of dust and gas in a galaxy** nebula
**cloud of flying drops** spray
**cloud of glory** halo, nimbus
**cloudy** befogged, clouded, confused, dark, depressive, dim, dismal, indistinct, lowering, muddy, murky, nebulous, obscure, opaque, overcast, shadowy
**clout** blow, box, buffet, clip, cuff, hammering, hit, knock, punch, rap, slap, smack, strike, thump, wallop, whack
**clove-flavoured herb** basil
**clove pink** carnation
**clover** trefoil
**cloverleaf** interchange
**clove-scented flower** pink
**clown** antic, buffoon, comedian, comic, dolt, fool, harlequin, jest, jester, joker, pierrot, prankster
**clownish** zany
**cloy** bore, deaden, dull, exhaust, glut, nauseate, numb, obtund, overdo, overfeed, sate, satiate, satisfy, saturate, stuff, surfeit
**cloying** fulsome, glutting, gorging, honeyed, luscious, mawkish, melting, nauseating, overfilling, satiating, sickly, stuffing, sugary, sweet(ened)
**cloying blandishments** treacle
**cloying sweetness** syrup
**club** association, bat, batter, bludgeon, circle, coterie, cudgel, organisation, set, shillelagh, society, stick
**club carrier** caddie
**club fee** due
**club foot** talipes
**club-footed person** taliped

**club for dancing** disco
**clublike weapon** mace
**club-moss** lycopod
**club-shaped** claviform
**club that plays pop music** disco
**club used in sport** bat
**club with a spiked metal head** mace
**club with heavy end** bludgeon
**clucking of hen** cackle
**clue** cue, discovery, evidence, guide, hint, imply, indicate, indication, indicator, inkling, insinuation, interpretation, lead, pointer, sign, suggest(ion), tip, tip-off, trace
**clued-up** knowledgeable
**clump** bumble, bunch, bundle, clomp, cluster, lumber, mass, stomp, thump, tramp, tuft
**clump of clay gouged out by a golf club** divot
**clumpy person** lummox
**clumsy** awkward, blundering, boorish, bumbling, bungling, clumpling, crude, dexterity, doltish, gauche, gawky, graceless, hamfisted, heavy, heavy-handed, hulking, ill-made, inelegant, inept, inert, insensitive, lacking, lumbering, lumpish, maladroit, oafish, rough, shapeless, tactless, uncoordinated, uncouth, ungainly, ungraceful, unhandy, unskilful, unskilled, untoward, unwieldy, wooden
**clumsy amphibian** toad
**clumsy boy** hobbledehoy
**clumsy baboon, brutish person** oaf
**clumsy country fellow** clodhopper
**clumsy failure** foozle
**clumsy fellow** boob, lubber, palooka
**clumsy fielder** butterfingers
**clumsy handwriting** scrawl, scribble
**clumsy lout** grobian, oaf
**clumsy oaf** lout
**clumsy person** boor, oaf
**clumsy player** dub
**clumsy serving** dollop
**clumsy ship** tub
**clumsy shoes** clogs
**cluster** assemblage, batch, bunch, clump, collection, congregate, cyme, flock, gathering, group, knot, mass, sorus, swarm, tuft
**clustered like grapes** aciniform
**clustered together** agminate
**cluster of bees** swarm
**cluster of islands in the sea** archipelago
**cluster of stars** nebula
**cluster of threads** tuft
**cluster of trees** clump
**clutch** brood, capture, catch, clasp, clench, embrace, grab, grasp,

grip(e), group, hold, seize, snag, snatch, youngling
**clutch at** grasp
**clutch firmly** grasp
**clutter** mess
**coach** advise, bogey, bus, car, carriage, carrier, chariot, coacher, cram, drill, educate, help, instruct(or), omnibus, prepare, saloon, stage, teach(er), train(er), tutor, vehicle
**coach dog** Dalmatian
**coachman** coachee, driver Jehu, whip
**coachman's seat** box
**coach privately** tutor
**coadjuster** assistant, auxiliary, helper
**coagulate** cake, clod, clot, cohere, congeal, convert, curdle, gel, harden, jell, set, solidify, thicken
**coagulated milk** curd
**coal** anthracite, ash, briquette, charcoal, cinder, clinker, coke, culm, ember, fuel, lignite, rock, torch
**coal after treatment** coke
**coal barge** keel
**coal bed** seam
**coal box** bin, bunker, hod
**coal bucket** hod
**coal car** corb, tender, tram
**coal chute** dock
**coal crib** bin
**coal deposit** soot
**coal digger** miner
**coal distillate** tar
**coal-dust** coom(b), culm, smut
**coaler** freighter
**coalesce** blend, clog, cohere, combine, consolidate, embody, fuse, integrate, join, merge, mingle, mix, unite
**coalfish** coley, cuddy, saithe
**coal fragment** ember
**coal holder** bin, bunker, hod
**coal in place** solid
**coal in small rounded lumps** cobbles
**coalition** affiliation, alliance, cartel, combination, consolidation, consortium, corporation, council, entente, faction, federation, fusing, fusion, incorporation, junction, junta, league, mass, merger, merging, partnership, trust, unification, union
**coal lifter** shovel
**coal measure** ton
**coalmine** colliery, pit
**coalmine gas** damp
**coalminer** collier
**coalmine shaft** adit, pit
**coalmining city of New South Wales** Lithgow
**coal oil** kerosene, petroleum
**coal pillar** stook
**coal product** tar

**coal receptacle** hod, scuttle
**coalscuttle** hod
**coal size** egg, nut, pea, stove
**coal slab** skip
**coalsmoke deposit** soot
**coal source** mine
**coal-tar derivative** dye, pitch
**coal-tar dye** indophenol
**coal-tar product** cresol, naphtha
**coal variety** cannel, lignite
**coal wagon** corb, tram
**coal weight** ton
**coalyard** ree
**coarse** base, bluff, boorish, brutish, common, crass, crude, dirty, earthy, faulty, foul-mouthed, graceless, gross, gruff, impure, indecent, indelicate, inelegant, inferior, loose, loutish, mean, obscene, ribald, rough, rude, textural, thick, uncivil, unpolished, unrefined, unsavoury, vile, vulgar
**coarse and hardy grass** kikuyu
**coarse and surly** chuffy
**coarse basket** skep
**coarse brutal person** swine
**coarse bulk food** roughage
**coarse canvas** burlap
**coarse cinnamon bark** cassia
**coarse cloth** baize, burlap, crash, fustian, hessian, leno, manta, scrim, shrouding, tapa
**coarse cloth of hemp** canvas
**coarse corundum** emery
**coarse cotton cloth** calico, denim, scrim, surat
**coarse cut tobacco** shag
**coarse fabric** bagging, crash, stamen, tat
**coarse fabric of hemp** sackcloth
**coarse fabric of silk** grogram
**coarse fibre** tow
**coarse file** rasp
**coarse fish** bream, tench
**coarse flax fibre** tow
**coarse-fleshed river fish** chub
**coarse floor-covering cloth** drugget
**coarse flour** meal
**coarse fodder** roughage
**coarse French tobacco** caporal
**coarse garment** brat, stroud
**coarse grain** meal, samp
**coarse grass** fag, reed, sedge, timothy
**coarse ground wheat** middlings
**coarse hair** shag
**coarse hair in wool** kemp
**coarse hemp** tow
**coarse hominy** grits, samp
**coarse in manners** vulgar

**coarse Italian water ice** granita
**coarse jute fabric** hessian
**coarse lace** macrame
**coarse linen cloth** buckram, lockram
**coarse linen fabric** crash, ecru, harn (Sc)
**coarsely ground corn** samp
**coarsely ground grain** grits
**coarsely ground maize** hominy, samp
**coarsely humorous** ribald, risqué, salacious, scabrous, scurrilous
**coarsely outspoken** raunchy
**coarsely woven fabric** hopsack
**coarse material** baize
**coarse matted wool** shag
**coarsen** impair, vulgarise
**coarse nap** shag
**coarse oatmeal** grits
**coarse outer cereal coat** bran
**coarse person** slob
**coarse person of bestial passion** yahoo
**coarse plain linen** crash
**coarse rigid hair** bristle, seta
**coarse rock** gneiss
**coarse rough shoe** brogue
**coarse rustic** boor
**coarse sacking** gunny
**coarse sand and small stones** gravel
**coarse sandstone** grit
**coarse seaweed** kelp, oarweed, tangle
**coarse silk** tusser, tussore
**coarse snuff** rappee
**coarse spiny-leaved Australian grass** porcupine grass, spinifex
**coarse stiffened cloth** buckram
**coarse tobacco** shag
**coarse towelling** terry
**coarse twilled fabric** drill
**coarse, vicious person** barbarian
**coarse weed** dock
**coarse weedy Malaysian grass** lalang
**coarse wool** baize, gare
**coarse woollen blanket** cotta
**coarse woollen cloth** baize, frieze, kersey, stammel, stroud
**coarse work shoe** brogue
**coarse woven cloth** bagging, sacking
**coarse woven fabric** scrim
**coarse woven material** matting
**coarse wrapping material** burlap
**coarse youth** yahoo
**coast** bank, beach, border, coastline, cruise, drift, freewheel, glide, laterality, littoral, ripa, run, sail, (sea)shore, seaside, skate, skip, slide, slip, strand, taxi, voyage
**coastal** littoral, marginal, seaside
**coastal area** tideland
**coastal inlet** bay, creek, ria
**coastal lake** lagoon
**coastal mound of sand** dune

**coastal mountain ranges of India** gha(u)t
**coastal region** littoral, seaboard, seashore, seaside
**coastal resort** seaside
**coastal resort in France** Nice
**coastal road with wide views** corniche
**coastal strip** beach, shore
**coastal wild duck** sheldrake, shelduk
**coast bird** gull, tern
**coaster** bob, mat, ship, sled, stand, vessel, winecup
**coaster waver** roller
**coasting** freewheeling
**coasting vehicle** bob, sled
**coastline** beach, border, (sea)shore, seaside, shoreline, strand
**coat** aba, apply, coating, cover, covering, fleece, fur, garment, hair, hide, husk, jacket, kirtle, layer, overcoat, overlay, pelt, plaster, rind, skin, smear, spread, tunic, wool, wrapping
**coat a building** paint
**coat collar** lapel
**coated with metal** tin-plated
**coat food** dredge
**coat hanger** peg
**coati** arctoid, narica, nasua, tejon
**coating** applying, blanket, covering, dusting, enamel, film, finish, lamination, layer, plastering, smearing, spreading, varnish, veneer
**coating eye round iris** sclerotic
**coating of the teeth** enamel
**coating on a cake** icing
**coat lining** sateen
**coat metal** anodise
**coat of animal** fur, pelage
**coat of armour** hauberk
**coat of arms** bearings, blazon, crest, heraldry
**coat of blood vessels** media
**coat of certain alloy** terne
**coat of eye** choroid
**coat of eyeball** sclera
**coat of gold** gild
**coat of hair** melote
**coat of mail** armature, armour, byrnie, corselet, cuirass, hauberk, panoply, protection
**coat of metal** plate
**coat of paint** layer
**coat of seed** bran, episperm
**coat of wool** fleece
**coat part** button, collar, lapel, skirt, sleeve
**coats teeth** enamel
**coat's turnback** lapel
**coat with aluminium** aluminise
**coat with crystallised sugar** candy
**coat with flour or sugar** dredge

**coat with gold** gild, plate
**coat with icing** glacé
**coat with metal** plate, terne
**coat with sugar** ice
**coax** allure, bait, beg, beguile, bribe, cajole, decoy, entice, flatter, inveigle, lure, manipulate, persuade, pet, soothe, tease, tempt, wheedle
**coax by flattery** cajole
**coaxial** conterminous
**coaxing** alluring, beguiling, cajolement, cajoling, decoying, enticing, flattering, persuading, soothing, wheedling
**coaxing talk** blarney, flattery
**cobalt bloom** erythrite
**cobber** chum, friend, mate, pal
**Cobbers and Sheilas** Australians
**cobbler** bootmaker, bootmender, snop
**cobbler's tool** awl, bradawl, last
**cobra** snake, viper
**cob's partner** pen
**cobweb material** fibroin
**cocaine** coke, snow
**cocaine course** coca
**cocaine, or other narcotic drug in powdered form** snow
**cocaine plant** coca
**cochleate** coiled, corkscrew, helical, spiral, turbinal, turbinate, volute
**cock** chanticleer, cockerel, rooster
**cock-a-hoop** gleeful
**cockatoo** galah, parrot
**cockatrice** basilisk
**cockerel** rooster
**cockeyed optimist** escapist
**cock fattened for eating** capon
**cockfight** spar
**Cockney** Londoner
**Cockney costermonger** pearly
**Cockney fruit seller** coster(monger)
**cock's comb** crest
**cockscomb** amaranth
**cocksure** arrogant, dogmatic, overconfident, presumptuous, self-confident
**cocktail** aperitif, appetiser, highball, martini, mixture, potion, sidecar
**cocktail containing whisky** manhattan
**cocktail garnish** olive
**cocktail maker** shaker
**cocktail room** lounge
**cocky** arrogant, brash, bumptious, conceited, lordly, parrot, saucy
**cocky person** bantam
**coconut fibre** coir
**coconut meat** copra
**coconut producing plant** palm tree
**coconut product** copra
**coconut shell** husk
**coconut tree** palm
**cocoon** pod

**cocoon for peas** pod
**cocoon silk** floss, thread
**cocoon stage of insect** chrysalis, pupa
**cocoon thread** silk
**cod** befool, tease
**coda** conclusion, end, epilogue, finale, postscript, tailpiece
**coddle** baby, brew, cocker, cosset, favour, fondle, gratify, humour, indulge, mollycoddle, overindulge, pamper, pet, poach, simmer, spoil, steep, stew
**code** canon, cipher, convention, cypher, ethics, etiquette, language, law, manners, maxim, principle, regulation, rule(s), system
**coded message** cryptograph
**code of behaviour** protocol
**code of beliefs** dogma
**code of honour** probity
**code of morality** ethos
**code of social conduct** etiquette
**code system** Morse
**codicil** addendum, addition, afterthought, appendix, coda, epilogue, extra, insert, postscript, pull-out, reconsideration, rider, sequel, subscript, supplement
**cod-like fish** hake
**coelenterate** acaleph(e), anemone, hydra, jellyfish, medusa, polyp, radiate
**coerce** abuse, bully, cause, compel, compulse, constrain, control, cow, curb, dominate, drive, exact, force, impel, impress, manage, override, press, threaten, torment, urge
**coerce compliance with** enforce
**coercion** abuse, browbeating, bullying, compulsion, constraint, control, duress, enforcement, force, inducement, insistence, intimidation, manipulation, menacing, obligation, pressure, requirement, sanctions, straint, terror, threats, twisting, violence
**coercion by threats** intimidation
**coexist with** accompany
**coffee** espresso
**coffee alkaloid** caffeine
**coffee bar** café
**coffee break** rest, recess
**coffee-chocolate flavour** mocha
**coffee cup** mug
**coffee grinder** mill
**coffee house** café
**coffee made under steam pressure** espresso
**coffee shop** café
**coffee's rival** tea
**coffee, stew or whiskey** Irish
**coffee style** espresso, expresso

**coffee vessel** pot, urn
**coffee with milk** café au lait (F)
**coffee without milk** café noir (F)
**coffer** casket, chest, container, crate, locker, receptacle, repository, safe, strongbox, trunk, vault
**coffers** assets, capital, exchequer, finances, funds, moneys, repositories, resources, revenues, treasury
**coffin** pall
**coffin carrier** hearse
**coffin cover** pall
**coffin stand** bier
**cog** gear(wheel), lie, notch, pawl, projection, ratchet, sprocket, tooth
**cogent** active, apropos, authorative, clear, coherent, compelling, consistent, convincing, credible, definite, dynamic, effective, efficient, energetic, evident, forceful, forcible, germane, impressive, logical, mighty, persuasive, pertinent, pithy, potent, powerful, rational, relevant, sound, strong, telling, valid, vigorous, weighty
**cogitate** cerebrate, concentrate, consider, contemplate, deliberate, evaluate, focus, imagine, meditate, ponder, surmise, think
**cogitative** contemplative, meditating, meditative, pensive, pondering, thoughtful
**cognac** brandy
**cognate** akin, alike, comparable, consistent, homogeneous, identical, kindred, related, similar, uniform, unvarying
**cognisance** awareness, consciousness, discernment, familiarity, knowledge, note, observation, perception, recognition, regardfulness, sensibility, sensitivity, urbanity, wariness, watchfulness
**cognisant** acquainted, admiring, alert, appreciative, apprised, attentive, awake, aware, cautious, conscious, conversant, enlightened, enthusiastic, familiar, informed, intelligent, knowing, knowledgeable, mindful, perceptive, percipient, pleased, respectful, responsive, sensible, sensitive, sentient, sharp, sophisticated, sympathetic, understanding, wise
**cognition** ability, apprehension, awareness, comprehension, consciousness, grasp, insight, intelligence, judg(e)ment, knowledge, notion, perception, recognition, sensation, understanding
**cogs on gearwheel** teeth

**cogwheel** gear, cog, pinion
**co-heir** parcener
**cohere** agree, bind, cement, cling, combine, conform, congeal, correspond, glue, jibe, join, set, stick, unite
**coherent** apparent, articulate, audible, clear, cogent, compact, comprehensible, connected, consistent, continuous, definite, distinct, eloquent, evident, explicit, express(ive), fluent, intelligible, logical, lucid, manifest, meaningful, obvious, palpable, patent, plain, pronounced, rational, recognisable, relevant, sound, unambiguous, unequivocal, united, valid, vocal
**cohesive and sticky** viscid
**coif** cap, skullcap
**coiffeur** hairdresser
**coiffure** bun, chignon, coif, haircut, hairdo, hairstyle, headdress, pompadour, set, tress
**coiffure cover** hairnet
**coil** convolute, curl, fuss, hubbub, loop, noise, snake, spin, spiral, tumult, twine, twist, writhe
**coil of false hair** hairpiece, postiche
**coil of hair** chignon
**coil of yarn** skein
**coin** bit, cash, change, compose, conceive, copper, create, currency, devise, fabricate, forge, form(ulate), gold, introduce, invent, launch, mint, money, mould, originate, piece, produce, silver, specie
**coin aperture** slot
**coin back** tail, verso
**coin box at Royal Mint** pyx
**coincide in time** synchronise
**coincidence** accident, accord, chance, coexistence, coextension, concurrence, consistency, consonance, egality, eventuality, fate, fluke, happenstance, harmony, luck, rapport, serendipity, simultaneity, uniformity, unity
**coincident** agreeing, alike, coinciding, congruent, equivalent, parallel
**coincidental** accidental, casual, chance, fluk(e)y, fortuitous, fortunate, lucky, unexpected, unforeseen, unpredictable
**coin collecting** numismatics
**coin collector** numismatist
**coin edging** milling, reeding
**coiner of words** neologist
**coin face** head, obverse
**coin factory** mint
**coin flip** toss
**coin-hole** slot
**coining of new words** neology

**coin money** specie
**coin new phrases** neologise
**coin of Afghanistan** abassi, afghani, amania, pul
**coin of Albania** franc, guintar, lek
**coin of South Korea** hwan, won
**coin of Venezuela** bolivar
**coin of Yemen** riyal
**coin of Yugoslavia** dinar, para
**coin of Zambia** kwacha
**coin opening** slot
**coin-operated machine** dispenser
**coin receptacle** metre, slot
**coins** cash, specie
**coin's edge** engrail
**coin-shaped** nummular
**coin-shaped object** disc
**coin-spin call** head, tail
**coir** matting
**colander** drainer, sieve, strainer
**cold** algid, aloof, arctic, bitter, callous, chill(y), cool, cruel, dead, detached, disdainful, distant, flu, formal, freezing, frigid, frosty, frozen, gelid, heartless, icy, indifferent, nipping, nippy, passionless, raw, reserved, sniffles, stiff, uncaring, unconcerned, unemotionable, unfriendly, uninterested, unresponsive, unsympathetic, wintry
**cold Adriatic wind** bora
**cold and cheerless** bleak
**cold and clammy** damp, dank
**cold and damp** clammy, dank, raw
**cold and slimy** clammy
**cold and unfriendly in manner** chilly
**cold-blooded** brutal, callous, cool, cruel, nonchalance, sangfroid, stoical, unfeeling, unimpassioned
**cold-blooded animal** ectotherm, fish, poikilotherm, reptile
**cold boned stuffed meat set in jelly** galantine (F)
**cold crystals** snow
**cold cubes** ice
**cold cuts** delicatessen
**cold dish** ice cream, salad
**cold drink** juice, lemonade, soda
**cold dry wind** bise
**coldest part of the southern hemisphere** Antarctic
**cold feet** fear, funk, nervousness
**cold in manner** frosty
**coldly** icily
**coldly hard** glassy
**cold meal** salad
**cold mix of vegetables** salad
**cold months** winter
**cold north wind in Adriatic** tramontane
**cold-producing** algific
**cold sea fog on east coast of Scotland** haar

**cold season** winter
**cold shoulder** cut, rebuff, snub, spurn
**cold south** Antarctic
**cold state** Alaska
**cold steel** bayonet
**cold stone** slab
**cold sufferer** sneezer
**cold symptom** sneeze
**cold Texas wind** norther
**cold weather garment** manta, overcoat, parka
**cold wind** bise, mistral
**cold wind in France** mistral
**cold zone** Arctic, Antarctic
**cole** cabbage, rape
**coleopterous insect** beetle
**coleseed** rape
**colewort** cabbage
**colic** bellyache, billary, flatulence, gripe
**collaborate** co-operate, collude, participate, unite
**collaborator** accessory, associate, co-operator, confederate, conspirator, contributor, double-dealer, participant, quisling, renegade, scab, traitor, turncoat
**collapse** breakdown, disintegration, downfall, failure, fall, fold
**collapse suddenly** crash
**collapsible boat** dinghy, flatboat
**collapsible shelter** tent
**collar** apprehend, appropriate, capture, catch, grab, seize, torques
**collarbone** clavicle
**collar button** stud
**collar fastening** stud
**collar for criminal** cang(ue)
**collar of flowers** garland, lei
**collars and ties** neckwear
**collate** appose, arrange, check, collocate, compare, juxtapose, match, sort, verify
**collateral** affiliated, assurance, attendant, bail, bond, concurrent, deposit, earnest, gage, guarantee, hostage, insurance, lateral, parallel, pawn, pledge, security, side, simultaneous, surety, warrant
**colleague** ally, associate, companion, comrade, confrère, helper, partner
**collect** accrue, accumulate, acquire, aggregate, amass, assemble, call, cluster, compile, compose, conduct, congregate, congress, contract, convene, converge, draw, garner, gather, group, heap, hoard, infer, jug, levy, muster, obtain, pile, pool, raise, rally, save, scramble, scrounge, secure, stockpile, uplift
**collectable knick-knack** curio
**collected** balanced, calm, composed, cool, nonchalant, peaceful, placid, poised, sedate, self-controlled, serene, steady, tranquil, undisturbed, unruffled, untroubled
**collect haphazardly together** grab, scrape, scratch
**collecting** accumulating, amassing, assembling, congregating, convening, converging, fetching, gathering, heaping, hoarding, rallying, retrieving, saving, stockpiling
**collect in quantity** amass
**collect in small quantities** glean
**collect into a sum** aggregate
**collection** accumulation, aggregation, alms, assembly, cluster, congregation, contribution, group, heap, hoard, series, set, variety
**collection and study of postage stamps** philately
**collection in a church service** offertory
**collection of ancient Icelandic poems** Edda
**collection of anecdotes** ana
**collection of animals** menagerie, zoo
**collection of books** library
**collection of choice poems** anthology
**collection of church writings** patrology
**collection of different things** variety
**collection of dried plants** herbarium
**collection of exotic objects** curiosa
**collection of facts** ana
**collection of families** clan
**collection of glosses** glossary
**collection of implements** kit
**collection of money at religious service** offertory
**collection of musical items** medley
**collection of papers** portfolio
**collection of people** crowd
**collection of plants** sertule, sertulum
**collection of poems** volume
**collection of poems of literary merit** anthology
**collection of pus** abscess
**collection of rainfall** catchment
**collection of records** archive
**collection of sayings** ana
**collection of scented flower petals** pot-pourri
**collection of sheaves** stook
**collection of sketches** ana
**collection of small bubbles in a liquid** foam, froth
**collection of table games** compendium
**collection of tents** camp
**collection of three** triad
**collection of tools** kit
**collection of turkeys** ratter
**collection of wild animals in captivity** menagerie, zoo

**collective farm in Russia** kolkhoz
**collective stakes in various games** pool
**collective unit** commune
**collector of books** bibliophil(e)
**collector of stamps** philatelist
**collect the crop** harvest, reap
**collect together** aggregate, amass, compile, muster
**college** academy, lyceum, school, university
**college acceptance exam** scholarship
**college cashier** bursar, treasurer
**college cheer** rah
**college discussion group** seminar
**college enrolment** intake
**college faculty head** dean
**college girl** coed
**college graduate** alumna, alumnus
**college graduates** alumnae, alumni
**college grounds** campus
**college head** principal, rector
**college near Berkshire** Eton
**college official** dean
**college permit for absence** exeat
**college servant** gyp, scout
**college session** semester
**college steward** manciple
**college teacher** lecturer, tutor
**college treasurer** bursar
**collide** clash, conflict, connect, contact, crash, differ, disaccord, disagree, encounter, impact, prang, ram, smash, strike
**collide violently** crash
**collide with** clash, crash, hit, ram, strike
**collie** sheepdog
**collie having a bluish-grey coat with speckles of black** (blue) merle
**collier** (coal)miner, sailor, ship
**colliery** (coal)mine, excavation, pit
**collision** accident, casualty, clash, conflict, convergence, crash, discord, encounter, friction, impact, impingement, meeting, quarrel, shock, wreck
**collision of several motor vehicles** pile-up
**collocate** arrange, place
**colloid** aerogel, emulsion, gel, gluey, mucin
**colloidal liquid** gel
**colloidal substance** gel, gum
**colloidal suspension** sol
**colloquial** chatty, everyday, folksy, homespun, homey, informal
**colloquial language** slang
**colloquial title** nickname
**colloquy** analysis, argument, chat, communion, conclave, conference, consideration, consultation, conversation, converse, debate, deliberation, dialogue, discourse, discussion, examination, exchange, gossip, meeting, parley, review, scrutiny, seminar, symposium, talk, tête-à-tête, word
**collusion** cabal, cahoots, complicity, connivance, conspiracy, covin, intrigue, scheme
**collusive alliance** cartel
**collywobbles** nervousness, stomach-ache
**Colombian cape** Aguja, Augusta, Marzo, Vela
**Colombian currency** peso
**Colombian gulf** Cupica, Darien, Tibuga, Tortugas, Uraba
**Colombian inlet** Tumaco
**Colombian language** Spanish
**Colombian plain** Llanos
**Colombian port** Cartagena, Lorica
**Colombian province** Arauca, Bolivar, Caldas, Cauca, Huila, Meta, Narino, Putumayo, Tolima, Valle
**Colombian religion** Roman Catholic
**Colombian volcano** Purace
**colonial governor** satrap
**colonial insect** ant
**colonial patriot** Revere
**colonial ruler** viceroy
**colonise** appropriate, dwell, establish, form, people, pioneer, populate, settle, subjugate
**colonist** colonial, homesteader, immigrant, pioneer, planter, settler
**colonnade** arcade, cloister, peristyle, portico
**colony** community, dependency, district, dominion, group, hamlet, homestead, mandate, outpost, possession, protectorate, province, satellite, settlement, stockade, territory, town, village
**colony insect** ant, bee
**colony of bees** hive
**colony of crows** rookery
**colony of rabbits** warren
**colony of social hornets** vespiary
**colophony** resin, rosin
**Colorado park** Estes
**Colorado ski city** Aspen
**colorant** colouring, dye, pigment, shade, tinge, tint
**colossal** delightful, enormous, gigantic, huge, immense, massive, monstrous, monumental, mountainous, prodigious, remarkable, splendid, titanic, tremendous, vast
**Colosseum sword-fighter** gladiator
**colossus** colosso, giant, monolith, statue, titan
**colostrum** beastings, beestings, biestings
**colour** beige, black, blue, brown, dye, green, hue, lilac, orange, red, tan, tint, violet, white, yellow
**colour blindness** achromatism, daltonism, protanopia, tritanopia
**colour changer** dye(r)
**coloured** dyed, stained
**coloured eye membrane** iris
**coloured flower leaf** petal
**coloured glass** schmelze, smalt(o)
**coloured handkerchief** bandanna
**coloured ice-cream** neapolitan
**coloured like a rainbow** iridescent
**coloured mosaic glass** smalt(o)
**coloured pencil** crayon
**coloured-stone picture** mosaic
**colourful** bright, brilliant, flamboyant, gaudy, lustrous, luxuriant, multicoloured, picturesque, quaint, striking, variegated, vivid
**colourful arc** rainbow
**colourful bird** peacock
**colourful fish** boce, opah, wrasse
**colourful Japanese sash** obi
**colourful procession** pageant
**colourful sash** obi
**colouring** dye, dyeing, paint
**colouring agent** dye, paint
**colouring matter** colourant, dye, pigment
**colouring matter of turmeric** curcumine
**colouring substance** pigment
**colourless** achromatic, ashen, drab, dreary, faded, insipid, pale, sickly, tame, vacuous, vapid, wan
**colourless gas** acetylene, ammonia, ethane, ketone, oxan(e)
**colourless gaseous element** nitrogen
**colourless gas with strong smell** ammonia
**colourless gem** diamond, topaz, white sapphire, zircon
**colourless hydrocarbon** ethane
**colourless inflammable gas** methane
**colourless liquid flavoured with aniseed** anisette
**colourless orange-flavoured liqueur** Cointreau
**colourless variety of opal** hyalite
**colourless volatile liquid** ether
**colour lightly** tinge, tint
**colour of horse** chestnut, roan
**colour of snow** white
**colour of the sky** azure
**colour of the sky at sunrise** aurora
**colour of traffic light** amber, green, red
**colour of unbleached linen** ecru
**colour of unbleached wool** beige

**colour-prejudiced** racial
**colour red in heraldry** gules
**colour shade** hue
**colour slightly** tincture, tinge, tint
**colours of beryl** blue, green, white, yellow
**colour system** PAL
**colour tone** shade
**colour value** tone
**colporteur** book-pedlar
**colt or filly** foal
**colubrine** snakelike
**Columbine's lover** Harlequin
**columbite** niobite
**Columbus's birthplace** Genoa
**Columbus's burial place** Seville
**Columbus's navigator** Pinzon
**Columbus's patron** Isabella
**Columbus's queen** Isabella
**Columbus's ship** Nina, Pinta, Santamaria
**column** monolith, obelisk, pilaster, pillar, shaft, stele
**column of numerical information** table
**column plinth** dado
**coma** drowsiness, lethargy, stupor, trance, unconsciousness
**comb** adjust, adorn, arrange, brush, clean, crest, disentangle, eliminate, examine, fix, groom, harrow, honeycomb, rake, search, separate, serration, smooth, untangle
**combat** action, battle, bout, clash, conflict, content(ion), contest, defy, duel, encounter, engage(ment), fight, fray, hostilities, joust, judo, karate, kung fu, oppose, oppugn, resist, skirmish, strive, struggle, war(fare), withstand
**combatant** battler, belligerent, contender, enemy, fighter, opponent, serviceman, soldier, warrior
**combatant in fight** dueller
**combat between knights** joust
**combat between two** duel
**combat unit** armament
**combat vehicle** tank
**combat with lances** joust
**combat zone** battlefield
**combination** alliance, amalgam(ation), association, blend, cabal, cartel, coalescence, coalition, composite, compound, confederacy, consortium, federation, merger, mix(ture), permutation, syndicate, unification, union
**combination of beams in a structure** trabeation
**combination of commercial firms** cartel, syndicate
**combination of events** conjuncture

**combination of groups acting together** consortium
**combination of notes sounded together in harmony** chord
**combination of tones** chord
**combine** add, alloy, ally, amalgamate, associate, bind, blend, cluster, co-operate, coalesce, commix, compose, compound, conglomerate, conjoin, connect, consolidate, incorporate, intermingle, join, link, meld, merge, mingle, mix, pool, unite
**combine augment** add, enlarge, subjoin, supplement
**combine chemically with water** hydrate
**combined action** synergy
**combined group of newspapers** syndicate
**combined spear and battle-axe** halberd, halbert
**combine in alliance** ally
**combine smoothly** blend
**combine tenets** syncretise
**combine with oxygen** oxidise
**combing** searching
**combining power** valency
**combining the serious and the comic** serio-comic, tragicomic
**combining two cultures** bicultural
**combustible** burnable, consumable, excitable, explosive, ignitable, incendiary, (in)flammable, nervous, spirited, temperamental, testy, touchy, volatile
**come** approach, arrive, attain, befall, cover, enter, extend, happen, issue, manage, near, occur, reach
**come about** arise, be, happen, occur, result, transpire
**come about as a result** eventuate
**come across** detect, discharge, discover, encounter, find, locate, meet, notice, unearth
**come after** ensue, follow
**come afterward** ensue, succeed
**come again** recur, repeat
**come all round** surround
**come along** arise, arrive, develop, happen, improve, mend, progress, rally, recover, recuperate
**come apart** break, crumble, disintegrate, separate, split, tear
**come around** accede, agree, bend, concede, grant, mellow, relent, revive, yield
**come as an addition** accrue
**come ashore** dock, land
**come as natural increase** accrue
**come at** assail, assault, attack, attain, beset, charge, discover, find, reach, rush, storm

**come at the end** last
**come back** boomerang, re-enter, reappear, rebound, rejoin, retort, return, riposte
**come-back** rally, re-appearance, rebound, recovery, resurgence, return, revival
**come back to a subject** revert
**come back to life** redivivus
**come before** appear, precede
**come between** alienate, disunite, divide, estrange, interfere, interpose, intervene, intrude, meddle, part, separate, split up
**come by** acquire, get, obtain, procure, secure, win
**come clean** acknowledge, admit, confess, reveal
**come close** advance, approach, near
**come closer** near(er)
**comedian** buffoon, clown, comic, dolt, droll, fool, harlequin, humorist, jester, joker, pierrot, prankster, wag, wit
**comedian Hope** Bob
**comedian's delight** laughter
**comedian's foil** stooge
**come down** alight, decline, degenerate, descend, deteriorate, fall, plunge, reduce, stumble, worsen
**come-down** anticlimax, blow, decline, deflation, degradation, demotion, descent, disappointment, humiliation, let-down, reverse
**come down in buckets** rain
**come down like a hawk** swoop
**come down off one's high horse** condescend
**come down on** criticise, disapprove, disfavour, oppose, protest, rebuke, reject, reprimand, veto
**come down with** catch, contract, sicken
**comedy** burlesque, farce, humour, lampoon, musical, pantomime, parody, satire, slapstick, travesty, vaudeville
**comedy sketch** skit
**comedy that involves horseplay** slapstick
**come face to face** meet
**come face to face with** confront
**come first** outshine, win, winner
**come forth** appear, emerge
**come forth suddenly** break, erupt
**come forward** advance, avaunt, volunteer
**come from** result
**come from cows** milk
**come from source** emanate
**come from Wales** Welsh
**come home to roost** boomerang

**come in** appear, arrive, enter, finish, infiltrate, inflow, penetrate, reach, show up
**come in again** re-enter
**come in contact** touch
**come in for** acquire, endure, receive, suffer
**come in last** lose
**come in sight** appear
**come into** acquire, enter, inherit, obtain
**come into accord** agreement
**come into being** appear, arise, begin, emerge, germinate, occur, originate
**come into collision** collide
**come into contact with** meet
**come into existence** arise
**come into one's mind** occur, realise, remember
**come into possession** acquire
**come into possession of** accrue, get
**come into sight** appear, emerge, loom
**come into the open** debouch
**come into view** appear, emerge
**comeliness** attractiveness, chasteness, decentness, decorousness, delicateness, exquisiteness, fitness, loveliness, niceness, pleasingness, politeness, presentableness, prettiness, properness, pureness, respectableness, seemliness, strikingness, suitableness
**comely** alluring, appropriate, apt, attractive, balanced, beautiful, becoming, bonny, charming, comme il faut (F), cultivated, decent, elegant, exquisite, fair, fit, good-looking, graceful, handsome, healthy, ladylike, lovely, mannerly, modest, nice, pretty, proper, radiant, refined, respectable, rosy, rosy-cheeked, sedate, winsome
**comely man** Adonis
**come near** approach, approximate
**come nearer to** approach
**come near in quality** approach
**come of age** mature
**come off** happen, occur, result, succeed, take place, transpire
**come off in layers** exfoliate
**come on** advance, appear, begin, develop, improve, proceed, progress, thrive
**come on scene** appear
**come on unexpectedly** sudden
**come out** appear, circulate, conclude, emerge, end, issued, result, spread, terminate
**come out against** defy, rebel
**come out even** draw, tie
**come out in a jet** spirt, spurt
**come out in a stream** pour

**come out into view** appear, emerge
**come out on enquiry** appear, emerge
**come out to the surface** emerge, outcrop
**come out with** acknowledge, admit, affirm, confess, declare, disclose, divulge, expose, own, reveal, say, state, unmask
**come over** annoy, bother, irritate, pester
**come round** accede, accept, acquiesce, allow, awake, concede, grant, recover, regain, relent, restored, revive, wake, yield
**come round again** recur
**come safely through** weather
**come short** miss
**comes out at night** bat, moon, nocturnal, owl
**comes out of an oyster** pearl
**come the time** until
**come through** accomplish, achieve, endure, prevail, succeed, survive, triumph, win, withstand
**come through alive** survive
**come through with flying colours** succeed
**come to** recover, revive, total
**come to a close** end
**come to an end** cease, conclude, die, expire, finish, quit, subside, terminate, vanish
**come to a point** taper
**come to a resolution** decide
**come to blows** brawl, dispute, fight, scuffle, skirmish, spar
**come to close quarters with** grapple
**come to full bloom** ripen
**come together** agree, amalgamate, assemble, coalesce, converge, gather, meet, unite
**come together and form one whole** coalesce
**come to grief** fail, miscarry
**come to grips with** encounter, face, handle
**come to have** acquire
**come to head** climax, crown, culminate, ripen, surmount
**come to life** awaken, revive, rouse
**come to life again** revive
**come to light** appear, arise, dawn, transpire
**come to mind** occur
**come to naught** abortive
**come to office** accede
**come to pass** appear, be, bechance, befall, betide, ensue, happen, occur
**come to perfection** bloom, ripen
**come to rest** alight, pause, settle, sit
**come to terms** agree, arrange
**come to the aid of** succour

**come to the end of one's life** die
**come to the surface** emerge
**come to understand** realise
**come true** happen, occur
**comet's path** orbit
**come tumbling down** fall, topple
**come uninvited** intrude
**come up** arise, happen, occur, reach
**come up as a consequence** arise
**come upon** discover, meet, visit
**come-uppence** chastening, desserts, dues, merit, punishment, rebuke, recompense, requital, retribution
**come up to** admit, approach, compare, match, meet, near, rival
**come up with** advance, approach, near, produce, propose, provide, reach, submit, suggest, supply
**come up with in pursuit** overhaul, overtake
**come what may** somehow
**comfort** aid, amenity, cheer, condolence, consolation, console, content, ease, encouragement, euphoria, help, pacify, reassure, refresh, relief, rest, revive, satisfaction, solace, soothe
**comfortable** adequate, cosy, cushy, easy, gemütlich (G), homely, relaxed, relaxing, restful, snug
**comfortable and warm** cosy
**comfortable seat** armchair
**comfortably easy** cushy
**comfortably situated** cosy, snug
**comfort in distress** solace
**comfort in grief** solace
**comic** amusing, droll, funny, humorous, risible, silly, wit
**comic actor in opera** buffo
**comical** absurd, amusing, charming, cheerful, comic, diverting, droll, enjoyable, entertaining, facetious, farcical, funny, hilarious, humorous, interesting, jocular, jocund, laughable, ludicrous, merry, odd, pleasant, priceless, puny, queer, ridiculous, side-splitting, silly, sportive, whimsical, witty
**comical act** jig
**comically idiotic** zany
**comic dog or planet** Pluto
**comic opera** opera buffa
**comic remark** gag
**comic's anecdotes** jokes
**comic strip** cartoon
**comic verse** doggerel, limerick
**coming** accession, advent, approach(ing), arrival, due, imminent, near, next
**coming before in time** prior
**coming events** future
**coming from abroad** peregrine

**coming in** entrance
**coming-out** debut
**comity** courtesy, friendliness
**command** adjure, administer, ascendancy, authority, authority, bade, beck, behest, bid, charge, coerce, commandment, compel, conduct, control, decree, demand, dictate, dictation, dictum, direct(ion), disposal, dominate, enjoin, exact, fiat, force, govern, hest, influence, injunction, instruct(ion), make, manage, mandate, mastery, obligate, officiate, order, overlook, oversee, possession, power, precept, prescribe, request, require, requisition, rule, sovereignty, subpoena, superintendence, supervise, supremacy, survey, tell
**commandeer illegally** hijack
**commander** leader
**commander in Algeria in former times** dey
**commander of a fleet in the Trojan war** Ajax
**commander of a troop** captain
**command of army** conduct
**command solemnly** adjure
**command to cow** soh
**command to dobbin** gee
**command to horse** gee, giddap, haw, huddup, hup, whoa
**command to turn left** haw
**command to turn right** gee, hup(p)
**comma-shaped bacterium** comma bacillus
**commemorate** celebrate, compliment, congratulate, consecrate, dedicate, eulogise, exalt, flatter, glorify, honour, observe, preserve, recall, remember, reverence, sanctify
**commemorate by adoption of name** eponymous
**commemorative award** medal
**commence** begin, inaugurate, initiate, open, originate, start
**commencement** advent, base, beginning, birth, foundation, genesis, inauguration, initiation, nascence, outset, overture, preamble, prelude, rudiment, start
**commencing move** initiative
**commend** acclaim, advise, applaud, assign, cheer, clap, commit, compliment, confide, deliver, endorse, entrust, eulogise, extol, flatter, invest, laud, magnify, praise, promote, recommend, sanction, transfer, trust, uphold
**commendable** admirable, approvable, blameless, creditable, deserving, estimable, excellent, good, just, laudable, meritorious, praiseworthy, respectable, superior, virtuous, worthy
**commendation** acclaim, acclamation, approbation, approval, award, citation, compliment, endorsement, eulogium, eulogy, extolment, flattery, kudos, laudation, laurels, panegyric, puffery, recognition, recommendation, reference, ribbon, sanction, testimonial, tribute
**commensuration** proportionment
**comment** annotate, annotation, criticism, elucidation, explain, explanation, exposition, note, observation, remark, speak, utter
**comment on** annotate
**commerce** bargaining, barter, business, dealings, exchange, fellowship, harmony, interchange, intercourse, marketing, trade, traffic, transaction, union
**commercial** (ad)vert, advertisement, business, financial, mercantile, sales, trade, trading, trafficking
**commercial agreement** contract
**commercial attaché** consul
**commercial battle** price war
**commercial conveyance** aeroplane, lorry, minibus, taxi(cab), taxi, truck, van
**commercial conveyance of goods** freightage
**commercial document** bill
**commercial iron** steel
**commercial operation** business
**commercial panic** scare
**commercial ship** liner
**commercial speculation** adventure, venture
**commercial success** boon, hit
**commercial traveller** bag-fox, bagman, drummer, representative, salesman
**commercial vehicle** lorry, van
**commercial writer** adman, copywriter
**commie** communist, red
**comminatory** denunciatory, threatening
**commiserate** comfort, condole, console, grieve, solace, sympathise
**commiserator** sympathiser
**commission** act, agency, appointment, authorise, certification, committee, conduct, document, duty, engage, name, percentage, power
**commission acting as regent** regency
**commissioner of oaths** notary
**commission to act for another** mandate
**commit** assure, conclude, confine, consign, depute, determine, do, engage, entrust, imprison, obligate, perform, perpetrate, place, pledge, plight, practise, promise, resolve, submit, surrender
**commit an offence** sin
**commit oneself** undertake
**committee** board, directorate, group, panel
**committee meeting** session
**committee of politicians governing a country** cabinet
**commit to memory** learn, memorise
**commit to paper** pen, write
**commit unreservedly** dedicate
**commodious** abounding, abundant, agreeable, ample, big, bountiful, broad, capacious, comfortable, convenient, copious, cosy, easy, enjoyable, expansive, extended, extensive, full, generous, great, homely, large, lavish, liberal, plentiful, plenty, profuse, rich, roomy, sizable, spacious, spacy, substantial, vast, wide
**commodities bought and sold** merchandise
**commodity** advantage, expediency, profit
**common** average, cheap, coarse, collective, commonplace, communal, correlative, customary, everyday, familiar, frequent, general, habitual, interactive, joint, lewd, low, mean, mediocre, mutual, ordinary, poor, prevalent, reciprocal, routine, stale, trite, uncouth, united, usual, vile, vulgar, widespread
**common Australian weed** cobbler's peg
**common benefit** commune bonum (L)
**common bird** sparrow
**common cheese** Cheddar
**common crowd** mob, ruck
**common example** byword
**common fellow** lout, jack
**common finch** linnet
**common flower** daisy
**common fund** pool, stokvel
**common gas** nitrogen, oxygen
**common ground squirrel** s(o)uslik
**common gull** mew
**common hirundine bird** chimney swallow
**common Indian bird** mynah
**common informer** delator
**common insect** ant
**common language** vernacular
**common law** usage
**common level** par
**common liquid** water
**common lodging-house** doss, kip
**common low shrub** fynbos, heather
**commonly approved** accepted

**commonly recognised text** vulgate
**common metal** iron
**common mica** muscovite
**common occurrence** commonality
**common pain tablet** aspirin
**common people** proletariat, rabble
**common pewter** ley
**commonplace** banal, boring, bromide, cliché, common, corny, daily, dreary, dry, dull, everyday, feeble, hackneyed, humdrum, maudlin, mundane, ordinary, pedestrian, regular, routine, sentimental, stale, stereotype, stock, trite, vapid
**commonplace remark** platitude
**common practice** procedure, rule
**common run** average
**common rush** floss
**common saying** adage
**common seal** sea-calf, sea-dog
**common seasoning** pepper, salt
**common sense** cleverness, discernment, nous, practicality, prudence, rationality, reasonableness, shrewdness, soundness, wisdom
**common snake** adder
**common table** mess
**common talk** gossip, rumour
**common to both** mutual
**common to both sexes** epicene
**common type of cartilage** hyaline cartilage
**common verb** are, be, is
**common viper** adder
**common vulgar person** pleb(eian)
**common weed** blackjack, khakibos, knapweed, nettle, yarrow
**common white corpuscle** lymphocyte
**common wild elm** witch-elm, wych-elm
**common yarrow** milfoil
**commotion** ado, agitate, agitation, brawl, bustle, confusion, din, disorder, disturbance, excitement, ferment, flare, flurry, fray, furore, fuss, hubbub, insurrection, kerfuffle, noise, pother, riot, ruction, rumpus, stir, stramash (Sc), to-do, tumult, turbulence, turmoil, uproar, welter
**communal** bourgeois, collective, common, communistic, community, general, joint, mutual, plebeian, public, shared, social
**communal farming settlement in Israel** kibbutz
**communal room** lounge
**commune in Italy** Asti, Milan, Padua
**commune in Netherlands** Ede
**commune with a god** pray
**communicate** acquaint, announce, connect, convey, correspond, declare, disclose, divulge, impart, inform, phone, proclaim, publish, report, reveal, signify, transmit, unfold
**communicate by letter** correspond
**communicate by wire** phone
**communicate in writing** write
**communicate news** impart
**communicate orally** speak, talk
**communication** connection, correspondence, disclosure, discussion, fellowship, information, interface, media, message, news, publication, speaking, transmittance, TV, word
**communication between minds** telepathy
**communication by canals and rivers** navigation
**communication by letters** correspondence
**communication by wire** telegram
**communication from one person to another** message
**communication instrument** telephone
**communication link** cable
**communications printer** Teletype
**communications satellite** Telstar
**communion cup** chalice
**communion plate** paten, patin(e)
**communion service** mass
**communion table** altar
**communiqué** announcement, aviso, bulletin, cable, communication, flash, intimation, message, news, notice, report, statement, telegram
**communist** Bolshevik, Bolshevist, collective, collectivist, leftist, Marxist, radical, red, revolutionary, socialist, totalitarian
**communist doctrines by Mao Tse-Tung** Maoism
**Communist newspaper** Izvestia, Pravda
**Communist policy body** Politburo
**community** city, co-operative, common(wealth), hamlet, identity, public, society, town
**community in nature or qualities** alliance
**community spirit** ethos
**commuter's travelling period** rush-hour
**Comora island** Mayotte, Moheli
**compact** agreement, arrangement, brief, compress, concise, condense(d), consolidate, contract, covenant, dense, firm, laconic, pact, short, solid(ify), stabilise, succinct, tamp, terse
**compact between nations** treaty
**compactly clustered** glomerate
**compactness** closeness, denseness, density, firmness, impenetrableness, impermeableness, solidness, thickness
**compact structure** density, firm
**companion** assistant, associate, bra, broer, comrade, escort, fellow, friend, mate, pal, partner
**companionable** affable, affectionate, amiable, amicable, attentive, beneficial, benevolent, benign, close, comradely, convivial, cordial, familiar, favourable, fond, friendly, genial, good, gregarious, helpful, intimate, kind(ly), neighbourly, outgoing, peaceable, propitious, receptive, sociable, sympathetic, warm, welcoming
**companion of Achilles** Patroclus
**companion of Caleb** Joshua
**companion of David** Jonathan
**companion of Hashabiah** Ezra
**companion of Hirah** Judah
**companion of Jonathan** David
**companion of neither** nor
**companion who shares one's activities** comrade
**company** assemblage, assemblance, assembly, association, body, circle, companionship, concourse, corporation, crowd, firm, gathering, group, partnership, party, society, troupe
**company account book** ledger
**company chief** boss
**company of actors** troupe
**company of animals** herd, pack
**company of herons** siege
**company of hunters** safari
**company of ladies** bevy
**company of lions** pride
**company of musicians** band, orchestra
**company of performers** troupe
**company of sailors** crew
**company of women** bevy
**company representative** agent
**company symbol** logo
**comparative** approximate, close, comparable, limited, modified, near, proximate, qualified, relative, restricted
**comparative conjunction** than
**comparatively lacking in hardness** soft
**comparatively unimportant** minor
**comparative part** proportion
**compare** appraise, collate, compete, confer, confront, contrast, correlate, criticise, differentiate, discern, discriminate, distinguish, equal(ise), juxtapose, liken, match, reason, resemble, separate, sieve, similar, sort, vie

**compare carefully** collate
**compare costs** price
**compare critically** collate
**compared with** vis-a-vis
**compare in detail** collate
**comparison** agreement, alliance, analogy, apposition, association, assonance, balance, closeness, collation, confrontation, confronting, contrast, equating, exemplification, identification, illustration, juxtaposition, likening, match, nearness, opposing, proximity, ratio, resemblance, separating, separation, similarity, study, synonymy, weighing
**compartment** apartment, cabin, division, roomette, section
**compartment for horse in stable** box
**compartment for one horse at a starting point** starting stall
**compartment for papers** pigeonhole
**compartment for the pilot and crew of an aircraft** cockpit
**compartment in a honeycomb** cell
**compartment in a stable** stall
**compartment of a lorry** cab
**compass** area, border, bound(ary), circuit, circumference, cycle, domain, enclosure, extent, field, frame, gamut, guide, limit, margin, needle, perimeter, range, reach, realm, region, register, round, scale, scope, section, sphere, stretch, territory, zone
**compass box** binnacle
**compass component** gyroscope
**compass direction of an aircraft** vector
**compass housing** binnacle
**compassion** clemency, feeling, kindness, mercy, pity, remorse, sorrow, sympathy, tenderness
**compassionate** caring, clement, humane, kind(ly), merciful, pitying, sympathetic, tender
**compass point** east, north, south, west
**compatible** adapted, agreeable, balanced, concordant, congenial, dulcet, equitable, euphonious, even, favourable, fit, friendly, genial, harmonious, just, kindly, matching, melodious, musical, pleasant, pleasing, proportional, simpatico, sympathetic
**compatriot** countryman
**compel** coerce, command, commit, conquer, constrain, direct, dominate, domineer, dragoon, drive, enforce, extort, force, hustle, impel, impress, make, motivate, necessitate, oblige, overpower, press(ure), provoke,
quash, quell, subdue, subject, suppress, urge
**compel by force** coerce
**compel departure** expel
**compelling** arousing, binding, casual, coercing, cogent, conclusive, convincing, driving, enforcing, exacting, forceful, hypnotic, impelling, influential, insistent, making, necessary, peremptory, powerful, restraining, unavoidable, urgent, urging, weighty
**compelling belief** cogent
**compelling fear** phobia
**compel obedience to** enforce
**compel observance of** enforce
**compel to leave** eject, expel
**compel without choice** necessitate
**compendium** abridgement, abstract, analect, analysis, assortment, batch, citation, collection, epitome, essay, kit, minute, outfit, précis, reduction, résumé, series, set, sketch, summary, tract, treatise
**compensate** balance, cancel, counteract, counterbalance, counterpoise, indemnify, offset, pay, recompense, recoup, recover, redeem, redress, refund, reimburse, remunerate, repay, requite, reward, satisfy
**compensate for** offset
**compensation** amends, atonement, payment, recompense, remuneration, reparation, reward, weighting
**compensation for inaccuracy** equation
**compensation for loss** indemnity
**compere** host
**compete** attempt, battle, challenge, clash, contend, contest, dispute, dual, emulate, encounter, fight, joust, meet, oppose, participate, rival, spar, strive, struggle, tussle, vie
**compete at speed with** race
**compete in a swimming contest** dive
**competence** ability, ableness, abundance, adequacy, aptitude, authority, capability, capableness, capacity, competency, efficacy, efficiency, eligibility, enough, expertise, facility, fitness, flair, force, knack, power, proficiency, readiness, saneness, skill, sufficiency, talent
**competent** able, acceptable, adept, adequate, adroit, apt, capable, creditable, effectual, efficacious, efficient, eligible, experienced, fit(ted), fitting, proficient, qualified, reputable, respectable, respected, responsible, satisfactory, trained
**competently** ably, adequately, expertly
**competent workman** journeyman
**compete with** rival
**competing** challenging, contending, contesting, emulating, fighting, rivalling, striving, struggling, vying
**competition** challenge, concourse, contention, contest, emulation, encounter, engagement, fight, game, match, meet, opposition, race, rivalry, struggle, tournament
**competition of speed** race
**competitive business** rat-race
**competitive event** championship, clash, contest, gala, match
**competitor** athlete, challenger, compeer, contender, contestant, entrant, fighter, opponent, opposition, rival
**competitor in judo** judoka
**competitor in karate** karateka
**compilation of dictionaries** lexicography
**compilation of poems** anthology
**compile** accumulate, amass, assemble, codify, collate, collect, cull, garner, gather, glean, order, organise, unite
**compiler of dictionary** lexicographer
**compiler of figures for study** statistician
**compiler of glossary** glossarist, glossator, glossist, glossographer
**compiler of synonyms** Roget
**compiler of thesaurus** Roget
**complacency** smugness
**complacent** affable, cheerful, complaisant, contented, cultivated, genteel, gratified, pleasant, pleased, satisfied, self-assured, serene, smug, suave, urbane
**complacent attitude** smugness
**complain** bemoan, bewail, carp, deplore, deprecate, disapprove, fret, fume, fuss, grieve, gripe, groan, grouse, growl, grumble, henpeck, lament, moan, mumble, murmur, mutter, nag, object, rail, squawk, wail, whine, whinge, yammer
**complain about** inveigh
**complain all the time** nag
**complainant** plaintiff, prosecutor
**complain bitterly** rail, wail
**complain childishly** whine
**complainer** squealer
**complain in low tones** murmur
**complain of** rebuke, remonstrate, reproach
**complain peevishly** grumble, pule
**complain pettily** carp
**complain repeatedly** beef

**complaint** accusation, affection, ailment, annoyance, disease, disorder, dissatisfaction, grievance, gripe, illness, plaint, wail
**complement** augment, companion, complete, enhance, supplement
**complete** absolute, accomplish, achieve, all, clear, clinch, close, conclude, concluded, consummate(d), crown, developed, discharge, do, done, end(ed), entire, essential, execute, filled, finalise, finish(ed), fulfilled, full, intact, integral, one, out-and-out, perfect, perform, plenary, realise, self-contained, settle, solid, sound, terminate, thorough, total, unabbreviated, unabridged, uncut, undivided, unedited, unexpurgated, unlimited, unreduced, utter, whole
**complete absence of hope** despair
**complete agreement** unison
**complete amount** total
**complete baby's outfit** layette
**complete bones of the body** skeleton
**complete certainty** conviction
**complete circle in fingerprint** whorl
**complete circuit** rounder
**complete collapse** debacle
**complete destruction** extinction
**complete disorder** chaos, fiasco
**complete divorce** a vinculo matrimonii (L)
**completed state** finish
**completed works** oeuvre
**complete failure** calamity, disaster, fiasco, flop
**complete failure of electricity supplies** black-out
**complete floor covering** fitted carpet
**complete happiness** bliss
**complete inability to speak** alalia, mutism
**complete in development** mature
**complete in itself** self-contained
**complete lack of sound** silence
**complete loss of hope** despair, despondency
**complete loss of strength** exhaustion
**completely** absolutely, all-out, comprehensively, entirely, exact, explicitly, fervently, flatly, fully, grossly, in toto (L), purely, radically, solidly, thoroughly, totally, truly, unreservedly, utterly, verily, wholly
**completely absorb in something** engross
**completely blind** bat, stone-blind
**completely clean** immaculate
**completely cold** icy, stone-cold
**completely complex** nonplus
**completely convincing** conclusive

**completely dark** black, pitch
**completely dependent** servile
**completely destroy** demolish, raze
**completely developed** mature, ripened
**completely drunk** stoned
**completely finished** all over
**completely perplexed** nonplussed
**completely soak** saturate
**completely taken aback** thunderstruck
**complete or partial removal of a tonsil** tonsillectomy, tonsillotomy
**complete reversal** changeover
**complete scale** gamut
**complete set of crockery** service
**complete suit of armour** panoply
**complete thing** whole
**complete trust** faith
**complete vegetarian** vegan
**complete verse of a poem** stanza
**completion of ebb** tide
**complex** complicated, complication, composite, compound, intricate, involved, perplexing, tangle(d)
**complexity** circuitry, complex, complicacy, complication, dilemma, implication, intricacy, labyrinth, network, obscurity, predicament, problem, quandary, riddle, unintelligibility
**complex of methods** system
**complex of rivermouth** delta
**complex whole** system
**compliance** acceptance, accession, accord, acknowledgement, acquiescence, admission, adoption, affirmation, agreement, approbation, approval, belief, compatibility, concert, concession, conformity, consent, docility, harmony, leave, mandate, meekness, obedience, obedient, observance, pliancy, recognition, sanction, similarity, submission, timidity, union, weakness, yielding
**compliant** adaptable, adjustable, complying, docile, dutiful, easy-going, favourable, flexible, gentle, kind, lenient, liberal, malleable, manageable, mild, modifiable, obedient, permissive, plastic, pliant, punctilious, respectful, submissive, tender, tractable, versatile
**compliant person** stooge
**complicate** confuse, entangle, interweave, involve, muddle
**complicated** complex, confused, difficult, elaborate, enigmatic, entangled, interlaced, intricate, involuted, involved, muddled, perplexing, problematic, puzzling, troublesome

**complicated form of blackgammon** tric-trac
**complicated network of passages** labyrinth, maze
**complicated procedure** rigmarole
**complicated scheme** plot
**complication** complexity, confusion, difficulty, drawback, intricacy, obstacle, problem, web
**complicity** guilt
**compliment** admiration, commend(ation), congratulate, felicitate, flatter(y), praise, regard, tribute
**complimentary** commendatory, fawning, flattering, free, fulsome, gratifying, gratis, gratuitous, honeyed, ingratiating, laudatory, sugary, time-serving, unpaid
**complimentary song** serenade
**comply** accede, accept, accommodate, accord, acquiesce, agree, assent, complete, concur, conform, consent, defer, discharge, execute, follow, fulfil, obey, oblige, observe, perform, relent, respect, satisfy, submit, succumb, surrender, yield
**comply with** acknowledge, agree, indulge, obey, submit
**comply with accepted standards** conform
**comply without protest** acquiesce
**component** adjunct, complement, composing, constituent, constituting, element, essential, factor, fraction(al), fundamental, influence, ingredient, inherent, integrant, module, part(ial), piece, portion, section(al), segment, unit
**component of army that fights on horseback** cavalry
**component part** element
**component part in mixture** ingredient
**compose** constitute, create, make, pacify, settle, soothe, write
**composed** calm, controlled, peaceful, placid, poised, quiet, sedate, serene, tranquil, unperturbed
**composed in rhythmic metre** metrical
**composed of cells** cellular
**composed of several races** multiracial
**composed of three consonants** triconsonantal
**composed of three parts** ternary
**composed *Tosca* and *La Boheme*** Puccini
**compose music for an orchestra** orchestrate
**composer** Abt, Arne, Auber, author, Bach, Bizet, Britten, Chopin, Coates, Copland, creator, Elgar, Enesco,

father, Foster, founder, Handel, Ibert, inventor, Lalo, Liszt, maker, mover, Nevin, originator, parent, planner, producer, Ravel, Sousa, Weber, writer
**composer, American** Barber, Bartlett, Bernstein, Cadmin, Copland, Fry, Gershwin, Harris, Herbert, MacDonald, Porter, Sousa, Weill
**composer, Argentinian** Castro
**composer, Austrian** Berg, Eybler, Hadyn, Heuberger, Mahler, Mozart, Schubert, Strauss, Webern, Wolf
**composer, Belgian** Benott, Campenhout, Dumont, Lemmens
**composer, Brazilian** Gomes, Villa-Lobos
**composer, Canadian** Brandscomb
**composer, Czech** Dvorak, Novak, Smetana
**composer, Danish** Hartman, Nielsen
**composer, Dutch** Arcadelt, Sweelinck, Wagenaar
**composer, English** Arne, Berkeley, Bliss, Blow, Britten, Byrd, Dyson, Elgar, German, Handel, Holst, Morley, Parry, Ravenscroft, Searle, Sullivan, Tallis, Taverner, Tippett, Vaughan, Williams, Walton, Wilbye, Wilson
**composer, Finnish** Kajanus, Pacius, Palmgren, Sibelius
**composer, French** Albert, Berlioz, Bizet, Boulanger, Delibes, Gounod, Halevy, Massenet, Monsigny, Offenbach, Ravel, Satie
**composer, German** Abt, Abert, Bach, Beethoven, Brahms, Flotow, Gieseking, Gluck, Henze, Hindmith, Hoffmann, Humperdinck, Mahler, Mendelsohn, Schumann, Schultz, Stockhausen, Telemann, Wagner, Weber, Weill
**composer, Hungarian** Bartok, Erikel, Joachim, Liszt, Romberg
**composer, Irish** Balfe, Field, Osborne, Wallace
**composer, Italian** Bellini, Leoncavallo, Mascagni, Puccini, Scarlatti, Verdi, Vivaldi
**composer, Norwegian** Grieg, Svendson
**composer of *Adriadne auf Maxos*** Strauss
**composer of *Aïda*** Verdi
**composer of a literary work** author
**composer of *Alzira*** Verdi
**composer of *Anna Bolena*** Donizetti
**composer of *Ariodante*** Handel
**composer of *Attila*** Verdi
**composer of *Barber of Seville*** Rossini
**composer of *Bartered Bride*** Smetana

**composer of *Battle of Legnano*** Verdi
**composer of *Billy Budd*** Britten
**composer of *Capriccio*** Strauss
**composer of *Caterina Cornaro*** Donizetti
**composer of *Cavalleria Rusticana*** Mascagni
**composer of *Clemenza Di Tito*** Mozart
**composer of *Consul, The*** Menotti
**composer of *Corsair, The*** Verdi
**composer of *Dalibor*** Smetana
**composer of *Damnation de Faust*** Berlioz
**composer of *Daphne*** Strauss
**composer of *Das Rheingold*** Wagner
**composer of *Daughter of the Regiment*** Donizetti
**composer of *Der Freischutz*** Weber
**composer of *Der Rosenkavalier*** Straus
**composer of *Die Feen*** Wagner
**composer of *Die Fledermaus*** Strauss
**composer of *Die Walkure*** Wagner
**composer of *Di Nurnberg*** Wagner
**composer of *Don Carlos*** Verdi
**composer of *Don Giovanni*** Mozart
**composer of *Donna Del Lago*** Rossini
**composer of *Donna Diana*** Reznicek
**composer of *Don Pasquale*** Donizetti
**composer of *El Ci*** Massenet
**composer of *Elektra*** Strauss
**composer of *Elisir D'Amore*** Donizetti
**composer of *Ernani*** Verdi
**composer of *Eugene Onegin*** Tchaikovsky
**composer of *Euryan, The*** Weber
**composer of *Evita*** Andrew Lloyd Webber
**composer of *Falstaff*** Verdi
**composer of *Faramondo*** Handel
**composer of *Faust*** Gounod
**composer of *Favola D'Orfeo*** Monteverdi
**composer of *Fedora*** Giordano
**composer of *Feminine Wiles*** Cimarosa
**composer of *Fidelio*** Beethoven
**composer of *Flying Dutchman, The*** Wagner
**composer of *Fra Diavolo*** Auber
**composer of *Gianni Schicchi*** Puccini
**composer of *Girl of the Golden West*** Puccini
**composer of *Guntram*** Strauss
**composer of *Il Duca D'Alba*** Donizetti
**composer of *Il Signor Bruschino*** Rossini
**composer of *Il Tabarro*** Puccini
**composer of *Il Trovatore*** Verdi
**composer of *Il Turco in Italia*** Rossini
**composer of *I Masnadieri*** Verdi
**composer of *I Puritani*** Bellini

**composer of *Koanga*** Delius
**composer of *La Cenerentola*** Rossini
**composer of *La Favorite*** Donizetti
**composer of *La Figlia Di Joria*** Pizetti
**composer of *La Finta Giardiniera*** Mozart
**composer of *La Forza Del Destino*** Verdi
**composer of *La Navarraise*** Massenet
**composer of *La Perichole*** Offenbach
**composer of *La Prophete*** Meyerbeer
**composer of *La Sonnambula*** Bellini
**composer of *La Straniera*** Bellini
**composer of *La Traviata*** Verdi
**composer of *Le Nozze Di Figaro*** Mozart
**composer of *Le Roi De Lahore*** Massenet
**composer of *Les Troyens*** Berlioz
**composer of *L'Italiana in Algieri*** Rossini
**composer of *Lodoletta*** Mascagni
**composer of *Lohengrin*** Wagner
**composer of *Lucia Di Lammermoor*** Donizetti
**composer of *Lucrezia Borgia*** Donizetti
**composer of *Luisa Miller*** Verdi
**composer of *Madama Butterfly*** Puccini
**composer of *Magic Flute, The*** Mozart
**composer of *Manon*** Massenet
**composer of *Manon Lescaut*** Puccini
**composer of *Martha*** Flotow
**composer of *Masked Ball*** Verdi
**composer of *Mazeppa*** Tchaikovsky
**composer of *Medium, The*** Menotti
**composer of melodies** melodist
**composer of *Merry Widow*** Lehar
**composer of *Mireille*** Gounod
**composer of *Murder in the Cathedral*** Pizetti
**composer of *Nerone*** Boito
**composer of *Night Bell*** Donizetti
**composer of *Norma*** Bellini
**composer of *Oberon*** Weber
**composer of oratorios** Handel
**composer of *Pagliacci*** Leoncavallo
**composer of *Parsifal*** Wagner
**composer of *Pearl Fishers, The*** Bizrt
**composer of *Pelleas et Melisande*** Debussy
**composer of *Peter Grimes*** Britten
**composer of *Rienzi*** Wagner
**composer of *Rigoletto*** Verdi
**composer of *Rule Britannia*** Arne
**composer of *Secret, The*** Smetana
**composer of *Semiramide*** Rossini
**composer of *Seraglio*** Mozart
**composer of *Shepherd King, The*** Mozart
**composer of *Shvanda the Bagpiper*** Weinberger

**composer of** *Sicilian Vespers, The* Verdi
**composer of** *Simon Boccanegra* Verdi
**composer of** *Snow Maiden, The* Rimsky-Korsakov
**composer of** *Stiffelio* Verdi
**composer of** *Sunken Bell* Respighi
**composer of symphonies** symphonist
**composer of** *Tales of Hoffmann* Offenbach
**composer of** *Tannhauser* Wagner
**composer of** *Thais* Massenet
**composer of** *Traviata* Verdi
**composer of** *Tristan und Isolde* Wagner
**composer of** *Tsar Saltan* Rimsky-Korsakov
**composer of** *Tsar's Bride, The* Rimsky-Korsakov
**composer of** *Turandot* Puccini
**composer of** *Two Widows, The* Smetana
**composer of** *Vakula the Smith* Tchaikovsky
**composer of verse** poet
**composer of** *William Tell* Rossini
**composer of** *Yolanta* Tchaikovsky
**composer, Polish** Chopin, Kolberg, Noskowski
**composer, Portuguese** Arneiro, Bomtempo, Portogallo
**composer, Romanian** Enesco, Otescua
**composer, Russian** Arenski, Godowsky, Rachmaninoff, Stravinsky, Tchaikovsky
**composer, Scottish** Gow, Spottiswoode
**composer, Spanish** Albeniz, Arboss, Barbier, Casals, Falla, Granados, Victoria
**composer, Swedish** Alfven, Atterberg, Hallstrom, Wennenberg
**composer, Swiss** Honegger, Martin
**composer, Venezuelan** Carreno
**composer, Welsh** Evans, Parry
**compose text** typeset
**composite photograph** montage
**composite picture** collage, montage
**composite plant** chicory, hawkweed, sneezeweed, succory
**composition** alloy, aria, arrangement, article, assortment, compound, comprisal, concord, conjunction, constitution, creation, design, draft, essay, form, integration, invention, layout, literary, making, manuscript, melody, novel, opus, song, structure, synthesis, theme, treatise, union, writing
**composition for eight** octet
**composition for five** quintet
**composition for four** quartet
**composition for full orchestra** symphony
**composition for nine** nonet
**composition for one** solo
**composition for one instrument** sonata
**composition for organ** toccata
**composition for practice** étude
**composition for seven** septet
**composition for six** sextet
**composition for solo instrument and orchestra** concerto
**composition for the dead** requiem
**composition for three** trio
**composition for two** duet, duo
**composition for virtuoso** étude
**composition in letter form** epistle
**composition in music** anthem, étude, hymn, opera, rondo, sonata, song
**composition in verse** poem
**composition of ballet** choreography
**composition of clay** lute
**composition of hymns** hymnody
**composition suggestive of the qualities of night** nocturne
**compositor** printer
**compos mentis** sane
**composure** calm(ness), control, dignity, ease, equanimity, poise, serenity
**compound** admixture, alloy, amalgam(ate), blend, camp, coalesce, colony, combination, combine, complex, composite, composition, concoct, court, courtyard, enclosure, fuse, fusion, intermingle, intricate, isomer, kampong, kraal, medley, mingle, mix(ture), quadrangle, residence, ring, settlement, unite
**compound in vitamin B** thiamine
**compound of alkali and oil** soap
**compound of carbon** carbide
**compound of different things** amalgam
**compound of hydrogen** hydride
**compound of mercury and another metal** amalgam
**compound of oxygen** oxide
**compound used in gunpowder** saltpetre
**comprehend** apprehend, assimilate, compose, comprise, conceive, contain, digest, discern, embody, embrace, grasp, include, know, perceive, read, realise, receive, see, sense, understand
**comprehend completely** realise
**comprehensive** blow-by-blow, broad, capacious, circumstantial, commodious, detailed, elaborate, exact, exhaustive, extensive, far-flung, far-reaching, full, general, great, huge, inclusive, intricate, large, lengthy, long, minute, particular, prevalent, protracted, spacious, specific, sweeping, thorough, universal, unlimited, vast, wholesale, wide-ranging, wide(spread)
**comprehensive glance** coup d'oeil (F)
**compress** bandage, condense, constrict, contract, crush, press, squeeze
**compressed into few words** brief, concise, succinct
**compress forcibly** telescope
**compress into a bundle** bale
**compress into pleats** crimp
**comprise** accommodate, comprehend, condense, consist, contain, cover, embody, embrace, envelop, imply, include, incorporate, involve, subsume
**comprising several items** omnibus
**comprising the whole** total
**compromise** accommodating, accord, adapt, adjust(ment), agree(ment), arbitrate, bargain, co-operation, concede, concession, discredit, dishonour, embarrass, expose, hazard, imperil, implicate, involve, jeopardise, negotiate, prejudice, retire, retreat, settle, trade-off, undermine, weaken
**compulsion by threat** duress
**compulsion to pull out one's hair** trichotillomania
**compulsive eating over a long period** hyperphagia
**compulsive overeating** hyperorexia
**compulsive stealing** kleptomania
**compulsory enrolment** conscript
**compute** ascertain, calculate, count, estimate, reckon
**computer** calculator, chip, mainframe, microcomputer, minicomputer, PC
**computer bug** virus
**computer code** ASCII
**computer connecting device** modem
**computer failure** crash
**computer gateway** port
**computer information** data
**computer inventor** Babbage
**computer language** Ada, Algol, BASIC, COBOL, FORTRAN, LISP, Pascal, PROLOG, SNOBOL
**computer memory** stack
**computer memory device** twister
**computer output** data
**computer program** DOS
**computer record** printout

**computer scanning device** optical character reader
**computer system** DOS
**compute sum of** add
**comrade** accomplice, ally, assistant, associate, bra, broer, buddy, chum, collaborator, colleague, comate, companion, compatriot, compeer, confidant, confrère, crony, fellow, friend, helper, mate, partner, peer
**comrade in arms** ally
**comradely** matey
**comradeship** association, brotherhood, camaraderie, circle, clan, club, companionship, company, fellowship, fraternity, friendliness, guild, kinship, league, set, sodality, union
**con** beguile, betray, cheat, cozen, deceive, delude, double-cross, dupe, ensnare, entrap, fool, hoax, hoodwink, know, learn, mislead, outwit, persuade, steer, study, swindle, trick
**concave** cupped, dished, hollow(ed), incurved, indented, sunken
**concave aerial for microwaves** dish
**concave ceiling** cupola
**concave moulding** scotia
**concavity** basin, bowl, cavity, concave, concha, cove, crater, cup, depression, dimple, dip, hole, hollow(ness), impression, incline, incurvature, incurvity, indent(ation), kneepan, pit, scoop, slope, venter
**conceal** bury, camouflage, cloud, cover, disguise, dissemble, ensconce, enshroud, hide, mask, obscure, screen, secrete, shelter, veil
**conceal defects** fake
**concealed** buried, closeted, covered, deep, hid(den), indiscernible, inner, invisible, latent, masked, privy, secreted, sheltered, unapparent, undiscoverable, unexposed, unknown, unrevealed
**concealed danger** pit(fall)
**concealed force** ambuscade
**concealed marksman** sniper
**concealed obstruction** snag, trap
**concealed rifleman** sniper
**concealed shelter** covert
**concealed talent** latent
**conceal in the hand** palm
**concealment** awning, blind, canopy, cloak, cover, defence, disguise, front, guard, guise, hedge, hiding, mantle, mask, masquerade, mimicry, place, protection, refuge, sanctuary, screen, secrecy, shade, shelter, shield, shroud, subterfuge

**concealment of one's actions** camouflage
**concealment of troops** ambush
**conceal true feelings** dissemble
**conceal with the hand** palm
**concede** accept, acknowledge, acquiesce, admit, agree, confess, grant, own, recognise, yield
**conceit** arrogance, assumption, cockiness, complacency, conceitedness, conception, ego(tism), fancy, idea, imagination, narcissism, notion, pride, self-conceit, self-esteem, self-importance, self-satisfaction, swagger, thought, vainglory, vanity
**conceited** arrogant, cocky, complacent, crowing, disdainful, egocentric, egotistic(al), haughty, inflated, proud, self-esteeming, self-important, smug, vain(glorious)
**conceited and arrogant** cocky
**conceited fellow** coxcomb
**conceited impertinent person** jackanapes
**conceited person** egotist, popinjay, prig, snob
**conceited smile** smirk
**conceited young man** puppy
**conceivable** apprehensible, believable, comprehensible, creatable, credible, imaginable, possible, realisable, supposable, thinkable, understandable
**conceivably possible** thinkable
**conceive** apprehend, believe, comprehend, create, devise, envisage, fancy, grasp, imagine, project, realise, think, understand
**conceived in the mind** idea
**conceived wrongly** mistaken
**concentrate** accumulate, amass, centre, clarify, cluster, collect, compact, compress, condense, constrict, contract, converge, crowd, focus, gather, intensify, muster, purify
**concentrated** centred, condensed, converged, deep, hard, intense, intensive, reduced, rich, strong, undiluted
**concentrated flavouring** essence
**concentrated juice** extract
**concentrated perfume** essence
**concentrated sauce made of soya beans and salt** tamari
**concentration** absorption, accumulation, application, cluster, consolidation, convergence, gathering, mass, thought
**concentration on local interests** parochialism

**concept** conception, conclusion, conjecture, conviction, hypothesis, idea, image, notion, opinion, persuasion, theory
**conception** design, idea, initiation, notion, origin, outset, plan
**conception of reason** idea
**conception of something that is perfect** ideal
**conceptualise** envisage, foresee
**concern** affair, affect, anxiety, appropriateness, attention, bearing, bother, burden, business, care, charge, company, consciousness, consideration, corporation, disquiet, distress, disturb, engage, enterprise, establishment, field, firm, heed, house, interest, involve(ment), job, matter, mission, organisation, perturb, regard, responsibility, solicitude, task, touch, trouble, worry
**concerned** active, affected, anxious, bothered, disquieted, distressed, disturbed, exercised, implicated, interested, involved, perturbed, regarded, touched, troubled, uneasy, upset, worried
**concerned chiefly with profit** commercial, financial
**concerned with** about, re
**concerned with an uncle** avuncular
**concerned with practical consequence** pragmatic
**concerned with promoting human welfare** humanitarian
**concerned with right and wrong conduct** moral
**concerned with smell** olfactory
**concerned with stones** lapidary
**concerning** about, anent, as, in re, of, on, re, regarding, respecting, to, touching
**concerning a barber** tonsorial
**concerning birth** natal
**concerning facts** factual
**concerning race** ethnic
**concerning speed greater than that of sound** supersonic
**concerning speed less than that of sound** subsonic
**concerning the matter** in re
**concerning urine** uric
**concern of editor** facts, news
**concern of Salus** health
**concern of shepherd** sheep
**concern oneself about** mind
**concern with set goals** organisation
**concert** accord(ance), administer, agreement, arrange, command, compatibility, compliance, concord, concurrence, conduct, conformity, congruity, consistency,

correspondence, direct, euphony, govern, harmony, manage, oversee, pitch, recital, rule, run, similarity, supervise, union, unison
**concerted action** crusade
**concerted gunfire** salvo
**concerted refusal to deal with** boycott
**concert hall** odeum
**concertina** squeeze-box
**concert manager** impresario
**concert waltz** valse
**concession** adjustment, assent, benefice, bestowal, capitulation, compromise, discount, exception, exemption, granting, limitation, offset, privilege, recognition, yielding
**conch** shell
**conciliate** appease, pacify, placate, propitiate, reconcile, soothe
**conciliatory** accommodative, accordant, agreeable, appeasing, disarming, dovish, forgiving, harmonious, irenic(al), pacific, pacifying, placative, placatory
**conciliatory gift** sop
**concise** abbreviated, abridged, abrupt, brief, brusque, compact, compendious, comprehensive, compressed, condensed, cryptic, curt, curtailed, direct, epigrammatic, laconic, pithy, short(ened), small, succinct, summary, synoptic, terse, tight
**concise and distinct** clean-cut
**concise drink** short
**concisely** briefly, compactly, laconically, pithily, shortly, succinctly, summarily, tersely
**conciseness** briefness, compactness, pithiness, shortness, succinctness, summariness, terseness
**conciseness of expression** brevity
**conclude** arrange, cease, clinch, close, complete, discontinue, end, expire, finish, halt, infer, resolve, seal, settle, stay, stop, suspend, terminate
**conclude from facts** infer
**conclude successfully** accomplish
**concluding section** coda, epilogue
**concluding speech** epilogue
**concluding TV programme** epilogue
**concluding word** amen
**conclusion** agreement, close, completion, consequence, culmination, conviction, decision, deduction, determination, end(ing), finale, finis(h), inference, issue, judg(e)ment, opinion, outcome, resolution, result, settlement, upshot, verdict
**conclusion of speech** peroration
**conclusion reached** decision

**conclusive** clinching, convincing, decisive, final, irrefutable, net(t), ultimate, unarguable
**conclusive stroke** coup de grâce (F)
**concoct** brew, contrive, fabricate, formulate, prepare
**concoction** blend, brew, compound, conception, creation, design, device, drink, invention, mix(ture), plan, plot, potion, preparation, scheme
**conconformist** disssenter, eccentric, heretic, iconoclast, individualist, maverick, oddball, protester, radical, rebel, secessionist
**concord** agreement, cohesion, compact, comradeship, concurrence, congeniality, consensus, consolidation, covenant, harmony, pact, peace, quiet(ude), serenity, treaty, truce, unison, unity
**concordant** agreeable, compatible, congruous, coordinated, dulcet, euphonious, harmonious, harmonising, matching, melodious, musical, tuneful
**concourse of hunters** meet
**concrete** actual, cement, certain, cohesive, compact, corporeal, definite, dense, discrete, distinct, explicit, express, factual, firm, material, particular, peculiar, real, sensible, singular, solid, specific, substantial, tangible, unique
**concreted sugar on cake** ice
**concrete ingredient** cement
**concrete mix** soup
**concrete worker** paver
**concretion formed in the bladder** stone
**concubine in harem** odalisque
**concubine of Abraham** Hagar
**concur** agree, assent, chime, coincide, collaborate, comply, conform, consent, contribute, cooperate, correspond, covenant, harmonise, help, jibe
**concur in** approve
**concurrence** accession, agreement, approval, assent, coincidence, combination, concord, concourse, conformation, congruity, conjugation, cooperation, harmony, interaction, junction, juncture, sanction, unanimity, union, unity
**concurrently with** during
**concurrent symptoms in disease** syndrome
**concur with** accept
**condemn** accuse, adjudge, blame, censure, charge, compel, convict, damn, demand, denounce, disapprove, doom, force, incriminate, indict, necessitate, objurgate, order, pronounce, punish, reprobate, require, sentence
**condemn as wrong** censure
**condemning publicly** denouncing
**condemn to exile** banish
**condensation** bind, brief, closeness, clot, cohesion, concentration, crushing, curd, density, dew, digest, gel, outline, précis, sketch, solidification, solidity
**condense** abbreviate, abridge, compact, compress, concentrate, consolidate, constringe, contract, cram, decrease, ram, reduce, shorten, squeeze, subtract, wedge
**condense book** abridge
**condensed** abridged, close, clotted, coagulated, compacted, compressed, concentrated, consolidated, contracted, crammed, crushed, curtailed, dried, hard, reduced, sere, shortened, shrunken, solid, squeezed, summarised
**condensed form** abridgement
**condensed moisture** dew, rain
**condensed oxygen** ozone
**condensed vapour** fog, steam
**condescend** accede, acquiesce, concede, conciliate, deign, descend, humble, pacify, patronise, respect, stoop, submit, unbend, vouchsafe, yield
**condescending** bending, deigning, disdainful, lofty, lordly, patronising, snobbish, snooty, supercilious, superior
**condescending manner** patronage
**condiment** allspice, caper, cayenne, cinnamon, clove, curry, garlic, ginger, mustard, onion, paprika, pepper(corn), pimento, rosemary, salt, seasoning, spice, turmeric
**condiment container** pepper-cellar, pepper-grinder, salt-cellar
**condiment jar** cruet
**condiment stand** cruet
**condition** abnormality, circumstance, consideration, determine, limit, plight, provision, proviso, requirement, requisite, situation, state, stipulation, term
**conditional** contingent, dependent, limitative, limited, probationary, provisional, provisionary, qualified, relative, restricted, tied
**conditionally released** on parole
**conditional pardon** parole
**conditional surrender** capitulation
**conditional word** however, if, or
**condition causing high temperature** fever

**condition giving young child nasty cough** croup
**conditioning researcher** Pavlov
**condition involving chest pain** angina
**condition in which the urine contains blood** haematuria
**condition in which thing is** state
**condition of being alone** solitude
**condition of being bow-legged** valgus
**condition of being poor** poverty
**condition of great distress** affliction
**condition of having long sight** hypermetropia
**condition of not being in use** abeyance
**condition of payment** term
**condition of race turf** going
**condition of rest** sleep
**condition of weightlessness** zero gravity
**condition requiring action** emergency
**condition resembling hell** inferno
**conditions of being a beggar** beggary
**conditions of life** environment
**condole** commiserate, compassionate, grieve, lament, pity, sympathise
**condone** disregard, excuse, forget, forgive, ignore, overlook, pardon, remit
**condor** vulture
**conducive to happiness** eud(a)emonic
**conducive to prosperity** auspicious
**conduct** action(s), administrate, administration, bearing, behave, behaviour, carriage, demeanour, deport(ment), direct, escort, execute, execution, guard, guide, guidance, lead, manners, mien, regulate, supervise, usher
**conduct a ceremony** officiate
**conduct financial operations** financier
**conduct fraudently** rig
**conduct oneself properly** behave
**conduct oneself well** behave
**conductor** bearer, boss, captain, chairman, chief, conveyor, director, executive, fugleman, guide, leader, maestro, manager, marshal, overseer, pilot, precentor, steersman
**conductor of musical band** bandmaster
**conductor of sitters** usher
**conductor of tour** guide
**conductor's stick** baton
**conduct the way** guide
**conduct to seat** usher
**conduct with no view to gain** profitmaking
**conduit** artery, cable, canal, channel, chimney, ditch, drain, duct, funnel, hose, main, moat, outlet, pipe,
runnel, sewer, sluice, trench, trough, tube
**conebearing tree** conifer
**cone-shaped** abconic(al), conic(al), conoid, pineal, turbinate
**cone-shaped hat** fez
**cone-shaped pile of straw or hay** cock
**cone-shaped structure** pyramid
**cone-shaped vessel ending in a tube** funnel
**cone-shape tent** te(e)pee
**confection** candy, preserve, sweet(meat)
**confectioner's place of work** sweetshop
**confection of little importance** trifle
**confederate** accomplice, ally, associate, colleague, combined, corporated, federal, federate, leagued, partner, rebel, supporter, unite(d)
**Confederate general** Lee, Meade
**confederate soldier** reb
**confederation** alliance, coalition, confederacy, federation, league, union
**confer** accord, afford, agree, allot, award, bestow, consult, converse, deliberate, discourse, discuss, donate, give, grant, ordain, palaver, parley, present, vouchsafe, yield
**confer credit on** accredit
**conference** analysis, caucus, colloquy, communication, consultation, convention, deliberation, diet, examination, forum, interview, meeting, palaver, parley
**conference between heads of states** summit
**conference of deeds** charter
**confer holy orders** ordain
**confer knighthood** dub
**conferment** adjudication, award, bestowal, bestowing, decision, decree, gift, granting, order, presentation
**conferral** award, bestowal, donation, investiture, offering, presentation
**conferring holy orders** ordination
**confer upon** bestow
**confer with** consult
**confess** acknowledge, admit, affirm, allow, assert, avouch, avow, betray, concede, confide, confirm, declare, disclose, divulge, expose, grant, manifest, own, profess, prove, recognise, reveal, show, swear, vow, warrant
**confession** acceptance, acknowledgement, admission, allowance, avowal, concession,
creed, disclosure, recognition, revelation
**confession of faith** credo, creed
**confession of guilt** peccavi
**confess to** admit, testify
**confide** admit, breathe, commend, commit, confess, consign, disclose, divulge, entrust, impart, reveal, whisper
**confidence** assurance, belief, courage, faith, reliance, trust
**confidence in someone** trust
**confidence of troops** morale
**confidence trick** bait, cheat, fraud, shenanigan
**confident** assured, certain, convinced, fearless, impertinent, positive, satisfied, secure, self-assured, self-confident, sure, unwavering
**confident and fearless** bold
**confident bearing** air
**confidential** esoteric, honourable, private, restricted, secret, trusted, trustworthy
**confidential hint** tip-off
**confidentially** aside, intimately, personally, privately, privily, secretly, sub rosa
**confidential remark to audience** aside
**confidential talk** tête-à-tête
**confidential warning or hint** tip-off
**confine** bind, boundary, cage, check, circumscribe, constrain, coop, (en)circle, enclose, immure, impound, limit(s), perimeter, periphery, quarantine, restrict, tie
**confine and contract** cramp
**confine behind bars** encage
**confined** bound(ed), caged, cloistered, cribbed, encaged, enclosed, entombed, immured, imprisoned, incarcerated, interned, kept, limited, narrow, pent, repressed, restrained, restricted
**confined person** captive, convict, detainee, hostage, inmate, internee, prisoner, slave
**confined to bed** ailing, bedridden, ill, indisposed
**confined to earth** earthbound
**confined to narrow area** parochial
**confined to select group** esoteric
**confine in small space** crib
**confinement** accouchement (F), astriction, childbed, custody, delivery, detention, enclosure, imprisonment, internment, isolation, labour, quarantine, restraint, restriction
**confine narrowly** cramp
**confine within limits** intern
**confine with rope** tether

**confining rope** tether
**confirm** accredit, approve, assure, attest, authenticate, brace, certify, corroborate, endorse, establish, evidence, fortify, prove, ratify, reinforce, strengthen, substantiate, testify, underwrite, validate, verify
**confirmed** absolute, accepted, approved, arrant, correct, decided, documented, endorsed, established, factual, habitual, inured, inveterate, official, ratified, right, rooted, seasoned, true, valid, verified
**confirmed by oath** affidavit
**confirmed drunkard** dronkie, sot
**confirmed in habit** inveterate
**confirm to shape** fit
**conflagration** arson, blaze, bonfire, combustion, fire, flame(s), furnace, holocaust, inferno, wildfire
**conflict** battle, clash, collide, collision, combat, contend, contention, contest, controversy, discord, disharmony, encounter, fight, interfere, oppose, opposition, strife, struggle, war
**conflict-minded?** headed for a show-down
**conflict of authority** antinomy
**conform** accept, accommodate, accord, acquiesce, adapt, adjust, agree, alter, answer, apply, assent, change, chime, coincide, comply, compose, concur, correspond, fit, habituate, harmonise, match, modify, prepare, qualify, reconcile, settle, shape, submit, tailor, yield
**conformal** orthomorphic
**conforming exactly with a standard** accurate
**conforming to a standard** normal
**conforming to a type** typical
**conforming to good taste** seemly
**conforming to standard type** legitimate
**conforming to what is usual** normal
**conform to** fulfil
**conform to shape** fit
**conform to the law** validate
**confound** amaze, astonish, astound, baffle, bemuse, bewilder, confuse, demolish, destroy, dumbfound, flummox, mystify, nonplus, obscure, perplex, puzzle, startle, surprise
**confront** accost, assail, attack, brave, challenge, compare, contradict, defy, encounter, face, meet, molest, oppose, pester, pursue, resist, show, tackle, threaten, thwart, withstand
**confuse** abash, addle, astonish, baffle, becloud, bedevil, befog, bemuse, bewilder, confound, demoralise, disarrange, discomfit, discompose, disconcert, discountenance, disorder, disorient, disturb, embarrass, embrangle, fluster, fuddle, intermingle, jumble, mix, mortify, mystify, nonplus, obfuscate, obscure, perplex, puzzle, shame, shock, upset
**confuse by strong light** bedazzle
**confused** abashed, addled, baffled, bemused, bewildered, blurry, bungled, chaotic, confounded, dazed, demoralised, deranged, disarranged, discomfited, discomposed, disconcerted, disordered, disorderly, disorganised, disoriented, dizzy, flummoxed, flustered, hazy, incoherent, indistinct, jumbled, mistaken, misunderstood, mortified, muddled, mystified, nonplussed, obscured, perplexed, puzzled, stupefied, tangled, unbalanced, uncertain, unclear, unsettled, untidy, upset
**confused bustle** alarum
**confused conflict** mêlée
**confused din** hubbab
**confused effect** blur
**confused fight** mêlée
**confused heap** imbroglio, jumble
**confused hurry** trepidation
**confused interwoven mass** tangle
**confused jumble** mess, welter
**confused mass** agglomerate
**confused mixture** hotchpotch, mishmash
**confused murmur** buzz
**confused noise** clamour, din, hubbub, hullabaloo, uproar
**confused situation** imbroglio, mix-up
**confused state** fuddle, maze
**confused statements** rigmarole
**confused struggle** mêlée, scrimmage, scuffle
**confused talk** galimatias
**confused uproar** brouhaha
**confused yelling of war-cry** hubbab
**confuse utterly** bewilder, mystify
**confuse with drink** fluster
**confusion** abashment, ado, astonishment, bedlam, bewilderment, bruise, bustle, chaos, commotion, consternation, disarrangement, disarray, disorder, distraction, ferment, medley, mélange, mess, panic, perplexity, psychopathy, shock, surprise, tangle, tumult, turmoil
**confusion of sounds** babel
**congeal** clot, coagulate, curdle, freeze, gel, harden, jell, set, solidify, stiffen, thicken
**congenial** agreeable, friendly, genial, kindly, kindred, pleasant, pleasing, suitable, suited, sympathetic
**congenital absence of limb** amelia
**congenital absence of teeth** anodontia
**congenital absence of tongue** aglossia
**congenital defect of spine** scoliosis, spina bifida
**congenital fissure of the upper lip** harelip
**congenital mark** mole
**congenital traits** heredity
**conger or moray** eel
**congest** bar, block, burden, clog, close, constrict, dam, hamper, hinder, impede, jam, obstruct, occlude, overpower, shackle, smother, stall, stick, stifle, stop, strangle, suffocate, suppress, throttle
**congested with blood** engorged
**congratulate** acclaim, applaud, bless, compliment, extol, felicitate, laud, praise, salute
**congratulate oneself** boast
**congratulation** acclaim, accolade, applause, approval, blessing, commendation, compliment(ing), eulogy, felicitation, gratulation, kudos, panegyric, plaudit, praise, tribute
**congregate** accumulate, amass, assemble, clump, cluster, collect, concentrate, conglomerate, convene, converge, convoke, crowd, flock, gather, mass, meet, muster, rally, rendezvous, throng
**congress** assembly, conference, convention, council, meeting
**congress of Welsh bards** eisteddfod
**congruent** accordant, consistent, suitable
**conical** funnel-shaped
**conical building enclosing kiln** hovel
**conical hat** fez
**conical hill** pap
**conical lodge** igloo, iglu, te(e)pee
**conical paper hat** dunce's cap
**conical pulley** fusee
**conical roll of thread** cop
**conical tent** te(e)pee, tipi
**conical wind instrument** trumpet
**conical wooden pin used in splicing** fib
**conifer** cedar, cypress, evergreen, fir, larch, pine, spruce, yew
**conifer of New Zealand** kauri
**coniferous tree** cedar, cypress, fir, larch, pine
**conjecture** guess, hypothesis(e), inference, opinion, presume,

suppose, supposition, surmise,
theorise, theory
**conjugal** bridal, connubial, epithalamic,
husbandly, marital, married,
matrimonial, nuptial, spousal,
wedded, wifely
**conjunction** accordance, affiliation,
agreement, alliance, amalgamation,
and, association, bonding, but,
combination, conjuncture, joinder,
juxtaposition, merger, neither, nor,
or, unification, union
**conjunction in German** und
**conjunction word** although, and, as,
since, therefore
**conjure** adjure, bewitch, charm, crave,
enchant, implore, importune, invoke,
juggle, pray, raise, summon,
supplicate
**conjurer** conjurator, enchanter,
evocator, illusionist, magician,
necromancer, prestidigitator,
sorcerer, theurgist, warlock, witch,
wizard
**conjure up** awaken, contrive, create,
evoke, excite, produce, recall,
recollect
**conjuring deception** hocus-pocus
**conjuring tricks** legerdemain
**conk out** faint
**connect** abut, adjoin, affix, ally,
articulate, associate, attach, bind,
cement, chain, clamp, coalesce,
cohere, combine, confederate,
conjoin, couple, fasten, fuse, identify,
impinge, join, link, meet, relate, sew,
solder, tie, truss, unite, weld
**connect by joints** articulate
**connected group** nexus
**connected series** sequel
**connected with** akin, related
**connected with birth** natal
**connected with fate** weird
**connected with residence** residential
**connected with seafaring** maritime
**Connecticut college** Yale
**connecting link** bond
**connecting neck of land** isthmus
**connecting tissue** commissure,
stroma, tendon
**connecting tissue in joint** ligament
**connection** acquaintanceship,
affiliation, affinity, alliance,
association, bond, conjunction,
connexion, coupling, joining, joint,
junction, liaison, link, relation(ship),
relative, tie, union, yoke
**connective tissue** epimysium
**connective word** conjunction
**connect with each other** interconnect,
join
**connivance** abettal

**connive** abet, bear, collude, complot,
condone, conspire, disregard,
endure, ignore, intrigue, machinate,
plot, scheme, suffer, tolerate
**connoisseur** aesthete, aficionado,
arbiter elegantiae (L), arbiter,
authority, buff, cognoscent, devotee,
expert, gourmand, gourmet, judge,
savant, specialist
**connoisseur of eating and drinking**
gastronome
**connoisseur of good food** gourmet
**connoisseur of wines** oenophile
**conquer** beat, defeat, overcome,
overpower, overwhelm, subdue,
subject, subjugate, surmount,
vanquish, win
**conquered territory** conquest
**conquering Hun** Atilla
**conqueror in contest** victor
**conquest** mastery, rout, seduction,
subjugation, triumph, vanquishment,
victory
**conscience stricken** guilty
**conscientious** careful, dedicated,
diligent, dutiful, faithful, honest,
incorruptible, painstaking,
scrupulous, straightforward, upright
**conscious** alert, awake, aware,
cognisant, intentional, knowing,
known, mindful, observant,
perceived, rational, reasoning,
sensible, sensitive, sentient
**consciously respectable** smug
**consciousness** apprehension,
awareness, knowledge, realisation,
recognition, sensibility
**consciousness of self** ego
**conscious of** aware
**conscious psyche** ego
**conscript** recruit
**consecrate** anoint, apotheosise,
beatify, bless, canonise, celebrate,
commit, dedicate, deify, devote,
elevate, esteem, exalt, hallow, laud,
ordain, pledge, sanctify, venerate,
vow
**consecrate as a priest** ordain
**consecrated** sacred
**consecrated oil** chris(o)m
**consecrated water** host
**consecrate with oil** anoint
**consecration** benediction, blessing,
dedication, grace, invocation,
sanctification, thanksgiving
**consecutive** continuous, progressive,
regular, serial, successive,
uninterrupted
**consent** accede, acceptance,
accord(ance), acquiesce(nce),
admit, agree(ment), allow, approval,
approve, assent, cede, compliance,

comply, concession, concur(rence),
confirm, go-ahead, grant, let,
permission, permit, sanction, submit,
yes, yield
**consenting reply** ay(e), yea, yes
**consent to** agree, approve
**consent to receive** acceptance
**consequence** aftermath, concern,
effect, importance, moment,
outcome, result, sequel, significance,
upshot, weight
**consequent clause of conditional
sentence** apodosis
**consequential** critical, crucial, grave,
great, heavy, important, momentous,
repercussive, resultant, resulting,
serious, significant, weighty
**consequently** accordingly, ergo,
hence, subsequently, therefore, thus
**conservative** careful, cautious,
conversational, die-hard, hardhat,
old-fashioned, orthodox, protecting,
prudent, reactionary, rearguard,
rightist, rightwing, stable, Tory,
traditional, unchanging
**conservative in British politics** Tory
**conservatives** rearguard
**conservatory** greenhouse
**conserve of fruit and sugar boiled
until thick** jam
**conserve of tomato** jam, ketchup,
paste, puree
**consider** adjudge, believe, bethink,
cogitate, consider, consult,
contemplate, deem, deliberate,
discuss, entertain, envisage,
envision, esteem, examine, heed,
honour, judge, measure, meditate,
observe, ponder, reflect, regard,
remember, repute, respect, revolve,
ruminate, study, suppose, think,
value, weigh
**considerable amount** lot, much,
quantity
**considerable number** many
**considerable portion** quantity
**considerable sum of money** packet
**considerably** abundantly, appreciably,
greatly, importantly, influentially,
largely, lavishly, markedly, much,
noticeably, plentifully, reasonably,
remarkably, significantly, substantial,
tidily, tolerably
**consider afresh** rethink
**considerate** charitable, concerned,
kind, patient, thoughtful,
well-disposed
**considerate in manner** courteous
**consideration** advisement, attention,
compensation, consequence,
contemplation, deliberation, fee,
importance, kindness, meditation,

patience, payment, recompense, reflection, regard, remuneration, rumination, significance, tact, thoughtfulness, weight
**consider carefully** deliberate
**considered opinion** estimation
**consider favourably** entertain
**considering that** as
**consider logically** reason
**consider the chances** weigh
**consign** assign, commit, convey, delegate, deliver, dispatch, entrust, freight, mail, post, relegate, remit, resign, send, ship, transfer, transmit, yield
**consignment** batch, cargo, delivery, goods, shipment, transfer
**consign to inferior position** relegate
**consign to the grave** bury, inearth, inter
**consist** comprise, include, incorporate, involve, lie, reside
**consistent** accordant, adhering, agreeing, assiduous, conforming, congruous, consonant, constant, dependable, faithful, harmonious, suitable, unchanging, undeviating, uniform, unwavering
**consisting in giving advice** advisory
**consisting of bone** osseous
**consisting of bristles** cetaceous
**consisting of eight** octave
**consisting of fat** adipose, fatty
**consisting of fire** fiery
**consisting of five leaflets** quinquefoliate
**consisting of flesh or muscle** sarcous
**consisting of four parts** quadripartite
**consisting of great stones** megalithic
**consisting of large particles** coarse
**consisting of layers** tiered
**consisting of many** multiple, numerous
**consisting of many individuals** multitudinous
**consisting of many items** numerous
**consisting of many volumes** voluminous
**consisting of molecules** molecular
**consisting of money** pecuniary
**consisting of muscle** sarcous
**consisting of standard units** modular
**consisting of three parts** tripartite, triple
**consisting of two atoms** diatomic
**consist of** contain, embody, embrace, hold, incorporate, involve
**consist with** agree, become, jibe, suit
**consolation** calming, comfort, commiseration, compassion, condolence, lessening, moderation, palliation, pity, relief, remission, solace, sympathy

**console** bracket, cabinet, calm, cheer, comfort, condole, encourage, ensemble, relieve, solace, soothe, stand, switchboard
**consolidate** amalgamate, combine, condense, federate, fortify, join, reinforce, secure, solidify, stabilise, strengthen, unify, unite
**consommé** soup
**consonant** accordant, agreeing, coherent, compatible, concordant, concurring, consentaneous, continuant, euphonious, fricative, harmonious, like-minded, melodious, monodic, musical, resonant, sibilant, sonant, sonorant, spirant, surd, unanimous
**consort** agree, harmonise, mate
**consort of Poseidon** Amphitrite
**consort of Vishnu** Sri
**consort of Zeus** Hera
**consort with others** socialise
**conspicuous** apparent, attracting, awesome, blatant, catching, celebrated, clear, discernible, eminent, evident, famous, garish, glaring, glorious, grand, impressive, manifest, marked, marvellous, noted, noteworthy, noticeable, observable, obvious, open, patent, perceptible, plain, prominent, radiant, recognisable, salient, stately, striking, visible, vivid, well-seen
**conspicuous act** deed
**conspicuous courage** gallantry
**conspicuous in society** smart, prominent
**conspicuous success** éclat
**conspiracy** collusion, complot, confederacy, connivance, contrivance, intrigue, machination, plot, scheme, stratagem, treachery, treason
**conspirator** abettor, accomplice, cabalist, collaborationist, collaborator, confederate, conspirer, intriguer, operator, plotter, schemer
**conspirator against government** Catilinarian
**conspirator against Julius Caesar** Brutus, Cassius
**conspire** combine, concur, contrive, intrigue, plot, revise
**constable** bobby, officer, policeman
**constable's truncheon** baton
**constant** assiduous, continual, continuous, devoted, firm, fixed, immutable, invariable, loyal, permanent, perpetual, persistent, regular, stable, steadfast, true, unchangeable, unchanging,

unending, unfailing, uniform, uninterrupted, unremitting, unvarying, unwavering
**constant attentions** assiduity
**constant desire** craving, itch, mania, obsession, yearning
**constant drinker** dronklap, tippler
**constant factor** modulus
**constant habit** usage
**constant in application** assiduous
**constantly cheerful** buoyant
**constantly recurring** chronic, eternal
**constant succession of changes** flux
**constant teasing desire** itch
**constellation** Apus, Aquarius, Aquila, Ara, Argo, Aries, Cancer, Canis, Cetus, Draco, Gemini, Leo, Libra, Lynx, Lyra, Mensa, Orion, Pavo, Phoenix, Pisces, Sagittarius, Scorpio, Taurus, Ursa, Vela, Virgo
**consternation** alarm, amazement, bewilderment, confusion, dismay, horror, panic, terror
**constituent** basic, component, element(al), essential, factor, ingredient, integral, part, principle, unit
**constituent matter** substance
**constituent of camphor oils** safrole
**constituent of eye drops** eserine
**constituent of food** protein, vitamin
**constituent of haemoglobin** haematin
**constituent part** component, element
**constitute** compose, comprise, establish, form
**constitution** charter, composition, disposition, formation, make-up, principle
**constrain** abuse, bind, bully, check, coerce, commandeer, compel, confine, curb, draft, drive, exact, extort, force, hustle, impel, impress, induce, instigate, necessitate, oblige, press(ure), provoke, restrict, suppress, swallow, taunt, tease, threaten, torment, urge
**constrain by force** duress
**constraint** bondage, captivity, check, coercion, compulsion, confinement, control, curb, detention, diffidence, duress, enforcement, force, imprisonment, necessity, obligation, persuasion, repression, requirement, restraint, restriction, slavery, suppression, urge
**constrict** arrest, bar, block, clog, compress, condense, contract, cram, cramp, curb, curtail, dam, delay, handicap, impede, inhibit, lesson, narrow, obstruct, overpower, press, prevent, purse, reduce, retard, shrink, squeeze, stall, stop, strangle,

**constricted** strangulate, suppress, throttle, tighten
**constricted** abridged, barred, blocked, clogged, close, closed, compact, compressed, concentrated, condensed, congested, contracted, crammed, cramped, crowded, curtailed, dammed, fast, firm, narrow(ed), obstructed, occluded, overpowered, pressed, reduced, rigid, secure, shrivelled, smothered, snug, stiff, stopped, strangled, stretched, suffocated, suppressed, taut, tense, throttled, tight, withered
**constrictive murderer** strangler
**construct** assemble, build, compose, create, design, edify, elevate, erect, fabricate, form(ulate), frame, invent, make, manufacture, produce, raise, rear
**construct again** rebuild
**construction beam** I-bar, I-beam
**construction set** kit
**construction worker** rigger
**constructor** builder, creator, erector, founder, inventor, originator, producer
**construe** adapt, clarify, comprehend, crack, decipher, decode, define, discover, elucidate, explain, expound, interpret, paraphrase, read, render, reproduce, restate, reveal, see. put, solve, take, transcribe, translate, understand, unfold, unravel
**consul's position** consulate
**consult** ask, confer, consider, debate, deliberate, interrogate, palaver, parley, question, regard, respect
**consult another doctor** take a second opinion
**consultative** advising, advisory, counselling, helping, recommending
**consult openly** affront
**consult together** confer, negotiate
**consumable** absorbable, edible, employable, exhaustible, expendable, usable, utilisable
**consume** absorb, burn, destroy, devastate, devour, dissipate, drain, drink, eat, empty, envelop, exhaust, expend, spend, squander, sup, swallow, use, waste
**consume by fire** cremate, incinerate
**consume food** eat
**consume in flames** burn
**consume meal** eat
**consumer** buyer, client, customer, emptor, habitué, marketer, patron, purchaser, regular, shopper, user
**consumer of food** diner, eater
**consume the whole of** exhaust

**consummate** accomplish, achieve, complete, do, execute, finish(ed), fulfil(led), perfect
**consumption** TB, tuberculosis
**consumption of the lungs** phthisis
**contact** communication, connection, junction, reach, touch
**contact by telephone** call, ring
**contact sport** boxing, rugby, soccer, wrestling
**contagious** catching, communicable, infectious, noxious, pestilential, poisonous
**contagious alarm** panic
**contagious disease** measles, mumps, smallpox
**contagious disease of birds** psittacosis
**contagious disease of horses** glanders
**contagious fear** panic
**contagious pustular disease of the skin** impetigo
**contagious skin infection** scabies
**contagious venereal disease** AIDS, gonorrhea, syphilis
**contagious viral disease** influenza, mumps
**contain** accommodate, admit, carry, comprise, control, embody, embrace, enclose, enfold, hold, include, incorporate, receive, repress, restrain
**contain a letter** envelope
**contained** accommodated, enclosed, held, in, incorporated, seated
**container** bag, basin, box, can, case, holder, jar, package, pot, receptacle, vat, vessel
**container for ashes** urn
**container for boiling water** kettle
**container for bread** bin
**container for hypodermic dose** ampoule
**container for implements** toolbox
**container for jam** jar
**container for letter** envelope
**container for mail** post-box
**container for packing** crate
**container for petrol** can, drum
**container for swept-up rubbish** dustbin, dustpan
**container for tape** cassette
**container for the bones of a corpse** ossuary
**container for voting slips** ballot box, voting-box
**container of toothed wheels** gearbox
**container top** lid
**container with handle** bucket
**container with lid** box, cannister
**containing abundance** copious, full

**containing aloes** aloetic
**containing and discharging pus** purulent
**containing a promise** promissory
**containing bivalent copper** cupric
**containing bones** ossiferous
**containing carbolic acid** carbolated
**containing gold** aureated, aurous
**containing iron** ferric, ferrous
**containing its own raising agent** self-raising
**containing lime** calcareous
**containing much salt** brine, saliferous, saline
**containing nothing** empty
**containing opium** opiate
**containing several objects** omnibus
**containing silver** argentic, lunar
**containing small grains** granular
**containing soap** saponaceous, soapy
**containing three consonants** triconsonantal
**containing vowels** vocalic
**containing water** aqueous, hydrous
**contains albumen** egg
**contains an edible kernel** nut
**contains blood** haematuria
**contaminate** abuse, befoul, besmear, besmirch, blight, corrupt, debase, defile, desecrate, dirty, envenom, foul, infect, influence, kill, mar, misuse, murder, pervert, poison, pollute, profane, smear, soil, spoil, stain, sully, taint, touch, vitiate
**contaminated by bacteria** septic
**contemplate** aim, attend, brood, consider, envisage, eye, heed, inspect, intend, mean, meditate, mind, muse, notice, observe, peer, ponder, pry, regard, resolve, revolve, ruminate, scan, view
**contemplative** meditative, musing, philosophical, reflective, studious, thoughtful
**contemporary** à la mode, coeval, coexistent, coexisting, compeer, concurrent, contemporaneous, current, existing, extant, fellow, living, modern, newfangled, peer, present, present-day, recent, simultaneous, synchronal, synchronous, up-to-date
**contempt** derision, disdain, disesteem, disgrace, dishonour, disregard, disrespect, ignominy, loathing, revulsion, scorn
**contemptible person** git, heel, peasant, pinhead, rabbit
**contemptible scoundrel** cur
**contemptibly small** measly
**contemptuous** abusive, arrogant, assuming, bad-mannered,

blustering, bold, cheeky, conceited, discourteous, disdainful, disrespectful, haughty, high-handed, ill-bred, imperious, impertinent, impolite, impudent, insolent, insulting, irreverent, lordly, misbehaved, overbearing, pert, pompous, presumptuous, pretentious, proud, rude, scornful, sneering, supercilious, uncivil
**contemptuous hoot** boo
**contemptuous look** fleer, sneer
**contemptuous reproach** taunt
**contend** argue, assert, battle, claim, combat, compete, cope, deal, debate, fight, grapple, maintain, strive, struggle, tussle, vie, wrestle
**contender** athlete, candidate, challenger, competitor, contestant, entrant, opposer, striver
**contender in a muscular test** athlete
**contend for a prize** compete
**contend in battle** fight
**contend in rivalry** compete, vie
**contend violently** quarrel
**contend with** antagonise, cope
**content** agreeable, appease, assenting, delightful, enjoy, gratify, humour, indulge, matter, pacify, please, reconcile, sanguine, satisfied, satisfy, willing
**contented sound** purr
**contention** argument, dispute, rivalry, strife
**contentious fellow** squarer
**contentiously** argumentatively, controversially, disputatiously
**contentious party** faction
**contentment** comfort, content, gladness, gratification, happiness, pleasure, serenity
**content of an atlas** map
**contents of the skull** brain, encephalon, grey matter
**content sound** purr
**conterminous** coaxial
**contest** against, altercation, argue, argument, battle, bout, challenge, combat, compete, competition, conflict, contend, contention, controversy, debate, dispute, doubt, encounter, fight, game, match, oppose, race, rivalry, struggle, tournament, tourney, vie
**contest again** replay
**contestant** athlete, campaigner, candidate, challenger, combatant, competitor, contender, disputant, entrant, litigant, opponent, opposer, rival, tussler
**contest at law** litigate
**contest between two** duel

**contest for recreation** game
**contest for two** duel
**contest judge** adjudicator, referee, umpire
**contest offering prizes** competition
**contest of five events** pentathlon
**contest of nations** war
**contest of skill** game, match, tournament
**contest of speed** race
**contest of team strength** tug of war
**context** atmosphere, background, circumstances, connection, element, environment, frame, setting, situation, surrounding
**contextual error** anachronism, misapplication, mislocation, misplacing
**contiguity** approximation, contract, junction, juxtaposition, touch, union
**continent** abstemious, abstinent, Africa, America, ascetic, Asia, austere, Australia, chaste, Eurasia, Europe, land, main(land), pure, region, sober, teetotal, temperate
**continental** epeiric, European
**continental buck?** eurodollar
**continental quilt** duvet
**continent around South Pole** Antarctica
**continent mainly within the Antarctic Circle** Antarctica
**contingency** casualty, chance, circumstance, event(uality), fortuity, happening, incident, likelihood, luck, occasion, possibility
**contingent** batch, bunch, group, mission, quota, section, set
**continual** ceaseless, constant, continuous, incessant, permanent, perpetual, recurrent, recurring, repetitious, repetitive, unceasing, unending, unremitting
**continually** always, constantly, endlessly, eternally, ever, persistently, repeatedly
**continually changing** floating
**continually recurring** constant
**continual rapid oscillation of eyeballs** nystagmus
**continuance** ceaselessness, connected, constant, extended, incessancy, persistence, prolonged, unbroken, unceasing, undivided, uneasingness, uninterrupted
**continue** abide, advance, endure, exist, extend, last, linger, maintain, perpetuate, persevere, persist, proceed, prolong, pursue, remain, resume, retain, stay, subsist, sustain, tarry
**continue a subscription** renew

**continue despite difficulty** persist
**continue determinedly** persist
**continued pain** ache, aching, agony
**continued steady efforts** perseverance
**continued story** serial, series
**continue firmly** persist
**continue in being** exist
**continue obstinately** persist
**continue steadfastly** persevere
**continue striving** persevere
**continue to live** survive
**continuing** abiding, enduring, lasting, ongoing, persisting, remaining, resting, staying, surviving, sustained
**continuing abuse** tirade
**continuing in the same state** permanent
**continuing on one tone** monotone
**continuing story** serial
**continuing three years** triennial
**continuing to exist** ongoing
**continuing to grow after flowering** accrescent
**continuing TV programme** series
**continuous** constant, extended, ongoing, prolonged, unbroken, undivided, uninterrupted
**continuous base under a building** podium
**continuous curve round a cylinder** spiral
**continuous discharge of firearms** fusillade
**continuous drinking** bout
**continuous heavy gunfire** cannonade
**continuous heavy rain** downpour
**continuously** de die in diem (L)
**continuously at equal distances** parallel
**continuous narration** epic
**continuous pain** ache
**continuous pain in the head** headache, migraine
**continuous record of events** history
**continuous section of wood along ship's side** strake, streak
**contort** convolute, deform, disfigure, distort, grimace, ripple, screw, shrink, shrivel, squirm, turn, twirl, twist, warp, whirl, wiggle, wrench, wrest, wriggle, wrinkle, writhe
**contort body** writhe
**contort the face** grimace
**contour** figure, line, lineament, outline, periphery, profile, silhouette
**contract** abbreviate, abridge, agreement, arrangement, bargain, compact, compress, concentrate, concordat, condense, constrict, convention, covenant, pact, reduce, shrink, stipulation, treaty
**contract bid** tender

**contracted** abstracted, clipped, compressed, condensed, constricted, constringed, decreased, dwindled, employed, lessened, narrow, pinched, reduced, summarised, tightened, wrapped-up
**contracting the blood vessels** styptic
**contract in wrinkles** purse
**contraction** abridgement, abstracting, binding, brief, clipping, condensing, constraint, cut, decrease, epitome, limitation, restriction, résumé, spasm, subtraction, systole
**contraction in size** shrinkage
**contract of insurance** policy
**contract of it is** tis
**contractor's estimate** quotation
**contract the brow** frown
**contract to** affiance
**contradict** abrogate, belie, challenge, controvert, deny, differ, disaffirm, dispute, dissent, gainsay, impugn, negate, nullify, rebut, refute, rescind, reverse, thwart
**contradiction between two laws** antinomy
**contradiction in terms** antilogy
**contradiction of ideas** antilogy
**contradictory statement** paradox
**contraption** apparatus, device, gadget, rig
**contrary** adverse, antagonistic, conflicting, contradictory, counter, disagreeable, headstrong, hostile, negative, obstinate, opposed, opposing, opposite, perverse, stubborn, unfavourable
**contrary opinion** opposite view
**contrary religious belief** heresy
**contrary to** against
**contrary to common sense** preposterous
**contrary to desire** adverse
**contrary to good manners** contra bonos mores (L)
**contrary to law** illegal, illicit
**contrary to logic** illegitimate
**contrary to reason** absurd, illogical, reasonless, unreasonable
**contrary to reasoning** illogical
**contrary to true** false, foul
**contrast** compare, comparison, difference, discriminate, distinguish, oppose
**contravene** belie, break, challenge, contradict, counter, counteract, deny, disobey, dispute, infringe, negate, oppose, transgress, violate
**contribute** accord, advance, afford, aid, bestow, donate, endow, forward, furnish, give, grant, offer, promote, provide, serve

**contribute to** add, aid, bring
**contribute to charity** donate
**contribute with** furnish
**contributory cause** factor
**contrite** apologetic, atoning, compunctious, embarrassed, guilt-ridden, humble, humbled, penitent, penitential, regretful, regretting, remorseful, repentant, rueful, self-reproachful, shamed, sorrowful, sorry, troubled
**contritely** apologetically, humbly, penitently, regretfully, remorsefully, repentantly, sorrily, sorrowfully
**contrition** penitence, remorse
**contrivance** apparatus, appliance, complot, conspiracy, coup, creation, design, device, gadget, gear, implement, instrument, intrigue, invention, machine, means, mechanism, plan, plot, scheme, stratagem, tactics, utensil
**contrivance to cut moorings of submerged mines** paravane
**contrive** concoct, conspire, construct, create, design, devise, effect, engineer, fabricate, frame, hatch, improvise, invent, manage, plan, plot
**control** check, command, constrain, curb, direct(ion), dominance, dominate, govern(ment), harness, manage(ment), mastery, prove, regulate, regulation, rein, restraint(t), rule, steer, test, verify
**control by machines** cybernation
**control course** steer
**controlled by fate** fateful
**control-lever of aeroplane** joystick
**controlling power** autocracy
**control oneself** abstain, avoid, refrain
**control over another** whiphand
**control rod** lever
**controls activities** manager
**controls self** exercises restraint
**control valve** poppet
**controversial** arguable, argumentable, contentious, controvertible, debatable, disputable, disputatious, disputed, polemic(al), suspicious, unsettled
**controversialist** eristic
**controversial public issue** cause célèbre
**controversy** altercation, argument, contention, debate, disagreement, dispute
**contumacious** adamant, contrary, disobedient, factious, headstrong, heady, intractable, obdurate, obstinate, persistent, pigheaded, rebellious, refractory, resistant, restive, stubborn, tenacious,

uncompromising, unruly, unyielding, wilful
**contumacy** breach, contrariety, disobedience, forwardness, intractableness, mutiny, obduracy, obstinacy, persistent, perverseness, perversion, perversity, rebellion, resolution, revolt, stubbornness, tenacity, violation, wilfulness
**contumely** abuse, arrogance, calumny, contempt, degradation, disdain, humiliation, incivility, indignity, insolence, insult, invective, pertiness, pomposity, roughness, rudeness, sarcasm, scorn
**contusion** blemish, bruise, bulge, bump, discoloration, injury, knob, lump, mark, swelling
**conundrum** acrostic, anagram, brain-teaser, charade, enigma, logograph, puzzle, rebus, riddle
**convalesce** heal, improve, mend, rally, recover, recuperate, revive
**convalescence** cure, improvement, incapacitation, recovery, recuperation, rehabilitation, remediation, restoration, treatment
**convene** assemble, collect, congregate, convoke, gather, meet
**convenience** adaptability, advantage, amenity, appliance, avail(ability), ease, expedience, facility, fitness, fittingness, handiness, leisure, opportuneness, suitability, use(fulness), utility
**convenient** accessible, appropriate, available, comfortable, easy, favourable, fit, handy, serviceable, suitable, useful
**convenient arrangement** accommodating
**convenient for carrying** portable
**conveniently within reach** handy
**convent** abbey, cloister, monastery, motherhouse, noviitiate, nunhood, nunnery, priory, sisterhood
**convent dining hall** refectory
**convent dweller** nun
**convent for nuns** nunnery
**convent head** abbess
**convent inhabitant** nun
**convention** agreement, assemblage, assembly, code, conference, congress, convocation, council, custom, deal, delegates, discussion, entente, etiquette, formality, gathering, meeting, pact, parley, practice, precedent, protocol, synod, tradition, treaty, usage
**conventional** accepted, common, correct, customary, decorous,

formal, normal, orthodox, proper, routine, stereotyped, traditional
**conventional act** amenity
**conventionality** orthodoxy, traditionalism
**conventionally accepted falsehood** fiction
**conventional opinion** idée reçue (F)
**conventional rules of manners** etiquette, protocol
**conventional rules of social behaviour** etiquette
**conventional usages of society** fashion
**convention-goer** delegate
**convent member** nun
**convent of nuns** nunnery
**convent sister** nun
**convent woman** nun
**converge** approach, assemble, blend, coincide, combine, concentrate, congregate, conspire, cooperate, correspond, focus, gather, group, intersect, join, meet, merge, mingle, unite
**conversant** abreast, acquainted, apprised, attentive, au fait (F), aware, briefed, cognisant, conscious, erudite, expert, familiar, informed, knowing, knowledgeable, mindful, posted, reliable, sensible, up, wise
**conversant with** au fait (F)
**conversation** chat, colloquy, communion, conference, connection, contact, converse, correspondence, dialogue, discourse, discussion, exchange, fellowship, gossip, meeting, palaver, parlance, sitting, talk, tête-à-tête
**conversational** candid, chatty, colloquial, communicative, conversable, discoursive, expansive, frank, free, open, straightforward, talkative, unreserved, unreticent, unsecretive, voluble
**conversation between two persons** dialogue, duologue
**conversation line** phone, telephone
**converse** antithesis, chat, confabulate, contrary, conversation, dialogue, discourse, discuss(ion), obverse, opposite, reverse(d), speak, talk, transposed
**converse informally** chat
**converse privately** whisper
**conversion** adaptation, adaption, alteration, change, modification, permutation, rebirth, reconstruction, reformation, regeneration, remaking, remodelling, transfiguration, transformation, translation, transmutation
**conversion of sugar to alcohol** fermentation
**convert** change, disciple, neophyte, proselyte, proselytise, redeem, transform
**convert and helper of St Paul** Titus
**converted heathen** neophyte
**converter** decoder
**convert for re-use** recycle
**convert from imperial system** metricate
**convertible to cash** negotiable
**convert into bone** ossify
**convert into cash** encash, redeem
**convert into fact** realise
**convert into forest** afforest
**convert into leather** tan
**convert into stone** petrify
**convert into wood** lignify
**convert to another religion** proselyte, proselytise
**convexity upon an upper surface** camber
**convex part** bulge
**convey** bear, bring, carry, cart, cede, communicate, deliver, demise, devise, disclose, dispatch, displace, divulge, fetch, grant, impart, mean, move, portage, relate, reveal, send, shift, transfer, transmit, transport
**conveyance** auto, bearing, bus, cab, carriage, carrying, cart, cartage, conveying, freightage, gig, hansom, hauling, lorry, lugging, portage, shipment, stagecoach, transfer, transit, transmission, transport, transportation, truck, vehicle
**conveyance by ferry** ferriage
**conveyance for the dead** bier, hearse
**conveyance for the sick** ambulance
**conveyance of estate** release
**conveyance of goods** transit
**conveyed by sea** seaborne
**conveyed through the air** airborne
**convey from one place to another** transport
**convey in boat across water** ferry
**conveying a command** mandatory
**conveying a warning** cautionary
**conveying sound** soniferous
**conveyor** bearer, carrier, deliverer, messenger, porter, revealer, runner, sender, servant, transmitter, transporter
**convey secretly** slip, smuggle
**conveys greetings** card
**convey through the air** waft
**convict** condemn, criminal, culprit, felon, imprison, inmate, lag, malefactor, prisoner, sentence
**conviction** assurance, belief, certainty, confidence, firmness, judg(e)ment, opinion, principle, reliance
**convict's warrant** mittimus
**convince** assure, confirm, influence, persuade, reassure, satisfy, sway
**convincing** assuring, cogent, conclusive, credible, impressive, likely, persuading, persuasive, plausible, powerful, probable, satisfying, swaying, telling
**convincing evidence** proof
**convincing quality** cogency
**convivial** affable, agreeable, amiable, befitting, celebrative, festive, gay, gregarious, hospitable, jolly, jovial, joyful, joyous, party, sociable, social
**conviviality** amiability, amity, amusement, cheerfulness, companionship, company, congeniality, exhilaration, exuberance, fellowship, fraternity, friendship, gaiety, glee, hilarity, jollification, jollity, kindliness, laughter, merriment, mirth, togetherness, warmth
**convolution** arc, bend, coil(ing), complexity, contortion, curve, gyrus, helix, intricacy, loop, meander, spiral, tortuousness, turn, twist, undulation, whorl, winding, zigzag
**convoy** accompany, attendance, escort, guard, protection
**convulse** agitate, disorder, disturb, excruciate, harrow, heave, shake, swirl, torment, twist, unsettle, upset, work, wring
**convulsion** agitation, attack, cataclysm, disturbance, explosion, fit, fury, outburst, paroxysm, rage, revolution, seizure, spasm, stroke, throe, turmoil, unrest, violence
**convulsive** agitated, berserk, crazed, distracted, distraught, excited, frantic, frenetic, frenzied, furious, hysterical, mad, maniacal, overwrought, rabid, raving, shudder, uncontrollable, uncontrolled, wild
**convulsive muscular contraction** spasm
**cony** coney, rabbit
**cooing bird** dove
**cook** bake, boil, braai, braise, broil, chef, concoct, falsify, fry, garble, grill, heat, prepare, roast, sauté, simmer, steam, stew, toast
**cook by boiling** seethe, simmer
**cook by dry heat** bake, braai, roast
**cook by slow simmering** stew
**cooked** done
**cooked dessert** pudding
**cooked enough** done

**cooked in a cream sauce** à la king
**cooked in juices** stewed
**cooked in olive oil with herbs** à la grecque (F)
**cooked insufficiently** rare, underdone
**cooked so as to be firm when eaten** al dente (I)
**cooked with cider and cream** à la normande (F)
**cooked with red wine** bourguignon (F)
**cooker** oven, stove
**cookery** cuisine
**cookery guide** recipe
**cook gently** brew, coddle, heat, poach, simmer, stew
**cook in fat in a pan** fry
**cook in fat in oven** roast
**cooking** board, bread, commons, cuisine, diet, edibles, fare, food, foodstuffs, larder, menu, nourishment, nutrition, provender, provisions, rations, refreshment, stores, sustenance, victuals
**cooking apparatus** rotisserie
**cooking area** kitchen
**cooking area in caravan** galley
**cooking art** cuisine
**cooking chamber** oven
**cooking dish** pan, pot
**cooking eggs** coddling
**cooking fat** lard, suet
**cooking formula** recipe
**cooking fuel** gas
**cooking instructions** recipe
**cooking method** braai, (deep-)fry, grill, roast
**cooking pan** skillet, wok
**cooking pot** olla, pan
**cooking range** stove
**cooking stand** trivet
**cooking stove** range
**cooking utensil** pot, pan
**cooking vessel** (frying) pan, pot, steamer
**cook in hot fat** fry
**cook in hot fat in the oven** roast
**cook in oil** fry
**cook in oven** bake, roast
**cook in skillet** fry
**cook's formula** recipe
**cook's garment** apron, hat
**cook's item** pan, pot
**cook slowly** simmer, stew
**cook's work garment** apron
**cook the books** fiddle
**cook too much** overdo
**cook up** brew, combine, concoct, contrive, devise, fabricate, improvise, invent, mix, plan, plot, prepare, scheme
**cook with it** electricity, fire, gas, microwave

**cook with oil** fry
**cool** abate, apathetic, audacious, calm, chill(ing), chilly, cold, dampen, deliberate, dispassionate, distant, freezing, frigid, impudent, indifferent, moderate, placid, quiet, repellent, self-possessed, temper, unconcerned, undisturbed, unexcited, unmoved, unruffled
**cool confidence** cheek
**cool courage** nerve
**cooler** fridge, icebox
**cooling device** fan, fridge, refrigerator
**cooling drink of diluted fruit-juices** sherbet, sorbet
**coolly** calmly, composedly, deliberately, imperturbably, level-headedly, nippily, placidly, quietly, refreshingly, relaxedly, serenely
**coolly unconcerned** nonchalant
**coolness in danger** courage, nerve
**cool spot** shade
**coomb** dale, dell, depression, dingle, glen, hollow, strath, vale, valley
**coop** aviary, box, cage, confine, corral, crawl, crib, dungeon, enclosure, henhouse, immure, imprison, intern, mew, pen, pound, vault
**coop dweller** hen
**cooped-up bird** cageling
**co-operate with enemy** collaborate
**co-operative** accordant, co-active, co-ordinated, coalition, company, concerted, concurrent, helpful, interactive, joint, mutual, obliging, partnership, unified, united
**co-operative action** synergism
**co-operative effort of a group** teamwork
**coop up** cage, detain, gaol, incarcerate
**cop** apprehension, arrest, capture, detention, peeler, policeman, seizure
**cope** contend, deal, handle, hurdle, manage, spar, strive, subsist, survive, tussle
**Copenhagen native** Dane
**Copenhagen park** Tivoli
**cope with** deal, encounter, handle, manage, struggle, tussle, weather, wrestle
**coping** managing, surviving
**copious discharge** spout
**copious stream** river
**copious supply** abundance
**cop-out** alibi, dodge, evasion, fraud, pretence, pretext
**copper alloy** brass, bronze
**copper coin** a(e)s, cent, para, pence, penny
**copper compound** cuprous
**copper money** a(e)s, cent, penny

**copper-tin alloy** bronze
**coppery** cupreous
**copper-zinc alloy** ormolu
**copse** thicket
**Coptic bishop** abba
**copy** ape, counterfeit, duplicate, echo, edition, emulate, facsimile, fake, follow, forgery, image, imitate, imitation, likeness, manuscript, mimic, mirror, model, parrot, pattern, photocopy, print, repeat, replica(tion), reproduce, reproduction, simulate, text, trace, transcribe
**copy a drawing** trace
**copy a paper** roneo
**copying** aping, counterfeiting, duplicating, echoing, emulating, following, imitating, insinuation, mimicking, mimicry, mirroring, photocopying, repeating, reproducing, simulating, transcribing
**copyist** artist, copier, copycat, imitator, penman, scribe, scrivener
**copy of book** edition
**copy of record** estreat
**copy out** extract
**coquette** flirt, heartbreaker, hoyden, hussy, jade, minx, philanderer, tease, tomboy, vamp, wanton
**coquettishly bashful** coy
**coral animal** polyp
**coral bank** reef
**coral creature** polyp
**coral island** atoll
**coral relief** cameo
**coral ridge** reef
**corbel** ancon, truss
**corb weevil** curculio
**cord** bind, bond, braid, connection, cordon, fasten, gut, lace, lanyard, ligature, line, link, nexus, ribbon, rope, strand, string, tape, thew, thread, tie, twine, yarn
**cordage fibre** istle, jute
**corded cloth** rep
**corded edging** fringe, macramé
**corded fabric** bengaline, pique, rep
**corded silk fabric** rep
**cord for corset** staylace
**cord for tying shoe** lace
**cord fringe** tassel
**cordial** affable, affectionate, agreeable, amiable, amicable, cheerful, courteous, earnest, friendly, genial, gracious, heartfelt, hearty, invogorating, sincere, sociable, warm, warm-hearted, whole-hearted
**cordial greeting** welcome
**cordiality** accessibility, affability, affection, amity, approachability, cheer, conviviality, friendliness,

happiness, heartiness, hospitality, informality, kindliness, love, sociability, tenderness, warmth, welcome
**cordial reception** welcome
**cord in candle** wick
**cordite** explosive, gunpowder
**cordless blower** radio-telephone
**cord of twisted gold or silver wire** purl
**cordon off** besiege, blockade, encircle, enclose, separate, surround
**cords by which a hammock is supported** clew
**core** centre, essence, heart, middle, nucleus, substance
**corium** derma, dermis, skin
**Cork river** Lee
**corkscrew shape** spiral
**corkwood** balsa
**corky layer** periderm
**corm** bulb
**cormorant** glutton, shag
**corn** ears, grain, kernel, maize, mealie, oats, papilloma, pickle, preserve, seed, wheat
**corn bread** pone
**corncob** ear, mealie
**corncob and briar** pipe
**corn ear** cob, mealie, spike
**corneous projection** horn
**corner** angle, bend, curve, elbow, hook, intersection, knee, monopolise, niche, nook, region, trap, turn
**corner brace** gusset
**corner of a wall** ancon
**corner of eye** canthus
**corner of sail** clew
**corner or narrow recess** nook
**cornerstone** coign(e), quoin
**corner support** gusset
**corner tower** bastion
**cornet** horn
**cornhead** ear
**corn husk** cap, chaff, shack
**cornmeal cake** pone
**corn pancake** fritter
**corn spike** ear
**corn to grind** grist
**Cornwall mine** bal
**corn-weed** tare
**corny** banal, dull, feeble, hackneyed, maudlin, stale, trite
**corollary** analogue, assumption, conclusion, conjecture, consequence, counterpart, deduction, duplicate, equal, inference, match, presumption, result, rider, surmise, twin
**corona** aura, halo, nimbus, radiance
**coroner's inquiry** autopsy, inquest

**coronet** chaplet, circlet, crown, diadem, fillet, garland, headdress, headgear, regalia, tiara, wreath
**coronet of a deer's antler** burr
**corporal** bodily, corporeal, earthly, fleshy, incarnate, material, mortal, physical, worldly
**corporal framework** skeleton
**corporate bond** debenture
**corporation** alliance, association, band, body, brotherhood, business, clique, club, co-operative, collection, company, concern, confederacy, (con)federation, congress, enterprise, establishment, fellowship, firm, fraternity, group, guild, league, order, organisation, partnership, society, syndicate, union
**corporation carrying on business** office
**corpse** ashes, body, cadaver, carcase, carcass, carrion, clay, corse, dust, relics, remains, skeleton, stiff
**corpse bearer** bier
**corpulent** burly, fat, obese, overweight, plump, rotund, stout, tubby
**corpulent beer** stout
**corral** capture, coop, enclosure, fold, imprison, kraal, pen, pound, stall, stockade, sty
**correct** accurate, adjust, admonish, amend, chastise, chide, cure, discipline, emend, exact, factual, faultless, flawless, improve, just, perfect, precise, proper, punish, readjust, rectify, redress, reform, regular, remedy, reprimand, reprove, right, strict, true, truthful, warn
**correct a manuscript** edit, revise
**correct an error** amend
**correct conduct** propriety
**correct in every detail** exact
**correction** adjustment, alteration, amendment, castigation, improvement, modification, rectification, reform, reproof
**correction of irregularities in teeth and jaws** orthodontics
**correctly** properly, rightly
**correctly reasoned** logical
**correctness** accuracy, exactitude, fidelity, preciseness, precision, rectitude, regularity, truth
**correctness of behaviour** propriety
**correct pitch of** tone
**correct response** answer
**correct spelling** orthography
**correct writing** edit
**correlative of nor** neither
**correlative of systolic** diastolic
**correspond** accord, agree, coincide, communicate, concur, conform,

dovetail, fit, harmonise, match, square, suit, tally
**correspondence** accordance, bulletins, closeness, comparison, concord, epistolary, epistolography, homology, likeness, mail, notes, post, postcards, reciprocity, similarity, uniformity
**corresponding thing** tally
**correspond to** match
**corridor** access, adit, aisle, arcade, causeway, colonnade, concourse, entrance, foyer, hall(way), lobby, passage(way), path, route, strip, vestibule, walk(way)
**corridors of power** bureaucracy
**corroborate** affirm, certify, confirm, document, endorse, substantiate, support, uphold, validate, verify
**corroboration** confirmation, validation
**corroboratory evidence** adminicle
**corrode** abrade, chafe, consume, corrupt, crumble, damage, degenerate, destroy, deteriorate, devour, disintegrate, erode, fragment, fret, gnaw, impair, oxidise, rust, waste, wear
**corroded** consumed, corrupted, eaten, eroded, gnawed, rusty
**corroding ulceration in mouth** canker
**corrosion** cankering, consuming, crumbling, decay, deposit, destruction, erosion, film, fraying, gnawing, harm, impairment, oxidation, patina, ravagement, ravaging, rust, wearing
**corrosion-protected** rustproof
**corrosion-resistant metal** iridium
**corrosive** abrasion, abrasive, acid(ic), acrid, ardent, biting, caustic, cauterant, cutting, destroyer, echarotic, erodent, erosive, harmful, incisive, mordant, sarcastic, trenchant, virulent, wasting, wearing
**corrosive acid used in making explosives** nitric
**corrosive agent** escharotic
**corrosive substance** acid
**corrugated** creased, crimped, fluted, furrowed, grooved, plaited, ridged, wrinkled, wrinkly
**corrugating machine** crimper
**corrupt** abandoned, adulterate(d), bent, bribe(d), contaminate, crooked, debase, defile(d), degenerate, demoralise, deprave(d), dishonest, dissolute, evil, false, fraudulent, immoral, impure, infect(ed), lure, pervert, pollute, reprobate, rotten, shady, sinful, spoil(ed), subvert, taint(ed), unethical, unprincipled,

**corrupt act** depravity
unscrupulous, untrustworthy, venal, wicked
**corrupt administration** malversation
**corrupt behaviour in position of trust** malversation
**corrupt dealing** jobbery
**corruptible** venal
**corrupting influence** bribe
**corruption** bribery, contamination, decay, defilement, depravity, dishonesty, dissolution, evil, immorality, perversion, pollution, rot, sinfulness, wickedness
**corruptly mercenary** venal
**corrupt morally** debauch
**corrupt practice** abuse
**corsac** corsak, fox
**corsage flower** orchid
**corset** bodice, girdle, stays
**corset bone** busk
**Corsica** Corse (F)
**Corsican pine** larch
**Corsican port** Ajaccio
**corticate** barklike
**corundum** emery
**coruscate** flare, flash, gleam, glimmer, glint, glisten, glitter, scintillate, shimmer, shine, sparkle, twinkle
**cosh** blackjack
**cosily** comfortably, intimately, securely, snugly, warmly
**cos lettuce** romaine
**cosmetic** lipstick, powder, rouge
**cosmetic case** etui
**cosmetic liquid** lotion
**cosmetic paste** mudpack
**cosmetic pencil** eye-liner
**cosmetic powder** kohl, rouge
**cosmetics** make-up
**cosmetic surgery** face-lift, redecoration, renovation, restoration
**cosmetic to darken eyelashes** mascara
**cosmetic treatment of hands and nails** manicure
**cosmic cycle** aeon
**cosmonaut** astronaut
**cosmopolitan** catholic, sophisticated, universal, urbane, well-travelled, worldly, worldly-wise
**cosmos** universe, world
**Cossack chief** ataman, hetman
**Cossack regiment** pulk
**Cossack whip** knout
**cost** account, afford, amount, charge, damage, dearness, detriment, disbursement, expenditure, expense, fare, loss, outlay, pain, payment, penalty, price, rate, value, worth, yield
**costa** midrib, rib, vein

**Costa Rican cape** Blanco, Elena, Velas
**Costa Rican currency** colón
**Costa Rican dance** Punto, Torito
**Costa Rican gulf** Dulce, Nicoya, Papagoya
**Costa Rican island** Coco
**Costa Rican lake** Arenal
**Costa Rican peninsula** Nicoya, Osa
**Costa Rican port** Limon, Puntarenas
**Costa Rican volcano** Irazu, Poas
**costing much** expensive
**costliness** dearness, expensiveness
**costly** dear, excessive, expensive, extravagant, gorgeous, high-priced, lavish, luxurious, opulent, precious, priceless, rich, steep, sumptuous, valuable
**costly fur** ermine, mink, sable, seal
**cost of borrowed money** interest
**cost of hiring** rental
**cost of warehousing** storage
**cost per unit** rate
**costume** attire, clothes, dress, garb, garment, habit, livery, mode, rig, uniform
**costume carnival** Mardi Gras, pageant
**costume of a monk** habit
**cost what it may** coûte que coûte (F)
**cosy** cheerful, comfortable, comfy, covering, easy, ensconced, homelike, homely, homey, intimate, relaxing, secure, sheltered, snug, warm
**cosy and warm** snug
**cosy contents** teapot
**cosy corner** nook
**cosy place** nest
**cosy retreat** nest
**cosy room** snuggery
**cosy spot** den, nest
**cosy talk** chat
**cot** bed, cradle, crib
**coterie** alliance, assembly, association, band, body, brotherhood, circle, clan, clique, club, community, company, crew, crowd, fraternity, gang, group, guild, horde, league, party, sect, society, troop, union, unit
**cotillion** cotillon, dance
**cottage** cabin, cot, hut, lodge, shack, shanty
**cotton and woollen cloth** wincey
**cotton bundle** bale
**cotton capsule** boll
**cotton carpet made in India** d(h)urrie
**cotton cloth** calico, cambric, drill
**cotton drill** denim
**cotton fabric** calico, cretonne, dimity, flannelette, galatea, nankeen, organdie, percale, poplin
**cotton fabric, glossy one side** sateen

**cotton fabric with a pile velvet** velveteen
**cotton fabric woven like satin** sateen
**cotton gauze** leno
**cotton gin inventor** Whitney
**cotton making** ginning
**cotton material to cover mattresses** ticking
**cotton pod** boll
**cotton seeding machine** gin
**cotton seed pod** boll
**cotton shoot** ratoon
**cotton spool** reel
**cotton starch** gomelin
**cotton textile centre in central Japan** Himeji
**cotton thread** lisle
**cotyledon** seedleaf
**couch** bed, divan, lounge, sofa
**couch with a back** settee
**cougar** panther, puma
**cough** bark, hack, hawk, hem, hoast (Sc)
**cough drop** lozenge, pastille, troche
**cough harshly** hack
**cough mixture** linctus
**cough mixture ingredient** ipecac(uanha)
**cough remedy** linctus
**cough up** deliver, surrender
**could do with** need
**council** advisors, assembly, board, cabinet, caucus, committee, conclave, conference, congregation, congress, convention, gathering, meeting, ministry, panel, senate, synod, trustees
**council of clergy** synod
**counsel** admonish, advice, adviser, advocate, attorney, barrister, caution, consideration, consultation, deliberation, direct(ion), exhort, forethought, guidance, guide, information, instruct, lawyer, opinion, plan, purpose, recommend(ation), rede, scheme, solicitor, suggest(ion), urge, warn
**counsel for the accused** defender
**counsellor** adviser, advocate, coach, confidant, guide, jurist, leader, mentor, solicitor, teacher, tutor
**count** amount, calculate, calculation, computation, compute, consider, depend, earl, enumerate, figure, number, quantity, regard, rely, score, sum, tally
**count calories** diet
**countenance** abet, aid, appearance, approval, aspect, assist(ance), complexion, encourage(ment), expression, face, favour, look, mien, patronise, sanction, support, visage

**countenance given by custom**
  sanction
**countenance giving no sign of emotion**
  poker-face
**counter** adverse, against, contrar(il)y, conversely, resist, respond, retaliate, teller
**counteract** annul, contravene, counterbalance, countervail, neutralise, offset, oppose, resist
**counteracting agent** antidote
**counteracts bacterial infection** antibiotic
**counteracts fever** antipyretic
**counteracts scurvy** antiscorbutic
**counterattack** retaliate
**counterbalance** balance, compensate, counterpoise, counterveil, equilibrate, equilibration, equipoise, offset, undo
**counterclockwise** anticlockwise, widdershins, withershins
**counterfeit** bogus, copy, dud, ersatz, fake, false, falsification, falsify, feign(ed), forged, forgery, fraudulent, imitation, mock, pretend(ed), sham, spurious
**counterfeit article** dud
**counterfeit note** forgery
**counterfeit weight** slang
**counterfoil** label, receipt, retainer, stub
**counterfoil of cheque** stub
**counter in pub** bar
**counter jumper** salesman, saleswoman
**counterpart** alternate, analogue, colleague, compeer, copy, ditto, duplicate, effigy, equal, equivalent, likeness, match, model, reflection, replica, rival, twin
**counterpoise** compensate, counterbalance
**counterpoison** antidote
**countertenor** alto
**counter used in various games** fish
**counting** calculating, checking, computing, (e)numerating, enumeration, estimating, mattering, numbering, reckoning, scoring, signifying, weighing
**counting device** abacus
**countless** endless, incalculable, infinite, innumerable, legion, limitless, measureless, myriad, uncounted, untold
**count of population** census
**count on** believe, rely, trust
**count out** disregard, eliminate, except, exclude, preclude
**countries' borders** international boundaries
**countries under one rule** empire

**countrified** agrarian, bucolic, country, country-born, homely, inurbane, provincial, rural, rustic, upcountry
**country** citizenry, homeland, land, landscape, nation, region, rural, rustic, scenery, state, terrain, territory
**country and western** hillbilly
**country aspect** landscape
**country bumpkin** hillbilly, yokel
**country dance** gavotte, reel
**country east of Syria** Iraq
**country fellow** jake, jasper
**country gentleman** squire
**country house** estate, grange, manor, villa
**country house in France** chateau
**country house with farm-buildings** grange
**country house with surroundings** place
**country in Africa** Niger, Uganda
**country in Arabia** Oman
**country in Asia** Iran, Iraq, Laos, Nepal, Syria
**country in East Africa** Kenya
**country in East Asia** Japan
**country in Europe** Italy
**country in Lhasa** Tibet
**country in North Africa** Chad, Morocco
**country in South America** Peru
**country in South East Asia** Laos
**country in southern Asia** Nepal
**country in the Balkans** Yugoslavia
**country in the Himalayas** Tibet
**country in West Africa** Ghana
**country in West Indies** Haiti
**country lane** byroad
**country leaver** emigrant, emigré
**countryman** bumpkin, compatriot, peasant, swain, yokel
**country north of China** Mongolia
**country of Lhasa** Tibet
**country on Yellow Sea** Korea
**country people** rustics
**country property** farm
**country residence** dacha, villa
**country ride on horseback** hack
**country road** lane
**country seat** estate
**country's gross earnings** GDP, GNP, national income
**countryside** landscape, outlook, panorama, picture, provinces, rural, scenery, sight, tableau, vista
**country villa in Russia** dacha
**country walk** hike
**country-wide** civil, governmental, national, public, state
**count up** add, enumerate, total
**count upon** anticipate, expect
**county** province, shire

**county bordering on North Wales** Cheshire
**county in England** Devon
**county in Wales** Anglesey, Flintshire, Glamorganshire
**county law officer** sheriff
**county of West Eire** Mayo
**coup** action, deed, exploit, feat, manoeuvre, masterstroke, stratagem, stroke, stunt, tour de force (F)
**coup de grâce** completion, deathblow, knockout
**coup d'état** coup, mutiny, overthrow, revolt, seizure, uprising
**couple** analogue, bi-, brace, conjoin, connect, duet, duo, dyad, join, link, marry, pair, partners, twin, two, twosome, unite, wed, yoke
**couple together** bracket
**coupling link** shackle
**courage** audacity, bold(ness), brave(ness), bravery, chivalry, daring, fearlessness, fortitude, gallantry, grit, guts, heart, heroism, intrepidity, mettle, mood, nerve, pluck, spunk, valiance, valour, virtue
**courage and courtesy** chivalry
**courage in battle** valour
**courageous** audacious, bold, brave, daring, fearless, gutsy, heroic, intrepid, plucky, resolute, stouthearted, valiant
**courageously and faithfully** animo et fide (L)
**courageous man** hero
**courageous person** lion-hearted
**courgette** baby marrow, zucchini
**courier** bearer, bellhop, callboy, carrier, conductor, express, guide, herald, leader, messenger, page, runner, transporter
**course** advance, bearing, behaviour, career, channel, direction, entrée, layer, method, mode, order, passage, path, procedure, process, progress, pursue, range, regularity, road, route, seminar, sequence, track, way
**course following main course** afters, dessert, sweet
**course in which anything moves or lies** direction
**course of action** career, mean, process
**course of action adopted** policy
**course of diet** dietary
**course of dinner** dessert, entrée, hors-d'œuvre, salad, soup
**course of life** curriculum vitae
**course of study at a university** curriculum

**course of teaching** syllabus
**course of travel** route
**course outline** syllabus
**course through life** career
**course travelled** route
**court** atrium, bar, bench, flatter, forum, homage, pursue, quad(rangle), respects, retinue, seek, staff, tribunal, woo, yard
**court action** assize, law, suit, trial
**court adjournment** recess
**court attendant** bailiff, clerk, courtier
**court buffoon** fool, jester
**court card** jack, king, queen
**courtcase** lawsuit, trial
**court dance** minuet
**court decision** verdict
**court defence** alibi
**courteous** affable, attentive, civil, courtly, elegant, gallant, gracious, mannerly, obliging, polished, polite, refined, respectful, urbane, well-bred, well-mannered
**courteous and helpful** obliging
**courtesan** fille de joie (F), harlot, hetaera, paramour, prostitute, quean, seductress, siren, trollop, whore
**courtesy** comity, friendliness
**court exhibit** evidence
**court game** tennis
**court hearing** trial
**courthouse surety** bail
**court injunction** writ
**court inquiry** hearing
**court jester** buffoon, fool
**courtliness** cajolery, ceremoniousness, ceremony, chivalrousness, civility, civilness, courteousness, decorum, dignity, diplomacy, elegancy, etiquette, flattery, formality, gallantness, gentlemanliness, politeness, refinedness, respect
**courtly gentleman** cavalier
**court meeting** session
**court officer in Scotland** macer
**court official** judge, magistrate, prosecutor
**court of justice** tribunal
**court of law** judicatory
**court order** bond, injunction, mandamus, subpoena, writ
**court order extract** estreat
**court panel** jury
**court penalty** fine, sentence
**court proceeding** trial
**courtroom declaration** plea
**courtroom event** trial
**courtroom official** usher
**court ruling** sentence
**court sitting** session

**court sport** netball, tennis
**court's verdict** judg(e)ment
**court with romance** woo
**courtyard** court, patio, quadrangle, yard
**courtyard of Arab house** hosh
**courtyard with a colonnade** piazza
**cousin** congener, cos, kin, kinsman, kinswoman, relative
**cousin of Absolom** Amasa
**cousin's father** uncle
**couth** cultured, well-mannered
**couture** dressmaking
**cove** anchorage, bay, creek, inlet, lagoon, ria, sound
**cover** asylum, cap, case, casing, clothe, coat(ing), conceal(ment), contain, counterbalance, couvert, covering, daub, defence, defend, disguise, dress, embrace, enshroud, envelop, enwrap, growth, guard, hide, insure, integument, lid, mask, offset, overlay, protect(ion), refuge, screen, secrete, shelter, shield, shroud, tegument, top, underbush, veil, woods
**cover and extend beyond** overlap
**cover cake in frosting** ice
**cover cake with sugar** ice
**cover charge** admission, fee, minimum
**covered** clad, cloaked, curtained, defended, described, detailed, disguised, guarded, hooded, insured, investigated, jacketed, masked, narrated, obscured, protected, recounted, reinforced, related, screened, shaded, sheltered, shrouded, veiled
**covered approach to entrance of building** porch
**covered by cloud** overcast
**covered by water** awash
**covered carriage** landau
**covered carriage drawn by two horses** cabriolet
**covered cloister** portico, stoa
**covered colonnade** stoa
**covered conduit** sewer
**covered dish** casserole
**covered drain** sewer
**covered entrance** porch
**covered entrance to a building** porte-cochere
**covered from the sun** shaded
**covered in band of colour** striped
**covered in moss** mossy
**covered passage** arcade
**covered pit for catching animals** pitfall
**covered porch** portico
**covered seat on elephant** haudah, howdah
**covered shopping walkway** arcade

**covered stall** kiosk
**covered thinly with gold** gilt
**covered trellis** pergola
**covered up** buried
**covered vehicle** van
**covered walk** arcade, cloister, pergola, portico, stoa
**covered walking surface** paving
**covered way** arcade
**covered with blood** gory
**covered with bristles** hispid
**covered with cedars** cedared
**covered with fur** furry
**covered with gold** aureate, gilded
**covered with grass** turfed, verdant
**covered with green vegetation** verdant
**covered with hair** pilose, pilous
**covered with paint** coated
**covered with pastry** pie
**covered with plants** overgrown
**covered with silky hair** sericeous
**covered with stiff hair** hispid
**covered with water** awash, flooded, inundated, sodden
**cover for bottle** lid
**cover for letter** envelope
**cover for light** lampshade
**cover for loose papers** folder
**cover for pot** lid
**cover for the bed** blanket, duvet, eider(down), quilt, sheet
**cover girl** model
**cover in flags** pave
**cover in folds** drape
**covering for ankle** gaiter, spat
**covering for a wound** dressing
**covering for face** mask, veil
**covering for foot** shoe
**covering for foot and lower leg** boot
**covering for hand** ga(u)ntlet, glove
**covering for head** beret, cap, coif, fez, hat
**covering for leg below knee** gaiter
**covering for shoulders** cape, shawl
**covering layer** coating
**covering of bud** calyx
**covering of canvas as shelter** awning, tent
**covering of cloth** gaiter
**covering of paint** coat
**covering of teeth** dentine
**covering of wheel** tyre
**covering on corn** husk
**covering over throne** canopy
**covering put over back and arms of chair** antimacassar
**covering the entire surface** all-over
**covering to keep the hands warm** glove, mitten, muff
**cover in paper** wrap

**coverlet** bedcover, counterpane, cover, duvet, eider(down), quilt
**cover of cooking utensil** lid
**cover of gramophone record** sleeve
**cover of mattress** ticking
**cover of the eye** eyelid
**cover oneself with** achieve, acquire, attain, collect, defend, guard, harvest, protect, receive, secure
**cover on pan** lid
**cover on wound** scab
**cover over window** shutter
**covers organ of sight** eyelid
**covers roof with straw** thatcher
**cover surface of** (over)spread
**covert** clandestine, concealed, disguised, hidden, secret(ive), unknown, veiled
**cover the inside of** line
**cover to keep teapot hot** cosy
**cover up** batten, camouflage, cloak, cloud, conceal, dissemble, enwrap, feign, hide, mask, obscure, repress, screen, secrete, shroud, suppress, whitewash, withhold
**cover-up** complicity, concealment, conspiracy, front, pretence, smoke-screen, whitewash
**cover wall with square slabs** tile
**cover with** anoint, smear
**cover with abuse** bespatter
**cover with alloy** braze
**cover with asphalt** pave, tar
**cover with bitumen** tar
**cover with cloth** drape
**cover with coating** encrust
**cover with concrete** pave
**cover with earth** bury
**cover with fabric** drape
**cover with firm surface** pave
**cover with first paint coat** prime
**cover with gems** bejewel
**cover with glass** glaze
**cover with plaster** parget
**cover with water** flood
**cover with wax** cere
**cover with zinc** galvanise
**covet** aspire, begrudge, crave, desire, envy, fancy, hanker, lust, ogle, want
**covetous** acquisitive, avaricious, desirous, envious, grasping, greedy, jealous, rapacious, selfish, stringy, yearning
**covetousness** acquisitiveness, appetite, ardour, avidity, craving, desire, eagerness, edacity, egocentricity, envy, graspingness, greed, gulosity, insatiability, itch, keenness, mania, passion, selfishness, thirst, yearning
**covin** collusion, conspiracy, deception, fraud

**cow** alarm, appal, awe, bovine, break, browbeat, bully, coerce, daunt, dishearten, dismay, domineer, frighten, heifer, intimidate, menace, oppress, overawe, overcome, petrify, scare, shock, subdue, terrify, threaten, tyrannise, unnerve
**coward** cad, chicken, cowardly, craven, dastard, faint-heart, milksop, papbroek, poltroon, renegade, sneak, timid
**cowardly** afraid, base, chicken-hearted, craven, dastardly, faint-hearted, fearful, frightened, poltroon, recreant, scared, spineless, timid, timorous, yellow
**cowardly buffoon** rascal, scaramouch
**cowardly colour** yellow
**cowardly fellow** caitiff, cur
**cowardly mammal** hy(a)ena
**cowardly person** sissy
**cow barn** byre, shed
**cowboy** bronco, buckaroo, cowpuncher, drover, gaucho, grazier, puncher, rider, vaquero
**cowboy event** rodeo
**cowboy gear** chaps
**cowboy greeting** howdy
**cowboy hat** stetson
**cowboy movie** Western
**cowboy of South America** gaucho
**cowboy's display** rodeo
**cowboy's footgear** boot
**cowboy's garment** chaps
**cowboy's hat** stetson
**cowboy show** rodeo
**cowboy's leather leggings** chaparajos, chaparejos, chaps
**cowboy's rope** lariat, lasso, riata
**cowboy's saddlebag** alforja
**cowboy's spade** loy
**cowboy's task** roping
**cowed** abject, alarmed, appalled, beaten, bullied, coerced, cringing, defeated, downcast, dragooned, frightened, frustrated, furtive, guilty, hangdog, humble, intimidated, overawed, overcome, overwhelmed, passive, petrified, scared, shocked, startled, terrified, tyrannised, unnerved, vanquished, wretched
**cower** crawl, cringe, crouch, fawn, flinch, grovel, quail, quake, shake, shiver, shrink, skulk, slink, slouch, sneak, stoop, toady, tremble, truckle, wallow, wince
**cowhide** leather
**cowhouse** byre, vachery
**cowl** canonicals, covering, headgear, hood
**cowlike** bovine
**cowlike African antelope** gnu

**cow noise** moo
**co-worker** ally, associate, collaborator, colleague, companion, compeer, comrade, confederate, equal, follower, friend, mate, member, partner, peer, team-mate
**cows** cattle
**cows and oxen** kine
**cow's call** moo
**cow's edible stomach lining** tripe
**cow shelter** byre
**cowslip** marigold, marsh, paigle
**cow's low** moo
**cow's mammary gland** udder
**cow's milk-sack** udder
**cow sound** low, moo
**cow's partner** bull
**cow talk** moo
**cow without horns** mul(l)ey
**coxcomb** jackanapes
**cox or pippin** apple
**coxswain** airman, aviator, captain, director, flier, guide, helmsman, leader, navigator, pilot, steersman
**coy** affected, arch, backward, bashful, coquettish, demure, diffident, evasive, flirtatious, flirty, kittenish, maidenly, meek, modest, philandering, prudish, reluctant, reserved, retiring, shrinking, shy, tame, timid, unassuming, unconfident, unpretentious, unsocial, virginal, withdrawn
**coyly** shyly
**coyote** prairie wolf
**coypu** nutria
**cozen** cheat, deceive
**cozener** cheater, deceiver
**cozy room** den
**crab** crosspatch, grouch, nag, pinnothere
**crabbed handwriting** illegible
**crab roe** coral
**crab's claw** chela
**crab shell** carapace
**crack** breach, break, chink, clap, crackle, crevice, fissure, flaw, fracture, pop, report, retort, rift, snap, splinter, split
**crack down on** check, end, stop
**cracked leaves** rimose
**cracked up** exaggerated, overpraised, overrated
**crack fighter pilot** ace
**crack in fissures of skin** chap
**crackling chest sound** rale
**crackling in sound** snappy
**crackpot** crank, nut, oddball
**cracksman** burglar
**crack up** break down, collapse
**cradle** cot, crib
**cradlesong** berceuse, lullaby

**cradling** holding, lulling, nestling, nursing, rocking, supporting
**craft** ability, aptitude, art, artfulness, artifice, boat, calling, cunning, deceit, dexterity, ingenuity, métier, plane, shrewdness, skill, subtlety, talent, trade, vocation
**craftier** slier
**craftily** artfully, astutely, calculatingly, cannily, cunningly, deceitfully, designingly, deviously, foxily, fraudulently, guilefully, knowingly, schemingly, sharply, shrewdly, slily, slyly, trickily
**craftiness** artfulness, astuteness, canniness, cunning(ness), deceitfulness, deviousness, foxiness, guile(fulness), knowingness, sharpness, shrewdness, slyness, subtleness, trickiness, wile, wiliness
**craft requiring skill** trade
**craftsman** artificer, artisan, artist, genius, hand, master, mechanic, producer, talent, workman
**craftsman in cloth** tailor, weaver
**craftsman in metal** smith
**craftsman in stone** mason
**craftsman in wood** carpenter
**craftsman of furniture** cabinet-maker
**crafty** artful, arty, astute, calculating, canny, crooked, cunning, deceitful, designing, devious, dishonest, foxy, fraudulent, guileful, insidious, knowing, plotting, scheming, sharp, shrewd, skilful, sleekit (Sc), sly, subtle, tricky, wily
**crafty animal** fox
**crafty competitor** gamesman
**craggy** asymmetrical, barbed, broken, bumpy, cleft, crooked, elliptic, irregular, jagged, lopsided, notched, pointed, ragged, rocky, rough, rugged, serrated, spiked, stony, unequal, uneven
**craggy hill** tor
**cram** cloy, compact, compress, condense, crowd, crush, fill, force, glut, jam, overcrowd, overfill, overindulge, pack, press, ram, satiate, shove, squeeze, stuff, surfeit
**cramp** abort, arrest, barrier, bridle, check, clamp, confine, convulsion, damper, direct, drive, fastening, hamper, hinder, hindrance, impede, incapacitate, obstruction, pang, preclusion, restrain, restrict(ion), secure, spasm, staple, steer, stopper, throe
**cramped** awkward, checked, circumscribed, clogged, confined, congested, crowded, encumbered, hampered, handicapped, impeded, narrow, obstructed, overcrowded, packed, restricted, squeezed, uncomfortable
**cramp in a muscle** myalgia
**cramp one's style** frustrate, hamper, impede, inhibit, obstruct
**cram together** bunch
**crane** bird, davit, derrick, elevator, hoist, lift, tackle, winch
**crane on board ship** davit
**crane support** gantry
**crane user** rigger
**cranial nerve** trigeminal
**cranial pain** headache
**cranium** brainpan, crown, head, noodle, pate, pericranium, poll, sconce, skull
**crank** crackpot
**crank of wheel** winch
**cranky** cross, crotchety
**cranny** breach, break, cavity, chap, chink, chip, cleft, crack, crevice, cut, fissure, fracture, gap, gash, groove, hole, interstice, interval, nook, opening, rent, rift, rut, slit, space, split, stria
**crapulence** drunkenness
**crash** accident, break, collapse, collide, collision, depression, failure, falling, impact, prang, shatter, smash
**crash against** hit
**crash helmet** skidlid
**crash into** ram
**crass** asinine, boorish, bovine, coarse, doltish, gross, oafish, obtuse, stupid, thick, unrefined, witless
**crassly** stupidly
**crater** abyss, caldera, cavity, cleft, cup, depression, dip, fovea, gulf, hole, hollow, niche, opening, pit, shell-hole
**crater in Hawaii** Kilauea
**crater lake near Naples** Averno
**cravat** scarf, tie
**crave** ask, beg, beseech, covet, demand, desire, dictate, entreat, fancy, implore, itch, need, petition, pray, require, seek, solicit, sue, supplicate, thirst, want, yearn
**crave for** covet, long
**craven** afraid, base, caitiff, coward(ly), dastard(ly), faint-heart(ed), fearful, lily-livered, milksop, nid(d)ering, poltroon, pusillanimous, recreant, renegade, scared, shrinking, sissy, sneak, soft, spineless, timid, timorous, weak(ling), yellow
**craven coward** poltroon
**craving** hunger, desire, concupiscence, hankering, longing, lust, thirst, urge, yearning, yen
**craving food** voracious
**craving for food** hungry, sitomania
**craving for intoxicating drink** dipsomania
**craving for liquid** thirst(y)
**craw** crop
**crawl** cower, creep, cringe, crouch, enclosure, fawn, grovel, inch, pedestrianism, pen, skulk, slide, slink, slither, sneak, worm
**crawling with pests** verminous
**crayfish** crawfish, crustacean, lobster
**crayfish egg** berry
**crayfish segment** metamere
**craze** dement, enrage, excite, fad, fancy, fascination, furore, infatuation, madden, mania, mode, passion, quirk, rage, session, unsettle, vogue, whim
**crazed** berserk, bewitched, broken, chipped, convulsive, cracked, crazy, cursed, defective, delirious, demented, deranged, distracted, distraught, faulty, fissured, flawed, frantic, frenzied, hysterical, imperfect, insane, irrational, lunatic, mad(dened), obsessed, overwrought, psychotic, rabid, raving, split, unbalanced, uncontrollable, unhinged, violent, wild
**craze for collecting books** bibliomania
**crazily ridiculous** zany
**crazy** absurd, bananas, batty, berserk, bonkers, confused, cracked, crazed, daft, demented, deranged, dippy, dotty, feebleminded, foolish, frantic, giddy, idiotic, impractical, inane, inconsequential, insane, irrelevant, loose, lunatic, mad, maniacal, nutty, potty, preposterous, raving, senseless, shaky, silly, stupid, weak, zany
**crazy person** nutter, wacky
**creak** grate, grind, grit, groan, jangle, jar, rasp, scrape, scratch, scream, screech, shriek, shrill, squeak, squeal, stridulate
**cream** balm, beat, best, choice, cosmetic, drub, élite, emulsion, flower, foam, liniment, lotion, oil, ointment, paste, pick, prime, prize, salve, skim, unguent, whip
**cream cake** éclair, gateau
**creamery** buttermaker
**cream-filled almond-flavoured pastry** frangipane
**cream of society** élite
**cream of the crop** best, choice
**cream protection for the skin** sun-tan lotion
**cream sauce with cheese flavouring** mornay

**creamy cheese** Brie, Camembert, Gervais
**creamy dessert** mousse
**creamy dish** mousse
**creamy meat sauce** velouté
**crease** clam, corrugate, crinkle, crumple, crunkle, fold, gaw, jumble, line, plait, pleat, ruck, ruga, suture, tuck, wrinkle
**crease in the skin** wrinkle
**create** cause, design, invent, make, manufacture, occasion, originate, produce
**create again** re-establish
**create by thought** invent
**created by imagination** fictive
**create enmity** embitter
**create in music** compose
**creates slippery surface** grease, ice, oil, soap
**creating dread** awesome
**creative** adept, artistic, arty, clever, constructive, endowed, fertile, formative, gifted, imaginative, ingenious, inventive, original, productive, prolific, resourceful, skilled, talented, visionary
**creative ability** imagination
**creative artist** poet
**creative craft** art
**creative impulse** afflatus, genius, inspiration
**creative poet** makar (Sc)
**creative pursuit** art
**creative skill** art
**creative thought** imagination
**creative work** art
**creator** architect, author, initiator, inventor, maker, originator
**creator of Sherlock Holmes** Doyle
**creature** animal, beast, being, bird, body, critter, dependent, entity, fellow, fish, human, individual, mammal, man, object, person, product, quadruped, reptile, somebody, someone, something, soul, thing, woman
**creature of Aboriginal myth** Bunyip
**creature's den** lair
**creature that lives in the soil** earthworm
**creature with shell** snail
**crèche** day-nursery, nursery
**credence** assurance, belief, confidence, credit(ability), dependence, faith, reliability, reliance, security, trust
**credit** acclaim, account, acknowledgement, ascribe, attribute, attribution, believe, confide, dueness, esteem, faith, glory, honour, kudos, loan, merit, rebate,
recognition, rely, repute, subvention, thank, trust
**creditable** estimable, honourable, meritorious, praiseworthy, reputable, respectable
**credit buying system** hire-purchase
**creditor in a mortgage** mortgagee
**credit side of trade balance** exports
**credit to** accredit, accuse, ascribe, assign, attribute, impute
**credo** code, creed, doctrine, motto, philosophy, tenet
**credulous** believing, deludable, gullible, naive, trustful, trusting, uncritical, undoubting, unsophisticated, unsuspecting, unsuspicious
**creed** -ism, articles, axiom, belief, canon, confession, conviction, credo, cult, denomination, doctrine, dogma, faith, Nicene, principles, religion, sect, tenet, theorem
**creek** bay(ou), brook, channel, cove, estuary, geo, gio, harbour, inlet, ria, rill, rivulet, strait, stream, tributary, watercourse
**creep** crawl, dawdle, drip, inch, jerk, sneak
**creeper** climber, ivy, rambler, runner, vine
**creeper-covered** ivied
**creeper sacred to Bacchus** ivy
**creeper's anchor** tendril
**creeper support** pergola
**creep forward** inch
**creeping palm** nipa
**creeping perennial grass** zoysia
**creeping plant** ipecac, kareao, kareau, pennywort, trailer
**creeping shoot** flagellum, runner
**creeping thing** reptile
**creepy** awful, disgusting, eerie, gruesome, horrible, menacing, scary
**creepy-crawly** insect
**cremation pile** pyre
**cremation vessel** urn
**cremation woodpile** pyre
**crematorium** cinerator
**crème de la crème** elite
**Cremona violin maker** Amati
**Creole dish** jambalaya
**crescent** bow-shaped, convexo-concave, crescine, curved, demilune, half-moon, hemicycle, increasing, lune, lunette, lunula, meniscus, scythe, semicircle, sickle, waxing
**crescent-shaped** lunate
**crescent-shaped bone forming part of the wrist** lunate
**crescent-shaped roll** croissant
**crest** apex, badge, cap, climax, comb, crista, crown, culmination, device, emblem, head, insignia, mane, peak, pinnacle, plume, ridge, summit, surmount, symbol, tassel, top, tuft
**crested bird** quez(t)al, trogon
**crested parrot** cockatoo
**crest of a cock** (cocks)comb
**crest of feathers** topknot
**crest of hill** knap
**Cretan bay** Canea, Kanca, Kisamo, Mesara, Suda
**Cretan cape** Buza, Liano, Lithinon, Salome, Sidero, Sidheros, Spatha, Stavros
**Cretan gulf** Khania, Merabello
**Cretan monster** minotaur
**Cretan port** Candia
**Cretan princess** Ariadne
**crevice** aperture, breach, break, chap, chasm, chink, cleft, crack, cranny, crevasse, ditch, fissure, fracture, furrow, gap, gash, gorge, groove, hole, interstice, narrow, opening, orifice, rent, rift, rupture, separation, slit, split, stria, sulcus, trench
**crew** force, gang, group, hands, pack, squad, team
**crib** bed, cheat, cot, cradle, manger, pilfer, pirate, plagiarise, purloin, steal
**cribbage score** peg
**cricket** grig
**cricket arbiter** umpire
**cricket ball** edger
**cricket bowl** googly, swerve, yorker
**cricket catch** dolly
**cricket club** bat
**cricketer** batsman, bowler, fielder
**cricketer on boundary** outfielder
**cricketers' building** pavilion
**cricket extra** bye
**cricket field** pitch
**cricket goal** wicket
**cricket ground in London** Lords
**cricket judge** umpire
**cricket-like insect** grasshopper
**cricket line** crease
**cricket official** umpire
**cricket pitch** wicket
**cricket position** leg, mid-on, slip
**cricket referee** umpire
**cricket score** runs
**cricket sequence** over
**cricket side** eleven, XI
**cricket sundry** extra
**cricket symbol** Ashes
**cricket team** eleven, XI
**cricket team's batting turn** innings
**cricket term** googly, over, tice, yorker
**cricket thrower** bowler
**cricket trophy** Ashes
**cricket wicket piece** bail, stump

**crime** assault, atrocity, battery, breach, embezzlement, fault, felony, infraction, misdeed, misdemeanour, offence, outrage, robbery, sin, theft, tort, transgression, trespass(ing), villainy, violation, wrong
**crime against state** treason
**crime by a public official** malfeasance
**crime file** dossier
**crime of fire-raising** arson
**crime of having two wives or husbands** bigamy
**crime provoked by sexual jealousy** crime passionel
**crime regarded by the law as grave** felony
**criminal** bent, convict, corrupt, crook, culpable, culprit, delinquent, desperado, evil-doer, felon, felonious, guilty, hoodlum, illegal, illicit, immoral, indictable, jailbird, lawbreaker, lawless, malefactor, nefarious, offender, outlaw, sinful, sinner, skolly, transgressor, tsotsi, unlawful, unrighteous, vicious, wicked, wrong
**criminal act** felony, infamy, murder, offence
**criminal activity** racket
**criminal deception** fraud
**criminal fire-setting** arson
**criminal group** gang
**criminal's escape** get away
**criminal undergoing imprisonment** convict
**criminal violence** thuggery
**crimped edging** frill
**crimson** bloody, blush, burgundy, cardinal, carmine, cerise, cramoisy, maroon, red, scarlet, vermilion
**crimson alkaline dye** magenta
**crimson colour** carmine, lake, magenta
**cringe** blench, cower, dodge, duck, flinch, grovel, quail, quiver, recoil
**cringe at** dread
**crinkly fabric** crêpe
**crinkly sheet of paper** crêpe
**crinky cabbage** kale
**cripple** amputee, becripple, damage, disable, enervate, handicap, impair, injure, invalid, lame, maim, maltreat, mangle, mar, mutilate, paralytic, ruin, scar, weaken
**crippled** bedridden, deformed, disabled, gammy, handicapped, lame, paralysed
**crises** emergencies
**crisis** calamity, catastrophe, climax, conjuncture, critical, crunch, dilemma, disaster, emergency, exigency, extremity, head, impasse, juncture, mess, pass, pinch, plight, predicament, rub, strait, trouble, turning-point
**crisp** bracing, breakable, brisk, brittle, chilly, cool, crumbly, crunchy, hard, lively, refreshing, resolved, spruce, stimulating, terse, unwilted
**crisp batter cake** waffle
**crisp bread in long thin strips** grissini
**crisp fruit** apple
**crispin** shoemaker
**crisping of the hair** frisure
**crisp knot-shaped salted biscuit** pretzel
**crisp lettuce** cos, iceberg
**crisp Mexican tortilla** taco
**crispness** briefness, briskness, brittleness, brusqueness, clearness, crispiness, firmness, freshness, incisiveness, pithiness, shortness, tartness, terseness
**crisp outside** crust
**crisp skin of roast pork** crackling
**crisp vegetable** celery, cos, lettuce
**criss-cross weave** plaid
**criteria** canons, gauges, measures, norms, principles, rules, standards, tests, yardsticks
**criterion** barometer, canon, code, example, gauge, guide(line), maxim, measure, model, norm, original, paradigm, pattern, principle, rule, scale, standard, test, touchstone, type, yardstick
**critic** carper, censor, connoisseur, fault-finder, judge, reviewer
**critical** accurate, acute, all-important, analytical, captious, carping, cavilling, censorious, crucial, dangerous, decisive, derogatory, determining, diagnostic, dire, disapproving, discerning, discriminating, disparaging, essential, exact, fastidious, fault-finding, grave, judicial, momentous, nit-picking, penetrating, perilous, precarious, precise, pressing, risky, serious, severe, uncomplimentary, urgent, vital
**critical examination** test
**critical remark** stricture
**critical trial** test
**criticise** adjudge, analyse, appraise, assess, attack, blame, carp, cavil, censure, condemn, denounce, disapprove, discriminate, disparage, evaluate, examine, flay, judge, malign, reproach, reprove, scan, slate, survey, treat, vilify
**criticise abusively** revile
**criticise harshly** attack
**criticise in a hostile manner** animadvert
**criticise mercilessly** roast, scarify
**criticise savagely** scalp
**criticise severely** castigate, clobber, fray, pan, slam, slate
**criticism** analysis, animadversion, appraisal, appreciation, assessment, blame, brickbat, censure, comment, commentary, critique, disapproval, disparagement, elucidation, evaluation, fault-finding, flak, judg(e)ment, knocking, notice, review, stricture
**critique of TV programme** review
**croaky** grating, gravelly, gruff, guttural, harsh, hoarse, husky, rasping, raucous, throaty
**crochet** tat
**crockery** china, dishes
**crockery item** cup, dish, plate, saucer
**Crockett's fort** Alamo
**crocodile** alligator, gavial, g(h)arial
**crocodilian** caiman, cayman
**Croesus's agent** Aesop
**Croesus's land** Lydia
**Cromwell's follower** Roundhead
**Cromwell's nickname** Noll
**crone** fury, hag, harridan, shrew, termagant, virago, vixen, witch
**crony** accomplice, ally, associate, bra, broer, chum, cohort, collaborator, colleague, companion, compeer, comrade, confederate, confidant(e), consort, familiar, fellow, friend, intimate, mate, pal, partner, peer, playmate
**crook** cheat, criminal, crosier, crozier, curve, gangster, hook, racketeer, robber, rogue, shark, shyster, swindler, thief, villain
**crooked** askew, awry, bent, crippled, curved, deceitful, deformed, devious, disfigured, dishonest, fraudulent, illegal, lopsided, misshapen, treacherous, twisted, unlawful, unscrupulous, wry
**crooked lawyer** shyster
**croon** breathe, hum, purr, sing, warble
**crop** clip, craw, curtail, cut, fruits, gathering, harvest, lop, mow, pare, produce, prune, reaping, reduce, shear, snip, top, trim, vintage, yield
**crop grain** reap
**crop hair** poll
**crop of bird or insect** craw
**crop of China** rice
**crop of fowl** maw
**crop of hawk** gorge
**cropped hair** stubble
**crop pest** locust
**crop protector** scarecrow
**crop up** appear, arise, arrive, emerge, happen, occur

**croquet arc** hood
**croquet stick** mallet
**croquet wicket** hoop
**crosier** criminal, crook, crozier, swindler, villain
**cross** angry, baffle, burden, cantankerous, churlish, contradict, cranky, frustrate, frustration, glowering, hybridise, intersect, irascible, irate, irritable, mean, misery, misfortune, moody, morose, oppose, opposing, opposition, peevish, petulant, resentful, spiteful, sullen, thwart(ing), touchy, traverse, trouble, unkind, unpleasant
**cross-aisle** transept
**cross and rude** surly
**crossbar of window** transom
**crossbeam** transom, trave
**cross between a tangerine, grapefruit and orange** ugli
**cross between he-ass and mare** mule
**crossbred** half-breed, hybrid, mongrel
**crossbred animal** hybrid, mule
**crossbred hunting dog** lurcher
**crossbred plant** hybrid
**crossbreed** blend, combination, cross, cur, hybrid(ise), interbreed, mix(ture), mongrel
**cross-connection of arteries** anastomosis
**cross-country horse-race** steeplechase
**cross-country race around a course marked by flags** point-to-point
**cross-country skiing** langlauf
**cross-fertilisation** xenogamy
**cross-fertilisation in flowering plants** allogamy
**crossing** blending, bridge, bridging, crisscrossing, crossbreeding, hybridising, interbreeding, intersecting, intersection, intertwining, lacing, meeting, mixing, plying, span(ning), traversing
**crossing-out** deletion
**crossing the ocean** transoceanic
**Cross inscription** INRI (Iesus Nazarenus Rex Iudaeorum)
**cross intricately** interlace
**Cross letters** INRI (Iesus Nazarenus Rex Iudaeorum)
**cross-lined pattern of squares** check, chequer
**cross one's heart** pledge, vow
**cross one's path** encounter
**cross out** cancel, delete, eliminate, erase, obliterate, remove
**cross over** bridge
**crosspatch** crab, grouch
**crosspiece of ladder** rung
**crosspiece on mast** yard-arm

**crosspiece on top of wicket in cricket** bail
**cross someone's palm** bribe, corrupt, entice, induce, influence, lure, suborn, tempt
**cross-stitch** herringbone
**cross-stitch embroidery on canvas** gros point
**cross-stroke on letter** serif
**cross swords** argue, battle, contend, disagree, dispute, fight, haggle, scuffle, struggle, wrangle
**cross-thread in weaving** weft
**crossways** angled, cross(wise), diagonal, oblique, slanting, transverse
**cross with one step** stride
**Cross words** INRI (Iesus Nazarenus Rex Iudaeorum)
**crotch** angle, bend, bifurcation, cleft, corner, crook, crotchet, crutch, cusp, divarication, division, edge, elbow, fork, grains, groin, intersection, knee, loins, nook, notch, point, post
**crotchet** caprice, eccentricity, fad, fancy, fault, fetish, oddity, quirk, singularity, trait, vagary, whim(sy)
**crotchety** awkward, contrary, cranky, cross, grumpy, irritable, peevish, testy
**crotchety behaviour** fantod
**Croton bug** German cockroach
**croton oil** tigline
**crouch** bend, bow, cower, cringe, duck, hunch, kneel, squat, stoop
**crouch with fear** cower, cringe, flinch
**crow** boast, brag, exult, gloat, raven, rook, strut, swagger, triumph, vaunt
**crowbar** jemmy, lever, pry
**crowd** assemble, audience, company, concourse, cram, herd, horde, masses, mob, multitude, pack, people, plebeians, populace, press, proletariat, rabble, shove, spectators, swarm, thrang (Sc), throng
**crowded** compressed, congested, dense, filled, jammed, milled, serried, thronged
**crowded collection** cluster
**crowded to capacity** packed
**crowded together** dense
**crowded untidy state** clutter
**crowd of children** smytrie (Sc)
**crowd of people** mass, multitude, press, throng
**crowd round** besiege
**crowd together** huddle, pack
**crowd trouble** riot
**crowfoot** orchis
**crowlike bird** raven

**crown** chaplet, circlet, coronal, diadem, distinction, honour, laurels, royalty, ruler, sovereign, tiara, trophy
**Crown colony** Hong Kong
**crowning mercy** godsend
**crown of athlete** laurel
**crown of head** pate, sconce
**crown-shaped headband of precious metal set with jewels** coronet
**crow's call** caw
**crow's relative** daw
**crucial** acute, central, critical, dangerous, decisive, demanding, determining, essential, fundamental, grave, important, intense, momentous, pivotal, serious, severe, urgent, vital
**crucial factor** key
**crucial moment** crisis
**crucial point** crux
**crucial time** crisis
**crucial turning point** crisis
**crucifix** cross, rood
**crucify** distress, excruciate, execute, harrow, persecute, rack, torment, torture, trouble, wring
**crude** awkward, blunt, boorish, clumsy, coarse, earthy, incomplete, raw, rough, rude, uncouth, undeveloped, unfinished, unpolished, unrefined, vulgar
**crude Australian** ocker
**crude conveyance** raft
**crude cream of tartar** argol
**crude fellow** stiff
**crude house** hut
**crude in artistic quality** raw
**crude metal** ore
**crude person** beast, boor, brute, bumpkin, clodhopper, clodpole, lout, peasant, ruffian, rustic, slob, swain
**crude potassium carbonate** potash
**crude sulphide mixture** matte
**crude tartar** argol
**crudity** bawdiness, churlishness, coarseness, commonness, crudeness, filth, impropriety, indecency, indelicacy, inelegance, lewdness, loudness, lowness, obscenity, offensiveness, prurience, rawness, rudeness, tactlessness, unrefinement, vulgarity
**cruel** barbarian, bitter, bloodthirsty, brutal, brutish, callous, ferocious, hard, heartless, inhuman, merciless, nasty, pitiless, relentless, ruthless, sadistic, savage, severe, truculent, unkind, unmerciful
**cruel and arbitrary use of authority** tyranny
**cruel and barbarous** inhuman
**cruel arsonist** Nero

**cruel biblical king** Herod
**cruel grasping woman** harpy
**cruel handling of a person**
    maltreatment
**cruel killing** butchery, hacking
**cruel king of Judea** Herod
**cruel person** fiend, ogre, sadist
**cruel Roman emperor** Nero
**cruel Roman fiddler** Nero
**cruel ruler** tyrant
**cruel Russian** Ivan
**cruelty** barbarity, bestiality, bloodthirstiness, brutality, brutishness, callousness, cold-bloodedness, depravity, devil(t)ry, diablerie, ferocity, grimness, hardheartedness, harshness, inhumanity, masochism, oppressiveness, ruthlessness, sadism, savagery, severity, spite(fulness), venom, viciousness
**cruise** coast, drift, sail, voyage
**crumb** atom, bit, dot, fragment, fritter, grain, minim, mite, molecule, morsel, nip, particle, pinch, scrap, seed, shred, sliver, snip(pet), soupçon, speck, splinter, trifle
**crumble** crush, decay, fragment, grate, powder, splinter
**crumble away** moulder
**crumbled building** ruin
**crumble easily** crisp, friable
**crumbly** breakable, brittle, crisp(y), crunchy, delicate, firm, fissile, fragile, frail, frangible, friable, powdery, shivery, short, soft, unwilted
**crumbly mixture** streusel
**crumbly stone** malm
**crumple** crease, crush, pucker, rumple, wrinkle
**crunch** bite, break, bruise, champ, chew, compress, crease, crisis, crush, crux, gnaw, grind, grip, mash, masticate, munch, nibble, nip, pierce, pinch, pound, rumple, seize, squeeze, tear, wound, wrinkle
**crunchy** crisp
**crunchy salad vegetable** celery
**crusade** campaign, cause, drive, jihad, movement, push
**Crusader's foe** Saracen
**crush** break, bruise, compress, conquer, crumble, disintegrate, infatuation, overpower, overwhelm, pound, powder, press, pulverise, quash, quell, smash, squeeze, subdue, swat, trample
**crushed** broken, bruised
**crushed coffee or cocoa beans** nib
**crushed maize** samp
**crush flat or to pulp** squash

**crushing** breaking, bruising, compressing, conquering, creasing, crumbling, crumpling, crunching, mashing, overcoming, overpowering, overwhelming, pounding, pulverising, quelling, repressive, rumpling, scotching, shattering, smashing, squeezing, subduing, vanquishing, wrinkling
**crushing of a calculus in the bladder by means of an instrument**
    lithotrity
**crushing plant** breaker
**crushing snake** anaconda, boa, python
**crushing tooth** molar
**crush inward** stave
**crush noisily** crunch
**crush out of shape** stave
**crush to powder** grind, pound
**crush underfoot** trample
**crush utterly** overwhelm
**crush with teeth** chew, grind
**crustacean** barnacle, crab, crayfish, isopod, krill, lobster, pedipalp, prawn, shrimp
**crustacean catcher** shrimper
**crustacean on ship hull** barnacle
**crustaceans, insects, etc.** arthropoda
**crustacean's tail** flapper
**crusted dessert or dish** pie
**crust formed over wound** scab
**crustiness** brittleness, brusqueness, captiousness, crisp(i)ness, crossness, curtness, friableness, gruffness, hardness, irritableness, peevishness, prickliness, shortness, surliness, testiness, touchiness
**crust of bread** heel
**crust of the earth** lithosphere
**crust on old port** beeswing
**crust on sore** scab
**crusty** brittle, brusque, captious, choleric, crabbed, crabby, crisp(y), cross, curt, friable, grouchy, gruff, hard, ill-humoured, irritable, peevish, prickly, short, short-tempered, snappish, snarling, surly, testy, touchy, well-baked, well-done
**crusty dessert** pie
**crusty growth on tree trunks** lichen
**crux** basics, centre, change, climax, core, crisis, crunch, essence, facts, focus, gist, heart, height, hub, kernel, marrow, mid(dle), nub, nucleus, pith, pivot, point, quintessence, reality, root, substance
**cry** announcement, appeal, bawl, bemoan, bewail, blubber, call, clamour, ejaculate, entreaty, exclaim, exclamation, greet (Sc), grieve, ho, howl, lament(ation), moan, outcry, proclaim,

proclamation, roar, rumour, scream, screech, shout, shriek, sob, sorrow, squall, vociferate, wail, weep, whimper, whoop, yell, yelp
**cry aloud** blart, grede
**cry and whine softly** whimper
**cry as a chick** chirp, peep
**cry as a sheep** bleat
**cry at bullfight** olé
**cry at the hunt** yoicks
**cry audibly** sob
**cry convulsively** sob
**cry down** belittle, cheapen, debase, denigrate, disparage, underrate
**cry feebly** mewl
**cry for again** encore
**cry for court silence** oyez
**cry for mercy** miserere
**cry for silence** oyez
**cry for truce** parley
**cry fretfully** grizzle
**cry heard at bullfight** olé
**cry hoarsely** croup
**cry in bullring** olé
**crying** demanding, flagrant, important, urgent, wailing, weeping
**crying like dog** yelling
**crying of hound** belling
**cry like dog** whine
**cry like elephant** barr, trumpet
**cry like pig** wrine
**cry like sheep** bleat
**cry loudly** bawl, howl, roar, shout, sob, wail
**cry noisily** squall, yell
**cry of amazement** ooh
**cry of ass** bray
**cry of approval** bravo, hurrah, olé
**cry of baby** mewl, pule
**cry of bacchanals** evoe
**cry of bat** chip
**cry of bird** birdcall, caw(k), chir(ru)p, clang, coo, pew
**cry of bittern** bill, boom
**cry of cat** mew, miaou, miaow
**cry of contempt** bah, boo
**cry of crow** caw, croak
**cry of deer** bell
**cry of delight** ah(a), oh
**cry of derision** catcall
**cry of disapproval** boo, catcall, hoot
**cry of disbelief** no, tut, what
**cry of discovery** aha, eureka
**cry of disgust** bah, boo
**cry of distress** moan, wail
**cry of dog** bark, bay
**cry of donkey** bray, heehaw
**cry of duck** quack
**cry of encouragement** yoicks
**cry of excitement** wow
**cry of exclamation** hosanna
**cry off** cancel, quit, withdraw

**cry of fox** bark
**cry of goat** bleat
**cry of goose** honk, yang
**cry of grief** alas
**cry of horse** neigh, whinny
**cry of hound** mute
**cry of hounds in pursuit** bay
**cry of jackal** pheal(e), pheeal
**cry of lion** roar
**cry of new-born child** vagitus (L)
**cry of owl** hoot, ululu
**cry of pain** ouch, ow, yelp
**cry of praise to God** hosanna
**cry of raven** cronk, qualm
**cry of revulsion** ugh
**cry of rutting buck** troat
**cry of sheep** baa, bl(e)at
**cry of snipe** scape
**cry of sorrow** alack, alas, ay, ullagone
**cry of surprise** aha, alas, oh
**cry of terror** scream
**cry of triumph** ah, voila
**cry of turkey** goggle
**cry of wild goose** honk
**cry of woe** alas
**cry out** ejaculate, exclaim, scream, yell
**cry out loudly** scream, sob, yell
**cry over** bewail
**crypt** catacomb, cavern, cell, cellar, chamber, grave, grotto, mausoleum, recess, sepulchre, tomb, undercroft, underground, vault
**cryptic** abrupt, arcane, brief, cab(b)alistic, concealed, curt, dark, elliptic(al), enigmatic, esoteric, hermetic, hidden, indefinite, ineffable, inexplicable, mysterious, mystic(al), nebulous, obscure, occult, secret, short, sibyllic, supernatural, terse, unclear, vague, veiled
**cryptogam** acrogen, moss
**cryptogamous cell** spore
**cryptogam's seed** spore
**cryptogram** cipher, code, crypt, enigma, puzzle
**cry shrilly** shriek
**crystal gaze** scry
**crystal gazing** scrying
**crystalline mineral** spar
**crystallised fruit** glacé
**crystallised sugar** candy
**cry to frighten animal** shoo
**cry weakly** pule
**cry with a loud voice** vociferate
**cub** apprentice, beginner, pup, reporter, youngling, youth
**Cuban bay** Broa
**Cuban cape** Cruz, Lucrecia
**Cuban capital** Habana (Sp), Havana
**Cuban castle** Morro
**Cuban cigar** Havana

**Cuban coin** centavo, cuarenta, peso
**Cuban dance** conga, danzon, guaracha, habanera, rumba
**Cuban dictator** Castro
**Cuban falls** Agabama, Caburni, Toa
**Cuban gourd instrument** maracas
**Cuban gulf** Anamaria, Batabano, Mexico
**Cuban island** Camaguey, Sabana
**Cuban leader** Castro
**Cuban money** peso
**Cuban Negro dance** rumba
**Cuban peasant dance** guajira
**Cuban province** Camaguey, Havana, Matanzas, Oriente
**Cuban seaport** Santiago de Cuba
**Cuban smoke** cigar
**Cuban swamp** Zapata
**Cuban tobacco** capa, vuelta
**cube** bar, block, brick, di(c)e, hexahedron, hunk, ingot, lump, mass, measure, six-sided square, slab, solid, square, tessera
**cubeb** cigarette
**cubed** diced
**cube of chance** di(c)e
**cube of ten** thousand
**cube of two** eight
**cube root of eight** two
**cube root of thousand** ten
**cube's side** square
**cubical block used in mosaic** tessera
**cubic capacity of ship** tonnage
**cubic content** capacity, volume
**cubicle** alcove, bay, bedroom, berth, booth, carriage, cavity, cell, chamber, compartment, dungeon, enclosure, hall, hollow, locker, niche, pigeonhole, room, section, stall
**cubicle for trying on garments** fitting room
**cubic measure** stere
**cubic metre** stere
**Cubist painter** Picasso
**cub scout group** pack
**cub shark** lamia
**cub's mother** lioness, tigress
**cuckoo** ani
**cuckoopint** arum
**cucumber-flavoured leaves** borage
**cucurbitaceous vine** melon
**cud-chewing animal** ruminant
**cuddle** caress, clasp, crouch, dandle, embrace, encircle, enfold, fondle, grasp, hold, huddle, hug, kiss, love, nestle, pat, pet, seize, snog, snug(gle), squeeze, stroke
**cuddling** nestling
**cuddly toy** teddy
**cuddy** ass, blockhead, closet, donkey, saloon, stupid

**cudgel** baton, batter, beat, cane, club, fustigate, maul, stave, thrash
**cudgel for killing fish** muckle
**cud holder** rumen
**cue** catchword, hint, incentive, key, nod, prompt(ing), reminder, sign(al), stimulus, suggestion
**cue game** billiards
**cue's blunt end** butt
**cuff** wristband
**cuff fastener** button, link, stud
**cuff heavily** clout
**cuff on the ear** box
**cuisine** cookery
**cul-de-sac** dead-end
**culinary art** cookery
**culinary berry** peppercorn
**culinary bulb** garlic
**culinary delight** pastry
**culinary directions** recipe
**culinary flavouring** aniseed, spice
**culinary herb** basil, marjoram, rosemary, sage, thyme
**culinary plant** celery, herb
**culinary sauce** gravy
**cull** amass, choose, collect, compile, crop, cut, extract, garner, gather, harvest, organise, pick, pluck, reap, remove, select, uproot, weed, winnow
**culled** hand-picked, picked
**culler** selector, weeder
**culm** coal-dust, fodder
**culminate** climax, close, complete, conclude, consummate, end, finish, pinnacle, surmount, terminate, tip, top
**culmination** acme, apex, apogee, climax, completion, conclusion, consummation, crown, finale, height, peak, perfection, pinnacle, summit, top, vertex, zenith
**culpability** blame, blameworthiness, censurability, delinquency, dereliction, fault, guilt, incrimination, liability, onus, responsibility
**culpable** blamable, blameworthy, criminal, faulty, guilty, immoral, laches, peccant, reprehensible, reprovable, sinful, transgressive
**culpable negligence** laches
**culprit** criminal, delinquent, evildoer, felon, malefactor, miscreant, offender, rascal, sinner, transgressor, wrongdoer
**cult** admiration, body, church, clique, craze, denomination, devotion, faction, faith, following, group, party, religion, reverence, school, sect, veneration, worship
**cult hero** idol
**cultivable** arable

**cultivate** aid, ameliorate, better, breed, cherish, develop, discipline, educate, elevate, encourage, farm, fertilise, grow, harvest, help, improve, plant, plough, prepare, pursue, raise, rear, tend, till
**cultivated area** tillage
**cultivated cabbage** kale
**cultivated cherries** duke
**cultivated forest** plantation
**cultivated garden border** flowerbed
**cultivated grass area** lawn
**cultivated hazel** filbert
**cultivated land** tillage
**cultivated plot** garden
**cultivate the soil** till
**cultivation** advocacy, agronomy, civility, culture, education, encouragement, fostering, gardening, gentility, manners, planting, promotion, pursuit, refinement, study, taste, tilling, working
**cultivation of flowers** floriculture
**cultivation of forest trees** silviculture
**cultivation of grapevines** viniculture, viticulture
**cultivation of miniature trees** bonsai (J)
**cultivation of trees or shrubs** arboriculture
**cultivator of land** cropper, farmer
**cult killing** ritual murder
**cultural** artistic, edifying, educative, enriching, ethnic, humane
**cultural revival** renaissance
**cultural spirit** ethos
**culture** accomplishment, art, breeding, civilisation, customs, education, elevation, enlightenment, erudition, improvement, learning, mores, polish, politeness, refinement, society, urbanity
**culture medium** agar
**cumbersome** awkward, bulky, burdensome, clumsy, heavy, hefty, inconvenient, massive, onerous, oppressive, troublesome, unmanageable, unwieldy
**cumin-flavoured liqueur** kummel
**cummerbund** band, kummerbund, sash, waist-sash, waistband
**cuneal** cuneate, cuneiform, wedge-shaped
**cuneate** cuneal, cuneiform, sphenoid, V-shaped, wedge-shaped
**cuneiform** cuneal, cuneate, wedge-shaped
**cunning** ability, adroitness, arch, art(ful), artifice, clever, craft(iness), crafty, deceitful, devious, finesse, foxy, guile, intrigue, shrewd(ness),
skilfulness, skill, sly(ness), trick(er)y, wily
**cunning deceit** guile
**cunning deception** legerdemain
**cunning demon** d(a)edal, imp, ogre
**cunning inquiry** loaded question
**cunningly** skilfully, slyly
**cunning manoeuvre to gain advantage** ploy
**cunning move** tactic
**cunning person** fox
**cunning strategy** finesse, tactics
**cunning way** wile
**cup** beaker, bowl, chalice, mug, tass(ie) (Sc), vessel
**cupboard** buffet, cabinet, case, closet, commode, counter, dresser, locker, wardrobe
**cupboard for storing food** larder
**cup dish** saucer
**cup edge** rim
**cup handle** ear
**cup holder** saucer
**Cupid** Eros
**cupidity** ardour, aspiration, avarice, avidity, breathlessness, desire, eagerness, edacity, greed, itch, keenness, longing, rapacity, ravenousness, stinginess, thirst, venality, yearning
**Cupid's dart** catananche
**Cupid's gift** love
**Cupid's shaft** arrow
**cup-like cavity** calix
**cup of assayer** cupel
**cup of flower** calyx
**cup of tea** cuppa, cupper
**cupola** dome
**cupped** concave
**cupping glass** artificial leech, ventose
**cupreous** coppery
**cup rim** lip
**cup's edge** rim
**cup-shaped mould** timbale
**cup-shaped organ** cupule
**cup-shaped stem sheath** achrea, ocrea
**cup stirrer** teaspoon
**cur** bitch, blend, cad, canine, combination, cross(breed), dog, hound, hybrid, knave, mixture, mongrel, mutt, polecat, pup(py), scoundrel, skunk, tike, tyke, viper, wastrel, wretch
**curable** treatable
**curate** clergyman
**curative** advantageous, beneficial, cure, healthy, medicinal, panacea, remedial, reparative, restorative, therapeutic
**curative drug** medicine
**curative mineral spring** spa
**curative tincture** iodine
**curb** barricade, barrier, border, boundary, brake, bridle, check, constrain, contain, control, deterrent, edge, enclosure, frame(work), hinder, hindrance, impede, inhibit, leniency, limitation, margin, moderate, muzzle, palisade, periphery, rein, repress, restrain(t), restrict, retard, subdue, suppress, tether, verge
**curbing** bridling, checking, constraining, containing, controlling, hindering, impeding, inhibiting, moderating, muzzling, repressing, restraining, restricting, retarding, subduing, suppressing
**curbing the secretion of sweat** anhidrotic
**curd food** yoghurt
**curdled** sour
**curdling agent** coagulator, rennet
**curds and whey** pinjane, slip
**cure** antidote, corrective, dose, heal, medication, medicine, nurse, preventive, recovery, relieve, remedy, restorative, salt, therapy, treat
**cure-all** balm, elixir, nostrum, panacea, remedy, theriac
**cure-all remedy** arcanum, elixir, panacea
**cured fodder** silage
**cured grass** hay
**cured herring** kipper
**cured pork** bacon, ham
**cured side of pig** bacon
**curer** healer
**curing flatulence** carminative
**curio** bric-a-brac, find, gem, ornament, pearl, rarity, treasure
**curios collectively** vertu, virtu
**curiosity** bygone, concern, curio, desire, freak, idiosyncrasy, ingenuity, inquiringness, inquisitiveness, interest, interrogation, knick-knack, marvel, miracle, monstrosity, nosiness, novelty, oddity, peculiarity, phenomenon, piquancy, prying, questioning, rarity, sight, snooping, spectacle, strangeness, trinket, wonder
**curious** agog, bizarre, exotic, extraordinary, foreign, inquiring, inquisitive, interested, meddlesome, meddling, mysterious, nosy, novel, odd, peculiar, peeping, peering, prying, puzzled, quaint, queer, questioning, rare, searching, singular, strange, unique, unorthodox, unusual
**curious custom** couvade

curious literature  impurity, pornography
curl  coil, convolute, corkscrew, entwine, ringlet, spiral, twist
curled ornament  scroll
curl hair  crimp
curling inwards  involution
curling target  tee
curl lip  sneer
curl up  huddle, nestle
curly  crisp, curled, frizzy, kinky, permed, squiggle, wavy
curly-haired  ulotrichous
curly-haired pet dog  poodle
curly-leaved chicory  endive
curly lock of hair  ringlet
curmudgeon  miser
currant  gadelle (F)
currant bun  black bun
currency  acceptance, (bank)notes, bills, cash, circulation, coin(age), commonness, diffusion, generality, money, prevalence, publicity, reign, run, spreading, transmission, universality, vogue
currency conversion charge  agio
currency unit of Afghanistan  afghani, pul
currency unit of Algeria  centime, dinar
currency unit of Australia  cent, dollar
currency unit of Bahamas  cent, dollar
currency unit of Barbados  cent, dollar
currency unit of Belgium  centime, franc
currency unit of Belize  cent, dollar
currency unit of Benin  centime, franc
currency unit of Bermuda  cent, dollar
currency unit of Bhutan  ngultrum, paisas, rupee
currency unit of British Honduras  cent, dollar
currency unit of Brunei  cent, dollar
currency unit of Burkina-Faso  centime, franc
currency unit of Burundi  centime, franc
currency unit of Cambodia  rial
currency unit of Cameroon  centime, franc
currency unit of Chad  centime, franc
currency unit of Chile  centesimo, escudo
currency unit of Costa Rica  centimo, colon
currency unit of Cyprus  cent, pound
currency unit of Czechoslovakia  haler, heller, korlina
currency unit of Denmark  krone, re
currency unit of Egypt  piastre, pound
currency unit of El Salvador  centavo, colon
currency unit of Ethiopia  birr, cent

currency unit of Fiji Islands  cent, dollar
currency unit of Finland  marrks, penni
currency unit of France  centime, franc
currency unit of Gabon  centime, franc
currency unit of Germany  Deutsche Mark, Deutschmark, pfennig
currency unit of Ghana  cedi, pesewa
currency unit of Greece  drachma, lepton
currency unit of Guatemala  centavo, quetzal
currency unit of Guinea  centime, franc
currency unit of Guyana  cent, dollar
currency unit of Haiti  centime, gourde
currency unit of Honduras  centavo, lempira
currency unit of Hong Kong  cent, dollar
currency unit of Hungary  fillér, forint
currency unit of Iceland  eyrir (pl. aurar), króna
currency unit of India  paisa, rupee
currency unit of Indonesia  rupiah, sen
currency unit of Iran  dinar, rial
currency unit of Iraq  dinar, fils
currency unit of Ireland  pence, pound
currency unit of Israel  agora, shekel
currency unit of Italy  lira
currency unit of Ivory Coast  centime, franc
currency unit of Jamaica  cent, dollar
currency unit of Japan  yen
currency unit of Jordan  dinar, fils
currency unit of Kampuchea  riel, sen
currency unit of Kenya  cent, shilling
currency unit of Kuwait  dinar, dirham, fils
currency unit of Laos  at, kip
currency unit of Lebanon  piastre, pound
currency unit of Libya  dinar, piastra
currency unit of Liechtenstein  centime, franc
currency unit of Luxembourg  centime, franc
currency unit of Madagascar  centime, franc
currency unit of Malaysia  cent, dollar, ringgit
currency unit of Mali  centime, franc
currency unit of Malta  pence, pound
currency unit of Mauritania  centime, franc
currency unit of Mauritius  cent, rupee
currency unit of Monaco  centime, franc
currency unit of Mongolia  mongo, tug(h)rik
currency unit of Morocco  dirham, franc
currency unit of Nepal  pice, rupee

currency unit of New Zealand  cent, dollar
currency unit of Nicaragua  centavo, cordoba
currency unit of Niger  centime, franc
currency unit of Nigeria  naira
currency unit of North Korea  chon, won
currency unit of Norway  krone, öre
currency unit of Omen  rial
currency unit of Pakistan  paisa, rupee
currency unit of Panama  balboa, centesimo
currency unit of Paraguay  centimo, guarani
currency unit of Poland  groszy, sloty
currency unit of Portugal  centavo, escudo
currency unit of Romania  ban, leu
currency unit of Rwanda  centime, franc
currency unit of San Marino  lira
currency unit of Saudi Arabia  riyal
currency unit of Senegal  centime, franc
currency unit of Seychelles  cent, rupee
currency unit of Sierra Leone  cent, leone
currency unit of Singapore  cent, dollar
currency unit of Somalia  cent, shilling
currency unit of South Africa  cent, rand
currency unit of South Korea  chon, won
currency unit of Soviet Union  kopeck, r(o)uble
currency unit of Spain  céntimo, peseta
currency unit of Sri Lanka  cent, rupee
currency unit of Sudan  piastre, pound
currency unit of Surinam  cent, g(u)ilder, gulden
currency unit of Sweden  krona, öre
currency unit of Switzerland  centime, franc
currency unit of Syria  piastre, pound
currency unit of Taiwan  cent, New Taiwan dollar
currency unit of Tanzania  cent, shilling
currency unit of Thailand  baht, satang
currency unit of the Netherlands  cent, gilder, guilder, gulden
currency unit of Tobago  cent, dollar
currency unit of Togo  centime, franc
currency unit of Trinidad  cent, dollar
currency unit of Tunisia  dinar, milli(e)me
currency unit of Turkey  lira, piastre
currency unit of Uganda  cent, shilling
currency unit of Uruguay  centimo, peso

**currency unit of Venezuela** bolivar, céntimo, morocota, real
**currency unit of Yemen** dinar, fils
**currency unit of Yugoslavia** dinar, para
**currency unit of Zaïre** centime, franc
**currency unit of Zambia** kwacha, ngwee
**currency unit of Zimbabwe** cent, dollar
**current** accepted, circulating, circulation, common, course, customary, draught, flow, general, in, jet, now, ongoing, popular, present, present-day, prevailing, prevalent, progress, recent, rife, river, stream, stylish, tide, up-to-date, widespread
**current events** news
**current fashion** mode, vogue
**current gauge** ammeter
**current liability** account payable
**current of air** blast, breeze, draught, wind
**current popular style** fashion
**current style** mode
**current unit** volt
**curried meat soup** mulligatawny
**curry** bruise, cajole, clean dress, comb, drub, groom, prepare
**curry accompaniment** rice
**curry a horse** clean, dress
**curry-flavoured soup of Anglo-Indian origin** mulligatawny
**curry powder** spice
**curse** accurse, afflict(ion), anathema, annoy(ance), bane, blaspheme, calamity, cuss, denounce, denunciate, denunciation, doom, drat, evil, execration, imprecate, imprecation, malediction, malison, misfortune, oath, plague, scourge, swear(word), thorn, torment, trouble, vex(ation)
**cursed** abominable, accursed, bedevilled, blighted, confounded, damned, detestable, devilish, doomed, excommunicated, execrable, execrated, fiendish, hateful, ill-fated, loathsome, odious, unholy, unsanctified, vile, villainous
**cursed thing** anathema
**curse of God** anathema
**cursive capital letter** uncial
**cursive writing** script
**cursory** brief, fleeting, hasty, hurried, inattentive, loose, passing, perfunctory, precipitate, quick, rapid, slight, superficial, swift, transient, unmeditated, unreflected
**curt** abrupt, blunt, brief, brusque, compact, concise, condensed, crisp, crusty, gruff, harsh, laconic, rude,
short, succinct, taciturn, tart, terse, uncivil, ungracious
**curtail** abbreviate, abridge, constrict, contract, cut, decrease, diminish, elide, lessen, nip, prune, reduce, restrict, shave, shorten, subtract
**curtail liberty** abridge
**curtain** concealment, cover, drape(ry), shade, shutter
**curtain cord** tieback
**curtain holder** rod
**curtain material** lace
**curtain of fire** barrage
**curtain pole** rod
**curtain rod** tringle
**curtain rod concealer** pelmet
**curtain screening women from men** purda(h)
**curtal axe** cutlass
**curtsy** bob, bow, greeting, nod, salaam, salute
**curvaceous** comely, elegant, graceful, shapely, well-formed
**curvature of aeroplane wing** camber
**curvature of the spine** kyphosis, lordosis, scoliosis
**curve** arc, arch, bend, bow, camber, coil, curvature, deflect, deviate, divert, epicycloid, ess, hook, horseshoe, hyperbola, incurve, inflect, loop, lunule, parabola, screw, sinus, spiral, swerve, trajectory, turn, twist, vault, vee, wind
**curve between lobes of leaf** sinus
**curved** arched, bent, bowed, coiled, convex, crooked, hooked, humped, inflected, rounded, sinuous, sweeping, turned, twisted, wound
**curved axe** adze
**curved bar put on horse's hoof** shoe
**curved bone** rib
**curved bone forming base of each half of pelvis** ischium
**curved cavalry sword** sabre
**curved elliptical path** orbit
**curved entrance** arch
**curved glass** lens
**curved hook** barb
**curved leg on furniture** cabriole
**curved letter** ess, S
**curved like a bow** arcuate
**curved like a sickle** falciform
**curved line** arc
**curved liquid surface** meniscus
**curved medieval sword** falchion
**curved moulding** ogee
**curved oriental sword** scimitar
**curved path of planet** orbit
**curved reaping hook** sickle
**curved roofing tile** pantile
**curved shape** arc
**curved structure** arch
**curved sword** cutlass, machete, sabre, scimitar
**curved symbol** hook
**curve formed at the intersection of two vaults** groin
**curve of beauty** sigmoid
**curve of coast** bight
**curves on hem** (e)scallops
**curve that spans an opening** arch
**curving** arc(h)ing, bending, bowing, coiling, hooking, inflecting, turning, twisting, winding
**cushion** absorb, bolster, check, pad, pillow, slow
**cushioned footstool** ottoman
**cushioned seat without back or arms** ottoman
**cushion for the head** pillow
**cushion-shaped** pulvinate
**cushion used as footstool** hassock
**cushy** comfortable, easy, soft
**cusp** angle, bend, corner, crook, crotch, edge, elbow, intersection, knee, nook, point
**cuspidor** spittoon
**cuss** curse, swear
**custodian** caretaker, concierge, janitor, keeper, superintendent, watchman
**custodian in library** librarian
**custodian of funds** treasurer
**custodian of museum** curator
**custody** care, charge, guardianship, holding, imprisonment, ownership, possession, preservation, safekeeping, security, trust, watch
**custom** convention, duty, etiquette, exaction, fashion, form, formality, habit, impost, law, manner, observance, observation, patronage, policy, practice, procedure, purchase, rate, rite, ritual, routine, routing, rule, style, tariff, tax, toll, tradition, usage, use, way, wont
**customary** accepted, accustomed, cliché, common, daily, established, everyday, familiar, fixed, frequent, general, habitual, natural, normal, ordinary, popular, prevailing, regular, rooted, routine, set, traditional, usual
**customary behaviour** norm
**customary benefit** perk
**customary methods** standard procedure
**customary mode** usage
**customary practice** ritual
**customary procedure** routine
**custom duty** impost
**customer** buyer, client(ele), marketer, patron(iser), punter, purchaser, shopper, vendee
**customer of** patronise
**customer's support** patronage

**custom-made** tailored
**custom of marriage to one wife or husband at a time** monandry, monogamy
**customs charge** duty
**customs duty** excise, impost, tariff
**cut** abbreviate, abridge, bisect, carve, chop, cleave, clip, crop, cross, curtail, dilute, diminish, divide, edit, fashion, fell, gash, hack, harvest, hew, hurt, incise, incision, insult, intersect, lower, make, mode, move, mow, pare, penetrate, pierce, prune, reduce, saw, sever(ed), shape, shear, shorten, slash, slit, snip, strait, thin, transect, trim, wound
**cut above** distinguished, outshine, reliable, trustworthy
**cut across** bisect, bridge, cross, ford, transcend, transect
**cut a figure eight** skate
**cut a log again** resaw
**cut and dried** automatic, prearranged, predetermined, settled
**cut and rip** lacerate
**cut and thrust** feint, jab, lunge, poke
**cut and title a film** edit
**cut apart** separate, sever
**cut apart to study** dissect
**cut artistically** carve
**cut a small piece off** snip
**cut at random** slash
**cut away** excise
**cut away branches** lop
**cut away rind** pare
**cut back** abbreviate, abridge, check, contract, crop, curb, curtail, cut, decrease, dock, drop, economise, economy, lessen(ing), lop, lower, prune, rationalise, reduce, reduction, retrench(ment), save, scrimp, shorten, slash, trim, truncate
**cut back business expenses** retrench
**cut bits off** snip
**cut bread** slice
**cut by fifty per cent** halve
**cut designs on metal plate** etch
**cut down** abridge, axe, chop, decrease, diminish, fell, hew, lessen, level, lop, lower, mow, reap, reduce
**cut down a tree** fell
**cut down expenses** axe, economise, save
**cut down grass** mow
**cut down on food intake** diet
**cute** adorable, appealing, attractive, beautiful, clever, lovable, pretty, sweet
**cutely** sweetly
**cut expenses** economise, save
**cut face of gem** facet
**cut first molar** teethe

**cut glass** crystal
**cut grass** mow
**cut hair** tonsure, trim
**cuticle** epidermis, integument, membrane, pellicle, skin
**cut in** interject, interpose, interrupt, intervene, intrude
**cut incisor** teethe
**cut in halves** bisect
**cut in pieces** chop, dice, hash, mince
**cut into a deep slope** escarp
**cut into bodies** surgery
**cut into cubes** dice
**cut into equal portions** halve
**cut into larynx from without** laryngotomy
**cut into long strips** slash
**cut into pieces** cantle, dice, dissect
**cut into small cubes** dice
**cut into small pieces** mince, shred
**cut into stripes** dag
**cut into strips** shred
**cut into three** trisect
**cut into trachea** tracheotomy
**cut into with a sharp instrument** pierce
**cut into with the teeth** bite
**cut in two** bisect, halve, sever, split
**cut in wood** carve
**cutis** skin
**cutlass** machete
**cut lawn** mow
**cut leather into layers** skive
**cutlery item** fork, knife, spoon, teaspoon
**cutlet** chop
**cut logs** saw
**cut loose** celebrate, depart, leave, quit
**cut lumber** chop, saw
**cut meat** slice, carve
**cut neatly** trim
**cut of beef** rump, sirloin, steak, topside
**cut of beef from the neck to the ribs** chuck
**cut off** abscind, amputate, apart, axed, ball, bereft, block, detach, disconnect, discontinue, disinherit, disown, end, excise, halt, intercept, interrupt, intersect, isolate, lop, obstruct, occlude, renounce, separate, sever, stop, suspend
**cut off a part of** curtail
**cut off beard** shave
**cut off by snipping** nip
**cut off by surgical operation** amputate
**cut off close** shave
**cut of fish** fillet
**cut off supply line** beleaguer, besiege, blockade, encircle
**cut off the head** behead
**cut off the rind** peel
**cut off the top** lop

**cut off top** truncate
**cut off with a shilling** disinherit
**cut off wool** shear
**cut of hair** bob, eton, trim
**cut of lamb** chop, leg, rib, shoulder
**cut of meat** brisket, chop, cutlet, flank, loin, rib, rump, shank, shoulder, steak, topside
**cut of pork** belly, ham, leg, loin, neck, sparerib
**cut open** dissect, slit
**cut open and examine** dissect
**cut or shape** trim
**cut or tear away** rip
**cut out** cease, contrive, debar, delete, eliminate, excise, exclude, exscind, exsect, extract, fail, oust, remove, sever, shape, stencil, stop, supersede, supplant
**cut out for** adapted, adequate, competent, designed, equipped, fitted, made, qualified, right, suitable, suited
**cut out part** resect
**cut-price disposal** sale
**cut roughly** hack
**cut short** abort, abridge, bob, clip, crop, curtail, dock, halt, interrupt, lop, sever, snip, stop, terminate, truncate
**cut slot in wood** mortise
**cut small** chop
**cut socially** snub
**cut someone's throat** harm, hurt, injure
**cutter** boat, brick, hewer, sled, sleigh, slicer, sloop, vessel, yacht
**cutter of gems** lapidary
**cut the edges from** pare, trim
**cut the grass** mow
**cut through** bisect, cleave, divide, intersect, sever, split
**cutting** acid, acrimonious, bit(ing), branch, carving, cleaving, clipping, edged, excavation, excerpt, honed, incisal, incisive, keen, leaf, limb, mordant, part(icle), piece, root, sarcastic, scything, secant, severance, severe, sharp(ened), shoot, slip, splitting, trenchant, wounding
**cutting beam** laser
**cutting blow** lash
**cutting edge** blade
**cutting implement** knife, panga, scissors, shears
**cutting instrument** knife, scissors, shears
**cutting into strips** dagging
**cutting into the trachea** tracheotomy
**cutting motion** slice
**cutting of teeth** dentition
**cutting part** blade

**cutting side of blade** edge
**cutting sound** swish
**cutting stroke** slice, chop
**cutting tool** adze, axe, chisel, froe, frow, knife, panga, saw, scissors, shears, slasher
**cutting tool for wood** adze
**cutting tooth** incisor
**cutting trees** felling
**cutting weapon** pole-axe, sword
**cuttlefish** spirula
**cuttlefish fluid** ink
**cuttlefish ink** sepia
**cut tobacco for making cigarettes** filler
**cut up** axe, carve, chop, criticise, dice, dissect, divide, injure, knife, lacerate, mince, slash, slice, wound
**cut up joint of meat** carve
**cut wildly** slash
**cut with a hand tool** saw
**cut with an axe** chop, hew
**cut with knife** carve, slash
**cut with scissors** snip
**cut with shears** clip, snip
**cut with sweeping strokes** slash
**cut wood** saw
**cut wool** shear
**cycle** aeon, age, bicycle, circle, epoch, era, frequency, pedal, period, progression, reappear, recur(rence), recurrent, return, revolution, rotation, round, scooter, sequence, series, succession, tandem, tricycle
**cycle of duty** rota
**cyclic recurrence** revolution
**cycling** riding
**cyclist** rider
**cycloid** arch
**cyclone** hurricane, tornado, typhoon
**cyclonic storm** hurricane, typhoon
**cylinder** geyser, platen, roller, spool, tube
**cylinder for spreading paint** roller
**cylinder of tobacco** cigar(ette)
**cylindrical military cap** shako
**cylindrical packet of coins** rouleau
**cylindrical saw** trepan
**cymbalo** dulcimer
**Cymric** Welsh
**Cymry** Kymry, Wales, Welsh
**cynic** dog-like, doubter, misanthrope, pessimist, sceptic, scoffer, snarling, surly
**cynical** acid, acrid, biting, captious, caustic, censorious, contemptuous, cross, cutting, derisive, disbelieving, distrustful, ironic, moody, mordant, pessimistic, petulant, pungent, sarcastic, satirical, scornful, sneering, sour, surly, unbelieving, waspish
**cynicism** heartlessness, misanthropy, surliness
**cynosure** centre, core, focus, headquarters, hub, target
**cypher** acrostic, calculate, cipher, code, count, cryptogram, cryptograph, decipher, decode, figure, reckon
**cypher system** code
**cyprinid** minnow
**cyprinoid fish** id(e), orf(e)
**Cypriote cape** Andreas, Gata, Greco, Zevgari
**Cypriote coin** para
**Cypriote underground** Eoka
**cyst** blister, abscess, bag, bladder, boil, canker, carbuncle, pimple, pouch, sac(cula), sore, swelling, theca, ulcer, utricle, vesicle, wen
**cyst containing watery fluid** hydatid
**cystlike bag** sac
**cyst on scalp** wen
**cytoid** cell-like
**Czech capital** Prague
**Czechoslovakian beer** pilson
**Czechoslovakian castle** Hradcany
**Czechoslovakian coin** crown, ducat, haler, heller, koruna
**Czechoslovakian dance** furiant, polka, redowa
**Czechoslovakian range** Tatra
**Czechoslovakian region** Bohemia, Moravia, Slovakia
**Czech writer** Kafka

# D

**dab** besmear, bit, blot, daub, jab, nip, pat, pinch, poke, rap, smudge, speck, tamp, tap, thump, touch, trace
**dabble** bathe, dampen, fritter, meddle, moisten, paddle, plash, play, plunge, potter, slop, splash, splatter, spray, sprinkle, tinker, wade, wallow, wet
**dabbler** amateur, dilettante, layman, unprofessional
**dabble with blood** engore
**dab hand** ace, champion, expert
**dad** daddy, father, pa(pa), parent, pater, pop, tata (Sp)
**dad's sister** aunt(ie), aunty
**daedal** complex, dedal, intricate, inventive, manifold, mazy, mysterious, skilful
**daffodil** Lent lily
**daft** barmy, berserk, crazy, demented, deranged, eccentric, empty, feeble-minded, foolish, frenzied, idiotic, inept, insane, irrational, loony, lunatic, mad, nuts, nutty, odd, raving, reckless, silly, stupid, void, wild
**daft about** crazy, doting, dotty
**dagga cigarette** reefer, zol
**dagger** anlance, bayonet, blade, bodkin, dirk, knife, krees, kris, kukri, poniard, rapier, sa(e)x, skean, stiletto, stylet
**dagger handle** hilt
**dagger holder** scabbard
**dagger of mercy** misericorde
**dagger with wavy blade** kreese, kris
**dagger, worn in the stocking** dhu, sgian-dhu, skean
**dagger wound** stab
**daily** char, circadian, common(ly), constant, customary, day-to-day, diurnal, everyday, frequent, habitual, often, ordinary, quotidian, regular, repeated, usual, wonted
**daily account** diary, journal
**daily fare** diet
**daily food and drink** fare
**daily grind** routine
**daily meals** board
**daily meeting** session
**daily news medium** (news)paper
**daily or weekly TV show** serial
**daily practice** routine
**daily publication** newspaper
**daily records of events** diary, journal
**daintily** charmingly, delicately, elegantly, finely, gracefully, neatly, prettily
**daintily odd** quaint
**daintily small** mignon
**dainty** beautiful, charming, delectable, delicacy, delicate, delicious, dinky, elegant, exquisite, fastidious, fine, finical, fussy, genteel, graceful, neat, (over)nice, particular, petite, precise,

**dainty food**

pretty, refined, scrupulous, squeamish, tasty, tender
**dainty food**  cake
**dainty morsel**  titbit
**dairy animal**  cow
**dairy cattle**  Ayrshires
**dairy farm device**  separator
**dairy product**  butter, cheese, cream, curd, milk, yogh(o)urt, yogurt
**dairy spread for bread**  butter
**dais**  estrade, platform, podium, rostrum, stage, stand
**daisy**  ox-eye
**daisy-like flower**  aster
**dale**  bottom, combe, coomb, dell, dingle, strath, vale, valley
**Dallas TV family**  Ewings
**dally**  caress, dawdle, delay, idle, inactive, lag, loiter, play, saunter, sport, tarry, toy, trifle
**Dalmatian's name**  Spot
**daltonism**  colour-blindness
**dam**  barrage, barricade, barrier, block, choke, embankment, mother, obstruction, weir
**damage**  break, deface, dent, deterioration, devastation, disaster, harm, havoc, hurt, impair, incapacitate, injure, injury, loss, maim, mar, misfortune, mutilate, ruin, scathe, spoil, suffering, weaken, wound, wreck
**damage by criticism**  maul
**damage by impact**  prang
**damaged by use of wear**  worn
**dam built across river**  barrage, weir
**dame**  female
**dam in Brazil**  Furnas, Itaipu, Peixoto
**dam in Egypt**  Aswan
**dam in Ghana**  Akosombo
**dam in Idaho**  Brownlee, Oxbow
**dam in Ivory Coast**  Dandama
**dam in Nile**  Aswan
**dam in Pakistan**  Tarbela
**dam in river**  barrage, weir
**dam in Tennessee**  Wheeler, Wilson
**dam in Washington**  Coulee
**damn**  abuse, blaspheme, blast, castigate, censure, condemn, criticise, curse, denounce, denunciate, doom, execrate, hoot, imprecate, iota, jot, pan, revile, sentence, slam, slate, swear, whit
**damnable**  accursed, blasted, despicable, detestable, hateful, infamous, infernal, loathsome, lost, reprobate, revolting, unhappy
**damp**  check, chill, dampen, dank(ness), extinguish, humid(ity), inhibit, moist(en), moisture, restrain, retard, soggy, steam(y), stifle, suffocate, vapour, wet(ness)

**damp and chilly**  dank
**damp and close**  muggy
**damp and cold**  dank, raw
**damp and dark**  dankish
**damp and sticky**  clammy, slimy
**damp and stifling**  muggy
**dampen**  abate, allay, bedew, check, cool, damp, daunt, deject, depress, diminish, disappoint, discomfort, discourage, dishearten, lessen, moisten, moisturise, retard, saturate, slow, temper, wet
**damsel**  girl, maiden
**damson**  plum
**dam up**  stem
**dance**  ball, ballet, bolero, bop, calypso, cancan, caper, conga, cotillion, fox-trot, frolic, gambol, hoof, hop, hula, jig, polka, prance, reel, rock, rumba, samba, schottische, shimmy, skip, social, spin, sway, swing, tango, tap, two-step, waltz, whirl
**dance about**  prance
**dance club**  disco
**dance drama of India**  kathakali
**dance for two in ballet**  pas de deux
**dance hall**  ballroom, disco
**dance like minuet**  gavotte
**dance like polka**  schottische
**dance like rumba**  mambo
**dance like tarantella**  bergamasque
**dance movement**  step
**dance of death**  dance macabre (F)
**dance of Israel**  hora
**dance of sailor**  hornpipe, jig
**dance of Waikiki**  hula
**dance performed by girls**  nau(t)ch
**dancer**  ballerina, danseur, danseuse, entertainer, figurant, jigger, tap-dancer, toe-dancer
**dancer's rail**  barre
**dance step**  pas, trot
**dance to jazz or rock music**  jive
**dancing**  reeling
**dancing on the toes in blocked shoes**  pointes
**dancing shoe**  pump
**dancing under a low pole**  limbo
**dandelion peduncle**  scape
**dander**  anger, indignation, temper
**dandified**  dandyish, foplike, foppish, ostentatious, showy
**dandle**  caress, cuddle, fondle, pat, pet, stroke
**dandruff**  scurf
**dandy**  beau, beauty, buck, coxcomb, dude, excellent, fop, superb, swell, toff
**Danes live there**  Denmark
**danger**  chance, endangerment, harm, hazard, imminence, injury, insecurity, jeopardy, liability,

menace, minacity, peril, precariousness, risk, threat, unsafety, vulnerability
**danger colour**  red
**dangerous**  critical, defenceless, dire, hazardous, imminent, insecure, ominous, parlous, perilous, precarious, risky, severe, threatening, uncertain, unsafe
**dangerously attractive woman**  femme fatale (F)
**dangerously fascinating woman**  siren
**dangerously steep**  precipitous
**dangerous mosquito**  aedes, anopheles
**dangerous movie feat**  stunt
**dangerous to tip**  canoe
**danger signal**  alarm, SOS, warning
**danger warning**  alert
**dangle**  brandish, depend, drag(gle), droop, flaunt, follow, hang, oscillate, sag, sway, swing, wave
**dangling cord ornament**  tassel
**Danish author of fairy tales**  Hans Christian Andersen
**Danish cheese**  tybo
**Danish coin**  krone, öre
**Danish composer**  Gade
**Danish dance**  sextur
**Danish fjord**  ise, lim
**Danish horn**  lur(e)
**Danish island**  Aaro, Aero, Als, Amager, Fano, Faroe, Fyn, Moen, Mors, Samso, Seeland
**Danish mathematician**  Erlang
**Danish measure**  alen, rode
**Danish money**  krone, öre
**Danish parliament**  Folketing, Landsting, Rigsraad
**Danish peninsula**  Jutland
**Danish possession**  Faroe, Greenland, Iceland
**Danish seaport**  Odense
**Danish strait**  Kattegat, Skagerrak
**Danish tribunal**  Rigsrad, Rigsret
**Danish weight**  eser, lod, ort
**danseuse (F)**  ballerina
**Dante's love**  Beatrice
**dapper**  active, brisk, dainty, natty, smart, spry, well-groomed
**darbies**  handcuffs
**dare**  affront, beard, brave, challenge, confront(ation), defy, encounter, endure, face, hazard, meet, opposition, provoke, risk, taunt, ultimatum, venture
**daredevil**  adventurer, desperado, madcap, stuntman
**daring**  adventurous(ness), audacious, audacity, bold(ness), brave(ry), courage(ous), fearless, heroic, heroism, impulsive, intrepidity,

plucky, reckless, undaunted, valiant, venturesome
**daring achievement** exploit
**daring act** escapade, stunt
**daring deed** feat
**daring enterprise** adventure
**daring feat** stunt
**daring project** enterprise
**daring stunt** feat
**daring woman** adventuress
**Darjeeling** tea
**dark** abstruse, bad, benighted, black, cheerless, concealed, dim, discouraging, disheartening, dismal, dusky, ebon, enigmatic, esoteric, evil, foul, gloomy, hidden, ignorant, infamous, infernal, inky, murky, mysterious, mystic(al), obscure, occult, puzzling, recondite, sad, secret, shadowy, shady, sinful, sullen, swarthy, uneducated, unenlightened, unintelligible, unlit, wicked
**dark and gloomy** murky
**dark beer** porter, stout
**dark blue colour** navy
**dark bread** rye
**dark-brown bitter beer** porter
**dark brown coffee** mocha
**dark brown fur** sable
**dark Chinese tea** oolong
**dark circle round the human nipple** aureola
**dark colour** dingy
**dark-coloured** dusky
**dark continent** Africa
**dark cream** beige
**dark dust** soot
**darker** inkier
**darker stage of twilight** dusk
**dark, fine-grained, hard extrusive rock** basalt
**dark fur** sable
**dark grey rain-bearing cloud** nimbostratus
**dark grey to black rock** basalt
**dark hours** night
**dark in colour** swart, swarthy
**darkish regions on Mars** mare
**dark kind of cured China tea** oolong
**darkness** blackness, dark, dimness, gloom, murk, night, obscurity, shadiness
**dark pigment in hair** melanin
**dark prison** dungeon
**dark red** cerise, claret, maroon, puce
**dark red resin** kino
**dark red wine** port
**dark skin** melanic
**dark-skinned** dusky, swarthy
**dark-skinned person** Negro
**dark spot** macula

**dark sticky substance** pitch
**dark sun-spot** macula
**dark sweet ale** porter
**dark sweet fortified wine** Marsala
**dark syrup** molasses, treacle
**dark time** night
**dark vitreous volcanic rock** obsidean
**dark wood** ebony
**dark yellow** amber
**darling** beloved, dear, favourite, idol, jewel, love, pet, skat, sweetheart, treasure, true love
**darling fruit?** clementine
**darn** embroider, mend, patch, repair, weave
**dart** arrow, barb, bolt, bound, cast, dash, flash, flight, fling, flit, fly, hurl, jaculate, javelin, launch, leap, missile, propel, quarrel, race, role, run, rush, scoot, scramble, send, shoot, sling, spring, sprint, start, tear, throw, thrust, toss, whistle, whiz
**dart along** flit
**dart off** bolt
**dart suddenly** dash
**dash** crash, dart, destroy, élan, fly, haste, hint, hurry, hurtle, hyphen, panache, race, ruin, shatter, slam, smash, soupçon, splash, sprint, spurt, strike, throw, thrust, touch, verve, vivacity
**dash against** batter, lash, ram
**dash at** charge
**dashboard** fa(s)cia
**dash down** slam
**dashing cavalryman** beau sabreur (F)
**dashing fellow** blade, buck
**dashing manner** panache
**dashing spirit** élan
**dashing style** élan, panache
**dash into violently** ram
**dassie** hyrax
**data** assumptions, documents, evidence, facts, figures, gen, information, input, memoranda, statistics
**data fed into computer** input
**data processor** computer
**date** age, appointment, engagement, epoch, era, escort, friend, meeting, partner, time
**date bearer** palm
**dated** archaic, obsolete, old, old-fashioned, outdated, outmoded, passé, passed, unfashionable
**date line on coin** exergue
**date to celebrate** anniversary
**date tree** palm
**dating from birth** natal
**dating from very long ago** ancient
**dating machine** dater
**datum** fact

**daub** begrime, besmear, blob, blotch, coat, colour, cover, deface, dirty, lay, mess, paint, patch, plaster, smear, smirch, smudge, soil, spatter, spot, stain
**daughter-in-law of Naomi** Ruth
**daughter of Abihail** Esther
**daughter of Abishalom** Maachah
**daughter of Acrisius** Danae
**daughter of Aeneas** Ilia
**daughter of Aeolus** Alcyone
**daughter of Agamemnon** Electra, Iphigenia
**daughter of Agenor** Europa
**daughter of Ahab** Athalia
**daughter of Bethuel** Rebekah
**daughter of Cadmus** Ino, Semele
**daughter of Caleb** Achsah
**daughter of Chaos** Nyx
**daughter of Chilion** Orpah
**daughter of David** Tamar
**daughter of Demeter** Kore, Persephone
**daughter of Eliab** Abihail
**daughter of Eliam** Bethsheba
**daughter of Ethbaal** Jezebel
**daughter of Ge** Tethys
**daughter of Haran** Iscah, Milcah
**daughter of Herod** Salome
**daughter of Herodias** Salome
**daughter of Jacob** Deborah, Rachel
**daughter of Jeremiah** Hamutal
**daughter of Jethro** Zipporah
**daughter of Laban** Leah, Rachel
**daughter of Lamech** Naamah
**daughter of last tsar** Anastasia
**daughter of Lear** Cordelia, Goneril, Regan
**daughter of Levi** Jochebed
**daughter of Loki** Hel
**daughter of Mahlon** Naomi
**daughter of Minos** Ariadne, Phaedra
**daughter of Pelias** Alcestis
**daughter of Philip III of Spain** Anne of Austria
**daughter of Polonius** Ophelia
**daughter of Rhea** Ceres, Juno, Vesta
**daughter of river god** Io
**daughter of Russian tsar** czarevna, tsarevna
**daughter of same parents** sister
**daughter of Saul** Michal
**daughter of Shakespeare** Hamnet, Judith, Suzanna
**daughter of Shylock** Jessica
**daughter of Spanish king** infanta
**daughter of Tantalus** Niobe
**daughter of Tzar Nicholas II** Anastasia
**daughter of Uranus** Rhea, Tethys
**daughter of Uriel** Maachah
**daughter of Zachariah** Abijah

**daughter of Zeus** Aphrodite, Charistes, Irene, Persephone
**daughter's brother** son
**daughter's husband** son-in-law
**daunt** alarm, appal, awe, deter, discourage, dishearten, dismay, dispirit, frighten, intimidate, overawe, scare, subdue, terrify, unnerve
**daunted** afraid, alarmed, cowed, deterred, discouraged, dismayed, dispirited, downcast, fearful, frustrated, intimidated, overawed, overcome, reluctant, subdued, unnerved
**daunting** alarming, appalling, awesome, cowing, dismaying, frightening, intimidating, overawing, scaring, subduing, terrifying
**dauntless soldier** hero
**dauntless woman** heroine
**David Copperfield character** Uriah Heep
**David Copperfield's father** Jesse
**David's victim** Goliath
**David's writings** Psalms
**David was one** psalmist
**dawdle** dally, delay, drag, idle, lag, loaf, loiter, poke
**dawdler** laggard, loafer, trailer
**dawn** advent, appear, arrival, aurora, begin, cockcrow, dawning, daybreak, dayspring, gleam, lighten, morn(ing), morningtide, open, prime, start, sun-up, (sun)rise
**day** age, cycle, daylight, dayshine, daytide, daytime, dia (Sp), diem (L), epoch, era, generation, interval, light, period, span, sunshine, Tag (G), time
**day after day** continually, endlessly, forever, monotonously, perpetually, persistently, regularly, relentlessly
**day before** eve
**day before today** yesterday
**day blindness** hemeralopia
**daybook** diary
**daybreak** cockcrow, dawn, dayspring, morning, sun-up, sunrise
**day by day** daily, gradually, progressively, steadily
**daydream** conceit, concept, envisagement, fantasise, fantasy, idea, imagination, imagine, mirage, muse, musing, phantasm, reverie, vagary
**daydreaming** mooning
**day-in-and-day-out** frequently, often, periodically
**day-labourer** peon
**day nursery** crèche
**Day of Atonement** Yom Kippur
**day of judgement** doomsday, finality

**day of recreation** holiday
**day of rest** Sabbath
**day of the month** date
**day on which one was born** birthday
**day's end** sunset
**days gone by** past
**days just before Lent** Shrovetide
**day's march** étape (F)
**days of old** history, yesteryear, yore
**days of yore** history, yesteryear
**day star** sun
**day's work** darg
**daytime nap** siesta
**day-to-day practice** routine
**daze** amaze, astonish, bewilder, confuse, dazzle, distraction, flabbergast, fog, numb, paralyse, shock, stagger, stun, stupefy, stupor
**dazed and staggering** groggy
**dazed condition or state** stupor, torpor, trance
**dazed with fear** petrified
**dazzling** amazing, astonishing, blinding, bright, brilliant, confusing, dazing, fascinating, fulgent, gleaming, gorgeous, impressing, overpowering, radiant, ravishing, sparkling, splendid, stunning, stupefying, vivid
**dazzling light** glare
**de-** away, down, from, out
**dead** absolute, apathetic, barren, callous, complete, deceased, defunct, departed, dull, entire, extinct, extinguished, frigid, inanimate, indifferent, inert, infertile, inoperative, late, lifeless, motionless, out, sterile, still, straight, unfeeling, unsympathetic, useless, utter
**dead and decaying flesh** carrion
**dead and gone** buried
**dead body** cadaver, carcase, carcass, corpse, remains, stiff
**dead deer's viscera** grallock
**deaden** alleviate, blunt, dope, drug, dull, mitigate, numb, subdue
**dead-end** cul-de-sac, impasse
**deadened sensibility** stupor, torpor
**dead flesh** carrion
**dead-heat** tie
**dead keen** avid
**dead language** Latin
**dead-leaf colour** filemot
**deadlock** bar, cease, cessation, checkmate, confound, confuse, curb, debar, dilemma, disable, embarrass, forestall, halt, hinder, impasse, impede, incapacitate, nonplus, obstruct, paralyse, perplex, predicament, quietus, stalemate, standstill, stop(page), stump, trammel, undermine

**deadly** destructive, fatal, fell, heinous, implacable, intense, lethal, malign, mortal, murderous, noxious, sanguinary, toxic
**deadly African snake** mamba
**deadly animal disease** rabies
**deadly Australian snake** taipan
**deadly combat** duel
**deadly contagious disease** plague
**deadly disease** AIDS, diphtheria, poliomyelitis, smallpox
**deadly fly** tsetse
**deadly grip** stranglehold
**deadly nightshade** belladonna, dwale
**deadly poison** aconite, arsenic, cyanide, strychnine
**deadly snake** cobra, mamba, taipan
**deadpan** blank, colourless, dry, dull, emotionless, enigmatic, expressionless, flat, inscrutable, lifeless, matter-of-fact, mundane, plain, prosaic, sober, vacant, wooden
**deadpan expression** poker face
**dead person** deceased, decedent, goner
**dead plant material** necron
**dead putrefying flesh** carrion
**Dead Sea land** Moab
**dead to the world** asleep, inert, lifeless, unconscious
**deal** act, amount, arrangement, assign, bargain, behave, contract, dealing, dispense, distribute, dole, extent, give, pact, quantity, sale, trade, traffic, transaction
**deal competently with** cope
**dealer** broker, chandler, distributor, handler, hawker, jobber, merchant, monger, peddler, salesman, shopkeeper, supplier, trader, tradesman, trafficker, vendor, wholesaler
**dealer in accessories of dress and sewing goods** haberdasher
**dealer in bills of exchange** cambist
**dealer in candles** chandler
**dealer in cloth** draper
**dealer in contraband** smuggler
**dealer in drugs** chemist, pharmacist, pusher
**dealer in fabrics** mercer
**dealer in fish** fishmonger
**dealer in food and household goods** grocer
**dealer in fruit** fruiterer
**dealer in furs** furrier
**dealer in hardware** ironmonger
**dealer in hides** fellmonger
**dealer in illegal drugs** pusher
**dealer in jewels** jeweller
**dealer in meat** butcher

**dealer in medicinal drugs** apothecary, chemist, pharmacist
**dealer in medicinal herbs** herbalist
**dealer in newspapers** newsagent
**dealer in poultry** poulterer
**dealer in provisions** grocer
**dealer in saddles** saddler
**dealer in securities** broker
**dealer in skins** fellmonger, furrier, skinner
**dealer in specified trade or merchandise** chandler
**dealer in stationery** stationer
**dealer in stocks and shares** stock-jobber, stockbroker
**dealer in stolen goods** fence
**dealer in supplies for ships** chandler
**dealer in textiles** draper, mercer
**dealer in tobacco and cigarettes** tobacconist
**dealer in writing materials** stationer
**deal evasively** palter
**deal in** sell, trade
**dealing out** apportionment
**dealing with** re, regarding
**dealing with adventures of rogues** picaresque
**deal in stolen goods** fence
**deal out** dispense, distribute, dole, mete
**deals with mental disorders** psychiatrist
**deal with** bank, concern, consider, cope, handle, manage, oversee, trade, treat
**deal with cruelly** maltreat
**deal with customer** serve
**deal with patient's ailments** treat
**deal with skilfully** manipulate
**deal with the case** treat
**dean's house** deanery
**dear** admired, angel, beloved, cherished, close, costly, darling, esteemed, excessive, expensive, familiar, favourite, high-priced, intimate, jewel, loved, precious, prized, profitless, respected, sweetheart, treasure(d), true-love, valuable, valued
**dearer** up
**dearly** affectionate, devotedly, earnestly, extremely, greatly, profoundly, tenderly
**dearness** costliness, expensiveness
**dearth** default, deficiency, deprivation, destitution, diet, drought, exiguity, failure, famine, fast, hunger, inadequacy, insufficiency, lack, meagreness, need, paucity, poorness, poverty, rareness, rarity, scantiness, scarceness, scarcity,
shortage, shortness, skimpiness, sparseness, starvation, stint, want
**dearth of food** famine
**dearth of petrol** fuel-shortage
**dear to each other** close
**death** decease, demise, departure, doom, end, mortality
**death announcement** obit(uary)
**death blow** coup de grâce (F)
**death by accident** fatality
**death is the gate of life** mors janua vitae (L)
**death levels all distinctions** omnia mors aequat (L)
**deathly** ashen, deadly, deathlike, fatal, gaunt, ghastly, grim, haggard, intense, pale, pallid, wan
**deathly pale** ashen, cadaverous, livid
**death mercy** euthanasia
**death notice** obit(uary)
**death of body tissue** gangrene
**death of cells in the body** necrosis
**death of one million people** megadeath
**death struggle** agony
**debacle** catastrophe, devastation, disaster, fiasco, havoc, reversal, ruin, shambles
**debar** arrest, ban(ish), bar, boycott, check, delay, deter, disallow, disentitle, dissuade, exclude, expel, forbid, hinder, interdict, intimidate, ostracise, outlaw, preclude, prevent, prohibit, proscribe, refuse, reject, restrain, restrict, snub, stop, veto
**debar from** exclude
**debar from enjoyment** deprive
**debar temporarily** suspend
**debase** adulterate, befoul, cheapen, contaminate, corrupt, defile, degrade, demean, depose, desecrate, devalu(at)e, disgrace, dishonour, humble, impair, lower, mar, pollute, reduce, shame, smudge, vitiate, weaken
**debased** abject, corrupt, degenerate, depraved, devalued, impaired, impure, inferior, lowered, reduced, soiled
**debatable** arguable, controversial, dubious, moot, uncertain
**debate** argue, argument, consider(ation), controversy, deliberation, discuss(ion), dispute, moot
**debating** arguing, contending, contesting, discussing, disputing, questioning, wrangling
**debating place** forum
**debauch** blacken, bribe, carousal, celebration, corrupt, debase, defame, degrade, demoralise,
deprave, disgrace, dishonour, entice, festivity, fix, jollification, lure, orgy, pervert, revelry, seduce, shame, spree, square, subvert, sully, vitiate
**debauched man** roué
**debauched party** orgy
**debauchee** carouser, Casanova, decadent, degenerate, deviant, harlot, lecher, libertine, pervert, profligate, prostitute, rake, reprobate, roué, seducer, sensualist, sybarite, wanton, wassailer, wastrel, womaniser
**debauchery** carousal, corruption, decadence, depravity, dissipation, dissoluteness, evil, excess, extravagance, gluttony, immortality, indulgence, intemperance, lewdness, licentiousness, lust, orgy, overindulgence, prodigality, profligacy, revel, riot, sin, vice, wantonness, wickedness
**debilitate** bankrupt, cripple, deplete, diminish, disable, drain, enervate, enfeeble, exhaust, fatigue, impair, impoverish, incapacitate, prostrate, reduce, sap, sink, tire, unbrace, undermine, undo, vitiate, weaken
**debilitative agent** enervator
**debility** adynamia, asthenia, astheny, atony, atrophy, caducity, castration, delicacy, enfeeblement, exhaustion, faintness, fatigue, feebleness, flaccidity, frailty, heaviness, impuissance, incapacity, infirmity, languor, lassitude, lethargy, limpness, listlessness, (over)tiredness, senility, sickliness, unmanning, weakness
**debility of nerves leading to fatigue** neurasthenia
**debit** arrears, bill, charge, commitment, debt, due, invoice, liability, obligation, score
**debonair** affable, buoyant, cheery, civil, courteous, debonnaire, elegant, gay, genial, genteel, graceful, gracious, jaunty, mannerly, merry, obliging, pleasant, refined, smooth, suave, urbane
**debris** bits, cast-offs, dross, flotsam, fragments, litter, pieces, refuse, remains, rubbish, rubble, ruins, waste, wreck(age)
**debris mound** moraine
**debt** account, arrears, claim, debit, deficit, due(ness), duty, liability, obligation, owing, responsibility, score
**debt certificate** debenture, IOU
**debt charge** debit

**debt collector** dun
**debt note** IOU
**debt of gratitude** obligation
**debtor** borrower, defaulter, insolvent
**debt still unpaid** arrear
**debt to equity ratio** gearing
**debut** entrance, introduction, opening, première, presentation
**decade** ten
**decadence** corruption, debasement, decay, decline, degeneracy, degeneration, deterioration, dissipation, dissolution, ebb, fall, perversion, recession, retrogression, wane
**decadent** carnal, corrupt, decaying, debased, debauchee, declining, degenerate, degenerating, degraded, degrading, depraved, deteriorating, dissipated, dissolute, hedonistic, immoral, rotten, sensuous, tainted, wasted
**decade of swing and bebop music** forties
**decamp** abandon, abscond, betray, bolt, defect, depart, desert, disappear, elope, escape, evacuate, exit, flee, fly, forsake, go, jilt, leave, maroon, migrate, quit, relinquish, remove, renounce, resign, retire, retreat, skip, vacate, vanish, withdraw
**decant** drain, pour, spill, splash, tap
**decapitate** behead, decollate, execute, guillotine, truncate
**decay** crumble, decadence, decline, decompose, decomposition, degenerate, degeneration, deteriorate, deterioration, disintegrate, fall, impairment, rot(ting), stagnate, wither
**decayed teeth** caries
**decayed vegetable matter** peat
**decayed wood used as tinder** punk
**decaying** crumbling, deteriorating, perishing, putrefacient, putrescent, rotten, rotting
**decay into dust** moulder
**decay of living tissue** necrobiosis
**decay of teeth** caries
**decay of tissue** gangrene
**decay to dust** moulder
**deceased** dead, defunct, departed, expired, finished, former, late, lifeless, lost
**deceased person** decedent
**deceit** cheating, chicanery, concealment, deceiving, deception, duplicity, falseness, fraud, guile, hypocrisy, perfidy, stratagem, treachery, trick(ery), wile
**deceitful** artful, bogus, counterfeit, crafty, crooked, cunning, deceiving, deceptive, delusive, devious, dishonest, fallacious, false, foxy, guileful, insincere, mock, pseudo, sly, snaky, treacherous, treasonable, twofaced, underhanded, unreal, untruthful, wily
**deceitful act** abuse
**deceitful appearance** phantom
**deceitful device** trick
**deceitful fellow** knave
**deceitfully alluring** meretricious
**deceitfulness** fraudulence
**deceitful pretence** hypocrisy
**deceive** bamboozle, beguile, bilk, bluff, cheat, con, cozen, decoy, defraud, delude, double-cross, dupe, enmesh, ensnare, entrap, fool, fox, gull, hoodwink, illude, lie, misguide, misinform, mislead, outwit, rook, victimise
**deceive by flattery** cajole
**deceive by trickery** dupe
**deceive by way of joke** hoax
**deceiver** charlatan, cheater, defrauder, deluder, dodger, duper, fraud, humbug, hypocrite, imposter, Judas, juggler, liar, quack, rogue, scoundrel, swindler, trickster
**decelerate** brake, check, halt, moderate, slow, stop
**deceleration pedal** brake
**December solstice** midsummer, midwinter
**decent** appropriate, decorous, fitting, proper, seemly, suitable, tasteful
**deception** bluff, cunning, deceit, fraud, guile, lie, ruse, sham, stratagem, treachery, trick, wile
**deceptive** deceitful, deceiving, (d)elusive, fallacious, false, misleading, specious
**deceptive act** feint
**deceptive appearance** facade, illusion
**deceptive display** window-dressing
**deceptively attractive appearance** gloss
**deceptive talk** humbug
**deceptive trick** ruse, sleight
**decide** conclude, determine, judge, opt, purpose, resolve, settle
**decide a dispute** arbitrate
**decided** absolute, categorical, certain, definite, distinct, emphatic, express, positive, resolute, undeniable, unquestionable
**decide democratically** vote
**decidedly** absolutely, definitely, evidently, obviously
**decided taste** penchant
**decide firmly** resolve
**decide judicially** adjust
**decide merits** judge

**decide upon** elect, resolve, settle
**deciding round in competition** final
**deciduous tree** elm, oak
**decimal base** ten
**decimal measuring system** metric
**decimal point** dot, comma
**decimal radix** ten
**decimal system** metric
**decimal unit** ten
**decipher** construe, crack, decode, disentangle, explain, interpret, read, render, reveal, solve, translate, understand, unfold, unravel
**decision** conclusion, determination, finding, judg(e)ment, resolution, verdict
**decision by authority** arbitrament, arbitration
**decision by direct voting** plebiscite
**decision of court of justice** judg(e)ment, sentence
**decision of jury** verdict
**decision of law-court** judg(e)ment, sentence
**decisive** conclusive, critical, determined, final, firm, incontrovertible, resolute
**decisive moment** crisis
**decisive point** culmination
**decisive point at issue** crux
**decisive point that settles argument** clincher
**decisive result** finish
**decisive win** landslide victory
**deck** adorn, attire, clothe, decorate, dress, embellish, garnish
**deck cleaning mop** swab
**decking** adorning, arraying, attiring, beautifying, clothing, decorating, dressing, embellishing, gracing
**deck out cheaply** bedizen
**deck up** prettify, prink
**deck with openwork fabric** belace
**deck with stellar shapes** enstar
**declaim** attack, decry, denounce, enunciate, harangue, lecture, orate, oration, perorate, proclaim, rant, rave, rebuke, recite, speak, spout, tirade, utter
**declaim bitterly** inveigh
**declaimer** lecturer, orator, rhetorician, speaker
**declaim publicly** orate
**declaim vehemently** rant, rave
**declamatory speech** tirade
**declaration** affirmation, announcement, assertion, attestation, averment, avowal, disclosure, document, manifestation, manifesto, notice, notification, proclamation, publication, revelation, statement, testament, testimony

**declaration of facts** statement
**declaration of intended marriage**
  banns
**declaration of intension to hurt** threat
**declaration of intent** manifesto
**declaration of objection** protest
**declaration to prove some fact**
  testimony
**declare** acknowledge, affirm, allege, announce, annunciate, assert, attest, aver, avouch, avow, broadcast, claim, confirm, cry, decide, decree, disclose, divulge, maintain, manifest, name, proclaim, profess, pronounce, publish, reveal, say, state, swear, tell, testify, utter, vow
**declare as true** assert, aver
**declare at cards** meld
**declare by general consent** vote
**declare formally** certify, state
**declare free from blame** exonerate
**declare innocent** acquit, clear
**declare invalid** annul
**declare loudly** exclaim
**declare not guilty** acquit
**declare null and void** cancel, repeal, withdraw
**declare officially to be a saint**
  canonise
**declare one's sins formally** confess
**declare openly** acquit, avow
**declare orally** nuncupate
**declare positively** assert, aver
**declare sacred** consecrate
**declare strongly** assert
**declare to be true** aver
**declare to be untrue** contradict, deny
**declare without proof** allege
**decline** abase, avoid, debase, declivity, degenerate, degeneration, deny, descend, diminish, dip, dissent, downhill, downward, ebb, enfeeblement, fail(ing), forgo, incline, languish, lapse, loss, negative, pale, protest, refuse, reject, repel, repudiate, sag, slope, slump, stoop, veto, weaken
**decline gradually** lapse, wane
**decline in brilliance** wane
**decline in quality** decay
**decline in status** comedown
**decline of life** age, oldness
**decline to take** forgo
**decline to use one's vote** abstain
**declining morality** going-to-the-dogs
**declivity** declension, decline, descent, dip, downgrade, drop, fall, incline, mount, rise
**decode** adapt, clarify, construe, crack, decipher, decode, decrypt, define, explain, interpret, read, render, solve, translate, understand, unravel
**decoder** converter
**decompose** addle, crumble, decay, disintegrate, dissect, dissolve, distil, divide, putrefy, reduce, resolve, rot, separate, spoil, stagnate
**decomposed rock** gossan
**decomposed vegetable substance**
  peat
**decontaminate** clean(se), disinfect, fumigate, purify, sterilise
**décor** furnishing, scenery
**decorative horizontal band** frieze
**decorate** accoutre, adorn, array, beautify, bedeck, cite, colour, deck, dress, embellish, emboss, embroider, furnish, garnish, gild, hang, honour, ornament, ornate, paint, paper, prettify, rubricate, scrimshaw, trim, varnish
**decorate a cake** ice
**decorate again** redo
**decorated and glaced earthenware**
  faïence
**decorated dart used during bullfight**
  banderilla
**decorated metal** tole
**decorate gaudily** prank
**decorate lavishly** adorn
**decorate the wall** paper
**decorate with needlework** embroider
**decorate with ribbons** festoon
**decorate woodwork** paint
**decoration** adornment, award, badge, bauble, beautification, colours, crown, elaboration, embellishment, emblem, enrichment, flourish, frill, garland, garnish, garter, laurel, medal, order, ornament(ation), ribbon, scroll, star, trimming
**decoration combining animal, human and plant forms** grotesque
**decoration for valour** medal
**decoration of stage** décor
**decorative** adorning, aesthetic, artistic, attractive, beautiful, beautifying, creative, cultivated, cultured, elegant, enhancing, exquisite, graceful, imaginative, ornamental, ornate, pretty, refined, sensitive, showy, stylish
**decorative addition** garnish
**decorative alloy** ormolu
**decorative band** frieze
**decorative brass** ormolu
**decorative curl** curlicue
**decorative earthenware** faïence
**decorative ensemble** décor
**decorative frill** ruche
**decorative object** ornament
**decorative plant** fern
**decorative ribbon** band, rib(b)and
**decorative scrolled tablet** cartouche
**decorative skirting** dado
**decorative tie** bow
**decorative tuft** tassle
**decorative work done with a tool**
  tooling
**decorous** appropriate, becoming, correct, decent, demure, dignified, polite, prim, proper, seemly, suitable
**decorous in manner and conduct**
  modest
**decorum** decency, dignity, etiquette, manners, politeness, propriety, seemliness
**decoy** allure, attack, attract(ion), bait, deceive, draw, ensnare(ment), entice(ment), entrap, induce(ment), lead, lure, magnet, seduce, tempt, trap
**decrease** abate(ment), contract, cutback, decline, deplete, diminish, diminution, dwindle, ebb, lessen(ing), reduce, reduction, shrinking, subside(nce), wane
**decrease by** deduct
**decrease in brilliance** wane
**decrease in force** abate
**decrease in size or power** wane
**decrease in speed** brake, slow-down
**decreasing** lessening, narrowing, receding, reducing, slackening, subsiding, waning
**decree** act, appoint, bull, canon, command, decide, dictate, dictum, edict, enact(ment), fiat, judgement, law, legislation, mandate, ordain, order, ordinance, rule, sanction, sentence, statute
**decree beforehand** predetermine
**decree by law** enact
**decreed** commanded, decided, determined, dictated, enacted, legislated, ordained, ordered, prescribed, proclaimed, ruled
**decree of Muslim ruler** irade
**decree of the Church** canon
**decrepit** aged, enfeebled, feeble, infirm, superannuated, weak
**decrepit old car** jalopy
**decrescendo** diminuendo
**decrescent** waning
**decry** accuse, beggar, calumniate, castigate, censure, condemn, curse, defame, defile, denigrate, denounce, deprecate, depreciate, deride, detract, discredit, dishonour, disparage, dispraise, impugn, jeer, libel, malign, mock, rail, reprove, revile, ridicule, smirch, taint, underestimate, underplay, underreckon, vilify

**decrypt** decode
**decussate** X-shaped
**dedicate** address, apply, bless, commit, consecrate, deify, devote, dignify, give, hallow, inscribe, name, offer, preface, sanctify
**dedicated by a vow** votive
**dedication festival** encaenia
**deduce** assume, conclude, derive, draw, evolve, gather, glean, guess, infer, presume, reason, remove, subtract, trace, understand
**deduce from** derive
**deducing** concluding, deriving, drawing, gathering, gleaning, inferring, reasoning, understanding
**deduct** abate, abstract, curtail, detract, devalu(at)e, diminish, discount, dock, lessen, lower, reduce, remove, subtract, weaken, withdraw
**deduct from** dock
**deduct from tally** discount
**deduct from wage** tax
**deduction** abridg(e)ment, abstraction, conclusion, consequence, corollary, curtailment, cutback, decrement, discount, exemption, induction, inference, judg(e)ment, logic, presumption, reasoning, rebate, reduction, refund, removal, subtraction, withdrawal
**deductive reasoning** logic
**deed** achievement, act(ion), document, exploit, fact, feat, gest(e), performance, prowess, reality, title(deed), transaction, truth
**deed in writing** act
**deed of trust** lien, mortgage, security
**deed of valour** valiance, valiancy
**deed of violence** outrage
**deedy** active, earnest, industrious
**deem** account, adjudge, believe, consider, hold, judge, regard, think
**deemster** dempster
**deep** absorbing, abstract, abstruse, abyss, astute, difficult, esoteric, extreme, grave, intelligent, intense, involved, mysterious, obscure, penetrating, profound, recondite, serious, shrewd, unfathomable, wise
**deep affection** love
**deep and long inlet of the sea** fiord, fjord
**deep bell sound** bong
**deep blue colour** azure, cobalt, ultramarine
**deep blue like clear sky** cerulean
**deep blue pigment** smalt
**deep boiling vessel** cauldron
**deep bowl** basin
**deep cavity in the ground** pothole
**deep chasm** abyss

**deep circular dish** basin
**deep continuous sound** rumble
**deep covered dish** tureen
**deep cuplike cavity on the side of the hipbone** acetabulum
**deep cut** gash, gouge
**deep dish** bowl
**deep distress** calamity
**deep ditch** trench
**deep drink** swig
**deepen** aggravate, amplify, augment, boost, cake, clot, concentrate, condense, congeal, dilate, dredge, emphasise, enhance, enlarge, excavate, expand, gel, grow, heighten, increase, intensify, jell, magnify, quicken, reinforce, set, sharpen, strengthen, thicken
**deepest part** bottom
**deepest within** in(ner)most
**deep feeling** emotion
**deep fissure in ice** crevasse
**deep-fried pieces of fish and vegetables** tempura
**deep-fried spicy chicken or pork dumplings** won ton
**deep furrow** trench
**deep gorge** canyon, ravine
**deep hole** pit
**deep hollow place in rocks** cavern
**deep humming sound** drone
**deep in thought** pensive
**deep laugh** ho
**deep long-handled spoon** ladle
**deep longing** yearning
**deep love** adoration
**deeply** acutely, artfully, deep, entirely, formidably, fully, gravely, greatly, immeasurably, impressively, intensely, intricately, mysteriously, powerfully, profoundly, resonantly, seriously, soundly, thoroughly, vastly, vividly
**deeply criminal** flagitious
**deeply distressing** afflicting, painful
**deeply grieved** heartbroken
**deeply instilled** ingrained
**deeply interested** absorbed, engrossed
**deeply loved** adored
**deeply mined** scored
**deeply moved** ardent, impassioned
**deeply moved by sorrow** affected
**deeply moving** poignant
**deeply respectful** reverent
**deeply sad** triste, tristful
**deeply thoughtful** pensive
**deep male voice** baritone, basso
**deep mourning worn by widow** weeds
**deep mud** mire
**deep narrow valley** ravine
**deepness** bottomlessness, broadness, depth, extremeness, farness,

graveness, greatness, intenseness, lowness, profoundness, sonorousness, wideness
**deep open crack** crevasse
**deep open cut** gash
**deep opening in earth** chasm
**deep pink colour** coral
**deep place** pit
**deep pleasure** gladness, joy
**deep purple** plum
**deep purplish red** magenta
**deep ravine** gorge, kloof
**deep recess** indentation
**deep red** carmine, crimson, maroon
**deep red gem** garnet, ruby
**deep red sweet wine** jerepigo, tent
**deep regret for wrong committed** remorse
**deep respect** veneration
**deep reverence** awe
**deep rift** chasm
**deep scarlet** cardinal
**deep scratch** gouge
**deep-sea fishing ground** haaf
**deep-seated** basic, deep-rooted, essential, in(ner)most, innate, inveterate, native, natural, profound, radical
**deep sleep** coma, sopor, stupor
**deep sleeplike state** trance
**deep sorrow** grief
**deep sound** oompah
**deep thought** cogitation
**deep tone** bass
**deep track made by the passage of wheels** rut
**deep unconsciousness** coma
**deep unnatural sleep** sopor
**deep valley** canyon, glen, ravine
**deep vessel for liquids** jug
**deep violet-blue** indigo
**deep waters** sea
**deep wide ditch around building** moat
**deep wooded valley** dingle
**deep wound** gash
**deer** buck, caribou, cervid, coward, doe, elk, hart, hind, moose, olen, roe, speeder, stag
**deer cry** bell, roar, saw
**deer flesh** venison
**deer horn** antler, balcon, bez, dag
**deer in its first year** fawn, kid
**deer in third year** sorel, spay
**deerlike** cervine
**deerlike mammal** okapi
**deerlike ruminant** antelope
**deer meat** venison
**deer of North America** caribou, moose
**deer scent** musk
**deerskin slipper** moccasin
**deerstalker** hat
**deer's track** spoor

**deer's winter coat** blue
**deer tail** flag
**deer track** slot, view
**deface** abuse, blacken, blemish, blight, blot, break, bruise, contuse, crush, cut, damage, deform, destroy, disable, disfeature, disfigure, efface, eliminate, eradicate, erase, expunge, harm, hurt, impair, injure, maltreat, mar, mutilate, obliterate, ruin, scar, score, soil, spoil, stain, taint, tarnish, trash, uglify, undermine, vitiate, weaken, wound, wreck, wrong
**defacer of public property** vandal
**de facto** actual(ly), existing, real(ly)
**defamation** aspersion, calumny, libel, obloquy, scandal, slander, smear, vilification
**defamatory** calumnious, critical, denigrating, disapproving, disgraceful, dishonourable, false, imputative, injurious, insulting, notorious, outrageous, shocking, slanderous, untrue
**defamatory statement** libel, slander
**defamatory writing** libel
**defame** asperse, belie, berate, denigrate, detract, discredit, disgrace, disparage, disprove, execrate, impugn, insinuate, libel, slander, smudge, soil, vilify
**default** absence, bilk, defect, deficit, defraud, dereliction, dishonour, evade, fail(ure), fault, forfeit, lack, lapse, loss, neglect, negligence, nonpayment, omission, renege
**defaulter** cheat, delinquent, nonpayer
**defeat** beat, check, conquer, downfall, foil, frustrate, frustration, loss, overcome, overthrow, overwhelm, rout, subdue, subjugate, thrash, thwart, vanquish(ment)
**defeat at chess** (check)mate
**defeat by majority of votes** outvote
**defeat easily** outclass
**defeated** ba(u)lked, beaten, checkmate, conquered, crushed, loser
**defeated person** overwhelmed, trounced
**defeat heavily** trounce
**defeat in battle** smite
**defeating** beating, conquering, crushing, mastering, overpowering, overthrowing, overwhelming, quelling, repulsing, routing, subduing, subjugating, vanquishing
**defeat totally** thrash
**defeat utterly** overwhelm, rout, trounce

**defect** betray, blemish, blot, deficiency, desert, fault, flaw, imperfection, lack, mar, revolt, want, weakness
**defect in a lens** aberration, abnormality
**defect in fabric** flaw
**defect in memory** amnesia
**defect in one's speech** impediment, lisp, stammer, stutter
**defect in timber** knot
**defective** faulty, impaired, imperfect, inadequate, lacking, unsound, wanting
**defective article** dud
**defective explosive** dud
**defective nutrition** dystrophy, malnourishment
**defective oxygenation of the blood** anoxaemia
**defective speech** lisp, stammer, stutter
**defect of the eye** astigmatism
**defector** absconder, deserter, escapee, fugitive, runaway, traitor, truant
**defence** armament, bastion, cover, deterrence, fortification, protection, resistance
**defenceless** assailable, exposed, helpless, insecure, invadable, naked, powerless, unarmed, uncovered, unguarded, unprotected, unsafe, unsheltered, vulnerable, weak, weaponless
**defence made of felled trees** abat(t)is
**defence used by accused** alibi
**defence work** redoubt
**defend** assert, fortify, guard, justify, maintain, preserve, protect, safeguard, screen, shelter, shield, uphold
**defendant in libel suit** libellee
**defendant's excuse** alibi
**defender** upholder
**defender of liberty** patriot
**defender of the faith** fidel defensor (L)
**defend from harm** protect
**defensible** holdable, justifiable, plausible, secure, tenable, valid
**defensible enclosure** boma
**defensive armour** aegis, mail
**defensive armour for forearm** vambrace
**defensive armour for the body** mail
**defensive barrier** barricade, stockade
**defensive bastion** fort
**defensive circle of water** moat
**defensive covering** armour, helmet, shield
**defensive ditch around castle** moat
**defensive enclosure** boma
**defensive footballer** back
**defensive garment** gambeson, jack
**defensive head covering** helmet

**defensive mound** rampart
**defensive plating on warship** armour
**defensive trench** foxhole
**defensive wall** parapet, rampart
**defer** adjourn, bow, comply, delay, deliver, entrust, postpone, prevent, procrastinate, put-off, refer, retard, shelve, submit, surrender, suspend, temporise, wait, yield
**defer action** procrastinate, wait
**deferential** acquiescent, adoring, awed, civil, complaisant, considerate, courteous, devout, docile, gentle, humble, loving, meek, mild, modest, obedient, obeisant, obsequious, passive, patient, peaceful, pious, polite, prostrate, respectful, reverent, soft, solemn, submissive, unpretentious, yielding
**defiance** antagonism, audacity, bearding, bravado, braveness, challenge, contumacy, daring, disobedience, disregard, insult, insurgency, intimidation, opposition, provocation, recalcitrance, resistance, revolt, scorn
**defiant** aggressive, challenging, contrary, disloyal, disobedient, disorderly, fierce, haughty, insolent, insubordinate, insurgent, intractable, mischievous, mocking, naughty, obstreperous, pugnacious, rebellious, recalcitrant, refactory, riotous, sarcastic, sneering, turbulent, undisciplined, unruly, wilful
**defiant behaviour** bravado
**deficiency** defect, deficit, flaw, inadequacy, lack, shortage
**deficiency disease** beriberi, pel(l)agra, rickets, scurvy
**deficiency of oxygen** anoxia, hypoxia
**deficient** defective, inadequate, inferior, insufficient, lacking, unsatisfactory, weak
**deficient in amount** meagre
**deficient in character** feeble
**deficient in consideration for others** selfish
**deficient in intelligence** feeble
**deficient in power** weak
**deficient in speed** slow
**deficient in strength** feeble, weak
**deficit** arrears, default, deficiency, loss, shortage, shortfall
**defier** darer
**defile** abuse, befoul, begrime, besmear, besmirch, blacken, blight, calumniate, canyon, cleft, contaminate, daub, decry, defame, denigrate, deprave, dirty, dishonour, draggle, fissure, foul, gorge, infect, malign, pass, poison, pollute, rape,

ravine, ravish, sacrilegiously, slander, smear, smirch, soil, stain, sully, taint, tarnish, traduce, vilify, vitiate
**defilement** contamination, dirt(iness), dung, excrement, excreta, faeces, filth(iness), foulness, garbage, grime, impurity, infection, muck, nastiness, ordure, pollution, refuse, sewage, slime, sludge, squalor, taint, uncleanness
**define** delineate, describe, enumerate, specify
**defined age** era
**defined area** zone
**definite** assured, certain, clear(ly), decided, defined, determined, exact, explicit, express, fixed, positive, precise, specific
**definite article** the
**definite locality** spot
**definitely unlawful** illicit
**definite thing** the
**definitive** absolute, archetypal, classic, clinching, conclusive, convincing, critical, crucial, decided, decisive, definite, determinate, exemplary, fateful, final, finished, ideal, influential, irrefutable, irrevocable, master, model, settled, significant, standard, ultimate, unanswerable
**deflate** chasten, collapse, compress, constrict, contract, dash, decompress, decrease, deplete, depreciate, depress, devalue, disconcert, dispirit, empty, exhaust, flatten, press, puncture, reduce, shrink, squash, squeeze, void
**deflated tyre** flat
**deflect** avert, bend, curve, deviate, divagate, diverge, divert, edge, flex, incline, parry, refract, shunt, shy, sidestep, sidetrack, sidle, swerve, switch, turn, twist, veer, warp
**deform** contort, disfigure, distort, maim, malform, mar, misshape, ruin, spoil
**deformation** denigration, distortion, slander, vilification, vituperation
**deformed** contorted, crippled, maimed, malformed, mangled, misshapen
**deformed flower** bullhead
**deformity** abnormality, defect, distortion, malformation, vileness
**defraud** beguile, bilk, bluff, cheat, delude, dupe, embezzle, fleece, hoodwink, mislead, mulct, outwit, pilfer, rob, rook, skin, swindle, trick, victimise
**defray in advance** prepay
**defrost** melt, thaw
**deft** adept, adroit, agile, apt, clever, dext(e)rous, expert, handy, skilful

**defunct** dead, deceased, departed, done-for, extinct, gone
**defy** baffle, beard, beat, brave, challenge, confront, dare, defeat, despise, disdain, disregard, elude, face, flout, foil, frustrate, provoke, repel, resist, scorn, slight, spurn, thwart, withstand
**defy contemptuously** mock
**defying lawful authority** rebellious
**defy orders** disobey
**degenerate** base, corrupt, debased, debauched, decadent, decay, decline, degenerated, degraded, depraved, derelict, deteriorate, dissolute, err, fail, fallen, ignoble, immoral, lapse, low, mean, regress, relapse, retrograde, retrogress, reverted, rot, sink, slip, worsen
**degenerating** decaying, declining, deteriorating, lapsing, regressing, retrograde, rotting, sinking, slipping, worsening
**degeneration** corruption, debasement, decadence, decline, degeneracy, depravation, depravity, descent, deterioration, evil, immorality, impurity, iniquity, lapse, perversion, retrogression, sinfulness, vice, viciousness, vitiation, wickedness
**degenerative disease of the brain** encephalopathy
**degradation** baseness, corruption, decadence, demotion, deposition, depravity, derogation, deterioration, discredit, disgrace, dishonour, disrepute, humiliation, ignominy, meanness, mortification, obloquy, vitiation
**degrade** abase, corrupt, debase, declass, defame, demean, demote, depose, deprave, depress, derogate, deteriorate, detract, disgrace, dishonour, disparage, disrate, downgrade, humble, humiliate, lower, shame
**degrade oneself** demean
**degree** angularity, certificate, class, diploma, extent, gradation, grade, level, measure, merit, quantity, rank, rate, series, stage, standard, state, status, step
**degree ceremony** graduation
**degree in a scale** grade
**degree in judo or karate** dan
**degree in rank** grade
**degree mentioned** such
**degree of eminence** stature
**degree of excellence** quality
**degree of heat** temperature
**degree of moisture** humidity
**degree of official standing** rank

**degree of progress** stage
**degree of quality** class, grade, mark, rating, standard, variety
**degree of remoteness** distance
**degree of value** rate
**degree of warmth** temperature
**degrees East or West** longitude
**dehiscent fruit** squirting cucumber
**dehorned cattle** mul(l)ey
**dehydrate** bake, deprive, desiccate, drain, dry, evaporate, exsiccate, parch, sear, sun-dry, thirst
**dehydrated** arid, barren, dried, dry, parched, sapless, seared, torrid, waterless
**deification of self** autotheism
**deified spirit or force** manito(u), manitu
**deify** admire, adore, adulate, celebrate, change, dignify, ennoble, esteem, exalt, glorify, hero-worship, honour, idealise, idolise, improve, increase, intensify, laud, lift, love, praise, renew, respect, revere(nce), transform, upgrade, uplift, upraise, value, venerate, worship
**deign** abase, belittle, bend, condescend, consent, debase, deem, degrade, demean, disgrace, humiliate, stoop, submit, vouchsafe
**deism** theism
**deity** divinity, genius, god(dess), godhead, icon, idol, immortal, joss, numen, spirit, supreme being
**deity of woods and flocks** faun
**deject** abash, allay, awe, check, chill, cool, crush, curb, damp(en), dash, daunt, deaden, demoralise, depress, desolate, diminish, discourage, discourse, dishearten, dismay, dispirit, dull, enervate, frighten, inhibit, intimidate, moderate, oppress, overawe, restrain, sadden, scare, stifle, tire, unnerve, weaken
**dejected** bad, crestfallen, despondent, disconsolate, dismal, doleful, down(cast), downhearted, droopy, gloomy, glum, low, melancholy, miserable, morose, mournful, pining, poor, sad, sombre, spiritless, sunk, unhappy
**de jure** legally, rightfully
**delay** dawdling, defer(ment), delaying, detain, hinder, impede, linger, loiter, postpone(ment), procrastinate, procrastination, retard, slow, stall, tarrying
**delay departure** linger
**delayed result** aftereffect
**delay in payment** moratorium
**delay progress** retard

**dele** cancel, delete, edit, erase, expunge, obliterate, omit, remove
**delectable titbit** bonne bouche (F)
**delegate** assign, commission, depute, deputy, entrust, envoy, representative
**delegated authority** power
**delegated power** authority
**delete** annul, cancel, dele, destroy, edit, efface, eliminate, eradicate, erase, exclude, expunge, obliterate, omit, remove
**deleterious** dangerous, destructive, detrimental, harmful, hurtful, injurious, ruinous
**deletion** abandonment, abolition, cancellation, elimination, erasure, excision, quashing, repeal, revocation
**deliberate** careful, cautious, cogitate, confer, conscious, consider(ed), consult, debate, designed, discuss, intentional, meditate, methodical, planned, ponder, premeditated, purposeful, purposive, reflect, studied, think, thoughtful, unhurried, weigh, wilful
**deliberate cruelty** torture
**deliberate deception** bluff, fraud
**deliberate extermination of a people** genocide
**deliberate insult** affront
**deliberately** calculatingly, consciously, emphatically, knowingly, resolutely, studiously, wilfully
**deliberately avoid** shun
**deliberately disregard** ignore, cold-shoulder
**deliberately emotionless** deadpan
**deliberately failing in one's duties** negligent
**deliberately go without food** fast
**deliberately ignore** snub
**deliberately set on fire** arson
**deliberate miscarriage** abortion
**deliberate pretence** affectation
**deliberate trouble-making** aggro
**deliberate wickedness** Satanism
**deliberation** advisement, care, debate, discussing, discussion, firmness, forethought, intention, leisureness, meditation, pondering, reasoning, review, slowness, thought(fulness), vigilance, wilfulness
**delicacy** accuracy, daintiness, dainty, fastidiousness, feebleness, fineness, finesse, frailty, lightness, precariousness, precision, respect, tact, tenderness, weakness
**delicate** accurate, airy, brittle, careful, critical, dainty, difficult, discrimination, ethereal, exquisite, fastidious, fine, fragile, frail, frangible, genteel, hypersensitive, luxurious, nice, painstaking, perishable, precarious, precise, sensitive, sheer, sheltered, skilful, slight, soft, subtle, tender, thin, transparent, weak
**delicate fabric** lace
**delicate filmy material** gossamer
**delicate food** cake
**delicate gauze** gossamer
**delicate gradation** nuance
**delicate indoor flower** cyclamen
**delicately** carefully, daintily, deftly, elegantly, skilfully, subtly, tactfully
**delicately pretty** dainty
**delicate manipulation** finesse
**delicate ornamental openwork** filigree
**delicate parsley-flavoured herb** chervil
**delicate perception** tact
**delicate shade** pastel
**delicate trim** lace
**delicate vine** smilax
**delicious** agreeable, appetising, aromatic, choice, dainty, delectable, delicate, enjoyable, epicurean, exquisite, fragrant, juicy, lekker, luscious, mouthwatering, nice, palatable, pleasant, pleasing, savoury, scrumptious, tasty, tender, titillating, toothsome
**delicious drink** nectar
**delight** amuse, charm, ecstasy, elate, elation, enchant, enjoyment, enrapture, felicity, gladness, glee, gratify, joy, please, pleasure, rapture, transport
**delightful** agreeable, amusing, captivating, charming, congenial, delectable, engaging, enjoyable, entertaining, entrancing, fascinating, frabjous, heavenly, joyous, pleasant, pleasing, pleasurable, ravishing, scrumptious, thrilling
**delightful abode** Eden
**delightful to look at** beautiful
**delight in** admire, love, revel
**delight intensely** enrapture
**Delilah's lover** Samson
**delineate** contour, depict, describe, design, diagram, draft, draw, figure, limn, outline, portray, sketch, trace
**delirious** crazy, demented, deranged, distracted, ecstatic, excited, febrile, frantic, frenzied, hysterical, insane, irrational, light-headed, mad, raving, unhinged, wild
**delirious excitement** frenzy
**deliriously happy** ecstatic
**delirious plucking of bed-clothes in fever** carphology

**delirium** agitation, ecstasy, excitement, ferment, fervour, fever, flush, frenzy, heat, hysteria, hysterics, madness, mania, panic, passion, phrenitis, turmoil, unreason, unrest
**delirium tremens** DTs, jim-jams
**deliver** announce, cast, cede, communicate, consign, direct, discharge, emit, impart, liberate, proclaim, promulgate, pronounce, ransom, redeem, release, relinquish, rescue, resign, save, surrender, transfer, utter
**deliver a discourse** speak
**deliver a homily** preach
**deliverance from a charge** acquittal
**deliver a sermon** preach
**deliver a speech** orate
**delivered by special service** express
**deliverer** defender, guardian, liberator, preserver, protector, rescuer, salvation, saviour
**deliver from danger** rescue
**deliver from evil** rescue
**deliver from sin** redeem
**deliver moral lecture** sermonise
**delivery** giving, liberation, presentation, transfer, transmittal
**delivery in trust** bailment
**delivery note** docket
**delivery of goods** bailment
**delivery vehicle** lorry, truck, van
**dell** combe, coomb, dale, dene, dingle, glen, ravine, slade, strath, vale, valley
**delta** estuary, tributary
**deltoid** triangular
**delude** beguile, betray, bluff, cheat, cozen, deceive, defraud, dupe, ensnare, entrap, fool, gammon, gull, hoax, hoodwink, juggle, misguide, misinform, mislead, outwit, rook, seduce, trick, victimise
**deluge** avalanche, cataclysm, catastrophe, downpour, flood, inundate, inundation, overflowing, overrun, overwhelm, rainstorm, spate, swamp, torrent
**delusion** blunder, daydream, deceit, deception, dream, erratum, error, fallacy, falsehood, fantasy, fault, flaw, hallucination, illusion, imagination, inaccuracy, mirage, misbelieve, misconception, mistake, reverie, solecism, sophism, speculation, trance, untruth, vision
**delusions of becoming large** macromania
**delusions of grandeur** megalomania
**delusive enticer** Pied Piper
**de luxe** choice, elegant, expensive, luxurious, special, superior
**de luxe car** limousine

**delve** burrow, dig, explore, investigate, probe, research, rummage, unearth
**demand** ask, challenge, claim, exact, extort, importune, impose, inquire, insist, lack, need, order, press, require, requisition, seek, solicit, sue, summon, supplicate, ultimatum, urge, want
**demand a price** charge
**demand a repetition** encore
**demand as being due** claim
**demand as one's property** claim
**demand earnestly** urge
**demanded repeat performance** encore
**demand firmly** insist
**demand for goods** market
**demanding task** challenge
**demand money with menaces** extort
**demand on physical energy** stress
**demand payment** dun
**demand payment for insurance policy** claim
**demand payment of** exact
**demand persistently** insist
**demand the presence of** summon
**demand to respond** challenge
**demand upon mental energy** stress
**demand with determination** insist
**demarcate** define, delimitate, determine, differentiate, distinguish, fix, mark, separate
**demarcated area** district
**demarcation** bound(ary), confine, delimitation, differentiation, distinction, division, enclosure, limit, line, margin, separation
**demean** abase, behave, conduct, debase, decry, degrade, demote, depreciate, discredit, disgrace, humble, lower, shame, vitiate
**demeaning** menial
**demean oneself** grovel, stoop
**demeanour** air, appearance, bearing, behaviour, conduct, countenance, deportment, manner, mien, physiognomy, visage
**demented** absurd, crazed, crazy, deranged, fatuous, frantic, frenetic, idiotic, illogical, insane, lunatic, mad, maniacal, non compos mentis (L), odd, queer, unbalanced
**demented person** maniac
**demented with worry** distraught
**dementia praecox** schizophrenia
**demigod** idol
**demigoddess** nymph
**demise** collapse, death, decease, expiration, passing, ruin
**demobilise** disband
**democracy** commonwealth, representative, republic

**democratic** autonomous, egalitarian, popular, populist, representative, self-governing
**demolish** annihilate, bulldoze, defeat, desolate, destroy, devastate, disassemble, dismantle, flatten, level, overthrow, overturn, precipitate, pulverise, raze, ruin, topple, undo, wreck
**demon** banshee, cruel, devil, evil, familiar, fanatic, fiend, genius, goblin, guide, imp, incubus, lamia, malignant, monster, ogre, rogue, succuba, succubus, tokoloshe, villain, warlock
**demoniac** demonic, devilish, diabolical, fiendish, frenzied, furious, hellish, infernal, mad, maniacal, possessed, satanic, wild
**demonic** accursed, aliéné (F), bedevilled, cacodemonic, damnable, demented, demoniac(al), demonian, deranged, devilish, diabolic, dire, fanatical, fiendish, fou (F), frantic, frenetic, furious, impious, lunatic, lycanthropic, mad, perverted, possessed, satanic, villainous, virulent
**demonic knowledge of devils** diablerie
**demon of man's dreams** succuba, succubus
**demon of nightmare** incubus, mara
**demon of the Arabs** Afreet, Afrit, Djinn, Genie, Ghul, Jinn
**demon of the Hindus** Rahu
**demon of the Zoroastrians** Dev
**demon of vanity** Asmodeus
**demon of woods** Leshy, Lesiy
**demon star** Algol
**demonstrate** describe, display, establish, evidence, exhibit, explain, illustrate, indicate, march, parade, protest, prove, rally, show, teach
**demonstration record** demo
**demonstrative pronoun** that
**demon who robs graves** ghoul
**demote** break, cashier, declass, degrade, depose, dethrone, dismiss, displace, dispossess, downgrade, exile, humble, reduce, relegate, uncrown, unseat
**demote team to lower division** relegate
**demotion** anticlimax, blow, comedown, decline, degrading, disappointment, downgrading, humiliation, relegation, reverse
**demount** dismantle
**demur** balk, cavil, demurral, disagree, disapprove, dispute, dissent, dodge, doubt, hesitate, object(ion), pause, protest, qualm, refusal, refuse,

remonstrance, remonstrate, scruple, waver
**demure** bashful, composed, coy, decorous, diffident, grave, mim, modest, prim, prissy, prudish, reserved, reticent, retiring, sedate, shy, sober, staid, straightlaced, unassuming
**den** cave, cloister, haunt, lair, retreat, sanctum, shelter, study
**denarius** penny
**denary** ten
**denatured alcohol** meths
**dendrite** dendron
**dendroid** tree-shaped
**dendron** dendrite
**dene** combe, coomb, dale, dell, dingle, down, dune, glen, ravine, slade, strath, vale, valley
**denegation** denial
**denial** answer, contradiction, declination, denegation, deprivation, disaffirmation, disagreement, disapproval, disavowal, disbelief, disclaimer, dismissal, dissent, distrust, doubt, gainsay, nay, negation, negative, no, prohibition, rebuff, refusal, rejection, renunciation, repudiation, repulse, retraction, turn down, unbelief, unsaying, veto
**denigrate** asperse, assail, blacken, calumniate, defame, impugn, revile, slander, smirch, soil, vilify
**denim** jean
**denim trousers** jeans
**denim trousers with bib** dungaree(s)
**denizen** aborigine, addressee, citizen, dweller, indweller, (in)habitant, inhabiter, inmate, native, occupant, occupier, resident, tenant
**denizen by birth** native
**denizen of hell** hellion, Satan
**den of otters** holt
**denomination** belief, breed, character, class, communion, designation, epithet, faith, group, identification, naming, nomenclature, order, religion, sect, type, variety
**denote** betoken, denominate, designate, express, imply, import, indicate, intimate, mark, mean, name, note, portend, represent, show, signify, suggest, symbolise, typify
**denoting air** aero-
**denoting approval** OK, okay
**denoting central part** mid
**denoting disgust** fie
**denoting doctrine** ism
**denoting either sex** epicene
**denoting English** Anglo-

**denoting final purpose** telic
**denoting four** quadri-
**denoting glands that secrete externally** eccrine
**denoting hesitation** er
**denoting laughter** haha
**denoting more than one** plural
**denoting number** numerical
**denoting one person or thing** singular
**denoting position in succession** ordinal
**denoting purpose** telic
**denoting the Miocene and Pliocene epochs** Neogene
**dénouement** catastrophe, climax, close, conclusion, consequence, culmination, effect, end, eventuality, evolution, finale, finish, outcome, peak, result, solution, termination, unravelling
**dénouement of drama** catastrophe
**denounce** accuse, arraign, assail, attack, blame, censure, condemn, denunciate
**denouncer** accuser, denunciator, discloser, informant, informer, talebearer, telltale
**dense** close, cohesive, compact, compressed, concentrated, condensed, consolidated, crammed, crass, crowded, dim, impenetrable, intense, massive, multitudinous, powerful, solid, stuffed, stupid, thick(set), tight, unintelligent
**dense aggregation** mass
**dense evergreen shrub** lonicera
**dense growth of trees** canebrake, forest, jungle
**densely matted fabric** felt
**densely populated area** city, town
**dense mass of trees** thicket
**dense mist** fog
**dense shrubbery** thicket
**dense smoke** smother, smudge
**dense thicket** jungle
**dense throng** press
**dense tuft of grass** tussock
**density** body, compactness, denseness, firmness, fixedness, inelasticity, massiveness, resistance, rigidity, solidity, solidness, stiffness, stupidity, thickness, tightness
**dent** chip, crater, depress(ion), dimple, dint, hollow, impression, indent, notch, tooth
**dental decay** caries
**dental hygiene** odontotherapia
**dental plug** amalgam, filling
**dental string** floss
**dentate** toothed
**dent in cheek** dimple
**dentine** ivory

**dentist's drill** burr
**dentist's plastic** cement
**dentures** teeth
**denude** bare, deforest, denudate, disrobe, divest, expose, strip, unclothe, uncover, undress
**denuded** bare, barren, bereft, deficient, destitute, devoid, disadvantaged, empty, exposed, forlorn, lacking, naked, needy, nude, peeled, poor, shorn, stripped, unclad, unclothed, uncovered, undressed, vacant, void, wanting, without
**denunciator** accuser, denouncer, discloser, informant, informer, taleteller, telltale
**deny** abjure, contradict, controvert, decline, disavow, disbelieve, disown, dispute, negate, nullify, object, oppose, refuse, refute, reject, reneg(u)e, renounce, repudiate, veto
**deny any connection with** disown
**deny existence** negate
**denying possibility of knowledge** sceptical
**deny oneself** abnegate, abstain
**deny pleasure to oneself** abnegate
**deny statement made by** contradict
**deny the truth of** negate
**deodar** cedar
**depart** avaunt, begone, bygone, decamp, decease, deviate, die, disappear, diverge, emigrate, escape, exit, flee, fly, go, leave, migrate, move, quit, remove, retire, retreat, scram, vamoose, vanish, vary, withdraw
**depart fast** scat, scoot, vamoose
**depart from** bypass, contrast, contradict, deviate, differ, diverge, quit, vacate
**depart hurriedly** vamoose
**departing** decamping, disappearing, escaping, exiting, going, leaving, migrating, outgoing, quitting, removing, retiring, retreating, vanishing, withdrawing
**departing from accepted standard** aberrant
**department** branch, bureau, decampment, district, division, domain, escapement, function, line, office, part, province, realm, region, retirement, section, sector, station, subdivision, unit
**department for things that are found** lost property
**department of Greece** Elia
**department of northern France** Oise
**department of southern France** Aveyron
**department within a university** faculty

**depart quickly** scat, skedaddle
**depart secretly** abscond, decamp
**departure** deviation, digression, egress, exit, going, ida (Sp), leaving, withdrawal
**departure of a crowd** exodus
**departure of actor** exit
**departure of Israelites from Egypt** Exodus
**depend** build, confide, correlate, count, dangle, droop, hang, hinge, lean, pend(ulate), reckon, rely, rest, suspend, swing, trust, turn
**dependable** certain, conscientious, faithful, honest, loyal, reliable, reliant, responsible, steady, sure, true, trustworthy, trusty, unfailing
**dependable supporter** stalwart
**dependence** addiction, confidence, connection, contingency, crutch, dependency, faith, pillar, relationship, reliance, subjection, subordination, support, trust
**dependence on drugs** addiction
**dependency of China** Tibet
**dependent** child, client, consequence, contingent, defenseless, dependant, follower, helpless, immature, inferior, minion, minor, pendent, pensioner, protégé(e), reliant, relying, retainer, secondary, servant, subject, subordinate, subservient, vulnerable, weak, youngster, youth
**dependent on chance** aleatoric, aleatory
**depend for subsistence** live
**depending** reliant
**depending on chance** aleatoric, aleatory, hazardous, precarious, uncertain
**depending on experience** empiric
**depending on uncertain event** aleatory, aleatoric
**depend on** believe, expect, rely
**depict** adorn, characterise, copy, decorate, define, demonstrate, describe, design, detail, display, draw, emulate, evidence, exemplify, exhibit, explain, express, illustrate, instance, limn, narrate, outline, paint, picture, portray, recount, reflect, report, represent, show, sketch, specify, trace
**depiction** cartoon, copy, effigy, facsimile, illustration, image, likeness, model, outline, picture, portrait, portrayal, replica, representation, sketch, study
**depiction of Christ** icon
**depiction of the beautiful** art
**deplete** bankrupt, bleed, consume, decrease, drain, empty, enervate,

evacuate, exhaust, lessen, reduce, spend, unload, weaken
**deplorable** calamitous, censurable, condemnable, dire, disastrous, disreputable, distressing, execrable, grievous, lamentable, miserable, opprobrious, pitiable, regrettable, reprehensible, sad, scandalous, shameful, unfortunate, wretched
**deplorably** sadly
**deplorably bad** sad
**deplore** bemoan, bewail, grieve, lament, mourn, regret
**deploy** display, unfold
**deploy military units** manoeuvre
**deponent** affiant, testifier, witness
**deport** banish, conduct, eject, evict, exclude, exile, expatriate, expel, ostracise, oust, outlaw, proscribe, repatriate, transport
**deportment** actions, air, aspect, attitude, bearing, behaviour, carriage, comportment, conduct, demeanour, etiquette, expression, guise, manners, mien, obedience, port, posture, semblance, ways
**depose** break, cashier, degrade, demote, dethrone, dismiss, displace, downgrade
**deposit** bank, coating, drop, hoard, lay, leave, lode, place, precipitate, put, rain, save, sediment, set, silt, snow, soot, store
**deposit as rubbish** dump
**deposit fish eggs** spawn
**deposit ice crystals** snows
**deposit in earth** bury, inter
**deposit in river** silt
**deposit of fine wind-blown soil** loess
**deposit of gold particles** placer
**deposit of sediment** silt
**deposit on floor of cave** stalagmite
**deposit on metal** rust
**deposit on purchase** down payment
**deposit on roof of cave** stalactite
**depository** bank, cashier, coffer, depositary, depot, fund, guardian, locker, magazine, repertory, repository, reserve, safe, savings, store(house), strongroom, treasurer, treasury, trustee, vault, warehouse
**depository for weapons** arsenal
**depot** depository, entrepôt, garage, repository, station, store(house), terminal, terminus, warehouse
**depot custodian** storekeeper
**deprave** corrupt, debase, debauch, degrade, demoralise, deteriorate, infect, pervert, seduce, subvert, vitiate
**depraved** bad, base, bestial, corrupt, debased, debauched, degenerate, dissolute, evil, immoral, lessen, licentious, lower, miscreant, preverted, rotten, shameless, shrewd, sinful, ugly, vicious, vile, wicked
**depraved person** rotter
**depravity** adulteration, corruption, immorality, lewdness, obscenity, perversion, sensuality, sin(fulness), turpitude, uncleanness, vitiation, vulgarity, wickedness
**depreciate** belittle, condemn, decry, denigrate, deplore, deprecate, depress, deride, devalue, discredit, disparage, lessen, lower, reduce, reject, underrate, undervalue
**depress** cheapen, dampen, debase, degrade, deject, devalue, discourage, dishearten, dispirit, humiliate, lower, oppress, reduce, sadden, weaken
**depressant drug** downer
**depressed** blue, concave, dented, disheartened, dispirited, down, indented, low, melancholy, sad, sunken, unhappy
**depressed by absence from home** homesick
**depressed in spirits** dysthymic
**depressed or bored state of mind** doldrums
**depressed when away from home** homesick
**depressing** bleak, daunting, dejecting, depressive, discouraging, heartbreaking, hopeless, melancholy, sad(dening), sombre, triste
**depression** blues, cavity, decline, dejection, dent, despondency, dimple, dint, dip, dumps, hollow, inactivity, indent(ation), melancholy, pit, recess(ion), sadness, slump, trough, valley
**depression between belly and thigh** groin
**depression between convolutions of brain** fissure
**depression between mountain peaks** col, dip
**depression in bottle bottom** kick
**depression in ear** scapha
**depression in fruits** eye
**depression in golf green** cup
**depression in mountain-chain** col
**depression in plank** knothole
**depression in range** pass
**depression in ridge** col
**depression worn by running water** gullet, ravine
**deprivation** bereavement, denial, deposition, deprival, dismissal, distress, divestment, expulsion, hardship, lack, loss, need, ousting, privation, removal, want, withholding
**deprive** bereave, commandeer, confiscate, debar, denude, deny, despoil, disallow, dispossess, divest, expropriate, refuse, remove, rob, strip, withhold
**deprive by deceit** cheat
**deprive by violence** rob
**deprived of** minus
**deprived of feeling** numb
**deprived of life** dead, lifeless
**deprive of ability** disable
**deprive of belongings** dispossess
**deprive of by deceit** mulct
**deprive of clothing** strip
**deprive of feeling** benumb
**deprive of food** starve
**deprive of judgment** infatuate
**deprive of life** kill, slay
**deprive of limb or other part** mutilate
**deprive of moisture** drain
**deprive of natural qualities** denature
**deprive of rank** demote
**deprive of reason** dement
**deprive of rights** attaint
**deprive of sacred character** desecrate
**deprive of sensation** stupefy
**deprive of shelter** unhouse
**deprive of sight** blind
**deprive of strength** weaken
**deprive of the vote** disfranchise
**deprive of vigour** enervate, weaken
**deprive of virginity** deflower
**deprive of vitality** enervate, deaden
**deprive of weapons** disarm, unarm
**deprive of wind** calm
**deprive priest of ecclesiastical rank** unfrock
**depth** abyss, complexity, deepness, profundity, timbre
**depute** accredit, appoint, authorise, certify, commission, commit, contract, delegate, depute, deputy, designate, empower, engage, entrust, guarantee, license, nominate, order, recognize, sanction, select, send
**deputised band** posse
**deputy** agent, ambassador, bureaucrat, comitatus (L), commissioner, consul, delegate, designated, diplomat, elected, emissary, envoy, legate, lieutenant, minister, posse, provost, proxy, representative, substitute, surrogate, viceroy
**deputy doctor** locum
**deputy of bishop** vicar
**derange** agitate, clutter, confuse, convulse, disarrange, discompose,

disorder, disorganise, displace, disturb, litter, misplace, move, ruffle, rumple, scatter, shake, shatter, shift, strew, tousle, transpose, twist, unhinge, untidy, work, wrinkle
**deranged** crazed, crazy, delirious, demented, distracted, frantic, frenzied, insane, irrational, lunatic, mad, maniacal, unbalanced, unhinged
**deranged in mind** moonstruck
**Derby entrant** horse
**Derby hat** bowler
**Derby is run here** Epsom
**derelict** abandoned, alone, bergie, careless, deserted, desolate, discarded, forlorn, hobo, neglected, negligent, outcast, rejected, relinquished, remiss, scorned, solitary, tramp, vagrant, wastrel
**dereliction** abandonment, apostasy, carelessness, default, defection, delay, desertion, disregard, fault, forgetfulness, forsaking, inaccuracy, inexactness, jilting, languidness, laxity, leaving, neglect, negligence, negligency, oversight, passiveness, rejection, remissness, slackness, sloppiness, transgression
**derelict person** bergie, hobo, tramp, vagrant
**deride** abuse, chaff, contemn, detract, disdain, fleer, gibe, hiss, jeer, jibe, lampoon, laugh, mock, rag, ridicule, satirise, scoff, scorn, slur, sneer, taunt, tease, twit, vilify
**derision** disdain, mockery, ridicule, scorn
**derisive** contemptuous, cynical, disdainful, disrespectful, flippant, impertinent, insulting, ironic, irreverent, misanthropical, mocking, pessimistic, ridiculous, sarcastic, sardonic, satirical, saucy, sceptical, scornful, sneering, taunting, unbelieving
**derisive sound** boo, hiss
**derivation of place names** eponomy
**derivative** copied, imitative, mock, onomatopoeic, parrotlike, plagiarised, put-on, secondhand, simulated, spin-off, unoriginal
**derivative of morphia** heroin
**derivative of phenol** anol
**derive** collect, deduce, draw, elicit, follow, gain, issue, obtain, originate, proceed, procure, trace
**derived by inference** illative
**derived from authority** official
**derived from direct descent** lineal
**derived from fat** adipic, sebacic
**derived from oil** oleic

**derived from the land** terrigenous
**derived from the name of its bearer's mother** metronymic
**derived from vinegar** acetic
**dermatitis from exposure to radiation** actinodermatitis
**dermis** corium, skin
**dernier** final, last
**derogatory** aspersive, base, captious, carping, cavilling, censorious, contemptible, critical, defamatory, disapproving, discreditable, disgraceful, dishonourable, disorderly, disparaging, disreputable, false, fault-finding, ignominious, infamous, injurious, insulting, libellous, low, malicious, mean, nagging, niggling, notorious, scandalous, scurrilous, shameful, shocking, slanderous, snide, traducing, unprincipled, untrue, vicious, vile, vituperative
**derogatory remark** slur, snide
**derrick** crane
**derrick pole** mast
**derrière** buttocks
**derry** ballad
**dervish's cap** taj
**descend** alight, degenerate, derive, issue, originate, plummet, sink, slant, tumble
**descend abruptly** plunge
**descendant** daughter, juvenile, kid, kin, lightie, minor, offshoot, progeny, protégé(e), toddler, tot, youngster
**descendant of Dan** Danite
**descendant of Ham** Hamite
**descendant of Jacob** Israelite, Levite
**descendant of Mohammed** Emir
**descendant of one of Noah's sons** Hamite
**descendant of Shem** S(h)emite
**descendant of white and Negro persons** mulatto
**descendants** babies, breed, children, daughters, family, heirs, infants, issue, juveniles, kids, lighties, lineage, minors, offshoots, offsprings, posterity, progeny, protégé(e)s, race, scions, seed, sons, toddlers, young, youngsters
**descendants of a common ancestor** family
**descend by rope** abseil
**descend freely** fall
**descend from same ancestor** consanguineous, akin
**descend from same forefather** agnate
**descending steeply** drop, precipitous, rapid
**descend to ground** alight

**descent** ancestry, attack, comedown, debasement, declination, decline, declivity, degradation, derivation, descending, drop, extraction, fall(ing), genealogy, heredity, inclination, incline, lineage, origin, parentage, plunge, raid, sink, slant, slope, swoop
**descent from parents** parentage
**describe** characterise, depict, narrate, portray, relate, represent, tell
**describe faintly** adumbrate
**describe grammatically** parse
**description** portrayal
**description of general features of universe** cosmography
**description of methods of lovemaking** erotology
**description of or treatise on organic tissues** histography
**description of reasons for award** citation
**description of stolen goods** hot
**description of teeth** odontography
**description of the character of the atmosphere** aerography
**description of the surface of the moon** selenography
**descriptive astronomy** uranography
**descriptive attribution** epithet
**descriptive science of metals** metallography
**descriptive writing** imagery
**descry** ascertain, catch, detect, determine, discern, disclose, discover, distinguish, encounter, espy, explore, expose, find, identify, locate, note, notice, observe, perceive, realise, recognise, reveal, see, spot, spy, uncover
**desecration of holy place** sacrilege
**desert** abandon, abscond, arid, barren, betray, defect, desolate, forsake(n), Gobi, infertile, Kalahari, leave, lonely, quit, relinquish, Sahara, solitude, uninhabited, unproductive, untilled, vacate, wasteland, wilderness
**desert animal** camel
**desert dweller** Arab, Bedouin, eremite
**deserted** bereft, derelict, desolate, empty, forlorn, forsaken, isolated, lonely, neglected, solitary, unfriendly, uninhabited, vacant
**deserted infant** foundling
**deserted place** ghost town
**deserted region** waste
**deserter** abdicator, absconder, apostate, betrayer, defector, delinquent, derelict, escapee, fugitive, malingerer, recreant,

renegade, runaway, shirker, traitor, truant, turncoat
**desert fox** Rommel
**desert illusion** mirage
**desert in Africa** Arabian, Elerg, Kalahari, Libyan, Namib, Nefund, Nubian, Sahara
**desert in Arabia** Ankaf, Nafud, Nefud, Rub al Khali
**desert in Asia** Gobi, Taklamakan
**desert in Australia** Simpson, Sturt
**desert in California** Colorado, Mojave
**desert in Chile** Atacama
**desert in China** Alashan, Gobi, Ordos, Shamo
**desert in Egypt** Libyan
**desert in Hawaii** Kau
**desert in India** Thar
**desert in Iran** Kerman
**desert in Israel** Negev
**desert in Libya** Fezzan, Murzuk
**desert in Mongolia** Gobi
**desert in Namibia** Kalahari, Namib
**desert in Peru** Sechura
**desert in Saudi Arabia** Nefud, Red, Rub-al-Khali
**desert in South America** Atacama
**desert in Sudan** Nubian
**desertion to the other side** defection
**desert lynx** caracal
**desert mainly in Botswana** Kalahari
**desert phenomenon** mirage
**desert plant** cactus
**desert rat** jerboa
**desert refuge** oasis
**desert region** erg
**desert state** Nevada
**desert train** caravan
**desert vision** mirage
**desert wanderer** nomad
**desert watering place** oasis
**desert wind** simoom, simoon, sirocco
**deserve** claim, earn, entitled, expect, gain, justify, merit(orious), procure, rate, warrant, win, worthy
**deserving** admirable, commendable, condign, creditable, estimable, excellent, exemplary, laudable, meriting, meritorious, praiseworthy, qualified, righteous, virtuous, worthful, worthy
**deserving blame** culpable, guilty
**deserving of admiration** estimable
**deserving respect** worthy
**deserving reward** merit
**deserving to be laughed at** absurd, foolish, ridiculous
**desiccate** dehydrate, drain, dry, dwindle, exhaust, fade, parch, sear, shrink, shrivel, wilt, wither, wizen
**desiccated** arid, dehydrated, drained, dry, dwindled, parched, seared,

sere, shrank, shrivelled, shrunk, wilted, withered, wizened, wrinkled
**desiccator** dryer
**design** arrangement, blueprint, condescend, create, devise, draw(ings), drift, end, intend, intention, mean(ing), object, outline, pattern, plan, project, proposal, propose, purpose, scheme, sketch, style
**design and bring into being** create
**designate** allot, appoint, assign, betoken, call, characterise, choose, christen, deem, define, delegate, denote, depute, describe, dub, earmark, entitle, import, indicate, label, mean, name, nominate, select, show, specify, stipulate, style, term
**designated for a building** site
**designated person** nominee
**designation** delegation, description, epithet, name, selection, title
**designation of place** address
**designed for male and female** unisex
**designed to beautify** cosmetic
**designed to be friendly** amicable
**designer** architect, artist, Chanel, Dior, planner
**designer of buildings** architect
**designer of fashionable styles** stylist
**designer of Parthenon** Callicrates, Ictinus
**designer of public utility works** engineer
**designer of the dancing in a ballet** choreographer
**designing** artful, astute, contriving, deceitful, scheming, tricky, unscrupulous, wily
**design in relief** emboss
**design in sunk relief** intaglio
**design on metal** etch
**design on skin** tattoo
**designs on wood made with a hot poker** xylopyrography
**design transfer** stencilling
**desirability** advantage, merit, profit, usefulness, value, worth
**desirable** admirable, agreeable, alluring, approvable, attractive, beneficial, charming, enviable, estimable, excellent, expedient, first-class, likable, lovable, pleasing, proper, recommendable, superb, superior, valuable, winning, worthy
**desirable residence** good address
**desire** appeal, appetence, appetite, ardour, ask, aspiration, aspire, care, covet(ousness), crave, craving, demand, emotion, fancy, feeling, greed, hankering, hunger, longing, lust, motive, need, passion, petition,

request, require, supplication, thirst, urge, want, will, wish, yearning, yen
**desire ambitiously** aspire
**desire and expect** hope
**desire anxiously** yearn
**desired standard** norm
**desire eagerly** aspire, covet
**desire for achievement** ambition
**desire for drink** thirst
**desire for food** appetite
**desire for success** ambition
**desire for water** thirst
**desire greatly** crave
**desire immoderately** covet
**desire intensely** crave
**desire to do good** benevolent
**desire to eat** appetite
**desire to gain** acquisitive
**desire to harm others** malice
**desire to know** curiosity
**desire to succeed** ambition
**desire to tease** malice
**desire to travel** wanderlust
**desire wrongfully** covet
**desiring food** hungry
**desirous to know** curious, inquisitive
**desist** abstain, arrest, avoid, cease, curb, curtail, deny, discontinue, end, eschew, halt, hold, interrupt, pause, reject, rest, shun, stay, stop
**desk** ambo, bureau, escritoire, secretaire
**desk for holding Bible in church** lectern
**desk with drawers** bureau
**desk worker** clerk
**desolate** abandoned, alone, barren, bleak, cheerless, depopulated, desert(ed), devastated, disconsolate, forlorn, (god)forsaken, inconsolable, lone(ly), lonesome, lorn, lost, miserable, ravaged, sad(dened), scorched, stark, unhappy, uninhabited, wild, wretched
**desolate looking** gaunt
**desolate region** desert, puna (Sp)
**despair** anguish, collapse, desperation, despondency, discouragement, disheartenment, gloom, hopelessness, inconsolableness, melancholy, misery, mope, ordeal, quit, surrender, trial, tribulation, wretchedness
**despair of** hopeless, irredeemable, lost
**despatch** dismiss, dispatch, expedite, express, hasten, hurry, perform, release, remit, send, transmit
**despatcher** sender
**desperado** bandit, buccaneer, criminal, cutthroat, felon, gangster, gunman, highwayman, hoodlum, lawbreaker,

malefactor, miscreant, outlaw, pirate, plunderer, raider, rapparee, robber, rover, rowdy, ruffian, terrorist, thief, thug, tough, tsotsi, villain
**desperate** acute, daring, despairing, dire, excessive, foolhardy, forlorn, frantic, grave, hopeless, prodigious, rash, reckless, urgent, wretched
**desperate appeal** SOS
**desperate course of action** pis aller (F)
**despicable** abhorrent, abject, base, beyond, cheap, contemptible, degrading, disgraceful, hateful, low, mean, nameless, pitiful, servile, shameful, sordid, vile, worthless, wretched
**despicable fellow** caitiff, hangdog
**despicable person** cad, cheapskate, fink, rotter, stinker
**despise** abhor, abominate, condemn, deride, detest, disdain, dislike, hate, jeer, loathe, mock, oppress, reject, ridicule, scoff, scorn, scout, shun, snub, spurn
**despite** against, aversion, malice, nevertheless, nonetheless, notwithstanding, outrage, spite, vex(ation)
**despite the fact** albeit, (al)though
**despoil** commandeer, confiscate, desolate, devastate, divest, maraud, pillage, plunder, poach, ravage, rob, ruin, snatch, spoliate, strip, thieve
**despondency** broken-heartedness, dejection, depression, despair, desperation, discouragement, down-heartedness, gloom, hopelessness, inconsolability, melancholy, misery, sadness, sorrow, wretchedness
**despondent period** blues
**despot** autarch, autocrat, dictator, emperor, lord, master, monarch, monocrat, oppressor, tsar, tyrant
**despotic** absolute, arbitrary, arrogant, authoritarian, autocratic, bossy, despotical, dictatorial, disdainful, doctrinaire, domineering, hard, harsh, haughty, high-handed, imperious, monocratic, oppressive, rigid, severe, sovereign, stern, strict, supercilious, tyrannical, unbounded, unconditional, unqualified
**despotic official** satrap
**despotism** absolutism, autarchy, autocracy, dictatorship, domination, imperialism, monocracy, oppression, sovereignty, supremacy, totalitarianism, tyranny
**dessert** afters, coupe, entremets, pudding, sweets

**dessert glass** coupe
**dessert nut** almond
**dessert shell** meringue
**dessert wine** marsala
**dessert with alcohol** trifle
**destination** bourn(e), goal, haven, harbour, landing-place, resting-place, station, stop, terminus
**destination of Titanic** New York
**destination on envelope** address
**destine** appoint, dedicate, design(ate), destinate, determine, devote, doom, earmark, fate, intend, mark, necessitate, ordain, predetermine, preordain, purpose, reserve, resolve, tag
**destined** booked, bound, directed, doomed, fated, intended, meant, preordained
**destined for death** dying
**destined for ruination** doomed
**destined to happen** in store
**destiny** chance, cup, decree, destination, doom, fate, fortune, future, goal, karma, kismet, lot, necessity, predestination, predetermination, stars
**destitute** depleted, distressed, impecunious, impoverished, indigent, needy, penniless, penurious, poor, poverty-stricken
**destitute of** devoid
**destitute of a tail** acaudal, anurous
**destitute of hair** bald
**destitute of knowledge** ignorant
**destitute of leaves** aphyllous
**destitute of strength** imbecile
**destitute of teeth** edentate
**destitute of vision** blind
**destitution** absence, beggary, dearth, default, depletion, distress, indigence, insolvency, lack, liquidation, mendicity, need, penury, poverty, starvation, want
**destroy** abolish, abrogate, absorb, annihilate, demolish, desolate, devastate, devour, end, eradicate, exterminate, extinguish, extirpate, gut, invalidate, kill, level, nullify, obliterate, rase, raze, rid, ruin, sabotage, slaughter, slay, smash, spoil, undo, waste, wreck
**destroy belief in** discredit, disprove, invalidate, refute
**destroy by wasting** consume, devour
**destroy completely** annihilate, eradicate
**destroyer of images** iconoclast
**destroy germs** sterilise
**destroy gradually** corrode, erode
**destroy insidiously** sap
**destroy one's affections** estrange

**destroy totally** annihilate, eliminate, exterminate, extirpate
**destroy work of art** vandalise
**destruction** annihilation, blast, death, demolition, desolation, devastation, downfall, ecocide, end, eradication, extermination, extinction, havoc, liquidation, massacre, overthrow, plague, ruin, shattering, slaughter, split, tear, vandalism, wrecking
**destruction of a ship by accident** wreck
**destruction of bacteria by antibodies** bacteriolysis
**destruction of life** holocaust
**destructive** adverse, antagonistic, calamitous, contradictory, deadly, deleterious, derogatory, disastrous, fatal, harmful, injurious, lethal, mischievous, obstreperous, opposed, opposing, pernicious, ravaging, ruinous, suicidal, unfriendly, unruly, vicious, violent
**destructive beetle** weevil
**destructive burning** fire
**destructive disease of trees and plants** blight, canker
**destructive emotion** hate
**destructive fire** conflagration
**destructive insect** locust, moth, termite, weevil
**destructively** balefully, calamitously, cataclysmically, catastrophically, deleteriously, detrimentally, fatally, harmfully, hurtfully, injuriously, lethally, perniciously, ruinously
**destructive person** vandal
**destructive sea wave** tsunami
**destructive winged insect** locust
**desultory** unmethodical
**detach** disconnect, disunite, isolate, separate, sever, unfasten
**detachable front part of gun carriage** limber
**detachable lock with a hinged hoop** padlock
**detached bell tower** campanile
**detached piece** fragment
**detached portion** piece
**detached state** isolation
**detail** appoint, assign, duty, enumerate, fact, item(ise), minutia, particular, service, specify
**detailed information** data
**detailed list** inventory
**detailed map or method** plan
**detailed report** dossier
**detailed version** elaboration
**detain** arrest, check, confine, delay, halt, hinder, hold, immure, impound, imprison, incarcerate, intern, keep,

pen, restrain, retain, retard, secure, slow, stay, stop, withhold
**detain during wartime** intern
**detainee** captive, convict, hostage, internee, prisoner, slave
**detain in wartime** intern
**detect** ascertain, catch, descry, determine, discern, disclose, discover, distinguish, espy, establish, expose, find, identify, learn, nose, notice, observe, perceive, recognise, reveal, see, sense, sight, spot, spy, trace, uncover, understand, unearth, unmask, unveil
**detecting system** radar
**detective** constable, cop, investigator, private eye, sleuth
**detective device** radar
**detective story** whodun(n)it
**detector** spotter
**detention** arrest, confinement, custody, delay(ing), detainment, hindrance, imprisonment, incarceration, quarantine, restraint, retaining, retardation, retention, stopping
**deter** daunt, discourage, dissuade, hinder, prevent, restrain, stop
**deterge** cleanse, mundify, purge
**detergent** abstergent, clean(s)er, cleansing, depurative, detersive, soap
**deteriorate** contaminate, corrupt, decay, decline, decompose, degenerate, disintegrate, fail, pervert, retrogress, rot, seduce, stagnate, worsen
**deteriorating** crumbling, decaying, declining, decomposing, degenerating, degrading, depraving, depreciating, ebbing, fading, lapsing, lowering, retrograde, spoiling, weakening, worsening
**deterioration** atrophy, corrosion, decline, decomposition, degeneration, demoralisation, descent, erosion, lapse, retrogression, seduction, slump, vitiation
**determinate portion** dose
**determination** backbone, drive, fortitude, persistence, resolution, resolve
**determine** ascertain, certify, check, conclude, condition, decide, establish, fix, resolve, settle, verify
**determine beforehand** predestine, predetermine
**determine boundaries** survey
**determine by common consent** agree

**determined** firm, resolute, rigid, staunch, steadfast, unfaltering, unflinching, unwavering
**determined by stars** sidereal
**determined in some belief** pertinacious
**determine position of** locate
**determine roughly** estimate
**determine the nature of** identify
**determine worth of** evaluate
**detest** abhor, abominate, deplore, despise, disesteem, disfavour, dislike, disrelish, execrate, hate, loathe, mislike, repudiate, spurn
**detestable** abominable, damnable, despicable, disgusting, foul, hateful, loathsome, mean, noisome, noxious, odious, putrid, repugnant, repulsive, revolting, scurvy, sickening, unlikable, unpleasant
**detestation** abhorrence, abomination, animosity, animus, aversion, bugbear, detesting, disfavour, dislike, displeasure, disrelish, hate, hatred, loathing, odium, repugnance
**detested person** anathema
**detested thing** abhorrence, anathema
**detest greatly** execrate
**detest utterly** abhor
**dethrone** demote, depose, displace, dispossess, downgrade, exile, expel, overthrow, uncrown, unseat
**detonate** bang, blast, bomb, burst, bust, discharge, eject, explode, fire, fulminate, hurl, ignite, kindle, launch, light, loose, rupture, shatter, shell, shiver, shoot, spark
**detonating device** fuse
**detour round** bypass
**detract from** impede
**detriment** damage, disadvantage, drawback, evil, harm, hurt, ill, impairment, injury, liability, loss, wrong
**detrimental** adverse, baleful, damaging, deleterious, destructive, harmful, hurtful, inimical, injurious, pernicious, prejudicial, unfavourable, untoward
**Detroit product** auto, car
**de trop** superfluous, unnecessary, unwanted, unwelcome
**deuce** two
**devalue** abase, cheapen, debase, decrease, deflate, degrade, deign, demean, depreciate, disgrace, dishonour, humble, lessen, lower, pervert, profane, reduce, shame
**devastate** abash, confound, demolish, desolate, despoil, destroy, disconcert, harry, mortify, plunder,

ravage, rifle, ruin, sack, strip, waste, wreck
**devastating** caustic, deadly, demolishing, destroying, effective, incisive, levelling, mordant, overpowering, overwhelming, pillaging, plundering, ravaging, ruining, ruinous, sacking, sardonic, satirical, savage, stunning, trenchant, wasting, wrecking
**devastation** adversity, blow, calamity, cataclysm, catastrophe, damage, demolition, desolation, despoilment, destruction, disaster, downfall, end, extermination, extirpation, failure, fiasco, harm, havoc, holocaust, loss, massacre, misfortune, obliteration, ravage(s), ruin(ation), suffering, tragedy, trouble, waste, wreckage
**develop** advance, amplify, bloom, breed, build, contract, cultivate, educe, enlarge, evolve, expand, explicate, exploit, extend, flower, generate, germinate, gestate, grow, improve, increase, magnify, mature, occur, promote, ripen, sprout, swell, uncover, widen
**develop by natural process** evolve
**developed aptitude** skill
**developer of anti-polio vaccine** Salk
**develop gradually** evolve
**develop in detail** elaborate
**develop in enthusiasm** warm
**developing** beginning, incipient, nascent
**developing a subject** topical
**developing from above downwards** basipetal
**developing from below upwards** acropetal
**developing insect** pupa
**develop into** become
**development** evolvement
**development of new hair** endysis
**develop rapidly** boom
**develop within** inbreed
**deviant** abnormal, atypical, bizarre, contradictory, curious, debauchee, degenerate, different, eccentric, exceptional, extraordinary, freak, funny, improper, incorrect, irregular, miscreant, odd, peculiar, perverse, pervert, quaint, queer, rare, rebellious, refractory, remarkable, singular, strange, troublesome, uncommon, unreasonable, untypical, unusual, villain, weird, whimsical, wrongdoer
**deviate** avert, depart, digress, diverge, err, part, stray, swerve, veer
**deviate from** bypass
**deviate from correct standard** err

**deviate from course** yaw
**deviate from what is proper** outré
**deviation** aberrancy, abnormality, alteration, anomaly, change, curve, declension, declinational, deflection, degeneracy, departure, digression, discrepancy, disparity, divergence, inconsistency, irregularity, oddness, shift, strangeness, swerve, turn, variance, variation, veer(ing)
**deviation from a fixed rule** abnormal, irregular
**deviation from course** drift
**deviation from norm** variation
**deviation from normal** aberrance
**device** artifice, bent, contrivance, design, desire, emblem, expedient, figure, gadget, inclination, invention, logotype, plan, project, ruse, shift, slogan, stratagem, trademark, trick, utensil, wile
**device controlling the relative humidity of the air** humidistat, hygrostat
**device copying pictures and diagrams to scale** pantograph
**device detecting objects deep underwater** hydroscope
**device detecting the presence of water** hydrostat
**device displaying radar signals** radarscope
**device for amplifying microwaves** maser
**device for automatic regulation of temperature** thermostat
**device for carrying injured people** stretcher
**device for catching animals** trap
**device for connecting several electric plugs to one socket** adaptor
**device for cooling air** air-conditioner, cooler, fan
**device for detecting vibration in ground** geophone
**device for dispensing spirits** optic
**device for displaying oscillations** oscilloscope
**device for extinguishing candle** snuffer
**device for holding boat** anchor
**device for holding things tightly** clamp
**device for holding things together** clip
**device for increasing speed** accelerator
**device for increasing volume of sound** amplifier
**device for interrupting an electric current** circuit breaker
**device for keeping temperature steady** thermostat

**device for making and breaking an electric circuit** switch
**device for measuring** rule(r)
**device for measuring energy expended** ergometer
**device for measuring sensitivity to light** sensitometer
**device for measuring spirit drink** optic
**device for opening tins** opener
**device for overturning ore trucks** tipple
**device for plucking guitar strings** plectrum
**device for raising chicks** brooder
**device for recording electric vibrations** oscillograph
**device for recording oscillation** oscillograph
**device for reducing noise** silencer
**device for revealing objects in the dark** snooperscope
**device for shaving** razor
**device for sucking milk from a bottle** teat
**device for unclosing** opener
**device for winnowing grain** fan
**device giving intense light** laser
**device giving protection from the rain** umbrella
**device helping in the study of the crystal structure of minerals** stauroscope
**device indicating speed of vehicle** speedometer
**device indicating the temperatures of remote locations** telethermoscope
**device maintaining constant pressure** barostat
**device observing optical spectra** spectroscope
**device photographing cloud patterns** nephograph
**device recording electrical activity in a muscle** electromyograph
**device recording electric currents as a graph** oscillograph
**device recording short time intervals** chronograph
**device recording speeds and times of use of vehicles** tachograph
**device regulating flow** valve
**device that flies aircraft on preset course** autopilot
**device that generates energy** dynamo
**device that gives assistance** aid
**device that holds tight** clamp
**device that records amount of fuel used** meter
**device to charge with gas** aerator
**device to clear windscreen** wiper
**device to control draught** damper
**device to deaden tone** mute

**device to fire a blast** detonator
**device to give artificial tan** sun-lamp
**device to grip** vise
**device to heat liquids** etna
**device to hoist large stones** lewis(son)
**device to keep wheel from turning** sprag
**device to prevent backward motion** detent
**device to reduce noise** damper
**device to regulate flow of liquid** valve
**device to secure object to bench** clamp
**device to separate fine from coarse** sieve
**device to stretch cloth** tenter
**device tracing the paths of high-energy particles** hodoscope
**device used by skin-divers** aqualung, scuba
**device used in echo location** sonar
**device used in the rain** umbrella
**device which produces a narrow beam of light** laser
**device with elastic for shooting small stones** catapult
**devil** beast, Beelzebub, Belial, brute, demon, fiend, Lucifer, monster, ogre, Old Nick, rogue, Satan, savage
**devilfish** devil ray, manta ray, octopus
**devilish** abominable, accursed, annoying, atrocious, corrupt, cruel, damnable, demoniac(al), demonic, detestable, diabolic(al), elfish, evil, fiendish, heartless, hellish, hideous, horrible, impious, impish, infernal, Mephistophelian, monstrous, satanic(al), sinful, sinister, troublesome, venomous, villainous, wicked
**devilry** deviltry, diablerie, evil, impishness, iniquity, malevolence, mischief, nefariousness, roguery, sorcery, viciousness, villainy, wickedness, witchcraft
**devil's advocate** advocatus diaboli (L)
**devil's three-pronged fork** trident
**devil's work** diablerie
**devil worshipper** satanist
**devious** calculating, crooked, cunning, deceitful, dishonest, dishonourable, evasive, excursive, indirect, insidious, insincere, scheming, sly, surreptitious, treacherous, tricky, underhand, wily
**devious excursion** vagary
**devise** bequeath, concoct, contrive, design, formulate, frame, imagine, invent, order, plan, plot, scheme, think, transfer
**devise secretly** plot

**devoid** bald, bare, barren, deficient, denuded, destitute, empty, lacking, vacancy, void, wanting, without
**devoid of emotion** dispassionate(ly)
**devoid of logic** illogical
**devoid of occupants** empty
**devoid of qualities** empty
**devoid of stipules** exstipulate
**devolved rule** decentralised government
**Devon border river** Exe
**devote** allocate, allot, apply, appropriate, assign, commit, consecrate, consign, dedicate, give, offer, pledge, reserve
**devoted** allotted, applied, appropriated, ardent, assigned, caring, committed, concerned, constant, dedicated, devout, enshrined, faithful, fond, loving, loyal, pledged, reserved, staunch, steadfast, true
**devoted admirer** idolater
**devoted follower** adherent, fidus Achates, servant
**devoted to eating** edacious
**devotee** -ist, addict, adherent, admirer, aficionado (Sp), believer, bigot, champion, chauvinist, disciple, enthusiast, fan(atic), follower, habitué, partisan, pious, promoter, religionist, supporter, votary, worshipper, zealot
**devotee of any sport or pastime** aficionado
**devotee of specified amusement** fan
**devotee of yoga** yogi
**devote oneself to** addict
**devotion** admiration, adulation, affection, ardour, attachment, consideration, constancy, craze, dedication, devotedness, devoutness, eagerness, edification, faith(fulness), fidelity, fondness, friendship, grace, integrity, love, loyalty, passion, piety, rapture, reverence, sanctity, staunchness, tenderness, veneration, warmth, worship
**devotional book** psalter
**devotional period** Lent
**devotional sisterhood** sorority
**devotional song** hymn, psalm
**devotion to the study of the beautiful** aestheticism
**devotion to women** gallantry
**devour** absorb, consume, cram, demolish, eat, engulf, gluttonise, gobble, gulp, ogle, ravage, raven, relish, scoff, subjugate, swallow, vreet
**devour greedily** gorge

**devout** angelic, ardent, devoted, earnest, faithful, fervent, godly, holy, orthodox, pietistic, pious, prayerful, pure, religious, reverent, saintly, seraphic, serious, sincere, solemn, vehement, worshipful
**devoutness** godliness, holiness, piety, piousness, pureness, religiousness, saintliness
**dew** condensation, damp(ness), darkness, drizzle, film, fog, haze, humidity, mist, moisture, smog, spray, steam, vapour
**dew measure instrument** drosometer
**dexterity** ability, adroitness, agility, ambidexterity, aptitude, art(istry), astuteness, craft, deftness, ease, expertise, facility, felicity, finesse, guile, handiness, ingenuity, keenness, knack, mastery, neatness, proficiency, quickness, shrewdness, skilfulness, skill, sleight, smartness, smoothness, tact, talent, touch, wittiness
**dexterous** able, acute, adept, adroit, ambidextrous, artful, clever, crafty, cunning, cute, deceitful, deft, dextrous, excellent, expert, handy, ingenious, intriguing, inventive, keen, masterful, masterly, neat, nimble, polished, practised, proficient, quick, resourceful, sharp, shrewd, skilful, skilled, slick, sly, subtle, versed
**dextrality** right, starboard
**dhobi** washerman, washerwoman
**dhoti** loincloth
**dia-** di-, through, throughout
**diablerie** demology, devilry, diabolism, magic, mischief, rascality, recklessness, sorcery
**diabolic** accursed, cacodemonic, damnable, demonic, detestable, devilish, diabolical, execrable, fiendish, ghoulish, hellish, hideous, infernal, monstrous, odious, satanic, villainous, wicked
**diabolically wicked** fiendish
**diacritical mark** accent, macron, punctuation, tilde
**diadem** chaplet, circlet, coronet, crown, fillet, headband, laurel, mitre, tiara, wreath
**diagonal band on shield** bend
**diagonal joining of two edges at a corner** mitring
**diagonal rib of a Gothic vault** ogive
**diagonal surface** bevel
**diagram** chart, drawing, figure, graph, illustration, layout, map, outline, plan, representation, schematic, sketch

**diagram of a building** plan
**diagram of star signs** zodiac
**dial** clock, face, horologe, ring, sundial, telephone, timepiece
**dialect** accent, argot, branch, cant, idiom, jargon, language, lingo, localism, patois, pidgin, speech, tongue, Twi, vernacular
**dialect sandwich** butty
**dialogue** argument, causerie, chat, communication, confabulation, conference, conversation, converse, debate, dialectic, discourse, discussion, meeting, parlance, polemic, talk
**dialysis** osmosis
**diameter of the inside of a gun barrel** calibre
**diamine oxidase** histaminase
**diamond** gemstone
**diamond dust** bort
**diamond-hard** adamant
**diamond lustre** adamantine
**diamond malformed in the making** bo(a)rt
**diamond scraps used in industry** bort
**diamond set by itself** solitaire
**diamond shape** rhomb(us)
**diamond-shaped pane of glass** quarrel
**diamond surface** facet
**diamond weight** carat
**diaper** nappy
**diaphanous** chiffon, clear, delicate, gauzy, gossamer, light, revealing, see-through, sheer, thin, translucent, transparent
**diaphanous dressing-gown** negligeé
**diaphragm** midriff, tympanum
**diaphragmatic** phrenic
**diaphragm between thorax and abdomen** midriff
**diarist** archivist, clerk, historian, Pepys, recorder, scorer, scribe
**diary** chronicle, daybook, journal, log
**diastase** amylase
**diastrophism** epeirogeny, orogeny
**diatomic valency** bivalent
**diatomite** tripoli
**diatonic scale** key
**diatribe** abuse, castigation, contumely, criticism, denunciation, disputation, harangue, invective, philippic, reviling, stricture, tirade, vituperation
**dib** dab, dap, dip, pat
**dice** carve, chop, divide, ivories, mince, reject, slice
**dice shape** cube
**dicey** chancy, dangerous, difficult, dubious, hairy, iffy, problematic, risky, tricky, unreliable

**dichotomy** biformity, doubleness, dualism, duality, duplexity, twosome
**dicing** carving, chopping, dividing, mincing, risking, slicing
**Dickens's miser** Scrooge
**dicker** agle-bargle (Sc), bargain, barter, chaffer, commute, haggle, hawk, higgle, negotiate, sell, swap, trade, vend
**dicta** acts, adages, aphorisms, axioms, commands, declarations, decrees, dictates, dictum, edicts, fiats, fundamentals, injunctions, judg(e)ments, laws, mandates, manifestos, maxims, orders, postulates, precepts, principles, pronouncement, regulations, rulings, truisms
**dictator** autocrat, caudillo, despot, Führer (G), oppressor, strongman, tyrant
**dictatorial** absolute, arrogant, authoritarian, autocratic, bossy, categorical, despotic, disciplinarian, dogmatic, domineering, emphatic, full, harsh, haughty, imperious, lofty, obdurate, oppressive, peremptory, proud, severe, sovereign, supreme, tyrannical, unconditional, unqualified, unrestrained, unrestricted
**dictatorial one-party system** totalitarianism
**dictator in Germany** Führer (G)
**diction** accent, argot, articulation, cant, dialect, elocution, intonation, jargon, patois, phraseology, pronunciation, stress, terminology, vocabulary
**dictionary** concordance, encyclop(a)edia, glossary, lexicon, vocabulary, wordbook
**dictionary-making** lexicography
**dictionary notation** anatomy, biology, botany, chemistry, dialect, plural, slang
**dictionary part** word
**dictum** act, adage, aphorism, axiom, byword, command, declaration, decree, dictate, edict, fiat, fundamental, injunction, judg(e)ment, law, mandate, manifesto, maxim, order, postulate, precept, principle, proclamation, pronouncement, proverb, regulation, ruling, saw, saying, statement, statute, truism
**didactic** abstruse, academic, bookish, donnish, educational, educative, formal, instructive, moral(ising), particular, pedagogic, pedant(ic), pompous, prescriptive
**didactic person** prig

**diddle** cheat, jog, rook, swindle
**did not pass an exam** failed
**dido** antic, caper, prank
**die** block, cease, cube, decay, decease, decline, dee (Sc), depart, end, expire, fail, finish, mould, perish, subside, succumb, vrek, weaken
**die away** evanesce, fade, vanish
**die down** abate, decrease, fade, subside
**die for making pipe** dod
**die from cold** perish
**die from immersion in liquid** drown
**die from lack of food** starve
**die in water** drown
**die languidly away** swoon
**die of hunger** starve
**die out** cease, eliminated
**diesel oil** derv
**diet** abstinence, chamber, commons, congress, convention, council, dietary, fare, fast, food, legislature, meeting, nourishment, parliament, provisions, rations, reduce, regime(n), sitting, slim, subsistence, sustenance, viands, victuals
**dietary nutrient** vitamin
**dieter's dish** salad
**dieting** reducing
**die without leaving a will** intestate
**differ** contrast, demur, disagree, dispute, dissent, vary
**difference** alteration, argument, cause, change, clash, contrast, contretemps, controversy, debate, deviation, differentiation, disagreement, discordance, discrepancy, disparity, dispute, distinction, divergence, diversity, idiosyncrasy, peculiarity, point, quarrel, question, squabble, strife, tiff, unlikeness, variation, wrangle
**difference of opinion** argue, argument, disagreement, dispute, dissent, dissidence
**different** assorted, changed, changeful, contrary, contrasted, deviating, differing, dissimilar, distinct, divergent, divers(e), exclusive, fraternal, miscellaneous, mixed, new, non-uniform, other, separate, several, some, sundry, unfamiliar, unidentical, unique, unlike, unusual, variant, various
**different aspects** facets, sides
**different from all others** exclusive
**differentiate** adapt, adjust, change, contrast, discriminate, distinguish, modify, separate
**different in nature** alien
**different in quality** distinct

**differently coloured in different parts** partcoloured, variegated
**different one** another
**different ones** other
**different person** another
**difficult** abstract, abstruse, arduous, awkward, baffling, complex, complicated, demanding, forbidding, formidable, hard, intractable, intricate, involved, laborious, obscure, obstinate, particular, perplexing, perverse, problematical, sticky, strenuous, stubborn, thorny, tiresome, tough, troublesome, trying, unaccommodating, unco-operative, uphill, wearisome
**difficult accomplishment** feat
**difficult breathing** dyspnoea
**difficult feat** stunt
**difficult journey** trek
**difficult question** poser, puzzler
**difficult situation** dilemma, fix, quandary, stymie
**difficult task** problem, teaser
**difficult to accomplish** hard
**difficult to bear** hard
**difficult to catch** elusive
**difficult to deal with** awkward, nasty, ticklish
**difficult to digest** indigestible
**difficult to endure** oppressive
**difficult to grasp mentally** elusory
**difficult to please** fussy, pernickety
**difficult to understand** ambiguous, illegible, indecipherable, knotty, obscure
**difficult trip** trek
**difficult undertaking** enterprise
**difficulty** dilemma, hassle, objection, obstacle, predicament, problem, quandary, reluctance, snag, stubborness, trouble
**difficulty in breathing** dyspnoea
**difficulty in emptying the bowels** constipation
**difficulty in passing urine** dysuria
**difficulty in speaking** dysphonia
**difficulty in swallowing** dysphagia
**diffidence** demureness, distrust, doubt, humility, lowliness, meekness, modesty, propriety, reserve, reticence, servility, shyness, submissiveness, timidity
**diffident** abash, aloof, bashful, constrained, coy, distant, doubtful, embarrassed, hesitant, insecure, meek, modest, quiet, reluctant, sheepish, shy, timid, unassertive, unsure
**diffuse** circulate, diffusive, disseminate, loose, meandering, prolix, scatter(ed), spread, vague

**diffuse throughout** imbue, permeate
**diffuse wildly** radiate
**diffusion** circulation, dissemination, distribution, prolixity, rambling, spread, verbiage, verbosity
**diffusion through membrane** osmosis
**dig** burrow, delve, excavate, gibe, gravel, grub, hoe, insult, investigate, jab, jeer, mine, penetrate, pierce, poke, probe, prod, punch, quarry, quip, research, scoop, search, shovel, taunt, thrust, till, tunnel, wisecrack
**dig deeply** delve
**digest** abridgement, absorb, abstract, assimilate, brief, classify, codify, compendium, compress, concoct, condense, consider, contemplate, dispose, dissolve, epitome, grasp, incorporate, master, meditate, ponder, précis, reduce, résumé, shorten, study, summarise, summary, synopsis, systematic, tabulate, understand
**digestant** digestive
**digestive** digestant, peptic
**digestive disease of horses** bot(s)
**digestive juice** pepsin, rennin
**digestive juice in the mouth** saliva
**digestive upset** dyspepsia
**digest of laws or rules** code
**dig for minerals** mine
**digger** burrower, dredger, excavator, miner, quarrier, sapper, spade, tunneller
**digger of ore** miner
**digging implement** hoe, spade
**digging in garden** spading
**digging instrument** spade
**digging scientist** archaeologist
**digging tool** spade, pickaxe
**digit** character, cipher, count, feeler, figure, finger, integer, number, numeral, phalange, sum, symbol, thumb, toe, total, unit
**digitalis** foxglove
**digit guard** thimble
**digit of the foot** toe
**dignified** august, decorous, distinguished, exalted, formal, grave, honourable, imposing, lofty, lordly, noble, orotund, sedate, solemn, stately
**dignified and tasteful** elegant
**dignified elderly lady** dowager
**dignify** adorn, advance, augment, beautify, bedeck, celebrate, deck, decorate, distinguish, elevate, embellish, enhance, ennoble, enrich, exalt, favour, festoon, garnish, glorify, grace, honour, illuminate, immortalise, invest, magnify, ornament, prefer, promote, raise, reward, upgrade
**dignity** augustness, courtliness, decorum, grandeur, gravity, hauteur, honour, importance, loftiness, majesty, nobility, nobleness, poise, propriety, solemnity, stateliness
**dignity of nobleman** earldom
**dig out** exhume, unearth
**digress** decant, deflect, deviate, divagate, diverge, drift, maunder, meander, roam, stray, swerve, veer, wander
**digression** aside, decanting, deflecting, departing, departure, detour, deviating, deviation, diversion, meandering, roving, swerve, tangent, variation
**digression in narrative** excursus
**dig sideways** tunnel
**dig up** discover, disinter, dredge, exhumate, exhume, expose, extricate, find, quarry, research, retrieve, study, uncover, unearth, uproot
**dig with snout** root
**dike** barrier, causeway, defence, ditch, embankment, moat
**dilapidate** crumble, decay, decline, decompose, deteriorate, erode, injure, mar, ruin, weather
**dilapidated** broken-down, crumbled, crumbling, damaged, decadent, decayed, decaying, decrepit, defaced, derelict, destroyed, deteriorated, disintegrated, impaired, marred, mouldy, neglected, ramshackle, rickety, ruined, ruinous, run-down, shabby, tumble-down, unimproved, weathered
**dilapidated condition** disrepair
**dilapidated old motor vehicle** jalopy
**dilapidation** collapse, corrosion, decomposition, decrepitude, destruction, deterioration, disintegration, disrepair, downfall, erosion, impairment, injury
**dilate** distend, engross, enlarge, expand, swell, widen
**dilated artery** aneurism, aneurysm
**dilated part of glass tube** bulb
**dilatory** avoiding, blocking, dallying, dawdling, deferring, indolent, laggard, late, lazy, lingering, preventing, prolonging, slagging, slow, sluggish, tardy
**dilemma** confusion, difficulty, embarrassment, hodge-podge, intricacy, jumble, mess, muddle, perplexity, pinch, plight, predicament, problem, puzzle, quandary, question, spot, strait, uncertainty
**dilettante** amateur, connoisseur, dabbler, layman, nonprofessional, trifler
**diligence** activity, application, assiduity, attention, attentiveness, care, constancy, earnestness, effort, exertion, industriousness, industry, intentness, perseverance, persistence, pertinacity
**diligent** active, assiduous, attentive, busy, conscientious, constant, earnest, indefatigable, industrious, laborious, painstaking, persevering, sedulous, studious
**diligent effort** application
**diligently** actively, assiduously, attentively, busily, carefully, conscientiously, constantly, earnestly, indefatigably, industriously, laboriously, perseveringly, persistently, sedulously, studiously, tirelessly
**dill plant or seed** anet
**dilute** adulterate, attenuate, decrease, diffuse, diminish, reduce, weaken
**diluted alcoholic beverage** punch
**diluted spirit, as an alcoholic drink** grog
**dilution** rarefaction, rarefication
**dim** adverse, blur(red), cloud, dark(en), dense, dull, dusky, efface, fade, faint, foggy, ill-defined, indistinct, obscure, shadowy, stupid, unclear, uncomplimentary, vague
**dim and blur** blear
**dim and drab** dingy
**dimension** amplitude, bore, bulk, calibre, capacity, expanse, extent, gauge, greatness, importance, largeness, length, magnitude, measure(ment), proportions, reach, scope, size, stretch, volume
**dimension of garment** size
**dimensions** extent, gravity, greatness, importance, magnitude, range, scope, seriousness, size, span, urgency, volume, weight
**diminish** (a)bate, cheapen, contract, cut, decrease, detract, dwarf, dwindle, ebb, fade, lessen, lower, reduce, shrink, sink, subside, taper, wane, wave
**diminish by constant loss** waste
**diminish gradually** taper
**diminish in value** depreciate, impair
**diminish in width** narrow
**diminish strength of** dilute
**diminish the number of** cull
**diminish the purity of** sully
**diminuendo** decrescendo

**diminutive** baby, bantam, compact, dinky, dwarf(like), elfin, lilliputian, little, microscopic, midget, mini(ature), minute, petite, puny, pygmy, short, slight, small, tiny, undersized, wee
**diminutive person** lilliputian, shrimp
**diminutive race** pygmy
**diminutive suffix** -ette
**dimly conscious** subconscious
**dimmer switch** rheostat
**dimness** bleariness, cloudiness, darkness, dinge, duskiness, faintness, greyness, indistinctness, shadowiness
**dimness of sight** scotoma
**dimness of the eyes** film
**dimness of vision** amblyopia
**dim perception** glimpse
**dim sight** astigmatism, caligo
**dimwit** idiot, ninny, schlemiel, schmo
**dim with tears** blear
**dimwitted** fatuous, feeble-minded, inane, stupid
**din** agitation, anarchy, babel, ballyhoo, bawl, bedlam, bellow, brawl, bray, cacophony, chaos, clamour, commotion, crash, fanfare, film, flurry, hubbub, hullabaloo, noise, outcry, pandemonium, racket, roar, row, scramble, shout, shouting, tumult, turmoil, uproar, vociferation, yell
**dine** banquet, breakfast, eat, essen (G), feast, feed, gourmandise, lunch, sup
**dine late** sup
**dine on** banquet, consume, eat, feast, feed
**dine outdoors** picnic
**diner** eater, restaurant, roadhouse
**diner's bill** tab
**dinghy need** oar
**dingo** warrigal
**dingy** colourless, dark, dim, dirty(-looking), discoloured, drab, dreary, dull(-coloured), dusky, faded, gloomy, grey, grimy, murky, obscure, seedy, shabby, soiled, sombre
**dining alcove** dinette
**dining hall of convent** refectory
**dining nook** dinette
**dining room** cenacle
**dining room furniture** buffet, chair, table
**dining surface** table
**dinkum** correct, genuine, right
**dinner** banquet, collation, feast, meal, refection, repast, spread, supper
**dinner bell** gong
**dinner course** dessert, entrée, hors-d'œuvre, salad

**dinner jacket** tuxedo
**diocese** archdiocese, bishopric, episcopacy, episcopate, prelacy, see
**diode** semiconductor
**dip** acclivity, cavity, dap, decline, dib, dive, drop, dunk, dyke, hollow, immerse, investigate, lade, pitch, plunge, sauce, sink, sop, submerge, torch, valley
**dip in liquid** sop
**dip into** browse
**dip into colour** dye
**diplomacy** artfulness, delicacy, discretion, finesse, intrigue, judiciousness, politics, prudence, sense, skill, statecraft, statesmanship, tact(fulness)
**diplomat** ambassador, arbitrator, attaché, chargé d'affaires, consul, emissary, envoy, go-between, intermediary, legate, mediator, middleman, moderator, negotiator, pacifier, peacemaker, plenipotentiary, politician, reconciler
**diplomatic** adept, astute, clever, consular, discreet, perspicacious, plenipotentiary, polite, politic(al), prudent, sensitive, subtle, tactful
**diplomatic agent** envoy
**diplomatic errand** mission
**diplomatic house** embassy
**diplomatic messenger** courier
**diplomatic minister** envoy
**diplomatic mission** legation
**diplomatic representative** minister
**diplomatic representative of the pope** nuncio
**dip out** ladle
**dipper** bail, bailer, bucket, ladle(r), ousel, ouzel, pail, scoop, shovel, spoon
**dipsomania** alcoholism
**dipteran** gadfly, dipteron, dipterous
**dipterous** dipteran
**dipterous insect** (house)fly
**dip the colours** salute
**dire** appalling, awful, calamitous, compelling, critical, crucial, desperate, direful, disastrous, dismal, dreadful, fearful, fearsome, frightful, grim, hideous, horrible, lamentable, ominous, outrageous, sad, sinful, sinister, terrible, urgent
**direct** advise, aim, bold, command, control, critical, direct, downright, evident, express, forthright, foursquare, frank, govern, guide, heart-to-heart, helm, immediate, instruct, lead, manage, order, outspoken, plain, point, regulate, send, simple, sincere, steer,

straight(forward), unambiguous, undeviating, unequivocal
**direct a course** steer
**direct action** revolt
**direct a ship** navigate
**direct assault by troops** storm
**direct attention to** refer
**direct a vehicle** steer
**direct a weapon** aim
**direct channel** pipeline
**direct course** pilot
**direct descent** lineal
**direct descent from an ancestor** lineage
**directed against a person** ad hominem (L)
**direct effort towards** aim
**direction** address, administration, aim, bearing, charge, command, control, course, current, directorate, government, guidance, instruction, label, leadership, line, management, order, oversight, path, road, route, run, sphere, subject, supervision, track, up, way
**direction finder on highway** signpost
**direction of movement** course
**direction of sunrise** East
**direction on a letter** address
**direction placard** sign
**directive** charge, command, decree, dictate, edict, injunction, instruction, notice, order, ordinance, ruling
**direct line of descent** lineal
**directly contrasted** antithetic(al)
**directly demonstrative** ostensive
**directly opposite** contrary, diametrical, fornenst (Sc)
**directly showing** ostensive
**direct one's way** wend
**direct opposite** antithesis
**direct opposition** contradiction
**director** administrator, boss, chief, choirmaster, commander, executive, governor, guide, head, leader, maestro, manager, official, overseer, precentor, principal, regulator, supervisor
**director of institution** superintendent
**director of orchestra** conductor
**director or producer of a ballet** regisseur
**directory** catalogue, list
**direct proceedings** preside
**direct the course of a vehicle** steer
**direct the steering of a ship** navigate
**direct to a wrong purpose** misguide
**direct towards object** aim
**direct upwards** raise
**direct wrongly** mislead
**dire fate** doom

**direly** alarmingly, awfully, calamitously, cruelly, disastrously, dismally, dreadfully, fearfully, gloomily, grimly, horribly, ominously, ruinously, sorely, terribly, woefully

**dirge** chant, dead-march, elegy, epicede, epicedium, jeremiad, keen, lament, monody, requiem, threnody, ululation

**dirgelike** monodic

**dirigible balloon** airship, Zeppelin

**dirigible gas** hydrogen, helium

**dirk** dagger

**dirt** dust, excrement, filth, grime, indecency, mire, muck, sand, slime, smut, soil

**dirt and water** mud

**dirt-cheap** low-cost

**dirt-free** clean

**dirtless** clean, pure, spotless, unsoiled, unstained

**dirt remover** clean(s)er, detergent, soap

**dirt settling on bottom** silt

**dirty** base, besmirching, contaminated, contemptible, dark(-coloured), defiled, despicable, dirtying, disagreeable, dull, filthy, foul, grimy, grovelling, grubby, immoral, indecent, licentious, mean, messy, mucky, nasty, obscene, shabby, sloppy, soil(ed), soiling, sordid, squalid, sullied, tainted, unclean, vile

**dirty brown** dunnish

**dirty coal** rash

**dirty fellow** brock, scab

**dirty foam** scum

**dirty line where child has washed** tidemark

**dirty liquid** slop

**dirty lock** frib

**dirty look** glower, reproach

**dirty place** sty

**dirty pool** sump

**dirty surface matter** scum

**disability** affliction, ailment, decrepitude, defect, disablement, disorder, handicap, impairment, impotence, impuissance, inability, inaptitude, incapacity, infirmity, lameness, malady, paralysis, senility, unfitness

**disable** cripple, damage, disqualify, eliminate, enervate, enfeeble, impair, incapacitate, indispose, invalidate, lame, maim, mar, mutilate, paralyse, prostrate, weaken

**disable by binding wings** pinion

**disabled person** invalid, paraplegic

**disabuse** correct, disenchant, disillusion, rid, unbeguile, undeceive

**disadvantage** damage, deprivation, detriment, disservice, drawback, handicap, harm, hurt, inconvenience, injury, liability, loss, prejudice

**disaffect** alienate, anger, annoy, antagonise, debauch, disillusion, embitter, envenom, estrange, insult, irritate, offend, poison, repel, sour

**disaffiliate** detach, dissociate, secede

**disagree** argue, bicker, bother, clash, conflict, contend, contest, contradict, contrast, counter, depart, deviate, differ, disaccord, dispute, dissent, distress, disturb, diverge, interfere, jar, object, offend, oppose, quarrel, sicken, spar, squabble, trouble, unlike, unsuitable, upset, vary, wrangle

**disagreeable** austere, cross, disgusting, displeasing, impolite, noisome, petulant, repel, repugnant, repulsive, sarcastic, uncourtly, unfriendly, unpleasant, unsavoury

**disagreeable person** misery, ratbag

**disagreeable sound** cacophony

**disagree in opinion** differ

**disagreement** argument, clash, conflict, debate, difference, discord, discrepancy, disparity, dispute, dissent, dissimilarity, divergence, diversity, division, incompatibility, incongruity, misunderstanding, quarrel, row, squabble, strife, tiff, unlikeness, variance, wrangle

**disagree openly** dissent

**disagree verbally** argue

**disappear** cease, depart, disperse, dissolve, ebb, end, evaporate, expire, fade, go, leave, perish, retire, retreat, retrocede, vanish, vaporise

**disappear from sight** vanish

**disappear gradually** fade

**disappearing** ceasing, departing, dissolving, ebbing, ending, escaping, evaporating, expiring, fading, fleeing, flying, going, passing, perishing, receding, retiring, vanishing, waning, withdrawing

**disappointment** discontent, disillusionment, failure, frustration, inefficacy, mortification, pain, sorrow

**disapproval sound** boo, hiss

**disapprove** condemn, criticise, dislike, refuse, veto

**disapproved** disapprobation, discountenance, displeasure, forbidden, taboo

**disapprove of** condemn, depreciate, taboo

**disapproving look** frown

**disarm** appease, confound, crush, deactivate, demobilise, depress, disband, discourage, dishearten, fluster, frighten, intimidate, melt, mollify, overthrow, paralyse, prostrate, reconcile, reduce, ruin, unarm, unman, unnerve, upset

**disarrange** confuse, disarray, disorder, disorganise, displace, disturb, mess, scramble, shake, shuffle, spoil, tousle, tumble, upset

**disarray** chaos, confusion, dismay, disorder, jumble, mess, muddle, untidiness, upset

**disassociate** dissociate, rebel

**disaster** accident, adversity, affliction, blow, calamity, casualty, cataclysm, catastrophe, convulsion, debacle, deluge, desolation, eruption, fiasco, flood, glitch, misadventure, mischance, misfortune, mishap, reversal, reverse, ruin, shock, stroke, tragedy, trouble, typhoon

**disastrous** appalling, calamitous, catastrophic, deplorable, destroying, dire(ful), dreadful, fatal, frightful, miserable, piteous, ruinous, shocking, tragic, unfortunate, unhappy, unlucky, wretched

**disastrous defeat** debacle

**disastrous flood** cataclysm

**disavow** contradict, defect, deny, disclaim, disinherit, disown, forswear, recall, reject, repudiate, retract, unsay

**disavowal** contradiction, denial, discarding, disclamation, disowning, renunciation, retraction

**disband** adjourn, burst, cleave, crumble, demobilise, dissipate, disintegrate, dismantle, dismiss, disorganise, dispel, disperse, disrupt, dissociate, dissolve, divide, divorce, end, fork, free, gape, inactivate, open, part, quit, release, retire, rout, scatter, separate, sever, shatter, split, spot, suspend, terminate, vanish

**disbelief in the existence of God** atheism, godlessness

**disbelieve** atheism, denial, discount, dissent, distrust, doubt, incredulity, infidelity, irreverence, nihilism, paganism, rejection, repudiation, scorn, unbelief

**disbeliever** agnostic, atheist, cynic, disbeliever, doubter, gentile, heretic, infidel, nonbeliever, nullifidian, pagan, sceptic, unbeliever

**disbeliever in God** heathen, pagan

**disburse** administer, allocate, allot, assign, consume, dispense, distribute, employ, expend, issue, mete, outlay, pay, share, spend

**disc** album, ball, band, circle, circumference, coil, cordon, cycle, dial, disk(ette), face, globe, lap, loop, orb, perimeter, plate, record(ing), release, revolution, ring, round, single, sphere, tape, turn, video

**discard** abandon, abolish, cancel, ditch, drop, dump, eject, eliminate, jettison, recall, reject, relinquish, remove, repudiate, revoke, scrap, shed, shelve

**discard as too old** superannuate
**discard as useless** scrap
**discarded** obsolete
**discarded articles** junk, rubbish
**discarded cargo** jetsam
**discarded material** scrap
**discarded paper** litter
**discern** ascertain, behold, descry, detect, determine, differentiate, discover, discriminate, distinguish, espy, judge, look, notice, observe, perceive, recognise, see, spy, understand

**discern beforehand** foresee
**discerner of the future** seer
**discernible** apparent, distinct, distinguishable, exposed, lucid, naked, observable, obvious, palpable, perceptible, revealed, unconcealed, uncovered, visible

**discernible throb of the heart** pulse
**discernment** acumen, acuteness, astuteness, awareness, care(fulness), caution, cleverness, comprehension, consideration, diplomacy, discrimination, grasp, ingenuity, intelligence, intuitiveness, judg(e)ment, keenness, knowledge, maturity, penetration, perception, perceptiveness, perspicacity, prudence, realisation, sense, sharpness, smartness, subtlety, taste, understanding, unsight, wisdom

**discernment of feeling** tact
**discern with eyes** see
**discharge** absolve, acquit, detonate, detonation, disburden, disburse, dismiss, dissolve, egest, eject(ion), emission, emit, excrete, execute, execution, exonerate, expel, fire, firing, fulfil(ment), honour, outflow, pay, perform, performance, pus, release, relieve, removal, remove, shoot(ing), unburden, unload, void

**discharge a debt** pay
**discharge a firearm** fire, shoot
**discharge as too old** superannuate
**discharge cargo** unload

**discharge copiously** pour
**discharged by expectoration** phlegm
**discharged obligation** paid, payment
**discharge from infection** pus
**discharge of a debt** acquittance, payment
**discharge of artillery** fusillade, salvo
**discharge of lightning** bolt
**discharge ovum from ovary** ovulate
**discharge workforce** pay-off
**disciple** adherent, apostle, follower, pupil, scholar, student, supporter
**disciple of Jeremiah** Baruch
**disciple of Jesus** Andrew, Bartholomew, James, John, Judas Iscariot, Mat(t)hew, Peter (Simon), Philip, Simon, Thaddaeus, Thomas
**disciple of Socrates** Plato
**disciple of Zeno** Stoic
**disciplinarian** coach, despot, dictator, formalist, martinet, taskmaster, teacher, trainer
**disciplinary action** punishment
**discipline** castigate, chastise, check, coaching, coerce, coercion, compulsion, control, coach, curriculum, enlighten, guide, indoctrinate, instruct(ion), inure, limitation, method, procedure, reprimand, train
**disclaimer** denial
**disclose** broadcast, communicate, confess, divulge, expose, leak, relate, reveal, show, tell, uncover, unveil, utter
**disclosure** exposé, exposure, revelation, uncovering, unmasking, unveiling
**disc of metal for a coin** planchet
**disco light** strobe
**discolour** bleach, distain, distort, mark, stain, tarnish, tinge, tint, varnish
**discoloured by bruise** livid
**discoloured like silver** tarnished
**discoloured spot** stain
**discomfit** abash, addle, chagrin, confound, confuse, conquer, defeat, demoralise, discompose, disconcert, discountenance, disorient, disturb, drip, embarrass, fluster, foil, frustrate, master, mortify, nonplus, obstruct, outmanoeuvre, outwit, overcome, overwhelm, perplex, rout, ruffle, shame, thwart, trounce, trump, upset, whip, worst
**discompose** abash, addle, agitate, confuse, derange, disarrange, discomfit, disconcert, disorder, disorient, disturb, embarrass, flurry, fluster, mortify, perplex, perturb, ruffle, scatter, shame, unbalance, unsettle, untidy, upset, worry

**disconcert** abash, agitate, annoy, baffle, ba(u)lk, bewilder, confuse, defeat, derange, disappoint, discompose, disorder, distract, disturb, embarrass, flurry, fluster, frustrate, jar, nonplus, perplex, perturb, rattle, ruffle, unbalance, unsettle, upset
**disconcerted** abashed, anxious, bewildered, confounded, confused, disturbed, embarrassed, perplexed, rattled, ruffled, uncomfortable, uneasy
**disconnect** abstract, break, cleave, detach, discontinue, disengage, (dis)sever, dissociate, divide, interrupt, isolate, part, quit, rend, segregate, separate, split, stop, sunder, uncouple, undo, unfasten, unlink
**disconsolate** blue, cheerless, dark, dejected, depressed, desolate, despairing, discouraged, dismal, dispirited, dreary, forlorn, gloomy, grief-stricken, heartbroken, hopeless, inconsolable, melancholy, miserable, sad, unhappy, woeful, wretched
**discontent** anger, angry, annoyed, chafed, cranky, disaffected, discontented, discontentment, disgruntled, displeasure, dissatisfaction, dissatisfied, envy, fretful, impatience, malcontent, petulant, restlessness, testy, uneasiness, vexed
**discontented** malcontent
**discontented person** grouch, misery
**discontinuance** adjournment, break, cessation, decay, delay, discontinuation, disruption, disuse, idleness, interruption, lull, neglect, pause, postponement, recess, respite, stop(page), suspension, termination
**discontinue** abandon, cancel, cease, desist, drop, end, finish, halt, intermit, interrupt, pause, quit, stop, suspend, terminate
**discord** conflict, disagreement, discordance, disharmony, dissonance, friction, strife
**discordant** absonant, dissonant, inharmonious, jarring, strident, tuneless, unmelodious, unmusical, untuneful
**discordant cry** squall
**discordant sound** cacophony
**discount** abatement, allowance, bargain, deduction, disbelieve, rebate, reduction

**discourage** daunt, deject, depress, deter, dishearten, dismay, dissuade, frighten, hinder, intimidate, obstruct, prevent, subdue
**discourage from acting** deter
**discourage through fear** deter
**discourse** address, chat, converse, descant, dialogue, discuss, essay, harangue, homily, lecture, orate, oration, palaver, rant, rave, screed, sermon, speech, talk
**discourse before audience** lecture
**discourse in honour of deceased person** eulogy
**discourse not addressed to any one** soliloquy
**discourse publicly** prelect
**discourser** conversationalist
**discourse to audience** address
**discourteous** abrupt, curt, disrespectful, ill-bred, impolite, rude, uncivil, ungracious, unmannerly
**discourteously brief** curt
**discourtesy** abruptness, affront, arrogance, crudity, impertinence, impoliteness, insolence, misbehaviour, pertness, rudeness, scowl, shortness, snub, tactlessness, tartness
**discover** ascertain, behold, cause, detect, determine, discern, disclose, espy, find, invent, learn, notice, obtain, see, show, spot, spy, tell, unearth
**discover by intuition** forebode, intuit, sense
**discover by searching** find
**discover by smell** nose
**discovered patch** stain
**discovered penicillin** Fleming
**discovered radium** Curie
**discoverer of America** Columbus
**discoverer of Australia** James Cook
**discoverer of Cape sea route** Dias
**discoverer of Greenland** Eric
**discoverer of Guam** Magellan
**discoverer of North Pole** Peary
**discoverer of smallpox vaccine** Jenner
**discoverer of South Pole** Amundsen
**discoverer of Tasmania** Tasman
**discoverer of the law of gravity** Newton
**discoverer of wine** Noah
**discoverer of X-rays** Roentgen, Röntgen
**discover exact place of** locate
**discover new places** explore
**discovery** apprehension, ascertaining, detection, espial, finding, idea, innovation, invention, locating, perception, unearthing

**discredit** cheapen, contempt, debase, decry, defame, deflate, degrade, denigrate, deny, detract, disbelief, disfavour, disgrace, disparage, dispute, distrust, doubt(fulness), humiliate, lampoon, libel, mockery, obloquy, question, refute, ridicule, shame, slur, smirch, suspicion
**discreet** alert, awake, aware, careful, cautious, chary, circumspect, considerate, diplomatic, discerning, guarded, heedful, judicious, politic, precautious, prudent, reserved, sagacious, sensible, tactful, wary, wise
**discrepancy** conflict, difference, disagreement, disparity, dissimilarity, dissonance, divergence, incongruity, inconsistency, variance, variation
**discrete** analytic, bitty, characteristic, diagnostic, disconnected, disjointed, dissecting, distinct, exclusive, fragmentary, identical, incomplete, inquiring, investigative, logical, own, partial, particular, peculiar, proper, questioning, rational, respective, searching, separate, several, singular, specific, studious, systematic, testing, unique
**discrete unit** fraction
**discretion** acumen, judg(e)ment, option, prudence, sagacity, tact, volition
**discretionary** elective, open, optional, unconditioned, unqualified, unrestrained, unrestricted, voluntary, volitional
**discriminate** critical, differentiate, discriminatory, distinguish(ing)
**discriminating** acute, assessing, astute, critical, cultivated, discerning, distinguishing, evaluating, fastidious, favouring, keen, particular, refined, selective, sensitive, separating, sifting, tasteful, victimising
**discriminating cognition** sense
**discrimination against the elderly** ag(e)ism
**discriminative** analytical, characteristic, chauvinistic, clear-eyed, (dia)critical, differential, disjunctive, distinctive, keen, peculiar, perceptive, preferential, racist, typical
**discuss** argue, confer, consider, consult, consume, contend, converse, debate, deliberate, discourse, dispute, dissect, dissert, examine, moot, parley, review, sift, study, treat, ventilate, weigh
**discuss casually** mention
**discuss formally** debate

**discuss idly** chat, natter
**discussion** argument, consideration, debate, dialogue, discourse, indaba, scrutiny, talk
**discussion list** agenda
**discussion meeting** indaba
**discus thrower** discobolus
**disdain** arrogance, condemn, contempt, despise, haughtiness, scorn, spurn
**disdainful** arrogant, blustering, conceited, condescending, contemptuous, deriding, derisive, despotic, dictatorial, haughty, high, imperious, insulting, lofty, mocking, overbearing, overweening, patronising, presumptuous, proud, satirical, scornful, snobbish, supercillious, superior, taunting
**disdainful look** moue (F)
**disdainful sound** snort
**disease** AIDS, ailment, cholera, complaint, derangement, distemper, fever, illness, infirmity, leprosy, lues, malady, polio, rickets, sickness
**disease accompanied by swelling** gout
**disease affecting large intestines** dysentery
**disease carrier** vector
**disease-carrying fly** tsetse
**disease caused by fungus** mycosis
**disease caused by the absorption of pus** py(a)emia
**disease causer** virus
**disease causing fits** epilepsy
**disease common among miners** nystagmus
**disease due to lack of vitamin B** beri-beri
**disease due to lack of vitamin C** scurvy
**disease in which malignant growth forms** cancer
**disease leaving scars** smallpox
**disease marked by tonic spasm** tetanus
**disease of a gland** adenopathy
**disease of animals** distemper, mange, rabies, rinderpest
**disease of apples** blotch, Cork
**disease of cattle** anthrax, nagana, redwater, rinderpest
**disease of cereals** ergot, smut
**disease of children** chickenpox, diphtheria, gastroenteritis, measles, mumps, polio(myelitis), scarlet fever, smallpox
**disease of corn** smut
**disease of diver** bends
**disease of domestic pigeons** ornithosis

**disease of ducks** keel
**disease of eyes** glaucoma
**disease of eyes in which they remain open during sleep** lagophthalmia
**disease of fowls** pip
**disease of grain** ergot, smut
**disease of horse's hock** spavin
**disease of liver** cirrhosis
**disease of livestock** nagana, rinderpest
**disease of Naaman** leprosy
**disease of nervous system** neuropathy
**disease of parrots** psittacosis
**disease of plants** scab
**disease of poultry** pip
**disease of rabbits** myxomatosis, snuffles
**disease of rye** ergot
**disease of sheep** anthrax, foot rot, gid
**disease of the eye** glaucoma, trachoma
**disease of the hair** trichoma
**disease of the toe** gout
**disease of tobacco** calico
**disease of unknown cause** idiopathy
**disease of wheat** bunt, cockle, rust
**disease source** virus
**disease that causes ulcerous sores in animals** canker
**disease very virulent** malignant
**disease with fits of somnolence** narcolepsy
**disease with glandular swellings** scrofula
**disease with inflammation in smaller joints** gout
**disembark** alight, arrive, debark, deplane, detrain, dismount, land, light, unload
**disembodied spirit** soul
**disencumber** discharge, disentangle, free, mitigate, release, relieve, remove, rid, unburden, unhamper, unload
**disentangle** detach, disconnect, extricate, free, loose, separate, sever, unravel, unsnarl, untangle, untwist
**disentangle wool** card
**disfigure** blemish, blotch, damage, deface, deform, disfeature, flaw, impair, injure, maim, mar, maul, ruin, scar, spoil, sully, trash, uglify, vandalise
**disfigurement** birthmark, blemish, blotch, damage, defacement, deformity, destruction, distortion, eyesore, frightfulness, impairment, imperfection, injury, monstrosity, n(a)evus, spot, stain, ugliness, unsightliness, vandalism

**disfiguring** maiming
**disgrace** baseness, degradation, degrade, disapprobation, disapproval, disapprove, disfavour, dishonour, disparagement, humiliate, ignominy, infamy, notoriety, obloquy, odium, opprobrium, scandal, shame, stain, stigma
**disgrace attaching to some act** opprobrium
**disgraceful** appalling, arrant, bad, blameworthy, defamatory, degraded, detestable, discreditable, dishonourable, disreputable, disrespectful, dreadful, evil, heinous, horrible, humiliating, inglorious, libellous, low, mean, obscene, odious, peccable, scandalous, shameful, shocking, unworthy, vile
**disgruntled person** sorehead
**disguise** camouflage, conceal, cover, deceive, dissemble, fake, mask, misrepresent, screen, shroud, veil
**disguise by embellishment** dress
**disguise for the face** mask
**disguise of Zeus** swan
**disgust** abhorrence, abomination, antipathy, aversion, cloy, detestation, dislike, displease, distaste, glut, hatred, irk, loath(ing), nausea(te), offend, outrage, repel, repugnance, repulse, repulsion, revolt, revulsion, satiate, scunner, shock, sicken, surfeit
**disgusting** abominable, detestable, distasteful, loathsome, noisome, obnoxious, obscene, odious, offending, offensive, repugnant, repulsive, revolting, sickening
**disgusting dirt and filth** squalor
**disgustingly abusive** foul
**dish** biriani, bowl, bredie, breyani, casserole, course, dessert, food, fritters, goulash, hotchpotch, mousse, plate, platter, ragout, risotto, salver, souffle, stew, tureen, vessel
**disharmony** discord, incongruity
**dishearten** crush, damp(en), dash, daunt, deject, depress, deter, discourage, dismay, dispirit, sadden
**dish eaten as first course** hors d'œuvre, starter
**dishes** crockery
**dishevelled** bedraggled, blowzy, botched, bungled, chaotic, cluttered, confounded, confused, dirtied, dirty, disarrayed, disordered, disorganised, entangled, fouled, frowzy, grubby, jumbled, littered, messy, mixed, muddled, polluted, ruffled, rumpled, scrambled, shuffled, slovenly, tangled, tousled, uncombed, unkempt, untidy
**dish for serving soup** tureen
**dish made from the stomach lining of a cow** tripe
**dish made of bread** panada
**dish of crackers and water** panada
**dish of dried fruit in syrup** compôte
**dish of eggs and milk** custard
**dish of fish, rice, eggs, etc.** biriani, kedgeree
**dish of flavoured melted cheese** fondue
**dish of green maize and beans boiled together** succotash
**dish of greens** salad
**dish of India** curry
**dish of maize and pepper** tamale
**dish of meat and vegetables** biriani, bredie, stew
**dish of noodles layered with spiced mincemeat** lasagna, lasagne
**dish of raw vegetables** salad
**dish of rice and meat** risotto
**dish of rice, fish, eggs, etc.** biriani, kedgeree
**dish of spicy fried mincemeat and crushed maize** tamale
**dish of the day** plat du jour
**dish of trotters** eisbein (G)
**dish of vegetables** salad
**dishonest** bent, cheating, corrupt, counterfeit, crafty, criminal, deceitful, deceiving, deceptive, designing, dishonourable, disreputable, double-dealing, faithless, false, fraudulent, guileful, hypocritical, immoral, lying, mendacious, perfidious, rascally, spurious, treacherous, two-faced, unethical, unfair, unjust, unprincipled, unscrupulous, untrustworthy, untruthful
**dishonest acquisition** graft
**dishonest dealing** hanky-panky
**dishonest person** knave, rascal, rogue
**dishonest trick** fraud
**dishonour** degrade, derogation, discredit, disfavour, disgrace, disrepute, ignominy, odium, shame
**dishonourable** degraded, discreditable, disgraceful, dishonest, flagrant, ignoble, ignominious, infamous, mean, shameful, shameless, shocking, treacherous, unfair, unprincipled, unscrupulous, unseemly, venal
**dishonoured** abused, affronted, assaulted, branded, defamed, discredited, disfavoured, disgraced, disparaged, insulted, invalidated,

raped, refuted, scandalised, seduced, smudged, stigmatised
**dish out** serve, inflict, allocate, distribute
**dish served before main course** entrée, hors d'œuvre, soup
**dish up** serve, ladle, spoon, scoop, prepare, produce
**dishwasher** plate-cleaner
**dishwasher cycle** dry, rinse
**disillusioned person** cynic
**disimprison** disenthrall, free, unbind, unchain, unharness, unmanacle, unmew, unshackle, untie, unyoke
**disinclination to exert oneself** lassitude
**disinclination to move** inertia
**disinclined** antipathetic, averse, indisposed, loath, opposed, recalcitrant, regret, reluctant, renitent, resistant, unwilling
**disintegrated rock** saprolite
**disinter** disentomb, exhume, unbury, unearth
**disinterested** fair, generous, impartial, neutral, unbias(s)ed, unprejudiced, unselfish
**disjoin** undo, separate, sever, disconnect, dissever, dislocate, remove, unravel, simplify, disunite, part
**disjoint** anatomise, dislimb, dislocate, dismember, dissect, divide, rend, sever
**dislike** abomination, antagonism, antipathy, aversion, detestation, disgust, distaste, hate, hatred, loathing, odium, phobia, repugnance, resent, satiety
**disliked person** erk
**dislike greatly** detest
**dislike intensely** abominate, detest, loathe
**dislike of children** misopaedia
**dislike of foreigners** xenophobia
**dislike of people** misanthropy
**dislike very strongly** abhor, loathe
**disliking work** indolent
**dislocate** anatomise, disjoint, dismember, dissect, divide, luxate, pull, rend, rip, sever, sprain, strain, stretch, tear, wrench
**dislodge** budge, dispel, displace, eject, expel, extricate, move, oust, remove, shift, uproot
**dislodged piece of turf** divot
**disloyal** subversive, traitorous, treacherous, treasonable, unfaithful, untrue
**disloyalty** apostasy, breach, deceit, estrangement, faithlessness, infidelity, recreancy, traitorousness, treason, unfaithfulness
**disloyalty to one's spouse** infidelity
**disloyalty to state** treason
**dismal** abysmal, bleak, cheerless, dark, depressing, doleful, drab, dreadful, drear(y), dull, ghastly, gloomy, grey, horrible, horrid, melancholic, miserable, nasty, rotten, sad, sombre, terrible
**dismally** bleakly, cheerlessly, darkly, depressingly, despondently, discouragingly, drearily, forlornly, gloomily, gruesomely, lugubriously, sadly, sombrely, sorrowfully
**dismalness** awfulness, dreariness, ghastliness, gruesomeness, horribleness, nastiness, rottenness, vileness, wretchedness
**dismantle** demount, dispossess, divest, strip, unrig
**dismantled ship** hulk
**dismay** abash, affright, agitation, alarm, anxiety, appal, apprehension, awe, chagrin, consternate, consternation, daunt, depress, discompose, disconcert, discourage, dishearten, disillusion, disturb, enervate, fear, frighten, funk, horrify, horror, intimidate, jar, jolt, mistrust, panic, perturb(ation), petrify, qualm, scare, shock, startle, terrify, terror, unnerve, upset
**dismay causing mental confusion** consternation
**dismaying** alarming, appalling, distressing, frightening, horrifying, paralysing, scaring, terrifying, unnerving
**dismiss** disband, discard, discharge, disperse, dissolve, expel, fire, free, oust, out, reject, release, remove, sack
**dismissal** adjournment, congé, discharge, end, notice, release
**dismiss all doubt** assure, confirm, ensure
**dismiss at the end of session without dissolution** prorogue
**dismissed like a batsman** out
**dismiss from employment** discharge
**dismiss from school** expel
**dismiss the batsman between wickets** run out
**dismount** alight, debark, detrain, dismantle, displace, unbuild, unmount, unrig, unsaddle
**Disney's deer** Bambi
**Disney's duck** Donald
**Disney's elephant** Dumbo
**Disney's mouse** Mickey
**disobedient** bad, contrary, defiant, fractious, headstrong, indocile, insubordinate, lawless, mischievous, naughty, nonobservant, obstinate, rebellious, refractory, stubborn, undutiful
**disobey** defy, disregard, infringe, resist, transgress, violate
**disobey openly** defy
**disorder** ailment, anarchy, chaos, complaint, confuse, confusion, derange(ment), disarrangement, disarray, discompose, disorderliness, disorganisation, disorganise, disturb(ance), illness, incoherent, irregularity, jumble, malady, mess, riot, sickness, tumult, turbulence, turmoil, unrest, unsettle, upset
**disordered and irrational** farrago
**disordered mess** tousle
**disordered situation** mare's nest
**disorder in a state** sedition
**disorderly** chaotic, disorganised, jumbled, lawless, messy, riotous, rowdy, unruly
**disorderly behaviour** riot
**disorderly collection** congeries
**disorderly crowd** mob, rabble
**disorderly group** gaggle
**disorderly haste** hurry-scurry
**disorderly medley** mess
**disorderly proceedings** scramble
**disorderly retreat** rout
**disorder of nervous system producing depression** neurosis
**disorder of the skin** nettle-rash
**disorganise** agitate, confound, confuse, derange, destroy, disarrange, discompose, dishevel, disorder, disrupt, disturb, entangle, jumble, misarrange, mix, muddle, scatter, shuffle, spoil, tangle, unsettle, untidy, upset
**disorganised** annoy, censure, chaotic, confused, criticise, debase, defame, denigrate, deprecate, deranged, detract, discredit, dishonour, disordered, disrupted, jumbled, lower, muddled, reduce, reproach, slur, unsystematic
**disparage** backbite, belittle, cheapen, criticise, debase, decry, defame, degrade, demean, denigrade, deprecate, depreciate, diminish, discredit, dishonour, downgrade, malign, reduce, reproach, traduce, underrate, undervalue, vilify
**disparagement** abuse, affront, belittlement, castigation, decrease, deflation, deprecation, detraction, devaluation, discredit, disrespect,

indignity, injury, insult, invective, outrage, reprimand
**disparaging** abusive, captious, caustic, censorious, condemning, cursing, derisive, derogatory, disapproving, fault-finding, insulting, ironical, libellous, maligning, mocking, nagging, reproachful, reviling, ridiculing, rude, sarcastic, sardonic, scathing, scolding, slanderous, taunting, traducing, upbraiding, vilifying
**disparaging remark** aspersion
**disparity** alteration, change, comparison, contrast, deflection, departure, difference, digression, discrepancy, dissent, dissimilarity, distinction, divergence, foil, imparity, inconsistency, inequality, irregularity, opposition, shift, variance, variation
**dispatch** communication, consign, correspondence, despatch, dismiss, do, eat, efficiency, express, forward, freight, haste, hurry, kill, mail, post, promptitude, quicken, rapidity, release, remit, report, send, settle, transmit
**dispatch bearer** messenger
**dispatch boat** aviso
**dispatch by certain way** route
**dispatcher** sender
**dispel** allay, banish, eliminate, expel, resolve, rout, scatter
**dispel any doubts** satisfy
**dispel apprehensions** reassure
**dispense** administer, allocate, allot, apply, apportion, assign, deal, direct, disburse, discharge, distribute, dole, enforce, execute, implement, operate, share, undertake
**dispense in small quantities** dole
**dispenser of alms** almoner
**dispense with** abolish, cancel, discard, disregard, forgo, ignore, omit, relinquish, waive
**disperse** banish, bestrew, circulate, diffuse, disappear, dismiss, dispel, disseminate, dissipate, dissolve, eject, evanesce, scatter, separate, sow, spatter, spread, vanish
**dispersion of the Jews** Diaspora
**dispirit** allay, break, check, cool, damp, dash, deaden, deject, demoralise, depress, desolate, deter, diminish, discourage, dishearten, disincline, dull, enfeeble, impair, moderate, prostrate, sadden, subdue, undermine, weaken, weary
**dispirited** cheerless, crestfallen, dejected, depressed, despondent, disconsolate, discouraged, disheartened, down(cast), gloomy,

glum, low, mopish, morose, sad, unhappy, weary
**displace** depose, dislocate, dismiss, move, oust, remove
**displaced person** evacuee
**displaced turf** divot
**display** arrange, array, demonstrate, evince, exhibit(ion), flaunt(ing), flourish, manifest(ation), parade, reveal, show, sight, sport, uncover, unfold
**displayed announcement** notice
**display feline content** purr
**display furniture** dresser
**display garments** model
**displaying pride** proud
**displaying shame** shamefaced
**displaying tender feelings** affectionate
**displaying wares** exhibitor
**display of computer tasks** menu
**display of cowboys' skill** rodeo
**display of exaggerated enthusiasm** gush
**display of fireworks** pyrotechnics
**display of live fish** aquarium
**display of skill** expertise
**display of wild temper** rampage
**display proudly** flaunt
**display scorn** sneer
**display sign** neon
**display stand** étagère (F)
**display-window thief** smash-and-grab thief
**displease** aggravate, anger, annoy, disgust, dissatisfy, exasperate, gall, incense, infuriate, irk, irritate, nettle, offend, pique, provoke, resent, rile, upset, vex
**displeasure** anger, annoyance, disapproval, dislike, dissatisfaction, distaste, dudgeon, embitterment, exasperation, indignation, ire, irritation, offence, pique, rancour, resentment, unhappiness, vexation, wrath
**disposable handkerchief** tissue
**disposal** arrangement, array, assignment, assortment, bestowal, clearance, command, conduct, discarding, dispensation, disposition, distribution, ejection, elimination, grouping, management, order(ing), placing, position, power, regulation, relinquishment, removal, riddance, scrapping, transaction
**disposal of the dead** funeral
**disposal problem** trash
**dispose** actuate, adjust, arrange, array, group, lead, prompt, range, tempt
**disposed** apt, given, liable, minded, prone, ready

**disposed to attack** aggressive
**disposed to do harm** malignant
**disposed to laugh** risible
**disposed to loving** amative
**disposed to mischief** mischievous
**disposed to quarrel** quarrelsome
**disposed to take risks** risky, venturesome
**dispose earlier** pre-arrange
**dispose for price** sell
**dispose of** decide, destroy, determine, discard, dump, jettison, kill, peddle, rid, scrap, sell, settle, transfer
**dispose of for money** sell
**disposition** arrangement, bent, bestowal, character, conclusion, control, disposal, distribution, grouping, humour, idiosyncrasy, inclination, liking, management, mood, nature, outcome, outlook, penchant, predisposition, readiness, result, spirit, temper(ament), tendency, turn, willingness
**disposition of estate** testament
**disposition to look on the bright side** optimism
**disposition to see things as they are** realism
**dispossess** bereave, commandeer, deprive, disinherit, eject, evict, exile, expel, oust, plunder, strip, supersede
**dispossess of** deprive
**disprove** belie, confute, deny, discredit, explode, negate, overthrow, puncture, rebut, squash
**dispute** altercation, argue, argument(ation), bicker, brawl, contention, contest, contradict, controversy, controvert, debate, deny, disagreement, discuss, feud, impugn, moot, oppose, quarrel, spat, squabble, wrangle
**dispute about words** logomachy
**disputed question** vexata quaestio (L)
**disputed territory** no-man's-land
**dispute excessively** argufy
**dispute hotly** altercate, wrangle
**dispute result** contest
**disquiet** alarm, anguish, anxiety, commotion, confusion, fuss, incommode, inquietude, nervousness, pain, restlessness, tumult, unease, unquietness, unrest, upset, worry
**disrate** demote, reduce
**disregard** affront, contempt, disfavour, dishonour, disobey, disrespect, forget, ignore, inattention, minimise, neglect, negligence, omission, overlook, oversight, rudeness, slight, snub, spurn, underestimate,

underrate, undervaluation, undervalue
**disregarding laws** lawless
**disregard one's superiority** condescend
**disregard temporarily** shelve
**disreputable** arrant, bad, base, contemptible, corrupt, crooked, derogatory, discreditable, disgraced, disgraceful, dishonourable, disorderly, heinous, ignominious, infamous, iniquitous, louche, low, mean, notorious, outrageous, raffish, rascally, scandalous, seedy, shady, shameful, shocking, slippery, unbecoming, unworthy, vicious, vile
**disreputable newspaper** rag
**disreputable person** rascal, rip
**disreputable woman** courtesan, harlot, jade, street-walker, strumpet, trollop
**disrepute** degradation, discredit, disesteem, disfavour, disgrace, ignominy, notoriety, odium, stigma, unpopularity
**disrespect** contempt, discourtesy, impoliteness, incivility, irreverence, rudeness
**disrespectful laugh** snigger
**disrobe** divest, doff, remove, shed, strip, unclothe, undrape, undress, unveil
**disrobing** undressing
**disruptive** confusing, disorderly, divisive, obstreperous, troublesome, unruly, upsetting
**dissect** analyse, anatomise, bar, disjoin, dismember, explore, inspect, investigate, probe, research, scalpel, scrutinise, search, unpiece, vivisect
**dissecting** analytical, anatomising, dismembering
**dissecting knife** scalpel
**dissection** analysis, anatomy, autopsy, breakdown, check, diagnosis, dissolution, division, enquiry, examination, inspection, investigation, scrutiny, search, separation, sifting, study, test, vivisection, zootomy
**dissection of arteries** arteriotomy
**dissection of corpses** necrotomy
**dissection of the brain** encephalotomy
**dissection of the head** cephalotomy
**dissection of the human body** anatomy
**dissection of the spleen** splenotomy
**dissector of dead bodies** anatomist, pathologist
**disseminate** broadcast, diffuse, disperse, promulgate, scatter, spread

**dissemination** circulation, diffusion, distribution, publication
**dissension** breach, demur, discord(ance), dispute, dissent, faction, objection, protest, strife, variance
**dissent** apostasy, decline, defect, differ(ence), disaffection, disagree, discard, discord, dispute, nonconformity, object(ion), protest, rebel, refuse, reject, renounce, resistance, schism
**dissenter** disputant, nonconformist, objector, protestant, rebel
**dissertation** address, column, commentary, critique, descant, discourse, disquisition, essay, exposition, homily, lecture, opinion, oration, sermon, speech, study, theme, thesis, treatise
**dissipate** debauch, disappear, disperse, scatter, squander, vanish, waste
**dissipation of energy** entropy
**dissociate** detach, disband, disconnect, disrupt, distance, divorce, isolate, quit, segregate, separate
**dissolute** abandoned, corrupt, debauched, dissipated, immoral, loose, wanton
**dissolute person** debauchee, libertine, profligate, rake(hell), rip, roué
**dissolution of marriage** divorce
**dissolvable** decomposable, diffusible, evaporable, fusible, meltable, perishable
**dissolve** adjourn, crumble, decline, decompose, deliquesce, destroy, die, diminish, disappear, disband, disfuse, disintegrate, dismiss, dispel, disperse, end, free, liquefy, loose(n), melt, perish, sever, terminate, thaw, vanish
**dissolved substance** solute
**dissolve in heat** melt
**dissuade** caution, deject, deprecate, deter, discourage, dishearten, disincline, influence, restrain, warn
**distance** aloofness, coldness, disassociate, gap, interval, remoteness, reserve, space
**distance above sea level** altitude
**distance between axles of vehicle** wheelbase
**distance between bridge supports** span
**distance between gear teeth** pitch
**distance between stops** stage
**distance between two landings** flight
**distance flown** flight
**distance from equator** latitude

**distance gun will effectively fire** range
**distance marker** metrestone, milepost, milestone
**distance measure** coss, cubit, kilometre, li, metre, mile, yard
**distance round a place** circuit
**distance round thing** girth
**distance runner** miler
**distance through** diameter
**distance travelled eastward** easting
**distance-viewing instrument** telescope
**distant** abroad, afar, aloof, apart, cool, detached, faint, far(-off), inaccessible, indistinct, obscure, outlying, remote, removed, separate, tele-, uncertain, yon(der)
**distant branch** outpost
**distant but visible** yon(der)
**distant event recorder** telemeter
**distant goal** destination, reach
**distantly superior** aloof
**distant past** antiquity, yore
**distant planet** Neptune, Pluto, Saturn, Uranus
**distant settlement** outpost
**distaste** abhorrence, antipathy, aversion, detestation, disapproval, disesteem, disfavour, disgust, dislike, displeasure, disrelish, horror, loathing, repugnance, revulsion
**distaste for food** asitia
**distasteful** abhorrent, aversive, disagreeable, disgusting, displeasing, hateful, nasty, nauseous, noisome, objectionable, obnoxious, offensive, rancid, repugnant, repulsive, sickening, undesirable, unfavourable, uninviting, unpalatable, unpleasant, unsavoury
**distemper** tempera
**distend** augment, bloat, bulge, dilate, enlarge, expand, extend, fatten, inflate, puff, spread, stretch, swell, tumely, widen
**distended bag** balloon, bladder
**distend with gas** inflate
**distilled beverage** ale, brew
**distilled spirit drink** brandy
**distilling vessel** retort
**distinct** apparent, audible, clear(-cut), decided, definite, different, discrete, dissimilar, distinguished, evident, explicit, individual, lucid, manifest, marked, notable, noticeable, obvious, palpable, patent, plain, rare, recognisable, separate, sharp, special, tangible, unconnected, unique, unlike, unmistakable, unusual, various, vivid, well-defined
**distinct from other things** single

**distinction** account, contrast, fame, feature, greatness, honour, renown, reputation, separation
**distinctive** aura, characteristic, colourful, distinguishing, exceptional, graphic, idiosyncratic, individual, lively, particular, peerless, picturesque, rare, remarkable, singular, special, specific, stimulating, symbolic, typical, uncommon, unique, unmatched, unusual, vivid
**distinctive air** aura
**distinctive aspect** visage
**distinctive character of a person** personality
**distinctive character of a people** ethos
**distinctive doctrine** -ism
**distinctive elegance of dress** style
**distinctive element** essence
**distinctive feature** motif
**distinctive feature of excellence** hallmark
**distinctive feature of style** mannerism
**distinctive flag** standard
**distinctive manner** style
**distinctive mark** badge, medal
**distinctive parts of face** features
**distinctive period** era
**distinctive quality** essence, speciality
**distinctive region** zone
**distinctive smell** aroma, odour
**distinctive system** -ism
**distinctive taste of substance** sapor
**distinctive things in a landscape** features
**distinctive way of doing something** style
**distinctly jointed** articulate
**distinctly stated** explicit
**distinct part** article, section, unit
**distinct possibility** likelihood
**distinct stage** phase
**distinct step in development** stage
**distinguish** characterise, classify, differentiate, discern, discriminate, mark, note, perceive, recognise, separate
**distinguished** august, celebrated, conspicuous, distinct, distingué, elegant, eminent, famous, grand, majestic, noble, notable, noted, noteworthy, pre-eminent, prestigious, prominent, remarkable, renowned, respected, salient, special, supreme
**distinguished Muslim in India** nabob, nawab
**distinguished person** notability
**distinguished scholar** savant
**distinguished soldier** warrior

**distinguishing feature** trait
**distinguishing mark** cachet, stamp
**distort** bias, buckle, contort, curl, deform, disfigure, falsify, garble, grimace, misshape, mumble, pervert, slant, torture, twist, warp, wrench, wrinkle
**distorted** askew, (a)wry, crooked, grained, lopsided, skew, twisted
**distorted facial expression** grimace
**distortion in a lens** astigmatism
**distract** amuse, bewilder, confuse, derange, disturb, divert, divide, draw, entertain, harass, infuriate, madden, perplex, worry
**distracted** absent-minded, bewildered, confounded, confused, delirious, deranged, distraught, frantic, frenzied, perplexed, phrenetic
**distracted with fear** frantic
**distraction** agitation, amusement, bewilderment, disturbance, diversion, interruption, recreation
**distrait** absent-minded, abstracted
**distraught with rage** frantic
**distress** ache, afflict, agonise, agony, alarm, angst, anguish, anxiety, dejection, grief, grieve, heartache, hurt, misery, oppress, pain, sadness, sorrow, suffering, torment, torture, tribulation, trouble, upset, woe, worry
**distress call** Mayday, SOS
**distress greatly** harrow
**distressing** affecting, afflicting, agonising, bothering, disturbing, grieving, grievous, harassing, harrowing, heart-breaking, hurtful, lamentable, painful, paining, perplexing, sad(dening), tormenting, troubling, upsetting, worrying, wounding
**distressingly inadequate** pathetic
**distress signal** alarm, flare, Mayday, siren, SOS
**distress signal rocket** flare
**distress with bodily suffering** afflict
**distress with extreme pain** agonise
**distribute** allocate, allot, apportion, arrange, assign, circulate, classify, codify, convey, deal, deliver, diffuse, dispense, disperse, dispose, disseminate, divide, dole, give, group, issue, mete, scatter, separate, share, spatter, spread, supply, tabulate
**distribute cards** deal(er)
**distribute evenly** equalise
**distribute in portions** allot
**distribute out** dole
**distribute shares** allot
**distribute unsuitably** miscast
**distribute with authority** allot

**distribution** allocation, allotment, circulation, diffusion, division
**distribution of gifts** largess(e)
**distribution rights** franchise
**distributor of alms** almoner
**district** area, canton, community, constituency, county, department, division, domain, locale, locality, neighbourhood, parish, precinct, province, quarter, realm, region, section, sector, sphere, state, territory, vicinity, ward, zone
**district governor in Nazi Germany** Gauleiter
**district in Algeria** Casbah, Kasba
**district in Iraq** Basra, Kurdistan
**district in London** Soho
**district in south-western France** Médoc
**district in West India** Goa
**district of France** department
**district under a priest** parish
**district under jurisdiction of a bishop** diocese, see
**district yielding petroleum** oilfield
**distrust** doubt, misgiving, mistrust, suspect, suspicion
**distrustful** alert, bleak, careful, chary, cynical, dark, dejected, depressed, doubtful, gloomy, guarded, hesitant, hopeless, mistrustful, morose, pessimistic, prudent, resigned, sad, sceptical, suspicious, unsure, vigilant, wary, watchful
**distrust of England** Anglophobia
**disturb** agitate, baffle, derange, disarrange, discommode, discompose, disconcert, disorder, disquiet, harass, interfere, interrupt, muddle, pester, plague, rile, trouble, unsettle, upset
**disturbance** ado, agitation, bustle, commotion, disorder, hubbub, perturbation, riot, ruckus, ruction, stir, tumult, turmoil, unrest
**disturbance by unruly mob** riot
**disturbance of mind** emotion
**disturbance of the peace** riot
**disturbances in radio reception** static
**disturb a public speaker** heckle
**disturb by handling** touch
**disturb composure** upset
**disturbed state** turbulence
**disturb emotionally** upset
**disturber of peace** rioter
**disturb greatly** perturb
**disturbing sound** noise
**disturb mentally** perturb
**disyllabic rousing cadence** iamb
**ditch** abandon, burrow, canal, channel, cloaca, conduit, culvert, dike, discard, duct, dugout, dyke,

excavate, moat, pit, rean, reen, sloot, trench, watercourse
**ditch around fortress**  moat
**dither**  bother, faff, falter, flap, fluster, haver, hesitate, indecision. panic, oscillate, quiver, shilly-shally, stew, teeter, tizzy, tremble, vacillate, waver
**ditherer**  waverer
**ditto**  likewise, same
**ditty**  air, anthem, ballad, carol, chant, chorus, dictate, doggerel, hymn, jingle, lay, lyric, melody, poem, psalm, saying, shanty, sing, song, strain, theme, verse, tune
**diurnal**  circadian, daily, day-to-day, everyday, quotidian
**diva**  heroine, prima donna, singer
**divalent atom**  diad
**divan**  couch, council, council-chamber, restaurant, smoking-salon, sofa
**dive**  dip, duck, jump, nose, plummet, plunge, submerge
**diver**  frogman, loon
**diverge**  bend, branch, cleave, depart, deviate, digress, dissect, disunite, divaricate, divide, divorce, drift, fork, meander, open, part, radiate, separate, sever, sklent (Sc), split, spread, stray, subdivide, swerve, turn, veer
**divergent line**  tangent
**divergent religious group**  sect
**diverging from straight line**  oblique
**divers**  assorted, different, manifold, many, mixed, numerous, several, sundry, varied, various
**diver's ailment**  bends
**diverse**  apart, assorted, different, dissimilar, distinct, divergent, miscellaneous, separate, several, sundry, unlike, variant, varied, various, varying
**diverse in character**  heterogeneous
**diverse item**  sundry
**diver's equipment**  scuba
**diversified in colour**  motley
**diversify**  alter, assort, change, expand, intersperse, variegate, variety, vary
**diversion**  alternative, amusement, deflection, detour, deviation, digression, distraction, divergence, entertainment, feint, joy, jubilation, manoeuvre, pastime, pleasure, recreation, trickery
**diversionary route**  detour
**diversion from reality**  escapism
**diversity**  assortment, contradiction, contrast, difference, disagreement, disparity, dissimilarity, divergence, diversification, heterogeneity, irregularity, medley, multiplicity, opposition, range, unevenness, unlikeness, variety, variance, variegation, variousness
**diversity of talent**  versatility
**divert**  absorb, abstract, amuse, avert, beguile, deflect, detract, distract, enliven, entertain, exhilarate, gladden, occupy, reroute, sidetrack, swerve
**divert attention**  distract
**divert fraudulently**  embezzle
**divest**  denude, deprive, despoil, devest, dispossess, disrobe, doff, remove, rid, strip, unclothe, undress
**divest of covering**  denude
**divide**  alienate, apportion, classify, distinguish, divorce, estrange, part, partition, separate, sever, share, split
**divide again**  subdivide
**divide and govern**  divide et impera (L)
**divide by chopping**  cleave
**divided by wall**  septate
**divided into equal vertical stripes**  paly
**divided into three**  trichotomous
**divided river mouth**  delta
**divided skirt**  culotte
**divide grammatically**  punctuate
**divide in halves**  bisect
**divide in three parts**  trisect
**divide into branches**  ramify
**divide into parts**  split
**divide into small pieces**  scantle
**divide into three**  trisect
**divided into three branches**  trifurcate
**divide into two branches**  bifurcate
**divide into two parts**  bisect, halve, split
**divide lengthwise**  split
**divide out in shares**  apportion
**divide proportionately**  average
**divides earth into North and South**  equator
**divide with others**  share
**dividing edge**  line, border
**dividing history into periods**  periodisation
**dividing line**  bisector
**dividing panel**  screen
**dividing wall**  partition, septum
**divination**  arithmancy, assumption, astrology, augury, clairvoyance, forecasting, foresight, foretelling, forewarning, geomancy, horoscope, incantation, intuition, magic, necromancy, omen, oracle, presage, soothsaying, sorcery, sortilege, speculation, spell, surmise
**divination by books**  bibliomancy
**divination by fire**  pyromancy
**divination by lots**  sortilege
**divination by means of communication with spirits**  psychomancy
**divination by means of lines**  geomancy
**divination by means of stones**  lithomancy
**divination by numbers**  numerology
**divination by smoke**  capnomancy
**divination by the flight and cries of birds**  ornithomancy
**divination by the interpretation of dreams**  oneiromancy
**divination by the stars**  astrology
**divination by water**  hydromancy
**divine**  angelic, beatific, celestial, exalted, foresee, godlike, godly, heavenly, hierologist, holy, marvellous, predict, prognosticate, prophesy, religious, sacred, scry, spiritual, supernatural, supreme, surmise, theologian, transcendent, wonderful
**divine attendant**  angel
**divine being or god**  deva
**divine by crystal gazing**  scry
**divine command**  precept
**divine favour**  grace
**divine impulse**  afflatus
**divine intervention**  theurgy
**divine law**  jus divinum
**divinely conferred power**  charisma
**divine messenger**  angel, apostle
**diviner**  astrologist, augur, clairvoyant, conjurer, explainer, guesser, interpreter, magician, oracle, prophet, reader, sangoma, seer, sibyl, soothsayer, theorist, witch
**divine status**  deity
**divine vengeance**  wrath
**divine wisdom**  theosophy
**diving bird**  auk, booby, coot, cormorant, darter, dopper, ducker, gannet, grayling, grebe, loon, murre, ouzel, penguin, razorbill, smew, tern
**diving gear**  fins, scuba, snorkel
**divinity**  deity, god(dess), godliness, guardian, numen, omnipotence, perfection, Scripture, spirit, Talmud, Torah
**divisible by two**  even
**division**  allotment, alternation, apportionment, boundary, demarcation, dichotomy, difference, disagreement, discord, distribution, disunion, estrangement, part(ition), rift, schism, section, separation, sharing, split
**division according to quality**  class
**divisional leader in the Mafia**  capo
**division by merit**  class
**division in a church**  schism
**division into three parts**  trichotomy
**division into two parts**  dichotomy
**division of a book**  chapter

**division of academic year** semester
**division of a cavalry regiment** squadron
**division of a country** canton, county, province
**division of a long poem** canto
**division of ancient Greece** Deme
**division of ancient Rome army** cohort
**division of a pound** ounce
**division of army** artillery, brigade, corps
**division of artillery** battery
**division of battle front** sector
**division of building** room
**division of calender year** day, month, week
**division of China** Manchuria
**division of city** precinct, ward
**division of corolla** petal
**division of creed** tenet
**division of Finnish poem** rune
**division of geological time** aeon
**division of geologic time** age
**division of highway** lane
**division of hospital** ward
**division of India** Agra
**division of mankind** race
**division of music** bar
**division of poem** canto, stanza, verse
**division of polo game** chukker
**division of school year** term
**division of society** caste, clan
**division of stained glass window** panel
**division of stock** shares
**division of target** inner
**division of the High Court of Justice** chancery
**division of the Koran** sura
**division of town** quarter
**division of word** morpheme, syllable
**division of year** day, month, season, semester, trimester, week
**divisive** damaging, disruptive, inharmonious, troublesome
**divisor** factor
**divorce** annul, breach, cancel, disjunction, dispart, disruption, dissociate, disunion, disunite, divide, partition, separate, separation, sever, split
**divorce allowance** alimony
**divorce and gambling state** Nevada
**divorce capital of the world** Reno
**divorce settlement** alimony, allowance
**divorce town in USA** Las Vegas, Reno
**divulge** bare, betray, blab, broadcast, communicate, confess, declare, disclose, exhibit, expose, impart, inform, leak, manifest, proclaim, publicise, publish, release, report, reveal, spread, tell, uncover, utter, voice
**divulge secrets** blab
**Dixieland music** jazz
**dizziness** faintness, giddiness, shakiness, vertigo, wobbliness
**dizzy** bemused, bewilder, changeful, confused, dazed, dazzled, distraught, faint, fool, giddy, light-headed, muddled, puzzled, scatterbrained, shaky, vertiginous, wobbly
**dizzy attack** spell
**do** accomplish, achieve, act, affair, arrange, commit, complete, create, effect, execute, fare, finish, operate, organise, perform, practise, prepare, produce, satisfy, suffice, suit, work
**do a beautician's job** comb, set
**do a favour for** oblige
**do again** iterate, recast, redo, rehash, repeat
**do alone** solo
**do an impression of** imitate
**do an injustice to** abuse, disrespect, mistreat
**do a number on** betray, cheat, deceive, defraud, shaft, swindle
**do a shoe-repairing job** resole
**do as one is asked** comply
**do as one is told** heed, listen, mind, obey, observe
**do away with** abate, abolish, annihilate, destroy, discard, discontinue, dispense, eliminate, end, expunge, exterminate, kill, liquidate, murder, obviate, remove, stop
**do bidding of** obey
**do breast-stroke** swim
**do business with** deal, patronise
**do butterfly stroke** swim
**docile** amenable, biddable, compliant, controlled, ductile, dutiful, educatable, manageable, manipulate, obedient, obliging, passive, pliable, pliant, quiet, responsive, submissive, tame, teachable, tractable, trainable
**dock** anchor, berth, dockage, harbour, jetty, marina, mole, moor, pier, quay, wharf
**docked tail** bobtail
**docket** bill, certificate, chit, counterfoil, file, index, mark, receipt, register, tab, ticket
**docket for round trip** return ticket
**dock for yachts** marina
**dock worker** stevedore
**doctor** adulterate, alter, botch, change, cobble, cook, cut, dentist, dilute, disguise, falsify, fix, forge, GP, medic, clinician, mispresent, osteopath, paediatrician, pervert, physician, repair, surgeon
**doctor and prophet of sixteenth century** Nostradamus
**doctor gaining experience** houseman, intern(e)
**doctor's aid** nurse
**doctor's business** practice
**doctor's charge** fee
**doctor's client** patient
**doctor's consulting room** surgery
**doctor's equipment** armamentarium
**doctor's examination** medical
**doctor skilled in psychiatry** psychiatrist
**doctors prescribe it** medicine
**doctor's stand-in** locum
**doctor who assists women at childbirth** accoucheur, obstetrician
**doctor who performs an operation** surgeon
**doctrinaire** -ismy, -ism
**doctrine** axiom, belief, canon, concept, conviction, credo, creed, dogma, doxie, doxy, gospel, knowledge, learning, lore, maxim, opinion, precept, principle, teachings, tenet, theory, thesis
**doctrine of angels** angelology
**doctrine of death and afterlife** eschatology
**doctrine of earthquakes** seismology
**doctrine of equality** egalitarianism
**doctrine of final causes** teleology
**doctrine of human welfare** gospel
**doctrine of innate ideas** nativism
**doctrine of non-killing or non-violence** ahimsa
**doctrine of salvation** soteriology
**doctrine that good must prevail in the end** optimism
**doctrine that there is only one God** monotheism
**doctrine that the universe is God** pantheism
**document** authenticate, certificate, certify, cite, corroborate, detail, form, instance, manuscript, paper, record, report, substantiate, support, validate, verify
**document amendment** rider
**documentary on travel** travelogue
**document carrier** attaché case
**document container** file
**document containing charge** indictment
**document giving authority** warrant
**document of proof** voucher
**documents case** attaché
**document signed by its author** autograph

**document stating alleged crimes** indictment
**document to be filled in** form
**document written by hand** manuscript
**dodder-grass** quaking-grass
**dodge** avoid, cringe, elude, equivocate, escape, evade, evasion, prevaricate, quibble, shun, sidestep, sidetrack, skulk, slyness, swerve, vacillate
**dodger** avoider, charlatan, cheat(er), deceiver, double-crosser, eel, idler, impostor, loafer, passenger, rogue, shark, sharper, shirker, slacker, swindler, trickster
**dodge the truth** prevaricate
**dodge work** shirk
**dodgy** tricky
**do down** belittle, criticise, discredit, humiliate
**do duty for** substitute
**doe** deer, hind, tag
**doe of first year** fawn
**doe's partner** buck, stag
**doff** abolish, delete, depose, detach, discard, discharge, dismiss, displace, drop, efface, eject, eliminate, erase, expel, extract, lift, move, oust, purge, raise, relegate, remove, shed, transfer, transport, undress, unseat, vail, withdraw
**dog** Aberdeen, Airedale, Alsatian, basset, bloodhound, boxer, bulldog, canine, Chihuahua, collie, corgi, cur, Dalmatian, Dane, dingo, Dobermann, dachshund, greyhound, hound, hund (G), husky, mastiff, mongrel, mutt, Pekin(g)ese, pooch, poodle, pug, pup(py), retriever, schipperke, setter, sheepdog, spaniel, spitz, terrier, track, whelp, whippet
**dog box** kennel
**dog-eat-dog** ferocious, fierce, ruthless, vicious
**dogged** constant, deliberate, determined, difficult, earnest, firm, fixed, haunted, hounded, inflexible, intent, obdurate, obstinate, persevering, persistent, pigheaded, plagued, purposeful, pursued, resistant, resolute, shadowed, sta(u)nch, steadfast, steady, stubborn, tenacious, tracked, trailed, troubled, unflagging, unshakable, unyielding
**dogged determination** persistence
**dogged dog** terrier
**doggedness** determination, determinedness, firmness, resoluteness, staunchness, steadfastness, steadiness, tenaciousness
**dog guarding the underworld** Cerberus
**doghouse** kennel
**dog in pain does this** yelp
**dog in Punch-and-Judy show** Toby
**dog in the manger** killjoy, meddler, misery, spoil-sport, wet blanket, wowser
**doglike** canine, cynic
**doglike carnivore** hy(a)ena
**dogma** axiom, belief, canon, cant, code, convictions, credendum, credo, creed, doctrine, -ism, maxim, opinion, precept, principles, teachings, tenet, theology, theory
**dog manager** handler
**dogmatic** assertive, authoritarian, authoritative, biased, bigoted, categorical, cocksure, credo, dictatorial, doctrinaire, doctrinal, dogmatical, domineering, downright, emphatic, fanatical, insistent, intolerant, magisterial, opinionated, oracular, overbearing, positive, thatic
**dogmatic in one's opinion** opinionated
**dogmatic principle** dictum
**dog named after a state in Mexico** Chihuahua
**dog noise** barking
**dog of a working breed** Alsatian
**dog of German origin** dachshund
**dog of mixed breed** mongrel
**dog of Pluto** Cerberus
**dog on leash** lym
**dog or cat** pet
**dog restraint** leash
**dog salmon** chum, keta
**dogsbody** drudge, factotum, skivvy
**dog's foot** paw
**dog's house** kennel
**dog's lead** leash
**dog's skin disease** mange
**Dog Star** Sirius
**dog's treat** bone
**dog's wagger** tail
**dogtooth violet** adder's-tongue
**dog-training collar** choker
**dog used to retrieve shot game** retriever
**dog wags this** tail
**dogwood plant** cornel, osier, sumach
**doily** antimacassar, doyley, mat, napkin
**doing PT** exercising
**doing time** in jail
**doit** copper coin, trifle
**do it in assent** nod
**do it to a top** spin
**dolce far niente** inactivity
**doldrums** apathy, blues, depression, dullness, dumps, inactivity, inertia, listlessness, malaise, torpor
**dole** allocation, allotment, allowance, deal, distribution, gratuity, lamentation, parcel, quota, share, sorrow, welfare
**dole cheque** giro
**doleful** afflicted, dismal, dreary, gloomy, joyless, lamentable, lugubrious, mournful, sad, sorrowful, unhappy, woeful
**doleful complaint** jeremiad, lamentation
**doleful sound** knell
**dole out** administer, allot, apportion, distribute, issue, ration
**dole out grudgingly** scant
**do little work** lazy
**dollar** buck
**dollar division** cent
**doll-like** cute
**doll on a string** puppet
**dolorous** doleful, grievous, lachrymose, lugubrious, melancholy, mournful, rueful, sad, sorrowful, tearful, woeful
**dolour** distress, grief, sorrow
**dolphin fish** dorado
**dolphinlike fish** inia
**dolphin's limb** flipper
**dolt** bonehead, clod, domkop, dunce, fool, idiot, ignoramus, imbecile, nitwit, oaf
**domain** area, arena, district, dominion, empire, estate, jurisdiction, kingdom, province, realm, region, section, sphere, territory
**domain of a baron** barony
**domain of an emir** emirate
**domain of devils** diablerie
**domain of supernatural beings** faerie
**domain of Thomas Hardy** Wessex
**dome** arch(way), cupola, curve, edifice, span, vault
**dome-roofed** apse, apsis
**dome-shaped hut** igloo, iglu
**dome-shaped tomb** tholos
**domestic** aboriginal, butler, domesticated, family, help, home(-loving), homebred, housekeeper, indigenous, inland, internal, local, native, servant, steward, tame, valet
**domestically produced** home-made
**domestic animal** cat, dog, pet
**domesticate** accustom, assimilate, break, domiciliate, gentle, habituate, (house)train, naturalise, pacify, tame
**domesticated** pacified, tame, trained
**domesticated animal** pet
**domesticated birds** poultry

**domesticated bovine** beast, cow, ox
**domesticated ox** zebu
**domesticated polecat** ferret
**domestic attendant** servant
**domestic basin** bowl
**domestic bird** chicken, duck, fowl, goose, hen, turkey
**domestic cock** capon
**domestic establishment** ménage
**domestic financial management** home-economy
**domestic fowl** goose, hen
**domestic fowls** poultry
**domestic help** maid
**domestic instrument** utensil
**domestic life** hearth
**domestic rodent** mouse, rat
**domestic servant** maid
**domestic spirit** kobold
**domestic waste** garbage
**domestic worker** cleaner, servant
**domicile** abode, accommodate, accommodation, address, barracks, billet, board, chambers, dwelling, establishment, habitation, harbour, home(stead), house, location, lodge, lodging, manor, mansion, nest, occupy, palace, place, quarters, residence, shanty, shelter, villa
**dominance** ascendancy, ascendency, authority, command, control, dominion, influence, lordship, mastery, power, predominance, primacy, rule, sovereignty, supremacy, sway
**dominant** central, controlling, paramount, pre-eminent, predominant, prevailing, prevalent, principal, prominent, regnant, ruling, superior, supreme
**dominant control** ascendancy, ascendency
**dominant custom** rule
**dominant feature** motif
**dominant person** mogul
**dominate** boss, command, control, denominate, designate, dictate, direct, domineer, govern, influence, intimidate, occupy, oppress, order, overbear, overlook, overpower, (over)rule, permeate, predominate, subdue, surpass, sway
**dominate by force** oppress
**dominating** controlling, directing, governing, leading, mastering, monopolising, overlooking, preponderating, ruling, surveying
**dominating idea** idée fixe (F)
**dominating theme** motif
**domineer** command, dominate, enthrall, govern, intimidate, master, oppress, regiment, rule, subjugate, suppress, surpass, tyrannise
**domineering** blustering, browbeating, bullying, hectoring, imperious, intimidating, masterful, menacing, overbearing, swaggering, threatening, tyrannical, tyrannising
**domineering woman** battle-axe, hussy
**Dominican Republic bay** Escocesa, Samana, Yuma
**Dominican Republic cape** Beata, Engano, Isabela, Macoris
**Dominican Republic island** Beata, Hispaniola, Saona
**Dominican Republic language** Spanish
**Dominican Republic lowland** Cibao
**Dominican Republic religion** Roman Catholic
**dominion** area, command, domain, empery, hegemony, jurisdiction, kingship, leadership, lordship, mastership, pre-eminence, rule, supremacy, territory
**domino face** ace
**domino spot** pip
**do more than duty requires** supererogation
**do more than is warranted** exceed
**don** academic, wear
**donate** award, bequeath, bestow, confer, contribute, extend, gift, give, grant, issue, leave, pledge, present, subscribe, yield
**donation** benefaction, contribution, gift, grant, gratuity, present
**donation for pious use** oblation
**donation of money to the poor** alm
**done** completed, cooked, finished, prepared, ready, through
**done at once** prompt
**done before the proper time** premature
**done by stealth** furtive, surreptitious
**done by the mind** mental
**done by way of trial** tentative
**donee** receiver, recipient
**do needlework** sew
**done for** beaten, broken, dashed, defeated, destroyed, doomed, exhausted, fatigued, finished, foiled, lost, ruined, tired, wrecked
**done in** bushed, dead, dog-tired, exhausted
**done in co-operation** concerted
**done indifferently** perfunctory
**done merely for sake of getting through a duty** perfunctory
**done on purpose** intended, intentional
**done openly** overt, unconcealed
**done secretly** clandestine, surreptitious
**done up** tired
**done with artful dexterity** sly
**done with care** careful
**done with careful attention** conscientious
**done with caution** wary
**done with enthusiasm** whole-hearted
**done without due consideration** ill-considered, rash
**done without exercise of will** involuntary
**done without forethought** casual
**done without pausing** non-stop
**done without preparation** extemporaneous
**done without skill** clumsy
**done with the hands** manual
**donga** gully, ravine
**donjon** keep
**donkey** ass, blockhead, burro, cuddy, dickey, dolt, dunce, fool, halfwit, idiot, jack(ass), jenny, moke, mule, Neddy, oaf, simpleton
**donkey call** bray
**donkey/horse offspring** mule
**donkey's cry** bray
**donkey's name** Ned(dy)
**donkey's snort** bray
**donkey-work** drudgery, groundwork, toil
**donnish person** pedant
**donor** almsgiver, benefactor, donator, giver, grantor, sponsor
**donor to a cause** benefactor
**do not admit** deny, ne admittas (L)
**do not be impetuous** festina lente (L)
**do not exaggerate** understate
**do not go beyond this point** ne plus ultra (L)
**do not heed** ignore
**do nothing** far nienta (I), idle
**do not include** omit
**do not pass exams** fail
**do not rub into wounds** salt
**do not take no for an answer** insist
**do not trust to appearances** fronti nulla fides (L)
**Don Quixote's donkey** Rosinante
**Don Quixote's lady** Dulcinea
**Don Quixote's squire** Sancho
**do office work** file
**doom** condemn(ation), death, decision, decree, destiny, fate, fore-ordain, fortune, ruin, sentence
**doomed** condemned, consigned, cursed, damned, decreed, destined, fated, fey, hopeless, ill-fated, ill-omened, judged, luckless, sentenced
**doomed person** goner
**doomed to be unlucky** ill-fated, ill-omened
**doom to ruin** damn

**do one's heart good** delight, excite, fulfil, satisfy
**do one's utmost** try one's best
**door** doorway, egress, entrance(way), entry, exit, portal
**door beam** lintel
**door catch** snib
**door curtain** portière
**door device** hinge
**door fastening** hasp, latch
**door frame upright** stile
**door handle** knob, pull
**door into the garden** French window
**door joint** hinge
**door-keeper** caretaker, concierge, custodian, doorman, guard, janitor, ostiary, porter, sentinel, tiler, turnkey, usher, warden, warder
**door knocker** rapper
**door lock** bolt, latch
**doorman** caretaker, gatekeeper, porter, usher
**door opener** key
**door part** lintel, panel, rail
**door pivot** hinge
**door post** anta, jamb(e)
**door rug** mat
**door signal** bell, knocker
**door-sill** threshold
**doorstep** threshold
**door timber** lintel
**door to control a flow of water** sluice
**door-to-door salesman** pedlar
**door to enter** entrance
**doorway curtain** portière
**do out of** ba(u)lk, bilk, cheat, con, deprive, fleece, rook, swindle, trick
**dope** blockhead, drugs, dunce, idiot, narcotic, opiate
**do penance** atone, suffer
**dopey** baffled, bemused, bewildered, confused, dazed, dizzy, fuddled, light-headed, muddled, numbed, perplexed, shocked, staggered, stunned, stupefied
**do PT** exercise
**dor** beetle
**dorado fish** dolphin
**dormancy** doze, hibernation, idleness, immobility, inaction, inactivity, inertia, nap, passivity, repose, rest, siesta, sleep, slumber, torpor, unemployment
**dormant** abed, abeyant, asleep, comatose, dull, fallow, hibernating, hidden, implicit, inactive, inert, latent, lethargic, lifeless, motionless, passive, pausing, potential, quiescent, quiet, resting, sleeping, sleepy, sluggish, stagnant, stationary, still, torpid
**dormant state** sleep

**dormer window** dormant, lucarne, luthern, oxeye
**dormitory** bedroom, cell, chamber, hostel, quarters, sleeping-room
**dormitory regulations** parietals
**dormitory sound** snore
**dormouse** loir
**dorp** hamlet, village
**dorsal** abaxia
**dorsal bones** ilia
**dory need** oar
**do's and don'ts** code, customs, etiquette, regulations, rules, standards
**dose** administer, draught, drench, gulp, measure, medicament, medicate, medicine, portion, potion, prescription, quantity, swallow, treat
**dose of medicine or poison** potion
**do something** act
**do something again** redo
**do something in return** repay
**doss** bed
**dossier** brief, case, data, diaries, documents, file, folder, information, letters, paper, portfolio, record
**do surface of road again** retar
**dot** dowry, iota, period, point, scatter, speck, spot, stipple
**do tailoring** sew
**dotard** fuddy-duddy
**dot/dash code** Morse
**dote** deranged, feeble-minded, infatuated, silly
**dote on** admire, adore, coddle, idolise, indulge, love, pamper, spoil, treasure
**do the bidding of** obey
**do the frug** dance
**do the washing and ironing** launder
**do this on April 1st** fool
**doting** childish, easy-going, extravagant, feeble-minded, fond, foolish, indulgent, lavish, lax, lenient, obliging, senile, soft, tenderhearted, unsound, weak
**dotingly fond of wife** uxorial
**dotted** piebald, pied, pinto, semé(e), spotty
**dotted cube** dice
**dotted in heraldry** semé(e)
**dotty** crazy, feeble-minded, senile
**double** bifold, comparable, copy, deceitful, doubly, dual, duplicate, equal, false, hypocritical, paired, proxy, replica, substitute, twice, twin
**double act** duo
**double agent** spy
**double-bass viol** violone
**double-bladed axe** twibill, twybill
**double button** stud

**double-cross** betray, cheat, con, defraud, hoodwink, mislead, swindle, trick, two-time
**double curve in architecture** ogee
**double-dealing** insincere, two-faced
**double entendre** ambiguity, anagram, innuendo, pun, vagueness
**double flower** burster
**double-handed sword** spadone
**double in poker** straddle
**double-marriage criminal** bigamist
**double meaning** ambiguity
**double mouldboard plough** lister
**double over** fold
**double prefix** di-
**double quartet** octet
**double-reed instrument** bassoon
**double refraction** birefringence
**double silk thread** tram
**double sulphate of aluminium** alum
**double tooth** molar
**double woven** two-ply
**doubling of a cord** loop
**doubt** ambiguity, apprehension, confusion, difficulty, dilemma, distrust, fear, hesitate, hesitation, incredulity, indecision, misgiving, mistrust, perplexity, problem, quandary, query, question, reservation, scepticism, suspect, suspicion, uncertainty, vacillate, waver
**doubter** agnostic, apostate, cynic, disbeliever, dissenter, iconoclast, pessimist, questioner, sceptic, scoffer, Thomas, unbeliever
**doubtful** ambiguous, confused, debatable, distrustful, dubious, hesitating, improbable, irresolute, obscure, precarious, sceptical, suspicious, unbelievable, uncertain, unconvinced, undecided, unreliable, unsettled, unsure, vacillating, vague, wavering
**doubtful meaning** equivocal
**doubtful story** rumour
**doubting** cynic, demurring, discrediting, distrusting, fearing, fluctuating, hesitating, incredulous, misgiving, mistrusting, querying, questioning, suspecting, vacillating, wavering
**doubting person** cynic
**doubt the innocence of** suspect
**dough raiser** yeast
**doughty** bold, brave, courageous, dauntless, determined, fearless, intrepid, stout, unafraid
**dough with savoury topping** pizza
**doughy cake** scone

**do up** decorate, fasten, modernise, pack, redecorate, renovate, repair, restore, tie, wrap
**dour** austere, dismal, dreary, forbidding, gloomy, grim, hard, humourless, inflexible, morose, obstinate, rigid, rigorous, severe, solemn, sour, stern, strict, sullen, unfriendly, unyielding
**douse** dip, dowse, drench, duck, dunk, extinguish, immerge, immerse, plunge, saturate, smother, snuff, soak, souse, steep, submerge
**dove** pigeon
**dove's call** coo
**dove's home** cote
**do violence to** outrage
**dowdily** frumpishly
**dowdily-dressed woman** frump
**dowdy** dingy, drab, frumpy, ill-dressed, old-fashioned, shabby, slovenly, tacky, tatty, unfashionable
**dowel** peg, pin
**do well** dow, prosper, succeed, thrive
**dowel used for pinning timber together** tre(e)nail
**dowel used to join timber** tre(e)nail, trunnel
**dowf** dull, flat, spiritless
**do what one is told to do** obedient, obey
**do without** decline, desist, eschew, forbear, for(e)go, relinquish, spare, waive
**down** bloom, de-, depressed, doon (Sc), drink, fell, floor, floss, fluff, gulp, low(er), nap, pile, sick, south, swallow, throw, topple
**down-and-out** beggar, derelict, destitute, forgotten, forsaken, impoverished, outcast, penniless, ruined, tramp, vagrant
**down at heel** destitute, disreputable, dowdy, impoverished, run-down, seedy, shabby, slovenly, worn
**downcast** sad, ruin, collapse, cheerless, dejected, discouraged, miserable, unhappy, daunted, despondent, crestfallen, gloomy, blue
**down duck** eider
**downfall** ruin, tiresome
**downhearted** blue, crestfallen, dejected, depressed, despondent, discouraged, disheartened, dismal, dispirited, downcast, gloomy, glum, low(-spirited), melancholy, sad, sorrowful, unhappy
**down in the dumps** blue, disconsolate, dispirited, mopish, sad, weary
**down in the mouth** blue, dejected, depressed, disappointed, disheartened, downcast, downhearted, heartsick, sad, unhappy
**down on** antagonistic, antipathetic, unsympathetic
**down payment** deposit
**downpour** cloudburst, deluge, flash, flood, inundation, rain, torrent, washout
**downright** candid, clear, explicit, frank, open, outspoken, positive, sheer, simple, straightforward, unequivocal, utter
**down source** eider
**Down's syndrome** mongolism
**down the drain** gone, lost, ruined, wasted
**down-to-earth** commonsense, hard-headed, matter-of-fact, no-nonsense, practical, realistic, sane, sensible
**down-to-earth person** realist
**down tools** strike
**down-trodden** abused, afflicted, distressed, exploited, helpless, oppressed, subjugated, subservient, tyrannised, victimised
**downturn** collapse, crash, decline, decrease, depression, drop, dwindling, failure, fall, fall-off, lessening, low, recession, reduction, reverse, slump, trough
**Down Under land** Australia
**down used for pillows** eider
**downward** declining, descend(ing), sliding
**downward bend** declination
**downward motion** descent
**downward rush** hurl
**downward slope** decline, declivity, descent, dip, downhill, hanging
**down with** à bas (F), defeat, destroy, exterminate, oust, overcome, revoke, squelch, supplant, terminate
**downy** clever, knowing
**downy bird** eider-duck
**downy duck** eider
**downy stone fruit** peach
**downy surface** nap
**downy tip tea** pekoe
**do wrong** err, offend, sin
**do wrong to** injure
**dowry** dot, dowage, dower, endowment, gift, inheritance, jointure, legacy, lobola, lobolo, portion, property, provision, share, talent, tocher
**dowser** water-diviner
**dowsing** rhabdomancy
**doze** catnap, drowse, kip, nap, nod, siesta, sleep, slumber, snooze, zizz
**dozen dozen** gross
**doze off** nod
**dozy** drowsy, half-awake, sleepy, somnolent, soporific, stupid, torpid
**drab** cheerless, colourless, dingy, dismal, drab, dreary, dull, flat, gloomy, grey, shabby, sombre, uninspired
**drab colour** dun
**drably dressed** dowdy
**drably dressed woman** frump
**Draconian** cruel, Draconic, harsh, rigorous
**Dracula's dentition** fangs
**Dracula's friends** bats, wolves, vampires
**Dracula's garment** cape
**Dracula's title** count
**draff** dregs, lees, remains, residue
**draft** breeze, check, compilation, compose, conscription, design, draw, formulate, induct, outline, plan, rough, sketch, swallow, version
**draft animal** horse, mule, ox
**drafter of documents** copyist, scrivener
**draft harness part** hame
**draft of an act of Parliament** bill
**draft of author** manuscript
**draft of law** bill
**drag** amplify, crawl, dally, draggle, dredge, expatiate, extend, haul, linger, loiter, lug, plod, prolong, protract, pull, schlep, shuffle, slow, tow, trawl, tug
**drag a car** tow
**drag along** entrain, trail
**drag along the ground** haul, trail
**drag artist** transvestite, female impersonator
**drag behind** trail
**drag by rope** tow
**drag forcibly** hale
**draggy** tedious, unpleasant
**drag loosely behind** trail
**drag of a wheel** skid
**dragon** wyvern
**drag one's feet** hobble, idle, lag, linger, procrastinate, shamble, shuffle, tarry
**dragon reputed to kill by its breath or look** basilisk
**dragon slain by Siegfried, in German mythology** Fafnir
**dragon slain by Beowulf** Grendel
**dragoon** browbeat, bully, coerce, compel, constrain, drive, force, impel, intimidate
**drag through mud** (be)smirch, stain
**drag wearily** trail
**drag with effort** lug

**drain** consume, debouch, exhaust, exude, sap, sewer, sinkhole, strain, weary
**drainage** discharge, effluence, gush, jet, outfall, outflow, outpouring, rush, sewage, spout
**drainage pipe** sewer
**drainage pit** sump
**drainage trench** ditch
**drain basin** sink
**drain dry** exsiccate
**drained of colour** blanch
**drainer** colander, sieve, strainer
**drain off** bail, bale
**drake** duck, mallard
**dram** draught, drop, finger, nip, portion, sip, soupçon, taste, tiff, tot
**drama company** troupe
**drama division** act, scene
**drama of mixed tragic and comic elements** tragicomedy
**dramatic** drama, exciting, expressing, graphic, histrionic, impressive, marked, noticeable, scenic, showy, significant, stagy, stirring, striking, sudden, surprising, theatrical, thespian, thrilling, vivid, wonderful
**dramatically** breathtakingly, emotionally, excitingly, melodramatically, sensationally, startlingly, suddenly, tensely, theatrically, thrillingly
**dramatic artist** actor
**dramatic composition with only one speaker** monologue
**dramatic division** scene
**dramatic entertainment in dumb show** pantomime
**dramatic performer** actor
**dramatic piece** monodram, skit
**dramatic portrayal** acting
**dramatic scene from history** pageant
**dramatic work** play
**dramatise** act, declaim, emote, enact, melodramatise, mount, overact, perform, produce, rant, roar, stage
**dramatised television based on real events** docudrama
**dramatis personae** cast
**dramatist** comedian, dramaturge, dramaturgist, melodramatist, playwright, screenwriter, tragedian
**dramatist, American** Albee, Anderson, Barker, Baum, Carroll, Miller, O'Neill, Williams
**dramatist, Australian** Chambers
**dramatist, Austrian** Blei, Collins, Muller, Neumann, Wildgans
**dramatist, Belgian** Maeterlink
**dramatist, Canadian** Rose
**dramatist, Czeck** Jerabeck, Jirasek

**dramatist, Danish** Bergstrom, Buchholtz, Ewald
**dramatist, Dutch** Coster, Emants, Feith, Vondel
**dramatist, English** Beaumont, Beddoes, Chapman, Fletcher, Fry, Granville-Baker, Johnson, Kenney, Kyd, Peele, Pinero, Rattigan, Shadwell, Shakespeare, Shirley, Stoppard, Tourneur, Travers, Udall, Vanbrugh, Webster
**dramatist, French** Blum, Claudel, Colle, Feydeau, Labische, Lesage, Meurice
**dramatist, German** Bab, Ganghoefer, Kind, Schiller, Toller, Wedekind, Zwerg
**dramatist, Greek** Euripides, Pherecrates, Sophocles, Sophron
**dramatist, Hungarian** Bessenyei, Doczi, Zilahy
**dramatist, Irish** Beckett, Behan, Colum, Gregory, Shaw, Synge, Wilde, Wills, Yeats
**dramatist, Italian** Alferi, Benelli, Goldoni, Marenco
**dramatist, Japanese** Chikamatsu
**dramatist, Mexican** Gamboa
**dramatist, Norwegian** Biester, Bjornson, Heiberg, Ibsen
**dramatist, Portuguese** Silva, Vicente
**dramatist, Russian** Alecsandri, Chekhov, Kapnist, Tolstoi
**dramatist, Scottish** Barki, Davidson, Robertson
**dramatist, South African** Fugard, Mhlophe, Slabolepszy, Themba
**dramatist, Spanish** Fernansez, Zamora
**dramatist, Swedish** Beskow, Edgrain, Strindberg
**dramatist, Swiss** Frisch, Wesker, Wycherley
**dramatist, Welsh** William
**dram of liquor** tot
**drape** apparel, array, attire, bedeck, clothe, conceal, cover, curtain, deck, decorate, dress, droop, drop, endow, enwrap, equip, festoon, fold, garb, garland, habit, hang(ing), hide, invest, outfit, rig, robe, screen, shroud, suspend, swathe, veil, vest, wrap
**draped border** valance
**draped garland** festoon
**drapery** blind(s), cloth, covering(s), curtain(s), hanging(s), tapestry
**drastic** desperate, dire, extreme, far-reaching, forceful, harsh, radical, severe, strong
**drat** curse, rot

**draught** cup, current, dose, drawing, drench, drink, flow, influx, movement, portion, potion, puff, quantity, traction
**draught animal** (dray)horse
**draught beer** bitter
**draught horse** shire
**draughtman's tool** T-square
**draught of liquor** swig
**draught of poison** potion
**draught of spirits** dram
**Dravidian language** Tamil
**Dravidian language of south-east India** Teluga
**draw** attract, compose, deduce, delineate, derive, draft, drag, drain, etch, form(ulate), frame, haul, inhale, limn, lottery, magnetise, prepare, pull, sketch, stretch, suck, tie, trace, tug, write
**draw a bead on** aim
**draw after** tow, trail
**draw along** drag
**draw as conclusion** derive
**draw attention** attract
**draw attention to** accentuate, refer
**draw away** divert
**drawback** defect, deficiency, detriment, difficulty, disability, disadvantage, discouragement, encumbrance, fault, flaw, handicap, hindrance, hitch, impediment, imperfection, inconvenience, interference, liability, limitation, minus, nuisance, obstacle, obstruction, snag, stumbling, trouble
**draw back** flinch, recede, recoil, retract, retreat, shrink, shy, withdraw
**draw back from pain** wince
**draw blood from** bleed
**draw breath** inhale
**draw by means of dots** stipple
**draw close** near
**draw comparisons** analogise
**drawee** acceptor
**drawer for money** till
**drawer of plans** draughtsman
**drawers** knickers
**draw forth** educe, elicit, evoke, extract, fetch
**draw from** abstract
**draw game** tie
**draw harshly over** scrape
**draw in** breathe
**draw in breath through the nose with a sharp hiss** sniff
**draw in dots** stipple
**drawing** attracting, cartoon, collecting, delineation, depiction, diagram, draughtmanship, extending, graphic, illustration, inhaling, lottery, outline, picture, portrait, portrayal, pulling,

representation, siphoning, sketch(ing), study, taking
**drawing close** nearing
**drawing in of breath** inhalation
**drawing instrument** crayon, pencil
**drawing on all sources** eclectic
**drawing pin** thumbtack, tintack
**drawing room** salo(o)n
**drawing together** astringent, styptic
**draw in silhouette** outline
**draw into the mouth** suck
**draw inward** attract
**draw liquid from** drain
**draw lots** ballot, choose
**draw near** approach, attract
**drawn game** tie
**drawn out** long
**drawn to** attracted
**draw off** broach, drain, exhaust, siphon
**draw off liquid** drain
**draw on** employ, exploit, extract, use
**draw out** continue, deracinate, educe, elicit, elongate, extend, extract, lengthen, prolong, stretch, uproot, withdraw
**draw out and twist into strands** spin
**draw out by suction** aspirate
**draw rein** halt
**draws and paints** artist
**draw sap from tree** bleed
**draw the line** bar, confine, fix, limit, object, part, prohibit, proscribe, restrict, stop
**draw through a bent tube** siphon
**draw through eyelets** lace
**draw tight** frap, tauten
**draw to** attract
**draw to a point** taper
**draw together** assemble, gather, join, knit, lace, pucker
**draw to oneself** attract
**draw towards** attract, pull
**draw up** arrange, array, compose, draft, formulate, frame, halt, prepare, redact, stop
**draw up plans again** redesign
**draw up the shoulders** shrug
**draw water** lade
**dread** alarm, apprehension, awe, bog(e)y, bugaboo, concern, consternation, dire, dismay, dreadful, fear(fulness), fright(ful), hesitation, horrible, horror, nervousness, panic, reverence, terrible, terror, timidity, uncertainty, worry
**dread awe** fear
**dreadful** abysmal, alarming, atrocious, awful, dare, dark, dire, disagreeable, distressing, dread, eerie, evil, fearful, fearsome, frightening, frightful, ghastly, grievous, grim, hideous, horrible, noxious, pernicious, repugnant, repulsive, terrible, terrific, terrifying, troublesome, villainous
**dreadful crime** enormity
**dreadful stench** miasma
**dread mingled with reverence** awe
**dread of books** bibliophobia
**dread of high places** acrophobia
**dread of open spaces** agoraphobia
**dread of pain** alhophobia
**dream** ambition, aspiration, daydream, delusion, design, desire, envisage, fancy, fantasy, goal, hope, illusion, imagination, imagine, incubus, nightmare, notion, oneiro-, rêve (F), reverie, speculation, stargaze, think, trance, vision, visualise, wish
**dreamer** daydreamer, fantast, idealist, idler, romancer, romantic, sleepwalker, somnambulist, visionary
**dream figure** phantasmagoria
**dream of** crave, itch, long, lust
**dream time** alchera, alcheringa
**dream up** conceive, concoct, contrive, create, devise, hatch, imagine, invent, spin
**dream world** Utopia
**dreamy** absent(-minded), abstracted, aerial, chimerical, comatose, daydreaming, dim, drowsy, dull, fantastic, faraway, listless, misty, musing, notional, oneiric, pensive, preoccupied, rapt, refreshing, romantic, shadowy, sleepy, thoughtful, tranquil, unreal, vague, whimsical
**dreamy musical piece** nocturne
**drear** bleak, cheerless, comfortless, depressing, dismal, doleful, downcast, dreary, forlorn, gloomy, glum, lonely, melancholy, mournful, solitary, sombre, sorrowful, wretched
**dreary** awful, bad, bleak, boring, cheerless, comfortless, depressing, dismal, doleful, dour, downcast, drab, drear, dull, forlorn, gloomy, glum, lifeless, lonely, melancholy, miserable, monotonous, mournful, routine, sad, solitary, sombre, sorrowful, tedious, tiresome, uneventful, wearisome, wretched
**dreary routine** treadmill
**dredge** cover, dust, powder, scatter, shower, spray, sprinkle, strew
**dredge to collect starfish** mop
**dregs** bums, debris, deposit, dross, fecula, garbage, grounds, lees, offal, outcast, rabble, refuse, remains, remnants, residue, residuum, riffraff, scum, sediment, trash
**dregs of molten glass** dribble
**drench** douse, drown, duck, flood, imbrue, inundate, saturate, soak, souse, steep, wet
**drenching rain** soaker
**drench with hot fat** baste
**dress** adorn, align, apparel, array, attire, clad, clothe(s), clothing, costume, fit, frock, garb, garments, gown, habiliment, habit, ornament, raiment, regalia, straighten, suit, vestments, vesture
**dressage position** pesade
**dress belt** sash
**dress carefully** preen, primp
**dress designer** couturier
**dress down** berate, castigate, rebuke, reprimand, reprove, scold
**dressed** attired, bandaged, changed, clad, clothed, donned, garbed, plastered, robed, treated
**dress edge** hem
**dressed kidskin** suede
**dressed pelt** fur
**dressed salad of raw cabbage** coleslaw
**dressed stone at the corner of a wall** quoin
**dresser in silk manufacturing** framer
**dresser of furs** furrier
**dress-fabric of crepe type made in silk** marocain
**dress feathers** preen
**dress fold** pleat
**dress gaudily** bedizen
**dress in** don
**dressing** attiring, bandage, bandaging, changing, clothing, donning, lint, plaster, plastering, togging, treating
**dressing for food** sauce
**dressing for making hair glossy** brilliantine
**dressing for wound** bandage, lint, plaster
**dressing gown** bathrobe, kimono, peignoir, robe
**dressing room** bedroom, boudoir
**dressing-table with a mirror** toile
**dress insertion** godet, gusset
**dressmaker** modiste, seamstress, sempstress
**dressmaking** couture
**dress neck strap** halter
**dress oneself up** prink
**dress ornament** brooch, clip, sash
**dress ostentatiously** overdress, prank, primp
**dress part** collar, panel, sleeve
**dress stone** nig
**dress to ostentation** prink
**dress trimming** braid, gimp, insertion, lace, piping, ruche, ruching

**dress up** adorn, beautify, deck, disguise, embellish, gild, improve, preen, titivate, tog
**dress with beak** preen
**dress with care** preen
**dress with too much formality** overdress
**dressy ornament** figgery
**dribble** drip, drivel, drizzle, drool, drop, leak, ooze, run, saliva, seep, slaver, slobber, spittle, trickle
**dribbling** dripping, dropping, leaking, oozing, running, seeping, slobbering, trickling
**dried and pounded meat pressed into cakes** pemmican
**dried beef** biltong, bucan
**dried brick** adobe
**dried bud used in seasoning** clove
**dried cassia seed** senna
**dried coconut kernels** copra
**dried cornstalks** straw
**dried flakes detached from the skin** scurf
**dried flower bud** clove
**dried flowers** brayera
**dried food for cattle** fodder
**dried fruit** apricots, peaches, prunes, raisins, sultanas
**dried fruit of a conifer** cone
**dried ginger** asarum
**dried grain stalks** straw
**dried grape** currant, raisin, sultana
**dried grass** hay
**dried ground starchy tubers of various orchids** salep
**dried hay** fodder
**dried kernel of coconut** copra
**dried leaves and flowers of hemp smoked as intoxicant** dagga, marihuana, marijuana
**dried leaves of purple foxglove** digitalis
**dried marjoram** oregano
**dried meat** biltong
**dried ones become raisins** grapes
**dried orchid tuber** salep
**dried-out** desiccated
**dried perspiration in wool** suint
**dried plum** prune
**dried pod of gourd used as rough sponge** loofah
**dried root of wild ginger** asarum
**dried sausage** saveloy
**dried shell of a plant** gourd
**dried spikes** cannabis
**dried strips of rolled dough** noodles
**dried strong-scented root of wild ginger** asarum
**dried-up** arid, parched, sere, shrunken
**dried-up appearance** weazen, wizened
**dried-up ditch** wadi

**dried wild marjoram as seasoning** oregano
**dried with heat** torrid
**drift** aim, bank, bias, coast, direction, drive, dune, float, ford, heap, impetus, impulse, inclination, intent, mass, meander, motion, penchant, pile, pressure, propensity, purpose, push, stray, tendency, tenor, trend, urge, waft, wander
**drift angle** leeway
**drifted accumulation** debris
**drifter** gypsy, itinerant, migrant, nomad, rambler, ranger, rover, stroller, tinker, transient, traveller, vagabond, vagrant, voyager, wanderer
**drifting** adrift
**drifting sand hill** dune
**drift on the surface of a liquid** float
**drifts sideways** crab
**drill** aerobics, auger, bit, bore, exercise, fabric, gore, gymnastics, habituation, initiate, instruct(ion), jackhammer, perforator, pierce, practice, practise, puncture, rehearsal, ritual, teach, textile, train(ing), tutor
**drill a hole** bore
**drill hall** armoury
**drilling tool** brace
**drill used in drilling rocks** aiguille
**drink** absorb, alcohol, beverage, booze, bumper, carouse, cocktail, down, drain, gulp, guzzle, highball, imbibe, indulge, intoxicant, lap, libation, liquid, liquor, nip, nogging, potation, potion, punch, quaff, refreshment, revel, sip, snort, spirits, stiffener, stimulant, sulk, sup, swallow, swig, swill, taste, tipple, tot
**drink alcohol** tipple
**drink and be merry** carouse
**drink another's health** pledge, toast
**drink before bed** nightcap
**drink by scooping up with tongue** lap
**drink constantly in small quantities** tipple
**drink deeply** quaff
**drink delicately** sip
**drink drunk after spirits** chaser
**drinker** alcoholic, boozer, carouser, dipsomaniac, dronklap, drunk(ard), guzzler, imbiber, inebriate, lush, tippler, toper, wino
**drink excessively** fuddle, tipple
**drink flavoured with juniper berries** gin
**drink for two** tea
**drink freely** carouse
**drink given to a departing rider** stirrup-cup

**drink greedily** guzzle, swill
**drink heavily** tope, quaff
**drink in** absorb, assimilate
**drinking age** adulthood, majority
**drinking-bottle** flask
**drinking bout** bender, binge, carousal, carouse, celebration, jag, orgy, potation, revelry, spree, wassail (Sc)
**drinking cup** beaker, horn, mug, quaich, stein, tankard, tass, tassie (Sc)
**drinking glass** braggart, goblet, rummer, schooner, scuttle, tumbler
**drinking house** pub, (wine)bar
**drinking mug** stein
**drinking place** grogshop, pub, (wine)bar
**drinking salute** toast
**drinking spree** binge
**drinking toast** bottoms up, cheers, prosit
**drinking tube** straw
**drinking tumbler** glass
**drinking vessel** beaker, (beer)tankard, chalice, cup, glass, goblet, gourd, mug, stein, tumbler
**drink in honour of** toast
**drink in large draughts** swig
**drink in small amounts** sip
**drink intoxicating liquor habitually** tipple
**drink made from apples** cider
**drink made from molasses** rum
**drink made from spirits** toddy
**drink made of wine and honey** oenomel
**drink much** bib
**drink noisily** slurp
**drink of sailor** grog, rum
**drink of spirit and water** grog
**drink of the gods** ambrosia, nectar, soma
**drink of whisky and soda water** peg
**drink regularly** tope
**drink sachet** teabag
**drinks are served here** bar, pub
**drinks counter** bar
**drink server** barman
**drink slowly** sip
**drink taken quickly** quickie
**drink the health of** pledge, toast
**drink to** pledge, salute, toast
**drink together** hobnob
**drink too much** tope
**drink to one's health** toast
**drink warily** sip
**drink with a fruit base** cordial
**drink with the tongue** lap
**drip** distill, dribble, dripple, drizzle, drop, exude, fall, filter, leak, percolate, plop, splash, sprinkle, trickle, weep

**drip saliva** drivel, slobber
**drive** avenue, compel, constrain, effort, energy, force, go, guide, hurl, impel, initiative, overtask, overwork, poke, press, propel, push, ride, rout, shove, task, travel, urge, vigour, whip
**drive a hard bargain** chaffer, haggle, negotiate
**drive apart** estrange
**drive at** aim, imply, indicate, infer, insinuate, intend, intimate, mean, signify, suggest
**drive at high speed** race
**drive away** banish, chase, dispel, repel, scat, shoo, voetsak, voetsek
**drive back** rebut, repel, repulse
**drive backwards** reverse
**drive ball into cup** hole
**drive before the wind** scud
**drive birds away** shoo
**drive down** tamp
**drive fast** speed
**drive forcibly** impel
**drive forth** propel
**drive forward** impel, propel
**drive-in hotel** motel
**drive insane** derange
**drive into motion** impel
**drivel** babble, dawdle, dote, dribble, drip, drool, foolish, fritter, gab, gibber(ish), idiotic, jargon, loiter, mucus, nonsense, ramble, rot, rubbish, saliva, silly, slabber, slaver, slobber, sniffle, snivel, sputum, squander, trash, trifle, twaddle
**drivel at length** spout
**drivelling** slavering
**drive mad** derange
**drive nail at angle** toe
**driven by lust** lustful
**drive off** repel, chase
**drive out** eject, exorcise, expel, (r)oust, rout
**drive out by force** expel
**drive out of office** eject, oust
**driver** chauffeur, conductor, handler, mechanic, technician, worker
**driver in the fairway** golfer
**driver of a chariot** charioteer
**driver of an elephant** mahout
**driver of motor car** chauffeur, motorist
**driver's compartment of lorry** cab
**driver's seat in a racing car** cockpit
**drive slantingly** toe
**drive strongly** urge
**drive too fast** speed
**drive up the wall** derange, exasperate, infuriate, irritate, madden
**drive with light blows** tamp
**driving as a hobby** motoring
**driving cylinder** piston
**driving force** guts, impetus, lifeblood

**driving forward** propulsion
**driving line** rein
**driving out** expulsion
**driving pedal** accelerator, brake
**driving shower** scud
**driving surface** road(way), street
**drizzle** rain, shower, smur (Sc), spit, spray, sprinkle
**drizzly** misty, rainy
**drizzly rain** smir(r), smur (Sc)
**droll** amusing, clown, comedian, comical, diverting, funny, jester, odd, queer, wag, waggish, witty
**drollery** absurdity, esprit, farce, foolery, humour, jest, mummery, prank, quip, ridiculousness, wit(ticism)
**droll fellow** wag
**drolly** amusingly, comically, divertingly, eccentrically, entertainingly, farcically, funnily, humorously, jocularly, ludicrously, oddly, quaintly, ridiculously, whimsically
**dromedary** camel, oont
**drone** buzz, hum, idler, lounger, murmur, parasite, sluggard, snail, thrum, whirring
**drone in the sleep** snore
**drone or queen** bee
**drongo** bird, twerp, twirp
**droning beetle** dor
**droning sound** hum
**drool** babble, blather, dribble, drivel, gibber, saliva(te), slabber, slaver, slobber, spit(tle), sp(l)utter
**droop** bend, bow, decline, dejected, despond, exhausted, fade, fall, fatigued, flag, hang, incline, languish, lop, nutate, sag, sink, slouch, weaken, weary, wilt, wither
**drooping** bending, dropping, lank, lop, nutant, sagging, sinking, slouching
**drooping-flowered shrub** fuchsia
**drooping of the upper eyelid** ptosis
**drop** abyss, bead, cease, dab, dash, decline, decrease, descent, diminish, drip, droop, droplet, dump, fall, globule, gutta, lower, nip, pearl, pinch, plunge, reduction, sag, sink, sip, smack, spot, taste, tear, tot, trace, trickle, tumble
**drop a hint** intimate
**drop an A-bomb on** nuke
**drop bait** dap, dip
**drop from aircraft by parachute** bail
**drop gently** dap
**drop in** call, visit
**drop in value** depreciation
**droplet** drip
**droplets** dew
**drop off** decline, decrease, deliver, diminish, doze, drowse, dwindle, leave, lessen, slacken, slant, slope, snooze
**drop of liquid** blob
**drop of moisture** bead
**drop of saline liquid** tear
**drop of sorrow** tear
**drop of wave** pitch
**drop out** abandon, forsake, leave, quit, renege, stop, withdraw
**drop-out** deviant, dissenter, hippie, loner, non-conformist, rebel, renegade
**dropsy** anasarca, oedema
**dropwort** meadowsweet
**dross** cinder, dregs, refuse, rubbish, scoria, scum, slag, sprue, trash, waste
**dross from metal-smelting** scoria
**dross of a metal** slag
**drove** assemblage, band, body, collection, company, covey, crowd, crush, flock, group, herd, horde, host, litter, mob, pack, rabble, shoal, swarm, throng
**drowned valley** ria
**drowse** catnap, doze, droop, nap, nod, rest, sleep, slumber, slump, snooze, snore, zizz
**drowsiness** oscitancy
**drowsy** asleep, comatose, dazed, dopey, dozy, druggy, dull, groggy, hypnotic, indolent, laz(il)y, lethargic, listless, lulled, nodding, opiate, oscitant, otiose, sleepy, sluggish, somniferous, somnolent, soporific, tedious, torpid
**drowsy person** sleepyhead
**drub** bang, batter, beat, belt, cane, clobber, cudgel, defeat, flog, hit, lash, leather, maul, overwhelm, pound, punish, rout, scourge, strike, thrash, trounce, whip
**drudge** dishwasher, factotum, grubber, hack, jackal, menial, plodder, scrubwoman, servant, skivvy, slave, sweater, toil(er), work(er)
**drudgery** bondage, chore, donkey-work, drudgism, fag, grind, hack-work, labour, moil, onerousness, serfdom, skivvying, slavery, slog, sweat, toil, travail, treadmill, turmoil, work
**drug** aloe, anaesthetic, anaesthetise, analgesic, antibiotic, cocain(e), deaden, depressant, dope, dose, drench, hemp, heroin, medicament, medicate, medication, medicine, morphia, morphine, narcotic, numb, opiate, opium, penicillin, poison, potion, remedy, snow, stimulant, stupefy, tranquilliser, treat

**drug addict** druggie, fiend, hype, junkie, junky, user
**drug causing forgetfulness of grief** nepenthes
**drug causing sleep** narcotic
**drug dealer** pusher
**drug dependence** addiction
**drug dependency** habit, monkey
**drug dose** hit
**drug experience** trip
**drug from coca** cocain(e)
**drug from plants** galenical
**drugged bliss** kaif, ke(e)f, ki(e)f
**drugged drink** hocus
**druggist** chemist, pharmacist
**drug-induced languor** kaif, ke(e)f, ki(e)f
**drug inducing sleep** phenobarbital
**drug made from juice of certain poppies** opium
**drug made from the dried leaves of hemp** b(h)ang
**drug plant** aloe
**drug prepared from dried foxglove leaves** digitalis
**drug pusher** peddler
**drug reaction** trip
**drug seller** dealer, pusher
**drugs kept for personal consumption** stash
**drug smuggler** mule
**drug tasting of iron** chalybeate
**drug that increases activity** stimulant
**drug that kills tapeworms** taeniacide
**drug that kills worms** vermicide
**drug that relieves pain** analgesic, anodyne, morphia, morphine
**drug used as cure** medication
**drug used to treat asthma** stramonium
**drug user** acidhead, addict, joypopper
**druid stone** boulder, graywether, sarsen
**drum** kettledrum, tambo(u)r, tomtom, tympan
**drum idly** thrum
**drum major's following** parade
**drummer** tympanist
**drumming** beating, pulsating, rapping, reverberating, tattooing, throbbing
**drumming sound** rataplan
**drum up** attract, canvass, collect, gather, obtain, petition, solicit
**drum with the fingers** thrum
**drunk** alcoholic, bender, binge, blotto, boozer, crapulous, dipsomaniac, dronklap, inebriate, inebrious, intoxicated, loaded, reveller, sloshed, smashed, sot, soused, sozzled, stoned, tight, tipsy
**drunk and whining** maudlin
**drunkard** alcoholic, alcy, alkie, bibber, boozer, dipsomaniac, drinker, dronkie, dronklap, elbow-crooker, inebriate, sot, souse, swillbelly, tippler, toper
**drunk as a lord** inebriated
**drunken fellow** boraccia (I), borachio
**drunken frolic** spree
**drunkenness** alcoholism, crapulence, dipsomania, inebriation, inebriety, insobriety, intemperance, intoxication, tipsiness
**drunkenness makes a man let out the truth** in vino veritas (L)
**drunken orgy** bacchanal
**drunken party** orgy
**drunken revelry** Bacchanal(ia), carousal, orgy
**drunken spree** orgy, spree
**drupaceous fruit** plum
**dry** arid, barren, biting, boring, dehydrated, desiccate, dreary, dull, evaporated, juiceless, moistureless, parched, plain, sapless, sarcastic, sec, sere, tedious, thirsty, tiresome, torrid, unadorned, uninteresting, waterless, xeric
**dryad** wood nymph
**dry and brittle** crisp
**dry as wine** brut, sec
**dry barometer** aneroid
**dry barren region** desert
**dry bed of stream** wadi, wady
**dry biscuit** cracker
**dry by rubbing** wipe
**dry cake** biscuit
**dry-cooked** roasted
**dry cooking** roasting
**dry cracking sound** crackle
**dry cut stalks of grain** straw
**dry dishes** wipe
**dry-eyed** tearless
**dry goods dealer** draper
**dry hay by loosening** ted
**dry inflammable matter** tinder
**drying agent** siccative
**drying cloth** towel
**drying oven** kiln, oast
**drying unit** oven
**dry lake basin** playa
**dry land** terra firma
**dry material for starting fire** kindling
**dryness** aridity, aridness, dehydration, drought, thirst
**dryness of the mouth** xerostomia
**dry out** dehydrate, parch
**dry out hay** ted
**dry period** drought
**dry, red Italian wine** Chianti
**dry red wine** claret
**dry region** desert
**dry riverbed** wadi, wady
**dry rough incrustation** scab
**dry savoury biscuit** cream-cracker
**dry scab** eschar
**dry scale of fern stem** palea
**dry scaly skin disease** psoriasis
**dry spell** drought
**dry stalk** straw
**dry tumour** xerodes
**dry up** cease, decrease, desiccate, exsiccate, harden, mummify, parch, sear, sere, shrivel, wilt, wither
**dry up and die** wither
**dry white wine** Alsace, chardonnay, Elsass (G), grand cru, moselle, riesling
**dry wine** brut, sec
**dry wit** salt
**dry with cloth** wipe
**dry wood** tinder
**dual** bi-, coupled, double, doubly, paired, twice, twofold
**duality** biformity, dichotomy, doubleness, dualism, duplexity, twoness
**dual monarchy** diarchy
**dual sound** chord
**dub** address, baptise, burnish, call, categorise, christen, denominate, designate, entitle, furbish, knight, label, level, (nick)name, scour, smooth, standardise, stereotype, style, tag, term, title, typecast
**dubbed** knighted
**dubious** alleged, ambiguous, apocryphal, debatable, doubtful, equivocal, hesitant, indefinite, obscure, problematical, questionable, shady, suspect, suspicious, uncertain, unclear, unconvinced, undecided, underhand, unsettled, unsure, wavering
**dubious and questionable** shady
**dubious apostle** Thomas
**dubious suspect** fishy
**duck** anas, avoid, dodge, drake, drake, eider, escape, evade, mallard, pekin, pintail, scaup, sidestep, smew, stoop, tarp, teal, tern
**duck-billed mammal** platypus
**duck call** quack
**duck down** eider
**duck feathers** down
**duck-like** anatine
**duck's cry** quack
**duck with soft down** eider
**duct** aperture, canal, channel, conduit, culvert, ditch, drain, funnel, furrow, groove, gutter, hose, main, outlet, passage, pipe, route, sewer, sink, sluice, strait, trench, trough, tube, vas, vent, watercourse
**ductile** docile, elastic, facile, fictile, flexible, formable, limber, lissome,

lithe, malleable, mouldable, plastic, pliable, pliant, shapeable, soft, springy, stretchable, stretchy, supple, teachable, tensile, tractable, trainable, willowy
**ductile solid** metal
**duct in the body** canal
**ductless gland** pancreas, pineal, pituitary, thymus, thyroid
**ductless gland near the root of the neck** thymus
**dud** failure, flop, useless, valueless, worthless
**dude** beau, breker, coxcomb, dandy, fop, lady-killer, pantsula, popinjay
**due** adequate, ample, anticipated, appropriate, attributable, awaited, becoming, deserved, expected, fee, fit, just, mature, merited, obligatory, outstanding, owing, payable, redeemable, scheduled, slated, suitable, unpaid
**due for payment** owing
**duel** affaire d'honneur (F), swordfight
**dueller** épéeist
**duelling sword** épée, sharp
**duenna** chaperon, companion, governess
**due statement** bill, voucher
**duet** cooperation, duo, two
**due to chance** accidental, fortuitous
**due to motion** kinetic
**due to the fact that** because
**duffle coat fastener** toggle
**dug deeply** delve
**dug for ore** mine
**dugong** manatee, sea-cow
**dugout** barricade, canoe, cave, ditch, dory, excavation, hovel, intrenchment, kayak, shelter, trench
**dugout canoe** banca, piragua, pirogue
**duke** baron, count, duc (F), earl, lord, marquess, nobleman, peer, viscount
**dulcet** agreeable, calm, canorous, compatible, concordant, congruous, delightful, enchanting, euphonious, fluent, harmonious, liquid, lyrical, matching, mellifluous, mellow, melodious, melting, musical, peaceful, pleasant, smooth, soft, solacing, soothing, sweet, symphonious, syrupy, tranquil, tuneful, winsome
**dulcimer** cymbalo
**dull** apathetic, bland, blunt(ed), boring, callous, colourless, dead, dense, depress, dim, dismal, dispirit, dowf, drab, dreary, drowsy, dry, dun, earthbound, flat, gloomy, grey, heavy, humdrum, inert, insensible, lifeless, listless, mat(t), monotonous, obscure, obtuse, overcast, plain, prosaic, slow, sluggish, spiritless, stagnant, stolid, stupid, tedious, thick, uneventful, unexciting, unimaginative, uninteresting, vapid, wan
**dull and heavy** leaden
**dull and motionless** glassy
**dull and tedious** prosy
**dull and uninteresting** stodgy
**dullard** blockhead, clod, dimwit, dunce, nitwit, num(b)skull, oaf
**dull, boring** monotonous
**dull brown** dun
**dull brownish-yellow** khaki
**dull by inaction** rust
**dull colour** drab, dun
**dull cry of pain** groan
**dulled to pleasure** blasé, jaded
**dull fellow** buff, chuff, drip, fog(e)y, humdrum
**dull finish** mat(t)
**dull from stillness** stagnant
**dull grey** leaden
**dull grey brown** dun
**dull heavy sound** thud, thump
**dull monotony** blandness, blankness, callousness, cloudiness, deadness, denseness, dimness, dreariness, dryness, dullness, emptiness, flatness, gloominess, heaviness, lifelessness, listlessness, mat(t), matte, plainness, prosaicness, sameness, slowness, sluggishness, stolidity, stolidness, stupidness, tediousness, thickness, tiresomeness, triteness, unintelligence
**dullness of colour** drabness
**dull of wit** slow-poke
**dull old fellow** fog(e)y
**dull pain** ache
**dull paint** matt(e)
**dull person** bore, dunce, log, zombie
**dull red** maroon
**dull routine** rut
**dull service** mat
**dull sound** thud
**dull-sounding blow** bump, thump
**dull sound of impact** phut
**dull statement** platitude
**dull stupid person** oaf
**dull surface of metal** matt(e)
**dull-tasting** bland
**dull thump** thud
**dull truism** platitude
**dull whitish tint** grey
**dull-witted person** dunce
**Dumas novel** *The Three Musketeers*
**dumb** aphonic, foolish, inarticulate, mum, mute, noiseless, quiet, reserved, reticent, silent, silly, soundless, speechless, still, stupid, taciturn, tongue-tied, unintelligent, voiceless, wordless
**dumbfound** amazed, astonish, astound, baffle, confound, confuse, dumfound, flabbergasted, nonplus, perplex, petrify, stagger, stun(ned), unbalance
**dumb person** mute
**dumb show** mime, pantomime
**dumbstruck** speechless
**dummy** artificial, blockhead, bogus, copy, counterfeit, dolt, dullard, duplicate, fake, false, figure, form, imitation, mannequin, mock, model, numskull, representation, reprint, sample, sham, simulated, substitute, teat
**dummy for display of clothes** mannequin
**dump** discharge, drop, eject, hovel, release, tip, unload
**dumped cargo** jetsam
**dun** auburn, brown, brunette, dusky, gloomy, hazel, mound, umber
**dunce** alec, ass, blockhead, dolt, dullard, ninny
**dun colour** ecru, grey, khaki, tan
**Dundee region** Tayside
**dune** bank, dean, dene, hill, hillock, knoll, mound, rise, sandhill
**dung** compost, contamination, defilement, dirt, dressing, droppings, excrement, excreta, faeces, feculence, fertiliser, filth(iness), foulness, garbage, grime, guano, manure, marl, muck, nastiness, ordure, pollution, refuse, sewage, slime, sludge, squalor, uncleanness
**dung beetle** dor, scarab
**dungeon cell** oubliette
**dunk** bathe, dip, douse, drench, duck, immerse, marinate, pickle, plunge, rinse, soak, souse, steep
**duo** brace, combination, couple, doublet, duet, match, pair, span, twins, two(some)
**dupe** bamboozle, befool, beguile, betray, bilk, bluff, butt, cheat, con, cozen, cully, deceive, defraud, delude, do, double-cross, embezzle, ensnare, fleece, fool, gudgeon, gull, hoax, hoodwink, humbug, impose, loser, mark, mislead, object, out-manoeuvre, outwit, patsy, pawn, pilfer, prey, puppet, push-over, rob, simpleton, stooge, subject, sucker, swindle, thwart, tool, trick, use, victim(ise)
**duple** double, duplicate, twofold
**duplicate** bifold, binary, bis, copy, ditto, double, dyad, encore, exact, facsimile, imitate, multiply, repeat,

replica, reproduce, reproduction, synonym, transcript, twain, twice, twin, twofold
**duplicate copy** estreat, stat
**duplicated cell** clone
**duplicate model** replica
**duplicate part** spare
**duplicity** artfulness, artifice, betrayal, craft, cunning, deceit, dishonesty, disloyalty, double-cross, double-dealing, faithlessness, falseness, fraud, guile, hypocrisy, improbity, perfidy, roguery, ruse, shrewdness, subtlety, treachery, treason, trickery, wiles
**durability** endurance, imperishability, permanence, persistence, strongness, sturdiness
**durable** abiding, constant, dependable, enduring, fast, firm, hardy, lasting, permanent, persistent, reliable, resistant, sound, stable, strong, sturdy, substantial, tough
**durable coating** enamel
**durable fabric** denim, scrim, serge
**durable wood** cedar, oak
**durable worsted fabric** serge
**duration** age, continuance, continuation, course, endurance, eternity, extension, extent, length, life(time), period, sentence, space, span, spell, stage, stretch, tenure, term, time
**duration measure** time
**duration of a life time** age
**duration of life** longevity
**duress** constraint
**during** continuing, in, meantime, meanwhile, on, over, pending, through(out), until, while, within
**during life** inter vivos (L)
**during pregnancy** antenatal, prenatal
**during the course of** in
**during the day** diurnally
**during the time** as
**during the time that** as, while
**during the time when** while
**during the trial** lite pendente (L)
**dusk** crepuscule, darkness, evenfall, eve(ning), eventide, fogginess, gloom, haziness, mistiness, obscurity, shade, shadow, sombreness, sundown, twilight
**dusky** cloudy, dark, dim, evening, eventide, foggy, gloomy, grey, hazy, inky, misty, murky, obscure, sable, shadowy, shady, sombre, sooty, sundown, swart, swarth(y), twilight, unlit, veiled
**dust** powder, grime, grit, particles, dirt, earth, commotion, racket, row, oose (Sc), wipe

**dusting powder** talc
**dust particle** mote
**dust remover** vacuum cleaner
**dusty** arid, chalky, crumbly, dirty, drab, dry, dull, filthy, granular, grubby, mucky, powdery, sandy, sooty, sprinkled, unclean, uninteresting, uninviting, unswept
**Dutch artist** Rembrandt van Rijn, Van Gogh, Vermeer
**Dutch bulb** tulip
**Dutch capital** Amsterdam
**Dutch cheese** Edam, Gouda
**Dutch city** Ede, Utrecht
**Dutch coin** stiver, doit
**Dutch ditch** dyke
**Dutch East Indies island** Java, Timor
**Dutch flower** tulip
**Dutch food** eel, herring
**Dutch geographer** Aa
**Dutch gold coin** guilder
**Dutch island** Aruba
**Dutch knife** snee
**Dutch liquid measure** aam, kan
**Dutch measure** aam, kop, vat
**Dutch measure of length** roede
**Dutch metre** el
**Dutch mister** mynheer
**Dutch port** Rotterdam
**Dutch pottery** Delft
**Dutch province** Friesland, Gelderland, Limburg, Utrecht, Zeeland
**Dutch river** Amstel
**Dutch round cheese** Edam
**Dutch silver coin** stooter
**Dutch wine measure** aam
**dutiful** adaptable, compliant, conscientious, courteous, deferential, devoted, docile, moral, obedient, obsequious, regardful, reliable, religious, respectful, reverent(ial), submissive, unassertive, yielding
**duty** charge, chore, custom, deference, devoir, fee, function, homage, impost, job, labour, levy, necessity, obligation, octroi, onus, rate, requirement, respect, responsibility, reverence, routine, service, tariff, task, tax, toll, trust
**duty list** rota, roster
**duty of subject to sovereign** allegiance
**duty on gifts** capital transfer tax
**duty on imports** tonnage
**duty on merchandise** custom
**duty paid on goods entering French cities** octroi
**duty register** rota, roster
**duty time** shift
**duvet** bedcover, bedquilt, bedspread, coverlet, pad, quilt

**dwale** belladonna
**dwarf** diminutive, gnome, little, manikin, midget, pigmy, pygmy, runt, small, stunted, tiny, undersized
**dwarf animal** runt
**dwarf-breed of dog** pug
**dwarfed tree** Bonsai
**dwarf European shrub** elderwort
**dwarf goblin** gnome
**dwarf plant** cumin, stunt
**dwarf variety of domestic fowl** bantam
**dwell** abide, bide, bivouac, continue, domicile, emphasise, encamp, inhabit, linger, live, nestle, ponder, remain, reside, sojourn, stay, stop, tarry, tenant
**dweller** resident
**dweller beyond the mountains** tramontane
**dwell in a place** abide
**dwelling** abode, apartment, bivouac, bungalow, camp, coop, cottage, den, domicile, flat, habitation, home, homestead, hospice, house, hut, kraal, pad, residence, residing, stable, tenement, tent
**dwelling addition** ell
**dwelling alone** eremitic
**dwelling house** residence, tenement
**dwelling in caves** spelaean
**dwelling in heaven** celestial
**dwelling in the underworld** chthonic
**dwelling place** abode, domicile, habitation, home, house, lodging, quarters, residence
**dwelling place on wheels** caravan
**dwell on** continue, elaborate, expatiate
**dwell permanently** live, reside
**dwell upon moodily** brood
**dwell upon the past** remember
**dwindle** abate, abbreviate, curtail, decay, decline, decrease, degenerate, deteriorate, diminish, disappear, ebb, evaporate, fade, lessen, reduce, shorten, shrink, shrivel, vanish, wane
**Dyak sword** parang
**dye** colour, colourant, eosin(e), pigment, stain, tincture, tinge, tint
**dye again** redye
**dye base** aniline
**dye deeply** engrain
**dyed-in-the-wool** complete, confirmed, entrenched, established, fixed, inveterate, settled, unshakable
**dye indigo** anil
**dyeing reel** wince
**dyeing tub** vat
**dyeing vat** tub
**dye one's hair again** retint

**dye plant** anil, madder, woad, wo(a)ld
**dye process using wax** bat(t)ick
**dye substance** aniline, sumac
**dye tank** vat
**dying coal** ember
**dying down** abating
**dying fire** embers
**dying out** disappearing, extinction
**dynamic** active, driving, electric, energetic, forceful, powerful, startling, thrilling, vigorous, vital
**dynamism** activity, ambition, animation, boisterousness, briskness, dash, determination, drive, energy, enterprise, force, gaiety, go, gusto, health, initiative, life, liveliness, might, pep, push, smartness, soundness, spirit, strength, verve, vigour, vim, virility, vitality, vivacity, zip
**dynamite** explosive(s)
**dynamite inventor** Nobel
**dynamo** generator
**dynamometer** ergometer
**dynamo part** armature
**dynast** ruler
**dynasty of Monaco** Grimaldi
**dyslexia** word-blindness
**dyslogistic** disapproving, opprobrious
**dyspepsia** indigestion

# E

**each** all, any, apiece, every, ilk(a) (Sc), individual, one, particular, per, personal, respective(ly), separate(ly), severally, singly
**each and every** all
**each of all** every
**each of four children born at one birth** quadruplet
**each of pair of small oars** scull
**each of the ends of the axis of the earth** pole
**each of the opposite ends of a magnet** pole
**each of two** either
**each one** all
**each segment of the backbone** vertebra
**each single** every
**each to each** separately
**each to his own taste** chacun à son goût (F)
**each year** annually
**eager** agog, anxious, ardent, athirst, avid, diligent, earnest, enthusiastic, fervent, greedy, hungry, impatient, industrious, intent, itching, keen, longing, passionate, raring, rath(e), zealous
**eager beaver** enthusiast
**eager desire** craving, longing, thirst, yearning
**eager desire to get or keep** avarice
**eager desire to travel** wanderlust
**eagerly** anxiously, earnestly, enthusiastically, fervently, greedily, hungrily, intently, keenly, longingly, zealously
**eagerly desirous** athirst, avid
**eagerly seeking knowledge** inquisitive
**eagerness** alacrity, amiability, ardour, cheer, cordiality, diligence, élan, fervour, fluster, heartiness, keenness, life, promptness, relish, sincerity, verve, vigour, vitality, zeal, zest
**eagerness for action** élan
**eagerness to possess** lust
**eager readiness** alacrity
**eager to fight** bellicose, warlike
**eager to know or learn** curious
**eager to win in discussion** agonistic
**eagle** ern(e)
**eagle nest** aerie
**eagle's claw** talon
**eagle's home** aerie, eyrie
**eagle's nest** aerie, eyrie
**eaglewood** agalloch, aloeswood, lign-aloes
**ear** attention, corncob, discrimination, hearing, heed, lug (Sc), notice, oto-, regard, sensitivity
**earache** otalgia, otitis
**ear and nose cavity** antrum
**ear auricle** pinna
**ear bone** anvil, incus, otolith, stapes
**ear cavity** saccule, sacculus, utricle, utriculus
**ear doctor** aurist, otologist
**eardrum** tympanum
**eared seal** otary
**earful** tongue-lashing
**earl** peer
**earlier** ago, before, previous, prior, sooner
**earlier born** elder
**earlier form of sonar** asdic
**earlier in time** prior, former
**earlier stage of chemistry** alchemy
**earlier than** before, ere, prior
**earliest** first
**earliest ancestor** primogenitor
**earliest in time of order** first
**earliest period of human culture** eolithic
**earliest trace of human handicraft** eolith
**ear lobe** earlop, lug
**early** ancient, beforehand, forward, initial, premature(ly), primal, soon, untimely
**early anaesthetic** ether
**early Arabic script or alphabet** Cufic, Kufic
**early artefact** eolith
**early Austrian hypnotist** Mesmer
**early bayonet** pike
**early beard** stubble
**early Briton** Celt, Pict
**early Central American** Aztec
**early central Italian** Sabine
**early Christian** Nazarene
**early church pulpit** ambo
**early counting device** abacus
**early Egyptian Christian** Copt
**early fable writer** Aesop
**early form of Arabic alphabet** Cufi, Kufic
**early form of bicycle** velocipede
**early form of helicopter** autogiro
**early form of ice hockey** bandy
**early form of motor coach** charabanc
**early form of sonar** asdic
**early Germanic tribesman** Saxon
**early harp** lyre
**early harpsichord** spinet
**early helmet** salade, sal(l)et
**early in day** betimes
**early in the day** matutinal
**early invader** Assyrian, Goth, Hun, Mongolian, Norseman, Roman, Vandal, Viking
**early Iranian inhabitant** Mede, Persian
**early last night** yestereen (Sc)
**early Mexican** Aztec
**early on** first
**early part of the day** morning

**early period of time** Stone Age
**early Persian** Mede
**early Peruvian** Inca
**early piano** dulcimer, harpsichord
**early sailor** Noah
**early Slavonic alphabet** Glagolitic
**early South African settlers** boers
**early typeface** Aldine
**early type of wig** peruke
**early warship** sloop, trireme
**early Xtian** Nazarene
**earn** acquire, collect, deserve, draw, gain, get, gross, make, merit, net, obtain, procure, rate, reap, receive, warrant, win
**earnest** ardent, assiduous, determined, devoted, diligent, eager, enthusiatic, faithful, fervent, fervid, firm, fixed, grave, heartfelt, impassioned, intent(ness), keen, passionate, pledge, purposeful, resolute, resolved, sedate, serious, sincere, sober, solemn, steady, true, urgent, warm, zealous
**earnest desire** longing
**earnest entreaty** obsecration, plea, prayer
**earnestly** closely, dearly, gravely, intently
**earnestly exhorted** urged
**earnest plea** obsecration
**earnest request** appeal, behest, entreaty, plea
**earnings** compensation, emolument, fee, honorarium, income, pay(ment), profits, remuneration, reward, salary, wages, yield
**earn one's living** work
**ear, nose and throat specialist** otolaryngologist
**earn with difficulty** eke
**ear of bear** auricle
**ear of corn** cob, mealie, spike
**ear of grain** spike
**ear of maize** mealie
**ear part** lobe
**earphones** headset
**ear shell** abalone, ormer, perlemoen
**earshot** hearing, range, reach, sound
**ear specialist** aurist, otologist
**ear-splitting** deafening, noisy
**earth** biosphere, clay, dirt, dust, globe, ground, humus, land, loam, marl, mould, planet, sod, soil, sphere, terra, terrene, topsoil, turf, world
**earth born** human, mortal, terrigenous
**earth-covered burial mound** barrow, tumulose, tumulous
**earthen vessel** pig
**earthenware** Delft, pottery
**earthenware beer mug** stein
**earthenware cooking dish** terrine

**earthenware jar** olla
**earthenware mug** stein
**earthenware pot** cruse, olla, terrine
**earthly** conceivable, imaginable, mortal, mundane, possible, profane, secular, temporal, terrestrial, worldly
**earthly love** Eros
**earthly paradise** Shangri-la
**earthmoving machine** grader
**earth pigment** ochre, sienna
**earthquake** cataclysm, earth-tremor, quake, seism, shake, tremor, upheaval
**earth's atmosphere** air
**earth's core** nife
**earth's crust** lithosphere
**earth sediment** silt
**earth-shaped** geoidal
**earth's pull** gravity
**earth's satellite** moon
**earth's shape** ellipsoidal
**earth's star** sun
**earth's surface** crust
**earth up plants** hill
**earthy** artless, basic, carnal, coarse, comfortable, crude, down-to-earth, dull, funky, hardboiled, hardy, lush, muddy, peasant, practical rustic, realistic, ribald, robust, sensual, sensuous, sexy, terrene, unpolished, unrefined, unsophisticated, untutored, virile, voluptuous
**earthy material** clay
**earthy pigment of a brownish-yellow colour** sienna
**eartuft of owl** plumicorn
**earwax** cerumen
**ease** abate, allay, alleviate, ameliorate, assuage, calmness, comfort, contentment, disburden, effortlessness, facilitate, informality, leisure, lessen, lighten, mitigate, naturalness, quiet, relax(ation), relieve, repose, rest, serenity, soothe, tranquillity
**ease burden** relieve
**easel** tripod
**ease off** abate, decrease, moderate, relent, slacken, subside, wane
**ease of reading** legibility, neatness, readableness
**ease pain** relieve
**easiest** clearest, lightest, simplest
**easily** calmly, certainly, effortlessly, freely, plainly, simply, smoothly, surely
**easily achieved but of little value** facile
**easily affected** irritable, sensitive
**easily agitated** nervy, uneasy
**easily alarmed** timid, timorous

**easily angered** choleric, iracund, irascible, short-tempered
**easily annoyed** bad-tempered, irascible, irritable, short-tempered
**easily bent** flexible, lithe, pliable, pliant, supple
**easily broken** brittle, crumbly, delicate, fragile, frail
**easily carried** portable
**easily convinced** gullible, pliable, weak
**easily crumbled** friable
**easily cut** tender
**easily deceived** gullible
**easily disgusted** fastidious
**easily done** effortless, facile
**easily excited** nervy
**easily frightened** timid
**easily handled** docile, malleable, manageable, pliant, tractable
**easily influenced** impressionable
**easily led** flexible, manageable
**easily managed** docile, gentle
**easily mislaid** losable
**easily mistaken for something else** deceptive
**easily moved** mobile
**easily moved by emotion** susceptible
**easily moved to love** amorous
**easily nauseated** squeamish
**easily noticed** manifest
**easily offended** squeamish
**easily perceived** clear, evident, manifest, obvious, palpable
**easily remembered** memorable
**easily scared** timid
**easily seen** noticeable, conspicuous
**easily seen through** transparent
**easily shocked** squeamish
**easily split rock** slate
**easily startled** jumpy, nervous, shy
**easily stretched** elastic
**easily tempted** frail, weak
**easily understood** clear, graspable, lucid, obvious, perspicuous, plain, simple
**easily vexed** fretful
**easing of strained relations between countries** detente
**East** Este (Sp), Orient
**East African country** Ethiopia, Kenya, Somalia, Tanzania
**East African cloth** kitenge
**East African drum** ngoma
**East African policeman** askari
**East African porridge** ugali
**East African port** Beira, Mombasa
**East African soldier** askari
**East African tree** podocarp
**East African tribe** Kikuyu, Ma(a)sai
**East Anglian marsh** fen
**East Asian country** Korea
**East Asian fibre palm** ramee, ramie

**East Asian palm and drink** nipa
**Easter gift** egg
**eastern** Asiatic, eoan, oriental
**Eastern Cape elephant park** Addo
**Eastern chief** emir, amir
**Eastern coach** araba
**Eastern continent** Asia
**Eastern country** China, Japan, India
**Eastern courtesy title** bey
**Eastern eye shadow powder** kohl
**Eastern female slave** odalisque
**Eastern flower** lotus
**Eastern food** rice
**Eastern garment** sari, sarong
**Eastern headdress** fez
**eastern hemisphere** orient
**Eastern hooka** narghile, nargile, nargilen
**Eastern inhabitant** Asian
**Eastern inn** serai
**Eastern inn for the reception of caravans** caravanserai
**Eastern instrument like a guitar** tambour
**Eastern language** Chinese, Indic, Japanese
**Eastern liquor** arak, arrack
**Eastern market** bazaar
**Eastern people** Chinese, Japanese, Malays
**Eastern potentate** sultan
**Eastern prince** maharaja(h), raja(h)
**Eastern religion** Buddhism, Islam, Taoism
**Eastern religious beggar** fakeer, fakir, faqir
**Eastern ruler** sultan
**Eastern sailor** lascar
**Eastern spirit distilled from rice** arak, arrack
**Eastern temple** pagoda
**Eastern Thrace** Turkey
**Eastern title** amir, emir, pasha
**Eastern tobacco pipe** kalian
**Eastern veil** yasmack
**Eastern weight** tael
**Eastern whip** chabouk
**Eastern wise man** magus
**East European** Slav
**East Europe Jewish language** Yiddish
**East Indian bean** urd
**East Indian fan-palm** talipot
**East Indian fig tree** banyan
**East Indian hempen matting** tat
**East Indian herb** sesame
**East Indian ox** g(a)yal
**East Indian palm tree** gomuti, nipa
**East Indian sailor** lascar
**East Indian tree** aloe, dhak, sal, teak, toon
**East Indian tree with red wood** toon
**East Indies island** Bali

**East London river** Buffalo
**East Mediterranean country** Egypt, Israel, Syria, Turkey
**East Mediterranean island** Crete, Cyprus
**East Sussex town** Rye
**east wind** Eurus
**easy** calm, carefree, casual, comfortable, compliant, effortless, facile, gentle, graceful, intelligible, lenient, light, pleasant, promiscuous, quiet, relaxed, simple, smooth, sociable, soft, tolerant
**easy and comfortable** cushy
**easy, bouncy gait** jogtrot
**easy catch in cricket** dolly
**easy chair** recliner, rocker
**easy death** euthanasia
**easy familiar talk** chat
**easy gait** amble, canter, trot
**easy gallop** canter
**easy-going** amenable, calm, carefree, casual, complacent, easy, even-tempered, indulgent, lenient, mild, nonchalant, patient, placid, relaxed, serene, tolerant, uncritical, unruffled
**easy of approach** accessible, affable
**easy pace** amble
**easy-paced horse** ambler, pad
**easy task** cinch, doddle
**easy to approach** accessible
**easy to be controlled** amenable
**easy to be spoken to** accessible, affable, courteous
**easy to converse with** affable
**easy to deal with** docile, tractable
**easy to do** facile, simple
**easy to get along with** diplomatic, suave, tactful
**easy to grasp** digestible
**easy to lift** light
**easy to manage** docile, wieldy
**easy to read** legible, neat, readable
**easy to talk to** affable, approachable
**easy to understand** obvious
**easy to use** accessible, handy
**easy victory** walk-over
**eat** chew, consume, corrode, devour, dine, feed, ingest, munch, sup, swallow
**eatable** chewable, comestible, consumable, dietetic, edible, esculent, foody, swallowable
**eatable fungus** mushroom
**eat a little** taste
**eat a meal** dine
**eat and drink sumptuously** feast
**eat as a glutton would** gorge, satiate
**eat a small portion** taste
**eat at night** supper

**eat away** bite, corrode, erode, erose, gnaw
**eat dinner** dine
**eaten into** etched
**eaten with bacon** egg
**eater** diner
**eat greedily** bolt, devour, glut, gobble, gorge, go(u)rmandise, gulp, gust, guzzle, scoff, stodge, stuff
**eat humble pie** apologise, recant
**eat hurriedly and noisily** gobble
**eating away** caustic, corrosive, erodent
**eating bees** apivorous
**eating car** diner
**eating food of both animal and vegetable origin** omnivorous
**eating greedily** voracious
**eating implement** fork, knife, spoon
**eating place** cafe, diner, inn, restaurant
**eating regimen** diet
**eating tool** fork, knife, spoon, teaspoon
**eating trough for horses** manger
**eating utensil** fork, knife, spoon
**eat in small amounts** nibble
**eat in style** dine
**eat into** corrode
**eat little by little** nibble
**eat meal** dine
**eat noisily** slurp
**eat no meat** vegetarian
**eat one's heart out** agonise, brood, crave, desire, despond, grieve, mope, mourn, regret, (re)pine, sorrow, want
**eat one's words** abjure, recant, rescind, retract
**eat or drink between meals** nosh
**eat outside** picnic
**eats** food, provisions, victuals
**eats anything** omnivorous
**eat sparingly** diet
**eat sumptuously** feast
**eat to excess** gorge
**eat to one's heart's content** feast
**eat up greedily** devour
**eat with much action of the jaws** munch
**eau de Cologne** perfume
**eaves** edge, overhang, projection, roof
**eavesdrop** curious, harken, inquisitive, listen, monitor, (over)hear, snoop, spy, wiretap
**eavesdropper** delator, informer, inquisitor, listener, snooper, spy
**eavesdropping** bug
**ebb** abate, decline, decrease, deterioration, outflow, recede, regress, retire, retrogression, sink, subside, tide, wane
**ebb and flow** tide
**ebbing and flowing** tidal
**ebb tide** nadir

**ebonite** vulcanite
**ebullient** aglow, boiling, enthusiastic, excited, exhilarated, exuberant, frothy, irrepressible, overflowing, sparkling, vivacious, zestful
**ebullition** boiling, explosion, fit, outbreak, outburst, overflowing, paroxysm, passion, rage, seething, spasm, storm, throe
**eccentric** batty, bizarre, character, crackpot, crank, elliptical, erratic, insane, irregular, odd(ball), oddity, outlandish, outré, parabolic, peculiar, quaint, queer, quirky, uncommon, unconventional, unique, unusual, weird
**eccentric behaviour** caper
**eccentricity** abnormality, anomaly, caprice, foible, idiosyncrasy, irregularity, nonconformity, oddity, oddness, peculiarity, quirk, singularity, strangeness, waywardness, weirdness
**eccentric person** crank, nut, oddball, quiz, weirdo
**eccentric wheel part** cam
**ecclesiastical** churchy, clerical, divine, holy, pastoral, priestly, religious, spiritual
**ecclesiastical area** parish
**ecclesiastical attendant** acolyte
**ecclesiastical banner** labarum
**ecclesiastical benefice** glebe
**ecclesiastical book** ordo
**ecclesiastical calendar of the months** menology
**ecclesiastical cap** barret, biretta, galerum, zucchetto
**ecclesiastical cape** amice, cappa, cope
**ecclesiastical close-fitting vestment** rochet
**ecclesiastical council** synod
**ecclesiastical court** classis, inquisition, Rota, runa
**ecclesiastical declaration of forgiveness of sins** absolution
**ecclesiastical decree** canon, decretal
**ecclesiastical garment** cassock, rochet, stole
**ecclesiastical headdress** mitre
**ecclesiastical hood** amice
**ecclesiastical law** canon
**ecclesiastical linen cloth** fanon
**ecclesiastical metropolitan** eparch
**ecclesiastical octave of feast** utas
**ecclesiastical office** prelacy
**ecclesiastical plate** patin(e)
**ecclesiastical reader** lector
**ecclesiastical residence** manse
**ecclesiastical scarf and vest** orale
**ecclesiastical seat** deanery, sedile

**ecclesiastical skull cap** biretta, callote
**ecclesiastical surplice** cetta
**ecclesiastical title** dom, father, fra, padre
**ecclesiastical unit** parish
**ecclesiastical vestment** alb, amice, chasuble, cope, orale, stole, vagas
**ecclesiastic without charge** abbé
**ecdysiast** stripper, stripteaser
**echelon** brand, category, class, condition, degree, grade, group, level, mark, notch, order, place, position, quality, rank, rung, size, stage, station, step
**echo** aftermath, allusion, ape, copy, recall, reflect, repeat, resemble, resound, reverberate
**echoing** repeating, resonance, resounding, reverberating
**echoism** onomatopoeia, sound-imitation
**Echo's idol** Narcissus
**echo sounder** asdic, sonar
**éclat** acclaim, acclamation, applause, approval, brilliance, celebrity, exhibition, fame, flourish, fuss, glory, lavishness, ostentation, ovation, pageantry, pomp, reputation, splendour
**eclectic** compound, diverse, free, liberal, manifold, many-sided, multiform, multiple, open, selecting, selective, synthetic, varied
**eclipse** cloud, darken, decline, diminution, dim(ming), dwarf, eradicate, erase, exceed, extinction, failure, fall, loss, mask, obscuration, obscure, outdo, outshine, overshadow, shading, shroud, surpass, transcend, veil
**economic** business, financial, fiscal, mercantile, profitable, solvent, trade
**economical** frugal, parsimonious, stingy, thrifty
**economical management** frugality, thrift
**economic analysis** dynamics
**economic declines** recession
**economic movement** syndic
**economise** conserve, husband, pinch, retrench, save, scrimp, skimp
**economy** conservation, control, curtailment, frugality, husbandry, limitation, maintenance, management, reservation, saving, system, thrift(iness)
**ecstasy** bliss, delight, élan, elation, Elysium, emotion, euphoria, exaltation, excitement, exhilaration, felicity, fervour, frenzy, gladness, happiness, joy, pleasure, rapture, reverie, rhapsody, sensation, sublimation, thrill, trance, transport
**ecstasy caused by desire of the unattainable** nympholepsy
**ecstatic** blissful, delirious, elated, enchanted, enraptured, enthusiastic, entranced, euphoric, exalted, excited, exultant, fervent, frenzied, glad, glorious, joyful, joyous, overjoyed, rapt, rapturous, rhapsodic, thrilled, transported
**ecstatically** blissfully, deliriously, elatedly, enthusiastically, fervently, joyfully, joyously, rapturously
**ecstatic delight** joy, rapture
**ecstatic joy** rapture, delight, bliss
**ecstatic review** rave
**ecstatic utterance** rhapsody
**ecto-** external, outer, outside
**ectoblast** ectoderm, epiblast
**Ecuador cape** Pasado, Puntilla, Rosa
**Ecuador coin** centavo, condor, sucre
**Ecuador island** Chaves, Isabela, Mocha, Pinzon, Wolf
**Ecuador islands** Galapagos, Colon
**Ecuador language** Jibaro, Quechua, Spanish
**Ecuador province** Azuay, Canar, Cotopaxi, Imbabura, Losrios
**Ecuador volcano** Sangay
**Ecuador waterfall** Agoyan
**ecumenical** oecumenical, universal, worldwide
**eczema** tetter
**Edam or Brie** cheese
**eddo** taro, root
**eddy** swirl, vortex, whirl(pool)
**eddying** swirling, whirling
**Eden** paradise
**Eden fruit** apple
**edentate** aardvark, anteater, armadillo, sloth
**edentulous** edentate, toothless
**edge** arris, border, bound(ary), brim, brink, brow, contour, flange, fringe, hem, inch, interest, lip, margin, perimeter, rim, side, sidle, verge, zest
**edge along** sidle
**edge between surfaces** arris
**edge closer** slide up
**edge forward** creep
**edgeless** borderless, fringeless, marginless, rimless
**edge of a cup** brim
**edge of a hill** brow
**edge of basket** foot
**edge of bird's bill** tomium
**edge of book cover** flap
**edge of cloth** hem
**edge of cloth finished to prevent ravelling out** selvage, selvedge
**edge of crater** lip

edge of garment  hem
edge of hat  brim
edge of highway  shoulder
edge of mouth  lip
edge of page  margin
edge of pavement  kerb
edge of road  wayside
edge of roadway  shoulder
edge of roof  eave
edge of skirt  hem
edge of square sail  leech
edge of street  kerb
edge of tooth  scalprum
edge of trousers  crease
edge sideways  sidle
edge up to  sidle
edging  adornment, binding, border, bordering, braid, decoration, embellishment, filing, flanking, frill, fringe, grinding, hem, honing, piping, sharpening, skirting, stropping, tassel, trimming, whetting
edging away  sidling
edging to prevent cloth from unravelling  selvage, selvedge
edgy  excitable, grouchy, growling, irascible, irritable, nervous, peevish, prickly, sensitive, sharp, snarling, tense, testy, touchy
edible  comestible, delicious, dietetic, eatable, esculent, good, gustable, harmless, nutrient, nutritive, palatable, succulent, wholesome
edible animal tissue  flesh
edible bean  broad, haricot, lima, ming, soya, sugar
edible bird  fowl
edible bivalve mollusc  clam, mussel, oyster
edible buds resembling tiny cabbage  Brussels sprouts
edible bulb  beet(root), carrot, garlic, onion, potato, radish, swede, sweet potato, turnip
edible crustacean  crayfish, lobster, prawn, shrimp
edible entrails  offal, tripe
edible fish  angel(fish), bass, cod, eel, geelbek, hake, halibut, kabeljou, kingklip, maasbanker, perch, salmon, sardine, snoek, sole, steenbras, stumpnose, tuna, weever
edible flat fish  sole
edible flesh  meat
edible flesh of sheep  mutton
edible freshwater fish  carp, trout
edible freshwater tortoise of North America  terrapin
edible fungus  agaric, blewit, cep, champignon, morel, mushroom, truffle
edible gland  liver

edible grain  cereal
edible grass  grain, hay, oat, rice, rye
edible innards  offal, tripe
edible innards of table fowl  giblets
edible Japanese berry  udo
edible jelly  gelatine
edible kernel  nut
edible kidney-shaped nut  cashew
edible leafstalk  celery, rhubarb
edible leguminous plant  bean
edible marine crustacean  crayfish, lobster, prawn, shrimp
edible mollusc  abalone, clam, mussel, ormer, oyster, perlemoen, snail, whelk
edible mushroom  blewit, cep, morel
edible offal of deer  (n)umbles
edible orange root  carrot
edible pancreas of lamb  sweetbread
edible part of grain  meal
edible part of nut  kernel
edible plant  asparagus, herb, okra, taro, vegetable
edible pod  okra
edible root  beet, carrot, potato, radish, swede, taro, yam
edible root orchid  salep
edible rootstock  taro
edible sea animal  eel, whale
edible sea mollusc  abalone, clam, mussel, oyster, perlemoen, whelk
edible seaweed  laver, kelp
edible seed  almond, bean, corn, hazelnut, kernel, nut, pea(nut), pecan, sesame
edible seeds of leguminous plants  pulse
edible shellfish  clam, cockle, crayfish, oyster, prawn, toheroa
edible shoot  asparagus
edible snail  escargot (F)
edible stem  eddo
edible tuber  oca, potato, yam
edible tuna found in warm seas  albacore
edible turtle  terrapin
edible vegetable flower  artichoke, cauliflower
edict  act, ban, command, declaration, decree, dictate, dictum, fiat, injunction, law, mandate, manifesto, order, ordinance, prescript, proclamation, pronouncement, regulation, ruling, statute, ukase
edification  breeding, cultivation, culture, discipline, education, enlightening, enlightenment, erudition, guidance, improvement, indoctrination, initiation, instruction, knowledge, scholarship, teaching, training, tutoring, uplift

edify  construct, educate, elevate, enlighten, guide, improve, inform, instruct, uplift
edit  alter, amend, annotate, assemble, censor, change, check, compile, correct, emend, redact, rephrase, revise, rewrite, select, splice
edited work  redaction
editing of a cinema film  montage
edition  copy, exemplar, impression, issue, number, printing, publication, version, volume
edition of a text with notes by several scholars  variorum
edition of magazine  issue
editor  annotator, compiler, journalist, redactor, reviser, writer
editor of scenario  scenarist
editor's concern  facts, grammar, news, spelling
Edo  Bini
educate  cultivate, drill, indoctrinate, instruct, school, teach, train
education  culture, instruction, knowledge, learning, schooling, tuition
educational institution  academy, school, seminary
educational unit  course
educe  cause, deduce, derive, develop, disclose, elaborate, elicit, enlarge, esteem, evoke, evolve, exact, expand, extort, extract, grow, increase, infer, mature, obtain, open, opine, progress, reason, surmise, unfold, unroll, wrest
eel  conger, moray, lamprey, dodger
eel basket  buck
eel-like aquatic animal  lamprey
eel-like fish  burbot, cusp, lamprey
eelpout  blenny, burbot
eel-shaped  anguilliform
eelworm  nematode, roundworm
eerie  awesome, creepy, eldri(t)ch, fearful, ghostly, gloomy, spectral, spooky, strange, uncanny, weird
eerily  weirdly
eeriness  weirdness
efface  annihilate, cancel, delete, destroy, dim, eradicate, erase, excise, expunge, humble, obliterate, rase, raze, timid
effect  accomplishment, achieve, consequence, consummate, do, efficacy, end, execution, import, intent, issue, operation, outcome, power, purport, result, signification, weight
effective  able, actual, alive, capable, causal, cogent, competent, direct, effectual, efficacious, efficient, existing, forceful, mean, potent, real,

remarkable, sovereign, sovran, striking, telling, trenchant, useful, valid, vigorous, virtual
**effectiveness** capability, efficacy, efficiency, force, potency, strength, success, validity, vigour, weight
**effect of a narcotic** narcosis
**effect of helm on ship** steerage
**effect of one person over another** influence
**effectually hinder** preclude, prevent
**effectuate** accomplish, effect
**effeminate** emasculate, epicene, feminine, flabby, flaccid, ladylike, limp, pampered, podgy, soft, unmanly, voluptuous, weak, womanish
**effeminate man** milksop, moffie, mollycoddle, nancy, ponce, sissy
**effeminate person** cissy, nelly
**efferent** centrifugal, radiating
**effervescence** animation, bubbling, buoyancy, eagerness, ebullience, energy, enthusiasm, excitement, exhilaration, exuberance, ferment(ation), foaming, gaiety, life, spirit, vigour, vitality, vivacity, zest
**effervescent** animated, bubbling, bubbly, buoyant, burbling, carbonated, delighted, ebullient, enthusiastic, excited, exhilarated, exuberant, fizzling, foaming, foamy, formenting, frothing, frothy, gay, happy, irrepressible, lively, merry, sparkling, vital, vivacious, zingy
**effervescent drink** lemonade, sherbet, soda(water)
**effete** barren, corrupt, debased, decadent, decayed, decrepit, degenerate, dissipated, drained, enervated, exhausted, feeble, sterile, weak
**effeteness** corruptness, decrepitness, degenerateness, dissipatedness, feebleness, ineffectualness, overrefinement, weakness
**efficacious** active, capable, competent, effective, effectual, efficient, energetic, operative, potent, powerful, successful, useful, working
**efficacy** ability, avail, benefit, bite, capability, cogency, convenience, effect(iveness), energy, fitness, force, influence, intensity, might, point, potency, power, practicality, profit, prowess, resolution, service, spirit, strength, sway, utility, validity, valour, vehemence, vigour, virtue, weight
**efficient** able, adept, businesslike, capable, competent, economic, effective, effectual, powerful, productive, proficient, ready, skilful, useful, well-conducted, well-organised, workmanlike
**efficient as food** nutritious
**effigy** appearance, carving, copy, depiction, drawing, dummy, engraving, facsimile, figure, guy, icon, idol, illustration, image, likeness, model, painting, photograph, picture, portrait, portrayal, print, reflection, replica, representation, resemblance, scarecrow, sketch, statue, study
**effloresce** bloom, blossom, burgeon, flourish, flower, mature, open, unfold
**effluvium** effluent, pollutant, sewage, waste
**effort** application, attempt, endeavour, energy, exertion, force, labour, pains, power, strain, stress, stretch, striving, struggle, toil, trouble, work
**effortless** cushy, easy, facile, flowing, inactive, inert, lucid, otiose, painless, passive, recumbent, simple, slack, sluggish, smooth, supine, uncomplicated, undemanding, unforced
**effortlessness** ease, easiness, facileness, painlessness, simpleness, smoothness
**effort to acquire knowledge** study
**effort to gain support** propaganda
**effrontery** abuse, arrogance, audacity, boldness, brassiness, brazenness, cheek, defiance, disrespect, front, gall, haughtiness, impertinence, impudence, incivility, insolence, insubordination, nerve, pertness, presumption, rashness, rudeness, sauciness, shamelessness
**effulgence** aureola, beam, blaze, brightness, brilliance, flame, flash, glance, gleam, glimmer, glint, glistening, glitter, glow, halo, illumination, iridescence, luminosity, lustre, nimbus, radiance, ray, refulgence, resplendence, scintillation, shimmer, shine, sparkle, sparkling, splendour, vividness
**effulgent** beaming, bright, brilliant, flashing, gleaming, glistening, glittering, glowing, illuminated, intense, lucid, luminous, radiant, resplendent, shining, sparkling, twinkling, vivid
**effusion** discharge, efflux, emanation, explosion, exuberance, gush, outburst, outflow, shedding
**effusion of blood into the pleural cavity** haematothorax
**effusive** copious, demonstrative, ebullient, enthusiastic, expansive, exuberant, generous, gushing, lavish, lyrical, sentimental, streaming, unreserved, unrestrained, verbose, warm, wordy
**effusively poetic** lyrical
**effusive person** gusher
**eft** afterwards, lizard, newt, salamander
**egest** discharge, eject, eliminate, evacuate, excrete, expel, void
**egg** goad, impel, incite, nit, oo-, ovi-, ovo, ovum, spawn, stimulate
**egg and milk dish** custard
**eggbeater** whisk
**egg bed** nest
**egg centre** yolk
**egg dish** omelette, soufflé
**egg drink** nog
**egged on** encouraged
**egg flip** nog
**egghead** genius, highbrow, intellectual
**egg layer** bird, hen
**egg meal** omelette, soufflé
**egg of a louse** nit
**egg on** abet, encourage, exhort, impel, incite, instigate, motivate, move, precipitate, prompt, push, spur, urge
**egg or island** Easter
**egg part** albumen, latebra, shell, white, yolk
**eggplant** aubergine, brinjal
**egg-producing organ** ovary
**egg repository** nest
**eggs** ova, roe
**egg shape** oval
**egg-shaped** oval, ovate, oviform, ovoid
**egg-shaped figure** oval
**egg-shaped flute** ocarina
**egg-shaped soft toy** gonk
**egg-shaped wind instrument** ocarina
**egg shell** shard
**eggs of fish** roe
**eggs of frogs** spawn
**egg white** albumen, glair
**egg yellow** yolk
**egg yolk thickening for sauces** liaison
**ego** individuality, personality, self(-importance)
**egoism** egocentricity, egotism, narcissism, self-absorption, self-centredness, self-conceit, self-concern, self-importance, self-love, self-regard, selfishness
**egoist** boaster, braggadocio, braggart, egomaniac, egotist, self-admirer
**egotism** bigheadedness, boastfulness, conceit(edness), egoism, egomania, narcissism, self-admiration, self-centredness, self-conceit,

self-importance, self-love, self-praise, superiority, vanity
**egotist** bighead, boaster, braggadocio, braggart, egoist, egomaniac, narcissist, self-admirer, swaggerer
**egotistic** bigheaded, boasting, bragging, conceited, egocentric, egoistic, egotistical, self-centred, self-important, superior, swollenheaded, vain
**egregious** abysmal, appalling, bald, blatant, bold, disgraceful, exceptional, extraordinary, flagrant, infamous, notable, notorious, outrageous, overt, remarkable, scandalous, shocking, striking
**egress** departure, emergence, escape, exit, exodus, issue, outlet, vent, withdrawal
**egret plume** osprey
**Egyptian** Copt
**Egyptian ancient deity** Ptah
**Egyptian bay** Foul
**Egyptian beer** bosa, bouza
**Egyptian bird** ibis
**Egyptian boat** baris
**Egyptian cadaver** mummy
**Egyptian calendar** Ahet, Apap, Choiak, Hathor, Mechir, Mesore, Pachons, Paophi, Payni, Shemu, Thoth, Tybi
**Egyptian canal** Suez
**Egyptian cape** Banas, Rasbanas
**Egyptian Christian** Copt
**Egyptian cigarette** gippy
**Egyptian cobra** asp, haje
**Egyptian coin** dinar, girsh, guinea, piaster, pound
**Egyptian cotton** maco, pima, sak(el)
**Egyptian cross** ankh
**Egyptian crown** atef, pschent
**Egyptian dam on the Nile** Aswan
**Egyptian dancing girl** almah, almes
**Egyptian deity of darkness** Set
**Egyptian deity of the dead** Amen-Ra
**Egyptian depression** Qattara
**Egyptian desert** Arabian
**Egyptian dog-headed ape** aani
**Egyptian dry measure** ardeb
**Egyptian dwarf god** Bes
**Egyptian fish** saide
**Egyptian funeral effigy** ushabti
**Egyptian goblin** oufe
**Egyptian god** Amen, Amon, Anubis, Aten, Atmu, Atum, Bes, Geb, Horus, Keb, Min, Nun, Osiris, Osiris, Ptah, Ra, Seb, Serapis, Set, Seth, Shu, Sothis, Tem, Thoth
**Egyptian goddess** Anta, Apet, Hathor, Isis, Ma, Maat, Nut
**Egyptian goddess of agriculture** Isis, Mut

**Egyptian goddess of evil** Ate
**Egyptian goddess of fertility** Isis
**Egyptian goddess of heaven** Nut
**Egyptian goddess of love** Hathor
**Egyptian goddess of right** Ma
**Egyptian goddess of truth** Ma, Maat
**Egyptian goddess of war** Nit
**Egyptian goddess of waters** Nun
**Egyptian god of air** Shu
**Egyptian god of creation** Ptah
**Egyptian god of earth** Geb, Keb
**Egyptian god of evil** Set, Seth
**Egyptian god of healing** Serapis
**Egyptian god of lower world** Osiris, Serapis
**Egyptian god of pleasure** Bes, Tem
**Egyptian god of procreation** Min
**Egyptian god of stars** Sothis
**Egyptian god of the underworld** Osiris
**Egyptian god of waters** Nun
**Egyptian god of wisdom** Thoth
**Egyptian granite** syenite
**Egyptian gulf** Salûm
**Egyptian heaven** Aalu, Aaru
**Egyptian hot wind** khamsin
**Egyptian isthmus** Suez
**Egyptian king** Akhenaton, pharaoh, Ptolemy, Ram(e)ses, Thutmose, Tutankhamen
**Egyptian king of gods** Amen(-Ra), Ammon, Amon, Amun
**Egyptian lake** Nasser
**Egyptian language** Coptic
**Egyptian lute** nabla
**Egyptian monument** sphinx
**Egyptian moon god** Yah
**Egyptian nature goddess** Isis
**Egyptian oasis** Farafra, Kharga, Siwa
**Egyptian peasant** fellah
**Egyptian peninsula** Sinai
**Egyptian port** Alexandria, Port Said, Rashid, Rosetta, Safaga, Suez, Tor
**Egyptian precious alloy** asem
**Egyptian province** Aswan, Beheira, Dumyat, Giza, Sohag
**Egyptian queen** Cleopatra, Nefertiti
**Egyptian queen of gods** Sati
**Egyptian river** Nile
**Egyptian ruins** Abydos, Thebes
**Egyptian sacred beetle** scarab
**Egyptian sacred bird** ibis
**Egyptian sacred bull** Apis
**Egyptian solar disc god** Aten, Aton
**Egyptian soldier** gippy
**Egyptian soul-survivor** ka
**Egyptian spiritual body** sahu
**Egyptian statue** sphinx
**Egyptian sun god** Amon, Amun, Horus, Ra, Tum
**Egyptian supreme sungod** Horus, Ra
**Egyptian symbol of eternal life** scarab
**Egyptian symbol of life** ankh

**Egyptian tomb** mastaba, pyramid
**Egyptian viper** asp
**Egyptian water lily** lotus
**Egyptian weight** kat
**Egyptian wind** kamsin, khamseen, sirocco
**Egyptian writing material** papyrus
**eider** down, duck, quilt
**eiderdown** coverlet
**eiderdown quilt** duvet
**Eiffel city** Paris
**eight** card, octa-, octad, octave, octo-
**eight-armed cephalopod** octopod, octopus
**eight bits** byte
**eighteenth-century French architecture** Rococo
**eighteenth-century hair style** pompadour
**eighteenth-century snuff** rappee
**eightfold** octuple
**eight furlongs** mile
**eight gallons** bushel
**eighth note** quaver
**eighth of a fluid ounce** drachm
**eighth of a gallon** pint
**eighth of a mile** furlong
**eighth part** octant
**eighth prime number** seventeen
**eighth satellite of Saturn** Iapetus
**eighth sign of Zodiac** Scorpio
**eight-hundredth anniversary** octocentenary
**eight-line poem** triolet
**eight-line stanza** octonary
**eight note span** octave
**eight performers** octet
**eight-shaped number system** octal notation
**eightsided** octagonal
**eight-sided figure** octagon
**eighty** fourscore
**eighty yards of wool** lea
**'e' in Morse** dot
**Einstein's theory** relativity
**Eire** Ireland
**Eisenhower's nickname** Ike
**eisteddfod** assembly, choir, competition
**either** or, any
**either of the two large hip muscles** psoas
**either of two books of the Apocrypha** Esdras I and II
**either of two small organs on each side of root of tongue** tonsil
**either of two upper cavities in the heart** atrium
**either one of two muscles that contract the brow in frowning** corrugator
**either part of bird's beak** mandible

**ejaculate** blurt, call, cry, discharge, eject, emit, exclaim, scream, shout, spurt, utter, yell
**ejaculation** blow, blurt, call, cry, egestion, emission, exclamation, expulsion, gasp, gulp, ha, pant, puff, release, unloading, vociferation, voidance, yell
**eject** banish, dart, deport, depose, discharge, disgorge, egest, emit, evict, exclude, excrete, expel, expropriate, extract, impel, omit, oust, remove, spew, spout, throw, void, vomit
**eject air and water** blow
**ejected by octopus** ink
**ejected saliva** spittle
**eject from school** expel
**eject from stomach through mouth** vomit
**eject from the mouth** spit
**eject violently** belch, spew, vomit
**eke** amplify, augment, enlarge, increase, inflate, lengthen, protract, stretch, supplement
**eke out** enlarge, husband, increase, stretch, supplement
**elaborate** adorn, baroque, better, complex, complicated, detailed, develop, exhaustive, flowery, improve, laborious, laboured, masterly, ornate, ostentatious, produce, refine, rococo, thorough
**elaborate and formal dinner** banquet
**elaborate architectural style** baroque
**elaborate embroidery** orphrey
**elaborate hairstyle** updo
**elaborately adorned** baroque, ornate
**elaborately attired** dressy
**elaborately cunning** Machiavel(l)ian
**elaborately decorated** ornate
**elaborately ornamental style** baroque, rococo
**elaborately performed** ceremonious
**elaborate meal** repast
**elaborate solo** aria
**elaborate speech** oration
**élan** ardour, brilliance, dash, enthusiasm, flair, impetuosity, verve, vivacity, zest
**elapse** go, lapse, pass
**elasmobranch** selachian
**elastic** accommodating, adaptable, buoyant, compliant, contractile, contractive, dilatable, ductile, flexible, garter, pliable, rebounding, recoil(ing), resilient, responsive, rubato, rubber(y), spongy, springy, stretchable, stretchy, supple, tensible, tolerant, volatile, yielding
**elasticated** stretching
**elastic fluid** gas

**elasticity** adjustability, agreeability, contractility, extensibility, flexibility, plasticity, recuperation, resilience, springiness, suppleness
**elastic knitted cloth** jersey
**elastic knitted material** stockinet
**elastic porous mass** sponge
**elate** brighten, cheer, comfort, console, elevate, encourage, exhilarate, gladden, hearten, overjoy, solace, warm
**elate beyond self-control** intoxicate
**elated** animated, blissful, cheered, delighted, ecstatic, elevated, euphoric, exalted, excited, exhilarated, exultant, glad, gleeful, happy, joyful, joyous, jubilant, overjoyed, pleased, proud, roused
**elation** buoyancy, euphoria, glee, joy, rapture, ruff
**elbow** bump, corner, crowd, jostle, knock, nudge, shove
**elbow bone** ulna
**elbow in pipe** ell
**elbow joint** toggle joint
**elbow protuberance** olecranon
**elbow room** ease, freedom, space
**elder** ainé(e) (F), ancient, centenarian, earlier, firstborn, master, nonagerian, octogenarian, older, patriarch, presbyter, prior, senior, septuagenarian, superior, veteran
**elder in a church** presbyter
**elderliness** age, ancientness, antiquity, decrepitness, greyness, oldness, senescence, venerableness
**elderly** aged, ageing, ancient, decrepit, grey-haired, grey-headed, hoary, old(ish), retired, senile, venerable
**elderly man** greybeard
**elderly relative** grandpa, gran(ny), ouma, oupa
**elderly rustic** gaffer
**elderly woman** biddy, crone, dowager
**elder son of Isaac and Rebecca** Esau
**eldest daughter of King Lear** Goneril
**eldest of children in a family** first-born
**eldest son of French king** dauphin
**eldest son of Russian emperor** czarevich, tsarevich
**El Dorado** fantasy
**eldritch** eerie, eldrich, hideous, unearthly, weird
**elect** adopt, appoint, ballot, choice, choose, chosen, co-opt, designate(d), determine, elite, first-class, hand-picked, opt, pick(ed), prefer(red), prime, prospective, quality, select(ed), vote
**elected governor of city** alderman
**elected head of republican state** president

**election** balloting, choice, choosing, co-option, decision, judg(e)ment, nomination, opinion, plebiscite, poll, preference, referendum, selection, voice, vote, voting
**election activity** hustling
**electioneering** analysing, campaigning, canvassing, examining, inspecting, investigating, polling, scanning, sifting, soliciting, studying, ventilating
**election official** scrutineer
**elector** balloter, chooser, constituent, selector, voter
**electoral support** mandate
**electric** breathtaking, charged, dynamic, electrified, electrifying, exciting, galvanic, jolting, moving, rousing, stimulating, stirring, tense, thrilling
**electrical contact** arc
**electrical current** amp(ere)
**electrical domestic device** appliance
**electrical force** volt
**electrical gauge** ammeter
**electrical instrument for measuring heat radiation** bolometer
**electrical isolation** insulation
**electrical item** bulb, plug
**electrically charged particle** ion
**electrical power** current
**electrical rectifier** diode
**electrical resistance** ohm
**electrical safeguard** fuse
**electrical unit** amp(ere), farad, volt, watt
**electrical unit of conductivity** MHO
**electrical unit of magnetic flux** maxwell
**electrical unit of quantity** coulomb
**electrical unit of resistance** ohm
**electric bus** tram
**electric cable** flex
**electric crank for engine** starter
**electric current rating** voltage
**electric doorbell** buzzer
**electric eye** photocell
**electric flex** wire
**electric generator** dynamo, magneto
**electrician** wirer
**electric insulator** mica
**electricity in atmosphere** static
**electricity resistance** ohm
**electric light glass** bulb
**electric light inventor** Edison
**electric particle** ion
**electric railway below the ground** subway
**electric razor** shaver
**electric unit** farad, ohm, volt, watt, weber
**electric unit of capacity** farad

**electric ventilating device** fan
**electrified particle** ion
**electrode** anode, cathode
**electrode giving off positive ions** anode
**electromagnetic unit** abampere, abfarad, maxwell
**electromotive unit** volt
**electro-negative ion** anion
**electronic device having three electrodes** triode
**electronic valve** triode
**electron tube** diode, vacuum
**elegance** balance, beauty, choiceness, courtliness, culture, dignity, distinction, exquisiteness, fashion, fineness, finery, gentility, grace, grandeur, luxuriousness, polish, purity, refinement, richness, style, stylishness, taste
**elegance in dress** chic, style
**elegance of manner** grace
**elegant** chic, choice, classy, dressy, excellent, fashionable, fine, graceful, luxurious, nice, posh, refined, stylish, tasteful, urbane
**elegant business establishment** salon
**elegant fashion** style
**elegant in dress** chic
**elegant in movement** graceful
**elegantly simple** neat
**elegantly stylish** chic, classy
**elegant water bird** swan
**elegy** dirge, Kaddish, keen, lament(ation), monody, ode, plaint, requiem, threnody
**element** component, constituent, environment, essential, habitat, ingredient, milieu, part, substance, unit
**elemental creature living in fire** salamander
**elementary** basic, fundamental, primary, rudimentary, simple, uncomplicated
**elementary particle** neutron
**elementary stages of a subject** rudiment
**elementary textbook** primer
**element in complex mechanism** unit
**element in organic matter** carbon
**element not tarnished by air** aluminium
**element that contributes to result** factor
**element used in medicine** iodine
**elemi** resin
**elephant** jumbo
**elephant driver** mahout
**elephant park** Addo
**elephant's cry** trumpet

**elephant's-ear** (Chinese) eddo, dasheen, taro
**elephant's tooth** ivory, tusk
**elephant's trunk** proboscis
**elephant's tusk** ivory, tooth
**elevate** advance, animate, better, cheer, crown, enhance, enliven, ennoble, erect, escalate, exalt, heighten, hoist, increase, intensify, lift, magnify, promote, raise, rear, refresh, rise, (up)heave
**elevated** advanced, aggrandised, exalted, heightened, hoisted, lifted, preferred, promoted, raised, tall, upgraded, up(lifted)
**elevated railway** el
**elevated region** altitude
**elevated step** stair
**elevate the hair** tease
**elevation** altitude, eminence, exaltedness, grace, grandeur, height, hill(ock), koppie, loftiness, mesa, mountain, nobility, nobleness, plateau, rise, salience, solemnity, stature, sublimity, tallness, upliftment, upslope
**elevation of earth or stones** mound
**elevator** chute, escalator, hoist, lift
**elevator inventor** Otis
**elevator well** shaft
**eleven-sided figure** hendecagon
**eleventh month of Hebrew civil year** Ab
**elf** brownie, fairy, gnome, goblin, hob, imp, leprechaun, newt, pixie, pixy, sprite
**elfin** elf(ish), pixie-like, puckish, sprite, urchin
**elicit** cause, deduce, derive, develop, educe, evoke, evolve, exact, extort, extract, obtain, wrench, wrest
**elicit affection** endear
**elicit report** debrief
**elide** blend, delete, omit, slur, syncopate
**eligible** fit, preferable, proper, qualified, suitable, suited, worthy
**Elijah's successor** Elisha
**eliminate** debar, deport, discard, discharge, dismiss, eject, evict, exclude, expel, exterminate, extrude, ignore, liquidate, obviate, omit, purge, reject, relegate, remove, suspend, terminate
**élite** aristocracy, best, choice, cream, elect, nobility, pick, selected
**elixir** amreeta, amrita, arcanum, basis, catholicon, essence, extract, invigorator, kernel, nostrum, panacea, pith, princip, quintessence, remedy, tincture
**elk** moose, sambar, sambur, wapiti

**elk-like animal** eland
**ellipse** orbit, oval
**elliptical** curved, egg-shaped, oval, ovate, ovoid
**elocution** declamation, diction, oratory, pronunciation, rhetoric
**elongate** extend, increase, lengthen, prolong, protract, remove, stretch
**elongated** hairlike, lank, linear, oblong, produced, prolate, slender
**elongated elephant's tooth** tusk
**elongated fish** eel, gar, pike
**elongated region** ridge
**eloquent speaker** orator
**eloquent speech** oratory
**El Salvador dance** pasillo
**El Salvador gulf** Fonseca
**El Salvador lake** Guija, Ilopango
**El Salvador point** Remedios
**El Salvador port** Acajutla, Cutuco
**El Salvador volcano** Izalco
**else** besides, different, instead, other(wise)
**elsewhere excuse** alibi
**elucidate** clarify, define, demonstrate, exhibit, explain, explicate, illuminate, illustrate, interpret, manifest, show, simplicity, specify
**elude** avoid, baffle, beat, bilk, confound, confuse, disappear, dodge, duck, escape, evade, flee, foil, outrun, puzzle, shirk, shun, stump, thwart, vanish
**elude by dodging** jink
**elude danger** escape
**elusive** baffling, deceptive, eely, elusory, equivocal, evasive, impalpable, inexplicable, intangible, shifty, slick, slippery, subtle, tricky, undefinable
**elusive person** will-o'-the-wisp
**elusory** baffling, bewildering, evasive
**elver** eel
**em** mut(ton), pica
**emaciate** atrophy, attenuate, consume, contract, enervate, erode, reduce, shrink, shrivel, starve, underfeed, waste
**emaciated** attenuate, bony, decayed, drawn, eroded, gaunt, lanky, lean, scraggy, shrivelled, slim, spare, tenuous, thin, withered, worn
**emaciated body** atomy
**emanate** arise, arrive, birth, come, derive, discharge, emerge, emit, flow, issue, originate, proceed, radiate, spring, stem
**emanation** discharge, drainage, effluent, effluvium, efflux, effusion, emergence, emerging, emission, exhaltation, issuance, issue, karma, leakage, proceeds

**emanation of the supreme deity** aeon
**emancipate** deliver, discharge, enfranchise, free, liberate, manumit, release, unfetter, unshackle
**emancipation** emancipating, liberation, manumission, manumitting, redeeming, release, rescue, unbinding, unyoking
**emancipator** liberator
**emasculate** asexualise, castrate, debilitate, enfeeble, soften, unman, weaken
**emasculated horse** gelding
**embalm** anoint, aromatise, enshrine, mummify, perfume, preserve, re-experience, relive, remember, reminisce, scent
**embalmed body** mummy
**embankment** balustrade, bridge, bulwark, causeway, dam, dike, dyke, jetty, levee, mound, palisade, pier, rampart, viaduct, wall, wharf
**embankment against river floods** levee
**embargo** ban, bar(rier), blockade, boycott, impediment, interdict, prohibition, stoppage
**embark** begin, board, commence, enter, institute, launch, sail, ship, undertake, voyage
**embark on** begin, commence, engage, enter, initiate, launch, start, undertake
**embark upon** start
**embarrass** abash, annoy, ashame, chagrin, complicate, confuse, discomfort, discompose, disconcert, hinder, impede, perplex, vex
**embarrassed through shame** sheepish
**embarrassing mistake** blooper
**embassy official** attaché
**embed** base, establish, fix, impact, implant, ingraft, inlay, install, locate, lodge, place, plant, set, surround
**embedded dirt** grime
**embellish** adorn, beautify, decorate, deepen, dignify, elaborate, embroider, enhance, enrich, exaggerate, garnish, glorify, grace, intensify, ornament, prettify, trim
**embellisher** adorner
**embellishment** adornment, array, attachment, beautification, decoration, enhancement, enrichment, festoons, filigree, frill, ornament(ation), prettification, spangle, trimming
**ember** ash, cinder, clinker, coal, slag
**embitter** acerbate, aggravate, annoy, disturb, exacerbate, infuriate, irritate, plague, poison, raise, rankle, sour

**embittered** angered, disaffected, disillusioned, envenomed, poisoned, sour(ed)
**embittered speech** acerbity
**embittering** angering, disillusioning, envenoming, poisoning, souring
**emblem** badge, figure, image, logo(type), sign, symbol, token
**emblematic hat** cap
**emblem of a business** logo
**emblem of authority** fasces
**emblem of Canada** maple (leaf)
**emblem of clan** totem
**emblem of honour and purity** ermine
**emblem of Ireland** shamrock
**emblem of morning** dew
**emblem of Nazi party** swastika
**emblem of office** badge
**emblem of peace** dove, olive branch
**emblem of remembrance** rosemary
**emblem of Scotland** thistle
**emblem of Wales** dragon, leek
**emblem of Western Province** disa
**embodiment** avatar, constitution, epitome, essence, exemplar, fusion, image, incarnation, inclusion, likeness, make-up, materiality, personification, portrayal, quintessence, recreation, representation, representative, semblance, substantiality, type, typifier, unification
**embody** amalgamate, coalesce, comprehend, comprise, consolidate, constitute, encompass, hold, incarnate, incorporate, materialise, merge, personify, substantiate, unite
**embody in flesh** incarnate
**embossed brooch** cameo
**embossed fabric** brocade
**embossed nail** stud
**embrace** adopt, caress, clasp, comprise, contain, cuddle, embody, encircle, enfold, espouse, grab, grasp, hug, include, squeeze, surround
**embraceable** acceptable, adoptable, kissable, receivable, squeezable
**embrace fondly** cuddle
**embrangle** confuse, entangle
**embrocation** liniment
**embroidered material** brocade
**embroidery** needlework
**embroidery frame** tabo(u)ret
**embroidery loop** picot
**embroidery stitch** featherstitch, herringbone, satin, smock
**embroidery with a repetitive pattern** blackwork
**embroidery yarn** crewel
**embroil** complicate, confound, confuse, disorder, disturb, enmesh,

entangle, implicate, incriminate, involve, mire, perplex, trouble
**embryo** beginning, commencement, egg, foetus, genesis, germ, nucleus, origin, ovum, seed, sprout
**emend** amend, correct, edit, improve, reform
**emendation** abridg(e)ment, alteration, correction, deletion, editing, expurgation, improvement, polishing, redaction, revision
**emerald** beryl
**emerald colour** green
**Emerald Isle** Erin, Ireland
**Emerald Isle draw** Irish Sweepstake
**emerge** appear, emanate, emit, issue, spread, surface
**emerge again** reappear
**emergence** advent, appearance, arrival, beginning(s), birth, cradle, dawn(ing), debut, foundation, genesis, inauguration, inception, infancy, introduction, launch, nascence, origin(s), outset, presence, rise, source, start
**emergence of young from body of mother** birth
**emergency** accident, conjuncture, crisis, difficulty, dilemma, exigency, extremity, impasse, juncture, necessity, needfulness, pass, pinch, predicament, strait, urgency
**emergency army** militia
**emergency exit** fire escape
**emergency vessel** lifeboat
**emergency way out** fire escape
**emerging** appearing, arising, developing, emanating, issuant, issuing, materialising, proceeding, rising, surfacing, transpiring
**emery** abrasive, Carborundum, corundum
**emery wheel** grinder
**emigrant** alien, colonist, émigré, exodist, expat(riate), foreigner, fugitive, itinerant, migrant, refugee, settler, vagrant, wanderer
**emigrant settlement** colony
**emigration** resettlement
**Emily Hobhouse's targets** concentration camps
**eminence** elevation, fame, note, prominence, renown, repute
**eminent** bossed, celebrated, conspicuous, distinguished, elevated, esteemed, exalted, famed, famous, great, high, lofty, marked, notable, noted, noteworthy, pre-eminent, prominent, raised, remarkable
**eminent conductor** maestro
**eminent musician** maestro

**eminent person** celebrity, notability
**emir** ameer, amir
**emissary** advocate, agent, ambassador, bearer, carrier, consul, courier, delegate, deputy, diplomat, envoy, factor, go-between, herald, intermediary, legate, messenger, minister, negotiator, plenipotentiary, rep(resentative), runner, substitute, surrogate
**emission** declaration, discharge, discharging, ejaculation, ejecta, ejection, eruption, evacuation, excretion, expression, exudation, issuance, issue, leaking, outpour, secretion, semen, utterance
**emission of rays** radiation
**emit** circulate, discharge, eject, eradiate, exhale, expel, exude, publish, radiate
**emit air** blow
**emit a shrill sound** skirl
**emit audibly** exclaim, utter
**emit breath with sudden convulsive spasm and noise** sneeze
**emit electromagnetic waves** radiate
**emit from centre** radiate
**emit light** glow, shine
**emit rays of colour** opalesce
**emit smoke** fume
**emit sparks** scintillate
**emit strong offensive smell** stink
**emitting an odour** odoriferous
**emitting light** fluorescent, shining
**emitting light without heat** luminescent
**emitting rays of light** radiant
**emit vapour** fume, reek
**emit wind noisily through mouth** belch
**emmet** ant, pismire
**emolument** allowance, benefits, earnings, gratuity, pay(ment), profit, remuneration, salary, wages
**emote** act, dramatise, exaggerate, gush, overact, perform, pretend, rant, rave
**emotion** affect(ion), feeling, love, passion, pathos, reaction, response, sensation, sentiment, sympathy
**emotional** ardent, demonstrative, emotive, enthusiastic, excitable, fervent, fervid, fiery, heated, hot-blooded, passionate, roused, sensitive, soulful, stirred, susceptible, temperamental, tender, warm, zealous
**emotional attitude** sentiment
**emotional bond** rapport
**emotional irregular piece of music** rhapsody
**emotionally aroused** excited

**emotionally disturbed** upset
**emotionally moving** touching
**emotionally strained** tense
**emotionally uninvolved** blasé, disinterested, impersonal
**emotionally upset** perturb
**emotional outburst** ebullition, hysterics
**emotional play** melodrama
**emotional release** catharsis, freeing, purgation
**emotional sensitivity** feeling
**emotional shock** trauma
**emotional situation** drama, tragic
**emotional strain** anxiety, stress, tension
**emotional thrill** frisson
**emotional tranquillity** ataraxia, ataraxy
**emotional weakness** sentiment
**emotive** dramatic, emotional, exciting, heady, impassioned, inspiring, lively, moving, rousing, spirited, stimulating, thrilling
**empathy** sympathy
**emperor** Kaiser, king, mogul, Rex, ruler, sovereign, czar, tsar
**emperor of Ethiopia** Negus
**emperor of Japan** Mikado
**emperor of Russia** czar, tsar
**emphasis** stress
**emphasise** accent, deepen, dramatise, intensify, mark, (over)stress, punctuate, spotlight, underline, underscore
**emphasises possession** own
**emphatic** ardent, assertive, critical, decided, determined, distinct, eminent, energetic, fervent, forceful, impassioned, impressive, marked, prominent, significant, spirited, stressed, striking, strong, vehement, vivid
**emphatically** absolutely, certainly, decidedly, definitely, directly, distinctly, earnestly, forcefully, forcibly, importantly, impressively, insistently, markedly, positively, powerfully, resoundingly, significantly, strikingly, strongly, vehemently, vigorously
**emphatic expression of approval** plaudit
**empire** authority, command, domain, kingdom, power, realm, Reich, rule, sovereignty, supremacy
**empire ruler** emperor
**employ** apply, commission, devote, engage, enlist, enrol, exercise, fill, handle, hire, manipulate, occupy, operate, place, retain, service, spend, use, utilise, wield
**employ again** re-engage, re-use, rehire
**employ delaying tactics** stall

**employ diligently** ply
**employee** agent, clerk, earner, hand, hireling, servant, staff, wage-earner, wager, worker, workman
**employee doing all kinds of work** factotum
**employees** hands, personnel, servants, staff, wage-earners, workers, (work)men
**employees of a company** staff
**employees' restaurant** canteen
**employer** boss, business, company, director, entrepreneur, establishment, firm, hirer, manager, master, organisation, owner, patron, proprietor, user
**employ for wages** hire
**employing** applying, engaging, enlisting, operating, using, utilising
**employment** agency, application, appointment, assignment, business, craft, duty, engagement, enlistment, exercise, exertion, hire, job, métier, mission, occupation, position, post, profession, service, trade, usage, use, work
**employ stratagems** manoeuvre
**emporium** bazaar, market, mart, shop, spaza, store
**empower** allow, authorise, commission, deputise, enable, license, qualify, warrant
**empress of Russia** czarina, czaritza, tsarina
**emptiness** barrenness, delusion, depletion, dullness, inanity, interim, lack, need, scarcity, senselessness, space, stupidity, uselessness, vacancy, vacantness, vacuum, verbosity, void(ness), wordiness
**empty** bare, blank, deplete, devoid, discharge, drain, evacuate, frivolous, hollow, inane, ineffective, meaningless, senseless, superficial, unburden, uninhabited, unload, unoccupied, unsatisfying, vacant, vacate, void
**empty boasting** fanfaronade
**empty-handed** unprovided, unsuccessful
**empty-headed** dull, foolish, frivolous, inane, obtuse, stupid, vacant, vacuous, witless
**empty-headed person** fool, nitwit, noddy
**empty-headed young woman** bimbo
**empty in the middle** hollow
**empty out** deplete
**empty out water from a boat** bail, bale
**empty place** space, vacuum, void
**empty pride** vanity
**empty promises** bunkum, lies

**empty sail of wind** spill
**empty shell** blank, casing, dud
**empty space** blank, gap, hollow, vacuum, void
**empty talk** blarney, bosh, chatter, flummery, gas, nonsense, palaver, prate, prattle, twaddle
**empty talker** chatterbox, gasbag
**empty the suitcase** unpack
**empty tomb** cenotaph
**empty turgid talk** rant
**emu** ratite, rhea
**emulate** ape, burlesque, challenge, clash, compete, contend, contest, cope, copy, duplicate, echo, equal, fight, follow, imitate, impersonate, jostle, litigate, match, mimic, mirror, mock, parody, personate, reflect, repeat, rival, simulate, skirmish, strive, struggle, vie
**enable** allow, authorise, capacitate, empower, fit, permit, prepare, warrant
**enact** act, authorise, command, decree, legislate, ordain, order, pass, perform, portray, proclaim, ratify, sanction
**enact laws** legislate
**enamour** allure, bewitch, captivate, charm, enchant, endear, enrapture, enthral, entrance, excite, fascinate, infatuate
**enamoured** épris (F)
**enate** maternal
**encamped** laagered
**encampment of wagons** laager
**enceinte** pregnant
**encephalalgia** headache
**encephalitis** phrenitis
**encephalon** brain
**enchant** allure, appeal, attract, bewitch, captivate, charm, delight, enrapture, ensnare, enthral, fascinate, hypnotise, mesmerise, spellbind, thrill, transport
**enchanted place** faerie, fairyland
**enchanter** conjurer, magician, mesmerist, necromancer, seer, soothsayer, sorcerer, spellbinder, thaumaturgist, witch, wizard
**enchantment** allure, bliss, charm, excitation, fascination, joy, magic, mesmerism, necromancy, rapture, sorcery, spell, witchcraft
**enchantress of Ulysses** Circe
**enchantress who lured sailors** Lorelei, siren
**enchiridion** handbook, manual, textbook, vade mecum (L)
**encircle** circumscribe, compass, embrace, enclose, encompass, enfold, (en)gird, environ, girdle, hedge, surround
**encircle waist** girt
**encircling strip of leather** belt
**enclave** cell, dovetailed
**enclose** bound, cage, circumscribe, cocoon, confine, corral, cover, encase, encircle, encompass, enter, envelop, fence, girdle, girt, hedge, immure, impound, include, insert, pen, picket, pound, ring, sheathe, surround, wrap
**enclosed** bounded, caged, confined, covered, encased, encircled, encompassed, enfolded, entered, fenced, hedged, in, included, inserted, penned, surrounded, wrapped
**enclosed area** yard
**enclosed area in school** classroom
**enclosed by** within
**enclosed car** sedan
**enclosed piece of land planted with fruit trees** orchard
**enclosed place** yard
**enclosed space screened for privacy** cubicle
**enclosed village** kraal
**enclose in a covering** envelop
**enclose in an orb** ensphere
**enclose in shell** encyst
**enclose in twists** coil
**enclose within walls** (im)mure, imprison
**enclosing a large space** spacious
**enclosing boundary** circumference, perimeter
**enclosure** arena, bawn, boundary, cage, cloister, compound, coop, corral, court, envelop, fence, hedge, insertion, kraal, mew, palisade, pen, receptacle, stockade, sty, yard
**enclosure containing fruit trees** orchard
**enclosure for cattle** corral, kraal, lair
**enclosure for child** playpen
**enclosure for convicts** barracoon
**enclosure for game** boma
**enclosure for pigs** sty
**enclosure for playing skittles** alley
**enclosure for storage** chest, locker
**enclosure for strayed animals** pound
**enclosure for wild animals** boma, corral
**enclosure in criminal court for accused** dock
**enclosure in which birds are kept** aviary
**enclosure of stakes** stockade
**encode** encipher
**encompass** begrid, comprehend, comprise, cover, embrace, (en)circle, enclose, ensphere, envelop, environ, gird, surround
**encounter** accost, attack, battle, bear, brawl, confront, contend, endure, experience, face, fight, front, meet(ing), spar, struggle, suffer, tussle, undergo
**encourage** abet, advance, aid, assure, cheer, foster, hearten, incite, inspire, inspirit, promote, reassure, second, stimulate, support, urge
**encourage in devilment** abet
**encourage offender** abet
**encouraging cry** cheer
**encroach** entrench, impinge, infiltrate, infringe, interfere, intrude, invade, irrupt, obtrude, overlap, transgress, trespass
**encroacher** trespasser
**encroachment** incursion, infiltration, influx, infringement, inroad, invasion, obtrusion, overrunning, transgression, trespass, usurpation, violation
**encroach unlawfully** intruder, transgressor, trespass
**encroach upon** impinge
**encrust** cake, fur
**encrusted** caked
**encrusted with sugar** iced, candied
**encumber** bar, bridle, burden, check, clog, constrain, cramp, cumber, embarrass, enladen, hamper, handicap, hinder, impede, inconvenience, obstruct, oppress, overload, retard, saddle, strain, trammel
**encumbrance** bar(rier), block, burden, check, deterrent, difficulty, disadvantage, drag, drawback, handicap, hindrance, hitch, impediment, let, liability, limitation, millstone, nuisance, obstacle, obstruction, restriction, shortcoming, snag, stoppage
**end** aim, attainment, bound, cease, close, closure, complete, conclude, conclusion, extreme, extremity, fin(ale), finis(h), intention, issue, limit, object(ive), peroration, purpose, result, stop, terminate, termination, terminus, wind-up
**endanger** commit, compromise, expose, hazard, imperil, involve, jeopardise, menace, risk, threaten, venture
**end crust of bread** heel
**endear** admire, attach, attract, bind, captivate, charm, enamour, engage, enjoy, esteem, treasure, win

**endearing** adorable, attractive, charming, engaging, lovable, sweet, winsome
**endeavour** aim, aspire, attempt, essay, seek, strive, struggle, try, undertake, work
**endemic** congenital, hereditary, inborn, inbred, indigenous, inherited, innate, instinctive, native
**ending** climax, close, completion, concluding, conclusion, consummation, culmination, end, final(e), finish(ing), gestation, resolution, terminating, termination
**ending doubt** conclusive
**ending in a short sharp point** apiculate
**ending in death** fatal
**endless** boundless, ceaseless, constant, continual, continuous, eternal, everlasting, immortal, incessant, infinite, interminable, monotonous, overlong, perpetual, persistent, unbounded, unbroken, undivided, undying, unending, uninterrupted, unlimited, whole
**endless life after death** eternity
**endless number** myriad
**endlong** lengthwise
**endocrine gland** pituitary
**end of a bus route** terminus
**end of a hammer** claw, peen
**end of a railway line** terminal
**end of a sentence** period, point
**end of a weaver's thread** thrum
**end of bread** crust, heel
**end of day** sunset
**end of daylight** nightfall
**end of life** death
**end of nuptial bliss** divorce proceedings
**end of prayer** amen
**end of Ramadan** Eid-ul-Fitr
**end of rugby game** no-side
**end of ship's yard** arm
**end of spine bones** sacra
**end of the day** midnight, nightfall, sunset
**end of time** death
**end of ulna** ancon(e)
**end of validity of thing** expiry
**end of war** peace
**end-of-world-battle** Armageddon
**endorse** advocate, affirm, approve, authorise, back, champion, confirm, countersign, favour, ratify, recommend, sanction, sign, support, sustain, warrant
**endorse, as a cheque** sign
**endorsement on passport** visa
**endorsor** signatory

**endow** award, bequeath, bestow, confer, endue, enrich, equip, give, grant, invest, leave
**endowed institution** foundation
**endowed with a voice** vocal
**endowment** ability, bequest, bounty, capability, capacity, gift, largess, power, quality, talent
**endpiece** tail
**end point** limit
**end prematurely** abort
**ends prayer** amen
**endue** clothe, endow, furnish, invest
**endurable** bearable, lasting, sufferable, sustainable, tolerable
**endurance** acceptance, bearing, continuance, durability, duration, fortitude, hardship, maintenance, misfortune, ordeal, patience, perseverance, persistence, resignation, resolution, stability, stamina, stoicism, strength, submission, sufferance, sustainment, tenacity, toleration, trial
**endure** abide, be, bear, continue, dree (Sc), encounter, experience, feel, last, persevere, persist, stand, submit, suffer, sustain, thole (Sc), tolerate, undergo, wear
**endure pain** suffer
**enduring** endless, everlasting, lasting, long-standing, persisting
**enduring an onslaught** running the gauntlet
**enduring energy** stamina
**enemy** adversary, antagonist, assailant, attacker, competitor, contender, contestant, foe, opponent, opposer, rival, vier
**enemy agent** saboteur, spy
**enemy of Christ** Antichrist
**enemy of the human race** hostis humani generis (L)
**energetic** active, aggressive, alive, ambitious, animated, brisk, devoted, diligent, dynamic, eager, effective, effectual, efficacious, efficient, electric, forceful, hard-working, high-powered, jumping, lively, potent, powerful, robust, spirited, strenuous, strong, tireless, vigorous, zealous, zippy
**energetically** actively, aggressively, ambitiously, briskly, determinedly, diligently, dynamically, eagerly, efficiently, emphatically, forcefully, lively, strenuously, vigorously
**energetic person** doer
**energy** activity, ambition, animation, drive, efficacy, enterprise, force, go, intensity, might, operation, pep, power, push, restlessness, spirit, stamina, strength, verve, vigour, vim, virility, vitality, zeal, zip
**energy manufacturing plant** gasworks
**energy material** fuel
**energy measure** entropy
**energy source** fuel
**enervate** cripple, debilitate, deplete, dilute, diminish, disable, enfeeble, exhaust, handicap, impair, impoverish, invalidate, reduce, sap, strain, tire, weaken
**enfeeble** blunt, break, cripple, damage, debilitate, demoralise, deplete, deteriorate, diminish, disable, enervate, exhaust, harm, impair, incapacitate, injure, lame, maim, mar, paralyse, spoil, subdue, tame, undermine, weaken
**enfold** clasp, embrace, enclose, envelop, enwrap, hug, (in)fold, swathe, wrap
**enfold in arms** embrace
**enforce** apply, cause, coerce, compel, complete, constrain, discharge, exact, execute, extort, force, impel, implement, impose, manage, oblige, oversee, perform, press, prosecute, reinforce, require, supervise, urge
**enforced banishment from one's country** exile
**enforced rule** law
**enforcer of hard work** taskmaster
**enforcing discipline** stern
**enfranchised person** voter
**engage** affiance, allure, amuse, appoint, assign, attract, betroth, bind, busy, contend, divert, employ, engross, enlist, enrol, entertain, hire, involve, oblige, occupy, participate, pledge, promise, require, scuffle, secure, wrestle
**engage as a soldier** enlist
**engage beforehand** bespeak
**engaged in** at
**engaged in warfare** militant
**engaged woman** fiancée
**engage for labour** hire
**engage for military service** enlist
**engage for pay** employ, hire
**engage for service** enlist
**engage for work** hire
**engage gear wheels** mesh
**engage in a bee** spell
**engage in advance** bespeak
**engage in altercation** wrangle
**engage in argument** spar
**engage in combat** fight
**engage in commerce** trade
**engage in festivities** celebrate
**engage in loud argument** wrangle

**engage in risky commercial transaction** speculate
**engage in stealing** thieve
**engagement** appointment, arrangement, assurance, betrothal, commitment, contract, date, meeting, oath
**engagement gem** diamond
**engaging in commerce** trading
**engaging in holiday activities** festal
**engine** agency, agent, apparatus, appliance, contraption, device, dynamo, instrument, locomotive, machine(ry), means, mechanism, motor, tool, turbine
**engine cylinder** piston
**engineer** construct, contrive, design(er), manage, plan, technician
**engineless aircraft** glider
**engine sound** chug
**engine turns** revs
**England** Albion, Angleterre (F), Anglia (L), Blighty, Britain, Britannia
**English** Anglo
**English admiral** Nelson
**English airport** Gatwick, Heathrow
**English architect** Wren
**English astronomer** Halley
**English bay** Bigbury, Falmouth, Lyme, Tor, Tremadoc, Wash, Weymouth
**English beverage** tea
**English billiards game** snooker
**English Bill of Rights** Magna C(h)arta
**English capital** London
**English caricaturist** Giles, Keene
**English cathedral city** Canterbury, Ely, Guildford, Truro, York
**English channel** Bristol, Solent, Spithead
**English channel island** Alderney, Guernsey, Herm, Jersey, Sark
**English cheese** Cheddar, Stilton
**English chinaware** Queen Anne, Royal Doulton, Spode
**English clown** Grimaldi
**English coin** bob, florin, farthing, guinea, pence, penny, pound
**English college** Balliol, Eton
**English colony** Carolina
**English composer** Arne, Britten, Elgar, Parry
**English conservative** Tory
**English county** Kent, Suffolk, Sussex, Yorkshire
**English cricket ground** Leeds, Lords
**English dance** hay, morris
**English dialect for pal** wack
**English dog** bulldog
**English elegist** Gray
**English emblem** lion, rose

**English film director** Attenborough, Branagh
**English flower** rose
**English-French battle** Crécy, Cressy, Poitiers
**English gold** rial
**English gun** sten
**English halfpenny** mag
**English historian** Bede
**English island** Bardsey, Holy(head), Lundy, Mersea, Sheppy, Tresco, Wight
**English islands** Channel, Farne, Scilly
**English jargon** pidgin
**English lady** dame
**English lake** Conistan
**English lexicographer** Murray
**English liberal** Whig
**English manufacturing city** Leeds
**English muffin** scone
**English name for Ursa Minor** Little Bear
**English nobleman** baron, earl
**English noblewoman** milady
**English order** Garter
**English patron saint** George
**English peninsula** Portland
**English person** pom(mie), rooinek, Sassenach (Sc)
**English philosopher** Ayer, Bacon, Hume, Russel, Spencer
**English playwright** Marlow, Shakespeare, Shaw, Stoppard
**English poet** Byron, Keats, Milton, Shakespeare, Tennyson, Wordsworth
**English policeman** bobby
**English political party** Conservative, Labour, Tory, Whig
**English porcelain** Queen Anne, Royal Doulton, Spode
**English potter** Wedgewood
**English prefix** Anglo-
**English public schoolboy** Etonian
**English queen** Elizabeth
**English racecourse** Ascot, Epsom
**English racecourse town** Esher
**English resort** Bath, Blackpool, Brighton
**English royal house** Hanover, Lancaster, Plantagenet, Stuart, Tudor, Windsor, York
**English royal racecourse** Epsom
**English school** Eton, Harrow, Rugby
**English sculptor** Epstein, Moore
**English sea** Irish, North
**English soldier** fusileer, khaki, redcoat, rooinek, tommy
**English statesman** Churchill, Cromwell, Disraeli, Gladstone, Pitt
**English strait** Dover
**English streetcar** tram

**English tavern** pub
**English title** baron, baronet, duchess, duke, prince(ss)
**English university** Cambridge, London, Oxford
**English version of advocate** barrister
**Englishwoman** Briton
**English woollen** tweed
**engram** (memory) trace
**engrave** carve, chisel, embed, etch, fix, grave, impress, imprint, incise, ingrain, inscribe, lodge, stamp, stipple
**engrave by use of acid** etch
**engraved design** intaglio
**engraved gemstone with a design in relief** cameo
**engraved gemstone with a sunken design** intaglio
**engraved on stone** lapidary
**engraved piece of art** etching
**engrave in dots** stipple
**engrave in metal** etch
**engrave on the memory** etch
**engraver** etcher
**engraver of stones** lapidarian, lapidary
**engraver on wood** xylographer
**engraver's tool** chisel, scauper, scorper, scraper
**engrave with acid** etch
**engraving** anaglyph(y), block, carving, cerograph, chasing, chiselling, cutting, etching, impression, inscribing, inscription, mark, plate, print, relief, stippling, woodcut
**engraving chisel** scauper, scorper
**engraving on wood** woodcut, xylograph
**engraving process producing tonal effects** mezzotint
**engraving tool** burin, chisel, graver, scauper, scorper, scriber
**engross** absorb, amuse, attract, consume, devour, divert, employ, engage, hold, immerse, obsess, pre(occupy)
**engross attention of** rivet
**engrossed** absorbed, deep, enthralled, fascinated, intent, lost, preoccupied, rapt, riveted
**engrossed in temporal pursuits** worldly
**engrossment** absorbing, absorption, abstraction, copy, devouring, devourment, employment, immersion, inscription, intensity, obsession, pre(occupation), thoughtfulness, transcript
**engross the mind** preoccupy
**engulf** bury, consume, deluge, dive, engorge, engross, entomb, flood, gulp, inundate, jump, leap,

overwhelm, plunge, sink, sound, submerge, submerse, swamp
**enhance** augment, beautify, better, embellish, enrich, heighten, improve, intensify, magnify
**enigma** conundrum, dilemma, mystery, plight, predicament, problem, puzzle, quandary, question, riddle, secret, unknown
**enigmatic** abstruse, arcane, baffling, blank, complicated, concealed, confusing, cryptic, dark, deadpan, deep, hard, hidden, impenetrable, incomprehensible, inconceivable, inscrutable, insoluble, intricate, knotty, mysterious, mystic, obscure, occult, opaque, perplexing, puzzling, recondite, secret, strange, thorny, unfathomable, unintelligible, weird
**enigmatic saying** parable
**enjoin** admonish, advise, ask, ban, bid, call, caution, charge, command, commend, compel, counsel, decree, demand, desire, dictate, direct, exhort, impose, instruct, invite, ordain, order, preclude, prescribe, prohibit, proscribe, recommend, require, solicit, suggest, summon, tell, urge
**enjoy** appreciate, experience, groove, have, like, own, possess, relish, savour, use
**enjoyable** delectable, delicious, delightful, entertaining, good, gratifying, great, nice, pleasant, pleasing, pleasurable, satisfying, toothsome
**enjoyable idleness** dolce far niente (I)
**enjoy a winter sport** skate, ski
**enjoy books** read
**enjoy greatly** relish
**enjoy in advance** anticipate
**enjoying the company of others** gregarious
**enjoyment** amusement, bliss, cheer, comfort, contentment, delectation, delight, ease, ecstasy, elation, entertainment, exhilaration, fun, gaiety, glee, gratification, happiness, jollity, joy, mirth, pleasure, recreation, satisfaction, thrill, zest
**enjoyment in doing things** gusto, zest
**enjoyment of cruelty to others** sadism
**enjoy taste of** savour
**enjoy the present day** carpe diem (L)
**enjoy with others** share
**enlace** entwine
**enlarge** add, amplify, augment, bloat, broaden, cumulate, develop, dilate, distend, double, eke, elaborate, elongate, expand, extend, gather, greaten, grow, heighten, increase, inflate, lengthen, magnify, mature, multiply, sprawl, spread, sprout, stretch, supplement, swell, wax, widen
**enlarge an opening** flare, ream
**enlarge by** add
**enlarged nasal tissue** adenoids
**enlarged thyroid** goitre
**enlarge hole** ream
**enlargement** addendum, addition, amplification, annexation, appendage, augmentation, doubling, increase, increment, magnification, supplementation, swelling, trebling
**enlargement in mine shaft** stasie, station
**enlargement in muscle** knot
**enlargement of gullet** crop
**enlargement of organ** struma
**enlargement of the thyroid gland** goitre
**enlighten** edify, educate, illuminate, inform, instruct, mitigate, teach
**enlightenment** culture, discipline, edification, education, guidance, initiation, instruction, knowledge, refinement, schooling, study, teaching, tuition, understanding
**enlist** engage, enrol, join, obtain, recruit, volunteer
**enlisted man** GI, private, recruit
**enliven** animate, brighten, cheer, exhilarate, inspire, invigorate, pep, stimulate
**en masse** together
**enmesh** bag, capture, catch, complicate, confound, confuse, corner, disorder, disturb, embroil, ensnare, entangle, entrap, hook, implicate, incriminate, intertwine, involve, knot, mire, net, perplex, snag, snare, snarl, take, tangle, trammel, trap, trouble
**enmity** acrimony, animosity, animus, antagonism, antipathy, aversion, bitterness, dislike, estrangement, hate, hatred, hostility, malice, malignity, odium, rancour, repugnance, spite, unfriendliness, venom
**ennoble** aggrandise, dignify, elevate, enhance, exalt, honour, raise
**ennui** boredom, dissatisfaction, doldrums, fatigue, languor, lassitude, lethargy, listlessness, melancholy, monotony, sluggishness, tedium, world-weariness
**enormous** abominable, astronomic, atrocious, colossal, disgraceful, egregious, evil, execrable, flagrant, gigantic, gross, horrendous, huge, ignominious, immense, large, mammoth, massive, mean, monstrous, outrageous, prodigious, shameful, sinful, stupendous, titanic, tremendous, vast, vile
**enormous creature** behemoth
**enormous thing** monster
**enough** abundant(ly), adequate(ly), ample, amply, enow, fairly, moderately, passably, plenty, reasonably, satisfactory, sufficient(ly), tolerably
**enough and to spare** ample
**enough now of this!** jam satis! (L)
**enough of words** satis verborum (L)
**enough rope** latitude, play, scope, swing, tolerance
**enough space** elbow-room
**enough to be measured** appreciable
**enquire** ask, examine, explore, inquire, inspect, investigate, probe, query, question, scrutinise, search
**enquire into** inspect, investigate, probe, scrutinise
**enquiry** analysis, audit, autopsy, examination, exploration, inquest, inspection, inquiry, inquisition, interrogation, investigation, probe, pursuit, query, quest(ion), research, review, scrutiny, search, study, survey, test
**enrage** aggravate, agitate, anger, (ex)acerbate, exasperate, incense, incite, inflame, infuriate, irk, irritate, madden, provoke, rile
**enrapture** beguile, bewitch, captivate, charm, delight, electrify, enamour, enchant, endear, enthral, entrance, excite, fascinate, gladden, gratify, hypnotise, move, overjoy, ravish, rejoice, spellbind, transport
**enrich** adorn, aggrandise, ameliorate, appreciate, augment, decorate, develop, elevate, embellish, endow, enhance, fatten, fertilise, grace, improve, lard, ornament, refine, satiate, supplement, upgrade, uplift
**enrichment** adornment, advancement, aggrandisement, appreciation, beautification, bestowment, betterment, conferment, decoration, development, edification, embellishment, endowment, enhancement, enlightenment, furtherance, improvement, investment, ornamentation, refinement, satiation, trimming, uplift
**enrich with any gift or faculty** endow
**enrol** accept, appoint, assemble, begin, bill, book, catalogue, chronicle, collect, commence, commission, congregate, convene, convoke, employ, engage, enlist,

enter, enumerate, file, gather, group, hire, index, inscribe, itemise, join, list, marshal, meet, muster, note, obtain, procure, record, recruit, register, retain, schedule, secure, start

**enrol again**  re-enlist
**enrol for a jury**  empanel, impanel
**enrol in armed services**  enlist
**enrol in army**  conscript
**enrol in the list of saints**  canonise
**en route**  in transitu (L)
**ens**  being, entity, essence
**ensanguined**  bloodstained, bloody
**ensconce**  camouflage, conceal, cover, entrench, hide, install, locate, nestle, place, screen, settle, shelter, shroud, veil
**ensemble**  aggregate, assembly, attire, company, costume, entirely, outfit, set, troupe
**enshrine**  allot, appropriate, assign, cherish, dedicate, devote, give, inshrine, pledge, reserve, treasure
**ensiform**  xiphoid
**ensign**  badge, banner, colours, crest, emblem, epaulette, escutcheon, flag, insigne, insignia, jack, pennant, pennon, ribbon, shield, sign, standard, streamer, symbol
**ensign of Othello**  Iago
**ensign's word to captain**  sir
**enslave**  addict, allure, attract, beguile, bewitch, bind, captivate, capture, catch, charm, conquer, (en)chain, enchant, ensnare, enthral, fascinate, fetter, habituate, handcuff, lure, manacle, mesmerise, overcome, restrain, seduce, shackle, subject, subjugate, tether, thrall, transport, trap, yoke
**enslavement**  bondage
**ensnare**  allure, beguile, captivate, catch, dupe, embroil, entangle, entrap, hoax, inveigle, mislead, net, seduce, snare, snarl, trap
**ensue**  arise, attend, befall, derive, emanate, eventuate, flow, follow, happen, issue, occur, proceed, result, seek, stem, succeed, supervene
**ensure**  ascertain, assure, attain, certify, confirm, effect, guarantee, insure, mind, secure, see, underwrite, warrant
**ensure observance of**  enforce
**entail**  cause, demand, impose, necessitate, occasion, require
**entangle**  catch, complicate, confuse, embroil, enlace, enmesh, ensnare, entrap, implicate, involve, jumble,

knot, muddle, perplex, puzzle, ravel, snag, snare, snarl, tangle, trap, twist
**enter**  approach, arrive, begin, board, commence, embark, enlist, enrol, insert, introduce, irrupt, join, journalise, list, log, note, offer, participate, penetrate, pierce, present, record, register, start, submit, tender, trespass
**enter an offence**  accede
**enter as an enemy**  invade
**enter forcibly**  irrupt
**enter in a register**  enrol
**entering upon**  accession
**enter into**  analyse, consider, examine, investigate, penetrate, probe, scrutinise, study
**enter into a league**  federate
**enter into an alliance**  unite
**enter into combat**  battle
**enter into the books**  validate
**enter on**  begin
**enterprise**  adventure, boldness, business, concern, drive, eagerness, endeavour, enthusiasm, establishment, initiative, operation, plan, programme, project, readiness, undertaking, venture, vigour, zeal
**enterprising businessperson**  entrepreneur
**enter speed contest**  race
**entertain**  absorb, admit, amuse, attend, charm, cheer, consider, contemplate, distract, divert, harbour, joke, mimic, please, ponder, receive, regale, treat, welcome
**entertain choicely with food**  regale
**entertainer**  acrobat, actor, actress, artiste, clown, comedian, host(ess), musician, speaker, stripper, tragedian
**entertain lavishly**  fête
**entertainment**  amusement, antic, carnival, celebration, dalliance, distraction, diversion, extravaganza, gala, lark, pleasantry, recreation, relaxation, sport, spree, tomfoolery
**entertain royally**  regale
**enter the picture**  appear
**enter uninvited**  intrude
**enter unlawfully**  trespass
**enter upon**  accede
**enter violently**  irrupt
**enthral**  allure, attract, becharm, beguile, bewitch, captivate, charm, dazzle, delight, enamour, enchain, enchant, engross, enrapture, enslave, excite, fascinate, grip, hypnotise, infatuate, inflame, intrigue, lure, mesmerise, rivet,

seduce, spellbound, subdue, subjugate, thrill, win
**enthralling**  brilliant, compulsive, impressive, memorable, superlative, wonderful
**enthuse**  absorb, effervesce, emote, excite, gush, impassion, inflame, interest, possess, rave, rhapsodise
**enthusiasm**  abandon, ardour, assurance, avidity, confidence, determination, devotion, eagerness, earnestness, ebullience, élan, emotion, energy, fervency, fervour, hopefulness, intensity, interest, passion, pep, spirit, verve, vitality, vivacity, warmth, willingness, zeal, zest
**enthusiasm that animates**  verve
**enthusiast**  addict, aficionado, buff, devotee, fan, zealot
**enthusiastic**  ardent, avid, devoted, eager, earnest, excited, fervid, keen, lyrical, zealous
**enthusiastic acclaim**  ovation
**enthusiastic admiration**  furore
**enthusiastic applause**  ovation
**enthusiastic supporter**  fan
**entice**  allure, attract, beguile, cajole, coax, decoy, draw, induce, inveigle, lure, persuade, seduce, sweet-talk, tantalise, tempt, wheedle
**entice a prey**  bait
**entice away**  lure
**enticement**  allure(ment), bait(ing), blandishment, cajolery, inveiglement, invitation, lure, seduction, temptation, trap, wheedling
**entice with bait**  lure
**entice with money**  bribe
**enticing**  alluring, attracting, beguiling, cajoling, coaxing, decoying, drawing, inveigling, luring, persuading, seducing, seductive, tempting, wheedling
**enticing look**  inviting smile
**enticing woman**  Lorelei, Mata Hari, siren, vamp
**entire**  complete, full, inclusive, intact, perfect, total, undiminished, undivided, unimpaired, unimpeded, universal, unlessened, unqualified, unreduced, unrestricted, whole
**entire amount**  all, total
**entirely**  absolutely, completely, fully, in toto (L), purely, thoroughly, totally, wholly
**entire range**  gamut, spectrum
**entire sum**  total
**entire thing**  integral
**entitle**  authorise, call, designate, dub, empower, name, qualify

**entitled to be chosen** eligible
**entity** article, being, core, creature, essence, existence, heart, kernel, life, nature, object, person, pith, presence, quantity, quiddity, soul, spirit, subsistence, substance, thing, unit
**entomb** inter, bury
**entomophagous** insectivorous
**entourage** ambience, ambit, attendance, attendants, bodyguard, convoy, cortege, court, environment, escort, followers, guard, milieu, precinct, retinue, safeguard, staff, suite, surroundings, train
**entrails** belly, bowels, gut(s), innards, insides, internals, intestines, inwards, offal, stomach, viscera, vitals
**entrails of deer** gralloch, umbles
**entrance** access, adit, admission, admittance, arrival, avenue, bewitch, captivate, charm, delight, door(way), enchant, enrapture, enthral, entrée, entry, fascinate, foyer, front, gate, ingress, inlet, introduction, mouth, opening, passage, porch, portal, ravish, transport
**entrance boring of mine** shaft
**entranced** bewitch, captivated, charmed, delighted, enchanted, enthralled, fascinated, rapt, ravished, transported
**entrance hall** foyer, lobby, vestibule
**entrance to building** door
**entrance to coal mine** pithead
**entrance to house** door
**entrance to mine** adit
**entrance to temple** propylaeum, propylon
**entranceway** door(way), gate, portal
**entrancing** alluring, charming, delightful, enchanting, fascinating, wonderful
**entrap** allure, bag, beguile, catch, embarrass, ensnare, entangle, entice, expose, implicate, involve, net, reveal, snare
**entrap adroitly** entice
**entrap by surrounding** besiege, circumvent, encircle
**entrapping network** web
**entreat** appeal, ask, beg, beseech, enjoin, entreat, impetrate, implore, importune, invoke, petition, plead, pray, request, sue, supplicate, urge, woo
**entreat earnestly** appeal, urge
**entreaty** adjuration, appeal, bid, call, cry, importunity, insistence, instance, instigation, invocation, obtestation, petition, plea, prayer, solicitation, suppliance
**entremets** afters, dessert, sweet
**entrench** anchor, barricade, base, brace, constitute, create, decree, defend, embed, enact, ensconce, establish, fasten, fence, fix, form, fortify, found, ground, implant, inaugurate, infringe, install, institute, maintain, moor, obtrude, plant, root, secure, set, settle, solidify, start, stick, trespass
**entresol** mezzanine
**entrust** assign, bequeath, charge, commend, commit, confide, consign, delegate, deliver, depute, invest, trust
**entrust a secret** confide
**entrusted with secrets** confidential
**entry** access, account, admission, admittance, appearance, attempt, brief, candidate, competitor, contestant, credit, debit, debut, description, door(way), effort, entrance, entrant, entrée, gate, ingress, initiation, inlet, introduction, item, note, opening, participant, passageway, player, portal, record, statement, submission
**entry of money owed** debit
**entry on a list** item
**entry permit** laissez passer (F), pass, visa
**entry rug** mat
**entwine** braid, embrace, enlace, entwist, interlace, intwine, plait, surround, twist, weave
**entwined hair** braid, plait
**enumerate** add, calculate, catalogue, compute, count, estimate, list, mark, name, narrate, numerate, reckon, recount, relate, specify, tabulate, tally
**enumerating** counting
**enunciate** accentuate, articulate, assert, asseverate, attest, aver, avow, blare, cry, declare, express, maintain, proclaim, say, state, utter, voice
**enunciation** accent(uation), affirmation, announcement, articulation, attack, averment, broadcast, delivery, emphasis, expressing, intonating, notice, presentation, pronouncing, pronunciation, protest, saying, stress
**envelop** blanket, cloak, conceal, cover, embrace, encase, encircle, enclose, encompass, enfold, engulf, (en)shroud, (en)wrap, enwreath, hide, obscure, pack, protect, shield, surround, swathe, veil
**envelope** case, casing, coating, cover(ing), jacket, sheath, shell, skin, wrapper, wrapping
**envelope inscription** address
**envelope part** flap
**envious** begrudging, covetous, desirous, discontent, green-eyed, grudging, hankering, itching, jaundiced, jealous, malicious, resentful, spiteful, unhappy, yearning
**environ** beset, encircle, enclose, encompass, engird, surround
**environment** ambience, circumstances, ecosystem, habitat, medium, milieu, situation, surroundings, terrain
**environmental party** Green
**envisage** anticipate, conceptualise, contemplate, envision, fancy, (fore)see, imagine, picture, predict, visualise
**envoy** agent, attaché, consul(ate), delegate, diplomat, embassy, emissary, legate, mediator, messenger, nuncio, plenipotentiary
**envoy to a minor country** chargé d'affaires
**envy** begrudge, covet(ousness), crave, cupidity, desire, discontent(ment), enviousness, fancy, grudge, hate, ill-will, jealousy, longing, malice, mortification, relish, resent(ment), rivalry, spite, unhappiness, want
**envy anyone the possession of** begrudge
**enwreath** encircle, surround
**enzyme** -ase, diastase, leaven, maltase, olease, pepsin, rennin
**enzyme group** esterase
**enzyme that digests elastin** elastase
**eoan** eastern
**épée** foil, rapier
**epéeist** dueller
**epergne** centrepiece, stand
**ephemeral** brief, brilliant, earthly, fast, flashing, fleeting, flying, fugacious, fugitive, human, impermanent, interim, meteoric, momentary, mortal, passing, provisional, rapid, short(-lived), sudden, swift, temporal, temporary, transient, transitory, worldly
**ephemerally** transitorily
**epic** bombastic, detailed, drama, epical, epopee, epos, excessive, fabulous, grand(iose), graphic, great, heroic, historical, history, huge, imposing, legend(ary), lofty, majestic, myth(ical), narrative, poem, saga, story, tale, vast, voluminous
**epicene** sexless, unisex
**epic of Troy** Iliad

**epic poem** *Beowulf*, epopee, epopoeia, epos, *Odyssey*
**epic poem attributed to Homer** *Odyssey*
**epic poem of Trojan War** *Iliad*
**epic poetry** epos
**epic song** ballad
**epic tale** saga
**epicure** aesthete, connoisseur, cormorant, debauchee, deipnosophist, epicurean, gastronome(r), gastronomist, glutton, gourmand, gourmet, hog, lecher, libertine, sensualist, sybarite, voluptuary
**epic writer** epicist
**epidemic** infestation, pandemic, plague, prevalent, rife, widespread
**epidemic disease of silkworms** pébrine
**epidermis** skin
**epidiascope** projector
**epigrammatic** amusing, brief, brilliant, clever, compact, concise, droll, facetious, fanciful, funny, gay, humorous, ingenious, jocular, laconic, lively, original, piquant, pithy, pointed, sparkling, succinct, terse, waggish, whimsical, witty
**epilepsy with loss of consciousness** grand mal
**episcopal headdress** mitre
**episcopal title** abba
**episode** affair, chapter, event, happening, incident, occurrence
**episodic story** serial
**epistaxis** nosebleed
**episternum** interclavicle
**epistle** communication, letter, message, missive, note
**epistle writer** Paul
**epitaph** hic jacet (L), inscription, motto, saying
**epithet** adjective, appellation, description, designation, nick(name), tag, title
**epithet of Aristotle** Stagirite
**epitome** abridg(e)ment, analects, analysis, bulletin, compilation, digest, embodiment, essence, example, exemplar, outline, personification, précis, prototype, representation, résumé, sketch, summary, syllabus, symposium, synopsis, type
**epizoon** parasite
**epoch** aeon, age, chronology, cycle, date, era, interval, period, season, space, span, stretch, time
**epoch of the tertiary period** Eocene
**Epsom horse race** Derby

**equable** agreeable, composed, even, placid, serene, tranquil, unchanging, uniform
**equal** able, adequate, alike, balanced, capable, co-ordinate, commensurate, comparable, competent, correspondent, counterpart, equivalent, even, fellow, fit, identical, iso-, like, match(ed), matching, mate, par, parallel, peer, proportionate, regular, sufficient, suitable, tantamount, uniform, unvarying
**equal amounts** ana
**equal footing** par
**equal in age** contemporary
**equal in any respect** peer
**equal in number** even
**equal in value** equivalent, tantamount
**equal in value or meaning** tantamount
**equalise** adapt, adjust, balance, compensate, equal, equate, even, fit, level, poise, regulate, smooth, symmetrise, tailor
**equaliser** leveller
**equality** agreement, balance, coincidence, conformity, égalité (F), equilibrium, equivalence, fairness, identity, impartiality, justice, oneness, par(ity), resemblance, sameness, unity
**equality between market and nominal value** par
**equality of score** tie
**equality of value** par
**equality of weight** equipoise
**equally** as
**equally adept with each hand** ambidext(e)rous
**equally balanced** even
**equally expert with each hand** ambidext(e)rous
**equally far from two extremes** mean
**equally strong** isodynamic
**equal part** half, moiety
**equal quantities** ana
**equal to zero** nilpotent
**equal value** par
**equanimity** aplomb, balance, calmness, composure, coolness, equability, inexcitability, meekness, peacefulness, placidity, poise, repose, resignation, serenity, temperance, tranquillity
**equation** formula
**equestrian** cavalier, cavalryman, Cossack, cowboy, dragoon, gaucho, horseman, hussar, knight, rider, trooper, vaquero
**equestrian sport** polo(crosse)
**equiangular polygon** isogon
**equidistant from extremities** middle

**equilateral figure** rhomb
**equilateral rectangle** square
**equilibrium** aplomb, assurance, balance, calm(ness), collectedness, composure, cool, deadlock, equality, (equi)poise, evenness, sedateness, self-possession, stability, steadiness, symmetry
**equine** ass, burro, charger, horse, mare, mule, stallion, steed
**equine colour** roan
**equine cover** saddle-cloth
**equine mammal** horse, quagga, zebra
**equine manoeuvres** dressage
**equine mom** mare
**equine quadruped** horse, quagga, zebra
**equine strap** martingale
**equine straps** reins
**equip** accoutre, adorn, arm, array, attire, clothe, deck, drape, dress, fit, furnish, gird, invest, kit, outfit, prepare, provide, purvey, rig, robe, stock, supply, trap
**equip for battle** arm
**equip for military service** accoutre
**equipment** accoutrement, apparatus, appliances, baggage, belongings, contrivances, furnishings, furniture, gear, habiliments, implements, kit, luggage, material, outfittings, paraphernalia, rig, supplies, tools, utensils
**equipment for a sport** gear
**equipment supplier** outfitter
**equipment used for gymnastics** apparatus
**equipoise** balance, ballast, compensation, counterbalance, counterpoise, counterweight, equilibrium, offset, requital, weight
**equip with engine** motorise
**equip with sails** rig
**equip with weapons** arm
**equitable** average, balanced, compatible, decent, detached, disinterested, dispassionate, equal, even(-handed), fair, honest, honourable, impartial, impersonal, just, lawful, neutral, outside, reasonable, unbiased, unprejudiced, unselfish, virtuous
**equitable portion** share
**equitation** horsemanship
**equity** assets, cash, fairness, investment, justice, justness, value
**equivalent** comparable, corresponding, counterpart, match, parallel, same, tantamount
**equivalent to** tantamount
**equivalent to eight bits** byte

**equivocate** avoid, cavil, deceive, dodge, duck, evade, fabricate, fake, falsify, fib, invent, lie, misrepresent, palter, perjure, prevaricate, quibble, shuffle, sidestep, stall
**equivocation** artifice, avoidance, chicane, compromise, cunning, deceit, deception, device, dodge, elusion, escape, evasion, evasiveness, excuse, expedient, falsehood, prevarication, qualification, resource, ruse, shuffling, stratagem, subterfuge, trickery, uncertainty, untruth, vagueness, wile
**era** aeon, age, century, days, epoch, interval, period, stage, time
**eradicate** abolish, annihilate, cancel, delete, demolish, destroy, devastate, efface, eliminate, erase, expunge, exterminate, extirpate, extract, obliterate
**erase** cancel, dele(te), deplete, destroy, dissolve, efface, eliminate, eradicate, expunge, expurgate, obliterate, remove
**erase in printing** delete
**eraser** rubber
**erasure** attrition, cancellation, deletion, elimination, eradication, expunction, extirpation, obliteration, removal
**ere** before
**erect** build, built, construct, establish, institute, (up)raise, upright, vertical
**erect annual grass** oat
**erection frames** scaffolding
**erection of any short body hairs** horripilation
**erelong** soon
**eremite** anchorite, hermit, recluse
**ergo** consequently, hence, so, therefore
**ergometer** dynamometer
**ergonomics** biotechnology
**ergot** rye
**ergotism** Saint Anthony's fire
**erica** fynbos, heath
**erigeron** fleabane
**Eritrean** Ethiopian
**erk** aircraftman
**ermine** stoat
**erne** sea-eagle
**erode** abrade, consume, corrode, decay, denude, deplete, destroy, deteriorate, disintegrate, eat, rust, spoil, wear
**Eros** Cupid
**erose** jagged, uneven
**erosion** abrading, abrasion, attrition, cankering, chafing, channelling, consuming, corrosion, damage, depreciation, detrition, fretting, friction, gnawing, grating, grooving, irritation, ravaging, resistance, rubbing, scrape, scraping, use, wear(ing)
**erotic** amorous, ardent, carnal, fervent, fiery, fond, infatuated, inflammatory, lovesome, lustful, passionate, prurient, rapturous, risqué, salacious, seductive, sensual, sexy, wanton
**erotic fondness of animals** zoophilia, zoophilism
**err** blunder, deviate, fail, goof, lapse, misbehave, miscalculate, misjudge, mistake, misunderstand, offend, sin, slip, stray, stumble, transgress, trespass, wander
**errand** assignment, business, commission, commitment, consignment, duty, entrustment, job, journey, mandate, message, mission, task, trip, trust, undertaking, work
**errand boy** bellhop, courier, messenger, page
**erratic** aberrant, abnormal, devious, eccentric, irregular, meandering, odd, queer, spasmodic, strange, unfixed, unpredictable, unstable, unusual, variable, wandering, whimsical
**erratically** aberrantly, abnormally, aimlessly, capriciously, changeably, digressively, fancifully, fitfully, indirectly, intermittently, irregularly, randomly, spasmodically, waywardly
**erring state** errancy
**erroneous** amiss, fallacious, false, faulty, flawed, illogical, inaccurate, incorrect, inexact, invalid, mistaken, spurious, unfounded, untrue, wrong
**erroneous legal proceeding** mistrial
**erroneous reading** falsa lectio (L)
**erroneous reckoning** miscast
**error** bloomer, blunder, fault, heresy, misdeed, mistake, peccadillo, slip(-up), wrongdoing
**error in chronology** parachronism
**error in computing of time** anachronism
**error in printing** erratum, misprint
**error in writing** erratum
**error of judgement** mistake
**ersatz** artificial, counterfeit, imitated, imitation, imitative, man-made, mock, pastiche, simulated, spurious, substitute, synthetic
**ersatz butter** margarine, oleo
**Erse** Gaelic, Irish
**erst** formerly, once
**erstwhile** bygone, former, late, old, one-time, past, previous, quondam, sometime
**erubescent** blushing, reddening
**eruct** belch, discharge, eject, regurgitate, vomit
**erudite** cultured, educated, knowledgeable, learned, lettered, literate, scholarly, well-read
**erudite judge** pundit
**erudite person** pedant, polymath, savant, scholar, student
**erudition** awareness, concepts, cultivation, data, doctrines, education, enlightenment, expertness, facts, information, instruction, intimacy, knowledge, learning, literature, precepts, refinement, scholarship, teachings, tuition
**erupt** burst, discharge, explode, gush, spout, vent, vomit
**erupting mountain** volcano
**erupting spring** geyser
**eruption** blast, detonation, discharge, dissilience, (earth)quake, ejection, explosion, flare-up, outbreak, outburst, tremor
**eruptive disorder of the skin** acne, lichen
**eruptive mountain** volcano
**Esau's nation** Edom
**Esau's twin** Jacob
**escalate** ascend, enlarge, expand, extend, grow, heighten, increase, intensify, mount, raise, rise
**escapade** adventure, antic, caper, fling, mischief, prank, revel, spree, trick
**escape** abscond, avoid, dodge, egress, elope, elude, evade, flee, flight, flow, fly, getaway, lam, leak(age), loophole, outflow, outlet, release, run, seep
**escape artist** Houdini
**escape, as fluid** leak
**escape by stratagem** elude
**escapee** absconder, defector, deserter, émigré, exile, fugitive, refugee, refugee, runaway, traitor, truant
**escape from** evade, elude
**escape hole** ventage
**escape of blood from a vessel** haemorrhage
**escape vent** outlet
**escaping air sound** hiss
**escapist** avoider, (day)dreamer, evader, fugitive, non-realist, optimist, rover, vagabond
**escapologist** Houdini
**escargot** snail
**eschalot** shallot
**eschew** avoid, disdain, disrelish, elude, evade, forbear, ignore, shirk, shun, snub

**escort** accompany, aide, attendant, bodyguard, chaperon, companion, company, conduct, convoy, cortege, date, entourage, guard(ian), guide, lead, partner, pilot, protect(ion), protector, retinue, safeguard, see, squire, suite, train, usher
**escort ship** corvette
**escritoire** (writing) desk
**esculent** edible
**escutcheon** arms, blazonry, crest, heraldry, insignia, shield
**esker** eskar, os
**Eskimo** Esquimau, Greenlander
**Eskimo assembly room** Kashim
**Eskimo boat** bidarka, k(a)iak, kayak, oomiak, umia(c)k
**Eskimo boot** kamik, mukluk
**Eskimo bus** sled
**Eskimo canoe** kayak
**Eskimo curfew** fute
**Eskimo delicacy** blubber
**Eskimo dog** husky, malamute, malemute, siwash
**Eskimo hut** igloe, igloo, iglu, topek, tupek, tupik
**Eskimo outer garment** parka, temiak
**Eskimo settlement** Etah
**Eskimo shelter** igloe, igloo, iglu, topek, tupek, tupik
**Eskimo skin jacket** parka
**Eskimo woman's knife** ulu
**esoteric** abstruse, ambiguous, arcane, confidential, confusing, cryptic, dark, deep, doubtful, enigmatic, hazy, hidden, insolvable, involved, mysterious, obscure, occult, opaque, private, privy, puzzling, recondite, secret, unclear, vague
**especial** distinctive, exceptional, extraordinary, individual, marked, notable, noteworthy, outstanding, particular, pre-eminent, special, specific, superior, uncommon, unique, unusual
**especial kindness** favour
**especially** chiefly, exceptionally, first(ly), mainly, markedly, notably, noticeably, particularly, predominantly, primarily, principally, remarkedly, significantly, specially, strikingly, uncommonly, unusually
**especially disliked person** bête noire (F)
**Esperanto variant** Ido
**espial** detection, discernment, discovery, espionage, following, intelligence, notice, observation, perception, recognition, reconnaissance, regard, spotting, spying, surveillance

**espionage** bugging, counter-intelligence, deception, eavesdropping, foxiness, infiltration, intelligence, investigating, operations, pretension, probing, prying, reconnaissance, reconnoitring, spying, surveillance, tailing, undercover
**espionage agent** informer, mole, spy
**esplanade** parade, promenade, walkway
**espousal** adoption, advocacy, betrothal, embracing, engagement, maintenance, support
**espouse** abet, adopt, advocate, assume, back, champion, choose, defend, elect, embrace, husband, maintain, marry, support, uphold, wed, wive
**esprit** acumen, brains, flair, ingenuity, initiative, insight, intuition, keenness, perspicacity, sagacity, sharpness, shrewdness, smartness, understanding, wisdom, wit
**esprit de corps** comradeship, morale, prejudice, solidarity, team-spirit, teamwork, togetherness
**espy** behold, descry, detect, discern, discover, notice, observe, perceive, recognise, see, spy, view, watch
**ess** curve, sigmoid, worm
**essay** aim, article, attempt, commentary, composition, critique, discourse, dissertation, effort, endeavour, exertion, experiment, manuscript, paper, strive, tackle, test, theme, thesis, treatise, trial, try, undertake, undertaking, venture
**essay for the English teacher** composition
**essay on a theme** thesis
**essence** attar, civet, core, cosmetic, entity, essentiality, extraction, gist, heart, incense, musk, nature, odour, perfume, pungency, quiddity, scent, spirit, verity
**essence of a thing** quiddity
**essence of real nature** entity
**essence of roses** attar
**essence or core** gist
**Essene** escetic, Hebrew, Jew, mystic
**essential** basic, characteristic, chief, constituent, crucial, definitive, elementary, fundamental, ideal, important, indispensable, intrinsic, key, main, necessary, necessity, needed, perfect, principal, pure, real, required, requisite, typical, vital
**essential character** spirit
**essential ingredient of the atom** positron
**essential in war** strategic

**essentiality** gravity, innately, materiality, matter, per se, reality, universe, vitality
**essential location** eye
**essential nature** entity, esse, quiddity
**essential part in a score** obbligato
**essential person** kingpin
**essential points of a speech** gist
**essential requirement** sine qua non (L)
**essential thing** need
**essential to existence** vital
**establish** appoint, ascertain, base, constitute, create, decree, enact, ensconce, entrench, fix, form, found, ground, implant, inaugurate, initiate, install, institute, organise, plant, root, secure, settle, start
**establish by law** enact
**establish co-operation** liaise
**established law** institute
**established method for doing something** formula
**established principle** axiom
**established quantity** measure, unit
**established rule** ordinance, rite, standard
**established standard** criterion, norm
**establish firmly** ensconce, entrench
**establishment** business, concern, creation, erection, factory, firm, formation, foundation, inauguration, installation, institution, invention, office, organisation
**establishment for treatment of invalids** sanatorium
**establishment of identity** identification
**establish peace** pacify
**establish the name of** identify
**establish the truth of** authenticate, issue
**estate** abode, area, assets, belongings, bequest, caste, chattels, class, condition, dignity, domain, effects, fortune, grade, holdings, home, lands, legacy, level, manor, place, position, possessions, property, residence, resources, standing, station, status, stratum, wealth, worth
**estate agent** realtor
**estate house** manor
**estate of a lord** manor
**estate of an insolvent debtor** assets
**estate of widow** dower
**esteem** admiration, admire, affection, appreciate, awe, cherish, commend, consider, credit, deem, favour, fondness, homage, honour, like, love, prize, regard, repute, respect, revere, reverence, treasure, valuation, value, venerate, veneration
**esteem of many persons** popularity

**Esther's uncle** Mordecai
**estimate** appraise, approximate, approximation, assess, calculate, calculation, computation, compute, count, estimation, evaluate, figure, gauge, guess, judge, judg(e)ment, measure, rate, reckon, valuate
**estimate amount of** appraise
**estimate beforehand** forecast, prophesy
**estimated price** quotation
**estimate general standard** average
**estimate incorrectly** misjudge
**estimate justly** appreciate
**estimate the worth of** cost
**estimate value of** assess, price
**estimate worth of** rate
**estimation** approximation, assessment, conclusion, esteem, feeling, honour, inference, judg(e)ment, mind, opinion, persuasion, respect, sentiment, surmise, thinking, viewpoint
**estop** bar, hinder, preclude, prevent, stop
**estrade** dais, platform, podium
**estragon** tarragon
**estrange** aggravate, alienate, anger, antagonise, destroy, disaffect, disunite, divide, drive, embitter, incense, part, provoke, quit, rupture, separate, sever
**estrangement** alienation, breach, dissociation, division, separation, withholding
**estuary** arm, creek, delta, drift, firth, f(j)ord, inlet, mouth, ria, sea-lock
**esurience** greed
**esurient** greedy, hungry, voracious
**étagère** whatnot
**etch** carve, corrode, cut, dig, engrave, furrow, groove, impress, imprint, incise, ingrain, inscribe, score, stamp
**etched design** intaglio
**etched metal sheet** copperplate
**etcher** engraver
**etching** carving, cut, impression, (im)print, sketch
**etching process producing tonal effects** aquatint
**eternal** abiding, ageless, always, ceaseless, constant, durable, endless, enduring, everlasting, frequent, immortal, incessant, infinite, interminable, lasting, perdurable, permanent, perpetual, relentless, stable, steady, timeless, unceasing, undying, unending, uninterrupted
**eternal city** Rome
**eternal death** perdition
**eternal punishment** damnation

**eternity** aeon, after-life, age, boundlessness, deathlessness, duration, endlessness, eternalness, everlastingness, futurity, heaven, immensity, immortality, immutability, infinity, paradise, perdurability, perpetuity, timelessness, vastness
**ether** air, gas, heavens, sky, space
**ethereal** aerial, airy, celestial, dainty, delicate, elusive, exquisite, fine, fragile, frail, heavenly, gaseous, gossamer, insubstantial, light, misty, rarefied, shadowy, spiritual, sublime, subtle, tenuous, thin, unearthly
**ethereal salt** ester
**ethical** conscientious, correct, decent, fair, good, honest, just, lofty, moral, noble, open, principled, proper, pure, righteous
**ethical story's lesson** moral
**ethical wrong** sin
**Ethiopian** Eritrean
**Ethiopian coin** amole, besa, girsh, piaster, talari, thaler
**Ethiopian dipterous insect** zimb
**Ethiopian emperor** negus
**Ethiopian falls** Blurnile, Tisisat
**Ethiopian garment** chamma
**Ethiopian island** Dahlak
**Ethiopian king** negus
**Ethiopian language** Amharic, Gallinya, Geez, Somali, Tigre, Titginya
**Ethiopian measure** farsakh, farsang, kuba, sinjer, sinzer, tat
**Ethiopian native** Afar, Falasha, Galla, Hamite, Semite, Somali, Tigrai
**Ethiopian port** Assab, Massawa
**Ethiopian prince** ras
**Ethiopian province** Arusi, Bale, Eritrea, Shewa, Sidamo, Tigre
**Ethiopian valley** rift
**ethmoid** sievelike
**ethnic** cultural, ethnological, human, indigenous, native, pagan, race, racial, traditional
**ethnical** racial
**ethnic bias** racism
**ethnic bigot** racist
**ethnic group** race
**ethnic hype** racist propaganda
**ethnic name of Croatia** Hrvatska
**ethnic slum** ghetto
**ethnography** anthropography
**ethnological group** tribe
**etiolated plant** albino
**etiquette** convention, decorum, dignity, manners, propriety, protocol
**etiquette requirement** formality
**Etna is one** volcano
**étrier** portable ladder
**eucalyptus** bloodwood, gum
**eucalyptus tree** (blue)gum

**eucalyptus tree on riverbank** coolabah, coolibah
**Eucharist** oblation, offering, offertory, sacrament
**eulogise** applaud, commend, extol, panegyrise, praise
**eulogy** acclaim, applause, exaltation, glorification, laudation, paean, panegyric, praise, tribute
**eunuch** castrato
**euphemistic word for devil** dickens
**euphonious** agreeable, dulcet, eloquent, lyric(al), mellifluent, mellifluous, mellow, melodious, musical, pleasing, rhythmical, rich, soft, soothing, tuneful
**euphonium** tuba
**euphoria** bliss, ecstasy, elation, elevation, exaltation, joy, jubilance, jubilation, nirvana, rapture, transport
**euphoric** blissful, cheered, contented, delighted, delirious, ecstatic, elated, elevated, enchanted, enthusiastic, excited, exhilarated, exultant, fervent, frenzied, glad, gleeful, gratified, happy, joyful, joyous, jubilant, pleased, proud, rapturous, roused, satisfied, thrilled, transported
**Eurasian duck** pigeon
**Eurasian flower** comfrey
**Eurasian fresh-water fish** bream
**Eurasian maple tree** sycamore
**Eurasian plant** asarabacca
**Eurasian strait** Dardanelles
**Eurasian tree** medlar
**Eurasion finch** siskin
**eureka red** puce
**European** continental, Croat, Dane, Finn, French, Greek, Lapp, Serb, Slav, Slovak, Swede, Swiss
**European bay** Biscay
**European bird** cuckoo, finch, hoopoe, merle, ousel, ouzel, starling
**European bison** auroch
**European blackbird** merl(e), ousel, ouzel
**European canal** Kiel
**European cavalry man** Cossack, Hussar, u(h)lan
**European cereal** rye
**European clover** alsike
**European coal basin** Saar
**European coastal area** Riviera
**European country** Britain, France, Germany, Italy, Portugal, Spain
**Europe and America** Occident
**Europe and Asia** Eurasia
**European deer** roe
**European defence pact** NATO, Warsaw
**European dish of fish, rice and eggs** kedgeree

**European dung beetle** dor
**European family of bankers** Rothschild
**European finch** serin
**European fish** bream, chub, dab, dace, dory, ide, orfe, roach, rudd, ruff, sennet, tench, tope
**European flat fish** plaice
**European freshwater fish** tench
**European grand duchy** Luxembourg
**European gulf** Riga, Bothnia
**European gull** mew
**European hawk** faller
**European herb** anise, balm, bennet, clary, dill, dittany, fennel, hyssop, mint, savory, tarragon
**European herring** sprat
**European honeysuckle** woodbine
**European industrial basin** Saar, Ruhr
**European in India** feringhee
**European kite** glead, gled(e)
**European lake** Como, Constance, Garda, Geneva, Ladoga, Lugano, Onega, Vattern, Zurich
**European language** Danish, Finnish, French, German, Italian, Norwegian, Portuguese, Spanish, Swedish, Ugric
**European lavender** aspic
**European married lady in India** memsahib
**European mountain range** Alps, Pyrenees
**European nation** Austria, Belgium, Bosnia, Croatia, Denmark, England, Finland, France, Germany, Greece, Holland, Hungary, Ireland, Italy, Liechtenstein, Luxembourg, Monaco, Norway, Poland, Portugal, Romania, Russia, Scotland, Slovakia, Spain, Sweden, Switzerland, Yugoslavia
**European oak** durmast, holm
**European peninsula** Crimea, Iberia, Italy
**European plain** steppe
**European polecat** fitch(et), fitchew
**European principality** Liechtenstein, Monaco
**European rabbit** con(e)y, leporid
**European republic** Eire, France
**European resort** Cannes, Nice
**European river** Danube, Elba, Oder, Rhine, Tisza, Ure, Yser
**European river flowing into the Baltic** Oder
**European shark** tope
**European snake** adder, asp, viper
**European songbird** redstart
**European sparrow** whitecap
**European strait** Bosp(h)orus, Dover, Kattegat, Skaggerrak

**European subway** metro, tube, underground
**European swallow** martin
**European thrush** ousel, ouzel
**European toy dog** griffon
**European viper** adder, asp
**European winter wind** mistral
**European wolf dog** Alsatian
**evacuate** discharge, egest, eject, excrete, expel, void
**evade** avoid, dodge, elude, equivocate, escape, parry, prevaricate, sidestep
**evade an obligation** welch, welsh
**evade by trickery** dodge
**evade meanly** shirk
**evade payment** bilk
**evade the truth** dodge, hedge, waddle
**evaluate** appraise, approximate, ascertain, assay, assess, balance, calculate, compute, determine, estimate, find, judge, measure, price, rate, reckon, survey, valuate, value, weigh
**evaluate anew** reassess
**evaluation** analysis, appraisal, appreciation, assessment, attempt, calculation, calibration, charge, comment, criticism, duty, estimation, guess, impost, judg(e)ment, levy, notice, opinion, ordeal, proof, rate, reckoning, study, survey, tax, toll, trial, valuation
**evaluator** arbiter, assessor, connoisseur, critic, judge
**evanesce** disappear, fade
**evangelical** biblical, campaigning, canonical, charismatic, crusading, divine, evangelistic, inspired, missionary, orthodox, proselytising, scriptural, textual, zealous
**evaporate** dehydrate, disappear, dry, fade, vanish, vaporise
**evaporating rapidly** volatile
**evasion** avoidance, dodging, equivocation, escape, prevarication, quibbling
**evasive** cagey, deceitful, deceptive, devious, oblique, shifty, slippery, tricky
**evasive creature** eel
**evasive stratagem** subterfuge
**evasive talk** circumlocution
**even¹** balance(d), calm, commensurate, composed, e'en, equable, equal, equitable, fair, flat, impartial, indeed, just, level, parallel, placid, quite, quits, regular, smooth, standard, steady, still, temperate, tranquil, uniform, yet
**even both ways** level
**even chance** toss-up
**even if** albeit, (al)though, granting

**evening** Abend (G), dusk, e'en, eve, gloaming, nightfall, sundown, twilight
**evening before** eve
**evening coat** cloak, wrap
**evening gathering** soiree
**evening light** dusk, gloaming, twilight
**evening meal** dinner, supper
**evening moisture** dew
**evening music** nocturne, serenade
**evening party** soiree
**evening prayer** vesper
**evening reception** soiree
**evening service** vespers
**evening shoe** pump
**evening song** evensong, nocturne, serenade
**evening star** Hesper(us), Venus, Vesper
**evening twilight** gloaming
**evenly balanced** equal
**evenly distribute weight** balance
**evenly proportioned** equal
**evenness of mind** equanimity
**even now** already, yet
**even of surface** smooth
**even so** nevertheless, nonetheless, quand même (F), still, yet
**evensong** vesper
**even supposing** albeit
**event** action, affair, business, circumstance, consequence, episode, experience, exploit, fact, happening, incident, matter, milestone, occasion, occurrence, outcome, rei (L), result, subsequence
**even temper** forbearance, patience
**eventful** active, busy, critical, exciting, fateful, important, momentous, notable, remarkable
**even the score** avenge, equalise, reciprocate, repay, requite
**even the score for** avenge
**even the smallest amount** any
**even though** if, albeit
**event in history** affair, episode, incident
**event in which persons compete** competition
**event that is unexpected** accident
**eventual** anticipated, approaching, closing, coming, concluding, conditional, consequent, contingent, decisive, dependent, destined, end(ing), ensuing, expected, extreme, fated, final, forthcoming, furthest, future, imminent, impending, inevitable, last, later, latest, likely, possible, prospective, subsequent, succeeding, terminating, ultimate, unborn
**eventuality** accident, case, chance, circumstance, coincidence,

contingency, crisis, emergency, event, fluke, happening, likelihood, luck, mishap, occurrence, outcome, possibility, probability
**eventual outcome** upshot
**eventuate** bechance, befall, betide, conclude, end, follow, happen, issue, occur, result
**even up** align
**eve of** erev
**ever** always, ay, constantly, continuously, e'er, eternally, everlasting, forever, frequently, persistently, relentlessly, repeatedly
**ever and anon** intermittently, occasionally, often, periodically, sometimes
**Everest mountain peak** Lhotse
**everglade** swamp
**everglade state** Florida
**evergreen** eternal, immortal, perpetual, unchangeable, young
**evergreen American tree** sapodilla
**evergreen bean** carob
**evergreen forest** pinewoods
**evergreen fragrant shrub** rosemary
**evergreen oak** holm, ilex
**evergreen shrub** box, furze, holly, juniper, magnolia, myrtle, oleander, rhododendron
**evergreen tree** balsam, carob, cedar, cryptomeria, fir, laurel, olive, pine, quassia, savin, spruce, yew
**ever in fashion** dateless
**everlasting** absolute, aeonian, ageless, boundless, constant, endless, enduring, eternal, eternity, immortal, imperishable, indestructible, infinite, keeping, lasting, perennial, permanent, perpetual, sempiternal, timeless, undying, unending
**everlasting flower** immortelle
**everlasting plant** orpine
**every** all, any, each, entire, ilk(a) (Sc), whatever, whole
**every bit of** all
**everybody** ones, all
**every car must have it** oil
**every day** daily, quotidian
**every eight years** octennial
**every item** all
**every night** nightly
**every ninth** nona-, enneadic
**every once in a while** infrequent, occasional, periodic
**every one** all, each, everybody, us
**everyone for himself** sauve qui peut (F)
**every one of** all
**every one taken separately** each

**everyone to his taste** chacun à son goût (F)
**every other** alternate
**every sennight** weekly
**everything** all, be-all, raison d'être (F)
**everything included** altogether
**everything in its right place** order
**every three months** quarterly
**every three years** triennially
**every time** always
**every time that** whenever
**every twenty-four hours** daily
**every two months** bimonthly
**every two years** biennial
**everywhere** about, always, around, extensively, invariably, omni-, omnipresently, pervasive, throughout, ubique (L), ubiquitously, uniformly, universally
**Eve's garden** Eden
**Eve's mate** Adam
**Eve's temptation** apple
**Eve's tempter** Satan, serpent
**evict** dislodge, dispossess, eject, expel, expropriate, foreclose, oust, remove, unhouse
**evicting officer** bailiff
**evidence** attest, certification, confirmation, denote, detonation, grounds, indication, information, manifest, mark, proof, show, sign, signal, support, testify, testimony, witness
**evidence giver** witness
**evident** apparent, apprehensible, clear, express, manifest, obvious, overt, palpable, patent, perceivable, perceptible, plain, salient, transparent, understandable, visible
**evil** amoral, bad(ness), base, corrupt, depraved, disaster, harm(ful), heinous, ill, immoral, iniquitous, iniquity, malevolent, malicious, malignant, misery, naughtiness, nefarious, pain, pernicious, sin(ful), sorrow, unfortunate, vicious, vile, wicked(ness), woe, wrong
**evil act** crime, maleficence, misdeed, sin
**evil deed** malefaction
**evil demon in Muslim mythology** afreet, afrit
**evil-doer** criminal, felon, malefactor, miscreant, sinner, villain
**evil evoked on other** curse
**evil goddess** Ate
**evil habit** vice
**evil in principle** wicked
**evil intent** malice
**evil Norse god** Loki
**evil Russian monk** Rasputin

**evil-smelling** malodorous, noisome, noxious, rank
**evil spell** hex
**evil spirit** (caco)demon, devil, fiend, ghoul, imp, poltergeist, Puck
**evil spirit of the sea** Davy Jones
**evince** argue, betoken, betray, demonstrate, denote, disclose, display, divulge, evidence, exhibit, expose, imply, indicate, manifest, open, present, render, reveal, show, signify, suggest, tell, uncover, unmask, unveil
**evince sorrow** weep
**Evita Bezuidenhout's ambassadorship** Bapetikosweti
**Evita Perón's country** Argentina
**evocative** arousing, awakening, educative, exciting, kindling, reminiscent, provocative, sensitive, stimulating, stirring, striking, suggestive
**evoke** adjure, antagonise, arouse, awaken, call, cause, educe, elicit, excite, induce, invite, obtest, produce, provoke, recall, rekindle, remind, stimulate, stir, suggest, summon
**evoke evil upon** excoriate, execrate, inveigh
**evoking pity** pathetic
**evolve** develop, educe, emit, enlarge, expand, generate, grow, increase, mature, unfold, unroll, yield
**evolve into** become
**evolvement** development, enlargement
**ewer** jug, pitcher, toilet-jug
**ewe's mate** ram
**ex** former, from, outdated
**exacerbate** aggravate, annoy, enrage, exaggerate, exasperate, heighten, incense, increase, inflame, infuriate, intensify, irritate, magnify, worsen
**exact** accurate, careful, close, compel, correct, demand(ing), exacting, extract, faithful, force, literal, orderly, precise, require, rigid, rigorous, scrupulous, severe, strict, true
**exact copy** duplicate, facsimile, image, replica
**exact copy of writing** facsimile
**exact counterpart** match, same
**exact likeness** image
**exactly** accurately, assuredly, definitely, indeed, perfectly, precisely, quite, scrupulously, strictly
**exactly alike** identical
**exactly like another example** duplicate
**exactly place** pinpoint
**exactly suitable** very
**exactly the same** identical
**exactly upright** perpendicular

**exactness** accurateness, carefulness, correctness, definiteness, exactitude, faithfulness, faultlessness, literalness, nicety, orderliness, precision, promptitude, regularity, rightness, rigorousness, scrupulousness, strictness, trueness, truth, veracity

**exact opposite** antipode, antithesis

**exact retribution for** revenge

**exaggerate** amplify, emphasise, exalt, magnify, overdo, overstate

**exaggerated fear of thunder and lightning** astraphobia, astrophobia

**exaggerated feeling of elation** euphoria

**exaggerated patriotism** chauvinism

**exaggerated statement not meant to be taken literally** hyperbole

**exaggerate the performance** overact

**exaggeration** amplification, exaltation, excess, overstatement, pretension

**exalt** appreciate, compliment, dignify, elate, elevate, encore, endorse, ennoble, extol, glorify, honour, intensify, please, praise, promote, raise, revere(nce), sanctify, sanction, stimulate, uplift

**exalted** commanding, dignified, elevated, eminent, ennobled, exultant, famed, glorified, grand, honourable, illustrious, incited, increased, inspired, joyous, lofty, renowned, stately, stimulated, sublime, triumphant

**exaltedness** augustness, elevation, grandness, highness, loftiness, prestigiousness

**exalted personage** panjandrum

**exalted state of feeling** ecstasy

**exalt in rank** elevate

**exalt maliciously** gloat

**exalt the spirits** elate

**examination** analysis, check-up, exam, exploration, inquiry, inquisition, inspection, investigation, observation, perusal, questioning, quiz, review, scrutiny, search, study, test, trial

**examination by X-rays** radioscopy

**examination glass** slide

**examination in court** trial

**examination in depth** study

**examination of accounts** audit

**examination of cadaver** autopsy

**examination of coins by an expert** shroffage

**examination of records** research

**examination of the urine** uroscopy

**examination of tissue cut from living body** biopsy

**examine** analyse, assess, explore, inquire, inspect, interrogate, investigate, look, peruse, probe, pry, research, scan, scrutinise, search, spy, study, survey, test, try, vet, weigh

**examine account books** audit

**examine again** reinspect

**examine and correct** revise

**examine and note** observe

**examine and set in order** overhaul

**examine and verify** audit

**examine by touch** feel, palpate

**examine critically** peruse, scan, scrutinise

**examine curiously** browse

**examine hastily** scan

**examine in court** question, try

**examine in detail** analyse, peruse

**examine minutely** scan, scrutinise, sift

**examine officially** inspect

**examine one's own thoughts** introspection

**examiner** censor, checker, critic, inquirer, inspector, investigator, overseer, researcher, reviewer, scrutineer, sleuth, supervisor, tester

**examiner of account** auditor

**examiner of votes** scrutineer

**examine searchingly** probe

**examine thoroughly** canvass

**example** case, criterion, experiment, ideal, illustration, instance, model, norm, paradigm, pattern, piece, precedent, problem, question, representative, sample, specific, specimen, test

**exasperate** anger, annoy, embitter, enrage, excite, gall, incense, inflame, infuriate, irk, irritate, madden, nettle, pique, provoke, rankle, rouse, vex

**excavate** burrow, channel, cut, delve, dig, disinter, dredge, exhume, extract, gouge, hollow, mine, quarry, scoop, tunnel, uncover, unearth

**exceed** beat, better, eclipse, excel, outdistance, outdo, outreach, outrun, outstrip, overdo, overtake, surmount, (sur)pass, top, transcend, transgress

**exceedingly** enormously, especially, exceptionally, extremely, greatly, highly, hugely, inordinately, superlatively, unusually, vastly, very

**exceedingly fine** superfine

**exceedingly important** essential

**exceeding the permitted limits** excessive

**exceed numerically** outnumber

**excel** beat, dominate, eclipse, exceed, outclass, outdo, outrank, outrival, outshine, outstrip, surmount, (sur)pass

**excellence** advantage, asset, distinction, eminence, feature, goodness, merit, plus, quality, superiority, virtue

**excellent** à la bonne heure (F), admirable, better, choice, classic, exceptional, fine, first-rate, good, grand, great, masterful, masterly, notable, perfect, pre-eminent, prime, rare, select, splendid, striking, super(b), superior, superlative, supreme, swell, top-notch, worthy

**excellent symbol** A

**excelling all others** best, pre-eminent

**except** bar(ring), besides, but, eliminate, excepting, exclude, excluding, lest, minus, omit(ting), reject, remove, save, spurn, unless

**except for** but

**except if** unless

**exception** anomaly, deviation, difference, disallowance, elimination, exclusion, exemption, inconsistency, omission, rarity, rejection, segregation, separation

**exceptional** aberrant, abnormal, especial, excellent, extraordinary, irregular, marvellous, outstanding, phenomenal, prodigious, rare, remarkable, special, superior, unusual

**exceptional ability** genius

**exceptionally** excellently, extraordinarily, marvellously, outstandingly, phenomenally, prodigiously, remarkably, specially, superiorly, unusually

**exceptional person** greatest, rara avis

**except on the condition that** unless

**except that mentioned** else

**except when** unless

**excess** debauchery, exceed, intemperance, nimiety, outrage, overactive, overindulgence, redundancy, remainder, spillover, superfluity, surplus

**excess baggage** overweight

**excess body water** dropsy

**excess fat** flab

**excess in eating** surfeit

**excessive** dear, exaggerated, exorbitant, extravagant, extreme, immoderate, inordinate, needless, redundant, superfluous, ultra, undue, unreasonable, vehement

**excessive adherence to law** legalism

**excessive admiration for books** bibliolatry, bibliomania

**excessive admiration of great person** hero-worship

**excessive amount** spate
**excessive amount of blood in an organ** hyperaemia
**excessive commotion** fuss
**excessive contraction of the pupil** miosis, myosis
**excessive craving after wealth** avarice
**excessive desire** erotomania
**excessive desire for wealth** greed
**excessive devotion to animals** zoolatry
**excessive dilation of the pupil** mydriasis
**excessive dose** overdose
**excessive dryness of the cornea and conjuctiva** xerophthalmia
**excessive eater** glutton
**excessive enlargement of artery** aneurism, aneurysm
**excessive enthusiasm** mania
**excessive erotic desire** erotomania
**excessive fear of heights** acrophobia
**excessive flattery** adulation
**excessive flow of words** logorrhoea
**excessive force** violence
**excessive growth of hands, feet and face** acromegaly
**excessive insistence on correct language** purism
**excessive labour** travail
**excessively** amazingly, copiously, enormously, exaggeratedly, exceedingly, extraordinarily, extravagantly, extremely, immoderately, inordinately, needlessly, outrageously, prodigally, profusely, superfluously, too, troppo, unduly, unnecessarily, unreasonably
**excessively attached to one's wife** uxorious
**excessively aware** hyperconscious
**excessively dry** arid
**excessively elevated** skyhigh
**excessively fashionable man** dandy, fop
**excessively fond of one's wife** uxorious
**excessively formal and conventional** stodgy
**excessively frugal** parsimonious
**excessively hot** canicular
**excessively particular about small details** meticulous
**excessively refined** alembicated, precious
**excessively respectful** obsequious
**excessively self-assertive** pushy
**excessively sensual person** debauchee, sybarite
**excessively sentimental film** tear-jerker
**excessively small** boxy

**excessive outward curvature of the spine** kyphosis
**excessive praise** adulation
**excessive pride in oneself** conceit
**excessive quantity of blood in tissues** hyperaemia
**excessive respect for English customs** Anglomania
**excessive sexual desire in men** satyriasis
**excessive sexual desire in women** nymphomania
**excessive tissue fluid** oedema
**excessive work** overwork
**excessive zeal** zealotry
**excess of blood in lower parts of organs** hypostasis
**excess of chances** odds
**excess of fluid in the tissues** oedema
**excess of nominal value** premium
**excess of red corpuscles in the blood** plethora
**excess sugar disorder** diabetes
**excess value of one currency over another** agio
**exchange** bandy, barter, Bourse, business, commerce, finance, (inter)change, market, mart, reciprocity, requite, shuffle, substitution, swap, switch, swop, trade, transfer
**exchange allowance** agio
**exchange blows** box
**exchange by way of barter** swap, swop
**exchange cheque** encash
**exchange for cash** sale, sell
**exchange for something else** commute
**exchange goods** barter
**exchange in commerce** trade
**exchange letters** correspond
**exchange of a commodity for money** sale
**exchange of ideas** dialogue
**exchange of merchandise** commerce
**exchange premium** agio
**exchequer** assets, capital, coffer, finances, funds, purse, resources, revenues, treasury, wealth
**excise** curette, cut, delete, erase, expunge, expurgate, kill, scratch
**excise-man** ga(u)ger, receiver
**excision** abolition, annihilation, death, extermination, extinction, obliteration, oblivion
**excision of a lung** lobectomy, pneumonectomy
**excision of lobe of an organ** lobectomy
**excitable** choleric, edgy, emotional, fiery, hasty, highly strung, irascible, nervous, passionate, sensitive, violent, volatile
**excite** affect, agitate, animate, arouse, awaken, discompose, disturb, elate, engender, evoke, fire, foment, galvanise, generate, ignite, impress, incite, induce, inflame, initiate, instigate, kindle, motivate, move, provoke, rouse, stimulate, stir, sway, thrill, touch, upset, waken, warm, whet
**excited** agitated, agog, discomposed, eager, elated, enthusiastic, keen, perturbed, red-hot, roused, ruffled, stimulated, thrilled
**excited activity** bustle
**excited feeling** sensation, thrill
**excited state of feeling** emotion
**excite emotionally** incite, stir
**excitement** ado, adventure, animation, elation, ferment, frenzy, interest, stir, thrill, tumult
**excite mirth** amuse
**excite pleasantly** titillate
**excite to action** impel
**excite to anger** irritate
**exciting** agitating, arousing, awakening, disturbing, electrifying, evoking, exhilarating, firing, fomenting, galvanising, heady, inciting, inflaming, inspiring, intoxicating, moving, provocative, provoking, quickening, rousing, sensational, stimulating, stirring, thrilling, titillating, wakening
**exciting novel** thriller
**exciting sneezing** ptarmic
**exclaim** bawl, bellow, ejaculate, shout, squall, vociferate, yell
**exclamation** ach, ah(a), call, cry, ejaculation, gee, oh, outcry, shout, (w)ow, yell
**exclamation for attention** ahem
**exclamation of contempt** tush
**exclamation of discovery** aha
**exclamation of disgust** pah, pshaw, ugh, yah, yuck
**exclamation of exertion** phew
**exclamation of grief** alas
**exclamation of joy** hurrah
**exclamation of pain** ouch, ow
**exclamation of pleasure** ah
**exclamation of praise to God** hallelujah, hosanna
**exclamation of questioning surprise** eh
**exclamation of relief** phew, whew
**exclamation of scorn** phooey
**exclamation of sorrow** alas
**exclamation of surprise** gee, hah, lor, oh, oops, wow

**exclamation of triumph** eureka, ha, voilà (F)
**exclamation of woe** alas
**exclamation to call attention** hey
**exclamation to stop** whoa
**exclamation to surprise a child** boo
**exclude** ban, (de)bar, depose, disallow, eject, eliminate, embargo, except, exile, expel, forbid, ignore, interdict, isolate, occlude, omit, ostracise, oust, preclude, prevent, prohibit, proscribe, refuse, reject, relegate, remove, repudiate, restrain, shut out, veto
**exclude from admission** debar
**exclude from consideration** eliminate
**exclude from society** exile, ostracise
**exclusion** ban(ishment), bar, constraint, debarment, denial, discharge, disenablement, disentitlement, dismissal, disqualification, ejection, elimination, eviction, exception, exile, expulsion, forbiddance, incompetence, ineligibility, injunction, obstruction, omission, preclusion, prevention, prohibition, proscription, rebuff, refusal, rejection, removal, repudiation, restriction, unconformity, veto
**exclusive** all, alone, antithetical, chic, choice, choosy, cliquish, complete, elect, elegant, entire, excluding, expensive, fancy, fashionable, high-priced, incompatible, individual, inimical, luxurious, narrow, omit, one, only, particular, posh, rare, restrictive, select(ive), single, snobbish, sole, special, swanky, total
**exclusive circle** clique, coterie
**exclusive group** clique, elect, elite
**exclusively** all, alone, entirely, only, singly, solely
**exclusive news story** scoop
**exclusive of** before
**exclusive person** snob
**exclusive possession of the trade in some commodity** monopoly
**exclusive right** prerogative
**exclusive set of people** clique, cabal, elect, elite
**excommunicate** anathematise, banish, deny, deport, depose, eject, eliminate, exclude, exile, expatriate, expel, forget, preclude, reject, relegate, repudiate, segregate, separate, unchurch
**excrement** contamination, defilement, dirt, droppings, dung, egesta, excreta, faeces, feculence, filth, filthiness, foulness, garbage, grime, manure, muck, nastiness, ordure, pollution, refuse, sewage, slime, sludge, squalor, stools, uncleanness
**excremental opening** anus
**excrescence** appendage, boil, branch, carbuncle, excretion, extension, lump, offshoot, outgrowth, pimple, pock, prominence, protuberance, pustule, swelling, whelk
**excrete** defecate, discharge, egest, eject, eliminate, emit, evacuate, expel, exude, pass, perspire, sweat, urinate, vent, void
**excrete from skin** sweat, perspire
**excretion** defecation, egestion, evacuation, extrusion, exudation, perspiration, secretion, smegma, sweat, urination, urine, voidance
**excretory cavity of birds** cloaca
**exculpate** absolve, acquit, clear, discharge, dismiss, excuse, exonerate, free, justify, pardon, release, vindicate
**excursion** airing, cruise, deviation, digression, drive, excursus, expedition, hike, jaunt, journey, junket, outing, ramble, ride, sightseeing, stroll, tour, trip, voyage, walk
**excursionist** reveller, sightseer, tourist, traveller, tripper
**excursive** devious, digressive, diverse
**excusable negligence** culpa levis (L)
**excuse** absolve, acquit, alibi, apology, clear, evasion, exculpate, exempt, exonerate, forgive, free, justification, justify, liberate, overlook, palliate, pardon, plea, pretence, release, vindicate
**excused liability** exempt
**excuse of any kind** alibi
**excuse used in court** alibi
**execrable** abominable, blighted, confounded, contemptible, damnable, deplorable, detestable, disreputable, doomed, foul, heinous, horrible, loathsome, obnoxious, opprobrious, repellent, repulsive, revolting, scandalous, shameful, terrible, unholy, unsanctified, vile, villainous
**execrate** abhor, abominate, curse, denounce, despise, detest, excoriate, hate, loathe, revile
**execute** achieve, administer, administrative, administrator, boss, director, effect(uate), enforce, finish, hang, kill, leadership, manager, perform, sign, supervisor
**execute in electric chair** electrocute
**executers** firing squad
**execute without trial** lynch
**execution by drowning** noyade
**execution by electricity** electrocute
**execution by petrol-soaked tyre** necklace
**executioner** annihilator, assassin, decapitator, executionist, exterminator, hangman, headsman, killer, lyncher, murderer, slaughterer, slayer
**executioner's rope** noose
**executive part of a government** administration
**executive team** management
**exemplary** admirable, cautionary, commendable, correct, epitomic, estimable, excellent, faultless, flawless, good, honourable, ideal, illustrative, laudable, meritorius, model, monitory, noble, outstanding, perfect, praiseworthy, quality, sample, sterling, typical, warning, worthy
**exemplify** demonstrate, depict, display, exhibit, illustrate, manifest, represent, show, typify
**exempt** absolve, clear, excuse, free, liberate, release, spare
**exemption from penalty** indemnity
**exemption from punishment** impunity
**exercise** action, activity, annoy, apply, discharge, discipline, drill, employ(ment), exert(ion), labour, operation, perform(ance), practise, procedure, ritual, schooling, train(ing), trouble, use, wield, work, worry
**exercise an opinion** opt
**exercise authority** preside
**exercise control** dominate
**exercised by person** spell
**exercise hall** gym(nasium)
**exercise horse on long rein** lunge
**exercise in a profession** practice
**exercise of reason** noesis
**exercise of skill** art
**exercise of the will** volition
**exerciser** gymnast
**exercise to keep one healthy** keep-fit
**exercise to prepare for exertion** limber up
**exercising delegated power** vicegerent
**exercising hall** gym(nasium)
**exercising sound judgement** prudential
**exercising the mind** thinking
**exert** apply, employ, exercise, expend, spend, use, utilise, wield
**exert control** predominate
**exert force** press
**exertion** action, activity, application, attempt, diligence, effort, employ,

exercise, industry, strain, stretch, struggle, toil, trial, use
**exertion of energy** action, activity
**exert oneself** attempt, concentrate, drive, drudge, endeavour, grind, labour, plod, push, slave, strain, strive, struggle, sweat, toil, work
**exert pressure on** squeeze
**exert to the utmost** strain, stretch
**exhalation** breath, effluvium, evaporation, mist, vapour
**exhale** belch, blow, breathe, discharge, dissipate, eject, emanate, emit, evaporate, expel, expire, exude, fan, gasp, huff, pant, puff, radiate, release, sigh, transmit, vent, waft, whiff
**exhale loudly through nostrils** snore, snort
**exhale noisily** sigh, snort
**exhaust** collapse, consume, deflate, deplete, dissipate, drain, empty, enervate, expend, extract, fag, fatigue, finish, fumes, lethargise, outlet, prostrate, sap, spend, spill, tire, vapour, waste, weaken, weary
**exhausted** beat, breathless, consumed, debilitated, depleted, disabled, dog-tired, drained, drowsy, effete, enervated, enfeebled, fatigued, feeble, haggard, overtired, run-down, spent, tired, weak, weary
**exhausted state** frazzle
**exhaust from rocket engine** jet-stream
**exhausting work** toil
**exhaustion** breakdown, collapse, debility, delicacy, depletion, disintegration, distress, enervation, failure, faint(ness), fatigue, feebleness, frailty, incapacity, languor, lassitude, lethargy, prostration, sickliness, tiredness, wastefulness, weakness, weariness
**exhaustion from lack of nourishment** inanition
**exhaust-pipe discharge** emission, fumes
**exhaust the strength** drain, enfeeble, impoverish
**exhibit** demonstrate, demonstration, disclose, display, evidence, exhibition, expose, exposition, express, offer(ing), reveal, show(ing)
**exhibiting sangfroid** nerveless
**exhibit intense anger** rage
**exhibition** demonstration, display, exhibit, expo(sition), fair, presentation, show
**exhibition example** showpiece
**exhibitionist** show-off
**exhibition of cowboy skills** rodeo
**exhibition of illusions** phantasm

**exhibition of products** fair
**exhibition room** gallery, museum, salon
**exhibit scorn** sneer
**exhilarate** animate, brighten, cheer, comfort, console, elate, elevate, encourage, enliven, excite, gladden, hearten, incite, inspire, invigorate, rejoice, rouse, solace, stimulate
**exhilarating** bracing, brisk, crisp, exciting, inspiring, lively, provocative, refreshing, rousing, sapid, sensational, stimulating, thrilling, tonic, vigorous
**exhort** advise, beseech, bid, encourage, entreat, goad, incite, persuade, spur, urge, warn
**exhume** disentomb, disinter, unbury, unearth
**exigency** constraint, crisis, demand, difficulty, emergency, extremity, hardship, necessity, need, pass, pinch, plight, predicament, quandary, requirement, strait
**exigent** clamorous, demanding, dogged, earnest, emphatic, exacting, forceful, importunate, insistent, persistent, pressing, urgent
**exiguous** meagre, scanty, slender, small
**exile** absence, alien, banish(ment), deport(ee), dislocate, displacement, ejection, émigré, evict(ion), exclusion, expatriate, expel, expulsion, fugitive, maroon, ostracise, oust, outcaste, outlaw, outlawry, penalty, poor, refugee, relegate, ruin, seclude, separation, uprooting
**exiled person** outcast
**exist** abide, am, are, be, befall, breathe, continue, endure, ensure, eventuate, happen, is, last, live, obtain, occur, prevail, remain, respire, stand, stay, subsist, survive
**existence** actuality, animation, being, breath, continuance, creation, duration, endurance, esse (L), life, reality, subsistence, survival
**existence of several meanings in a single word** polysemy
**existent** active, actual, alive, animate, current, existing, extant, functioning, live, living, operative, prevailing, vital
**existent thing** reality
**existing** alive, being
**existing alone** single
**existing at same period** coeval
**existing at the same time** concurrent, simultaneous
**existing but not developed** latent
**existing condition** actuality

**existing for a time but not lasting** transitory
**existing for many years** long-standing
**existing from the beginning** original, primordial
**existing from the first** original
**existing in fact** actual
**existing in great quantity** much
**existing in large amounts** copious
**existing in name only** nominal
**existing in plentiful supply** abundant
**existing in space** spatial
**existing in the mind** abstract, ideal
**existing in the present** actual
**existing only in name** nominal
**existing since a person's birth** congenital
**existing thing** reality
**exist on small pittance** eke
**exist together** coexist
**exist widely** prevail
**exit** departure, egress, escape, exodus, going, outlet, retirement, retreat
**exodus** departure, emigration, escape, evacuation, exit, fleeing, flight, hegira, hejira, leaving, migration, recession, retirement, retreat, withdrawal
**ex officio** honorary
**exonerate** absolve, acquit, clear, condone, discharge, dismiss, except, exculpate, excuse, exempt, free, justify, liberate, pardon, release, relieve, vindicate
**exorbitant** enormous, exceeding, excessive, extravagant, inordinate, unreasonable
**exorbitant price** steep
**exorcise** adjure, disenchant, expel, purify, unspell
**exotic** alien, bizarre, curious, extrinsic, fascinating, foreign, introduced, naturalised
**exotic flower** orchid
**exotic objects** exotica
**exotic ocean bird** sea-coot
**expand** accrue, aggrandise, amass, amplify, boost, develop, dilate, distend, enhance, enlarge, exaggerate, extend, grow, increase, inflate, open, reinforce, spread, strengthen, stretch, supplement, swell, unfold
**expanse** abyss, amount, area, breadth, capacity, chasm, degree, desert, extension, extent, field, immensity, largeness, leeway, plain, quantity, range, scope, space, stretch, sweep, tract, vastness, void, waste
**expanse of salt water** ocean, sea
**expanse of the universe** space

**expanse of water** dam, lake, sea
**expansion** broadening, diffusement, dilation, enhancement, enlargement, growth, increase, magnification, widening
**expatriate** banish, castaway, deport, dismiss, emigrant, émigré, exclude, exile, expel, isolate, oust, outcast, outlaw, pariah, proscribe, refugee, relegate, seclude
**expect** anticipate, assume, await, forecast, hope, imagine, presume, reckon, surmise, wish
**expectant** abiding, agape, agog, eager, enceinte, eventual, expected, expecting, gravid, imminent, pregnant, ready, vigilant
**expectation** belief, confidence, fear, hope, promise, reliance, trust, wish
**expectation of trouble** foreboding
**expected now** due
**expecting things to go well** sanguine
**expectorate** cough, discharge, eject, eruct, excrete, expel, hawk, hiss, spit, splutter
**expect that results will be good** optimism
**expect with desire** hope
**expediency** advisability, appropriateness, aptness, benefit, convenience, effectiveness, fitness, helpfulness, pragmatism, profitability, prudence, suitability, usefulness, utility
**expedient** advantageous, advisable, appropriate, convenient, helpful, pragmatic, source
**expedite** accelerate, despatch, dispatch, hasten, precipitate, quicken
**expedition** despatch, dispatch, exploration, haste, journey, promptness, safari, speed
**expel** banish, deport, depose, discard, discharge, dismiss, dispossess, egest, eject, eliminate, evict, exclude, excrete, exile, extrude, oust, reject, relegate, remove, turn, void
**expel air from lungs** cough, exhale
**expel by legal process** evict
**expend** consume, disburse, dissipate, drain, empty, exhaust, invest, spend, squander, use
**expenditure** application, charge, consumption, cost, disbursement, expense, outgo, outlay, output, pay(ment), price, recompense, remuneration, reward, spending, use
**expenditure of energy** work
**expenditure of time** cost
**expend strength** exert
**expend uselessly** waste

**expense** amount, charge, consumption, cost(liness), depletion, disbursement, drain, exhaustion, expenditure, fare, fee, loss, outlay, output, overheads, price, quotation, rate, sacrifice, spending
**expense schedule** budget
**expensive** costly, dear, excessive, exorbitant, extravagant, high-priced, immoderate, inestimable, lavish, precious, rich, unreasonable, valuable, wasteful
**expensive fur** mink, sable
**experience** adventure, bear, contact, doing, encounter, endure, episode, event, evidence, exposure, face, feel, incident, know(ledge), observation, proof, sophistication, suffer, taste, test, try, undergo, wisdom
**experienced** able, competent, felt, master, skilled, trained, versed, veteran, wise
**experienced actor** trouper
**experienced and trusted adviser** confidante, mentor
**experienced flier** ace
**experienced sailor** salt
**experience pain** suffer
**experience teaches fools** experienta docet stultos (L)
**experiment** assay, examination, examine, research, test, trial, try
**experimental** conjectural, empirical, exploratory, hypothetical, indefinite, pending, preliminary, probative, provisional, questionable, speculative, tentative, test, theoretic, trail, untried
**experimental workshop** laboratory
**expert** able, ace, acquaint, adept, adroit, advise, apt, authority, champion, clever, cognoscente (I), connoisseur, critic, educate, experienced, genius, learned, maestro, master(ful), mavin, notify, prodigy, proficient, pundit, quick, skilled, specialist, trained, versed
**expert airman** ace
**expert aviator** ace
**expert cook** chef
**expert in financial exchange** cambist
**expert in Hebrew** Hebraist
**expert in Jewish law** dayan
**expert in judo** judoka
**expert in karate** karateka
**expert in linguistics** grammarian, linguist
**expert in logic** logician
**expert in natural history** naturalist
**expert in precious stones** gemmologist

**expert instructor at golf club** pro
**expertise** ableness, adroitness, aptness, art, cleverness, command, deftness, dexterity, expertness, facility, judg(e)ment, knack, know-how, knowledge, mastery, proficiency, prowess, skilfulness, skill, virtuosity
**expert judge** connoisseur
**expert knowledge** expertise
**expert level in karate** dan
**expertly** ably, adeptly, adroitly, aptly, cleverly, deftly, handily, knowledgeably, proficiently, skilfully
**expertness** adeptness, adroitness, aptness, cleverness, deftness, dexterity, handiness, judg(e)ment, mastery, proficiency, skilfulness, skill
**expert of law** lawyer
**expert on past** historian
**expert person** dab
**expert pilot** ace
**expiate** atone, offset, pay, recompense, redeem, remedy, shrive
**expiation** amends, atonement, compensation, indemnity, quittance, redemption, redress, reparation, requital, satisfaction
**expiator** penitent, atoner
**expiration** bereavement, death, decease, demise, departure, dying, end, exit, loss, passing, quietus, release
**expiration of air** exhalation
**expire** cease, complete, conclude, decease, die, discontinue, elapse, emit, end, exhale, extinct, finish, lapse, pant, pass, perish, respire, sigh, stop, terminate, void
**expiring** ceasing, closing, concluding, departing, dying, ending, finishing, lapsing, perishing, stopping, terminating
**explain** answer, clarify, decode, define, delineate, describe, elucidate, explicate, expound, interpret, justify, reveal, simplify, solve, unravel, warrant
**explain a word** define
**explain by example** demonstrate, illustrate
**explain in detail** expound
**explanation** account, definition, elucidation, explication, interpretation, meaning, reason, solution
**explanation of conduct** account
**explanation of passage of Scripture** exegesis
**explanatory comment added to text** gloss
**explanatory example** illustration

**explanatory note** annotation, comment
**explanatory text** key
**explicable** accountable, definable, describable, explainable, intelligible, interpretable, resolvable, understandable
**explicit** categorical, certain, clear, definite, direct, distinct, exact, express, frank, open, outspoken, patent, plain, positive, precise, specific, stated, unambiguous, unequivocal, unqualified, unreserved
**explode** blast, burst, detonate, discharge, discredit, disprove, erupt, fulminate, invalidate, pop, puncture, rebut, refute, repudiate, ridicule, shatter, shoot
**explode softly** pop
**explode with sudden force** detonate
**exploding star** nova
**exploit** abandon, accomplishment, achievement, advance, adventure, coup, cozen, deed, feat, further, improve, manoeuvre, maximise, milk, misuse, promote, stroke, stunt, trick, use, utilise
**exploit selfishly** use
**explore** analyse, examine, inspect, investigate, probe, prospect, research, scout, scrutinise, search, travel
**explore by touch** feel, palpate
**explosion** bang, blast, burst, clap, crack, detonation, discharge, eruption, fit, outburst, paroxysm, report
**explosion of a bomb in the air** airburst
**explosive** amatol, ammunition, bad, cordite, critical, dangerous, dynamite, emotional, fulminant, gelignite, grenade, gunpowder, inflammable, loaded, perilous, powder, pyrotechnic, strained, TNT, touchy, trinitrotoluene, unstable, volatile, volcanic
**explosive detonator** fuse
**explosive firework** cracker, petard
**explosive head of missile** warhead
**explosive mixture** dualin, firedamp, gunpowder, nitroglycerine
**explosive noise** bam, bang
**explosive projectile** bomb, shell
**explosive rating** megaton
**explosive shell** grenade
**explosive sound** bang, blast, pop
**explosive substance** gelignite, pyroxylin
**explosive toy** popgun
**ex-plum** prune
**exponent** advocate, backer, champion, defender, illustration, indication, interpreter, performer, presenter, promoter, spokesman, supporter, upholder
**export illegally** smuggle
**exposé** bare, disclosure, exposure, revelation, uncovering, unmasking, unveiling
**expose** air, bare, detect, disclose, display, endanger, exhibit, jeopardise, manifest, open, present, reveal, show, subject, uncover, unmask, unveil
**exposed to air** aerated, naked
**expose skin to sun** tan
**expose to air** aerate
**expose to danger** endanger, imperil, jeopardise
**expose to sun** insolate
**expose to view** disclose, open, reveal, show
**exposition** annotation, critique, demonstration, desertion, disclosure, discourse, display, exegesis, exhibition, explanation, explication, exposure, fair, helplessness, market, performance, presentation, revelation, review, thesis, treatise
**exposure** abandonment, admission, airing, avowal, baring, broadcast, desertion, disclosure, display, divulgement, experience, exposé, exposition, forsaking, hazard, jeopardy, leak, liability, orientation, presentation, publication, report, revelation, risk, susceptibililty, uncovering, unmasking, unveiling, vulnerability
**exposure to injury** peril
**exposure to public scorn** pillory
**express** assert, asseverate, clear, courier, declare, definite, denote, designate, direct, distinct, exact, exhibit, explicit, expose, fast, indicate, manifest, obvious, outlet, particular, plain, rapid, represent, show, signify, singular, speak, state, swift, true, utter, vent, voice
**express a belief** opine
**express abhorrence** execrate
**express agreement** assent, subscribe
**express amusement** laugh
**express a negative reply** no
**express an opinion** opine
**express appreciation for** acknowledge
**express approval** applaud, cheer, clap, praise
**express audibly** utter
**express a view** opine
**express boredom** yawn
**express by action** gesture, signal
**express contempt** bah, boo, flout, hiss, scorn
**express derision** boo
**express disapproval** deprecate, object, protest, sneer
**express discontent** complain, nag
**express dissatisfaction** complain
**expressed in few words** terse
**expressed in one language** monolingual
**express fully in speech** state
**express gratitude** acknowledge, thank
**express grief by shedding tears** weep
**express highway** freeway
**express in different words** paraphrase, rephrase, reword
**express indirectly** allude, hint, imply
**express in English** anglicise
**express in fewer words** condense, summarise
**expressing a cause** causative
**expressing a desire** optative
**expressing a view** venturing an opinion
**expressing disgust** fie
**expressing duty** ought
**expressing elevated feeling** soulful
**expressing mild annoyance** flipping
**expressing mirth** laughing
**expressing motion** gesture
**expressing negation** not
**expressing opposition** adversative
**expressing pleasure** glad
**expressing rebuke** tut-tut
**expressing regret** apologetic, apologise, rueful
**expressing remorse** sorry
**expressing sharp pain** ouch
**expressing sorrow** rueful
**expressing sorrow by wearing black clothes** mourning
**expressing surprise** eh, golly, good heavens, gosh
**expressing threat** minatory
**expressing wish** optative
**express in words** state, utter, verbalise
**expression** announcement, assertion, communication, delivery, diction, discourse, explanation, idiom, indication, language, locution, mention, phrase, remark, saying, show, sign, speaking, speech, statement, symbol, term, token, utterance, word
**expression by hand motions** gesticulation
**expression in words** statement
**expressionless** blank, dead-pan, dry, dull, empty, hidden, inexplicable, inscrutable, mysterious, straight-faced, unimaginative, vacuous, wooden
**expression of affection** caress
**expression of alarm** cor
**expression of apology** sorry

**expression of approval** OK, okay, plaudit
**expression of contempt** sneer
**expression of denial** no
**expression of disapproval** censure
**expression of disbelief** aw, garn, nonsense
**expression of disgust** fie, pah, ugh, yuck
**expression of emphatic denial** (h)aikona
**expression of gratitude** thanks(giving)
**expression of grief** alas, lament
**expression of pain** groan, ouch, ow
**expression of pity** alas
**expression of refusal** no
**expression of scorn** sneer
**expression of sorrow** alas
**expression of surprise** eh, gee, golly, good heavens, gosh
**expressive gesture** nod, shrug
**expressly stated** explicit
**express manager** courier
**express mirth** laugh
**express objection** protest
**express one's view** opine
**express open disapproval of** decry
**express or hold the opinion** opine
**express permission** sanction
**express pity** alas
**express pleasure** purr, smile
**express pleasure at happiness** congratulate
**express position** at
**express regret** apologise
**express strong approval** applaud
**express strong disapproval** condemn
**express sympathy** condole, sympathise
**express the opinion** opine
**express utter disapproval of** condemn
**express verbally** speak, utter
**express view** opine
**expulsion** banning, bouncing, dismissal, ejection, evacuation, eviction, excretion, exile, isolation, ouster, removal
**expunge** abolish, cancel, dele(te), demolish, edit, efface, eliminate, eradicate, erase, excise, extirpate, obliterate, omit, quell, ravage, ruin, strike
**expunger** eraser
**expurgate** bowdlerise, censor, cleanse, cut, debilitate, delete, purge, remove, soften, weaken
**exquisite** admirable, appealing, beautiful, charming, choice, consummate, dainty, delicate, discriminating, elegant, keen, poignant, polished, precious,
priceless, rare, refined, select, sensitive, valuable
**exquisitely beautiful** lovely
**ex-serviceman** vet(eran)
**extant** active, actual, alive, current, existent, existing, functioning, live, living, operative, present(-day), prevailing
**extempore** ad lib, freely, impromptu, improvised, impulsively, offhand, spontaneously, suddenly, unprepared
**extemporise** ad lib, create, improvise, invent
**extend** attenuate, bestow, broaden, confer, continue, dilate, elongate, enlarge, expand, impart, increase, inflate, lengthen, lie, maintain, offer, perpetuate, present, prolong, protract, reach, sprawl, spread, stretch, submit, widen
**extendable tape** elastic
**extend across** bridge, cover, span
**extend a loan** renew
**extend downwards** dip
**extended family** ménage
**extended journey** tour, voyage
**extended view** panorama
**extended written contract** pact, treatise
**extend in duration** prolong
**extending far** far-reaching, great
**extending far down** deep
**extending uniformly in same direction** straight
**extend into territory of others** encroach
**extend over** cross, ford, lap, span, wade
**extend the upper beyond the lower** overlap
**extend to** reach
**extensive** broad, comprehensive, far-reaching, large, spacious, thorough, vast, wide
**extensive grassy treeless plain** llano
**extensively** widely
**extensive maze** labyrinth
**extensive treeless plain in Europe** steppe
**extensive view** panorama
**extensive voyage** peregrination
**extensor muscle** triceps
**extent** ambit, amount, amplitude, area, bounds, breadth, bulk, compass, degree, dimension, duration, expanse, length, limit, magnitude, measure, play, quantity, range, reach, scope, size, space, span, sphere, stretch, sweep, term, time, volume, width
**extent of divergence** angle
**extent of influence** incidence
**extent of land** acreage
**extent of pitch of musical instrument** range
**extent of reportage** coverage
**extent of surface** area
**exterior** appearance, extrinsic, face, foreign, mien, outer, outside, outward
**exterior curve of an arch** extrados
**exterior wall coating** pebble-dash
**exterminate** abolish, annihilate, destroy, eliminate, eradicate, extirpate
**extermination of a race** genocide
**external** alien, exterior, foreign, independent, outer, outward
**external angle** cant
**external angle of a building** quoin
**external appearance** guise
**external boundary** outline
**external corner of a wall** coign(e), cornerstone, quoin
**external covering** dress
**external form** figure, shape
**external part** outside
**external part of ear** auricle
**external shell of motor vehicle** bodywork
**external structure of a building** shell
**external to the mind** objective, real
**ex-Thai money** tical
**extinct** dead, ended, extinguished, obsolete, out, over, terminate
**extinct animal like an elephant** mammoth
**extinct bird** aepyornis, auk, dodo, jibi, moa, offbird, roc
**extinct bird of Mauritius** dodo
**extinct elephant** dinothere, mammoth, mastodon
**extinct European wild horse** tarpan
**extinct flightless New Zealand bird** moa
**extinct flying reptile** pterodactyl
**extinct gigantic sloth** mylodon
**extinct jumbo** mammoth
**extinct mammal** mastodon
**extinct ratite** moa
**extinct reptile** brontosaur(us), dinosaur, pterodactyl, pterosaur, tyrannosaurus
**extinct rhinoceros** toxodon
**extinct species of elephant** mammoth
**extinct volcano in Japan** Fuji
**extinct volcano in New Zealand** Egmont
**extinct wild ox** aurochs, urus
**extinct winged reptile** pterodactyl
**extinct zebra-like mammal** quagga
**extinguish** abolish, annihilate, destroy, douse, expunge, exterminate, kill, quench, smother, stifle

**extirpate** abolish, crush, deracinate, dissolve, eliminate, eradicate, excise, exterminate, overturn, purge, quash, remove, subdue, terminate, uproot, vanquish
**extol** acclaim, applaud, celebrate, commend, compliment, eulogise, exalt, glorify, laud, panegyrise, praise
**extol the attributes of** praise
**extort** ask, blackmail, bleed, coerce, command, compel, enjoin, exact, extract, force, make, milk, request, squeeze, threaten, wrench, wrest, wring
**extortionate lender** usurer
**extortionate lending** usury
**extortionist** blackmailer, extortioner, bloodsucker, wringer, exacter, vulture, vampire
**extort money** blackmail
**extort money from** bleed, squeeze
**extra** added, additional, ancillary, auxiliary, bye, especially, etcetera, further, more, odd, over, plus, redundant, spare, special, superfluity, supplementary, surplus
**extra amount** bonus
**extra card** joker
**extra clause** codicil
**extract** abstract, choose, citation, cite, compound, concentrate, cull, decoction, deduce, derive, develop, distil(late), divine, draw, educe, elicit, elixir, essence, evoke, evolve, exact, excerpt, express, extort, gather, get, glean, obtain, pull, quotation, quote, reap, remove, select(ion), tincture, understand, uproot, withdraw, wrest, wring
**extracted passage** excerpt
**extracted virtues of any drug** essence
**extract from book** excerpt
**extracting tool** pliers
**extract metal from ore** smelt
**extract money by fraudulent means** mulct
**extract of important ingredient** essence
**extract of the adrenal glands** adrenalin
**extract ore** mine
**extracurricular activities** moonlighting
**extra dividend** bonus
**extra hours of work** overtime
**extra in cricket** bye
**extra large** outsize
**extra long** maxi
**extraneous** absurd, conflicting, contradictory, contrary, discordant, immaterial, impertinent, improper, inapplicable, inapposite, inapt, incoherent, incongruous, inconsistent, inessential, insignificant, irrelevant, outer, trifling, trivial, unbecoming, unimportant, unrelated, unsuitable
**extraordinarily large** enormous
**extraordinary** abnormal, amazing, egregious, exceptional, fantastic, marvellous, notable, noteworthy, particular, peculiar, phenomenal, rare, remarkable, significant, singular, special, strange, striking, surprising, uncommon, unimaginable, unique, unprecedented, unusual, wonderful
**extraordinary in size** giant, huge
**extraordinary thing** oner
**extra pay** bonus
**extra pay in special cases** weighting
**extra payment** bonus, premium
**extra performance** encore
**extra run in cricket** bye
**extra-sensory perception** ESP
**extra song** encore
**extra supply** reserve, reservoir
**extra treat** bonus
**extra tyre** spare
**extravagance** exaggeration, excess, exorbitance, folly, improvidence, lavishness, outrageousness, overspending, overspending, preposterousness, prodigality, profligacy, profusion, recklessness, squandering, unrestrained, waste(fulness), wildness
**extravagant** absurd, bizarre, costly, excessive, exorbitant, expansive, fanciful, fantastic, flamboyant, flashy, foolish, garish, gaudy, grandiose, imprudent, lavish, ornate, ostentatious, outrageous, overpriced, preposterous, pretentious, prodigal, profligate, reckless, showy, spendthrift, unreasonable, wasteful, wild
**extravagant coarse satirical humour** Pantagruelism
**extravagantly fanciful** fantastic
**extravagantly odd** outré
**extravagantly ornamented** baroque, rococo
**extravagant person** spender, spendthrift, squanderer, waster, wastrel
**extreme** acute, arrant, dire, drastic, excessive, extravagant, fanatical, final, greatest, immoderate, intense, last, outermost, radical, rarest, remotest, superfluous, ultimate, ultra-, uncompromising, undue, utmost, utter(most)
**extreme anger** wrath
**extreme contempt** scorn
**extreme dirt** filth
**extreme dislike** aversion, hatred
**extreme displeasure** anger
**extreme distress** misery
**extreme edge** verge
**extreme emotion** love, rage
**extreme fear** horror, terror
**extreme force** intensity
**extreme heat** sizzle
**extreme imbecility** idiocy
**extreme in views** radical
**extreme joy** delight
**extreme limit** end
**extremely angry** furious, livid, wrathful
**extremely attractive** stunning
**extremely bad** abysmal, atrocious
**extremely badly** abysmally
**extremely beautiful** exquisite
**extremely cold** arctic
**extremely comfortable** luxurious
**extremely conscientious** scrupulous, thorough
**extremely cruel** atrocious, barbaric
**extremely delighted** overjoyed
**extremely dirty** filthy
**extremely distasteful** repugnant
**extremely eager** avid
**extremely foolish** insane, tomfool
**extremely frightened** terrified
**extremely funny** hilarious
**extremely good** excellent
**extremely great** monumental, stupendous
**extremely high fever** hyperpyrexia
**extremely improbable** impossible, inconceivable, marvellous
**extremely injurious** virulent
**extremely large** gigantic, huge
**extremely ornate** giddy
**extremely poor** beggarly, needy
**extremely rare bird** rare avis in terris (L)
**extremely reckless** lunatic
**extremely remarkable** astounding, phenomenal
**extremely rich person** billionaire, millionaire
**extremely short time** nanosecond
**extremely small** microscopic, minuscule, minute, nano-
**extremely small person** midget
**extremely strong** Atlantean, herculean
**extremely tense and nervous** highly-strung
**extremely tidy** immaculate
**extremely ugly** hideous
**extremely unusual** outré
**extremely well behaved** as good as gold
**extremely wicked** atrocious, nefarious
**extremely wicked person** fiend
**extreme mental imbecility** idiocy

**extreme mental suffering** agony
**extreme misfortune** calamity
**extreme pain or misery** anguish, agony
**extreme partisan** zealot
**extreme poverty** beggary, penury
**extreme scarcity of food** famine
**extreme suffering** agony
**extreme terror** horror
**extreme tiredness** fatigue
**extreme top** tiptop
**extreme wickedness** atrocity
**extremity** acme, ambit, apex, boundary, consummation, edge, end, excess, extreme, finale, finger, foot, frontier, horizon, limb, limit, nadir, pinnacle, tail, terminal, terminus, tip, toe, top, ultimate, verge, zenith
**extremity of line** end
**extricate** deliver, detach, disembarrass, disencumber, disengage, disentangle, disjoin, emancipate, extract, free, liberate, release, relieve, rescue, save, untangle, untie
**extrovert** loudmouth, mingler, outgoing, socialiser
**exuberance** animation, copiousness, ebullience, generosity, lavishness, liberalism, liberality, liveliness, luxuriance, prodigality, profusion, richness, teemingness, unlimitedness, vitality, yeastiness
**exuberant** abundant, animated, boisterous, buoyant, ebullient, extravagant, generous, high-spirited, lavish, liberal, lively, overflowing, plentiful, profuse, rich, unlimited, vivacious, yeasty, zestful
**exuberantly plentiful** profuse
**exude** discharge, emit, jet, ooze, outpour, secrete, spew, spurt, squirt
**exude liquid** bleed
**exude moisture** ooze
**exuding moisture** sweating
**exult** gloat, glory, jubilate, rejoice, revel, triumph
**exultant** delighted, ecstatic, elated, flushed, gleeful, joyful, joyous, jubilant, rejoicing, triumphant

**exultantly** gleefully, jubilantly
**exult over** gloat
**exult riotously** maffick
**eye** aim, attention, discernment, ee (Sc), estimation, eyeball, gaze, glance, glimpse, inspect, iris, look, observe, oculus, ogle, opinion, optic, orb, orifice, peeper, perception, regard, respect, see, sight, survey, taste, view, vision, watch
**eye amorously** ogle
**eye askance** leer, ogle
**eyeball** orb
**eyeball coat** cornea
**eyeball movement** vergence
**eyebrow** brow, supercilium, wriggle
**eye cavity** orbit, socket
**eye coat** conjunctiva, cornea, retina, sclera
**eye colour** blue, brown, hazel, green
**eye coloured portion** iris
**eye cosmetic** kohl, mascara
**eyecup** eyeglass
**eye defect** astigmatism, cataract
**eye disease** glaucoma, iritis
**eye doctor** oculist, opthalmologist
**eyedrop** tear
**eyedrop element** eserine, physostigmin(e)
**eye dropper** pipette
**eye flap** blinker, visor
**eye flirtatiously** ogle
**eye-for-an-eye** justice, reprisal, retaliation, retribution, revenge, vengeance
**eye glass** lens, lorgnette, lorgnon, monocle, ocular, specs, spectacle(s)
**eyeglasses on hand** lorgnette
**eyeglasses with spring to clip nose** pince-nez
**eyeglass for one eye** monocle
**eyeglass frame** rim
**eye globe** eyeball
**eye infection** sty(e)
**eye inflammation** conjunctivitis, iritis, pinkeye, sty(e)
**eyeing** contemplating, inspecting, ogling, perusing, regarding, scanning, scrutinising, studying, surveying, viewing, watching
**eye inner coat** retina

**eyelash** cilium, winker
**eyelash colouring** dye, mascara
**eyelashes** cilia
**eyelash make-up** mascara
**eye layer** chor(i)oid, uvea
**eyelet** fastening, grommet, hole, loophole, ocellus, orifice
**eyelet in sail** cringle
**eyelet-making tool** bodkin, stiletto
**eye level** eyeline
**eyelid droop** ptosis
**eyelid infection** sty(e)
**eye-like** ocular
**eye lustfully** ogle
**eyeman** oculist
**eye mask** domino
**eye medicinal instrument** eyedropper
**eye membrane** cornea, iris, retina, sclera
**eye muscle** iris
**eye of bean** hila, hilum
**eye of fruit** nose
**eye of hinge** gudgeon
**eye of insect** stemma
**eye of seed** hilum
**eye opening** pupil
**eye part** cornea, fovea, iris, lens, pupil, retina, uvea
**eyepiece of telescope** power
**eye protectors** goggles
**eyers** oglers, watchers
**eyes burn when peeling these** onions
**eyeshade** blinder, opaque, visor
**eye shield** goggles, patch
**eyeshot** eyesight, range, reach
**eyesight** light, sight, view, vision
**eye signal** wink
**eye socket** orbit
**eye sore** sty(e)
**eyesore** deformity, dump, fright, pigsty
**eye specialist** oculist
**eyestalk** peduncle, stipe
**eyetooth** canine, cuspid, fang
**eye trouble** cataract
**eyewash** baloney, nonsense, rubbish
**eyot** ait, holm, island, isle(t)
**eyra** jaguarondi, jaguarundi
**eyrie** aerie, house, nest
**eyrie dweller** eagle

# F

**fable** allegory, fabricate, fabrication, fairy, falsehood, fantasy, fib, fiction, figment, invent(ion), legend, lie, myth, narrative, parable, romance, saga, story, tale, untruth, yarn
**fabled** fabricated, fabulous, famed, famous, fictional, legendary, mythical, pretended, renowned, speculated
**fabled animal** unicorn
**fabled cave dweller** troll
**fabled city of gold** Eldorado
**fabled fish** mah
**fabled monstrous bird** roc
**fabled South American city** Eldorado
**fabric** building, calico, candlewick, challis, chenille, chiffon, cloth, constitution, construction, contrivance, corduroy, cotton, devise, dome, drill, edifice, erection, flannel, foundations, framework, holland, infrastructure, leno, linen, lisle, loom, make-up, material, muslin, nankeen, nap, net, nylon, organisation, outline, pile, poplin, sarcenet, sateen, satin(et), satinette, serge, silk, structure, stuff, taffeta, tamine, tamis, tapestry, textile, texture, tissue, toile, towelling, tower, tulle, tweed, twill, velour, voile, weave, web, whipcord
**fabricate** assemble, build, concoct, construct, create, devise, erect, fake, falsify, fashion, feign, forge, form, invent, lie, make, manufacture, shape
**fabricated word** neologism
**fabrication** assemblage, assembly, building, compose, constructing, construction, creation, deceit, design, edifice, erect(ion), fable, fabric, fake, falsehood, fancy, fantasy, fib, fiction, forgery, form, imagination, invention, lie, manufacture, mendacity, produce, production, sham, skeleton, structure, untruth, yarn
**fabricator** coiner, constructor, creator, designer, faker, falsifier, fibber, forger, liar, manufacturer, perjurer, prevaricator, storyteller
**fabric for uniforms** khaki
**fabric made from cellulose** rayon
**fabric made of flax** linen
**fabric made of waste silk** schappe
**fabric of coarse fibre** mat
**fabric of silk and mohair** grogram
**fabric of wool and cotton** par(r)amatta

**fabric pattern** paisley
**fabric plant** cotton, flax
**fabric press** iron
**fabric ridge** wale
**fabric stiffener** starch
**fabric-stretching machine** stenter
**fabric with gold or silver thread interwoven** lamé
**fabric with long soft nap** plush
**fabric with long velvety pile** chenille
**fabric with velvety finish** velour
**fabulist** Aesop
**fabulous** absurd, amazing, astonishing, celebrated, extreme, fabricated, fictional, imaginary, incredible, invented, marvellous, mythical, prodigious, unbelievable, unreal, untrue, wonderful
**fabulous animal** basilisk, cockatrice, griffin, gryphon, unicorn
**fabulous bird** garuda, lightning bird, phoenix, roc, simurg
**fabulous composite animal on Chinese and Japanese pottery** kylin
**fabulous creature** bunyip
**fabulous griffin-like creature with body of horse** hippogriff, hippogryph
**fabulously wealthy king** Croesus
**fabulously wealthy man** midas
**fabulous monster half-man half-horse** centaur
**fabulous monster of swamps and lagoons** bunyip
**fabulous monster with one horn** unicorn
**fabulous small fire-breathing dragon** basilisk
**fabulous winged horse** Pegasus
**façade** affectation, appearance, camouflage, challenge, countenance, defy, disguise, exterior, face, front(age), guise, illusion, mask, pretence, put-on, show, veneer
**façade of building** frontage
**face** air, appearance, aspect, cheek, confront, countenance, cover, dial, effrontery, encounter, expression, exterior, facade, features, front, frown, grimace, image, look, meet, mien, outside, physiognomy, prestige, pretence, reputation, scowl, semblance, show, sight, surface, visage
**face boldly** confront

**face-cloth** flannel
**face covering** domino, mask, veil, visor, yashmak
**face in hostility** confront
**face of building** front
**face of coin** obverse
**face of tyre** tread
**face of watch** dial
**face part** brow, cheek, chin, eye, forehead, mouth, nose
**face-powder case** compact
**facet** angle, aspect, characteristic, detail, element, face, factor, feature, item, pane, part, particular, phase, plane, point, side, slant, surface, templet, twist
**face the pitcher** bat
**facetious** amusing, blithe, comical, flippant, frivolous, funny, humorous, jesting, jocose, jocular, joking, jovial, kidding, ludicrous, playful, pleasant, sportive, tongue-in-cheek, unserious, witty
**facetious person** wag
**face to face** confronting, opposite, tête-à-tête, vis-à-vis
**facet of compound eye** ocellus
**face up to** accept, acknowledge, confront, recognise
**face value of share** par
**face veil** yashmak
**face without ornamentation** sans serif, sanserif
**facial characteristic** feature
**facial disguise** mask
**facial distortion** grimace
**facial expression of scorn** sneer
**facial feature** chin, eye, lip, mouth, nose
**facial frill** earring
**facial hair** beard, moustache
**facial mask** visor
**facial neuralgia** tic
**facial painting and powdering** make-up
**facial part** feature
**facial spasm** tic, twitch
**facial twitch** spasm, tic
**facial wrinkle** line
**facile** adroit, artful, deft, dexterous, docile, easy, effortless, flexible, flowing, fluent, free, glib, hasty, light, masterly, mild, obedient, plausible, pliant, proficient, ready, simple, skilful, skilled, slick, smooth, suave, superficial, urbane, voluble, yielding

**facilely** adeptly, adroitly, easily, effortlessly, fluently, lightly, quickly, readily, skilfully, smoothly

**facilitate** abet, accelerate, advance, aid, allay, alleviate, assist, assuage, clear, disburden, ease, encourage, expedite, forward, foster, further, help, lessen, promote, reduce, relieve, smooth, support, sustain

**facilities** amenities, conveniences, equipment, means, opportunities, prerequisites, resources, services

**facility** ability, adroitness, advantage, aid, amenity, benefit, bent, building, capability, complex, dexterity, ease, easiness, easy, edifice, efficiency, effortlessness, expertness, feasibility, fluency, gift, knack, means, network, operation, pliancy, pliant, proficiency, quickness, readiness, resource, services, simpleness, skilfulness, skill, smoothness, structure, system, talent, unimpeded

**facing** braving, confronting, defying, encountering, experiencing, meeting, opposing, opposite, overlooking, partnering

**facing away from the stem** abaxial

**facing the stem** adaxial

**fact** act(uality), certainty, circumstance, contingency, datum, deed, detail, element, event, factor, factuality, fait accompli (F), feature, gospel, happening, incident, information, item, occurrence, particular, performance, point, reality, specific, truth, validity, verity

**faction** action, behaviour, bloc, camp, clique, coalition, combination, complot, conflict, contingent, controversy, coterie, crowd, deed, disagreement, discord, dispute, dissession, division, fighting, friction, gang, ginger, group, infighting, intrigue, junta, junto, lobby, minority, party, plot, pressure, quarrel(ling), rebellion, revolt, scheme, section, sect(or), set, side, stratagem, strife, tumult, turbulence

**factitious** affected, artificial, bogus, built, constructed, contrived, counterfeit, crafted, fabricated, fake, insincere, manufactured, pinchbeck, rigged, sham, simulated, unauthentic, ungenuine, unnatural

**fact of being final** finality

**fact of being first-born child** primogeniture

**fact of belonging to particular nation** nationality

**fact of exceeding** excess

**fact of having only one single meaning** monosemy

**factor** agent, aspect, banker, cause, circumstance, component, consideration, constituent, detail, devisor, element, facet, financier, gene, influence, ingredient, instrument, item, lend, parameter, part, point, proxy, reason, sponsor, supporter, thing

**factory** facility, forge, manufactory, mill, plant, shop(floor), works, workshop

**factory machinery** plant

**factory restaurant** canteen

**factory whistle** hooter

**factory worker** operative

**facts** acts, actualities, certainties, data, deeds, details, dope, events, happenings, incidents, information, occurrences, performances, realities, truths

**facts collection** ana, data

**facts given** data

**fact that must be kept in mind** consideration

**factual** absolute, accurate, actual, authentic, bona fide, close, correct, detailed, exact, faithful, genuine, legitimate, literal, natural, objective, positive, precise, pure, real(istic), straight, sure, true, unbiased, undistorted, unfictitious, unimaginary, unquestionable, valid, veracious

**faculty** ability, academicians, academics, aptitude, authorisation, bent, brain-power, capability, capacity, cleverness, competence, department, dexterity, discipline, disposition, facility, flair, force, genius, gift, instructors, knack, lecturers, licence, means, pedagogues, power, prerogative, privilege, proclivity, profession, proficiency, property, readiness, resources, right, school(masters), sense, skilfulness, skill, staff, talent, teacher, technique, virtue, vocation

**faculty for power of speech** voice

**faculty head** dean

**faculty of breathing** breath

**faculty of expression** language

**faculty of perceiving sounds** hearing

**faculty of perception** acuteness, hearing, sight, smell, taste, touch

**faculty of prophet** prophecy

**faculty of reason** thought

**faculty of reasoning** intellect

**faculty of recalling to mind** memory

**faculty of seeing** sight

**faculty of speaking** speech

**faculty of speech** language

**faculty party** drinks, tea

**fad** affectation, craze, fancy, fashion, infatuation, mania, mode, rage, style, trend, vogue, whim

**faddish behaviour** fantod

**fade** blanch, bleach, blench, decline, decrease, deteriorate, die, dim, diminish, disappear, discolour, disperse, dissolve, droop, dull, dwindle, ebb, fail, languish, lessen, moderate, pale, perish, shrivel, vanish, wane, wilt, wither, yellow

**fade away** dwindle, evanesce, fail, wither

**faded and worn** dilapidated, shabby, tatty

**fade from sight** evanesce

**fading** bleaching, blenching, dimming, disappearing, discolouring, dispersing, dissolving, drooping, dulling, dwindling, ebbing, failing, falling, flagging, languishing, paling, perishing, shrivelling, vanishing, wilting, withering

**faff** dither, fuss

**fag** cigarette, droop, drudge, exhaust, fatigue, flag, gofer, jade, labourer, menial, moiler, prostrate, slave, tire, toil, weary

**fag end** butt, stompie, stub

**fag end holder** ashtray

**fail** abandon, bust, cease, crash, decline, desert, deteriorate, die, disappoint, dwindle, fade, fall, flag, flop, flummox, flunk, fold, forget, forsake, founder, languish, leave, miscarry, miss, neglect, sink, wane, waste, weaken

**fail at gaming** lose

**failed** phut

**fail in ability** unable

**fail in duty** remiss

**failing** abandoning, blemish, defect, deficiency, disappointing, drawback, error, failure, fault, flaw, foible, fruitless, imperfection, misfiring, misfortune, neglecting, omitting, shortcoming, unproductive, weakness

**failing to achieve a purpose** abortive

**failing to produce the desired effect** inefficacious

**fail in mind** senile

**fail in spirit** quail

**fail to achieve purpose** abortive

**fail to appear** abscond, absent

**fail to care for** neglect

**fail to comply** violate

**fail to develop** stagnate

**fail to distinguish between** confuse

**fail to do** neglect, omit

**fail to fulfil obligation** welch, welsh

**fail to give due care to** neglect
**fail to hit** miss
**fail to hold a straight course** yaw
**fail to ignite** misfire
**fail to include** omit
**fail to justify** belie
**fail to keep** lose
**fail to keep a secret** tattle
**fail to keep contact with friend** lose touch
**fail to notice** overlook
**fail to pay proper care** neglect
**fail to recall** forget
**fail to remain compact** straggle
**fail to win** lose
**failure** absence, bankruptcy, breakdown, bust, collapse, crash, decay, decline, default, defeat, deficiency, dereliction, deterioration, disappointment, disaster, downfall, dud, failing, fiasco, flop, frustration, incompetent, insolvency, insufficiency, lack, loser, loss, miscarriage, neglect, negligence, no-hoper, nonexistence, nonperformance, nonstarter, omission, overthrow, ruin, shortcoming, slip-up, stoppage, unsuccessfulness, wash-out, wreck
**failure in examination** fail
**failure in secretion of urine** anuria
**failure of blood to clot normally** haemophilia
**failure of energy** anergy
**failure of firearm** stoppage
**failure of issue** defectus sanguinis (L)
**failure of mental abilities** dotage, senility
**failure of milk secretion** agalactia
**failure of muscle** achalasia
**failure of vitality** deliquium
**failure to act** default
**failure to correspond** discrepancy
**failure to function in normal manner** malfunction
**failure to note something** oversight
**failure to pay** default
**failure to reach required standard** shortcoming
**failure to understand** incomprehension
**failure to win** loss
**faineance** sloth
**faineant** idle, lazy
**faint** blackout, bland, bleached, collapse, cowardly, dim, distant, dizzy, drop, dull, exhausted, faded, faltering, fearful, feeble, flag, gentle, giddy, half-hearted, hazy, hushed, ill-defined, indistinct, irresolute, languid, lethargic, light, low, mild, muffled, pusillanimous, remote, sick, slight, soft, subdued, swoon(ing), syncope, unconsciousness, vague, weak, woozy
**faint from heat** swelter
**faint from hunger** leery
**faint halo or light around sun or moon** corona
**faint-hearted** timid
**faint in colour** dim, pale, vaal, whitish
**faint light** gleam, glim(mer)
**faintly coloured** pale
**faintly indicate** adumbrate
**faintly lit** dim
**faint of scent** cold, waugh
**faint smell** whiff
**faint tinge** shade
**fair** adequate, attractive, auspicious, average, beautiful, blond(e), bright, clean, clear, cloudless, comely, decent, deserved, direct, disinterested, distinct, equal, equitable, even, exhibit(ion), favourable, honest, honourable, hopeful, impartial, just, legitimate, light, middling, moderate, open, pale, passable, promising, proper, rather, reasonable, somewhat, spotless, square, sunny, tolerable, tolerate, unbiased, unprejudiced, untarnished, white
**fair and calm** settled
**fair and just** equitable
**fair and sincere in behaviour** honest
**fair-and-square** correct, dinkum, honest, just
**fair and sunny** clear
**fairer sex** women
**fairground vehicle** dodgem-car
**fairground wheel** Ferris
**fair-haired** blonde
**fair in action** just
**fair in shade** light
**fairly** averagely, cleanly, decently, deservedly, equally, equitably, honestly, honourably, impartially, legitimately, lightly, properly, reasonably, squarely
**fairly cold** cool
**fairly great in amount** considerable
**fairly late** latish
**fairly massive** largish
**fairly new** newish
**fairly old** oldish
**fairly quickly** allegretto
**fairly well in health** middling
**fairly young** youngish
**fair-minded** disinterested, even(-handed), impartial, just, unbiased, unprejudiced
**fairness** decency, equity, justice, legitimacy, rightfulness
**fair ride** carousel, merry-go-round, roundabout
**fair treatment** right
**fairway sportsperson** golfer
**fair weather** sunshine
**fairy** brownie, elf, fay, leprechaun, nix, pixie, pixy, sprite
**fairy godmother** benefactress
**fairy king** erlking, Oberon
**fairylike** elfin
**fairy-like creature** elf
**fairy queen** Titania
**fairy's rod** wand
**fairy tale** fable, fabrication, fantasy, invention, romance, untruth
**fairy-tale aircraft** Persian carpet
**fairy-tale figure** elf, witch
**fairy-tale giant** ogre
**fairy-tale start** once
**faith** allegiance, assurance, belief, church, communion, confidence, conviction, credence, credit, creed, denomination, dependence, doctrine, dogma, faithfulness, fidelity, honesty, honour, hope, loyalty, persuasion, pledge, promise, reliance, religion, sincerity, tenet, trust, truth(fulness), vow, word
**faithful** accurate, adherents, believable, believers, brethren, close, communicants, congregation, conscientious, constant, convinced, credible, dependable, devoted, exact, followers, loyal, precise, reliable, stalwarts, staunch, steadfast, strict, supporters, thorough, true(-blue), true-hearted, trustworthy, trusty, truthful
**faithful follower** loyalist
**faithful friend** dog, fidus Achates
**faithful in both** in utroque fidelis (L)
**faithful representation of truth** accuracy
**faithful servant** retainer
**faith in oneself** assured, confidence, pride, vanity
**faith pledged** affiance
**fake** act, affect(ed), artificial, assume(d), bluff, bogus, charlatan, copy, counterfeit, fabricate, false, falsify, feign, forge(d), forgery, fraud, hoax, imitation, impostor, mock, phoney, pretend(ed), pseudo, reproduction, ruse, sham, simulate(d), simulation, spurious, trick
**fake jewels** paste
**fakery** hokum
**falcon** harrier, hawk, kestrel, tercel
**falconary** hawking
**falconer** hawker, ostreger
**falcon in first year** sore(hawk)
**falcon or hound** harrier
**falconry** hawking

**Falkland penguin** rockhopper
**fall** abate, autumn, cadence, capitulate, capitulation, collapse, crash, death, decline, decrease, defeat, depreciate, descend, die, diminish, dive, downfall, drop, dwindle, ebb, err, flag, gravitate, incline, lessen(ing), lowering, occur, overthrow, pitch, plunge, plummet, reduction, resign, sink, slide, slope, slump, stumble, submit, subside, succumb, surrender, topple, trip, tumble, wane, yield
**fall abruptly** dump
**fallacious** absurd, amiss, crafty, deceitful, designing, disingenuous, double-dealing, erroneous, false, fraudulent, hypocritical, illogical, illusory, inaccurate, inconsistent, inexact, insincere, invalid, irrational, mistaken, senseless, specious, spurious, treacherous, tricky, two-faced, underhand, unsound, untrue, untrustworthy, wrong
**fallacious argument** captious, paralogism
**fallacious reasoner** sophist
**fallacy** bubble, chimera, deceit, deception, delusion, error, falsehood, fantasy, flaw, illusion, misbelief, misconception, mistake, myth, non sequitur, solecism, sophism, untruth
**fall apart** break, collapse, crumble, decay, decompose, disband, disintegrate, disperse, dissolve, disunite, rot, shatter
**fall as frozen rain** sleet
**fall asleep** doze off, nod off
**fall away** collapse, decadence, defect, ebb, lapse
**fall back** lapse, recede, relapse, resort, retreat
**fall back again** relapse
**fall back on** use, employ
**fall behind** trail, lag, straggle
**fall behind others** lag
**fall down** cave, collapse, disappoint, fail, flop, swap, swither
**fall due** accrue, befall
**fallen meteor** meteorite
**fallen timber** log
**fallen woman** harlot, hussy, slut
**fall fast** hop
**fall flat in worship** prostrate
**fall for** accept, desire, swallow
**fall from clouds** rain
**fall from grace** backslide, lapse
**fall from horse** purl
**fall from repute** degradation
**fall gradually** ebb, sag
**fall guy** dupe, scapegoat, victim

**fall headlong** pitch, topple
**fallible** faulty, flawed, imperfect, mortal, unreliable
**fall ill again** relapse
**fall in** collapse, crumble, sink
**fall in a heap** tumble
**fall in drips** drop
**fall in drops** dribble, drip, spatter, trickle
**fall in folds** drape
**falling flakes** snow
**falling mass of snow** avalanche
**falling of bodies to earth** gravitation
**falling slush** sleet
**falling star** comet, meteor
**fall in price** sag
**fall into disfavour** discredit, disesteem, disgrace
**fall into disuse** lapse
**fall into error** slip, stumble
**fall into ruin** decadent, decay, deteriorate, wither
**fall into slumber** drowse
**fall in value** depreciate
**fall in with** accept, assent, comply, meet, support
**fall of bodies to earth** gravitation
**fall of earth and rocks** landslide
**fall off** decelerate, decline, decrease, deteriorate, drop, retreat, slump, yield
**fall of water** cascade
**fall on** assail, assault, attack, snatch
**fall open** gap
**fall out** altercate, argue, bicker, clash, differ, disagree, dispute, fight, quarrel, squabble
**fall over** tumble
**fallow deer** fawn
**fallow land** ley
**fall season** autumn
**fall short** disappoint, fail, miss
**fall short of** sub-
**fall short of expectations** disappoint
**falls in Cuba** Agabama, Caburni, Toa
**falls in Ethiopia** Blue Nile, Tisisat
**falls in Nile** Ripon
**falls in Zimbabwe** Victoria
**fall suddenly** drop, slump
**fall through** collapse, fail, founder, miscarry
**fall to** begin, commence, start, tackle, undertake
**fall to lower level** decline, subside
**fall upon** assail, assault
**fall upon violently** attack
**fall with a thump** flop
**false** artificial, bogus, counterfeit, deceitful, deceiving, deceptive, dishonest, disloyal, erroneous, faithless, fake, fallacious, faulty, feigned, forged, fraudulent, hypocritical, imitation, improper, inaccurate, inconstant, incorrect, inexact, insincere, invalid, lying, mendacious, misleading, mistaken, mock, perfidious, phoney, pretended, sham, simulated, spurious, substitute, supplementary, synthetic, treacherous, two-faced, unreal, unreliable, untrue, untruthful, wrong
**false argument** sophism
**false belief** delusion, fallacy, illusion
**false charge** calumny
**false claim** pretension
**false claimant** pretender
**false defamatory statement** libel
**false display** affectation
**false form** pseudomorph
**false fruit** accessory fruit, pseudocarp
**false god** Baal, idol
**false hair made up into coil** postiche
**falsehood** deceit, deception, dishonesty, dissimulation, fib, fiction, lie, perjury, story, untruth
**false image** idol
**false impression** delusion, illusion, misconception
**false lure** decoy
**false name** pseudonym
**falseness** deceit, disloyalty, untruthfulness
**false plea** pretext
**false pretence** affectation
**false pronunciation of words** cacoepy
**false reason** excuse, pretext
**false report** canard, furphy, slander
**false show** bubble, colour, illusion, pretence
**false statement** lie
**false statement about a person** slander
**false step** faux pas
**false teeth** dentures
**false topaz** citrine
**false to promises** faithless
**falsifier** forger, liar
**falsify** adulterate, alter, belie, conceal, concoct, confute, contradict, counterfeit, deceitfulness, dissimulate, distort, doctor, exaggerate, fabrication, faithlessness, fake, falsehood, feign, forge, garble, lie, misrepresent, misstate, oppose, overcolour, pervert, pretend, prevaricate, sham, untrustworthiness, untruth
**falsify cheques** forge, fraud
**falter** hesitate, stammer, stumble, stutter, tremble, vacillate, waver
**faltering and staggering** tottering
**fame** acclaim, admiration, celebrity, distinction, eminence, esteem, estimation, glory, greatness, honour,

illustriousness, name, notability, note, notoriety, opinion, prestige, prominence, rank, renown, reputation, repute, respect, stardom, vogue

**famed** acclaimed, celebrated, distinguished, eminent, famous, great, illustrious, noted, notorious, recognised, renowned, well-known

**famed horse race** Derby, July

**famed person** notable, star

**familiar** abreast, accustomed, acquainted, associate, au fait (F), aware, close, common, companion, confidential, conversant, everyday, free(-and-easy), frequent, friend(ly), household, informal, intimate, knowledgeable, ordinary, presuming, presumptive, presumptuous, recognisable, relaxed, routine, social, tame, thick, unceremonious, versed, well-acquainted, well-known, well-versed

**familiar name** diminutive, epithet, sobriquet

**familiar with** au fait (F)

**family** ancestor, ancestry, birth, blood(-children), breed, brood, category, child(ren), clan, class, classification, descendant, descent, dynasty, extraction, folk, forebears, genealogy, gens, group, home, house(hold), ilk, issue, kin(dred), kinsmen, line(age), offspring, parent(age), parental, pedigree, people, progeny, race, relations, relatives, tribe

**family animal** pet

**family car** sedan

**family chronicle** saga

**family circle** hearth

**family clan** tribe

**family feud** vendetta

**family heraldic devices** arms

**family maxim** motto

**family member** aunt, brother, daughter, father, grandparent, mother, sis(ter), son, uncle

**family name** nomen, surname

**family of Italian violin makers** Amati, Stradivari

**family servant** retainer

**family shield** escutcheon

**family symbol** crest

**family treasure** heirloom

**family tree** genealogy, lineage

**family trip** outing

**famished** craving, edacious, hollow, hungry, malnourished, peckish, ravenous, starved, starving, undernourished, voracious

**famous** acclaimed, brilliant, celebrated, distinguished, eminent, exalted, excellent, (far-)famed, glorious, great, honoured, illustrious, legendary, lustrous, memorable, notable, noted, popular, pre-eminent, prominent, remarkable, renowned, respected, signal, venerable, well-known

**famous American fighting unit** Green Berets, Marines

**famous American hotel** Hilton, Sheraton

**famous canal** Panama, Suez

**famous cathedral** Chartres

**famous Christian drama** Oberammergau Passion Play

**famous college in Berkshire** Eton

**famous composer** Bach, Beethoven, Brahms, Chopin, Delius, Grieg, Lehar, Liszt, Strauss

**famous construction in Berlin** wall

**famous designer** Chanel, Dior

**famous dramatist** Ibsen, Marlow, O'Neill, Shakespeare, Stoppard, Williams

**famous English field-marshal** Alexander, Kitchener, Montgomery

**famous English spa** Bath

**famous fabler** Aesop

**famous falls location** Niagara, Victoria

**famous female singer** diva

**famous fiction sleuth** Hercule Poirot, Sherlock Holmes

**famous for apple-growing** Ceres

**famous for his fables** Aesop

**famous game reserve** Kruger National Park, Londolozi, Mala Mala

**famous gardens** Kew, Kirstenbosch

**famous Greek mathematician** Euclid, Pythagoras

**famous Indian building** Taj Mahal

**famous lawsuit** cause célèbre

**famous leaning tower** Pisa

**famous lioness** Elsa

**famous loch** Ness

**famous make of china and porcelain** Chelsea, Dresden, Rosenthal, Royal Doulton, Wedgwood

**famous miser** Scrooge

**famous painting** Mona Lisa

**famous person** celebrity, notable, personality

**famous person's signature** autograph

**famous predictor** Nostradamus

**famous racecourse** Ascot

**famous rock in Australia** Ayers

**famous Roman orator** Cicero

**famous sailor** Noah

**famous scientist** Einstein

**famous Spanish palace** Alhambra

**famous tower** Pisa

**famous traveller** Polo

**famous vehicle in Durban** ricksha(w)

**famous Venetian bridge** Rialto

**famous waterfall** Iguassu, Niagara, Victoria

**famous whale** Moby Dick

**fan** adherent, admirer, agitate, air-condition(er), air-cool, arouse, blow(er), buff, cool, devotee, enthusiast, excite, fanatic, follower, freak, friend, increase, lover, propeller, provoke, refresh, rouse, stimulate, stir, supporter, vane, ventilate, ventilator, winnow

**fanatic** activist, addict, bigot, crazed, devotee, enthusiast, extravagant, extremist, freak, frenetic, friend, lunatic, maniac, militant, partisan, phrenetic, radical, sectarian, unreasonable, visionary, votary, zealot, zealous

**fanatical** bigoted, burning, crazed, enthusiastic, extravagant, extreme, fervent, frantic, frenzied, mad, maniacal, obsessive, overenthusiastic, passionate, rabid, radical, unreasonable, visionary, wild, zealous

**fanatical behaviour** fanaticism

**fanaticism** ardour, bigotry, chauvinism, craze, dedication, enthusiasm, extremism, fervour, fondness, infatuation, intolerance, keenness, madness, monomania, narrow-mindedness, obsessiveness, passion, prejudice, racialism, racism, radicalism, rage, zeal

**fancied** dreamt, ideal, imaged, imaginary, imagined, opined

**fancies in sleep** dream

**fanciful** airy(-fairy), bizarre, capricious, curious, extravagant, fabulous, fairy-tale, fantastic, fictitious, grotesque, humorous, imaginary, imaginative, inventive, legendary, mythical, romantic, shadowy, unusual, vaporous, visionary, whimsical, wild

**fanciful composition** extravaganza

**fanciful notion** conceit, reverie, whimsy

**fancy** believe, capricious, choice, conceive, conception, conjecture, craving, decorate, desire, dream, elegant, envision, fantasy, favour, fine, fondness, guess, hallucination, hankering, idea, imagination, imagine, impression, inclination, irregular, judg(e)ment, like, liking, notion, ornamental, ornate, picture, prefer(ence), quirk, reckon, rococo, sensitivity, suppose, taste, thinking, thought, urge, vagary, whim(sical)

**fancy bread** cake
**fancy-dress ball** bal paré (F), masquerade
**fancy knot** bow
**fancy twist** curlicue
**fancy vision** phantom
**fane** sanctuary, temple
**fanfare** dash, display, flourish, hooray, parade, shaking, show, tantara, trumpets, tucket
**fan out** spread
**fantast** dreamer, visionary
**fantastic** absurd, amazing, bizarre, brilliant, enormous, excellent, exotic, extreme, fanciful, fictitious, first-rate, grandiose, great, illusory, imaginary, imaginative, incredible, irrational, marvellous, odd, outlandish, overwhelming, ridiculous, sensational, strange, superb, tremendous, unbelievable, visionary, weird, wonderful
**fantastic notion** pipe dream
**fantastic proceeding** caper
**fantastic success** succès fou (F)
**fantasy** aberration, apparition, aspiration, conception, (day)dream, delusion, fancy, fantasia, figment, hallucination, illusion, image, imagination, imaginativeness, imagine, insubstantiality, invention, mirage, misconception, nightmare, phantasm, phantom, pipe-dream, reverie, shadow, speculation, unreality, vapour, vision
**fantasy in sleep** dream
**fantasy world** fairyland
**fantoccini** marionettes
**far** comprehensive, considerably, decidedly, deep(ly), distant(ly), extremely, far-flung, far-off, far-removed, faraway, further, greatly, incomparably, long, miles, much, opposite, other, out-of-the-way, outlandish, remote(ly), removed, tele-
**far and away** incomparably
**far and near** everywhere
**far and wide** abroad, broadly, everywhere, extensively, ubiquitous, widely
**far apart** distant, remote
**farce** absurdity, comedy, interpolation, joke, liturgical, mockery, nonsense, parody, ridiculousness, satire, sham, slapstick, travesty
**farcical boastful coward** scaramouch
**far cry** discrepant, distant, faraway, remote(ly)
**far down** deep
**fare** be, board, charge, cost, diet, do, eatables, fee, food, go, happen, journey, manage, meals, menu, pass(age), passenger, pick-up, price, proceed, prosper, provisions, rations, sustenance, table, travel(ler), wayfarer
**Far Eastern temple** pagoda
**Far Eastern unit of weight** tael
**fare for Jack Horner** pie
**farewell** adieu, adios, aloha, au revoir (F), auf Wiedersehn (G), ave, bye(-bye), cheerio, cheers, ciao (I), congé, departure, goodbye, parting, sayonara (J), send-off, tata, totsiens, vale(diction)
**fare well** bloom, flourish, prosper
**farewell gesture** wave
**farewell party** send-off
**farewell speech** epilogue, valediction, valedictory
**far-flung** (a)broad, (a)far, extensive, far-off, far-reaching, faraway, general, great, huge, large, lengthy, long, out-of-the-way, outlying, prevalent, protracted, remote, rife, spacious, thorough
**far from centre** outlying, remote
**far from straightforward** tortuous
**far from the mark** wide
**farm** acreage, acres, croft, cultivate, farmhold, farmstead, grange, hacienda, homestead, land, lease, manor, manure, plaas, plantation, plough, ranch(o), smallholding, station, sublet, till
**farmable** arable
**farm and its buildings** farmstead
**farm animal** cow, fowl, horse, pig, sheep
**farm animal enclosure** corral
**farm bird** duck, fowl, goose, turkey
**farm building** barn, cowshed, shed, silo, stable
**farmer** agriculturist, agronomist, boer, bumpkin, countryman, crofter, cultivator, exciseman, gaffer, grower, hobnail, husbandman, maker, peasant, peon, ploughman, producer, rustic, smallholder, sodbuster, taxman, tiller, yeoman, yokel
**farmer's need** seed
**farmer who raises livestock** stockbreeder
**farm helper** hand
**farming** agriculture, crofting, cultivating, husbandry, operating, planting, renting
**farming job** harvesting, milking, planting, ploughing, sheep-shearing
**farming machine** baler, harvester, thresher, tractor
**farming system** crop rotation
**farming vehicle** cart, harvester, tractor
**farm labourer** peasant, peon, serf
**farm products** eggs, grain, maize, vegetables
**farm shed** barn
**farm structure** silo
**farm tool** fork, shovel, spade
**farm worker** hand, labourer
**farmyard bird** chicken, duck, goose, turkey
**farmyard manure** mis, muck
**far-off** afar, distant, remote, tele-
**far out** extreme, radical, ultra, unconventional, unique, unusual
**farrago** confused, gemors, hodgepodge, hotchpotch, jumble, mash, medley, mélange (F), mess, miscellany, mishmash, mixture, olio, potpourri
**far recessed** deep
**farrier's work** shoeing
**far superior** streets ahead
**farther aft** after
**farther away** beyond
**farther forward** ahead
**farthest** extreme, longest, remotest
**farthest aft** sternmost
**farthest from centre** extreme
**farthest planet** Pluto
**fascinate** absorb, allure, attract, beguile, bewitch, captivate, charm, delight, enchant, engross, enrapture, enthrall, entice, entrance, hypnotise, impress, infatuate, influence, intrigue, lure, mesmerise, pull, rivet, seduce, spellbind, tantalise, transfix
**fascinating** captivating, charming, delighting, enchanting, engrossing, enthralling, entrancing, hypnotising, infatuating, intriguing, irresistible, riveting, transfixing
**fascinating relic** curio
**fascination** allure(ment), appeal, attraction, attractiveness, charm, enchantment, enticement, entrancement, glamour, hypnotism, infatuation, interest, lure, magic, magnetism, mesmerism, pull, seduction, sorcery, spell, witchery
**fashion** accommodate, adapt, adjust, alter, appearance, approach, attitude, bon ton (F), clothing, conformity, construct, conventionality, craze, create, custom, cut, design, fad, figure, fit, forge, form, frame, hold, kind, latest, line, look, make, manner, method, mode, model, mould, pattern, rage, shape, society, sort, style, suit, tailor, tone, trend, type, vogue, way
**fashionable** à la mode, chic, contemporary, cool, current,

customary, dashing, elegant, gallant, genteel, in, jaunty, latest, modern, modish, popular, posh, prevailing, ritzy, smart, stylish, swell, swish, trendsetting, trendy, up-to-date, usual, vogue, with it
**fashionable beach**  plage
**fashionable dressmaker**  modiste
**fashionable in style**  à la mode
**fashionable people collectively**  society
**fashionable person**  trendy
**fashionable reception**  salon, soiree
**fashionable resort**  spa
**fashionable society**  beau monde, haut monde
**fashion craze**  fad, trend
**fashion designer**  Arendz, Chanel, couturier, couturière, Dior, Levin, Rosenwerth, St Laurent, stylist
**fashion direction**  trend
**fashioned again**  remade
**fashion leader**  trendsetter
**fashion mode**  trend
**fashion plate**  beau, dandy
**fast**  abstain, accelerated, active, alert, apace, brisk, deceptive, deep, diet, dissolute, enduring, energetic, eternal, extravagantly, faithful, famish, fastened, firm(ly), fixed(ly), fleet, flying, hasty, hurried, impregnable, inescapable, inextricable, insincere, lasting, loyal, nippy, permanent, presto, profligate, quick(ly), rapid(ly), reckless(ly), reduce, resistant, secure, speedily, speedy, starve, staunch, steadfast, strong, swift, tied, unchaste, unreliable, wild
**fast animal**  cheetah
**fast bike**  racer
**fast bowler**  seamer
**fast car**  racer
**fast cat**  cheetah
**fast coach**  flier, flyer
**fasten**  affix, anchor, attach, bind, bolt, chain, clinch, close, connect, fix, glue, grip, join, lace, link, lock, nail, paste, peg, pin, rivet, seal, secure, snib, stick, tack, tether, tie, unite, weld
**fastened cluster**  bunch
**fastener**  binding, bolt, buckle, button, catch, clamp, clasp, clip, hasp, hatpin, holder, hook, latch(et), link, lock, nail, nut, padlock, peg, pin, rivet, screw, securer, staple, staylace, stud, tack, tendril, toggle, zip(per)
**fastener for nappy**  safety-pin
**fastener for washing**  peg
**fastener on duffel coat**  toggle

**fasten firmly**  rivet, seal
**fasten horseshoe**  nail
**fastening**  buckle, button, catch, clamp, clasp, copula, fastener, hasp, hinder, hook, lock, pin, rivet, screw, spike, staple, vinculum, yoke
**fastening device**  zipper
**fastening on gate**  latch
**fastening pin**  nail
**fastening rod**  bolt, rivet
**fasten rope**  reeve
**fasten securely**  bolt, brace, clinch, lock, nail, seal
**fasten ship with ropes**  moor
**fastens shoes**  lace
**fasten thing to another**  attach
**fasten tightly**  brace
**fasten together**  connect, tie
**fasten with cord**  tie
**fasten with gum**  glue, paste, seal
**fasten with shoestrings**  lace up
**fasten with thread**  sew
**fastest land animal**  cheetah
**fastest shearer**  ringer
**fast food item**  bunny chow, (ham)burger, fish and chips, hot dog, pizza
**fast food stall**  hot-dog stand
**fast glance**  peek
**fast heavily-armed warship**  destroyer
**fast highway**  expressway, freeway
**fast horse**  clipper
**fastidious**  affected, critical, dainty, dandy, demanding, difficult, exacting, finical, finicky, fussy, overdelicate, overexacting, (over)nice, particular, refined, squeamish
**fastidious about trifles**  pernickety
**fastidious diner**  epicure
**fastidious person**  fusspot
**fasting period**  Lent
**fast lively dance**  jive
**fast military aircraft**  fighter
**fast pace of horse**  gallop
**fast plane**  jet
**fast postal service**  airmail, fastmail, priority
**fast runner**  sprinter
**fast-running plover-like bird**  courser
**fast sailing ship**  clipper, dromon(d)
**fast, straight downhill run in skiing**  schuss
**fast train**  express, limited
**fast unintelligent talk**  gabble
**fast warship**  cruiser
**fat**  abundant, adipose, broad, copious, corpulent, dull, extended, fatty, fertile, flab, fleshy, fruitful, grease, lard, lucrative, obese, oil, overweight, plentiful, plump, podgy, portly, productive, remunerative,

rich, schmal(t)z, sluggish, stout, stupid, thick, wide
**fatal**  calamitous, catastrophic, damned, deadly, decisive, destructive, disastrous, doomed, fateful, ill-advised, important, inevitable, lethal, mortal, ruinous, terminal
**fatal drug intake**  overdose
**fatality**  calamity, casualty, catastrophe, collision, death, decease, disaster, lethality, malignancy, misfortune, mortality, pile-up
**fatal poison**  bane
**fatal to self**  suicidal
**fat and flour mixture**  roux
**fate**  chance, death, destine, destiny, destruction, divine, doom, end, foreordain, fortune, future, horoscope, inevitability, issue, karma, kismet, lot, luck, outcome, predestination, predestine, providence, result, ruin, stars, unavoidability, upshot, will
**fated**  destined, doomed, inescapable, inevitable
**fated to die**  doomed, fey
**fateful**  critical, crucial, deadly, decisive, disastrous, fatal, ominous
**fat fellow**  glutton, hind
**fat from wool**  lanolin(e)
**father**  beget, dad(dy), pa(pa), pater, père (F), pop, sire
**father and mother**  parents
**father and ruler of family**  patriarch
**Father Christmas**  Santa Claus, St Nicholas
**fathered**  procreated, sired
**father-in-law of Mohammed**  Abu-Bekr
**father-in-law of Tutankhamen**  Akhnaton
**father-in-law of Wagner**  Liszt
**fatherland**  homeland
**fatherly**  benign, kind, paternal, protecting, protective, tender
**father of Aaron**  Amram
**father of Abas**  Celeus, Lynceus
**father of Abel**  Adam
**father of Abia**  Jeroboam, Rehoboam, Samuel
**father of Abiathar**  Ahimelech
**father of Abida**  Midian
**father of Abiezer**  Gilead
**father of Abihail**  Eliab, Huri
**father of Abihu**  Aaron
**father of Abijah**  David, Jeroboam, Rehoboam, Samuel
**father of Abimelech**  Abiatha, Gideon
**father of Abinadab**  Jesse, Saul
**father of Abiram**  Eliab
**father of Abishua**  Phineas
**father of Abner**  Ner
**father of Abraham**  Terah

| | | |
|---|---|---|
| father of Absalom  David | father of David  Jesse | father of Huram  Bela |
| father of Acacallis  Minos | father of Delaiah  Mehetabeel | father of Huz  Nahor |
| father of Acarnan  Alcmaeon | father of Dinah  Jacob | father of Ibneiah  Jeroham |
| father of Acastus  Pelias | father of Ebed  Jonathan | father of Ichabod  Phinehas |
| father of Achilles  Peleus | father of Elaida  David | father of Iddo  Zecharaih |
| father of Achim  Sadoc | father of Elam  Shem | father of Igal  Joseph |
| father of Achsah  Caleb | father of Eleazar  Aaron | father of Ilia  Numitor |
| father of Acis  Faunus | father of Eliphal  Ur | father of Imnah  Asher |
| father of Acrisius  Abas | father of Eliphalet  David | father of Ira  Bela |
| father of Addar  Belah | father of Eliphaz  Esau | father of Irad  Enoch |
| father of Adonijah  David | father of Elisha  Shaphat | father of Irene  Jupiter |
| father of Aeacus  Jupiter, Zeus | father of Elishama  David | father of Iris  Thaumus |
| father of Aegaeon  Uranus | father of Elishua  David | father of Isaac  Abraham |
| father of Aeneas  Anchises | father of Eliud  Achim | father of Iscah  Haran |
| father of a family  paterfamilias | father of Elkanah  Korah | father of Ishbak  Abraham |
| father of Agamemnon  Plisthenes | father of Elon  Zebulun | father of Ishboseheth  Saul |
| father of Agave  Cadmus | father of Elpalet  David | father of Ishmael  Abraham |
| father of Agenor  Antenor, Neptune, Poseidon | father of Enos  Seth | father of Ishui  Saul |
| father of Ahiam  Sharar | father of Ephraim  Joseph | father of Isis  Saturn |
| father of Alcyone  Aeolus, Atlas | father of Ephron  Zoar | father of Issachar  Jacob |
| father of Alexander  Priam, Simon | father of Er  Jose | father of Jaasiel  Abner |
| father of Aloeus  Neptune, Poseidon | father of Eri  Gad | father of Jaazaniah  Jeremiah |
| father of Amalek  Eliphaz | father of Esau  Isaac | father of Jachin  Simeon |
| father of Amnon  David | father of Ethnan  Ashur | father of Jacob  Isaac |
| father of Amon  Manasseh | father of Ezekiel  Busi | father of Jahaziel  Hebron |
| father of Amram  Bani | father of Ezer  Ephraim | father of Jair  Kish |
| father of Ananias  Nedebaeus | father of Gaal  Ebed | father of Jalaam  Esau |
| father of Anax  Uranus | father of Gad  Jacob | father of Jalon  Ezra |
| father of Andrew  Jonas | father of Gaham  Nahor | father of Janna  Joseph |
| father of Aphrodite  Jupiter, Zeus | father of Galahad  Lancelot | father of Japhet  Noah |
| father of Apollo  Jupiter, Zeus | father of Gazez  Caleb | father of Japhia  David |
| father of Ares  Jupiter, Zeus | father of Gershom  Moses | father of Jarib  Simeon |
| father of Arges  Uranus | father of Gether  Aram | father of Javan  Japheth |
| father of Aridai  Haman | father of Gideon  Joash | father of Jemima  Job |
| father of Asenath  Potipherah | father of Gilead  Machir | father of Jemuel  Simeon |
| father of Ashbel  Benjamin | father of Gog  Shemaiah | father of Jephthan  Gilead |
| father of Asher  Jacob | father of Gomer  Japheth | father of Jeremiah  Hilkiah |
| father of Atlas  Iapetus | father of Haggi  Gad | father of Jesaiah  Hananiah |
| father of Azor  Eliakim | father of Ham  Noah | father of Jesher  Caleb |
| father of Bacchus  Jupiter, Zeus | father of Hamlet  Claudius | father of Jesse  Obed |
| father of Barak  Abinoam | father of Hammoleketh  Machir | father of Jessica  Shylock |
| father of Basmath  Solomon | father of Hamnet  Shakespeare | father of Jesui  Asher |
| father of Bathsheba  Eliam | father of Hamutal  Jeremiah | father of Jewish nation  Abraham |
| father of Bedan  Gilead | father of Hanniel  Ephod | father of Jezebel  Ethbaal |
| father of Bernice  Herod | father of Hanoch  Reuben | father of Jezer  Naphtali |
| father of Bethuel  Nahor | father of Haran  Caleb | father of Jezreel  Hosea |
| father of Bezaleel  Uri | father of Hareph  Caleb | father of Jidlaph  Nahor |
| father of Bimhal  Japhlet | father of Hasadiah  Zerubbabel | father of Job  Issachar |
| father of Boaz  Salmon | father of Hashubah  Zerubbabel | father of John  Zebedee, Zachariah |
| father of Buz  Nahor | father of Hathath  Othniel | father of John the Baptist  Zachariah |
| father of Cain  Adam | father of Hazo  Nahor | father of Jokshan  Abraham |
| father of Cainan  Enos | father of Hebron  Kohath | father of Jonan  Eliakim |
| father of Caleb  Hezron | father of Hermes  Zeus | father of Jonathan  Saul |
| father of Canaan  Ham | father of Hermia  Egeus | father of Joseph  Jacob |
| father of Chesed  Nahor | father of Herodias  Aristobulus | father of Joshua  Nun |
| father of Chileab  David | father of Herson  Reuben | father of Josiah  Amon |
| father of Copreus  Pelops | father of Hezekia  Ahaz | father of Jotham  Gideon |
| father of Cordelia  Lear | father of Hilkia  Hosah | father of Juda  Joseph |
| father of Croesus  Alyattes | father of Hophni  Eli | father of Judah  Jacob |
| father of Daniel  David | father of Hosea  Nun | father of Judith  Shakespeare |
| father of Dathan  Eliab | father of Hul  Aram | father of Kezia  Job |
| | father of Hupman  Benjamin | father of Kish  Jehiel |

father of Kohath Levi
father of Korah Esau
father of Laban Bethuel
father of Laertes Arcesius, Polonius
father of Leah Laban
father of Levi Jacob
father of Lud Shem
father of Maachah Nahor
father of Maaz Ram
father of Madai Japhet
father of Magog Japheth
father of Malchishua Saul
father of mankind Adam
father of Massa Ishmael
father of Matthew Alphaeus
father of Medan Abraham
father of Melech Micah
father of Meonothai Othniel
father of Mephibosheth Saul Jonathan
father of Merab Saul
father of Merari Levi
father of Mesech Japhet
father of Mesha Caleb
father of Methuselah Enoch
father of Mibsam Simeon
father of Micha Mephibosheth
father of Michal Saul
father of Midian Abraham
father of Mikloth Jehiel
father of Minos Jupiter, Lycastus
father of Miranda Prospero
father of Misham Elpaal
father of Mishma Ishmael
father of Mizzah Reuel
father of Mordecai Jair
father of Moses Amram
father of Naam Caleb
father of Naamah Lamech
father of Nadab Aaron
father of Nahson Amminadab
father of Nehemiah Azbuk
father of Nepheg David
father of Nethaneel Jesse
father of Noah Ishmael
father of Nogah David
father of Nohah Benjamin
father of Obadiah Azel, Jehiel, Shemaiah
father of Obal Joktan
father of Obed Boaz, Jahra, Shemaiah
father of Odysseus Laertes, Sisyphus
father of Omar Eliphaz
father of Omri Becher, Michael
father of Onam Jerameel, Shobal
father of Onan Judah
father of one's husband father-in-law
father of Ophelia Polonius
father of Orestes Agamemnon
father of Othni Shemaiah
father of Ozem Jesse
father of Ozni Gad
father of Pallu Reuben

father of Parmashta Haman
father of Parshandatha Haman
father of Peleth Jonathan
father of Peter Jonas
father of Pharez Judah
father of Phinehas Eli
father of Phuvah Issachar
father of Pildash Nahor
father of Pluto Saturn
father of Pollux Zeus
father of Poseidon Cronos, Kronos
father of Rachel Laban
father of Raddai Jesse
father of Reaia Micah
father of Rebekah Bethuel
father of Rehabiah Eliezer
father of Rehoboam Solomon
father of Rekem Hebron
father of Rephah Ephraim
father of Resheph Ephraim
father of Reuben Jacob
father of Reuel Esau
father of Rhea Uranus
father of Rhesa Zorobabel
father of Rosamunda Cunimond
father of Rosh Benjamin
father of Rufus Simon
father of Salmon Nahshon
father of Salome Herod
father of Samson Manoah
father of Samuel Elkanah
father of Sarah Asher
father of Saturn Uranus
father of Saul Kish
father of Seb Shu
father of Sered Zebulun
father of Seth Adam
father of Sethur Michael
father of Shaaph Caleb
father of Shamariah Rohoboam
father of Shammah Jesse
father of Shammua David
father of Shaul Simeon
father of Sheber Caleb
father of Shehariah Jehoram
father of Shelah Judah
father of Shem Noah
father of Sherah Ephraim
father of Sheva Caleb
father of Shillem Naphtali
father of Shimea David
father of Shimma Jesse
father of Shobab David
father of Shuah Abraham
father of Shuham Dan
father of Shuni Gad
father of Simeon Jacob
father of Simon Mattathias
father of Suzanna Shakespeare
father of Tamar David
father of Tantalus Amphion, Jupiter, Thyestes

father of Taphath Solomon
father of Tarea Micah
father of Tebah Nahor
father of Tema Ishmael
father of Teman Eliphaz
father of Themis Uranus
father of Theseus Aegeus
father of Tiras Japheth
father of Titans Uranus
father of Tola Issachar
father of Triton Neptune, Poseidon
father of Tubal Japheth
father of Tyr Odin
father of Ulysses Laertes
father of Uriel Tahath
father of Vashni Samuel
father of Zachariah Jeroboam
father of Zacharias Barachias
father of Zara Judah
father of Zaza Jonathan
father of Zebadiah Ishmael
father of Zebulun Jacob
father of Zedekiah Josiah
father of Zeruah Nebat
father of Zimeon Abraham
father of Ziporah Jethro
father of Zohar Simeon
father of Zophai Elkanah
father of Zur Jehiel
father of Zuriel Abihail
father or mother parent
father's boy son
father's brother uncle
father's father grandpa
father's sister aunt
fatigue drain, ennui, exertion, exhaust(ion), fag, hardship, lassitude, misuse, oppress, overtire, sleepiness, tedious, tire, tiredness, toil, weakness, weariness, weary, whack
fat in bones marrow
fatlike substance lipid(e)
fat melted from roasting meat dripping
fatty adipose, fat, greasy, lipid(e), oily, oleaginous, rich, sebaceous, slick, slimy, slippery, suety
fatty acid amino-
fatty blood alcohol cholesterol
fatty deposit within artery atheroma
fatty part of milk cream
fatty substance suet, tallow
fatty substance in cavities of bones marrow
fatuous absurd, asinine, crazy, foolish, idiotic, inane, mindless, puerile, purposeless, witless
fatuously absurdly, brainlessly, densely, dully, foolishly, idiotically, inanely, ludicrously, mindlessly, stupidly
fatuous person goof

**faucet** (pet)cock, robinet, spigot, stopcock, tap, valve
**faucet leak** drip
**faucet trouble** drip, leak
**fault** blemish, defect, delinquency, demerit, error, failing, flaw, imperfection, indiscretion, misdeed, mistake, offence, shortcoming, sin, weakness, wrong
**fault-finder** critic
**fault-finding in petty way** nit-picking
**fault in computer's system or program** bug, virus
**faultless** accurate, blameless, classic, correct, impeccable, innocent, perfect, pure, sinless, unspotted
**faulty** bad, culpable, defective, dys-, imperfect, incomplete, reprehensible
**faulty assumption** misinterpretation
**faulty reasoning** syllogism
**faulty structure** deformity, malformation, malformed
**fauna** animals
**fauna and flora** nature
**fauna on Australian ten-cent coin** lyrebirds
**faux pas** blunder, clanger, error, gaffe, indiscretion
**favour** aid, approbation, approval, approve, assistance, badge, boon, champion, choose, commend, courtesy, esteem, gift, goodwill, grace, help, honours, indulge, influence, kindness, liking, oblige, regard, repute, souvenir, support, vantage
**favourable** advantageous, approving, auspicious, beneficial, benign, comfortable, conducive, eager, effective, effectual, encouraging, fit, good, propitious, rewarding, salutary, serviceable, suitable, sympathetic, understanding
**favourable attention** ear, study
**favourable bias** err, favouritism
**favourable condition** advantage
**favourable for a purpose** opportune
**favourable occasion** opportunity
**favourable opinion** esteem
**favourable outcome** success
**favourable outcome of illness** lysis
**favourable position for observation** coign(e)
**favourable purchase** bargain
**favourable state** advantage
**favourable to health** salubrious
**favourable verdict** absolvitor, acquittal
**favourable vote** ay(e), yea, yes
**favouring of family** nepotism
**favouring social equality** democratic
**favour in return** quid pro quo

**favourite** beloved, best, brat, choice, darling, dear(est), esteemed, favoured, god, hero, ideal, idol, pet, popular, predilection, preference, preferred, selected, sweetheart, Utopian
**favourite animal** pet
**favourite child** minion
**favourite one** pal, pet
**favourite remedy** nostrum
**favourite residence of Queen Victoria** Osborne House
**favourite wife of Mohammed** Aisha, Ayesha
**favour to relatives** nepotism
**fawn** adulate, brown, cajole, caress, coax, cringe, deer, doe, flatter, grovel, servility, youngling
**fawn-coloured** cervine
**fawning person** flunk(e)y
**fawn shade** beige
**fay** fairy
**FBI man** agent
**fealty** allegiance, constancy, faith, fidelity, loyalty, truth
**fear** afraid, alarm, angst (G), anxiety, apprehensiveness, awe, concern, dismay, dread, emotion, fright(ened), hesitant, horror, panic, phobia, piety, shrink, solicitude, terror, timorousness, trepidation, uneasy, venerate
**fear and wonder** awe
**fearful** afraid, annoying, apprehensive, august, awesome, awful, cautious, cowardly, dire, dread(ful), frightened, macabre, nervous, ominous, panicky, reluctant, revered, sacred, terrible, terrified, terrifying, timid, timorous, tremulous, trepid, unwilling, venerable
**fear greatly** dread
**fearing open spaces** agoraphobic
**fearless** bold, brave, confident, courageous, daring, gallant, heroic, indomitable, intrepid, plucky, unafraid, undaunted, valiant, valorous
**fearless person** dreadnought
**fear of aeroplanes or flying** aerophobia, pterophobia
**fear of animals** zoophobia
**fear of bees** apiphobia, melissophobia
**fear of being alarmed** phobophobia
**fear of birds** ornithophobia
**fear of blood** haematophobia, haemophobia
**fear of blushing and the colour red** erythrophobia
**fear of bridges or crossings** gephyrophobia
**fear of burial alive** taphophobia

**fear of cats** ailurophobia, gatophobia
**fear of certain sexual preferences** homophobia
**fear of children** paedophobia
**fear of choking** pnigophobia
**fear of closed areas** claustrophobia
**fear of clouds** nebulaphobia
**fear of cold** cheimophobia, cyrophobia, psychrophobia
**fear of colours** chromophobia
**fear of confined spaces** claustrophobia, clithrophobia
**fear of contamination** mysophobia
**fear of crossing bridges** gephydrophobia
**fear of crossing streets** dromophobia
**fear of crowds** demophobia, ochlophobia
**fear of darkness** achluophobia, lygophobia, nyctophobia, scotophobia
**fear of death or dead bodies** necrophobia, thanatophobia
**fear of depths or deep places** bathophobia
**fear of deserts or dry places** xerophobia
**fear of dining and the conversation there** deiphnophobia
**fear of dirt** rupophobia
**fear of dogs** cynophobia
**fear of draughts of air** aerophobia
**fear of dust** amathophobia
**fear of dying** thanatophobia
**fear of enclosed spaces** claustrophobia, clithrophobia
**fear of experiencing bodily pains** algophobia
**fear of fires** pyrophobia
**fear of fish** ichthyophobia
**fear of flying** aerophobia, pterophobia
**fear of foreigners** xenophobia
**fear of germs** microbiophobia
**fear of ghosts** phasmophobia
**fear of good news** euphobia
**fear of heat** thermophobia
**fear of heights** acrophobia
**fear of horses** hippophobia
**fear of ideas and reason** ideaphobia
**fear of illness** nosophobia, pathophobia
**fear of injury** traumatophobia
**fear of insects** entomophobia
**fear of lightning** astrapophobia, keraunophobia
**fear of loneliness** autophobia, eremiophobia, monophobia
**fear of madness** lyssophobia, maniaphobia
**fear of men and boys** androphobia
**fear of mice** musophobia

**fear of name or particular word** onomatophobia
**fear of noise** phonophobia
**fear of novelty** neophobia
**fear of number thirteen** triskaidekaphobia
**fear of objects on the left side** levophobia
**fear of old age** gerascophobia
**fear of open spaces** agoraphobia, kenophobia
**fear of pain** algophobia, odynophobia
**fear of particular place** topophobia
**fear of peanut butter clogging in the mouth** arachibutyrophobia
**fear of people** anthropophobia
**fear of poisoning** iophobia, toxicophobia
**fear of pregnancy** maieusiophobia
**fear of public speaking** glossophobia, lalophobia
**fear of reptiles** bactraphobia
**fear of riding in a vehicle** amaxophobia
**fear of sea** thalassophobia
**fear of shadows** sciophobia
**fear of sharks** galeophobia
**fear of sitting down** cathisophobia
**fear of sleep** hypnophobia
**fear of slime** blennophobia
**fear of snakes** ophidiophobia
**fear of speaking aloud** phonophobia
**fear of speed** tacophobia
**fear of spiders** arachnaphobia
**fear of staining** cromophobia
**fear of strangers and all things foreign** xenophobia
**fear of surgery** ergasiophobia, tomophobia
**fear of technology** technophobia
**fear of the English** Anglophobia
**fear of the night** nyctophobia
**fear of the ocean** thalassophobia
**fear of the Russians** Russophobia
**fear of thunder** brontophobia, keraunophobia, tonitrophobia
**fear of trains** siderodromophobia
**fear of travel** hodophobia
**fear of wasps** spexsophobia
**fear of water** aquaphobia, hydrophobia, hygrophobia
**fear of women and girls** gynophobia
**fear of worms** helminthophobia, scoileciphobia
**fearsome** alarming, awe-inspiring, awesome, formidable, horrifying, menacing, unnerving
**fearsome person** ogre, tartar
**fearsome woman** ogress, virago
**feasible** attainable, likely, possible, practicable, reasonable, viable, workable

**feasible within bounds** viable
**feast** bacchanal, banquet, carousal, carouse, celebrate, celebration, ceremony, collation, debauch, delight, dine, entertain(ment), event, festival, festivity, fête, frolic, gathering, gorge, gourmandise, gratification, indulge, jubilee, lark, occasion, orgy, partake, party, regale, remembrance, repast, revel, ritual, spread, treat, whirl
**feast in open air** picnic
**feast of Hawaiian food** luau
**Feast of Lanterns** Bon
**feast one's eyes upon** gaze, glance, look, observe, regard
**feast royally** regale
**feat** accomplishment, achievement, act(ion), adroit, adventure, attainment, deed, dextrous, enterprise, exploit, neat, performance, prowess, smart, stunt, trick
**feathered friend** bird
**feathered missile** arrow
**feather filament** dowl(e)
**feather in one's cap** acclaim, accomplishment, distinction, garland, honour, laurels, praise, prestige
**feather pen** quill
**feathers** down, plumage, plumes
**feather scarf** boa
**feathers of bird** plumage
**feather used as pen** quill
**feathery** downy, fleecy, flowing, fluid, pinnate, rounded, silky, smooth, soft, velvety
**feathery frond** fern
**feathery-leafed herb** feverfew
**feathery quilt** duvet, eiderdown
**feat of daring** stunt
**feat of endurance** marathon
**feat of strength or skill** tour de force

**(F)**

**feature** aspect, characteristic, component, display, dramatise, form, mien, movie, part, peculiarity, quality, sketch, speciality, trait
**featureless** blank, nondescript
**features of land-area as seen in broad view** landscape
**febrile** feverish
**February 29 period** leap year
**feckless** aimless, feeble, futile, hopeless, incompetent, ineffectual, inefficient, shiftless, useless, weak, worthless
**fecund** fertile, fertilising, fructious, fruit-bearing, fruitful, generative, lush, potent, productive, profuse, prolific, rich

**fecundate** fertilise
**fecundity** abundance, bounty, copiousness, creativity, fertility, fruitfulness, lushness, luxuriance, productiveness, prolificality, richness, wealth
**federation** amalgamation, coalition, confederating, confederation, league, syndicate, union, uniting
**federation of states** commonwealth
**fedora** hat
**fed up** annoyed, bored, depressed, discontented, dismal, dissatisfied, gloomy, glum, tired, weary
**fee** charge, compensation, consideration, fare, pay(ment), price, remuneration, salary, wage
**feeble** debilitated, declining, delicate, dim, doddering, effete, enervated, enfeebled, exhausted, failing, faint, frail, inadequate, incompetent, indecisive, ineffective, ineffectual, infirm, lame, languid, poor, powerless, puny, shilpit, sickly, tame, thin, weak(ened)
**feeble character** nincompoop
**feeble creature** weakling
**feeble imitation** parody
**feeble in character** chinless, gormless
**feeble in health** infirm
**feeble-minded** anile, deficient, dotty, dull(-witted), retarded
**feeble-minded person** idiot, moron
**feeble-minded senility** dotage
**feeble-minded through old age** senile
**feeble person** namby-pamby, weakling
**feeble sentimentality** mush
**feebly humorous** corny
**feebly sentimental** lackadaisical, languishing, mawkish, mushy
**feebly submissive person** doormat
**fee charged for passage on ferry** ferriage
**feed** board, browse, cater, crop, devour, dine, eat, edibles, engorge, fodder, food, forage, foster, gorge, gratify, nourish, nurture, partake, please, provision, sate, satiate, satisfy, subsist, sustain, victuals
**feed a fire** stoke
**feedbag item** oats
**feed from the breast** suckle
**feed greedily** gorge
**feeding bottle mouthpiece** teat
**feeding mainly on insects** entomophagous, insectivorous
**feeding on animals** zoophagous
**feeding on both plants and flesh** omnivorous
**feeding on carrion** necrophagous
**feeding on decaying matter** saprophagous

**feeding on dung** scatophagous
**feeding on fish** ichthyophagous
**feeding on flesh** carnivorous
**feeding on grain** granivorous
**feeding on grass and cereals** graminivorous
**feeding on plants** herbivorous
**feeding on wood** hylophagous, lignivorous
**feed on** eat
**feed on shoots and leaves** browse
**feed with fuel** stoke
**fee from employment** emolument, salary
**feel** appear, believe, bent, caress, composition, consider, empathise, endure, enjoy, experience, feeling, finger, finish, fondle, fumble, grope, handle, impression, judge, knack, know, notice, observe, perceive, quality, reckon, seem, sense, suffer, surface, sympathise, texture, think, touch, undergo, understand, vibes
**feel attracted to** like
**feel bitter** resent
**feel certain** know, realise
**feel compassion** pity
**feel concern** care
**feel contempt** despise
**feel contrition** repent, rue
**feel disgust** revolt
**feel dissatisfaction** resent
**feel dull pain** ache
**feeler** advance, antenna, barometer, experiment, inquiry, leak, offer, overture, palp(us), probe, proposal, random, sample, sensor, tentacle
**feel for** bleed, condole, grieve, lament, pity
**feel great joy** rejoice
**feel guilt** shame
**feel guilt about something** ashamed
**feel hatred** loathe
**feel hostility toward** execrate
**feel hot and bothered** perspire
**feel hurt** resent
**feel ill** ail
**feeling** consciousness, emotion(al), empathy, impression, opinion, passion(ate), sensation, sensibility, sensitive, sensitivity, sentient, sentiment(ality), sympathy
**feeling at ease** comfortable
**feeling braced** tingling
**feeling confused** dizzy, giddy
**feeling convinced** certitude
**feeling deeply** intense
**feeling dejected** glum
**feeling effects of disease** sick
**feeling envy** envious
**feeling extreme ill will** malignant
**feeling for another in pain** sympathy

**feeling great guilt** contrite
**feeling malicious satisfaction** gloating
**feeling nausea** queasy
**feeling no hope** hopeless
**feeling no remorse** unrepentant
**feeling of annoyance** chagrin, offence
**feeling of appreciation** gratitude
**feeling of being ill at ease** dysphoria
**feeling of belonging together** togetherness
**feeling of certainty** boldness, certitude, confidence, self-reliance
**feeling of cold** shiver
**feeling of confusion** consternation
**feeling of depression** malaise
**feeling of desire** hope
**feeling of disapproval** objection
**feeling of discouragement** chill
**feeling of doubt** dubiety, misgiving, scruple
**feeling of general happiness** euphoria
**feeling of great unhappiness** misery
**feeling of horror** shivers
**feeling of ill will** grudge
**feeling of inadequacy** inferiority complex
**feeling of regret** remorse
**feeling of remorse** conscience, regret
**feeling of romance** stardust
**feeling of sickness** malaise, nausea
**feeling of trust** hope
**feeling of uneasiness** malaise
**feeling of well-being** euphoria
**feeling or emotion** sentiment
**feeling pity** sorry
**feeling regret** sorry
**feeling sharp pain** smarting
**feeling slightly hungry** peckish
**feeling sorrow** rueful
**feeling stupefied** dazed, muzzy
**feel like** desire, fancy, want
**feel pain** suffer
**feel regret** rue
**feel remorse** repent
**feel repentant about** regret
**feel slight pricking sensation** tingle
**feel sore** smarting
**feel sorrow** grieve
**feel sorry** mourn, regret
**feel sorry for** commiserate, pity, regret
**feel strong desire for** long
**feel strong hatred for** loathe
**feel the want** miss
**feel tingling pain** smart
**feel unwell** ail
**feel very cold** freeze
**feel with fingers** palpate, touch
**feign** affect, assume, bluff, concoct, contrive, copy, counterfeit, deceive, delude, emulate, fabricate, fake, forge, imitate, impersonate, invent, lie, make-believe, mimic, mislead,

perform, pose, posture, pretend, seem, sham, simulate
**feign confidence** bluff
**feigned sickness** malingery
**feign illness** malinger
**feign strength** bluff, deceive, fake, mislead, pretend
**feldspar with pearly appearance** moonstone
**felicitations** blessings, cheers, compliments, congratulations, greetings, joy, salutations, toasts, well-wishing
**felicity** aptness, bliss, delight, ecstasy, fitness, gladness, happiness, harmony, joy, justness, pertinence, rapture, relevance, relevancy, suitability
**feline** canny, cat(-like), cattish, crafty, cunning, felid, genet, graceful, insidious, jaguar, leonine, lynx-like, ocelot, ounce, pussycat, seductive, sensual, sinuous, slinky, sly, smooth, sneaky, stealthy, subtle, tiger, tricky, wily
**feline animal** cat, cheetah, eyra, jaguarondi, jaguarundi, lion, lynx, ocelot, tiger
**feline hybrid** tigon
**feline pelt** leopard skin, tiger skin
**feline pet** cat
**feline predator** cheetah, leopard, lion, lynx, tiger
**feline sound** purr
**feline treat** catnip
**fell** cut, demolish, descended, flatten, level, prostrate, raze
**fellow** acquaintance, affiliate(d), akin, allied, ally, ami (F), amigo, analogue, associate, bloke, boy, bozo, bra, broer, buddy, caballero, chap(pie), chum, co-worker, codger, colleague, companion, compeer, comrade, counterpart, crony, don, equal, esquire, friend, gentleman, guy, hidalgo, hombre, individual, lad, male, man, mate, oke, ou, pal, person, related, resemblant, squire, twin
**fellow boarder** room-mate
**fellow communist** comrade
**fellow countryman** compatriot, friend, native
**fellow feeling** benevolence, co-operation, comradeship, condolence, friendliness, humanity, identification, participation, pity, sympathy
**fellow member of profession** confrère
**fellow members of religious society** brethren
**fellow official** colleague

**fellow sailor** shipmate
**fellow scholar** classmate
**fellowship** association, brotherhood, camaraderie, club, communion, companionship, familiarity, fraternity, guild, intimacy, kindliness, league, order, sisterhood, sociability
**fellowship and loyalty among intimate friends** camaraderie
**fellow traveller** pinker
**fellow worker** colleague, mate
**fell sick** ailed
**felon** criminal, cruel, malicious, malignant, murderous, whitlow, wicked
**felony** crime, sin, wickedness
**felony is one** crime
**felt cap** beret
**felt hat** fedora
**felt material** baize
**felt sun hat** Terai
**female** dame, delicate, distaff, effeminate, feminine, girl, lady, she, woman(ly)
**female adult** woman
**female adviser** Egeria
**female announcer** commère
**female antelope** doe
**female ass** jenny
**female baboon** babuina
**female badger** sow
**female bed attire** negligee, nightie, pyjamas, teddy
**female bird** hen
**female cat** grimalkin, puss, she-cat, tabby
**female chauffeur** chauffeuse
**female chicken** hen
**female child** daughter, girl
**female clairvoyant** seeress
**female comedian** comedienne
**female deacon** deaconess
**female deer** doe, hind, roe
**female deer in second year** teg
**female deity** goddess
**female demon** hag, lamia, succubus
**female dog** bitch
**female domestic servant** skivvy
**female donkey** jenny, she-ass
**female elephant** cow
**female equine** mare
**female ferret** bitch, gill, jill
**female figure representing Britain** Britannia
**female film player** actress
**female fish** raun, spawner
**female foal** filly
**female fowl** hen
**female fox** bitch, vixen
**female friend** amie (F)
**female gamete** egg, ootid
**female garment** dress

**female germ cell of animals** ovum
**female germ cell of seed plants** ovule
**female giant** giantess, ogress
**female goat** doe, nanny
**female graduate** alumna
**female hare** doe, puss
**female hawk** lanner
**female head of abbey of nuns** abbess, mother superior
**female head of household** mistress
**female heir** heiress
**female hero** heroine
**female herring** raun
**female hormone** oestrogen
**female horse** dam, filly, mare
**female horse rider** equestrienne
**female inheritor** heiress
**female kangaroo** doe, gin
**female killer** murderess
**female kin** aunt, daughter, (grand)mother, niece, sister
**female lead** heroine
**female leopard** leopardess
**female lobster** hen
**female lover** inamorata
**female massager** masseuse
**female maturity** womanhood
**female minister** priestess
**female monster** harpy, Lamia, ogress, Scylla
**female night-club singer** chanteuse
**female offspring** daughter
**female of the black grouse** grey-hen
**female organ** ovary, uterus, womb
**female organ of flower** pistil
**female otter** bitch
**female ovum** egg
**female parent** mother
**female partner** wife
**female party giver** hostess
**female peafowl** peahen
**female pig** sow, gilt
**female polecat** gill, jill
**female pop singer** Annie Lennox, Brenda Fassie, Cher, Madonna, Tina Turner, Yvonne Chaka-Chaka
**female professional singer** canatatrice (F)
**female pronoun** she
**female rabbit** doe
**female ray** maid
**female red deer** hind
**female relative** aunt, daughter, grandmother, mother, niece, sister
**female reproductive organ** ovary
**female rhinoceros** cow
**female ruff** ree(ve)
**female ruler** empress, queen
**female ruminant** cow, ewe
**female salmon** baggit, hen, raun
**female sandpiper** reeve
**female seal** cow

**female servant** maid(servant)
**female sex hormone** oestrogen
**female sheep** ewe
**female sibling** sister
**female singer of lowest range** contralto
**female singing voice** alto, contralto, soprano
**female slave in Turkish sultan's seraglio** odalisque
**female sovereign** queen
**female spirit** banshee
**female spouse** wife
**female stage performer** actress
**female star** actress, heroine
**female statue used as column** caryatid
**female suffix** -ess
**female swan** pen
**female swine** sow
**female teacher** mistress
**female Thespian** actress
**female tiger** tigress
**female title** madam
**female treble** soprano
**female voice** alto, contralto, soprano
**female walrus** cow
**female warrior** Amazon
**female whale** cow
**female who inherits great wealth** heiress
**female wizard** witch
**female wolf** bitch, she-wolf
**female zebra** mare
**feminine** delicate, distaff, effeminate, female, ladylike, womanly
**feminine equivalent of satyr** nymphomaniac
**feminine pronoun** her, she
**feminine sex** female
**feminine suffix** -ette
**feminine title** dame, lady(ship), madam(e), milady, princess
**femme fatale (F)** charmer, Circe, enchantress, seductress, siren, vamp
**femur** thighbone
**fen** bog, marsh(land), morass, quagmire, slough, swamp
**fence** balustrade, barricade, barrier, enclose, enclosure, encompass, guard, hedge, palisade, pen, protect, rail, rampart, reset, safeguard, screen, surround, wall
**fence door** gate
**fenced village** kraal
**fence feature** gate
**fence in** enclose, pen
**fence in with stakes** impale
**fence of iron railings** palisade
**fence opening** gate
**fence part** gatepost
**fence post** stake

**fencer's foil** épée
**fence's horizontal bar** rail
**fence stake** picket
**fence steps** stile
**fencing** swordplay
**fencing foil** épée
**fencing material** wire
**fencing posture** septime
**fencing rapier** foil
**fencing sword** épée, foil, rapier, saber
**fencing thrust** botte (F), hay, lunge, punto, remise, riposte
**fend** avert, debar, forestall, guard, hinder, inhibit, parry, prevent, protect, screen, shelter, shield, ward
**fender mishap** bump, dent, rent
**fend for** maintain, support, sustain
**fend off** avert, check, defend, deflect, parry, rebuff, repel, repulse, resist
**feral** brutal, savage, uncultivated, untamed, wild
**ferment** agitate, agitation, boil, brew, bubble, commotion, concoct, excite(ment), fester, fever, foam, foment, frenzy, froth, glow, heat, incite, inflame, leaven, provoke, rise, rouse, seethe, smoulder, stew, stir, tumult, turmoil, unrest, uproar, work, yeast
**fermentation** zymosis
**fermentation tank** vat
**fermented apple juice** cider
**fermented cabbage** sauerkraut
**fermented cider-like drink made from pears** perry
**fermented grape juice** wine
**fermented liquor** ale
**fermented malt** beer
**fermented malt liquor** ale
**fermented milk** yogh(o)urt
**fermenting agent** barm, leaven, yeast
**ferment in gastric juice** pepsin
**fern garden** fernery
**fern leaf** frond
**fern spores** nardoo
**fern with delicate stalks and frond** maidenhair
**ferocious** acute, barbaric, beastly, bestial, brutal, cruel, demonic, diabolic, feral, fierce, great, harsh, heartless, inhuman, intense, lupine, merciless, monstrous, murderous, pitiless, rapacious, ruthless, sanguinary, savage, sharp, truculent, untamed, vicious, violent, vivid, wild
**ferocious act** ferocity
**ferocity** barbarity, brutality, cruelty, fierceness, inhumanity, savageness, savagery, viciousness
**ferret** ferule, polecat
**ferret about** hunt, rummage, search

**ferret out** scrounge
**ferric metal** iron
**ferric oxide as ore** haematite
**ferrous metal** iron
**ferrule** ferrel
**ferry** boat, carrier, carry, convey, ferryboat, ford, ply, pont, ship, traject, transport
**ferry dock** slip
**ferryman of the Styx** Charon
**fertile** abundant, fat, fecund, flowering, fruitful, luxuriant, plenteous, plentiful, productive, prolific, rich, teeming, yielding
**fertile area** oasis
**fertile area of Sahara** Fezzan
**fertile deposit in river valleys** loess
**fertile desert spot** oasis
**fertile place** oasis
**fertile soil** loam
**fertilisation** endogamy, porogamy, xenigamy
**fertilisation by cross-pollination** xenogamy
**fertilisation of flowers** pollination
**fertilise** compost, dress, enrich, fecundate, feed, fructify, impregnate, manure, mulch
**fertilised egg** oosperm
**fertiliser** carnallite, compost, dressing, droppings, dung, guano, manure, marl, urea
**fertilising dust of flower** pollen
**fertilising organ** stamen
**fertility** abundance, fecundity
**ferule** ferret, polecat
**fervent** alight, animated, ardent, ardour, brilliant, burning, eager, earnest, enthusiastic, excited, fervid, fiery, flaming, frantic, glowing, heated, hot, impassioned, impetuous, inflamed, intense, loving, nervous, parching, passionate, pietistic, radiant, sensitive, tense, touchy, upset, warm, zealous
**fervent devotee** partisan
**fervent supporter of cause** chauvinist
**fervid** ardent, devout, eager, ecstatic, excited, fervent, impassioned, passionate, warm, zealous
**fervour** animation, ardour, eagerness, earnestness, enthusiasm, excitement, fervency, flame, glow, gusto, heat, intense, intensity, passion, vehemence, warmth, zeal, zest
**festal** carnival, celebratory, cheery, convivial, feative, gay, happy, hearty, jolly, jovial, joyful, joyous, jubilant, merry, mirthful, sportive
**festal day** festival

**fester** agitate, burn, chafe, decay, decompose, excite, ferment, foment, grow, heat, incite, inflame, mortify, necrose, pique, provoke, putrefy, rage, rankle, rot, rouse, seethe, simmer, smoulder, stagnate, suppurate, ulcerate
**festering** angry, bad, corrupt, decayed, decomposed, fermenting, f(o)etid, fomenting, heated, inflamed, perished, putrid, rank, red, rotten, septic, sore, stinking
**festering sore** abscess
**festival** carnival, celebration, Easter, feast, fête, fiesta, gala, Mardi Gras
**festival of Shrove Tuesday** Mardi Gras
**festival of the Resurrection** Easter
**festive** festal, gala, gay, jolly, joyous, larkish, lighthearted, merry, sportive
**festive celebration** festivity
**festive gathering** fair, gala, shindig
**festive occasion** beanfeast, gala, wassail
**festive wear** finery
**festivity** amusement, celebration, festival, fiesta, fun, gaiety, gala, jollification, joviality, joyfulness, merriment, mirth, party, pleasure
**festoon** adorn, array, bedeck, deck, decorate, drape, garland, hang, lei, swag, swathe, wreathe
**festoon of ornamental fruit or flowers** swag
**fetch** afford, bag, bring, capture, catch, conduct, delight, deliver, dodge, draw, ensnare, entrap, get, go, grab, grasp, obtain, procure, reach, retrieve, seize, stretch, trick, wraith, yield
**fetching** alluring, attractive, crafty, cunning, pleasing, scheming, sweet, taking, winning, winsome
**fetch up** arrive, come, finish, halt, reach, stop
**fête** bazaar, carnival, celebration, entertainment, fair, feast, festival, frolic, gala, lionise, Mardi Gras, party, social, treat
**fetid** foetid, foul, fusty, gamy, malodorous, mouldy, musty, niffy, noisome, offensive, olid, putrid, rancid, rank(-smelling), rotten, smelly, stale, stinking, tainted, unclean, unpleasant, whiffy, yeasty
**fetish** amulet, charm, compulsion, crotchet, eccentricity, fixation, idée fixe (F), kink, mania, obsession, periapt, talisman, totem
**fetor** stench
**fetter** bind, bond, captivity, chain, check, curb, detain, duress, gyve, handcuff, hinder, hindrance, impede,

imprison, iron, manacle, restrain(t), shackle, tie, truss
**fetter for the hand** handcuff, manacle
**feud** animosity, argument, broil, contention, difference, discord, dispute, enmity, falling-out, hostility, quarrel, strife, vendetta
**feudal estate** manor
**feudal lord** chieftain, liege, master, seigneur, suzerain
**feudal overlord** suzerain
**feudal slave** serf
**feudal superior** lord
**feudal tax** scutage
**feudal villein** serf
**feuding** quarrelling
**fever** agitation, ague, ailment, ardour, delirium, desire, ecstasy, excitement, febricity, febrile, fervour, feverishness, heat, illness, infection, inflammation, intensity, passion, pyrexia, restlessness, temperature, turmoil, unrest, urgency
**feverish** ardent, boisterous, chaotic, distracted, excited, febrile, fervent, fevered, fitful, flurrying, flushed, frantic, frenetic, frenzied, heated, hectic, hot, impatient, inflamed, obsessive, passionate, pyretic, restless, riotous, turbulent, wild
**feverish chill** ague
**feverish cold** chill
**feverishly active** hectic
**fever transmitted by mosquito bite** malaria
**fever tree** acacia
**fever with shivering** ague
**few** limited, meagre, oligo-, rare, scant, scarce, several, some, wheen (Sc)
**few and far between** infrequent, meagre, rare, scanty, scarce, scattered, scattering, sparse, uncommon, unusual
**fewer** less, rarer, scantier, scarcer, sparser, thinner
**fey** clairvoyant, doomed, elfin, fairylike, other-worldly, strange, visionary, whimsical
**fez-like cap** tarboosh
**fiancé** betrothed, boyfriend, bridegroom-to-be, husband-to-be, intended, sweetheart
**fiancée** betrothed, bride-to-be, girlfriend, intended, sweetheart, wife-to-be
**fiasco** abortion, botch, catastrophe, debacle, disaster, failure, inefficacy, mess, nonsuccess, rout, ruin, scrape
**fiat** act, decree, edict, order, sanction
**fib** fabrication, falsehood, falsity, fiction, invention, lie, misrepresentation, palter,

prevaricate, prevarication, story, taradiddle, untruth, whopper
**fibber** cheater, liar, misleader, perjurer, prevaricator
**fibre** ambari, ambary, bast, character, coir, eruc, fibril, filament, hemp, istle, jute, mould, nature, pita, raffia, ramie, roughage, sisal, staple, strand, texture, thread
**fibre for rope** sisal
**fibre from coconut** coir
**fibre from leaves of agave** sisal
**fibre from outer husk of coconut** coir
**fibre knot** nep
**fibre made by larvae of certain moths** silk
**fibre of South American aloe** sisal
**fibre plant** aloe, cajun, flax, hemp, pita, ramie, sisal
**fibres of flax** harl
**fibre split up into fibrils** fibrilate
**fibre used for cord** istle
**fibre used for cordage** sisal
**fibre used for robes** manil(l)a
**fibre used for sacking** jute
**fibre used for stuffing** kapok
**fibrous bone-connecting tissue** ligament
**fibrous mineral which does not burn** asbestos
**fibrous tumour** fibroma
**fibrous weaving material** raffia
**fickle** capricious, changeable, disloyal, faithless, inconstant, irresolute, mutable, treacherous, uncertain, unfaithful, unpredictable, unreliable, unstable, unsteady, unsure, vacillating, variable, volatile, wavering
**fickleness** capriciousness, changeableness, fancifulness, fitfulness, impulsiveness, inconstancy, irresoluteness, irresolution, mutability, uncertainty, unfaithfulness, unstableness, unsteadiness, untrustworthiness
**fickle person** chameleon
**fico** trifle
**fiction** concoction, fable, fabrication, falsity, fantasy, figment, imagination, improvisation, lie, myth, novel, parable, romance, unreality, yarn
**fictional** imaginary, invented, literary, mythical, non-existent, unreal
**fictional book** novel
**fictional plantation** Tara
**fiction work** novel
**fiction writer** novelist
**fictitious** apocryphal, artificial, assumed, bogus, false, fanciful, feigned, imaginary, imagined, improvised, invented, mythical, unreal, untrue

**fictitious bird** phoenix, lightning bird
**fictitious country rich in gold** Eldorado
**fictitious name** pseudonym
**fictitious narrative** tale
**fictitious person** myth
**fictitious reason** pretext
**fictitious story** invention
**fiddle** cheat, con, diddle, fasify, fidget, fix, fraud, gerrymander, graft, healthy, interfere, juggle, manoeuvre, meddle, monkey-business, play, racket(eer), rip-off, sound, strong, swindle, tamper, tinker, toy, trifle, violin, wangle
**fiddle around** peddle
**fiddle-de-dee** nonsense
**fiddler** cheat, fiddle-player, swindler, violinist
**fiddlesticks** balderdash, eyewash, fiddle-de-dee, fiddle-faddle, nonsense, rubbish
**fiddling** contemptible, futile, petty, trivial
**fiddling emperor** Nero
**fiddly** awkward, intricate
**fidelity** accuracy, adherence, allegiance, closeness, constancy, correspondence, devotion, exactness, faithfulness, fealty, integrity, loyalty, piety, precision, reliability, staunchness, troth, trustworthiness, truth
**Fidel's country** Cuba
**fidget** bustle, chafe, fiddle, fret, squirm, twitch, uneasy, worry, wriggle
**fidget with thumbs** twiddle
**fidgety** impatient, jerky, nervous, restive, restless, uneasy
**Fido's treat** bone
**field** area, battleground, catch, expanse, handle, lea, meadow, paddock, pasture, realm, speciality, territory, veld
**field diversion** sport
**fielder** catcher
**field event** athletics, cricket, discus, javelin, jump, rugby, shooting, soccer, throw
**fieldfare** thrush
**field game** basketball, bowls, football, hockey, jukskei, lacrosse, rugby, soccer
**field glasses** binoculars
**field mammal** hare, mole, yak
**field of battle** battlefield
**field of conflict** arena
**field sport** athletics, cricket, discus, javelin, jump, rugby, shooting, soccer, throw
**field surface** turf
**field where rice is grown** paddy(-field)

**field-work** lunet(te), redan
**field worker** labourer
**fiend** barbarian, beast, brute, demon, devil, hellhound, incubus, monster, succubus
**fiendish** abominable, accursed, barbaric, brutal, cruel, cursed, damnable, damned, demoniac(al), demonic, detestable, devilish, hateful, infamous, infernal, inhuman, loathsome, malicious, monstrous, odious, satanic, savage, vicious, vile, wicked
**fiendish person** Mephistopheles
**fierce** aggressive, ardent, barbaric, bestial, brutal, brutish, cruel, dangerous, eager, fell, ferocious, furious, impetuous, intense, murderous, passionate, sanguinary, savage, truculent, untamed, vehement, violent, wild
**fierce American Indian** Apache
**fierce anger** outrage
**fierce attack** onset, onslaught
**fierce indignation** saeva indignatio (L)
**fierce look** glare
**fiercely** brutally, cruelly, ferociously, fiercely, frenziedly, furiously, intensely, menacingly, murderously, savagely, tempestuously, threateningly, viciously, wildly
**fierce person** drago(o)n, tartar
**fierce swashbuckler** Drawcansir
**fiery** ablaze, afire, alight, ardent, avid, berserk, burning, dyspeptic, eager, enthusiastic, fervent, fervid, fierce, flaming, gleaming, glowing, heated, ignited, impassioned, inflamed, intense, passionate, red, roused, tempestuous, torrid, vehement, warm, zealous
**fiery bullet** tracer
**fiery colour** crimson, orange, red, vermilion
**fiery particle** spark
**fiery red** minium
**fiery red precious stone** carbuncle
**fiery scaled, seven-headed sea serpent described in the book of Job** leviathan
**fiesta** anniversary, carnival, fair, feast, festival, festivity, fête, gala, holiday, Mardi Gras, party, remembrance
**fifth anniversary** quinquennial, quinquennium
**fifth columnist** quisling, spy
**fifth power of a quantity** sursolid
**fifth satellite of Jupiter** Amalthea
**fifth sign of the Zodiac** Leo
**fiftieth anniversary** jubilee
**fifty-seven degree angle** radian
**fifty-third card** joker

**fight** affray, argue, argument, assault, battle, bicker, box, brawl, close, combat, conduct, conflict, contend, contest, defy, dispute, encounter, engage(ment), feud, fray, grapple, joust, oppose, prosecute, resist, row, scrap, scrimmage, scuffle, skirmish, spar, squabble, strive, struggle, tilt, tussle, war, withstand, wrangle, wrestle
**fight against** combat, oppose, oppugn, resist
**fight back** contain, control, curb, reply, repress, resist, restrain, retaliate, retort, suppress
**fight between armies** battle
**fight between small groups** skirmish
**fight division** round
**fight down** control, curb, repress, restrain, suppress
**fighter** aggressor, assailant, assaulter, attacker, boxer, brave, cavalryman, champion, combatant, contender, contestant, disputant, dragoon, duellist, fencer, gladiator, man-at-arms, mercenary, militant, militarist, prizefighter, pugilist, soldier, swordsman, trouper, warrior, wrestler
**fighter in the ring** boxer, wrestler
**fighting** aggressive, assaulting, battling, belligerent, boxing, brawling, clashing, closing, combating, combative, conflicting, contending, contentious, disputatious, engaging, feuding, grappling, hawkish, jousting, martial, militant, pugnacious, rumbling, sparring, struggling, tilting, truculent, tussling, warlike, wrestling
**fighting between nations** war
**fighting fish** betta, leervis, marlin, plakat, tigerfish
**fighting force** army
**fighting spirit** morale
**fighting vessel** warship
**fighting with shadows** sciamachy, sciomachy, skiamachy
**fighting with the fists** fisticuffs
**fight in public** affray
**fight off** rebuff, repel, repress, repulse, resist, rout
**fight shy of** avoid, disdain, dodge, elude, escape, eschew, evade, shun, sidestep, spurn
**fight with lances** joust
**fight with swords** fence
**figment** canard, concoction, delusion, fable, fabrication, falsehood, fiction, hoax, idea, ideality, illusion, imagination, invention, myth, story

**figment of the imagination** fabrication, hallucination, illusion, mockery
**figurative illustration** imagery
**figurative use of a word** trope
**figure** amount, believe, calculate, calculation, character, compute, count, digit, drawing, form, guess, icon, judge, number, numeral, ornament, price, shape, total
**figured muslin** organdie
**figure-hugging dress** sheath
**figure of a god** idol
**figure of a small child or cherub** amoretto, amorino, putto
**figure of speech** conceit, epagoge, figure, image(ry), metaphor, personification, simile, trope, turn of phrase
**figure of worship** idol
**figure out** calculate, compute, decipher, disentangle, explain, fathom, reckon, resolve, see, solve, understand
**figure problem** sum
**figure with jointed limbs controlled by wires** marionette, puppet
**figure with many sides and angles** polygon
**figure with seven sides and angles** heptagon
**figure with twelve angles and sides** dodecagon
**figurine** carving, gimcrack, knick-knack, model, ornament, statue(tte), tanagra, trinket
**Fijian** Vitian
**Fijian bay** Mbya, Natewa, Ngaloa, Savusavu
**Fijian chestnut** rata
**Fijian fish** ongu
**Fijian point** Vuya
**Fiji discoverer** Tasman
**Fiji group** Lau, Ra
**Fiji island** Eld, Kambara, Kia, Koro, Mali, Mango, Naiau, Ngau, Ono, Ovalau, Totoya, Vitelevu
**filament** fibre, hair, harl, strand, thread
**filbert** cob(nut), hazelnut
**filch** abstract, embezzle, misappropriate, pilfer, purloin, steal, take, thieve,
**file** abrade, apply, burnish, case, classify, data, document, dossier, enter, folder, follow, furbish, grate, information, march, papers, polish, portfolio, queue, rasp, record, refine, register, row, rub, scrape, shape, smooth, store
**file a suit** litigate
**file of papers** dossier
**file wrongly** misfile

**filibuster** adventurer, delay, harangue, pillager
**filiform stem** runner
**filing drawer** tray
**filing envelope** folder
**Filipino native** Ata, Igorot, Moro, Tagalog
**fill** execute, fulfil, function, infuse, occupy, pervade, provide, sate, satiate, satisfy, saturate, sufficiency, surfeit
**fill adequately** supply
**fill again** refill, reload
**fill a suitcase** pack
**fill by sewing** darn, patch
**fill completely** charge, saturate
**fill container with liquid again** top-up
**fill cup to brim** bumper, crown
**filled pastry** pie
**filled tortilla** taco
**filled with air** pneumatic
**filled with alarm** dismayed
**filled with anger** irate
**filled with fear** afraid
**filled with joy** glad
**filled with mistaken zeal** fanatic(al)
**filled with passion** ardent
**filled with repentance** remorseful
**filled with respect and awe** reverent
**filled with shame** ashamed
**filled with sorrow** rueful
**fillet between flutes of column** stria
**fillet steak served with a coating of pâté** tournedos Rossini (I)
**fillet under the ovolo of a capital** orle
**fill full** force, stuff
**fill in** acquaint, advise, answer, brief, complete, deputise, inform, replace, represent, substitute, understudy
**fill in ballot** vote
**fillip** animate, arouse, awaken, incentive, incite, induce(ment), motivate, prick, prod, prompt, provocation, snap, stimulate, stimulus, tonic, urge
**fill joints between tiles** grout
**fill like a cushion** stuff
**fill out** complete, diffuse, dilate, enlarge, expand, stretch, stuff, swell
**fill overfull** cram
**fill the mind** obsess
**fill to excess** cram, glut
**fill up** replenish, replete, sate, stop, stuff
**fill with air** aerate, inflate
**fill with apprehension** alarm
**fill with bitterness** envenom
**fill with cargo** load, stow
**fill with cement** grout
**fill with courage** hearten
**fill with creative enthusiasm** inspire
**fill with dismay** consternate

**fill with eagerness** enthuse
**fill with ennui** bore
**fill with exhilaration** elate
**fill with fear** alarm, appal
**fill with high spirits** elate
**fill with holes** perforate
**fill with hope** inspire
**fill with inhabitants** populate
**fill with joy** elate, gladden
**fill with mortar** grout
**fill with optimism** elate
**fill with pride** elate, swell
**fill with surprise** astonish
**fill with terror** consternate, terrify
**fill with wonder** amaze, awe
**filly or colt** foal
**film** blanket, blur, coat(ing), cover, covering, gauze, haze, integument, layer, membrane, mist, movie, peel, photograph, scum, sheet, shoot, skin, spill, take, veil, web
**film appearing on metals** patina
**film award** Artes, Oscar
**film maker** producer
**film part** role
**film sequence** shot
**film's text** script
**film theatre** bioscope, cinema, moviehouse
**film with fast-moving plot** actioner, thriller
**filmy crust on old port wine** beeswing
**filter** clarify, clear, exude, filtrate, leach, leak, ooze, percolate, percolator, purify, refine, screen, seep, sieve, strain(er)
**filth** corruption, depraved, dirt, dregs, foul, garbage, grime, grubby, impurity, lewd, manure, mire, mud, nasty, obscene, obscenity, offal, pollution, putrid, refuse, scummy, sediment, slimy, slop, sludge, slush, smudge, smut, squalor, trash, vile(ness), vulgarity
**filthy** dirty, foul, obscene, squalid, unclean, vile
**filthy place** sty(e)
**filtration** purification
**final** absolute, certain, closing, coming, complete, completing, concluding, conclusive, decided, decisive, definitive, definite, determinate, end(ing), eventual, finished, finishing, fixed, inevitable, irrevocable, last, latest, settled, sure, terminal, terminating, ultimate
**final cessation of the menses in women** menopause
**final cessation of vital functions** death
**final demand** ultimatum

**finale** climax, conclusion, culmination, curtain, end, finis(h), terminus
**final hymn** recessional
**finally** absolutely, conclusively, decidedly, decisively, definitely, definitively, enfin (F), eventually, incontrovertible, irrevocably, lastly, ultimately
**final move at chess** checkmate
**final outcome** dénouement, upshot
**final part of thing** tailpiece
**final proposal** ultimatum
**final purpose** goal
**final reckoning** showdown
**final resolution in play** dénouement
**final result** conclusion, outcome, upshot
**final result of match** score
**final school examination** matriculation
**final snooker target** black ball
**final stage** finish
**final stage of chess match** endgame
**final word** amen, ultimatum
**finance** account, back, banking, business, capitalise, commerce, economics, float, fund, guarantee, investment, money, subsidise, support, underwrite
**financial** banking, budgeting, commercial, economic, fiscal, monetary, money, pecuniary
**financial accounting loss** debit
**financial aspects** economics
**financial consultant** accountant
**financial depression** slump
**financial institution** bank, building society
**financial means** resources
**financial need** poverty
**financial officer** treasurer
**financier** baron, businessperson, capitalist, employer, entrepreneur, executive, industrialist, magnate, merchant, mogul, potentate, tradesperson, tycoon
**finch** bunting, junco, linnet, moro, serin, siskin, tarin, towhee
**find** attain, bargain, decide, detect, determine, discover(y), encounter, expose, locate, recover, uncover
**find and bring in** retrieve
**find answer to** solve
**find a second buyer** resell
**find a way out** escape, exit
**find a way round** circumvent
**find capital for** finance
**finder** detector
**find exact place of** locate
**find fault** carp, cavil, complain, condemn, gripe, grumble, quarrel, reproach, reprove, ridicule
**find fault continually** annoy, nag

**find fault in a petty way** niggle, nitpick
**find fault noisily** scold
**find fault persistently** annoy, nag
**find fault with** blame, complain, criticise, impeach, quarrel, quibble
**find gold** strike
**find guilty of crime** convict
**finding general favour** popular
**finding no rest** restless
**finding of total** summation
**find innocent** acquit
**find mass of** weigh
**find not guilty** acquit
**find out** ascertain, detect, determine, disclose, discover, expose, learn, note, observe, perceive, realise, reveal, stalk, trial, unmask
**find out a secret** detect
**find out for certain** ascertain
**find out suddenly** realise
**find position of** locate
**find purchaser** sell
**find repugnant** abhor
**find substitute for** replace
**find sum of** add
**find the answer** solve
**find the arithmetic mean** average
**find the depth of** sound
**find the explanation** solve
**find the place** locate
**find the total** add
**find the weight of** weigh
**find under Christmas tree** gifts, presents
**find way round** circumvent, evade
**fine** accomplished, admirable, affected, amerce, beautiful, braw (Sc), choice, elegant, excellent, exceptional, exquisite, fancy, first-rate, forfeit, great, keen, little, magnificent, masterly, minute, mulct, ornate, penalise, penalty, perfect, powdered, punish, rare, refined, select, sharp, skilled, small, superior, ticket
**fine and transparent** sheer
**fine appearance** resplendence
**fine arts** beaux-arts
**fine bet is an advantage** benefit
**fine bran** pollard
**fine cloth like serge** say
**fine cloth of goat's hair** mohair
**fine coal** duff, screenings
**fine coffee** mocha
**fine cord** string
**fine cotton** lisle
**fine cotton fabric** muslin, nainsook, organdie
**fine cotton thread** lisle
**fine crack** hairline
**fine curtain material** net
**fine cut tobacco** shag

**fine delicately woven cotton fabric** muslin
**fine deportment** bel air (F)
**fine dinnerware** china
**fine display** array
**fine distinction** subtlety
**fine drops of water** drizzle, spray
**fine dry earth** dust
**fine dust** powder
**fine earthenware** china, porcelain
**fine embroidery on canvas** needlepoint
**fine eyes, good looks** beaux yeaux (F)
**fine fabric** lawn, linen, mohair, muslin, percale
**fine feathers** plumage
**fine fellow** bawcock
**fine flexible leather of goatskin** morocco
**fine for breach of rules** forfeit
**fine gauzy fabric** chiffon, tissue
**fine glazed Italian pottery** majolica
**fine goat's wool** cashmere
**fine-grained micaceous sandstone** itacolumite
**fine in texture** delicate
**fine linen** batiste, cambric, lawn
**fine literature** belles-lettres, classics
**finely formed** shapely
**finely ground meal** flour
**finely ribbed corduroy fabric** needlecord
**finely shaded** refined, subdued, subtle, tasteful
**finely stranded pasta** angelhair, vermicelli
**fine metal open-work** filigree
**fine misty rain** drizzle, smir(r), smur
**fine muslin** organdie
**fine net fabric** tulle
**fine network spun by spider** cobweb
**fine open-work of silver wire** filigree
**fine parchment** vellum
**fine particles** powder
**fine plaited straw** leghorn
**fine plaster used on interior and exterior walls** stucco
**fine point** detail
**fine porcelain** bone china
**fine powder** talc, dust
**fine quality of coffee** mocha
**fine rain** drizzly
**fine ravellings** lint
**fine-ribbed dress material** bengaline
**finery** additions, adornments, decoration, dress, equipment, extras, fittings, fixtures, frilliness, frills, frippery, fuss, gaudery, gear, livery, mannerisms, ornamentation, ostentation, panoply, regalia, trappings, trimmings, trumpery
**fine sediment** silt

**fine silk** crin, cypress, tulle
**fine silk fabric** sarcenet
**fine silky fabric** ninon
**fine smooth cotton thread for stockings** lisle
**fine soft wool** cashmere
**fine sort of leather** morocco
**finesse** adeptness, adroitness, artfulness, artifice, artistry, bluff, cleverness, craft, delicacy, diplomacy, discretion, feint, manoeuvre, polish, quickness, ruse, savoir-faire, skill, subtlety, tact, trick, wile
**finest** balmiest, best, brightest, choicest, clearest, daintiest, driest, fairest, greatest, keenest, nicest, purest, rarest, subtlest, sunniest
**fine stone particles** gravel, sand
**fine straw hat** panama
**fine translucent muslin** organdie
**fine-tune** adjust, readjust
**fine white china clay** kaolin
**fine white linen** cambric
**fine wire in electric light bulb** filament
**fine wool for knitting** fingering
**fine woven silk** sarcenet
**finger** digit, feel, handle, manipulate, maul, touch
**finger-band** ring
**finger bone** phalange
**fingernail** una (Sp)
**fingernail care** manicure
**finger or toe** digit
**finger part** nail
**finger protector** thimble
**finger-speech** chirology, dactylology
**finger to elbow length** cubit
**finicky** choosy, critical, dandy, dapper, delicate, difficult, faddy, fastidious, finical, foppish, fussy, hypercritical, meticulous, nitpicking, overnice, particular, pernickety, picky, precise, scrupulous
**finish** accomplish, attain, cease, close, complete, completion, conclude, conclusion, consume, consummate, culminate, discontinue, elegance, end, execute, fulfil, over, polish, suspend, terminate, termination
**finished** accomplished, complete(d), condemned, consummated, done, doomed, ended, experienced, fulfilled, ideal, impeccable, over, past, perfect, polished, practised, proficient, refined, ruined, settled, terminated
**finished food** ate, eaten
**finished without result** deadlock, draw, stalemate
**finishing** accomplishing, achieving, ceasing, closing, completing,

concluding, discharging, doing,
ending, executing, finalising,
fulfilling, settling, terminating
**finishing blow** coup de grâce (F)
**finishing line of race** tape
**finishing tool** reamer
**Finland** Suomi
**Finland island** Hailuto, Karlo, Vallgrund
**Finn** Cheremis, Fioun, Ingerman,
Ostiak, Ostyak, Swekoman
**Finnish bath** sauna
**Finnish coin** markka, penni
**Finnish dialect** Karelian
**Finnish division** Ijore, Villipuri
**Finnish epic poem** *Kalevala*
**Finnish harp** kantela, kantele
**Finnish islands** Åland
**Finnish isthmus** Karelia
**Finnish lake** Inari, Saimaa
**Finnish name for the Åland islands**
Ahvenanmaa
**Finnish parliament** Eduskunta
**Finnish poem** rune
**Finnish port** Abo, Pori, Porvoo, Turku
**Finnish province** Hame, Kuopio,
Kymi, Mikkel, Oulu, Uusimaa
**Finnish runner** Paavo Nurmi
**Finnish-style steam bath** sauna
**Finnish underworld** Tuonela
**Finno-Ugric language** Lapp, Magyar,
Ostyak, Vot
**fipple flute** recorder
**fir** conifer, (fir)tree
**fire** ardour, arouse, barrage, blaze,
burn, combustion, conflagration,
cremate, detonate, discharge,
dismiss, eject, élan, energy,
enthusiasm, excite, explode, flame,
gusto, hail, heat, holocaust, hurl,
ignite, ignition, incite, inferno,
inflame, inspire, kindle, launch, light,
loose, sack, salvo, shell(ing), shoot,
sniping, spark, stir, vim, volley
**fire a gun** shoot
**firearm** blunderbuss, carbine, flintlock,
fusil, (hand)gun, machinegun,
Mauser, musket, pistol, revolver,
rifle, shotgun, six-shooter, weapon
**firearm missile** bullet
**fire at from cover** snipe
**fire attack** bombardment
**fireback** macartney, reredos
**firebrand** agitator, demagogue,
fomenter, incendiary, inciter,
instigator, rabble-rouser,
revolutionary, troublemaker
**fire-breathing monster** dragon
**fire-bug** arsonist, fire-raiser, incendiary
**fire crime** arson
**firedog** andiron
**fire escape** emergency exit
**fire extinguisher** sprinkler

**fire frame** cresset
**fire from artillery** enfilade
**fire fuel** charcoal, coal, logs, peat
**fire in hearth** ingle
**fireman** stoker
**fireman's need** hose, water
**fireman's scaling ladder** pompier
**fire missile** shoot
**fireplace** grate, hearth, ingle
**fireplace pincer** tong
**fire plug** hydrant
**fireproof material** asbestos, uralite
**fire raiser** arsonist, firebug, incendiary,
pyromaniac
**fire raising** arson, incendiarism
**fire residue** ash
**fire retardant** borax
**fire-setting** arson
**fireside** abode, family, hearth,
home(stead), household, inglenook,
place, residence
**fireside tool** prong, tong
**fire stirrer** poker
**fire upon** bombard
**fire warden** ranger
**firewood** kindling, logs
**firewood support** andiron
**firework** Catherine wheel, cracker,
rocket, squib
**fireworks display** pyrotechnic
**fireworks item** sparkler
**fireworks show** pyrotechnic display
**firing lever** trigger
**firing of weapons in unison** salvo
**firing pin** striker
**firing squad** executors
**firm** adamant, anchored, association,
business, committed, compact,
company, compressed,
concentrated, concern, confirmed,
constant, convinced, corporation,
definite, dense, dependable,
determined, dogged, embedded,
enterprise, established,
establishment, fast(ened), fixed,
grounded, hard, house, immovable,
inflexible, institution, motionless,
organisation, partnership, reliable,
resolute, rigid, secure, set(-up),
settled, solid, stable, stationary,
staunch, steadfast, steady, stiff,
strict, strong, sturdy, sure, syndicate,
true, unshakable, unwavering,
unyielding
**firmament** air, cerulean, empyrean,
heaven, infinity, sky, space,
stratosphere, universe, vault
**firm dealing in medicinal drugs**
pharmacist
**firm elastic tissue in the body**
cartilage
**firm ground** terra firma

**firm hold** cinch, grip
**firm in principle** staunch
**firm juicy fruit** apple, pear
**firmly** immovably, motionlessly,
securely, staunch, steadfastly,
strictly, unshakably
**firmly fixed** rigid, set, stable, steady
**firmly implanted** rooted
**firmly laid down** positive
**firmness** balance, callosity, certainty,
density, durity, fastness, hardness,
perseverance, persistence,
resolution, rigidity, solidity, stability,
steadfastness, steadiness,
toughness
**firmness of character** backbone, grit
**firmness of mind** constancy
**firm of London underwriters** Lloyd's
**firm place in bog** hag
**firm's leader** boss, entrepreneur
**firm-stemmed marsh plant** reed
**firm trust** confidence
**fir or pine timber** deal
**fir seed bearer** cone
**first** basic, beforehand, chief,
commencement, earliest, eldest,
elementary, foremost, fundamental,
head, highest, initial(ly), introductory,
key, leading, main, oldest, opening,
original(ly), paramount, pre-eminent,
predominant, preference, premier,
primary, prime, primeval, primitive,
primo (I), principle, prior, ruling,
senior, sooner, sovereign, start,
uppermost
**first among equals** primus inter pares
(L)
**first and foremost** primarily
**first appearance in public** debut
**first-born** elder, eldest
**first born** Cain
**first British woman MP** Lady Astor
**first caliph of Islam** Abu-Bekr
**first Christian monk** Anthony
**first Church Council** Nicene
**first citizen** mayor
**first city** Ur
**first-class** A-one, excellent, OK
**first coat of paint** primer
**first coat of tin** blue
**first course of a meal** appetiser,
entrée, hors-d'œuvre, starter
**first cruise** maiden voyage
**first cry of new-born baby** vagitus (L)
**first day of Lent** Ash Wednesday
**first day of the week** Sunday
**first division of ruminant's stomach**
tripe
**first eight books of Bible** Octateuch
**first finger** index
**first five books of Old Testament**
Pentateuch

**first garden** Eden
**first-hand** unused
**first high priest of the Israelites** Aaron
**first in quality** prime
**first in rank** prime
**first in series of books** volume one
**first king of Egypt** Menes
**first king of Hebrews** Saul
**first king of Hejaz** Husein ibn-Ali
**first king of Israel** Saul
**first king of Thebes** Ogyges
**first lady** Eve, Pandora
**first leaf produced by plant embryo** cotyledon
**first letter of name** initial
**first letter of the Hebrew alphabet** aleph
**first letter of word** initial
**first light** dawn
**first light of day** daybreak
**firstly** basically, cardinally, chiefly, elementary, fundamentally, initially, maidenly, originally, primarily, primitively, primordially, principally
**first man** Adam
**first man in space** Yuri Gagarin
**first man to swim Channel** Webb
**first meal course** appetiser, hors-d'œuvre, starter
**first meal of the day** breakfast
**first milk of mammal after parturition** colostrum
**first move** initiative
**first murderer** Cain
**first murder victim** Abel
**first name** baptismal name, Christian name, forename, given name
**first night** premiere
**first Northwest Passage ship** Gjoa
**first note of the scale** do, ut
**first number** one
**first of month in ancient Roman calendar** calends
**first page of book** fly-leaf, title page
**first part** front
**first part of day** morn
**first patriarch of Hebrew nation** Abraham
**first performance of film or play** premiere
**first period of play** opening-session
**first person** I
**first person pronoun** I, me, my
**first person singular** I
**first place of exile of Napoleon** Elba
**first player** opener
**first pope** Peter
**first Prime Minister of India** Nehru
**first principle** basis, element
**first-rate** à la bonne heure (F), best, good, prime, super(ior), supreme
**first reader** primer

**first Roman emperor** Augustus
**first series of book** volume one
**first set of animal teeth** milk teeth
**first shoots** braid
**first showing** premiere
**first sign of crying** tear-drop
**first sign of Zodiac** Aries
**first Sunday in Lent** Quadragesima
**first television satellite** Telstar
**first thing** betimes
**first undersketch of painting** macchia
**first-violin player** leader
**first woman** Eve, Pandora
**first woman in space** Valentina Tereschkova
**first year buck** fawn
**first-year college student** fresher, freshman
**firth** coppice, estuary, frith, inlet, kyle
**fir tree** conifer, pine
**fiscal** bread-and-butter, budgetary, economic, financial, monetary, money, pecuniary, sumptuary
**fiscal estimate** budget
**fiscal matters** economics, fiscality
**fish** angel fish, angle, baardman, barbel, barracuda, bass, blacktail, bream, capelin, carp, cast, chub, clam, cod, dace, dageraad, darter, eel, eelpout, elf, flounder, galjoen, gar, grunter, gurnard, haarder, haddock, hake, hottentot, id(e), ikan, kabeljou, kingklip, leervis, ling, loach, maasbanker, mackerel, marlin, monkfish, mullet, musselcracker, net, opah, perch, pike, pilchard, piranha, plaice, ray, roman, salmon, sardella, sardine, scad, scrod, search, seine, sennet, seventy four, shad, shark, snapper, sole, spin, sprat, steenbras, sturgeon, tarpon, tetra, trawl, troll, trout, tuna, tunny, wrasse
**fish and rice dish** kedgeree
**fish appendage** fin
**fish bait** fly, worm
**fish basket** cauf, caul, cawl, corf, cran, creel, hask, pot, rip, slath, weel, wicker
**fish bin for salting** canch, kench
**fish box** trunk
**fish-breeding station** fishery
**fish briner** cobberer
**fish by trolling** drail
**fish catcher** angler, net
**fish-catching animal** otter
**fish-catching bird** auk, fish eagle, heron, kingfisher, osprey, pelican, penguin, sea eagle
**fish cleaner** giller, scaler
**fish condiment** paste
**fish delicacy** caviar, roe

**fish dish** kedgeree
**fish dresser** idler
**fish-eating bird** auk, fish eagle, heron, kingfisher, osprey, pelican, penguin, sea eagle
**fish-eating hawk** fish eagle, osprey
**fish-eating mammal** bear, dolphin, otter, seal, whale
**fish eggs** roe, spawn
**fisher** angler, bird, marten, pekan, piscator, prawner, seiner, wejack
**fisher for congers** eeler
**fisherman** angler, fisher, piscator(ian), seiner
**fisherman apostle** Peter
**fisherman's aid** bait, line, worm
**fisherman's basket** creel, weel
**fisherman's hat** squam
**fisherman's haul** catch
**fisherman's item** pole
**fisherman's large wicker basket** creel
**fisherman's lure** bait, fly, spinner
**fisherman's spear** lance
**fishes migrating up rivers from the sea in order to breed** anadromous
**fish farming** aquaculture
**fish for eels** grig, sniggle
**fish for salmon** snigger
**fish from boat** angle, harl, trawl, troll
**fish from moving boat** trawl, troll
**fish-glue** gelatin, isinglass
**fish having nests of seaweed** goby
**fish-hawk** osprey
**fish-hook** angle, barb, drail, drail, gaff, gape, gig, kirby
**fish-hook array** gig, trotline
**fish-hook line-leader** snell
**fish-hook money** lari(n)
**fish-hook part** barb, fly
**fish horde** school, shoal
**fish illegally** poach
**fishiness** improbity
**fishing appurtenance and device** net
**fishing bait** chokka, fly, hellgramite, sardine, tjokka, worm
**fishing bait resting on bottom** ledger
**fishing basket** creel, sla(r)th
**fishing bird** auk, fish eagle, heron, kingfisher, osprey, pelican, penguin, sea eagle
**fishing boat** coracle, dogger, dory, smack, trawler, trow
**fishing boot** wader
**fishing buoy** dan
**fishing cord** line
**fishing device** float, fly, line, net, otter, pole, reel, rod, trotline, weir
**fishing eagle** osprey
**fishing equipment** tackle
**fishing expedition** drave
**fishing gear** fly, hook, line, net(s), reel, rod, tackle, tew

**fishing grounds** banks, haaf
**fishing hazard** snag
**fishing hook arrangement** gig
**fishing line** gut, trot
**fishing line cork** bob, float, quill
**fishing line cork and line float** bob
**fishing line leader** snell
**fishing line weight** sinker
**fishing mesh** net
**fishing need** creel, gaff, hook, line, net, rod
**fishing net** flue, fyke, sagene, seine, spiller, trawl
**fishing pole** rod
**fishing port in England** Falmouth
**fishing port in France** St Tropez
**fishing reel** winch
**fishing right** piscary
**fishing rod** pole
**fishing sloop** smack
**fishing snare** net
**fishing spear** gaff, leister
**fishing spool** reel
**fishing stick** pole, rod
**fishing tackle** tew
**fishing with baited hook trailing behind boat** trolling
**fishing worm** crawler, tagtail
**fish lightly** dib
**fish-like** ichthyic
**fish like an eel** lamprey
**fish-like mammal** dolphin, orc, porpoise, whale
**fish-like skin** ichthyosis
**fish-like vertebrate** ichthyoid(al), ray
**fish line** snell, trawl, troll, trot
**fish line cork** bob
**fish louse** gisler
**fish lure** bait
**fish measure** barrel
**fishmonger** pressoner
**fish nest** redo
**fish net** flue, sagene, seine, setnet, spiller, trawl
**fish netted** lift
**fish net user** seiner
**fish not undersized** count, keeper
**fish of Atlantic** cusk, escolar, hake, herring, menhaden, scup, shad, tautog
**fish of carp family** bream, roach
**fish of zodiac** Pisces
**fish organ** fin
**fish out** extract, extricate, find, produce
**fish ovary** roe
**fish part** bone, fin, scale
**fish pickle** alec
**fish pitching prong** gaff, pew
**fish plate** scale
**fish poison and insecticide** cube
**fish-poison tree** assaca, bito, cube, cuspa, hura, kumu, neka

**fish pond** piscina, stew, vivarium, viver
**fish pool** stew(pond), trunk
**fish portion** fil(l)et, loins, steak
**fish prong** gaff, pew, pugh
**fish propeller** fin, tail
**fish relish** botargo, caviar, garum
**fish resembling the sardine** sardelle
**fish sauce** alec, garum
**fish's body part** fin
**fish's breathing organ** gill
**fish scraper** scaler
**fish's gill-cover** operculum
**fish similar to the herring** alewife
**fish's ovary** roe
**fish spear** gaff, gig, harpoon, leister, waster
**fish stew** bouillabaisse
**fish studies** ichthyology
**fishtail** urosome
**fish that can travel on land** anabas, mudskipper
**fish through ice** chug
**fish trap** eelpot, net, weel, weir
**fish underwater** goggle, spearfish
**fishway** pass, raceway
**fish which clings to another fish** remora
**fish whisker** barbel
**fishwife** shrew
**fish with a mayfly** dap
**fish with hands** guddle, gump
**fish with hook and line** angle
**fish with long spearlike snout** gar(fish)
**fish with moving line** trawl, troll
**fish with net** seine, trawl
**fish without ventral fins** apod
**fish with skin which soils fingers like wet coal** saithe
**fish with spinning bait** troll
**fishy** dishonest, dull, funny, glassy, questionable, smelly, vacant
**fissile rock** shale
**fissure** breach, break, chasm, chink, cleft, crack, cranny, crevice, gap, hole, interstice, rent, rift
**fissured lip** harelip
**fissure in glacier** crevasse
**fist** clasp, clench, grab, grasp, grip, mitt, nieve (Sc), seize
**fistical** pugilistic
**fit** adjust, agree, appropriate, apt, athletic, capable, competent, equip, harmonise, healthy, proper, seizure, shape, spasm, suitable, well
**fit and able** dow (Sc)
**fit and healthy** well
**fit and well** hale
**fit as a fiddle** blooming, fit, healthy, robust, sound, strong
**fit for consumption** edible
**fit for food** esculent

**fit for ploughing** arable
**fit for service in the air** airworthy
**fit for tillage** arable
**fit for use on roads** roadworthy
**fitful** broken, desultory, erratic, fluctuating, haphazard, impulsive, intermittent, irregular, restless, spasmodic, sporadic, variable
**fit gem in gold** mount
**fit in** belong
**fit metal on horse's hoof** shoe
**fitness** admissibility, applicability, aptness, compatibility, competency, congruity, eligibility, haleness, pertinence, preparation, relevancy, robustness, suitability
**fit of abstraction** muse
**fit of anger** fret, fume, rage, rampage, tantrum, temper, wax
**fit of depression** blues, hump, jim-jams, mulligrubs
**fit of fury** rage
**fit of hysterics** crise de nerfs (F)
**fit of ill humour** tiff
**fit of ill temper** pet
**fit of petulance** huff
**fit of shivering** ague
**fit of temper** tantrum, paddy
**fit one inside another** nest
**fit out** accommodate, accoutre, arm, array, attire, equip, outfit, prepare, provide, rig, supply
**fit plate to horse's foot** shoe
**fit snugly** nestle
**fitted garment** reefer
**fitter** abler, better, healthier, readier, seemlier, trimmer, worthier
**fitting** accordant, adapted, apparatus, appropriate, apt, becoming, befitting, cohesive, consistent, equipment, expedient, feasible, fixture, furniture, harmonious, meet, opportune, pat, proper, right, seemly, suitable, suited, timely
**fitting close to the skin** skin-tight
**fitting or appropriate** pertinent
**fitting return** meed
**fitting together** assembly
**fit to be chosen** eligible
**fit to be eaten** edible
**fit to be seen** presentable
**fit to be sold** saleable
**fit to eat** comestible, eatable, edible, esculent
**fit together** articulate
**fit to put to sea** seaworthy
**fit up with** furnish
**fit with fists** box
**five** cinq (F), penta-
**five-cent piece** nickel
**five-dollar bill** fin
**five dozen** tally

**five faculties** senses
**fivefold** quintuple
**five-franc piece** écu
**five hundred sheets of paper** ream
**five-hundredth anniversary** quin(que)centenary
**five long bones between wrist and fingers** metacarpus
**five-note scale** pentatonic scale
**five-pointed star** pentagram
**five shillings** crown
**five-sided figure** pentagon
**five years' anniversary** quinquennial
**fix** adjust, affix, anchor, arrange, assign, attach, correct, determine, dilemma, establish, fasten, implant, mend, plant, plight, predicament, repair, secure, set, settle, specify, stabilise, stick, tie
**fix amount of** assess
**fix a tax** assess
**fixation** complex, crotchet, delusion, eccentricity, fancy, fetish, monomania, notion, obsession, oddity, quirk
**fix attention on** focus
**fix closely** rivet
**fix deeply** imbed
**fixed** agreed, attached, bound, definite, immovable, invariable, permanent, resolved, rigid, secure, set, stuck
**fixed allowance** ration
**fixed amount of work** stint
**fixed annual allowance** annuity
**fixed at focal point** centred
**fixed basin** sink
**fixed charge** fee, rate
**fixed form of public worship used in churches** liturgy
**fixed landing-stage** quay
**fixed law** statute
**fixed look** gaze, stare
**fixed payment made by employer** salary
**fixed posture** pose
**fixed price** rate, fee
**fixed quantity** constant
**fixed relation** ratio
**fixed roof of car** hardtop
**fixed routine** rote, rut
**fixed seat in church** pew
**fixed stare** gaze
**fixed starting point** datum
**fix firmly** anchor, entrench, rivet
**fix in** implant
**fixing** anchoring, attaching, binding, cementing, connecting, coupling, embedding, establishing, fastening, glueing, implanting, installing, linking, locating, mending, pinning, placing, planting, positioning, rooting, securing, setting, sticking, tying
**fix in mind** imprint
**fix in position** immobilise
**fix limits** demarcate
**fix safely** fasten
**fix the eyes upon** pore
**fix the mind on** intend
**fix the time** set
**fix the value** assess
**fix together** bond
**fix up** arrange, equip, fix, furnish, mend, organise, plan, produce, provide, reconcile, resolve, settle, solve, supply
**fizzle** bubble, fizz, sparkle
**fizzle out** abort, collapse, fail
**fizzy** aerated, bubbling, bubbly, carbonated, effervescent, frothy, gassy, sparkling
**fizzy drink** Coke, cola, (cream) soda, ginger ale, lemonade
**fizzy water** soda
**fizzy wine** perlé
**fjord** creek, estuary, fiord, firth, inlet, mouth, ria
**fjord in Iceland** Breidha, Eski, Jsa, Siglu, Skaga, Vopna
**flab** fat, flabbiness
**flabby body fat** blubber
**flaccid** drooping, feeble, flabby, limp, relaxed
**flack** ack-ack
**flag** abate, alert, banderole, banner, colours, dangle, decline, die, droop, ebb, ensign, fade, fail, faint, fall, guidon, jack, languish, pennant, pennon, sag, signal, sink, slump, standard, streamer, succumb, sway, tire, wane, wave, weaken, weary, wilt
**flag bearing a device** banner
**flag down** hail
**flagellate** whip
**flagellum** cilium
**flag flower** iris
**flagged** abated, declined, died, drooped, ebbed, faded, failed, fainted, fallen, pined, sagged, sank, slumped, sunk, waned, weakened, wilted
**flagman** warner
**flag officer's boat** barge
**flag of the armed forces** ensign
**flagon** bottle
**flag-pole** mast
**flagrant** atrocious, blatant, coarse, conspicuous, crying, disgraceful, egregious, evident, gross, impudent, notorious, outrageous, rank, scandalous, wicked
**flagrantly disobey** flout
**flagstaff** mast, pole
**flag stripe** bar
**flail** beat, thrash, thresh, windmill
**flair** ability, adroitness, aptitude, aptness, capability, chic, dexterity, discernment, discrimination, élan, elegance, endowment, facility, finesse, genius, gift, instinct, knack, mastery, odour, panache, penchant, perception, skill, style, talent, taste, verve
**flake of soot** smut
**flake out** collapse, faint, tire
**flakes of dead skin** dandruff, scurf
**flakes of ice** snow
**flaky mineral** mica
**flamboyance** boldness, dash, éclat, élan, flourish, ostentation, panache, self-assurance, spirit, style, verve
**flamboyant** arabesque, brave, brilliant, colourful, dashing, dazzling, elaborate, exciting, extravagant, fancy, flashy, florid, flowery, fussy, gaudy, gay, glamorous, grandiose, jaunty, ornate, ostentatious, rich, rococo, showy, striking, stylish, swashbuckling, theatrical
**flamboyant manner** panache
**flamboyant person** mountebank
**flamboyant style** panache
**flame** ardour, blaze, burn, conflagration, fervour, fire, flash, glow, heat, inflame, passion, zeal
**flame up** fume, seethe, sizzle
**flank** border, edge, fringe, haunch, hip(-ham), loin, side, skirt, wall, wing
**flank position in hockey, football, rugby or soccer** wing
**flannel** face-cloth
**flap** agitate, apron, beat, cover, dither, flail, flutter, fly, fold, fuss, lapel, panic, shake, skirt, swing, swish, tab, tail, thrash, thresh, vibrate, wag, wave
**flapjack** pancake
**flap of shoe** tongue
**flap on aircraft** aileron
**flared up** flaring, heated, raging
**flare out** broaden, splay, widen
**flare up** blaze, burn, erupt, explode, ignite, kindle, light
**flaring** blazing, dazzling, flickering, fluttering, glaring, wavering, widening
**flash** counterfeit, flame, flare, flashy, flaunting, gaudy, glance, glare, gleam, glint, glitter, instant, ostentation, ostentatious, outburst, pretentious, scintillate, sham, showy, spark(le), spilt-second, streak, twinkling
**flashlight** torch
**flash like lightning** fulminate, explode
**flash of lightning** streak

**flash of lightning with crash of thunder** thunderbolt

**flashy** celebrated, cheap, chromatic, coruscant, flamboyant, flaunting, garish, gaudy, glittery, laudable, loud, meretricious, obtrusive, ostentatious, pretentious, showy, sparkling, splendid, sporty, superb, tasteless, tawdry, tinselly

**flask** thermos

**flat** absolute, apartment, boring, collapsed, definitely, delayed, dull, even, horizontal, insipid, level, lifeless, low, peremptory, plane, positively, prone, prosaic, prostrate, smooth, spiritless, stale, supine, tasteless, tedious, tenement, uninteresting, unqualified

**flat area of East England** Fens

**flat bean** lima

**flatboat** barge, pram, scow

**flat bottle** (hip-)flask

**flat-bottomed barge** lighter, scow

**flat-bottomed boat** barge, pontoon, punt, scow

**flat-bottomed freight boat** barge

**flat-bottomed rowing boat** dory

**flat-bottomed skiff** dory

**flat-bottomed vessel** keel

**flat bread** chapati, paratha, pita, poori

**flat bread-roll** bap

**flat candlestick with handle** sconce

**flat cap** beret, tam

**flat case for carrying documents** briefcase

**flat case for face powder** flapjack

**flat chocolate squares with nuts** brownies

**flat circular plate** disc, platter

**flat club** bat

**flat cooking surface** griddle

**flat cushion** pad

**flat disc** platter, record

**flat dish** plate, platter, saucer

**flat failure** dud

**flat fish** brill, dab, flounder, fluke, halibut, plaice, skate, sole, (sting)ray, turbot

**flat for rent** tenement

**flat hat** beret

**flat iron plate of baker** griddle

**flat land** holm

**flat like a disc** discoid

**flatly** absolutely, blandly, bluntly, categorically, completely, deadly, drably, dully, evenly, horizontally, insipidly, levelly, lifelessly, lowly, monotonously, point-blank, positively, prosaically, recumbently, smoothly, spiritlessly, stalely, tediously, unconditionally, unhesitatingly, uniformly, vapidly, weakly

**flat many-stringed musical instrument** zither

**flat of the foot** sole

**flat of the hand** palm

**flat on one's back** bedridden, defenceless, destitute, helpless, hospitalised, impotent, powerless, strengthless, supine, unwell

**flat out** all out, double-quick

**flat pearshaped leaf** blade

**flat piece of earth with grass** sod

**flat piece of wood** splat

**flat piece of wood used as tile** shingle

**flat pocket-bottle** flask

**flat roofing-tile** tegula

**flat round piece** disc, disk, plate, puck

**flat, round plate** disc

**flat ruler used for punishing boys** ferule

**flat section** panel

**flat server** tray

**flat slab of stone** flag

**flat, soft cap** beret

**flat support for pan on stove** hob

**flat surface** area, plane

**flat surface of gem** table

**flat tableland** mesa, veld

**flatten** compress, even, iron, level, plaster, raze, roll, squash, trample

**flattened and having two edges** ancipital

**flattened at poles** oblate

**flattened fold** pleat

**flattened part of oar** blade

**flatten with machine** bulldoze

**flatter** adulate, beautify, blandish, cajole, caress, charm, coax, compliment, court, duller, enhance, fawn, humour, imitate, inveigle, lower, oil, (over)praise, palp, persuade, pet, please, puff, smooth, soft-soap, staler, sweet-talk, weaker, wheedle

**flatterer** adulator, sycophant, toady

**flattering** complimentary

**flattering notice** write-up

**flattering speeches** sawder

**flatter obsequiously** adulate

**flatter oneself** boast

**flatter servilely** adulate

**flattery** adulation, blarney, cajolery, celebration, compliment, eulogium, eulogy, exaltation, extolment, glorification, humouring, laudation, magnification, overpraising, palaver, praise, puffery, salute, sawder, tribute, trumpetry

**flat thin cheek-muscle** buccinator

**flat thin sheet of metal** plate

**flat-topped cap** kepi

**flat-topped hill** mesa, moor, plateau

**flat-topped mountain on sea bed** guyot

**flat-topped straw hat with brim** boater

**flat tyre** blow-out

**flatulence** fas, flatus, pomposity, wind(iness)

**flatulent** boastful, bombastic, discursive, empty, gas-producing, gassy, inflated, long-winded, pompous, pretentious, shallow, turgid, vain, windy

**flatworm** cestode, tapeworm

**flaunting style** panache

**flavour** acidness, aspect, aura, blandness, essence, gusto, nature, piquancy, saltiness, sapidity, sapor, savour, season(ing), smack, sourness, spirit, style, sweetness, tang, taste, tastiness, tone, touch

**flavoured liqueur** Advocaat, Amaretto, Anis(ette), Bénédictine, Chartreuse, Cointreau, Crème de Menthe, Curaçao, Drambuie, Galliano, Grand Marnier, Kummel, Maraschino, ratafia, Sambuca, Sprega, Tia Maria, Van der Hum

**flavoured milk drink** shake

**flavoured water-ice** sorbet

**flavoured with seeds** spiced

**flavourful** agreeable, delectable, délicieux (F), delicious, enjoyable, epicurean, flavoursome, nice, palatable, piquant, sapid, spicy, tasty

**flavourful sauce** dressing

**flavouring herb** basil, mint, oregano, parsley, rosemary, thyme

**flavouring liquor extracted from barley and almonds** orgeat

**flavouring plant** herb

**flavouring substance** angostura, aniseed, chili, essence, grenadine, licorice, seed, spice, vanilla

**flavourless** bland, insipid, jejune, mawkish, mild, stale, tasteless, unappetising, unpalatable, vapid, watery

**flavour with salt or condiments** season

**flaw** blemish, blot, break, crack, defect, fault, fracture, imperfection, spot

**flaw in logic** fallacy

**flaw in stocking** ladder

**flaw in timber** dauk

**flawless** faultless, ideal, immaculate, impeccable, perfect, pure, spotless, unblemished, untarnished

**flawlessly** accurately, correctly, exactly, exquisitely, faultlessly, guiltlessly, immaculately, impeccably, innocently, justly,

**flax**     278     **flighty**

perfectly, precisely, purely, regularly, rightly, spotlessly, strictly, virtuously
**flax** linen, plant, tow
**flax fabric** linen
**flax oil** linseed
**flaxseed** linseed
**fleabane** erigeron
**flea-colour** puce
**fleck** atom, besmirch, blot, circle, dab, dirty, dot, iota, jot, mark, mite, mote, point, soil, spatter, speck(le), splodge, spot, stain, sully, taint, tarnish
**fledermaus** bat
*Fledermaus* opera
**fledging bird** fledgeling, squab
**flee** abandon, abscond, avoid, bolt, cease, decamp, depart, desert, disappear, elope, escape, exit, fly, hasten, lam, leave, run, scatter, shun, skedaddle, skip, speed, vanish, withdraw
**fleece** clip, shear, wool
**fleece cutter** shearer
**fleeced** beguiled, bled, cheated, deceived, defrauded, deluded, double-crossed, drained, duped, exhausted, extorted, extracted, fooled, hoaxed, milked, misled, outwitted, reduced, robbed, sheared, swindled, thwarted, victimised
**fleece from goat** angora, mohair
**fleece holder** woolsack
**fleecy** woollen
**fleecy mass** flocculus
**flee from danger** scurry, scuttle
**flee from the law** abscond
**flee hastily** lam
**fleer** deride, gibe, jeer, mock, ridicule, scoff, sneer, taunt, twit
**fleet** agile, argosy, armada, division, fast, flotilla, navy, nimble, quick, rapid, speedy, squadron, swift(-footed), vessels, warships, winged
**fleet animal** deer
**fleeting** brief, ephemeral, evanescent, flitting, flying, fugitive, impermanent, momentary, passing, short(-lived), temporary, transient, transitory, vanishing
**fleetingly** briefly
**fleet of armed ships** armada
**fleet of merchant ships** argosy
**fleet of small ships** flotilla
**fleet of warships** armada
**flee to wed** elope
**Flemish copper coin of small value** mite
**Flemish painter** Bruegel, Eyck, Goes, Mabuse, Mor, Rubens, Teniers, Van Dyck, Weyden

**Flemish port** Antwerp, Ostend
**Flemish Ypres** leper
**flesh** beef, blood, family, fat, humanity, kin(ship), man, meat, muscle, mutton, pork, relations, tissue, veal
**flesh-coloured** incarnadine
**flesh-eating** carnivorous
**flesh-eating animal** carnivore
**flesh-eating fish** piranha
**flesh formation** sarcosis
**flesh of animal used as food** meat
**flesh of calf as food** veal
**flesh of cow, ox as food** beef
**flesh of fruit** pulp
**flesh of pig as food** pork
**flesh of sheep as food** mutton
**flesh of swine** pork
**flesh out** colour, embody, fill, incorporate, pad, substantiate
**fleshy back part of the leg below the knee** calf
**fleshy compound fruit** sorosis
**fleshy edible leaf stalks** asparagus, celery, chicory, endive, rhubarb
**fleshy fruit** apple, gourd, pear, pome, quince
**fleshy hinder part of leg below knee** calf
**fleshy part of ear** lobe
**fleshy part of side between hips and ribs** flank
**fleshy pome fruit** apple, pear, quince
**fleshy projection** papilla
**fleshy rock plant** sedum
**fleshy tropical American plant** agave
**fleshy tumour** sarcoma
**fleur-de-lis** flower, iris, lily, liss, lys
**flex** bend, bow, buckle, cable, contort, curve, diverge, genuflect, incline, lean, stoop, swerve, turn, twist, veer, warp
**flexibility** adaptability, affable, agreeable, complaisance, compliant, docile, ease, elasticity, obedience, pliability, pliancy, resilience, springiness, stretch, suppleness, tractility, willing, yielding
**flexibility of tempo** rubato
**flexibilty** adaptability, complaisance, elasticity, resilience, springiness
**flexible** adaptable, affable, complaint, complaisant, conformable, docile, elastic, limber, lithe, loose-limbed, manageable, pliable, pliant, springy, supple, versatile, wieldy, yielding
**flexible bamboo cane** whang(ee)
**flexible disk** diskette, floppy disk
**flexible joint** hinge
**flexible leather strip** belt, strap
**flexible link** tie
**flexible part of whip** lash
**flexible pipe** hose

**flexible putty** mastic
**flexible rod** raddle, wattle
**flexible shoot** bine
**flexible shoot cut from tree** switch
**flexible tube conveying water** hose
**flexible twig** osier, rattan, wicker, withe
**flexible twig used for binding** withe, withy
**flexibly** amenably, docilely, elastically, limberly, lithely, openly, pliably, responsively, rubato, supplely, supply, tractably, variably
**flexion of a limb** anaclasis
**flexuous** anfractuous, bending, circuitous, convoluted, crooked, curving, indirect, meandering, roundabout, serpentine, sinuous, spiral, tortuous, turning, twisting, winding, zigzag
**flicker** breath, drop, flare, flash, flutter, gleam, glimmer, quiver, spark, trace, vestige, vibrate, waver
**flickering softly over a surface** lambent
**flicking game** tiddly-wink
**flick of the finger** fillip
**flick through** scan, skim, thumb through
**flier** aeronaut, airman, aviator, bird, flyer, kite, pilot, plunge
**flight** absconding, aviation, cloud, dart, dash, departure, distance, eloping, escape, exit, exodus, extent, fleeing, formation, journey, migration, race, range, retreat, route, running, sailing, scud, soaring, span, speed, squadron, stairway, trip, unit, voyage
**flight cost** airfare
**flight from danger** hegira, hejira
**flight from reality** escape
**flight landing place** airport
**flightless bird** bubbling, callow, dodo, emu, kiwi, moa, nestler, nestling, ostrich, penguin, ratite, rhea
**flightless New Zealand bird** kiwi
**flightless sea-bird** auk
**flight of missiles** volley
**flight of steps** stair, staircase
**flight of steps down to a river** ghat
**flight path** track
**flight staff** crew
**flight terminal** airport
**flighty** airy, anile, capricious, careless, changeable, contrary, crazy, cross-grained, deviative, disobedient, dizzy, erratic, explosive, faithless, fickle, fitful, frivolous, giddy, impulsive, irresponsible, lawless, light-headed, mad, scatter-brained, skittish, stray, thoughtless, unbalanced, unstable, unsteady, volatile, wayward, whimsical

**flighty fool** idiot
**flighty girl** goosecap
**flighty person** flibbertigibbet
**flimsy** delicate, diaphanous, feeble, foolish, fragile, frail, frivolous, implausible, inadequate, insignificant, insubstantial, light, makeshift, meagre, poor, rickety, shaky, shallow, slight, superficial, tenuous, thin, transparent, trivial, unconvincing, unsatisfactory, unsubstantial, weak
**flimsy nightwear** negligee
**flimsy web** gossamer
**flinch** avoid, blench, cower, cringe, crouch, quail, quake, recoil, retreat, shirk, shiver, shrink, shy, start, swerve, wince
**fling** attempt, binge, booze-up, cast, catapult, chuck, heave, hurl, indulgence, jerk, launch, lob, pitch, precipitate, propel, send, shoot, shot, shy, sling, slug, spree, stab, tear, throw, toss, try, whirl
**fling away** discard, dump, unload
**fling forcibly** catapult, precipitating, propelling, sending, shying, slinging, throwing, tossing
**fling out** explode, fulminate
**fling with violence** hurl
**flint glass** crystal
**flint-like form of quartz** chert
**flip** dab, eggnog, fillip, flick, flop, flounce, heave, impulse, jerk, pat, propel, snap, somersault, spin, strike, throw, toss, touch, trip, turn, twirl, twist
**flip a coin** toss
**flip a pancake** toss
**flip over** capsize, overturn, somersault
**flippancy** archness, cheekiness, flightiness, frivolity, impertinence, irreverence, levity, lightness, pertness, sauciness, volatility
**flippant** aggressive, airy, audacious, bold, brash, brazen, cocky, disrespectful, forward, frivolous, glib, impertinent, impudent, insolent, irreverent, pert, rude, saucy, superficial
**flipper** feeler, fin, limb, wing
**flip through** browse
**flip through the pages** scan, skim, spot-check
**flirt** coquet(te), dally, fillip, heart-breaker, jilt, ogle, philander(er), tease, wanton, wink
**flirtatious** amorous, coquettish, coy, flirty, teasing
**flirtatious girl** coquette, minx
**flirt with** consider, entertain, try

**flit** bob, dance, dart, depart, flash, flicker, flitter, flutter, fly, gad, move, pass, quiver, remove, skim, slip, speed, volitant, waver, whisk, wing
**float** buoy, cork, drift, fluctuate, glide, hover, inundate, launch, levitate, raft, rest, suspend, swim, waft
**float-board of a water wheel** awe
**floating** afloat, bobbing, buoyant, fluctuating, free, migratory, movable, natant, sailing, swimming, transitory, unattached, uncommitted, unsinkable, variable, wandering
**floating at random** adrift
**floating bag** balloon
**floating barrier of timber** boom
**floating filth** scum
**floating free** adrift
**floating frozen mass** iceberg
**floating garden** Chinampa
**floating ice-mass** iceberg
**floating ice-sheet** floe
**floating in water** afloat
**floating leaves of water lily** lily pad
**floating log platform** raft
**floating marker** buoy
**floating mass of frozen water** iceberg
**floating mooring** buoy
**floating on the surface** supernatant
**floating pier** pontoon
**floating plants of the Nile** sudd
**floating population** boat people, flotsam
**floating sheet of ice** floe
**floating structure of timber** raft
**floating timber** driftwood
**floating wreckage** flotsam
**float of logs** raft
**float up** ascend, rise
**flock** bevy, brood, company, crowd, drove, flight, group, herd, litter, pack, school, swarm, troop
**flock of birds** bevy, flight
**flock of coots** covert
**flock of geese** gaggle, skein, team, wedge
**flock of goats** herd
**flock of larks** bevy
**flock of pheasants** eye, nide, nye
**flock of quails** bevy
**flock of wild geese in flight** skein
**flock together** congregate
**flock with the company** troop
**flog** beat, cane, chastise, drive, flail, flay, hide, lash, oppress, overtax, punish, push, scourge, sell, strain, strap, strike, tax, thrash, trounce, whack, whip
**flood** abundance, alluvial, cataract, cloudburst, copiousness, deluge, downpour, drown, engulf, excess, fill, glut, gush, immerse, inundate,

inundation, overabundance, (over)flow, oversupply, overwhelm, plenteousness, profusion, rush, satiety, spate, stream, submerge, surge, surplus, swarm, sweep, tide, torrent
**flooded** awash, choked, deluged, drowned, engulfed, filled, gushed, immersed, inundated, (over)flowed, overwhelmed, rushed, submerged, surged, swamped, swarmed, swept
**floodgate** barricade, conduit, faucet, obstacle, outlet, sluice, tap, turnstile, weir
**flood of light** refulgence
**flood of words** effusion
**flood survivor** Noah
**flood with light** illuminate, irradiate, lighten
**floor** base, bottom, fell, least, minimum
**floor cleaner** broom, mop
**floor covering** carpet, lino(leum), mat, rug, tile
**floor covering piece** tile
**flooring of wooden blocks** parquet
**floor inlay** parquetry
**floormat** rug
**floor of fireplace** hearth
**floor pad** mat
**floor shiner** polish
**floorshow** cabaret
**floor supervisor** floor-walker, shopwalker
**floor-swab** mop
**flop** collapse, drop, dud, fail(ure), fall, fiasco, misfire, tumble
**flop about** lollop
**floppy disk** diskette, flexible disk
**flora and fauna** biota
**flora and fauna found at bottom of sea** benthos
**floral buttonhole** corsage
**floral display** arrangement
**floral emblem of New South Wales** waratah
**floral emblem of South Africa** protea
**floral emblem of Victoria** heath
**floral tribute** garland, lei
**Florence Nightingale was one** nurse
**Florentine navigator in the New World** Amerigo Vespucci
**florid** adorned, blowzy, blushing, flamboyant, flushed, frilly, glowing, high-coloured, lurid, ornate, ostentatious, radiant, red(dish), rhetorical, rococo, rubicund, ruddy, showy, tropical
**florid architectural style** rococo
**Florida resort** Miami
**floridly decorated** flamboyant
**florilegium** anthology
**floss silk** filoselle

**floating goods** flotsam
**flotilla** armada, fleet, navy, shipping
**flotsam** cast-offs, debris, jetsam, junk, refuse, rubbish, scum, sweepings, vagrants, wreckage
**flounce or trimming on dress** falbala
**flounder** blunder, falter, flop, hesitate, hobble, limp, shamble, stagger, struggle, stumble, waver
**flour** bran, dust, farina, meal, powder, speckle, sprinkle
**flour dough** pasta
**flour factory** mill
**flour from a cereal grain** farina
**flour glue** paste
**flourish** abound, adorn(ment), advance, bloom, blossom, boast, boom, brag, brandish(ing), dash, decoration, develop, display, embellish, fanfare, flaunt, floreat (L), flower, gesture, grow, increase, luxuriate, ornament, panache, parade, progress, prosper, shake, show, succeed, sweep, swing, swish, thrive, twirl(ing), vaunt, wave, wax, wield
**flourish after signature** paraph
**flourishing** blooming, blossoming, booming, burgeoning, developing, flowering, increasing, lush, luxuriant, prospering, prosperous, rampant, succeeding, successful, thriving
**flourishing excessively** rampant
**flourishing green vegetation** verdure
**flourish in writing** quirk
**flourish of trumpets** fanfare
**flour of cereal** farina
**flour-shaker** dredger
**flout** abhor, beard, brave, chaff, challenge, confront, dare, defy, deride, despise, detest, disdain, disparage, disregard, face, gibe, insult, jeer, loathe, mock, neglect, provoke, revile, ridicule, scoff, scorn, slight, sneer, spurn, taunt
**flow** abound, current, discharge, flood, gush, jet, outpouring, overflow(ing), pour, proceed, river, run, stream, teem, tide
**flow away** ebb
**flow back** ebb, recede, subside
**flower** aster, azalea, beauty, bloom, blossom, boronia, bud, candytuft, cowslip, develop, disa, elite, geranium, grow, hyacinth, hydrangea, iris, lilac, lily, lupin, nasturtium, orchid, pansy, peony, petunia, phlox, primula, prosper, protea, reproduce, rose, snapdragon, strelitzia, tulip, unfold, violet
**flower beds** garden

**flower beetle** chafer
**flower border** bed
**flower bract** pale(a)
**flower bud** knot
**flower bud used as a spice** clove
**flower bunch** bouquet, nosegay, posy
**flower-bush** hydrangea
**flower centre** eye
**flower child** beatnik, bohemian, hippie, hippy
**flower-cluster** corymb, raceme, umbel
**flower container** pot, urn, vase
**flower cultivator** gardener
**flower dealer** florist
**flower dust** pollen
**flower-eating** anthophagous
**flower emanation** aroma, fragrance, perfume, smell
**flower envelope** perianth
**flower essence** attar, ottar, otto
**flower field** gowan
**flower garland** anadem, chaplet, lei
**flower goddess** Flora
**flower grown from tuber** canna, dahlia, tulip
**flower head** capitulum
**flower holder** vase
**flowering fodder plant** lupin
**flowering herb** hepatica, lavender
**flowering more than once in a single season** remontant
**flowering plant** hawthorn, holly, hop, larkspur, orchid, poppy, rose, violet
**flowering shrub** azalea, erica, fuchsia, oleander, rhododendron, seringa
**flowering tree** jacaranda, lilac, magnolia, mimosa
**flowering vine** jasmine, wisteria
**flowering water plant** lotus, water-lily
**flower jug** vase
**flower leaf** bract, petal, sepal
**flowerless** ananthous
**flowerless plant** acrogen, fern, fungus, ivy, lichen, moss
**flowerlike** anthoid
**flower necklace** garland, lei
**flower of bean family** wisteria
**flower of forgetfulness** lotus
**flower or eye part** iris
**flower organ** pistil, stamen
**flower part** anther, bract, calyx, carpel, corolla, filament, ovary, pericarp, petal, pistil, receptacle, sepal, spadix, spur, stamen, stem, stigma, style
**flower pistil** carpel
**flower plot** bed, garden
**flower pot** jardinière (F), vase
**flower-power drop-out** hippie, hippy
**flower receptacle** torus, vase
**flowers also called heart's-ease** wild pansy

**flowers collectively** flora
**flower section** petal
**flower seed** ovule
**flower seller** florist
**flower-shaped ornament** rosette
**flower site** bed
**flower spike** ament, catkin, spadix
**flower stalk** pedicel, petiole, scape, stem
**flower stand** epergne
**flowers' visitor** bee
**flower syrup** nectar
**flower that never fades** amaranth
**flower tree** catalpa, mimosa
**flower turning to sun** heliotrope, sunflower
**flower vessel** vase
**flower with six segments** sexfoil
**flow freely** pour
**flow in a slow stream** trickle
**flowing** abounding, cascading, continuous, effusive, facile, fluent, running, rushing, smooth, streaming, sweeping, swollen, teeming, uninterrupted
**flowing and ebbing** tidal
**flowing back of the tide** ebb
**flowing body of water** stream
**flowing easily** fluent
**flowing freely** affluent
**flowing garment** robe
**flowing into each other** interfluent
**flowing out** effluent
**flowing smoothly** profluent
**flowing smoothly and sweetly** mellifluous
**flowing together** confluent
**flowing towards a point** afflux
**flowing water** current, river, stream
**flow-off** drainage
**flow of language** copia verborum (L)
**flow of volcanic mud** lahar
**flow out** issue, leak, ooze, seep
**flow out from** emanate
**flow out slowly** ooze
**flow out violently** gush
**flow-rate measure** metre
**flow slowly** ooze
**flows through Pisa and Florence** Arno
**flow windingly** meander
**flow with a burbling sound** purl
**flu** influenza
**fluctuate** alter(nate), change, equivocate, float, hesitate, irregular, move, oscillate, seesaw, shift, shuffle, sway, swing, undulate, unstable, vacillate, vary, veer, wave, waver
**fluctuate in opinion** vacillate
**fluency of speech** eloquence, volubility
**fluent** articulate, balanced, copious, easy, eloquent, euphonious, flowing,

glib, graceful, liquid, proportioned, ready, smooth, streaming, voluble, well-spoken
**fluent and effective use of language** eloquence
**fluent in speech** voluble
**fluently** eloquently, smoothly
**fluff** down, dust, fuzz, lint, muddle, nap, oose (Sc)
**fluffy dish** soufflé
**fluffy fibre** baru
**fluffy mass of spun sugar** candyfloss
**fluffy potatoes** mash
**fluid** flexible, gaseous, liquid, vapour, watery
**fluid dram** drachm
**fluid ejected by octopus** ink
**fluid excreted by the kidneys** urine
**fluid-filled sac** bursa
**fluid for writing** ink
**fluid from rubber tree** latex
**fluid in a plant** sap
**fluid in the gall bladder** bile
**fluid loss** leakage, seepage
**fluid of blood** plasma
**fluid of plants** latex
**fluid produced by bees** honey
**fluid rock** lava
**fluid said to flow in the veins of the gods** ichor
**fluid secreted by the liver** bile
**fluid shed** spillage
**fluid surrounding the foetus in the womb** amniotic fluid
**fluid unit** litre, pint
**fluke** barb, blessing, chance, coincidence, flat-fish, flounder, fortuity, gamble, happenstance, harpoon, helminth, nematode, potluck, risk, serendipity, trematode, windfall
**fluke worm** plaice
**flummox** bewilder, confound, disconcert, stump
**flung drops of water** spray
**flunk** fail
**flunkey** flunky, footman, lackey, manservant, minion, slave, snob, toady, underling, valet
**flurry** ado, bustle, commotion, confuse, disturb(ance), flutter, gust, hassle
**flush** abundant, bloom, blush, burn, cleanse, colour, crimson, discover, disturb, drench, eject, empty, evacuate, even, expel, flame, flat, freshness, full, generous, glow, go red, hose, lavish, level, moneyed, overflowing, plane, prosperous, redden, redness, rich, rinse, rolling, rosiness, rouse, smooth, square, start, suffuse, swab, syringe, true, uncover, vigour, wash, wealthy, well-heeled, well-off
**flushed** aglow, blushing, crimson, feverish, rosy, ruddy
**flushed with shame** red
**flush with water** sluice
**fluster** agitate, bother, confuse, disconcert, excite, flurry, hurry, perturb, upset
**flute** channel, cutting, fife, furrow, groove, gutter, hollow, pipe, rut, score, trench
**fluted border** frill
**flute-like musical toy** ocarina
**flute-player** flautist
**flutter** agitate, flap, flit, fluctuate, flurry, fluster, hover, quiver, ripple, tremble, tremor, tumult, vibrate, wave
**flutter like a bird** flacker
**flutter of disturbance** agitation
**flutter one's eyelashes** blink, nictitate, wink
**fluvial island** eyot
**fly** aviate, bolt, career, control, display, elapse, flit, float, flutter, glide, hasten, hover, hurry, manoeuvre, mount, operate, pass, pilot, race, scamper, scoot, shoot, show, soar, speed, sprint, tear, wing
**fly about** flit
**fly aloft** soar
**fly alone** solo
**fly an airplane** aviate
**fly at** assail, assault, attack, charge, rush, strike
**fly before the wind** scud
**fly-by-night** chancer, crooked, debt-skipper, dishonest, dishonourable, fleecer, inconstant, jackleg, momentary, shady, sharp, shifty, short-lived, swindler, transient, transitory, unreliable, unstable, unsteady
**fly-catching warbler** redstart
**fly causing sleeping sickness** tsetse
**flyer** aviator, pilot
**flyer who tests out planes** test pilot
**fly high** soar
**fly in aircraft** aviate
**flying** abandoning, aviation, brief, careering, controlling, dashing, deserting, disappearing, displaying, drifting, elapsing, express, fast, fleeing, fleet(ing), flight, flitting, gliding, hasty, hovering, hurried, hurrying, mercurial, mobile, operating, rapid, rushed, scampering, soaring, speeding, speedy, temporary, vanishing, volitant, waving, winged
**flying about rapidly** volitant
**flying aid** wing
**flying fish** gurnard, gurnet, saury
**flying gaggle** skein
**flying insect** bee, dor, fly, gnat, mosquito, moth, wasp
**flying machine** aeroplane
**flying mammal** bat
**flying mouse** bat
**flying plaything** kite
**flying saucer** UFO
**flying service** airline
**flying squid** sea-arrow
**flying squirrel** taguan
**flying toy** kite
**fly in pieces** shatter
**fly in the face of** contravene, controvert, cross, defy, disobey, disregard, ignore, oppose
**fly in the ointment** difficulty, drawback, flaw, hitch, inconvenience, problem, snag
**fly killer** swatter
**fly like a butterfly** flit
**fly off the handle** explode
**fly on sheep** ked
**fly or move lightly and quickly** flit
**flyover** overpass
**fly quickly** flit
**fly's larva** screwworm
**fly that bites cattle** gadfly
**fly the coop** abscond, escape, flee
**fly up** ascend
**fly upwards** soar
**foal's mother** mare
**foam** bubbles, froth, lather, spray, spume, suds
**foam and swell of sea** surf
**foam at the mouth** boil, rage
**foam formed by soap and water** lather
**foaming at the mouth** raging
**foam of breaking waves** surf
**foamy** barmy, effervescent, fizzy, foaming, foamlike, frothy, lathery, mousseux (F), soapy, sparkling, spumy, yeasty
**foamy drink** ale
**foamy froth** lather
**foamy top of beer** head
**foamy wave** whitecap
**fob off** deceive, dump, foist, get rid of, impose, inflict, unload
**focal point** climax, focus, heart, highlight, hub
**focus** centre, concentrate, converge, core, heart, middle
**focus exclusively** concentrate
**focus of attention** cynosure
**fodder** ammunition, encouragement, ensilage, feed, food(stuff), forage, fuel, grain, grass, hay, herbage, incitement, material, means, nourishment, pasturage, pasture, provender, provocation, rations,

roughage, silage, stock, store, stover, straw, vert
**fodder bin** silo
**fodder-grass** hay, lucerne, timothy
**fodder pit and tank** silo
**fodder plant** alfalfa, clover, lucerne, tare, vetch
**fodder rack** cratch
**fodder store** silo
**fodder stored in silo** hay, silage
**fodder to store** ensilage, ensilate, ensile, ensilo
**fodder tower** silo, tank
**fodder trough** bin, crib, manger
**foe** adversary, antagonist, assailant, attacker, competitor, enemy, ill-wisher, opponent, rival
**foetus-to-be** embryo
**fog** becloud, bewilder, blur, brume, cloud, confusion, darken(ing), daze, dim, haze, miasma, mist, muddle, smog
**fogey** fogy, fuddy-duddy
**foggy** blurred, brumous, cloudy, dim, grey, hazy, indistinct, misted, misty, murky, nebulous, obscure, vaporous, wintry
**foible** abnormality, anomaly, bent, caprice, crotchet, eccentricity, fault, fetish, habit, idiosyncrasy, irregularity, mannerism, nonconformity, oddity, peculiarity, quirk, singularity, strangeness, trait, trick, twist, vagary, waywardness, weirdness
**foil** antithesis, baffle, ba(u)lk, blade, check, contrast, contravene, counter, defeat, disconcert, elude, épée, film, frustrate, hamper, hinder, impede, lamina, leaf, nip, nullify, outsmart, outwit, parry, prevent, rapier, repulse, setting, staging, steel, stooge, stop, thwart, vanquish
**fold** bend, crease, crumple, double, enclose, envelop, flock, furrow, gather, intertwine, layer, overlap, pen, pleat, ply, tuck, turn, wrap, wrinkle
**fold and press** crimp
**folded-back part of coat** lapel
**folded-down corner of a page** dog's-ear
**folded, filled tortilla** taco
**folder** file, folio
**fold in** tuck
**fold in cloth** crease, pleat
**folding** pleating, telescoping
**folding bed** cot, stretcher
**folding chair** faldstool
**folding mark** crease
**folding money** note
**folding pocketknife** penknife

**folding stool** faldstool
**folding-table framework** trestle
**fold in material** pleat
**fold line** crease
**fold of cloth** pleat
**fold of coat** lapel
**fold of garment** lappet
**fold of sail** reef
**fold of string** loop
**fold on animal's throat** dewlap
**fold or circle** loop
**fold over** lap
**fold over and stitch** hem
**fold under** tuck
**foliage** foliation, foliature, frondescence, greenery, leafage, leaves, vegetation, vernation
**foliage colour** green
**foliage item** leaf
**foliage of bay tree** laurel
**folio** page
**folk dance** Highland fling, hornpipe, sword dance
**folk legend** lore, myth
**folklore** custom, fable, habit, institution, legend, lore, myth(ology), ritual, story, superstitions, tradition, usage
**folklore monster** ogre
**folk tale** legend, myth, saga
**follicle** crypt, sac
**follicle inflammation** sycosis
**follow** accompany, adopt, chase, comply, copy, ensue, heed, imitate, mimic, mind, obey, observe, proceed, pursue, replace, result, simulate, succeed, supplant, trace, trail
**follow a clue** sleuthed, track
**follow after** pursue, tail, trail
**follow a trail** trace
**follow a winding course** meander
**follow backward** retrace
**follow close behind** tag, tail
**follow closely** dog, ensue, heel, shadow, supervene, tag, tail
**follow commands** obey
**follow course of** trace
**follower** acolyte, adherent, companion, disciple, partisan, pursuer, servant, supporter
**follower in fashion** modist(e)
**follower of a leader** disciple
**follower of Attila** Hun
**follower of Bacchus** Maenad, satyr
**follower of Christ** Christian, disciple
**follower of fashion** modist(e)
**follower of Greek philosophy** Eleatic
**follower of Islam** Moslem, Muslim
**followers** adherents, fans, retinue, train
**follow example** emulate
**following** adherents, admirers, after, attendance, attendants, below,

clientele, dependants, ensuing, entourage, fans, métier, next, patrons, resulting, retinue, sect, sequent(ial), subsequent, succeeding, tailing, train
**following after** next
**following as a result** consequent(ial)
**following at once** next
**following closely** dogging, stalking
**following day** (to)morrow
**following in order** succession
**following in time** after
**following next** ensuing
**following one's own inclination** libertine
**following on from** after
**following reason** logical
**following word for word** literal
**follow in place of** supersede
**follow in sequence** ensue, rotate
**follow in turn** alternate
**follow on** ensue
**follow one another** alternate
**follow orders** obey
**follows midday** afternoon
**follow stealthily** tail
**follow suit** comply, concur, copy, echo, emulate, imitate, mimic, parallel
**follow the outline** trace
**follow-through** effectuation, sequel, sustain
**follow tracks** trail
**follow-up** sequel
**folly** absent-mindedness, absurdity, absurdness, confusion, extravagance, fatuity, foolishness, idiocy, imbecility, instability, irrationality, lunacy, madness, nonsense, nonsensicality, recklessness, senselessness, silliness, stupidity, thickness, vacancy
**foment** actuate, agitate, arouse, bathe, boil, breed, brew, contrive, disturb, embrocate, encourage, evoke, excite, ferment, fester, incite, inflame, initiate, instigate, poultice, prompt, provoke, rouse, suscitate, urge
**fomenter** inciter, instigator
**fond** adoring, affectionate, amorous, caring, devoted, doting, loving
**fondant** sweetmeat
**fondle** caress, cuddle, dandle, embrace, hug, nuzzle, pat, paw, pet, stroke
**fondly devoted to one's wife** uxorious
**fond manner** dearly
**fondness** affection, amorousness, amour, attachment, care, desire, devotion, dotingness, fancy, kindness, liking, love, lovingness, partiality, penchant, predilection,

**fondness for** susceptibility, taste, tenderness, warmness, weakness
**fondness for** weakness
**fondness for women** philogyny
**fondness of travelling** wanderlust
**fond of** partial
**fond of books** literary
**fond of chatting** chatty
**fond of company** gregarious
**fond of eating** gourmand
**fond of finding fault** captious
**fond of old ways** old-fashioned
**fond of one's wife** uxorious
**fond of the open air** outdoor
**fond remembrance of past** nostalgia
**fond way of greeting** kiss
**font** laver, source
**fontanelle opening** vacuity
**food** bread, diet, eats, fare, kai, meal, menu, nosh, nourishment, nutriment, nutrition, pabulum, provisions, regimen, sustenance, tucker, viands
**food additive** tartaric acid
**food and drink for meal** repast
**food bit** ort
**food can** tin
**food container** basin, can, plate
**food cooked over charcoal in tandoor** tandoori
**food cupboard** larder
**food distributed in charity** dole
**food dye** saffron, turmeric
**food eaten** repast
**food element** carbohydrate, mineral, protein, vitamin
**food farinaceous** sago
**food fish** cero, cod(ling), flathead, haddock, hake, kabeljou, kingklip, ling, mackerel, mullet, perch, pilchard, pompano, robalo, scad, shad, snapper, snoek, trout, tuna, whiting
**food flavouring** spice
**food for animals** forage
**food for cattle and horses** forage
**food for colt** mare's-milk
**food for re-chewing** cud
**food for soldiers** ration
**food fragment** ort
**food from heaven** manna
**food grain** millet
**food intake expert** dietician
**food left over** leavings, ort, scraps
**food material** bean, corn, rice, sago, tapioca, wheat
**food menu** list
**food merchant** butcher, grocer, victualler
**food mixture** filling
**food of certain bees and beetles** ambrosia, nectar
**food of hawk** rat

**food of love** music
**food of owl** mouse
**food of the gods** ambrosia
**food of the indolent** lotus
**food of wild turkey** pecan
**food plant** taro, vegetable
**food poisoning** ptomaine
**food portion** ration
**food prepared and served according to Jewish dietary laws** kosher
**food prepared from fermented milk** yogh(o)urt
**food producer** farmer
**food programme** menu
**food provided** fare
**food-raiser** farmer
**food receptacle** tray
**food refuse** swill
**food regimen** diet
**food remnant** scrap
**food retailer** grocer
**food scrap** ort
**food shortage** famine
**foodshredder** grater
**food starch** arrowroot, cornflour, sago, tapioca
**food store** larder
**foodstuff in India** d(h)al
**food tin** can
**food-tinning factory** canning
**food to entice prey** bait
**food to satisfy** square meal
**fool** alec, ass, befool, blockhead, boob(y), buffoon, cheat, clot, clown, cozen, dally, dawdle, deceive, delude, dolt, domkop, droll, dunce, dunderhead, dunderpate, dupe, footle, gaby, goat, gudgeon, hoax, hoodwink, humorist, idiot, ignoramus, imbecile, jest(er), madman, moron, nincompoop, ninny, nit(wit), noodle, nut, oaf, play, sap, simp(leton), toy, trick, twaddle, twit, zany
**fool around** deplete, exhaust, jive, lallygag, misspend, philander, skylark, squander, waste
**fool away** fribble
**foolery** barney, game, horseplay, motley, nonsense
**foolhardy** bold, brash, headlong, impetuous, madcap, rash, reckless, venturous
**fooling** banter, mummery
**foolish** absurd, asinine, balmy, daft, dotted, dull, dumb, fatuous, idiotic, idle, imprudent, inane, irrational, mad, ridiculous, senseless, silly, sot, stupid, thoughtless, unwise, vacant, vain, vapid, void, witless, zany
**foolish act** dido, idiotism
**foolish action** folly, foppery, ineptitude

**foolish behaviour** antic, frivolity
**foolish chatterer** magpie
**foolish fellow** dummy, gaby, gander, noodle, sap, simp, sop, widgeon, zany
**foolish girl** tawpie, tawpy
**foolish ideas** moonshine
**foolish, lacking reason** senseless
**foolishly** absurdly, apishly, fondly, idly, simple, simply
**foolishly dreamy** moony
**foolishly fond** dotes
**foolish mistake** goof
**foolishness** absurdity, absurdness, asininity, barney, buncombe, bunkum, craziness, dumbness, fatuity, folly, foolish, frivolity, idiocy, illogically, imprudence, inanity, incautiousness, indiscreetness, indiscretion, irresponsibility, lunacy, mischief, nonsense, prankishness, punk, sappiness, senselessness, short-sightedness, silliness, stupidity, tommyrot, weakness
**foolish person** ass, chump, dotard, goof, idiot, nincompoop, ninny, nitwit, noodle, omadhaun, sap, simp(leton), stupe, twit
**foolish pretender to knowledge and wisdom** wiseacre
**foolish remark** inanity
**foolish talk** baloney, blah, blether, boloney, chatter, drivel, gibberish, nonsense, prattle, wishwash
**fool's gold** pyrite
**fool's headdress** cap-and-bells
**fool's paradise** delusion, illusion
**fool's parsley** kex
**fool's stitch** tricot
**foot** base, bottom, iamb, inhibit, paw, ped-, pedestal, pes
**foot ailment** bunion, callus, corn, wart
**foot and mouth disease** murrain
**football** soccer
**football association** league
**footballer's aim** goal
**football field** arena, gridiron, oval, stadium
**football game** rugby, soccer
**football kick** punt
**football misplay** fumble
**football official** linesman, ref(eree)
**football pass** lateral
**football rest time** half(-time)
**football score** goal, try
**football shoe part** cleat
**football supporter** fan
**football team** side
**football throw** ground
**football umpire** ref(eree)
**foot beat** tread
**foot bone** tarsus

**foot bottom** sole
**foot consisting of two short syllables** pyrrhic
**foot covering** boot, galosh, plimsoll, sandal, shoe, slipper, sock
**foot digit** toe
**footed** cleared, compensated, discharged, honoured, liquidated, met, offered, pedate, recompensed, reimbursed, remitted, remunerated, rendered, requited, rewarded, settled
**footed vase** urn
**footfall** gait, step, tread
**footgear** boots, sandals, shoes
**foot grip for climber** toe-hold
**foot it** pace, saunter, step, stroll, walk
**foot-joint** ankle
**footless** apod(al), free
**footless animal** apod(al)
**foot lever** pedal, treadle
**footlike part** pes
**footman** flunk(e)y, manservant, valet
**footman in livery** flunk(e)y
**foot of beast having claws** paw
**foot of four syllables** paeon
**foot of three syllables** anap(a)est, dactyl(ic)
**foot of two syllables** iamb(ic), pyrrhic, spondee, trochee
**foot of wolf** pad
**foot-operated lever** pedal
**foot part** arch, heel, instep, sole, toe
**footpath edge** kerb
**footpath of canal** towpath
**foot pedal** lever, treadle
**footprint mould** moulage
**foot racer** runner
**foot rest of saddle** stirrup
**foot's digit** toe
**foot soldier** footman, infantryman, legionnaire, mercenary, peltast, private, regular
**foot sole** plantar
**footstalk** pedicel, petiole, strig
**foot support** stirrup
**foot swelling** bunion
**foot the bill** treat
**foot therapist** chiropodist
**foot traveller** hiker, pedestrian, tramp
**foot treatment** pedicure
**foot verse** iamb
**footway** path, trail, walk
**footway along canals** towpath
**footwear** boot, galosh, plimsoll, sandal, shoe, slipper, socks
**footwear craftsman** shoemaker
**footwear item** shoe, sock
**footwear of soft deerskin** moccasin
**footwiper** mat
**fop** beau, cavalier, coxcomb, dandy, dude, gallant, pantsula, popinjay, poseur, prig, spark, strutter

**foppish** dandified, dandyish, finicky, fop-like, gaudy, ornate, ostentatious, vain
**for** as, because, by, concerning, during, para (Sp), por (Sp), pro-, since, to, toward
**for a brief period** awhile
**forage** hay
**forage plant** alfalfa, rape
**for a little while** awhile
**for all future time** evermore
**for all intents and purposes** practically
**for all one knows** perhaps
**for all that** nevertheless
**for all time** ever(more), forever, permanently
**foramen** orifice, perforation
**for a moment** awhile
**for a particular purpose** expressly
**for a particular purpose only** ad hoc
**for a short time** awhile
**forasmuch as** because
**foray** assault, attack, charge, forage, incursion, inroad, invasion, irruption, offensive, onslaught, pillage, raid, ransack, ravage, skirmish, sortie, storm
**forbade** outlawed, precluded, prohibited, vetoed
**forbear** abide, abnegate, abstain, avoid, cease, decline, desist, endure, eschew, forgo, omit, pause, quit, refrain, renounce, restrain, sacrifice, shun, stop, suffer, tolerate, withhold
**forbearance** abstinence, avoidance, clemency, desisting, endurance, forbearing, indulgence, leniency, long-suffering, longanimity, meekness, mercy, mildness, patience, pity, resignation, restraint, self-denial, submission, sufferance, temperance, tolerance, toleration
**forbearing** abstaining, avoiding, ceasing, declining, desisting, easy, eschewing, forgiving, indulgent, lenient, merciful, mild, moderate, omitting, patient, pausing, refraining, stopping, tolerant, withholding
**forbid** arrest, ban, curb, (de)bar, deter, disallow, discourage, eliminate, enjoin, exclude, hinder, impede, inhibit, interdict, oppose, outlaw, preclude, prevent, prohibit, proscribe, refuse, reject, repel, stop, taboo, tabu, vent, veto
**forbidden** disallowed, disapprove, ejected, illicit, proscribed, refused
**forbidden act** crime
**forbidden by law** illegal, illegitimate, illicit
**forbidden city** Lhasa

**forbidding** banning, debarring, disallowing, excluding, hindering, inhibiting, outlawing, precluding, prohibiting, proscribing, stern, vetoing
**forbid flatly** veto
**forbid passage through** stop
**forbid use of** interdict
**for boiling water** kettle
**for burning a body** pyre
**for carrying objects** tray
**force** coerce, coercion, compel, compulsion, constrain, dint, drive, effect, efficacy, efficiency, energy, impel, intensity, might, necessitate, oblige, overcome, (over)power, potency, pressure, propel, strength, vehemence, vigour, violence, vis (L), weightiness
**force air through nose** snore, snort
**force along** boost, push, shove, urge
**force a way into** penetrate
**force back** repel
**force causing rotation** torque
**force down** detrude, oppress, ram, tamp, trample
**force from behind** vis a tergo (L)
**forceful** cogent, convincing, dynamic, effective, intense, pithy, potent, telling, vigorous
**forceful blow** sock, wham
**forceful constraint** duress
**forceful man** go-getter
**forceful rush** jet
**force in** intrude
**force in operation** energy
**force into action** impel
**force into doing something** press-gang
**force into motion** impel
**force of attack** brunt
**force of constables** posse
**force of men** army, commando, corps, posse
**force of moving body** momentum
**force of nature** element, weather
**force one's way** muscle
**force onward** urge
**force or urge out** extrude
**force out** eject, oust
**forcer** coercer
**force that twists** torsion, torque
**force to abdicate** dethrone
**force too much into** overstuff
**force to produce rotation** torque
**force with legal authority** posse
**force with which body moves** impetus
**forcible** active, assertive, coercive, cogent, compelling, compulsory, drastic, effective, efficient, energetic, forceful, imposed, impressive, intense, irresistible, mighty, potent,

powerful, required, strong, urgent, valid, weighty
**forcible push** thrust
**forcible restraint** duress
**forcible seizure** reprisal
**forcible stream of air** blast
**forcibly put an end to** quell
**for clearing river-bed** dredger
**for common use** communal
**ford** bridge, cross, drift, meet, negotiate, paddle, ply, span, splash, surmount, traverse, wade, zigzag
**ford a stream** wade
**for dear life** desperately, quickly, urgently
**for dressing wounds** lint
**for each** apiece, per
**fore-and-aft rigged vessel** schooner, sloop
**forearm bone** radius, ulna
**forebear** ancestor, forefather, predecessor
**forebode** augur, betoken, forecast, foreshadow, foretell, foretoken, indicate, intuit, omen, portend, predict, presage, presignify, prognosticate, promise, sense, vaticinate
**foreboding** anxiety, apprehension, auguring, augury, betokening, chill, dread, fear, forecast, foresight, foretelling, indicating, menacing, misgiving, omen, ominous, portending, portent, prediction, premonition, premonitory, presentiment, prophesy, sign, warning
**foreboding disaster** dire
**foreboding evil** ominous
**forebrain** prosencephalon
**forecast** anticipate, augur, conjecture, estimate, foresight, foretell, forethought, guess, plan, prearrange, predict(ion), prescience, project
**forecast course of disease** prognosis
**fore end of a ship** bow
**forefather** ancestor, forebear, originator, parent, patriarch, (primo)genitor, procreator, progenitor, sire
**forefatherly** ancestral
**forefinger** index finger
**forego** abandon, abnegate, abstain, cede, forgo, relinquish, renounce, resign, sacrifice, surrender, waive, yield
**foregone** abandoned, ceded, relinquished, renounced, resigned, sacrificed, surrendered, waived, yielded
**forehead** brow, face, front, sinciput

**forehead strap** tumpline
**for eight people** eightsome
**foreign** alien, dissimilar, exotic, extraneous, imported, inappropriate, inconsistent, irrelative, irrelevant, remote, strange, unrelated, xeno-
**foreign agent** spy
**foreign body** impurity
**foreign-born resident** alien
**foreign country** outland
**foreign customs-house** douane (F)
**foreigner** alien, émigré, immigrant, non-native, outsider, stranger
**foreign language** lingo, xenoglossia
**foreign priest** abbé
**foreign woman** madame, signora
**foreman** administrator, boss, chief, director, employer, executive, gaffer, ganger, gangsman, governor, head, leader, manager, master, overseer, owner, steward, supervisor
**foreman of jury** chancellor
**foreman printer** clicker
**foremost** chief, essential, first, leading, main, paramount, supreme, vital
**foremost in rank** first
**foremost part of advancing army** vanguard
**foremost part of a ship** stern
**forenoon** morning
**foreordain** allot, consecrate, dedicate, destine, determine, doom, intend, mean, ordain, predecide, predestinate, predestine, predetermine, purpose, resolve, set
**fore part** front
**fore part of aeroplane** nose
**fore part of ship** bow, prow, stem
**forerunner** ancestor, avant-coureur (F), envoy, foregoer, foretoken, herald, indication, leader, precursor, predecessor
**forerunner of fridge** icebox
**forerunner of sonar** asdic
**foreshadow** augur, betoken, bode, forebode, foretell, foretoken, indicate, omen, predestine, prefigure, presage, presignify
**foresight** care, clairvoyance, farsightedness, forecast, foreknowledge, forethought, glimpse, judg(e)ment, judiciousness, precaution, preconception, prescience, presentiment, preview, prospect, prudence, readiness, sagacity, vision
**forest** copse, grove, timberland, woodland, wood(s)
**forestage** apron
**forestall** anticipate, avert, avoid, divert, for(e)see, frustrate, hinder, intercept,

obstruct, obviate, parry, pre-empt, preclude, prevent, thwart
**forest clearing** glade, sartage
**forest divinity** dryad, nymph, Pan, Silvanus, Sylvanus
**forester** woodsman
**forest god** Pan, Silvanus, Sylvanus
**forest growth** tree
**forest humus** mor
**forestless tract** steppe
**forest official** ranger
**forest path** trail
**forest patrol warden** ranger
**forest plant** tree
**forest tree** ash, beech, pine
**foretell** adumbrate, augur, (fore)bode, forecast, foresee, foreshadow, forewarn, indicate, insee, portend, predict, presage, prognosticate, prophesy, signify, soothsay, spae (Sc), vaticinate
**foreteller** prophet, seer
**forethought** anticipation, care, precaution, providence, provision, prudence
**forever** always, ceaselessly, constantly, continually, endless(ly), eternally, eternity, ever(lasting), evermore, in aeternum (L), incessantly, indefinitely, permanently, perpetually, persistently, sine die (L), unceasingly, undyingly
**for ever and ever** in saecula saeculorum (L)
**for every** each, per
**foreword** dedication, exordium, introduction, lead-in, opening, overture, preamble, preface, preliminary, prelude, proem, prologue
**for example** as, eg, so, vide
**forex charge** agio
**for fear that** lest
**forfeit** charge, cheat, damages, default, escheat, estreat, fine, forfeiture, lose, loss, mulct, penalty, relinquish, renounce, surrender
**forfeited soldier** perdu(e)
**forfeiture** déchéance (F)
**for free** complimentary, gratis
**for fun** blithely, facetiously, gaily, jokingly, laughingly, mischievously, playfully, teasingly, wittily
**for further consideration** ad referendum (L)
**forge** beat, cast, coin, compose, copy, counterfeit, create, drudge, fake, falsify, fashion, feign, fireplace, foundry, hearth, imitate, invent, mould, produce, smithy

**forger** con, contriver, counterfeiter, creator, devisor, fabricator, faker, falsifier, liar
**forgery** charlatan, coining, copy, counterfeit(ing), crimen falsi (L), dud, duplicate, facsimile, fake, fraud(ulence), hoax, image, imitation, imposter, likeness, model, pattern, phoney, photocopy, print, replica, reproduction, sham
**forget** disregard, neglect, overlook
**forgetfulness of the past** Lethe
**forget oneself** deviate, err, misbehave, offend, transgress, trespass
**forging block** anvil
**forgivable** condonable, excusable, pardonable, remittable, venial
**forgive** absolve, acquit, amnesty, condone, exculpate, excuse, exempt, exonerate, ignore, nullify, overlook, pardon, remit, reprieve, shrive, waive
**forgiveness** absolution, absolving, acquittal, amnesty, clemency, compassion, excusal, exoneration, forbearance, grace, humanity, lenience, leniency, lenity, mercifulness, mercy, pardon(ing), remission, vindication
**forgiving** absolutory, absolving, acquitting, clement, compassionate, condoning, excusing, excusive, exonerating, humane, indulgent, lenient, merciful, mild, pardoning, placable, reconcilable, remitting, soft-hearted, tolerant
**forgo** abandon, abstain, cede, complete, forfeit, relinquish, renounce, resign, sacrifice, surrender, waive, yield
**forgo food** fast
**forgone** sacrificed, surrendered, waived, yielded
**for good** finally, irrevocably, permanently
**for good measure** additionally, gratis, gratuitously
**forgotten state** oblivion
**for instance** as, par exemple (F), say
**forked bone between head and breast of bird** merrythought, wishbone
**forked rod** crutch
**for keeps** conclusively, determinedly, permanently, resolutely, seriously, sincerely
**fork for lifting hay** pitchfork
**forking in three** trichotomous
**fork out** pay
**fork part** prong, tine
**fork prong** tine
**fork-shaped piece between fingers of a glove** fourchette

**fork tine** prong
**fork used for digging potatoes** graip
**for lack of anything better** faute de mieux (F)
**for life** lasting, lifelong, lifetime, permanent
**forlorn** abandoned, abject, alone, desolate, destitute, disconsolate, dreary, forsaken, helpless, miserable, unhappy, woebegone, wretched
**forlorn and wretched** desolate
**forlorn hope** enfants perdus (F)
**for love** freely, gratis, pleasurably
**form** application, approach, arrange(ment), ceremony, combine, conformity, construct, contrive, convention, create, design, discipline, document, educate, fabric(ate), fashion, figure, formula, frame, genre, genus, group, idea, invent, kind, make, manner, method, model, mould, order, outline, paper, practice, procedure, produce, ritual, rule, scheme, shape, sort, species, style, system, texture, variety
**form a barrier** door
**form a cluster** agglomerate
**form after a model** imitate
**form a harmonious compound** blend
**formal** approved, ceremonial, distant, exact, explicit, express, fixed, lawful, legal, methodical, official, perfunctory, precise, prescribed, prim, regular, rigid, ritualistic, set, solemn, starchy, stiff, strict
**formal account** statement
**formal accusation** indictment
**formal act** ceremony
**formal address** lecture, oration
**formal address for woman** madam
**formal admission into society** initiation
**formal agreement** contract
**formal agreement between nations** treaty
**formal and precise** prim
**formal announcement** declaration
**formal assembly** conclave, congress, diet, synod
**formal base element** metal
**formal choice** election, vote
**formal command** edict
**formal curse** anathema
**formal dance** ball
**formal debate** deliberation
**formal decree** edict
**formal denunciation of a doctrine** anathema
**formal discourse** lecture
**formal discussion** debate
**formal document** charter, indenture

**formal dress** gown
**formal essay** monograph, treatise
**formal etiquette** protocol
**formal examination of accounts** audit
**formal exercise enthusiast** gymnast
**formal farewell** congé
**formal forgiveness of sin** absolution
**formal gesture of greeting made by women** curts(e)y
**formal gown** robe
**formal greetings conveyed in a message** compliments
**formal international agreement** treaty, pact
**formality and hypocrisy in religion** pharisaism
**formal judgement** sentence
**formal letter** missive
**formally accept** approve, endorse, recognise, support, uphold
**formally prohibit** ban
**formally question** examine
**formally regular** solemn
**formally withdraw** secede
**formal meeting of delegates for discussion** congress
**formal objection** protest
**formal offer for job** tender
**formal official agreement** treaty
**formal permission** authorisation, licence, license
**formal person** precisian
**formal politeness** ceremony
**formal practice** rite
**formal praise** encomium
**formal procedure** ceremony, protocol
**formal proclamation** edict
**formal proposition** thesis
**formal record** act, document, minutes
**formal request to authorities** petition
**formal robe** gown
**formal setting-free from guilt** absolution
**formal social presentation** debut
**formal speech** address, allocution, oration
**formal statement** pronouncement
**formal talk** address
**formal test** exam(ination)
**formal warning** caveat
**formal welcome** reception
**formal written defence of a cause** apologia
**formal written supplication** petition
**form a mental picture of** imagine, invent
**form an estimate** calculate
**form an opinion of** estimate
**form a row** align, aline
**formation of charged atoms** ionisation
**formation of rings** annulation
**formation of tissues** histogenesis

formation of troops  echelon, parade
formation of words that imitate what they stand for  onomatopoeia
form a wrong opinion about  mistake
form a wrong opinion of  misjudge
form border to  edge
form connecting link between  mediate
for measuring atmospheric pressure  barometer
formed beneath earth's surface  hypogene
formed by lines  geometric
formed by trees  arboreous
formed during festering  pus
formed into bundles  baled
formed like a letter H  zygal
for men only  stag
former  above, aforementioned, ancient, antecedent, anterior, bygone, departed, earlier, erstwhile, ex-, foregoing, foregone, lapsed, last, late, old, old-time, one-time, past, precedent, preceding, previous, prior, quondam, sometime, whilon
former Anglo-Saxon kingdom  Mercia
former bicycle  pennyfarthing
former British Airline  BOAC
former British coin  farthing, florin
former British colony in the East  Aden
former Briton  Pict
former capital of Corsica  Bastia
former capital of Pakistan  Karachi
former capital of Vietnam  Saigon
former cavalryman  lancer
former cavalry weapon  lance
former Chinese capital  Peking
former Chinese leader  Mao
former Chinese nurse  amah
former church representative  pardoner
former cloth measure  ell
former coin of India  anna
former copper coin of the Netherlands  doit
former days  ago, eld, past(s), yore
former Dutch coin  ducat, stiver
former earthen dwelling  rath
former Eastern leader  shah
former Egyptian president  Sadat
former emperor  czar, tsar
former English coin  groat
former European coin  ducat
former farmer  yeoman
former Flemish coin  mite
former freeholders  yeomanry
former French coin  sou, écu
former ganglord  Capone
former gold coin  ducat, mohur, moidore, pistole
former gold coin of France  napoleon

former gold coin of India  mohur
former gold coin of Portugal  moidore
former gold coin of Spain  pistole
former husband or wife  ex
former Indian coin  anna
former Indian groom  saice, sice, syce
former Indian prime minister  Desai, Nehru
former Indian servant  s(a)ice, syce
former Indian soldier  sepoy
former Iranian ruler  shah
former Italian coin  scudo, soldo
former Japanese money  sen
former Japanese outcast  eta
former kingdom in Ethiopia  Amhara
former king of Norway  Haakon
former king of Saudi Arabia  Saud
former Libyan province  Cyrenaica
formerly  aforetime, before, erst, heretofore, hitherto, lately, once, previously, yore
formerly Arbela  Arbil, Erbil, Irbil
formerly Burma  Myanmar
formerly Ceylon  Sri Lanka
formerly Formosa  Taiwan
formerly gall  bile
formerly LM  Maputo
formerly Persia  Iran
formerly Rangoon  Yangon
formerly Siamese  Thai
formerly Zend  Avestan
formerly Madagascar  Malagasy Republic
former Malawi capital  Zomba
former measure of land, about two acres  morg(en)
former Mexican  Aztec
former mistress  courtesan
former musical instrument like oboe  shawm
former name for endoplasmic reticulum  ergastoplasm
former name for lipid  lipoid
former name for radon  niton
former name for scrofula  king's evil
former name for topology  analysis situs
former name for whisky  usquebaugh (Sc)
former name of Algeria  Numidia
former name of Botswana  Bechuanaland
former name of Denmark  Thule
former name of Dhaka  Dacca
former name of Djakarta  Batavia
former name of Edirne  Adrianople
former name of Egypt  United Arab Republic
former name of Erbil  Abrela
former name of Ethiopia  Abyssinia
former name of Hawaii  Sandwich Islands

former name of Iran  Persia
former name of Iraq  Mesopotamia
former name of Iskenderun  Alexandretta
former name of Istanbul  Constantinople
former name of Jerez  Xeres
former name of Kafiristan  Nuristan
former name of Kampuchea  Cambodia
former name of Kananga  Luluabourg
former name of Kiribati  Gilbert Islands
former name of Lüda  Dairen
former name of Malawi  Nyasaland
former name of Mali  French Sudan
former name of Namibia  South-West Africa
former name of Nauru  Pleasant Island
former name of Sri Lanka  Ceylon
former name of Surinam  Dutch Guiana
former name of Taiwan  Formosa
former name of Tanzania  Tanganyika
former name of Thailand  Siam
former name of Toamasina  Tamatave
former name of Tokyo  Edo, Yeso
former name of Twi  Ashanti
former name of Vietnam  Annam
former NATO general  Haig
former Nazi deputy  Hess
former noble  thane
former operation to correct squints  strabotomy
former ostler  s(a)ice, syce
former Ottoman governor  bey
former Paris fortress  Bastille
former payment by freeholder  quitrent
former pope  Pius
former Portuguese president  Eanes
former Portuguese province in India  Goa
former Portuguese territory  Angola
former pot mender  tinker
former public announcer  crier
former pupil or student  alumna, alumnus, apostle, disciple, graduate
former regime  ancien régime (F)
former rifleman  fusilier
former royal arms of France  fleur-de-lis
former royal palace in Paris  Tuileries
former ruler  czar, tsar
former ruler of Hyderabad  nizam
former ruler of Iran  shah
former Russian emperor  czar, tsar
former Shah's surname  Pahlavi
former Siam  Thailand
former Siamese  Thai
former small coin  farthing
former small French coin  sou
former South African heavyweight  Kallie Knoetze

**former Soviet police** Ogpu
**former Spanish coin** real
**former Spanish dictator** Franco
**former Spanish gold coin** doblon, doubloon
**former spouse** ex
**former student, as of an alma mater** alumna, alumnus
**former Syrian nomad** Saracen
**former table covering** tapis
**former Thai money** tical
**former time** past
**former times** antiquity, eld
**former trade allowance** tret
**former trading vessel** crare, crayer
**former Turk** Osmanli
**former Turkish soldier** nizam
**former Turkish title** dey
**former unit of luminance** lambert
**former USSR council** Soviet
**former Venetian gold coin** sequin
**former Venetian ruler** doge
**form glossy surface on** enamel
**formicary inhabitant** ant
**formidable** awesome, dangerous, difficult, dreadful, fearful, frightful, great, mighty, strong
**form ideas** ideate
**form in a cluster** group
**forming an exception** exceptional
**forming a reserve** funding
**forming a unit** en suite (F)
**forming no angle** agonic
**forming steam** vaporescent
**form in layers** laminate
**form in the mind** ideate, shape
**form into alternate ridges and grooves** corrugated
**form into fabric** knit, weave
**form into jelly** gel, jell, set
**form into ringlets** curl
**form in which a book is published** edition
**formless** amorphous, chaotic, confused, indefinite, nebulous, shadowy, shapeless, undefined, unformed, unshaped, vague
**formless matter** plasma
**form of a** an
**form of address** madam, sir
**form of address as mark of respect** tuan
**form of address for a man** mister
**form of architecture** Ionic
**form of asdic** sonar
**form of a verb functioning as a noun** gerund
**form of basalt** tachylyte
**form of baseball** softball
**form of boxing practice** spar
**form of carbon** (char)coal
**form of chalcedony** sard

**form of cloud** cirrus, nimbus, stratus
**form of communication** radio, telephone, television, TV
**form of crane** derrick
**form of dancing** ballet, modern, tap
**form of diversion** cards
**form of early Japanese drama** No(h)
**form of energy** electricity
**form of entertainment** revue
**form of Esperanto** Ido
**form of expression** diction
**form of freehold** udal
**form of gambling** lottery, pools, sweepstake
**form of government** democracy, monarchy
**form of greeting** bow, handclasp, handshake, kiss, nod, wave
**form of humour** pun
**form of I** myself
**form of is** are, be, was, were
**form of Japanese unarmed combat** karate
**form of jazz** trad
**form of jelly** gel
**form of language** dialect, prose
**form of language used by an individual person** idiolect
**form of lottery** tombola
**form of lotto** bingo
**form of mental disease** paranoia, schizophrenia
**form of music composition** fugue, nocturne, symphony
**form of oxygen** ozone
**form of prayer** litany
**form of public transport** bus, train
**form of public worship** liturgy
**form of punishment** penalty
**form of quartz** agate
**form of Sanskrit** Vedic
**form of the** ye
**form of type** boldface, cursive, italic, roman
**form of unarmed combat** judo
**form of worship** liturgy, ritual
**form of wrestling** tag
**form of writing** drama, poetry, prose
**form of yoga** hatha
**form premature judgement on** prejudge
**form pus** fester, suppurate
**form rings** annulate
**form rounded grooves** flute
**formula** method, precept, prescription, recipe, rule, saying
**formula for solution** hypothesis, key
**formula of religious faith** creed
**formulate** devise, invent, order, organise, outline, systematise
**formulator of law of gravity** Newton
**form variation in species** cline

**form words from letters** spell
**form words into compounds** agglutinate
**for nothing** free, gratis
**for one** each, per
**for one eye** monocular
**for one's country** pro patria (L)
**for one's own part** personally
**for producing typed copies** stencil
**for purpose of** to
**for recording transactions** ledger
**for roof** tile
**forsake** abandon, desert, discard, disown, forgo, jettison, jilt, leave, quit, recant, reject, relinquish, renounce, repudiate
**forsake entirely** abandon, desert
**forsaken** abandoned, alone, bereft, derelict, deserted, desperate, destitute, isolated, neglected, outcast, rejected, solitary
**forsaken by one's love** lovelorn
**forsaker of the faith** apostate
**forsake ship** abandon
**forsake utterly** abandon
**for sale** accessible, attainable, available, obtainable
**for shame!** fi donc! (F), fib, fie
**for smoothing clothes** iron
**for so much** pro tanto (L)
**for space of** during
**forswear oneself** lie
**Forsyth file** Odessa
**fort** blockhouse, camp, castle, citadel, fortress, garrison, redoubt, station, stronghold
**forte** aptitude, blade, eminency, endowment, faculty, gift, loud(ly), métier, skill, stark, strength, strong(-point), talent, technique
**for that** therefore
**for that reason** accordingly, because, consequently, therefore
**for the birds** absurd, ridiculous, unbelievable, unworthy
**for the future** in futuro (L)
**for the initiated only** esoteric
**for the meantime** ad interim
**for the most part** chiefly, essentially, generally, largely, mainly, mostly, principally
**for the present** ad interim, provisionally, temporarily
**for the public good** pro bono publico (L)
**for the reason that** because
**for the sake of example** exempli gratia (L)
**for the sake of honour** honoris causa (L)

**for the time being** ad interim, meantime, meanwhile, pro tempore (L), temporarily
**for this occasion** pro hac vice (L)
**for this particular purpose** ad hoc
**for this reason** ergo, hence, so
**fortification** bastion, battlement, bolstering, bracing, bulwark, buttress, citadel, defence, dugout, earthwork, fort(ifying), lunette, moat, mound, parados, parapet, rampart, redan, redoubt, sconce, stockade, strengthening, stronghold
**fortification ditch** escarp, foss(e), moat, scarp, trench
**fortification of two parapets at a salient angle** redan
**fortified building** fortress
**fortified place** bastion, castle, fort(ress), garrison, stronghold
**fortified residence** castle, dun
**fortified seaport in Italy** Taranto
**fortified tower** bastion
**fortified village** pa(h)
**fortified white wine** Madeira
**fortified wine** port, sherry
**fortify** arm, boost, buttress, embattle, enrich, man, reinforce, resolve, strengthen
**fortify against attack** embattle
**fortify with spirits** lace
**fortissimo** loud(ness)
**fortitude** courage, endurance, hardiness, mettle, nerve, pluck, resolution, tenacity
**for travelling over snow** ski
**fortress** alcazar, barrier, Bastille, bastion, borough, burg, buttress, casbah, castle, chateau, citadel, fort(ification), kasbah, strength, stronghold, tower
**fortress city in France** Metz, Strasbourg
**fortress ditch** moat
**fortress in Texas** Alamo
**fortress overlooking a city** citadel
**fortress town in France** Toul
**fortuitous** accidental, aleatory, casual, chance, contingent, fortunate, haphazard, happy, inadvertent, incidental, involuntary, occasional, random, serendipitous, unanticipated, undeliberate, undesigned, unexpected, unintentional, unlooked for, unplanned
**fortuitously** coincidentally
**fortuitous risk** chance
**fortunate** advantageous, auspicious, benign(ant), blessed, bright, favourable, favoured, fortuitous, golden, halcyon, happy, lucky, prosperous, providential, rich, rosy, succeeding, successful, thriving, timely, well-off
**fortunately** feliciter (L), luckily, successfully
**fortunate trait** felicity
**fortune** circumstances, destiny, fate, luck, riches, wealth
**fortune card** tarot
**fortune favours fools** fortuna favet fatuis (L)
**fortune-hunter** adventurer
**fortunes** accidents, adventures, assets, biography, chances, destinies, escapades, experiences, fates, hazards, means, possessions, properties, prospect, riches, treasures, wealth
**fortune-teller** astrologer, augur, diviner, geomancer, horoscoper, oracle, prophet, sangoma, seer, sibyl, stargazer
**fortune-telling** divination
**fortune-telling by playing-cards** cartomancy
**fortune-telling card** tarot
**fortune-telling from the lines on the palm of the hand** palmistry
**for two** à deux (F)
**forty days' isolation** quarantine
**forty-eight zeros after a number** octillion
**forty-five degree angle** octant
**forty-five inches** ell
**forty winks** catnap, doze, nap, rest, siesta, snooze
**forum** agency, arena, assembly, bar, bench, channel, colloquy, conference, congress, consultation, convention, convocation, court, debate argument, discussion, focus, judicature, judiciary, market(-place), mart, medium, meeting, mouthpiece, organ, seminar, symposium, talk, teach-in, tribunal
**for uniting substances** glue
**for use on snow** sled(ge), sleigh, toboggan
**for want of any better alternative** faute de mieux (F)
**forward** advanced, ahead, aid, bold, brazen, confident, direct, eager, early, earnest, en avant (F), forth, fro(ntward), future, hurry, impertinent, impudent, intelligent, on(ward), out, pert, precocious, preliminary, presumptuous, progressive, promote, prompt, radical, ready, redirect, relay, send, sincere, speed, support, to(ward), willing, zealous
**forward by stages** relay
**forward charge** onrush
**forward curvature of the spine** lordosis
**forward edge of ship's prow** cutwater
**forward girl** strap
**forward momentum** impetus
**forward movement** advancement
**forwardness** earliness, impudence, pertness, precociousness, prematureness, progressiveness
**forward payment** remit
**forward position** front
**forward swell** onrush
**forward thrust** lunge
**for what reason?** why
**for wide circulation** encyclical
**foss** canal, fosse, moat
**fossa** cavity, pit
**fossil** bones, footprint, impression, petrification, relics, spoor, track
**fossil ammonite** snakestone
**fossil animal** zoolite
**fossil coral** fungite
**fossil crab** crabite
**fossil crinoid** stone-lily
**fossil expert** palaeontologist
**fossil fish** ichthyolite
**fossil footprint** ichnite
**fossil fruit** lithocarp
**fossil fuel** coal, peat
**fossilise** ossify
**fossilised resin** amber
**fossil of a coil-shaped shell** ammonite
**fossil of biped dinosaur** tyrannosaur
**fossil plant** calamite
**fossil remains** exuviae
**fossil resin** amber
**fossil resin used for jewellery** amber
**fossil wood** pinite
**fossil worm track** cast
**foster** adopt, breed, encourage, favour, forward, further, nourish, nurse, nurture, patronise, promote, rear, sustain
**fosterage** adoption, nursery
**fostering care** nurture
**foul** abominable, besmirch, caught, clog, defile, dirty, disgrace, disgusting, dishonourable, filthy, f(o)etid, gross, impure, jammed, loathsome, low, noisome, obscene, offensive, pollute(d), profane, putrid, rainy, repellent, repulsive, sinful, soil(ed), squalid, stain(ed), stinking, stormy, sullied, tainted, tangled, tarnished, tempestuous, unclean, unfavourable, vile, vulgar, wicked
**foul and putrid water** addle
**foul and stuffy** frowsty
**foul breath** halitosis
**foul language** filth, ordure
**foul-mouthed** profane, scurrilous

**foul odour** rancidity, reek, stench, stink
**foul play** business, chicanery, corruption, crime, deception, double-dealing, duplicity, fraud, funny, injustice, jiggery-pokery, murder, roguery, treachery, villainy
**foul smell** stench
**foul up** botch, bungle, mangle, muddle
**foul watery discharge from a wound or ulcer** ichor
**foumart** polecat
**found** base, discovered, equipped, establish, eureka, ground, institute, originate
**foundation** base(ment), basis, creation, endowment, establishment, foothold, footing, groundwork, motive, purpose, root, rudiment, settlement, source, substructure
**foundation garment** corset
**foundation of Marxism** *Communist Manifesto*
**foundation of sauces** roux
**foundation structure of a tyre** carcass
**foundation timber** sill
**found at sea bottom** demersal
**found at some dances** stagline, wallflower
**found beyond wrist** hand
**founded in truth** valid
**founded on experiment** empirical
**founder of antiseptic method in surgery** Lister
**founder of Bolshevik Party** Lenin
**founder of Buddhism** Buddha
**founder of first city** Cain
**founder of Greek drama** Thespis
**founder of hypnotism** Mesmer
**founder of Methodism** Wesley
**founder of Nineveh** Ninus
**founder of psychoanalysis** Freud
**founder of Rome** Romulus
**found in abscess** pus
**found in apiary** bee
**found in beehive** honeycomb
**found in Champ de Mars** Eiffel Tower
**found in chimneys** soot
**found in deserts** sand
**found in high seas** oceanic
**found in hives** bees
**found in oyster** pearl
**found in park** swan
**found in pod** pea
**found in polar seas** iceberg
**found in pure state** native
**found in school lunchbox** sandwich
**found in the laundry** suds
**found in veins** blood
**found in wood** tree
**foundling** castaway, changeling, derelict, orphan, outcast, stray, waif
**found on coat** lapel

**found on fish hooks** bait
**found on grape farm** vineyard
**found on ground** epigean
**found on oak tree** acorn
**found on roof** tile
**found out** discovered
**foundry** factory, workshop
**found wanting** culpable, guilty, inadequate
**fountain drink** malt, soda
**fountain nymph** naiad
**four** tetra-, tetrad
**four-cornered sail** lug
**four-cornered sail on yard** lugsail
**four corners of baseball diamond** bases
**four-fifths of atmosphere** nitrogen
**fourfold** quadruple, quadruplicate
**four-footed animal** beast, quadruped
**four gills** pint
**four-headed muscle at front of thigh** quadriceps
**four-horsed chariot** quadriga
**four-hundredth anniversary** quadricentennial, quartercentenary
**four inches** hand
**four-in-hand** ascot, carriage, tie
**four-in-hand coach** tally-ho
**four-leaved figure** quatrefoil
**four-legged** quadruped
**four-legged friend** dog, horse
**four-legged reptile** caiman, cayman, dinosaur, lizard, turtle
**four-letter word** tetragram
**four-line stanza** quatrain
**four-lobed ornamental, opening in Gothic stonework** quatrefoil
**four pecks** bushel
**fourpenny piece** groat
**four-poster** bed
**four-pound loaf** quartern-loaf
**four seasons** year
**four-sided court in a building** quadrangle
**four-sided figure** quadrangle, quadrilateral, rectangle, square, tetragon
**four-sided pillar** obelisk
**four-sided plane figure** rectangle
**four-sided plane figure with opposite sides parallel** parallelogram
**four-sided polygon** quadrilateral, tetragon
**four-sided shape** rectangle
**four-sided stele** obelisk
**four-sided tapering pillar** obelisk
**foursquare** bold, direct
**fourteen-line poem** quatorzain
**fourteen-line poem with a rhyme system** sonnet
**fourteen pounds** stone

**fourteenth February** Saint Valentine's Day
**fourth caliph of Islam** Ali
**fourth dimension** time
**fourth estate** press
**fourth of eight parrying positions in fencing** quart
**fourth part** quarter
**fourth sign of the Zodiac** Cancer
**fourth stomach in a ruminating animal** abomasum
**fourth year buck** sore
**four-toed anteater** tamandu(a)
**four weeks before Christmas** Advent
**four-wheeled carriage** berlin, fiacre, landau, phaeton, surrey, tarantass
**four-wheeled carriage with folding top** barouche
**four-wheeled horse-drawn carriage** barouche, landau
**four-wheeled Russian vehicle** tarantass
**four-wheeled vehicle** auto(mobile), berlin, brougham, landau, phaeton, surrey, trap, victoria, wagon
**four-wheeled vehicle for heavy loads** wag(g)on
**four-winged insect** moth
**four-winged insect living near water** caddis fly
**four year period** quadrennial
**fowl** capon, chook(ie), cock, hen
**fowl enclosure** coop
**fowl perch** roost
**fowl pox** roup
**fowl run** coop
**fowls** poultry
**fowl's entrails** giblets
**fowl's stomach** craw, crop
**fowl tick** tampan
**fox** corsac, deceive, dissemble, fennec, jackal, puzzle, quadruped, tod (Sc), trick
**fox-fire** will-o'-the-wisp
**foxglove** digitalis
**fox-hunter's halloo** yoicks
**fox-hunting dog** hound, terrier
**fox's den** lair
**foxtrot** dance
**fox with large ears** fennec
**foxy** artful, astute, calculating, canny, crafty, cunning, deceitful, designing, devious, fraudulent, guileful, scheming, sharp, shrewd, sly, subtle, titian, tricky, wily
**foyer** antechamber, anteroom, lobby, vestibule
**fra** friar, monk
**frabjous** delightful, joyous
**fracas** altercation, brawl, broil, commotion, discord, disorder, dispute, fight, melée, quarrel, riot,

**fraction**           291           **fraternity**

row, scramble, spat, squabble, tumult, turmoil, uproar, wrangle
**fraction** bit(e), crumb, division, equation, fragment, grain, half, morsel, part, piece, (pro)portion, quantity, ratio, remnant, section, segment, share, slice, sliver, soupçon, taste
**fractional currency** scrip
**fraction of a foot** inch
**fraction of yen** sen
**fractions of pound** ounce, pence
**fraction term** denominator, numerator
**fracture** breach, break(age), cleft, crack, fissure, gap, opening, rent, rift, rupture, schism, splinter, split
**fracture support** plaster cast
**fragile** breakable, brittle, crumbly, dainty, delicate, elegant, exquisite, feeble, fine, flimsy, frail, frangible, friable, infirm, slight, trivial, weak
**fragment** bit, chip, crumb, disintegrate, divide, fraction, iota, morsel, part(icle), piece, rag, remnant, sample, scrap, section, segment, shard, sherd, shred, sliver, smithereen, snatch, snippet, splinter, trace, vestige, wisp
**fragment of bread** crumb
**fragment of broken pottery found in an excavation** pot(sherd)
**fragment of cloth** rag, shred
**fragment of lava** cinder
**fragment of pottery** ostracon, shard, sherd
**fragment of sail** hullock
**fragment of song** snatch
**fragments of exploded bombs or shells** shrapnel
**fragments of literary material** ana, miscellany
**fragments of uneaten food** leavings, scraps
**fragrance** aroma, attar, balm(iness), bouquet, cologne, extract, fragrancy, fume, odour, ottar, otto, perfume, redolence, sachet, scent, smell, spice, sweetness
**fragrant** ambrosial, aromatic, balmy, odoriferous, odorous, perfumed, redolent, scented, spicy, sweet-scented
**fragrant brown balsam** tolu
**fragrant climber** jasmine
**fragrant extract** attar, cloves, ottar, otto
**fragrant flower** carnation, jasmine, lilac, rose
**fragrant grass** vetiver
**fragrant grass mat** tatty
**fragrant green or yellow liqueur** chartreuse
**fragrant gum resin** bdellium

**fragrant herb** anise, balm, mint, rosemary, thyme
**fragrant liquid** perfume
**fragrant oil** attar, ottar, otto
**fragrant ointment** balm, balsam, (spike)nard, valerian
**fragrant plant used in medicine** angelica
**fragrant resin** elemi, myrrh
**fragrant rootstock** orrice, orris
**fragrant shrub** frangipani, lilac, tiara
**fragrant smell** redolence
**fragrant tea** jasmine, pekoe, rooibos
**fragrant West indian tree** bayberry
**fragrant wood** agalloch, aloe, cedar, mimosa
**frail** breakable, brittle, decrepit, delicate, feeble, flimsy, fragile, infirm, insubstantial, puny, slight, tender, unchaste, unsound, vulnerable, weak
**frail person** weakling
**frailty** defect, delicacy, delicateness, failing, fallibility, fault, feebleness, foible, fragility, imperfection, infirmity, peccability, puniness, suggestibility, susceptibility, thinness, weakness
**frame** anatomy, assemble, build, casing, character, chassis, constitute, contour, disposition, erect, fabric(ate), form(ulate), framework, institute, invent, make, model, mount(ing), plan, rack, rafters, scaffolding, scheme, shape, shell, skeleton, sketch, structure, support, system, temperament, texture
**framed mirror** cheval
**frame for bearing the dead** bier
**frame for embroidery** tambour
**frame for stretching cloth** tenter
**frame of bars** grate
**frame of bed** bedstead
**frame of car** chassis
**frame of mind** attitude, habit, humour, mood, spirit, temper
**frame of reference** objectivity, perspective
**frame of saddle** saddletree
**frame of ship** hull
**frame once used as punishment** stocks
**frame outside a ship's gunwale** outrigger
**frame round a hearth** fender
**frame to support a blackboard** easel
**frame-up** conspiracy, plot, set-up, trap
**frame used to support clay or other materials in modelling** armature
**frame which joins oxen together** yoke
**frame with branches for holding lights** chandelier

**framework** cadre, carcass, lattice, skeleton
**framework for animal's fodder** crib
**framework for carrying luggage** roof rack
**framework of a window** casing
**framework of bed** bedstead
**framework of crossing laths** lattice
**framework of regiment** cadre
**framework of slats** crate
**framework supporting a bridge** trestle
**France's longest river** Loire
**France's patron saint** Denis
**France's symbol** cock, Marianne
**Franciscan friar** Minorite
**Franciscan monk** friar
**Franciscan nun** Clare
**Franco adherent** Falangist
**francolin** partridge
**frangible** breakable, brittle, fissile, flimsy, fragile, frail, friable, unstable, unsteady, weak, wobbling
**frank** bold, candid, free, honest, ingenuous, mark, nonrestrictive, open, outright, signature, sincere, truthful, undisguised, uninhibited, unreserved, unrestrained, unrestricted
**frank and outspoken** candid
**frank attitude** openness
**frankfurter** sausage, wiener
**frankincense** olibanum
**Frankish law-book** Salic
**frankly** artlessly, bluntly, candidly, clearly, directly, forthrightly, freely, generously, honestly, indeed, openly, plainly, sincerely, straight(forwardly), transparently, truthfully, undoubtedly, unreservedly
**frankness** artlessness, bluntness, candidness, candour, guilelessness, ingenuousness, openness, plainness, sincerity, straightforwardness, truthfulness, veracity
**frantic** berserk, crazy, delirious, desperate, distracted, distraught, fraught, frenetic, frenzied, furious, hectic, insane, mad, maniacal, overexcited, overwrought, phrenetic, raging, raving, wild
**frantically** distraughtly, frenziedly, furiously, wildly
**frantic rush** stampede
**frantic state** frenzy
**frate** friar
**fraternal** brotherly
**fraternal handshake** grip
**fraternise with** befriend
**fraternity** alliance, assemblage, association, brotherhood, circle, clan, clique, club, coalition,

companionship, company,
comradeship, consanguinity, coterie,
fellowship, group, guild, kinship,
league, propinquity, relatedness,
relationship, set, society, sodality,
union
**fraternity for mutual help**
Freemasonry
**fraternity pin letter** iota
**fraud** artifice, charlatan, cheat,
counterfeit, deceit, deception,
double-dealing, duplicity, fake,
forgery, guile, hoax, sham,
swindling, treachery, trick(ery)
**fraudulence** deceitfulness
**fraudulent device** trick
**fraudulently alter** falsify, forge
**fraudulently convert money** embezzle
**fraudulently take** steal
**fraudulent secret understanding**
collusion
**fraught with danger** dangerous,
hazardous, perilous, risky
**fraught with destiny** fateful
**fray** abash, altercation, brawl, conflict,
confuse, decompose, discomfit,
dispute, exasperate, fatigue, fight,
fracas, fret, fuss, melée, quarrel,
ravel, scuffle, shred, skirmish,
squabble, strife, tatter, tussle, wear,
wrangle
**frayed** chafed, fretted, rubbed, torn,
wore, worn
**frayed end** frazzle
**freak** abnormality, anomaly,
malformation, mutant, odd(ity), queer
**freakish idea** whim
**freak of nature** lusus naturae
**free** clear, complimentary, deliver,
disengage, easy, emancipate,
exempt, exonerate, familiar, frank,
generous, gratis, independent,
informal, lavish, liberal, liberate,
licentious, loose, open, outspoken,
release, relieve, rid, swift,
unattached, unceremonious,
unchecked, unconstrained,
uncontrolled, unencumbered,
unfettered, unimpeded, uninhibited,
unobstructed, unregulated,
unreserved, unrestrained,
unrestricted, unreticent, unstinted
**free admission** avowal
**free and easy** breezy, casual,
footloose, impertinent, informal,
lenient, relaxed, tolerant
**freebooter** pirate, sea-rover
**free card of admission** pass
**free choice** liberum arbitrium (L)
**freed from** exempt
**freedom** autonomy, deliverance, ease,
emancipation, emotion, franchise,
frankness, immunity, impunity,
independence, informality, leeway,
liberty, looseness, openness,
opportunity, play, power,
presumption, privilege, range,
release, scope, self-government,
uhuru
**freedom from agitation** sang-froid
**freedom from captivity** liberty
**freedom from constraint** ease
**freedom from danger** safety
**freedom from error** inerrancy
**freedom from liability** exemption,
immunity
**freedom from malice** candour
**freedom from narrowness** latitude
**freedom from pain** ease
**freedom from physical pollution** purity
**freedom from prejudice** liberality
**freedom from restraint** latitude
**freedom from restrictions**
emancipate, latitude
**freedom from risk** safety
**freedom from war** peace
**freedom from worry** abandon
**freedom of access** entrée
**freedom of choice** option
**freedom of manner** abandon
**freedom seeker** escaper
**freedom to act as one pleases**
autonomy
**freedom to choose** option
**free excursion** treat
**free from** absolve, de-, rid
**free from agitation** calm
**free from an obligation** exempt
**free from anxiety** carefree, reassure
**free from any moral wrong** innocent
**free from bacteria** aseptic, sterile
**free from blame** absolve, clear,
exculpate, exonerate, vindicate
**free from blemishes** clear
**free from captivity** rescue
**free from care** careless, secure
**free from clouds** clear
**free from colour** achromatic
**free from concern** insouciant
**free from cost** gratis
**free from danger** rescue, safe
**free from deceit** sincere
**free from deduction** nett
**free from dirt** clean
**free from discount** nett
**free from disease** heal
**free from doubts** sure
**free from drug addition** clean
**free from dullness** clear
**free from emotion** dispassionate
**free from enemy occupation** liberated
**free from error** amend
**free from germs** aseptic, sterile
**free from illusion** disenchant
**free from impurities** refine
**free from indecency** clean
**free from micro-organisms** sterile,
aseptic
**free from moisture** dried
**free from national limitations**
cosmopolitan
**free from obligation** acquit, excuse,
exempt
**free from obscurity** clear
**free from pain** comfortable
**free from payment** ransom, scot-free
**free from penalty** absolve
**free from physical desire** platonic
**free from prejudice** candid
**free from pretence** sincere
**free from punishment** amnesty,
exempt
**free from restraint** abandoned,
emancipate, loosen, unbend, unleash
**free from restrictions** emancipate
**free from risk** safe
**free from sepsis** aseptic
**free from strife** friendly, nonviolent,
peaceful
**free from tainting** pure
**free from tension** relaxed
**free from water** anhydrous
**free hand** authority, carte blanche,
discretion, freedom, latitude, liberty,
permission, power, scope
**freeholder** scope
**freehold land possession** udal
**freehold system** udal
**freeing** disentangling, exempting,
extricating, redeeming, releasing,
relieving, rescuing, ridding,
unburdening, undoing, unleashing
**freeloader** bloodsucker, cadger,
hanger-on, leech, parasite,
scrounger, sponger
**freely** abundantly, amply, bountily,
candidly, easily, extravagantly,
frankly, generously, lavishly,
liberally, openly, plainly, readily,
spontaneously, unreservedly,
voluntary, willingly
**freely critical** candid
**freely given** voluntary
**freely invited** welcome
**free market** perfect competition
**free-moving blood cell** corpuscle
**free of** lacking, rid, without
**free of action** independence
**free of bacteria** aseptic
**free of charge** complimentary, free,
gratis
**free of danger** safe
**free of germs** aseptic
**free-style fight** all-in wrestling bout
**free-swimming larva of a crab** zo(a)ea

**freethinker** agnostic, atheist, cynic, disbeliever, doubter, empiricist, heathen, infidel, libertine, nullifidian, pagan, questioner, schismatic, sceptic, unbeliever
**freethinker on religion** libertine
**free throw** foul
**free ticket** pass
**free time** holiday, leisure, liberty
**free to act** voluntary
**free to move** mobile
**freeway** expressway
**freewheel** coast
**free will** volition
**freeze** benumb, chill, congeal, frost, glaciate, harden, ice, limit, refrigerate, stiffen, stop, suspend
**freeze one's blood** frighten
**freezer** icebox
**freezing** arctic, benumbing, biting, chill, congealing, cutting, frigid, frost-bound, frosty, glacial, hardening, icing, icy, inhibiting, numbing, pegging, penetrating, polar, stopping, suspending, wintry
**freezing compartment in fridge** icebox
**freezing rain** sleet
**freight** baggage, burden, cargo, cartage, conveyance, load, luggage, portage, shipment, transportation
**freight boat** ark, barge, flatboat, oiler, scow, tanker
**freight carrier** goodstrain
**freight charge** railage
**freight of a ship** cargo
**freight train** rattler
**French** Franco-, Gallian, Gallic(an), Gaul, Romance
**French abbé** abbot
**French abbot** abbé
**French aeroplane inventor** Louis Bleriot
**French again** encore
**French airline** Air France
**French airplane** avion
**French airport** Charles de Gaulle, Orly
**French air squadron** escadrille
**French anthem** 'Marseillaise'
**French article** la, le, un(e)
**French artist** Boucher, Cézanne, Corot, Degas, Duchamp, Ingress, La Tour, Manet, Matisse, Monet, Renoir, Toulouse-Lautrec
**French astrologer** Nostradamus
**French at home** chez
**French attendant** concièrge
**French aviator** Bleriot
**French bacteriologist** Pasteur
**French baggage-wagon** fourgon
**French baked pastry** quiche
**French bay** Arachon, Biscay
**French bean** haricot

**French before** avant
**French between** entre
**French blue** bleu(e), nattier, ultramarine
**French blue cheese** Roquefort
**French bond** rente
**French bookbinding style** Grolier
**French brandy** Armagnac, Cognac, eau-de-vie, fine, marc
**French bronze coin** sou
**French burgundy** Mâcon
**French cabbage** chou
**French cake** baba, gateau
**French Canadian** Canuck
**French cap** beret
**French carriage** fiacre
**French castle** château
**French cathedral city** Aix, Amiens, Reims, Sen
**French chalk** talc
**French cheese** bleu, Bonbel, Brie, Camembert, cantal, ervy, gex, Munster, Roquefort
**French chemist** Pasteur
**French chicken** poule
**French china** Limoges
**French chocolate** mousse
**French clergyman** abbé, père
**French cleric** abbé, curé
**French cloth cap** beret
**French coarse cloth** bure
**French coast** Riviera
**French coin** blanc, centime, denier, ecu, franc, obole, sou
**French colony** Algeria
**French comic actor** Tati
**French common soldier** poilu
**French composer** Auber, Bizet, Debussy, Gonoud, Ibert, Lalo, Lully, Massanet, Ravel
**French connective** et
**French country house** château
**French couturier** Chanel, Dior, St Laurent
**French criminal investigation department** Sûreté
**French currency** franc
**French dance** bal, boutade, branle, canary, farandole, gavot(te), tambourin
**French deal** donne
**French department** Aisne, Ardèche, Ardennes, Aude, Aveyron, Basses-Pyrénées, Corrèze, Côte-d'Or, Doubs, Isère, Mayenne, Meuse, Moselle, Oise, Orne, Rhône, Savoie, Seine, Tarn, Vienne, Yonne
**French depot** orne
**French desert soldier** legionnaire
**French designer** Chanel, Dior, St Laurent
**French detective force** Sûreté

**French dialect** patois
**French district** Alsace, Arrondissement
**French donkey** ane
**French dugout** abri
**French duke** duc
**French dynasty** Bourbon, Capet, Merovingian, Orleans, Valois
**French east** est
**French ecclesiastic** abbé, curé, monseigneur, prêtre
**French elegance** luxe
**French emblem** fleur-de-lis
**French emperor** Napoleon
**French equal** pareil(e)
**French explorer** Cartier, Jolliet, Lasalle, Radisson
**French farewell** adieu
**French father** pére
**French fire** feu
**French form of bowls** boule
**French form of the totalisator** Parimutuel
**French for summer** été
**French friend** ami(e)
**French fries** chips
**French general** De Gaulle, Napoleon, Pétain, Weygand
**French gold coin** écu
**French grain ear** epi
**French here** ici
**French high fashion** couture
**French his** ses, son
**French house** maison
**French idiom** Gallicism
**French Impressionist painter** Cézanne, Corot, Degas, Manet, Monet, Renoir
**French income** rente
**French infantryman** poilu
**French is** est
**French island** Cite, Corsica, Groix, Hyere, If, Oleron, Re, Ushant, Yeu
**French lace** alencon, cluny, val
**French lake** Annecy, Cazaux
**French lavender** stechados
**French law functionary's cap** mortier
**French leather** cuir
**French leave** AWOL, hooky, lam
**French legal cap** mortier
**French length measure** aune
**French liqueur** anniset, chartreuse
**French literary prize** Goncourt
**French loaf** baguette
**French machine gun** mitrailleuse
**French mail** poste
**Frenchman's hat** beret
**French market town** Agen
**French me** moi
**French meat dish** entrecôte, pâté, salmi(s)
**French menu** carte
**French metropolis** Paris

**French military academy** Saint Cyr, St Cyr
**French military cap** kepi
**French mister** monsieur
**French mixed with English** Franglais
**French monetary unit** franc, sol
**French mother** mere
**French motor track** Le Mans
**French motorway** autoroute
**French mountain range** Alps, Cevennes, Ecrins, Jura, Maritimes, Pyrenees, Vosges
**French mrs** madame
**French name for Antwerp** Anvers
**French name for Brittany** Bretagne
**French name for Morocco** Maroc
**French national anthem** 'Marseillaise'
**French naval station** Brest, Toulon
**French needlepoint lace** alencon
**French no** non
**French nobleman** duc, marquis
**French nose** nez
**French novelist** Victor Hugo
**French opera** Carmen, Faust, Lakme, Manon
**French painter** Boucher, Cézanne, Corot, Degas, Duchamp, Ingress, La Tour, Manet, Matisse, Monet, Renoir, Toulouse-Lautrec
**French palace** palais
**French pancake** crêpe
**French pantomime character** Columbine, Harlequin, Guignol, Pierette, Pierrot
**French parliament** House, Senat
**French pastry** eclair, millefeuille (F)
**French patron saint** Denis
**French peasant's shoe** sabot
**French perfume** Chanel, Dior, Worth
**French philosopher** Pascal
**French playwright** Anouilh
**French policeman** gendarme
**French porcelain** Limoges, Sèvres
**French pork** sale
**French port** Bordeaux, Brest, Caen, Calais, Cherbourg, Dunkerque, Marseilles, Toulon
**French preposition** des
**French prison** Bastille
**French private soldier** poilu
**French pronoun** ces, elle, ils, mes, te, toi
**French Protestant** Huguenot
**French province** Alsace, Artois, Brittany, Comtat, Foix, Limousin, Lorraine, Poitou, Touraine
**French race track** Auteuil, Longchamps
**French region** Alsace, Picardy
**French resort** Antibes, Cannes, Menton, Nice, Pau, Riviera

**French resort with sulphurous springs** Aix-les-Bains
**French restaurant** bistro
**French revolutionary hymn** 'Marseillaise'
**French round, flat hat** beret
**French royal family** Bourbon
**French royal palace** Louvre, Tuileries, Versailles
**French sailor** matelot
**French saint** Joan, Martin
**French school** école, institute, lycée
**French scoundrel** roué
**French sculptor** Duchamp, Rodin
**French sea** mer
**French seaport** Bordeaux, Brest, Calais, Cherbourg, Marseilles, Nantes
**French secondary school** lycée
**French servant** bonne, valet
**French sheep dog** briard
**French shop** boutique
**French shop girl** grisette
**French shrine** Lourdes
**French silk** soie
**French sleeping car** wagon-lit
**French soldier** chasseur, poilu, zouave
**French-speaking person** francophone
**French stately dance** minuet
**French stock exchange** Bourse
**French stocking** bas
**French stoneware** gres
**French strait** Bonifacio
**French street** rue
**French subway** metro
**French summer** été
**French symbol** fleur-de-lis, fleur-de-lys, lily
**French tapestry** gobelin
**French thank you** merci
**French that** ce(la), cet(te), que, qui
**French there** voila
**French tobacco** tabac
**French tomato-flavoured consommé** madrilène
**French town** Agen
**French underwater explorer** Cousteau
**French upon** sur
**French verb** être
**French verse form** rondel, virelai
**French vineyard** cru
**French waiter** garçon
**French waterfall** Gavarnie
**French wind** mistral
**French wine** Alsace, Beaujolais, Bergerac, Bordeaux, Bourgogne, Burgundy, Chablis, Champagne, Côtes-du-Rhône, Entre-deux-Mers, Mâcon, Médoc, muscadel(le), muscatel, Pontac, Sauterne, vin

**French wine district** Alsace, Bordeaux, Burgundy, Champagne, Medoc
**Frenchwoman's title** madame
**French wooden shoe** sabot
**French working girl** grisette
**French writer** Camus, Flaubert, Rabelais, Voltaire
**frenetic** agitated, berserk, boisterous, chaotic, convulsive, demented, deranged, distracted, distraught, excited, flurrying, frantic, frenzied, furious, heated, hectic, hysterical, insane, mad, maniacal, overwrought, rabid, raging, raving, turbulent, uncontrolled, wild
**frenzied** agitated, amok, angry, berserk, convulsive, delirious, distracted, distraught, excited, frantic, frenetic, furious, hectic, hysterical, mad, maniacal, rabid, uncontrolled, wild
**frenziedly violent** berserk
**frenzied person** frenetic
**frenzied woman** m(a)enad
**frenzy** agitate, agitation, anger, arouse, delirium, derange(ment), disarrange, disquiet, enrage, enrapture, enthusiasm, excite(ment), furore, fury, incite, infuriate, ire, madden, madness, mania, paroxysm, perturb, rage, raving, ruffle, stimulate, tantrum, transport, upset, wrath
**frenzy caused by desire of the unattainable** nympholepsy
**frequency of tone** pitch
**frequent** attend, common, constant, continual, habitual, haunt, iterative, many, numerous, often, ordinary, perpetual, persistent, recurrent, regular, repeated, several, usual, visit
**frequented abode** haunt
**frequented by ghost** haunted
**frequenter** addict, conformist, conventionalist, devotee, fan, habitué, regular
**frequently** commonly, constantly, continually, customarily, familiarly, habitually, much, numerously, oft(en), persistently, recurrently, repeatedly, usually
**frequent use** practice
**frequent visitor** habitué
**fresh** anew, artless, cool, healthy, inexperienced, invigorating, new, novel, pure, raw, recent, refreshing, unadulterated, uncultivated, untrained, vigorous, youthful
**fresh air** ozone
**fresh and bracing** crisp
**fresh as if new** pristine
**fresh, as lettuce** crisp

**freshen** aerify, (en)liven, perk, purify, recover, refresh, renew, revive, rouse, sanitate, stimulate, ventilate
**freshet** billow, flood, heave, spate, surge, swell
**fresh fodder** soilage
**fresh from the factory** modern, new-fashioned, up-to-date
**fresh information** news
**freshly** additionally, anew, bloomingly, brightly, briskly, cleanly, clearly, coolly, crisply, differently, healthily, modernly, newly, novelly, originally, purely, recently, refreshingly, rosily, stiffly, sweetly, unusually
**freshness** bloom, brightness, cleanness, newness, novelty, vigour
**fresh trial** retrial
**freshwater carp** chub
**freshwater catfish** pout
**freshwater crayfish** yabbie, yabby
**freshwater crustacean** cray(fish)
**freshwater duck** teal, widgeon
**freshwater fish** bass, blenny, bream, carp, catfish, dace, darter, eelpout, ide, perch, pope, pout, powan, rainbow, roach, tench, trout, turbot
**freshwater fish allied to carp** ide
**freshwater lobster** crayfish
**freshwater mammal** beaver, otter
**freshwater mussel** clam
**freshwater nymph of classical mythology** naiad
**freshwater snail** neritine
**freshwater tortoise** terrapin
**freshwater white fish** gwyniad
**fret** affront, agonise, anguish, annoy(ance), brood, corrode, corrosion, erode, fume, gnaw(ing), grieve, harass(ment), irritate, needle, nettle, provoke, repine, stew, taunt, tease, torment, vex(ation), worry
**fret away** gnaw
**fretful** angry, anxious, captious, careful, churlish, concerned, cross, crotchety, disagreeable, distressed, edgy, fearful, ill-tempered, impatient, irritable, nervous, peevish, pettish, petulant, querulous, snappish, sullen, tense, testy, touchy, troubled, uneasy, vexed, watchful, worried
**friar** abbé, abbot, almsman, beggar, brother, cleric, father, frater, mendicant, monastic, monk, padre, priest, regular, religious
**friar of fiction** Tuck
**friar's cowl** capouch, capuche
**friar's title** fra
**friary** abbey, cloister, convent, house, monastery, nunnery, priory
**fricative** buzz, consonant, durative, hiss, sonant, spirant

**fricative consonant** spirant
**friction** abrasion, antagonism, chafing, conflict, resistance, strife
**fridge** refrigerator
**fried food item** bacon, egg, fritter, vetkoek
**fried meatball** frikkadel, rissole
**fried oblong strip of potato** chip
**fried quickly** sauté
**fried roll of potato** croquette
**fried tortilla** taco
**fried tortilla served with hot chili sauce** enchilade
**friend** acquaintance, ally, ami(e) (F), amigo, associate, backer, bra, broer, buddy, chum, colleague, companion, comrade, confidant, confrère, crony, helper, intimate, mate, pal, pardner, patron, sympathiser
**friend and follower of Aeneas** Achates
**friend in war** ally
**friendliness** amicability, comity, courtesy
**friendly** advantageous, affable, amiable, amicable, benevolent, brotherly, chummy, compatible, cordial, devoted, faithful, fast, favourable, firm, fraternal, genial, gentle, hearty, helpful, intimate, kind(ly), loyal, matey, pally, sisterly, sympathetic, thick, trustworthy, warm
**friendly alliance** consociation
**friendly associate** ally
**friendly discussion** symposium
**friendly dwarf of myths** troll
**friendly fellowship** companionship
**friendly greeting** hello
**friendly hint** tip
**friendly informal conversation** chat
**Friendly Islands** Tonga
**friendly letter** screed
**friendly ocean mammal** dolphin
**friendly regard** favour
**friendly relationship** amity
**friendly talk** chat
**friendly teasing** banter, persiflage
**friendly understanding** entente
**friend of Achilles** Patroclus
**friend of Jonathan** David
**friend of Othello** Iago
**friend of Quixote** Sancho Panza
**friend of Sherlock Holmes** Watson
**friend of the court** amicus curiae
**friend of the human race** amicus humani generi (L)
**friends and neighbours** kith
**friendship** accord, affection affinity, amicability, amity, comradeship, concord, cordiality, esteem, familiarity, friendliness, harmony, intimacy, love, peace, unity
**frigate necessity** sail

**fright** alarm, anguish, anxiety, apprehension, bête noire (F), consternation, discomfort, dismay, dread, fear, horror, monster, nightmare, ogre, panic, quaking, quivering, scare, shock, terror, trepidation
**frighten** affright, agitate, alarm, appal, awe, cow, daunt, deter, discourage, dismay, dissuade, flabbergast, fright, haunt, horrify, intimidate, overawe, panic, rattle, scare, startle, stun, terrify, threaten, torment, unnerve
**frighten away** appalled, chase, cowed, daunted, intimidated, petrified, scare, shocked, shoo, terrified, unnerved
**frightened suddenly** startled
**frighten from** deter
**frighten greatly** terrify
**frightening** alarming, appalling, awesome, cowing, daunting, dreadful, fearful, fearsome, intimidating, petrifying, scaring, scary, shocking, startling, terrifying, unnerving
**frighteningly weird** eerie
**frighten off** deter
**frighten severely** terrify
**frighten suddenly** startle
**frightful** appalling, awful, dire, dreadful, fearful, ghastly, grim, grisly, gruesome, harrowing, hideous, horrible, lurid, macabre, petrifying, shocking, terrible, terrifying, traumatic, unnerving
**frightful giant** ogre
**frigid** apathetic, austere, callous, chilling, cold, freezing, frosty, gelid, glacial, icy, insensitive, insipid, snowy, stoical, uncaring, unemotional, unfriendly, unromantic
**frigidity** apathy, austerity, coldness, formality, frozenness, gelidity, hardness, iciness, inertia, primness, rawness, reserve, reticence, severity, sharpness
**frilled collar** ruff
**frilled lace** ruche
**frilling, sometimes of lace** ruche
**frill made by pressing pleats** gauffer, goffer
**frill or gathering of lace** ruche
**frill worn round the neck** ruff
**frilly nightie** negligee
**fringe** binding, bonus, border(line), edge, edging, extra, filigree, frill, hem, limits, march, margin, ornament, perimeter, periphery, plus, ruff, surround, tassel, trimming
**fringe area** hinterland
**fringe benefit** perk(s), perquisite(s)

**fringed cord** tassel
**fringed prayer shawl worn by Orthodox Jewish men** tallis, tallith
**fringe of hair** bang
**fringe of hair above the eye** eyebrow
**frisky** bouncy, coltish, frolicsome, lively, rollicking, sportive
**frisky movement** caper, capriccio
**fritter** dissipate, misspend, shred, squander, waste
**fritter away** squander
**fritter one's time away** frivol, idle, peddle
**fritter time away** linger
**frivol away** squander
**frivolity** childishness, folly, fun, gaiety, jest, levity, nonsense, silliness, triviality
**frivolous** asinine, childish, dizzy, empty-headed, facetious, flighty, flippant, foolish, giddy, idle, immature, impertinent, inane, insignificant, irresponsible, juvenile, light(-minded), petty, puerile, scatterbrained, silly, slight, superficial, trifling, trivial, unimportant
**frivolous objection** cavil
**frizzy** crimped, crisp, curled, curly, frizzed, wiry
**frizzy hairstyle** afro
**frock** anoint, appoint, blouse, call, cassock, coat, consecrate, costume, dress, elect, ensemble, garb, garment, gown, habit, invest, nominate, ordain, outfit, robe, smock, suit, vestment
**frog** toad
**frog-hopper** spittle-bug
**froglike creature** toad
**frogman** (skin-)diver
**frogman's footwear** flipper
**frog noise** croak
**frog pool** froggery
**frogs and toads** anurans
**frog's eggs** spawn
**frog's larva** tadpole
**frog's relative** toad
**frog's sound** croak
**frolic** amusement, antic, caper, cavort, conviviality, enjoyment, escapade, festivity, frisk, fun, gaiety, gambol, game, jollity, joyous, lark, laughter, merriment, mirth, play, prank, recreation, revel(ry), rollick, romp, skylark, sport(ive), spree, trick
**frolicky action** romp
**frolic or binge** spree
**frolicsome** coltish, frisky, frolicky, gay, kittenish, lively, merry, playful, sportive, sprightly
**frolicsome leap** caper

**from** ab-, back, da (I), de (F), de-, fro, of, von (G)
**from a great distance** afar
**from a pig** ham
**from a region of south-west China** Tibetan
**from Athens** Greek
**from A to Z** lock, stock and barrel
**from bed and board** a mensa et toro (L)
**from beginning to end** through
**from Beijing** Chinese
**from Cardiff** Welsh
**from Cathay** Chinese
**from cause to effect** a priori
**from Cork** Irish
**from day to day** daily, de die de diem (L)
**from Dublin** Irish
**from dusk to dawn** overnight
**from each** apiece
**from eighty to eighty-nine years old** octogenarian
**from Eire** Irish
**from end to end** along, among, throughout
**from eternity** ab aeterno (L)
**from fifty to fifty-nine years old** quinquagenarian
**from forty to forty-nine years old** quadragenarian
**from France** French
**from hand to mouth** improvidently, insecurely, meagrely, scantily, uncertainty, unstably
**from head to foot** cap-à-pie
**from here** hence
**from home** away
**from hundred and more years old** centenarian
**from it** thence
**from largest continent** Asian
**from Malaya** Malayan
**from memory** ex capite (L)
**from Moscow** Muscovite, Russian
**from ninety to ninety-nine years old** nonagenarian
**from now on** henceforth, hereafter
**from oak** acorn
**from one side to the other** across
**from one's own viewpoint** personally
**from outside** ab extra (L)
**from outside the earth** extraterrestrial
**from particular view-point** angle
**from place to place within** through
**from Rangoon** Burmese
**from Scandinavia** Norse
**from seventy to seventy-nine years old** septuagenarian
**from side to side** across, thwart
**from sixty to sixty-nine years old** sexagenarian

**from stern to stern** completely, solidly, soundly, thoroughly, totality
**from Switzerland** Swiss
**from Tel Aviv** Israeli
**from that** thereof
**from that day** a die (L)
**from that place** thence
**from that place onward** thenceforth, thenceforward
**from that time** since
**from that time on** thenceforth, thenceforward
**from the Arctic** polar
**from the beginning** a principio (L), ab initio (L), ab ovo (L), anew
**from the books** ex libris
**from the bottom of one's heart** deeply, heartily, imo pectore (L), sincerely
**from the commencement** ab origine (L)
**from the first** beginning, inception, outset, start
**from the horse's mouth** first hand
**from the interior** out
**from the marriage bond** a vinculo matrimonii (L)
**from then till now** since
**from the Orient** Eastern
**from the origin** ab origine (L)
**from there** thence
**from the same family** related
**from the side** obliquely, sidelong
**from the time when** since
**from the very beginning** ab ovo (L)
**from thirteen to nineteen** teenage
**from this day** hence(forth), hereafter
**from this place** hence
**from this time on** evermore, hence(forth), hereafter
**from time to time** occasionally, sometimes
**from what place** whence
**from when** since
**from which** whence
**from within** ab intra (L)
**from within ship into water** overboard
**from without** ab extra (L)
**from Zurich** Swiss
**frond** leaf
**fronded plant** fern
**front** anterior, bearing, demeanour, exterior, facade, face, first, fore(most), frontage, head, mask, van
**frontage** exterior, facade, face, (fore)front
**front edge of book** face
**frontier** backwoods, border(line), bound(ary), edge, extreme, limit, march, outpost, outskirts, pale, rim
**frontiersman** pioneer

**fronting** facing, overlooking
**front lower guard of helmet** beaver
**front of army** van(guard)
**front of boat** prow
**front of building** facade
**front of fireplace** hearth
**front of foot** toe
**front of head** face
**front of leaf** recto
**front of leg below knee** shin
**front of lower jaw** chin
**front of mouth** preoral
**front of saddle** fore-bow, pommel
**front of ship** prow
**front of shoe** toe
**front of tibia** shin
**front on** face
**front part** fore
**front part of helmet** nasal, visor
**front part of missile** nosecone
**front part of shoe** toecap
**front-row rugby forward** hooker
**front seat in a theatre** stall
**front seats** parquet
**front view** facade
**front wheels of auto** camber
**frost** chill, hoarfrost, ice, rime
**froster** icer
**frostiness** iciness
**frosting** icing
**frosting device** freezer, icer
**frost-resistant** hardy
**frosty** icy
**froth** bubbles, effervescence, ferment(ation), fizz, foam, frothiness, moisture, scum, spume, suds, yeast
**froth from soapsuds** lather
**froth-like** spumy, yeasty
**froth of beer** head
**froth of soap and water** suds, lather
**froth on top of beer** head
**frothy drink** ale, beer
**frothy egg-dish** soufflé
**frothy material** tulle
**frothy sweat** lather
**frown** anger, disapprove, discourage, dislike, displeased, furrow, glare, gloom, glower, grimace, lour, lower, pout, scowl, sullen
**frown ill-temperedly** scowl
**frown on** disapprove, disfavour, dislike, prohibit
**frown upon** decline
**frowsty** airless, close, decayed, fusty, heavy, mildewed, mouldy, muggy, musty, old, oppressive, smelly, stale, stuffy, sultry, unventilated
**frowsty warmth** fug
**frowzy** blowzy, dirty, messy, shabby, slatternly, sloppy, slovenly, ungroomed, untidy, unwashed
**frowzy woman** dowdy

**frozen** clogged, gelid, icebound, iced, numb, refrigerated
**frozen confections** ices
**frozen crystals** snow
**frozen delicacy** frappé, ice (cream), mousse, sherbet, sorbet, spumoni
**frozen dessert** ice cream
**frozen dew** frost, rime
**frozen drip** icicle
**frozen figure** snowman
**frozen floating mass** iceberg
**frozen liquid** ice
**frozen rain** hail, sleet, snow
**frozen raindrops** hail
**frozen slush** snow-ice
**frozen spike** icicle
**frozen vapour** frost, rime
**frozen vapour which falls in flakes** snow
**frozen wasteland** tundra
**frozen water** ice
**fructify** fertilise
**frugal** abstemious, abstinent, careful, chary, conservative, economic(al), meagre, miserly, niggardly, parsimonious, saving, scant(y), scrimpy, self-controlled, self-denying, skimpy, small, sparing, stingy, temperate, thrifty
**frugally** abstemiously, carefully, economically, meagrely, parsimoniously, prudently, sparingly, thriftily
**frugal person** economiser, Scrooge, Spartan
**fruit** advantage, apple, apricot, avocado, banana, berry, cherry, consequent, crop, fig, grape, guava, kiwi, kumquat, lemon, lime, mango, melon, na(a)rtjie, nut, offspring, olive, orange, outcome, papaya, papino, pawpaw, peach, pear, pineapple, plum, pomegranate, product, quince, revenue, strawberry, tangerine, tomato, yield
**fruit akin to apple** medlar
**fruit basket** chip, pottle, punnet
**fruit candied and preserved in syrup** succades
**fruit centre** Ceres, core
**fruit cluster** bunch
**fruit conserve** jam
**fruit container** crate
**fruit cooked in syrup** compote
**fruit course** dessert
**fruit decay** blet, mildew, mould, rot
**fruit dot** sorus
**fruit drink** ade, cider, lemonade, perry, punch, ratafia
**fruit-eating beetle** borer
**fruit-eating bird** mousebird, starling, toucan

**fruit enclosed in jelly** chartreuse
**fruit extract** juice
**fruit-flavoured water ice** frappé
**fruit flesh** pulp
**fruit for jelly** quince
**fruit for making gin** sloe
**fruit for marmalade** orange
**fruit formed other than from ovary** pseudocarp
**fruitful** abundant, fertile, plentiful, productive, prolific, rich
**fruit fungi** aecidium, aecium, telium
**fruit ingredient of perry** pears
**fruit juice drink** ade
**fruit kernel** core, pit, seed, stone
**fruit knife** corer
**fruitless** abortive, futile, idle, pointless, profitless, unavailing, unfruitful, useless, vain
**fruitlessly** vainly
**fruit like small apple, eaten when decayed** medlar
**fruit like tangerine** satsuma
**fruit liquid** juice
**fruit-loving beetle** borer
**fruit of beech tree** mast
**fruit of blackthorn** sloe
**fruit of elm** samara
**fruit of fir** cone
**fruit of gourd** melon
**fruit of gourd family** pepo
**fruit of hawthorn** haw
**fruit of horse chestnut tree** conker
**fruit of nut** kernel
**fruit of oak tree** acorn
**fruit of palm tree** coconut, date
**fruit of pine tree** cone
**fruit of rose** hip
**fruit of sambucus** elder(berry)
**fruit of sapodilla** naseberry
**fruit of tropical cactus** prickly pear
**fruit of tropical palm tree** coconut
**fruit of vine** grape
**fruit party drink** punch
**fruit pastry** tart
**fruit peel** rind, skin
**fruit pickles** chutney
**fruit pie** tart
**fruit pie topped with scones** cobbler
**fruit pit** pyrene
**fruit preserve** jam
**fruit pulp** puree
**fruit punch** ade
**fruit refuse** marc
**fruit resembling tangerine** mandarin
**fruit seed** pip
**fruit's flowers** blossoms
**fruit skin** peel, rind
**fruit stewed with sugar** compote
**fruit stone** pip, pit
**fruit sugar** fructose, levulose
**fruit-tree disease** gumming

**fruit trees** orchard
**fruit used in jelly** cherry, plum, quince
**fruit with hard shell** coconut, gourd, litchi, nut
**fruit with pip** cherry
**fruity, nutty and nice** nougat
**frumpish** bedraggled, dowdy, old-fashioned, out-of-date, shabby, slatternly, slovenly, unkempt, untidy
**frumpishly** dowdily
**frumpish state** dowdiness
**frustrate** baffle, ba(u)lk, block, cancel, check, circumvent, confront, counter, defeat, depress, disappoint, discourage, dishearten, foil, forestall, inhibit, neutralise, nullify, outwit, ruin, spike, stymie, thwart
**frustrated by opposition** thwarted
**frustrator of plans** marplot
**fry** boil, ferment, sauté, sizzle
**fry fast** sauté
**frying pan** skillet, spider
**frying pan utensil** spatula
**fry lightly in a little heat** sauté
**fuddle** confuse
**fuddled** confused, drunk, muddled, muzzy, tipsy
**fuddy-duddy** conservative, dodo, dotard, fog(e)y, fossil, square
**fuel** butane, coal, diesel, gas(oline), oil, petrol(eum), wood
**fuel conveyor** oil tanker
**fuel for braai** charcoal
**fuel from bogs** peat
**fuel from coal** coke
**fuel oil** kerosene
**fuel transporting vessel** coaler
**fuel used in heavy road-vehicles** derv
**fugacious** ephemeral, evanescent, fleeting, transitory
**fugitive** apostate, deserter, escapee, escapist, exile, itinerant, outlaw, refugee, renegade, rover, runaway, vagrant
**fugitive from justice** outlaw
**fugitive from reality** escapist
**fugitive from Sodom** Lot
**fugitive of foreign country** émigré
**fugitive slave** maroon
**fulcrum** bait, glut, pivot, prop, support
**fulcrum oar** lock, thole
**fulfil** accomplish, achieve, answer, complete, conclude, do, end, execute, finish, meet, obey, perfect, realise, reform, satisfy, terminate
**fulfil expectations** satisfy
**fulfilling all the necessary conditions** valid
**fulfil the needs of** satisfy
**full** ample, complete, comprehensive, exactly, filled, flush, loaded, mature, maximum, packed, perfectly, plenary, replete, rich, saturated, stuffed, teeming, thorough, total, unabridged, very, voluminous, whole
**full after eating** replete
**full authority** carte blanche
**full bloom flower** anthesis
**full-bosomed** buxom
**full development** maturity
**full discretionary power** carte blanche
**full extent** gamut
**full extent from end to end** span
**full force** impact
**full game of golf** round
**full glass** bumper
**full-grown** adult
**full-length** maxi
**full-length apron** pinafore
**full-length mirror** cheval
**full measure** limit, maximum, utmost
**fullness** abundance, ampleness, broadness, completeness, comprehensiveness, copiousness, entireness, entirety, extensiveness, generousness, intactness, plenitude, plenteousness, repleteness, richness, satiety, sufficiency, thoroughness, vastness
**fullness of tone** volume
**full of** -ose
**full of ambition** ambitious
**full of anger** wrath
**full of beans** energetic, lively
**full of bitter mockery** sardonic
**full of bitterness** acrimonious
**full of bloodshed** gory
**full of chinks or cracks** rimose
**full of common sense** cool, prudent, sound
**full of complaints** querulous
**full of confidence** trustful
**full of depressions** pitted
**full of energy** spirited
**full of evasions** shifty
**full of excitement** agog
**full of fears** timorous
**full of feeling** expressive
**full of fight** scrappy
**full of foliage** leafy
**full of glee** songfull
**full of gossip** chatty, gossipy
**full of hazard** adventurous
**full of health** buxom
**full of ideas** creative, inventive
**full of incidents** eventful
**full of keen desire** eager
**full of laughter** merry
**full of life** alive, animated, energetic, intense, lively, vigorous, vital, zestful
**full of light** luminous
**full of meaning** pregnant
**full of mischief** mischievous
**full of mystery** mysterious
**full of nervous tension** all on edge
**full of nuts** nutty
**full of pep** alert, brisk, ebullient, lively, sharp, snappish
**full of pips** pippy
**full of pores** porous
**full of power** live
**full of pranks** frolic
**full of risk** perilous
**full of roots** rooty
**full of sad longing** wistful
**full of sediment** feculent
**full of sharp points** prickly
**full of short broken waves** choppy
**full of small lumps** nubbly
**full of small spaces** porous
**full of spirit** feisty, volatile
**full of vim and vigour** fresh
**full of vitality** robust, vigorous, vivacious
**full of vivacity and spirit** animated, lively
**full of weeds** weedy
**full of windings** tortuous
**full of zest** snappy
**full powers** carte blanche
**full river** banker
**full-sized** adult, ripe
**full-sounding** sonorous
**full stop in punctuation** period
**full suit of armour** panoply
**full sweep** gamut
**full theatre notice** SRO (standing room only)
**full up** replete
**full value** amount
**full warranty** unconditional guarantee
**fully absorbed** rapt
**fully acquainted with** au courant (F)
**fully acquiesce** accede
**fully attended** plenary
**fully attended meeting** plenum
**fully developed** adult, ripe
**fully grown** adult, mature, ripe
**fully informed** au courant de (F), au fait (F)
**fully maintained** unabated
**fully satisfied** sated
**fully sufficient** adequate
**fulminate against** condemn, criticise, decry, denounce, denunciate, depreciate, disapprove, discredit, inveigh, vastness
**fumble** bumble, grope, muff, paw, spoil
**fume** boil, chafe, exhalation, fret, rage, rank, rave, reek, seethe, smoke, smoulder, storm, stream, vaporise, vapour
**fume angrily** rage
**fumer** seether
**fumes** exhaust, haze, reek, smog, smoke, stench, vapour

**fumigate** cleanse, disinfect, purify, reek, sterilise
**fuming sulphuric acid** oleum
**fun** amusement, enjoyment, frolic, gaiety, joking, joy, play, pleasure, sport
**funambulist** rope dancer, rope walker, wire walker
**fun and games** horseplay
**function** act, affair, capacity, ceremony, do, duty, employment, fête, forte, gala, go, interest, job, matter, métier, mission, operate, operation, party, perform, post, purpose, realm, role, run, serve, task, use, work
**functional** functioning, going, hard-wearing, operational, plain, practical, running, serviceable, useful, utilitarian, utility, working
**functional body part** organ
**functionally** operationally, practically, usefully
**functionless** otiose
**function of an advocate** advocacy
**function of the ear** hear
**functions of living things** biotics
**fund** accumulation, capital, collection, endow(ment), grant, invest(ment), kitty, money, reserve, resource, savings, stack, stock, store, supply, vein
**fundamental** basic, central, elementary, essential, main, necessary, original, primary, principle, rule
**fundamental idea** keynote
**fundamentalist** hardliner
**fundamental law** principle
**fundamentally** au fond (F), basally, basically, essentially
**fundamental nature** essence
**fundamental part** root
**fundamental quantity** unit
**fundamental reason** rationale
**fundamental tone in music** key
**fundamental truth** principle
**fundamental unit** base
**fundamental unit of capacitance** farad
**fundi** pundit
**fund of money for communal use** kitty
**fundraising sale of goods** bazaar
**funeral** burial, interment, obsequies
**funeral announcement** obit(uary)
**funeral attendant** mute
**funeral bell** knell
**funeral car** hearse
**funeral ceremony** dirge, exequy, obsequy
**funeral director** embalmer, mortician, undertaker
**funeral fire** pyre

**funeral garland** wreath
**funeral hymn** dirge, elegy, requiem, threnody
**funeral lament** dirge
**funeral notice** obit(uary)
**funeral ode** epicedium
**funeral oration** éloge, eulogy
**funeral pile for burning corpse** pyre
**funeral poem** elegy
**funeral procession** cortege
**funeral pyre** balefire
**funeral rite** obsequy
**funeral service in its solemn forms** dirge
**funeral song** dirge, elegy, keen, requiem
**funeral stack** pyre
**funeral tune** dirge
**funeral undertaker** mortician
**funeral vehicle** hearse
**fungal growth** mildew
**fungal reproductive body** ascospore
**fungoid infection of throat** thrush
**fungoid plant** sarcina
**fungous excrescence in a horse's foot** canker
**fungus** blight, canker, decay, disease, fungous, infestation, lichen, mildew, mould, mushroom, pest, phycomycete, rot, rust, smut, toadstool, truffle
**fungus affecting cereals** ergot
**fungus cells** asci
**fungus disease** ergot
**fungus disease of plants** scab
**fungus growth** mildew, mould, wart
**fungus plant** uredinium, uredium
**fungus sac** ascus
**fungus stem** stipe
**fungus such as mushroom** agaric
**funicular** cableway
**funicular lift** ski-lift
**funk** coward
**funnel-like anchor** drogue
**funnel-shaped** conical
**funnel-shaped flower** arum (lily), petunia
**funny** absurd, amusing, bizarre, comic(al), curious, droll, dubious, entertaining, facetious, fantastic, farcical, grotesque, hilarious, humorous, laughable, mysterious, odd, peculiar, perplexing, puzzling, queer, remarkable, ridiculous, silly, strange, unusual, weird, witty
**funny and risque** ribald
**funny bone** olecranon
**funny business** sham, trickery
**funny character** card
**funny end of joke** punch-line
**funny fellow** wit

**funny person** comedian, comedienne, comic
**fun word** anagram
**fur** beaver, civet, coat, ermine, fleece, genet, hair, hide, mink, pelage, pelt, sable, skin, wool
**fur animal** beaver, calabar, calaber, ermine, genet, marten, mink, otter, sable, seal
**fur cape** palatine, pelerine
**fur coat** anorak
**fur collar** boa
**furculum** furcula, merrythought, wishbone
**fur cylinder** muff
**fur dealer** furrier
**fur-edged coat** pelisse
**fur for the neck** necklet
**fur from lambs** karakul
**fur garment for neck** necklet
**fur hat worn by Hussars** busby
**fur hunter** trapper
**Furies** Alecto (the unresting), Erinyes, Megaera (the jealous), Tisiphone (the avenger)
**Furies in Greek mythology** Erinyes, Eumenides
**furious** distraught, enraged, fierce, flaming, frantic, frenzied, fuming, inflamed, infuriated, irate, ireful, livid, mad, provoked, rabid, raging, ranting, red-hot, ropable, seething, storming, violent, wrathful
**furious driver** Jehu
**furiously angry** livid
**furious passion** wreak
**furious storm** hurricane, tempest, typhoon
**furious tumult of events** maelstrom
**furious woman** m(a)enad
**furl** coil, roll
**fur like astrakhan** caracul
**fur-lined mantle** pelisse
**furlough** congé, dismissal, layoff, leave, vacation
**fur mat** rug
**furnace** burner, crematorium, destructor, fumarole, heater, incinerator, kiln, oast, oven, smelter, stove, volcano
**furnace draft regulator** damper
**furnace escapee** Abednego
**furnace flue** chimney, pipe, tewel
**furnace for firing pottery** kiln
**furnace for metal** forge
**furnace fuel** coal
**furnace process** smelting
**furnace tender** stoker
**furnace vent** taphole
**fur neckpiece** boa
**furnish** appoint, decorate, equip, lend, outfit, provide, purvey, supply

**furnish a crew** man
**furnish a service** execute, render
**furnish for service** equip, fit, supply
**furnishing** affording, appointing, bestowing, décor, decorating, endowing, equipping, giving, granting, offering, presenting, providing, revealing, rigging, stocking, storing, supplying
**furnishing of stage** décor
**furnish with** endow
**furnish with authority** vest
**furnish with feathers** fledge
**furnish with food** cater, feed
**furnish with gift** endow
**furnish with money** endow
**furnish with new weapons** rearm
**furnish with ornament** adorn
**furnish with shoes** shod
**furnish with something that is required** supply
**furnish with weapons** arm
**furniture maker** cabinet-maker, joiner
**furniture truck** van
**furniture van** pantechnicon
**furniture wheel** caster, castor
**furniture wood** balsa, cedar, ebony, imbuia, oak, pine, stinkhorn, tambotie, teak
**fur of beaver** plew
**fur of coypu** nutria
**fur of grey squirrel** calabar, calaber
**furore** abandon, ardour, commotion, craze, delirium, disturbance, élan, excitement, fad, fervour, fit, frenzy, fury, gusto, hysteria, mania, outburst, outcry, paroxysm, rage, rapture, riot, stir, tantrum, temper, uproar, verve, zeal
**furred aquatic fish-eating mammal** otter
**furriness** hairiness
**furrow** channel, cleft, fissure, groove, rut, sulcus, track, trench, trough
**furrow in a road** rut
**furrow-like crease** wrinkle
**furrow made by a wheel** rut
**furry animal** ermine, mink, rac(c)oon, sable
**furry aquatic mammal** otter, seal
**furry foot** paw
**furry fruit** peach
**furry growth found on old bread** mould

**furry marten** sable
**furry-skinned fruit** peach
**fur scarf** boa, tippet
**fur skin** pelt
**further** additional(ly), advance, aid, also, besides, beyond, extra, farther, furthermore, longer, more(over), oblige, other, promote, supplementary, support, too, urge, yonder
**further disavowal** redenial
**further down** deeper, lower
**further from the centre** outer
**furthermore** additionally, also, and, besides, likewise, moreover, too, yet
**further on** onward(s)
**further than** beyond
**further too** also
**furthest** ultimate, utmost
**furthest aft** aftermost
**furthest back** backmost, rearmost
**furthest back in time** earliest
**furthest behind** hindmost
**furthest limit** uttermost
**furthest north** northernmost
**furthest part** tip
**furthest to the left** leftmost
**furthest to the right** rightmost
**furthest within** in(ner)most
**fur throat-wrap** boa
**furtive** clandestine, covert, crafty, cunning, foxy, hidden, secret(ive), skulking, sly, sneaking, sneaky, stealthy, undercover, underhand, wily
**furtive behaviour** stealth
**furtive glance** peep
**furtive in character** shifty
**furtive look** peep, sneakily, stealthily, surreptitiously
**furtiveness** stealth
**furtive type** sneak
**furtive wanderer up to no good** prowler
**furuncle** boil
**fury** anger, frenzy, furore, hag, ire, passion, rage, termagant, vehemence, violence, virago, vixen, wrath
**furze** gorse, whin
**fuse** absorb, amalgamate, assimilate, bind, blend, bond, co-operate, coalesce, combine, compound, connect, consolidate, dissolve, embody, fasten, glue, gum, homogenise, incorporate, integrate, intermingle, (inter)mix, link, liquefy, marry, melt, merge, mingle, paste, pool, synthesise, unify, unite, weld
**fused** blown
**fused head and thorax of spider** cephalothorax
**fused metal and refuse** slag
**fused volcanic rock** obsidian
**fuse together** weld
**fusible alloy** solder
**fusible substance** metal
**fusillade** barrage
**fusion in one whole** coalition
**fusion worker** welder
**fuss** activity, ado, agitate, agitation, annoy, argument, bother, bustle, commotion, dispute, disturb, excitation, flurry, fluster, fret, irritate, kerfuffle, perturb, pester, pettiness, pother, row, to-do, unrest, worry
**fuss over details** niggle
**fussy** demanding, finical, finicky, meticulous, ornate, particular, punctilious
**fussy decoration** frou-frou
**fussy excitement** ado
**fustigate** cudgel
**fusty** ill-smelling, mouldy, muggy, musty, rank, stale
**futile** frivolous, fruitless, ineffective, ineffectual, meaningless, trifling, trivial, unavailing, unimportant, unproductive, unprofitable, unsuccessful, useless, vain
**futile combat** sciamachy, sciomachy, skiamachy
**futility** emptiness, frivolity, inanity, triviality, unreality, uselessness, vanity
**future** coming, impending, offing, opportunity, prospective, tomorrow
**future insect** larva
**future life** afterlife
**future misery** perdition
**future spouse** fiancé(e)
**futuristic** ultramodern
**fuzz** fluff
**fuzz up** bungle, confuse, muddle
**fuzzy fruit** peach
**fuzzy ravellings** lint
**fylfot** swastika

# G

**gab** chatter, gossip, prattle, talk, twaddle
**gad** gallivant, rove, wander
**gad about** gallivant, meander, promenade, ramble, range, roam, rove, saunter, shuffle, stroll, traipse, wander
**gadabout** gallivanter, rambler, rover, wanderer
**Gaddafi's state** Libya
**gadfly** dipteran, dipteron, dipterous, horse-fly
**gadget** device, gismo, utensil
**Gael** Celt, Kelt, Scot
**Gaelic** Celt, Erse, Highlander, Keltic, Scot
**Gaelic dagger** skean, skene
**Gaelic delicacy** oatcake
**Gaelic dialect** Erse
**Gaelic eisteddfod** mod
**Gaelic funeral dirge** coronach
**Gaelich poem** duan
**Gaelic Ireland** Eire
**Gaelic sea god** Ler
**Gaelic water sprite** kelpie
**gaffer** boss, chief, director, employer, executive, foreman, governor, head, leader, manager, master, overseer, owner, rube, supervisor
**gag** choke, curb, gasp, hoax, jest, joke, pant, puke, silence, suppress, throttle, wisecrack
**gaga** fatuous, foolish, senile
**gage** bail, bond, captive, challenge, collateral, dare, defiance, deposit, gauntlet, guarantee, hostage, pawn, pledge, prisoner, security, surety, token, warrant
**gaggle** geese
**gaggle member** goose
**gag or silence** muzzle
**gaiety** animation, buoyancy, cheer(fulness), delight, elation, flashiness, fun, gaudiness, gayness, gladness, glee, hilarity, jollity, joviality, joyfulness, joyousness, jubilation, laughter, life, liveliness, merriment, mirth, pleasure, vivacity
**gaily** blithely, brilliantly, cheerfully, exultantly, garishly, gaudily, gleefully, happily, joyfully, joyously, jubilantly, merrily, showily
**gain** accrue, achieve, acquire, acquisition, advance, approach, attain, benefit, better, capture, clear, collect, earn, gather, get, harvest, improve, increase, make, near, obtain, produce, profit(s), progress, prosper, reach, reap, secure, thrive, win(nings), yield
**gain access** enter
**gain advantage** benefit
**gain a point in sport** score
**gain as clear profit** net(t)
**gain a victory** win
**gain by effort** attain
**gain by endeavour** achieve
**gain by threats** extort
**gain by work** earn
**gain exemption** excuse
**gain from hard work** earn
**gainful** beneficial, constructive, edifying, enriching, fat, fruitful, fulfilling, good, gratifying, helpful, lucrative, paying, pleasing, productive, profitable, remunerative, rewarding, satisfying, useful, valuable, well-paid, worthwhile
**gain in competition** win
**gain knowledge** learn
**gain mastery** prevail
**gain on** approach, outdistance, outstrip, overtake
**gain one's end** succeed
**gain over expense** net(t)
**gain payment by work** earn
**gain points** score
**gain possession of** secure
**gain profit** earn
**gainsay** confute, contradict(ion), denial, deny, disaffirm, disagree, disbelieve, disclamation, disproof, dissent, impugn, negate, negation, nullify, object(ion), prohibit, protest, refute, unsaying, veto
**gain strength** improve
**gain supremacy** prevail
**gain the confidence of** convince
**gain the favour of** propitiate
**gain the mastery** prevail
**gain the upper hand over** awe, browbeat, intimidate, subdue
**gain time** delay, postpone, procrastinate, stall, temporise
**gain victory** beat, win
**gait** amble, gallop, job, pace, run, saunter, step, stride, strut, swagger, trot, walk
**gaited horse** pacer
**gaiter** legging, spat
**gait of horses** canter, gallop, pace, rack, trot
**gait setter** pacer
**gala** carnival, celebration, festival, festive, festivity, fête, gay, jamboree, jovial, joyful, jubilee, merry, pageant, party, procession
**Galápagos lizard** iguana
**Galápagos reptile** tortoise
**gale** blast, cyclone, explosion, fit, hurricane, outbreak, outburst, peal, shriek, squall, storm, tempest, tornado, typhoon
**Galilean town** Cana, Nazareth
**Galileo dropped stones from this tower** Pisa
**gall** annoy, asperity, cheek, humiliate, impertinence, insolence, nerve, rancour, vex
**gall and wormwood** anger, annoyance, exasperation, irritation, resentment
**gallant** bold, brave, chivalrous, courageous, courteous, courtly, daring, fearless, gay, heroic, obliging, plucky, polite, resolute, showy, stalwart, suitor, valiant, valorous, wooer
**gallant lover** squire
**gallant person** cavalier
**gallantry** audacity, boldness, bravery, courage, daring, fearlessness, heroism, intrepidity, manliness, mettle, nerve, pluck, prowess, spirit, valiance, valour
**galleon cargo** oro (Sp)
**gallery** ambulatory, arcade, audience, balcony, colonnade, hall, loggia, mezzanine, piazza, portico, salon, spectators
**gallery custodian** curator
**gallery in a fort** caponier
**galley** bireme, kitchen, proof, pull, ship, slip, trireme
**Gallic** French
**Gallic race** French
**gallinule** pukeko
**gallivant** gad, rove, wander
**gallivanting person** gadabout
**galloon** lace, trimming
**gallop** bolt, canter, career, dart, dash, fly, hasten, hie, hurry, lope, race, run, rush, scamper, scud, scuttle, shoot, spank, speed, sprint, tear, whisk, zoom
**gallop at full speed** career
**gallop faster than** outride
**gallop gently** canter
**gallows** gibbet, halter, noose, scaffold
**gallows platform** scaffold

**galore** (a)plenty
**galosh** overshoe
**galvanise** arouse, electrify, excite, fire, inspire, invigorate, jolt, move, prod, provoke, quicken, shock, spur, stimulate, stir, vitalise
**gamble** back, bet(ting), chance, dare, game, gaming, hazard, lavish, lottery, play, potshot, punt, risk, speculate, speculation, squander, stake, uncertainty, venture, wager(ing), waste
**gambler** adventurer, adventurist, backer, better, bettor, gamester, punter, speculator, wagerer
**gamble recklessly** plunge
**gambling** cards, dice
**gambling assistant** croupier, tout
**gambling card game** baccarat, faro, loo, poker, twenty-one
**gambling chances** odds
**gambling counter** chip
**gambling cube** di(c)e
**gambling game** craps, fah-fee, faro, roulette
**gambling house** cas(s)ino
**gambling losses** losings
**gambling place** casino
**gambling wheel** roulette
**gambling with two coins** two-up
**gambol** caper, cavort, dance, frisk, frolic, hop, jump, prance, rollick, romp, skip, spring
**game** adventure, amusement, bold, bowls, brave, competition, contest, cricket, diversion, fearless, football, fun, hide-and-seek, hockey, joke, jukskei, ludo, match, plan, play, plucky, prey, quarry, resolute, rugby, scheme, skittles, soccer, sport, strategy, tag, tennis, undertaking, willing
**game at cards** baccarat, bridge, loo, pinochle, poker, rummy
**game at marbles** taw
**game being played in casino** baccarat, bingo, chemin, fir, lotto, roulette, twenty-one
**game between two pairs of players** doubles
**game bird** grouse, guinea-fowl, partridge, pheasant, quail, snipe
**game club** bat
**game dog** retriever, setter, spaniel
**game fish** king fish, marlin, tiger fish, trout
**game for one** patience, solitaire
**game for two** chess
**game in pub** darts
**gamekeeper** keeper, warden
**game like baseball** rounders
**game like bingo** ke(e)no, kino, quino

**game like croquet** (pall-)mall
**game like hockey** bandy
**game like hockey played by men on ponies** polo
**game marble** agate, taw
**game of cards** baccarat, bridge, loo, pinochle, poker, rummy
**game of chance** bingo, faro, ke(e)no, kino, lottery, lotto, quino, roulette
**game of feigning death** possum
**game of hare and hounds** paper chase
**game of marbles** taw
**game of princes** polo
**game of skill** chess, pool
**game of snooker** frame
**game played in a pool** water polo
**game played on a lawn** bowls, croquet
**game played on horseback** polo(crosse)
**game played on ship's deck** shovelboard
**game played with nine balls and cue** bagatelle
**game played with sticks** hockey
**game resembling backgammon** pachisi
**game reserve near St Lucia** Hluhluwe
**game similar to bingo** lotto
**game similar to hockey** shinty
**games of strength** athletics
**games player** sportsperson
**game tally** score
**game thief** poacher
**game with rings** hoop-la
**game with small wooden discs** squail
**game with special pieces** dominoes
**gamin** brat, ragamuffin, stroller, urchin, waif
**gaming cube** di(c)e
**gaming house** cas(s)ino
**gaming stake** ante
**gaming table official** croupier
**gamp** umbrella
**gamut** area, compass, field, range, scale, scope, series, spectrum, sweep
**gander's mate** goose
**Gandhi's garb** dho(o)ti, dhuti
**Gandhi's nation** India
**Gandhi's policy of non-violent resistance to British rule** satyagraha
**Gandhi's title** Mahatma
**gang** band, bunch, cabal, circle, clique, club, coffle, company, core, coterie, crew, crowd, faction, group, herd, horde, lot, mob, pack, party, ring, school, set, shift, squad, team, troupe
**ganger** boss, foreman, leader, overseer
**Ganges country** India
**ganglion** cerebrum, cyst, swelling, tumour

**gang of miners** core
**gang of witches** coven
**gangplank** brow, gangway, ramp
**gangrene** necrosis
**gangrene of jawbone** phossy
**gangster** apache, bandit, brigand, cowboy, criminal, crook, desperado, gunman, heavy, highbinder, hoodlum, mafioso, mobster, mug, murderer, offender, racketeer, robber, rough, ruffian, skollie, skolly, thug, tough, tsotsi
**gangsterism** thuggery
**gang up** congregate, cooperate
**gang up on** ambush, attack, surround
**gangway** aisle, alleyway, gangplank, lane, passage(way), walkway
**gaol** bagnio, calaboose, confine, custody, detain, detention, guardhouse, immure, impound, imprison, incarcerate, inside, intern, jail(house), jankers, limbo, lock-up, nick, pen(itentiary), prison
**gap** aperture, breach, break, chasm, cleft, difference, disparity, hiatus, hole, interim, interruption, lacuna, opening, space, void
**gape** crack, dehisce, gawk, gaze, mollusc, ogle, open, part, split, stare, wonder, yawn
**gape at** ogle, stare
**gape with drowsiness** yawn
**gap in armour** chink
**gaping** broad, cavernous, cracking, goggling, great, open(ing), ringent, splitting, staring, vast, wondering, yawning
**gaping hollow** chasm
**gap in mountains** col, pass
**gap where something is missing** hiatus
**garage** carport, lock-up, petrol station
**garb** array, attire, clothes, clothing, costume, dress, fashion, garments, habiliments, habit, mode, style
**garbage** debris, detritus, filth, junk, litter, offal, rubbish, scraps, slops, swill, trash
**garbage collector** dustman
**garble** confuse, distort, doctor, falsify, jumble, misquote, misreport, misrepresent, mistranslate, muddle, mutilate, pervert, slant, twist
**garb of bagpiper** kilt
**garden** area, backyard, bed, border, estate, grounds, orchard, park(land), patch, plot, row, strip, woodland, yard
**garden basket** trug
**garden bird** thrush
**garden blaze** bonfire
**garden bug** ant
**garden cultivator** horticulturist

**garden cutters** shears
**garden designing** landscaping
**garden digging tool** spade
**garden elf** gnome
**gardener's hand tool** trowel
**gardener's underground friend** earthworm
**garden figure** dwarf, gnome
**garden flower** aster, dahlia, daisy, petunia, poppy, rose, violet
**garden herb** mint, parsley, rosemary, tarragon, thyme
**gardening implement** fork, hoe, hose, mattock, rake, secateurs, shears, spade, trimmer, trowel
**garden in Athens where Aristotle taught** Lyceum
**garden insect** ant
**garden lake** pond
**garden moisture** dew
**garden mollusc** snail
**garden nuisance** weed
**garden of betrayal** Gethsemane
**garden of delight** Eden
**garden of fruit trees** orchard
**garden of golden apples** Hesperides
**garden of paradise** Eden
**garden ornament** dwarf, gnome
**garden outhouse** shed
**garden pest** aphid, earwig, greenfly, plant louse, slug, snail
**garden plant** lily, shrub, verbena
**garden plant with slipper-shaped flower** calceolaria
**garden plot** bed
**garden scraper** rake
**garden seat enclosed by branches** arbour
**garden shack** shed
**garden soil** dirt, loam
**garden sprinkler** spray
**garden statue** dwarf, gnome
**garden tool** fork, hoe, hose, mattock, rake, secateurs, shears, spade, trimmer, trowel
**garden track** path
**garden tree with dangling yellow blossoms** laburnum
**garden wall** ha-ha
**garden where Plato taught** Academy
**gare** covetous, miserly
**garish** brassy, cheap, flashy, flaunting, gaudy, glaring, glittering, loud, raffish, showy, tasteless, tawdry, vulgar
**garish sign** neon
**garland** anadem, bay, chaplet, coronal, coronet, crown, decoration, diadem, fascia, festoon, flowers, headband, honours, laurels, lei, loop, wreath
**garland for the head** anadem
**garland of flowers** lei

**garlic mayonnaise** aïoli
**garlic mustard** jack-by-the-hedge
**garlic segment** clove
**garment** aba, apparel, blouse, cape, cloak, coat, costume, cymar, dho(o)ti, dhuti, dress, frock, garb, gown, jersey, kanga, kitenge, robe, saree, sari, sarong, shirt, simar, skirt, slip, stole, tunic, ulster, vest, wrap
**garment arm** sleeve
**garment edge** hem
**garment fastener** button, clasp, pin, zipper
**garment fold** pleat
**garment for bishop** chimar, chimere
**garment for priest** alb, amice, cassock, ephod
**garment for the dead** shroud
**garment hanging from the hips** hipster
**garment identifier** tab, tag
**garment insert** gore, gusset
**garment maker** seamstress, tailor
**garment measurement** size
**garment nuisance** lint
**garment of herald** tabard
**garment of Malaysia** sarong
**garment of servant** livery
**garment part** bodice, collar, cuffs, lapel
**garments** apparel, attire, clothes, outfit, uniform
**garment to sleep in** nightie, pyjamas
**garment worn by bishops** rochet
**garner** accumulate, achieve, amass, bank, cache, collect, crib, deposit, depot, earn, gather, granary, reap, safe, silo, stock, store, vault
**garnet berry** currant
**garnet cut in a concave cabochon** carbuncle
**garnish** adjunct, adorn(ment), decorate, decoration, embellish, enhance, grace, ornament(ation), savour, trim
**garnished ice cream** coupe
**garnished with vegetables** jardinière
**garnishing herb** parsley
**garnish of toast** crouton, sippet
**garniture** adornment, appurtenance, embellishment
**garçon** attendant, server, steward, waiter
**garotte** asphyxiate, choke, garrot(t)e, inhibit, repress, smother, stifle, strangle, suffocate, suppress, throttle
**garret** attic, clearstory, clerestory, cockloft, dormer, housetop, loft, mansard
**garrison** barracks, base, camp, command, defend, detachment, encampment, fort(ification), fortress, guard, man, mount, occupy, place,

position, post, protect, station, stronghold, troops, unit
**garrulity** babble, babbling, chatter, chattiness, gabbiness, prating, talkativeness, verbosity
**garrulous** babbling, loquacious, prating, prolix, talkative, verbose
**Gary Player's game** golf
**gas** acetylene, aer-, butane, carbon dioxide, carbon monoxide, ether, fuel, fume, gasoline, helium, hydrogen, laughing gas, methane, miasma, nitrogen, oxygen, ozone, petrol, propane, reek, smoke, vapour
**gasbag** balloon, chatterbox, chatterer
**gaseous element** argon, chlorine, helium, hydrogen, krypton, neon, nitrogen, oxygen, radon, xenon
**gaseous hydrocarbon** ethane
**gaseous mixture** air
**gas forming part of the air** argon, ozone
**gash** cleave, cleft, cut, gouge, incise, incision, lacerate, laceration, notch, rend, rent, score, slash, slit, split, tear, wound
**gas in the atmosphere essential to life** oxygen
**gas jet** burner
**gas lighter fluid** butane
**gas measure** therm
**gas meter reader** gasman
**gasoline** gasolene, petrol
**gasp** aspirate, blow, breathe, choke, cry, exclaim, gulp, heave, huff, labour, pant, puff, rasp, snort, sop, strain, swelter, utter, wheeze
**gasp convulsively** sob
**gasp for breath** pant
**gas-ring** furnace, range, stove
**gastralgia** stomach ache
**gastronomy** cookery, cuisine, diet, epicureanism, gluttony, gourmandism, gulosity
**gastropod** abalone, limpet, mollusc, ormer, perlemoen, snail, whelk
**gastropod shell** cowrie, perlemoen
**gas unit** therm
**gas used in fluorescent tubes** argon
**gas used in lasers and illuminated signs** neon
**gat** firearm, pistol, revolver
**gate** barrier, door(way), entrance, exit, gateway, hatchway, opening, passage, portal, spigot, tap, valve, yett (Sc)
**gate at railway station** barrier
**gateau** cake
**gate-crash** intercede, interrupt, intrude, obtrude
**gate-crasher** infiltrator, interloper, intruder

**gatehouse** bar, lodge
**gateway** barway, door, entrance, gate, inlet, mouth, opening, orifice, port(al), propylaeum, (pro)pylon, rim, torii
**gateway of Egyptian temple** pylon
**gateway of Shinto temple** torii
**gather** accrete, accumulate, aggregate, amass, assemble, assume, collect, conclude, condense, deduce, fold, garner, glean, grow, harvest, hoard, increase, infer, learn, meet, muster, pleat, pluck, reap, thicken, tuck, understand
**gather after a reaper** glean
**gather and bind** sheave
**gather by bits** glean
**gather crops** harvest, reap
**gathered border** frill
**gathered flounce** falbala
**gathered into a mass** conglomerate
**gathered together** agminate
**gather facts** examine, research, study
**gather harvest** reap
**gather in a crowd** flock
**gather in crops** harvest, reap
**gathering** assemblance, assembly, boil, collection, company, concourse, congregation, congress, convention, convocation, crowd, get-together, group, jamboree, mass, meeting, party, rally, round-up, throng, turn-out
**gathering dust** idle
**gathering implement** rake
**gathering nuts** nutting
**gathering of company directors** board meeting
**gathering of grapes** vintage
**gathering of pus** abscess
**gathering of Scouts** jamboree
**gathering of witches** coven
**gather in great quantity** amass
**gather into a crowd** congregate
**gather into a mass** agglomerate, aggregate
**gather into creases** pucker
**gather in vertical pleats** kilt
**gather knowledge** learn
**gather leaves** rake
**gather scattered grain** glean
**gather slowly** glean
**gather speed** accelerate
**gather together** assemble, congregate
**gauche** awkward, clumsy, gawky, graceless, ignorant, ill-bred, ill-mannered, indelicate, inelegant, inept, insensitive, maladroit, ordinary, tactless, uncouth, uncultured, ungainly, ungentlemanly, unladylike, unpolished, unskilful, unsophisticated, vulgar

**gaucho** cowboy, herdsman
**gaucho knife** bolo
**gaucho lariat** bola(s)
**gaucho weapon** bola(s), bolo, machete
**gaudily adorned** tawdry
**gaudy** bright, brilliant, flash(y), florid, garish, gay, glaring, glitzy, loud, lurid, ostentatious, raffish, showy, tasteless, tawdry, unsubtle, vulgar
**gaudy show** bravery, hoopla
**gauge** adjudge, appraise, ascertain, assess, basis, bore, calculate, capacity, count, depth, determine, estimate, evaluate, example, extent, guess, guide, height, indicator, judge, magnitude, measure, meter, model, pattern, rate, reckon, sample, scope, size, span, standard, test, value, weigh, width, yardstick
**gauge in a car** mileometer, speedometer
**gauge in airplane** altimeter
**gauge indicator** arm, hand, needle
**Gauls' priest** druid
**gaunt** angular, blare, bleak, bony, cadaverous, deathly, denuded, desolate, dismal, dreary, emaciated, forlorn, grim, haggard, harsh, hollow-eyed, lank(y), lean, meagre, peaked, scraggy, scrawny, shrivelled, skeletal, skinny, spare, stalky, stark, starved, stern, thin, wasted, weedy, withered
**gaunt and pale** cadaverous
**gauntlet** glove
**gauntlet spike** gad
**gauzy fabric** chiffon, leno, tissue, tulle
**gavel** hammer, mallet
**gavel of judge** mace, mallet
**gavial** crocodile
**gawk** bear, boggle, boor, bumbler, bumpkin, bungler, churl, clod, dolt, dunderhead, fool, gape, gawp, gaze, goggle, ignoramus, look, lout, lubber, marvel, oaf, simpleton, stare, watch, wonder, yahoo
**gawky** awkward, clownish, clumsy, gauche, loutish, lumbering, lumpish, maladroit, oafish, uncouth, ungainly
**gay** airy, blithe, cheerful, convivial, dissipated, glad, gleeful, good-humoured, happy, homosexual, jolly, jovial, joyful, joyous, licentious, light-hearted, lively, merry, riant, showy, sprightly, urning, vivacious
**gay colour** red
**gay, colourful clothes** trappings
**gay dog** playboy
**gay, flighty person** butterfly
**gay woman** femme galante (F)
**Gaza victor** Allenby

**gaze** contemplate, eye(ful), gape, gawk, goggle, observe, ogle, peer, peruse, scrutinise, stare, study, watch, wonder
**gaze askance** leer
**gaze at** eye, ogle
**gaze at fixedly** stare
**gaze attentively** pore
**gazebo** alcove, balcony, belvedere, pavilion, pergola, recess, summerhouse, trellis, turret
**gaze exultingly** gloat
**gaze fiercely** glare
**gaze fixedly** stare
**gaze intently** pore, stare
**gazelle** ariel, deer, goa, impala, kudu, springbok
**gaze narrowly** peer
**gaze out the window** (day)dream, muse
**gaze rudely** stare
**gaze upon** behold
**gaze with malevolent smugness** gloat
**gaze with malicious joy** gloat
**gear** accessories, accoutrements, affair, apparatus, apparel, array, attire, baggage, belongings, cam(wheel), clothes, clothing, cog(wheel), doings, dress, equipment, garb, garments, gearing, gearwheel, get-up, habit, harness, instruments, kit, luggage, machinery, mechanism, outfit, paraphernalia, possessions, stuff, supplies, tackle, things, togs, tools, trappings, traps, wear, workings, works
**gear for sport** equipment
**gear tooth** cog
**gear wheel** driven, helical, pinion
**gear with teeth** cog
**gecko** lizard
**gee** golly
**gel** cake, clot, condense, congeal, deepen, jell, set, thicken
**gelatine case for a dose of medicine** capsule
**gelatinous** congealed, gluey, glutinous, gooey, gummy, jellied, jelly(-like), mucilaginous, rubbery, sticky, viscid, viscous
**gelatinous dessert** jelly
**geld** alter, asexualise, castrate, emasculate, neuter, spay, weaken
**Gelderland city** Ede
**gelding** horse
**gelid** algid, arctic, cold, cool, freezing, frigid, frosty, ice-cold, icy, polar, snappy, snowy, wintry
**gelling agent** pectin
**gem** agate, almandine, amethyst, beryl, diamond, emerald, flower, garnet, gemstone, iolite, jade,

jasper, jewel, masterpiece, onyx, opal, pearl, peridot, pick, pièce de résistance, prize, ruby, sapphire, sard(ine), sardius, sparkler, spinel, stone, topaz, treasure, zircon
**gem-bearing shellfish** oyster
**gem carved in relief** cameo
**gem cutter** lapidary
**gem cut with a flat top** table-cut
**gem cut with design** intaglio
**gemel** double, twin
**gem face** collet, facet
**gem polisher** lapidary
**gemsbok** oryx
**gemstone surface** facet
**gemstone weight** carat
**gen** background, data, details, facts, info(rmation), low-down
**gendarme** policeman
**gender** feminine, masculine, neuter, sex
**genealogical diagram** tree
**genealogical relation** filiation
**genealogy** ancestry, background, beginning, birth, blood, breeding, derivation, descendancy, descent, etymology, extraction, family, foundation, heredity, line(age), nobility, origin, parentage, pedigree, race, root, source, stemma, stock, strain, stirps, tree
**general** common, customary, ill-defined, impartial, inexact, lax, miscellaneous, ordinary, overall, prevailing, prevalent, regular, universal, unspecialised, usual, vague, widespread
**general admission** admittedly, allowedly
**general agreement in opinion** consensus
**general applause** éclat
**general applicability** generality
**general aspect of landscape** scenery
**general confusion** welter
**general consent** unanimity
**general course of action** career, trend
**general decorative effect** décor
**general direction and tendency** trend
**general drift** tenor, trend
**general effect of items of dress** ensemble
**general existing** prevalent
**generalised idea** concept
**generality** abstraction, approximateness, body, breadth, bulk, commonness, comprehensiveness, concept, extensiveness, generalisation, idea, impreciseness, indefiniteness, looseness, majority, mass, most, notion, statement, sweeping,

theorem, theory, thought, universality, vagueness
**generally** commonly, often, ordinarily, usually
**generally accepted** accredited
**generally prevailing rate** average
**general manumission** abolition of slavery
**general meaning** drift
**general mixture** salmagundi, salmagundy
**general of David** Abner, Joab
**general of Saul** Abner
**general pardon** amnesty
**general practitioner's visit** house call
**general principle** canon
**general purport** tenor
**general purpose vehicle** jeep
**general remedy** panacea
**general rise in prices** inflation
**general sketch** outline
**general slaughter** massacre
**general's personal assistant** aide
**general summary** synopsis
**general survey** overview
**general truth** maxim
**general type** average, mean
**general weather** climate
**generate** beget, breed, cause, create, engender, evolve, father, form, initiate, make, originate, produce, propagate, spawn
**generate heat** boil
**generating heat** thermal
**generation** age, breed(ing), creation, crop, epoch, era, evolution, formation, genesis, issue, kin, lineage, offspring, origination, period, procreation, progeny, propagation, race, reproduction, strain, time(s)
**generator** dynamo
**generosity** abundance, altruism, amplitude, benefaction, beneficence, benevolence, big-heartedness, bounteousness, bountiful, bounty, charity, donation, goodness, grant, gratuity, kindness, largeness, largess(e), lavishness, liberality, magnanimity, munificence, nobleness, plenitude, plethora, unselfishness
**generosity in giving** bounty
**generosity in giving to the needy** charity
**generous** abundant, altruistic, ample, beneficent, benevolent, big, bounteous, bountiful, charitable, copious, honourable, humane, kind, large, liberal, magnanimous, munificent, noble, overflowing, plenteous, plentiful, unselfish

**generous giving** largess(e)
**generous in giving** open-handed
**generous in giving to the needy** charitable
**genesis** beginning, birth, commencement, formation, origin, outset, source, start
**Genesis woman** Eve
**genet** fur, genette
**genetic change** mutation
**genetic inheritance** heredity
**genetic replica** clone
**Geneva in German** Genf
**genial** affable, agreeable, amenable, amiable, amicable, benign, cheerful, cheery, convivial, cordial, courteous, debonair, easygoing, encouraging, enlivening, friendly, gay, good-humoured, gracious, happy, hearty, jolly, jovial, kind(ly), lively, merry, mirthful, pleasant, sunny, warm, willing
**geniality** amiability, blitheness, bonhomie, buoyancy, cheerfulness, congeniality, conviviality, exuberance, friendliness, gaiety, gayness, gladness, joyousness, kindliness, light-heartedness, optimism, sociability, warmth
**genially** affably, agreeably, amiably, benignly, cheerfully, cheerily, convivially, cordially, enliveningly, happily, heartily, jovially, joyously, kindly, merrily, pleasantly, sunnily, warmly
**genie** djinni, djinny, goblin, jinnee, jinni, sprite
**genipap tree** genip, lana
**genitourinary** urogenital
**genius** ability, adept, aptitude, bent, brain, brightness, brilliance, capacity, daemon, double, endowment, expert, faculty, flair, genie, gift, inclination, intellect, knack, maestro, master-hand, mastermind, pastmaster, propensity, spirit, talent, turn, virtuoso
**genre** appearance, approach, brand, breed, cast, category, class, custom, family, fashion, genus, kind, name, order, school, sort, species, style, type, variety
**gent** gentleman, man
**genteel** aristocrat(ic), arrogant, cavalier, civil, courteous, courtly, cultured, dainty, debonair, decorous, delicate, elegant, fashionable, flashy, formal, gallant, gentle, gentlemanly, graceful, gracious, ladylike, mannerly, noble, patrician, polished, polite, pompous, refined, respectable, snobbish, stylish,

urbane, well-born, well-bred, well-mannered
**Gentile** goy, non-Jew
**Gentile convert to Jewish faith** proselyte
**gentle** clement, courteous, cultivated, gentle-hearted, high-born, honourable, humane, kind-hearted, kind(ly), lenient, light, manageable, meek, merciful, mild, moderate, pacific, peaceful, polished, polite, respectable, soft, soothing, temperate, tender, tractable, well-born, well-bred
**gentle and easy death** euthanasia
**gentle and tractable** tame
**gentle blow under the chin** chuck
**gentle breeze** aura, zephyr
**gentle canter** trot
**gentle gallop** canter
**gentle golf stroke** putt
**gentle grin** beam, smile
**gentle in manner** bland, mild
**gentle knock** tap
**gentle laughter** chuckle
**gentleman** amateur, aristocrat, attendant, butler, caballero, don, duke, honest, lord, man, noble, patrician, peer, reputable, sir, sport, squire
**gentleman-at-arms** pensioner
**gentleman of the highest rank** grandee
**gentleman's personal attendant** valet
**gentleness** amiableness, balminess, blandness, calmness, easiness, humaneness, kind(li)ness, lightness, meekness, mercifulness, mildness, peacefulness, placidness, quietness, tenderness
**gentle or suave in manner** bland
**gentle poke** nudge
**gentle slope** glacis
**gentle wind** aura, breeze
**gentlewoman** lady
**gently** airily, delicately, evenly, faintly, gradually, lightly, moderately, progressively, slightly, slowly, softly, steadily, tenderly, timidly
**gentry** aristocracy, best, cream, crème de la crème (F), elect, elite, nobility, noblesse, patricians, patriciate, peerage, pick, quality, society
**genu** knee
**genuflect** bend, curts(e)y, kneel, stoop, worship
**genuine** actual, approved, authentic, bona fide, certified, complete, dinkum, earnest, honest, inartificial, just, lawful, legal, legitimate, licit, natural, open, original, plain, pukka, pure(bred), real(istic), rightful, simple, sincere, solid, sound, sterling, thorough, true(-blue), unadulterated, unaffected, valid, veritable, warranted
**genuineness** honesty, legitimateness, naturalness, pureness, realness, soundness, trueness, veridity
**genus** brand, breed, caste, category, character, class, collection, denomination, department, description, division, family, genre, grade, group(ing), ilk, kind, league, logic, make, nature, order, quality, race, rank, set, sort, species, sphere, stamp, status, style, tribe, type, value, variety
**genus of gastropods having external ovoid shell** scaphander
**genus of toads comprising American spadefoot** scaphiopus
**geo** creek, gio
**geode** cavity, druse, nodule
**geodesy** geography, uranometry
**geographical index** gazetteer
**geographic location** seat
**geography** geodesy
**geoidal** earth-shaped
**geological age** C(a)enozoic, epoch, era, period, Pliocene, system
**geological epoch** eocene
**geological interval** age
**geological period** era
**geomancy** prophecy
**geometric** cubist(ic)
**geometrical line** chord, tangent
**geometrical measure** parallel
**geometrical solid** cone, cube, cylinder, ellipsoid, prism
**geometric curve** cycloid, evolute, folium, helix, parabola, spiral
**geometric figure** circle, cone, cube, ellipse, lune, polygon, prism, rhomb, square
**geometric proportion** ratio
**geometric rule** theorem
**geometric shape** oblong, prism
**geometric solid** cone
**geometric theory** conics
**geophagy** pica
**geoponic** bucolic, farming, husbandry, rural, rustic
**George Cross island** Malta
**George Formby's instrument** ukulele
**George Gershwin's brother** Ira
**germ** bacteria, begining, bud, bug, cause(r), egg, embryo, micro-organism, microbe, nucleus, origin, ovule, ovum, root, rudiment, seed, source, spark, spore, sprout, virus
**German** Hegel, Teuton(ic)
**German Air Force** Luftwaffe
**German-American physicist** Einstein
**German apple pastry** strudel
**German army camp** Stalag
**German army tank** panzer
**German astronomer** Kepler
**German beer mug** stein
**German brandy** kirschwasser
**German breed of dog** dachshund, Rottweiler, weimaraner
**German cavalryman** u(h)lan
**German coffee cake** stollen
**German coin** mark, pfennig
**German composer** Bach, Beethoven, Brahms, Handel, Wagner, Weber
**German dance** allemande
**German dialect** Yiddish
**German dictator** Hitler
**German dish of chopped pickled cabbage** sauerkraut
**German dry white wine** moselle
**German emperor** kaiser
**German empire** Reich
**German folklore spirit** kobold
**German for I** ich
**German for one** ein
**German gent** herr
**German god of thunder** Donar
**German health resort** Kursaal
**German highway** autobahn
**German hunting dog** weimaraner
**Germanic** Teutonic
**Germanic alphabet** runic
**Germanic peoples** Teutonic
**German industrial valley** Ruhr
**German Jewish language** Yiddish
**German king** kaiser
**German lady** Frau
**German leader** Adolph Hitler, Erhard, Fuehrer, Führer
**German light machine gun** spandau
**German married woman** Frau
**German measles** roseola, rubella
**German miss** Fräulein
**German mister** Herr
**German money** mark, pfennig
**German motorway** autobahn
**German Mrs** Frau
**German National Socialist** Nazi
**German naval base** Kiel
**German nobleman** baron
**German parliament** Reichstag
**German pistol** luger, mauser
**German poet** Goethe
**German porcelain** Dresden, Meissen
**German port** Atona, Hamburg
**German port on the Ems** Emden
**German prisoner-of-war camp** Stalag
**German pronoun** du, ich, sie, uns
**German psychologist** Wundt
**German pub** stube
**German reformer** Martin Luther

**German region** Sudeten
**German rifle** mauser
**German sausage** wurst
**German secret police** Gestapo
**German shepherd dog** Alsatian
**German silver** albata
**German softly** leise
**German soldier** Jerry
**German soldier's spiked helmet** pickelhaube
**German songs** lieder
**German spinster** Fräulein
**German spirit** geist
**German state** Bavaria
**German steel city** Essen
**German submarine** U-boat
**German telegraphic press pioneer** Reuter
**German title** graf, herr, von
**German toast** prosit
**German trout** huck
**German valley** Ruhr
**German warplane** Fokker, Stuka
**German wheat** emmer, spelt
**German white wine** hock
**German wholemeal rye bread** pumpernickel
**German wine** hock, Liebfraumilch, Moselle, Nierstein, Riesling, Sekt, Silvaner
**German woman** Frau
**German young lady** Fräulein
**germ cell** gonad, ovule, ovulum
**germ-free** aseptic, clean, disinfected, healthy, hygienic, immaculate, pure, sanitary, spotless, sterile, unadulterated, uncontaminated, unpolluted, untainted, wholesome
**germ-free form** asepsis
**germicide** antiseptic, bactericide, disinfectant, fumigant, fumigator, microbiocide, purifier, steriliser
**germinate** bud, develop, generate, grow, originate, shoot, sprout, swell
**germinated barley** malt
**germinating plant** spire
**germ-killing substance** streptomycin
**germ of a plant or animal** embryo
**gerontology** geriatrics, gerontotherapy, nostology, therapy
**gestation** conception, development, drafting, evolution, incubation, maturation, planning, pregnancy, ripening
**gesticulate** gesture, indicate, motion, nod, point, sign(al), signalise, wave
**gesticulation** motion, sign(al), wave
**gesture** act(ion), courtesy, formality, gesticulate, gesticulation, indicate, indication, motion, point, sign(al), wave

**gesture expressing submission** obeisance
**gesture for peace** V-sign
**gesture showing agreement** nod
**gesture showing indifference** shrug
**gesture to express victory** V-sign
**get** achieve, acquire, apprehend, attain, become, beget, breed, capture, catch, contract, earn, engender, gain, generate, induce, influence, obtain, persuade, prepare, procure, produce, provide, reach, receive, secure, understand, win
**get aboard** flip
**get about** navigate
**get across** communicate, convey, cross, impart, negotiate, reach, transmit, traverse
**get a degree** graduate
**get ahead** advance, flourish, progress, prosper, succeed, thrive
**get a load of** behold, glance, glimpse, listen, observe, peep, sneak, view, witness
**get along** accord, agree, cope, develop, do, fare, fettle, harmonise, manage, progress, prosper, shift, succeed, survive
**get a move on** commence, haste(n), hurry, hustle, rush, start
**get angry** bridle
**get a rash** break out
**get around** bypass, circumvent, coax, entertain, flatter, outflank, outsmart, outwit
**get at** accessible, acquire, annoy, ascertain, attack, attain, bribe, corrupt, criticise, discover, find, hint, imply, impose, influence, insinuate, intend, mean, nag, reach, suggest, tamper
**get away** decampment, depart, disappear, elude, escape, evade, flee, flight, leave, scram, slip
**get back** reclaim, recoup, recover, redeem, regain, repossess, retain, retaliate, retire, retrieve, return, revert, revisit
**get back together** regroup
**get behind** endorse, finance, promote, push, support
**get benefit of** use
**get better** recuperate
**get better of** best, convalesce, daunt, down, heal, improve, mend, overcome, rally, recover, recuperate, revive, surmount
**get by** bypass, circumvent, cope, exist, manage, overtake, round, subsist, survive
**get by begging** cadge
**get by cheating** fiddle

**get by force** extort
**get by pressure** extract
**get by sponging** cadge
**get clear of** strip
**get close** near
**get comfy** cuddle up
**get down** alight, depress, descend, disembark, dishearten, dismount, dispirit, sadden, weary
**get down to pray** kneel
**get estate** inherit
**get even** avenge, reciprocate, repay, requite, retaliate, revenge
**get even for** avenge
**get far ahead of** outdistance
**get free** escape
**get free of restriction** escape
**get from** derive
**get going** begin, start
**get hold of** acquire
**get in** appear, arrive, collect, come, embark, enter, include, infiltrate, insert, interpose, land, penetrate
**get information** learn
**get in one's hair** annoy, exasperate, harass, irritate, plague
**get in rut** stultify
**get in the way** de trop (F), intercede, interfere, interpose, obtrude
**get into train** entrain
**get in touch with** contact
**get it** understand
**get lost** beat it, scat, scram, shoo, stray, voetsak, voetsek
**get lucky** hit
**get metal from ore** smelt
**get money for** sell
**get more and more of** accumulate
**get off** alight, debark, depart, deplane, descend, detach, detrain, disembark, dismount, escape, exit, leave, remove, separate, shed
**get off feet** sit
**get off on** appreciate, enjoy, savour
**get off one's feet** sit
**get off on the right foot** auspicate
**get off safely** escape
**get off track** derail
**get off your feet** sit
**get old** age
**get on** accord, advance, agree, ascend, board, concur, embark, manage, mount, progress, succeed, survive
**get on aircraft** board
**get one's back up** anger, exasperate, irk, irritate, provoke, vex
**get one's bearings** orientate
**get one's hackles up** incense
**get on horseback** mount
**get on in years** elderly

**get on one's nerves** aggravate, annoy, exasperate, irritate, upset
**get on to chair** sit
**get on to train** board
**get on well** like
**get out** alight, broadcast, circulate, decamp, deliver, depart, eject, escape, evacuate, expel, flee, flit, go, leave, produce, publicise, publish, quit, scarper, scat, scram, split, vacate, withdraw
**get out of** avoid, dodge, escape, evade, shirk, skive
**get out of sight** hide
**get out of town** lam
**get over** accomplish, communicate, convey, cross, defeat, explain, impart, overcome, pass, recover, recuperate, surmount, survive, traverse
**get past** beat, hurdle
**get pay** earn
**get ragged** fray
**get ready** prepare, rehearse
**get rid of** banish, depose, dispose, eject, eliminate, eradicate, exclude, expel, obviate, remove, shed
**get round** bypass, cajole, circumvent, coax, convert, edge, evade, outmanoeuvre, overcome, persuade, skirt
**get soap out** rinse
**get temporary use of** borrow
**get the benefit of** use
**get the better of** beat, best, defeat, outdo, outwit, overcome
**get the hang of** comprehend, grasp, understand
**get the message** understand
**get there** arrive
**get the rope** hang
**get the upper hand** predominate
**get through** complete, end, endure, finish, terminate
**get through to** penetrate
**getting on** elderly
**getting the better of** overcoming
**get to** arrive
**get together** accumulate, agree, amass, assemble, band, collaborate, collect, compile, compromise, congregate, converge, gather, join, meet, rally, reunion, unite, visit
**get to know** ascertain, learn
**get to one's feet** arise, stand
**Gettysburg loser** Lee
**Gettysburg orator** Everett
**Gettysburg victor** Meade
**get under one's skin** annoy, chafe, excite, grate, impress, inspire, irk, irritate, penetrate
**get under way** inaugurate, initiate

**get up** arise, arouse, arrange, ascend, climb, fake, increase, mount, organise, rise, scale, stir, study
**get up and go** ambition, bounce, desire, energy, initiative, oomph, vigour, vitality
**get up on your feet** stand
**get used to** acclimatise, accustom
**get used to again** reaccustom
**get weary** tire
**get well** recover
**get wind of** scent
**get wrong** misinterpret
**gewgaw** trinket
**geyser** cylinder, heat, hot, spring, stream
**geyser mouth** crater
**Ghanaian coin** pessewa
**Ghanaian currency** cedi
**Ghanaian dam** Akosombo
**Ghanaian lake** Ashanti, Brongahafo, Volta
**Ghanaian money** cedi, pesewa
**Ghanaian port** Tema
**Ghanaian wind** Harmattan
**ghastly** awful, cadaverous, deathly, dreadful, frightful, ghostly, grim, gruesome, hideous, horrible, horrid, loathsome, lurid, macabre, pale, repellent, shocking, terrible, terrifying
**ghetto** slum
**ghost** apparition, demon, devil, eidolon, fallacy, ghoul, goblin, hallucination, hint, illusion, image, impression, phantom, poltergeist, revenant, shade, shadow, soul, spectre, spirit, spook, suggestion, wraith
**ghostliness** eeriness
**ghostly** eerie, ghastly, illusive, illusory, insubstantial, mysterious, pale, phantasmal, phantom, shadowy, spectral, spooky, strange, supernatural, uncanny, unearthly, unreal, weird, white
**ghostly being** ghoul, vampire
**ghost or apparition** wraith
**ghost-ridden** haunted
**ghost town near Lüderitz** Kolmanskop
**ghoul at fair** geek
**ghoulish** black, grisly, gruesome, macabre, morbid, revolting, sadistic, sick, unhealthy, unwholesome
**giant** behemoth, colossal, colossus, enormous, gigantic, Goliath, Hercules, huge, immense, jumbo, king-size, large, mammoth, monster, monstrous, ogre, stupendous, titan(ic), tremendous, vast
**giant cactus** saguaro
**giant clam** tridacna
**giant crushed by Hercules** Antaeus

**giant dog** mastiff
**giantess** Argante, Norn
**giant hero** Goliath
**giant hunter** Orion
**giantism** acromegaly
**giant killed by Apollo** Otus
**giant killed by David** Goliath
**giant killer** Apollo, David, Jack
**giant living on human flesh** ogre
**giant monster** afreet, afrit
**giant of Palestine** Anak
**giant perch** barramundi
**giant planet** Jupiter, Neptune, Saturn, Uranus
**giant's dance** Stonehenge
**giant's mother** Gaea, Gaia, Ge
**giant, tropical grass** bamboo
**gibber** babble, blab, cackle, chatter, gabble, jabber, prattle
**gibberish** babble, balderdash, blather, drivel, gabble, jabber, nonsense, prattle, twaddle
**gibbet** gallows, scaffold
**gibe** derision, jape, jeer, jibe, mockery, sarcasm, scoff, scorn, sneer, taunt
**giddiness** dizziness, faintness, light-headedness, unsteadiness, vertiginousness, vertigo
**giddy** careless, dizzy, faint, flighty, frivolous, impulsive, inconstant, intoxicating, light(-headed), silly, unstable, unsteady, vacillating, vertiginous, wild
**gift** ability, allowance, alms, bequest, boon, bounty, capability, contribution, donation, dower, endowment, genius, grant, gratuity, inheritance, largess(e), legacy, offering, power, present, presentation, subsidy, talent
**gifted** able, accomplished, ace, acute, adept, adroit, agile, apt, au fait (F), bright, brilliant, capable, clever, competent, dext(e)rous, expert, ingenious, intelligent, masterful, masterly, skilful, skilled, smart, talented
**gifted with prophetic power** fatidical
**gift for Dad** shirt, socks, tie
**gift giver** donor, Santa
**gift hose** Christmas stocking
**gift left in a will** legacy
**gift of God** grace
**gift of money** baksheesh, bonsella, gratuity, pouch
**gift of nature** dower, dowry
**gift of talent** dower
**gift of the gab** eloquence, loquacity
**gift of the Magi** frankincense, gold, myrrh
**gift of tongues** glossolalia
**gift recipient** donee

**gifts freely given** largess(e)
**gift showing respect** tribute
**gift sock** Christmas stocking
**gifts to the poor** alms
**gift to develop** talent
**gift to waiter** tip
**gift voucher** token
**gigantic** colossal, enormous, giant, herculean, huge, immense, infinite, mammoth, prodigious, stupendous, titanic, tremendous, vast
**gigantic crocodile** gavial
**gigantic New Zealand coot** notornis
**gigantic person** titan
**gigantic statue** Colossus
**gigantic stork from India** argala
**giggle** amusement, cackle, chortle, chuckle, ha-ha, laugh(ter), snicker, snigger, tee-hee, titter, twitter
**gild** adorn, array, aur(e)ate, aurify, beautify, bedeck, bedizen, brighten, camouflage, caparison, coat, conceal, deck, decorate, electro-plate, embellish(ed), embroider(ed), enamel, enhance(d), enrich(ed), furbish, garnish(ed), gilt, gold-plate, grace(d), inaurate, lacquer, paint, plate, prettify
**gilded** gilt, gold, golden
**gilded bronze** ormolu
**gilded metal** vermeil
**gilded youth** jeunesse dorée (F)
**gilder** tracer
**gills of oyster** beard
**gilt** begild, gild
**gilt alloy** ormolu
**gimcrack** bauble, curiosity, gadget, gewgaw, gimmick, memento, souvenir, tawdry, trifle, trinket
**gimmick** attraction, contrivance, device, dodge, gadget, gambit, manoeuvre, ploy, scheme, stratagem, stunt, trick
**gin** alcohol, bait, crane, decoy, drum, ensnarement, hoist, hook, liquor, lure, net, noose, pitfall, pump, rummy, snare, spirit, toil, trap, tripod
**gin cocktail** martini
**gin-flavouring berry** juniper
**ginger beer** pop
**gingerbread of oatmeal and treacle** parkin
**ginger cookie** snap
**gingiva** gum
**gin, lime and soda cocktail** rickey
**gin type** absinthe
**giraffe** camelopard
**giraffe-like animal** okapi
**girdle** band, belt, bind, bound, cincture, cingulum, corset, cummerbund, encircle, enclose, encompass, environ, fillet, hem, ring, sash, surround, waistband, zone
**girdlecake** crumpet, girdlescone, pancake
**gird one's loins** arm, brace, prepare, ready, steel
**girl** chick, child, chit, colleen, dame, damsel, daughter, dell, domestic, female, Fräulein (G), gal, girlfriend, lass(ie), mademoiselle, maid(en), minx, miss, schoolgirl, sis(ter), sweetheart, wench, youngster
**girl at mirror** primper
**girl Friday** secretary
**girlfriend** steady, sweetheart, sweetie
**girlfriend of Zeus** Io
**girl from Russia** Olga
**girl graduate** alumna
**girl hunter** wolf
**girl relative** niece, sister
**girl's plaything** doll, jacks, skipping-rope
**girl's title** Miss
**girl student** co-ed
**girl who behaves boisterously** hoyden
**girl with mischievous charm** gamine
**girt** bind, encircle
**girth** (belly-)band, bulk, circumference, measure, saddle-band, size, strap
**girth measurement** waist
**gist** core, direction, drift, essence, force, idea, import, marrow, matter, meaning, nub, pith, point, quintessence, sense, significance, substance, tenor
**git** bastard, fool
**gittern** guitar
**give** accord, afford, assume, bestow, communicate, contribute, deliver, donate, emit, endow, gie (Sc), hand, impart, issue, offer, perform, present, pronounce, provide, recede, retire, supply, tender, vouchsafe, yield
**give absolution to** shrive
**give access** admit
**give access to** open, unbolt, unlatch, unload
**give account of** describe, narrate, relate, report, state
**give a command** order
**give a damn** care, mind
**give added support** reinforce, strengthen
**give a definite structure** organise
**give advance notice** bill
**give advice to** admonish, counsel
**give a fright** frighten
**give a fright to** startle
**give a hand** assist
**give aid to** assist, help, succour
**give air to** vent

**give a leg up** advance, aid, assist, boost, help, succour, support
**give a meal to** feed
**give an account** describe, report
**give and take** barter, compromise, swap
**give-and-take** adaptability, flexibility, goodwill, willingness
**give an earlier date to** antedate
**give a new title** rename
**give an example** illustrate
**give a nickname to** dub
**give an opinion** advise, pronounce
**give another exam** retest
**give a picture in words** describe
**give approval to** endorse
**give a prize** award
**give a rank to** rate
**give a reason** account
**give a receipt for** acknowledge
**give a rightful claim** entitle
**give as due share** allot
**give a speech** address, orate
**give assent** approve
**give a suggestive look** leer
**give a tenth part** tithe
**give a title to** entitle
**give attention to** hear, notice, tend
**give authority** authorise
**give away** betray, disclose, divulge, expose, leak, relent, reveal, uncover, yield
**give away part of** share
**give a wide berth** avoid, boycott, shun
**give back** refund, remise, remit, restore, return
**give birth to** bear, beget, deliver, originate, spawn
**give birth to a calf** calve
**give birth to lamb** (y)ean
**give brief look at** glance
**give character to** endue, indue
**give claim to** entitle
**give comfort** solace
**give confidence to** (re)assure
**give consent** accede, agree
**give continuous account** narrate
**give counsel to** advise
**give deceptive information to** mislead
**give decision** determine
**give deep sorrow** grieve
**give deep thought to** ponder
**give details of** explain
**give direction to a weapon** aim
**give discomfort to** ail
**give ear to** heed
**give effect** enforce
**give emphasis** stress
**give energy to** energise
**give erroneous information to** misinform
**give evidence** affirm, attest, testify

give example illustrate
give expression to vent
give false account of misrepresent
give false notion of belie
give food to feed
give for a time lend, loan
give for good service tip
give form shape
give formally present
give for safekeeping entrust
give for temporary use lend
give forth afford, conceive, emit, proclaim, speak, warp, yield
give forth doleful sound knell
give freely contribute
give free of charge complimentary, gratis
give free rein to indulge, oblige
give fresh strength renew
give ground relent
give grounds justify
give grudgingly stint
give guarantee assure
give guidance to counsel
give guns to arm
give heed to attend, listen
give help assist
give holy orders ordain
give image of reflect
give imitation repeat
give in admit, capitulate, collapse, comply, concede, quit, relent, submit, succumb, surrender, yield
give in detail itemise
give in exchange swap, swop
give in response to question answer
give in to submit, yield
give into someone's care consign
give knowledge inform
give leave to allow, authorise, let, permit
give legal assent sanction
give letter verbally dictate
give life to animate, birth, enliven, vivify
give light shine
give lip to sass
give manifest evidence radiate
give meaning interpret
give meaning of explain
give money pay
give moral training educate
given accorded, addicted, administered, allowed, apt, awarded, bestowed, (con)ceded, conferred, contributed, displayed, disposed, donated, entrusted, furnished, granted, inclined, indicated, lent, liable, likely, manifested, permitted, presented, prone, provided, relinquished, supplied, yielded
give name to denominate
given as a tribute tributary

given condition data, premise
given facts data
give nickname to dub
given in trust fiduciary
given name forename
give notice apprise, resign
give notice to notify
given over to addicted
given quantity allowance, portion, quote, ration
given the sack fired
given to airs and graces affected, lackadaisical, languishing
given to caution wary
given to constant anxiety insecure
given to drinking bibulous
given to fighting pugnacious
given to jesting facetious
given to meditation reflective
given too little to eat underfed
given to question answer
given to trifling frivolous
give off belch, discharge, divide, emit, evolve, excrete, exhale, exude, produce, release, separate, shed, vent
give off bubbles effervesce
give offence insult
give off flashing light coruscate
give off vapour steam
give on credit lend
give one's word promise
give one's word to assure
give one the creeps disgust, frighten, horrify, scare, terrify
give on loan lend
give on to overlook
give opinion opine
give orderly structure to organise
give out advertise, allot, announce, assign, broadcast, communicate, deal, discharge, disseminate, distribute, emit, exhale, exude, impart, issue, notify, produce, publish, release, stop, transmit, utter
give out a strongly offensive smell stink
give out breath expire
give out vapour steam
give pause bewilder, deter, disconcert, dismay, frighten, worry
give permission assent, consent
give personally hand
give priority prefer
give prior warning of presage
give prolonged cry howl, ululate
give prominence to feature, highlight
give proof of attest
give public address orate
give public notice of advertise

giver backer, benefactor, contributor, donator, donor, grantor, helper, supporter
give reluctantly (be)grudge
give rest ease
give right to entitle
give rise to beget, engender, induce
giver of expert advice consultant
giver of gift donor
giver of Golden Fleece Phrixus
giver of information at race meeting tipster
give satisfaction atone
give short measure skimp
gives inside information tipster
give strength to support
give support to aid
give temporarily lend
give temporary relief from respite
give testimony depose, testify, witness
give thanks to bless
give the eye ogle
give the facts explain
give the lie to belie, challenge, contradict, controvert, deny, dispute, explode, impugn, negate, overthrow, refute
give the once-over inspect
give the stick to cane
give to charity donate
give too much importance to overplay
give too much medicine overdose
give trouble to ail, bother
give umbrage to displease, insult
give unwillingly begrudge
give up abandon, abdicate, abnegate, abstain, break, capitulate, cease, cede, chuck, discontinue, forfeit, forgo, forsake, quit, relinquish, remit, render, renounce, resign, stop, submit, surrender, waive, yield
give up altogether abandon
give up by oath abjure
give up evil ways reform
give up power abdicate
give up tenure of vacate
give up the ghost die, pass away
give up to another cede
give up treacherously away, betray
give up wholly devote
give vent to air, discharge, emit, issue
give visual attention look
give vitality to invigorate
give voice to utter
give warning alert
give warning of portend
give way accede, buckle, budge, burst, cede, collapse, crack, crumble, crumple, disintegrate, fall, falter, reclaim, sink, succumb, surrender, yield
give way to indulge, ratify, submit

**give way to anger** fume
**give way to anxiety** worry
**give weapons** arm
**give wrong information to** misinform
**giving a pleasant smell** fragrant, odorant
**giving a wild berth to** avoiding
**giving contentment** satisfactory
**giving false testimony** perjury
**giving freely** donating, generous
**giving full details** circumstantial
**giving in** ceding
**giving in large quantities** lavish
**giving medical attention** treating
**giving milk** milch, suckle
**giving much information concisely** compendious
**giving much information in a few words** concise
**giving notice of danger** caution, warning
**giving one thing and receiving another** exchange
**giving out deep sound** resonant, sonorous
**giving partial relief** palliative
**giving pleasure** pleasurable
**giving relief** merciful
**giving serious attention and thought** careful
**giving tranquillity to** restful
**giving trouble** cumbrous
**giving up** abandonment, abnegation, ceding, cession
**Giza sight** pyramid, sphinx
**gizzard of fowl** giblets
**glabrous** bald, hairless, slick, smooth
**glacial chasm** crevasse
**glacial deposit** moraine, placer, tail
**glacial division** sérac
**glacial epoch** ice age, glacial period
**glacial fissure** crevasse
**glacial gravel ditch** escar, eskar, esker
**glacial gravel ridge** escar, eskar, esker
**glacial hill** kame
**glacial hollow** corrie, cirque
**glacial ice** sérac
**glacial mass** ice
**glacial mound** escar, eskar, esker
**glacial period** ice age
**glacial ridge** arête, escar, eskar, esker, os
**glacial snow** névé
**glacial waste deposit** drift
**glacier crack** crevasse
**glacier division** sérac
**glacier fissure** crevasse
**glacier pinnacle** sérac
**glad** blithe, bright, cheerful, cheery, contented, delighted, elated, fain, gay, gleeful, gratified, happy, jocund, jovial, joyful, joyous, merry, overjoyed, pleased, willing
**gladden** animate, brighten, cheer, delight, elate, enhearten, enliven, exhilarate, please, pleasure, rejoice, vivify
**gladdon** stinking iris
**glade** clearing
**glade shaded by trees** arbour
**gladiator armed with a net and trident** retiarius
**gladiator's weapon** sword, trident
**gladly** cheerfully, cheerily, delightedly, exuberantly, fain, gaily, gleefully, happily, heartily, joyfully, joyously, lief, merrily, mirthfully, smilingly, unreluctantly, vivaciously, willingly
**gladness** delight, gaiety, jollity, joy(fulness), pleasure
**glair** albumen, albumin, egg-white
**glamorous** alluring, attractive, beautiful, captivating, charming, dazzling, elegant, enchanting, exciting, fascinating, glossy, gorgeous, lovely, smart
**glamour** allure, appeal, attraction, beauty, charm, chic, fascination, glitter, magic, prestige, romance
**glance** cast, flash, gleam, glimpse, glisten, glitter, look, reflect
**glance at** browse, scan, skim
**glance over** browse, scan
**glance over quickly** scan
**glance quickly** peek, peep
**glance slyly** leer
**glance through** scan, skim
**glance with lascivious expression** leer
**glancing at** eyeing, ogling
**glancing blow** (side)swipe
**glancing rebound** ricochet
**gland** breast, endocrine, liver, milt, parotid, prostate, thymus, thyroid
**gland enlargement** goitre
**gland near stomach** pancreas
**gland secreting through duct** exocrine
**gland-shaped** adenoid
**glandular fever** infectious mononucleosis
**glare** brilliance, dazzle, flash, frown, gleam, glitter, gloat, glower, scowl, shine, showiness, stare
**glare at** ogle
**glare longer than** outstare
**glaring** audacious, blatant, blinding, brilliant, chromatic, conspicuous, distinct, fixing, flagrant, flaring, frowning, glimmering, glittering, gross, harsh, immodest, intense, lustrous, manifest, moping, obvious, open, outstanding, overt, rank, scowling, vacillating, visible, vivid
**glaring blunder** howler
**glaringly obvious** blatant
**glass** barometer, cup, goblet, lens, mirror, pane, potion, transparency, tumbler
**glass artisan** glazier
**glassblower** mumbler
**glass bottle** carafe
**glass bubble** bleb
**glass capsule** ampoule, phial, vial
**glass coloured blue with cobalt** smalt
**glass container** bottle, jar
**glass container for wine** bottle, carafe
**glass cover of food** bell, cloche
**glasses** eyeglasses, goggles, shades, specs, spectacles
**glass fitter** glazier
**glass flask** mat(t)rass
**glass for mosaic** tessera
**glass for paste jewels** strass
**glass for refracting light rays** lens
**glass fragments** cullet
**glass handling rod** punty
**glass ingredient** potash, sand, silica, silicon
**glass in state of fusion** metal
**glass in window** pane
**glass jar** tallboy, carboy
**glasslike** vitric
**glasslike coating** enamel
**glassmaker's oven** leer, lehr
**glass-maker's rod** pontil, punty
**glass mirror** looking-glass
**glass of beer** brew
**glass of brandy** sneaker
**glass of spirits** chasse
**glass of whisky** rubdown
**glass of wine** apéritif
**glass only partly fused** frit(t)
**glass orb** marble
**glass panel** pane
**glass rod** cane
**glass screen** window
**glass scum** gall
**glass showcase** vitrine
**glass sliver** shard
**glass tempering** annealing
**glass to assist the eye** eyeglass
**glass toy ball** marble
**glass tube** pipette
**glass used in laboratory** beaker, pipette, retort, test-tube
**glass vessel** ampoule, bottle, carboy, flask, jar, phial, vial
**glassware** crystal, glass
**glassware resistant to heat** Arcoflam, Corningware, Pyrex
**glass water-bottle** carafe
**glass wine-bottle** carafe, decanter, flagon
**glass with marbled effect** schmelze

**glassworker** glassman, glazier, servitor, snapper
**glass-wort** kali, kelpwort, marsh samphire, saltwort
**glassy** blank, clear, cold, dazed, dull, empty, expressionless, fixed, glasslike, glazed, glossy, hyaline, hyaloid, icy, lifeless, shiny, slippery, smooth, transparent, vacant, vitreous
**glassy rock** obsidian, quartz
**Glaswegian** Scot
**glaze** burnish, coat(ing), enamel, finish, gloss, lacquer, lustre, patina, polish, shine, varnish
**glazed cotton** chintz
**glazed earthenware from Holland** Delft, delftware
**glazed fissures in china** crackle
**glazed pottery** ceramic
**glazed with a caramelised sugar** brulée
**glaze on Chinese porcelain** eelskin
**glazier** glassworker
**glazier's tack** brad
**gleam** beam, flare, flash, glance, glimmer, glint, glisten, glitter, glow, ray, shimmer, shine, sparkle
**glean** achieve, acquire, advance, attain, capture, collect, conclude, deduce, derive, draw, elicit, evoke, extract, follow, gain, gather, get, improve, infer, obtain, procure, reap, reason, receive, trace, understand
**glee** bliss, buoyancy, cheer, delight, elation, felicity, gaiety, gladness, happiness, hilarity, joviality, joy, jubilation, merriment, mirth, pleasure, song
**gleeful chuckle** chortle
**gleeful sound** chuckle
**glen** combe, coomb, dale, dell, strath, valley
**glia** neuroglia
**glib** artful, easy, fluent, garrulous, loquacious, plausible, prolix, quick, ready, slick, smooth(-tongued), suave, talkative, unctuous, voluble
**glib in speech** voluble
**glib person** sophist
**glib talker** spieler
**glib urbanite** city slicker
**glide** coast, drift, elapse, float, flow, fly, glissade, graze, issue, lapse, prceed, roll, run, sail, skate, ski, skim, slide, slip, soar, stream
**glide away** elapse
**glide by** fleet, pass
**glide off** exit
**glide over** lambent
**glide over ice** skate, ski, slide
**glide over snow** ski
**glide over water** sail, skim, surf

**glider** biplane, sailplane, scooter
**glide swiftly** scrieve, sweep
**gliding dance** courante
**gliding of the voice** drag
**glimmer** beam, blink, effulge, flicker, fulgurate, glare, gleam, glint, glisten, glitter, glow, grain, hint, inkling, ray, shimmer, shine, sparkle, stream, suggestion, trace, twinkle
**glimpse** espy, feeling, glance, inkling, look, peek, peep, sight(ing), spot, spy, view
**glint** flash, gleam, glimmer, glitter, reflect, shine, sparkle, twinkle, twinkling
**glissade** descent, slope
**glisten** flash, glance, glare, gleam, glimmer, glint, glister, glitter, shimmer, shine, sparkle, twinkle
**glistening moisture** dew
**glitter** beam, brightness, coruscate, flare, flash, glare, gleam, glimmer, glint, glisten, lustre, radiance, scintillate, sheen, shimmer, shine, spangle, sparkle, twinkle
**glittering** clinquant, coruscating, flaring, flashing, gleaming, glimmering, glinting, glistening, scintillating, shimmering, shining, sparkling, twinkling
**glittering with colours** iridescent
**glittering with tinsel** clinquant
**glittery strings** tinsel
**gloat** boast, crow, enjoy, exult, eye, glare, leer, ogle, rejoice, triumph, vaunt
**global** all-inclusive, all-encompassing, comprehensive, encyclopaedic, exhaustive, general, globular, globulous, inclusive, international, orbital, planetary, rotund, round, spherical, spheroidal, thorough, total, ubiquitous, universal, unlimited, vast, whole, world(-wide)
**globate** spheroidal
**globe** earth, (eye)ball, globoid, globule, orb, oval, planet, round, sphere, spheroid, spherule, terra, terrene, world
**globular base of stem** bulb
**globular drop of liquid** blob
**globular wine-bottle** flagon
**globule** bead, bubble, drop(let), particle, pearl, pellet
**gloom** blackness, blues, cloud(iness), dark(ness), dejection, depression, despair, despondency, dimness, drear, dullness, dusk, greyness, melancholy, misery, murk(iness), obscurity, sadness, shade, shadow, sorrow, twilight, unhappiness, woe
**gloomily** eerily

**gloomily threatening** lurid
**gloomy** awesome, bad, black, blue, cheerless, dark(some), dejected, depressed, depressing, despondent, dim, disheartened, dismal, dispirited, downhearted, dreary, dull, dusky, eerie, glum, joyless, melancholy, mope, morose, murky, obscure, overcast, pessimistic, sad, saturnine, shaded, shadowy, sombre, stygian, unlit
**gloomy about future** pessimistic
**gloomy and strange** eerie
**gloomy and unsociable** morose
**gloomy mood** dumps, sulks
**gloomy person** saturnine
**gloomy state of mind** melancholy
**glorify** admire, boost, commend, deify, dignify, elevate, esteem, exalt, extol, hail, honour, idealise, idolise, increase, intensify, praise, recommend, renew, revere, sanctify
**gloriole** aureole, halo, nimbus
**glorious** admirable, beautiful, bright, brilliant, celebrated, dazzling, delightful, distinguished, divine, eminent, enjoyable, famed, famous, gorgeous, heavenly, illustrious, majestic, radiant, renowned, triumphant, wonderful
**glory** ad gloriam (L), adoration, beauty, blessing, brilliance, celebrity, delight, dignity, distinction, eminence, exult, fame, grandeur, gratitude, greatness, heaven, homage, honour, illustriousness, immortality, kudos, magnificence, majesty, pomp, praise, prestige, radiance, rejoice, relish, renown, resplendence, splendour, triumph, worship
**glory around idealised person** halo
**glory-of-the-snow** chionodoxa
**glory to God in the highest** Gloria in Excelsis Deo
**glory to the Father** Gloria Patri
**gloss** analysis, annotate, annotation, appearance, comment(ary), critique, exegesis, explain, explanation, front, glaze, interpretation, lustre, polish, sheen, shine, varnish
**glossary** concordance, dictionary, encyclopedia, language, lexicon, vocabulary, wordbook
**gloss on old wood** patina
**gloss over** camouflage, conceal, disguise, hide, mask, varnish, veil, veneer, whitewash
**glossy** deceptive, elegant, false, feigned, glistening, glowing, imitation, luminous, lustrous, satiny, shiny, silken, sleek, synthetic, unreal, velvety

**glossy and smooth** sleek
**glossy black** raven
**glossy black bird** drongo, raven
**glossy cotton fabric** sateen
**glossy fabric** alpaca, gloria, sateen, satin, sharkskin, silk, taffeta
**glossy finish** enamel
**glossy material** satin
**glossy paint** enamel
**glossy silk cloth** lustring, lutestring
**glossy transparent paper** glassine
**glove** gauntlet, mitt(en)
**glove box** cubby
**glove leather** kid, napa, suede
**glow** ardour, blush, brighten, brightness, brilliance, burn(ing), colour, effulgence, enthusiasm, excitement, fervour, fill, flush, gleam, glimmer, gusto, intensity, light, passion, phosphorescence, radiance, radiate, redden, shine, smoulder, splendour, thrill, tingle, vehemence, vividness, warmth
**glower** frown, fume, glare, look, scowl, stare
**glow faintly** gleam
**glowing** aglow, beaming, blushing, bright(ening), burning, colouring, filling, flaming, florid, flushed, flushing, gleaming, glimmering, radiant, radiating, red(dening), rich, shining, smouldering, suffused, thrilling, tingling, vivid, warm
**glowing appearance** radiance
**glowing cinder** ember
**glowing piece of coal** ember, gleed
**glowing with feeling** ardent
**glowing with good health** radiant
**glowing with heat** incandescent
**glowing with soft radiance** lambent
**glue** adhesive, agglutinate, attach, cement, fasten, fixative, gum, join, mortar, paste, plaster, putty, sealant, solder, stick, stucco, viscidity
**glue on** adhere
**glue shut** seal
**gluey** colloid
**gluey mud** slime
**gluey substance** colloid
**gluey tree sap** resin
**glum** churlish, crabbed, crestfallen, crusty, doleful, down, moody, sad, serious, sulky, sullen, surly
**glumness** crustiness, dejectedness, dolefulness, gloominess, gruffness, grumpiness, lowness, moodiness, moroseness, saturnineness, sourness, sulkiness, sullenness
**glut** choke, excess, gorge, overabundance, oversupply, pleroma, sate, saturation, superabundance, superfluity, surfeit, surplus
**glutinous** adhesive, cohesive, gluey, gummy, sticky, viscous
**glutinous edible part of the turtle** calipash, calipee
**glutted state** satiety
**glutton** cormorant, eater, gobbler, gorger, go(u)rmand, go(u)rmandiser, guzzler, hog, omnivore, pantophagist, pig, whale
**gluttony** go(u)rmandising, go(u)rmandise, go(u)rmandism, greed(iness), insatiability, piggishness, rapacity, voracity
**gnarled** contorted, distorted, gnarly, knotted, knurled, lined, rough, rugged, shrivelled, shrunken, twisted, weather-beaten, withered, wizened, wrinkled
**gnarly** gnarled, knotty, lined, rugged, shrivelled, shrunken, twisted, withered, wrinkled
**gnash teeth** gnarl
**gnat** midge, mosquito, muggie
**gnaw** bite, chew, consume, devour, eat, erode, fret, harry, haunt, munch, nag, nibble, niggle, plague, prey, trouble, wear, worry
**gnawing animal** rodent
**gnawing rodent** mouse, rat
**gnome** dwarf, elf, goblin, imp, leprechaun, pixie, pixy, sprite, troll
**gnomon of sundial** style
**gnu** wildebeest
**go** advance, agree, belong, depart, disappear, elapse, energy, extend, fare, function, gae (Sc), gang (Sc), jibe, journey, leave, move, pass, proceed, progress, reach, result, retreat, scram, shoo, travel, try, vamoose, vanish, voetsak, voetsek, walk, withdraw, work
**go aboard** embark
**go about** act, address, approach, begin, circulate, perform, tackle, travel, undertake, wander, work
**go about as a vagrant** tramp
**go about begging** cadge
**go about dreamily** moon
**go about idly** gad
**go about pilfering** maraud
**go about restlessly** flutter
**go abroad** migrate
**go a-courting** woo
**goad** anger, ankus(ha), annoy, arouse, crook, dare, drive, egg, exhort, harass, hound, impel(ling), impetus, incense, incenting, incite(ment), inciting, instigate, instigating, irritate, irritating, irritation, jolt, lance, lash(ing), motivation, persecute, pique, poke, pole, pressure, prick(ing), prod(ding), prompt(ing), propel(ling), rod, rowel, ruffle, spear, spur(ring), stave, stick, stimulate, stimulating, stimulation, stimulus, sting(ing), taunt, thrust, urge, urging, worry(ing)
**goading remark** taunt
**go after** follow
**go against** oppose
**go ahead** advance, agreement, assent, begin, clearance, consent, continue, lead, move, permission, precede, proceed, progress, sanction
**go-ahead** agreement, ambitious, assent, authorisation, clearance, consent, enterprising, leave, OK, permission, pioneering, progressive, sanction, up-and-coming
**go aimlessly** drift, roam, stray, wander
**goal** aim, ambition, aspiration, bourn(e), design, destination, destiny, end(point), ideal, intent(ion), limit, mark, object(ive), purpose, score, target, terminal, terminus
**goaler** captor, guard, jailer, keeper, screw, warden, warder
**go along** accompany, agree, assent, escort, follow, join, travel
**go a long way round** circuitous, indirect
**go along with** accompany, assent, escort, join
**go around** bypass, circumvent, skirt, via
**go as a guard** escort
**go ashore** disembark, land
**go astray** backslide, err
**goat** Amalthae, Amaltheia, argue, attack, billy, blame, criticise, fool, nanny
**go at a great speed** pace
**goat call** baa, bleat
**go at easy gallop** canter
**go at easy speed** lope
**goatee** beard
**goat god** Pan
**goat-hair cloth** camlet, mohair
**goat-like antelope** chamois
**goatlike Asian mammal** tahr, thar
**goat-like Greek deity** Pan, satyr
**goat's cry** bleat
**goatskin leather** morocco
**goat's-milk cheese** feta
**goatsucker** nighthawk, nightjar, whippoorwill
**goat's wool** cashmere
**go at top speed** sprint
**go away** begone, decamp, depart, disappear, exit, flee, leave, recede, retreat, scat, scram, shoo, vanish, voetsak, voetsek, withdraw
**go away from** quit

**go away secretly** abscond
**go AWOL** desert
**gob** clot, mouth, sailor, spit, tar
**go back** backslide, desert, ebb, forsake, recede, regress, reneg(u)e, repudiate, retract, retreat, return, reverse, revert
**go back on** betray, contradict, disavow, forsake, reneg(u)e, repudiate, retract
**go back on a promise** reneg(u)e
**go back over** retrace
**go back to** reverse
**go bad** addle, fester, putrefy, rot, suppurate
**go bankrupt** fail
**gobble** bolt, consume, cram, devour, eat, gorge, gulp, guzzle, stuff, swallow
**gobbler** go(u)rmandiser, turkey-cock
**go before** antecede, precede
**go before in rank** precede
**go below the surface** sink
**go beneath water** submerge
**go berserk** rampage
**go-between** agent, arbiter, bawd, broker, contact, dealer, factor, informer, intermediary, liaison, means, mediator, medium, messenger, middleman, pander
**go beyond** exceed, (sur)pass
**go beyond the limit** exceed
**Gobi desert** Hanhai, Shamo
**Gobi desert lake** Hara
**goblet** beaker, chalice, draught, drink, (drinking-)cup, glass, hanap, jeroboam, potion, rummer, skull, tallboy, tass(ie) (Sc), teacup, trophy, tumbler, wineglass
**goblin** apparition, bogey(man), brownie, demon, devil, elf, fiend, genie, gnome, gremlin, hobgoblin, imp, kobold, leprechaun, nis, pixie, pixy, pooka, Puck, red-cap, spectre, spirit, sprite, troll
**goblin of Arabian tales** genie, jinnee
**go brown** tan
**go bust** break, fail, insolvent
**go by** adopt, elapse, exceed, flow, follow, heed, observe, pass, proceed, trust
**go by air** fly
**go by bus** ride
**go by car** drive, motor, ride
**go by plane** fly
**go by ship** sail
**go by vehicle** ride
**god** deity, dieu (F), divine, icon, idol, image, numen, spirit, supreme
**God** Adonai, Almighty, Elohim, Jehova(h)
**God be willing** Deo volente (L)

**God be with you** Deus vobiscum (L)
**goddesses inspiring learning and the arts** muses
**goddess of abundance** Ops
**goddess of agriculture** Bau, Ceres, Demeter, Ops
**goddess of air** Aura, Hera
**goddess of arts** Athena, muse
**goddess of beauty** Freya, Lakshmi, Shree, S(h)ri, Venus
**goddess of chance** Fortuna
**goddess of childbirth** Ilithyia, Levana, Lucina
**goddess of corn** Ceres
**goddess of crops** Anena, Annona, Anona
**goddess of dawn** Aurora, Eos, Etain, Matuta, Thesan, Ushas
**goddess of dead** Freyja, Nut
**goddess of destiny** Fates, Nona, Norn, Urd
**goddess of dew** Herse
**goddess of discord** Ate, Discordia, Eris
**goddess of earth** Arura, Ceres, Dana, Dione, Eos, Ge(aea), Ops, Papa, Tari, Tellus, Terra, Themis
**goddess of evil** Ate
**goddess of faithfulness** Fides
**goddess of fate** Moerae, Nona, Norn, Parca
**goddess of fertility** Astarte, Danu, Don, Frija, Ishtar, Isis, Ma, Ops, Serapis, Tellus
**goddess of fire** Brigit, Hestia
**goddess of flowers** Chloris, Flora, Nanna
**goddess of fortune** Fortuna, Lakshmi, Tyche
**goddess of fruit** Pomona
**goddess of fruitful earth** Demeter
**goddess of fruitfulness** Freya
**goddess of grain** Ceres
**goddess of harvest** Carpo, Ceres, Ops
**goddess of healing** Brigit, Eir, Gula, Hina
**goddess of health** Damia, Hygeia, Salus, Valetudo
**goddess of hearth** Frigg, Hestia, Vesta
**goddess of history** Saga
**goddess of hope** Spes
**goddess of horses** Epona
**goddess of hunting** Artemis, Diana
**goddess of justice** Astraea, Dike, Maat, Themis
**goddess of light** Cupra
**goddess of love** Aphrodite, Astarte, Athor, Dwyn, Freyja, Hathor, Isis, Venus
**goddess of magic** Hecate
**goddess of marriage** Frigg, Hera
**goddess of maternity** Apet, Mut

**goddess of memory** Mnemosyne
**goddess of mercy** Kwannon
**goddess of mischief** Ate, Eris
**goddess of moon** Aah, Artemis, Astarte, Chia, Diana, Isis, Losna, Luna, Moon, Phoebe, Selena, Susanoo
**goddess of motherhood** Isis
**goddess of music** Benten
**goddess of nature** Artemis, Cybele, Isis, Nymph
**goddess of night** Nox, Nyx, Ratri
**goddess of ocean** Nina
**goddess of peace** Eirene, Irene, Pax
**goddess of plenty** Nehalennia, Ops
**goddess of poetry** Brigit, Sarasvati
**goddess of prosperity** Salus
**goddess of purity** Astraea
**goddess of rainbows** Iris, Ixchel
**goddess of retribution** Ara, Ate, Nemesis
**goddess of revenge** Nemesis
**goddess of rivers** Anqet, Boann
**goddess of rumour** Fama
**goddess of sea** Amphitrite, Doris, Eurynome, Nina, Ran, Tethys, Thetis
**goddess of sky** Juno, Nut
**goddess of sorcery** Hecate
**goddess of sorrow** Mara
**goddess of speech** Vach
**goddess of storms** Ran
**goddess of sun** Amaterasu, Shapash
**goddess of truth** Ma, Maat
**goddess of underworld** Allatu, Gerd
**goddess of vegetation** Ceres, Cora, Cotys, Kore, Ops
**goddess of vengeance** Nemesis
**goddess of victory** Nike, Victoria
**goddess of volcanoes** Pele
**goddess of war** Alea, Anatu, Bellona, Enyo, Minerva, Morrigan, Tiu, Tyr, Vacuna
**goddess of wealth** Fortuna, Lakshmi, Ops
**goddess of wisdom** Athena, Minerva, Pallas, Ushas
**goddess of witchcraft** Hecate
**goddess of woods** Artemis, Diana
**goddess of youth** Hebe, Idunn, Juventas
**god-forsaken** desolate
**god killing** deicide
**godless** atheistic, depraved, evil, heathen, impious, irreligious, irreverent, pagan, profane, sacrilegious, ungodly, unholy, unrighteous, wicked
**godless person** atheist
**godlike** deific, divine
**godly** blameless, devout, divine, God-fearing, good, holy, innocent,

pious, pure, religious, righteous, saintly, virtuous
**god of agriculture** Faunus, Ogmios, Picus, Tamu, Urash
**god of altar fire** Agni
**god of ancient Egypt** Amen
**god of ancient Memphis** Ptah
**god of Arcadia** Pan
**god of arts** Apollo, Siva
**god of atmosphere** Hadad
**god of censure** Momus
**god of chaos** Nu(n)
**god of childbirth** Bes
**god of commerce** Mercury
**god of corn** Cat
**god of craftsmen** Goibniu, Gwydion, Lug, Ptah, Vulcan, Weland
**god of culture** Odin
**god of dance** Bes, Siva
**god of darkness** Dylan, Erebus, Loki, Set
**god of dawn** Bochica
**god of day** Horus
**god of dead** Mot, Odin, Orcus, Yama
**god of destruction** Loki, Siva
**god of dreams** Morpheus
**god of earth** Bel, Dagan, Enlil, Geb, Jord, Seb, Tellus
**god of eloquence** Mercury
**god of erotic desire** Kama
**god of evening star** Hesperus
**god of evil** Ahriman, Bes, Fomor, Set, Seth
**god of fertility** Frey, Ninib, Rongo, Shango
**god of fields** Faun, Pan, Silvanus, Telipinu
**god of fire** Agni, Nusku, Rudra, Vulcan
**god of flocks** Pan, Tammuz, Veles
**god of flocks and pastures** Pan
**god of fortune** Ganesha
**god of Hades** Dis, Pluto
**god of happiness** Hotei, Jurojin
**god of harvests** Akakanet, Cronus, Min
**god of healing** Aesculapius, Apollo
**god of herds** Faun
**god of households** Lares
**god of hunting** Gwynn, Ulir
**god of justice** Forsete, Forseti, Ptah
**god of learning** Imhotep
**god of light** Amida, Apollo, Balder, Horus, Mithras
**god of love** Amor, Angus, Ares, Bhaga, Cupid, Eros, Freyer, Frikko, Kama
**god of manly youth** Apollo
**god of marriage** Hymen
**god of medicine** Aesclapius, Asclepus
**god of Memphis** Apis, Ptah
**god of mirth** Comus, Izume, Komos, Momus
**god of mischief** Lok, Loki

**god of moon** Mannar, Sin, Soma, Thoth
**god of music** Apollo, Bes, Bran
**god of nature** Mamtou, Marsyas, Min
**god of ocean** Oceanus
**god of pastures** Pan
**god of peace** Forseti
**god of pleasure** Bes, Besa
**god of poetry** Brage, Bragi, Bran
**god of prosperity** Frey, Jessis
**god of rain** Baal, Indra, Parjanya, Rongo, Tlaloc
**god of rain and thunder** Indra
**god of revelry** Comus, Komos
**god of ridicule** Momus
**god of rivers** Alpheus, Hapi
**god of roads** Dosojin
**god of sea** Aegir, Antaeus, Dylan, Ea, Hler, Ler, Manannan, Neptune, Poseidon, Susanoo, Triton, Yam
**god of shepherds** Pales, Pan
**god of sky** Anu, Indra, Tien, Tiu, Tyr, Uranus, Zeus, Zio, Ziu
**god of sleep** Morpheus
**god of storm** Adad, Addu, Rudra
**god of sun** Amen, Amon, Aten, Helios, Lugh, Mithras, Phoebus, Ra, Sol, Susanoo, Tum, Vishnu
**god of thunder** Adad, Dis, Donar, Perun, Shango, Thor, Zeus
**god of underworld** Bile, Dis, Hades, Math, Pluto, Pwyll, Serapis
**god of victory** Tyr
**god of war** Ares, Ashur, Coel, Er, Indra, Mars, Odin, Skanda, Thor, Tiu, Tyr, Woden
**god of wealth** Daikoku, Platus, Plutus
**god of wind** Adad, Aeolus, Huracan, Odin, Typhon
**god of wine** Bacchus, Dionysus
**god of wisdom** Ea, Marduk, Nebo, Odin, Tat, Thoth
**god of wisdom and war** Odin, Wotan
**god of woods** Dryad
**god of youth** Apollo
**go door-to-door** peddle
**god or goddess** deity
**go down** collapse, decline, decrease, degenerate, descend, deteriorate, disappear, drop, fail, fall, founder, lose, set, sink, submerge, submit, succumb, suffer, vanish
**go down freely** fall
**godparent** sponsor
**God protect you** Dieu vous garde (F)
**God's acre** cemetery, churchyard, graveyard, necropolis
**God's elect** Israel
**godsend** benediction, blessing, bonanza, boon, manna, miracle, windfall
**God willing** Deo volente (L)

**God wills it** Deus vult (L)
**goes like a rocket** zooms
**goes with a suit** tie
**goes with neither** nor
**go far** advance, progress, succeed
**go fast** gee, run, speed
**go faster** gee (up)
**go faster than** outpace, outstrip
**go first** lead
**go fly a kite** drag, scram, split
**go for** admire, aim, attack, choose, enjoy, favour, fetch, like, obtain, prefer, reach, seek, stretch
**go for and bring** fetch
**go forth** egress, exit
**go forward** advance, proceed
**go from one country to another** migrate
**go from one place to another** tour, travel
**go from place to place** peripatetic
**go furtively** sneak, steal
**go-getter** planner
**goggle** eye, gape, gawk, gaze, glare, leer, marvel, ogle, stare, wonder
**goggle box** television, TV
**go hand in hand with** attend
**go hastily** rush, speed
**go hungry** fast, starve
**go in** adopt, embrace, engage, enter, ingress, penetrate, practise, undertake
**go in again** re-enter
**go in for** adopt, choose, embrace, enter, follow, practise, pursuit, undertake
**go in for competition** enter
**go in front** lead
**go in front again** relead
**going about** afoot
**going to a worse condition** retrogress
**go in peace** vade in pace (L)
**go in pursuit** chase
**go in search for** quest
**go in search of pleasure** gad
**go into** analyse, begin, consider, develop, discuss, dissect, enter, examine, investigate, probe, pursue, review, scrutinise, study, undertake
**go into action** start
**go into detail** amplify
**go into hiding** isolate, seclude
**go into raptures** rave
**go into red** overdraw
**go into ruin** deteriorate
**goitre** enlargement, struma, swelling, tracheocele
**gold** affluence, assets, aurum, bullion, cash, chrys, coin, fortune, funds, gilt, jewels, money, opulence, or (F), oro, plenty, property, resources, riches, treasure, valuables, wealth

**gold and silver lace trimming**
    passementerie
**gold bar** ingot
**gold-bearing** auric
**gold before coining** bullion
**gold cast in a mould** ingot
**gold coin** dobln, doubloon, ducat,
    eagle, cu, guilder, guinea, gulden,
    Krugerrand, lois d'or, moidore,
    napoleon, pahlavi, pistole, solidus,
    sovereign
**gold coin of Ancient Persia** daric
**gold coin of Iran** pahlavi
**gold-coloured** aureate
**gold-coloured alloy** ormolu
**gold-coloured alloy of copper and zinc**
    oroide
**gold-coloured fish** dory
**gold-coloured ide** orf
**gold-coloured medium-sweet cherry**
    oloroso
**gold-coloured metal** ormolu
**gold embroidery** orphrey
**golden** advantageous, aureate, auric,
    best, blond(e), bright, brilliant,
    excellent, fair, favourable, gilt,
    glorious, happy, (in)valuable, joyful,
    lustrous, mellow, precious, priceless,
    promising, prosperous, resplendent,
    rich, rosy, shining, successful,
    tanned, timely, yellow
**golden beaker** saga
**golden bug** ladybird
**golde-calf maker** Aaron
**golden crowfoot** buttercup
**goldeneye** whistle-duck
**golden oriole** loriot
**Golden State** California
**golden syrup** treacle
**golden-touch king** Midas
**golden yellow bird** oriole
**gold filling** inlay
**goldfish** orfe
**gold French coin** cu
**gold in heraldry** or(e)
**gold inlay on steel** damascene
**gold mass** ingot, nugget
**gold or silver lace** orris
**gold paint** gilt
**gold-plate** gild
**gold quality unit** carat
**gold-rush city of Alaska** Nome
**gold seeker in Alaska** klondiker
**goldsmith's mandril** triblet
**gold-threaded material** lam
**gold-touch king** Midas
**gold unit** carat
**gold unit of Lithuania** lit
**gold-weight unit** carat, ounce
**golf attendant** caddie, caddy
**golf ball support** tee

**golf club** brassie, cleek, driver, iron,
    mashie, midiron, niblick, putter,
    spoon, wedge, wood
**golf-club with deep iron head** niblick
**golf course** links
**golf course cry** fore
**golf course depression** cup
**golf course parts** bunker, fairways,
    greens, rough, tees, trap
**golf cup** hole, ryder
**golf device** iron, tee
**golfer** legman, teer
**golf error** hook, pull, slice
**golfer's attendant** caddie, caddy
**golfer's dream** hole-in-one
**golfer's objective** hole
**golfer's porter** caddie
**golfer's start** tee
**golfer's target** cup
**golfer's warning shout** fore
**golf gadget** tee
**golf handicap** half-one
**golf holes unplayed** bye
**golfing cry** fore
**golfing hazard** bunker, rough,
    sand-pit, trap, water hole
**golfing standard** par
**golfing start** tee
**golf instructor** pro
**golf iron for lob shots** mashie
**golf peg** tee
**golf position** stance
**golf score** ace, birdie, bogey, eagle,
    hole-in-one, par, stroke
**golf score of one stroke over par for**
    **the hole** bogey
**golf score of one stroke under par for**
    **the hole** birdie
**golf score of three strokes under par**
    **for the hole** albatross
**golf score of two strokes under par for**
    **the hole** eagle
**golf scratch** par
**golf starting point** tee
**golf stick** club
**golf stroke** baff, chip, drive, loft, putt,
    sclaff
**golf term** lie
**golf tournament anyone may enter**
    open
**golf trolley** buggy, cart
**goliard** jester, minstrel
**Goliath's foe** David
**Goliath's slayer** David
**go like a fish** swim
**golly** gee, gosh
**go mad** rave
**gondolier's boat song** barcarol(l)e
**gone** ago, away, lost, off, out, past
**gone before** past
**gone beyond recall** irrevocable
**gone by** ago, past

**gone off** rancid
**gone out of use** extinct, obsolete
**gone to bed** abed
**gone up** risen
*Gone with the Wind* **hero** Rhett Butler
*Gone with the Wind* **heroine** Scarlett
    O'Hara
**gonfalon** banner, eagle, flag, labarum,
    standard, vexillum
**gong** bell
**goober** peanut
**good** à la bonne heure (F), able,
    admirable, agreeable, beneficent,
    beneficial, benevolent, capable,
    capital, clever, commendable,
    compete, competent, conscientious,
    deserving, efficient, excellent,
    exceptional, exemplary, expert,
    favourable, fit, friendly, genuine,
    gracious, heedful, honest,
    honourable, humane, immaculate,
    kind(ly), merit(orious), moral, nice,
    obedient, obliging, pious, qualified,
    ready, reliable, righteous, safe,
    satisfactory, suitable, suited,
    unblemished, unimpeached, upright,
    valid, valuable, virtue, virtuous,
    well-behaved, well-disposed, worthy
**good breeding** bon ton (F)
**goodbye** adieu, adios, aloha,
    arrivederci (I), au revoir (F), ave,
    cheerio, ciao (I), dismissal, farewell,
    leave, sayonara (J), ta-ta, totsiens,
    valediction
**good chance** opportunity
**good condition** kilter, kelter
**good day** bonjour (F)
**good digestion** eupepsia
**good faith** bona fides, sincerity
**good feelings** amity, friendship,
    goodwill
**good fellow** brick, hearty, sport,
    Trojan, trump
**good fellowship** affability,
    camaraderie, clubbiness,
    comradeship, congeniality,
    friendliness, mateship,
    pleasantness, sociability
**good-for-nothing fellow** idler,
    Jackeen, layabout, lazy-bones,
    loafer, rapscallion, reprobate,
    scal(l)awag, scallywag, useless,
    wastrel
**good fortune** bonne fortune (F), hap,
    hit, luck, prosperity, weal, welfare,
    well-being, windfall
**good health!** cheers, prosit (G), slàinte
    (Sc), slànte mhath (Sc)
**good housekeeping** husbandry
**good humour** affability, amiability,
    cheerfulness, jollity, joviality,
    joyousness, vivacity

**good-humoured** affable, amiable, approachable, cheerful, (con)genial, expansive, good-tempered, happy, jovial, pleasant
**good-humoured chortle** chuckle
**good-humoured parody** spoof
**good judgment** commonsense
**good-looking** alluring, attractive, beautiful, comely, elegant, enchanting, fair, glamorous, handsome, personable, pretty, rosy-cheeked, seemly, tasteful, well-favoured
**good looks** beauty, comeliness, attractiveness, glamour, handsomeness, loveliness, prettiness
**good loser** sport
**good luck** benefaction, blessing, boon, fortune, jackpot, luck, prosperity, windfall
**good luck charm** mascot, talisman
**good luck to you!** prosit (G)
**good manners** breeding, courtesy
**good meal** feast
**good moral conduct** morality
**good-morning** bonjour (F), good-day
**good name** honour
**good nature** affability, amiability, bonhomie (F)
**good-natured** amiable, pleasant
**good-naturedly frank and hearty** bluff
**goodness** benevolence, essence, excellence, generosity, integrity, kindness, morality, probity, quality, strength, value, virtue, worth
**good-night** bonsoir (F)
**good old days** past, yesteryear
**good opinion** approval
**good opinion of oneself** self-esteem
**good or ill fortune** luck
**good place to keep cash** safe
**good poker hand** fullhouse
**good prospect** likelihood
**good quality** virtue
**good quoit throw** ringer
**good reason** logic, sense
**good reception** bon accueil (F)
**good reputation** credit
**good riddance** relief, rubbish
**goods** advantages, avails, belongings, benefits, chattels, commodities, effects, freight, furnishings, furniture, gains, gear, interests, merchandise, merits, moralities, movables, paraphernalia, possessions, profits, property, rights, services, stock, stuff, things, uses, virtues, wares, worths
**Good Samaritan** humanitarian
**goods are taken on this for trial** appro
**goods as shipped** invoice
**goods at reduced prices** sale

**goods carried on ship or aircraft** cargo
**goods cast adrift** lagan, ligan
**goods cast overboard** jetsam
**good seat** ringside
**good sense** reason, sanity
**goods for sale** merchandise, wares
**good soil** loam
**goods on hand** stock
**good spirit** genie
**goods shipped** shipment
**goods shipped by public carrier** freight
**goods sold** sales
**goods thrown overboard** jetsam
**goods transport charge** airfreight, ferriage, railage
**good style** bon ton (F)
**goods vehicle** lorry, truck, van
**goods washed ashore** flotsam
**good taste** goût (F), elegance
**good thing** beauty
**good to eat** comestible, yummy
**good turn** favour
**goodwill** acquiescence, affection, amity, benevolence, compassion, favour, friendliness, friendship, generosity, heartiness, humanity, kindness, loving-kindliness, sincerity, sympathy, zeal
**good wish** Godspeed
**good wishes** compliments, congratulations, felicitations, greetings
**good working order** kelter, kilter
**good year** vintage
**goody-goody** pious, priggish, sanctimonious, self-righteous
**gooey** sticky
**goof** blunder, botch, err, idle, mistake
**go off** abscond, bang, burst, decamp, depart, deteriorate, detonate, discharge, dislike, erupt, explode, fire, fulminate, happen, leave, loathe, occur, part, pop, proceed, putrefy, quit, rot, turn, vanish
**go off course** deviate, veer, yaw
**go off in changed direction** swerve
**go off with a bang** explode
**goofy** infatuated, silly
**go on** abide, begin, chatter, commence, continue, en-, endure, happen, last, occur, persist, proceed, progress, restart, stay, waffle
**go on a diet** slim
**go on after interruption** resume
**go on a horse** ride
**go on all fours** crawl
**go on and off** intermit
**go on a ship** board
**go on a voyage** sail

**go on bent knee to ask** beg, beseech, implore
**go on board** embark
**go on continually** ceaseless
**go on foot** pedestrian
**go on foot laboriously** trudge
**go on for ages** secular
**go on horseback** ride
**go on one's knees** kneel
**go on pension** retire
**go on sea** sail
**go on stage** act
**go on without pause** segue
**goose** nene
**goose cry** honk, crackle
**goose flesh** horripilation, pimples
**goose genus** Anserinae (L)
**goose sound** honk
**go out** depart, exit, expire, leave, outward
**go out buying** shop
**go out of one's way** detour, deviate, willing
**go out of sight** disappear
**go out of use** obsolete
**go out with** date
**go over** audit, check, detail, examine, inspect, list, peruse, read, recall, rehearse, repeat, review, revise, scan, skim, study
**go overboard** overdo, overreact
**go over carefully** scan
**go over the main points again** recap(itulate)
**go past** circumvent
**go places** advance, proceed, progress, succeed, tour, travel
**go quickly** fly, hasten, hie, scoot, speed
**go rapidly** run
**gore** blood(shed), butchery, carnage, slaughter
**gorge** abyss, bolt, canyon, chasm, cleft, clough, cram, defile, devour, disgust, feed, fill, fissure, gap, glut, gobble, go(u)rmandise, gully, gulp, guzzle, hog, overeat, pass, ravine, sate, stuff, surfeit, swallow, wolf
**gorgeous** attractive, beautiful, brilliant, dazzling, delightful, enjoyable, fine, glamorous, glorious, good(-looking), grand, lovely, luxurious, magnificent, pleasing, ravishing, resplendent, rich, showy, splendid, stunning, sumptuous, superb
**Gorgon** Euryale, Medusa, Stheno
**gormandiser** glutton
**go round** revolve, rotate
**go round about** circumambient
**go round continuously** circulate
**go round the flank of** outflank
**gorse** furze, whin

**gory** blood-soaked, bloodstained, bloody, brutal, disgusting, ghastly, grim, gruesome, lurid, macabre, murderous, red, revolting, sanguinary, sanguine, savage, violent
**gosh** gee, golly
**go spare** enrage, mad
**gospel** certainty, credo, creed, doctrine, fact, message, news, revelation, teaching, testament, tidings, truth, verity
**gospel preacher** evangelist
**gospel writer** evangelist, John, Luke, Mark, Matthew
**gossamer** airy, cobwebby, delicate, fine, flimsy, gauzy, insubstantial, light, sheer, shimmering, silky, thin
**gossamer-like** wispy
**gossip** babbler, bavardage (F), blab, blether, busybody, chatterbox, chinwag, (chit)chat, gabble, gossip-monger, hearsay, jaw, prate, prattle(r), quidnunc, report, rumour(-monger), scandal(monger), talebearer, tattle(r), telltale, tittle-tattle, whisper(er), yarn
**gossip idly** prate, tattle
**gossipy** chatty, newsy
**gossipy person** flibbertigibbet
**go suddenly** scoot
**go swiftly** run
**go the rounds** patrol
**go through** audit, bear, brave, check, consume, discuss, endure, examine, exhaust, experience, explore, face, hunt, investigate, look, perform, rehearse, scan, scrutinise, search, squander, suffer, tolerate, undergo, use, withstand
**go through logical processes** ratiocinate
**go to** attend
**go to and fro** swing
**go to a restaurant** eat out
**go to bat** advocate, champion, defend, support
**go to bed** retire
**go to court** litigate
**go together** accord, agree, court, date, fit, harmonise, match, see, woo
**go together with** accompany
**go to law** litigate, proceed, sue
**go to live in another country** emigrate
**go too fast** speed
**go to one's head** dizzy, excite, intoxicate
**go too quickly** speed
**go too slow** lag
**go to pieces** break, crumple, decompose, disintegrate, shatter
**go to pot** deteriorate

**go to ruin** degenerate
**go to see** visit
**go to the dogs** degenerate, deteriorate
**go to the wall** collapse, fail, fall
**go toward sunrise** east
**gouge** cheat, chisel, claw, cut, dig, extract, force, furrow, gash, groove, hack, hollow, incise, incision, notch, scoop, score, scratch, slash, swindle, trench
**gouge out** bore
**gouging chisel** scorper
**goulash** stew
**go under** collapse, default, die, drown, fail, fold, founder, sink, submerge, succumb
**go under an assumed name** incognito
**go underground** hide
**go unsteadily** yaw
**go up** ascend, bounce, climb, leap, mount, rise, spring, uprise
**gourd** calabash, melon, pepo, pumpkin, squash, vegetable
**gourd fruit** cucumber, melon, pepo
**gourd shell serving as liquid holder** calabash
**gourmand** bon vivant (F), epicure, gastronome, glutton(ous), gorger, gourmet, guzzler, hog, pig
**gourmet** bon vivant (F), bon viveur, connoisseur, epicure(an), gastronome(r), go(u)rmand
**gout in the foot** podagra
**gout in the head** cephalagra
**gouty** arthritic
**govern** check, command, conduct, contain, control, decide, determine, direct, discipline, dominate, guide, influence, lead, manage, master, order, oversee, pilot, preside, quell, regulate, reign, restrain, rule, steer, subdue, superintend, supervise, sway, tame
**governed by bishops** episcopal
**governed by the movements of the sea** tidal
**governess** amah, ayah, bonne (F), companion, duenna, gouvernante (F), guide, instructress, mentor, nanny, nurse(maid), teacher, tut(o)ress
**govern harshly** oppress
**governing** commanding, reigning, ruling
**governing body** senate
**governing upper house** senate
**government** administration, authority, charge, command, conduct, control, direction, domination, dominion, establishment, executive, guidance, law, management, ministry, powers-that-be, régime, regulation,

restraint, rule, sovereignty, state, superintendence, supervision, surveillance, sway
**government by a few** oligarchy
**government by all members of a community** pantisocracy
**government by bishops** episcopacy, episcopate
**government by citizen possessing property** timocracy
**government by eight rulers** octarchy
**government by elderly men** gerontocracy
**government by élite** aristocracy
**government by force** coercion
**government by holy persons** hagiocracy
**government by one person** monocracy
**government by paupers** ptochocracy
**government by priests** hagiarchy, hierocracy, theocracy
**government by seven rulers** heptarchy
**government by the army** stratocracy
**government by the best in birth** aristocracy
**government by the mob** ochlocracy
**government by the nobility** aristocracy
**government by the people** democracy
**government by the rich** plutocracy
**government by the workers** ergatocracy
**government by three rulers** triumvirate
**government by women** gynarchy, matriarchy
**government department** bureau
**government department in charge of the revenue** exchequer, finance
**government departments of Vatican** Curia
**government employee** official
**government envoy** emissary
**government gratuity** grant
**government leaders** cabinet
**government levy** tax
**government messenger** emissary
**government ministers' group** cabinet
**government of a prince** principality
**government of bishops** episcopacy
**government permit** licence
**government representative** consul
**government tax** VAT
**governor** administrator, bureaucrat, chief, director, executive, head, magistrate, officer, potentate, president, principal, regent, regulator, ruler, satrap, viceroy
**governor of a prison** alcaide
**govern unjustly** misrule
**govern with tyranny** oppress
**go well** blend

**go well with** suit
**go with** accompany, accord, agree, belong, blend, complement, correspond, fit, harmonise, match, suit
**go with irregular slipping motion** slither
**go with me** vade mecum
**go without** abstain, forgo, lack, spare, want
**go without food** diet, fast, starve
**go with speed** run
**gown** dress, frock, robe
**go wrong** backfire, degenerate, err, fail, misfire, sin, stray
**goy** Gentile, non-Jew
**grab** annex, appropriate, bag, capture, catch, clutch, collar, commandeer, grasp, grip, hent, hold, impress, nab, pluck, rap, seize, snatch, strike
**grab at** clasp, clutch, grasp, gripe, snatch
**grabber** snatcher
**grace** adorn, attractiveness, beautify, beauty, benignity, charm, clemency, comeliness, deck, devoutness, dignify, ease, elegance, embellish, enhance, favour, gracefulness, holiness, kindness, leniency, piety, polish, refinement, symmetry
**grace at table** benedicite
**graceful** agile, beautiful, becoming, elegant, natural, refined, tasteful
**graceful animal** gazelle
**graceful being** fairy, peri
**graceful bird** swan
**graceful branch** spray
**graceful female dancer** ballerina
**graceful flowing melody** cantilena
**graceful furniture** sheraton
**graceful girl** nymph, sylph
**graceful horse** Arab
**graceful in appearance** elegant
**gracefully** agilely, beautifully, becomingly, charmingly, easily, elegantly, finely, flowingly, grazioso, naturally, pleasingly, smoothly, tastefully
**gracefully slender** svelte
**gracefully thin** slender
**graceful rhythm** lilt
**graceful tree** elm
**graceful woman** sylph
**graceless** artless(ness), awkward, blundering, boorishness, brutishness, bungling, clownish(ness), clumsy, coarse, crudeness, degenerate, disrespectful, gauche(rie), gawkiness, gawky, grossness, ham-fisted, ignorant, ill-bred, ill-mannered, impudent, inelegant, inept(ness), inexpert(ness), insensitive, lost, lowness, lumbering, maladroit(ness), oafish(ness), roughness, rude(ness), savageness, stiff(ness), tactless(ness), unco-ordinated, uncoordination, uncouth(ness), uncultured, ungainliness, ungainly, ungraceful, unpolished, unrefined, unskilled, unskilful(ness), unsophisticated, vulgarness

**grace note one step below the principal note** acciaccatura
**gracious** accommodating, amiable, beneficent, benevolent, benign, charming, chivalrous, civil, compassionate, condescending, considerate, courteous, courtly, friendly, gentle, hospitable, indulgent, kind, merciful, mild, patronising, pleasing, polite, tender, well-disposed
**gracious woman** lady
**grackle** blackbird, (jack)daw
**grade** arrange, blend, brand, categorise, category, class(ify), condition, degree, evaluate, group, incline, label, level, mark, notch, order, place, position, qualify, quality, range, rank, rate, rung, shade, size, slope, sort, stage, standard, station, step, type, upgrade, value
**grade school papers** mark
**gradient** bank, degree, grade, hill, inclination, incline, indicator, mark, point, ramp, rate, rise, slope
**gradual** cautious, continuous, deliberate, easy, even, gentle, gradational, inchmeal, leisurely, measured, methodic, moderate, paced, progressive, regular, slow(ly), snail-like, steady, step-by-step, successive, systematic, unhurried
**gradual change** drift
**gradual loss of vigour** decline
**gradually** continuously, progressively
**gradually decrease** taper
**gradually disappear** fade
**gradually disappearing** obsolescent
**gradually enervate** sap
**gradually increase in speed** accelerando
**gradually quicken** accelerando, stringendo
**gradually reduce in speed** diminuendo
**gradual slowing of tempo** rallentando, ritardando
**graduate** accommodate, adapt, adjust, alumna, alumnus, arrange, bachelor, calibrate, classify, dispose, grade, group, licentiate, order, pass, proportion, qualify, range, rank, regulate, sort
**graduated glass tube** burette
**graduate of a college** alumna, alumnus
**graduation certificate** diploma
**graft** allurement, bribe(ry), bribing, bud, corruption, demoralisation, dishonesty, engraft, enticement, extortion, fraud, implant, implantation, incentive, inducement, insert, jobbery, join, pay-off, profiteering, scion, shadiness, shoot, splice, sprout, transplant, venality
**grain** atom, barley, bit, cereal, corn, crumb, fibre, fragment, granule, grist, groats, iota, jot, kernel, maize, marking, mealie, millet, mite, modicum, molecule, morsel, oats, particle, pattern, piece, rice, rye, scrap, seed, speck, surface, texture, trace, weave, wheat
**grain bag** sack
**grain-beating instrument** flail
**grain bin** garner
**grain bristle** awn
**grain chaff** bran
**grain crop** corn, maize, wheat
**grain disease** ergot
**grained leather** roan
**grain for grinding** grist
**grain fungus** ergot
**grain grinder** miller
**grain ground to powder** meal
**grain husks** bran
**grain insect** weevil
**grain measure** bushel
**grain mite** acarus
**grain of a plant** seed
**grain of quartz** crystal
**grain of wheat** kernel
**grain plant** tef(f)
**grain pudding** semolina
**grain refuse** chaff
**grain shell** husk
**grain slide** chute
**grains of quartz** sand
**grain stalk** straw
**grain store** granary, silo
**grain type** rice
**grain used for brewing** malt
**grain used in making whiskey** malt, rye
**grain warehouse** elevator
**graminaceous plant** grass
**grammar component** adjective, adverb, conjunction, noun, preposition, pronoun, verb
**grammatical arrangement of words** syntax
**grammatical fault** solecism
**grammatical part** noun
**grammatical relationship** syntax

**grammatical tabulation** paradigm
**grammatical term** adjective, adverb, conjunction, noun, preposition, pronoun, verb
**grammatical understatement** litotes
**grammatical unit** clause, junction, phrase
**gramophone** record-player
**gramophone needle** style, stylus
**gramophone record** disc
**granadilla** grenadilla, passion-fruit
**grand** august, complete, comprehensive, dignified, distinctive, elevated, eminent, exalted, excellent, fine, glorious, grandiose, great, imposing, impressive, large, lofty, magnificent, main, majestic, palatial, pretentious, princely, principal, royal, splendid, stately, sublime, superb
**Grand Canal bridge** Rialto
**Grand Canyon river** Colorado
**Grand Canyon state** Arizona
**granddaughter of Augustus** Agrippina
**grand division of time** aeon, epoch
**grandeur** dignity, eminence, exaltation, excellence, glamour, glory, greatness, immensity, importance, loftiness, magnificence, majesty, nobility, pomp, splendour, state(liness), sublimity
**grandfather of Abraham** Nahor
**grandfather of Achilles** Aeacus
**grandfather of Agamemnon** Atreus
**grandfather of Eleazer** Merari
**grandfather of Enos** Adam
**grandfather of Eran** Ephraim
**grandfather of Heber** Asher
**grandfather of Heman** Samuel
**grandfather of Hul** Shem
**grandfather of Ichabod** Eli
**grandfather of Irad** Cain
**grandfather of Laadah** Judah
**grandfather of Mizzah** Esau
**grandfather of Noah** Methuseleh
**grandfather of Phinehas** Aaron
**grandfather of Rehabiah** Moses
**grandfather of Samuel** Korah
**grandfather of Tubal** Noah
**grandiloquent** bombastic, flowery, high-flown, high-sounding, inflated, lofty, magniloquent, oratorical, pompous, pretentious, rhetorical, swollen, turgid
**grandiose** affected, ambitious, bombastic, extravagant, flamboyant, grand, high-flown, imposing, impressive, lofty, magnificent, majestic, monumental, ostentatious, pompous, pretentious, showy, stately, weighty
**grand, like a palace** palatial

**grand mal** fit, epilepsy
**grand manner** panache
**grandmother** granny, nan, ouma
**grandparent** grandfather, grandmother, granny, ouma, oupa
**grand slam in cards** vole
**grandson of Abraham** Esau, Jacob
**grandson of Adam** Enos
**grandson of Boaz** Jesse
**grandson of Esau** Mizzah
**grandson of Eve** Enos
**grandson of Genghis Kahn** Kublai
**grandson of Hur** Bazaleel
**grandson of Matthan** Joseph
**grandson of Noah** Aram
**grandson of Numitor** Remus, Romulus
**grandson of Odin** Volsung, Wolsung
**granny** grandmother, nan, ouma
**grant** accept, accord, admit, allot, allow(ance), alms, award, bequeath, bequest, bestow, boon, (con)cede, concession, confer, consent, convey, donate, dower, gift, give, impart, indulge, lead, permission, permit, portion, (re)mise, stipend, subvention, supply, transfer, transmit, vouchsafe, yield
**grant absolution** shrive
**grant a permit** license
**grant authority to** authorise, commission
**grant by treaty** cede
**granted** yes
**granted thing** axiom, premise
**grantee** assignee, beneficiary, cessionary, recipient
**granter** conferrer
**grant independence** decolonise
**grant of money from government** subsidy, subvention
**grant of rights** charter, deed, franchise, patent
**grant per head** capitation
**grant permission** allow, dispense
**grant relief** forgive
**grant temporary use of** lease
**grant use of** lend
**granular** crumbly, grainy, granulated, gritty, rough, sandy
**granular farinaceous food** tapioca
**granular limestone** oolite
**granular snow** névé
**granular snowfield** firn, névé
**granulate** grain, kern, pulverise, roughen
**granulated snow** névé
**grape** uva
**grape and wine** muscat
**grape bunch** bob
**grape conserve** jam, jelly, moskonfyt
**grape drink** brandy, wine

**grape fermentation stimulant** must, stum
**grapeflower** hyacinth
**grape for malmsey** malvasia
**grapefruit** pomelo, shaddock
**grape-growing** viticulture
**grape harvest** vintage
**grape hyacinth** musk
**grape ivy** rhoicissus
**grape juice** dibs, must, ptisan, sapa, stum
**grape pest** phylloxera
**grape pigment** (o)enin
**grape plant** vine
**grape pomace** rape
**grape product** brandy, juice, sugar, syrup, vinegar, wine
**grape refuse** bagasse, marc, mash
**grape remains** marc
**grape seed** acinus
**grape sugar** dextrose, glucose
**grape used for wine** bukettraube, cabernet sauvignon, chenin blanc, cinsaut, colombard, gamay, gewürztraminer, hanepoot, merlot, muscadel, muscat, pinotage, riesling, semillon, shiraz, steen
**grape-wort** baneberry
**graph** blueprint, chart, curve, diagram, drawing, grid, map, mathematics, outline, picture, sketch, table
**graphic** detailed, diagrammatic, picturesque, striking, telling, vivid
**graphic symbol** character
**graphite** lead, moderator, pencil, plumbago, wad
**graphite rod** pencil
**grapple** attack, catch, clash, clasp, clinch, clutch, combat, confront, content, cope, encounter, engage, face, fasten, fight, grab, grasp, grip, hold, hug, seize, snatch, struggle, tackle, tussle, wrestle
**grapple for oysters** tong
**grapple with** battle, clash, combat, encounter, struggle, tackle, wrestle
**grappling fighter** wrestler
**grasp** ability, catch, clasp, clinch, close, clutch, comprehend, comprehension, embrace, extent, follow, garb, grapple, grip, hold, knowledge, learn, mastery, nab, perception, possession, reach, realisation, realise, retention, scope, see, seize, snatch, take, tenure, understand(ing)
**grasper** taker
**grasp firmly** clasp
**grasping** acquisitive, avaricious, catching, clasping, clinching, covetous, following, grappling, greedy, gripping, mean, miserly,

rapacious, seeing, seizing, selfish, snatching, stingy, tightfisted, understanding, venal
**grasping appendage** tab
**grasping instrument** tong(s)
**grasp mentally** comprehend
**grasp tightly** clench, grip
**grass** bamboo, dagga, esparto, grazing, lawn, marijuana, meadow, nark, pasturage, pasture, poa, reed, sward, turf
**grass and other plants** herbage
**grass basket** otate
**grass border along a road** verge
**grass bristle** awn
**grass colour** green
**grass-covered earth** lawn, sward
**grass-cutter** (lawn-)mower
**grass-cutting implement** scythe
**grass disease** ergot
**grassed area** lawn
**grass for thatching** bango
**grass growing among corn** darnel
**grass growing in cold regions** poa
**grasshopper** grig, katydid, locust
**grasshopper-like insect** cicada
**grass joint** culm, stem
**grassland** lea, llano, meadow(land), pampas, pasture, prairie, savanna(h), steppe, veld
**grasslands in Argentina and Uruguay** pampas
**grassland with low trees** bushveld
**grass leaf** blade
**grass/leaf mixture** mulch
**grass-like** gramineous
**grass-like herb** rush, sedge
**grass-like marsh plant** reed
**grass-like moor plant** sedge
**grass-like wheat** rye
**grass rug** mat
**grass section** turf
**grass stem** culm, haulm, stalk
**grass used in paper making** esparto
**grass variety** brome, fescue, reed, rye
**grass widow** divorcee
**grassy area** lawn
**grassy open place in forest** glade
**grassy plain** llano, pampas, prairie, savanna(h), steppe
**grassy plain with few or no trees** savanna(h)
**grate** abrade, aggravate, annoy, bars, creak, discordant, exasperate, fireplace, fret, furnace, grid, grind, harsh, irk, irritate, jar, mince, peeve, pulverise, rasp, reduce, rub, scrape, scratch, shred, vex, wear
**grated spice** nutmeg
**grateful** agreeable, appreciative, gratifying, indebted, mindful, obligated, obliged, pleasant, satisfying, sensible, thankful, welcome
**grateful recognition** appreciation
**grate harshly** rasp
**grate harshly over** scrape
**grater** rasper
**gratify** bribe, content, delight, favour, fulfil, give, gladden, humour, indulge, please, pleasure, recompense, reward, sate, satisfy
**gratify fully** sate, satiate
**grating** abrasive, aggravating, annoying, croaky, displeasing, disturbing, galling, grid, grinding, gritting, harsh, hoarse, irksome, irritating, jarring, rasping, raucous, rusty, scraping, screeching, strident, unmelodic, vexatious, wearing
**grating in a jail door** grille
**grating sound** rasp
**grating utensil** grater
**gratis** chargeless, complimentary, costless, expenseless, free(ly), gratuitous(ly), unpaid, voluntary
**gratitude** acknowledgement, appreciation, gratefulness, obligation, recognition, thankfulness, thanks(giving)
**gratuitous** complimentary, free, gratis, groundless, irrelevant, needless, superfluous, unasked for, uncalled for, unjustified, unnecessary, unprovoked, unsolicited, unwarranted, voluntary, wanton
**gratuity** award, bonus, dividend, donation, douceur, extra, fee, gift, honorarium, perk(s), perquisite, plus, pourboire (F), present, reward, tip
**grave** acute, consequential, critical, crucial, crypt, dangerous, death, deep, dignified, dour, dull, earnest, eventful, gloomy, grim, hazardous, heavy, important, leaden, long-faced, mausoleum, momentous, muted, perilous, pit, pressing, quiet, sedate, sepulchre, serious, severe, sober, solemn, sombre, staid, subdued, thoughtful, threatening, tomb, unsmiling, vault, vital, weighty
**grave and thoughtful** serious
**graveclothes** cerement, shroud
**grave crime** felony
**grave-digger** sexton
**grave doubt** fear
**gravelly** grainy, granular, granulated, grating, gritty, gruff, guttural, harsh, hoarse, husky, pebbly, raspy, raucous, rocky, sandy, shingly, stony, throaty
**gravel particles** grit

**gravel ridge** escar, eskar, esker, sowback
**gravel ridge left by glacier** escar, eskar, esker
**grave marker** tombstone
**graven image** idol
**grave robber** body snatcher, ghoul
**graveside monument** tombstone
**graveyard** burial-ground, burial-place, cemetery, churchyard, necropolis
**graveyard inscription** epitaph
**gravid** pregnant
**gravitate** descend, drop, fall, incline, lean, move, precipitate, settle, sink, tend
**gravity** acuteness, consequence, danger, demureness, dignity, earnestness, exigency, importance, perilousness, reserve, restraint, sedateness, seriousness, severity, significance, sobriety, solemnity, sombreness, thoughtfulness, urgency
**gravy** jus (F), sauce
**gravy dish** boat
**graze** abrade, abut, adjoin, bark, blemish, browse, brush, caress, claw, collide, contact, converge, crop, cut, damage, deface, devour, eat, etch, fare, feed, feel, flay, flick, fondle, gash, glance, gouge, grass, grate, pasture, rub, score, scrape, scratch, touch, wound
**graze cattle for payment** agist
**grazed skin** abrasion
**graze lightly** scuff
**grazing animal** herbager
**grazing ground for cattle** shiel(ing)
**grazing land** lea, pasture
**grazing prairie** range
**grease** adhesive, bribe, butter, drippings, fat, lard, lubricate, oil, tallow, wax
**grease for instance** lubricant
**grease from wool** lanolin(e)
**grease someone's palm** bribe, corrupt, induce, influence
**grease the hand** bribe
**grease wheels** aid, expedite
**greasewood** chico, greasebush
**greasy** facile, fatty, lardaceous, lardy, oily, pinguid, saponaceous, sebaceous, slimy, slippery, slithery, smeary, smooth, unctuous, waxy
**greasy and wet** slimy
**greasy mud** slime
**greasy preparation for healing** ointment
**greasy slope** shoot
**great** big, chief, considerable, countless, distinguished, eminent, enormous, exalted, famous, fine, gigantic, glorious, grand, huge,

illustrious, immense, important, large, leading, lofty, marvellous, momentous, notable, noted, numerous, principal, prominent, remarkable, super, unusual, vast, wonderful
**great abundance** profuse, scads
**great actor** star
**great admirer** idolater
**great affection** love
**great affliction** tribulation
**great amount** abundance, lot(s), much
**great and destructive fire** conflagration
**great anger** rage, wrath
**great ant-eater** tamanoir
**great artery** aorta
**great artist** master
**great ash tree of Norse mythology** Igdrasil, Ugdrasil, Yggdrasil
**great astonishment** amazement
**great barracuda** picuda
**Great Barrier Island** Otea
**Great Basin river** Sevier
**Great Basin state** Nevada
**Great Bear** Ursa Major
**great body of water surrounding the land of the globe** ocean, sea
**Great Britain** Albion, Britannia
**great calamity** catastrophe, disaster
**great change** cataclysm
**great circle of the earth** equator
**greatcoat** overcoat, paletot
**great composer** maestro
**great Comrades champion** Bruce Fordyce
**great conductor** maestro
**great crowd** horde
**great deal** lot, much
**great deal in a little space** magnum in parvo (L)
**great desert** Gobi, Hinnai, Sahara, Thar
**great desire for drink** dipsomania, thirst
**great disaster** catastrophe
**great disgrace brought by shameful conduct** opprobrium
**great disorder** chaos, havoc
**great distance** (a)far
**great eagerness** enthusiasm
**great enemy of man** Satan
**great entertainment** fête
**great enthusiasm** gusto, zeal
**greater** major
**greater in quantity** more
**greater in value** major
**greater part** bulk, majority, mass
**greater than a right angle** obtuse
**greater than zero** positive
**greatest amount** maximum, most
**greatest distance from sun** apsis
**greatest Egyptian god** Osiris

**greatest in size** largest, most
**greatest possible degree** utmost
**greatest possible number** maximum
**great fear** dread, terror
**great feat of skill** tour de force (F)
**great flood** deluge
**great folly** lunacy
**great force** violence
**great fuss** ado
**great generosity** munificence
**great good** magnum bonum (L)
**great-grandson of Noah** Nimrod, Hul
**great happiness** bliss, felicity
**great haste** hurry, speed
**great Hindu sage** maharishi
**great hunger** voracity
**great hunter of the Bible** Nimrod
**great hurry** rush
**great in number** many, numerous
**great joy** elation, glee
**great king of Persia** Darius, Xerxes
**Great Lake** Erie, Huron, Michigan, Ontario, Superior
**Great Lake explorer** Champlain
**great lake of India** Erle
**great lie** whopper
**great liking** love
**great love** devotion
**great lover** Romeo, Juliet
**greatly** abundantly, bulkily, chiefly, colossally, considerably, decidedly, enormously, exceedingly, extensively, extremely, grandly, highly, hugely, immensely, lengthily, mainly, mightily, much, notably, powerfully, primarily, principally, prominently, protractedly, remarkably, sorely, stupendously, superiorly, tremendously, vastly, very, voluminously
**greatly desire** crave
**greatly developed** advanced
**greatly enjoy** relish
**greatly exaggerated** hyperbolic
**greatly exceeding others** pass
**greatly fear** dread
**greatly lamented** regrettable
**greatly puzzle** perplex
**greatly varying weight** maund
**great man** hero
**great many** scores
**great misfortune** calamity
**great multitude** throng
**great musical composer** maestro
**greatness** abundance, amplitude, attainment, distinctiveness, eminence, enormity, immensity, importance, influence, intensity, largeness, liberality, magnanimity, magnitude, majesty, mass, notoriety, renown, scope, solemnity, sufficiency, vastness

**greatness of extent** amplitude, magnitude
**great number** host, lac, lakh, lots, many, much, multitude, myriad, shoal
**great ocean** Atlantic, Pacific
**great pain** agony
**great personage** grandee, mogul, nabob
**great pleasure** delight
**great plenty** abundance
**great poem** epic
**great power** might
**great quantity** abundance, much, oodles, sea, slew, superabundance
**great reader** bookworm
**great realm** empire, kingdom
**great relish** gusto, verve, zest
**great respect** awe, honour
**great river** Amazon, Congo, Rhine
**great sacrifice** hecatomb
**great scholar** polymath
**Great Sea** Mediterranean
**great skill** expertise
**great slaughter** carnage
**great speaker** orator
**great success** éclat, hit
**great sufferer** martyr
**great surprise and anxiety** consternation
**great swelling wave** billow
**great tendon** hamstring
**great toe** hallux
**great tower of castle** donjon
**Great Trail terminus** Detroit
**great trial** ordeal
**great undertaking** magnum opus
**great unhappiness** misery
**great unknown** death
**great volcano** Etna, Vesuvius
**great wave** billow
**great whirlpool** maelstrom
**Great White Way** Broadway
**great wickedness** enormity
**great woman singer** diva, prima donna
**great wonder** awe
**Grecian covered walk** stoa
**Greece** Achaia, Attic, Ellas, Helene, Hellas, Hellenic
**greed** acquisitiveness, appetence, avarice, avidity, covetousness, craving, cupidity, desire, eagerness, edacity, esurience, fervency, gluttony, graspingness, greediness, hunger, impatience, insatiability, itch, keenness, longing, meanness, miserliness, parsimony, passion, rapacity, ravenousness, selfishness, venality, voraciousness, voracity, yearning
**greed for gain** avarice, cupidity
**greed for wealth** avarice

**greediness** desire, edacity, gluttony, selfishness, voracity
**greediness of appetite** voracity
**greediness of gain** avarice
**greedy** acquisitive, aspiring, avaricious, avid, covetous, craving, desirous, eager, edacious, esurient, gluttonous, grabby, grasping, hoarding, hungry, impatient, insatiable, miserly, niggardly, penurious, piggy, rapacious, ravenous, selfish, voracious
**greedy eater** glutton, go(u)rmand
**greedy fellow** shark
**greedy in eating** ravenous, voracious
**greedy moneylender** usurer
**greedy person** glutton, hog, Midas, pig
**Greek** Athenian, Attic, Hellenic
**Greek amphitheatre** odeum
**Greek architectural order** Corinthian, Doric, Ionic
**Greek army unit** taxis
**Greek assembly** Agora, Apella, Ecclesia, Pnyx
**Greek athletic contest** Agon
**Greek avenging spirit** Erinys
**Greek bay** Akritas, Eleusis, Krios, Malea, Matapan, Spada, Tainaron
**Greek bread** pit(t)a
**Greek chariot** quadriga
**Greek cheese** feta
**Greek chicken and lemon soup thickened with beaten egg** avgolemono
**Greek choric hymn** dithyramb
**Greek citadel** Acropolis
**Greek city-state** Corinth, Sparta, Thebes
**Greek coin** diobolon, drachma, hecte, lepton, obol(o), stater
**Greek colony** Byzantium, Syracuse
**Greek column** Corinthian, Doric, Ionic
**Greek commune** deme
**Greek country** Elis
**Greek Cupid** Eros
**Greek currency** diobol, drachma, ducat, lepta, lepton, obol(us), stater
**Greek dance** bouzouki, chorus, gerandos, kordax, phyrric, rommaika, syrtos
**Greek dawn goddess** Eos
**Greek deity** satyr
**Greek department** eleia
**Greek dialect** Achaean, Aeolic, Arcadian, Attic, Coan, Doric, Elean, Eolic, Ionic, Melian, Theran
**Greek dish** baklava, mous(s)aka, taramasalata
**Greek district** Arcadia, Argolis, Attica, Chios, Corinth, Crete, Epirus, Kastoria, Kilkis, Laconia, Laris(s)a, Lesbos, Messenia, Pella, Phocis, Rhodope, Serrai
**Greek drama** mime, tragedy
**Greek dramatist** Euripides
**Greek drinking cup** cotyle, hoimos
**Greek drink of aniseed-flavoured spirits** ouzo
**Greek earthenware jar** amphora
**Greek epic** *Iliad, Odyssey*
**Greek epic poet** Homer
**Greek equivalent of Cupid** Eros
**Greek equivalent of Neptune** Poseidon
**Greek fable writer** Aesop
**Greek festival** Delia
**Greek festival city** Nemea, Olympia
**Greek flask** olpe
**Greek fortified hill** Acropolis
**Greek garment** chiton, chlamys, peplos, tunic
**Greek girl** haidee
**Greek god** Aeolus, Apollo, Ares, Auster, Bacchus, Boreas, Comus, Dionysus, Dis, Eros, Eurus, Hades, Helios, Hephaestus, Hermes, Kronos, Momus, Nereus, Pan, Pluto, Poseidon, Triton, Zeus
**Greek goddess** Amphitrite, Aphrodite, Ara, Artemis, Ate, Athena, Chloris, Clotho, Cybele, Demeter, Eir, Eos, Eris, Ge, Hebe, Hecate, Hera, Hestia, Horae, Irene, Moira, Nemesis, Nike, Pallas, Rhea, Selene, Upis
**Greek goddess of dawn** Eos
**Greek goddess of death** Ker
**Greek goddess of evil** Ate
**Greek goddess of flora** Chloris
**Greek goddess of fortune** Tyche
**Greek goddess of health** Hygeia
**Greek goddess of hunting** Artemis
**Greek goddess of justice** Themus
**Greek goddess of love and beauty** Aphrodite
**Greek goddess of magic** Hecate
**Greek goddess of peace** Irene
**Greek goddess of rainbows** Iris
**Greek goddess of retribution** Nemesis
**Greek goddess of the earth** Gae, Gaia, Ge
**Greek goddess of the moon** Artemis
**Greek goddess of the sea** Amphitrite
**Greek goddess of the underworld** Hecate, Hekate
**Greek goddess of victory** Nike
**Greek goddess of war** Enyo
**Greek goddess of wisdom** Athena, Athene
**Greek goddess of youth** Hebe
**Greek god of death** Hades
**Greek god of dreams** Morpheus
**Greek god of healing** Asclepius
**Greek god of love** Eros
**Greek god of marriage** Hymen
**Greek god of medicine** Asclepius
**Greek god of nature** Pan
**Greek god of sleep** Hypnos
**Greek god of sowing** Cronos, Kronos
**Greek god of the forests** Pan
**Greek god of the north wind** Boreas
**Greek god of the seas** Poseidon
**Greek god of the west wind** Zephyrus
**Greek god of the wind** Aeolus
**Greek god of war** Ares
**Greek god of wine** Bacchus, Dionysus
**Greek governor** toparch
**Greek group of islands** Bodecanese, Cyclades, Ionian, Sporades, Strophades
**Greek gulf** Argolis, Athens, Corinth, Kavalla, Laconia, Lepanto, Mesara, Patrai, Salonika, Saronic, Toronaic
**Greek harp** lyre
**Greek hero** Achilles, Ajax, Cadmus, Heracles, Hercules, Jason
**Greek holiday island** Crete
**Greek home of gods** Olympus
**Greek huntress** Atalanta
**Greek idiom** Graecism
**Greek island** Corfu, Crete, Delos, Icaria, Idra, Ithaca, Lemnos, Lesbos, Maxos, Mikonos, Milos, Paros, Patmos, Rhodes, Rhodos, Samos, Santorini, Skyros, Thasos, Zante
**Greek islander** Corfiot, Cretan, Ithacan
**Greek lake** Copais, Karla, Kastoria, Prespa, Tachinos, Topolia, Vistonis, Volve
**Greek leather flask** olpe
**Greek liqueur** ouzo
**Greek love god** Eros
**Greek magistrate** archon
**Greek market-place** agora, agore
**Greek mathematician** Archimedes, Euclid
**Greek measure of distance** stadium
**Greek measure of length** bema
**Greek messenger of the gods** Hermes
**Greek military formation** phalanx
**Greek monk** caloyer
**Greek monster** Chimera, Sphinx
**Greek mountain of the gods** Olympus
**Greek muse** Calliope, Clio, Erato, Euterpe, Melpomene, Polyhymnia, Terpsichore, Thalia, Urania
**Greek musical instrument** aulos, barbitos, bouzouki, cithara, lyre, syrinx
**Greek mythical monster** Minotaur
**Greek mythological giant** Orion
**Greek nymph** Oenone, oread
**Greek one-eyed giant** Cyclops
**Greek oracle** Delphi, Dodona

**Greek order of architecture** Corinthian, Doric, Ionic
**Greek paradise** Elysium
**Greek parliament** boule
**Greek peninsula** Acte, Akte, Akti, Chalcidice, Morea, Peloponnesus, Sithonia
**Greek philosopher** Aristotle, Democritus, Heraclitus, Plato, Pythagoras, Socrates, Thales
**Greek philosopher and poet** Xenophanes
**Greek pillar** stela, stele
**Greek pitcher** olpe
**Greek poem** epic, epode, *Iliad*, *Odyssey*
**Greek poet** Homer
**Greek port** Corfu, Corinth, Enos, Kavalla, Patrai, P(e)iraeus, Salonika, Syra, Syros, Volos
**Greek portico** stoa, xystus
**Greek priest** myst(agogue)
**Greek protector of herds** Ares
**Greek province** Nome
**Greek red wine** retsina
**Greek region** doris
**Greek river god** Alpheus
**Greek ruins** Acropolis, Corinth, Delos, Eleusis, Elevsis, Pella, Samos
**Greek runner** Atalanta
**Greek sanctuary** sekos
**Greek sea** Aegean, Crete, Euxine, Ionian, Mirtoon
**Greek seagod** Triton
**Greek silver coin** drachma
**Greek sleeveless vest** exomion
**Greek soldier** hoplite
**Greek soldiers' ceremonial white pleated skirt** fustanella
**Greek soup made with eggs, lemon juice and rice** avgolemono
**Greek state** Phocis
**Greek supreme god** Zeus
**Greek supreme goddess** Hera
**Greek temple** naos
**Greek tribal area** deme
**Greek underground** Elas
**Greek urn** stamnos
**Greek valley** Nemea
**Greek vase** amphora, lecythus, pelike
**Greek version of Cupid** Eros
**Greek version of the Old Testament** Septuagint
**Greek war cry** alala
**Greek war god** Ares
**Greek warrior** Ajax
**Greek warrior at the siege of Troy** Mirmidon
**Greek warship** cataphract, trireme
**Greek weight** drachma, oke
**Greek wine** retsina
**Greek writer of comedies** Menander
**Greek writer of fables** Aesop, Babrius
**green** blooming, budding, common, covetous, emerald, envious, flourishing, fresh, grassy, gullible, ignorant, immature, inexperienced, jealous, lawn, leafy, lime, naïve, new, olive, park, raw, recent, resentful, sward, tender, undecayed, undeveloped, unripe, unseasoned, unsophisticated, untrained, verdant, young
**green algae** stonewort
**green amphibian** frog
**green bean** haricot
**green beryl** emerald
**green-blue** cyan
**green colour** celadon, emerald, jade, loden, terre-verte
**green colouring matter of plants** chlorophyll
**green culinary vegetable** broccoli, cabbage, lettuce, pea, spinach
**green deposit on copper or brass** verdigris
**green desert spot** oasis
**greenery** foliage, greenness, vegetation, verdure
**green film on copper** patina
**greenfly** aphid
**green foliage** greenery
**green gem** alexandrite, amazonite, aquamarine, beryl, emerald, heliotrope, jade, malachite, topaz, tourmaline
**green glass found in Bohemia** moldavite
**green grasshopper** katydid
**greenheart** bebeeru, tree
**greenhorn** amateur, apprentice, beginner, fledg(e)ling, ignoramus, initiate, jay, learner, mug, neophyte, novice, recruit, rookie, simpleton, softhorn, starter, student, sucker, tenderfoot, trainee, tyro
**greenhouse** conservatory, glasshouse, hothouse, nursery, pavilion, vinery
**green insect** mantis
**greenish-blue** aqua(marine), cyan, teal, turquoise
**greenish colour** eau-de-Nil
**greenish fluid** bile
**greenish yellow** olive
**Greenland airbase** Thule
**Greenland and northern part of USA** Nearctic
**Greenland bay** Baffin, Disko, Melville
**Greenland cape** Bismarck, Farewell, Grivel, Jaal, Lowenorn, Walker
**Greenland discoverer** Eric
**Greenland division** Kome
**Greenlander** Eskimo
**Greenland Eskimo** Agto, Ita, Kaladlit, Nugsuak
**Greenland polar base** Etab
**Greenland settlement** Etah
**Greenland strait** Davis, Denmark
**green light** approval, blessing, clearance, confirmation, leave, liberty, permission
**green lining material** baize
**green mineral** epidote, malachite
**greenness** inexperience, innocence, simplicity, trustfulness, verdancy, verdure, youthfulness
**green parrot** kea
**green pasture** meadow
**green patina formed on copper** verdigris
**green peppermint liqueur** crème de menthe
**green pigment** bice
**green pigment in plants** chlorophyll
**green plover** lapwing
**green pod used for thickening** okra
**green precious stone** beryl, emerald
**green quartz** prase
**green rock** ophite
**green rust on bronze and copper** patina, verdigris
**greens** vegetables
**greens club** putter
**green spot in desert** oasis
**green stone** beryl, emerald, jade, olivine
**green Swiss cheese** sapsago
**green tea** hyson
**green variety of olivine** peridot
**green vegetable** bean, broccoli, lettuce, pea, spinach
**green vegetation** verdure
**green woodpecker** yaffle
**greeny blue** teal
**greet** accost, acknowledge, address, approach, ave, hail, hello, hi, meet, receive, salute, signal, smile, wave, welcome
**greeting** accost, address, approach, ave, hail, hello, hi, how, letter, message, note, receive, salutation, salute, smile, speak, telegram, tiding, wave, welcome, wire
**greetings** compliments, devoirs, regards, respects
**gregarious** affable, amicable, brotherly, chummy, convivial, cordial, extrovert, friendly, genial, hearty, kindly, neighbourly, outgoing, sociable, social, warm(-hearted)
**grenade trigger** pin
**Gretel's brother** Hansel
**grey** ashen, ashy, bleak, bloodless, cheerless, cloudy, colourless, dark, depressing, dim, dismal, drab,

## greyback herring — gritty

**dreary**, dull, gloomy, leaden, livid, murky, neutral, overcast, pale, pallid, sunless, unclear, unidentifiable, wan
**greyback herring** cisco
**greybeard** elder, patriarch
**grey-brown** dun
**grey colour with brownish tinge** taupe
**grey duck** gadwall
**grey-faced** ashen
**grey goose** greylag
**grey-headed** hoar(y)
**greyhound** whippet
**greyhound in first year** sapling
**greyish** dun
**greyish-blue colour** perse
**greyish-brown** dun, taupe
**greyish-brown duck** pintail
**greyish colour** ashy, ecru
**greyish-fawn colour** oatmeal
**greyish-red** azalea
**greyish-tan** beige
**greyish-white** hoar
**greyish-yellow** écru, Isabel(la), Isabelline, sand
**grey-looking** ashen
**grey matter** brain
**grey metallic element** zirconium
**grey mineral, found in hydrothermal veins** galena, galenite
**grey nerve matter** cinerea
**grey or fawn colour** neutral
**grey warbler** riro-riro
**grey whale** baleen
**grey with age** hoar(y)
**grey with tinge of another colour** taupe
**grid** arrangement, channels, complex, fretwork, grating, grille, lattice, maze, mesh, network, organisation, structure, system, trellis, web
**griddle** hot-plate
**griddle cake** crumpet
**gridiron** grill
**grief** affliction, agony, anguish, austerity, bereavement, blow, burden, dejection, desolation, distress, dolour, grievance, heartache, heartbreak, melancholy, misery, misfortune, mourning, ordeal, pain, penitence, regret, remorse, repentance, sadness, sorrow, suffering, teen, tribulation, trouble, woe, worry
**grief of bereavement** mourning
**grievance** accusation, affliction, allegation, calamity, charge, complaint, damage, distress, grief, grudge, hardship, indignity, injury, injustice, moan, outrage, resentment, sorrow, trial, tribulation, unfairness, unhappiness, wrong

**grieve** ache, afflict, agonise, bemoan, bewail, complain, crush, deplore, depress, distress, hurt, injure, lament, mourn, regret, rue, sadden, sorrow, suffer, wail, weep, wound
**grieve for** mourn
**grieve over** deplore
**grieve over someone's death** mourn
**grievous** calamitous, deplorable, distressing, dreadful, heinous, lamentable, painful, regrettable, sad, severe, shameful, sorrowful
**grievous bodily harm** mayhem
**grievous disaster** calamity
**grill** arrangement, barbecue, broil, burn, catechise, complex, cross-examine, fry, grate, grid(dle), interrogate, maze, network, pump, quiz, scald, structure, system, toast, torment, torture, web
**grille** grating
**grilled bread** toast
**grim** cruel, depressing, dire, dour, dreadful, fearsome, ferocious, fierce, forbidden, forbidding, frightening, frightful, ghostly, gloomy, gruesome, hard, harsh, horrible, horrid, joyless, merciless, morose, repellent, resolute, severe, shocking, sinister, stern, surly, terrible, unattractive, uncompromising, unpleasant, unrelenting, unyielding
**grimace** contort, frown, glare, grin, mop, pout, scowl, smirk, sneer
**grimace when sulking** pout
**grime** begrime, contaminate, dirt(y), dust, filth, mire, muck, scum, smirch, smudge, smut, soil, soot, tarnish
**grim fate** doom
**grimly jocular** sardonic
**grimy** besmeared, filthy, foul, grubby, smutty, soiled, sooty, unclean
**grin** beam, grimace, laugh, simper, smile, smirk, twinkle
**grind** abrade, bray, core, crush, drudgery, exertion, file, gnash, grate, grit, harass, labour, mill, mince, oppress, persecute, polish, pound, powder, pulverise, round, routine, rub, sand, scrape, sharpen, slavery, smooth, sweat, task, toil, torment, whet
**grind away** labour, lucubrate, read, study, toil
**grind coarsely** kibble
**grind down** afflict, consume, corrode, crush, destroy, deteriorate, erode, harass, hound, oppress, persecute, plague, spoil, trouble
**grind food with teeth** masticate
**grinding instrument** pestle
**grindingly wretched** abject, miserable

**grinding machine** mill
**grinding material** abrasive
**grinding organ of a bird** gizzard
**grinding tooth** molar
**grinding wheel** shell
**grind into a smooth paste** levigate
**grind into small parts** crush
**grind noisily** grate
**grind teeth** gnash
**grind teeth together** gnarl
**grind to a fine powder** triturate
**grind with teeth** chew, gnash, masticate
**grip** absorb, acquaintance, catch, clasp, clutch, compel, comprehension, control, divert, embrace, engross, enthrall, fascinate, grasp, handle, hold, influence, involve, keeping, mastery, mesmerise, power, rivet, seize, spellbind, sway, tenure, thrill, traction, understanding
**gripe** ache, affliction, clasp, clutch, colic, complain(t), contract, control, cramp(s), distress, fret, grasp, grievance, grumble, indigestion, oppress, pain, secure, seize, spasm, stomach-ache, twinge
**grip like a vice** clamp
**gripping device** vice
**gripping tool** pincer, tongs, vice
**grip tight** hold fast
**grip tightly** pinch
**grisette** canker, fungus, toadstool
**grisly** abhorrent, abominable, appalling, awful, dangerous, detestable, dreadful, frightful, ghastly, gory, grim, gruesome, harsh, hideous, horrendous, horrible, horrid, macabre, odious, offensive, ominous, repugnant, shocking, sickening, terrible, threatening, ugly, unyielding
**grist flower** mill
**gristle** cartilage
**grit** bravery, clench, courage, determination, doggedness, dust, fortitude, gameness, gnash, grail, grate, gravel, grind, guts, lock, nerve, pebbles, perseverance, pluck(iness), resolution, sand, shingle, spirit, stamina, tenacity, toughness
**gritty** arenaceous, bold, brave, courageous, daring, dauntless, determined, dusty, firm, game, grained, grainy, granular, gravelly, heroic, indomitable, intrepid, lionhearted, mettlesome, pebbled, pebbly, plucky, powdered, pulverous, resolute, sandlike, sandy,

spirited, stalwart, staunch, sturdy, unwavering, valiant
**gritty textured fruit** pear, guava
**grivet** monkey
**grizzle** cry, fret, sniffle, snivel, snuffle, whimper, whine, whinge, worry
**grizzled** grey(-haired), grey-headed, greying, grizzly
**grizzly** bear, grey(-haired), greyish
**grizzly animal** bear
**groan** bemoan, complain, fret, grouse, grumble, grunt, lament, moan, murmur, sniffing, sob, wail, weep, whine
**grog** booze
**groggy** jolly, screwed
**grommet** becket, eyelet, loop, ring, washer
**groom** adjust, adorn, arrange, bridegroom, brush, clean, consort, curry, disentangle, do, dress, drill, educate, equerry, fix, (h)ostler, neaten, nuture, partner, preen, prepare, rub, saice, school, smarten, smooth, spouse, stableboy, stableman, syce, tend, tidy, train, untangle
**groomed beauty** glamour
**grooming tool** comb
**groom's partner** bride
**groom the nails** manicure
**groove** channel, convention, cut, enjoy, flute, furrow, habit, hollow, notch, place, procedure, routine, rut, scarf, score, slot, stria, swing, trench, usage
**groove caused by wheel** rut
**grooved face** diglyph
**grooved joint** rabbet, rebate
**grooved wheel** pulley, sheave, shiver
**groove left by wheel** rut
**grooves on rock** striae
**groovy** attractive, fashionable
**groovy player** gramophone
**grope** feel, finger, fish, flounder, fumble, grabble, probe, scrabble, search
**grope about** fumble
**gross** accumulate, aggregate, all-inclusive, big, blatant, body, bring, broad, bulk(y), coarse, colossal, complete, crude, dense, earn, entire(ly), fat, flagrant, foul, glaring, grievous, heavy, huge, hulking, improper, impure, inclusive, indecent, indelicate, large, lewd, mass, obscene, obvious, offensive, outrageous, outright, overweight, plain, rude, serious, shameful, sheer, shocking, sum, tasteless, thick, total(ity), utter, vulgar, whole
**gross income** revenue

**gross injustice** iniquity
**grossly abusive** scurrilous
**grossly cruel** outrageous
**grossly excessive** exorbitant
**grossly lustful man** satyr
**grossly offensive** outrageous
**grossly overweight** corpulent, obese
**grossly stupid** crass
**gross offence** enormity
**grosso modo** approximately, roughly
**gross revenue** turnover
**grotesque** absurd, bizarre, deformed, distorted, extravagant, fanciful, fantastic, freakish, hideous, incongruous, macabre, malformed, misshapen, monstrous, odd, outlandish, ridiculous, strange, ugly, unnatural, unsightly, weird
**grotesque action** antic
**grotesque animal** monster
**grotesque figure** gargoyle
**grotesque misapplication of words** malapropism
**grotesque posture** antic
**grotto** catacomb, cave(rn), chamber, grot, hollow, recess, subterranean, tunnel
**grouch** complainer, grumble, mope(r), spoilsport
**grouchy** abrupt, bad-tempered, bearish, bilious, brusque, cantankerous, cross, crotchety, fractious, grouchy, grumpy, irascible, irritable, peevish, surly, testy, touchy, uncivil
**grouchy fellow** crab
**grouchy person** crank
**ground** account, base, cause, consideration, earth, establish, factor, fix, found(ation), instruct, land, motive, mould, premise, rationale, reason, sediment, settle, sod, soil, terrain
**ground attached to a sacred building** precinct
**ground beef** mince
**ground beetle** scarab
**grounded** based, coached, established, fixed, founded, informed, initiated, instructed, prepared, set(tled), taught, trained, tutored
**ground for belief** evidence
**ground for horse-racing** racecourse
**ground grain** meal
**ground ivy** gill
**groundless** baseless, empty, false, idle, illusory, imaginary, uncalled-for, unfounded, unjustified, unprovoked, unsubstantial, unsupported, unwarranted
**groundless assumption** hypothesis

**ground maize** mealiemeal
**groundnut** peanut
**ground occupied by rabbits** warren
**ground of war** casus belli (L)
**ground on which battle is fought** field
**ground on which cattle graze** pasture
**ground pine** foxtail
**ground-plan of building** ichnography
**ground plan of railway** alignment, alinement
**grounds** account, acres, area, argument, base, basis, call, cause, country, deposit, district, domain, dregs, estate, excuse, factor, fields, foundation, gardens, holding, inducement, justification, land, lees, motive, occasion, park, principle, property, realm, reason, score, sediment, surroundings, terrain, territory, tract, vindication
**grounds for a suit** case
**grounds of university or college** campus
**ground squirrel** gopher
**ground wheat** flour
**ground wheat husks** bran
**group** arrange, association, band, bunch, catalogue, category, circle, class, clique, cluster, collection, company, congregation, crowd, ensemble, genus, grade, marshal, organisation, organise, party, place, school, sect, set, sort, troop
**group having similar views** sect
**group hired to applaud** claque
**group in charge of club** committee
**group member** insider
**group of activists** cadre
**group of actors** troupe
**group of aides** retinue
**group of animals** drove, flock, genus, herd
**group of badgers** cete
**group of beauties** bevy
**group of bees** hive, swarm
**group of binary digits in computer** byte
**group of biota** ecospecies
**group of birds** covey, flight, flock
**group of bits** byte
**group of bitterns** sedge, siege
**group of buildings** block
**group of Canary Islands** Ferro, Gomera, Graciosa, Hierro, Lanzarote, Palma, Roca, Tenerife
**group of cattle** drove, herd, mob
**group of citizen-soldiers** militia
**group of computer jobs** batch
**group of coots** covert, raft
**group of corn-sheaves in field** shock
**group of cows** herd
**group of cranes** sedge, siege

**group of crows** hover, rookery
**group of decorative ivy** Aralia
**group of doves** flight
**group of eagles** convocation
**group of eels** swarm
**group of eight** octad, octave, octet, octonary, ogdoad
**group of elephants** herd
**group of employees** staff
**group of extinct languages of ancient Italy** Osco Umbrian (Oscan, Umbrian, Sabellian)
**group of facts** data
**group of falcons** cast
**group of fish** shoal, school
**group of five** cinquain, pentad, quintet
**group of fixed stars** constellation
**group of four** mess, quartet, quaternion, tetrad
**group of four dramas** tetralogy
**group of four persons** foursome
**group of four related literary works** tetralogy
**group of four voices** quartet
**group of foxes** skulk
**group of friends** bunch, clique
**group of fruit trees** orchard
**group of furnished cabins** motel
**group of geese** flock, gaggle, nide, nye
**group of genera** family
**group of giraffes** herd
**group of girls** bevy
**group of graduates** alumnae, alumni
**group of graduate students** seminar
**group of grouse** covey
**group of gulls** colony
**group of hawks** cast, leash
**group of herons** sedge, siege
**group of hives** apiary
**group of hoodlums** gang
**group of horses belonging to one owner** string
**group of hounds** cry, kennel, pack
**group of houses** borough
**group of hundred** chiliad
**group of huts** kraal
**group of islands** archipelago, atoll
**group of islands along the coast of south-eastern Alaska** Alexander Archipelago
**group of islands in Indian Ocean** Seychelles
**group of islands in Indonesia** Ar(r)u
**group of islands in the Gulf of Bothnia** Åland
**group of islands in the Mediterranean** Balearic
**group of islands in the West Indies** Caicos, Greater Antilles, Leeward, Lesser Antilles, Windward

**group of islands off the east coast of Africa** Comoros
**group of islands off the west coast of Africa** Canary, Cape Verde
**group of kangaroos** mob, troop
**group of ladies** bevy
**group of larks** bevy
**group of lines of verse** stanza
**group of lions** pride
**group of listeners** audience
**group of military rulers** junta
**group of Moslem scholars** ulema
**group of mountains in Australia** Snowy
**group of musicians** band, ensemble, orchestra
**group of nine** ennead, nonary, nonet
**group of North African languages** Hamitic
**group of particular levels** echelon
**group of peacocks** muster
**group of pedigree animals** stud
**group of penguins** colony, rookery
**group of people** crowd, idiom
**group of pheasants** bouquet, eye, nide, nye
**group of picked flowers** bunch
**group of pigeons** flight, flock
**group of plants** garden, plot
**group of plants including seaweed** algae
**group of players** company, team
**group of poems with a theme** epos
**group of puppies** litter
**group of quails** bevy
**group of racehorses** stable, string
**group of regiments** brigade
**group of related things** brood, set
**group of retorts** setting
**group of rhymed lines** stanza
**group of roe deer** bevy
**group of Scouts** troop
**group of seals** pod
**group of seven** hebdomad, heptad, septenary, septet
**group of sheep** flock
**group of ships** fleet
**group of similar things** set
**group of singers** choir, chorus
**group of six** hexad, senary, sextet
**group of small furry marsupials** phalangers
**group of soldiers** troop
**group of South Pacific islands** Samoa
**group of species** genus
**group of spectators** audience, crowd, gallery
**group of starlings** murmuration
**group of stars** asterism, constellation, Orion
**group of students** class, seminar

**group of supporting dancers in ballet** corps de ballet
**group of symbols** formula
**group of symptoms** syndrome
**group of ten** decad(e), denary
**group of ten notes** decuplet
**group of tents** camp, canvas
**group of things** genus
**group of three** triad, trine, trinity, trio, triumvirate, triune
**group of three lines in verse** tercet
**group of three literary works** trilogy
**group of three persons** threesome
**group of thugs** gang
**group of trained singers** choir, chorus
**group of trees** forest, grove, plantation
**group of trout** hover
**group of twelve** dozen
**group of twelve islands in south-eastern Aegean** Dodecanese
**group of twenty** score
**group of two** brace, couple, diarchy, dyad, pair
**group of two vowels** digram, digraph
**group of utensils** tea set
**group of verses** poem
**group of voices** choir, chorus
**group of whales** pod
**group of wolves** pack
**group of women** bevy
**group of words** phrase, sentence
**group spirit** esprit de corps, morale
**group therapy** est
**group together** assemble, gather
**group who regularly eat together** mess
**group with a common aim** bloc
**group with common ancestors** clan
**group with like outlook** party, sect
**grouse** carp, complain(t), grievance, grumble, henpeck, moan, mumble, mutter, nag, objection, whine, yammer
**grout** dregs, lute, sediment
**grove** academy, bluff, boscage, camp, copse, covert, dell, forest, hurst, island, orangery, orchard, pinery, shaw, spinney, spring, stand, thicket, toft, tope, wild(wood)
**grovel** cower, crawl, creep, cringe, crouch, defer, fawn, flatter, kowtow, sneak
**grove of fruit trees** orchard
**grove of mango trees** tope
**grove of osiers** holt
**grove of small trees** copse
**grove of sugar maples** camp
**grow** advance, arise, become, breed, cultivate, develop, enlarge, evolve, expand, extend, farm, flourish, flower, germinate, improve,

increase, issue, originate, produce, progress, proliferate, propagate, prosper, raise, rise, shoot, spread, spring, sprout, stretch, swell, turn
**grow ashen** pale
**grow better** amend, heal, improve
**grow bigger** enlarge
**grow calm** quiesce
**grow cordial** thaw
**grow dark** darken, gloam, gloom
**grow dim** bleach, blear, blur, dull, fade, pale
**grow drowsy** nod, tire
**grow dull** pall, tarnish
**grow exuberantly** luxuriate, vegetate
**grow faint** appal, die, weaken
**grow fat** batten, fatten
**grow genial** thaw
**grow gradually less** taper
**grow in clusters** racemose
**growing along ground** decumbent
**growing among rocks** saxatile
**growing angry** rascent
**growing closely together** thickset
**growing directly from the stem** sessile
**growing from a peduncle** pedunculate
**growing in air** aerial
**growing in clumps** tufted
**growing in clusters** acervate, racemose
**growing in dry conditions** xeric
**growing in heaps** acervate
**growing in meadows** campestral
**growing in moist places** hygrophilous
**growing in pairs** binate
**growing in rubbish** ruderal
**growing in sand or sandy places** arenicolous
**growing in sevens** septenate
**growing in snow** nival
**growing in wastes** ruderal
**growing in water** aquatic
**growing luxuriantly** exuberant
**growing naturally without cultivation** spontaneous
**growing old** ageing, elderly, senescent
**growing on a stem** cauline
**growing out** enate
**growing out of something abnormally** excrescent
**growing plants** greenery
**growing profusely** luxuriant
**growing rapidly** booming
**growing rice** paddy
**growing-season** spring
**growing together** adnate, symphysis
**growing to manhood** adolescent
**growing towards the light** heliotropic
**growing under snow** nival
**growing under water** submerged, submersed
**growing up** adolescent

**growing vegetation** verdure
**growing vigorously** thrifty
**growing wild** agrarian, agrestal, savage
**grow in length** elongate
**grow in size** swell
**grow into** advance, progress
**grow into a mass** accumulate, agglomerate
**grow irregularly** scramble
**growl** complain, crab, gnarl, gripe, groan, grouse, grumble, howl, lament, moan, mumble, murmur, rumble, snarl, yap, yelp
**grow large** expand, swell, wax
**grow less** abate, assuage, decrease, diminish, ebb, shrink, slake, wane
**grow less severe** relent
**grow light** dawn
**grow luxuriantly** thrive
**growl viciously** snarl
**growl with bared teeth** snarl
**grown in a paddy** rice
**grown to maturity** adult, full-grown
**grown-up** adult, full-grown, fully-fledged, (gentle)man, lady, mature, woman
**grown-up kid** goat
**grown-up person** adult
**grown-up tadpole** frog
**grow old** age, mature, ripen, senesce
**grow older** age, mature, mellow
**grow on** accept, effect, impress, influence, stir, touch
**grow on vine** grape
**grow out** enate
**grow out of** abandon, discard, outgrow
**grow over** invade
**grow pale** blanch, bleach, blench, fade
**grow profound** deepen
**grow rich** fatten
**grow sick** ail
**grow slimmer** slenderise
**grow smaller** shrink
**grow sound** heal
**grow still** hush
**growth** agriculture, corn, crop, cyst, development, expansion, increase, produce, product, result, shoot, swelling, tumour
**growth and development of cancer** carcinosis
**growth caused by dampness** mildew, mould
**growth chart** graph
**grow thin** peak
**growth of capital by continued interest** accumulation
**growth of trees** wood
**growth on rhino** horn
**grow to be** become
**grow together** accrete, coalesce, knit

**grow to increase** accrue
**grow too big for** outgrow
**grow to stalk** spindle
**grow uninteresting** pall
**grow up** accrue, appear, arise, bloom, burgeon, develop, stem
**grow vigorously** flourish, thrive
**grow wan** pall
**grow wearisome** bore, pall, wear-out
**grow weary** tire
**grow young again** rejuvenesce
**groyne** breakwater, jetty, mole, pier
**grub** burrow, caterpillar, chrysalis, delve, dig, explore, ferret, food, forage, hunt, investigate, larva, maggot, nosh, nymph, probe, pupa, root, rummage, scour, toil, unearth, uproot, worm
**grubby** dirty, dusty, filthy, grimy, messy, mucky, scruffy, seedy, shabby, slovenly, soiled, squalid, unclean, untidy, unwashed
**grudge** animosity, antagonism, aversion, begrudge, bitterness, covet, dislike, enmity, envy, grievance, hate, hatred, ill-will, jealousy, malice, mind, rancour, regret, resent(ment), spite, stint, suffer, umbrage, venom, yield
**grudging** cautious, guarded, half-hearted, hesitant, reluctant, secret, unenthusiastic, unwilling
**grudging admiration** envy
**grudging feeling** envy
**grudging giver** niggard
**grudgingly admire** envy
**gruel** oatmeal
**gruelling** arduous, backbreaking, brutal, crushing, demanding, difficult, exhausting, hard(-going), harsh, laborious, punishing, severe, stern, strenuous, taxing, tiring, tough, trying
**gruesome** abominable, awful, fearful, gaunt, ghastly, grim, grisly, hideous, horrible, horrific, horrifying, macabre, monstrous, morbid, repellent, repugnant, repulsive, shocking, spine-chilling, terrible
**gruesomely imaginative** macabre
**gruff** bad-tempered, brusque, coarse, crusty, grumpy, harsh, hoarse-voiced, impolite, rough, rude, sour, surly, uncivil
**gruff bark of dog** woof
**gruff noise** groan
**grumble** bleat, carp, complain(t), grievance, gripe, grouch, grouse, growl, henpeck, moan, mumble, murmur, mutter, nag, object(ion), rumble, whine, yammer
**grumble like a dog** growl

**grumpy** annoyed, bad-tempered, bearish, brusque, cantankerous, captious, contrary, crabbed, crabby, crestfallen, cross, crotchety, crusty, dejected, difficult, disagreeable, discontented, disgruntled, displeased, doleful, down, glum, grouchy, gruff, ill-tempered, irascible, irritable, malcontent, moody, morose, peevish, perverse, petulant, quarrelsome, saturnine, sulky, sullen, surly, testy, vexed
**Guam is one** island
**Guam port** Piti
**guanaco** llama
**guanidine** carbamidine
**guarantee** assurance, assure, attestation, bond, certainty, certify, collateral, contract, covenant, endorsement, ensure, guaranty, indemnity, insurance, insure, oath, pledge, promise, secure, security, surety, testimonial, undertaking, vouch(er), warrant(y), word
**guarantor** backer, ensurer, guarantee, indemnitor, insurer, obligator, patron, sponsor, supporter, surety, voucher, warrantor
**guaranty** agreement, assurance, bond, collateral, covenant, deposit, endorsement, gage, guarantee, oath, obligation, pawn, pledge, promise, security, sponsor, surety, undertaking, voucher, warrant(y), word
**guard** bulwark, defence, defend(er), escort, guardian, preserve, protect(ion), protector, safety, save, security, sentinel, sentry, shield, watch(man)
**guard against** beware
**guard at the Tower of London** beefeater
**guarded** cagey, careful, cautious, covered, defended, discreet, non-committal, reserved, restrained, reticent, secretive, suspicious, watchful, way
**guarded locality** post
**guardian** attendant, champion, conserver, curator, custodian, defender, escort, guard, keeper, minder, preserver, protector, trustee, warden, warder
**guardian of minor** tutor
**guardian of morals** custos morum (L)
**guardian saint** patron
**guardian's care** tutelage, wardship
**guardian's charge** ward
**guardianship** protectorate, wardship
**guardian spirit** angel
**guardian's ward** protégé(e)

**guarding against disease** prophylactic
**guard position in fencing** septime
**guardrail** ox-fence, oxer
**guardsman** grenadier
**guard's van in a goods train** caboose
**Guatemala coin** centavo, peso, que(t)zal
**Guatemala currency** que(t)zal
**Guatemala dance** elson, guarimba
**Guatemala department** Escuintla, Izabal, Jalaa, Peten, Quiche, Solola, Zacapa
**Guatemala fruit** anay
**Guatemala gulf** Honduras
**Guatemala insect** kelep
**Guatemala lake** Atitlan, Dulce, Guija, Izabal, Peten
**Guatemala port** Barrios, Livingston, Ocos
**Guatemala ruins** Tikal
**Guatemala volcano** Agua, Pacaya, Tacana, Tajumulco
**guerdon** recompense, reward
**Guernsey** Jersey
**Guernsey lily** amaryllis
**guerrilla** freedom-fighter, irregular, partisan, resistance, sniper
**guess** assume, assumption, belief, believe, conjecture, deem, estimate, estimation, fancy, fathom, feel(ing), hazard, hypothesis, imagine, intuition, judge(ment), judgment, notion, opinion, penetrate, predict(ion), reckon(ing), solve, speculate, speculation, subject, suppose, surmise, suspicion, theory, think
**guess at a future event** forecast
**guessing game** bluff, charade, coffeepot
**guesswork** approximation, assumption, conclusion, conjecture, estimate, estimation, fancy, guess, hypothesis, inference, intuition, notion, presumption, presupposition, reckoning, speculation, supposition, surmise, suspicion, theory
**guest** caller, company, customer, patron, visitor
**guest brought by an invited person** parasite, umbra
**guesthouse in monastery** xenodochium
**guest receiver** welcomer
**guffaw** bellow, cachinnation, horse-laugh, howl, laugh, roar, shriek
**guidance** admonition, advice, charge, control, counselling, direction, disposal, exhortation, guideline, help, illumination, indication, instruction, leadership, management, navigation,

persuasion, pointers, recommendation, regulation, rule, steerage, steering, teaching, warning
**guide** accompany, advise, attend, command, conduct(or), control, convoy, direct(or), drive, educate, escort, indication, influence, instruct, lead(er), manage, mark, navigate, pilot, regulate, sign(al), steer(sman), supervise, usher
**guide a ship** steer
**guidebook for tourists** Baedeker
**guide by rudder** steer
**guided trip** tour
**guide in Middle Eastern countries** dragoman
**guide of coach horses** postboy
**guide or interpreter in Arabic countries** dragoman
**guide to visitors of antiquities** cicerone
**guide vehicle** steer
**guide who shows visitors round a place** cicerone
**guide wrongly** mislead
**guiding in discovering** heuristic
**guiding spirit of a group** ethos
**guiding star** cynosure
**guild** association, brotherhood, chapel, club, company, corporation, fellowship, fraternity, league, lodge, order, organisation, society, union
**guild president** dean
**guile** artfulness, artifice, cheat, chicanery, craft(iness), cunning, deceit, deception, dole, duplicity, fallacy, finesse, fraud, knavery, perfidy, shrewdness, slickness, slyness, treachery
**guilefully persuade** entice, inveigle, tempt
**guileless** artless, bold, candid, explicit, fair, frank, genuine, honest, ignorant, ingenuous, innocent, just, naïve, open(-hearted), plain, simple, sincere, straightforward, trustful, trustworthy, undeceiving, unequivocal, unguarded, unwary
**guillemot** puffin, razorbill
**guillotine victim's cart** tumbrel, tumbril
**guilt** blame, conscience, contrition, culpability, delinquency, disgrace, dishonour, guilty, infamy, iniquity, misconduct, regret, remorse, responsibilty, self-condemnation, self-reproach, shame, sinfulness, stigma, wickedness, wrong(doing)
**guiltless** blameless, clean, clear, immaculate, impeccable, innocent, irreproachable, pure, sinless, spotless, unimpeachable, unspotted, untainted, untarnished

**guilty** amiss, criminal, culpable, demeritorious, erring, evil, felonious, heinous, illegal, illegitimate, illicit, lawless, nolo contendere, peccant, regretful, remorseful, repentant, sinful, unlawful, wicked, wrong
**guilty of crime** criminal
**guilty of fraud** fraudulent
**guilty of offence** culprit
**guilty of treason** traitor, treasonable
**guilty party** culprit
**Guinea bight** Benin
**Guinea cape** Verga
**Guinea coin** franc
**Guinea currency** sily
**Guinea island group** Los
**Guinea lake** Tombo, Tristao
**Guinea mountains** Loma, Nimba
**guinea pig** cavy, paca
**guinea pig male** boar
**Guinea squash** eggplant
**Guinevere's husband** Arthur
**Guinevere's lover** Lancelot
**guise** air, appearance, aspect, attire, blind, camouflage, cast, cloak, clothes, clothing, concealment, costume, cover, demeanour, device, disguise, dress, effect, excuse, exterior, façade, face, fashion, front(age), garb, garments, habit, image, impression, look, manner, mask, masquerade, mimicry, ploy, pretence, ruse, screen, semblance, show, subterfuge, veil, veneer, way
**guitar** gittern
**guitar device** capo
**guitar-like instrument** balalaika, bouzouki, lute, mandolin, sitar, ukulele
**guitar sound** twane, twang
**guitar string plucker** plectrum
**guitar with three strings** samisen
**gulch** abysm, abyss, arroyo, canyon, chasm, cleft, crack, crevasse, crevice, defile, fissure, gap, gorge, gulf, gully, ravine, valley
**gulf** abyss, basin, bay, bight, breach, chasm, cleft, gap, gorge, opening, rift, separation, split, yoid
**gulf in Africa** Aden, Guinea
**gulf in Arabian Sea** Oman
**gulf in Baltic Sea** Bothnia, Riga
**gulf in Bulgaria** Bulgas
**gulf in Burma** Martaban
**gulf in Chile** Arauco, Guafo, Penas, Uncud
**gulf in China** Liaotung, Pechili, Pohai, Pohai, Tonkin
**gulf in Colombia** Cupica, Darien, Tibuga, Tortugas, Uraba
**gulf in Costa Rica** Dulce, Nicoya, Papagayo

**gulf in Crete** Khania, Merabello
**gulf in Cuba** Ana-Maria, Batabano, Mexico
**gulf in Djibouti** Tadjoura
**gulf in Egypt** Aqaba
**gulf in El Salvador** Fonseca
**gulf in France** Aegina
**gulf in Greece** Aegina, Athens, Laconia, Rendina, Salonika, Thermaic
**gulf in Guatemala** Honduras
**gulf in Haiti** Gonave
**gulf in Honduras** Fonseca
**gulf in India** Cambay, Kutch, Mannar
**gulf in Indonesia** Bone, Tolo, Tomini
**gulf in Israel** Aqaba
**gulf in Italy** Gaeta, Genoa, Oristano, Orosei, Salerno, Taranto
**gulf in Libya** Sidra, Sirte
**gulf in New Guinea** Huon, Papua
**gulf in New Zealand** Hauraki
**gulf in North America** Alaska
**gulf in North Vietnam** Tonkin(g)
**gulf in Panama** Chiriqui, Darien, Mosquito, Sunblas
**gulf in Sardinia** Oristano, Orosei
**gulf in Siberia** Ob
**gulf in Sicily** Catania, Noto
**gulf in Sri Lanka** Mannar
**gulf in Sweden** Bothnia
**gulf in the Mediterranean** Taranto
**gulf in Tunisia** Gabes, Hammemet, Tunis
**gulf in Turkey** Antalya, Cos
**gulf in Venezuela** Paria
**gulf in Yugoslavia** Kvarner
**Gulf state** Oman
**gull** befool, bird, cheat, cozen, deceive, delude, dupe, fool, Lari, mew, rook, simpleton, skua, swindle, tern
**gullet** gore, gusset, oesophagus, throat, water-channel
**gullible** credulous, foolish, green, innocent, naïve, silly, trusting, unsceptical
**gullible person** sap
**Gulliver's country** Lilliput
**gull-like bird** skua, tern
**gull's cry** maw, mew
**gull's relative** tern
**gully** abyss, canyon, corridor, crevasse, donga, fissure, gorge, gulch, gulf, passage, ravine, sloot, valley
**gully formed by rain** sloot
**gulp** bolt, choke, devour, gasp, gobble, guzzle, quaff, stuff, swallow, swig, swill, wolf
**gulp for air** gasp
**gum** adhesive, cement, clog, exudate, fix, gingiva, glue, paste, resin, seal, stick

**gumbo** okra
**gumboil** abscess
**gum got from certain trees** mastic
**gum of various trees** kino
**gumption** astuteness, audacity, backbone, boldness, cleverness, common sense, courage, daring, energy, enterprise, gameness, guts, initiative, judg(e)ment, mettle, nerve, nous, pluck, resolution, resourcefulness, shrewdness, spirit, stamina, vigour, wisdom
**gum resin** bdellium, copal, la(b)danum, myrrh, resinoid, tacamahac
**gum resin used in perfumes** myrrh
**gum used in tanning** kino
**gun** cannon, firearm, gat, pistol, rifle
**gun belt** holster
**gun dog** retriever, setter
**gunfire sound** bang, report
**gun firing shells** mortar
**gun inventor** Bren, Colt, Remington
**gunlock catch** sear
**gunlock hammer** doghead
**gunman** assassin, bandit, brigand, butcher, criminal, crook, cutthroat, desperado, enforcer, executioner, exterminator, freebooter, gangster, killer, murderer, ruffian, shooter, sniper, terrorist, thug
**gun missile** bullet
**gun muffler** silencer
**gunner** artilleryman
**gun salute** salvo
**guns, bombs, etc.** ammo
**gunshot sound** bang, report
**gun tube** barrel
**gurgle** babble, bubble, burble, crow, lap, murmur, ripple, splash
**gurnet fish** gurnard
**guru** swami
**gush** babble, burst, cascade, chatter, drivel, effuse, emanate, emote, enthuse, exuberance, flood, flow, gabble, issue, jabber, jet, outburst, outflow, outpouring, overflow, pour, run, rush, spout, spurt, stream, surge, swell, tattle, tide, torrent, yabble
**gushing** bursting, cascading, ebullient, effusive, emanating, emitting, expansive, flooding, flowing, glib, jetting, pouring, running, rushing, slick, spouting, spurting, streaming, unctuous, unreserved, verbose, warm, zealous
**gush out** flow
**gusset** inset
**gust** blast, blow, breeze, burst, fit, flavour, flaw, flurry, gale, passion,

puff, relish, rush, squall, surge, taste, zest
**gusto** appetite, appreciation, brio, delight, élan, enjoyment, enthusiasm, exhilaration, exuberance, fervour, fondness, liking, pleasure, relish, satisfaction, savour, taste, verve, zeal, zest
**gust of laughter** gale
**gust of wind** blast
**gusty** airy, blowy, blustering, blustery, boisterous, breezy, dirty, draughty, foul, fresh, gustful, light, lofty, open, raging, rough, spacious, squally, stormy, tempestuous, turbulent, uncluttered, well-ventilated, wild, windy
**gut** abdomen, audacity, backbone, belly, bowel(s), catgut, colon, courage, daring, despoil, disembowel, entrails, innards, insides, intestines, pillage, plunder, pouch, raid, ransack, stomach, vitals
**gut pain** gastralgia
**gut part** ileum

**guts** audacity, bowels, bravery, courage, daring, endurance, entrails, fearlessness, innards, intestines, nerve, offal, pluck, stamina, tenacity, viscera
**gutter** channel, conduit, ditch, donga, drain, duct, groove, passage, pipe, rone, runnel, sloot, sluice, trench, trough, tube
**gutteral** rasping, rough, thick, throaty
**gutter step** kerb
**gutter to carry off rain from roof** rone
**gutter urchin** stroller, waif
**guttural** deep, grating, gravelly, gruff, harsh, hoarse, husky, low, rasping, rough, thick, throaty
**guttural sound of anger** growl
**guy** bloke, boy, caricature, chap, fellow, individual, lad, man, mock, oke, ou, person, ridicule, youth
**guy to support** stay
**guzzle** bolt, carouse, cram, devour, drink, gobble, gorge, go(u)rmandise, quaff, stuff, swill, tope, wolf
**gymnasium** akhara

**gymnast** exerciser
**gymnastics** acrobatics, athletics, calisthenics, exercises, high-vaulting, somersaulting, sport, tumbling
**gymnastics movement** kip, pike, tuck
**gym pad** mat
**gypsy** drifter, explorer, gipsy, hiker, itinerant, migrant, migratory, nomad(ic), passenger, rambler, ranger, roamer, Romany, rover, roving, shifting, stroller, tinker, tourist, transient, traveller, tripper, unsettled, vagabond, vagrant, voyager, wanderer, wayfarer
**gypsy gentleman** rye
**gypsy language** Romany
**gypsy man** rom
**gypsy's card** tarot
**gypsy's home** caravan
**gyrate** circle, circulate, grind, gyre, pirouette, revolve, roll, rotate, spin, spiral, swirl, swivel, twirl, wheel, whirl, wind

# H

**haberdasher** clothier, costumer, furrier, hosier, outfitter, seamstress, shopkeeper, tailor
**habile** dext(e)rous, skilful
**habit** addiction, array, bent, cloth, conduct, conformity, custom, disposition, dress, equip, familiarity, garb, instinct, knack, practice, regularity, routine, rule, temperament, tendency, tradition, trait, trick, usage, use(r), way, wont
**habitat** abode, domain, domicile, element, environment, haunt, home, locale, locality, milieu, quarters, realm, region, surroundings, terrain, territory, zone
**habitation** abiding, address, camper, colony, community, domicil(e), dwelling, habitancy, home, house, living, location, lodging, nest, occupancy, quarters, residence, residency, residing, settlement, society, villa
**habit of abstaining from pleasure** abstinence
**habit of action** knack
**habit of eating earth** geophagy

**habit of marrying only once** monogamy
**habit of pairing with a single mate** monogamy
**habitual** accustomed, common, customary, established, familiar, fixed, natural, normal, ordinary, persistent, recurrent, regular, routine, standard, traditional, usual, wonted
**habitual act** exercise
**habitual criminal** bloubaadjie, gaolbird, jailbird, prisoner, recidivist
**habitual doing** practice
**habitual drinker** tippler
**habitual drug user** addict, roker
**habitual drunkard** dronkie, dronklap, inebriate, sot
**habitual drunkenness** crapulence, inebriety
**habitual food** diet
**habitual loafer** layabout
**habitually forgetful** absent-minded
**habitually hopeful** sanguine
**habitually on the look-out** wary
**habitually silent** taciturn
**habitually truthful** veracious
**habitual scoffer** cynic

**habitual sleeplessness** insomnia
**habituate** acclimatise, accommodate, accustom, adapt, adjust, alter, anneal, apply, change, comply, condition, conform, domesticate, drill, educate, enure, equip, familiarise, fit, inure, make, match, modify, naturalise, prepare, qualify, ready, remodel, season, shape, suit, tailor, temper, train
**habitue of track** gambler, race-lover
**hack** bark, chop, commonplace, cough, cut, gash, hackney, haggle, hew, kick, lease, let, mangle, mediocre, mercenary, mutilate, nag, notch, old, overdone, pedestrian, poor, rent, slash, stereotyped, trite, undistinguished, unoriginal, used
**hackbut** (h)arquebus
**hackney coachman** jarvey, jarvie
**hackneyed** banal, clichéd, common(place), corny, dull, humdrum, inane, insipid, overdone, overworked, pedestrian, prosaic, simple, stale, stereotyped, stock, threadbare, tired, trite, uninspired, vieux jeu (F), worn-out
**hackneyed phrase** cliché

**hackneyed quotation** tag
**had a golden touch** Midas
**had best** should
**had better** should
**haddock** scrod
**Hadean river** Acheron, Lethe, Styx
**Hades** hell, underworld
**Hades river** Acheron, Lethe, Styx
**had food** ate
**haecceity** individuality
**haemoglobin deficiency** anaemia
**haemoglobin deficient** anaemic
**haemophiliac** bleeder
**haemorrhage** bleed
**haemorrhoids** piles
**hag** beldam(e), crone, fury, haggard, harridan, hellcat, shrew, sibyl, termagant, virago, vixen, wench, witch
**haggard** careworn, drawn, emaciated, gaunt, ghastly, meagre, pale, pinched, shrunken, thin, wan, wasted, wild-looking, worn, wrinkled
**haggard or ill-tempered woman** harridan
**Haggard title** She
**haggle** annoy, argue, argument, badger, bargain, barter, cavil, dicker, disagreement, dispute, hack, haggling, harass, higgle, mangle, negotiate, worry, wrangle
**hail** acclaim, accost, acknowledge, address, applaud, assail, ave, barrage, batter, bombard(ment), call, cheer, cry, esteem, exalt, extol, greet, honour, pelt, rain, receive, salute, salvo, shout, shower, storm, torrent, volley, wave, welcome
**hail and rain** sleet
**hailer** loudspeaker
**hailing call** cooee
**hails from Delhi** Indian
**hails from Denmark** Dane
**hair** bristle, filament, locks, pelo (Sp), tresses
**hair bleach** peroxide
**hair clip** slide
**haircloth** cilice
**hair cream** pomade
**hair cropped short in the manner of a schoolboy** Eton crop, shingle
**haircut** tonsure
**hair cut short and standing stiffly upright** crewcut, en brosse (F)
**hair decoration** snood
**hairdresser** barber, beautician, coiffeur, coiffeuse, friseur, haircutter, (hair)stylist
**hairdresser's premises** salon
**hair dye** henna, rinse, tint
**hair-end splitting** distrix
**hair fastener** clip

**hair fringing the eyelid** eyelash
**hair groomer** comb
**hair-holder** clip
**hairiness** bristleness, crinosity, furriness, hirsuteness, pilosity, shagginess, woolliness
**hairless** bald(headed), baldpated, beardless, clean-shaven, glabrous, shaven, shorn, tonsured
**hairlike** trichoid
**hairlike growth** villus
**hair net** snood
**hair of Angora goat** mohair
**hair oil** brilliantine, pomade
**hair on brush** bristle
**hair on horse's neck** mane
**hair on man's chin** beard
**hair on man's face** whisker
**hair on man's upper lip** moustache
**hairpiece** postiche, toupee, wig
**hair-raising** alarming, bloodcurdling, eerie, exciting, frightening, horrifying, scary, shocking, spine-chilling, startling, terrifying, thrilling
**hair rinse** henna
**hair-setting jelly** gel
**hair soap** shampoo
**hair straightener** comb
**hairstyle** coiffure
**hairstyle cut short and even all round the head** bob
**hairstyle for long hair** ponytail
**hairstyle piled up by backcombing** beehive
**hairstyle with a curled fringe across the head** frizette
**hairstylist** coiffeur, coiffeuse, hairdresser
**hair wash** shampoo
**hairy** bearded, bushy, dangerous, difficult, fleecy, frightening, furry, hirsute, nerve-racking, pilose, risky, scaring, shaggy, stubbly, woolly
**hairy arch** eyebrow
**hairy dog** Afghan
**hairy hedgehog** moon-rat
**hairy man** Esau
**Haitian dance** juba
**Haitian evil spirit** baka
**Haitian island** Gonave, Hispaniola, Navassa, Tortue, Tortuga, Vache
**Haitian island group** Caymites
**Haitian lake** Saumatre
**Haitian magic** obeah, obi
**Haitian money** gourde
**Haitian outlaw** caco
**Haitian plain** Cayes, Gonaives, Jacmel, Leogane, Nord
**Haiti cape** Foux
**Haiti channel** St Marc, Sud
**Haiti deity** Loa
**Haiti gulf** Gonave

**hajji's robes** ihram
**hake** whiting
**halcyon** balmy, calm, fortunate, glorious, happy, joyous, kingfisher, mild, moderate, peaceful, placid, pleasant, prosperous, quiet, reposeful, restful, serene, still, stormless, temperate, thriving, tranquil, unagitated, warm
**hale** drag, draw, healthy, pull, robust, strong, vigorous
**hale and hearty** healthy
**half** bisect(ion), demi-, division, fraction(al), half-share, hemi-, hemisphere, imperfectly, incomplete(ly), limited, moiety, part(ial), partially, portion, section, segment, semi-, share, slightly, some
**half a circle's diameter** radius
**half a laugh** ha
**half an em** en
**half a pica** en
**half a pint** cup
**half a quart** pint
**half a real** picayune, picayunish
**half a score** ten
**half asleep** dopey, drowsy, nodding, sleepy, somnolent
**half a sphere** hemisphere
**half a toy** yo
**half-baked** crazy, foolish, ill-conceived, impractical, short-sighted, stupid
**half-bull, half-man** Minotaur
**half-caste** hybrid, metis, mulatto
**half diameter** radius
**half-done** incomplete, uncompleted, undone, unfinished, unfulfilled
**half-dozen** six
**half-dress** skirt
**half glass** split
**half-hearted** apathetic, cool, feeble, indifferent, listless, lukewarm, neutral, passive, perfunctory, spiritless, tame, uninterested
**half-human, half-beast** satyr
**half-human sea creature** mermaid, triton
**half-light** evening, sunset, twilight
**half-man, half-bull** Minotaur
**half-man, half-goat Greek god** Pan, Faunus
**half-man, half-horse** centaur
**half-melted snow** slush
**half month** fortnight
**half-moon** arc
**half-note** minim
**half of diameter** radius
**half of sword** forte
**half of the cheek** chap
**half quart** pint
**half-sister of Amnon** Tamar
**half sphere** hemisphere

**half step** semitone
**half-suppressed laugh** chuckle, snigger
**half-tamed horse** bronco
**half-tamed polecat** ferret
**half the celestial sphere** hemisphere
**half the earth** hemisphere
**half the width of an em** en
**half-turn movement in dressage** caracole
**halfway** central, equidistant, imperfectly, incomplete(ly), intermediate, mid(dle), midway, moderately, nearly, partial(ly), partly, rather
**halfway house** inn
**halfway submerged** waist-deep
**halfway to the horizon** middle-distance
**halfway up** midair
**halfwit** dullard, dunce, fool, idiot, imbecile, incompetent, moron, nitwit, simpleton, zany
**half-witted person** simpleton
**half-woman, half-fish** mermaid
**half-year course** semester
**halibut steak** flitch
**halite** rock-salt
**hall** antechamber, anteroom, aula (G), corridor, entry, hallway, lobby, passage, salle (F), vestibule
**Halley's discovery** comet
**hall for assemblies** saloon
**hall for lectures** theatre
**hallmark** badge, brand-name, device, emblem, endorsement, indication, mark, seal, sign, stamp, symbol, trademark
**hallow** anoint, bless, dedicate, enshrine, sanctify
**hallowed** adored, blessed, consecrated, holy, sacred, sanctified, venerated, worshipped
**hallowed place** shrine
**Halloween outfit** costume
**hallucinate** (day)dream, fantasise, imagine
**hallucination** aberration, apparition, delusion, dream, fantasy, figment, illusion, mirage, phantasm(agoria), vision
**hallucinogen** LSD
**halo** aureola, aureole, corona, gloriole, nimbus
**halt** arrest, ba(u)lk, boggle, brake, cease, crippled, crush, defect, desist, discontinue, end, falter, hesitate, hold, lame, limp, pause, quell, quit, respite, rest, stammer, stand, stem, stop(page), stumble, stutter, terminate, waver, whoa
**halter** noose, rope, strap, tether
**haltere** balancer, halter

**halter for breaking in horses** hackamore
**halting** awkward, broken, faltering, hesitant, imperfect, laboured
**halt in hostilities** cease-fire
**halve** apportion, bisect, divide, equalise, share
**ham** amateur, tyro
**hamburger garnish** gherkin, onion
**hamburger roll** bun
**ham it up** overact
**hamlet** burg, community, crossroads, dorp, town, village
**Hamlet's home** Elsinore
**hammer** bang, batter, beat, beetle, club, drive, fashion, forge, form, gavel, hit, kevel, knock, make, mallet, maul, pelt, pound, pummel, shape, sledge, strike, tamper, tap(per)
**hammer away** drudge, labour, persevere, persist
**hammered spike** nail
**hammerer** panelbeater
**hammer handle** helve
**hammer head part** peen
**hammer out** accomplish, chisel, complete, create, fashion, finish, generate, manufacture, model, mould, negotiate, produce, reconcile, roughcast, settle, shape
**hammer part** peen, helve
**hammer's pal** nail
**hammer with a large head** mallet
**hamper** basket, cramp, curb, curtail, encumber, frustrate, hamstring, handicap, hinder, impede, obstruct, prevent, restrain, restrict, shackle, thwart
**hamstring** hock
**hand** aid, art(istry), assist(ance), chiro-, clap, conduct, convey, craftsman, danny, deliver, direction, employee, fist, give, guide, help, influence, labourer, lead, ovation, palm, part, pass, relief, script, share, skill, support, touch, worker, workman, writing
**hand across** pass
**hand axe** chopper
**handbag** bag, briefcase, purse, satchel, valise, wallet
**hand bomb** grenade
**handbook** atlas, booklet, chart, directory, enchiridion, guide(book), itinerary, manual, map, notebook, plan, vade-mecum
**handcart** wheelbarrow
**hand-clapping** applause
**hand covering of boxer** glove

**handcuff** fetter, frustrate, hinder, impede, inhibit, manacle, shackle, thwart
**handcuffs** bracelets, cuffs, darbies, manacles
**hand digit** finger, thumb
**hand down** bequeath, communicate, deliver, give, grant, impart, transfer, transmit, will
**handed down** hereditary
**handfed calf** pod
**hand gesture** wave
**hand-gun** pistol, revolver
**hand-held firework** sparkler
**hand-held hammer drill** jackhammer
**hand held light** torch
**handicap** barrier, block, burden, constraint, curb, defect, difficulty, disability, disadvantage, drawback, encumber, encumbrance, hamper, hinder, hindrance, impairment, impede, impediment, inconvenience, limit(ation), obstacle, obstruction, penalty, restraint, restrict(ion), shortcoming, stumbling-block
**handicap stroke to be taken when desired** bisque
**handicraft** art(isanship), craft(smanship), handiwork, skill, workmanship
**hand in again** resubmit
**hand-in-glove** allied
**hand-in-hand** closely, concurrently, conjunct, jointly, together
**hand in whist** misère
**handiwork** achievement, artefact, creation, design, doing, (handi)craft, invention, product(ion), result, work
**hand joint** wrist
**handkerchief** bandanna, hanky, mouchoir (F), tissue
**handle** act, administer, ansa (L), balustrade, carry, command, control, cope, direct, employ, feel, finger, govern, grasp, grip, guide, hold, knob, manage, manipulate, market, operate, peddle, sell, touch, trade, transact, treat, utilise, wield
**handle awkwardly** fumble, paw
**handle carelessly** maul
**handle of a dagger** haft, hilt
**handle of pail** bail
**handle of scythe** snath(e)
**handle of sword** hilt
**handle of weapon** helve
**handle of whip** whipstock
**handle on machine** lever
**handle on vase** ansa (L)
**handler** agent, coach, wielder
**handler of wild animals** tamer
**handle roughly** maltreat, maul, mishandle

**handle roughly or rudely** tousle
**handle rudely** paw
**handle the helm** steer
**handling** administration, approach, conduct, direction, management, manipulation, running, treatment, usage
**hand measure** span
**hand-me-down** second-hand, used, worn
**hand-mill for grinding grain** quern
**hand motion** gesture
**hand of cards without court card** carte blanche
**hand on** relay
**hand on hip** akimbo
**hand ornament** ring
**hand out** disburse, dispense, disseminate, distribute, mete
**hand-out** alms, bulletin, charity, circular, dole, freebie, issue, largess(e), leaflet, literature, share(-out), statement
**hand out cards** deal
**hand out punishment** mete
**hand over** cede, deliver, donate, impart, present, release, relinquish, surrender, yield
**hand over fist** easily, steadily, swiftly
**hand over for a price** sell
**hand over money** pay
**hand part** finger, knuckle, palm, thumb
**hand-picked** chosen, called, elect, recherché, select(ed)
**hand reaper** scythe, sickle
**hand-reared lamb** cosset
**hands** authority, care, charge, command, control, crew, guidance, possession, power, supervision
**hands down** absolutely, easily, effortlessly, incontestably, undeniably
**hand signal** wave
**handsome** abundant, admirable, ample, attractive, comely, considerable, elegant, generous, good-looking, graceful, gracious, large, liberal, majestic
**handsome man** Adonis, Apollo
**handsome-plumaged bird** bullfinch
**handsome youth** Adonis
**hands on hips** akimbo
**hand starter for car** crank
**hand-thrashing implement** flail
**hand-thrown explosive** grenade
**hand-thrown spear** javelin
**hand tool for cutting** axe
**hand warmer** muff
**hand-worker's implement** tool
**handwriting** cacography, calligraphy, chirography, fist, (long)hand, penmanship, scrawl, scribble, script

**handwriting on the wall** foreboding, forewarning, omen, premonition, warning
**handwritten document** manuscript
**handy** accessible, adept, apt, available, beneficial, convenient, deft, dext(e)rous, easy, expedient, expert, helpful, manageable, nearby, practical, tractable, useful, versatile
**handyman** do-all, factotum, jack-of-all-trades, odd-jobber, rouseabout, roustabout
**hang** adhere, adorn, cover, dangle, decorate, depend, drape, execute, float, gibbet, hesitate, hold, hover, impend, incline, linger, lynch, rely, rest, stick, suspend, swing, trail
**hang about** dally, haunt, hover, linger, loiter, resort, roam
**hang about idly** loiter
**hang above** hover
**hang and arrange in folds** drape
**hang around** dally, dawdle, frequent, haunt, hover, idle, linger, loiter, potter, remain, stay
**hang back** crouch, demur, flinch, hesitate, lag, recoil, shirk, shy
**hang down** dangle, droop, sag
**hang down loosely** slouch
**hanger-on** dependant, follower, lackey, minion, parasite, sponger, sycophant, toady
**hang fire** delay, procrastinate, vacillate
**hang freely** dangle
**hang illegally** lynch
**hang in air** hover
**hang in folds** drape
**hanging** dangling, drooping, execution, flapping, floppy, gibbeting, loose, lynching, nutant, pendancy, pendulousness, suspended, suspension, swinging, unattached, unsupported
**hanging back** doubtful, hesitant
**hanging bandage for a wounded limb** sling
**hanging bed** hammock
**hanging border of drapery** valance
**hanging cover** canopy
**hanging down** flabby, flaccid, limp
**hanging drapery** curtain
**hanging fire** abeyant, delayed, pending, postponed, unsettled
**hanging freezing water** icicle
**hanging locket** pendant
**hanging lock of wool** daglock
**hanging loop** noose
**hanging loop on garment** tab
**hanging loose** flabby, flaccid, limp
**hanging loosely** baggy, dangling, floppy, pendulous
**hanging ornament** pendant

**hangings** arras, artwork, curtain, drapery, paintings, pictures, tapestry
**hanging spike of frozen water** icicle
**hang in the air** hover
**hang limply** sag, lop
**hang loose** flow
**hang loosely** dangle
**hangman** beheader, decapitator, executioner, garrot(t)er, lyncher
**hangman's halter** noose
**hangman's scaffold** gallows
**hang on** absorb, adhere, append, cling, cohere, continue, endure, grasp, grip, linger, persevere, persist, remain, rest, wait
**hang on the cross** crucify
**hang on to** favour, follow, support
**hang out at** frequent
**hang over** approach, impend, loom, menace, threaten
**hangover** after-effects, babbala(a)s, crapulence
**hang rope** noose
**hang sideways** sag
**hang suspended** hover
**hang the lip** sulk
**hang up** block, disconnect, obstruct, restrict, retard, suspend
**hang without trial** lynch
**hank** coil, loop, skein
**hanker** ache, aim, aspire, burn, covet, crave, desiderate, desire, dream, hope, hunger, itch, long, lust, need, pant, pine, pursue, seek, starve, thirst, want, wish, yearn
**hanker after** crave, desire
**hanker for** covet, crave, desire, hunger, thirst, want
**hankering** appetite, ardour, craving, desire, hunger, itch, longing, lust, passion, thirst, urge, weakness, wish, yearning
**Hanoi is there** Vietnam
**Hansel's partner** Gretel
**Hansen's disease** leprosy
**Hansen's disease sufferer** leper
**haphazard** accidental, aimless, arbitrary, careless, casual, chance, disorderly, disorganised, hit-or-miss, indiscriminate, random, slapdash, slipshod, unstructured, unsystematic
**haphazard manner** slapdash
**hapless** ill-fated, luckless, unfortunate, unlucky
**happen** appear, arise, become, befall, betide, chance, come, ensue, eventuate, fall, intervene, issue, occur, result, supervene, transpire, uncover, unearth
**happen afterwards** ensue
**happen again** re-occur, recur
**happen again and again** recur

**happen as an interruption** supervene
**happened to** befell
**happening** accident, adventure, affair, befalling, case, chance, chancing, developing, ensuing, episode, event, experience, incident, occasion, occurrence, occurring, phenomenon, resulting, scene
**happening before** previous
**happening before birth** antenatal, prenatal
**happening before marriage** antenuptial
**happening by chance** accidental, casual, fortuitous
**happening during the day** diurnal
**happening every eight years** octennial
**happening every third year** triennial
**happening every two years** biennial
**happening in fits and starts** intermittent, spasmodic
**happening irregularly** occasionally
**happening now** current(ly)
**happening often** frequent
**happening once every year** annual
**happening once in a hundred years** centennial
**happening repeatedly** recurrent, constant
**happens afterwards** ensue
**happens by chance** accidental
**happens next** ensue
**happen to** befall, betide
**happen together** coincide, concur
**happily** agreeably, appropriately, cleverly, delightedly, elatedly, enthusiastically, fortunately, freely, gladly, gracefully, heartily, lief, seasonably, sincerely, tactfully, willingly
**happiness** beatitude, blessedness, bliss, contentment, delight, elation, gladness, joy, jubilation, pleasure, rejoicing, satisfaction
**happy** appropriate, befitting, blessed, blissful, blithe, cheerful, contented, delighted, enviable, favoured, felicitous, fortunate, gay, glad, joy(ful), joyous, jubilant, lucky, merry, pleased, propitious, satisfied
**happy accident** serendipity
**happy-go-lucky** blithe, carefree, casual, devil-may-care, easy-going, heedless, irresponsible, light-hearted, reckless
**happy nature** joyous
**happy state of mind** elation
**happy with what one has** contend
**hara-kiri** seppuku (J)
**harangue** address, bombast, declaim, diatribe, exhort(ation), lecture, orate, oration, preach, rant, speech, spiel, spout, screed, tirade
**harass** annoy, badger, bait, bedevil, beleaguer, beset, bother, disturb, exasperate, exhaust, fatigue, fret, gall, harry, hound, irk, molest, nag, oppress, perplex, persecute, pester, plague, tease, tire, torment, trouble, vex, weary, worry
**harassment** aggravation, annoyance, badgering, bedevilment, bother, irritation, molestation, nuisance, persecution, pestering, torment, trouble, vexation
**harass with shells** strafe
**harbinger** adumbrate, announcer, augury, auspice, betoken, clue, forebode, foreshadow, herald, omen, portend, precursor, predict, premonition, prophecy, spell, symptom, usher, warner
**harbour** anchorage, bay, board, cherish, cove, cover, destination, entertain, haven, hold, house, lodge, maintain, port, refuge, retreat, sanctuary, seaport, security, shelter
**harbour a grudge** resent
**harbour boat** tug
**harbour city** port
**harbour for yachts** marina
**harbour in Corsica** Bastia
**harbour in Hawaii** Pearl
**harbour in Guam** Apra
**harbour jetty** wharf
**harbour marker** buoy
**harbour town** port
**harbour vessel** scow, towboat, tug
**hard** adamant(ine), arduous, austere, burdensome, callous, compact, complex, complicated, difficult, exacting, exhausting, firm(ly), gallingly, grinding, hard-hearted, harsh, impenetrable, incessantly, indifferent, inflexible, intently, irrefutable, laborious, oppressive, perplexing, puzzling, relentless, resistant, rigid, rough, severe(ly), solid, spirituous, stormy, strict, tough, unfeeling, unkind, unrelenting, unsentimental, unsparing, unsympathetic, unyielding, vigorous, violent(ly)
**hard acid fruit** quince
**hard and fast** binding, fixed, inflexible, rigid, set, strict, stringent, unalterable, unchangeable
**hard and lumpy** knobbly
**hard animal fat** lard, suet
**hard aromatic resin** copal
**hard at work** busy
**hard-baked bread** rusk
**hard-bitten** callous, cold, hard-boiled, hard-headed, hard-nosed, hardened, hardhearted, heartless, indifferent, insensitive, matter-of-fact, obdurate, practical, ruthless, shrewd, soulless, thick-skinned, tough, uncaring, unfeeling, unresponsive, unsympathetic
**hard black vulcanised rubber** ebonite, vulcanite
**hard black wood** ebony
**hard blow** oner, slug, sock
**hard blow with the hand** clout
**hard but fragile** brittle
**hard by** close, near
**hard carcinoma** scirrhus
**hard coating** crust
**hard cooking fat** lard, suet
**hard-core** dedicated, die-hard, extreme, rigid, staunch, steadfast
**hard deposit that forms on the teeth** tartar
**hard drawn** taut, tense
**hard drink** spirit
**hard drinker** alcoholic, dipsomaniac, dronkie, dronklap, drunkard, soaker, sot, toper
**hard dry formation** crust
**harden** anneal, cake, coagulate, compress, confirm, fortify, fossilise, gel, habituate, indurate, inure, ossify, petrify, reinforce, season, set, solidify, stabilise, starch, steel, strengthen, temper, toughen, vitrify, vulcanise
**hardened against moral influence** obdurate
**hardened place** callosity, callus
**hardening of the walls of arteries** arteriosclerosis
**harden oneself** steel
**harden the heart** estrange
**harden to** enure, inure
**hard exterior covering nut** (nut)shell
**hard fact** undeniable truth
**hard facts** basics, essentials, fundamentals, practicalities
**hard fat** lard, suet, tallow
**hard fat of kidneys** suet
**hard feelings** bitterness, grudge, hate, ill-will, malice, resentment
**hard fruit** quince, sloe
**hard glassy mineral** spinel
**hard glazed roll** bagel
**hard glossy finish** enamel, lacquer
**hard grains left after milling of flour** semolina
**hard growth on the skin** wart
**hardhack** spirea, steeplebush
**hard-headed** clear-thinking, hard-boiled, level-headed, practical,

pragmatic, sensible, shrewd, tough, unsentimental
**hard-hearted** adverse, aloof, callous, cold, cruel, distant, hard, heartless, inhuman, intolerant, merciless, obdurate, passionless, pitiless, soulless, stern, stony, uncaring, uncompassionate, unconcerned, unfeeling, unmerciful, unmoved, unsympathetic, untouched
**hard hit** oner, smack
**hard hitter** slugger
**hard igneous rock** basalt
**hardiness** fortitude
**hard knock** oner
**hard labour** toil
**hardline** definite, extreme, immoderate, intransigent, militant, tough, uncompromising
**hardliner** fundamentalist
**hard lump** callosity, callus
**hard lump on horse's back, from galling of saddle** warble
**hardly** barely, nearly, rigorously, scarcely, severely, unkindly
**hardly any** few, scant, scarce, sparse
**hardly ever** rarely
**hard mark to remove** stain
**hard metal** iron, steel
**hard mineral** emery
**hard money** cash, coins, money, specie
**hardness** cruelty, firmness, grimness, harshness, inclemency, indifference, inelasticity, insensibility, intractability, ossification, petrification, pitilessness, rigidity, rigor, stiffness, tightness, toughness
**hardness scale** Mohs
**hard of hearing** deaf
**hard outer cover** crust, shell
**hard outer part of bread** crust
**hard outer part of fruit** shell
**hard painful boil** carbuncle
**hard question** conundrum, poser, puzzler, riddle, teaser
**hard resin** copal
**hard ring-shaped bread roll** bagel
**hard rock** granite
**hard round cheese** Edam
**hard rubber** ebonite, vulcanite
**hard sea-reef** coral
**hard seed of fruit** stone
**hard-shelled fruit** nut
**hard-shelled insect** beetle
**hardship** adversity, affliction, austerity, desolation, difficulty, duress, harm, hurt, misadventure, mishap, need, predicament, privation, prostration, rigour, suffering, trial, tribulation, visitation, want
**hard smooth timber** boxwood

**hard solid mass** concretion
**hard stone** adamant, flint, granite
**hard stone containing silica** flint
**hard straw under-mattress** palliasse
**hard substance in sea** coral
**hard substance of tusks of elephant** ivory
**hard sweet** butterscotch, jawbreaker
**hard swelling** node, scirrhus
**hard teaklike wood** afrormosia
**hard thickened part of skin** callosity, call(o)us
**hard times** adversity
**hard tissue of coral** sclerenchyma
**hard tissue of teeth** dentine
**hard to accomplish** arduous
**hard to bear** burdensome
**hard to capture** fugacious
**hard to climb** steep
**hard to deal with** intractable, parlous
**hard to do** arduous
**hard to endure** severe
**hard to excite** stolid
**hard to find** elusive, scarce
**hard to grasp** slippery, transient
**hard to handle** awkward
**hard to make out** illegible, obscure, unreadable
**hard to pin down** evasive
**hard to please** fastidious, fussy, nice
**hard to solve** elusory
**hard to understand** abstruse, profound
**hard-up** bankrupt, broke, bust, impoverished, penniless, pinched, poor, short
**hard variety of coal** anthracite
**hardware** ironmongery
**hardware dealer** ironmonger
**hard water** ice
**hard-wearing** durable, resilient, rugged, stout, strong, sturdy, tough
**hard white pottery** ironstone
**hardwood club used by Aborigines** nulla-nulla
**hardwood tree** ash, blackbutt, ebony, elm, maple, oak
**hard work** application, grind, labour, moil, ply, slave, slog, strain, sweat, toil
**hard worker** toiler
**hard-working** assiduous, busy, conscientious, devoted, diligent, earnest, energetic, industrious, tireless, zealous
**hardy** bold, courageous, daring, durable, robust, sound, strong, sturdy, vigorous
**hardy breed of pig** Gloucester Old Spot
**hardy cabbage** kale, savoy
**hardy cabbage with wrinkled leaves** savoy

**hardy cereal** barley, oat
**hardy dog** terrier
**hardy ruminant** goat
**Hardy's comedy partner** Laurel
**Hardy's first name** Oliver, Thomas
**hardy variety of cauliflower** broccoli
**hare** leporid, rabbit
**harebrained** brainless, careless, crackpot, crazy, daft, doltish, fatuous, flighty, foolish, giddy, half-baked, halfwitted, idiotic, imbecile, inane, ludicrous, mad(cap), rash, reckless, ridiculous, scatterbrained, senseless, silly, simple, stupid, weak, witless
**harelike** leporine
**harem** seraglio, zenana
**harem girl** odalisk, odalisque
**harem guard** eunuch
**harem member of sultan** odalisk, odalisque
**harem room** oda
**hare's tail** scut
**hark** attend, hear, h(e)arken, heed, list(en), mark, notice, recall
**hark back** recall, recollect, regress, remember, retrogress, revert
**harlot** hussy, prostitute, streetwalker, tart
**harm** abuse, blemish, damage, detriment, evil, hurt, ill(-treat), ill-use, impair(ment), injure, injury, loss, maltreat, mar, mischief, misfortune, molest, ruin, scathe, spoil, wickedness, wound, wrong
**harm caused by overflowing water** flood damage
**harmful** baleful, deleterious, detrimental, hurtful, injurious, malefic, mischievous, nocuous, noxious, pernicious
**harmful element** danger
**harmful exhalations from marshes** miasma
**harmful gossip** scandal
**harmful substance** poison
**harmful to health** deleterious
**harmless** beneficial, benign, blameless, canny, fearless, gentle, humble, impotent, innocent, innocuous, innoxious, inoffensive, insipid, manageable, mild, powerless, safe, soft, tame, unharmed, unhurtful, weak
**harmless lie** fib
**harmless tumour** benign
**harmonic unit** cell
**harmonious** agreeable, amicable, balanced, co-ordinated, compatible, concordant, congruous, cordial, dulcet, euphonious, friendly, harmonising, matching, melodious,

musical, sweetsounding, sympathetic, tuneful
**harmonious combination of tones** chord
**harmonious sound** music
**harmonise** accede, accommodate, accord, adapt, adjust, agree, arrange, assent, attune, blend, compose, co-ordinate, correspond, match, reconcile, regulate, resemble, suit, tone
**harmonium** organ
**harmony** accord, agreement, amicability, balance, co-operation, co-ordination, compatibility, concord, conformity, congruence, consistency, consonance, correspondence, euphony, friendship, like-mindedness, melody, order, parallelism, peace, rapport, suitability, symmetry, sympathy, tune(fulness), unanimity, understanding, unison, unity
**harmony of sounds** symphony
**harm the dignity of** humiliate
**harness** accoutrement, apply, bonds, bridle, control, couple, employ, equipage, equipment, framework, gear, inspan, restrain, saddle, tack(le), trappings, utilise, yoke
**harness hook** spirket
**harness oxen** inspan
**harness part** bit, blinds, bridle, collar, halter, hame(s), rein, saddle, trace
**harness strap** rein
**harp** aeolian, arpa (I), cithara, kithara, lyre
**harp at** bother, harass, pester
**harp constellation** Lyra
**harpist of Saul** David
**harplike ancient Greek instrument** lyre
**harp on** labour, press, push, reiterate, renew, repeat, stress
**harpoon** arrow, barb, dart, spear
**harpsichord** clavicembalo
**harp upon** carp, nag, press, repeat
**harpy** cheater, harridan, mercenary, shrew, termagant, virago
**harridan** beldam(e), crone, hag, harpy, hellcat, shrew, tartar, termagant, virago, vixen, witch, Xanthippe
**harried** pestered, plagued, teased, tormented, troubled, vexed, worried
**harrier** falcon
**Harris fabric** tweed
**harrow** alarm, appal, astound, crucify, cultivate, daunt, delve, dibble, dig, dismay, distress, disturb, execute, frighten, harry, hoe, horrify, outrage, panic, persecute, perturb, petrify, plough, rack, raft, rake, scare, shock, spade, terrify, torment, torture, unnerve
**harrowing experience** ordeal
**harry** annoy, badger, chivvy, distress, disturb, fret, gall, harass, harrow, haunt, irk, molest, pester, pillage, plague, ravage, tease, torment, trouble, vex, worry
**harsh** abrupt, acrimonious, astringent, bad-tempered, blatant, brusque, brutal, crude, cruel, curt, discordant, dissonant, grating, grim, grinding, ill-natured, jarring, raucous, rigorous, rough, rude, rugged, severe, stern, strident, uncivil, unfeeling, unharmonious, unkind
**harsh and high-pitched** shrill
**harsh and sharp** acerbic
**harsh breathing** râle, stridor
**harsh critic** impugner
**harsh cry of duck** quack
**harsh cry of rook** craw
**harsh discordant scream** squall
**harsh discordant sound** cacophony
**harsh high-pitched scream** screech
**harsh in tone** shrill, strident
**harsh light** glare
**harshly loud** raucous
**harsh metallic sound** jangle
**harshness** abusiveness, acerbity, acrimony, asperity, austerity, bitterness, bleakness, brutality, coarseness, crudeness, cruelness, grimness, hardness, ill-temper, raucousness, relentlessness, rigour, ruthlessness, severeness, severity, sternness, unkindness, unpleasantness
**harshness of sound** asperity
**harshness of tone** stridence, stridency
**harsh overseer** slave-driver
**harsh piercing scream** screech
**harsh shrill sound** stridor
**harsh sound** jar, rasp, stridor
**harsh-sounding** raucous
**harsh sound made by ducks** quack
**Hart's-tongue fern** scolopendrium
**harvest** abundance, agriculture, benefits, collect, crop, earnings, fruit, gather, glean, ingathering, output, pick, product, quantity, reap, result, store, supply, take, vintage, yield
**harvest crop of** reap
**harvester** agriculturist, collector, cultivator, farmer, gatherer, peasant, reaper, thresher, tiller
**harvest grain** reap
**has** owns, possesses
**has a bearing on** affects
**has a debt** owes
**has a few** tipples
**has a gut feeling** suspects
**has ambition** aspire
**has a meal** dine, eat
**has a price of** costs
**has a repast** eat
**has as consequence** entails
**has a yen for** fancy
**has been** was
**has bitter juice** aloe
**has expert knowledge** professional
**has faith in** trust
**hash** confusion, jumble, medley, muddle, shambles, stew
**has high opinion of** admire
**hashish** cannabis, boom, dagga, dope, ganja, grass, hash, hemp, marihuana, marijuana, pot
**has horn on nose** rhinoceros
**has in mind** intend
**has mewing cry** catbird
**has nothing to do with** shuns
**has one leg on each side of** straddle
**has permission** may
**has refined tastes** epicure
**has sharp point** thorn
**hassle** ado, annoy, argument, bother, difficulty, dispute, fight, harass, nuisance, problem, quarrel, trial, trouble, wrangle
**haste** alacrity, dispatch, expedition, flurry, hurry, need, precipitancy, rapidity, speed, suddenness, swiftness
**hasten** accelerate, advance, animate, canter, drive, expedite, flee, fly, gallop, goad, haste, hie, hurry, hustle, incite, inspire, instigate, move, outstrip, precipitate, quicken, race, run, rush, scurry, scuttle, speed, spur(t), stimulate, urge
**hasten away** flee, scat, scoot
**hasten occurrence of** precipitate
**hasten slowly** festina lente (L)
**hastily erected rampart** barricade
**hastily prepared** rough-and-ready
**hastiness** briskness, eagerness, fastness, fleetness, hurriedness, impatience, promptness, rapidness, speediness, swiftness
**has to** must
**hasty** brief, brisk, brusque, cursory, eager, expeditious, fast, headlong, heedless, hotheaded, hurried, impatient, impetuous, impulsive, prompt, quick, rapid, rash, reckless, rushed, short, snappy, speedy, swift, thoughtless, urgent
**hasty act** fling
**hasty and careless** slapdash
**hasty attempt** fling
**hasty pen-stroke** dash
**has weapons** armed

**hat** beret, brim, cap, chapeau, deerstalker, derby, fedora, fez, headgear, helmet, job, panama, role, toque, trilby

**hatch** breed, brood, cover, design, devise, incubate, plan, plot, scheme, shade, (trap-)door

**hatchet** axe, chopper, tomahawk

**hatchet man** assassin, bravo, cut-throat, debunker, desperado, destroyer, detractor, ruffian

**hatching apparatus** incubator

**hate** abhor(rence), abominate, abomination, animosity, antagonism, aversion, despise, detest, disfavour, dislike, enmity, execrate, hatred, hostility, loathe, loathing, malice, odium, phobia, repugnance, resentment, revulsion

**hat edge** brim

**hated thing** anathema

**hate extremely** abhor, detest, loathe

**hateful** abhorrent, aversive, despicable, detestable, execrable, heinous, hideous, horrid, loathsome, malevolent, malicious, obnoxious, odious, repulsive, spiteful, unbearable, unlikeable, wicked

**hateful person** cur

**hater of foreigners** xenophobe

**hater of mankind** misanthrope, misanthropist

**hater of marriage** misogamist

**hater of women** misogynist

**hate very much** detest

**hat made of fine straw-like material** panama

**hat material** felt, straw

**hat of sailor** sou(wester)

**hat of soldier** busby, helmet, kepi, shako

**hat plume** aigret

**hatred** abomination, animosity, animus, antagonism, antipathy, aversion, bitterness, detestation, disfavour, dislike, enmity, execration, grudge, hate, horror, loathing, malice, malignity, odium, repugnance, revenge, revulsion, venom

**hatred among physicians** odium medicum (L)

**hatred among theologians** odium theologicum (L)

**hatred of books** bibliophobia

**hatred of God** misotheism

**hatred of marriage** misogamy

**hatred of reason or knowledge** misology

**hatred of strangers** xenophobia

**hatred of women** misogyny

**hatred or fear of foreigners** xenophobia

**hatter** milliner

**hat with strings** bonnet

**hat worn by Sherlock Holmes** deerstalker

**haughtily** loftily

**haughtily distant** aloof

**haughtiness of manner** hauteur

**haughty** aloof, arrogant, assuming, cavalier, commanding, conceited, contemptuous, disdainful, imperious, indifferent, lofty, lordly, presumptuous, proud, remote, scornful, self-important, snobbish, snooty, stuck-up, supercilious, superior, vain

**haul** capture, carry, cart, catch, convey, convoy, drag, draw, hale, heave, loot, lug, net, pull, shift, strain, tote, tow, traction, transport, tug, yield

**haul along ground** drag

**haul by rope** heave

**haul down sail** lower

**hauled vehicle** caravan

**hauling cart** dray

**haul into court** hale

**haul or lug** drag

**haul up** hoist

**haul up sail** trice

**haunches** buttocks, thighs

**haunt** beset, burden, den, frequent, harass, lair, nest, obsess, oppress, place, plague, possess, recur, refuge, rendezvous, repair, resort, retreat, sanctuary, spot, torment, trouble, visit, walk, worry

**haunted** beset, cursed, eerie, frequented, ghosted, ghostly, ghostridden, jinxed, lingered, molested, obsessed, plagued, possessed, recurred, repaired, resorted, spooky, tormented, troubled, visited, walked, worried

**haunting fear** nightmare

**haunting idea** obsession

**hautboy** haubois, oboe, strawberry

**hauteur** affectation, affectedness, airs, arrogance, bluster, conceit, contempt, courtliness, decorum, derision, dignity, disdain, dislike, grandeur, gravity, haughtiness, insolence, loftiness, lordliness, majesty, nobility, pomposity, pompousness, presumption, pretensions, pretentiousness, pride, propriety, scorn(fulness), sneering, solemnity, stateliness, superciliousness, swagger

**Havana is there** Cuba

**have** accept, acquire, assert, bear, befool, cheat, comprehend, compromise, contain, endure, enjoy, experience, feel, gain, get, got, hae (Sc), hold, include, incorporate, keep, maintain, obtain, occupy, opine, own, permit, possess, procure, receive, retain, suffer, sustain, take, undergo

**have a bearing on** impinge, influence, infringe

**have a breather** pause, stop

**have a crack** attempt

**have a desire** wish

**have a dialogue** parley

**have a drink** imbibe

**have a finger in** nose, pry, snoop

**have a funny feeling** forebode

**have a go** try

**have a good opinion of** approve

**have a high opinion** admire

**have a liking for** fancy

**have altercation** dispute

**have ambition** aspire, strive

**have a meal** dine, eat

**have a nap** sleep

**have an argument** argue

**have an aversion to** execrate

**have another court case** retrial

**have an undulating shape** wave

**have an upright position** stand

**have a propensity** lean

**have a rest** sit

**have a row** argue

**have as a purpose** intend

**have a share in** partake

**have a shot** attempt, tackle, try

**have a strong aversion to** hate

**have a vision** dream

**have a word with** converse, talk

**have brief view of** glimpse

**have bright aspect** smile

**have by heart** remember

**have characters in common with two groups** osculate

**have common boundary** abut

**have concern** care

**have confidence in** believe, trust

**have debts** owe

**have done with** cease, desist, stop

**have doubts** suspect

**have doubts about** mistrust

**have effect** count, tell, weigh

**have elasticity** stretch

**have equal weight** balance

**have every appearance of** seem

**have excess flow of saliva** drool, slaver

**have existence** be

**have faith in** believe, trust

**have feet** pedate

**have free passage into each other** intercommunicate

**have fun** disport, frisk, frolic, gambol, jol, lark, play, rollick, romp
**have good judgement** discriminate
**have granted to one** obtain
**have hard feelings about** resent
**have high regard for** esteem
**have in common** share
**have in mind** intend, mean
**have in prospect** await
**have life** be, is, live
**have liking for** affect
**have lunch** eat
**have mercy** forgive, spare
**have mercy upon me** miserere mei (L)
**haven** anchorage, asylum, goal, harbour, lee, oasis, port, refuge, retreat, safety, sanctuary, sanctum, shelter
**have noisy drinking-party** carouse
**have-not** lack, need, pauper, want
**have obligations** owe
**have on** tease, trick, wear
**have one foot in the grave** dying, expiring, fading, going, slipping
**have partial fall** stumble
**have permission** may
**have place in reality** exist
**have power to** can
**have presence** be
**have recourse** resort
**have regard for** affection
**have rightful place** belong
**haversack** back-pack, bag, knapsack, pack
**have same opinion** agree
**have scruples** demur
**have similarity to** resemble
**have some food** eat
**have some origin** cognate
**have strong wish for** desire
**have success** succeed
**have the ability to** can
**have the best** benefit, conquer, defeat, subdue, win
**have the eyes turned in different directions** squint
**have the fortune to be** happen
**have the management of** superintend
**have the mastery of** possess
**have the means to** can
**have the power** can
**have to** compel, must, ought, should
**have to do with** appertain
**have too high an opinion of** overrate
**have to take it before shooting** aim
**have unfavourable opinion** disapprove
**have victory** win
**have want of** need
**have wrong idea** misconceive
**have wrong opinion of** misdeem, misjudge

**having a bad name** disreputable, ignominious, infamous, notorious
**having ability** able, competent
**having a blue colour** caesious
**having abnormally low body-temperature** hypothermia
**having a branchlike shape** ramiform
**having a broad end with a central depression** retuse
**having a certain ability** capable
**having a certain madness** manic
**having a commanding influence over** dominate
**having a common boundary** coterminous
**having a common centre** concentric
**having a corolla and calyx** dichlamydeous
**having a crooked tail** curvicaudate
**having a curved form** unciform
**having a deep sound** sonorous
**having a dignified mien** portly
**having a distinctive smell** odorous
**having a double shell** bivalve
**having a dull edge** blunt
**having a fair appearance** specious
**having a false name** pseudonymous
**having a feeling of dizziness** swim
**having affinity for water** hydrophilic
**having a flushed complexion** florid
**having a foundation** based
**having a friendly nature** amiable
**having agreeable flavour** sapid
**having a handle** ansate
**having a head** cephalate, cephalous
**having a hissing sound** sibilant
**having a keel** carinate(d)
**having all its parts** complete
**having all power** Almighty, omnipotent
**having all sides equal** equilateral
**having almond-shaped eyes** sloe-eyed
**having a long thin tail** leptocercal
**having a low boiling point** volatile
**having a meal** dining, eating
**having a meaning** significant
**having a minute bore** capillary
**having ample space** roomy, spacious
**having an affinity for lipids** lipophilic
**having an agreeable pungent taste** piquant
**having a nap** asleep
**having an appetite** peckish
**having a narrow skull** leptocephalic, leptocephalous
**having an aversion to something** allergic
**having an effect** operative
**having an even number of toes** artiodactyl
**having angles** angulate
**having animal life** zoic

**having a notched edge** emarginate(d)
**having an underlying purpose** tendentious
**having an unnatural gaiety of spirit** fey
**having a pectoral ailment** chesty
**having a pleasant nature** amiable
**having a poor sense of smell** microsmatic
**having a radiate form** actinoid
**having a rightful claim** entitled
**having a sawlike edge** serrated
**having a scent** odorous
**having a sharp cutting edge or point** keen
**having a single set of unpaired chromosomes** haploid
**having a smooth reflecting surface** specular
**having a snack** eating
**having aspirations beyond true worth** pseud(o)
**having a spore case** thecate
**having a strong desire for achievement** ambitious
**having a strong smell** odorous, redolent
**having a tendency to laugh** risible
**having a thorax** chested
**having a twang** nasal
**having authority** magisterial
**having a valency of four** quadrivalent, tetravalent
**having a valency of two** divalent
**having a valid will** testate
**having a veil** velate
**having a voice** vocal
**having a will** testate
**having bony skeleton** osseous
**having branched antennae** ramiform
**having branches** ramose, ramous
**having breasts** mammiferous
**having brio** vigorous
**having bristles** setiferous, setigerous, setose
**having broad rounded end** spatulate
**having broad views** broad-minded, eclectic
**having burning desire** fervid
**having caudal appendage** tailed
**having colour** coloured
**having committed offence** guilty
**having common sense** sensible
**having constant entropy** isentropic
**having corolla and calyx** dichlamydeous
**having cover** insured
**having curved leaves** curvifoliate
**having curved ribs** curvicostate
**having cutting edge** trenchant
**having delusions** paranoiac
**having died out** extinct

having direct spiritual significance
  mystical
having divergent rays  radiate
having ears like a hare's  lagotic
having eight feet  octopod
having elegance  graceful
having enough money to meet one's liabilities  solvent
having equal angles  equiangular
having equal atmospheric pressure  isobaric
having equal entropy  isentropic
having equal sides  equilateral
having esoteric knowledge  gnostic
having extremely keen sight  hawk-eyed
having eyes with pale irises due to disease  wall-eyed
having feathers  pinnate
having feeling  sensitive
having feet  pedate
having fewer restraints  freer
having few or no teeth  edentate
having fingers  digitate
having fixed limits  mensurable
having flavour  sapid
having flavour of game  gamy
having foot digits  toed
having foreknowledge  prescience
having foresight  prescient
having four divisions  quadrifid
having four parts  quadruple, quaternary
having four sides  quadrilateral
having furrow  fluted, grooved, guttered
having gained  up
having goatee  bearded
having gone bad  off
having good digestion  eupeptic
having good judgement  sagacious, wise
having good manners  polite
having good memory  retentive
having good name  reputable
having good vision  keen-eyed
having great ability  talented
having great importance  momentous
having great influence  influential, mighty, puissant
having great power  mighty, puissant
having great variety  multifarious
having had the cerebrum removed  decerebrate
having hair  piliferous
having hard continuous shell  testaceous
having harmful effect  mischievous
having harsh voice  hoarse
having healing properties  medicinal
having husky voice  hoarse
having infinite power  omnipotent
having insight into future  foresighted

having intelligence and knowledge  wise
having its origin in a dry habitat  xerarch
having kinship  kindred
having knowledge  aware, cognisant, cognizant, wise
having lasted a hundred years  centennial
having leaves  foliate
having left  gone, off
having left a valid will at death  testate
having less colour  paler
having liberty  free
having life  alive
having little length  short
having little money  poor
having little or no yoke  alecithal
having little weight  light
having lived for a long time  old
having lobes  lobate
having long slender leaves  leptophyllous
having lost the power of motion and feeling  torpid
having made and left a will  testate
having many clefts  rimose
having many different skills  versatile
having many mountains  mountainous
having many openings  porous
having many parts  multiple
having many sides  multilateral
having many trees  arboreous
having maximum extent  complete
having mental gifts  talented
having moderate heat  warm
having money penalty  pecuniary
having more assets than liabilities  solvent
having more than one possible meaning  ambiguous
having much knowledge  well-informed
having mutual resemblance  similar
having narrow oval eyes  almond-eyed
having nasty odour  smelly
having neck hair  maned
having no ability to move  inert
having no cavity  solid
having no children  childless
having no clear outline  ill-defined
having no compassion  unsympathetic
having no definite form  nebulous
having no definite shape  amorphous
having no equal  peerless, unrivalled
having no established key  atonal
having no feet  apod(al)
having no fingers or toes  adactylous
having no fixed habitation  vagabond
having no flipper  finless
having no flowers  ananthous
having no gender  it
having no gills  abranchial, abranchiate

having no goal  aimless
having no head  acephalous
having no interest  indifferent, supine
having no joints or articulated limbs  anarthrous
having no key  atonal
having no limit  boundless
having no mind of one's own  acquiescent, cowering, cringing, henpecked, spineless
having no money  impecunious, penniless, poor, skint
having no moral quality  amoral, nonmoral
having no name  anonymous
having no nationality  stateless
having no occupant  vacant
having no opinions  viewless
having no parallel  unique
having no petals  apetalous
having no pity  ruthless
having no placenta  aplacental
having no power  ineffective
having no religious belief  nullifidian
having no shelter  houseless
having no special purpose  idle
having no spine  spineless
having no stalk  sessile
having no stamens  anandrous
having no strength  weak
having no tail  acaudal
having no troubles  carefree
having no value  worthless
having no visible stem  acaulescent
having no weak points  airtight
having no weight  imponderable
having no will  intestate
having occult powers  psychic
having one ear  mohaural
having one thread  unifilar
having one wife  monogamy
having organs like leaves  foliaceous
having outline of egg  elliptical, oval
having pleasant manners  debonair
having pods  leguminous
having power  able
having power of resistance  strong
having prickles  aculeate
having private interest  interested
having projecting jaws  prognathic, prognathous
having prongs  tined
having properties of oil  oleaginous
having ribs (of leaf)  nervate
having same age  coeval
having same osmotic pressure  isotonic
having second sight  clairvoyant
having semiconductors  transistorised
having separate fingers or toes  digitate
having seven divisions  septenate

**having seven parts** heptamerous, septuple, sevenfold
**having several functions** multirole
**having sharp points** aculeate
**having similar qualities** kindred
**having six angles** hexangular
**having six sides and six angles** hexagonal
**having small compartments** cellular
**having special beauty** exquisite
**having spinal column** vertebrate
**having spines** acanthus
**having spokes** radial
**having stomata on both surfaces** amphistomatal, amphistomatic
**having strong acid taste** tangy
**having strong taste** pungent
**having success** successful
**having sufficient power** able, capable, skilful
**having ten legs** decapod
**having the appearance of glass** vitriform
**having the appearance of wood** ligniform
**having the effect of** virtual
**having the effect of sneezing** sternutatory, sternutative
**having the eyes distinctly separate** dichoptic
**having the faculty of perception** perceptive, percipient
**having the form of an ear** auriform
**having the form of a thread** filiform
**having the gift of the gab** voluble
**having the intent to deceive** fraudulent
**having the lustre of a diamond** adamantine
**having the nature of vinegar** acetic
**having the outline of an egg** elliptical, oval
**having the power of thinking** cogitative
**having the power to do** able
**having the qualities of soap** saponaceous
**having the quality of destroying** pernicious
**having the same centre** concentric
**having the same meaning** equivalent
**having the same origin** cognate
**having the same viewpoint** synoptic
**having the sepals all united** monosepalous
**having the shape of an almond** amygdaloid
**having the shape of a strap** ligulate
**having the shape or form of an eel** anguilliform
**having the stamens in three bundles** triadelphous
**having the wrong role** miscast

**having thick undergrowth** scroggy
**having three apses** triapsal
**having three axis** triax(i)al
**having three branches** trifurcate
**having three capsules** tricapsular
**having three carpels** tricarpous
**having three cusps** tricorn
**having three fingers or toes** tridactyl
**having three horns** tricorn
**having three leaflets** ternate
**having three legislative chambers** tricameral
**having three points** tricuspid
**having three prongs** tridental, tridentate
**having three rays** triact
**having three ribs** tricostate
**having three sides** triangular
**having three tail-like processes** tricaudate
**having three toes** tridactyl
**having three valencies** tervalent, trivalent
**having three wives at once** trigamous
**having to account for something** answerable
**having toes** digitate
**having too high an opinion of one's qualities** conceited
**having tufts of hair** comate, comose
**having tufts of long hairs** barbate
**having twenty parts** twentyfold
**having two angles** biangular
**having two colours** dichromatic
**having two feet** bipedal
**having two foci** bifocal
**having two hands** bimanous, bimanual
**having two heads** bicephalous, dicephalous
**having two languages** bilingual
**having two leaves** bifoliate
**having two legislative chambers** bicameral
**having two or more colours** pied
**having two or more possible meanings** ambiguous
**having two parts** bipartite
**having two poles** bipolar
**having two sides equal** isosceles
**having two spouses at the same time** bigamy
**having two stable states** bistable
**having two tapering points** biacuminate
**having two valencies** divalent, bivalent
**having two wings** dipterous
**having unequal sides** scalene
**having unrestricted power** despotic
**having value specified** worth
**having variables equal to zero** trivial
**having variegated lines** striped
**having various forms** variform

**having venae** veined
**having very extensive knowledge** omniscient
**having very great power** omnipotent
**having very marked veins** venose
**having vigour** punchy
**having weapons** armed
**having well-developed muscles** muscular
**having windows** fenestrated
**having wings** alate, alar
**having woolly or curling hair** ulotrichous
**having zero as limit** null
**having rounded projections** lobate(d)
**havoc** carnage, chaos, confusion, damage, desolation, destruction, devastation, disorder, disruption, ravages, ruin, slaughter, waste, wreck
**Hawaiian acacia** koa
**Hawaiian beach** Waikiki
**Hawaiian bird** io, oo
**Hawaiian city** Honolulu
**Hawaiian coffee** kona
**Hawaiian common** noa
**Hawaiian county** Honolulu, Kauai, Maui
**Hawaiian dance** hula(-hula)
**Hawaiian dish** poi
**Hawaiian fabric** kapa, tapa
**Hawaiian farewell** aloha
**Hawaiian feast** luau
**Hawaiian fibre** pulu
**Hawaiian fish** ahi, aku(le), au, awa, moano, ulua
**Hawaiian fly catcher** elepaio
**Hawaiian food** poi
**Hawaiian frigate bird** iwa
**Hawaiian garland** lei
**Hawaiian goose** nene
**Hawaiian greeting** aloha
**Hawaiian guitar** ukulele
**Hawaiian harbour** Pearl
**Hawaiian hawk** io
**Hawaiian hello** aloha
**Hawaiian honey-eater** kioca, ooaa
**Hawaiian instrument** uke(lele), ukulele
**Hawaiian island** Hilo, Kahoolawa, Kauai, Kaula, Lanai, Maui, Molokai, Niihau, Oahu
**Hawaiian loincloth** malo
**Hawaiian mountain range** Kohala, Koolau, Waianae
**Hawaiian musical instrument** pua, uke(lele), ukulele
**Hawaiian palm-lily drink** (k)ava
**Hawaiian royal chief** alii
**Hawaiian seaport** Hilo
**Hawaiian shrub** aalii
**Hawaiian song** mele
**Hawaiian starch** apii

**Hawaiian state bird** goose
**Hawaiian state flower** hibiscus
**Hawaiian state tree** candlenut
**Hawaiian taro dish** poi
**Hawaiian temple** heiau
**Hawaiian veranda** lanai
**Hawaiian volcano** Hualalai, Kilauea, Maunakea, Maunaloa
**Hawaiian welcome** aloha
**Hawaiian woman** wahine
**Hawaiian women's dance** hula(-hula)
**Hawaiian word for hello or goodbye** aloha
**hawk** bargain, bark, belligerent, bird, caracara, cheater, cough, eagle, eruct, falcon, goshawk, hack, harrier, hem, kestrel, kite, market, militant, militarist, offer, osprey, peddle, sell, tout, trade, vend, vulture, warmonger
**hawk carrier** cad
**hawker** bargainer, colporteur, concessionaire, crier, dealer, falconer, haggler, higgler, huckster, merchant, pedlar, salesman, seller, vendor
**hawker of books** colporteur
**hawker with small commodities** pedlar
**hawk-eyed** observant, perceptive, sharp-sighted, vigilant, watchful
**Hawkeye State** Iowa
**hawk goods** cadge
**hawking** falconry
**hawk-leash line** creance
**hawk-like seabird** skua
**hawk moth** sphinx
**hawk's cage** mew
**hawk's leash** lune
**hawk's nest** eyrie, aery
**hawk's ring** varvel, vervel
**hawk trainer** falconer
**hawser** cable, mooring, rope
**hawthorn** may (tree), mayflower
**hawthorn berry** haw
**hawthorn flower** may(flower)
**hawthorn fruit** haw
**hay** fence, forage, hedge, straw
**hay bundle** bale
**hay bundler** baler
**hayfever** rhinitis
**haying implement** binder, tedder
**hay-rack** stable-rack
**haystack** (hay)rick, stack
**haywire** awry, chaotic, confused, crazy, disordered, disorganised, mad, tangled, topsy-turvy, wild, wrong
**hazard** accident, adventure, ante, bet, chance, contingency, dare, (en)danger, enterprise, experience, exploit, fate, fortune, gamble, imperil, incident, jeopardy, luck, occurrence, offer, peril, pledge, risk, speculate, speculation, stake, undertaking, venture, wager
**hazardous** casual, chancy, dangerous, dicey, difficult, dire, insecure, jeopardous, ominous, perilous, random, risky, rum, speculative, treacherous, uncertain, undecided, unpredictable, unsafe, unsettled, venturesome
**haze** cloud, dimness, film, fog, mist, obscurity, smog, smokiness, steam, torment, unclearness, vagueness, vapour
**hazelnut** cob(nut), filbert
**hazelnut flavour** noisette
**hazelnut liqueur** noisette
**hazy** cloudy, dim, foggy, misty, muddled, muzzy, obscure, overcast, smoky, vague
**head** apogee, authority, beginning, cape, caput, cardinal, cephalo-, chief, climax, command(er), conclusion, cranium, crisis, culmination, director, dome, excel, first, foam, foremost, front, froth, genius, govern, intellect, leader, leading, mind, noddle, origin, outdo, pate, poll, precede, principal, rise, rule, skull, source, summit, tête (F), tip, top, wisdom, wit, zenith
**headache** annoyance, bane, bother, (en)cephalalgia, hassle, hemialgia, inconvenience, migraine, neuralgia, nuisance, problem, trouble, vexation, worry
**headband** fillet, ribbon, snood, taenia
**head-burrowing bird** ostrich
**head cook** chef, chef de cuisine (F)
**head cooler** icebag
**head count** census
**head covering** beret, bonnet, cap, hair, hat, helmet, turban
**head covering attached to a coat** hood
**headdress** bonnet, cap, coiffure, cowl, hairdo, hat, headgear, tiara, turban
**headdress for monarch** crown
**headed bolt** rivet
**headgear** beret, cap, fez, hat, helmet, tam
**head gesture** nod
**head harness** bridle
**heading** capping, caption, category, class, commanding, controlling, crowning, directing, division, governing, guiding, headline, leading, managing, name, preceding, rubric, ruling, running, section, supervision, title, topic, topping
**heading of an article** caption
**heading upward** skyward
**head in Hawaii** Diamond
**headland** bill, cape, chersonese, cliff, foreland, head, hook, mull, ness, peninsula, point, promontory, ridge, sandbar, sandpit, spit, spur
**headland or cape** mesa, promontory
**headland projecting into the sea** cape
**headless metal or wooden pin** dowel
**headless nail** sprig
**headless pin** dowel
**headless tack** sprig
**headline writer** sub
**headlong** ahead, breakneck, dangerous, Gadarene, hastily, hasty, head-first, heedlessly, hurriedly, impetuous, impulsive, pell-mell, precipitate(ly), ramstam, rank, rashly, reckless, steep, thoughtlessly, wildly
**headlong plunge into water** dive
**headlong rush** stampede
**headman** captain, chief, leader, ruler
**headman's implement** axe
**head monk** abbot
**head movement** nod
**head of abbey** abbot
**head of adult tapeworm** scolex
**head of advisory council** president
**head of Arab tribe** sheik(h)
**head of cattle** neat
**head of certain colleges** provost
**head of chapter of canons** dean
**head of comet** coma
**head of convent** abbess
**head of corn** ear
**head of diocese** bishop
**head of empire** emperor
**head off** avert, catch, deflect, distract, divert, forestall, inhibit, intercept, interpose, intervene, prevent, stay, stop
**head of faculty** dean
**head of gang** captain, boss
**head of household** master, mistress
**head of military unit** commanding officer
**head of monastery** abbot
**head of municipality** mayor
**head of museum** curator
**head of nuns** abbess
**head of publishing department** editor
**head of republic** president
**head of Roman Catholic Church** Pope
**head of sheaf of oats** awn
**head of ship** captain
**head of society** president
**head of state** king, president, ruler
**head of synod** moderator
**head of town** mayor
**head of university faculty** dean

**head organ** brain, ear, eye, mouth, nose
**head over heels** completely, earnestly, intensely, passionately, uncontrollably, utterly, vehemently
**headpiece of a column** capital
**head protector** bonnet, hat, helmet
**headquarters of International Red Cross** Geneva
**headquarters of regiment** depot
**headquarters of the London metropolitan police** Scotland Yard
**head-rest** pillow
**headscarf tied under chin** babushka
**headset** earphones
**head-shaving style** tonsure
**head side of coin** obverse
**head skin** scalp
**headstrong** adamant, bullheaded, difficult, disobedient, dogged, fractious, inflexible, intractable, obdurate, obstinate, perverse, pigheaded, refractory, stubborn, unruly, wilful
**head support** brace, neck
**head to foot** top to bottom
**headwear** beret, busby, cap, hat, helmet
**headwear securer** hatpin
**heady** exciting, exhilarating, hasty, potent, rash, reckless, stimulating, strong, thoughtless
**heal** cleanse, conciliate, cure, disinfect, improve, mend, pacify, purge, purify, reconcile, recover, recuperate, regenerate, rehabilitate, remedy, repair, restore, settle, soothe, subdue
**healer** curer
**healer by rubbing** masseur
**healer of Naaman** Elisha
**healing action** treatment
**healing agent** balsam
**healing art** medicine
**healing by manipulation** chiropractic
**healing goddess** Eir
**healing mark** scar
**healing ointment** balm, salve
**healing plant** sanicle
**healing pool in Jerusalem** Bethesda
**healing root** ginseng
**health** condition, constitution, fitness, form, haleness, heal(thiness), heartiness, potency, robustness, salubrity, shape, soundness, state, strength, tone, vigour, vitality, welfare, well-being
**health bath** spa
**health-food fat** lecithin
**healthily red** ruddy
**health resort** spa
**health worker** doctor, nurse

**healthy** able-bodied, active, beneficial, blooming, bracing, desirable, fine, fit, flourishing, good, hale, hardy, hearty, invigorating, nourishing, nutritious, positive, prosperous, robust, salubrious, sound, strong, sturdy, thriving, viable, vigorous, well, wholesome
**healthy and strong** lusty
**healthy condition** fitness
**healthy-looking** bonny
**healthy practice** hygiene
**healthy red** ruddy
**healthy spot** spa
**heap** accumulate, accumulation, amass, bank, bestow, burden, collect(ion), confer, gather, hoard, increase, lavish, load, lot, mass, mound, mountain, pile, shower, stack, stockpile, store
**heap of combustible material** pyre
**heap of earth** mound
**heap of stones** cairn
**heap of wood for fire** pyre
**heap together** accumulate, amass
**heap up** accumulate, acervate, amass, collect, compile, garner, gather, hoard, stock(pile)
**heap upon** assign, bestow, burden, confer, load, supply
**hear** acknowledge, ascertain, attend, catch, discover, eavesdrop, examine, find, gather, hark, hearken, heed, investigate, judge, learn, listen, overhear, perceive, regard, try, understand
**hearable** audible
**hear case again** retry
**hear confession of** shrive
**heard in opera** aria
**heard twice** echo
**hearer** listener
**hearing aid** amplifier, ear(-piece), ear-trumpet, megaphone, otoscope, stethoscope
**hearing device** headphone
**hearing distance** earshot
**hearing organ** ear
**hearing range** earshot
**hearken** attend, hear, heed, list(en), notice, obey, observe, regard
**hearsay** buzz, chatter, dirt, gossip, grapevine, news, report, rumour, story, tale, talk, tittle-tattle, word
**hearsay story** rumour
**heart** affection, boldness, bravery, centre, character, coeur (F), compassion, cor (L), corazon (Sp), core, courage, crux, cuore (I), disposition, emotion, essence, feeling, fortitude, guts, herz (G), hub, love, middle, mind, nature, nerve, centre, nub, nucleus, pity, resolution, seat, sentiment, soul, source, spirit, sympathy, temperament, tenderness, ticker
**heartache** affliction, agony, anguish, anxiety, bereavement, bitterness, dejection, desolation, despair, discomfort, distress, grief, grievance, heartbreak, misery, mourning, pain, regret, remorse, sadness, sorrow, suffering, torment, torture, trial, tribulation, trouble, unhappiness, woe, worry, wretchedness
**heart and soul** absolutely, completely, cordially, devotedly, eagerly, entirely, gladly, unreservedly, wholeheartedly, willingly
**heart artery** aorta
**heartbeat** diastole, pulse, systole
**heartbeat controller** pacemaker
**heartbeat discernible to the touch** pulse
**heartbroken** broken-hearted, crestfallen, crushed, dejected, desolate, despondent, disappointed, disconsolate, dispirited, downcast, grieved, miserable
**heartburn** dyspepsia, gastric, pyrosis, water brash
**heart chamber** atrium, auricle, ventricle
**heart disease** angina, myocarditis
**heart drug** digitalis
**hearten** assure, brighten, buoy, cheer, comfort, console, convince, ease, elate, elevate, embolden, encourage, enliven, exhilarate, gladden, incite, inspire, inspirit, invigorate, persuade, reassure, refresh, relieve, solace, soothe, strengthen, uplift, warm
**heartening** affecting, assuring, auspicious, brightening, cheerful, confronting, convincing, encouraging, exciting, exhilarating, gladdening, hopeful, inspiring, moving, persuading, promising, propitious, reassuring, rosy, rousing, soothing, stimulating, stirring, uplifting
**heartfelt** ardent, cordial, deep, devout, earnest, fervent, genuine, honest, profound, sincere, unfeigned, warm, wholehearted
**heartfelt cry** cri de coeur
**hearth** birthplace, family, fire(place), fireside, hearthstead, home(stead), household
**hear the other side** audi alteram partem (L)
**hearth fire** ingle
**hearth rod** poker
**heart illness** angina

**heartily** affably, agreeably, ardently, avidly, earnestly, ebulliently, energetically, favourably, feelingly, genuinely, gladly, passionately, pleasingly, profoundly, spiritedly, willingly,
**heartless** brutal, callous, cold(-hearted), cruel, frigid, hard, harsh, inexorable, inhuman, insensitive, merciless, passionless, pitiless, relentless, remorseless, ruthless, savage, stern, stony, uncaring, unfeeling, unkind, unsympathetic
**heart-rending** aching, affecting, depressing, disheartening, distressing, harrowing, heartbreaking, heavy, lamentable, moving, painful, pathetic, piteous, pitiful, poignant, rueful, sad, tragic
**heart-shaped** cordate
**heart specialist** cardiologist
**heart-throb** idol, pin-up, star
**heart-warming** affecting, cheering, encouraging, heartening, moving, pleasing, rewarding, satisfying, touching, warming
**hearty** animated, authentic, avid, cheerful, cordial, deep, earnest, exuberant, fervent, friendly, genuine, hale, healthy, passionate, robust, vigorous, zealous
**hearty and persistent effort** zeal
**hearty enjoyment** gusto
**hear wrongly** mishear
**he assists** helper
**he assists the umpire** linesman
**heat** animate, ardour, earnestness, excite(ment), fervour, fever, fieriness, flush, fury, glow, hotness, impetuosity, inflame, intensity, passion, reheat, rouse, sizzle, stimulate, stir, sultriness, swelter, toast, vehemence, violence, warm(th), zeal
**heat content** enthalpy
**heated** acrimonious, angry, animated, bitter, excited, fierce, fiery, flushed, frenzied, furious, glowed, impassioned, intense, passionate, raging, reheated, stormy, tempestuous, vehement, violent
**heated discussion** argument, quarrel, squabble
**heated wine with sugar** glühwein, mulled
**heater** fireplace, forge, furnace, kiln, microwave, oven, radiator, stove, toaster
**heater or range** stove
**heater wire** element
**heat fat** clarify

**heath** erica, moor
**heathen** Antichrist, atheist(ic), backslider, barbarian, barbarous, cynical, disbeliever, doubter, Gentile, godless, heathenish, heretic, iconoclast, infidel, irreligious, misbeliever, pagan, Philistine, unbeliever, unenlightened, unsaved
**heathen image** idol
**heather** erica, heath
**heath genus** erica
**heathland** fynbos, moor
**heating apparatus** stove
**heating channel** duct
**heating coil** element
**heating fuel** gas
**heat ore to extract metal** smelt
**heat producer** fuel
**heat-proof vessel** casserole
**heat source** coal, fuel, sun
**heat spreader** radiator
**heat to almost boiling point** scald
**heat to a sufficient temperature to kill germs** pasteurise
**heat-treated coal** coke
**heat unit** therm
**heat up** parboil, precook, reheat, warm
**heat wine with sugar and spices** mull
**heave** breathe, bulge, cast, chuck, drag, elevate, exhale, fling, groan, haul, hitch, hoist, hurl, lever, lift, palpitate, pant, puff, pull, raise, retch, rise, send, sigh, sob, surge, throw, toss, tug, vomit
**heaven** afterlife, atmosphere, bliss, delight, ecstasy, Eden, empyrean, firmament, happiness, hereafter, infinity, millennium, paradise, pleasure, rapture, sky, Utopia
**heavenly** angelic, beautiful, blessed, blissful, celestial, cherubic, delightful, divine, entrancing, ethereal, exquisite, glorious, holy, lovely, paradisiacal, rapturous, ravishing, seraphic, sublime, wonderful
**heavenly being** (arch)angel
**heavenly body** comet, luminary, meteor, moon, orb, planet, satellite, star, sun
**heavenly creature** angel
**heavenly food** manna
**heavenly instrument** harp
**heavenly joy** blessedness
**heavenly place** paradise
**heavenly region** sphere
**heavenly state** bliss
**heavenly sweet** angelic
**heavenly twins sign** Gemini
**heaven resident** angel
**heavens** aerosphere, ether, firmament, sky
**heave up** heeze

**heaviest metal** osmium
**heavily armed foot soldier in ancient Greece** hoplite
**heavily armed warship** battleship, destroyer
**heavily clouded** overcast
**heavily defeat** hammer
**heavily loaded** laden
**heavily populated** crowded
**heaviness** weightiness
**heaviness of an object** weight
**heaviness of mind** gloom
**heavy** boring, burdensome, cloudy, clumsy, coarse, concentrated, crestfallen, cumbersome, depressed, depressing, difficult, disconsolate, distressing, down-hearted, gloomy, grave, hefty, important, louring, lowering, momentous, mournful, onerous, oppressive, ponderous, sad, slow, sorrowful, stodgy, thick, tiresome, unleavened, weighty
**heavy and clumsy** lumpish
**heavy and moist** sodden
**heavy antelope** eland
**heavy army overgarment** greatcoat, petersham
**heavy artillery piece** cannon
**heavy blacksmith's hammer** sledge(hammer)
**heavy black wood** ebony
**heavy blow** bang, clout, dunt (Sc), oner, slosh, slug, smash, thump, welt
**heavy blow with hand** thump
**heavy book** tome
**heavy burden** load
**heavy butcher's knife** cleaver
**heavy club** bludgeon, cudgel
**heavy coach** drag
**heavy common pottery** stoneware
**heavy cord** rope
**heavy cotton fabric** cretonne
**heavy curtains** drapes
**heavy curved knife** kukri
**heavy dark medium-sweet sherry** oloroso
**heavy downpour** deluge
**heavy drinker** alcoholic, alkie, alky, dipsomaniac, dronkie, dronklap, lush, sponge, toper
**heavy element** lead
**heavy fabric for tents** duck
**heavy fall** gutser
**heavy fall of rain** deluge, downpour
**heavy flood** spate
**heavy fog** brume
**heavy food** stodge
**heavy fortified dessert wine** jerepigo
**heavy glove** gauntlet
**heavy greatcoat** petersham
**heavy gun** cannon

**heavy hammer** maul, sledge
**heavy-handed** autocrat(ic), awkward, domineering, graceless, harsh, insensitive, oppressive, overbearing, tactless, thoughtless, unsubtle
**heavy-headed nail for bootsoles** hobnail
**heavy-headed stick** bludgeon
**heavy-hearted** sad
**heavy inert gas** xenon
**heavy javelin** pilum
**heavy knife** machete, panga
**heavy lace** guipure
**heavy mass** weight
**heavy metal** lead, rock
**heavy metal industry** steel works
**heavy mist** fog
**heavy mop of hair** mane
**heavy motor vehicle** camion
**heavy neck scarf** muffler
**heavy oil engine** diesel
**heavy overcoat** greatcoat, petersham, ulster
**heavy perfume** chypre
**heavy polished metal** chromium
**heavy rain** storm
**heavy ringing sound** clang
**heavy-scented bitter drug** opium
**heavy shadow** gloom
**heavy shoe** boot, brogan, brogue
**heavy spar** barite
**heavy starchy food** stodge
**heavy timber beam** sleeper
**heavy volume** tome
**heavy wagon** dray, truck, van
**heavy walk** trudge
**heavy walking boot** Balmoral
**heavy weight** monkey, ton
**heavy wood** beech, ebony, hickory, jarrah, larch
**heavy wooden hammer** maul
**heavy wooden mallet** beetle
**heavy wool fabric** moreen, worsted
**he became an Egyptian pharaoh while still a boy** Tutankhamen, Tutankhamun
**he betrayed Jesus** Judas
**hebetude** dullness, lethargy
**Hebrew** Israelite, Jew, Rabbinic, Semite
**Hebrew alphabet** aleph-beis, aleph-bet
**Hebrew avenger** Goel
**Hebrew coin** shekel
**Hebrew commentary** biur
**Hebrew dance** hora
**Hebrew drum** toph
**Hebrew dry measure** epha(h), homer, kor, omer
**Hebrew high priest** Aaron, Eli
**Hebrew horn** shifar, shophar
**Hebrew judge** Eli
**Hebrew king** David, Saul, Solomon
**Hebrew kingdom** Israel, Judah

**Hebrew lawgiver** Moses
**Hebrew lyre** asor
**Hebrew measure** cor, ephah, hen, hin, kab, ker, kor, log, omer
**Hebrew musical instrument** asor, toph
**Hebrew name for God** Adonai, El(ohim), Jahveh, Jahweh, Yahveh, Yahweh
**Hebrew nation** Israel
**Hebrew patriarch** Abraham, Isaac, Jacob
**Hebrew plural ending** -im
**Hebrew prayer book** Mahzob
**Hebrew praying mantle** tallith
**Hebrew precept** tora
**Hebrew prophet** Amos, Elijah, Elisha, Ezekiel, Habakkuk, Hosea, Isaiah, Jeremiah, Joel, Malachi, Micah, Nahum, Nathan, Obadiah
**Hebrew religion** Judaism
**Hebrews** Israelites
**Hebrew t** teth
**Hebrew teacher** rab(bi), reb
**Hebrew underworld abode of the dead** Sheol
**Hebrew unit of capacity** hin
**Hebrew unit of dry measure** epha(h)
**Hebrew vowel** kamets, tsere
**Hebrew weight** gerah, omer
**Hebrides island** Iona, Skye
**he cannot do without drugs** addict
**he cannot speak** mute
**he can put people in a trance** hypnotist
**he checks the company's books** auditor
**he chirps** bird
**heckle** bait, barrack, disrupt, gibe, interrupt, jeer, pester, taunt
**he comes first** winner
**he comes last** loser
**he competes in physical exercises** athlete
**he controls money** financier
**he crossed Alps with elephants** Hannibal
**hectic** boisterous, busy, chaotic, excited, fast, fevered, feverish, flurrying, frantic, frenetic, frenzied, furious, heated, riotous, turbulent, wild
**hectic city routine** rat race
**hectic social life** whirl
**hector** boast, bully, harass, intimidate, provoke, threaten
**he defeated the Christians near Tiberias** Saladin
**hedge** barrier, block, border, boundary, confine, dodge, edge, enclose, equivocate, evade, fence, hedgerow, hinder, insurance, obstruct, prevaricate, protect(ion), quibble,

quickset, restrict, screen, sidestep, stall, surround, temporise, windbreak
**hedge in** besiege
**hedge plant** dog rose, privet
**hedge puzzle** maze
**hedgerow flower** vetch
**hedgerow tree** hawthorn
**hedge shrub** myrtle, privet
**hedge sparrow** dunnock, titling
**hedge-tree** hawthorn
**he died** obiit
**he died at Spandau Prison** Rudolf Hess
**he dissects** anatomist
**he does experiments** scientist
**he does it in Switzerland** yodel
**he does not believe in God** atheist
**he does nothing** idler
**hedonist** bon vivant (F), epicurean, glutton, go(u)rmand, indulger, libertine, profligate, rake, roué, sensualist, sybarite, utilitarian, voluptuary
**he draws up deeds** notary
**heed** attention, care, caution, consider(ation), listen, mark, mind, note, notice, obey, regard, vigilance, watchfulness
**heedful** attentive, cautious, mindful, observant, prudent, vigilant, watchful
**heedfulness** caution
**heedless** blind, blithe, careless, casual, deaf, distracted, distrait, headlong, imprudent, impulsive, inadvertent, inattentive, incautious, negligent, oblivious, precipitate, rash, reckless, regardless, thoughtless, unalert, unmindful
**heedless of duty** negligent
**heehaw** bray
**heel bone** calcaneum, calcaneus
**heelless slipper** mule
**heel tendon** Achilles
**he fell in love with his reflection** Narcissus
**he fiddled while Rome burned** Nero
**he fits teeth** dentist
**hefty** ample, awkward, beefy, bulky, burly, colossal, forceful, heavy, husky, massive, ponderous, powerful, robust, stalwart, strong, sturdy, substantial, weighty
**he gets the notes right** tuner
**he gives out the cards** dealer
**he gives twice who gives speedily** bis dat qui cito dat (L)
**he goes in front** leader
**he goes to sea** sailor
**he grunts** pig
**he hails from Teheran** Iranian
**he hangs upside down in a cave** bat
**he has two wives illegally** bigamist

**he himself has said it**  ipse dixit (L)
**heifer**  cow
**height**  acme, altitude, apex, ceiling, climax, crest, crown, culmination, degree, dignity, elevation, eminence, extremity, exultation, grandeur, highness, length, limit, loftiness, maximum, mountain, peak, pinnacle, prominence, stature, summit, tallness, top, ultimate, utmost
**height above sea level**  altitude, elevation
**heighten**  aggravate, amplify, elevate, enhance, exalt, increase, magnify, raise, strengthen, uplift
**heighten the level of**  raise
**height gauge**  altimeter
**height of activity**  career
**he initiates**  launcher
**heinous**  abominable, atrocious, evil, flagrant, hateful, infamous, reprehensible, villainous, wicked
**heinous deed**  atrocity
**heir**  beneficiary, co-heir, heiress, inheritor, scion, successor
**he is a beneficiary**  heir
**he is absent**  abest (L)
**he is aimed at**  target
**he is amusing**  comic
**he is between a marquis and a viscount**  earl
**he is canonised**  saint
**he is centre of romance**  man
**he is companionless**  loner
**he is cruel**  brute
**he is disloyal to his country**  traitor
**he is doomed**  goner
**he is elsewhere**  absent(ee)
**he is from the largest continent**  Asian
**he is from the Philippine islands**  Filipino
**he is from Stockholm**  Swede
**he is ill**  aegrotat
**he is in charge**  boss
**he is inexperienced**  amateur, beginner, greenhorn
**he is in possession**  owner
**he is no mumbler**  enunciator
**he is no rocker**  mod
**he is not an altruist**  egoist
**he is not involved**  bystander
**he is not loyal**  traitor
**he is not present**  absentee
**he is no troopie**  civilian
**he is not to be believed**  liar
**he is really stupid**  idiot
**he is stingy**  miser
**he is unskilful**  amateur
**held at Oberammergau**  Passion Play
**held for ransom**  hostage
**held in bondage**  captive
**held in private ownership**  proprietary

**helicopter**  whirlybird
**helicopter blade**  rotor
**helicopter landing spot**  helipad
**helicopter vane**  rotor
**Helios**  sun god
**he lives on the Tiber**  Roman
**helix**  coil, corkscrew, curl(icue), loop, ringlet, screw, spiral, tendril, thread, twist, volute, whorl
**hell**  abyss, agony, anguish, condemnation, desolation, despair, Dys, Erebus, Gehenna, Hades, inferno, limbo, misery, pandemonium, pang, perdition, Sheol, suffering, throe, torment, underworld, woe
**Hellas**  Greece
**hellbent**  determined, fixed, intent, resolved, set(tled)
**Hellene**  Greek, Ionian
**Hellenic**  Greek
**Hellenic land**  Greece
**hellish**  abominable, accursed, atrocious, cruel, damnable, damned, detestable, devilish, diabolical, dreadful, fiendish, infernal, monstrous, vicious, wicked
**hello**  hi, ciao (I)
**helm**  armour, command, control, direction, directorship, government, guidance, helmet, leadership, reins, rudder, rule, saddle, steer, tiller, wheel
**helmet**  casque, headdress, headpiece, morion
**helmet-shaped**  galea
**helmet visor**  ventail
**helminth**  fluke, nematode
**helmsman**  wheelman
**helmsman of racing shell**  cox
**Heloise's lover**  Pierre Abèlard
**he loved Beauty**  beast
**help**  abet, advice, advise, aid, alleviate, ameliorate, assist(ance), avoid, back(ing), befriend, co-operate, cure, ease, encourage, foster, further, helper, improve, lend, promote, relief, relieve, remedy, save, shun, succour, support
**helper**  acolyte, adjunct, adjutant, aide, ally, assistant, attendant, auxiliary, coadjutor, collaborator, colleague, deputy, mate, second, servant, subsidiary, supporter
**helper in time of need**  Samaritan
**help forward**  promote
**helpful**  advantageous, assisting, beneficial, caring, considerate, constructive, convenient, co-operative, fortunate, friendly, kind, neighbourly, obliging, practical, serviceable, supporting, supportive, sympathetic, useful, willing
**helpful hint**  tip
**helpful person**  Samaritan
**help in difficulty**  alleviating, assisting, backing, co-operating, curing, easing, healing, improving, mitigating, promoting, relieving, saving, succour(ing), supporting
**helping**  amount, dollop, piece, plateful, portion, ration, serving, share
**helping hand**  aide
**helping in a subsidiary way**  ancillary
**helping to learn**  heuristic
**helping to sail**  crewing
**help in something bad**  abet
**helpless**  abandoned, aidless, defenceless, dependent, destitute, disabled, empty, exposed, faint, feeble, forlorn, friendless, guideless, impotent, incapable, incompetent, incurable, inept, infirm, lost, paralysed, powerless, unfit, unprotected, unsupported, useless, vulnerable, weak, worthless
**helpless amazement**  stupor
**helpless mental weakness**  imbecility
**help signal**  SOS
**help-yourself eats**  buffet
**helter-skelter**  carelessly, confused(ly), disordered, disorganised, haphazard, hastily, headlong, higgledy-piggledy, hit-or-miss, hurriedly, impulsively, jumbled, muddled, pell-mell, random, rashly, recklessly, rushed, topsy-turvy, unsystematic, wildly
**Helvetian**  Swiss
**Helvetic**  Swiss
**hem**  border, edge, fringe, margin, trim, verge
**he made a good end**  bene decessit (L)
**he makes beer**  brewer
**he makes bread**  baker
**he makes men's clothes**  tailor
**hem and haw**  hesitate, stammer
**he married Guinevere**  Arthur
**he married Juliet**  Romeo
**he may be in the team**  possible
**hem in**  beset, besiege, confine, enclose, restrict, surround
**hemispherical roof**  dome
**hemp**  abaca, ambari, b(h)ang, charas, dagga, fibre, ganja, ke(e)f, kief, marihuana, marijuana, pita, ramie, sisal, tow
**hemp drug**  hashish
**hemplike fibre**  sunn
**hemp plant**  cannabis, fimble
**hemp used as narcotic**  b(h)ang, dagga, hashish, marihuana, marijuana

**hen** fowl
**hence** away, ergo, therefore, thus
**henceforth** in futuro (L)
**hence these tears** hinc illae lacrimae (L)
**henchman** accessory, accomplice, aide, ally, assistant, associate, attendant, auxiliary, backer, bodyguard, cohort, collaborator, colleague, confederate, creature, crony, flatterer, flunk(e)y, follower, heavy, helper, helpmate, hireling, lackey, minder, minion, partner, pet, sidekick, subordinate, supporter, toady
**hen fattened for eating** poulard
**hen house** coop
**henna** dye, privet, shrub
**hennery** coop, henhouse
**henpeck** annoy, badger, chivvy, complain, goad, grouse, grumble, harass, harry, mumble, mutter, nag, pester, plague, provoke, scold, vex, whine, worry, yammer
**henpecked** annoyed, badgered, browbeaten, bullied, cowering, dominated, goaded, harassed, harried, meek, pestered, provoked, scolded, spineless, subjugated, timid
**hen's perch** roost
**hen's product** egg
**he opposes order** nihilist
**hepatic juice** bile
**hepatic organ** liver
**he performs domestic duties** manservant, valet
**he plays a part** actor
**he plays for love** amateur
**heptad** septet
**her** sa (F)
**herald** announce, augury, courier, crier, envoy, forerunner, foretoken, harbinger, indicate, indication, intuition, messenger, omen, precede, precursor, predecessor, prediction, proclaim, runner, sign(al), token
**heraldic band** fess(e)
**heraldic design** orle
**heraldic device** emblem
**heraldic gold** or
**heraldic monster** griffin, gryphon
**heraldic shield** escutcheon
**heraldic sign** fess(e)
**heraldic triangulation** gironny, gyronny
**herald of Greek gods** Hermes
**heraldry design** orle
**herald's sleeveless coat** tabard
**herb** aloe, anise, basil, catnip, clary, coriander, dill, dittany, fennel, leek, mace, medic, mint, moly, oregano, parsley, rosemary, rue, sage, savory, sedum, tansy, tarragon, thyme, wort, yarrow
**herbaceous garden plant allied to petunia** salpiglossis
**herbaceous plant** iris, lupin
**herbage** grass, pasturage
**herbal** botany, vegetal
**herbal hair dye** henna
**herbal medicine** muti
**herb as part of a bouquet garni** bay leaf, parsley, thyme
**herb for seasoning meat** rosemary
**herb growing near marshes** marsh mallow
**herb of carrot family** anise
**herb of grace** rue
**herb of mustard family** cress
**herb of pea family** lotus, mimosa
**herb of remembrance** rosemary
**herb of rose family** avens
**herb seed** sesame
**herb used in stuffing and meat dishes** parsley, sage, thyme
**herb with sweet leaves used in vinegar** tarragon
**herd** assemble, associate, bunch, cage, cluster, collect, congregate, corral, crowd, crush, drive, flock, force, gather, guide, horde, lead, mass, mob, multitude, muster, pack, press, protect, rabble, rally, shepherd, swarm, throng, wrangle
**herd instinct** crowd
**herd of buffaloes** gang
**herd of horses** band
**herd of roes** bevy
**herd of whales** gam, pod
**herd of wild swine** sounder
**herdsman** cowboy, drover, gaucho, herder, vaquero, wrangler
**here** aca (Sp), hither, ici (F), now
**hereafter** eternally, eventually, finally, forever, future, hence(forth), perpetually, presently, subsequently, then, ultimately
**here and everywhere** hic et ubique (L)
**here and now** immediately, quickly
**hereditary** ancestral, bequeathed, congenital, customary, family, genealogical, genetic, inborn, inbred, inheritable, inheritance, inherited, lineal, passable, traditional, transmitted, tribal, willed
**hereditary disease** haemophilia
**hereditary genes** germ plasm
**hereditary ruler** dynast
**heredity determinant** gene
**heredity factor** gene
**here I am and here I stay** j'y suis et j'y reste (F)
**here lies** ci-gît (F), hic jacet (L)
**heresy** agnosticism, apostasy, atheism, conversion, delusion, disloyalty, dissent, error, heterodoxy, iconoclasm, idolatry, impiety, irreligion, scepticism, schism, superstition, unorthodoxy
**heretic** agnostic, apostate, denier, deserter, dissenter, doubter, heathen, iconoclast, idolater, infidel, nonbeliever, nonconformist, pagan, rationalist, renegade, renouncer, repudiator, sceptic, sectarian, separatist, unbeliever, unorthodox
**heretical doctrine** heresy
**heretic religion** gnosticism
**heretofore** earlier, ere, formerly, hitherto, previously
**heritage** ancestry, background, bequest, birthright, bloodline, endowment, estate, family, history, inheritance, legacy, lineage, lot, past, patrimony, pedigree, portion, share, tradition
**hermaphrodite** bisexual, epicene, gynandroid, intersex, monoclinous, monoecious, unisexual
**hermaphroditism** abnormality
**Hermes** Mercury
**hermetic** airtight, sealed, shut, watertight
**hermit** anchoret, anchorite, ancress, ascetic, eremite, loner, monk, nun, recluse, solitaire, solitarian, solitary, troglodyte
**hermitage** abbey, ark, ashram, bungalow, cenoby, cloister, convent, cottage, covert, friary, grotto, mew, monastery, nunnery, priory, refuge, retreat, sanctum, shanty, shelter, villa
**hernia** rupture
**hernia of the brain** encephalocele
**hero** celebrity, champion, conquerer, conqueror, dignitary, examplar, gallant, goody, heart-throb, idol, paladin, paragon, personage, protagonist, stalwart, (super)star, valiant, victor, warrior
**heroic** bold, brave, courageous, daring, dauntless, determined, drastic, epic, fearless, gallant, heroical, lionhearted, resolved, stalwart, staunch, unwavering, unyielding, valiant, valorous, virile, worshipful
**heroic in style** epic
**heroic narrative** saga
**heroic Norse legend** saga
**heroic poem** epic, epos, work
**heroic song** *Edda*
**heroic tale** epic, gest(e), saga
**heroic woman** Amazon, virago
**heroin** horse, junk, scag, skag, smack

**heroine** celebrity, champion, conquerer, dignitary, diva, goddess, goody, ideal, idol, paragon, personage, protagonist, (super)star
**heroism** boldness, bravery, courage, daring, fearlessness, fortitude, gallantry, intrepidity, prowess, spirit, valour
**heron** bittern, crane, egret, hern, rail
**hero of Homer's *Iliad*** Achilles
**hero of Trafalgar** Nelson
**hero's hall** Valhall(a), Walhall(a)
**hero worship** admiration, adulation, apotheosis, awe, deification, exaltation, extolment, idolatry, idolisation, idolise, veneration
**herpes** shingles
**herring** alec, anchovy, brit, pilchard, sill, sprat
**herring barrel** cade
**herringbone** cross-stitch
**herring-like fish** sprat, shad
**herring measure** cran
**he settles disputes at games** umpire
**he sings alone** soloist
**hesitancy** ambiguity, aversion, confusion, dislike, distaste, doubt, indecision, irresolution, loathing, perplexity, quandary, reluctance, repugnance, reservation, scepticism, uncertainty, unpredictability, vacillation, wavering
**hesitant** delaying, diffident, dithery, doubtful, dubious, evasive, faltering, hovering, indecisive, irresolute, pausing, reluctant, sceptical, tardy, tentative, uncertain, undecided, unresolved, unsure, wavering
**hesitate** alternate, boggle, delay, demur, dither, doubt, evade, falter, fumble, halt, hover, mutter, pause, procrastinate, scruple, stammer, stumble, stutter, think, vacillate, wait, waver
**hesitating sound** um
**hesitation** delay, doubt, err, faltering, fumbling, indecision, irresolution, misdoubt, misgiving, pause, qualm, reluctance, scruple, stammering, stumbling, stuttering, uncertainty, unwillingness, vacillation
**he slept for twenty years** Rip van Winkle
**he speaks** loquitur (L)
**Hesperian** Western
**Hesperus** Venus
**hessian bag** sack
**he studies bird's eggs** oologist
**he studies heavenly bodies** astronomer
**he studies mosses** bryologist
**he studies wines** oenologist

**het** agitated, annoyed, excited
**he takes an oath** juror
**he tends horses** groom
**heteroclitic** heteroclite, irregular, unusual
**heterogeneous mass** conglomeration
**heterogeneous mixture** stew
**he throws people out of clubs** bouncer
**he tills fields** farmer
**he treats teeth** dentist
**he undergoes suffering for a cause** martyr
**hew** axe, carve, chop, cut, fashion, fell, form, hack, lop, make, model, sculpt(ure), sever, shape, smooth, split
**he wanders about** rover
**he was Hollywood's legendary dancer** Fred Astaire
**he was invulnerable except for his heel** Achilles
**he was killed in the Battle of Trafalgar** Nelson
**he was the doubter** Thomas
**he was thrown into the lion's den** Daniel
**hewn stone for building** ashlar
**he works it** operator
**he works on cars** mechanic
**he works on the land** farm-hand, farmer
**he wrote fables** Aesop
**hex** spell, witch
**hexagonal** sexangular
**hexagonal tile** favus
**heyday** bloom, flowering, peak, pink, prime, vigour
**hi** hello
**Hialeah event** race
**hiatus** aperture, breach, break, cavity, chasm, cleft, disruption, fissure, gap(e), incision, interruption, interval, lacuna, opening, orifice, rift, separation, slot, space, trench, vacuum
**hibernal viral infection** cold
**hibernation** dormancy, idleness, immobility, inaction, inactivity, inertia, laziness, passivity, shiftlessness, sloth, sluggishness, torpor, unemployment, winter sleep
**Hibernian** Irish
**hiccup** hics
**hick** bumpkin, countryman, farmer, provincial, yokel
**hickory** pecan
**hidden** abstruse, clandestine, close, concealed, covered, covert, cryptic, dark, ensconced, latent, mysterious, mystical, obscure, occult, secret,
shrouded, ulterior, underlying, unseen, veiled
**hidden danger** pitfall
**hidden explosive device** booby-trap
**hidden in hand** palmed
**hidden marksman** sniper
**hidden matter** mystery
**hidden obstacle** snag
**hidden passenger** stowaway
**hidden shooter** sniper
**hidden stock** hoard
**hidden store** cache
**hidden supply** hoard
**hidden treasure** trove
**hidden weapons store** cache
**hide** abscond, bark, block, bury, cache, camouflage, cloak, closet, cloud, coat, conceal, cover, disguise, dissemble, fell, fleece, fur, harbour, hoodwink, hull, jacket, leather, lurk, mask, obscure, obstruct, peel, pelt, retire, safeguard, screen, secrete, shroud, skin, stow, strike, suppress, veil, whip, withdraw
**hideaway** cave, cloister, concealed, cover, disguised, dugout, haven, hermitage, hidden, hide-out, hiding-place, lair, mew, nest, refuge, retreat, sanctuary
**hide before tanning** pelt
**hidebound** conventional, entrenched, narrow(-minded), rigid, set, strait-laced, ultra-conservative
**hide from view** obscure
**hide of calf or lamb** kip(skin)
**hide of ox** oxhide
**hide of young animal** kip(skin)
**hideous** appalling, awful, beastly, disgusting, dreadful, frightful, ghastly, grim, grisly, grotesque, gruesome, heinous, horrible, horrid, macabre, monstrous, odious, offensive, repulsive, revolting, shocking, terrible, terrifying, ugly, vile
**hideous monster** ogre, ghoul
**hide-out** asylum, cave(rn), cavity, corner, cranny, den, harbour, haunt, haven, hideaway, hole, lair, niche, nook, recess, refuge, resort, retreat, shelter
**hiding** beating, burying, caching, caning, cloaking, concealing, covering, disguising, drubbing, eclipsing, flogging, masking, obscuring, screening, secreting, sheltering, spanking, thrashing, veiling, whipping
**hiding place** ambush, cache, cover, hideaway, lair, retreat, shelter, trap
**hiding to attack by surprise** ambuscade
**hidrosis** perspiration, sweat

**hie** hasten, hurry, urge
**hiemal** hibernal, wintry
**hierarchy** caste, class, degree, echelon, gradation, grade, grading, graduation, ladder, order, position, progression, rank(ing), register, scale, sequence, series, spectrum, spread, status, steps, strata
**hieroglyphic** enigmatical, figurative, obscure, symbolic
**hi-fi system** stereo(gram)
**higgledy-piggledy** anyhow, confused(ly), disorderly, disorganised, haphazard(ly), helter-skelter, indiscriminate(ly), jumbled, muddled, pell-mell, topsy-turvy
**high** acute, arrogant, capital, chief, costly, dear, distinguished, early, elated, elevated, eminent, energetic, exalted, expensive, haughty, high-priced, hilarious, important, intense, intensified, lofty, lordly, main, pre-eminent, principal, prominent, proud, remote, serious, sharp, shrill, skyscraper, strong, tall, towering
**high and dry** abandoned, aground, beached, bereft, helpless, stranded
**high and low** everywhere, exhaustively
**high and mighty** arrogant, cavalier, conceited, haughty, imperious
**high and narrow chest of drawers** chiffonnier
**high ball in tennis** lob
**high bay window** oriel
**high body temperature** fever
**highbrow** aesthete, bluestocking, bookish, cultivated, deep, egghead, intellectual, mastermind, savant, scholar
**high card** ace
**high chest of drawers** tallboy
**high-class** choice, classy, deluxe, exclusive, first-rate, (high-)quality, posh, select, superior, top-flight, upper-class
**high-class cooking** haute cuisine (F)
**high-class dressmaking** haute couture (F)
**high craggy hill** krans, tor
**high crime** treason
**high distinction** renown
**high ecclesiastical dignitary** prelate
**higher** loftier, up
**higher course** seminar
**higher in place** above, over, superior
**higher in rank** above, senior, superior
**higher levels** brass
**higher position** up, precedence
**higher rank than viscount** earl
**higher school** academy

**higher than** above, over, superior
**highest** costliest, greatest, loftiest, sharpest, steepest, strongest, supreme, tallest, topmost, up(per)most
**highest adult male voice** alto, countertenor
**highest age of teenager** nineteen
**highest amount** maximum
**highest authoritarian** supremo
**highest authority** supremacy
**highest card in loo** pam
**highest degree** summit, utmost
**highest endeavour** best
**highest European volcano** Etna
**highest excellence** tip-top
**highest female voice** soprano
**highest heights** transcendency
**high estimation** repute
**highest in authority** supreme
**highest lake** Titicaca
**highest level** summit
**highest male adult voice** alto, countertenor
**highest mountain** Everest
**highest mountain in Australia** Kosciusko
**highest mountain in Japan** Fuji-san, Fujiyama, Mount Fuji
**highest mountain in Tasmania** Ossa
**highest mountain in the Alps** Mont Blanc
**highest part** tip, top
**highest part of ship's mast** masthead
**highest peak in England** Scafell Pike
**highest peak in Ireland** Carrauntoohill
**highest peak of attainment** Everest
**highest pitch** pinnacle
**highest point** acme, apex, apogee, summit, top, vertex, zenith
**highest point of excellence** tip-top
**highest point reached by a star** meridian
**highest possible** maximal, maximum
**highest rank in British army** field marshal
**highest stage** acme
**highest storey** attic
**highest top** acme, summit, zenith
**highest university degree in any faculty** doctorate
**highest value** maximum
**highest volcano in Europe** Etna
**high explosive** amatol, gelignite, melinite, TNT, trinitrotoluene, trinitrotoluol
**high fashion** haute couture (F)
**high-fashion model** mannequin
**high feeble sound** peep
**high-fibre ingredient** bran

**high-flown** elaborate, exaggerated, extravagant, florid, grandiose, lofty, overblown, pretentious
**high-flown rhetorical style of writing** euphuism
**high-flying songster** lark
**high grassland in central Asia** Pamirs
**high-handed** arbitrary, autocratic, bossy, despotic, dictatorial, domineering, imperious, inconsiderate, oppressive, overbearing, self-willed, tactless, tyrannical
**high hat** topper
**high hill** tor
**high hit** lob, skier, skyer
**high in pitch** alt
**high in stature** tall
**high intellectual ability** brains
**high in the hip** iliac
**high IQ society** Mensa
**high jinks** frolic
**high-kicking dance** cancan
**highland** highveld, plateau
**Highland cap with pointed front** glengarry
**Highland dagger** dirk (Sc), skean-dhu (Sc), sgian-dhu (Sc)
**Highland dance** fling
**Highlander** Scot
**Highlander garment** kilt
**Highlander pouch** sporran
**Highlander's cloth** tartan
**Highlander's knife** dirk (Sc), sgian-dhu (Sc), skean-dhu (Sc)
**Highlander's pouch** sporran
**Highlander's sword** claymore
**Highland Games event** caber
**Highland manservant** gillie
**Highland dance** fling
**Highland drink** scotch
**Highland sword** claymore
**high leather riding boot** Wellington
**high-level land** highveld, plateau
**highlight** accent(uate), best, climax, cream, emphasise, feature, focal point, focus, illuminate, peak, spotlight, stress, underline
**highly accomplished** finished, proficient, skilful
**highly amuse** regale
**highly coloured** colorific
**highly coloured monkey** douc
**highly competent in a job** professional
**highly confidential** secret
**highly curious** agog
**highly dangerous and corrosive acid** sulphuric
**highly developed** elaborate
**highly distinguished** illustrious
**highly distinguished female singer** diva

**highly emotional music** rhapsody
**highly emotional situation** drama
**highly esteemed** honoured
**highly excellent** expert
**highly excited** agog
**highly immoral character** reprobate
**highly impatient, eager or curious** agog
**highly inflammable petroleum** napalm
**highly intelligent person** intellectual
**highly magnetic rock** lodestone
**highly offensive** unheard of
**highly original** seminal
**highly pleasing** delicious
**highly poisonous alkaloid** strychnine
**highly poisonous gas** arsine
**highly poisonous substance** strychnine
**highly practised and skilful** expert
**highly reprehensible** sinful
**highly-seasoned dish** olio, olla
**highly-seasoned dried sausage** saveloy
**highly-seasoned Mexican dish** tamale
**highly-seasoned sausage** boerewors, salami, saveloy
**highly-seasoned soup** mulligatawny
**highly-seasoned stew** biriani, breyani, goulash, ragout
**highly sensitive** exquisite
**highly skilled** adept
**highly skilled in any achievement** ace
**highly-strung** edgy, excitable, nervous, nervy, tense
**highly-strung condition** nerves
**highly talented** brilliant
**highly unpleasant** nasty
**highly unsuitable** indecent
**highly valued** dear, precious
**high male singing voice** alt, (counter)tenor
**high mental ability** talent
**high-minded** bold, brave, chivalrous, courteous, courtly, decent, disinterested, ethical, fair, gallant, generous, gentlemanly, good, heroic, honest, honourable, idealistic, knightly, law-abiding, lofty, magnanimous, moral, noble, principled, pure, reliable, reputable, righteous, scrupulous, scrupulous, true, trustworthy, trusty, truthful, unselfish, upright, valiant, veracious, virtuous, worthy
**high mountain** Alp, Everest, Himalayas
**high mountain peak** alp
**high musical note** alt
**high narrow window** lancet
**high noon** midday
**high officer of state** marshal
**high official** dignitary

**high official in the Ottoman Empire** beg, bey
**high performance touring car** gran turismo
**high-pitched** acute, alt, shrill, strident
**high-pitched bark** yelp
**high-pitched cry** squeal
**high-pitched flute** fife
**high-pitched radio signal** bleep
**high-pitched voice** treble
**high plain** highveld, plateau
**high playing card** ace
**high point** acme, apex, climax, peak, summit, zenith
**high-pointed hill** tor
**high praise** eulogy
**high priest** pontiff
**high priest of Israel** Eli
**high projection** tor
**high public regard** honour
**high-quality tea** pekoe
**high railway** el
**high range of mountains with jagged peaks** sierra
**high rank** dignity, eminence, purple
**high-ranking card** ace
**high-ranking churchman** cardinal
**high-ranking naval man** admiral
**high-ranking officer such as a bishop or cardinal** prelate
**high reading desk** ambo
**high regard** esteem
**high repute** éclat, reputation
**high respect** esteem, honour
**high-rising shoe** topboot
**high rocky hill** tor
**high rocky tableland** mesa
**high-sounding** affected, artificial, extravagant, flamboyant, grandiose, high-flown, ostentatious, pompous, pretentious, stilted, strained
**high speed driver** racer
**high-speed measurement** Mach
**high-spirited** boisterous, bold, bouncy, daring, dashing, ebullient, effervescent, energetic, exuberant, frolicsome, fun-loving, gallant, lively, mettlesome, peppy, sparkling, spirited, vibrant, vital, vivacious
**high-spirited behaviour** shenanigan
**high-spirited escapade** caper
**high-spirited horse** steed
**high-spirited romping girl** tomboy
**high spirits** animation, buoyancy, cheer, elation, exuberance, exuberant, gaiety, glee, happiness, hilarity, joie de vivre (F), merriment
**high-stepping trot in dressage** passage
**high stiff collar** choker
**high temperature** fever, hot
**high temperature gauge** pyrometer

**high temperature of body** heat
**high title of sovereignty** emperor
**high Turkish official** pasha
**high up** aloft
**high volley** lob
**high-water mark** gauge, limit
**high waterproof boot** wader
**highway** expressway, freeway, (high)road, interstate, thoroughfare, throughway, turnpike
**highway barricade** roadblock
**highway charge** toll
**highway curve** ess, S
**highway division** lane
**highway edge** shoulder
**highwayman** bandit, brigand, burglar, cheat, fraud, land-pirate, marauder, outlaw, pirate, plunderer, raider, robber, stealer, thief
**highway marker** sign
**highway robber** bandit
**highway round city** ring road
**highway surface** asphalt
**highway word** route
**high wind** gale
**hijack** commandeer, expropriate, kidnap, seize, seizure, skyjack, snatch, steal, stick-up
**hijacker's victim** hostage
**hike** back-pack, march, plod, ramble, tramp, trek, trudge, walk
**hiker** (bush-)walker, explorer, gypsy, migrant, nomad, rambler, rover, tourist, traveller, tripper, voyager, wanderer, wayfarer
**hiker's satchel** rucksack
**hilarious** amusing, comical, convivial, entertaining, funny, gay, happy, humorous, hysterical, jolly, jovial, joyful, merry, noisy, rollicking, side-splitting, uproarious
**hilarity** amusement, boisterousness, cheerfulness, conviviality, entertainment, exhilaration, exuberance, frivolity, gaiety, glee, jollification, jollity, joviality, joyousness, laughter, levity, merriment, mirth
**hill** brae (Sc), climb, down, drift, elevation, eminence, fell, gradient, height, hillock, hilltop, incline, knoll, krans, mound, mount, prominence, rise, slope, tor
**hillbilly** country and western
**hill-building insect** ant, termite
**hill country** highland
**hill dugout** abri, cave, grotto
**hill-dwelling insect** ant, termite
**hill in Rome** Aventine, Caelian, Quirnal
**hillock** barrow, hummock, knap, knoll, monticule, mound, tumulus
**hill of loose sand** dune

**hill-range** ridge
**hillside** brae (Sc)
**hillside debris** scree
**hillside shelter** abri
**hill-slope** brae (Sc)
**hilltop outpost** redoubt
**hilt** grip, haft, handgrip, handle, helve
**him** le (Sp)
**Himalayan bear** panda
**Himalayan cedar** deodar
**Himalayan country** Nepal
**Himalayan goat** goral, serow
**Himalayan guide** sherpa
**Himalayan kingdom** Nepal
**Himalayan mammal** panda
**Himalayan mountain** Annapurna, Dhaulagiri, Everest, Kangchenjunga, Lhotse, Makalu, Manaslu
**Himalayan state** Nepal
**Himalayan wild goat** markho(o)r
**Himalayan wild sheep** bharal, burhel
**himself** se (L)
**hind** after, back, hinder, rear, tail
**hinder** abort, bar, block, check, contravene, counteract, cramp, cumber, defer, delay, deter, disallow, encumber, fetter, forbid, frustrate, hamper, hamstring, handicap, impede, inhibit, interfere, interrupt, limit, obstruct, oppose, preclude, prevent, prohibit, retard, stop, thwart
**hinder effectively** prevent
**hinder progress of** impede
**hind-limb muscle in vertebrates** gluteus
**hindmost** tail
**hindmost part** rear
**hindmost part of animal** tail
**hindmost section of brain** medulla
**hind part** back, rear
**hind part of boat** stern
**hind part of insect** abdomen
**hind part of saddle** cantle
**hind part of the head** occiput
**hindquarters** rump
**hindquarters of a horse** croup, crupper
**hindrance** bar(rier), check, deterrent, difficulty, drag, drawback, encumbrance, handicap, hitch, impediment, impeding, limitation, obstacle, obstruction, prevention, restraint, snag, stoppage, stopping
**Hindu** Indian
**Hindu adept** mahatma
**Hindu ascetic** fakir, yogi
**Hindu asceticism** yoga
**Hindu bible** shaster, s(h)astra
**Hindu class** caste
**Hindu clerk** babu
**Hindu dancing girl** bayadere

**Hindu deity** Brahma, Dev(a), Ganesha, Indra, Krishna, Shira, Vishnu
**Hindu demon** Rahu
**Hindu devotional incantation** mantra
**Hindu exercises** yoga
**Hindu festival** Diwali
**Hindu Festival of Lights** Deepavali
**Hindu fire god** Agni
**Hindu garment** saree, sari
**Hindu gate tower** gopuram
**Hindu ghat** pyre
**Hindu god** Deva
**Hindu god of fire** Agni
**Hindu god of rain and thunder** Indra
**Hindu hereditary class** caste
**Hindu holy books** Veda
**Hindu honorific** Sri
**Hindu idol** swami
**Hindu incarnation** avatar
**Hindu influential teacher** guru, swami
**Hindu loincloth** dhoti
**Hindu moral law** dharma
**Hindu mystic** yogi
**Hindu mystical and magical writings** tantra
**Hindu philosopher** yogi
**Hindu philosophy** sankhya, yoga, yogi
**Hindu poet** Tagore
**Hindu police officer** tanadar
**Hindu priest** brahmin
**Hindu princess** ranee, rani
**Hindu queen** (maha)ranee, rani
**Hindu religious ascetic** fakir
**Hindu religious instructor** swami
**Hindu religious philosophy** yoga
**Hindu religious rite** pooja, puja
**Hindu religious teacher** swami
**Hindu retreat** ashram
**Hindu sacred writings** Veda
**Hindu saint** (maha)rishi
**Hindu spiritual leader** guru, maharishi
**Hindu spiritual teacher** guru, swami
**Hindustani** Urdu
**Hindu teacher** guru, swami
**Hindu title** acharya, aya, babu, mahatma, pandit, pundit, sri(mati), swami
**Hindu title of honour** Sri
**Hindu trader** banian, banyan
**Hindu wandering holy man** Sad(d)hu
**Hindu woman's garment** saree, sari
**hinge** basis, centre, depend, elbow, hang, joint, knee, pivot, premise, rest, rotate, rule, turn
**hinged barrier** gate
**hinged cover** lid
**hinged fastener** hasp
**hinged flap on aeroplane wing** aileron
**hinged legs** trestle
**hinged metal strap** hasp
**hinged nautical steering gear** rudder

**hinged padlock clasp** hasp
**hinged panel** door
**hingelike joint in body** ginglymus
**hint** advice, allude, allusion, breath, clue, cue, dash, help, implication, imply, indicate, indication, inkling, innuendo, insinuate, insinuation, intimate, intimation, mention, pointer, prompt, refer, reminder, sign(al), soupçon, speck, suggest(ion), suspicion, taste, tinge, tip(-off), touch, trace
**hint at** broach, imply, intimate
**hint obliquely** insinuate
**hint of danger** warning
**hint slyly** insinuate
**hint to actor** cue
**hip** ilia
**hipbone** ilium
**hipbone section** ilium, pubis
**hip-cavity** acetabulum, cotyle
**hip joint** coxa, enarthrosis
**hip nerve** sciatic
**hippie's bankroll** bread
**hippie's home** pad
**hippies' shared home** commune
**hippo is one** pachyderm
**hippopotamus** sea-cow
**hippopotamus-like beast described in the Book of Job** behemoth
**hippy** beatnik, bohemian, drop-out, flower child, hippie
**hip socket** acetabulum, cotyle, hip-cavity
**hire** allowance, appoint, book, bribe, charge, charter, commission, compensation, cost, employ, engage, fare, fee, lease, let, pay, price, procure, rend, rent(al), reserve, retain, salary, stipend, toll, wages
**hire by contract** charter
**hire-car** taxi(-cab)
**hired cab** taxi
**hired girl** biddie, biddy
**hired killer** bravo
**hired man** hand, labourer
**hired mourner** keener, mute, wailer, weeper
**hired ruffian** bravo, myrmidon
**hired soldier** mercenary
**hired worker** hand
**hire of a ship** freight
**hire out** let, rent
**hire out again** relet
**hirer** boss, employer, lessee, renter
**hiring cab** taxi
**hirsute** bearded, bristled, downy, hairy, prickly, shaggy, unshaven, unshorn, whiskered
**hirsute growth** mane
**his** ses (F)

**his and her** their
**hispid** bristly, shaggy
**hiss** boo, buzz, catcall, condemn, contempt, damn, decry, deride, derision, hissing, hoot, jeer, mock(ery), rasp, revile, ridicule, shrill, sibilance, sibilate, wheeze, whirr, whistle, whiz(z)
**hissing** booing, catcalling, condemning, damning, decrying, deriding, hooting, jeering, mocking, rasping, reviling, ridiculing, shrilling, wheezing, whirring, whistling, whizzing
**hiss in pan** sizzle
**historic** celebrated, consequential, epoch-making, extraordinary, famed, famous, momentous, notable, outstanding, remarkable, renowned, significant
**historic age** era
**historical accuracy** synchronism
**historical circuit court** eyre
**historical documents' home** archives
**historical era** age
**historical figure** Napoleon
**historical period** era, time
**historical poem** epic
**historical record** annals, chronicle, story
**historical time period** era
**historical truth** historicity
**historic event** epic
**historic period** era
**history** account, anecdote, annals, archive, chronicle, depiction, dossier, experiences, facts, information, lore, memories, narrative, news, past, preterition, record, relation, report, story, study, tale, tradition, yesteryear
**history and description of books** bibliography
**history of martyrs** martyrology
**history of scandals** chronique scandaleuse (F)
**history record** annal
**histrionic** affected, bogus, dramaturgic, emotive, false, insincere, (melo)dramatic, operatic, scenic, sensational, sham, stagy, theatrical, thespian, unnatural
**his wife turned into a pillar of salt** Lot
**hit** accomplish, achieve, arouse, attain, bang, batter, beat, blow, club, cuff, effect, flog, jab, klap, knock, lam, lob, pelt, pound, punch, reach, slap, slug, smack, smite, sock, strike, stroke, struck, swat, thrash, thump, wallop, whack, win, zap
**hit a baseball** bat
**hit a fly** swat
**hit back** reciprocate, retaliate

**hit ball high** lob
**hit by bullet** shoot
**hit by shooting** snipe
**hitch** attach, bind, catch, clamp, connect, fasten, harness, hindrance, impediment, jerk, join, knot, lash, lift, ligature, limp, move, noose, obstacle, obstruction, pull, setback, shift, snag, stagger, string, tether, tie, tug, unite
**hitch a lift** thumb
**Hitchcock thriller** *Psycho*
**hit hard** bat, donder, klap, lam, slam, slog, slug, swat, swipe, thrash
**hitherto** ago, before, ere, here, until now, yet
**hitherto unknown** novel
**Hitler's deputy** Hess
**Hitler's follower** Nazi
**Hitler's special force** SS
**Hitler's title** Führer
**hit lightly** pat
**hit man** assassin, killer, murderer
**hit off** capture, catch, impersonate, mimic, represent
**hit on** discover, guess, invent, realise
**hit one's foot on the ground** stamp
**hit on the head** conk
**hit or miss** aimless, casual, incidental, indiscriminate, random, undirected, uneven
**hit out** assail, attack, condemn, criticise, denounce, lash, rail
**hit sharply** rap
**hit smartly** swat
**hit soundly** batter, pound, pummel, trounce
**hit the jackpot** succeed
**hit the roof** bridle, explode, rage, rave, storm
**hit the sack** nap, retire, snooze
**hitting with a club** bludgeoning
**hit up** loft
**hit upon** discover, guess, invent, realise
**hit with a sweeping stroke** swipe
**hit with fist** punch
**hit with hand** slap
**hit with heavy blow** thwack
**hit with heavy blows** slog
**hit with open hand** smack
**hit with the hand** slap
**hive** accumulate, amass, cache, collect, deposit, garner, gather, hoard, hub, save, stockpile, store, treasure
**hive dweller** bee
**hives symptom** welt
**hoard** accumulate, amass, assemblage, assemble, cache, collect(ion), deposit, fund, garner, gather, harvest, heap, hive, lay-up, mass, pile, reserve, save, scrape,

stash, stock(pile), store, supply, treasure
**hoard away** stash
**hoarded wealth** treasure
**hoarder** amasser, churl, collector, miser, niggard, skinflint
**hoard of precious gems** treasure
**hoard of riches** treasure
**hoar-frost** rime
**hoarse** croaking, croaky, dry, grating, gravelly, gruff, guttural, harsh, husky, rasping, raspy, raucous, rough, roupy, scratchy, stertorous, straining, throaty, voiceless, wheezy
**hoarse cry** croak
**hoarsely breathing** stertorous
**hoarsely resonant** throaty
**hoarse rattling noise in breathing during sleep** snore
**hoarse-voiced black bird** raven, rook
**hoary** age-old, aged, ancient, antediluvian, antiquated, antique, archaic, early, elderly, frosty, grey(-haired), grizzled, old(-fashioned), olden, out-of-date, senescent, silver(y), snowy, superannuated, timeworn, venerable, white(-haired)
**hoax** bamboozle, bilk, cheat, con, deceive, deception, delude, fake, fool, fraud, gag, hoodwink, hum, joke, leg-pull, prank, rumour, ruse, scheme, sham, spoof, string, swindle, trick(ery)
**hobble** delay, falter, fetter, halt, hamper, hinder, hitch, hop, impede, jerk, limp, pause, retard, shamble, shuffle, stagger, stumble, tether, toddle, totter, trammel
**hobby** amusement, avocation, diversion, divertissement, entertainment, game, interest, pastime, play, pursuit, recreation, relaxation, sideline
**hobby of collecting cigarette cards** cartophily
**hobby of collecting postcards** deltiology
**hobnailed shoe** tacket
**hobo** bergie, bum, tramp, vagrant
**hobo's food** grub
**Ho Chi Minh City** Saigon
**hock** hamstring, pawn, pledge
**hockey-like game** lacrosse
**hockey puck** rubber
**hockey puck destination** goal
**hockey score** goal
**hock of horse** gambrel
**hocus** befool, beguile, cheat, contaminate, corrupt, deceive, drug, dupe, falsify, hoax, hoodwink,

mislead, mystify, narcotise, numb, stupefy, trick(ery)
**hodge-podge** gallimaufry, hash, hotchpotch, olio
**hoe** burrow, cultivate, delve, dibble, dig, excavate, grub, harrow, mine, penetrate, pierce, quarry, rake, scoop, scour, scrape, scratch, scuffle, spade, till, trowel, tunnel, weed
**hoe's target** weed
**hog** pig, swine, boar
**hog-like animal** peccary
**hogwash** pigswill
**hoi polloi** admass, commonage, commonality, demos, plebeians, rabble, ragtag, riffraff
**hoist** crane, derrick, elevate, elevator, erect, heave, heeze, heft, hoick, launch, lift, raise, sway, weigh, winch, windlass
**hoisting bucket** kibble
**hoisting crane** davit
**hoisting machine** crane, winch
**hoisting rope** gantline
**hoist on shoulder** hump
**hoity-toity person** arrogant, haughty, snob
**hokum** bosh, bunkum, drivel, fakery, flapdoodle, humbug, nonsense, rot, rubbish, trash, tripe
**hold** adhere, avast, bear, believe, bind, celebrate, clasp, cling, clutch, cohere, consider, contain, continue, control, detain, embrace, endure, espouse, esteem, grasp, grip, harbour, have, judge, keep, last, observe, occupy, own, persist, possess, regard, remain, retain, retention, stay, stop, support, sustain, think, use, wait
**hold a believe** suppose
**hold a brief for** approve, defend, favour, promote, propound, sanction
**hold a conference** confer, gather, meet, sit
**hold-all** bag, valise
**hold aloof** refrain
**hold and use** wield
**hold a session** gather, meet, sit
**hold as precious** treasure
**hold as property** own, possess
**hold as sacred** enshrine, inshrine
**hold as true** accept
**hold attention** interest
**hold a view** opine
**hold back** arrest, check, contain, control, curb, dam, delay, deny, desist, detain, deter, detract, handicap, hinder, inhibit, refrain, refuse, rein, repress, restrain, retain, retard, stifle, stop, suppress, withdraw, withhold
**hold back by force** restrain
**hold back on leash** trash
**hold by right** own, possess
**hold closely** cradle, cuddle
**hold closely in one's arms** embrace, hug
**hold closely to** adhere
**hold consultation** advise
**hold conversation about** discuss
**hold dear** cherish, love, treasure
**hold different belief** dissent
**hold down** contain, pinion
**hold due to war** capture, intern
**holder** bearer, box, case, champion, container, cover, crate, custodian, handle, housing, incumbent, keeper, occupant, owner, possessor, proprietor, purchaser, receptacle, rest, sheath, stand, tenant
**holder for loose papers** folder
**holder for new work** in-tray
**holder for one or more candles** candlestick
**holder of a bursary** bursar
**holder of a mandate** mandatary
**holder of church living** beneficiary
**holder of commission** officer
**holder of concession** concessionaire
**holder of lease** lessee
**holder of property** owner, proprietor
**hold fast** adhere, clench, clinch, cling, fix, hook, pin, secure, support, tenacious
**hold firmly** clutch, grasp, grip, insist
**hold formal argument** debate
**hold for questioning** detain
**hold for reason** kidnap
**hold forth** advance, declaim, descant, discourse, extend, harangue, offer, orate, spiel, submit
**hold for trial** remand
**hold from** abstain
**hold good** apply, prevail, serve, stand
**hold in** restrain
**hold in abeyance** postpone
**hold in abomination** hate
**hold in check** compesce, govern, rein, repress
**hold in common** share
**hold in contempt** scorn
**hold in custody** confine, jail
**hold in deep respect** revere
**hold in favour** prefer
**holding all it can** full
**holding back** restraining
**holding currently accepted views** orthodox
**holding device** vice
**holding fast** grasp, tenacious
**holding fill** full
**holding firmly** tenacious
**holding property** proprietary
**holding tightly** tenacious
**holding together** solidarity
**holding tool** vice
**holding up** embargo, seizure
**hold in high regard** appreciate
**hold in place** anchor
**hold in readiness** poise
**hold in regard** esteem, respect
**hold in war** capture, intern
**hold in wrestling** armlock, (half-)nelson, headlock
**hold items together** clip, pin, staple
**hold no more** brim
**hold off** avoid, defer, delay, postpone, rebuff, refrain, repel, suspend, wait
**hold office** function, rule
**hold on** (a)bide, continue, perpetuate
**hold on course** fetch, stand, stem
**hold one's ground** resist, stand, stick
**hold one's own** compete
**hold on tightly** cling
**hold out** continue, endure, extend, give, last, offer, oppose, persevere, persist, present, resist, (with)stand
**hold out to give** offer
**hold over** adjourn, defer, delay, waive
**hold person for ransom** kidnap
**hold royal office** reign
**holds academic degree** graduate
**hold same view** agree, concur
**holds back water** dam
**holds baptismal water** font
**holds egg cell** ovule
**holds hair in place** clip
**holds milk** udder
**hold spellbound** enthral
**holds teeth** jaw
**holds up a curtain** rod
**hold suspended** dangle, poise
**hold sway** predominate, prevail, reign, rule, run
**hold the fort** defend, maintain, uphold
**hold the opinion** opine
**hold tight** grip, squeeze
**hold tightly** clip, grip, stick
**hold to be true** aver
**hold together** bond, clamp, cohere, consist, fasten
**hold to ransom** blackmail, capture, hijack, kidnap
**hold under spell** bewitch, charm, enchant
**hold up** bear, brace, buttress, delay, detain, display, erect, exhibit, expose, flaunt, halt, hamper, hinder, impede, lift, raise, retard, rob, show, stand, stop, support, sustain, unroll, uphold
**hold-up** bottleneck, delay difficulty, detention, freebooting, heist, hitch,

interruption, jam, obstruction, piracy, robbery, setback, slowdown, snag, stick-up, stoppage, trouble, wait
**hold up for adoration** elevate
**hold up to ridicule** mock
**hold with** accept, countenance, support
**hole** abyss, aperture, basin, bore, burrow, cavity, concavity, cove, den(t), donga, drill, fault, flaw, gap, gash, gorge, gully, hollow, hovel, incision, inlet, mouth, opening, orifice, perforation, pit, retreat, rut, sinus, tunnel, vent
**hole-and-corner** backstairs, clandestine, covert, secret, underhand
**hole-boring tool** gimlet
**hole dug for burial of corpse** grave
**hole for coin** slot
**hole for something to fit into** socket
**hole in bow of ship** hawse
**hole in earth spewing lava** volcano
**hole in one** ace
**hole in ship's bow** hawse
**hole in ship's side to carry off water from deck** scupper
**hole in the road** pothole
**hole of a needle** eye
**hole played in three strokes under par** albatross
**holiday** celebration, feast, fête, fiesta, gala, leave, recess, vacation
**holiday accommodation** hotel, time-share
**holiday away from home** outing
**holiday complex** camp, hotel
**holiday gala** fête
**holiday house** cottage, rondavel, villa
**holiday hut** chalet
**holiday-maker** tourist
**holiday of newly-married couple** honeymoon
**holiday place** resort
**holiday resort** spa
**holiday traveller** tourist
**holiday weekend** Easter
**holiest city of Islam** Mecca
**holiness** blessedness, devoutness, divineness, divinity, faithfulness, godliness, piety, piousness, pureness, purity, religiousness, sacredness, saintliness, sanctity, spirituality, virtuousness
**Hollands gin** Schiedam, schnap(p)s
**holler** bawl, call, cheer, clamour, cry, hail, halloo, holla, hollo(a), howl, roar, scream, shout, shriek, squeal, whoop, yell, yelp
**hollow** artificial, basin, bottom, bowl, cave, cavern(ous), cavity, channel, concave, concavity, crater, cup, deceptive, deep, dent, depressed, depression, dimple, empty, false, flimsy, fruitless, futile, groove, indentation, indented, insincere, meaningless, pit, reverberant, socket, spacious, sunken, toneless, unfilled, useless, void, worthless
**hollow amongst hills** lap
**hollow and inflated** tyre
**hollow between hills** valley
**hollow conduit** pipe
**hollow cylinder** drum, pipe, tube
**hollow depression** basin
**hollow dish** basin, bowl
**hollowed-tree coffin** cist
**hollow-eyed** haggard
**hollow glass vessel** bottle, jar
**hollow grass** cane, reed
**hollow-horned ruminant** goat
**hollow in belly** navel
**hollow in cheek** dimple
**hollow in coil of cable** tier
**hollow in hill** clash, combe, coom(b), corrie
**hollow in surface** dent
**hollow in tile** key
**hollow in which water collects** vlei
**hollow mark** dent
**hollow metal vessel** pot, bell
**hollow muscular organ** heart
**hollowness** concavity, inanity, vacuity, vanity
**hollow object in which metal is cast** mould
**hollow of arm** armpit
**hollow of horse's tooth** mark
**hollow of knee** ham
**hollow of roof** valley
**hollow out** cave(rn), cut, dig, excavate, excise, howl, mine
**hollow part of organ** ventricle
**hollow place in rock** cave, grotto
**hollow rock nodule** geode
**hollow rod** tube
**hollow stem** cane
**hollow stem of feather** quill
**hollow tile** backing
**hollow tropical grass** bamboo
**hollow tube** pipe
**hollow within a solid body** cavity
**holly** ilex, inkberry
**holly's Christmas partner** ivy
**Hollywood** Tinseltown
**Hollywood film award** Oscar
**Holmes's hat** deerstalker
**holm-oak** ilex
**holomorphic** analytic
**holothurian eaten by the Chinese** sea-slug, trepang
**holy** beatific, blessed, blest, chaste, consecrated, deiform, devout, divine, dreadful, ecstatic, faithful, godly, hallowed, pietistic, pious, religious, reverent, sacred, sainted, saintly, sanctus (L), spotless, unstained, untainted
**holy book of Christianity** Bible
**Holy City** Jerusalem
**holy city of Islam** Mecca
**holy garden** Eden
**holy image** icon
**holy immersion** baptism
**holy joy** beatitude
**holy lady** nun
**Holy Land** Israel
**holy man** sad(d)hu, saint
**holy man of Lhasa** lama
**holy person** martyr, saint, venerable
**holy picture** icon
**holy place** altar, church, sanctuary, sanctum, shrine, temple
**holy platter** grail
**holy scripture of Islam** Koran
**holy scripture of Christianity** Bible
**holy sister** nun
**holy song** hymn
**holy statue** icon
**holy Ukrainian city** Kiev
**holy war** crusade, jihad
**holy-water font** stoup
**holy-water receptacle** font
**Holy Willie** hypocrite
**homage** acknowledgement, admiration, adoration, adulation, allegiance, awe, deference, devotion, duty, esteem, faithfulness, fidelity, honour, loyalty, praise, recognition, regard, respect, reverence, service, tribute, veneration, worship
**home** abode, birthplace, bungalow, central, close, country, direct, domestic, domicile, dwelling(-place), familiar, family, fireside, habitat(ion), hearth, homeland, homestead, house(hold), intimate, native, near, nest, origin, pied-à-terre, refuge, residence, retreat, root, shelter, territory
**home and lands of a lord** manor
**home building** house
**home-dweller** resident
**homefolks** family
**home for bees** hive
**home for dog** kennel
**home for hamster** cage
**home for pet bird** cage
**home for poor** hospice
**home for traveller** hotel, inn, motel
**home fuel** gas
**home ground** familiarity, focus
**home in *Gone with the Wind*** Tara
**homeland** fatherland, mother country, motherland
**home leaser** tenant

**homeless** abandoned, cheerless, derelict, deserted, desolate, destitute, disconsolate, disinherited, displaced, dispossessed, dossers, down-and-out, exiled, forlorn, forsaken, helpless, houseless, itinerant, lonely, lost, miserable, outcast, pathetic, pitiable, pitiful, roaming, squatters, stray, tramps, travellers, unhappy, unsettled, vagabond, vagrants, wandering, wretched
**homeless and helpless person** waif
**homeless animal** maverick, stray, waif
**homeless child** gamin, street Arab, stroller, urchin, waif
**home life** seclusion
**homelike** cheerful, comfortable, cordial, cosy, domestic, easy, familiar, friendly, homebred, homespun, homy, hospitable, informal, intimate, peaceful, pleasant, quiet, relaxing, restful, serene, snug, tranquil, warm
**homely** agreeable, ample, coarse, comfortable, commodious, common(place), convenient, cosy, delightful, domestic, easy, enjoyable, everyday, frugal, homespun, inelegant, plain, primitive, simple, snug, ugly, uncomely, unpretending, unpretentious
**homely speech** vernacular
**home movie** video
**home of Abraham** Ur
**home of bees** hive
**home office** study
**home of Greek god, Pan** Arcadia
**home of Irish kings** Tara
**home of Lazarus** Bethany
**home of Manxman** Isle of Man
**home of muses** Helicon
**home of National Botanic Gardens in South Africa** Kirstenbosch
**home of Odysseus** Ithaca
**home of pharaohs** Egypt
**home of recluse** hermitage
**home of Saul's witch** Endor
**home of Scarlett O'Hara** Tara
**home of Shakespeare** Stratford-on-Avon
**home of swarm of bees** beehive
**home of the gods** Asgard, Olympus
**home of William Tell** Altdorf
**home of Zeno** Elea
**home-owner's document** deed
**homer** (homing) pigeon
**home reserve** Landwehr (G), militia, territorials
**home retreat** den

**Homeric** colossal, epic, heroic, Homerian, imposing, magnificent, monumental, titanic, towering
**Homer's epic** *Iliad, Odyssey*
**home rule** autonomy, independence, liberty, Swaraj, uhuru
**homesickness** desire, longing, maladie du pays (F), nostalgia, yearning
**homesickness as a disease** nostalgia
**homespun** amateurish, artless, coarse, crude, folksy, home-made, homely, inelegant, plain, rough, rude, rustic, unpolished, unrefined, unsophisticated
**home statue** lar
**home sweet home** hearth
**homicidal** berserk, bloody, deadly, killing, lethal, maniacal, mortal, murderous
**homicide** assassin(ation), killer, manslaughter, murder, parricide, regicide, silencer, slaying, sniper
**homiletic passage of the Talmud** Aggadah
**homily** address, descant, discourse, essay, lecture, lesson, oration, parable, preaching, preachment, salutation, screed, sermon, talk, teaching, thesis, treatise, valedictory
**homing bird** pigeon
**hominy** samp
**homogeneity** accordance, agreement, comparability, consistency, consonancy, identicalness, identity, likeness, oneness, parallelism, regularity, sameness, similarity, uniformity, uniformness
**homogeneous** akin, alike, analogous, cognate, comparable, consistent, consonant, harmonious, identical, kindred, similar, uniform, unvarying
**homologous** accordant, akin, allied, comparable, consistent, constant, correspondent, corresponding, like, parallel, regular, relative, similar, uniform
**Homo sapiens** human(ity), man
**homosexual** catamite, effeminate, gay, homophile, invert, lesbian, moffie, pederast, queer, tribadic, urning
**Honduras coin** centavo, lempira, peso
**Honduras port** Tela
**Honduras ruins** Tenampua
**Honduras sea** Caribbean
**hone** abrade, civilise, cultivate, edge, elevate, file, grind(stone), improve, perfect, point, polish, rasp, refine, sharpen, strop, temper, wheel, whet(stone)
**honest** authentic, candid, chaste, decent, ethical, fair, frank, genuine, good, guileless, incorrupt, just, moral, open, principled, sincere, straight(forward), true, trustworthy, trusty, truthful, unreserved, upright, upstanding, veracious, virtuous
**honesty** candour, equity, explicitness, fairness, faithfulness, fidelity, frankness, genuineness, honour, integrity, justness, morality, objectivity, openness, outspokenness, rectitude, scrupulousness, sincerity, straightforwardness, trustworthiness, truth(fulness), veracity, virtue
**honey** compliment, mel, molasses, nectar, praise, sweetness, syrup
**honey badger** ratel
**honey base** nectar
**honey bear** kinkajou, sun bear
**honeybird** wattlebird
**honey-collector** bee
**honey 'depot'** hive
**honeydew melon** muskmelon, spanspek
**honey drink** mead, mulse
**honey-eater** iao, manuao, moho, tui
**honeyed wine** oenomel
**honey-gland of a flower** nectary
**honey ingredient** nectar
**honey insect** bee
**honey liquor** mead
**honey of flowers** nectar
**honey producer** bee
**honey wine** mead
**Hong Kong bay** Mirs, Repulse, Sheko
**Hong Kong coin** cent, dollar
**Hong Kong district** Wanchai
**Hong Kong gardens** Tigerbalm
**Hong Kong island** Lantao
**Hong Kong peninsula** Kowloon
**honk** oink
**honking bird** goose
**Honolulu's island** Bahu
**Honolulu suburb** Waikiki
**honorary** complimentary, ex officio, formal, free, gratuitous, honorific, intentional, nominal, optional, spontaneous, titular, unforced, unofficial, unpaid, voluntary, willing
**honorary canon** prebendary
**honorary crown of victory** bay, laurel
**honorary name** title
**honoris causa** honorary
**honour** acclaim, acknowledgement, admiration, adoration, authority, credit, dignity, distinction, esteem, eulogy, exalt, fame, garland, glory, homage, honesty, integrity, justness, laurels, notability, praise, pride, privilege, rank, regard, renown, reputation, repute, respect,

**honourable** reverence, reward, tribute, venerate, veracity, virginity, worship
**honourable** distinguished, eminent, ethical, fair, great, honest, illustrious, just, moral, noble, notable, prestigious, principled, proper, renowned, reputable, respectable, respected, revered, right(eous), sincere, true, trustworthy, trusty, upright, upstanding, venerable, virtuous, worthy
**honourable fame** glory
**honourably discharged** emeritus
**honour a debt** pay
**honour with** bestow
**hood** bonnet, calash, caléche, capote, capouch, capuche, cloak, coif, conceal, cover, cowl, curtain, disguise, eclipse, envelop, gangster, hat, headcloth, headdress, headgear, hooligan, mantilla, mask, muffle, ruffian, scarf, screen, shroud, thug, tsotsi, veil
**hooded cloak** domino
**hooded coat** capote
**hooded fur or cloth jacket** parka
**hooded garment** cowl, parka
**hooded jacket** anorak, parka
**hooded overcoat worn by troops** parka
**hooded robe worn at masked balls** domino
**hooded snake** cobra
**hooded wicker cradle** bassinet
**hoodlum** assassin, barbarian, brawler, brute, bully, burglar, criminal, crook, desperado, gangster, garroter, goon, hooligan, knave, mafioso, mobster, mugger, murderer, racketeer, rascal, rowdy, ruffian, scoundrel, slayer, terrorist, thief, thug, tough, tsotsi, vandal, villain, wretch
**hood of cloak** cowl
**hood on an Eskimo woman's parka for carrying a child** amaut, amowt
**hood on monk's garment** cowl
**hoodoo** affliction, annoy, blight, calamity, conjure, curse, distress, evil, fetish, harass, harm, hex, imp, jinx, misfortune, scourge, torment, trouble, vexation, voodoo
**hoodwink** bamboozle, befool, cheat, deceive, defraud, delude, dupe, gull, hoax, impose, outwit, swindle, trick, victimise
**hoof** boot, dance, eject, extremity, (fore)foot, hand, kick, pad, paw, prance, step, trample, trotter, unguis, ungula, walk
**hoofed** cloven-hoofed, ungulate, ungulous
**hoofed mammal** ungulate

**hoof sound** clop
**hook** amo (I), bag, barb, brace, catch, clamp, clasp, collar, curve, (en)snare, entangle, entrap, fasten(er), fix, grab, hasp, heel, hitch, holder, link, lock, loop, noose, peg, sabre, secure, sickle, snag, trap, trick
**hook a fish** catch
**hook-billed bird** shrike
**hooked claw** talon
**hooked like an eagle's beak** aquiline
**hooked nail** tenter
**hooked nose** beak
**hooked peg for hanging harness on** spirket
**hooked pole for hauling large fish aboard or ashore** gaff
**hooked staff of bishop** crook, crosier
**hooked user** addict
**hook for fish** drail, gaff, gig
**hook, line and sinker** completely, entirely, thoroughly, totally, utterly, wholly
**hook-up** annexe, connect, harness, inspan, lace, lash, picket, tether, tie
**hook up** alliance, coalition, confederation, connecting, coupling, entente, junction, rejoinder, unification
**hooligan** bovver, boy, delinquent, hoodlum, larrikin, lout, mobster, rough, rowdy, ruffian, skollie, thug, tough, tsotsi, vandal, yob
**hoop** bail, band, circle(t), girdle, loop, ring, round, wheel
**hooped petticoat** farthingale
**hoop handle of kettle** bail
**hoot** boo, honk, toot
**hooter** horn, megaphone, owl, signal, siren, whistle
**hop** bounce, frisk, jump, leap, prance, romp, spring, vault
**hop and step** skip
**hop-bine** stem
**hop-drying kiln** oast
**hope** ambition, anticipate, anticipation, aspiration, aspire, assume, assurance, await, belief, confidence, contemplate, conviction, desire, dream, expect(ation), faith, foresee, hopefulness, long(ing), optimism, promise, prospect, rely, trust, want, wish
**hope earnestly** trust
**hope for** crave, desire
**hopeful** anticipative, assured, auspicious, bright, bullish, buoyant, cheerful, confident, encouraging, expectant, favourable, heartening, optimistic, promising, reassuring, rosy, sanguine

**hopeful disposition** optimism
**hopefulness** faith, hope, optimism
**hopeful person** aspirer
**hopeless** deadly, despairing, despondent, disconsolate, fatal, forlorn, grave, irredeemable, irremediable, irreparable, irrevocable, lost, remediless, serious
**hopelessness** dejectedness, despair, desperateness, downheartedness, forlornness
**hopeless one** goner
**hop extract** lupulin
**hop kiln** oast
**hop lightly** skip
**hopper** toad
**hopping marsupial** kangaroo, wallaby
**hopping parasite** flea
**hopscotch** peevers (Sc)
**hopscotch tile** peever(s)
**horde** army, band, bevy, concourse, crew, crowd, drove, flock, gang, herd, host, mob, multitude, pack, press, swarm, throng, troop
**horizon** azimuth, compass, confines, outlook, perspective, prospect, range, realm, scope, skyline, sphere, stretch, verge, view, vista
**horizontal** flat, level, plane, prone, supine
**horizontal band across shield** fess(e)
**horizontal bar** rail
**horizontal line** level
**horizontal opening into a mine** adit
**horizontal spar for ship's sail** yardarm
**horizontal stripe across the middle of a shield** fess(e)
**horizontal timber across top of door or window** lintel
**hormone** adrenalin(e), stimulant, testosterone
**hormone affecting circulation** adrenaline
**hormone maker** gland
**hormone that stimulates the nervous system** adrenaline
**horn** antler, bugle, callous, corn(et), cornu, crest, plume, pommel, projection, quill, spike, tentacle, topknot, trombone, trumpet, tuba, tuft
**horned animal** buck, goat, rhinoceros
**horned ruminant** deer, goat
**horned ungulate** deer
**horned wild sheep** mouf(f)lon
**hornless cow** mul(l)ey
**horn on foot digit** toenail
**horn's sound** beep
**horny** bicorn(ate), bony, callous, ceratoid, corneous, corniculate, cornute(d), indurate, ossified, thick-skinned, tough
**horny foot casing** hoof

**horny growth in sole of horse's foot**
frog
**horny place on skin** corn
**horny shield of the ends of fingers**
nail
**horologe** clock, dial, timepiece, watch
**horologist** watchmaker
**horologium** clocktower, horologion
**horoscope based on the time of one's birth** nativity
**horrible** abominable, appalling, awful, bad, deplorable, disgusting, dreadful, frightening, frightful, ghastly, horrendous, horrid, horrifying, loathsome, macabre, nasty, odious, repellent, repulsive, shocking, sickening, terrible
**horrible to see** horribile visu (L)
**horrible to tell** horribile dictu (L)
**horrid** awful, bad, bristling, cruel, disagreeable, disgusting, dreadful, frightful, gloomy, hideous, horrible, nasty, objectionable, odious, offensive, repulsive, revolting, shocking, sickening, terrible, terrifying, unkind, unpleasant
**horrific** appalling, awful, dreadful, formidable, frightening, ghastly, grim, harrowing, hideous, horrid, odious, repulsive, revolting, scaring, shocking, terrifying
**horrify** appal, daunt, disgust, dishearten, nauseate, petrify, revolt, shock, terrify
**horror** abhorrence, alarm, antipathy, apprehension, aversion, awfulness, consternation, disgust, dismay, dread, fear, fright(fulness), ghastliness, hatred, hideousness, loathing, outrage, panic, repugnance, revulsion, shock, terror
**horror-struck** aghast
**hors de combat** disabled, hamstrung, helpless, incapacitated, indisposed
**hors d'oeuvre** antipasto (I), apéritif, appetiser, entrée, relish, snack, starter
**horse** Arab, broodmare, charger, equine, filly, foal, gee-gee, gelding, hack, mare, mount, mustang, nag, palfrey, palomino, pony, quadruped, roan, sire, stallion, steed, stud, trotter, Waler, yearling
**horse attendant** (h)ostler, groom
**horseback sport** polo(crosse)
**horse barn** stable
**horse blanket** manta
**horse breed** Appaloosa, Arab(ian), Palomino, pony, thoroughbred
**horse-breeding farm** stud
**horse-chestnut fruit** conker
**horse colour** chestnut, grey, roan

**horse command** gee
**horse-doctor** farrier, vet(erinary)
**horse-drawn cab** hansom
**horse-drawn carriage** cabriolet, landau
**horse-drawn vehicle** cart, chariot
**horse event** point-to-point
**horse farm** stud
**horse-fly** cleg, gadfly, tabanid
**horse food** oats
**horse for ordinary riding** hack(ney)
**horse for steeplechasing** chaser
**horse hair** mane
**horse kept for breeding** stud
**horse leg part** cannon, fetlock, hock, pastern
**horseman** cavalier, cavalryman, cowboy, cuirassier, dragoon, equerry, equestrian, gaucho, groom, (h)ostler, hussar, jockey, knight, lancer, postilion, rider, stableboy, trainer, trooper
**horseman's goad** spur
**horsemanship** equestrianism, equitation, manège
**horse muster** roundup
**horse not castrated** stallion
**horse not placed in first three in race** also-ran
**horse of Achilles** Balios, Xanthus
**horse of a small breed** pony
**horse of Copreus** Arion
**horse of mixed colour** roan
**horse of Quixote** Rosinante
**horse pace** trot
**horseplay** buffoonery, capers, clowning, fooling, pranks, rag, romping, rumpus, skylarking
**horse prod** spur
**horserace** Derby, July, Met, steeplechase
**horserace over obstacles** steeplechase
**horse racing devotee** turfite, turfman
**horse-racing track** turf
**horse rider** jockey
**horse-rider's foot** stirrup
**horse's abode** stable
**horse's cry** neigh, whin(n)ey
**horse sense** judg(e)ment, practicality, soundness
**horse's eye-screens** blinkers
**horse's feed container** nosebag
**horse's foot** frog, hoof
**horse's frisky leap** curvet
**horse's gait** canter, gallop, pace, race, rack, run, trot, walk
**horse shed** stable
**horseshoe crab** limulus
**horse-shoer** farrier
**horse show** gymkhana
**horse-show event** dressage
**horse's leather straps** harness

**horse's mane** crest
**horse's neck hair** mane
**horse-soldier** cavalryman, trooper
**horse-soldiers** cavalry
**horse sound** neigh
**horse's pace** canter, gallop, trot
**horse sprinkled with white hairs** roan
**horse's sound** neigh
**horse's stall** stable
**horse strap** halter, harness, rein
**horse that has never won a race** maiden
**horse trained for racing** pacer
**horse training** dressage
**horse used for breeding** broodmare, stallion
**horsewhip** chabouk
**horse with high action** stepper
**horse with human body** centaur
**hortatory discourse** homily
**hose** channel, conduit, dampen, drench, duct, hosiery, irrigate, line, main, moisten, outlet, pantihose, pipe, soak, socks, souse, spray, sprinkle, stockings, tights, tube
**hosiery item** pantihose, sock, stocking
**hosiery mishap** ladder, run
**hospital** asylum, clinic, infirmary, lazaret, retreat, sanatorium
**hospital division** ward
**hospital for lepers** lazaret(te), lazaretto
**hospital inmate** patient
**hospitality** amicability, benignancy, congeniality, cordiality, easiness, friendliness, generosity, geniality, kindheartedness, kindliness, receptiveness, sociability, warmth
**hospital operating room** theatre
**hospital porter** orderly
**hospital room** ward
**hospital sister** nurse
**hospital transport** ambulance
**hospital unit** ward
**hospital vehicle** ambulance
**hospital worker** nurse, orderly
**host** anchor-man, announcer, army, array, band, company, compere, drove, entertainer, horde, innkeeper, introduce, landlord, legion, multitude, myriad, present(er), proprietor, swarm, throng
**hostage** leverage, pawn, pledge, prisoner, security
**hostage holder** captor
**hostel** boarding-house, doss-house, guest-house, hostelry, hotel, inn, residence
**hostelry** inn
**hostile** adverse, against, aggressive, alien, antagonistic, anti-, bellicose, belligerent, combative, contrary, fighting, inhospitable, inimical,

malevolent, mean, militant, opposed, repugnant, ugly, unfavourable, unfriendly, unkind, unsympathetic, unwelcoming, warlike
**hostile act** blow
**hostile action** opposition
**hostile attack** assault, raid
**hostile criticism** animadversion
**hostile expedition** warpath
**hostile feeling** antagonism, enmity, ill will
**hostile feeling towards** antipathy
**hostile incursion** inroad, irruption
**hostile look** scowl
**hostile opposition** confrontation
**hostile person** enemy
**hostile spirit** ghoul
**hostile to** against
**hostilities** battles, conflict, contention, fighting, militancy, raids, sieges, strife, war(fare)
**hostility** animosity, animus, antagonism, battle, belligerence, bickering, combat, conflict, contention, contest, disaffection, disapprobation, duel, enmity, feud, grudge, hate, hatred, malice, odium, opposition, scuffle, truculence, war(fare)
**host to cochineal** nopal
**hot** ardent, biting, blistering, burning, excitable, fervent, fervid, fiery, furious, heated, het, irascible, peppery, pungent, sharp, spicy, sultry, torrid, tropical
**hot air** blather, blether, bosh
**hot-air balloon** montgolfier
**hot and bothered** confused
**hot and close** sultry
**hot and humid** sweltering
**hot and moist** humid
**hot and steamy** torrid
**hot Arabian wind** samiel, simoom, simoon
**hotbed** breeding-ground, cradle, den, hive, nest, nidus, nursery, school, seedbed, womb
**hot bedtime drink** cocoa, milo
**hot beverage** cocoa, coffee, tea
**hot-blooded** ardent, demonstrative, eager, emotional, excitable, fervent, fiery, heated, high-spirited, hold, impetuous, impulsive, lustful, passionate, rash, sensitive, sensual, spirited, susceptible, temperamental, tender, warm(-blooded), wild
**hotch-potch** collection, confusion, gemors, jumble, mess, miscellany, mishmash, mix, mixture, potpourri
**hot condiment** cayenne
**hot contempt** scorn
**hot desert wind** sirocco

**hot dip food** fondue
**hot drink** chocolate, cocoa, coffee, tea
**hot dry Mediterranean wind** sirocco
**hot dry wind that blows from the Arabian desert** simoom, simoon
**hotel** hostel(ry), house, inn, motel, pub(lic house), tavern
**hotel cook** chef
**hotel employee** bellboy, chef, manager, receptionist, valet, waiter
**hotel errand-boy** bellboy, bellhop, page
**hotelier** innkeeper
**hotel manager** maitre d'hôtel
**hotel patron** guest
**hotel porter** doorman
**hotel worker** barmaid, barman, waiter, waitress
**hot flame apparatus** torch
**hothead** daredevil, desperado, hotspur, madcap, madman, tearaway, terror
**hot-headed** excitable, fiery, hasty, headstrong, hot-tempered, impetuous, impulsive, passionate, quick-tempered, rash, reckless, volatile
**hothouse** conservatory, glasshouse, greenhouse, nursery, plant-house, vinery
**hothouse for oranges** orangery
**hot Indian dish** curry
**hot milk curdled as by wine** posset
**hot moist wind in southern Europe** sirocco
**hot mulled wine** glühwein, negus
**hot North African wind** g(h)ibli
**hot of climate** (sub)tropical, torrid
**hot off the press** brand-new, latest, recent, red-hot
**hot oppressive wind** berg wind, sirocco
**hotplate** griddle
**hotpot** stew
**hot pungent spice** peri-peri
**hot rod event** race
**hot season** summer
**hot spice** chilli, mustard, pepper, peri-peri
**hot spiced rum drink** toddy
**hot, spicy dish** curry
**hot spring** geyser
**hot spring mineral** opal
**hot sweetened wine with water** negus
**hot tea holder** urn
**hot-tempered** irascible
**hot under the collar** angry, enraged, irate, upset
**hot vapour** steam
**hot-water spring** geyser
**hot weather** heat
**hound** addict, badger, canine, chase, chervy, chiv(v)y, devotee, dog, drive,

goad, harass, hector, hunt, impel, persecute, persue, pester, prod, provoke, pursue, ride
**hound used for hunting hares** harrier
**hour** hora (S), time
**hour given on radio** time-signal
**hourglass contents** sand
**hourly** done, horal, occurring, periodic
**house** abode, business, casa (Sp), company, concern, cottage, domicile, dwelling, edifice, establishment, firm, home, hotel, hovel, hut, inn, khaya, lodge, maison (F), manor, mansion, pondok, residence, rondavel, shelter, structure, tavern, villa, whare (M)
**house break** burgle
**housebreaker** burglar, robber, stealer, thief
**house-breaking tool** jemmy
**house chamber** room
**housecoat** robe
**house covering** roof
**house endowed for poor persons** almshouse
**house extension** ell
**house finch** linnet
**household** average, common, conventional, domestic, family, hearth, home(spun), homestead, house, kraal, ménage, ordinary, repeated, ritual, routine, standard, typical, usual
**household animal** pet
**householder** freeholder, home-owner, landlady, landlord, occupant, owner, proprietor, resident, tenant
**household gadget** appliance
**household god** lar
**household gods** lares et penates (L)
**household gods of the ancient Romans** penates
**household item** broom, duster, iron
**household linen** napery
**household pest** fly
**household servant** menial
**household task** chore
**household tip** hint
**house in Mexico** casa
**housekeeper's storeroom** still room
**house lizard** gecko
**housemaid** bonne (F), cleaner
**house number** address
**house occupied by religious order** monastery
**house of a minister** manse
**house of business** establishment
**house of cathedral head** deanery
**house of dean** deanery
**house of debauchery** seraglio
**house of ill fame** bordel(lo), brothel, cathouse

**house of minister** manse
**house of the dead** mortuary, ossarium
**house on the level** bungalow
**house on wheels** caravan, trailer
**house part** bathroom, kitchen, roof, room
**house pet** canary, cat, dog, parrot
**house plant** aspidistra, cactus, fern, ficus
**house provided for a minister** manse
**house renter** tenant
**houses garden tools** shed
**house shoes** slippers
**house steward** butler
**house style** ranch
**houses tympanum** ear
**houses vehicle** garage
**house-top** roof
**housewife** Hausfrau (G)
**house wing** ell, annexe
**house with outbuildings and land** messuage
**housey-housey** bingo, lotto
**housing** accommodating, billeting, boarding, dwellings, harbouring, homes, houses, lodging, quartering, quarters
**housing development** estate
**housing for vehicle** garage
**housing loan** mortgage
**Houston stadium** Astrodome
**hovel** bower, cabin, coop, corral, cottage, den, dump, dwelling, enclosure, hole, hut(ch), outhouse, (pig)sty, scum, shack, shanty, shed, slum
**hover** fluctuate, flutter, hang, pause, poise, waver
**how** whereby
**how come?** why
**however** anyhow, but, nevertheless, nonetheless, notwithstanding, still, though, yet
**howl** bawl, bay, bark, bellow, caterwaul, clamour, cry, groan, hoot, lament, outcry, roar, scream, screech, shout, shriek, ululate, wail, weep, yell, yelp, yowl
**howl at the moon** bay
**howling animal** wolf
**howls like a hound** bays
**hoyden** clown, lout, romp, tomboy
**H-shaped** zygal
**hub** axis, bosom, centre, core, crux, cynosure, depths, essence, focus, headquarters, heart, hinge, hive, interior, kernel, marrow, mid(dle), midst, nucleus, pith, pivot, quintessence, root, target
**hubbub** ado, bedlam, brouhaha, chaos, clatter, commotion, din, disorder, disturbance, noise, pandemonium, racket, riot, stir, tumult, turbulence, unrest, uproar
**hub of a wheel** nave
**Huck Finn's transportation** raft
**Huckleberry Finn's creator** Clements, Twain
**huddle** clump, cluster, clutch, conclave, congregate, converge, crouch, crowd, cuddle, disorder, flock, gather, gravitate, heap, hunch, jumble, knot, mass, meet, muddle, nestle, press, snuggle, throng
**huddle up** crouch, cuddle, nestle, snuggle
**hue** aspect, bellow, blush, cast, chroma, clamour, colour, complexion, cry, dye, flush, light, nuance, outcry, shade, tinge, tint, tone, whoop, yell, yowl
**hue and cry** ballyhoo, brouhaha, clamour, furore, hullabaloo, pandemonium
**huff** anger, annoyance, bad mood, blow, breathe, displeasure, gasp, grudge, heave, irritation, mood, offence, pant, passion, pique, puff, resentment, sulk, throb, tiff, umbrage, vexation, wheeze
**huff and puff** bluster, hector, pant
**hug** cherish, clasp, clinch, cling, clutch, cuddle, embosom, embrace, enclose, enfold, follow, grip, hold, lock, monopolise, nurse, retain, snuggle, squeeze
**huge** big, colossal, elephantine, enormous, extensive, gargantuan, giant, gigantic, great, immense, large, mammoth, massive, mountainous, prodigious, stupendous, titanic, tremendous, vast
**huge creature** dinosaur, giant, Goliath, leviathan, mammoth, monster, ogre, whale
**huge floating mass of ice** iceberg
**huge Florida marsh** Everglades
**huge oil carrier** supertanker
**huge person in fairy tales** giant
**huge quantity** vast
**huge self-service store** hypermarket
**huge stone used in the building of prehistoric monuments** megalith
**huge victory at election** landslide
**hulk** body, bruiser, debris, derelict, lout, lubber, oaf, prison, ruin, ship(wreck), skeleton, vessel, wreck
**hulking** awkward, big, bulky, burly, colossal, corpulent, dense, enormous, extensive, fat, gigantic, great, gross, heavy, huge, immense, large, mammoth, massive, overgrown, prodigious, sizable, spacious, substantial, ungainly, vast, voluminous
**hull** casing, coat, (corn-)husk, crust, framework, legume, peel, pod, rind, shell, shuck, skeleton, skin, structure
**hulled wheat** groats
**hulled wheat boiled in milk and sweetened** frumenty
**hum** bombilate, bombinate, boom, buzz, croon, drone, move, mumble, murmur, noise, pulsation, pulse, purr(ing), sing, stir, throb, thrum, tune, vibrate, vibration, whirr, whizz, zoom
**human** being, body, child, compassionate, considerate, creature, fallible, fleshly, homo sapiens, humane, individual, kind(ly), man(like), mortal, natural, person(al), reasonable, soul, susceptible, understandable, understanding, woman(ly)
**human being** earthling, individual, man, one, person, woman
**human beings** humanity, humans, (hu)mankind, people
**human being with power to become a wolf** werewolf
**human bones** skeleton
**human breast** bosom
**human dregs** riff-raff
**humane** benevolent, charitable, compassionate, forbearing, forgiving, gentle, good(-natured), human, kind(-hearted), kindly, lenient, loving, merciful, mild, polite, sympathetic, tender, understanding
**human female** woman
**human-flesh eater** cannibal
**human fossil** anthropolith
**human frame** body, skeleton
**human gland** pituitary, thyroid
**human haunches** buttocks, derrière
**human in form** anthropomorphos
**humanise** better, civilise, domesticate, edify, educate, enlighten, improve, polish, reclaim, refine, soften, tame, temper
**humanitarian** almoner, almsgiver, altruist(ic), benefactor, benevolent, benignant, charitable, compassionate, gracious, humane, kind, munificent, philanthropist, philanthropic, public-spirited
**humanitarianism** benevolence, charitableness, charity, compassionateness, generosity, goodwill, humanism, loving-kindness, philanthropy
**humanity** benevolence, benignity, charity, civilisation, compassion, flesh, goodness, (hu)mankind,

kindness, man, mercy, mortality, people, pity, public, sensuality, society, sympathy, tolerance
**human-like animal** gorilla, monkey
**human male** man
**human nature** humanity
**human or animal waste** excreta
**human race** humanity
**human resources** helpers, members, personnel
**human skill** artifice
**human skill as opposed to nature** art
**human skull** death's-head
**human sound** voice
**human species** (hu)mankind
**human trunk** torso
**humble** abase, abash, common(place), crush, debase, deferential, demean, insignificant, low(er), lowly, meek, modest, obedient, ordinary, plain, polite, reduce, respectful, self-effacing, servile, simple, subdue, submissive, subservient, timid, unassuming, unimportant, unostentatious, unpretentious
**humble attitude of mind** humility
**humble dependant** vassal
**humble entreaty** supplication
**humble oneself** grovel
**humble servant** lackey
**humbly submissive** meek
**humbug** charlatanism, cheat, deception, falseness, fraud, hoax, imposition, impostor, imposture, nonsense, pretence, sham, swindle, trick
**humdinger** daisy, dinger, jewel, lulu, oner, pip, ripsnorter, snorter
**humdrum** banal, boring, dreary, dull, flat, monotonous, mundane, ordinary, tiresome, trivial, uneventful, unexciting, wearisome
**humid** clammy, damp, dank, moist, muggy, steamy, sticky, sultry, wet
**humiliate** abase, abash, ashamed, chagrin, chasten, crush, debase, degrade, demote, discomfit, disgrace, dishonour, downgrade, embarrass, humble, mortify, shame, subdue, vitiate
**humiliating treatment** indignity
**humiliation** abasement, abashment, anticlimax, awkwardness, bashfulness, blow, chagrin, comedown, compunction, confusion, decline, demotion, distress, embarrassment, ignominy, mortification, reverse, shame
**humility** deference, diffidence, humbleness, lowliness, meekness, modesty, respect, self-abasement, submissiveness, unpretentiousness

**hummingbird** thornbill
**humming insect** dor
**humorist** clown, comedian, comedienne, comic, entertainer, ironist, teaser, wag, wisecracker, wit
**humorous** amusing, comic(al), funny, jocular, laughable, ludicrous, witty
**humorous entertainer** comedian, comedienne
**humorous five-line stanza** limerick
**humorous imitation** parody
**humorously indecent** bawdy
**humorous performer on stage** comedian, comedienne
**humorous ridicule** badinage
**humorous speech** pleasantry
**humorous stage play** comedy
**humorous topical drawing** cartoon
**humorous use of words** pun
**humorous verse written in a jumble of languages** macaronic verse
**humour** banter, caprice, comedy, fancy, farce, flatter, funniness, inclination, irony, jest, jocularity, mood, pamper, pleasure, pun, quip, sal (Sp), sarcasm, spoil, temper(ament), vagary, whim, wisecrack, wit(ticism), wittiness
**humourless** austere, boring, dour, dry, dull, glum, grave, heavy-going, morose, serious, sober, solemn, tedious, thick
**hump** bulge, bump, knob, lump, mound, projection, prominence, protuberance, swelling
**hump-backed** crookbacked, crooked, deformed, humped, hunchbacked, hunched, misshapen, stooped
**humped animal** camel, dromedary
**humped ox** zebu
**humpless camel** llama
**humpy** noded, warty
**hun** barbarian, destroyer, savage, vandal
**hunch** arch, bend, crouch, curve, feeling, guess(work), huddle, hump, idea, impression, inkling, intuition, premonition, presentiment, shrug, squat, stoop, suspicion, tense
**hunch or natural drive** instinct
**hundred** hecto-, hect-
**hundred-and-fifty years anniversary** sesquicentennial
**hundred cubed** million
**hundred dinars** rial
**hundred-handed giant** Briareus, Cottus, Gyges
**hundred make yen** sen
**hundred runs** century
**hundred sen** riel, yen
**hundred square metres** are
**hundredth anniversary** centenary

**hundredth of rouble** copeck, kope(c)k
**hundred thousand rupees** lakh
**hundredth part of a dollar** cent
**hundredth part of an are** centare, centiare
**hundredweight** quintal
**hundred-year-old person** centenarian
**hundred years** centenary
**hundred years and over** centenarian
**Hungarian** Magyar
**Hungarian breed of hunting dog** vizsla
**Hungarian canal** Sarviz, Sio
**Hungarian city** Eger
**Hungarian coin** bals, filler, forint, korona, leno
**Hungarian currency** balas, fillerr, forint, gara, pengo
**Hungarian dance** czardas, kos
**Hungarian dish** goulash
**Hungarian dog** kuvasz, puli
**Hungarian dynasty** Angevin, Arpad
**Hungarian forest** Bakony
**Hungarian gypsy** tzigane
**Hungarian horseman** hussar
**Hungarian hunting dog** vizsla
**Hungarian lake** Balaton, Blatensee, Ferto, Velevce
**Hungarian light cavalry soldier** Hussar
**Hungarian mountain range** Bukk, Carpathian, Matra, Mecsek
**Hungarian musical instrument** cembalo, tarogato
**Hungarian plain** Puszta
**Hungarian red pepper** paprika
**Hungarian regime** Kadar
**Hungarian region** Banat
**Hungarian stew** goulash
**Hungarian turnip** kohlrabi
**Hungarian wine** Eger, Szekszard, Tokay
**hunger** appetite, crave, desire, famine, greed, longing, want, yearn, yen
**hunger for** crave, desire
**hunger pain** pang
**hungry** appetitive, desirous, esurient, famished, famishing, gaunt, longing, malnourished, needing, peckish, pining, ravening, ravenous, starved, starving, underfed, undernourished, unfed, wanting, yearning
**hungry for human flesh** cannibalistic
**hunk** block, chunk, clod, dollop, lump, mass, piece, slab, wedge
**hunt** chase, dog, forage, hound, investigate, investigation, prey, pursue, pursuit, quest, rummage, scour, search, seek, track, trail
**hunt down** hound, persecute, pursue
**hunt eagerly** badger
**hunted animal** prey

**hunter** Ahab, chaser, deerstalker, explorer, falconer, gunner, hawker, huntsman, Nimrod, pursuer, searcher, seeker, shikaree, shikari, stalker, tracker
**hunter constellation** Orion
**hunter's cap** deer-stalker
**hunter's hideaway** lie
**hunter's prey** game
**hunter's snare** trap
**hunt for** scrounge
**hunt for criminal** hue and cry
**hunt illegally** poach
**hunting cry** tally-ho, tantivy
**hunting dog** basset, beagle, courser, harrier, hound, setter, wild dog
**hunting enthusiast** Nimrod
**hunting expedition** safari
**hunting guide in Scotland** gillie
**hunting hound** basset, beagle, harrier, retriever
**hunting knife** bowie
**hunting leopard** cheetah
**hunting trip** safari
**hunting whip** crop
**huntsman's cry to hounds** tally-ho
**hurdle** barricade, barrier, complication, difficulty, fence, handicap, hedge, hindrance, impediment, jump, obstacle, obstruction, problem, snag, stumbling-block, wall
**hurdy-gurdy** barrel organ
**hurl** cast, dart, dash, explode, fire, fling, heave, launch, pelt, pitch, project, propel, shy, sling, throw, toss
**hurling weapon** assegai, boomerang, spear
**hurly-burly** action, activity, animation, bustle, chaos, commotion, confusion, disorder, exertion, furore, hubbub, hustle, labour, life, liveliness, motion, movement, stir, work
**hurrah** arriba (S), viva, Vrystaat, whoopee, yippee
**hurricane** cyclone, gale, squall, tempest, tornado, typhoon, whirlwind, (wind)storm
**hurricane centre** eye
**hurried activity** bustle
**hurried writing** scrawl, scribble
**hurry** accelerate, alacrity, bustle, celerity, commotion, confusion, dash, dispatch, expedite, expedition, flurry, flutter, fly, goad, haste(n), hie, precipitation, promptitude, quicken, quickness, race, run, rush, scurry, speed, urge(ncy)
**hurry on foot** run
**hurt** ache, afflict, annoy, bruise, burn, cut, damage, detriment, disable, disadvantage, distress, grieve, harm(ed), impair, injure, injury, lesion, loss, maim, maltreat, mar, pain, sadden, slash, smart, spoil, sting, strike, suffer, throb, torture, upset, wound, wrong
**hurt by wrenching** sprain
**hurt deeply** wound
**hurt dully** ache
**hurtful** abrasive, abusive, annoying, bad, biting, brutal, catty, caustic, cruel, cutting, damaging, dangerous, derogatory, destructive, detrimental, galling, grating, harmful, humiliating, injurious, irritating, malicious, mean, nasty, pernicious, rough, ruinous, scathing, sharp, spiteful, unkind, unpleasant, upsetting, vicious, wounding
**hurtful remark** barb
**hurtle** charge, chase, crash, dash, fly, plunge, race, rattle, rush, scoot, scramble, shoot, speed, spin, spur, tear
**hurt the pride of** pique
**husband** benedict, breadwinner, budget, conserve, consort, custodian, economise, groom, hoard, hubby, man, mari (F), mate, partner, ration, save, spouse, store
**husband-and-wife** couple, mates, spouses
**husband and wife team who discovered radium** Curie
**husband of Abia** Herzon
**husband of Abigail** David, Jether, Nabal
**husband of Abihail** Abishur, Rohoboam
**husband of Achsah** Othniel
**husband of adulteress** cuckold
**husband of Agave** Echion
**husband of Amphitrite** Poseidon
**husband of Andromache** Hector
**husband of Andromeda** Perseus
**husband of Anne** Shakespeare
**husband of Anne Boleyn** Henry VIII
**husband of Aphrodite** Vulcan
**husband of Asenath** Joseph
**husband of Azubah** Caleb
**husband of Bashemath** Esau
**husband of Bathsheba** David, Uriah
**husband of Elisabeth** Zacharias
**husband of Elisheba** Aaron
**husband of Enid** Geraint
**husband of Ephratah** Caleb
**husband of Esther** Ahasuerus
**husband of Evita** Pèron
**husband of Frigga** Odin
**husband of Gomer** Hosea
**husband of Haggith** David
**husband of Hamutal** Josiah
**husband of Hannah** Elkanah
**husband of Helen of Troy** Menelaus
**husband of Helga** Hagar
**husband of Hera** Zeus
**husband of Herodias** Herod
**husband of Isis** Osiris
**husband of Jedidah** Amon
**husband of Jehosheba** Jehoiada
**husband of Jerioth** Caleb
**husband of Jessica** Lorenzo
**husband of Jezebel** Ahab
**husband of Jochebed** Amram
**husband of Judith** Esau
**husband of Leah** Jacob
**husband of Leda** Tyndareus
**husband of loose wife** cuckold
**husband of Maacah** David
**husband of Maachah** Rehoboam
**husband of Mahalath** Esau, Rehoboam
**husband of Merab** Adriel
**husband of Michaiah** Rehoboam
**husband of Michal** David
**husband of Milcah** Nahor
**husband of Naarah** Ashur
**husband of Naomi** Elimelech
**husband of Orpa** Chilion
**husband of Prisca** Aquila
**husband of Queen Victoria** Albert
**husband of Rachel** Jacob
**husband of Rebecca** Isaac
**husband of Rhea** Saturn
**husband of Rosamunda** Alboin
**husband of Ruth** Boaz
**husband of Sarah** Abraham
**husband of Tethys** Oceanus
**husband of Thetis** Peleus
**husband of Titania** Oberon
**husband of Xanthippe** Socrates
**husband of Zilpah** Jacob
**husband of Ziporah** Moses
**husband or father** man
**husband or wife** consort, mate, spouse
**husbandry** agriculture, agronomics, agronomy, conservation, cultivation, economy, farming, frugality, management, saving, sparingness, thrift(iness), tillage, tilth, viticulture
**husband's survivor** widow
**hush** allay, calm, mollify, mute, quiet, shush, silence
**hush money** blackmail, bribe, extortion, grease, protection, sop
**hush up** conceal, cover-up, smother, squash, suppress
**husk** bark, bract, bran, case, chaff, coating, corn, covering, hull, legume, lemma, pea pod, peel, rind, scale, shell, shuck, skin, tegument
**husk of fruit** glume, lemma
**husk of nut** bolster, shack
**husk of oats** flight
**husk or outer covering** hull

**husks of corn** chaff
**husks of grain** bran
**husks separated in threshing** chaff
**husky** beefy, brawny, burly, croaking, croaky, gruff, guttural, harsh, hefty, hoarse, low, muscular, powerful, rasping, raucous, rough, rugged, stocky, strapping, strong, sturdy, thickset, throaty, tough
**Hussar's jacket** dolman
**hussy** coquette, flirt, harridan, hoyden, jade, minx, quean
**hustle** bundle, bustle, commotion, con, drive, elbow, energy, force, hasten, hurry, jog, jostle, push, rush, shove, thrust
**hustler** swindler
**hut** booth, cabin, cottage, den, hovel, khaya, lean-to, shack, shanty, shed, shelter
**hyacinth** grapeflower
**hyaenid** aardwolf
**hyaline** glasslike, transparent, vitreous
**hyaloid** glassy
**hybrid** amalgam, combination, combine, composite, compound, conglomerate, cross(-breed), half-breed, heterogeneous, heterogeny, mixed, mixture, mongrel, mule, mutt
**hybrid animal** mule
**hybrid citrus fruit** ugli
**hybridise** cross
**hybrid language** jargon, tsotsitaal
**hybrid of pansy** viola
**hybrid of tangerine and grapefruit** tangelo
**hybrid rose** floribunda
**hybrid vigour** heterosis
**hybrid yak** (d)zo, zdo
**hydrangea** Christmas flower, flower bush
**hydrated magnesium silicate** talc
**hydrocarbon** naphthalene
**hydrocarbon obtained from coal-tar** benzene, benzine
**hydrocarbon oil** petroleum
**hydropathy** water-cure
**hydrophobia** rabies

**hydroxic suffix** -ol
**hygiene** cleanliness, disinfection, purity, sanitation, sterility, wholesomeness
**hygienic** aseptic, clean, disinfected, germ-free, harmless, healthy, pure, salubrious, sanitary, sterile, wholesome
**hygroscope** weather-house
**hylic** material
**hymen** maidenhead, maidenhood, virginity
**hymn** anthem, carol, psalm, sanctus, song
**hymnal** psalter
**hymn of praise** psalm
**hymn of praise to God** doxology
**hymn sung in alternate parts** antiphon
**hymn tune** chorale
**hype** racket
**hyperbole** bombast, embellishment, emphasis, enlargement, exaggeration, excess, extravagance, inflation, magnification, overstatement, pretension, pretentiousness, rant, rhetoric, verbosity, wordiness
**hypercritical** defamatory, denunciatory, derogatory, exacting, fussy, overcensorious, overcritical, overdiligent, pedantic, scurrilous, severe, strict, trenchant
**hyperoptic** farsighted
**hypersensitive** allergic, delicate, hyperreactive, oversensitive, oversusceptible, volatile, volcanic, waspish
**hyphen** bond, dash, punctuation
**hypnotic** compelling, irresistible, magnetic, mesmeric, mesmerising, sleep-inducing, soporific, spellbinding
**hypnotic drug** barbiturate
**hypnotic state** mesmerism, trance
**hypnotise** absorb, benumb, bewitch, captivate, drug, enrapture, enthral, entrance, fascinate, involve, magnetise, mesmerise, stupefy
**hypnotism** hypnosis, mesmerism, suggestion

**hypnotist** enchanter, enchantress, Mesmer, mesmeriser, mesmerist, Rasputin, spellbinder, Svengali
**hypocrisy** affectation, cant, chicanery, deceit(fulness), deception, dishonesty, dissembling, duplicity, faking, falseness, falsity, fraud, insincerity, lip-service, mendacity, pharisaism, pretence, pretext, quackery, sophistry
**hypocrite** charlatan, deceiver, dissembler, fraud, imposter, pharisee, phoney, pretender
**hypocritical** deceitful, deceptive, dissembling, double-faced, false, fraudulent, hollow, insincere, misleading, pharisaic(al), phoney, pretending, sanctimonious, self-righteous, specious, spurious, two-faced
**hypocritical in speech** double-tongued
**hypocritically** dissemblingly, fraudulently, hollowly, sanctimoniously, speciously, spuriously
**hypocritical talk** cant
**hypodermic instrument** syringe
**hypothesis** assumption, postulate, premise, proposition, theory, thesis
**hypothetical** academic, conjectural, imagined, inferred, notional, presumed, presumptive, questionable, speculative, supposed, suppositious, surmised, theoretical
**hyrax** (klip)dassie
**hysteria** agitation, delirium, frenzy, hysterics, madness, neurosis, panic, unreason
**hysterical** berserk, comical, crazed, demented, farcical, frantic, frenzied, hilarious, mad, neurotic, overwrought, priceless, raving, side-splitting, uncontrollable, uproarious
**hystricomorph rodent** porcupine

# I

**I am not what I once was** non sum qualis eram (L)
**I am present** adsum
**I and my king** ego et rex meus (L)
**Ian Smith declared it** UDI
**I assure you** really
**iatric** iatrical, medical, medicine
**iatrical** medical
**Iberian** Portuguese, Spanish
**Iberian country** Portugal, Spain
**Iberian unit of length** vara
**ibidem** ibid
**Ibsen character** Ase, Ellida, Hedda, Nora
**Ibsen's doll** Nora
**ice abode** igloo, iglu
**ice barrier** snow-fence
**ice boot** skate
**icebox** freezer
**ice-cold** arctic, chilled, frigid, frozen, gelid, icebound, icy, numb
**ice cream cake containing fruit and nuts** cassata
**ice cream container** carton, cone, tub
**ice-cream cornet** cone
**ice cream covered with baked meringue** baked Alaska
**ice cream flavour** caramel, coffee, strawberry, vanilla
**ice cream glass** slider
**ice cream holder** cone
**ice cream in layers** neapolitan
**ice cream shell** cone
**ice cream wafer** cone
**ice cream with various toppings** sundae
**ice crystal** snowflake
**ice crystals** snow
**iced** frozen
**iced beverage** tea
**iced cream cake** éclair
**iced drink** frappé
**iced drink of wine, sugar and lemon** cobbler
**iced or hot drink** tea
**ice dwelling** igloo, iglu
**ice grasping tool** tong
**ice hut** igloo, iglu
**Iceland bay** Faxa, Huna
**Icelandic ballad** rimur
**Icelandic bard** scald, skald
**Icelandic dish** bloomor, Harofisk, skyr
**Icelandic epic** Edda, saga
**Icelandic fjord** Breidha
**Icelandic geyser** gryla
**Icelandic giant** Atli

**Icelandic glacier** Hofsjokull, Langjokul, Vatnajokull
**Icelandic harp** langspil
**Icelandic narrative** Edda, saga
**Icelandic parliament** Althing
**Icelandic tale** saga
**Iceland lake** Myvatn, Thorisvatn
**Iceland money** aurar, eyrir, krona
**Iceland republic** Lyoveldio
**Iceland volcanic island** Surtsey
**Iceland volcano** Askia, Eldfell, Hekla, Laki
**Iceland waterfall** Detti(foss), Gull(foss)
**ice lolly** popsicle
**ice mass** berg, floe
**ice or sugar server** tongs
**ice performer** skater
**ice pinnacle** sérac
**icer** froster
**ice sheet floating in sea** floe
**ice skating venue** rink
**iciness** chilliness, frigidity, frostiness, indifference
**icing** frosting
**icon** appearance, effigy, figure, idol, ikon, image, likeness, painting, picture, pietà, portrait, reflection, semblance, statue, symbol
**iconoclast** dissenter, nonconformist, radical, rebel, upstart
**iconology** symbolism
**icons collectively** iconology
**icterus** jaundice
**icy** aloof, arctic, biting, bitter, chilling, chilly, cold, distant, forbidding, freezing, frigid, frosty, gelid, glacial, hostile, ice-cold, indifferent, raw, steely, stony, unfriendly
**icy coating** rime
**icy cold** arctic, freezing, frigid, gelid
**icy downpour** hailstorm
**icy ground cover** snow
**icy rain** sleet
**idea** belief, brainstorm, clue, concept(ion), impression, inkling, intention, interpretation, notion, objective, opinion, plan, sentiment, thought, view
**idea developed throughout a work** theme
**idea formed in advance** preconception
**ideal** conception, consummate, epitome, illusory, imaginary, impractical, intention, model, object(ive), paragon, perfect, standard, unpractical, unreal, visionary

**ideal excellence** beau idéal
**ideal glory investing person** halo
**idealist** dreamer, ideologist, optimist, perfectionist, philosopher, romantic, spiritualist, Utopian, Utopiast, visionary
**idealistic campaign** crusade
**ideally rustic** Arcadian
**ideal place to live** Cockaigne, Cockayne, Utopia
**ideal state** Utopia
**ideas used only to win applause** claptrap
**ideate** conceive, imagine
**idée fixe** obsession
**identical** alike, corresponding, duplicate, equal, equivalent, indistinguishable, interchangeable, like, matching, precisely, self(same), twin, uniform
**identical in size** equal
**identical relatives** twins
**identical sibling** twin
**identifiable** ascertainable, classifiable, detectable, diagnosable, discernible, distinguishable, known, namable, noticeable, perceptible, recognisable, unmistakable
**identifiable music** themes
**identification** association, credentials, detection, diagnosis, documents, empathy, fellow-feeling, involvement, labelling, naming, papers, pinpointing, rapport, recognition, relationship, sympathy
**identification of God with the universe** pantheism
**identify** associate, catalogue, classify, connect, detect, determine, diagnose, distinguish, know, label, name, notice, pinpoint, place, recognise, specify, spot, tag
**identify disease** diagnose
**identifying paper flap** tab, tag
**identity** distinctiveness, existence, individuality, likeness, name, nature, oneness, particularity, personality, sameness, self(hood), singularity, title, unanimity, uniqueness, unity
**identity card** identification
**identity for sheep** earmark
**ideological prejudice** -ism
**ideologue** theorist, visionary
**ideology** approach, avenue, axioms, beliefs, convictions, course, credence, credo, creed, doctrine, dogma, faith, gospel, ideals, method,

**idiocy** fatuity, fatuousness, folly, foolishness, imbecility, insanity, lunacy, senselessness, silliness, stupidity
philosophy, policy, position, practice, principles, procedure, program(me), scheme, system, teachings, tenets, theory, thesis, thinking, values, viewpoint

**idiom** argot, brogue, cant, cliché, collocation, colloquialism, dialect, expression, idiolect, jargon, language, lingo, locution, parlance, patois, phrase(ology), phrasing, saying, slang, speech, style, tongue, usage, vernacular

**idiomatic** colloquial, dialectal, grammatical, vernacular

**idiomatic expression** phrase

**idiosyncrasy** affectation, allergy, attribute, characteristic, constitution, eccentricity, feature, foible, habit, intolerance, mannerism, mood, nature, peculiarity, property, quality, quirk, sensitivity, singularity, temperament, trait, trick, twist, weakness

**idiosyncratic** abnormal, anomalous, bizarre, capricious, characteristic, distinctive, eccentric, erratic, freakish, individual, irregular, novel, odd, offbeat, outlandish, peculiar, quirky, singular, strange, typical, uncommon, unconventional, unorthodox, unusual, weird

**idiot** ass, blockhead, booby, cretin, dimwit, dolt, domkop, dunderhead, fool, half-wit, ignoramus, imbecile, jerk, moron, nerd, nincompoop, nitwit, simpleton

**idiotic** asinine, crazy, daft, dumb, fatuous, foolhardy, foolish, harebrained, imbecile, inane, insane, lunatic, moronic, stupid, unintelligent

**idle** dawdle, fruitless, futile, groundless, inactive, indolent, jobless, laggard, languid, lazy, listless, loafing, loiter, saunter, shiftless, slack, slothful, sluggish, trivial, unavailing, unemployed, unfilled, unoccupied, useless, vacuous, vain, waste(ful), workless, worthless

**idle away time** loaf

**idle boast** bluff

**idle chatter** gossip

**idle fancy** dream

**idle fellow** fainéant, footer, skulker

**idleness** dawdling, ease, hibernation, inaction, inactivity, inertia, inertness, inoccupation, lassitude, leisure, lethargy, loafing, loitering, shiftlessness

**idle pleasantly** while

**idler** beggar, bench warmer, clock watcher, dawdler, do-nothing, drifter, drone, fainéant, good-for-nothing, laggard, layabout, lazybones, loafer, loiterer, lounger, shirker, skiver, slacker, sloth, slouch, sluggard, sponger, tramp, truant, vagrant

**idle talk** chat(ter), chitchat, chitter-chatter, froth, gossip, palaver, poppycock, skinder

**idle thinker** dreamer

**idle time away** moon

**idle wanderer** vagabond

**idly** abundantly, copiously, free(ly), lazily, loosely

**idly scribble** doodle

**idocrase** vesuvianite

**idol** Baal, celebrity, darling, deity, delusion, dream, effigy, fallacy, favourite, fetish, fondling, hero, icon, ikon, illusion, image, jewel, likeness, lion, misbelief, miscalculation, pet, satyr, spectre, statue, symbol, vision

**idolise** admire, adore, deify, exalt, glorify, herd-worship, lionise, love, revere(nce), venerate, worship

**idyll** bucolic, eclogue, fantasy, fiction, legend, melodrama, novel, pastoral, romance, story, tale

**idyllic** bucolic, charming, delightful, halcyon, happy, heavenly, idealised, pastoral, peaceful, perfect, picturesque, rural, rustic, simple, unspoiled

**idyllic poem** eclogue

**I exist** am

**if** although, condition, granting, provided, providing, though, whether, yet

**if not** alternatively, unless

**if not, then** else

**if one had one's way** ideally

**if possible** perhaps

**if you go this you share expenses** dutch, scotch

**igloo inhabitant** Eskimo

**igneous** fiery, magmatic

**igneous crystalline rock** granite

**igneous rock** diorite

**ignite** burn, conflagrate, detonate, enkindle, fire, glow, heat, illuminate, incandesce, inflame, kindle, light

**ignoble** abject, base, common, crude, debased, degraded, despicable, detestable, disgraceful, dishonourable, ignominious, inferior, low(born), lowly, mean, obscure, petty, shabby, small, vulgar

**ignominious** abject, degrading, despicable, discreditable, disgraceful, dishonourable, disreputable, humiliating, indecorous, inglorious, mortifying, scandalous, shameful, sorry, undignified

**ignominious failure** fiasco

**ignominy** abasement, contempt, discredit, disgrace, dishonour, disrepute, infamy, mortification, obloquy, odium, opprobrium, reproach, scandal, scorn, shame, stigma

**ignorance** benightedness, blindness, confusion, darkness, denseness, dumbness, greenness, illiteracy, innocence, nescience, simplicity, stolidness, stupidity, unawareness, unenlightenment, unintelligence

**ignorant** benighted, blind, crude, dark, illiterate, inexperienced, innocent, naïve, nescient, stupid, superficial, unacquainted, unaware, uncultivated, uneducated, unenlightened, uninformed, uninstructed, unlearned, unscholarly, untaught, untutored, unwitting

**ignorant person** fool, ignoramus, mutt

**ignore** cold-shoulder, cut, disregard, elide, neglect, omit, overlook, pass, reject, skip, slight, snub

**ignore correction or alteration** stet

**ignored person** Cinderella

**ignore orders** disobey

**ignoring of reality** escapism

**iguana** lizard

**iguanodon** dinosaur

**I had** I'd

**I have** I've

**I have it!** eureka

**I hope for better things** spero meliora (L)

**I hope in the Cross** in cruce spero (L)

**ilex** holly, inkberry

**ilk** brand, breed, cast, class, extraction, family, genre, genus, kind, line(age), order, pedigree, progeny, race, sort, species, stamp, stock, strain, tribe, type, variety

**ill** afflicted, ailing, ailment, bad(ness), calamity, disease(d), evil, faulty, harm, hurt, improperly, indisposed, iniquitous, injury, misfortune, naughty, poor(ly), sick, trouble, unfavourably, unfortunately, unhealthy, unkindly, unsatisfactory, unwell, wicked, wrong

**ill-adapted for use** awkward

**ill-advised** abrupt, brash, careless, daft, foolish, hasty, heedless, ill-considered, ill-judged, ill-suited, imprudent, inappropriate, indiscreet, injudicious, irresponsible, misguided, perverse, precipitate, rash, reckless, short-sighted, thoughtless, unadvised, unseemly, unwary, unwise, wild

**ill-assorted** discordant, incompatible, inharmonious, mismatched, unsuitable, unsuited

**ill at ease** anxious, awkward, disturbed, edgy, embarrassed, fidgety, hesitant, nervous, restless, unquiet, unsure

**ill-balanced** lopsided

**ill-bred** brusque, crude, disrespectful, ill-mannered, impolite, impudent, inconsiderate, insolent, rude, tactless, uncivil, uncouth, ungallant, ungracious

**ill-bred dog** cur, mongrel

**ill-bred person** boor, cad, churl, larrikin

**ill-disposed** against, antagonistic, averse, disinclined, hostile, loath, opposed, reluctant, unco-operative, unfavourable, unfriendly, unsympathetic, unwelcoming, unwilling

**ill-disposed towards others** malevolent

**illegal** actionable, adulterine, banned, bootleg, contraband, criminal, felonious, forbidden, foul, illegitimate, illicit, outlawed, prohibited, unauthorised, unconstitutional, under-the-counter, unlawful, unlicensed, wrongful

**illegal act** crime, offence, transgression

**illegal alien** immigrant

**illegal exaction** extortion

**illegal gambling game** fah-fee

**illegal game-hunter** poacher

**illegal groom** bigamist

**illegal holding back of a horse by its jockey** pulling

**illegally seize aircraft** hijack

**illegal radio station** pirate

**illegal seizure** usurpation

**illegal seizure of power** coup d'etat

**illegal seller of drugs** pusher

**illegal setting on fire** arson

**illegal trafficker** smuggler

**illegible** faint, indecipherable, indistinct, obscure, scrawled, unreadable

**illegible handwriting** indecipherable, scrawl

**illegitimate** fatherless, illegal, illicit, illogical, incorrect, misbegotten, unlawful

**ill-fated** doomed, hapless, luckless, unfortunate, unhappy, unlucky

**ill-fated ship** Birkenhead, Flying Dutchman, Grosvenor, Lusitania, Marie Celeste, Titanic, Waratah

**ill-favoured** objectionable, unattractive

**ill feeling** animus, bitterness, enmity, rancour, resentment

**ill health** ailment, indisposition, sickness

**ill humour** acerbity, anger, bitterness, crankiness, crossness, fume, grumpiness, irascibility, petulance, pique, spleen, surliness, tartness, temper, testiness, touchiness

**illiberal** benighted, bigoted, hidebound, ignorant, intolerant, mean, miserly, narrow-minded, niggardly, parsimonious, petty, prejudiced, reactionary, repressive, small-minded, tight(fisted), uncultured, untaught, untutored

**illicit** black(-market), clandestine, contraband, criminal, forbidden, furtive, guilty, ill-gotten, illegal, illegimate, immoral, improper, lawless, prohibited, secret, sneaky, unauthorised, underhanded, unlawful, unlicensed, unsanctioned, wrong

**illicit affair** amour

**illicit liquor shop** speakeasy

**illicit love affair** adultery, amour, liaison

**illicit lover of married man or woman** paramour

**illicit spirit** poitin, poteen

**illicit trader in liquor** bootlegger

**illicit whisky** hooch

**illiterate** analphabetic, benighted, ignorant, nescient, uncultured, uneducated, unenlightened, uninformed, unlearned, unlettered, unscholarly, unschooled, untaught, unversed

**ill-mannered** discourteous, ill-bred, impolite, insolent, rude, uncivil, uncouth, ungallant

**ill-mannered child** brat

**ill-mannered young man** cub

**ill-natured** cantankerous, crotchety, nasty

**ill-natured churlish fellow** curmudgeon

**illness** affliction, ailment, attack, breakdown, colic, collapse, complaint, complication, condition, disability, disease, disorder, distemper, handicap, ill-being, ill-health, indisposition, infirmity, malady, sickness, weakness

**illogical** absurd, contradictory, fallacious, incongruous, irrational, sophistic, unproved, unreasoning, unsound, untenable, wrong

**illogical inference** non sequitur

**ill-omened** accursed, bad, bedevilled, bewitched, black, blighted, condemned, cursed, damned, discouraging, doomed, fated, hapless, hopeless, ill-fated, inauspicious, luckless, ominous, ruined, undone, unfortunate, unhappy, unlucky, unpropitious, wretched

**ill-planned urban areas** subtopia

**ill-repute** disesteem, disfavour, disgrace, dishonour, disrepute, ignominy, infamy, notoriety, obloquy, shame, unpopularity

**ill-smelling** noisome

**ill-supplied with red blood cells** anaemia

**ill temper** anger, annoyance, asperity, curtness, grouchiness, impatience, irascibility, irritability, moodiness, petulance, spleen, tartness, tetchiness

**ill-tempered** acrimonious, annoyed, choleric, churlish, cranky, cross, curt, displeased, enraged, exasperated, furious, grumpy, heated, hot, ill-humoured, impatient, incensed, indignant, infuriated, irascible, irate, ireful, irritable, irritated, outraged, passionate, piqued, provoked, raging, resentful, snappy, touchy, wrathful

**ill-tempered woman** harridan, she-fox, vixen

**ill-timed** awkward, foolish, hasty, ill-advised, ill-judged, ill-suited, improper, imprudent, inappropriate, inauspicious, incongruous, inconvenient, indiscreet, inexpedient, injudicious, inopportune, malapropos, rash, tasteless, unbecoming, unbefitting, unfit(ting), unseasonable, unseemly, unsuitable, unthinking, untimely, unwelcome, unwise

**ill-treat** abuse, bruise, bully, damage, disrespect, harass, harm, harry, hurt, injure, maltreat, mishandle, mistreat, misuse, oppress, wrong

**illude** cheat, deceive, mock, trick

**illuminate** adorn, beam, beautify, brighten, colour, decorate, elucidate, enhance, enrich, garnish, gleam, highlight, interpret, irradiate, light(-up), manifest, scintillate

**illuminated again** relit

**illuminated bullet** tracer

**illuminated-sign gas** neon

**illuminated writing on scrolls** Fraktur

**illuminating** gaslight

**illumination** awareness, beaming, clarification, edification, education, enlightenment, glitter, glowing, insight, knowledge, learning, light(ing), lightness, luminosity, radiance, radiation, sapience, twinkle, understanding, wisdom
**illumine** illuminate, irradiate
**illusion** belief, chimera, conceit, deception, delusion, error, fallacy, fantasy, fear, hallucination, haunt, mirage, misbelief, misconception, myth, perception, phantasm(agoria), phantom, show, sleight, vagary, vapour, whim
**illusionist** conjurer, magician
**illusive images** phantasmagoria
**illusive remark** innuendo
**illusory** apparent, beguiling, deceitful, delusive, delusory, dreamlike, dreamy, erroneous, fallacious, false, fanciful, illusionary, illusive, imaginary, imagined, misleading, mistaken, quixotic, sham, tricky, unfactual, unreal, untrue
**illusory reward** carrot
**illusory riches** mine
**illusory thing** mirage
**illustrate** adorn, clarify, decorate, demonstrate, depict, draw, elucidate, emphasise, exemplify, exhibit, explain, illuminate, interpret, ornament, picture, show, sketch
**illustrate with hands** gesticulate
**illustration** analogy, artwork, cartoon, case, clarification, comparison, decoration, depiction, design, diagram, drawing, elucidation, example, exemplar, exemplification, explanation, figure, graphic, image, instance, interpretation, painting, photograph, picture, representation, sample, sketch, specimen
**illustrative** archetypal, characteristic, descriptive, diagrammatic, exemplary, explanatory, graphic, ideal, model, paradigmatic, perfect, pictorial, representative, sample, specimen, standard, symbolic, typical
**illustrator in *Punch*** Keene
**illustrious** brilliant, celebrated, distinguished, eminent, exalted, excellent, famed, famous, glorious, great, magnificent, noble, notable, noted, outstanding, prestigious, prominent, remarkable, renowned, signal, splendid
**illustrious warrior** hero
**ill will** animosity, antagonism, antipathy, aversion, dislike, enmity, envy, grudge, hatred, hostility, invidiousness, malevolence, malice, malignity, rancour, resentment, spite, unfriendliness
**I love** amo (L), je taime (F)
**image** appearance, concept(ion), copy, counterpart, delineation, depict, effigy, envisage, facsimile, figure, form, icon, idea, idol, ikon, impression, likeness, notion, perception, photograph, picture, portrait, reflection, replica, represent(ation), semblance, similarity, statue, visage
**image breaker** iconoclast
**image formed by rays of light** spectrum
**image of a god** idol
**images collectively** imagery
**image with solid construction** idol
**image worship** idolatry
**imaginable** believable, comprehensible, conceivable, creatable, credible, framable, likely, plausible, possible, thinkable
**imaginary** abstract, chimerical, dreamy, extravagant, fanciful, fictitious, fictive, ghostly, idealistic, illusory, imagined, legendary, nightmarish, phantasmagoric, phantasmal, phantom, preposterous, spectral, unreal, visionary
**imaginary combat** sciamachy, skiamachy
**imaginary creature** basilisk, griffin, tokoloshe, unicorn
**imaginary flower that never fades** amaranth
**imaginary imp** gremlin
**imaginary kingdom** Ruritania
**imaginary land of great wealth** Eldorado
**imaginary line round the earth** equator
**imaginary one-horned animal** unicorn
**imaginary paradise on earth** Shangri-la
**imaginary perfect place** Utopia
**imaginary small being** elf, fairy, gnome, leprechaun, pixie, pixy, sprite, tokoloshe
**imaginary unfading flower** amaranth
**imagination** conception, creativity, enterprise, fancy, idea, illusion, image, imaginativeness, ingenuity, insight, inspiration, inventiveness, mind's eye, notion, originality, resourcefulness, supposition, vision, wit
**imaginative** clever, constructive, creative, descriptive, dreamy, enterprising, fanciful, fantastic, fertile, fictional, fictitious, figmental, imaginary, ingenious, innovative, inspired, inventive, mythical, original, resourceful, visionary, vivid
**imagine** assume, believe, conceive, conjecture, conjure, create, devise, envisage, fancy, frame, invent, picture, plan, pretend, project, realise, scheme, suppose, suspect, think, visualise, ween
**imagined source of emotional control** nerves
**imagined state of perfection** beau idéal
**imagine to be guilty** suspect
**imago** insect
**imam** caliph, imaum
**imbalance** asymmetry, bias, disparity, disproportion, fickleness, fluctuation, fluidity, frailty, imparity, inequality, insecurity, instability, insufficiency, lopsidedness, partiality, restlessness, unevenness, unfairness, unsteadiness, vacillation, variability, volatility, weakness
**imbecile** absurd, ass, backward, blockhead, bungler, crazy, cretin, defective, deficient, dolt, domkop, dope, dotard, dull(ard), dummy, fatuous, feeble-minded, fool(ish), half-witted, idiot(ic), ignoramus, inane, moron(ic), nitwit, retardate, retarded, silly, simple(ton), stupid, thick(head), vacant, witless
**imbecilic** asinine, brainless, crazy, doltish, foolish
**imbibe** absorb, assimilate, consume, drink, ingest, receive, swallow
**imbiber** drinker, tippler
**imbibition** absurdity, brainlessness, feeblemindedness, incompetency, senselessness
**imbroglio** complexity, entanglement, involvement, misunderstanding, quandary
**imbue** affect, animate, charge, diffuse, encourage, enliven, extend, flavour, hearten, impregnate, influence, infuse, inspire, inspirit, instil, lace, leaven, penetrate, percolate, permeate, pervade, saturate, season, spice, spur, stimulate, suffuse
**imitate** affect, ape, assume, burlesque, caricature, copy, counterfeit, duplicate, echo, emulate, follow, forge, impersonate, mimic, mirror, mock, parody, parrot, personate, repeat, reproduce, sham, simulate, spoof
**imitate a donkey** bray
**imitate conditions of** simulate
**imitating** copying, counterfeiting, emulating, impersonating,

mimicking, mirroring, mocking, parodying, personating, repeating, simulating

**imitation** aping, artificial, caricature, copy, counterfeit, dummy, echoing, ersatz, fake, forgery, fraud, impersonation, impression, likeness, mimicking, mimicry, mock(ery), mocking, parody, reflection, replica, reproduction, resemblance, sham, simulated, simulation, substitution, synthetic, travesty

**imitation child** doll
**imitation diamond** rhinestone, zirconium
**imitation gem** paste
**imitation gold** ormolu, oroide, pinchbeck
**imitation leather** leatherette
**imitation pearl** olivet, paste
**imitation stone** scagliola
**imitative** copied, copying, derivative, mimicking, mock, onomatopoeic, parrot-like, plagiarised, pseudo, put-on, second-hand, simulated, unoriginal
**imitator** actor, aper, conformist, copycat, copyist, echo, epigon(e), faker, feigner, forger, impersonator, mimic, parrot, plagiarist, portrayer, pretender, simulator
**immaculate** aseptic, blameless, clean, correct, faultless, flawless, ideal, impeccable, incorrupt, innocent, neat, perfect, pure, sinless, speckless, spotless, spruce, stainless, unblemished, undefiled, unpolluted, unsoiled, unspoiled, unsullied, untainted
**immaculately** flawlessly, spotlessly
**immanent** connate, enwrought, hereditary, inborn, indwelling, ingrained, inherent, innate, intrinsic, inveterate, inwrought, natural, rooted
**immaterial** extraneous, impertinent, inapposite, incorporeal, inessential, insignificant, irrelevant, minor, trifling, trivial, unimportant, unnecessary
**immaterial part of person** soul, spirit
**immature** adolescent, babyish, callow, childish, crude, early, fledg(e)ling, imperfect, infantile, jejune, juvenile, naïve, nascent, puerile, raw, rudimentary, sophomoric, teenage, un(der)developed, unready, unripe, untimely, young, youthful
**immature and inexperienced** callow
**immature animal** larva
**immature cucumber** gherkin
**immature egg** ovule

**immature female gamete that develops into an ovum** ootid
**immature frog** tadpole
**immature insect state** larva
**immeasurable** bottomless, boundless, endless, immense, incalculable, inestimable, inexhaustible, infinite, limitless, unbounded, unlimited, vast
**immeasurable depth** abyss
**immeasurable period** aeon, eternity
**immeasurably large** immense
**immediacy** directness, imminence, instantaneity, nearness, simultaneity, swiftness
**immediate** abrupt, actual, adjacent, close, current, direct, existing, instant(aneous), near(est), next, personal, present, pressing, primary, prompt, proximate, recent, running, simultaneous, up-to-date, urgent
**immediate but subsidiary cause** occasion
**immediate insight** intuition
**immediate involuntary response** reflex
**immediately** adjacently, closely, directly, forthwith, instantaneously, instantly, nearly, now, promptly, pronto, straightaway, unhesitatingly
**immediately following** next
**immediately payable** due
**immediately previous** preceding
**immense** astronomical, boundless, broad, capacious, colossal, enormous, expansive, extensive, gigantic, great, huge, infinite, large, massive, measureless, monstrous, staggering, titanic, vast
**immense period of time** aeon
**immense statue** colossus
**immensity** abyss, amplitude, bulk, enormity, expanse, extent, fullness, greatness, hugeness, immenseness, infinity, largeness, scope, spaciousness, vastness
**immerse** absorb, amuse, attract, baptise, bathe, bury, captivate, cleanse, deluge, dip, dive, divert, douse, drench, drown, duck, engage, engross, fascinate, fill, flood, inundate, involve, lustrate, marinate, moisten, plunge, (pre)occupy, purify, rinse, rivet, sink, soak, submerge, swamp
**immerse again** redip
**immerse for a time** dip
**immerse in boiling water** scald
**immerse in liquid** dip, marinate
**immerse in water** bathe, dip
**immigrant** alien, entrant, foreigner, incomer, newcomer, nonnative, outsider, settler, tramontane

**immigrant worker** Gastarbeiter (G)
**immigration to Israel** aliyah
**imminence** approach, immediacy, instancy, menace, nearness, threat
**imminent** afoot, approaching, brewing, brooding, close, (forth)coming, gathering, immediate, impending, looming, menacing, near, nigh, overhanging, proximate, threatening, toward
**immobile** fixed, frozen, immovable, inert, motionless, rigid, riveted, rooted, stable, static, stationary, stiff, still, stolid, unmoving
**immobilise** cripple, disable, fix, freeze, halt, paralyse, stop, transfix
**immobilised by ice** icebound
**immoderate** exaggerated, excessive, exorbitant, extravagant, extreme, inordinate, lavish, outrageous, overblown, ultra, unbridled, uncalled-for, uncontrolled, uncurbed, undue, unreasonable, unrestraint, unwarranted
**immodest** arrogant, bold, brazen, cheeky, coarse, dirty, disrespectful, forward, immoral, impertinent, improper, impudent, impure, indecent, lascivious, lewd, obscene, promiscuous, pushy, revealing, risqué, shameful, shameless, smutty, undignified, wanton
**immodesty** impudicity, shamelessness
**immoral** abandoned, bad, corrupt, debauched, degenerate, depraved, dishonest, dissipated, dissolute, evil, foul, impure, indecent, lewd, licentious, nefarious, obscene, pornographic, profligate, reprobate, sinful, unchaste, unethical, unprincipled, vicious, vile, wanton, wicked, wrong
**immoral habit** vice
**immorality** deathlessness, dissipation, heinousness, indecency, sinfulness, timelessness, turpitude, wickedness
**immorally pure** immaculate
**immoral man** rake
**immoral trait** vice
**immoral woman** hussy, tart, tramp
**immortal** abiding, aeonian, ceaseless, constant, deathless, durable, endless, enduring, eternal, everlasting, imperishable, incorruptible, indestructible, interminable, lasting, permanent, perpetual, timeless, undiminished, undying, unfading
**immortalise** celebrate, commemorate, enshrine, memorialise, perpetuate
**immovable** adamant, constant, determined, fast, firm, fixed,

**inflexible**, jammed, obdurate, obstinate, resolute, rooted, secure, set, stable, stationary, steadfast, stuck, unshakable, unwavering, unyielding

**immune** clear, exempt, free, insusceptible, invulnerable, proof, protected, resistant, safe, unaffected, unsusceptible

**immunise** inject, inoculate, protect, safeguard, vaccinate

**immunity** amnesty, charter, exemption, franchise, freedom, indemnity, insusceptibility, liberty, licence, prerogative, privilege, release, right

**immure** cage, commit, confine, constrain, detain, encage, enclose, gaol, impound, imprison, incarcerate, intern, jail, mew, restrain, restrict

**immutable** binding, changeless, consistent, constant, even, firm, fixed, habitual, incontrovertible, inflexible, invariable, permanent, perpetual, regular, rigid, set, stable, steadfast, steady, stringent, unbroken, unchangeable

**imp** demon, (d)jinni, djinny, goblin, spirit, sprite, urchin

**impact** collision, crash, effect, force, jolt, thrust

**impact between two balls** kiss

**impair** adulterate, attenuate, blacken, botch, cripple, damage, damnify, debase, deface, derange, diminish, disable, disfigure, distort, enervate, enfeeble, handicap, harm, hurt, injure, lessen, mar, meddle, mutilate, scar, shatter, spoil, undermine, weaken, worsen

**impaired ability to read** alexia

**impaired co-ordination of speech** dysphasia

**impaired value of** damaged

**impaired vision with no discernible damage to the eye or optic nerve** amblyopia

**impair fatally** mar

**impairment due to use** wear

**impairment of activity** paralysis

**impairment of the ability to speak normally** dysphonia

**impair the strength of** debilitate

**impale** bore, eviscerate, gut, lance, perforate, pierce, pink, prick, puncture, skewer, spear, spike, spit, stab, stick, transfix

**impalpable** airy, ambiguous, blurred, clouded, cloudy, dreamlike, esoteric, ethereal, fleeting, imperceptible, imponderable, insubstantial, intangible, mysterious, obscure, recondite, secret, subtle, tenuous, unclear, unreal, unworldly, vague, wispy

**impart** bestow, communicate, confer, contribute, convey, disclose, discover, divulge, give, grant, lend, offer, relate, reveal, tell, yield

**impartial** detached, disinterested, dispassionate, equitable, equity, even, fair(ness), just, legal, neutral, objectivity, true, unbiased, unbigoted, uninfluenced, unprejudiced

**impart knowledge to** inform

**impassable** blocked, closed, impenetrable, inaccessible, obstructed, remote, unapproachable, unattainable, unnavigable, unpassable

**impasse** blockage, cessation, check(mate), cul-de-sac, deadlock, dilemma, draw, halt, nonplus, perplexity, predicament, quietus, snag, stalemate, stand-off, standstill, stop(page), tie

**impassioned** animated, ardent, blazing, fervent, fervid, furious, inflamed, inspired, intense, vehement, violent, vivid, warm

**impassive** aloof, apathetic, calm, composed, cool, dispassionate, emotionless, expressionless, indifferent, reserved, sedate, stoic(al), stolid, unconcerned, unemotional, unexcitable, unfeeling, unmoved, unruffled

**impassive person** stoic

**impatience** agitation, eagerness, haste, heat, impetuosity, intolerance, irritability, nervousness, rashness, restlessness, shortness, snappishness, uneasiness, vehemence

**impatience under affliction** dysphoria

**impatient** abrupt, brusque, demanding, edgy, fretful, hasty, hot-tempered, impetuous, intolerant, irritable, precipitate, restless, snappy, sudden, uneasy, unquiet

**impatient and nervy** restive

**imp causing mechanical problems** gremlin

**impeach** accuse, allege, arraign, assail, assign, blame, censure, challenge, charge, delate, denounce, discredit, disparage, implicate, impugn, incriminate, indict, revile, tax

**impeachable** taxable

**impeachment** accusation, arraignment, charge, denouncement, disparagement, indictment

**impeccable** blameless, exact, exquisite, faultless, flawless, immaculate(ly), innocent, irreproachable, perfect(ly), precisely, pure(ly), scrupulous, sinless, spotlessly, stainless, unblemished, unerring

**impecunious** bankrupt, destitute, impoverished, indigent, insolvent, needy, penniless, penurious, poor, short

**impede** arrest, bar, block, check, clog, confound, contravene, corner, delay, deter, encumber, estop, frustrate, hamper, handicap, hinder, inhibit, intercept, interfere, interrupt, intervene, obstruct, obviate, preclude, prevent, retard, sabotage, slow, stall, stop, thwart, undermine

**impede breathing** suffocate

**impede growth** stunt

**impediment** bar(rier), check, clog, curb, encumbrance, fault, hesitance, hindrance, hitch, obstacle, obstruction, restrain, restriction, snag, stammer, tether

**impeding** delaying, hampering, hindering, obstructing, restraining, retarding, stopping

**impel** actuate, coerce, compel, drive, exhort, force, goad, impress, incite, lash, move, nudge, poke, prick, prod, propel, push, send, shove, spur, thrust, urge, whip

**impelling force** stress

**impend** alarm, appear, approach, bulk, bully, emerge, frighten, hang, hover, imminent, intimidate, loom, lour, lower, menace, suspend, terrorise, threaten

**impending** brewing, coming, hovering, imminent, looming, menacing, near(ing), oncoming

**impenetrable** dense, elusive, impervious, insensible, insoluble, inviolable, obscure, sealed, solid, thick

**impenetrable to sight** opaque

**impenitent** abandoned, callous, hard, indurate, insensible, inured, irreclaimable, irrepentant, lost, miscreant, obdurate, remorseless, unrepentant

**imperative** arbitrary, command(ing), compulsory, dogmatic, essential, inescapable, liability, masterful, necessary, needful, obligatory, required, responsibility, urgent, vital

**imperative need** necessity

**imperceptible** faint, gradual, inaudible, inconsiderable, indiscernible, indistinct, insensible, invisible, microscopic, minute, shadowy, slight, subtle, tiny, unapparent, undetectable, unnoticeable, unseeable

**imperceptible margin** hairbreadth, hair's breadth

**imperfect** defective, faulty, incomplete, rudimentary, un(der)developed

**imperfect control of one's bodily movements** ataxia

**imperfection** blemish, blotch, defect, deficiency, failing, fallibility, fault, flaw, frailty, inadequacy, infirmity, shortcoming, stain, taint, weakness

**imperfectly crystallised diamond** bort

**imperfectly transparent** translucent

**imperfect nutrition** malnutrition

**imperial** august, exalted, grant, great, high, kingly, lofty, magnificent, majestic, noble, princely, queenly, regal, royal, sovereign, superior, supreme

**imperial distance** mileage

**imperialism** acquisitiveness, adventurism, colonialism, empire-building, expansionism

**imperial land-measure** acre

**imperial ruler** emperor

**imperial Russian ruler** czar, tsar

**imperil** bare, compromise, endanger, expose, gamble, hazard, jeopardise, menace, peril, risk, threaten

**imperious** arbitrary, arrogant, assuming, commanding, conceited, despotic, disdainfully, dogmatic, domineering, haughty, high-handed, insolent, lordly, masterful, necessary, needful, overbearing, peremptory, pompous, presumptuous, proud, required, urgent, vital

**imperishable** abiding, constant, deathless, durable, endless, enduring, eternal, everlasting, immortal, incorruptible, indelible, indestructible, indissoluble, infinite, interminable, lasting, never-ending, perennial, permanent, perpetual, timeless, undying, unfading

**impermeable to air** airtight, hermetic

**impersonal** aloof, bureaucratic, businesslike, cold, detached, dispassionate, distant, faceless, formal, frosty, glassy, inhuman, neutral, objective, remote

**impersonate** act, ape, caricature, enact, imitate, mimic, mock, parody, personate

**impertinence** absurdity, audacity, boldface, boldness, effrontery, forwardness, freshness, immaterially, impoliteness, incivility, insolence, intrusiveness, irrelevance, pertness, ridiculousness, rudeness, shamelessness, upstart

**impertinent** arrogant, cheeky, disrespectful, flippant, fresh, frivolous, impolite, impudent, inappropriate, incongruous, insolent, insulting, intrusive, irrelevant, pert, presumptuous, ridiculous, rude, saucy, trivial, uncivil

**impertinently insulting** insolent

**impertinent speech** cheek

**imperturbable** balanced, calm, collected, complacent, composed, cool, dispassionate, easy-going, even-tempered, inexcitable, nonchalant, peaceful, placid, poised, sedate, serene, tranquil, unflappable, unmoved, unperturbed, unruffled, untroubled

**impervious** closed, damp-proof, hermetic, immune, impenetrable, impermeable, invulnerable, proof, repellent, resistant, scaled, sealed, sound, strong, tight, treated, unaffected, unmoved, untouched

**impervious to harm** invulnerable

**impervious to sound** soundproof

**impervious to water** waterproof

**impetuosity** bustle, dash, élan, force, haste, hurry, hustle, impatience, impulsiveness, intolerance, rashness, recklessness, rush, shortness, vehemence, violence

**impetuous** abrupt, brash, careless, eager, fervid, fiery, foolhardy, forceful, furious, hasty, hot, impulsive, obstinate, passionate, precipitate, quick, rash, reckless, spirited, spontaneous, ungovernable, unreasoned, unruly, vigorous, violent

**impetuous beginning** onset

**impetuous onset** surge

**impetuous person** hothead

**impetuous rush** élan

**impetus** catalyst, energy, force, goad, impulse, incentive, momentum, motivation, power, pressure, push, spur, stimulus

**impetus gained by movement** momentum

**impiety** apostasy, blasphemy, curse, cursing, desecration, error, execration, heresy, impiousness, irreligiousness, irreverence, malediction, mockery, obscenity, profanation, profaneness, profanity, sacrilege, schism, swearing, swearword, ungodliness, unorthodoxy, violation

**impinge** affect, clash, encroach, enter, hit, influence, infringe, intrude, invade, overstep, trench, trespass, usurp, violate

**impinge upon** affect, clash, collide, infringe, touch

**impious** blasphemous, desecrative, diabolic, godless, immoral, indevout, iniquitous, irreligious, irreverent, pharisaical, profane, sacrilegious, sanctimonious, satanic, sinful, ungodly, unholy, wicked

**impious talk** blasphemy

**impish** devilish, elfin, imp-like, mischievous, naughty, playful, prankish, puckish, roguish, sportive

**implacable** barbarous, bitter, brutal, callous, cold-blooded, cruel, deadly, ferocious, fierce, grim, hard(-hearted), harsh, heartless, hellish, inclement, inexorable, inflexible, inhuman(e), intransigent, malevolent, merciless, painful, pitiless, ravenging, raw, relentless, remorseless, ruthless, sadistic, savage, severe, spiteful, unfeeling, unkind, vengeful, vicious

**implacably hostile** irreconcilable

**implant** graft, imbed, imbue, impregnate, impress, inculcate, infix, influence, infuse, inject, inseminate, insert(ion), insinuate, inspire, instil, introduce, plant, sow

**implant firmly** engrain

**implant living tissue** transplant

**implausible** absurd, deceptive, delusive, dubious, fallible, false, far-fetched, feeble, flimsy, frivolous, impossible, improbable, inaccurate, inadequate, inconceivable, incredible, poor, preposterous, suspect, thin, transparent, trivial, unbelievable, uncertain, unconvincing, unimaginable, unlikely, unreliable, unsatisfactory, unthinkable, weak

**implement** accomplish, achieve, activate, apparatus, appliance, begin, cause, contrivance, device, enforce, equipment, execute, fulfil, gadget, install, instrument, invention, perform, realise, supplement, tool, utensil

**implement for cutting furrows** plough

**implement for playing a violin** bow

**implement for shelling nuts** nutcracker

**implement for shooting stones** catapult

**implement for turning up soil** plough
**implements for eating food** cutlery
**implements of war** artillery
**implicate** associate, compromise, concern, connect, embroil, ensnare, entangle, include, incriminate, inculpate, involve
**implication** acclusion, association, conclusion, connection, consequence, effect, inference, innuendo, insinuation, intimation, involvement, meaning, outcome, repercussion, significance, suggestion
**implicit** absolute, complete, full, hinted, implied, innate, staunch, suggested, tacit, total, understood, unqualified, unquestioning, unreserved, unspoken, utter, wholehearted
**implied** betokened, connoted, entailed, evidenced, hinted, imported, included, indicated, inherent, insinuated, intimated, meant, unexpressed, unspoken
**implied without being stated** tacit
**implore** adjure, ask, beg, beseech, conjure, crave, demand, entreat, importune, insist, invoke, obsecrate, obtest, plead, pray, press, request, seek, solicit, sue, supplicate, urge
**imply** betoken, connote, denote, entail, evidence, hint, import, include, indicate, infer, insinuate, intimate, involve, mean, presuppose, require, signify, suggest
**imply guilt of someone** incriminate
**implying respect** honorific
**impolite** abrupt, bad-mannered, boorish, coarse, cross, discourteous, disrespectful, ill-bred, ill-mannered, insolent, rough, rude, uncivil, unpolished, unrefined
**imponderable** baffling, imperceptible, inconsiderable, minute, tenuous, ungraspable, unimageable, unimaginable, unmeasurable, unponderable
**import** bearing, drift, gist, implication, intention, introduce, land, meaning, message, moment, purport, sense, significance, thrust
**importance** concern, consequence, consideration, distinction, eminence, esteem, import, influence, interest, moment(ousness), prestige, pretentiousness, prominence, self-esteem, significance, standing, status, substance, usefulness, value, weight(iness), worth
**importance attached** emphasis
**important** chief, consequential, critical, distinctive, essential, far-reaching, foremost, great, heavy, high-level, high-ranking, influential, key(note), leading, main, major, material, meaningful, momentous, necessary, notable, noteworthy, outstanding, powerful, pre-eminent, primary, principal, prominent, relevant, salient, seminal, serious, significant, substantial, urgent, valuable, vital, weighty, worthwhile
**important date** era
**important happening** event, incident
**important harbour** port
**important individual** personage
**importantly placed** high-ranking
**important period** era
**important person** bigwig, eminence, mogul
**important source of flour for bread** wheat
**import illegally** smuggle
**import inspector** custom
**import or export illegally** smuggle
**importunate creditor** dun
**importune** badger, beg, beseech, coax, entreat, imprecate, inveigle, pester, petition, plague, ply, press, solicit, sue, supplicate, tax, urge, vex, wheedle
**impose** apply, charge, command, demand, dictate, direct, enjoin, exact, exert, foist, force, inflict, insinuate, interfere, interrupt, intrude, levy, obtrude, prescribe, set, superpose, trouble
**impose a monetary penalty** fine
**impose a penalty on** penalise
**impose as a burden** saddle
**impose a task on** charge
**impose authoritatively** prescribe
**impose by necessity** entail
**impose charges** tax
**impose on** abuse, beguile, deceive, exploit, hoax, hoodwink, misapply, misuse, pervert
**impose tax** levy
**impose upon** hoodwink, obtrude, sting
**imposing** august, dignified, enormous, gigantic, grand, lofty, majestic, mighty, stately, stupendous, titanic, towering, tremendous
**imposing arrangement** array
**imposing building** edifice
**imposition** application, artifice, burden, charge, cheating, constraint, deception, decree, duty, encroachment, exaction, fraud, hoax, infliction, introducing, intrusion, levying, liberty, lines, presumption, promulgation, punishment, stratagem, task, tax, trickery
**impossible** absurd, hopeless, impracticable, inadmissible, inconceivable, insoluble, ludicrous, outrageous, preposterous, ridiculous, unacceptable, unachievable, unattainable, unobtainable, unreasonable, unthinkable, unworkable
**impossible to miss** conspicuous, egregious, flagrant, prominent
**impost** assessment, charge, custom(s), demand, duty, evaluation, excise, fee, homage, levy, offering, payment, ransom, rates, rating, subsidy, tariff, tax(ation), tithe, toll, tribute
**impostor** charlatan, cheat, deceiver, fake, fraud, hypocrite, impersonator, mountebank, phoney, pretender, quack, rogue, sham, swindler, trickster
**impotent** disabled, feeble, frail, helpless, inadequate, incapable, incapacitated, incompetent, ineffective, infirm, nerveless, paralysed, powerless, unable, weak
**impoverish** bankrupt, beggar, break, denude, deplete, diminish, drain, exhaust, reduce, ruin, sap, weaken
**impoverished** destitute, distressed, drained, empty, impecunious, needy, poor, poverty-stricken, reduced
**impracticable** awkward, impossible, impractical, inconvenient, inoperable, unachievable, unattainable, unfeasible, unserviceable, unsuitable, unworkable, useless
**impractical** absurd, academic, ideal(istic), impossible, impracticable, inefficacious, inoperable, inoperative, ivory tower, quixotic, romantic, speculative, starry-eyed, unbusinesslike, unrealistic, unserviceable, unworkable, useless, visionary, wild
**impractically idealistic** quixotic
**impractical person** dreamer
**imprecation** anathema, ban, curse, excommunication, execration, expletive, imprecation, jinx, malediction, oath, profanity
**imprecise** ambiguous, approximate, careless, cloudy, confused, disorderly, equivocal, estimated, fluctuating, hazy, ill-defined, inaccurate, incorrect, indefinite, indeterminate, indistinct, inexact, loose, rough, unexplicit, untrue, vague
**impregnable** absolute, certain, faultless, flawless, imperishable,

**impregnable defence** aegis
**impregnate** fertilise, fill, fructify, imbue, infuse, inseminate, permeate, pervade, saturate, soak, steep, suffuse, wet
 invincible, invulnerable, mighty, perfect, powerful, safe, secure, solid, stable, staunch, strong, sturdy, unassailable, unattackable, unbeatable, undefeatable, undeniable
**impregnated with salt** saline
**impregnate with carbon dioxide** aerate, carbonate
**impregnate with medicinal substances** medicate
**impregnate with nitrogen** nitrify
**impregnate with semen** inseminate
**impregnate with sweet smell** perfume
**impregnate with water** hydrate
**impress** affect, arrogate, cajole, coax, confiscate, conscript, convince, crimp, disturb, draft, engrave, enlist, establish, impression, imprint, influence, install, mark, move, oblige, persuade, press, print, seal, stamp, strike, wheedle
**impress a mark on** stamp
**impress clearly** etch
**impress deeply** engrave
**impressed with fear** afraid
**impression** dent, effect, feeling, impact, imprint, indentation, influence, mark, opinion, sense, stamp, understanding
**impressionable** dewy-eyed, emotionable, formative, gullible, impressionable, malleable, maudlin, mouldable, naïve, nostalgic, open, overemotional, pathetic, pliant, receptive, responsive, romantic, sensitive, sentimental, soft-hearted, susceptible, tearful, tender, vulnerable
**impression of the tip of a finger** fingerprint
**impressive** awesome, effective, exciting, forcible, grand, imposing, majestic, memorable, moving, outstanding, powerful, riveting, stirring, striking, touching
**impressive display** array
**impressive quality** charisma
**imprint** badge, brand, engrave, establish, etch, fix, impress(ion), indentation, logo, mark, print, sign, stamp
**imprinted mark** stamp
**imprint vividly** etch
**imprison** bury, confine, detain, embar, entomb, incarcerate, intern, jail, lock-up, quod, seclude, shut-up

**imprisonment** confinement, custody, detainment, detention, duress, incarceration, internment
**improbability** doubt, dubiety, uncertainty, unlikelihood, unlikeliness
**improbable** doubtful, dubious, illogical, implausible, uncertain, unforeseeable, unlikely, unreasonable, weak
**improbable hope** dream
**improbable tale** tall story
**impromptu** ad lib(itum), extempore, improvised, impulsive, off-hand, spontaneously, sudden, unexpected, unprepared, unrehearsed, unscripted
**improper** abnormal, amiss, erroneous, false, faulty, illicit, immoral, impolite, inaccurate, inappropriate, inapt, incorrect, indecent, indecorous, indelicate, inelegant, inexact, irregular, lewd, mistaken, outré, risqué, smutty, suggestive, tactless, unbecoming, unfit(ting), ungenteel, unseemly, unsuitable, untoward, untrue, unused, vulgar, wrong
**improper behaviour** indecorum
**improper disclosure of secrets** leakage
**improve** ameliorate, amend, better, civilise, correct, elevate, embellish, emend(ate), enhance, gain, grow, meliorate, mend, perfect, rearrange, rectify, recuperate, redeem, redo, reform, rehabilitate, repair, revamp, revise, upgrade
**improve by adding detail** embellish
**improve condition** upgrade
**improved fortification** barrier
**improve in rank** advance
**improvement** advance, amelioration, amendment, correction, development, edification, enhancement, furtherance, gain, increase, progress, rally, recovery, rectification, refinement, reform(ation), repair, rise, upswing
**improvement in appearance** facelift
**improve morally** edify
**improver** ameliorant
**improve the mind** edify
**improve the time** carpe diem (L)
**improvident** careless, imprudent, neglectful, prodigal, thoughtless, thriftless, wasteful
**improving** correcting, developing, helping, increasing, mending, polishing, progressing, rallying, rectifying, reforming, rising, upgrading
**improvise** ad lib, coin, concoct, contrive, devise, extemporise, invent
**improvise on stage** ad lib

**imprudent** brash, careless, flippant, foolish, heedless, ill-advised, impetuous, incautious, inconsiderate, indiscreet, irresponsible, rash, reckless, thoughtless, unwary, unwise, wild
**impudence** audacity, boldness, brass, brazenness, cheek(iness), cockiness, disrespect, effrontery, flippancy, forwardness, guff, impertinence, incivility, insolence, nerve, officiousness, pertness, presumption, rudeness, sass(iness), sauciness, shamelessness, unmannerliness
**impudent** audacious, bold(-faced), brassy, brazen, cheeky, forward, impertinent, insolent, insulting, pert, presumptive, presumptuous, rude, sassy
**impudent behaviour** presumption
**impudent boldness** nerve
**impudent girl** minx, strap
**impudent lie** bounce
**impudent repartee** backchat
**impudent speech** cheek
**impudent talk** lip
**impudicity** immodesty, shamelessness
**impugn** abuse, accuse, arraign, attack, blame, castigate, censure, challenge, charge, condemn, contradict, denounce, deny, dispute, doubt, impeach, incriminate, malign, proscribe, question, revile, stigmatise, vilify
**impuissant** impotent, weak
**impulse** boost, desire, emotion, force, goad, inclination, instinct, itch, mania, prompting, spur, stimulation, tendency, urge, want
**impulse fibre** nerve
**impulse to light fires** pyromania
**impulse to steal** kleptomania
**impulsive** emotional, hasty, headlong, impetuous, instinctive, intuitive, passionate, precipitate, quick, rash, spontaneous, unpremeditated
**impulsive action** stampede
**impulsive thief** kleptomaniac
**impunity** amnesty, dispensation, exemption, freedom, immunity, liberty, licence, permission, privilege, security
**impure** adulterated, alloyed, contaminated, corrupt, debased, defiled, diluted, dirty, foul, immodest, indecent, infected, obscene, polluted, tainted, unclean, unrefined
**impure mass of metal** regulus
**impurities in metal** dross
**impurity** adulteration, contaminant, contamination, corruption,

defilement, dirt(iness), filth, foulness, grime, immodesty, immorality, indecency, infection, licentiousness, mark, mixture, obscenity, pollution, scum, spot, stain, unchastity, vulgarity
**imputation attaching to person's reputation** stigma
**impute** accuse, allot, ascribe, assign, attribute, blame, censure, charge, credit, incriminate, indict, lay, recriminate, refer, relate, tax
**imputer** accuser, betrayer, informer
**in** accordingly, amid, among, approved, chic, coming, en (F), encircled, inside, internally, popular, prevalent, regarding, standard, within
**in ABC sequence** alphabetical
**in abeyance** abeyant, pending, shelved, suspended
**inability** disability, disqualification, handicap, impotence, inadequacy, incapability, incapacity, incompetence, powerlessness, weakness
**inability to breathe** apnoea
**inability to chew** amesesis
**inability to concentrate** aprosexia
**inability to construct sentences** acataphasia
**inability to differentiate tones** amusia
**inability to feed** aphagia
**inability to feel** anaphia, anaesthesia
**inability to feel pain** analgesia, analgia
**inability to focus images on the retina** ametropia
**inability to hear** deaf
**inability to identify objects** agnosia
**inability to learn** ineducability
**inability to move** inertia, paralysis
**inability to pronounce words** alexia, aphemia, aphonia
**inability to read** alexia
**inability to resist something** weakness
**inability to see clearly in bright light** hemeralopia
**inability to see near objects clearly** hyperopia
**inability to sleep** insomnia
**inability to smell** anosmia
**inability to speak** alalia, aphonia, aphony, dumbness
**inability to stand up** astasia
**inability to swallow** aphagia
**inability to take action** ab(o)ulia
**inability to taste** ageusis
**inability to understand speech** aphasia
**inability to vocalise** alalia
**inability to walk** abasia, crippled
**inability to write** agraphia, dysgraphia

**inability to write coherently** dysgraphia
**in a bland manner** blindly
**in abnormal place** ectopic
**in a body** en masse
**in absence of** without
**in abundance** ample, galore, oversupplied, plenty
**in a catastrophic way** disastrously
**inaccessible** impassable, isolated, obscure, remote, unapproachable, unattainable, unfrequented
**in accord** agreeable, en rapport (F), united
**in accordance** along
**in accordance with** per
**in accordance with the law** de jure
**inaccuracy** blunder, carelessness, defect, erratum, error, fault(iness), imprecision, inexactness, miscalculation, mistake, slip, unfaithfulness, unreliability
**inaccurate** careless, defective, erroneous, faulty, imprecise, incorrect, inexact, loose, mistaken, out, unfaithful, unreliable, unsound, unspecific, wild, wrong
**in a circle** around
**in a coma** comatose, drowsy
**in action** active, afoot, idleness, immobility, inactively, inertia, on, rest, stagnation, torpor
**inaction** idleness, inertness, sluggishness
**inactive** apathetic, dormant, fallow, idle, immobile, indifferent, indolent, inert, inoperative, lazy, passive, sedentary, sluggish, stagnant, still, supine, unenthusiastic, uninterested, unmoved, unmoving
**inactive as during sleep** dormant
**inactive form of an insect** pupa
**inactive job** sinecure
**in active opposition** antagonistic
**inactivity** dormancy, inaction, indolence, inertia, inertness, quiescence, sloth, torpor, unemployment
**in actual being** in esse
**in addition** additionally, again, also, and, besides, else, further, moreover, thereto, too, yet
**in addition to** also, and, else, plus
**in addition to that already said** moreover
**in a delicate manner** airily
**in a delightful way** wonderfully
**inadequacy** dearth, defect(iveness), deficiency, failing, fault(iness), imperfection, inability, inaptness, incompetence, incompetency, ineffectiveness, inefficacy,

insufficiency, lack, meagreness, paucity, poverty, scantiness, shortage, shortcoming, skimpiness, unfitness, unsuitableness, want, weakness
**inadequate** bare, defective, deficient, imperfect, inapt, incapable, incommensurate, incompetent, incomplete, inefficient, inferior, insufficient, meagre, mediocre, scant(y), short, skimpy, unable, unequal, unfit, unqualified, unsuitable
**inadequate amount** deficiency
**in a different way** afresh, anew, otherwise, timidly
**in a direct line** lineal, linear
**inadmissible** disallowed, immaterial, inappropriate, incompetent, irrelevant, prohibited, unacceptable, unallowable, unqualified
**in a doomed way** fatally
**in advance** ahead, before(hand), earlier, early, first, forward, prematurely, previously, prior, sooner
**in advance of** ahead, before
**inadvertent** accidental, careless, casual, chance, forgetful, heedless, inattentive, indifferent, negligent, offhand, regardless, remiss, slack, thoughtless, unconscious, unintended, unintentional, unplanned, unpremeditated, unthinking
**inadvertently** carelessly, casually, forgetfully, heedlessly, inattentively, inconsiderately, indifferently, neglectfully, negligently, randomly, remissly, slackly, thoughtlessly, unawares, unconsciously, undesignedly, unintentionally, unmindfully, unthinkingly, unwarily, unwittingly
**inadvertent mistake** oversight
**inadvisable** daft, foolish, ill-advised, impolitic, imprudent, indiscreet, inexpedient, injudicious, misguided, unwise
**in a dying state** moribund
**in a few words** briefly
**in a fickle manner** capriciously
**in a flutter** pit-a-pat
**in a foreign country** abroad
**in a free and lively manner** capriccioso
**in a frenzy** amok, amuck, frantic
**in a gaudy manner** garishly
**in a gay manner** gaily
**in a high degree** extremely, very
**in a higher place** above
**in a higher position** upper
**in a human manner** humanly
**in a jaunty manner** airily

**inalienable** absolute, inherent, inviolable, non-negotiable, non-transferable, permanent, positive, sacrosanct, unassailable, unforfeitable, untransferable
**in a line** arow
**in a little while** anon
**in all but name** virtual
**in all conscience** assuredly, certainly, honestly
**in all directions** around
**in all haste** amain
**in alliance** united
**in all places** everywhere, ubiquitous
**in all seriousness** au grand sérieux (F)
**in a lower place** beneath
**in a lower position** under
**in a middle position** between
**in a minute** immediately, presently, shortly, soon
**inamorato** lover
**in a more excellent manner** better
**in an agitated manner** agitato
**in an appropriate manner** accordingly
**in a natural or unrefined state** crude
**in and out** irregular, through
**inane** daft, empty, fatuous, foolish, frivolous, futile, idiotic, inept, mindless, nutty, obtuse, puerile, senseless, silly, stupid, trifling, unimaginative, unintelligent, vacuous, vain, vapid, void, worthless
**in an elated manner** ecstatically
**inanely foolish** fatuous
**in a nervous way** tensely
**in an extreme degree** extremely
**inanimate** dead, defunct, inert, lifeless, spiritless
**inanimate object** it
**inanimate object worshipped by savages** fetish
**in an inconsistent and unpredictable way** erratically
**in an inferior condition** worse
**in an instant** jiffy, trice
**in an oblique direction** askew
**in another place** elsewhere, in alio loco (L), there
**in another way** differently
**in an out-of-way place** isolated
**in anticipation** beforehand
**in an undertone** sotto voce
**in an unfitting manner** inappropriately
**in an unhealthy manner** insalubriously
**in an unintelligent manner** stupidly
**in a nutshell** briefly
**in any case** anyhow, en tout cas (F)
**in any manner** anyhow
**in a place** at
**inapplicable** inapposite, inappropriate, inapt, irrelevant, unsuitable, unsuited

**inappropriate** ill-suited, impractical, improper, inapt, incompatible, incongruous, inexpedient, irrelevant, tactless, unapt, unfair, unfit, unjust, unseemly, unsuitable, unsuited, untimely, untoward
**inappropriate lack of seriousness** levity
**in a proper manner** duly
**inapt** awkward, clumsy, dull, gauche, ill-fitted, ill-suited, ill-timed, inapposite, inappropriate, incapable, inept, slow, stupid, tactless, unfit, unfortunate, unhappy, unsuitable, unsuited
**in a roundabout way** indirectly, obliquely
**in arrears** behind, late, overdue, owed, payable, unpaid
**inarticulate** blurred, dumb, faltering, halting, hesitant, incoherent, incomprehensible, indistinct, muffled, mumbled, mute, silent, tongue-tied, unclear, unintelligible, unspoken, unuttered, unvoiced, voiceless, wordless
**in a rut** stultified
**in a short time** anon, presently, soon
**in a singing manner** cantabile
**in a skilful manner** ably
**inasmuch as** because, since
**in association with** among(st)
**in a state** agitated, anxious, distressed, disturbed, flustered, ruffled, upset
**in a state of coma** comatose
**in a state of eager expectation** agog
**in a state of mental confusion** mixed up
**in a state of motion** agoing
**in a state of nature** bare, exposed, in puris naturalibus (L), naked, nude, unclothed, uncovered, undressed
**in a state of pupillage** in statu pupillari (L)
**in a state of suspension** abeyance
**in a stir** agitated
**in a straight line** alignment
**in a strange manner** queerly
**in a superior way** better
**inattention** absent-mindedness, abstraction, carelessness, daydreaming, default, disregard, failure, forgetfulness, inadvertence, indifference, laxity, neglect, negligence, omission, oversight, preoccupation, remoteness, shortcoming, slackness, thoughtlessness
**inattentive** absent-minded, careless, distracted, distrait, dreamy, heedless, negligent, preoccupied, regardless, remiss, thoughtless, unheeding, unmindful, vague
**inaudible** faint, imperceptible, indistinct, low, muffled, mumbled, muted, noiseless, silent, stifled
**inaugural** dedicatory, first, initial, introductory, launching, maiden, opening
**inaugurate** begin, commence, commission, consecrate, dedicate, enthrone, establish, induct, initiate, install, instate, institute, introduce, invest, launch, open, ordain, originate, start
**inauspicious** bad, black, discouraging, ill-omened, ominous, threatening, unfavourable, unfortunate, unlucky, unpromising, unpropitious
**in a vacuum** in vacuo (L)
**in a venetian blind** slat
**in a vertical line** apeak
**in a very hungry manner** ravenously
**in a violent frenzy** beserk
**in a way** as, partly
**in bad faith** mala fide
**in bad taste** indecent, offensive
**in battle array** embattle
**in bed** abed, resting
**in between** intermediate
**in black and white** clear, evident, explicit, plain, positive, unmistakeable
**inborn** congenital, connate, genetic, hereditary, inbred, ingrained, inherent, inherited, innate, instinctive, native, natural
**inborn character** nature
**inbred** constitutional, incrossed, ingrained, inherent, innate, native, natural
**in brisk time** allegro
**Inca** Quechuan, Atahualpa
**Inca administrator** curaca
**incalculable** countless, dubious, inestimable, infinite, innumerable, uncertain, uncountable, unpredictable, untold
**incantation** chant, charm, enchantment, magic, mesmerism, necromancy, occultness, repetition, ritual, sorcery, spell, spiritualism, verbalism, verbosity, witchcraft
**incapable** disqualified, feeble, helpless, inadequate, incompetent, ineffective, inept, insufficient, powerless, unable, unfit(ted), unqualified, unsuited, weak
**incapable of attention** giddy
**incapable of being avoided** ineluctable
**incapable of being dissolved** insoluble
**incapable of being educated** ineducable
**incapable of being heard** inaudible

**incapable of being implemented** inoperable
**incapable of being satisfied** insatiable
**incapable of effort** nerveless
**incapable of error** infallible
**incapable of feeling** adamant
**incapacity** disability, disqualification, feebleness, inability, inadequacy, impotence, incapability, incompetency, ineffectiveness, powerlessness, unfitness, weakness
**incapacity to move or feel** paralysis
**incarcerate** check, commit, confine, constrain, constrict, embar, enclose, impound, imprison, intern, jail, restrain
**incarceration** bondage, confinement, imprisonment, restraint
**incarnate** bodily, corporal, corporeal, earthly, embodied, fleshly, mortal, personified, physical, typified
**incarnation** avatar, embodiment, exemplification, manifestation, personification, type
**in case** if, lest, provided
**in case that** if, lest, so
**incautious** careless, hasty, heedless, ill-judged, improvident, imprudent, impulsive, inconsiderate, indiscreet, negligent, precipitate, rash, reckless, thoughtless, unthinking
**incendiary** agitator, arsonist, combustible, demagogue, fire-raiser, firebrand, firebug, flammable, inciting, inflammable, inflammatory, insurgent, provocative, pyromaniac, rabble-rouser, rabble-rousing, revolutionary, seditious, subversive
**incendiary liquid** napalm
**incense** affront, agitate, anger, appreciation, aroma, arouse, balm, enrage, exasperate, excite, fragrance, goad, homage, inflame, infuriate, insult, irk, irritate, joss-stick, madden, offend, perfume, provoke, respect, rile, scent, tribute, worship
**incensed** angry, enraged, frantic, furious, inflamed, infuriate, irate, mad, overwrought, raging, unrestrained, wrathful
**incentive** fillip, goad, impulse, incitement, inducement, motive, spur, stimulus
**incessant** ceaseless, constant, continual, continuous, eternal, frequent, perpetual, relentless, repeated, steady, unceasing, unending, unrelenting, unremitting
**incessantly** endlessly, perpetually
**inch** budge, crawl, creep, dawdle, dislodge, drag, ease, edge, loop, move, pass, propel, push, remove, roll, shift, slide, slither, stir, string, thread, wind, wriggle, writhe
**in character** normal, proper, suitable
**in charge of company funds** treasurer
**in charge of magazines** editor
**inches** crawls, creeps, dawdles, drags, eases, edges, loops, passes, slides, slithers, stirs, writhes, winds
**incidence** amount, commonness, degree, extent, frequency, occurrence, prevalence, range, rate
**incident** act, adventitious, affair, circumstance, circumstantial, concern, doing, episode, event(uality), happening, matter, occasion, occurrence, phenomenon, proceeding
**incidental** accidental, accompanying, ancillary, attendant, casual, chance, contingent, contributory, fortuitous, minor, nonessential, odd, random, related, secondary, subordinate, subsidiary, supplementary
**incidental opinion** obiter dictum
**incinerate** bake, burn, char, cremate, overbake, parch, roast, scorch, scorify, smelt, torrefy
**incineration of body** cremation
**incinerator** crematorium
**in cipher** coded
**incipient** basic, beginning, commencing, developing, early, elementary, genetic, inaugural, inceptive, inchoate, nascent, newborn, original, primal, prime, rudimental, starting
**in circulation** afloat, afoot
**in circumference** around
**incise** carve, chisel, chop, claw, cleave, cut, damage, divide, engrave, etch, furrow, gash, grate, graze, groove, lacerate, mark, nick, notch, penetrate, pierce, rend, rub, score, scrape, scratch, sculpt, sever, slash, slice, slit, split, tear, wound
**incised gem** intaglio
**incision** cleft, cut, gash, nick, notch, opening, scarification, score, scotch, scratch, slash, slit, snick
**incision in colon** colotomy
**incision into white tissue of frontal lobe of brain** lobotomy
**incision in trachea** tracheotomy
**incision in vagina** vaginotomy
**incisive** acerbic, acid, acrid, acute, alert, astringent, astute, biting, caustic, censorious, cutting, cynical, disparaging, ironic, judicious, keen, mordant, penetrating, perceptive, perspicacious, piercing, sarcastic, sardonic, satirical, severe, sharp, smart, stinging, tart, trenchant
**incite** abet, actuate, agitate, arouse, back, drive, edge, egg, encourage, excite, foment, goad, hound, impel, influence, instigate, prod, prompt, provoke, push, rouse, spur, stimulate, stir, thrust, urge
**incite by encouragement** abet
**incitement** encouragement, excitement, goad, hounding, impetus, impulse, instigation, motivation, motive, provocation, spur, stimulus
**inciter** agitator, demagogue, firebrand, fomenter, instigator, rabble-rouser, revolutionary, setter-on, troublemaker
**incite to action** egg
**incite to sin** tempt
**inciting** inflaming, instigating, prompting, provoking, rousing, spurring, stimulating, urging
**incivility** acerbity, affront, aspersion, bluntness, brusquerie, coarseness, discourteousness, discourtesy, disrespect, impertinence, impoliteness, indecorum, insult, misbehaviour, provocation, rudeness, snub, unmannerliness, vulgarity
**inclement** bad, bitter, boisterous, cruel, foul, grim, harsh, implacable, intemperate, pitiless, remorseless, rigorous, rough, severe, stormy, tempestuous, unkind, unrelenting, violent, windy
**inclination** aptness, bent, bevel, bias, cant, cast, drift, fondness, grade, gradient, leaning, love, passion, penchant, predilection, predisposition, preference, proclivity, proneness, propensity, rake, slant, slope, tendency, tilt, trend, turn, will
**inclination of mind** propensity
**inclination to believe too readily** credulity
**inclination to vomit** nausea
**incline** acclivity, angle, ascent, bank, bend, bevel, cant, choose, descent, deviate, dip, drop, fall, grade, hill, inclination, lean, motivate, pitch, ramp, rise, slant, slope, sway, tend, tilt, tip, trend, turn, veer
**incline beforehand** predispose
**inclined** angled, apt, aslope, atilt, bearing, bevelled, descending, diagonal, disposed, given, graded, leaning, leant, likely, liable, oblique, pitched, rising, sagging, slanted, sloped, sloping, steep, swerving, tilting, verging, willing
**inclined path** ramp
**inclined to** prone
**inclined to be aloof** offish

**inclined to be friendly** sociable
**inclined to be sympathetic**
    well-disposed
**inclined to be thin** lean
**inclined to delay** dilatory
**inclined to disbelieve** sceptical
**inclined to fear** timid
**inclined to fighting** bellicose
**inclined to laugh** risible
**inclined to sickness** queasy
**inclined to sue** litigious
**inclined to suspend judgement**
    sceptical
**inclined to vomit** nauseous, sick
**inclined trough** chute
**inclined walkway** ramp
**incline from perpendicular** bend
**incline from the vertical** hade
**incline head** nod
**incline to one side** list
**in close order** serried
**in close proximity** near
**include** comprehend, comprise,
    contain, embrace, entail, involve
**included Aegean isles** Ionian
**inclusion** addition, incorporation,
    insertion, involvement
**inclusive** compendious,
    comprehensive, comprising,
    embracing, encircling, enclosing,
    extensive, general, surrounding
**inclusive of all** overall
**incogitant** thoughtless
**incognito** alias, anonymous, cloaked,
    covert, disguised, fake, false,
    feigned, masked, nameless,
    obscure, pretend, pseudonym,
    unacknowledged, unindentified,
    unknown, unmarked, unnamed,
    unrecognisable, unrecognised,
    unsigned, unsung, veiled
**incognizant** careless, heedless,
    ignorant, inattentive, innocent,
    napping, thoughtless, unaware,
    unconscious, unenlightened,
    uninitiated, unmindful, unprepared,
    unsuspecting
**incoherence** brokenness, confusion,
    contrariness, deviation, difference,
    discord, disjointedness, illogicality,
    inarticulateness, incompatibleness,
    inconsistency, mumbling, rambling,
    unconnectedness, unintelligibility,
    variance, wildness
**incoherent** confused, contradictory,
    contrary, detached, different,
    disconnected, discrepant,
    disordered, illogical, inarticulate,
    irrational, loose, muddled,
    murmured, scrambled, straying,
    unconnected

**incoherent speech** gibberish, jargon,
    mutter
**in cold blood** brutally, deliberately,
    intentionally, knowingly
**income** earnings, gain, interest,
    means, pay, proceeds, profits,
    receipts, return, revenue, salary,
    stipend, takings, wages
**income from taxes** revenue
**incomer** outsider
**in commission** operating, running,
    working
**in commotion** wroth
**in compact formation** serried
**in company** together
**incomparable** brilliant, exceptional,
    exquisite, inimitable, matchless,
    paramount, peerless, rare, superb,
    superior, superlative, supreme,
    transcendent, unequalled, unique,
    unmatchable, unmatched,
    unparalleled, unrivalled
**incompatible** adverse, antagonistic,
    contradictory, contrary, discordant,
    factious, hostile, ill-assorted,
    inconsistent, inconsonant,
    irreconcilable, opposed, opposite,
    unbecoming, uncomplementary,
    uncongenial, unsuitable, unsuited
**incompatibly** conflictingly,
    discordantly, incongruously,
    inconsistently, unsuitably
**incompetence** bungling, disability,
    disenablement, disentitlement,
    disqualification, elimination,
    exclusion, feebleness, frailty,
    impotence, inability, inadequacy,
    incapability, incapacity, inefficiency,
    ineligibility, ineptness, infirmity,
    paralysis, rejection, stupidity,
    uselessness, weakness
**incompetent** awkward, clumsy,
    deficient, helpless, ignorant,
    inadequate, incapable, ineffective,
    ineffectual, inefficient, inept,
    inexpert, insufficient, maladroit,
    unable, unapt, unequal, unfit(ted),
    unhandy, unqualified, unskilful,
    useless
**incompetent athlete** bum
**incompetently** ineffectually,
    inefficiently, ineptly, inexpertly,
    insufficiently, unskilfully, uselessly
**incomplete** broken, defective,
    deficient, fragmentary, imperfect,
    insufficient, lacking, part(ial), short,
    sketchy, undeveloped, undone,
    unfinished, wanting
**in complete agreement** unanimous
**incomplete development of an organ**
    aplasia, hypoplasia
**incomplete skull** calvaria

**incomprehensible** baffling, enigmatic,
    impenetrable, inconceivable,
    inscrutable, mysterious, obscure,
    opaque, perplexing, puzzling,
    unfathomable, unintelligible
**inconceivable** implausible, impossible,
    incredible, mind-boggling,
    staggering, unbelievable, unheard
    of, unimaginable, unknowable,
    unthinkable
**in concert** collectively, concertedly,
    jointly, mutually, prearranged,
    together, united
**in conclusion** eventually, finally, lastly,
    ultimately
**inconclusive** ambiguous, indecisive,
    indeterminate, open, uncertain,
    unconvincing, undecided,
    unsatisfying, unsettled, vague
**in confidence** entre nous, sub rosa
**in conflict** inconsistent, irreconcilable
**in confusion** hugger-mugger,
    hurry-scurry
**incongruity** abnormality, absurdity,
    anomaly, conflict, craziness,
    departure, eccentricity, exception,
    folly, foolishness, idiocy,
    inappropriateness, incompatibility,
    inconsistency, irrationality,
    irregularity, joke, ludicrousness,
    nonsense, oddity, peculiarity, rarity,
    senselessness, silliness, stupidity,
    unsuitability, variance
**incongruous** absurd, alien,
    anomalous, arbitrary, contradictory,
    contrary, defiant, deviating,
    disagreeing, discordant, discrepant,
    disparate, displaced, dissonant,
    extraneous, inappropriate, inapt,
    incompatible, inconsistent,
    inconsonant, independent,
    inharmonious, rigid, sullen,
    unconformable, unfitting, unknown,
    unreasonable, unseemly, unsuitable
**incongruous mixture** motley
**in conjunction with** together
**in consequence** accordingly, because,
    consequently, following, hence,
    thereby
**in consequence of that** thereby
**inconsequential** commonplace,
    everyday, extraneous, frivolous,
    immaterial, impertinent, inapposite,
    incidental, inconsiderable,
    inessential, insignificant, irrelevant,
    little, meaningless, minor, negligible,
    paltry, petty, puny, slight, small,
    trifling, trite, trivial, unimportant,
    valueless, worthless
**inconsequential talk** prattle
**inconsiderable** exiguous, few, flimsy,
    infrequent, insignificant, insufficient,

irrelevant, light, meagre, meaningless, mere, minor, minute, negligible, nugatory, paltry, petty, rare, scant(y), scarce, scattered, small, sparse, sporadic, thin, tiny, trifling, trivial, unimportant, unsubstantial

**inconsiderate** careless, harsh, ill-advised, inattentive, indiscreet, injudicious, insensitive, intolerant, misguided, rash, reckless, regardless, rude, self-centred, selfish, severe, tactless, thoughtless, unkind, unthinking, unthoughtful, unwise

**inconsiderate** careless, impolite, insensitive, rude, tactless, thoughtless

**inconsistency** confusion, contrast, difference, disagreement, discrepancy, disparity, dissonance, divergence, inconstancy, instability, mutability, paradox, unsteadiness, variance

**inconsistent** changeable, contradictory, discrepant, divergent, erratic, fickle, inappropriate, incoherent, incompatible, incongruous, inconstant, inharmonious, paradoxical, reasonless, unsteady, volatile

**inconsistent and unpredictable** erratic

**inconsolable** anxious, brokenhearted, crestfallen, dejected, depressed, desolate(d), despairing, desperate, despondent, devastated, disappointed, disconsolate, downcast, frantic, grief-stricken, heartbroken, hopeless, melancholy, miserable, mournful, prostrated, sorrowful, suicidal, wretched

**inconsolable bereaved woman** Niobe

**inconspicuous** camouflaged, hidden, insignificant, low-key, modest, muted, ordinary, plain, quiet, retiring, unassuming, unobtrusive, unostentatious, unremarkable, unspectacular

**inconstant** capricious, changeable, fickle, inconsistent, mercurial, moody, uncertain, unstable, volatile

**inconstant person** chameleon, weathercock

**in contact with** against

**in contrast to** against

**incontrovertible** certain, clear, established, incontestable, indisputable, indubitable, irrefutable, positive, self-evident, sure, undeniable, unquestionable, unshakable

**inconvenience** annoyance, awkwardness, bother, burden, cumber, difficulty, disadvantage, discomfort, disruption, disturbance, drawback, fuss, hindrance, impede, nuisance, trouble, uneasiness, unfitness, unsettle, untimeliness, upset, vexation

**inconvenient** annoying, awkward, disadvantageous, inopportune, troublesome, untimely, vexatious

**inconvenient in size or weight** cumbersome

**incorporate** absorb, amalgamate, assimilate, blend, coalesce, combine, consolidate, contain, embody, fuse, include, integrate, merge, mix, organise, subsume, unite

**incorporate as member** enrol

**incorporated senior member of college** fellow

**incorporation** absorption, amalgamation, assimilation, association, blend, coalition, company, conversion, digestion, federation, fusion, inclusion, insertion, integration, merger, society, transformation, unification, unifying, union

**incorrect** amiss, erroneous, false, faulty, flawed, improper, inaccurate, inexact, mistaken, out, specious, unfitting, unsuitable, untrue, wrong

**incorrect count** error, miscount, mistake

**incorrectly** faulty, improperly, incorrectly, inexactly, mistakenly, speciously, unsuitably

**incorrectly reasoned** illegitimate

**incorrect mark** X

**incorrect name of item** misnomer

**incorrect pronunciation** cacology

**incorrect sum** miscalculation

**incorrect term** misnomer

**incorrect understanding** misperception

**incorrigible** hardened, hopeless, incurable, intractable, inveterate, irredeemable, unteachable

**incorruptible** everlasting, honest, honourable, imperishable, just, straight, trustworthy, unbribable, undecaying, upright

**incorruptible judge** Rhadamanthys

**increase** addition, advance, augment, deepen, eke, enlarge(ment), escalate, expand, extend, extension, flourish, gain, greater, grow(th), improve, increment, intensify, issue, multiply, raise, rise, spread, step-up, swell, upturn, wax

**increase by** add
**increase by growth** accrue
**increase by natural growth** accretion
**increase by stages** escalate
**increased activity of heart due to exertion** palpitation
**increase gravity of** aggravate
**increase in bulk** expand
**increase in extent** escalate
**increase in quality** enhance
**increase in salary** rise
**increase in scope** extend
**increase in size** enlarge
**increase in volume** swell
**increase rapidly in numbers** proliferate
**increase the wealth of** aggrandise
**increasing at the summit** acrogenous
**increasing in heat** incalescent
**increasing in reputation** rising
**increasing the secretion of milk** galactopoietic

**incredible** absurd, amazing, astonishing, astounding, extraordinary, fantastic, far-fetched, great, implausible, impossible, improbable, inconceivable, preposterous, remarkable, superb, unbelievable, unimaginable, unthinkable, wonderful

**incredibly absurd** priceless

**incredulity** amazement, apprehension, astonishment, disbelief, disquiet, distrust, doubt(ing), dubiety, fear, misgiving, mistrust, qualm, scepticism, surprise, suspicion, unbelief, wonder

**incredulous** disbelieving, distrustful, doubtful, doubting, dubious, sceptical, suspicious, unbelieving, uncertain, unconvinced

**increment** accretion, addition, advancement, augmentation, enlargement, extension, gain, growth, increase, supplement

**incriminate** accuse, arraign, blame, charge, impeach, implicate, inculpate, indict, involve, recriminate

**incubus** demon, nightmare, spirit

**inculcate** advise, coach, direct, drill, educate, enlighten, guide, impart, implant, infix, inform, infuse, instil, instruct, sow, teach, train, tutor

**inculpate** accuse, affect, associate, charge, concern, connect, implicate, incriminate, indict, involve, touch

**incumbent** beneficiary, cleric, in, obligatory, official, possessor, pressing, reclining, resident, responsible, resting, sojourner, tenant

**incur** acquire, arouse, assume, contract, discover, draw, earn, ensure, experience, incite, invite, procure, provoke, run-up, undergo, welcome

**incurable** contractible, drawable, fatal, hopeless, incorrigible, inducible, inveterate, irrecoverable, irremediable, terminal

**incurably bad** incorrigible

**incur debts** owe

**incur disadvantage** lose

**incursion** arrival, assault, attack, charge, flow, foray, impingement, inflow, influx, inroad, inrush, invasion, irruption, offensive, onset, onslaught, penetration, raid, rush, sally, seizure, sortie, strike

**incus of the ear** anvil

**in days of yore** heretofore

**in debt** accountable, behind, bound, liable, owe, owing, responsible, straitened

**indebted** answerable, appreciative, bankrupt, beholden, grateful, insolvent, liable, liquidated, obligated, obliged, outstanding, owed, owing, responsible, thankful, unpaid

**indebtedness** answerability, appreciation, debit, debts, default, failure, gratitude, insolvency, liabilities, obligation, score

**indebted to** owe

**indecency** carnality, crudity, dissipation, filthiness, immodesty, impropriety, indecorum, indelicacy, inelegance, obscenity, repulsivity, rudeness, shamelessness, unaptness, uncivility, uncouthness, unmannerliness, unsuitability, vileness, vulgarity, vulgarness, wantonness

**indecent** coarse, crude, dirty, distasteful, filthy, foul, gross, immodest, improper, impure, indelicate, lewd, licentious, obscene, offensive, outrageous, pornographic, shocking, unrefined, unseemly, vulgar

**indecent in a very offensive way** obscene

**indecent language** scurrilous

**indecent literature** pornography

**indecent pictures** pornography

**indecipherable** cramped, illegible, indistinct, tiny, unclear, unintelligible, unreadable

**indecision** ambivalence, doubt, hesitancy, hesitation, indecisiveness, irresolution, uncertainty, vacillation, wavering

**indecisive** doubtful, faltering, hesitating, inconclusive, indefinite, indeterminate, irresolute, tentative, uncertain, unclear, undecided, undetermined, unsure, vacillating, wavering

**in declamatory style** parlando

**indeed** actually, admittedly, assuredly, aye, certainly, definitely, doubtlessly, exactly, forsooth, positively, precisely, really, strictly, surely, truly, undeniably, verily, yea, yes

**in deep despair** de profundis (L)

**indefatigable** active, assiduous, attentive, brisk, busy, careful, conscientious, constant, determined, diligent, dynamic, earnest, energetic, forceful, forcible, hard-working, immovable, industrious, laborious, lively, obdurate, obstinate, persevering, persistent, pertinacious, potent, powerful, resolute, spirited, steady, strenuous, stubborn, studious, tenacious, tireless, unremitting, unwearying, vigorous

**in default of something better** faute de mieux (F)

**indefensible** defenceless, faulty, inadmissible, inexcusable, insupportable, specious, submissive, surrendering, unarguable, unarmed, unforgivable, unjustifiable, unpardonable, untenable, unwarrantable, weaponless, wrong

**in defiance of** against

**indefinable but distinctive quality** je ne sais quoi (F)

**indefinite** boundless, confused, confusing, dim, doubtful, endless, equivocal, incalculable, indistinct, inexact, infinite, limitless, obscure, undefined, undetermined, unlimited, unsettled, unspecific, vague

**indefinite article** a, an

**indefinite large number** zillion

**indefinitely** ad infinitum, confusedly, continually, doubtfully, endlessly, equivocally, eternally, evasively, generally, imprecisely, inexactly, permanently

**indefinitely many** myriad, umpteen

**indefinite number** any, several, some

**indefinite object** it

**indefinite period** aeon

**indelible** enduring, indestructible, ineffaceable, ineradicable, ingrained, lasting, permanent

**indelicate** coarse, crude, embarrassing, gross, immodest, improper, indecent, low, obscene, off-colour, offensive, risqué, rude, shocking, suggestive, tasteless, unseemly, vulgar

**in demand** admired, celebrated, fashionable, needed, popular, requested

**indemnity** amends, amnesty, atonement, charter, compensation, cover, damages, exemption, fine, franchise, freedom, guarantee, immunity, insurance, liberty, payment, prerogative, privilege, protection, reimbursement, release, remuneration, reparation, restitution, reward, right, satisfaction, security

**indent** bruise, cut, deface, depress, dimple, furrow, gouge, graze, groove, mar, mark, nick, notch, scallop, scratch, serrate, slash, srape

**indented parapet** battlement

**independence** autonomy, emancipation, freedom, individualism, liberty, manumission, self-determination, self-government, self-rule, separation, sovereignty, swaraj, uhuru

**independent** absolute, autonomous, decontrolled, free, impartial, individual(istic), liberated, non-aligned, self-contained, self-determining, self-governing, self-reliant, self-sufficient, self-supporting, separate, sovereign, unaided, unbiased, unconnected, unconstrained, uncontrolled, unconventional, unrelated

**independent community** autonomy, commonwealth

**independent existence** entity

**independent-minded person** maverick

**independent operator** freelance

**independent state in Rome** Vatican City

**independent system of stars** galaxy

**in depth** comprehensively, exhaustively, extensively, intensively, thoroughly

**indescribable** indefinable, ineffable, inexpressible, unutterable

**in despair** au désespoir (F)

**in detail** comprehensively, exhaustively, thoroughly

**indeterminate** imprecise, inconclusive, indefinite, inexact, open-ended, uncertain, undecided, undefined, undetermined, unfixed, unspecified, unstated, vague

**index** clue, director(y), forefinger, guide, hand, indication, indicator, list, mark, needle, pointer, sign, symptom, table, token

**index of matters** index rerum (L)

**index of words** index verborum (L)

**India** Bharat
**Indian aborigine** Bengali
**Indian alcoholic drink** arak, arrack, nipa
**Indian antelope** blackbuck, goral, nilgai, nilghau, nylghau, sasin
**Indian ascetic** fakir
**Indian ballet dance** nau(t)ch
**Indian bamboo mat** tatty
**Indian bird** minah, myna(h)
**Indian boat** d(h)oni
**Indian boy's name** Ali
**Indian buffalo** arnee, arni
**Indian butter** ghee, ghi
**Indian cape** Comorin
**Indian carriage** gharri, gharry
**Indian caste** Ahir, Gaddi, Gola, Jat, Mali, Rajput
**Indian cigarette** biri
**Indian city noted for gem cutting** Golconda
**Indian clarified butter from milk of buffalo or cow** ghee, ghi
**Indian class system** caste
**Indian coast** Malabar
**Indian coin** anna, lac, paisa, rupee, tara
**Indian college** Tol
**Indian condiment** curcuma
**Indian corn** gram, kanga, maize, samp
**Indian cotton carpet** durrie, satrangi
**Indian currency** rupee
**Indian curtain** d(h)urrie
**Indian custom** dastur
**Indian dance** nau(t)ch
**Indian desert** Thar
**Indian dialect** Hindo(o)stani
**Indian dish** curry
**Indian district** Goa, Malabar, Mofussel, Nasik, Patna, Satara, Sibi, Simla, Zillah
**Indian dress** saree, sari
**Indian elephant** hathi
**Indian fabric** shela(h)
**Indian festival** mela
**Indian fig** banian, banyan, bunyan
**Indian fish** flatfish
**Indian flat unleavened bread** roti
**Indian flour** at(t)a
**Indian foodstuff** d(h)al, dholl, ghee, lentils
**Indian foot soldier** peon
**Indian form of address for man** Lala, sahib
**Indian game** pachisi
**Indian garment** banian, banyan, dhoti, kurta, saree, sari
**Indian gesture in dances** mudra
**Indian gown** saree, sari
**Indian grant** cowle, enam, jaghir, sasan
**Indian grass** dura
**Indian groom** sais, sice, syce

**Indian guide** shikari
**Indian guitar** yina
**Indian guitar-like instrument** sitar
**Indian gulf** Cambay, Kutch, Mannar
**Indian guru** swami
**Indian gymnasium** akhara
**Indian hand-spun cloth** khaddar
**Indian hardwood** sal
**Indian harem** zenana
**Indian hat** topi
**Indian headdress** topknot, turban
**Indian hemp** bhang, dagga, ganja, ke(i)f, kif, marijuana, ramie, sunn
**Indian hemp plant** bhang
**Indian holy man** sad(d)hu
**Indian hunter** shikari
**Indian island** Chilka, Diu
**Indian king** maharaja(h), raja(h)
**Indian kingdom** Nepal
**Indian lady** begum, memsahib
**Indian lake** Chilka, Colair, Dhebar, Sambahr, Wular
**Indian language** Bengali, Gujarati, Hindi, Marathi, Pali, Sanskrit, Tamil, Telugu, Urdu
**Indian language of south** Tamil
**Indian leader** Mohandas Gandhi
**Indian leather sandal** chappal
**Indian loin cloth** d(h)oti, lungee, lungi
**Indian loose-fitting shirt** banian, banyan
**Indian lotus** nelumbo
**Indian lute** sitar
**Indian mahogany** rohan, toon
**Indian man's loincloth** lungi
**Indian meal** atta, curry
**Indian men's high-collared coat** sherwani
**Indian millet** dari, doura, dourah, durra, ragi, sorghum
**Indian moccasin** pac
**Indian monkey** rhesus
**Indian monument** Taj Mahal
**Indian music** raga
**Indian musical instrument** sitar, vina
**Indian muskrat** ondatra
**Indian nurse** amah, ayah, dhai
**Indian Ocean gulf** Aden
**Indian Ocean island** Mahe, Mauritius, Reunion
**Indian Ocean islands** Comoros, Maldives, Nicobar, Seychelles
**Indian ocean vessel** dhow
**Indian of lowest Hindu caste** Harijan, Pariah, Shudra, untouchable
**Indian of Mexico** Aztec, Mam, Opato, Otomi, Toltec
**Indian of Peru** Inca, Kechua, Quechua, Quichua
**Indian orchid** faam
**Indian or Chinese** Asiatic
**Indian ox** zebu

**Indian palm tree** nipa
**Indian peasant** ryot
**Indian percussion instrument** tabla
**Indian physician** hakeem, hakim
**Indian plant yielding fragrant oil** pa(t)chouli, patchouly
**Indian port** Calcutta, Madras
**Indian Portuguese possession** Goa
**Indian potato** sunflower, yam
**Indian prince** maharaja(h), raja(h)
**Indian prince in former times** nawab
**Indian princess** (maha)rani, ranee
**Indian pulse** d(h)al, dholl
**Indian queen** ranee, rani
**Indian rainy season** monsoon, varsha
**Indian red wood** toon
**Indian region** Malabar
**Indian religion** Hindu, Moslem, Muslim
**Indian religious teacher** guru, (maha)rishi, swami
**Indian rhythmic music** tala
**Indian rice dish** biriani, biryan
**Indian river fish** mahseer
**Indian robber** dacoit
**Indian robe** saree, sari
**Indian rock snake** krait
**Indian rubber** caoutchouc
**Indian rural worker** ryot
**Indian sacred city** Banaras, Benares, Varanasi
**Indian sailor** lascar
**Indian servant** s(a)ice, syce
**Indian sir** sahib
**Indian's light turban** puchree, puggaree, pug(g)ree
**Indian social class** Brahmin, caste, Kshatriya, Sudra, Vaisya, varna
**Indian social custom** dharma
**Indian social system** caste
**Indian soldier** Jawan, lascar, peon, sepoy
**Indian soldier formerly serving under British command** sepoy
**Indian song** raga
**Indian spice** cardamom
**Indian sports ground** maidan
**Indian spotted deer** axis
**Indian stag** sambar, sambur
**Indian state** Assam, Bihar, Gujarat, Kerala, Manipur, Mysore, Orissa, Punjab
**Indian statesman** Gandhi, Nehru
**Indian stringed instrument** sarangi, sitar, tamboura
**Indian tailor** durzi
**Indian temple** pagoda
**Indian tenant farmer** ryot
**Indian timber tree** sal
**Indian title** saheb, sahib, Sri
**Indian tobacco plant** lobelia
**Indian tongue** Tamil

**Indian tree** emblica, gaub, margosa, palay, toon
**Indian tribe** Ao, Awan, Bheel, Bhil, Turi, Wea
**Indian trooper** sowar
**Indian turban** pugree, seerband
**Indian vocal music without words** alap
**Indian washerman** dhobi
**Indian water vessel** lota(n), loto
**Indian wayside stop** parao
**Indian weaver bird** baya
**Indian weight** tola
**Indian wet nurse** amah
**Indian wheat** sujee, suji
**Indian wild buffalo** arna, arnee, arni
**Indian wild dog** dhole
**Indian woman's dress** saree, sari
**Indian woman's short-sleeved bodice** choli
**Indian woman's veil** purdah
**indicate** betoken, connote, denote, designate, disclose, display, evidence, evince, express, imply, manifest, mark, point, read, record, register, reveal, show, signal, signify, specify, state, suggest, tell
**indicate as guilty** incriminate
**indicate assent** nod
**indicated earlier** aforegiven, aforesaid, aforestated
**indicates direction** to
**indicates position** at
**indicates twelve** dodeca-
**indicate with finger** point
**indicate wrongly** misdirect
**indicating a cell** cyto-
**indicating a diseased condition** -(i)asis
**indicating a dream** oneiro-
**indicating a tumour** -oma
**indicating dryness** xero-
**indicating external** ecto-
**indicating fear** timid, timorous
**indicating fermentation** zym(o)-
**indicating lack** dis-
**indicating love** affectionate
**indicating medical care or treatment** -iatric
**indicating outside** ecto-
**indicating presence of divinity** numinous
**indicating relationships** of
**indicating removal or release** dis-
**indicating reversal** dis-
**indicating the brain** encephal(o)-
**indicating the colour green** chloro-
**indicating unmarried name** née
**indication** betoken, clue, denomination, denote, denotation, evidence, evince, explanation, hint, imply, index, indicate, inkling, intimation, manifest(ation), mark, note, omen, reveal, show, sign(al), signify, suggest(ion), symptom, warning
**indication of illness** symptom
**indication of something to come** omen, presage
**indication of something undesirable coming** threat
**indication to convey some meaning** sign
**indicative** average, characteristic, classic, eloquent, essential, expressive, knowing, meaning, model, normal, orthodox, representative, significant, standard, stock, suggestive, symptomatic, typical, usual
**indicative sign** pointer
**indicator** blinker, display, gauge, guide, index, mark(er), meter, pointer, sign(al), signpost, symbol, winker
**indicator disc** dial
**indicator of an alternative** or
**Indic language** Hindi, Urdu
**indict** accuse, arraign, attain, charge, complain, frame, impeach, litigate, prosecute, punish, sue, summons, tax
**indictable offence** misdemeanour
**indict before tribunal** arraign
**indictment** accusation, acte d'accusation (F), allegation, arraignment, charge, impeachment, incrimination, prosecution, summons
**indifference** aloofness, apathy, callousness, carelessness, coldness, coolness, detachment, disinterestedness, disregard, equity, inattention, negligence, neutrality, nonchalance, triviality, unconcern, unimportance
**indifference in religion** adiaphorism
**indifferent** aloof, apathetic, average, blasé, callous, careless, cold, cool, detached, distant, fair, heedless, impervious, inattentive, insensible, mediocre, middling, moderate, neutral, nonchalant, ordinary, passable, perfunctory, poco curante (I), regardless, unconcerned, unimpressed, uninspired, unmindful, unmoved, unresponsive
**indifferent and haughty** supercilious
**indifferent to criticism** thick-skinned
**indigence** bankruptcy, beggary, depression, destitution, indebtedness, insolvency, lack, need(iness), pauperism, pennilessness, penury, poverty, slum(p), starvation, want

**indigenous** aboriginal, congenital, endemic, immanent, implanted, inborn, ingenerate, ingrained, innate, intrinsic, local, native, original, rooted
**indigenous inhabitant** aborigine, native
**indigent** bankrupt, barefoot, beggar(ly), destitute, impoverished, lacking, necessitous, needy, pauper(ised), penniless, penurious, poor, poverty-stricken, ragged, ruined, wanting
**indigestion** cardialgia, dyspepsia, heartburn, hyperacidity, nausea, queasiness
**indignant** angry, annoyed, disgruntled, exasperated, fuming, furious, heated, incensed, irate, livid, mad, outraged, resentful, riled, scornful, wrathful
**indignation** anger, exasperation, fury, ire, (out)rage, resentment, scorn, umbrage, wax, wrath
**indignity** abuse, affront, contempt, contumely, disgrace, dishonour, disrespect, humiliation, injury, insolence, insult, offence, opprobrium, outrage, reproach, rudeness, scorn, shock, slight, snub, violation, violence
**indigo** anil, dye, pigment, woad
**indirect** ancillary, circuitous, crooked, devious, implicit, incidental, meandering, oblique, rambling, roundabout, secondary, subsidiary, tortuous, unintended, wandering, winding, zigzag
**indirect and cagey** evasive
**indirect consequence** repercussion
**indirect course** detour
**in direction of** towards
**in direct relation** en rapport (F)
**indirect route** detour
**indiscernible** ambiguous, bleary, blurred, confused, dim, doubtful, faint, hazy, hidden, imperceptible, indefinite, indeterminate, indistinct, invisible, minute, misty, obscure, shadowy, tiny, unapparent, unclear, undiscernible, unfathomable, unintelligible, unseen, vague, weak
**indiscreet** bold, brash, foolhardy, foolish, harebrained, hasty, ill-advised, ill-judged, immodest, impolitic, improper, imprudent, indecent, indelicate, mindless, precipitate, rash, thoughtless, uncircumspect, unseemly, untactful, unwise
**indiscreet act** gaffe
**indiscreet action** faux pas

**indiscretion** absurdity, boob, brick, carelessness, error, faux pas, folly, foolishness, gaffe, idiocy, imbecility, imprudence, inaccuracy, irrationality, irresponsibility, lunacy, madness, mistake, neglect, negligence, nonsense, omission, rashness, recklessness, remissness, silliness, slackness, slip, stupidity, tactlessness, thoughtlessness
**indiscriminate** aimless, careless, confused, desultory, general, haphazard, indiscriminating, miscellaneous, mixed, motley, promiscuous, random, sweeping, uncritical, undiscriminating, undistinguishable, undistinguishing, unmethodical, unselective, unsystematic, wholesale
**indiscriminate collector** magpie
**indiscriminate killing** massacre
**in disguise** incognito, unidentified, unknown
**in disorder** haywire
**in disorderly haste** helter-skelter
**in disorderly manner** anyhow
**indispensability** essentiality
**indispensable** basic, certain, compulsory, crucial, essential, fundamental, imperative, important, key, material, necessary, needed, obligatory, pressing, required, requisite, rudimentary, substantive, unavoidable, urgent, vital
**indispensable condition** conditio sine qua non (L)
**indisposed** ailing, averse, ill, laid up, loath, reluctant, sick, unwell
**indisposed to activity** indolent
**indisposed to exertion** indolent, languid, lazy
**indisposition** ailment, illness, sickness
**indisputable** absolute, apparent, certain, evident, incontestable, incontrovertible, irrefutable, manifest, obvious, positive, sure, unanswerable, undeniable, unquestionable
**in dispute** antagonistic
**in disrepair** dilapidated
**in distant past** long ago
**indistinct** ambiguous, blurred, confused, dim, distant, doubtful, dubious, faded, faint, feeble, fuzzy, hazy, ill-defined, indefinite, misty, mumbled, nebulous, obscure, shadowy, uncertain, unclear, undefined, unintelligible, vague
**indistinctly** faintly, hazily, indefinitely, mistily, obscurely, unintelligently, vaguely, weakly
**indistinctly felt** dull

**indistinct vision of near objects in old age** presbyopia
**indite** compose, correspond, dictate, draft, draw, edit, formulate, frame, pen, redact, redo, revise, scrawl, scribble, transcribe, type, write
**individual** being, bloke, body, chap, character(istic), creature, custom, discreet, distinct, exclusive, fellow, identical, man, mortal, oke, one, ou, own, particular, party, peculiar, person(al), private, proper, respective, separate, several, single, singular, somebody, soul, special, specific, type, unique, unit
**individual animal or plant** organism
**individual example** specimen
**individual human being** person
**individuality** character, distinction, haecceity, originality, personality, uniqueness
**individual nature of a person** character
**individual performance** solo
**individual performer** soloist
**individual taste** fancy
**indoctrinate** brainwash, coach, discipline, drill, educate, ground, imbue, induct, initiate, instate, instruct, introduce, invest, prepare, prime, school, teach, train, tutor, verse
**indoctrination** brainwashing, breeding, civilisation, cultivation, culture, development, discipline, edification, education, enlightenment, erudition, improvement, instruction, knowledge, scholarship, training, tutoring
**Indo-European person** Slav
**indolence** dullness, heaviness, idleness, inactivity, indolence, inertia, lassitude, laziness, slackness, sloth, slowness, stagnation, tardiness, vegetation
**indolent** apathetic, dilatory, drowsy, idle, inactive, inert, lackadaisical, languid, lazy, lethargic, listless, otiose, resting, slack, slothful, slow, sluggish, soporific, stagnant, torpid
**indolent person** lazy-bones, shirker, slacker
**indomitable** indefatigable, invincible, invulnerable, resolute, unconquerable, unyielding
**indomitable courage** grit
**Indonesian boat** prau
**Indonesian dish** satay
**Indonesian island** Aroe, Aru, Bali, Borneo, Java, Madura, Sumatra, Timor
**Indonesian island group** Kai, Obi

**Indonesian money** sen
**indoor display area** showroom
**indoor plant** aspidistra, cactus, fern, ficus
**indoor shoe** slipper
**in doubt** in dubio (L)
**in drinking person's health** prosit (G)
**indubitable** certain, evident, incontrovertible, indisputable, irrefutable, obvious, sure, unarguable, undeniable, undoubted
**indubitably** incontrovertibly, indisputably, unarguably, undoubtedly, unquestionably
**induce** actuate, cause, convince, effect, impel, incite, inspire, instigate, motivate, move, occasion, persuade, produce, prompt, propel, seduce
**inducement** cause, encouragement, impetus, incentive, influence, inspiration, instigating, lure, motive, occasion, persuasion, provocation, reason, stimulus
**inducement of sleep** hypnosis
**induce to give up habit** wean
**inducing disease** peccant
**inducing drowsiness** somnolent
**inducing flow of saliva** sialagogue, sialogogue
**inducing indolence** lazy
**inducing milk secretion** galactagogue
**inducing sleep** narcotic, somniferous, somnific, soporific
**inducing vomiting** emetic
**induction** admission, baptism, conclusion, consecration, debut, deduction, enthronement, generalisation, inauguration, inference, initiation, installation, institution, introduction, investiture, launch, ordination, presentation
**induction ceremony** initiation
**in due course** eventually, finally
**indulge** allow, coddle, cosset, favour, foster, gratify, humour, mollycoddle, pamper, permit, pet, regale, satiate, satisfy, spoil, suffer
**indulge in nostalgia** reminisce
**indulgence** courtesy, excess, extravagance, favour, fondness, forbearance, intemperance, kindness, leniency, luxury, partiality, patience, profligacy, spoiling, tolerance, understanding
**indulgent** compliant, easy-going, favourable, fond, forbearing, generous, gentle, gratifying, kind, lenient, liberal, mild, permissive, tender, tolerant, understanding
**indulge oneself** bask, luxuriate, wallow
**indulging in personal whims** faddish

**indurate** brace, buttress, fortify, gird, harden, nerve, reinforce, steel, strengthen, toughen
**indurated** bony, hard, sclerous
**industrial city in Germany** Solingen
**industrial city in Japan** Amagasaki
**industrial diamond** bo(a)rt
**industrialist** boss, builder, capitalist, constructor, magnate, manufacturer, producer, tycoon
**industrial product** output
**industrial strike** walk-out
**industrious** assiduous, brisk, busy, diligent, dynamic, energetic, enterprising, forceful, hard-working, intense, persevering, persistent, pertinacious, sedulous, studious, vigorous, virtuous, worksome
**industrious insect** ant, bee
**industrious person** busy bee
**industry** activity, attention, business, commerce, craft, determination, devotedness, diligence, dynamism, effort, employment, enterprise, fabrication, labour, manufacture, manufacturing, occupation, production, sedulity, toil, trade, virtue, work
**in eager excitement** agog
**in eager haste** hotfoot
**in early life** young
**in early stage** beginning, incipient
**inebriate** alcoholic, alkie, boozer, dipsomaniac, dronkie, dronklap, drunk(ard), soak, sot, sponge, tippler, toper, wino
**inebriated** drunk(en), fuddled, intoxicated, maudlin, merry, sozzled, tight, tipsy, well-oiled
**inebriety** alcoholism, bibulousness, dipsomania, drunkenness, imbibing, insobriety, intemperance, intoxication, sottedness, tipsiness, toping
**inedible** deadly, disgusting, fatal, fetid, harmful, hurtful, inconsumable, injurious, lethal, noisome, noxious, offensive, poisonous, rotten, uneatable, unedible, unhealthy
**inedible mushroom** toadstool
**ineffable** incommunicable, indefinable, indescribable, inexpressible, nondescript, unnamable, unspeakable, unutterable
**in effect** actually, basically, effectively, en effet (F), essentially, really, truly, virtually
**ineffective** barren, bootless, feeble, fruitless, futile, idle, impotent, inadequate, ineffectual, inefficient, inept, lame, powerless, unavailing, unproductive, unsuccessful, useless, vain, void, weak, worthless
**in effect, though not in fact** virtual
**ineffectual** futile, impotent, ineffective, pointless, powerless, unavailing, useless, weak
**ineffectual person** wimp
**ineffectual thing** dud
**inefficiency** carelessness, disorganisation, incompetence, muddle, negligence, slackness, sloppiness, waste(fulness)
**inefficient** disorganised, feeble, incapable, incompetent, ineffective, ineffectual, inept, inexpert, money-wasting, negligent, slipshod, sloppy, time-wasting, unworkmanlike, wasteful, weak
**inelastic** close-grained, compact, compressed, concentrated, dense, firm, hard, inflexible, rigid, set, solid(ified), stiff, taut, tense, tight, unbending, unyielding
**inelegant** abrupt, artificial, artless, awkward, bombastic, bungling, coarse, common, constrained, countrified, crude, forced, formal, gauche, graceless, homely, ignorant, inept, inexpert, insensitive, jerky, maladroit, plain, primitive, rude, stiff, tactless, turgid, uncouth, undignified, ungraceful, unpolished, unrefined, unsupple
**in elevated position** high, up
**ineligible** disqualified, improper, incompetent, unacceptable, undesirable, undesirable, unequipped, unfit(ly), unqualified, unseemly, unsuitable, unworthy
**ineluctable** inescapable, relentless
**in empty space** in vacuo (L)
**in England he is a bobby** policeman
**inept** absurd, anomalous, awkward, clumsy, foolish, inane, inappropriate, inapt, incompetent, meaningless, ridiculous, unfit, unhandy, unskilful, unsuitable, unsuited
**inept actor** ham
**inept through lack of practice** rusty
**inequality** bias, difference, disparity, disproportion, dissimilarity, diversity, imparity, irregularity, odds, prejudice, unequalness, unevenness
**in equal quantities** ana
**inequilibrium** disproportion, imbalance
**inequitable** bad, biased, bigoted, close-minded, illegitimate, intolerant, narrow-minded, one-sided, partial, partisan, prejudiced, unfair, unjust(ifiable), unlawful, unreasonable, wrong
**inequity** abuse, bias, bigotry, discrimination, favouritism, grievance, hurt, injustice, maltreatment, mistreatment, partiality, prejudice, unfairness
**in error** wrong
**inert** apathetic, comatose, dead, dormant, dull, idle, immobile, inactive, inanimate, indolent, lazy, lifeless, listless, motionless, passive, senseless, sleepy, sluggish, somnolent, stagnant, stationary, still, torpid, unmoving, unresponsive
**inert gas** actinon, argon, neon, radon, xenon
**inertia** apathy, deadness, drowsiness, dullness, idleness, immobility, inaction, inactivity, indolence, inertness, laziness, lethargy, lifelessness, listlessness, motionlessness, passiveness, passivity, slackness, sloth, sluggishness, stillness, stupor, torpidness, torpor, unresponsive(ness)
**inescapable** certain, destined, fated, inevitable, inexorable, irrevocable, sure, unalterable, unavoidable
**in essence** basically, essentially, materially, substantially
**inessential** accessory, accidental, appendage, dispensable, disposable, expendable, extra(neous), immaterial, impertinent, inapposite, inconsequentially, insignificant, irrelevant, needless, non-essential, optional, redundant, replaceable, secondary, spare, superfluity, superfluous, surplus, trifling, trimming, trivial, unasked for, uncalled for, unimportant, unnecessary
**in eternal remembrance** memoria in aeterna (L)
**in every place** everywhere
**in every respect** comprehensively, fully
**in every truth** verily
**inevitable** absolute, assured, automatic, certain, conclusive, decreed, definite, destined, fatal, fated, fixed, incapable, inescapable, inexorable, involuntary, irrefutable, irrevocable, mechanical, necessary, ordained, settled, sure, unalterable, unavoidable, unchangeable, undeniable, undisputed
**inevitable result** nemesis
**inexact** amiss, approximate, borderline, concocted, doubtful, erroneous, estimated, fallacious, false, faulty, imprecise, inaccurate,

incorrect, indecisive, indefinite, indeterminate, invalid, loose, marginal, mistaken, rough, spurious, unreal, untrue, wrong
**in exactly the same words** verbatim
**in excess** over
**in excess of normal number** supernumerary
**in excess of what is needed** spare
**in exchange against** for
**in exchange for** against
**in excited eagerness** agog
**inexcusable** blameworthy, condemnable, discreditable, flagitious, ignoble, immoral, inatoneable, indefensible outrageous, iniquitous, irremissible, nefarious, unexcusable, unexpiable, unforgivable, unjustifiable, unpardonable, unwarrantable, wicked, wrongful
**inexhaustible** absolute, abundant, all-embracing, boundless, endless, enormous, eternal, immense, incalculable, indefatigable, inestimable, infinite, interminable, limitless, measureless, never-ending, never-failing, numberless, perpetual, stupendous, total, unbounded, unconfined, uncounted, undaunted, unending, unfailing, unflagging, unlimited, untiring, untold, unwearied, unwearying, vast, wide
**in existence** alive, extant
**inexorable** binding, cruel, destined, fated, firm, hard, implacable, inescapable, inflexible, obdurate, pitiless, relentless, remorseless, ruthless, severe, strict, unavoidable, unbending, unfeeling, unyielding
**inexorably** adamantly, certainly, compulsory, consequently, determinedly, firmly, fixedly, immovably, inevitably, inflexibly, insistently, naturally, obdurately, perforce, resolutely, rigidly, stiffly, stubbornly
**inexpedient** adverse, conflicting, detrimental, foolish, hostile, ill-advised, impolite, imprudent, inadvisable, indiscreet, injudicious, inopportune, misguided, opposing, rash, reluctant, repugnant, senseless, stupid, unadvisable, undesirable, unfortunate, unpropitious, unshrewd, unthinking, unwise
**inexpensive** bargain, budget, cheap, discounted, economical, half-price, low-cost, low-priced, modest, reasonable, reduced, wholesale

**inexperience** greenness, ignorance, inexpertness, innocence, naïvety, newness, rawness, strangeness, unfamiliarity
**inexperienced** amateur, callow, fresh, green, immature, inexpert, innocent, naïve, new, raw, unaccustomed, unacquainted, unfamiliar, uninitiated, unpractised, unschooled, unseasoned, unskilled, unsophisticated, untrained, unversed
**inexperienced actress** ingénue
**inexperienced person** greenhorn
**inexpert actor** ham
**inexplicable** baffling, enigmatic, incomprehensible, incredible, inscrutable, insoluble, miraculous, mysterious, mystifying, puzzling, strange, unaccountable, unfathomable
**inexpressible** inconceivable, indefinable, indescribable, ineffable, nameless, unbelievable, unimaginable, unspeakable, unutterable, wonderful
**in extremis** dying
**inextricably** indissolubly, indistinguishably, inseparably, intricately
**in fact** actually, de facto, indeed, really
**infallible** accurate, certain, dependable, fail-safe, faultless, foolproof, impeccable, inerrant, omniscient, perfect, reliable, sure(-fire), trustworthy, unerring, unfailing, unfaltering, unimpeachable
**infamous** bad, base, detestable, disgraceful, dishonourable, disreputable, hateful, heinous, ignominious, ill-famed, iniquitous, knavish, loathsome, monstrous, nefarious, notorious, odious, outrageous, scandalous, scurvy, shameful, shocking, vile, villainous, wicked
**infamous Roman emperor** Nero
**infamous Russian monk** Rasputin
**infamous traitor** Judas
**infamy** discredit, dishonour, disrepute, ignominy, notoriety, opprobrium, scandal, shame
**infancy** arising, babyhood, beginning, commencement, dawn, nascence, onset, origin, outset, start
**infant** babe, baby, bairn, bantling, child(ish), chrisom, dawning, developing, early, emergent, growing, immature, initial, juvenile, lightie, minor, new, newborn, rudimentary, suckling, toddler, tot, young, youthful
**infant food** milk, pap

**infanticide** babykilling
**infantile** adolescent, babyish, child-like, childish, immature, infantile, jejune, juvenile, puerile, sophomoric, tender, undeveloped, weak, young, youthful
**infantile paralysis** polio(myelitis)
**infantryman's gun** musket
**infantry side-arm** rifle
**infant's garment** bunting, crawler, diaper, nappy, pantywaist, sleeper
**infant's plaything** ball, doll, rattle
**infant's room** nursery
**infant that is being suckled** nurseling
**in fashion** à la mode, modish
**in fasting time** Lenten
**infatuate** beguile, besot, bewitch, enchant, enrapture, fascinate, mislead, obsess, stupefy
**infatuation** adulation, affection, ardour, besottedness, craze, crush, devotion, dotage, enthusiasm, fad, fanaticism, fascination, fixation, folly, fondness, friendship, infatuation, keenness, liking, love, madness, mania, mode, novelty, obsession, passion, rage, rapture, regard, tenderness, thing, trend, vogue, warmth, zeal
**in favour of** for, pro
**in fear** afraid
**infect** affect, afflict, blight, contaminate, corrupt, defile, enthuse, infest, influence, inspire, pervert, poison, pollute, sicken, spoil, taint, touch
**infection** contagion, contamination, corruption, defilement, disease, epidemic, illness, inflammation, influence, pestilence, poison, pollution, taint, virus
**infection caused by contaminated water** cholera
**infection caused by fungus** mycosis
**infectious** catching, communicable, contagious, contaminating, corrupting, deadly, defiling, epidemic, infective, pestilential, poisoning, polluting, spreading, transmissible, virulent
**infectious bacterial fever** typhoid
**infectious disease** AIDS, cholera, measles, mumps, (para)typhoid, pest, whooping cough, TB, tuberculosis, zymosis
**infectious disease affecting the bowels** cholera
**infectious disease in cattle** murrain
**infectious disease of horses** dourine, surra
**infectious disease of oriental tropics** kala-azar

**infectious disease with red spots**
  chicken-pox, measles
**infectious disorder caused by parasitic mites** mange
**infectious febrile disorder** influenza
**infectious fever** typhus
**infectious fright** panic
**infectious germ** virus
**infectious mononucleosis** glandular fever
**infectious skin disease** scabies
**infectious terror** panic
**infectious tropical fever** blackwater fever, breakbone fever, dandy, dengue
**infectious virus disease marked by red rash** measles
**infecund** barren, childless, effete, fallow, fruitless, infertile, sterile, unfruitful, unprolific
**infer** calculate, conclude, conjecture, construe, deduce, derive, estimate, gather, guess, imply, indicate, insinuate, intimate, presume, reason, show, tell, understand
**inference** assumption, conclusion, conjecture, consequence, construction, corollary, deduction, extrapolation, illation, implication, interpretation, presumption, reading, surmise
**inferior** bad, humble, junior, lesser, lousy, low(er), mediocre, menial, minion, minor, poor, second-class, second-rate, secondary, shoddy, slipshod, subordinate, subsidiary, substandard, third-rate, underling, underneath, unsatisfactory, vassal, worse
**inferior actor** shine
**inferior anthracite** culm
**inferior cloth** shoddy
**inferior deity** godkin, godling
**inferior end of neck of mutton** scrag
**inferior grade of diamond** bo(a)rt, bortz
**inferior horse** nag, rip
**inferiority** humbleness, imperfection, inadequacy, insignificance, lowliness, meanness, mediocrity, shoddiness, slovenliness, subordination, subservience
**inferior kind of cinnamon** cassia
**inferior legal practitioner** pettifogger
**inferior liquor** swill
**inferior metal mixed with gold or silver** alloy
**inferior remnant** fag
**inferior satin** satinet
**inferior set of people** rabble
**inferior specimen** rogue
**inferior to** below, beneath

**inferior verse-writer** poetaster
**inferior whiskey** redeye
**inferior wine** plonk
**infernal** abominable, accursed, atrocious, barbaric, brutal, condemned, cruel, cursed, damnable, damned, despicable, detestable, devilish, diabolic, doomed, fiendish, hateful, hellish, infamous, inhuman, loathsome, lost, malevolent, malicious, monstrous, odious, pernicious, pestilential, reprobate, revolting, ruthless, satanic, savage, underworld, unhappy, vicious, vile, wicked
**inferno** conflagration, Hell
**infertile** acarpous, arid, barren, dried-up, fallow, impotent, infecund, non-productive, parched, sterile, unbearing, unfructuous, unfruitful, unproductive
**infertility** aridness, effeteness, fallowness, fruitlessness, impotence, infecundity, unfruitfulness, unproductiveness
**infest** alive, beset, crawling, invade, overrun, plagued, ridden, teeming
**infestation with roundworms** ascariasis
**infestation with tapeworms** taeniasis
**infested with lice** louse-infested, lousy, pediculous
**in festivity** en fête (F)
**infidel** agnostic, atheist, disbeliever, freethinker, gentile, giaour, godless, heathen(ish), heretic, idolater, idolatrous, irreligionist, irreligious, nullifidian, pagan, scoffer, unbeliever
**infidelity** adultery, betrayal, cheating, deceitfulness, disbelief, disloyalty, double-dealing, duplicity, faithlessness, falseness, falsity, inconstancy, perfidy, treachery, treason, unbelief, unfaithfulness
**infield hit** bunt
**infiltrate** filter, insinuate, intrude, penetrate, percolate, permeate, pervade, sift
**infiltrator** intruder, mole, penetrator, spy, subversive, subverter
**in fine feather** healthy
**in fine fettle** hale, hardy, hearty
**infinite** absolute, bottomless, boundless, ceaseless, countless, endless, enormous, eternal, fathomless, immeasurable, immense, incalculable, incomputable, indefinite, inestimable, inexhaustible, limitless, myriad, never-ending, perennial, perpetual, stupendous, total, unbounded, uncountable, unending, unfathomless, unlimited, unmeasured, untold, vast, wide
**infinite age** aeon
**infinitesimal** atomic, diminutive, dwarf, elfin, faint, fine, gradual, imperceptible, inappreciable, inaudible, inconsiderable, insensible, insignificant, invisible, little, microscopic, mini(ature), miniscule, minute, negligible, petite, pygmy, shadowy, short, slender, slight, small, subtle, teeny, tiny, wee
**infinite time** eternity
**infinity** boundlessness, countlessness, endlessness, eternity, everlasting, immeasurableness, immensity, inexhaustibility, interminableness, limitlessness, perpetuity, vastness
**infirm** ailing, anile, bedridden, decrepit, feeble, frail, ill, inconstant, indisposed, insecure, rickety, senile, sick, unstable, weak, withered
**infirmary** clinic, hospice, hospital
**infirmity** affliction, ailment, complaint, condition, debility, defect, disability, disease, disorder, exhaustion, feebleness, frailty, handicap, ill(ness), impairment, incapacity, indisposition, languor, malady, malaise, sickliness, sickness, upset, weakness
**in fits and starts** spasmodic
**inflame** aggravate, agitate, anger, arouse, embitter, enrage, exasperate, excite, fan, fire, foment, fuel, heat, ignite, impassion, incense, incite, increase, infuriate, intensify, ire, kindle, madden, provoke, rile, rouse, stimulate, worsen
**inflamed** angry, chafing, festering, hot, red, septic, sore, swollen
**inflamed by anger** afire
**inflamed eyelid** sty(e)
**inflamed skin** eczema
**inflamed sore** blain
**inflamed sore on finger** whitlow
**inflamed swelling on edge of eyelid** sty(e)
**in flames** aflame
**inflame with love** enamour
**inflammable** burnable, combustible, flammable, incendiary
**inflammable adhesive** resin
**inflammable gel** napalm
**inflammable hydrocarbon** methane
**inflammable liquid** oil
**inflammable oil distilled from coal** naphtha
**inflammable poisonous gas** cyanogen
**inflammation** abscess, bruise, bulge, bump, burning, dilation,

enlargement, heat, infection, lump, protuberance, rash, redness, sore(ness), swelling, tenderness
**inflammation of appendix** appendicitis
**inflammation of artery** arteritis
**inflammation of bladder** cystitis
**inflammation of bone** osteomyelitis
**inflammation of bone substance** osteitis
**inflammation of bowel** colitis, enteritis
**inflammation of brain** (en)cephalitis
**inflammation of breast** mastitis
**inflammation of bursa** bursitis
**inflammation of cerebral membrane** meningitis
**inflammation of colon** colitis
**inflammation of conjunctiva** conjunctivitis
**inflammation of cornea** keratitis
**inflammation of cow or ewe's udder** garget
**inflammation of duodenum** duodenitis
**inflammation of ear** otitis
**inflammation of eardrum** tympanitis, tympany
**inflammation of endocardium** endocarditis
**inflammation of eye** conjunctivitis, iritis, ophthalmia, ophthalmitis, pink-eye, sty(e)
**inflammation of eyelid** sty(e)
**inflammation of eye membrane** retinitis
**inflammation of fallopian tubes** salpingitis
**inflammation of fibrous connective tissue** fibrositis
**inflammation of gland** adenitis
**inflammation of gums** gingivitis, pyorrhoea
**inflammation of hair follicles** sycosis
**inflammation of heart** carditis
**inflammation of horse's frog** thrush
**inflammation of ileum** ileitis
**inflammation of inner coat of artery** endarteritis
**inflammation of intestines** enteritis, gastroenteritis
**inflammation of iris of eye** iritis
**inflammation of joints** arthritis, synovitis
**inflammation of kidneys** nephritis
**inflammation of larynx** laryngitis
**inflammation of ligaments** desmitis
**inflammation of lining membrane of middle ear** tympanitis
**inflammation of lining of colon** colitis
**inflammation of lining of womb** endometritis
**inflammation of liver** hepatitis
**inflammation of long bone** epiphysitis
**inflammation of lungs** pneumonia

**inflammation of lymphatic glands** adenitis
**inflammation of mammary gland** mammitis
**inflammation of marrow of bone** osteomyelitis
**inflammation of mastoid process** mastoiditis
**inflammation of membrane lining the heart** endocarditis
**inflammation of membrane of mouth** stomatitis
**inflammation of membrane round lungs** pleurisy
**inflammation of meninges** meningitis
**inflammation of mesentery** mesenteritis
**inflammation of mucous membrane** catarrh
**inflammation of mucous membrane lining the womb** endometritis
**inflammation of muscles** myositis
**inflammation of myocardium** myocarditis
**inflammation of nerves** neuritis
**inflammation of nose** rhinitis
**inflammation of ovaries** oophoritis, ovaritis
**inflammation of pancreas** pancreatitis
**inflammation of periosteum** periostitis
**inflammation of peritoneum** peritonitis
**inflammation of pharynx** pharyngitis
**inflammation of pleura** pleurisy
**inflammation of prostate glands** prostatitis
**inflammation of renal pelvis** pyelitis
**inflammation of retina** retinitis
**inflammation of sclera** scleritis, sclerotitis
**inflammation of sinus** sinusitis
**inflammation of skin** dermatitis
**inflammation of smooth membrane lining the heart** endocarditis
**inflammation of spinal cord** myelitis
**inflammation of spine** spondylitis
**inflammation of spleen** splenitis
**inflammation of stomach and intestines** gastro-enteritis
**inflammation of substance of lungs** pneumonia
**inflammation of throat** quinsy
**inflammation of thyroid gland** thyroiditis
**inflammation of tongue** glossitis
**inflammation of tonsils** quinsy, tonsillitis
**inflammation of trachea** bronchitis, tracheitis
**inflammation of uvula** uvulitis
**inflammation of vagina** vaginitis
**inflammation of veins** phlebitis
**inflammation of vertebrae** spondylitis

**inflammation of voice box** laryngitis
**inflammation of womb** metritis, uteritis
**inflammation suffix** -itis
**inflammatory** explosive, fiery, provocative, rabble-rousing, riotous, seditious
**inflatable mattress** airbed, lilo
**inflatable toy** ball(oon)
**inflate** aerate, amplify, balloon, bloat, boost, dilate, distend, enlarge, escalate, exaggerate, expand, increase, prolong, swell
**inflated** bloated, blown, bombastic, distended, escalated, extended, high-flown, ostentatious, pretentious, puffed, raised, tumid, turgid
**inflated language** bombast
**inflated with air** pneumatic
**inflation** distention, enlargement, hyperinflation, increase, rise, spread
**inflectional morphology** accidence
**inflexibility** decision, determination, firmness, fixity, hardness, immovability, inelasticity, intransigence, obstinacy, pertinacity, rigidity, rigidness, rigor, steadfastness, stiffness, stringency, stubbornness, tenacity
**inflexible** adamant, firm, fixed, headstrong, immovable, implacable, inexorable, intractable, iron(clad), obdurate, relentless, resolute, rigid, rigorous, set, solid, steadfast, steely, strict, stringent, stubborn, unbending, undeviating, unyielding
**inflexibly** inexorably, intractably, relentlessly, resolutely, steadfastly, strictly, stringently, stubbornly, unbendingly
**inflict** administer, afflict, apply, burden, deal, deliver, enforce, exact, force, impose, impose, lay, levy, perpetrate, visit, wreak
**inflict a penalty on** penalise, punish
**inflict injury in retribution** revenge
**inflict in return** retaliate
**infliction of capital punishment** execution
**inflict retribution** avenge
**inflict sharp pain** stab
**inflow** arrival, flow, incursion, influx, inrush, invasion, rush
**inflow of tide** flow, flux
**influence** activate, affect, agency, arouse, authority, bias, control, count, credit, direct(ion), dispose, domination, effect, guidance, guide, hold, impel, importance, impress, incite, incline, induce, instigate, leverage, manipulate, mastery, modify, move, persuade, power, predispose, predominance,

**influence deeply** impress
**influence of women** feminism
**influential** absolute, arch, authoritative, charismatic, chief, compelling, conclusive, considerable, controlling, critical, crucial, decisive, definite, definitive, dominant, dominating, effective, eminent, exalted, fateful, final, guiding, high, important, instrumental, leading, momentous, moving, noteworthy, persuasive, potent, powerful, prominent, renowned, ruling, significant, strong, superior, telling, weighty, well-placed pressure, prestige, prompt, rule, spell, sway, weight
**influential person** mandarin, mogul
**influential person behind the scenes** éminence grise (F)
**influenza** cold, flu
**influx** arrival, entry, infiltration, inflow, ingress, inundation
**in focus** clear, distinct, sharp-edged
**in force** alive, binding, current, effective, valid
**in foreign land** abroad
**inform** accuse, acquaint, advise, animate, apprise, arouse, blab, brief, broadcast, caution, communicate, disclose, divulge, edify, enlighten, enliven, illuminate, imbue, impart, inspire, instil, instruct, notify, quicken, relate, tell, warn
**inform against** denounce
**informal** ad lib, bohemian, casual, colloquial, common, everyday, familiar, fluent, humdrum, irregular, lax, nonconforming, offhand, original, plain, simple, unique, unorthodox, unusual, vernacular
**informal diplomatic message** memorandum
**informal discussion** pourparler (F)
**informal friendly gathering** social
**informal friendly understanding between nations** entente cordiale
**informal gathering for dancing and music** ceilidh (Sc)
**informal gathering for singing** singsong
**informal greeting** ciao (I), hello
**informal hello** hi, howdy
**informal letter** memorandum
**informal meeting** get-together
**informal name for medical practitioner** doc
**informal name of Mars** Red Planet
**informal note** chit
**informal party** braai, clambake
**informal photograph** snap
**informal shoes** sneakers, tackies
**informal speech** vulgate

**informal talk** chat
**informal word to mother** ma, mom, mum
**informal written message** memorandum
**informant** announcer, apprise(r), authority, instructor, mouthpiece, newsmonger, notifier, reporter, source, spokesman, spokeswoman
**information** advice, blurb, briefing, bulletin, circumstances, clues, communication, communiqué, counsel, data(bank), database, dossier, facts, gen, illumination, input, instruction, intelligence, knowledge, message, news, notice, report, wisdom, word
**information about recent events** news
**information storage device** disk
**information stored** input
**informative** chatty, communicating, communicative, constructive, educational, enlightening, expansive, explanatory, forthcoming, free, gossipy, helpful, illuminating, instructive, newsy, open, revealing, sociable, talkative, unreserved, useful, valuable
**informative talk** lecture
**informed** abled, abreast, acquainted, au courant (F), au fait (F), authoritative, aware, briefed, conversant, enlightened, erudite, expert, familiar, knowledgeable, learned, posted, primed, reliable, trained, up, versed, well-informed, well-reached, well-read
**informed about** enlightened
**informer** accuser, betrayer, denouncer, denunciator, discloser, impimpi, informant, Judas, mole, sneak, spy, squealer, (super)grass, talebearer, telltale
**inform on** accuse, betray, blab, denounce, grass, incriminate, sneak, spy, squeal
**in forward direction** onwards
**infract** break, disobey, disregard, infringe, transgress, violate
**in French** Gallice
**in French it is le** the
**infrequent** casual, exceptional, few, incidental, inconstant, irregular, meagre, occasional, rare, scant, scarce, seldom, sporadic, uncommon, unusual, unwonted
**infringe** breach, break, contravene, defy, disobey, disregard, encroach, flout, ignore, impinge, infract, intrude, invade, overstep, poach, squat, transgress, trespass, undue, violate

**infringement** abuse, breach, contravention, crime, defiance, encroachment, error, evasion, grievance, infraction, injury, injustice, interruption, intrusion, invasion, misdeed, offence, poaching, sin(fulness), transgression, trespass, violation, wickedness, wrong
**infringement in soccer** hands
**infringement of the rules of sport** foul
**in front** ahead, before, leading, preceding
**in front of** afore, ahead, before, leading, preceding
**in full** completely, entirely, in pleno (L), unabridged, wholly
**in full dress** en grande tenue (F)
**in full force** amain, strong
**in full measure** richly
**in full ownership** own
**in full swing** animated, lively
**in full view** exposed, overt, public
**in funds** solvent, well-off, well-supplied
**infuriate** aggravate, anger, annoy, antagonise, chafe, enrage, exasperate, incense, inflame, irritate, madden, offend, provoke, rile, rouse, vex, wrath
**infuriating** aggravating, angering, exasperating, incensing, infuriating, irritating, maddening, mortifying, pestilential, riling, vexatious
**infuse** animate, boil, brew, draw, encourage, enliven, ferment, flavour, galvanise, hearten, imbue, implant, inculcate, infiltrate, infix, influence, inject, insert, insinuate, inspire, inspirit, instil, interject, introduce, lace, leaven, make, saturate, season, seethe, soak, sow, spice, spur, steep, stew, stimulate, tinge
**infusion** bath, dip, immersion, impregnation, income, injection, macerating, permeation, saturation, shade, soak, stain, steeping, submerge, tea, tincture, tinge, transfusion
**infusion of fresh or dried herbs** tisane
**infusion of leaves** tea
**infusion of malt** ale, grout, wort
**in general** mostly, usually
**ingenious** adroit, bright, brilliant, clever(ness), crafty, creative, dext(e)rous, fertile, gifted, imaginative, innovative, intricate, inventive, knack, masterly, original, ready, resourceful, shrewd, skilful, skill, subtle
**ingeniously simple and effective** elegant
**ingenuity** ability, adroitness, aptitude, art, bent, capability, capacity,

cleverness, competence, craft, creativeness, daring, dexterity, enterprise, expertise, facility, finesse, flair, genius, gift, imagination, initiative, insight, inventiveness, knack, knowledge, mastery, method, newness, originality, resource, shrewdness, skill, talent, technique, trade, virtuosity, vision, wit

**ingenuous** artless, candid, frank, genuine, guileless, innocent, naïve, open, simple, sincere, straightforward, trustful, undeceitful, unstudied, unwary

**ingenuousness** candidness, childlikeness, fairness, frankness, freeness, honesty, justness, naïveness, plainness, simpleness, sincereness, sincerity, trustfulness, unwariness

**ingest** absorb, consume, devour, drink, eat, gulp, imbibe, incept, inhale, swallow, swill, take

**ingesting** absorbing, consuming, devouring, drinking, eating, gulping, imbibing, inhaling, swallowing, swilling, taking

**ingle** fireplace

**in God have I trusted** in Deo speravi (L)

**in good condition** fit, sound, taut

**in good faith** bona fide, honestly, honour, lawfully, pledge, sincerity

**in good health** fit, sound, well

**in good manner** well

**in good order** orderly, shipshape, tidy

**in good part** cheerfully, cordially, good-naturedly, well

**in good shape** healthy

**in good spirits** cheerful, cheery, contented, elated, happy, high

**in good taste** artistic, elegant, tasteful

**in good time** betimes, early, punctual, rapidly, speedily, swiftly

**ingrained** basic, deep-rooted, deep-seated, embedded, engrained, entrenched, essential, established, fixed, fundamental, habitual, hereditary, immovable, inborn, inbred, inbuilt, incorrigible, inedible, ineffaceable, ineradicable, inexpungible, inherent, inherited, innate, inveterate, rooted, stubborn, thorough, unchangeable

**ingrained dirt** grime

**in grand style** artistic

**ingratiate** blandish, crawl, fawn, flatter, grovel, insinuate

**ingratiate oneself** grovel

**ingratiating** bootlicking, crawling, fawning, humble, obsequious, servile, smarmy, smooth-tongued, sycophantic, unctuous

**in great demand** recherché

**in great difficulties** in extremis (L)

**in great need of food** destitute, starving

**in great numbers** galore

**ingredient** component, constituent, element, factor, part

**ingredient in brewing** yeast

**ingredient of concrete** cement, grit, sand

**ingredient of plastic** resin

**ingress** access, aperture, approach, arcade, arrival, avenue, corridor, door(way), entrance, entrée, entry, exit, inflow, influx, inroad, intrusion, lane, means, passage, penetration, porch, portico, roadway, route, vestibule, walkway

**inhabit** abide, domicile, dwell, in, live, locate, lodge, nest(le), occupy, people, populate, possess, remain, reside, settle, squat, stay, tenant

**inhabitant** -ite, aborigine, cit(izen), denizen, (in)dweller, inmate, lodger, native, occupant, occupier, resident, settler, tenant

**inhabitant of Denmark** Dane

**inhabitant of Greenland** Eskimo

**inhabitant of heaven** celestial

**inhabitant of Malaysia** Malay

**inhabitant of New England** Yankee

**inhabitant of Philippines** Filipino, Tagalog

**inhabitant of South West Asia** Arabian

**inhabits Saudi Arabia** Arab

**inhalation** air, breath(ing), exhalation, gasp, gulp, inhalement, inspiration, insufflation, pant, puff, respiration, sniff(le), snuffle, suction, wheeze

**inhale** breathe, consume, drag, drain, draw, drink, eat, gasp, gulp, imbibe, inbreathe, ingest, inspire, puff, pull, respire, smell, smoke, sniff(le), snuff(le), suck, swallow, waft, whiff

**inhale a drug** snort

**inhale and exhale** breathe, respire

**inhale audibly** sniff

**inhale sharply** gasp

**in half** two

**inharmonious** absonant, absurd, antagonistic, atonal, discordant, dissonant, rugged, strident, tuneless, unmelodious, unmusical

**inharmonious relationship** outs

**in harness** active, busy, working

**in heaven is rest** in caelo quies (L)

**in heraldry a bird without feet** martlet

**inhere** abide, belong, compose, connect, constitute, correspond, dwell, inhabit, live, make, occupy, pertain, reside, stay

**inhere in** appertain

**inherent** basic, congenital, essential, fundamental, hereditary, immanent, inborn, inbred, indigenous, ingenerate, ingredient, innate, inseparable, intrinsic, native, natural, permanent, radical, substantial

**inherit** assume, receive

**inheritance** bequest, birthright, decent, estate, heredity, heritage, legacy, patrimony, succession

**inheritance of firstborn** birthright

**inheritance that brings more burden than profit** damnosa hereditas (L)

**inherited estate** fee

**inherited item** heirloom

**inheritor** beneficiary, children, coheir, devisee, donee, follower, heir(ess), heritor, heritress, heritrix, offspring, recipient, spawn, successor

**inhibit** arrest, bridle, check, constrain, curb, (de)bar, deter, discourage, forbid, frustrate, gag, hinder, hold, impede, obstruct, prevent, prohibit, repress, restrain, restrict, stanch, stem, stop, suppress, thwart

**inhibit from** deter

**inhibition** bar, check, embargo, hang-up, hindrance, impediment, interdict, obstacle, obstruction, prohibition, repression, reserve, restraint, restriction, reticence, self-conscious, shyness

**in high dudgeon** angry, fuming, indignant, resentful, vexed

**in higher position** up(wards)

**in high spirits** elated, exultant, frisky, proud

**in honour of** for

**in-house phone** intercom

**inhuman** animal, barbaric, barbarous, bestial, brutal, callous, cold-blooded, cruel, diabolical, fiendish, heartless, inhumane, merciless, pitiless, remorseless, ruthless, savage, sublime, unfeeling, vicious

**inhumane** brutal, callous, cold-hearted, cruel, heartless, inhuman, insensitive, pitiless, unfeeling, unkind

**in human form** incarnate

**inhumanly cruel** diabolic

**in ignorance** unknowingly

**inimical** adverse, against, alien, antagonistic, anti, baleful, clashing, conflicting, contradictory, contrary, contrasted, counter, deleterious, destructive, detrimental, discordant, dissentient, diverse, harmful, hostile, hurtful, inhospitable, injurious, malevolent, opposed, opposite,

**inimitable** pernicious, prejudicial, reverse, unfavourable, unfriendly, unkind, unlike, warlike
**inimitable** consummate, distinctive, exceptional, extraordinary, incomparable, matchless, notable, outstanding, paramount, peerless, perfect, rare, remarkable, special, superlative, supreme, uncommon, unequalled, unique, unmatched, unparalled, unrivalled
**iniquitous** abominable, evil, nefarious, sinful, unjust, vicious, wicked
**iniquity** blame, corruption, crime, decadence, degeneration, delinquency, depravity, error, evil(doing), guilt, immorality, impurity, misconduct, misdeed, offence, perversion, responsibility, sin(fulness), trespass, vice, viciousness, wickedness, wrong(doing)
**in isolation** aside
**in it** therein
**initial** beginning, commencing, early, elementary, first, fundamental, inaugural, incipient, initiating, introductory, nascent, opening, original, primary, prime, starting
**initial action** first step
**initial letter** bloomer
**initial move** gambit
**initial movie print** rush
**initials used as Christian emblem** IHS
**initial work** spadework
**initiate** begin(ner), cause, coach, commence, establish, freshman, inaugurate, indoctrinate, induce, induct, instate, instigate, institute, instruct, introduce, invest, launch, open, originate, pioneer, pledge, prompt, start, stimulate, teach, train
**initiate or set up** found, institute
**initiation** access, admission, appearance, baptism, beginning, birth, bow, commencement, début, dedication, enrolment, entrance, entrée, entry, inauguration, inception, installation, instruction, introduction, investiture, onset, opening, origin, outset, preface, prelude, primordium, reception, rise, rudiments, source, start
**initiative** action, aggressiveness, ambition, démarche (F), drive, dynamism, energy, enterprise, gumption, inventiveness, lead(ership), originality, pluck, recommendation, resourcefulness, statement, step, suggestion
**in itself** per se (L)

**in its natural state** au naturel (F)
**in its original place** in situ (L)
**inject** add, bring, drive, fill, force, imbue, (in)fix, infuse, inoculate, insert, instil, interject, introduce, jab, shoot, steep, vaccinate
**injected beneath the skin** hypodermic
**injected dose of a drug** shot
**injection** booster, clyster, dose, enema, fix, hypo, inoculation, insertion, introduction, lavement, shot, therapy, vaccination, vaccine
**injection into the rectum** enema
**injection of blood into a patient** transfusion
**inject seed into** inseminate
**injunction** behest, charge, command(ment), demand, dictate, dictation, dictum, directive, enjoinment, exaction, exhortation, imperative, instruction, mandate, ordainment, prescript, requirement, requisition, ultimatum, will
**injure** break, cripple, damage, deface, disfigure, enervate, enfeeble, harm, hurt, ill-treat, impair, lame, maim, mangle, mar, mistreat, mutilate, ruin, scathe, scotch, smirch, spoil, stain, waste, weaken, wound, wrong
**injure by hot fluid** scald
**injure the self-respect** humiliate
**injure with a horn** gore
**injurious** abusive, bad, calamitous, calumnious, caustic, corruptive, damaging, defamatory, deleterious, dire, false, harmful, peccant, pernicious, ruinous, scandalous, wrongful
**injurious act** spoil
**injurious corn-weed** tare
**injuriously** badly, balefully, calamitously, catastrophically, dangerously, deleteriously, detrimentally, fatally, hurtfully, lethally, perniciously, roughly, ruinously
**injury** abuse, annoyance, bruise, damage, evil, grievance, harm, hurt, ill, impairment, injustice, insult, lesion, loss, mischief, ruin, scathe, trauma, wound, wrong
**injury by blow to body** bruise
**injury to brain caused by heavy blow** concussion
**injustice** bias, discrimination, disparity, favouritism, inequality, iniquity, one-sidedness, oppression, partiality, partisanship, prejudice, unfairness, unlawfulness, wrong
**inkberry** holly, ilex
**in keeping** agreeable, tallying

**in keeping with accepted standards** comme il faut (F)
**inkfish** cuttle, squid
**in kind** correspondingly, like(wise), similarly
**inkling** allution, clue, cue, desire, faintest, glimmering, hint, idea, inclination, indication, innuendo, intimation, notice, notion, pointer, sign, suggestion, suspicion, whisper
**ink stain** blot
**inlaid** enamelled, enchased, inset, lined, mosaic, ornamented, set, studded, veneered
**inlaid flooring** parquet
**inlaid mosaic panel** (in)tarsia
**inlaid work in wood or ivory** marqueterie, marquetry, parquetry
**inlaid work of brass and tortoiseshell** boul(l)e, boul(l)ework, buhl
**inland port in north-eastern Peru** Iquitos
**inland region** interior
**inland sea of Russia** Aral, Azov, Caspian
**in large numbers** galore
**in leaf throughout the year** evergreen
**in league with** allied, amalgamated, co-operating, coactive, collaborating, jointly, leagued
**inlet** admission, bay, bight, cove, creek, entrance, estuary, fiord, firth, fjord, fleet, hope, ingress, opening, passage, ria, strait, valve
**inlet of the sea** ria
**inlet on sea-coast** creek
**in lieu** instead
**in life** alive
**in light of** considering
**in like manner** also, as, even, so
**in limbo** suspended
**in line** aligned, level, plumb, straight, true
**in logical order** consecutive
**in love** amorous, besotted, charmed, enamoured, enraptured, smitten
**in low spirits** despondent
**inly** closely, deeply, internally, inwardly
**in many cases** commonly, often
**in many colours** colourful, polychrome
**in many instances** often
**inmate** insider, occupant, prisoner
**in memory of** in memoriam
**in mental or moral darkness** benighted
**in mint condition** unused
**in moderately slow tempo** andante
**in moral darkness** benighted
**inmost** central, deep(est), essential, innermost, intimate, personal, secret
**inmost recess** bosom

**in motion** astir, functioning, moving, working
**in murderous frenzy** amok, amuck
**in music, allegro** briskly
**inn** auberge, boardinghouse, (caravan)serai, haven, hostel(ry), hotel, khan, lodge, lodging, motel, pension, posada (Sp) pub(lic-house), rest-house, roadhouse, tavern
**in name only** nominal
**innards** bowels, guts, intestines, offal, viscera
**innate** basic, congenital, essential, fundamental, hereditary, immanent, impulsive, inborn, inbred, ingenerate, inherent, in(ner)most, instinctive, intrinsic, native, natural, spontaneous
**innate ability** talent
**innate character** nature
**innately** congenitally, essentially, inherently, instinctively, intrinsically, intuitively, natively, naturally
**inner** hidden, inside, interior, internal, private, spiritual
**inner being** entity, soul
**inner circle** cadre
**inner coat of eye** retina
**inner coffin** shell
**inner contour of an arch** archivolt
**inner covering** lining
**inner eye coat** retina
**inner framework of fire** grate
**inner layer of an organ** intima
**inner layer of skin** derma
**inner lining of the bark of exogenous trees** bast, bass, liber, phloem
**inner mass of cell material** endoplasm
**innermost membrane enclosing foetus** amnion
**innermost part** core
**innermost part of a temple** adytum
**innermost planet** Mercury
**inner nature** inwardness
**inner part** interior
**inner part of hand** palm
**inner part of nut** kernel
**inner personality** anima
**inner portion of cigar** filler
**inner portion of egg** yolk
**inner room** bower, ben (Sc)
**inner room of a classical temple** cella, naos
**inner skin layer** dermis
**inner sole** sock
**inner spirit** anima
**inner upper surface** ceiling
**inn in Turkey** khan
**innkeeper** aubergiste (F), caterer, host(ess), hotelier, hotelkeeper, hotelman, inn-holder, landlady, landlord, padrone, publican, taverner
**innocence** blamelessness, guiltlessness, inculpability, naïveté, naïvety, purity, sinlessness
**innocent** artless, blameless, chaste, childlike, clear, credulous, dewy-eyed, faultless, frank, fresh, green, guileless, guiltless, gullible, harmless, honest, immaculate, impeccable, incorrupt, innocuous, inoffensive, irreproachable, naïve, natural, open, pure, righteous, simple, sinless, spotless, stainless, trustful, upright, virtuous
**innocently** artlessly, blamelessly, chastely, clearly, credulously, faultlessly, frankly, guiltlessly, honestly, immaculately, impeccably, naïvely, openly, purely, righteously, spotlessly, uprightly, virginally
**innocuous** bland, domesticated, dovelike, dull, gentle, harmless, innocent, inoffensive, insipid, irreproachable, jejune, mild, moderate, safe, soft, tame, uninspiring, unobjectionable, unobnoxious
**innocuously** gently, moderately, safely
**in no key** atonal
**in no manner** never, no way, not
**in no time** quickly, rapidly, readily, speedily, swiftly
**innovation** alteration, change, departure, introduction, modernisation, modernism, neologism, newness, novelty, progress, reform, variation
**innovative** adventurous, bold, daring, different, drastic, enterprising, experimental, fresh, fundamental, go-ahead, imaginative, inventive, modernising, new, novel, original, progressive, radical, reforming, resourceful, revolutionary
**innovator** developer, founder, leader, pioneer
**in no way** no ways, nohow, not
**innuendo** aspersion, hint, implication, imputation, insinuation, intimation, slant, slur, suggestion, whisper
**innumerable** countless, incalculable, infinite, many, myriad, numberless, numerous, umpteen, uncountable, unnumbered, untold
**inoculate** imbue, immunise, inculcate, indoctrinate, infuse, inject, instruct, protect, safeguard, shield, teach, vaccinate
**inoculation fluid** vaccine
**in-off** jenny
**inoffensive** harmless, humble, innocent, innocuous, mild, peaceable, quiet, retiring, unassertive, unobtrusive, unoffending
**in one's dotage** senile
**in one's favour** beneficial, helpful, well-disposed
**in one's own person** in propria persona (L)
**in one's own view** personally
**in one's right mind** compos mentis (L)
**in one's second childhood** childish, daft, senile
**in one's shirt sleeves** jacketless
**in one's true colours** en déshabillé (F)
**in one way or another** somehow
**in one word** briefly
**in open court** in curia (L)
**inoperable** impracticable, unworkable
**in operation** active, afoot, effective, functioning, on, operative
**inoperative** abeyant, absent, broken-down, cancelled, collapsed, defective, dilapidated, dormant, finished, gone, idle, immobile, inactive, ineffective, inert, jobless, latent, nonfunctioning, off, old, postponed, unavailable, unemployed, unoccupied, unserviceable, unused, unworkable, useless
**inopportune** ill-timed, inauspicious, malapropos, mistimed, unpropitious, untimely
**in opposition to** against, anti-, con
**in order** acceptable, allowed, appropriate, arranged, correct, done, fitting, neat, OK, orderly, permitted, proper, right, straight, suitable, tidy
**in order of merit** seeded
**in order that** so
**inordinate** disproportionate, excessive, exorbitant, extravagant, great, immense, immoderate, intemperate, undue, unreasonable, unwarranted
**inordinate desire to possess** cupidity
**inorganic** mineral
**in other countries** abroad
**in other words** namely
**in our presence** coram nobis (L)
**in outline** briefly
**in pain** aching
**in part** comparatively, moderately, partially, partly, relatively, slightly, tolerably
**in particular** distinctly, especially, exactly, expressly, particularly, specifically
**in part payment** à compte (F)
**in passing** accidentally
**in past ages** heretofore
**in peace** in pace (L)

**in perfect health** as right as a trivet
**in perpetuum** always
**in person** bodily, in propria persona (L), personally
**in pieces** broken, dilapidated, disintegrated, fragmentary, shattered, smashed
**in place** arranged, at, ordered
**in place of** instead, lieu
**in place of a parent** in loco parentis (L)
**in plain words** nudis verbis (L)
**in plentiful supply** ample, easy, galore
**in plenty** abundant
**in point of fact** actually, certainly, doubtlessly, indeed
**in poor condition** ill
**in poor health** ailing, ill
**in poor spirits** depressed, despondent, low
**in praise** eulogy
**in preference** first
**in preparation** afoot
**in presence of** before
**in primitive state** savage
**in principle** ideally, theoretically
**in print** available, obtainable, out, printed, published
**in private** confidentially, intimately, privately, secretly
**in process of birth** nascent
**in process of rotting** putrescent
**in progress** afoot, en train (F), happening, occurring, on(going), proceeding
**in proportion** pro rata
**in proportion to the estimated value of the goods taxed** ad valorem
**in prospect** close, near, planned, projected
**in public** coram populo (L)
**in pursuit of power** Machiavel(l)ian
**input** capture, code, data, details, documents, facts, figures, information, insert, materials, process, statistics, store
**in quarantine** isolated
**in question** debatable, problematic, questionable
**inquest officer** coroner
**in quick tempo** presto
**inquire** ask, assay, enquire, examine, explore, interrogate, investigate, probe, pry, quaere (L), query, question, quiz, research, scan, scout, scrutinise, search, spy, study, unearth
**inquire intensively** delve
**inquire into** examine, explore, investigate
**inquirer into death** coroner
**inquiring** inspecting, probing, scrutinising

**inquiry** examination, interrogation, investigation, query, question(ing), study
**inquisition** (cross-)examination, cross-questioning, grilling, inquest, inquiry, interrogation, investigation, question(ing), quizzing, witch-hunt
**inquisitive** curious, eager, eavesdropping, inquiring, interested, intrusive, investigative, meddlesome, meddling, nos(e)y, persistent, prying, questioning, scrutinising, snooping, snoopy
**inquisitive person** rubberneck
**in rags** ragged, seedy, shabby, tattered, tatty
**in rapid tempo** allegro
**in readiness** beforehand, fit, prepared, ready, set, waiting
**in reality** actually, de facto, really
**in recent times** lately, recently
**in regard to** about, apropos, concerning
**in regard to place** local
**in relation to** vis-à-vis
**in requital of** for
**in reserve** aside, spare
**in respect of** anent, apropos, regarding
**in retrospect** reconsidering
**in return** again
**in reverse** backward
**in reversed order** vice versa
**inroad** assault, attack, charge, entrance, foray, incision, incursion, intrusion, invasion, irruption, offensive, onset, onslaught, penetration, piercing, puncturing, raid, rush, strike
**in rows** tiered
**in sackcloth and ashes** atoning, chastened, compunctious, contrite, disturbed, embarrassed, penitent, remorseful, sorrowful, sorry
**insalubrious** detrimental, dirty, fatal, injurious, jejune, lethal, noxious, pestiferous, unclean, unhealthful, unhealthy, unhygienic, unnutritive, unpleasant
**in same plane** coplanar
**in same straight line** collinear
**ins and outs** corners, crannies, curves, details, features, habits, intricacies, peculiarities, traits, turns
**insane** absurd, barmy, berserk, bedonderd, beneek, Corybantic, crazed, crazy, delirious, demented, deranged, distracted, distraught, eccentric, fatuous, feeble-minded, frantic, frenetic, hysterical, irrational, loony, lunatic, mad, maniacal, mental, non compos mentis (L), nonsensical, nuts, provoked,

psychotic, schizophrenic, senseless, stupid, tempestuous, unbalanced, violent
**insane person** lunatic, nut-case
**insanity** absurdity, anility, asininity, carelessness, delirium, dementia, derangement, dipsomania, dotage, eccentricity, foolishness, franticness, frenzy, idiocy, imbecility, ineptness, insaneness, lunacy, madness, neurosis, oddness, psychosis, recklessness, senility, senselessness, unbalance
**insatiable** greedy, immoderate, incontrollable, inordinate, intemperate, persistent, rapacious, ravenous, unquenchable, unsatisfiable, voracious
**insatiable greed** avarice
**inscribe** address, blaze, carve, cut, dedicate, engrave, enlist, enrol, enscroll, enter, etch, impress, imprint, incise, mark, record, register, sign, stamp, write
**inscription** autograph, caption, dedication, engraving, epitaph, label, legend, lettering, saying, signature, words
**inscription on a tomb** epitaph
**inscription on Christ's cross** INRI (Iesus Nazarenus Rex Iudaeorum)
**inscrutable** baffling, blank, cryptic, deadpan, deep, enigmatic, hidden, impenetrable, incomprehensible, inexplicable, mysterious, unexplainable, unfathomable, unintelligible, unsearchable
**inscrutable monster of Greek mythology** sphinx
**inscrutable person** sphinx
**in second place** runner-up
**in secret** incognito, secretly, slyly, surreptitiously
**insect** anopheles, ant, aphid, bee, beetle, bug, butterfly, cicada, cockroach, creepy-crawly, cricket, dragonfly, earwig, emmet, flea, fly, gadfly, gnat, gogga, grasshopper, imago, locust, louse, maggot, mite, mosquito, moth, nit, pest, termite, vermin, wasp, weevil
**insect antenna** feeler
**insect bite** sting
**insect case** cocoon
**insect, creepy-crawly** gogga
**insect expert** entomologist
**insect feeler** antenna
**insect flying with loud humming noise** CMR beetle, Christmas beetle, dor, rose beetle
**insect foot** tarsus

**insecticide** acaricide, aldrin, anthelmintic, fumigant, miticide, pesticide, poison, vermicide
**insect in the stage between egg and pupa** larva
**insectivorous** entomophagous
**insect killer** insecticide
**insect larva** grub
**insect on a dog** flea
**insect's feeler** antenna, palp
**insect's nest** nidus
**insect's organ of touch** feeler
**insect's proboscis** stinger
**insect's resinous secretion** lac
**insect's sensors** palp
**insect's stomach** ventriculus
**insect stage** imago, larva, pupa
**insect that injures stored grain** weevil
**insect that makes a sound by scraping** stridulator
**insect that swarms** bee
**insect with showy wings** butterfly
**insecure** afraid, anxious, dangerous, defenceless, exposed, flimsy, frail, hazardous, infirm, insubstantial, loose, precarious, rickety, risky, rocky, shaky, uncertain, unconfident, unguarded, unprotected, unreliable, unsafe, unsound, unstable, unsteady, unsure, vulnerable, weak
**insensibility** apathy, coma, coolness, deadness, dullness, forgetfulness, impassivity, indifference, listnessness, neglect, numbness, oblivion, paralysis, passivity, somnolence, stoicism, stupor, torpor, trance, unawareness, unconcern, unconsciousness, unfeelingness, unresponsiveness
**insensible** benumbed, callous, comatose, dull, hard, inert, inured, numb(ed), stupid, torpid, tough, unaware, unconscious, unperceiving
**insensible state** narcosis
**insensitive** thick-skinned, crass, callous, cruel, thick, emotionless, tough, numb, dead, insentient, immune, impervious, unreactive, nonallergic, mean, nasty, heartless, unaware, uncultured, uncultivated, insensible
**inseparable** bosom, close, devoted, indissoluble, indivisable, inextricable, inseverable, intimate
**inseparable friends** David and Jonathan
**insert** add(ition), enter, entry, imbed, implant, inclusion, inject, inlay, inset, interlard, interpolate, interpose, introduce, introduction, intrusion, place, put, set, supplement
**insert extemporary variations** ad lib

**insert film into camera** load
**insertion** addition, entry, implant, inclusion, insert, inset, interpolation, introduction, intrusion, panel, supplement
**insert new film** reload
**inset** gusset, inlay, insert
**in seventh heaven** rapturous
**inshore trading ship** coaster
**in short** briefly, enfin (F)
**in short supply** few, inadequate, insufficient, scarce
**in shreds or rags** tattered
**in shy manner** coyly
**inside** belly, bowels, concrete, entrails, gut(s), in(doors), innards, inner(most), interior, internal, inward, organs, stomach, vitals, within
**inside a house** indoors
**inside covering** lining
**inside information** tip
**inside of building** interior
**inside of coat** lining
**inside out** backward, completely, reversed, thoroughly
**insider** inmate
**insides** belly, bowels, entrails, gut(s), innards, interiors, organs, stomach, viscera
**inside that** therein
**insidious** artful, beguiling, corrupting, crafty, crooked, cunning, deceitful, deceptive, designing, devious, duplicitous, entrapping, foxy, guileful, slick, sly, smooth, sneaking, stealthy, subtle, surreptitious, treacherous, tricky, wily
**insidious narcotic** alcohol, tobacco
**insight** acuity, acumen, awareness, comprehension, discernment, discrimination, imagination, inspection, intellect, interpretation, intuition, look, penetration, perception, perceptiveness, perspicacity, sagacity, understanding, wisdom
**insignia** award, badge, brand, chevron, crest, decoration, distinction, emblem, ensign, heraldry, mark, medal(lion), regalia, signet, signs, symbol, tab, token
**insignia of royalty** regalia
**insignificant** flimsy, inconsequential, inconsiderable, insubstantial, irrelevant, meaningless, minor, negligible, non-essential, nugatory, paltry, petty, scanty, tenuous, tiny, trifling, trivial, unimportant, unimpressive, unportentous, unsubstantial
**insignificant person** nobody
**in silence** sub silentio (L)

**insincere** artificial, crafty, devious, dishonest, disingenuous, disloyal, dissimulating, double-dealing, fulsome, incandid, lying, treacherous, tricky, two-faced, unfrank, wily
**in sincere manner** sincerely
**insincere praise** flattery
**insincere support** lip-talk
**insincere talk** bunkum, cant, jargon, lies
**in single file** one by one
**in single sequence** uniserial
**insinuate** advert, allude, clue, cue, hint, imply, inculcate, indicate, infiltrate, infuse, inject, instil, intimate, introduce, suggest, whisper
**insinuate oneself** ingratiate, sidle, work, worm
**insinuation** allusion, aspersion, hint, infusion, injection, innuendo, slur
**insipid** arid, banal, barren, bland, drab, empty, inane, jejune, lifeless, stupid, tame, tasteless, uninteresting, vapid, wishy-washy
**insipidity** banality, dullness, emptiness, flatness, flavourlessness, inexpressiveness, jejuneness, lifelessness, monotony, spiritlessness, staleness, tameness, tastelessness, tedium, tiredness, vapidity, vapidness
**insipid person** drip, wet
**insist** advise, allege, assert, assure, aver, avow, claim, command, contend, counsel, demand, exhort, expostulate, hold, maintain, persist, predicate, proclaim, profound, pronounce, reiterate, repeat, request, require, solicit, stress, suggest, swear, testify, underline, underscore, uphold, urge, vouch, vow
**insistence on a right** assertion
**insistence upon details** realism
**insistent** accentuated, adamant, demanding, emphatic, exigent, forceful, importunate, incessant, obstinate, persevering, persistent, recurrent, repeated, stubborn, tenacious, uncompromising, unfaltering, urgent
**insistent person** stickler
**insist on** demand, exact
**insist on requittal** demand satisfaction
**insist on urgently** press
**insist upon** assert, exact
**in slumber** asleep
**in small particles** fine
**in smooth manner** legato
**insobriety** alcoholism, bibulousness, crapulence, dipsomania, drinking,

drunkenness, inebriety, intemperance, intoxication, tipsiness
**in so far as** inasmuch, qua
**insolence** abuse, audacity, boldness, brashness, cockiness, disrespect, effrontery, forwardness, gall, impertinence, impoliteness, impudence, incivility, insubordination, intrusiveness, pertness, presumption, rudeness, sass, side
**insolent** abusive, arrogant, bold, brazen, cheeky, contemptuous, defiant, disrespectful, forward, fresh, impertinent, impudent, insubordinate, insulting, pert, presumptuous, rude, sassy, saucy, uncivil
**insolent menace** bravado
**insolent person** jackanapes
**insolvent** bankrupt, broke, bust, defaulting, destitute, failed, impecunious, indebted, moneyless, ruined
**insolvent person** bankrupt
**in so many words** in totidem verbis (L)
**in some degree** partly
**in some measure** somewhat
**in some order** alphabetical
**in some place** somewhere
**in some unknown way** somehow
**in some way** somehow
**insomnia** insomnolence, restlessness, sleeplessness, wakefulness
**insomnious** sleepless
**insouciant** airy, blithe, bright, carefree, casual, cheerful, easy-going, gay, glad, gleeful, happy-go-lucky, heedless, improvident, jaunty, jolly, light-hearted, merry, nonchalant, playful, sans souci (F), smiling, sunny, unconcerned, untroubled, unworried
**inspan** harness
**inspect** audit, check, examine, investigate, oversee, scan, scrutinise, search, study, superintend, supervise, survey, vet, visit
**inspection** examination, investigation, observation, scrutiny, study
**inspection of business accounts** audit
**inspection of the trachea** tracheoscopy
**inspection point** checkpoint
**inspector** examiner, tester
**inspector of accounts** auditor
**inspiration** afflatus, animus, arousal, aspiration, awakening, causation, contrivance, creation, encouragement, excitation, idea, influence, inspiring, intuition, muse, prompting, revelation, spur, stimulus, thought
**inspire** affect, animate, arouse, assure, cause, educate, encourage, energise, engender, enhearten, enlighten, enliven, enthuse, excite, explain, fill, fire, fortify, hearten, imbue, impel, influence, infuse, inhale, inspirit, instigate, instil, motivate, produce, respire, restore, reveal, snuff, stimulate, stir, transform, uplift
**inspire a belief** flatter
**inspire affection** endear
**inspired utterance** prophecy
**inspire passion** kindle
**inspirer of poets** muse
**inspire with foolish passion** infatuate
**inspire with love** enamour
**inspire with prejudice** animating, bias, encouraging, enlivening, galvanising, imbuing, influencing, moving, rousing, spurring, stimulating, stirring, uplifting
**inspiring devotion** charisma
**inspiring friendliness** amiable
**in spite of** despite, notwithstanding, regardless, yet
**in spite of oneself** malgré soi (F)
**in spite of the fact that** albeit, nevertheless, notwithstanding
**in spite of this** nevertheless
**install** establish, found, inaugurate, induct, initiate, plant, site, station
**install a bishop** enthrone
**install again** reinstate
**installation in office** investiture
**install formally** invest
**install in office** seat
**instalment** chapter, division, episode, establishment, investment, part, payment, placement, portion, repayment, section
**instalment of book** fascic(u)le, fasciculus
**instalment repayment** amortisation
**instance** case, citation, example, exemplification, illustration, occasion, precedent, quotation, specific, time
**instant** abrupt, breath, burst, crack, direct, fast, flash, immediate, jiffy, minute, moment, occasion, prompt, quick, second, speedy, trice, twinkling, urgent
**instantaneous photograph** snapshot
**instant house** prefab
**in state of disrepair** dilapidated
**instead** alternatively, else, preferably, rather
**in step** coinciding, conforming, conformity
**instep bone** metatarsal
**in stern of ship** aft
**instigate** abet, actuate, agitate, animate, (a)rouse, constrain, dispose, encourage, entice, excite, generate, impel, incite, induce, initiate, inspire, jog, jolt, persuade, press, prick, prompt, provoke, spur, tempt, thrust
**instigator** fomenter, inciter
**instigator of revolt** ringleader
**instil** bias, charge, educate, engender, engraft, fill, gradually, imbue, implant, impress, inculcate, infect, infix, inflame, infuse, ingrain, insinuate, instruct, introduce, penetrate, permeate, saturate, steep, stir, teach, train, tutor
**instinct** ability, aptitude, awareness, empathy, faculty, feeling, flair, gift, habit, impulse, intuition, predisposition, prompting, talent, tendency
**instinctive** automatic, congenital, hereditary, immanent, impulsive, inborn, inherent, innate, intuitive, involuntary, native, natural, spontaneous, untaught
**instinctive appreciation** flair
**instinctive belief** intuition
**instinctive good taste** flair
**instinctive impulses of the individual** id
**instinctive knowledge** intuition
**institute** appoint, commence, constitute, enact, establish, found, inaugurate, initiate, introduce, ordain, undertake
**institute legal proceedings** litigate, prosecute, sue
**institution** association, asylum, company, constitution, corporation, establishment, foundation, initiation, institute, museum, ordainment, sanatorium, society, syndicate
**institution for the care of orphans** orphanage
**institution for the insane** asylum
**in store** approaching, coming, destined, imminent, impending
**in store for** awaiting
**in straight line** collinear
**in strict confidence** confidentially, intimately, secretly, sotto voce
**instruct** brief, direct, discipline, edify, educate, indoctrinate, inform, order, prescribe, school, teach, train
**instruction** command, cultivation, culture, direction, edification, education, guidance, initiation, learning, order, schooling, teaching, training, tuition, tutelage, tutoring

**instruction book** enchiridion, handbook, manual, textbook, vade mecum
**instruction period** lecture, lesson, tutorial
**instructions for dish** recipe
**instructions to delete** dele
**instruction to a computer** command
**instructive** cultural, didactic, doctrinal, edifying, educative, homiletic, humanistic, informative, instructional, moralistic, propaedeutic, scientific
**instructive discussion** seminar
**instructive example** lesson
**instructor** adviser, coach, master, mentor, preceptor, teacher, trainer, tutor
**instructor in sports** coach
**instruct privately** tutor
**instrument** agent, appliance, barometer, broker, cello, contraption, contrivance, device, drum, gadget, implement, invention, mandolin, means, mechanism, medium, ocarina, robot, tool, utensil, violin, zither
**instrumental** active, assisting, auxiliary, conducive, contributory, helpful, influential, involved, subsidiary, useful
**instrumental composition** sonata
**instrumentalist** cellist, flautist, pianist, trumpeter, violinist, violist
**instrumentality** action, agency, aid, assistance, avail, effectiveness, efficacy, help, helpfulness, influence, manner, means, mediation, method, power, service, strategy, support, system, utility, value, way
**instrumental passage before soloist** intro(duction)
**instrumental solo for virtuoso** étude
**instrument ascertaining the intensity of radiant heat** pyroscope
**instrument examining light refraction in the eye** retinoscope
**instrument for boring holes in rocks** aiguille
**instrument for boring small holes** awl
**instrument for combing flax** heckle
**instrument for copying maps** pantograph
**instrument for counting corpuscles in the blood** haemocytometer
**instrument for cracking nuts** nutcracker
**instrument for cutting skin for grafting** dermatome
**instrument for delivering babies** forceps
**instrument for determining tints** tintometer

**instrument for determining densities of oil** oleometer
**instrument for determining hardness of materials** sclerometer
**instrument for determining time and latitude** almacantar, almucantar
**instrument for draining or injecting fluids** cannula
**instrument for estimating degrees of sensitiveness to pain** algometer
**instrument for estimating the dustiness of the air** koniscope, zymometer
**instrument for etching on glass** hyalograph
**instrument for examining a wound** probe
**instrument for examining hollow organs such as the bowel** endoscope
**instrument for examining the eye** ophthalmoscope
**instrument for examining the cervix** colposcope
**instrument for examining the interior of the stomach** gastroscope
**instrument for examining tissues and organs** fibrescope
**instrument for finding direction** compass
**instrument for holding open a surgical incision** retractor
**instrument for lifting and holding blood vessels** tenaculum
**instrument for listening to body sounds** stethoscope
**instrument for making incisions in surgery** lancet, scalpel
**instrument for making small surgical incision** bistoury
**instrument for measuring altitudes** almacantar, almucantar
**instrument for measuring amount of dew deposited** drosometer
**instrument for measuring an electric current in amperes** ammeter
**instrument for measuring angles** callipers, octant, pantometer, protractor
**instrument for measuring astronomical declination** declinometer
**instrument for measuring atmospheric pressure** barometer
**instrument for measuring blood pressure** sphygmomanometer
**instrument for measuring curved lines** opisometer
**instrument for measuring density of liquids** hydrometer
**instrument for measuring dust in the air** konimeter

**instrument for measuring earthquakes** seismograph
**instrument for measuring heat radiation** bolometer
**instrument for measuring heights** altimeter
**instrument for measuring high temperatures** pyroscope
**instrument for measuring humidity** hygrometer
**instrument for measuring humidity of air or gas** hygrometer
**instrument for measuring intensity of colour** colorimeter
**instrument for measuring intensity of radiation** actinometer
**instrument for measuring sharpness of hearing** audiometer
**instrument for measuring slopes** clinometer
**instrument for measuring small electric currents** galvanometer
**instrument for measuring temperature** thermometer
**instrument for measuring the force of wind** anemometer
**instrument for measuring the velocity of the blood flow** galvanometer, rheometer
**instrument for measuring the volume of solid bodies** stereometer
**instrument for measuring turbidity of liquid** nephelometer
**instrument for measuring very small distances** micrometer
**instrument for opening a body passage for inspection** speculum
**instrument for pressing the tongue down** spatula
**instrument for propelling boat** oar
**instrument for removing discs of bone from the skull** trepan, trephine
**instrument for removing hook from fish** disgorger
**instrument for removing liquids from a body cavity** aspirator
**instrument for removing tumours by tightening a wire loop** écraseur
**instrument for restoring heart rhythm by electric shock** defibrillator
**instrument for retarding the motion of a wheel** brake
**instrument for ringing** bell
**instrument for scraping bones** raspatory, xyster
**instrument for showing force of earthquake** seismograph
**instrument for summoning diners** gong
**instrument for testing the density of gas** dasymeter

**instrument for varying an electric resistance** rheostat
**instrument for winding** key
**instrument for writing** pen(cil)
**instrument imitating peal of bells** carillon
**instrument indicating the humidity of air** hygroscope
**instrument magnifying small objects** microscope
**instrument marking musical time at selected time** metronome
**instrument measuring altitude** altimeter
**instrument measuring magnetic intensity** magnetometer
**instrument of call** gong
**instrument of investigation** probe
**instrument of punishment** gallows, guillotine, tumbrel, tumbril
**instrument of torture** pilliwinks, rack
**instrument panel** facia
**instrument panel in car** dashboard
**instrument recording brain activity** electroencephalograph
**instrument recording heartbeats** electrocardiograph
**instrument recording muscle activity** electromyograph
**instrument recording time** chronograph
**instrument recording variations in blood pressure** kymograph
**instrument removing stones from the bladder** gorget
**instrument shaped like a sliced pear** lute
**instruments of war** arms
**instruments played by striking** percussion
**instrument that amplifies small sounds** phonendoscope
**instrument that measures electric current** ammeter
**instrument that throws picture on screen** projector
**instrument to measure the strength of wind** anemometer
**instrument to show speed of moving vehicle** speedometer
**instrument to warn ships in mist** foghorn
**instrument used in auscultation of heart and lungs** stethoscope
**instrument used in navigation** sextant
**instrument used to measure vapour pressure** isoteniscope
**instrument with mighty keys** organ
**instrument with which things are pounded in a mortar** pestle
**in style of** à la
**insubordinate** contumacious, cross-grained, defiant, disobedient, disorderly, dissenter, insurgent, insurrectional, lawless, mutineer, mutinous, noncooperative, opposed, perverse, protester, rebel(lious), recalcitrant, recusant, refractory, resistant, restive, revolutionary, rioter, riotous, seditious, striker, turbulent, undisciplined, undutiful, unruly, upriser
**in subsequent time** afterward
**in substance** basically
**insubstantial** aerial, airy, dainty, delicate, ethereal, fanciful, fantastic, feeble, fictitious, flimsy, fragile, frail, gossamer, idle, illusory, imaginary, immaterial, incorporeal, insignificant, light, makeshift, nominal, nugatory, petty, poor, puny, rickety, scant, shaky, shallow, slight, spectral, spiritual, superficial, tenuous, trifling, unimportant, unreal, vaporous, watery, weak
**in succession** en suite (F)
**in such a way** so
**insufficient** deficient, exiguous, imperfect, impotent, inadequate, incapable, incompetent, lacking, minus, needful, penniless, penurious, poverty-stricken, scant(y), scant, scarce, short, spare, wanting
**insufficiently factual** abstract
**insufficient nutrition** malnutrition
**in suitable manner** properly
**insular** alone, blinkered, closed, detached, illiberal, isolated, limited, narrow, parochial, petty, provincial, restricted, segregated, separate, separative
**insular terrain** island, isle
**insulate** isolate, pad, protect, screen, shelter, weatherproof
**insulated cord** flex
**insult** abuse, affront, aspersion, condemn, contempt, denounce, discredit, disdain, disgrace, disoblige, fling, humiliate, ignominy, incivility, indignity, injure, insolence, jeer, lampoon, libel, offence, offend, outrage, rebuff, revile, ridicule, rudeness, scoff, scorn, slander, slight, slur, snub, throw
**insulting** abusive, aloof, arrogant, brusque, churlish, cool, denunciation, derogatory, disgraceful, disparaging, flippant, ill-bred, neglectful, obtrusive, offensive, rude, scouting, snobby, uncivil, unrefined
**insulting remark** slur
**insulting speech** abuse

**insult openly** affront
**insult to sovereign** lese-majesty, treason
**in supporting position** onside
**insurance** assurance, covenant forethought, indemnification, indemnity, pledge, precaution, safeguard, security, warranty
**insurance certificate** policy
**insurance evaluator** assessor
**insurance man** agent, sales rep(resentative)
**insurance protection** coverage
**insure** assure, certify, cover, ensure, guarantee, indemnify, underwrite, warrant
**insurgent** anarchist, brawler, insurrection(ary), malcontent, mutineer, rebel, resister, revolter, revolutionary, revolutionist, rioter, riotous, seditionist
**insurmountability** insuperability
**insurrection** insurgency, mutiny, rebellion, revolt, riot, uprising
**insurrection at sea** mutiny
**in suspense** agog, anxious
**in sympathy** en rapport (F)
**intact** complete, entire, sound, unaltered, unimpaired, whole
**intaglio** carving, engraving, etching, rotogravure
**intake** quota
**intake of air** breath
**intangible** airy, ambiguous, bodiless, cloudy, dim, discarnate, dreamlike, esoteric, ethereal, evanescent, faint, ghostly, illusory, imaginary, immaterial, impalpable, insubstantial, microscopic, mysterious, nebulous, obscure, phantom, psychical, spectral, spooky, subtle, tenuous, undefined, unnoticeable, unreal, untouchable, vague, wispy
**intarsia** marquetry, tarsia
**in tears** blubbering, crying, distressed, sobbing, weeping
**integral** basic, complete, component, constituent, entire, essential, full, intact, undivided, unimpaired, whole
**integrate** articulate, assimilate, blend, cohere, combine, consolidate, desegregate, melt, merge, mingle, unify, unite
**integrity** decency, goodness, honesty, honour, justness, morality, principle, probity, rectitude, uprightness, virtue, wholeness
**integument** bag, coat, container, cover, crust, envelope, husk, membrane, peeling, pod, poke (Sc),

rind, sack, sheath, skin, wrapper, wrapping
**intellect** aptitude, brainpower, brains, cognition, consciousness, genius, insight, intelligence, intuition, judg(e)ment, (master)mind, mentality, nous, reason, sense, thinker, thought, understanding
**intellectual** academic, bookish, brain, egghead, highbrow, intelligent, mental, noetic, professor, rational, scholarly, studious, thoughtful
**intellectual attitude** pose
**intellectual contradiction** antinomy
**intellectual flight** soaring
**intellectual gifts** ability
**intellectual hold** grip
**intellectually clever** brainy
**intellectual person** egghead
**intellectual relish** palate
**intelligence** acumen, alertness, aptitude, brains, capacity, cleverness, mind, news, power, reason, sense, understanding
**intelligence agent** spy
**intelligent** acute, adroit, agile, alert, apt, bright, brilliant, clever, comprehending, conscious, deft, discerning, ingenious, intellectual, keen, lucid, luminous, sagacious, sane, sapient, sharp, shrewd, smart, wise
**intelligent breed of dog** border collie, sheepdog
**intelligible** apparent, appreciable, clear, comprehensible, discernible, evident, knowable, legible, lucid, manifest, obvious, penetrable, perspicuous, plain, simple, translucent, understandable, unobscure
**intelligible to outsiders** exoteric
**intemperate** abandoned, crude, dipsomaniacal, drunken, exaggerated, excessive, extortionate, extreme, free-living, immoderate, incontinent, inordinate, lavish, licentious, loose, prodigal, profligate, rash, satyric, self-indulgent, severe, sweltering, torrid, undue, unreasonable, unrestrained, violent, wanton, wild
**intend** aim, calculate, contemplate, contemplate, design, desire, earmark, expect, mean, meditate, plan, (pre)determine, (pre)destine, project, propose, purpose, pursue, resolve, scheme, will
**intended** deliberate, precontrived, premeditated, studious
**intended proceedings** plan
**intended to punish** punitive

**intended to reach** for
**intended to sell quickly** catchpenny
**intending goodwill** benevolent
**intend to be** mean
**in tennis, 40-all** deuce
**intense** acute, bitter, caustic, concentrated, crucial, deep, devoted, ecstatic, emotional, energetic, excitable, extreme, fervent, fierce, great, hot, impulsive, incisive, inflamed, keen, passionate, poignant, profound, rancorous, rapt, sarcastic, sharp, strong, studious, tart, tense, violent, volatile
**intense agitation** fever
**intense beam** laser
**intense desire** longing, yearn, yen
**intense dislike** animosity, animus, hate, hatred, horror
**intense dislike of wood** hylephobia
**intense dismay** horror
**intense effort** force
**intense expectancy** suspense
**intense fear** terror
**intense gloom** murk
**intense gunnery bombardment** cannonade
**intense happiness** felicity
**intense heat** fervour
**intense ill will** hatred
**intense intermittent pain in nerves of face and head** neuralgia
**intense light beam** laser
**intense longing** yen
**intensely disliked** detestable
**intensely engaged** absorbed
**intensely hot** fiery
**intensely interested** afire
**intensely interesting** absorbing
**intensely passionate** torrid
**intensely sweet** cloying, saccharine
**intense urge to steal** kleptomania
**intensify** aggravate, augment, boost, concentrate, deepen, emphasise, enhance, enrich, escalate, exaggerate, extend, fire, fuel, heighten, increase, magnify, overstress, quicken, raise, reinforce, sharpen, stimulate, strengthen, thicken, worsen
**intensive attack** blitzkrieg
**intensive inquiry** inquisition
**intensive teacher** crammer
**intent** absorbed, aim, alert, attentive, avid, committed, concentrated, contemplative, decided, determined, eager, earnest, fixed, intense, intention, observant, occupied, plan, preoccupied, purpose, rapt, resolute, resolved, steadfast, steady, watchful
**intention** aim, ambition, bent, bourn(e), decision, design, destination,

direction, end, gist, goal, idea, ideal, implication, intent, mark, meaning, motive, object, objective, plan, point, project, proposal, purport, purpose, resolution, resolve, scope, set, target, undertaking, view
**intentional** deliberate, devised, intended, meant, planned, plotted, prearranged, predetermined, purposive, schemed, wilful
**intentional cough** hawk
**intentional error** deliberate mistake
**intentional false statement** lie
**intentional killing of oneself** suicide
**intentionally offensive** derogatory
**intentional self-slaughter** suicide
**intentional violation of truth** lie
**intent look** gaze
**intently** attentively, closely
**intents and purposes** concentrated, determined, virtually
**inter** bury, entomb, inhume, sepulchre
**interbreeding of races** miscegenation
**intercede** adjure, appease, arbitrate, enjoin, entreat, implore, (inter)mediate, interpose, moderate, negotiate, obtest, pacify, propitiate, represent, solicit
**intercept** ambush, block, catch, seize, stop
**interchange** alternate, bandy, barter, change, cloverleaf, communication, connection, contact, conversion, convert, crossing, crossroads, displace, exchange, intersection, intersperse, junction, liaison, oscillate, reciprocate, remove, replace, rotate, substitute, substitution, swap, switch, trade, transmit, transpose, vary
**interclavicle** episternum
**intercontinental ballistic missile** rocket
**interdict** ban, bar(rier), blockage, check, debar, embargo, exclude, forbid, hindrance, impediment, inhibition, interdict, obstacle, prohibit(ion), proscribe, refuse, restriction, stoppage, veto
**interest** absorb, advantage, attention, attract, benefit, concern, curiosity, dividend, holding, involve, pursuit, stake, yield
**interested in** into
**interested in the obscene** prurient
**interested spectator** observer
**interesting and controversial public affair** cause célèbre
**interestingly odd** bizarre
**interestingly old-fashioned** quaint
**interesting period** episode
**interesting relic** curio

**interesting spread** array
**interfere** arrest, barricade, block, clash, collide, conflict, contravene, cramp, disrupt, encumber, frustrate, hamper, handicap, hinder, impede, inhibit, intercede, interrupt, intervene, intrude, meddle, molest, obstruct, prevent, pry, restrain, tamper, trammel
**interim** acting, interval, intervening, meantime, meanwhile, preliminary, provisional, stopgap, temporary
**interim monarch** regent
**interim ruling group** regency
**interior** centre, civil, core, heart, hidden, in(ner)most, inland, inner, inside, internal, intimate, inward, local, mental, middle, non-coastal, nucleus, personal, secret, veiled
**interior decoration** decor, paint, wallpaper
**interior design** decor
**interior layer** lining
**interior part** inside
**interject** infuse, insert, instil, interfere, interpose, interrupt, intervene, introduce, intrude
**interjecting** infusing, injecting, inserting, instilling, introducing, intruding
**interjection** cry, ejaculation, exclamation, imbedding, infusion, insertion, interpolation, interposition, remark, statement, utterance
**interlace** alter, blend, braid, combine, crisscross, entwine, (inter)mingle, (inter)twist, knit, lace, mix, plait, pleat, remodel, scramble, transform, twine, variegate, vary, weave
**interlace, as on a loom** weave
**interlaced hair** plait
**intermediary** advocate, agent, ambassador, arbiter, broker, buffer, bumper, courier, cushion, dealer, delegate, diplomat, emissary, envoy, factor, fender, go-between, judge, liaison, mediator, messenger, middleman, minister, negotiator, peacemaker, referee, representative, safeguard, screen, shield, umpire
**intermediate** halfway, intervening, mean, mesne, mid(way), middle
**intermediate between black and white** grey
**intermediate in time** mean
**intermediate number** some
**intermeshing system** network
**interminable** ceaseless, dragging, endless, eternal, everlasting, infinite, limitless, long(-drawn-out), long-winded, never-ending, perpetual, protracted, unbounded, unlimited, wearisome
**intermission** abeyance, arrest, cease, cessation, delay, discontinuance, halt, interim, interlude, intermittence, interval, lull, pause, recess, rest, stop, suspension
**intermittent** broken, erratic, fitful, flickering, fluttering, inconstant, infrequent, irregular, jerky, occasional, periodic, punctuated, recurring, remittent, spasmodic, sporadic, uneven, unsteady, wavering
**intermittent fever** ague
**intermittent hot spring** geyser
**intermittent light** glimmer
**intermittently rainy** showery
**intermix** blend
**intern** confine, detain, hold
**internal** civil, domestic, immanent, implanted, in-house, inherent, innate, inner, inside, interior, intimate, inward, mental, private, state, subjective, true
**internal content of a concept** intention
**internal evidence of authenticity** cachet
**internal organs** viscera
**internal organs of the body** viscera, viscus
**internal part of a dome** cupola
**internals** entrails, guts, innards, insides, intestines
**internal sac** cyst
**internal secretion** hormone
**internal spy** mole
**internal telephone system** intercom
**international** cosmopolitan, ecumenical, general, global, intercontinental, interstate, nonsectarian, universal, worldwide
**international agreement** cartel, treaty
**international cricket match** test
**international distress signal** Mayday, SOS
**international humanitarian society** Red Cross
**international language** Esperanto
**international match** test
**international overlooking** amnesty
**International Phonetic Alphabet** IPA
**international police** Interpol
**international soccer body** FIFA
**international telegram** cable
**international thawing of relations** detente
**interplanetary craft** spaceship
**interpolate** alter, amend, edit, inject, insert, insinuate, intercalate, interline, interrupt, intervene, introduce, revise, rewrite
**interpolation** addendum, addition, annotation, codicil, footnote, implant, inclusion, insert(ion), inset, insinuation, interlining, introduction, postscript, scholium, supplement
**interpose** insert, insinuate, interfere, interject, interrupt, intervene, introduce, intrude, mediate, offer, thrust
**interpose on behalf of another** intercede, plead
**interpret** clarify, construe, elucidate, explain, explicate, translate, understand
**interpretation of a text** eisegesis, exegesis
**interpreter** annotator, commentator, exponent, interlocutor, translator
**interpreter of dreams** oneirocritic
**interpret incorrectly** misconceive, misinterpret, misread
**interpreting** adapting, clarifying, construing, deciphering, decoding, defining, elucidating, explaining, expounding, paraphrasing, reading, rendering, solving, taking, translating
**interpret spoken word like deaf person** lip-read
**interpret wrongly** misconstrue
**interrogate** ask, cross-examine, examine, grill, inquire, interpellate, investigate, probe, query, question, quiz, test
**interrogate after mission** debrief
**interrupt** discontinue, disturb, interfere, interpose, intervene, intrude, obtrude, stop, suspend
**interrupter wheel** ticker
**interruption** break, disconnection, discontinuance, disruption, disturbance, division, halt, hiatus, hindrance, hitch, impediment, intrusion, obstacle, obstruction, pause, separation, stop(page), suspension
**interruption in continuity** hiatus
**intersect** crisscross
**intertwine** abut, adjoin, bisect, cleave, connect, converge, decussate, disconnect, divide, halve, intercept, (inter)cross, interrupt, join, lace, meet, split, sunder, touch, unite
**intersection of two roads** crossroad
**interstice** blank, breach, break, chink, cleft, crack, cranny, crevice, divide, fissure, gap, hiatus, hole, intermission, interruption, interval, lacuna, lull, nook, opening, pause, recess, rent, rift, space, void
**intertwine** adorn, affix, ally, bend, bind, blend, braid, coil, connect, contract, convolute, crease, (criss)cross,

crumple, double, (en)fold, enlace,
entangle, entwine, fasten, festoon,
fuse, gather, heal, inosculate,
(inter)lace, (inter)twist, (inter)weave,
(inter)wreathe, intermingle, intersect,
introduce, inweave, join, knit, link,
loop, mend, merge, overlap, plait,
pleat, secure, slice, surround, tie,
tuck, twirl, unite, wind, wrap
**interval**   break, delay, distance, interim,
intermission, meantime, pause,
period, rest, space, spell, wait
**interval between acts of a play**
entr'acte
**interval in cinema**   intermission
**interval of calm**   lull
**interval of inaction**   pause
**interval of octave**   ottava
**interval of quiet**   lull
**interval of rest**   respite
**intervene**   arbitrate, bargain, conciliate,
disrupt, disturb, intercede, intercept,
interfere, interpose, interrupt,
intrude, meddle, mediate, negotiate,
placate, tamper, umpire
**intervene and make ineffective**
override
**intervening period**   interim, meantime,
meanwhile
**intervening space**   interstice
**intervening time**   interim, meantime,
meanwhile
**intervention**   break, inroad, insertion,
insinuation, interference, interval,
intrusion, mediation, ministry,
negotiation, obtrusion, pause,
peacemaking
**interview**   consultation, discussion,
examination, interrogate,
question(ing), verbal
**interweave**   associate, entwine,
integrate, interlace, intermingle,
intertwine, mesh, plait
**interweave wool**   knit
**intestinal**   central, enteric, essential,
inner, inside, interior, internal,
inward, middle
**intestinal disease**   diarrhoea,
dysentery, gastro-enteritis
**intestinal fortitude**   guts, nerve
**intestinal part**   bladder, bowel(s),
duodenum, entrails, ileum, kidney,
liver, spleen, stomach
**intestinal roundworm**   ascarid
**intestines**   bowel(s), colons, entrails,
guts, insides, internals, inwards,
viscera, vitals
**in that direction**   to
**in that manner**   thus
**in that place**   there
**in that respect**   therein

**in the absence of the accused**
absente reo (L)
**in the act**   redhanded
**in the air**   afoot, close, imminent
**in the ascendant**   ascending, climbing,
commanding, dominant, dominating,
flourishing, increasing, prevailing,
rising, supreme, winning
**in the background**   inconspicuous,
offstage, unnoticed, unobtrusive,
unseen
**in the bag**   assured, certain, definite,
sure
**in the balance**   pending, undecided
**in the beginning**   first
**in the best of health**   fit
**in the black**   solvent
**in the blood**   congenital, inherited,
innate
**in the buff**   bare, naked, nude, unclad
**in the capacity of**   qua
**in the case of**   if, whether
**in the centre**   (a)mid, amidst, central,
core
**in the class of**   among(st)
**in the clear**   blameless
**in the clouds**   absent-minded,
abstracted, bemused, dreaming,
faraway, impractical, in nubibus (L),
irrational, unrealistic
**in the company of**   among(st)
**in the course of**   amid, during
**in the current fashion or style**   modish
**in the dark**   benighted, ignorant, in
tenebris (L), invisible, uninformed
**in the dark about**   ignorant
**in the direction of**   at, towards
**in the direction of the apex**   acropetal
**in the distance**   far, yonder
**in the doldrums**   dispirited, mopish,
weary
**in the end**   finally, lastly
**in the face of**   against
**in the fashion**   à la mode, fashionable,
mod(ish)
**in the field**   afield
**in the first part**   early
**in the first place**   imprimis, primarily
**in the flesh**   here, present
**in the foreground**   ahead, conspicuous
**in the future**   henceforth, later
**in the grave**   buried, dead, deceased
**in the highest**   in excelsis (L)
**in the increase**   developing, expanding,
growing, multiplying, spreading
**in the intervening period of time**
meanwhile
**in the land of Nod**   asleep
**in the last place**   lastly
**in the latest fashion**   à la page (F)
**in the lead**   ahead
**in the light of**   considering

**in the long run**   eventually, finally,
generally, ultimately
**in the main**   chiefly, mostly, principally
**in the manner of**   à la, alla (I), so
**in the manner of a skit**   satirically
**in the manner of Shylock**   usuriously
**in the manner that**   as
**in the market for**   lacking, wanting,
without
**in the matter of**   (in) re
**in the meantime**   interim
**in the middle**   amid(st), among(st),
between, central, equidistant,
halfway, mid(st), through
**in the middle of two**   between, betwixt
**in the midst**   amidst, among(st), during
**in the mind**   id, mentally
**in the mire**   entangled
**in the money**   affluent, rich, wealthy,
well-off
**in the morning**   antemeridian
**in the name of**   in nomine (L)
**in the name of Christ**   in Christi
nomine (L)
**in the name of the king**   de par le roi
(F)
**in the natural or raw state**   crude
**in the nature of things**   in rerum natura
(L)
**in the near future**   anon, presently,
shortly, soon
**in the neighbourhood**   locally
**in the neighbourhood of**   about,
approximately, around, close, near
**in the news**   current, topical
**in the offing**   afoot, imminent, near
**in the open**   out(side)
**in the open air**   à la belle étoile (F),
alfresco (I), outside
**in the past**   ago, gone, once, over,
past, since, yesteréen, yesteryear
**in the pink**   hale
**in the pipeline**   brewing, coming
**in the place cited**   in loco citato (L)
**in the place of**   in loco (L)
**in the place of a parent**   in loco
parentis (L)
**in the place quoted**   loco citato (L)
**in the process of rotting**   putrescent
**in the proximity of**   near
**in the ratio of one to two**   subduple
**in the raw**   naked
**in the rear**   (be)hind
**in the recent past**   yesterday
**in the red**   bankrupt, indebted,
insolvent, overdrawn
**in the region of**   approximately
**in the role of**   as
**in the same book**   ibid(em) (L)
**in the same manner**   as
**in the same place**   ibid(em) (L)
**in the same state as**   in statu quo (L)

**in the same way** as
**in the second place** secondly
**in these parts** hereabouts, locally
**in these times** nowadays
**in the sky** overhead
**in the style or fashion of** à la
**in the thick** amid(st), among(st), mid(st)
**in the third place** thirdly
**in the time that** while
**in the trial stages** experimental, probative
**in the very act** flagrante delicto (L)
**in the vicinity** around, local(ly)
**in the way that** as
**in the wind** afoot, approaching, coming, imminent, impending
**in the womb** in utero (L)
**in the work cited** opere citato (L)
**in the world** existent
**in the wrong** culpable, guilty, liable, mistaken
**in the year after the birth of Christ** anno post Christum natum (L)
**in the year of man's redemption** anno humanae salutis (L)
**in the year of our Lord** anno Domini (L)
**in the year of the reign** anno regni (L)
**in the year of the world** anno mundi (L)
**in this manner** thus
**in this place** be, here(in), hoc loco (L)
**in this usual way** more suo (L)
**in this way** as, so, thus
**in three languages** triglot
**in threes** ternary
**intimate apparel** lingerie
**intimate associate** friend
**intimate conversation** tête-à-tête
**intimate friend** alter ego, crony, pal
**intimate group** coterie
**intimation** allusion, clue, hint, implication, indication, inference, inkling, insinuation, reference, suggestion, whisper
**intimation of disdain** bah, contempt
**in time** eventually, someday, sometime, ultimately
**in time gone by** ago
**in time past** ago, heretofore
**intimidate** alarm, appal, browbeat, bulldoze, bully, coerce, cow, dishearten, dismay, dispirit, dissuade, frighten, overawe, scare, subdue, terrify, terrorise, threaten
**intimidation** alarm, arm-twisting, browbeating, bullying, coercion, daunting, dismay, disquietude, dread, fear, fright, menaces, menacing, pressure, terror(isation), terrorising, threats, tremor, tyranny
**intimidatory remark** threat

**into** within
**into error** astray
**intolerable** abhorrent, insufferable, insupportable, unbearable, unendurable
**intolerant** biased, bigoted, chauvinistic, close-minded, cynical, fanatical, illiberal, impatient, inconsiderate, insular, jaundiced, jingoistic, narrow-minded, opinionated, prejudiced, prescriptive, racist, sexist, small-minded, uncharitable, unforbearing, unindulgent, unreasonable, warped
**intolerant of waiting** impatient
**intolerant person** bigot
**intonation** accent, articulation, bend, bow, chant, curvative, diction, elocution, enunciation, inflection, modulation, pronunciation, speech, stress, tone
**intone** carol, chant, chime, croon, emit, inflect, intonate, modulate, murmur, pronounce, recite, say, sing, speak, utter, whisper
**intoner** chanter
**into parts** apart
**into reserve** aside
**into the bargain** addition, also, too
**into the very midst of the business** in medias res (L)
**into the wind** leeward
**into vein** intravenous
**intoxicant** alcohol
**intoxicate** exhilarate, fuddle, inebriate, inflame
**intoxicated** blotto, drunk(en), oiled, pissed, sloshed, smashed, tight, tipsy, wrecked, zonked
**intoxicating** alcoholic, heady, inebriant, intoxicant, strong, thrilling
**intoxicating drink** ava
**intoxicating drink used in Vedic ritual** soma
**intoxicating liquor** alcohol
**in traces only** vestigial
**intransigent** adamant, contrary, determined, die-hard, firm, fixed, headstrong, immovable, inexorable, inflexible, insistent, intractable, obdurate, perverse, reactionary, resolute, rigid, set, stiff, strict, stubborn, unbending, uncompromising, unrelenting, unshakable, unyielding, wilful
**intransitive** neuter
**intravascular coagulation of blood** thrombosis
**intra-** inside, within
**intrepid** audacious, bold, brave, courageous, daring, dashing, dauntless, dreadless, fearless, firm,

hardy, heroic, nervy, plucky, resolute, staunch, sturdy, unafraid, unalarmed, undaunted, unfaltering, unfearing, valiant
**intrepid warrior** hero
**intricacy** complexity, conundrum, enigma, intricateness, knottiness, perplexity, puzzle, puzzlement, riddle, tortuosity, web
**intricate** baroque, complex, convoluted, difficult, elaborate, fancy, involute, involved, obscure, tangled, tortuous
**intricate threadwork** lace
**intrigue** absorb, adultery, affair, amour, arrest, attract, baffle, cabal, conspiracy, conspire, enthral, fascinate, impress, interest, lewdness, liaison, pique, plot, ruse, scheme, secret, seduce, spy, stimulate, titillate, tryst, wangling
**intriguer** conspirator, plotter, schemer
**intrinsic** basic, built-in, central, congenital, essential, genuine, inborn, inbred, inherent, innate, native, natural, real, true
**intrinsic nature** essence
**introduce** acquaint, admit, advance, announce, befriend, begin, harbinger, inaugurate, initiate, launch, lead, mention, offer, originate, present, promote, propose, sponsor, suggest, usher
**introduced from abroad** exotic
**introduced from outside** foreign
**introduce formally** present
**introduce fundamental change to** revolutionise
**introduce new words** neologise
**introduces alternative** or
**introduction** beginning, implementation, installation, institution, opening, orientation, preamble, preface, prelude, presentation, proem, reference, start
**introduction to a book** preface, proem
**introductory** antecedent, basic, early, elementary, explanatory, first, fundamental, inaugural, incipient, initial, initiative, leading, opening, prefatory, preliminary, prelusive, preparatory, primary, starting
**introductory book** isagoge
**introductory chapter** preface
**introductory discourse** proem
**introductory movement** overture
**introductory part of discourse** exordium
**introductory performance** prelude
**introspective** absorbed, brooding, concentrating, contemplative, deliberative, engrossed, introverted,

# intrude — invest

**intrude** (cont.) inward-looking, meditative, musing, occupied, pensive, pondering, preoccupied, rapt, reflective, ruminant, speculative, thoughtful
**intrude** encroach, infringe, interfere, obtrude, trespass, violate
**intrude illegally** trespass
**intruder** attacker, burglar, busybody, crasher, interferer, interloper, invader, meddler, newcomer, outsider, parvenu, prowler, raider, squatter, thief, trespasser
**intrude stealthily** encroach
**intrude without right** trespass
**intrusion** infringement, inroad, interruption, invasion, trespass, usurpation, violation
**intrusive** annoying, forward, incursive, interfering, intruding, invasive, irksome, irritating, irruptive, meddling, nosy, obtrusive, prying, pushing, worrisome
**intrusively helpful** officious
**intrusive rock formed at great depth** plutonic
**in truth** actually, frankly, really, truthfully
**intuit** apprehend, comprehend, conjecture, deduce, discern, discover, feel, foretell, grasp, guess, infer, ken, know, perceive, realise, see, sense, suppose, surmise, suspect, understand
**intuition** discernment, feeling, gut, hunch, insight, instinct, perception, precognition, presentiment, sixth sense
**intuitive discernment** flair
**intuitive feeling** hunch
**in tune** harmonious
**in twenty-four hours' time** tomorrow
**in two minds** ambivalent, undecided
**in unbroken order** consecutive
**inundate** bury, choke, cover, deluge, drench, drown, engulf, flood, glut, overflow, overpower, overrun, overspread, overwhelm, sate, saturate, soak, submerge, swamp
**in unending supply** galore
**in unison** together
**inure** acclimatise, accommodate, accustom, adapt, adjust, condition, drill, educate, enure, equip, exercise, familiarise, habituate, naturalise, practise, prepare, ready, season, train
**in use** in usu (L)
**inutility** fruitlessness, futility, inadequacy, inanity, ineffectuality, inefficacy, ineptitude, inoperativeness, meritlessness, unproductivity, uselessness, valuelessness, worthlessness

**in utter confusion** pell-mell, topsy-turvy
**invade** assail, assault, attack, beset, besiege, blitz, encroach, enter, infest, infringe, interrupt, intervene, intrude, irrupt, occupy, overrun, overspread, penetrate, permeate, pervade, raid, seize, storm, transgress, violate
**invader** intruder, marauder, raider, usurper, violator
**in vain** futile
**invalid** cripple, disabled, handicapped, illegitimate, null, useless, valetudinarian, void
**invalidate** annul, cancel, confute, controvert, debunk, destroy, disable, disapprove, discredit, disprove, disqualify, eliminate, end, eradicate, explode, expose, expunge, extinguish, extirpate, incapacitate, invalidate, negate, nullify, obliterate, overthrow, overturn, quash, rebut, refute, repudiate, rescind, revoke, subvert, suppress, terminate, undo, void
**invalidating defect in document** flaw
**invalidation** (ab)negation, abrogation, annulment, cessation, confutation, defeasance, disablement, discarding, discredit, dismissal, dissolution, enervation, overturn, paralysis, refutation, repeal, repudiation, rescinding, rescindment, revocation, spoiling, subversion, termination, undoing, vitiation, voidance, weakening, withdrawal
**invalid's oatmeal food** gruel
**invalid's toilet** bedpan, bottle
**invaluable** costly, dear, essential, excellent, exceptional, expensive, exquisite, incalculable, indispensable, inestimable, matchless, needful, peerless, precious, priceless, rare, unequalled, unique, unusual, useful, valuable
**invariable** changeless, invariant, unchangeable, unchanging, uniform, unvarying
**invariable quantity** constant
**invasion** assault, attack, encroachment, infringement, intrusion, irruption, penetration, raid
**invasion by air** raid
**invasion day** D-Day
**invective** abusive, accusation, calumnious, censorious, contumely, damnatory, denunciation, denunciatory, depreciation, derogatory, diatribe, disparagement, disparaging, insulting, railing, reproach, scorn, tirade, vituperation

**inveigh** abuse, attack, berate, censure, curse, decry, denigrate, depreciate, disparage, execrate, impugn, lambast(e), oppugn, protest, rebuke, vituperate
**inveigle** allure, attract, bait, beguile, blandish, cajole, coax, compliment, court, deceive, decoy, draw, entice, flatter, humour, lure, mislead, persuade, praise, puff, seduce, tempt, wheedle
**invent** coin, compose, conceive, conjure, create, design, devise, discover, fabricate, fantasise, imagine, indulge, license, mint, originate, produce, register, spin, varnish
**invented statement** fiction, figment
**invented word** neologism
**invention** brainchild, coinage, contraption, contrivance, creation, creativity, deceit, design, development, device, discovery, fabrication, fake, falsehood, fantasy, fib, fiction, forgery, gadget, genius, imagination, lie, originality, prevarication, sham, story, untruth, yarn
**invention copyright** patent
**invention of Hermes** lyre
**invention of the mind** figment
**inventive** complex, creative, daedal, fertile, gifted, imaginative, ingenious, inspired, mysterious, original, resourceful, skilful
**inventive ability** contrivance
**inventor** architect, artist, author, builder, coiner, contriver, craftsman, creator, designer, deviser, discoverer, establisher, father, generator, initiator, maker, originator, planner, producer
**inventor of the centigrade scale** Celsius
**inventor of the radiation gauge** Geiger
**inventor's right** patent
**inverse** contrary, inverted, opposite, reverse, transposed
**inversion of the eyelashes** trichiasis
**invert** capsize, introvert, overset, overturn, reverse, transpose, upset, upturn
**invertebrate** spineless, worm
**invertebrate creature** insect
**in very good health** as fit as a fiddle
**in very high spirits** cock-a-hoop
**invest** array, attire, bestow, clothe, cover, disburse, donate, dress, employ, encircle, enclose, endow, endue, entrust, expend, give, imbue, induct, instate, lay, ordain, place,

**investigate** risk, spend, stake, store, subsidise, supply, venture, vest
**investigate** analyse, consider, examine, explore, inspect, look into, probe, ransack, research, rummage, scour, scrutinise, search, sift, study
**investigate with stealth** snoop
**investigation** analysis, enquiry, examination, exploration, hearing, inquest, inquiry, inspection, probe, research, review, scrutiny, search, study, survey
**investigation of pedigrees** genealogy
**investigator** analyst, detective, fact-finder, inquisitionist, inspector, researcher, reviewer, scrutiniser
**invest in** buy
**investiture** admission, apparel, attire, chairing, consecration, coronation, crowning, enthronement, establishment, inauguration, induction, installation, instatement, introduction, mantle, ordination, robe, vestment
**investment** contribution, input, share, stake
**investment list** portfolio
**invest unwisely** misplace
**invest with** attach, endue
**invest with a title** dub
**inveterate bitterness** rancour
**in vicinity** local
**in view** visible
**in view of fact that** whereas
**in view of the fact that** inasmuch as
**invigorate** activate, animate, boost, cheer, energise, enliven, excite, fortify, freshen, inflame, intensify, kindle, nerve, pep, quicken, refresh, rouse, stimulate, strengthen, vitalise
**invigorating** chilly, energising, fresh, healthful, remedial, restorative, stimulating, tonic, vivifying, wholesome
**invigorating air** ozone
**invigorating thing** tonic
**invincible** impenetrable, indomitable, insuperable, insurmountable, irrepressible, unvanquishable
**inviolable** hallowed, holy, inalienable, sacred, sacrosanct, unalterable
**invisible** absent, camouflaged, concealed, dark, disappearing, disguised, hidden, imperceivable, imperceptible, infinitesimal, latent, obscure, screened, secret, unapparent, undivulged, unnoticeable, unobserved, unrevealed, unseen, unsighted, vanished, veiled
**invisible to the naked eye** atomlike, microscopic

**invite** adjure, (al)lure, ask, attract, beseech, bid, call, draw, encourage, entice, implore, incite, induce, plead, request, summon, tantalise, tempt
**invited visitor** guest
**invoice** account, bill, charge, reckoning, statement, tally
**invoke happiness on** bless
**invoke with tears** implore
**involuntary** automatic, instinctive, reflex, reluctant, uncontrolled, unwilled
**involuntary expiration** sneeze
**involuntary response** reflex
**involuntary urination** enuresis
**involute** intricate, involved
**involuted** abstruse, complicated
**involve** absorb, accuse, combine, commit, complicate, comprehend, comprise, concern, confuse, connect, contain, embrace, enclose, enfold, engage, entail, entangle, implicate, imply, include, incriminate, inculpate, indicate, perplex, preoccupy, require, signify, suggest, surround, typify
**involved as a result** entailed
**involve deeply** immerse
**involve in an accusation** incriminate
**involve in conflict** embroil
**involvement in wrongdoing** complicity
**involving bloodshed** gory
**involving three parties** tripartite
**involving four parties** quadripartite
**involving great risk** hazardous
**involving light** optical
**involving personal relationships** interpersonal
**involving risk** adventurous, dangerous
**involving the crime of treason** treasonable
**involving the supernatural** occult
**involving two or more countries** international
**in want** needy
**inward looking** egotistic, introspective, self-centred
**in whatever way** however
**in what manner?** how
**in what place?** where
**in what position?** where
**in which current is measured** ampere
**in witness** in testimonium (L)
**iodine analysis** iodometry
**iodine-treated** iodised
**Ionian island** Corfu
**ion with a negative charge** anion
**ion with a positive charge** cation
**iota** atom, jot, particle, scintilla, scrap, spark, tittle, trace
**ipecac** ipecacuanha
**ipecacuanha alkaloid** emetine

**IQ society** Mensa
**Iranian** Persian
**Iranian coin** rial
**Iranian donkey** onager
**Iranian language of Pathans** Pashto
**Iranian money** rial
**Iranian Moslem leader** ayatollah
**Iranian parliament** Majlis
**Iranian rugs** Persian carpets
**Iraqi money** dinar, dirham
**irascible** acrimonious, angry, astringent, bitter, cantankerous, caustic, censorious, choleric, cross, crusty, cutting, fierce, grumpy, hasty, hot-tempered, ill-humoured, impatient, irritable, mordant, passionate, peevish, petulant, prickly, pungent, quarrelsome, quick-tempered, rancorous, ratty, sarcastic, severe, sharp, short-tempered, snappish, spiteful, sullen, tart, temperamental, testy, touchy, trenchant
**irate** angry, cross, enraged, fuming, furious, ireful, irritable, irritated, livid, piqued, provoked, rabid, ranting, raving, riled, ropable, wrathful
**ire** acerbity, acrimony, anger, animosity, disapproval, displeasure, dudgeon, enmity, fury, irritation, passion, rage, spleen, vexation, virulence, wrath
**Ireland** Eire, Emerald Isle, Erin, Hibernia
**Ireland's national airline** Aer Lingus
**irenic** conciliatory, peaceful
**iridaceous plant** ixia
**irides** fleur-de-lis, irises
**iridescence** changeability, dazzling, glimmer(ing), glisten(ing), lustre, lustrousness, opalescence, polychromaticism, reflection, reflectivity, shimmer, shine, shininess, variance, variedness
**iridescent** kaleidoscopic
**iridescent gem** opal
**iridescent like an opal** opalescent
**iris** fleur-de-lis, rainbow, xyrid
**irises** fleur-de-lis, irides
**iris flower** fleur-de-lis, rainbow
**Irish** Erse, Hibernian, Milesian
**Irish accent** brogue
**Irish and Welsh travelling tinkers' cant** Shelta
**Irish boy** gossoon
**Irish charm** blarney
**Irish clan** sept
**Irish clover-like symbol** shamrock
**Irish county** Armagh, Kerry, Leitrim, Mayo, Meath, Sligo, Tyrone
**Irish cudgel** shillelagh
**Irish dagger** sgian-dhu, skean-dhu

**Irish dance** fading, jig
**Irish drinking den** shebean, shebeen
**Irish elf** leprechaun
**Irish emblem** harp
**Irish funeral song** keen
**Irish Gaelic** Erse
**Irish game like hockey** hurling
**Irish goblin** leprechaun
**Irish illicit spirit** poitin, poteen
**Irish island group** Aran
**Irish lament** ulla-lulla
**Irish language** Celtic, Erse, Keltic
**Irish lassy** colleen
**Irish liqueur flavoured with coriander** usquebaugh
**Irish lower house** Dáil
**Irishman** Malesian, Paddy
**Irish member of parliament** teachta
**Irish moss** carrageen
**Irish mourning party** wake
**Irish parliament** Dáil (Eireann), Oireachtas
**Irish poet** Joyce, Moore, Yeats
**Irish dramatist** Synge, Yeats
**Irish political group** IRA, Provos, Sinn Fein
**Irish Protestant** Orangeman, Ulsterman
**Irish province** Munster
**Irish racecourse** Curragh
**Irish republic** Eire
**Irish sprite** leprechaun
**Irish sweater** aran
**Irish symbol** harp, shamrock
**Irish tenant** cott(i)er
**Irish whiskey** usquebaugh
**irk** abhor, afflict, aggravate, anger, annoy, bedevil, bore, bother, discompose, disgust, displease, dissatisfy, distress, disturb, enrage, exasperate, fret, frustrate, gall, harass, harry, incense, ire, irritate, madden, molest, needle, nettle, pester, pique, plague, provoke, rile, ruffle, tease, tire, torment, trouble, vex, weary, worry
**irksome** annoying, boring, bothersome, burdensome, disagreeable, exasperating, irritating, tedious, tiresome, troublesome, unwelcome, vexatious, vexing, wearisome
**iron** determined, ferrous, flatiron, harsh, ironlike, metal, powerful, press, steel, stern, strong, unyielding, vigorous
**iron bar used as lever** crowbar
**iron block on which a smith hammers metal** anvil
**iron-bound** inflexible, rigid, rigorous, rugged, unyielding

**iron bracket strengthening angle of construction** gusset
**Iron Chancellor** Bismarck
**iron-clad ship** monitor
**iron collar for punishing offenders** jougs (Sc)
**iron cooking pot** skillet
**ironer** presser
**iron for casting** mitis
**iron framework** cradling
**iron-headed golf club** cleek
**iron hoisting-bucket** kibble
**ironic** acidulous, acrid, burlesque, contemptuous, contradictory, cynical, derisive, figurative, incongruous, ironical, mocking, mordant, paradoxical, ridiculing, sarcastic, sardonic, satirical, scoffing, scornful, sneering, surprising, unexpected, unforeseen, wry
**ironical** derisive, figurative, ironic, paradoxical, sarcastic, sardonic, satirical, sneering, wry
**ironically ambiguous** left-handed
**ironic humour** sarcasm
**iron lung** respirator
**ironmongery** hardware
**iron or lead** metal
**iron out** eliminate, erase, finalise, perfect, reconcile, resolve, settle, simplify, solve, unravel
**iron out and smooth off** flatten
**iron oxide** rust
**iron oxide red** agate
**iron prong for cooking** spit
**iron rod** bar
**irons** constraint, fetters, gyves, hampers, pinions, restraint, trammels
**iron-toothed instrument for combing wool** card
**irony** contrariness, derision, facetiousness, incongruity, mockery, paradox, sarcasm, satire
**Iroquois' home** te(e)pee, tipi
**irradiate** animate, brighten, cheer, clarify, edify, educate, enlighten, exalt, flash, gleam, illuminate, illumine, indoctrinate, inform, initiate, instil, light(en), shimmer, shine
**irrational** aberrant, absurd, brainless, crazy, demented, foolish, illogical, injudicious, insane, mindless, nonsensical, senseless, silly, unreasonable, unreasoning, unthinking, unwise, wild
**irrational fear** phobia
**irrational number** surd
**irredeemable** incontestable, incontrovertible, indisputable, irreclaimable, undeniable

**irrefutable** absolute, apparent, clear, conclusive, definite, evident, final, indisputable, indubitable, manifest, obvious, palpable, patent, unassailable, undeniable, undisputed, unquestionable
**irregular** aberrant, abnormal, asymmetric(al), bending, circuitous, devious, eccentric, erratic, heteroclite, heteroclitic, lawless, lumpy, nonconforming, nonconformist, random, rough, spasmodic, sporadic, unequal, uneven, unmethodical, unsystematic, unusual, variable
**irregular in behaviour** erratic
**irregularity** aberration, abnormity, abortion, anomalism, anomaly, asymmetry, bumpiness, circuitry, confusion, cragginess, crookedness, eccentricity, erraticism, freak, inconsistency, monstrosity, oddity, oddness, ruggedness, singularity, strangeness, systemless, unequality, unevenness, variation
**irregularity marked with black and white** piebald
**irregularly formed word** heteroclite, heteroclitic
**irregular mass** agglomeration
**irregular rotating shaft** cam
**irregular soldier** guer(r)illa
**irregular sonnet** quatorzain
**irregular triangle** scalene
**irrelevant** alien, extraneous, foreign, illogical, immaterial, impertinent, inapplicable, inappropriate, incongruous, inconsequent, inconsistent, insignificant, peripheral, tangential, unconnected, unessential, unnecessary, unrelated, unwarranted
**irrelevant conclusion** non sequitur
**irreproachable** blameless, correct, errorless, ethical, flawless, ideal, immaculate, impeccable, infallible, moral, perfect, principled, respectable, sinless, spotless, stainless, unblameworthy, unblemished, unimpeachable
**irresistible** alluring, compelling, imperative, inescapable, inexorable, overpowering, potent, seductive, urgent
**irresistible desire to steal** kleptomania
**irresistible force** constraint, juggernaut
**irresistible tendency to steal** kleptomania
**irresistible urge** compulsion
**irresolute** changeable, cowardly, diffident, doubtful, faithless, faltering, fearful, feeble, fickle, hesitant,

hesitating, inconsistent, mercurial, perplexed, pliant, reluctant, sceptical, squeamish, submissive, suspicious, tentative, timid, uncertain, unconvinced, undecided, unfaithful, unresolved, unsettled, vacillating, variable, volatile, yielding

**irresponsible** capricious, careless, changeable, erratic, flighty, frivolous, giddy, immature, inconsiderate, inconstant, irresolute, lawless, rash, reckless, self-centred, thoughtless, unanswerable, undecided, unreliable, unruly, unstable, untrustworthy, volatile, wavering, wild

**irresponsible person** enfant terrible (F), flibbertigibbet

**irreverence** blasphemy, cheek(iness), contempt, derision, discourtesy, dishonour, disregard, disrespect, flippancy, frivolity, heresy, impertinence, impiety, impoliteness, impudence, insolence, levity, mockery, pertness, profanation, rudeness, sacrilege, sauce, sauciness, violation

**irreverent** discourteous, disrespectful, impertinent, impious, impolite, insolent, profane, undevout, unholy, unpious, unreligious

**irreversible fact** fait accompli (F)

**irrigate** dampen, drench, flood, inundate, moisten, spray, sprinkle, supply, (s)wash, water, wet

**irrigation ditch** drain, flume, sloot, sluice

**irritable** bearish, cantankerous, crabbed, cross, edgy, excitable, fiery, fretful, grouchy, grumpy, hasty, high-strung, impatient, irascible, narky, nervous, peevish, querulous, ratty, resentful, snappish, snappy, testy, tetchy, touchy, waspish

**irritable person** crank, grouch

**irritable temper** spleen

**irritably brusque** snappy

**irritate** aggravate, anger, annoy, bug, chafe(d), enrage, exacerbate, excite, fret, gall, grate, harassed, incense, inflame, infuriate, ire, irk, itch, needle, nettle, niggle, peeve, pestered, pique, plagued, rankle, rasp, red, rile(d), ruffle, sensitive, smarting, sore, stimulate, tease, tormented, vex(ed), worry

**irritate intensely** exasperate

**irritate playfully** tease

**irritate severely** rankle

**irritating** acrid, aggravating, agitating, angering, displeasing, disturbing, galling, irksome, irritant, maddening, nettling, provoking, tiresome, troublesome, vexatious

**irritating desire** itch

**irritating insect** gnat, mosquito, muggie

**irritating person** gadfly

**irritating sound** noise

**irritation** aggravation, anger, annoyance, chafing, crossness, discontent, displeasure, dissatisfaction, exasperation, fury, impatience, indignation, irritability, irritant, itch, nuisance, pain(fulness), pique, provocation, resentment, stimulation, vexation

**irritation skin** itch

**is** abides, be, breathes, endures, est (L), exists, inhabits, lives, prevails, stands, survives

**is able to** can

**is able to preserve** can, tin

**is ahead** leads

**is an integral part of** inheres

**is aware** knows

**is consequence of** result

**is curious** wonders

**is deficient** lacks

**is delirious** raves

**is drowsy** nods

**is fond of** cares, likes, loves

**is friendly** fraternises

**I shall rise again** resurgam (L)

**I shudder as I tell the story** horresco referens (L)

**is important** matters

**is inclined to** tends

**is indebted to** owes

**is in force** prevails

**isinglass** mica

**is innate** inheres

**is in pain** aches

**is in session** sits

**is insistent** persists

**is in the majority** outnumbers

**is in vogue** prevails

**is it clear and truthful?** realistic

**Islamic Bible** Koran

**Islamic call to prayer** azan

**Islamic centre** Mecca

**Islamic chief** ameer, amir, emir

**Islamic evil jinni** Eblis

**Islamic house of worship** masjid, mosque

**Islamic law** ada(t), bai, sharia, sheri(at)

**Islamic leader** ayatollah, ima(u)m

**Islamic prince** sherif

**Islamic ruler** ameer, amir, bey, caliph, emir, sultan

**Islamic Sabbath, falling on Friday** Juma

**Islam robes** ihram

**Islam sacred scriptures** Koran

**island** ait, atoll, cay, enclave, eyot, floe, haven, holm, iceberg, île (F), isle(t), key, oasis, reef, refuge, sanctuary

**island and sea** Timor

**island at centre of Earth** Meru

**island awarded George Cross** Malta

**island belonging to the Netherlands** Aruba

**island group** archipelago, atoll

**island group in the Indian Ocean** Aldabra, Comoros, Maldives, Seychelles

**island group off Alaska** Aleutian, Andreanof, Pribilof, Rat

**island group off Guam** Maraianas

**island group off Taiwan** Matsu, Mazu, Penghu, Pescadores, Quemoy

**island group off Tonga** Haapai, Tofua, Vavua

**island in a lake** holm

**island in Alaska** Adak, Afognak, Atka, Attu, Diomede, Kodiak, Nunivak, Umnak, Unimak

**island in a river or lake** holm

**island in China** Matsu, Quemoy

**island in Galway Bay** Aran

**island in Indonesia** Alor, Bali, Java, Sumba

**island in Ireland** Aran, Rathlin, Saltee, Tory

**island in New York harbour** Ellis

**island in San Francisco Bay** Alcatraz

**island in the Atlantic** Madeira

**island in the Baltic Sea** Åland

**island in the eastern Mediterranean** Crete, Cyprus

**island in the Inner Hebrides** Iona

**island in the Ionian group** Corfu, Ithaca, Levkas, Paxos, Zante

**island in the Irish Sea** Man

**island in the North Sea** Texel

**island in the Saronic Gulf** Aegina

**island in the South Pacific** Fiji

**island in the West Indies** Barbados, Trinidad

**island in the West Pacific** Borneo

**island in Torres Strait** Thursday

**island in Tunisia** Djerba

**island noted for its monolithic statues** Easter

**island off Alaska** Kodiak

**island off China** Quemoy

**island off France** Corsica, If, Re, Sark, Ushant, Yeu

**island off Ireland** Achill, Aran, Rathlin, Tory

**island off Italy** Capri, Elba, Ischia, Lipari, Sardinia, Sicily

**island off Jutland** Laeso, Samso

**island off New York** Coney

**island off Scotland** Arran, Tiree

**island off Sicily** Stromboli

**island off Sumatra** Bangka, Nias
**island off Tuscany** Elba
**island of Grenada** Carriacon
**island of Guam** Cabras
**island of Italy** Elba
**island of Macao** Coloane, Taipa
**island of Malta** Comino, Gozo
**island of Mauritius** Agalega, Gabriel, Rodriguez
**island of Samoa** Manua, Ofu, Olosega, Rose, Savaii, Tau, Tutuila, Upolu
**island of Sicily** Egadi, Lipari, Ustica
**island of Solomon Islands** Buka, Florisa, Russell, Savo, Tulagi
**island of South Yemen** Kamaran, Perim, Socotra
**island of the Cyclades** Delos, Kea, Melos
**island of the Orkney Islands** Hoy, Pomona, Rousay, Sanday, Stronsay
**island of the Seychelles** Ladigue, Mahe, Praslin
**island of Western Samoa** Apolima, Manono, Savaii
**island resort near Venice** Lido
**island(s)** Aldabra, Aleutian, Antipodes, Ascension, Azores, Bahamas, Bermuda, Bounty, Cape Verde, Caroline, Chatman, Comoros, Coney, Cook, Corsica, Crete, Cyprus, Delos, Elba, Ellice, Falkland, Fiji, Gilbert, Hainan, Hawaiian, Keeling, Majorca, Maldive, Malta, Manihiki, Marquesas, Marshall, Mauritius, Melos, Mikonos, Molucca, North, Palau, Palau, Paros, Pátmos, Philippine, Phoenix, Réunion, Revilla, Rhodes, Samoa, Sardinia, Seychelles, Sicily, Society, Solomon, South, Sri Lanka, St Helena, Tahiti, Taiwan, Tasmania, Tokelau, Tristan da Cunha, Tubaai, Vancouver
**islands north of Cuba** Bahamas
**islands off Scotland** Orkneys
**island source of marble** Paros
**isle** island
**Isle of Man** Mona
**isle of Napoleon** Corsica, Elba, St Helena
**Isle of Wight strait** Solent
**islet** ait, eyot
**is like a cat on hot bricks** fidget
**ism** doctrine
**is noisy** roils
**is nostalgic** reminisce
**is not** ain't, isn't, isnae (Sc), isne (Sc)
**is of concern** interest, relevant
**is of consequence** matters
**is of use** avails
**isogram** isoline, isopleth

**isolate** abstract, alienate, banish, boycott, confine, detach, disconnect, divide, divorce, exclude, exile, expatriate, identity, imprison, insulate, ostracise, outlaw, quarantine, remove, seclude, segregate, separate, sequester, sever, single
**isolated** abnormal, alone, anomalous, detached, disconnected, divorced, freak, hidden, insulated, lonely, outlying, quarantined, remote, retired, secluded, segregated, separated, sequestered, sporadic, unfrequented
**isolated article** oddment
**isolated ground** island
**isolated hill** mesa
**isolated land tract** island
**isolated tract** island
**isolate oneself** secede, withdraw
**isolation** aloofness, detachment, disconnection, loneliness, quarantine, retirement, seclusion, separation, solitude, withdrawal
**isolation of person to prevent the spread of infection** quarantine
**isoline** isogram, isopleth
**is on the go** gads
**isopleth** isogram, isoline
**is outstanding** excels
**is paid for work** earns
**is present** attends
**is present at** attends
**is profitable** pays
**is prosperous** thrives
**Israel** Beulah
**Israeli** sabra
**Israeli airport** Lod
**Israeli dance** hora
**Israeli desert** Negev
**Israeli money** agora, shekel
**Israeli parliament** Knesset
**Israeli patriot** Zionist
**Israeli port** Eilat
**Israeli study centre** Ulpan
**Israelite leader** Moses
**Israelites** Hebrews
**Israelites rested here after crossing the Red Sea** Elim
**Israeli weapon** Uzi
**is seated** sits
**is situated** lies
**issuance** diffusion, discharge, distribution, ejection, emission, exhalation, issue, promalgation, radiation
**issue** children, circulate, come, conclusion, consequence, copy, crux, deliver(y), discharge, distribute, edition, effect, effuse, egress, emanate, emerge, emit, end, event, issuance, offspring, ooze, originate, outcome, outflow, percolate, point, pour, problem, proceed, proclamation, product, progeny, publication, publish, question, result, seep, sending, supply, version
**issue again** reprint
**issue a permit** license
**issue forth** emanate, emerge, emit
**issue from** emanate
**issue that has been settled in court** iudicata (L)
**is suitable to** fits
**isthmus** narrowness, neck, peninsula, strait
**isthmus in Chile** Ofoui
**isthmus in Egypt** Suez
**isthmus in Malaysia** Kra
**is upright** stands
**is upset through discontent** repines
**is victorious** wins
**it** es (G)
**Italian** Florentine, Milanese, Neapolitan, Piedmontese, Roman, Tuscan, Venetian
**Italian active volcano** Vesuvius
**Italian actress** Duse, Lollobrigida, Loren
**Italian Adriatic island** Lido
**Italian adventurer** Casanova
**Italian and Spanish dance with sudden skips** saltarello
**Italian aristocratic family** Orsini
**Italian arm of the Mediterranean** Adriatic
**Italian art centre** Florence, Siena
**Italian astronomer** Galileo, Secchi
**Italian atelier** bottega
**Italian cab** vettura
**Italian calcareous rock** scaglia
**Italian carriage** chaise
**Italian cathedral** duomo
**Italian cathedral city** Florence, Milan, Rome
**Italian champagne** asti, spumante
**Italian cheese** bitto, bra, mozzarella, parmesan, ricotta, romano
**Italian chief** duce
**Italian chief magistrate** doge
**Italian city on the Arno** Florence
**Italian city on the Po** Turin
**Italian coffee** capuccino, espresso
**Italian composer** Bellini, Donizetti, Monteverdi, Puccini, Rossini, Scarlatti, Verdi, Vivaldi
**Italian condiment mixture** tamara
**Italian countess** contessa
**Italian currency** lira, lire, soldo
**Italian dance** forlana, furlana, rigoletto, saltarello, tarantella, volta
**Italian department** calabria

**Italian dialect spoken in Florence** Tuscan
**Italian dish** cannelloni, lasagne, osso buco, pasta, pizza, ravioli, risotto
**Italian dish of rice with stock** risotto
**Italian distance** canna
**Italian dog with fox-like appearance** volpino
**Italian drink** bevere
**Italian ewe-milk cheese** pecorino
**Italian family** Cenci, Doria, Este, Medici
**Italian family royal name** Este
**Italian flute** zuffolo
**Italian food** pasta
**Italian futurist painter** Severini
**Italian gambling game** mora
**Italian gentleman** signor(e)
**Italian girl** signorina
**Italian gold coin** ducat
**Italian goodbye** addio, ciao
**Italian greeting** ciao
**Italian guerrilla general** Garibaldi
**Italian holiday** festa, feste
**Italian hors d'oeuvre** antipasto
**Italian house** casa, casino
**Italian hurrah** viva
**Italian ice-cream** cassata, spumone
**Italian inn-keeper** padrone
**Italian inventor** Marconi
**Italian island** Capri, Cos, Elba, Ischia, Lido, Lipari, Sardinia, Sicilia, Sicily
**Italian islander** Sardinian, Sicilian
**Italian lady** donna, signora
**Italian lake** Como
**Italian little** poco
**Italian lover** amoroso
**Italian measure** braccio, canna, orna, palma, tavola
**Italian millet** buda, moha, tenai
**Italian miss** signorina
**Italian money** lira, lire, soldo
**Italian monk** padre
**Italian motorway** autostrada
**Italian mountain peak** Cima
**Italian mountains** Apennines
**Italian musician** Toscanini
**Italian name for Italy** Italia
**Italian one** uno
**Italian opera** *Aïda, Norma, Pagliacci*
**Italian opera house** La Scala
**Italian operatic baritone** Gobbi
**Italian operatic composer** Mascagni, Puccini
**Italian operatic soprano** Tebaldi, Tetrazzini
**Italian operatic tenor** Caruso, Pavarotti
**Italian painter** Botticelli, Da Vinci, Francesca, Giotto, Masaccio, Michelangelo, Raphael, Tintoretto, Titian
**Italian palace** palazzo

**Italian pasta** cannelloni, farfalle, macaroni, ravioli, spaghetti, tagliatelle
**Italian pie** pizza
**Italian poet** Alighieri, Ariosto, Betti, Boiardo, Carducci, Dante, Leopardi, Petrarch, Tasso, Ungaretti
**Italian policeman** carabiniere, sbirro
**Italian political party** Fascist
**Italian porridge** polenta
**Italian port** Bari, Cagliari, Genoa, Pola, Rimini, Salerno, Trani, Trieste, Zadar, Zara
**Italian pottery** majolica
**Italian princely family** Este
**Italian province** Alba, Como, Este, Parma, Piedmont, Pisa, Pola, Roma, Tuscany, Zara
**Italian red wine** Chianti
**Italian region** Umbria
**Italian resort** Alassio, Capri, Lido, Locarno, Pesaro, San Remo, Syracuse
**Italian restaurant** trattoria
**Italian rice dish** risotto
**Italian royal family** Este, Savoy
**Italian ruler** duce
**Italian saint** Neri
**Italian sausage** mortadella, salami
**Italian sculptor** Bernini, Lombardo, Michelangelo, Sansovino
**Italian seaside resort** Lido
**Italian secret society** Maf(f)ia, Camorra
**Italian shoemakers** succi
**Italian silver coin** lire
**Italian snack** pizza
**Italian somebody** uno
**Italian soup** minestrone
**Italian sparkling wine** asti, spumante
**Italian street** calle, strada, via
**Italian style of art in the 17th century** seicento
**Italian time** tempo
**Italian town or city** Aosta, Bra, Dego, Firenze, Gela, Genoa, Lodi, Marsala, Milano, Ostia, Pavia, Roma, Sorrento, Trieste, Venezia
**Italian university city** Balogna, Bari, Padua, Pisa
**Italian vegetable soup with bacon and rice or pasta** minestrone
**Italian vermouth** Cinzano, Martini
**Italian violinist** Paganini, Tartini
**Italian violin maker** Amati, Guarneri, Stradivari
**Italian volcano** Etna, Stromboli, Vesuvius
**Italian white-and-green marble** cipolin
**Italian white wine** Asti, Orvieto
**Italian wicker-covered bottle** flask
**Italian wine** Asti, Barbera, Bardolino, Barolo, Chianti, Dolcetto, Frascati, Lumbrusco, Marsala, Orvieto, Soave, Sylvaner, Tocai, Vapolicella
**Italian yes** si
**Italic language** Latin
**it appears that** apparently
**it becomes an ovum** ootid
**it can be flown in the wind** kite
**it cancels a debit** credit
**it can lead to famine** food shortage
**it can make a cuppa** teabag
**it carries blood** vein
**itch** ache, crave, creep, desire, hanker, irritation, prickle, tickle, yearn
**itching sensation** urtication
**itch remover** backscratcher
**itchy** eager, edgy, fidgety, impatient, restive, restless, scratchy, unsettled
**it contains psalms** psalter
**it contains vitamin C** guava, orange, tomato
**it converts AC to DC** diode
**it could be a goatee** beard
**it could be laid by tortoise** egg
**it does not follow** non sequitur (L)
**it does not please me** non libet (L)
**item** article, detail, notice, point, thing, unit
**item in an auction** lot
**item in a sum** addend
**item in auction** lot
**item in diary** entry
**itemise** bill, book, catalogue, cite, count, declaim, detail, enrol, enter, enumerate, file, index, list, mention, name, narrate, note, number, perform, quote, recite, record, recount, register, rehearse, relate, schedule, specify, tell
**itemised bill** invoice
**itemised record** list
**item lacking** need
**item of cutlery** fork, knife, spoon, teaspoon
**item of food** viand
**item of footwear** boot, galosh, sandal, shoe, slipper, tackie
**item of furniture** bed, bureau, chair, dresser, table
**item of headwear** beret, cap, doek, hat, helmet, scarf
**item of mail** letter, postcard
**item of stationery** envelope, (writing-)pad
**item recorded in diary** entry
**it ended World War 1** Treaty of Versailles
**iterate** echo, make, quote, recapulate, recite, recount, refer, rehearse, reiterate, relate, renew, repeat, replay, reproduce, restate, retell, reword, say, stress
**it explodes** bomb

it flies by night  bat
it follows Shrovetide  Lent
it goes off as a warning  alarm
it goes with a mortise  tenon
it grunts  hog, pig
it has been proved  probatum est (L)
it helps motorist to find the way  road map
it holds cartridges in recorder  tape-deck
it holds documents together  paper-clip, staple
it holds thread in sewing machine  shuttle
it illuminates  candle, flare, lamp, lantern, torch
it indicates end of rugby match  final whistle
itinerant  adventurer, bergie, drifter, explorer, gallivanting, gypsy, hobo, journeying, migratory, nomad(ic), peripatetic, pilgrim, preaching, rambler, rambling, roamer, roaming, Romany, rootless, roving, stroller, thumbing, tramp, travelling, vagrant, wanderer, wandering, wayfarer, wayfaring
itinerant musician  piper
itinerary  agenda, arrangements, calender, chart, circuit, course, diary, journal, journey, log, logbook, map, passage, plan, program(me), prospectus, record, route, schedule, timetable, tour
it intercepts light  lampshade
it is  it's, 'tis
it is affixed to a letter  stamp
it is denied  negatur (L)
it is finished  consummatum est (L)
it is futile to rush  more haste, less speed
it is ground  meal
it is, in short  it's, 'tis
it is not theirs  ours
it is often driven  golf ball
it is permitted  licet (L)
it is proved as you go along  solvitur ambulando (L)

it is shortly  it's
it is so  ita est (L)
it is spoken in Oslo  Norwegian
it is used for cooking  oil
it keep hands warm  glove, muff
it laces and is flexible  elastic
it links equal temperatures  isotherm
it lubricates  oil
it makes dough rise  yeast
it makes one remember  reminder
it makes waste  haste
it marks the spot  X
it may be  perhaps, possibly
it may sting unless dead  nettle
it measures  ruler
it measures distance walked  pedometer
it might be Havana  cigar
it neighs  horse
it pricks  needle, pin
it propels a boat  oar
it removes moisture from clothes  drier, tumbler
it rings  bell
its  ses (F)
it is a division  partition
it is a gamble  bet
it is a hint  innuendo
it is a puzzle  enigma
it is a semi-solid solution  gel
it is between back of nose and throat  adenoids
it is built on the beach  castle
it is chewed  gum
it is flown in the wind  kite
it is frightening  ghost
it is funny  cartoon, comedy
it is greasy  oil
it is hearsay  rumour
it is hung when decorating  curtain, wallpaper
it is limbless  snake
it is located between one's waist and thigh  hip
it is not made public  confidential information
it is not made to be broken  rule
it is not true  denial

it is only a pleasure  certainly
it is over us all  sky
it is planted to grow  seed
it is read to children at night  bedtime story
it is round  circle
it is run  race
it is set up to catch criminal  roadblock
it is sworn  oath
it is thrown at weddings  confetti, rice
it is tied  knot
it is trained to carry missives  pigeon
it is very small  atom
it is worn round waist  belt, sash
its capital is Addis Ababa  Ethiopia
its capital is Boise  Idaho
its capital is Jerusalem  Israel
its capital is Port-au-Prince  Haiti
its capital is Rangoon  Burma
its capital is Stockholm  Sweden
its capital is Vientiane  Laos
it seems that  apparently
it seems to me  methinks
itself  ipso
it sells gifts for children  toy shop
it smells  nose
it sticks  adhesive, glue, gum
it stings  nettle
it stretches  elastic
it supports artist's painting  easel
it swings on clock  pendulum
it times sports events  stop watch, time watch
it twinkles  star
itty-bitty  wee
it warms  heater
it was conquered by Hillary  Everest
it will  it'll
'I've found it'  eureka
ivories  keyboard
ivory  dentine, ebur (L), tusk
ivory source  elephant, tusk, walrus
ivory tissue  dentine
Ivy League college  Harvard, Yale
I will not contest it  nolo contendere (L)

# J

**jaçana** lily-trotter
**jab** dig, hook, lunge, nudge, plunge, poke, prod, punch, rap, thrust, thump, uppercut, whack
**jabber** babble, burble, chaffer, chat(ter), clack, clatter, gab(ble), gibberish, gossip, hocus-pocus, jargon, jobber, maunder, mumble, nonsense, palaver, patter, prate, prattle, ramble, sputter, talk, tattle, twaddle, yabber, yak, yap
**jabber inarticulately** gibber
**jabberwocky** nonsense, rigmarole, tune
**jacaranda city** Pretoria
**jacinth** hyacinth
**jack** banner, boost(er), colours, ensign, erect, flag, hoist, lift(er), pennant, pennon, raise, sailor, standard, streamer, upheave, uplift
**jackal** bloodsucker, creature, doormat, drone, drudge, dupe, fawner, hack, hanger-on, hireling, lackey, minion, parasite, pawn, puppet, slave, stooge, sycophant, toady, tool
**jackanapes** coxcomb
**jacket** anorak, blazer, case, casing, coat, enclosure, envelope, mackinaw, reefer, sheath, skin, tunic, wrapper, wrapping
**jacket and trousers** suit
**jacket fold** lapel
**jacket material** tweed, wool
**jacket worn over armour** tabard
**jack in playing cards** knave
**jack rabbit** hare
**jackstraws** spillikins
**Jack Tar** sailor
**jack up** boost, elevate, heave, hoist, lift, raise
**Jacob had twelve** sons
**Jacob's third son by Leah** Levi
**Jacob's twin** Esau
**jactation** boasting
**jade** crock, gemstone, hack, harridan, hussy, jadestone, nag, nephrite, roarer, shrew, slattern, trollop, vixen, wench, whistler
**jaded** allayed, corrupt, debauched, dissipated, dissolute, dog-tired, dulled, exhausted, numbed, profligate, satiated, wanton, worn-out
**Jaffa in Hebrew** Yafo
**jag** barb, break, cog, cut, gash, indent, knurl, load, nick, notch, projection, quantity, ratchet, scallop, scarify, scrap, serrate, slash, snag, spree, sprocket, spur, tear, tooth
**jagged** barbed, broken, cleft, craggy, erose, notched, pointed, ragged, ridged, rough, serrate, spiked, toothed, uneven
**jagged-edged** serrated
**jagged projecting point** snag
**jai alai** pelota
**jail** confine, gaol, guardhouse, imprison, lock up, penitentiary, prison, quod
**jailed dissident** political prisoner
**jailer** captor, gaoler, guard, (jail)keeper, screw, turnkey, warden, warder
**jail inmate** prisoner
**jail room** cell
**jail window** grill(e)
**Jainist scripture** Sutra
**jalopy** auto(mobile), car, junk, tjorrie, wreck
**jam** affix, conserve, crowd(ing), crush, fix, force, host, multitude, pack, predicament, preserve, push, spread, squeeze, stick, stoppage, throng, thrust, wedge
**Jamaican ebony** cocuswood
**Jamaican liquor** rum
**Jamaica pepper** allspice, pimento
**jam pastry** tart
**Jane Austen heroine** Anne Elliot, Elizabeth Bennet, Emma Woodhouse
**Jane's jungle mate** Tarzan
**jangle** argue, argument, cacophony, clang(our), clank, clatter, conflict, contend, discord, feud, fight, meeting, quarrel, rattle, row, skirmish, squabble, struggle, wrangle
**janitor** caretaker, concierge, custodian, doorkeeper, porter
**January** Enero (Sp)
**Japan** Nippon
**Japanese aboriginal** Ainus
**Japanese art of fencing** kendo
**Japanese art of flower arrangement** ikebana
**Japanese art of folding paper** origami
**Japanese art of growing miniature trees** bonsai
**Japanese art of paper folding** origami
**Japanese art of self-defence** aikido, judo, jujitsu, karate
**Japanese basket-work palanquin slung on pole** kago
**Japanese bay** Ise, Tokyo, Yedo
**Japanese bean** soya
**Japanese board-game** go
**Japanese bream** tai
**Japanese capital** Tokyo
**Japanese carriage** ricksha(w), sado
**Japanese carved toggle** netsuke
**Japanese cedar** cryptomeria, sugi
**Japanese city bombed in 1945** Hiroshima, Nagasaki
**Japanese classic drama** no(h)
**Japanese cooking utensil** hibachi
**Japanese currency** sen, yen
**Japanese dance** bugaku, kagura
**Japanese dancing girl** geisha
**Japanese deer** sika
**Japanese dish** sashimi, sukiyaki, sushi, tempura
**Japanese dog** Akita
**Japanese drama** kabuki, no(h)
**Japanese dwarf tree** bonsai
**Japanese edible berry** udo
**Japanese emperor** mikado
**Japanese female companion** geisha
**Japanese five-line poem of thirty-one syllables** tanka
**Japanese flower arrangement** ikebana
**Japanese form of fencing** kendo
**Japanese form of pinball** pachinko
**Japanese form of self-defence** akido
**Japanese garment** haori, happi, kimono, mino, obi
**Japanese gateway to Shinto temple** torii
**Japanese girl trained to entertain men** geisha
**Japanese guitar-like instrument** samisen
**Japanese harp** koto
**Japanese hostess** geisha
**Japanese liquor made from rice** saké, saki
**Japanese long loose robe worn with sash** kimono
**Japanese maple genus** acer
**Japanese mat** tatami
**Japanese military class** samurai
**Japanese military commander** shogun
**Japanese money unit** sen, yen
**Japanese outcast** (y)eta
**Japanese padded floor mattress** futon
**Japanese paper folding art** origami
**Japanese parliament** diet
**Japanese poem of seventeen syllables** haiku, hokku
**Japanese poem of thirty-one syllables** tanka
**Japanese popular traditional theatre** kabuki

**Japanese port** Osaka, Otaru, Yahata, Yawata
**Japanese portable charcoal grill** hibachi
**Japanese pottery** awata, satsuma
**Japanese prince** daimio, daimyo
**Japanese quince** japonica
**Japanese religion** Shinto, Zen Buddhism
**Japanese religion revering ancestors and nature spirits** Shinto
**Japanese retainer** samurai
**Japanese rice wine** saké, saki
**Japanese ritual suicide by disembowelling** hara-kiri, seppuku
**Japanese ruler** shogun
**Japanese sandal** zori
**Japanese sash** obi
**Japanese sauce** soy
**Japanese Shinto temple gateway** torii
**Japanese ship** maro, maru
**Japanese singing girl** geisha
**Japanese slippers** flip-flops
**Japanese snack of cold rice flavoured and garnished** sushi
**Japanese sport** aikido
**Japanese standard-sized mat** tatami
**Japanese stringed instrument** koto
**Japanese sword** cat(t)an, katana, wacadash
**Japanese system of unarmed combat** aikido, jujitsu, karate
**Japanese tea ceremony** chanoyu
**Japanese three-lined poem of seventeen syllables** haiku, hokku
**Japanese three-stringed guitar** samisen
**Japanese title** kami
**Japanese traditional puppet theatre** bunraku
**Japanese translucent sliding door made of paper** shoji
**Japanese tree** cedar
**Japanese variety of soy sauce** tamari
**Japanese verse form** haiku, hokku, tanka
**Japanese wall-picture** kakemono
**Japanese warrior** samurai
**Japanese woman diver** ama
**Japanese woman trained to entertain men** geisha
**Japanese wooden-soled sandal** geta
**Japanese wrestling** sumo
**Japan's capital** Tokyo
**jape** banter, chaff, crack, drollery, fleer, fool, gag, gibe, humour, jeer, jest, joke, mock, pun, quip, squib, tomfoolery, trick, twit, wisecrack, witticism
**japer** clown, comedian, joker, prankster
**japonica** camellia
**japonica fruit** quince

**jar** agitate, annoy, bicker, bottle, canister, clash, container, contend, crock, cruset, decanter, demijohn, disagree, disturb, ewer, flagon, flask, grate, interfere, irk, irritate, jolt, jug, nettle, offend, oppose, pitcher, pot, quarrel, rasp, scratch, shake, urn, vase, vessel, vibrate, wrangle
**jargon** abracadabra, argot, babble, balderdash, cant, dialect, diction, gibberish, gobbledegook, idiom, language, lingo, lingua franca, nonsense, parlance, patois, phraseology, pidgin, rubbish, slang, terminology, tongue, usage
**jargon associated with officials** officialese
**Jason's crew** Argonauts
**Jason's father** Aeson
**Jason's rival** Creusa
**Jason's ship** Argo
**Jason's teacher** Ch(e)iron
**Jason's uncle** Pelias
**Jason's wife** Medea
**jaundice** disapproval, disbelief, doubt, envy, icterus, idée fixe (F), jealousy, pedantry, prejudice, prenotion, presumption, suspicion
**jaundiced** blasé, covetous, cynical, doubting, envious, hostile, jealous, satiated, sceptical
**jaunt** airing, excursion, joyride, junket, outing, picnic, promenade, ramble, stroll, tour, trip
**jaunty** airy, breezy, buoyant, dapper, gay, lively, perky, showy, smart, trim
**jaunty rhythm** lilt
**Javanese arrow-poison** upas
**Javanese badger** teledu
**Javanese poison tree** upas
**Javanese printing** bat(t)ik
**Javanese tree** upas
**Java plum** duhat, jambul
**javelin** arrow, assegai, dart, harpoon, lance, missile, spear
**jaw** cheek, dewlap, jowl, mandible
**jaw bone** mandible
**jawbreaker** boiled sweet, jaw-crusher
**jaw part** chin
**jaws of an animal** chops
**jazz dance** jive
**jazz singing** scat
**jazz up** animate, enhance, improve
**jealous** attentive, begrudging, covetous, defensive, desirous, displeased, distrustful, envious, grudging, insecure, malcontent, mindful, precautious, resentful, solicitous, suspicious, vigilant, watchful, yearning
**jealousy** anxiety, bitterness, defensiveness, distrust, doubt, envy, grudge, mistrust, paranoia, resentment, spite, suspicion, vigilance
**jeans** corduroys, denims, dungarees, pants, slacks, trousers
**jeans fabric** denim
**jeer** boo, catcall, deride, derision, despise, gibe, heckle, hiss, hoot, hound, jab, jape, mock, revile, ridicule, scoff, scorn, sneer, spurn, tackle, taunt, tease
**jeer at** boo, gibe, taunt
**jeering remark** jest, skit
**jejune** arid, banal, childish, diluted, dry, ignorant, immature, inane, insipid, juvenile, meagre, naïve, prosaic, senseless, skimpy, tasteless, tedious, thin, tiresome, unanimated, uninformed
**jell** brace, cake, clot, coagulate, cohere, condense, congeal, curdle, deepen, gel(atinate), harden, jellify, reinforce, set, solidify, starch, stiffen, tauten, tense, thicken
**jellied meat stock** aspic
**jellied petrol** napalm
**jelly** confection, confiture, conserves, gelatine, gelée (F), jam, konfyt
**jellyfish** medusa, polypus, quarl
**jellyfish cell** cnidoblast
**jelly from seaweeds** agar
**jelly glass** jar
**jelly ingredient** gelatine
**jellylike candy** paste
**jellylike colloid** gel
**jellylike stuff** gel, goo, jam
**jellylike substance** gel
**jelly-making fruit** apple, quince
**jemmy** crowbar, lever
**jennet** ass, donkey
**jeopardise** chance, endanger, expose, gamble, hazard, risk, stake, venture
**jeremiad** complaint, cry, groan, lament(ation), moan, sob, wail
**jerk back** recoil
**jerk lightly** jiggle
**jerky** bouncy, bumpy, convulsive, fitful, jolty, palsied, rough, shaky, spasmodic, spastic, tremulant, tremulous, uncontrolled
**jerky eye movement** saccade
**jerky movement** flounce, twitch
**jeroboam** double-magnum, wine bottle
**jersey** cattle, gansey, pullover, sweater, textile, vest
**jersey with multicoloured design** fair-isle
**Jerusalem oak** ambrosia
**jest** banter, chaff, crank, deride, fun, gibe, hoax, humour, jape, jeer, joke, kid, mock, play, pleasantry, prank,

quip, quirk, raillery, sally, scoff, sneer, sport, tease, witticism
**jester** buffoon, clown, comedian, fool, harlequin, joker, madcap, mime, mummer, pantaloon, Pierrot, quipster, wag, wit, zany
**jester's dress** motley
**jester's stick** bauble
**jesting** facetious, humorous, jocund, kidding, laughing, merry, mocking, nonsensical, playful, quipping, roguish, rollicking, scoffing, silly, sneering, teasing
**Jesus** Immanuel
**Jesus the Saviour of men** Iesus Hominum Salvator (L)
**jet** black, ebony, flow, fountain, geyser, gush, inky, jetliner, nozzle, raven, spout, spray, spring, sprinkler, spurt, squirt, stream, turbojet, well
**jet-bath** spa
**jet for example** aeroplane
**jet plane** airbus, jumbo
**jetsam** debris, flotsam, junk, sweepings, wreckage
**jet stream** spurt
**jettage** quayage, wharfage
**jetting hot spring** geyser
**jetty** breakwater, dock, groin, groyne, mole, pier, protection, quay, shelter, wharf
**Jew** Hebrew, Israeli
**Jew converted to Christianity** Marrano
**jewel** charm, find, gem, opal
**jewelled collar** carcanet
**jewelled headband** diadem, tiara
**jewelled head-dress** crown, tiara
**jewelled necklace** carcanet
**jeweller** artist, craftsman, engraver, gemmologist, glyptographer, horologist, lapidary, watchmaker
**jeweller's eyepiece** loupe
**jeweller's paste** strass
**jeweller's small magnifying glass** loupe
**jewellery item** bangle, bracelet, brooch, (ear)ring, necklace
**jewellery made from artificial gemstones** diamanté
**jewellery stone** opal
**jewel set by itself** solitaire
**Jewish** Judaic, Semitic
**Jewish autumn thanksgiving festival** Sukkoth
**Jewish boy's thirteenth birthday** Bar Mitzvah
**Jewish bread roll** bagel, beigel
**Jewish commentary** haggada
**Jewish communal agriculture settlement** kibbutz
**Jewish day of fasting** Day of Atonement, Yom Kippur

**Jewish dialect** Yiddish
**Jewish doctor of law and religion** rabbi
**Jewish doxology** kaddish
**Jewish ecclesiastic** rabbi
**Jewish feast** Passover, Pesach
**Jewish feast day** Chanukkah, Hanukkah
**Jewish festival** Purim, Seder, Sukkoth, Yomtov
**Jewish festival commemorating their escape from Egypt** Passover, Pesach
**Jewish greeting** shalom
**Jewish holiday** Chanukkah, Hanukkah, Pesach, Purim, Rosh Hashanah, Seder, Shabuoth, Shavuot, Sukkoth, Yom Kippur
**Jewish house of worship** synagogue
**Jewish language** Hebrew, Ladino, Yiddish
**Jewish law** Torah
**Jewish lawgiver** Moses
**Jewish law-maker** rabbi
**Jewish liturgical prayer** Kaddish
**Jewish measure of capacity** cab
**Jewish meeting-place for worship** synagogue
**Jewish militia** hagana
**Jewish minister** rabbi
**Jewish month** Ab (Av), Adar(-Sheni), Bul, Elul, Etanim, Kuslewe, Marheshran (Heshvan), Nisan, Sebat (Shevat), Sif, Siwan (Sivan), Tammuz (Tammuz), Tebet (Tevet), Tishri
**Jewish name for non-Jew** goy
**Jewish nation** Israel
**Jewish New Year** Rosh Hashanah, Shavuot
**Jewish Pentecost** Shabuoth
**Jewish prayer book** mahzor, siddur
**Jewish prayer shawl** tallith
**Jewish priest** rabbi
**Jewish priestly vestment** ephod
**Jewish religious leader** rabbi
**Jewish salutation** shalom
**Jewish school** yeshiva
**Jewish silver coin** shekel
**Jewish skull-cap** yamilke, yarmulke
**Jewish spiritual figure** rabbi
**Jewish teacher of the law** scribe
**Jewish title** rab(bi), reb(be)
**Jewish weight and coin** shekel
**Jew of central or eastern European descent** Ashkenazi
**Jew of Spanish or Portuguese descent** Sephardi
**Jew's harp** trump
**Jews' homeland** Israel
**Jews or Jewish communities living outside Israel** Diaspora

**jib** ba(u)lk, recoil, refuse, retreat, shrink
**jibe** deride, derision, flout, jeer, mock(ery), ridicule, sarcasm, scoff(ing), scorn, sneer, taunt, twit
**jiffy** trice
**jig or reel** dance
**jilt** betray, desert, forsake, reject, relinquish, spurn, tergiversator
**jingled, as a bell** rang
**jinnee** imp
**jinx** annoyance, bewitch, bog(e)y, curse, demon, evil, hex, hoodoo, imp, imprecation, incubus, invocation, misfortune, plague, scourge, spell, torment, trouble, vexation, voodoo, witch
**jive** (be)bop, boogie, jol, swing
**job** assignment, career, chore, position, profession, responsibility, situation, task, work
**job chitchat** shoptalk
**job done while sitting** sedentary
**job hunter** applicant, candidate, competitor
**jobless** idle, inactive, unemployed, unoccupied
**job of work** task
**job opening** vacancy
**job permanency** tenure
**jobs for pals** nepotism
**job side benefit** perk
**job to do** task
**jockey** beguile, deceive, delude, equestrian, horseman, horsewoman, outwit, rider, trainer, trick, victimise
**jockey whip** bat
**jocose** absurd, arch, comical, entertaining, facetious, farcical, funny, humorous, jesting, jocular, joking, kidding, laughable, nonsensical, playful, ridiculous, silly, sportive, teasing, waggish, whimsical, witty
**jocular** facetious, humorous, jocose, jolly, light-hearted
**jocular person** wag
**jodhpurs** riding breeches
**jog** bounce, canter, dent, dislodge, flick, gallop, jag, jerk, jiggle, joggle, jolt, jostle, knob, lope, nick, nub, nudge, poke, prod, push, run, shake, slash, trot, wobble
**jogging along** ajog
**jogging gait** trot
**jog on horse** trot
**jog the memory** remind
**Johannesburg region** PWV, Rand
**John Hop** policeman
**joie de vivre** ebullience, enjoyment, gaiety, gusto, joy, pleasure, relish, zest

**join** abut, accompany, add, adhere, adjoin, agglutinate, ally, amalgamate, annex, append, assemble, attach, bind, cement, chain, coalesce, cohere, combine, confederate, conjoin, connect, contact, converge, couple, embody, enlist, enrol, enter, fasten, fuse, interlock, intersect, knit, link, marry, mass, match, meet, merge, pair, pool, seam, sew, splice, tie, union, unite, weld, yoke
**join a flight** enplane
**join army** enlist
**join as increase** add
**join by fusion** weld
**join by interweaving strands** splice
**join cloth** sew
**join college** enrol
**joined together** conjunct
**joined writing paper** pad
**join forces** ally, unite
**join forces with** attach
**join in** co-operate, contribute, help, partake, participate
**join in an alliance** confederation
**join in fabric** seam
**joining company** merger
**joining strip** isthmus
**joining together** conjugation
**joining word** and
**join in pursuit of common interests** alliance
**join into one** unite
**join in wood** mitre, mortice, mortise, tenon
**join of side and bottom of ship** chine
**join of two edges** butt
**join register** enrol
**joint** angularity, ankle, butt, co-, connect(ion), corporate, couple, den, divide, elbow, hinge, hip, junction, knee, link, mutual, node, seam, tenon, union
**joint above hock** stifle
**joint at right angle** knee, ell
**joint between hand and arm** wrist
**joint between two bones** commissure
**joint business** partnership
**joint cavity** bursa
**joint component** mortice, mortise, tenon
**joint concern** syndicate
**joint connecting foot and leg** ankle
**joint disease** osteoarthritis
**jointed** arthrous, articulate, hinged
**jointed stem** culm
**joint formed by talus** ankle
**joint fund** kitty
**join the army** enlist, enrol
**joint heir** parcener
**joint heirship** parcenary

**joint in arm** elbow
**joint inheritor** co-heir
**joint in hind leg of horse** hock
**joint in leg** ankle, knee
**joint investor** partner
**joint lubricator** synovia
**joint of arm** elbow, shoulder, wrist
**joint of beef** brisket, chuck, chump, neck, roast, rump, short-rib, steak, topside
**joint of bird's wing** flexure
**joint of finger** knuckle
**joint of leg** ankle, hip, knee
**joint of meat** baron, loin, saddle
**joint of mutton** leg, loin, neck, saddle
**joint of ship** chase
**joint of stem** node
**joint of two pieces of wood** mitre
**join together** affix, associate, attach, bind, coalesce, combine, conjugate, connect, couple, fasten, fix, fuse, knit, link, merge, paste, solder, splice, tie, unify, unite, weld, yoke
**join together with heat** weld
**joint on which door swings** hinge
**joint ownership** community
**joint part** mortice, mortise, tenon
**joint-stock** corporate
**jointure** dower, estate
**join up** enlist, enrol, enter
**join up again** re-enlist
**join with** accompany, associate
**join wood** butt, rabbet
**joke** banter, chaff, deride, frolic, fun, gag, gambol, jape, jest, lark, mock, play, prank, pun, quip, quirk, ridicule, sally, sport, taunt, tease, witticism, yarn
**joker** buffoon, chap, clown, comedian, comic, expedient, guy, hoax, humorist, japer, jester, kidder, punster, quipster, smarty, wag, wise-guy, wisecracker, wit
**joking** badinage, bantering, chaffing, deriding, frolicking, gambolling, jesting, mocking, quipping, ridiculing, taunting, teasing
**jollification** amusement, beano, boisterousness, carousal, celebration, cheerfulness, conviviality, debauch, exhilaration, exuberance, festivity, gaiety, glee, hilarity, jollity, joviality, joyousness, laughter, levity, merriment, mirth, revel
**jollity** amusement, blitheness, cheer(fulness), delight, distraction, diversion, elation, enjoyment, entertainment, felicity, frolic, fun, gaiety, gladness, glee, hilarity, joie de vivre (F), joviality, joy, junketing, liveliness, merriment, mirth,

pleasure, recreation, romp, sport, treat, vivacity
**jolly** blithe, buoyant, cheerful, festive, frolicsome, gay, glad, happy, jovial, joyful, joyous, jubilant, merry, mirthful, party, playful, riant, spirited, sportive, sunny
**jonquil** narcissus
**Jordanian mountain** Nebo
**Jordan's outlet** Dead Sea
**Jordan's source** Hermon
**Josip Broz** Tito
**jostle** bump, butt, crowd, elbow, force, hustle, jog(gle), jolt, press, push, scramble, shake, shoulder, shove, squeeze, throng, thrust
**jot** ace, atom, bit, detail, dot, enter, fraction, freckle, grain, iota, list, mite, molecule, note, particle, record, register, scribble, small, spark, speck, tad, tittle, trace, trifle, whit, write
**jot down** list, note, record, register, scribble, write
**jotted notes** jotting
**jotter** (note) pad, notebook
**jotting** clip(ping), cutting, excerpt, list, memo(randum), message, note, record, tally
**jotting taken for future reference** note
**journal** book, chronicle, daily, date book, daybook, diary, gazette, ledger, log, magazine, memoir, minutes, monthly, (news)paper, periodical, publication, record, register, review, scrapbook, tabloid, weekly, yearbook
**journal entry** item
**journalise** enter
**journalism** broadcasting, composition, copy-writing, correspondence, coverage, editing, feature-writing, news, press, recording, reportage, reporting, writing
**journalist** broadcaster, columnist, commentator, contributor, correspondent, diarist, editor, (feature-)writer, gazetteer, hack, newswriter, news(paper)person, pressman, reporter, scribe, stringer
**journalist's credit** byline
**journal keeper** diarist
**journal seller** newsagent
**journey** course, excursion, expedition, fare, fly, gallivant, go, iter (L), itinerary, jaunt, outing, passage, peregrinate, pilgrimage, proceed, progress, ramble, range, roam, route, rove, safari, tour, tramp, travel, traverse, trek, trip, voyage, wander(ings), wend
**journey down** descent

**journey for a definite purpose**
expedition
**journey for pleasure** tour
**journey in aircraft** flight
**journeyman** artisan
**journey on foot** hike, tramp
**journey round** circuit
**journey segment** leg
**journey's end** destination
**journey stage** leg
**journey through** cruise, sail, tour, travel
**journey to a sacred place** pilgrimage
**joust** altercation, assault, battle, bout, box, brawl, clash, combat, conflict, contend, contest, duel, encounter, engage(ment), feud, fight, grapple, match, mêlée, riot, scuffle, skirmish, spar, struggle, tilt, tourney, tussle, war, wrestle
**jovial** affable, airy, blithe, boon, buoyant, cheery, convivial, cordial, gay, glad, happy, jocular, jolly, joyous, jubilant, merry, mirthful
**jovial fellow** blade
**jowl** cheek, chop, jaw, muzzle
**joy** blessedness, bliss, buoyancy, charm, delight, ecstasy, elation, euphoria, exultation, felicity, festivity, fun, gaiety, gladness, glee, gratification, happiness, joyfulness, pleasure, rapture, ravishment, satisfaction, transport, treasure, wonder
**Joy Adamson's lion** Elsa
**joyful** animated, blessed, blissful, blithe(some), buoyant, cheerful, delighted, delightful, elated, enrapture, excited, gay, glad, gratified, happy, jocund, jolly, jovial, jubilant, merry, mirthful, overjoyed, pleased, satisfied, thrilled
**joyful cry of infant** crow
**joyful hymn** carol
**joyful religious festival** feast
**joyful song** carol
**joyless** depressed, dismal, downcast, dreary, gloomy, grim, miserable, sad, unhappy
**joy of living** joie de vivre (F)
**joyous** animated, blissful, blithe, bright, carefree, cheerful, debonair, delighted, delirious, ecstatic, elated, enthusiastic, euphoric, fervent, festive, frenzied, gay, genial, glad, gleeful, happy, heartening, hilarious, jolly, jovial, joyful, lively, merry, overjoyed, rapturous, sparkling, sunny, transported, vivacious
**joyous ecstasy** rapture
**joyously** animated, blissful, blithe, carefree, debonair, delirious, ecstatic, elated, enthusiastic, euphoric, fervent, frenzied, glad, gleeful, hilarious, jolly, jovial, joyful, joyous, lively, merry, overjoyed, rapturous, sparkling, sunny, transported, vivacious
**joyous song** carol
**joyous time** gala
**joy ride** spin
**JR's series** *Dallas*
**jubilant** elated, enraptured, excited, exuberant, exultant, glad, joyous, overjoyed, rejoicing, thrilled, triumphant
**jubilation** beatitude, blessedness, bliss, celebration, cheer(fulness), cheeriness, contentment, delight, ecstasy, elation, enjoyment, euphoria, excitement, exultation, felicity, festivity, gaiety, gladness, happiness, joy, merriment, merrymaking, pleasure, prosperity, rejoicing, revelry, satisfaction, triumph
**jubilee** anniversary, carnival, carousal, celebration, commemoration, festival, festivity, fête, gala, holiday, revelry, treat
**Judaean king** Herod
**Judas kiss** betrayal, double-cross
**Judas tree** gallows
**judge** adjudicate, adjudicator, appreciate, arbiter, arbitrate, arbitrator, ascertain, assess(or), authority, conclude, condemn, connoisseur, consider, critic(ise), decide, decree, deem, determine, discern, distinguish, doom, esteem, estimate, evaluate, evaluator, examine, expert, find, gauge, justice, magistrate, mediate, mediator, moderator, rate, reckon, referee, regard, review, rule, sentence, sit, try, umpire, value
**judge before hearing** prejudge
**judge in matters of taste** arbiter elegantiarum (L)
**judge in Muslim country** cadi, kadi
**judgement** appraisal, arbitration, ascertainment, assessment, belief, conclusion, conviction, damnation, decision, decree, determination, diagnosis, discernment, discretion, discrimination, doom, enlightenment, estimate, fate, finding, intelligence, judgment, mediation, misfortune, opinion, order, outcome, penalty, penetration, perspicacity, prudence, punishment, result, retribution, ruling, sense, sentence, shrewdness, taste, understanding, valuation, verdict, view, wisdom
**judgement in court** decree
**judgement of work** estimation
**judge of good eating and drinking** gastronome
**judge's bench** bank
**judge's black cap** coif
**judge's garment** robe
**judge's gown** toga
**judge's hammer** gavel, mace
**judge's headgear** wig
**judge's private room** chambers
**judge's seat** bema, bench, bima(h)
**judge the pace** time
**judge the worth of** estimate
**judging character by face** physiognomy
**judging standard** criterion
**judicial** critical, discrimination, distinguished, forensic, impartial, judge-like, judiciary, judicious, juridical, legal, magistral, official
**judicial board** tribunal
**judicial decision** award, judg(e)ment, verdict
**judicial sentence** adjudication
**judicial trial** case
**judicial writ issued as command to inferior court** mandamus
**judicial writ ordering an officer to arrest** capias
**judicious** acute, astute, careful, cautious, circumspect, considered, diplomatic, discerning, discreet, expedient, informed, politic, prudent, rational, reasonable, sage, sane, sensible, shrewd, skilful, sober, sound, thoughtful, well-advised, well-judged, wise
**judo grade** dan
**judo room** dojo
**Judy's puppet partner** Punch
**jug** carafe, churn, container, crock, ewer, flagon, jar, mug, pitcher, toby, urn, vessel
**jug for ale** toby
**juggins** blockhead, dolt, simpleton
**juggle** alter, change, conjure, disguise, doctor, manipulate, manoeuvre, modify, rearrange, rig
**jug handle** ear
**juice** beverage, essence, extract, fluid, latex, liquid, liquor, lush, moist, nectar, sap(py), secretion, serum
**juicy** colourful, interesting, lush, moist, naughty, provocative, racy, risqué, sappy, sensational, spicy, succulent, suggestive, vivid, watery
**juicy fruit** grape, orange, pear, strawberry
**juicy gourd** melon
**juicy pear** Bartlett
**juicy stone fruit** peach
**Juliet's partner** Romeo

**jumble** chaos, clutter, collection, confound, confuse, confusion, conglomeration, disarrange, disarray, dishevel, disorder, disorganise, entangle, hodge-podge, hotchpotch, litter, medley, mélange, mess, miscellany, mishmash, mistake, mix(ture), muddle, scramble, shuffle, tangle, welter
**jumbled pile of printer's type** pi(e)
**jumbled word** anagram
**jumble of articles** rummage
**jumbo** aeroplane, behemoth, colossal, colossus, Cyclopean, elephant(ine), enormous, gargantuan, giant, gigantic, huge, immense, jet, king-size, large (airliner), leviathan, mammoth, massive, mighty, monster, monstrous, outsize, oversize(d), titanic, vast, whopper
**jumbuck** sheep
**jump** advance, agitation, appreciate, ascend, avoid, boost, bounce, bound, buck, bypass, caper, cavort, clear, digress, disregard, escalate, evade, flinch, frisk, frolic, gain, gambol, hop, hurdle, ignore, increase, interval, jerk, jig, jolt, leap(frog), miss, mount, omit, overjump, overlook, pole-vault, pounce, prance, recoil, rise, skip, spiral, spring, spurt, start, surge, switch, vault, wince
**jump about** frisk, gambol, rollick, romp
**jump about playfully** caper, gambol
**jump at** catch, grab, snatch
**jumper** jersey, pullover, sweat-shirt, sweater, trampolinist, woolly
**jump high** leap
**jumpily** anxiously, fidgetiness, nervously, restlessly, tensely
**jumping action in skating** axel
**jumping insect** flea
**jumping marsupial** kangaroo
**jumping movement in skating** axel
**jumping pest** flea
**jump in mirth** caper
**jump in surprise** start
**jump into** interject, interrupt, intrude
**jump off** alight, descend, dismount, land, undertake
**jump off the high board** dive
**jump on one leg** hop
**jump out quickly** dart
**jump over rope** skip
**jump repetitively** skip
**jumpy** agitated, anxious, apprehensive, edgy, fidgety, jittery, nervous, nervy, restless, shaky, tense
**junction** adhesion, association, combination, concourse, confluence, connecting, connection, convergence, coupling, crossing, intersection, join(er), joining, joint, juncture, juxtaposition, linking, meeting-point, nexus, pivot, seam, terminal, terminus, unification, union, uniting
**junction at top of roof** ridge
**juncture** alliance, aspect, chapter, combination, conjuncture, connection, coupling, crisis, crux, edge, emergency, exigency, hour, instant, joint, junction, linking, moment, occasion, period, phase, point, position, seam, stage, state, step, time, union, weld
**June bug** dor, June beetle, May beetle, May bug
**jungle** desert, waste, wilderness
**jungle animal** ape, tiger
**jungle cat** Leo, lion
**jungle climber** liana
**jungle journey** safari
**jungle king** lion
**jungle knife** machete
**jungle queen** lioness
**jungle swinger** ape, liana
**jungle vine** liana
**junior** inferior, lesser, lower, minor, secondary, subordinate, subsidiary, younger
**junior actress** starlet
**junior bingo** lotto
**junior Boy Scout** Cub
**junior diplomat** attaché
**junior Girl Guide** Brownie
**junior hospital doctor** houseman, intern
**junior naval officer** ensign
**juniper spirit** gin
**juniper tree** cade
**junk** clutter, debris, dregs, garbage, leavings, litter, oddments, refuse, rubbish, rummage, scrap, trash, waste, wreckage
**junkie** addict, dope-fiend, junky, user
**Jupiter's satellite** Callisto, Europa, Ganymede, Io
**jurisdiction** area, authority, bounds, command, control, domination, dominion, field, influence, orbit, power, prerogative, province, range, reach, rule, say, scope, sovereignty, sphere, sway, zone
**jurisdiction of a bailiff** bailiwick
**jurisdiction of an emir** emirate
**jury** adjudgers, appraiser, arbiter, critic, estimators, inquest, judges, judicator, jurers, jurymen, jurywomen, justice, mediator, panel, peers

**just** accurate, barely, blameless, conscientious, correct, deserved, due, equitable, evenhanded, exact(ly), fair(-minded), fitting, good, honest, honourable, impartial, irreproachable, lawful, legal, legitimate, merely, merited, normal, only, positively, precise, proper, pure, reasonable, regular, right(eous), rightful, soon, true, unbiased, unprejudiced, upright, virtuous, well-deserved
**just about** almost, approximately, nearly, practically, well-nigh
**just a little bit** slightly
**just as soon** gladly, preferably, willingly
**just beginning** nascent
**just claim** right
**just coming into existence** nascent
**justice** amends, appropriateness, correction, equitableness, equity, fairness, honesty, impartiality, integrity, judge, justifiableness, justness, law, legality, legitimacy, magistrate, penalty, reasonableness, recompense, rectitude, redress, reparation, right(fulness), rightness, satisfaction
**justice bringing deserved punishment** nemesis
**justifiable** acceptable, confirmable, defendable, defensible, excusable, explainable, explicable, fit, forgivable, justified, lawful, legitimate, maintainable, pardonable, proper, reasonable, right, sound, supportable, sustainable, tenable, understandable, valid, vindicable, warrantable, warranted, well-founded
**justifiable claim** pretension
**justification** apology, approval, basis, cause, defence, excuse, explanation, extenuation, foundation, grounds, mitigation, plea, rationalisation, reason, substance, vindication, warrant
**justify** absolve, acquit, approve, confirm, defend, establish, exculpate, excuse, exonerate, explain, forgive, legalise, maintain, pardon, substantiate, support, sustain, uphold, validate, vindicate, warrant
**just now** anon, immediately, recently, soon
**just open** ajar
**just right for job** ideal
**just so** exactly, quite
**just started** incomplete, unprepared, unready
**just the same** nevertheless, nonetheless, notwithstanding

**jut** bulge, extend, obtrude, overhang, poke, project, protrude, show
**jute for sacking** burlap
**jut out** bulge, extend, overhang, poke, project, protrude
**jutting out** prominent, salient
**jutting rock** krans, tor

**juvenile** adolescent, babyish, boy, callow, child(ish), childlike, girl, green, immature, inexperienced, infant(ile), jejune, minor, preteen, puerile, teenaged, teenager, tender, underage, unsophisticated, young(ster), youth(ful)
**juvenile delinquent** hoodlum, skollie

**juxtaposed** adjacent, appose, balance, collate, collocate, compare, contrast, match, partner, weigh
**juxtaposition** adjacency, balance, closeness, contact, contiguity, contrast, immediacy, nearness, proximity, vicinity

# K

**Kaiser's folk** Germans
**kale** cabbage
**kaleidoscopic** iridescent
**Kampuchean currency** riel
**Kampuchean lake** Tonlesap
**Kampuchean money** riel
**Kampuchean plain** Joncs
**Kampuchean ruins** Angkor(wat)
**kangaroo** boomer, euro, flier, flyer, wallaby, (walla)roo
**kangaroo rat** potoroo
**kapok** ceiba
**karate grade** dan
**karma** destiny, fate, kismet
**karyokinesis** mitosis
**karyoplasm** nucleoplasm
**Katmandu is there** Nepal
**kayak** canoe
**Keats's speciality** ode
**kebab stick** skewer
**keelless boat** canoe
**keel-like part** carina
**keel over** capsize, careen, collapse, drop, faint, fall, founder, heel, overturn, stagger, swoon, upset
**keen** acute, anxious, ardent, astute, avid, bewail, biting, bitter, caustic, clever, desiring, devoted, diligent, dirge, discerning, eager, earnest, enthusiastic, excited, fervid, fine, fond, honed, incisive, industrious, intense, lament, nice, penetrating, perceptive, piercing, poignant, pungent, quick, red-hot, sensitive, severe, sharp, shrewd, strong, trenchant, utter, vivid, wise, yare, zealous
**keen and well-dressed** smart
**keen ballet-lover** balletomane
**keen dry north wind in Switzerland** bise
**keen-edged** sharp
**keen enjoyment** zest
**keen-eyed** seeing
**keen insight** acumen

**keenness** acuity, acumen, eagerness, edge, genius, sharpness, talent
**keen resentment** ire
**keen sight** sharp eyes
**keen-sighted** lyncean, lynx-eyed
**keep** arrest, conceal, defend, detain, donjon, dungeon, dwell, fort, guard, have, hide, hold, honour, lodge, maintain, maintenance, manage, observe, own, preserve, protect, provide, refrain, remain, reserve, retain, stronghold, subsistence, support, tower
**keep afloat** buoy
**keep air moving** fan
**keep alive** sustain
**keep aloof from** avoid
**keep apart** isolate, quarantine, seclude, segregate, separate
**keep at** complete, continue, drudge, endure, finish, grind, labour, maintain, persevere, persist, pursue, remain, slave, stay, toil, trail
**keep at a distance** cold-shoulder, ignore, rebuff, reject
**keep away** absent
**keep away from** abstain, avoid, circumvent, evade
**keep back** censor, check, conceal, constrain, control, curb, delay, detain, hide, impede, limit, prohibit, repress, reserve, restrain, restrict, retain, retard, stifle, stop, suppress, withhold
**keep clear of** avoid, shun
**keep company with** consort, hobnob
**keep down** check, control, repress
**keeper** custodian, gaoler, guard(ian), jailer, protector, warden
**keeper of brothel** bawd
**keeper of elephant** mahout
**keeper of golf-course** green-keeper
**keeper of prison** gaoler, jailer, provost, warden
**keeper of rabbit reserve** warrener

**keeper of the purse** treasurer
**keep finding fault** carp
**keep fixed** nail
**keep for future** safekeep
**keep for future use** store
**keep for later use** reserve
**keep from** abstain, desist, refrain, withhold
**keep from decay** preserve
**keep from falling** support
**keep from happening** prevent
**keep going** continue, endure, maintain, perpetuate, persevere
**keep grass short** lawnmower
**keep hidden** conceal
**keep in** conceal, confine, control, detain, hide, inhibit, quell, restrain, retain, stifle, suppress
**keep in check** arrest, bridle, contain, control, rein, restrain, withhold
**keep in custody** detain
**keeping** agreement, care, carrying, charge, conformity, conserving, consistency, controlling, custody, depositing, garnering, harmony, heaping, maintaining, patronage, piling, placing, possessing, possession, preserving, protection, safekeeping, trust
**keeping of birds** aviculture
**keeping of custom** observance
**keep in hold** stay, withhold
**keep in mind** hold, remember, retain
**keep in motion** agitate, stir
**keep in one's heart** cherish
**keep in one's service** employ
**keep in store** stock
**keep intact** preserve
**keep in the hand** hold
**keep in view** await, consider
**keep in warehouse** store
**keep off** parry, rebuff, reject
**keep off alcohol** abstain

**keep on** continue, endure, maintain, persevere, persist, prolong, remain, retain, stay
**keep on at** badger, harass, harry, importune, nag, pester, pursue
**keep oneself from action** forbear, refrain
**keep one's eye on** guard, monitor, observe, scrutinise, survey
**keep on limited allowance** stint
**keep out** bar, exclude, seclude, separate
**keep out of sight** hide
**keep possession of** retain
**keep regular stock for sale** carry
**keep safe from decay** preserve
**keepsake** emblem, favour, memento, memory, relic, remembrance, reminder, souvenir, symbol, token
**keep secret** conceal, hide, withhold
**keep someone back** hinder
**keep supplied** maintain
**keep supplies of** stock
**keeps the sea out of Holland** dyke
**keeps you dry** raincoat, umbrella
**keep to rules** conform
**keep track of** follow, monitor, oversee, watch
**keep under** repress
**keep under control** bridle, harness, rein, repress, rule, withhold
**keep under one's thumb** dominate
**keep up** balance, compete, contend, continue, emulate, equal, maintain, match, persevere, preserve, rival, support, sustain, vie
**keep watch** spy
**keep within limits** contain
**keg** barrel, butt, cask, drum, tun, vat
**kelp** seaweed
**ken** acquaintance, eyeshot, know(ledge), purview, recognition, sensibility, sight, visibility, vision
**kennel** doghouse
**Kentucky race** Derby
**Kenyan person** Kikuyu, Ma(a)sai
**Kenyan soldier** askari
**Kenyan warrior tribe** Ma(a)sai
**kepi** cap
**kept from general knowledge** secret
**kept man** gigolo
**kept secret** clandestine, esoteric, occult, undisclosed
**kerb** wayside
**kerfuffle** commotion, fuss
**Kermit is one** frog
**kernel** basis, being, centre, core, cream, crux, egg, embryo, entity, essence, germ, gist, grain, grist, heart, hub, keynote, life(blood), marrow, meat, middle, nature, nitty-gritty, nub, nucleus, nut, ovum,
pith, pivot, point, principle, quick, quintessence, root, seed, soul, spirit, stone, substance
**kernel's hard covering** nutshell
**kernel used as cookery seasoning** nutmeg
**kestrel** windhover
**ketch** boat, jack, ship, vessel, yacht
**kettledrum** timbal, tymbal
**kettledrummer** timpanist, tympanist
**kettle of fish** mess
**key** answer, cay, essential, fit, fundamental, important, indication, opener, quay, solution, translation
**keyboard** ivories
**keyboard instrument** accordion, clavichord, concertina, harpsichord, marimba, organ, piano(forte), spinet, xylophone
**keyboard percussion instrument** celesta, celeste
**keyboard player** organist, pianist
**key group** cadre
**key in** capture, enter, input, load, store
**keylike cross of old Egypt** ankh
**key man** gaoler
**key of outer door** latchkey
**key of pianoforte** note
**key personnel** cadre
**key player in basketball** pivot
**keystone** quoin
**key to fit most locks** master-key, skeleton-key
**khaki colour** drab
**khan** caravanserai
**Khan** Imran
**Khomeini's land** Iran
**kick** animation, boot, drop-kick, force, funk, harshness, hit, intensity, life, pep, power, punch, pungency, punt, push, rebound, resist, shove, sparkle, strength, strike, tang, tap, toe, verve, vim, vitality, zest
**kick a football** punt
**kick around** abuse, debate, maltreat, mistreat, misuse
**kick in** contribute, give
**kicking one's heels** inactive, latent
**kick off** begin, commence, inaugurate, initiate, introduce, open, start
**kickoff** beginning, commencement, outset, start
**kick out** discharge, dismiss, eject, evict, expel, oust, reject, remove, sack
**kick over the traces** defy, disobey, mutiny, rebel, resist, revolt, rise
**kick up a fuss** squawk
**kick with front of foot** toe
**kid** baby, bairn, boy, child, cozen, fool, girl, hoodwink, infant, joke, lad, lightie, mock, plague, rib, ridicule,
stripling, tease, teenager, tot, trick, youngster, youth
**kiddies' game** catch, hide and seek, tag, tig
**kidnap** abduct, appropriate, capture, commandeer, detain, expropriate, hijack, pirate, pluck, remove, seize, skyjack, snatch, steal
**kidnap by force** abduct
**kidnap demand** ransom
**kidnapper** abductor, crook, hijacker, rapist, robber, skyjacker, thief
**kidnapper's demand** ransom
**kidney ailment** nephritis
**kidney disease** uraemia
**kidney disorder** anuria
**kidney enzyme** renin
**kidney excretion** urine
**kidney secretion** renin
**kidney-shaped** reniform
**kidney-shaped nut** cashew
**kidney tube** ureter
**kidskin** vellum
**kid with a route** paperboy, papergirl
**kill** annihilate, assassinate, behead, butcher, cancel, cease, decapitate, decollate, destroy, dispatch, electrocute, erase, execute, exterminate, extinguish, extirpate, hang, lapidate, liquidate, massacre, murder, necklace, obliterate, poison, quash, quell, ruin, shoot, slaughter, slay, smother, strangle, throttle, veto
**kill a fly** swat
**kill animal as prescribed by Muslim law** hal(l)al
**kill animals for food** slaughter
**kill as sacrifice** immolate
**kill by cutting throat** jugulate
**kill by squeezing the windpipe** strangle
**kill by stoning** lapidate
**killed by an arrow in his heel** Achilles
**killed by Joab** Absalom
**killed by other animal for food** prey
**killed by Paris** Achilles
**killed for one's beliefs** martyred
**killer** assassin, butcher, executioner, exterminator, gunman, murderer, slaughterer, slayer, strangler
**killer disease** AIDS, cancer
**killer of a tyrant** tyrannicide
**killer whale** orc
**kill flies** swat
**kill for food** slaughter
**killing** assassination, bloodshed, bonanza, carnage, coup, elimination, execution, extermination, fatality, fortune, gain, hit, homicide, liquidation, (man)slaughter, massacre, murder, profit, slaying, success, winner

**killing a human being unintentionally**
  manslaughter
**killing of a king**  regicide
**killing of infant soon after birth**
  infanticide
**killing of many people**  carnage
**killing of one person by another**
  homicide, manslaughter, murder
**killing of one's brother**  fratricide
**killing of oneself**  suicide
**killing of one's father**  patricide
**killing of one's mother**  matricide
**killing of one's sister**  sororicide
**killing of one's wife**  uxoricide
**kill inhumanly**  murder
**killjoy**  complainer, dampener, damper, misery, pessimist, spoil-sport
**kill oneself**  suicide
**kill someone like vigilantes**  lynch
**kill wickedly**  murder
**kiln**  drier, furnace, oast, oven, stove
**kiln-dried barley**  malt
**kiln for drying hops**  oast
**kiln lining**  firestone
**kilt**  fil(l)ibeg, petticoat, philibeg, piupiu, plaid, skirt, wraparound
**kimono sash**  obi (J)
**kin**  affinity, blood, connection, family, kindred, kinship, kith, lineage, near, related, relation(ship), relatives, sib
**kind**  accommodation, affectionate, agreeable, amiable, beneficent, benevolent, brand, breed, category, character, class, compassionate, congenial, cordial, courteous, description, essence, family, friendly, generous, genre, gentle, good, gracious, humane, ilk, kindly, loving, manner, mild, mould, nature, persuasion, pleasant, race, set, sort, species, sympathetic, temperament, tender, type, variety
**kind and helpful**  benevolent
**kind deed**  favour, generosity
**kindergarten system**  Fröbelism, Froebelism, Montessori, Waldorf
**kind-hearted**  amicable, compassionate, considerate, generous, good-hearted, good-natured, humane, humanitarian, obliging, sympathetic, warm-hearted
**kindle**  animate, arouse, awaken, excite, fan, fire, ignite, incite, induce, inflame, inspire, light, provoke, rouse, sharpen, stimulate, stir, thrill
**kindling**  (char)coal, firewood, firing, fuel, ignition, leaves, lighting, log, quickening, tinder, twigs
**kindly**  benevolent, benign, compassionate, (con)genial,
  cordially, gentle, good-natured, mild, pleasant, politely, sympathetic
**kindly care of God**  providence
**kindly disposed**  friendly
**kindly feeling**  goodwill
**kindness**  aid, beneficence, benevolence, charity, favour, generosity, grace, humanity
**kind of**  fairly, rather, somewhat
**kind of acid**  amino, boric
**kind of admiral**  rear
**kind of angle**  acute
**kind of apple**  golden delicious, granny smith, russet, starking
**kind of artistic work**  genre
**kind of axe**  adze
**kind of back**  hardback, softback
**kind of barge**  wherry
**kind of bean**  haricot, kidney, mung, sugar
**kind of beer**  draught, lager, Pils(e)ner, stout
**kind of beetle**  CMR, Christmas, dung, rose, scarab
**kind of beet with edible leaves and stalks**  chard
**kind of biscuit**  garibaldi, ginger, Marie
**kind of bookbinding**  yapp
**kind of branched tumour**  polypus
**kind of brooch**  cameo
**kind of bun**  Chelsea, raisin
**kind of cake**  beestings, chocolate, madeira, sponge
**kind of carp**  ide
**kind of celery with turnip-like root**  celeriac
**kind of cereal**  bran, oats, wheat
**kind of chalcedony with coloured layers**  onyx
**kind of chinaware**  Limoges, Royal Doulton, Spode
**kind of clear soup**  julienne
**kind of coffee**  capuccino, drip, espresso, instant, percolated
**kind of cotton cloth**  calico
**kind of cuckoo**  ani
**kind of dagger**  dirk
**kind of dark tea grown in China**  oolong
**kind of dark volcanic rock**  trap
**kind of disinfectant**  carbolic
**kind of drinking cup**  quaich, quaigh, qualch
**kind of driver**  backseat, racing
**kind of duck**  eider
**kind of fabric**  cotton, lisle, linen, rayon, viscose
**kind of fastener**  (hat)pin, paperclip, staple
**kind of fighter**  wrestler
**kind of fine pottery**  delftware, Wedgwood
**kind of fine silk**  sarcenet, sarsenet
**kind of firework**  Catherine wheel, rocket, serpent, sparkler
**kind of foxtrot**  onestep
**kind of freehold right**  udal
**kind of fuel**  diesel, gas, petrol(eum)
**kind of fungus**  mushroom, toadstool
**kind of fur**  fox, mink, sable
**kind of gourd or pumpkin**  calabash
**kind of grass**  buffalo, kikuyu, tef(t)
**kind of grass used as pasture and fodder**  fescue, lucerne
**kind of green tea from China**  hyson
**kind of gun**  AK 47, Beretta, Colt, Kalashnikov, RN, shotgun, Sten
**kind of hand in velvet glove**  iron
**kind of hard white pottery**  ironstone
**kind of hawk**  merlin
**kind of hound**  basset
**kind of house**  bungalow, chalet, semi
**kind of iris**  orris
**kind of jazz dance**  shimmy
**kind of jewel**  diamond, emerald, pearl
**kind of lace**  galloon
**kind of large baboon**  mandrill
**kind of large dog**  Alsatian, Dobermann, Newfoundland
**kind of large pea**  marrowfat
**kind of large violin**  viola
**kind of laurel**  bay
**kind of lettuce**  cos, iceberg, red oak
**kind of light beer**  lager
**kind of lily**  arum, St Joseph's
**kind of linen tape**  inkle
**kind of liquor**  brandy, malt, rum
**kind of llama with long woolly hair**  alpaca
**kind of long-leaved lettuce**  cos
**kind of lottery**  tombola
**kind of man's hat**  bowler, deerstalker, fez, trilby
**kind of mead flavoured with mulberries**  morat
**kind of melon**  cantaloup(e), spanspek
**kind of modelling clay**  plasticine
**kind of motorcar**  bakkie, convertible, limousine, sedan, tjorrie, van
**kind of neuralgia**  tic
**kind of old pistol**  flintlock
**kind of opal**  cacholong
**kind of ottoman or hassock**  pouf(fe)
**kind of paint**  enamel, PVA
**kind of pancake**  crêpe, waffle
**kind of peach with smooth downless skin**  nectarine
**kind of pick-axe**  mattock
**kind of picture puzzle**  rebus
**kind of pier**  anta
**kind of pine**  pinon
**kind of plant**  sedge
**kind of poplar**  aspen

**kind of practitioner** dentist, doctor, therapist
**kind of primrose** cowslip
**kind of public transport vehicle** (mini)bus, tram, taxi
**kind of race** marathon, relay, sprint
**kind of raisin** sultana
**kind of revolver** Colt
**kind of rolled currant bun** Chelsea
**kind of rose** floribunda, noisette
**kind of sail** jib, lateen, main, royal
**kind of sailing boat** sloop, yacht
**kind of sailing boat with two masts** yawl
**kind of sauce prepared from a bean** soy
**kind of sausage** boerewors, chipolata, polony, salami, vienna
**kind of saw** fret, tenon
**kind of sherry** amontillado
**kind of shovel** scoop
**kind of skittles** ninepins
**kind of slow polka** schottische
**kind of small falcon** merlin
**kind of small fowl** bantam
**kind of small orange** clementine, mandarin, na(a)rtjie
**kind of small seagull** kittiwake
**kind of small shark** dogfish
**kind of small trout** char
**kind of smoked pork sausage** cervelat
**kind of smoked salmon** lox
**kind of snooker rest** spider
**kind of soft cheese** Brie, Camembert, ricotta
**kind of soil** clay, sand
**kind of sole** Dover, West Coast
**kind of sorcery** obeah, obi
**kind of sorghum** doura(h), durra
**kind of sound** dental, glottal, palatal
**kind of soup** bean, onion, oxtail, pea, tomato, vegetable
**kind of spanner with adjustable jaws** monkey-wrench
**kind of sponge cake** angel
**kind of sprouting broccoli** calabrese
**kind of squirrel fur** vair
**kind of stork** ibis, marabou
**kind of strong gin** schnapps
**kind of style** genre
**kind of sweetmeat** caramel, mebos
**kind of syrup** golden, maple
**kind of thistle** ceanothus
**kind of toad** natterjack
**kind of trap** gin
**kind of tree** alder, ash, baobab, beukenhout, cedar, elder, elm, fir, gum, oak, olive, pine, poplar, redwood, sandalwood, sapodilla, sloe, tambotie, yellowwood
**kind of trumpet** clarion
**kind of tyre** retread

**kind of volcano** active, dormant
**kind of watch chain** albert
**kind of watered silk** tabby
**kind of wattle** myall
**kind of weasel** ermine, stoat
**kind of wild duck** mallard
**kind of wine** port, red, rosé, white
**kind of witchcraft** obeah, obi
**kind of writing** copperplate, italic, round hand
**kind of writing desk** davenport
**kind of xylophone** marimba
**kind of yarrow** sneezewort
**kindred** agnate, allied, associated, brood, cognate, family, foster, hearth, ilk, kinfolk, related, sib(ling), tribe
**kind to guests** hospitable
**kine** cattle, cows, oxen
**king** monarch, rex, roi (F), royal, ruler, sovereign
**King Arthur's abode** Aval(l)on, Camelot
**King Arthur's birthplace** Tintagel
**King Arthur's burial place** Aval(l)on
**King Arthur's court** Camelot
**King Arthur's father** Uther Pendragon
**King Arthur's fool** Dagonet
**King Arthur's killer** Modred
**King Arthur's magic sword** Excalibur
**King Arthur's mother** Igerna, Igerne, Igraine, Ygerne
**King Arthur's place of death** Camlan
**King Arthur's son** Modred
**King Arthur's wife** Guenever, Guinever(e)
**King Arthur's wizard** Merlin
**king beater** ace
**King David** psalmist
**kingdom** country, domain, dominion, dukedom, dynasty, earldom, empire, monarchy, nation, principality, realm, sovereignty, sphere, state, territory
**kingdom in Arabia** Yemen
**kingdom in South Asia** Nepal
**kingdom in South East Asia** Laos
**kingdom in the Himalayas** Bhutan
**kingdom of Agamemnon** Mycenae
**kingdom of Alexander** Macedonia
**kingdom of Pluto** Hades, underworld
**kingdom of Ulysses** Ithaca
**kingfish** opah
**kingfisher** halcyon
**king killed by Samuel** Agag
**King Kong** ape
**kingly** assured, autocratic, commanding, despotic, dignified, domineering, imperial, imperious, majestic, mighty, noble, poised, princely, proud, regal, royal, stately
**kingly power** reign
**king of Basan** Og

**king of beasts** lion
**king of dwarfs** Alberich
**king of elves** Erl
**king of fairies** Oberon
**king of Hebrews** David, Saul, Solomon
**king of Israel** Ahab, David, Jeroboam, Saul, Solomon
**king of Israel married to Jezebel** Ahab
**king of Juda** Asa
**king of Judea** Herod
**king of Macenae** Atreus
**king of Mercia** Offa
**king of the cats** Leo, lion
**king of the Jews** Herod
**king of the jungle** lion
**king of Troy** Priam
**king's abode** palace
**king's daughter** princess
**king's deputy** viceroy
**king's eldest son** dauphin, prince
**king's grant to son** ap(p)anage
**kingship** regency
**king's home** castle, palace
**king's lady** queen
**king's officer in charge of horses** equerry
**king's retinue** court
**king's son** prince
**king's stand-in** regent
**king topper** ace
**king with golden touch** Midas
**kinkajou** honey bear, lemur, potto
**kinky** bizarre, depraved, eccentric, odd, outlandish, peculiar, perverted, queer, strange, weird
**kin of shallot** leek
**kinship** affinity, bearing, connection, relationship, tie
**kinsman** brother, compatriot, daughter, enate, relation, relative, sib(ling), sister, son, tribesman
**kin to weasel** polecat, stoat
**kiosk** bay, bookstall, carrel(l), closet, compartment, coop, counter, covering, cubby, cubicle, enclosure, news stand, pen, protection, room, shelter, (snack) booth, stall, stand, table
**Kipling book for children** Puck of Pook's Hill, The Jungle Books
**Kipling novel** Kim, Stalky and Co, The Light that Failed
**Kipling poem** 'If', 'Recessional'
**kirtle** coat, cover, gown, skirt, tunic
**kismet** destiny, fate, karma
**kiss** accolade, brush, buss, caress, contact, graze, greet, impact, osculate, peck, salute, smack, smooch, sweet, touch
**kissable** appealing, charming, cute, fetching, lovable, lovesome, personable

**kissing** lipwork, osculating
**kissing sprig** mistletoe
**kiss of peace** pax
**kiss wetly** slobber
**kit** apparatus, equipment, gear, instruments, outfit, provisions, rig, set, supplies, tackle, tools, utensils
**kitchen annexe** scullery
**kitchen appliance** refrigerator
**kitchen basin** sink
**kitchen container** canister, tea caddy
**kitchen counter** bar
**kitchen cupboard** dresser
**kitchen gadget** grater
**kitchen garment** apron
**kitchen herb** mint, parsley, thyme
**kitchen implement** grater, kettle, pan, pot, toaster, utensil
**kitchen in aircraft** galley
**kitchen in ship** galley
**kitchen kiln** oven
**kitchen linen** apron, dishcloth, towel
**kitchen mixer** blender
**kitchen on ship's deck** caboose
**kitchen pinny** apron
**kitchen rag** dishcloth
**kitchen range** stove
**kitchen sideboard** dresser
**kitchen spreader** spatula
**kitchen stove** range
**kitchen under-servant** scullion
**kitchen utensil** colander, corer, grater, kettle, ladle, mixer, opener, pan, peeler, pot, spatula, toaster
**kitchen utensil store** scullery
**kitchen vessel** dish, kettle, pan, pot
**kitchen wash basin** sink
**kit out** accoutre, arm, dress, equip, furnish, outfit, prepare, supply
**kitten** bear, cat, kit(ty), pussy, youngling
**kitten's cry** mew
**kitty** award, bank, bonanza, capital, endowment, foundation, funds, jackpot, pool, pot, prize, reserve, reward, stakes, stock, store, supply, winnings
**kiwi** apteryx, fruit
**klaxon** honk, horn, megaphone, siren
**knack** ability, adroit(ness), apt(itude), aptness, art, competence, dexterity, endowment, finesse, gift, habit, hang, proficiency, qualification, skill, talent, trick
**knaggy** knotty, rugged
**knapsack** rucksack
**knave** betrayer, blackguard, bounder, cad, charlatan, cheat, cheater, churl, dastard, devil, evildoer, jack, louse, miscreant, rascal, renegade, rogue, rotter, ruffian, scamp, scapegrace, scoundrel, skollie, swindler, traitor, tsotsi, varlet, villain, wretch

**knavish** deceitful, deceptive, dishonest, lying, rascally, roguish, tricky, villainous
**knead body** massage
**knee** angle, bend, corner, crook, crotch, cusp, edge, elbow, genu (L), intersection, joint, nook, point, stifle
**kneecap** patella
**kneel** bend, bow, curts(e)y, genuflect, kowtow, stoop, worship
**kneeling desk for prayer** prie-dieu
**knickers** drawers, knickerbockers, underclothes, undies
**knife** blade, cut, dagger, kris, lacerate, slash, stab
**knife handle** haft
**knife thrust** stab
**knife used as weapon** dagger
**knife wound** stab
**knight** cavalryman, chessman, dub, equestrian, fighter, gallant, gentleman, horseman, sir, soldier, warrior, younker
**knightly champion** paladin
**knightly conduct** errantry
**knight of a French order** chevalier
**knight of King Arthur** Dinadin, Galahad, Gawain, Kay, Lancelot, Modred
**knight of the road** bergie, hobo, itinerant, nomad, stroller, tramp, vagabond, walker
**knight of the Round Table** Dinadin, Galahad, Gawain, Kay, Lancelot, Modred
**knight errant** paladin
**knight's garment** jacket, mail, tabard
**knight's horse** steed
**knight's jacket** tabard
**knight's spear** lance
**knight's title** sir
**knight's wife** dame, lady
**knit** affix, ally, bind, connect, contract, crotchet, fasten, fold, furrow, gather, heal, hook, interlace, intertwine, (inter)weave, join, knot, link, loop, mend, mesh, purl, secure, tie, unite, wrinkle
**knitted garment** jersey, jumper, pullover, sweater
**knitted jacket** cardigan
**knitted jumper** jersey, pullover
**knitted pattern looking like twisted rope** cable
**knitted pullover** jersey, jumper
**knitted sweater** guernsey
**knitted vest** spencer
**knit the brows** frown
**knitting pin** needle
**knives and forks** cutlery

**knob** bulge, bunch, grip, handle, hold, knop, lump, node, nodule, nub, protrusion, stud, swelling, tumour
**knob of a sword hilt** pommel
**knob on root or branch** node
**knob or lump** node
**knock** bang, beat, belittle, blame, blow, complaint, criticise, criticism, deprecate, disparage, hit, propulsion, rap, strike, stun, tap, thump
**knock about** abuse, associate, bash, batter, bruise, buffet, damage, hit, hurt, maltreat, manhandle, mistreat, ramble, range, roam, rove, saunter, traipse, travel, wander
**knock around** gallivant, jaunt, ramble, range, rove, stroll, traipse, wander
**knock down** batter, bludgeon, clout, demolish, destroy, devastate, fell, floor, level, pound, prop, raze, smash, wallop, wreck
**knocked out** inert, unconscious
**knock gently** tap
**knocking shop** brothel, cathouse
**knock into** bump
**knock off** assassinate, cease, complete, conclude, deduct, filch, finish, kill, murder, nick, pilfer, pinch, quit, rob, slay, steal, stop, terminate, waste
**knock on door** rap
**knock out** defeat, flatten, floor, overthrow, prostrate, stun, trounce
**knockout** bestseller, hit, KO, sensation, smash(-hit), stunner, success, triumph, winner
**knock senseless** stun
**knock sharply** rap
**knock to the ground** floor
**knock unconscious** stun
**knock up** batter, bliksem, bruise, damage, donder, hurt, impair, injure, mar, neuk, pound, rap, thump, wound
**knoll** anthill, bulge, bump, dune, elevation, eminence, height, hill(ock), hummock, hump, knob, koppie, mound, mount, prominence, rise, sand-hill, tor
**knot** bend, body, bow, clique, cluster, company, complexity, conundrum, crowd, entangle, epaulette, fasten, frog, group, interlacement, intertwine, join, knar, knob, knur(r), loop, lump, node, nodule, perplexity, problem, puzzle, slipknot, tangle, tie, tuft, twist, unite
**knot again** retie
**knot and mix together** tangle
**knot in thread of wood** burl
**knot in wood** knag, knar, knur(r)
**knot laces** tie

**knot of hair** bob
**knot-shaped biscuit** pretzel
**knotted lace** tatting
**knotted mess** tangle
**knotted whip** knout
**knotty** baffling, baroque, circuitous, complex, complicated, confusing, difficult, enigmatic, gnarled, gnarly, intricate, involved, labyrinthine, mysterious, nodose, nodous, nodulous, obscure, perplexing, strange, tangled, tortuous, weird
**knotty point** nodus
**knot used to shorten rope temporarily** sheepshank
**know** apprehend, comprehend, discern, distinguish, experience, fathom, ken (Sc), perceive, realise, recognise, see, understand
**know again** recognise
**know-all** bookworm, genius, pundit, savant, scholar
**know by instinct** intuit(ion)
**know by intuition** intuit
**know how to** can
**knowing** astute, aware, clever, competent, discerning, eloquent, expert, intelligent, leery, sagacious, shrewd, significant, skilful
**knowing everything** omniscient
**knowing look** leer

**knowingly** deliberately
**knowing nothing** skilless, unskilled
**knowing the facts** informed
**know instinctively** intuit,
**knowledge** apprehension, awareness, data, discernment, education, enlightenment, erudition, facts, gossip, information, ken, learning, lore, news, -ology, perception, rumour, scholarship, science, skill, tuition, understanding, wisdom
**knowledgeable** academic, acquainted, adept, aware, clued up, conscious, educated, erudite, experienced, expert, familiar, intelligent, learned, sagacious, sensible
**knowledgeable from practice** experienced
**knowledge acquired by study** learning
**knowledge brought in proof** witness
**knowledge of appropriate behaviour** savoir-faire
**knowledge of spiritual mysteries** gnosis
**knowledge of the heart** cardiology
**knowledge of the structure of the earth** geognosy
**knowledge of woodland conditions** woodcraft
**known for something bad** notorious

**known only to connoisseurs** recherché
**known to many** well-known
**known without doubt** certain
**know the ropes** knowledgeable
**knuckle of pork** eisbein (G), hock
**knuckle under** accede, acquiesce, bidding, capitulate, defer, submit, succumb, surrender, yield
**koala** carbora
**kobold** brownie, dwarf, gnome, goblin, hobgoblin, imp, knurl, nis, spirit, sprite
**Kodiak** bear
**Korean currency** won
**kudos** acclaim, accolade, acknowledg(e)ment, applause, approval, bays, celebrity, commendation, congratulation, credit, crown, deference, dignity, distinction, eminence, eulogy, exaltation, fame, garland, glory, homage, honour, immortality, laurels, merit, panegyric, plaudit, praise, prestige, prize, recognition, regard, renown, respect, reverence, thanks, tribute, trophy
**kyat** 100 pyas
**kylie** boomerang, kiley
**Kyongsong** Seoul
**kyphosis** hunchback

# L

**label** class, company, designate, docket, epithet, marker, name, sticker, tag, tally, ticket, trademark
**labial malformation** harelip
**labile** fluctuating, unstable
**labium** lip, maxilla, mouth
**laboratory** atelier, studio, study, workroom, workshop
**laboratory examination** analysis
**laboratory flask** Erlenmeyer
**laboratory tube** burette, pipette
**laboratory vessel** beaker, bell-jar, flask, retort
**laborious** active, arduous, assiduous, back-breaking, burdensome, crushing, difficult, diligent, fatiguing, gruelling, hard, heavy, Herculean, industrious, onerous, punishing, tedious, tiresome, toilsome, troublesome, trying, wearisome, weary
**laborious effort** toil

**labour** assignment, childbirth, commission, confinement, difficulty, drudge, duties, effort, employment, exert(ion), fatigue, grind, heave, job, livelihood, mission, moil, obstetrics, overwork, slavery, strive, struggle, sweat, task, toil, travail, work
**labourer** blue-collar, drudge, earner, employee, hand, help, professional, servant, toiler, white-collar, worker, workman
**labour hard** toil
**labour in childbirth** travail
**labour overcomes all difficulties** labor omnia vincit (L)
**Labrador dog** retriever
**lab sample** specimen
**labyrinth** anfractuosity, coil, complexity, convolution, entanglement, intricacy, jungle, maze, puzzle, riddle, tortuosity, windings

**lac** encrustation, incrustation, lacquer, resin, shellac, varnish
**lace** attach, bind, bootlace, braid, close, cord, crochet, embroider, fasten, fortify, intertwine, interweave, mesh(-work), net(ting), openwork, shoelace, shoe(string), thread, tie
**lace cape** mantilla
**lace collar** vandyke
**Lacedaemon** Laconia, Sparta
**lace frill** ruche
**lace-hole** eyelet
**lace loop** picot
**lace loophole** eyelet
**lacerate** afflict, claw, cut, deface, distress, gash, harm, hurt, injure, jag, maim, mangle, mutilate, pain, rend, rip, shred, slash, slice, stab, tear, torment, torture, wound
**lacerated** aching, bruised, gashed, injured, slashed, tormented

**lace scarf worn by Spanish woman** mantilla
**lace trimming** edging
**lacework** tatting
**lachrymal drop** tear
**lachrymator** tear gas
**lachrymose** crying, dolorous, lugubrious, mournful, sad, tearful, weeping, weepy, woeful
**lack** absence, dearth, deficiency, deficit, insufficiency, need, paucity, scarcity, shortage, want
**lackadaisical** abstracted, affected, apathetic, blasé, carefree, dreamy, dull, half-hearted, idle, impassive, inactive, indifferent, inert, laggard, languid, languishing, lazy, lethargic, limp, listless, neuter, neutral, numb, otiose, somnolent, spiritless, unemotional, unenthusiastic
**lackey** attendant, butler, creature, dependant, domestic, equerry, flatterer, flunk(e)y, follower, footman, hanger-on, henchman, hireling, (h)ostler, jackal, leech, livery, minion, page, parasite, pet, retainer, satellite, scullion, seneschal, servant, squire, steward, supporter, sycophant, toady, valet, vassal, waiter, yeoman
**lacking** defective, deficient, impaired, inadequate, incompetent, incomplete, insufficient, mediocre, missing, requiring, sans, shy, unfinished, unqualified, without
**lacking ability** unable
**lacking a definite shape** amorphous
**lacking a dwelling place** homeless
**lacking ambition** unaspiring
**lacking aspiration** unambitious
**lacking a sternum** asternal
**lacking a tail** acaudate, anurous, tailless
**lacking a will** intestate
**lacking breadth** narrow, thin
**lacking care** careless, crude
**lacking colour** pale, toneless
**lacking colour or vitality** toneless
**lacking confidence** doubtful, hesitant, insecure
**lacking courage** pusillanimous, timid
**lacking creativity** inartistic
**lacking definition** blurred
**lacking desire for food** asitia
**lacking distinctive characteristics** nondescript
**lacking due decency** immodest
**lacking elegance** clumsy, graceless
**lacking energy** gutless
**lacking expertise** inexpert
**lacking flavour** insipid, tasteless

**lacking fluency of expression** ineloquent
**lacking foresight for the future** improvident
**lacking foundation** baseless
**lacking fresh air** airless, stuffy, sultry
**lacking freshness** stale
**lacking friends** friendless, lonely
**lacking fullness** meagre, slight, ullage
**lacking generality** ad hoc
**lacking good manners** ill-behaved, ill-bred
**lacking grace** clumsy
**lacking heat** cold, cool
**lacking identity** nameless
**lacking in imagination** earthbound
**lacking in power** impotent, ineffectual
**lacking in regard for other's feelings** brusque, inconsiderate
**lacking in respect** disrespectful, irreverent
**lacking in sensibility** senseless, stupid
**lacking in seriousness** flippant, pert, trifling
**lacking in spiritual awareness** soulless
**lacking in taste** flavourless, insipid, vulgar
**lacking intelligence** feeble-minded, stupid
**lacking in variety** monotonous
**lacking knowledge** ignorant
**lacking life** dead, lifeless
**lacking lustre** dull
**lacking moderation** intemperate
**lacking moral restraints** unashamed
**lacking noble qualities** soulless
**lacking passion** unromantic
**lacking power of sight** blind
**lacking professional skill** amateurish
**lacking rainfall** arid
**lacking reality** insubstantial
**lacking reason** illogical, inept, irrational
**lacking self-assurance** shy, timid
**lacking sensation** numb
**lacking sense** foolish, gormless
**lacking sharp edge** blunt
**lacking sight** blind
**lacking strength** feeble, weak
**lacking strength of character** feeble, spineless
**lacking the necessities of life** needy
**lacking the skill** unable
**lacking the usual attachment** floating
**lacking ventilation** stuffy
**lacking vigour** flaccid, languid, nerveless, spiritless
**lacking vitality** effete, toneless
**lacking warmth** cold, impersonal
**lacking zest** vapid
**lacklustre** cheerless, dark, dense, dingy, doltish, dull, dusky, insipid, monotonous, muddy, muted, obscure, ordinary, passionless, prosaic, shabby, simple, soiled, stupid, tarnished, tasteless, tedious, uneventful, unintelligent, vacuous, vapid
**lack of** deficiency
**lack of activity** inertia
**lack of adequate food** malnutrition
**lack of adornment** austerity, simplicity
**lack of agreement** inconsistency
**lack of appetite for food** anorexia
**lack of balance** disparity, imbalance, imparity, inequality, inequilibrium, unevenness
**lack of beauty** ugliness
**lack of care** negligence
**lack of clarity** vagueness
**lack of comfort** discomfort
**lack of contentment** discontent
**lack of difficulty** ease
**lack of dignity** indecorum
**lack of dutifulness** impiety
**lack of education** ignorance, illiteracy
**lack of effectiveness** futility
**lack of emotion** detachment
**lack of energy** anergy, flatness, languor, lassitude
**lack of feeling** anaesthesia, apathy, deadness, dispassion, insensibility, insensitivity, insentience, numbness
**lack of food** dearth, famine, starvation
**lack of fullness in cask** ullage
**lack of government** anarchy
**lack of grace** indecorum, inelegance
**lack of harmony** discord
**lack of interest** apathy, indifference
**lack of knowledge** ignorance
**lack of light** darkness
**lack of meaning** futility
**lack of obedience** indiscipline
**lack of optimism** negativity, pessimism
**lack of oxygen in blood** asphyxia
**lack of oxygen in tissues** anoxia
**lack of pigment in skin** alphosis
**lack of power** adynamia, atony, incapacity
**lack of power of the muscles in walking** abasia
**lack of pride** humility
**lack of progress** stasis
**lack of proper care** carelessness, negligence
**lack of purpose** futility
**lack of red blood cells** anaemia
**lack of refinement** crudeness, raunch
**lack of resolve** hesitancy
**lack of respect** disrespect, irreverence
**lack of restraint** incontinence
**lack of self-control** indiscipline
**lack of sense** nonsense
**lack of serious thought** frivolity, levity

**lack of skill** inability, inertia
**lack of sophistication** simplicity
**lack of strength** hyposthenia
**lack of success** failure
**lack of the sense of taste** ageusia
**lack of thoughtfulness** inconsideration
**lack of vitality** languish, languor, lethargy
**lack of wisdom** incipience
**lacks strength** weakling
**lack vitality** languish
**Laconia** Lacedaemon, Sparta
**laconic** biting, blunt, brief, compact, concise, crisp, elliptical, incisive, keen, neat, pointed, quiet, reticent, sharp, short, silent, succinct, taciturn, terse, trenchant, untalkative
**lacquer** burnish, coat, colophony, enamel, face, finish, gild, glaze, gloss, lac, lustre, mitigate, oleoresin, paint, palliate, patina, polish, resin, rosin, shellac, shine, soften, stain, texture, varnish, veneer, wax
**lacrimal globule** tear(drop)
**lacy fabric** netting
**lacy plant much used by florists** fern
**lacy serviette** doily
**lacy shawl** mantilla
**lad** boy, chap, fellow, guy, juvenile, kid, lightie, schoolboy, stripling, tad, youngster, youth
**ladder** ascent, companionway, disjunction, rigging, run, rungs, scale, series, stairs, stepladder, steps
**ladder between decks** companionway
**ladder formation** echelon
**ladder in hosiery** run
**ladderlike** scalar
**ladder step** rung
**lade** cram, fill, freight, heap, load, pack, pile, stack, stuff
**laden** burdened, charged, encumbered, loaded
**ladies' fingers** kidney vetch, okra
**ladies' garment** dress
**ladies' man** admirer, beau, Casanova, Don Juan, dotard, libertine, philanderer, playboy, rake, Romeo, roué, Valentino
**ladle** dip, scoop, spoon
**ladled** bailed, baled, dipped, dug, emptied, excavated, gouged, hollowed, scooped, scraped, shovelled, spooned
**ladle out** disburse, dish out, distribute, hand out
**lad's partner** lass
**lady** aristocrat, baroness, begum, countess, czarevna, czarina, czaritza, dame, Don(n)a, duchess, empress, female, feminine, gentlewoman, helpmate, madam(e), mademoiselle, Madonna, (maha)ranee, (maha)rani, marchioness, mate, matron, memsahib, milady, miss, mistress, noblewoman, partner, peeress, princess, queen, ranee, senora, signorina, signorita, spouse, tsarevna, tsarina, tsaritsa, wife, woman
**lady attending on the sovereign** lady-in-waiting
**ladybird** beetle, insect, ladybug, ladycow, ladyfly, vedalia
**Lady Bountiful** benefactor
**ladybug** beetle, ladybird, vedalia
**Lady Day** annunciation day
**ladyfish** bonefish, tenpounder, wrasse
**lady-killer** Casanova, coxcomb, dandy, flirt, libertine
**ladylike** aristocratic, considerate, correct, courteous, courtly, cultured, decorous, dignified, elegant, female, feminine, genteel, gracious, mannerly, matronly, noble, polished, refined, stately, well-behaved, well-bred, well-mannered, well-spoken, womanish, womanlike, womanly
**ladylove** amante (F), amour (F), beloved, covivante (F), darling, flame, heart-throb, jewel, lover, minion, mistress, paramour, precious, sweetheart, truelove
**lady of high rank** begum
**lady of house** goodwife
**lady of the lake** Ellen, Vivien
**lady of the sea** mermaid
**lady's bow** curts(e)y
**lady's bower** clematis
**lady's escort** squire
**lady's finger** bhindi
**lady's handbag** cabas, purse
**lady's hat** bonnet
**lady's headdress** chapeau, coif, crown, diadem, mantilla, tiara, wimple
**lady's maid** abigail
**lady's mantle** rocaceous plant
**lady's outer garment** robe
**lady's partner** gentleman
**lady's private sitting-room** boudoir
**lady's short fur-trimmed jacket** cymar, simar
**lady's slipper** cypripiedium, duck, moccasin flower, nervine, orchid, yellows
**lady's smock** cuckoo-flower
**lady's sunshade** parasol
**lady's thumb** redshank
**lady's tresses** orchid
**lady superior of a nunnery** abbess
**lady's very short jacket** bolero
**lady teacher** mistress
**lady winner** victrix (L)
**lag** bandiet, bloubaadjie, convict, dawdle, falter, felon, follower, idle, imprison, linger, loiter(er), offender, prisoner, retardation, slow-down, slowing, tarry, trail
**lag behind** loiter, straggle, trail
**lager beer** Pils(e)ner
**lag from metal-smelting** scoria
**laggard** dawdler, idler, loafer, loiterer, lounger, saunterer, slowcoach, sluggard, snail, straggler
**lagoon** basin, bayou, bight, cove, fiord, fjord, gulf, lake, loch, pond, pool, shoal, swamp, tarn
**Lagos is there** Nigeria
**Lahore native** Pakistani
**laic** civil, earthly, lay(man), non-clerical, nonpastoral, nonreligious, profane, secular(istic), state, temporal, unreligious, worldly
**laid-back** calm, casual, cool, easygoing, relaxed, unflappable, unhurried, untroubled, unworried
**laid food** egg
**laid up** bedridden, disabled, housebound, ill, immobilised, incapacitated, indisposed, injured, sick
**laid-up stock** store
**lair** burrow, cavern, den, haunt, hide-out, hideaway, hole, lie, nest, retreat, sanctuary
**lair of fox** den, kennel
**lair of otter** holt, hover
**lair of wild boar** sounder
**laissez-faire** indifference, individualism, non-interference, non-intervention, unconcern
**laity** assembly, brethren, congregation, crowd, fellowship, flock, host, laymen, multitude, nonecclesiastics, parish, people, seculars, throng
**lake** Athabasca, basin, bayou, Chad, dam, Kariba, lagoon, lakelet, loch (Sc), Malawi, mere, Nyasa, Placid, pond, pool, reservoir, Salt Lake, Tanganyika, tarn, Titicaca, Torrens, vlei, Winnipeg
**lake between America and Canada** Erie
**Lake City** Chicago
**Lake Constance** Bodensee
**lake-dwelling** crannog(e), palafitte
**lake-dwelling in Scotland or Ireland** crannog(e)
**lake fish** vendace
**lake in Afghanistan** Helmand
**lake in Africa** Albert, Chad, Congo, Kariba, Malawi, Nyasa, Rudolf, Tanganyika, Turkana, Victoria, Volta

**lake in Alabama**  Martin
**lake in Alaska**  Iliamna, Naknek
**lake in Albania**  Ohrid(sko), Prespa, Scutari, Ulze
**lake in Argentina**  Cardiel, Fagnano, Musters, Viedma
**lake in Armenia**  Sevan, Urmia, Van
**lake in Asia**  Aral, Balkhash, Baykal, Caspian, Urmia
**lake in Australia**  Amadeus, Bulloo, Cowan, Eyre, Torrens
**lake in Bolivia**  Coipasa, Poopo, Rogagua, Titicaca
**lake in Botswana**  Dow, Ngami
**lake in Brazil**  Aima, Feia, Mirim
**lake in Burundi**  Rugwero, Tshohoha
**lake in California**  Almanor, Berryessa, Clear, Eagle, Mono, Owens, Salton, Soda, Tahoe, Tulare
**lake in Cambodia**  Tonlesap
**lake in Canada**  Abitibi, Bear, Cree, Dubawnt, Garry, Kootenay, Louise, Nipigon, Okanagan, Rainy, Seul, Simcoe, Slave, Winnipeg
**lake in Chad**  Chad
**lake in Chile**  Puyehue, Ranco, Rupanco, Toro, Yelcho
**lake in China**  Bamtso, Bornor, Chaling, Chao, Ebinor, Erhhai, Hungste, Kaoyu, Khanka, Lopnor, Montcalm, Namtso, Oling, Poyang, Tai, Telli, Tsinghai, Tungting
**lake in Congo**  Leopold, Mweru, Tumba, Upemba
**lake in Costa Rica**  Arenal
**lake in Egypt**  Burullus, Edku, Idku, Manzala, Mareotis, Maryut, Moeris
**lake in El Salvador**  Guija, Ilopango
**lake in England**  Coniston, Ullswater, Windermere
**lake in Estonia**  Peipus
**lake in Ethiopia**  Abaya, Abe, Rudolf, Shola, Stefanie, Tana, Zeway
**lake in Europe**  Balaton, Como, Constance, Garda, Geneva, Ladoga, Lugano, Maggiore, Malaren, Onega, Peipus, Scutari, Vanem, Vattern, Zurich
**lake in Finland**  Hauki, Inari, Juo, Kalla, Kemi, Koitere, Lappa, Lesti, Muo, Nasi, Nilakka, Oulo, Pielinen, Puru, Puula, Pyha, Saimaa, Simo
**lake in Florida**  Apopka, Arbuckle, Dora, Harney, Jessup, Kissimmee, Ledwith, Newnan
**lake in France**  Annecy, Casaux
**lake in Gabon**  Anengue
**lake in Georgia**  Bankhead, Harding, Hartwell, Lanier, Martin, Nottely, Sinclair
**lake in Ghana**  Bosumtwi, Volta

**lake in Greece**  Copais, Karla, Kastoria, Kopais, Prespa, Tachinos, Topolia, Vistonis, Volve
**lake in Guatemala**  Atitlan, Dulce, Guija, Izabel, Peten
**lake in Haiti**  Saumatre
**lake in Honduras**  Brewer, Criba, Yojoa
**lake in Hungary**  Balaton, Blatensee, Ferto, Velence
**lake in Iceland**  Myvatn, Thorisvatn
**lake in Idaho**  Bear, Grays, Priest
**lake in Illinois**  Michigan
**lake in India**  Chilka, Colair, Dhebar, Sambahr, Wular
**lake in Indiana**  Manitou, Michigan, Monroe, Wawasee
**lake in Indonesia**  Ranau, Towuti
**lake in Iowa**  Clear, Spirit, Storm
**lake in Iran**  Maharlu, Nemekser, Niris, Niriz, Sahweh, Sistan, Tasht, Tuzlu, Urmia, Urumiyeh
**lake in Ireland**  Boderg, Carra, Conn, Cooter, Derg, Doo, Dromore, Ennell, Erne, Gowna, Key, Mask, Oughter, Ramor, Ree, Sheelin, Tay
**lake in Israel**  Huleh, Tiberias
**lake in Italy**  Albano, Bolsena, Bracciano, Como, Garda, Iseo, Lesina, Lugano, Maggiore, Perugia, Varano
**lake in Japan**  Chuzenji, Inawashiro, Kutchawa, Shikotsu, Towada, Toya
**lake in Kampuchea**  Tonlesap
**lake in Kansas**  Cheney, Kirwin, Milford, Neosho
**lake in Kentucky**  Cumberland
**lake in Kenya**  Magadi, Naivasha, Rudolf, Victoria
**lake in Louisiana**  Borgne, Clear, Darbonne, Iatt, Larto, Maurepas, Saline
**lake in Madagascar**  Alaotra, Itasy
**lake in Maine**  Chesuncook, Grand, Moosehead, Rangeley, Schoodic, Sebago, Sebec
**lake in Malawi**  Nyasa
**lake in Massachusetts**  Onota, Quabbin, Rohunta, Webster
**lake in Mexico**  Chapala
**lake in Michigan**  Burt, Houghton, Torch
**lake in Minnesota**  Bemidji, Itasca, Leech, Superior
**lake in Mississippi**  Barnett, Enid, Grenada, Okatibbee, Sardis
**lake in Missouri**  Ozarks, Tablerock
**lake in Montana**  Flathead, Fortpeck, Hebgen, Medicine
**lake in Montenegro**  Scutari, Shkoder
**lake in Nevada**  Mead, Mud, Pyramid, Ruby, Tahoe, Walker, Winnemucca
**lake in New York**  Cayuga, Conesus, Erie, George, Honeoye, Oneida, Ontario, Otisco, Otsego, Placid, Saranac, Saratoga, Schroon, Seneca, Success
**lake in New Zealand**  Breunner, Hawea, Ohau, Pukaki, Pupuke, Rotorua, Taupo, Te Anau, Tekapo, Wakatipu, Wanaka
**lake in Nicaragua**  Managua
**lake in North America**  Athabasca, Erie, Huron, Manitoba, Michigan, Nettiling, Nipigon, Ontario, Reindeer, Superior, Winnipeg
**lake in Norway**  Alte, Femund, Ister, Mjosa, Rostvatn, Rotstavn, Snasa, Tunnsjo
**lake in Oklahoma**  Eufaula, Oologah
**lake in Oregon**  Albert, Crater, Harney, Klamath, Malheur, Waldo
**lake in Panama**  Gatun
**lake in Paraguay**  Vera, Ypacarai, Ypoa
**lake in Peru**  Titicaca
**lake in Philippines**  Lanao, Taal
**lake in Poland**  Goplo, Mamry, Sniardwy
**lake in Puerto Rico**  Caonillas, Carite, Loiza
**lake in Romania**  Sinoe
**lake in Russia**  Aral, Balkhash, Baykal, Chany, Elton, Ilmen, Ladoga, Neva, Onega, Sego, Selety, Taymyr, Tengiz, Zaysan
**lake in Rwanda**  Kivu
**lake in Scotland**  Katrine, Laggan, Linnhe, Lomond, Morar, Ness, Rannoch, Tay
**lake in South Africa**  Sibaya, St Lucia, Umsingazi
**lake in South America**  Titicaca
**lake in South Australia**  Eyre
**lake in South Carolina**  Catawba, Hartwell, Marion, Moultri, Murray, Wateree
**lake in South Dakota**  Bigstone, Oahe, Traverse
**lake in Sudan**  No
**lake in Sweden**  Dalalven, Hjalmaren, Malaren, Silja, Storavan, Vanern, Vattern
**lake in Switzerland**  Ageri, Bienne, Brienz, Geneva, Hallwil, Leman, Lucerne, Lugano, Lungern, Morat, Sarnen, Thun, Uri, Vierwald, Wallen, Zug, Zurich
**lake in Syria**  Djeboid, Tiberias
**lake in Tanzania**  Rukwa
**lake in Tasmania**  Echo, Sorrel
**lake in Tennessee**  Cherokee, Douglas, Reelfoot, Wattsbar
**lake in Texas**  Amistad, Falcon, Texoma
**lake in Tibet**  Aru, Bam, Bum, Dagtse, Garhur, Jagok, Jiggitai, Kashun, Kyaring, Mema, Nam, Seling, Tabia,

Tangra, Terinam, Tosu, Tsaring, Yamdok, Zilling
**lake in Tunisia** Djerba
**lake in Turkey** Beysehir, Egridir, Tuz
**lake in Uganda** Albert, Edward, George, Kyoga, Victoria
**lake in Uruguay** Difuntos, Merin, Mirim
**lake in Utah** Salt Swan, Sevier
**lake in Venezuela** Maracaibo
**lake in Vermont** Caspian, Champlain, Dunmore, Seymour
**lake in Wales** Bala, Vyrnwy
**lake in Washington** Chelan
**lake in West Virginia** Lynn
**lake in Wisconsin** Mendota, Poygan, Winnebago, Wissota
**lake in Wyoming** Jackson
**lake in Yugoslavia** Ohrid, Prespa, Scutari
**lake in Zaire** Kivu, Mweru, Tanganyika
**lake in Zambia** Bangweulu, Kariba, Mwera, Tanganyika
**lake near Manila** Taal
**lake of volcanic origin** maar
**lake poet** Wordsworth
**Lake State** Michigan
**lam** batter, beat, birch, bolting, break, donder, escape, flail, flog, hit, horsewhip, jailbreak, klap, lash, pound, scourge, strike, thrash, thresh, wallop, whip
**lama-land** Tibet
**lama monastery** lamasery
**lamb** yean(ling)
**lambaste** beat, cane, donder, klap, thrash, whip
**lamb chop** cutlet
**lambent** aglow, dancing, flitting, glowing, (in)candescent, licking, luminant, quivering, skipping, suffused
**lamb's cry** bleat
**lamb's fleece** astrakhan
**lamb's mother** ewe
**Lamb's pen name** Elia
**lame** crippled, defective, disabled, handicapped, hobbled, hobbling, inadequate, limping, poor, unconvincing, weak
**lame duck** cheapskate
**lament** bellyache, bemoan, bewail, beweep, complain(t), condole(nce), coronach, cry, deplore, dirge, disapprove, elegy, grieve, jeremiad, knell, lamentation, moan(ing), mourn, obsequies, outcry, pine, plaint, regret, requiem, rue, sigh, snivel, sob, sorrow, suffer, threnody, wail, wake, weep, whimper, whine
**lamentable** deplorable, doleful, inadequate, meagre, mournful, niggardly, petty, piteous, pitiable, plaintive, poor, regrettable, sad, tragic, unfortunate
**lamentation** blubbering, cry, distress, elegy, grief, howl, keening, lament, mourning, pain, regret, sadness, snivel(ling), sob(bing), sorrow(ing), tears, wailing, weep(ing), woe
**lament for** bemoan
**lament for the dead** dirge, elegy, keen, mourn
**lament in writing** elegise
**lame person** cripple, invalid, paraplegic
**laminate** coat, (ex)foliate, layer, overlay, overspread, separate, stucco, veneer
**laminated granite** gneiss
**laminated material** plywood
**laminated rock** shale
**lamp** beacon, bulb, candle, flare, lantern, light, star, taper, torch
**lamp-cover** shade
**lamp dimmer** switch
**lamp magician** genie, genius, (d)jinni
**lamp oil** kerosene
**lamp on car** headlight
**lampoon** burlesque, caricature, defame, derision, iambic, malign, mock(ery), parody, pasquinade, revile, ridicule, satire, satirise, send-up, skit, spoof, squib, take-off, vilify
**lamp part** wick
**lamp producing white light** arc
**lamprey** cyclostome, eel
**lamprey fisherman** eeler
**lanai** veranda
**Lancashire seaport** Preston
**lance** fling, launch, spear
**lance-corporal's sign of rank** stripe
**Lancelot's lady** Elaine, Guinever(e)
**lancet arch** ogive
**lancet fish** serra
**land** acres, ager (L), alight, arrive, berth, catch, country, debark, descend, dirt, disembark, district, dock, earth, estate, ground, loam, nation, property, province, realty, region, secure, soil, terra firma, territory, tract
**land and water creature** amphibian
**land area** acreage
**land close to sea** sea-shore
**land drained by a river** basin
**landed class** gentry
**landed estate** manor
**landed home** estate
**landed property** estate
**landed proprietor** laird
**landed widow** dowager
**land fish** anabas, mud-hopper
**land forces** army
**land from a ship** alight, debark
**land going with parson's living** glebe
**land grant** ap(p)anage
**land granted as benefice** glebe
**land held in payment of rent** feu
**land held in return for services** feod, feud
**land held under feudal system** fief
**landing flight** stair
**landing in sea** ditching
**landing path of aircraft** runway
**landing pier** dock, jetty
**landing place** levee, quay
**landing place for helicopter** heliport
**landing place of the Ark** Ararat
**landing slip** pier
**landing strip** runway
**landlord** innkeeper, lessor
**landlord of inn** host, innkeeper, taverner
**landlord of pub** licensee
**landlord's charge** rental
**landlord's contract** lease
**landlord's income** rent(al)
**land management** husbandry
**landmark near Giza** Sphinx
**landmark of stone** cairn
**land measure** a(c)re, decare, metre, ro(o)d
**land of lakes** Michigan
**land of milk and honey** Utopia
**Land of Nod** sleep
**land of pasta** Italy
**land of the rising sun** Japan
**land of the shamrock** Eire, Erin, Ireland
**land opposed to water** shore
**landowner** laird (Sc), landlady, owner, proprietor, titleholder
**land parcel** lot
**landscape** aspect, countryside, cyclorama, outlook, paesaggio (I), panorama, paysage (F), picture, prospect, representation, scene(ry), scenography, sketch, tableau, view, vista
**landscape features** scenery
**landscape gardener** topiarist
**landscape painting** paysage (F)
**lands down under** antipodes
**landslide** avalanche
**land slope** versant
**Landsmål** Nynorsk
**land snail with no shell** slug
**land-steward** bailiff
**land suitable for crops** arable
**land surrounded by water** island, isle
**land tax** cess (Sc)
**land temporarily under grass** ley
**land tenure** socage
**land that adjoins sea** shore
**land under one rule** empire
**land unit** acre

**land used by aeroplanes** aerodrome, airstrip
**land worker** farmer, peasant, tiller
**lane** alley, course, passage, path, track, way
**laneway** alley
**lang syne** ago, past, yore
**language** argot, communication, dialect, diction, discourse, expression, idiom, jargon, lingo, patois, speech, style, tongue, tsotsitaal
**language based on Esperanto** Ido
**language form** dialect
**language intended to confuse** mumbo-jumbo
**language of a country** idiom
**language of Afghanistan** Balochi, Baluchi, Dari, Pashto, Pushto, Pushtu
**language of ancient Iberia** Iberian
**language of ancient Rome** Latin
**language of Andorra** Catalan
**language of Angola** Kimbundu
**language of a people** idiom
**language of Belgium** Flemish
**language of Bhutan** Dzongkha
**language of biblical times** Aramaic
**language of Cambodia** Khmer
**language of Cicero** Latin
**language of Ecuador** Jibaro, Spanish
**language of Flanders** Flemish
**language of Germany** Deutsch, German
**language of Ghana** Fanti
**language of India** Hindi, Sanskrit, Tamil, Telugu, Urdu
**language of Iran** Pahlavi, Zend
**language of Java** Javanese
**language of Kampuchea** Khmer
**language of Kenya** Swahili
**language of Malaysia** Tagalog
**language of Mali** Bambara, Dogon, Malinke, Mande, Songhai
**language of Monaco** French
**language of North India** Hindi
**language of Norway** Norwegian
**language of Pakistan** Baluchi, Bengali, Punjabi, Pushtu, Sindhi, Urdu
**language of Paraguay** Guarani
**language of Paris** French
**language of Peru** Aymara, Quechua
**language of Philippines** Bicol, Ibanag, Ilocano, Moro, Tagalog, Visayan
**language of Polynesia** Tagalog, Uvea
**language of Rwanda** Kirundi, Swahili
**language of Scotland** Erse, Lallan(d)
**language of Sierra Leone** Krio, Mende, Temne
**language of South Africa** Afrikaans, English, North Sotho, Pedi, SiNdebele, SiSwati, South Sotho, Tswana, Xhosa, Zulu
**language of southern Ghana** Twi
**language of South India** Tamil
**language of South Vietnam** Cham, Khmer, Rhade
**language of Sri Lanka** Tamil
**language of Sudan** Efik, Ewe, Ga, Ibo, Kru, Mandingo, Mole, Tshi, Yoruba
**language of the Ivory Coast** Dioula
**language of the Philippine Islands** Tagalog
**language of the Talmud** Hebrew
**language of thieves** argot
**language of Tibet** Bodskad
**language of Wales** Celtic, Cymraeg, Keltic, Welsh
**language of Zaïre** Kikongo, Kingwana, Lingala, Swahili, Tshiluba
**language of Zambia** Bemba, Lozi, Nja, Nyanja, Tonga
**language of Zimbabwe** Ndebele, Shona
**language without meaning** nonsense
**languid** dull, feeble, inert, lazy, lethargic, limp, listless, sluggish, spiritless, torpid, weary
**languish** ail, brood, decline, desire, deteriorate, diminish, droop, fade, fail, faint, flag, grieve, hanker, hunger, long, lovelorn, melancholic, mope, pine, sicken, sigh, sink, sorrow, suffer, sulk, wane, want, waste, weaken, wilt, wither, yearn
**languishing with love** lovesick
**languish with oppressive heat** swelter
**languor** apathy, debility, dullness, ennui, faintness, fatigue, feebleness, indolence, inertia, inertness, insensitivity, languidness, lassitude, laxity, silence, slackness, spiritlessness, stillness, strain, tiredness, tranquillity, weakness
**laniferous** lanigerous, wool-bearing
**lank** drooping, dull, emaciated, gaunt, lanky, lean, lifeless, limp, long, scrawny, skinny, slender, slim, spare, straggling, thin
**lanky** angular, bony, gaunt, rangy, spare, tall, thin, weak, weedy
**lantern** beacon, bulb, candle, flare, gaslight, lamp(ion), light, star, taper, torch
**lantern fly** Fulgora
**lantern on top of a dome** cupola
**Laotion money** at
**lap** circle, circuit, cover, distance, enfold, envelop, orbit, overlay, round, swaddle, tour, turn, twist, wrap
**lap dog** Maltese, Pekin(g)ese, pom(eranian), poodle, pug
**lapidate** kill, stone

**Lapsang Souchong** tea
**lapse** decline, deteriorate, error, expire, fall, interval, mistake, oversight, pause, recess, slip, terminate
**lapse morally** backslide
**lapse of memory** blackout
**lap up** absorb
**lapwing** pe(e)wit
**lar** idol
**larcenist** burglar, robber, stealer, thief
**larcenous** thieving
**larceny** burglary, fraud, hold-up, pilfering, pillage, plunder, raid, rapine, robbery, stealing, swindle, theft
**lard** fat
**larder** buttery, cuddy, pantry, spence, storeroom
**larding strip** lardo(o)n
**large** abundant, ample, big, broad, bulky, copious, elephantine, enormous, extensive, full, generous, gigantic, grand, great, hefty, huge, immense, jumbo, liberal, long, macroscopic, man size, massive, makulu, megalithic, outsize, plentiful, sizable, spacious, vast, weighty, wide
**large amount** lots, mass, much, plenty, raft, scads, spate, wad
**large and heavy** massive
**large and luxurious car** limousine
**large and thick of build** burly
**large animal** elephant, hippo(potamus)
**large antelope** addax, eland, kudu
**large antelope of Africa** addax, eland, gnu, sassaby
**large antlered animal** reindeer
**large ape** gorilla, orang-outang, orang-utan
**large area** extent, tract
**large area of trees** forest, plantation, wood
**large Australian kingfisher** kookaburra
**large baboon** mandrill
**large bag** holdall, (ruck)sack
**large bag filled with gas** balloon
**large barrel** vat
**large basket** hamper, pannier
**large bear-like mammal** panda
**large bedroom** dormitory
**large beer cask** tun
**large beer mug** stein, tankard
**large being** monster
**large-billed bird** pelican
**large bird** condor, eagle, emu, heron, ostrich, pelican, rhea, roc, stork
**large bird cage** aviary
**large bird dog** setter
**large bird enclosure** aviary
**large bird of prey** eagle
**large bird preying on fish in inland waters** osprey

**large bird with long neck and legs** flamingo
**large bivalve mollusc** cockle, mussel, perlemoen
**large black bird** raven
**large black dog** Dobermann, Rottweiler
**large black dung beetle** scarabaeus
**large black sea-bird** cormorant
**large black spider** tarantula
**large block of stone** monolith
**large blunt needle** bodkin
**large body of soldiers** army
**large body of water** lake, sea, vlei
**large boiling vessel** cauldron
**large book** tome
**large bottle** demijohn, flagon, magnum
**large bowl-shaped metal pan used in Chinese cooking** wok
**large box** crate
**large branched candlestick** candelabrum
**large brass wind instrument** trombone
**large breed of dog** Great Dane, wolfhound
**large breed of domestic pigeon** runt
**large brilliant parrot** macaw
**large brown Alaska bear** Kodiak
**large brownish-black kangaroo** wallaroo
**large brown seaweed** kelp
**large building** edifice
**large building for storing grain** barn, silo
**large bundle** bale
**large cabinet** armoir
**large cage for birds** aviary
**large car** limousine
**large carnivore** bear
**large carriage** coach
**large cask** butt, hogshead, tun
**large cat** cheetah, cougar, leopard, lion, puma, tiger
**large cave** cavern
**large chocolate pastry** torte
**large church** cathedral
**large citified area** conurbation
**large civet** zibet
**large clan** tribe
**large clasp-knife** jackknife
**large closed van for moving furniture** pantechnicon
**large coarse roofing slate** rag
**large coloured handkerchief** bandanna
**large commercial establishment** warehouse
**large container** tank, vat
**large container for washing** tub
**large continent** Africa, Asia, Eurasia, Europe
**large convoy of ships** armada, fleet
**large corvette** frigate

**large country house** manor
**large crested parrot** cockatoo
**large crow** raven
**large crowd of people** mass
**large cup** mug
**large cupola** dome
**large daily paper** broadsheet
**large dark-coloured monitor lizard** perentie, perenty
**large, deep opening in the ground** pit
**large deep pot** cauldron
**large deer** caribou, eland, elk
**large desert** Sahara
**large destructive fire** conflagration, inferno
**large destructive rat** bandicoot
**large dish** platter
**large dog** Great Dane, komondor, mastiff, wolfhound
**large domestic bird** goose, turkey
**large doorway** portal
**large drinking bowl** jorum
**large drinking cup** beaker, goblet, scyphus, tankard
**large drinking glass** rummer, tumbler
**large drinking room** beer hall
**large drinking vessel** beaker
**large duck** muscovy, sheldrake, shelduck
**large duck of New Zealand** paradise duck
**large early form of mandolin** mandola
**large earthenware mug for beer** stein
**large earthworm used as fishing-bait** lobworm
**large edible sea fish** cod, snoek, tuna
**large edible shellfish** abalone, crayfish, kreef, perlemoen
**large enclosure for birds** aviary
**large erf** smallholding
**large Eskimo boat** umiak
**large evergreen tree** cedar
**large expanse of water surrounded by land** lake, vlei
**large extinct elephant** dinothere, mammoth, mastodon
**large extinct herbivorous dinosaur** brachiosaurus, brontosaurus, iguanodon, ultrasaurus
**large extinct mammal** mastodon
**large extinct marine reptile** elasmosaurus
**large falcon** gyrfalcon
**large farm** ranch
**large feather** penna, plume
**large feather of wing or tail** quill
**large fern** bracken
**large firm cushion used as a seat** pouf(fe)
**large fish** cabezon(e), marlin, snoek, sturgeon, tuna
**large fish-eating waterfowl** pelican

**large fishing net** seine
**large fish-shaped marine mammal** whale
**large flat area on the moon** mare
**large flatfish** halibut, ray, skate
**large flat plate** ashet
**large fleet** armada
**large flightless bird** emu, ostrich
**large flying beetle** CMR beetle, cockchafer, May beetle, May bug
**large food dish** platter
**large-footed** megapod
**large formal assembly** convention
**large fortified building** castle
**large free-standing stone or monolith** menhir
**large French country house** chateau
**large fronded fern** osmund(a)
**large fruit** pineapple, spanspek, (water)melon
**large game fish** marlin, maskalonge, maskanonge, muskellunge, wahoo
**large gastropod** conch
**large gathering** crowd, rally
**large gathering of Boy Scouts** jamboree
**large gland round neck of bladder** prostate
**large glandular organ** liver
**large glass bottle protected by a wicker casing** carboy
**large goblet for holding wine** chalice
**large gourd used as food** pumpkin
**large grand house** mansion
**large grass** bamboo
**large, grassy plain with small trees in Brazil** campo
**large green grasshopper** katydid
**large group** crowd, gang, horde, mass, mob
**large group of Boy Scouts** troop
**large group of fish** shoal
**large group of musicians** orchestra
**large group of people** crowd
**large gulp** swig
**large gun** cannon
**large hairy tropical spider** tarantula
**large hall for physical training** gym
**large hammer** sledge
**large hand** paw
**large handkerchief** bandanna
**large hard sweet for sucking** gob
**large hat** sombrero, stetson
**large hawk** osprey
**large-headed match** fusee
**large-headed nail** stud, tack
**large headline** banner
**large heavy book** tome
**large heavy gun** cannon
**large heavy knife** machete, panga
**large heavy Malay knife** parang
**large heavy rope** hawser

large heavy shoes clodhoppers
large heavy vehicle juggernaut
large highly venomous snake cobra, fer de lance
large hole pit
large horned animal buffalo, rhino(ceros)
large house mansion
large house section wing
large house spider cardinal
large humped bovine yak
large Hungarian dulcimer cimbalom, cymbalom
large in area extensive
large Indian antelope nilgai, nylghau
large infantry unit battalion
large inn hotel
large in size enormous, gigantic, great, huge, massive
large iron mining bucket kibble
large jug ewer, pitcher
large jug with handle pitcher
large kangaroo wallaroo
large kettle ca(u)ldron
large kind of fern bracken
large kind of goldfish orfe
large kind of hazelnut cob
large kind of wasp hornet
large landed estate manor
large land mammal elephant, rhino(ceros)
large light-coloured antelope addax
large liquid container vat
large lizard goanna, iguana
large long-armed ape orang-utan
large male kangaroo boomer
large mammal elephant, hippo(potamus), rhinoceros, tiger
large maple sycamore
large marble taw
large marine duck merganser
large marine fish noted for its ferocity wolffish
large marine worm used as bait lug(worm)
large meal feast
large measure of quantity last
large medal medallion
large Mediterranean fish maigre
large merchant-vessel argosy
large meteor bolide, fireball
large milk can churn
large monkey ape, baboon
large moth with egg-shaped cocoon eggar, egger
large motorboat launch
large mug jug, pot, tankard
large muscular body mesomorph
large nail spike
large natural stream river
largeness of mind liberality

large North American deer moose, wapiti
large number host, manifold, many, numerous
large number of scads
large number of insects swarm
large nut with wrinkled shell walnut
large ocean mammal whale
large open basket scuttle
large orange navel
large ornamental feather plume
large oval bottle flagon
large oval dish platter
large overpowering force juggernaut
large padded sofa chesterfield
large parrot macaw
large passenger aircraft airliner
large pebble stone
large perennial plant tree
large petrel nelly
large piano grand
large pick mattock
large piece hunk
large piece of ice detached from an iceberg calf
large piece of linen to cover bed sheet
large pigeon runt
large pill bolus
large pitcher ewer
large plant tree
large playing marble alley, bonce, jack, king, queen
large pond lake
large pool for keeping sea animals oceanarium
large portion lot, much
large possum phalanger
large possum of Australia cuscus
large powerful anthropoid ape gorilla
large powerful dog mastiff
large prawns scampi
large property estate
large public building hall
large public exhibition exposition
large pulpit ambo
large quantity dollop, mass, reams, scads, swag
large quantity of paper ream(s)
large rabbit hare
large ray manta
large reception room saloon
large reddish kangaroo euro
large reed bamboo
large reptile alligator, crocodile
large retail shop emporium
large ribbed apple custard
large rich cream cake gateau
large rifled guns artillery
large river reptile crocodile
large rock boulder
large roll of money wad

large room hall
large rough-haired terrier Airedale
large round bottle surrounded by a protective framework carboy
large rounded vessel for holding liquids flagon
large round stone boulder
larger quantity more
larger than above
large safe strongroom
large sailing ship galleon, windjammer
large saurian crocodile
large-scale conflict Armageddon
large-scale destruction holocaust
large-scale manufacture mass production
large-scale raid invasion
large scoop shovel
large sea-animal with long tusks walrus
large sea-bird gannet, skua
large sea-bird like a goose gannet, solan
large sea-duck scoter
large sea-eel conger
large sea-fish ray, shark, skate
large sea-fish of West Indies barracuda
large sea-going vessel ship
large seawall dyke
large serpent boa, python
large serving dollop
large sheet of floating frozen water ice floe
large shellfish clam, lobster
large ship aircraft carrier, galleon, warship
large shoes gumboots
large shop store
large showy flower dahlia, peony, protea, strelitzia
large shrimp prawn, scampi
large silvery game-fish tarpon
large-sized letter capital
large sleeve dolman
large slice of cake slab
large smile beam
large snake anaconda, boa (constrictor), python
large social gathering party, rout
large sofa davenport
large soft bread roll bap
large soft travelling bag holdall
large South American bird rhea
large South American lake Titicaca
large South American snake anaconda, boa (constrictor)
large space area
large species of deer elk
large species of dormouse loir
large species of tunny albacore
large spider tarantula

large spoon ladle
large spotted animal leopard
large square shield pavis(e)
largess aid, allotment, allowance, alms-giving, altruism, beneficence, bounty, charity, contribution, donation, endowment, generosity, gift, largesse, liberality, offering, present, stipend, subsidy
largest amount maximum
largest artery in the body aorta
large stately building edifice
largest bat known kalong
largest bat species in UK noctule
largest bird ostrich
largest boat carried by sailing ship longboat
largest continent Asia
largest deer elk
largest desert Sahara
largest European bird of prey lammergeier, lammergeyer
largest Greek island Crete, Kriti
largest island of the Inner Hebrides Skye
largest lake in Scotland Lomond
largest land animal elephant
largest living bird ostrich
largest living rodent capybara
largest mammal whale
largest Mediterranean island Sicily
largest natural lake in Wales Bala
largest North American ring-plover killdeer
largest office block Pentagon
largest of the British isles Great Britain
largest of the Mariana islands Guam
largest of the salivary glands below each ear parotid
largest of the satellites of Uranus Titania
large stone megalith
large storage jar pithos
large store emporium
largest Quebec city Montreal
large stream river
large stream of water river
large striped feline tiger
largest river in France Loire
largest river in Ireland Shannon
large strong bag sack
large strong box chest, coffer
large strong dog mastiff
largest Scottish loch Lomond
largest species of petrel nelly
largest US state Alaska
large succulent aloe
large sums of money fortune
large swallow swig
large sweater sloppy joe
large teapot urn

large tear in garment rent
large tent marquee
large terrier dog Airedale
large thick old-fashioned watch turnip
large town city
large tract of grassland without trees prairie
large tree ash, beech, cedar, jacaranda, liquidambar, oak, yellowwood
large treeless area of grassland prairie, veld
large treeless plains in South America pampas
large triangular sail spinnaker
large tropical aquatic mammal manatee
large tropical snake anaconda, boa (constrictor)
large tub vat
large tusked animal elephant, hippo(potamus), walrus
large-tusked whale narwhal
large ungulate takin
large van used for removing furniture pantechnicon
large vase urn
large vegetable pumpkin
large vehicle bus, lorry
large veil worn by Muslim and Hindu women chadar, chador, chuddah, chuddar, chudder
large venomous lizard Gila monster
large venomous snake cobra, fer-de-lance, mamba, (puff)adder, rinkhals, taipan
large vessel urn
large vessel for boiling ca(u)ldron
large vessel for tea urn
large vessel with handle, spout and lid flagon
large violin viola
large volume tome
large voracious sea-fish shark
large vulture condor, griffon
large wading bird adjutant, stork
large wardrobe armoire
large wasp hornet
large water-bird pelican, swan
large waterfall cataract
large water-jug ewer
large water-pipe main
large watertight case caisson
large wave billow, breaker, surge, tsunami
large wax candle burned before the alter cerge
large weasel stoat
large weight ton
large weighty book tome
large Welsh river Severn
large white bear polar

large white sturgeon beluga
large wide-mouthed instrument saxophone
large wild-sheep of Asia argali, bighorn
large winebottle rehoboam
large wineglass braggart, rummer
large wingless horned grasshopper weta
large wooded area forest
large wooden hammer mall
large woody plant tree
large yacht sail spinnaker
lariat halter, lasso, leash, line, noose, (picketing) rope, tether, thong
lark antic, caper, fling, frolic, fun, gambol, game, jape, mischief, prank, revel, rollick, romp, spree
lark about play, romp, skylark, sport
lark-like bird pipit
larrikin hooligan, skollie
larva caterpillar, grub, maggot, nymph
larval oyster spat
larva of botfly bot
larva of coelenterate planula
larva of dipterous fly screwworm
larva of insect grub, maggot
larva of toad or frog tadpole
lascivious abandoned, bawdy, carnal, coarse, concupiscent, debauched, degenerate, depraved, dissolute, erotic, impure, lecherous, lewd, libidinous, lurid, lustful, obscene, promiscuous, ribald, sadistic, salacious, scurrilous, sensual, vile, vulgar, wanton
lasciviousness appetite, concupiscence, debauchedness, desire, impureness, laxness, lechery, lewdness, libido, licentiousness, lust(fulness), passion
lascivious talk smut
lash affix, attack, beat, bind, blow, censure, criticise, fasten, flay, flog, hammer, hit, join, lambast(e), pour, rope, scold, scourge, secure, strap, strike, stripe, stroke, swipe, teem, tether, thrash, tie, upbraid, wag, whip
lash into fury enrage, infuriate, madden
lass damsel, girl, lassie, maiden, meisie, miss, schoolgirl
lassitude apathy, deadness, debility, drowsiness, dullness, exhaustion, fatigue, feebleness, frailty, heaviness, idleness, inaction, inactivity, incapacity, indolence, inertia, infirmity, languidness, languor, laziness, lethargy, listlessness, numbness, oscitance, sickliness, sleepiness, sloth(fulness), slowness, sluggishness, stagnancy,

stagnation, stupor, tiredness,
torpidity, torpidness, torpor,
vegetation, weakness
**lasso** lariat, lash, leash, line, noose,
rope, shackle, tether, thong
**lasso loop** noose
**lass on page one** cover girl
**last** conclusive, continue, definite,
end(ing), endure, extreme, final,
hindmost, latest, lowest, mould,
omega, perpetuate, remain(ing),
stay, terminal, ultima(te), unlikely,
unsuitable, unwilling, utmost
**last a long time** endure
**last battle of Napoleon** Waterloo
**last but one** penultimate
**last but two** antepenultimate
**last compartment of ruminants'
stomach** abomasum
**last course of a meal** dessert
**last examination** final
**last Greek letter** omega
**last honours** burial
**lasting** abiding, ceaseless,
changeless, constant, continuing,
dateless, (en)durable, enduring,
eternal, everlasting, immortal,
incessant, interminable, ongoing,
permanent, persisting, stable,
steadfast, surviving, unaging,
unending
**lasting a long time** chronic, everlasting
**lasting eight years** octennial
**lasting five years** quinquennial
**lasting for a lifetime** lifelong
**lasting for an age** secular
**lasting forever** eternal, perpetual
**lasting forty days** Lenten,
quadragesimal
**lasting four years** quadrennial
**lasting ill will** spite
**lasting mutual hostility** feud
**lastingness** durability, durableness,
enduringness
**lasting only a moment** momentary
**lasting only for a day** ephemeral
**lasting period** duration
**lasting six years** sexennial
**lasting through the year(s)** perennial
**lasting two years** biennial
**last in succession** lattermost
**last king of Egypt** Far(o)uk
**last king of Iraq** Faisal
**last king of Troy** Priam
**last longer than** outlast
**last meal of the day** supper
**last-mentioned** latter
**last-minute items of news** stop press
**last name** surname
**last offer** ultimatum
**last of its kind** omega
**last of the Stuarts** Anne

**last outpost** Natal
**last over the fence** tail
**last portion of small intestines** ileum
**last remaining bit** dreg
**last resort** pis aller (F), refuge
**last resource** dernier ressort (F)
**last retreat** redoubt
**last sheep to be shorn** cobbler
**last six lines of sonnet** sestet
**last stage of insect** imago
**Last Supper chalice** grail
**last syllable** ultima
**last things** finality
**last trace** vestige
**last under use** wear
**last word** amen
**last year's snow** firn
**Las Vegas feature** strip
**Las Vegas state** Nevada
**latch** bolt, catch, sneck
**latch on to** apprehend, comprehend,
understand
**late** deceased, delayed, dilatory,
former, lasting, modern, overdue,
recent, slow, tardy
**late breakfast** brunch
**lateen-rigged Arabian Sea ship** dhow
**late learner** opsimath
**lately acquired** new
**late meal** supper
**late middle-aged** elderly, old
**late news item** stop press
**late night wish** good night,
sweet-dreams
**latent** abeyant, concealed, covert,
dormant, hidden, inactive, passive,
potential, sleeping, unaroused
**latent ability** potential
**later** after(wards), behind, next,
presently, since, subsequently,
tardily, thereafter
**lateral** edgeways, flanking, side(ward),
sideways
**lateral boundary** side
**lateral curvature of the spine** scoliosis
**lateral extension** wing
**lateral part** side
**lateral shoot** arm
**lateral supporting structure of bridge**
abutment
**lateral surface** side
**later in time** after
**later reflection** afterthought
**later than** after, behind, beyond
**later than expected** tardy
**latest** current, fashionable, final, in,
last, modern, new(est), now,
slowest, ultimate, up-to-date
**latest fashion** dernier cri (F)
**latest information** news
**lath** batten, panel, rail, slat, splat,
spline, strip

**lathe operator** turner
**lather** beat, bubbles, cane, donder,
foam, froth, lambast(e), soap(suds),
suds, thrash, whip
**lathe-worker** turner
**lath used by harlequin in old comedy**
slapstick
**Latin** Roman
**Latin American currency** peso
**Latin American dance** conga, rumba,
samba, tango
**Latin American shawl** serape
**Latin name for ancient Troy** Ilium
**Latin name for bear** ursa
**Latin name for England** Anglia
**Latin speaker** Roman
**Latin version of Bible** Vulgate
**latitude** breath, clearance, compass,
elbow-room, extent, field, freedom,
indulgence, leeway, liberty, licence,
play, range, reach, room, scope,
space, span, spread, sweep,
unrestrained, unrestrictedness, width
**latter** closing, last, later, latest, modern,
recent, second
**latter part** end
**latter part of day** evening
**latter part of Tertiary period** Neocene,
Neogene
**latter part of the day** evening
**lattice** fretwork, grate, grating, grid,
grill(e), herse, mesh, network,
reticulation, trellis, twine, web
**lattice of cross-bars** trellis
**lattice on which trees are trained**
espalier
**lattice-work** treillage, trellis
**Latvian** Lett
**Latvian coin** lat
**laud** acclaim, applaud, approve,
celebrate, clap, commend,
compliment, congratulate, eulogise,
exalt, extol, felicitate, glorification,
glorify, honour, hymn, magnify,
praise, proclaim, rejoice, salute,
toast, welcome
**laudable** admirable, approvable,
blameless, commendable,
creditable, estimable, excellent,
good, just, meritorious, praiseworthy,
unimpeachable
**laudatory act** coup
**laudatory discourse** eulogy, panegyric
**laudatory notice** puff
**laugh** chortle, chuckle, giggle, grin,
guffaw, smile, snicker, snigger, titter
**laughable** absurd, amusing, comical,
derisive, derisory, diverting, droll,
farcical, funny, hilarious, humorous,
ludicrous, nonsensical,
preposterous, ridiculous

**laugh at** belittle, deride, disdain, jeer, lampoon, mock, parody, ridicule, scoff, scorn, taunt, tease
**laugh contemptuously** snort
**laugh covertly** giggle, titter
**laugh furtively** snigger
**laugh impudently** fleer
**laugh in a quiet manner** chuckle, titter
**laughing all the way to the bank** earning very well
**laughing animal** hy(a)ena
**laughing gull** pewit
**laughing jackass** kookaburra
**laughing predator** hy(a)ena
**laughing stock** mock, sport, target, victim
**laugh in small half-suppressed bursts** giggle
**laugh loudly** cachinnate, roar
**laugh mockingly** fleer, jeer
**laugh off** dismiss, disregard, ignore, minimise, overlook, ridicule
**laugh out loudly** roar
**laugh quietly** chuckle
**laugh rudely** jeer
**laugh scornfully at** deride
**laugh slyly** snigger
**laughter** amusement, chuckling, giggling, glee, hilarity, laughing, merriment, mirth, riant, tittering
**laughter sound** ha
**laugh throatily** chuckle
**launch** begin, establish, float, hurl, inaugurate, propel, start, take-off
**launch out at** attack
**launder** bath(e), clean(se), disinfect, dust, iron, moisten, mop, purge, purify, rinse, scour, scrub, shower, sluice, sponge, swab, sweep, trunk, wash, wet, wipe
**launderer** washerman
**launder with a long rod** poss
**laundry** laundrette, wash-house, washing
**laundry appliance** iron, tumble dryer, washing machine
**laundry chore** ironing
**laundry day** wash-day
**laundry employee** ironer
**laundry fastener** peg
**laundry holder** basket
**laundry location** line
**laundry need** iron, soap, starch, washing powder
**laundry stiffener** starch
**laurel** bay(-tree)
**laurel-like tree** sassafras
**lava** aa, andesite, ashes, basalt, coulee, granite, lapillous, magma, obsidian, pumice, scoria, verite
**lava hill** volcano
**lava source** volcano
**lava stone** pumice
**lavation** ablution, clean(s)ing, lavage, wash(ing)
**lavatory** convenience, gents, ladies, latrine, loo, toilet, WC
**lava vent** volcano
**laver** font
**lavish** abundant, bestow, excessive, expend, extravagant, prodigal, profuse, prolific, spendthrift, superabundant, unrestrained, unstinted, wasteful
**lavish meal** feast
**law** act, canon, charter, code, codification, commandment, covenant, custom, decree, edict, enactment, jurisprudence, justice, order, ordinance, postulate, principle, regulation, rule, statute
**law-breaker** convict, criminal, delinquent, miscreant, offender, skellum, skelm, skollie, transgressor, trespasser, tsotsi, violator
**law court** bar
**lawful** allowable, authorised, constitution, forensic, judicial, jural, juristic, just, legal(ised), legitimate, licit, mandated, obedient, proper, rightful, sanctioned, statutory, valid, warranted
**lawless** anarchic, chaotic, defiant, dishonest, disorderly, illegal, illicit, insubordinate, insurgent, miscreant, mutinous, nefarious, rebellious, reckless, riotous, roguish, scampish, unlawful, unrestrained, unruly, wicked, wild
**lawlessness** anarchy, chaos, confusion, crime, disorder, illegality, mutiny, piracy, revolt, riot, unruly, unscrupulousness, vicious, violence
**lawless violent person** outlaw
**law man** barrister, sheriff
**lawn** cloth, common, fabric, field, grass (plot), green(ery), greensward, linen, material, meadow, pasturage, sod, sward, textile, turf, verdure
**lawn game** bowls
**lawn greenery** grass
**lawn moisture** dew
**lawnmower** grass-cutter
**lawn tool** mower, rake
**law passed by legislative body** statute
**law report** case
**laws made** legislation
**lawsuit** action, argument, case, cause, contest, dispute, litigation, persecution, suit, trial
**lawsuit that attracts much interest** cause célèbre
**lawyer** advocate, amicus, attorney, barrister, bencher, case, cause, contest, counsel(lor), dispute, intercessor, judge, judicator, jurist, legalist, legist, mouthpiece, pleader, prosecution, prosecutor, sergeant, silk, solicitor, suit, trial
**lawyer's charge** fee
**lawyer's fee** retainer
**lax** backward, careless, casual, dilatory, disorderly, drooping, flabby, flat, heedless, inadvertent, inattentive, inexact, injudicious, lenient, listless, loose, neglectful, negligent, promiscuous, relaxed, remiss, slack, thoughtless, unrigorous, unstrict, vague, weak
**laxative** aperient, cathartic, dose, ipecac, physic, purgation, purgative, purge, salts, senna
**laxative plant** senna
**lax in morals** dissolute
**lay** allay, amateur, appease, arrange, ascribe, bet, calm, charge, deposit, dilettante, devise, impose, impute, laic(al), locate, nonclerical, place, poem, position, prepare, put, quiet, secular, set, song, stake, still, suppress, unclerical, wager
**lay-about** deadbeat, idler, pike(r)
**lay about one** assail, assault, attack, harass, proceed, scramble, start
**lay a fine** impose
**lay a ship over on her side** careen
**lay aside** abandon, discard, dismiss, drop, postpone, reject, renounce, repudiate, shelve, store
**lay a trap** set
**lay at the door of** attribute, credit, impute
**lay away** amass, collect, hoard, pile, stack, store, treasure
**lay back** recline
**lay bare** divest, exhibit, expose, narrate, open, strip, uncover, unearth, unfold, unveil
**lay brother** frater
**lay church official** elder
**lay claims** demand
**lay claim to** profess
**lay desolate** waste
**lay down** affirm, assert, assume, cede, deposit, discard, drop, establish, formulate, give, leave, ordain, pose, prescribe, quit, relinquish, state, stipulate, submit, surrender, yield
**lay down arms** capitulate, surrender
**lay down the law** command, control, dictate, dogmatise, emphasise, govern, mandate, pontificate, regulate
**layer** bark, base, bed, blanket, casing, coat(ing), course, cover(ing), envelope, film, hen, lame, lamina,

level, lining, mantle, membrane, overcoat, peel, plate, ply, range, region, scab, scum, seam, sheath, sheet, shell, skin, stratum, table, thickness, tier, touch, veneer, zone
**layer a surface** adsorb
**layer at back of eyeball** retina
**layered crystalline rock** schist
**layered garden** terrace
**layered row** tier
**layered wood** plywood
**layer of atmosphere above troposphere** stratosphere
**layer of bone** lamella
**layer of cake** tier
**layer of earth** stratum
**layer of earth's crust** sima
**layer of eggs** hen
**layer of paint** coat
**layer of skin below epidermis** dermis
**layer on outside of tree** bark
**layers of small broken stone** macadam
**layer underneath** substratum
**lay eyes on** behold, encounter, observe, see
**lay figure** effigy, image, mannequin, model, puppet
**lay footpath** pave
**lay for** ambush, await, ensnare, lurk, prowl
**lay hands on** acquire, assault, attack, discover, find, grab, grasp
**lay heads together** consult
**lay hidden** lurk, hide
**lay hold of** catch, clasp, clinch, grab, grasp, grip, seize, snag, snatch, twist
**lay in** accumulate, amass, collect, gather, glean, hoard, srockpile, store
**laying fowl** hen
**laying out of grounds** landscape gardening
**lay in ruins** blast, destroy, ruin, spoliate, wreck
**lay into** assail, assault, attack, lambast(e)
**lay in wait** ambush
**lay it on** boast, embroider, exaggerate
**lay like a trap** set
**lay like the table** set
**layman** amateur, catechumen, civilian, dilettante, ignorant, laic, laity, layperson, learner, non-clergyman, non-professional, novice, ordinand, outsider, parishioner, postulant, seminarist
**lay off** axe, cease, chuck, desist, discharge, dismiss, drop, fire, oust, quit, stop, withhold
**lay official in church** deacon

**lay on** cater, colour, contribute, furnish, give, provide, stage, stress, supply, underline
**lay on the line** endanger, imperil
**lay open** disclose, reveal, unveil
**lay out** arrange, chart, contribute, demolish, design, disburse, display, exhibit, expend, fell, flatten, give, invest, outline, pay, plan, prepare, spend
**layout** aggregation, arrangement, blueprint, chart, collection, display, disposal, format, formula, group, map, outline, set, sketch, spread
**lay out garden** landscape
**lay out in lavender** admonish, berate, chide, demolish, reprove, scold, scorch
**lay out money** invest
**lay over** defer, overnight, postpone, stop, table
**layperson** amateur, catechumen, civilian, dilettante, ignorant, laic, laity, learner, non-clergyman, non-professional, novice, ordinand, outsider, parishioner, postulant, seminarist
**lay stress upon** demand, enforce, impress, urge
**lay the base of** found
**lay to rest** bury, inter
**lay up** accumulate, ail, amass, disable, droop, fail, hoard, hospitalise, incapacitate, keep, languish, put away, save
**lay waste** despoil, destroy, devastate, pillage, ravage, spoil
**laze** idleness, lounge
**laze around** loaf
**lazily** drowsily, languidly, lethargically, sleepily, slowly, sluggishly, somnolently, torpidly
**laziness** carelessness, dullness, languor, laxity, lethargy, listlessness, lumpishness, sleepiness, torpor
**lazy** apathetic, averse, dormant, drowsy, dull, idle, inactive, indolent, inert, languid, lethargic, lifeless, listless, loafing, otiose, slack, sleepy, slothful, slow, sluggish, somnolent, supine, tired, torpid, work-shy
**lazy creature** sloth
**lazy person** idler, layabout, loafer, lounger, scamp, shirker, skiver, slug(abed), sluggard
**lea** field, grassland, meadow, pasture (land)
**leach** drain, extract, filter, filtrate, percolate, seep, strain
**leach for hawks** lune
**lead** advance, advantage, cause, clue, command, conduct, direct(ion),

dispose, draw, edge, escort, example, govern, guidance, guide, head, hint, incline, indication, induce, influence, leadership, leash, manage, margin, model, outdo, outstrip, pass, persuade, pilot, precede(nce), prevail, principle, priority, prompt, start, steer, suggestion, supervise, surpass, transcend, undergo, usher
**lead and tin alloy** terne
**lead assault** spearhead
**lead astray** bewilder, pervert, seduce
**lead away** abduce, seduce
**lead away from virtue** debauch
**lead character** hero(ine), protagonist
**leader** boss, captain, chief(tain), commander, conductor, councellor, director, duce (I), editorial, forerunner, guide, head, manager, pacemaker, pacesetter, principal, ringleader, ruler, skipper, superior
**leader in fashion** trendsetter
**leader of attack** spearhead
**leader of chorus** coryphaeus
**leader of group** top dog
**leader of sect** guru
**leader of singing** precentor
**leader of the government** prime minister
**leader of Tibetan Buddhists** Dalai Lama
**leadership** administration, authority, captaincy, command, control, direction, directorship, domination, guidance, influence, initiative, management, pre-eminence, premiership, running, superintendency, supremacy, sway
**lead glass** strass
**lead in** usher
**leading** causing, chief, commanding, conducting, directing, disposing, dominant, drawing, escorting, first, foremost, governing, greatest, guiding, heading, highest, inclining, inducing, influencing, main, managing, number one, outstanding, persuading, pre-eminent, preceding, prevailing, primary, principal, ruling, steering, superior, supreme, ushering
**leading actor** hero, star
**leading article** editorial
**leading attack force** spearhead
**leading ballet dancer** coryphée, prima ballerina
**leading case** precept
**leading character** protagonist
**leading family** dynasty
**leading female singer in an opera** prima donna

**leading lady**  diva, heroine, premiere, star
**leading male character**  hero
**leading note**  tonic
**leading nowhere**  blind, cul-de-sac
**leading player**  hero(ine), protagonist, star
**leading position**  vanguard
**leading sheep of flock with bell on neck**  bellwether
**lead off**  begin, commence, inaugurate, initiate, open, start
**lead on**  allure, beguile, deceive, delude, entice, hoodwink, inveigle, lure, mislead, persuade, seduce, tempt, trick
**lead ore product**  wulfenite
**lead source**  galena
**lead strap**  leash
**lead the thrust**  spearhead
**lead the way**  actuate, broach, conduct, inaugurate, initiate, institute, launch, open, originate
**lead up to**  approach, build up, imply, insinuate, intimate, introduce, overture, preface
**leaf**  frond, page
**leaf aluminium**  tinfoil
**leaf arrangement in bud**  vernation
**leaf drink**  tea, tisane
**leafless plant**  dodder
**leaflet**  advert, booklet, brochure, circular, handbill, pamphlet, tract
**leaf-living moth genus**  tortricid
**leaf of betel**  pan
**leaf of book**  page
**leaf of calyx**  sepal
**leaf of fir or pine**  needle
**leaf of palm or cycad**  frond
**leaf of paper**  folio
**leaf of three leaflets**  trefoil
**leaf-scraper**  rake
**leaf-shaped ornament on Gothic pinnacles and gables**  crocket
**leaf's stalk**  petiole
**leafstalks fruit**  rhubarb
**leaf through**  browse
**leaf vein**  rib
**leafy arbour**  bower
**leafy beverage**  tea, tisane
**leafy fence**  hedge
**leafy nook**  bower
**leafy salad ingredient**  chard, cos, lettuce, spinach
**leafy shelter**  bower
**leafy vegetable**  cabbage, chard, cos, endive, kale, lettuce, romaine, spinach
**league**  alliance, coalition, combine, confederate, covenant, federation, union, unite
**Leah's maidservant**  Zilpah

**leak**  aperture, chink, crack, crevice, discharge, disclose, disclosure, divulge(nce), drip, escape, exude, fissure, hole, leakage, leaking, ooze, oozing, opening, pass, percolation, percolate, perforation, puncture, reveal, revelation, seep(age), spill, tell, trickle
**leakage**  drain, drip, efflux, emission, escape, gush, leak, outflow, percolation, seepage, spurt
**leak out**  escape, filter
**leak slowly out**  ooze
**leaky**  cracked, holey, leaking, perforated, permeable, porous, punctured, split, waterlogged
**lean**  angular, barren, bend, bony, confide, deficient, depend, emaciated, favour, gaunt, inadequate, incline, lank, list, meagre, prefer, prop, raw-boned, recline, rely, repose, rest, scanty, scrawny, skinny, slant, slender, slim, slope, spare, tend, thin, tilt, toward, trust
**lean and bony**  scraggy
**lean and long-limbed build**  asthenic
**lean and sinewy**  muscular, powerful, strong, wiry
**lean and skinny person**  scrag
**lean beef cut**  fillet, topside
**lean-bodied person**  ectomorph
**leaned**  sloped, tilted, tipped
**lean flesh**  brawn
**lean forward**  stoop
**lean in a lazy manner**  inclining, lollant, propping, reclining, reposing, resting, slanting, sloping, tilting, tipping
**leaning**  aptitude, bent, bias, disposition, inclination, penchant, proneness, taste, tendency
**leaning over**  beetle, overhanging
**leaning tower city**  Pisa
**lean lazily**  loll
**leanness**  bareness, barrenness, gauntness, lankness, meagreness, pitifulness, poorness, ranginess, scantiness, skinniness, slenderness, slimness, spareness, sparseness, thinness, wiriness
**lean on**  blackmail, force, persuade, pressurise
**lean or bony**  angular
**lean over**  heel, list
**lean over backwards**  sacrifice
**lean over to one side**  list
**lean part of loin of pork**  griskin
**lean person**  scrag
**lean-to**  addition, annexe, booth, building, cabin, den, hovel, hut(ch), pen, refuge, shanty, shed, shelter, stall, structure, sty
**leap**  advance, bounce, bound, caper, cavort, clear, escalate, escalation, frisk, gambol, hasten, hop, hurry, hurtle, increase, jump, reach, rise, rocket, rush, skip, soar, spring, (up)surge, upswing, vault
**leap about**  prance
**leap from one leg to the other in ballet**  jeté
**leap headlong**  dive
**leaping amphibian**  frog, toad
**leaping marsupial**  kangaroo
**leap lightly or hop**  skip
**leap made by a horse without advancing**  capriole
**leap on one foot**  hop
**leap over**  vault
**learn**  absorb, acquire, apprehend, ascertain, assimilate, attain, comprehend, detect, determine, discern, discover, disinter, gain, gather, glean, grasp, hear, master, memorise, pat, perceive, realise, receive, see, study, trace, uncover, understand, unearth
**learn by concentrated study**  mug, swot
**learn by heart**  con, memorise
**learned**  academic, cultivated, cultured, deep, educated, erudite, expert, highbrow, informed, knowledgeable, literate, profound, scholarly, skilled, versed, wise
**learned Brahman**  Brahmin, pandit, pundit
**learned expert**  pandit, pundit
**learned Hindu**  pandit, pundit
**learned person**  polymath, savant, scholar, student
**learned society in India**  Akademi
**learner**  amateur, apprentice, beginner, neophyte, novice, pupil, scholar, student, tiro, trainee, tyro
**learner tradesman**  apprentice
**learn from experience**  assay
**learning**  cultivation, culture, data, edification, education, enquiry, erudition, exploring, facts, hunting, information, inquiry, investigating, knowledge, lore, quest, scholarship, search, study, wisdom
**learning of lessons heard during sleep**  hypnopaedia
**learnt in class**  lesson
**lease**  agreement, charter, hire, let, license, loan, rent(al), sublet
**leased again**  re-let
**leased by tenant**  sub-let
**leased property**  rental
**lease-giver**  lessor

**leaseholder** holder, inhabitant, lessee, occupier, resident, tenant
**lease out** hire
**lease payment** rental
**leash** check, control, curb, fasten, hold, lead, rein, restrain, suppress, tether
**leash for hawks or falcons** lune
**leasing** chartering, hiring, letting, loaning, renting
**least** fewest, last, littlest, lowest, meanest, merest, minimum, minutist, poorest, slightest, smallest, tiniest
**least amount** rap
**least amount possible** minimum
**least civil** rudest
**least comely** ugliest
**least common** rarest
**least complex** simplest
**least costly** cheapest
**least dangerous** safest
**least fancied competitor** underdog
**least harsh** mildest
**least possible** minimal
**least quantity** minimum
**leather** beat, belt, calfskin, cane, chastise, donder, lash, punish, scourge, spank, suede, trounce, whip
**leather band** belt, strap, thong
**leather case for a weapon** holster
**leather covers to prevent a horse seeing sideways** blinkers
**leather cuirass** lorica
**leather factory** tanning
**leather fold on book spine** tailcap
**leather footwear** (jack)boot, sandal, shoe
**leather from buffalo skin** buff
**leather from oxhide** buff
**leather from sheepskin** roan
**leather from young goat skin** chevrette, kid
**leather garment** buff
**leather glove** gauntlet
**leather jacket padded with mail** acton
**leather leggings** chaparajos, chaparejas, chaps, puttee, putty
**leatherneck** marine, soldier
**leather-processing works** tannery
**leather screens on bridle** blinkers
**leather shorts** lederhosen
**leather splitting** skiving
**leather strap** strop, taws(e) (Sc), thong
**leather strap supporting body of vehicle** thorough-brace
**leather strip** strap
**leather strip in the heel of a shoe** rand
**leather thong** riempie, strap
**leather tool** awl
**leather with a nap** suede
**leather works** tannery

**leathery** coarse, durable, inflexible, resistant, rigid, rough, rugged, strong, tough
**leave** abandon, allowance, bequeath, cease, depart, desert, forbear, forget, go, holiday, omit, permission, quit, relinquish, renounce, stop, vacate, vacation
**leave as a legacy** will
**leave as it is** stet
**leave a union** secede
**leave behind** abandon, desert, forsake, renounce
**leave by will** bequeath
**leave desolate** bereave
**leave destitute** abandon, maroon, strand
**leave employment** resign, retire
**leave empty** vacate
**leave for** repair to
**leave furtively** steal
**leave hastily** skedaddle
**leave helpless** strand
**leave hurriedly** flee
**leave illegally** abscond, desert
**leave in the lurch** abandon, desert, forsake, jilt, quit, reject
**leave it** stet
**leave job** resign
**leaven** adjust, affect, alterer, baking powder, barm, catalyst, convert, determinant, enhearten, enzyme, ferment, infect, influence, inspire, leavening, lighten, maltase, pepsin(ate), pervade, qualify, raise, self-raising flour, soda, suffuse, yeast, zymogen
**leave no chance** prevent, prohibit
**leave no choice** necessitate
**leave no clear traces of** obliterate
**leave no option** necessitate
**leave no vestige** expunge
**leave no void** permeate, pervade
**leave of absence** congé, exeat, furlough
**leave off** abstain, cease, desist, discontinue, end, halt, quit, refrain, rest, stop, terminate
**leave one place and settle in another** migrate
**leave one's own country to settle in another** emigrate
**leave out** bar, delete, disregard, elide, eliminate, except, exclude, ignore, neglect, omit, overlook, reject, repudiate, skip
**leave out in the cold** disregard, forget, ignore, overlook, reject, shun, snub
**leaves** abandons, allots, allowances, assigns, blades, cedes, concessions, consents, consigns, decamps, departs, disappears, exits,

foliage, folios, goes, holidays, liberties, needles, pages, quits, refers, retires, sanctions, sheets, vacations
**leaves collectively** foliage
**leaves hair curly** perm
**leave ship** disembark
**leaves of plants** leafage
**leave-taking** congé, exit, parting
**leave the stage** exeunt
**leave the straight and narrow** backslide
**leave to by will** bequeath
**leave to enter** admission
**leave to one's fate** maroon
**leave uncared for** neglect
**leave undone** neglect, omit
**leave unmolested** tolerate
**leave unoccupied** vacate
**leave unprotected** expose
**leave vehicle in bay** park
**leave without paying** do a moonlight flit
**leave workforce** retire
**leaving a will** testate
**leaving no room for complaint** satisfactory
**leaving no room for hope** desperate
**leaving no slack** tight
**leaving no will** intestate
**leavings** debris, deposit, dregs, droppings, dross, dung, embers, excrement, guano, lees, leftover, litter, muck, offal, orts, refuse, remainder, remains, residue, rubbish, rubble, ruins, rummage, scrapings, scum, sediment, silt, trash, wastage, waste
**leaving valid will** testate
**Lebanese capital** Beirut
**Lebanese town** Sidon
**Lebanese tree** cedar
**Lebanese Uniat** Maronite
**Lebanese valley** Bekaa, Beqaa
**lecher** Casanova, debauchee, harlot, libertine, playboy, profligate, prostitute, rake, reprobate, roué, seducer, slut, trollop, wanton, whore, womaniser
**lecherous look** leer
**lecherous man** roué
**lecherous wood god** satyr
**lechery** appetite, carnality, concupiscence, crudity, depravity, desire, impurity, indecency, lasciviousness, lewdness, libido, lust(fulness), obscenity, passion, profligacy, salacity, unchastity
**lectern** ambo, book-stand, desk, dias, escritoire, holder, platform, podium, pulpit, rostrum, stand, support

**lecture** address, admonish, apologue, berate, castigate, censure, chide, discourse, dissertation, earbashing, expound, harangue, homily, instruct(ion), lesson, parable, rate, rebuke, reflection, reprimand, reproof, reprove, scold, sermon, speak, speech, talk, teach, warning
**lecture in public** prelect
**lecture room** lyceum
**ledge** foothold, mantle, offset, outcropping, projection, ridge, shelf, sill, step
**ledge at back of altar** gradin(e)
**ledger entry** credit, debit, item
**lee** covering, protection, shelter
**leech** annelid, barnacle, bloodsucker, dependant, follower, freeloader, gill, hanger-on, healer, lackey, minion, parasite, physician, sail, sponger, sycophant, usurer, worm
**leek-green** porraceous
**leek-green quartz** prase
**leer** basilisk, eye, fleer, gloat, goggle, grin, ogle, smirk, squint, stare, watch, wink
**leery** careful, cautious, chary, distrustful, heedful, hesitant, knowing, mistrustful, observant, shy, sly, suspicious, uncertain, unsure, untrustful, wary
**lees** deposit, dregs, leavings, refuse, rubbish, sediment
**left** anarchistic, communist, gone, heirloom, leftwing, liberal, portside, progressive, sinister, sinistral, sinistrous, went
**left alone** deserted, desolate
**left- and right-handed** ambidextrous
**left bank** bohemian
**left close** unopen
**left desolate** bereft
**left-handed** awkward, careless, clumsy, dextrosinistral, dubious, fumbling, gauche, indistinct, maladroit, paradoxical, sardonic, sinistral, tactless
**left-handed person** lefty
**left-handed side of ship** larboard, port
**left-hand page of open book** verso
**left helpless without resources** stranded
**leftist** Red
**left-over** balance, carry-over, dross, excess, fragments, junk, leavings, legacy, oddment(s), ort, refuse, remainder, remains, remanent, remnant(s), residual, residue, residuum, rest, rubbish, rubble, ruins, rummage, scraps, scum, shards, spoils, sprue, superfluity, surplus(age), survivor, trash, waste

**left-over scrap** orts, remanent
**leftovers meal** hash
**left, right and centre** everywhere
**left side of account** debit
**left side of ship** larboard, port
**left to choice** optional
**left to the imagination** unspoken
**left-winger** radical
**leg** brace, fibula, fraction, horse, lap, limb, member, part, pillar, portion, prop, section, sector, segment, shank, shin(bone), stage, stretch, stump, support, tibia, trestle, underpinning, upright
**legacy** ancestry, bequeathal, bequest, bestowal, birthright, devise, endowment, estate, gift, heirloom, hereditament, heritage, (in)heritance, patrimony, tradition
**legal** above-board, adjudicatory, allowable, allowed, authorised, constitutional, forensic, judicial, lawful, legalised, legitimate, licit, permissible, proper, rightful, sanctioned, valid, warrantable
**legal advisor** adviser, advocate, attorney, council, counsel, lawyer, solicitor
**legal arrest** caption
**legal claim** demand, lien
**legal code** pandect
**legal command from superior** mandate
**legal contest** trial
**legal disqualification** incapacity
**legal dissolution of marriage** divorce
**legal document** contract, deed, writ
**legal example** precedent
**legal expenses** costs
**legal expert** legist
**legal information** evidence
**legal inquiry** inquest
**legally** lawfully
**legally acceptable** valid
**legally bound** liable
**legally permitted** licit
**legally preclude** estop
**legally responsible** liable
**legally sound** valid
**legal man** lawyer
**legal matter** res
**legal maturity** age
**legal medico** coroner
**legal offence** crime, delict, felony, violation
**legal official** fiscal
**legal order** writ
**legal order of dismissal** nonsuit
**legal paper** document
**legal possessor** owner
**legal power of right** authority
**legal process** action

**legal prosecution** suit
**legal proviso** caveat
**legal representative** advocate, attorney, lawyer
**legal restraint** interdict
**legal right** lien
**legal rule** law
**legal successor** heir
**legal summons** writ
**legal support** maintenance
**legal voter** elector
**legal wrong** tort
**leg armour** greave, jambart, jambeau, jamber
**legate** bequeath, delegate, emissary, envoy, messenger
**legatee** heir
**legation** commission, contingent, delegates, delegation, deputation, embassy, envoys, mission
**leg bone** femur, fibula, shin, thigh, tibia
**legend** allegory, caption, celebrity, commentary, fable, fiction, (folk-)tale, historical, inscription, key, luminary, motto, myth, narrative, parable, phrase, saga, story, tradition, wonder
**legendary** acclaimed, chimerical, dreamy, eidetic, exalted, extravagant, fabled, fabulous, famed, fanciful, fantastic(al), fictitious, heroic, idealistic, illustrious, imaginary, immortal, invented, lustrous, mythic(al), popular, quixotic, radiant, renowned, romantic, storied, strange, supernatural, traditional
**legendary bird** lighting bird, roc
**legendary birthplace of Romulus and Remus** Alba Longa
**legendary British king** Lear
**legendary daughter of Tentalus** Niobe
**legendary figure** Magog
**legendary hero** Paladin
**legendary hunter** Orion
**legendary illustrative part of the Talmud** Haggadah
**legendary island** Avalon
**legendary king** Solomon, Midas
**legendary rat killer** Pied Piper of Hamelin
**legendary sailor** Sinbad
**legendary singing siren** Lorelei
**legendary sword** Balmunc, Balmung, Excalibur
**legendary tale** fable, myth, saga
**legendary Tibetan creature** abominable snowman, yeti
**legerdemain** juggling, sophistry, trickery
**legible** clear, decipherable, definite, discernible, distinct, distinguishable, explicit, intelligible, lucid, neat,

perceptible, plain, readable, salient, tidy, typed
**legislate** authorise, charter, codify, coerce, constitute, decree, dragoon, enact, establish, fix, force, formulate, necessitate, oblige, ordain, order, prescribe, reconstitutionalise, regulate, require, set
**legislation** codification, dictate, law(making), ordinances, prescript, statutes
**legislative** congressional, judical, law-giving, law-making, ordaining, parliamentary, senatorial
**legislative body** assembly, chamber, congress, diet, legislature, parliament, senate
**legislative building** House of Parliament, Statehouse
**legislator** congressman, director, lawgiver, lawmaker, parliamentarian, politician, senator, Solon, statesman
**legislature** assembly, caucus, chamber, congress, convention, council, diet, parliament, senate, session
**legitimate** authorise, correct, justify, lawful, legal(ise), logical, normal, proper, regular, sanctioned
**legitimate power to command** authority
**leg joint** ankle, hip, knee
**leg of mutton** gigot
**leg part** ankle, calf, foot, knee, shin, thigh
**leg-puller** humorist, trickster
**leg rest on saddle** crutch
**legume** beans, capsule, hull, loment, lupin, peas, pericarp, pods, pulse, seed case, vetch
**legume feast** beano
**legume grown for food** lentil
**legume plant** trefoil
**leguminous** fabaceous
**leguminous bean** haricot, lima, soya, sugar
**leguminous fodder** sainfoin
**leguminous herb** lupin, sainfoin
**leguminous plant** bean, lentil
**leg up** assistance, boost, help, support
**lei** garland
**leisure** comfort, dolce vita, ease, free(dom), holiday, inactivity, liberty, opportunity, pause, quiet, recreation, relaxation, respite, rest, retirement, unemployment, unoccupied, vacation
**leisure activity** hobby
**leisure hours** horae subsecivae (L)
**leisurely** carefree, comfortable, deliberate, easily, easy, gentle, laid-back, lazy, loose, premeditated, relaxed, restful, slow, tranquil, unhasty, unhurried
**leisurely studying of something** perusal
**leisurely walk** amble, loiter, promenade, saunter, stroll
**leisure pursuit** hobby, pastime
**leman** beloved, lover, mistress, sweetheart
**lemonade** pop
**lemonade with beer** shandy
**lemon-coloured** citrine
**lemon drink suffix** -ade
**lemon-scented leaves** balm
**lemur** loris
**lend** accommodate, advance, contribute, furnish, give, help, loan, provide, spend
**lend a hand** aid, assist, help
**lend aid** help
**lend an ear** hearken, listen
**lend itself to** fit, suit
**lend oneself to** agree, co-operate, consent, espouse, support
**length** distance, duration, extent, measure, period, piece, portion, reach, section, segment, space, span, stretch, term
**length across centre of circle** diameter
**length and breadth** all
**lengthen** attenuate, continue, eke, elongate, expand, extend, increase, prolong, protract, stretch
**lengthen out** attenuate, prolong
**length expressed in feet** footage
**length measure** ell, foot, inch, (kilo)metre, mile, span, yard
**length measured in yards** yardage
**length of decorative frill** ruche
**length of film** footage
**length of life** age
**length of metal links** chain
**length of rails** track
**length of sawn timber** plank
**length of service** longevity
**length of step** pace
**length of time one can remember** memory
**length of twenty-two yards** chain
**length times width** area
**length unit** metre, yard
**lengthwise** (end-)long
**lengthwise threads in a loom** warp
**lengthy** diffuse, digressive, elongated, extended, extensive, interminable, lengthened, (long-)drawn-out, long(-winded), overlong, prolix, prolonged, protracted, rambling, talkative, tedious, verbose, windy, wordy
**lengthy and earnest speech** harangue
**lengthy letter** epistle
**lengthy rebuke** earful
**lengthy story** chronicle, epic, saga
**lengthy text** screed
**lengthy treatment of subject** discourse
**lenience** clemency, compassion, forbearance, gentleness, indulgence, lenity, mercy, mildness, tenderness, tolerance
**leniency** clemency, forbearance, gentleness, indulgence, mercy, mildness, permissiveness, tolerance
**lenient** charitable, clement, compassionate, easy, gentle, humane, kind, merciful, mild, moderate, softhearted, soothing, sympathetic, tender, tolerant, understanding
**leno** fabric, weave
**lens** meniscus
**lens defect** astigmatism
**lens for defective eye** eyeglass
**lens for looking through** eyepiece
**lens-shaped** lenticular, lentoid
**lens-shaped seed** lentil
**lentigo** freckle
**lentil-shaped** lenticular, lentiforum
**lento** slow
**Leo animal** lion
**leonine** animal, beautiful, lion-like
**leopard-like feline** cheetah, ocelot
**Leo's sign** lion
**leper** lazar, lepra, leprosy, outcast
**leper hospital** lazaret(to), spital
**leper island** Molokai
**leper king** Baldwin
**lepid** jokey, witty
**lepidolite** mica
**Lepidoptera** moth
**leporid** hare, leveret
**leporine** harelike
**leprechaun** dwarf, elf, fairy, fay, gnome, gremlin, imp, kobold, sprite
**leprosy** disease, lazary, lepra, scall
**leprous** decayed, diseased, lepridote, leprose, leprotic, scabby, scaly, unclean
**Lesbos sea** Aegean
**lese-majesty** iconoclasm, insurrection, laesa majestas (L), sedition, treason
**lesion** abnormality, bruise, contusion, cut, defacement, disorder, harm, impairment, injury, laceration, rip, slash, sore, tear, trauma, wound
**less** fewer, immaterial, imperfect, inferior, lacking, meagrely, minor, minus, second-rate, secondary, shorter, smaller, subordinate, unimportant, without
**less adulterated** purer
**less attractive** uglier
**less colour** paler

**less convincing** lamer
**less difficult** easier
**lessee** boarder, dweller, hirer, holder, lodger, occupant, occupier, renter, tenant
**lessen** abate, abridge, allay, alleviate, appease, contract, curtail, de-escalate, deaden, decline, decrease, degrade, depreciate, diminish, disparage, dwindle, ease, erode, fail, flag, impair, lighten, lower, minimise, mitigate, moderate, narrow, reduce, shrink, slack, weaken
**lessen force** geld
**lessen greatly** deplete
**lessening of pace** slowdown
**lessen in severity** ease
**lessen in value** cheapen, shrink
**lessen sensitivity** dull
**lessen strength** wear
**lessen tension** relax
**lessen the lustre of** tarnish
**lessen the severity of** mitigate
**lessen the tension** ease
**lessen velocity** deaden
**lesser** imperfect, inferior, junior, less, lower, mediocre, minor, minute, narrower, petit, second-rate, secondary, shorter, slighter, smaller, subaltern, subordinate
**lesser anteater** tamandu(a)
**Lesser Antilles** Caribbees
**lesser goddess** nymph
**lesser number** minority
**lesser white heron** egret
**less good** worse
**less hazardous** safer
**less ill** better
**less important** minor
**less in number** fewer
**less jaded** fresher
**lesson** class, coaching, deterrent, drill, example, exemplar, exercise, instruction, lecture, message, moral, period, precept, punishment, reading, rebuke, schooling, task, teaching, tutoring, warning
**lesson of fable** moral
**lessor** lease-giver
**less populous** sparser
**less restrained** freer
**less risky** safer
**less than** beneath, hardly
**less than deadly** nonfatal
**less than elegant** seedy
**less than full amount** ullage
**less than normal** hypo-, subnormal
**less than twice** once
**less tight** looser
**less true** falser
**less undignified** soberer

**less well** iller, worse
**less well off** poorer
**lest** except, unless
**let** abandon, allow, assign, authorise, commission, disappoint, empower, enable, encumbrance, fail, favour, grant, hindrance, hire, impediment, lease, license, obstruct, omit, permit, relinquish, rent, sublet, suffer, tolerate, warrant, yield
**let air out** deflate
**let aside** forget, ignore, neglect
**let become known** spill
**let down** abandon, abate, betray, desert, dib, disappoint, disenchant, disillusion, dissatisfy, fail, jilt, lower, reduce, relax, slacken, strike, submit, vail
**let-down** anticlimax, blow, come-down
**let fall** depose, drop, vail
**let fall off** shed
**let fly** bolt, cast, emit, fire, fling, hurl, launch, peg, propel, throw, toss, vent, wing
**let go** deliver, demise, disband, discard, discharge, disengage, dismiss, disperse, dissolve, drop, emancipate, fire, free, liberate, loose(n), manumit, quit, release, relinquish, unarm, uncage, unchain, unfetter, unhand, unleash, unseize, untie
**let go to pot** neglect
**lethal** dangerous, deadly, destructive, disastrous, fatal, killing, leprous, malignant, mortal, mortiferous, murderous, noxious, poisonous, ruinous, septic, suicidal, toxic, venomous, virulent
**lethalise** destroy, kill
**lethal nerve gas** sarin
**lethargic** comatose, drowsy, dull, inert, languid, lazy, listless, sleepy, slothful, sluggish, torpid
**lethargy** apathy, coma, drowsiness, dullness, inaction, indifference, indolence, inertia, inertness, lassitude, laziness, listlessness, sleepiness, slowness, sluggishness, sopor, stupidity, stupor, torpidity, torpor
**let head droop in drowsiness** nod
**let him take who can** capiat qui capere possit (L)
**let in** accept, adhibit, admit, embrace, greet, include, incorporate, insert, install, open, receive, welcome
**let in again** re-admit
**let it stand** keep, retain, stet
**let it stay as written** stet
**let know** acquaint
**let land** gavelkind

**let loose** bellow, emit, explode, free, liberate, relax, release, rescue, slip, unchain, yell
**let off** absolve, acquit, clear, detonate, discharge, dispense, disregard, emit, excuse, exempt, exonerate, explode, exude, fire, forgive, ignore, leak, liberate, neglect, overlook, pardon, release, spare, vindicate
**let on** betray, broadcast, disclose, divulge, impart, leak, proclaim, publish, reveal, tell
**let oneself down with a rope** abseil
**let one's hair down** relax
**let original form stand** stet
**let out** betray, blab, break, discharge, disclose, divulge, emit, expose, free, give, leak, liberate, loosen, produce, release, reveal, spill, utter
**let out a moan** groan
**let remain** leave, stet
**let sink** vail
**let slide** abandon, drop, forget, ignore, neglect
**let slip** disclose, divulge, forego, lapse, reveal
**let someone use** lend
**let spittle flow from mouth** slaver
**let stand** stet
**letter** ABC, abecedary, acknowledgement, alphabet, answer, breve, character, chit, communication, correspondence, dispatch, envelope, epistle, grapheme, hieroglyphic, ideogram, ideograph, italic, learning, line, mail, meaning, message, missive, note, reply, scholarship, sign, substance, syllabary, symbol
**letterbox** mailbox, postbox
**letter by letter** literatim
**letter carrier** connection, intermediary, postman
**letter from pope** brief, bull, encyclical
**letter H** aitch
**letterhead** stationery
**letter holder** letterbox, postbox
**lettering cut-out** stencil
**letter lever on typewriter** key
**letter of challenge** cartel, defy
**letter of debt** IOU
**letter of defiance** cartel, defy
**letter of general distribution** circular
**letter of indebtedness** IOU
**letter of introduction** credential
**letter of marque** mart
**letter of marque recipient** privateer
**letter of permission** exeat
**letter of the alphabet other than a vowel** consonant
**letter or word added to end of word** suffix

**letter puzzle**  anagram
**letter representing a word**  logogram
**letters**  belles-lettres, books, communication, correspondence, culture, diaries, dossier, education, erudition, file, handwriting, humanities, information, knowledge, learning, literature, longhand, lore, packages, paper, parcels, post, records, research, schooling, scholarship, script, study, tuition, wisdom, writing(s)
**letter's cross stroke**  serif
**letter sent by the pope to bishops in all countries**  encyclical
**letter sibilant**  ess
**letters meaning let it stand**  stet
**letters of adulation**  fan mail
**letters of language**  alphabet
**letters on Christ's cross**  INRI
**letters received**  incoming mail
**letters standing for chemical element**  symbol
**letter stroke**  serif
**letter writer**  correspondent
**letter writing**  correspondence
**let the doer beware**  caveat actor (L)
**let the purchaser beware**  caveat emptor (L)
**let there be light**  fiat lux (L)
**let there be no ill omen**  absit omen (L)
**let the traveller beware**  caveat viator (L)
**lettuce**  cos, iceberg, red oak, romaine, salad, vegetable
**lettuce dish**  salad
**let-up**  abate(ment), cease, cessation, decrease, diminish, end, halt, interval, moderate, recess, relax, remission, rest, slacken, stop, subside
**let up**  abate, decrease, diminish, ease, mitigate, stop, subside, terminate
**let up on**  loosen, relax, slacken
**let violence give place to law**  cedant arma togae (L)
**levant**  abscond, bolt, flee
**Levantine garment**  caftan, kaften
**Levantine headdress**  fez, turban
**Levantine lute**  oud
**Levantine madder**  Alizari
**Levantine measure**  dra, pik
**Levantine vessel**  bum, dhow, saic, settee, xebec
**Levantine wind**  etesian, khamsin
**levee**  assembly, dike, durbar, dyke, embankment, gathering, pier, quay, reception
**level**  aim, aligned, balanced, bulldoze, calm, class, degree, demolish, destroy, devastate, direct, echelon, elevation, equable, equal(ise),

equality, equivalent, even, flat(ten), flush, grade, height, horizontal, layer, line, plain, plane, point, position, rank, raze, smooth, stable, stage, standard, standing, status, steady, storey, straight, stratum, tier, uniform, zone
**level after ploughing**  bush
**level a rafter**  edge
**level cut on hillside**  terrace
**level grassy plain**  steppe
**level-headed**  balanced, calm, collected, composed, cool, dependable, even-tempered, reasonable, sane, self-possessed, sensible, steady, unflappable
**level-headedness**  sagacity
**levelled**  bent
**leveller**  destroyer, equaliser
**levelling piece**  shim
**level of command**  echelon
**level of electric pressure**  potential
**level off**  bulldoze, hammer
**level of hotness**  temperature
**level of seating**  tier
**level of ship**  deck
**level of society**  stratum
**level of stage**  study
**level open area**  esplanade
**level piece of ground**  area
**level score**  par
**level surface**  plane
**level surface of**  scrape
**level to ground**  raze
**level tract of country**  plain, veld
**level treeless plain**  steppe, veld
**level with**  abreast
**Leven**  lake, Loch
**lever**  (crow)bar, dislodge, force, handle, heave, jemmy, joy-stick, move, pedal, prise, pry, purchase, raise, shift, tappet
**leverage**  authority, control, force, influence, pry, purchase, strength, support, vantage
**leveret**  leporid
**lever in a gun**  cock
**lever in a loom**  lam
**leviathan**  colossus, giant, (sea) monster, titan
**levity**  buoyancy, facetiousness, flightiness, flippancy, frivolity, giddiness, irreverence, jocularity, light-heartedness, silliness, skittishness, triviality
**levy**  assessment, charge, collect(ion), contribution, demand, duty, exact(ion), excise, fee, gather(ing), impose, imposition, raise, subscription, tariff, tax, toll
**levy a fee**  tax

**lewd**  bawdy, blue, dirty, impure, indecent, lascivious, libidinous, licentious, loose, lustful, obscene, pornographic, profligate, promiscuous, salacious, smutty, unchaste, vile, vulgar, wanton, wicked
**lewd man**  lecher
**lewd talk**  smut
**Lewis Carroll's girl**  Alice
**lexicographer**  compiler, drudge, editor, etymologist, linguist, onomastic, wordperson
**lexicography**  dictionary-making, etymology, glossography, lexicology, onomastics, onomatology
**lexicon**  dictionary, thesaurus, vocabulary, wordbook
**lexicon language**  Arabic, Greek, Hebrew, Syriac
**lexis**  vocabulary, words
**Lhasa is there**  Tibet
**Lhasa native**  Tibetan
**Lhasa palace**  Potala
**liability**  accountability, arrears, burden, debit, debt, disadvantage, drag, drawback, duty, encumbrance, handicap, hindrance, impediment, indebtedness, millstone, nuisance, obligation, obstacle, onus, responsibility
**liability to error**  fallibility
**liability to harm**  danger
**liable**  accountable, amenable, answerable, apt, bound, chargeable, exposed, inclined, likely, obligated, obliged, open, prone, responsible, subject
**liable to**  subject
**liable to become involved in accidents**  accident prone
**liable to change**  labile, mutable, variable
**liable to cross one's fingers**  superstitious
**liable to decay**  perishable
**liable to err**  fallible
**liable to erratic behaviour**  temperamental
**liable to error**  fallible
**liable to rot**  perishable, unstable
**liable to sin**  peccable
**liable to suspicion**  equivocal
**liaison**  affair, alliance, amour, bond, co-operation, communication, connection, contact, go-between, hook-up, interchange, intrigue, link, mediator, romance, union
**liar**  cheat(er), deceiver, fabricator, fake, falsifier, fibber, fibster, fraud, hedger, hypocrite, imposter, libeller, misleader, perjurer, pretender,

**prevaricator**, storyteller, swindler, yarner
**libation** beverage, cocktail, decoction, draught, drink, drunkenness, intoxicant, liquid, nightcap, noggin, oblation, potation, potion, sacrifice, tribute
**libel** aspersion, blacken, calumny, culumniate, defamation, defame, malign, revile, slander, slur, smear, traduce, vilification, vilify
**libellous** accusable, aspersive, caustic, critical, culpable, defamatory, depraved, derogatory, disapproving, disgraceful, false, injurious, malicious, maligning, satirical, scurrilous, slanderous, soiling, tainting, traducing, untrue, vilifying, vitriolic, vituperative
**liber** bass, bast, phloem
**liberal** abundant, advanced, altruistic, ample, bountiful, broad-minded, charitable, copious, free(-handed), generous, handsome, kind, lavish, lenient, libertarian, magnanimous, moderate, munificent, open-handed, open-minded, plentiful, profuse, progressive, radical, reformist, rich, tolerant, unprejudiced, unstinting
**liberal arts** humanities
**liberal Buddhist school of Tibet** Mahayana
**liberal gift** largess(e)
**liberality** altruism, ampleness, big-heartedness, bounty, breadth, broad-mindedness, candour, charity, compassion, generosity, impartiality, indulgence, kind-heartedness, kindness, largess(e), latitude, magnanimity, munificence, neutrality, open-heartedness, philanthropy, plenty, prodigality, toleration
**liberally** abundantly, altruistically, bountifully, charitably, copiously, handsomely, kindly, lavishly, munificently, plentifully, profusely, richly, unstintingly
**liberal or radical** leftist
**liberate** deliver, discharge, disengage, disunite, divide, emancipate, extricate, free, loose, quit, ransom, redeem, release, remit, rescue, separate, sever, unbind, unchain, unfetter, unshackle, unslave, unthrall, untie
**liberator** deliverer, emancipator, freer, manumitter, rescuer, saviour
**liberator of Hebrews** Moses
**liberties** audacity, disrespect, familiarity, forwardness, impertinence, impudence, insolence, overfamiliarity, presumption
**libertine** adulterer, corrupt, debauchee, debaucher, decadent, dissipator, dissolute, gallant, gigolo, humanist, independent, lecher, liberal, Lothario, philanderer, playboy, prodigal, profligate, rake, rakish, reprobate, roué, sensualist, tolerant, unbiased, wanton
**liberty** authorisation, autonomy, carte blanche, dispensation, emancipation, franchise, freedom, immunity, independence, leave, liberation, licence, permission, privilege, release, right, sanction, self-determination, sovereignty
**liberty of choosing** option
**libidinous** bawdy, bestial, blue, carnal, degenerate, dirty, immoral, impure, indecent, intemperate, lascivious, lewd, licentious, loose, lubricious, lustful, obscene, pornographic, salacious, sensual, smutty, unchaste, vile, vulgar, wanton
**libido** aphrodisia, erotism, lubricity, lust, oestrus, rut, salacity, sensuality, sexuality
**library** ambry, archives, athenaeum, bibliothéque (F), bookery, collection, reading-room, reference-room, series, stack, study
**library of Oxford University** Bodley
**library rack** bookshelf
**library sign** silence
**library user** reader
**librate** balance, poise, quiver, sway
**Libyan currency** dinar
**licence** abandon, anarchy, audacity, authorisation, authority, certificate, charter, disorder, dispensation, dissipation, dissoluteness, entitlement, excess, exemption, freedom, immoderation, immunity, imprimatur, impropriety, independence, indulgence, irresponsibility, latitude, lawlessness, leave, liberty, nonconformity, permission, permit, privilege laxity, right, unruliness, warrant
**licence for absence** exeat
**license** accredit, allow, authorise, certify, commission, empower, entitle, permit, sanction, warrant
**licensee** permit-holder
**licentious** abandoned, amoral, debauched, disorderly, dissolute, free, immoral, impure, lascivious, lawless, lax, lecherous, lewd, liberal, libertine, loose, lustful, profligate, promiscuous, ribald, sensual, uncontrollable, unruly, wanton, wild
**licentious man** goat, libertine
**licentious party** orgy
**licentious person** libertine
**licentious talk** ribaldry
**licit** allowable, allowed, authentic, authorised, constitutional, genuine, just, lawful, legal(ised), legitimate, moral, permissible, proper, real, rightful, sanctioned, statutory, true, valid
**lick** brush, dart, flick(er), lap, smear, taste, tongue, touch, wash
**lick one's lips** anticipate, enjoy, relish, savour
**lick the dust** grovel, kowtow, toady, truckle
**lick up** lap
**lid** bung, cap, cork, cover, plug, stopper, top
**lid fastener** hasp
**lidlike structure in plant** operculum
**lido** pool
**lie** be, belong, consist, deceit, deception, dwell, equivocate, exist, extend, fabricate, fabrication, falsehood, falsification, falsity, fib, fiction, invent(ion), location, mendacity, misrepresent(ation), myth, perjure, perjury, place, position, prevaricate, prevarication, recline, remain, repose, rest, stretcher, untruth, whopper
**lie about** bask, loll
**lie about small matter** tarradiddle
**lie alongside** accost
**lie around** compass
**lie at anchor** moor
**lie at ease** bask, loll
**lie at full length** stretch
**lie concealed** darkle
**lie contiguous** confine
**lie detector** polygraph
**lie dormant** hibernate, latent, sleep
**lie down** charge, couch, laze, lean, lounge, recline, repose, rest
**lie down for sleep** kip
**lief** agreeable, beloved, gladly, willingly
**lie face down** pronate
**lie face up** supinate
**lie fallow** stagnate
**lie flat on belly** grovel
**liege** chieftain, feudal, lady, lord, loyal, master, mistress, sovereign, superior, vassal
**lie head to wind** try
**lie heavily upon** oppress
**lie hidden** lurk
**lie in ambush** ambuscade, hide, hugger, lurk
**lie in court** perjure
**lie in one's throat** calumniate, defame, libel, slander, traduce

**lie in the grave** sleep
**lie in wait** ambush, await, couch, lurk, skulk, waylay
**lie in warmth and sunshine** bask
**lie in water** douse, drown
**lie low** couch, elude, hide, lurk, prowl
**lien** attachment, entailment, mortgage, right, security
**lie next to** adjoin
**lie obliquely** slant
**lie opposite to** subtend
**lie over** cover
**lie prone** grabble, grovel
**lie quiet** snudge
**lie snug** cuddle
**lie stretched out** sprawl
**lie unevenly** sag
**lieutenant** two-pipper
**lieutenant of Othello** Cassio
**lie with** unite
**lie with limbs spread out** sprawl
**lie with sails furled** hull
**life** anima (L), animation, bio-, energy, existence, sparkle, spirit, verve, vigour, vita (L), vitality, vivacity
**lifeboat crane and support** davit
**life everlasting** eternity, heaven
**life force** nature, vitality
**life-giving gas** oxygen
**life-giving juice of plants** sap
**life history** biography
**life in the absence of free oxygen** anaerobiosis
**life in the presence of free oxygen** aerobiosis
**lifeless** azoic, breathless, buried, cold, dead, deceased, defunct, dull, extinct, heavy, inactive, inanimate, inert, insipid, listless, passive, sluggish, spiritless, stiff, stillborn, tame, torpid
**life of pleasure and luxury** dolce vita
**life span** longevity
**life story** biography
**lifetime** aeons, age, career, centuries, course, existence, generations, longevity, period, perpetuity, span, time, years
**life to come** heaven, hereafter
**life-work** calling, career, interest, profession, vocation
**lift** annul, ascend, boost, cancel, climb, disappear, disperse, dissipate, doff, drive, elevate, elevator, encouragement, end, escalator, exalt, fillip, heave, heft, hoist, lever, loft, manifest, mount, paternoster, pick-me-up, raise, rear, reassurance, relax, remove, rescind, revoke, ride, rise, run, stop, terminate, transport, upheave, uplift, upraise, upright, vanish

**lift a finger** contribute, help
**lift an elbow** booze, drink, imbibe
**lifting** ascending, cancelling, climbing, ending, mounting, relaxing, removing, rescinding, rising, terminating
**lifting device** crane, derrick, hoist, winch, windlass
**lift inventor** Otis
**lift one's hat** doff
**lift the spirits** elate
**lift up** adorn, augment, dignify, elevate, enhance, ennoble, glorify, heave, heighten, hoist, illuminate, immortalise, magnify, raise, (up)lift, upraise
**lift up your hearts** sursum corda (L)
**lift with effort** heave
**ligament** bond, fr(a)enum, tendon, tie
**ligation** bandage, compress, dressing, ligature
**ligature** bandage, bandaging, bind, bond, bow, braid, colligate, compress, connection, cord, couple, joint, knot, ligation, line, link, loop, rosette, strap, string, thong, tie
**light** agile, airy, angel, approach, aspect, blanched, brightness, brilliance, buoyant, carefree, cheerful, cheery, dawn, daybreak, daylight, descend, flimsy, gossamer, happy, humorous, ignite, illumination, inconsiderable, insubstantial, kindle, lamp, land, nimble, pale, radiance, shallow, slight, sunrise, trifling, trivial, unsubstantial, viewpoint, volatile, whitish
**light afternoon meal** tea
**light after sunset** afterglow
**light again** rekindle
**light aircraft without engine** glider
**light amusing play** comedy
**light and airy** ethereal
**light and heat source** sun
**light and lively musical composition** humoresque
**light and shade effects in nature** chiaroscuro
**light-attracted insect** moth
**light axe** hatchet, tomahawk
**light beam** ray
**light beer** bock, lager, Pils(e)ner
**light bit for a horse** snaffle
**light blow** clap, dab, flick, flip, pat
**light blow with something broad** flap
**light blunt-edged sword used in fencing** foil
**light boat** canoe, sculler, shallop, skiff, wherry
**light boat used on the Bosporus** caïque

**light breeze** air
**light brown** bay, beige, ecru, fawn, sorrel, tan
**light brown horse** sorrel
**light brown spot on skin** freckle
**light-bulb wire** filament
**light cabaret** revue
**light cake** scone, sponge
**light camel** dromedary
**light cannon** falconet
**light canvas shoe with a plaited sole** espadrille
**light carriage** chaise
**light cart** buggy
**light cavalryman in the French army** chasseur
**light clear red** cerise
**light colour** tint
**light conversation** chit-chat
**light cream pastry** éclair
**light crown** diadem
**light dancing shoe** pump
**light dessert** mousse
**lighten** brighten, cheer, disburden, ease, gladden, illume, illumination
**light entertainment** revue
**lighter-than-air craft** aerostat
**lighter upper layer of earth's crust** sial
**lightest element** hydrogen
**lightest metal** lithium
**light evening meal** supper
**light explosion** pop
**light fabric** net, voile
**light fall of rain** shower
**light fawn colour** ecru
**light fencing sword with tapering blade** sabre
**light fitting** chandelier
**light flat-bottomed Venetian canal boat** gondola
**light fleecy piece** flake
**light flitting over marshes** will-o'-the-wisp
**light fog** mist
**light-footed** active, nimble
**light footwear** sandal, slipper
**light green** jade
**light grey** ecru
**light gymnastic exercises** callisthenics
**light hair tint** rinse
**light-headed** delirious, dizzy, giddy, thoughtless, unsteady
**light-hearted** blithe, breezy, buoyant, carefree, cheerful, debonair, delighted, elated, gay, gladsome, happy, jolly, jovial, jubilant, optimistic, sunny, untroubled
**light helmet with outward-curving rear part** sallade, sal(l)et
**light hooded raincoat** cagoule, kagaul, kagoule

**lighthouse** beacon, beam, bonfire, flare, lightship, lookout, Pharos, sign(al), watchtower
**light humorous play** farce
**light in colour** fair
**light in darkness** lux in tenebris (L)
**light indoor shoe** slipper
**lighting** brightening, ignition, illuminating, illumination, (ir)radiation, kindling
**lighting bug** firefly
**lighting device** candle, flare, (gas) lamp, lantern, torch
**lighting fixture** lamp
**light intensity** albedo
**light into** assail, attack, lambast(e)
**lightless state** darkness
**light lunch or snack** tiffin
**lightly** gently
**lightly armed foot soldier of ancient Greek** peltast
**lightly built** svelte
**lightly touching** lambent
**light machine gun** Sten
**light meal** collation, snack
**light morning meal** continental breakfast
**light motorcycle** moped, scooter
**light musical drama** operetta
**light musket** fusil
**light narrow boat propelled by paddle** canoe
**lightness of heart** gaieté de coeur (F)
**lightning attack** blitzkrieg
**lightning bolt** streak
**light of heel** agile, fleet, light-footed
**light on** detect, discover, encounter, find
**light open boat** canoe
**light open boat for shallow waters** shallop
**light open four-wheeled carriage** phaeton
**light open two-wheeled carriage** curricle
**light opera** operetta
**light orchestral work** extravaganza
**light overcoat** topcoat
**light part** bulb
**light pastry** choux, puff, phyllo
**light piece of satire** burlesque, skit
**light pink wine** rosé
**light porous kind of lava** pumice
**light purple** lavender
**light racer** go-cart
**light raft** balsa
**light rainfall** shower
**light rap** tap
**light reddish-brown colour** sorrel
**light round flat cake** muffin
**light round teacake** crumpet, pikelet
**light rowing boat** paddle ski

**light royal crown** diadem
**light rubber-soled shoe with a cloth upper** dap, gym shoe, plimsoll, sneaker, tackie, takkie
**light sailing ship** pinnace
**light sailing vessel** yacht
**light scarf** bandanna
**light screen** shade
**light shade of purple or lavender** palatinate
**light shallow rowing boat** wherry
**light shoe** sandal, tackie, takkie
**light shoe for dancing** pump
**light shoes** slippers
**light short-handled axe** hatchet
**light silk** ninon
**light sleep** slumber
**light soft-soled shoe** espadrille, sneaker, tackie, takkie
**light source** bulb, candle, electricity, lamp, moon, sun
**lights out** dark, taps
**light spear** assegai, javelin
**light spongy dish** mousse, soufflé
**light sporting gun** shotgun
**light springing gait** lilt
**light steel helmet** basinet
**light stroke** pat
**light sweet wine** canary, Sauterne
**light-switch word** off, on
**light talk** banter
**light tap** pat
**light timber** balsa
**light time** day
**light-tube gas** neon
**light two-wheeled carriage** gig, shandrydran
**light two-wheeled horse-drawn vehicle** tonga
**light umbrella** parasol
**light unlined jacket** blazer
**light up** brighten, clarify, illuminate, illumine
**light wagon** cart
**light weapon** side-arm
**lightweight corner stand with three or more open shelves** étagère (F), whatnot
**lightweight machine gun** Sten
**lightweight material made from camel hair** aba
**lightweight wind-resistant jacket** windbreaker
**light wind** breeze
**light wine** chardonnay, grand cru, Marsala, Moselle, riesling
**light wispy clouds** cirrus
**light wood** balsa
**light yellowish-brown** fawn
**lignaloes** eaglewood
**Ligurian port** Genoa

**like** admire, akin, analogous, approve, as, choose, comparable, counterpart, disposed, enjoy, equal, favour, love, prefer, probably, relish, resembling, same, similar, sort, wish
**like a beast** bestial
**like a berry** baccate
**likeable** agreeable, amiable, appealing, appreciable, attractive, charming, complaisant, engaging, enjoyable, friendly, genial, nice, pleasant, pleasing, simpático (Sp), sympathetic, winning, winsome
**like a book** completely, entirely, thoroughly, wholly
**like a bull** taurine
**like a cancerous growth** scirrhous
**like a child** babyish
**like a chorus** choric
**like a duck** anatine
**like a feeble old woman** anile
**like a fox** vulpine
**like a gale** windy
**like a goose** anserine
**like a group of sheep** flock
**like a harp** lyre
**like a heathen** atheistic, pagan
**like a horse** equine, horsy
**like a key spanner** allem
**like a lion** leonine
**like a lizard** saurian
**like an angel** cherubic
**like an automaton** robotic
**like an eagle** aquiline
**like an egg** ovular
**like a new person** fresh
**like an oblong** rectangular
**like an ostrich** struthious
**like a number not divisible by two** odd
**like anything** extremely, intensely, terrifically
**like a palace** palatial
**like a parrot** psittacine
**like a parrotfish** scaroid
**like a pig** porcine
**like a pipe** tubular
**like a pixie** elfin
**like a play** dramatic
**like a rabbit** hare
**like a river delta** deltoid
**like a sage** wise
**like a sheet of glass** icy
**like a shot** eagerly, hurriedly, immediately, instantly, quickly, speedily, unhesitatingly
**like a small trumpet** bugle
**like a spiral** spiroid
**like a statue** immobile, motionless, rigid
**like a stepmother** novercal
**like a stone** lithoid
**like a story** narratively
**like a teacher** pedagogic

**like a tendon** desmoid
**like a trooper** earnestly, enthusiastically, vigorously, wholeheartedly, zealously
**like a tyrant** despotical
**like a weak old woman** anile
**like a wing** alar
**like better** prefer
**like burnt dust** ashy
**like cancer** cancroid
**like cats and dogs** disagreeing, incompatible, irreconcilable
**like cheese** caseous
**like clockwork** invariably, methodically, regularly, smoothly, systematically
**like copper** cupreous
**like crazy** ardently, devotedly, excitedly, furiously, intensely, passionately, recklessly
**liked by many people** popular
**like deer** cervine
**like ducks' toes** webbed
**like fibrous tissue** fibroid
**like for like** retaliation, talion
**like glass in hardness** vitreous
**like grass** graminaceous
**like hare** rabbit
**like leather** coriaceous
**likelihood** chance, liability, likeliness, possibility, probability, prospect, verisimilitude
**like lobes** lobate
**likely** acceptable, applicable, apposite, appropriate, apt, believable, credible, hopeful, liable, plausible, possible, probable, promising, prospective, relevant, suitable
**likely story** tale
**likely to be difficult** formidable, serious
**likely to cause argument** contentious
**likely to succeed** hopeful
**likely to turn out well** promising
**like mad** energetically, excitedly, fanatically, furiously, madly, quickly, speedily, vehemently, violently, wildly
**like magic** quickly
**like man** anthropoid, humanoid
**like marble** marmoreal
**like mice** murine
**liken** alliterate, analogise, associate, compare, correlate, equate, imitate, juxtapose, link, match, parallel(ise), portray, relate
**likeness** affinity, agreement, alikeness, analogy, canvas, copy, delineation, depiction, draft, drawing, duplicate, effigy, facsimile, homogeneity, icon, identicalness, illustration, image, model, photograph, picture, portrait, portrayal, replica, reproduction, resemblance, sameness, semblance, similarity, sketch, study, uniformity
**likeness in respects** analogy
**likeness in sculpture** image
**likening** comparing, comparison, matching, relating
**like nylons** sheer
**like Paradise** Edenic
**like periodically improving fevers** intermittently
**like serum** serous, watery
**like silver in colour** silvery
**like snow** cold, white
**like soap** saponaceous, soapy
**like some vegetables** leafy
**like tapeworms** taenioid
**like Telly Savalas** bald
**like that** so
**like the Andes** Andean
**like the wind** swiftly
**like tufts of wool** flocculent
**like vinegar** acetic
**like water** aqueous
**likewise** also, ditto, moreover, similarly, too
**liking** affection, affinity, appreciation, attraction, bias, desire, disposition, favour, fondness, inclination, leaning, penchant, predilection, predisposition, preference, proclivity, propensity, tendency
**liking better** preference
**liking the society of other people** sociable
**liliaceous plant** aloe, asparagus, aspidistra, hyacinth
**lilt** accent, beat, cadence, dance, flow, lyric, measure, melody, movement, pattern, pulsation, pulse, rhythm, sway, swing, tempo, time, tune, wave
**lilting** cadent, dulcet, lyrical, melodious, musical, tuneful
**lily** aloe, arum, calla, ixia, lis, lotus, tulip, yucca
**lily-livered** cowardly, timid
**lily-producer** bulb
**lilytrotter** jaçana
**Lima is there** Peru
**limb** appendage, arm, border, bough, branch, child, descendant, edge, extremity, hand, heir, leg, manus, margin, member, part, piece, projection, shoot, spur, wing
**limber** agile, bendable, ductile, extensible, extensile, fictile, flexible, lissom(e), malleable, pliable, pliant, resilient, supple, tractile
**limber up** exercise, prepare
**limbless creature** serpent, snake, worm
**limbo** banning, blackness, committal, confinement, darkness, eclipse, exclusion, imprisonment, internment, isolation, limbus, nirvana, oblivion, quarantine, segregation, separation, slavery, void
**limb of a tree** branch
**limb used by turtle in swimming** flipper
**lime drink** -ade
**limestone** marble
**limestone grained loosely** oolite
**lime sulphate** gypsum
**lime tree** basswood, linden, tilleul (F)
**limit** bar, border, bound(ary), bridle, ceiling, check, compass, confine, curb, deadline, edge, end, extent, fix, forbid, frontier, hinder, maximum, mete, outline, outpost, perimeter, periphery, prohibit, rein, restrain(t), restrict(ion), rim, specify, stay, termination, ultimate, utmost, verge
**limitation** barrier, block, boundary, bounds, control, deterrent, drawback, handicap, impediment, inability, liability, limit, obstruction, restraint, restriction
**limitation of supply** stint
**limited** bound, cramped, curbed, demarcated, dull, girded, obtuse, reined, restrained, scant, vacuous, witless
**limited period of time** term
**limited property right** easement
**limited to a district** territorial
**limiting factor** parameter
**limit line** boundary
**limits of application** extent
**limit supplies** ration
**limousine** auto(mobile), car
**limp** debilitated, exhausted, falter, flabby, flaccid, halt, hobble, lameness, lank, pliable, relaxed, shamble, shuffle, spent
**limpid** bright, brilliant, clear, comprehensible, crystal-clear, crystalline, diaphanous, distinct, evident, explicit, filmy, glassy, intelligible, liquid, lucent, lucid, obvious, pellucid, plain, pure, shining, still, translucent, transparent, vitreous
**linchpin** axle-pin
**line** align, aline, ancestry, border, cable, contour, file, goods, mark, occupation, phrase, policy, product, queue, rank, rope, row, rule, stance, stock, streak, stripe, tier
**line about which something rotates** axis
**line above the staff** le(d)ger
**line across middle of circle** diameter

**lineage** ancestry, birth, descent, parentage
**lineal** ancestral, family, hereditary, linear, matriarchal, parental, patriarchal, racial
**linear extent** length
**linear mark on surface** stria
**linear measure** centimetre, foot, inch, metre, millimetre, yard
**linear unit** inch, metre, yard
**line at school dance** stag
**line caused by folding** crease
**line diagonal to the selvedge of a fabric** bias
**line enclosing an area** circuit
**line enclosing circle** circumference
**line for hoisting** halyard
**line for holding hawk** lune
**line from circle centre** radius
**line in printing** serif
**linen** cloth, damask, fabric, material, textile
**linen colour** ecru
**linen fluff** lint
**linen for shirts** sark
**linen garment** line
**linen plant** flax
**linens** bedclothes, bedding, face cloths, napkins, pillowcases, sheets, tablecloths, towels, washcloths
**linen tape** inkle
**linen used for dressing wounds** lint
**linenware** napery
**line of ancestors** ancestry
**line of approach** avenue
**line of battle** front
**line of coast** seaboard, seashore
**line of colour** streak
**line of communication** road
**line of conduct** course
**line of defence** alibi
**line of descent** ancestry, pedigree
**line of English kings** Plantagenet, Stewart, Tudor
**line of equal heat** isotherm
**line of guards** cordon
**line of hereditary rulers** dynasty
**line of juncture** seam
**line of longitude** meridian
**line of poetry** verse
**line of rotation** axis
**line of sewing** seam
**line of six metrical feet** hexameter
**line of travel** route
**line of verse** stich
**line of verse composed of eight syllables** octosyllable
**line of verse consisting of four feet** tetrameter
**line of verse of three measures** trimeter
**line of waiting persons** queue

**line on a map linking places of equal temperature** isotherm
**line on largest sail** mainsheet
**liner** aeroplane, aircraft, airplane, boat, hydroplane, steamer, (steam)ship
**liner attendant** steward(ess)
**lines in circle** radii
**lines inside of orange rind** pith
**lines of a play** script
**lines of verse** poem, stanza
**lines on a map** grid
**lines through one line** ray
**line that intersects a curve** secant
**line that is not straight** curve
**line touching circle** tangent
**line up** align, aline, arrange(ment), array, indigent, obtain, prepare, secure, straighten
**line-up** arrangement, array, row, team
**line where land meets the sea** coast
**line with plaster** ceil
**ling** burbot, heath(er)
**linger** dally, dawdle, delay, idle, lag, loaf, loiter, loll, lounge, meander, procrastinate, remain, saunter, slouch, stroll, tarry, totter, wander
**linger behind** straggle
**linger furtively** lurk
**lingerie** bra(ssière), finery, nightie, nighty, slip, underclothes, undergarments, underwear, undies
**lingerie edging** lace
**lingering glow** phosphorescence
**linger on the way** loiter
**lingua franca** cant, dialect, jargon, koine, language, patois, terminology
**linguistic science** philology
**linguistic scientist** etymologist
**liniment** arnica, embrocation
**liniment made with soap and camphor** opodeldoc, soap-liniment
**lining of timber** brattice
**lining up** alignment
**link** ally, annexe, articulation, attach, bind, bond, bridge, chain, (con)catenate, conjoin, connect(ion), connective, copula, couple(r), fasten, filler, hook, impugn, interlock, join(t), knot, liaison, lock, loop, measure, nexus, pin, pivot, rabbet, relate, relation, ring, span, splice, tie, unite, uniting, yoke
**link firmly** knot
**linking two pieces of chain** schackle
**link of chain** toggle
**links in sewing** stitches
**links sport** golfing
**link together** concatenate, confederate, couple, league, shackle, unionise
**linseed** flaxseed
**linseed plant** flax

**lintel** transom
**lionise** celebrate, fête, praise
**lion-like** leonine
**lion-like sound** roar
**lion's abode** den
**lion's cry** roar
**lion's glory** mane
**lion's growl** roar
**lion's home** den
**lion sign** Leo
**lion's noise** roar
**lion's ruff** mane
**lion's share** preponderance
**lip** edge, labium
**lip caress** kiss
**lip-curling jeer** sneer
**lip-held ornament** labret
**lipoid** fatty, lipoidal
**lip service** artificiality, duplicity, falseness, hypocrisy, insincerity, uncandidness
**liquefied by heat** fuse, molten
**liquefy** condense, dissolve, fluidise, flux, fuse, heat, liquidise, melt, permeate, render, run, saturate, smelt, soak, souse, suspend, thaw
**liqueur** kirsch
**liqueur distilled from cherries** maraschino
**liqueur flavoured with almonds** ratafee, ratafia
**liqueur flavoured with caraway and cumin seeds** kümmel
**liqueur flavoured with naartjies** Van der Hum
**liqueur flavoured with peel of bitter oranges** Curaçao
**liqueur flavoured with wormwood** absinthe
**liqueur from brandy flavoured with nut kernels** noyau
**liqueur having a raw egg base** advocaat
**liquid** beverage, drink, fluid, juice, melted, potable, thawed
**liquidator** sequestrator
**liquid carrier** bucket, hose, pail
**liquid container** bottle, bucket, can, cup, jug, mug, vat, vessel
**liquid content of fruit** juice
**liquid food** soup
**liquid food for pigs** swill
**liquid for colouring fabric** dye
**liquid for drinking** beverage
**liquid for writing** ink
**liquid holder** vat
**liquid injected into body** enema
**liquid loss** ullage
**liquid measure** drachm, litre, pint, quart
**liquid measure of four pints** pottle
**liquid metal** mercury
**liquid mud** slush

**liquid obtained by distillation** spirit
**liquid part of blood** plasma
**liquid passing through membrane** permeant
**liquid perfume** scent
**liquid portion of the nucleus of a cell** karyolymph
**liquid preparation for the skin** lotion
**liquid prepared for drinking** beverage
**liquid put into body** enema
**liquid secreted in the mouth** saliva
**liquid soap for hair** shampoo
**liquid spilt** ullage
**liquid unit** litre
**liquid used as a foundation of soup** stock
**liquid used by scent makers** citral
**liquid vessel** can, cup, kettle, mug, pot, tank, trough, tub, vial
**liquid which forms in the mouth** saliva
**liquid with something dissolved in it** solution
**liquor** akvavit, ale, aquavit, bitters, bourbon, brandy, gin, grog, liqueur, mampoer, rum, scotch, spirit, vodka, witblits, whisky
**liquor banner** prohibitionist
**liquor dependant** alcoholic, alkie
**liquor glass** gun
**liquorice flavour** anise
**liquorice-flavoured liqueur made from aniseed** anisette
**liquorice-flavoured spice** aniseed
**liquor with juniper berries** gin
**lissom** agile, flexible, lissome, lithe, nimble, supple, svelte
**list** agenda, arrange, attendance, band, bill, book, border, cant, careen(ing), catalogue, chart, classify, codify, directory, enlist, enrol, enter, enumerate, file, group, incline, index, inventory, invoice, itemise, lean, note, notify, program(me), record, register, roll, roster, schedule, series, syllabus, tally, tilt(ing), tip
**listed** catalogued, enrolled, entered, enumerated, filed, indexed, noted, recorded, registered, scheduled
**listen** attend, concentrate, hark, hear(ken), heed, mind, obey, observe
**listen attentively** hark, hearken
**listener** ear, hearer
**listeners** audience
**listener's permit** radio licence
**listen in** bug, eavesdrop, wiretap
**listening device** bug
**listening organ** ear
**listen secretly** eavesdrop
**listen to** hear, heed, obey
**listen to utter rumour** hearsay
**listen with both ears** hark, hearken

**list in detail** itemise
**list individually** itemise
**listless** apathetic, careless, heavy, heedless, inattentive, languid, lethargic, lifeless, limp, mopish, torpid, vacant
**listlessness** apathy, drowsiness, dullness, enervation, ennui, fatigue, heaviness, indolence, inertia, inertness, kef, lackadaisicalness, languidness, lassitude, lethargy, limpness, passivity, phlegmaticness, sleepiness, sluggishness, sluggishness, supineness, torpidness
**listless or feeble** nerveless
**list of actors** cast
**list of annotations** glossary
**list of candidates** slate, leet (Sc)
**list of cargo** manifest
**list of charges** tariff
**list of contents of book** index
**list of dishes available at meal** menu
**list of dramas** repertoire
**list of duties** roster, rota
**list of events** calendar, programme
**list of figures** table
**list of goods shipped** invoice
**list of grievances** screed
**list of items** catalogue, schedule
**list of items for meeting** agenda
**list of personnel** roster, rota
**list of prices** tariff
**list of signatures on public appeal** petition
**list of things to be done** agenda, agendum, itinerary
**list of top records** hit parade
**list one by one** itemise
**list showing turns of duty** roster, rota
**list singly** itemise
**list to be answered** questionnaire
**lit** aglow, alight, burning, drunk, gleaming, glowing, ignited, illuminated, inebriated, intoxicated, lighted, luminous, on, sottish
**literal** accurate, exact, faithful, scrupulous, truthful, verbatim
**literally** actually, au pied de la lettre (F), exactly, plainly, really, strictly, truly, verbatim
**literary assistant** amanuensis
**literary collection** ana, miscellany
**literary composition** article, effusion, essay
**literary criticism** critique, review
**literary critique** recension
**literary drudge** hack
**literary extracts** anthology
**literary genre** drama, novel, poetry
**literary gossip** ana
**literary name for Ireland** Erin, Hibernia
**literary parody** burlesque

**literary pseudonym** nom de plume, pen-name
**literary ridicule** satire
**literary satire** lampoon
**literary scraps** ana
**literary word for swimming** natation
**literary work in verse** poem
**literary works** drama, novels, poetry
**literate** articulate, book-learned, clear, correct, cultivated, cultured, educated, erudite, grammatical, informed, instructed, intelligent, learned, legible, lettered, literary, lucid, punditic, refined, scholarly, schooled, skilful, trained, tutored, (well-)versed
**literature** belles-lettres, books, classics, humanities, letters, works, writings
**literature relating to the lives of saints** hagiography, hagiology
**lithe** flexible, limber, lissom(e), loose-jointed, loose-limbed, pliable, pliant, supple
**lithe and slender** graceful, willowy
**litheness** agility, flexibleness, lissomness, pliableness, pliantness, suppleness
**lithograph in oil-colours** oleograph
**lithology** petrology
**litigious** actionable, aggressive, argumentative, bellicose, controversial, disputable, dissentious, eristic(al), exceptive, litigable, polemic, pugnacious, quarrelsome
**litotes** understatement
**lit sign** neon
**litter** brood, confusion, debris, derange, disarrange, disorder, fragments, mess, muck, palankeen, palanquin, rubbish, scatter, shreds, stretcher, strew, untidiness
**litter of pigs** farrow
**little** babyish, barely, brief, diminutive, fleeting, inconsiderable, infant, infinitesimal, insignificant, insufficient, junior, meagre, mean, microscopic, miniature, minor, minute, modicum, negligible, niggardly, paltry, passing, petite, petty, scant, selfish, short, skimpy, slender, slight(ly), small, tiny, trivial, unimportant, weak, wee
**little advertisement** ad
**little arrow** dart
**little auk** dovekey, dovekie, guillemot, puffin, razorbill
**little barb** barbule
**little baronet** bart
**little bedroom** cubicle
**little bit** poco (Sp)

**little bite** nip
**little bit of soda** dash, splash
**little bits** smithereens
**little boy** lad, nino (Sp), outjie, piccanin, pik(k)enien, umfaan
**little by little** imperceptibly, slowly, unnoticeably
**little child** baby, bairn, kleintjie, toddler, tot
**little cloudiness** nebula
**little creature** elf
**little devil** imp
**little dome** cupola
**little drink** tot
**little fairy** elf
**little finger** pinkie
**little fish** fingerling, fry, minnow, sardine, smelt
**little floor covering** rug
**little girl** cookie, cooky, sis(sy)
**little girl's hair ornament** ribbon
**little island** islet
**little lace loop** picot
**little look** peep
**little lump** knobble, nodule
**little man** dwarf, manikin
**little measure** inch
**little one** tot
**little orphan girl** Annie
**little people** dwarfs, elves, fairies, gnomes, imps, leprechauns, midgets, nymphs, sprites, trolls
**little pie** patty
**little pot** pottle
**little purple flower** violet
**little quarrel** spat
**little rodent** mouse
**little short of being** almost
**little sister** sis
**little spot** speckle
**little thanks** ta
**little tongue** uvula
**little valley** slade
**littoral** beach(front), coast(al), coastline, coastwise, inning, plage (F), riparian, sands, seacoast, seashore, seaside, shore(line), strand
**liturgical** ceremonial, ceremonious, eucharistic, formal, liturgic, paschal, ritual, sacerdotal, sacramental, solemn
**liturgical act** lavabo
**liturgical formula of praise to God** doxology
**liturgy** celebration, ceremony, formality, function, litany, liturgiology, observance, practice, rite, ritual, sacrament, service, solemnity, worship

**live** active, alive, animate, be, dwell, endure, exist, flourish, fresh, persist, reside, subsist, survive, vita (I)
**live a fast life** pace
**live coal** ember, gleed
**live craftily at the expense of others** sponge
**live in** act, behave, dwell, occupy, reside, tenant
**live in a tent** camp
**live in concord** agree
**live in the past** remember, reminisce
**live it up** celebrate
**livelihood** activity, business, capacity, career, diet, fare, job, keep, living, maintenance, means, nourishment, nutriment, occupation, position, profession, regimen, subsistence, support, sustenance, trade, upkeep, venture, vocation, work
**live like the devil** evil
**liveliness** animation, ardour, élan, energy, exultation, felicity, fervour, fire, gaiety, jollity, jubilee, merriness, mirth, perkiness, quickness, revelry, sanguineness, spark, spirit, sportiveness, vivacity, zeal
**livelong** entire, lifelong, unbroken, undivided, whole
**live longer than** outlast, outlive
**livelong plant** orpine
**lively** active, agile, alert, animated, breezy, bright, brilliant, brisk, buoyant, clear, effective, energetic, eventful, fresh, gay, high-spirited, moving, piquant, quick, spirited, sprightly, spry, strong, telling, vigorous, vivacious, vivid, vivo (mus.)
**lively action** jig
**lively and cheerful** perky
**lively and quick** brisk
**lively and vigorous** zippy
**lively cadence** lilt
**lively dance** farandole, gal(l)opade, galop, hoe-dance, hornpipe, jig, polka, reel
**lively dance for two persons** rigadoon, riguadon
**lively French dance** can-can, cotill(i)on
**lively frolic** spree
**lively joy** glee
**lively jumping dance** jig
**lively musical composition** scherzo
**lively Neapolitan dance** tarantella
**lively Polish dance** maz(o)urka
**lively Scottish dance** reel
**lively Spanish dance** bolero, cachuca, fandango, jota, zapateado
**lively stage-dance with high kicking** can-can
**lively wit** esprit
**live monotonously** vegetate

**liven** activate, animate, arouse, boost, brighten, cheer, elate, encourage, enkindle, fortify, goad, incite, inspire, kindle, motivate, move, promote, rouse, stimulate, stir, waken
**liven up** animate, brighten, energise, enliven, invigorate, rouse, vitalise
**live on** augment, feed, flourish, increase, subsist, thrive
**live peaceably together** coexist
**liver atrophy** lupinosis
**liver-based spread** pâté
**liver disease** hepatitis
**liver dish** pâté, terrine
**liveried attendant** page
**liveried servant** flunk(e)y, footman
**liver inflammation** hepatitis
**liver of lobster** tomalley
**Liverpool venue of Beatles** Cavern
**liver secretion** bile
**livery boy** page
**livery servant** flunk(e)y
**lives** is
**lives in cloister** nun
**lives in igloo** Eskimo
**lives in seclusion** anchorite, eremite, hermit, recluse, stylite
**live together as husband and wife** cohabit
**live together in peace** coexist
**live up to** honour
**live with** accompany
**livid** angry, ashen, bloodless, bluish, bruised, contused, discoloured, enraged, fuming, furious, ghastly, greyish, incensed, indignant, infuriated, ireful, pale, pallid, purple, rabid, wan, waxen, wrathful
**living** active, alive, existing, extant, live(ly), subsistence, surviving, sustenance, vigorous
**living alone** solitary
**living among trees** arboreal
**living being** creature
**living body of human being** person
**living both on land and in water** amphibian, amphibious
**living for ever** immortal
**living in communities** social
**living in flocks** gregarious
**living in isolation** anchorite, eremite, hermit, recluse, stylite
**living in or on the soil** terricolous
**living in or on wood** lignicole, lignicolous
**living in snow** nival
**living in water** aquatic
**living museum town** Matjiesfontein, Pilgrim's Rest
**living near the sea** maritime
**living on fish** piscivorous
**living or growing in water** aquatic

**living place** abode
**living quarters** habitation
**living room** lounge
**living space** lebensraum
**living thing** organism
**living together in herds or flocks** gregarious
**living under canvas** camping
**living under stones** lapidicolous
**living unit in hotel** suite
**lizard** chameleon, gecko, iguana, salamander, saurian, skink
**lizard that changes colour** chameleon
**llama** guanaco
**llama-like animal** alpaca
**lo** behold
**load** albatross, assignment, boatload, burden, charge, contents, cross, duty, encumbrance, freight, goods, incubus, lade, merchandise, obligation, onus, pack, routine, shipload, strain, stuff, task, tax, weight
**load cargo** lade
**load mark** Plimsoll line
**load of herring** cran
**load the dice** fix, prearrange, predesign, rig
**loaf** bread, cake, cereal, dally, dawdle, delay, idle, lag, laze, lie, loiter, loll, lounge, mooch, repose, saunter, sit, tarry
**loafer** bum, cadger, dodger, good-for-nothing, idler, laggard, larrikin, layabout, lazybones, loiterer, lounger, malingerer, passenger, shirker, shoe, slacker, slipper, sluggard, vagrant, wastrel
**loaf of pig's offal** ha(r)slet
**loam** clay, dirt, dust, earth, ground, land, mud, sand, silt, sod, (top)soil, turf
**loam deposit** loess
**loan** accommodate, advance, allow(ance), credit, grant, lend, moneylending, mortgage, oblige, transaction, trust, usury
**loaner** moneylender
**loan note** IOU
**loan on the security of a ship** bottomry
**loan shark** usurer
**loan sharking** usury
**loath** against, antipathetic, averse, backward, detest, disinclined, grudging, hesitant, hostile, ill-disposed, indisposed, inimical, loth, opposed, reluctant, resistant, resisting, slow, unenthusiastic, unfavourable, unwilling
**loathe** abhor, abominate, contempt, deplore, deride, despise, detest, disapprove, disdain, disfavour, disinclined, dislike, disregard, execrate, flout, hate, nauseate, neglect, revile, scorn, shun, slight, unwilling
**loathing** abhorrence, abominating, abomination, aversion, detestation, disgust, distaste, enmity, hate, hatred, nausea, odium, ranking, repugnance, repulsion
**loathing of food** anorexia
**loathness** averseness
**loathsome** abhorrent, abominable, appalling, atrocious, deplorable, despicable, detestable, disgusting, dislikable, execrable, foul, hateful, heinous, horrid, intolerable, loathly, nasty, nauseating, nauseous, obnoxious, obscene, odious, offensive, rank, repellent, repulsive, sickening, ugly, unendurable, vile
**loathsome dirt** filth
**loathsome person** insect, toad
**lob** bang, batter, beat, cast, chuck, drive, drop, fling, flog, hit, hurl, impel, knock, launch, pitch, shed, shy, slap, smack, sock, strike, swat, throw, thrust, thump, toss, whack
**lobby** antechamber, anteroom, anteroom, corridor, entreé, entry, foyer, hall(way), influence, passage, porch, pressure, solicit, vestibule
**lobe of ear** lap
**lobe ornament** earring
**lob off** sned (Sc)
**lobster claw** chela
**lobster ovary** roe
**lobster shell** carapace
**lobster's weapon** claw
**local** community, confined, district, edaphic, home, indigenous, limited, narrow, native, neighbourhood, parish, parochial, provincial, regional, restricted, sectional, topical, vicinal
**local accent** dialect
**local branch of society** chapter
**local bulletin** regional news
**local colour** accuracy
**local custom** lex loci
**local deity** numen
**local dialect** patois
**local dropsy** oedema
**locale** area, local(ity), location, place, position, precinct, scene, section, setting, site, venue, zone
**local expression** idiom
**local geology** geognosy
**local inflammation of the skin** erysipelas
**localise** concentrate, confine, delimit, encircle, identify, limit, pinpoint, place, position, quarantine, restrain, restrict, situate, surround
**localised vector** rotor
**locality** area, district, habitat, locale, locus, place, point, region, scene, site, situation, spot, stead, venue, vicinity
**local levies** rates, taxes
**locally** close(by), here(abouts), limitedly, narrowly, nearby, parochially, provincially
**local office** branch
**local ordinance** by(e)-law
**local political boss in Latin America** cacique, cazique
**local position** site
**local rather than general** sectional
**local regulation** by(e)-law
**local relationship** ubiety
**local resident** native
**local saying** idiom
**local taxes** rates
**locate** assign, bestow, descry, detect, determine, discern, discover, espy, establish, find, fix, live, localise, mark, occupy, pinpoint, pitch, place, position, reside, settle, site, situate, spot, stand, trace, uncover, unearth
**located inside** inner
**located off the highway** devious
**locate elsewhere** relocate, resite
**locating equipment using radio pulses** radar
**locating system** sonar
**location** amenity, area, collocation, colony, disposition, district, domestication, emplacement, fixation, homestead, installation, locale, nearness, neighbourhood, pinpointing, place(ment), placing, position, province, region, seat, settlement, settling, site, situation, spot, standing, station, territory, ubiety, venue, vicinity, zone
**location of an event** venue
**location of home** address
**loch** lake
**Loch Lomond sight** Brae
**Loch Ness monster** Nessie
**loch of the monster** Ness
**lock** bolt, clasp, close, conduit, confine, curl, dag, drag, embrace, fasten, hair, hasp, hug, link, padlock, ringlet, seal, secure, shut, strand, tress, tuft, unite
**lockable bag for mail** pouch
**lock aperture** keyhole
**lock clasp** hasp
**locker** box, cabinet, case, chest, compartment, cupboard, safe, trunk
**locket** jewellery, pendant
**lock improperly** bind

**lock inventor** Yale
**lockjaw** tetanus, trismus
**lock mechanism** detent
**lock of hair** cot, curl, frizzle, ringlet, skein, tag, tangle, tress
**lock of wool** frib, staple, tag
**lock opener** code, key
**lock out** ban, banish, (de)bar, exclude, exclusion, exile, ostracise, strike
**locks** hair, tresses
**lock unfastener** key
**lock up** cabinet, cage, calaboose, confine, detain, gaol, imprison, jail, jug, prison, stow
**loco** frenzied, locomotive, lunatic, nuts
**loco driver** engineer
**locomotive** diesel, puffer, (steam) engine, train
**locomotive and coaches** train
**locomotive crane** jenny
**locomotive that transfers goods** freight train
**locomotive wheel** driver
**locust** destroyer, false acacia, glutton, grasshopper, hopper, insect, orthopteran, vermin, weta
**locust tree** carob, false acacia
**locution** dialect, expression, idiom, language, phrase(ology), saying, term, word
**lode of ore** reef
**lodestone** magnet
**lodge** association, cabin, cottage, deposit, embed, habitation, harbour, house, place, quarter, settle, shelf, shelter, society
**lodge deeply** embed
**lodge in temporary quarters** camp
**lodge in tents** encamp
**lodger** boarder, encumbent, guest, inmate, lessee, occupant, renter, resident, roomer, tenant
**lodging** accommodating, billeting, boarding, entertaining, habitation, harbouring, quarterage, sheltering, sticking
**lodging for travellers** hospice
**lodging home** digs
**lodging house** hostel, hotel, inn, tenement
**lodging place** room
**lodgings** abode, accommodation, apartments, billet, boarding, digs, dwelling, pad, quarters, residence, rooms, shelter
**loft** attic, balcony, cockloft, gallery, garret, hay-loft, mansard, pigeon-house
**lofting golf-club** iron
**lofty** aerial, dignified, elevated, eminent, epic, exalted, haughty, high, imposing, proud, sublime, tall

**lofty and disdainful** haughty
**lofty building** skyscraper
**lofty flight** soaring
**lofty peak** pinnacle
**lofty slender turret on a mosque** minaret
**lofty standard** ideal
**lofty structure** tower
**lofty superiority** superciliousness
**log** account, amass, beam, branch, chart, cover, daybook, diarise, diary, gauge, gear, journal, logarithm, logbook, note, piece, record, register, report, tally, timber, trunk
**logarithmic unit** bel
**log float** raft
**log for veneer** peeler
**loggia** gallery
**log hut** cabin
**logic** argument, coherence, deduction, dialectics, foresight, link, logistics, organisation, polemics, rationale, rationally, reason(ing), relationship, sense, thought, wisdom
**logical** analytic, clear, cogent, deducible, deductive, dialectic, inferential, necessary, obvious, pertinent, philosophic, possible, rational, reasonable, relevant, sensible, sound, tenable, valid, wise
**logical analysis** syllogism
**logical basis** rationale
**logical proposition** theorem
**logical refutation** elenchus
**logo** badge, cipher, emblem, ensign, figure, sign, symbol, (trade)mark
**log sledge** sloop
**log support** firedog
**log used in trial of strength** caber
**log vessel** raft
**Lohengrin's love** Elsa
**loin** lumbus
**loincloth** dhooti(e), dhoti, dhuti, waistcloth
**Loire port** Nantes
**loiter** amble, dally, dawdle, delay, idle, lag, linger, loaf, loll, meander, persist, potter, remain, saunter, shamble, slouch, stay, stroll, tarry, vegetate
**loiter about** mooch
**loiterer** dawdler, idler, lingerer, slowcoach
**loll** dangle, depend, drag(gle), droop, flap, flop, hang, languish, lean, lie, loaf, loiter, lounge, oscillate, recline, relax, rest, sag, slouch, slump, sprawl, sway, swing, trail, vegetate, vibrate
**lolly** lollipop, sweet
**Lombardy capital** Milan
**London airport** Gatwick, Heathrow

**London art gallery** National, Tate
**London association of underwriters** Lloyds
**London bar** pub
**London borough** Ealing, Greenwich, Lambeth, Sutton
**London Bridge river** Thames
**London district** Chelsea, Soho
**Londoner** Cockney
**London exhibition hall** Olympia
**London football ground** Wembley
**London gallery** National, Tate
**London Gardens** Kew
**London insurance company** Lloyds
**London market** Billingsgate
**London nightclub area** Soho
**London park** Hyde
**London prison** clink, Marshalsea, Newgate
**London river** Thames
**London shopping place** Bond Street, Fortnum and Mason, Harrods
**London square** Trafalgar
**London station** Paddington, Victoria, Waterloo
**London street** Baker, Bond, Harley, Lombard
**London streetcar** tram
**London thoroughfare** Pall Mall
**London W1 district** Soho
**lone** alone, apart, deserted, isolated, lonesome, one, only, separate, separated, single, sole, solitary, solo, unaccompanied, unattached, unattended
**lone flight** solo
**loneliness** desolation, dreariness, forlornness, lonesomeness, seclusion, solitude
**lonely** abandoned, alone, apart, deserted, dreary, estranged, forlorn, forsaken, friendless, lone(some), outcast, remote, secluded, separately, sequestered, single, solely, solitary, uninhabited, withdrawn
**lonely place** solitude
**loner** alien, anchoress, anchorite, eremite, hermit, individualist, marabout, nonconformist, nun, outcast, outsider, pariah, pillarist, recluse, solitary, solitudinarian, troglodyte
**Lone Star State** Texas
**lone wolf** individualist, loner, maverick
**long** ache, attenuated, crave, extensive, lang (Sc), lengthy, overlong, prolix, prolonged, stretched, wordy, yearn
**long adventure** epic
**long adventurous journey** odyssey
**long ago** erst, once, yore

**long and bitter hostility between two families** feud, vendetta
**long and flaccid** lank
**long and limp** lanky
**long and narrow opening** fissure
**long and serious letter** missive
**long and short foot metre** trochee
**long and slender** reedy
**long and slippery** eel
**long and tedious** lengthy
**long and tedious letter** screed
**long and tiresome** tedious
**long angry speech** tirade
**longanimity** forbearance, long-suffering, sufferance
**long appendage of nerve cell** axon
**long Arabic tunic with a sash** caftan, kaftan
**long arm of crane** jib
**long arm of sea** fiord, fjord
**long backed bench** pew
**long baggy sweater** sloppy joe
**long-beaked sea fish** saury
**long bed-like seat** sofa
**long-billed marsh bird** snipe
**long-bladed hatchet** cleaver
**long blouse** tunic
**long-bodied dog** Dachshund
**long-bodied carrier pigeon type** scandaroon
**long bounding stride** lope
**long burning fuse** slowmatch
**long canine tooth** fang
**long cannon** culverin
**long claw** talon
**long cloak** capote
**long coat** jukbah, maxi
**long cross country journey** overland
**long curl of hair** ringlet
**long cut** slash, slit
**long dagger** dirk
**long dash** em dash
**long deep cut** gash
**long, difficult journey** trek
**long discord** descant, tirade
**long-distance road race** marathon
**long doleful cry of dog** howl
**long drawn-out** lengthy
**long-drawn wail** whine
**long dress** maxi, robe, tunic
**long dress worn by a monk or nun** habit
**long drink** schooner
**long-eared dog** basset, spaniel
**long-eared mammal** hare, rabbit
**long easy stride** lope
**longer than broad** oblong, oval
**longest note in common use** semibreve
**longest river** Nile
**longest river in China** Yangtze
**longest river in Europe** Volga

**longest river in France** Loire
**longest river in Great Britain** Severn
**longest river in Italy** Po
**long eventful journey** odyssey
**longevity** seniority, tenure
**long exhausting work** slog
**long firearm** rifle
**long fish** eel
**long flower-stalk coming directly from root** scape
**long flowing garment** robe
**long for** aspire, covet, crave, desire, hope, pine, want, wish, yearn
**long fur or furlined cloak** pelisse
**long garment** himation, jubka, kanzu, pelisse, stole
**long garment worn by certain clergymen** cassock
**long-grained rice** patna
**long-haired dog of Chinese breed** chow
**long-haired Tibetan ox** yak
**long hair on neck of animal** mane
**long hair rolled into a knot or bun at the back** chignon
**long-handled sickle** scythe
**long-handled spoon** ladle
**long harangue** tirade
**long hard journey** trek
**long harsh speech** tirade
**long heavy hair** mane
**long heavy wave** roller
**long heroic story** saga
**long Highland shawl** plaid
**long high-pitched cry of a horse** neigh
**long hilltop** ridge
**long hollow** groove
**long hooded Arabic cloak** burnous
**long hooded cloak worn by Muslim women** burka
**longhorn beetle** longicorn
**longing** ambition, aspiration, coveting, craving, desire, desiring, hankering, hungering, itch(ing), lusting, nostalgia, pining, thirst, urge, wanting, wish, yearning
**longing for** sighing
**long in the teeth** aged, ancient, elderly, old
**long involved story** saga, yarn
**longish skirt** midi
**longitudinal cleft** scissure
**long journey** odyssey, tour, trek
**long knife** couteau, whittle
**long-lasting** abiding, constant, continuing, durable, enduring, imperishable, lasting, lifelong, long-standing, perennial, permanent, persistent, prolonged, protracted, unchanging, unfading

**long leather leggings worn by cowboys** chaparajos, chaparejos, chaps
**long-leaved plant** fern
**long leg** stilt
**long-legged bird** crane, flamingo, heron, stilt, stork, wader
**long-legged hen** shanghai
**long lettuce** cos
**long life** longevity
**long limbless reptile** snake
**long-lived** durable, enduring, (long-)lasting, long-standing
**long lock** tress
**long lock of hair on the forehead** lovelock
**long loose collarless Indian shirt** k(h)urta
**long loose overcoat** ulster
**long mantle for woman** capote
**long mirror mounted on swivels in a frame** cheval
**long movie** epic
**long-napped rough cloth** shag
**long narrative poem** epic
**long narrow band** stripe
**long narrow bone** rib
**long narrow canoe** piragua, pirague
**long narrow channel** groove
**long narrow cleft** fissure
**long narrow coastal inlet** ria
**long narrow crack in rock** fissure
**long narrow cut** slit
**long narrow drum** tambourine
**long narrow flag** pennant, pennon, streamer
**long narrow flag with cleft end** banderole
**long narrow furrow** groove
**long narrow inlet** ria
**long narrow muscle across front of thigh** sartorius
**long narrow open receptacle for water** trough
**long narrow piece** strip
**long narrow room** gallery
**long narrow roughly-made cigar** stog(e)y
**long narrow-sailed canoe** proa, prua
**long narrow seed-vessel** siliqua, silique
**long narrow shaft of stone** obelisk
**long narrow sledge** toboggan
**long narrow strip of material to wear round neck** scarf
**long narrow sword** rapier
**long narrow underwater bank** spit
**long-necked bird** crane, duck, flamingo, goose, ostrich, stork, swan
**long-necked bulbless onion** scallion
**long-necked lute with extra bass strings** theorbo

**long-necked Persian lute** pandora, pandore
**long-nosed fish** gar(fish)
**long-nosed kangaroo rat** potoroo
**long nose of animal** snout
**long novel** saga
**long outer garment** robe
**long overcoat** chesterfield
**long overland journey** trek
**long padded seat with back** sofa
**long period of financial and industrial slump** depression
**long period of time** aeon, century, epoch, era
**long piece split off** sliver
**long pillow** bolster
**long pillow across bed** bolster
**long pipelike ulcer** fistula
**long plaintive cry** howl
**long poem** ode
**long pointed hood** capuche
**long pointed shoe** winkle-picker
**long pointed spear** javelin, lance
**long pointed streamer** pennon
**long pointed tooth** fang, tush, tusk
**long pointed weapon** lance, spear
**long rein used for exercising and training horses** lunging rein
**long restlessness** itch
**long ridge of post-glacial gravel in river valleys** escar, eskar, esker
**long riding breeches** jodhpurs
**long river** Amazon, Danube, Loire, Nile, Volga
**long rounded piece of wood** pole
**long run** marathon
**long scaly limbless reptile** snake
**long scarf** stole
**long scolding speech** harangue, tirade
**long seat** bench, settee
**long seaworm** nereis, ragworm
**long seed container** pod
**long shaggy overcoat** capote
**long-shaped boat** coracle, currach, cur(r)agh (Sc)
**long shot** bet, outside chance, outsider
**long side whiskers** dundreary
**long-sightedness incident to old age** presbyopia
**long silky wool** angora
**long since** yore
**long skirt-like garment** dhooti(e), dhoti, dhuti
**long slender cigar** manatella
**long slender fish** ling
**long slender food-fish of South Pacific** barracouta, barracuda
**long slender sword** rapier
**long snout** proboscis
**long-snouted animal** tapir
**long song for one voice** aria
**long spar** boom, mast

**long spear** lance
**long spectacular film** epic
**long speech** descant, oration, screed
**long speech by one person** monologue
**long squared piece of wood** beam
**long-standing** abiding, enduring, established, long-established, long-lasting, long-lived, time-honoured, traditional
**long steep slope at edge of plateau** escarpment
**long-stemmed grass** reed
**long-stemmed rice** aman
**long step** stride
**long story** saga
**long stride** lope
**long-striding run** lope
**long strip of leather** strap
**long surgical knife with a narrow blade** bistoury
**long sword** spathe
**long-tailed monkey of Asia** langur
**long tale** saga
**long tall bridge** viaduct
**long tedious letter** screed
**long tedious period** siege
**long tedious procedure** rigmarole
**long thick hair** mane
**long, thin and wiry** beanpole
**long thin stripe** streak
**long three-stringed Japanese guitar, played with plectrum** samisen
**long timber of ship** keel
**long time** aeon, ages, years
**long tooth** fang, laniary, tusk
**long tunic worn by priests** cassock
**long Turkish robe** dolman
**long Turkish tobacco-pipe** chibouk, chibouque
**long-tusked sea mammal** walrus
**long upholstered seat** ottoman
**long US river** Mississippi
**long, usually rhymed, heroic poem** ode
**long vacation** extended leave
**long vehement speech** harangue, tirade
**long vertical rod in basket-making** stake
**long vessel** canoe, piragua, pirogue, raft
**long voyage** tour
**long way** far
**long way off** distant, far
**long way to** Tipperary
**long weak twig** sarmentose
**long white neckerchief worn with formal riding dress** stock
**long white rootcrop** parsnip
**long wide scarf** stole
**long-winged British bird** swallow

**long-winged seabird** albatross
**long word** mouthful
**long writing** screed
**loo** bathroom, closet, convenience, latrine, lavatory, outhouse, privy, toilet, urinal, WC, washroom
**look** anticipate, appear(ance), aspect, await, expect, face, gaze, glance, lo, mien, search, see(k), seem, sight, vide (L), view, watch
**look about furtively** snoop
**look after** attend, guard, mind, nurse, protect, supervise, tend, watch
**look after sick person** nurse
**look-alike** clone, doppelgänger, double, replica, ringer, spit, twin
**look angrily** glower
**look as if** seem
**look askance** glim, leer, skew
**look at** envisage, eye, observe, ogle, see, view
**look at amorously** ogle
**look at carefully** scan
**look at closely** examine, observe, peruse, scrutinise
**look at critically** eye
**look at curiously** quiz
**look at fondly** ogle
**look at knowingly** leer
**look at minutely** study
**look at suggestively** leer
**look attentively at** consider
**look at with contempt** scorn
**look back** ponder, recall, recollect, reflect, reminisce, review, ruminate
**look better than** outshine
**look briefly** glance
**look closely** espy, peer, pry, scan
**look closely at** examine
**look curiously** peer, pry
**look daggers** frown, glare, scowl
**look down on** contemn, despise, disdain, disparage, loathe, patronise, scorn, sneer, spurn
**look down upon** despise, snob
**looker** eyewitness, goggler, observer, ogler, peeper, seeker, seer, spectator, viewer, watcher, witness
**looker-on** beholder, bystander, observer, (sight)seer, spectator, watcher, witness
**look fiercely** glare
**look fixedly** gaze, glare, stare
**look for** anticipate, await, expect, pursue, search, seek
**look for a missing person** trace
**look for as due** expect
**look for scraps** scavenge
**look for something** search
**look for the woman** cherchez la femme (F)

**look forward** await, envisage, envision, expect, foresee, hope
**look forward to** anticipate, await, envisage, envision, expect, hope
**look furtively** peek, peep
**look high and low** hunt, search
**looking a sickly yellow colour** sallow
**looking exhausted from prolonged worry** haggard
**looking glass** mirror
**looking strained** drawn
**looking thin and sickly from illness** peakish
**looking tired** worn
**looking worn** wan
**look inquisitively into** pry
**look intently** pore, scan
**look into** examine, explore, fathom, inspect, investigate, plumb, probe, (re)search, scrutinise, study
**look into things inquisitively** pry
**look lecherously** leer
**look like** resemble
**look narrowly** peer
**look obliquely** squint
**look of deep thought** frown
**look of scorn** sneer
**look of things** circumstance
**look on** consider, eye, judge, observe, reckon, regard, speculate, take, view, watch
**look on as likely to happen** expect
**look on with wonder and pleasure** admire
**look out** beware, watch out
**lookout** beacon, future, guard, outlook, readiness, scout, vigil, watchtower
**look-out** affair, business, concern, guard, post, problem, sentinel, sentry, tower, vigil, watch-tower, watch(man), worry
**look out on** face, front, overlook
**lookout turret** bartizan
**look over** browse, check, examine, inspect, monitor, peruse, scan, survey, view
**look over and correct** edit, revise
**look over quickly** scan
**look poetically** lo
**look quickly** glimpse, peek, peep
**look round** browse
**looks** appearance
**look shyly** peep
**look slyly** leer, peep
**look sneakingly** pry
**look steadily** con, gaze, scan, stare
**look sullen** pout
**look through** search
**look to the end** respice finem (L)
**look up** ameliorate, esteem, find, gain, improve, progress, ransack, research, visit

**look upon** regard
**look up to** admire, esteem, exalt, extol, honour, idolise, respect, revere, worship
**look with greedy pleasure** gloat
**look with half-closed eyes** blink
**look with pleasure on** admire
**look with wide-open eyes** goggle
**loo mask** loup
**loom up** appear, emerge, rise
**loop** bend, bow, coil, connect, curl, curve, (en)circle, enclose, encompass, eyelet, fold, girdle, hoop, join, kink, knot, loophole, noose, ring, roll, spiral, stitch, turn, twirl, twist
**loop by ice-skater** spoon
**looped neck scarf** ascot
**looped rope** noose
**loop for hanging** tab
**loophole** aperture, avoidance, escape, evasion, excuse, eyelet, opening, plea, pretext, slot
**loop in a lace edge** picot
**loop in rope with running knot** noose
**loop of a rope** bight
**loop of chain** link
**loop of leather round Scout's neckerchief** woggle
**loop on lace** picot
**loop with running knot** noose
**loose** baggy, careless, dissolute, ease, free, general, ill-defined, immoral, imprecise, indefinite, indistinct, inexact, lax, liberate, loosen, negligent, release(d), slack(en), unbind, unbound, unfasten(ed), unfettered, unleash, unlock, unrestrained, unrestricted, untied, wanton
**loose, backless, strapless slipper** mule
**loose blood** bleed
**loose brightly coloured dress** muu-muu
**loose cape** talma
**loose change** coins
**loose Chinese suit for women** samfoo
**loose cloak** mantle, paletot
**loose cloth on back of chair** antimacassar
**loose coat** cassock, inverness, paletot
**loose coil** skein
**loose dress** tea gown
**loose earth** mould
**loose-fitting dress** chemise
**loose flannel jacket** banian, banyan
**loose flowing garment** gown
**loose garment** chasuble, robe, smock, wrap
**loose garment worn by Arabs** aba

**loose garment worn in South America** poncho
**loose gown** kimono, negligee, negligée
**loose hanging rag** tatter
**loose hooded cloak** jellaba, jellobah
**loose jacket** reefer
**loose Japanese robe** kimono
**loose-jointed** lanky
**loose-limbed** flexible, lissom(e), lithe
**loose liver** lecher, libertine, roué
**loosely** slack, slackly
**loosely-twisted string** fillit
**loosen** deliver, detach, free, liberate, mitigate, relax, release, separate, slacken, soften, unbind, undo, unfasten, unloose(n), unstick, untie
**loose neckwear** scarf
**loose net for woman's back hair** snood
**loosen hay** ted
**loosening hay for drying** tedding
**loosening-up exercises at the barre in ballet** battement
**loosen knots** untie
**loosen soil** hoe
**loosen up** lessen, moderate, relax, soften, unbend, weaken
**loose outer garment** blouse, cloak, robe
**loose overall** smock
**loose overcoat with a removable cap** inverness
**loose robe** simar
**loose robe worn over armour** surcoat
**loose scrum** maul
**loose skin on throat** dewlap, jowl
**loose sleeveless cloak or overcoat** mantle
**loose sleeveless garment** cape
**loose-stoned slope** scree
**loose-topped boot** wellington
**loose trousers** slacks
**loose tunic, as worn by African men** dashiki
**loose upper garment** blouse
**loose white vestment worn by clergy** surplice
**loose woman** harlot, prostitute, slut
**loose wool** fluff
**loot** abduct, boodle, boot(y), bounty, capture, depredate, despoil, goods, haul, kidnap, maraud, pillage, plunder, prize, raid, ransack, ravage, riches, rifle, rob, sack, seize, snatch, spoil(s), spoliate, steal, swag, swindle
**looter** pillager, plunderer, predator
**lop** abbreviate, abridge, clip, contract, crop, curtail, cut, dawdle, decrease, dock, hang, hew, lessen, level, mow, pare, prune, reduce, shear, shorten, slouch, snip, top, trim
**lope** bound, gallop, swing

**lop off** amputate
**lopsided** askew, awry, crooked, squint, tilting, unbalanced, unequal, uneven
**lopsidedness** asymmetry, crookedness, unevenness
**loquacious** garrulous, long-winded, talkative, talky, windy, wordy
**lord** commander, earl, governor, laird (Sc), leader, master, noble(man), peer, potentate, prince, ruler, seigneur, sovereign, superior, viscount
**lord it over** browbeat, domineer, repress, tyrannise
**lordly** disdainful, grand, haughty, imperious, lofty, magnificent
**lords and ladies** nobility, peerage
**lore** beliefs, doctrine, experience, knowledge, learning, myth(o)s, sayings, scholarship, teaching, tradition, wisdom
**loris** lemur
**lorn** desolate, forlorn
**lorry** truck
**lose** dodge, duck, elude, escape, evade, fail, fall, forfeit, forget, lap, mislay, misplace, miss, outstrip, overtake, pass, succumb, yield
**lose as a penalty** forfeit
**lose blood** bleed
**lose colour** bleach, fade, pale, whiten
**lose consciousness** faint, swoon
**lose courage** falter
**lose energy** wilt
**lose fluid** leak
**lose footing** slip
**lose freshness** fade, wilt, wither
**lose girth** slim
**lose hair** bald
**lose heart** despair, despond
**lose heat** cool
**lose hope** despair
**lose identity** merge
**lose importance** decline, degenerate, dwindle
**lose keenness** go sour
**losel** useless, wasteful, worthless
**lose lustre** bleach, pale, tarnish
**lose memory of** forget
**lose milk teeth** wissel
**lose moisture** dry
**lose no time** rush, scramble
**lose one's colour** pale
**lose one's equilibrium** overbalance
**lose one's head** explode, rage
**lose one's nerve** panic
**lose one's way** stray
**loser at Hastings** Harold
**loser at Majuba** British
**lose something in the translation** misinterpret, misread, mistranslate

**lose strength** decline, falter, lag, slacken, wane
**lose temporarily** mislay
**lose track of** lose, misplace
**lose value** depreciate
**lose vigour** flag
**lose vitality** wither
**lose weight** reduce, slim
**losing one's faculties** senile
**losing one's temper** flying off the handle
**loss** bereavement, cost, damage, debit, defeat, deprivation, destruction, detriment, disadvantage, failure, harm, hurt, injury, losing, misfortune, privation, ruin, waste
**loss by use** wastage
**loss of ability to feel pain while still conscious** analgesia
**loss of ability to focus images on the retina** ametropia
**loss of ability to interpret sensations** agnosia
**loss of ability to speak or write** aphasia
**loss of ability to write** agraphia
**loss of appetite** anorexia
**loss of consciousness** apoplexy, blackout, coma, faint
**loss of control** rampage
**loss of eyelashes** madarosis
**loss of feeling** anaesthesia, insensibility
**loss of friendship** alienation
**loss of hair** alopecia, baldness
**loss of hair of the eyebrows** madarosis
**loss of life on a large scale** mortality
**loss of memory** amnesia
**loss of one's faculties** dotage, senility
**loss of position** come-down
**loss of power of articulate speech** aphasia
**loss of red corpuscles** anaemia
**loss of rights through conviction** attainder
**loss of sensation** anaesthesia
**loss of sense of direction** disorientation
**loss of sense of smell** anosmia
**loss of speech** aphasia
**loss of speed** deceleration
**loss of strength** asthenia, debility
**loss of the ability to speak coherently** anarthria
**loss of the ability to write** agraphia
**loss of vital power** adynamia
**loss of voice** aphonia
**loss of willpower** abulia
**loss or wrong** damnum
**loss through damage** breakage

**lost** abandoned, bewildered, confused, corrupt, defeated, destroyed, dissipated, gone, hardened, irreclaimable, irredeemable, misplaced, missed, missing, misspent, profligate, ruined, shameless, wasted
**lost animal** stray
**lost in thought** absent-minded, absorbed, bemused, dreamy, musing, reflective, wistful
**lost liquid** ullage
**lost owing to crime** forfeit
**lost pet** stray
**lost possession of ball** turnover
**lost speed** slowed
**lot** array, assortment, batch, bundle, circumstance, cluster, collection, consignment, crowd, destiny, fate, group, many, mass(es), much, parcel, part, piece, portion, quantity, quota, role, set, share, tract
**lotion** liniment
**lotion for rubbing limbs** embrocation
**lot of goods sold to highest bidder** auction
**lots** many, myriads, oodles, plenty
**lots and lots** tons
**lottery** chance, draw, gamble, hazard, raffle, risk, sweepstake, venture
**lottery ticket not drawing a prize** blank
**lotto** housey-housey
**lottolike game** ke(e)no, kino, quino
**louche** disreputable, oblique, shifty
**loud** blatant, boisterous, bold, clamorous, coarse, crude, deafening, earsplitting, emphatic, flashy, forte, fortissimo, gaudy, loud-voiced, noisy, obtrusive, raucous, resounding, ribald, roaring, rude, showy, snazzy, sonorous, stentorian, uncivilised, vociferous, vulgar
**loud and distracting noise** din
**loud and harsh** strident
**loud and hoarse** raucous
**loud and insistent in speech** vociferous
**loud and pompous** bombastic
**loud and showy** brash
**loud coarse laugh** heehaw
**loud commotion** uproar
**loud complaint** squawk
**loud cry** shout, yell
**loud deep sound** roar
**loud eager cry** whoop
**loud gleeful chuckle** chortle
**loudhailer** megaphone
**loud harsh cry** squawk
**loud homage** acclamation
**loud horn noise** blare, klaxon

**loud kiss** smacker
**loudly** brashly, brazenly, coarsely, crudely, forte, raucously, resoundingly, rowdily, sonorously, stridently, strongly, tumultuously, turbulently, vehemently, vulgarly
**loudly obtrusive** blatant
**loudmouth** boaster, brag(gart), gasbag, swaggerer, windbag, windgat
**loudness unit** sone
**loud noise** ballyhoo, bang, din, fuss, roar
**loud noise from exhaust** backfire
**loud protest** clamour, outcry
**loud quarrel** broil
**loud revelry** riot
**loud ringing sound** clang
**loud shout** bellow
**loud silly laugh** cackle
**loud sound** bang, noise
**loud sound of bells** peal
**loudspeaker** hailer, stentor, tweeter, woofer
**loud-voiced** stentorian
**loud wailing cry** yowl
**lounge** couch, dawdle, day-room, drawing-room, idle, laze, living-room, loaf, loiter, loll, parlour, recline, relax, saunter, sitting-room, slump, sofa, sprawl
**lounge about** loaf
**lounging about** lolling
**lounging room** den
**loup** loo mask
**lour** alarm, browbeat, bully, frighten, frown, gloominess, impend, intimidate, loom, lower, menace, scowl, sullenness, terrorise, threaten
**louse** aphid, cad, cootie, nit, parasite, slater, vermin
**louse egg** nit
**louse-infested** pedicular, pediculous
**lousy** bad, detestable, inadequate, inferior, lice-infested, mean, shoddy, sloppy, slovenly, vile, wretched
**lout** barbarian, blunderer, brute, cad, churl, clodhopper, clown, dolt, gawk, oaf, ox, ribald, skollie, skolly, thug, yahoo, yobbo
**loutish** awkward, bad-mannered, bluff, boorish, brusque, churlish, clownish, coarse, curt, discourteous, foul-mouthed, gauche, gawky, ill-mannered, impolite, indecorous, insolent, lumpish, maladroit, oafish, rough, rude, uncivil, uncouth, ungainly, ungracious, unmannerly
**loutish person** chuckle-head, oaf
**louvre** slat, slit, turret, vent
**lovable** adorable, alluring, amiable, angelic, appealing, attractive, beautiful, captivating, charming, cuddly, cute, delightful, deserving, divine, endearing, engaging, fetching, intriguing, irresistible, lovely, pleasing, sweet, winsome
**love** adoration, adore, adulate, adulation, affection, amor (L), amorousness, appreciate, ardour, aroha, attachment, attraction, benevolence, cherish, delight, desire, devotion, dote, enjoy(ment), fancy, fondness, friendliness, friendship, idolise, inclination, infatuation, kindness, like, liking, passion, rapture, regard, taste, tenderness, treasure, value, warmth, weakness, worship
**love affair** affaire (F), affaire d'amour (F), affaire de coeur, amour, ardour, betrothal, devotion, engagement, fervour, intrigue, passion, relationship, romance, tryst
**love and admire** worship
**love apple** tomato
**love child** bastard
**love deeply** adore
**love excessively** idolise
**love feast** agape
**love foolishly** dote
**love greatly** adore
**love-in-idleness** wild pansy
**love intensely** adore
**love intrigue** amour, affair
**love letter** billet-doux
**lovely** adorable, agreeable, attractive, beautiful, charming, delightful, elegant, enchanting, enjoyable, exquisite, graceful, gratifying, handsome, marvellous, nice, pleasant, pleasing, pretty, sweet, winning, wonderful
**lovely lady** belle
**lovely maiden** nymph
**lovely to look at** beautiful
**love of animals** zoophilia, zoophilism
**love of archery** toxophilism
**love of Caesar** Servilia
**love of country** allegiance, amor patriae (L), chauvinism, jingoism, nationalism, patriotism
**love of cruelty** sadism
**love of fellow man** charity
**love of fine arts** vertu, virtu
**love of mankind** humanity, philanthropy
**love of one's country** amor patriae (L), patriotism
**love of oneself** narcissism
**love of the arts** dilettantism
**love of wisdom** philosophy
**lover** admirer, adorer, amorist, beau, belle amie (F), beloved, bon ami (F), boyfriend, cicisbeo (I), courter, devotee, fan, fiancé(e), gigolo, girlfriend, inamorata, inamorato, leman, mistress, paramour, philanderer, Romeo, suitor, swain, sweetheart, wooer
**lover of Acis** Galatea
**lover of Aeneas** Dido
**lover of Aïda** Radames
**lover of archery** toxophilite
**lover of art** aesthete
**lover of beauty** aesthete
**lover of books** bibliophil(e)
**lover of Clytemnestra** Aegisthus
**lover of food** gourmand, gourmet
**lover of Guinevere** Lancelot
**lover of Hero** Leander
**lover of Lancelot** Elaine, Guinever(e)
**lover of learning** philomath
**lover of one's country** patriot
**lover of Pyramus** Thisbe
**lover of statue** Pygmalion
**lover of the nymph Arethusa** Apheus
**lover of things foreign** xenophile
**lover of wine** oenophile
**lover's appointment to meet** tryst
**lovers' archer** Cupid
**lovers' meeting** tryst
**lovers' row** tiff
**lovers' tiff** spat
**love song** serenade
**loves the foreign** xenophilia
**love story** romance
**love tenderly** dote
**love to excess** idolise, dote
**love-token** gage d'amour (F)
**loving** adoring, affectionate, amorous, appreciating, ardent, caressing, cherishing, cordial, cuddling, dear, desiring, devoted, embracing, fancying, fond(ling), friendly, idolising, kind, kissing, liking, tender, treasuring, warm, worshipping
**loving infatuatedly** doting
**loving kindness towards others** charity
**lovingly** ardently, dearly, kindly, tenderly, warmly
**loving touch** caress
**low** abject, base, crude, dead, deep, degraded, dejected, depressed, disgraceful, dishonourable, dispirited, disreputable, dying, grovelling, humble, ignoble, lowly, menial, miserable, moo, poor, profound, prone, prostrate, sad, servile, sinking, sordid, supine, unbecoming, undignified, unelevated, unhappy, vile, vulgar, weak
**low and harsh** gruff
**low, as a cow** moo

**low ball** liner
**low bark** woof
**low basin** bidet
**low blood pressure** hypotension
**low-bred dog** cur
**low budget movie** quickie
**low cart** dray
**low-class lawyer** pettifogger
**low cloud** mist
**low couch** divan
**low-crowned felt hat** billycock
**low-cut neck of woman's garment** décolletage
**low-cut shoe** anklet, buskin, slipper, sock
**low deck of ship** orlop
**low deep sound** groan
**low dull sound** thud
**lower** darken, debase, decrease, degrade, demean, depress, diminish, dip, down, drop, frown, glower, humble, humiliate, inferior, lessen, nether, reduce, sink, soften, vail
**lower and raise head** nod
**lower animal** brute
**lower appendages** feet
**lower back** loin
**lower back joint** sacroiliac
**lower case letter** minuscule
**lower classes** rabble
**lower corner of square sail** clew
**lower dignity of** demean
**lower edge of dress** hemline
**lower edge of sail** clew
**lower end of mast** heel
**lower floor of building** ground
**lower for a moment** dip
**lower headlights** dip
**lower in dignity** demean
**lower in estimation** abase
**lower in position** subjacent, subordinate, under
**lower in price** reduce
**lower in quality** cheapen, debase
**lower in rank** abase, demote, downgrade, inferior
**lower in social class** declass
**lower in value** debase
**lower in worth** devalue
**lower jaw** chin
**lower jaw in mammals** mandible
**lower joint of ham** hock
**lower joint of leg of cooked fowl** drumstick
**lower leg covering** gaiter, puttee
**lower leg joint** ankle
**lower limb** leg
**lowermost** lowest
**lower oneself** condescend, stoop
**lower opening of bowels** anus
**lower part** bottom

**lower part of abdomen** pubes
**lower part of alimentary canal** intestine
**lower part of an interior wall** dado
**lower part of arm** forearm
**lower part of face** chin
**lower part of human trunk** abdomen
**lower part of insect's mouth** labium
**lower part of intestines** ileum
**lower part of leg** shank, shinbone
**lower part of pistil** ovary
**lower part of visor** beaver
**lower part of wall** dado
**lower part of woman's dress** skirt
**lower pinna** earlobe
**lower side** bottom
**lower square member of base of column** plinth
**lower surface of a room** floor
**lower than** below, beneath
**lower than normal mental development** amentia
**lower the dignity** meek
**lower world** Hades, Tartarus
**lowest** cheapest, commonest, crudest, deepest, gloomiest, glummest, grossest, humblest, last, least, littlest, low(er)most, lowliest, meanest, meekest, nethermost, paltriest, plainest, poorest, primary, puniest, quietest, roughest, rudest, saddest, shallowest, shoddiest, shortest, simplest, smallest, softest, unhappiest, vilest
**lowest cardinal number** one
**lowest class of a community** proletariat
**lowest commissioned officer in navy** ensign
**lowest deck** orlop
**lowest ebb** nadir
**lowest female operatic voice** contralto
**lowest female singing voice** alto
**lowest form of wit** pun
**lowest in level** basic
**lowest level** bottom, floor, hardpan
**lowest limit** minimum
**lowest male voice** bass
**lowest note of a chord** fundamental
**lowest of four great Hindu castes** Sudra
**lowest-order mammal** monotreme
**lowest part** bottom
**lowest part in music** bass
**lowest part of a building** foundation
**lowest part of anything** bottom
**lowest point** base, bottom, minimum, nadir, perigee, root, zero
**lowest positive integer** one
**lowest quarter of ship** steerage
**lowest rank** scouring
**lowest sail** course

**lowest storey of a building** basement
**lowest throw at dice** ambsace, amesace
**lowest throw of dice** deuce
**lowest tide** neap
**lowest whole number** one
**low fellow** rascal, varlet
**low flat land near a river** holm
**low-growing herb with broad leaves** plantain
**low-growing shrub** arctic willow
**low-growing willow** sallow
**low hill** burrow, hillock, hummock, knap, knoll, kopje, koppie, monticule, mound
**low in cost** cheap
**lowing** mooing
**low in price** cheap
**low in spirits** blue, depressed
**low in temperature** cold
**low island** cay, key
**low islet of coral or sand** cay
**lowland** carse (Sc), flatland, grassland, meadow, pampas, plain, plateau, prairie, savanna(h), steppe, tableland, tundra, veld
**lowland reclaimed from sea** polders
**lowland Scot** Sassenach
**lowly** common, docile, dutiful, earth-born, homely, humble, meek, menial, modest, obedient, peaceful, plain, plebian, poor, reserved, restrained, unequal, unknown, unpretending
**lowly female servant** skivvy
**low-lying land** fen, marsh
**low moan** groan, croon
**low neckline** décolletage
**lowness of spirits** spleen
**low noise** hum
**low organ note** subbass
**low-pitched** deep
**low-pitched brass wind instrument** tuba
**low pitched sound** bass
**low place between hills** dale
**low platform** dais
**low-quality diamond** bo(a)rt
**low rail-truck** bogey
**low-ranking noble** baron
**low seat** tabo(u)ret
**low section of a city** slum
**low shoe** pump
**low shoes** loafers
**low sound** drone, hum, moan, murmur, rumble
**low spirits** blues, depressed, doldrums, dumps, gloom
**low stool** cricket, tabo(u)ret
**low storey between others** mezzanine
**low tide** neap

**low-value British coin** penny, tuppence, twopence
**low voice** bass
**low wall** parapet
**low wash-basin** bidet
**low water** neap-tide
**loyal** allegiant, dedicated, dependable, devoted, faithful, honest, leal (Sc), liege, obedient, patriotic, pledged, reliable, staunch, steadfast, true, trustworthy, trusty, unbribed, unwavering
**loyal friend** Achates
**loyalist** adherent, admirer, conservative, defender, devotee, maintainer, partisan, patriot, supporter, sustainer, Tory, votary
**loyal subject** liege
**loyalty** allegiance, devotion, faithfulness, fidelity, lealty (Sc), patriotism
**lozenge** pastille
**lozenge to sweeten breath** cachou
**lubricant** castor, cleanser, glycerine, graphite, grease, oil, ointment, plumbago, salve, unguent, vaseline, wax
**lubricate** bribe, daub, grease, lard, oil, pomade, smear, smooth, soap, wax
**lubricate with oil** grease
**lubricious** lascivious, lewd, oily, slippery
**lucent** clear, diaphanous, filmy, limpid, lucid, shining, translucent, transparent
**lucerne** alfalfa
**lucid** bright, brilliant, clear, distinct, evident, intelligible, limpid, obvious, perspicuous, plain, radiant, rational, reasonable, sane, transparent, understandable, unmistakable
**lucidity** clarity, sanity
**Lucifer** Beelzebub, Devil, Satan
**luck** accident, casualty, cess, chance, coincidence, destiny, fate, felicity, fortunateness, fortune, karma, kismet, lot, opportunity, prosperity, prosperousness, serendipity, success
**luckily** fortunately, happily, opportunely, providentially
**lucky** advantageous, auspicious, benign, expedient, favourable, felicitous, fortuitous, fortunate, happy, opportune, profitable, prosperous, successful, timely
**lucky accidental stroke** fluke
**lucky chances** odds
**lucky charm** amulet, mascot, periapt, talisman
**lucky dip** grab-bag
**lucky find** trouvaille (F), windfall
**lucky number** seven

**lucky stroke** fluke
**lucrative** advantageous, desirable, fat, favourable, fecund, fructuous, fruitful, gainful, moneymaking, paying, productive, profitable, prosperous, remunerative, rewarding, well-paid, worthwhile, yielding
**lucre** gain, mammon, money, pelf, profit, riches, spoils, wealth
**ludicrous** absurd, amusing, bombastic, burlesque, comic(al), crazy, derisible, droll, extravagant, fallacious, fantastic, farcical, funny, idiotic, improper, inane, incorrect, jocular, laughable, nonsensical, odd, outrageous, peculiar, preposterous, quaint, queer, ridiculous, sarcastic, satirical, silly, sportive, untrue, witty, zany
**ludicrous comedy** farce
**ludicrous failure** fiasco
**lues** pestilence, plague
**lug** bear, bring, carry, conduct, convey, drag, draw, ear, fetch, hale, haul, heave, jerk, lift, move, pull, relay, take, tow, trail, transfer, transmit, transport, tug, wrench, yank
**luggage** baggage, bags, (suit)cases, trunks
**luggage holder** boot
**luggage item** case
**luggage shelf** rack
**lugubrious** dark, dirgelike, disconsolate, disheartening, dismal, doleful, dreary, elegiac, forlorn, funereal, gloomy, joyless, melancholy, miserable, morose, mournful, rueful, sombre
**lukewarm** balmy, blood-warm, dispassionate, impassive, indifferent, irresolute, listless, mild, summery, temperate, tepid, uncommitted, unconcerned, uninterested, unresponsive, warm
**lull** abate, allay, calm, cease, compose, diminish, hush, lullaby, pacify, pause, quell, slacken, soothe, subside
**lumbago** backache
**lumbar region** loin
**lumber factory** sawmill
**lumberjack's cry** timber
**lumber source** tree
**lumbus** loin
**luminary** celebrity, dignitary, idol, lead, name, notable, personage, personality, somebody, (super)star, VIP, worthy
**luminescence produced by friction** triboluminescence

**luminous** aglow, bright, clear, illuminated, intelligent, intelligible, lighted, lit, lucid, perspicacious, radiant, resplendent, shining, smart
**luminous atmospheric phenomenon** aurora
**luminous beetle** firefly
**luminous body around which the earth revolves** sun
**luminous bridge** arc
**luminous element** radium
**luminous light round saint's head** halo
**luminous ring** halo
**lummox** fumbler, lout, lubber, oaf
**lump** bubo, bump, clot, clump, compile, gob, goitre, group, growth, knob, lob, mass, node, nodule, nub, swelling, tumour, wad
**lumpish** awkward, clownish, clumsy, gauche, gawky, heavy, loutish, maladroit, oafish, stupid, uncouth
**lump of blood** clot
**lump of chewing tobacco** quid
**lump of coal** nubble
**lump of dirt** clod
**lump of dough** bread
**lump of gold as found in the earth** nugget
**lump of gum** wad
**lump of rock** stone
**lump of tobacco for chewing** quid
**lump of turf** divot, sod
**lump on skin** wen
**lump on tree** knot
**lump reducer** ice bag
**lump sum** settlement
**lumpy** agitated, anxious, apprehensive, bumpy, cloggy, clotted, curdled, edgy, fidgety, grainy, granular, knobby, nervous, nervy, nodular, tense
**lumpy swelling** bubo, node
**lunar appearance** moonrise
**lunar body** moon
**lunar crater** linne
**lunar phase** crescent
**lunar plain** mare
**lunar valley** rill(e)
**lunate** crescent(-shaped), crescentoid, moon-shaped, semilunar
**lunatic** bedonderd, beneek, crazy, daft, demented, demoniac, deranged, fanatic, irrational, loony, mad(man), maniac, non compos mentis (L), psychopath
**lunatic asylum** bedlam
**lunch hour** midday break
**lunch time** noon
**lung disease** emphysema, phthisis, pneumonia, silicosis, tuberculosis

**lunge** bound, charge, cut, dash, dive, feint, jab, jump, leap, pass, pitch, plunge, poke, pounce, spring, stab, swing, swipe, thrust
**lung infection** pneumonia, tuberculosis
**lung inflammation** pneumonia
**lungs of sheep and pigs used as food for pets** lights
**lupine creature** wolf
**lupine man** werewolf
**lurch** careen, incline, jerk, keel, lunge, pitch, reel, roll, slant, stagger, stumble, sway, swerve, tilt, totter
**lure** allure, attract(ion), bait, bribe, cajolery, decoy, draw, entice(ment), snare, tempt(ation), trap
**lure into a trap** decoy
**lurid** aglow, ardent, ashen, awful, crimson, dire, disgusting, dreary, dusky, fierce, fiery, garish, gaudy, ghastly, gloomy, gory, graphic, grim, gruesome, horrifying, intense, macabre, melodramatic, murky, pale, pallid, revolting, savage, scarlet, sensational, shocking, somber, startling, stimulating, terrible, violent, vivid, vulgar
**lurk** ambush, darkle, elude, escape, hide, loiter, prowl, skulk, slink, sneak, steal, underlie, waylay
**lurking place** retreat
**luscious** appetising, attractive, creamy, dainty, delectable, delicious, delightful, dulcet, elegant, enjoyable, epicurean, fine, fragrant, fulsome, grand, honeyed, juicy, lush, luxurious, palatable, refined, rich, succulent, superb, sweet, tangy, tasty, tempting, tender, voluptuous
**lush** dense, elaborate, elegant, fancy, flourishing, grand, luxuriant, luxurious, ornate, prolific
**lust** appetite, avidity, carnality, concupiscence, covetousness, crave, craving, cupidity, demand, desire, eagerness, lechery, lewdness, libidinousness, libido, license, longing, lubricity, need, passion, prurience, sensuality, want
**lust after** covet, crave, desire, need, want

**lustful** avid, carnal, desiring, desirous, greedy, lascivious, lecherous, lewd, piggish, prurient, ravenous, robust, salacious, unsated, voracious
**lustful man** lecher
**lustily** healthily, powerfully, robustly, stalwartly, stoutly, strongly, sturdily, vigorously
**lustre** brightness, brilliance, burnish, effulgence, gleam, gloss, glow, honour, luminosity, merit, notability, radiance, radiation, refulgence, sheen, shimmer, shine, splendour
**lustreless** dull, mat
**lustre of surface** gloss
**lustrous** beamy, bright, celebrated, gleaming, glossy, gorgeous, illustrious, iridescent, luminous, radiant, refulgent, renowned, shining, shiny, splendid, splendorous, twinkling
**lustrous fabric** sateen, satin, silk, taffeta
**lustrous fur** mink, sable
**lustrous gem** opal, pearl
**lustrous mineral found in Greenland** cryolite
**lusty** bulky, energetic, hale, healthful, healthy, large, lively, lustful, powerful, robust, stout, strong, vigorous, virile
**Lutetian** Parisian
**lute with eleven strings** theorbo
**luxate** dislocate
**luxuriant** abundant, ample, copious, elaborate, fancy, fertile, florid, fruitful, lavish, lush, opulent, ornate, plentiful, profuse, prolific, rich, rococo, thriving
**luxuriant and succulent** lush
**luxurious** abounding, comfortable, copious, costly, de luxe, easy, extravagant, gorgeous, inordinate, lush, luxuriant, opulent, ornate, ostentatious, pleasurable, plush, posh, rich, self-indulgent, sensual, splendid, sumptuous, sybaritic, voluptuous, wealthy
**luxurious and voluptuous** sybaritic
**luxurious motor car** limousine
**luxurious person** sybarite

**luxury** elegant, expensive, extravagance, indulgence, luxurious, ritzy, treat, wealth
**Luzon native** Ata
**lycanthrope** werewolf
**lying** deceit(ful), dishonest(y), double-dealing, duplicity, fabrication, false, falsity, fibbing, guile(ful), mendacious, perjury, treacherous, two-faced, untruthful(ness)
**lying against** alongside, anent
**lying at full length** flat, prostrate
**lying beyond** ulterior
**lying close to** adjacent
**lying dormant** latent
**lying down** recumbent
**lying face downwards** prone, prostrate
**lying face upwards** supine
**lying flat** prone, prostrate, supine
**lying inactive** dormant, hibernating, latent
**lying inactive as in sleep** dormant
**lying in store for** awaiting
**lying in wait** ambush, lurking
**lying lengthwise** longitudinal
**lying near to** adjacent
**lying off a ship's centre** abeam
**lying on the back** supine
**lying outside** external
**lying under a curse** accursed
**lying under oath** perjury
**lying with face to ground** prostrate, prone
**lying witness** perjurer
**lymphoid organ near base of neck** thymus
**lynx** caracal, wildcat
**lynx-eyed** keen-sighted
**Lyra star** Vega
**lyric** air, anthem, ballad, carol, chant, chorus, ditty, hymn, lay, melody, ode, poem, poetic, psalm, rhyme, song, sonnet, strain, tune, verse
**lyrical** dulcet, ecstatic, effusive, elegiac, emotional, enthusiastic, expressive, impassioned, inspired, lilting, melodious, metrical, passionate, poetic, rapturous, rhapsodic, tuneful
**lyric poem** (ep)ode
**lyric poet** odist

# M

**ma** mamma, mom(ma), mother
**mac** mack(intosh), raincoat
**macabre** abhorrent, anaemic, ashen, atrocious, awful, brutal, cadaverous, cruel, deathly, dire(ful), dread(ful), eerie, fearsome, fierce, frightening, frightful, gaunt, ghastly, ghostly, gory, grim, grisly, grotesque, gruesome, haggard, hideous, horrendous, horrid, horrific, inhuman, monstrous, morbid, odious, ogreish, pallid, repugnant, sadistic, savage, scary, sinister, skeletal, unearthly, wan, weird, white
**macabre state** grisliness
**macadam** stones, tar
**Macaque monkey** rhesus
**macaw** ara, arar(a), maracan, parrot
**mace** bar, baton, birch, cane, club, pole, rod, sceptre, shaft, staff, stick, truncheon, wand
**machete** cutlass
**machine** apparatus, appliance, association, contraption, device, engine, mechanism, organisation, system
**machine for lifting heavy equipment** crane
**machine for raising water** pump
**machine for rolling washed linen** mangle
**machine for separating cream from milk** separator
**machine for shaping wood** lathe
**machine for spinning wool** spinning-jenny
**machine for squeezing moisture from clothes** wringer
**machine for washing dishes** dishwasher
**machine for weaving** loom
**machine fretsaw** jigsaw
**machine gun** AK47, Bren, Maxim, Sten, Tommy, Uzi, Vickers
**machine in speed contest** racer
**machine knob** lever
**machine pedal** treadle
**machinery for grinding corn** mill
**machine to wind a cable** capstan
**machinist** artisan, craftsman, electrician, engineer, mechanic, technician
**machismo** brawn, grit, hairiness, insensitivity, manliness, masculinity, sexism, virility
**macho** virile
**macho person** he-man

**mackerel** shiner
**mackerel-like fish** cero, tinker, tunny
**mackerel shark** porbeagle
**mackintosh** mac(k), raincoat
**macrocosm** cosmos, empyrean, entirety, firmament, galaxy, globe, heavens, nature, sky, totality, universe, world
**macula** blackhead, freckle, macule, mark, pimple, pit, pockmark, scar, speck, spot
**mad** amok, angry, absurd, ardent, avid, barmy, bedonderd, berserk, crazed, crazy, dangerous, demented, deranged, distracted, enraged, exasperated, excessive, excited, fanatical, foolish, frantic, fuming, furious, harmful, ill-advised, incensed, infatuated, infuriated, insane, irate, irrational, livid, loony, ludicrous, lunatic, maniacal, nonsensical, nutty, perilous, preposterous, provoked, rabid, reckless, unbalanced, unhinged, unreasonable, violent, wild, wrathful
**Madagascan primate** babacoote, indri, lemur, sifaka
**Madame Tussaud's nationality** Swiss
**mad as a hatter** crazy, demented, insane
**madcap** adventurer, adventurous, audacious, bold, dangerous, daredevil, daring, death-defying, desperado, desperate, determined, eccentric, foolhardy, frantic, furious, harebrained, hasty, headstrong, impetuous, imprudent, impulsive, incautious, irresponsible, lively, mad, pantaloon, rash, rattlebrained, reckless, risky, scatterbrained, show-off, tearaway, violent, wild, zany
**madden** aggravate, anger, annoy, craze, dement, derange, distract, enrage, exasperate, frenzy, harass, incense, inflame, infuriate, irritate, provoke, unhinge, upset, vex
**maddening** annoying, (en)raging, fierce, flagrant, furious, immoderate, infuriating, intense, irritating, notorious, outrageous, passionate, perturbing, vehement, violent
**madder-root pigment** rubiate
**made by a cartographer** map
**made by churning cream** butter
**made by fletcher** arrow
**made effective from earlier** backdated

**made for special service** express
**made from fermented malt** beer
**made into honey** nectar
**mad emperor** Nero
**made of animal skin** leather
**made of baked clay** earthen
**made of black** ebon
**made of bronze** brazen
**made of cereal grass** oaten
**made of clay** ceramic, earthen
**made of flax** linen (cloth)
**made of fleece** woollen
**made of interwoven osiers** basket
**made of iron** powerful, solid, steely, strong
**made of oak** oaken
**made of oats** oaten
**made of pressed curds** cheese
**made of wood** treen(ware), wooden
**made thing** artefact, artifact
**made to measure** bespoke, tailored
**made-up** fabricated, fairy-tale, false, fictional, imaginary, invented, make-believe, mythical, unreal, untrue
**made up of parts** composite
**made up of three parts** trine
**made with meat and vegetables** stew
**mad frolic** prank
**madhouse** asylum, bedlam, nuthouse, turmoil, uproar
**madly seeking to kill** amok
**madman** demoniac, fool imbecile, headcase, idiot, loony, lunatic, maniac, nut(case), psychopath, psychotic
**madness** absurdity, anility, craziness, daftness, dementia, dipsomania, folly, insanity, lunacy, mania, melancholia, neurosis, ridiculousness, senselessness, silliness, unbalance
**madness confined to one subject** monomania
**Madrid is there** Spain
**mad Roman emperor** Nero
**mad with rage** frantic
**Mafia members** Mafiosi
**Mafia official** padrone
**magazine** arsenal, depot, journal, monthly, ordnance, pamphlet, paper, periodical, powder-room, quarterly, store(house), warehouse, weekly
**magazine model** cover girl
**magazine official** editor
**magazine of stores for warfare** arsenal

**magazine with nude women** girlie
**magenta** bluish-red
**maggot** botfly, caprice, caterpillar, grub, humour, larva, whim, worm(il)
**maggot of the bluebottle, used as bait** gentle
**magic** art, astrology, augury, bewitching, charming, conjuring, craft, deceit, demonology, diablerie, enchanting, enchantment, exorcism, fascinating, foreboding, hocus-pocus, illusion, incantation, influence, jiggery-pokery, jinx, marvellous, necromancy, obi, obsession, occult(ism), occultness, omen, rite, sorcery, spell(binding), thaumaturgy, trickery, voodoo, witchcraft, witchery
**magical** amazing, astonishing, astounding, dreamy, extraordinary, incredible, marvellous, miraculous, phenomenal, supernatural, unreal, wonderful
**magical hope** wish
**magical influence** hex, spell, witchcraft, witchery
**magical science of Neoplatonists** theurgy
**magic beverage** potion
**magic formula** abracadabra, incantation, nostrum, presto, spell
**magician** archimage, clairvoyant, conjurer, conjuror, fortuneteller, illusionist, juggler, magus, medium, mesmerist, necromancer, sorcerer, sorceress, thaumaturgist, theurgist, witch, wizard
**magician's attendant** famulus
**magician's rod** wand
**magic potion** elixir, arcanum
**magic spell** hex, incantation
**magic symbol** caract
**magic wand of Aaron** rod
**magic words of Ali Baba** open sesame
**magistrate** alca(l)de, constable, doge, governor, judge, justice, mayor, prefect, provost, reeve, syndic
**magistrate of ancient Rome** praetor
**magistrate of Venice** doge
**magma** lava
**magma gusher** volcano
**magmatic** igneous
**magnanimity** benevolence, bigness, chivalry, easiness, generosity, justness, kindness, largeness, leniency, liberalness, nobleness, patience, selflessness, tolerance
**magnanimous** altruism, beneficent, bounty, charitable, elevated, exalted, fair, forgiving, generous, high-minded, humanitarian, just, lenient, liberal, lofty, noble, tolerant, unbiased, unresentful, unselfish
**magnate** baron, bigwig, mogul, noble, personage, plutocrat, tycoon
**magnesium silicate** talc
**magnet** allure, appeal, attractant, invitation, lodestone, lure, paramagnet, solenoid, temptation
**magnetic** alluring, appealing, attracting, attractive, catching, charismatic, dynamic, enthralling, forceful, grabbing, gripping, irresistible, mesmeric, potent, pulling, tugging, vital
**magnetic oxide of iron** loadstone
**magnetic record** floppy, disk
**magnetic tape** cassette
**magnetism** affinity, allure, appeal, attraction, attractiveness, capillarity, charisma, charm, enchantment, fascination, glamour, gravitation, gravity, grip, hypnotism, inclination, interest, magic, mesmerism, power, spell, sympathy, tendency
**magnification** amplification, blow-up, boost, build-up, embellishment, emphasis, enhancement, enlargement, exaggeration, excess, expansion, hyperbole, increase, inflation, intensification, overstatement, pretension, pretentiousness
**magnificence** brilliance, elegant, excellent, fine, glorious, glory, gorgeous, grand(eur), imposing, impressive(ness), lavishness, luxuriousness, luxury, majestic, majesty, nobility, opulence, outstanding, plush(ness), pomp, posh, rich, solemnity, splendid, splendour, state(liness), sublimity, superb, swankness
**magnificent** brilliant, dazzling, dignified, elegant, excellent, extraordinary, fine, gorgeous, grand, imposing, impressive, lavish, majestic, princely, radiant, rich, splendid, stately, sublime, sumptuous, superb, superior
**magnificently false** splendide mendax (L)
**magnificently generous** munificent
**magnificent tomb** mausoleum
**magnifico** baron, grandee, hidalgo, lord, magnate, merchant, nobleman, notable, patrician, peer, personage, prince
**magnify** amplify, augment, boost, deepen, dilate, dramatise, enhance, enlarge, exaggerate, expand, greaten, heighten, increase, inflate, intensify, overdo, overemphasise, overplay, overstate, praise
**magnifying** dilating, enhancing, exaggerating, expanding, heightening, increasing, inflating, intensifying, overdoing
**magnifying glass** loupe
**magniloquence** arrogance, boastfulness, bombast, braggadocio, fustian, grandiosity, haughtiness, pomposity, tumidity, vainglory
**magniloquent** arrogant, bombastic, braggart, bragging, declamatory, exalted, grandiose, haughty, inflated, lofty, orotund, pompous, pretentious, turgid
**magnitude** abundance, bulk, consequence, copiousness, dimensions, enormousness, extent, fame, greatness, immensity, importance, largeness, mass, measure, plentitude, plenty, quantity, significance, size, vastness, volume
**magpie** blabber, chatterbox, chatterer, driveller, gabbler, gusher, jabberer, palaverer, payet, payot, popinjay, prater, prattler, pyat, skinderbek
**magpie lark** peewee
**Mahayama form of Buddhism of Tibet and Mongolia** Lamaism
**maiden** celibate, chaste, damsel, first, fresh, girl, initial, lass(ie), maid, miss, new, nymph, pure, single, spinster, spouseless, unmarried, untried, unused, unwed, virgin, wench
**maidenhair tree** gingko, ginkgo
**maidenhood** celibacy, maidhood, singleness, virginity
**maidenly** becoming, chaste, decent, decorous, feminine, immaculate, ladylike, modest, proper, pure, spotless, virtuous, womanish, womanlike, womanly
**maiden name** née
**maidservant** amah, ayah
**mail** address, consign, correspondence, da(w)k, dispatch, forward, letter, package, post, send, transmit
**mail charge** postage
**mailman's superior** postmaster
**mail worker** sorter
**maim** cripple, damage, disable, disfigure, dismember, hurt, impair, incapacitate, injure, lame, mangle, mar, mutilate, savage, wound
**main** cable, capital, cardinal, central, channel, chief, conduit, critical, crucial, direct, downright, duct, entire, essential, extensive, first, force, foremost, general, great, head(most), idea, leading, line,

necessary, outstanding, paramount, particular, pipe, power, pre-eminent, predominant, primary, prime, principal, pure, sheer, special, supreme, vital
**main actor** hero(ine), star
**main artery** aorta
**main body** mass
**main church of diocese** cathedral
**main city** capital, metropolis
**main colour on the Greek flag** blue
**main colour on the Japanese flag** white
**main colour on the Swiss flag** red
**main commodity** staple
**main door** front entrance
**main Indonesian isle** Java
**main ingredient** basis
**mainland Europe** Continent
**mainly** chiefly, commonly, especially, essentially, generally, largely, mostly, overall, particularly, primarily, principally, routinely, substantially, usually
**main male character in story** hero
**main meal** dinner
**main operational camp** base
**main part** essence
**main part of a tree** trunk
**main part of column** shaft
**main passage** corridor
**main point** gist, nub
**main road** expressway, highway, mainway, thoroughfare
**main role** lead
**main room in great house** hall
**main route** highway
**mainspring** cause, fountain head, incentive, inspiration, motivation, motive, origin, source
**main stalk** stem
**mainstay** anchor, Atlas, backbone, base, bulwark, buttress, foundation, linchpin, pillar, prop, security, staff, substructure, support
**main stem of deer's antlers** beam
**main stem of tree** trunk
**main storey of large house** piano nobile (I)
**mainstream** accepted, conventional, established, general, normal, orthodox, received, regular, standard
**main substance of a matter** gist
**main support of structure** backbone
**maintain** affirm, allege, assert, asseverate, aver, avow, back, champion, claim, confine, conserve, contend, continue, declare, defend, finance, hold, insist, justify, keep, nurture, perpetuate, preserve, profess, prolong, provide, retain, state, supply, support, sustain, uphold, vindicate
**maintain against an opponent** fight
**maintain by reasoning** argue
**maintain effort** persevere, persist
**maintain persistently** insist
**maintenance** aliment, alimony, allowance, bread, care, continuation, conversation, defence, food, keep(ing), livelihood, living, nurture, perpetuation, preservation, protection, provisions, repairs, running, subsistence, supply, support, sustenance, upkeep
**maintenance man** janitor
**main theme of a book** subject matter
**main vein of leaf** midrib
**main vessel from the heart** aorta
**maize** corn, mealie
**maize bread** mealiebread, pone
**maize whiskey** bourbon
**majestic** august, dignified, distingué, distinguished, grand, imperial, kingly, lofty, lordly, magnificent, monarch(i)al, noble, pompous, princely, proud, regal, royal, splendid, stately
**majesty** augustness, authority, dignity, exaltedness, glory, grandeur, impressiveness, kingliness, loftiness, magnificence, monarchy, nobility, pomp, regality, regalness, resplendence, royalty, sovereignty, splendour, state(liness), sublimity, supremacy
**major** capital, chief, extreme, foremost, greater, greatest, highest, key, large(r), main, predominant, prime, principal, superior, supreme, utmost
**Majorcan resort** Palma
**major cricket match** test
**major diatonic scale** gamut
**majority** adulthood, bulk, commonality, mass, maturity, more, most, plurality, populace, preponderance, proletariat, seniority, superiority, (wo)manhood
**majority of** most
**majority view** consensus
**major part** bulk
**major planet** Jupiter, Neptune, Saturn, Uranus
**major's musical partner** minor
**major work of a writer** magnum opus
**make** accomplish, acquire, brand, build, cause, change, compel, compose, constitute, construct, create, design, disposition, do, earn, effect, estimate, execute, fabricate, fashion, force, form, gain, induce, judge, manufacture, mould, name, nature, obtain, perform, procure, produce, product(ion), prompt, render, secure, shape, structure, transform, win
**make a bet** wager
**make a blunder** err
**make a booking** reserve
**make a cannon** carambole
**make a cardigan** knit
**make acceptable** validate
**make a choice between** opt
**make acknowledgement** confess
**make a coin** strike
**make a copy of** reproduce
**make acquaintance** meet
**make acquaintance of** befriend
**make a cross** vote
**make active** energise
**make a cut in** incise
**make a declaration against** protest
**make a design in relief** emboss
**make a determined demand** insist
**make a dirty mark on** smudge
**make a distinction** differentiate
**make a dull heavy sound** thud
**make advances** flirt
**make advances to** approach
**make a federal case of** exaggerate
**make a fool of** dupe, guy, hoodwink, insult, twit
**make a furrow** plough
**make again** re-create
**make a getaway** flee
**make a god of** deify
**make a grasping sound** rasp
**make a great effort** exert, strive
**make agreement** arrange
**make a hash of** botch, bungle, mishandle, mix, muddle
**make a hissing sound** sizzle
**make a hole** bore, excavate, pierce
**make a hooting cry** ululate
**make a horsy noise** snort
**make a humming sound** drone
**make a jersey** knit
**make a journey** tour, travel
**make a lady of** ladify, ladyfy
**make a law** enact, legislate
**make a list of** itemise
**make allowance for** consider
**make allusion** refer
**make a loan** lend
**make amends** apologise, appease, atone, compensate, expiate, recompense, recoup, redeem, reimburse, repay
**make amends for** atone, expiate
**make a mess of** botch, bungle, mix
**make a mistake** slip up
**make a movie** film
**make a muck of** bungle, muff, ruin
**make an addition to** add
**make an appearance** arrive, come

**make an attack on** assault
**make an attempt** bid, endeavour
**make an earnest appeal** plead
**make an effort** attempt, essay, exert
**make an entreaty** beg, implore, plead, pray, sue
**make a nest** nidificate, nidify
**make angry** enrage, incense, rile, vex
**make an offer** bid
**make a noise** clamour
**make a notch in** nick
**make answer** respond
**make anxious** rattle
**make a phone call** dial, phone
**make a picture of** portray
**make a plaintive cry** whine
**make a play** chase, court, pursue, serenade, woo
**make a plundering raid** maraud
**make a pot of tea** brew
**make appeals to** solicit
**make a prisoner of** capture
**make a quick grab** snatch
**make a recording** tape
**make a replica of** duplicate
**make a request** solicit
**make artificial** sophisticate
**make, as a profit** realise
**make a serious mistake** blunder
**make ashamed** abash
**make a sharp abrupt sound** clap
**make a short high-pitched sound** squeak
**make a show of** overact
**make as if** affect, feign, feint, pretend
**make a smile** amuse
**make a solemn declaration** testify
**make a sound of distress** moan
**make a speech** orate
**make a squeaking sound** creak
**make a stab at** attempt, endeavour, essay
**make a stand** insist
**make a start** approach
**make a statement** say
**make a statement of money** account
**make a statute** enact
**make as though** affect, feign, pretend, seem
**make a summoning sign** beckon
**make a sweater** knit
**make a tour of inspection** look over
**make a violent attack** assault
**make a voyage** sail
**make a wailing feline noise** caterwaul
**make aware of** acquaint
**make away** abscond, depart, flee, scoot
**make away with** destroy, finger, kill, murder, palm, pilfer, purloin, rob, slaughter, slay, squander, steal, swipe
**make bad use of** abuse, misuse

**make barren** sterilise
**make beautiful** embellish
**make beer or tea** brew
**make believe** assume, charade, dream, enact, envision, fantasy, imagination, imagine, invent, play(-acting), pretence, pretend, role-play, suppose, unreality
**make-believe purpose** pretence
**make beloved** enamour, endear
**make best of** exploit
**make best use of** eke, optimise
**make better** ameliorate, amend, improve, reform
**make bid** offer
**make big effort in game** play-up
**make bigger** enlarge
**make bitter** acerbate, embitter
**make book** bet, gamble, stake, wager
**make both ends meet** economise, endure, survive
**make braver** embolden
**make bright** illuminate, irradiate, lighten
**make bright by rubbing** burnish
**make brighter** brighten
**make broader** widen
**make brown** tan
**make bubbly** aerate
**make by hand** craft
**make by placing parts together** construct
**make cakes** bake
**make callous** indurate
**make calm** appease, pacify
**make capable** capacitate
**make ceremonially clean** purify
**make certain** ascertain, ensure, insure
**make changes** alter
**make charge repeatedly** iterate
**make chemically active** activate
**make choice** decide, opt
**make clear** clarify, elucidate, explain, illustrate
**make clear by examples** illustrate
**make clearer** clarify
**make cloth on a loom** weave
**make coins** mint
**make cold(er)** chill, refrigerate
**make comfortable** ease
**make competent** qualify
**make conflicting statements** equivocate, tergiversate
**make conform** adjust
**make confused** addle, bemuse
**make contact** meet
**make content** satisfy
**make cool** refrigerate
**make corrections** amend
**make counter-attack** react, retaliate
**make curious** intrigue
**make current** update
**make deep research** delve

**make deletions or changes in** censor, edit
**make designs on metal** etch
**make diary entry** log
**make different** alter, change, commute, dissimilate, vary
**make dirty** befoul, smirch , soil
**make do** cope, eke, endear, improvise, manage
**make dots** stipple
**make dough** knead
**make dove calls** coo
**make drunk** intoxicate
**make dry** parch
**make earnest request** appeal
**make easier** alleviate
**make easier to understand** clarify
**make easy** facilitate
**make effervescent** aerate
**make equal** even, square
**make evasive statements** prevaricate, tergiversate
**make even** level
**make evident** evince
**make excessive demands on** overtax
**make excessive profits** profiteer
**make explosive sound** sneeze
**make eyes at** ogle
**make famous** celebrate
**make fast** belay, fix, latch, secure
**make faulty** vitiate
**make favourable impact** impress
**make feeble** emaciate
**make feline sounds** purr
**make firm** fix
**make fizzy** aerate, carbonate
**make flat** level
**make for** advance, approach, assault, charge, ensure, facilitate, forward, further, near, promote, raid
**make formal request** apply
**make formal statement of** certify
**make foul** pollute
**make free** rid, affranchise
**make fresh ascent** remount
**make fruitful** fecundate
**make full** fill
**make fun of** banter, burlesque, deride, disparage, fleer, jeer, lampoon, mock, parody, quiz, rag, rib, ridicule, taunt, tease
**make furious** enrage, infuriate
**make furrows in** plough
**make furtive enquiries** pry
**make game of** deride, gibe, jeer, lampoon, parody, rag, ridicule, satirise, taunt
**make generally available** release
**make generally known** advertise, publish
**make gentle** tame
**make gloomy** darken, deject

**make glorious** glorify
**make good** accomplish, correct, expiate, prosper, recompense, recoup, rectify, remunerate, renew, repay, succeed
**make great contribution** redound
**make great demands** exacting
**make greater** aggrandise, increase, magnify
**make great progress** steam
**make guesses** speculate
**make happy** beatify, bless, brighten, cheer, elate, gladden
**make haste** hasten, hurry, speed
**make hazy** blur
**make headway** advance, develop, forge, gain, go, proceed, progress, roll
**make heavy demands on** tax
**make hermetic** seal
**make higher offer** outbid
**make hole in** dibble, perforate
**make hollow** dish
**make holy** hallow, sanctify
**make hot again** reheat
**make hot and very dry** parch
**make humble** humiliate
**make humming sound** drone
**make illegal** ban, debar, deface, proscribe, veto
**make immovable** fix, rivet
**make immune** vastate
**make impact** impinge
**make impassable** obstruct
**make impervious** seal, stop
**make impossible** prevent, prohibit
**make impracticable** preclude
**make impure** adulterate
**make incursion** invade
**make indistinct** blur
**make inroads upon** consume
**make insane** derange
**make insensitive** deaden
**make into a law** enact
**make into an island** enisle
**make into a saint** canonise
**make into a statute** enact
**make into bundles** bale
**make into law** enact
**make invalid** vitiate
**make it** prosper, succeed, survive
**make it possible** enable
**make joyful** elate
**make knot** tie
**make knotted lace** tat
**make known** acquaint, advertise, advise, air, announce, blare, convey, disclose, divulge, impart, indicate, mention, notify, proclaim, publish, relate, reveal, signify, uncover
**make known by words** express
**make known in detail** explain

**make known publicly** announce
**make known to the public** promulgate
**make lace** tat
**make large quantities of articles for sale** manufacture
**make larger** augment, enlarge, expand, increase
**make last longer** protract
**make lawful** legalise
**make lean** emaciate
**make legal** legitimise
**make legally competent** capacitate
**make less** abate
**make less blameworthy** extenuate
**make less concentrated** dilute
**make less difficult** ease, facilitate, simplify
**make less glaring** subdue
**make less severe** mitigate
**make less wide** narrow
**make liable** subject
**make light** alleviate, ease
**make like crossword** compile
**make lines** rule
**make liquid turbid by stirring** roil
**make longer** elongate, extend, increase, lengthen, prolong, protract, stretch
**make lovable** endear
**make love to** court, smooch, vry, woo
**make love with** spoon
**make loving sounds** coo
**make lucid** elucidate, illuminate
**make meaningless marks with a pen** scribble
**make menace** threaten
**make mention of** refer
**make merry** banquet, caper, carouse, celebrate, frisk, frolic, gambol, revel, romp
**make minor alterations** amend
**make mistake** err
**make money** earn, gain, mint, profit, succeed
**make morally bad** deprave
**make more bearable** ease
**make more easily borne** mitigate
**make more extreme or intense** heighten
**make more lively** enliven
**make more modern** update
**make more tight** tighten
**make much ado about nothing** overreact
**make much of** cajole, cherish, embroider, exaggerate, indulge, magnify, overstate, stress
**make narrow** constrict
**make neat** trim
**make new** renovate
**make noble** exalt
**make notes upon** annotate

**make obeisance** bow, curts(e)y, kneel, stoop
**make observations** annotate
**make occur at same time** synchronise
**make of** construe, explain, interpret
**make off** abscond, bolt, decamp, depart, flee, fly, leave
**make offer** bid
**make official entry** endorse, indorse
**make off quickly** absquatulate, scoot, scram
**make off secretly** abscond, decamp, elope
**make off with** abduct, appropriate, filch, pilfer, pinch, rob, steal
**make off with celerity** scoot
**make of rattan** cane
**make one** unify
**make one's flesh creep** frighten, horrify, repel, repulse, revolt, scare, terrify
**make one's hackles rise** afraid, anger, annoy
**make one's hair stand on end** frighten
**make one sick** appal, nauseate, repel, revolt, sicken
**make one's mark** prosper, succeed
**make one's own** adopt
**make one's own decisions** self-determined
**make one's way** advance, proceed, progress
**make one's way by jostling** elbow
**make one's way to** proceed
**make orderly** tidy
**make out** assert, claim, complete, decipher, demonstrate, describe, descry, detect, discern, discover, distinguish, espy, fare, fathom, follow, grasp, identify, imply, infer, maintain, manage, note, perceive, progress, prove, read, realise, recognise, see, succeed, understand
**make out of nothing** create
**make out scantily** eke
**make over** alter, ameliorate, amend, assign, cede, improve, polish, rectify, redecorate, redo, rehash, transfer
**make pale** blanch
**make pale by shutting out light** etiolate
**make parallel** align
**make partial changes** modify
**make part of** among
**make pastries** bake
**make peace** appease, intercede
**make physically clean** purge
**make plundering raid** maraud
**make plywood** veneer
**make points** score
**make poisonous** envenom

**make possible** certify, enable, equip, strengthen, validate
**make powerless by look** fascinate
**make preparation** provide
**make present of** donate
**make pretty** adorn
**make prisoner** arrest, capture
**make progress** improve, recover, recuperate
**make prominent** accentuate
**make prostrate** lay
**make public** air, blazon, break, proclaim
**make pus** fester
**make quips** gag
**maker** author, builder, constructor, creator, fabricator, framer, manufacturer, producer
**maker and mender of locks** locksmith
**make ready** prepare
**make reasoned protest** expostulate
**make remarks** comment
**make reparation for** atone, redress
**make resentful** embitter
**make reservations** book
**make resolute** steel
**make restitution** compensate
**make right** correct
**maker of alcoholic liquor** distiller
**maker of arms** armourer
**maker of arrows** fletcher
**maker of artificial eyes** ocularist
**maker of a speech** orator
**maker of a will** testator
**maker of barrels** cooper
**maker of beer** brewer
**maker of candles** chandler
**maker of carts** cartwright
**maker of earthenware** potter
**maker of medals** medallist
**maker of saddles** saddler
**maker of tallow** chandler
**maker of wagons** wainwright
**maker of white leather** tawer
**maker of yarn** spinner
**make safe** assure
**make self-conscious** embarrass
**make sense** coherent
**make sense of** fathom
**make short** abbreviate
**make short flights** flit
**make shrill howl of cat** caterwaul
**make silly mistake** boob
**make slanting** splay
**make slightly acid** acidulate
**make slower** decelerate
**make small** belittle
**make small changes in** modify
**make smaller by cutting** razee
**make small hole in** prick
**makes men's clothes** tailor
**make smooth** even

**make smooth and glossy** polish
**make sniffing sounds** snuffle
**make snorelike sounds** stertorous
**make soft** pad
**make someone laugh** amuse
**make somewhat acid** acidulate
**make sound of disbelief** snort
**make soundproof** deaden
**make soundtrack for** dub
**make sour** acerbate
**make speech** orate
**make speed slowly** festina lente (L)
**make steady** stabilise
**make stronger** strengthen
**make subdued continuous sound** murmur
**make suitable** adapt, adjust, prepare
**make superficial incisions** scarify
**make supple** massage, rub
**make sure of the trick** ruse
**makes your eyes water** onion
**make taut** strain, stretch
**make tense** tauten
**make test** experiment
**make the acquaintance of** meet
**make the best of** manage, tolerate
**make the first attack** aggressive
**make the grade** accomplish, achieve, pass, qualify, succeed
**make the most of** optimise
**make theories** guess, speculate
**make the rounds** patrol
**make the scene** participate
**make thin** attenuate
**make things go smooth** oil
**make thinner** dilute, weaken
**make thoroughly clean** cleanse
**make thoroughly wet** soak
**make tidy** clear, groom, preen
**make to know** acquaint
**make to laugh** amuse
**make too small or short** scrimp
**make to smile** amuse
**make tracks** depart, disappear
**make trial of** test
**make trouble** stir
**make turbid** perturb, rile, roil
**make typographical errors** misprint
**make ugly** uglify
**make unable to see** blind
**make undying** immortalise
**make uneasy** perturb
**make unfriendly** alienate, estrange
**make unhappy** sadden
**make uniform** standardise
**make unintelligible** obscure
**make untidy** mess, muss, rumple
**make up** arrange, collect, complete, compose, comprise, concoct, constitute, construct, create, devise, fabricate, fill, form(ulate), invent,

meet, originate, prepare, repair, supplement, supply
**make-up** arrangement, assembly, character, composition, configuration, constitution, construction, cosmetics, figure, form(at), formation, nature, organisation, paint, powder, structure, style, titivate
**make up for** atone, balance, redeem, redress
**make-up for eye lashes** mascara
**make up of mixed ingredients** concoct
**make up one's mind** choose, conclude, decide, determine, resolve, select, settle
**make up to** court, flatter, woo
**make-up worn on the face** base, blusher, eye shadow, foundation, lipstick, rouge
**make used to** accustom, habituate
**make useless** destroy
**make use of** avail, employ, utilise
**make visual search** look
**make void** abrogate, annul, quash
**make warm** heat
**make way through** filter
**make weaker** attenuate, dilute
**make wealthy** endow, enrich, improve, upgrade
**make weary** fag, tire
**make well** heal
**make whistlestop tour** barnstorm
**make white** bleach
**make with the hands** fists
**make worse** aggravate
**make young again** rejuvenate
**making projection for mortise** tenoning
**maladjusted person** misfit
**maladroit** awkward, clumsy, coarse, crude, gauche, graceless, incompetent, inefficient, inelegant, inept, inexpert, inhabile (F), loutish, oafish, rough, rude, rustic, tactless, unfit, ungraceful, unskilful, unsuited
**malady** ache, ailment, derangement, disability, disease, disorder, distemper, feebleness, fever, hurt, illness, indisposition, infection, insanity, madness, malaise, pain, sickness, weakness
**malaria** ague, delirium. disease, illness, sickness
**malaria fever, with cold, hot and sweating stages** ague
**malarial** paludal
**malarial fever** ague
**malaria parasite causing tertian fever** vivax

**malarkey** baloney, blather, bunkum, drivel, flummery, foolishness, humbug, nonsense, (tommy)rot
**Malayan boat** prau, proa
**Malayan dagger** crease, creese, kris
**Malayan garment** sarong
**Malayan gaur** seladang
**Malayan gibbon** siamang
**Malayan island** Bali, Borneo, Java, Sumatra, Timor
**Malayan knife** crease, creese, kris
**Malayan royal palace** istana
**Malayan small pill-like sweetmeat** cachou
**Malayan tree** terap
**Malayan wild buffalo** gaur, seladang
**malcontent** concerned, contrary, discontent, disgruntled, dissatisfied, factious, gloomy, perverse, rebellious, unhappy, unquiet
**mal de mer (F)** seasickness
**male** bachelor, beau, bloke, boy, chap, esquire, fellow, gentleman, guy, he, him, man(like), manly, mannish, masculine, oke, ou, parent, paternal, staminate, unfeminine, unwomanly, virile
**male address** mister, sir
**male animal** bull, ram
**male announcer** compere
**male ant** aner
**male ass** jackass
**male attendant** squire
**male badger** boar
**male bee** drone
**male bird** cock
**male cat** tom
**male chicken** rooster
**male child** boy, lad, outjie, son, umfaan
**male deer** hart, roebuck, stag
**male deer in fourth year** sore, staggard
**male deer in second year** pricket
**male descendant** son
**male domestic fowl** cock, rooster
**male donkey** dicky, jack(ass)
**male duck** drake
**male elephant** bull
**malefaction** breach, crime, felony, horror, infringement, offence, outrage, transgression, trespass, violation, wrong(doing)
**malefactor** criminal, evil-doer
**male falcon** t(i)ercel
**male family member** cousin, father, nephew, son, uncle
**male feline** tom-cat
**male ferret** hob(b)
**malefic** baleful, harmful
**maleficent** antagonistic, atrocious, debased, deleterious, depraved, destructive, evil, foul, harmful,
hostile, hurtful, inhuman, injurious, malevolent, malign, (ob)noxious, perilous, pernicious, poisonous, toxic, unfriendly
**male fish-eggs** milt
**male foal** colt
**male fox** dog
**male friend** ami (F)
**male goat** billy(-goat), buck, ram
**male goose** gander
**male gypsy** rom
**male hare** buck, jack
**male hawk** jack, tassel, t(i)ercel
**male heir** son
**male Hindu garment** dho(o)ti, dhootie, dhuti
**male hog** boar
**male honeybee** drone
**male horse** colt, gelding, stallion, steed, stud
**male hospital attendant** orderly
**male issue** son
**male kangaroo** boomer, buck
**male lobster** cock
**male lover** inamorato
**male monarch** king
**male mouser** tom
**male neckwear item** cravat, tie
**male noble** lord
**male offspring** son
**male organ of flower** stamen
**male otter** dog
**male parent** father, sire
**male part of flower** stamen
**male peafowl** peacock
**male person** he
**male pig** boar, hog
**male polecat** hob(b)
**male professional singer** cantatore
**male progeny** son
**male pronoun** he
**male rabbit** buck
**male red deer** hart, stag
**male relative** brother, father, nephew, uncle
**male rhinoceros** bull
**male royal** prince
**male salmon** buck, cock, gib
**male salmon in spawning season** kipper
**male seal** bull
**male servant** manservant, valet
**male sheep** ram, tup
**male sibling** brother
**male singing voice** alto, baritone, bass(o), tenor
**male sovereign** emperor, king
**male specie** man
**male stage performer** actor
**male statue used as a column** atlas, telamon
**male swan** cob
**male swine** boar
**male teacher** master
**male title** mister, sir
**male turkey** tom
**male vocalist** tenor
**male voice** alto, baritone, bass(o), tenor
**malevolent** baleful, begrudging, evil(-minded), hateful, hostile, malicious, malign(ant), rancorous, resentful, spiteful
**malevolent fairy** goblin
**malevolent ghost** duppy
**malevolent person** snake
**malevolent spirit** ghoul
**male walrus** bull
**male whale** bull
**male wild duck** mallard
**male witch** warlock
**male wolf** dog, he-wolf
**male zebra** stallion
**malformation** abortion, asymmetry, deformity, disfigurement, distortion, eyesore, imperfection, monstrosity, ugliness
**malformation of body or limb** deformity
**malformed animal** teratism
**malformed diamond** bo(a)rt
**malice** anger, animosity, animus, bitterness, enmity, envy, grudge, hate, hatred, hostility, ill will, ire, malevolence, malignity, meanness, pique, rancour, resentment, revenge, spite(fulness), venom, wrath
**malicious** abusive, baleful, bitter, catty, defamatory, false, hateful, ill-natured, injurious, malevolent, malign(ant), nasty, pernicious, rancorous, resentful, slanderous, snide, spiteful, untrue, vengeful, vicious, wanton
**malicious burning** arson
**malicious chatter** gossip, skinder(y)
**malicious destruction** sabotage
**malicious fabrication** smear
**malicious female** bitch, skinderbek
**malicious gossip** scandal, skinder(y)
**maliciousness** balefulness, bitterness, injuriousness, rancorousness, resentfulness, spite(fulness), vengefulness, viciousness
**malicious person** shrew
**malicious publication** libel
**malicious remark** aspersion
**malicious report** slander
**malicious satire** lampoon
**malicious setting on fire** arson
**malicious talk** scandal, skinder(y)
**malign** abuse, bad, baleful, baneful, calumniate, defame, denigrate, disparage, evil, harm(ful), hostile,

**malignant** hurtful, injure, injurious, libel, malevolent, pernicious, revile, slander, smear, traduce, vicious, vilify, wicked
**malignant** dangerous, deadly, evil, fatal, harmful, hurtful, lethal, malevolent, malicious, perilous, virulent
**malignant cancer** carcinoma, melanoma
**malignant disease in cattle** anthrax
**malignant growth** cancer
**malignant hate** rancour
**malignant tumour** sarcoma
**malignant tumour of epithelial tissue** epithelioma
**maligner** asperser, caviller, censor, critic, defamer, denigrator, denouncer, derogator, detractor, impugner, liar, libeller, reprover, satirist, slanderer, traducer, vilifier
**malignity** acrimony, anger, animosity, bitterness, enmity, ferocity, frenzy, fury, grudge, hate, hatred, hostility, ire, malevolence, malignancy, rage, rancour, spite, venom, violence, wrath
**malinger** abandon, avoid, default, duck, evade, fail, loaf, neglect, procrastinate, shirk, slack
**malison** curse
**Mali town** Bamba, Gao, Kati, Kayes, Mopti, Nara, Niono, Nioro, San, Segou, Sikasso
**malleable** adaptable, adjustable, docile, domesticable, ductile, educable, extensile, fictile, governable, impressionable, lissom(e), mobile, movable, pliable, sensitive, suasible, tractable, tractile, yielding
**malleable metal** tin
**malleable metallic element** aluminium
**mallee fowl** lowan
**mallet** beetle, club, gavel, hammer, pounder, rammer, stick, tamper, tapper
**malnutrition** boniness, emaciation, enfeeblement, exhaustion, gauntness, haggardness, prostration, scrawniness, starvation, undernourishment
**malodorous** disagreeable, fetid, foul, fusty, mouldy, musty, nauseating, noisome, odorous, putrid, rancid, rank, reeking, reeky, rotten, sickening, smelly, stenchful, stinking, stuffy, unfresh, unpleasant
**malted beverage** ale, beer
**malt extract** wort
**malt liquor** ale, beer

**maltreat** abuse, afflict, aggrieve, damage, disrespect, harm, hurt, ill-treat, injure, manhandle, maul, mishandle, mistreat, misuse, torture, wrong
**malt vinegar** alegar
**malvaceous treelike plant** tree mallow
**mama's mate** papa
**mamilla** nipple, teat
**mamma** breast, ma(m), mama, mom, mother
**mammal** animal, ass, bat, bison, cat, cow, dog, dugong, elephant, horse, manatee, mink, mole, monotreme, moose, otter, ox, pig, racoon, reindeer, rhinoceros, seacow, seal, walrus, whale, yak
**mammal of Madagascar** lemur
**mammal of Peru** alpaca
**mammalogy** therology
**mammal with a pouch** kangaroo, wombat
**mammal with laughing cry** hyena
**mammal with tawny fur** hare
**mammary gland** udder
**mammon** avarice, greed
**mammoth** dinothere, enormous, gigantic, huge, immense, mastodon, monstrous, monumental
**man** chap, guy, humanity, male, mankind, oke, ou, people, person
**man about town** beau, Casanova, dandy, debauchee, fop, playboy, rake, roué, socialite, womaniser
**manacle** bind, bond, chain, check, curb, fetter, hamper, hamstring, handcuff, inhibit, iron, restrain, shackle, tie
**manage** accomplish, administer, arrange, contrive, control, cope, direct, dominant, handle, manipulate, rule, run, steward, succeed, superintend, supervise
**manageable** amenable, compliant, conductible, contrivable, controllable, convenient, directable, docile, easy, governable, handy, manipulable, operable, pliable, submissive, tameable, tractable, wieldy
**manage affairs** conduct
**manage awkwardly** botch, bungle
**manage badly** maladminister
**manage craftily** manipulate
**managed to do** did
**manage in a skilful way** wangle
**management** accomplishment, address, administration, adroitness, arrangement, board, bosses, capability, care, charge, command(ment), conduct, control, deftness, direction, directorate, directors, employers, executives, government, guidance, leadership, oversight, regulation, skill, superintendence, supervision, surveillance, treatment
**management of a business** admin(istration)
**management of affairs** husbandry
**management of land** agronomy
**management of money** finance
**manage on one's income** make ends meet
**manager** administrator, agent, boss, chief, controller, director, executive, governor, helmsman, intendant, leader, master, overseer, pilot, steward, superintendent, supervisor, treasurer
**manager of another's estate** trustee
**manager of farm** farmer
**manage thriftily** economise, husband
**man appointed to kill bull in bullfight** matador
**man armed with halberd** halberdier
**man as an epitome of the universe** microcosm(os)
**manchester goods** linen
**Manchurian seaport** Ilan
**mandarin** bureaucrat, na(a)rtjie, tangerine
**mandate** act, behest, charge, colony, command, commission, decree, dependency, dictate, edict, fiat, injunction, instruction, order, ordinance, protectorate, province, requirement, requisite, ruling, state, statute, ukase, ultimatum, warrant, writ
**mandatory** binding, compelled, compulsory, demanded, essential, exigent, imperative, necessary, obligatory, preceptive, required, requisite, urgent
**man devoted to expensive dissipation** playboy
**mandible** jaw(bone)
**mandolin-like Greek folk instrument** bouzouki
**mandrel** spindle
**mandrill** ape, baboon
**man-eater** anthropophagite, cannibal, ghoul, lion, monster, ogre(ss), shark, tiger, vampire
**man-eating monster** ogre
**manège** horsemanship
**man employed to carry luggage** door-keeper, porter
**man from Copenhagen** Dane
**man from Finland** Finn
**man from Stockholm** Swede
**manger** box, crèche, crib, hutch, rack, stall, tray, trough

**mangle** destroy, disfigure, lacerate, maim, mar, maul, mutilate, ruin
**mangy** abject, base, contemptible, deteriorated, dilapidated, dire, dirty, diseased, disgraceful, disreputable, hateful, ignominious, itchy, mean, miserable, odious, poor, scabby, scaly, scruffy, seedy, shabby, sorry, squalid, tatty, wretched
**manhandle** abuse, batter, beat, bully, carry, haul, heave, hector, hit, hump, maltreat, maul, mistreat, misuse, pelt, pommel, pull, pummel, push, shove, slap, smack, strike, thrash, trounce, tug
**man-hater** anchorite, ascetic, cynic, eremite, hermit, misanthrope, misanthropist, monk, recluse, solitary
**Manhattan skyline features** towers
**manhole** hatch(way), hole, opening, scuttle
**manhood** bravery, courage, firmness, masculinity, maturity, mettle, resolution, spirit, strength, valour, virility
**mania** craze, craziness, delirium, derangement, disorder, fad, frenzy, infatuation, insanity, lunacy, madness, rage
**maniac** ass, cuckoo, enthusiast, fanatic, loony, lunatic, madman, monomania, nitwit, nutcase, phrenetic, psychopath, simpleton, zealot
**maniacal** bizarre, beneek, beneuk(s), crazy, demented, deranged, infatuated, insane, lunatic, mad, maniac, non compos mentis (L), odd, peculiar, psychotic, queer, unbalanced, unsafe
**mania for cleanness** mysophobia
**mania for dancing** tarantism
**mania for work** ergomania
**manic** agitated, excited, frantic, frenzied, hyperactive, hysterical, perturbed
**manifest** apparent, clear, conspicuous, declare, demonstrate, disclose, distinct, evident, evince, glaring, noticeable, obvious, open, palpable, patent, plain, reveal, unmistakable, visible
**manifestation** disclosure, display, exhibition, exposure, instance, mark, materialisation, revelation, show, sign, symptom, token
**manifestation of Christ to the Magi** epiphany
**manifest repugnance against** rebel
**manifold** multifaceted, multifarious, multiple, multiply, multitudinous, numerous, varied, various

**manifold variety** multiplicity
**Manila Bay island** Corregidor
**Manila hemp** abaca
**man in armed forces** serviceman, troopie
**man in charge of workers** foreman
**man in drag** transvestite
**manioc** cassava, manioca
**manipulate** control, direct, employ, guide, handle, influence, manoeuvre, negotiate, operate, ply, rig, steer, use, wangle, wield, work
**manipulate in a fraudulent way** rig
**manipulate to one's advantage** gerrymander
**manipulator of a hoe** hoer
**mankind** civilisation, flesh, folks, humanity, humankind, man, menfolk, people, proletariat, society
**manlike woman** virago
**manly** bold, brave, courageous, male, manful, masculine, undaunted, valiant, virile
**man-made** artificial, manufactured, synthetic
**man-made element** fermium
**man-made fibre** rayon, nylon
**man-made human-like creature of Jewish legend** golem
**man-made stone implement** artefact, artifact
**man-made waterway** canal
**man-made yarn** nylon
**manned carriage** ricksha(w)
**mannequin** dummy, manikin, model
**manner** appearance, aspect, bearing, behaviour, carriage, character, custom, demeanour, habit, kind, look, method, mien, mode, sort, style, way
**mannerism** affection, air, artifice, characteristic, earmark, fashion, formality, habit, idiosyncrasy, individualism, kink, manneredness, mark, overelegance, overnicety, pose, pretence, quirk, stamp, stiffness, tic, trademark, trick, unnaturalness, way
**manner of acting** mode
**manner of doing things** style
**manner of dress** vogue
**manner of expression** diction, phraseology
**manner of forward motion of horse** gait
**manner of speaking** accent, façon de parler (F)
**manner of speech peculiar to a district** accent
**manner of thinking** thought
**manner of treating** usage
**manner of walking** gait

**manner of weaving** texture
**manner of writing** style
**mannish woman** butch
**manoeuvre** action, dodge, intrigue, machination, manipulate, ploy, stratagem, subterfuge, tactic, trick
**man of authority and great wealth** aga
**man of courage** hero
**man of great strength and agility** Tarzan
**man of great wisdom** sage
**man of honour** galant homme (F)
**man of learning** sage
**man of means** billionaire, capitalist, mammonist, millionaire, moneybags, nabob, plutocrat
**man of superhuman achievement** superman
**man of the church** bishop, clergyman, deacon, dean, dominee, priest
**man of the hour** hero
**man of the road** tramp
**man of the sea** sailor
**man of valour** hero
**man of wealth** nabob
**man of wit** bel esprit (F)
**man on his wedding day** (bride)groom
**manor** abode, area, barony, court, domain, dwelling, estate, habitation, hall, holdings, lands, mansion, palace, property, residence, seat, villa
**man or ape** primate
**manor grounds** demesne
**man paid by a woman for his attentions** gigolo
**man powerful from wealth** plutocrat
**man proposes and God disposes** l'homme propose et Dieu dispose (F)
**man's broad tie** ascot
**man sent out to reconnoitre** scout
**manservant** attendant, butler, factotum, footman, garçon, gillie (Sc), lackey, squire, steward, valet
**manservant in livery** flunk(e)y
**man's felt hat** trilby
**man's figure as a pillar** telamon
**man's formal evening wear** tuxedo
**man's garment** jacket, shirt, trouser(s), underpants, vest
**man's hat** bowler, fez, sombrero, trilby
**mansion** chateau, estate, manor, manse, palace, palazzo (I), villa
**man's lowest voice** bass
**man's neck-scarf** cravat
**man's personal attendant** valet
**man's pocket-book** wallet
**man's pointed beard** goatee
**man's servant** valet
**man's shoe with a very pointed toe** winkle-picker
**man's sleeveless vest** singlet

**man's small light knotted scarf** ascot, cravat
**man's stiff white kilt worn in Albania and Greece** fustanella
**man's suit part** jacket, vest
**man's tunic** kirtle
**man's undershirt** singlet
**man's wig** toupee
**manta ray** devil-fish
**mantle** awning, blanket, blind, canopy, cape, carpet, cloak, cloud, coat(ing), conceal(ment), cover(ing), curtain, dim, disguise, envelope, film, front, guard, hedge, hide, hood, layer, mask, obscure, pretext, screen, shade, shawl, sheet, shelter, shield, shroud, veil, wrap(per), wrapping
**man to look up to** hero
**manual** companion, enchiridion, guide(book), hand-operated, handbook, human, instructions, non-automatic, physical, primer, textbook, vade-mecum
**manual digit** finger, thumb
**manual skill** (handi)craft
**manual training system** sloid, sloyd
**manual worker** hand, labourer
**manual workplace** workshop
**manufacture** assemble, assembly, build, compose, concoct, construct(ion), contrive, create, creation, develop, devise, fabricate, fabrication, facture, forge, form(ation), frame, hatch, invent, make, (mass-)produce, (mass-)production, shape
**manufactured goods** products
**manufacture from raw materials** produce
**manufacturer** builder, constructor, creator, fabricator, factory-owner, industrialist, maker, producer
**manufacture's union** cartel
**manufacturing plant** factory
**manumission** delivery, discharge, emancipation, enfranchising, freeing, liberating, liberation, loosing, manumitting, redemption, release, rescue, unbinding, untying
**manumit** affranchise, deliver, discharge, dismiss, emancipate, free, liberate, ransom, redeem, rescue, unmanacle, unshackle
**man unduly devoted to smartness** dandy, pantsula
**manure** compost, dressing, dung, excrement, excreta, fertilizer, guano, marl, muck, ordure, organic, sleech, stools, worthing
**manuscript** deed, documemt, handwriting, parchment, scroll, text, vellum

**manuscript volume** codex
**man who acts as midwife** accoucheur (F)
**man who attends to horses at inns** (h)ostler
**man who lives off prostitute's earnings** pimp, ponce
**man who pays excessive attention to dress** dandy, fop, pantsula
**man who repairs steeples** steeplejack
**man who serves at a table** waiter
**man who tends sheep** shepherd
**man who unloads ships** stevedore
**man who washes clothes** dhobi
**man with the white feather** coward, niddering, poltroon, underling
**many** abundant, copious, countless, frequent, innumerable, lots, manifold, myriad, numerous, profuse, several, sundry, varied, various
**many and various** manifold, multifarious
**many a time** commonly, frequently, often, regularly, routinely
**many children of one parent** quiverful
**many colours** polychromatic, polychrome
**many happy returns** congratulate, felicitate
**many-headed mythological monster** Hydra
**many-legged creature** centipede, millipede, songololo
**many millions** billion, trillion, zillion
**many-sided figure** polygon
**many times** oft, often
**many times over** repeatedly
**Maori alcoholic drink** wairepo
**Maori amulet** tiki
**Maori camp** pa(h)
**Maori canoe** waka
**Maori ceremonial war dance** haka
**Maori demon** Atua, Taipo
**Maori food** kai
**Maori fort** pa
**Maori funeral** tangi
**Maori greenstone charm** tiki
**Maori hut** whare
**Maori mat or cloak** pake
**Maori skirt** piupiu
**Maori talisman** tiki
**Maori village** kaik, pa
**Maori war club** mere
**Maori weapon** patu
**Maori woman** wahine
**map** arrange, atlas, cartograph, chart, course, detail, diagram, graph, guidebook, itinerary, outline, plan, plot, projection, route, sketch, way
**map book** atlas
**map-drawing** cartography

**maple genus** acer
**map line** contour (line), isobar
**mapmaker** cartographer, topographer
**map of region** ichnography
**mapping** cartography
**mapping of regions** chorography
**map pressure line** isobar
**mar** damage, deface, deform, disfigure, harm, hurt, impair, injure, maim, mangle, mutilate, ruin, scar, spoil, tarnish, temper, wreck
**maraud** despoil, loot, pillage, plunder, raid, ransack, ravage
**marauder** attacker, bandit, brigand, corsair, crook, desperado, forager, freebooter, gangster, gunman, highwayman, hijacker, invader, outlaw, pirate, plunderer, raider, robber, rover, thief, tsotsi
**marble** agate, Carrara, chalcedony, harsh, icy, limestone, quartz, rigid, steely, taw
**marble-like stone** alabaster
**marble of real alabaster** ally
**marble tomb** sarcophagus
**marble with green bands** cipolin
**march** advance, borderland, boundary, confines, demo(nstration), development, evolution, file, footslog, frontier, hike, marshland, pace, parade, passage, procession, progress, stalk, step, stride, tread, trek, walk
**march in a procession** parade
**march in front of** lead
**marching soldiers** infantry
**march on display** parade
**march on show** parade
**march plant** reed
**march stiffly** goose step
**Mardi Gras** carnival
**mare's nest** chaos, confusion, deception, delusion, disarray, fake, imitation, jumble, mess, mock, sham
**margarine container** tub
**margin** allowance, border, bound(ary), brim, brink, confine, edge, extra, latitude, leeway, limit, perimeter, periphery, play, rim, room, scope, side, skirt, space, surplus, verge
**marginal** bordering, borderline, coastal, minimal, negligible, peripheral, slight, small
**marginal explanation** footnote, gloss
**marginal note** annotation, (a)postil, gloss, scholium
**margin of a river** bank
**marijuana** bhang, cannabis, charas, dagga, dope, ganja, grass, hashish, hemp, kaif, ke(e)f, ki(e)f, pot
**marijuana cigarette** reefer, zol

**marinate** drench, dunk, immerse, pickle, soak, steep
**marine** fleet, nautical, naval, oceanic, sailor, sea(faring), seascape, shipping, soldier, tonnage
**marine animal** seal, walrus
**marine bird** auk, cormorant, penguin, (sea)gull
**marine borer** gribble, piddock, shipworm
**marine channel** strait
**marine creature** fish, shark, turtle, whale
**marine crustacean** barnacle, crab, crayfish, kreef, prawn
**marine decapod** crab, squid
**marine decapod crustacean** shrimp
**marine diving bird** auk, penguin
**marine duck** smew
**marine eel** conger, moray
**marine expanse** sea
**marine fish** bonito, hake, kingklip, sea-bass, snoek, tarpon
**marine fluctuation** tide
**marine fossil** trilobite
**marine gastropod** periwinkle, whelk
**marine gem** pearl
**marine growth** coral, sponge
**marine hazard** reef
**marine ice** (ice) floe
**marine mammal** dolphin, seal, whale
**marine map** chart
**marine painting** seascape
**marine plant** kelp, seaweed
**mariner** sailor, salt, seafarer, seaman
**marine railway** slipway
**marine reptile** seasnake, turtle
**marine shell** conch, cowrie, perlemoen
**marine snail** periwinkle
**marine surface organisms** plankton
**marine tortoise** turtle
**marine turtle** caret
**marine worm** sea mouse
**marionette** doll, dummy, fantoccio (I), puppet
**marionettes** fantoccini (I)
**marish** boggy, marshy, mire, swampy
**marital** conjugal, married, matrimonial, nuptial, spousal, wedded
**maritime** aquatic, coastal, estuarine, marine, nautical, naval, navigational, oceanic, sea(faring), seagoing, seamanly, tidal
**maritime province of the Netherlands** Zeeland
**mark** badge, blemish, blot, brand, characterise, characteristic, consequence, cut, destine, distinction, eminence, heed, importance, impression, imprint, indicate, indication, inscription, label, line, note, notice, object, observe, point, purpose, regard, scar, sign, spot, stain, stamp, symbol, tag, target, token, trace, trait
**mark as correct** tick
**mark as incorrect** cross
**mark a trail** blaze
**mark branded on slave** stigma
**mark cattle** brand
**mark down** book, decrease, depreciate, note, reduce, slash, undercut
**marked accent** brogue
**marked area for tennis** court
**marked by denial** negative
**marked by happiness** felicitous
**marked by intelligence** able
**marked by refinement** elegant
**marked by wavy lines** flamboyant
**marked dissimilarity** contrast
**marked in two different colours** piebald
**marked lack of cordiality** snub
**marked like a tiger** tigrine
**markedly eccentric** potty
**markedly neglect** slight
**marked ski run** piste
**marked with rings** annulate
**marker made of stones** cairn
**market** bazaar, Bourse, business, fair, hawk, marketplace, mart, merchandise, outlet, peddle, promote, retail, sell, shop, store, trade
**market for goods** outlet
**market in Venice** Rialto
**marketplace** agora, forum, mart
**marketplace entertainer** mountebank
**marketplace in Greece** agora
**marketplace in Muslim countries** souk, sug
**mark for insertion** caret
**mark indicating standard of gold** hallmark
**marking the end of the pilgrimage to Mecca** Eid-ul-Adha
**mark left by damage** scar
**mark left by foot on ground** step
**mark left from a wound** cicatrice, cicatrix, scar
**mark left on flesh by the blow of a whip** wale, weal
**mark of a pen** stroke
**mark of caste** purdah
**mark of disgrace** stigma
**mark off** delete
**mark off limit** demarcate
**mark of infamy** stigma
**mark of interrogation** query
**mark of omission** caret
**mark of social disgrace** stigma
**mark of the lash** stripe
**mark of the plough** furrow
**mark on quoits** hub
**mark on skin** birthmark, naevus, scar
**mark on wound dressing** bloodstain
**mark out** define, depict, outline, pace, portray, profile, represent, shape, sketch, trace
**mark out limits of** define
**mark placed over vowels** accent, diaeresis, umlaut
**marks a noun** a(n), the
**marksman** bersagliere, deadeye, marker, pluffer, rifleman, (sharp)shooter, shootist, shot(man), sniper
**mark the limits of** circumscribe
**mark the skin** tattoo
**mark to let stand** stet
**mark to shoot at** target
**mark track of** trace
**mark up** boost, double, escalate, increase, inflate, raise
**mark with branding iron** sear
**mark with small scars** pit
**mark with spots** dabble
**marlin** spearfish
**marmoreal** statuesque
**maroon** abandon, desert, enisle, forsake, isolate, leave, seclude, strand
**marquetry** (in)tarsia
**marriage** alliance, amalgamation, association, bridal, confederation, consolidation, coupling, link, match, matrimony, merger, nuptials, spousal, union, wedding, wedlock
**marriageable** adult, developed, full-grown, marriable, mature, nubile, ripe
**marriage after first spouse** digamy
**marriage at advanced age** opsigamy
**marriage below position** hypogamy
**marriage ceremony** matrimony, nuptials, wedding, wedlock
**marriage contract** affiance
**marriage gift** dowry, lobola
**marriage maker** developer, enterpriser, go-between, matchmaker, planner, promoter
**marriage notice** ban(n)s
**marriage of convenience** mariage de convenance (F)
**marriage offer** proposal
**marriage partner** mate
**marriage settlement** dowry, lobola, tocher
**marriage to person of equal class** hypergamy
**marriage vow** I do, pledge, troth
**marriage within group** endogamy
**marriage with one wife** monogyny
**married** bridal, conjugal, connubial, coupled, joined, marital, matched,

mated, matrimonial, nuptial, one, spousal, united, wed(ded), yoked
**married Italian woman** signora
**married Italian woman's lover** cicisbeo
**married man** husband
**married Spanish woman** senora
**married state** wedlock
**married woman** matron
**marrow** core, cream, essence, gist, heart, kernel, pith, quick, substance
**marrow of bone** medulla
**marry** affiance, affiliate, ally, associate, betroth, bond, couple, espouse, herd, hitch, join, link, match, mate, merge, partner, unify, unite, wed
**marry a second time** rewed
**marsh** bayou, bog, everglade, fen, mire, moor(land), morass, mud, quag(mire), quicksand, slobland, slough, slush, sullage, swamp(land), vlei, wallow, wetland
**marshal** align, arrange, array, assemble, collect, convoke, deploy, director, gather, gather, manager, order, rank, sheriff, supervisor
**marshal of Napoleon** Ney
**marsh bird** bittern, rail, snipe, sora, stilt
**marsh gas** methane
**marsh grass** reed, sedge
**marshland** fen, wetland
**marshland grass** reed
**marsh overflowed by sea** salting
**marsh plant** buckbean, bulrush, calla, cattail, fern, juncus, reed, rush, sedge
**marsh pool** plash
**marsh samphire** glasswort, saltwort
**marsh tree** alder
**marsh wading bird** snipe
**marshy area** mire, wetland
**marshy ground** bog, fen, morass, vlei
**marshy offshoot of river** bayou
**marshy pine forest** taiga
**marshy place** quag, slough, swale
**marshy region in USA** Everglades
**marshy river inlet** bayou
**marshy spot** quag
**marshy tract** bog, fen, quag(mire)
**Mars is one** planet
**marsupial** bandicoot, cuscus, kangaroo, koala, opossum, possum, wombat
**marsupial kangaroo-rat** potoroo
**mart** emporium, market(place)
**marten** fisher, martrix, sable, sobol
**martial** aggressive, antagonistic, belligerent, brave, combative, courageous, inimical, lionhearted, militant, military, pugnacious, truculent, valiant, warlike
**martial art** aikido, j(i)ujitsu, judo, jujutsu, karate, kung fu, savate, wu-su

**martinet** disciplinarian, drillmaster, stickler, taskmaster
**Martini garnish** olive
**Martini necessity** gin
**mart part** store
**martyr** afflict, distress, harass, hound, hunt, ill-treat, immolate, impale, injure, maltreat, molest, oppress, persecute, pursue, stone, torment, torture, victimise
**marvel** gape, gaze, genius, goggle, miracle, phenomenon, portent, prodigy, whiz(z), wonder
**marvellous** amazing, astonishing, astounding, breathtaking, excellent, extraordinary, fabulous, fantastic, improbable, incredible, sensational, smashing, surprising, wonderful, wondrous
**marvellous thing** prodigy, portent
**Marxism** Communism
**marzipan flavour** almond
**mascot** amulet, charm, periapt, talisman
**masculine** courageous, daring, dreadless, dynamic, hardy, he, iron-hearted, macho, male, manly, mannish, mighty, muscular, powerful, robust, sinewy, stalwart, strong, unafraid, vigorous, virile
**masculine woman** Amazon
**mash** beat, break, bruise, champ, compress, condense, crease, crumble, crumple, crunch, crush, distort, flatten, grind, hash, jam, mince, mixture, mush, paste, pound, press, pulp, pulverise, pummel, push, reduce, rumple, smash, squash, squeeze, stuff, wrinkle
**mash or pulp fruit or vegetables** purée
**masjid** mosque, musjid
**masjid's tower** minaret
**mask** conceal(ment), disguise, evasion, masquerade, pretence, pretext, revel, ruse, shroud, subterfuge, veil
**masked ball** masquerade
**ma's mate** pa
**mason** stoneworker
**masonic doorkeeper** tiler
**Masonic meeting place** lodge
**masonry** stonework
**masonry joint** joggle
**masonry of smooth, squared stones** ashlar
**Mason's branch** lodge
**mason's tool** trowel
**mason's work** masonry
**masquerade as** impersonate, mimic
**mass** aggregate, aggregation, amass, assemble, bunch, cluster,

collect(ion), combination, conglomeration, convoke, gather, general, heap, hoi polloi, magnitude, majority, massa (I), massiveness, pile, proletariat, public, quantity, widespread
**Massachusetts citizen** Bostonian
**massacre** annihilation, assassinate, bloodbath, bloodshed, butcher(y), carnage, decimate, decimation, destruction, eradicate, execution, exterminate, genocide, holocaust, killing, liquidate, murder, pogrom, slaughter, slay
**massage** acupressure, align, attrition, friction, handle, knead(ing), manipulate, manipulation, palming, palpate, palpation, reflexology, rub(-down), rubbing, shiatsu (J), stimulate, stroke, tough
**mass book** missal
**mass departure** exodus
**Mass for the dead** Requiem
**massive** bulky, colossal, enormous, extensive, gigantic, huge, immense, leviathan, mammoth, monster, vast, weighty
**massive boxer** heavyweight
**massive breakwater** mole
**mass meeting** rally
**mass murder** butchery, carnage, decimation, genocide, holocaust
**mass of bubbles** foam
**mass of burning fuel** fire
**mass of bushes** shag
**mass of cast metal** ingot
**mass of coal** jud
**mass of different things put together** conglomeration
**mass of dislodged snow** avalanche
**mass of eggs in a female fish's ovary** bevy
**mass of eggs in fish** roe
**mass of floating ice** (ice)berg
**mass of floating water-plants** sudd
**mass of hair** mop, shock
**mass of ice** floe, glacier
**mass of lava** clinker
**mass of material** heap
**mass of metal** ingot
**mass of minerals formed into one rock** aggregate
**mass of molten glass** parison
**mass of particles in soil** aggregate
**mass of rock** massif
**mass of salt water** sea
**mass of slag or lava** clinker
**mass of snow and ice** avalanche
**mass of snow-ice** névé
**mass of spectators** crowd
**mass of trees and shrubs** boscage, boskage, thicket

**mass of water** sea
**mass protest** demo(nstration)
**mast** flag-pole, spar
**master** ace, adept, baas, boss, bwana, captain, cardinal, chief, commander, defeat, dominating, employer, expert, govern, head, main, overcome, overpower, oversee, predominant, prime, principal, rule, skilful, skilled, subjugate
**masterful** domineering
**master hand** expert
**master key** pass key, passe-partout
**masterly** adept, adroit, clever, excellent, exquisite, proficient, skilful, skilled, superior, supreme
**masterly stroke** tour de force (F)
**mastermind** architect, authority, conceive, direct, expert, genius, intellect, maestro, organise, plan, virtuoso
**master of a manor** lord
**master of a merchant ship** captain
**Master of Arts** artium magister (L), MA
**master of ceremonies** announcer, chairman, chairperson, compere, emcee, host, magister ceremoniarum (L), verger
**master of music** virtuoso
**master of the suspense thriller** Alfred Hitchcock
**master of Toby** Punch
**master of yoga** yogi
**masterpiece** chef-d'oeuvre (F), jewel, magnum opus, masterwork, piece de résistance (F), prize, show-piece
**master-stroke** coup
**masticate** bite, bray, champ, chew, crumble, crunch, crush, disintegrate, gnaw, levigate, liquefy, mumble, munch, nibble, remasticate
**masticator** chewer, tooth
**masticatory stimulant** betel
**mat** dull, lustreless, rug
**matador** bullfighter
**matador's sword** estoque
**match** adapt, affiliation, agree, alliance, ally, bout, combination, compare, contest, copy, correspond, counterpart, couple, double, duet, duplicate, equal, equivalent, event, fit, game, harmonise, join, marriage, mate, oppose, pair, peer, replica, rival, suit, tally, test, trial, twin, union, vesta, vie
**match against** oppose
**matched articles** set
**matched duo** pair
**matched group** set
**matching boudoir linen** bedset
**matching pair** set

**matching sweater and cardigan** twinset
**matchmaker** Cupid
**mate** bra, broer, buddy, chum, cobber, companion, consort, copulate, couple, friend, marry, match, pair, pal, partner
**matelot** matlo(w), sailor, seaman
**mate of he** she
**material** barathea, challis, cloth, corporeal, denim, element, essential, fabric, ground, hylic, important, ingredient, linen, lint, matter, momentous, nankeen, nylon, real, satin, stuff, substance, taffeta, tangible, textile, unspiritual, velvet
**material covering billiard table** baize
**material covering bottom surface of room** flooring
**material deposited by water** driftwood, jetsam
**material edge** hem
**material for burning** fuel
**material for imitation gems** paste
**material for sailor's suits** galatea
**material for starting a fire** dry wood, kindling, straw
**material gain** acquisition
**materialistic** avaricious, covetous, grasping, greedy, money-grubbing, selfish, wordly
**material source of help** aid
**material thing** object
**material to** appertaining, apposite, apropos, involving, pertinent, relevant
**material to conceal the face** veil
**material to cover mattresses** ticking
**material used for making jeans** denim
**material with nap** suede
**material world as a whole** nature
**matériel** accoutrements, apparatus, appliances, contrivances, equipment, furnishings, furniture, gear, implements, machinery, paraphernalia, tools, utensils
**maternal** affectionate, caring, devoted, enate, fond, fostering, gentle, guardian, kind, loving, matronal, motherly, parental, possessive, protecting, protective, shielding, tender, vigilant, warm, watchful
**maternal relationship** enation
**maternal relative** enate
**maternity** gentleness, kindness, maternalism, motherhood, motherliness, parenthood, protectiveness, tenderness, warmth
**matey** comradely, fellow, friend(ly), intimate
**mat for a glass** coaster
**mathematical problem** sum
**mathematical relationship** parity

**mathematical symbol** factor, operand, pi, placeholder, sign
**mathematician** algebraist
**maths branch** algebra
**maths chart** graph
**maths study** algebra, geometry, trigonometry
**mating** breeding, copulating, coupling, joining, marrying, matching, pairing, wedding, yoking
**matrimonial** conjugal, marital, married, nuptial, spousal, wedded, wedding
**matrimonial alliance** match
**matrimony** marriage, match, nuptials, together, union, wedding, wedlock
**matrix** die, example, forge, format, frame, last, model, mould, origin, pattern-guide, punch, source, stamp, template, womb
**matt** dull, lustreless, mat, non-gloss
**matted lock** cot(t), daglock
**matted wool** shag
**matter** affair, consequence, count, difficulty, importance, material, question, reason, significance, signify, stuff, subject, substance, thing, topic
**matter conveyed by post** mail
**matter floating on liquid** scum
**matter flowing from volcano** lava
**matter from distillation** extract
**matter from sore** pus
**matter of course** practice
**matter-of-fact** deadpan, dry, dull, emotionless, flat, lifeless, mundane, plain, prosaic, sober, unsentimental
**matters to be attended to at meeting** agenda
**matter that has been decided** chose judgée (F)
**matter that remains a secret** mystery
**matter that settles to bottom of liquid** sediment
**matter thrown out by volcano** ejecta, lava
**matter under discussion** issue
**matter under inquiry** case
**matting fibre** coir, raffia
**matting grass** esparto
**mattress** futon, pallet, palliasse
**mattress covering** ticking
**mattress filled with liquid** water bed
**mattress filling** bedstraw, coir
**mattress parasite** bedbug
**mattress stuffing** ceiba, coir, flock, kapok
**maturation** changes, forming, growing, meiosis, pubescence
**mature** adult, age, autumn, bold, complete, decoct, develop, due, experienced, fit, full(-grown), fully-developed, grey, grow,

**mature beyond** outgrow
grown(-up), manly, marriageable, maturate, mellow, old, perfect, prime, ready, refined, reliable, responsible, ripe, ripen(ed), season(ed), womanly, worldly
**mature beyond** outgrow
**matured** adult, formed, grown, homogamy, mellow, seeded
**matured female sheep** ewe
**mature insect** imago
**mature person** adult
**mature reproduction cell** egg, gamete, germ, sperm
**mature too early** precocious
**maturing** ag(e)ing, blooming, developing, mellowing, perfecting, ripening, seasoning
**maturing agent** ager
**maturing early** rathe-ripe
**maturity** adulthood, age, completion, consummation, dependability, development, heyday, judiciousness, matureness, mellowness, nubility, perfection, plumpness, prudence, puberty, pubescence, readiness, reliability, responsibility, responsibleness, ripeness, roundness, sagacity, softness, wiseness, (wo)manhood
**matutinal** early, matinal, morning
**maudlin** emotional, feeble, lachrymose, mawkish, over-emotional, (sickly-)sentimental, slushy, soupy, susceptible, tearful, tender, weak, weepy
**maul** abuse, batter, beat, claw, ill-treat, lacerate, mangle, manhandle, molest, paw, pummel, thrash
**Mau-Mau leader** Kenyatta
**maundy money** largess(e)
**mauser** rifle
**mausoleum** shrine, Taj Mahal, tomb
**mauve** lilac
**maverick** dissenter, eccentric, enfant terrible (F), heretic, nonconformist, protester, radical, rebel
**mavis** blackbird, (song) thrush, throstle
**mawkish** banal, cloying, commonplace, corny, dull, feeble, foul, hackneyed, maudlin, nauseating, nauseous, old-fashioned, putrid, sentimental, sickening, sickly, smelly, sour, stale, trite, unpleasant, vomitory
**maxillary sinus** antrum
**maxim** adage, aphorism, axiom, cliché, dictum, dogma, gnome, homily, item, moral, motto, precept, prescript, proverb, rule, saw, saying, slogan, truism, truth, witticism
**maxim adopted as rule of conduct** motto

**maximum** greatest, highest, paramount, supreme, top, utmost
**maximum security prison** penitentiary
**maxisingle** EP
**may** might
**maybe** mayhap, peradventure, perchance, perhaps, possibly, probably
**mayfly** dun, ephemera, ephemerid, ephemeropteran
**mayhem** chaos, commotion, disorder, havoc, trouble, violence
**may he or she rest in peace** requiescat in pace (L)
**may it last for ever** esto perpetua (L)
**may not** refusal
**may you travel safely** Godspeed
**maze** confusion, intricacy, labyrinth, meander, perplexity, puzzle, snarl, uncertainty
**me** moi (F), myself
**meadow** field, grassland, lea, ley, mead(owland), pasturage, pasture(land), wong
**meadow flower** cowslip
**meadowland** field, grassland, lea, ley, pasturage
**meadowsweet** dropwort
**meagre** deficient, exiguous, hungry, inadequate, insubstantial, lean, little, measly, negligible, paltry, poor, puny, scant(y), scarce, scrimpy, short, skimpy, slender, slight, small, spare, sparse, thin, weak
**meagre allowance** pittance
**meagre distribution** sparseness
**meagreness** bareness, boniness, inadequacy, insufficiency, leanness, paucity, pettiness, scarceness
**meal** agape, banquet, beanfeast, bran, breakfast, brunch, cereal, cornmeal, cuisine, dinner, farina, festivity, flour, food, lunch, menu, picnic, refreshment, repast, sandwich, snack, spread, supper, tea, victuals
**meal additive** sauce
**meal combining breakfast and lunch** brunch
**mealie** maize
**meal instructions** recipe
**meals list** menu
**meal starter** hors-d'œuvre, soup
**mealtime prayer** grace
**mealy-mouthed** equivocal, evasive, flattering, glib, indirect, over-squeamish, plausible, prim, reticent, smooth-tongued
**mean** aim, average, backing, base, coarse, common, contemplate, contemptible, convey, denote, design, despicable, destine, dispensable, express, foreordain, foul, humble, ignoble, imply, inconsequent, indicate, inferior, inglorious, insignificant, intend, intermediate, little, low, make, mercenary, method, midpoint, mingy, miserly, nasty, niggardly, nonessential, paltry, parsimonious, penurious, petty, plebeian, poor, predestinate, purpose, represent, revenue, rude, selfish, signify, stingy, suggest, tight, unclean, undignified, unessential, ungenerous, unimportant, unimposing, vulgar, way
**mean, contemptible person** scullion
**meander** circle, intricacy, labyrinth, loop, maze, ramble, rove, snake, stray, stroll, turn, wander, wind, zigzag
**mean dwelling** hovel, shack, shanty
**mean fellow** cad, coward, cur, dog, skunk
**mean figure** average
**meaning** connotation, definition, denotation, expressive, gist, idea, import, intent(ion), interpretation, knowing, meaningful, poignant, point, purport, purpose, sense, significance, signification, trend
**meaning half** semi-
**meaningless** absurd, aimless, empty, futile, hollow, inane, nonsensical, pointless, purposeless, senseless, trifling, trivial, useless, vain, worthless
**meaningless cipher group** null
**meaningless repetition of speech** echolalia
**meaningless ritual** mumbo-jumbo
**meaningless string of words** rigmarole
**meaningless words** nonsense
**meaning life** bio-
**meaning to kill** murderous
**meanly parsimonious** abjectness, cheapness, contemptibility, evil, miserliness, parsimoniousness, pettiness, sinfulness, stinginess
**meanness** degradation, evil, hostility, malice, parsimony, servility, tight-fistedness
**mean person** miser, Scrooge
**mean roughly-built dwelling** shanty
**means** affluence, agency, avenue, contrivance, course, estate, finances, fortune, funds, income, instrument, manner, medium, method, mode, money, process, property, resources, riches, substance, way, wealth, wherewithal
**means by which one lives** subsistence
**means by which something is judged** criteria

**means of access** door, gateway, key, portal
**means of approach** adit
**means of attack kept for surprise** secret weapon
**means of communication** media, radio, telephone
**means of control** rein
**means of conveyance** aircraft, bus, car, ship, train, tram, transport, vehicle
**means of deceiving enemy observation** camouflage
**means of entry** access
**means of escape** loophole, outlet
**means of examining** test
**means of support** sustenance
**means of transforming** alembic
**meantime** coincidentally, concurrently, during, interim, meanwhile, simultaneously, throughout, while
**mean to** intend
**meant to be amusing** facetious
**meant to escape notice** furtive
**meanwhile** ad interum, break, delay, gap, interim, interlude, intermission, interval, meantime, opening, pause, period, playtime, rest, season, space, spell, temporarily, term, time, wait
**mean with money** miserly, parsimonious, tight
**measles** morbilli, rubeola
**measly** contemptible, inferior, meagre, paltry, worthless
**measure** act, amount, appraise, balance, capacity, compass, consider, criterion, dimensions, ell, evaluate, expanse, gauge, lea, magnitude, means, mete, method, metre, plan, plummet, quantity, range, rule, scale, scheme, scope, size, sound, standard, test, weight
**measured distance** (kilo)metre, mile
**measured electricity usage** metered
**measure depth** plumb
**measured in hundreds** centesimal
**measured monotonous song** chant
**measured movement of sound** cadence
**measured portion** dose
**measured precipitation** rainfall
**measured quantity** dose
**measure, equal to four inches of a horse's height** hand
**measure for capacity** bushel
**measure for herrings** cran
**measure in length and breadth** dimension
**measurement** altitude, appreciation, assessment, calculation, calibration, dimension, estimation, evaluation, gauging, mensuration, reading, reckoning, size, survey, valuation
**measurement in printing** em
**measurement of electricity** amp(ere)
**measurement of land** acre, hectare, morgen, rood
**measurement of mental abilities** psychometry
**measurement of the human body** anthropometry
**measurement of weight** gravimetry
**measure of Afghanistan** jerib, karoh
**measure of Algeria** pik, rebis, tarri, termin
**measure of beer** middy
**measure of capacity** tun (252 wine gallons)
**measure of cloth** ell
**measure of cut wood** cord
**measure of dagga** zol(l)
**measure of distance** kilo(metre), mile, odometer
**measure of gold's purity** carat
**measure of heat** temperature
**measure of herrings** cran
**measure of land** acre, hectare, morgen, rood
**measure of medicine** dose
**measure of paper** ream
**measure of perfume** dram
**measure of six feet** fathom
**measure of spirits** jigger
**measure of stacked timber** stere
**measure of the purity of gold** carat
**measure of time** span
**measure of weight** carat, centigram, decigram, decagram, dram, grain, gram, hectogram, kilogram, milligram, ounce, pound, stone, ton
**measure of weight for precious stones** carat
**measure of wood** cord
**measure of yarn** lea
**measure out** allot, apportion, assign, dispense, distribute, divide, issue, mete
**measures radiation** Geiger counter
**measures time** clock
**measure the depth of water** sounding
**measure the heaviness of** weigh
**measure to which others must conform** standard
**measure-unit of twelve points** em
**measure up** answer, correspond, equal, match
**measure up to** equal, match, meet, rival, touch
**measure used for comparison** yardstick
**measure water-depth** fathom
**measuring distance travelled by wheeled vehicle** odometer
**measuring instrument** gauge, meter, ruler, vernier
**measuring strip** ruler
**measuring worm** looper
**meat** beef, flesh, lamb, pork, veal, venison
**meat and herb paste** paté
**meat axe** cleaver
**meatball** frikkadel, rissole
**meat braised with vegetables in wine** à la mode
**meat broth** pot-au-feu
**meat chop** cutlet
**meat chopper** cleaver
**meat cooked on skewer** kebab, sosatie
**meat cut** chop, fillet, roast, silverside, T-bone, thickrib, topside
**meat cut into chunks and grilled on a skewer** en brochette (F)
**meat cutlet** chop
**meat dish** braai, bredie, breyani, chops, roast, stew
**meat entrails** offal
**meat jelly** aspic
**meat joint** leg, loin, roast
**meat of pig** ham, pork
**meat or fowl boiled with rice** pilaf(f), pilao, pilau, pilaw
**meat paste** paté
**meat pin** skewer
**meat retailer** butcher
**meat roasted on skewers** kebab, sosatie
**meat sauce** gravy
**meat seller** butcher
**meat shop** butchery
**meat slicer** carver
**meat stew dish** bredie, goulash, stroganoff
**meat stuffed into a tube** sausage
**meat vendor** butcher
**meaty** savoury
**meaty drink** beef tea
**meaty snack** pasty
**mechanic** artificer, artisan, craftsman, craftsperson, engineer, fitter, machinist, repairman, workman
**mechanical contrivance** engine
**mechanical discharging apparatus** ejector
**mechanical excavator** digger
**mechanical instrument** tool
**mechanical man** automaton, robot
**mechanical memory** rote
**mechanical model of the solar system** orrery
**mechanical plough** tractor
**mechanical repetition** rote
**mechanical skill in art** technique
**mechanical slave** robot
**mechanical source of power** engine

**mechanised man** robot
**mechanism that moves on a gantry**
   traveller
**mechanism to increase speed**
   accelerator
**medal** award, decoration, emblem,
   insignia, medallion, recognition,
   reward, star, trophy
**medallion stone** cameo
**meddle** impose, interfere, interpose,
   intervene, intrude, peep, pry, snoop,
   tamper
**meddler** busybody, gossip, interferer,
   interloper, intruder, peeper, snoop,
   snoop(er)
**meddlesome** interfering, intrusive,
   officious, pragmatic, prying
**meddlesome person** busybody
**meddle with** finger, molest
**meddling** hindrance, interception,
   interference, interruption, intrusion,
   meddlesomeness, obstruction
**media interview** press conference
**median strip** mall
**mediate** arbitrate, intercede, interpose,
   reconcile, settle
**mediator** advocate, agent, arbiter,
   counsellor, go-between, interagent,
   interceder, intermediary,
   intermediate, internuncio, intervener,
   middleman, moderator, pacifier,
   paraclete, peacemaker, reconciler,
   umpire
**medical** analeptic, corrective,
   febrifugal, healing, iatric(al),
   medicinal, palliative, remedial,
   restorative, sanative, therapeutic,
   tonic
**medical assessment** prognosis
**medical care** iatrics
**medical care centre** clinic, hospital
**medical certificate for ill student**
   aegrotat
**medical element** iodine
**medical emblem** staff of Esculapius
**medical examination of dead body**
   post mortem
**medical expert who performs**
   **operations** surgeon
**medical herb** arnica
**medical institution** sanatorium
**medical instrument** endoscope,
   forceps, scalpel, spatula,
   stethoscope, syringe
**medical instrument for examining the**
   **larynx** laryngoscope
**medical orderly** medic
**medical person** doctor
**medical photographic beam** roentgen
   rays
**medical science concerned with the**
   **rectum** proctology

**medical snuff** errhine
**medical student** intern, medic
**medical suffix** -itis
**medical transfer to specialist** referral
**medical use of sunshine** solarium
**medicate** administer, anoint, attend,
   bathe, doctor, dose, dress, drug,
   embrocate, nurse, oil, palliate,
   plaster, relieve, remedy, restore,
   salve, treat
**medicated drink** julep
**medicated sweetmeat** lozenge
**medication** drug, medicine
**medication for asthma** bronchodilator
**medication for constipation** cathartic
**medication for coughs** antitussive
**medication for mouth ulcers**
   demulcent
**medication for tumours** cytotoxin
**medication placed on sores** poultice
**medicinal** analeptic, analgesic,
   aseptic, assuasive, balmy, bracing,
   curative, healing, laxative, narcotic,
   preventive, remedial, restorative,
   reviving, roborant, sedative,
   soothing, stimulating, therapeutic
**medicinal and cooking plant** herb
**medicinal applier** doser
**medicinal bark** chinchona, pereira
**medicinal bloodsucker** leech
**medicinal cure** remedy
**medicinal element** iodine
**medicinal flower** aloe, poppy, rue
**medicinal herb** aloe, arnica, senna
**medicinal measure** dose
**medicinal pellet** pill
**medicinal plant** aconite, aloe, arnica,
   boneset, camomile, catmint, catnip,
   erica, herb, ipecac, lobelia
**medicinal plant leaves** senna
**medicinal spring** spa
**medicinal submersion** mud bath
**medicinal tablet** pill
**medicine** drug, medicament,
   medication, physic, remedy, tonic
**medicine amount** dosage, dose
**medicine ball** pill
**medicine bottle** vial
**medicine container** ampoule, capsule
**medicine for headache** cephalalgic
**medicine for phlegm in the**
   **air-passages** expectorant
**medicine holder** capsule
**medicine inducing the flow of saliva**
   sialogogue
**medicine man** powwow, sangoma
**medicine measure** dose
**medicine that causes vomiting** emetic
**medicine to allay fever** antipyretic
**medicine to reduce fever** febrifuge
**medicine used to counteract poison**
   antidote

**medico** doctor
**medieval catapult** onager
**medieval chemistry** alchemy
**medieval class structure** feudalism
**medieval dagger** an(e)lace
**medieval four-stringed guitar** gittern
**medieval garment** chausses, dalmatic,
   gambeson, rochet
**medieval guitar** lute
**medieval Irish clan** sept
**medieval Irish foot soldier** kern
**medieval jacket** acton
**medieval language of Egyptians**
   Coptic
**medieval musical stringed instrument**
   viol
**medieval musician** minstrel,
   troubadour
**medieval prose narrative** saga
**medieval soldier** knight
**medieval soldier armed with a halberd**
   halberdier
**medieval story** saga
**medieval torture device** iron maiden
**medieval warrior** knight
**medieval weapon** gisarme
**mediocre** acceptable, adequate,
   admissible, amateurish, average,
   fair, indifferent, inferior, insignificant,
   meagre, mean, middling, moderate,
   modest, negligible, neutral, ordinary,
   passable, run-of-the-mill, scant,
   so-so, tolerable, trifling,
   undistinguished, unexceptional,
   uninspired
**mediocrity** adequateness,
   indifference, inferiority,
   insignificance, moderateness,
   neutrality, nobody, nonentity,
   normality, obscurity, ordinariness,
   poorness, triviality, unimportance
**meditate** aim, brood, cabal, cogitate,
   concoct, contemplate, deliberate,
   devise, evaluate, muse, plan, plot,
   ponder, reflect, ruminate, speculate,
   study, theorise, think
**meditation routine** yoga
**meditative** abstracted, concentrating,
   contemplating, contemplative,
   (ex)cogitative, intent, lucubrative,
   mulling, musing, pensive, reflective,
   ruminant, ruminative, thoughtful
**Mediterranean boat** caique, xebec
**Mediterranean country** Algeria,
   France, Greece, Italy
**mediterranean fever** brucellosis
**Mediterranean fruit tree** olive
**Mediterranean group of islands**
   Balearic
**Mediterranean island** Capri, Corsica,
   Crete, Cyprus, Elba, Gibraltar, Lipari,
   Majorca, Malta, Sardinia, Sicily

**Mediterranean locust tree** carob
**Mediterranean port** Algiers, Marseilles
**Mediterranean principality** Monaco
**Mediterranean resort** Lido, Monte-Carlo, Nice, Riviera
**Mediterranean sailing vessel** caique, xebec
**Mediterranean sea** Adriatic, Aegean, Ionian
**Mediterranean volcano** Etna
**Mediterranean wind** Etesian, tramontana
**medium** agency, air, atmosphere, avenue, average, centre, channel, condition, environment, fair, form, influence, instrument(ality), intermediate, mean(s), mediocre, middle, middling, mode, organ, psychic, way
**medium dry Spanish sherry** amontillado
**medium of exchange** money
**medium-sized sofa** settee
**medley** cento, confusion, fantasia, farrago, goulash, hash, hodge-podge, hotchpotch, jumble, kedgeree, melange, mess, miscellany, mixture, mosaic, motley, oddments, olio, olla, paraphernalia, pastiche, pot-pourri, revue, tangle, variation
**medusa** gorgon, jellyfish, quarl
**meek** adaptable, compliant, deferential, docile, forbearing, gentle, humble, mild, modest, obliging, pacific, passive, patient, peaceful, reserved, servile, shy, soft, spiritless, subdued, submissive, tame, timid, tolerant, unresisting
**meek animal** lamb
**meekness** acquiescence, compliance, deference, docility, gentleness, humbleness, humility, mildness, modesty, patience, peacefulness, resignedness, softness, submission, tameness, timidity, weakness
**meerschaum** mineral, sea foam, sepiolite
**meet** adapted, agree, answer, appropriate, assemble, collect, conflict, confront, conjoin, contest, convene, converge, cross, discharge, encounter, gather, gratify, join, match, muster, oppose, proper, satisfy, settle, suitable, unite, visit
**meet boldly** face
**meet debt** pay
**meet defeat** lose
**meet equally in contest** match
**meet face to face** affront, confront
**meet for discussion** confer

**meet halfway** accommodate, adjust, arbitrate, axial, compromise, concede, imperfect, intercede, intermediate, limited, mean, medial, medium, mid, moderate, negotiate
**meeting** assembly, conference, connection, date, encounter, engagement, gathering, get-together, indaba, joining, junction, kgotla, rendezvous, reunion, session, tryst, union
**meeting a curved line** tangent
**meeting, as of headmen** indaba
**meeting between leaders of opposing forces** parley
**meeting for a discussion** conference
**meeting for boat races** regatta
**meeting house** basilica, cathedral, church, mosque, oratory, sanctuary, synagogue, temple, vestry
**meeting of a court** session
**meeting of cardinals to elect a new pope** conclave
**meeting of old friends** reunion
**meeting of spiritualists** seance
**meeting of witches** coven
**meeting place** hall, kgotla, venue
**meeting place in ancient Rome** forum
**meeting to have informal chat and coffee** Kafeeklatsch (G)
**meet in hostility** encounter
**meet the needs of** suffice
**meet together** assemble
**meet up again** reunite
**meet with** encounter, endure, experience, receive, undergo
**megalocardia** cardiomegaly
**Meissen porcelain** Dresden
**melaleuca tree** paperbark
**melancholy** adust, blue(s), dejected, dejection, depression, despondency, despondent, dispirited, doleful, downcast, gloominess, gloomy, hypochondria, inconsolable, lugubrious, miserable, pensiveness, sad(ness), sober, sobriety, sombre, sorrowful, thoughtful(ness), unhappy
**melancholy Portuguese song** fado
**mélange** assortment, confusion, jumble, medley, miscellany, mix(ture)
**meld** blend, combine, merge
**mêlée** affray, battle, brawl, brush, chaos, clamour, dispute, disturbance, donnybrook, encounter, fight, fracas, fray, pandemonium, quarrel, riot, row, rumpus, scrap, scuffle, skirmish, storm, unrest, wrangle
**meliorate** ameliorate, better, improve, mend, recover
**mellow** age(d), cheerful, cordial, creamy, delicate, delicious, dulcet,

easy, full-flavoured, genial, gentle, happy, improved, jolly, jovial, juicy, luscious, mature, mellifluous, melodious, mild, perfect, placid, pleasant, relaxed, rich, ripe, rounded, serene, smooth, soft, soften(ed), sweet, tender, tranquil, tuneful
**melodic** ariose, melodious, songlike, tuneful
**melodic sounds** music
**melodic tune** melisma
**melodious** accordant, appealing, concordant, dulcet, euphonic, golden, harmonious, lyrical, melic, melodic, musical, pleasant, rhythmical, silvery, sweet-sounding, symphonic, tuneful
**melodious sounds** euphony, music
**melodrama** emotionalism, fantasy, fiction, histrionics, idyl, legend, novel, sensationalism, story, tale, theatrics
**melodramatic** blood-and-thunder, exaggerated, extravagant, histrionic, maudlin, mawkish, overdramatic, overemotional, sensational, sentimental, theatrical, treacly
**melodramatic display** histrionic
**melody** accord, air, aria, cantabile, carol, chant, concord, descant, ditty, harmony, lyric, melodiousness, music, song, strain, theme, tune
**melon** cantaloupe, charentais, gallia, honeydew, ogen, spanspek
**melon-shaped vegetable** pumpkin
**melt** assuage, blend, colliquate, defrost, deliquesce, diffuse, disarm, dissolve, dwindle, fade, flux, fuse, gentle, liquefy, liquidise, mediate, mollify, placate, propitiate, relax, soften, thaw, unfreeze
**melt, as snow** thaw
**melt away** disappear, disperse, dissolve, evaporate, fade, vanish
**melted butter** ghee
**melting-pot for metals** crucible
**melting snow** slosh, slush
**melt together** fuse
**member** arm, branch, component, constituent, division, ear, element, foot, fragment, hand, inhabitant, initiate, leg, limb, nose, organ, part, paw, portion, segment, tongue, wing
**member of African tribe** Ibo, Igbo, Kikuyu, Masai, Matabele, Ndebele, Shona, Sotho, Xhosa, Zulu
**member of armed gang** bandit
**member of ancient-Jewish ascetic sect** Essene
**member of cathedral chapter** canon

**member of charitable organisation**
  Rotarian
**member of choir** chorister
**member of Church of Jesus Christ of Latter-day Saints** Mormon
**member of clan** tribesman
**member of clergy** cleric
**member of clique** insider
**member of college** collegian
**member of David's council**
  Achitophel, Ahithophel
**member of deputation** delegate
**member of dissident political group**
  Adullamite
**member of dynasty** dynast
**member of electorate** voter
**member of embassy** attaché
**member of family** relation
**member of gang of armed robbers**
  dacoit
**member of Hindu sect** Sikh
**member of Homo sapiens** (wo)man
**member of hospital staff** almoner
**member of Indian monotheistic sect**
  Sikh
**member of indigenous group of people**
  native
**member of infantry regiment**
  grenadier
**member of international association of women's club** soroptimist
**member of Jamaican sect** rastafarian
**member of Jewish sect** Pharisee
**member of jury** juror
**member of labouring class in Egypt**
  fellah
**member of learned society** fellow
**member of legion** legionnaire, legionary
**member of Levi's tribe** Levite
**member of low caste** pariah
**member of lower nobility in Spain**
  hidalgo
**member of lowest hereditary order of British nobility** baronet
**member of military caste in Japan**
  samurai
**member of mixed Arab and Berber race** Moor
**member of monastery** monk
**member of monastic community**
  coenobite
**member of moral and social fraternity**
  Freemason
**member of outcast class in Japan** eta
**member of Oxford University** Oxonian
**member of parliament** lawmaker, parliamentarian
**member of partnership** partner
**member of patrol** scout
**member of peerage** noble
**member of Pope's council** cardinal
**member of quartet** tenor
**member of religious order** ab, friar, monk, nun, priest
**member of religious sect** Mormon
**member of senate** elder, senator
**member of Slavonic language group**
  Slav
**member of Society of Friends** Quaker
**member of Society of Mary** Marist
**member of strictly conservative Muslim sect** Wah(h)abi
**member of string section** cellist, violinist
**member of Upper House** senator
**member of tribe roaming from place to place** nomad
**membership** adherence, allegiance, associates, body, chair, constituency, fellow(ship), members, place, seat
**membership fee** dues
**members of a profession** faculty
**membrane** coating, covering, diaphragm, film, gauze, layer, scum, skin, tissue, veil
**membrane bag** sac
**membrane between toes of waterfowl**
  web
**membrane enclosing foetus** caul
**membrane enveloping skull**
  pericranium
**membrane enveloping the lungs**
  pleura
**membrane expelled after birth**
  afterbirth
**membrane lining cavity of abdomen**
  peritoneum
**membranes that envelop the brain and spinal cord** meninges
**membranous sac enclosing the heart**
  pericardium
**memento** celebration, cue, keepsake, memorandum, monument, note, record, relic, remembrance, reminder, souvenir, testimonial, token, trophy
**memoir** biography, essay, narrative, record, register
**memoir of one's life** autobiography
**memoirs** accounts, annals, autobiography, biographies, chronicles, confessions, diary, essays, experiences, journals, life (story), lives, memories, narratives, recollections, records, reminiscence
**memo item** pad
**memorable** catchy, celebrated, distinguished, extraordinary, famous, historic, illustrious, important, impressive, notable, noteworthy, outstanding, remarkable, significant, striking, unforgettable
**memorable flower** forget-me-not
**memorable part** highlight, peak
**memorable period** era
**memorandum** agenda, chit, letter, list, memo, message, minute, notation, note, record, record, reminder
**memorial** cenotaph, commemorative, headstone, mausoleum, memento, monument(al), obituary, petition, plaque, pyramid, record, remembrance, shrine, souvenir, statue, stone, tombstone
**memorial inscription** epitaph
**memorial of a nation's great dead**
  pantheon
**memorial service** obit(uary)
**memorial structure** monument
**memorise** get, learn, remember, retain
**memory** capacity, computer, mind, recollection, remembrance, retention
**memory aid** mnemonic
**memory gap** amnesia
**memory loss** amnesia
**memory on computer chip** RAM, ROM
**memory trace** engram
**men** adults, attendants, beings, bodies, employees, gentlemen, hands, humanity, individuals, males, mankind, ones, people, personages, persons, retainers, servants, soldiers, souls, subjects, valets, vassals, workers, workmen
**menace** alarm, annoyance, bully, danger, frighten, hazard, impend, intimidate, intimidation, jeopardy, loom, minaciousness, minacity, nuisance, peril, pest, plague, scare, terror(ise), threat(en), troublemaker, warning
**menacing boy** Dennis
**ménage** commune, family, household, housekeeping, kin, stewardship
**menagerie** zoo
**mend** ameliorate, amend(ment), correct, darn, emend, fix, heal, improve(ment), recover, rectification, rectify, renew, repair, restore
**mendacious** corrupt, crafty, deceitful, deceiving, deceptive, dishonest, fallacious, false, fraudulent, guileful, lying, perfidious, perjured, treacherous, unfair, unreliable, untrue, untruthful
**mendacious person** fibber, liar
**mendacity** crookedness, deceit, deception, distortion, evasion, falsehood, falseness, falsity, fib, fiction, guilefulness, hypocrisy, lie, perjury, prevarication, untruth(fulness)
**mend by stitching** darn

**mend clumsily** patch
**mender of pots and pans** tinker
**mender of shoes** cobbler
**mendicant** almsman, bankrupt, beggar, begging, bergie, borrower, cadger, cadging, drifter, friar, hobo, insolvent, moocher, parasite, pauper, scrounger, scrounging, sponger, stroller, supplicant, tramp, vagrant
**mendicant friar** frater
**mend one's ways** reform
**mend roughly** cobble
**mend shoes** cobble
**mend socks** darn
**mend with thread** darn
**menial** assistant, attendant, beggarly, boring, cringing, degrading, demeaning, domestic, dull, equerry, flunk(e)y, footman, groom, helper, helping, humble, humdrum, ignominious, lackey, low(ly), maidservant, mean, minion, peon, routine, servant, servile, serving, skiv(v)y, slave, stableman, subordinate, underling, unskilled, valet, waiter, yeoman
**menial worker** drudge
**men in general** menfolk
**menology** calendar, chronogram
**men only party** stag
**men's baggy knickerbockers clasped below the knees** plus fours
**men's loo** gents
**mensuration of plane surface** planimetry
**menswear article** cravat, jacket, shirt, tie, trousers, vest
**mental** bedonderd, beneek, beneuk(s), cerebral, deranged, disturbed, insane, intellectual, lunatic, noetic, psychiatric, unbalanced, unstable
**mental ability** brainpower, ingenuity, mentality
**mental activity** brainwork, conceit
**mental acuteness** acumen
**mental agitation** emotion
**mental anguish** heartache, torment
**mental attainment** acquirement
**mental attitude** outlook, sense
**mental calm** peace
**mental communication** telepathy
**mental composure** equanimity
**mental concept** idea
**mental connection** association of ideas
**mental darkness** ignorance
**mental defect** amentia, imbecile, incompetent
**mental deficient** dullard, dunce, halfwit, idiot, imbecile, incompetent, moron, simpleton

**mental deficiency** amentia, idiocy, imbecility, senility
**mental depression** melancholia, melancholy, the vapours
**mental disorder** aberration, mania, paranoia, psychosis, schizophrenia
**mental disorder marked by depression and ill-founded fears** melancholia
**mental disorder producing depression** neurosis
**mental distress** sorrow
**mental disturbance** delirium, neurosis
**mental dullness** hebetude, stupor
**mental faculty** wit
**mental feeling** sentiment
**mental flaw** neurosis
**mental illusion** phantom
**mental image** fantasy, idolum
**mental indolence** apathy
**mental lapse** aberration
**mental laziness** languor
**mental lethargy** hebetude
**mentally acute** sagacious, shrewd
**mentally deranged** manic, non compos mentis (L)
**mentally disturbed** perturbed
**mentally dull** slow
**mentally feeble** imbecile
**mentally handicapped** ament, moron
**mentally hazy** muzzy
**mentally ill** demented, insane, manic
**mentally incapable of managing one's own affairs** non compos mentis (L)
**mentally infirm** decrepit, senile
**mentally quick** agile
**mentally sound** rational, sane
**mentally stimulating** piquant, pungent
**mentally unwholesome** morbid
**mentally upset** disturb(ed)
**mentally weak through old age** senile
**mental pain** anguish
**mental perplexity** study
**mental picture** image
**mental preference** predilection
**mental prospect** vista
**mental regard** eye
**mental relish** palate
**mental representation** image
**mental reservation** arrière-pensée (F)
**mental retardation** dullness, imbecility, incompetency
**mental spirit** morale
**mental state of balance** equilibrium
**mental state of over-excitability** hypomania
**mental strain** stress, tension
**mental strength** vigour
**mental suffering** anguish, torment
**mental tendency** bias
**mental training** education, study
**mental turmoil** distraction

**mental twist** kink
**mental unsoundness** lunacy
**mental view** perspective, prospect
**mental weariness** ennui
**mention** adduce, allusion, broach, citation, cite, communicate, declare, disclose, divulge, impart, indication, intimate, name, note, recognition, recount, remark, report, reveal, say, state, tell, tribute
**mention definitely** specify
**mention in despatches** citation
**mention in detail** particularise
**mention in order** recite
**mention one by one** enumerate
**mention particularly** specify
**mentor** adviser, coach, confidant, counsellor, educator, expert, guide, guru, instructor, master, monitor, oracle, pandit, pundit, sage, teacher, therapist, tutor
**menu** board, bread, carte, charges, commons, cooking, cuisine, diet, eatables, edibles, fare, food(stuffs), larder, meals, meat, nourishment, nutrition, provender, provisions, rations, refreshment, schedule, stores, sustenance, table, tariff, victuals
**menu listing dishes available on a particular day** carte du jour
**men working together** crew, gang, shift, team
**mepacrine** quinacrine
**mercantile analyst** economist
**mercenary** acquisitive, avaricious, bought, bribable, covetous, freelance, grasping, greedy, hired, hireling, paid, selfish, sordid, venal
**mercenary person** huckster
**mercenary soldiers** condottiere
**mercenary worker** hireling
**merchandise** belongings, commodities, effects, goods, market, sell, stock, wares
**merchandise of a chandler** candles, chandlery
**merchant** broker, businessperson, dealer, industrialist, salesperson, shopkeeper, trader
**merchantable** marketable, saleable
***Merchant of Venice* villain** Shylock
**merchant sailing-ship** windjammer
**merciful** benign, clement, compassionate, forbearing, forgiving, generous, gracious, humane, humanitarian, kind(-hearted), large, lenient, liberal, mild, pitying, soft, sparing, sympathetic, tender-hearted

**merciless** cruel, fell, inexorable, pitiless, relentless, ruthless, uncompassionate, unfeeling
**mercurial** adaptable, adjustable, capricious, changeable, erratic, express, faithless, fast, fickle, fitful, fleet, flexible, flighty, floating, fluid, inconstant, indefinite, irregular, irresolute, mobile, mutable, protean, rapid, shifting, speedy, uncertain, unfaithful, unpredictable, unreliable, unsettled, unstable, unsteady, vacillating, variable, versatile, volatile, wavering, winged
**mercury** quicksilver
**mercury alloy** amalgam
**Mercury's winged sandals** talaria
**mercy** benevolence, blessing, clemency, compassion, consideration, discretion, forbearance, forgiveness, gentleness, grace, humanity, kindness, lenience, leniency, pity, placability, tenderness
**mercy killing** euthanasia
**mere** bare, entire, inconsiderable, lake, only, pool, pure, scant, sheer, simple, trifling, trivial
**mere assertion** ipse dixit (L)
**mere chance** haphazard
**merely** absolutely, barely, but, completely, entirely, hardly, just, only, purely, scanty, scarcely, simply, solely, utterly
**mere scrap** iota
**mere show** bluff, phantom
**meretricious** bold, cheap, counterfeit, deceitful, dodgy, elusive, false, garish, gaudy, insincere, loud, ornate, showy, specious, spurious, tawdry
**merganser** duck, goosander, herald, nun, sawbill, sheldrake, shelduck, smee, smew, weaser
**merge** amalgamate, associate, blend, coalesce, combine, consolidate, fuse, (inter)mix, join, meet, mingle, unite, wed
**merge in** admix, blend, bond, cement, cohere, combine, fuse, glue, intertwine, mix
**merger** amalgamation, association, cartel, coalition, combination, confederation, conglomerate, consolidation, fusion, incorporation, monopoly, syndicate, syndication, union
**meringue cake with cream and fruit** pavlova
**merit** advantage, asset, attribute, claim, credit, desert, deserve, due, earn, excellence, good(ness),

gratitude, integrity, justice, justification, justify, morality, purity, quality, recompense, reward, right, talent, value, virtue, warrant, worth(iness)
**meritorious** admirable, capital, champion, choice, commendable, creditable, deserving, distinguished, estimable, excellent, exemplary, exquisite, fine, first-class, first-rate, good, great, honourable, laudable, notable, noted, outstanding, praiseworthy, prime, rare, reputable, respectable, select, superb, superior, superlative, valuable, wonderful, worthy
**merrily** amusingly, comically, facetiously, funnily, humorously, joyfully, joyously, light-heartedly, vivaciously
**merriment** amusement, celebration, cheer, conviviality, exhilaration, festivity, folly, frivolity, frolic, fun, gaiety, glee, hilarity, jocularity, joviality, joy, jubilee, laughter, mirth, revelry, sport
**merry** beamish, blithesome, buoyant, cheerful, cheery, convivial, delighted, easy-going, elated, festive, gay, genial, glad, gleeful, happy, hilarious, jolly, jovial, joyful, light-hearted, lively, mirthful, sunny, tipsy, untroubled
**merry and bright** cheerful
**merry drinking party** carousal
**merry fellow** wag
**merry frolic** revel, spree
**merry-go-round** carousel, roundabout, whirligig
**merrymaker** reveller
**merrymaking** carousing, celebration, festivity, fun, jollification, merriment, party, revelry
**merry play** frolic, fun, game, play, sport
**merry tune** lilt
**mesa** alp, butte, highveld, hillock, mount(ain), peak, plateau, tableland, upland
**mesh** combine, engage, ensnare, entanglement, fishnet, interlock, knit, lace(work), net(ting), network, plexus, snare, toils, tracery, trellis, weaving, web(bing)
**mesh fabric** net
**mesmerise** benumb, bewitch, captivate, constrain, enrapture, enthrall, entrance, fascinate, grip, hypnosis, hypnotise, induce, insensibility, magnetise, numbness, spell(bind), stupefaction, stupefy, trance, unconsciousness
**mesmerism** hypnotism

**mess** clutter, confuse, confusion, dirtiness, disorder, gemors, hodge-podge, hotchpotch, jumble, litter, medley, miscellany, muddle, pickle, predicament, spill, unpleasantness, untidiness
**mess about** dabble, footle, interfere, meddle, play, tamper, trifle
**message** cable(gram), communication, errand, information, letter, mission, note, notice, point, postcard, radiogram, report, signal, statement, telegram, theme, transmit, wire, word
**message flasher** heliograph
**message in code** cryptogram
**message received** roger
**message transmitter** telex
**mess around** fiddle
**messenger** agent, ambassador, apostle, bearer, carrier, courier, emissary, envoy, errand-boy, go-between, harbinger, herald, legman, nuncio, runner
**messenger of Zeus** Iris
**mess up** botch, bungle, disrupt, jumble, muddle, spoil, tangle
**messy** bedraggled, chaotic, dirty, dowdy, filthy, grubby, jumbled, muddled, nasty, piggy, rotten, sloppy, slovenly, turbid, unkempt, untidy
**messy place** sty
**metal** alloy, aluminium, barium, brass, chrome, cobalt, copper, element, gold, hardness, iron, lead, mineral, money, nickel, ore, silver, steel, tin, uranium, zinc
**metal alloy** amalgam, brass, bronze, solder
**metal analyst** assayer
**metal band** hoop
**metal bar** ingot, rail, rod
**metal bar on house door** hasp
**metal bar screen** grille
**metal beam** girder
**metal-bearing compound** ore
**metal-bearing rock** ore
**metal-bearing vein** lode
**metal bolt** rivet
**metal box** canister
**metal cap to strengthen end of stick** ferrule
**metal case** canister
**metal casting** ingot, pig
**metal cement** solder
**metal circlet** armlet, ring
**metal coating** patina, rust
**metal container** can(ister), drum, pail, pot, tin
**metal cord** wire
**metal currency** coin

**metal disk** coin, gong, medal, paten, sequin
**metal dross** slag
**metal eyelet** grommet, grummet
**metal fastener** hasp, nail, nut, pin, rivet, screw, zip
**metal fastening pin** nail, rivet
**metal flask** canteen
**metal frame held in front of one walking** walker, zimmer
**metal framework for fire** grate
**metal goods** cutlery, hardware
**metal-headed war club** mace
**metal in mass** bullion
**metal in sheets** foil, leaf, plate
**metal leaf** foil
**metallic** argentine, burnished, clinking, firm, glossy, hard, iron, lustrous, metalline, reflective, shiny, solid, steely, tempered, tinny
**metallic cement** solder
**metallic chemical element** arsenic
**metallic cloth** lamé, tinsel
**metallic element** cobalt, gallium, gold, iron, lead, platinum, radium, rhenium, ytterbium, yttrium, zinc
**metallic fabric** lamé
**metallic mineral** ore
**metallic missile** bullet
**metallic mixture** alloy, bronze
**metallic money** coins
**metallic noise** bam
**metallic plate** alloy
**metallic rock** ore
**metallic seal** capsule
**metallic sound** chime, clank, clink, ding, dong
**metallic thread** cord, wire
**metallic wrapping** (tin)foil
**metallic zinc** spelter
**metal marker** stake
**metal mass** ingot, pig
**metal merchandise** hardware
**metal missile** bomb, grenade, shell, torpedo
**metal mixture** alloy
**metal nugget** prill
**metal ornament with inlaid gold or silver** damascene
**metal pattern** template
**metal peg** pin
**metal piece of money** coin
**metal pin** nail, rivet
**metal pivot** hinge
**metal refuse** dross, scoria, scum, slag
**metal related to nickel** cobalt
**metal rim of wooden wheel** strake
**metal rod** bar
**metal rod for poking a fire** poker
**metal shaft** rod
**metal sheet** foil, leaf, plate
**metal shell** bomb

**metal source** ore
**metal spacer in printing** lead, slug
**metal spicule** nail
**metal spike** nail, needle
**metal stand** trivet
**metal strand** wire
**metal suit** armour, mail
**metal support for a weak or injured leg** calliper
**metal symbol** badge
**metal tag at end of shoelace** a(i)glet
**metal thread** cable, wire
**metal threaded fabric** lamé
**metal-to-metal sound** clank
**metal tracks** railroad
**metal urn** samovar
**metal used for roofing** zinc
**metal vessel** can
**metal wheel** fil(l)et
**metal wind instrument** sarrusophone
**metal wood fastener** nail
**metalworker** forger, riveter, smith, welder
**metalworking block** anvil
**metalworking tool** swage
**metamere** somite
**metamorphic rock** gneiss
**metamorphosis** alteration, amendment, change(-over), conversion, difference, diversification, innovation, modification, (per)mutation, rebirth, revision, revolution, shift, transfiguration, transformation, transition, transmutation, variance, variation
**mete** allocate, allot, apportion, border, distribute, frontier, limit, measure
**meteor** comet, fire-ball, meteorite, meteoroid, shooting star
**meteor hole** crater
**meteoric** brief, brilliant, dazzling, ephemeral, fast, flashing, fleeting, instantaneous, momentary, overnight, rapid, spectacular, speedy, sudden, swift
**meteoric stone** aerolite
**meteorological instrument** radiosonde
**meteorologist** weather man
**meteorology** aerography, climate, climatology, weather
**mete out** administer, allot, apportion, assign, dispense, distribute, portion
**metered vehicle** cab, taxi
**methane** gas
**method** approach, arrangement, course, design, disposition, fashion, form, manner, mode, order, pattern, plan(ning), practice, procedure, programme, regularity, routine, rule, scheme, structure, style, system, technique, way

**methodical** business-like, deliberate, disciplined, efficient, exact, laborious, methodic, meticulous, neat, ordered, orderly, organised, painstaking, planned, precise, regular, scrupulous, structured, systematic, tidy, uniform
**methodical compendium of a body of laws** Digest
**methodical thought** logic
**Methodist** Wesleyan
**method of action** plan
**method of cell division** mitosis
**method of dating past events by analysis of tree rings** dendrochronology
**method of detecting aircraft** radar
**method of operation** process
**method of performance** technique
**method of preservation** storage
**method of procedure** mode
**method of proceeding with a task** modus operandi
**method of rapid writing** shorthand
**method of rotary printing** letterset
**method of transferring money** giro
**method of voting** ballot
**method of wall-painting** fresco, stereochromy
**methods and techniques of escaping** escapology
**methods and techniques of escaping from confinement** escapology
**method used to achieve aim** tactics
**meticulous** accurate, careful, cautious, demanding, detailed, exact, fastidious, finical, finicky, fussy, painstaking, precise, punctilious, scrupulous, strict, thorough
**métier** concentration, craft, field, forte, job, line, living, major, occupation, profession, pursuit, skill, speciality, sphere, trade, vocation, work
**metre** measure, prosody
**metrical composition** poem, verse
**metrical foot** anapest, dactyl, iamb(us), paeon, spondee, trochee
**metrical foot of three short syllables** tribrach
**metrical foot of two syllables** iamb(us)
**metrical scanning** scansion
**metrical stress** ictus
**metrical unit consisting of four feet** tetrapody
**metric measure** are, centi-, deca-, deci-, gram, hect-, kilo-, litre, metre, milli-, stere
**metric measure of volume** litre
**metric measure of length** metre
**metric square measure** are
**metric suppression** elision
**metric system** algorism, algorithm

**metric ton** tonne
**metric unit** are, gram, litre, metre, stere
**metric unit of capacity** kilolitre, litre, millilitre
**metric unit of distance** kilometre, metre
**metric unit of land measure** are, hectare
**metric unit of length** centimetre, kilometre, metre, millimetre
**metric unit of mass** centigram, decagram, gram, kilogram, tonne
**metric volume** litre
**mettle** ardour, backbone, boldness, bravery, character, courage, daring, determination, fibre, firmness, fortitude, gallantry, grit, hardihood, heroism, intrepidity, nerve, pluck, resolution, spirit, steadfastness, tenacity, valour, will
**meu** baldmoney, spignel
**mew** cage, confine, coop, embar, enclosure, gull, howl, moult, pen, pule, purr, shed, skin, slough, squall, stable, whine
**Mexican** Aztec, Chicano, Mayan
**Mexican amphibian** axolotl
**Mexican bean** frijol
**Mexican blanket** serape
**Mexican border river** Rio Grande
**Mexican bread** tortilla
**Mexican cactus** mescal, peyote
**Mexican cattle farm** rancho
**Mexican coin** peso
**Mexican corn mush** atole
**Mexican cotton cloth** manta
**Mexican crisp pancake** taco
**Mexican dance** raspa
**Mexican dish** enchilada, taco, tamale, tortilla
**Mexican drink** mescal, pulque, tequila
**Mexican fermented drink** pulque, tequila
**Mexican fibre** istle, ixtle, pita, sisal
**Mexican food** enchilada, taco, tamale, tortilla
**Mexican friend** amigo
**Mexican hat** sombrero
**Mexican hut** jacal
**Mexican Indian** Alais, Cora, Maya, Tlascalan, Xova
**Mexican labourer** peon, serf
**Mexican liquor from agave** tequila
**Mexican liquor from cactus tops** peyote
**Mexican mammal** ocelot
**Mexican money** peso
**Mexican pancake** tortilla
**Mexican peasant** peon
**Mexican peninsula** Yucatan
**Mexican persimmon** chapote
**Mexican plant** chapote, jalap

**Mexican plant with scarlet bracts** poinsettia
**Mexican prairie wolf** coyote
**Mexican province** Yucatan
**Mexican pyramid temple** teocalli
**Mexican ranch** hacienda, rancho
**Mexican rodent** tucan
**Mexican shawl** serape
**Mexican slave** peon
**Mexican spiny tree** retamo
**Mexican spirit** tequila
**Mexican state** Colima, Durango, Hidalgo, Leon, Tlaxcala, Veracruz, Yucatan
**Mexican wind instrument** clarin
**mezzanine** entresol
**miasma** exhalation, f(o)etor, mephitis, mofette, pollution, reek, stench
**mica** glist, isinglass, lepidolite, talc
**mica-bearing rock** domite
**Michaelmas flower** daisy
**Michelangelo sculpture** Pietà
**Mickey's surname** Mouse
**microbe** amoeba, bacillus, bacterium, bug, gamete, germ, micro-organism, pathogen, spirochaete, virus
**micro-organism living only in presence of free oxygen** aerobe
**micro-organisms that cause disease** bacteria
**microphone** dictaphone, hailer, loudspeaker, mike
**microscopic anatomy** histology
**microscopic creature** animalcule, animalculum
**midcalf length** midi
**midday** meridian, noon(day), noontide, noontime
**midday break** lunch hour
**midday meal** dinner, lunch(eon)
**midday rest** siesta
**midden** bin
**middle** central(ity), centre(most), centric, epicentre, equidistant, halfway, interjacent, intermediate, mean, medial, median, medium, mesal, mid(point), midriff, midst, midway, waist(line)
**middle age** adulthood, maturity
**middle class** bourgeoisie, citizenry, commonality
**middle course** via media (L)
**middle ear** tympanum
**middle ear bone** stapes
**Middle Eastern cloak** jellaba(h)
**Middle Eastern country** Iran, Iraq, Israel, Jordania, Kuwait, Lebanon, Saudi Arabia, Syria
**Middle Easterner** Arab, Iranian, Iraqi, Israeli, Jordanian, Kowaiti, Kuwaiti, Lebanese, Syrian
**Middle Eastern export** oil

**Middle Eastern ex-ruler** shah
**Middle Eastern gulf** Aden
**Middle Eastern lake** Dead Sea
**middle estimate** average
**middleman** broker, distributor, entrepreneur, intermediary, wholesaler
**middleman in dispute** mediator
**middle of human trunk** waist
**middle of magazine** centre spread
**middle of oar** loom
**middle-of-the-road** centre, compromise, median
**middle part** centre, core
**middle part of a country** midland
**middle part of pork loin** tenderloin
**middle quality** medium
**middle soprano** mezzo
**Middle Stone Age** Mesolithic
**middle traffic light colour** amber
**middling** adequately, average, everyday, fair, grade, mean, median, mediocre, medium, moderate(ly), passable, so-so, somewhat, tolerable, tolerably, unexceptional, unremarkable
**middling quality** mediocre
**Mid-East canal** Suez
**midge** gnat, muggie
**Midlands beer** nog
**mid-length skirt** midi
**midpoint** average, centre
**midpoint of a shield** fess(e) point
**midshipman** cadet
**midst** amid, among, arena, between, centre, core, middle, thick
**midweek** Wednesday
**midwife** accoucheur (F), accoucheuse (F), deliverer, obstetrician
**midwifery** delivery, obstetrics, parturition, tocology
**mien** air, appearance, aspect, attitude, aura, bearing, behaviour, carriage, cast, climate, colour, complexion, composure, conduct, countenance, demeanour, deportment, expression, favour, feature, gesture, manner, poise, position, posture, presence, style, visage
**might** ability, capability, capacity, energy, force, main, may, potency, power, puissance, strength, sway, valour, vigour
**mighty** enormous, forceful, hardy, huge, potent, powerful, puissant, robust, stalwart, stout, strong, sturdy, tremendous, vigorous
**migrant** commuter, drifter, emigrant, expatriate, globe-trotter, gypsy, immigrant, itinerant, mariner, migrating, migrator, mover, nomad,

rover, roving, stroller, tinker, traveller, vagrant, voyager, wanderer
**migrate** emigrate, immigrate, journey, move, relocate, resettle
**migration** emigration, journey, roving, travel, trek, voyage, wandering
**migration to a new gold field** gold rush
**migratory** deracinated, displaced, emigrant, errant, floating, going, gypsy, homeless, immigrant, itinerant, journeying, moving, nomad(ic), peregrine, roaming, rootless, roving, travelling, unsettled, wandering, wayfaring
**migratory bird** bobolink, cuckoo, goose, ibis, plover, ruff, stork, swallow, swift, tern, visitor
**migratory duck** gadwall
**migratory worker** itinerant
**mike** amplifier, microphone
**mild** affable, amiable, balmy, benedict, benign, bland, clement, docile, emollient, genial, gentle, humble, indulgent, kind, lenient, meek, merciful, mollifying, pacific, placid, shy, smooth, soft, soothing, tame, temperate, tranquil
**mild antiseptic** borax
**mild cheese** Gouda
**mild cigar** claro
**mild crumbly white cheese** Caerphilly
**mild Dutch cheese** Edam
**mild explosion** pop
**mild form of cancer** cancroid
**mild form of imprecation** drat
**mild gentle breeze** zephyr
**mild in judging** lenient
**mild in speech** soft-spoken
**mildly** blandly, docilely, forbearingly, gently, kindly, meekly, mercifully, moderately, peaceably, placidly, pleasantly, serenely, smoothly, softly, temperately, tenderly, tranquilly, warmly
**mildly indecent** naughty
**mild mental disorder** neurosis
**mildness** clemency, docility, indulgence, leniency, placidity, tenderness, tranquillity, warmth
**mild, not excessive** moderate
**mild oath** gar, good heavens
**mild repugnance** distaste
**mild sickness** malaise
**mild, sweet pepper for spicy meat dishes** paprika
**mild-tasting** bland
**mild temper** mansuetude
**mileage** coverage, distance, payment, service, truckage, usage, use, wear
**mileage recorder** odometer
**Milesian** Erse, Irish(man)

**milestone** juncture, mark(er), milepost, pointer, progress, (sign)post
**milfoil** herb, yarrow
**milieu** ambience, atmosphere, aura, background, class, element, environment, environs, locale, medium, neighbourhood, setting, sphere, surroundings, vicinity
**military** army, combative, contingents, fighting, forces, legions, martial, militant, militarist, naval, recruits, reinforcements, service, soldiers, soldiery, troops, warlike
**military academy in France** St Cyr
**military aircraft** fighter
**military art** tactics
**military assistant** aide(-de-camp), attaché
**military attack** offensive
**military badge** star
**military body** army
**military canteen** NAAFI
**military cap** beret, kepi, shako
**military chaplain** padre
**military chief in India** sirdar
**military coat** buff coat
**military coat-fastening** frog
**military college** academy
**military colour** khaki
**military command** at-ease, fire
**military courier** estafette
**military detention area** stockade
**military dining room** mess
**military display** parade
**military division** brigade, corps, legion, unit
**military engineer** sapper
**military ensign** pennon
**military equipment** armament
**military exercise** tattoo
**military fête by night** tattoo
**military field-ration package** ratpack
**military fieldwork** redan
**military flag** standard
**military flute** fife
**military foe** enemy
**military force** army, commando, corps, legion, militia, troop
**military gesture of respect** salute
**military gong** medal
**military government** stratocracy
**military grade** rank
**military group** army
**military guard** sentry
**military habit** uniform
**military headgear** bearskin, beret, busby, cap, helmet, kepi, shako
**military imprisonment** detention
**military intake** roofie(s)
**military jacket** tunic
**military jumper** paratroop
**military leader** caudillo

**military leave** furlough
**military lodging** barracks
**military man** martialist
**military manoeuvre** operation
**military manoeuvres** drill, ops, strategy, tactics
**military marksman** sniper
**military meal tray** varkpan
**military music** march
**military nucleus** cadre
**military obstacle** abat(t)is
**military officer** brigadier, captain, colonel, commander, general, lieutenant, major
**military officer of the highest rank** field marshal
**military operation** siege
**military pageant** tattoo
**military policeman** MP, redcap
**military post** base, boma, command, garrison, station
**military precision** snap
**military prison** brig, DB, stockade
**military projectile** ammunition, arrow, ball, bomb, grenade, missile, shell, spear
**military quarters** camp
**military rampart** aggar
**military rank** airman, brigadier, captain, colonel, cornet, corporal, general, grade, lieutenant, major, private, sergeant
**military rule-breaker** defaulter
**military rulers** junta
**military school student** cadet
**military science** strategy
**military shelter** barracks, bunker, tent
**military shoe** caliga
**military standard** vexillum
**military storehouse** arsenal, depot, etape
**military stores** ammunition, ordnance
**military strength** force
**military stripe** chevron
**military stronghold** fortress
**military student** cadet
**military subunit** platoon
**military supplies** ordnance
**military survey of enemy territory** reconnaissance
**military sword** sabre
**military symbol of rank** star
**military toilet** latrine
**military trumpet** bugle
**military uniform** tunic
**military unit** army, battalion, brigade, cohort, commando, corps, detachment, division, group, platoon, regiment, section, squad(ron)
**military vehicle** jeep, tank, troop-carrier
**military wake-up** reveille
**military weapons** (am)munition, arms

**milium** whitehead
**milk** lac (L), lait (F), latte (I), leche (Sp), milch (G)
**milk can** churn
**milk component** lactose
**milk container** bottle, udder
**milk curdler** rennet
**milk farm** dairy
**milk fat** cream
**milk food** yog(h)urt
**milk gland** udder
**milkiness** lactescence
**milking farm** dairy
**milk jelly dessert** blancmange
**milkmaid's chair** stool
**milk organ** udder
**milk preparation** yog(h)urt
**milk protein** casein(ogen)
**milk pudding** sago
**milk shop** dairy
**milksop** coward, dastard, sissy, weakling
**milk sugar** lactose
**milk supplier** dairy, udder
**milk thickened by acid** curd
**milk-wort plant** senega
**milky appearance** lactescence
**milky bedtime drink** chocolate, cocoa
**milky fluid of plant** latex
**milky gem** opal
**milky juice of an American tree, used in chewing gum** chicle
**milky stone** opal
**Milky Way** galaxy
**milky-white gem** opal
**mill around** linger
**mill ditch** leat
**millennium** aeon, aspiration, chillad, golden age, millenary, Utopia
**milliner** hatter
**millinery** hats
**millinery container** bandbox, hatbox
**millinery item** hat
**million million** billion
**million raised to seventh power** septillion
**million raised to third power** trillion
**millionth part of metre** micron
**million tons** megaton
**millipede** duisendpoot, milleped(e), songololo
**mill's water ditch** leat
**mill trench** leat
**mill wheel** pirn
**milter salmon** eke
**mime** mimic, mummery, pantomime
**mimed performance** charade
**mimic** actor, ape(r), caricature, caricaturist, copy(-cat), echo, feign, imitate, imitative, imitator, impersonate, impressionist, mime, mirror, mock, parody, parrot, represent, satirise, sham, simulate
**mimicking bird** parrot
**mimicry** aping, blind, burlesque, camouflage, caricature, concealment, copy(ing), counterfeit, deception, disguise, echoing, farce, imitation, impersonation, lampoon, likeness, mask, masquerade, mime, mimicking, mockery, parody, pretence, resemblance, ridicule, satire, screen, sham, simulation, subterfuge, travesty
**mimosaceous tree** acacia, mimosa
**mina bird** myna(h), starling
**mince** chop, cut, diminish, extenuate, grind, palliate
**minced meat packed into skin** sausage
**minced meat rolled in bacon and fried** kromesky
**minced oath** egad
**mincer** ponce
**mince the truth** dodge, fudge, hedge, waffle
**mind** attend, belief, bent, bias, brain, care, consideration, contemplation, disposition, heed, inclination, intellect, intelligence, intent(ion), judg(e)ment, memory, note, nous, obey, object, opinion, proclivity, purpose, reason, recollection, regard, sentiments, tend, understanding, will, wish, wont
**mindful** alert, aware, careful, chary, respectful, sensible, watchful
**mindless** absurd, blind, brainless, careless, dense, dull, empty, fatuous, foolish, frivolous, futile, hasty, idiotic, impetuous, inane, inept, irrational, ludicrous, puerile, rash, reckless, senseless, silly, stupid, thoughtless, unintelligent, unthinking, violent, wild, witless
**mindlessness** absurdness, blindness, brainless(ness), dullness, fatuousness, foolishness, hastiness, heedlessness, illogicalness, impetuousness, indiscreetness, ineptness, irrationalness, ludicrousness, perfunctoriness, rashness, recklessness, senselessness, silliness, stupidness, wildness, witlessness
**mindless wrecker** vandal
**mind one's manners** behave
**mind out** beware, watch
**mind reader** telepath
**mind the sick** nurse
**mine** colliery, excavate, excavation, hoard, my, pit, shaft, stock, tunnel, unearth, vein
**mine and thine** meum et tuum (L)
**mine car** cocopan, golovan, skip
**mined element** mineral
**mined material** ore
**mine entrance** adit
**mine of wealth** golconda
**mine partition** brattice
**mine passage** adit, shaft
**mine placed against wall** limpet
**mine pool** sump
**mine product** coal, gold, mica, ore, platinum, tin
**miner** coal miner, collier, pitman, pitworker
**mineral** apatite, barite, crystal, fluorite, inorganic, iolite, marl, metal, ore, silica
**mineral aggregate** ore
**mineral bath** spa
**mineral-bearing rock** ore
**mineral consisting mainly of magnesia** periclase
**mineral constituent of granite** hornblende
**mineral deposit** lode, mine
**mineral found in glittering scales** mica
**mineral fuel** coal
**mineral oil** petroleum
**mineral related to dolomite** ankerite
**mineral resort** spa
**mineral rock** ore
**mineral spring** spa, well
**mineral substance used as electrical insulator** mica
**mineral vein** lode
**mineral water** seltzer
**mineral water resort** spa
**miners' disease** pneumo(no)coniosis, silicosis
**miners' language** Fanagalo, Fanakalo
**miner's safety lamp** Davy lamp
**miner's sieve** griddle
**miner's sledge** mallet
**mine shaft** adit, pit
**mine shaft lining** tubbing
**mine's level entrance** adit
**mine support** stull
**mine tunnel** shaft
**mine worker** cager, collier, miner
**mingle** associate, blend, combine, compound, conjoin, connect, consolidate, fuse, hobnob, intermingle, (inter)mix, join, merge, participate, socialise, unify, unite
**mingy** mean, miserly, niggardly, stingy
**miniature** baby, bantam, designed, diminutive, epitome, little, manikin, microcosm, microscopic, midget, mini, minim, minute, model, picture, pocket, reduced, reduction,

represented, small, teeny, tiny, toy, wee(ny)
**miniature case for memento** locket
**miniature dog** toy
**miniature hour-glass device** egg-glass
**miniature violin** kit
**mini bikini** tanga
**minimal tide** neap
**minimum** admission, base, bottom, depth, fee, least, limit, lowest, margin, modicum, nadir, slightest, smallest
**minimum size of meeting** quorum
**mining basket** corf
**mining chisel** gad
**mining in steps** stoping
**mining joint** cleat
**mining level** gallery, gangway, head, kip
**mining product** coal, gold, mineral, ore, platinum
**mining sieve** trommel
**minion** assistant, courtier, creature, dainty, elegant, flatterer, flunk(e)y, follower, hanger-on, hireling, idol, inferior, lackey, leech, parasite, pretty, slave, sponge, subordinate, sycophant, toady, wheedler
**minister** abbé, chaplain, clergyman, cleric, dominee, deacon, dean, delegate, diplomat, envoy, padre, pastor, preacher, predikant, priest, rabbi, reverend, vicar
**minister of Ahasuerus** Haman
**minister's house** manse
**ministers of religion** clergy
**minister's residence** manse, vicarage
**minister to** aid, furnish, help, serve, supply, tend
**mink** fur
**mink-like animal** weasel
**mink or sable** fur
**Minnelli movie** Cabaret
**minor** child, inconsiderable, inferior, insignificant, junior, lesser, negligible, peripheral, petty, secondary, slight, small(er), subordinate, trifling, trivial, underage, unimportant, ward
**minor details** trivia
**minor earthquake** tremor
**minor illness** ailment
**minority group** faction
**minority protest** dissent
**minor literary work** opuscule
**minor mistake** slip
**minor nobleman** hidalgo (Sp)
**minor occupation** avocation
**minor offence** delinquency, misdemeanour
**minor quake** tremor
**minor river** bayou

**minor road** byway
**minor under care of a guardian** ward
**Minotaur** monster
**minster** cathedral
**minstrel** balladeer, bard, chorister, crooner, epicist, lyrist, musician, poet, singer, skald, songster, troubadour, vocalist
**minstrel's song** lay
**mint** brand-new, brew, cast, coin, compose, concoct, construct, create, die, excellent, fabricate, first-class, fresh, germinate, invent, make, new, perfect, produce, stamp, strike, uncancelled, unused
**mintage fee for coining money** brassage
**mintlike plant of which cats are fond** catmint, catnep, catnip, nepeta
**mint or sage** herb
**minty oil** menthol
**minus** deficiency, deficit, disadvantage, lack(ing), less, liability, short, subtract
**minute** critical, detailed, diminutive, infinitesimal, instant, memorandum, moment, note, proceedings, record, small, teeny, tiny
**minute amount** scintilla
**minute animal** mite
**minute animal and vegetable organisms** plankton
**minute branch of bronchus** bronchiole
**minute cavity** vacuole
**minute crevice between things** interstice
**minute crustacean** ostracod
**minute detail of conduct** punctilio
**minute grains** sand
**minute living being** microbe
**minutely worked out** elaborate
**minute opening** pore
**minute organism** corpuscle
**minute organism causing disease** bacillus, virus
**minute orifice in epidermis of leaf** stoma
**minute particle** atom
**minute particle charged with electricity** electron
**minute part of body cell** chromosome
**minute portion** atom, grain
**minute portion of matter** particle
**minute skin opening** pore
**minx** belle, coquette, demirep, drab, flirt, hag, harlot, harridan, hoyden, hussy, jade, jilt, prostitute, quean, shrew, tomboy, trollop, vamp, wanton
**miracle** marvel, omen, phenomenon, portent, prodigy, rarity, sign, spectacle, thaumaturgy, wonder
**miracle making** theurgy

**miraculous** incredible, marvellous, preternatural, supernatural, wonderful, wondrous
**miraculous divine action** theurgy
**miraculous token** sign
**mire** addle, begrime, bog, entangle, fen, involve, marsh, morass, muck, mud(dy), ooze, quag(mire), slime, slough, slush, stall, swamp(land)
**mirror** copy, depict, echo, emulate, exampler, glass, image, imitate, likeness, looking-glass, manifest, mimic, reflect(or), replica, represent, reproduce, reproduction, speculum, twin
**mirror backing** tain
**mirrored likeness** image
**mirror in telescope** speculum
**mirror tinfoil** tain
**mirth** buoyancy, cheer, conviviality, elation, enjoyment, felicity, fun, gaiety, gayness, glee, hilarity, jocundity, jollity, joyfulness, joyousness, laughter, levity, merriment, noise, rejoicing, revelry
**mirthful** amusing, beamish, cheerful, debonair, exultant, humorous, jolly, jovial, jubilant, laughing, lively, ludicrous, overjoyed, pleased, riant, ridiculous, smiling, untroubled
**miry place** slough, swamp, vlei
**misanthropic** alienated, antisocial, reserved, retiring, unfriendly, unsociable, withdrawn
**misapprehension of true state of affairs** illusion
**misappropriate money** defalcate
**misbegotten** dishonest, illegitimate, illicit, natural, unlawful
**misbehave** break, defy, disobey, err, infringe, offend, overstep, sin, slip, transgress, trespass, violate
**miscalculate** blunder, err, misjudge, overrate, underrate
**miscarry** abort, agley, fail, misfire
**miscellaneous** assorted, confused, diverse, diversified, heterogeneous, indiscriminate, jumbled, many, mingled, mixed, motley, promiscuous, sundry, varied, various
**miscellaneous collection of articles** salmagundi, salmagundy
**miscellaneous curios** bric-à-brac
**miscellaneous extras** etceteras
**miscellaneous items** odds and ends
**miscellaneous mixture** medley
**miscellaneous people** odds and sods
**miscellany** ana(lecta), analects, assortment, collection, compendium, extracts, medley, mess, mixture, notes, oddments, pieces, varia

**mischief** devil, evil, harm, hurt, imp(ishness), injury, misbehaviour, misfortune, naughtiness, roguery, shenanigan
**mischievous** annoying, arch, baleful, calamitous, destructive, elfish, evil, harmful, hurtful, impish, injurious, malefic, malevolent, noxious, rascally, roguish, ruinous, scatheful, sinister, sly, teasing, waggish, wanton
**mischievous act** prank
**mischievous adventure** escapade
**mischievous boy** gamin
**mischievous child** elf, imp, jackanades, puck, rogue, scamp, urchin
**mischievous creature** elf, goblin
**mischievous elf** leprechaun
**mischievous fairy** sprite
**mischievous girl** cutty, hussy
**mischievous goblin** gremlin
**mischievous kid** imp
**mischievous lad** gamin
**mischievous little devil** imp
**mischievous person** rascal, rogue
**mischievous practical jokes** monkey-tricks
**mischievous rogue** scamp
**mischievous sprite** gremlin, hobgoblin, puck
**mischievous troublemaker** gremlin
**misconstrue** miscalculate, misconceive, misinterpret, misjudge, misread, misreckon, misunderstand
**miscreant** rascal, rogue, scamp, villain, wretch, wrongdoer
**misdeed** crime, fault, felony, misconduct, misdemeanour, misdoing, offence, peccadillo, sin, transgression, trespass, wrong(doing)
**misdirected reverence** superstition
**miser** cheapskate, curmudgeon, hoarder, hunks, meanie, meany, moneygrabber, nabal, niggard, pennypincher, pinchpenny, scrimp, Scrooge, skinflint, tightwad
**miserable** abject, awful, bad, bleak, catastrophic, deplorable, destitute, distressed, doleful, dreary, forlorn, heart-broken, luckless, mean, needy, penniless, pitiful, sad, uncomfortable, uneasy, unfortunate, unhappy, wretched
**miserable abode** doghole
**miserable creature** wretch
**miserable dwelling** hovel
**miserably inadequate** pathetic
**miserly** greedy, meagre, mean, niggardly, parsimonious, penurious, scrimping, selfish, stingy, tight, ungenerous
**misery** anguish, bale, desolation, grief, sadness, sorrow, suffering, torment, tribulation, unhappiness, woe, wretchedness
**misfile** mislay
**misfortune** adversity, affliction, blow, calamity, catastrophe, disaster, distress, evil, fluke, happening, hardship, harm, hazard, ill, misadventure, mischance, mishap, reverse, ruin, trial, tribulation, trouble, woe, wrong
**misgiving** anxiety, care, concern, disquiet, distrust, doubts, fear, feeling, mistrust, nervousness, premonition, question, scruple, suspicion, uncertainty
**mishap** accident, adversity, calamity, casualty, contretemps, disaster, fiasco, misadventure, mischance, misfortune, snag
**mishmash** hodge-podge, hotchpotch, jumble, mess
**misinform** deceive, misdirect, misguide, mislead
**misinformed** mistaken
**misinterpret** confuse, garble, misapprehend, miscalculate, misconceive, misconstrue, misjudge, misread, misreckon, misrepresent, misteach, misunderstand
**mislaid** absent, astray, disappeared, displace, forfeited, gone, lacking, lost, misplaced, missing, strayed, vanished, wayward
**mislay** derange, dislocate, displace, disremember, drop, forget, lose, misfile, misplace, miss
**mislead** deceive, delude, misconduct, misdirect, misguide
**mislead as to one's strenght** bluff
**misleading argument** fallacy, sophism
**misleading talk** humbug
**mislead purposely** deceive
**misogynist** anti-feminist, bigot, egoist, hermit, male chauvinist, narcissist, recluse, sexist, woman-hater
**mispickel** arsenopyrite
**misplace** derange, dislocate, displace, lose, misapply, misbestow, misdirect, misfile, mislay
**misplay** lose
**misprint** erratum, typo
**misproportioned** asymmetrical
**misread** distort, misapprehend, misconceive, misconstrue, misinterpret, misjudge, mistake, mistook, mistranslate, misunderstand
**misrepresent** belie, disguise, distort, embarrass, exaggerate, falsify, garble, misstate, mock, parody, pervert, ridicule, twist, understate
**miss** avoid, blunder, err, escape, evade, fail(ure), forego, lack, lose, mademoiselle, mistake, omit, overlook, skip, slip, spinster, want
**miss deliberately** skip
**misshapen animal** monster
**missile** arrow, bullet, dart, grenade, javelin, lance, projectile, rocket, spear, strategic weapon
**missile store** silo
**missile weapon** arrow, ballista, bola(s), catapult, gun, onager, rifle, slingshot
**missing** absent, astray, discontinuous, displaced, gone, lacking, lost, minus, mislaid, misplaced, needed, nowhere, required, wanting
**missing part in manuscript** lacuna
**missing without permission** AWOL
**mission** aim, assignment, charge, commission, contingent, delegation, embassy, errand, goal, job, legation, mandate, ministry, office, pursuit, quest, task, trust, undertaking
**missive** answer, card, communication, dispatch, epistle, letter, line, mail, message, note, post(card), reply, report, screed, telegram
**Miss Ono** Yoko
**miss the mark** err
**Miss West** Mae
**mist** bewilderment, brume, cloud, drizzle, fog, haze, perplexity, smog
**mistake** bloomer, blunder, boner, bungling, clanger, err(atum), error, failure, fault, howler, inattention, incorrect, lapse, malentendu (F), misapprehend, misapprehension, misconception, misjudg(e)ment, misprint, misunderstand, oversight, slip, wrong
**mistake due to inadvertence** oversight
**mistaken** erroneous, inaccurate, incorrect, misconceived, wrong
**mistaken belief** delusion, fallacy
**mistaken idea** fallacy
**mistaken in one's opinions** misguided
**mistaken notion** fallacy
**mistake noted for correction** erratum
**mistake the meaning of** misconstrue
**mister** Effendi, esquire, Herr, master, monsieur, senor, signore, sir(e)
**mistreat** abuse, aggrieve, damage, disrespect, ill-treat, injure, maltreat, manhandle, maul, mishandle, misuse, persecute, pound, torture, wrong
**mistress** madam, lover
**mistress of a wealthy man** courtesan
**mistress of castle** chatelaine

**mistress of Toby** Judy
**mistrust** apprehend, beware, distrust, doubt, fear, suspect, wariness
**misty** blurred, blurry, cloudy, dewy, foggy, fuzzy, hazy, indistinct, murky, overcast, vague
**misunderstand** err, misapprehend, misconceive, miscount, misinterpret, misjudge, misread, mistake, misuse
**misunderstanding** error, malentendu (F), misapprehension, misconceiving, misconstruction, misconstruing, misinterpreting, misjudging, misjudg(e)ment, misreading, mistake, mistaking, mix-up
**misuse** abuse, aggrieve, batter, defraud, desecrate, exploit, force, ill-treat, ill-use, impair, maltreat, manhandle, misapply, misemploy, mishandle, misrule, mistreat, pollute, ravish, torment, torture, violate, waste
**misuse of words** malapropism
**mite** acari, atom(y), bit, dot, fleck, iota, jot, minimun, molecule, pittance, point, smidgen, speck, tick, trace
**mitigate** allay, appease, assuage, calm, check, lighten, moderate, placate, relieve, remit, temper, tranquillise
**mitigating circumstances** extenuation
**mitosis** karyokinesis
**mitral** valve
**mitten** glove, mitt, muff(etee)
**mittens of a pugilist** boxing gloves
**mix** alloy, amalgam(ate), associate, assortment, blend, coalesce, combination, combine, commix, composite, compound, concoction, confuse, conglomerate, consort, cross, dash, fold, fraternise, fuse, hobnob, homogenise, incorporate, interfuse, intermingle, intermix, intertwine, interweave, join, jumble, mingle, mixture, socialise, stir, synthesis, union, unite
**mix and stir when wet** pug
**mix as eggs** beat, scramble
**mix briskly** stir
**mix by hand** knead, manipulate
**mix by means of a spoon** stir
**mix clay with water by revolving machinery** blunge
**mix confusedly** ambivalent, associated, blended, broiled, coalesced, compounded, diverse, fused, intermingled, joined, joint, merged, mingled, motley, uncertain, united, varied
**mixed alcoholic drink** cocktail
**mixed bag** medley, olla
**mixed blood** Creole, mestizo

**mixed chalice** krasis
**mixed composition** miscellaneous
**mixed dish** hodge-podge, hotchpotch, olio, salad, stew
**mixed drink** cocktail, negus, nog, toddy
**mixed drink sometimes called nog** egg-flip
**mixed European and Asiatic descent** Eurasian
**mixed fabric of silk and wool** sayette
**mixed fight** mêlée
**mixed horse colour** roan
**mixed language** Creole, Fanagalo, Fanakalo, jargon, pidgin, tsotsitaal
**mixed marriage** exogamy
**mixed metaphor** catachresis
**mixed pickle** piccalilli
**mixed raw vegetables** salad
**mixed salad dish** salmagundi, salmagundy
**mixed school** co-ed
**mixed spices** tamara
**mixed twilled fabric** zanella
**mixed type** pi(e)
**mixed up** bewildered, complicated, confused, disordered, disoriented, distracted, distraught, disturbed, entangled, haywire, jumbled, mistaken, muddled, perplexed, puzzled, scrambled, upset
**mixed vegetables used as salad** macedoine
**mixed with foreign matter** impure
**mixer drink** lemonade, soda
**mix in crowd** (inter)mingle
**mixing implement** agitator, beater, mixer
**mix ingredients** stir
**mix liquors** brew
**mix of herbs tied or wrapped together** bouquet garni
**mix of spices used in Indian cooking** garam masala
**mix plaster** ga(u)ge
**mix tea** bulk
**mix thoroughly** blend
**mix together** blend, commingle, compound, stir
**mixture** amalgam, assortment, blend, combination, composition, compound, conglomeration, diversity, hash, hodge-podge, hotchpotch, medicine, medley, melange, miscellany, olio, pot-pourri, preparation, salmagundi, salmagundy, selection, stew
**mixture added to wine** dosage
**mixture attractive to pigeons** salt-cat
**mixture for cake** batter
**mixture for dressing leather** dubbin(g)
**mixture of ale and oatmeal** stoory
**mixture of alkaloids** adonidin, jaborine

**mixture of barks** tonga
**mixture of beer and lemonade** shandy
**mixture of black and white** grey, grizzle
**mixture of butter and flour** roux
**mixture of cement and stones** concrete
**mixture of cement, sand and water** mortar
**mixture of cement with sand and gravel** concrete
**mixture of clay and rock** body
**mixture of clay and sand** loam
**mixture of dried rose petals and spices** pot-pourri
**mixture of drugs** species
**mixture of elements** didymium
**mixture of feeds** mash
**mixture of fruit or vegetables** macedoine
**mixture of gases we breathe** air
**mixture of left-overs** hash
**mixture of liquorice sweets** all-sorts
**mixture of mercury with a metal** amalgam
**mixture of metals** alloy
**mixture of minerals** magma
**mixture of oats and barley** dredge
**mixture of principles** euonymin
**mixture of proteins** crotin
**mixture of religions** theocrasy
**mixture of salts** soyate
**mixture of sand and gravel** hoggin(g)
**mixture of sawdust and glue** badigeon
**mixture of slag and ore** browse
**mixture of smoke and haze** smaze
**mixture of spices** garam masala
**mixture of spirits and water** grog, highball
**mixture of stout and champagne** black velvet
**mixture of two or more metals** alloy
**mixture of vinegar and honey** oxymel
**mixture of vitamins** bios
**mixture of white and black** grey, grizzle
**mixture of wine, honey and spices** clary
**mixture to whiten bread** hards
**mix-up** confusion, disorder, fight, hash, jumble, melange, mêlée, mess, mistake, misunderstanding, muddle, muss, pi, scramble, tangle
**mix up** bewilder, blend, combine, complicate, confound, confuse(d), disturb, entangle, garble, implicate, involve, jumble, mix, muddle, perplex, puzzle, upset
**mix up cards in pack** shuffle
**mix when wet** pug
**mix wine** part
**mix with** adulterate

**mix with hands** knead
**mix with opium** opiate
**mix without distinction** promiscuous
**mix with spoon** stir
**mix with yeast** barm
**mnemonic** reminder
**mnemonic subject** memory
**Moabite king** Mesha
**Moab mountain** Nebo
**moan** bemoan, complain, dirge, grieve, groan, lament, lamentation, mourn, threnody, wail
**moaning Minnie** crybaby
**moan over** bemoan
**moat** barricade, canal, channel, conduit, defence, ditch, drain, dyke, fence, foss(e), furrow, graff, gully, trench, trough, watercourse
**mob** assemblage, bandits, barbarians, body, collections, crowd, drove, flock, gang(sters), gathering, group, herd, hoodlums, horde, host, jostle, legion, mass(es), multitude, overrun, pack, press, proletariat, public, rabble, rout, surge, surround, swarm, syndicate, throng
**mob disperser** teargas
**mobile** active, changeable, ever-changing, expressive, flexible, fluid, itinerant, migrant, motile, movable, peripatetic, portable, travelling, wandering
**mobile home** caravan, trailer
**mobile table** trolley
**mob killing of accused outside the law** lynching
**mob of hair** tousle
**mob rule** anarchy, chaos, lawlessness, mobocracy, ochlocracy, riot, terrorism, vigilantism, violence
**mobster** gangster
**mob up** swab, wipe
**mob violence** riot
**moccasin** larrigan, loafer, pac, shoe, snake, viper
**mocha** fine coffee
**mock** ape, banter, chaff, cheat, deceive, defy, deride, derision, disappoint, dupe, ersatz, fake, flout, fool, gibe, guy, imitate, insult, jeer, jibe, lampoon, leer, mimic, mislead, mockery, ridicule, satirise, scoff, scorn, sneer, tantalise, taunt, tease, twist
**mock attack** feint
**mocked by fate** ironic
**mocker** scoffer, taunter
**mockery** burlesque, caricature, contempt, contumely, deception, derision, disdain, disrespect, farce, imitation, insults, jeering, lampoon, mimicry, parody, pretence, ridicule,
sarcasm, satire, scoffing, scorn, sham, travesty
**mocking** contemptuous, cynical, derisive, derisory, disdainful, disrespectful, impudent, insulting, ironic, irreverent, sarcastic, sardonic, satiric(al), scoffing, scornful, snide, taunting
**mocking smile** sneer
**mocking words** scoff
**mock moon** paraselene
**mock orange** syringa
**mock pearl** olivet
**mock sun** parhelion
**mode** appearance, approach, configuration, craze, fashion, form, gradation, kind, look, manner, means, method, modality, modification, mould, pattern, practice, procedure, rule, shape, style, system, technique, variety, vogue, way, wise
**model** archetype, base, carve, cast, copy, design, dummy, epitome, example, exemplar, facsimile, fashion, form, gauge, ideal, image, imitation, mannequin, mock-up, mould, original, paradigm, paragon, pattern, plan, poser, prototype, replica, representation, sculpt, shape, show, sitter, specimen, standard, subject, type, typical
**model construction set** kit
**model design** pattern
**model displaying clothes** mannequin
**model for imitation** pattern
**modelled in wax** ceroplastic
**model of excellence** paragon
**model of person** effigy
**model of shoemaker** last, tree
**model of soundness** bell
**model of the human body** manikin
**model on a small scale** miniature
**Model T** tin-lizzie
**mode of conducting business** procedure
**mode of dealing with** treatment
**mode of existence** life
**mode of expression** idiom, phrase(ology)
**mode of formation** figuration
**mode of singing** chant
**mode of speaking** diction
**mode of walking** pace
**mode of writing with a style** stylography
**moderate** abate, allay, alleviate, appease, assuage, average, calm, chair, check, conservative, control(led), cool, curb, cushion, decrease, deliberate, diminish, disciplined, dwindle, ease, equable,
fair, gentle, indifferent, judicious, lessen, limited, mediocre, medium, mild, mitigate, modest, modify, modulate, ordinary, pacify, peaceable, qualify, quiet, reasonable, reduce, referee, regulate, repress, restrain(ed), sensible, sober, soften, specify, steady, steady, subdue, tame, temper(ate), umpire, usual, well-regulated
**moderate in intensity** calmly, deliberately, equably, limitedly, mezzo, mild(ly), modestly, passably, peaceably, rather, restrainedly, soberly, somewhat, steadily, temperately
**moderately good** middling, so-so
**moderately hot** warm
**moderately slow** andante
**moderately warm** lukewarm, tepid
**moderately wealthy** well-to-do
**moderately well** assez bien (F)
**moderate red** cerise
**moderate socialist in Russia** menshevik
**moderation** abstemiousness, alleviation, calmness, caution, composure, control, coolness, decrease, discretion, equanimity, fairness, justice, mildness, reasonableness, reduction, restraint, sedateness, self-control, sobriety, temperance
**modern** advanced, avant-garde, contemporaneous, contemporary, current, existing, fashionable, fresh, futuristic, immediate, late(st), modernistic, neonomian, neoteric, new(est), novel, present(-day), progressive, recent, revolutionary, topical, untraditional, up-to-date
**modern airliner** jet
**modern Ashanti** Twi
**modern dance** bop, break dancing, jitterburg, jive, rock 'n roll, shuffle, twist
**modern dance hall** disco(theque)
**modern detector** radar
**modern English-sounding rune** wen
**modern Greek name for Crete** Kriti
**modernise** do-up, improve, progress, redesign, reform, refresh, refurbish, regenerate, remake, remodel, renew, renovate, restyle, revamp, streamline, transform, update
**modernist** apostate, avant-gardist, innovationist, maverick, pacesetter, reformer, trendsetter
**modern Jewish state** Israel
**modern music** mbqanga, pop, rap
**modern name of Arbela** Ebril

**modern Persia** Iran
**modern Persian** Iranian
**modern Siamese** Thai
**modern tune** pop song
**modest** bashful, becoming, blushful, chaste, decent, decorous, demure, humble, mediocre, meek, moderate, nervous, prim, proper, prudish, reserved, retiring, timid, unassuming, unboastful, unextravagant, unimposing, unobtrusive, unpretentious, unseen, virtuous
**modest contribution** mite
**modest farm** smallholding
**modest girl** blusher
**modesty** bashfulness, coyness, decency, demureness, diffidence, humbleness, humility, meekness, propriety, prudery, pudency, quietness, reserve, reticence, self-effacement, shyness, simplicity, timidity
**mod fashion** fad
**modicum** allowance, atom, bit, bite, chip, crumb, drop, fraction, fragment, grain, granule, iota, jot, little, mite, molecule, nip, particle, pittance, ration, scrap, smattering, smithereens, speck, splinter, tittle, trifle, whit
**modification** adjustment, refinement, revision, variant, variation
**modification of Esperanto** Ido
**modified for different purpose** adapted
**modify** adapt, adjust, alter, balance, change, convert, decrease, diminish, dulcify, improve, limit, moderate, qualify, recast, redesign, redo, reduce, reform, remould, reorganise, (re)shape, restrain, restrict, revise, soften, temper, transform, transmute, vary
**modify for different purpose** adapt
**modish** fashionable, in
**mod style** fad
**modulate** accentuate, adapt, adjust, alleviate, assuage, attune, chime, diversify, harmonise, intonate, key, pitch, regulate, stress, temper, tone, tune, vary
**modulation** accent, adaptation, alteration, cadence, change, emphasis, enunciation, modification, pitch, reduction, rhythm, stress, throb, tonality, tone, transition, variation
**modulation of the voice** cadence, inflection, intonation
**mofified leaf** sepal
**moggy** cat, mog
**Mogul** Mongolian

**mogul** baron, celebrity, lord, magnate, notable, official, personage, tycoon
**mohair** angora, fabric, garment, textile
**mohair source** angora
**Mohammedanism** Islamism, Muslimism
**Mohammed's birthplace** Mecca
**moiety** bisection, chip, crumb, division, fraction, half, hemisphere, portion, ration, segment, semisphere
**moist** clammy, damp, dank, dewy, drizzly, humid, muggy, rainy, wet(tish)
**moist and cold** clammy
**moisten** anoint, bedew, damp(en), dew, humidity, imbrue, irrigate, lap, lick, moisture, ret, saturate, soak, sodden, spill, splash, sponge, spray, sprinkle, vaporise, wash, water, wet
**moisten flax** ret
**moisten while cooking** baste
**moisture** clamminess, condensation, damp(ness), dankness, dew(iness), fluid, fog, humidity, hygr-, moistness, ooze, perspiration, rain, saliva, sogginess, steaminess, sweat, teardrops, tears, vapour, water, wet(ness)
**moisture-extracting machine** drier
**moistureless** arid, desiccated, dry
**moisture oozing from the skin** sweat
**moke** ass, donkey
**molar** grinder, (wisdom) tooth
**molasses** treacle
**molasses spirit** rum
**mole** barrier, birthmark, blotch, breakwater, discolouration, dock, groyne, jetty, mar, naevus, patch, pier, pimple, spot, spy, wart, wharf
**molest** annoy, assail, attack, bother, discommode, harass, hector, irritate, plague, torment, torture, trouble, vex, worry
**Moliére character** miser
**mollify** allay, appease, assuage, calm, compose, conciliate, cushion, ease, lessen, lull, mellow, mitigate, moderate, modify, pacify, placate, quell, quiet, reduce, relax, relieve, soften, soothe, subdue, temper
**mollusc** abalone, alikreukel, bivalve, chokka, clam, cowrie, cuttlefish, decapod, gastropod, limpet, mussel, nautilus, octopus, oyster, periwinkle, perlemoen, sea-ear, shellfish, slug, snail, squid, univalve, whelk
**mollusc's anchor** byssus
**mollusc that bores ships** teredo
**mollusc with distinct tentacled head** cephalopod
**mollycoddle** baby, chicken, coddle, cosset, crybaby, effeminate, humour,

(over)indulge, pamper, pet, sissy, softy, spoil, spoon-feed, weakling
**molten rock** lava, magma
**mom** ma(ma), mamma, mother, mum(my)
**moment** consequence, consideration, drive, flash, force, gravity, instant, jiff(y), minute, second, significance, trice, twinkling
**momentary** brief, brilliant, ephemeral, fast, flashing, fleeting, flying, fugitive, hasty, little, meteoric, passing, quick, rapid, short(-lived), sudden, swift, temporary, transient, transitory
**momentary show** flash
**momentous** consequent, critical, crucial, decisive, eventful, fateful, grave, historic, important, serious, significant, vital, weighty
**momentum** drive, energy, force, impact, impetus, impulse, incentive, power, pressure, push, speed, stimulus, strength, thrust, urge, velocity
**mom or dad** parent
**Monaco princess** Caroline, Stephanie
**monarch** autocrat, czar, despot, dictator, dynast, emperor, empress, Kaiser, king, majesty, potentate, prince(ss), queen, rex, ruler, sovereign, tsar, tyrant
**monarchal ruler** potentate
**monarchist** royalist
**monarch of Iran** shah
**monarch's headwear** crown
**monarch's period of rule** reign
**monarch's residence** palace
**monarch's seat** throne
**monarch's spouse** consort
**monarch's symbol** sceptre
**monarchy** anarchy, autocracy, command, control, crown, despotism, direction, domain, dominion, duchy, dukedom, dynasty, emperor, empire, empress, government, influence, king(dom), kingship, legality, management, monarch, power, principality, principate, realm, reign, rule, sovereignty, sway, tyranny
**monarchy supporter** royalist
**monastery** abbey, abode, ashram, bonzery, cenoby, charterhouse, cloister, convent, friary, hermitage, hospice, lamasery, mandra, monkery, nunnery, priory, residence, seminary
**monastery church** abbey, minster
**monastery head** abbot
**monastery yard** garth

**monastic** ascetic, austere, celibate, cloistered, contemplate, recluse, secluded, withdrawn
**monastic arcade** cloister
**monastic chapel** abbey
**monastic deputy** prior
**monastic house** cloister
**monetary** budgetary, capital, cash, economic, financial, fiscal, money, nummary, nummular, pecuniary
**monetary penalty** fine
**monetary settlement** endowment
**monetary unit** bill, coin, dollar, note, rand, rupee
**monetary unit of Alaska** dollar
**monetary unit of Albania** lek
**monetary unit of Algeria** dinar
**monetary unit of Angola** kwanza
**monetary unit of Argentina** peso
**monetary unit of Bangladesh** taka
**monetary unit of Belgium** franc
**monetary unit of Bolivia** peso boliviaro
**monetary unit of Brazil** cruzeiro
**monetary unit of Bulgaria** lev
**monetary unit of Burkina-Faso** franc
**monetary unit of Burundi** franc
**monetary unit of Cameroon** franc
**monetary unit of Chad** franc
**monetary unit of China** yuan
**monetary unit of Colombia** peso
**monetary unit of Congo** franc
**monetary unit of Cuba** peso
**monetary unit of Dahomey** franc
**monetary unit of Denmark** krone
**monetary unit of Dominican Republic** peso
**monetary unit of Ecuador** sucre
**monetary unit of El Salvador** colon
**monetary unit of Finland** markka
**monetary unit of France** franc
**monetary unit of Gabon** franc
**monetary unit of Ghana** cedi
**monetary unit of Greece** drachma
**monetary unit of Grenada** dollar
**monetary unit of Guatemala** quetzal
**monetary unit of Guinea** franc
**monetary unit of Haiti** gourde
**monetary unit of Honduras** lempira
**monetary unit of Hungary** forint
**monetary unit of India** rupee
**monetary unit of Iran** rial
**monetary unit of Israel** pound
**monetary unit of Italy** lira
**monetary unit of Ivory Coast** franc
**monetary unit of Kampuchea** riel
**monetary unit of Kenya** shilling
**monetary unit of Lichtenstein** franc
**monetary unit of Luxembourg** franc
**monetary unit of Madagascar** franc
**monetary unit of Malaysia** ringit
**monetary unit of Mali** franc
**monetary unit of Mauritania** ouguiya
**monetary unit of Mauritius** rupee
**monetary unit of Mexico** peso
**monetary unit of Morocco** dirham
**monetary unit of Netherlands** guilder
**monetary unit of Nicaragua** cordoba
**monetary unit of Niger** franc
**monetary unit of Nigeria** naira
**monetary unit of Panama** balboa
**monetary unit of Papua New Guinea** kina
**monetary unit of Peru** sol
**monetary unit of Poland** zloty
**monetary unit of Portugal** escudo
**monetary unit of Romania** leu
**monetary unit of Russia** r(o)uble
**monetary unit of Rwanda** franc
**monetary unit of Senegal** franc
**monetary unit of Saudi Arabia** riyal
**monetary unit of Sierra Leone** leone
**monetary unit of Soviet Union** grivna, kope(c)k, r(o)uble
**monetary unit of Spain** peseta
**monetary unit of Sri Lanka** rupee
**monetary unit of Swaziland** lilangani
**monetary unit of Sweden** krona
**monetary unit of Switzerland** franc
**monetary unit of Tahiti** franc
**monetary unit of the Philippines** peso
**monetary unit of Togo** franc
**monetary unit of Uruguay** peso
**monetary unit of Venezuela** bolivar
**monetary unit of Vietnam** dong
**monetary unit of Zambia** kwacha
**monetary unit of Zimbabwe** dollar
**money** affluence, assets, banknotes, capital, cash, change, coin, coppers, currency, dough, finances, funds, gain, lucre, mazuma, means, mint, note, pocket, profit, prosperity, rhino, riches, specie, tin, wealth
**money advancer** lender
**money affairs** finance
**money back** refund
**money bag** purse
**money beads** wampum
**money-case** purse, wallet
**money collected in a religious service** offertory
**money compensation** solatium
**money-drawer** till
**money due** debt
**money earned** earnings, income
**moneyed** rich
**moneyer's weight** droit
**money-exchange charge** agio(tage)
**money extorted by threats of exposure** blackmail
**money factory** mint
**money for charity** alms
**money for expenses** allowance
**money for incidental expenses** kitty, petty cash
**money for the poor** alms
**money gained through gambling** winnings
**money gains** profit
**money given in recognition of service** gratuity
**money-grabber** materialist, miser
**money granted** subsidy
**money-grubbing** materialistic
**moneyholder** purse, wallet
**money in account** credit
**money in advance** surety
**money in coin or notes** cash
**money in kitty** ante
**money in till** float, takings
**money in use in a country** currency
**money invested in a concern** stock
**moneylender** broker, financier, loaner, usurer
**moneylending establishment** pawnshop
**money lent** loan
**money lost in gambling** losings
**moneymaker** mint
**moneymaking** advantageous, gainful, lucrative, paying, profitable, remunerative, worthwhile
**money matters** finance
**money off** rebate
**money-off voucher** coupon
**money on account** credit, payment
**money on hand** cash, funds
**money order** draft
**money-order on a banker** cheque
**money overdue** arrears
**money owed** arrears, debt
**money paid as instalment** earnest
**money paid by a passenger** fare
**money paid for release** ransom
**money penalty** fine
**money placed in bank** deposit
**money pouch** purse
**money resources** finance, funds, means
**money roll** wad
**money saved for future use** nest-egg
**money set aside** savings
**money support for an undertaking** finance
**money user** spender
**money vault** safe
**money wagered** stake
**Mongolian** Mogul
**Mongolian Buddhist priest** lama
**Mongolian capital** Ulan Bator
**Mongolian desert** Gobi
**Mongolian priest** shaman
**Mongolian tent** yurt
**Mongolian warrior** ta(r)tar
**mongrel** bastard, bigener, brak, cross, crossbre(e)d, cur, dog, feist, fice, half-breed, half-caste, hybrid,

ill-defined, limer, métis (F), mixed, mulatto, mule, mutt, offshoot, piebald, quadroon, tike, tyke
**mongrel dog**  brak, cur, mutt
**monies received**  takings
**monitor lizard**  goanna
**monk**  abbé, abbot, Bernadine, brother, celibate, c(o)enobite, eremite, friar, monastic, prior, religious
**monkey**  ape, baboon, chimp(anzee), gorilla, grivet, langur, primate, simian, waag
**monkey bread tree**  baobab
**monkey business**  chicanery, clowning, dupery, foolery, foolishness, mischief, naughtiness, pranks, rascality, tomfoolery, tricks
**monkey-like animal**  lemur
**monkey of Tarzan**  Cheeta
**monkey-wrench**  spanner
**monk of Lamaism**  lama
**monk of last Tsar's court**  Rasputin
**monk's garment**  scapular
**monk's haircut**  tonsure
**monk's head**  abbot
**monk's home**  monastery
**monk's hooded garment**  cowl
**monkshood plant**  aconite, wolfsbane
**monk's room**  cell
**monk's title**  abbot, brother, Dom, Fra
**monoclinous**  hermaphrodite
**monocracy**  absolutism, autocracy, czarism, despotism, dictatorship, monarchy, sovereignty, tsarism, tyranny
**monodic**  dirgelike
**monody**  dirge, epicedium, jeremiad, lament, threnode, threnody, ululation
**monolith**  Ayers Rock, column, monument, needle, obelisk, pillar, shaft
**monologue**  address, harangue, lecture, monodrama, oration, philippic, recitation, sermon, soliloquy, speech
**monopolise**  absorb, appropriate, arrogate, consume, control, dominate, own, pre-empt
**monosepalous**  gamosepalous
**monotheistic sect**  Sikhism
**monotonous**  banal, bland, basic, boring, colourless, common, dreary, droning, dull, flat, humdrum, plodding, practical, prosaic, repetitious, repetitive, routine, same, soporific, tedious, tiresome, toneless, unchanging, undeviating, uneventful, uniform, uninflected, uninteresting, unvaried, unvarying, vapid, wearisome
**monotonous buzz**  drone
**monotonous chanting**  sing-song

**monotonous song**  chant
**monotonous sound**  drone
**monotonous speaker**  drawler
**monotony**  boredom, colourless, dullness, ennui, flatness, repetitiveness, routine, sameness, tediousness, tedium, uniformity
**monster**  anomaly, bog(e)y, brute, centaur, demon, devil, dragon, fiend, freak, gargoyle, giant, griffin, hippogriff, hippogryph, horror, huge, Minotaur, miscreant, monstrosity, monstrous, ogre, sadist, savage, sphinx, teratism, tokoloshe, tyrant, villain, werewolf
**monster breathing fire**  dragon
**monster killed by Zeus**  Typhoeus
**monster living in the swamps of central Australia**  bunyip
**monster of myth**  ogre
**monster slain by Hercules**  Hydra
**monster's Loch**  Ness
**monster with hundred eyes**  Argus
**monster with hundred hands**  Briareus
**monstrosity**  abberation, abnormality, anomaly, atrocity, colossus, deformity, demoniac, evil, eyesore, freak, frightfulness, giant, horribleness, horror, malformation, miscreation, monster, obscenity, ogre(ss), savageness, sight, spectacle, terror, titan
**monstrous**  colossal, enormous, gigantic, great, hideous, horrendous, horrible, huge, immense, large, outrageous, prodigious, shocking, terrible, tremendous
**monstrous beast**  leviathan
**monstrous creature of classical mythology**  orc
**monstrous lie**  strammer
**monstrous wickedness**  enormity
**montane**  mountain-dwelling
**Monte Carlo is there**  Monaco
**Monterrey pine**  macrocarpa
**month**  mensis (L), mes (Sp), mese (I), mois (F), monat (G)
**monthly**  mensal, per mensum (L)
**monthly pay**  salary
**monthly payment**  instalment
**monument**  cenotaph, crypt, gravestone, mausoleum, memorial, reliquary, remembrance, shrine, statue, testament, testimonial, tomb(stone), vault
**monumental**  awesome, big, bulky, classic, colossal, enduring, enormous, historic, immense, immortal, important, jumbo, lasting, majestic, mammoth, massive, memorable, monstrous, outstanding,

prodigious, significant, staggering, towering, unforgettable
**monumental Egyptian structure**  pyramid, Sphinx
**monumental gateway**  pylon
**monumental inscription**  epitaph
**monumental structure**  pyramid, ziggurat, zik(k)urat
**monument consisting of a single stone**  monolith
**monument to the dead**  cenotaph
**moo**  low
**mood**  attitude, blues, cast, consciousness, disposition, dumps, feeling, humour, melancholy, mind, mode, nature, opinion, perception, position, spirit, temper(ament), vein
**moodily**  angrily, crestfallenly, crossly, crustily, curtly, dismally, dolefully, dourly, frowningly, gloomily, glumly, irritably, lugubriously, miserably, morosely, pensively, petulantly, sadly, sulkily, sullenly, temperamentally, testily, touchily
**mood of vexation**  peeve
**moody**  broody, captious, fretful, gloomy, intractable, irritable, perverse, snappish, splenetic, stubborn, sulky, sullen, testy
**mooing**  lowing
**moon**  luna (L), month, satellite
**moon about in low spirits**  mope
**moon age at beginning of calendar year**  epact
**moon beam**  ray
**moon-calf**  dolt, idiot
**moon-faced**  round
**moonflower**  angel's tears
**moon god**  Enzu, Sin
**moon goddess**  Artemis, Cynthia, Hecate, Isis, Luna, Phoebe, Selene
**moon hole**  crater
**moon inhabitant**  selenite
**moon point furthest from earth**  apogee
**moon's first quarter**  crescent
**moon shadow**  umbra
**moon-shaped**  crescent
**moonshine**  booze, nonsense
**moonshine detective**  Cuff
**moonstruck**  crazed, lunatic
**moon valley**  rill(e)
**moonwort**  honesty, lunaria
**moony**  dreamy, listless, moonlit, weak
**moor**  affix, anchor, attach, berth, dock, fasten, fen, heath, marsh, moorland, muir, navigate, place, secure, tie, upland, wasteland
**Moor**  Arab
**moored security**  girt
**mooring post**  bollard
**mooring weight**  anchor

**moor in suitable place** berth
**Moorish kettle-drum** atabal
**moorland bird** curlew
**moorland shrub** heather
**Moor of Venice** Othello
**moose** elk
**moot** debatable, debate, discuss, disputable, disputed, doubtful, subject, unsettled
**mop** clean, sponge, swab, tangle, wash, wipe
**mope** agonise, brood, despair, droop, fret, grieve, idle, lament, languish, lower, meditate, muse, pine, pout, repine, sulk
**mop the deck** swab
**mop up** absorb, clean, clear, eliminate, neutralise, secure, sponge, swab, wash, wipe
**moral** blameless, chaste, decent, ethical, ethics, good, honest, honourable, innocent, just, lesson, meaning, message, morality, noble, principled, proper, pure, right(eous), significance, standards, upright, virtuous
**moral attitude** standpoint
**moral campaigner** crusader
**moral code** ethics
**moral corruption** depravity, gangrene, wickedness
**moral deterioration** corruption
**morale** attitude, condition, confidence, esprit de corps, feelings, heart, mettle, mood, nerve, resolution, resolve, spirit, state, temper, zeal
**moral excellence** goodness, uprightness, virtue
**moral fable** apologue
**moral fall** lapse
**moralising lecture** homily
**morality** constancy, decency, decorum, equity, ethics, faithfulness, goodness, honesty, integrity, justice, loyalty, morals, rectitude, righteousness, trustworthiness, virtue
**moral laxity** decadence, innocently, justly, nobly, properly, purely, righteously, rightly, uprightly, virtuously
**morally accountable for actions** responsible
**morally bad** evil, wicked
**morally better** nobler
**morally binding** incumbent
**morally correct** ethical
**morally corrupt** decadent
**morally debased** abject
**morally depraved** corrupt
**morally evil** vicious
**morally good** virtuous
**morally impure** unclean

**morally lax** dissolute
**morally low** base
**morally pure** chaste
**morally repugnant** obscene
**morally strict** austere, puritanical
**morally undefiled** pure
**morally weak** frail
**morally wrong** immoral
**morally wrong act** crime
**moral obligation** bond, duty
**moral offence** sin
**moral of story** epimyth
**moral or mental snare** net
**moral philosophy** ethics
**moral principle** ethic
**moral quality** thew
**moral rule** ethic, principle
**morals** conduct, customs, ethics, ethos, ideals, integrity, manners, morality, mores, principles, probity, rectitude, scruples, standards
**moral sense of right and wrong** conscience
**moral slip** lapse
**moral snare** net
**moral taint** stain
**moral to a story** tag
**moral trial** probation
**moral uprightness** virtue
**moral value** ideal
**moral wrong** evil, harm, sin
**morass** bog, fen, marsh, quagmire, slough, swamp, vlei, wetland
**moray** eel
**morbid** diseased, extreme, gloomy, gruesome, macabre, perverse, sensitive, sick, tainted, vitiated
**morbid absorption in fantasy** autism
**morbid anxiety** dysthymia
**morbid aversion to food** sitophobia
**morbid aversion to strangers** xenophobia
**morbid condition of the urine** dysuria
**morbid contraction** stricture
**morbid craving for** narcomania
**morbid craving for alcoholic liquor** dipsomania
**morbid daintiness of the appetite** opsomania
**morbid depression without real cause** hypochondria
**morbid dislike of foreigners** xenophobia
**morbid dread of being alone** monophobia
**morbid dread of confined places** claustrophobia
**morbid dread of contracting disease** nosophobia
**morbid dread of heights** acrophobia
**morbid dread of open places** agoraphobia

**morbid dread of water** hydrophobia
**morbid drowsiness** lethargy
**morbid egotism** egomania
**morbid erotic desire** erotomania
**morbid fear** phobia
**morbid hardening of tissue** scleroma
**morbid hunger** bulimia
**morbid interest in excrement** scatology
**morbid liking for some particular kind of food** opsomania
**morbidly self-opinionated** egomaniac
**morbid repugnance to food** sitophobia
**morbid restlessness** dysphoria
**morbid sensitiveness of nerves** hyperaesthesia
**morbid state resulting from overmuch tea-drinking** theism
**morbilli** measles, rubeola
**mordant** abrupt, acid, acrid, bitter, caustic, cynical, derisive, disdainful, edged, erosive, impolite, insulting, ironic, mocking, moody, mordacious, morose, peevish, pungent, sarcastic, sardonic, snappish, surly, teasing, unfriendly
**mordant mineral salt** alum
**mordent** pralltriller
**more** added, additamentary, additional, additory, adjunct, appendage, besides, better, else, extra, fresh, further(more), increase, increment, longer, moreover, new, other, spare, supplement(ary)
**more advantageous** better
**more ancient** older
**more and more** increasingly, progressively
**more appealing** cuter
**more arduous** harder
**more arid** drier
**more awkward** lumpier
**more compact** firmer
**more competent** abler
**more conclusively** a fortiori (L)
**more costly** dearer
**more crafty** slier, slyer, wilier
**more delicate** finer
**more distant** farther, further
**more distant part of sea in view** offing
**more envious** greener
**more extended** longer
**more facile** easier
**more fortunate** luckier
**more garish** gaudier
**more graceful** statelier
**more gritty** sandier
**more haste, less speed** festina lente (L)
**more irritable** testier
**more isolated** lonelier
**more mature** older

**more or less** approximately, roughly
**more ornamental** fancier
**moreover** additionally, again, also, and, au reste (F), besides, ditto, further(more), too
**more overbearing** bossier
**more pleasant** nicer
**more potent** stronger
**more prudent** wiser
**more recent** later, nearer, newer
**more recently** later
**more remote** ulterior
**more sage** wiser
**more slanting** steeper
**more sloppy** messier
**more splendid** finer
**more stylish** classier, niftier
**more suitable** better
**more than** above, super-
**more than enough** abundant, ample, galore, plentiful, plenty, superfluous, surplus, too
**more than expected** extra
**more than half** bulk, majority, mass
**more than is needed** superfluous
**more than more** most
**more than once** twice
**more than one** plural
**more than one magus** magi
**more than one man** men
**more than ordinary** especial
**more than sufficient** abundant, ample
**more than sufficiently** amply, fully, generously
**more than sufficient quantity** abundance
**more than ten** umpteen
**more than two** several
**more than usual** extra
**more to the front** anterior
**more unusual** rarer
**morgue** crematorium, crematory, mortuary
**Mormon** Latter-day Saint
**Mormon administrator** apostle
**Mormon state** Utah
**Mormon state aborigine** Utahan
**morning** dawn, daybreak, daylight, forenoon, morn, sun-up, sunrise
**morning meal** breakfast
**morning moisture** dew
**morning poetically** morn
**Morning Prayer** matin
**morning prayer service** matins
**morning star** daystar, Lucifer, Phosphorus, Venus
**morning twilight** aurora
**morning vapour** dew
**Moroccan city** Rabat
**Moroccan enclave** Ceuta
**Moroccan port** Rabat
**Moroccan robe** caftan, kaftan

**Morocco leather** levant, maroquin
**Moro chief** dato
**moron** dullard, idiot, imbecile, num(b)skull, retard(ate)
**moronic** asinine, brainless, crazy, deficient, dense, dim, doltish, dull, fatuous, feeble(-minded), foolish, gullible, half-witted, idiotic, imbecile, inane, insane, lunatic, naïve, obtuse, senseless, shallow, silly, simple, sluggish, stolid, stupid, thick, unintelligent, witless
**morose** blue, churlish, cross, dismal, doleful, gloomy, grim, grouchy, lugubrious, moody, mopish, morbid, perverse, sad, sombre, sour(-tempered), stern, sulky, sullen, surly, unhappy, unsocial
**morosely irritable** grumpy
**moroseness** acerbity, austerity, morbidity, petulence, saturnity, severity, silence, spleen, taciturnity
**morose sneerer** cynic
**Morse code dot** dah, dit
**Morse code symbol** dash, dot
**morsel** bit, bite, crumb, drop, flavour, fraction, fragment, grain, hunk, iota, modicum, mouthful, nibble, nip, piece, ration, scrap, section, segment, sip, slice, snack, soupçon, taste, titbit, whit
**morsel out** allocate, apportion, dispense, distribute, divide
**mortal** being, body, deadly, destructive, earthling, earthly, ephemeral, fatal, final, human, individual, killing, lethal, murderous, person, temporal, transient, (wo)man, worldly
**mortality** death(-rate), destruction, humanity, man, (hu)mankind, massacre, mortalness, pandemic, society
**mortal life viewed as a journey** pilgrimage
**mortally** fatally, intensely
**mortar** cannon, carronade, cement, clay, composition, concrete, daubing, howitzer, plaster
**mortar carrier** hod
**mortgage** bond, debenture, guaranty, lien, obligate, pledge, security, warranty
**mortice insert** tenon
**mortician** undertaker
**mortification** awkwardness, bashfulness, chagrin, confusion, disappointment, discontent, discouragement, disenchantment, disillusionment, displeasure, dissatisfaction, distress,

embarrassment, failure, frustration, humiliation, regret, shame
**mortification of flesh** gangrene
**mortification of the flesh** asceticism
**mortified** abashed, affronted, annoyed, ashamed, crushed, dead, deflated, displeased, embarrassed, horrified, humbled, humiliated, shamed, vexation
**mortify** abase, abash, agitate, annoy, deject, discourage, disgust, dishearten, displease, embitter, gangrene, humble, humiliate, offend, shame, subdue, upset, vex
**mortify intentionally** snub
**mortify the flesh** crucify
**mortise filler** tenon
**mortuary** crematorium, crematory, morgue
**mosaic glass tile** tessera
**Mosaic law** Torah
**mosaic piece** tile
**Mosaic sibling** Miriam
**mosaic work** parquetry
**Moscow citadel** Kremlin
**Moses was found in the river** Nile
**mosey** amble, saunter, stroll
**Moslem** dervish, Islamic, Mohammedan, Muslim, Saracen
**mosque** masjid, mesked, musjid
**mosque prayer leader** ima(u)m
**mosque tower** minaret
**mosquito** aedes, anopheles, culex, culicid, dipteran, dipterous, fly, gnat, insect, skeeter
**moss** lichen, liverwort, lycopod(ium)
**moss-like plant** hepatic, lichen
**moss or liverwort** bryophyte
**most** best, maximum
**most advanced in position** foremost
**most advantageous** best
**most ancient** oldest
**most astute** smartest
**most attractive** loveliest
**most beloved** dearest
**most bloody** goriest
**most central** inner
**most considerate** nicest
**most corrosion-resistant metal known** iridium
**most courageous** bravest
**most desirable** best
**most difficult** toughest
**most direct line of descent in skiing** fall-line
**most dismal** dreariest
**most distant** farthest
**most dizzy** giddiest
**most docile** tamest
**most essential part of any substance** quintessence
**most exalted** noblest

most excellent best
most expensive dearest
most facile easiest
most favourable best, optimum
most frugal thriftiest
most honourable noblest
most humble least, lowest
most important main, prime
most important part alpha and omega
most important people kingpins
most inferior worst
most inquisitive nosiest
most inward in(ner)most
most junior youngest
most keen sharpest
most lazy idlest
mostly chiefly, commonly, customarily, especially, generally, largely, mainly, normally, ordinarily, particularly, predominantly, primarily, principally, typically, usually
most mature oldest, ripest
most meagre barest
most miserly meanest
most modern latest, newest
most nervous edgiest
most noticeable salient
most opulent richest, wealthiest
most outstanding best
most peculiar oddest, strange
mostrance ostensory
most recent last, latest, newest
most remote ultima
most sacred sacrosanct
most sacred part of a temple adytum
most sacred shrine in Mecca Caaba, Kaaba
most secretive cagiest
most secure safest
most senior oldest
most sharply inclined steepest
most slender leanest
most sluggish slowest
most solemn day of Jewish year Day of Atonement, Yom Kippur
most spiteful nastiest
most squalid sleaziest
most thoughtful kindest
most uncertain vaguest
most unpleasant worst
most unstained cleanest
most unusual rarest
most up-to-date latest
most vicious meanest
most widely used metal iron
most youthful youngest
motel inn
moth lepidopteran
moth and rust decomposition, dilapidation
moth collector lepidopterist

mother cherish, cosset, dam, foster, indulge, ma, madre (Sp), mam(m)a, mater (L), mere (F), mom(my), mum(my), nurse, nurture, overprotect, pamper, produce, protect, raise, rear, spoil, tend
mother and father parents
mother country homeland
mother horse mare
mother-in-law of Ruth Naomi
motherless calf dog(e)y, dogie
motherly affectionate(ly), caring, comforting, fond, gentle, innately, kind(ly), loving, maternal, natively, naturally, protective, tender, warm
mother of Aaron Jochebed
mother of Abas Hypermnestra, Metanira
mother of Abel Eve
mother of Abihu Elisheba
mother of Abishai Zeruiah
mother of Absalom Maachah
mother of Acacallus Pasiphae
mother of Acarnan Callirrhoe
mother of Achilles Thetis
mother of Acis Symaethis
mother of Acrisius Aglaia
mother of Adonijah Haggith
mother of Aeacus Aegina
mother of Aegaeon Gaea, Ge
mother of Agave Harmonia
mother of Agenor Libya
mother of Alexander Olympias
mother of Aloeus Canace
mother of Amalek Timnah
mother of Anax Gaea, Ge
mother of animal dam
mother of Aphrodite Dione
mother of Apollo Leto, Leton(i)a
mother of Arges Gaea, Ge
mother of Artemis Leto
mother of Asher Zilpa
mother of Bacchus Semele
mother of Benjamin Rachel
mother of Bethuel Milcah
mother of Buz Milcah
mother of Caesar Aurelia
mother of Cain Eve
mother of Chileab Abigail
mother of Chilion Naomi
mother of Copreus Hippodamia
mother of Cupid Venus
mother of Daniel Abigail
mother of Dinah Leah
mother of Don Juan Inez
mother of Eliphaz Adah
mother of Ephraim Asenath
mother of Esau Rebecca, Rebekah
mother of Ethnan Helah
mother of Gad Zilpah
mother of Gaham Reumah
mother of Galahad Elaine

mother of Gazez Ephah
mother of Gershom Zipporah
mother of Hamlet Gertrude
mother of Haran Ephah
mother of Hazo Milca
mother of Hector and Paris Hecuba
mother of Helen of Troy Leda
mother of Hercules Alcmene
mother of Hermes Maia
mother of Horus Isis
mother of Irene Themis
mother of Iris Electra
mother of Isaac Sarah
mother of Ishbak Keturah
mother of Ishmael Hagar
mother of Ishui Ahinoam
mother of Isis Rhea
mother of Issachar Leah
mother of Jacob Rebecca
mother of Jesus Mary
mother of John Elisabeth, Salome
mother of Jokshan Keturah
mother of Joseph Rachel
mother of Josiah Jedidah
mother of Jotham Jerushah
mother of Judah Leah
mother of King Arthur Igraine, Ygerne
mother of Mary Anne
mother of Medan Keturah
mother of Mephibosheth Rizpah
mother of Mesha Hodesh
mother of Midian Keturah
mother of Mikloth Maachah
mother of Minos Europa
mother of Moses Jochebed
mother of Naamah Zillah
mother of Nadab Elisheba
mother of Napoleon Hortense
mother of Nero Agrippina
mother of Obed Ruth
mother of Onam Atarah
mother-of-pearl nacre
mother of Pharez Tamar
mother of Pildash Milcah
mother of Pollux Leda
mother of Poseidon Rhea
mother of Rajiv Gandhi Indira
mother of Rehoboam Naamah
mother of Reuben Leah
mother of Reuel Bashemath
mother of Rhea Gaea
mother of Salome Herodias
mother of Samuel Hannah
mother of Seb Tefnut
mother of Seth Eve
mother of Shaaph Maachah
mother of Shammua Bathsheba
mother of Sheber Maachah
mother of Sheva Maachah
mother of Shobab Azubah, Bathsheba
mother of Shuah Keturah
mother of Simeon Leah

**mother of Solomon** Bathsheba
**mother of Tantalus** Niobe, Pluto
**mother of Teman** Adah
**mother of Tethys** Terra
**mother of the Virgin Mary** Saint Anne
**mother of Titan** Gae(a), Gaia
**mother of Triton** Amphitrite
**mother of Ulysses** Anticlea
**mother of Venus** Dione
**mother of Zebulon** Leah
**mother of Zeus** Rhea
**mother of Zimran** Keturah
**mother or father** parent
**mother sheep** ewe
**mother's mother** grandma
**'mother's ruin'** gin
**mother's sister** aunt
**mother wit** brains, judgement, savvy
**moths and butterflies** lepidopterous
**moth whose larva feeds on apples** codling
**moth with crescent-shaped spots on wings** luna
**motif** air, argument, concept, decoration, design, device, feature, figure, form, idea, leitmotif, leitmotiv, logo, matter, melody, notion, ornament, patter, pattern, shape, song, strain, subject, text, theme, topic, tune
**motion** action, beckon, change, deportment, direct, dynamics, flow, flux, gesticulate, gesture, inclination, mechanics, mobility, move(ment), nod, passage, passing, progress, proposal, proposition, recommendation, sign(al), suggestion, transit, travel, usher, wave
**motionless** calm, dead, fixed, idle, immobile, immovable, inactive, inanimate, inert, lifeless, passive, quiescent, quiet, resting, silent, sleeping, stagnant, static, stationary, still, tranquil, unmoved, unmoving
**motionless through lack of wind** becalmed
**motion making towards some goal** move
**motion picture** movie
**motion picture award** Oscar
**motion picture sequence** scene
**motion roused by being taken unawares** surprise
**motivate** actuate, arouse, bring, cause, draw, drive, encourage, enkindle, excite, goad, impel, incite, induce, inspire, kindle, lead, move, persuade, prompt, propel, provoke, push, rouse, spur, stimulate, stir, trigger, urge

**motivation** ambition, desire, drive, hunger, impulse, incentive, incitement, inspiration, interest, motive, persuasion, spur, stimulus, wish
**motive** active, cause, desire, enticement, goad, impulse, incentive, inducement, influence, intent(ion), motivation, object, purpose, reason, spur, stimulating, stimulus, target, wish
**motive for action** cause
**motley** assorted, dissimilar, diversified, mingled, mixed, unlike, varied
**motor** aeromotor, auto(car), car, drive, dynamo, engine, generator, machine, ride, tour, travel, vehicle
**motorbike attachment** sidecar
**motorboat built for high speeds** speedboat
**motor caravan** camper
**motorcar fender** bumper
**motorcoach** bus, charabanc
**motorcycle attachment** sidecar
**motorcycle manoeuvre** wheelie
**motorcyclist** biker
**motoring competition** rally
**motorist** driver
**motorist's aid** map
**motorist's hotel** motel
**motorless aircraft** glider
**motor part** armature, cam, piston, plug
**motor-racing obstacle** chicane
**motor-racing stable** écurie
**motor-racing track** circuit
**motor truck** lorry
**motor vehicle** auto, bakkie, car, (mini)bus, tractor, van
**motor vehicle frame** chassis
**motorway** Autobahn (G), autostrada (I), avenue, course, highway, lane, path, pathway, road(way), route, street, thoroughfare, track, way
**mottled** blotchy, chequered, dappled, flecked, marbled, piebald, pied, speckled, stippled, streaked, variegated
**mottled citrus** ugli
**motto** adage, byword, catchword, cry, dictum, formula, gnome, maxim, precept, rule, saw, saying, slogan, watchword
**mould** arrangement, blight, brand, build, cast, character, construct(ion), cut, design, die, dirt, dust, fit, forge, form(at), frame, fungus, ground, humus, ilk, influence, loam, make, matrix, mildew, model, mouldiness, mustiness, pattern, quality, sculpt, shape, shed, soil, stamp, structure, style, template, work

**mouldable** creatable, fashionable, forgeable, makable, plastic, workable
**moulded metal** castiron
**mould for casting** matrix
**moulding** ogee, cyma
**moulding compound** plastic
**moulding in the form of a ring** annulet
**moulding of a cornice** cyma
**moulding round a column** cincture
**mould in relief** emboss
**mouldy** blighted, decayed, decaying, decomposed, fusty, mildewed, musty, putrid, rotting, spoiled, stale, stinky, stuffy, unfresh
**mound** bank, bump, butte, drift, dune, elevation, embankment, foothill, haystack, heap, hill(ock), hummock, hump, inselberg, knoll, koppie, lump, monticule, pile, ridge, rise, stack
**mound forming Roman rampart** agger
**mound of bread** loaf
**mound of rough stones as monument** cairn
**mound of sand** dune
**mound over ants' nest** anthill
**mount** accumulate, arise, ascend, bestride, build, climb, display, escalade, exhibit, frame, grow, hill, horse, increase, intensify, launch, mountain, multiply, prepare, produce, raise, ready, rise, scale, soar, stage, steed, support, swell, tower
**mountain** alp, elevation, eminence, escarpment, height, mons (L), mount, oro-, peak, pinnacle, promontory, spur, tor, upland
**mountain ash** rowan
**mountain cleft** couloir, dredge, kloof, ravine
**mountain climber** alpinist
**mountain crest** arête
**mountain debris** moraine
**mountain-dwelling** montane
**mountaineer** climber
**mountaineering spike** crampon
**mountain goat** ibex
**mountain home of Greek gods** Olympus
**mountain hut** chalet
**mountain in Afghanistan** Chagai, Himalayas, Koh, Pamirs, Safeo, Sulaiman
**mountain in Africa** Atlas, Drakensberg, Elgon, Karas, Kareeberg, Karisimbi, Kenya, Kilimanjaro, Langeberg, Maloti, Malutiberg, Meru, Rasdashan, Roggeveldberg, Soutpansberg, Stormberg, Swartberg, Teide, Toubkal

**mountain in Alabama** Cheana, Look Out, Raccoon
**mountain in Alaska** Ada, Bona, Brooks, Chugach, Crazy, Kaiyuh, Kilbuck, Wrangell
**mountain in Albania** Korab, Koritnik, Pindus, Shala
**mountain in Algeria** Ahaggar, Aissa, Atlas, Bumidia, Dahra, Djurjura, Mouydir, Tahat
**mountain in Angola** Loviti
**mountain in Antarctica** Erebus, Markham, Prince Charles
**mountain in Arabia** Horeb, Nebo, Sinai
**mountain in Argentina** Aconcagua, Andes, Conico, Maipu, Porto
**mountain in Armenia** Ara, Ararat, Taurus
**mountain in Asia** Altal, Everest, Himalaya, Lebanon
**mountain in Australia** Augustus, Bruce, Cradle, Gregory, Kosciusko, Legge, Magnet, Mulligan, Olga, Stuart
**mountain in Austria** Hochgolling, Kitzbuhel, Stubai, Wildspitze, Zugspitze
**mountain in Belgium** Ardennes, Botrange
**mountain in Bermuda** Pegu Yoma
**mountain in Bolivia** Andes, Illampu, Jara, Sajama, Zapaleri
**mountain in Botswana** Tsodilo
**mountain in Brazil** Bandeira, Itatiaia, Urucum
**mountain in Bulgaria** Balkan, Botev, Musala
**mountain in Burma** Nattaung, Popa, Saramati, Victoria
**mountain in California** Muir, Shasta, Whitney
**mountain in Canada** Logan, Mackenzie, Robson, Royal, Stikine, Tremblant, Vancouver, Waddington
**mountain in Canary Islands** Elcumbre, La Curux, Lacruz, Tenerife, Teyde
**mountain in Chad** Tibesti
**mountain in Chile** Cochrane, Conico, Maca, Paine, Pular, Torre, Velluda, Yogan
**mountain in China** Everest, Kundelungu, Muztabh, Nan Shan, Omei, Omi, Pobeda, Sung
**mountain in Colombia** Abibe, Andes, Baudo, Chamusa, Cocuy, Oriengal, Perija, Tunahi
**mountain in Corsica** Cinto, Rotondo
**mountain in Costa Rica** Blanco, Chirripo
**mountain in Crete** Dikte, Ida, Juktas, Lasthi, Theodore

**mountain in Cuba** Turquino
**mountain in Cyprus** Troodos
**mountain in Czechoslovakia** Ore, Sudeten, Tatra
**mountain in Dominican Republic** Duarte, Gallo, Tina
**mountain in Ecuador** Andes, Cayambe, Cotopaxi, Sangay
**mountain in Egypt** Ghabib, Katherina, Sinai
**mountain in England** Cumbrian, Helvellyn, Peak, Scafell, Skiddaw, Snowdown
**mountain in Ethiopia** Talo
**mountain in Europe** Carpathian, Etna, Jungfrau, Matterhorn, Nadelhorn, Ore, Zugspitze
**mountain in Fiji** Monavatu, Nararu
**mountain in Finland** Haltia
**mountain in France** Auvergne, Blanc, Cenis, Cevennes, Dore, Forez, Jura, Puy, Pyrenees, Ventoux, Vosges
**mountain in Gabon** Iboundji, Mpele
**mountain in Georgia** Kennesaw, Stone
**mountain in Germany** Feldberg, Venusberg, Watzmann
**mountain in Ghana** Afadjato
**mountain in Greece** Athos, Elikon, Helicon, Hymettus, Ida, Olympus, Ossa, Parnassus, Parnon, Pelion, Pentelicus, Pilion, Pindus, Taygetos, Vuranon
**mountain in Greenland** Forel, Gunnbjorn, Khardyu, Payer
**mountain in Guam** Lamla, Tenjo
**mountain in Guatemala** Agua, Atitlan, Pacaya, Tacana, Tajamulco, Toliman
**mountain in Guinea** Tamgue
**mountain in Haiti** Cahos, Lahotte, Laselle, Noires, Nord, Troudeau
**mountain in Hawaii** Kaala, Kamakou, Kohala, Lanaihale
**mountain in Hong Kong** Castle, Victoria
**mountain in Hungary** Bakony, Carpathian, Kekes, Mecsek
**mountain in Iceland** Hekla, Jokul
**mountain in India** Ghats, Kamet, Kanchinjunga, Meru, Siwalik, Suleiman, Tankse
**mountain in Indonesia** Bulu, Katopasa, Kerinci, Menjapa, Niapa, Rindjani, Slamet, Talakmau
**mountain in Iran** Ararat, Cush, Demavend, Elburz, Hamunt, Hindu, Khormuj, Khosf, Sabalan, Zagros
**mountain in Ireland** Antrim, Donegal, Kennedy, Kippure, Leinster, Mourne, Ox, Wicklow
**mountain in Israel** Atzmon, Carmel, Meron, Nafh, Sagi, Sinai

**mountain in Italy** Apennines, Bernina, Cimone, Ortles, Rosa, Sabine, Vesuvius
**mountain in Ivory Coast** Nimba
**mountain in Japan** Asahi, Asama, Fujiyama, Hakusan, Kiusiu, Tokachi, Yariga, Yesso, Zao
**mountain in Java** Gede, Murjo, Semeroe, Semeru, Slamet, Soembing
**mountain in Jordan** Bukka, Darab, Mubrak, Nebo
**mountain in Kampuchea** Aural, Pan
**mountain in Kansas** Sunflower
**mountain in Kenya** Cheptulil, Elgon, Kenya, Kulal, Logonot, Matian
**mountain in Laos** Atwat, Bia, Copi, Khat, Lai, San, Tiubia
**mountain in Lebanon** Hermon
**mountain in Lesotho** Maloti, Maluti
**mountain in Liberia** Niete, Nimba, Uni, Wutivi
**mountain in Libya** Bette
**mountain in Liechtenstein** Rhatikon
**mountain in Louisiana** Driskill
**mountain in Maine** Bigelow, Cadillac, Katahdin
**mountain in Malawi** Kirk, Mchinji, Mulanje
**mountain in Malaysia** Binaija, Bulu, Murjo, Niapa, Raja
**mountain in Mali** Manding, Mina
**mountain in Mexico** Blanco, Bufa, Orizaba, Perote
**mountain in Morocco** Anti, Atlas, Toubkal
**mountain in Mozambique** Chimanimani, Gorongosa, Himalaya
**mountain in Namibia** Erongo, Hakos, Huns, Naukluft, Waterberg
**mountain in Nepal** Everest
**mountain in New Guinea** Albert, Victoria
**mountain in New Hampshire** Monadnock, Moriah, Waumbek
**mountain in New Mexico** Wheeler
**mountain in New York** Bear, Marcy
**mountain in New Zealand** Aspiring, Chope, Cook, Eamshaw, Egmont, Flat, Franklin, Pihanga, Stokes, Tutamore
**mountain in Nicaragua** Medera, Mogoton
**mountain in Nigeria** Tamgak
**mountain in North America** Appalachian, Elbert, Marcy, Rocky
**mountain in North Ireland** Antrim
**mountain in Norway** Galdhöpiggen, Kjolen, Numedal, Snohetta, Telemark
**mountain in Oman** Hafit, Harim, Sham
**mountain in Pakistan** Trichmir

**mountain in Panama** Chico, Columan, Gandi, Santiago
**mountain in Peru** Coropuna, Huamina, Huascaran
**mountain in Philippines** Apo, Banahao, Iba, Mayon, Pulog
**mountain in Poland** Rysy, Sudeten, Tatra
**mountain in Portugal** Acor, Etrela, Gerez, Marao, Monchique, Mousa, Peneda, Petrosul
**mountain in Romania** Bihor, Caliman, Codrul, Negoi, Pietrosu, Rodnei
**mountain in Russia** Belukha, Pobeda
**mountain in Rwanda** Karisimbi
**mountain in Samoa** Fito, Matafao, Savaii
**mountain in Sardinia** Ferry, Gallura, Limbara, Linas, Rasu, Vittoria
**mountain in Scotland** Attow, Ben Lomond, Grampian, Hope, Macdhui, Merrick, Nevis
**mountain in Sicily** Erei, Etna, Ibrei, Moro, Nebrodi, Sori
**mountain in Sierra Leone** Loma
**mountain in Somalia** Surudad
**mountain in South Africa** Drakensberg, Lebombo, Stormberg, Swartberg, Table
**mountain in South America** Acarahy, Aconcagua, Andes, Baia, Goiaz, Parima
**mountain in South Korea** Chiri
**mountain in South Vietnam** Badinh, Knontran, Tchepone
**mountain in Spain** Gata, Montseny, Mulhacen, Nethou, Penalara, Perdido, Pyrenees, Rouch, Teide, Teleno
**mountain in Sudan** Kinyeti
**mountain in Sweden** Ammar, Helags, Sarjek, Sarv
**mountain in Switzerland** Bernina, Eiger, Jungfrau, Jura, Pilatus, Rigi, Rosa, Weisshorn, Wetterhorn
**mountain in Syria** Hermon, Libanus
**mountain in Tahiti** Orohena
**mountain in Taiwan** Hsinkao, Tzukao, Yushan
**mountain in Tanzania** Gelai, Hanang, Kilimanjaro, Kisigo, Livingstone, Pare
**mountain in Tasmania** Barron, Cradle, Drome, Grey, Humboldt, Nevis
**mountain in Thailand** Khieo, Maelamun
**mountain in Tibet** Bandala, Everest, Kailas, Kamet, Sajum
**mountain in Togo** Agou
**mountain in Turkey** Ak, Ararat, Bingol, Bolgar, Erciyas, Hasan, Karacal, Suphan, Taurus
**mountain in Uganda** Elgon, Margherita

**mountain in USSR** Alagoz, Belukha, Caucasus, Elbrus, Ural
**mountain in Venezuela** Cuneva, Icutu, Parima, Pava, Roraima, Yavi
**mountain in Wales** Cambrian, Plynlimmon, Snowdon
**mountain in West Scotland** Ben Nevis
**mountain in Yugoslavia** Durmitor, Triglav
**mountain in Zaïre** Ditemba
**mountain in Zambia** Chifukunya, Mpangwe
**mountain lake** tarn
**mountain lion** puma
**mountain nymph** oread
**mountain nymph of classical mythology** oread
**mountain of Muses** Helicon, Parnassus
**mountain or hill** berg
**mountainous district in Greece** Arcadia
**mountainous region** highland, highveld, plateau, sierra, uplands
**mountain panther** ounce
**mountain pass** col, gap, gha(u)t, nek
**mountain passage** tunnel
**mountain pass in Austria** Arlberg
**mountain peak** alp, ben (Sc)
**mountain peak in Australia** Woodroffe
**mountain peak shaped like a needle** aiguille
**mountain pool** tarn
**mountain railway** funicular
**mountain range** Adirondacks, Alaska, Alleghenies, Alps, Altai, Andes, Appalachians, Atlas, Cascades, Chizarira, Drakensberg, gha(u)t, Grampians, Himalayas, Pamir, Pennine, Pyrenees, Sierra Madre, Sierra Nevada, Sierra Tarahumane, Snowy, Ural
**mountain range in Alaska** Baird, Brooks, Chugach, Crazy, Kaiyuh, Kilbuck, Wrangell
**mountain range in America** Appalachian, Sierra
**mountain range in Australia** Stirling, Tomkinson
**mountain range in Canada** Cariboo, Laurentian, Pembina, Skeena, Stelias
**mountain range in Chile** Almeida, Andes, Darwin, Domeyko
**mountain range in China** Atlay, Bogdoula, Himalaya, Kunlun, Tanglha
**mountain range in Colorado** Rocky
**mountain range in Cuba** Cristal, Maestra, Organos, Trinidad
**mountain range in Ethiopia** Ahmar, Choke

**mountain range in Europe** Alps, Tatra
**mountain range in France** Cevennes
**mountain range in Germany** Alps, Hardt, Harz, Hunsruck, Ore, Rhön
**mountain range in Greece** Pindus
**mountain range in Hungary** Bukk, Carpathian, Matra, Mecsek
**mountain range in Idaho** Cabinet, Selkirk
**mountain range in India** Aravalli, Himalaya, Satpura, Vindhya
**mountain range in Ireland** Comeragh, Galty, Stacks
**mountain range in Italy** Alps, Apennines, Maritimes, Ortles
**mountain range in Kirgiz** Alai
**mountain range in Luxembourg** Ardennes
**mountain range in Massachusetts** Berkshire
**mountain range in Minnesota** Cuyuna, Mesabi, Misquah
**mountain range in Montana** Bigbelt, Crazy, Lewis, Pocky
**mountain range in Morocco** Atlas, Rif
**mountain range in Nepal** Himalaya
**mountain range in New Hampshire** White
**mountain range in Pakistan** Makran
**mountain range in Panama** Veragua
**mountain range in Russia** Alai, Caucasus, Ural, Yablonoi
**mountain range in Rwanda** Mitumba
**mountain range in Scotland** Cairngorms
**mountain range in Siberia** Altai, Ural
**mountain range in Somalia** Guban
**mountain range in South America** Andes
**mountain range in South Africa** Cedarberg, Drakensberg, Soutpansberg, Stormberg
**mountain range in Thailand** Dawna
**mountain range in Tibet** Himalaya, Kailas, Kunlun
**mountain range in Turkey** Ala, Dagh, Taurus
**mountain range in Uganda** Ruwenzori
**mountain range in Utah** Uinta
**mountain range in Yugoslavia** Dinaric
**mountain range in Zaïre** Mitumba, Ruwenzori, Virunga
**mountain range in Zambia** Muchinga
**mountain ravine** kloof
**mountain ridge** arête
**mountain sickness** puna
**mountainside railway** funicular
**mountains in Andorra** Pyrenees
**mountains in Europe** Alps
**mountains in Peru** Andes
**mountains in Switzerland** Alps
**mountains in Tennessee** Smokies

**mountain sound** yodel
**mountain tobacco** arnica
**mountain top** peak
**mountaintop nest** aerie
**mountain tree** ash
**mountain where Moses received commandments** Sinai
**mountain wild-goat** ibex
**Mountbatten's title** Earl
**mountebank** allurer, charlatan, hoaxer, pitchman, pretender, quack, rascal, rogue, swindler
**mounted guns** ordnance
**mounted herdsman in South American pampas** gaucho
**mounted infantryman armed with a carbine** dragoon
**mounted lancer** u(h)lan
**mounted man with lance in bullfight** picador
**mounted on a horse** equestrian
**mounted people** cavalcade
**mounted policeman** trooper
**mounted sentry placed in advance of an outpost** vedette, vidette
**mounted soldier** cavalryman, equestrian
**mounted soldier in India** sowar
**mounted troops** cavalry
**mount from which Zeus watched Trojan War** Ida
**mount of hard snow on a ski slope** mogul
**mount up** accrue, ascend, collect, increase, multiply
**mourn** ache, bemoan, bewail, cry, deplore, despair, grieve, howl, keen, lament, languish, miss, moan, regret, repine, rue, sob, sorrow, suffer, wail, weep, yearn
**mourn for** bewail, lament
**mournful** cheerless, depressing, discouraged, dismal, doleful, downhearted, dreary, gloomy, grievous, lachrymose, long-faced, lugubrious, melancholic, plaintive, regrettable, sad, sorrowful, triste, woeful
**mournful poem** elegy
**mournful song** dirge
**mournful sound** knell
**mournful verse** elegy
**mourning garment** sable
**mourn loudly** wail
**mouse-coloured** dun
**mouse deer** chevrotain
**mouselike animal** gerbil, rat, shrew
**mouselike flying animal** bat
**mouser** cat
**mouse sound** squeak
**mouth** aperture, boating, braggadocio, cavity, door(way), entrance, entrée,
entry, estuary, gateway, gob, hatch, inlet, jawbone, jaws, lips, mandible, maxilla, opening, orifice, oro-, ostiole, outfall, outlet, passage, portal, postern, rim, stoma, vaunting
**mouthful of liquid** sip
**mouth gland** tonsil
**mouthlike opening** orifice
**mouth of cavity** aperture, orifice, vent
**mouth of Niger** Nun
**mouth of river** estuary, wetland
**mouth of volcano** crater
**mouth organ** harmonica
**mouth part** jaw, lip
**mouthpiece of horse's bridle** bit
**mouth sore** ulcer
**mouth's roof** palate
**mouth-to-stomach passage** throat
**movable** changeable, detachable, mobile, operable, portable, portative, transferable, transportable, transposable, turnable, walkable
**movable barrier** door, gate
**movable cover** lid
**movable double button** stud
**movable frame of loom** batten, lay, sley
**movable goods** bona mobilia (L)
**movable hospital** ambulance
**movable house** caravan, trailer
**movable joint** hinge
**movable partition** screen
**movable portal** door, gate
**movable possession** chattel
**movable rail at junction** switch
**movable shed** bail
**movable stand on which coffin rests** bier
**move** act(ivate), actuate, advance, affect, agitate, arouse, astir, awaken, bear, betake, budge, carry, change, convey, deed, dispatch, disperse, essay, excite, gesture, go, gyrate, impel, incite, induce, influence, jerk, lead, locomote, manhandle, march, migrate, motion, operate, proceed, progress, prompt, propel, propound, pull, push, put, remove, roll, rotate, rouse, scatter, send, shake, shift, shove, stir, stratagem, suggest, tactics, touch, transfer, transport, transpose, trundle, tug, turn, twitch, walk, wheel
**move about** converse, displace, roll, shuffle
**move about furtively** lurk, prowl, slink
**move about in disorder** jumble
**move about noisily** clatter
**move about restlessly** fidget, flutter
**move abruptly** flounce
**move a camera** pan, track
**move across** traverse, thwart
**move actively** yank
**move ahead steadily** forge, press on, progress
**move aimlessly** drift, poke
**move along** mosey, sashay, slog
**move apart** spread
**move around** stir
**move around busily** bustle
**move aside** skew
**move, as liquid** flow
**move at easy gallop** canter
**move at easy pace** amble, stroll
**move at top speed** lick
**move away** decamp, mog, recede, sheer
**move away from** ebb, recede, shy
**move awkwardly** hodge, lop, lumber, shamble
**move back** ebb, recede, recur, retire, retreat, retrocede, withdraw
**move back and forth** flap, (see)saw, sway, swing, wag, wave(r)
**move backwards** regress, retrogress, reverse
**move body with short twists** wriggle
**move briskly** breeze, squirt, stir, trance, travel, trot
**move by crawling** scramble
**move by jerks** jigget, jiggle, jinkle
**move by short shocks** jog
**move cautiously** creep
**move chess piece** develop
**move clumsily** flop, galumph, lumber, stumble
**move computer video display** scroll
**move confusedly** mill
**move crabwise** sidle
**moved guiltily** slunk
**move diagonally** cater
**move down** decline, descend, lower, stoop
**move downward** descend
**move easily** flow, glide
**move elusively** jink
**move erratically** flit
**move foot** step
**move forcibly** shove
**move forward** advance, break, come, progress
**move forward slowly** nose
**move friskily** caper
**move from one place to another** migrate
**move from place to place** ambulant, transfer
**move from secure position** dislodge
**move furtively** glide, leer, prowl, sidle, skulk, slink, sneak, steal
**move gradually** edge
**move hastily** scramble, skirr
**move head** nod
**move heavily** (f)lump, lug, lumber

**move heavily on wheels** trundle
**move helically** spiral, twirl
**move house** resettle
**move hurriedly** scamper, scurry
**move idly about** gad
**move impulsively** scamper
**move in a circle** swirl, eddy
**move in awkward manner** gangle
**move in buoyant manner** lilt
**move inch by inch** edge
**move in chess** gambit
**move in circle** gyrate
**move in circles** eddy, mill, purl, swirl
**move in circular orbit** revolve
**move indolently** loll
**move in jerks** flip
**move in large waves** surge, swell
**move in reverse** back(up)
**move in small degrees** inch
**move in sneaking manner** slink
**move in undulations** wave
**move in ungainly bounds** lollop
**move in ungainly way** flop
**move in water** swim
**move in waves** undulate
**move languidly** maunder
**move lazily** hulk, idle, snail
**move leisurely** amble
**move lightly** brush, flit, skip, skit
**move lightly and quickly** flit
**move like snake** slither
**movement** act(ion), activity, advancement, beat, campaign, cause, change, division, drive, exercise, flow, gesture, group, moment, motion, move, operation, pace, part, party, passage, progress, rhythm, section, shift, stir(ring), swing, taxis, tempo, transfer, trend, tropism
**movement in ballet** battement, cabriole, développé, entrechat, glissade, jeté, pas, pirouette, plié
**movement in dancing** figure
**movement in dressage** volte
**movement in fencing** parry, passado, volt(e)
**movement of attack** offensive
**movement of earth's crust** diastrophism
**movement of feet** gait
**movement of panicky group** stampede
**movement of sea** tide, wave
**movement of tide** ebb
**movement of troops** evolution, manoeuvre
**movement of vehicles** traffic
**movements of trained horse** manège
**movement sound** rustle
**move nervously** dither
**move noisily** clatter, gallumph, tramp

**move obliquely** sidle, skew
**move off** mosey
**move off quickly** scoot
**move off the main track** shunt
**move on** go, mog, onrush, succeed, vamp
**move on casters** truckle, trundle
**move on hands and knees** crawl
**move onward** progress
**move onwards** pass, proceed
**move on wheels** roll, skate
**move out** blow, leave, vacate
**move over lightly** skim, glide, fly, skate, slide, coast
**move over snow** mush, ski, sled
**move quickly** bob, dart, flash, flit, run, scat, scud, shift, skite, speed, squib, wallop, zap
**move quickly to one side** dodge
**move quietly** creep, slip
**mover** author, composer, creator, founder, inventor, maker, originator, parent, planner, producer, proposer, writer
**move rapidly** career, clatter, dart, fly, hurtle, jump, race, rip, run, scour, scud, speed
**move restlessly** fidget
**move restlessly about** gad
**move rhythmically** dance, march, oscillate, waggle
**mover of scenery** stagehand
**move round and round** eddy, swirl, twirl
**move round axis** rotate
**move round swiftly** swirl
**move round the edge** skirt
**mover's truck** pantechnicon, van
**move secretly** sneak
**move shakily** totter
**move sideways** crab, edge, sidle, skid, slent
**move silently** creep, steal, tiptoe
**move slightly** budge, stir
**move slowly** crawl, creep, dawdle, drag, drawl, inch, lag, linger, pant, worm
**move slowly along** inch
**move slowly and stealthily** creep
**move slowly towards** inch
**move slyly** slink
**move smoothly** float, flow, glide, glissade, sail, sleek, slide, slip
**move spasmodically** twitch
**move spirally** gyrate, twist
**move steadily** forge
**move stealthily** creep, glide, prowl, pussifoot, pussyfoot, skulk, slink, sneak, steal
**move suddenly** bolt, dart, flit, flounce, lash, run, start, jerk

**move swiftly** career, course, dart, fly, leap, rake, run, spin
**move swiftly and suddenly** shoot
**move tail** wag
**move the feelings** affect
**move the feet without lifting them** shuffle
**move the head** nod
**move things about** rearrange
**move through air** fly
**move through water** sail, swim, wade
**move timidly** sidle
**move to and fro** rock, sway, swing, wave
**move to another place** switch, transfer
**move to music** dance
**move to new home** resettle
**move towards** approach
**move uneasily** fidget
**move unsteadily** bicker, dodder, flounder, hobble, stumble, teeter, toddle, totter, wobble
**move up** promote, raise
**move up and down** bob, dance, rebound
**move up to a higher rank** promote
**move up to next standard** pass
**move upward** arise, ascend, fly, rise, soar
**move upwards** arise, ascend
**move very slowly** inch
**move vigorously** bestir, flog, stir, stray
**move violently** dash, flog, leap
**move wildly** career
**move wings** flap
**move wings up and down** flap
**move with a lever** prise, pry
**move with an eddying motion** swirl
**move with beating motion** flap
**move with bounding strides** lope
**move with current** drift
**move with difficulty** wade
**move with dragging feet** shuffle
**move with effort** ache, heave
**move with quick steps** patter
**move with short twisting movements** wriggle
**move with slight jerk** hitch
**move with speed** run
**move with stealth** prowl, tiptoe
**move with the times** progress
**move with tide** drift
**movie** bioscope, cinema, feature, film, picture
**movie award** Oscar
**movie celebrity** film star
**movie collie dog** Lassie
**movie eats** candy, popcorn
**movie format** cinerama
**movie house** bioscope, cine(ma), theatre
**movie personality** star

**movie serial division** episode
**movie shot** close-up
**movie synopsis** scenario
**movie tape** video
**movie theatre** cine(ma)
**movie visitor from space** ET
**moving** activating, advancing, affecting, arousing, astir, budging, drifting, emotional, going, impelling, leaving, marching, migrating, motile, motivating, proceeding, progressing, pushing, quitting, shifting, stirring, switching, touching, transferring, walking
**moving about** ambulant, astir, stirring
**moving about rapidly** volitant
**moving at a comfortable space** easy-going
**moving at a low rate of speed** slow
**moving away from the centre** centrifugal
**moving backwards** retrograde, reverse
**moving crowd** stream
**moving footway** escalator, travolator
**moving force** agent, impetus, spirit
**moving forward** progressive
**moving furtively** sneaking
**moving herd of cattle** drove
**moving ice layer** glacier
**moving lattice** apron
**moving machinery part** mechanism
**moving mass of ice** glacier
**moving outwards** centrifugal
**moving part** axle, rotor, screw
**moving part of cylinder** piston
**moving picture** bioscope, cinema, film, movie
**moving seat** rocking-chair
**moving staircase** conveyor, escalator, lifter
**moving towards the centre** centripetal
**moving truck** pantechnicon, van
**moving violently** impetuous
**moving water** river, stream
**moving with ease** nimble
**mow down** butcher, decimate, massacre, slaughter
**Mozart opera** The Marriage of Figaro
**MP's constituency** seat
**MP without office** backbencher
**Mr Claus** Santa
**Mr in Madrid** señor
**Mrs in Madrid** señora
**Mrs Thatcher's nickname** Iron Lady
**much** abundant, ample, considerable, considerably, copious, decidedly, exceedingly, excessively, frequently, great(ly), indeed, nearly, often, plenteous, plenty, rather, regularly, somewhat, substantial, sufficient, tons, very
**much in little** multum in parvo (L)

**much loved** beloved, revered
**much ornamented** ornate
**much prized fish** salmon
**much smaller than normal** miniature
**much speed** haste
**much travelled** beaten
**much troubled in mind** distraught
**much-used** old
**much-worn automobile** jalopy
**muck** compost, contamination, debris, defilement, dirt, droppings, dung, dust, excrement, excreta, faeces, filth(iness), foulness, fragments, garbage, gook, grime, impurity, litter, manure, mire, mud, nastiness, ordure, pollution, refuse, rubbish, sewage, shreds, slime, sludge, smudge, squalor, stain, tarnish, uncleanness
**muck up** bungle, mar, muff, ruin, spoil
**mucky** dirty
**mucous discharge** rheum
**mucous membrane connecting eyeball and inner eyelids** conjunctiva
**mucus** phlegm
**mud** clay, dirt, mire, ooze, silt, slime, sludge
**mud brick** adobe
**mud deposit** silt
**muddle** addle, becloud, bewilder, chaos, clutter, confound, confuse, confusion, daze, derange, disarrange, disarray, disorder, ensnarl, jumble, mess, mix(-up), nonplus, perplex, scramble, spoil, stupefy, tangle, tumble
**muddled state** fuddle
**muddle through** contrive, manage
**muddy** boggy, cloudy, confused, dirty, marshy, slushy, soiled, vague
**muddy place** slough
**muddy pool** letch
**mud volcano** salse
**muff** bungle
**muffetee** glove, mitt(en), muff
**muffler** collar, scarf, silencer
**muffle up** disguise, envelop, shroud, stifle, swathe
**mufti** civvies
**mug** beaker, cup, flagon, jug, pot, tankard, toby
**Mugabe's party** ZANU
**muggins** simpleton
**Muhammed Ali's nickname** Greatest
**mulct** amerce(ment), bilk, cheat, confiscate, defraud, fine, fleece, forfeit, penalise, penalty, punish, swindle
**mule-driver** muleteer
**mule's shoe** planch

**mulish** adamant, bull-headed, callous, capricious, contrary, cross-grained, disobedient, dogged, erratic, fickle, firm, fixed, flighty, hard, headstrong, implacable, incorrigible, inexorable, inflexible, iron, obdurate, obstinate, perverse, pig-headed, relentless, self-willed, stiff-necked, stubborn, stupid, tenacious, unbending, uncompromising, ungovernable, unpredictable, unruly, unshakable, unyielding, wayward, wilful, wilful
**mull** brood, confuse, consider, fumble, muddle, ponder, ruminate, speculate, study, weigh
**mulled wine** negus
**mull over** brood
**multicoloured** bright, brilliant, colourful, flecked, intense, iridescent, marmoreal, motley, opaline, pavonine, polychromatic, prismatic, rich, speckled, spectral, striated, tartan, variegated, versicolour, vivid
**multicoloured quartz** onyx
**multifarious mixture** salmagundi, salmagundy
**multiple** collective, manifold, many, numerous, plural, several, sundry, various
**multiple electrical plug** adapter
**multiplied by four** quadruplicate
**multiply** augment, boost, breed, burgeon, double, duplicate, enlarge, expand, extend, generate, increase, intensify, magnify, manifold, procreate, propagate, raise, redouble, reproduce, spread
**multiply by four** quadruple
**multiply by seven** septuple
**multiply by three** treble
**multiply by two** double
**multispeaker sound system** stereophonic
**multitude** bunch, collection, confluence, congregation, crowd, crush, drove, group, host, mass, multiplicity, myriad, party, school, shoal, swarm, throng, tons
**mum** ma(ma), mom(my), mother, mummy, silent
**mum and dad** parents
**mumble** babble, complain, gabble, gibber, grouse, grumble, henpeck, jabber, mump, murmur, mutter, nag, patter, speak, whine, yammer
**mummify** anoint, embalm, preserve, shrivel
**mummy's wrapping** bandage
**mum or dad** parent
**mum's sister** aunt
**munch** champ, chew, chomp, crunch, gnaw, nibble

**munch noisily** champ
**mundane** banal, carnal, common(place), corporeal, earthly, everyday, humdrum, ordinary, prosaic, routine, secular, temporal, terrene, terrestrial, trite, typical, usual, worldly
**Munich is there** Germany
**municipal** borough, city, civic, civil, public, town, urban
**municipal area** borough, ward
**municipal chief** mayor
**municipality** city, constituency, district, metropolis, precinct, suburbs, town(ship)
**municipality head** mayor
**munificent** abundant, altruistic, ample, beneficent, benevolent, bounteous, bountiful, extravagant, generous, liberal, luxuriant, plentiful, profuse, rich, sumptuous, unsparing
**munitions** ammunition, armaments, artillery, battery, bombs, bullets, cannon, dum-dums, equipment, explosives, firearms, guns, implements, instruments, material, mines, missiles, ordnance, provisions, rockets, supplies, tackle, things, tools, torpedoes, weapons
**munitions storehouse** arsenal
**mural tapestry** arras
**murder** assassinate, assassination, destroy, homicide, kill(ing), manslaughter, slay
**murderer** assassin, butcher, decapitator, executioner, exterminator, filicide, fraticide, garotter, gunman, hangman, homicide, impaler, infanticide, killer, knifer, lyncher, matricide, parricide, patricide, slaughterer, slayer, sniper, sosoricide, strangler, thug, triggerman, tyrannicide, uxoricide, vaticide
**murder of a child** filicide, prolicide
**murder of an infant** infanticide
**murder of a parent** parricide
**murder story** thriller
**murine** mouse, rat(like)
**murk** dark(ness), dense, misty
**murky** bleak, cheerless, cloudy, cryptic, dark, desolate, dirty, dismal, dreary, dusky, enigmatic, foggy, gloomy, grave, grim, heavy, hidden, joyless, misty, nebulous, obscure, occult, opaque, perplexing, puzzling, rainy, secret, solemn, sombre, vague, veiled
**murmur** complaint, grumble, mumble, mutter, susurration, susurrus, whimper, whisper
**murmur of brook** music

**murmur of dove** coo
**murmur softly** coo
**murrey** purple-red
**muscle** adductor, biceps, brawn, core, exertion, flexor, gist, muscularity, pennon, potency, power, restore, rotator, sinew, sphincter, substance, tendon, tensor, thew, tissue
**muscle around pupil** iris
**muscle in** jostle, shove
**muscle of shoulder lifting upper arm** deltoid
**muscle of upper arm** biceps
**muscle spasm** cramp, tic
**muscle tremor** twitch
**muscle trouble** cramp
**muscle with double attachment** biceps
**muscology** bryology
**Muscovite** Russian
**muscular** able, active, aggressive, brawny, broad-shouldered, bustling, emphatic, energetic, hefty, mighty, rugged, stalwart, staunch, strapping, sturdy, wholesale
**muscular contraction** convulsion, cramp, crick, pang, spasm, stitch, throe, tic
**muscular debility** myasthenia
**muscular man** he-man
**muscular pain** ache
**muscular rheumatism** fibrositis
**muscular substance of heart** myocardium
**muscular twitch** tic
**muse** brood, cerebrate, chew, cogitate, conjecture, consider, contemplate, deliberate, dream, evaluate, examine, meditate, ponder, reflect, review, revolve, ruminate, speculate, study, surmise, think, weigh
**Muse of astronomy** Urania
**Muse of comedy and pastoral poetry** Thalia
**Muse of dance and of choral song** Terpsichore
**Muse of epic poetry** Calliope
**Muse of history** Clio
**Muse of love poetry** Erato
**Muse of lyric poetry and music** Euterpe
**Muse of singing, mime and sacred dance** Polyhymnia
**Muse of tragedy** Melpomene
**museum custodian** curator
**museum display** art, diorama
**museum employee** guide
**museum official** curator
**mush** pulp
**mushroom** agaric, appear, brief, burgeon, cep, chanterelle, develop, flourish, fungus, grow, morel,

multiply, proliferate, puffball, quick, spread, sprout, temporary, toadstool, transitory, truffle
**mushy** doughy, maudlin, mawkish, pulpy, romantic, sentimental, sloppy, slushy, soft, squishy, sugary, syrupy
**music** euphony, harmony, melody, score, song, tune
**music accompanying film** theme
**musical** accordant, dulcet, euphonic, harmonious, lilting, lyric(al), melic, melodic, melodious, operatic, pleasant, resonant, rhythmical, symphonic, tuneful, vocal
**musical accent** beat
**musical arrangement** scale
**musical arrangement of words** melody
**musical beat** rhythm, tempo
**musical caprice** capriccio
**musical character** clef
**musical chord** major, minor
**musical comedy** operetta
**musical composition** fugue, opus, rhapsody, rondo, sonata
**musical composition for eight performers** octet
**musical composition for singers** cantata
**musical composition for solo voices** oratorio
**musical conclusion** coda
**musical drama** oper(ett)a
**musical eightsome** octet
**musical eulogy** heroic song
**musical finale** coda
**musical form** fugue
**musical genius** maestro
**musical group** band, quartet, quintet, sextet, trio
**musical half note** minim
**musical instrument** accordion, bazooka, bugle, cello, chord, clarion, clavier, concertina, drum, dulcimer, flute, harp, lute, maraca, marimba, oboe, ocarina, organ, piano(forte), recorder, spinet, tambourine, tuba, viol(in), xylophone
**musical instrument of ancient Greece** kithara
**musical instrument of ancient Egypt** sistrum
**musical instrument of pipes worked by bellows** organ
**musical instrument with one string** monochord
**musical introduction** prelude
**musically poetic** lyrical
**musically slow** andante
**musical medley** pot-pourri
**musical melody** aria

**musical movement played slowly** lento
**musical note** breve, minim
**musical ornament** trill
**musical pace** tempo
**musical performance** concert, recital
**musical piece** étude
**musical pitch** tone
**musical play** opera
**musical preface** prelude
**musical production** revue
**musical program** recital
**musical reed** oat
**musical shaker** maraca
**musical show** opera, revue
**musical sign** clef, note
**musical sound** note, tone, tune
**musical study** étude
**musical succession of notes** scales
**musical symbol** clef, note
**musical term** allegro, andante, largo, leger, presto
**musical threesome** trio
**musical time** tempo
**musical timer** metronome
**musical tone** note
**musical toy** ocarina
**musical twosome** duo
**musical work** opera, opus, oratorio
**music conductor's baton** wand
**music for nine singers** nonet
**music for one performer** solo
**music for solo instrument** étude
**music for virtuoso** étude
**music hall** odeon, odeum
**musician** accompanist, artist, composer, conductor, harpist, instrumentalist, minstrel, performer, pianist, player, singer, virtuoso, vocalist
**musician ridding town of rats** Pied Piper
**music-lover's purchase** album
**music originally intended for performance in the morning** aubade
**music pipe** reed
**music played between two acts of a play** entr'acte
**music symbol** clef
**music with refrain** rondo
**music writer** composer
**musing** absorbed, absorption, brooding, cogitating, concentrating, (day)dreaming, deliberating, dreamy, introspection, meditating, meditation, meditative, pensive, pondering, rapt, reflecting, reflective, reverie, ruminating, ruminative, speculating, thinking, thoughtful, weighing, wistful
**musk cat** civet
**musk-flavoured grape** muscat

**musk melon** cantaloupe, spanspek
**musk-yielding cat** civet
**Muslim** Islamic, Shiite
**Muslim bible** Koran
**Muslim building at Mecca** Caaba, Kaaba
**Muslim caller to prayer** muezzin
**Muslim call to prayer** adan, azan
**Muslim cap** fes, taj
**Muslim chief civil and religious ruler** caliph
**Muslim chief in Phillippines** dato
**Muslim code of religious law** shariah, sheriah
**Muslim crier** muezzin
**Muslim decree** irade
**Muslim dervish** Mahdi
**Muslim evil spirit** Mahound
**Muslim faith** Islam
**Muslim fast** Ramadan
**Muslim festival** Bairam
**Muslim garment** jubbah
**Muslim god** Allah
**Muslim governor in the Middle East** emir
**Muslim harem** seraglio, serail
**Muslim hat** fez, taj
**Muslim headwear** turban
**Muslim holy book** Koran
**Muslim holy city** Mecca
**Muslim house of worship** masjid, mosque, musjid
**Muslim Indian** Mogul
**Muslim judge** cadi, kadi
**Muslim lady of high rank** begum
**Muslim leader** ayatollah, bey, caliph, imam(u)m, shaikh, sheik(h), shereef, sultan
**Muslim learned in Islamic theology and sacred law** mollah, moulana(h), mullah
**Muslim magistrate** cadi, kadi
**Muslim mendicant** dervish
**Muslim messiah** Mahdi
**Muslim monk** dervish
**Muslim name** Ali
**Muslim name of God** Allah
**Muslim noble** ameer, amir, emir
**Muslim nymph** houri
**Muslim official** ima(u)m
**Muslim official under Mogul empire** nabob, nawab
**Muslim place of worship** masjid, mosque, musjid
**Muslim prayer** Fatiha(h)
**Muslim prayer leader** ima(u)m
**Muslim priest** ima(u)m, mufti
**Muslim prince** ameer, amir, caliph, emir, sultan
**Muslim princess** begum
**Muslim religious ascetic** fakeer, fakir, faqir

**Muslim religious leader** caliph, sheik(h)
**Muslim religious mendicant** fakir
**Muslim ruler** ameer, amir, caliph, emir, sultan
**Muslim ruler's wife** sultana
**Muslim sacred building at Mecca** Caaba, Kaaba
**Muslim scholar** mollah, mulla(h), ulema
**Muslims collectively** Islam
**Muslim sect** Shia(h), Shiite, Sunni
**Muslim's head-dress** turban
**Muslim shrine at Mecca** Caaba, Kaaba
**Muslim slaughter** hal(l)al
**Muslim sovereign** sultan
**Muslim spirit** (d)jinn, djinny, genie, jinnee
**Muslim's red flat-topped cap with tassel** fez
**Muslim's thirty days fast, from sunrise to sunset** Ramadan
**Muslim student** ulema
**Muslim temple** mosque
**Muslim title** aga, ali, mollah, mulla, say(y)id, sharif, shereef, sherif
**Muslim under vows** dervish
**Muslim warrior of high rank** ghazi
**Muslim weight** rotl
**Muslim who has been to Mecca as pilgrim** hadji, haj(j)i
**Muslim who knows the Koran by heart** hafiz
**Muslim woman ruler** begum
**Muslim woman's veil** yashmak, yasmack
**Muslim women's quarters** harem
**Muslim world** Islam
**muss** agitation, confusion, disarray, disorder(liness), disruption, heap, jumble, mess, muddle, rumple, scramble, tousle, tumult, turbulence, turmoil, untidiness, upset
**Mussolini's country** Italy
**must** duty, essential, frenzy, imperative, mandatory, mould, necessary, necessity, need, obligation, requirement, requisite
**mustang** bronco
**mustard family plant** cress
**mustard plaster** sinapism
**muster** assemblage, assemble, assembly, collect(ion), compilation, conference, congregation, congress, convene, convention, convocation, convoke, gather(ing), group, marshal, meeting, mobilise, number, rally, statistics, summon, turnout
**muster of witches** coven
**muster troops for inspection** parade
**musty** aged, ancient, apathetic, close, corrupt, decaying, dull, foul, frowzy,

fusty, hoary, indifferent, insipid, listless, malodorous, mif, moss-grown, mouldy, rancid, rank, reeky, sluggish, sour, spoiled, stagnant, stale, stuffy, turned, vapid
**musty smell** fusty
**mut** em
**mutable** adaptable, alterable, capricious, changeable, changing, fickle, flexible, inconstant, irresolute, uncertain, unstable, unsteady, vacillating, volatile, wavering
**mutation** alteration, change, conversion, deviation, exchange, modification, modulation, move, permutation, reversal, transition, translation, umlaut, variation
**mute** deaden, dumb, inarticulate, mum, noiseless, quiet, reticent, silence, silent, speechless, still, subdued, taciturn, uncommunicative, unexpressed, unpronounced, unspoken, voiceless, wordless
**mutilate** blemish, butcher, cripple, damage, deface, deform, destroy, detruncate, disable, discolour, disfigure, dismember, garble, geld, harm, impair, injure, lacerate, lame, maim, mangle, mar, misshape, ruin, scar, spoil, stab, torture, uglify
**mutilate by blows** mangle
**mutineer** agitator, anarchist, defier, demonstrator, protestor, rebel, resister, revolter, rioter, striker, traitor, trouble-maker
**mutinous** bolshie, disobedient, insubordinate, insurgent, insurrectionary, rebellious, revolutionary, riotous, seditious, subversive, turbulent, unruly
**mutiny** defiance, disobedience, disobey, insubordination, insurrection, protest, putsch, rebel(lion), resist(ance), revolt, revolution, riot, rising, sedition, strike, uprising
**mutter** complain, grouse, grumble, mumble, murmur, slur, stutter, whine, whisper, yammer
**mutton** em, mut
**mutual** balanced, common, complementary, correlative, exchanged, interactive, interchangeable, interchanged, joint, reciprocal, returned, shared
**mutual agreement** pact, unity

**mutual aid pact** alliance
**mutual civility** comity, courtesy
**mutual concession** compromise
**mutual concord** peace
**mutual dependence** solidarity, symbiosis
**mutual effect** interaction
**mutually destructive** internecine
**mutually reliant** interdependent, symbiotic
**mutual pact** bilateral agreement
**mutual relationship** symbiosis, symmetry, term
**mutual tolerance** compatibility
**mutual transference** permutation
**mutual trust and friendship** camaraderie
**mutual understanding** affinity, agreement, amity, friendship, goodwill
**muzzle** bit, censor, choke, curb, gag, guard, jaws, mouth, nose, restrain, silence, snout, stifle, suppress
**my** mea (L)
**mynah bird** mina, starling
**myopia** near-sightedness, short-sightedness
**myopic** half-blind, near-sighted, short-sighted
**myriad** countless, immeasurable, infinite, innumerable, legion, limitless, multiple, numerous, scores, thousands, various
**myriapod** centipede, millipede, millepede, songololo
**myself** I, me
**mysterious** abstruse, arcane, concealed, daedal, eerie, enigmatic(al), esoteric, inexplicable, inscrutable, mystical, obscure, recondite, secret, uncanny, unexplainable, unfathomable, unintelligible, weird
**mysterious force** od, odyl(e)
**mysteriously puzzling** enigmatic
**mysterious person** enigma
**mystery** conundrum, enigma, problem, puzzle, question, riddle, secrecy, secret
**mystic** abstruse, arcane, close, concealed, covert, cryptic, dark, deep, enigmatic, esoteric, hidden, masked, mysterious, mystical, obscure, occult, orphic, recondite, secret, shrouded, symbolic, unknowable, unseen, veiled

**mystical** abstruse, close, concealed, covert, cryptic, dark, hidden, masked, metaphysical, mysterious, mystic, obscure, occult, otherworldly, paranormal, preternatural, recondite, secret, shrouded, supernatural, transcendental, unseen, veiled
**mystical atmosphere** aura
**mystic art** alchemy, cab(b)ala, voodoo
**mystic writing** rune
**mystify** baffle, bamboozle, bewilder, elude, perplex, puzzle, stump
**myth** epic, fable, fallacy, fiction, legend, lore, saga, story, tradition
**mythical** fabulous, feigned, fictitious, historical, idealistic, imaginary, imagined, immortal, legendary, mythic, mythological, visionary
**mythical beast** dragon, unicorn
**mythical being** gnome, goblin, spirit, werewolf
**mythical bird** lightning bird, phoenix, roc
**mythical chief evil jinny** Eblis
**mythical Chinese pheasant** fum, fung
**mythical creature of the sea** mermaid
**mythical drink of the gods** nectar, soma
**mythical Greek hero** Heracles, Herakles, Hercules
**mythical horned creature** unicorn
**mythical horse** Pegasus, unicorn
**mythical hunter** Orion
**mythical king of Attica** Ogyges
**mythical king of Britain** Lud
**mythical maiden** Antiope, Callisto, Danae, (hama)dryad, Io, Leda, maenad, naiad, nymph, Semele
**mythical monster** basilisk, chimera, cyclops, dragon, Gorgon, griffin, harpy, hydra, minotaur, ogre, orc, sphinx, tokoloshe, wyvern
**mythical monster, half man, half horse** centaur
**mythical Roman twins** Romulus and Remus
**mythical sea being** mermaid
**mythical sea monster** orc
**mythical stream** Styx
**mythical submerged island** Atlantis
**mythological giant** titan
**mythology** anthropology, fable, folk-tales, folklore, legend, lore, myths, stories, tradition
**myths collectively** mythology

# N

**naartjie** mandarin, tangerine
**nab** apprehend, arrest, bag, capture, catch, clutch, seize, snatch
**nacre** (mother-of-)pearl
**nadir** bathos, bedrock, bottom, deepest, depths, minimum, zero
**naevus** birthmark, lesion, mole, patch
**nag** annoy, badger, carp, goad, grumble, hack, harass, heckle, hector, horse, irritate, m(a)enad, nettle, niggle, pester, pony, scold, shrew, termagant, torment, vex
**nagging woman** scold
**nagging worry** anxiety
**nag pettily** carp
**naiad** water nynph
**nail** arrest, attach, beat, brad, claw, fasten, fingernail, fix, hammer, hook, join, peg, pin, pincher, rivet, secure, skewer, spike, tack, talon, toenail, unguis
**nail down** batten, resolve, settle
**nailed at foot** toed
**nailfile material** emery
**nailhead** stud
**nail polish** enamel
**nail to the cross** crucify
**nail up** mount
**nail with large head sticking out** stud
**naïve** artless, candid, childish, credulous, explicit, frank, genuine, green, guileless, immature, ingenuous, innocent, open, plain, raw, simple, sincere, trustful, unaffected, undeveloped, uninitiated, unsophisticated, unspoiled, unwise, unworldly
**naïve girl** ingénue
**naïvety** artlessness, candidness, candour, credulity, directness, frankness, guilelessness, honesty, ingenuousness, innocence, naïveness, naïveté, openness, rawness, simplicity, sincerity, trustfulness, trustworthiness, undeceptiveness
**naked** bare, blunt, defenceless, destitute, evident, exposed, manifest, mere, nude, sheer, simple, stripped, unadorned, unarmed, uncoloured, undressed, unexaggerated, unfurnished, unguarded, unprotected, unsheathed
**naked boy representing a cupid** amoretto, amorino, putto
**naked figure** nude

**nakedness** baldness, bareness, nudity, openness, simplicity, undress
**naked runner** streaker
**namby-pamby** affected, anaemic, colourless, coward, effeminate, indecisive, insipid, mincing, moffie, prim, prissy, sissy, vapid, watery, weak, weakling
**name** appellation, character, cite, classify, credit, denominate, denomination, designate, designation, distinction, eminence, entitle, epithet, esteem, fame, honour, identify, indicate, nickname, nom (F), nomen (L), nominate, note, -onym, praise, renown, reputation, repute, soubriquet, specify, term, title
**name a person's illness** diagnose
**name as authority** cite, quote
**name at birth** née
**named** baptised, chosen, christened, designated, dubbed, entitled, identified, selected, styled, termed, yclept
**named before** aforesaid
**name derived from father or ancestor** patronymic
**name expressly** specify
**name for a donkey** Ned(dy)
**name for an office** designate
**name for Hades** Dis
**name for office** nominate
**name for some orchestras** philharmonic
**name full of meaning** epithet
**name given to the Devil** Apollyon, Lucifer, Satan
**name-giver** announcer, eponym, namer, nomenclator, onomatologist, terminologist, toastmaster
**name in grammar** noun
**nameless** allonym, anonymous, cryptonymous, horrible, incognito, indescribable, insignificant, obscure, renownless, undesignated, undistinguished, unidentified, unknown, unmentionable, unnamed, unspeakable, untitled
**name letters in a word** spell
**namely** chiefly, explicitly, mainly, scilicet, specifically, to wit, viz
**name of book** title
**name of eight kings of England** Henry
**name of English royal house** Plantagenet, Stuart, Tudor
**name of God in Old Testament** Jehovah, Yahveh, Yahweh

**name of painting** title
**name of person** signature, surname
**name of something** noun
**name of three emperors of Russia** Alexander
**name replacing an ordinary name** nickname
**names of people considered untrustworthy** blacklist
**name word** noun
**Namibian region** Damaraland, Etosha
**Namibian tribe** Herero
**Namibia's ghost town** Kolmanskop
**naming** addressing, calling, denomination, designation, eponymy, nomenclature, nominating, terminology
**naming word** noun
**nan** grandmother, granny, nanny, ouma
**nan bread** naan
**nancy** effeminate, homosexual, moffie
**Nancy or Ronnie** Reagan
**nanny** domestic, goat, grandmother, keeper, nurse(maid)
**nanny's charge** kid
**nanny's domain** nursery
**nap** catnap, down, doze, drowse, fabric, fibre, forty winks, fuss, kip, nod, repose, rest, siesta, sleep, slumber, snooze, texture, weave
**nape** cuff, niddick, nucha, poll, scruff, scurf
**napery** linen(ware)
**naphthalene** hydrocarbon
**napkin** cloth, diaper, serviette
**Napoleon's birthplace** Corsica
**Napolean's marshal** Murat
**Napoleon's prison island** Elba
**Napoleon was defeated at this battle** Waterloo
**nap on cloth** pile
**napped cloth** plush
**napping** asleep, dozing, drowsing, nodding, resting, sleeping, snoozing
**nappy** diaper, downy, fleecy, fluffy, furry, fuzzy, hairy, napkin, peachy, shaggy, soft, thick, velutinous, velvety
**narcissism** airs, conceit, ego, egotism, immodesty, ostentation, self-admiration, self-interest, self-love, swank, vanity
**narcissistic** conceited, egocentric, egoistic, egomanical, egotistic, self-centred, selfish, smug, vain
**narcissus** jonquil

**narcotic** alcohol, anaesthetic, analgesic, anodyne, barbiturate, belladonna, cannabis, cocaine, dagga, drug, hemp, heroin, hypnotic, marijuana, morphine, nicotine, opiate, opium, painkiller, relaxant, sedative, soother, soporific, tranquilliser
**narcotic and emetic plant** mandragora, mandrake
**narcotic constituent of opium** morphia, morphine
**narcotic hemp** b(h)ang
**narcotic in opium** narceine
**narcotic plant with large yellow fruit** mandragora, mandrake
**narcotics seller** pusher
**nard** balsam
**nares** nose, nostrils
**nark** annoy, bad-tempered, blabber, informer, infuriate, irritable, irritate, snitch, snoop, spoilsport, spy, squeaker, squealer, tattle, tease, upset
**narrate** describe, detail, disclose, mention, portray, recapitulate, recite, recount, rehearse, relate, repeat, report, reveal, review, state, tell, unfold
**narrating continuously** epic
**narration** account, annals, chronicle, description, diary, epic, explanation, fable, history, legend, memoir, myth, portrayal, record, relation, report, saga, sketch, story, summary, tale, telling
**narrative** account, chronicle, description, drama, epic, episode, history, myth, novel, opus, parable, play, romance, saga, story, tale, theme, work
**narrative part of Buddhist literature** Sutra
**narrative poem** epic, epos, lay
**narrative song** ballad
**narrator** anecdotist, annalist, author, bard, chronicler, commentator, delineator, raconteur, reciter, relator, reporter, storyteller, writer
**narrow** biased, bigoted, clannish, close, confined, constricted, cramped, diminish, dogmatic, illiberal, inflexible, intolerant, limit(ed), meagre, partial, pinched, prejudiced, reduce, restrict(ed), scanty, simplify, slender, slim, small-minded, stingy, strait, straiten(ed), tight
**narrow alley in a town** lane, wynd (Sc)
**narrow and intense ray of light** laser beam
**narrow aperture** chink, slit

**narrow band** belt, orle, tape
**narrow band in suit material** pinstripe
**narrow band round the edge of shield** orle
**narrow band worn round head** bandeau, fillet
**narrow base of petal** unguis
**narrow beam of light** ray
**narrow braid of silk** galloon
**narrow-brimmed felt hat** homburg
**narrow brooch** pin
**narrow canoe** kayak, proa, prua
**narrow channel** gut, kyle (Sc)
**narrow coastal inlet** ria
**narrow connecting strip** isthmus
**narrow cord** string
**narrow cotton strip** tape
**narrow crack** crevice, fissure
**narrow cut** slit
**narrow cut in the earth** trench
**narrow elevation** ridge
**narrower part of bottle** neck
**narrow fillet** taenia
**narrow fissure** crevice
**narrow footway** catwalk
**narrow groove** slot
**narrow horizontal projection** ledge
**narrowing of a passage in the body** stenosis
**narrowing to a sharp point** acuminate
**narrow inlet** geo, gio, ria
**narrow inlet of sea** firth
**narrow inlet of sea between steep cliffs** fiord, fjord
**narrow inlet of the sea coast** ria
**narrow lane** alley, wynd (Sc)
**narrowly** barely, carefully, closely, illiberally, intolerantly, just, limitedly, meagrely, nearly, precisely, scantily, scarcely, strictly, tightly
**narrow mark** stripe
**narrow-minded** biased, bigoted, close-minded, conservative, constricted, fanatical, hidebound, illiberal, insular, intolerant, mean, myopic, one-sided, parochial, petty, prejudiced, purblind, short-sighted, small, unreasonable, warped
**narrow miss** shave
**narrow moulding** bead
**narrow mountain passage** pass, poort
**narrow mountain valley** glen
**narrowness of outlook** provincialism
**narrow opening** chink, crack, crevice, fissure, slat, slit, slot
**narrow opening between hills** gorge
**narrow orle** tressure
**narrow part of tennis racket** handle
**narrow passage** alley(way)
**narrow path** lane
**narrow pennant** pennon, streamer
**narrow piece of land** slype, strip

**narrow piece of land connecting two larger bodies of land** isthmus
**narrow piece of wood** slat
**narrow raised strip** ridge
**narrow ribbon** tape
**narrow road** lane
**narrow sea** channel
**narrow sea channel** kyle
**narrow sea inlet** ria
**narrow seaway** strait
**narrow shelf** ledge
**narrow spade with a single footrest** loy
**narrow strait** kyle, gorge
**narrow street** alley, lane, wynd (Sc)
**narrow strip** shred
**narrow strip of hide used as lash of whip** thong
**narrow strip of wood** slat
**narrow sword** tuck
**narrow track** lane
**narrow trimming** edging, hemming, piping
**narrow valley** dene, glen, ravine, wynd (Sc)
**narrow water passage** strait
**narrow way** lane
**narrow wooded valley** dene
**nasal** nose-guard, rhinal, twangy
**nasal aperture** nostril
**nasal catarrh** coryza
**nasal cavity** sinus
**nasal release of air** sneeze
**nasal sound** snort
**nasal tone** twang
**nasal vowel sign** tilde
**nascent** advancing, beginning, budding, developing, evolving, growing, immature, young
**naseberry** sapodilla
**nasty** cruel, defiled, dirty, disagreeable, disgusting, filthy, foul, horrible, ill-natured, impure, inclement, indecent, indelicate, lascivious, licentious, loathsome, malicious, nauseous, obnoxious, obscene, offensive, repellent, repulsive, ribald, smutty, spiteful, ugly, vile
**nasty grin** leer
**nasty person** meanie
**nasty remark** nip
**nasty smell** reek
**natal labour** confinement
**Natal pass** Sani
**Natal resort** Durban, Margate
**natant** floating, swimming
**natatorial** natatory, swimming
**nation** clan, commonwealth, community, confederacy, confederation, country, dynasty, empire, family, federation, kingdom, land, nationality, natives, pais (Sp),

people, population, principality, public, race, realm, republic, state, tribe

**national** chauvinistic, citizen, civic, civil, countrywide, domestic, federal, general, governmental, inhabitant, internal, nationwide, native, patriotic, public, resident, social, state, subject, tribal, widespread

**national anthem of France** 'Marseillaise'
**national betting machine** tote
**national dance of Poland** polonaise
**national emblem of Ireland** shamrock
**national flower of South Africa** protea
**national gathering for musical competitions** eisteddfod
**national guard of France** garde nationale
**nationalism** allegiance, chauvinism, jingoism, loyalty, nationality, patriotism
**nationalistic** allegiant, jingoistic, loyal, patriotic
**nationality** ancestry, birth, citizenship, clan, descent, heredity, heritage, history, lineage, nation, parentage, race, tribe
**national park in Canada** Yoho
**national park in South Africa** Kruger
**national park in Tennessee** Shiloh
**national police force of Spain** Guardia Civil
**national pride** nationalism
**national socialism** fascism, Nazism
**national song** anthem
**national symbol** emblem
**national treasury** exchequer
**nation's spirit** ethos
**nationwide** countrywide, extensive, general, interstate, national, overall, widespread,
**native** aboriginal, aborigine, autochthon, congenial, genuine, inborn, indigenous, inhabitant, inherent, intrinsic, -ite, local, natal, nation, natural, original, raw, tellurian, tribal, tribe, unadorned, voter
**native Australian companion bird** brolga
**native-born Israeli** Sabra
**native country** homeland
**native drum** tom-tom
**native gold** nugget
**native inhabitant** aborigine
**native Israeli** Sabra
**native land** birthplace, home
**native language of Canton or Kwantung provinces** Cantonese
**native mineral** ore
**native of Afghanistan** Afghan

**native of Alaska** Ahtena, Aleut, Eskimo, Ingalik, Koyukon, Tlingit
**native of Albania** Albanian
**native of Algeria** Algerian, Algerine, Berber, Kabyle
**native of Andorra** Andorran
**native of Angola** Angolian
**native of Ankara** Turk
**native of Arabia** Arab
**native of Arctic areas** Eskimo
**native of Argentina** Argentine, Argentinian
**native of Armenia** Armenian
**native of Athens** Greek
**native of Australia** Aboriginal, Aborigine, Australian
**native of Austria** Austrian
**native of Azerbaijan** Azerbaijani, Azeri
**native of Baghdad** Iraqi
**native of Bahamas** Bahamian
**native of Bahrein** Bahrani, Bahreni
**native of Bangladesh** Bangladeshi
**native of Barbados** Barbadian
**native of Belgium** Belgian
**native of Belize** Belizean
**native of Benin** Beninese
**native of Bermuda** Bermud(i)an
**native of Berne** Swiss
**native of Bhutan** Bhutanese
**native of Borneo** Dyak
**native of Brazil** Brazilian
**native of Brittany** Breton
**native of Bulgaria** Bulgarian
**native of Cameroon** Cameroonian
**native of Canada** Canadian
**native of Cape Town** Capetonian
**native of Cape Verde Islands** Cape Verdean
**native of Cayman Islands** Cayman Islander, Caymanian
**native of Chad** Chadian
**native of Chile** Chilean
**native of China** Chinese
**native of Colombia** Colombian
**native of Comore** Comoran
**native of Congo** Congolese
**native of Costa Rica** Costa Rican
**native of Croatia** Croat
**native of Cuba** Cuban
**native of Cyprus** Cypriot(e)
**native of Czech Republic** Czeck
**native of Denmark** Dane
**native of Denpasar** Balinesi
**native of Djibouti** Djiboutian
**native of Dominica** Dominican
**native of Ecuador** Ecuadorean, Ecuadorian
**native of Egypt** Egyptian
**native of El Salvador** Salvadorean
**native of Elsinore** Dane
**native of England** English(wo)man
**native of Estonia** Estonian

**native of Ethiopia** Ethiopian
**native of Fiji** Fijian
**native of Finland** Finn
**native of Flanders** Flemish
**native of France** French(wo)man
**native of Gabon** Gabonese
**native of Gambia** Gambian
**native of Georgia** Georgian
**native of Germany** German
**native of Ghana** Ghanian
**native of Gibraltar** Gibraltarian
**native of Glasgow** Glaswegian, Scot
**native of Great Britain** Briton
**native of Greece** Greek
**native of Grenada** Grenadian
**native of Guatemala** Guatemalan
**native of Guinea** Guinean
**native of Guyana** Guyanese
**native of Haiti** Haitian, Haytian
**native of Hondura** Honduran
**native of Hungary** Hungarian
**native of Iceland** Icelander
**native of India** Indian
**native of Indiana** Indianian
**native of Indonesia** Indonesian
**native of Iran** Iranian
**native of Iraq** Iraqi
**native of Ireland** Hibernian, Irish(wo)man
**native of Isle of Man** Manx(wo)man
**native of Israel** Israeli
**native of Italy** Italian
**native of Jamaica** Jamaican
**native of Japan** Japanese
**native of Jordan** Jordanian
**native of Kampuchea** Cambodian
**native of Kazakhstan** Kazak(h)
**native of Kenya** Kenyan
**native of Kurdistan** Kurd
**native of Kuwait** Kowaiti, Kuwaiti
**native of Laos** Laotian
**native of Latvia** Latvian, Lett
**native of Lebanon** Lebanese
**native of Lesotho** Basotho
**native of Liberia** Liberian
**native of Libya** Libyan
**native of Lichtenstein** Lichtensteiner
**native of Lithuania** Lithuanian
**native of Liverpool** Scouse(r)
**native of Louisiana** Cajun
**native of Luxembourg** Luxemburger
**native of Macedonia** Macedonian
**native of Malawi** Malawian
**native of Malaysia** Malay
**native of Maldives** Maldivian
**native of Mali** Malian
**native of Malta** Maltese
**native of Mauritania** Mauritanian
**native of Mauritius** Mauritian
**native of Media** Mede
**native of Mexico** Mexican
**native of Micronesia** Micronesian

**native of Moldavia** Moldavian
**native of Monaco** Monegasque
**native of Mongolia** Mongolian
**native of Montenegro** Montenegrin
**native of Montserrat** Montserratian
**native of Morocco** Moroccan
**native of Mozambique** Mozambican
**native of Myanmar** Burmese
**native of Namibia** Namibian
**native of Naples** Neapolitan
**native of Nauru** Nauruan
**native of Nepal** Nepalese
**native of New Zealand** Maori, New Zealander
**native of Nicaragua** Nicaraguan
**native of Nigeria** Ibo, Nigerian
**native of Northern Ireland** Ulster(wo)man
**native of North Korea** North Korean
**native of Norway** Norman, Norse, Norwegian
**native of Oman** Omani
**native of Oslo** Norwegian
**native of Pakistan** Pakistani
**native of Panama** Panamanian
**native of Paraguay** Paraguayan
**native of Peru** Peruvian
**native of Philippines** Filipina, Filipino
**native of Poland** Pole
**native of Portugal** Portuguese
**native of Preston** Lancastrian
**native of Puerto Rico** Puerto Rican
**native of Qatar** Qatari
**native of Rio de Janeiro** Carioca(n)
**native of Romania** Romanian
**native of Rome** Italian, Roman
**native of Russia** Russian
**native of Samos** Samiote
**native of Santiago** Chilian
**native of Saudi Arabia** Saudi (Arabian)
**native of Scandinavia** Northman
**native of Scotland** Scot, Scots(wo)man
**native of Senegal** Senegalese
**native of Serbia** Serb
**native of Singapore** Singaporean
**native of Slovakia** Slovak
**native of Slovenia** Slovene
**native of Smyrna** Smyrniot
**native of Somalia** Somali
**native of South Africa** South African
**native of South Korea** South Korean
**native of Spain** Spaniard
**native of St Helena** St Helenian
**native of St Lucia** St Lucian
**native of St Vincent** Vincentian
**native of Sudan** Sudanese
**native of Suomi** Finn
**native of Surinam** Surinamer
**native of Swaziland** Swazi
**native of Sweden** Swede
**native of Switzerland** Swiss
**native of Sybaris** Sybarite

**native of Syria** Syrian
**native of Taiwan** Taiwanese
**native of Tajikistan** Tajik
**native of Tangier** Tangerine
**native of Tanzania** Tanzanian
**native of Tasmania** Tasmanian
**native of Tel Aviv** Israeli
**native of Thailand** Thai
**native of the Western world** Occidental
**native of Togo** Togolese
**native of Tonga** Tongan
**native of Troy** Trojan
**native of Tunisia** Tunisian
**native of Turkey** Turk
**native of Turkmenistan** Turk(wo)man
**native of Tuvalu** Tuvaluan
**native of Tyneside** Geordie
**native of UAR** Arab
**native of Uganda** Ugandan
**native of Ukraine** Ukrainian
**native of United Kingdom** Briton
**native of Uruguay** Uruguayan
**native of Uzbekistan** Uzbek
**native of Venezuela** Venezuelan
**native of Vietnam** Vietnamese
**native of Wales** Welsh(wo)man
**native of Warsaw** Pole
**native of Western Samoa** Western Samoan
**native of Yemen** Shafai, Yemeni, Zaidi
**native of Yugoslavia** Yugoslav
**native of Zambia** Zambian
**native of Zaïre** Zaïrean
**native of Zimbabwe** (Ma)shona, Matabele, Zimbabwean
**native soil** homeland
**native zinc sulphide** blende, sphalerite
**nativity** ancestry, childbearing, (child)birth, crèche, delivery, descent, heritage, parentage, parturition
**nativity setting** Bethlehem, stable
**natrium chloride** chloride, sodium, salt
**natter** babble, blather, chat(ter), chinwag, chitchat, conversation, gabble, gap, gossip, jabber, jaw, palaver, prattle, talk, yak
**natty** chic, dapper, elegant, fancy, fashionable, sleek, smart, snazzy, spruce, stylish, well-dressed
**natural** average, disinterested, genuine, impartial, inbred, inherent, innate, instinctive, nonpartisan, normal, regular, unadulterated, unaffected, unbiased, unforced, uninvolved
**natural ability** aptitude, flair, talent
**natural accompaniment** ap(p)anage
**natural aptitude** flair, talent
**natural ardour** mettle
**natural cover-up on statue** fig leaf

**natural division of fish's flesh** flake
**natural dye** henna
**natural elevation** eminence
**natural environment of animal or plant** habitat
**natural father** genitor
**natural filament** fibre
**natural fool** innocent
**natural force** agent
**natural fuel** gas
**natural gift** talent
**natural grease in sheep's wool** lanoline, suint
**natural guardian** parent
**natural height** stature
**natural hole in ground** pit
**natural home of animal or plant** habitat
**naturalised citizen** immigrant
**naturalism** realism
**naturalistic** graphic, lifelike, natural, photographic, realistic, representational, true-to-life
**natural kind of farming** organic
**natural landscape** scenery
**natural liking** affinity, attraction, inclination
**natural location** habitat
**natural lump of gold** nugget
**naturally abnormal** illegitimate
**naturally inclined to love** amorous
**naturally inherent** inborn
**naturally unpleasant and mean** ill-natured
**natural mass of stone** rock
**natural mineral** ore
**naturalness** ease
**natural peak** pinnacle
**natural pigment** ochre
**natural product** outgrowth
**natural satellite of the earth** moon
**natural science** physics
**natural simplicity** naïveté, naivety
**natural skill** knack
**natural talent** aptitude, flair, gift
**natural tendency** propensity
**natural underground reservoir** cenote
**natural vault** dome
**nature** character(istic), class, composition, constitution, cosmos, creation, disposition, esse, formation, genius, genre, grain, individuality, kind, matter, mood, personality, propensity, qualification, quality, reality, species, spirit, temperament, type, universe, world
**nature demon** genius
**nature goddess** Nymph
**nature of God** divine
**naturist** gymnosophist, nudist, sunworshipper

**naught** aught, cipher, defeat, destruction, disaster, duck, failure, nil, nix, nobody, none, nothing(ness), nought, nullity, ought, ruination, zero, zilch
**naughty** annoying, defiant, delinquent, disobedient, frolicsome, immoral, impish, improper, indecent, insubordinate, lewd, misbehaved, mischief, mischievous, playful, prankish, ribald, roguish, sportive, teasing, vulgar, wayward, wicked
**naughty kid** brat, imp
**nauseated from travelling** carsick
**nausea** abhorrence, aversion, biliousness, detestation, disgust, dislike, distaste, hatred, loathing, qualm, queasiness, repugnance, retching, revulsion, sickness, vomiting
**nauseate** abominate, biliousness, disgust, horrify, loathe, offend, reject, repel, repulse, revolt, sicken, upset
**nauseous** bilious, ill, indisposed, nauseated, queasy, sick, uncomfortable
**nautical** boating, marine, maritime, naval, navigational, oceanic, sailing, seafaring, seagoing, yachting
**nautical accommodation** cabin
**nautical anchorage** port
**nautical cleat** kevel
**nautical cry** ahoy
**nautical direction** aport
**nautical disaster** shipwreck
**nautical greeting** ahoy
**nautical knot** granny
**nautical measure** fathom
**nautical mile** knot
**nautical shout** ahoy
**nautical term** alee, tack
**nautical waiter** steward
**nautical windlass** capstan
**Navajo cabin of logs and mud** hogan
**naval colour** navy blue, white
**naval force** armada, convoy, fleet
**naval jacket** reefer
**naval mess** wardroom
**naval NCO** yeoman
**naval officer** admiral, commander, ensign
**naval officer of highest rank** admiral
**naval personnel** ratings
**naval petty officer** yeoman
**naval petty officer in charge of steerage** coxswain
**naval pinnace** barge
**naval rank** admiral, commander
**naval rating** erk
**naval rebellion** mutiny
**naval vessel** battleship
**nave** hub

**navel** bellybutton, middle, omphalos, orange, umbilicus
**navigable channel** fairway, waterway
**navigate** approach, aviate, captain, cross, cruise, direct, drive, fly, guide, journey, manage, manoeuvre, pilot, plot, sail, skipper, steer, traverse, voyage, yacht
**navigate a ship** sail
**navigation** aviation, boating, cruising, flying, helmsmanship, pilotage, piloting, sailing, seamanship, steering, voyaging, yachting
**navigational instrument** compass
**navigation skill** seacraft
**navigator** airman, aviator, captain, coxswain, director, flier, guide, helmsman, leader, marine(r), pilot, sailor, salt, seafarer, seaman, steersman
**navvy** digger, labourer, worker, workman
**navy** argosy, armada, destroyers, fleet, flotilla, lazuline, ships, submarines, warships
**navy chief** admiral
**navy construction worker** Seabee
**nay** no
**Nazi concentration camp** Auschwitz, Bergen-Belsen, Dachau, Treblinka
**Nazi leader** Hitler
**Nazi secret police** Gestapo
**Nazi symbol** fylfot, Hakenkreuz, swastika
**Nazi war-camp** Stalag
**Nazi war criminal** Eichmann
**Neanderthal** primitive, reactionary, ultraconservative, uncivilised
**neap** tide, ebb
**neap and ebb** tide
**Neapolitan dance** tarantella
**Neapolitan ice cream with candied fruit and nuts** cassata
**near** about, abutting, adjoining, allied, approach(ing), at, by, close, connected, contiguous, faithful, familiar, forthcoming, imminent, literal, narrow, nearby, nigh, related, stingy, tight, touching
**near a centre** inner
**near a fireplace** hob
**near at hand** local
**nearby** accessible, adjacent, adjoining, around, at, beside, close, convenient, handy, near, neighbouring
**near death** comatose, dying, moribund, stagnant, static
**nearer the beginning** early
**nearer the rear** after
**nearest** closest
**nearest in place** next

**nearest orbital point** perigee
**nearest the end** endmost
**nearing correctness** approximate
**near in position** nearby
**near in relationship** close
**near in time** about
**nearly** about, almost, approximately, closely, comparatively, near, practically, roughly, virtually, (well-)nigh
**nearly all** bulk
**nearly hopeless** desperate
**nearly resembling** approximate
**nearness** adjacency, affection, availability, closeness, comradeship, dearness, familiarity, fellowship, fondness, handiness, intimacy, proximation, proximity, tenderness, vicinity
**nearness in space or time** propinquity, proximity
**near shore** inshore
**near-sighted** biased, bigoted, hidebound, illiberal, insular, mope-eyed, myopic, narrow(-minded), parochial, partial, provincial, purblind, rooted, settled, short-sighted
**near-sightedness** myopia
**near that place** thereabouts
**near the coast** coastal, inshore
**near the end** ad fin (L)
**near the kidneys** adrenal
**near the shore** coastal, inshore
**near to** about, nigh
**near to the actual** approximate
**neat** adroit, apt, attic, brief, cattle, clean, clear, clever, deft, dext(e)rous, effective, efficient, elegant, epigrammatic, homy, methodical, nice, orderly, plain, precise, prim, pure, shipshape, simple, skilful, sleek, smart, spick-and-span, spruce, straight, tidy, trig, trim, unadorned, undiluted, unmixed, unornamented, unpretentious, well-groomed, well-planned, witty
**neat and elegant** snappy
**neat and precise** dapper
**neat and smart** natty
**neat as a conifer** spruce
**neat as a new pin** clean, immaculate
**neater** trimmer
**neat in dress and appearance** smart, spruce
**neatly** accurately, adeptly, adroitly, agilely, aptly, cleverly, daftly, daintily, dext(e)rously, efficiently, effortlessly, elegantly, fastidiously, gracefully, handily, methodically, nicely, nimbly,

precisely, purely, skilfully, stylishly, systematically, trimly
**neatly arranged** tidy
**neatly dodge** sidestep
**neatness** accuracy, adroitness, agility, aptness, daintiness, efficiency, effortlessness, elegance, expertness, grace, niceness, nicety, orderliness, precision, skilfulness, skill, smartness, stylishness, tidiness, trimness
**neb** beak, bill, nose, point, snout, spout, tip
**nebulous** abstract, ambiguous, amorphous, astral, celestial, cloud-like, cloudy, confused, dim, faint, formless, fuzzy, hazy, heavenly, imprecise, indefinite, indistinct, misty, murky, obscure, overcast, shadowy, shapeless, turbid, uncertain, unclear, vague
**nebulous body** comet
**necessarily stringent** drastic
**necessary** basic, compulsive, elementary, essential, fated, forced, fundamental, important, indispensable, instant, necessity, needed, needful, occasioned, required, requisite, rudimentary, unavoidable, urgent, vital
**necessary outfit** equipment
**necessary want** need
**necessitate** bind, coerce, compel, constrain, demand, dictate, entail, exact, force, impel, intimidate, make, oblige, press, require, tie
**necessities** essentials, fundamentals, indispensables, needs, requirements
**necessity** compulsion, demand, destiny, essential, exigency, extremity, fate, fundamental, indispensability, inevitability, karma, kismet, necessary, need(fulness), obligation, poverty, (pre)requisite, requirement, want
**necessity knows no law** necessitas non habet legem (L)
**neck** cape, cervix, channel, isthmus, nape, peninsula, scruff, strait, tongue
**neck and neck** abreast, alongside, equal, even, parallel
**neckband** bandanna, collar, fichu, kerchief, neckerchief, ruff, scarf, stole
**neck frill** ruff
**neck hair** mane
**necklace** amulet, beads, chain, choker, locket, medallion, necklet, pendant, riviére, torque
**necklace ball** bead
**necklace of twisted metal** torque
**necklace part** bead
**neck of land** isthmus

**neck of mutton** scrag
**neck of the uterus** cervix
**neck of the woods** locality, neighbourhood, region, vicinity
**neck stiffness** crick
**neck support** headrest
**neck swelling** goitre
**neckwear** ascot, bow tie, choker, cravat, jabot, kerchief, scarf, tie
**necrology** martyrology, obit(uary)
**necromancer** astrologer, charmer, dowser, enchanter, exorcist, incantator, magician, magus, obeah, occultist, prophet, sangoma, sorcerer, sorceress, spiritualist, witch, wizard
**necromancy** conjure, demonology, diabolism, exorcism, hoodoo, horoscopy, magic, obi(ism), soothsaying, sorcery, theurgy, voodoo, witchcraft, witchery, wizardry
**necropolis** catacomb, cemetery, churchyard, columbarium, graveyard, ossuary, urnfield
**necrosis** gangrene
**nectar** ambrosia, honey
**nectar-gathering bird** colibri, honey-eater, hummingbird
**neddy** burro, donkey, (jack)ass, moke
**née** born, formerly, heretofore, previously
**need** demand, desideratum, destitution, distress, emergency, essential, exigency, extremity, inadequacy, lack, longing, miss, necessitate, necessity, neediness, paucity, poverty, privation, require(ment), requisite, shortage, urgency, want, wish
**needed** demanded, lacked, missed, necessary, necessitated, required, wanted
**needed for life** vital
**need for water** thirst
**needful thing** necessity
**needing expiation** piacular
**needing lubrication** unoiled
**needing much perserverance** laborious
**needle** aggravate, annoy, auger, bait, bit, bodkin, borer, bristle, darner, drill, graver, harass, indicator, irk, irritate, mock, perforator, piercer, pin, provoke, punch, puncturer, rile, scauper, scorper, spicule, spike, stylus, tag, tease, tip, tool, trocar
**needlecase** étui
**needle eye** hole
**needle-fish** gar(fish), pipefish
**needle hole** eye
**needle monument** obelisk

**needle-shaped** acicular, dendritic, spicular, tapering
**needless** causeless, excessive, gratuitous, groundless, nonessential, pointless, purposeless, redundant, superfluous, uncalled-for, undesired, unessential, unnecessary, unneeded, unwanted, useless, verbose
**needless accumulation of words** verbiage
**needless bustle** fuss
**needless to say** naturally, necessarily, obviously
**needle therapy** acupuncture
**needlework** crocheting, embroidery, fancywork, knitting, lacework, needlecraft, needlepoint, petit point, sewing, smock(ing), stitching, tapestry, tat(ting), trimming
**needleworker** crewelworker, crocheter, embroiderer, knitter, needlewoman, sewer, stitcher, tatter
**need of a rider** reins, saddle
**needs airing** musty
**need to pay** owe
**needy** beggarly, bankrupt, deprived, destitute, disadvantaged, impecunious, impoverished, indigent, insolvent, lacking, moneyless, necessitous, penniless, pinched, poor, poverty-stricken, wanting
**neep** turnip
**nefarious** atrocious, cursed, demonic, detestable, evil, flagitious, foul, gruesome, heinous, ignoble, infamous, iniquitous, insidious, low, malevolent, notorious, obdurate, odious, satanic, sinful, vicious, villainous, wicked
**nefarious deeds** skul(l)duggery, trickery
**negate** annul, cancel, contradict, decline, deny, disagree, discharge, discredit, dispute, forbid, invalidate, nullify, object, oppose, override, overrule, prohibit, refute, reject, repeal, rescind, revoke, suppress, traverse, vacate, veto, void
**negating adverb** no
**negation** absence, contravention, declination, denegation, denial, disallowance, disapproval, disproof, dissent, dream, illusion, nonentity, nothing, objection, protest, refusal, repulse, turndown, unsaying, veto, void
**negation of request** refusal
**negation prefix** non-
**negative** against, contrary, cynical, deny(ing), dissenting, dubious,

forbidding, mopy, negate, no(t), nullify, observe, opposing, opposite, pessimistic, refute, sceptical, veto
**negative adverb** not
**negative answer** no
**negative electrode** cathode
**negatively charged atom** ion
**negatively charged ion** anion
**negative particle** ion
**negative prefix** non-
**negative reply** no
**negative statement** negation
**negative vote** nay, no
**negative word** no(t)
**neglect** carelessness, default, dereliction, disdain, disregard, disrespect, evade, failure, forget, heedlessness, ignore, indifference, neglect, negligence, omission, omit, overlook, procrastinate, rebuff, scorn, slight, spurn, unconcern
**neglected calf** dog(e)y, dogie
**neglected one** Cinderella
**neglectful** cunctatory, derelict, disregardant, inadvertent, inattentive, laggard, lax, negligent, sloppy, unaware, unwatchful
**neglecting to show courtesy** inattentive
**neglect of duty** delinquency
**neglect to do** omit
**neglect to include** omit
**negligee** bathrobe, caftan, décolletage, gown, kaftan, kimono, nightdress, peignor, robe, robe-de-chambre (F)
**negligence** carelessness, default, dereliction, disregard(fulness), failure, heedlessness, inadvertence, inadvertency, inattention, incaution, indifference, laxity, omission, oversight, remissness, shortcoming, slackness, thoughtlessness
**negligent** careless, casual, cursory, forgetful, inattentive, indifferent, lax, neglectful, nonchalant, offhand, remiss, slack, thoughtless, unconcerned, unheeding, unsolicitous, unstudied
**negligently** carelessly, forgetfully, heedlessly, inadvertently, inattentively, indifferently, remissly, slackly, thoughtlessly, unthinkingly
**negligible** inappreciable, inconsequential, inferior, insignificant, negatory, paltry, petty, small, unimportant, worthless
**negotiate** adjudicate, arrange, assign, bargain, circulate, clear, commute, compromise, conclude, deal, endorse, intercede, settle, transfer, treat
**negotiate a deal** transact

**negotiator** advocate, agent, arbiter, arbitrator, conductor, deputy, diplomat, emissary, envoy, factor, go-between, haggler, interceder, intermediary, judge, mediator, mediatrix, merchant, moderator, negotiant, peacemaker, peddler, politician, referee, rep(resentative), salesperson, seller, substitute, surrogate, transactor, umpire, vendor
**Negro hymn** spiritual
**neigh** baa, bleat, brae, bray, call, cry, wail, whinny
**neighbour** acquaintance, associate, friend
**neighbourhood** approach, area, community, district, locale, locality, nearness, outskirts, proximity, quarter, region, suburbs, vicinity
**neighbourhood pub** local
**neighbouring** adjacent, adjoining, bordering, connecting, near(by), nearest, next, surrounding
**neighbourly** affectionate, amiable, amicable, attentive, beneficent, beneficial, benevolent, benign, bounteous, brotherly, charitable, close, companionable, compassionate, comradely, congenial, considerate, convivial, cordial, courteous, familiar, favourable, fond, fraternal, friendly, genial, good, helpful, hospitable, intimate, kind(ly), obliging, outgoing, peaceable, propitious, receptive, sociable, sympathetic, welcoming, well-disposed
**neigh softly and gently** snigger
**neither** nor
**neither bad nor good** mediocre
**neither early nor late** punctual
**neither good nor bad** indifferent, mediocre, so-so
**neither here nor there** irrelevant, nowhere
**neither masculine nor feminine** neuter
**neither more nor less** equal, sheer
**neither rich nor elaborate** plain
**neither's correlative** nor
**Nelson's blood** rum
**nemesis** defeat, destiny, destruction, fate, punishment, requital, retribution, ruin, vanquishment, vengeance
**nenuphar** white water-lily
**neolith** artefact, artifact
**neolithic** secular
**neology** neologism, neoterism
**neon** gas
**neophyte** abecedarian, amateur, apprentice, beginner, convert, disciple, learner, newcomer, novice, probation, proselyte, protégé(e), pupil, recruit, roofie, rookie, student
**Nepal** Sherpaland
**Nepalese** Sherpa, Kha
**Nepalese soldier** Gurkha
**Nepal money** rupee
**nephew of Aaron** Hur
**nephew of Abraham** Lot
**nephew of Daedalus** Talus
**nephew of David** Amasa
**nephew of Shallum** Jeremiah
**nephew's sister** niece
**nephrite** jade
**ne plus ultra (L)** acme, culmination, height
**nepotism** bias, inequity, injustice, partiality, patronage, prejudice, unfairness
**Neptune** Poseidon
**nereis** ragworm
**nerve** audacity, bravery, cheek, courage, daring, determination, endurance, fearlessness, fortify, fortitude, gall, might, pluck, resolution, steadfastness, steel, strength, tenacity, vigour
**nerve cell** neuron
**nerve cell process** axon(e)
**nerve centre** ganglion
**nerve centre in the skull** brain
**nerve condition** palsy
**nerve doctor** neurosurgeon
**nerve fibre** axon(e)
**nerveless** confident, diffuse, disabled, feeble, frail, helpless, impotent, incapable, ineffective, inert, infirm, listless, paralysed, powerless, unable, weak
**nerve network** plexus, rete, retia
**nerve pain** neuralgia, sciatica
**nerve-racking** distressing, exhausting, harrowing
**nerve-tract bend** genu
**nerve white matter** alba
**nervine** drug, soothing
**nervous** aflutter, agitable, agitated, alarmed, anxious, apprehensive, disquieted, distressed, disturbed, edgy, excitable, excited, fearful, fidgety, flustered, fretful, frightened, irritable, itchy, jumpy, perturbable, perturbed, restless, scared, strained, tense, timid, timorous, uneasy, upset, worried
**nervous breakdown** collapse, crack-up, neurasthenia
**nervous bustle** fuss
**nervous debility** adynamia, neurasthenia
**nervous disorder** chorea, epilepsy, tic
**nervous disorder of horses** stringhalt
**nervous excitement** fever

**nervous frenzy**  amok
**nervous haste**  flurry
**nervously shy**  timid
**nervous malady**  aphasia, neuritis, tic
**nervousness**  agitation, angst, anxiety, dread, excitability, excitement, fluster, fright, funk, hypertension, nerves, perturbability, restlessness, shaking, strain, tenseness, tension, timidity, touchiness, trembling, twitching, unrest, upset, worry
**nervous person**  jitterbug
**nervous reaction**  shakes
**nervous substance in interior cavity of tooth**  pulp
**nervous substance in skull**  brain
**nervous tension**  stress
**nervous tremor of emotion**  thrill
**nervous twitch**  tic
**nervy**  agitated, apprehensive, brave, brawny, cheeky, courageous, fidgety, gallant, insolent, jittery, nervous, powerful, restless, robust, spirited, strong, tense, uptight, valiant, vivacious
**nescience**  blindness, confusion, cynicism, darkness, disbelief, dumbness, idiocy, ignorance, illiteracy, imbecility, inexperience, innocence, simplicity, stupidity, unawareness, unbelief, unconsciousness
**nescient**  agnostic, ignorant
**ness**  cape, headland, promontory
**nest**  aerie, asylum, bevy, bower, breeding-ground, brood, burrow, cloister, coop, covey, den, dwelling, earth, eyrie, flock, form, haunt, hermitage, hideaway, home, hotbed, house, lair, nidus, nook, pen, perch, refuge, resort, retreat, roost
**nest builder**  ant, bee, bird, hornet, mouse, wasp
**nest egg**  cache, deposit, reserve, savings, store
**nestle**  cuddle, enfold, ensconce, nest, settle, snug(gle)
**nestle closely**  huddle
**nestle together**  cuddle
**nestling**  chick, cuddling, eyas, youngling
**nest of bird of prey**  aerie, eyrie
**nest of spiders**  nidus
**nest of termites**  termitarium
**nest of wasps**  vespiary
**Nestor**  adviser, councillor, leader, patriarch, sage
**net**  bag, capture, catch, clear, closing, conclusive, earn(ings), (en)mesh, (en)snare, (en)tangle, final, gain, income, lacework, lattice, make, mesh-work, netting, network, profit, realise, reap, reticulation, take-home, total, tracery, trap, tulle, web
**net a goal**  score
**net fabric**  malines, tulle
**net fisher**  seiner
**net for catching birds or fish**  trammel
**net game**  tennis, volleyball
**nether**  basal, base, beneath, bottom, buried, low(-hanging), low-lying, lower, nadir(al), submerged, under(ground), unelevated
**Netherlands dialect**  Frisian, Frunkish
**Netherlands gin**  geneva, schnapps
**Netherlands language**  Dutch
**Netherlands liquid measure**  aam, aum
**Netherlands reclaimed land**  polder
**Netherlands townhall**  stadhuis
**nether world**  Avernus, Hades, hell, underworld
**net-like**  retiary, reticular
**net-making**  retiary
**net profit distribution**  dividend
**net spun by spider**  web
**nett**  clear, conclusive, final, gain, net, reap
**netted fabric**  netting
**netting**  gauze, lace, mesh
**nettle**  angry, annoy, goad, harass, irk, irritate, pique, provoke, ruffle, sting, tease, vex
**nettle rash**  hives, uredo, urticaria
**net used for veils**  tulle
**net used on fishing boat**  trawl
**network**  arrangements, complex, grid, grill(e), jungle, labyrinth, lace(work), mat(ting), maze, meander, mesh, methodology, net, organisation, plexus, rete, reticulation, system, wattle, web
**network fabric**  mesh
**network of fine threads**  reticle
**network of lines on map**  grid
**network of nerves**  plexus
**network of paths**  labyrinth, maze
**network of small cracks in a painting or its varnish**  craquelure
**networks of venae**  veinings
**net worth**  assets, value
**neural**  dorsal, nerve, nervous
**neuralgia of hip and thigh**  sciatica
**neuroglia**  glia
**neuron**  (nerve) cell, neurone
**neurosis**  abnormality, deviation, disease, hysteria, irregularity, malady, obsession, phobia, psychopathy, sickness
**neurotic**  abnormal, anxious, compulsive, confused, deranged, deviant, disordered, disturbed, hypochondriac, hysterical, insane, irrational, mad, maniac, nervous, psychopathic, unstable
**neurotic or hysterical symptom**  topalgia
**neuter**  asexual, castrate, disinterested, effeminise, eunuch, geld(ing), generic, impartial, it, neutral, sexless, spay, sterile, sterilise, unbiased, unman, unsexed
**neuter pronoun**  it
**neutral**  disinterested, dull, expressionless, impartial, indifferent, neuter, nonaligned, peaceful, toneless, unbiased, uncommitted
**neutrality**  aloofness, detachment, dispassion, impartiality, independence, neutralism, objectivity, pacifism, peaceableness
**neutral particle**  neutron
**neutral tone**  grey
**never**  nary, ne'er, nevermore, not
**never a one**  none
**never ceasing**  perpetual
**never despair**  nil desperandum (L)
**never-ending**  boundless, ceaseless, constant, continual, eternal, everlasting, incessant, nonstop, perpetual, relentless, unbroken, unceasing, uninterrupted, unremitting
**never growing old**  ageless
**never hit target**  missed
**never mind**  disregard
**never satisfied**  insatiate
**never say die**  nil desperandum (L)
**never still**  restless
**never stopping**  endless
**nevertheless**  but, however, nonetheless, notwithstanding, quand même (F), regardless, still, though, yet
**never to be heard again**  unrepeatable
**new**  additional, current, fresh, further, late, modern, neo-, neoteric, novel, recent, unexercised, unfamiliar, unused
**new actress**  starlet
**new and strange**  novel
**newborn's outfit**  layette
**new convert**  neophyte, novice
**new dad**  stepfather
**new device**  innovation
**new discovery**  invention
**new doctrine**  neologism, neology
**New Englander**  Yankee
**new growth of plant**  shoot
**New Guinea city**  Lae
**New Haven tree**  elm
**New Haven university**  Yale
**new information**  news
**new interpretation**  neologism, neology
**newly**  afresh, anew, chicly, fashionably, freshly, just, lately,

modernistically, modernly, recently, smartly
**newly and ostentatiously rich person** nouveau riche (F)
**newly-baked** fresh
**newly-coined word** neologism, neology
**newly-hatched fish** fry
**newly-hatched salmon** alevin, pink
**newly-married man** groom
**newly-married woman** bride
**newly-ordained priest** neophyte
**newly-rich person** nouveau riche (F), upstart
**New Mexican pine** pinon
**new Mrs** bride
**newness** freshness, novelty
**New Orleans music** jazz
**new recruit** greenhorn, roofie, rookie
**news** account, announcement, article, bulletin, communiqué, data, facts, information, message, newscast, newspaper, release, report, scandal, statement, story, tidings
**news account** report
**news article** item
**news banner** headline
**news chief** editor
**news disseminators** media
**new settler** migrant
**new shoot** sprout
**news journal** (news)paper
**newsmonger** busybody, gossipmonger, quidnunc, skinderbek, tattler, telltale
**New South Wales horse** Waler
**newspaper** annually, daily, gazette, journal, monthly, organ, periodical, publication, quarterly, rag, tabloid, weekly
**newspaper article** editorial, feature, item
**newspaper article of rumours about town** gossip column
**newspaper chief** editor
**newspaper cutting** clipping
**newspaper employee** reporter
**newspaper in concentrated form** tabloid
**newspaper section** roto
**newspaper seller** news vendor
**news paragraph** item
**news put into newspaper at latest possible moment** stop press
**newsreader** announcer
**news report** bulletin, flash, scoop
**news sheet** paper
**news statement** release
**news story title** headline
**new star** nova
**New Stone Age** Neolithic
**news vendor** newspaper seller

**newt** amphibian, eft, evet, salamander, triton
**new translation** neologism, neology
**new wine** must
**new word** neologism, neology
**New World** America
**New Year's Day** jour de l'an (F)
**New Year's Eve** Hogmanay
**New Year's Eve gift** hagema, hogmanay
**New York city district** Bronx, Brooklyn, Harlem, Manhattan, Queens
**New York city island** Staten
**New Zealand beetle** huhu
**New Zealand bird** apteryx, huia, kaki, kea, kiwi, moa, ratite, tui
**New Zealand district** Otago
**New Zealander** Kiwi, Maori
**New Zealand flax** phormium
**New Zealand honey-eater** tui
**New Zealand iguana** tuatara
**New Zealand laughing owl** whekau
**New Zealand native** Maori
**New Zealand native settlement surrounded by paddock** pa(h)
**New Zealand operatic soprano** Kiri Te Kanawa
**New Zealand palm** nikau
**New Zealand parrot** kaka, kea
**New Zealand Polynesian** Maori
**New Zealand sheep-killing parrot** kea
**New Zealand soldier** Anzac
**New Zealand spa resort** Rotorua
**New Zealand starling** huia
**New Zealand tree** karui
**New Zealand tribe or clan** ngati
**next** adjacent, after(ward), alongside, consequent, ensuing, following, later, nearest, neighbouring, proximate, sequential, subsequent, succeeding, successive
**next after first** second
**next after second** third
**next before last** penultimate
**next day** tomorrow
**next door** adjacent, neighbour
**next door to** beside
**next in line** heir, successor
**next to** abreast, alongside, beside, by, near(-hand), nearby
**next to last syllable** penult
**next to radius** ulna
**next world** afterworld, heaven, nirvana, paradise
**nexus** bond, link
**nib** apex, beak, bill, extremity, neb, peak, pen point, summit, tip, top, vertex
**nibble** assay, bite, browse, chew, clamp, crop, crunch, crush, eat, gnaw, graze, grip, munch, nip,

pasture, peck, pierce, relish, rend, sample, savour, seize, sip, snap, taste, tear, test, titbit, try, worry, wound
**Nicaraguan poet** Dario
**Nicaraguan rebel** Sandinista
**nice** accurate, agreeable, amiable, exact, good, likeable, pleasant, pleasing, precise, skilled, tactful, tasty
**nicely groomed** well-kept
**nice to hug** cuddly
**nicety** accuracy, aspect, attribute, daintiness, delicacy, detail, distinction, exactness, facet, factor, finesse, instance, item, meticulousness, minuteness, nuance, precision, refinement, respect, subtlety, triviality
**niche** alcove, coin (F), compartment, corner, cove, cranny, cubby(hole), nook, pigeonhole, place, recess
**niche in wall** alcove
**Nicholas of Russia** czar, tsar
**nick** chip, cut, damage, gash, gouge, groove, hollow, incision, indent, mark, notch, scar, score, slash, snick, split, spot
**nickname** agnomen, appellation, byname, cognomen, diminutive, dub, epithet, label, miscall, moniker, sobriquet
**nicotinic acid** niacin
**nictitate** blink, wink
**nictitating membrane** haw, third eyelid
**nide** eye, nye
**nidified** nested
**nifty** agile, clever, excellent, fine, good, quick, smart, spruce, stylish
**Nigerian** Bini, Edo, Ibibio, Ibo, Igbo
**Nigerian famine region** Biafra
**Nigerian money** naira
**Nigerian state** Bauchi, Imo, Lagos, Ogun, Ondo, Oyo, Sokoto
**Nigerian tribe** Aro, Edo, Ibo
**Nigerian walled city** Kano
**niggard** churl, curmudgeon, harpy, hoarder, hunks, miser, scrooge, skinflint
**niggardly** beggarly, cheap, cheese-paring, close, covetous, frugal, grudging, hardfisted, meagre, mean, mercenary, miserable, miserly, paltry, parsimonious, penny-pinching, penurious, poor, scanty, skimpy, sordid, sparing, stingy, tightfisted
**niggardliness** chariness, covetousness, extortion, frugality, misanthropy, nearness, penuriousness, scrimpiness, selfishness, skimpiness, sordidness,

**niggle** tenacity, tightness, ungenerosity, unyieldingness

**niggle** annoy, carp, cavil, complain, criticise, fuss, gripe, irritate, nag, object, rankle, trifle, worry

**niggling** complicated, detailed, foolish, fussy, idiotic, insignificant, intricate, minor, numb, ornate, petty, puny, silly, trifling, trivial, unimportant, useless, worthless

**nigh** about, almost, anon, approximately, close(ly), convenient, direct, imminent, looming, near(by), nearly, quick, short, soon, straight

**night** dark(ness), dusk, evening, nightfall

**night and day** ceaselessly, continually, endlessly, incessantly, indefatigably, interminably, tirelessly, unceasingly, unremittingly

**night attire** nightclothes, nightdress, nightgown, nightshirt, nightie, nighty, pyjamas

**night before** eve

**nightbird** nightingale, owl

**night blindness** nyctalopia

**nightclothes** nightdress, nightgown, nightie, nightshirt, nighty, pyjamas

**nightclub entertainment** cabaret

**nightfall** crepuscule, dusk, evenfall, evening, eventide, gloaming, moonrise, night, sundown, sunset, twilight

**night-flyer** bat, moth, owl, nightjar

**nightguard** watchman

**nightlight** moon

**nightly** night-time, octurnally

**nightmare** (caco)demon, duress, hallucination, horror, incubus, ordeal, phantasm(agoria), succubus, torture, trial, tribulation

**night music** nocturne

**night of the present day** tonight

**night sound** snore

**night stick** baton

**night study** lucubration

**night watch** vigil

**night watchman** sentinel, sentry

**nightwear** dressing gown, nightclothes, nightdress, nightgown, nightie, nightshirt, nighty, pyjamas

**nihilist** anarchist, insurgent, rebel, revolutionary, terrorist

**nihility** non-existence, nothingness, nullity, trifle

**nil** duck, goose-egg, love, naught, none, nothing, zero

**Nile boat** nuggar

**Nile dam site** Aswan

**Nile sailing boat** dahabe(ey)ah, dahabiah

**nilgai** nylghau

**nil in tennis** love

**Nilotic people** Nubas

**nim** game

**nimble** active, acute, adroit, agile, alert, awake, brisk, deft, energetic, intelligent, light-footed, lithe, lively, nippy, proficient, prompt, quick(-witted), rapid, ready, smart, speedy, sprightly, spry, swift

**nimble and quick** deft

**nimbleness** acuteness, address, agility, alertness, braininess, cleverness, esp(i)rit, fineness, fleetness, grace, ingenuity, legerity, lightness, skill, swiftness, wittedness

**nimble performer** acrobat

**nimbus** ambience, atmosphere, aura, aureole, cloud, corona, glow, halo, lustre, quality, radiance

**nine-angled figure** nonagon

**nine-day prayer** novena

**ninefold** nonuple

**nine-headed monster** Hydra

**nine inches** span

**nine inspiring ladies** Muses

**ninepins** skittles

**nine-sided figure** nonagon

**nineteen twenties hairstyle** marcel, shingle

**nine year cycle** juglar

**ninny** ass, dolt, domkop, dummy, dunce, fondling, fool, idiot, saphead, simpleton, twerp

**ninth month of Muslim year** Ramadan

**ninth planet of solar system** Pluto

**ninth sign of the Zodiac** Archer, Sagittarius

**niobite** columbite

**nip** bite, catch, check, clip, dram, draught, drop, grip, nibble, pinch, portion, shot, sip, snag, snip, squeeze, swallow, taste, tot

**nipa palm** atap

**nip in the bud** extinguish, quell, stop, suppress

**nipper** lightie, pikkie, youngster

**nippers** clincher, forceps, holder, pinchers, pliers, tweezers, vice

**nipping** acerbic, biting, bitter, chilling, chilly, cold, freezing, insulting, jeering, keen, nasty, nippy, numbing, pinching, sarcastic, scoffing, severe, sharp, snippy, tart, taunting

**nipple** breast, dug, mamilla, pap(illa), teat, tit, udder

**Nippon** Japan

**nippy** active, agile, biting, chilly, fast, nimble, nipping, quick, sharp, speedy, sprightly, spry, stinging

**nip with fingers** pinch

**niton** radon

**nit-picking** captiousness, carping, cavilling, censoriousness, critical, fault finding, finicky, fussy, hair-splitting, hypercritical, insignificant, minor, nagging, niggling, pedantic, pettifogging, petty, piddling, quibbling, trifling, unimportant

**nitrate** fertiliser

**nitre** saltpetre

**nitrogenous compound** protein

**nitrogen trihydrate** ammonia

**nitroglycerine explosive** gelignite

**nitrous oxide** laughing gas

**nitty-gritty** core, crux, gist, heart, kernel, marrow, nucleus, pith, root, substance

**nitwit** dolt, domkop, dope, dummy, fool, halfwit, idiot, nincompoop, ninny, simpleton, twerp

**nix** nobody, nothing, water elf, water sprite

**no** denial, dissent, nae (Sc), nay, negative, nein (G), nix, non (F), refusal, rejection

**Noah's boat** ark

**Noah's mountain** Ararat

**Noah's third son** Japheth

**Noah's time** Noachian

**Noah's transportation** ark

**no amateur** pro

**no bid** pass

**nobility** aristocracy, dignity, élite, eminence, excellence, generosity, gentry, grandeur, greatness, honour, illustriousness, integrity, lords, magnificence, majesty, nobleness, nobles, peerage, stateliness, superiority, uprightness, virtue, worthiness

**nobility of a state** aristocracy

**noble** admirable, aristocrat, aristocratic, earl, edel (G), elevated, generous, great, high-born, honourable, illustrious, lofty, lord(ly), magnanimous, peer, stately, superior, titled

**noble birth** gentility

**noble estate** earldom

**noble extraction** birth, blood

**noble in spirit** gallant

**noble Italian family** Este

**noble lady** peeress

**nobleman** aristocrat, baron(et), count, czar, don, duke, earl, emperor, gentleman, grandee, hidalgo, khan, king, lord, (maha)rajah, marquis, noble, patrician, peer, prince, sheik, viscount

**nobleman's estate** manor

**nobleness** augustness, dignity, generousness, grandness,

**nobleness of character** greatness, honour(ableness), impressiveness, lordliness, stateliness, virtuousness, worthiness
**nobleness of character** nobility
**noble of ancient Athens** eupatrid
**noble of ancient Rome** patrician
**noble people must behave nobly** noblesse oblige
**noble red wine** cabernet sauvignon
**noble's title** lord
**noblewoman** aristocrat, baroness, countess, czarina, donna, duchess, empress, gentlewoman, lady, (maha)ranee, (maha)rani, noble, peer(ess), princess, queen
**nobody** also-ran, cipher, cypher, menial, no-one, none, nonentity, nothing
**nobody on earth** none
**no business** irrelation
**nocent** baleful, baneful, deleterious, injurious, noisome, noxious, pernicious
**noctambulist** nightwalker, noctambule, sleepwalker, somnambulant, somnambulist
**nocturnal** night(-time), nightly, noctivagant, noctivagous
**nocturnal animal** aardvark, aardwolf, ant bear, badger, bat, coon, lemur, opossum, porcupine, possum, ratel
**nocturnal bird** nightjar, owl
**nocturnal chick** owlet
**nocturnal enuresis** bed-wetting
**nocturnal fantasy** dream
**nocturnal flying mammal** bat
**nocturnal hours** night
**nocturnal insect** moth
**nocturnal isopod** sea slater
**nocturnally** nightly
**nocturnal vision** dream
**nocturne** composition, dreamy, lullaby, serenade
**nocuous** destructive, disastrous, harmful, hurtful, lethal, malignant, morbific, noisome, noxious, pernicious, poisonous, prejudicial, toxic, venomous
**nod** acknowledge(ment), agree, assent, bob, cue, doze, gesture, greeting, indicate, salute, sign(al), sleep
**noddle** brains, head
**node** bulge, bump, burl, connection, gnarl, growth, joint, junction, knob, knot, link, lump, nodule, nub(ble), projection, prominence, protuberance, swelling, tuberosity
**noded** humpy, warty
**nod or curtsy** bow
**nodose** knotted, knotty

**nodular** blemished, bulging, gnarly, knaggy, knobbed, knobby, knotty, nodous, nubby, papular, pimpled, protruding, raised, rough, tuberous, tumorous, uneven, verrucose, verrucous, warty
**no effects** nulla bona (L)
**no end** considerably
**no end of** infinite
**noetic** abstract, conceptual, mental, theoretical
**noetic rating** IQ
**no extent** not
**no feeling** numb
**no final verdict made** open question
**no flies on** alert, knowing, sharp, smart
**nog** egg-flip
**no gender** it, neuter
**noggin** cup, dram, libation, mug, nip, tot
**no go** futile, hopeless, impossible
**no good** dud, hopeless, useless
**no goods** nulla bona (L)
**no hope** despair
**noise** ballyhoo, bawl, bedlam, cacophony, clamour, clangour, clatter, commotion, din, discord, dissonance, fracas, grunt, hubbub, jabber, outcry, pandemonium, racket, rattle, roar, row, rumour, rumpus, scream, sound, stridulation, thunder, tumult, turmoil, uproar, yell
**noiseless** aphonic, hush(ed), mum, mute, quiet, reticent, silent, speechless, still, taciturn, unsounded, voiceless
**noiselessly implied** tacitly
**noise of cat** purr, meow, miaow
**noise of hooter** beep
**noise of snake** hiss
**noisily exuberant** boisterous
**noisily resisting control** obstreperous
**noisome** contaminated, dirty, disagreeable, disgusting, evil-smelling, fetid, filthy, grisly, harmful, ill-smelling, impure, loathsome, nasty, nauseating, objectionable, (ob)noxious, odious, offensive, polluted, putrid, rank, repellent, repulsive, rotten, sickening, squalid, stinking, sullied, unclean, unpleasant, vile
**noisy** babbling, blaring, blatant, boisterous, cacophonous, chattering, clamorous, deafening, dissonant, ear-splitting, harsh, loud, pandemonic, piercing, rackety, riotous, rowdy, screeching, stentorian, strident, tumultuous, turbulent, uproarious, vocal, vociferous
**noisy acclaim** riot
**noisy and disorderly** rowdy
**noisy and riotous** nag
**noisy and unprincipled propaganda** ballyhoo
**noisy argument** wrangle
**noisy breathing** snoring, stertor
**noisy chatter** cackle
**noisy chatterer** magpie
**noisy confused situation** bedlam
**noisy, continuous and trivial talk** yak
**noisy crowd of people** rabble
**noisy dance** tap
**noisy display** splurge
**noisy disturbance** commotion, confusion, fracas, rumpus, uproar
**noisy festivity** bacchanalia, orgy
**noisy fight** brawl
**noisy fireworks** bangers
**noisy footfall** thud
**noisy party** shindig
**noisy public disturbance** affray
**noisy publicity** ballyhoo
**noisy quarrel** affray, barney, brawl, broil, fracas, fray, row, squabble
**noisy rabble** rout
**noisy riotous fight or brawl** mêlée
**noisy rush** scutter
**noisy serpent** rattlesnake
**noisy sleeper** snorer
**noisy toy** rattle
**noisy, unhealthy breathing** rale, wheeze
**noisy vibration** rattle
**noisy wedding serenade** charivari, shivaree
**no joke** reality, seriousness
**no kidding** really
**no longer active** retired
**no longer alive** dead, deceased, late
**no longer burning** extinct, out, quenched
**no longer existing** defunct, extinct, obsolete
**no longer fresh** stale
**no longer here** gone
**no longer in existence** extinct
**no longer in use** obsolete
**no longer living** dead, extinct
**no longer married** divorced
**no longer sleeping** awake
**no longer taking place** off
**no longer used** antiquated, obsolete
**no longer working** retired
**noma** stomatitis
**nomad** Bed(o)uin, drifter, gypsy, itinerant, migrant, migrator, rambler, roamer, rover, strayer, stroller, traveller, vagabond, wanderer

**nomadic** ambulant, bohemian, drifting, itinerant, migratory, pastoral, rambling, roaming, roving, straggling, straying, transitory, vagabond, vagrant, wandering
**nomadic life** vagrancy
**nomadic race of Arabs** Bed(o)uin
**nomad of the Syrian Desert** Saracen
**no matter how many** any
**no matter which** any(thing), either
**no matter who** anybody, anyone
**nom de guerre** alias
**nom de plume** alias, assumed, nom de guerre, (pen) name, pseudonym
**no meat on religious day of abstinence** maigre
**nomenclature** classification, codification, phraseology, taxonomy, terminology
**nominal** formal, insignificant, insubstantial, minimal, official, ostensible, pretended, professed, puppet, purported, self-called, self-styled, small, so-called, supposed, symbolic, theoretical, titular, token, trifling, trivial, would-be
**nominal suffix** -ier
**nominal value** par
**nominal word** noun
**nominate** appoint, assign, choose, designate, elect, empower, invest, name, recommend, suggest, tag
**nominating** naming
**nomination** appointment, assignment, designation, inauguration, induction, installation, ordainment, ordination, presentation, proposal, selection
**nominator** namer
**nominee** appointer, aspirant, assignee, candidate, choice, consignee, contestant, delegate, favourite, protégé(e), runner, selectee
**nomogram** abac, nomograph
**no more than** but, just, mere, only
**nomothetic** legislative, nomothetical
**nonage** adolescence, childhood, immaturity, infancy, juniority, juvenility, minority, youth
**nonagon** enneagon
**nonamateur** pro
**nonattendance** absence
**nonattender** absentee, malingerer, truant
**nonbarking dog** basenji
**nonbeliever** agnostic, atheist, cynic, disbeliever, doubter, sceptic
**nonbituminous coal** anthracite
**nonce** paedophile
**nonchalance** apathy, balance, calm(ness), casualness, collectedness, composure, cool(ness), easiness, equanimity, indifference, neutrality, placidity, poise, serenity, steadiness, tranquillity, unconcern, unsolicitude
**nonchalant** airy, apathetic, balanced, calm, casual, collected, composed, cool, easygoing, indifferent, neutral, placid, poised, serene, steady, tranquil, unconcerned, unexcited, unmoved
**nonclerical** laic, lay
**nonclerical male** layman
**noncommissioned sailor** rating
**non compos mentis** crazy, demented, unbalanced
**nonconformist** dissenter, heretic, individualist, protester, rebel
**nonconformist chapel** Bethal, Bethesda
**nonconformist doctrine** heresy
**noncorrosive** rustproof
**non cross-ply tyre** radial
**nondealer** pone
**nondeciduous shrub** evergreen
**nondescript** amorphous, nothing, odd, peculiar, strange, unclassifiable
**nondrinker** abstainer, ascetic, hydropot, nephalist, prohibitionist, puritan, teetotaller, water drinker
**none** neither, nil, no-one, nobody, none, not any, not one, nothing, zero
**nonentity** air, chimera, cipher, delusion, dummy, eidolon, fantasy, illusion, insignificancy, jackstraw, maya, mediocrity, mirage, mist, naught, nobody, nothing, nullity, obscurity, phantasmagoria, phantasmagory, runt, scrub, smoke, squirt, vapour, zero
**nonerasable** indelible
**nonessential thing** luxury
**nonetheless** nevertheless, notwithstanding
**nonexistent thing** nonentity
**nonferrous alloy** Tula(work)
**nonflowering plant** fern
**nonfunctional claw in dogs** dewclaw
**nongloss** matt
**nonhuman thing** it
**noninclusion** exception, exclusion, nonadmission, omission, preclusion
**noninterference** laisser faire, laissez faire
**noniron fabric** dripdry
**non-Jew** goy
**non-Jewish girl** shiksa
**non-Jewish people** gentiles
**nonmagnetic compass** gyro(compass), gyroscope
**nonmajor** junior
**nonmember of some circle** outsider
**nonmetallic element** argon, helium, iodine, neon, silicon, xenon
**nonmigratory** resident
**nonmilitary person** civilian
**non-Muslim** giaour
**nonnative resident** immigrant
**no noise** calm, quiet, still
**nonpermanent staff** freelance, temp(orary)
**nonphysical** incorporeal, platonic, spiritual, unfleshly
**nonplus** amaze, astound, baffle, bewilder, confound, confuse, confusion, disconcert, dumbfound, embarrass, impasse, perplex, perplexity, plight, predicament, puzzle, stump, stupefy, vexation
**nonprofessional** amateur(ish), dabbler, dilettante, laic(al), layperson, unskilled
**nonrotating part of a motor** stator
**nonsense** absurdity, balderdash, bosh, drivel, eyewash, fiddle-de-dee, fiddlesticks, folly, hogwash, humbug, kibosh, malarkey, moonshine, piffle, rot, rubbish, shenanigan, tommy-rot, tosh, tripe, twaddle
**nonsensical** absurd, aimless, crazy, derisory, empty, farcical, fatuous, foolish, futile, halfwitted, hollow, idiotic, illogical, inane, incongruous, insignificant, irrational, laughable, ludicrous, mad, meaningless, mindless, pointless, preposterous, ridiculous, senseless, silly, stupid, trifling, trivial, useless, vain, worthless
**nonskilled worker** labourer
**nonstandard** variant
**nonstandard language** slang
**nonstick material** Teflon
**nonstop** ceaseless, constant(ly), continual, continuous, direct, endless, frequent, habitual, incessant, ongoing, persistent, regular, relentless, repeated, steady, unbroken, unceasing, unending, uninterrupted, unremitting
**nonuser of drugs** straight
**nonverse text** prose
**nonworking male of honeybee** drone
**no objection** accept, OK, okay, yes
**noodles** pasta
**noodles cooked with tomato and basil** napolitana (I)
**nook** alcove, cavity, corner, cranny, hide-out, neuk (Sc), niche, recess, retreat
**noon** midday, noonday, noontide, noontime
**noonday rest** nap, siesta
**no-one** none
**noose** ambush, bend, bond, circle, coil, curl, curve, eyelet, fastening, gin, halter, hitch, hook, kink, lariat, lasso,

ligature, loop, pitfall, ring, snare, spiral, springe, tie, trap, twirl
**no person** nobody
**no points** duck, love
**nor** neither, ni (F)
**Nordic** Norse
**Nordic person** Arian, Aryan
**no recollection** amnesia, blankness
**Noriega's country** Panama
**norm** average, criterion, mean, model, pattern, rule, standard, type, yardstick
**normal** average, characteristic, common, conventional, customary, daily, general, medium, natural, ordinary, prevailing, regular, routine, sane, standard, typical, unchanging, universal, usual
**normal ability to experience sensation** aesthesia
**normal abode** habitat
**normal dilatation of the pupil of the eye** mydriasis
**normal mentally** sane
**Norman sword** spatha
**no room to swing a cat** cramped, incommodious
**Norse** Norwegian
**Norse alphabet** runic
**Norse chieftain** jarl, yarl
**Norse epic** *Edda*
**Norse fire demon** Surtr
**Norse god** Aegir, Aeser, Alcis, Asa, Balder, Brage, Bragi, Donat, Er, Frey, Hler, Hoder, Hoth(r), Lok(i), Odin, Thor, Tiu, Ty, Tyr(r), Ull, Vali, Van(ir), Wodan, Woden, Wotan, Zio, Ziu
**Norse goddess** Eir, Erda, Fre(y)a, Fria, Hel, Idun, Nanna, Norn, Ran, Urd
**Norse goddess of beauty** Fre(y)a
**Norse goddess of destiny** Urd
**Norse goddess of flowers** Nanna
**Norse goddess of healing** Eir
**Norse goddess of love and beauty** Freya
**Norse goddess of spring** Idun
**Norse god of evil** Lok
**Norse god of fertility** Frey
**Norse god of light** Balder
**Norse god of mischief** Loki
**Norse god of poetry** Bragi
**Norse god of the sea** Aegir, Hler
**Norse god of the sky** Tiu, Ty(r)
**Norse god of thunder** Thor
**Norse god of war** Odin, Ty(r)
**Norse god of wisdom** Odin
**Norse home of gods** Asgard
**Norse legend** *Edda*, saga
**Norse minstrel** scald, skald
**Norse mythological king** Atli

**Norse mythological sword** Gram
**Norse mythological tree** Igdrasil, Yg(g)drasil
**Norse mythological wolf** Fenrir, Fenris
**Norse poem** rune
**Norse poetry** *Edda*
**Norse saint** Olaf II, Olan II
**Norse sea god** Aegir
**Norse sea rover** Viking
**Norse tale** saga
**Norse warrior fighting in a drugged frenzy** berserker
**North African antelope** addax
**North African chieftain** emir, ameer
**North African citadel** casbah, kasbah
**North African city** Algiers, Cairo
**North African country** Algeria, Egypt, Libya, Morocco, Sudan
**North African desert** Sahara
**North African dish of coarse grain** couscous
**North African gazelle** dibatag
**North African lute-like instrument** oud
**North African mongoose** ichneumon
**North African Muslim** Berger, Moor
**North African sheep** aoudad, arui
**North American adult male** siwash
**North American amphibious mole** star-nosed mole
**North American burrowing marmot** woodchuck
**North American cocktail** Harvey Wallbanger, Manhattan, prairie oyster
**North American country** Canada, USA
**North American deer** moose, wapiti
**North American desert** Mohave, Mojave
**North American elk** moose, wapiti
**North American fish** alewife
**North American flower** dogbane
**North American hut** shebang
**North American Indian** Abnaki, Apache, Arapaho, Comanche, Cree, Mohawk, Osage, Pawnee, Seminole, Seneca, Sioux, Ute
**North American Indian child** pap(p)oose
**North American Indian shoe** moccasin
**North American Indian symbol** totem
**North American Indian tribal chief** sachem, sagamore
**North American Indian war-axe** tomahawk
**North American Indian woman** squaw
**North American large covered wagon** prairie-schooner
**North American lizard** anole
**North American marshy land** muskeg
**North American moraceous tree** Osage orange

**North American name for wolverine** carcajou
**North American nation** Canada, USA
**North American orchid** adam-and-eve, puttyroot
**North American pink-flowered shrub** rhodora
**North American porridge of maize meal** mush
**North American prairie-wolf** coyote
**North American rail** sora
**North American reindeer** caribou
**North American shrub** sagebrush
**North American small rodent** prairie-dog
**North American stag** wapiti
**North American team game** lacrosse
**North American tree** bay rum bayberry, maple
**North American tree related to walnut** hickory
**North American tribes** Abnaki, Apache, Arapaho, Comanche, Cree, Mohawk, Osage, Pawnee, Seminole, Seneca, Sioux, Ute
**North American wild cat** lynx
**North Atlantic fish** torsk
**North Atlantic islands** Faeroes
**North Australian port** Darwin
**northerly** arctic, boreal, north(ern), northward, septentrional
**northern** arctic, boreal, northerly, septentrional
**northern country** Alaska, Finnland, Norway, SIberia
**northern diving sea-bird** auk
**Northern Ireland** Ulster
**northern sea** Baltic
**northern sea duck** eider
**North Sea arm** Skagerrak
**North Sea port** Blyth
**north Sotho** Pedi
**north Spanish border town** Irum
**north-west African capital** Algiers
**northwestern Chinese** Uig(h)ur
**northwestern French wind** mistral
**northwestern German port** Hamburg
**north-west German port** Kiel
**north wind** mistral
**north wind in Italy** tramontana
**north zone** Arctic
**Norway and Sweden** Scandinavia
**Norwegian** Norse(man)
**Norwegian arctic explorer** Nansen
**Norwegian composer** Grieg
**Norwegian dance** halling
**Norwegian dramatist** Ibsen
**Norwegian inlet** fiord, fjord
**Norwegian language** Norse
**Norwegian parliament** Storting
**Norwegian poet** Ibsen
**Norwegian sea loch** fiord, fjord

**Norwegian tongue** Norse
**Norwegian whirlpool** maelstroom
**no score** duck, love, nil
**nose** beak, bec (F), neb, snoot, snout
**nose around** prowl, seek
**noseband with a lunging rein, used in horses' training** cavesson
**nosebleed** epistaxis
**nose cartilage** septum
**nose dive** dive, drop, plummet, plunge
**nosegay** bouquet, posy
**nose inflammation** rhinitis
**nose noise** snore
**nose opening** nostril
**nose partition** vomer
**nose shape** pug, Roman, sharp
**nose-to-lip hair** moustache
**nose-wiper** handkerchief, hanky, tissue
**nosh** drink, eat
**nostalgia** homesickness, longing, regret, remembrance, wistfulness, yearning
**nostalgic** homesick, longing, regretful, wistful
**nostology** gerontology
**Nostradamus** prediction-monger
**nostril** ala, blowhole, naris, spiracle, thrill
**nostrils** nares, nose
**nostrum** arcanum, cure, drug, medication, medicine, panacea, potion, proprietary, remedy, treatment
**nosy** curious, eavesdropping, inquisitive, interfering, nosey, prying
**nosy person** busybody, nosyparker, prier
**not** na (Sc), nae (Sc), neither, non-, un-
**not a bean** broke, skint
**nota bene** heed, mark, observe
**notable** alert, capable, careful, celebrity, conspicuous, diligent, distinguished, eminent, especial, extraordinary, famed, major, memorable, noted, noteworthy, notorious, prominent, remarkable, signal, thrifty, uncommon, unusual
**not able** unable
**notable achievement** feat
**notable age** epoch, era
**notable case on trial** cause célèbre
**notable deed** exploit, feat, gest(e)
**notable occurrence** event
**notable person** notability
**not able to be burnt by fire** incombustible
**not able to be transferred** inalienable
**not able to be travelled over** impassable
**not able to produce offspring** sterile
**not absent** present
**not absolute** arbitrary, conditional

**not abstract** concrete, solid
**not absurd** reasonable
**not abundant** light, rare, scant, spare
**not accompanied** a cappella, solo
**not according to due form** informal
**not according to rule** false
**not accurate** impure, inexact
**not accurately known** uncertain
**not acid** alkaline
**not a coastal person** inlander
**not acquired** intrinsic, native
**not acting** static
**not active** inert, resting, retired, static
**not actuated** trabeated
**not a favourite** outsider
**not affording comfort** incommodious
**not a friend** enemy
**not a genuine fruit** pseudocarp
**not agitated** calm, tranquil
**not a Jew** Gentile
**not alfresco** indoors
**not all** some, few
**not allowable** illicit, impermissible
**not allowed** forbidden, illicit, out
**not allowing the passage of light** opaque
**not a marriage of convenience** love match
**not amateur** pro(fessional)
**not ample** skimpy
**not an altruist** egoist
**not analytic** synthetic(al)
**not an egoist** altruist
**not anonymous** onymous
**not any** nary, no(ne), nothing
**not anything** naught, nothing
**not anywhere** nowhere
**not apart** joined, together, united
**not a play for minors** adult show
**not apparent to eye** invisible
**not appropriate** inapt
**not a professional** amateur
**not artificial** natural
**not a sailor** landlubber
**not as big** smaller
**not a service man** civilian
**not as fancy** plainer
**not as good** worse
**not as hard** easier
**not asleep** awake
**not as many** fewer
**not as much** less
**not as old** newer, younger
**not assumed** sincere
**not as tight** looser
**not as young** older
**not at all** never, noways, nowise
**not at any time** never
**not at home** abroad, away, leave, out
**not attained** unachieved
**not attending** abstracted
**not attentive** absent, dreamy

**not attractive** homely, plain, ugly
**not at work** off
**not awake** asleep
**not away** present
**not backed by written authority** imperceptible
**not bad** average, fair, passable, respectable, so-so
**not balanced** unequal
**not bankrupt** solvent
**not barefoot** shod
**not based on moral standards** amoral
**not bashful** confident, unshy
**not BC** AD
**not behaving well** naughty
**not behind** abreast
**not being used** idle
**not belonging** extraneous, extrinsic
**not better** worse
**not beyond** within
**not beyond endurance** tolerable
**not binding** null, void
**not bitter** unresentful
**not blunt** sharp, whetted
**not bold** faint
**not bound** free, unrestrained
**not bound by rules** arbitrary
**not bright** dim, dull, grey
**not brightly** dimly
**not broad** narrow, thin
**not broken up** whole
**not bumpy** flat
**not busy** empty, free, idle, slack
**not by a long sight** hardly
**not by degrees** outright
**not by means of cash** in kind
**not candid** disingenuous, insincere
**not carefree** burdened, concerned, worried
**not careful** careless
**not caring** pococurante
**not causing pain** painless
**not cautious** unwary
**not ceasing** ceaseless
**not central** acentric
**not certain** undecided, undetermined, unsure
**not certifiable** sane
**notch** cleft, cog, crease, crenel(tate), cut, degree, dent, dimple, gash, grade, groove, incision, indent(ation), level, nick, nock, score, scratch, serrate, slash, stigma, tooth
**notched like the teeth of a saw** serrated
**notch up** achieve, gain, make, record, register, score
**not clean** dirty, soiled
**not clear** dark, dim, muddy, obscure, thick, turbid
**not clearly expressed** obscure, vague

not clerical　lay
not clever　dunceish
not closed　open
not clothed　naked, nude
not coarse　fine
not commodious　cramped
not common　rare
not communicative　reticent
not compact　loose
not compassionate　stern, strict
not competent　inept
not complete　partial
not completely　part(ial)ly
not complex　simple
not complicated　simple
not complimentary to　alien
not compulsory　optional
not concealed　overt
not concentrated　diffuse
not concerned　carefree
not concerned with morals　amoral
not concrete　abstract
not confident　uncertain
not confined　free, loose, unrestrained
not conforming to type　atypical
not conscious　asleep, unaware
not consistent　erratic
not constrained　voluntary
not containing a liquid　aneroid
not continuous　intermittent
not contradictory　consistent
not contrite　unrepentant
not controlled by will　involuntary
not cooked　raw
not copied　original
not corporeal　immaterial
not corrupt　pure
not costly　cheap
not counting　apart
not covered　bare, naked, open, uninsured
not created　uncaused
not crude　civil
not dangerous　cushy, harmless
not dark at night　moonlit
not dead　alive
not deciduous　evergreen
not deep　shallow
not deficient　faultless, perfect
not definite　tentative, vague
not dense　sparse
not deserved　unearned
not detailed　broad
not determined　indefinite
not dexterous　maladroit
not different　same, unchanged, unvarying
not difficult　easy, simple
not discordant　pure
not discovered　unknown
not diseased　sound
not disposed to severity　lenient

not distributable among a number　indivisible
not divisible by two　odd
not documented　ahistorical
not doing anything　idle
not domestic　foreign
not down　up
not drunk　sober
not dry　wet
not dual　singular
not due to conscious volition　spontaneous
not dull　sharp
not dumb　bright, smart
note　answer, card, chit, chronicle, comment, currency, debt, distinguish, draft, enter, examine, information, letter, memo(randum), mention, message, minutes, money, notice, observe, record, reminder, renown, reply, semibreve, write
not easily agitated　phlegmatic
not easily broken　strong
not easily converted into cash　illiquid
not easily described　indefinite, indeterminate, nondescript
not easily disturbed　equable, placid
not easily excited　phlegmatic, stoic, stolid
not easily grasped by the mind　impalpable
not easily persuaded　obstinate
not easily perturbed　imperturbable, unruffled
not easily understood　obscure
not easy　complex, difficult, stiff
notebook　pad
not ecclesiastical　civic, laic, profane, secular, temporal
note certifying that a student is sick　aegrotat
not economical　wasteful
noted　acclaimed, alluded, brilliant, catalogued, celebrated, cited, designated, detected, distinguished, eminent, esteemed, exalted, fabled, famed, famous, glorious, heeded, illustrious, indicated, marked, mentioned, notable, noticed, observed, popular, prominent, recognised, recorded, registered, remarked, renowned, venerable, well-known, well-liked, witnessed
note in margin　gloss, postil
note in the sol-fa scale　doh, fah, la, mi, re, soh, te
not either　neither, nor
not elevated　low
not elusive　tangible
not emitting articulate sound　mute
not employed　idle
not endorsed　unsigned

not endowed with reason　irrational
not enduring with composure　impatient
not enough　inadequate, insufficient
not enough to meet amount required　undersubscribed
not entirely　part(ial)ly
note of charges　bill
note of contract　memorandum
note of excuse　aegrotat
not ephemeral　long-term
not equal for some task　unable
noter　observer
note stating student is ill　aegrotat
note systematically　observe
note-taker　stenographer
note the speed　time
note the time　date
note to chemist　prescription
note to help memory　memorandum
not even　odd, rough
not ever　never
not evergreen　deciduous
note well　nota bene (L)
noteworthy　eminent, exceptional, extraordinary, meaningful, notable, noticeable, outstanding, remarkable, signal, significant, single, unusual
noteworthy achievement　feat
noteworthy things　memorabilia
not exactly divisible　odd
not exaggerated　level-headed, practical, pragmatic, sensible, sober, uncoloured
not exalted　low
not excessive　moderate, modest, reasonable
not excited　calm, relaxed
not exciting　boring, pale, tame
not exclusive in opinion　eclectic
not exempt　liable
not existing before　new, fresh
not expecting too much　reasonable
not extreme　bland, conservative, mild, moderate
not false　real, true
not familiar　strange
not famous　inglorious, unknown
not fancy　plain
not far away　near(by)
not far-fetched　natural
not far from　almost
not far off　approximate
not fast　slow
not fat　lean, slim
not feeling emotion　apathetic
not few　many
not figuratively　literally
not filled　blank, empty
not fine　coarse
not firm　floppy, limp, shaky, unstable, unsteady

**not fit** ineligible
**not fit for consumption** inedible
**not fitting** inapt
**not fit to be eaten** inedible
**not fixed** ambulatory, mobile
**not fixed in extent** indeterminate
**not flexible** renitent, rigid, stiff
**not flowing freely** viscous
**not fluid** solid
**not FM** AM
**not following logically** inconsequent
**not follow suit** reneg(u)e
**not forbidden** allowed, licit, permitted
**not for competition** hors concours (F)
**not foreign** domestic
**not free** bound
**not fresh** old, stale
**not from** to
**not fully** partly
**not fully capable** inefficient
**not fully developed** immature, undeveloped, unformed, unripe, youthful
**not fully formed** imperfect, incomplete
**not fully grown** immature
**not fussy** easy-going
**not general** especial, homely, local, particular, personal
**not generally intelligible** esoteric
**not generous** illiberal, mean, niggardly
**not genuine** fake, fictitious, imitation, phoney, pseudo, sham, spurious
**not given to drink** sober
**not giving milk** dry, eild (Sc)
**not giving vent to** suppress
**not gloss** matt(e)
**not going straight to the point** indirect, prevaricate
**not going to extremes** moderate
**not good to look at** ugly
**not gradually** outright
**not green** ripe, experienced
**not growing old** ageless
**not guilty** innocent
**not hard** easy, soft
**not harsh** kind, lenient, mild
**not hasty** slow
**not having** lack, need
**not having feet** apod
**not having knowledge** nescient
**not having made a will before death** intestate
**not having predetermined axes** isotropic, isotropous
**not having sufficient ability** unable
**not headlong** sideways
**not healthful** morbid, sick, toxic
**not heavy** light
**not here** absent, away, otherwhere, out, there
**not heterodox** orthodox
**not hiding one's thoughts** candid

**not high** low
**nothing** nada (Sp), naught, nil, nobody, none, nonentity, nowt, nullity, rien (F), rubbish, trivia, void, zero, zilch
**nothing better** best
**nothing else than** mere
**nothing further** ne plus ultra (L)
**nothing in it** empty
**nothing is great unless good** nil magnum nisi bonum (L)
**nothing more than** mere
**nothing short of** absolutely, completely, totally
**nothing to do with it** irrelevant
**not holding any rank** private
**not hollow** solid
**not home** out
**not hostile** amicable
**notice** account, ad(vertisement), advice, announcement, attention, bill, comment, communication, consideration, criticism, detect, discern, distinguish, espy, heed, information, instruction, intelligence, intimation, mark, mind, news, note, notification, observation, observe, order, perceive, poster, regard, remark, review, see, sign, spot, warning
**noticeable** appreciable, clear, conspicuous, detectable, distinct, evident, manifest, notable, obvious, perceivable, perceptible, plain, prominent, striking
**notice of danger** alarm, warning
**notice of death** obituary
**notice of intention to marry** banns
**not identical** distinct
**not idle** occupied
**notify** acquaint, apprise, inform, tell
**not illegal** lawful
**not illuminated** dark, unlit
**not imaginary** real
**not imitative** original
**not immediately obvious** subtle
**not implying limitation** aorist
**not imported** home-produced
**not imposing in appearance** mean, shabby
**not in** out
**not in alphabetical order** analphabetic
**not in a million years** never
**not in any place** nowhere
**not inapt** suitable
**not in bondage to another** free
**not inclined to give information** reserved, uncommunicative
**not included in a rule** exception
**not including** except
**not independent** subject
**not indigenous** exotic

**not indoors** alfresco
**not inexact** accurate
**not influenced by involvement** disinterested
**not informed** unaware
**not in good health** poorly
**not inhabited** vacant, empty
**not in harmony** dissonant
**not in its place** missing, lost
**not injured or harmed** untouched
**not in keeping with** alien
**not innocent** guilty
**not in one's own country** foreign
**not in one's right mind** non compos mentis (L)
**not in open court** in camera
**not in operation** off
**not inside** outside
**not in style** outmoded, passé
**not intellectual** lowbrow
**not interesting** dull
**not in the mood** averse, disinclined, reluctant, unwilling
**not in the right direction** wry
**not in use** disused, idle, spare
**not invited** unasked
**not involving risk** safe
**notion** attitude, belief, caprice, conceit, concept(ion), desire, fad, fancy, fantasy, idea, image, impression, impulse, inkling, invention, judg(e)ment, knowledge, observation, opinion, percept, phantasy, reflection, sentiment, slant, supposition, theory, view, whim, wish
**notional** abstract
**not iron or steel** nonferrous
**not irritating** bland
**not italic** roman
**not jesting** serious
**not Jewish** gentile
**not joined** apart
**not justifiable** indefensible
**not keen** loth, reluctant
**not knowing** nescience, unaware
**not kosher** tref, treif(a)
**not lacking anything** complete
**not ladies** gentlemen
**not late** punctual, timeously
**not later** immediately, now
**not lax** rigid, strict
**not lean** fat
**not learned** instinctive
**not leaving a will** intestate
**not legal** illegal
**not legally binding** void
**not legible** obscure
**not lenient** severe
**not level** rough, uneven
**not liable** exempt
**not liable to decay** aseptic

**not liable to pain** impassible
**not liable to sin** impeccable
**not liberal** restricted
**not likely** improbable
**not lit** dark
**not literal** figurative, metaphorical
**not local** azonic, express, general
**not locked up** free
**not long ago** lately, recent(ly)
**not long delayed** speedy, swift
**not long past** recent
**not long since** recently
**not loose** tight
**not lucid** opaque
**not mad** sane
**not many** few, infrequent, meagre, occasional, rare, scant, scarce, skimpy, sporadic
**not marketable** unsaleable
**not married** single, unwed
**not matched** odd, orra (Sc)
**not mean** generous
**not merely superficial** thorough
**not methodical** casual
**not mild** harsh
**not mind** acquiesce, indifferent, uncaring
**not mixed** sincere
**not monastic** secular
**not moving** firm, inactive, inert, motionless, static, stationary, statuelike, unmoving
**not much to look at** ugly
**not native** alien, exotic
**not natural** artificial, factitious
**not naturalised** alien
**not naturally belonging** extraneous
**not near** off
**not necessary** inessential
**not needed** needless, unnecessary
**not negative** positive
**not negligible** considerable, serious
**not new** second-hand, used
**not nice** horrible, mean
**not noticed** hidden, invisible, unseen
**not noticing anything** unobservant
**not nourishing** lean
**not now** eventually, later, then
**not objectionable** inoffensive
**not obligatory** optional
**not obscene** decent
**not observed** unseen
**not obtuse** acute, alert, sharp
**not obvious** deep, doubtful, inner, secret, subtle
**not occupied** idle
**not odd** even
**not off** on
**not of practical relevance** academic
**not of primary importance** subsidiary
**not of sound mind** non compos mentis (L)

**not often** barely, rarely, seldom
**not of the mind** somatic
**not old** new
**not on** off
**not on centre** acentric, eccentric
**not one** nobody, none, zero
**not one of the batting side** fielder
**not one or the other** neither
**not one's own** alien, strange
**not on purpose** unintentional
**not on speaking terms** bad friends
**not on time** late, overdue
**not onymous** anonymous
**not on your life** nay, never
**not opaque** transparent
**not open** closed, reticent
**not operating** off
**not optimistic** pessimistic
**notoriety** celebrity, discredit, disgrace, dishonour, disrepute, eminence, escutcheon, esteem, favour, glory, greatness, honour, infamy, obloquy, opprobrium, praise, publicity, reputation, respect, stain, stigma, superiority, supremacy
**not original** second-hand
**not originating within the body** heterogenous
**notorious** blatant, disgraceful, dishonourable, disreputable, distinguished, fabled, famed, flagrant, glaring, grand, historical, ignominious, immortal, infamous, legendary, memorable, notable, obvious, open, overt, prominent, scandalous, shameful
**notoriously vile** infamous
**notorious Russian monk** Rasputin
**not orthodox** heterodox
**not out** in, no
**not out of doors** inside
**not outside** indoors, inside
**not outspoken** mealy-mouthed
**not outstanding** average
**not overt** covert
**not overweight** slim
**not paid at the right time** overdue
**not painful** indolent
**not paired** odd
**not partial** complete
**not particular** general
**not partitioned** undivided
**not partly** entirely, wholly
**not part of a set** odd
**not passive** active, reacting
**not permanent** casual, irregular, temporary, transient
**not permitted** forbidden, illicit, unlawful
**not personal** public
**not pertinent** irrelevant
**not perused** unread
**not pessimistic** optimistic

**not plain** fancy, ornamental
**not plainly marked** indistinct
**not pleasant in appearance** uncomely
**not pleasurably entertained** unamused
**not plentiful** insufficient, scant, scarce
**not plump** lean, thin
**not plural** singular
**not poetic** prosaic
**not positive** negative
**not practicable** visionary
**not practical** abstract
**not practising solitary life** social
**not precise** faulty, inexact
**not prejudiced** liberal
**not prepared to wait** impatient
**not prepared** unready
**not prepared to wait** impatient
**not present** absent, away, elsewhere
**not private** public
**not producing** sterile
**not professional** amateur, laic
**not profound** shallow
**not progressing** moribund, static
**not public** personal, private
**not published** inedited
**not punctual** late
**not put off** undaunted, undeterred
**not qualified** incompetent, unfitted
**not quarried** live
**not quick** slow
**not quite** almost, nearly, scarcely
**not quite dry** tacky
**not rambling in speech** coherent
**not rapid** gradual
**not rare** well done
**not reacting** passive
**not ready** unprepared
**not real** false, fictitious, ideal, illusory, imaginary
**not recent or modern** old
**not refined** crude
**not regular** casual
**not related to history** ahistoric(al)
**not relaxed** nervous, taut
**not repeated** one-off
**not required** needless, otiose
**not requisite** adscititious
**not resilient** inelastic
**not respectable in character** disreputable
**not responding to friendliness** sullen
**not responsive** immune
**not restricted** liberal
**not revealed** undisclosed
**not rhythmical** ragged
**not rich** plain, poor
**not right** wrong
**not rigid** lax
**not ripe** green, immature
**not robust** delicate, sickly, weak(ly)
**not rough** even, gentle, smooth

**not roughly** tenderly
**not round** angulate
**not rubbed out** unerased
**not sacred** profane, secular
**not said to a goose** boo
**not sanctioned** unapproved
**not sane** insane, mad
**not saying all that one knows** reserved, reticent
**not scarce** plentiful
**not seeing clearly** dim
**not sensitive to reproach** thick-skinned
**not serious** casual, frivolous
**not settled** undecided, undetermined
**not severe** lenient, mild
**not severed** uncut, united
**not sexual** platonic
**not sharp** dull, obtuse
**not shedding tears** tearless
**not showing emotion** impassive
**not shut** open
**not sideways** headlong
**not silently** aloud
**not simple** complex
**not slack** taut, tight
**not slow** fast, quick
**not small** big
**not smooth** abrupt, choppy, jerky, rough
**not sober** drunk
**not sociable** antisocial
**not social** asocial
**not soft** hard
**not so great** fewer, less, smaller
**not soiled** clean
**not solid** hollow
**not so much** less
**not so old** younger
**not sorry** impenitent
**not so soon** later
**not sound** ailing, weak
**not specific** general, generic, overall, vague
**not spiritual** carnal, secular
**not spoken** unsaid
**not spotted** immaculate
**not stable** astatic
**not stale** fresh
**not stationary** mobile, portable
**not steady** unstable
**not steep** gradual
**not stereospecific** atactic
**not stiff** limp
**not stimulating** bland
**not stout** slender
**not straight** bent, crooked, curved
**not straightforward** crooked, devious, evasive, shifty
**not strict** lax
**not strictly true** inexact
**not strong** fragile

**not strong or positive** neutral
**not subject to** exempt
**not subject to a feudal superior** liegeless
**not submitting to authority** insubordinate
**not substantial** slight
**not sufficient** scant
**not suitable** inapt, unapt, unsuitable
**not sullied** untainted
**not superficial** thoroughgoing
**not sure** confused, doubtful, uncertain
**not surprisingly** naturally
**not susceptible** immune
**not susceptible to control or authority** recalcitrant
**not sweet** acrid, bitter, pungent, sour
**not swift** slow
**not taking account** irrespective
**not tall** short
**not tamed** feral, wild
**not tarnished** unsullied
**not taut** slack
**not telling the truth** lying
**not temporary** permanent
**not tender** tough
**not tested** untried
**not that** this
**not the less for** nevertheless, notwithstanding
**not the main egress** side exit
**not the one or the other** neither
**not there** here, mad, out
**not the real name** agnomen, nickname, nom de plume, pseudonym
**not the same** another, different, exclusive, other, separate
**not the same kind or type** heterogeneous
**not these** those
**not thinking** incogitant, thoughtless
**not this** other, that
**not those** these
**not thought out** ill-considered
**not tight** lax, loose
**Nottingham football team** Forest
**not to be annulled** inalienable, permanent
**not to be conveyed** untransferable, inalienable, unconsignable
**not to be doubted** certain
**not to be entered** barred
**not to be escaped from** ineluctable, unescapable
**not to be in time for** miss
**not to be made void** inalienable, permanent
**not to be recovered** irretrievable
**not to be taken lightly** serious
**not to be thought of** impossible, inconceivable

**not to be trusted** treacherous
**not to be violated** sacred
**not together** apart
**not to mention** besides
**not too cold, not too hot** lukewarm, temperate, tepid
**not too much** ne nimium (L)
**not to one's liking** disagreeable
**not tough** tender
**not to understand** mistake
**not trained** unschooled
**not transferable** inalienable, permanent
**not transmitting light** opaque
**not transparent** cloudy, opague, unclear
**not trifling** earnest
**not true** false, lie
**not turbid** clear, limpid
**not typical** atypical
**not ugly** attractive
**not understood** confused, unclear
**not unequal** uniform
**not uniform** inequable, unequal
**not universal** subaltern
**not unruly** orderly
**not unstable** steady
**not unto us** non nobis (L)
**not unwary** cautious
**not up** down
**not up to** incapable, unfit, unqualified
**not used** untouched
**not usual** abnormal
**not usually** boldly, brazenly, curiously, eminently, famously, fragrantly, importantly, interestingly, notoriously, oddly, prominently, strangely, supremely, unexpectedly, uniquely, unusually
**not uttered** mute
**not vague** definite
**not valid** nugatory, null, void
**not varying** equable
**not veracious to do this** lie
**not verified** unproven
**not vertical** unplumb
**not very clear** obscure
**not very deep** shallow
**not very good** so-so, indifferent
**not very often** seldom
**not very wide** narrow
**not wanted** undesired, superfluous
**not warranted** undue
**not wasteful** economical
**not wearing a yashmak** veilless
**not well** ailing, ill, sick, unfit
**not wet** dry
**not what it purports to be** spurious
**not wholly** part(ial)ly
**not wide** narrow
**not wild** tame
**not windy** calm

**not wisely** silly
**not within** beyond, out
**not with others** alone, single
**notwithstanding** although, nevertheless, nonetheless
**notwithstanding that** although
**notwithstanding this** his non obstantibus (L)
**not working** idle, off, unusable
**not working freely** rigid, stiff
**not worth mentioning** insignificant, slight, trifling, unimportant
**not worthy** ineligible
**not written** oral, verbal
**not written on** blank
**not yet constructed** unbuilt
**not yet decided** undetermined
**not yet disclosed** ulterior
**not yet fully developed** inchoate
**not yet mature** nascent
**not yet paid** overdue
**not yet payable** undue
**not yet revealed** latent
**not yet tested** untried
**not yet twenty** nineteen
**not yet used** new, untapped
**not yet weaned** suckling
**not young** old
**nought** blank, duck, naught, nil, nobody, none, nothing(ness), nullity, zero
**noughts and crosses** tic(k)-tac(k)-toe
**nounal suffix**
**noun ending**
**noun suffix** -ade, -en, -es(e), -ier
**nourish** feed, foment, foster, help, nurse, nurture, promote, succour, support, sustain
**nourish and rear** nurture
**nourishing** alible, alimentative, attending, contributive, feeding, fostering, healthful, healthy, helpful, life-sustaining, nursing, nurturing, nutritious, nutritive, promoting, supplying, supportive, sustaining, tending, wholesome
**nourishing decoction** ptisan, tisane
**nourishing food** nutriment
**nourishing substance** nutrient
**nourishment** aliment(ation), edibles, food(stuffs), meals, nutriment, nutrition, pabulum, provisions, rations, sustenance, viands
**nous** alertness, common sense, gumption, intellect, intelligence, mind, reason, sense, talent, wit
**nouveau riche** newly-rich, parvenu(e), upstart
**no value** null, void
**novel** account, chronicle, creative, different, drama, fiction, fresh, intrigue, latest, literature, modern, mystery, narrative, neoteric, new, prose, rare, recent, refreshed, renewed, romance, saga, shocker, story, strange, tale, thriller, unknown, unusual, western
**novel published in instalments** serial
**novel relating the early development and education of the hero** Bildungsroman (G)
**novelty** bauble, freshness, innovation, newness, oddity, trinket, uniqueness
**novercal** stepmotherly
**novice** abecedarian, acolyte, amateur, apprentice, beginner, canonical, convert, debutant, entrant, fledgeling, greenhorn, intern, layman, layperson, learner, neophyte, newcomer, noviciate, novitiate, probationer, pupil, recruit, roofie, rookie, student, tiro, trainee, tyro, waister
**now** anon, current, immediately, instantly, nowadays, promptly, since, soon, straightaway, today
**nowadays** today
**now Alsace** Alsatia
**now and again** occasionally, often, periodically, sometimes
**now and then** infrequently, intermittently, occasionally, periodically, randomly, sometimes, sporadically
**no way** never
**now called Day of Goodwill** Boxing Day
**now Gweru** Gwelo
**now Kisangani** Stanleyville
**now Luvuei** Lumai
**now Nuristan** Kafiristan
**now Shah Faisalabad** Lyallpur
**now Sri Lanka** Ceylon
**now Thailand** Siam
**now Vadodara** Baroda
**now Zimbabwe** Rhodesia
**noxious** baneful, corrupting, deleterious, disastrous, fatal, harmful, hurtful, injurious, malignant, mortal, murderous, noisome, pernicious, pestilential, poisonous, prejudicial, toxic, unhealthy, vicious
**noxious emanation** mephitis
**noxious plant** weed
**noxious weed** loco
**nuance** dash, distinction, finesse, gradation, hint, nicety, refinement, shade, subtlety, suggestion, suspicion, tinge, touch, variation
**nub** bulge, bump, gist, hump, knob, knot, lump, node, nodule, nubble, pommel, protuberance, swelling, tubercle, tumour

**nubile** adult, developed, full-grown, marriageable, mature, ripe
**nuclear** atomic, central, dynamic, inner
**nuclear beams** radiation
**nuclear bomb** nuke
**nuclear container** reactor
**nuclear device** bomb, reactor
**nuclear particle** atom
**nuclear reaction** fission, fusion
**nuclear shutdown warmth** afterheat
**nuclear vessel** reactor
**nucleus** centrality, centre, core, germ, heart, kernel, pith, soul
**nucleus of deuterium atom** deuteron
**nude** bare, denuded, divested, exposed, naked, plain, stark-naked, unadorned, unattired, unclad, unclothed, uncovered, undecked, undecorated, undressed
**nude runner** streaker
**nudge** bump, dig, elbow, jab, jog, jostle, kick, poke, prod, prompt, push, touch
**nudist** gymnosophist, naturist, sunworshipper
**nudity** bareness, nakedness, undress
**nuisance** affliction, annoyance, bore, bother, disadvantage, handicap, hassle, inconvenience, menace, offence, ordeal, pest, plague, problem, tiresome, trial, trouble, vexation, worry
**null** ineffectual, invalid, nonexistent, useless, valueless, void
**nullah** ravine, sloot, stream, watercourse
**null and void** abolished, invalid, nullified, renounced, repudiated, rescinded, revoked
**nullifidian** atheist, disbeliever, gentile, nonbeliever, pagan, sceptic, unbeliever
**nullify** abjure, abolish, annul, avoid, cancel, counteract, discharge, dissolve, eliminate, invalidate, negate, neutralise, overrule, recall, renounce, repeal, repudiate, rescind, terminate, undo, vacate, veto, void
**nullification** neutralising, quashing, repealing, rescinding, revoking, vetoing, voiding
**numb** apathetic, benumbed, dazed, deaden, drugged, dull, dumb, frozen, insensate, insensible, insensitive, inured, mindless, obtuse, paralysed, paralytic, sensationless, senseless, stun, torpid, unaware, uncaring, unemotional, unfeeling
**number** beat, collection, company, compute, count, digit, edition, enumerate, figure, include, issue,

many, numeral, numerate, quantity, rhythm, sum, total
**numbered musical work** opus
**number five as on dice** cinque
**number in a baker's dozen** thirteen
**number in cricket team** eleven
**number in duet** two
**number in football side** eleven
**number in quartet** four
**number in trio** three
**number of baseball players in side** nine
**number of beasts** herd
**number of bricks** clamp
**number of cakes baked at one time** batch
**number of cat's lives** nine
**number of cattle** herd
**number of copies of a book printed at one time** edition
**number of fish** school
**number of guns or cannons** battery
**number of hawks** cast
**number of inhabitants** population
**number of lines of writing** acrostic
**number of miles travelled** mileage
**number of nuts in text** ennage
**number of persons available for military service** manpower
**number of points made in a game** score
**number of sheep** flock
**number of shops under the same owner** chain
**number of Snow White's friends** seven
**number of things grouped together** bunch
**number of threads per inch** pitch
**number of years** age
**number pages of a book** paginate
**number represented by one and thirty noughts** nonillion
**numbers pool** gambling, lottery
**number system with base eight** octal
**number ten iron** (sand) wedge
**number that divides another without a remainder** submultiple
**number the pages of** paginate
**numbness** anaesthesia, apathy, callousness, deadness, disregard, dullness, frozenness, insensibility, insensitiveness, paralysis, passionless, shock, stupor, torpidity, torpidness, torpor, unconsciousness
**numeral** cipher, digit, figure, fraction, integer, number, numero (Sp), symbol
**numerical data** statistics
**numerical symbol** figure
**numerous** abundant, copious, large, many, multifarious, numberless, plentiful, populous, profuse, several, sundry, various
**numerous and varied** manifold
**nummular** circular, coin-shaped, disc-shaped
**numnah** numdah, saddle-cloth
**numskull** ass, blockhead, idiot, numbskull
**nun** abbess, anchoress, aspirant, beguinage, beguine, canoness, canonical, clergywoman, cloistress, mother, novice, pigeon, postulant, prioress, recluse, religious, sister(hood), smew, virgin, votaress
**nunnery** abbey, cloister, convent, monastery, novitiate, priory
**nun's cap** coif
**nun's dress** habit
**nun's headdress** veil, wimple
**nun's home** convent, nunnery
**nuptial** bridal, conjugal, connubial, genial, hymeneal, marital, marriage, matrimonial, spousal, wedded, wedding
**nuptial ceremony** wedding
**nuptial vacation** honeymoon
**Nuremberg** Nürnberg (G)
**nurse** amah, attend, cherish, encourage, feed, help, nanny, nourish, nurture, promote, rear, succour, tend
**nurse a grievance** sulk
**nurse excessively** coddle, pamper
**nursemaid** amah, ayah, bonne (F), nanny
**nurse or nun** sister
**nursery** créche, fosterage
**nursery plant** seedling
**nursery poem** rhyme
**nursery rhyme** doggerel
**nursery rhyme character** Humpty Dumpty, Mother Goose
**nurse's boss** matron

**nurseling** baby, bairn (Sc), bambino (It), bébé (F), changeling, cub, enfant (F), foal, fostering, foundling, infant, kitten, kitty, neonate, newborn, nursling, papoose, pup(py), suckling, supporting, toddler, tot, weanling
**nurture** advance, aid, breed, cherish, cultivate, encourage, feed, foster, help, maintain, mother, nourish, nurse, parent, promote, raise, rear, stimulate, sustain, teach, tend
**nut** almond, areca, brazil, cashew, crackpot, eccentric, en, hazel, kernel, litchi, lunatic, macadamia, madman, nutcase, peanut, pecan, seed, senses, stone, walnut
**nut-flavoured brandy liqueur** noyau
**nut-meat candies** pralines
**nutmeg appendage** aril
**nut of areca palm** betel
**nut of cultivated hazel** filbert
**nut of hickory tree** pecan
**nut of turpentine tree** pistachio
**nut-pine tree** pinon
**nutria** coypu
**nutrition** aliment, food, nourishment, nutriment, subsistence, sustenance
**nutritional disease of children** kwashiorkor
**nutritious** alimental, beneficial, healthful, nourishing, nutritive, wholesome
**nutritious bean** soya
**nutritious starch** arrowroot
**nuts and bolts** basics
**nut tightener** spanner
**nutty** crazy, mad
**nutty confection** nougat, praline
**nutty liqueur** noyau
**nut used in cake** almond, pecan, walnut
**nut usually keeps it in place** bolt
**nye** eye, nide
**nylghau** nilgai
**nylon item** stocking
**nylon net** tulle
**nymph** (hama)dryad, houri, naiad, nereid, oceanid, oread, sylph
**nymph-chaser** satyr
**nymph of Muslim paradise** houri
**nymph of the woods** (hama)dryad
**Nynorsk** Landsmål

# O

**oaf** blockhead, bonehead, boob, buffoon, cad, clodpate, deadhead, dolt, dullard, dunce, fool, gawk, goon, loggerhead, lout, lummox, ninny, nitwit, num(b)skull, simpleton
**oafish** boneheaded, bovine, clumsy, dense, doltish, heavy, loutish, stupid
**oak seed** acorn
**oar** blade, paddle, scull
**oar blade** palm, peel
**oar fulcrum** thole
**oar holder** rowlock
**oar or paddle** row
**oar part** loom
**oar pin and rester** thole
**oar-propelled ship** bireme, galley, trireme
**oarsman** rower
**oar used over the stern** scull
**oasis** asylum, haven, refuge, resort, retreat, sanctuary, sanctum, shelter, spa, springs, wadi, wady
**oasis in Egypt** Bahariya, Dakhla, Kharga, Siwa
**oasis in Iraq** Maniya
**oasis in Niger** Kaouar
**oasis in the Sahara** Biskra
**oast** furnace, heater, kiln, ost, oven
**oath** affirmation, assurance, avowal, curse, cuss, egad, guarantee, imprecation, malediction, pledge, promise, swear(word), troth, vow, warrant, word
**oath breaking** forswearing, perjury
**oath of fidelity** troth
**oat husk** flight, shood
**oatlike grass** brome
**oatmeal** cereal, farina, gruel, must, oats, porridge, pottage, stodge
**oatmeal porridge** pottage
**obduracy** constancy, firmness, inflexibility, intransigence, resolution, resolve, staunchness, steadfastness, strictness
**obdurate** adamant, callous, dogged, firm, fixed, graceless, hard(-hearted), hardened, implacable, inexorable, inflexible, intransigent, iron, mulish, obstinate, pigheaded, relentless, reprobate, shameless, stubborn, unbending, unshakable, unyielding
**obeah** obi
**obedience** acceptance, acquiescence, adaptability, agreement, allegiance, compliance, conformity, deference, docility, duty, fawning, obeisance, observance, pliancy, respect, servility, submissiveness, subservience, yielding
**obedient** abiding, amenable, behaved, biddable, compliant, dedicated, deferential, disciplined, docile, dutiful, faithful, good, law-abiding, loyal, peaceful, submissive, subservient, willing
**obeisance** bow, curts(e)y, deference, esteem, estimation, homage, honour, kneeling, passivity, regard, resignation, respect, salute, servility, sycophancy, worship
**O be joyful in the Lord** jubilate Deo (L)
**obelisk** column, guglia, monolith, monument, needle, pillar, pylon, shaft
**obese** bulky, chubby, corpulent, fat, heavy, lumpish, outsize, overweight, paunchy, plump, podgy, portly, pudgy, roly-poly, rotund, round, stout
**obesity** bulk, corpulence, fatness, fleshiness, grossness, overweight, portliness, stoutness, tubbiness
**obey** accept, acknowledge, adapt, complete, comply, follow, grant, heed, mind, observe, perform, react, relent, respect, satisfy, stoop, succumb, surrender
**obfuscate** (be)dim, bewilder, cloud, confuse, darken, obscure, overshadow, stupefy, veil
**obi** obeah
**obituary** necrology, obit
**object** aim, argue, article, base, body, butt, complain, demur, design, end, entity, expostulate, fact, focus, goal, grumble, idea, intent(ion), it, item, mind, motive, objective, oppose, phenomenon, point, protest, purpose, reality, reason, recipient, res (L), target, thing, victim
**object aimed at** target
**object causing embolism** embolus
**object formally** protest
**object in family for generations** heirloom
**objection** but, cavil, censure, challenge, complaint, demur, doubt, exception, niggle, opposition, protest, remonstrance, scruple
**objection raised** demurral
**objective** aim, aspiration, butt, chase, clinical, desire, destination, end, equitable, fair, goal, ideal, impartial, intent, just, mark, neutral, point, prey, purpose, quarry, target, termination, trophy, true, unbiased
**objective case of he** him
**objective case of they** them
**objectively** clinically, detachedly, dispassionately, even-handedly, fairly, impartially, impersonally, judicially, justly
**objectivity** broad-mindedness, disinterest, fairness, impartiality, indifference, justice, materiality, otherness, reality, tangibility
**object of affection** idol
**object of aim** butt, target
**object of annoyance** bugbear
**object of ardent desire** passion
**object of bowlike curvature** arc
**object of bric-à-brac** curio
**object of considerable age** antique
**object of contempt** scorn
**object of derision** jest
**object of devotion** idol
**object of dislike** aversion, bête noire (F)
**object of excessive devotion** fetish
**object of great beauty** gem
**object of irrational devotion** fetish
**object of laughter** jest
**object of sight** spectacle
**object of terror** bugbear
**object of worship** idol, totem
**object serving as souvenir** memento
**object shaped like a ship** nef
**object to** depreciate, resent
**objet d'art** bric-à-brac
**obligate** bind, coerce, command, compel, constrain, drive, force, fundamental, impel, impose, indebt, make, necessary, necessitate, oblige, overcome, pledge, press(ure), primary, require, urge
**obligation** accountability, appreciation, bond, burden, care, charge, command, commission, commitment, constraint, contract, covenant, deal, debt, deed, demand, devoir, duress, duty, enforcement, function, indebtedness, liability, necessity, oath, onus, pact, pressure, promise, responsibility, task, treaty, trust
**obligation not to marry** celibacy
**obligations imposed by honour or rank** noblesse oblige
**oblige** accommodate, benefit, bind, coerce, compel, constrain, favour, force, gratify, impel, indulge, make, obligate, require, serve

**obliged** appreciative, beholden, bound, compelled, grateful, indebted, thankful
**obliged to** owe
**obliging** amiable, cheerful, complaisant, co-operative, courteous, friendly, helpful, polite, solicitous
**oblique** abaxial, angled, arcane, askew, aslant, awash, awry, bias, canting, covert, deceptive, deflectional, diagonal, evasive, immoral, inclined, indicular, indirect, perverse, rhomboid, scalene, sidelong, skew, slanting, slash, sloped, sloping, sly, squint, tortuous, transverse, underhand, veiled
**oblique cut** bevel
**oblique look** leer
**obliquely** askance, aslant, diagonally, evasively, sidelong, slantwise
**oblique opening through wall of church affording view of altar** squint, hagioscope
**oblique position** slant
**oblique rays** abaxial
**oblique stroke** solidus
**obliquity** amphibology, artfulness, bias, cant, carnality, confusion, criminality, deviation, deviousness, dishonesty, enigma, inclination, incline, obscurity, perplexity, perversity, puzzle, ramp, scramble, sinfulness, slant, slope, sneakiness, sway, tilt, tip, ungoodness, wryness
**obliterate** annihilate, cancel, dele(te), destroy, efface, eradicate, erase, expunge, extirpate, rase, raze
**oblivious** amnesic, careless, confusion, disregardful, forgetful, heedless, neglectful, negligent, obscurity, thoughtless, unclarity, vagueness
**oblong** elliptical, elongated, longitudinal, rectangle
**oblong mass of melted metal** pig
**obnoxious** annoying, answerable, exposed, fulsome, hateful, liable, loathsome, nauseous, objectionable, odious, offensive, open, subject, unbearable
**obnoxious person** nuisance
**oboe** hautboy, szopelka
**obscene** coarse, filthy, gross, immodest, immoral, impure, indecent, lewd, lubricious, offensive, pornographic, prurient, ribald, salacious, vulgar
**obscene literature** scatology
**obscenely coarse person** yahoo
**obscene material** pornography
**obscene talk** smut

**obscenity** atrocity, bawdiness, carnality, dirt(iness), dissipation, filth(iness), foulness, impurity, indecency, indelicacy, lewdness, pornography, profanity, salaciousness, salacity, scatology, shamelessness, smut, unseemliness, vileness, vulgarity
**obscure** becloud, blur(ry), clouded, confuse, darken, dim, doubtful, gloomy, imperfect, indefinite, indistinct, murky, mysterious, nebulous, obfuscate, opaque, recondite, remote, secluded, secret, shadowy, uncertain, unclear, unknown, unnoted, unnoticed, vague, veiled
**obscure in meaning** cryptic
**obscurely** dimly
**obscure outline of** smear
**obscure thing** mystery
**obscurity** ambiguity, confusion, darkness, dimness, doubtfulness, dubiousness, haziness, indistinctness, nullity, profoundness, sombreness, uncertainty, vagueness
**obsequies** burial, entombment, exequies, funeral, internment
**obsequious** compliant, cringing, deferential, docile, dutiful, fawning, flattering, grovelling, ingratiating, mean, menial, obedient, oily, servile, slavish, smarmy, submissive, subservient, sycophantic, toadying, tractable, unassertive, unctuous, whining
**obsequious flattery** smarm
**obsequious follower** satellite
**observant** alert, attentive, aware, curious, devoted, dutiful, interested, keen, law-abiding, loyal, mindful, moral, nice, obedient, perceptive, quick, sharp-eyed, vigilant, watchful
**observation of birds by augurs** ornithoscopy
**observe** celebrate, comment, comply, detect, discover, espy, eye, follow, keep, mark, mention, nota (L), note, notice, obey, perceive, regard, remark, see, solemnise, spot, watch, witness
**observe as holy** sanctify
**observe carefully** note
**observe closely** watch
**observe duly** celebrate
**observe narrowly** eye
**observer** bystander, commentator, eyewitness, noter, onlooker, spectator, viewer, watcher, witness
**obsess** bedevil, engross, grip, haunt, possess, preoccupy, torment

**obsession** complex, compulsion, enthusiasm, fetish, fixation, hallucination, idée fixe (F), impulse, irresistible, maggot, mastery, (mono)mania, passion, phobia, possession
**obsessional devotion to ecclesiastical tradition** ecclesiolatry
**obsession for anything foreign** xenomania
**obsession of Ahab** Moby Dick, whale
**obsession of mind by one idea or interest** monomania
**obsessive** besetting, compulsive, consuming, fixed, gripping, haunting, manic
**obsessive desire to do things on a grand scale** megalomania
**obsessive love for oneself** egomania
**obsolete** ancient, antiquated, archaic, bygone, dated, defunct, démodé (F), discarded, extinct, musty, old, outmoded, outworn, passé
**obsolete form** anachronism, antique
**obsolete German silver coin** t(h)aler
**obsolete gold coin** doubloon
**obsolete Greek letter** digamma
**obsolete phrase** archaism
**obsolete stringed instrument** psaltery
**obstacle** bar(ricade), barrier, block(ade), blockage, bottleneck, bunker, check, cul-de-sac, deadlock, drawback, handicap, hazard, hindrance, hurdle, impasse, impediment, inconvenience, interference, jam, limitation, obstruction, retardation, snag, stalemate, stay, stop, stoppage, tie
**obstacle on golf course** hazard
**obstacle race in canoes** slalom
**obstetrician** accoucheur (F), accoucheuse (F)
**obstetrics** midwifery, tocology, tokology
**obstinacy** dourness, firmness, inflexibility, persistence, pertinacity, perverseness, resoluteness, stubbornness, tenaciousness, tenacity, unpliability, wilfulness
**obstinate** asinine, aversion, cussed, firm, headstrong, inflexible, intractable, mulish, obdurate, persistent, perverse, recalcitrant, resolute, stubborn, unbending, uncontrollable, unyielding, wilful
**obstinate and stupid** asinine
**obstinate animal** mule
**obstinate behaviour** contumacy
**obstinate in opinion** dogmatic, opinionated
**obstinately determined** dogged
**obstinately disobedient** recalcitrant
**obstinately wrong** perverse

**obstinate person** mule
**obstreperous** blatant, boisterous, brawly, clamorous, disorderly, loud, noisy, rackety, rampageous, recalcitrant, restive, riotous, rowdy, tempestuous, truculent, tumultuous, uncontrolled, unrestrained, unruly, vociferous
**obstruct** arrest, bar(ricade), block, check, choke, clog, cumber, curb, frustrate, hamper, hamstring, hide, hinder, impede, inhibit, interrupt, mask, obscure, occlude, prevent, restrict, slow, stop
**obstruction** ban, bar(ricade), barrier, bottleneck, curb, hindrance, hitch, limitation, obstacle, prohibition, snag, stop(page), veto
**obstruction of an artery by a blood clot** embolism
**obstruction of the intestine/ ileum** ileus
**obstructive** awkward, blocking, delaying, hindering, inhibiting, occlusive, preventative, restrictive, stalling, unco-operative, unhelpful
**obstructive official routine** red tape
**obtain** acquire, attain, capture, derive, earn, gain, get, prevail, procure, purchase, reign, rule, secure, seize, win
**obtainable** accessible, attainable, available, convenient, present, reachable
**obtain against a person's will** extract
**obtain appointment** land
**obtain as reward of labour** earn
**obtain by care** procure
**obtain by intimidation** extort
**obtain by request** impetrate
**obtain by threats** extort
**obtain by trickery** wangle
**obtain control of** take
**obtain cover for** insure
**obtained by leaching** lye
**obtained from apple juice** malic
**obtain illegally** ill-gotten
**obtain laboriously** eke
**obtain loan** borrow
**obtain money by demands** extort
**obtain on loan** borrow
**obtain possession of** acquire
**obtain through labour** earn
**obtain with difficulty** eke
**obtrude** bulge, encroach, extend, gatecrash, infringe, intercede, interfere, interpose, interrupt, intrude, jut, meddle, poke, project, protrude, pry, show, trespass, violate
**obtrusively bright** garish, gaudy, showy
**obtrusively vulgar** blatant

**obtuse** blind, blunt, boneheaded, dopey, dormant, dull, dumb, insensate, insensitive, lethargic, numb, opaque, retarded, slow, stupid, thick(-skinned), unfeeling, unintelligent, unpointed, vacuous, vapid
**obtuse angle** bullnose, heel
**obverse of coin** head, man
**obviate** anticipate, avert, avoid, forestall, preclude, prevent
**obvious** apparent, clear, conspicuous, definite, distinct, evident, liable, manifest, open, overt, patent, perceptible, plain, prominent, showing, unblurred, undisguised, unhidden, unmistakable, visible
**obvious facts** truism
**obviously** apparently, conspicuously, evidently, manifestly, openly, overtly, perceptibly, transparently, visibly
**obviously planned** contrive
**obviously true** undeniable
**occasion** case, cause, celebration, chance, convenience, creative, event, evoke, excuse, generate, incident, induce(ment), instance, justification, motivate, motive, occurrence, opening, opportunity, party, persuade, produce, prompt, provoke, reason, time
**occasional** casual, desultory, incidental, infrequent, intermittent, irregular, odd, periodic, rare, sporadic, uncommon
**occasional profit from office** vail
**occasion for rejoicing** festivity
**occasion when food is eaten** meal
**Occident** West
**occidental** Western
**occipital protuberance** inion
**occlude** bar(ricade), block, burden, choke, clog, close, congest, constrict, dam, debar, embolise, enclose, hamper, hinder, impede, jam, obstruct, oppilate, overpower, prevent, prohibit, seal, shackle, shut, smother, stifle, stop, strangle, suffocate, suppress, throttle
**occult** arcane, cabalistic, concealed, cryptic, hidden, inexplicable, inscrutable, mysterious, mystic(al), mystifying, preternatural, puzzling, shrouded, supernatural, undisclosed, unknown
**occultism** (black) magic, enchantment, mysticism, sorcery, spell, spiritualism, supernaturalism, witchcraft
**occultist** enchantress, magician, sorceress, witch
**occult sign** omen

**occupant** colonist, (house)holder, inhabitant, lessee, lodger, native, occupier, renter, resident, settler, squatter, tenant, user
**occupant of a place** tenant
**occupant of a prison** inmate
**occupation** activity, business, calling, capture, career, conquest, control, craft, employ(ment), habitation, holding, invasion, job, living, métier, occupancy, possession, post, profession, pursuit, residence, seizure, skill, takeover, tenancy, tenure, trade, use, vocation, work
**occupation pursued for pleasure** hobby
**occupied in preparation** preparatory
**occupy** absorb, amuse, busy, capture, concern, control, cover, defeat, divert, employ, engage, engross, fill, hold, inhabit, interest, invade, involve, keep, overrun, own, permeate, possess, preoccupy, reside, seize, settle, subjugate, use
**occupy a seat** sit, preside
**occupy chair of authority** preside
**occupy completely** fill
**occupying equal time** isochronous
**occupying one day** diurnal
**occupying the whole of** fill
**occupy one's attention completely** engross
**occupy pleasantly** amuse
**occupy same position** coincide
**occupy the same portion of space** coincide
**occupy wholly** engross
**occur** appear, be, betide, chance, come, emerge, ensue, eventuate, follow, happen, intervene, issue, result, transpire
**occur afterward** ensue
**occur as outcome** result
**occur at irregular intervals** sporadic
**occur at stated intervals** regular
**occur at the same time** coincide, synchronise
**occur before** antedate
**occurred together** coincided
**occurrence** adventure, affair, afloat, coincidence, contingent, current, doing, encounter, episode, event(uality), happening, incident(al), instance, occasion, phenomenon, proceeding, realisation
**occurrence of a thing** event
**occurrence of events simultaneously** coincidence
**occurrence requiring immediate action** emergency
**occurring about once per day** circadian

**occurring at intervals** sporadic
**occurring at intervals of three months** quarterly
**occurring at last** eventual
**occurring at once** immediate
**occurring at sunset** acronyc(h)al
**occurring at the same time** coinciding, concurrent, simultaneous, synchronic, synchronous
**occurring before birth** antenatal
**occurring by chance** accidental, casual, incidental
**occurring by turns** alternating
**occurring every eight days** octan
**occurring every four years** penteteric, quadrennial
**occurring every hundred years** centennial
**occurring every third day** quartan, tertian
**occurring every three hundred years** tercentennial
**occurring every three years** triennial
**occurring every twenty years** vicennial
**occurring every two hundred years** bicentennial
**occurring every two years** biannual
**occurring frequently** common
**occurring in an instant** instantaneous
**occurring in between** intercurrent
**occurring in fact** real
**occurring in its usual place** entopic
**occurring in outer space** cosmic
**occurring in pairs** binary, binate
**occurring in spring** vernal
**occurring in winter** hibernal
**occurring irregularly** episodic, sporadic
**occurring often** frequent
**occurring once every five years** quinquennial, quinquennium
**occurring once every six years** sexennial
**occurring only here and there** sporadic
**occurring regularly** periodic
**occurring too early** prematurely
**occurring twice a year** biannual
**occurring unexpectedly** sudden
**occurring unintentionally** accidental
**occur with** accompany
**ocean** abundance, Antarctic, Arctic, Atlantic, brine, expanse, flood, Indian, main, multitude, North Atlantic, Pacific, sea, Southern
**ocean bird** auk, cormorant, erne, penguin, petrel, (sea)gull, skua
**ocean east of Africa** Indian
**ocean east of Italy** Adriatic
**ocean floating matter** algae, flotsam

**ocean god** Neptune, Poseidon
**oceanic** aquatic, endless, enormous, expansive, large, limitless, marine, maritime, nautical, naval, pelagic, saltwater, sea(faring), unbounded, vast
**ocean ingredient** salt
**ocean liner** ship
**ocean location device** sonar
**ocean lying between the Americas and Asia** Pacific
**ocean movement** tide
**ocean nymph** Oceanid
**ocean organisms** plankton
**ocean phase** tide
**ocean rip** undertow
**ocean route** lane
**ocean's motion** tide
**ocean traveller** seafarer, voyager
**ocean west of Africa** Atlantic
**Ocotea bullata** stinkwood
**ocotillo** cactus
**Octavia's husband** Nero
**octavo** eights
**octet** octave
**October birthstone** opal
**octopus** cephalopod
**octopus arm** tentacle
**octuple** eightfold
**ocular** ophthalmic, optical, visual
**ocular muscle** iris
**ocular organ** eye
**oculist** eyeman, ophthalmologist
**odd** abnormal, bizarre, curious, different, eccentric, extra(ordinary), fantastic, freakish, infrequent, occasional, offbeat, orra (Sc), peculiar, quaint, queer, rare, remarkable, rum, singular, strange, uncommon, unequal, uneven, unique, unmatched, unusual, variable, weird
**odd article** oddment
**oddball** character, crackpot, deviator, eccentric, exception, freak, individual, loner, misfit, oddity, rarity, solitary, sport, weirdie, weirdo
**odd behaviour** antic, eccentricity
**oddity** abnormality, anomaly, character, curiosity, eccentricity, freak, idiosyncrasy, irregularity, misfit, peculiarity, phenomenon, quirk, rarity
**odd job** chore
**odd-jobber** handyman
**odd-jobman** orra
**oddly amusing** droll
**oddly flecked or streaked** freaked
**odd-man-out** exception, maverick, misfit, nonconformist, outsider
**oddment** bit, bric-à-brac, chip, fragment, keepsake, (k)nick-(k)nack,

left-over, relic, remembrance, reminder, remnant, token
**odd or whimsical** eccentric
**odds** advantage, chances, difference, edge, handicap, inequality, inferiority, irregularity, lead, likelihood, predominance, probability, supremacy
**odds and ends** bits, debris, etceteras, extras, fragments, incidentals, junk, leavings, modicums, morsels, oddments, ort, pickings, refuse, remnants, rubbish, scraps, seconds, snatches, tags
**odds and ends lying about** litter
**odds and ends of equipment** paraphernalia
**odds and ends of profits** pickings
**odd things** oddments
**ode** ballad, carol, elegy, encomium, epicedium, lay, lyric, panegyric, poem, serenade, song
**ode or song of lamentation** threnody
**Oder in Polish** Odra
**ode writer** poet
**Odin's brother** Ve, Vili
**Odin's eight-footed horse** Sleipner, Sleipnir
**Odin's son** Thor, Tyr
**odious** abhorrent, abominable, accursed, baneful, despicable, detestable, disliked, execrable, hateful, loathsome, nauseous, obnoxious, offensive, repellent, repulsive
**odist** poet
**odium** abhorrence, animosity, antipathy, bitterness, detestation, discredit, disdain, disgrace, disgust, dislike, execration, hate, hatred, hostility, loathing, opprobrium, rancour
**odontalgia** toothache
**odontoid** toothlike
**odorimetry** olfactometry
**odorous** fragrant
**odour** air, aroma, atmosphere, aura, bouquet, breath, character, complexion, emanation, essence, fetor, flavour, fragrance, hint, perfume, redolence, savour, scent, smell, spirit, stench, stink, tone, trace, trail
**odourless tasteless gas** hydrogen
**Odysseus's dog** Argos
**oedema** dropsy
**oesophagus** gullet
**oestrus** heat
**of** about, by, concerning, de (F), from
**of a bear** ursine
**of a bird** avian
**of a bishop** episcopal

of a bronze colour aeneous
of a building's interior indoor
of a cause causal
of a centenary centennial
of a certain printing lithographical
of acid taste tart
of a city urban
of a cuckoo cuculiform
of a cultural group ethnic
of a deeper pitch lower
of a duke ducal
of a faction factious
of a father paternal
of a feast festal, festive
of a female her
of a fox vulpine
of age adult, grown-up, mature
of a ghostly quality eerie
of a gland adenoid
of a goat caprine
of a golden colour aureate
of a goose anserine, anserous
of agreement contractual
of a group of stars galactic
of a gull larine
of a hare leporine
of a high degree intense
of a horse equine
of a hunch intuitional
of aircraft aero-
of a line linear
of a lizard saurian
of all sorts omnifarious
of a lobe lobar
of a marsh paludal
of a mayor mayoral
of amber succinic
of a mind apt
of a musical mode modal
of an ancient alphabet hieroglyphic, runic
of ancient Greece Ionian
of an editor editorial
of an embryo embryonal, embryonic
of an empire imperial
of an enemy hostile
of a nerve neural
of a net retiary
of a new kind novel
of animals faunal
of an island insular
of an object its
of an ordered structure organisational
of a notary public notarial
of another time anachronism
of a noun nounal
of a numen numinous
of a parish parochial
of a particular area local
of a piece alike, consistent, identical, uniform
of a pig porcine

of a pontiff pontifical
of a profession professional
of a pugilist punch-drunk
of arctic region polar
of a region areal, regional
of a region adjoining a glacier periglacial
of Argos Argive
of a river fluvial, fluviatile, riparian
of a rule regnal
of a sheriff shrieval
of Asia Asiatic
of Asia Minor Anatolian
of a snake colubrine
of a son or daughter filial
of a state treasury fiscal
of a stem pedicular
of a tail caudal
of a tailor or to tailoring sartorial
of a televised image video
of a title titular
of atom arrangement steric(al)
of atomic power nuclear
of atoms isotopic
of a tortoise testudinal
of aura aural
of a velum velar
of a virus viral
of a wall mural
of a web retiary
of a wing alar
of a wolf lupine
of a zone zonal
of bears ursine
of bees apian
of betrayal treasonable
of birds avian
of birth natal
of blessed memory beatae memoriae (L)
of bluish leaden colour livid
of blunt shape obtuse
of bodily endurance staminal
of bone osseous, osteal
of boxing fistic
of brain study bionic
of breathing out expiratory
of Brittany Breton
of building tectonic
of burial mortuary
of candle grease stearic
of cardiac dilation diastolic
of cats feline
of Caucasoid origin Nordic
of Cerene Cerenaic
of cervix cervical
of cheerful disposition sonsy (Sc), sonsie (Sc)
of childbirth intrapartum, puerperal
of church unity ecumenic
of cities urban
of citrus fruits citric

of clan tribal
of class rule hegemonic
of clay earthen
of clerks clerical
of coins numismatic
of colour chromatic
of comedy comedic
of command to horse gee(-ho), gee-up
of common occurrence rife
of considerable size big
of consummate art artistic
of course! bien entendu (F), certainly, naturally, obviously, undoubtedly, yes
of course not! no
of courts of law forensic
of deer cervine
of delicate beauty dainty
of delicate constitution fragile
of delicate frame fragile
of Denmark Danish
of deposits sedimentary
of descent lineal
of different kinds diverse
of digestion peptic
of dinner prandial
of dogs canine
of double meaning ambiguous
of doubtful honesty shady
of doubtful meaning ambiguous
of dreams oneiric
of dye tinctorial
of early period in culture archaic
of earthquakes seismic
of easy address affable
of easy virtue immoral, sinful
of ebb and flow tidal
of edible grain cereal
of elephants elephantine
of elves elfin
of equal force equipollent
of equal measure isometric
of equal size isometric
of ethnicicity ethonological
of Europe and Asia Eurasian
of evidence evidential
of evil omen sinister
of external origin extraneous
of extra quality superfine
of extreme beauty exquisite
of extreme degree intense
of eyeball membrane corneal,
off -ab, absent, aff (Sc), apo-, away, cancelled, finished, gone, kill, missing, mouldy, sour, stale, turned, unsatisfactory, vacation, void, wrong
of fair social standing respectable
offal carcass, debris, dregs, dross, garbage, junk, leavings, litter, lumber, refuse, remains, residue, rubbish, scrap, trash, tripe, waste
offal of fish gurry, stosh

**off and on** intermittently, occasionally, periodically, sometimes, sporadically
**of farming** agriculture
**of fat** adipose
**off-beat** bizarre, curious, eccentric, extraordinary, fantastic, freakish, grotesque, ludicrous, odd, outlandish, outré, peculiar, queer, strange, unconventional, unusual, wacky, weird, zany
**off-centre** acentric
**off-colour** ill, peaky, poorly, queasy
**off course** adrift
**off duty** free, off
**of feet** pedal
**offence** action, aggressive, annoyance, assault, attack(ing), aversion, dereliction, detestation, disgust, displeasure, enmity, misdemeanour, resentment, sin, transgression, trespass, umbrage, violence
**offence against etiquette** solecism
**offence against grammar** solecism
**offence against morality** evil, crime
**offence against social convention** faux pas
**offence against the law** delict
**offence in soccer** offside
**offence when horse won't jump** refusal
**offend** affront(ed), annoy(ed), chafe, disgust(ed), displease, err, fret(ted), hurt, insult(ed), irritate(d), miff, mortify, outrage, pain(ed), provoke, repel(led), rile(d), sickened, sin, snub(bed), transgress, upset, vex(ed), violate, wound, wrong
**offender** criminal, culprit, delinquent, lawbreaker, malefactor, miscreant, sinner, transgressor, wrongdoer
**offending by excess** fulsome
**offend moral feelings** scandalise
**offend morally** sin
**offend the dignity of** affront
**offensive** abominable, annoying, assailant, detestable, disagreeable, disgusting, displeasing, distasteful, embarrassing, hateful, impertinent, insolent, insulting, intolerable, invading, irritating, loathsome, nasty, noisome, objectionable, obnoxious, odious, rancid, rank, repugnant, repulsive, rude, shocking, unpleasant, vexing, vile
**offensive act** affront
**offensive breath** halitosis
**offensive language** abuse
**offensively** aggressively, disagreeably, disgustingly, insultingly, irritatingly, nastily, obnoxiously, odiously, repellently, revoltingly, rudely, sickeningly, uncivilly, unpleasantly, vilely
**offensively assertive** brash
**offensively bright** garish
**offensively contemptuous** insolent
**offensively showy** brash
**offensive operation** attack, siege
**offensive or defensive instrument** weapon
**offensive smell** stench
**offensive to senses** foul
**offensive weapon** sword
**offer** approach, bid, extend, immolate, motion, overture, pose, present(ation), presentment, proffer, proposal, propose, proposition, provide, recommend, sacrifice, submission, submit, suggest(ion), tender, volunteer
**offer a price** bid
**offer as guarantee** gage
**offer a soft touch** tender
**offer at auction** bid
**offered** advanced, moved, presented, proposed, provided, showed, submitted, suggested, volunteered
**offer excuse** alibi
**offer for consideration** propose, propound
**offer for sale** expose, hawk, vend
**offering good value for the price** inexpensive
**offering helpful suggestions** constructive
**offering of goods** sale
**offering opposition** resistant
**offering problems that test one's ability** challenging
**offer in sacrifice** immolate
**offer in writing** tender
**offer marriage** propose
**of fermentation** zymotic
**offer objections** demur
**offer of hospitality** invitation
**offer of marriage** proposal
**offer of terms** proposition
**offeror** presenter, profferer
**offer reasons** argue
**offer solemnly** pledge
**offer to pay** bid
**of fever** febrile
**of few years** young
**off-form** stale, unfit
**off guard** incognizant, napping, suddenly, tardy, unawares, unexpectedly
**offhand** abrupt, airy, aloof, brusque, careless, casual, cavalier, curt, glib, impromptu, perfunctory, unconcerned, uninterested
**offhand in manner** brusque

**office** agency, authority, bureau, business, department, duty, function, group, headquarters, job, jurisdiction, occupation, organisation, position, post, quarters, section, staff, station, workshop
**office chief** boss, manager
**office communication** memo, phone
**office crew** staff
**office directive** memo
**office furniture** desk
**office head** manager
**office note** memo
**office of abbot** abbacy
**office of ambassador** embassy
**office of archbishop** primacy
**office of bishop** archbishopric, episcopate, lawn
**office of clergyman** ministry
**office of deacon** diaconate
**office of dean** deanery
**office of director** directorate
**office of Islamic ruler** emirate
**office of judge** bench
**office of king or queen** royalty
**office of mininster of state** portfolio
**office of nuncio** nunciature
**office of pontifex** pontificate
**office of pope** papacy
**office of president** presidency
**office of primate** primacy
**office of professor** chair
**office of secretary** secretariat
**office of sheriff** shrievalty
**officer** admiral, agent, brigadier, bureaucrat, captain, colonel, command(er), executive, general, major, official, pilot, policeman, representative, rule, skipper
**officer authorised to certify deeds** notary
**officer commanding brigade** brigadier
**officer commanding household of great noble** chamberlain
**officer commanding warship** captain
**officer of British royal household** equerry
**officer's servant** batman
**officer who attends a general** aide-de-camp
**officer who keeps accounts on ship** purser
**officer who makes public announcements** crier
**office seeker** aspirant, candidate, suitor
**office table** desk
**office without work** sinecure
**office worker** clerk, secretary, typist
**official** administrator, authorised, authoritative, executive, formal
**official act** acta

official at boxing match    referee
official at sports event    steward
official at wedding    usher
official authentication    attestation
official award    citation
official bureaucratic procedure    red tape
official certificate    notary
official command    edict, mandate
official count of the population    census
official declaration    promulgation
official decree    edict, ukase
official denial    démenti
official distributor of alms    almoner
official document    indenture
official duty    function
official examination of accounts    audit
official examiner    censor, inspector
official formality and etiquette    protocol
official gown    robe, toga
official holder of an office    functionary
official in court    judge
official investigator    inquisitor
official journal    gazette
official language of Ethiopia    Amharic
official language of Kampuchea    Khmer
official language of Pakistan    Urdu
official language of Yugoslavia    Serbo-Croat(ion)
official letter    brief, missive
official list of names    register
officially administrative    bureaucratic
officially approve    endorse
officially declare    certify
officially view    inspect
official managing a racecourse    steward
official message    brevet
official minister of religion    clergyman, dominee, pastor, priest, reverend, vicar
official mission    embassy
official negation    veto
official note    memo
official notice    bulletin, citation, edict, proclamation, summons
official numbering of population    census
official of certain churches    elder
official opinion    decree, ruling
official order    indent
official order having legal force    decree
official paper    document
official Parliamentary reports    Hansard
official premises of a consul    consulate
official printed statement giving certain facts    certificate

official proving of will    probate
official record    logbook
official recorder    registrar
official record of inhabitants    census
official rejection    veto
official report    bulletin, Hansard
official residence of sovereign    palace
official sanction    fiat
official scrutiniser    censor
official scrutiny of accounts    audit
official seal    cachet
official sitting    session
official stamp    chop, seal
official stave    mace
official story    report
official transaction    acta
official visit of inspection    visitation
officiate as bishop    pontificate
of figures    digital
of films    cinematic
of fine appearance    splendid
of finer quality    better
of fire    igneous
of fireworks    pyrotechnic
of fish    piscatorial, piscine
off one's guard    asleep, napping, unalert, unprepared, unready, unwary, unwatchful
of forbidding countenance    austere
of foreign origin    heterogenous
of forests    sylvan
offset    counterbalance
off-shade of white    bone
offshoot    addition, aftermath, annex, bough, branch, child, consequence, daughter, derivative, descendant, heir, issue, kin, leafstalk, offspring, outgrowth, ramification, relation, relative, result, runner, shoot, son, sprout, spur, stem, supplement, tendril
offshore territory    island, isle
offspring    brood, child(ren), daughter, descendants, issue, progeny, seed, son
offspring of mixed race    mulatto, quadroon, sambo
offspring of Poseidon    Pegasus
offspring of she-ass and stallion    hinny
offspring of tiger and lioness    tigon
off the cuff    confidentially, extempore, impromptu, offhand
off-the-cuff remark    ad lib, extempore, extemporise, impromptu, offhand
off the hook    acquitted, cleared, exonerated, vindicated
off the mark    amiss, astray, awry, off, wide, wrong
off the path    astray

off the record    confidential, confidentially, private(ly), unofficial, unofficially, unofficially
off the track    adrift, astray, digressing, mistaken, wandering
off the track of human thought    abstruse
of full age    major
of full age and capacity    independent, sui juris (L)
of full weight    pucka, pukka
off-white    alabaster, bisque, cream, ecru, eggshell, oyster, putty
of galaxy    galactic
of gloomy temperament    saturnine
of gold    auric, or
of good appearance    personable, presentable, specious
of good character    moral
of good digestion    eupeptic
of good judgment    sound
of good omen    de bon augure (F)
of good quality    pucka, pukka
of good social standing    respectable
of great delicacy    exquisite
of greater age    elder, older
of great magnitude    large
of great price    costly, precious
of great renown    famous, illustrious
of great significance    weighty
of great size    terrific
of great value    precious
of great virtue    excellent
of great worth    valuable
of Greece    Greek
of hard texture    scleroid
of hares    leporine
of harvest    foliar
of hearing    aural
of heat    caloric, thermal
of hedgehogs    erinaceous
of hell    infernal
of heraldic arms    armorial
of herbs    herbaceous
of hidden meaning    mystic
of high birth    noble
of highest status    supreme
of high mountains    alpine
of high quality    delicate, fine
of high temperature    boiling, hot
of high tension    entonic
of himself, herself, itself    sui (L)
of his or her age    aetatis suae (L)
of his own accord    motu proprio (L)
of Homer    Homerian, Homeric
of horse-riding    equestrian
of human form    anthropoid
of hundred years    centenary
of hunting    venatic
of ill repute    discreditable, ill-famed, infamous, notorious
of immersion    baptismal

of imposing appearance noble
of inactivity inertial
of India Indian
of inexhaustible energy tireless
of inferior quality schlock, trash
of inferior rank subaltern
of infirm health valetudinarian
of insects insectean
of Ireland Irish
of it its
of Italy Italian
of its own kind sui generis, unique
of joints articular
of kidneys nephritic
of kind disposition good-tempered
of land agrarian, praedial, terrestrial
of language lingual
of last month ultimo
of late lately, latterly, recently
of Later Stone Age Neolithic
of law courts judicial
of laws statutory
of leaves foliaceous, foliar
of leaves having veins nervate
of legal authority jurisdictional
of length linear, longitudinal
of less importance secondary
of light photic
of lions leonine
of litle age young
of little account immaterial, trifling, trivial
of little breadth narrow
of little depth shallow
of little importance frivolous, petty, trivial
of little length short
of little weight light
of living organisms biotic
of living things organic
of lofty character noble
of long ago yore
of low character ignoble
of lower rank subordinate
of low position ignoble
of machines mechanical
of majestic height lofty
of manganese manganic
of many colours multicoloured
of many-sided ability versatile
of marble marmoreal
of marriage conjugal, connubial, marital, nuptial
of me my
of meaning in language semantic
of measurement dimensional
of measures mensural
of medicine Aesculapian
of medium strength moderate
of melody melodic
of mental creative ability imaginative
of method stylar

of metrical feet iambic
of mice murine
of middle line of body medial, mesial
of middling quality mediocre
of milk galactic, lacteal, lactic
of mind noetic
of mind and body psychosomatic
of mine my
of minor importance secondary
of mixed colours roan
of mom and dad parental
of more than average height tall
of morning song matinal
of Moscow Muscovite
of Moses Mosaic
of motion dynamic, kinetic
of motive force dynamic
of mountainous regions montane
of mouths oscular
of names onomastic
of Naples Neapolitan
of navigation nautical
of neat appearance tidy
of neck cervical, jugular
of neglected appearance dishevelled, unkempt, untidy
of nerves neural
of newborn child neonatal
of new kind novel
of next month proximo
of nitrogen nitric
of no account inferior, negligible, petty
of no avail idle
of no effect invalid, null, void
of no essential consequences immaterial
of no great weight insignificant
of no help useless
of no importance immaterial, insignificant, trivial
of no matter or concern insignificant
of no particular colour neutral
of no real value nugatory
of northern Europe Nordic
of north polar region Arctic
of northwestern France Breton
of northwestern winds etesian
of not long ago recent
of no use functionless, ineffective, otiose
of obscure antiquity Ogagian, prehistoric
of ocean ebb and flow tidal
of office work clerical
of old erst, formerly, olden
of old age senile
of one mind harmonious, unanimous
of one opinion consentient
of one part unary
of one's birth natal
of one's own personal
of one's own accord proprio motu (L)

of one's own free will voluntarily
of one year annual
of only one colour monochrome
of open fields campestral
of open texture cellular
of optimum period ephebic
of or between two à deux (F)
of order tactic
of or due to motion kinetic
of or like an ostrich struthious
of or on the shore littoral
of Orpheus Orphic
of outstanding quality best
of owners proprietary
of parrots psittacine
of past times former
of peaceful disposition pacific
of period before childbirth prenatal
of plane aero-
of plants vegetal
of pleasant flavour tasty
of pleasure hedonic
of poor quality inferior, lean, putrid, shoddy
of postage stamps philatelic
of posterior part of body caudal
of pottery fictile
of preliterate groups tribal
of present times modern
of preventive action precautionary
of priesthood sacerdotal
of profound wisdom sagacious, sage
of puberty hebetic
of public revenue fiscal
of public speaking oratorical
of punishment penal
of pure breed thoroughbred
of quakes seismic
of questionable character eccentric, odd, queer, strange
of questionable value dubious
of recent origin new
of red tape bureaucratic
of refined luxury elegant
of refined taste nice
of regular shape geometric
of reptiles herpetologic
of right mind sane
of rituals ceremonial
of river-banks riparian
of sailors nautical
of salt saline
of same age coeval
of same genus congeneric
of same kind similar
of scanty appearance meagre
of seamen nautical
of seed seminal
of seeing visual
of sensation sensory
of serious writing literary
of service advantageous

of settlements colonial
of sexual love amatory, erotic
of sheep ovine
of ships nautical, naval
of short duration brief, transient
of sight optic(al), visual
of silver colour argent
of six senary
of size quantitative
of skeleton osteal
of skin dermoid
of small dainty build petit(e)
of smaller quality less
of small inland seas thalassic
of small stature short
of small value trivial
of small width narrow
of Socrates Socratic
of sorts adequate, admissible, passable, tolerable, unnotable
of sound acoustic(al), audio, sonic
of sound mind compos mentis (L), rational, sane
of sound waves sonar, sonic
of south polar region Antarctic
of space spatial
of speed measurement tacheometrical, tachymetrical
of spring vernal
of stamp collection philatelic
of stars astral, stellar
of steady and sober character staid
of stone lithic
of summer aestival
of superior quality choice
of suspected character dubious
of Sweden Swedish
of swimmimg natatorial, natatory
of Swiss mountains Alpine
of systematic study scientific
of tailors sartorial
of tannin tannic
of TB hectic
of tears lachrymal
of teeth dental
often commonly, customarily, frequent(ly), generally, habitually, much, periodically, regularly, repeatedly, usually
of ten decimal
of tender years young
often pierced lobe
often worn apron, sash
of that thereof
of that kind such
of that thing its
of the affairs of a state pragmatic
of the age preceding the Palaeolithic age Eolithic
of the Andes Andean
of the anus anal
of the armed forces military

of theatre operation surgical
of the Austrian capital Viennese
of the back dorsal, tergal
of the belly coeliac
of the bile biliary
of the bladder cystic
of the blood haemal
of the bodily organs organic
of the body physical, somatic
of the brain cerebral, encephalic
of the breasts mammary
of the capacity to reason intellectual
of the cheek malar
of the chest pectoral
of the chin genial
of the Christian church ecclesiastical, ecumenic
of the city urban
of the civet family viverrine
of the clergy clerical
of the colon colonic
of the colour of verdigris aeruginous
of the country rural
of the currency in use monetary
of the darkest colour black
of the decimal system metric
of the desires orectic
of the devil diabolic, satanic
of the diatonic system tonal
of the ear aural, otic
of the earliest age of the world prim(a)eval
of the early part of the Stone Age Palaeolithic
of the earth terrene, terrestrial
of the earth as a planet telluric
of the earth's surface geographical
of the eight-hundredth anniversary octocentenary
of the embryo foetal
of the Emerald Isle Irish
of the essence crucial, essential, indispensable, vital
of the eucharist sacramental
of the evening vespertine
of the extreme Protestants in Ireland Orange
of the eye ocular, ophthalmic, optic
of the eyelids palpebral
of the eye or sight ocular
of the eye socket orbital
of the face facial
of the fifth degree quintic, sursolid
of the fiftieth anniversary quinquagenary
of the first citizen mayoral
of the first importance primary
of the first magnitude celebrated, important, major, notable, prominent, significant
of the first stage primary
of the first water excellent

of the five-hundredth anniversary quincentenary
of the forearm cubital
of the forehead metopic
of the genes genetical
of the glottis glottal
of the god Pan Pandean
of the greatest degree utmost
of the gums gingival
of the head cephalic
of the heart cardiac
of the highest class classic(al)
of the highest degree superlative
of the highest intensity extreme
of the highest order perfect, supreme, transcendent
of the highest quality best
of the hip sciatic
of the human body corporal
of the ileum ileac, ileal
of the ilium iliac
of the immediate surroundings ambient
of the intellect noetic
of the intestines enteric
of the iris iridic
of the Isle of Man Manx
of the jaw gnathic
of the Jewish Passover paschal
of the kidneys renal, nephritic
of the largest continent Asiatic
of the larynx laryngeal
of the later Stone Age Neolithic
of the least size minimal
of the leg crural
of the lips labial
of the liver hepatic
of the loins lumbar
of the love of things Greek philhellenic
of the lowlands of Scotland Lallan
of the lungs pulmonary
of them their
of the mail postal
of the meaning of words semantic
of the media journalistic
of the Middle Ages medi(a)eval
of the mind mental, noetic
of the moon lunar
of the mouth buccal, oral, oscular
of the nature of a horse horsy
of the nature of lime calcareous
of the nature of wood ligneous
of the nature or colour of wine vinaceous
of the neck cervical
of the nerves neural
of the Netherlands Dutch
of the night nocturnal
of the Nile Nilotic
of the north boreal
of the north polar region Arctic
of the nose nas (L), nasal

of the nostrils narial
of the number seven septimal
of the object its
of the occult mystical
of the ocean oceanic
of the ocean motion tidal
of the open sea pelagic
of the optic membrane corneal
of the Orient eastern
of the ox bovine, oxlike
of the palate palatal, palatine
of the pampas pampean
of the Passover paschal
of the past historic
of the period before the fall prelapsarian
of the physical and chemical condition of the soil edaphic
of the pig family suilline
of the poles polar
of the pope apostolic
of the present and recent times modern
of the present day hodiernal
of the press journalistic
of the pulse sphygmic
of the quest for perfection idealistic
of the reign of James Jacobean
of the relationship between husband and wife conjugal, connubial
of the ribs costal
of the river-bank riparian
of the roots radical
of the sacrum sacral
of the same age coetaneous, coeval, contemporary
of the same clan agnate
of the same era contemporary
of the same family cognate, related
of the same generation coeval
of the same kind such(like)
of the same mind ad idem
of the same shape isomorphic
of the sartorious sartorial
of the scapula scapular
of the science of medicine medical
of the sea marine, thalassic
of the second degree quadric
of the second geological era Mesozoic
of the sense of hearing aural
of the sense of light optical
of the senses sensual
of the skin cutaneous
of the skull cranial
of the sky celestial
of the soul or mind psychic(al), spiritual
of the south polar regions Antarctica
of the spleen lienal, splenic
of the stars astral, sidereal, stellar
of the stomach gastric

of the study of birds ornithological
of the summer aestival
of the sun solar
of the tail caudal
of the teeth dental
of the thigh femoral
of the third order tertiary
of the throat guttural
of the tongue glossal, glottic
of the top 100 m of the ocean epipelagic
of the units of heredity genic
of the universe cosmic
of the USA American
of the voice vocal
of the weather climatic, meteorological
of the whole world mondial
of the wind (a)eolian
of the woman feminine, her
of the womb uterine
of the woods silvan, sylvan
of the words of a language lexical
of the world secular
of the wrist joint carpal
of this hereof
of this life temporal
of this world earthly, mundane, sublunary, worldly
of three components ternary
of three dimensions cubic
of times long past ancient
of tin tinny
of tiresome duration lengthy
of tissues surrounding the teeth periodontal
of tone tonal
of tones tonic
of toothache odontalgic
of touch tactile
of trade mercantile
of tree growing arboricultural
of trivalent iron ferric
of Troy Trojan
of twilight crepuscular
of two dual
of two metals bimetallic
of two minds dithering, hesitant, uncertain, unsure, wavering
of two parts duple
of two sides bilateral
of uncertain classification ambiguous
of uncertain nature equivocal
of understanding empathetic
of undisputed origin authentic, genuine
of uniform consistency smooth
of units unitary
of unknown name anonymous
of unmixed descent pure
of unsound mind crazy, demented, insane, non compos mentis (L)
of uric acid salts uratic

of urine uric, urinary
of us our
of USSR Soviet
of various kinds miscellaneous
of varying quality unequal
of vast extent broad, spacious
of verse poetic(al)
of very great age Ogygian, prehistoric
of very high quality superb
of viewpoint opinionative
of vinegar acetic
of violet colour violaceous
of vocal inflection tonetic
of vocal sounds phonetic
of voice vocal
of Wales Welsh
of walls mural
of war martial
of warships naval
of wasps vespine
of water aqueous
of wave motion tidal
of weak health sickly
of weak intellect addle-headed
of what kind it may be whatever
of wine vinous
of wine, at room temperature chambré
of wings alar
of wisdom sapiential
of wolves lupine
of woman feminine, her
of woods silvan, sylvan
of word meanings semantic
of wretched appearance forlorn
of yore bygone, erst
of you your
of you and me our
of yttrium yttric
ogee moulding, talon
ogee-shaped ogival
ogival ogee-shaped
ogle eye, fleer, gaze, glance, glare, gloat, glower, goggle, leer, peer, scan, scrutinise, sneer, squint, stare, wink
ogre basilisk, bogey(man), demon, devil, gangster, giant, hoodlum, incubus, malefactor, manslayer, miscreant, monster, ruffian, scoundrel, skollie, spectre, tokoloshe, tsotsi, tyrant, villain
oil attar, fuel, lubricant, lubricate, otto
oil bottle cruet
oil can oiler
oil-carrying ship tanker
oilcloth waxcloth
oil container drum
oiler tanker
oilfield of Kuwait Bahrah, Burgan, Minagish, Raudhatain, Sabriya, Wafra
oil from oranges neroli

**oil from sheep's wool** lanolin(e)
**oilless paint** tempera
**oil of bitter orange** neroli
**oil of roses** attar, otto
**oil painting of Christ on a wooden panel** icon
**oil-producers' cartel** OPEC
**oil-rich Asiatic legume** soya bean
**oil-seed** rape
**oilskin coat** slicker
**oil states** OPEC
**oil tree** eboe
**oil well** gusher
**oily** fatty, greasy, pinguid, sebaceous, servile, unctuous
**oily fruit** olive
**oil-yielding nut** peanut
**oily-livered fish** cod
**oily mud** sludge
**oily wood** teak
**ointment** balm, cerate, cosmetic, cream, emulsion, liniment, lotion, nard, oil, paste, salve, unguent
**ointment base** lanolin(e)
**ointment source** nard
**okay** all right, alright, OK, yes
**okra** gumbo, ladies' fingers, plant, vegetable
**old** adroit, aged, alt (G), ancient, antique, auld (Sc), decayed, decrepit, dilapidated, elderly, experienced, familiar, former, intelligent, olden, past, primitive, senile, sensible, stale, thoughtful, unfashionable
**old age** agedness, ancientness, anility, antiquity, dotage, eld, elderliness, feebleness, imbecility, maturity, oldness, senescence, senility, seniority, weakness
**old aircraft** biplane
**old and feeble** decrepit
**Old and New Testament** Bible
**old and unspoiled** pristine
**old, as bread** stale
**Old Blue Eyes** Sinatra
**old bone** fossil
**old boys** alumni
**old car** clunker, jalopy, tin lizzie, tjorrie
**old card game for four players** quadrille
**old cat** grimalkin
**old Chinese porcelain** Ming
**old Chinese weight** liang
**old city** Ur, Zimbabwe
**old cloth** rag
**old clothes merchant** fripper
**old cloth measure** ell
**old coat** mummock
**old coin** ducat, farthing, penny
**old convict** bloubaadjie, lag
**old cooker** stove

**old crock** banger
**old dagger** snee
**old dark lock-up** dungeon
**old district ruler** toparch
**old Dutch cargo-boat** gal(l)iot
**old Dutch copper coin** doit
**olden** bygone
**olden days** antiquity
**old English coin** farthing, guinea, shilling
**old English dance** hornpipe
**old enough to marry** marriageable
**older** alder, ancestor, elder, senior, staler
**older form of oboe** hautboy
**older person** elder
**older relative** aunt, grandpa, granny, ouma, oupa, uncle
**oldest colonial city in Peru** Piura
**oldest man** Methuselah
**oldest member of a group** matriarch, patriarch
**oldest of the Pleiades** Maia
**oldest son of Aaron** Nadab
**old European coin** ducat
**old ewe** crone
**old experienced sailor** salt, shellback
**old-fashioned** ancient, archaic, dated, musty, obsolete, outdated, outmoded, quaint
**old-fashioned brooch** cameo
**old-fashioned person** fog(e)y
**old fellow** gaffer
**old film-star legend** Gable, Garbo, Monroe, Valentino
**old fish** mossback
**old Flemish coin of very small value** mite
**old fogy** anachronism, conservative, fogey, fogram, stick-in-the-mud
**old French** Gaul
**old French coin** écu, sou
**old gold coin** ducat
**old golf club** baffy
**old Greek coin** obol
**old Greek hero** Achilles, Ajax, Herakles, Hercules, Nestor
**old Greek theatre** Odeon
**old guitarlike instrument** lute
**old hag** witch
**old hand** stager, veteran
**old hat** antiquated, archaic, banal, stale
**old horse** nag
**old Indian coin** anna
**old Indian weight** pala
**old instrument** lyre
**old Ireland** Erin
**old language** Latin
**old liquid measure** anker
**old love song** amoret
**old lute** rebec(k)
**old maid** spinster

**old man** centenarian, elder, father, geezer, grandfather, greybeard, octogenarian, old-timer, patriarch, sexagenarian, venerable
**old man's beard** clematis
**old maxim** saw
**old measure** ell
**old name for Ireland** Erin
**old name for Thailand** Siam
**old name for trombone** sackbut
**old name of Singapore** Temasek
**old Nick** demon, devil, Satan
**old Norse poems** *Edda*
**old overworked horse** hack, jade, nag
**old Paris prison** Bastille
**old part-song** madrigal
**old Persia** Iran
**old photo shade** sepia
**old porcelain** Ming
**old pub** ale-house
**old rag** tatt
**old remnant** relic
**old Roman road** iter
**old Russian emperor** czar, tsar
**old sailing vessel** galleon
**old sailor** sea dog
**old saying** adage, maxim, proverb, saw
**old she-cat** grimalkin
**old ship** hulk
**old shoe** bauchle (Sc)
**old Siam** Thailand
**old Slavic musical instrument** balalaika
**old soldier** veteran
**old Spanish coin** peso
**old Spanish dance** fandango
**old Spanish gold coin** doblón, doubloon
**old stately dance** minuet, pavane
**Old Stone Age** Palaeolithic
**old stringed instrument** bandore, lute, pandora, pandore
**old-style shoe protector** spat
**Old Testament archangel** Gabriel
**Old Testament character** Aaron, Abraham, Benjamin, David, Isaac, Jacob, Joseph, Moses, Noah, Samuel, Solomon
**Old Testament priest** Eli
**Old Testament prophet** Nahum
**old threshing tool** flail
**old-time** yore
**old-timer** veteran
**old-time Spanish vessel** galleon
**old-time you** ye
**old unit of length** ell
**old vixen** harridan
**old witch** hag
**old wive's tale** fable
**old woman** cailleach, crone, gammer
**old womanish** anile
**Old World finch** linnet

**Old World monkey** langur
**old writing implement** quill, style
**old yes** yea
**old you** ye
**oleaceous tree** olive
**oleander** rosebay
**olefine gas** ethylene
**oleic acid salt** oleate
**olein** triolein
**olfactometry** odorimetry
**olfactory organ** nose
**olid** fetid, foul-smelling, rank-smelling, smelly, stinking
**oligarch or sachem** ruler
**olio** conglomeration, farrago, fricassee, goulash, hodgepodge, hotchpotch, medley, mélange, miscellany, mishmash, mixture, potpourri, ragout, scramble, stew, variety
**olive-brown** drab
**olive-green song bird** siskin
*Oliver Twist* **character** Artful Dodger, Fagan, Nancy
**olive-shaped** olivary, oval
**Olympic event** athletics, boxing, canoeing, games, races, triathlon, wrestling
**omelette base** egg
**omelette filled with minced pork** foo yo(a)ng, foo yung, fu yung
**omen** augur(y), auspice, bode, danger, feeling, foreboding, forecast, foretell, foretoken, (fore)warning, harbinger, indication, portent, predict, presage, prognostic, prophetic, sign, soothsay, token, vaticinate
**omen drawn from the action of birds** auspice, ornithoscopy
**ominous** bodeful, dark, dismaying, evil, fateful, foreboding, forecasting, forewarning, ill-omened, looming, malign, menacing, oracular, portent(ous), predictive, presage, prognostic, prophetic, sign, sinister, threatening, unlucky, vaticinal
**omission** avoidance, caret, default, delinquency, disregard, erasure, exception, exclusion, failure, ignoring, interval, lack, neglect, negligence, nonadmission, noninclusion, nonperformance, oversight, preclusion
**omission in law** loophole
**omission mark** caret
**omission of a letter or a word in writing** lipography
**omission of end of a word** apocope
**omission of letter from word** syncope
**omit** delete, exclude, forget, ignore, neglect, overlook, skip
**omit in printing** dele(te)
**omit in pronunciation** elide

**omit through carelessness** neglect
**omit to do something** neglect
**omnipresent** attendant, everywhere, present, ubiquitous
**on** about, above, active, ahead, around, at, atop, auf (G), beside, beyond, by, fast, forward, near, onward, operating, touching, upon
**on account of** because, for
**on a chair** seated
**onager** ass, catapult
**on a level with** beside
**on a level with the water** awash
**on all occasions** always, regularly
**on all sides** about, around
**on all sides of** around, surrounding
**on and off** discontinuously, intermittently, periodically, remittently, sometimes, spasmodically
**on and on** continually, continuing, continuously, endlessly, (for)ever, monotonous, running, tedious, unceasingly
**on an incline** sloping
**on an occasion** once
**on an upper floor** upstairs
**on a par** equal, level, well-matched
**on approval** experimental, pending
**on a previous occasion** earlier
**on a ship** aboard
**on a single occasion** once
**on a small scale** petty
**on average** generally, normally, typically, usually
**on a wall** mural
**on back of fish** dorsal fin
**on basis of seven** septenary
**on behalf of** for
**on boarding house terms** en pension (F)
**on board ship** afloat, asea
**on both sides** ambidextrous, amphi-
**once** definitely, erst, ever, former(ly), just, nearly, only, previously, quondam, semel (L), someday, whenever
**once again** afresh, anew, encore, over
**once a month** monthly
**once and for all** conclusively, decidedly, decisively, definitively, determinately, finally, permanently, positively, ultimately
**once around a racetrack** lap
**once a week** weekly
**once a year** annual(ly), yearlong, yearly
**once for all** outright
**once in a blue moon** hardly, rarely, seldom
**once in a while** occasionally, otherwhiles, periodically, sometimes
**once in three weeks** tri-weekly

**once more** afresh, again, anew, encore
**once or twice** infrequently, sporadically
**once round the track** lap
**once upon a time** previously
**on circuit** itinerant
**on condition that** if, provided, so
**on day on which abstinence of meat is ordered** maigre
**on dry land** ashore
**on duty** busy, engaged, working
**one** ace, adult, ae, agreed, ain, alone, an, ane (Sc), any(body), anyone, being, body, ein (G), individual, integer, isolated, joined, lone(ly), man, married, only, person, single, sole, solitary, un (F), une (F), uni-, unit, united, uno (I), you
**one account of a matter** version
**one-act opera** operetta
**one addicted to luxury** voluptuary
**one after another** following, seriatim, succession, tandem
**one alone** odd
**one and all** each, jointly, severally
**one and only** exclusive, sole
**one and the same** identical
**one appointed to act for another** deputy
**one as stated** any
**one at a time** individually, separately, singly
**one at cards** ace
**one-bagger** single
**one before another** tandem
**one beyond help** goner
**one beyond the protection of the law** outlaw
**one born in a place** native
**one bound to a master to learn a trade** apprentice
**one by himself** loner
**one by one** apiece, individually, overhead, personally, separately, singly
**one captured in war** prisoner
**one casting a ballot** voter
**one-celled microscopic animal** protozoan, protozoon
**one chosen to transact business for others** syndic
**one circuit of a racecourse or track** lap
**one claiming a right of voting** suffragist
**one coming at the end** tail-ender
**one confined to an institution** inmate
**one cubic foot per second** cusec
**one cubic metre** stere
**one dainty in eating and drinking** epicure
**one dependent on charity** pauper
**one deprived of something** loser

**one deputed to speak for others** spokesman
**one devoted to his or her country** patriot
**one devoted to monastic life** oblate
**on edge** agitated, avid, eager, edgy, frayed, frazzled, intent, jumpy, nervous, ragged, restless, threadbare, uneasy
**one difficult to dislodge** limpet
**one-dimensional** linear, flat
**one easily imposed on** mug
**one-eighth of a mile** furlong
**one employed in cleaning streets** scavenger
**one employed in working with machinery** mechanic
**one engaged in medicine** practitioner
**one executing a headlock or half-nelson** wrestler
**one-eyed** monocular
**one-eyed giant** Argus, Cyclops, Polyphemus
**one favoured** pro
**one first in rank** primate
**one floor of building** storey
**one followed by eighteen zeros** trillion
**one followed by hundred zeros** googol
**one followed by nine zeros** milliard
**one followed by six zeros** million
**one followed by thirty-six zeros** sextillion
**one followed by thirty zeros** quintillion
**one followed by twelve zeros** trillion
**one followed by twenty-four zeros** quadrillion
**one fond of good living** bon vivant (F)
**one for whom a married person has illicit love** paramour
**one fully skilled in an art** adept
**one gainfully employed** earner
**one game of snooker** frame
**one given up to something** addict
**one guilty of arson** incendiary
**one guilty of crime** felon
**one habitually untidy** sloven
**one-half tile** head
**one having a meal** diner
**one having gigantic strength** titan
**one held for security** hostage
**one holding an office** official
**one-horned animal** monoceros, unicorn
**one-horned rhinoceros** badak
**one-horse carriage** brougham, chaise, gig, hansom, rig, shay
**one-humped camel** dromedary
**one hundred and forty-four** gross
**one hundred ares** hectare
**one-hundred-eyed giant** Argus
**one-hundred percent** all

**one-hundredth** centi-
**one-hundredth of a pound** pence, penny
**one-hundredth of a yen** sen
**one hundred years** century
**one impervious to pain or pleasure** stoic
**one in a million** unique
**one in annual meteor shower** Leonid
**one in cards** ace
**one in charge** boss, manager
**one in charge of cavalry horses** farrier
**one in charge of collected funds** treasurer
**one in charge of horses** groom
**one in charge of nursing in a hospital** matron, superintendent
**one in charge of the commercial affairs of a ship** supercargo
**one in constant suffering** martyr
**one in control** master
**one indefinitely** any
**one in formal discussion** debater
**one in gunfight** duellist
**one inheriting from will** devisee
**one in second childhood** dotard
**one in subordinate position** assistant
**one in the ear or mouth is very painful** abscess
**one in the know** insider
**one in the lead** pacemaker
**one in time saves nine** stitch
**one item in auction** lot
**one item on sports programme** event
**one kept in prison** prisoner
**one kept in the hands of the enemy** hostage
**one lately arrived** newcomer
**one less than par** birdie
**one liable to render account** accountant, creditor
**one living in a place** resident
**one loop of chain** link
**one losing a struggle** underdog
**one makes this in a diary** entry
**one making a will** devisor, testator
**one-masted vessel** cutter, sloop
**one may be eaten for breakfast** egg, rasher
**one million million** billion
**one-millionth of a metre** micron
**one-millionth of a second** microsecond
**one more** again, another
**one more than one** two
**one named after another** namesake
**one named for office** nominee
**on end** continuously, serially, successively, together
**oneness** agreement, changelessness, harmony, identity, sameness, singleness, singularity, union, uniqueness, unity, wholeness
**one newly risen into notice or power** parvenu
**one new to anything** novice
**one not backed to win** underdog
**one-oar-bank galley** unireme
**one obtaining retribution** avenger
**one of a flight of stairs** stair, step
**one of a group of Turkish soldiers of 19th-century** bashibazouk
**one of a kind** distinctive, rare, singular, special, unique, unusual
**one of a mob** rioter
**one of a pair of similar things** doublet
**one of Columbus's ships** Nina, Pinta, Santa Maria
**one of couple in relationship** partner
**one of eight racers** oar
**one of five** quin
**one of five children born at a birth** quin(tuplet)
**one of four children born at a birth** quad(ruplet)
**one of four joint rulers** tetrarch
**one of gigantic size** titan
**one of high birth** noble
**one of Job's comforters** Elihu
**one of low origin** filius terrae (L)
**one of mixed breed** Métis, mongrel
**one of Neptune's trumpeters** Triton
**one of pair used in slalom** ski
**one of pleasant countenance** smiler
**one of porcupine's spines** quill
**one of Robin Hood's men** Friar Tuck
**one of same class** fellow
**one of Santa's reindeer** Blitzen, Dancer, Donder, Fixen, Prancer, Rudolf
**one of set of bones between wrist and fingers** metacarpus
**one of set of bones between ankle and toes** metatarsus
**one of seven children born at a birth** septuplet
**one of several units** tier
**one of six children born at a birth** sextuplet
**one of the bones behind a deer's foot** dew-claw
**one of the Channel Islands** Sark
**one of the common people** plebeian
**one of the divisions of the calyx** sepal
**one of the four cardinal points** East, North, South, West
**one of the four sets in a pack of cards** suit
**one of the great lakes** Erie, Huron, Michigan, Ontario, Superior
**one of the highest towns in the world** Cerro de Pasco

**one of the Muses** Calliope, Clio, Erato, Euterpe, Melpomene, Polyhymnia, Terpsichore, Thalia, Urania
**one of the old block** chip
**one of the pieces forming a cask** stave
**one of the ribs in the frame of a wooden vessel** futtock
**one of the same rank** peer
**one of the senses** hearing, sight, smell, taste, touch
**one of the seven deadly sins** anger, covetousness, envy, gluttony, lust, pride, sloth
**one of the Seven Dwarfs** Bashful, Doc, Dopey, Grumpy, Happy, Sleepy, Sneezy
**one of the Seven Wonders** Colossus of Rhodes, Hanging Gardens of Babylon, Tomb of Mausolus, Pharos of Alexandria, Pyramids of Egypt, Statue of Zeus, Temple of Artemis
**one of the small beads on a rosary** ave
**one of the suits at cards** club, diamond, heart, spade
**one of the surfaces of an object** side
**one of the Three Graces** Aglaia, Euphrosyne, Thalia
**one of the three sections of the hipbone** ischium
**one of the two** either
**one of the two parts of a thing** moiety
**one of the two peaks of Mount Sorata** Ancohuma, Illampu
**one of the uprights of the wicket at cricket** stump
**one of thirty-six in a yard** inch
**one of those who sign a document** signatory
**one of three children born at a birth** triplet
**one of three equal parts** third
**one of Three Musketeers** Aramis, Athos, Porthos
**one of three sharing supreme power** triumvir
**one of two** either
**one of two children born at a birth** twin
**one of two cross-pieces over stumps in cricket** bail
**one of two openings of nose** nostril
**one of two parts** half, moiety
**one of us** me, you
**one of US great lakes** Erie, Huron, Michigan, Superior, Tahoe
**one omitted** out
**one on cards or dice** ace
**one only** single
**one opposed** anti
**one or the other** either

**one other** another
**one over par** bogey
**one owed money** creditor
**one part of journey** leg
**one part of play** act
**one-piece garment** bodysuit, catsuit, overall
**one placed on guard** sentinel
**one pound note** oncer
**one pound sterling** quid
**one programme of soap** episode
**one put to death** martyr
**one responsible for club funds** treasurer
**onerous** back-breaking, burdensome, demanding, difficult, exacting, exigent, grave, hard, heavy, oppressive
**one sank the Titanic** iceberg
**one's attendance** presence
**one's attendants** entourage
**one's best work** masterpiece
**one's blood relations** kinsfolk
**one's bounds** purlieu
**one's closest relative** next of kin
**one's competitor** opposition
**one score** twenty
**one's country** fatherland, homeland, motherland
**one's daily round** routine
**one's duty** obligation
**one seeing the bright side** optimist
**one segment of compound eye** facet
**one segment of spinal column** vertebra
**one's employment** occupation
**one sent to preach the Gospel** apostle
**one's equal** peer
**one serving in an army** soldier
**one's family** kinsfolk
**one's forte** métier
**one's habitual associates** entourage
**one's happiest profession** métier
**one's home** abode, domicile, residence
**one's house** home
**one-sided** biased, prejudiced, unfair, unilateral, unjust
**one-sided inclination** bias
**one side of a leaf of a book** page
**one's individuality** identity
**one skilled at strategy** tactician
**one skilled in accounts** accountant
**one skilled in arithmetic** arithmetician
**one skilled in international law** publicist
**one skilled in languages** linguist
**one skilled in magic** magician
**one skilled in obstetrics** obstetrician
**one skilled in science** scientist
**one skilled in the science of exchange** cambist
**one's lot in life** allotment

**one slow at learning** dullard, dunce
**one's native country** fatherland, homeland, motherland
**one's natural language** mother tongue, native tongue
**one's natural life** lifelong
**one's nearest pub** local
**one's old university** alma mater
**one's own** personal
**one's own flesh and blood** blood, family, kin(dred), relations, relatives
**one's own handwriting** autography
**one's own individuality** self
**one's own man** bachelor, independent, unconfined, ungoverned, unmarried, unrestrained, unrestricted
**one's parent's parent** grandparent
**one spike of a fork** prong, tine
**one's possessions** belongings
**one-spot card** ace
**one-spot domino** ace
**one's relations** kindred
**one's relative** kin
**one's relatives** family, kinsfolk
**one's right wits** senses
**one's school** alma mater
**one's second self** alter ego
**one's speciality** forte
**one's strongest point** forte
**one who steals cattle** rustler
**one-storey house** bungalow
**one's trade** métier
**one suffering from mental derangement** psychopath
**one suffering greatly for his beliefs** martyr
**one's university** alma mater
**one superior to humans in intellect and morality** superman
**one taken prisoner** captive
**one taking a share** partaker
**one taught in school** scholar
**one-tenth** deci-, tithe
**one-tenth of a legion** cohort
**one thing on list** item
**one-third of mile** li
**one-thousand million** milliard
**one-thousand-millionth of a second** nanosecond
**one-thousandth** milli-
**one-thousandth of an inch** mil
**one thousand thousand** million
**one thousand years** chiliad
**one time only** once
**one to feed the flames** stoker
**one told by Aesop** fable
**one tooth on gear-wheel** cog
**one to whom a legacy is bequeathed** heir, legatee
**one to whom allotment is made** allottee

one to whom bequest is made  legatee
one to whom debt is due  creditor
one to whom secrets are told
   confidant
one track circuit  lap
one under care of another  protégé(e)
one under par  birdie
one under the orders of another
   subordinate
on even terms  quit
one versed in law  jurist
on every occasion  always
on every side of  ambient, around,
   surrounding
one Wall Street concern  bond
one-way gear  ratchet
one way or another  somehow
one way to cook  boil, braai, fry, roast,
   stew
one wears bracelet round this  wrist
one-wheeled bike  unicycle
one who acts disloyally  traitor
one who acts for another  agent
one who acts in a dumb-show
   mummer
one who acts irrationally  wack(o)
one who administers wills  executor
one who advocates changes
   turnabout
one who advocates greater political
   freedom  liberal
one who annoys  pest
one who answers for an infant at
   baptism  godfather, godmother,
   sponsor
one who appeals to a higher court
   appellant
one who apprises  enlightener
one who arranges marriages for
   payment  marriage broker
one who asks questions  querist
one who assails cherished beliefs
   iconoclast
one who assumes a false identity
   imposter
one who attends to the secular affairs
   of the church  deacon
one who avoids human society
   misanthrope
one who avoids military service by
   obtaining government work
   embusqué (F)
one who avows his religion  confessor
one who bargains  negotiator
one who believes in strict discipline
   disciplinarian
one who bellows  roarer
one who bequeaths  legator
one who blocks new laws
   obstructionist
one who botches things  bungler
one who breaks law  felon

one who brings a charge against
   impeacher
one who brings bad luck  Jonah
one who brings good luck  mascot
one who builds with stone  mason
one who buys and sells for others
   broker
one who calculates insurance risks
   and premiums  actuary
one who calls  hailer
one who cannot be believed  liar
one who cannot pay his debts
   bankrupt
one who carries a message
   messenger
one who carries out  executor
one who carries out death sentence
   executioner
one who changes sides  turncoat
one who chases another  pursuer
one who chokes  splutterer
one who cleans and thickens cloth
   fuller
one who cleans the streets  scavenger
one who climbs mountains
   mountaineer
one who collects postage stamps
   philatelist
one who collects things of interest
   collector
one who comments on current events
   commentator
one who commits sabotage  saboteur
one who commits treason  traitor
one who compels by force  coercer
one who competes  contestant
one who conducts periodicals  editor
one who damages  vandal
one who deals in flowers  florist
one who deals in furs  furrier
one who deifies himself  autotheist
one who designs buildings  architect
one who dies for a cause  martyr
one who digs  digger
one who disclaims  recanter
one who does all kinds of work
   factotum, girl Friday,
   jack-of-all-trades
one who does not believe in religion
   atheist, infidel
one who does not fight  noncombatant
one who doesn't drink alcohol
   abstainer, teetotaller
one who dresses and colours tanned
   leather  currier
one who dresses flashily  pantsula,
   spiv
one who drinks overmuch tea  theine
one who drives cattle to market
   drover
one who eats  eater
one who eats human flesh  cannibal

one who eats no animal produce
   vegan
one who employs  engager
one who enjoys good living  epicure
one who enters hostile territory to
   observe and report  spy
one who entertains  host(ess)
one who entraps  ensnarer
one who erases  effacer
one who excels  ace
one who explores caves for sport
   spelunker
one who extorts money  racketeer
one who faces facts  realist
one who fancies oneself an invalid
   malade imaginaire (F)
one who feeds cattle for market
   grazier
one who feigns illness  malingerer
one who fells lumber  lumberjack
one who fights  combatant
one who first originates  pioneer
one who fishes for shrimps  shrimper
one who flees  escaper
one who flies aircraft  aviator
one who foretells future events
   prophet, soothsayer
one who gives  donator, donor
one who gives evidence in a law court
   witness
one who gives professional massage
   masseur, masseuse
one who gives up easily  quitter
one who gives written evidence
   deponent
one who grades things  sorter
one who grinds grain  miller
one who habitually stays away
   absentee
one who has committed a crime
   culprit
one who has information  knower
one who has made a will  testator
one who has visions  seer, prophet
one who hates all women  misogynist
one who hearkens  listener
one who helps others  altruist
one who hides in a ship to obtain
   passage  stowaway
one who holds that baptism should be
   for adults only  anabaptist
one who inclines to disbelieve  sceptic
one who infringes copyright  pirate
one who injects heroin into himself
   junkie, junky
one who introduces TV programs
   presenter
one who invests for high profits
   speculator
one who is curious  quidnunc
one who is for  pro
one who is in the know  insider

one who is not in favour  opposer
one who is opposed  anti
one who is skilled  proficient
one who is slow to learn  dunce
one who is uncertain about his belief in God  agnostic
one who is versed in educational methods  education(al)ist
one who is versed in languages  polyglot
one who journeys to a sacred place  pilgrim
one who judges by rank rather than merit  snob
one who keeps financial accounts  accountant, bookkeeper
one who kills a king  regicide
one who kills a parent  parricide
one who kills by treacherous violence  assassin
one who kills himself intentionally  suicide
one who kills one's brother or sister  fratricide
one who kills one's father  patricide
one who kills one's mother  matricide
one who kills his wife  uxoricide
one who knows  cognoscente
one who knows only one language  monoglot
one who leads another astray  seducer
one who learns only late in life  opsimath
one who leases from a tenant  sub-lessee
one who leaves a will  testator
one who listens secretly  eavesdropper
one who listens to and records foreign broadcasts  monitor
one who litters  litterbug
one who lives luxuriously  bon vivant (F)
one who lives near a city  suburbanite
one who lives near another  neighbour
one who lives on another  parasite, sponger
one who looks on dark side  pessimist
one who loves beauty  aesthete
one who loves his or her country  patriot
one who maintains doubt  sceptic
one who makes an affidavit  affiant
one who makes an appeal  appellant
one who makes a study of love  amorist
one who makes barrels  cooper
one who makes clothes  tailor
one who makes continual efforts  trier
one who makes knives  cutler
one who makes optical instruments  optician

one who makes women's hats  milliner
one who manages another's property  steward
one who moans  groaner
one who moves out of the country  emigrant
one who occupies vacant premises without leave  squatter
one who offers service  volunteer
one who opposes changes in policy  standpatter
one who opposes reform  obscurant
one who overcharges  profiteer
one who overruns a country  invader
one who owes  debtor
one who plays an organ  organist
one who pleads another's cause  advocate
one who plunders  despoiler
one who practises any of the fine arts  artist
one who practises massage  masseur, masseuse
one who praises the good old days  laudator temporis acti (L)
one who precedes another in an office  predecessor
one who predicts a person's future  fortune-teller
one who presents personal accounts  autobiographer
one who presides  chairman
one who provides massage professionally  masseur, masseuse
one who puts ideas into practice  ideopraxist
one who puts an edge  sharpener
one who puts parts together  assembler
one who raises scares  scaremonger
one who receives  recipient
one who receives stolen property  fence
one who rejects authority in religion  freethinker
one who rejects societal values  nihilist
one who rejects war  pacifist
one who relapses into crime  recidivist
one who remains  survivor
one who rents a house  tenant
one who returns accusations  recriminator
one who riots  rioter
one who robs at sea  pirate
one who rows  oarsman
one who rules for another  regent
one who salts and smokes fish  fish-curer
one who scourges himself in penance  flagellant
one who screams  shrieker

one who seeks an appointment  candidate
one who seeks to cause war  warmonger
one who seems to have no mind or will  zombie
one who sees something  witness
one who sells  hawker, merchant, vendor
one who sells candles  chandler
one who sells fish  fishmonger
one who settles an account  payer
one who settles on land without title  squatter
one who shirks duty  truant
one who shoes horses  farrier
one who shoots with a bow and arrow  archer
one who shuttles  commuter
one who steals  burglar, crook, lifter, robber, smuggler, stealer, taker, thief
one who steals cattle  rustler
one who steals from shops  shoplifter
one who steers ship  helmsman
one who stirs things up  troublemaker
one who stockpiles  collector
one who studies  scholar, student
one who studies agronomy  agronomist
one who studies moral or mental science  philosopher
one who studies plants and animals  naturalist
one who studies the Middle Ages  medi(a)evalist
one who succeeds another  success
one who sues  suitor
one who sues in a law court  plaintiff
one who supports another  backer
one who supports national rights  nationalist
one who takes an oath  juror
one who takes part in conversation  interlocutor
one who takes part in election  voter
one who takes the initiative  leader
one who tempts  tempter
one who tends a fire  stoker
one who testifies  witness
one who transgresses  sinner
one who treats diseases of the feet  chiropodist
one who treats diseases of horses  farrier
one who treats diseases of the mind  psychiatrist
one who tries to go faster  hastener
one who uses something  user
one who utters falsehood  liar
one who warns or advises  monitor
one who watches a game  spectator
one who weeds  hoer

**one who weeps** crier
**one who works for wages** employee
**one who works in gold** goldsmith
**one who writes about books** bibliographer
**one who writes to dictation** amanuensis
**one with indigestion** dyspeptic
**one with loud voice** stentor
**one with no practical sense** muff
**on farther side** beyond
**on fire** ablaze, afire, aflame, alight, ardent, blazing, burning, fiery, fired, flaming, ignited
**on foot** à pied (F), afoot, jogging, on fore, running, skipping, sprinting, walking
**on friendly terms** peaceful
**ongoing** accepted, advancing, circulating, common, continuing, continuous, current, customary, due, enduring, general, growing, increasing, intensifying, lasting, open, outstanding, owing, payable, pending, popular, present, prevailing, prevalent, progressive, rife, sustained, unpaid, unsettled, widespread
**ongoing story** serial
**on guard** alert, awake, wary
**on hand** accessible, along, available, handy, imminent
**on high** aloft
**on hold** pending
**on horseback** à cheval (F), mounted
**on in years** elderly
**onion-like vegetable** chive, leek, shallot
**onion sauce** béchamel, soubise
**on land** ashore
**onlooker** bystander, examiner, eyewitness, gawker, gazer, inspector, observer, scrutiniser, spectator, viewer, watcher, witness
**only** alone, barely, but, distinct, exclusively, however, just, mere, singly, sole(ly), uniquely
**only a moment** momentary
**only a small lake** mere
**only English pope** Adrian
**only just** barely, scarcely
**only other choice** alternative
**only talk** gossip, hearsay
**only two** á deux (F)
**only with difficulty** hardly
**on neither side** neutral
**on next page** overleaf
**on no account** nay, never
**on no occasion** never
**on occasion** occasionally, sometimes
**on occasion of** at

**onomatopoeia** echoism, sound-imitation
**onomatopoeic** copied, derivative, echoic, imitative, mock, parrotlike, plagiarised, put-on, second-hand, simulated, unoriginal
**on one occasion** once
**on one's guard** careful, cautious, mindful, vigilant, wary, watchful
**on one side** aside, ipsilateral, unilateral
**on one's last legs** dying, failing
**on one's own** alone, autonomous, independent(ly), personally, self-reliant, separately, single, solely
**on one's own initiative** de proprio motu (L)
**on one's toes** alert
**on one's uppers** broke, penniless, ruined
**on paper** ideally, theoretically, written
**on pins and needles** agitated, anxious, tenterhooks, uneasy
**on purpose** deliberately, expressly, intentionally, knowingly, purposely, wilfully, wittingly
**on right-hand side** dexter
**on river-bank** riparian
**onrush** career, cascade, dash, deluge, drive, efflux, effusion, flood, fountain, gush, issuance, jet, millrace, Niagara, outflow, (out)rush, push, race, rapids, sally, spout, spurt, stampede, stream-current, surge, swell, wave
**on same footing** equal
**onset** assault, attack, beginning, charge, inception, onrush, start
**on ship** aboard
**on show** exposed, undisguised
**onslaught** assault, attack, blitz, bombardment, charge, coup de main (F), foray, fusillade, invasion, onset, raid, rush, salvo, sortie, strike
**on stage alone** solo, solus
**on strike** out
**on summit of** atop
**on tap** available, ready,
**Ontarian capital** Toronto
**Ontario Indian** Cree
**on that account** hence
**on the alert** awake
**on the average** generally, typically, usually
**on the ball** adroit, alert, astir, awake, competent, quick, vital
**on the beach** ashore
**on the best of terms** au mieux (F)
**on the blink** broken, faulty, malfunctioning
**on the boil** seething
**on the breadline** needy
**on the brink of** almost, verge

**on the cards** afoot, apt, destined, imminent, impending, liable, ordained, probable
**on the contrary** again, au contraire (F), but, per contra, rather
**on the cross** crosswise
**on the dot** dabble, exactly, precisely, promptly, punctually, stipple, stud
**on the double** briskly, immediately, posthaste, quickly, straightaway, tantivy
**on the downgrade** declining, depressed, falling, sagging, sinking, sliding, slumping, weakening
**on the extreme outside** outermost
**on the face of it** apparently, seemingly
**on the face of the earth** everywhere
**on the fence** impartial, irresolute, neutral, uncommitted, undecided
**on the fly** hastily, hurriedly, quickly, speedily, swiftly
**on the foot** afoot
**on the go** active, afoot, busy
**on the high** aloft
**on the house** complimentary, free, gratis
**on the increase** expanding, multiplying, spreading
**on the inside** inwardly
**on the instant** forthwith, immediately, instantly, now
**on the lam** escaped, escaping, fled, fleeing, flown, hiding, scot-free
**on the left side** (a)port, sinister
**on the level** aboveboard, even, fair, genuine, honest, open, straight
**on the line of** along
**on the lookout** alert, awake, wakeful, watchful
**on the loose** escaping, free, runaway, unconfined
**on the lower floor** downstairs
**on the make** advancing, increasing, rising
**on the march** advancing, afoot, marching, progressing
**on the market** accessible, attainable, available, obtainable, purchasable
**on the mend** better, convalescent, convalescing, improving, recovering, recuperating
**on the move** afoot, astir, journeying, travelling, voyaging
**on the nose** exactly, perfectly, precisely, promptly
**on the ocean** asea
**on the offensive** advancing, aggressive, attacking, invading, invasive
**on the other hand** again, alternatively, although, but, however
**on the other side** across, over

**on the other side of a bridge** transpontine
**on the other side of page** overleaf
**on the outs** alienated, estranged, unfriendly
**on the outside** external, outwardly
**on the part of** for
**on the quiet** confidentially, privately
**on the rampage** amok, amuck, berserk, destructive, raging, rampant, riotous, violent, wild
**on the rear side of** behind
**on the right-hand side** dexter, starboard
**on the road** cruising, driving, en route, journeying, travelling
**on the rocks** aground
**on the run** defeated, escaping, fugitive, hastily, hurriedly, hurrying, quickly, swiftly
**on the same level** par
**on the scrap heap** discarded, ditched, redundant
**on the shelf** inactive, inoperative, nonfunctioning, unoccupied, unusable, unused, useless
**on the sheltered side of ship** lee
**on the ship** aboard
**on the sinistral side** left-hand
**on the sly** secretly
**on the spot** in loco (L)
**on the spur of the moment** hastily, impetuously, impromptu, impulsively, offhand, precipitately, recklessly, suddenly, unexpectedly
**on the stick** active, alert, aware, bustling, keen, quick
**on the subject of** about, regarding
**on the summit** atop
**on the surface** apparently, ostensibly, outwardly, superficially
**on the take** avaricious, covetous, grasping, greedy, mercenary
**on the trot** consecutively
**on the verge of tears** teary, weepy
**on the very top** uppermost
**on the wane** decadent, declining, decreasing, decrescent, degenerating, deteriorating, diminishing, dropping, dwindling, dying, ebbing, fading, lessening, obsolescent, subsiding, weakening, withering
**on the watch** alert
**on the way** agate, en route, in transitu (L), threatening
**on the whole** altogether, generally, mostly, overall, predominantly, usually
**on the wing** flying
**on the wrong track** mistaken
**on thin ice** unsafe, vulnerable

**on this** hereupon
**on this account** for
**on time** exact, precisely, prompt, punctual(ly), sharp
**on to** upon
**on top** upon, winning
**on top of** above, aloft, atop, onto, upon
**on top of that** also
**on top of the world** ecstatic, elated, exultant, happy
**on trial** experimental, provisional
**on two occasions** twice
**onus** burden, charge, cross, debt, demand, disadvantage, duty, guilt, hindrance, impediment, liability, load, obligation, obstruction, responsibility, task, tribulation, weight, worry
**on vacation** away, off
**onward** advanced, advancing, ahead, forward, improved
**onward movement** advancement, progress
**onward rush** birr, onrush, surge
**onwards** ahead
**onwards in time** forth
**on welfare** beggary, lacking, moneyless, needy, penniless, poverty-stricken
**on what account** why
**on which small articles are carried** tray
**on which smith works metal** anvil
**on which the wheel turns** axle
**onyx** chalcedony
**oodles** lots, quantities
**oof** cash, money
**oolong** tea
**oomph** brio, drive, energy, enthusiasm, (get-up-and-)go, gusto, it, life, pep, punch, sex appeal, spirit, verve, vigour, vim, vitality, zest
**oont** camel, dromedary
**ootheca** ovisac
**ooze** bleed, discharge, drain, drip, drop, emit, escape, exudation, exude, filter, flow, leach, leak, marsh, mire, moisture, mud, percolate, seep, seip, sipe, slime, strain, sweat, sype, transude, trickle, weep
**ooze out** exude, seep
**ooze through** percolate
**ooze through pores** transude
**oozy** slimy
**oozy mud** slime
**opacity of photographic image** density
**opah** kingfish
**opalescent glass** opaline
**opaque** backward, blurred, clouded, cloudy, confused, cryptic, dim, dubious, dull, lumpish, obtuse, simple, slow-witted, stupid, turbid, unintelligent, vacuous, vague
**opaque glass** hyalite
**open** accessible, available, begin, candid, exposed, fair, frank, ope, overt, public, sincere, start, unclosed, uncovered, undecided, undo, unfilled, unlock, unobstructed, unoccupied, unreserved, unrestricted, unroll, unseal
**open a beer keg** tap
**open again** re-open
**open air** outdoor, outside
**open-air fire to express joy** bonfire
**open-air market** entrepôt, flea market, mart
**open-air meal** braai, picnic
**open-air swimming pool** lido
**open and genuine** sincere
**open-and-shut** obvious, simple, straightforward
**open and shut eyes** blink
**open and sincere** genuine, naïve, open-hearted, undeceptive
**open arcade** loggia
**open, as a door** dup
**open-backed sandal** mule
**open balcony in a theatre** loggia
**open car without rear seats** roadster
**open, clearly honest** candid
**open corridor** loggia
**open country** veld
**open courtyard within a Roman house** atrium
**open cylindrical vessel** pail
**open day** at-home
**open declaration** avowal
**open defiance** affront
**open disobedience** defiance
**open end of firearm** muzzle
**opener** (latch)key
**open-eyed look** stare
**open fabric** gauze, net
**open fire** bombard
**open footwear** sandal
**open forest space** glade
**open framework** lattice
**open gallery** loggia
**open grassland** lea, veld
**open-handed** bountiful, free, generous, large-hearted, lavish, liberal
**open-handed blow** slap
**opening** aperture, canal, cave, cavity, crack, eyelet, gap, inlet, intro(duction), lacuna, leak, mouth, opportunity, orifice, passage, puncture, slit, space, split, stoma, vent
**opening above door** transom
**opening for coins** slot

**opening giving access to sewer**
   manhole
**opening in cloud** rift
**opening in clouds** rent
**opening in fence** gap, gate
**opening in nose** naris, nostril
**opening in ship's deck for lowering cargo** hatchway
**opening in side of ship** port(hole)
**opening in the middle of the eye** pupil
**opening in the skin** pore
**opening into mine** adit
**opening in wall** door, window
**opening in wall for cannon** embrasure
**opening mouth of a cavity** orifice
**opening of exhibition of paintings**
   vernissage
**opening of negotiations** overture
**opening piece played by an orchestra**
   overture
**opening show jitters** first-night nerves
**opening to allow entrance** gate
**open inner court-yard** patio
**open Italian pie** pizza
**open knots** untie
**open knowledge** daylight
**open land** lea, veld
**open level country** campagna, champaign
**openly** airily, arguably, barely, blatantly, brazenly, clearly, coram populu (L), extensively, freely, gapingly, generally, obviously, overtly, passably, plainly, publicly, shamelessly, spaciously, sweepingly, unashamedly, unreservedly, visibly, wantonly, widely, yawningly
**openly done** overt, unconcealed
**open main court of a Roman house**
   atrium
**open market** fair
**open moor** fynbos, heath
**open-mouthed** agape, clamorous, greedy, ravenous, vociferous
**open mouth wide** gape
**open onto** adjoin
**open pastry** flan, quiche
**open place in a forest** glade
**open place where cows are milked**
   loan
**open portico** veranda(h)
**open receptacle** tray
**open region** savannah, veld
**open resistance to authority**
   defiance, rebellion
**open revolt against authority** mutiny
**opens a lock** key
**open-shelved cabinet** étagère (F)
**open shoe** sandal
**open-sided gallery** loggia
**open-sided shelter for a car** carport

**open sore** ulcer
**open space** area, gap
**open space for movement of aircraft**
   airport, aerodrome
**open space in forest** glade
**open space surrounded by buildings**
   piazza, square
**open tart** flan
**open tart with savoury filling** quiche
**open to argument** controvertible
**open to attack** assailable, attackable, defenceless, vulnerable
**open to bribery** corruptive, venal
**open to choice** optional
**open to correction** corrigible
**open to danger** exposed, vulnerable
**open to discussion** debatable, moot, negotiable
**open-toed shoe** sandal
**open to general use** public
**open to objection** exceptionable
**open-topped wine-flask** carafe
**open to question** disputable
**open to suggestion** amenable
**open to suspicion** questionable
**open to the sky** hypaethral, roofless
**open to view** overt
**open tract in forest** glade, slash
**open tract of country** campagna, champaign
**open up** broach, broaden
**open valley** dale
**open wagon** dray
**open way** road
**open wide** gape, yawn
**open woodland space** glade
**openwork fabric** lace, net
**openwork shoe** sandal
**open wound** sore
**opera box** lodge
**opera by Beethoven** Fidelio
**opera by Bellini** Norma
**opera by Bizet** Carmen
**opera by Britten** Gloriana
**opera by Donizetti** Don Pasquale, Lucia di Lammermoore
**opera by Dvorak** Rusalka
**opera by Gounod** Faust
**opera by Mascagni** Cavalleria Rusticana, Pagliacci
**opera by Massenet** Manon, Thaïs
**opera by Mozart** Cosi fan tutte, Don Giovanni, Figaro, Idomeneo, Seraglio
**opera by Puccini** Edgar, La Bohéme, Madame Butterfly, Tosca, Turandot
**opera by Rachmaninov** Aleko
**opera by Rossini** Barber of Seville, Semiramide, Tancredi, William Tell
**opera by Schubart** Fierabras
**opera by Schumann** Genoveva
**opera by Smetana** Bartered Bride, Dalibor

**opera by Strauss** Bat, Salome
**opera by Tshaikovsky** Mazeppa
**opera by Verdi** Aïda, Don Carlos, Falstaff, il Travatore, La Traviata, Macbeth, Nabucco, Otello, Rigoletto
**opera by Wagner** Flying Dutchman, Lohengrin, Parsifal, Rienzi, Siegfried, Tannhäuser, Tristan and Isolda
**opera by Weber** Euryanthe, Freischütz, Oberon
**opera extra** supper
**opera glasses** binocular, lorgnette
**opera hat** gibus, topper
**opera highlight** aria
**opera house** La Scala, Met(ropolitan)
**opera libretto** text
**opera solo** aria
**opera star** diva
**operate** act, cause, conduct, effect, elicit, employ, engineer, evoke, function, go, handle, manage, manipulate, perform, produce, run, serve, use, utilise, work
**operate a car** drive
**operate a loom** weave
**operate a machine** run, use
**operate a vehicle** drive
**operate on skull** trepan
**operates the controls** pilot
**opera text** libretto
**operatic air** aria
**operatic Japanese emperor** Mikado
**operatic singer** basso
**operatic solo** aria
**operating at high speed** express
**operating doctor** surgeon
**operating from without** extrinsic
**operating in several countries**
   multinational
**operating room** theatre
**operating smoothly** floating
**operation** action, agency, business, effect, efficacy, employment, enactment, execution, handling, manipulation, manoeuvre, performance, potency, procedure, process, transaction, undertaking, virtue
**operational flight by military aircraft**
   sortie
**operation to cut into the bladder to remove stone** lithotomy
**operation to cut into the brain**
   encephalotomy
**operation to remove appendix**
   append(ic)ectomy
**operation to remove the uterus**
   hysterectomy
**operation to remove the stomach**
   gastrectomy

**operative** active, artisan, effective, efficient, exerting, functional, hand, investigator, key, mechanic, operating, operator, relevant, serviceable, worker, workman

**operator** actor, administrator, conductor, contractor, dealer, director, doer, executor, handler, machinist, manager, manipulator, mechanic, operant, operative, performer, practitioner, punter, surgeon, technician, trader, wheeler-dealer, worker

**operator of controls** pilot

**operose** active, arduous, astir, assiduous, boring, busy, constant, difficult, endless, exacting, hard-working, industrious, intent, laborious, onerous, strenuous, tedious, tireless, toilsome, troublesome, unflagging, wearisome

**opiate** drug, soporific, stupefy

**opine** suppose, think

**opine as paper chief** editorialise

**opinion** advice, assessment, belief, conclusion, conjecture, credo, estimate, estimation, evaluation, feeling, idea, impression, judg(e)ment, notion, persuasion, principle, sentiment, tenet, theory, thought, view(point)

**opinionated** adamant, dogmatic, obdurate, overbearing, prejudiced, stubborn, uncompromising

**opinion formally expressed** report

**opinion given** advice

**opinion survey** poll, Gallup

**opium derivative** heroin

**opium narcotic** narceine

**opponency** antagonism, opposition

**opponent** adversary, antagonist, challenger, competitor, contestant, disputant, dissident, enemy, foe, objecter, opposer, opposition, rival

**opponent of political change** reactionist

**opponent of the Crusaders** Saladin

**opportune** appropriate, convenient, favourable, felicitous, fit(ted), suitable, timely

**opportune gift** Godsend

**opportunist** chancer

**opportunity** break, chance, contingency, convenience, freedom, juncture, leisure, liberty, means, occasion, opening, possibility, range, room, scope, space, time

**opportunity for buying and selling** market

**oppose** anti-, combat, confront, contrast, contravene, gainsay, hinder, interfere, prevent, refuse, resist, rival, thwart, veto, withstand

**oppose boldly** beard

**opposed** adverse, against, averse, contrary, contrasted, diametric, hostile, opposite

**opposed in nature** contrary

**opposed to** adverse, against, anti-, averse

**opposed to anion** cation

**opposed to change** conservative, dogmatic, narrow-minded

**opposed to express** tacit, local

**opposed to gross** net

**opposed to sacred** profane, secular

**opposed to specific** general

**opposed to wholesale** retail

**opposing** antagonistic, combatant, conflicting, enemy, opposed, resisting, rival

**opposite** adverse, antithesis, antonym, conflicting, contradiction, contradictory, contrary, contrasted, converse, corresponding, diverse, facing, fronting, hostile, incompatible, inconsistent, inimical, inverse, irreconcilable, opposed, refractory, reverse, unlike

**opposite middle ship side** abeam

**opposite of abscissa** ordinate

**opposite of add** subtract

**opposite of alee** aweather

**opposite of allopathy** homeopathy

**opposite of anima** persona

**opposite of anode** cathode

**opposite of apathetic** emotional

**opposite of apogean** perigean

**opposite of apogee** perigee

**opposite of autonym** pseudonym

**opposite of aweather** alee

**opposite of brevity** prolixity

**opposite of cathode** anode

**opposite of chaos** order

**opposite of close** open

**opposite of collateral** lineal

**opposite of composed** frantic

**opposite of credit** debit

**opposite of debit** credit

**opposite of dele** stet

**opposite of either** neither

**opposite of emotional** apathetic

**opposite of enclave** exclave

**opposite of epilogue** prologue

**opposite of exclave** enclave

**opposite of fat** lean

**opposite of flotsam** lagan, ligin

**opposite of frantic** calm, composed

**opposite of hither** yon(der)

**opposite of hollow** solid

**opposite of homeopathy** allopathy

**opposite of hook** slice

**opposite of lagan** flotsam

**opposite of lean** fat

**opposite of lee** stoss

**opposite of leeward** windward

**opposite of left** right

**opposite of lineal** collateral

**opposite of maxi** mini

**opposite of mini** maxi

**opposite of nadir** zenith

**opposite of neither** either

**opposite of no** yes

**opposite of ontology** phenomenology

**opposite of open** close

**opposite of oral** written

**opposite of order** chaos

**opposite of ordinate** abscissa

**opposite of our** their

**opposite of perigean** apogean

**opposite of perigee** apogee

**opposite of phenomenology** ontology

**opposite of plutocracy** ptochocracy

**opposite of printed** verbal, written

**opposite of prolixity** brevity

**opposite of prologue** epilogue

**opposite of pseudonym** autonym

**opposite of ptochocracy** plutocracy

**opposite of rear** van

**opposite of retail** wholesale

**opposite of right** left, wrong

**opposite of slice** hook

**opposite of solid** hollow

**opposite of stet** dele

**opposite of stoss** lee

**opposite of subtract** add

**opposite of taboo** acceptable, permitted

**opposite of tense** flexible, loose, slack

**opposite of their** our

**opposite of us** others, them, those

**opposite of van** rear

**opposite of wane** wax

**opposite of wax** wane

**opposite of wholesale** retail

**opposite of windward** leeward

**opposite of written** oral, printed

**opposite of wrong** right

**opposite of yes** no

**opposite of yonder** hither

**opposite of zenith** nadir

**opposite to** anti-

**opposition** adversary, antagonism, combating, competition, contrast, difference, objection, offset, opponency, opposing, resistance, resisting

**oppositionist** anti-

**opposition to all constituted authority** nihilism

**opposition to the divine will** theomachy

**opposition to war** pacifism

**oppress** abuse, afflict, anguish, break, burden, crush, depress, dispirit,

**oppressed** drive, embitter, grieve, harass, harry, maltreat, overbear, overburden, overload, overpower, persecute, repress, sadden, strain, subdue, subjugate, suppress, torment, trouble, vex, wrong
**oppressed** abused, crushed, downtrodden, harried, maltreated, overpowered, persecuted, subdued, subjugated, suppressed, vexed, wronged
**oppressed person** drudge, serf
**oppressive** brutal, burdensome, cruel, depressing, despotic, harsh, inhuman, onerous, repressive, severe, sultry, tyrannical, unbearable, unjust
**oppressive humid heat** swelter
**oppressively hot and humid** sweltering
**oppressive person** incubus
**oppressive ruler** tyrant
**oppressive stillness** languor
**oppressor** autocrat, bully, despot, dictator, intimidator, master, persecutor, scourge, slave-driver, taskmaster, tormentor, tyrant
**opprobrious** abusive, hateful, infamous, insolent, insulting, reproachful
**opprobrium** belittlement, censure, debasement, deflation, degradation, derogation, devaluation, disapprobation, disapproval, discredit, disgrace, dishonour, disrepute, ignominy, infamy, ingloriousness, notoriety, odium, shame
**opt** choose, decide, elect, pick, prefer, select
**optic** eyepiece, lens, ocular, ophthalmic, optical, visual
**optical** ocular, optic, visual
**optical device** telescope
**optical glass** lens
**optical illusion** fallacy, fata morgana (I), mirage
**optical instrument** sextant
**optical instrument measuring magnifying power** auxometer
**optical maser** laser
**optical measurement** dioptre
**optical toy** kaleidoscope
**optic cover** eyelid
**optic orb** eyeball
**optic organ** eye
**optimism** anticipation, buoyancy, cheerfulness, confidence, encouragement, expectancy, faith, hope(fulness), reliance, sanguineness, trust

**optimistic** assured, auspicious, buoyant, carefree, cheerful, cheery, confident, dreamy, encouraging, energetic, expectant, favourable, hopeful, idealistic, impractical, promising, reassuring, romantic, sunny
**optimum** best
**optimum era** heyday
**opting for** selecting
**option** acceptance, adoption, alternative, answer, assignment, choice, co-option, commitment, desire, determination, discretion, election, equivalent, espousal, nomination, opinion, partiality, pleasure, possibility, preference, recourse, replacement, selection, solution, substitute, surrogate, taste, vote, will, wish
**opulence** abundance, affluence, bounty, cornucopia, elegance, fortune, lavishness, luxuries, luxury, plenty, prosperity, riches, richness, wealth
**opulent** abundant, affluent, copious, luxuriant, luxurious, moneyed, prosperous, rich, sumptuous, wealthy
**opulent father** rich daddy
**or** alternative, aut (L), either
**ora** stomata
**oracle** answer, astrologer, augur, foreseer, forewarning prophecy, fortune, fortuneteller, horoscoper, judg(e)ment, necromancer, prediction, predictor, presage, prophet, revelation, soothsayer, sorcerer, wise-man
**oracular** absolute, allegorical, arbitrary, arcane, augural, cryptic, enigmatic, gnomic, grave, imperious, judicial, judicious, latent, obscure, pontifical, positive, predictive, prescient, prognostic, pythonic, sibyllic, solemn, sybelline, sybillic, vague, vatic
**oral** mouthed, said, spoken, unwritten test, uttered, verbal, viva voce, vocal
**oral communication** talking
**oral contract** assumpsit
**oral fluid** saliva
**oral history** folklore, traditions
**oral promise** parole
**orange and black starling** baltimore
**orange colour** ochre
**orange-coloured vegetable** butternut, carrot, pumpkin
**orange drink** -ade
**orange dye** henna
**orange essence** neroli (oil)
**orange-flavoured liqueur** Curaçao
**orange flower oil** neroli

**orange jam** marmalade
**orange of traffic light** amber
**orange-pink fruit** apricot
**orange-pink gem** coral
**orange plum-like fruit** loquat
**orange-red** carroty
**orange-red cornelian** sard
**orange-red pigment** realgar
**orange-rind spread** marmalade
**orange seed** pip
**orange skin** peel
**orange variety** navel
**orange vegetable** butternut, carrot, pumpkin
**orange-yellow colour** saffron
**orangutan** pongo
**orate** address, declaim, deliver, descant, discourse, do, eulogise, evangelise, exhort, harangue, lecture, perform, perorate, preach, prelect, rail, read, recite, rehearse, render, repeat, rodomontade, say, sermonise, speak, speechify, talk
**oration** address, declamation, discourse, harangue, lecture, rhetoric, speech
**orator** Cicero, declaimer, demagogue, elocutionist, lecturer, preacher, prelector, rhetor(ician), speaker, speechmaker
**orator at a funeral** eulogist
**oratorio composer** Handel
**orator's platform** dais
**oratory** declamation, eloquence, rhetoric
**orb** (eye)ball, globe, globule, sphere
**orbicular** annular, circular, cycloid, cylindrical, egg-shaped, global, globate, globelike, orbiculate, oval, pyriform, round, spheral, spherelike, spheric(al), spheroidal, spheroidic, spherular
**orbit** ambit, circle, circumgyration, circumvent, compass, course, cycle, domain, ellipse, eye-socket, influence, orb, path, pattern, range, reach, revolution, revolve, rotate, rotation, round, scope, sphere, sweep, track, trajectory
**orbital extremity** apsis
**orb of sight** eye
**orc** grampus, killer-whale, ogre, orca, sea-monster
**orchard** grove
**orchestra area** pit
**orchestra conductor** director
**orchestral brass instrument** horn
**orchestral composition** concerto
**orchestral kettledrum** timpano, tympano
**orchestral piece** overture

**orchestral piece suggesting a rural scene** pastorale
**orchid** aerides, arethusa, calanthe, coralroot, cymbrid, disa, faham, labellum, odontoglossum, pogonia, slipper, vanilla
**orchid root** salep
**orchid tea** fa(h)am
**orchid with fragrant leaves** fa(h)am
**orchis** crakefeet, crowfoot, crowtoe
**Orczy hero** Scarlet Pimpernel
**ordain** appoint, call, confer, declare, decree, destine, dictate, direct, doom, enact, enjoin, establish, fate, inaugurate, induct, instate, instruct, invest, legislate, nominate, order, predestine, prescribe, proclaim, rule, select, warrant
**ordeal** affliction, agony, calamity, deprivation, distress, grief, infliction, misery, sorrow, suffering, test, torment, torture, tragedy, trial, tribulation, trouble, woe
**order** adjust, arrangement, behest, class, command, demand, direct(ion), directive, disposition, edict, genus, grade, harmony, hest, injunction, instruct(ion), kind, mandate, prescription, regularity, regulate, sequence, society, sort, symmetry, tribe, ukase
**ordered** adjured, adjusted, arranged, booked, catalogued, charged, classified, commanded, controlled, decreed, directed, enacted, engaged, grouped, instructed, neatened, ordained, organised, prescribed, regulated, requested, required, reserved, tabulated, tidied
**ordered arrangement** array
**ordered by canon law** canonical
**orderly** business-like, methodical, neat, normally, regular, systematic, trim
**orderly arrangement of ideas** method
**orderly in appearance** neat
**orderly progress** procession
**orderly statement of facts** exposé
**order not to do** forbid
**order obliging people to stay indoors within certain hours** curfew
**order of architecture** Composite, Corinthian, Doric, Ionic, Tuscan
**order of brown algae** fucales
**order proclaimed by authority** edict
**order that forbids** prohibition
**order to return** recall
**ordinal number** first, second, third
**ordinance** assize, ceremony, declaration, decree, dictation, dictum, edict, guideline, mandate, proclamation, sacrament, ukase

**ordinary** accepted, accustomed, acknowledged, average, common(place), conventional, current, customary, domestic, general, habitual, homely, indifferent, inferior, informal, median, mediocre, mundane, natural, norm(al), plain, prevalent, regular, routine, run-of-the-mill, simple, so-so, standard, stereotypical, typical, unastonishing, usual, workaday
**ordinary handwriting** longhand
**ordinary in quality** mediocre
**ordinary language** prose
**ordinary seaman** matelot, rating
**ordinary standard** average
**ordinary stitch in knitting** garter, plain, purl
**ordination** appointment, charging, classification, collocation, commandment, composition, conferment, consecration, construction, designation, empowering, induction, initiation, investiture, ordaining, ordainment, tabulation
**ordnance** ammunition, armaments, arms, artillery, firearms, guns, munitions, weaponry, weapons
**ordnance depot** arsenal
**ore** bullion, element, metal, mineral
**ore deposit** lode
**oregano-like herb** basil
**or else** otherwise, treat
**ore pit** mine
**ore refinery** smelter
**ore shoot** bonanza
**ore vein** lode
**ore washing trough** buddle
**ore-yielding tungsten** wolfram
**orfe** goldfish, ide
**organ** ear, eye, harmonium, hypothalamus, kidney, lung, spleen, stomach
**organ defect** dysfunction
**organ desk** console
**organ grinder** busker
**organic** animate, biotic, fundamental, innate, integral, integrated, live, natural, structural, systematic, systematised, vital
**organic manure** compost
**organic soil** humus
**organic substance of bones** ossein
**organise** arrange, combine, constitute, construct, co-ordinate, dispose, frame, harmonise, order
**organised band of singers** choir
**organised crime** underworld
**organised massacre** pogrom
**organised notes** music

**organised ramified power** octopus
**organise labour** unionise
**organiser of a ballet** impresario
**organism** animal, association, being, body, cell, company, creature, entity, fellow, human, individual, league, something, structure, union
**organism modified by its environment** ecad
**organ keyboard** manual
**organ of balance** ear
**organ of breathing** lung
**organ of fish** fin
**organ of hearing** ear
**organ of locomotion** fin
**organ of sight** eye
**organ of smell** nose
**organ of song in birds** syrinx
**organ of touch** palpus
**organ stop** gamba, quint, salicet, sext
**organ stop consisting of reed pipes** krummhorn
**organ stop with soft reedy tone** salicional
**orgy** binge, carnival, carousal, carouse, compotation, debauch, festival, festivity, fling, frolic, grope, party, revelry, revels, rouse, saturnalia, spree, wassail
**oriel** window
**Orient** East
**orient** acclimate, adapt, adjust, align, arrange, condition, conform, direct, face, glossy, glowing, habituate, iridescent, locate, lustrous, nacred, opalescent, oriental, orientate, pearly, regulate, situate, tailor, train, true, turn
**Oriental** Asian, Asiatic, Chinese, Eastern(er), Levantine
**oriental boat** sampan
**oriental child's nurse** amah
**oriental council-chamber** divan
**oriental curved sword** scimitar
**oriental direction** East
**oriental drum** tom-tom
**oriental fabric** baft
**oriental footwear** soy
**oriental gown** kimono
**oriental greeting** salaam
**oriental head-dress** fez, turban
**oriental market** bazaar
**oriental nymph** houri
**oriental palm sap spirit** arak
**oriental pipe** hooka(h)
**oriental plant** udo
**oriental porter** hamal
**oriental prison** bagnio
**oriental queen** (maha)ranee, (maha)rani
**oriental rice dish** pilau
**oriental sailor** lascar

**oriental salutation** salaam
**oriental sauce** soy
**oriental small boat** sampan
**oriental staple** rice
**oriental title** baba
**oriental tobacco-pipe** hookah
**oriental vessel** junk
**oriental wagon** araba
**oriental weight** catty, tael
**oriental wheeled carriage** araba
**orifice** aperture, cleft, mouth, opening, perforation, vent
**orifice in volcanic region** fumarole
**origen suffix** -ese
**origin** aboriginal, creative, earliest, fertile, genesis, initial, inventive, opening, primitive, primordial, rise, root, source
**original** archetypal, authentic, creative, earliest, endemic, fertile, first, fresh, fundamental, genuine, inborn, incipient, ingenious, initial, intrinsic, introductory, inventive, master, model, native, new, novel, opening, pattern, precedent, primary, primordial, pristine, prototype, radical, resourceful, rudimentary, special, standard, starting, type, unknown, untried, unusual
**original explorer** pioneer
**original inhabitant of a country** aborigine, autochthon, indigene, native
**originality of design** creativity
**original manuscript** urtext
**original model** prototype
**original pattern** archetype
**original Swiss canton** Uri
**original uniform of a fascist** black shirt
**originate** arise, author, begin, cause, create, discover, emanate, establish, found, initiate, introduce, invent, launch, lead, proceed, produce, spring, start, stem
**originate from** emanate
**originating** nascent
**originating in a dry habitat** xerarch
**originating in hospital** nosocomial
**originator** architect, author, creator, founder, inventor, pioneer
**origin of biblical woman** rib
**origin of the universe** cosmogony
**orison** devotion, litany, prayer, supplication
**Orkney fishing ground** Haaf
**ormer** abalone, perlemoen, sea-ear
**ornament** accessory, adorn, adornment, bauble, bedeck, bric-à-brac, curio, decorate, decoration, detail, grace, tassel, trim, trinket
**ornamental ankle chain** anklet

**ornamental arrangement of flower beds** parterre
**ornamental badge** brooch
**ornamental band** obi (J), sash
**ornamental band worn round the head** circlet
**ornamental bone in lip** labret
**ornamental border of threads or tassels** fringe
**ornamental braid** lace
**ornamental brooch** plaque
**ornamental candlestick with several branches** candelabrum
**ornamental case** locket
**ornamental centrepiece for a table** epergne
**ornamental clasp** brooch
**ornamental clipping** topiary
**ornamental cover over curtain rail** pelmet
**ornamental edge** frill, fringe
**ornamental fabric** lace
**ornamental feather** plume
**ornamental figure** fret
**ornamental fish** koi, orfe
**ornamental frill of lace worn on front of shirt** jabot
**ornamental ground** garden
**ornamental hair clasp** barrette
**ornamental hanging tuft** tassel
**ornamental headband** tiara
**ornamental holder for a hot coffee cup** zarf
**ornamental knot of ribbon** bow
**ornamental knot or loose threads** tassel
**ornamental lining for a book cover** doublure
**ornamental loop** knop, picot
**ornamental pattern on side of stocking** clock
**ornamental pendant** a(i)glet
**ornamental pin** brooch
**ornamental plant** agave, aloe, azalea, strelitzia
**ornamental pot for display of growing flowers** jardinière
**ornamental pouch** sporran
**ornamental precious stones** jewellery
**ornamental ribbon** chou
**ornamental screen covering wall behind altar** reredos
**ornamental shoulder piece** epaulette
**ornamental sphere** orb
**ornamental staff as a symbol of royal power** sceptre
**ornamental stand** epergne
**ornamental stem** stave
**ornamental stone** onyx
**ornamental stonework in the upper part of a Gothic window** tracery
**ornamental thread loop** picot

**ornamental tuft** tassel
**ornamental wall border** dado
**ornamentation by designs** figuration
**ornament at the apex of a gable** finial
**ornament for ankle** anklet
**ornament for the arm** bracelet
**ornament for the middle of a dining table** epergne
**ornament inlaid with gold or silver** damascene
**ornament round neck** necklace
**ornament with needlework** embroider
**ornate** adorned, arabesque, busy, elaborate, elegant, embellished, fancy, flashy, florid, flowery, gaudy, grandiose, involved, lofty, pompous, rococo, showy, splendid
**ornate ceiling** plafond
**ornate show** flubdub
**ornis** avifauna
**ornithology** bird-watching
**orogeny** diastrophism, epeirogenesis, epeirogeny
**Orontes** Asi
**orotund** bombastic, booming, dignified, imposing, magniloquent, pompous, pretentious, resonant
**orphan** foundling, outcast, parentless, stray, waif
**Orphic** esoteric, mysterious, mystic, oracular
**orra** miscellaneous, occasional, odd, supernumerary, unmatched
**orraman** odd-jobman
**orrery** planetarium
**or's partner** either
**ort** fragments, leavings, left-over, odds and ends, refuse, scrap, waste
**or then** otherwise
**orthodox** approved, conventional, devout, official, ordinary, standard, traditional
**orthodox practice of medicine** allopathy
**orthodoxy** accordance, authenticity, belief, compliance, conformity, conservatism, conventionality, credo, creed, doctrinalness, faith, firmness, obduracy, obedience, purism, rightness, strictness, tradition(alism), truth
**orthomorphic** conformal
**orthopteran** locust
**orthopterous insect** mantis
**oryx** gemsbok
**os** bone, eskar, esker, mouth, opening, oral, orifice
**oscillate** alternate, debate, equivocate, falter, fluctuate, sway, swing, tergiversate, vacillate, vary, vibrate, waver
**oscillation of earth's axis** nutation

**oscitant** dull, negligent, sleepy, yawning
**oscitation** drowsiness, inattention, negligence, yawning
**osculate** adjoin, connect, embrace, greet, hug, kiss, meet, run, salute, skim, touch
**osier** willow
**osier plantation** holt
**Oslo's country** Norway
**Osmani title of respect** aga
**osmosis** dialysis
**osprey** ossifrage, pygarg, sea hawk
**osseous** bony
**ossify** callous, fossilise, harden, indurate, petrify, stiffen
**ostensible** apparent, assumed, avowed, clear, distinct, external, feigned, lucid, nominal, obvious, ostensive, outward, patent, plain, plausible, pretended, professed, prominent, reputed, seeming, specious
**ostensible meaning** purport
**ostensory** monstrance
**ostentation** boasting, display, éclat, flashiness, flourish, pomp, pretence, pretension, semblance, showiness
**ostentatious** boastful, conspicuous, extravagant, fantoosh (Sc), flamboyant, gaudy, loud, pompous, pretentious, showy, vain, vulgar
**ostentatious activity** fuss
**ostentatious charitable woman** lady bountiful
**ostentatious defiance** bravado
**ostentatious display** splash
**ostentatiously smart** ritzy
**ostentatious show** display
**ostler** groom, hostler, stableboy, stableman
**ostracise** banish, (de)bar, discard, disenfranchise, disregard, exclude, excommunicate, exile, expatriate, ignore, isolate, neglect, refuse, reject, repudiate, shun, spurn
**ostrich-like bird** emu, rhea
**otalgia** earache
**Othello's false friend** Iago
**Othello was one** Moor
**other** added, additional, additory, alia (L), alternate, alternative, ancient, annexed, auxiliary, contrary, different, distinct, earlier, else, extra, extrinsicality, former, further, ither (Sc), more, opposite, otra (Sp), previous, prior, separate, spare, supplementary, unidentical, unlike, variant
**other name** alias
**other option** alternative
**other side** observe

**other than** except
**other things being equal** ceteris paribus
**otherwise** alias, besides, contrarily, conversely, different(ly), else(where), excluding, inversely, or, without
**otherwise known as** alias
**otic** aural
**otic jewellery** earrings
**otic organ** ear
**otic ornament** earring
**otic pain** earache
**otic stopper** earplug
**otiose** functionless, futile, lazy, purposeless, sterile, superfluous, unemployed, unnecessary, unwanted, useless
**Ottawa is there** Canada
**otto** attar
**Ottoman** footstool, Osmanli, sofa, Turk(ish)
**Ottoman court** (Sublime) Porte
**Ottoman governor** bey, pacha, pasha
**Ottoman lord** aga
**Ottoman official** dey, pacha, pasha
**Ottoman title** ag(h)a
**ought** should
**ounce** feline, wild cat
**our planet** Earth
**our source of light and heat** sun
**oust** ban(ish), deport, discard, discharge, dislodge, dismiss, disown, displace, eject, evict, exile, expel, extrude, fire, overthrow, remove, repudiate, sack, supersede, supplant, suspend
**ouster** ejector, eviction, evictor
**ousting** defeat, discarding, discharging, discomfiture, dismissing, disowning, displacement, (down)fall, ejecting, end, expelling, overthrow, overthrowing, repudiating, rout, ruin, sacking, undoing
**oust tenant** evict
**out** absent, away, completely, concluded, dismiss, elapsed, empty, exhausted, from, fully, hence, issued, lacking, maximally, missing, openly, publicly, removed, unabashedly
**out-and-out** absolute, blatant, complete, confirmed, downright, exhaustive, express, going, hardened, outright, perfect, radical, sheer, thorough, total, umcompromising, unconditional, unequivocal, unmitigated, unmodified, unqualified, unrestricted, utter

**out at the elbow** beggarly, impoverished, needy, seedy, shabby, shoddy, tattered
**outbreak** display, epidemic, eruption, (out)burst, riot, upsurge
**outbreak of disease** pandemic
**outbreak of emotionalism** hysteria
**outbreak of lawlessness** riot
**outbuilding** shed
**outburst** access, agitation, anger, attack, bang, blast, blow-up, burst, cascade, clamour, clap, commotion, complaint, crack, crash, cry, detonation, discharge, disturbance, ejection, eruption, excitement, explosion, fit, flare-up, flash, flood, flow, frenzy, furore, fury, gush, howl, indignation, ire, jet, noise, outbreak, outcry, paroxysm, passion, spasm, storm, surge, tantrum, tirade
**outburst of anger** passion
**outburst of emotion** gust
**outburst of feeling** ebullition
**outcast** bergie, castaway, derelict, evictee, exile(d), expatriate, expelled, fugitive, hobo, itinerant, leper, nomad, nonperson, ousted, outlaw, pariah, refugee, rejectee, reprobate, ronin, rover, runaway, scavenger, stray, stroller, tramp, unperson, untouchable, vagabond, vagrant, waif, wanderer, wretch
**outcome** aftereffect, aftermath, conclusion, consequence, development, effect, end, harvest, issue, outgrowth, pay-off, product, repercussion, result, sequel, upshot, wake, yield
**outcry** clamour, complaint, cry, howl, noise, outburst, protest, scream, screech, uproar, yell
**outdated** passé
**outdo** beat, best, break, cap, conquer, cover, crown, defeat, dominate, dwarf, eclipse, exceed, excel, finish, outclass, outdistance, outgo, outrate, outreach, outrun, outstrip, outwalk, overcome, overrule, subdue, surpass, top, transcend, trump, upstage, vanquish
**outdo in sales** outsell
**outdoor** open-air
**outdoor entertainment** fête champetre (F)
**outdoor fry-up** barbecue, braai
**outdoor function with sale of goods** fête
**outdoor garment** cloak, coat, windbreaker, windcheater
**outdoor meal** braai, picnic
**outdoor pastime** sport

**outdoor sport** cricket, hockey, polo, rugby, soccer, tennis, volleyball
**outdoor staircase** perron
**outdoor theatre** drive-in
**outer** ecto-, exposed, exterior, external, extrinsic, foreign, fringe, objective, out(lying), outside, outward, peripheral, physical, remote, surface, utter
**outer Arabian garment** hai(c)k
**outer area of town** outskirts
**outer boundary** perimeter
**outer casing of aeroplane's engine** nacelle
**outer circle of wheel** felloe, felly
**outer coating of prawns** peel
**outer coat of pollen grain** extine
**outer covering** husk, skin
**outer covering of the eyeball** sclera
**outer covering of the skull** scalp
**outer covering of tooth** enamel
**outer door** oak
**outer edge** fringe, rim
**outer garment** brat, coat, frock, gown, himation, overslop, paletot, parka, robe, sweater, wrap
**outer grain husk** bran
**outer grey matter of brain** cortex
**outer layer** peel, rind, skin
**outer layer of egg** shell
**outer layer of fruit** rind
**outer layer of skin** epidermis
**outer limit** extremity
**outer line of fortification** bail
**outermost** distant, extreme, furthest, outmost, remote(st), ultimate, uttermost, yonder
**outermost edge of spine of shoulder blade** acromion
**outermost layer of pericarp** epicarp
**outer part of cricket or baseball pitch** outfield
**outer part of flower** perianth
**outer part of orange** rind
**outer piece sawn from log** slab
**outer ring of wheel** rim
**outer room** anteroom
**outer seed coating** testa
**outer seed cover** aril
**outer skin** epidermis
**outer skins of fruit** epicarp
**outer sleevelees garment worn by Arabs** aba
**outer space** azure, cerulean, firmament
**outer wall of castle** bailey
**outfit** accoutrements, attire, clothing, costume, coterie, ensemble, equip, kit, rig out, set-up, shebang, suit
**outfitter** tailor
**outflow** bleeding, discharge, drainage, ebb, efflux, emanation, issue, jet, leak(age), outgo, outstream, overflow, seepage, spurt
**out front** vanward
**outgoing** departing
**outgoing person** extrovert
**outhouse** backhouse, barn, chamber, coop, lean-to, (out)building, privy, shack, stable, toolhouse, (tool)shed
**outing** excursion, expedition, jaunt, picnic, spin, trip
**outlandish** alien, barbarous, eccentric, exotic, fantastic, outré, queer
**outlaw** bandit, brigand, buccaneer, criminal, deserter, desperado, felon, fugitive, highwayman, pirate, privateer, robber, rover, runaway, rustler, thief
**outlawed** hors de la loi (F)
**outlay** charge, cost, disbursement, expenditure, expense, investment, outgo(ings), payment, price, spending
**outlay of money** cost
**outlet** channel, duct, egress, exit, opening, orifice, vent
**outlet of river** mouth, outfall
**outline** cartoon, contour, draft, drawing, figure, frame, lay-out, plan, profile, résumé, rough, shape, silhouette, skeleton, sketch, summary, synopsis, trace
**outline of closed figure** perimeter
**outline of course of study** syllabus
**outline of future development** scenario
**outline of play** scenario
**outline of something as seen from the side** profile
**outline of the earth** map
**outline seen against the light** silhouette
**outlive** outlast, survive
**outlook** aspect, attitude, belvedere, disposition, future, humour, interpretation, lookout, mood, observatory, panorama, perspective, picture, prospect, scene, spectacle, standpoint, temper, view(point), vista
**out loud** audible, clear, distinct, hearable
**outlying district of city** suburb
**outlying settlement** outpost
**outlying trading station** fort
**outmoded** antique, dated, obsolete, passé, square, unusable
**out of** ex (L), ex-, from
**out of a clear blue sky** abruptly, rapidly, suddenly, unexpectedly
**out of action** hors de combat (F)
**out of a hundred** per cent
**out of bed** astir, up
**out of bounds** banned, barred, forbidden, impolite, improper, meat of pig, off-limits, prohibited, rude
**out of breath** agasp, breathless, panting, puffed, winded
**out of character** inappropriate, unfit, unsuitable
**out of commission** deactivated, disabled, inactive, injured, invalid
**out of condition** unfit
**out of control** chaotic, confused, haywire, topsy-turvy, ungovernable
**out-of-control fear** hysteria
**out of country** abroad
**out of danger** safe
**out of date** antiquated, archaic, corny, dated, démodé (F), discarded, elapsed, expired, extinct, invalid, lapsed, obsolete, old(-fashioned), outdated, passé
**out of debt** afloat
**out-of-doors** alfresco, outdoors, outside
**out of earshot** inaudible, unheard
**out of fashion** démodé (F), outmoded
**out of focus** blurred, fuzzy, indistinct, muzzy, shadowy, unclear
**out of goodness** ex gratia (L)
**out of hand** uncontrolled
**out of harmony** ajar, alien
**out of health** ill, sick
**out of hearing** aside
**out of joint** disjointed, dislocated, ill-timed, inappropriate, portentous, unjointed, unpromising
**out of keeping** incongruous
**out of line** discrepant, divergent, incongruous, unconformable
**out of mind** aside
**out of minority** major
**out of one's mind** crazy, demented, insane
**out of one's wits** mad
**out of order** amiss, broken(-down), burst, haywire, improper, inappropriate, indecorous, inoperative, kaput, nohow, unfit, unsuitable, wrong
**out of place** disarranged, disorderly, improper, inappropriate, inapt, incongruous, irrelevant, tactless, topsy-turvy, unbecoming, unfitting, unseemly, unsuitable, unsuited, unwarranted
**out of practice** rusty
**out of print** unavailable, unobtainable
**out of puff** panting
**out of question** inconceivable
**out of reach** beyond, inaccessible
**out of sight** imperceptible, invisible, remote, sightless, unseeable

**out of sorts** bilious, cheerless, crotchety, dejected, depressed, downcast, ill, melancholy, mopish, nohow, queasy, queer, seedy, weary
**out of step** erratic, inconsistent
**out of style** (out)dated, old
**out of the blue** abruptly, promptly, suddenly, unexpectedly
**out of the corner of one's eyes** askance
**out of the country** rural
**out of the depths** de profundis (L)
**out of the fight** disabled, hors de combat (F), incapacitated
**out of the ordinary** different, eccentric, exceptional, exclusive, extraordinary, few, quaint, rare, scarce, singular, strange, uncustomary, unfamiliar, unorthodox, unusual, weird
**out of the ordinary way of nature** abnormal, preternatural
**out of the question** absurd, forbidden, impossible, impracticable, inconceivable, ridiculous, unattainable, unthinkable
**out of the right way** astray
**out of the usual course** extraordinary
**out of the way** afield, aside, away, distant, inaccessible, isolated, remote, secluded
**out of the woods** clear, safe, secure
**out of this world** excellent, exceptional, fantastic, incredible, marvellous, outre, unbelievable, wonderful
**out-of-towner** immigrant
**out of turn** amiss
**out of view** invisible
**out of whole cloth** created, fabricated, feigned, fictitious, imaginary, invented, untrue
**out of work** disengaged, idle, inactive, jobless, unemployed, unoccupied
**outpace** outrun
**output** data, information, produce, production, yield
**outrage** abuse, affront, atrocity, barbarism, brutality, cruel, disgrace, enormity, evil(-doing), indignity, injure, insult, malefaction, maltreat, offend, scandal, shock, violation, violence
**outrageous** atrocious, egregious, excessive, exorbitant, extreme, horrifying, monstrous, outré, scandalous, shocking
**outrageous event** scandal
**outrageous thing** montrosity
**outré** bizarre, curious, eccentric, exaggerated, extraordinary, extravagant, fantastic, freakish, grotesque, improper, indecorous, ludicrous, odd, off-beat, outlandish, outrageous, outraging, peculiar, queer, strange, unconventional, unusual, weird
**outrun** beat, better, conquer, defeat, eclipse, elude, evade, exceed, excel, outdistance, outdo, outpace, overcome, overtake, pass, subdue, surmount, surpass, top, vanquish
**outset** beginning, commencement, inception, onset, start
**outshine** becloud, dwarf, eclipse, excel, outclass, outdazzle, override, overrule, overshadow, preponderate, surpass, upstage
**outside** covering, exterior, external, face, foreign, obscure, remote, surface
**outside a curriculum** extramural
**outside auditorium** amphitheatre
**outside bull's-eye** inner
**outside coating** crust
**outside covering** wrapper
**outside gallery** piazza, veranda(h)
**outside normal courses** extramural
**outside of** besides, excepting
**outsider** alien, visitor
**outside show** varnish
**outside the walls** extra muros (L)
**outside toilet** outhouse
**outside window shutters** persiennes
**outspoken** blunt, candid, direct, explicit, forth-right, frank, free(-spoken), open, plain-spoken, pointed, sharp, unchecked, unconstrained, uninhibited, unreserved, unreticent
**outstanding** bold, conspicuous, due, eminent, excellent, impressive, memorable, notable, prominent, salient, sensational, smashing, striking, super(b), superior, unforgettable, unmistakable, unsettled
**outstanding ability** prowess
**outstanding amount** arrear(s)
**outstanding bill** debt
**outstanding debt** arrear(s)
**outstanding endowment** talent
**outstanding feat** tour de force (F)
**outstanding in size** lulu, makulu
**outstanding item** pièce de résistance (F)
**outstandingly bad** egregious
**outstanding performer** star
**outstanding person** oner
**outward appearance** exterior, external, front, similitude, surface
**outward covering** garment
**outward movement of tide** ebb
**outward sea current** riptide
**outward show** appearance, focus, visage
**ouzo flavour** aniseed
**ouzo flavouring plant** anise
**ova** eggs
**oval** egg-shaped, ellipse, ellipsoidal, elliptical, oviform, ovoid
**oval acid fruit** lemon
**oval body** egg
**oval muff** egg-cosy
**oval-shaped figure** ellipse
**oval window** oxeye
**ovary of female fish filled with matured eggs** roe
**oven** furnace, kiln, microwave, oast
**oven-cooked** roasted
**oven for hops** oast
**oven for pottery** kiln
**ovenproof dish with a close-fitting lid** casserole
**over** above, accessory, across, additional, again, aloft, atop, besides, beyond, completed, concluded, dead, done, during, ended, epi-, exceeding, excess, excessive, extinct, extra, finished, kaput, leftover, more, o'er, odd, of, on, outstanding, overhead, past, repetition, residual, super-, superfluous, sur-, surplus, terminated, unused, upon
**overabundance** congestion, excess, glut, overflow, overfullness, overplenty, overspill, redundance, superabundance, surfeit, surplus
**overact** affect, counterfeit, emote, exaggerate, magnify, overdo, overplay, overstate, overstress, sham, stretch
**over again** afresh, anew
**overall** blanket, complete, comprehensive, dungaree, entire, extended, general, inclusive, panoramic, total, umbrella, unbroken, universal, whole
**overall material** denim
**over and above** addition(al), besides, extra, moreover, plus
**over and done with** past
**over and over** continually, endlessly, frequently, often, repeatedly
**over a period of five years** quinquennial, quinquennium
**over average height** tall
**overawe** awe, bully, compel, control, cow, daunt, disconcert, dismay, dominate, domineer, impress, intimidate, oppress, repress, restrain, threaten
**overbearing** arrogant, dictatorial, domineering, haughty, imperious, supercilious

**overbearing woman** termagant, virago
**overcast** clouded, cloudy, dismal, dreary, dull, hazy, murky, sombre, sunless
**overcoat** ulster
**overcome** attack, beat(en), capture, conquer, crush, defeat, deprive, discomfit, master, overpower, override, prevail, quell, rout, storm, subdue, surmount, triumph, victorious, win
**overcome by effort** conquer
**overcome by force of numbers** overwhelm
**overcome by greater ingenuity** outwit
**overcome by physical exhaustion** prostrate
**overcome problems** cope
**overcome with fear** fearful, panic-stricken, startled
**overcome with guilt or remorse** ashamed
**overcome with wonder** awestruck
**over-confident of oneself** cocksure
**overdo** exaggerate
**overdo it** overburden, overload, overwork
**overdrawing of bank account** overdraft
**overdue** arrear, behind(hand), belated, delayed, deserved, dilatory, just, late, outstanding, owed, owing, payable, slow, tardy, unpaid, unpunctual, unsettled
**overdue debt** arrear(s)
**overeat** bolt, cram, devour, feed, fill, glut, gobble, gorge, gulp, guzzle, surfeit, swallow, vreet, wolf
**over-elaborate treatment of gardens** Godwottery
**over-emotional play** melodrama
**over-enthusiastic** manic
**overfed feeling** satiety
**over fifty percent** majority
**overfill** cloy, compact, cram, crush, force, glut, gorge, jade, jam, nauseate, overcrowd, pack, press, ram, sate, satiate, shove, squeeze, stuff
**overflow** cover, deluge, drown, flood, inundate, inundation, soak, spill, submerge, surplus, swamp
**overflow of water** flood
**over-fluent** voluble
**over-full of facts** stodgy
**over-fussy** pedantic
**over garment** apron, overall
**overgrown** abandoned, awkward, blundering, bovine, clumsy, derelict, heavy, hulking, lumbering, neglected, ponderous, ungainly, unwieldy, weedy

**overhanging edge of roof** eaves
**overhanging shelter** canopy
**over-hasty** rash
**overhaul** examine, fix, inspect, overrun, recondition(ing), redo, renew, repair, restore, service
**overhead** above, aerial, aloft, atop, skyward, up(per), upward
**overhead projecting window** oriel
**overhead train** el
**overhead transport system** telferage, telpherage
**overhear** eavesdrop
**over-indulge** dandle, favour, glut, gorge, humour, over-imbibe, overdrink, pamper, spoil, surfeit
**overjoyed** cock-a-hoop, delighted, ecstatic, elated, enraptured, euphoric, excited, glad, gleeful, happy, joyful, jubilant, rapturous, rejoicing, thrilled, transported
**overland journey** trek
**overlay** cover, lap
**overlay painting** scumble
**overlay with fine wood** veneer
**overlay with gold** gild
**overlook** condone, disregard, excuse, forget, forgive, ignore, miss, neglect, omit, pass, slight, superintend
**overlook intentionally** pretermit
**overlying** blanketing
**over-meticulous** fussy, pedantic
**over-particular** fussy
**overpass** flyover
**over period of five years** quinquennial
**overpopulated** crowded
**overpower** conquer, defeat, overcome, overwhelm, rout, subdue, vanquish
**overpowering** compelling, forceful, irresistible, overwhelming, strong, unbearable
**overpower with light** dazzle
**overpower with sound** deafen
**over-praise** adulate, flatter
**over-precise** pedantic
**over-prolonged** long-drawn-out
**over-quick** hasty
**over-refine** alembicate
**over-refined** alembicated
**over-refinement** effeteness
**over-refinement in art** preciosity
**overrule** disallow, influence, nullify, repeal, repudiate, rescind
**overrun** assail, attack, besiege, cover, devastate, encroach, exceed, impinge, infest, invade, loot, overspread, pillage, raid, ravage, sack, saturate, swarm
**overseas** abroad
**overseas telegram** cable
**oversee** superintend, supervise

**overseer** boss, chief, commander, foreman, foreperson, headman, headperson, manager, monitor, overlooker, proctor, protector, superintendent, supervisor, taskmaster, teacher
**overseer at parties** chaperon
**over-sensitive** neurotic
**over-sentimental** maudlin, mawkish, mushy
**overshadow** bedim, blacken, conspicuous, darken, dim, dominate, eclipse, exceed, obscure, outshine, overcloud, predominate, screen, shade, surpass, veil
**overshoe** galosh
**oversight** blunder, care, charge, control, erratum, fault, lapse, management, mistake, slip, superintendence
**overspread with a tint** suffuse
**overstate** amplify, exaggerate, expand, magnify, overdo, overstress
**overstatement** exaggeration
**overstepping limits of moderation** excess
**overt** apparent, clear(-cut), conspicuous, definite, evident, explicit, exposed, manifest, obvious, open, plain, public, showing, unconcealed, unhidden, unmistakable, unobscured, visible
**overtake** catch, chase, engulf, exaggerate, outdo, outstrip, overhaul, overwhelm, pass, reach, strike, surprise
**overtaken by night** benighted
**overtaken by time** belated
**over that period** then
**over the moon** happy
**over there** yonder
**over the top** excessive, immoderate, inordinate
**overthrow** capsize, conquer, defeat, destroy, dethrone, disenact, evert, fall, oust, overcome, overpower, overset, overturn, overwhelm, raze, reverse, ruin, subjugate, subvert, uncrown, unseat, upset, usurp, vanquish
**overtone** association, connotation, feeling, flavour, hint, implication, inference, innuendo, intimation, meaning, nuance, presumption, sense, significance, signification, suggestion, undercurrent
**overture** advance, approach, introduction, invitation, offer, opening, prelude, proposal, signal, tender
**overturn** abolish, annul, capsize, conquer, countermand, depose,

**destroy, founder, invalidate,
overbalance, overthrow, quash,
repeal, rescind, reverse, roll, spill,
topple, tumble, unseat, upend,
upset, upturn**
**over-waistcoat of knitted wool**
cardigan
**overweight** chubby, corpulent,
distorted, fat(ness), fleshy,
imbalance, inequality, obese,
obesity, offset, outsize, overbalance,
overheaviness, plumpness,
preponderance, rotundity, stout
**overweight condition** obesity
**overwhelm** awe, bury, confuse, cover,
crush, defeat, deluge, destroy,
drown, engulf, flood, inundate,
overburden, overload, overpower,
overrun, stagger, stun, stupefy,
subdue, submerge, swamp
**overwhelming defeat** rout
**overwhelming feeling of joy** ecstasy
**overwhelm with astonishment**
flabbergast
**overwhelm with kisses** smother
**overwhelm with wonder** amaze
**ovi-** egg, ovum
**ovine** sheep-like
**ovipositor** terebra
**ovisac** ootheca
**ovoid** egg-shaped, ellipsoid, elliptical,
obovate, oval, ovate, oviform, ovular
**ovule** egg, germ, ovum, seed

**ovum** egg, embryo, germ, grain,
kernel, seed, sperm, spore
**owed** arrear, mature, outstanding,
(over)due, owing, payable, unpaid,
unsettled
**owing** ascribable, debited,
encumbered, imputable, indebted,
liable, obliged, outstanding,
overdrawn, (over)due, owed,
payable, unpaid, unsettled
**owing an account** debit
**owing money to** indebted
**owing obedience** subject
**owing obligation** indebted
**owing to** because
**owing to others** debts
**owl's call** hoot
**own** accept, acknowledge, admit,
agree, ain (Sc), allow, concede,
confess, have, hold, maintain,
possess, preserve, retain, use
**owned by you** your(s)
**owned up** confessed
**owner** holder, (land)lord, master,
mistress, possessor, proprietor
**ownerless mongrel of the East**
pi(e)-dog, pye-dog
**owner of country estate** laird (Sc)
**owner of dog** master
**owner of factory** entrepreneur,
manufacturer
**owner of farm** farmer
**owner of inn in Italy** padrone

**owner of land bordering a river**
riparian
**owner's mark on sheep** earmark
**owning** having
**owning allegiance** subject
**own** has
**own the truth of** admit
**own up** acknowledge, admit, avow,
confess, expose, profess, reveal
**Oxbridge teacher** don
**oxer** guard-fence, guardrail, ox-fence
**ox-eye** daisy
**ox fat** suet
**ox-fence** guardrail, oxer
**Oxford college** Balliol, Magdalen, Oriel
**oxidation** corrosion, rust
**oxide of copper** cuprite
**oxidise** discolour, oxygenate, rust
**oxlike antelope** eland, gnu
**oxlike quadruped** bison, yak
**ox of Celebes** anoa, goa
**ox of Tibet** yak
**oxpecker** tick-bird
**ox stomach as food** tripe
**oxter** armpit, axilla, hug
**oxygenate** aerate, oxidise
**oxygen compound** oxide
**oxygen transporter in blood**
haemoglobin
**oyster bed** layer
**oyster gem** pearl
**oyster reared in artificial bed** native
**oyster spawn** spat

# P

**pa** dad
**Paarl feature** Berg River
**pabulum** aliment(ation), bite, bread,
cereal, edibles, food(stuffs), fuel,
groceries, meals, meat, menu, mess,
nourishment, nutriment, nutrition,
prog, rations, refection, regimen,
snack, subsistence, support,
sustenance, victuals
**pace** amble, foot, gait, gallop, go, jog,
measure, motion, plod,
progress(ion), quickness, rate, rove,
run, space, speed, step, stride,
synchronise, tempo, time, travel,
traverse, tread, trot, trudge, velocity,
walk
**pace hastily** stride
**pacemaker** leader
**pace restlessly** prowl

**pachyderm** elephant, hippo(potamus),
rhino(ceros)
**pacific** appeasing, calm, clement,
conciliatory, easy, good-natured,
halcyon, irenic, lenient, merciful,
motionless, noncombative,
nonviolent, peace-loving, peaceable,
peaceful, placating, placid,
propitiable, quiet, restful, serene,
tolerant, tranquil, unbellicose,
unruffled
**Pacific aroid** taro
**pacificate** pacify
**pacification** appeasement, calming,
comfort, compromise, conciliation,
consolation, consoling,
disarmament, mediation,
moderation, mollification, pacifying,
pact, peacefulness, reconcilement,
reconciliation, relieving, rest,
soothing, subdual, treaty
**pacificator** appeaser
**Pacific country of many islands** Fiji
**Pacific discoverer** Balboa
**Pacific island** Ara, Atoll, Bali, Ducie,
Ellice, Fiji, Guam, Komodo, Lau,
Leyte, Mariana, Munga, Nauru,
Niue, Okinawa, Rapa, Saipan,
Samoa, Sulu, Tahiti, Tasmania,
Truk, Upola, Uvea, Wake, Yap
**Pacific island cloth** tapa
**Pacific islander** Fijian, Samoan,
Tahitian
**Pacific island group** Fiji, Pelew,
Samoa
**Pacific peninsula** Baja, Korea
**Pacific pine** hala, ie, matsu
**Pacific republic** Nauru

**Pacific root vegetable** taro
**Pacific salmon** chum, coho, sockeye
**Pacific shrub** salal
**Pacific tree** (Chinese) eddo, dasheen, elephant's ear, taro
**pacifier** appeaser, bribe, comforter, dummy, inducement, lure, mollifier, nipple, placater, reward, sop, sweetener
**pacifism** nonviolence, pacificism, passive, resistance
**pacifist** dove, pacificist, peace lover, peacemonger
**pacify** adjust, allay, alleviate, appease, arbitrate, assuage, calm, comfort, compose, conciliate, dulcify, ease, gap, hush, intervene, lull, mollify, palliate, placate, propitiate, quiet(en), relieve, smooth, soften, soothe, tranquillise
**pack** bundle, burden, compress, cram, gang, haversack, knapsack, load, package, parcel, set, stow
**package** amalgamation, bale, box, bundle, carton, case, combine, container, entity, pack(et), parcel, receptacle, unit
**pack animal** ass, camel, donkey, llama
**pack cargo** stow
**pack donkey** burro
**pack down tightly** tamp
**packed** brimful, chock-a-block, (chock-)full, overflowing
**packet** bag, carton, case, container, pack(age), parcel, wrapper, wrapping
**pack firmly** tamp
**pack goods away** stow
**pack in** attract, cram, draw, stop
**packing box** crate
**packing cloth** soutage
**packing container** crate
**packing material** gasket
**packing ring** gasket
**pack in tightly** cram, wedge
**pack into a small space** compact
**pack neatly** stow
**pack of wild dogs** gang
**pack up** stall, stop, store
**pact** agreement, alliance, arrangement, assurance, bargain, bond, commitment, compact, concord, covenant, deal, league, oath, pledge, promise, protocol, treaty, troth, truce, understanding, undertaking, vow, word
**pad** block, buffer, cushion, fill, foot(print), jotter, notepad, pack, pillow, protect(ion), stuff(ing), wad, walk, writing pad
**padded coverlet** quilt
**padded garment** truss
**padded seat** sofa
**padded waterproof jacket** anorak
**padding** amplifying, augmenting, bombast, eking, filling, inflating, lengthening, protracting, shaping, stretching, verbosity, waffle, wordiness
**padding for a coat** wad
**paddle** beat, dabble, drive, lever, oar, ply, propel, pull, row, scull, shuffle, splash, steer, whip
**paddling** canoeing, dabbling, propelling, pulling, rowing, sculling, slopping, wading
**paddock** camp, corral, field
**Paddy** Irish(man)
**paddy** fit, rage, rice-field, temper
**paddy crop** rice
**pad of surgical wool** swab
**pad out** amplify, augment, elaborate, expand, inflate, stretch
**padre** chaplain, cleric, curate, divine, dominee, father, minister, parson, pastor, priest, rabbi, rector, reverend, vicar
**paedophile** nonce
**pagan** agnostic, antichrist, atheist, disbeliever, dominee, doubter, fetishist, gentile, heathen, hedonist, heliolater, iconoclastic, idolater, idolatrous, infidel, irreligionist, irreligious, nihilistic, pantheist, paynim, unbeliever
**pagan god** idol
**paganism** agnosticism, atheism, disbelief, godlessness, heathenism, heliolatry, iconolatry, idolatry, irreligion, nonbelief, scepticism, unbelief, worldliness
**pagan prophetess** sibyl
**pagan symbol** idol
**page** announce, attendant, bellboy, bid, call, chapter, episode, epoch, era, event, flyleaf, folio, footboy, footman, incident, leaf, pageboy, paginate, period, phase, point, porter, seek, servant, sheet, side, squire, stage, summon, time, typescript, verso
**pageant** display, exhibition, extravaganza, float, gala, panorama, pantomime, parade, presentation, procession, production, review, ritual, scene, show, spectacle, tableau
**pageantry** ceremony, display, drama, extravagance, flourish, glamour, glitter, glory, grandeur, greatness, magnificence, majesty, melodrama, nobility, parade, pomp, show, spectacle, splendour, state, sublimity, theatricality, triumph
**pageboy in a hotel** attendant, bellboy, footboy
**page edge** margin
**page in account book** folio
**page number** folio
**paginate** foliate
**paging** calling, leafing, seeking, summoning
**paging device** bleeper
**pagoda top** tee
**pagoda tree** Sophora
**paid athlete** pro(fessional)
**paid driver of private vehicle** chauffeur
**paid mourner** weeper
**paid out money** spent
**paid performer** pro(fessional)
**paid sportsman** pro(fessional)
**paid worker** earner
**paigle** cowslip
**pail** bail, basin, bucket, can, container, holder, pitcher, pot, receptacle, tub, vessel
**paillette** spangle
**pain** ache, afflict, agony, displease, disquiet, distress, efforts, grieve, harm, hurt, irritate, misery, pang, soreness, suffering, throe, torment, torture, trouble, twinge, worry
**pained bark** yelp
**pained sigh** moan
**pain from running** stitch
**painful** aching, achy, arduous, difficult, distressful, distressing, excruciating, hurtful, insufferable, laborious, pestering, sore, stinging, throbbing, tormenting, troublesome, unacceptable, unpleasant, vexing, worrying
**painful exertion** travail
**painful inflammation of finger or toe** whitlow
**painful inflammation of joints or muscles** arthritis, rheumatism
**painful joints** arthritis
**painful labour** travail
**painful obstruction of ileum** ileus
**painful sensation caused by want of food** hunger
**painful sigh** groan
**painful spot** sore
**painful stomach ailment** gastro-enteritis
**painful to touch** sore
**painful urination** dysuria
**painful wound** sore
**pain in back** notalgia
**pain in chest** angina
**pain in head** encephalalgia, headache
**pain in hip** coxalgia
**pain in inner ear** earache
**pain in kidney** nephralgia

**pain in lower back** lumbago
**pain in muscle** myalgia
**pain in neck** crick
**pain in nerves** neuralgia
**pain in or near the heart** cardialgia
**pain in sciatic nerve** sciatica
**pain in side of body** stitch
**pain in stomach** gastralgia
**pain intensity unit** dol
**pain interjection** ouch, ow
**painkiller** anaesthetic, analgesic, anodyne, aspirin, assuasive, balm, codeine, barbiturate, cocaine, depressant, drug, hypnotic, liniment, lotion, morphine, narcotic, ointment, opiate, opium, paracetomol, paregoric, remedy, salve, sedative, soporific
**painless** easy, effortless, fast, pain-free, quick, simple, trouble-free, undemanding
**painless death** euthanasia
**pain limited to one side of the body** hemialgia
**pain of mind** grief, sorrow
**pain relayer** nerve
**pain restricted to particular spot** topalgia
**pains** aches, ails, bother, care, diligence, effort, industry, labour, trouble
**painstaking** assiduous, careful, conscientious, correctly, dedicated, devoted, diligent(ly), earnest(ly), exactly, hardworking, industrious, intensely, meticulous, persevering, persistently, precisely, punctilious, scrupulous(ly), sedulous, strenuous(ly), thorough(ly)
**paint** adorn, coat(ing), colourant, delineate, depict, describe, distemper, draw, dye, embellish, enamel, figure, lacquer, limn, pigment, portray, represent, rouge, sketch, stain, tincture, tint, varnish, whitewash, woad
**pain tablet** aspirin
**paint again** repaint
**paint badly** daub
**paint car again** respray
**paint coarsely** daub
**painted or carved ornament in Arabian design** arabesque
**painter** artist, cable, colourist, delineator, dilettante, drawer, illustrator, monochromist, picturist, portrayer, rope, sketcher
**painter of animal subjects** animalier
**painter of miniatures** miniaturist
**painter of people** portraitist
**painter's medium** acrylic, gouache, oil, tempera, watercolour

**painter's stand** easel
**paint in dots** stipple
**painting** canvas, chromo, fresco, illustration, landscape, miniature, mural, oil (painting), picture, portrait, representation, scene, still-life, watercolour
**painting, especially altarpiece of two panels** diptych
**paint in glowing terms** doctor, falsify
**painting made using transparent watercolours** aquarelle
**painting medium** acrylic, gouache, oil, tempera, watercolour
**painting of Christ** icon
**painting of circular form** tondo
**painting on dry plaster on a wall or ceiling** secco
**painting on fresh plaster on a wall or ceiling** fresco
**painting on wall or ceiling** fresco, mural, secco
**paintings** art
**painting that portrays rural life** pastoral
**paint in watercolour** limn
**paint pigment** cobalt, umber
**paint solvent** acetone
**paint the town red** celebrate, revel
**paint thickly** impaste, impasto
**paint thinner** acetone
**paint with gold** gilding
**paint with short strokes** stipple
**pair** analogue, brace, bracket, combination, combine, couple, diad, doublet, duad, duet, duo, dyad, engaged, group, harness, join, link, marry, match, mate, set, span, splice, team, twin(s), two(some), unite, wed, yoke, zygo-
**pair again** rematch
**paired** matching, twinned, wed(ded), yoke
**pair of artistes** duo
**pair of earphones** headset
**pair off** associate, consort, co-operate, espouse, fraternise, intermarry, partner
**pair of forceps** pincette
**pair of horses** team
**pair of oxen** yoke
**pair of performers** duet, duo
**pair of scales** balance
**pair of small drums played with hands** tabla
**pair of tweezers** pincette
**pair of units treated as one** dyad
**Pakistani language** Baluchi, Bengali, Punjabi, Putshu, Sindhi, Urdu
**Pakistani province** Baluchistan, Punjab, Sind

**pal** bra, broer, buddy, chum, companion, crony, friend, mate
**palace** basilica, castle, chateau, château, court, dome, hall, manor, mansion, palais (F), palazzo (I), residence, schloss, seat, villa
**palace in Grenada** Alhambra
**palace in Paris** Elysée, Louvre, Tuileries, Versailles
**palace of sultan** seraglio
**palaeontologist's find** fossil
**palatable** agreeable, ambrosial, appetising, delectable, delicious, delightful, gourmet, gustatory, luscious, mouth-watering, pungent, sapid, satisfying, savoury, spicy, sweet, tasty, toothsome
**palate** appetite, enjoyment, gusto, liking, relish, taste, zest
**palatial** elegant, fancy, grand, luxurious, magnificent, majestic, massive, ostentatious, splendid, stately, sumptuous, swanky
**palatial door** portal
**palaver** audience, cajolery, chatter, colloquy, confer(ence), consultation, converse, discussion, gossip, interview, meeting, negotiate, nonsense, parley, talk
**pale** anaemic, ashen, ashy, blanch, bleached, boundary, bounds, chalky, colourless, dim, dull, enclosure, fade(d), faint, feeble, fence, light, lily-livered, limits, obscure, pallid, pasty, picket, poor, sallow, thin, wan, wash-out, weak, white(n), whitish
**pale and drawn** wan
**pale and sickly looking** anaemic
**pale as a ghost** numb, panic-stricken
**pale beer** Pils(e)ner
**pale brown** beige, ecru, fallow
**pale colour** pastel
**pale-coloured** light
**pale green** Nile
**pale green colour** celadon
**pale greyish colour** ashy
**pale greyish-yellow colour** nankeen, nankin
**pale in colour** anaemic
**pale mauve** lilac
**paleness** dimness, faintness, feebleness, inadequateness, lightness, poorness, sallowness, thinness, weakness
**paleontologist's find** fossil
**pale pinkish-violet** lilac
**pale purple** lavender, lilac, mauve
**pale red in colour** pink
**pale red wine** rosé
**pale shade** pastel
**Palestinian city** Haifa, Samaria

**Palestinian mountain** Carmel, Gilead, Horeb
**Palestinian plain** Sharon
**pale yellow** flaxen, lemon
**pale yellowish-brown** ecru
**palfrey** horse
**palindromic word** boob, ere, eve, eye, kayak, madam, noon, pop, refer, tat
**palisade** barricade, barrier, bluff, bulwark, corral, defence, enclose, enclosure, fence, fortification, fortify, guard, hedge, impound, kraal, paddock, paling, pen, pound, railings, rampart, shield, stockade, wall, yard
**pall** annoy, casket, cerements, check, cloud, cloy, coffin, covering, damper, dismay, gloom, glut, gravity, irk, jade, mantle, melancholy, overdo, overfeed, sarcophagus, sate, satiate, shadow, shroud, sicken, sombreness, tire, veil, weary
**palliasse** mattress, pallet
**palliate** abate, allay, alleviate, appease, assuage, calm, comfort, ease, lessen, mitigate, moderate, modify, pacify, quiet, relax, relieve, remit, reprieve, soothe, subdue
**palliation** abatement, alleviation, apology, appeasement, comfort, diminution, ease, excuse, exoneration, extenuation, justification, qualifying, reduction, relief, relieving, remedy, respite, solace, soothing, varnish, veneer, vindication
**palliative** alleviate, calmative, calming, mitigatory, mollifying, sedative, soothing
**pallid** anaemic, ashen, ashy, average, boring, cadaverous, colourless, drained, dull, insipid, lifeless, livid, pale, pasty(-faced), sallow, sapless, sickly, spiritless, sterile, tame, tedious, tired, uninspired, vapid, wan, waxen, waxy, whitish
**pallor** anaemia, ashenness, bloodlessness, ghastliness, ghostliness, lividness, paleness, sickliness, wanness
**pally** friendly
**palm** bays, crown, fame, glory, hand, honour, laurels, merit, mitt, paw, plant, prize, success, triumph, trophy, victory
**palm civet** palm-cat, paradoxure
**palm cockatoo** ara(ra)
**palm fibre** raffia
**palm food** coco(nut), date, nut, sago
**palmistry** augury, chiromancy, divination, foretelling, fortunetelling, prediction, prognostication, prophecy, vaticination
**palm juice** sura
**palm leaf** frond, ola, ole
**palmlike tree** burrawang, cycad
**palm off** impose, offload, thrust, unload
**palm off as genuine** foist
**palm of hand** thenar, volar
**palm sap** toddy
**palm stems used in basketwork** rattan
**palm tree** nipa, ti
**palm tree fibre** raffia, raphia
**palmy** balmy, enchanting, enjoyable, fabulous, flourishing, halcyon, marvellous, peaceful, promising, prosperous, serene, sunny, thriving, victorious
**palp** feel, handle, palpate
**palpable** apparent, appreciable, blatant, clear, concrete, conspicuous, corporeal, distinct, evident, exposed, manifest, material, obvious, open, perceptible, plain, professed, real, solid, substantial, tactile, tangible, touchable, unmistakable, unveiled, visible
**palpitate** beat, drum, flutter, patter, pound, pulsate, pulse, quake, quiver, shake, shiver, throb, thump, tremble, twitter, vibrate
**palpitating** beating, drumming, fluttering, pulsating, pulsing, shivering, tremour, tumult, turbulency
**palpus** antenna, feeler, tentacle
**palsied** arthritic, crippled, disabled, helpless, immobile, incapacitated, lame, numb, paralysed, paralytic, rheumatic, shivering, trembling
**palsy** immobility, paralysis, Parkinsonism
**palsy sufferer** spastic
**paltry** base, beggarly, derisory, despicable, inconsiderable, insignificant, low, meagre, mean, measly, minor, miserable, petty, pitiful, poor, puny, slight, small, sorry, trifling, trivial, unimportant, worthless, wretched
**paludal** malarial
**pampas grass** paspalum
**pamper** baby, caress, cocker, coddle, cosher, cosset, dandle, favour, fondle, gratify, humour, mother, (over-)indulge, pet, spoil
**pamphlet** booklet, brochure, circular, essay, folder, leaflet, monograph, program(me), tract
**pan** censure, circle, container, criticise, flay, follow, move, pot, saucepan, scan, skillet, sweep, swing, track, turn, vessel, wok
**panacea** bezoar, catholicon, cure(-all), elixir, ginseng, heal-all, nepenthe, nostrum, remedy, solace
**panache** brilliance, chic, crest, dash, decoration, distinction, éclat, élan, elegance, enthusiasm, feathers, flair, flamboyance, flourish, grandness, gusto, magnificence, nobility, ornament, ostentation, plume, smartness, spirit, style, swagger, taste, tuft, verve, vigour, zest
**Panama seaport** Colon
**panatella** cigar
**pancake** crêpe, flapjack, omelet(te)
**pancake frying-pan** griddle
**pancreatic cells** islets of Langerhans
**panda** bear(cat), wah
**Pandects of Justinian** Digest
**pandemonium** anarchy, bedlam, brawl, cacophony, chaos, commotion, confusion, disorder, fracas, frenzy, fury, rage, riot, ruckus, rumpus, tumult, turbulence, turmoil, uproar
**pander** bawd, exploiter, go-between, leech, madam, pimp, procurer, provider, runner, scavenger, scrounger, smuggler, solicitor, supplier, sycophant, toady
**pander to** attend, gratify, humour, indulge, kneel, kowtow, please, satisfy, slither, toady
**panegyric** acclaim, accolade, announcement, applause, approval, citation, credit, discourse, eulogium, eulogy, extolment, flattery, homage, hurrah, oration, paean, praise, recognition, recommendation, reverence, testimonial, tribute
**panelbeater** hammerer
**panel for switches** console
**panel member** juror, panellist
**panel of judges** jury
**panel of magistrates** bench
**pang** ache, agony, anguish, discomfort, distress, pain, stab, sting, throb, throe, twinge
**pangs of childbirth** travail
**pangs of death** agony
**panic** agitation, alarm, consternation, dismay, fear, flap, fright(en), horror, hysteria, overact, scare, terrify, terror(ise)
**panicmonger** alarmist
**panic-stricken** aghast, alarmed, appalled, fearful, frenzied, frightened, goose-pimply, horrified, horror-stricken, hysterical, nervous, numb, overwhelmed, panic-struck, petrified, stunned, stupefied, terrified, terror-stricken
**panic-stricken rush** stampede

**pan of balance** scale
**panoply** adornment, array, attire, covering, decoration, display, dress, garb, ornamentation, parade, regalia, show
**panorama** cyclorama, landscape, overview, perspective, prospect, range, scene(ry), sight, spectacle, survey, tableau, view, vision, vista
**panoramic** bird's-eye, comprehensive, extensive, far-reaching, general, inclusive, overall, scenic, sweeping, universal, wide(spread)
**panoramic view** vista
**pan out** happen, result, yield
**pant** blow, desire, gasp, long, pech (Sc), puff, pulsate, thirst, throb, yearn
**pant for breath** gasp
**pan to burn incense** censer, thuribe
**pantoffle** panto(u)fle, slipper
**pantomime clown** pierrot
**pantry** ambry, buttery, cuddy, cupboard, larder, spence, storage
**pantry item** bottle, can, jar
**pants** briefs, drawers, knickers, panties, shorts, slacks, trousers, trunks, underpants, undershorts, undies, Y-fronts
**papal ambassador** legate, nuncio
**papal cape** orale
**papal court** curia
**papal decree deciding a point of canon law** decretal
**papal edict** bull
**papal envoy** nuncio
**papal letter** breve, brief, bull, encyclical, tome
**papal messenger** nuncio
**papal palace** Vatican
**papal representative** legate
**papal rescript** mandate
**papal system** papacy
**papal veil** orale
**papaya** papino, pa(w)paw
**paper** bond, certificate, document, essay, journal, manuscript, newspaper, periodical, report, tissue
**paper bag** sack
**paper chief** editor
**paper discs** confetti
**paper drying frame** tribble
**paper fastener** clip, staple
**paper fastening machine** stapler
**paper-folding art** origami
**paper for printing newspapers on** newsprint
**paper-glazing machine** calender
**paper hanky** tissue
**paper holder** clip, spike
**paper-making grass** esparto
**paper measure** ream, quire
**paper missile** pellet

**paper money** cheque, draft, note
**paper napkin** serviette
**paper quantity** bundle, quire, ream
**paper's exclusive story** scoop
**paper size** demy, din, folio, foolscap, octavo, quarto
**paper's official comment** editorial
**paper-thin pastry with chopped nuts and honey** baclava, baklava
**paper thrown at weddings** confetti
**paper vendor** newsboy
**paper web** roll
**papilionaceous plant** bean
**paprika** capsicum
**par** average, balance, equality, evenness, identity, normal, parity, stability, standard, usual
**parable** adage, allegory, aphorism, apologue, axiom, chronicle, cliché, dictum, exemplum, fable, history, homily, legend, lesson, maxim, myth, narrative, platitude, proverb, saying, sermon, story, tale, truism
**parachute soldier** aeronaut, parachutist, paratrooper
**parachute sport** skydiving
**parachute straps** harness
**parachutist** skydiver
**paraclete** advocate, mediator
**parade** air, array, autocade, blazon, brandish, ceremony, column, cortege, display, exhibit, fete, file, flaunt, grandeur, march, ostentation, pageant(ry), pomp, process(ion), promenade, review, show, spectacle, splash, strut, succession, swagger, train, troop, vaunt(ing)
**parade of horsemen** cavalcade
**parade sight** float
**parade vehicle** bandwagon, float
**paradigm** archetype, criterion, design, epitome, example, exemplar, gauge, ideal, model, mould, original, paragon, pattern, perfection, prototype, standard, type
**Paradise** Eden
*Paradise Lost* **poet** Milton
**paradise on earth** Shangri-la
**paradoxical** antagonistic, antithetical, conflicting, contradictory, contrary, incompatible, incongruous, inconsistent, ironic(al), opposite
**paraffin** alkane, kerosene, kero(sine)
**paragon** archetype, champion, criterion, epitome, exemplar, ideal, jewel, lovely, masterpiece, model, paradigm, pattern, prototype, quintessence, standard, ultimate
**paragraph in a contract** clause
**parallel** analogous, correspondent, corresponding, counterpart,

like(ness), match, resembling, similar(ity)
**parallel grooves** stria
**parallel to** alongside
**paralyse** anaesthetic, arrest, benumb, cripple, debilitate, disable, freeze, halt, immobilise, incapacitate, lame, numb, petrify, stun, stupefy, transfix
**paralysed** arrested, benumbed, crippled, disabled, hemiplegic, incapacitated, lamed, numb, paraplegic, quadriplegic, tetraplegic
**paralysing disease** polio
**paralysing poison extracted from wourali root** curare, curari
**paralysis** arrest, breakdown, halt, immobility, palsy, paraplegia, quadriplegia, shutdown, stagnation, standstill, stoppage, torpor
**paralysis limited to a single part** monoplegia
**paralysis of all four limbs** quadriplegia, tetraplegia
**paralysis of arms and legs** quadriplegia
**paralysis of one side of the body** hemiplegia
**paralysis of the lower part of the body** paraplegia
**paralytic** canned, crippled, disabled, drunk, immobile, immobilised, incapacitated, inebriated, intoxicated, lame, numb, palsied, paralysed, quadriplegic
**parameter** boundary, criterion, framework, guideline, indication, limit(ation), restriction, specification, variable
**paramount** capital, cardinal, champion, chief, dominant, eminent, first, foremost, greatest, highest, main, matchless, pre-eminent, primary, prime, principal, significant, sovereign, superior, superlative, supreme, top(most), unequalled, unsurpassed
**paranoia** delusions, dementia, derangement, insanity, lunacy, madness, (megalo)mania, monomania, obsession, psychosis
**paranoid** crazy, demented, deranged, distracted, insane, lunatic(al), mad(man), possessed, unbalanced
**parapet** barricade, bastion, breastwork, bulwark, buttress, embankment, fortification, palisade, rampart
**paraphernalia** accessories, accoutrements, apparatus, appliances, appointments, baggage, belongings, effects, equipage, equipment, fixture, gear, implements, instruments, material,

possessions, properties, rigging, tackle, turnout
**paraphrase** explain, quotation, recapitulate, recapitulation, rendering, rephrase, restate(ment), reword(ing), summary, translate, translation, version
**parasite** appendage, beggar, bloodsucker, bur, cestode, dependant, drone, epizoon, flatterer, flea, flunk(e)y, fungus, hanger-on, helminth, idler, leech, louse, mite, sponge, sucker, sycophant, tick, toady
**parasite of man** roundworm, tapeworm
**parasitic** bloodsucking, cadging, leechlike, sponging
**parasitic insect** bug, flea, ked, louse, tick
**parasitic person** sycophant
**parasitic plant** mistletoe
**parasitic worm** bot, fluke, helminth
**parasol** sunshade, umbrella
**paratrooper** aeronaut, parachutist
**parcel** apportion, bundle, distribute, divide, group, lot, pack, package, packet, plot, quantity, tract
**parcel out** allocate, allot, apportion, disperse, distribute, divide
**parcener** co-heir
**parch** dehydrate, desiccate, dry, evaporate, roast, sear, shrink, shrivel, toast, wilt, wither
**parched** adust, arid, barren, browned, dehydrated, desiccated, dry, evaporated, exsiccated, juiceless, roasted, sapless, sear, sere, shrivelled, sterile, thirsty, toasted, unwatered, waterless, wilted, withered
**parched by sun** torrid
**parchment** charter, constitution, contract, deed, degree, manuscript, palimpsest, paper, papyrus, scroll, sheepskin, stationery, title, vellum
**parch with heat** burn, scorch
**pardon** absolution, absolve, acquit(tal), allowance, amnesty, clear, condone, discharge, exculpate, excuse, exonerate, forgive(ness), free, grace, indulgence, overlook, release, remission, remit, reprieve, spare, venia (L)
**pardonable** allowable, condonable, defensible, endurable, exculpable, excusable, forgivable, harmless, justifiable, minor, nugatory, remittable, reprievable, supportable, tolerable, trivial, unblamable, understandable, unimportant, venial
**pare** clip, cut, diminish, lessen, peel, reduce, shave, trim, whittle

**parent** ancestor, dam, father, genitor, guardian, mater, mother, pater, sire
**parentage** ancestry, birth, descent, extraction, lineage, origin, pedigree
**parentless** orphan
**parentless child** orphan, waif
**parent's brother** uncle
**parent's sister** aunt
**parer** peeler
**pare with a knife** whittle
**par for the course** average, commonplace, mediocre, ordinary, predictable, standard, typical, usual
**pariah** beggar, bergie, castaway, exile, fugitive, hobo, leper, outcast, outlaw, refugee, rejectee, rover, runaway, tramp, untouchable, vagabond, vagrant, wretch
**Paris airport** Orly
**Paris designer** Chanel, Dior, St Laurent, Worth
**parish** brethren, church(goers), community, congregation, district, flock, fold, parishioners, see
**Paris headwear** beret
**parish officer** beadle
**parish priest** vicar
**Parisian** Lutetian
**Paris shopgirl** midinette
**Paris museum and art gallery** Louvre
**Paris palace** Elysée
**Paris river** Seine
**Paris ruffian** apache
**Paris salesgirl** midinette
**Paris stock exchange** Bourse
**Paris suburb** Asnières
**Paris tower** Eiffel
**Paris underground** metro, subway
**parity** accordance, affinity, agreement, analogy, (co)equality, comparison, consistency, correspondence, evenness, identity, levelness, likeness, monotony, par, parallelism, sameness, similarity, uniformity, unity
**park** common, field, gardens, green, heath, place, preserve
**parka** anorak
**parka part** hood
**park in California** Yosemite
**parking place** lot, bay
**parking place for aircraft** apron
**park in New York city** Battery, Bryant, Grant
**Parkinson's disease** palsy
**park-keeper** ranger
**park seat** bench
**park supervisor** warden
**park warden** ranger
**parky** chilly, cold
**parlance** argot, brogue, cant, dialect, diction, discussion, idiom, jargon,

language, phraseology, speech, tongue, vernacular
**parley** confer(ence), conversation, converse, discourse, discussion, negotiate, negotiation, talk
**parliament** assembly, congress, convocation, council, diet, house, legislature, senate
**parliamentary** congressional, deliberative, democratic, governmental, lawmaking, legislatorial, legislative, representative, senatorial, synodical
**parliamentary body** cabinet
**parliamentary break** recess
**parliamentary closure** gag
**parliamentary discussion** debate
**parliamentary records** Hansard
**parliamentary vote of money** appropriation
**parliament of Afghanistan** Shura
**parliament of Denmark** Folketing, Landsting, Rigsraad
**parliament of Finland** Eduskunta
**parliament of Greenland** Landstraad
**parliament of Iceland** Althing
**parliament of Isle of Man** Tynwald
**parliament of Israel** Knesset
**parliament of Netherlands** States Generaal
**parliament of Norway** Lag(h)ting, Odelst(h)ing, Storting
**parliament of Poland** Sejm, Senat, Seym
**parliament of Portugal** Cortes Geraes
**parliament of Republic of Ireland** Dáil (Eireann), Oireachtas
**parliament of Russia** Duma
**parliament of South Africa** Volksraad
**parliament of Spain** Cortes
**parliament of Sweden** Riksdag
**parliament of Turkey** Porte
**parlour** anteroom, chamber, den, foyer, hall, lounge, sala (Sp), salon, sitting-room, study, vestibule
**parlour game** charades
**parlous** awkward, clever, cunning, dangerous, difficult, extremely, perilous, shrewd, trying, venturesome
**parochial** biased, bigoted, blinkered, closed, confined, district, doctrinaire, exclusive, factional, hidebound, illiberal, insular, intolerant, isolated, limited, local, narrow(-minded), parish, petty, provincial, regional, restricted, sectarian, sectional, verkramp, zonal
**parody** amphigory, ape(ry), apology, burlesque, caricature, exaggeration, farce, imitation, lampoon, mimic(ry), mockery, pasquinade, satire, satirise, skit, spoof, take-off, travesty

**paroxysm** attack, contraction, convulsion, cramp, epilepsy, eruption, explosion, fit, jactation, outburst, qualm, shakes, stroke, tantrum, throe, twitching, upheaval
**paroxysmal form of arthritis** gout
**paroxysmal headache** migraine
**paroxysm of desire** orgasm
**par plus one** bogey
**parquetry** checkering, decoration, marquetry, ornamentation, tessellation, tiling
**parr** fingerling, grilse, salmon, samlet, smolt
**parrot** ape, ara, caricaturist, cockatoo, copy, echo, emulate, follow(er), imitate, imitator, impersonator, impressionist, lorikeet, macaw, mimic, mirror, parodist, polly, rehearse, reiterate, repeat, shadow, simulate
**parrot-fashion** automatically, mechanically, mindlessly, unthinkingly
**parrot fever** psittacosis
**parrot-like** psittacine
**parrot-like learning** rote
**parry** avert, avoid, block, deflect, divert, dodge, duck, elude, evade, fence, field, obviate, preclude, prevention, quibble, rebuff, shun, sidestep
**parsimonious** begrudging, carking, close, economical, frugal, grasping, mean, miserable, miserly, niggardly, penny-pinching, penurious, prudent, saving, scrimpy, sparing, stingy, stinting, thrifty, tight(fisted)
**parsimony** carefulness, closeness, cupidity, economy, extortion, frugality, husbandry, meanness, miserliness, niggardliness, providence, prudence, restraint, saving, selfishness, skimpiness, stinginess, thrift, tight-fistedness, usury, venality
**parson** churchman, clergyman, cleric, divine, dominee, ecclesiastic, incumbent, minister, padre, pastor, preacher, predikant, priest, rector, reverend, theologian, vicar
**parsonage** curacy, deanery, diocese, pastorate, presbytery, rectory, see, vicarage
**parson bird** tui
**parson's house** parsonage
**part** allot, charge, component, divide, division, duty, element, estrange, fraction, fragment, function, ingredient, interest, lot, member, piece, portion, quarter, region, rôle, section, sector, segment, separate, sever, share, sunder

**part above ground** top
**partake** enjoy, participate, sample, share
**partaker** associate, coheir, coheiress, colleague, communicant, copartner, housemate, participant, participator, partner, roommate, sharer
**partaker in guilt** accomplice
**partake too freely** indulge
**part allotted** share
**part broken off** fragment
**part company** conflict, depart, disagree, dissociate, disunite, oppose, separate
**part connecting head and torso** neck
**part cut off** section, segment
**parted from** bereft
**part exchange deal** trade-in
**partial** biased, component, crude, fractional, fragmentary, immature, imperfect, inadequate, incomplete, influenced, interested, limited, local, meagre, one-sided, partisan, prejudiced, scanty, sectional, slight, tendentious, unfair, unfinished, unjust
**partial aspect of thing** side
**partial blindness** cecutiency, meropia
**partial darkness** gloom, shade
**partial dictionary** glossary
**partial fasting** abstinence
**partiality** attachment, attraction, bias, disposition, fancy, favour(itism), humour, inclination, injustice, leaning, liking, love, nature, predilection, preference, prejudice, prepossession, temperament, tendency
**partially burnt coal** soot
**partially dried grape** raisin
**partially intoxicated** tipsy
**partially opened flower** (rose)bud
**partially unconscious** subconscious
**partial or total loss of sight** amaurosis
**partial paralysis** paresis
**partial refund** rebate
**partial shadow** penumbra
**partial similarity of things** analogy
**partial to** favour, mad about
**partible** dividable, divisible, reducible, separable, splittable
**participant** associate, coheir, colleague, communicant, contributor, helper, member, part, partaker, partaking, participator, partner, party, shareholder, sharer, sharing, worker
**participant in symposium** symposiast
**participate** engage, partake, perform, share
**participation** assistance, co-operation, collaboration, contact, contribution, direction, doing, evidence, experience, exposure, familiarity,

give-and-take, helpfulness, influence, involvement, knowledge, observation, part, partnership, practice, proof, responsiveness, share, sharing, teamwork, training, trial, under-standing, unity
**particle** atom, bit, electron, grain, iota, mite, molecule, mote, neutrino, neutron, piece, quark, scrap, shred, snippet, speck, whit
**particle in blood** embolus
**particle of bread** crumb
**particle of dirt** smut
**particle of dust** mote
**particle of fire** spark
**particle of matter** atom, quark
**particle of stone** grit
**particular** careful, certain, circumstance, critical, dainty, demanding, detail, discriminating, distinct, especial, exact, express, fact, finicky, fussy, item, marked, notable, one, peculiar, precise, remarkable, separate, single, singular, special, specific(ation), strict, uncommon, unusual
**particular and exceptional** special
**particular area** spot
**particular calling or career** vocation
**particular duty** special assignment
**particular example** instance
**particular instance** case
**particularise** cite, delineate, depict, designate, detail, differentiate, enumerate, indicate, itemise, mark, mention, narrate, note, portray, recount, relate, separate, specify
**particularly** critically, daintily, demandingly, discriminatingly, distinctly, especially, exactly, expressly, fastidiously, fussily, notably, peculiarly, precisely, remarkably, specially, specifically, uncommonly
**particular part** article
**particular part of space** place, spot
**particular physical weakness** infirmity
**particular place** location, spot
**particular point** detail
**particular portion of time** period
**particular system of units** metrology
**part in film** role
**parting** adieu, departure, division, farewell, going, goodbye, partition, rift, rupture, separation, split
**parting of the ways** schism, watershed
**part in play** role
**partisan** adherent, backer, biased, champion, devotee, factional, follower, guer(r)illa, irregular, partial, prejudiced, stalwart, supporter, upholder, votary, zealot

**partition** allotment, barrier, distribution, divide(r), division, part, portion, screen, section, separate, separation, share, wall
**partitioned** septate
**partition for ventilation in a mine** brattice
**partition that separates two cavities** septum
**partly** comparatively, halfway, incompletely, partially, partway, relatively, slightly, somewhat
**partly blind** dim-sighted, purblind
**partly coincide** overlap
**partly cooked by boiling** parboil
**partly detached house** semi-
**partly divine being** demigod
**partly frozen rain** sleet
**partly fused glass** frit(t)
**partly melted snow** sleet
**partly open** ajar
**partly submerged** emersed
**partly sunk into a wall** engaged
**partly thawed snow** sleet
**part man, part bull** minotaur
**part man, part horse** centaur
**partner** accompany, accomplice, aide, ally, associate, attendant, co-worker, cohort, colleague, comrade, consociate, consort, counterpart, husband, mate, pal, participant, spouse, wife
**partner in crime** abettor, accomplice
**partnerless woman at dance** wallflower
**partner of countess** earl
**partners carrying on business** firm, partnership
**partnership** affiliation, alliance, association, brotherhood, combination, companionship, company, corporation, firm, fraternity, interest, syndicate, union
**partnership in wrongdoing** complicity
**part of accepted doctrine** dogma
**part of act** scene
**part of aircraft** nacelle
**part of alimentary canal** intestine
**part of amniotic sac** caul
**part of anchor** arm, crown, eye, fluke, head, palm, pee, ring, throat
**part of apron** bib
**part of atlas** map
**part of bagpipe** drone
**part of basket** border, fitch, foot, handle, rand, rim, slew, stake, upset
**part of bicycle** bell, handle, pedal, spoke, wheel
**part of blood** corpuscle, serum
**part of bloom** petal
**part of body** arm, foot, hand, head, hip, leg, organ, torso

**part of body between ribs and hips** waist
**part of body containing the heart and lungs** chest
**part of body enclosed by ribs** chest
**part of body inside ribcage** thorax
**part of brain** medulla, thalamus
**part of bridge** arch
**part of Britain** England, Ireland, Scotland, Wales
**part of burning cigarette** ash
**part of button** shank
**part of cake** layer
**part of camera** lens, trigger
**part of car containing the back seats** tonneau
**part of car's exhaust** manifold
**part of car's ignition** magneto
**part of cereal plant** ear
**part of chain** link
**part of chancel** altar
**part of chest wall** rib
**part of china set** cup, plate, saucer, teapot
**part of church** apse
**part of church near altar** chancel
**part of circle** segment, arc
**part of circumference of a circle** arc
**part of clergyman's benefice** glebe
**part of coat** button, collar, lapel, lining, sleeve
**part of comb** teeth
**part of cone-shaped solid next to the base** frustrum
**part of contract** clause
**part of cornice** facia
**part of curve** arc(h)
**part of day** eve(ning), morn(ing), noon
**part of distributor** rotor
**part of dog's leg** paw
**part of door frame** jamb(e)
**part of dresser** drawer
**part of ear** canal, helix, incus, lobe, membrane, pinna, tube, tympanum
**part of earth's crust** sial
**part of egg** white, yolk
**part of electric motor** armature
**part of eye** conjuctiva, cornea, fovia, iris, lens, ligament, macula, pupil, retina, sclera
**part of eyeball** uvea
**part of face** beard, cheek, chin, eye, features, jaw, lip(s), mandible, (pre)maxilla, moustache, mouth, nose
**part of face above eyebrow** forehead
**part of factory** shop-floor
**part of feather** harl, herl, vane
**part of finger** nail
**part of Firth of Lorn** Oban
**part of fish** fin, scale

**part of flower** anther, carpel, filament, leaf, ovary, petal, pistil, receptacle, sepal, stamen, stem, stigma, style
**part of flower's corolla** petal
**part of foot** heel, inch, instep, sole, tarsus, toe
**part of garment** sash
**part of glove** godet
**part of grate** hob
**part of Greek tragedy between choric songs** episode
**part of ground where wickets are set up** pitch
**part of guitar** fret
**part of hand** finger, knuckle, palm, thumb
**part of harp** base, board, body, foot, neck, pedal, pillar, string
**part of head** scalp
**part of headset** earpiece
**part of helmet** nasal, visor
**part of hi-fi** tuner
**part of Highland costume** plaid
**part of horse's foot between fetlock and hoof** pastern
**part of horse's leg** fetlock
**part of Iberia** Spain
**part of India** Assam, Bihar, Delhi, Goa, Kerala, Mysore, Nagaland, Orissa, Pondicherry, Punjab
**part of intestine** ileum
**part of jacket front** lapel
**part of jaw** chin, gonion
**part of journey** leg
**part of kitchen** scullery
**part of lamp** bulb
**part of leg** ankle, foot, knee, shin
**part of leg between hip and knee** thigh
**part of lock** rewet, strike
**part of long poem** canto
**part of lower intestine** colon
**part of lyric ode** epode
**part of meadow** lea
**part of minute** second
**part of mouth** lip
**part of neck** throat
**part of necklace** bead
**part of nun's dress** wimple
**part of nun's headdress** barb
**part of orchid** anther
**part of organ** tissue
**part of organisation** network
**part of personal computer** microprocessor
**part of pinna** ear lobe
**part of plant** branch, leaf, root, stem
**part of play** act, epitasis, scene
**part of plough in which share is fixed** share-beam
**part of poem** stanza, verse
**part of portion** share
**part of pound weight** ounce

**part of priest's attire** amice
**part of program** event
**part of revolver** backstrap, barrel, butt, cylinder, gate, grip, latch, muzzle, rod, slide
**part of rigging** topsail
**part of roof** eaves
**part of saddle** pommel
**part of sail** bunt, clew, cringle, foot, head(board), panel, pocket, seam, tabling, window
**part of scale** doh, fah, lah, me, re, soh, te
**part of school year** term
**part of see** parish
**part of sentence** clause
**part of sequence** episode
**part of serial** episode
**part of shaft** saddle
**part of ship** deck
**part of ship above main deck** superstructure
**part of ship allotted to passengers paying lowest fair** steerage
**part of ship's bow** forecastle
**part of shoe** arch, eyelet, flap, heel, instep, nose, shoelace, sole, tip, tongue, upper, vamp, welt
**part of skeleton** arm, foot, leg, rib, skull
**part of skirt looped up** pannier
**part of skull enclosing brain** cranium
**part of sleeping berth** bedroom
**part of sleeve** cuff
**part of speech** adjective, (ad)verb, conjunction, preposition, (pro)noun, word
**part of spiral gear** helical tooth
**part of stage in front of the drop-scene** proscenium
**part of stairs** riser
**part of step** riser
**part of stocking** leg, toe
**part of Stone Age** Neolithic
**part of stove** oven
**part of target** inner
**part of temple above columns** entablature
**part of theatre behind the stalls** pit
**part of theology concerned with death anf final destiny** eschatology
**part of threadcutting tool** diestock
**part of tobacco pipe** bowl, stem
**part of trunk** waist
**part of trunk between neck and abdomen** thorax
**part of typewriter** key
**part of unconscious** id
**part of United Kingdom** England, Northern Ireland, Scotland, Wales
**part of upper deck used by officers** quarterdeck
**part of varnish** resin

**part of walrus tusk** ivory
**part of ward** precinct
**part of waterway** channel
**part of week** day
**part of West Indies** Bahamas
**part of wheel** ratchet, tyre
**part of wheel that touches ground** tread
**part of wicket** bail, stumps
**part of window** bead, brickmould, casing, counterweight, frame, rail, sash, skirt, strip, (window)pane
**part of window frame** lintel
**part of year** autumn, fall, spring, summer, winter
**part of Yugoslavia** Serbia
**part played** role
**partridge** francolin
**partridge flock** covey
**part song** glee, madrigal
**part taken as example** specimen
**part-time employee** temp(orary)
**part-time labourer** hired hand
**part to play** role
**parturition** accouchement (F), (child)birth, confinement, delivery, genesis, labour, nativity, parturiency, travail
**part used to typify a whole** specimen
**part with** abandon, cede, discard, dismiss, forsake, jettison, release, relinquish, renounce, sacrifice, yield
**part with cash** pay
**part wth** abandon, discard, forgo, jettison, relinquish, renounce, sacrifice, surrender, yield
**party** alliance, association, beano, celebration, contestant, detachment, entertainment, faction, festivity, function, gathering, group, litigant, participant, reception, social, soiree, squad, team
**party badge** rosette
**party concerned about environment** green
**party drink** punch
**party for men only** stag
**party-giver** host(ess)
**party of persons sent** mission
**party opposed to that in power** opposition
**party to a lawsuit** litigant
**party to celebrate new home** house-warming
**party under Hitler** Nazi
**party who brings suit into lawcourt** plaintiff
**parvenu** adventurer, arrivé, arriviste, arrogant, audacious, brash, cocky, feigning, forward, impertinent, insolent, newly-rich, nobody, plebeian, pretender, snob, upstart

**Paschal festival** Easter, Pesach
**pa's mate** ma
**pasque flower** anemone
**pass** approve, channel, circulate, condition, defile, depart, die, disappear, disregard, elapse, enact, end, exceed, excel, expire, fade, go, ignore, laisser passer (F), laissez passer (F), lapse, leave, move, nek, occur, okay, overtake, passport, proceed, pronounce, send, skim, spend, stage, surpass, terminate, transfer, transmit, utter, vanish
**pass across** transit
**passage** affair, aisle, alley, avenue, byway, channel, clause, cross, dispute, journey, line, movement, paragraph, pass(ing), road, route, section, text, thoroughfare, tour, transit(ion), trip, voyage
**passage across** transit
**passage between buildings** alley
**passage between cliffs** gat
**passage between forest trees** glade
**passage between seats** aisle
**passage between terraced houses** entry
**passage for fluid** duct
**passage for surplus water from dam** spillway
**passage from mouth to stomach** throat
**passage from throat to lungs** windpipe
**passage in a building** corridor
**passage in the body** meatus
**passage money** fare
**passage of goods** transit
**passage of scriptures** text
**passage of water joining seas** strait
**passage out** egress, exit
**passage outward** outlet
**passage quoted** citation, quotation
**passage to be played very softly** pianissimo
**passage underground** tunnel
**passageway** aisle, alley, lane
**pass along** relay
**pass a rope through** reeve
**pass away** decease, die, disappear, elapse, expire, perish, vanish
**pass between hills** defile
**pass between peaks** col
**pass by** disregard, elapse, forget, ignore, leave, miss, neglect, omit, overlook, pass over, pretermit
**pass criticism** animadvert
**passé** aged, antiquated, antique, archaic, bygone, dated, démodé, faded, forgotten, grey, hoary, obsolete, old-fashioned, outdated, outmoded, outworn, rejected

**passed away** died
**passed bill** act
**passed from one end to the other** through
**passenger** commuter, cruiser, encumbrance, equestrian, fare, hitchhiker, journeyer, pillion(-rider), rider, tourist, traveller, voyager, wayfarer
**passenger carriage on lines** train, tram(car)
**passenger carrier** aeroplane, aircraft
**passenger plane** airliner
**passenger room** cabin
**passenger seat on motorbike** pillion
**passenger ship** liner
**passenger vehicle** minibus, taxi, tram(car), (trolley)bus
**passerine bird** finch, starling
**pass for** impersonate, masquerade, play
**pass from place to place** circulate
**pass from sight** disappear
**pass hand gently along surface** stroke
**passing** approving, brief, casual, cursory, departing, elapsing, exceeding, excelling, fleeting, flowing, going, graduating, hasty, leaving, momentary, moving, outdoing, proceeding, qualifying, quick, running, short, succeeding, superficial, surmounting, temporary, transient, transitory
**passing craze** fad
**passing hollow** crescent
**passing on of family traits** heredity
**passing reference** allusion
**passing with time** transient
**pass into** enter
**pass into unfrozen state** thaw
**passion** affection, anger, ardour, attachment, desire, emotion, excitement, fear, feeling, fervour, fury, heat, hope, joy, love, rapture, transport, vehemence, warmth, wrath, zeal
**passionate** ardent, ecstatic, emotional, excited, fervent, fervid, furious, impassioned, intense, vehement
**passionate appeal** complaint, cri de coeur, protest
**passionate desire** lust
**passionate enthusiasm for ballet** balletomania
**passionate expression of grief** elegy, lament
**passionately fond of** crazy, dote, infatuated
**passion for appearing important** megalomania
**passion for writing verses** metromania
**passion fruit** granadilla, grenadilla

**passive** dispassionate, fainéant, faint, feeble, inactive, inert, patient, receiving, receptive, resigned, stoic, submissive, torpid, unagitated, uninterested, unresisting
**passive female principle of universe** Yin
**passively resentful** sullen
**passive state** inertia
**pass judgement** arbitrate
**pass judgement before trial** prejudge
**pass judgement on** criticise
**passkey** master-key
**pass laws** legislate, prescribe
**pass lightly over** flit, skim
**pass, like time** elapse
**pass off** counterfeit, disappear, emit, fake, feign, happen, occur, vanish, vaporise
**pass off in vapour** evaporate
**pass on** bequeath, impart, relate, relay, reveal, transmit
**pass oneself off as** (im)personate
**pass on news** report
**pass out** die, distribute, drop, faint, swoon
**pass over** cross, disregard, ford, forget, ignore, neglect, omit, overlook, skip, wade
**Passover festival** Pesach
**pass over lightly** skim, slur
**pass over with one step** stride
**passport** access, admission, admittance, authorisation, card, carte d'entrée (F), certificate, clearance, credentials, deed, diploma, docket, entrée, entry, identification, liberty, license, missive, pass, passe-partout, permission, permit, recommendation, reference(s), release, safe-conduct, sanction, testimonial, ticket, title, visa, voucher, warrant
**passport endorsement** visa
**pass quickly** sweep
**pass round** bypass
**pass slowly through** ooze
**pass standard ten** matriculate
**pass the end of a rope through** reeve
**pass the hand lightly over** stroke
**pass the time of day** chat, converse, speak, talk
**pass thread through** sew
**pass through** negotiate
**pass through a hole** reeve
**pass through a sieve** sift
**pass through pores** percolate, permeate
**pass up** decline, discard, discount, dismiss, forgo, ignore, miss, neglect, refuse, reject, waive

**past** ago, (a)gone, ancient, antiquated, beyond, by(gone), elapsed, eld, expected, expired, finished, forgotten, history, lapsed, over, preterition, previous, spent, yesterday, yore, youth
**pasta** cannelloni, farfalle, fetuccini, lasagna, lasagne, macaroni, noodles, ravioli, spaghetti, tagliatelle
**past due time for payment** overdue
**paste** adhere, adhesive, attach, bind, bond, cement, cling, connect, cream, dough, fasten, fix, fuse, glue, gum, hitch, lash, lotion, ointment, rope, salve, secure, stick, strap, tie, unguent
**pasteboard square** card
**pastel flower** sweet-pea
**paste made of crushed sesame seeds** tahina, tahini
**paste used to fix glass** putty
**past, gone by** ago
**pastille** bonbon, candy, confection, lozenge, pill, tablet, troche
**pastime** amusement, diversion, entertainment, excursion, fun, game, hobby, interest, jaunt, leisure, play, pleasure, recreation, relaxation, sport, treat
**past master** artist, expert, virtuoso, wizard
**past of 'to be'** were
**pastor** clergyman, dominee, minister
**pastoral** bucolic, country, harmonious, idyllic, innocent, irenic, peaceful, quiet, restful, rural, rustic, serene, tranquil, uncomplex
**pastoralist** cattle-farmer, sheep-farmer
**pastoral poem** eclogue, idyll
**pastoral scene** idyll
**pastor's office** pastorate
**past recall** bygone
**pastry** Danish, éclair, flaky, phyllo, pie, puff, tart
**pastry dish** pie
**pastry seller** pieman
**pastry shop** patisserie
**past tense** aorist
**past tense suffix** -ed
**past the expected time** late, overdue
**past the prime** faded, passé
**pasturage** feed, fodder, forage, grass(land), herbage, lea, pasture, provender, range
**pasture** browse, camp, field, fodder, grass(land), grazing, lea, meadow, pasturage, range
**pasture for hire** agist
**pastureland** lea, ley
**pasture on a mountain side** alp
**pasture rate** agist
**pasture sound** moo

**pasty substance** putty
**pat** caress, dab, fondle, pet, tap, touch
**patch** correct, fix, mend, repair, settle, smooth
**patches of shade** shadow
**patch up again** revamp
**pâté** crown, head, liver, paste, patty, terrine
**pâté made from duck and goose liver** pate de foie gras
**patella** kneecap, kneepan, limpet, rotula
**patellar region** joint, knee, stifle
**patent** apparent, blatant, certify, clear, conspicuous, copyright, create, discover, evident, flagrant, glaring, grant, indisputable, invent(ion), manifest, obvious, open, overt, permit, trademark, unhidden, unmistakable, unveiled
**patent medicine** nostrum
**paternal** benevolent, concerned, father-like, fatherly, indulgent, patrimonial, protective, solicitous, vigilant
**paternal inheritance** patrimony
**path** alley, avenue, boulevard, byway, circuit, course, device, direction, (foot)path, (foot)way, highway, idea, island, lane, loop, manner, means, median, method, passage(way), pavement, procedure, ramp, road, route, run(way), sidewalk, strategy, street, strip, towpath, track, trail, trajectory, walk(way)
**pathetic** affecting, distressing, doleful, emotional, grievous, lamentable, melting, moving, piteous, pitiable, pitiful, plaintive, poignant, rueful, sad, sorrowful, tender, touching, woeful
**path of planet or satellite** orbit
**pathological** bad, contaminated, diseased, gangrened, infected, morbid, mortified, poisoned, septic
**pathological enlargement of the spleen** splenomegaly
**pathologist** diagnostician
**pathology** bacteriology, diagnostics, etiology, nosogenesis, nosography, nosology, pathobiology, pathogenesis, pathognomy, symptomatology
**path round a heavenly body** orbit
**pathway** direction, footway, path, road
**patience** amenability, aplomb, assiduity, composure, constancy, diligence, endurance, equanimity, equilibrium, forbearance, fortitude, inexcitability, perseverance, persistence, quiet, repose, resignation, restraint, serenity, stamina, stoicism, sufferance, tenacity, tolerance, tractability
**patient** calm, diligent, invalid, passive, persevering, persistent, quiet, resigned, sedulous, serene, stoical, submissive, susceptible, unexcited
**patient man** Job
**patient not residing in hospital** outpatient
**patient's medical history** anamnesis
**patient suffering** endurance
**patina** appearance, burnish, coat, enamel, film, finish, glaze, gloss, grain, lacquer, lustre, polish, sheen, shine, smoothness, surface, texture, varnish
**patio** cloister, court(yard), piazza, porch, terrace
**pat lightly** dab
**pat of butter** dab
**patois** accent, argot, cant, dialect, idiom, jargon, language, parlance, patter, pronunciation, provincialism, slang, speech, tongue, usage, vernacular
**pat on the back** assure, commend, congratulate, encourage, hearten, praise, reassure
**patrician** aristocratic, noble
**patriotic** allegiant, chauvinist(ic), flag-waving, jingoistic, loyal, nationalist(ic)
**patriotism** allegiance, amor patriae (L), chauvinism, faithfulness, fidelity, jingoism, loyalty, nationalism, staunchness, steadfastness, trustiness
**patrol vessel** vedette, vidette
**patron** advocate, benefactor, client, customer, defender, protector, supporter
**patronage** aid, assistance, attendance, auspices, backing, business, buying, clientele, commerce, condescension, custom, defence, encouragement, financing, help(ing), marketing, promoting, promotion, shopping, sponsorship, support, trade, trading, traffic, visits
**patroness and adviser** Egeria
**patronise** aid, approve, assist, back, befriend, condescend, contemn, cultivate, descend, discredit, dishonour, encourage, favour, foster, frequent, fund, guard, help, insult, maintain, preserve, promote, slur, sponsor, support, tolerate, underestimate, yield
**patronising** condescending, disdaining, haughty, high-handed, overbearing, snobbish, stooping, superior
**patron saint of cripples** Giles
**patron saint of England** George
**patron saint of fertility** Yaksha
**patron saint of fisherman** Peter
**patron saint of France** Denis
**patron saint of Ireland** Patrick
**patron saint of lepers** Giles
**patron saint of Norway** Olaf
**patron saint of Russia** Nicholas
**patron saint of sailors** Elmo
**patron saint of Scotland** Andrew
**patron saint of shoemakers** Crispin
**patron saint of Spain** James, Santiago
**patron saint of travellers** Christopher
**patron saint of Wales** David
**pattern** archetype, copy, decoration, design, example, follow, guide, imitate, model, mould, norm, order, paradigm, prototype, sample, specimen, style
**pattern cut out in metal** template
**patterned floor** parquet
**pattern for shaping** mould
**pattern-guide** matrix, template
**pattern of excellence** paragon
**pattern of striae** striation
**pattern of wood** grain
**pattern on skin** tattoo
**pattern plate** stencil
**pattern set in surface** inlaid design
**pattern stencil** template
**paucity** dearth, deficiency, fewness, inadequacy, insufficiency, meagreness, poorness, scantiness, scarcity, shortage, sparseness, sparsity, thinness
**paunch** abdomen, boep, breadbasket, (pot)belly, stomach, tummy
**pauper** almsman, bankrupt, beggar, bergie, debtor, hobo, insolvent, tramp, vagrant
**pause** arrest, break, cease, delay, deliberate, demur, desist, halt, hesitate, hesitation, intermission, intermit, interrupt(ion), interval, lull, respite, rest, stop, suspension, wait, waver
**pause in doubt** hesitate
**pause in movement** stay
**pause in the Psalms** selah
**pause or break within a line of verse** caesura
**pause through doubt** hesitate
**pause upon** dwell, linger, loiter, tarry
**pave a road** tar
**paved area** patio
**paved area adjoining house** yard
**paved courtyard** patio
**paved road** street
**pavement** alley, avenue, footpath, lane, path(way), promenade, trail, walk

**pavement at side of street** trottoir
**pavement edge** kerb
**pavement for roads** macadam
**pave the way** herald
**pave the way for** facilitate, ready
**paving block** set(t)
**paving material** bricks, tar, tiles
**paw** abuse, attack, caress, feel, finger, fondle, foot, forepaw, grab, hoof, ill-treat, manipulate, maul, molest, pad, scrape, scratch, sole, strike, stroke, touch, trotter, unguis
**pawn** chessman, guarantee, hock, pledge, security
**pawnbroker** loaner, (money)lender, uncle, usurer
**pawnbroker's pledge** hock
**pawnbroker's shop** spout
**pawnbroker's speciality** loan
**paw of fox** pad
**pawpaw** papaw, papaya, papino
**pay** compensate, discharge, earning, fee, income, indemnify, liquidate, payment, punish, recompense, reimburse, remunerate, repay, requite, retaliate, revenge, reward, salary, satisfy, settle, suffer, wages, yield
**payable** ascribable, claimable, deserved, due, earned, entrenched, legitimate, merited, owed, owing, profitable, rightful
**pay a call** visit
**pay a debt** settle
**pay a grant to** subsidise
**pay a short visit** call
**pay attention to** court, hearken, heed, listen, note, observe, tend
**pay back** avenge, chasten, punish, reciprocate, recompense, refund, reimburse, repay, retaliate, square
**pay beforehand** advance
**pay court to** woo
**payee** endorse, endorser, holder
**pay for** atone, buy, compensate, finance, purchase, suffer
**pay for all** treat
**pay for service rendered** remunerate
**pay for the use of a car** hire
**pay half each** go fifty-fifty
**pay in advance** prepay
**paying** benefiting, bestowing, granting, lucrative, profiting, recompensing, reimbursing, remunerating, rendering, requiting, settling, yielding
**paying back** reprisal
**paying client** customer
**paying point** tollgate
**payment** deposit, disbursement, expenditure, expense, fee, instalment, outlay, pay, premium, refund, reimbursement, remittance, remuneration, settlement, share, tribute
**payment back** rebate
**payment demand** dun
**payment for professional services** fee
**payment for work done** salary, wages
**payment in acknowledgement of subjection** tribute
**payment made by tenant** rental
**payment of cash on purchase** spot-cash
**payment of means of support** alimony
**payment of pilot** pilotage
**payment received** receipt
**payment slip** receipt
**payment to a doctor** fee
**payment to an author** royalty
**payment to public revenue** duty
**payment to the infirm** disablement benefit
**pay no attention to** disregard, neglect
**pay no intention to** ignore, reject
**pay off** acquit, clear, discharge, dismiss, fire, graft, liquidate, retaliate, sack, satisfy, settle, square, suborn, succeed, work
**pay-off** climax, conclusion, consequence, crunch, culmination, judg(e)ment, outcome, punch-line, result, reward, upshot
**pay off old scores** avenge, repay, requite, retaliate
**pay on arrival** COD
**pay one's share** ante
**pay out** disburse, expend, render, retaliate, spend
**pay out money** spend
**pay postage beforehand** prepay
**pay respect to officer** salute
**pay road fee there** tollgate
**pay the bill** settle, treat
**pay the penalty of** atone, expiate
**pay to landlord** rent
**pay too little attention** neglect
**pay way** toll road
**pea** legume
**peace** accord, agreement, calm(ness), composure, conciliation, concord, contentment, harmony, hush, order, pax (L), quiet, relaxation, repose, rest, security, serenity, silence, tranquillity, treaty, truce
**peace be with you** pax vobiscum (L)
**peace bird** dove
**peace disturbance** riot
**peaceful** amicable, calm, compatible, dignified, friendly, gentle, gracious, halcyon, harmonious, irenic, nonviolent, pacific, placatory, placid, quiescent, quiet, reposeful, restful, serene, still, tranquil, unagitated, unexcited, unruffled

**peaceful and happy** idyllic
**peaceful person** pacifist
**peaceful relations** amity
**peace lover** pacifist
**peacemaker** advocate, appeaser, arbiter, arbitrator, conciliator, go-between, interceder, intercessor, intermediary, judge, mediator, negotiator, peacemonger, referee, umpire
**peace offering** homage, irenics, libation, offering, offertory, sacrifice, tribute
**peace of mind** ataraxia, ataraxy, contentment, serenity
**peace pipe** calumet
**peace prize** Nobel
**peace symbol** dove
**peace treaty** nonagression pact
**peace tribunal's seat** The Hague
**peach dessert** melba
**peachwort** persicaria
**peacock's mate** peahen
**peacock's pride** tail
**pea holder** pod
**peak** acme, alp, apex, ben, bulge, cap, climax, crag, crest, cusp, hill, horn, meridian, pinnacle, piton, point, precipice, promontory, ridge, shade, spire, summit, tilt, tip, top, tor, vertex, visor, zenith
**peaked military hat with plume** shako
**peak in the Himalayas** Everest
**peak of a cap** visor
**peal** carillon, chime, clamour, clang, clap, clash, crack, crash, resonate, resound(ing), reverberation, ring(ing), roar, rumble, sound, toll, vibrate
**pealing of bells** tintinnabulation
**peal or chime** ring
**peanut** goober, groundnut
**pearl** nacre
**pearl-bearing shellfish** oyster
**pearling boat** lugger
**pearling town of Western Australia** Broome
**pearl maker** oyster
**pearl millet** bajra
**'Pearl of the Antilles'** Cuba
**pearl source** oyster
**pear-shaped chemical vessel** aludel
**peasant** boor, churl, cotter, countryman, lout, oaf, provincial, rustic, serf, yokel
**peasant in Arab countries** fellah
**peasant in India** ryot
**peas are found in it** pod
**pea-shaped** pisiform
**pea shell** pod
**peat** turf
**peat bog** marsh

**pebble** gem, gravel, hardness, jackstone, pellet, rock, scree, stone
**pebbles on the shore** shingle
**pecan** hickory-nut
**peccadillo** error, indiscretion, misdeed
**peccary** boar
**pech** pant
**peck** bite, blow, depress, dig, food, (in)dent, jab, kiss, knock, poke, prick, rap, scrape, scratch, strike, stroke, tap
**pecking order** hierarchy
**peculiar** bizarre, curious, distinctive, eccentric, exceptional, extraordinary, odd, particular, proper, queer, singular, special, strange, uncommon, unique, unusual, weird
**peculiar charm** aroma
**peculiar dialect** cant, lingo
**peculiarity** abnormality, attribute, characteristic, distinction, earmark, eccentricity, foible, hallmark, idiocrasy, idiosyncrasy, kink, mannerism, mettle, oddity, oddness, queerness, quip, quirk, rarity, strangeness, temper, trait, twist, whim
**peculiarity of behaviour** quirk
**peculiarity of phraseology** idiom
**peculiar lustre of a pearl of the finest quality** orient
**peculiar notion** fad
**peculiar person** weirdo
**peculiar speech** idiom
**peculiar thing** oddity
**peculiar to oneself** private
**peculiar trait** oddity
**pecuniary** financial, fiscal, monetary, nummular
**pecuniary gain** profit
**pecuniary gain as motive** lucre
**pedagogue** dogmatist, educationist, educator, instructor, mistress, pedant, professor, schoolmaster, (school)teacher, tutor
**pedal** (foot-)lever, treadle
**pedal bike** cycle
**pedal digit** toe
**pedal gout** podagra
**pedal-operated pleasure-boat** pedalo
**pedal that controls speed of engine** accelerator
**pedant** bookworm, casuist, dogmatist, literalist, purist, quibbler, sophist
**pedantic** abstruse, conceited, didactic, dogmatic, erudite, formal, haughty, ostentatious, (over-)fussy, pompous, preachy, pretentious
**pedantic teacher** pedagogue
**pedate** footed
**peddle** dawdle, daydream, dispense, distribute, fiddle, fribble, hawk, idle, loaf, market, merchandise, niggle, procrastinate, promote, retail, scatter, sell, strew, trade, vend
**pedestal** base, bottom, column, foot, foundation, mounting, pier, pillar, platform, plinth, rest, stand, support, understructure
**pedestal base** plinth
**pedestal part** dado
**pedestrian** banal, boring, commonplace, dull, flat, footslogger, indifferent, mediocre, mundane, ordinary, plodding, prosaic, stodgy, uninspired, walker, walking
**pedestrian walk** mall
**pedicular** louse-infested, pediculous
**pedigree** ancestry, bloodline, derivation, descent, genealogy, heritage, line(age)
**pedigreed mount** hot-blooded, thoroughbred
**pedlar** chapman, colporteur, coster(monger), gutter-man, haggler, hawker, higgler, itinerant, monger, peddler, salesman, shopman, (street-)seller, street-trader, vendor, walker
**peek** blink (Sc), coup d'oeil (F), glance, glimpse, observe, peep, peer, see, spy, view, witness
**peel** bark, decorticate, denude, doff, excoriate, flay, husk, layer, pare, rind, scale, skin, split, strip, uncover
**peeler** cop, parer
**peel of deer's horn** fraying
**peel off** flake, flay
**peep** blink, consider, contemplate, emerge, examine, eye, gaze, glance, glimpse, inspect, issue, look, observe, peek, peer, regard, scan, scrutinise, see, sight(ing), snoop, spy, squint, study, survey, view, watch
**peep about** snoop
**peeper** eye
**peeping Tom** voyeur
**peep inquisitively into** pry
**peep out** peer
**peepshow** raree (show)
**peep slyly** peek
**peer** baron, compeer, duke, earl, equal, gaze, lord, marquess, match, nobleman, peep, viscount
**peerage** aristocracy, barony, nobility, peers
**peer group rivalry** keeping up with the Joneses
**Peer Gynt's mother** Ase
**peer inquisitively** pry
**peerless** best, classic, excellent, first-rate, greatest, highest, incomparable, inimitable, matchless, nulli secundus (L), paramount, perfect, prime, sans pareil (F), select, sovereign, sublime, superior, supreme, unequalled, unexcelled, unparalleled, unprecedented
**peer of the lowest rank** baron
**peer of the realm** earl
**peeve** annoy, bother, chafe, disquiet, exasperate, fret, gall, grate, grievance, gripe, harass, irk, irritant, irritate, jar, nettle, nuisance, ordeal, pest(er), provoke, rankle, ruffle, trial, vex(ation)
**peeved** annoyed, displeased, exasperated, galled, harassed, indignant, irked, irritated, miffed, nettled, offended, passionate, piqued, provoked, riled, sore, vexed
**peevish** bitter, captious, cavilling, crabby, cross, crotchety, dyspeptic, fretful, grumpy, hateful, hostile, ill-humoured, impatient, irritable, liverish, mean, moody, pettish, petulant, querulous, snappy, spiteful, splenetic, sulky, touchy, waspish
**peevishly impatient** petulant
**peevish person** crab
**peewit** lapwing, pewit
**peg** dowel, hob, marker, nob, pin, plug, tee
**peg away** persevere, persist
**peg for a hole in a cask** spigot
**peg of wood** nog
**pejorative** belittling, contemptuous, deprecatory, depreciative, disdainful, disparaging, disrespectful, downgrading, humiliating, insolent, insulting, irreverent, lessening, lowering, mortifying, rude, sornful
**pekoe** tea
**pelage** coat, fleece, fur, hair, hide, pelt, pile, skin, wool
**pelf** assets, capital, finances, fortune, lucre, means, money, opulence, profit, property, riches, wealth
**pelican's feature** beak
**pellet** ball, bead, capsule, globule, grain, marble, oval, pea, pearl, pebble, pill, seed, shot, spheroid, spherule, stone, tablet
**pellet rifle** air gun
**pellets of frozen rain** hail
**pellicle** blanket, caul, cover(ing), cuticle, enamel, epidermis, epithelium, facing, film, flake, foam, integument, lamina, layer, membrane, peel, scale, scum, sheet, skin, varnish, veneer
**pellucid** bald, bare, blunt, clear, cogent, coherent, comprehensible, crystal(line), diaphanous, glassy, intelligible, limpid, lucid, naked,

**obvious**, rational, simple, straightforward, translucent, transparent, understandable, vitreous
**pelt** batter, beat, blow, fur, hide, pepper, skin, stroke
**pelt with stones** lapidate
**pelvic bone** ilium, sacrum
**pelvic cavity** cloaca
**pelvic joint** hip
**pelvis** hip
**pen** ballpoint, cage, camp, compose, compound, corral, draft, enclosure, kraal, pound, stockade, sty, stylus, write
**penal** correctional, corrective, disciplinary, penalising, punitive, retributive
**penal institution** penitentiary, prison, reformatory
**penalty** disadvantage, fine, forfeit(ure), infliction, price, punishment, retribution
**penalty payment** fine
**penance** atonement, mortification, penalty, reparation, (self-)punishment
**penchant** affinity, bent, bias, disposition, flair, fondness, inclination, leaning, liking, partiality, predilection, proclivity, proneness, propensity, taste, tendency, turn
**pencil end** stub
**pencil rubber** eraser
**pendant** hanging, locket, necklace, necklet, overhanging, pendent, pending, pendulous, pensile, projecting, undecided, whence
**pendant of ice** icicle
**pendant ornament** tassel
**pendent** dangling, drooping, flapping, floppy, hanging, loose, pendulous, suspended, swinging, unattached, unsupported
**pending** awaiting, forthcoming, hanging, imminent, impending, undecided, undetermined, unsettled
**pendulous** hesitate, swing, undecided, vacillating, vibrate, waver
**pendulous double chin** jowl
**pendulous part** lobe
**pendulum motion** swing
**pen end** nib
**penetrable** accessible, apprehensive, fathomable, intelligible, open, passable, permeable, pervious, porous, pregnable, vulnerable
**penetrate** augur, bore, comprehend, discern, enter, gore, percolate, perforate, permeate, pervade, prick, probe, puncture, spear, stab, touch, (trans)pierce, understand
**penetrate throughout** permeate

**penetrating** acute, boring, critical, diffusing, ear-splitting, entering, harsh, incisive, infiltrating, intelligent, keen, mordant, observant, perceptive, permeating, pervading, piercing, pointed, pricking, probing, profound, pungent, quick, sharp, shrewd, shrill, stabbing, strong
**penetrating headlight** foglamp
**penetration of fluids through porous particles** osmosis
**penetrative** piercing
**pen for cattle** camp, corral, kraal
**pen for pigs** sty
**pen for small animals** hutch
**pen for swine** sty
**peninsula** cape, chersonese, foreland, head(land), hook, mull (Sc), neck, point, promontory, spur, tongue
**peninsula in the Adriatic** Istria
**peninsula of Alaska** Kenai, Seward
**peninsula of Chile** Hardy, Lacuy, Tumbes
**peninsula of Costa Rica** Nicova, Osa
**peninsula of Denmark** Jutland
**peninsula of Egypt** Sinai
**peninsula of England** Portland
**peninsula of Europe** Balkan
**peninsula of Greece** Acte, Chalcidice, Morea, Sithonia
**peninsula of Guam** Orote
**peninsula of Hong Kong** Kowloon
**peninsula of Manchuria** Liaotung
**peninsula of Mexico** Baja, Yucatan
**peninsula of New Zealand** Mahia, Otago
**peninsula of Panama** Azuero
**peninsula of Russia** Crimea, Kamchatka, Karelia, Kola
**peninsula of South-west Europe** Iberia
**peninsula of West Alaska** Seward
**penitence** compunction, contrition, regret, remorse, repentance, self-reproach, shame, sorrow
**penitent** abject, amending, apologetic, atoning, conscience-stricken, contrite, humble, regretful, remorseful, repentant, rueful, sorrowful, sorry
**penitential garment** cilice
**penitential psalm** Miserere
**penitentiary** jail, lockup, prison, reformatory
**penman** author, scribe, writer
**penman's palsy** writer's cramp
**pen name** alias, allonym, anonym, nom de guerre, nom de plume, pseudonym
**pen name of Dickens** Boz
**pen name of Lamb** Elia

**pennant** banderole, banner, burgee, ensign, flag, insignia, jack, pennon, standard, streamer
**penniless** bankrupt, broke, depleted, destitute, impecunious, indigent, moneyless, needy, pauperised, poor, ruined, skint
**penniless person** pauper
**Pennine river** Trent
**pennon** banner, ensign, flag, insignia, jack, pennant, standard, streamer
**penny** denarius
**penny-pincher** hoarder, miser, niggard, skinflint
**penny-pinching** close, frugal, grasping, mean, miserable, miserly, niggardly, parsimonious, penurious, saving, scrimpy, sparing, stingy, tightfisted
**pen or cob** swan
**pen pal** correspondent
**pen-point** nib
**pens and papers** stationery
**pensioner** annuitant, beadsman, beneficiary, dependant, gentleman-at-arms, pensionary
**pension off** superannuate
**pensive** bemused, bewailing, contemplate, dreaming, gloomy, grieving, immersed, lamenting, meditative, moody, musing, reflective, ruminative, sober, thinking, thoughtful, wistful
**pensive sadness** melancholy
**pent** caged, confined, cooped, imprisoned, penned
**Pentateuch** Torah
**pen tip** nib
**pent-up** caged, checked, confined, curbed, restrained, suppressed
**pentyl** amyl
**penurious** beggarly, bereft, chary, cheap, destitute, drained, frugal, impecunious, inadequate, mean, miserly, moneygrubbing, niggardly, restricted, skinflinty, stingy, thrifty, tight, ungenerous
**penury** deficiency, destitution, inadequacy, indigence, insolvency, lack, need, poverty, privation, ruin, scarceness, scarcity, shortage, want
**peon** attendant, labourer, serf, soldier, traveller
**peonism** peonage
**people** clan, commonalty, crowd, demos, folks, gentes (L), humanity, humans, masses, mortals, persons, populace, public, race, us, we, (wo)men
**people dance round this with streamers** maypole
**people employed** personnel

**people in attendance** retinue
**people in general** public, we
**people in team of judges** panel
**people next below nobility** gentry
**people not of a specific occupation** laity
**people of a district** community, neighbourhood
**people of good family** gentlefolk
**people of Kampuchea** Khmer
**people of Philippine Islands** Tagalog
**people of same social level** class
**people of same status** equals
**people of state** nation
**people that pay tribute** tributary
**pep** ambitious, animation, élan, energy, force, go, initiative, power, spirit, stamina, verve, vigour, vim, vivacity, zest
**pepper** capsicum, cayenne, condiment, kava, pelt, spice
**pepper grinder** mill
**pepper's companion** salt
**pepper shrub** (c)ava, kava
**peppery** biting, caustic, fiery, hot(-tempered), irascible, irritable, piquant, pungent, sarcastic, snappish, spicy, stinging, testy, touchy, trenchant, waspish
**pep talk** motivational speech
**pep up** animate, energise, enliven, excite, exhilarate, fortify, inspire, invigorate, quicken, rouse, stimulate, vitalise, vivify
**per** by, each, for, the, through
**peradventure** chance, doubt, perhaps, uncertainty
**perambulator** pram
**per annum** annually
**perceive** appreciate, apprehend, conceptualise, deduce, descry, discern, discover, distinguish, espy, feel, imagine, know, note, notice, observe, realise, reason, recognise, remark, see, sense, think, understand
**perceive a sound** hear
**perceive by the nose** smell
**perceive clearly with mind** discern
**perceived by the senses** sensate
**perceived by touch** tactile
**perceive intuitively** sense
**perceive with eyes** see
**percentage** commission, fraction, part, (pro)portion, segment
**perceptible** apparent, appreciable, cognisable, discernible, perceivable, understandable
**perceptible by touch** tactile, tangible
**perceptible to the ear** audible
**perceptible to the eye** visible

**perception** acuteness, awareness, cognition, concept, consciousness, feeling, flair, grasp, idea, image, insight, intelligence, knowledge, percept, revelation, sensation, sense, understanding, view, wisdom
**perception without objective reality** hallucination
**perceptive** acute, alert, alive, astute, aware, cognizant, discerning, discriminating, impressible, intelligent, observant, penetrating, percipient, perspicacious, piercing, quick, responding, responsive, sagacious, sapient, sensitive, sharp, shrewd, smart, wise
**perch** alight, bar, branch, dwell, measure, nest(le), place, pole, repose, rest(ing), roost, seat, settle, sit
**perch for the night** roost
**perch-like fish** darter
**percoid fish** scat
**percolate** charge, diffuse, discharge, distil, drain, drip, extract, exude, fill, filter, imbue, (in)filtrate, leach, leak, lixiviate, ooze, pass, penetrate, permeate, pervade, purify, saturate, seep, sieve, strain, trickle
**percolate slowly** seep
**percolator** cauldron, filter, strainer
**percussion disc** gong
**percussion instrument** cymbal, drum
**perdition** damnation, destruction, downfall, hell, ruin
**peregrinate** ambulate, cruise, drift, gallivant, hike, itinerate, jaunt, journey, meander, perambulate, proceed, ramble, range, roam, rove, straggle, stray, stroll, travel, traverse, voyage, wander
**peregrine** alien, exotic, foreign, migrating, peculiar, strange, transatlantic, travellling, unindigenous, wandering
**peremptory** absolute, arbitrary, arrogant, authoritative, binding, categorical, commanding, compelling, decisive, decretory, despotic, dictatorial, dogmatic, domineering, final, imperative, imperious, insistent, intolerant, jussive, mandatory, obligatory, obliging, oppressive, overbearing, perceptive, pontifical, positive, tyrannical, undeniable, urgent
**perennial** chronic, constant, continual, enduring, eternal, everlasting, immortal, unceasing, undying
**perennial grass** timothy
**perennial herb** acanthus
**perennial plant** carex, sedum

**perfect** accomplished, complete(d), consummate, excellent, expert, faultless, finished, flawless, full, ideal, pure, skilled, spotless, thorough, typical, unqualified
**perfect diamond** paragon
**perfect female bee** queen
**perfect for the job** ideal
**perfect happiness** bliss
**perfection** ability, accuracy, acme, actuality, adroitness, exactness, expertness, faultlessness, goodness, ideal(ity), intactness, justness, ne plus ultra (L), pre-eminence, pureness, stainlessness, thoroughness, truth, verity, virtue
**perfectionism** accuracy, care, completeness, daintiness, demandingness, exactness, fastidiousness, fineness, finicality, finicalness, niceness, rigidness, severity, strictness
**perfectionist** academic, conscientious, exacting, formalist, idealist, meticulous, particular, pedant, precise, precisionist, purist, scrupulous, selective
**perfectly** à merveille (F), admirably, altogether, certainly, completely, consummately, entirely, exactly, explicitly, faultlessly, flawlessly, fully, ideally, plenarily, positively, precisely, purely, quite, radically, superbly, superlatively, supremely, thoroughly, totally, truly, utterly, verily, wholly
**perfectly clean** immaculate
**perfectly in tune** pure
**perfect model** ideal
**perfect mystery** thummim
**perfect place** Utopia
**perfect state** nirvana
**perfect thing** ideal
**perfidious** deceitful, disloyal, faithless, traitorous, treacherous, untrustworthy
**perfidy** betrayal, corruption, criminality, crookedness, deceit(fulness), deviousness, dishonesty, disloyalty, double-cross, duplicity, faithlessness, falseness, fraud, graft, hypocrisy, infidelity, mendacity, traitorousness, treachery, treason, trickery, wiliness
**perforate** bore, cut, drill, enter, honeycomb, nick, penetrate, permeate, pierce, prick, punch, puncture, rupture, slash, slit, stab
**perforated bowl** colander
**perforated metal** stencil
**perforation in surgical instrument** fenestra

**perforce** automatically, certainly, compellingly, compulsorily, consequently, inevitably, inexorably, naturally, necessarily, needfully, needs, requisitely, surely, unavoidable, unavoidably, willy-nilly

**perform** accomplish, achieve, act, aid, assist, commit, discharge, do, effect, enact, execute, fulfil, help, minister, operate, participate, patronise, perpetrate, play, promote, render, serve, subserve

**perform again** redo, reenact
**perform alone** solo
**perform an action** do
**perform an autopsy** anatomise, dissect, inspect, vivisect

**performance** achievement, act(ion), appearance, attainment, audition, comic, completion, conduct, deed, discharge, drama, entertainment, execution, exhibit(ion), exploit, feat, opera, operation, pageant, piece, play, portrayal, premiere, presentation, production, redemption, rendition, show, tragedy, vaudeville

**performance by one** solo
**performance by skater** ice show
**perform an unscrupulous trick** pull a fast one
**perform a public reading** recite
**perform a service** officiate
**perform as in a play** act
**perform clumsily** botch, bungle
**perform divine service** officiate
**performed in a set manner** pro forma

**performer** actor, actress, agent, artist(e), dancer, doer, entertainer, player, trouper

**performer guide** cue
**performer of spectacular gymnastic feats** acrobat
**performer on a horse** equestrian, equestrienne
**perform function** serve
**performing functions of nutrition** alimentary
**perform in special shoes** ballet, tap-dancing
**perform in theatre** act
**perform mean duties** sutler
**perform on a musical instrument** play
**perform on ice** skate
**perform on stage** (en)act
**performs rhythmical steps** dancer
**perform surgery on** operate
**perform the duties of an office** officiate
**perform the part of** act
**perform with choir** sing

**perfume** aroma, attar, balm, bouquet, cologne, cosmetic, eau de Cologne, essence, extract, fragrance, fragrancy, incense, musk, odour, otto, redolence, scent

**perfume bag** sachet
**perfumed** aromatic, balmy, fragrant, odorous, pungent, savoury, (sweet-)scented
**perfumed powder** talc
**perfume made from sandalwood** chypre (F)
**perfume-making resin** benzoin
**perfume source** flower, musk, whale
**perhaps** conceivably, feasibly, maybe, mayhap, peradventure, perchance, possibly
**periapt** amulet, charm
**peril** danger, endanger, hazard, imperil, insecurity, jeopardy, menace, risk, vulnerability
**perilous** acute, alarming, chancy, critical, crucial, dangerous, deciding, exposed, grave, hazardous, insecure, momentous, parlous, pivotal, precarious, risky, serious, severe, threatening, treacherous, unsafe, unsure, urgent, vital
**perimeter** ambit, border, boundary, bounds, circumference, confines, edge, limit

**period** aeon, age, cycle, date, days, decade, dot, duration, epoch, era, hour, interval, lesson, moment, months, portion, quarter, quinquennium, season, semester, session, space, span, spell, stage, stretch, term, time, weeks, while, years

**period after midday** afternoon
**period after sunset** night
**period before midday** morning
**period between** since
**period between anniversaries** year
**period between childhood and maturity** youth
**period between wars** peace
**periodic** broken, consistent, constant, continued, discontinuous, even, fitful, fixed, frequent, habitual, intermittent, irregular, occasional, ordered, punctuated, recurrent, regular, set, spasmodic, sporadic, stated, steady, systematic, uniform
**periodical** journal, magazine, monthly, organ, paper, publication, quarterly, review, serial, weekly
**periodical gathering for trade** fair
**periodical publication containing news** newspaper
**periodic payment** annuity
**period in development** stage

**period in history** era
**period in polo** chukka, chukker
**period in which primitive stone implements were used** Palaeolithic
**period of being a novice** noviciate, novitiate
**period of celebration** festival
**period of confinement** accouchement (F)
**period of darkness** night
**period of dawn of the mammals** Eocene
**period of fasting** Lent
**period of five years** lustrum, pentad, quinquennium
**period of four years** quadrennium
**period of greatest splendour** meridian
**period of high economic growth** boom
**period of history** age, era
**period of human life** age
**period of immense duration** aeon
**period of inactivity** doldrums
**period of indulgence in activity** jag
**period of instruction** lessons
**period of nonoperation of power supply** blackout, outage
**period of one hundred years** century
**period of one thousand years** millennium
**period of play in polo** chukka, chukker
**period of prison sentence** stretch
**period of school year** term
**period of seven days** week
**period of sovereignty** reign
**period of tenure** term
**period of ten years** decade, decennial, decennium
**period of the flappers** twenties
**period of the revolution of the moon** month
**period of three days** triduum
**period of time** aeon, age, cycle, day, era, hour, minute, month, session, spell, week, year
**period of two years** biennium
**period of wakefulness at night** watch
**period of watch** vigil
**period of youth** nonage
**period preceding the Palaeolithic age** Eolithic
**periods of history** age
**peripatetic** itinerant, journeying, peregrinating, travelling, wayfaring
**peripatetic buyer** shopper
**peripheral** borderline, exterior, external, marginal, minor, shallow, skin-deep, superficial
**periphery** borderline, edge, fringe, limits, march(es), margin, outskirts, perimeter, sideline

**perish** atrophy, corrode, decay, decease, degenerate, die, disappear, dissolve, end, expire, vanish, wane, wither
**perish from hunger** starve
**perish in water** drown
**perissodactyl** horse, rhino(ceros), tapir
**periwig** peruke, wig
**perjurer** falsifier, fibber, forswearer, liar, prevaricator
**perjury** dishonesty, falsehood, forswearing, mendacity, prevarication, untruthfulness
**perk up** brighten, improve, rally, recover, recuperate, revive
**perky** active, agile, airy, alert, blithe, breezy, brisk, carefree, cheerful, chirpy, confident, gay, (high-)spirited, jaunty, joyous, keen, lively, nimble, pert, playful, quick, saucy, self-assertive, showy, smart, sprightly, spruce, spry, trim, vigorous
**permanent** constant, durable, enduring, everlasting, invariable, lasting, perpetual, unaltered, unchanged, unchanging
**permanent abnormal dilation of an artery** aneurism, aneurysm
**permanent dweller** resider
**permanently present in something** indwelling
**permanent military station** camp
**permanent stock** fund
**permeate** blend, diffuse, engrain, enter, fill, imbue, impregnate, infiltrate, infuse, leaven, osmose, penetrate, perforate, pervade, saturate, soak
**permissible** acceptable, acknowledgeable, admissible, allowable, appropriate, approvable, apt, authorised, excusable, justifiable, lawful, legal, legitimate, licit, pardonable, permitted, proper, suitable, tolerable, tolerated
**permission** allowance, approbation, authorisation, blessing, clearance, consent, franchise, freedom, grant, indulgence, leave, liberty, permit, sanction, tolerance, warrant
**permission for temporary absence** exeat
**permission to be absent from duty** leave
**permit** accord, allow, approve, authorise, bless, charter, consent, empower, enable, endure, entitle, give, grant, legalise, let, licence, license, nod, permission, sanction, suffer, tolerate, validate, vouchsafe, warrant
**permit for entering a country** passport

**permit-holder** licensee
**permitted by law** legal
**permitted leeway** tolerance
**permitted to trade** licensee
**permit use of** lend, loan
**permutation** alteration, change, combination, difference, innovation, metabolism, mutation, revolution, transformation, transition, translation, translocation
**pernicious** baleful, baneful, damaging, deadly, deleterious, destructive, detrimental, evil, fatal, harmful, hurtful, injurious, lethal, malevolent, malign, noxious, pestiferous, ruinous, venomous, wicked
**per one** each
**Pèron musical** *Evita*
**perorate** conclude, discourse, expatiate, orate, recapitulate, recount, rodomontade, speechify
**perpendicular** abrupt, erect, morality, plumb, precipitous, rectitude, right-angular, standing, upright, vertical
**per person** per capita
**perpetrate** actuate, always, do, effect, (en)act, enduringly, execute, perform, permanently, practice, pursue, transact
**perpetrate injustice against** aggrieve
**perpetual** aeonian, ageless, constant, continuous, dateless, durable, endless, eternal, frequent, immortal, infinite, interminable, permanent, timeless, unceasing, unending
**perpetual lease at fixed rent** feu
**perpetually** agelessly, constantly, continuously, datelessly, unceasingly, uninterruptedly
**perpetually young** ageless
**perplex** baffle, befuddle, bewilder, bother, complicate, confound, confuse, discourage, dum(b)found, hamper, harass, mystify, nonplus, puzzle, rattle, snarl
**perplexingly complicated** intricate
**perplexity** astonishment, bewildered, confusion, consternation, conundrum, doubt, dubiety, enigma, mistrust, nonplus, puzzle(ment), riddle, stupefaction, uncertainty, worry
**per se** alone, apart, immanently, individually, inherently, innately, intrinsically, separately, solitary
**persecute** afflict, annoy, bother, crucify, harass, molest, oppress, punish, torment, torture
**persecution complex** paranoia
**persecution of the Jews** pogrom

**persecutor** autocrat, bully, despot, oppressor, scourge, tormentor, tyrant
**perseverance** continuance, decision, determination, devotion, doggedness, endurance, indefatigability, patience, persistence, pertinacity, resolution, resolve, stamina, steadfastness, tenacity
**persevere** continue, contrary, disobedient, headstrong, intractable, last, obstinate, persist(ent), perverted, stubborn, unyielding, wayward, wilful
**persevering self-assertion** push
**Persia** Iran
**Persian** Iranian
**Persian carpet** Kirman
**Persian coin** rial
**Persian fairy** peri
**Persian gazelle** cora
**Persian governor** satrap
**Persian harp** sang
**Persian lamb** caracul, karakul
**Persian language** Farsi, Pahlavi, Zend
**Persian lynx** caracal
**Persian poet** Hafiz, Omar
**Persian ruler** shah
**Persian silver coin** rial
**Persian sprite** peri
**Persian sword** acinaces
**Persian tile** kashi
**Persian title** Mirza
**Persian unit of distance** parasang
**Persian water wheel** noria
**Persian wild ass** onager
**persicaria** peachwort
**persiflage** banter, raillery
**persist** abide, accept, await, bear, continue, endure, expect, insist, keep, last, linger, persevere, remain, reside, stay, suffer, tarry, tolerate
**persistence** continuance, decision, determination, endurance, obstinacy, patience, perseverance, pertinacity, stamina, steadfastness, tenacity
**persistent** constant, continual, continuous, enduring, indefatigable, lasting, obstinate, persevering, pertinacious, repeated, resolute, steadfast, stubborn, tenacious, unyielding
**persistent abnormal fear of something** phobia
**persistent absence from work** absenteeism
**persistent attack** siege
**persistent horse** stayer
**persistent idea dominating person's mind** obsession
**persistent illness** ailment

**persistently annoy** harass
**persistent sensation of numbness and tingling in hands and feet** acroparaesthesia
**person** being, body, chap, character, creature, customer, entity, fellow, folk, guy, human, individual, lad, lass, life, mortal, object, oke, one, ou, persona, personage, self, somebody, someone, soul, spirit, (wo)man
**person able to do odd jobs** handyman
**person accused in a lawsuit** defendant
**person accused of offence** culprit
**person acting for another** proxy
**person actively hostile to another** enemy
**person addicted to working** workaholic
**person admired by fan** idol
**personal** bodily, individual, intimate, own, particular, private
**personal ability** accomplishment
**personal accomplishment** attainment
**personal appearance** presence
**personal attendant** maid, valet
**personal belongings** clobber, effects, paraphernalia
**personal benefit** sake
**personal charm** charisma
**personal clerk** private secretary
**personal clothes** clobber
**personal consequence** dignity
**personal consideration** importance
**personal effects** belongings, property
**personal enrichment** self-aggrandisement
**personal equipment** kit
**personal estate** effects
**personal file** dossier
**personal height** stature
**personal helper** attendant
**personal idiosyncrasy or whim** fad
**personal interest** affairs, self
**personality** affection, celebrity, character, charisma, difference, dignitary, disposition, identity, individuality, lik(e)ability, luminary, magnetism, make-up, nature, notable, personage, pleasantness, psyche, star, temperament, uniqueness
**personal journal** diary
**personal knowledge** acquaintance
**personal liberty** freedom
**personally** alone, especially, exclusively, expressly, idiosyncratically, in propria persona (L), independently, individually, intimately, particularly, peculiarly, privately, solely, specially, subjectively
**personal observation** autopsy
**personal outlook** philosophy
**personal pronoun** her, him, his, me, my, our, she, us, we
**personal property** effects
**personal quality** charisma
**personal record** diary
**personal satire** lampoon
**personal strong point** forte
**person always keeping an eye on the time** clock-watcher
**persona non grata** outcast
**person appointed by testator to carry out terms of will** executor
**person at an auction** bidder
**person at the helm** steersman
**person authorised to act for another** agent, proxy
**person bearing blame due to others** scapegoat
**person bearing heavy burden** camel, donkey
**person belonging to a group** member
**person betrothed** fiancé(e)
**person bringing good luck** mascot
**person competing against another** rival
**person conducting a business** manager
**person considered suitable for an office** candidate
**person converted from one opinion to another** proselyte
**person decamping in secret** fly-by-night
**person dedicated to monastic work** oblate
**person delegated to act for another** deputy
**person deprived of protection of law** outlaw
**person detained in custody** detainee
**person directing an enterprise** master-mind
**person directing circus performance** ringmaster
**person displaying paedophilia** paedophile
**person easily deceived** sucker
**person eating** diner
**person employed at a bar** tapster
**person employed for wages** employee
**person employed to carry luggage** porter
**person employed to copy manuscripts** amanuensis
**person employed to drive a car** chauffeur
**person employed to protect game** gamekeeper
**person employed to take care of horses** groom
**person employed to write for newspaper** journalist
**person engaged in research** academic, boffin
**person filled with excessive enthusiasm** fanatic
**person formidable to both friend and foe** Drawcansir
**person from another country** foreigner
**person from Antipodes** Aussie
**person from eighty to eighty-nine years old** octogenarian
**person from fifty to fifty-nine years old** quinquagenarian
**person from forty to forty-nine years old** quadragenarian
**person from hundred and over** centenarian
**person from ninety to ninety-nine years old** nonagenarian
**person from seventy to seventy-nine years old** septuagenarian
**person from sixty to sixty-nine years old** sexagenarian
**person from the East** Asian
**person from the same country as another** compatriot
**person given to crazes** faddist
**person given to gossip** newsmonger, quidnunc, skinderbek
**person giving evidence** witness
**person giving sworn testimony** witness
**person guilty of an offence** culprit
**person guilty of wickedness** villain
**person having admiration for England** Anglophil(e)
**person having authority** power
**person having control** master
**person having special knowledge** expert
**person having the same name as another** namesake
**person held in custody** detainee, prisoner
**person helping to carry coffin at funeral** pallbearer
**person holding a university degree** (post-)graduate
**person holding highest hereditary title of nobility** duke
**person holding high rank** dignitary
**person holding property by lease** lessee
**personification** acting, appearance, conceit, delineation, duplication, embodiment, epitome, example, image, impersonation, incarnation, likeness, metaphor, representation
**personification of health** Hygeia

**personify** characterise, embody, exemplify, express, represent, symbolise
**person in book** character
**person in charge** boss, manager
**person in charge of a state department** minister
**person in charge of funds** treasurer
**person in charge of gambling-table** croupier
**person in charge of museum** curator
**person in charge of prisoner** jailer
**person in charge of stabling horses at inn** (h)ostler
**person in custody** detainee
**person in effective control** entrepreneur
**person in Greenland** Eskimo
**person in place of another** substitute
**person in ragged dirty clothes** ragamuffin
**person inspired by violent enthusiasm** nympholept
**person in teens** teenager
**person in tent** camper
**person interested in expressions** phraseologist
**person in the know** insider
**person in the street** layman
**person in whom one confides** confidant
**person killed in accident** casualty
**person known** acquaintance
**person lacking courage** coward
**person lacking normal colouring** albino
**person learned in history** historian
**person living in Greenland** Eskimo
**person loyal to his country** patriot
**person making excursion** tripper
**person named** nominee
**person named after another** namesake
**personnel** associates, employees, force, group, staff, workers
**personnel nucleus** cadre
**personnel of vessel** crew
**person next door** neighbour
**person not acceptable** persona non grata (L)
**person not present** absentee
**person not serving in the armed forces** civilian
**person obsessively addicted to work** workaholic
**person of austere fortitude** stoic
**person of consequence** magnifico
**person of equal standing** compeer
**person of erudite tastes** highbrow
**person of extreme strictness in morals** puritan
**person of fiery temper** spitfire

**person of greater age** elder
**person of great importance** somebody
**person of great mental ability** wit
**person of great patience** Job
**person of great self-control** stoic
**person of great size** giant
**person of great strength** Samson
**person of great strength or size** titan
**person of great wickedness** monster
**person of importance** somebody
**person of infallible wisdom** Daniel, Solomon
**person of low birth** churl
**person of lower classes** pleb(eian)
**person of mature age** adult
**person of mixed blood** metis, mulatto
**person of noble birth** patrician
**person of no importance** nonentity
**person of property** (free)holder, possessor, proprietor
**person of rank** eminence, magnate, magnifico, personage
**person of refined tastes** epicure
**person of relatively liberal views** verligte
**person of ridiculous appearance** quiz
**person of secluded habits** anchoress, anchoret, anchorite, hermit, recluse
**person of taste** connoisseur, dilettante
**person of ultra-conservative views** verkrampte
**person of unknown abilities** dark horse
**person of varied learning** polymath
**person of wealth** magnate, nob
**person of white and black parentage** mulatto
**person on diet** slimmer
**person one does not know** stranger
**person one hundred or more years old** centenarian
**person one knows slightly** acquaintance
**person on regimen** dieter
**person on trial** defendant
**person on vacation** holidaymaker
**person operating machine** operator, user
**person opposed to war** dove, pacifist
**person or thing worthy of imitation** model
**person out of harmony with period** anachronism
**person over one hundred years old** centenarian
**person owing money** debtor
**person persevering** trier
**person possessing a million rands** millionaire
**person practising teetotalism** teetotaller
**person producing an effect** agent

**person prominent in fashionable society** socialite
**person put in authority** prefect
**person recently arrived** newcomer
**person regarded as eligible for marriage** match
**person regarded as identical with another** clone
**person regarded with affection** pet
**person rejected by society** outcast
**person removed** evacuee
**person renting property** tenant
**person responsible** culprit
**person ruined mentally or physically** wreck
**person's animating principle** anima, animus, spirit
**persons banded together** cohort
**person's bearing** mien
**person's behaviour** conduct
**person's calling in life** mission
**person's competitor** rival
**persons comprising nation** people
**person's death** demise
**person's distinguishing personality** character
**person's double** ringer
**person sent away from place of danger** evacuee
**person sent to seek military information** scout
**persons grouped together** cohort
**person's height** stature
**person's identity** name
**persons in attendance** retinue
**person's individual nature** character
**person skilled in geometry** geometer
**person skilled in Hebrew** Hebraist
**person skilled in languages** linguist
**person skilled in maintaining machinery** mechanic
**person skilled in music** musician
**person skilled in physics** physicist
**person skilled in shooting** marksman
**person skilled in sinology** sinologue
**person skilled in surgery** surgeon
**person's mental ability** mentality
**person's moral nature** character
**person's name used in signing** signature
**persons of the same family** kin, relatives
**person's particular like or dislike** craze, fad
**person's partner in marriage** spouse
**person's physical condition** health
**person's private room** sanctum, snuggery
**person's property** estate
**person's right** due
**person's self** ego

person's sensitive feelings susceptibility
person's speciality métier
person's sphere of operataion fief
person's strong point forte, métier
person stupefied by habitual drunkenness dronkie, sot
person suffering chronic mental disorder psychopath, schizophrenic
person suffering from leprosy lazar, leper
person's wraith or double fetch
person that is doomed goner
person that seems to cause bad luck jinx
person to whom a legacy is bequeathed legatee
person to whom another is protector protégé(e)
person to whom a transfer of property is made alienee
person to whom money is owed creditor
person to whom something is allotted allottee
person travelling from place to place itinerant
person travelling on skis skier
person under instruction trainee
person under medical treatment patient
person under twenty-one minor
person unduly anxious about his health valetudinarian
person unknown quidam
person unnamed so-and-so, such-and-such
person used by another as a tool cat's-paw
person versed in law legist
person who accepts things as they are realist
person who acts as a judge judicator
person who acts for other people agent
person who always expects the worst pessimist
person who announces items in a broadcast announcer
person who assists women in child-birth accoucheur (F), accoucheuse (F)
person who behaves affectedly poseur
person who behaves dishonourably cad
person who behaves humorously comedian
person who belongs to a club member
person who bets money gambler
person who buys consumer

person who carries a golf player's clubs during play caddie, caddy
person who casts metal founder
person who cleans the chimney sweep
person who coaches singers or ballet dancers répétiteur (F)
person who collects fares in public transport conductor
person who collects moths and butterflies lepidopterist
person who commits piracy pirate
person who cuts precious stones lapidary
person who deals in animal skins fellmonger
person who decides a question judge
person who designs buildings architect
person who dislikes cats ailurophobe
person who draws a cheque drawer
person who dresses stone mason
person who drives cattle drover
person who effects seeming impossibilities wizard
person who enjoys good food gourmet
person who enjoys luxurious living bon vivant (F)
person who entertains quests host
person who entices others to follow him Pied Piper
person who examines scrutator
person who extorts profit from others leech
person who fishes with rod and line angler
person who flies in a lighter-than-air craft aeronaut
person who gains unauthorised access to a computer hacker
person who gives a talk speaker
person who gives counsel counsellor
person who gives evidence in court witness
person who grants a lease of property lessor
person who grows plants gardener
person who has arrived recently newcomer
person who has a wild social life raver
person who has defeated all others champ(ion)
person who has had a limb amputated amputee
person who has made a will testator
person who has nonintellectual tastes lowbrow
person who has risen suddenly from humble position upstart

person who has urinary disorder diabetic
person who hates foreigners xenophobe
person who hates or fears England or its people Anglophobe
person who hates strangers xenophobe
person who hates women misogynist
person who hides on a ship stowaway
person who hoards wealth miser
person who interprets dreams oneirocritic
person who introduces artistes at variety show compère
person who introduces speakers at dinner toastmaster, toastmistress
person who is a fashion leader trendsetter
person who is afraid of cats ailurophobe
person who is against war pacifist
person who is a vigorous campaigner crusader
person who is chronically sick valetudinarian
person who is deceived patsy
person who is drunk inebriate
person who is engaged to be married fiancé
person who is intermediate between an extrovert and an introvert ambivert
person who is legal property of others slave
person who is master of dinner-table conversation deipnosophist
person who is nominated by another nominee
person who is permanently lame cripple
person who is rejected outcast
person who is ridiculed patsy
person who is self-taught autodidact
person who is shipwrecked castaway
person who is taught pupil
person who is under the patronage of another protégé(e)
person who is unsuited to his work misfit
person who is victimised patsy
person who keeps an aviary aviarist
person who keeps bees apiarist
person who kills his or her parent parricide
person who lags behind laggard, procrastinator
person who learns only late in life opsimath
person who likes cats ailurophile
person who likes foreigners xenophile

**person who like to stir things up**
troublemaker
**person who lives in a place** occupier
**person who lives in Arctic circle**
Lap(lander)
**person who lives in a suburb**
suburbanite
**person who lives in seclusion**
anchoress, anchoret, anchorite,
hermit
**person who lives next door** neighbour
**person who looks after affairs of**
**entertainer** manager
**person who looks after a place**
caretaker
**person who looks after horses** groom
**person who loves his country** patriot
**person who makes and sells women's**
**hats** milliner
**person who makes candles** chandler
**person who manages property for**
**another** trustee
**person who massages** masseur,
masseuse
**person who mends shoes** cobbler
**person who notifies actors when to go**
**on stage** callboy
**person who observes Sabbath strictly**
Sabbatarian
**person who operates machine**
machinist, operator, user
**person who owns land on a river bank**
riparian
**person who performs menial tasks**
flunk(e)y
**person who plays the alto saxophone**
altoist
**person who plays the lute** lutenist
**person who plays the lyre** lyrist
**person who plays the oboe** oboist
**person who practices sodomy**
sodomite
**person who predicts the future**
prophet
**person who presides over meeting**
chairman
**person who processes film** developer
**person who protects and supports**
**another** patron
**person who provides eat and drink**
caterer
**person who puts designs on skin**
tattooist
**person who receives something**
recipient
**person who refuses to acknowledge**
**an awkward truth** ostrich
**person who refuses to take an oath**
nonjuror
**person who repairs chimneys**
steeplejack

**person who rescues someone from**
**harm** saviour
**person who says much of little value**
windbag
**person who schools animals for racing**
horse trainer
**person who searches assiduously**
ferret
**person who sees visions** prophet,
seer
**person who selects** selector
**person who sells candles** chandler
**person who sells goods abroad**
exporter
**person who sells newspapers**
newsvendor
**person whose name one has forgotten**
thingamy, thingumajig, thingummy,
thingy, whomever
**person who shoes horses** farrier
**person who shrinks from danger**
coward
**person who speaks Bini** Edo
**person who spoils other people's**
**pleasure** killjoy
**person who spreads malicious gossip**
scandalmonger
**person who stirs up trouble** firebrand
**person who studies past events**
historian
**person who studies plants** botanist
**person who supports his or her**
**country** patriot
**person who takes an oath** juror
**person who takes care of horses**
(h)ostler
**person who takes revenge** avenger
**person who talks wittily** wit
**person who tells** narrator, teller
**person who tells lies** liar
**person who thinks he or she has**
**knowledge of everything** know-all
**person who traps and sells rabbits**
rabbiter
**person who uses bow and arrow**
archer, toxophilite
**person who uses LSD** acidhead
**person who watches bathers** lifeguard
**person who works on steadily** plodder
**person who writes a novel** author,
novelist
**person who writes for newspaper**
columnist
**person who writes the words for a**
**song** lyricist
**person with antiquated ideas** fog(e)y
**person with biased views** bigot
**person with compact muscular body**
mesomorph
**person with congenital mental**
**deficiency** ament

**person with exclusive information**
insider
**person with experience of the**
**supernatural** mystic
**person with expert knowledge of**
**science** scientist
**person with fat and heavy body build**
endomorph
**person with fiery temper** spitfire
**person with fortune of several millions**
multimillionaire
**person with his or her head in the**
**clouds** dreamer
**person with improbable hopes**
dreamer
**person with IQ between 50 and 70**
moron
**person with lean body** ectomorph
**person with leprosy** leper
**person with more than one spouse**
bigamist
**person with morning delivery**
postman
**person with muscular body build**
mesomorph
**person with nervous disorders**
neurotic
**person without a country** refugee,
stateless
**person without equal** non(e)such
**person without freedom and personal**
**rights** slave
**person with outgoing personality**
extrovert
**person without melanin** albino
**person without professional**
**knowledge** layman
**person without regular work** vagrant
**person with outstanding intellect**
mastermind
**person with pigment deficiency** albino
**person with powerful voice** stentor
**person with sly look** leerer
**person with some marvellous gift**
prodigy
**person with speech defect** stutterer
**person with the same appearance**
doppelgänger, look-alike
**person with thin body build**
ectomorph
**person with Titian hair** redhead
**person with university degree**
(post-)graduate
**person you don't know** stranger
**perspective** viewpoint
**perspicacious** alert, aware, clever,
observant, penetrating, perceptive,
sagacious, shrewd
**perspicacity** acuity, acumen,
acuteness, apprehension,
astuteness, awareness, brains,
clairvoyance, discrimination, esprit,

flair, ingenuity, insight, intelligence, judg(e)ment, keenness, knowledge, notice, perceptiveness, percipience, prudence, sagaciousness, sagacity, sense, shrewdness, skill, smartness, understanding
**perspicuous** astute, certain, clear, distinct, evident, intelligible, lucid, plain, pointed, tangible, unmistakable, unqualified, well-defined
**perspiration** hidrosis, sweat
**perspire** drip, secrete, sweat, swelter
**persuade** actuate, advise, affect, allure, bend, bribe, coax, compel, convert, convince, counsel, enlist, entice, exhort, force, impel, incline, induce, influence, inspire, inveigle, lure, motivate, move, prompt, satisfy, seduce, sway, tempt, urge
**persuade by flattery** cajole
**persuade by offer of reward** entice
**persuade gradually** coax
**persuade of what is false** deceive
**persuade to believe firmly the truth** convince
**persuade to do some sin or folly** seduce
**persuasion** admonition, advice, affiliation, belief, bribery, consequence, conversation, credo, creed, force, group, inducement, interest, opinion, potency, seduction, weight
**persuasive talk** rhetoric
**pert** audacious, bold, bouncy, brash, brassy, flippant, forward, fresh, impertinent, impolite, impudent, insolent, jaunty, lively, peppy, perky, presumptuous, rude, sassy, saucy, sprightly, vivacious
**pertaining to a royal court** aulic
**pertaining to** about
**pertaining to abbey** abbacy
**pertaining to abbot** abbatial
**pertaining to abdomen** alvine, ventral
**pertaining to action** practical
**pertaining to actors** histrionic, thespian
**pertaining to advertisement** publicity
**pertaining to Aeolus** Aeolian
**pertaining to aerial navigation** aeronautic(al)
**pertaining to age** geriatric, senile
**pertaining to air** aerial
**pertaining to alchemy** spagyric(al)
**pertaining to ambassador** legatine
**pertaining to anagram** anagrammatical
**pertaining to ancestry** lineal
**pertaining to ancient Italy** Italic
**pertaining to angels** angelic
**pertaining to animals** zoic
**pertaining to ankle** talaric, tarsal

**pertaining to aphids** aphidian
**pertaining to apples** malic
**pertaining to archbishop** archiepiscopal
**pertaining to area** areal, regional
**pertaining to arm** brachial
**pertaining to armbone** ulnar
**pertaining to armed ship** naval
**pertaining to armpit** axillar(y)
**pertaining to army** military
**pertaining to art of cutting gems** lapidary
**pertaining to ashes** cinerary
**pertaining to asses** asinine
**pertaining to atoms** atomic
**pertaining to aura** aural
**pertaining to back** dorsal, lumbar
**pertaining to back of skull** occipital
**pertaining to baked clay** earthen
**pertaining to banks of a river** riparian
**pertaining to barber or his art** tonsorial
**pertaining to bath** balneal, balneary
**pertaining to bears** ursine
**pertaining to bees** apian
**pertaining to bell** campanular
**pertaining to belly** coeliac
**pertaining to biology** biologic(al)
**pertaining to birds** avian, ornithic, oscine
**pertaining to birth** natal
**pertaining to bishops** episcopal
**pertaining to blood** haemal
**pertaining to blood vessel** arterial, venous
**pertaining to body** corporeal, physical, somatic
**pertaining to bone** osseous, oste-, osteal, osteo-
**pertaining to both sexes** unisex
**pertaining to brain** cerebral, encephaloid
**pertaining to branch** ramal, ramose, ramular, ramulose
**pertaining to bread** panary
**pertaining to bristle** setal
**pertaining to building** tectonic
**pertaining to bull** taurine
**pertaining to calf** vitular
**pertaining to calf of the leg** sural
**pertaining to carving** glyphic, glyptic
**pertaining to cats** feline
**pertaining to caves** spelaean
**pertaining to cell** cytoid
**pertaining to centre** central, focal
**pertaining to chamber** cameral
**pertaining to cheek** malar
**pertaining to cheek-bone** jugal
**pertaining to cherubs** cherubic
**pertaining to child** filial
**pertaining to childbirth** puerperal

**pertaining to children and their diseases** paediatric
**pertaining to choirs** choral
**pertaining to circle** circular
**pertaining to cities** urban
**pertaining to city** urban
**pertaining to clan** clannish
**pertaining to coins or coinage** numismatic, nummary
**pertaining to commodities** staple
**pertaining to construction** tectonic
**pertaining to cookery** culinary
**pertaining to cork** suberic
**pertaining to coughs** tussive
**pertaining to country** rural, rustic
**pertaining to cremation** crematory
**pertaining to dancing** Terpsichorean
**pertaining to dawn** auroral, eoan
**pertaining to death anniversary** obitual
**pertaining to deer** cervine, damine
**pertaining to desire** orectic
**pertaining to diaphragm** phrenic
**pertaining to diet** dietary
**pertaining to digestive system** peptic
**pertaining to dinner** prandial
**pertaining to diocese** diocesan
**pertaining to divination** mantic
**pertaining to doctrine** dogmatical
**pertaining to dogs** canine
**pertaining to dove** peristeronic
**pertaining to drama** histrionic, thespian
**pertaining to dress** vestiary
**pertaining to drinking** potatory
**pertaining to duke** ducal
**pertaining to ear** aural, otic
**pertaining to earth** earthy, geo-, terrene, terrestrial
**pertaining to earthquakes** seismic
**pertaining to Easter** Paschal
**pertaining to ecclesiastical chapter** capitular
**pertaining to Egypt** Coptic
**pertaining to empire** imperial
**pertaining to end of a period** latter
**pertaining to energy** actinic
**pertaining to evening** vesper
**pertaining to exercises** gymnastics
**pertaining to eyebrows** supercilliary
**pertaining to eyelid** palpebral
**pertaining to eyes** ocular, optic
**pertaining to face** facial
**pertaining to fat** adipose, sebaceous
**pertaining to fathers** paternal
**pertaining to fermentation** zymotic
**pertaining to fireworks** pyrotechnic
**pertaining to first principles of learning** elemental
**pertaining to fish** finny, ichthyal, ichthyic, piscatory, piscine
**pertaining to fishing** halieutic, piscatorial

pertaining to five  quinary
pertaining to fixed camp  stative
pertaining to flower  floral
pertaining to food  alimentary
pertaining to food plants  vegetal
pertaining to foot  pedal, podal
pertaining to forest  nemoral, silvan, sylvan
pertaining to form  modal
pertaining to foxes  vulpine
pertaining to fruit  carpo-
pertaining to fugue  fugal
pertaining to fungi  agaric
pertaining to garments  vestiary
pertaining to genus  generic
pertaining to glass  vitreous, vitric
pertaining to goat  caprine
pertaining to gold  auric
pertaining to gonads  gonadic
pertaining to goose  anserine
pertaining to grain  oaten
pertaining to grapes  acinic
pertaining to grass  graminaceous
pertaining to group of singers  choral
pertaining to grove  nemoral
pertaining to hair  pileous
pertaining to hanger-on  parasitical
pertaining to head  cephalic
pertaining to headache  cephalalgic
pertaining to healing art  therapeutic
pertaining to hearing  acoustic
pertaining to heart  cardiac
pertaining to heat  caloric, thermal, thermic
pertaining to Hebrew  Hebraic
pertaining to herring  clupeoid
pertaining to hip  sciatic
pertaining to home  domestic
pertaining to horizon  mundane
pertaining to horsemanship  equestrian
pertaining to hunting  venatic
pertaining to hurling and flight of projectiles  ballistic
pertaining to ileum  ileac, iliac
pertaining to India  Indic
pertaining to inferior animals  bestial
pertaining to island  insular
pertaining to Isle of Man  Manx
pertaining to kidneys  renal
pertaining to kitchen  culinary
pertaining to knee  genual
pertaining to knowledge  epistemological, sciential
pertaining to lake  lacustrine
pertaining to land  agrarian, geoponic
pertaining to law  canonic
pertaining to Leo  Leonine
pertaining to life  biotic
pertaining to lion  leonine
pertaining to lips  labial

pertaining to liturgies or public worship  liturgical
pertaining to loins  lumbar
pertaining to love  amatory, amorous, erotic
pertaining to lungs  pulmonic
pertaining to lungs and stomach  pneumogastric
pertaining to mail  postal
pertaining to mankind  human
pertaining to marriage  marital, nuptial
pertaining to marshes  paludal
pertaining to master  magisterial
pertaining to measurement by volume  volumetric
pertaining to messenger  emissary
pertaining to middle  median, mesial
pertaining to midwifery  obstetric
pertaining to milk  lacteal, lactic
pertaining to Milky Way  galactic
pertaining to mind  mental, noetic
pertaining to mirrors  specular
pertaining to money  nummary, pecuniary
pertaining to moon  lunar
pertaining to moon  lunar, selenic
pertaining to mothers  maternal
pertaining to motion  kinetic
pertaining to movement of the eye  oculomotor
pertaining to name  onomastic
pertaining to names  nominal
pertaining to navel  umbilical
pertaining to nervous system  neural
pertaining to nobleman  ducal
pertaining to nose  nasal
pertaining to nostril  narial, narine
pertaining to number eight  octal
pertaining to number sixty  sexagenary
pertaining to oceans  pelagic
pertaining to ode  odic
pertaining to old age  geriatric, senile
pertaining to Old World  European
pertaining to one ear  monaural
pertaining to organic tissues  histo-
pertaining to outside  external
pertaining to palm of hand  volar
pertaining to Passover  paschal
pertaining to period of pregnancy  antenatal
pertaining to pertinent  appurtenance
pertaining to pineapple  anonaceous
pertaining to Plato  Platonic
pertaining to poles of a cell  polar
pertaining to pope  papal
pertaining to present day  hodiernal
pertaining to public worship  liturgic(al)
pertaining to pugilism  fistic
pertaining to punishment  penal, punitive

pertaining to race  ethnic
pertaining to rain  pluvial
pertaining to rays  actinic, radial
pertaining to reason  noetic
pertaining to religious law  canonic
pertaining to resistance  resistive
pertaining to ribs  costal, costate
pertaining to ridge  cardinal
pertaining to right side of a vessel  starboard
pertaining to rites  ritual
pertaining to river  potamic, riparian, riverine
pertaining to river Styx  Stygian
pertaining to runes  runic
pertaining to sad story  tragic
pertaining to sailors  nautical
pertaining to saints or holy things  hagio-
pertaining to saliva  sialic
pertaining to salvation  soterical
pertaining to sandstone  arenilitic
pertaining to science  scientific
pertaining to Scriptures  Scriptural
pertaining to sea  marine
pertaining to seals  phocine
pertaining to seashore  littoral
pertaining to sense of hearing  auricular
pertaining to sense of smell  olfactory
pertaining to sense of touch  haptic, tactile
pertaining to sensual pleasure  voluptuous
pertaining to serpent  anguine, ophic
pertaining to serum  serous
pertaining to sexual love  amatory
pertaining to sheep  ovine
pertaining to shepherds  pastoral
pertaining to ships  nautical, naval
pertaining to shore  littoral
pertaining to shoulder  humeral, scapular
pertaining to side  lateral
pertaining to siege  obsidional
pertaining to sight  optic, visual
pertaining to six  senary
pertaining to skin  dermatic
pertaining to skull  cranial, cranio-
pertaining to smell  olfactory
pertaining to Smyrna  Smyrniot
pertaining to snakes  herpetological, ophidian, ophioid
pertaining to soft palate  velar, uvular
pertaining to soil  edaphic
pertaining to sound  sonant, sonar, sonic, tonal
pertaining to space  spatial
pertaining to speech  vocal
pertaining to spinal cord  myeloid
pertaining to stars  astral, sidereal, stellar

**pertaining to stomach** gastric
**pertaining to stones** lapidary
**pertaining to subsidy** subsidiary
**pertaining to sugar** saccharin(e)
**pertaining to suicide** suicidal
**pertaining to summer** estival
**pertaining to sun** solar
**pertaining to sundial** sciatheric
**pertaining to surface** superficial
**pertaining to swimming** natatorial, natatory
**pertaining to Switzerland** Swiss
**pertaining to symptoms** sem(e)iotic, semiological
**pertaining to systems** systemic
**pertaining to table** mensal
**pertaining to tailor** sartorial
**pertaining to tallow or fat** sebaceous
**pertaining to Tasmania** Tasmanian
**pertaining to tears** lachrymal
**pertaining to teeth** dental
**pertaining to tension** tensile
**pertaining to the Alps** Alpine
**pertaining to the Angles** Anglian
**pertaining to the Copts** Coptic
**pertaining to the East** eoan, oriental
**pertaining to the heavens** uranian
**pertaining to the Mediterranean Sea** Mediterranean
**pertaining to the North Pole** Arctic
**pertaining to the Orkney islands** Orcadian
**pertaining to the South** austral
**pertaining to Thespis** Thespian
**pertaining to thigh** femoral
**pertaining to thirty years** tricennial
**pertaining to this life** temporal
**pertaining to throat** guttural, jugular
**pertaining to thunder and lighting** ceraunic
**pertaining to tides** tidal
**pertaining to time** temporal
**pertaining to tin mines** stannary, stannous
**pertaining to today** diurnal
**pertaining to toe** digital
**pertaining to town** civic, urban
**pertaining to tragedy** thespian
**pertaining to trees** arboreal
**pertaining to Troy** Trojan
**pertaining to twenty** icosian, vicenary
**pertaining to twilight** crepuscular
**pertaining to tympanum** tympanic
**pertaining to uncle** avuncular
**pertaining to underworld and the deities inhabiting it** chthonian
**pertaining to universe** cosmic, cosmo-, universal
**pertaining to veal** vituline
**pertaining to vehicles** vehicular
**pertaining to veins** venous
**pertaining to vinegar** acetic

**pertaining to vision** optic(al)
**pertaining to voice** vocal
**pertaining to volcano** volcanic
**pertaining to vowels** vocalic
**pertaining to wall** mural, parietal
**pertaining to wandering Arabs** Bedouin
**pertaining to war** martial
**pertaining to warmth** thermal, thermic
**pertaining to warships** naval
**pertaining to wasps** vespine
**pertaining to water** aquatic, hydraulic
**pertaining to weight** baric
**pertaining to whales** cetic
**pertaining to widows** vidual
**pertaining to wind** (a)eolian
**pertaining to window** fenestral
**pertaining to wine or grapes** vinaceous
**pertaining to wings** alar
**pertaining to winter** boreal, hibernal, hiemal, wintry
**pertaining to wives** uxorial
**pertaining to wolves** lupine
**pertaining to women** feminine
**pertaining to woods** sylvan
**pertaining to word meanings** semantic
**pertaining to words** lexical, lexicon
**pertaining to world** mundane
**pertaining to worship** liturgic
**pertaining to wrist** carpo-
**pertaining to yesterday** hesternal, yester
**pertaining to youth or pubescence** hebetic
**pert fellow** jackanapes
**pert girl** chit, hussy, minx
**pertinacious** determined, dogged, firm, immovable, importunate, indefatigable, intractable, obstinate, persistent, perverse, recalcitrant, resolute, self-willed, steadfast, stubborn, tenacious, tireless
**pertinacity** constancy, contumacy, dedication, diligence, endurance, firmness, grit, inflexibility, insistence, intransigence, mulishness, obstinacy, perseverance, persistence, pluck, resoluteness, resolution, rigidity, stamina, sternness, stubbornness, tenacity, wilfulness
**pertinence** appositeness, aptness, congruousness, consonance, fitness, harmoniousness, harmony, relevance, suitability, suitableness
**pertinent** apposite, appropriate, apropos, apt, fitting, proper, relating, relevant, suitable, valid
**perturb** agitate, arouse, bother, confuse, derange, discompose, disconcert, disorder, disquiet, distract, disturb, excite, fluster, irritate, rouse, suscitate, tease, torment, trouble, upset, vex
**perturbation of mind** trepidation
**pertussis** whooping cough
**peruke** (peri)wig
**perusal** analysis, browse, catechism, check(up), examination, exploration, inquiry, inquisition, inspection, interrogation, investigation, overview, probe, questioning, quiz, read(ing), review, scrutiny, search, study, survey, test, trial
**peruse** browse, check, examine, inspect, read, scan, scrutinise, study
**peruser** inspector, reader, scanner
**Peruvian camel** llama
**Peruvian dance** cachua, cueca, kaswa
**Peruvian Indian** Inca
**Peruvian money** centavo, dinero, libra, sol
**Peruvian sheep** alpaca
**Peruvian volcano** Misti
**pervade** affect, charge, diffuse, extend, fill, honeycomb, imbue, (in)fuse, in(ter)osculate, leaven, merge, osmose, penetrate, percolate, permeate, saturate, suffuse, transfuse
**perverse** abnormal, contrary, depraved, deviant, dogged, forward, ironic, pig-headed, wayward
**perverse behaviour** waywardness
**perversion** abuse, corruption, decadence, degeneration, depravity, evil, immorality, impurity, iniquity, malapropism, misuse, profanation, sinfulness, solecism, vice, viciousness, waste, wickedness
**pervert** abase, allure, avert, corrupt, deflect, distort, divert, exploit, misinform, mislead, misuse, reduce, shunt
**perverted** aberrant, abnormal, corrupt, deviate, distorted, evil, false, faulty, immoral, kinky, ludicrous, misguided, monstrous, ridiculous, seduced, twisted, unsound, vitiated
**pervert from morality** debauch
**pesky plant** weed
**pessimist** alarmist, complainer, cynic, defeatist, depressor, doubter, dropout, grumbler, hypochondriac, moper, worrier
**pest** annoyance, bane, bore, bug, curse, epidemic, nuisance, pain, plague, scourge, vexation
**pester** annoy, badger, bedevil, bother, bug, disturb, gall, harass, harry, hector, molest, nag, nettle, plague, tease, trouble, vex, worry
**pestering** harassment

**pester verbally** nag
**pestilence** lues, plague
**pest killer** insecticide
**pests** vermin
**pet** caress, cherished, choice, dear, favourite, fondle, pat, preferred, stroke
**pet aversion** bête noire (F)
**pet cat** pussy
**peter out** cease, dwindle, ebb, evaporate, fade, fail, stop, wane
**pet food** bird seed
**pet idea** fad
**petite** bantam, charming, dainty, delicate, diminutive, elegant, fine, graceful, little, midget, miniature, minute, neat, petit, pretty, pygmy, small, tiny
**petition** address, adjure, appeal, application, beg, beseech, entreat(y), impetrate, obtest, pray(er), request, requisition, solicit, sue, suit, supplicate
**petition hearing** oyer
**petition of protest** remonstrance
**pet lamb** cade
**petrified remains** fossil
**petrify** alarm, appal, arrest, astound, awe, benumb, cow, daunt, dismay, freeze, frighten, halt, harrow, horrify, intimidate, lapidify, numb, outrage, paralyse, scare, shock, startle, stun, stupefy, terrify, terrorise, transfix, unman, unnerve
**pet rodent** gerbil, hamster, mouse, rat
**petrol** fuel, gas(oline)
**petrol bowser** pump
**petroleum** gas, oil
**petroleum before it has been refined** crude oil
**petrol grading** octane
**petrology** lithology
**petrol pump** bowser
**petrol rating** octane, regular, super
**petrol source** oil
**petrol station** garage
**petrol tanker** bowser
**petticoat** (half-)slip, lingerie, undergarment, underskirt, underwear
**pet title** nickname
**petty** diminutive, inconsiderable, inferior, insignificant, lesser, little, mean, minor, nugatory, paltry, small, stingy, trifling, trivial, ungenerous, unimportant
**petty and over-elaborate** niggling
**petty contrivance** knack
**petty criminal** spiv
**petty demon** imp
**petty details** trifles, trivia(lities)
**petty falsehood** fib
**petty formality** punctilio

**petty gossip** tittle-tattle
**petty liar** fibster
**petty lie** nonsense, taradiddle
**petty love affair** amour(ette)
**petty objection** cavil
**petty offence** peccadillo, slip
**petty officer on a merchant ship** bos'n, boatswain, bosun
**petty practitioner in any activity** pettifogger
**petty quarrel** fuss, spat, squabble, tiff, tracasserie
**petty ruler** princeling
**petty schoolmaster** pedant
**petty sum** driblet
**petulant** acrimonious, captious, cross, huffy, irascible, irritable, peevish, snappish, testy, tetchy, touchy, vexatious, waspish
**pew** bench, seat
**pew cushion** hassock
**pewit** lapwing, peewit
**pewter alloy** bidri
**pewter cup** goddard
**pewter drinking-vessel** tankard
**phalanger** arboreal, cuscus, marsupial, (o)possum
**phalanx** assemblage, assembly, association, audience, battalion, brigade, contingent, council, division, escadrille, faction, gathering, group, legion, levy, platoon, squadron, synod
**phallic symbol** linga(m)
**phantasm** apparition, chimera, daydream, delusion, demon, eidolon, fantasy, Fata Morgana, figment, ghost, hallucination, illusion, incubus, shade, soul, spirit, vision
**phantasmagoria** dreamy, ghostly, hallucination, illusory, imaginary, nightmarish, phantasmal, spectral, surreal, unreal
**phantom** apparition, chimera, eidolon, ghost, hallucination, illusion, image, imaginary, incubus, mirage, nightmare, revenant, shadow, spectre, spirit, umbra, vision
**phantom of the mind** apparition, delusion, illusion
**phantom pregnancy** pseudocyesis
**phantom ship** Flying Dutchman
**Pharisee in New Testament** Nicodemus
**pharmacist** apothecary, chemist, druggist, pharmacopoeist, posologist
**pharmacy** apothecary, dispensary, pharmacology, pharmacopoeia, posology
**pharyngeal tonsil** adenoid
**phase** appearance, aspect, chapter, condition, development, facet, feature, level, period, point, position, season, spell, stage, state, step, time, view
**phase in** include, incorporate, insert, insinuate, interject, introduce
**phase out** close, deactivate, eliminate, remove, replace, terminate, withdraw
**pheasant's nest** nide
**phenomena** miracles, prodigies, rarities, sensations, sights, spectacles
**phenomenal** amazing, astounding, breathtaking, curious, exceptional, extraordinary, fantastic, freakish, miraculous, odd, peerless, rare, remarkable, uncommon, unfamiliar, unmatched, unusual, weird
**phenomenon** appearance, circumstance, curiosity, episode, event, exception, experience, fact, happening, incident, marvel, miracle, occasion, occurrence, prodigy, rarity, sensation, sight, spectacle, wonder
**phial** ampoule, bottle, cruet, vial
**philander** coquet, cruise, dally, debauch, flirt, gallivant, toy, trifle, wanton, womanise
**philanderer** Casanova, debauchee, flirt, playboy, roué, trifler, woman-chaser, womaniser
**philanthropic** alms-giving, altruistic, benevolent, big-hearted, bountiful, charitable, generous, humanitarian, kind, lavish, liberal, munificent, princely, public-spirited, rich
**philanthropist** almsgiver, altruist, benefactor, contributor, donator, donor, financier, humanitarian, mainstay, patron, sponsor
**philanthropy** agape, almsgiving, altruism, beneficence, benevolence, benignancy, benignity, bounty, caritas (L), charitableness, charity, generosity, helpfulness, humanity, kind-heartedness, kindliness, kindness, liberality, ministry, munificence, patronage, pity, sympathy
**philately** timbrology
**philippic** abusive, admonition, aspersion, calumny, censure, condemnation, contumely, curse, diatribe, invective, jeremiad, malediction, reprimand, reproval, revilement, satire, screed, tirade
**Philippine lake** Lake Taal
**Philippine monkey** machin
**Philippine one-edged knife** bolo
**Philippine palm** nipa
**Philippine plant** abaca
**Philippine port** Manila
**Philippine rice** macan

**Philippine skirt** saya
**Philippine's major city** Manila
**Philistine god** Dagon
**Philistine slain by David** Goliath
**philosopher** Confucius, guru, ideologist, intellectual, Kant, logician, metaphysician, Plato, pundit, rationalist, reasoner, sage, Socrates, theoriser, theorist, thinker
**philosophic doubt** scepsis
**philosophy** beliefs, doctrine, forbearance, logic, rationalism, reasoning, stoicism, theory, thought
**philosophy of causation** (a)etiology
**philosophy of law** jurisprudence
**philosophy of morals and moral choices** ethics
**philosophy of Plato** Platonism
**philosophy recognising only matters of fact** positivism
**phlebotomy** blood-letting
**phlegm** mucus
**phlegmatic** apathetic, cold, composed, dormant, dull, emotionless, frigid, insentient, languid, lethargic, listless, lymphatic, numb, stoical, stolid, torpid, unmoved, untouched
**phloem** liber
**phobia** angst, anguish, anxiety, distrust, dread, fear, horror, misgiving, panic, qualm, suspicion, terror, worry
**phone** call, ring, telephone
**phone book** directory
**phone directory assistant** operator
**phonetic** articulated, character, hiragana, intonated, oral, phenomena, sounded, sounding, spoken, symbol, uttered, verbal, vocal, voiced
**phoney** assumed, bogus, charlatan, cheat, deceiver, empiric, fake, false, flash, forged, fraudulent, hoax, imitator, pinchbeck, pretender, quack, ruse, sham, swindle
**phonograph record** disc, disk, single
**phony** charlatan, deceiver, empiric, hoax, imitator, pretender, quack, ruse, swindle
**photo** print, snap(shot)
**photo cell** electric eye
**photocopy process** diazo
**photo finish** dead heat
**photograph** collotype, daguerreotype, (dia)positive, exposure, image, negative, photo, pic(ture), portrait, print, snap
**photographic cubicle** darkroom
**photographic device** camera
**photographic fluid** toner
**photographic process** platinotype
**photograph of a cloud** nephogram

**photograph produced from negative** print
**photography** xerography
**photography using X-rays** roentgenography
**photo machine** camera
**photo sensitivity rating** din
**photo taker** camera, photographer
**photo within a photo** inset
**phrase** call, clause, designate, express(ion), idiom, locution, mode, motto, name, part, passage, saying, sentence, style, term, unit, verse, voice, word
**phraseology** expression, idiom, inflection, language, parlance, speech, style, syntax, verbiage, wording
**phrase on coat of arms** motto
**phthisis** tuberculosis
**phut** failed
**phylactery** tefillah, tephillah
**physical** bodily, corporal, corporeal, material, mortal, sensible
**physical basis of mental phenomena** psychophysics
**physical bearing** deportment
**physical character of ground** terrain
**physical deformity** bow-leg
**physical exertion** exercise
**physical geography** geonomy, physiography
**physically attractive** nubile
**physically destructive** pestilent
**physically disabled** handicapped, lame
**physically weak** feeble, frail, infirm
**physically strong** athletic
**physical torture** anguish
**physical weariness** languor, lassitude
**physician** doc(tor), healer
**physicist** Einstein
**physics** astrophysics, pneumatics, science
**physiognomy** appearance, brow, contour, countenance, demeanour, expression, facade, features, mien, visage
**piano adjuster** tuner
**piano-key material** ivory
**piano music** sonata
**piano repairman** tuner
**pica** em
**picador** bullfighter
**picaroon** bandit, buccaneer, corsair, felon, freebooter, hoodlum, mischief-maker, miscreant, pirate, rascal, recreant, rogue, ruffian, scoundrel, skollie, thief, thug, tsotsi
**piece of live coal** ember
**pick** acquire, choice, choose, collect, criticise, cull, get, peck, pilfer, reap, rob, select, steal

**pick at** nibble, peck
**pick carefully** cull
**picked quality** choice
**picket fence** paling
**picketing worker** striker
**picking and choosing** eclectic
**picking from the bill of fare** à la carte
**pick into separate fibres** tease
**pickle** brine, chili, chowchow, chutney, cornichon, crisis, difficulty, dilemma, dill, exigency, fix, gherkin, marinade, marinate, mess, mischief, predicament, preserve(r), problem, quandary, relish, sauce, scrape, season, souse, steep, store, trouble
**pickle brine** souse
**pickled cabbage** sauerkraut
**pickled cucumber** gherkin
**pickled flower buds** capers
**pickled roe of sturgeon** caviar(e)
**pickled rosebud** caper
**pickle in brine** souse
**pickling cucumber** gherkin
**pickling herb** dill
**pick-me-up** tonic
**pick off** detach, drill, drop, fell, hit, plug, remove, shoot, strike
**pick on** badger, bait, blame, bully, criticise, goad, nag, needle, quibble with, tease, torment
**pick out** choose, cull, discriminate, distinguish, except, excise, hand-pick, notice, perceive, recognise, remove, select, separate, sight, spot
**pickpocket** bandit, burglar, cheat, dip, housebreaker, plunderer, robber, shoplifter, stealer, swindler, thief
**pick up** acquire, arrest, buy, catch, collect, contract, elevate, fetch, gain, gather, get, glean, grasp, handle, hoist, improve, learn, lift, master, mend, nab, nick, obtain, progress, purchase, raise, rally, recover, resume, uplift
**pick-up** van
**pick up speed** accelerate
**picnic bottle** flask
**picnic pest** ant
**picture** describe, description, drawing, image, imagine, likeness, movie, paint(ing), photo(graph), represent(ation), semblance, tableau
**picture border** frame
**picture composed of a number of individual pictures** montage
**picture drawer** illustrator
**picture holder** frame
**picture house** cinema
**picture of Christ wearing crown of thorns** Ecce Homo

**picture of interlocking pieces** jigsaw puzzle
**picture of landscape** panorama
**picture of night scene** nocturne
**picture of sexy woman** pin-up
**picture of the dead Christ** pietà
**picture of variety of materials pasted onto a surface** collage
**picture of Virgin Mary** icon, Madonna
**picture puzzle** jigsaw, rebus
**picturesque** attractive, beautiful, charming, colourful, graphic, idyllic, intense, lively, pretty, quaint, scenic, striking, vivid
**picturesque poem** idyll
**picturesque presentation** tableau
**picturesque scene** idyll
**picture support** easel
**picture theatre** bioscope, cinema
**picture to oneself** image
**picture unrolled before spectator** panorama
**pidgin** jargon
**pie** pastry, quiche, tart
**piebald** blotchy, brindled, checked, chequered, dappled, flecked, many-coloured, marble(d), motley, mottled, multicoloured, parti-coloured, pied, pinto, polychromatic, speckled, spotted, stippled, streaked, striped, variegated
**piebald horse** pinto
**piece** article, augment, bit, complete, enlarge, essay, example, fragment, instance, mend, paper, part, patch, portion, quantity, scrap, section, segment, shred, story, thing
**piece broken off** fragment
**piece cut off** section, segment
**pièce de résistance** jewel, masterpiece, masterwork, showpiece
**piece for one voice** solo
**piece introducing a larger work** prelude
**piece let in** inset
**piecemeal** fragmentary, gradually, unsystematic
**piece of advice** tip
**piece of armour** tasse
**piece of bad luck** misadventure
**piece of badminton equipment** shuttlecock
**piece of bitter criticism** diatribe
**piece of bread soaked in liquid** sop
**piece of bric-à-brac** curio
**piece of burlesque** skit
**piece of business performed** transact
**piece of cheating** fiddle, swindle
**piece of cloth** rag
**piece of cloth sewed on a garment** patch
**piece of cloth used for mending** clout

**piece of crockery** cup, dish, plate, saucer
**piece of crude metal** slug
**piece of cunning** artifice
**piece of curved ship's timber** stemson
**piece of cutlery** (dessert)spoon, fork, knife, tablespoon, teaspoon
**piece of eight** peso
**piece of enclosed ground** yard
**piece of equipment** appurtenance, implement
**piece of evidence** clue
**piece of fabric** cloth
**piece of finery** fallal
**piece of fish** fil(l)et
**piece of fishing equipment** rod
**piece of fishing tackle** rod
**piece of fried bread** crouton
**piece of furniture** chair, cupboard, sofa, table, whatnot
**piece of glass in the form of a thread** fibre
**piece of glowing coal** ember, gleed
**piece of good luck** windfall
**piece of gossip** on dit (F)
**piece of grassland** meadow
**piece of ground** acre, area, lot, plot
**piece of ground described geologically** terrain
**piece of hot glass** bit
**piece of humorous mimicry** skit
**piece of information** datum
**piece of jewellery** bangle, bracelet, brooch, (ear)ring, watch
**piece of land** lot
**piece of land almost surrounded by water** peninsula
**piece of land for development** tract
**piece of land planted with fruit trees** orchard
**piece of land surrounded by water** island
**piece of land surrounded by water on three sides** peninsula
**piece of land used as pasture** field
**piece of leather for sharpening a razor** strop
**piece of legislation** bill
**piece of live coal** ember
**piece of luck** fluke
**piece of luggage** bag, (suit)case, trunk
**piece of lumber** board
**piece of material left over** remnant
**piece of material sloping to an edge** wedge
**piece of meat** chop, rib, steak
**piece of mischief** prank
**piece of music** étude, rondo, sonata
**piece of narrow cord** string
**piece of news** item
**piece of nonsensical writing in verse** amphigory, amphigouri

**piece of office furniture** desk
**piece of ordnance** gun
**piece of ornamental jewellery** bangle, bracelet, brooch, (ear)ring, watch
**piece of paper** sheet
**piece of pasta** noodle
**piece of pastry** puff
**piece of rebaked bread** rusk
**piece of reckless adventure** escapade
**piece of rising ground** eminence
**piece of rock** stone
**piece of sacred music** anthem
**piece of satire** skit
**piece of scurrilous satire on person** lampoon
**piece of shot** pellet
**piece of snow** flake
**piece of soap** bar
**piece of solid upright masonry** pier
**piece of strategy** tactic
**piece of studio equipment** camera
**piece of tilled land** acre
**piece of timber** board
**piece of tobacco for chewing** quid
**piece of turf** divot, sod
**piece of wet spongy ground** bog, marsh, swamp, vlei
**piece of whole** portion
**piece of wood** log, plank
**piece of wood for levelling concrete** screed
**piece of wood torn from tree** sliver
**piece of work** job, task
**piece out** augment, eke, enhance, enlarge, expand, supplement
**piece shaped to fit into mortise** tenon
**piece together** assemble, attach, compose, connect, fit, fix, join, mend, patch, reconstruct, repair, restore, unite
**pie dough** pastry
**Pied Piper's river** Weser
**pie fruit** apple
**pie-in-face humour** slapstick
**pie-in-the-sky** delusions, illusions, self-deceit, self-deception, utopia
**pie-in-the-sky fantasy** pipe dream
**pier** brace, breakwater, buttress, column, dock, foundation, groyne, jetty, jutty, landing, levee, mole, pillar, post, promenade, quay, support, wharf
**pier base** plinth, socle
**pierce** affect, apprehend, bore, drill, gore, grasp, impale, lance, lancinate, move, penetrate, perforate, prick, puncture, riddle, stab, strike, thrill, touch, transpierce, understand
**piercer** awl
**pierce slightly** prick
**pierce slightly with a sword** pink
**pierce through** transfix

**pierce with a stake** empale, impale
**pierce with a weapon** stab
**pierce with horn** gore
**pierce with many holes** riddle
**pierce with tusk** gore
**piercing cry** scream
**piercing in tone** shrill
**piercing tool** awl
**piercing wound** stab
**piety** devotion, devoutness, dutifulness, duty, faith, godliness, grace, holiness, religion, respect, reverence, sanctity, veneration
**piffle** twaddle
**pig** barbarian, boar, boor, eater, frump, glutton, grunter, hog, piglet, pigling, porker, sloven, sow, swine, vulgarian, warthog
**pigeon** barb, carrier, dove, fantail, isabel, jacobin, nun, pidgin, piper, pouter, roller, ruff, squab, trumpeter, tumbler, turbit, wonga
**pigeon blood** garnet
**pigeon call** coo
**pigeon coop** cote
**pigeon food** pea, salt-cat
**pigeon grass** foxtail
**pigeon hawk** merlin
**pigeonhole** alcove, compartment, cubby(hole), defer, file, label, locker, niche, nook, partition, place, postpone, receptacle, section, shelve, slot
**pigeon-house** columbary, cote, dooket, dovecote, loft, rook(ery)
**pigeon nestling** squab
**pigeon pea** d(h)al, dholl
**pigeon sound** coo
**pigeon with the power of inflating its crop** pouter
**pigeon woodpecker** flicker
**pig fat** lard
**pig flesh** pork
**pig food** swill
**pig house** sty
**piglet's mom** sow
**pig-like mammal** tapir
**pig meat** bacon, ham, pork
**pigment** colour(ing) matter, dye(stuff), hue, ochre, paint, sepia, stain, tincture, tint
**pigment for paint** ochre
**pigment for woodwork** korowai
**pigment found in plants** xanthein
**pigment in butterfly wing** pterin
**pigment like ochre** umber
**pigment made from soot** lampblack
**pigment user** dyer
**pigpen** sty
**pig raised for pork** porker
**pig's abode** sty
**pig's fat** lard

**pig's feet** trotters
**pig's flesh** bacon, ham, pork
**pig's foot** trotter
**pig's grease** mort
**pig's grunt** oink
**pig's ham cured like bacon** gammon
**pig's home** pen, sty
**pig's meat** bacon, ham, pork
**pig sound** oink
**pig's pen** sty
**pigtail** plait, queue
**pike** assegai, autobahn, causeway, fee, freeway, gar, harpoon, highway, javelin, lance, payment, poleaxe, shaft, spear, speedway, spontoon, toll(booth), tollgate, turnpike
**piked shoe** beaker
**pike-like fish** gar(fish)
**pikestaff topped by an axe-like blade and spike** gisarme, halberd
**pilaster** anta, pier
**pile** accumulate, accumulation, amass(ment), assemblage, assemble, batch, beam, building, bulk, bunch, bundle, collect(ion), column, down, edifice, haemorrhoid, heap, hoard, lump, mass, pier, pillar, pyre, stack, stake, stock, supply, texture, wealth, wedge, wool
**pile fabric with loops uncut** terry
**pile high** stack
**pile of bricks for burning** clamp
**pile of hay** stack
**pile of stones** cairn
**pile of wood for burning the dead** pyre
**pile one on top of another** stack
**piles** haemorrhoids
**pile up** accumulate, amass, compile, heap, hoard, smash, stack
**pilfer** filch, lift, pinch, pirate, rob, scavenge, shoplift, sponge, steal, swipe, thieve
**pilferer** filcher, robber, stealer, thief
**pilgrim** crusader, palmer, sojourner, traveller, wanderer, wayfarer
**pilgrimage** excursion, expedition, journey, tour, trip
**pilgrimage to Mecca** hadj, hajj
**pilgrim from the Holy Land** palmer
**pill** capsule, lozenge, pastille, pellet, tablet
**pillage** booty, despoil, forage, loot, maraud, pickeer, plunder, raid, ransack, rape, rapine, rifle, rob(bery), sack, spoil, steal
**pillager** looter, plunderer
**pillar** caryatid, colonnade, column, mainstay, peristyle, pier, pilaster, pole, post, prop, pylon, shaft, stele, support

**pillow** bolster, cushion, pad, prop, support
**pillow cover** case, tick
**pillow which can be inflated** air cushion
**pilot** aeronaut, airman, aviator, boss, captain, conduct(or), control, coxswain, direct(or), drive, escort, flier, fly(er), guide, handle, helmsman, lead(er), manage, navigate, navigator, operate, run, steer(sman)
**pilot an aircraft** aviate
**pilothouse** wheelhouse
**pilot's compartment** cockpit
**pimento** allspice
**pimp** pander, ponce
**pimping** feeble, puny, sickly, small
**pimple** blackhead, blotch, eruption, furuncle, lump, monticle, papilla, papule, pockmark, pustule, spot
**pimples** acne
**pimply** blotchy, spotty
**pimply disorder** acne
**pin** bolt, brooch, cotter, dowel, fasten(ing), fix, peg, secure
**pinafore** apron
**pinball word** tilt
**pincers** extractor, forceps, nippers, pincher, pliers, tongs, tweezer
**pinch** bind, compress, nick, nip, pain, predicament, scrimp, squeeze, steal, tighten, trace
**pinch sharply** nip
**Pindar output** ode
**pin down** bind, compel, constrain, detect, determine, force, hold, identify, immobilise, locate, make, nail, pinpoint, press, pressurise, specify, tie
**pine** abate, ache, burn, covet, crave, decline, desire, die, droop, ebb, fade, fail, faint, fall, flag, fret, grief, grieve, hala, hanker, hunger, itch, lament, languish, lim, long, lust, mope, mourn, pant, sigh, sink, torment, wane, want, waste, weaken, wither, wilt, yearn
**pineal** cone-shaped, conical
**pineapple** ananas
**pine away** dwindle, macerate, waste
**pine-cone** strobile, strobilus
**pine-cone-shaped** pineal
**pine extract** amber, resin, rosin
**pine for** grieve, long, yearn
**pine fruit** cones
**pine leaf** needle
**pine nut** pinon
**pine or fir timber** deal
**pine product** resin, rosin, turpentine
**pine sap** resin, rosin
**pine tree** conifer, fir

**pine tree exudation** resin, rosin
**Pine Tree State** Maine
**pine wood** deal
**pin for hanging** peg
**pin for holding meat** skewer
**pin for securing tent** peg
**ping-pong** table tennis
**ping-pong need** ball, bat, net, paddle, racket, table
**pinguid** fatty, greasy, oily, soapy
**pinheaded** silly, stupid
**pining amorously** lovelorn
**pin in gunwale of boat as fulcrum for oar** thole
**pin in nave of wheel** axle
**pinion** bind, chain, fasten, manacle, shackle, tie
**pink** rosy
**pink-coloured bird** flamingo
**pink-fleshed fish** salmon
**pink flower** azalea
**pink-flowered herb** sainford
**pinkish-brown bird** hoopoe
**pinkish-violet colour** lilac
**pink long-necked bird** flamingo
**pink tinge** blush
**pink to yellowish tan colour** bisque
**pinna** auricle, ear
**pinnacle** acme, apex, climax, crest, culmination, eminence, pad, peak, summit, top, tor, tower, turret, zenith
**pinnate** feathery
**pinned down** fixed, trapped, unmovable
**pinning down** nailing
**pinniped mammal** pinnipedian, seal, sealion, walrus
**pinnothere** crab
**pin of sundial** gnomon
**pin ornament** brooch
**pintail** duck
**pintail duck** smee
**pinto** blotchy, flecked, mottled, piebald
**pioneer** colonist, developer, explorer, frontiersman, innovator, leader, settler, Voortrekker
**pioneer aviator** Bleriot
**pioneer in any art** avant-garde
**pioneer psychologist** Freud
**pious** angelic, clean-minded, dedicated, devoted, devout, godly, good, holy, humble, moral, pietistic, religious, reverent(ial), righteous, sacred, saintly, sanctimonious, spiritual, unctuous, venerative, virtuous, worshipful
**pious fraud** fraus pia (L)
**piously** pietistically, spiritually, unctuously
**piously humble and submissive** meek
**pip** seed

**pipe** cheep, conductor, conveyor, duct, hooter, horn, hose, meerschaum, peep, pipeline, reed, tube, twitter
**pipeclay used by dressmakers** tailor's chalk
**pipe coupling** nipple
**pipe down** hush, silence
**pipe dream** chimera, daydream, fantasy, reverie, vagary
**pipe for carrying rainwater from roof to drain** downpipe
**pipe for waste** drain
**pipe-like ulcer** fistula
**pipe on a roof** gutter
**pipe to chimney** uptake
**pippin** apple
**piquancy** acidity, appeal, aroma, bewitchery, bite, bitterness, crispness, essence, excitement, flavour, gusto, intensity, interest, keenness, liveliness, mordancy, pep, pungency, relish, savour, seasoning, sharpness, smack, spiciness, sting, tang, tartness, taste, vehemence, vitality, zest
**piquant** attractive, biting, brisk, burning, clever, curried, fascinating, interesting, intriguing, lively, peppery, poignant, pungent, quick, racy, sharp, smart, snappy, sparkling, spiced, spicy, stimulating, tang(y), tart, tasty, vigorous, zestful, zesty
**pique** affront, annoy(ance), displease, displeasure, excite, grudge, huff, incense, interest, irk, irritable, irritate, irritation, miff, mortify, nettle, offence, offend, prick, provoke, resentment, rile, spur, stimulate, sting, umbrage, vex(ation), wound
**pirate** buccaneer, corsair, filibuster, freebooter, picaroon, plunderer, sea-rover
**pirate of Algeria** corsair
**pirate ship** corsair, gallivat, picaroon, privateer
**pirouette** circle, pivot, reel, revolution, revolve, roll, rotate, rotation, spin, swirl, turn, twirl, twist, wheel, whirl
**piscina** fish-pond
**piscine** bathing pool
**piscine organ** fin, gill
**piscine ovary** roe
**pisiform** pea-shaped
**pismire** ant, emmet
**pistillate plant** female
**pistil of a flower** carpel
**pistol** Beretta, Colt, dag, gat, (hand)gun, Luger, pop, revolver
**pistol-armed soldier** pistoleer
**pistolero** gunslinger
**piston** ram

**pit** cavity, crater, depression, excavation, hole, hollow, indentation, mine, seed, stone, trap
**pit against** match, oppose, set against
**pitch** arena, asphalt, bitumen, cant, cast, cobble, cover, crown, crumple, decline, degree, distance, erect, extent, grade, heave, intensity, key, launch, pave, peak, place, resin, rocking, rosin, shake, shoot, slope, summit, tar, throw, tilt, timbre, tone, top(ple), toss, tumble, zenith
**pitch a ball** bowl
**pitch a camp** encamp
**pitchblende** ore
**pitcher** bottle, container, creamer, crock, cruse, ewer, flinger, hurler, jar, jug, mug, olla, samovar, shot-putter, stein, tankard, thrower, toby, tosser, urn, vessel
**pitcher spout** lip
**pitchfork prong** tine
**pitch in** assist, contribute, help, participate, tackle
**pitch into** abuse, assail, assault, attack, beset, besiege, harass, importune, revile
**pitch on** choose, determine, elect, pick
**pitch suddenly to one side** lurch
**pitch tent** camp
**piteous** deplorable, distressing, doleful, miserable, mournful, moving, pathetic, pitiable, rueful, sad, sorrowful
**pitfall** catch, danger, deadfall, difficulty, downfall, hazard, peril, pit, snag, snare, springe, trap
**pith** consequence, core, crux, depth, elixir, essence, focus, force, fundamental, gist, graveness, gravity, heart, import(ance), kernel, marrow, matter, meat, moment, nub, nucleus, point, power, quintessence, significance, soul, spirit, strength, substance, support, value, weight
**pith helmet** topee, topi
**pithy** brief, cogent, concise, laconic, meaty, succinct, terse, trenchant
**pithy jointed stem** stave
**pithy maxim** apophthegm
**pithy reply** retort
**pithy saying** aphorism, mot
**pithy witticism** bon mot
**pitiable** affecting, calamitous, cheerless, deplorable, deserted, destitute, dire, distressing, forlorn, grievous, helpless, homeless, hopeless, lamentable, lonely, miserable, pathetic, pitiful, poignant, regrettable, sad(dening), touching, unfortunate, unhappy, wretched

**pitiful** abject, contemptible, deplorable, despicable, dismal, doleful, dolorous, low, mean, miserable, niggardly, paltry, pathetic, piteous, pitiable, pitying, sad, scanty, skimpy, sorry, squalid, unimportant, vile, woeful, wretched
**pitiless** cruel, inexorable, mean, merciless, ruthless, unmerciful
**pitman** miner
**pit of theatre** parterre
**pit tunnel** shaft
**pit viper** copperhead, rattlesnake
**pitworker** miner
**pity** abomination, benevolence, commiseration, compassion, condole(nce), console, gentleness, humaneness, humanity, kindliness, lament, mercy, regret, relent, remorse, ruth, sympathy, tenderness
**pity-evoking quality** pathos
**pivot** axis, axle, centre, circle, focus, fulcrum, gimbal, gyrate, hinge, pin, pintle, pirouette, reel, revolve, rotate, slue, somersault, spin, spindle, spool, swing, swivel, thole(pin), toe, traverse, trunnion, turn, twist, wheel, whirl
**pivotal** axial, basic, capital, central, critical, crucial, exigent, focal, fundamental, important, momentous, polar, pressing, primary, radical, significant, supreme, trochoid, urgent
**pivotal point** axis, fulcrum, knuckle
**pivot bearing** jewel
**pivoted catch** ratchet
**pivoting** dishrag
**pivot on** depend, hinge, rely
**pivot on chair** swivel
**pivot pin** pintle
**pivot stand** pedestal
**pixie** dwarf, elf, fairy, gnome, goblin, imp, pixy
**pixie-like** elfin
**pizza** pie
**placard** poster
**placate** alleviate, appease, assuage, calm, conciliate, ease, humour, lull, moderate, mollify, pacify, please, propitiate, quiet, reconcile, relieve, satisfy, soothe, subdue
**placation** reassurance
**placatory concession** sop
**place** area, circumstances, collocate, deposit, domicile, dwelling, function, house, job, lay, lieu, locale, locality, locate, location, locus, occasion, office, opportunity, position, post, put, rank, region, residence, sector, set, site, situation, space, spot, stead
**place alone** isolate
**place among records** file

**place apart** isolate
**place aside for a purpose** earmark
**place at disadvantage** handicap
**place at intervals** space
**place at rest** holiday resort
**place at risk** endanger
**place before** prefix
**place between** interpose
**place confidence in** believe, trust
**place containing fabulous riches** Aladdin's cave
**placed diametrically opposite** anitpodal
**placed lengthways** longitudinal
**place finder** map
**place for animals** zoo
**place for bees** apiary
**place for camping** site
**place for children and their nurses** nursery
**place for clothes when travelling** (suit)case
**place for cultivating trees** arboretum
**place for dancing** disco(theque)
**place for depositing the ashes of the dead** cinerarium
**place for dining out** restaurant
**place for doing business** office
**place for entering** entrance
**place for evening entertainment** nightclub
**place for goatee** chin
**place for growing ferns** fernery
**place for hiring horses** livery
**place for keeping birds** aviary
**place for keeping goods** store(-house)
**place for keeping pigs** piggery, sty
**place for keeping small land animals** terrarium
**place for killing animals for food** abattoir, slaughterhouse
**place for learning** college, school, university
**place for little bout** arena
**place for making money** mint
**place for manufacturing** workshop
**place for open discussion** forum
**place for private worship** oratory
**place for public amusements** casino, theatre
**place for public records** archives
**place for retailing** shop
**place for sick people** hospital
**place for sitting** seat
**place for special worship** chapel, church, mosque, oratory, sanctuary, shrine, synagogue, temple
**place for sports meeting** venue
**place for stores** depot, storeroom
**place for teenagers to meet** youth club
**place for the sale of retail goods** shop
**place for washing clothes** laundry

**place for washing dishes** scullery
**place for watching stars** observatory
**place for workout** gym(nasium)
**place frequented by criminals** haunt
**place high in rank** exalt
**place in attitude** pose
**place in box** encase
**place in different position** relocate
**place in high rank** exalt
**place in line** align
**place in middle** centre
**place in mutual relationship** correlate
**place in new order** rearrange
**place in order** arrange, array
**place in pickle** souse
**place in position** install, put, situate
**place in recumbent posture** lay
**place in safe-keeping** store
**place in storehouse** store
**place in urn** inurn
**place in which one lives** abode, home, house
**place in which the bodies of the dead are kept** charnel house, morgue, mortuary
**place in with something else** enclose
**place it** put
**place name** toponym
**placenta** afterbirth
**place of abomination** Gehenna
**place of action** arena, scene
**place of activity** hive
**place of bliss** Eden
**place of concealment** hide-out
**place of confinement** cage, prison
**place of contentment** Eden
**place of debauchery** den, sty
**place of detention** prison
**place of distribution of alms** almonry
**place of duty** post
**place of education** college, school, seminary, technikon, university
**place of event** venue
**place off the beaten track** backwater
**place of great abundance** El Dorado
**place of great disorder** shambles
**place of growing plants** garden
**place of hermit's retreat** hermitage
**place of higher education**
**place of learning** college, school, technikon, university
**place of misery** hell
**place of Napoleon's first exile** Elba
**place of origin** source
**place of public contest** arena
**place of refreshment** café, inn, restaurant
**place of refuge** abri, asylum, haven, shelter
**place of residence** home
**place of rest for Israelites** Elim
**place of sacrifice** altar

**place of safety** haven
**place of seclusion** retreat
**place of storage** storehouse
**place of study** academy, college, school, university
**place of the dead** Sheol
**place of total privacy** sanctum
**place of trade** agora, marketplace, mart
**place of uproar** bedlam, pandemonium
**place of victory for Napoleon** Ligny, Lodi
**place of work** office
**place of worship** altar, chapel, church, mosque, oratory, sanctuary, shrine, synogogue, temple
**place on computer** key in
**place on official list of saints** canonise
**place on order** indent
**place on royal seat** throne
**place over** superimpose
**place overgrown with ferns** brake
**place providing accommodation** boarding-house, hotel, inn
**place reliance in** trust
**place seed in ground** sow
**place set aside for treating the sick** sickbay
**place side by side** collocate, juxtapose
**place someone with legs and arms outstretched** spread-eagle
**place that cultivates crops** farm
**place that sells equestrian equipment** saddlery
**place to change** dressing room
**place to drive** tee
**place together** collocate
**place to hang one's coat** cloakroom
**place to live in** habitation
**place to moor vessel** anchorage
**place to observe** window
**place to park car** garage
**place to put the mail** letter box, postbox
**place to rest** bed, seat
**place to see a doctor** clinic
**place to shop in** hypermarket, store
**place to sit** bench, chair, seat
**place to sleep on a ship** berth
**place to stay** home
**place to store tools** shed
**place to view fish** aquarium
**place to where letters are sent** address
**place to which person is going** destination
**place to work out** gym(nasium)
**place tree in ground** plant
**place under arrest** capture, nab
**place under water** submerge
**place unnamed** somewhere
**place upon** lay

**place used for Christian worship** chapel
**place where actor prepares** dressing room
**place where alcoholic liquor is distilled** distillery
**place where beer is made** brewery
**place where bees are kept** apiary
**place where candles are kept** chandlery
**place where cats are boarded** cattery
**place where corpses are cremated** crematorium
**place where documents and records are kept** archive(s)
**place where earthenware is made** pottery
**place where fishing takes place** fishery, piscary
**place where food is prepared and cooked** kitchen
**place where frogs are kept** froggery
**place where goods are sold** market, shop
**place where government records are kept** archive(s)
**place where grapes are grown** vineyard
**place where helicopters take off and land** heliport
**place where hides are tanned** tannery
**place where money is coined** mint
**place where nerve-cells join** synapse
**place where one hangs one's hat** hearth
**place where one lives** home
**place where one resides** residence
**place where people meet** rendezvous
**place where planes land** airport
**place where provisions are kept** store
**place where railway lines meet** junction
**place where river may be crossed by foot** drift, ford
**place where sheep are kept** camp, kraal, pen
**place where ship is moored** berth
**place where ships are built** dockyard, shipyard
**place where ships may anchor safely** anchorage
**place where skins are dressed** tannery
**place where snakes are kept** ophidarium
**place where souls are cleansed of sin** purgatory
**place where swans are kept** swannery
**place where tame rabbits are kept and bred** rabbitry
**place where things are made** workshop

**place where treasure is kept** treasury
**place where turf or peat is dug** turbary
**place where two rivers meet** confluence
**place where vessel is anchored** anchorage
**place where washing is done** laundry
**placid** balanced, calm, collected, composed, cool, demure, easy-going, equable, gentle, halcyon, inexticable, mild, moderate, motionless, pacific, passive, patient, peaceful, quiescent, quiet, reposeful, sedate, serene, steady, tame, timid, tolerant, tranquil, undisturbed
**plague** affliction, annoyance, calamity, curse, disease, epidemic, evil, harass, lues, nuisance, pestilence, torment, trouble, vexation
**plague epidemic** pestilence
**plague outbreak** epidemic
**plaid material** tartan
**plain** apparent, clear, direct, distinct, downright, evident, homespun, intelligible, lucid, manifest, obvious, open, ordinary, pampa(s), patent, prairie, simple, ugly, unambiguous, understandable, unequivocal, unmistakable, veld
**plain as day** clear(-cut), evident, overt
**plain circle worn in pierced ear** sleeper
**plain clothes as distinguished from uniform** civ(v)ies, mufti
**plain dealing** candour, straightforwardness
**plain figure with twelve sides** dodecagon
**plain in Central America** prairie
**plain in Hungary** Puszta
**plain in Lebanon** Elbika
**plainly and simply** tout court (F)
**plainly evident** obvious
**plain sailing** smooth
**plains in Argentina** pampas
**plainsong sign** neum
**plaintiff** accused, accuser, complainant, litigant, prosecutor, suer, suitor
**plaintive** crying, discontented, discouraged, doleful, elegiac(al), grieving, heartbroken, melancholy, miserable, mournful, sad, sobbing, sorrowful, unhappy, wistful
**plaintive cry** bleat, mourn, whine
**plaintive sound** moan
**plaintive writer** elegist
**plain, upright type** roman
**plain weave** tabby
**plain-woven cotton cloth** gingham
**plait** braid, crease, crimp, dart, flute, fold, furrow, gather, groove, pigtail,

plat, pleat, plication, plicature, queue, ridge, ruck, ruffle, shirr, tress, tuck, twill, weave, wrinkle
**plaited cord** braid
**plaited frill** ruche
**plaited straw** leghorn, sennit
**plaited trimming** ruche
**plait of hair** pigtail, queue, tress
**plan** arrange(ment), aspire, blueprint, conception, concoct, design, devise, diagram, draft, drawing, hatch, idea, intend, intention, lay-out, map, method, model, plot, prearrange, procedure, program(me), project, proposal, purpose, scale, scheme, skeleton, sketch, strategy, system, tactics, theory
**plan beforehand** calculate, premeditate
**plane** aircraft, airliner, airplane, flat, float, glide, homaloid, plateau, sail, skate, skim, skyline, soar
**plane curve** ellipse, parabola
**plane-detecting device** radar
**plane engine casing** nacelle
**plane flap** aileron
**plane handle** tote
**plane of gem** facet
**plane part** flap, nose, tail, wing
**plane port** aerodrome
**plane's electronics** avionics
**plane's staff** crew
**plane surface** area
**planet** civilisation, Earth, Jupiter, mankind, Mars, Mercury, moon, Neptune, Pluto, Saturn, star, Uranus, Venus, world
**planetarium** orrery
**planetary** global, migratory, moving, peripatetic, rambling, roving, sublunary, terrestrial, travelling, universal, unsettled, vagabond, wandering
**planetary path** orbit
**planetary satellite** moon
**planet discovered by Herschel** Uranus
**planet farthest from the sun** Pluto
**planet nearest to the sun** Mercury
**planet next beyond Earth** Mars
**plane tree** platan
**planet's path** orbit
**planet we live on** Earth
**plane with eight sides and angles** octagon
**plane with five sides and angles** pentagon
**plane with four sides and angles** tetragon
**plane with nine sides and angles** enneagon, nonagon
**plane with seven sides and angles** heptagon

**plane with six sides and angles** hexagon
**plane with ten sides and angles** decagon
**plan for deceiving enemy** stratagem
**plan formed by thinking** idea
**plan in advance** premeditate
**plank** beam, board, girder, joist, panel, rafter, slat, spar, support, timber
**plank on wheels** skateboard
**plan mentally** meditate
**planned** aimed, contemplated, envisaged, intended, invented, meant, organised, outlined, plotted, prepared, proposed, purposed, represented, schemed
**planned attempt to gain public support** campaign
**planned cleverly** engineered
**planned earlier** premeditated
**planned undertaking** project, scheme
**planner** mastermind
**planning garden** landscaping
**plan of action** course, line, procedure
**plan of travel** itinerary, route
**plan secretly** intrigue, plot, scheme
**plan secretly with others** conspire
**plant** aloe, apparatus, bury, bush, engender, equipment, establish, factory, fix, flower, found, foundry, gear, herb, inlay, insert, inset, instil, inter, lodge, machinery, mill, myrtle, root, scatter, seed(ing), set(tle), shop, shrub, sow, station, transplant, tree, vegetable, vegetation, weed, works, workshop, yard
**plant adapted to dryness** cactus, xerophyte
**Plantagenet** Angevin
**plantain** abaca, banana, buckhorn, cock, finger, fleawort, netleaf, pala, ribgrass, (road)weed, sitfast, snakeweed
**plantain eater** splitbeak, touraco
**plantain lily** funkia
**plant akin to buttercup** anemone
**plant akin to spurge** croton
**plantar** foot, sole
**plantation of conifers** pinetum
**plantation of shrubs** shrubbery
**plantation of vines** vineyard
**plant axis** stem
**plant bearing grapes** vine
**plant bristle** awn, seta
**plant bud** camas(s), cammas, cion
**plant bug** capsid
**plant-burning bush** wahoo
**plant by spading** spit
**plant cell** spore
**plant change of form** ecad
**plant container** (flower)pot

**plant cooked and used as fruit** rhubarb
**plant covered with stinging hairs** nettle
**plant cutting** slip
**plant deeply** heel
**plant disease** blight, necrosis, uredo
**plant dust** pollen
**plant-eating animal** herbivore
**plant embryo** seed
**plant expert** botanist
**plant family** genus
**plant feeder** root
**plant fibre** flax
**plant firmly** brace
**plant fluid** sap
**plant food** nutrient
**plant fungus** ergot, mildew
**plant furnishing aniseed** anise
**plant germ** seed
**plant gland** nectary
**plant growing in water** bilders, hydrophyte
**plant growing in wet or waterlogged soil** hygrophyte
**plant growing where it is not desired** weed
**plant-growth in relation to gravity** geotropism
**plant harvested** crop
**plant-honey** nectar
**plantigrade mammal** bear
**planting device** drill, seeder
**plant in rows** drill
**plant insect** aphid, mite
**plant joined to another** graft
**plant juice** sap
**plant keeping shape and colour when dry** everlasting
**plant life** flora, vegetation
**plant like bracken** fern
**plant-like sea animal** sea anemone
**plant living on decayed organic matter** saprophyte
**plant louse** aphid, mite, psylla
**plant manure** mulch
**plant of meadows** poophyte
**plant of mint family** oregano
**plant of the dead** asphodel
**plant of the pansy family** viola
**plant of the parsley family** anise
**plant organ** leaf, pistil, stoma
**plant origin** seed
**plant or leaf outgrowth** enation, ovule
**plant ovule** seed
**plant part** leaf, pistil, shoot, stem, stoma
**plant pigment** cyanin
**plant pod** boll
**plant prickle** thorn
**plant root** radix
**plant rooted in ground** liana, liane

**plants** factories, flora, foundries, mills, shops, yards
**plant's climbing shoot** tendril
**plant secretion** resin, rosin
**plant seed** ovule, sow
**plants growing at high altitudes** alpestrine, subalpine
**plants growing wild** agrarian
**plant shoot** cion, graft, rod, sprig, stolon, sucker
**plant shop** nursery
**plant's lifeline** root
**plant's main stem** caulis
**plant's nectar-secreting organ** nectary
**plants of a particular region** flora
**plant source of oil** olive
**plant's second crop** etch
**plant stalk** stem
**plant stem** bine
**plant stem joint** node, phyton
**plant store** nursery
**plant-sucking insect** aphid
**plant's underground part** root
**plant's unit of reproduction** seed
**plant that grows entirely in the air** aerophyte
**plant that grows in waterlogged soil** hygrophyte
**plant that grows on rocky ground** lithophyte
**plant that has no stamens or pistils** cryptogam
**plant that lasts** perennial
**plant that likes damp ground** moss
**plant that lives off another one** parasite
**plant that lives only a year** annual
**plant that produces nicotine** tobacco
**plant tissue** xylem
**plant trees on** afforest
**plant used as food flavouring** fennel
**plant used as soap** amole
**plant used for cigars** tobacco
**plant used for its seeds** sesame, sunflower
**plant used in salads** lettuce
**plant used in sauce for fish** parsley
**plant with aromatic seeds** caraway
**plant with bell-shaped flowers** foxglove
**plant with bitter juice** aloe
**plant with edible leaves** cress
**plant with feathery leaves** yarrow
**plant with fragrant creamy-white flowers** tuberose
**plant with fronds** fern
**plant with hooked thorns** wait-a-bit
**plant with narcotic leaves** coca, tobacco
**plant with no distinct members** thallus
**plant without stem and leaves** lichen
**plant with pungent bulb** garlic, onion

**plant with showy flowers** peony
**plant with spicy seeds** caraway
**plant with stinging hairs on the leaves** nettle
**plant with strong smell** catmint
**plant with succulent root** beet
**plant with three pistils** trigyn
**plant with three stamens** triander
**plant with trees** afforest
**plant with yellow flowers** mustard
**plant yielding aniseed** anise
**plant yielding bitter juice** aloe
**plant yielding blue dye** woad
**plan with skill** contrive
**plaque** atheroma, brooch, medal, ornament, plate, stele, tablet, tartar, trophy
**plaster** bedaub, cement, coat, daub, dressing, gypsum, mortar, smear, spread, stucco
**plasterer's mortarboard** hawk
**plastering tool** trowel
**plaster moulding** stucco
**plaster of Paris** gypsum
**plaster support** lath
**plastic** compliant, creative, docile, ductile, easy, fictile, flexible, impressionable, inventive, labile, malleable, manageable, mouldable, pliable, receptive, responsive, soft, spineless, supple, tractable, unformed, yielding
**plastic material** vinyl
**plastic mixture of any substances** amalgam
**plastic mug** beaker
**plastic resin** polyester
**plastic surgery** anaplasty, face-lift, redecoration, restoration
**plate** anode, course, cover, dish, electroplate, laminate, panel, platter, portion, print
**plateau** highland, highveld, mesa, stability, stage, tableland, upland
**plateau face** escarpment
**plateau in Uganda** Ankole
**plateau of land** tableland
**plateau with steep sides** mesa
**plate-cleaner** dishwasher
**plated** chromed, ironclad
**plated metal** electro
**plate-like ornament** plaque
**plate of food** dish
**plate on insect** tergum
**platform** arena, bema, bima(h), dais, deck, landing, principles, pulpit, rostrum, stage, tribune
**platform for corpse** bier
**platform for discussion** forum
**platform for goods** pallet
**platform for guns** emplacement
**platform for preacher** pulpit

**platform for public speaking** rostrum
**platform for speaker** dais, platform, pulpit, rostrum, stage
**platform in synagogue** bema, bima(h)
**platform on which loaded vehicles are weighed** weighbridge
**platform projecting from the wall of a building** balcony
**platform supporting a classical colonnade** stylobate
**plating of warships** armour
**platitude** banality, bromide, chestnut, cliché, commonplace, dullness, inanity, insipidity, monotony, plainness, staleness, stereotype, triteness, triviality, truism
**platonic** calm, cool, ideal, incorporeal, intellectual, nonphysical, objective, philosophical, rational, serene, spiritual, tranquil, transcendant, unfleshly
**platter** charger, dish, mortarboard, palette, plate, record, salver, tray
**plaudit** acclaim, acclamation, accolade, applause, approval, cheers, commendation, compliment, congratulation, éclat, eulogy, kudos, laudation, ovation, panegyric, praise, tribute
**plausible** convincing, deceiving, deceptive, fairspoken, glib, specious
**play** activity, amusement, comedy, diversion, exercise, frolic, fun, game, jest, (melo)drama, movement, operation, pastime, piece, recreation, show, tactic, tragedy, trifling
**play a guitar** strum
**play a high shot** lob
**play a part** act, impersonate, personate
**play around** dally, flirt, fool, philander, trifle, womanise
**play a sly trick** pull a fast one
**play at** affect, assume, feign, pretend, simulate
**play at bridge** finesse
**play at courtship** philander
**play at love** flirt
**play badly** misplay
**play boisterously** rollick, romp
**playboy** debauchee, lady-killer, libertine, philanderer, rake, roué, socialite, womaniser
**playboy's routine** line
**play by ear** extemporise, improvise
**play division** act, scene
**play down** belittle, decry, derogate, disparage, minimise, soft-pedal, underplay, underrate, undervalue
**played as desired** ad libitum

**played out** banal, completed, dull, ended, fatigued, finished, insipid, overused, tired, weary
**played with bow** violin
**played with mallets** croquet
**played with rackets** tennis
**player** actor, actress, artist, competitor, contestant, entertainer, gambler, musician, performer, trouper, virtuoso, wagerer
**player in film** actor
**player in the brass section** trombonist, trumpeter
**player in the string section** cellist
**player of barrel-organ** organ-grinder
**player of percussion instrument** drummer
**player's stake in poker** ante
**player's turn to bid** call
**player who cuts cards** pone
**play first card** lead
**play for admiration** show-off, swank
**play for money** gamble(r)
**play for time** delay, hang, procrastinate, stall, temporise
**playful** amusing, cheerful, elfish, frisky, frolicsome, gamesome, gay, humorous, impish, jesting, lively, merry, mischievous, prankish, puckish, rollicking, scampish, skittish, spirited, sportive, sprightly, vivacious, witty
**playful action** frolic, fun
**playful amusement** fun
**playful banter** badinage, joking
**playful bite** nip
**play full of sensational happenings** melodrama
**playfully ribbing** teasing
**playfully torment** tease
**playful mischief** roguery
**playful or humorous composition** humoresque
**playful ridicule** badinage
**playful talk** chaff, badinage
**playful teasing** banter
**playful touch** chuck
**play games of chance for money** gamble
**playground gear** roundabout, see-saw, slide, swing
**play guitar** strum
**play Hamlet** act
**play havoc** confuse, demolish, destroy, disrupt, wreck
**play havoc with** damage, disorganise, injure, mutilate, ruin, unsettle, upset
**playhouse** amphitheatre, auditorium, hall, odeum, theatre
**play idly** strum
**playing card** ace, deuce, jack, joker, king, queen, tarot, ten, trey

**playing card's jack** knave
**playing card suit** clubs, diamonds, hearts, spades
**playing cube** di(c)e
**playing field** arena
**playing marble** agate
**playing on a surface** lambent
**playing the leading role** starring
**playing tile** domino
**play it by ear** ad lib, extemporise, improvise
**play lightly over** lambent
**play monotonously** strum
**play on** abuse, exploit, misuse, utilise
**play on stringed instrument** thrum
**play on words** pun, quibble
**play out** complete, conclude, consume, exhaust, expend, finish, resolve, squander, terminate
**play-practice** rehearsal
**play role** act
**play rough jokes on** rag, tease, torment
**play roughly** romp
**play segment** act
**play setting** scene
**play tenpins** bowl
**play the fool** daff, footle
**play the game** compromise, conform, defer, temporise, yield
**play the lead** star
**play the part of** act
**plaything** ball, doll, teddy bear, top, toy
**playthings store** toy shop
**play to excite laughter** farce
**play to the gallery** dramatise
**play truant** malinger
**play up** accentuate, annoy, bother, emphasise, exaggerate, highlight, hurt, magnify, malfunction, misbehave, pain, spotlight, stress, trouble, underline
**play up to** cajole, fawn, flatter, inflate, soft-soap, toady, wheedle
**play wildly** romp
**play with** jiggle, toy, waggle, wiggle
**play without words** mime
**play with songs** musical
**playwright** dramaturge, farceur (F), (melo)dramatist, scriptwriter, tragedian
**play writer** dramatist, playwright
**play wrongly** renege
**plaza de toros** bullring
**plea** apology, appeal, entreaty, excuse, overture, petition, prayer, pretext, request, suit, supplication
**plead** allege, apologise, appeal, argue, ask, assert, avow, beg, beseech, declare, entreat, exhort, implore, maintain, persuade, pray, proclaim, request, seek, supplicate, urge

**plead in favour of** advocate
**plead in protest** expostulate, remonstrate
**plead passionately** entreat
**pleasant** acceptable, agreeable, amiable, amusing, cheerful, enjoyable, eu-, fair, friendly, humorous, jocose, jocular, merry, nice, pleasing, sunny, welcome, witty
**pleasant and easy** cushy
**pleasant bazaar** fair
**pleasant idleness** dolce far niente (I)
**pleasant journey** bon voyage
**pleasantly** affably, amiably, charmingly, cheerfully, congenially, engagingly, finely, gratifyingly, nicely, refreshingly, satisfyingly
**pleasantly odd** quaint
**pleasantly stimulating** piquant
**pleasantly warm** genial
**pleasantness** agreeableness, amenity, enjoyableness, pleasurableness
**pleasantness of sounds** euphony
**pleasant odour** aroma, fragrance
**pleasant song** lilt
**pleasant sounds** music
**pleasant to eat** moreish
**pleasant to look at** comely
**pleasant to the taste** palatable
**please** amuse, charm, cheer, content, delectate, delight, divert, elect, entertain, gladden, gratify, humour, indulge, like, mollify, opt, pacification, rejoice, satisfy, select, suit, tickle, want
**please by compliance** gratify
**pleased** glad, gratified, happy, thankful
**pleased as punch** delighted
**pleased interjection** aha
**please greatly** delight, enthral
**please reply** répondez s'il vous plait (F), RSVP
**pleasing** agreeable, amiable, amusing, attractive, charming, cheering, contenting, delightful, delighting, enjoyable, entertaining, gladdening, good, gratifying, humouring, indulging, lekker, likeable, nice, polite, rejoicing, satisfying, suiting, tickling
**pleasing in behaviour** personable
**pleasing in flavour** tasty
**pleasing sound** euphony, music
**pleasing to the eye** artistic, attractive, beautiful, handsome, lovely
**pleasing to the senses** sensuous
**pleasurable** agreeable, amusing, beautiful, comfortable, delectable, enjoyable, genial, heavenly, lovable, lovely, melodious, pleasant, pleasing, welcome

**pleasurable activity** game, play, recreation
**pleasurable contemplation** admiration
**pleasurable journey** trip
**pleasure** amusement, bliss, cheer, delight, desire, diversion, elation, enjoyment, entertainment, fun, gaiety, gladness, happiness, joy, luxuriousness, merriment, mirth, option, predilection, purpose, treat, wish, zest
**pleasure boat** launch, yacht
**pleasure carriage** chaise, surrey
**pleasure craft** barge, boat, canoe, cruiser, yacht
**pleasure excursion** jaunt
**pleasure excursion including a meal out of doors** picnic
**pleasure in others' misfortune** schadenfreude (G)
**pleasure-loving** hugging, sensuous, voluptuous
**pleasure seeker** fainéant, hedonist, playboy, playgirl, sport
**pleasure-seeking** hedonism
**pleasure ship** yacht
**pleasure trip** excursion, jaunt, outing, tour, treat, vacation
**pleasure voyage** cruise
**pleasure walker** hiker
**pleasure-weary** blasé
**pleat** bend, crease, crimp, crumple, double, flute, fold, furrow, gather, intertwine, layer, overlap, pinch, plait, plucker, tuck, turn, wrinkle
**pleated frill** ruche
**pleated skirt** kilt
**plea that a person was elsewhere when an act occurred** alibi
**pleat vertically** kilt
**plebeian** base, blue-collar, coarse, common, gauche, humble, ignoble, inferior, low(-class), lower class, mean, obscure, pleb(e), proletarian, roturier (F), rude, shabby, tawdry, uncouth, unrefined, untitled, vulgar, working class
**plebiscite** ballot, election, poll, referendum, vote
**plectrum of harp** fescue
**pledge** assurance, bail, bind, bond, contract, covenant, deposit, (en)gage, guarantee, mortgage, oath, pawn, promise, secure, security, surety, swear, undertake, undertaking, vouch, vow, warrant, word
**pledge a chesspiece** pawn
**pledge of eternal love** troth
**pledge to tell the truth** oath
**plenary** absolute, complete, entire, full

**plenitude** abundance, ampleness, bounty, broadness, capacity, completeness, completion, comprehensiveness, entirety, extensiveness, exuberance, fullness, overfulfilment, plenty, pleroma, plethora, refill, replenishment, satiety, saturation, sufficiency, totality, vastness, wealth, wholeness
**plenteous** abounding, abundant, affluent, ample, copious, exuberant, fertile, generous, inexhaustible, lavish, liberal, luxuriant, plentiful, productive, rich
**plentiful** abound, abundant, ample, copious, enough, exhaustless, exuberant, fertile, fruitful, galore, generous, great, inexhaustible, lavish, liberal, luxuriant, numerous, opulent, overflowing, plenteous, profuse, rich, uberous, unsparing
**plenty** abundance, affluence, ample, amplitude, bait, bountiful, copious, enough, exuberant, fullness, galore, lots, much, opulence, plenitude, plethora, profusion, prosperity, quite, riches, superfluity, wealth, won
**plenty of space given** wide berth
**plexus** complication, mesh, network
**pliable** compliant, deferential, docile, extensible, flexible, flexile, formable, lissom(e), malleable, manageable, obedient, passive, persuasible, pliant, stretchable, supple, susceptible, teachable, tractable, trainable
**pliant** adaptable, bendable, biddable, compliant, ductile, facile, flexible, impressionable, limber, lithe, manageable, persuadable, plastic, pliable, supple, susceptible, tractable, yielding
**pliant leather** buff
**pliers** extractor, forceps, nippers, pincers, pinchers, tongs
**plight** condition, dilemma, pledge, predicament, situation, state
**plight one's troth** affiance, espouse
**plimsoll** canvas shoe, pump, sandshoe, sportshoe, tackie, tacky
**plinth** base, block, foot(stall), foundation, mounting, orle, pedestal, pier, socle, stand, support
**plinth of column** dado, socle
**plod** drudge, labour, lumber, moil, overdo, pace, persevere, shuffle, slave, slog, struggle, sweat, toil, tramp(le), trudge, walk
**plod heavily** trudge
**plonk** rotgut
**plot** action, allotment, area, cabal, calculate, chart, collude, concoct, conspiracy, conspire, contrive, design, devise, draft, draw, erf, frame, green, ground, hatch, intrigue, lay, locate, lot, manoeuvre, map, narrative, outline, parcel, patch, plan, project, scenario, scheme, story, stratagem, subject, theme, thread, tract
**plot of building land** site
**plot of flowers** bed
**plot of ground** erf, lot, plat
**plot of play** scenario
**plotter** cabalist, conniver, conspirator, conspirer, intriguer, map maker, planner, schemer, slyboots, strategist
**plot together** conspire
**plough** cultivate, dig, furrow, ridge, till
**plough beast** ox
**plough blade** coulter, share
**ploughed trench** furrow
**plough handle** stilt
**plough the soil** cultivate, delve, dig, farm, furrow, hoe, prepare, rake, spade, till
**ploy** artful, artifice, craft, dodge, feint, gambit, game, manoeuvre, ruse, scheme, stratagem, subterfuge, tactic, wile
**pluck** bravery, collect, courage, determination, harvest, jerk, nerve, pull, resolution, snatch, spirit, tear
**plucked instrument, with four pairs of strings** mandolin
**pluck up** annihilate, demolish, dissolve, eliminate, eradicate, exterminate, extirpate, gut, muster, ravage, smash, summon, wreck
**pluck up courage** cheer
**plucky** adventurous, audacious, aweless, bold, brave, cheerful, courageous, daring, dashing, dauntless, energetic, fearless, firm, game, gay, great-hearted, gritty, lion-hearted, lively, mettlesome, resolute, spirited, stalwart, staunch, steadfast, sturdy, unafraid, unalarmed, valiant, valorous, vigorous, vivacious
**plug** bung, cork, pigtail, spigot, stopper, stopple, stuff
**plug fitting a cylinder** piston
**plug for closing a bottle** cork, stopper
**plug in** charge, connect
**plug of hemp** wad
**plum** damson, fruit, gage, lomboy, orleans, prune, sloe
**plumage** crest, down, feathering, feathers, hackle, panache, plumosity, topknot, tuft, tussock
**plum as a fruit** drupe
**plumb** bang, delve, directly, downright, exactly, explore, fathom, gauge,

**lead**, measure, perpendicularly, precisely, probe, search, slap, sound, vertically, weigh(t)
**plumbing system** drainage
**plumbing tube** pipe
**plume** aglet, aigret(te), aiguillette, boast, brag, crow, egret, exult, feather, knot, panache, preen, pride, quill
**plumed heron** egret
**plume of feathers used as head-dress** panache
**plume oneself on** boast about, pride oneself
**plum-like fruit** sloe
**plummet** collapse, descend, dive, drop, fall, float, hurl, lead, lunge, lurch, nosedive, plop, plumb, pounce, swoop, weight
**plump** blunt, burly, buxom, chubby, corpulent, direct, dumpy, fat, fleshy, full, obese, podgy, portly, rotund, round, sonsie, sonsy (Sc), stout, tubby, well-fed
**plump and comely** buxom
**plump and round** chubby
**plump celluloid doll** kewpie
**plump-faced** chubby
**plump for** back, choose, favour, select, support
**plumpness** burliness, buxomness, chubbiness, dumpiness, embonpoint (F), fullness, portliness, pudginess, puffiness, rotundity, rotundness, roundness, stoutness, top-heaviness, tubbiness fatness
**plum-sized orange-like fruit** cumquat, kumquat
**plum used in gin** sloe
**plunder** booty, despoil, devastate, loot, maraud, pillage, prey, raid, ransack, rape, ravage, rob(bery), sack, spoils, strip, theft
**plunderer** aggressor, attacker, bandit, brigand, burglar, cheat, embezzler, forager, fraud, highwayman, housebreaker, invader, looter, marauder, pickpocket, pirate, raider, reiver, robber, shoplifter, spoiler, stealer, swindler, thief, trespasser
**plundering raid** reive
**plunge** baptise, bathe, descend, dip, duck, hasten, immerse, inundate, jump, leap, (nose-)dive, plummet, plump, rush, scramble, scurry, sink, skydive, submerge
**plunge briefly into liquid** dip
**plunge headfirst into water** dive
**plunge into water** souse
**plural ending** -en, -es

**plus** additional, and, auxiliary, extra, helpful, more, spare, supplementary, with
**plush** costly, lavish, luxurious, opulent, rich, sumptuous
**plush fabric** velour(s)
**Pluto** Dis
**plutocracy** government, ruling
**plutocrat** aristocrat, Croesus, Midas, nabob
**plutonic** abyssal
**ply** apply, assail, assault, attraction, besiege, bias, bombard, charge, exercise, exploit, follow, lavish, partiality, pommel, practice, practise, prejudice, provide, pursue, raid, replenish, satiate, supply, surfeit, torment, torture, treat, trounce, twist, undertake, use, utilise, wield
**plying** exercising, following, practising, pursuing, selling
**ply the needle** sew
**pneuma** breath, soul, spirit
**pneumatic tyre inventor** Dunlop
**pneumatic wheel** tyre
**poach** infringe, intrude, plunder, rob, steal, trespass
**poacher's dog** lurcher
**pocket** bag, compact, compartment, concise, little, miniature, pouch, receptacle
**pocket a ball in snooker** pot
**pocketbook** wallet
**pocket bottle** (hip) flask
**pocket clock** watch
**pocket watch** fob
**pockmarked** pitted
**pod** case, cocoon, hull, husk, legume, shell
**podded vegetable** pea
**podgy** burly, buxom, chubby, corpulent, fat, fleshy, gross, heavy, obese, outsize, overweight, plump, portly, stout, tubby
**podiatrist** chiropodist
**podium** bema, bima(h), dais, platform, rostrum, stage
**pod of peas** hull
**pod vegetable** bean, pea
**poem** ballad, ditty, eclogue, elegy, epic, idyll, limerick, lyric, ode, rhapsody, rhyme, rondelet, song, sonnet, verse, villanelle
**poem addressed to a person** ode
**poem describing pastoral scenes** idyll
**poem division** canto
**poem for singing** ballad, song
**poem in the form of a letter** epistle
**poem lamenting a dead person** elegy
**poem meant to be sung** ode
**poem of five verses** quinzaine
**poem of fourteen lines** sonnet

**poem of heroism** epic
**poem of lament** elegy, ode
**poem or song with a regularly repeated refrain** roundelay
**poem recited before a play** prologue
**poem set to music** ballad, ode, song
**poem with fourteen lines** sonnet
**poem with six stanzas** sestina
**poem with ten or thirteen lines** rondeau
**Poe's bird** raven
**poet** bard, elegist, idyllist, imaginist, lyricist, lyrist, minstrel, odist, rhymer, rhymester, rhymist, scald, skald, sonneteer, vers-librist, versemaker, versifier
**poetic** artistic, elegiac, graceful, lyric(al), melodic, melodious, metrical, rhythmical
**poetical frenzy** furor poeticus (L)
**poetical over** o'er
**poetical rhythm** measure, meter
**poetic anger** ire
**poetic foot** iamb(ic), ionic
**poetic lines** verse
**poetic muse** Calliope, Erato
**poetic name for Ireland** Emerald Isle
**poetic rhythm** meter
**poetic word for between** tween
**poetic word for curse** malison
**poetic word for the sun** sol
**poet of ancient Greece** Pindar
**poetry** meter, numbers, poesy, rhythm, verse
**poetry muse** Calliope, Erato
**poetry reading** recital
**poignant** acute, agonising, biting, bitter, caustic, distressing, hurtful, intense, keen, moving, painful, piercing, piquant, pointed, pungent, sad, sarcastic, serious, severe, sharp, sincere, strong, touching, upsetting
**point** aim, aspect, cusp, demonstrate, detail, direct, feature, heart, indicate, juncture, meaning, moment, object, particular, prong, purpose, res (L), score, sense, stage, suggest, tip, unit
**point aimed at** scope
**point at back of head** inion
**point at the target** aim
**point at top of nose** nasion
**point at which an orbiting object is closest to the earth** perihelion
**point a weapon** aim
**point by point** seriatim
**pointed** acerose, aciform, barbed, craggy, cuspidal, cuspidate, directed, effective, focused, impressive, peaked, penetrating, sagittate, sagittiform, serrate, sharp,

spear-headed, spinous, succinct, terse, thorny, toothed, xiphoid
**pointed arch** ogee, ogive
**pointed beard** goatee
**pointed end** cusp, tip
**pointed end of heart** apex
**pointed goad** rod
**pointed instrument** awl, prod, stiletto
**pointed like a needle** acerose
**pointed metal** nail, pin
**pointed missile** arrow, dart
**pointed outgrowth on plant** thorn
**pointed part** prong
**pointed part of church roof** steeple
**pointed part of steeple** spire
**pointed saying** epigram
**pointed stem** spire
**pointed tip of spear** spearhead
**pointed tool** awl, eyeleteer
**pointed tooth** canine
**pointed upwards** apeak
**pointed weapon** assegai, spear
**pointed wheel** tracer
**pointer** adage, arrow, caution, charge, clue, compass, guide, hint, index, indicant, indicator, key, landmark, law, lodestar, mark, motto, needle, polestar, recommendation, reference, rule, sign, suggestion, tip, warning
**pointer on dial** needle
**point gun at target** aim
**point in dispute** issue
**pointing backwards** retrorse
**pointing inwards** re-entrant
**pointing outwards** salient
**point in orbit of a planet nearest to sun** perihelion
**point in orbit of a planet farthest from sun** aphelion
**point in question** issue
**pointless** alien, blunt, edgeless, empty, illogical, impertinent, inane, irrational, irrelevant, meaningless, nonsensical, senseless, unessential, unsharp, vain
**pointless sword** curtana, curtein, épée
**point of antler** tine
**point of argument** gist
**point of breast** nipple
**point of concentration** centre, focus
**point of convergence** focus
**point of crossing** intersect(ion)
**point of development** stage
**point of entry** portal
**point of greatest interest** clou
**point of high land jutting out into sea** headland, promontory
**point of intersection** vertex
**point of lace** tag
**point of land** cape, spit
**point of pen** nib

**point of perfection** acme, apex, culmination, zenith
**point of planet's orbit farthest from the sun** aphelion
**point of rotation** axis, pivot
**point of story** nub
**point of the sun's orbit farthest from the earth** apogee
**point of time** date
**point of view** angle, approach, aspect, attitude, belief, context, judg(e)ment, opinion, outlook, perspective, position, slant, standpoint, view(point)
**point on compass** rhumb
**point one's pencil** sharpen
**point on fork** prong
**point on head** inion
**point on which a lever is placed for support** fulcrum
**point opposite the zenith** nadir
**point out** denote, designate, elucidate, explain, identify, indicate, mention, remind, reveal, show, specify
**point out the way** direct
**point scored after deuce in tennis** advantage
**point the finger at** blame, incriminate
**point to** indicate, reveal
**point to possible danger** warn
**point to target** aim
**poise** aplomb, assurance, balance, behaviour, collectedness, composure, confidence, control, correspondence, counterpoise, demeanour, equality, equilibrium, equipoise, equivalence, evenness, float, hover, levelness, mien, par, parallelism, parity, savoir-faire, stability, steadiness, steady, suaveness, suspense, symmetry, uniformity, urbanity, weigh
**poison** acaricide, arsenic, bane, blight, contaminate, contamination, corrupt(ion), cyanide, dope, envenom, fungicide, germicide, infect(ion), intoxicant, kill, malignancy, miasma, murder, pesticide, pollute, ruin, strychnine, toxicant, toxicity, toxin, venom, virus
**poisonous** baneful, contagious, dangerous, deadly, fatal, harmful, infective, injurious, lethal, malicious, malign(ant), morbific, mortal, nocuous, noxious, septic, toxic, unhealthy, venomous, viperous, virulent
**poisonous alkaloid found in putrefying matter** ptomaine
**poisonous bean** calabar
**poisonous element** arsenic
**poisonous evergreen shrub** oleander

**poisonous extract** violin
**poisonous fluid of snakes** venom
**poisonous fungus** toadstool
**poisonous gas** arsine, stibine
**poisonous mushroom** agaric, amentia, toadstool
**poisonous oily liquid extracted from tobacco** nicotine
**poisonous plant** aconite, cowbane, deathin, loco, oleander, samnitis
**poisonous shrub** cube, gifblaar, laburnum, lithi, sumac
**poisonous snake** adder, asp, boomslang, cobra, krait, mamba, puffadder, rinkhals, taipan, viper
**poisonous stench** mephitis
**poisonous substance found in tobacco** nicotine
**poisonous tree** upas
**poisonous vine** sumac
**poisonous viper** asp
**poisonous weed** loco
**poison used in insecticides** aldrin
**poke** dab, intrude, jab, meddle, nose, nudge, prod, punch, push, snoop, stab, tamper, thrust, thump
**poke around** root
**poke fun at** chaff, deride, guy, jeer, mock, needle, rib, ridicule, taunt, tease
**poke one's nose in** interfere, snoop
**poke roughly** jab
**poker stake** ante
**poker word** pat
**poke with elbow** nudge
**poke with something pointed** prod
**poky** confined, cramped, crawling, graceless, indecisive, late, lingering, mean, messy, narrow, relaxed, restraining, shabby, sloppy, slow, small, stuffy, tardy, tiny, uncertain, unkempt
**Poland** Polska
**polar** arctic, boreal, central, cold, contrary, crucial, directing, freezing, frigid, fundamental, guiding, hostile, icebound, inimical, pivotal, principal, repugnant, telluric
**polar bear** nanook
**polar cover** icecap
**polar jacket** anorak
**polar light** aurora
**polar region** Arctic
**polar shipping hazard** iceberg
**pole** bar, caber, mast, post, rod, shaft, spar, staff, standard, stick
**polecat** ferret, foumart, skunk, stinker, zoril
**poled boat** punt
**pole for propelling a boat** quant
**pole for rowing** oar
**pole for supporting sails** mast

**polemic** argument, case, contention, controversy, debate, defence, dialectic, discussion, dispute, dissension, ground(s), logic, polemical, quarrel, reason(ing), squabble, strife, wrangle
**polemics** argumentation, controversy, litigation
**polemist** controversialist, debater, disputer, pilpulist
**pole on which flag is hoisted** flagstaff
**poles apart** different, disagreeing, distinct, incompatible, incongruous, irreconcilable, separate
**pole separating horses in a stable** bail
**poles for walking** stilts
**pole used on board a vessel** boathook
**pole with toothed crossbar** rake
**police** constabulary, cop, guard, inspector, officer, patrol, protect, regulate, sheriff
**police barrier** cordon
**police cordon** dragnet
**police district** precinct
**police force** constabulary
**police force of the Republic of Ireland** Garda Síochána
**police 'grass'** informer
**police identification** badge
**police informer** Askari, grass, impimpi, nark
**police klaxon** siren
**police look for it** clue
**policeman** bluecoat, bobby, carbiniere (I), constable, cop(per), detective, gendarme(rie), gendarmery, john hop, officer, patrolman, walloper
**police officer** inspector
**police perambulation** beat
**police spy** Askari, grass, impimpi, informer, nark
**police staff** truncheon
**police trainee** cadet, student
**Police vocalist** Sting
**police weapon** truncheon
**policy** approach, astuteness, discretion, expediency, handling, management, procedure, prudence, rule, sagacity, skill, stratagem, tactic
**policy of non-interference** individualism, laisser faire (F), laissez faire
**policy of racial segregation** apartheid
**policy of separation** separatism
**policy reversal** volte-face
**polio** infantile paralysis, poliomyelitis
**polish** beeswax, beeswing, brighten, brightness, buff, burnish, civilise, clean, elegance, enhance, finesse, finish, glaze, gloss, grace, lustre, poise, refine(ment), rub, sheen, shine, smooth, style, varnish, wax

**polish a surface** buff
**polish by rubbing** burnish
**Polish currency** zloty
**Polish dance** krakowiak, mazurka, polacca, polka, polonaise
**polished silk fabric** ciré
**polisher of gems** lapidary
**Polish governor** vaivode, voivode, waywode
**polish hard** scour
**polishing abrasive** emery
**polishing material** beeswax, emery, pumice, rabat, rouge, sand, wax
**polishing wheel** bob, buff(er), scaife, skaif, skeif
**polish nails** buff
**Polish Nobel prize winner** Curie
**polish off** bolt, consume, devour, down, eat, eliminate, finish, gobble, liquidate, murder, shift, stuff, wolf
**Polish pianist** Chopin
**polish with brush** scrub
**polite** civil, complaisant, courteous, courtly, elegant, formal, gracious, mannerly, pleasant, polished, refined, respectful, sociable, suave, tactful, urbane
**polite amusing remark** pleasantry
**polite expression of praise** compliment
**polite request** invitation
**polite term of address** madam, sir
**political adventurer** carpetbagger
**political and economic theory of Karl Marx** Marxism
**political campaigning** hustings
**political clique** cabal, faction, junta
**political combination** bloc
**political committee** caucus
**political conservatism** rightism
**political disorder** anarchy
**political division of Switzerland** canton
**political dogma** ideology
**political economy** plutonomy
**political exile** émigré
**political fugitive** refugee
**political gathering** rally
**political group** bloc, party
**political hawk** militarist
**political intrigue** imbroglio, wire-pulling
**political killing** assassination
**political leader** fugleman
**politically aggressive** hawkish
**politically organised people** state
**political pamphlet** tract
**political plot** cabal
**political predecessor** progenitor
**political rebel** Frondeur
**political scandal** Watergate
**political spreader of panic** terrorist
**political subdivision** ward

**political system** ideology
**political theorist** ideologue
**political wisdom** policy
**polka** dance
**poll** ballot, canvass, census, count, cranium, demography, election, enumeration, figures, Gallup, head, nape, pate, register, roster, sampling, skull, statistics, survey, tabulation, tally, vote, voting
**pollen-bearing organ of a flowering plant** stamen
**pollen-bearing organ of plants** anther
**pollinated by animals** zoophilous
**pollination by snails** malacophily
**polling place** booth
**poll tax** capitation
**pollute** abuse, befoul, contaminate, corrupt, debase, defile, desecrate, despoil, destroy, devalue, dirty, foul, maculate, misuse, profane, ravage, soil, stain, sully, unhallow, violate, vitiate
**polluted** cankerous, contaminated, corrupted, damaged, dirty, f(o)etid, harmed, impure, morbific, noisome, noxious, odious, poisoned, rank, smoky, soiled, sooty, tainted, unclean, unhygienic, violated
**polluted air** smog
**pollution** contamination, defiling, fouling, foulness, impurity, miasma, smog, soiling
**polo team** four
**Polska** Poland
**poltroon** coward, craven, dastard, faint-heart, invertebrate, mouse, recreant, renegade, sissy, sneak, weakling, wheyface
**polyester fibre** dacron
**polygonal** prism
**polygonal recess** apse
**polygon having eight sides** octagon
**polygon having five sides** pentagon
**polygon having four sides** tetragon
**polygon having nine sides** enneagon, nonagon
**polygon having seven sides** heptagon
**polygon having six sides** hexagon
**polygon having ten sides** decagon
**polygon having three sides** triangle
**Polynesian chestnut** rata
**Polynesian dance** hula
**Polynesian garland of flowers** lei
**Polynesian island** Bali
**Polynesian taro paste** poi
**Polynesian tree** ti
**polyphonic composition** fugue
**polyps' reef growth** coral
**pome fruit** apple
**pomelo** grapefruit

**pomp** brilliance, ceremonial, ceremoniousness, ceremony, dignity, display, éclat, flourish, formality, grandeur, magnificence, ostentation, pageant(ry), parade, pomposity, (ritual) show, solemnity, splendour, state, style
**pompon** cockade, feather, panache, rosette, tassel, topknot
**pompous** arrogant, blatant, boastful, bombastic, bumptious, cocky, conceited, consequential, egotistical, grand(iloquent), grandiose, haughty, histrionic, illustrious, immodest, imperious, magnificent, orotund, ostentatious, perky, pretentious, prideful, self-important, selfish, sententious, snobbish, splendid, stiff, stilted, stuck-up, turgid, vain(glorious)
**pompous gait** strut
**pompous in expression** grandiloquent
**pompous language** bombast
**pompously dogmatic** pontifical
**pompously solemn** portentous
**pompous official** panjandrum
**pompous show** pageant, parade
**pompous speech** harangue
**pompous type** prig
**pompous walk** strut
**ponce** libertine, mincer, pimp
**poncho** cloak, cycling cape
**pond** millpond, pool, tarn, water hole
**pond amphibian** frog, newt
**pond bird** duck, goose, swan
**ponder** brood, cerebrate, cogitate, consider, contemplate, deliberate, mull, muse, reflect, ruminate, think, weigh
**ponder morbidly** brood
**ponderous** bulky, heavy, important, massive, momentous, weighty
**pond flower** lily
**pone ingredient** cornmeal
**pontiff** bishop, pope
**pontificate** bishopric, declaim, diocese, episcopate, harangue, lecture, mitre, moralise, orate, papacy, papality, papism, perorate, popedom, preach, prelacy, prelature, see, sermonise
**pony** bronco, colt
**pool** ante, bank, billiards, carr, cartel, coalition, combine, consortium, dib, dike, dump, (fish)pond, funds, group, jackpot, kitty, lagoon, lake, league, lin(n), mere, merge, pot, puddle, share, splash, stake, syndicate, tarn, team, trust, union
**pool at Jerusalem** Bethesda
**pool below waterfall** lin(n), llyn
**pool in bog** hag
**pool of money** kitty
**pool room** billiards parlour

**pool stick** cue
**pool tree** dilo, keena
**pool without outlet** stagnum
**poor** base, common, deficient, destitute, distressed, doomed, faulty, gaunt, humble, impecunious, impoverished, inadequate, indigent, inferior, lacking, lank, lean, luckless, meagre, needy, penniless, reduced, seedy, shabby, substandard, underfed, valueless, worthless
**poor and diseased person** lazar, leper
**poor as a church mouse** beggary, lacking, needy, penniless
**poor city area** slum
**poor condition** bad shape
**poor diet** malnutrition, undernourishment
**poor fellow** beggar
**poor handwriting** cacography, scribble
**poor horse** cayuse
**poorly** insufficiently, meagrely, pitiably, rottenly, shabbily, shoddily, sparsely, weakly
**poorly done** shoddy
**poorly dressed** shabby
**poorly lit** dim
**poorly matched** ill-assorted, incompatible, mismatched, unsuitable, unsuited
**poorly suited** crook
**poorly supplied** scant
**poor old tired horse** hack
**poor painting** daubery
**poor performer at sport** palooka
**poor person** pauper
**poor sleeper** insomniac
**poor visibility** darkness, dimness, murk
**poor worn-out horse** jade
**poor wretch** caitiff
**pop** bang, boom, burst, cola, crack, detonate, explode, explosion, fulminate, insert, lemonade, noise, push, put, report, shove, slip, snap, soda, stick, thrust, tuck
**pop dancing venue** disco(theque)
**pope** bishop, pontiff
**Pope's epic poem** *Dunciad*
**pope's palace** Vatican
**pope's triple crown** tiara
**Popeye's girl** Olive
**Popeye's tonic** spinach
**popinjay** coxcomb, fop
**pop like a balloon** burst
**poppycock** babble, baloney, bombast, chaff, drool, falderal, fiddle-de-dee, folly, foolishness, froth, fustian, gibberish, havers, hocus-pocus, jargon, nonsense, rant, refuse, rigmarole, rubbish, stuff, tommyrot, trash, twaddle, twattle
**poppy drug** opium

**poppy seed** maw seed
**pop the question** propose
**populace** commoners, demos, inhabitants, mob, peasantry, people, proletariat, residents, riffraff
**popular** approved, faddish, favourite, prevailing, received, (well-)liked
**popular book** best-seller
**popular cheese** Cheddar, sweetmilk
**popular dessert** ice cream, pie
**popular drink** coffee, tea
**popular figure** heroine
**popular flower** rose
**popular girl** belle
**popular leader** tribune
**popular Mediterranean resort area** Riviera
**popular novel** potboiler
**popular pet** cat, dog, goldfish
**popular pot plant** aspidistra
**popular report** rumour
**popular saying** proverb
**popular song** ballad
**popular style** vogue
**popular success** hit
**popular to eat during summer** salad
**popular tree** abele, aspen
**popular type of plum** victoria
**popular whim** craze, fad, rage
**popular woman** belle
**population count** census
**pop-up grill** toaster
**porbeagle** shark
**porcelain** celadon, ceramics, china(ware), Delft, delicate, earthenware, faience, fragile, Imari, ju, ko, Limoges, Meissen, pottery, Sèvres, Spode
**porcelain from China** ju, ko
**porcelain from Egypt** faience
**porcelain from England** Royal Doulton, Spode
**porcelain from France** Limoges, Sèvres
**porcelain from Germany** Meissen
**porcelain from Holland** Delft
**porcelain from Japan** imari, kutani
**porcelain from the Orient** celadon
**porcelain ingredient** clay, kaolin, petuntse
**porcelain insulator** cleat
**porch** anta, galilee, gallery, logia, portico, solarium, stoa, stoop, veranda(h), vestibule
**porcine adipose** fatback
**porcine animal** hog, pig, swine
**porcine leather** pigskin
**porcine sound** oink
**porcupine anteater** echidna
**porcupine spine** quill
**pore in leaf** stoma
**pore in plants** hydathode

**pore over** study
**porifer** sponge
**pork and veal mixture** scrapple
**porker** pig
**pork fat** lard
**porkfish** sisi
**pork infested with tapeworm** measly
**pornographic** bawdy, coarse, dirty, erotic, filthy, foul, indecent, lewd, obscene, offensive, prurient, ribald, salacious, smutty, vile, vulgar
**pornographic books** curiosa, erotica
**pornography** bawdry, dirt, filth, indecency, obscenity, ribaldry, sexploitation, smut
**porous** absorbent, bibulous, cellular, cribriform, cribrose, cushioned, cushiony, elastic, honeycombed, light, penetrable, perforated, permeable, pervious, pitted, sievelike, spongelike, spongy, springy
**porous metal** sponge
**porous rock** tufa, tuff
**porous substance** sponge
**porpoise** sea-hog
**porpoise-like creature** dolphin
**porraceous** leek-green
**porridge** mealie-meal, oatmeal, oats, pap, parritch (Sc), putu
**porridge flakes** oats
**porridge ingredient** mealie-meal, oatmeal
**porridge made from Indian corn** samp
**porridge made of maize** mealie-meal, polenta
**port** air, anchorage, attitude, cast, conduct, gateway, harbour, haven, larboard, manner, mien, presence, refuge, seaport, shelter, temperate, town, wine
**portable athletics barrier** hurdle
**portable bed** carrier, cot
**portable canopy** parasol, umbrella
**portable case** hold-all
**portable case for loose papers** portfolio
**portable chair** sedan
**portable dwelling** yurt
**portable fireplace** barbecue, braai
**portable light** lamp, lantern, torch
**portable rain shelter** umbrella
**portable rocket gun** bazooka
**portable sitting bath** hip-bath
**portable steps** ladder
**portable stove** primus
**portable tub** tosh
**portage** carriage, cartage, conveyance, demand, fare, ferriage, freight(age), haulage, porterage, shipment, toll, towage, transport, truckage, waftage

**portal** access, adit, door(way), entrance, entrée, entry(way), gate(way), ingress, inlet, opening
**port drink** negus
**portend** augur, betoken, (fore)bode, forecast, foretell, forewarn, harbinger, omen, predict, presage, prognosticate, prophesy, threaten, warn
**portending evil** ominous
**portent** augury, foreshadowing, harbinger, indication, marvel, miracle, omen, phenomenon, premonition, presage, prodigy, sensation, sight, sign, spectacle, token, warning, wonder
**portentous** breathtaking, extraordinary, fabulous, foreboding, grave, inauspicious, looming, miraculous, ominous, serious, threatening, unfavourable, unfortunate
**porter** baggageman, bearer, caddie, caretaker, carrier, commissionaire, concierge, door-keeper, doorman, gatekeeper, janitor, port(e)ress, receptionist, watchman
**porter or stout** ale
**portico** arcade, colonnade, loggia, porch, stoa, veranda(h)
**port in Algeria** Oran
**port in Arabia** Aden
**port in Argentina** Rosario
**port in Athens** P(e)iraeus
**port in Bahamas** Nassau
**port in Belgium** Antwerp, Ostend
**port in Black Sea** Odessa
**port in Brazil** Belem, Rio, Salvador
**port in Burma** Akyab, Bassein, Henzada, Moulmein
**port in Chile** Arica, Coquimbo, Lota, Tome
**port in China** Amoy, Canton, Chefoo, Dairen, Kongmoon, Ningpo, Pakhoi, Shasi, Shangai, Swatow, Wuhu
**port in Colombia** Cartagena, Lorica
**port in Corsica** Ajaccio
**port in Cyprus** Famagusta
**port in Denmark** Nykøbing
**port in East Africa** Beira
**port in Egypt** Alexandria, Dumyat, Ouseir, Port Said, Rosetta, Safaga, Tor Suez
**port in El Salvador** Acajutla, Cutuco
**port in England** Birkenhead, Falmouth, Goole
**port in Ethiopia** Assab, Massawa
**port in France** Bordeaux, Brest, Caen, Calais, Cherbourg, Dunkerque, Dunkirk, Marseille, Toulon
**port in Germany** Altona, Hamburg
**port in Ghana** Tema

**port in Guatemala** Barrios, Livingston, Ocos
**port in Honduras** Laceiba, Trujillo
**port in Illinois** Peoria
**port in India** Bombay
**port in Iran** Bushire, Jask, Pahlevi
**port in Iraq** Basra, Fao
**port in Israel** Ashdod, Eilat
**port in Italy** Bari, Genoa, Pola, Salerno, Trieste, Zara
**port in Japan** Kobe, Otaru, Yahata, Yawata
**port in Jordan** Akaba, Aqaba
**port in Maryland** Baltimore
**port in Montenegro** Antivari, Bar, Dulcigno, Ulcinj
**port in Morocco** Agadir, Ceuta, Larache, Mazagan, Mogador, Saffi, Safi, Tangier, Tentuan
**port in Mozambique** Beira
**port in Namibia** Lüderitz, Walfish Bay, Walvis Bay
**port in New Guinea** Daru, Lae, Madang, Wewak
**port in New Zealland** Gisborne
**port in Nicaragua** Corinto
**port in Nigeria** Calabar, Lagos
**port in North Chile** Iquique
**port in North Vietnam** Haiphong, Tonkin
**port in Pakistan** Chalna, Karachi
**port in Panama** Colon, Cristobal
**port in Poland** Danzig, Gdansk
**port in Portugal** Setubal
**port in Rome** Ostia
**port in Russia** Anapa, Eisk, Odessa
**port in Scotland** Ayr
**port in South Africa** Cape Town, Durban, East London, Port Elizabeth
**port in south-east Italy** Taranto
**port in South Ireland** Cobh
**port in South Vietnam** Danang, Nhatrang, Quinhon, Saigon
**port in South Yemen** Aden
**port in Spain** Abdera, Adra, Alicante, Almeria, Barcelona, Cadiz, Gadir, Malaga, Noya
**port in Sweden** Malmö
**port in the Philippines** Legaspi, Manila
**port in Tunisia** Bizerte, Gabes, Sfax, Sousse, Tunis
**port in Wales** Cardiff
**port in West Australia** Fremantle
**port in West Indonesia** Jambi Djambi
**port in Yemen** Aden, Mocha, Moka
**port in Yugoslavia** Belgrade, Dubrovnik, Kotor, Novisad, Rijeka, Split
**portion** allot(ment), bit, dab, distribute, divide(nd), division, dole, dowry, lot, part, piece, quota, section, segment, serving, share, whit

portion of actor's part   length
portion of arrow   breast
portion of bowling green   rink
portion of butter   pat
portion of estate   legitim(e)
portion of food   gobbet, helping, mess
portion of food remaining uneaten
   leftover
portion of land   acre, area, division, lot
portion of land nearly surrounded by
   water   peninsula
portion of liturgy   anaphora, cataphora
portion of medicine   dose
portion of play   scene
portion of Scripture   lesson
portion of time   distance, span
portion of tobacco   cud
portion of tongue   blade
portion of veld fenced for pasture
   camp
portion out   allot, dole, mete
portly   bloated, burly, chunky,
   corpulent, heavy, obese, overweight,
   paunchy, rotund, stalwart, stout,
   tubby
portmanteau   chest
port of arrival   destination
port on the Mediterranean   Tyre
portrait done in solid black on white
   silhouette
portrait of oneself by oneself
   self-portrait
portray   act, delineate, depict, describe,
   draw, enact, limn, paint, picture,
   represent, sketch
portrayal   account, acting, appearance,
   cartoon, character, depiction,
   description, detail, dramatics,
   drawing, embodiment, explanation,
   illustration, image, impersonation,
   likeness, narrative, outline, part,
   performance, performing, persona,
   picture, report, role, show, sketch
portray emotionally   dramatise
portray falsely   misrepresent
portray in colours   paint
portraying   describing, painting,
   picturing, rendering, representing,
   sketching
portray without speaking   mime
Portugal and Spain   Iberia
Portugal as a Roman province
   Lusitania
Portuguese airline   TAP
Portuguese coin   crusado, johannes,
   rei
Portuguese country in India   Goa
Portuguese dance   fado
Portuguese folk-song   fado
Portuguese gentleman   senhor, señor
Portuguese money   conto, cruzeiro,
   escudo

Portuguese navigator   Dias, Gama
Portuguese nobleman   grandee
Portuguese title   dom, dona
Portuguese wine   Aveleda, Dao,
   Douro, Madeira, Mateus Rosé, Rioja
pose   act, affect, allege, allocate,
   arrange, assert, assume, attitude,
   baffle, bluff, boast, deceive, declare,
   embarrass, fake, feign, interrogate,
   model, mystify, perplex, place,
   position, posture, predicate, pretend,
   profound, puzzle, sit, state, stump,
   submit, swank
pose for painting   sit
Poseidon   Neptune
pose in ballet   arabesque
poser   brainteaser, braintwister,
   dilemma, enigma, intricacy, model,
   mystery, perplexity, problem, puzzle,
   question, riddle, sitter, stumper,
   subject, teaser
posh   classy, elegant, exclusive,
   fashionable, grand, high-class,
   la-di-da, lavish, luxurious, refined,
   select, smart, stylish, swanky
position   circumstance, condition, job,
   location, on, opinion, order, place,
   plight, pose, post, posture, rank, site,
   situation, stance, station, status,
   vantage, viewpoint
position directly behind the
   wicket-keeper   longstop
position from which there is no escape
   impasse
position in army   rank
position in life   station, estate
position in paid employment   job
position in society   station
position of authority   seat
position of flag showing respect
   half-mast
position of golf ball   lie
position of high rank   eminence
position of public attention   limelight
position of superiority   advantage
position of the feet in certain games
   stance
position of the sun at noon   meridian
position of work   job
position particularly for someone
   niche
position taken for stroke in golf
   stance
position without duties   sinecure
positive   absolute, assured, certain,
   clear, (cock)sure, convinced,
   definite, determined, direct, explicit,
   express, firm, plus, practical,
   precise, stated, stubborn
positive answer   ay(e), yea, yes
positive electrode   anode
positive in judgement   decided

positively charged ion   cation
positive particle   proton
positive person   optimist
positive pole   anode
positive reply   ay(e), yea, yes
positive statement   assertion, averment
positive terminal   anode
possess   acquaint, acquire, command,
   constrain, contain, control, embrace,
   gain, get, govern, has, have, hold,
   impart, maintain, obtain, occupy,
   own, receive, retain, secure
possess ambition   aspire
possessed by an evil spirit   demoniac
possesses ability   can
possessing a flat breastbone   ratite
possessing an untrimmed edge
   deckled
possessing a pile   napped, rich
possessing a special ability   skilled
possessing being   extant
possessing courage   brave
possessing feeling   sentient
possessing feet   pedate
possessing hooves   ungulate
possessing knowledge   aware,
   knowing
possessing landed property   acred
possessing leaflets   foliolate
possessing leaves   foliate, leafy
possessing life   animate(d)
possessing no heat   cold
possessing no limits   boundless,
   infinite
possessing ribs   costate
possessing rows   tiered
possessing stateliness   majestic
possessing supreme power
   all-powerful, omnipotent
possessing taste   sapid, savoury
possessing tendons   sinewed
possessing wings   alar, alate
possession   asset, aught, care, colony,
   control, custody, demesne,
   dependency, dominion,
   engrossment, enjoyment, estate,
   grasp, heritage, heritance, hold,
   occupation, ownership, patrimony,
   property, protection, protectorate,
   province, retention, tenure, territory,
   title, wealth
possession in law   seisin
possession of a mind   mentality
possession of common features
   affinity
possession of feudal property   sasine
possession of knowledge   science
possession of land by freehold   seisin
possession of value   asset
possessions   assets, belongings,
   chattels, controls, custodies, effects,
   estates, goods, movables,

**possessions of mine** paraphernalia, property, riches, things, wealth
**possessions of mine** my
**possessive adjective** their
**possessive pronoun** her(s), his, its, mine, my, our(s), their(s), your(s)
**possessor** bearer, custodian, holder, incumbent, keeper, landlord, master, mistress, occupant, owner, proprietor, purchaser
**possible** conceivable, credible, feasible, imaginable, likely, practicable
**possible culprit** suspect
**possible event** eventuality, possibility
**possible in practice** practicable
**possible result** eventuality
**possibly** maybe, mayhap, perchance
**post** account, advertise, announce, assign, canter, catalogue, column, correspondence, courier, file, inform, job, locate, mail, newel, palisade, pillar, placard, place, pole, position, record, register, runner, scamper, send, shaft, situate, situation, stake, standard, station, support, upright
**postage item** letter, stamp
**postbox** mailbox
**poster** affiche (F), placard
**posterior** aftermost, buttocks, consequent, haunches, hind(most), hindquarters, later, rear, succeeding, tail
**posterior lobe of the pituitary gland** neurohypophysis
**posterior opening** anus, cloaca
**poster word** wanted
**post exchange** canteen
**postgraduate scholarship** fellowship
**post helping to support rail** baluster
**postmortem** autopsy, consequent, embalmment, ensuing, necropsy, post-obit, retrospect, review, subsequent
**post-op wound** scar
**post par avion** airmail
**postpone** adjourn, dally, defer, delay, discontinue, intermit, procrastinate, prorogue, rank, recess, reserve, shelve, stall, subject, subordinate, suspend, table, temporise, waive
**postpone execution** respite
**postpone punishment** reprieve
**post sack** mailbag
**postulate** adjure, advance, ask, assume, beg, beseech, conclude, deduce, deem, gather, guess, judge, plead, posit, predicate, presume, propose, speculate, suppose, surmise, theorise
**posture** affect, attitude, bearing, condition, deform, demeanour, orientation, poise, pose, position, predicament, set, situation, stance, state, tendency
**posture in ballet** arabesque
**posture in yoga** asana
**post with movable arms for signalling** semaphore
**posy** blossoms, bouquet, festoon, flowers, garland, nosegay, spray, wreath
**pot** container, dagga, grass, jar, marijuana, olla, urn, vase, vessel
**potassium carbonate** potash
**potassium nitrate** nitre
**potato** spud, tater
**potato and leek soup** vichyssoise
**potato bud** eye
**potato chip** crisp
**potato crisps** chips
**potato disease** blight
**potato hole** eye
**potato seed-bud** eye
**potato slice** chip
**Potato State** Idaho
**pot cover** lid
**potency** capacity, control, efficacy, energy, might, power, strength, vigour
**potent** authoritative, cogent, commanding, compelling, convincing, dominant, dynamic, effective, efficacious, forceful, influential, mighty, moving, persuasive, powerful, puissant, pungent, strong, telling, vigorous
**potent drink from Polynesian shrub** kava
**potent green alcoholic drink** absinth(e)
**potent home-brewed alcoholic drink** mampoer, skokiaan, witblits
**potential** ability, capacity, dormant, hidden, imaginable, implicit, inactive, latent, likely, possibility, possible, promise, prospect(ive)
**potential oak** acorn
**potholer** caver
**potion** beaker, beverage, brew, chalice, concoction, cup, cure, dose, draught, drench, drink, drug, elixir, goblet, libation, liquid, measure, medicine, mixture, nostrum, philtre, portion, potation, prescription, quaff, quantity, refreshment, remedy, specific, stimulant, teacup, tonic, trophy
**potion portion** dose
**potoroo** kangaroo rat
**pot plant** aspidistra, bonsai, fern, ficus, lantana, peperomia
**pot-pourri** hotch-potch, mixture, olio, selection
**potter's clay** argil
**potter's material** clay
**potter's oven** kiln
**potter's stuff** clay
**potter's tool** pallet
**potter's wheel** disc, disk, kick, lathe, pallet, throw
**pottery** ceramics, Delft, earthenware
**pottery fragment** ostracon, (pot)sherd, shard
**pottery glaze** slip
**pottery made of coarse baked clay** earthenware
**pottery oven** kiln
**pottery with a pale grey-green glaze** celadon ware
**potto** kinkajou, lemur
**pouch** bag, container, pocket, purse, reticule, sack, sporran
**pouch-beaked bird** pelican
**pouchlike bag** reticule
**pouchlike hat** snood
**pouchlike part in animal** sac
**pouch worn in front of the kilt** sporran
**poultice** application, bandaging, cataplasm, compress, dressing, embrocate, embrocation, epithem, foment(ation), malagma, plaster, pledget, quilt, sinapism, stupe
**poultry** chickens, ducks, fowls, geese, hens, turkeys
**poultry breed** bantam, Dorking, Houdan, leghorn, Orpington
**poultry disease** pip
**poultry enclosure** coop
**poultry food** mash, mealies
**poultry product** egg
**poultry seasoning** sage, thyme
**pounce** ambush, assault, attack, jump, leap, strike, swoop
**pounce down on** swoop
**pounce on** grab, nab, seize
**pound** baste, batter, beat, bray, bruise, confine, crush, cudgel, doghouse, donder, enclosure, imprison, kennel, klap, nicker, oncer, pen, pommel, powder, pulverise, pummel, strike, thrash, thump, trap, yard
**pound at a slant** toe
**pound down** tamp
**pound for stray cattle** pinfold
**pound heavily and insistently** batter
**pound note** oncer
**pound with fists** pummel
**pour** cascade, cataract, course, decant, deluge, discharge, disgorge, downpour, emit, expel, flood, flow, gush, outflow, rain(storm), run, rush, spill, splash, spout, spurt, stream, tamp, teem, throng, torrent
**pour around** circumfuse
**pourboire** gratuity, tip

**pour down** rain, teem
**pour excessive love upon** dote
**pour forth** debouch, disembogue, effuse, emit, shed
**pouring edge** lip
**pouring out** effusion
**pouring vent** spout
**pouring with rain** pelting
**pour melted fat over roasting meat** baste
**pour off, leaving sediment** decant
**pour oil on troubled waters** allay, calm, pacify, quiet, soothe
**pour out** effuse, spill, spout, teem
**pour out in a rush** gush
**pour out into another vessel** transfuse
**pour over** suffuse
**pour water over** sluice, swill
**pour with rain** teem
**pout** brood, frown, glower, grimace, lower, mope, moue (F), scowl, sulk
**pouting look** moue (F)
**poverty** absence, aridity, bareness, beggary, dearth, deficiency, destitution, distress, hardship, impoverishment, indigence, infertility, insolvency, insufficiency, lack, meagreness, necessitousness, necessity, need(iness), paucity, pennilessness, penury, peonage, peonism, privation, scantiness, scarceness, scarcity, shortage, skimpiness, sterility, straits, unfruitfulness, want
**powder** ash, bran, cosmetic, dust, explosive, flour, granulate, gun powder, meal, particles, pollen, pounce, pulverise, sand, sawdust, soot, sprinkle, talc
**powdered ferric oxide** rouge
**powdered tobacco** snuff
**powder of cacao seeds** cocoa
**powder produced by seed-bearing plant** pollen
**powder used to darken eyelids** kohl
**powdery earth** dust
**powdery product of combustion** ash
**powdery substance** farina
**power** ability, authority, capability, command, competence, control, dominion, energy, force, influence, might, potency, rule, strength, vis (L)
**power-cable support** pylon
**power-cell** battery
**power cut** blackout
**power-driven abrasive disc** sander
**powered flight** aviation
**powered vessel** steamship
**power existing from eternity** aeon
**power failure** blackout
**powerful** cogent, commanding, dominant, effective, effectual, eminent, energetic, firm, forceful, forcible, great, hardy, impressive, influential, mighty, potent, predominant, prevailing, puissant, reputable, robust, rugged, stalwart, staunch, stiff, strong, sturdy, supreme, tough, vehement, vigorous, virile, weighty
**powerful alkali** potash
**powerful and mighty** puissant
**powerful astringent** adrenalin
**powerful beam** spotlight
**powerful blow** swat
**powerful businessperson** tycoon
**powerful dog** mastiff
**powerful electric horn** claxon, klaxon
**powerful evil demon of Arab mythology** afreet, afrit
**powerful in effect** effective
**powerful lamp** klieg
**powerfully active** energetic
**powerful person** mogul
**powerful ship** tug
**power group** bloc
**powerless** abrogated, crippled, defenceless, disabled, disarmed, exposed, feeble, frail, harmless, helpless, impotent, inactive, incapable, ineffective, invalid, obsolete, strengthless, unable, unarmed, unfit, unskilful, useless, void, weaponless
**power of containing** capacity
**power of determining** volition
**power of domination** supremacy
**power of effective action** clout
**power of endurance** stamina
**power of exciting tender emotions** pathos
**power of flying** flight
**power of hearing** audition
**power of imagination** fancy, fantasy
**power of lever** leverage
**power of seeing** eyesight, sight
**power plant** hydro
**power pole** pylon
**power source** atom, electricity, generator, motor
**power station device** generator
**powers that be** authorities, establishment
**power that acts** agent
**power to do anything** ability
**power to enforce obedience** authority
**power to influence** prestige
**power to inspire devotion and enthusiasm** charisma
**powwow** assembly, carnival, caucus, celebration, ceremony, confer, congress, consult, convene, deliberation, dialogue, discourse, discussion, festival, festivity, fête, forum, indaba, kgotla, meeting, negotiation, palaver, rite, ritual, summit, talk
**practicability** achievability, advantage, feasibility, handiness, possibility, practicality, use(fulness), viability
**practicable** attainable, do-able, feasible, performable, possible, realistic, viable, workable
**practical** business-like, commonplace, crafty, do-able, down-to-earth, efficient, empirical, factual, mundane, pragmatic, proficient, prosaic, qualified, realistic, seasoned, sensible, skilled, sound, tedious, trained, usable, useful, utilitarian, valuable
**practical ability** cleverness, skill
**practical dilemma** quandary
**practical intelligence** sense
**practical joke** hoax, jape, leg-pull, prank, trick
**practical joker** hoaxer
**practicalness** empiricalness, factualness, hard-headedness, mudaneness, pragmatism
**practical outlook** realism
**practical person** pragmatist
**practical skill** art, knowledge
**practical tool** utensil
**practical unit of quantity in electricity** ampere-hour
**practical wisdom** philosophy, sense
**practice** action, application, convention, custom, discipline, drill, effect, exercise, experience, habit, method, operation, performance, policy, procedure, rehearsal, repetition, routine, run through, study, system, tradition, training, usage, use, way
**practice of being married to one person at a time** monogamy
**practice of collecting postage stamps** philately
**practice of cultivating the ground** agriculture
**practice of disputation** eristic
**practice of eating earth, clay and sand** geophagia, geophagism, geophagy
**practice of eating excrement for religious rites** scatophagy
**practice of having more than one wife at once** polygamy
**practice of hypnosis** hypnotism
**practice of naming parent from child** teknonymy
**practice of praying to God** prayer
**practice of self-discipline** ascesis
**practice of showing undue preference** favouritism
**practice of spying** espionage

**practice of sword play** fence
**practice of using spies** espionage
**practice of witchcraft** witchery
**practise** action, apply, custom, do, drill, execute, exercise, experience, follow, habit, implement, observe, perfect, perform(ance), plot, ply, polish, prepare, process, pursue, rehearse, repeat, stratagem, study, train, undertake, wont
**practise beforehand** rehearse
**practise boxing** spar
**practise crystal gazing** scry
**practised ability** skill
**practise deceit** juggle
**practise for** exercise
**practise for performance** rehearse
**practise husbandry** farm
**practise legal chicanery** pettifog
**practise theft** thieve
**practising pillage** rapacious
**practitioner of terrorism** terrorist
**pragmatic** assiduous, business-like, busy, effective, efficient, industrious, meddlesome, occupied, practical, realistic, sensible, utilitarian, vigorous, wise
**pragmatically** efficiently, practically, realistically, sensibly
**pragmatic person** realist
**pragmatism** practicality
**pragmatist** realist
**Prague native** Czech
**prairie dweller** plainsman
**Prairie State** Illinois
**prairie wolf** coyote
**praise** acclaim, acclamation, accolade, admiration, adoration, applaud, approbation, celebrate, cheer, commend, compliment, congratulate, congratulation, devotion, éloge (F), esteem, eulogium, eulogy, exalt(ation), extol(ment), flatter, glorify, gratitude, honour, laud(ation), revere, worship
**praise be to God** laus Deo (L)
**praise enthusiastically** extol
**praise highly** adulate, eulogise, exalt, extol, laud
**praise insincerely** flatter
**praise lavishly** extol
**praise loudly** applaud
**praise oneself** boast
**praise too highly** adulate
**praiseworthy** admirable, approvable, blameless, choice, creditable, deserving, estimable, excellent, exemplary, honourable, laudable, magnificent, meritorious, splendid, superfine, virtuous, wonderful, worthy
**praising highly** eulogising
**praline ingredient** pecan

**pralltriller** mordent
**pram** perambulator
**prance** bluster, boast, bob, bounce, bound, brag, bully, caper, capriole, cavort, dance, flit, frisk, frolic, gambol, hector, hop, hurdle, jig, jump, leap, parade, play, pounce, romp, skip, spring, stalk, swagger
**prang** crash
**prank** antic(s), banter, bedaub, bedeck, caper, cheat, deception, dido, distraction, entertainment, escapade, fling, fraud, frolic, fun, gambol, game, hoax, hobby, jape, jest, joke, juggle, lark, mischief, overdecorate, pastime, play, quip, recreation, revel, romp, ruse, sport, spree, stunt, swindle, trick, witticism
**prankster** buffoon, clown, comedian, dolt, fool, harlequin, jester, joker, pierrot
**prat** bungler
**prate** blab, bleat, blether, chat(ter), converse, drivel, gab(ble), gossip, natter, palaver, patter, prattle, ramble, say, skinder, speak, talk, tattle, twattle, utter
**prattle** babble, blather, blether, chatter, drivel, gabble, jabber, prate, twaddle, twitter
**prawn dish** scampi
**pray** ask, beg, beseech, crave, entreat, implore, importune, invoke, petition, plead, request, solicit, sue, supplicate, urge, worship
**pray and work** ora et labora (L)
**prayer** appeal, beseechment, communion, devotion, doxology, entreaty, glorification, impetration, invocation, litany, magnification, obtestation, orison, petition, plea, praise, request, solicitation, suit, supplication, thanksgiving
**prayer beads** rosary
**prayer bench** prie-dieu
**prayer book** breviary, evangeliary, evangelistary, formulary, lectionary, litany, missal, ordo, pontifical
**prayer ending** amen
**prayer for the dead** requiem
**prayer of thanks** grace
**prayer room** oratory
**prayer rug** asana
**prayer's last word** amen
**prayer tower** minaret
**pray for us** ora pro nobis (L)
**praying desk** prie-dieu
**praying insect** mantis
**preach** address, admonish, advice, advocate, chastise, counsel, disseminate, evangelise, exhort, harangue, homilise, lecture, moralise, orate, predicate, prelect, press, profess, propagate, reprimand, sermonise, urge
**preacher** bishop, canon, chaplain, churchman, clergyman, cleric, curate, dean, dominee, ecclesiastic, evangel(ist), exhorter, homilist, lecturer, liturgiologist, liturgist, minister, missionary, moraliser, parson, pastor, predicant, predikant, priest, rabbi, rector, reverend, ritualist, sermoniser, sermonist, vicar
**preaching of the gospel** evangelism
**preach noisily** harangue, rant, rave
**preach the gospel to** evangelise
**pre-adulthood** adolescence
**preamble** exordium, foreword, introduction, overture, preface, preliminary, prelude, proem, prologue
**pre-birth** antenatal
**precarious** baseless, doubtful, dubious, hazardous, insecure, risky, uncertain, unreliable, unstable, unsteady, unsure
**precaution** care, foresight, forethought, providence, prudence, wariness
**precede** antecede, antedate, forego, forerun, head, herald, introduce, lead, preface, usher
**precede in time** antedate
**precedence** antecedence, authority, earliness, hegemony, importance, precedent, predominance, pre-eminence, prefixion, prerogative, previousness, primacy, priority, privilege, rank, right, seniority, superiority, supremacy, urgency
**precedence in rank** seniority
**precedent** authority, barometer, criterion, custom, example, exemplar, instance, measure, model, pattern, rule, ruling, standard
**precedes a storm** thunder
**precedes specific noun** the
**preceding action** prelude
**preceding all others** first
**preceding day** dawn, morn(ing)
**preceding night** eve(ning)
**preceding something else** prevenient
**preceding today** yesterday
**pre-Christian** pagan
**precinct** ambit, area, borough, bound, canton, community, confine, constituency, country, department, diocese, district, division, enclosure, limit, parish, province, quarter, region, section, state, territory, ward, zone
**precincts** environs, habitat, milieu, mise en scène (F), surroundings

**precious** beloved, cherished, costly, dear, fine, golden, invaluable, priceless, select, valuable
**precious fur** ermine, mink, sable
**precious metal** gold, silver
**precious stone** agate, amethyst, aquamarine, asteria, beryl, carbuncle, chrysolite, diamond, emerald, garnet, gem, jewel, lazuli, moonstone, opal, ruby, sapphire, sard(ine), sardius, topaz, turquoise, zircon
**precious thing** curio, jewel, pearl, relic
**precipice** bluff, brink, cliff, crag, escarpment, height, incline, kloof, krans, palisades, promontory, ridge, steep, tor
**precipitate** abrupt, advance, dispatch, expedite, hasten, hasty, headlong, hurry, rash, speed, sudden, violent
**precipitation** dive, downpour, hail, haste(ning), heave, impulsiveness, plunge, rain, recklessness, rush, scramble, scurry, snow, suddenness, thrust
**precipitous** abrupt, ascending, bluff, careless, cliffy, craggy, declining, downhill, hasty, hurried, perpendicular, rash, sheer, steep, sudden, uphill
**précis** abridgement, abstract, compendium, condensation, condense, digest, outline, résumé, rundown, sketch, summary, survey, syllabus, synopsis
**precise** accurate, authentic, close, correct, defined, definite, demanding, distinct, exact, explicit, factual, flawless, particular, prim, real, right, rigid, severe, specific, strict, unconditional, unerring, veracious
**precise information** facts
**precisely** definitely, expressly, fixedly, literally, particularly, perfectly, specifically
**precisely corresponding** parallel
**precisely limited** strict
**precisely on time** on the dot
**preciseness** accurateness, correctness, definiteness, exactness, fixedness, literalness, strictness
**precise person** purist
**precisian in speech** prig
**precision** accuracy, accurateness, adherence, carefulness, correctness, definiteness, exactitude, exactness, faultlessness, fidelity, nicety, particularity, preciousness, preciseness, rigorousness, unerringness
**precision of reproduction** fidelity

**preclude** debar, exclude, hinder, inhibit, obviate, restrain
**preclude legally** estop
**preclude self-contradiction** estop
**preconceived opinion** prejudice
**precursor** ancestor, antecedent, author, creator, explorer, foregoer, forerunner, founder, innovator, messenger, missionary, originator, pioneer, predecessor, progenitor, vanguard
**predacious cat** cheetah, leopard, lion, tiger
**predator** bloodsucker, carnivore, lion
**predatory** bestial, carnivorous, devouring, fierce, hunting, injurious, lupine, marauding, pillaging, plundering, predacious, rapacious, raptorial, ravaging, robbing, voracious, vulturine, wolfish
**predatory incursion** raid
**predatory seabird** skua
**predetermined** agreed, destined, fateful, fixed, foredoomed, foregone, intentional, meant, meditated, ordained, prearranged, predecided, predestined, preplanned
**predicament** condition, crisis, dilemma, distress, embarrassment, entanglement, impasse, intricacy, muddle, plight, problem, puzzle, quandary, situation, state, trial
**predicate** advance, allege, assert, assume, aver, contend, declare, express, imply, maintain, postulate, proclaim, profess, propose, signify, suggest, suppose
**predict** augur, auspicate, envision, forebode, forecast, foresee, foreshadow, forespeak, foretell, forewarn, harbinger, indicate, portend, presage, prognose, prognosticate, project, promise, prophesy, soothsay
**prediction** augury, divination, forecast, prognosis, prophecy, soothsaying
**prediction-monger** Nostradamus
**prediction of a person's future** horoscope
**prediction yearbook** almanac
**predilection** affection, aptitude, aptness, attachment, bias, bigotry, cast, choice, desire, drift, fancy, fondness, inclination, leaning, liking, partiality, passion, penchant, ply, prejudice, proclivity, set, taste, temperament, tendency, turn, warp, weakness
**predisposition** propensity, tendency
**predominate** dominate, outweigh, overrule, preponderate, prevail, surpass

**pre-eminence** distinction, excellence, fame, incomparability, matchlessness, predominance, prestige, prominence, renown, repute, superiority, supremacy, transcendence
**pre-eminent** chief, distinguished, excellent, exceptional, foremost, incomparable, inimitable, leading, matchless, outstanding, passing, peerless, predominant, prominent, renowned, superior, superlative, supreme, surpassing, transcendent, unequalled, unmatched, unrivalled, unsurpassed
**pre-eminently** conspicuously, emphatically, greatly, incredibly, largely, notably, par excellence (F), particularly, strikingly, unusually
**pre-empt** acquire, anticipate, appropriate, arrogate, assume, (pre)occupy
**preen** adorn, array, bejewel, paint, plume, powder, prettify, primp, prink, titivate, trim
**preface** avant-propos (F), exordium, foreword, introduction, overture, preamble, preliminary, prelude, proem, prologue
**prefatory** antecedent, early, elementary, exordial, first, inaugural, initial, introductory, opening, preceding, precursory, preliminary, prelusive, preparatory, proemial, starting
**prefer** adopt, advance, back, choose, desire, elect, fancy, favour, lodge, opt, pick, press, proffer, promote, rather, recommend, select, support, want
**preferably** choicely, gladly, lief, rather, sooner, willingly
**preference** advantage, bent, bias, choice, desire, favourite, favouritism, inclination, liking, option, partiality, penchant, pick, precedence, predilection, predisposition, prejudice, priority, selection, superiority, vantage, want
**preferred above others** favourite
**preferring the company of others** social
**prefer to** rather
**prefix** arch-, cognomen, de-, designation, di-, en-, epithet, exa-, name, preface, prelude, tele-
**prefix forming verbs** de-, em-, en-
**prefix for reversal of something** de-
**prefix indicating internal** endo-
**prefix indicating lacking** im-
**prefix indicating new** neo-
**prefix indicating next to** ad-

**prefix indicating one-hundredth** centi-
**prefix indicating one million** mega-
**prefix indicating one million million** tera-
**prefix indicating one-millionth** micro-
**prefix indicating one-tenth** deci-
**prefix indicating one thousand million million** peta-
**prefix indicating one thousand million** giga-
**prefix indicating one thousand** kilo-
**prefix indicating one-thousandth** milli-
**prefix indicating one trillion** exa-
**prefix indicating ten** deca-
**prefix indicating three** tri-
**prefix indicating two** bi-
**prefix meaning not** anti-, im-, in-, ir-, li-, non-, un-
**pre-frog stage** tadpole
**pregnant** abundant, creative, crucial, enceinte, fertile, fraught, gestational, gravid, ingenious, inventive, prolific, replete
**prehistoric** Ogygian
**prehistoric English ruins** Stonehenge
**prehistoric flint instrument** eolith
**prehistoric hill-fort** rath
**prehistoric house built on piles** palafitte
**prehistoric man** Neanderthal
**prehistoric painting** pictogram, pictograph
**prehistoric people** cavemen
**prehistoric reptile** dinosaur, saurian
**prehistoric tool** artefact, artifact
**prejudice** bend, bias, bigotry, damage, dispose, drawback, impede, incline, injure, injury, intolerance, jaundice, liability, loss, narrowmindedness, one-sidedness, parti pris (F), preconception, predisposition, prejudg(e)ment, prepossession, slant, sway, turn, twist, warp
**prejudiced person** bigot
**prelate** abbot, (arch)bishop, archdeacon, canon, cardinal, dean, diocesan, dominee, hierarch, pastor, pontiff, pope, primate, prior, rector, vicar
**preliminary** inaugural, introductory, preface, prelude, preparation, prior
**preliminary discourse** prologue
**preliminary discussion** pourparler
**preliminary essay** prolusion
**preliminary learning** propaedeutic
**preliminary matter** avant-propos (F)
**preliminary model for a sculpture** maquette
**preliminary observations** prolegomena
**preliminary plan** outline
**preliminary proposition** lemma

**preliminary remarks** avant-propos (F)
**preliminary statement** preamble
**preliterate social group** tribe
**prelude** beginning, commencement, exordium, foreword, introduction, overture, preface, preliminary, proem, prologue, start
**prelude to a meal** gong
**pre main meal** entrée
**premature** early, hasty, ill-considered, immature, impulsive, incomplete, raw, unripe, unseasonable, untimely
**premature birth** abortion, miscarriage
**premeditate** consider, deliberate, plan, plot, prearrange, preconsider, precontrive, predeliberate, predetermine, predevise, scheme
**premier** arch, cardinal, chancellor, chief, earliest, first, foremost, head, highest, initial, leading, main, oldest, original, pre-eminent, president, primary, prime, principal, supreme, top(most)
**premise** assumption, axiom, basis, foundation, inference, lemma, point, postulate, postulation, surmise, theorem, thesis
**premises** building, data, establishment, facts, grounds, introduce, preface, prelude, proof, property
**premium** agio, award, benefit, bonus, bounty, consideration, deduction, discount, fee, gift, gratuity, prize, rebate, recompense, refund, requisite, reward, tip
**premium on money in exchange** agio
**premonition** anxiety, augury, dread, fear, feeling, foreboding, forecast, forewarning, harbinger, hunch, idea, intuition, omen, portent, presage, presentiment, prognostic, sign, suspicion
**preoccupation** absorption, abstraction, daydreaming, distraction, immersion, insensibility, intensity, oblivion, obliviousness, obsession, unattentiveness, unheedfulness
**preoccupied** absent-minded, absorbed, concentrating, engrossed, inattentive, meditative, pondering
**preoccupied with one's own concerns** egoistic, narcissistic, self-centred
**pre-operation drug** anaesthetic
**preordain** allot, dedicate, designate, destine, doom, fate, mean, ordain, predetermine, purpose
**preparation** alertness, arrangement, compound, concoction, development, medicine, mixture, preparing, readiness, tincture

**preparation for washing carpets** shampoo
**preparation for washing hair** shampoo
**preparation for water retention** diuretic
**preparation of ammonia** sal volatile
**preparation of potato starch** tapioca
**preparation that arrests bleeding** styptic
**preparatory measure** arrangement
**prepare** anticipate, arrange, compose, construct, contrive, devise, equip, fit, form, groom, make, manufacture, order, plan, prime, provide, set
**prepare an ambush** set a trap
**prepare a trap** set
**prepare beer** brew
**prepare by intense study** cram
**prepared barley** malt
**prepare dough** knead
**prepared to serve with milk** au lait
**prepared track** road
**prepare fish** bone, gut, scale
**prepare food** cook
**prepare for action** alert
**prepare for boxing match** train
**prepare for exam** cram, study, swot
**prepare for growth** plant
**prepare for holiday** pack
**prepare for publication** edit, redact
**prepare for sports event** train
**prepare for starting** prime
**prepare for use** make
**prepare for war** arm
**prepare land for seed** till
**prepare leather** tan
**prepare letters for printing** typeset
**prepare manuscript for publication** edit, revise
**prepare mentally** psych up
**prepare photograph from negative** develop
**prepare prescription** dispense
**prepare table for meal** set
**prepare text** edit
**prepare the way** pave
**prepare to hit golf ball** address
**prepare to pray** kneel
**prepare to publish** edit
**prepare to testify** swear
**preparing for something** get ready
**preponderance** ascendancy, authority, bulk, control, dominance, domination, extensiveness, force, greatness, hegemony, leadership, majority, mass, power, primacy, rule, sovereignty, strength, superiority, supremacy, weight
**preponderate** prevail
**preposition** adjunct, after, at, atop, by, ere, for, from, in(to), mid, near, of,

on(to), out, over, per, re, till, to, under, until, unto, up, via, with
**preposition of direction** into
**preposition of location** on
**preposition of place** at
**preposition of possession** of
**preposition of source** from
**preposterous** absurd, asinine, extravagant, foolish, irrational, perverse, ridiculous
**prerogative** advantage, allowance, authority, birthright, choice, claim, demand, due, exception, exemption, franchise, grant, immunity, liberty, license, permission, precedence, privilege, right, sanction
**presage** adumbrate, augur(y), betoken, forebode, foreboding, foreshadow, foreshow, foretell, imply, indicate, omen, portend, portent, predict, presentiment, prognosticate, promise, signify
**prescribe** assign, authorise, codify, command, constrain, decree, demand, dictate, direct, enjoin, establish, impose, institute, ordain, order, predetermine, proclaim, pronounce
**prescribed** absolute, thetic
**prescribed amount** dose
**prescribed food** diet
**prescribed penalty** fine, sentence
**prescribed quantity** dose
**prescribed selection of food** diet
**prescriber of spectacles** optometrist
**prescription** direction, formula, mixture, preparation, recipe, remedy
**presence** accompaniment, adjacency, attendance, bearing, being, closeness, company, ease, eidolon, elegance, entity, existence, ghost, impression, life, nearness, neighbourhood, personality, poise, proximity, refinement, residence, spirit, ubiety, urbanity, wraith
**presence of albumin in urine** albuminuria
**presence of fat in urine** lipuria
**presence of mind** alertness, aplomb, collectedness, control, dispassion, equilibrium, intelligence, poise, quickness, saneness, sang-froid, sanity, stability, steadiness
**presence of pus in urine** pyuria
**present** afford, announce, benefaction, bestow, bonus, confer, current, donate, donation, endow, existing, extant, gift, give, grant, here, imitate, introduce, near(by), now, personate, point, represent, show, yield
**presentation** appearance, arrangement, award, bestowal, ceremony, conferral, delivery, demonstration, display, donation, exhibition, grant, investiture, offer(ing), performance, presentment, production, proposal, show, staging, submission, tender
**presentation tray** salver
**present-day Roman** Italian
**presenter** compere, (pr)offerer
**present for public to see** exhibit
**present indicative of 'be'** are, is
**present itself** arise, offer
**presently** anon, currently, directly, forthwith, immediately, instantly, now(adays), readily, shortly, soon
**presentment** advancement, offer, presentation, proposal, statement, tender
**present one person to another** introduce
**present time** now(adays)
**present within a localised area** endemic
**preservative** jam
**preserve** can, continue, guard, jam, keep, maintain, pickle, protect, save, shelter, sustain, uphold
**preserve corpse with spices** embalm
**preserved bone** fossil
**preserved corpse** mummy
**preserve dead body** embalm
**preserved in brine** corned
**preserved in sugar** candied
**preserve from decay** embalm
**preserve meat with salt** corn
**preserve of citrus fruit** marmalade
**preserve of fruit** confiture
**preserver** attendant, brine, caretaker, champion, curator, custodian, defender, deliverer, escort, gaoler, governor, guard(ian), jailer, keeper, liberator, lifeguard, lifeline, lifesaver, overseer, preservative, protector, rescuer, salt, salvation, saviour, steward, trustee, vinegar, warden, warder
**preserving against poison** alexipharmic
**preserving memory** memorial
**preside** administer, chair, conduct, control, direct, govern, head, lead, manage, officiate, run, superintend
**president** administrator, chairman, chief, controller, director, executive, leader, manager, presider, principal
**president of symposium** symposiarch
**preside over** administer, enforce, oversee, supervise
**presiding bishop of Scottish Episcopal Church** primus
**presiding officer** speaker
**press** burden, condense, crowd, crush, dun, hurry, implore, iron, mash, plead, pressure, push, reduce, squeeze, stress, trouble, urge
**press agency in Russia** Tass
**press agent** publicist
**press and TV** media
**press briefly with sponge without rubbing** dab
**press charges** prosecute, sue
**press clothes** iron
**press down** tamp
**pressed fruit remains** marc
**pressed woollen fabric** felt
**presser** ironer
**press exposure** publicity
**press fingers along** rub
**press for payment** dun
**press forward** thrust
**press hard** drive
**pressing** acute, burning, compelling, critical, crucial, demanding, emergent, eventful, exigent, grave, imperative, important, importunate, pivotal, profound, serious, significant, urgent, vital
**pressing claim** demand
**pressing implement** iron
**pressingly** acutely, gravely, hazardously, importantly, perilously, pivotally, precariously, riskily, seriously, severely, threateningly, vitally, weightily
**pressing machine** mangle
**pressing need** exigency
**press, like the washing** iron
**press the doorbell** ring
**press upon** urge
**press upon unduly** obtrude
**pressure** compress(ion), force, harassment, impetus, influence, momentum, push, squeeze, strain, stress, tension, urge(ncy)
**pressure change** allobar
**pressure cooker** steamer
**pressure device** barometer
**pressure gauge for gases** aerodensimeter
**pressure line on map** isobar
**pressure pack can** aerosol
**pressure ratio** psia
**pressure stabiliser** barostat
**press with the nose** nuzzle
**prestidigitation** chicanery, conjuring, deceit, deception, dupery, fraud(ulence), hocus-pocus, jugglery, juggling, magic, quick-fingeredness, thaumaturgy, trickery
**prestidigitator** artist(e), conjurer, juggler, legerdemainist, magician, trickster, wizard

**prestige** authority, celebrity, distinction, importance, influence, kudos, notability, (pre-)eminence, predominance, renown, reputation, repute, stature, supremacy, weight

**presto** behold, brisk, express, fast, hastily, immediate, instant, promptly, quick(ly), rapid(ly), speedily

**presume** arrogate, assume, believe, conclude, conjecture, dare(say), deem, guess, infer, judge, opine, postulate, predicate, (pre)suppose, speculate, undertake, usurp, venture

**presume true** believe

**presumingly free in speech** pert

**presumption** anticipation, arrogance, assumption, assurance, audaciousness, audacity, bias, boldness, brazenness, cheek, conceit, confidence, conjecture, contumely, deduction, effrontery, evidence, expectation, face, forwardness, ground, guess, haughtiness, hauteur, hope, hubris, hypothesis, immodesty, impudence, inference, inkling, insolence, overconfidence, pedantry, pertness, pomposity, posit, (pre)supposition, pretentiousness, priggishness, probability, proposition, reason, sauciness, self-conceit, shamelessness, surmise, suspicion, temerity, theory, thought, trust, view

**presumptuous** arrogant, assuming, assured, audacious, bold, brash, brazen, bumptious, cocky, confident, dictatorial, disrespectful, domineering, egotistical, forward, fresh, imperious, impertinent, impudent, insolent, insulting, rash, rude, satisfied, snobbish, sure, unwarranted, vain

**presumptuous person** upstart

**pretence** act(ing), air, charade, claim, cloak, creation, deceit, deception, delusion, excuse, façade, faking, falsehood, fantasy, feigning, feint, fib, fiction, fraud, guise, hoax, lie, mask, motive, pretending, pretext, ruse, semblance, sham, show, subterfuge, swindle, veneer, wile

**pretend** act, affect, allege, assume, counterfeit, create, dissemble, dissimulate, fabricate, fake, feign, image, invent, lie, profess, sham, simulate

**pretended science** pseudo-science

**pretender** actor, cheater, fibber, hypocrite, imposter, liar, masquerader, prevaricator, quack, trickster

**pretend illness** malinger

**pretend not to notice** connive
**pretend to** assume
**pretend to be** (im)personate, sham, simulate
**pretend to be ill to escape duty** malinger
**pretend to make love** flirt
**pretentious** affected, alleging, arrogant, arty, baroque, boastful, bombastic, elaborate, extreme, fantoosh (Sc), haughty, inflated, ornate, ostentatious, overwrought, pompous, showy, spectacular
**pretentious behaviour** grandeur
**pretentious display** ostentation
**pretentiously artistic** arty
**pretentious talk** claptrap
**pretermit** disregard, ignore, neglect, omit, overlook
**Pretoria-Witwatersrand-Vereeniging (Area)** PWV
**prettiest** bonniest, cutest, fairest, loveliest
**pretty** appealing, attractive, beautiful, bonny, charming, clever, comely, cute, dainty, dear, delicate, delightful, elegant, fair(ly), fine, good-looking, handsome, lovely, melodious, moderately, neat, nice(-looking), pleasant, pleasing, somewhat, tasteful, trim, tuneful, velvety, very
**pretty blue garden flower** cornflower, scabious
**pretty gas sign** neon
**pretty girl** beauty, bunny, prim
**pretty up** adorn
**prevail** abide, abound, conquer, convince, defeat, dispose, dominate, endure, govern, incline, influence, last, lead, obtain, overcome, overrule, persist, persuade, predominate, preponderate, prompt, reign, rule, succeed, sway, triumph, win
**prevailing** affecting, dominant, effective, forceful, persuasive, pre-eminent, predominant, prevalent, principal, rife, ruling, vigorous
**prevailing course** tenor
**prevailing craze** mania
**prevailing fashion** mode, vogue
**prevailing idea in a speech** keynote
**prevailing mode** ton, fashion
**prevailing order** regime
**prevailing spirit** ethos
**prevailing system** regimen
**prevailing tone** keynote
**prevailing trend of opinion** mainstream

**prevail on** dispose, importune, incline, influence, inspire, motivate, persuade, wean
**prevail over** affect, dominate, outweigh, overcome
**prevail upon** convince
**prevail upon to refrain** dissuade
**prevalent** brief, common, current, customary, endemic, epidemic, frequent, general, popular, potent, powerful, predominant, rampant, regnant, rife, widespread
**prevaricate** belie, cavil, counterfeit, deceive, dissemble, dodge, elude, equivocate, euphemise, evade, fake, falsify, fence, fib, hedge, lie, mislead, misrepresent, palter, quibble, shift, shy, tergiversate, weasel
**prevarication** artfulness, chicanery, equivocalness, equivocation, evasion, evasiveness, fable, falsehood, falsity, fencing, invention, lie, myth, quibble, story, untruth, yarn
**prevaricator** beguiler, bluffer, canter, casuist, dodger, equivocator, evader, fabricator, falsifier, fibber, hoaxer, hypocrite, liar, perjurer, quibbler, seducer, sophist, storyteller
**prevent** arrest, avert, block, check, constrain, contravene, (de)bar, deter, (e)stop, foil, forestall, frustrate, hamper, hinder, impede, interfere, interrupt, obstruct, obviate, preclude, prohibit, retard, thwart, veto
**prevent blood clotting** anticoagulant
**prevent entry** debar
**prevent from acting** deter
**prevent from being seen** hide
**prevent from publishing** censor, gag
**prevent from speaking** muffle
**preventing convulsions or epilepsy** anticonvulsant
**prevent in law** estop
**prevention** avoidance, bar, check, elimination, hindrance, obstacle, obviation, safeguard
**preventive** antidote, constraining, constraint, deterrent, embargo, hindering, impeding, interruptive, obstruction, obstructive, preventative, prevention, protection, protective, remedy, restraint, restrictive, setback, veto
**preventive coat of paint** sealer
**preventive treatment against diseases** prophylaxis
**prevent progress** hinder, obstruct
**prevents clothes from creasing** hanger
**prevents floods** dam
**previous** ancient, earlier, early, erstwhile, ex, feu, foregoing,

foregone, former, past, precedent,
preceding, preliminary, prior, recent
**previous day** eve, yesterday
**previous example** precedent
**previously** above, already, before,
erewhile, formerly, hitherto, once,
theretofore, ultimo
**previously described** aforementioned,
aforesaid
**previously unknown** unheard of
**previous name of Kisangani**
Stanleyville
**previous name of Thailand** Siam
**previous to** before, ere, preceding,
prior
**prewar** antebellum
**prey** catch, devour, eat, exploit, kill,
prize, quarry, target, victim(ise)
**prey of cats** birds, mice, rats
**prey on** burden, devour, distress,
haunt, hunt, oppress, seize, trouble,
worry
**price** amount, assess, charge,
consequence, cost, damage,
dearness, demand, duty, estimate,
expenditure, expense, fine, hire,
invoice, levy, outlay, payment,
quotation, rate, rent(al), result, tariff,
valuation, value, worth
**price after discount** net(t)
**price charged to passenger on public
transport** fare
**priceless** costly, expensive,
inestimable, invaluable,
irreplaceable, prized, rare
**priceless vase** Ming
**price list** tariff
**price of entry** admission
**price of passage** fare
**price of redemption** ransom
**price paid to travel on bus** fare
**price per unit** each, rate
**price quoted for work to be done**
estimate
**pricker** thorn
**pricking instrument attached to
horse-rider's heel** spur
**pricking of conscience** compunction
**pricking tool** awl
**prickle** barb(ule), cusp, flick, itch,
needle, nick, pink, point, prick,
prong, snag, spike, spur, stick, sting,
thorn, tickle, tine, tingle
**prickly** barbed, bristly, complicated,
edgy, fractious, grumpy, irritable,
peevish, pettish, petulant, scratchy,
sharp, snappish, spiny, stinging,
tetchy, thorny, ticklish, tricky, waspish
**prickly bush** gorse
**prickly creature** hedgehog, porcupine
**prickly herb** nettle
**prickly pear** cactus, opuntia, tuna

**prickly plant** acanthus, briar, brier,
cactus, cardoon, nettle, teasel, thistle
**prickly rodent** porcupine
**prickly shrub** bramble, briar, brier,
caper, gorse
**prickly weed** blackjack, thistle
**pride** arrogance, conceit, haughtiness,
hauteur, hubris, hybris, lions,
presumption, self-respect, vanity
**pride and joy** boast
**pride oneself on** boast, brag, exult,
glory, revel, vaunt
**prier** pryer, snooper
**priest** abbé, cassock, chaplain,
churchman, clergyman, cleric(al),
curate, curé, dean, dominee,
ecclesiastic, evangelist, father, fra,
lama, liturgist, minister, missionary,
padre, parson, pastor, preacher,
predikant, rabbi, vicar
**priestly** Aaronic, canonical, churchly,
clerical, ecclesiastic, ministerial,
pastoral, prelatic, priestlike,
sacerdotal
**priestly garment** alb
**priestly government** hierarchy
**priest of ancient Celtic religion** Druid
**priest of ancient Persia** magus
**priest of Tibet** lama
**priest-ridden state** sacerdotage
**priest's ankle-length garment** cassock
**priest's assistant** curate
**priest's cap** biretta
**priest's cloth** amice
**priests collectively** clergy
**priest serving a bishop** chancellor
**priest's garment** alb, stole
**priest's helper** curate
**priest's home** vicarage
**priest's vestment** alb, amice, cassock,
chasuble, cope, ephod, maniple
**prig** affecter, bluenose, carper,
euphemist, faultfinder, formalist,
fusspot, pedant, prude, purist,
puritan, snob
**prim** demure, exact, fastidious, formal,
precise, priggish, prudish, rigid,
scrupulous, squeamish, starched,
stiff(-necked)
**prima ballerina** heroine
**prima donna** diva, heroine
**prima donna's forte** aria
**prim and precise** starchy
**primarily** au fond (F), basically,
capitally, cardinally, chiefly,
especially, essentially, firstly,
fundamentally, generally, initially,
mainly, mostly, originally,
predominantly, principally, radically
**primary** capital, cardinal, central, chief,
direct, earliest, elementary, first,
fundamental, genetic, head, highest,

initial, main, major, ordinate, original,
paramount, prime, principal
**primary colour** blue, red, yellow
**primary leaf of plant** cotyledon
**primary number** one
**primary root** radicle
**primary social unit** family
**primary source** origin
**primary type of a series** prototype
**primate** anthropoid, ape, (arch)bishop,
archpriest, baboon, cardinal,
dignitary, ecclesiarch, lemur, human,
monkey, simian, suffragan, tarsier
**prime** basic, chief, elementary, first,
fundamental, primary, principal
**prime cut of beef** rump, sirloin
**primed** fitted, groomed, informed,
notified, prepared, told
**prime minister** premier
**prime minister of Irish Republic**
Taoiseach
**prime minister of Louis XIII** Richelieu
**prime mover** agent, architect, author,
begetter, beginning, builder, cause,
constructor, creator, designer, father,
founder, framer, genesis, God,
initiator, inventor, mainspring, maker,
motor, origin(ator), producer, root,
source, spring
**prime of life** heyday
**primeval** first, original, primary, prime,
primigenial, primitive, primordial
**primeval epoch** eocene
**primitive** antediluvian, archaic,
atavistic, barbarian, barbaric, crude,
earliest, elemental, elementary,
eolithic, first, Neanderthal, original,
plain, preadamite, prehistoric,
primary, primeval, primordial,
pristine, rough, rude, savage,
simple, uncivilised, uncomplicated,
uncouth, uncultured, unpolished,
unrefined, vernacular, wild
**primitive drum beaten with the hands**
tom-tom
**primitive religion** animism
**primitive stone tool** eolith
**primitive tool** artefact, artifact
**primordium** inception, initiation
**primp** adorn, beautify, decorate,
garnish, groom, plume, preen, prink,
smart, tidy, titivate
**primulaceous plant** saltwort, sea
milkwort
**princely** bounteous, generous,
gracious, grand, imperial, lavish,
liberal, noble, royal, stately
**princely Italian family** Este
**Prince of Wales** Charles
**prince or lord** atheling
**prince's crown** coronet

**princess** infanta, monarch, potentate, sovereign
**princess of Britain** Anne, Diana, Margaret
**Princess of Wales** Diana
**principal** actor, actress, capital, central, chief, dean, director, dominant, first, foremost, head(master), headmistress, highest, leader, leading, main, paramount, pre-eminent, prime, rector, ruler, staple, star
**principal actor** hero, protagonist, star
**principal bullfighter who kills the bull** matador
**principal church of a diocese** cathedral
**principal commodity** staple
**principal division of country** province
**principal female character** heroine
**principal food** staple
**principal government ministers** cabinet
**principal lecturer** professor
**principally interested in one's own thoughts** introverted
**principal magistrate of Scottish burgh** provost
**principal male character** hero
**principal manservant** butler
**principal part of brain** cerebrum
**principal performer** protagonist
**principal person** captain, chief(tain), commander, head, master, mistress, principal, ruler
**principal spring of watch** mainspring
**principal town** capital, city, metropolis
**principle** axiom, belief, canon, code, criterion, doctrine, dogma, ethic, formula, goodness, honesty, honour, integrity, law, main, maxim, morality, opinion, precept, probity, proposition, rectitude, rule, standard, tenet, test, theorem, truth
**principle church of a diocese** cathedral
**principled** blameless, chaste, conscientious, correct, decent, ethical, fair, fitting, good, honest, honourable, innocent, just, lofty, moral, noble, proper, pure, right(eous), true, trustworthy, trusty, upright, upstanding, virtuous
**principle dancer in a ballet company** premier danseur (F), première danseuse (F), prima ballerina
**principle front of a building** façade
**principle land** continent, mainland
**principle of absolute government** absolutism
**principle of doctrine** dogma

**principle of indifference** equiprobability
**principles** conscience, ethics, fairness, honesty, ideals, innocence, integrity, loyalty, morals, piety, respectability, righteousness, standards, trustworthiness, virtue
**principles of bell-ringing** campanology
**principles of maintaining health** hygiene
**print** brand, engrave, imprint, lettering, mark, photo, publish, stamp
**printed advertising leaflet** circular
**printed at bottom of page** footnote
**printed below** subscript
**printed cotton cloth** calico
**printed fabric** batik
**printed greeting** card
**printed journal** daily, (news)paper
**printed matter** literature
**printed placard** poster
**printed publication containing news** (news)paper
**printed symbol** mark
**printed volume** book
**printer** compositor, linotype, pressman, typesetter, typographer
**printer's annual feast** wayzgoose
**printer's mark** caret, stet
**printer's measure** em, en, pica
**printer's mistake** erratum, typo
**printer's proof** galley, proof-sheet
**printer's proof-corrector** reader
**printer's space** em, en, pica
**printer's star** asterisk
**print for the blind** Braille
**printing** edition, typography, xerography
**printing chaos** pie
**printing error** erratum, typo
**printing errors** errata
**printing fluid** ink
**printing for blind inventor** Braille
**printing house** press
**printing machine** press
**printing measure** em, en
**printing mistake** erratum, typo
**printing plate** stereotype
**printing type** bold, italic, roman
**prior** abbot, antecedent, before, earlier, former, pre-existing, preceding, precursory, prefatorial, prefatory, previous
**prior accomplishment** anticipation
**prior condition** prerequisite
**prior decree** preordination
**prior event** antecedent
**prior in origin** elder
**prior instance** precedent
**priority** antecedence, consequence, foregoing, important, influence, level, pre-eminence, precedence,

precedency, preceding, predating, preface, preference, prelude, previousness, rank, right, seniority, superiority, supremacy, urgency, weightiness
**prior judicial decision** precedent
**prior to** above, before, earlier than, ere, preceding
**prior to the period in which history begins** prehistoric
**prior to this time** hitherto
**prior warning** tip-off
**priory** abbey, cloister, convent, friary, monastery, nunnery
**prise** force, lever(age), purchase
**prising device** crowbar
**prising tool** crowbar
**prism** polygonal
**prison** dungeon, gaol, jail(house), lockup, pen(itentiary), quod, stir
**prison camp** stalag
**prison cell** dungeon
**prisoner** bandiet, bloubaadjie, captive, convict, detainee, hostage, inmate, internee, jailbird
**prisoner at the bar** accused
**prisoner's conditional release** parole
**prisoner's court** dock
**prisoner sentenced to life imprisonment** lifer
**prison guard** warder
**prison in England** Broadmoor
**prison inmate** convict
**prison in USA** Alcatraz, Sing Sing
**prison keeper** warder
**prison official** captor, gaoler, governor, guard, jailer, keeper, warden, warder
**prison quarters** cells
**prison room** cell
**prison runaway** escapee
**prison term** sentence
**prison warder** screw
**prissy** prim, prudish
**prissy person** prig
**pristine** ancient, antique, archaic, bygone, chaste, earliest, early, first, fundamental, immaculate, immemorial, impeccable, incorrupt, initial, innocent, introductory, maiden, old, opening, original, premier, primary, prime, primeval, primigenial, primitive, primordial, pure, remote, righteous, rudimentary, sinless, spotless, stainless, starting, unspoiled, unspoilt, upright, virginal
**pristine garden** Eden
**privacy** concealment, covertness, hiddenness, intimacy, isolation, loneness, obscurity, reclusion, reservedness, reticence, retirement,

**private** retreat, seclusion, secrecy, secretness, separation, silence, slyness, solitude

**private** alone, apart, closed, concealed, confidential, covert, esoteric, especial, exclusive, hermitic, individual, particular, peculiar, personal, privy, secluded, secret(ive), singular, solitary, special, unaccessible

**private cabinet** camarilla
**private chamber of a judge** camera
**private chapel** oratory
**private conversation** tête-à-tête
**private detective** investigator, PI
**private door** postern
**private dwelling** house
**private eye** investigator, PI
**private hospital** clinic
**private instructor** tutor
**private investigator** detective, PI, sleuth

**privately** alone, aside, clandestinely, covertly, individually, intimately, off-camera, personally, secretively, separately, slyly, sneakingly, specially, stealthily, sub rosa

**private meeting-place** conclave
**private phone link** tie-line
**private place** nest
**private room** cabinet, closet, sanctum
**private teacher** governess, tutor

**privation** beggary, confiscation, difficulty, distress, forfeiture, hardship, indigence, mendicity, necessity, need, poverty, predicament, strait, want

**privet border** hedge

**privilege** advantage, benefit, birthright, claim, concession, due, entitlement, franchise, freedom, immunity, liberty, licence, permission, prerogative, right, sanction, title

**privileged class** aristocracy
**privilege due to older age** seniority
**privilege entails responsibility** noblesse oblige
**privilege granted** indulgence
**privilege of admission** entrée

**privy** cloaca, close, closet, confidential, exclusive, hidden, individual, intimate, lavatory, loo, outhouse, private, restricted, secret, WC

**prize** appraise, appreciate, award, esteem, premium, reward, treasure, trophy, value

**prize at horse event** rosette
**prize at Olympic Games** bronze, gold, silver
**prized fish** trout
**prized fur** ermine, mink, sable
**prized violin** Stradivarius

**prize fight** bout
**prize fighter** boxer, combatant, contestant, fighter, pugilist
**prize in contest** stake
**prize in sporting contest** cup
**prizes in horseracing** sweepstake
**pro** expert, for

**probable** apparent, apt, believable, conceivable, credible, foreseeable, liable, likely, logical, ostensible, plausible, possible, potential, predictable, presumable, presumptive, reasonable, supposed, viable

**probably true** likely, verisimilar
**probationer** abecedarian, aspirant, candidate, novice, novitiate, postulant

**probe** ask, audit, delve, enquire, examination, examine, experiment, exploration, explore, inquest, inquire, investigate, investigation, penetrate, question, review, scrutinise, scrutiny, search, trial

**probe the mind** psychoanalysis
**probing bullet** tracer
**probing legation** fact-finding mission
**probing reportage** investigative journalism

**probity** chastity, decency, excellence, fairness, fidelity, good(ness), honesty, honour, innocence, integrity, merit, morality, purity, rectitude, reputability, straightness, uprightness, veracity, virginity, virtue, worth

**problem** conundrum, delinquent, difficult(y), dispute, doubt, enigma, hassle, intractable, poser, predicament, puzzle, quandary, question, riddle, snag, trouble, uncertainty, unruly

**problematic idea** nodous
**problem drinker** alcoholic, alkie, dipsomaniac
**problem fixer** troubleshooter
**proboscis** nose, trunk
**procedural stage** degree

**procedure** act(ion), approach, bureaucracy, conduct, course, custom, deed, form, groove, guidelines, line, management, manner, manoeuvre, method(ology), modus operandi, operation, performance, policy, practice, process, routine, rule, scheme, step, strategy, style, system, technique, transaction

**procedure of doing something** method
**procedure regularly followed** ritual

**proceed** advance, arise, come, continue, emanate, evolve, flow, go, improve, issue, move, pass, progress, prosper, result, roll, stream, travel, wend

**proceed briskly** trot

**proceeding** account, act(ion), affairs, annals, archives, dealings, deed, doing(s), manoeuvre, matters, measure, minutes, move, ongoing, operation, process, records, report, step, undertaking, venture

**proceeding by eights** octal
**proceeding by inquiry** investigating, zetetic
**proceeding from** emanation
**proceeding inconspicuously but harmfully** insidious
**proceedings at a parliamentary election** hustings
**proceedings in court** acta
**proceed without effort** saunter

**process** course, manage, method, practice, prepare, procedure, proceeding, technique, treat

**process between wash and dry** rinse

**procession** cavalcade, column, cortège, course, file, march, motorcade, pageant, parade, promenade, round, run, sequence, series, stream, string, succession, train

**process of boiling** ebullition
**process of breaking down food** digestion
**process of doing** act(ion)
**process of drawing out and twisting into threads** spinning
**process of dressing** toilet
**process of dyeing with several colours** batik
**process of etching on zinc** zincography
**process of extracting coal** mining
**process of fermentation** zymolysis, zymosis
**process of formation of mountains** orogenesis, orogeny
**process of giving birth** parturition
**process of learning** education
**process of numbering** numeration
**process of taking a photograph** photofluorography
**process set up by yeast** fermentation

**proclaim** advertise, announce, annunciate, bill, blare, broadcast, declare, decree, disclose, herald, ordain, predicate, profess, promulgate, pronounce, publish, signal, state

**proclaim publicly** declare

**proclamation** announcement, command, decree, dictum, edict, enouncement, fiat, manifesto, notice, notification, order, promulgation, rule, ukase
**proclamation of marriage** banns
**proclivity** ability, affection, aptitude, aptness, bent, bias, craving, desire, drift, fancy, fondness, gift, idiosyncrasy, impulse, inclination, instinct, intuition, itch, liking, longing, partiality, passion, penchant, predilection, predisposition, preference, proneness, propensity, readiness, resolve, skill, susceptibility, talent, taste, tendency, tending, urge, verging, weakness, wish, zeal
**procrastinate** adjourn, dawdle, defer, delay, (dilly-)dally, loiter, postpone, prolong, protract, respite, retard, table, temporise, wait, waive
**procure** acquire, cause, effect, gain, get, obtain, secure, win
**prod** aggravate, annoy, dig, drive, elbow, goad, jab, needle, nudge, persecute, pester, poke(r), prick, provoke, punch, rouse, shove, spur, stick, stir, torment
**prodigal** abundant, copious, extravagant, playboy, plenteous, plentiful, reckless, spendthrift, wasteful, waster, wastrel
**prodigal person** spendthrift
**prodigious** abnormal, colossal, enormous, extraordinary, gigantic, huge, immense, mammoth, marvellous, stupendous, titanic, tremendous, uncommon, unusual, wonderful, wondrous
**prodigy** abnormality, champion, exemplar, freak, genius, intellect, marvel, miracle, mutation, paragon, spectacle, talent
**prod onward** urge
**produce** bear, beget, cause, compose, create, demonstrate, effect, fruits, generate, make, manufacture, occasion, originate, product, show, supply, yield
**produce a book** print
**produce a current of air** blow
**produce a jersey** knit
**produce a play** stage
**produce by labour** elaborate
**produced by art** artificial
**produced by germ** septic
**produced by putrefaction** saprogenic
**produced by volcanic action** igneous
**produced on earth's surface** epigene
**produced under surface of earth** hypogene

**produce eggs** lay, ovulate, spawn
**produce milk** lactate
**produce offspring** breed
**produce ova** ovulate
**producer of female gametes** ovary
**produces stamen** tassel
**producing abundantly** fertile, fruitful
**producing a desired result** efficacious
**producing a temporary increase of energy** stimulant
**producing fever** pyretic
**producing good effects** salutary
**producing heat** calorific, pyrogenic
**producing much** prolific
**producing no fruit** acarpous
**producing oil** oleaginous
**producing one fruit** hapaxanthic, monocarpic, monocarpous
**producing or transmitting light** luminiferous
**producing sound** soniferous
**producing sweat** sudoriferous
**producing warmth** calefactory
**producing young by means of eggs hatched within the body** ovoviviparous
**product** artefact, artifact, consequence, construction, creation, effect, fruit, goods, invention, issue, legacy, line, merchandise, offshoot, result, returns, service, upshot, ware, work, yield
**production** assemblage, book, building, composition, concert, construction, creation, direction, disclosure, display, execution, exhibition, fabrication, formation, management, manufacture, movie, musical, offerings, opening, opera, origination, output, preparation, presentation, producing, publication, revelation, shaping, staging, turnout, volume
**production of raw silk** sericulture
**production of sound** audio
**productive** creative, fecund, fertile, fruitful, fruitive, generative, pregnant, profitable, prolific, shaping, yielding
**productive cell** spore
**product of a number multiplied by itself** square
**product of bees** honey
**product of coal-tar** aniline
**product of combustion** ash
**product of fire** ash
**product of oyster** pearl
**product of same kind** edition
**product of two equal factors** square
**prod with elbow** jostle, nudge
**profanation of anything holy** sacrilege
**profane** blasphemous, common, debase, defile, desecrate, heathen, impious, impure, irreligious, irreverent, low, mean, misuse, pollute, sacrilegious, secular, ungodly, unholy, unredeemed, vulgar, wicked
**profane behaviour** profanity
**profess** allege, assume, aver, claim, dissemble, offer, purport, simulate
**professed** alleged, avowed, declared, ostensible, pretended, proclaimed, self-confessed
**professed admirer of the beautiful** aesthete
**profession** assertion, avowal, business, career, declaration, job, occupation, vocation
**professional boxer** pugilist
**professional business** practice
**professional care of hands** manicure
**professional charge** fee
**professional clown** jester
**professional cook** chef
**professional customer** client
**professional gambler** blackleg, scab
**professional in massage** masseur, masseuse
**professional joker** jester
**professional killer** assassin
**professional male dancing partner** gigolo
**professional misconduct** malpractice
**professional name** pseudonym
**professional poet** bard
**professional preacher** pulpiteer
**professional psalm** introit
**professional remuneration** fee
**professional rider in horseraces** jockey
**professional swindler** chevalier d'industrie (F)
**proffer** adduce, advance, allege, bestow, bid, cite, commit, declare, demonstrate, display, enter, estimate, evidence, expound, extend, give, grant, indicate, manifest, offer, overture, pay, pose, present, propose, provide, refer, register, relate, render, show, state, submit, suggest, table, tender, volunteer
**proficiency** ability, aptitude, competence, expertise, facility, skilfulness, skill, talent
**proficient** able, accomplished, adept, apt, competent, conversant, experienced, finished, masterly, skilful, skilled
**profile** analysis, biography, characterisation, chart, contour, diagram, drawing, examination, features, figure, form, graph, outline, picture, portrait, review, shape, side

view, side-face, silhouette, sketch, study, survey, vignette, visage
**profit** advance, advantage, avail, benefit, earnings, emoluments, gain, good, improve(ment), interest, lucre, net(t), proceeds, receipts, return, revenue, surplus, takings, use, value, win(nings), yield
**profitable** aiding, beneficial, conducive, economic, fat, fructuous, gainful, invaluable, lucrative, opportune, prolific, remunerative, rewarding, serviceable, suitable, useful
**profit by** exploit, use, utilise
**profit from transaction** proceeds
**profit's counterpart** loss
**profit seeker** investor
**profits of sown land** emblements
**profligate** debauched, degenerate, depraved, extravagant, immoderate, immoral, libertine, licentious, loose, rake, reckless, reprobate, roué, shameless, spendthrift, vicious, wasteful, wicked
**profound** abstruse, abysmal, cavernous, complex, deep, depth, discerning, erudite, esoteric, extreme, hard, intense, knowledge, learned, penetrating, recondite, sagacious, serious, skilled, solemn, strong, subtle, thoughtful, unqualified, vivid, weighty, wise
**profoundly wise** sage
**profound reverence** adoration
**profundity** abstractness, abstrusity, abyss, cabalism, cavity, complexity, crater, deepness, depth, difficulty, erudition, hardness, hole, hollow, mysticity, pit, sagacity, shaft
**profuse** ample, copious, excessive, generous, lavish, liberal, luxuriant, plentiful, teeming
**profuse bleeding** haemorrhage
**profusely elaborate architectural style** rococo
**profusion** abundance, excess, extravagance, galaxy, glut, multiplicity, multitude, piles, plenitude, plenty, quantity, surplus, waste, wealth
**progenitor** ancestor, begetter, forefather, forerunner, model, mother, original, parent, predecessor, primogenitor
**progeny** breed, brood, calves, children, cubs, cuttings, descendants, family, heirs, issue, kids, kin, kittens, lambs, litter, offshoots, offspring, outcome, posterity, product, scions, seed, shoots, sprigs, sprouts, stock, succession, young

**prognosis** augury, calculation, divination, estimation, forecast, prediction, prognostication, prophecy
**prognostic** augury, auspice, divination, fatidic(al), feeling, foreboding, foretoken, forewarning, indication, omen, oracular, prediction, predictive, presage, prescient, prophetic, sign, token
**prognosticate** forebode, forecast, foreshadow, foretell, portend, predict, presage, prophesy
**program** agenda, approach, attack, bulletin, calculate, calendar, formulate, menu, outline, performance, plan, play, prepare, programme, project, range, schedule, scheme, scroll, show
**program by one musician** recital
**program in serial** episode
**programme of space exploration** Star Trek
**program of a business meeting** agenda
**program of enforced economy** austerity
**program presenter** announcer
**programs for computer** programmes, software
**progress** advance(ment), course, develop(ment), evolve, forward, gain, go, grow(th), hasten, headway, improve(ment), increase, journey, march, milestone, modernise, motion, movement, onward, proceed, progression, prosper, recoup, recover, tour, travel
**progress slowly but with perseverance** plod along
**progress through life** career
**progress towards a climax** crescendo
**prohibit** abrogate, ban, block, censor, check, countermand, (de)bar, deny, disallow, enjoin, exclude, forbid, hinder, impede, inhibit, interdict, kill, obliterate, obstruct, outlaw, preclude, prevent, proscribe, quash, refuse, reject, repress, restrain, restrict, segregate, stop, subdue, suppress, taboo, veto
**prohibited** banned, barred, forbidden, taboo, vetoed
**prohibited trade** contraband
**prohibit from doing** debar
**prohibiting court order** interdict
**prohibition** ban, bar(rier), constriction, denial, embargo, exception, exile, forbiddance, hindrance, injunction, interdict(ion), interference, nay, negation, no, obstacle, preclusion, prevention, rejection, restriction, segregation, veto

**prohibitionist** abolitionist, abstainer, ascetic, hydropot, nephalist, puritan, teetotaller, water-drinker
**prohibition of marriage outside one's tribe** endogamy
**prohibitive** confining, constraining, exclusive, forbidding, inhibitory, interdictive, preventive, prohibitory, restrictive, selective, separative, suppressive
**prohibit legally** estop
**prohibitor** vetoer
**project** activity, aim, cast, contrive, design, devise, extend, frame, homework, jut, plan, plot, proposal, propose, protrude, scheme, throw, toss
**projected image** shadow
**projected law** bill
**projected missile** rocket
**projected photo** slide
**projected weapon** missile
**projectile** arrow, bullet, missile, rocket, shell
**projecting** jutting, protruding, protrusive, protuberant, salient
**projecting collar** flange
**projecting corner** coign
**projecting crag** scar
**projecting edge** brim, lip
**projecting flat rim** flange
**projecting fortification** bastion
**projecting joint of finger** knuckle
**projecting lower edge of roof** eaves
**projecting mountain range** spur
**projecting mouth and nose of an animal** muzzle
**projecting outwards** prominent
**projecting part of fortification** bastion
**projecting part of wall immediately above ground** plinth
**projecting part of wheel** cam
**projecting polygonal recess with a window** oriel
**projecting remnant of cut tree** stump
**projecting rim of wheel** flange
**projecting roof edge** eave
**projecting tube for pouring a liquid** spout
**projection** diagram, estimation, forecast, ledge, map, overhang, promontory, protrusion, ridge
**projection at rear of saddle** cantle
**projection from ear** lobe
**projection on leg of cock** spur
**projector** epidiascope
**project outwards** bulge
**proliferate** abound, advance, augment, boost, breed, crowd, dilate, enhance, enlarge, escalate, expand, extend, flourish, grow, increase, inflate, intensify, luxuriate, multiply,

mushroom, prolong, propagate, raise, reproduce, snowball, spread, strengthen, swarm, teem, thrive
**prolific** abounding, abundant, creative, exuberant, fecund, fertile, fructuous, fruitful, fruitive, lavish, luxurious, plenteous, producing, productive, profuse, progenitive, rich, teeming, yielding
**prolix** bombastic, long-winded, tedious, wearisome, wordy
**prolong** extend, lengthen, protract
**prolong departure** linger
**prolonged and unnatural sleep** coma, lethargy
**prolonged applause** ovation
**prolonged argument** controversy
**prolonged assault** siege
**prolonged bitter hostility** feud, vendetta
**prolonged cry of horse** neigh
**prolonged deep unconsciousness** coma
**prolonged dull pain** ache
**prolonged feud** vendetta
**prolonged fight between armed forces** battle
**prolonged high-pitched cry** wail
**prolonged quarrel** feud
**prolonged unconsciousness** coma
**prolong the agony** martyr
**promenade** arcade, avenue, boulevard, broadwalk, esplanade, gallery, lane, mall, parade, passage, path, pier, road, saunter, street, stroll, strut, walk
**prominence** bulge, celebrity, cliff, conspicuousness, crag, crest, cusp, distinction, eminence, fame, greatness, height, importance, jutting, mound, name, pinnacle, precedence, prestige, rank, reputation, rise, salience, spur, swelling, weight
**prominent** arrant, chief, conspicuous, distinguished, eminent, evident, famous, flagrant, important, jutting, main, marked, noticeable, obvious, outstanding, pointed, principal, projecting, pronounced, salient, showing, striking, unique, well-marked
**prominent aspect** feature
**promiscuous** careless, casual, debauched, dissipated, dissolute, fast, heedless, hodge-podge, immoral, indiscriminate, intermingled, irresponsible, lax, loose, mingled, miscellaneous, mixed, nonselective, random, tarty, uncritical, unselective, wanton, wild

**promise** ability, agree, assurance, assure, augur, bond, commitment, compact, contract, covenant, denote, engage, guarantee, indicate, oath, parole, pledge, plight, stipulate, suggest, swear, undertake, undertaking, vouch, vow, warrant, word
**promised deliverer of Jews** Messiah
**promise on oath** swear
**promise solemnly in marriage** affiance
**promise to marry** betroth
**promise to meet at a given time** appointment
**promising possibility** potential
**promissory note** IOU
**promontory** bluff, cape, cliff, foreland, head(land), hill, isthmus, ness, overhang, peninsula, point, projection, spur, tongue, tor
**promote** advance, advertise, advocate, aid, assist, back, boost, champion, elevate, encourage, endorse, exalt, forward, foster, further, help, honour, nurture, plug, popularise, publicise, push, recommend, sell, sponsor, stimulate, support, upgrade, urge
**promoter of change** catalyst
**promoting growth of hair** trichogenous
**promoting health or safety** salutiferous
**promoting perspiration** sudatory
**promoting strength and beauty** callisthenic
**promotion** advancement, advertising, encouragement, hype, marketing, promulgation, publicity, raise, upgrading
**promotional description** blurb
**promotion in rank** advancement
**prompt** alert, assist, brisk, cause, cue, eager, early, elicit, exactly, expeditious, goad, help, impel, incite, induce, influence, inspire, instant, instigate, log, motivate, move, occasion, prod, provoke, punctual(ly), quick, rapid, ready, remind(er), sharp, smart, speedy, spur, stimulate, stimulus, swift, timely, unhesitating, urge, willing
**prompted by no motive** spontaneous
**prompting** admonition, assisting, cueing, eliciting, evoking, forcing, incitation, inciting, inducing, inspiring, instigating, motivating, moving, persuading, prodding, provoking, pushing, reminding, rousing, spurring, stimulating, urging
**promptly** anon, directly, immediately, instantly, now, pronto, punctually, quickly, rapidly, shortly, soon, speedily, swiftly, unhesitatingly

**prompt to undertake** enterprising
**prone** apt, bent, disposed, eager, even, flat, inclined, leaning, level, liable, likely, lying, oblique, predisposed, prostrate, ready, recumbent, slant, sloping, sprawling, supine, tending
**prone to anger** iracund
**prone to encroachment** aggressive
**prong** arm, bayonet, branch, fork, hook, lance, nail, nib, pierce, point, projection, spike, spur, stab, tine, tip, tooth
**pronged implement** fork
**pronged salmon spear** leister
**prong of fork** tine
**pronoun** he, her, him, it, its, itself, me, our, ours, she, sua (L), they, we, you
**pronounce clearly** enunciate
**pronounce free** absolve
**pronounce guilty** condemn, convict
**pronounce holy** bless
**pronounce indistinctly** mumble, slur, stutter
**pronounce judicially** adjudge
**pronouncement** allocution, announcement, bull, command, declaration, decree, dictum, edict, fiat, judg(e)ment, law, order, ordinance, proclamation, rule, statement, ukase
**pronounce not guilty** absolve
**pronounce through the nose** nasalise
**pronounce unfit for use** condemn
**pronto** directly, immediately, instantly
**pronunciation** accentuation, articulation, delivery, diction, elocution, enunciation, intonation, modulation, phonation, presentation, utterance, voice
**proof** certification, demonstration, evidence, examination, impenetrable, scrutiny, test(imony), trial
**proof given in court** evidence
**proof of a will** probate
**proof of payment** receipt
**proofreader's mark** caret, dele, stet
**proof that one was elsewhere** alibi
**prop** bolster, brace, buttress, lean, (main)stay, maintain, rest, set, shore, stand, support, sustain, truss, uphold
**propagate** beget, breed(ing), broadcast, circulate, disseminate, engender, generate, increase, multiply, procreate, produce, promote, promulgate, publicise, reproduce, reproduction, spread
**propagative segment of tapeworm** proglottis

**propel** actuate, compel, discharge, drive, eject, force, heave, hurl, impel, launch, move, press, project, push, shoot, spur, start, throw, thrust, toss, urge
**propel a bicycle** pedal
**propel a boat** row
**propeller** blade, fan, oar, rotator, rotor, screw, shaft
**propeller shaft** driving shaft
**propelling organ of fish** fin, tail
**propels bicycle** pedal
**propels boat** oar
**propel with oars** row
**propensity** bent, bias, disposition, drift, idiosyncrasis, idiosyncrasy, inclination, inclining, leaning, likeliness, penchant, predilection, predisposition, temperament, tendency, tending, turn, weakness
**proper** accurate, adapted, appropriate, apt, befitting, convenient, correct, decent, decorous, dignified, due, exact, fit(ting), formal, meet, normal, peculiar, polite, precise, prim, respectable, right, special, specific, suitable, suited, tasteful
**properly arranged** orderly
**proper place for anything** berth
**property** assets, attribute, belongings, characteristic, chattel, effects, estate, fixtures, goods, land, luggage, merchandise, ownership, personality, possession, quality, reality, wares
**property attachment** lien
**property available** assets
**property contract** lease
**property document** deed
**property inherited from one's father** patrimony
**property of value** assets
**property or money brought by a bride to her husband** dowry, lobola
**property owned** demesne
**property owner** deedholder, landlady, landlord, proprietor, titleholder
**property owner's document** deed
**property receiver** assignee
**property reverting to government** escheat
**property right** easement
**property saved from wreckage** salvage
**property tax** rates
**property title** deed
**property where tea is cultivated** estate
**prophecy** forecast, geomancy, prediction, prognosis, soothsaying
**prophesy** announce, augur, conjecture, divine, envision, forecast, foresee, foreshadow, forespeak, foretell, forewarn, guess, harbinger, portend, predict, presage, prognosticate, signify, soothsay, speculate, vaticinate
**prophesy from cast earth** geomancy
**prophet** advocate, apostle, augur, clairvoyant, diviner, Eli, evangelist, Ezekial, forecaster, foreteller, medium, occultist, oracle, preacher, predictor, prognosticator, revealer, sangoma, seer, sibyl, sorcerer, warner
**prophetess** Cassandra, Deborah, pythoness, sibyl
**prophetic sign** omen
**prophetic similitude** type
**prophetic utterance** prophecy
**prophet of disaster** Cassandra
**prophet of the Bible** Amos, Daniel, Elisha, Esau, Ezekiel, Ezra, Haggai, Hosea, Isaiah, Jeremiah, Joel, Jonah, Micah, Nahum
**propinquity** affinity, agnation, agreement, closeness, cognation, enation, identity, juxtaposition, kinship, nearness, neighbourhood, nighness, presence, proximity, rapport, relationship, understanding, unity, vicinity
**propitiate** accommodate, adjust, appease, assuage, atone, compromise, concede, conciliate, defuse, mollify, placate, reconcile, reunite, soothe, submit, surrender, yield
**propitious** agreeable, auspicious, beneficent, beneficial, benign, compassionate, conducive, congenial, fair, favourable, fit, fortunate, friendly, gracious, kind, merciful, opportune, pleasing, profitable, suitable, understanding
**prop mover in the theatre** stagehand
**proportion** adjust, arrange, balance, comparison, dimensions, distribution, extent, harmony, part, ratio, redistribute, regulate, relation, size, symmetry
**proportional** accordant, akin, balanced, complementary, connective, consistent, correlated, correspondent, corresponding, equivalent, harmonious, matching, parallel, related, relative, symmetrical
**proportional distribution of seats in a legislative body** apportionment
**proportionally** pro rata
**proportionate** balanced, commensurate, comparable, compatible, consistent, correspondent, corresponding, equitable, equivalent, even, just, proportional
**proportion between parts** symmetry
**proportionment** commensuration
**proposal** approach, bid, design, motion, offer, overture, plan, presentation, presentment, proffer, program(me), project, scheme, suggestion, tender, terms
**proposal in a meeting** motion
**propose** bid, design, intend, name, nominate, offer, plan, present, profound, purpose, recommend, suggest, tender
**propose as candidate** nominate
**propose as payment** offer
**proposed arrangement** schema
**proposed marriage notice** banns
**proposer** advocate, backer, campaigner, champion, counsellor, defender, mover, promotor, speaker, spokesman, supporter, upholder
**proposition** lemma, motion, plan, premise, project, proposal, protasis, recommendation, scheme, suggestion, supposal, tender, theorem, thesis
**proposition in logic** obverse
**proposition leading to conclusion** premise
**proposition to be maintained or proved** thesis
**propound** advance, advocate, postulate, predicate, present, proffer, propose, submit, suggest, tender
**proprietor** deedholder, feudatory, (free)holder, innkeeper, landholder, landlady, landlord, landowner, lord, manager, master, mistress, owner, possessor, restaurateur, squire, taverner, titleholder, vendee
**proprietor of an inn** padrone (I)
**propriety** conformity, decency, decorum, dignity, etiquette, fitness, grace, modesty, politeness, properness, protocol, refinement, seemlishness, suitableness
**propriety in conduct** decorum
**propriety of behaviour** decency
**propulsive** impulsive
**prop up** buttress, support
**prosaic** banal, boring, commonplace, dry, dull, everyday, flat, humdrum, mundane, ordinary, routine, stale, tedious, unimaginative, uninteresting, wearisome
**prosector** anatomiser
**prosecute** arraign, charge, conduct, consummate, indict, persevere, persist, sue, summon
**prosencephalon** forebrain

**prospect** anticipation, contemplating, expectance, outlook, search, survey, view, vista
**prospective chance** expectancy
**prospector's companion** ass, mule
**prosper** advance, bloom, flourish, flower, gain, luxuriate, profit, progress, succeed, thrive
**prosperity** affluence, boom, fortune, plenty, rich, success, wealth, welfare
**prosperous** auspicious, favourable, flourishing, fortunate, rich, successful, thriving, wealthy
**prostitute** abuse, bawd, cheapen, courtesan, debase, demire, femme galante (F), harlot, hooker, misuse, moll, paramour, seductress, siren, slut, streetwalker, trollop, trull, wanton, whore
**prostrate** abase, abject, cringe, defenceless, dejected, depressed, desolate, disarmed, exhausted, flat, grovel, helpless, inconsolable, kneel, kowtow, lying, overcome, paralysed, powerless, prone, reduced, spent, submit
**prostrate oneself** cringe, grovel, kneel, kowtow, submit
**prostrate with grief** heartbroken, heartsick, inconsolable
**protect** befriend, bless, chaperone, conceal, conduct, conserve, cover, defend, ensconce, escort, forfend, foster, hide, house, keep, maintain, patronise, preserve, (safe)guard, save, screen, secure, shelter, shield, veil
**protect against disease** inoculate
**protect by divine power** sain
**protect clothes** apron, overalls
**protected against disease** immune
**protected bird** eagle, swan
**protected from light** shady
**protected with weapon** armed
**protect from danger** defend
**protect from harm** shield
**protect from sun** shade
**protecting barrier** bulkhead
**protecting bracket** sponson
**protecting charm** amulet, periapt
**protecting covering of animals** skin
**protecting shelter** lee
**protecting soldier** guardsman
**protection** (a)egis, barrier, buffer, care, custody, defence, guardianship, preservation, preserver, safety, security, shelter
**protection against damage or loss** indemnity
**protection against rain** umbrella
**protection against splashes** mudguard, splatterdash

**protection for houseworker** apron
**protection from bad weather** shelter
**protection from collision** bumper, fender
**protection from danger** shelter
**protection money** bribe
**protection of warrior** armour, helmet, shield
**protective bar** fender
**protective care** custody
**protective covering** armour, shield
**protective covering for head** helmet
**protective covering for knee** kneecap
**protective covering of animals** skin
**protective ditch** moat
**protective garment** apron, overall
**protective headgear** helmet
**protective layer** coating, integument
**protective piece on shoe heel** tap
**protective plate or screen** shield
**protective rim** bank
**protect lovingly** cherish
**protector** bodyguard, counsel, defender, guard(ian), patron
**protectorate** guardianship
**protects clothes in kitchen** apron
**protects finger while sewing** thimble
**protects organ of sight** eyelid
**protégé** pupil, smike, ward
**protein catalyst** enzyme
**protein found in milk** casein
**protein-rich bean** soya
**protein substance found in bone and tissue** collagen
**protest** affirm, announce, argue, assert, attest, aver, avow, complain, declare, disapproval, disapprove, dissent, exception, expostulate, object(ion), oppose, outcry, protestation, remonstrate, tut-tut
**protest at** depreciate
**protestation** complaint, oath, objection, pledge, protest, remonstrance, vow
**protest excitedly** squeal
**protesting list of names** petition
**protocol** conventions, decorum, etiquette, formalities, pact, treaty
**protoplasmic contents of ovum** vitellus
**protozoan** amoeba, foram, monad, moner, paramecium, protist, protozoon, radiate, stentor
**protract** adjourn, continue, defer, delay, eke, elongate, extend, lengthen, postpone, procrastinate, prolong, shelve, stall, stretch, suspend, table, temporise
**protracted** acute, broad, capacious, close, concentrated, deep, dragging, endless, everlasting, extensive, extreme, far-flung, fierce, forceful,

general, great, huge, infinite, intense, large, lengthy, limitless, long, powerful, prevalent, profound, severe, spacious, strained, thorough, unbounded, universal, unlimited, vast, wide(spread)
**protracted speech** tirade
**protrude** bulge, excurve, extend, extrude, goggle, jut, obtrude, pout, project, protuberate, swell
**protrude lips** pout
**protruding belly** boep, paunch
**protruding rock formation** outcrop
**protrusion** bulge, bulk, bump, growth, knob, knot, lump, nub, projection, snag, stud, swelling, tumour
**protrusion of eyeball** exophthalmia, exophthalmus
**protuberance** bleb, blister, gnarl, jut, knob, lump, node, prominence, protrusion, swelling, tuberosity, wart
**protuberance from deer's head** antler, horn
**proud** arrogant, conceited, contented, creditable, disdainful, haughty, imperious, majestic, overconfident, overweening, presumptuous, snooty, stately, vain
**prove** ascertain, confirm, establish, evidence, justify, show, substantiate, test, try, verify
**prove beyond doubt** evince, manifest
**prove by reasoning** argue
**proved by chain of reasoning** theorem
**Provençal stew of vegetables** ratatouille
**proverb** adage, aphorism, apothegm, axiom, byword, catchword, cliché, dictum, epigram, gnome, maxim, motto, precept, prescript, saw, saying, slogan
**proverbial back-breaker** straw
**proverbial saying** saw
**proverbial truth** axiom
**prove to** convince, satisfy
**prove to be false** disprove, refute
**provide** accord, add, afford, award, bestow, bring, cater, consider, contribute, distribute, donate, endow, endue, equip, furnish, give, impart, invest, lavish, lend, offer, outfit, prepare, present, produce, render, serve, supply, yield
**provided** added, afforded, brought, catered, equipped, furnished, given, if, imparted, lent, presented, rendered, served, supplied, yielded
**provided that** if, so
**provide entertainment** cater, treat
**provide for** cater, endow, fend, keep, maintain, nourish, nurture, support, sustain

**provide funds for** finance
**provide grudgingly** scant
**provide help** avail
**provide loans** lend
**provide lodging for** accommodate
**provide meals** cater
**provide money for** finance
**provide refuge** harbour
**provider of financial cover** insurer
**provider of food for a party** caterer
**provide schooling for** educate
**provides heat** sun
**provide temporarily** lend
**provide weapons** arm
**provide what is needed** cater
**provide with** endow
**provide with a ceiling** ceil
**provide with another edge** rehem
**provide with answers** spoon-feed
**provide with capital** finance
**provide with defensive works** fortify
**provide with equipage** accoutre
**provide with money** fund
**provide with permanent income** endow
**provide with the means** enable
**provide with weapons** arm
**providing for future needs** provident
**providing maintenance** alimentary
**providing nourishment** nutrient
**province** area, assignment, canton, capacity, colony, concern, constituency, county, department, district, division, dominion, duty, estate, function, jurisdiction, line, locale, occupation, orbit, profession, region, responsibility, section, sphere, state, territory, tract, trade, zone
**province of Afghanistan** Farah, Kapisa, Kunar, Kunuz, Logar, Mazar, Parwan, Wardak, Zabul
**province of Belgium** Antwerp, Brabant, Flanders, Liege, Namur
**province of Canada** Alberta, Manitoba, Newfoundland, Ontario, Quèbec, Saskatchewan
**province of China** Chekiang, Fukien, Honan, Shansi, Tibet, Tsinghai
**province of Cuba** Camagüey, Havana, Matanzas
**province of Ethiopia** Arusi, Bale, Eritrea, Gojam, Shewa, Tigre
**province of Indonesia** Bale, Bengkulu, Djambi, Jambi, Jaya, Maluku
**province of New Zealand** Auckland, Canterbury, Otago, Taranaki, Wellington
**province of northern Ethiopia** Eritrea
**province of Northern Ireland** Ulster
**province of South Africa** Eastern Cape, Eastern Transvaal, Free State, KwaZulu/Natal, North West, Northern Cape, Northern Transvaal, PWV, Western Cape
**province of Spain** Aragon, Avila, Granada
**province of Uganda** Buganda
**province of western Austria** Tyrol
**province of Yugoslavia** Banat
**province of Zaïre** Equator, Kasai, Kivu, Shaba
**provincial** bucolic, countrified, divisional, dogmatic, domestic, intolerant, local, parochial, plebeian, prejudiced, regional, rural, rustic, sectional
**provincial dialect** patois
**provincial governor of ancient Persia** satrap
**provision** condition, food, if, proviso, stipulation, supplies, supplying, viands
**provisional** conditional, experimental, impermanent, incidental, interim, pro tempore (L), provisionary, substitute, temporary, tentative, transitional
**provisional conviction** opinion
**provisionally** dependently, limitatively, restrictedly, substitutionally, tentatively, transitionally
**provisioner to an army post** sutler
**provision of chairs** seating
**provision of false teeth** prosthodontia
**provisions** eatables, eats, edibles, foodstuff, groceries, rations, supplies, viands, victuals
**provisions cupboard** larder
**proviso** clause, condition, limitation, mandate, provision, qualification, requirement, stipulation, string, terms, ultimatum
**provocative** aggravating, alluring, arousing, challenging, disturbing, erotic, exciting, goading, insulting, outrageous, seductive, stimulating, suggestive, tempting
**provoke** affront, aggravate, anger, annoy, arouse, enrage, exacerbate, exasperate, excite, incense, incite, induce, inflame, infuriate, instigate, irritate, needle, nettle, rouse, stimulate, tease, vex
**provoke by jokes** tease
**provoke to fury** enrage
**prow** beak, bow, gallant, ram, rostrum, stem, worthy
**prowl** ambush, crouch, creep, follow, forage, hide, hunt, loiter, lurch, lurk, plunder, prey, pursue, pussyfoot, ramble, roam, rove, scavenge, scour, seek, skulk, slinked, sneak, snoop, steal, trail, traverse, wander
**prowl about suspiciously** lurch

**prowl in search of something** mouser
**proximity** adjacence, adjacent, approach, approximation, closeness, contiguity, edge, juxtaposition, nearness, neighbourhood, nighness, presence, proximateness, verge, vicinity
**proximity of blood** kinship
**proxy** agent, alternate, deputy, permit, representative, surrogate, understudy, vice regent, warrant
**prude** affecter, bluenose, Bowdler, censor, euphemist, fanatic, moralist, pedant, prig, prude, puritan, rigorist, zealot
**prudence** care, caution, discretion, foresight, judg(e)ment, planning, precaution, preparedness, providence, saving, thrift, vigilance, wariness, wisdom
**prudent** careful, cautious, circumspect, discreet, farsighted, foreseeing, frugal, judicious, precautious, provident, sensible, shrewd, sparing, thrifty, vigilant, wise
**prudent conduct** policy
**prudent foresight** precaution
**prudery** coyness, formality, overmodesty, priggishness, prissiness, prudishness, severity, strictness
**prudish** coy, demure, nice, (over)modest, priggish, prim, prissy, proper, pure, queasy, reserved, squeamish, strai(gh)t-laced
**prudishness** coyness, archness, backwardness, bashfulness, prissiness, demureness, evasiveness, reservedness, shyness, timidness, squeamishness, delicateness, fastidiousness, scrupulousness
**prudish person** prig
**prune** clip, cut, dock, lop, reduce, sned (Sc), snip, trim
**pruning scissors** secateurs
**pruning tool** shears
**Prussian cavalryman** u(h)lan
**Prussian leather** spruce
**pry** excavate, force, inquire, inspect, interfere, interrogate, intervene, intrude, lever, meddle, nose, obtrude, open, peep, poke, probe, query, scan, search, separate, snoop, survey, wrest
**pry bar** lever
**prying** agape, eager, eavesdropping, examining, forward, gawking, impertinent, inspecting, interfering, intruding, intrusive, investigative, meddlesome, meddling, nosy, ogling, peeking, peeping, peering,

persistent, poking, prowling, scanning, scrutinising, snooping, spying, studying, surveying
**prying bar** lever
**pry into other's private affairs** snoop
**psalm** carol, chant, doxology, hymn, melody, paean
**psalter** hymnal, hymn book
**psalterium** omasum
**pseudo** artificial, assumed, bogus, counterfeit, ersatz, factitious, fake, false, feigned, forged, fraudulent, imitation, mock, phoney, pretended, sham, spurious, synthetic, unreal
**pseudo-artistic** arty
**pseudocarp** accessory fruit, apple, false fruit, fig, strawberry
**pseudonym** alias, allonym, byname, cognomen, epithet, nickname, nom de plume, sobriquet
**pseudoscience** alchemy
**psittacine** parrot-like
**psyche** anima, ego, individuality, intellect, mind, personality, pneuma, self, soul, spirit, subconscious
**psychiatric disorder** amnesia, anorexia nervosa, autism, schizophrenia
**psychiatrist** alienist, analyst, psychoanalyser
**psychic** arcane, esoteric, extrasensory, ghostly, intellectual, magical, mental, mystic(al), occult, phantom, psychological, spectral, spiritual, supernatural, telepathic, unearthly, unknown, unreal
**psychical research** parapsychology
**psychological shock** trauma
**psychopath** lunatic, maniac, nutcase, psychotic, sociopath
**pteric** alar, winged, winglike
**pteridophyte** fern, horsetail
**ptisan** barley-water, tisane
**Ptolemy** pharaoh
**pub** alehouse, bar, Brauhaus (G), honky-tonk, dive, hotel, inn, local, roadhouse, saloon, shebeen, tavern
**pub drink** ale, beer
**pub game** darts
**pub item** ale, beer
**public** civic, civil, community, general, national, social, universal, unrestricted
**public address** speech
**public apology** amende honorable (F)
**public assembly in ancient Greece** agora
**publication** announcement, broadcast, editing, edition, issue, journal, magazine, newspaper, printing, production, promulgation, pronouncement, publishing

**publication manager** editor
**publications inspector** censor
**public auction** outcry, rummage sale
**public bath** lido, therm
**public building for gambling** casino
**public carriage** cab
**public ceremony** function
**public convenience** latrine
**public conveyance** (mini)bus, train, tram
**public crier's cry** oyes, oyez
**public debate** forum, indaba, kgotla
**public declaration of policy** manifesto
**public decree** edict
**public dining room** saloon
**public discussion** debate, forum
**public disgrace** ignominy
**public disorder** mêlée, riot
**public display** scene
**public disturbance** riot
**public document** archive
**public drain** sewer
**public esteem** repute
**public executioner** hangman
**public eye** limelight, recognition
**public garden** park
**public gathering** forum, meeting
**public guardian** police
**public hall for dancing** palais
**public-house** bar, hotel, inn, local, pub, tavern
**public image** persona
**publicise** advertise, announce, broadcast, circularise, disseminate, herald, placard, post, promote, promulgate, propagate, publish, report, ventilate
**publicity** advertising, hype, information, news, plug, promotion, propaganda
**publicity feat** stunt
**publicity stunt** gimmick
**public lodging house** hotel
**publicly** openly, publice (L)
**publicly applaud** acclaim
**publicly show** display
**public meeting** forum
**public meeting to protest** demo(nstration)
**public notice** ad(vertisement), edict
**public occasion** function
**public official** notary
**public open-air swimming pool** lido
**public opinion** consensus, vox populi
**public outcry** furore
**public passage** road
**public performance of music** recital
**public performer** artiste
**public place for debate** forum, indaba, kgotla
**public place for dirty linen** launderette
**public place for walking** promenade

**public prison** gaol
**public procession** parade
**public promenade** esplanade
**public protest** demo(nstration)
**public recreation ground** park
**public regard** repute
**public report** fame
**public road** street
**public room** hall
**public sale** auction
**public sale official** auctioneer
**public scale** tron
**public servant** bureaucrat
**public service** utility
**public shame** ignominy
**public show** exhibition, expo(sition), spectacle
**public slaughterhouse** abattoir
**public speaker** declaimer, orator, rhetor, speechmaker
**public speaker who entrances his or her audience** spell-binder
**public speech** oration
**public spirit** patriotism
**public-spiritedness** almsgiving, charity, generosity
**public square** piazza, plaza
**public statement** announcement
**public swimming pool** lido
**public transport** (mini)bus, omnibus, train, tram
**public treasury of ancient Rome** fisc
**public tree-planting time** Arbor Day
**public tumult** riot
**public vehicle** cab, (mini)bus, taxi, taxicab
**public vote** election
**public walk** alameda, mall, promenade
**public watchdog** ombudsman
**public way** avenue, lane, road, street
**public weighing machine** tron
**public writer** scrivener
**publish** advance, advertise, announce, broadcast, circulate, declare, disclose, distribute, divulge, edit, exhibit, issue, print, proclaim, produce, promote, publicise, report, reveal, sponsor, tell
**publish again** reissue
**published after author's death** posthumous
**published announcement of death** obit(uary)
**published copy** edition
**published in instalments** serial
**published mistake** erratum
**publish illegally** pirate
**publishing exclusively** copyright
**publishing official** editor
**publish text** print
**publish without permission** pirate
**pub nearest home** local

**pub order** ale, beer
**pub snack** peanut
**pub's storage place** tap-room
**Puccini opera** La Boheme, Madame Butterfly, Tosca, Turandot
**puccoon** alkanet, alkannin, anchusin, bloodroot, gromwell
**puce** flea-colour, purple-brown
**pucker** crease, fold, purse, wrinkle
**pucker up** crinkle
**puckish** elfin
**pudding** blancmange, custard, dessert, mousse
**pudding ingredient** rice, sago, semolina, tapioca
**pudding mixture** batter
**pudding starch** rice, sago, tapioca
**puddle** bungler, muddle, pool
**pudency** modesty, shame
**puerile** adolescent, babyish, boyish, childish, foolish, girlish, immature, inane, jejune, juvenile, naïve, petty, silly, sophomoric, trivial, weak
**puerility** childishness, dimness, dullness, flippancy, folly, fun, gaiety, giddiness, girlishness, jest, levity, nonsense, obtuseness, shallowness, silliness, simplicity, stupidity, triviality
**Puerto Rican island** Culebra, Mona, Vieques
**puff** blast, blow, breath(e), commendation, drag, draught, emanation, exhale, gasp, gulp, gust, inflate, inhale, pant, smoke, suck, swell, wheeze, whiff
**puff and blow** pant
**puffed out** baggy
**puffed up** arrogant, bigheaded, boastful, conceited, high and mighty, pompous, proud, swollen-headed
**puffing** dragging, drawing, inhaling, panting, smoking, sucking, wheezing
**puffing billy** locomotive
**puff noisily** chug
**puff of air** breeze, whiff
**puff out** enlarge, expand, inflate
**puff pastry case with a savoury or sweet filling** bouchée
**puff up** bloat
**pug** carlin, (lap)dog
**pug dog** mops
**pugilist** boxer, bruiser, fighter, pug
**pugilistic** fistical
**pugnacious** aggressive, combative, contentious, hot-tempered, irascible, irritable, quarrelsome
**pugnacious behaviour** belligerence
**puissant** mighty, powerful
**pukeko** gallinule
**pull** appeal, drag, draw, haul, influence, jerk, lug, lure, stretch, tow, trail, tug, yank

**pull a boner** goof
**pull about roughly** tousle
**pull a face** grimace
**pull a fast one** cheat, deceive, defraud, delude, hoodwink, mislead, swindle, trick
**pull along** drag, draw, lug, tow
**pull a long face** sulk
**pull along with force** drag
**pull apart** attack, criticise, dismember, flay, knock, part, separate, tear
**pull behind** drag, tow
**pull down** bulldoze, demolish, destroy, dismantle, remove
**pulled candy** taffy, toffee
**pulley wheel** sheave
**pull forcibly** haul
**pull forcibly apart** tear
**pull hard** tug
**pull in** arrest, arrive, attract, clear, draw, earn, gain, gross, make, nail, net, park, reach, stop
**pulling** culling, dislocating, drawing, enticing, gathering, luring, plucking, rending, ripping, straining, tearing, uprooting, weeding, yanking
**pulling force** traction
**pull jerkily** yank
**Pullman car** sleeper
**pull off** accomplish, achieve, detach, doff, manage, remove, succeed, swing, wrench
**pull oneself together** rally
**pull one's legs** chaff, joke, rag
**pull one's weight** co-operate
**pull one vehicle behind another** tow
**pull out** abandon, depart, discontinue, evacuate, extract, leave, quit, retreat, stretch, withdraw
**pullover** dashiki, jumper, sweater
**pull plant from soil** uproot
**pull round** rally
**pull someone's leg** banter, chaff, deceive, fool, gibe, jeer, misguide, mislead, mock, rag, rib, taunt, tease, trick
**pull strenuously** heave
**pull suddenly** yank
**pull the trigger** shoot
**pull the wool over one's eyes** deceive, delude, dupe, fool, hoodwink, humbug, trick
**pull through** rally, recover, recuperate, survive, weather
**pull together** co-operate, collaborate
**pull to pieces** tear
**pullulate** bud, develop, multiply, sprout, swarm, teem
**pull up** brake, criticise, halt, rebuke, reprimand, stop, uproot
**pull violently** tear, tug
**pull with a jerk** tug, yank

**pull with effort** heave
**pulmonary organ** lung
**pulp** cheap, flesh, lurid, marrow, mash, mush, pomace, purée
**pulped fish** pomace
**pulped food** purée
**pulped fruit** purée
**pulped potatoes** mash
**pulpit** ambo, bema, bima(h), clergy, desk, dias, estrade, lectern, platform, rostrum, soap-box
**pulpit discourse** sermon
**pulpit in mosque** mimbar
**pulpit lecture** sermon
**pulp of vegetables** purée
**pulp product** paper
**pulpy** cushioned, elastic, gelatinous, mushy, soft, spongy, squashy, swampy, yielding
**pulpy edible red fruit** tomato
**pulpy food** mess
**pulsate** beat, palpitate, pound, pulse, quaver, quiver, reverberate, shiver, shudder, throb, thump, tick, tremble, vibrate
**pulsation of the heart** heartbeat, throb
**pulse** bean, (heart)beat, lentils, oscillation, peas, pulsate, pulsation, throb, vibration
**pulse-beat absence** acrotism
**pulse on radar screen** blip
**pulverise** bray, crush, destroy, donder, granulate, grind, mill, pound, smash, triturate, wreck
**pulverised glass** frosting
**pulverised tobacco** snuff
**puma** cougar
**pummel** batter, beat, claw, donder, klap, lacerate, mangle, pound, thrash
**pumping engine part** piston
**pumping organ** heart
**pumpkin eater** Peter
**pump out** deflate, drain, empty, extract, remove
**pump up** bloat, dilate, enlarge, expand, inflate
**pun** quip, witticism
**punch** blow, bore, box, bump, cut, drive, elbow, hit, impact, jab, knock(out), pierce, point, poke, prick, prod, push, slam, smash, stamp, strike, stroke, thump, uppercut, verve, vigour
**Punch and Judy character** puppet
**Punch's dog** Toby
**punctilious person** precisian, prig
**punctual** early, exact, precise, prompt, strict, timely
**punctuation mark** brace, bracket(s), breve, colon, comma, dash, diacritic, dot, full stop, hyphen, parenthesis, period, point, semicolon, space

**punctum** dot, speck
**puncture** leak, perforate, perforation, pierce, rupture
**punctured tyre** flat
**pundit** academician, analyst, arbiter, authority, bookworm, brain, commentator, connoisseur, critic, expert, fundi, genius, highbrow, intellectual, judge, maestro, pantologist, philosopher, prodigy, reviewer, sage, savant, scholar, talent
**pungency** acidity, acridity, bitterness, keenness, nip, painfulness, pathos, piquancy, poignance, sadness, saltiness, severity, snap, sourness, spirit, tang, wittiness
**pungency of flavour** heat
**pungent** acrid, biting, bitter, caustic, cutting, hot, keen, mordant, penetrating, peppery, piercing, piquant, poignant, sarcastic, sardonic, sharp, stimulating, tangy, trenchant
**pungent bud** clove
**pungent bulb** garlic, onion
**pungent colourless gas** ammonia
**pungent condiment** pepper
**pungent edible bulb** onion, garlic
**pungent edible plant** nasturtium
**pungent edible root** garlic, onion, radish
**pungent flavouring** spice
**pungent flower** nasturtium
**pungent gas with strong alkaline reaction** ammonia
**pungent odour** tang
**pungent pepper** cayenne, tabasco
**pungent plant** pepper
**pungent pod used in pickles** chili
**pungent root vegetable** radish
**pungent salad ingredient** onion
**pungent salad root** radish
**pungent sauce** tabasco, worcester
**pungent seasoning** spice
**pungent smell** tang
**pungent vegetable** onion
**Punic faith** fides Punica (L)
**punish** castigate, chasten, chastise, correct, discipline, penalise, reprove, scourge
**punishable by death** capital
**punish a child** spank
**punish by a fine** amerce
**punish by beating** chastise
**punish by paddling** spank
**punish for a wrong** avenge
**punish for speeding** fine
**punish in any way** amerce
**punishment** beating, chastening, chastisement, correction, criticism, discipline, fine, imprisonment, maltreatment, overexertion, penalty, penance, sanction, sentence
**punishment for breach of law** penalty
**punishment rod** cane, ferule
**punish severely** castigate, chastise, trounce
**punitive** castigatory, correctional, corrective, disciplinary, harsh, hurtful, penal, punishing, retributive, revengeful, severe
**punning retort** clinch
**punt** back, bet, gamble, garvey, hit, kick, lay, poy, quant, skerry, stake, wager
**punter** backer, gambler, punt
**puny** delicate, denourished, emaciated, feeble, frail, inferior, scrubby, shallow, small, trivial, underdeveloped, underfed, undersized, unimportant
**pup** cub, doggy, puppy, whelp, youngling
**pupa** chrysalid, chrysalis, egg, flaxseed, instar, puppet, tumbler, wriggler
**pupil** beginner, disciple, learner, neophyte, novice, probationer, scholar, schoolboy, schoolgirl, student, trainee
**pupil dilation** mydriasis
**pupil in a military academy** cadet
**pupillage** minority, nonage, schooldays
**pupil of Plato** Aristotle
**pupil with position of authority** prefect
**puppet** creature, doll, dupe, figurehead, instrument, Judy, marionette, mouthpiece, pawn, Punch, stooge, tool
**puppet show** grand guignol
**puppy** canine, cub, cur, dog(gy), pup, tyke, whelp, youngling
**puppy bite** nip
**purchase** acquire, acquiring, acquisition, bargain, buy(ing), get, hire, leverage, obtain(ment), possession, procure(ment), purchasing, raise, rent, secure, tackle
**purchase and use of goods** consumption
**purchase certificate** coupon
**purchaser** buyer, client, consumer, customer, marketer, patron, shopper, vendee
**purchasing agent** buyer, purchaser
**purchasing power** value
**pure** absolute, chaste, clean, faultless, guileless, immaculate, innocent, pedigreed, spotless, sterling, true, unadulterated, undefiled, unmixed, unsullied, untainted, untarnished, utter
**pure beauty** aesthetic
**pure-bred animal** pedigree
**puree** pulp
**pure honey** mel
**pure in heart** good, moral, righteous, saintly, virtuous
**purely imaginary thing** figment
**purely verbal argument** quibble
**purest and most perfect form** quintessence
**pure water** lymph
**purgation** absolution, acquittal, cleansing, epuration, expurgation, freeing, justification, lavage, penance, purging, purification, release, riddance, vindication, washing
**purgative** Epsom salts, laxative
**purgative drug** aloe, jalap, senna
**purgative plant** turpeth
**purge** absolve, clarify, clean sweep, clean up, clean(se), clear, crushing, dismiss, eject(ion), eliminate, elimination, eradicate, eradication, exonerate, expel, expiate, exterminate, forgive, kill, liquidate, liquidation, oust, pardon, purify, removal, remove, suppression, wash
**purging** absolving, cleansing, clearing, dismissing, ejecting, eradicating, exonerating, expelling, exterminating, forgiving, killing, pardoning, purifying, removing, washing
**purification** absolution, clarification, clean(s)ing, decontamination, defecation, depurating, depuration, detersion, disinfecting, disinfection, exculpation, expurgation, filtration, freshening, lustration, purgation, purging, refining, sublimating, washing
**purified potash** pearl ash
**purify** absolve, acquit, antisepticise, bathe, clarify, clean(se), consecrate, decontaminate, deterge, disinfect, distil, filter, freshen, fumigate, redeem, refine, sanctify, sanitise, shrive, vindicate, wash
**purify by sacrifice** lustrate
**purify from sin** sanctify
**purify of sin** cleanse
**purist** stickler
**Puritan leader** Pym
**purity** abstinence, blamelessness, chasteness, chastity, clarity, cleanliness, cleanness, clearness, decency, delicacy, distinction, faultlessness, genuineness, honour, immaculacy, immaculateness, innocence, integrity, modesty, morality, piety, polish, pureness, sanctity, simplicity, truth,

untaintedness, uprightness, virtue, wholesomeness
**purloin** appropriate, arrogate, counterfeit, finger, pilfer, pocket, rob, scavenge, shoplift, sponge, steal, swipe, take, thieve
**purple and violet gem** almandine, amethyst, garnet, spinel
**purple-berried wild tree** elder
**purple-brown** puce
**purple colour** amaranth
**purple gem** amethyst
**purple or violet dyeing-powder** cudbear
**purple-red** magenta, murrey
**purple seaweed** laver
**purple shade** lilac, mauve, puce, violet
**purple-white flower tree** magnolia
**purplish brown** puce
**purplish colour** lilac, mauve, violet
**purplish flower** lilac
**purplish red** claret, lake, magenta, murrey
**purport** aim, allege, aver, claim, contend, convey, declare, effect, idea, import, indicate, intent, maintain, meaning, plan, point, proclaim, purpose, relevance, sense, tenor
**purpose** aim, concern, consequence, constancy, dedication, deliberation, design, determination, devotion, effect, end, function, goal, idea, intent(ion), issue, mind, motive, object(ive), outcome, persistence, plan, point, principle, propose, question, rationale, reason, resolution, resolve, result, sake, single-mindedness, spirit, steadfastness, talk, target, tenacity, topic, use, view, vision, why, will, zeal
**purposely mislead** deceive
**purposely overlook** connive, disregard, ignore
**purpose of duty** function
**purpose of existence** raison d'être (F)
**purpose or goal** end
**purse** award, coffer, contract, exchequer, finances, funds, gather, gift, handbag, means, money(-bag), moneyholder, pouch, present, prize, pucker, resources, reward, sporran, tighten, treasury, wallet, wealth, wringler
**purser** cashier
**purse snatcher** pickpocket
**purse strings** budget, finance
**pursue** attend, chase, court, desire, dog, follow, harpy, haunt, hound, hunt, maintain, perform, persecute, practise, proceed, quest, search,
seek, shadow, stalk, trace, track, trail, woo
**pursued animals** game
**pursue game** stalk
**pursuer** follower, hunter
**pursuer of fox** hound, huntsman
**pursuer of perfection** idealist
**pursue stealthily** stalk
**pursuit** aim, aspiration, chase, continuance, desire, effort, employment, end, execution, goal, hobby, intent, interest, objective, occupation, pastime, probe, searching, tracking, trailing, venture, work
**pursuit of some branch of knowledge** study
**pursy** corpulent, fat, overweight, short-winded
**purulent inflammation of the end joint of a finger** felon, whitlow
**purvey** cater, equip, furnish, outfit, provide, provision, purvey, render, retail, sell, supply, supply, transmit, victual
**purvey food** cater
**push** advertise, attack, barge, boost, depress, determine, drive, effort, ejection, elbow, exert, force, impel, impulse, instigate, jostle, motivate, nudge, persuade, press, propel, shoulder, shove, thrust, urge
**push a boat** barge
**push around** bully
**push aside** shunt
**push-bike** (bi)cycle
**pushchair** stroller
**push down** press
**push for** demand
**push forward** incite, nudge, precipitate, prod, propel, urge
**push from below** boost
**push from position** budge
**push gradually** nudge
**push in** press
**push in where unwanted** obtrude
**push off** depart, launch, leave
**push on** advance, continue, drudge, endeavour, hurry, labour, persevere, persist, plod, proceed, progress
**push roughly** barge, hustle, jostle
**push rudely** elbow
**push up** boost, lift
**push upwards** boost
**push vigorously** shove
**push violently** hush
**push with a jerk** jog
**push with the elbow** nudge
**push with the head or horns** butt
**pushy** aggressive, ambitious, assertive, bold, brash, brassy, brazen, bumptious, cheeky, cocky,
domineering, forceful, forward, insolent, loud, obtrusive, officious, peremptory, presumptuous, self-assertive, self-seeking
**pusillanimous** cowardly, craven, fearful, feeble, gutless, timid, timorous
**pus in the body** sepsis
**pussyfoot** creep, equivocate, prevaricate, prowl, sneak, tiptoe
**pustule** abscess, blister, bump, carbuncle, furuncle, gumboil, inflammation, lesion, papule, pimple, pock(mark), spot, ulcer
**put** deposit, express, impose, place, render, set, translate
**put across** communicate, convey, explain, express
**put a damper on** dishearten
**put a hedge round** fence
**put air into** aerate
**put air into tyre** inflate, pump
**put a layer on a surface** spread
**put a match to** ignite
**put an edge on** sharpen
**put an end to** abolish, cease, quash, scotch, squash, stop, terminate
**put apart** separate
**put aside** abandon, bury, cache, deposit, discard, disregard, forget, hoard, ignore, keep, reserve, retain, save, shelve, stash, stockpile, store, stow
**put aside for the time** postpone
**put aside or postpone** shelve
**put a stop to** end
**put a stop to affection** estrange
**put at a disadvantage** penalise, upstage
**putative** academic, accepted, alleged, assumed, conjectural, established, fabled, hypothetical, imaginary, imputed, presumed, pretended, reputed, soi-disant (F), supposed
**put at risk** endanger, jeopardise
**put away** bestow, certify, commit, consume, deposit, devour, discard, drink, eat, hoard, imprison, institutionalise, remove, replace, return, save, slaughter, store, stow, tidy
**put away for future use** store
**put away in safe place** stash
**put away sword** sheathe
**put back** defer, delay, postpone, replace, reschedule, restore
**put back a grade** demote
**put ball into play** kick-off, serve
**put behind bars** confine, detain, imprison, jail
**put between** insert
**put beyond doubt** manifest

**put burden on** load, strain
**put by** save, store
**put by itself** isolate
**put cash into shares** invest
**put down** condemn, contemn, crush, defeat, deflate, degrade, deposit(ed), deprecate, depress, despise, destroy, disdain, dismiss, dispraise, disvalue, enter, humble, humiliate, inscribe, kill, laid, lay, log, mortify, note, quell(ed), record, register, reject, report, repress, ridicule, shame, silence, slight, snub, squash, stamp, state, suppress, topple, transcribe, whither
**put down tiles** lay
**put down to** attribute
**put forged bank notes into operation** utter
**put forth** advertise, assert, exert, insist, present, propagate, propose, submit, use
**put forth effort** exert
**put forth flowers** blossom
**put forth shoots** sprout
**put forward** advance, allege, assert, introduce, move, nominate, offer, present, press, propose, recommend, submit, suggest, table, tender
**put forward as a possibility** suggest
**put forward for consideration** propose, submit
**put forward to conceal the reality** ostensible
**put in** consume, enter, induct, initiate, inject, input, insert, insinuate, install, interject, interpose, introduce, ordain, spend, submit
**put in an appearance** attend
**put in case** encase
**put in chains** manacle
**put in charge** entrust(ed)
**put in cipher** encode
**put in circulation** publish
**put in dossier** file
**put in envelope with letter** enclose
**put in force** legislate
**put in forgotten place** mislaid
**put in gathers** shirr
**put in good word for** recommend
**put in harm's way** endanger
**put in hiding place** secreted
**put in jeopardy** imperil
**put in mind** connote, recall, remind, suggest
**put in order** arrange, array, neaten, settle, sort
**put in place** position, set, situate
**put in plain English** paraphrase, translate
**put in position** posit, set

**put in quarantine** isolate
**put in row** align
**put in scabbard** bayonet, sword
**put in seed** sow
**put in service** use
**put in storage** bin, store
**put in straightjacket** restrict
**put in the ground** inter, plant
**put in the shade** outshine
**put into action** activate, actuate, practise, start, use
**put into cipher** encode
**put into circulation** issue
**put into danger** imperil
**put into difficulty** embarrass
**put into effect** actioned, enforce, implement
**put into liquid** dip, immerse
**put into motion** actuate
**put into operation** actuate, implement, use
**put into print** publish
**put into required order** arrange
**put into rhyme** versify
**put into secret store** stash
**put into service** use
**put into words** express, say, speak
**put into working order** organise
**put in trance** hypnotise, mesmerise
**put in type** print, set
**put in vessel** pot
**put knife away** sheathe
**put life into** animate, inspirit
**put money in account** deposit
**put money on** bet
**put more bullets in** reload
**put off** adjourn, avoid, confuse, daunt, defer, delay, demoralise, deter, disconcert, discourage, dishearten, dismay, dissuade, distract, distress, divert, forestall, hinder, nauseate, postpone, procrastinate, repel, reschedule, retard, shelve, unsettle
**put off till tomorrow** procrastinate
**put off track** derail, mislead
**put off until later** postpone, procrastinate
**put on** act, add, affect, affix, anoint, apply, assume, attach, attire, back, bet, clothe, deceive, depict, dissemble, do, don, dramatise, dress, fake, falsify, feign, gain, impose, mislead, mount, overact, perform, place, present, pretend, produce, provide, sham, simulate, smear, stage, stake, wager
**put on airs** pose
**put on belt** girt
**put on board ship** embark
**put on burst of speed** sprint
**put on cake** icing
**put on clothes** dress, don

**put on desert island** maroon
**put on different course** reroute
**put on display** array(ed), exhibit, illuminate, mount, show
**put one's feet up** rest
**put one's finger on** find, identify, recall, remember
**put one's foot down** insist
**put one's foot in one's mouth** blunder
**put one's mind to** cogitate, focus
**put one's shoulder to the wheel** endeavour, strive
**put one's signature to** sign
**put on guard** alert, warn
**put on island** enisle
**put on pedestal** dignify, exalt, glorify, idealise, idolise, worship
**put on short allowance** scant
**put on show** exhibit
**put on tape** record
**put on the air** broadcast
**put on the Ritz** peacock, pose, posture
**put on the shelf** defer, delay, postpone, prorogue, shelve
**put on to** inform
**put on to ledge** shelve
**put on trial** arraign
**put on weight** fatten, gain
**put out** anger, announce, annoy, badger, bother, broadcast, circulate, confound, disadvantage, disconcert, dismiss, disturb, douse, embarrass, evict, exasperate, expel, extinguish, hurt, inconvenience, irk, irritate, issue, offend, oust, peeved, pester, publish, quench, release, smother, trouble, upset, vexed
**put out forged banknotes** utter
**put out of action** immobilise, stop
**put out of existence** destroy
**put out of joint** dislocate, luxate
**put out of place** displace, mislay
**put out of shape** distort
**put out of sight** hide
**put out of tune** detune, scordato
**put pen to paper** write
**put poison in** envenom
**put pressure on** press
**put pressure on to extort** bite
**putrefaction** decay, decomposition, disintegration, rot
**putrefy** addle, curdle, decay, decompose, defile, deteriorate, disintegrate, fester, moulder, rot, spoil, stale, suppurate, taint
**putrefying** septic
**putrefying flesh** carrion
**putrescent** decaying, decomposing, rotten, rotting, stinking
**putrid** bad, contaminated, corrupt, decayed, decomposed, dirty, faecal, feculent, f(o)etid, filthy, foul, impure,

loathsome, mouldy, musty, nasty, nauseating, noisome, noxious, off, offensive, polluted, rancid, rank, rotten, slimy, sour, spoiled, squalid, sullied, unclean, vile
**putrid flesh** carrion
**putrid odour** f(o)etor, stench
**put right** (a)mend, correct, rectify, redress
**put round** wrap
**put sample in the mouth** taste
**put side by side** juxtapose
**put six feet under** bury, inter
**put someone in his or her place** humble, humiliate, mortify
**put someone into the shade** beat, exceed, excel, outrival, outstrip, overshadow, trump
**put something on** add
**put strain on** task
**put tennis ball into play** serve
**put the finger on** betray, tattle
**put the pressure on** necessitate
**put the top on** cap
**put the wind up** alarm, discourage, frighten, panic, scare
**put things into suitcase** pack
**put thought into words** express
**put through** accomplish, achieve, compass, complete, conclude, dispatch, execute, finalise, finish, manage, realise, terminate
**putting area** green
**put to a purpose** use
**put to death** crucify, execute, kill, murder
**put to extreme pain** torment
**put to flight** crush, discomfit, disperse, overrun, overthrow, overwhelm, panic, rout, scatter, stampede, subdue, trample
**put together** add, adjust, assemble, compile, frame, mix, synthesise
**put together clumsily** botch
**put together in a box** pack

**put together roughly** cobble
**put to inconvenience** trouble
**put to purpose** use
**put to rest** allay
**put to shame** abash, disgrace, eclipse, exceed, excel, outclass, outdo, outshine, outstrip, override, surpass
**put to some purpose** use
**put to the proof** assay, examination, experiment, ordeal, scrutiny, test, trial
**put to the question** ask, inquire, interrogate, query
**put to the sword** butcher, execute, kill, massacre, murder, slaughter, slay
**put to the test** examine
**put to trial** tempt
**put to trouble** inconvenience
**put to use** apply, utilise
**put under ground** bury
**put under lock and key** confine, detain, imprison, incarcerate
**put under the hammer** auctioned
**put up** accommodate, advance, affix, assemble, board, build, construct, entertain, erect, fabricate, fit, float, give, house, invest, nominate, offer, pay, pledge, present, propose, provide, raise, recommend, set, shelter, submit, supply
**put up a bet** ante
**put up a fight** resist
**put up for sale** expose, offer
**put up for sale again** resell
**put up money for** sponsor
**put upon** exploit, impose, inconvenience, obtrude, use
**put-upon** abused, beleaguered, exploited, inconvenienced, persecuted, used
**put up picture** hang
**put up tent** camp
**put up to** abet, drive, encourage, goad, incite, instigate, prompt, urge
**put up with** abear, abide, accept, acquiesce, allow, bear, brook,

condone, endure, stand, stomach, suffer, swallow, take, tolerate
**put wise** alert, notify, tell, warn
**put with** add, tolerate
**put within** enclose, inclose
**puzzle** acrostic, anagram, bewilder, confound, conundrum, crossword, dilemma, disconcertment, enigma, jigsaw, logogriph, mystery, mystify, perplex, pose, predicament, problem, puzzlement, quandary, question, riddle, uncertainty
**puzzled state** perplexity
**puzzle entry** word
**puzzle out** crack, decipher, decode, resolve, see, solve, unravel, untangle, work out
**puzzling** abstract, abstruse, bewildering, complicated, concealed, cryptic, curious, difficult, enigmatic(al), esoteric, evasive, indistinct, inexplicable, insoluble, insolvable, knotted, knotty, masked, mysterious, mystifying, nebulous, odd, peculiar, perdu, perplexing, problematic, queer, riddling, secret(ive), unexplainable, veiled
**puzzling question** poser, riddle
**puzzling situation** enigma, quandary
**puzzling technique** mystique
**puzzling thing** enigma
**pyaemia** blood-poisoning
**Pygmalion's statue** Galatea
**pygmy** bantam, dwarf, lilliputian, midget, runt
**pygmy falcon** falconet
**pygmy weapon** blowpipe
**pylon** gateway
**pyramidal heap of stones** cairn
**pyramid site** El Gîza
**pyrexia** fever
**pyromania** arson
**pyromaniac** arsonist, fire-setter, incendiary, pyrophile
**pyrosis** heartburn

# Q

**quack** assumed, bungler, cackle, charlatan, clack, cozener, crocus, empiric, fake(r), fraud, gaggle, honk, humbug, imposter, masquerader, mountebank, phoney, pretended, pretender, pseudo, swindler, ululate
**quack doctor** crocus
**quack grass** couch grass

**quack medicine** nostrum
**quadri-** tetra-
**quadrilateral** tetragon
**quadruped** ass, beast, deer, four-legged, goat, horse, sheep
**quadruped carnivore** hy(a)ena, jackal, leopard, lion
**quadruple** fourfold, quadruplex

**quadruplex** fourfold, quadruple
**quaere** query, question
**quaff** bolt, consume, devour, drain, drink, gobble, gulp, guzzle, imbibe, sip, suck, sup, swallow, swill, wolf
**quagmire** bog, difficulty, entanglement, fen, impasse, marsh, mire, morass, moss, pass, pinch, plight,

predicament, quag, quandary, quicksand, slough, swamp

**quail** blanch, blench, cower, cringe, droop, faint, falter, flinch, quake, recoil, shake, shrink, shudder, tremble

**quaint** antiquated, bizarre, charming, curious, cute, droll, eccentric, fanciful, odd, old-fashioned, outdated, outmoded, peculiar, picturesque, queer, singular, strange, twee, unique, unusual, whimsical

**quaint humour** drollery
**quaintly artistic** arty
**quaintly pleasing** cute
**quaint object** curio
**quair** book (Sc)
**quake** convulse, convulsive, cower, move, pulsate, quaver, quiver, shake, shudder, tremble, tremor, vibrate, waver, wobble
**quaking-grass** dodder-grass
**qualification** ability, accomplishment, allowance, aptitude, capability, capacity, caveat, competence, eligibility, exception, exemption, fitness, knowledge, limitation, proficiency, requirement, skill, stipulation, suitability, training
**qualified** able, accomplished, adept, adequate, au fait (F), capable, cautious, certified, competent, conditional, contingent, efficient, eligible, equipped, equivocal, experienced, expert, fit, knowledgeable, licensed, polished, practised, proficient, provisional, skilful, talented, trained, worthy
**qualified dispenser of prescribed medicine** chemist
**qualified practitioner of medicine** doctor, physician
**qualified to be chosen** eligible
**qualify** adapt, adjust, authorise, call, categorise, characterise, classify, define, delimit, describe, designate, diminish, distinguish, ease, empower, endow, equip, fit, graduate, lessen, limit, mitigate, moderate, modify, name, permit, prepare, reduce, regulate, restrain, restrict, sanction, shape, soften, soothe, suit, temper, train, vary, weaken
**quality** aspect, attribute, calibre, character(istic), class, condition, constitution, deal, description, essence, feature, grade, kind, make, mark, merit, nature, peculiarity, property, sort, superiority, trait
**quality arousing pity** pathos

**quality ascribed to person** attribute
**quality black tea** pekoe
**quality giving stability** ballast
**quality of being amusing** humour
**quality of being chaste** modesty
**quality of being funny** humour
**quality of being pious** piety
**quality of being selective** selectivity
**quality of character** mettle
**quality of compassion** mercy
**quality of deserving well** merit
**quality of mind** mentality
**quality of outline** contour
**quality of sound** tone
**quality of tone** resonance, timbre
**quality of voice** timbre
**quality suffix** -ancy
**qualm** agony, anxiety, apprehension, disbelief, disquiet, distrust, doubt, fear, hesitation, incredulity, jealousy, misgiving, mistrust, queasiness, question, reluctance, scepticism, scruple, suspicion, twinge, uncertainty, uneasiness, wariness, worry
**quandary** bewilderment, difficulty, dilemma, doubt, dubiousness, enigma, fix, intricacy, perplexity, plight, predicament, quagmire, strait, trouble, uncertainty, wavering
**quantitative** metric, numerical
**quantity** aggregate, allotment, allowance, amount, batch, breadth, bulk, capacity, content, degree, expanse, extent, greatness, length, lot(s), magnitude, mass, measure(ment), number, part, (pro)portion, quota, share, substance, sum, unit, weight, whole
**quantity allotted** quota
**quantity by which multiplicand is multiplied** multiplier
**quantity for drawing on** stock
**quantity having magnitude** scalar
**quantity lost by decrease** decrement
**quantity more than enough** abundance
**quantity of coal** keel
**quantity of electricity** unit
**quantity of fish** catch, draft
**quantity of food at moment of swallowing** bolus
**quantity of food for one person** serving
**quantity of matter** mass
**quantity of medicine** dosage, dose
**quantity of money** sum
**quantity of paper** bundle, quire, ream
**quantity of sugar** cupful, (tea)spoonful
**quantity of yarn** ball, hank, skein
**quantity to be multiplied by another** multiplicand

**quantum leap** breakthrough
**quarantine** aloofness, detach(ment), disconnect, divorce, exile, insulate, interdict, isolate, isolation, loneliness, restrain, retirement, seclusion, segregate, segregation, separate, separation, sequester, solitude
**quarantine signal** yellow jack
**quarrel** altercation, argue, argument, bicker, brawl, breach, broil, carp, clash, commotion, conflict, contend, contention, controversy, coolness, differ(ence), disagree(ment), dispute, dissent, dissession, disturbance, feud, fight, fracas, misunderstanding, quarry, row, rupture, schism, spar, spat, squabble, strife, tiff, tumult, vendetta, wrangle
**quarreling** disagreeing, disputing, fighting, rowing, wrangling
**quarrel noisily** wrangle
**quarrel pettily** bicker
**quarrelsome** argumentative, cantankerous, cross, irascible, irritable, pugnacious, querulous, scrappy
**quarrelsome woman** termagant, vixen
**quarry** aim, excavation, game, goal, kill, mine, object(ive), pit, prey, prize, quarrel, raven, target, victim
**quart** carte, fourth, measure
**quarter** accommodate, area, bed, billet, board, country, direction, district, division, foursome, fourth, house, locality, neighbourhood, part, place, point, position, province, region, section, sector, side, spot, station, term, terrain, territory, vicinity, zone
**quarter acre** rood
**quarter circle** quadrant
**quarterly payment** quarterage
**quarter penny** farthing
**quarter phase** diphase
**quarter pint** gill
**quarter round** ovolo
**quarters** abode, accommodation, barracks, camp, casern(e), chambers, chummery, dwellings, hostel, housing, lodging, rooms, shelter
**quarters for mineworkers** compound
**quarters for troops** canton
**quarter soldiers** billet
**quarter year** trimester
**quartet** foursome, quaternity, tetrad
**quartz** agate, jasper, silica
**quartz piece** crystal
**quash** abrogate, annul, beat, cancel, destroy, disannul, discharge,

extirpate, invalidate, nullify, overrule, overturn, quell, recant, reject, rescind, reverse, revoke, subdue, supersede, undo, void
**quash action** abate
**quaver** flicker, flutter, oscillate, quiver, shake, shudder, thrill, tremble, vibrate, warble, waver, wobble
**quavering tone** vibrato
**quavering voice** tremolo
**quay** anchorage, berth, breakwater, dock, harbour, haven, jetty, levee, mole, pier, port, waterfront, wharf
**quayage** wharfage
**queasy** anxious, bilious, dainty, disgusting, dizzy, faint, fastidious, fussy, giddy, green, groggy, ill, indisposed, nauseated, nauseating, nauseous, nervous, off-colour, qualmish, queer, repulsive, revolting, sick, squeamish, uncomfortable, uneasy, unwell, worried
**Québec district** Levis
**Québec peninsula** Gaspe
**Québec vehicle** caleche
**queen** beauty, belle, consort, doyenne, empress, goddess, idol, Königin (G), mistress, monarch, princess, regina, reina (Sp), reine, ruler, sovereign
**queen Anne's lace** wild carrot
**queen city** Cincinnati
**queen of Carthage** Dido
**queen of fairies** Mas, Titania, Una
**queen of Sparta** Leda
**queen's attendants** ladies-in-waiting
**queen's daughter** princess
**queen's female offspring** princess
**queen's male offspring** prince
**queen's residence** palace
**queer** bizarre, crazy, curious, dizzy, eccentric, faint, funny, gay, giddy, ill, light-headed, mysterious, odd, peculiar, puzzling, queasy, reeling, remarkable, rum, singular, strange, unbalanced, uncommon, unconventional, unnatural, unsound, unwell, weird
**queer notion** kink
**queer person** oddity
**quell** abate, abort, allay, alleviate, appease, calm, compose, conquer, crush, defeat, dull, extinguish, overcome, overpower, overwhelm, pacify, palliate, quash, quiet, silence, squelch, stifle, subdue, subjugate, suppress, tranquillise, vanquish
**quench** allay, appease, conquer, cool, crush, destroy, extinguish, nip, quash, sate, satiate, satisfy, slake, smother, subdue, subvert, suffocate
**querulous** censorious, complaining, cross, discontented, faultfinding,

finicky, fractious, fretful, fussy, ill-natured, irritable, peevish, petulant, quarrelsome, testy, touchy, waspish, whining
**query** analyse, ask, confusion, dilemma, dispute, examine, inquire, inquiry, interrogatory, investigate, object, poser, protest, quandary, question
**quest** adventure, aim, crusade, enquiry, enterprise, excursion, expedition, exploration, following, game, goal, hunt, investigation, journey, mission, pilgrimage, prey, pursuit, search, seeking, tracking, undertaking, venture, voyage
**question** argument, ask, challenge, contention, cross-examine, debate, difficulty, disbelieve, dispute, doubt, enquire, enquiry, examine, inquire, inquiry, interrogate, interrogation, interview, investigation, issue, misgiving, mistrust, motion, oppose, probe, problem, query, quiz, subject, suspect, theme, topic
**questionable** confusing, controversial, controvertible, cryptic, debatable, disputable, doubtful, dubious, mysterious, mystifying, obscure, oracular, problematic(al), puzzling, uncertain, unconvincing, undecided, vague
**questionable authenticity** apocryphal
**question ambiguously worded** riddled
**questioner** agnostic, disbeliever, doubter, enquirer, examiner, interrogator, interviewer, investigator, sceptic
**question exhaustively** grill
**questionnaire** answer-sheet, test, quiz, form
**questions drawn up for formal answer** questionnaire
**quest of Ahab** Moby Dick
**queue** chain, file, line, order, pigtail, procession, row, sequence, series, string, succession, tail(back), train
**quibble** argue, bicker, carp, cavil, equivocate, evade, evasion, fence, nag, niggle, quip, spar, subterfuge
**quick** active, acute, agile, alert, fast, fleet, hasty, hurried, immediate, impatient, instantaneous, keen, lively, presto, prompt, rapid, sharp, short, snappish, snappy, speedy, sudden, swift, vigorous
**quick anatomy** vivisection
**quick and light in action** nimble, agile
**quick assets** cash
**quick at noticing things** observant
**quick blast** toot, jig
**quick blow** swat, rap

**quick counterstroke** riposte
**quick drink** snort, nip
**quicken** accelerate, activate, advance, animate, arouse, dispatch, energise, enliven, excite, expedite, galvanise, hasten, hurry, impel, incite, inspire, invigorate, precipitate, reactivate, refresh, revive, rouse, sharpen, speed, stimulate, strengthen
**quickened** accelerated, aroused, excited, expedited, hastened, hurried, impelled, incited, inspired, revived, stimulated
**quicken motion** accelerate
**quick examination** once-over
**quick-firing gun** pom-pom
**quick forward movement** career
**quick humour** wit
**quick in learning** apt, smart, intelligent
**quick in movement** agile, nimble
**quick jerk** yank
**quick light meal** snack
**quick, light, tapping feet** patter
**quick look** peep, glance, peek, glimpse, scry
**quickly** abruptly, allegro, apace, cito (L), directly, erelong, hurriedly, immediately, instantly, instantaneously, presto, promptly, pronto, rapidly, slapdash, straight away, swiftly
**quickly accomplished** rapid
**quickly fading** evanescent
**quickly fried in hot pan with little fat** sauté
**quickly passing away** transient
**quick meal** snack
**quick movement** dart
**quick movement to avoid something** dodge
**quick-moving** agile
**quickness of perception** acumen
**quickness of understanding** intelligence
**quick on the feet** nimble
**quick punch** jab, clip
**quick response** reflex
**quick return thrust in fencing** riposte
**quick, sharp reply** riposte
**quick, sharp sound** snap
**quicksilver** mercury
**quick snooze** (cat)nap
**quick stroke** dab
**quick swim** dip
**quick tempered** irascible, moody
**quick to evaporate** volatile
**quick to learn** apt, smart
**quick to notice** observant
**quick to take advantage** smart
**quick twisting movement** wriggle
**quick witticism** sally
**quick witty reply** repartee

**quid of tobacco** cud
**quid pro quo** compensation, equivalent, exchange, reprisal, retaliation
**quiescence** inactivity
**quiescent** calm, dormant, inactive, latent, placid, resting, serene, undisturbed, unmoving
**quiescent state** repose
**quiet** calm, composed, contended, dumb, even-tempered, gentle, hush(ed), inaudible, low, lull, mild, motionless, noiseless, pacific, pacify, peace(ful), placid, reserved, rest(ful), retiring, serene, sh, shy, silence, silent, smooth, soft, soundless, still(ness), subdued, thoughtful, tranquil, uncommunicative, undisturbed, unforthcoming, untroubled
**quiet and inconspicuous** sober
**quiet and serious** staid
**quiet arrogance** cheek
**quiet attitude to life** quietism
**quieten** allay, appease, blunt, compose, dull, hush, muffle, quell, silence, stifle, still, subdue
**quieting pain** analgesic
**quiet laugh** chuckle
**quietness** calm, noiselessness, peace, quietude, rest, serenity, silence, stillness, tranquillity
**quietness of mind** peace
**quiet period** lull
**quill-feather of bird's wing** flag
**quilt** bed quilt, bedcover, bedspread, caddow, counterpane, cover(let), duvet, eider(down), pad
**quilting made by filling stitched areas with padding** trapunto
**quilt stuffed with eider feathers** duvet, eiderdown
**quinacrine** mepacrine
**quinine source** cinchona
**quinine water** tonic
**quintal** hundredweight
**quintessence** backbone, core, elixir, essence, essentiality, exemplar, extract, heart, kernel, marrow, perfection, pith, quiddity, spirit, truth
**quintet** duet, five(some), orchestra, pentad, quintuplet
**quintuple** fivefold
**quip** badinage, epigram, equivocation, gibe, jape, jest, joke, mot, pleasantry, pun, quibble, repartee, retort, squib, witticism
**quirk** aberrance, aberration, abnormality, chicanery, contortion, convolution, curve, elusion, idiosyncrasy, manoeuvre, oddity, particularity, rarity, sham, spiral, subterfuge, trait, twist, whim
**quirky** eccentric
**quisling** betrayer, collaborationist, conspirator, deceiver, deserter, informer, Judas, rebel, renegade, subversive, traitor, turncoat
**Quisling's crime** treason
**quit** abandon, cease, decamp, depart, desert, desist, disappear, discontinue, drop, end, evacuate, exit, forsake, free, go, halt, leave, liberated, released, relinquish, renege, renounce, repudiate, resign, retire, rid, stop, surrender, suspend, vacate, vanish, withdraw
**quite** certainly, completely, entirely, exceedingly, extremely, fairly, highly, indeed, perfectly, positively, rather, remarkably, totally, truly, utterly, vastly, very, wholly
**quite a few** several
**quite a knack** talent
**quite blind** stone-blind
**quite clear** lucid, obvious, plain, simple
**quite convinced** cocksure
**quite enough** ample, plenty
**quite firm** adamant
**quite openly** overtly
**quite saleable** commercial
**quite tasty** palatable
**quit** ceases, discontinues, drops, ends, halts, resigns, retires, stops, surrenders, suspends, withdraws
**quits** equal, even, level, square
**quit the premises** vacate
**quiver** beat, convulse, flop, fluctuate, jerk, move, oscillate, oscillation, palpitate, pound, pulsate, quake, quaver, shake, shiver, shudder, throb, toss, tremble, trembling, tremor, twitch, undulate, vibrate, vibration, waggle, wave
**quivering motion** tremor
**quiver with fear** tremble
**quixotic** dreamy, high-flown, idealistic, imaginary, impracticable, improbable, romantic, theoretical, unrealistic, unworkable, utopian, visionary, whimsical, wild
**quiz** ask, catechise, catechism, cross-examine, debrief, enquire, examination, examine, grill, inquire, interrogate, investigate, investigation, pump, question(ing), questionnaire, test
**quiz in court** cross-examine
**quiz judge** panellist
**quiz jury** panel
**quizzical** aberrant, absurd, comical, deviate, eccentric, fanciful, lost, odd, outlandish, peculiar, perplexed, queer, sarcastic, sardonic, satirical, strange, weird, whimsical, wry
**quod** court, imprison, jail, prison
**quod erat demonstrandum** QED
**quoin** coign(e), cornerstone
**quoit that falls round peg** ringer
**quota** aggregate, allocation, allotment, allowance, intake, limit, lot, part, percentage, (pro)portion, quantity, quantum, ration, share
**quotation** charge, citation, classicus, cost, cutting, estimate, excerpt, extract, figure, passage, piece, price, quote, rate, reference, tender
**quote** adduce, allege, allude, cite, demand, duplicate, evaluate, example, excerpt, exemplify, extract, illustrate, instance, mention, note, price, recall, recollect, refer, repeat, retell, substantiate
**quote as authority** cite
**quotient of two numbers** ratio

# R

**Ra** sun-god
**Rabat is there** Morocco
**rabbis collectively** rabbinate
**rabbit** angora, bunny, con(e)y, cottontail, hare, jack rabbit
**rabbit colony** warren
**rabbit coop** hutch
**rabbit fever** tularaemia
**rabbit fur** con(e)y
**rabbit hut** hutch
**rabbit's home** hole, warren
**rabbit's kin** hare
**rabbit's tail** scut
**rabble** commoners, crowd, dregs, gang, herd, hoi-polloi, horde, mob, peasantry, proletariat, ragtag, riff-raff, rout, scene, scum, surge, swarm, throng, trash, vermin
**rabble-rouser** agent provocateur (F), agitator, demagogue, fomenter, incendiary, inciter, instigator, insurgent, provoker, rebel, ringleader, troublemaker
**rabble-rousing** demagoguery, sedition
**rabid** ardent, berserk, fanatical, fervent, frenzied, furious, headstrong, hydrophobic, livid, mad, maniacal, raging, unreasoning, violent, wild, zealous
**rabid devotee** fan
**rabies** hydrophobia
**raccoon-like animal** coati, panda
**race** advance, ancestry, breed, children, clan, class, competition, contest, course, descent, family, folk, generation, genus, hasten, humanity, humankind, hurry, lap, line, marathon, nation, people, progeny, progress, rally, relay, run, scurry, species, speed, sprint, spurt, steeplechase, stream, tribe, wisk
**race an engine** rev
**racecourse** circuit, circus, course, hippodrome, lap, race(track), round, route, speedway, track, turf
**racecourse circuit** lap
**racecourse official** steward
**raced** galloped, hurried, ran, sped, speeded, tore, torn
**race faster than** outrun
**racehorse unlikely to win** outsider
**race in which extra weight is carried by some horses** handicap
**race murder** genocide
**race of women warriors** Amazon
**racer** flier, mudder, speeder, trotter
**racetrack** speedway

**racetrack fence** rail
**racetrack tipster** tout
**racial** ancestral, ethnic(al), ethnological, folk, genealogical, genetic, inherited, national, tribal
**racial enclave** ghetto
**racial segregation** apartheid
**racial slum** ghetto
**raciness** headiness, liveliness, ribaldry, spiritedness
**racing bird** pigeon
**racing boat** scull
**racing circuit** lap
**racing dog** greyhound, whippet
**racing great** Fangio, Piggott, Senna
**racing tout** urger
**racing vehicle** kart
**racism** chauvinism, fanaticism, intolerance, prejudice, racialism, unfairness
**rack** agonise, agony, crib, distress, force, frame(work), strain, torment, torture, wrest
**racket** ballyhoo, bat, business, commotion, con, deception, din, dissipation, disturbance, dodge, excitement, fiddle, fraud, fuss, gaiety, game, hilarious, hubbub, hullabaloo, hype, intimidation, loudness, merrymaking, noise, outcry, pandemonium, proceeding, racquet, row, scheme, shouting, swindle, trick, tumult, uproar, violence
**racket game** badminton, squash, tennis
**racket game venue** court
**raconteur** anecdotist, fabulist, narrator, romancer, storyteller
**racoon-like flesh-eating mammal** coati
**racy** animated, boisterous, breezy, broad, buoyant, dubious, dynamic, energetic, entertaining, enthusiastic, exciting, exhilarating, heady, indecent, indelicate, lively, naughty, ribald, rich, risqué, sharp, sparkling, spicy, spirited, strong, suggestive
**radar beacon** racon
**radar display** scan
**radar image** blip
**radial bar of wheel** spoke
**radially symmetrical** actinomorphic
**radial or retread** tyre
**radiance** brightness, brilliance, delight, gaiety, glare, gleam, glitter, glow, happiness, incandescence, joy, light, lustre, pleasure, rapture, resplendence, shine, splendour, warmth

**radiant** aglow, alight, beaming, bright, brilliant, delighted, ecstatic, effulgent, gleaming, glittering, glorious, glowing, happy, illuminated, joyful, joyous, luminous, lustrous, resplendent, shining, sparkling, splendid, sunny
**radiant gloss** lustre
**radiate** beam, circulate, diffuse, disperse, disseminate, divaricate, diverge, emanate, emit, glitter, glow, irradiate, issue, pour, scatter, scintillate, shine, sparkle, spread, twinkle
**radiating** centrifugal, efferent
**radiation** beam, diffusion, discharge, ejection, emanation, emission, exhalation, gleam, glimmer, glint, glow, issuance, issue, ray, shaft, streak, stream
**radiation with a frequency of under one metre** microwave
**radiator** heater
**radical** basic, complete, deep-seated, entire, essential, excessive, extreme, extremist, fanatical, fundamental, innate, left-winger, militant, native, natural, original, profound, severe, sweeping, thorough, violent
**radical acid** ac(et)yl
**radical derived from ethane** ethyl
**radical person** extremist
**radical socialism** leftism
**radicle** root(let)
**radio** air, beam, broadcast, radiocast, radiotelegraph, receiver, relay, send, shortwave, show, televise, transistor, transmit, wireless
**radio acknowledgement** roger
**radioactive element** actinium, plutonium, radium, thorium, uranium
**radioactive gas** radon
**radioactive isotope of carbon** radiocarbon
**radioactive ore** uranium
**radio award** Artes
**radio crackling** static
**radio detecting instrument** radar
**radio disturbance** static
**radio inventor** Marconi
**radiology** roentgenology
**radio navigational system** loran
**radio receiving set** wireless
**radio static** interference
**radio telegram** aerogram
**radio telescope reflector** dish
**radiotherapy** actinotherapy

**radio, TV and press** media
**radio user** listener
**radio valve** diode
**radio wave reflected from the ionosphere** sky wave
**radio worker** announcer, DJ
**radius times two** diameter
**radix** base, etymon, radicle, root
**radix of the decimal system** ten
**radon** niton
**raffish** disorderly, disreputable, dissipated-looking
**raffle** draw, lot(tery), sweep(stake), tombola
**raft** catamaran, float, pontoon, rowing boat
**rafter** beam, cantilever, crossbeam, girder, joist, lintel, plank, spar, support, timber
**raft of floating logs** catamaran
**rag** admonish, annoy, badger, berate, bully, chaff, chide, irritate, jive, remnant, reproach, ridicule, scold, scrap, shmatte (Y), shred, tat(ter), taunt, tease, torment, upbraid
**rag doll** golliwog, moppet
**rage** anger, ardour, craze, desire, destruction, enthusiasm, eruption, fad, fashion, frenzy, fume, fury, infatuation, ire, libido, mania, mode, paddy, rant, rave, storm, temper, tumultuousness, turbulence, vehemence, violence
**rage for writing** furor scrinendi (L)
**ragged** disorganised, erratic, fragmented, frayed, irregular, jagged, mean, notched, poor, rent, ripped, rough, scraggy, scruffy, serrated, shabby, tattered, tatty, threadbare, torn, uneven, unkempt, worn-out
**ragged article** tat
**ragged clothes** tats
**ragged fellow** tatterdemalion
**raging** ebullient, enraged, fanatical, feverish, flaming, frantic, frenzied, fretting, fuming, furious, incensed, infuriated, irate, ireful, irrational, rabid, raving, savage, seething, storming, tempestuous, upset, violent, wild
**raging fire** blaze, conflagration, inferno, wildfire
**raging stream** torrent
**ragout** bredie, goulash, haricot, salmi(s), stew
**ragtime piano music** honky-tonk
**ragweed plant** ira
**ragworm** nereis
**rah!** cheer
**raid** assail, assault, attack, charge, desolate, forage, foray, incursion, inroad, intrude, invade, invasion, irruption, loot, maraud, onset, onslaught, pillage, plunder(ing), ransack, seizure, sortie, strip, trespass
**raider** attacker, brigand, despoiler, forager, invader, looter, marauder, pirate, plunderer, ransacker, reiver, robber, sacker, thief
**rail** balustrade, banister, banter, bar, complain, crosspiece, denounce, deterrent, hindrance, impediment, inveigh, line, obstacle, paling, pole, rant, rave, rod, scoff, shaft, stake, stick, stop, track
**rail against** inveigh, revile
**rail bird** sora
**railing** balustrade, barrier, berating, bulasters, fence, fencing, inveighing, nagging, paling, palisade, parapet, rails, ranting, reviling, scolding, stakes, upbraiding
**rail in law-court** bar
**raillery** badinage, banter, burlesque, chaff, derision, drollery, fun, gibe, humour, irony, jeer, lampoon, laughter, levity, mockery, parody, persiflage, pleasantry, repartee, ridicule, sarcasm, satire, teasing, waggery, wit, wordplay
**rail of cart** rave
**rail on stairs** banister
**railroad locomotive** engine
**railroad support** trestle
**rail round ship's stern** taffrail
**rail support** sleeper
**railtracks** tramlines, tramways
**rail transport** train, tram
**rail vehicle** funicular, train, tram
**railway** line, metro, railroad, rails, subway, track, tramway, tube, underground
**railway carriage** coach
**railway control building** signalbox
**railway engine** locomotive
**railway maintenance worker** fettler
**railway official** stationmaster
**railway saloon car with luxurious equipment** Pullman
**railway system** network
**railway track supporter** sleeper
**railway truck** wagon
**railway worker** porter, shunter
**raiment** apparel, attire, clothes, clothing, costume, dress, ensemble, garb, garments, gear, habits, outfit, ray, togs, vestments, vesture, wardrobe, wear
**rain** bucket, cloudburst, deluge, downpour, drizzle, drop, fall, flood, hail, pour, precipitation, raindrops, rainfall, shower, spit, squall, stream, teem, thunderstorm, torrent
**rain and snow** sleet
**rain boot** galosh
**rainbow** arc(h), iris
**rainbow effect in sea spray** seabow
**rainbow fish** guppy, maori
**rain cloud** nimbus
**raincoat** gaberdine, mac, mack(intosh), slicker
**rain freezingly** sleet
**rain gauge** pluviometer, udometer
**rain gust** squall
**rain heavily** pour, teem
**rain icily** sleet
**rainless period** drought
**rain lightly** mist
**rain queen of the Lobedu tribe** Mojadji, Mujaji
**rain shield** umbrella
**rainstorm** cloudburst, deluge, downpour, flood, inundation
**rainy** bad, blustery, clammy, damp, dank, dewy, disagreeable, drenched, drippy, drizzly, foggy, foul, humid, misty, moist, murky, pouring, raining, rough, showery, soaked, stormy, teeming, wet(tish), wild
**rainy season of South Asia** monsoon
**raisable river crossing** drawbridge
**raise** advance, amplify, animate, arouse, assemble, awake(n), boost, breed, construct, cultivate, elevate, engender, enhance, erect, excite, gather, grow, heave, hoist, increase, intensify, invigorate, lift, originate, produce, promote, propagate, rear, rise, rouse, setup, uplift
**raise a child** rear
**raise aloft** hoist
**raise an army** recruit
**raise and then dash the hopes of** tantalise
**raise, as a family** rear
**raise by assessment** levy
**raise by hand** nob
**raise by mechanical means** hoist
**raise children** rear
**raised cloth fibres** nap
**raised couch** sofa
**raised earth along river's edge** bank
**raised edge** flange, ridge, rim
**raised fibres** nap
**raised flat bank** terrace
**raised floor or platform** stage
**raised letters** Braille
**raised level space** terrace
**raised level surface** platform
**raised narrow pathway** catwalk
**raised pathway** causeway
**raised platform** dais, podium, stage, stand

**raised print for blind**  Braille
**raised ridge**  welt
**raised road**  causeway, viaduct
**raised road across piece of water**  causeway
**raised strip**  ridge
**raised wooden shoe**  patten
**raise flag**  hoist
**raise from the dead**  resurrect, resuscitate, revive, revivify
**raise in price**  enhance
**raise in rank**  ennoble, exalt, promote
**raise in spirits**  elate
**raise in status**  upgrade
**raise intellectually**  elevate
**raise in value**  upgrade
**raise livestock**  breed
**raise morale**  boost
**raise objection**  except
**raise objections**  boggle, cavil, demur
**raise one's glass to**  toast
**raise pedigreed dogs**  breed
**raise petty objections**  carp, cavil
**raise shoulders**  shrug
**raise the roof**  complain, gripe, grumble, grump
**raise the shoulders**  shrug
**raise the spirits of**  elate
**raise to a higher rank**  promote
**raise to a noble rank**  ennoble
**raise to heights**  exalt
**raise to the third power**  cube
**raise up**  elate, elevate, exalt, extol
**raising agent**  yeast
**raising pattern**  embossing
**raj**  rule, sovereignty
**rajah's wife**  ranee, rani
**rake**  accumulate, amass, collect, debauchee, drag, examine, forage, gather, graze, grub, harrow, hoe, hunt, implement, lecher, libertine, loosen, playboy, profligate, ransack, rascal, remove, roué, scan, scour, scrape, scratch, scrutinise, search, sport, strafe, sweep
**rake in**  (a)mass, collect, gather
**rally**  assemble, collect, convene, convocation, gather(ing), marshal, meeting, muster, organise, re-form, reassemble, recover, recuperate, regroup, renewal, reunion, revive, stand, summon, unite
**rallying cry**  slogan
**rally of Boy Scouts**  jamboree
**ram**  Aries, beat, butt, cram, crash, crowd, dash, drive, drum, force, hammer, hit, impact, jam, pack, piston, pound, push, smash, strike, stuff, thrust, tup
**ramble**  amble, excursion, gad, gallivant, meander, roam, rove, saunter, stray, stroll, walk, wander

**rambler**  drifter, globetrotter, hiker, roamer, rover, stroller, walker, wanderer, wayfarer
**rambling**  circuitous, digressive, disconnected, drifting, incoherent, irregular, long-drawn-out, long-winded, ranging, roaming, roving, sauntering, sprawling, spreading, straggling, trailing, wordy
**rambling composition**  rhapsody
**rambling talk**  rigmarole
**ramification**  branch(ing), complication, configuration, consequence, derivative, development, division, effect, end, eventuation, extension, forking, implication, limb, offshoot, radiation, repercussion, result, sequel, sprig, sprout, subtlety, twig, upshot
**rammed earth**  pisé
**ramose**  branched, branching
**ramp**  ascent, declivity, dip, grade, gradient, incline, plane, rise, slope
**rampage**  amok, destruction, frenzy, fury, rage, rant, rave, roar, rush, storm, tear, tempest, tumult, turmoil, uproar, upset, violence
**rampager**  rioter
**rampant**  aggressive, dominant, excessive, flagrant, outrageous, riotous, unbridled, ungovernable, unrestrained, vehement
**rampart**  abat(t)is, agger, barbican, barricade, bastion, battlement, breastwork, bulwark, defence, fence, fort(ification), guard, line, parapet, rampier, security, stronghold, vallum, wall
**ramshackle**  crumbling, decrepit, derelict, deteriorating, dilapidated, flimsy, haywire, jerry-built, rickety, shaky, tottering, tumbledown, unsafe, unsteady
**ram's-horn trumpet used in Jewish religious ceremonies**  shofar, shophar
**ram's mate**  ewe
**ranch**  estate, farm, hacienda, plantation, station
**rancher**  cattleman
**ranch house**  homestead
**rancid**  bad, decayed, decomposed, f(o)etid, foul, fusty, mouldy, musty, off, putrid, rank, rotten, sour, spoiled, stale, tainted, turned
**rancorous**  bitter, implacable, malevolent, malicious, resentful, spiteful, vindictive, virulent
**rancour**  acrimony, anger, animosity, aversion, bitterness, distaste, enmity, fury, gall, hate, hatred, indignation, malevolence, malice, resentment, spite, venom

**Rand**  Reef
**randan**  spree
**random**  accidental, aimless, aleatory, arbitrary, careless, casual, chance, disorganised, fortuitous, haphazard, incidental, irregular, occasional, orderless, serendipitous, sporadic, spot, stray, unarranged, undesigned, unplanned
**random few**  some
**rands and cents**  money
**randy**  beggar, boisterous, disorderly, lustful, riotous, scold, vagrant, virago
**range**  align, amplitude, area, arrange, array, bounds, class(ify), compass, dispose, distance, domain, extend, extent, field, gamut, kind, latitude, lie, limits, line, margin, occupy, opportunity, orbit, order, queue, race, rank, reach, register, roam, rove, row, run, scope, sort, span, stove, sweep, trace, wander
**range about**  prowl
**range from which to choose**  selection
**range of activity**  scope
**range of arrow**  flight
**range of food**  fare
**range of frequencies**  spectrum
**range of gun**  carry, gunshot, random
**range of hills**  backbone, chain, ridge, sierra
**range of knowledge**  ken
**range of physical vision**  purview
**range of sight**  eyeshot, ken, scan
**range of tones**  key, scale
**range of voice**  alto
**range of wavelength**  band
**range over**  sweep
**ranger**  bushfighter, forester, keeper, warden, warder
**Rangoon is there**  Burma
**rank**  absolute, abundant, align, arrange(ment), array, body, class(ify), complete, dignity, dispose, distinction, division, eminence, exuberant, gamy, level, line, membership, noxious, offensive, order, position, pungent, rancid, range, row, series, sort, standing, station, tier, utter, vigorous
**rank above army captain**  major
**rank above colonel**  general
**rank and file**  commonalty, community, majority, mass(es), participants, populace, soldiers, troops
**rank between marquis and viscount**  earl
**rank imposes obligations**  noblesse oblige
**rank in tennis**  seed

**rankle** anger, annoy, chafe, embitter, fester, gall, irk, irritate, nettle, rile
**rank next under abbot** prior
**rank of angels** seraphim
**rank of Islamic ruler** emirate
**rank of society** class
**rank of tribal patriarch** patriarchate
**rank or order of persons** class
**rank-smelling** f(o)etid, olid, smelly
**rank-tasting** rancid
**ransack** comb, gut, loot, pillage, plunder, raid, ravage, rifle, rummage, sack, scour, search, strip
**ransom** compensation, deliver, deliverance, extricate, fine, free(ing), liberate, liberty, payment, penalty, price, recoupment, redeem, redemption, release, reprieve, rescue, restoration, restore
**rant** bellow, bluster, bombast, cry, declaim, diatribe, discourse, expound, fume, harangue, orate, perorate, rage, rave, rhetoric, scolding, shout, speechify, tirade, tumidity, turgidity, vociferation, yell
**rant and rave** rage, seethe
**ranting** fuming, yelling
**rap** bang, bash, bat(ter), beat, blow, box, buffet, bump, clatter, crash, hammer, hit, knock, pound, punch, slam, smack, strike, stroke, swat, thump, wallop, whack
**rapacious** avaricious, devouring, extortionate, grasping, greedy, looting, marauding, pillaging, plundering, predacious, predatory, preying, ravenous, voracious, wolfish
**rapacious bird** hawk, jaeger, skua
**rapacious fish** piran(h)a
**rapacious person** harpy, shark
**rape** abuse, assault, cole(-seed), deflower, maltreatment, oil-seed, rapine, ravish(ment), violate, violation
**rape plant** colza
**rapid** active, agile, agitated, brisk, express, fast, fleet, flying, galloping, hasty, headlong, hurried, mosso, precipitate, presto, prompt, quick, speedy, sudden, swift
**rapid change of pitch** tremolo
**rapid explosive noise** chug
**rapid gasp** pant
**rapid glance** coup d'oeil (F)
**rapid heartbeats** palpitations
**rapidity** abruptness, acceleration, agility, apace, briskness, celerity, dispatch, expedition, fastness, fleetness, haste, hurry, pace, promptness, quickness, race, run, rush, scamper, scramble, scurry, speed, swiftness, urgency, velocity

**rapidity of movement** celerity, quickness, speed
**rapid keyboard composition** toccata
**rapidly** directly, double-quick, expeditiously, headlong, hurriedly, instantly, rashly, speedily, suddenly, unexpectedly
**rapidly-growing plant** filler
**rapidly-swirling water** whirlpool
**rapid population increase** explosion
**rapid rise or swell** upsurge
**rapid speech** patter
**rapid succession of questions** barrage
**rapid survey of a subject** apercu
**rapier** épée, sword
**rapine** burglary, depredation, despoilment, fraud, freebooting, hijacking, hold-up, larceny, pillage, piracy, plagiarism, plunder, raid, rape, raven, robbery, sack, stealing, swindle, theft
**rap over knuckles** reprimand
**rapping sound** rat-tat(-tat)
**rapport** affection, affinity, alliance, amity, attachment, benevolence, bond, closeness, communication, companionship, compatibility, concord, connection, conviviality, empathy, familiarity, fellowship, fondness, fraternity, friendship, harmony, intimacy, love, regard, relationship, sympathy, togetherness, understanding
**rapt** absorbed, abstracted, bewitched, captivated, charmed, consumed, delighted, ecstatic, elated, enchanted, engrossed, enraptured, enthralled, entranced, fascinated, gripped, happy, held, immersed, intent, jubilant, occupied, ravished, spellbound, transported
**rapt in thought** absorbed, engrossed, reflective
**rapture** beatitude, bliss, delectation, delight, ecstasy, elation, elysium, enchantment, euphoria, exaltation, excitation, exhilaration, felicity, fun, gladness, happiness, heaven, joy, pleasure, spell, thrill, transport, Utopia
**rapturous** blissful, charmed, content, delighted, ecstatic, elated, enchanted, enraptured, enthusiastic, euphoric, excited, felicitous, gratified, orgasmic, pleased, ravished, satisfied, transported
**rapturous happiness** bliss
**rare** admirable, excellent, exceptional, exquisite, extraordinary, incomparable, infrequent, inimitable, precious, scarce, singular, sparse, sporadic, super(lative), uncommon, underdone, unique, unusual
**raree** peepshow, raree show
**rarefied** clannish, cleansed, cliquish, eminent, esoteric, exclusive, high, lofty, noble, private, prominent, refined, select(ive), snobbish, sublime
**rarefy** attenuate, clarify, cleanse, distil, filter, process, purify, refine, subtle
**rare hard white metallic element** ruthenium
**rare inert gaseous element** distinctively, exceptionally, krypton, notably, remarkably, wonderfully
**rare meat** underdone
**rare metal** molybdenum
**rare object** curio(sum)
**rare pleasure** treat
**rare vulture** lammergeier, lammergeyer
**raring** agog, anxious, ardent, athirst, desperate, eager, earnest, enthusiastic, fervent, greedy, hungry, impatient, intent, itching, keen, longing, ready, willing, yearning, zealous
**raring to go** panting
**rarity** abnormality, anomaly, curiosity, greatness, infrequency, occasionalness, oddity, rareness, scantness, tenuity, uniqueness, value, wonder, worth
**rascal** blackguard, cad, cur, dastard, devil, disgrace, dishonest, imp, knave, mean, miscreant, paltry, rake, rapscallion, reprobate, rogue, scalawag, scallywag, scamp, scapegrace, scoundrel, skelm, spalpeen, trickster, varlet, villain, wag, wastrel
**rascally** arch, disreputable, elfin, good-for-nothing, impish, knavish, mischievous, naughty, puckish, reprobate, roguish, scoundrelly, sportive, unscrupulous, villainous, waggish, wicked
**rascally lawyer** pettifogger
**rase** demolish, destroy, erase, level, raze
**rash** adventurous, audacious, careless, dermatitis, eczema, epidemic, eruption, foolhardy, hasty, headlong, headstrong, heady, heedless, hotheaded, ill-advised, ill-considered, impetuous, imprudent, impulsive, incautious, indiscreet, outbreak, plague, reckless, thoughtless, unguarded, unthinking, unwary
**rash impetuous person** hothead
**rashness** carelessness, hastiness, heedlessness, hot-headedness,

impetuosity, impetuousness, impulsiveness, incautiousness, recklessness

**rash speed** haste

**rasp** abrade, agitate, burnish, creak, croak, disturb, file, furbish, grate, grating, grind(ing), groan, harshness, hiss, hoarseness, irk, irritate, jar, jolt, offend, polish, refine, rock, rub, sand, scour, scrape, scratch, screech, shape, shrill, sibilate, smooth, squeak, squeal, vibrate, wheeze, whirr, whistle, whiz

**rasp noisily** grate

**rat** blackleg, betray, bilk, default, defraud, dodge, evade, fail, neglect, rodent, scab, swindle

**ratable value** ratal

**ratchet catch** click

**rate** assess(ment), basis, berate, charge, class(ification), classify, consider, cost, count, degree, esteem, estimate, evaluate, figure, grade, measure, pace, percentage, position, price, proportion, quality, rank, rating, ratio, reckoning, relation, scale, scold, speed, standard, status, tariff, value

**rate for the job** wage

**rate highly** appreciate

**rate of activity** tempo

**rate of ascent** grade

**rate of motion** speed

**rate of movement** pace, tempo

**rate of occurrence** frequency

**rate of progress** speed

**rate of turning** spinning, strobic

**rate per hundred** percentage

**rater** assessor

**rate too low** underestimate

**rather** bit, fairly, instead, moderately, noticeably, prefer(ably), pretty, quite, relatively, significantly, slightly, somewhat, sooner, very

**rather cold** coldish

**rather ill** poorly

**rather large** considerable

**ratified agreement** treaty

**ratify** accredit, affirm, approve, attest, bind, clinch, confirm, corroborate, endorse, establish, sanction, seal, secure, substance, support, testify, validate, verify, warrant

**rating** appraising, assessing, class(ification), classing, considering, counting, degree, designation, estimate, estimating, evaluating, evaluation, grade, grading, measuring, order, placing, position, rank(ing), rate, reckoning, regarding, sort, standing, status, valuing, weighing

**rating in the navy** quartermaster

**ratio** arrangement, balance, correlation, correspondence, equation, fraction, percentage, proportion, rate, relation(ship)

**ration** allocate, allocation, allot(ment), allowance, amount, apportion, budget, conserve, control, deal, dispense, distribute, dole, food, helping, issue, limit, measure, part, portion, provision, quota, restrict, save, share, stores, supplies, supply

**rational** analytic, credible, dialectic, fair, feasible, judicious, just, logical, mental, normal, possible, reasonable, responsible, sagacious, sage, sane, sound, wise

**rationale** excuse, exegist, exposition, ground, illustration, link, logic, pretense, reason, relationship, theory, thesis

**rationalise** excuse, justify, reorganise, streamline, vindicate

**rational number** integer

**rational thought** logic

**ration out** allot, apportion, dole

**ratite bird** cassowary, cassowary, emu, kiwi, moa, ostrich, rhea, struthian

**rat-kangaroo** potoroo

**ratlike** murine

**ratlike hibernating rodent** hamster

**ratlike Australian marsupial** bandicoot

**rat poison plant** oleander

**rattan's stem** cane

**rattle** bang, blather, blether, bounce, bump, chatter, clank, clash, clatter, clink, clitter, confuse, disconcert, disturb, fluster, frighten, hurtle, jangle, jar, jiggle, jolt, rap, scare, shake, upset, vibrate

**rattlebrained** addled, addlepated, bewildered, confused, giddy, madcap, muddled, scatterbrained, unable, unstable, vague

**rattle off** list, recite, repeat

**rattle on** cackle, chatter, gab, gibber, jabber, prattle

**rattler** clatterer, rattlesnake

**rattlesnake** belltail, cascabel, sidewinder

**rattling noise** rattle

**ratty** angry, annoyed, crabbed, cross, impatient, irritable, peeved, short-tempered, snappy, touchy

**raucous** grating, harsh(-sounding), hoarse, husky, loud, noisy, rasping, rough, rowdy, strident

**raucous cry** catcall

**raucous laugh** cackle

**raunchy** earthy, lecherous, lusty, slovenly, smutty, vulgar

**ravage** damage, deflower, demolish, desolate, despoil, destroy, destruction, devastate, devastation, eat, forage, foray, havoc, loot, pillage, plunder, populate, prey, ransack, riot, ruin, sack, spoil, spoliate, waste

**rave** complimentary, compliments, enthuse, enthusiastic, excellent, fantastic, favourable, praise, rage, ramble, rant, storm, trendy, wonderful

**ravel** complicate, confuse, decipher, entangle, explicate, fray, interlace, intertwine, involve, knotted, muddle, plait, shred, snarl, tangle, twist, unfold, warrant, winnow

**Ravel composition** *Bolero*

**ravel out** disentangle, unravel

**raven** black(ish), corbie, crow, dark, ebony, inky, jet, nigrescent, nigritudinous, pitch-black, pitch-dark, sable, unlit

**ravenous** devouring, edacious, famished, greedy, hungry, lupine, marauding, plundering, predatory, preying, rapacious, raptorial, starved, starving, voracious, wolfish

**rave-up** blow-out, celebration, do, orgy, party

**ravine** abyss, canyon, chasm, cleft, coulee, crevasse, crevice, defile, gorge, gulf, gully, kloof, pass

**ravine bridge** viaduct

**raving** berserk, crazed, crazy, delirious, frantic, frenzied, furious, hysterical, insane, irrational, mad, rabid, raging, wild

**ravish** abuse, amuse, bewitch, captivate, charm, cheer, delight, divert, electrify, enchant, enrapture, enthral, entrance, fascinate, gratify, move, outrage, overjoy, please, rape, rejoice, satisfy, spell-bind, thrill, transport, violate

**ravishing** agreeable, beautiful, bewitching, blissful, brilliant, charming, congenial, dazzling, delectable, delightful, elegant, enjoyable, exquisite, glorious, gorgeous, grand, heavenly, irresistible, lovely, luxuriant, magnificent, opulent, pleasant, pleasurable, provocative, radiant, rapturous, seductive, showy, specious, splendid, stunning, sublime, sumptuous, superb, wonderful

**raw** bare, basic, bloody, bold, brutal, candid, chilly, cold, crude, fresh, grazed, green, harsh, inexperienced, naked, natural, open, plain, pure, realistic, rough, rude, scraped,

scratched, sensitive, sore, tender, uncooked, unfinished, unmade, unpractised, unprepared, unprocessed, unrefined, unripe, unskilled, untrained, untreated
**raw army recruit** roofie, rookie
**rawboned** angular, attenuated, bony, cadaverous, emaciated, gaunt, haggard, lank, lean, meagre, pinched, scraggy, scrawny, shrivelled, skinny, spare, thin, wasted
**raw fish** sashimi
**raw gold** nugget
**rawhide** birch, cane, cat, crop, horsewhip, lash, parfleche, quirt, scourge, sjambok, switch, thong, whip
**rawhide shoe** vel(d)skoen, vellies
**rawhide thong** riem(pie)
**raw material** grist, ore, staple
**raw mineral deposit** ore
**raw porridge** oats
**raw recruit** greenhorn, ignoramus, roofie, rookie, simpleton
**raw skin of sheep** pelt
**raw, smoked ham** prosciutto
**raw sugar** beet
**raw vegetable dish** salad
**ray** bar, beam, flash, flicker; glance, gleam, glint, glitter, idea, light, radiance, radiation, radius, shaft, skate, spark(le), streak, sunbeam, sunray, trace
**ray of sun** sunbeam
**ray of moonlight** moonbeam
**rayon** viscose
**rayon fabric** surah
**raze** bulldoze, demolish, destroy, devastate, dismantle, eradicate, erase, exterminate, flatten, level, obliterate, precipitate, prostrate, rase, ruin, terminate, topple
**razor** shaver
**razor blade feature** edge
**razor sharpener** strop
**re** about, concerning, on, reference, regarding, relating, respecting
**reach** accomplish, achieve, approach, arrive, attain, busy, distance, equal, extend, extent, gain, grasp, impress, influence, match, outstretch, overtake, scope, seize, span, stretch, touch
**reach across** overstride, span
**reach a destination** arrive
**reach an end** stay
**reach an understanding** agree
**reach a total** amount
**reach by effort** attain
**reach forth** extend
**reach high level** soar
**reach its highest point** culminate

**reach of thought** wisdom, wit
**reach out** spread, stretch, utter
**reach the top** arrive
**reach the zenith** peak
**reach to** line
**reach with end** abut
**react** acknowledge, answer, behave, (counter)act, ebb, function, hinder, operate, oppose, proceed, recede, reciprocate, recoil, reneg(u)e, repay, reply, respond, retort, work
**react excessively to something** overreact
**reaction** acknowledg(e)ment, answer, backlash, compensation, conservatism, counter-revolution, counteraction, counterbalance, feedback, recoil, reflex, reply, resistance, response, reversion
**reaction after impact** repercussion
**reactionary** conservative, counter-revolutionary, diehard, obstructive, reactionist, right-winger, rightist
**reactionary person** ultraconservative, verkrampte
**reaction time** latency
**reactive substance** reagent
**react to** acknowledge, respond
**read** announce, comprehend, construe, decipher, declaim, deliver, discern, discover, display, indicate, interpret, note, peruse, present, recite, record, register, scan, see, show, speak, study, understand, utter
**readable** clear, comprehensible, compulsive, construable, decipherable, deliverable, discoverable, enjoyable, entertaining, gripping, intelligible, interesting, interpretable, legible, plain, pleasant, scannable, speakable, understandable
**read carefully** peruse, scrutinise
**read carelessly** skim
**read here and there** browse
**readily touched with emotion** susceptible
**readiness** aptness, dexterity, facility, handiness, maturity, preparation, preparedness, promptitude, ripeness
**reading** analysis, announcing, decoding, diagnosis, edition, education, elucidation, enquiry, erudition, examination, exercise, explanation, grasp, homework, homily, impression, inquiry, inspection, interpretation, lecture, lesson, perusal, perusing, print, quest, recital, recitation, rendering, review, scanning, scrutiny, sermon,

study(ing), task, text, treatment, understanding, unlocking, version
**reading desk** ambo, lectern
**reading glasses** specs, spectacles
**reading list of names** roll-call
**reading matter** book, magazine, newspaper
**reading stand** ambo, lectern
**read into** assume, infer, insert, interject, interpolate, misconstrue
**readjust** accommodate, accord, adapt, integrate, poise, readapt, rearrange, reconcile, reorientate, reset, restore
**read letter by letter** spell
**read lightly** browse
**read off** dictate
**read quickly** scan
**read rapidly** dip, gobble, skim
**read slowly** spell
**read studiously** pore
**read systematically** frequent
**read thoroughly** peruse, scrutinise
**ready** accessible, adjusted, adroit, agreeable, alert, arrange(d), astute, available, cheerful, completed, convenient, disposed, eager, equip(ped), fitted, game, geared, handy, happy, inclined, keen, near, order, organise(d), present, perceptive, prepare(d), prompt, quick, ripe, set, sharp, willing
**ready a computer** boot
**ready for action** arm, expedite
**ready for anything** prepared, primed, set
**ready for marriage** nubile
**ready for picking** ripe
**ready for use** available
**readying a horse for riding** saddling
**ready-made** bought, sale
**ready-made clothing** slop
**ready money** cash
**ready perception** acumen
**ready to act** agile
**ready to be hanged** gallows-ripe
**ready to be reaped** ripe
**ready to betray** treacherous
**ready to cry** weepy
**ready to drop** tired
**ready to eat** cooked, ripe
**ready to find fault** captious, hypercritical, pedantic, priggish
**ready to go** bound, prepared, primed, set
**ready to harvest** ripe
**ready to make amends** penitent
**ready to shoot** loaded
**ready to undertake** willing
**ready to wash** soaped
**ready to wear** off the peg
**ready to wed** nubile

**ready to yield to someone's wishes** indulgent
**ready when wanted** forthcoming
**ready with words** fluent
**real** absolute, actual, authentic, bona fide, certain, essential, factual, genuine, heartfelt, honest, intrinsic, legitimate, positive, right(ful), sincere, substantial, substantive, tangible, true, unaffected, unfeigned, valid, veritable
**real estate** property, realty
**real ground of complaint** grievance
**realise** accomplish, achieve, acquire, answer, aware, complete, comprehend, conclude, conscious, discharge, do, effect(uate), execute, fill, fulfil, grasp, image, imagine, know, observe, perform, recognise, see, understand
**realism** actuality, fact, practicality, pragmatism, rationality, reality, sanity, sensibleness, truth, validity, verity
**realist** pragmatist
**realistic** authentic, commonsense, exact, faithful, genuine, lifelike, natural, no-nonsense, practical, pragmatic, rational, sensible, unidealistic, veracious
**reality** fact, genuineness, realism, truth, validity
**really** absolutely, actually, authentically, categorically, certainly, factually, genuinely, honestly, indeed, intrinsically, literally, positively, rightfully, rightly, sincerely, surely, truly, unfeignedly, validly
**really remarkable** tremendous
**realm** area, arena, battleground, bound(ary), capacity, circuit, commonwealth, community, compass, country, demesne, department, district, domain, dominion, dynasty, empire, enclosure, estate, extent, field, function, ground, kingdom, limit, locality, monarchy, nation, neighbourhood, orbit, patch, people, plot, principality, province, race, range, reach, sphere, world
**realm of fabulous richness** El Dorado
**real name** autonym
**real thing** entity
**re a nose job** rhinoplastic
**reap** acquire, collect, cut, derive, gain, garner, gather, get, harvest, obtain, win
**reaped** acquired, collected, cut, derived, gained, garnered, gathered, got, harvested, scythed, won
**re a period of ten years** decadal

**reaping hook** scythe, sickle
**reappraise** reassess
**rear** after, back(ground), behind, breed, buck, build, construct, cultivate, educate, elevate, end, erect, fabricate, following, foster, grow, hind(most), last, lift, nurse, nurture, raise, rearguard, stern, tail, train
**rear carefully** tiddle
**rear children** bear, beget
**rear end** tail
**rear gate** postern
**rearing of birds** aviculture
**rearing of fish** pisciculture
**rearing place for plants** nursery
**rear of aircraft** empennage
**rear of saddle** cantle
**rear of ship** stern
**rear orifice** anus
**rear part of male fowl's back** saddle
**rearrange** reorganise, shuffle
**reason** aim, argue, cause, convince, design, end, excuse, explanation, incentive, intellect, intelligence, intention, judg(e)ment, justification, justify, logic, logos, mind, motive, nous, objective, persuade, purpose, ratiocinate, rational(e), sanity, sense, understanding, wits
**reasonable** average, fair, fit, honest, inexpensive, intelligent, judicious, just, logical, moderate, modest, plausible, practical, proper, rational, right, sane, satisfactory, seasoned, sensible, sober, sound, tolerable, viable, well-advised, well-thought-out, wise
**reason against** argue, expostulate, object, protest, remonstrate
**reasoned exposition** rationale
**reasoned thought** logic
**reason for action** active, motive
**reason for existing** raison d'être (F)
**reason for pride** boast
**reason from facts** deduce
**reasoning** analysis, argument(ation), assumption, case, deduction, exegesis, induction, lemma, logic, proof, rationalisation, supposition, theory, thinking, thought
**reason with** argue, debate, dispute, move, persuade, protest, remonstrate, talk, urge
**reassemble** rally, re-form, regroup, reorganise, unite
**reassess** re-examine, reconsider, rethink, revalue, review, revise
**reassurance** aid, boost, cheer, consolation, encouragement, favour, help, inspiration, lift, placation, stimulation, stimulus, succour, support, uplift, urging

**reassure** assure, bolster, cheer, comfort, embolden, encourage, hearten, inspire, inspirit, satisfy, support, uplift
**rebate** allow(ance), cutback, decrease, deduct(ion), discount, reduction, refund, repay(ment), rollback, share, subtract
**rebel** agitator, apostate, brawler, defy, disobey, dissent(er), flinch, heretic, insurgent, insurrectionist, mutineer, mutinous, mutiny, nonconformist, rebellious, recoil, resist, revolt(er), revolutionary, revolutionist, rioter, schismatic, secessionist, sectarian, seditionist, shrink, traitor, turncoat
**rebel army member** guer(r)illa
**rebellion** disobedience, insurrection, resistance, revolt, revolution, rising, sedition, uprising
**rebellion against authority** mutiny
**rebellious** defiant, difficult, disloyal, disobedient, disorderly, incorrigible, insubordinate, insurgent, mutinous, obstinate, obstreperous, rebel, resistant, revolutionary, riotous, seditious, subversive, treasonable, turbulent, unruly
**rebellious seaman** mutineer
**rebel noisily** riot
**rebind a book** recover
**rebind a trunk** restrap
**rebirth** neogenesis, regeneration, renaissance, renascence, renewal, resurrection, revival
**reborn** redivivus
**rebound** bounce, dap, ebb, misfire, recoil, refection, reflex, repercussion, resonate, resound, return, ricochet
**rebound, as elastic** resile
**rebroadcast** relay
**rebuff** check, cold-shoulder, cut, decline, denial, deny, disallowance, discourage(ment), ignore, negation, opposition, refusal, refuse, reject(ion), repel, repulse, repulsion, resist, slight, snub, spurn
**rebuke** admonish, berate, blame, castigation, censure, charge, chide, chiding, disapprove, lecture, rating, reprehend, reprehension, reprimand, reproach, reproof, reprove, scold(ing), slating, snub
**rebuke severely** keelhaul
**rebuking sound** tut
**rebury** reinter
**rebut** argument, check, contradict, defeat, deny, discredit, disprove, expose, negate, refute, repel, retort, riposte, thrust
**rebuttal** alibi, answer, case, declaration, defence, denial,

**recalcitrant** exposing, negation, parry, plea(ding), puncturing, refutation, response, retaliation, retort, testimony
**recalcitrant** awkward, captious, crabby, cross, defiant, disobedient, disorderly, fractious, fretful, insubordinate, irritable, opposing, peevish, rebellious, refractory, renitent, resistance, resistive, riotous, seditious, testy, touchy, turbulent, uncompliant, undisciplined, unruly
**recall** annul, countermand, impeachment, memory, recant(ation), recollection, remember, repeal, retract, revoke, withdraw
**recall fondly** cherish
**recall memories** reminisce
**recall the course** retrace
**recant** abjure, deny, disavow, disown, recall, repudiate, retract, unsay
**recap** perorate, summarise
**recapitulate** enumerate, narrate, perorate, recite, recount, reiterate, repeat, review, reword, summarise
**re cardiac contractions** diastolic, systolic
**recede** abate, decrease, diminish, ebb, leave, regress, retire, retract, retreat, retrocede, retrograde, retrogress, reverse, submit, subside, wane, withdraw, yield
**recede as tide** ebb
**receipt** acceptance, acknowledgement, counterfoil, delivery, receiving, reception, slip, stamp, stub, taking, ticket, voucher
**receipt in full** acquittance
**receipts** earnings, emoluments, gain, gate, income, interest, means, pay(ment), proceeds, profits, remuneration, return, revenue, reward, salary, stipend, surplus, take, takings, wages, winning, yield
**receive** accept, acquire, admit, approve, collect, derive, endure, entertain, experience, gain, get, greet, inherit, obtain, pocket, realise, take, welcome
**receive a legacy** inherit
**receive an academic degree** graduate
**receive and transmit** relay
**receive as adequate** accept
**receive as guest** entertain
**receive as reward** reap
**receive by bequest** inherit
**received account** asset
**received by the ear** aural
**received gladly** welcome
**receive from lottery** draw

**receive information** hear
**receiver** beneficiary, container, grantee, legatee, payee, receptacle, recipient, repository
**receiver in bankruptcy** sindico
**receiver of a cheque** payee
**receiver of a gift** donee
**receiver of benefits** beneficiary
**receiver of bequest** legatee
**receiver of income** earner
**receiver of mandate** mandatary
**receiver of stolen goods** fence, lock
**receive with applause** acclaim
**receive with pleasure** gratify
**receiving willingly** acceptant, receptive
**recent** brand-new, current, fresh, late(st), latter, modern(istic), neo(teric), new, novel
**recent arrival** newcomer
**recently** currently, freshly, lately, latterly, modernly, newly, novelly
**recently cut** mown
**recently deceased** late
**recently made** new
**recently-married couple** newly-wed
**receptacle** bin, container, holder, pocket, repository, vessel
**receptacle for ashes** urn
**receptacle for bones of dead** ossarium, ossuary
**receptacle for butter** ruskin
**receptacle for coal** bunker
**receptacle for holding frozen food** freezer
**receptacle for holy water** font
**receptacle for ore-crushing** mortar
**receptacle for poker chips** kitty
**receptacle for relics** reliquary
**receptacle for sacred relics** sepulchre, shrine, tablet
**receptacle for ship's compass** binnacle
**receptacle of baker** breadpan, cake tin
**reception** acceptance, acknowledg(e)ment, admission, affair, entertainment, fête, function, greeting, hello, levee, party, reaction, receipt, receiving, recognition, response, soirée, treatment, welcome
**reception hall of an Indian prince** durbar
**receptionist** greeter
**reception of sound** audio
**reception room** hall, parlour, salon
**receptive** accessible, alert, amenable, approachable, bright, favourable, friendly, hospitable, interested, open(-minded), perceptive, responsive, sensitive, suggestible, susceptible, sympathetic, welcoming

**recess** adjourn(ment), alcove, apse, bay, break, cavity, cell, corner, cove, depression, dissolve, gulf, harbour, holiday, hollow, indentation, intermission, interval, niche, nook, prorogue, recede, respite, rest, terminate, vacation
**recessed space** alcove
**recessed window** oriel
**recesses** corner, depths, heart, interior, reaches
**recess for family records** tablinum
**recess for hinge leave** pan
**recess for piece of sculpture** ancona
**recess in church** apse
**recess in church wall** ambry
**recess in colon** haustrum
**recess in Japanese house** tokonoma
**recess in mountain** cirque
**recess in mountain range** bay
**recess in rock** hitch
**recess in room-wall** alcove
**recess in side of hill** corrie
**recess in side of room** ala
**recess in synagogue** ark
**recess in wall** niche, alcove
**recession** decline, depression, downturn, retreat, slump
**recess on stage** canopy
**recipe** directions, formula, ingredients, instructions, means, method, precept, prescription, procedure, process, program(me), receipt, rule, system, technique
**recipe measure** cup, tablespoon, teaspoon
**recipient** beneficiary, conferree, donee, legatee, receiver, taker
**recipient bequest** legatee
**recipient of gift** donee
**recipient of legacy** legatee
**recipient of pension** pensionary, pensioner
**recipient of undelivered letter** sender
**reciprocal** allied, analogous, answering, bilateral, common, complement(ary), connected, contingent, correlate, correlative, corresponding, counterpart, dependent, equivalent, identical, interactive, interchangeable, interrelated, joint, matching, mutual, related, relative, respective, returned, shared, similar, synonymous
**reciprocal action** interplay
**reciprocal influence** interaction
**reciprocal of viscosity** fluidity
**reciprocate** alternate, barter, correspondent, equal, exchange, interchange, match, reply, requite, respond, return, swap, trade

**recital** account, chronicle, communication, concert, count, delineation, delivery, detail, entertainment, history, monologue, musicale, narrate, narration, narrative, performance, picture, reading, recitation, record, recount, rehearsal, relate, rendering, repeat, repetition, report, show, soliloquy, speech, staging, statement, story, tale, talk, telling, version
**recital of prayer** geulah, hamotzi, kedushah
**recitation** lecture, narration, passage, performance, piece, reading, recital, rendering, telling
**recite** compute, count, declaim, deliver, depict, describe, detail, enumerate, figure, intone, itemise, narrate, orate, perform, portray, quote, reckon, recount, rehearse, relate, render, repeat, review, say, share, sketch, speak, state, tell
**recite metrically** scan
**recite numbers** count
**reciter of epic poems** rhapsode, rhapsodist
**recite tiresomely** thrum
**recite to secretary** dictate
**recite with great ease** rush
**recite words from a book** quote
**reckless** brash, careless, desperate, hasty, heedless, imprudent, incautious, indiscreet, irresponsible, madcap, negligent, rash, regardless, wild
**reckless from despair** desperate
**recklessly daring person** daredevil
**recklessly extravagant** profligate
**recklessly wasteful** prodigal
**reckless person** tearaway
**reckless risk-taker** daredevil, rantipole
**reckless ruffian** desperado
**reckless state of mind** desperation
**reckon** account, add, appraise, assess, assume, believe, calculate, compute, conjecture, consider, count, deem, enumerate, esteem, estimate, evaluate, expect, fancy, figure, gauge, guess, hold, imagine, judge, number, rate, regard, suppose, surmise, tally, think, total
**reckon erroneously** miscast
**reckoning** account, addition, bill, calculation, charge, computation, computing, count, doom, due, enumeration, estimate, judg(e)memt, retribution, score, settlement
**reckoning by the year** annual
**reckoning by twelves** duodecimal
**reckoning by twenties** vigesimal

**reckoning of debit and credit in money account**
**reckoning of value** estimation
**reckon mathematically** compute
**reckon up** calculate, compute
**reckon with** anticipate, consider, contemplate, cope, expect, face, foresee, handle, treat
**reclaim** object, protest, recall, recapture, recover, redeem, reform, regain, regenerate, rehabilitate, reinstate, rescue, restore, retrieve, salvage, subdue, tame
**reclaimed land** carr, polder, thwaite
**reclaim from savage state** civilise
**recline** couch, lean, lie, loll, lounge, repose, rest, sprawl
**recline comfortably** lounge
**reclining** accumbent, recumbent
**recluse** anchoret, anchorite, ascetic, eremite, hermit, isolated, loner, monk, reclusive, secluded, solitary, stylite, withdrawn
**reclusive** cloistered, companionless, eremitic, friendless, isolated, lonely, lonesome, private, remote, retired, secluded, sheltered, solitary, unsociable, unsocial
**recognisable** identifiable
**recognisance** bail
**recognise** acknowledge, admit, appreciate, apprehend, approve, avow, comprehend, confess, detect, distinguish, endorse, honour, identify, know, own, ratify, realise, recall, recollect, re-identify, remember, respect, reward, support, tell, understand, uphold, validate, warrant
**recognised by law** lawful
**recognised procedure** routine
**recognised superiority** eminence
**recognised truth** axiom
**recognise sound** hear
**recognise the authority of** acknowledge
**recognition** acceptance, acknowledg(e)ment, admission, allowance, appreciation, approval, avowal, awareness, confession, detection, discovery, gratitude, greeting, honour, identification, notice, perception, realisation, recall, recollection, remembrance, respect, salute, understanding
**recognition of achievement** citation, laurel
**recognition of error** resipiscence
**recoil** back(lash), boomerang, falter, flinch, kick, quail, react, rebound, resonance, retreat, reverberate, revulsion, shrink, shy, spring

**recoil from** abhor, abominate
**recollect** commune, concentrate, contemplate, evoke, meditate, place, ponder, pray, recall, remember
**recollection** image, impression, memory, mind, recall, remembering, remembrance, reminiscence, souvenir
**recolour** dye
**recommend** advise, advocate, applaud, approve, commend, condone, counsel, endorse, entrust, eulogise, extol, praise, suggest
**recommend a line of conduct** advise
**recommendation** advice, advocacy, appeal, approval, blessing, caution, counsel, credential, direction, endorsement, guidance, hint, idea, letter, opinion, order, praise, proposal, reference, referral, remonstrance, sanction, suggestion, teaching, testimonial, tip, urging, warning
**recommended drug for remedy** prescribe
**recompense** amends, brokerage, commission, compensate, compensation, damages, indemnification, indemnify, indemnity, pay, reimburse, remunerate, remuneration, repay(ment), requital, requite, reward, salary, satisfy, wage
**reconcile** accept, accommodate, accord, adjust, appease, compose, conciliate, content, convince, harmonise, pacify, placate, propitiate, rectify, resign, resolve, reunite, settle, square, submit, yield
**reconcile oneself** acquiesce
**reconciliation** accommodation, adjustment, agreement, appeasement, compromise, conciliation, détente, forgiveness, harmony, pacification, propitiation, reunion, settlement, understanding
**recondite** abstract, abstruse, arcane, cabalistic, concealed, cryptic, dark, deep, esoteric, hidden, incognisable, involved, mysterious, mystic(al), obscure, occult, profound, secret, supernatural
**recondition** adjust, condition, correct, mend, overhaul, rectify, refinish, reinforce, renew, renovate, repair, restore, service
**reconnoitre** examine, explore, inspect, invigilate, observe, patrol, probe, scan, scout, scrutinise, snoop, spy, survey, view
**reconstruct** reassemble, rebuild, recall, recollect, recompose,

recondition, refabricate, refashion, remember, restore, revamp
**record** account, annals, catalogue, chronicle, copy, date, diary, disc, docket, enrol, enter, graph, history, introduce, log, mark, memoir, memorandum, note, page, platter, prick, scroll, slip, tape, title, transcribe, warble
**record a debt** debit
**record again** retape
**record book** journal, ledger, log
**record by notches** score
**record cover** jacket, sleeve
**record dissent** moan, protest
**recorded events of one year** annal
**recorded proceedings** acta
**recorder** accountant, administrator, agent, amanuensis, annalist, archivist, booker, bookkeeper, cassette, chronicler, clerk, copyist, diarist, dictaphone, flute, gauge, historian, marker, notary, notator, noter, register, registrar, scorer, scribe, secretary, seismograph, speedometer, stenographer, tape, teleprinter, turnstile
**record formally** register
**record from the past** oldie
**recording** cut, disc, documenting, enrolling, gramophone, logging, performance, record, release, tape, video
**recording device** cassette, tape
**recording mouthpiece** fipple
**recording ribbon** tape
**record kept by golfer** score-card
**record name of** enter
**record of building society account** passbook
**record of car movement** jumbo
**record of daily events** diary
**record of dealings** acta
**record of document** protocol
**record of events** annal, history, memoir
**record of family background** genealogy
**record of footprints** stibogram
**record of heart movement** cardiogram
**record of investigation** dossier, file, report
**record of journey** journal, log
**record of loan** charge
**record of meeting** minutes
**record of Mohammed's sayings** hadit
**record of muscular work** ergogram
**record of one year** annal
**record of past events** history
**record of patient** chart
**record of proceedings** acta, iter, journal, minutes
**record of sum owed** debit

**record of travel** itinerary
**record of voyage** log
**record on magnetic strip** tape
**record-player** gramophone
**record-player needle** stylus
**records** annals, archives, chronicles
**record set** album
**records of events set down year by year** annals
**record speed** time
**record with camera** film
**recount** communicate, depict, describe, detail, enumerate, narrate, portray, recite, rehearse, relate, repeat, report, tell
**recount events** narrate
**recoup** recall, recapture, recover, redeem, regain, repair, repossess, rescue, restore, retake, retrieve, salvage, save
**recourse** access, alternative, application, backup, choice, cloister, fortress, option, plea, preference, refuge, request, reserve, resource, retreat, sanctum, selection, substitute, support
**recourse in difficulty** refuge
**recover** acquire, convalesce, find, mend, rally, recall, recapture, reclaim, recoup, recuperate, redeem, regain, reinsure, repair, rescue, restore, retrieve, salvage, save, secure
**recover after illness** rally
**recovered wreckage** flotsam
**recover health after illness** convalesce
**recovery** betterment, healing, improvement, mending, rally, restoration, revival, upturn
**recreant** apostate, base, cowardly, craven, dastardly, faithless, false, renegade, traitor, treacherous, unfaithful, untrue
**recreate** copy, reconstruct, redo, reform, remake, remodel, renovate, reproduce
**recreation** activity, amusement, distraction, diversion, entertainment, exercise, fun, games, hobby, impression, leisure, memory, pastime, play, pleasure, recall, relaxation, reminiscence, sport
**recrimination** accusation, bickering, counterattack, countercharge, quarrel, retaliation, retort, squabbing
**recruit** apprentice, augment, beginner, conscript, convert, draft(er), engage, enlist, enrol, helper, hire, impress, initiate, learner, levy, mobilise, muster, novice, procure, raise, refresh, reinforce, renew, restore,

roofie, rookie, strengthen, supply, trainee
**rectangle** oblong
**rectangular** angular, foursquare, oblong, quadrate, square
**rectangular column set into a wall for ornament** pilaster
**rectification** adaptation, adjustment, alteration, amelioration, amendment, arrangement, arranging, betterment, correction, fitting, fixing, gain, improvement, modification, ordering, redress, regulation, remodelling, repair, setting, tuning
**rectify** adjust, align, amend, attune, correct, cure, emend, fix, focus, improve, mend, redress, reform, regulate, remedy, repair, revise, right, square, straighten
**rector** abbé, bishop, canonist, chaplain, clergyman, confessor, curé, dean, dignitary, dominee, ecclesiastic, evangelist, father, minister, monsignor, parson, pastor, preacher, predikant, prelate, priest, reverend, theologian, vicar
**rector's house** rectory
**recuperate** convalesce, heal, improve, mend, rally, recover, regenerate, rejuvenate, restore, resuscitate, revive, revivify
**recur** badger, continue, harass, intermit, persevere, persist, re-occur, reappear, repeat, resume, return, revert, vex
**recurrent** continued, frequent, habitual, haunting, periodic, recurring, regular, repeated, repetitive
**recurrent loss of vision in twilight** nyctalopia
**recurrent period** cycle
**recurring every eight years** octennial
**recurring every five years** quinquennial
**recurring every four years** quadrennial
**recurring every night** nightly
**recurring every ninth day** nonan(e)
**recurring every seventh day** septan
**recurring every seven years** septennial
**recurring every ten years** decennial
**recurring every third day** tertian
**recurring every three years** triennial
**recurring every two years** biennial
**recurring every year** annual
**recurring pattern** cycle, recurrence, rhythm
**recurring theme, as in a novel** leitmotif, leitmotiv
**recurring yearly** annual
**recycle** reclaim, reconstitute, reprocess, reuse, salvage, save

**red** blushing, Bolshevik, carmine, cherry, cochineal, Communist, crimson, fiery, maroon, rose, rosso (I), rubious, ruddy, scarlet, socialist, solferino, vermilion
**Red** Commy, Leftist
**redact** edit, rephrase, rewrite
**redactor** editor, reviser, rewriter
**red admiral insect** butterfly
**red and inflamed** bloodshot
**red and pink gem** almandine, beryl, carbuncle, garnet, jacinth, quartz, rose, ruby, rutile, spinel
**red baneberry** redberry, toadroot
**red bank balance** overdraft
**red-bellied woodpecker** chab
**red birthmark** naevus
**red blood-corpuscle** erythrocyte
**red-breasted bird** robin
**red cedar** juniper, sabina, savin
**red complexion** rosy
**red cosmetic** blusher, rouge
**red deer** brocket, olen, spay
**redden** blush, brighten, burn, colour, crimson, flame, flush, gleam, glimmer, glow, shine, smoulder, suffuse
**reddening** blushing, erubescent
**red denotes it** danger
**reddish** bay, bloodshot, blooming, blushing, cerise, chestnut, flaming, flesh, flushed, foxy, fresh, glowing, pink, red, rose(ate), rosy, rubicund, ruddy, russet, salmon, sandy, titian
**reddish-brown** auburn, bay, brick, chestnut, ferruginous, ginger, henna, mahogany, roan, russet, rust, sepia, sienna, sorrel, terracotta, titian, vermilion
**reddish-brown feline** eyra
**reddish-brown horse** sorrel
**reddish-brown horse** bay, chestnut
**reddish-brown wood** mahogany
**reddish colour** cerise, rosy, rubicund, russet
**reddish dye** henna
**reddish gem** saro
**reddish hair tint** henna
**reddish-orange gem** jacinth
**reddish-purple colour** amaranth, burgundy, cerise, magenta, maroon, puce
**reddish stone with embedded crystals** porphyry
**reddish-yellow** fallow
**red dye** eosin, madder, kermes, purpurin
**rede** advise, counsel, explanation
**redecorate** rearrange, redo
**redeem** absolve, acquit, change, defray, deliver, discharge, emancipate, exchange, free, fulfil, keep, liberate, meet, offset, outweigh, perform, ransom, reclaim, recoup, recover, recuperate, regain, repurchase, rescue, retrieve, salvage, save
**redemption** atonement, compensation, conversion, deliverance, escape, exchange, expiation, fulfilment, liberation, preservation, ransom, re-establishment, rebirth, reclamation, rehabilitation, release, rescue, restitution, restoration, retrieval, salvation, saving
**red entry** debit
**red-eyed fish** rudd
**red-faced** blowsy, blowzy, florid, flushed, ruddy
**redfish** drum, fathead, perch, rosefish, salmon
**red food dye** cochineal
**red furniture wood** mahogany
**red garden flower** canna
**red garnet** almandine
**red gem** garnet, ruby
**red grouse** moorfowl
**red gum** eucalypt, jarrah
**red hair-dye** henna
**red-haired** carroty
**red-handed** in flagrante delicto
**red hue** cerise
**redingote** coat
**red jewel** ruby
**red-legged crow** chough
**red-letter day** occasion
**red-light district** brothel
**red mercuric sulphide** cinnabar
**redness of skin, usually occuring in patches** erythema
**redness of sky** aurora
**Red Norse navigator** Eric
**redo** redecorate, restyle, rework
**red ochre** ruddle
**redolence** aroma, balm, bouquet, essence, fragrance, incense, odorousness, odour, perfume, reek, savour, scent, smell
**redolent** ambrosial, aromatic, evocative, fragrant, odoriferous, odorous, perfumed, pungent, reeking, savoury, scented, smelly, suggestive, sweet-smelling
**redolent wood** cedar
**red osier** willow
**redo unskilfully** botch
**red pepper** capsicum, cayenne, paprika, tabasco
**red pigment** arumin, haem, lake, puccoon, sandyx, sinopia, vermilion
**red pimples** acne
**red planet** Mars
**redress** adjust, amend, atonement, compensation, correct, rectify, relief, remedy, repair, reparation, restitution, restoration, right, satisfaction
**red-rind cheese** Edam, Gouda
**red salad item** tomato
**red salmon** sockeye
**red sandalwood** chandam, sanders
**Red Sea peninsula** Sinai
**red smoked pork sausage** saveloy
**red stone fruit** cherry
**red stopper** eugenia, ironwood
**red tape** bureaucracy, documentation, formality, legalism, motion, nonsense, paperwork, procedure, protocol, red-tapism, research, rigidity, rigmarole
**red traffic signal** stoplight
**reduce** abridge, adjust, allay, attenuate, conquer, contract, control, curtail, debase, decrease, degrade, deplete, depress, diminish, ebb, lessen, lower, overpower, shorten, subdue, subjugate, suppress
**reduce activity of** depress
**reduce amount of** retrench
**reduce burden** ease
**reduce by** deduct
**reduce by cutting** pare
**reduce by mental analysis** resolve
**reduced to system** science
**reduce expenditure** economise
**reduce in bulk** thin
**reduce in character** degrade
**reduce in degree** detract
**reduce in force** attenuate
**reduce in rank** abase, demote
**reduce in size** shrink
**reduce intensely** moderate
**reduce in thickness by rolling** planish
**reduce numbers of** deplete
**reduce pressure** decompress
**reduce price** cheapen
**reduce prices greatly** slash
**reduce sail** reef
**reduce someone to tears** upset
**reduce speed** brake, decelerate, slacken, slow
**reduce the number of animals** cull
**reduce to a means** average
**reduce to ash** incinerate
**reduce to ashes** cremate, incinerate, scorify
**reduce to carbon** char
**reduce to dross** scorify
**reduce to fine articles** atomise, micronise
**reduce to fine state** refine
**reduce to flat surface** level
**reduce to fluid** liquefy
**reduce to insensibility** stun
**reduce to lime or ash** calcine
**reduce to lower rank** degrade, demote

**reduce to nothing** annihilate, annul, discreate, exterminate, obliterate
**reduce to order** methodise
**reduce to powder** grind, pulverise
**reduce to pulp** crush, mash
**reduce to smallest part** minimise
**reduce to subjection** master
**reduce to submission** defeat, overpower
**reduce weight of** disburden, lighten
**reducing in rank** abasing
**reducing worth** devaluing
**reduction** allowance, bargain, concession, condensation, curtailment, cut(back), decline, decrease, deduction, discount, ebb, economy, giveaway, lessening, loss, lowering, rebate, retrenchment, saving, shrinkage, snip, subsidence
**reduction in price** concession, saving
**reduction of A-bombs** nuclear disarmament
**reduction of blood supply to part of body** isch(a)emia
**redundancy** dismissal, excess, repetition, sacking, superfluity, surplus, tautology, unemployment, uselessness, wordiness
**redundant** copious, diffuse, excessive, exorbitant, extra, immoderate, overmuch, periphrastic, profuse, repetitious, superfluous, surplus, unnecessary, useless, verbose, windy, wordy
**reduplicate** ape, copy, ditto, double, duplicate, facsimile, imitate, iterate, repeat
**red usually denotes this** danger
**red vegetable** beet, tomato
**red-violet pigment** turacin
**red wine** beaune, cabernet sauvignon, cinsaut, claret, gamay, malmsey, merlot, pinotage, port, shiraz
**re early 19th century art** neoclassic
**re-echo** rebound, resonate, resound, reverberate, ring
**reed** bolt, dart, flight, quarrel, shaft
**reedbird** bobolink, ricebird
**reed canary grass** spire
**reed end** tongue
**reed for winding thread** spool
**reed in organ** vibrator
**reed instrument** clarinet, oboe
**reed instrument of brass** sarrusophone
**reedlike** arundinaceous
**reed of loom** comb
**reed organ** harmonium, melodeon
**reed organ player** accordionist
**reed pipe** mirliton
**reed warbler** pitbird
**reedy** frail, thin, twilled, weak

**reedy plant** sprit
**reef** bedrock, cay, coral, fold, kay, key, lode, mange, pitfall, reefer, rock, saddle, scar, shoal, tombolo
**Reef** Rand
**reef growth** coral
**reek** fume, odour, smell, stench, stink
**reel** axle, bobbin, falter, lurch, oscillate, pin, pirn, pitch, revolve, rock, roll, rotate, shake, spin, spindle, spool, stagger, stumble, sway, swim, swing, swirl, totter, twirl, unsteadiness, waver, wheel, whirl
**reel for drawing silk** filature
**reel for winding yarn** bobbin, pirn, spool, swift
**reel off a story** scrieve
**reel used for yarn** crib
**reeve** bailiff, steward
**re eye lining** retinal
**ref** referee, umpire
**refectory in monastery** frater
**refer** advert, allude, apply, ascribe, assign, attribute, belong, cite, commit, concern, consult, credit, deliver, direct, go, guide, hint, impute, mention, pertain, point, recommend, relate, send, submit, transfer
**referee** abjudicator, adjudicate, arbiter, arbitrate, arbitrator, arbitress, decide(r), decree, determiner, intercede, intervene, judge, mediator, negotiate, negotiator, peacemaker, placate, ref, umpire
**referee's assistant** linesman
**reference** allusion, bearing, character, citation, concern, introduction, mention, note, quotation, recommendation, regard, relation, remark, respect, testimonial
**reference book** dictionary, encyclopaedia
**reference list for text** index
**reference manual** handbook
**referendum** plebiscite
**refer indirectly** allude
**referring to** re
**referring to separately priced dishes** à la carte
**refers to decay** off, putrefaction, putrid
**refer to** allude
**refer to briefly** mention
**refer to by name** mention
**refer to higher court** appeal
**refill** fill, furnish, provide, recharge, reload, replace(ment), replenish, restock, restore, supply
**re finance** economic
**refine** cavil, civilise, clarify, cleanse, complete, depurate, discriminate, distil, elaborate, improve, lave, mature, perfect, prevaricate, process, purify, rarefy, ripen, wash
**refined** chaste, choice, civil(ised), clarified, courteous, courtly, cultivated, cultured, debonair, decent, delicate, discriminating, elegant, exact, exquisite, fine, formal, fussy, genteel, gentle, gentlemanly, graceful, ladylike, nice, noble, polished, polite, precise, punctilious, pure, sensitive, sophisticated, subtle, tasteful, urbane, well-bred, well-mannered
**refined and genteel** dainty
**refined expletive** egad
**refined grace** elegance
**refined in manner** genteel
**refined in manners** courtly
**refined loveliness** elegance
**refined petroleum** petrol
**refined woman** lady
**refinement** breeding, chivalry, civilisation, civility, clarification, culture, discrimination, distinction, elegance, fineness, finesse, finicality, grace, improvement, lustration, nuance, preciseness, purification, sophistication, suavity, tastefulness
**refine metal** smelt
**reflect** communicate, consider, contemplate, deliberate, demonstrate, depict, display, echo, exhibit, express, imitate, indicate, manifest, meditate, mirror, muse, ponder, portray, rebound, reproduce, reveal, ruminate, show, think
**reflectance ratio** albedo
**reflect deeply** meditate
**reflected image** shadow
**reflected sound** echo
**reflection** attention, cerebration, copy, counterpart, deliberation, duplicate, image, imitation, impression, likeness, mirror, opinion, picture, replica, thought, twin, view
**reflection after an act** afterthought
**reflection of snow in the sky** snow-blink
**reflection of sound** echo
**reflective** absorbed, contemplate, dreaming, dreamy, forlorn, grave, imitative, intent, longing, meditative, melancholy, mournful, musing, pensive, pondering, resounding, ruminant, ruminative, sad, serious, sober, solemn, thoughtful, wistful, yearning
**reflect light** shine
**reflect on** muse
**reflector of polished metal** speculum

**reflexive pronoun** herself, himself, itself, myself, oneself, ourselves, thyself
**reform** ameliorate, amend(ment), better, correct(ion), improve(ment), rectify, regroup, repair, restore
**reformation** amendment, betterment, correction, improvement, reform
**reformed prostitute** magdalen(a)
**refractory** contrary, contumacious, disobedient, fractious, headstrong, intractable, mulish, obstinate, obstreperous, perverse, pigheaded, rebellious, recalcitrant, restive, stubborn, uncontrollable, ungovernable, unmanageable, unruly, wilful, wrongheaded
**refractory pot in which gold or silver is refined** cupel
**refrain** abstain, arouse, avoid, cease, cheer, chorus, desist, discontinue, forbear, kindle, leitmotif, leitmotiv, melody, motif, quit, relinquish, renew, renounce, renovate, restore, restrain, revivify, sacrifice, stop, tune, verse, withhold
**refrain from** abstain, avoid, boycott, forbear, forgo
**refrain from alcohol** abstain
**refrain from giving** bury, conceal, hide, withhold
**refrain from voting** abstain
**refraining from speech** mute, silence
**refresh** enliven, invigorate, renew, renovate, repair, restore, revive, stimulate
**refreshing drink** tonic
**refreshing odour** ozone
**refreshment** drinks, enlivenment, freshening, reanimation, reinvigoration, renewal, renovation, repair, restoration, revitalisation, revival, snacks, stimulation, titbits
**refreshment interval at work** tea break
**refreshment on a journey** bait
**refrigerant gas** ethane
**refrigerate** chill, congeal, cool, freeze, ice
**refrigerator** fridge, icebox
**ref's blower** whistle
**refuge** asylum, custody, evasion, harbour, haven, hiding, mew, oasis, preservation, privacy, protection, resort, retreat, safety, sanctuary, sanctum, seclusion, security, shelter, tactic
**refugee** absconder, alien, deserter, eloper, émigré, escapee, exile, fugitive, outlaw, stranger
**refund** rebate, recompense, reimburse, remit(tance), remunerate, repay(ment), restore, return

**refund in part** rebate
**refurbish** continue, extend(ing), face lift, fix(ing), mend, modernise, modernising, overhaul, reaffirm(ing), rebuild, recondition, recover(ing), recreate, refinish, refit(ting), rejuvenate, rejuvenating, remodel, renew(ing), renovate, renovating, reopen(ing), repair(ing), repeating, replace, replacing, restock(ing), restore, restoring, resume, resuming, resurrect, resuscitate, retouch, revamp, service, transform(ing), treat
**refusal** choice, consideration, denial, negation, no, nonacceptance, nonconsent, opportunity, option, rebuff, regrets, rejection, repudiation, veto
**refusal to take food** sitiophobia
**refuse** cast-offs, chaff, confute, counter, debris, decline, deny, discredit, disprove, dregs, dross, flotsam, garbage, husks, jetsam, junk, lees, leftovers, litter, negate, offal, rebuff, rebut, reject, repudiate, rubbish, scum, sediments, slobs, trash, waste
**refuse abruptly** ba(u)lk
**refuse access to** deny
**refuse admission** close
**refuse approval** veto
**refuse attentions** spurn
**refuse coal** breeze
**refuse consent** veto
**refuse container** dustbin
**refuse dealings with** repudiate
**refuse-eating beetle** scavenger
**refuse fish** chum, shack
**refuse from melting metals** dross, scoria, slag
**refuse from threshing** husk
**refuse glass** calx, cullet
**refuse holder** bin
**refuse in wine making** marc
**refuse left by boring insects** frass
**refuse matter** soil
**refuse near dwelling** midden
**refuse of burned coals** cinder
**refuse of coffee beans** triage
**refuse of grain** bran, husks
**refuse of grapes after wine-making** rape
**refuse of oil mills** shode
**refuse of plants** ross
**refuse of smelted metal** slag
**refuse of wool** backings
**refuse remover** dustman
**refuse separated by sifting** screenings
**refuse to accept** reject
**refuse to acknowledge** deny
**refuse to approve** veto
**refuse to associate with** ostracise

**refuse to believe** discredit
**refuse to commit oneself** hedge
**refuse to deal in as protest** boycott
**refuse to deal with** boycott
**refuse to give** deny, withhold
**refuse to grant** deny
**refuse to have dealings with** boycott
**refuse to move** ba(u)lk
**refuse to notice** disregard, ignore
**refuse to obey** defy, mutiny, rebel
**refuse to recognise** disclaim, disown, repudiate
**refuse to take notice of** ignore
**refuse to talk** dummy
**refusing forgiveness** unrepentant
**refutation** rebuttal
**refute** answer, belie, confound, confute, contradict, controvert, counter, debunk, demolish, deny, discredit, disprove, explode, expose, gainsay, invalidate, negate, oppose, overthrow, rebut, repugn, ruin
**refute by argument** rebut
**regain** find, re-establish, reattain, recall, recapture, reclaim, recoup, recover, redeem, reinstate, reobtain, repossess, reseize, resume, retake, retrieve
**regain health after illness** convalesce
**regain one's strength** recuperate
**regain ownership of** repossess
**regain strength** rally
**regal** imperial, kingly, magnificent, noble, princely, proud, queenly, royal, sovereign, stately
**regale** amuse, banquet, beguile, captivate, celebrate, charm, cheer, comfort, cram, delight, divert, enchant, enliven, enrapture, entertain, entrance, fascinate, feast, fête, glut, gratify, honour, indulge, occupy, please, recreate, salute, satiate, toast, treat
**regal fur** ermine
**regalia part** orb, sceptre, tiara
**regard** account, affection, attention, care, concern, consider(ation), deem, deference, detail, esteem, estimation, eye, hear, heed, hold, honour, interest, judge, liking, look, note, notice, observe, particular, rate, reference, repute, respect, suppose, thought, value
**regard amorously** ogle
**regardant** watchful
**regard as** see
**regard as equivalent** equate
**regard as hopeless** deplore
**regard as inferior** despise
**regard as irrelevant** discount
**regard as likely** expect

**regard as object of great interest** lionise
**regard as perfect** idealise
**regard as proper** accept
**regard as true** believe
**regard as valuable** esteem
**regarded as being** putative
**regarded as holy** sacramental
**regarded as pious** saintly
**regard favourably** approve
**regard for others as a principle of action** altruism
**regardful** acquiescent, advertent, alert, amenable, attentive, biddable, careful, circumspect, concentrating, docile, duteous, dutiful, heedful, meticulous, mindful, obedient, observant, particular, precise, prudent, respectful, studious, submissive, watchful, well-trained
**regard highly** admire, approve, consider, deem, esteem, honour, rated, respect
**regarding** about, anent, apropos, in re, re, respecting
**regarding mankind as the centre of existence** anthropocentric
**regarding one's own race as the most important** ethnocentric
**regarding things as they are** realistic
**regardless** careless, deaf, disregardful, heedless, inattentive, indifferent, indiscreet, neglectful, nevertheless, nonchalant, reckless, unguarded, unmindful, unthoughtful, unwary, unwise
**regardless of that** but
**regard reverently** adore
**regards** beholds, compliments, deems, eyes, greetings, marks, notices, observes, remarks, respects, views, watches
**regard studiously** con
**regard to** anent
**regard too favourably** overrate
**regard to others as a principle of action** altruism
**regard with affection** love
**regard with blind adoration** idolise
**regard with deep respect** venerate
**regard with disgust** abhor
**regard with displeasure** disesteem, disfavour, dislike
**regard with esteem** admire
**regard with favour** approve
**regard with hatred and disgust** loathe
**regard with honour** respect, venerate
**regard with indifference** disdain
**regard with profound respect** revere, venerate
**regard with repugnance** abhor, abominate, despise, detest

**regard with utmost respect and affection** adore
**regard with veneration** revere
**regard with wonder** admire
**regatta** meeting, race
**regency** kingship, queenship
**regenerate** better, improve, rebuild, reconstitute, reconstruct, recreate, reform, rehabilitate, rejuvenate, remodel, repair, replace, reproduce, reshape, restore, revive
**regime** administration, control, direction, dominion, governance, government, leadership, management, regimen, regulation, reign, rule, system
**regimen** course, diet, fashion, manner, means, method, mode, regime, regulation, reign, rule, style, system, therapy, treatment, way
**regiment** assimilate, band, body, company, contingent, corps, crew, detachment, discipline, division, domineer, mass-produce, organise, squad(ron), standardise, systematise, team, troop, unit
**regimental flag** ensign
**regimental pet** mascot
**regimented** methodical, severe, stern, strict, systematic
**regiment member** grenadier, soldier
**regina** queen
**region** ambit, area, arena, belt, district, domain, dominion, jurisdiction, locale, location, orb(it), part, portion, province, quarter, section, site, space, sphere, spot, terrain, territory, tract, vicinity, zone
**region above mouth** epistoma, epistome
**regional** continental, country, district, insular, local, municipal, parochial, peninsular, provincial, rural, sectional, state, subdivisional, suburban, territorial, town, urban, zonal
**regional manner of pronunciation** accent
**regional manner of speaking** dialect
**regional plant** flora
**regional weather condition** climate
**region beyond atmosphere** space, stratosphere
**region far away** strand
**region near equator** doldrums
**region of amplitude** antinode
**region of bishop** diocese, see
**region of body just above waist** midriff
**region of ocean** country, land
**region of origin** cradle
**region of shifting sand** erg

**regions round the South Pole** Antarctic
**region where Gaelic is usually spoken** Gaeltacht
**register** almanac, annals, archives, betray, catalogue, chronicle, demonstrate, diary, display, enlist, enrol(ment), enter, entry, evince, exhibit, express, file, indicate, inscribe, ledger, list, log, manifest, mark, memorandum, note, read, record, registration, registry, reveal, roll, roster, say, schedule, show
**register of deaths** death-roll, necrology
**register of martyrs** martyrology
**regorge** disgorge, vomit
**regress** backslide, decline, degenerate, ebb, fade, fail, recede, relapse, retire, retrograde, retrogress, return, reverse, revert, subside
**regret** anxiety, bemoan, bewail, contrition, deplore, deprecate, dole, fret, grief, grieve, lack, lament(ation), miss, mourn, need, regretfulness, remorse, repent(ance), repine, rue, shamefulness, sorrow, want, woe, worry
**regret absence** miss
**regret deeply** deplore
**regret for sins** penance
**regretful** abject, apologetic, conscience-stricken, contrite, dejected, despondent, disappointed, homesick, humble, lamenting, longing, mortified, nostalgic, penitent, regretful, remorseful, repentant, rueful, sad, shamefaced, sorrowful, sorry, unhappy
**regretful acknowledgement** apology
**regretful memory of earlier time** nostalgia
**regret strongly** lament
**regrettable** affecting, awful, deplorable, disappointing, discouraging, disheartening, distressful, distressing, doleful, lamentable, moving, pitiable, pitiful, sad(dening), shameful, unfortunate, unlucky, woeful
**regrettable fact** pity
**regrettable mistake** blunder
**regret the absence of** miss
**regretting the death of** bewailing, grieving, mourning
**regroup** rally, reassemble, reform, reorganise, unite
**regular** conforming, constant, customary, established, even, fixed, formal, general, habitual, methodical, normal, periodic,

recurrent, systematic, uniform,
 unvarying, usual
**regular accommodation payment** rent
**regular aircraft route** airway
**regular churchgoer** attender
**regular course of action** habit
**regular course of procedure** routine
**regularise** standardise
**regularity** cadence, constancy,
 continuity, habit, method, monotony,
 order(liness), rhythm, routine, rule,
 sameness, system, tedium, tradition,
 uniformity, unison, unity
**regular job** employment
**regularly existing** endemic
**regularly produced for market** staple
**regularly shaped** symmetrical
**regular meeting place** rendezvous
**regular oval** eclipse
**regular patron** habitué
**regular ship** liner
**regular trade or business** custom
**regular weather conditions** climate
**regulate** adjust, administer, arrange,
 balance, catalogue, conduct, control,
 direct, dispose, fix, govern, manage,
 moderate, order, organise, rule,
 standardise
**regulated by the will** voluntary
**regulate food** diet
**regulating expenditure** sumptuary
**regulating wheel of a watch**
 balance-wheel
**regulation** accepted, adjustment,
 administration, arrangement,
 commandment, control, customary,
 decree, dictate, direction,
 disposition, edict, formal, law,
 legislation, management, normal,
 official, order, ordinance, ordinary,
 precept, prescribed, procure,
 required, requirement, rule, statute,
 supervision, usual
**regulation of price** assize
**regulator** valve
**regurgitate** burp, ejaculate, eject,
 heave, recapitulate, redo, regorge,
 reissue, repeat, restate, resurge,
 vomit
**regurgitated food** cud
**rehash** alter, change, rearrange(ment),
 rejig(ging), reshuffle, rework, rewrite
**rehearsal** account, catalogue,
 description, drill, enumeration, list,
 narration, practice, preparation,
 reading, recital, relation, runthrough,
 telling
**rehearse** act, describe, drill, narrate,
 practise, recite, relate, repeat, train
**rehoboam** bottle, bowl, wine-bottle
**Rehoboam** king

**reign** administer, command, control,
 dominion, empire, govern, influence,
 jurisdiction, monarchy, power,
 predominate, prevail, regency,
 regime, rule, sovereignty,
 supremacy, sway
**reigning** administering, au courant (F),
 chief, commanding, controlling,
 dictatorial, fashionable, governing,
 head, influencing, modish, popular,
 prevailing, rampant, regnant, rife,
 ruling, stylish, supreme, universal
**reigning beauty** belle
**reigning queen** regina
**reign in India** raj
**reign supreme** preside
**reimburse** atone, clear, compensate,
 discharge, foot, give, honour,
 indemnify, liquidate, meet, offer, pay,
 recompense, recoup, redress,
 refund, remit, remunerate, render,
 repay, requite, restore, reward,
 satisfy, settle, square
**rein** brake, bridle, check, control, curb,
 govern, guide, halter, harness, hold,
 line, moderator, restrain(t),
 restrict(ion), rule, strap, tether
**reindeer** caribou, cervid, cervine,
 cervoid, deer, rangifer, rein, tarand
**reindeer man** Lapp
**reindeer moss** sward
**reinforce** amplify, augment, bar,
 bolster, brace, emphasise, enlarge,
 fortify, harden, increase, nervate,
 prop, recruit, steel, stiffen,
 strengthen, stress, supplement,
 support, toughen, underline, uphold
**reinforce footwear** tap
**rein in** restrain
**reinstate** re-establish, reappoint, recall,
 rehabilitate, reinstall, replace,
 restore, return
**reinstate a deletion** stet
**reiterate** repeat, restate
**reiver** raider, thief
**reject** abnegate, castaway, castoff,
 contradict, decline, demur, deny,
 disallow, disapprove, disbelieve,
 discard, eject, eliminate, exclude,
 expel, forbid, jettison, negate,
 negative, refuse, regurgitate, repel,
 spurn, veto, vomit
**reject as not valid** quash
**reject as one's heir** disinherit
**reject as untrue** deny
**reject as unwanted** discard
**reject disdainfully** spurn
**rejected by betrothed** jilted
**reject in an examination** pluck
**reject in contempt** spurn
**rejection** avoiding, brush-off,
 contradiction, denial, denying,
 desertion, disallowance, disbelief,
 dismissal, disregard, elimination,
 exclusion, ignoring, interdiction,
 negating, negation, omission, rebuff,
 refusal, renunciation, repelling,
 repudiation, repulse, slighting,
 turndown, veto
**rejection of all religious and moral**
 **principles** nihilism
**rejection of doctrine** heresy
**reject scornfully** scout
**reject with contempt** spurn
**rejoice** celebrate, delight, exult, glory,
 joy, jubilate, revel, triumph
**rejoice greatly** exult
**rejoice noisily** maffick
**rejoice with** congratulate
**rejoicing** celebrating, celebration,
 cheer, delight(ing), elation,
 exultation, festivity, gladness,
 glorying, happiness, joy, jubilation,
 merrymaking, revelry, triumph
**rejoicing in another's misfortune**
 malevolent
**rejoin** acknowledge, answer, counter,
 echo, explain, quip, react,
 reciprocate, reply, resolve, respond,
 retaliate, retort, return, riposte, solve
**rejoinder** answer, comeback,
 contradiction, repartee, reply,
 response, retort, return, riposte
**rejuvenate** brace, continue, cure,
 energise, enliven, exhilarate, extend,
 fortify, freshen, galvanise, harden,
 invigorate, mend, modernise,
 overhaul, quicken, reaffirm,
 reanimate, recharge, recruit, refresh,
 regenerate, reinvigorate, rekindle,
 remake, remodel, renew, renovate,
 repair, restore, resuscitate, revamp,
 revive, stimulate, strengthen, update
**relapse** backslide, degenerate,
 deteriorate, fade, fail, lapse,
 recurrence, regress(ion), relapse,
 retrogression, reversion, revert,
 setback, sicken, sink, weaken(ing),
 worsen
**relapse into bad ways** backslide
**relate** ally, announce, associate,
 broadcast, connect, delineate,
 describe, detail, disseminate,
 divulge, impart, marry, narrate,
 recite, recount, regard, rehearse,
 repeat, represent, respect, tell, tie,
 wed
**relate again** retell
**relate as story** narrate
**relate circumstantially** detail
**related** affinitive, agnate, akin, alike,
 allied, appropriate, apropos,
 cognate, connected, correlated,

## related by blood — 622 — relating to the skeleton

coupled, equivalent, kin(dred), lashed, sealed, united, wedded
**related by blood** (a)kin, kindred
**related group** family, series
**related in any way** agnate, cognate
**related inversely** reciprocal
**related on father's side** agnate, paternal
**related on mother's side** cognate, enate, enatic
**related social group** family
**related to alpaca** llama
**related to cassowary** emu
**related to hearing** aural
**related to pig** tapir
**related to sound** acoustic
**related to the ostrich** struthious
**related to tribology** friction, lubrication, wear
**related to volume** cubical
**related to watches** horological
**relate in full** recite
**relate in verse** versify
**relate to** (ap)pertain, belong, refer
**relating to** about, against, of, re
**relating to algae** algoid
**relating to almonds** amygdalate
**relating to an archbishop** archiepiscopal
**relating to Andes** Andean
**relating to angels** angelic
**relating to animal life** zoic
**relating to archery** toxophilite
**relating to art of medicine** Aesculapian
**relating to a see** diocesan
**relating to Asia** Asiatic
**relating to basalt** trappean
**relating to bathing** balneal
**relating to bees** apian
**relating to bile** biliary
**relating to birds** avian
**relating to birth** natal
**relating to body of customs** traditional
**relating to bone** osteal
**relating to brain** encephalic
**relating to brain fibres** pontal
**relating to breeding of bees** apiarian
**relating to burial of the dead** funeral
**relating to central government** federal
**relating to children and their diseases** p(a)ediatric
**relating to church meeting** congregational
**relating to church unity** ecumenical
**relating to city** civic
**relating to colouring** tinctorial
**relating to comedy** comic
**relating to connotations of words** semantic
**relating to continents** epeiric
**relating to cookery** culinary

**relating to correct use of eyes** orthoptic
**relating to craft of potters** fictile
**relating to cultivated land** agrarian
**relating to deer** cervine
**relating to digestion** peptic
**relating to dreams** oneiric
**relating to duty** deontic
**relating to eagles** aquiline
**relating to earthly matters** temporal
**relating to earthquakes** seismic
**relating to ebb and flow** tidal
**relating to education** scholastic
**relating to England and France** Anglo-French
**relating to England and India** Anglo-Indian
**relating to electrodes** anodic
**relating to elegy** elegiac
**relating to financial planning** budgetary
**relating to fire** igneous
**relating to fish** piscatorial, piscine
**relating to force of attraction** gravitational
**relating to forefathers** ancestral
**relating to glass** vitreous
**relating to goats** capric
**relating to hearing** auditive, auditory
**relating to high mountains** alpine
**relating to horses** equestrian
**relating to immediate surroundings** ambient
**relating to induction** inaugural
**relating to infectious diseases** zymotic
**relating to insomnia** agrypnotic
**relating to intellect** noetic
**relating to inward feelings** visceral
**relating to islands** insular
**relating to Japan** Nipponese
**relating to kissing** oscular
**relating to knowledge** epistemic
**relating to landed property** agrarian
**relating to lands** agrarian
**relating to latent forces of the earth** geodynamic
**relating to law** juridical
**relating to Lent** Quadragesimal
**relating to lice** pedicular
**relating to life** biotic
**relating to long-legged wading birds** grallatorial
**relating to love** amatory, amorous
**relating to lymph** lymphatic
**relating to main fund of a business** capital
**relating to males** masculine
**relating to marriage** hymeneal, marital
**relating to meals** prandial
**relating to medicine** iatric(al)
**relating to mercury** mercurial
**relating to Middle Ages** mediaeval

**relating to milk** galactic
**relating to missiles or projectiles** ballistic
**relating to money** pecuniary
**relating to morals** ethic
**relating to names** onomastic
**relating to Negros** Negritic
**relating to nerves** neural
**relating to night** nocturnal
**relating to Nile** Nilotic
**relating to noon** meridian
**relating to number sixty** sexagesimal
**relating to open sea** pelagic
**relating to oracles** oracular
**relating to Orient** Asiatic, oriental
**relating to part of ear** lobar
**relating to part of eyeball** uveal
**relating to Peter** Petrine
**relating to pharmacy** pharmaceutic
**relating to pillars** columnar
**relating to place of learning** academic
**relating to pregnancy** (ante)natal, prenatal
**relating to proper names** onomastic
**relating to punishment** penal
**relating to pure motion** kinematic
**relating to royal house** aulic
**relating to science** metric
**relating to sea** oceanic
**relating to servant in house** menial
**relating to sexual love** erotic
**relating to shapes** figural
**relating to ships** nautical
**relating to sight** optic
**relating to soil** edaphic
**relating to son or daughter** filial
**relating to sound** acoustic
**relating to stars** astral, sidereal
**relating to St Francis of Sales** Salesian
**relating to stone workers** masonic
**relating to swimming** natatorial, natatory
**relating to tailors** sartorial
**relating to tears** lac(h)rymal, lacrimal
**relating to the back** dorsal
**relating to the ear** otic
**relating to the end** latter
**relating to the eye** optic
**relating to the head** capital
**relating to the heart and blood vessels** cardiovascular
**relating to the heart and lungs** cardiopulmonary
**relating to the jaw** maxillary
**relating to the liver** hepatic
**relating to the lungs and stomach** pneumogastric
**relating to the mind** noetic
**relating to the nose** nasal
**relating to the side** lateral
**relating to the skeleton** osteal

**relating to the soul** inner
**relating to the tongue** lingual
**relating to time to come** future
**relating to tonsils** amygdaline
**relating to trade** mercantile
**relating to trees** arboreal, arboreous
**relating to trustee** fiduciary
**relating to two** dual
**relating to universe** cosmic
**relating to virus** viral
**relating to vision** optic
**relating to vocabulary** lexical
**relating to war** martial
**relating to wasps** vespine
**relating to wax modelling** ceroplastic
**relating to wife** uxorial
**relating to wings** alar
**relating to wolves** lupine
**relation** account, association, connection, description, kin, narration, narrative, reference, regard, relating, relationship, report, respect, story, telling
**relation between species** affinity
**relation by marriage** affinity
**relation of likeness** analogy
**relation of plant growth to gravity** geotropism
**relationship** affair, bond, conjunction, connection, exchange, kinship, liaison, link, proportion, ratio, similarity, tie-up
**relationship between cause and effect** causality
**relationship by descent from the same ancestor** consanguinity
**relation to sentence** parse
**relative** affiliated, applicable, associated, aunt, brother, comparable, comparative, connected, cousin, family, germane, kin, nephew, niece, related, relation, relevant, sib, sister, uncle
**relative bigness** size
**relative by marriage** in-law
**relative importance** status
**relative in proportion** size
**relatively far out** outer
**relatively short** abbreviated
**relatively short and strongly built** stocky
**relative on father's side** agnate
**relative quality** class
**relative quantity** degree
**relative speed** rate
**relative to** re
**relativity rule** Einstein's law
**relax** abate, calm, diminish, ease, ebb, enfeeble, laze, lessen, loosen, lower, mitigate, moderate, reduce, relax, relieve, remit, rest, slacken, soften, tranquillise, unbend, unwind, weaken
**relaxation** calmness, dolce far niente (I), ease, holiday, intermission, leave, leisure, lull, pause, peace, quietude, recess, repose, rest, tranquillity, vacation
**relaxation of international tension** détente
**relaxed** abated, calm, carefree, casual, collected, composed, cool, eased, easy-going, even-tempered, informal, mild, unhurried
**relaxed in style** easygoing, laid-back, unhurried
**relax from labour** rest
**relaxing** restful
**relaxing political strain** détente
**relax severity** relent
**relay** carry, communicate, communication, despatch, dispatch, message, (re)broadcast, relief, send, shift, spread, supply, transmission, transmit, turn
**relay of workers** shift
**release** acquit(tal), advertise, assoil, broadcast, deliver(ance), discharge, disclose, disengage, dismiss(al), emancipation, exempt(ion), free(dom), issue, liberate, liberation, loose, manumit, proclaim, publish, relieve, rescue, rescuing, televise, unhand, unleash, unloose, unpen, unshackle, untie
**release conditionally** parole
**release emotion** abreast
**release from a promise** acquit
**release from blame** absolve
**release from bonds** unfetter
**release from debt** freith
**release from duty** relieve
**release from guilt** absolution
**release from obligation** acquit, exempt
**release from restraint** unfetter
**release from servitude** affranchise
**release from tension** relieve
**release gas from** deflate
**release of person not found guilty in court** acquittal
**release on bond** parole
**release the grip of hands** unclasp
**release through pores** exude
**release without charge** free
**relegate** abolish, delete, demote, depose, detach, discharge, dismiss, displace, doff, efface, eject, eliminate, erase, expel, extract, move, oust, purge, remove, shed, transfer, transport, unseat, withdraw
**relent** capitulate, forbear, melt, relax, slacken, slow, soften, unbend, weaken, yield

**relentless** bloodthirsty, cruel, ferocious, grudging, inexorable, inhuman, obdurate, persistent, pitiless, stern, undaunted, unforgiving, unkind, unrelenting, unremitting, unsparing, unyielding
**relentless control** clutch
**relentless tracker** hound, sleuth
**relevance** application, bearing, bond, communication, connection, consequence, correspondence, function, import(ance), intercourse, link, marriage, matter, moment, pertinence, practice, purpose, relation(ship), significance, tie-in, use, value, weight
**relevant** admissible, applicable, appropriate, apropos, apt, fitting, germane, material, opposite, pertinent, proper, related, significant, suited
**reliable** authoritative, certain, conscientious, consistent, dependable, genuine, honourable, infallible, observant, steady, sure, trustworthy, trusty, unchangeable, unfailing
**reliable friend** ally
**reliable person** Atlas, mainstay
**reliable support** anchor
**reliance** assurance, belief, confidence, credence, credit, dependence, faith, trust
**reliance on truth** trust
**reliant** dependable, dependent, depending, trusting
**relic** debris, embers, fragments, keepsake, memento, pieces, remains, remembrance, reminder, remnant, rubble, ruins, scrap, souvenir, survival, token, trace, trophy, vestige, wreckage
**relic of former times** antique
**relics** bones, cadaver, carcass, corpse, fossil, fragments, keepsake(s), memento, petrification, remembrance, remnants, scraps, souvenir, stiff, tokens, traces, vestiges
**relics gallery** museum
**relict** widow
**relief** aid, alleviation, assistance, balm, break, comfort, cure, deliverance, diversion, ease, embrocation, help, liberation, liniment, medicine, mitigation, opiate, palliation, relaxation, release, remedy, remission, rescue, respite, rest, softening, solace, succour, support, treatment
**relief carving** cameo
**relief in sculpture** relievo

**relief of** rid
**relief office worker** temp
**relief of pain** ease
**relief of strong feelings** catharsis
**relieve** abate, aid, allay, alleviate, assist, assuage, calm, comfort, correct, disburden, ease, exempt, help, lessen, mitigate, mollify, pacify, reduce, relax, release, remedy, rid, slacken, solace, soothe, subdue, succour, support, sustain, unburden
**relieves blocked nasal psassages** decongestant
**relieved sigh** phew
**relieves hay fever** antihistamine
**relieves muscular tension** massage
**relieves pain** analgesic
**relieve someone's anxiety** reassure
**relieves stomach and gullet ulcers** antacid
**relieve without curing** palliate
**relieving** aiding, assisting, consoling, curing, dulling, easing, helping, mitigating, mollifying, relaxing, softening, solacing, soothing, succouring, supporting, sustaining
**relieving burden** lightening
**relieving pain** analgesic, anodyne
**relieving shift of workers** relay
**religieuse (F)** nun
**religieux (F)** padre, priest
**religion** belief, canons, Church, creed, deism, denomination, divinity, doctrine, dogma, faith, pantheism, persuasion, piety, sect, spirituality, Taoism, theism, theology, theosophy, worship
**religion of Jews** Judaism
**religion of Muslims** Islam
**religions and beliefs** Bahaism, Buddhism, Christianity, Hinduism, Islam, Jainism, Judaism, obi, Shamanism, Shintoism, Sikhism, Taoism
**religious** conscientious, devotional, devout, divine, doctrinal, dutiful, exacting, faithful, God-fearing, holy, nun, pious, pure, reverent, righteous, rigid, sacred, scriptual, scrupulous, spiritual, strict, theological, unswerving
**religious address** sermon
**religious adherence to laws** nomism
**religious allegory** parable
**religious anniversary** feast
**religious assemblage** congregation
**religious awakening** revival
**religious belief** creed, doctrine, dogma, faith, persuasion, tenet
**religious book** psalter
**religious brother** monk
**religious brotherhood** fraternity

**religious campaign** crusade, jehad, jihad
**religious capital of Islam** Mecca
**religious ceremony** mass, rite
**religious circle of beads** rosary
**religious circular** tract
**religious class of people** sect
**religious congregation** flock
**religious conversion** salvation
**religious denomination** church, sect
**religious deviant** heretic
**religious deviation** heresy
**religious devotion** piety
**religious discipline** asceticism, penance
**religious dogma** tenet, doctrine
**religious establishment** abbey
**religious expedition** rite
**religious faith** Baha'i, Buddhism, Christianity, Confucianism, Hinduism, Islam, Judaism, religion, Zoroastrianism
**religious female** nun
**religious festival** Christmas, Easter, Eid-ul-Fitr, fiesta, Mela, Purim
**religious follower** disciple
**religious group** cult, sect
**religious head** pope
**religious hermit** monk
**religious house** abbey, church, cloister, convent, friary, monastery, mosque, nunnery, priory, synagogue, temple
**religious hymn** canticle
**religious hymns collectively** hymnody
**religious inspiration** afflatus
**religious journey** pilgrimage
**religious leader** dominee, hierarch, ima(u)m, moulana(h), mullah, pope, priest, rabbi, reverend
**religious lecture** homily, sermon
**religious legalism** nomism
**religious madness** theomania
**religious morning service** matins
**religious music** cantata
**religious musical composition** anthem, cantata, hymn, motet, oratorio
**religious novice** neophyte
**religious observance** rite
**religious offshoot** sect
**religious opinion** doxy
**religious outpost** mission
**religious painting** icon
**religious pamphlet** tract
**religious pastorate** parish
**religious period** Lent, Ramadan
**religious picture** icon
**religious poll** theological survey
**religious possession** power
**religious recluse** anchorite, hermit, monk, nun

**religious representation** icon
**religious rite** mystery, ordinance
**religious science** theology
**religious sect** denomination, Hare Krishna, Moonies
**religious sister** nun
**religious solemn day** fast
**religious song** anthem, cantata, chant, hymn, psalm
**religious songbook** hymnal, psalter
**religious speech** sermon
**religious story** parable
**religious superior** abbot, mother, provincial
**religious symbol** icon
**religious war** crusade, jehad, jihad
**religious woman** nun
**religious writing of doubtful authenticity** apocrypha
**religious zealot** fanatic
**relinquish** abandon, abdicate, abjure, abnegate, abscond, allow, betray, capitulate, cease, cede, clear, commit, decamp, defect, deliver, depart, desert, desist, despair, devote, disappear, discard, disclaim, discontinue, disgorge, ditch, drop, evacuate, exit, forbear, forfeit, (for)go, forsake, forswear, give, grant, jettison, jilt, leave, lend, liberate, lose, maroon, move, quit, reject, release, renounce, repudiate, resign, surrender, waive, yield
**relinquish a job** resign
**relinquish a position** retreat
**relish** appetiser, appreciate, appreciation, aspic, condiment, delight, desire, enjoy(ment), fancy, flavour, fondness, gusto, like, liking, love, palate, pleasure, predilection, preference, satisfaction, savour, taste, wish, zest
**relish for food** chaw
**relish tray item** olive
**relocate** resite
**reluctance** aversion, disinclination, hesitance, loathing, repugnance, unwillingness
**reluctance to move** inertia
**reluctant** adverse, antagonistic, averse, cautious, circumspect, demurring, disapproving, disinclined, faltering, grudging, hesitant, indisposed, leery, lo(a)th, opposed, resistant, resisting, slow, struggling, unwilling
**reluctant through fear** fearful
**reluctant to hear** earless
**rely** bank, bet, count, depend, hope, lean, reckon, rest, swear, trust
**relying** dependent, reckoning
**relying on experience** empiric

**rely on** believe, depend, trust
**remain** abide, bid(e), cling, continue, delay, dwell, endure, last, linger, outlast, outlive, perdure, persevere, persist, prevail, remnant, rest, scrap, sojourn, stand, stay, succeed, survive, tarry, wait
**remain awake** vigilate
**remainder** balance, carry-over, difference, dregs, effect, excess, leavings, outstanding, overplus, remnant, residuals, residue, residuum, rest, result(ant), superfluity, surplus, trace
**remain in a place during summer** aestivate
**remaining** abiding, clinging, continuing, delaying, dwelling, enduring, lasting, lingering, outstanding, prevailing, resting, standing, surviving, tarrying, unfinished, waiting
**remaining attached to the plant when withered** marcescent
**remaining choice** alternative
**remaining neutral** non-committal
**remaining part of felled tree** stump
**remaining piece** remnant
**remaining trace** vestige
**remaining unmarried** celibate
**remain in one place in the air** hover
**remain in readiness** wait
**remain motionless** stagnate
**remain on one's feet** stand
**remains** ash(es), discards, fragments, garbage, leavings, leftovers, oddments, orts, refuse, relics, remainder, remnants, residue, rest, ruins, rummage, truck, vestiges
**remains in pipe bowl** topper
**remains of anything ruined** wreck
**remains of bolted flower** semolina
**remains of cane** bagass(e)
**remains of combustion** ash
**remains of destroyed ship** wreck
**remains of fire** ash
**remains of food** scrap
**remains of old building** ruins
**remain suspended in one place** hover
**remain too long** outstay, overstay
**remain torpid** hibernate
**remain undeveloped** abort
**remain united in a mass** cohere
**remain unused** lie
**remain upright** stand
**remake** alter, convert, rebuild, reconstruct, redo, reform, remodel, renew, repair, reshape, revamp, revise
**remark** acknowl(e)dgement, assertion, comment, consideration, declaration, declare, heed, mention, note, notice, observation, observe, opinion, perceive, regard, say, see, state(ment), utter(ance)
**remarkable** amazing, astounding, conspicuous, distinguished, eminent, exceptional, extraordinary, famous, impressive, notable, noteworthy, prodigious, prominent, singular, strange, striking, uncommon, unusual, wondrous
**remarkable achievement** feat
**remarkable event** miracle
**remarkable happening** phenomenon
**remarkable occurrence** miracle
**remarkable period** epoch
**remarkable person** humdinger
**remarkably learned** erudite
**remarkably rare objects** exotica
**remarkably small** diminutive, tiny
**remarkably strange** exotic
**remark about** mention
**remark briefly** glance
**remediable** (a)mendable, correctable, curative, emendable, fixable, recoverable, rectifiable, redeemable, restorable
**remedial** beneficial, corrective, curative, healthful, helpful, restorative, salutary, wholesome
**remedial treatment** cure, therapy
**remedy** antidote, antitoxin, correct, cure, heal, medicament, medication, medicine, ointment, panacea, relief, remove, repair, restorative, restore, right, treatment
**remedy for all diseases** catholicon, panacea
**remedy for a particular ailment** specific
**remedy for jaundice** icteric
**remedy for reducing fever** febrifuge
**remember** bethink, commemorate, memorialise, memorise, muse, place, recall, recognise, recollect, reidentify, reminisce, retain, retrospect, review
**remember an event very vividly** relive
**remembrance** anamnesis, keepsake, memento, memorial, memory, recollection, relic, remembering, reminder, reminiscence, retrospect(ion), shrine, souvenir, thought, token
**remind** hint, prompt
**reminder** clue, cue, evocator, hint, keepsake, memo(randum), mnemonic, note, prompting, souvenir, token
**remind one of** resemble
**reminiscence** anecdote, memoir, memory, recall, recollection, reflection, remembrance, retrospection, review
**reminiscent** evocative, nostalgic, remindful, similar, suggestive
**remiss** careless, delinquent, derelict, fainéant, forgetful, heedless, inattentive, indolent, laggard, lax, lazy, loose, negligent, shiftless, slack, sloppy, slothful, slow, tardy
**remission** abatement, absolution, decrease, diminution, discharge, forgiveness, indulgence, lessening, mitigation, pardon, pause, relaxation, release, relinquishment, respite, subsidence
**remissness** carelessness, dilatoriness, forgetfulness, heedlessness, inattentiveness, laxness, negligence, slackness, tardiness, thoughtlessness
**remit** abate, absolve, cancel, diminish, forgive, forward, overlook, postpone, replace, restore, return, send
**remittance** allowance, consideration, dispatch, fee, payment, sending
**remnant** balance, bit, end, fragment, hangover, leftovers, oddment, offcut, piece, remainder, remains, residue, residuum, rest, scrap, shred, survival, trace, vestige
**remnant of anything** stub
**remnant of fire** ash
**remnant of tree** stump
**remnant of unburnt tobacco in pipe** dottle
**remnants of something destroyed** debris
**remnants of wreck** wreckage
**remodel** rebuild, redo, remake, reproduce, restore, revamp
**remonstrance** admonition, blame, castigation, caution, censure, denial, deprecation, disagreement, disclaimer, dissent, dissuasion, expostulation, grievance, noncompliance, objection, protest(ation), rebuke, remonstration, reprimand, scolding
**remonstrate** argue, castigate, censure, chide, denounce, dispose, expostulate, protest, rebuke, reprimand, reproach, scold, suppose, upbraid, vituperate
**remorse** angst, anguish, compassion, compunction, contrition, grief, guilt, penitence, pity, regret, shame, sorrow
**remorseful** apologetic, contrite, penitent, regretful, repentant, sad, sorry
**remorseless** callous, cruel, hard(-hearted), harsh, inexorable,

inhumane, merciless, pitiless, relentless, ruthless, savage, stern, unforgiving, unmerciful, unrelenting, unstoppable
**remote** abstracted, afar, alien, aloof, detached, different, distant, faint, far(-off), faraway, foreign, furthermost, inaccessible, indifferent, indirect, isolated, lonely, negligible, out-of-the-way, outlying, removed, secluded, separated, slender, slight, slim, unconnected, uninvolved, unlikely, vague, withdrawn
**remote allusion** hint
**remote-controlled ship** drone
**remote fort** outpost
**remote from observation** obscure
**remote from sea** inland
**remote in time** long ago
**remoteness** distance
**remote settlement** outpost
**remount** reset
**removable cover** lid
**removal** de-, departure, dislodgment, dismissal, dispossession, ejection, elimination, eradication, expulsion, extraction, move, relocation, stripping, subtraction, transfer, uprooting, withdrawal
**removal of** de-
**removal of any part of the body** ablation
**removal of Fallopian tubes** tubectomy
**removal of fat from the body by suction** liposuction
**removal of ice from glacier** attrition
**removal of loosened rock** scaling
**removal of ship's spars** dismastment
**removal of the appendix** append(ic)ectomy
**removal of the womb** hysterectomy
**removal prefix** de-
**remove** abolish, abstract, amputate, de-, dele(te), destroy, diminish, disburden, dislodge, displace, eliminate, expose, extract, extricate, kill, rebate, replace, rip off, separate, shed, steal, strip, subtract, take, transfer, uncover, uproot
**remove air from** de-aerate, deflate
**remove all clothes** strip
**remove all traces** eradicate, erase
**remove apple centre** core
**remove bit by bit** scamble
**remove bone from** fillet
**remove cargo** unload
**remove clothing** disrobe, doff, strip, undress
**remove colour** bleach
**remove cork** open
**remove corneous growths** dehorn
**remove cover** uncap

**remove covering from** strip
**remove cream** skim
**remove creases from clothes** iron
**remove curbs** unbridle
**remove detonator from bomb** defuse
**remove dirt** dust, sweep
**remove dirt from** cleanse
**remove entirely** uproot
**remove errors from** correct, emend, erase
**remove excess metal** cut
**remove fleece** shear
**remove forcibly from power** overthrow
**remove from account** debit
**remove from active service** retire
**remove from fixed position** dislodge
**remove from office** depose, dethrone, oust, unseat
**remove from one place to another** transfer
**remove from power** depose, dethrone
**remove from sight** seclude
**remove from the truck** unload
**remove gas** degas
**remove hair** (d)epilate
**remove hair from face and chin** shave
**remove hat as a sign of respect** vail
**remove head skin** scalp
**remove husks and chaff** geld
**remove ice** de-ice
**remove impurities** refine
**remove ink** eradicate
**remove insides of fish** gib, gip
**remove knot** undo, untie
**remove laundry fasteners** unpeg
**remove lid** open
**remove limb** amputate
**remove mast** unstep
**remove moisture from** dehydrate, desiccate, dry
**remove objectionable parts** expurgate
**remove obstruction from** unblock
**remove one's clothes** strip
**remove ore** extract
**remove or take out** eliminate
**remove particles of gold leaf** skew
**remove peel** pare
**remove pencil mark** erase
**remove pins** unpeg
**remove poisons** decontaminate
**remove potatoes** grabble
**remove powdery matter** dust
**remove pretensions** debunk
**remove queen bee** demaree
**remove quietly** abstract
**remove restraints from** unbridle
**remove rind** peel
**remove salt from** desalinate
**remove seed from flax** ribble
**remove seeds** stone
**remove skin** excoriate, hull, husk, pare, peel

**remove skin of almonds** blanch
**remove soap** rinse
**remove sound from tape** blip
**remove stamens** castrate
**remove stitch** decrease
**remove surface cream** skim
**remove tablecloth** draw
**remove to lower class** relegate
**remove to safety** evacuate
**remove water** dehydrate, desiccate
**remove weapon** unarm
**remove weeds** hoe
**remove wool** belly
**remove wrinkles from clothes** iron
**remunerate** benefit, compensate, earn, fee, gain, indemnify, net, profit, recompense, redress, reimburse, (re)pay, return, reward, satisfy, yield
**remuneration** bribe, compensation, earnings, emolument, fee, gratuity, income, payoff, recompense, remittance, (re)payment, salary, settlement, stipend, tip, wages
**Remus's twin** Romulus
**renaissance** awakening, re-emergence, rebirth, rekindling, renascence, renewal, resurgence, resurrection, revival
**renal** nephritic
**renal pain** colic
**renal tube** ureter
**renascent** awakenened, awakening, reanimated, reappearing, reborn, regenerative, renewed, resurgent, revived
**rend** anatomise, batter, bite, branch, break, burst, chew, clamp, claw, cleave, crack, crash, crunch, crush, cut, demolish, destroy, detach, disband, disjoint, dislimb, dislocate, dismember, dissect, distress, disunite, diverge, divide, fracture, fragment, fray, gash, gnaw, grip, hack, hold, incise, jag, lacerate, maim, mangle, mince, nibble, nip, open, pain, part, peel, pierce, pinch, pull, quarter, rack, rip, rive, rupture, scramble, scratch, separate, sever, slash, split, sunder, tear, wound, wrench, wrest, wring
**rend apart** abscind, divulse
**render** afford, contribute, deliver, demonstrate, do, exhibit, give, interpret, make, perform, present, restore, submit, supply, surrender, translate
**render active** activate, animate, enliven
**render assistance to ship** foy
**render bomb harmless** defuse
**render capable** activate, capacitate
**render desolate** destroy, ruin
**rendered hog fat** lard

**render fit** adapt
**render gloomy** sadden
**render incapable of procreating children** sterilise
**render ineffective** vitiate
**rendering null and void** defeasance
**rendering plant** knackery
**render insane** derange
**render muddy** roil
**render neutral** neutralise
**render null and void** cancel, (dis)annul, frustrate, negate, neutralise, nullify
**render sparkling** aerate
**render suitable** adapt
**render to** bestow
**render turbid** roil
**render unconscious** stun
**render unfeeling** numb
**render useless** null(ify)
**render verdict** pass
**render void** annul, defeat, nullify
**render weak** enervate
**rendezvous** appointment, assemble, assignation, collect, date, engagement, gather, meet(ing), muster, tryst
**rending** anatomising, battering, cleaving, cracking, demolishing, dissecting, fracturing, lacerating, separating, severing, smashing, snapping, wounding
**rendition** arrangement, construe, decoding, enactment, execution, interlinear, interpretation, lection, paraphrase, performance, production, recital, rendering, reproduction, restatement, transcription, translation, understanding, variation, version
**renegade** apostate, backslider, betrayer, fugitive, impimpi, insurgent, outlaw, quisling, rebel, recreant, slacker, traitor, turncoat
**renegue** decline, deny, refuse, renege, renounce
**renew** iterate, re-establish, recondition, recreate, redo, refresh, regenerate, reiterate, remake, renovate, repair, repeat, replenish, restore, resume, resupply, resurrect, revive, update
**renewal** enlivenment, freshening, improvement, rally, reappearance, reawakening, rebirth, reconditioning, reconstitution, recovery, recreation, refreshment, refurbishment, rehabilitation, reinvigoration, renaissance, renascence, renovation, repair, restoration, resuscitation, revitalisation, revival, stimulation

**renewing** continuing, extending, mending, modernising, overhauling, reaffirming, recreating, refitting, regenerating, rejuvenating, repairing, replacing, restocking, resuming, transforming
**renew the circuit** rewire
**renounce** abandon, abdicate, abjure, abnegate, avoid, avow, decline, deny, desert, disavow, discard, disclaim, disown, eliminate, eschew, forgo, forsake, forswear, leave, quit, recant, refuse, relinquish, reneg(u)e, repudiate, resign, vacate, waive
**renovate** do up, mend, overhaul, recondition, redo, reform, refresh, refurbish, rehabilitate, remodel, renew, repair, restore, resuscitate, revamp, revive
**renown** acclaim, bays, celebrity, distinction, éclat, eminence, fame, favour, glory, importance, kudos, notability, popularity, pre-eminence, prestige, primacy, prominence, reputation, repute, stardom, vogue
**renowned** acclaimed, celebrated, distinguished, eminent, famed, famous, illustrious, notable, noted
**renowned explorer** Cook, Livingstone, Park, Polo, Stanley
**rent** cleft, crack, fissure, gap, gorge, hire, laceration, lease, let, opening, payment, rental, return, rift, rip, schism, separation, split, tore, torn
**rental agreement** lease
**renter** hirer, holder, lessee, tenant
**rent out** lease
**rent out of pasture** agist
**rent payer** tenant
**rent rooms to** lodge
**rent under contract** lease
**renunciation** capitulation, contradiction, delivery, denial, destruction, disavowal, dismissal, dissent, loss, negation, oblation, prohibition, refusal, rejection, repudiation, repulse, resignation, sacrifice, submission, surrender, veto
**reorganise** change, edit, emend, overhaul, realign, rearrange, reconstruct, recreate, rectify, redevelop, redo, refashion, regroup, remake, restore, revamp
**repair** adjust(ment), amend(ment), condition, darn, fix, form, heal, improve(ment), mend, overhaul, patch, recondition, rectification, rectify, redo, redress, refit, remake, remedy, remodel, renew, renovate, resole, restoration, restore, retrieve, revive, shape, state, stitch, tar
**repair badly** botch

**repair boat** careen
**repair clumsily** botch
**repair road** skid
**repair worn tyre** recap
**reparation** amends, atonement, compensation, indemnification, recompense, recoupment, redemption, redress, renovation, repair, repayment, requital, retribution, solatium
**repartee** answer, badinage, banter, counterblast, counterstroke, drollery, jesting, jocularity, joking, persiflage, pleasantry, quip, raillery, reply, return, riposte, sally, waggery, wit(tiness), wordplay
**repast** banquet, board, dinnertime, feast, food, lunchtime, meal(time), mess, provision, refection, refreshment, snack, suppertime, table, victuals
**repay** avenge, compensate, indemnify, reciprocate, recompense, refund, reimburse, remunerate, requite, restore, retaliate, return, revenge, reward, square
**repayable on demand** callable
**repay in kind** retaliate
**repayment** compensation, rebate, recompense, refund, reimbursement, remuneration, requitement, restitution, reward
**repay with good or evil** requite
**repeal** abolish, abrogate, annul(ment), countermand, nullify, recall, rescind, reverse, revoke, withdraw
**repeat** again, ditto, duplicate, echo, emphasise, ingeminate, iterate, iteration, memorise, mimic, parrot, quote, recap(itulate), recite, reconstruct, recreate, recur, redo, reduplicate, regurgitate, rehearse, reiterate, repetition, rephrase, report, reproduce, rerun, restate
**repeat aloud** recite
**repeat by request** encore
**repeated bifurcation** dichotomy
**repeated drumming** tattoo
**repeated dull explosive sound** chug
**repeated from point indicated** dal segno
**repeated knocking** ratatat
**repeatedly** always, ceaselessly, constantly, continually, continuously, eftsoons, frequently, incessantly, often, recurrently
**repeatedly annoy** pester
**repeated movie** rerun
**repeated musical phrase** ostinato
**repeated sound** echo
**repeat game** replay
**repeating decimal** repetend

**repeat marks** ditto
**repeat offender** malefact
**repeat of pattern** gait
**repeat passages from** quote
**repeat performance** encore, rerun
**repeat prefix** re-
**repeat someone's opinion** echo
**repeat someone's concurring statement** re-echo
**repeat sound** echo
**repeat tiresomely** din
**repel** decline, deflect, disgust, disperse, foil, nauseate, rebuff, refuse, reject, repulse, revolt, sicken, spurn, withstand
**repellant** centrifugal
**repellent** abominable, base, contemptible, corrupt, decaying, despicable, dirty, disgusting, distasteful, execrable, f(o)etid, foul, hateful, heinous, horrible, horrid, impure, loathsome, mean, nasty, nauseating, noisome, obnoxious, obscene, odious, offensive, putrid, reeking, repugnant, repulsive, resistant, revolting, rotten, sickening, unbearable, vile
**repent** atone, bemoan, deplore, lament, regret, rue, yield
**repentance** bitterness, compunction, contriteness, contrition, disappointment, dole, embarrassment, grief, guilt, lamentation, penitence, regret, remorse(fulness), rue(fulness), self-blame, self-denunciation, shame, sorriness, sorrow, woe
**repentant** apologetic, ashamed, contrite, penitent, regretful, rueful, sorry
**repent of** rue
**repercussion** backlash, concussion, consequence, echo, effect, impact, kickback, rebound, recoil, result, reverberation, shock, upshot
**repertory** collection, list, range, repertoire, repository, reserve, reservoir, stock, store, supply
**repetition** duplication, echo, recital, recurrence, repeat, restatement, return, rote
**repetition of sound** echo
**repetition of the same thing in different words** tautology
**repetitive** boring, colourless, droning, dull, flat, humdrum, mechanical, monotonous, plodding, recurrent, repetitious, samey, soporific, tedious, tiresome, toneless, unchanging, uniform, uninflected, unvaried, wearisome
**repetitive theme** rondo

**repine** agonise, bemoan, bewail, brood, complain, fret, fuss, groan, grumble, lament, languish, meditate, moan, mope, mourn, murmur, muse, pine, regret, rue, ruminate, sigh, sulk, weaken
**replace** follow, oust, re-establish, refund, reinstate, repay, replenish, reset, restore, substitute, succeed, supersede, supplant, supply
**replace a gem** reset
**replace bullet** reload
**replacement** double, fill-in, proxy, re-establishment, reinstatement, stand-in, substitute, successor, surrogate, understudy
**replenish** fill, furnish, provide, recharge, refill, refuel, reload, renew, restock, revictual, (re)store, supply
**replete** abounding, abrim, bursting, cloyed, complete, crammed, filled, full, gorged, jammed, packed, profuse, rampart, sated, satiated, stuffed, surfeited
**replica** copy, duplicate, facsimile, imitation, model, reproduction, twin
**replication** answer, copy, counterfeit, duplicate, echo, facsimile, forgery, image, imitation, likeness, model, pattern, photocopy, print, recital, recurrence, rehearsal, rejoinder, relation, renewal, repeat, replica, replying, reproduction, tautology
**reply** acknowledge, answer, antiphon, back-chat, correspond, echo, password, reaction, rejoin(der), replication, respond, response, results, retort, return, riposte
**reply in kind** reciprocate, retaliate
**reply of assent** ay(e), yea, yes
**reply to** acknowledge, answer
**reply to answer** replication
**report** account, analysis, announce(ment), appear, article, brief, compte rendu (F), declaration, denounce, description, detail, disclose, dispatch, gossip, hearsay, message, news, note, paper, record, relate, reveal, rumour, sound, state(ment), story, summary, tale, talk, tell, tidings, word, write-up
**reporter** announcer, correspondent, hack, journalist, newscaster, newshound, newsman, newspaperman, newspaperwoman, pressman, writer
**reporter's exclusive story** scoop
**reporter's word** where
**report in detail** document
**report minutely** detail
**report of events** news

**repose** breath, dormant, ease, hibernate, hush, idleness, nod, peace, quiet, recess, relax, relief, respite, rest(fulness), serenity, siesta, sleep, slumber, somnolence, tranquillity, vegetate
**repose on bed** lie
**repository for bodies** morgue
**repot** reset
**represent** act, denote, depict, describe, designate, embody, enact, evoke, exemplify, exhibit, express, figure, illustrate, image, mean, outline, perform, personify, picture, portray, produce, render, reproduce, show, sketch, stage, symbolise, typify
**representation** account, bust, committee, delegates, delegation, description, exhibition, explanation, idol, illustration, image, likeness, model, narration, performance, picture, play, portrait, portrayal, production, relation, show, sight, sketch, spectacle, statue
**representation of child or angel** putto
**representation of Mary with the body of Jesus** pietà
**representation of one colour** monochrome
**representation of the Crucifixion** Calvary
**representative** agent, attorney, consignee, delegate, deputy, diplomat, embodiment, emissary, envoy, factotum, proctor, proxy, sample, specimen, spokesman, substitute, surrogate, trustee, type, typical, understudy
**representative at a conference** delegate
**representative of pope** legate
**representative portion** sample
**represent by marks** notate
**represented by an x** ten
**represent in drawing** limn
**representing the whole Christian world** ecumenical
**representing vocal sounds** phonetic
**represent in outline** adumbrate
**represent on stage** act
**represent too favourably** flatter
**repress** arrest, check, command, conceal, control, curb, curtail, enthral, govern, inhibit, quash, quell, reduce, restrain, squelch, subdue, subjugate, suppress, temper
**repress anger** smoulder
**repress by power** overbear
**repression** authoritarianism, censorship, coercion, constraint, control, denial, despotism, domination, gagging, inhibition,

restraint, subjugation, suffocation, suppression, tyranny
**repressive** absolute, authoritarian, autocratic, brutal, coercive, cruel, despotic, dictatorial, forbidding, grinding, harsh, heavy, onerous, oppressive, prohibitive, restraining, restrictive, severe, suppressive, tough, tyrannical, unjust
**reprieve** abate, acquittal, allay, alleviate, amnesty, deliverance, forgiveness, indulge, mitigate, mitigation, palliation, relaxation, relief, remission, remit, respite, suspend, suspension
**reprimand** admonition, blame, castigate, castigation, censure, check, chide, chiding, criticism, disparagement, lecture, rating, rebuff, rebuke, reprehension, reproach, reproof, reproval, row, scold, upbraid, warning, wigging
**reprint** reissue
**reprisal** compensation, counterattack, counterstroke, indemnity, redress, repayment, requital, restitution, retaliation, retribution, revenge, vendetta, vengeance
**reproach** abuse, blame, censure, chide, condemn(ation), criticise, criticism, disapproval, discredit, expostulation, ignominy, indignity, infamy, opprobrium, rebuke, remonstrance, reprehend, reprehension, reprimand, reproof, reprove, scold, shame, upbraid(ing)
**reproachful** abusive, censorious, critical, disappointed, disapproving, disparaging, fault-finding, hurt, insulting, libellous, maligning, offensive, opprobrious, reproving, reviling, rude, scathing, scolding, slanderous, stung, traducing, upbraiding, upset, vilifying, vituperative, wounded
**reproachful language** exprobration
**reproach stingingly** taunt
**reprobate** amoral, caitiff, corrupt, depraved, despicable, devil, hopeless, miscreant, outcast, rogue, scoundrel, sinful, traitor, troublemaker, unprincipled, villain, wicked, wretch
**reproduce** breed, copy, duplicate, echo, generate, imitate, match, mirror, multiply, print, proliferate, propagate, recreate, repeat, replicate, spawn
**reproduction** breeding, copy, duplicate, imitation, procreation, propagation, replica
**reproduction unit** seed

**reproduction without fertilisation** apomixis
**reproductive** generative, genital, sex(ual)
**reproductive cell** gamete
**reproductive organ** ovary
**reproof** admonition, blame, censure, condemnation, criticism, rebuke, reprimand, reproach, scolding, upbraiding
**reprove** abuse, accuse, admonish, berate, blame, castigate, censure, charge, chide, condemn, criticise, denounce, disapprove, rate, rebuke, reprehend, reprimand, reproach, scold, tax, upbraid
**reprove firmly** admonish
**reprove severely** rag, scold
**reprove sharply** rebuke
**reprove solemnly** admonish
**reproving** abusing, blaming, castigating, chastising, condemning, correcting, criticising, denouncing, disapproving, lecturing, punishing, reprimanding, reproaching, scolding
**reptile** lizard, snake, saurian, turtle, iguana, serpent, crocodile, alligator, gavial, caiman, tortoise, terrapin, tuatara
**republic in Africa** Botswana, Cameroon, Senegal, South Africa, Sudan, Tanzania, Tunisia, Zimbabwe
**republic in Arabia** Yemen
**republic in North Africa** Algeria, Libya, Tunisia
**republic in North America** Mexico
**republic in South America** Argentina, Bolivia, Brazil, Chili, Colombia, Ecuador, Peru, Venezuela
**republic in southeastern Asia** Laos
**republic in southwestern Asia** Iran
**republic in the Levant** Syria
**republic in West Africa** Congo, Ghana, Niger, Senegal
**Republic of Ireland** Eire
**republic on the Mediterranean** Syria
**republic on the Red Sea** Yemen
**repudiate** abandon, abolish, abrogate, annul, cancel, condemn, contradict, deny, desert, disapprove, disavow, discard, disclaim, disobey, disown, forsake, gainsay, ignore, neglect, nullify, recall, recant, reject, renounce, rescind, spurn, transgress, veto, void
**repugnance** aversion, conflict, detestation, discrepancy, disgust, disharmony, horror, nausea, objection, offence, opposition, reluctance, resistance, revulsion
**repugnant** abhorrent, abominable, adverse, antagonistic, averse,

contradictory, contrary, despicable, distasteful, fulsome, hostile, incompatible, inimical, loath, objecting, objectionable, obnoxious, odious, reluctant, repellent, unfriendly
**repulse** avoid, beat, check, conquer, crush, defeat, disregard, overpower, overthrow, quell, rebuff, refusal, refuse, reject, repel, rout, shun, snub, spurn(ing), subdue, subjugate, vanquish
**repulsive** abhorrent, abominable, detestable, disgusting, distasteful, ill-natured, loathsome, objectionable, odious, offensive, repellent, repugnant, unpleasant
**repulsive in appearance** ugly
**repulsively fat** gross
**repulsively filthy** squalid
**reputable** creditable, dependable, excellent, good, honourable, irreproachable, legitimate, principled, reliable, respectable, trustworthy, upright, worthy
**reputation** character, credit, distinction, esteem, estimation, fame, honour, infamy, name, opinion, position, renown, repute, standing, stature
**repute** account, allege, assume, celebrity, consider, credit, dignity, distinction, eminence, esteem, estimation, excellence, fame, glory, greatness, honour, importance, merit, name, notability, note, prestige, prominence, quality, rank, regard, renown, reputation, stardom, superiority, suppose, worth
**reputed** apparent, assumed, likely, logical, plausible, presumed, professed, purported, putative, reasonable, seeming, supposed
**request** appeal, ask, behest, beseech, demand, entreaty, implore, intercession, invite, invocation, obsecration, obtest(ation), petition, plea, require, solicit(ation), suggest, supplicate, supplication
**request as one's right** claim
**request earnestly** adjure, implore
**request for donation** appeal
**request to attend** invite
**require** ask, beg, claim, demand, depend, dictate, direct, enjoin, lack, miss, necessitate, need, obligate, order, request, urge, want
**required amount** quantum
**required by law** legal
**required by social custom** de rigueur (F)
**required standard** norm
**require expiation** piacular

**requirement** claim, command, demand, directive, injunction, mandate, must, need, requisition, ukase
**require much effort** strenuous
**require urgently** exact
**requiring care and adroitness** tricky
**requiring exact performance** strict, stringent
**requiring great effort** strenuous
**requiring great patience** demanding
**requiring much** exigent
**requisite for farming** stock
**requisites for an undertaking** equipage
**requisition** application, appropriate, appropriation, call, commandeer(ing), confiscate, demand, occupation, occupy, order, request, seize, seizure, summons, take(over), use
**requital** compensation, justice, reckoning, recompense, redress, reparation, repayment, reprisal, retaliation, retribution, revenge, reward, satisfaction, vengeance
**requite** atone, avenge, barter, compensate, discharge, exchange, honour, indemnify, liquidate, meet, offer, pay, punish, reciprocate, recompense, refund, reimburse, render, repair, repay, respond, restore, retaliate, revenge, reward, satisfy, settle, swap
**reredos** brazier, drapery, fireback, reardos, retablo, screen
**re-rent one's suite** sub-let
**re repetitious use of words** tautological
**res** point, thing
**rescind** abolish, abrogate, annul, cancel, delete, destroy, dissolve, efface, eliminate, end, eradicate, erase, expunge, extinguish, invalidate, nullify, obliterate, override, overthrow, quash, repeal, repudiate, retract, reverse, revoke, subvert, suppress, terminate, void
**rescind officially** repeal
**rescue** deliver(ance), extricate, free, liberate, liberation, preserve, ransom, recover(y), redeem, redemption, release, relief, salvage, salvation, save, saving
**rescued by Hercules** Hesione
**rescuer** defender, deliverer, guardian, liberator, preserver, protector, salvager, salvation, saviour
**rescuer of wrecked ships** salvager
**research** analyse, analysis, delve, enquire, enquiry, examination, examine, experiment(ation),
exploration, explore, groundwork, inquire, inquiry, investigate, investigation, probe, scrutinise, scrutiny, search, study
**researcher** analyst, boffin, enquirer, examiner, fieldworker, inquirer, inspector, investigator, reviewer, scientist, sleuth, student
**researcher's milieu** lab(oratory)
**resemblance** affinity, analogy, closeness, comparison, conformity, correspondence, facsimile, image, kinship, likeness, parallel, parity, sameness, semblance, similarity
**resemblance of sounds** alliteration, assonance
**resemblance to ancestors** atavism
**resemble** approach, duplicate, echo, favour, mirror, parallel
**resembling almonds** amygdaline
**resembling another** similar
**resembling arrow** sagittal
**resembling bears** ursine
**resembling bees** apian
**resembling birds** avian
**resembling carbon** carbonaceous
**resembling circle** cycloid
**resembling coins** nummular
**resembling comb** pectinal
**resembling ducks** anatine
**resembling eagles** aquiline
**resembling eggs** ovularian
**resembling egg yolk** vitelline
**resembling fat** lipoid(al)
**resembling fibres** fibroid
**resembling fish** ichthyoid(al)
**resembling fungi** fungoid
**resembling goose** anserine
**resembling grapes** uveous
**resembling hair in tenuity** capillary
**resembling hares** leporine
**resembling hawks** accipitrine
**resembling horse** equoid
**resembling human being** android
**resembling human being in form** anthropoid
**resembling in sound** assonant
**resembling ivory** eburnean, eburneoid, eburneous
**resembling ladder** scalariform
**resembling leather** coriaceous
**resembling lobes** lobate(d)
**resembling long hair** piliform
**resembling man** anthropoid
**resembling marble** marmoreal
**resembling mite or tick** acaroid
**resembling oil** oleaginous
**resembling old woman** anil
**resembling paradise** paradisaical, paradisiac(al)
**resembling pea** pisiform
**resembling pearl** nacreous, pearly
**resembling pillar** stelar
**resembling reed** arundinaceous
**resembling sac** saccular
**resembling salt** haloid
**resembling snake** anguine, snaky
**resembling snow** niveous
**resembling spines** acanthoid
**resembling star** stellate(d)
**resembling starch** amylaceous
**resembling swallows** hirundine
**resembling the brain** encephaloid
**resembling tree** arboreal
**resembling wall** mural
**resembling water** hydrotoid
**resembling wolf** lupine
**resembling wood** ligneous
**resent** (be)grudge, dislike
**resenter** begrudger
**resentful** aggravated, angered, angry, annoyed, bitter, embittered, hostile, indignant, irate, ireful, irked, irritated, peeved, revengeful, wrathful
**resentful contemplation** envy
**resentful displeasure** umbrage
**resentful through envy** jealous
**resentment** anger, animosity, bitterness, displeasure, dudgeon, fury, grudge, huff, hurt, indignation, ire, irritation, malice, pique, rage, umbrage, vexation, vindictiveness, wrath
**reservation** booking, condition, demur, doubt, enclave, hesitation, homeland, park, preserve, proviso, qualification, reserve, sanctuary, scepticism, scruple, stipulation, territory, tract
**reserve** constraint, earmark, hold, keep, order, qualification, reservation, restraint, retain, retention, reticence, save, silence, store, supply
**reserved** aloof, appointed, composed, engaged, formal, frigid, modest, restrained, retained, reticent, retiring, rigid, secretive, shy, silent, snobbish, taciturn, unapproachable, uncommunicative, unforthcoming, unresponsive, unsociable, unsocial, withdrawn
**reserved in speech** taciturn
**reserve fund** savings
**reserve supplies** store
**reserve tyre** spare
**reservoir** basin, cistern, dam, millpond, pool, receptacle, store, sump, supply, tank, well
**reservoir of thermometer** bulb
**reset** restore, return
**resettlement** emigration
**resettlement of a plant** ecesis
**reshowing movie** rerun

**reshuffle** (inter)change, realign(ment), rearrange(ment), redistribute, redistribution, regroup(ing), reorganisation, reorganise, restructure, restructuring, revise, revision, shake-up, shift, shuffle, upheaval
**reshuffle the cards** redeal
**reside** abide, domicile, domiciliate, dwell, ensconce, exist, habituate, inhabit, inhere, lie, live, lodge, occupy, remain, settle, squat, stay, tenant
**reside briefly** sojourn
**reside in** inhabit, occupy
**residence** abode, domicile, dwelling, habitation, hall, home, hostel, house(hold), lodging, manor, mansion, occupation, pad, palace, place, quarters, seat, sojourn, stay, villa
**residence of ambassador** embassy
**residence of archbishop** palace
**residence of clergyman** manse
**residence of community of monks** monastery
**residence of consul** consulate
**residence of ecclesiastic** curatage, deanery, manse
**residence of envoy** embassy
**residence of farmer** farm, grange
**residence of French president** Elysée
**residence of sovereign** palace
**residence of students** hostel
**residence of sultan** seraglio
**residence of vicar** vicarage
**residency** agency, area, home
**resident** citizen, denizen, (in)dweller, inhabitant, living, local, lodger, settled
**residential** commuter, suburban
**residential area** belt, commuter, dormitory, estate, settlement, suburb(ia)
**resident of Hawaii** Kamaaina
**resident of Newfoundland** Livyer
**resident physician** intern
**resident theatre company** rep
**reside temporarily** stay
**residual** excessive, extra, extreme, leftover, needless, outstanding, over(abundant), profuse, redundant, remaining, remanent, residuary, spare, surplus, unnecessary, unneeded
**residue** ash, balance, dregs, remainder, remains, remnant, residuum, rest, surplus
**residue of coal** cinder
**residue of pressed grapes** marc
**residuum** balance, dregs, excess, leavings, remainder, residual, residue, rest, surplus, trace

**resign** abandon, abdicate, demit (Sc), forgo, forsake, leave, quit, relinquish, renounce, secede, sede, submit, surrender, vacate, yield
**resignation** abandonment, cession, compliance, docility, endurance, meekness, obedience, passiveness, reconciliation, renouncing, renunciation, resignedness, resigning, submission, sufferance, toleration, yielding
**resigned** abandoned, abdicated, ceded, cheerful, collected, compliant, complying, composed, dispassionate, forsake, humble, left, long-suffering, meek, mild, obedient, patient, quit, reconciled, relinquished, stoical, subdued, submissive, tolerant, unperturbed, unresisting, vacated, yielded
**resigned gesture** shrug
**resigned person** stoic
**resign from** quit
**resign office** demit
**resign oneself** accept, acquiesce, bow, comply, reconcile, submit, yield
**resign oneself to** accept
**resile** bounce, rebound, recoil
**resilience** airiness, bounce, buoyancy, cheerfulness, elasticity, extensibility, flexibility, give, lightness, liveliness, perkiness, plasticity, recoil, rubberiness, snap
**resilient** adaptable, bendable, bouncy, buoyant, carefree, contractive, elastic, flexible, lively, plastic, pliable, rebounding, rubbery, springy, strong, supple, tough
**resilient plastic** melamine
**resin** adhesive, alkyd, animé, bitumen, dammer, elemi, ether, gum, jalap, lac(quer), nard, resinoid, rosin, saran, shellac, tar, varnish
**resin-flavoured Greek wine** retsina
**resin from hemp** charas
**resin from insects** lac
**resin from turpentine tree** alk
**resin in solid form** rosin
**resin of fir tree** blob
**resinous aromatic substance** balsam
**resinous hemp extract** hashish
**resinous powder used as a sedative** lupulin
**resinous substance** balsam, lac
**resinous tree** fir, pine
**resin used for waxing thread** cobbler's wax
**resin used in varnish** elemi
**resist** against, assail, assault, attack, avoid, battle, breast, cancel, check, combat, confront, counteract, countervail, curb, defy, dispute, face, forgo, hinder, impugn, neutralise, oppose, rebuff, recalcitrate, refuse, reluct, repel, repress, repulse, strive, thwart, weather, withstand
**resistance** battle, combat, contention, counteraction, defiance, fight(ing), hindrance, impediment, obstruction, opposition, refusal, struggle
**resistance to authority** contumacy, rebelliousness
**resistance to disease** premunition
**resistance to rust** stainless
**resistance to sea-sickness** sea-legs
**resistance unit** ohm
**resistant** abiding, antagonistic, antipathetic, averse, clear, constant, defiant, dependable, disinclined, dissident, durable, enduring, fast, firm, immune, impervious, indisposed, loath, opposed, persistent, reliable, reluctant, sound, stable, strong, sturdy, substantial, tough, unwilling, unyielding
**resistant to force** renitent
**resistant to ordinary treatment** refractory
**resistant to rust** stainless
**resistant to wind and rain** weatherproof
**resist authority** rebel
**resist boldly** defy
**resister of change** standpatter
**resisting** confronting, defying, opposing
**resisting wear** durable
**resist openly** defy
**resist stoutly** entrench
**resist strongly** oppose
**resolute** adamant, bold, constant, courage, determined, firm, fixed, obstinate, persevering, stalwart, staunch, stubborn, unshaken
**resolute endurance** fortitude
**resoluteness** determination, firmness, perseverance, persistence, steadfastness, tenacity
**resolution** aim, boldness, decision, determination, end, firmness, intention, perseverance, proposal, resolve, unravelling
**resolve** analyse, clear, confirm, convert, decide, determination, determine, establish, explain, explicate, intention, purpose, reduce, resolution, separate, transform
**resolve grammatically** parse
**resonant** full, orotund, resounding, reverberant, rich, ringing, sonorous, thunderous, vibrant
**resort** aid, assemble, asylum, contrivance, den, employ, frequent, haunt, help, lair, option, recourse,

refuge, retreat, sanctuary, spa, spot, use, utilise
**resort in Colorado** Aspen
**resort in Florida, USA** Miami
**resort in France** Deauville, Nice, Cannes, Riviera, Menton, Pau
**resort in Hawaii** Waikiki
**resort in Switzerland** St Moritz
**resort island off Java** Bali
**resound** announce, bellow, boom, clang, peal, (re-)echo, repeat, resonate, reverberate, ring, rumble, thunder, tintinnabulate, vociferate
**resounding** conclusive, decisive, full, powerful, resonant, rich, sonorous, thorough, vibrant, vocal
**resounding kiss** smacker
**resounding noise** wham, whang
**resource** ability, aid, asset, capability, cleverness, course, device, expedient, help, hoard, holdings, ingenuity, initiative, means, possessions, recourse, reserve, resort, source, stockpile, supply, support, talent, wealth
**resourceful** able, bright, capable, clever, creative, fertile, imaginative, ingenious, innovative, inventive, originative, quick-witted, sharp, talented
**resources** abilities, assets, capabilities, capital, courses, devices, expedients, funds, hoards, holdings, initiatives, materials, means, money, property, reserves, resorts, riches, sources, stockpiles, supplies, talents, wealth
**respect** admiration, admire, affection, approbation approval, aspect, attend, bearing, connection, consider(ation), deference, detail, discrimination, esteem, estimation, feature, heed, homage, honour, matter, notice, partiality, particular, point, preference, reference, regard, relation, veneration
**respectability** aristocracy, decency, dignity, etiquette, fitness, honour, loyalty, morality, nobility, respectableness, status, virtue
**respectable** acceptable, adequate, clean-living, considerable, decent, dignified, estimate, fair, honest, honourable, moderate, passable, reputable, respected, tolerable, trustworthy, upright, worthy
**respect deeply** honour, revere
**respected** competent, creditable, reputable, respectable
**respect for oneself** self-respect
**respectful** amiable, civil, considerate, courteous, formal, genial, gracious, mannerly, obedient, obeisant, obliging, polite, regardful, reverent, suave, submissive, subservient, thoughtful
**respect highly** admire
**respective** corresponding, individual, own, particular, personal, relevant, separate, several, special, specific, various
**respects** aspects, compliments, considerations, esteems, greetings, honours, regards
**respirator** iron lung
**respiratory disorder** asthma
**respiratory infection** pneumonia
**respiratory organ** gill, lung
**respiratory spasm** hiccough, hiccup
**respiratory system disease** consumption, emphysema, parrot fever, phthisis, pleurisy, pneumoconiosis, psittacosis, quinsy, tuberculosis
**respire** breathe, evacuate, exhale, exhaust, expire, gasp, inhale, pant, puff, recover, respite, rest, sigh, suspire
**respite** acquit, adjourn, allay, break, delay, intermission, interval, lapse, let-up, lull, palliate, pause, postpone(ment), relief, relieve, remit, repose, rest, truce, wait
**resplendent trogon** que(t)zal
**respond** acknowledge, answer, confirm, counter, react, rebut, reciprocate, recognise, rejoin, reply, retort, return
**responding** replying, retorting, returning
**respond more strongly than justified** over-react
**respond to alarm** awake
**respond to stimulus** react
**response** acknowledg(e)ment, answer, comeback, communiqué, confirmation, emotion, letter, note, pathos, react(ion), rejoinder, repartee, replication, reply, respondence, retaliation, retort
**response prayer** litany
**response to a charge** plea
**response to external stimulus** tropism
**response to gravity** geotaxis
**response to liturgy** antiphon
**response to stimulus** reaction
**responsibility** accountability, answerability, authority, blame, burden, care, conscientiousness, culpability, dependability, duty, fault, guilt, importance, job, liability, maturity, obligation, onus, power, reliability, sense, soberness, stability, trust(worthiness)
**responsible** accountable, administrative, amenable, answerable, authoritative, bound, capable, chargeable, compos mentis (L), conscientious, creditable, culpable, dependable, dutiful, duty-bound, executive, guilty, high, honest, liable, moral, obligated, rational, reasonable, reliable, reprehensible, sane, subject, trustworthy
**responsive** acquiescent, admiring, agreeable, amenable, appreciative, approving, complying, concurring, conscious, consenting, mindful, open, perceptive, persuadable, susceptible, sympathetic, willing
**responsive feeling** reaction
**rest** abstain, cease, ease, inaction, lie, nap, pause, peace, place, recline, relax, relaxation, remainder, remnant, reply, repose, respite, siesta (Sp), sit, sleep, stability, unemployment, wait
**rest against** lean
**restart** continuation, continue, proceed, renewal, reopen(ing), restart, resume, resumption, resurgence
**restate** construe, explain, interpret, outline, put, recount, render, repeat, reproduce, review, summarise, transcribe, translate
**restate as summary** recap
**restaurant** automat, beanery, bistro, brasserie, buffet, cabaret, café, cafeteria, canteen, chisanyama, coffee house, diner, dinette, eatery, eating house, grill, hosteria (Sp), inn, luncheonette, lunchroom, roadhouse, tavern, teahouse, trattoria
**restaurant car** diner
**restaurant employee** waiter, waitress
**restaurant-keeper** restaurateur
**restaurant patron** diner, eater
**restaurant serving beer and food** brasserie
**restaurant show** cabaret
**restaurant with no waiters** cafeteria, self-service, take away
**restaurant worker** chef, cook, kitchen-hand, maître d'hôtel, waiter, waitress
**rest day** Sabbath
**rest for spear or lance** faucre, fewter, queue
**rest for tympan** gallows
**restful** calm, comfortable, languid, peaceful, placid, quiet, relaxed, relaxing, serene, sleepy, unhurried
**restful ease** leisure
**rest idly** slug

**resting** abed, dormant, dozing, laying, leaning, lying, napping, propping, reclining, relaxing, reposing, sitting, sleeping, slumbering, standing
**resting on fluid** floating
**resting on one's oars** idling
**resting on the genua** kneeling
**resting place** bed, billet, den, grave, lair, nest, perch
**rest in peace** RIP
**rest in snooker** spider
**restitution** compensation, recompense, redress, remuneration, reparation, repayment, satisfaction
**restive** impatient, itchy, nervous, obstinate, recalcitrant, refractory, restless, stubborn, uneasy, unquiet
**restless** agitated, anxious, astatic, awake, discontent, excitable, fidgety, hyperactive, impatient, incessant, insomniac, itching, itchy, moving, nervous, nomadic, perturbable, restive, roaming, uneasy, unhappy, unquiet, unrestful, unsatisfied, unstable, wandering, worried
**restless condition** fidget
**restless desire** itch
**restless mood** fidget
**restlessness** agitation, anxiety, concern, dissatisfaction, edginess, fidgetiness, fidgets, fitfulness, fretfulness, fuss, impatience, insomnia, itch(iness), jumpiness, nervosity, nervousness, restiveness, sleeplessness, stir, strain, tension, transientness, uneasiness, unrestfulness, unstableness, unsteadiness, upset, wakefulness, worry
**restless person** flibbertigibbet
**restock** refill
**rest on cushion of air** hover
**rest on seat** sit
**rest on surface** lie
**rest on the knees** kneel
**rest on water** float
**restoration** amends, compensation, copy, imitation, rebirth, reconstruction, recovery, refreshment, regeneration, rehabilitation, renewal, renovation, repair, replacement, restitution, resurrection, resuscitation, return, revival, revivification
**restoration of harmony** rapprochement, reunion
**restoration to former position** rehabilitation
**restore** fix, heal, mend, recover, refresh, regenerate, rehabilitate, reinstate, renew, renovate, repair,
replace, repone (Sc), reset, return, revive
**restore confidence** reassure
**restored to right position** righted
**restore to equilibrium** stabilise
**restore to former position** reinstate, reset
**restore to good condition** renovate
**restore to health** cure, recuperate
**restore to life** resuscitate, revive, revivify
**restore to original state** renew
**restore to sound condition** mend
**restore to state of activity** reactivate
**restore to strength** reinforce
**restore to unity** reintegrate
**restore to youthful vigour** rejuvenate
**restore to zero** reset
**restore what was taken** refund
**restrain** abate, arrest, bate, bridle, check, circumscribe, confine, constrain, control, curb, delay, deter, govern, hamper, hinder, impede, inhibit, keep, obstruct, regulate, rein, repress, restrict, retard, slow, stem, stop, subdue, suppress, tether, trammel
**restrain by force** arrest, coerce
**restrained** calm, discreet, mild, moderate, muted, quiet, reticent, soft, steady, subdued, tasteful, temperate, undemonstrative, unemphatic, unobtrusive
**restrained and cool in manner** reserved
**restrained laugh** tehee, titter
**restrained quality** modesty
**restrain in scope** restrict
**restrain oneself** abstain
**restraint** aplomb, arrest, blockage, bondage, captivity, check, command, confines, constraint, control, detention, embargo, grip, limit, manacles, moderation, reserve, restriction, subtlety, suppression
**restraint between states** nonaggression
**restraint on instincts** inhibition
**restrict** bind, bound, cage, circumscribe, confine, constrain, constrict, contain, cramp, curb, delimit, demarcate, diminish, gate, hamper, handicap, impede, impound, inhibit, limit, modify, narrow, pen, qualify, regulate, rein, restrain, tether, tie
**restricted in one's views** narrow-minded, verkramp
**restricted menu** diet, regimen
**restricted to campus** gated
**restricted to one direction only** one-way
**restricting rope** leash, tether
**restriction** clause, confinement, delimitation, imprisonment, limit(ation), narrowness, proscription, provision, specification, tightness
**restriction on movements** curfew
**restructure** reorganise
**rest upright** stand
**rest with confidence** depend, rely, trust
**restyle** remodel
**result** answer, appear, arise, backwash, conclusion, consequence, culminate, decision, denouement, derive, determination, develop(ment), effect, emerge, end(-product), ensue, event(ually), finish, flow, follow, fruit, happen, issue, originate, outcome, proceed, produce, product, reaction, resolution, resolve, sequel, solution, spring, stem, terminate, termination, turnout, upshot, verdict
**result from** sue
**result given by dividing one quantity by another** quotient
**result in** cause
**result in contributing** redound
**resulting indirectly** consequential
**resulting in the end** eventual
**result of addition** sum, total
**result of action** effect
**result of cause** effect
**result of division** quotient
**result of match** score
**result of multiplication** product
**result of subtraction** remainder
**result of too much drink** babbala(a)s, hangover
**result of vote** election, mandate
**result produced by some action** consequence
**results** aftermath, appears, arises, consequences, decisions, develops, effects, ends, ensues, follows, fruits, issues, outcomes, products, sequels, stems
**resume** advance, continue, proceed, recommence, restart
**résumé** abstract, analysis, biography, bulletin, compendium, condensation, cuttings, epitome, summary, synopsis
**resume original shape** resile
**resuming normal shape after distortion** elastic
**resumption** continuation, re-establishment, renewal, reopening, restart, resurgence
**resurface a tyre** recap, retread
**resurrect** disinter, reactivate, reintroduce, renew, restore, revive

**resurrection** comeback, reactivation, reappearance, rebirth, renaissance, renewal, restoration, resurgence, resuscitation, return, revival
**resurrection festival** Easter
**resurrection plant** selaginella
**resuscitate** reanimate, refresh, renew, rescue, restore, resurrect, revive, revivify, save
**resuscitation** katsu, renewal, revival, revivification
**retag** relabel
**retail** handle, market, peddle, sell, stock, vend
**retail as a hawker** peddle
**retailer of fish** fishmonger
**retailer of fruit and vegetables** greengrocer
**retail market** outlet
**retail shop** store
**retail store** shop, warehouse
**retail trader** merchant
**retain** clasp, clutch, detain, employ, engage, grasp, hold, keep, maintain, preserve, recollect, remember, reserve, restrict, save, secure, stet
**retainer** advance, attendant, dependant, deposit, domestic, fee, flunk(e)y, footman, lackey, servant, supporter, valet, vassal
**retaining leaves all year** evergreen
**retaining wall** revetment
**retain momentum** drift
**retain possessions** keep
**retaliate** reciprocate
**retaliation** counterblow, reciprocation, repayment, reprisal, requital, revenge, vengeance
**retaliation in kind** eye for an eye
**retaliatory action** counterattack
**retaliatory attack** countercharge
**retard** backward, check, decelerate, delay, impede, obstruct, slow
**retard by obstruction** hinder, impede
**retard growth** stunt
**retard in movement** impede
**retard progress** obstruct
**retch** gag, heave, puke, regorge, regurgitate, sick, spew, vomit
**reticence** avoidance, bashfulness, diffidence, muteness, quietness, reserve, restraint, shyness, silence, speechlessness, taciturnity, unobtrusiveness, unsociability
**reticent** close-lipped, close-mouthed, mealy-mouthed, mum, mute, quiet, reserved, restrained, secretive, shy, silent, speechless, taciturn, tight-lipped, uncommunicative, unforthcoming, unobtrusive
**reticle** lattice, network
**reticulation** network

**reticule** pouch
**reticule closer** drawstring
**retinue** attendant, convoy, cortege, employees, entourage, escort, followers, personnel, procession, retainer, suite, train
**retire** leave, recede, retreat, retrocede, withdraw
**retired and retaining title as honour** emeritus
**retired person** pensioner
**retired person's income** pension
**retired servant** emeritus
**retirement allowance** pension
**retirement income** annuity, pension
**retire to the country** rusticate
**retiring** aloof, bashful, cenobitic, coy, demure, departing, diffident, distant, eremitical, humble, leaving, meek, modest, private, quiet, reclusive, reserved, reticent, shy, taciturn, timid, timorous, unassertive, unassuming, unobtrusive, unpretentious, unsociable, unsocial, withdrawing
**retiring from office** outgoing
**retort** acknowledge, alembic, answer, argue, contradict, counter(blast), counterclaim, countershare, cylinder, furnace, phial, purify, quip, rebut(tal), reciprocate, refute, rejoin(der), repartee, repay, replication, reply, respond, response, retaliate, return, riposte, sally, say, vessel, vial, witticism
**retrace one's steps** reverse, untread
**retract** deny, disavow, recant, recede, repeal, retreat, revoke, unsay, withdraw
**retreaded tyre** recap
**retreat** asylum, back-pedal, den, depart(ure), ebb, flight, haunt, haven, hermitage, leave, privacy, recede, recoil, refuge, resort, retire(ment), retrocede, sanctuary, seclusion, shrink, withdraw(al)
**retreat in disorder** rout, flee
**retribution** amends, nemesis, penalty, recompense, requital, retaliation, revenge, vengeance
**retributive justice** nemesis
**retrieve** fetch, free, liberate, ransom, re-establish, recall, recapture, reclaim, recoup, recover, rectify, redeem, regain, rehabilitate, reinstate, repair, replace, rescue, restore, retake, return, salvage, save
**retrieving** recouping, redeeming, repairing, rescuing, restoring, salvaging

**retrograde** declining, degenerating, deteriorating, inverted, recede, reversed
**retrogress** backslide, degenerate, deteriorate, fail, (re)lapse, retrogression, revert, weaken
**retrogression** decline, degeneration, ebb, recession, reflux, regress, relapse, retirement, senility, vitiation, withdrawal
**retrospect** afterthought, consideration, contemplation, hindsight, meditation, memory, overview, recollection, reflection, rememoration, reminiscence, review, survey, view
**retry** rehear
**retrying of a case** retrial
**return** backslide, crisis, earn, ebb, gain, give, homecoming, income, interest, profit, reappear(ance), receipt, recoil, recur(rence), regress, reject, relapse, render, repatriate, repay, reply, restitution, restore, retaliate, retort, revert, vote, yield
**return blow** tit
**return for the worse** relapse
**returning missile** boomerang
**return like for like** retaliate
**return of ball before it reaches the ground** volley
**return of criminal to country where offence was convicted** extradition
**return of good sense** resipiscence
**return on investment** dividend, interest, profit
**return punch** counter
**return quickly** rebound
**return tennis ball** rally
**return thrust** riposte
**return tit-for-tat** retaliate
**return to custody** remand
**return to former state** revert
**return to health** recover
**return to live** revive
**return to mind** recur
**return to native land** repatriate
**return to office** re-elect
**return to original condition** recycle
**return to usual state** normalise
**return to zero** reset
**re-usable spacecraft** shuttle
**re-use** reclaim, reconstitute, recycle, rehash, rework
**re-used letters** anagram
**re-used material** hash
**revalue** reassess, rethink, revaluate
**reveal** announce, bare, betray, communicate, declare, detect, disclose, disclosure, display, divulge, evince, exhibit, exhume, expose, impart, inform, proclaim, relate,

show, state, tell, uncover, unearth, unmask, unveil, utter
**revealed spiritual knowledge** gnosis
**reveal secrets** tattle
**reveal the age of** dates
**revel** appreciate, carnival, carouse, celebrate, celebration, debauch, drink, enjoy, feast, gloat, glory, indulge, jol, orgy, relish, roister, savour, wallow, wassail
**revelation** admission, announcement, betrayal, broadcast, bulletin, confession, detection, disclosure, discovery, display, exhibition, exposition, exposure, info(rmation), leak, manifestation, news, prophecy, publication, report, reveal, secret, surprise, telling, unmasking, vision
**reveller** carouser, celebrator, hedonist, joller, libertine, merrymaker, rioter, roisterer, rollicker, sybarite
**revel noisily** roister
**revelry** celebration, debauch, festivity, jol, jollification, jollity, merrymaking, spree
**revenge** reprisal, requital, requite, retaliate, retaliation, retribution, satisfaction, vengefulness, vindicate
**revengeful** implacable, malevolent, malicious, malignant, resentful, vindictive
**revenge oneself** retaliate
**revenue** earnings, funds, income, profit, return
**revenue stamp** fiscal, tax-paid
**reverberate** (re-)echo, rebound, recoil, reflect, report, resound, return, ring, roll, rumble, thunder, vibrate
**reverberation** echo(ing), noise, report, resounding, roll, rumble, rumbling
**revere** admire, adore, awe, beatify, esteem, exalt, glorify, hallow, honour, respect, reverence, sanctify, treasure, venerate, worship
**revered** venerated, worshipped
**revere greatly** idolise
**reverence** admiration, adoration, awe, bow, devotion, esteem, estimation, homage, honour, humility, prayer, regard, respect, revere, sacrifice, veneration, worship
**reverent** adoring, awed, decorous, deferential, devout, humble, loving, meek, obsequious, pious, proper, religious, reserved, respectful, reverential, saintly, serious, solemn, spiritual, subdued, submissive, worshipful
**reverential veneration** awe
**reverie** (day)dream, delusion, extravagance, fantasy, musing, quixotism

**reversal** abolition, bolting, defection, inversion, nullification, rejection, repeal, repudiation, rescission, retraction, revocation, turn-about, upset, voidance, withdrawal
**reverse** back, change, check, contrary, converse, countermand, counterpart, defeat, invert, misadventure, misfortune, opposite, overthrow, rear, rescind, revoke, setback, transport, veto
**reverse curve** ess, S-curve
**reversed in order** converse
**reverse fault** thrust
**reverse oars** sheave
**reverse page of book** (re)verso
**reverse side of coin** pile, tail, verso
**reversion** backlash, backslide, ebb, reaction, rebound, recoil, recurrence, reflex, reflux, regress, relapse, repercussion, return, reversal, reversing, throwback, turnabout
**reversion to type** atavism
**revert** backslide, degenerate, fail, lapse, persist, reappear, rebound, recur, regress, relapse, repair, repeat, resume, retreat, return, revisit, weaken
**review** abstract, cavalcade, cogitation, commentary, criticism, critique, epitome, essay, evaluation, examination, inspect(ion), investigation, judg(e)ment, pageant, re-examine, recitation, reconsider, reduction, revision, spectacle, study, summary, survey, symposium, synopsis, theme, thesis, tract
**reviewer** arbiter, commentator, critic, essayist, judge
**review of something in the paper** write-up
**review unfavourably** pan
**revile** abuse, assail, attack, belabour, calumniate, curse, defame, execrate, exprobate, lambast(e), malign, oppugn, scoff, traduce, vilify, vituperate
**revise** alter, amend, change, correct, cram, edit, emend, memorise, modify, overhaul, re-examine, recast, reconsider, reconstruct, rectify, redraft, repair, retouch, revamp, review, rework, rewrite, update
**revise and correct** chastise
**revival** reawakening, rebirth, recrudescence, renaissance, renewal, restoration, resurgence, resurrection, resuscitation
**revival of Greek ideals** neo-Hellenism
**revive** animate, awaken, cheer, comfort, cure, invigorate, quicken,

rally, reactivate, reanimate, reawake, recover, refresh, regenerate, reinvigorate, rejuvenate, rekindle, renew, renovate, repeat, restore, resuscitate, revitalise, rouse, service, valet
**revivification** resuscitation
**revoke** abrogate, annul, cancel, countermand, disclaim, invalidate, negate, nullify, quash, recall, recant, reneg(u)e, repeal, repudiate, rescind, retract, reverse, withdraw
**revoke a legacy** adeem
**revoke at cards** reneg(u)e
**revoke formally** abrogate
**revolt** abhor, aversion, bolt, confront, detest, disgust, dislike, disobey, horrify, insurrection, mutiny, nauseate, rebel(lion), repel, repulse, revolution, riot, rising, secede, sedition, uprising, violate
**revolution** change, circuit, overthrow, rebellion, revolt, rotation, uprising
**revolutionary colour** red
**revolutionary entombed in Red Square** Lenin
**revolutionary song** 'Marseillaise'
**revolutionary song adopted by socialists** 'Internationale'
**revolve** cerebrate, circle, circulate, circumvolve, consider, gyrate, orbit, pirouette, pivot, ponder, reel, roll, rotate, spin, swivel, turn, weigh, wheel
**revolve mentally** agitate
**revolver** gat, gun, pistol, rod
**revolve rapidly** spin
**revolve with changing inclination** wobble
**revolving apparatus** rotator
**revolving body** planet, satellite
**revolving cylinder** rotor
**revolving cylinder of angler's reel** spool
**revolving gate** turnstile
**revolving part** rotator, rotor
**revolving part of dynamo** armature
**revolving pulley/spindle** capstan
**revolving toy** yo-yo
**revue humour** burlesque, satire
**revulsion** aversion, disgust, dislike, distaste, execration, odium, offence, repellence, repugnance, repulsion
**revving** acceleration, pick-up, response, running, speed-up
**reward** award, benefaction, bonus, bounty, compensate, compensation, compliment, desert, douceur, emolument, grant, gratuity, honorarium, meed, merit, pay(ment), payoff, premium, prize, recompense, reimburse, remunerate,

remuneration, repay, requital, salary, tribute, wages
**reward given for success in competition** prize
**reward of victory** crown
**rework** alter, amend, change, correct, edit, emend, redo, rehash, review, revise, rewrite, update
**rewrite** edit, rectify, revise, reword
**rhabdomancy** divining, dowsing
**rhamphoid** beaklike
**rhapsodic** beaming, blissful, delighted, delirious, ecstatic, elated, enthusiastic, joyful, overcome, overjoyed, ravished, thrilled
**rhapsodise** enthuse
**Rhenish wine** hock
**rhetoric** bombast, eloquence, hyperbole, oratory, rant, verbosity
**rhetorical** bombastic, flamboyant, flashy, florid, pretentious, showy, verbose
**rhetorical question** erotema, eroteme, erotesis
**rheum** catarrh
**rheumatic affliction in muscles** lumbago
**rheumatic pain in tissues** fibrositis
**rhinal** nasal
**Rhine** Rhein
**Rhine city** Basel, Bonn, Mainz, Mannheim
**Rhine siren** Lorelei
**Rhine wine** hock, moselle, riesling, traminer
**rhinoceros bird** oxpecker
**rhizome** root(stalk), rootstock, stem, tuber
**Rhode Island bay** Narragansett
**Rhode Island harbour town** Newport
**Rhode Island state flower** violet
**Rhodesia declared it** UDI
**Rhodes statue** Colossus
**Rhône city** Arles, Lyon, Lyons
**Rhône delta** Camargue
**Rhône valley wind** mistral
**rhymed lyric** ode
**rhyme or reason** logic, meaning, method, plan
**rhyming couplet** distich
**rhyming game** crambo
**rhyming stanzas** poetry
**rhythm** accent, balance, beat, cadence, emphasis, fluctuation, jingle, lilt, measure, movement, pulsation, pulse, recurrence, stress, swing, symmetry, tempo, time
**rhythmical throbbing** pulse
**rhythmic cadence** lilt
**rhythmic call** chant
**rhythmic flow** cadence

**rhythmic or metrical pattern of a verse** scansion
**rhythmic pattern of Indian music** tala
**rhythmic rise and fall** heave
**rhythm in sound** cadence
**rhythm of verse** metre
**rhythm or beat** pulse
**ria** entrance, inlet, recess
**riant** cheerful, gay, laughing, laughter, smiling
**riata** lariat, lasso, reata
**rib** costa, line, purling, ridge, strip, tease
**ribald** abusive, coarse, dirty, gross, indecent, irreverent, loose, mocking, obscene, scurrilous, vulgar, wanton
**ribaldry** bawdiness, coarseness, crudeness, crudity, indelicacy, raciness, roughness, rudeness, smut, tawdriness, uncouthness, unevenness, vulgarity
**ribbed cotton fabric** whipcord
**ribbed fabric** cord(uroy), faille, pique, rep, twill
**ribbed trousers** cords
**ribbon** cestos, cestus, cordon, cummerbund, (head)band, sash, tape, waistband
**ribbon across finishing line** tape
**ribbon as badge of honour** cordon
**ribbon award** rosette
**ribbon fern** pteris
**ribbonfish** guapena, serrana
**ribbon for border** lisere
**ribbon-like in form** cestoid
**ribbon-like intestinal worm** cestode
**ribbon-like scroll bearing inscription** banderole
**ribbon snake** garter
**ribbon tree** ho(u)here, lacebark, ribbonwood
**ribbon used to bind a curtain** tieback
**ribbonwood** lacebark
**ribgrass** ribwort
**rib of insect wing** vein
**rib of leaf** vein
**rib of ship** wrong
**rib of violin** bout
**rib playfully** chaff, rag, tease
**ribs of umbrella** frame
**rice** arroz (Sp), oryza (L), Reis (G), riso (I), riz (F)
**ricebird** bobolink, reedbird
**rice boiled with meat** pilaf(f), pilao, pilau, pilaw
**rice dish** biriani, paella (Sp), pilau, pilaw, risotto
**rice field** paddy, sawah
**rice grass** barit, cord-grass
**rice husk** bran
**rice in the husk** paddy
**rice liquor** sake, saké, saki

**rich** abounding, abundant, affluent, ample, aromatic, bounteous, bountiful, copious, costly, deep, estimable, expansive, fertile, fruitful, full, harmonious, luxuriant, moneyed, opulent, plenteous, plentiful, precious, productive, valuable, vivid, wealthy
**rich and costly** sumptuous
**rich and lush** luxuriant
**rich and showy** exotic
**rich and smooth** creamy
**rich and sweet liqueur** crème
**rich beef stew containing beer** carbonade
**rich black fur** sable
**rich blue-veined cheese** Stilton
**rich brown pigment** mummy, sepia
**rich cake** dariole, gateau, madeleine, torte
**rich clay soil** loam
**rich cream cake** torte
**rich crumbly biscuit** shortbread
**rich deep blue** mazarine
**rich entertainment** banquet
**riches** affluence, assets, fortune, gold, money, plenty, property, resources, substance, treasure, wealth
**rich fabric** brocade, lamé, panne, silk
**rich frozen pudding** cassata, nesselrode
**rich fur** ermine
**rich gold and silver embroidery** tambour
**rich in-crowd member** jet-setter
**rich in detail** ornate
**rich in oil** fat, greasy
**rich in resources** fertile
**rich in vowels** vocalic
**rich king** Croesus, Midas
**rich layer cake** gateau, torte
**richly coloured** gorgeous
**richly decorated tapestry** arras
**richly embroidered band** offray, orphrey
**richly fruitful** prolific
**richly-laden ship** argosy
**richly sweet in taste** luscious
**richly verdant** lush
**rich man** capitalist, Croesus, Midas, millionaire, nabob, plutocrat
**rich part** cream, fat
**rich people** haves
**rich reddish-brown colour** sepia
**rich retired Anglo-Indian** nabob
**rich sherry wine** madeira
**rich silk fabric** brocade
**rich soup made from shellfish** bisque
**rich source of iron** liver
**rich sponge-cake soaked in rum syrup** baba
**rich sweet cake** madeira, torte

**rich tapestry** arras
**rich trappings for horse** caparison
**rich wine** madeira
**rich womaniser** playboy
**rich yeast roll** brioche
**rick** stack
**rickety old vehicle** rattletrap, tjorrie
**rickshaw pulled by cyclist** pedicab
**rid** clear, deliver, disabuse, disburden, divest, free, purge, relieve
**riddle** conundrum, enigma, mystery, perforate, poser, problem, puncture, puzzle, sieve
**riddled** filtered, holey, parted, percolated, purified, screened, seeped, separated, sifted, strained
**ride** control, drive, float, go, handle, jaunt, journey, lift, manage, move, outing, pester, progress, sit, steer, travel, trip
**ride a bike** cycle
**ride at easy pace** amble, hack
**ride bicycle** pedal
**ride down** overtake
**ride high** waft
**ride out** bear, endure, suffer, withstand
**rider** addition, amendment, annex, appendage, appendix, cavalier, cavalryman, codicil, commuter, corollary, cowboy, equestrian, equestrienne, estafette, horseman, horsewoman, jockey, passenger, sitter, supplement, trainer
**rider's footrest hung from saddle** stirrup
**rider's goad** spur
**rider's need** reins, saddle
**rider's seat** saddle
**ride waves** surf
**ridge** apex, arris, bank, billow, breaker, bulge, crease, crest, crimp, crinkle, crista, crown, crumple, cultivate, dig, embankment, fold, furrow, groove, head, heap, height, hill, knoll, line, mass, mound, overlap, peak, pile, pinnacle, plough, promontory, pucker, reef, rib, rim, ripple, rise, ruck, rumple, seam, shelf, summit, swell, till, top, tuck, weal, welt, wrinkle
**ridge and trough on water** wave
**ridge between horse's shoulder blades** withers
**ridge between mouldings** arris
**ridge face** escarp(ment)
**ridge in cloth** rib, wale, welt
**ridge of drifted sand** dune
**ridge of earth** rideau
**ridge of glacial drift** esker, escar, kame, os
**ridge of hill** saddle
**ridge of rock** dike, reef
**ridge of sand** dene, dune

**ridge of the occiput** inion
**ridge on shoe** welt
**ridge on woven fabric** wale
**ridge over the eyes** brow
**ridge raised on flesh by stroke of whip or rod** weal
**ridge-shaped structure** carina
**ridicule** banter, burlesque, chaff, deride, derision, gibes, jeers, lampoon, mock(ery), pillory, raillery, sarcasm, satire, satirise, scorn, taunts, twit
**ridicules vice and folly** satire
**ridiculous** absurd, asinine, comical, cynical, derisible, derisory, farcical, ironical, laughable, ludicrous, mindless, nonsensical, preposterous, risible, satirical, senseless, stupid
**ridiculous ceremonial** mummery
**ridiculous failure** fiasco
**ridiculous show** farce
**riding academy** manège
**riding animal** camel, elephant, horse, pony
**riding breeches** jodhpurs
**riding coat** joseph
**riding costume** habit
**riding horse** hack, rouncy
**riding on horseback** equitation
**riding pants** jodphurs
**riding school** manège
**riding seat** saddle
**riding shoe** solleret
**riding show** rodeo
**riding stick** crop
**rife** abounding, accepted, circulating, common, copious, current, customary, epidemic, general, multitudinous, numerous, ongoing, overflowing, pervasive, plentiful, popular, present, prevailing, prevalent, profuse, rampant, swarming, sweeping, thronged, universal, widespread
**riff-raff** hoi-polloi, rabble, scum
**rifle** assault, attack, burgle, carbine, cheat, defraud, demolish, despoil, dispossess, foray, gut, gyp, invade, loot, maraud, pillage, plunder, raid, ransack, ravage, rob, ruin, rummage, sack, strip
**rifle blade** bayonet
**rifle bore** calibre
**rifle firing-pin** tige
**rifleman** soldier
**rifleman's predecessor** musketeer
**rifle's kickback** recoil
**rifle spear** bayonet
**rifle sport** skeet
**rifle strap** sling

**rifle through** hunt, ransack, rummage, search
**rifling through** assaulting, attacking, burgling, demolishing, gutting, gypping, invading, pilfering, plundering, raiding, ravaging, robbing, stripping, swindling
**rift** aperture, argument, break, cavity, chink, cleavage, cleft, crack, cranny, crevasse, crevice, cut, disjoint, dispute, fissure, fracture, gap, gash, hiatus, interval, lacuna, lapse, nick, opening, orifice, ostiole, pause, quarrel, reave, recess, rip, rupture, schism, scission, scissure, sever, slit, split
**rig** accoutre, engineer, equip(ment), fake, fixtures, furnish, gear, juggle, kit, livery, manipulate, outfit, provide, stack, supplies, supply, tackle
**rigged contest** set-up
**rigged vessel** sailer
**right** accurate, actually, advantageously, appropriate, becoming, befitting, claim, comme il faut (F), correct, de rigueur (F), direct(ly), due, equitable, equitably, fair, genuine, good, honest, immediately, justice, just(ify), lawful(ly), lawfulness, legitimate, lien, normal, ownership, prerogative, principal, proper, quite, seemly, sound, straight, suitable, suitably, title, true, truly, upright, virtue
**right and left** ubiquitous
**right-angle joint** ell, knee, tee
**right as command to horses** ree
**right away** directly, forthwith, immediately, instantly, now, pointblank, promptly, pronto, quickly, speedily, straightaway, summarily
**right behaviour** dharma
**right belonging to a person** privilege
**righteous** blameless, equitable, faultless, good, guiltless, holy, incorrupt, innocent, justifiable, moral, noble, scrupulous, stainless, unerring, unsoiled, unspotted, upright, virtuous
**right-handed** dextral
**right-hand page of open book** outpage, recto
**right-hand person** adviser, assistant
**right-hand side of ship** starboard
**right inherited from ancestors** patrimony
**right next to** alongside
**right of admission** entrée, entry
**right of choice** option
**right of entry** entrée, ticket
**right off the bat** immediately, now, quickly

**right of going out** egress, exit
**right of ownership** title
**right of presentation to benefice** advowson
**right of retention** lien
**right of self-government** autonomy
**right of shaving the head** tonsure
**right of sovereign** prerogative
**right of voting in political elections** suffrage
**right of way** access
**right side** offside, starboard
**right to another's property** lien
**right to demand payment** recourse
**right to do as one pleases** liberty
**right to enter** entrance
**right to fish in certain waters** piscary
**right to go in** ingress
**right to hold a local court** soke
**right to retain property** lien
**right to speak** say
**right to vote** adulthood, suffrage
**rigid** firm, formal, hard, immovable, inelastic, inflexible, intense, iron-bound, set, severe, starchy, stiff, strict, stringent, taut, unbending, unmoving, unyielding
**rigid hair** bristle, seta
**rigidity** austerity, density, economy, firmness, fixedness, hardness, inelasticity, inflexibility, resistance, rigidity, self-denial, set, solidity, stiffness, stringency
**rigidity of cells, due to uptake** turgor
**rigidly** stiffly
**rigidly conventional** hidebound, narrow-minded
**rigid stick** ramrod
**rigid support** buttress, prop, strut
**rigorous** absolute, accurate, arduous, austere, autocratic, challenging, cold, demanding, despotic, exact(ing), firm, fixed, hard, harsh, immovable, inflexible, merciless, nice, nippy, nonflexible, nonpliant, pitiless, precise, rigid, rough, scientific, scrupulous, set, severe, spartan, stern, stiff, strict, stringent, tough, trying, tyrannical, unflexible, wintry
**rigorously** badly, bleakly, extremely, firmly, hardly, inflexibly, sternly, strictly, toughly
**rigour** harshness, severity, strictness
**rig-out** apparel, attire, clobber, clothe, costume, dress, furnish, garb, outfit, supply, togs
**rig out** accoutre, arm, array, attire, clothe, equip, fit, furnish
**rig up** arrange, assemble, build, construct, erect, improvise

**rile** aggravate, agitate, anger, annoy, disturb, embitter, incense, irk, irritate, madden, peeve, pester, roil, taunt, torment, vex
**rill** beck, brook, burn, course, current, drift, flow, rivulet, run(nel), stream(let), surge, tide, torrent, tributary, watercourse
**rim** border, bound(ary), brim, brink, circumference, confine, edge, flange, fringe, hem, lip, margin, outline, perimeter, periphery, skirt, verge
**rime** (hoar-)frost
**rim-like part** flange
**rim of basket** hoop
**rim of ear** helix
**rim of horseshoe** web
**rim of wheel** felloe, felly, strake
**rind** casing, cover, crust, epicarp, hull, husk, integument, peel, pellicle, pod, scale, sheath, shell, skin, tegument
**rinderpest** cattle-plague
**rind of fruit** peel
**rind of ham** skin
**rind of roasted pork** crackling
**rind of tree** bark
**ring** announce, arena, circle(t), clique, competition, contest, cordon, coterie, encircle, hoop, jingle, league, loop, mob, peal, phone, proclaim, resonate, resound, reverberate, rink, set, surround, syndicate, telephone, toll, vibrate
**ring a bell** sound familiar
**ring around nipple** areola
**ring around saint's head** halo
**ring bell** toll
**ringed** circled, circular, disk-like, encircled, enclosed, hooped, round, streaked, striped, surrounded
**ringed boa** aboma
**ringed planet** Saturn
**ringer** bell
**ring for securing bird** vervel
**ring for training horses** longe, lunge
**ringing in ears** tinnitus
**ringing instrument** bell
**ringing of bells** peal, tintinnabulation
**ringing sound** tinkle
**ringlet** curl
**ring loudly** peal
**ring-necked duck** dogy, moonbill, ringbill, scaup
**ring of bells** peal
**ring of dots around edge of coin** graining
**ring of flowers** wreath
**ring of light** aura, aureola, aureole, halo, nimbus
**ring of muscles closing and opening orifice** sphincter

**ring of wagons** corral, la(a)ger
**ring on target** inner, outer
**ring out** peal
**Ringo was one** Beatle
**ring recipient** bride, fiancé, groom
**ring road** bypass
**ring seal** signet
**ring-shaped** annular, circinate, circular, cricoid
**ring-shaped bread roll** bagel
**ring-shaped coral island** atoll
**ring supporting lampshade** gallery
**ring-tailed mammal** lemur, raccoon
**ring that is whirled around the body** hula hoop
**ring through which driving reins pass** terret
**ring up** phone
**ringwise** annularly
**ring with deep sound** toll
**ringworm** fungus, mycosis, serpigo, tetter, tinea
**rinse** bathe, clean(se), splash, swill, wash, wet
**rinse mouth and throat with a liquid** gargle
**Rio bay** Guanabara
**Rio beach** Copacabana
**Rio mountain** Sugarloaf
**Rio peak** Corcovado
**riot** amok, brawl, carouse, commotion, confusion, disorder, disturbance, festivity, fight, fray, hubbub, melee, mêlée, outbreak, tumult, uprising, uproar
**riotous** rebellious, uproarious
**riotous action** rampage
**riotous amusement** carnival
**riotous crowd** mob
**riotous party** orgy, spree
**riot repellent** tear-gas
**rip** cheat, cleavage, cleave, crack, cut, divide, fissure, lacerate, laceration, libertine, movement, nag, open, overfall, rake, rend, rent, rogue, rupture, rush, saw, score, screw, separate, shred, slash, slit, split, strip, tear, wave
**ripe** consummate, developed, finished, full, grown, mature, prepared, ready, ruddy
**ripen** age, become, develop, evolve, mature, mellow, prepare, season, soften, transform
**ripening early** rareripe, rath(e), rathe-ripe
**rip off** cheat, con, defraud, diddle, do, dupe, exploit, fleece, lift, overcharge, pilfer, pinch, rob, steal, sting, swindle, swipe, thieve, trick
**rip-off** cheat, con, diddle, exploitation, fraud, robbery, swindle, theft

**riposte** acknowledg(e)ment, answer, barb, comeback, counterblow, quip, rejoin(der), repartee, reply, respond, response, retaliate, retaliation, retort, return, sally
**ripped** dislocated, hacked, pulled, scored, slashed, slit, sprained, strained, stretched, tore, torn, wounded, wrenched
**ripper** tearer
**ripple** agitate, curl, purl, ruffle, undulate, undulation, wave(let)
**rip to pieces** tear apart
**rise** advance, appear, arise, ascend, ascent, augmentation, beginning, climb, close, enlarge, grow, happen, increase, increment, issue, occur, oppose, origin(ate), proceed, promotion, resist, revolt, rising, soar, source, stand, succeed, swell
**rise above** bestride, overlook, overtop, surmount, tower, transcend
**rise abruptly** thrust, zoom
**rise again** resurge
**rise and fall** fluctuate, loom, welter
**rise and fall of the sea** tide
**rise as vapour** steam
**rise from bed** get up
**rise high** tower
**rise in rank or status** promotion
**rise in rebellion against authority** revolt
**rise in revolt** mutiny
**rise in sea level** eustasy
**rise in the air** soar
**rise in value** appreciation, enhance, improve
**rise of tide** flow
**rise of water** flood
**rise of wave** s(c)end
**rise precipitously** sky
**rise steeply** soar
**rise to great height** tower
**rise to notice** emerge
**rise up** ascend, insurrect
**rise upwards** upheave
**risible** absurd, amusing, comic(al), diverting, droll, eccentric, entertaining, facetious, farcical, funny, hilarious, humorous, jocular, jolly, laughable, ludicrous, odd, quaint, rich, ridiculous, riotous, silly, slapstick, waggish, whimsical, witty
**rising** advancing, appearing, ascending, climbing, emanating, emergent, emerging, enlarging, eventuating, flowing, growing, improving, increasing, intensifying, issuing, lifting, mounting, occurring, originating, progressing, prospering, rebellion, revolution, soaring, springing, surfacing, swelling, waxing

**rising above others** eminent
**rising agent** mos, yeast
**rising air** updraught
**rising by degrees** gradient
**rising current of warm air** thermal
**rising sharply** abrupt
**rising volume and intensity** crescendo
**rising with a slope** acclivitous, acclivous, ascending
**risk** attempt, chance, danger, dare, endanger(ment), exposure, gamble, hazard, imperil, insecurity, jeopardise, jeopardy, liability, menace, peril, speculate, speculation, venture
**risk covered by insurance policy** coverage
**risked money** bet
**risky** chancy, dangerous, daredevil, daring, hazardous, perilous, precarious, uncertain, unsafe, venturesome
**risky act** gamble
**risky investment** speculation
**risky to physical fitness** unhealthy
**risky undertaking** gamble, venture
**risotto** rice (dish)
**risqué** crude, indecent, indecorous, indelicate, off-colour, racy, salty, suggestive, tasteless, unrefined
**rissole** frikkadel, meatball
**rite** act, ceremony, communion, custom, form(ality), liturgy, ordinance, procedure, ritual, usage
**rite of marriage** matrimony
**rite of passage** adolescence, baptism, marriage
**ritual** ceremonial, ceremony, commemoration, convention(al), custom, display, form, formal(ity), function, habit, observance, parade, practice, procedure, rite, rubric, service, solemn(ity), stately, tableau, tradition
**ritual cleansing** purification
**ritual foolery** trumpery
**ritual for first night of Passover** Seder
**ritually accepted by Muslims** hal(l)al
**ritually prepared food** hal(l)al, kosher
**ritually unfit to be eaten** tref, treif(a)
**ritual suicide with a sword** hara-kiri (J), hari-kari, seppuku
**ritual table** altar
**rivage** bank, coast, shore
**rival** antagonist, challenger, compete, competitive, competitor, contestant, emulate, equal, foe, match, opponent, opposed, opposing, vie
**rivalry** bout, challenge, competition, conflict, contest, emulation, encounter, engagement, fight, meeting, opposition, tournament

**rive** claw, cleave, crack, dissect, distress, divide, injure, mangle, part, rend, rip, rupture, scratch, sever, shred, slice, splinter, split, sunder, tear, wound
**river** Avon, channel, creek, current, estuary, gutter, inlet, lee, rio (Sp), rivulet, Rubicon, stream, torrent, waterway
**river animal** beaver, crocodile, hippo(potamus), otter
**river bank** brae (Sc), levee, ripa, ripe
**river barrier** dam, weir
**river bend** heck
**river boat** barge, cog, foist, pulwar
**river branch that forms backwater** billabong
**river channel** alveus, bed, cat
**river chute** rapids
**river crossed by Caesar** Rubicon
**river crossing** drift, ford
**river-crossing operator** ferryman
**river curve** bend
**river dam** weir
**river dragon** crocodile
**river duck** eider, greenwing, mallard, teal, widgeon
**river edge** bank, levee
**river feeder stream** tributary
**river fish** blay, catfish, dace, trout
**river-flood** spate
**river flowing into the Dead Sea** Jordan
**river front** dockside
**river gauge** nilometer
**river horse** hippopotamus
**river in Afghanistan** Harut, Helmand, Indus, Kaboel, Kandu, Khash, Lora, Murghab, Oxus
**river in Africa** Benue, Blue Nile, Caledon, Congo, Gambia, Kagera, Kasai, Kei, Limpopo, Niger, Nile, Orange, Senegal, Shire, Tana, Uele, Vaal, Volta, White Nile, Zambezi
**river in Alabama** Mobile, Pea, Tallapoosa, Tombigbee, Warrior
**river in Alaska** Chena, Chulitna, Colville, Copper, Kobuk, Koyukuk, Noatak, Porcupine, Susitna, Tanana, Yukon
**river in Albania** Bojana, Drin, Erzeni, Mat, Osum, Seman, Semeni, Shkumbi, Vijose
**river in Algeria** Cheliff, Medjerda, Shelif
**river in America** Allegheny, Amazon, Arkansas, Colorado, Columbia, Gila, Hudson, Mississippi, Missouri, Ohio, Pecos, Penodscot, Platte, Tennesee, Teton, Yellowstone
**river in Angola** Cassai, Chicapa, Cuango, Cuanza, Cuito, Kunene, Longa, Zenza

**river in Argentina** Blanco, Chubut, Colorado, Grande, Negro, Paraná, Plata, Salado
**river in Arizona** Colorado, Gila, Salt, Verde
**river in Asia** Amur, Asi, Ganges, Indus, Mekong, Oorontes, Salween, Tigris
**river in Australia** Ashburton, Barcoo, Barwon, Darling, Diamantina, Fitzroy, Fortescue, Leichhardt, Macquirie, Murchison, Murray, Paroo, Swan
**river in Austria** Danube, Donau, Drau, Inn, Kamp, Raab, Rhine, Thaya, Traun
**river in Bavaria** Isar, Lech, Main
**river in Belgium** Bouco, Dyle, Lesse, Lys, Maas, Mark, Meuse, Rupel, Sambre, Scheldt, Yser
**river in Bhutan** Amochu, Machu, Manas
**river in Bolivia** Benecito, Beni, Grande, Guapore, Machupo, Orton, Parapeti, Yacuma, Yata
**river in Botswana** Boteti, Botlethe, Chobe, Cuando, Limpopo, Macloutsi, Molopo, Nata, Okavango, Okwa, Putumayo, Taokne
**river in Brazil** Amazon, Guaporé, Ica, Iguacu, Jacul, Madeira, Negro, Pará, Paraná, Parnahiba, Purus, Putumayo, Tapajos, Tocantins, Xingo
**river in Bulgaria** Danube, Isker, Marica, Maritsa, Mesta, Ogosta, Osma, Struma
**river in Burma** Chindwin, Hka, Irrawaddy, Kaladan, Malikha, Pegu, Salween, Salwin
**river in Burundi** Akanyaru, Kagera, Malagarazi, Ruvubu, Ruzizi
**river in California** Eel, Feather, Pit, Sacramento, Stony, Trinity
**river in Cambodia** Bassac, San, Sen, Srepok, Tonlesap
**river in Cameroon** Ekela, Sanaga
**river in Canada** Fraser, Knife, Liard, Mackenzie, Nelson, Niagara, Ottawa, Peace, Pelly, Slave, St Lawrence, Yukon
**river in Central Africa** Congo, Uele
**river in central Bolivia** Mamoré
**river in Central Europe** Elbe, Inn, Isar, Oder
**river in Chad** Bahraouk, Chari, Logone
**river in Chile** Alhue, Bio-bio, Bravo, Bueno, Camina, Colina, Loa, Maipo, Puelo, Valdivia
**river in China** Fenho, Han, Hwang Ho, Manass, Peiho, Salween, Si Kiang, Sungari, Tarim, Tung, Urungu, Wei, Yangtze

**river in Colombia** Amazon, Caqueta, Casanare, Isana, Magdalena, Meta, Pauto, Putumayo, Sinu, Truando, Upia, Uva
**river in Congo** Congo, Lubilash, Lulua, Sanga, Ubangi, Wamba
**river in Corsica** Golo, Gravone, Taravo
**river in Costa Rica** Irazu, Matina, Poas, Sixaola, Tarcoles
**river in Cuba** Cauto, Zaza
**river in Cyprus** Pedias, Pedieos
**river in Czechoslovakia** Elbe, Isar, Lebe, March, Moldau, Morava, Torysa, Vag
**river in Denmark** Asa, Guden, Gudenaa, Holm, Lonborg, Skive, Stor(aa), Susaa, Vorgod
**river in Devon** Exe
**river in Dominican Republic** Ozama, Yuna
**river in Ecuador** Curaray, Daule, Mira, Napo, Pindo, Tumbes, Zamora
**river in Egypt** Nile
**river in El Salvador** Jiboa, Lapaz, Lempa
**river in England** Aire, Avon, Cam, Coquet, Dee, Dove, Exe, Itchen, Lune, Mersey, Nene, Orwell, Ouse, Severn, Swale, Tamar, Tee, Tees, Thames, Trent, Tyne, Ure, Usk, Wye
**river in Estonia** Ema, Kasari, Narva, Parnu
**river in Ethiopia** Akobo, Atbara, Baro, Dawa, Fafan, Hawash, Omo, Takkaze, Web
**river in Europe** Danube, Dnieper, Don, Douro, Elbe, Inn, Loire, Maas, Oder, Ouse, Po, Rhine, Rhône, Saar, Seine, Thames, Tiber, Tisza, Vistula, Volga, Yser
**river in Finland** Lapuan, Lotta, Muonio, Oulu, Teno, Tornio
**river in Florence** Arno
**river in Florida** Aucilla, Banana, Indian, Manatee, Ochlawaha, Scambia, Suwanee
**river in France** Adour, Aisne, Allier, Charente, Cher, Dordogne, Durance, Garonne, Gironde, Isère, Loire, Marne, Meuse, Oise, Rhône, Saone, Seine, Somme, Tarn, Yser
**river in French Guiana** Maroni
**river in Gabon** Abanga, Ivindo, Ogooué, Ogowe
**river in Geneva** Rhône
**river in Georgia** Etowah, Flint, Pea, Pigeon, Satilla
**river in Germany** Eder, Elbe, Ems, Fulda, Main, Mosel, Neckar, Oder, Rhein (G), Rhine, Ruhr, Saar, Spree, Weser

**river in Ghana** Afram, Ankobra, Daka, Kulpawn, Ofin, Oti, Tano, Volta
**river in Greece** Arda, Axios, Eurotas, Evros, Kephisos, Lerna, Peneus, Rhouphia, Roufias, Saranta, Struma
**river in Guatemala** Azul, Belize, Dulce, Lapaz, Negino, Polochic, Samala
**river in Guinea** Bafing, Falema, Konkoure, Niger, Senegal, Tinkisso
**river in Guyana** Berbice, Cuyuni, Essequibo
**river in Hades** Acheron, Lethe, Styx
**river in Haiti** Artibonite, Guayamouc
**river in Honduras** Aguan, Coco, Lempa, Negro, Patuca, Santiago, Segovia, Ulua, Wanks
**river in Hungary** Drava, Duna, Henrad, Ipoly, Kapos, Körös, Maros, Mura, Rabca, Theiss, Vistula, Zala
**river in Iberia** Mino
**river in Iceland** Hvita, Jokulsa, Thjorsa
**river in Idaho** Lochsa, Payette, Salmon, Snake
**river in India** Cauvery, Chenab, Ganges, Gogra, Hooghly, Indus, Jumna, Kistna, Luni, Mahanadi, Penganga, Ravi, Sutlej
**river in Indiana** Ohio, Wabush
**river in Indonesia** Barito, Digul, Hari, Kajan, Kampar, Kapuas, Mahakam, Musi, Pawan
**river in Iran** Araks, Atrek, Euphrates, Haliri, Mashkel, Mund, Rabch, Sefid, Shur
**river in Iraq** Euphrates, Tigris, Zab
**river in Ireland** Annelee, Avoca, Bandon, Blackwater, Boyne, Brosna, Erne, Inny, Lee, Liffey, Nore, Shannon
**river in Israel** Faria, Jordan, Lakhish, Malik, Qishon, Yarkon
**river in Italy** Adda, Adige, Arno, Nera, Piave, Po, Reno, Sangro, Tiber
**river in Ivory Coast** Cavally, Komoe, Sassandra
**river in Jamaica** Black, Cobre, Minho
**river in Java** Brantas, Liwung, Solo
**river in Jordan** Jordan, Yarmuk
**river in Kampuchea** Bassac, Mekong, Porong, San, Srepok, Tonlesap
**river in Kansas** Arkansas, Missouri, Saline, Solomon
**river in Kenya** Athi, Keiro, Lak, Tana, Turkwell
**river in Laos** Done, Khong, Namhou, Noi, Sebang
**river in Latvia** Dvina, Gauja, Lielupe, Ogre, Salaca
**river in Lebanon** Damour, Hasbani, Joz, Litani, Lycos, Orontes
**river in Lesotho** Caledon, Orange
**river inlet** bayou, ria

**river in Liberia** Cess, Loffa, Manna, Mano, Morro, San Pedro, St John, St Paul
**river in Lithuania** Dubysa, Neman, Nemunas, Pregolya, Venta
**river in London** Thames
**river in Louisiana** Amite, Boeuf, Red, Sabine, Tensas
**river in Maine** Aroostook, Kennebago, Penobscot, Saco
**river in Malawi** Bua, Dwanga, Lilongwe, Shire
**river in Malaysia** Barito, Kutai, Pahang, Perak
**river in Mali** Bagoe, Bakoy, Bani, Niger, Senegal
**river in Manila** Pasig
**river in Mauritius** Grand, Poste, Rempart
**river in Melbourne** Yarra
**river in Mexico** Balsas, Bravo, Lerma, Panuco, Santiago, Yaqui
**river in Minnesota** Rainy, St Croix
**river in Monaco** Vesubie
**river in Mongolia** Kerulen, Orhon, Selenge
**river in Montana** Kootenai, Milk, Missouri, Tongue
**river in Morocco** Dra, Moulouya, Sebou, Tensift, Wadi
**river in Mozambique** Buzi, Incomati, Komati, Masintoto, Muira, Mupal
**river in Munich** Isar
**river in Namibia** Auob, Huab, Kwando, Nossob, Olifant, Omaruru, Swakop, Ugab
**river in Natal** Tugela, Umgeni, Umsunduzi, Umzimkulu
**river in Nebraska** Dismal, Elkhorn, Logan, Niobrara, Platte
**river in Nepal** Babai, Bheri, Gandak, Karnali, Rapti, Sarda
**river in Nevada** Humbolt, Reese, Truckee
**river in New Guinea** Amberno, Fly, Hamu, Kikori, Purari, Sepik
**river in New Hampshire** Bellamy, Israel, Merrimack, Saco, Souhegan
**river in New Mexico** Gila, Pecos, San Jose, Ute
**river in New York** Genesee, Hoosic, Hudson, Mohawk, Niagara, Oswego, Tioga
**river in New Zealand** Clarence, Hurunui, Manawatu, Mokau, Oreti, Rangitikei, Tamaki, Waiau, Waihou, Waikato, Waipa, Wairoa
**river in Nicaragua** Coco, Escondido, Grande, Tuma, Wanks
**river in Nigeria** Benue, Gana, Gongola, Kaduna, Komadugu, Niger, Oli, Yobe

**river in North Ireland** Mourne
**river in North Italy** Rubicon
**river in North Korea** Nam, Taedong, Tumen, Yalu
**river in North Vietnam** Bo, Ca, Chay, Chu, Koi, Nhiha
**river in Norway** Alta, Ena, Glomma, Namsen, Oi, Orkla, Otter, Rana, Reisa, Tana
**river in Oxford** Isis
**river in Pakistan** Ganges, Indus, Jamuna, Jhelum, Kundar, Nal, Ravi, Zhob
**river in Papua New Guinea** Fly
**river in Paraguay** Acaray, Confuso, Parana, Ypani
**river in Paris** Seine
**river in Perth** Swan
**river in Peru** Amazonas, Apurimac, Huallaga, Maranon, Morona, Napu, Pastaza, Rimac, Tigre, Ucayali, Urabamba
**river in Philippines** Agno, Agusan, Bro, Laoang, Magat, Mindanao, Pampanga, Pasig
**river in Poland** Brda, Bug, Drana, Lyna, Narew, Niemen, Notec, Oder, San, Vistula, Warta, Wistoka
**river in Portugal** Douro, Guadiana, Mino, Mira, Mondego, Sabar, Seda, Sor, Tago, Tamega, Tua, Vouga, Zezere
**river in Puerto Rico** Anasco, Camuy, Fajardo, Tanama, Yauco
**river in Queensland** Cloncurry, Flinders, Leichhardt, Thomson
**river in Romania** Aluta, Arges, Buzdu, Crasna, Danube, Mures, Prut, Siret, Somesul, Timis, Vedea
**river in Rome** Tiber
**river in Russia** Abgara, Bo, Desna, Dn(i)eper, Donets, Dvina, Irtysh, Kama, Kolyma, Lena, Neman, Neva, Ob, Oka, Ural, Volga
**river in Rwanda** Akanyaro, Kagera, Luvironza
**river in Sardinia** Flumendosa, Lascia, Mannu, Samassi, Tirso
**river in Scotland** Annan, Beauly, Clyde, Dee, Doon, Esk, Ettrick, Farra, Findhorn, Garry, Nith, Oykell, Spey, Tay, Teviot, Tweed
**river in Senegal** Casamance, Faleme, Gambia, Senegal
**river in Siberia** Aldan, Amur, Ili, Lena, Maya, Ob, Olekma, Onon, Sobol, Taz
**river in Sicily** Belice, Platani, Salso, Simeto, Torto
**river in Sierra Leone** Jong, Moa, Mongo, Rokkel, Scarcy, Waanje
**river in Singapore** Seletar, Sungei

**river in Somalia** Juba, Nogal, Scebeli
**river in South Africa** Breë, Caledon, Crocodile, Fish, Gamtoos, Gourits, Kei, Keiskamma, Komati, Krom, Letaba, Limpopo, Olifants, Orange, Sabie, Storms, Tugela, Umgeni, Umzimdusi, Vaal, Wilge
**river in South America** Amazon, Japurá, Madeira, Orinoco, Paraná, Purus
**river in South Asia** Indus
**river in South Korea** Han, Naktong, Somjin, Yongsan
**river in South Vietnam** Ba, Dongnai, Mekong, Song
**river in Southwest Asia** Asi, Orontes, Tigris
**river in Spain** Alagon, Duero, Ebro, Esla, Guadalquiver, Guadiana, Jucar, Mino, Riaza, Segura, Sil, Tagus, Ter
**river in Sudan** Bahr-el-Ablad, Bahr-el-Atbara, Blue Nile, Ghazal, White Nile
**river in Surinam** Suriname
**river in Swaziland** Komati, Mhlatzu, Umbulozi, Usutu
**river in Sweden** Dal, Gota, Klar, Lainio, Lule, Torne, Ume
**river in Switzerland** Aar, Doubs, Inn, Linth, Maggia, Pratigau, Rhine, Rhône, Sarine, Thur
**river in Syria** Asi, Barada, Euphrates, Jordan, Orontes
**river in Taiwan** Choshui, Haulien, Tachia, Tanshui, Wuchi
**river in Tanzania** Kagera, Kilombero, Kipengere, Kisigo, Malagarasi, Mara, Mbemkuru, Pangani, Wembere
**river in Tasmania** Derwent, Tamar
**river in Thailand** Chi, Mekong, Menam, Meping, Nan
**river in the Netherlands** Dintel, Dommel, Eems, Kromme, Maas, Meause, Waal, Yssel
**river in Tibet** Indus, Matsang, Nak, Nau, Salween, Sutlej
**river in Togo** Anie, Haho, Mono, Oti
**river in Transkei** Bashee
**river in Transvaal** Crocodile, Komati, Letaba, Mogalakwena, Olifants, Pongola
**river in Tunisia** Medjerda
**river in Turkey** Athi, Dicle, Gediz, Kizil, Mesta, Sakarya, Sarus, Seyhan
**river in Uganda** Aswa, Kafu, Katonga, Pager
**river in Uruguay** Cebolati, Cuareim, Malo, Mirim, Negro, Ulimar, Yaguaron

**river in Venezuela** Caroni, Caura, Guanare, Meta, Orinoco, Ventuari
**river in Vienna** Danube, Donau
**river in Wales** Dee, Severn, Taff, Teifi, Teme, Towy, Usk, Vyrnwy, Wye
**river in West Africa** Niger, Senegal
**river in Yugoslavia** Bosna, Danube, Drim, Drina, Ibar, Neretva, Raska, Sava, Tamis, Una, Vardar
**river in Zaïre** Aruwimi, Bomokandi, Bomu, Ebola, Epulu, Kafubu, Kasai, Kibali, Kwango, Kwilu, Lindi, Lomela, Luvua, Tshuape
**river in Zambia** Chongwe, Dwonge, Kabompo, Kafue, Kalomo, Lunga, Luongo, Luswishi, Machili, Makondo, Manyinga, Mlembo, Mombezhi, Mwambwa
**river in Zimbabwe** Limpopo, Lundi, Sabi, Sanyati, Zambezi
**river island** ait
**river mammal** beaver, otter
**river mouth** delta, estuary
**river nymph** naiad
**river of Attica** Ilissus
**river of Charon** Styx
**river of Damascus** Pharpar
**river of fire** Phlegethon
**river of forgetfulness** Lethe
**river of Kubla Khan** Alph
**river of the underworld** Styx
**river of woe** Acheron
**river Orontes** Asi
**river outlet** bayou, mouth
**river-oyster** etheria
**river path** course
**river rights** riparian
**river's edge** bank
**riverside** bank
**riverside quay** levee
**river source** creek, rill, spring
**rivers of Hades** Acheron, Lethe, Phlegethon, Styx
**river's path** course
**river to the Seine** Oise
**river transport** ferry
**river turbulence** rapid
**river valley** dale, poort, wadi, wady
**river vessel** barge
**rivet head** cuphead
**riveting** absorbing, alluring, arresting, beguiling, captivating, charming, compulsive, enchanting, engaging, engrossing, enthralling, entrancing, exciting, fascinating, fixing, gripping, hypnotising, immersing, interesting, intriguing, spellbinding, thrilling
**riviera** coast, shore
**riviére** necklace
**rivulet** beck, brook, burn, rill, stream(let), watercourse

**road** artery, avenue, (clear)way, course, expressway, highway, lane, motorway, path(way), route, rua (P), rue (F), street, thoroughfare, trail, turnpike, via
**road across water** causeway
**road bar of payment point** tollgate
**road chart** map
**road covering** tar(mac)
**road designed for fast traffic** autobahn (G), freeway, highway, motorway
**road end** cul de sac
**road hazard** pot-hole
**roadhouse** inn, diner
**road levy** toll
**road lined with houses** street
**road locomotive** steamer
**road machine** grader, scraper
**road material** macadam, tar(mac)
**road open at both ends** thoroughfare
**road provided for passing along** way
**road rules** highway code
**road's curve** camber
**road shoulder** berm(e)
**roadside hotel** motel
**road slope** grade
**road surface** asphalt, cement, macadam, tar(mac)
**road taken** route
**road tax** toll
**road transporter** hauler
**road users** traffic
**road vehicle** auto, bakkie, car, lorry, (mini)bus, van
**roadway** avenue, lane, street
**roam** browse, go, loiter, meander, ramble, range, rove, saunter, stray, stroll, trek, walk, wander, wend
**roamer** nomad, rover, stroller, wanderer
**roaming** exploring, straying, traversing, wandering
**roaming from pasture to pasture** nomad
**roam stealthily** prowl
**roar** bawl, bay, bellow, boom, bray, cry, growl, grunt, guffaw, howl, laugh(ter), noise, rave, rumble, scream, shout, shriek, snarl, squall, thunder, ululate, uproar, vociferate, wail, yell, yowl
**roaring beast** lion
**roaring trade** boom
**Roaring Twenties** era
**roar like a bull** bellow
**roar like wind** hurl
**roast** bake
**roasted mutton leg** gigot
**roasting chamber** oven
**roasting fowl** capon
**roasting rod** pin, spit
**roast in the open** barbecue, braai

**roast slightly** parch
**roast stick** skewer
**rob** cheat, crook, defraud, deprive, plunder, rifle, rook, steal
**robber** bandit, burglar, cheat, dacoit, gangster, looter, plunderer, raider, stealer, thief
**robbery** depredation, filching, fraud, heist, holdup, larceny, pillage, raid, rapine, ravin, stealing
**robbery at sea** piracy
**robbery by an armed gang** dacoity
**robbery under arms** hold-up
**robe** apparel, attire, drape, dress, garb, garment, gown, habit, housecoat, peignoir, toga, wrapper
**robe reaching the ankles** talar
**robes worn by pilgrims to Mecca** ihram
**robe worn by bishop** chimer(e)
**robin** red-breast
**Robin Hood's beloved** Marian
**Robin Hood's forest** Sherwood
**Robin Hood's Friar** Tuck
**Robin Hood's refuge** Greenwood
**robin's home** nest
**Robinson Crusoe's friend** Friday, Xurie
**rob of courage** unnerve
**rob of judgement** blind
**rob of life** bereave
**robot** android, automatic, automaton, smart
**rob systematically** plunder
**robust** boisterous, brawny, burly, coarse, crude, energetic, hale, hardy, healthy, hearty, hefty, lively, lusty, powerful, rambunctious, riotous, rough, rude, rugged, stalwart, staunch, stout, strong, sturdy, vigorous, virile
**rock** agitate, anchor, astonish, astound, basalt, boulder, bulwark, daze, jar, lurch, mainstay, pitch, protection, reef, reel, roll, shake, shale, shock, stagger, stone, support, sway, swing, toss
**rock angle** dièdre
**rock-badger** hyrax, (klip)dassie
**rock-bed forming a trough** syncline
**rock bottom** basics, nadir, zero
**rock-cavity lined with crystals** vug
**rock climbing** mountaineering
**rock-climbing method** layback
**rock clinger** limpet
**rock composed of angular fragments** breccia
**rock composed of sand** sandstone
**rock composed of volcanic fragments** agglomerate
**rock drill** stoper
**rock-dwelling** saxatile

**rocket** capsule, firework, missile, projectile, satellite, skyrocket, spacecraft, spaceship, weapon
**rocket compartment** capsule
**rocket game** badminton
**rocket range** Woomera
**rockfish** rena
**rock formed from volcanic ashes** tuff
**rock fragments** gravel
**rock fuel** coal
**Rockies wind** chinook, snow eater
**rocking cot** cradle
**rock in sea** stack
**rock musician** guitarist
**rock of calcium magnesium** dolomite
**rock of mixed minerals** aggregate
**rock or strait** Gibraltar
**rock-rabbit** hyrax, (klip)dassie
**rock-salt** halite
**rock that has solidified from molten rock** igneous rock
**rock to and fro** quake, sway, swing
**rock unsteadily** wobble
**rock used for building** granite
**rock-wall builder** stonemason
**rock with many small cavities formed from lava** pumice
**rocky** craggy, rock-like, rough, rugged, shaky, solid, stony, unstable, unsteady
**rocky desert ravine** donga, wadi, wady
**rocky edge** reef
**rocky eminence** incline, palisades, precipice
**rocky headland** escarpment, scarp, tor
**rocky hill** krans, tor
**rocky island** skerry
**rocky ravine** arroyo, kloof
**rocky recess** cave
**rocky ridge** reef
**rocky table-land** mesa
**rocky watercourse in North Africa** wadi, wady
**rod** bar, baton, cane, dowel, mace, pole, sceptre, shaft, spindle, staff, stick, wand
**rod as symbol of office** verge
**rod a yard long** yardstick
**rodent** ag(o)uti, agouty, bandicoot, beaver, capybara, chinchilla, guinea-pig, hamster, hare, lemming, mammal, marmot, mole, mongoose, mouse, porcupine, rabbit, rac(c)oon, rat, squirrel, vermin, vole
**rodent snare** mousetrap
**rode roughshod over** trot
**rod for discipline** fer(r)ule, yard
**rod for firearm bore** wiper
**rod for holding hot glass** punty
**rod for holding meat** skewer, spit
**rod forming handle of golf club** shaft
**rod for punishment** birch, cane

**rod in cricket** stump
**rod in spinning wheel** spindle
**rod of Aaron** mullein
**rod of any substance** bar
**rodomontade** bluff, bluster, boast(ful), boasting, bombast, brag(gadocio), bragging, bravado, bunkum, crow, extravagance, fanfaronade, fustian, gasconade, magniloquence, overstate, prate, puff, rant, roister, self-praise, tumidity
**rod on which a wheel turns** axle
**rod pointed at both ends** skewer
**rod-shaped** rhabdoid, virgulate
**rod to immerse sheep** crutch
**roe** caviar
**roe male fish** milt
**roentgenology** radiology, röntgenology
**Roentgen ray** roentgenogram, röntgenogram, X-ray
**roe of beluga** caviare
**roe of male fish** milt
**roe of sturgeon** caviar
**roe-stone** oolite
**rogue** charlatan, cheat, devil, imp, knave, mischief-maker, miscreant, mountebank, picaro, quack, rapscallion, rascal, rotter, scamp, scapegrace, scoundrel, shirker, skollie, swindler, vagrant, villain, wag, wretch
**roguish** arch, artful, comical, elfin, facetious, frolicsome, funny, high-spirited, humorous, impish, jocular, jolly, jovial, knavish, knowing, mischievous, naughty, pert, playful, puckish, rascally, saucy, sly, sportive, teasing, vexatious, waggish, witty
**roguish child** urchin
**roguishness** artfulness, badness, comicalness, frolicsomeness, funniness, humorousness, impishness, jocularity, knavishness, knowingness, mischief, mischievousness, naughtiness, pertness, perverseness, playfulness, roguery, sauciness, shenanigan(s), sinfulness, slyness, waggishness, waywardness, wiliness, wittiness
**roil** aggravate, agitate, anger, annoy, becloud, bedevil, bewilder, blunder, discountenance, disorder, disquiet, disturb, exasperate, foul, harass, irk, irritate, muddle, peeve, perturb, pique, plague, provoke, rile, vex
**roiled** turbid
**roister** badger, bluster, bouse, brag, brawl, bully, carouse, fight, flaunt, puff, rampage, revel, riot, strut, swagger, uproar

**rôle** capacity, characterisation, function, part, pose, post, service, work
**roll** bagel, bap, beigel, bun, catalogue, cylinder, enfold, envelop, gyrate, list, register, revolve, rock, roller, rotate, scroll, spin(dle), sway, swing, trundle, turn, undulate, wrap
**roll a ball** bowl
**roll about** sc(r)amble
**roll around** wallow
**roll as a ship** lurch, sway
**rolled paper thrown at party** streamer
**rolled smoke** cigar
**rolled, stuffed meat** roulade
**rolled tea** cha
**roller coaster** big dipper
**roller in a typewriter** platen
**roller machine** calender
**rollerskating venue** rink
**roll eyes about** goggle, squint
**roll gently** paddle
**rollicking** blithe, boisterous, bouncy, carefree, cheerful, clamorous, convivial, festive, frolicsome, gay, gleeful, impetuous, impish, jolly, joyful, light-hearted, loud, merry, mischievous, noisy, playful, puckish, riotous, spirited, sportive, sprightly, unrestrained, unruly, vociferous
**rolling grassland** prairie, veld
**roll of banknotes** wad
**roll of cloth** bolt
**roll of film** reel
**roll of hair or silk** rowel
**roll of long hair** chignon
**roll of minced meat** frikkadel, rissole
**roll of money** wad, bankroll
**roll of names** list
**roll of parchment** scroll
**roll of roulette wheel** coup
**roll of tobacco** carot, cigar
**roll of wallpaper** bolt
**rolls of pasta containing meat** cannelloni
**rolls of veal and ham, cooked in wine** saltimbocca
**roll together** convolve
**roll up** curl, furl
**roll up sleeves** reeve
**Roman** Italian, Latin
**Roman alphabet as used to transliterate Japanese** romaji
**Roman amphitheatre** Colosseum
**Roman arena fighter** gladiator
**Roman Catholic anthem** motet
**Roman Catholic book** missal
**Roman Catholic church** Basilica
**Roman Catholic dignitary** (arch)bishop, cardinal, nuncio, pope
**Roman Catholic ecclesiastic's skull-cap** zucchetto

**Roman Catholic head** pope
**Roman Catholic missionary** Jesuit
**Roman Catholic nine-day of prayer** novena
**Roman Catholic religious service** Mass
**Roman Catholic supreme ecclesiastical court** Rota
**romance** affair, amour, attachment, charm, excitement, extravagance, fable, falsehood, fantasy, fascination, fiction, glamour, idyll, intrigue, legend, liaison, melodrama, novel, passion, relationship, sentiment, story
**Roman city** Iasi
**Roman coin** as, denarius, quinarius
**Roman conspirator** Brutus, Casca
**Roman date** calends, ides, nones
**Roman deity** Janus, Juno, Jupiter, Lar, Mars, Mercury, Minerva, Pluto, Saturn, Venus
**Roman despot** Nero
**Roman dictator** Caesar, Sulla
**Roman dress** toga
**Roman emperor** Augustus, Caesar, Caligula, Claudius, Commodus, Hadrian, Nero, Nerva, Tiberius, Trajan
**Roman emperor's privy purse** fisc
**Roman equivalent of Hades** Dis
**Roman equivalent of Poseidon** Neptune
**Roman festival** saturnalia
**Roman festival calender** fasti
**Roman fiddler** Nero
**Roman fountain** Trevi
**Roman garment** lacerna, palla, planeta, stola, toga, tunic
**Roman general** Caesar
**Roman god** Amor, Apollo, Bacchus, Comus, Cupid, Dis, Eurus, Faunus, Janus, Jove, Komus, Lar, Mars, Morpheus, Mors, Neptune, Orcus, Penates, Pluto, Sol, Somnus, Volcanus, Vulcan
**Roman goddess** Annona, Aurora, Ceres, Dea, Dian(a), Epona, Fauna, Flora, Hestia, Iris, Juno, Lua, Luna, Nona, Nox, Nyx, Ops, Phoebe, Pomona, Proserpina, Salus, Spes, Terra, Venus, Vesta
**Roman goddess of agriculture** Ceres
**Roman goddess of arts** Minerva
**Roman goddess of childbirth** Lucina
**Roman goddess of crops** Annona
**Roman goddess of dawn** Aurora
**Roman goddess of fertility** Fauna
**Roman goddess of fields** Fauna
**Roman goddess of fire** Vesta
**Roman goddess of flowers** Flora
**Roman goddess of fortune** Fortuna

**Roman goddess of fruit** Pomona
**Roman goddess of health** Salus
**Roman goddess of hearth and home** Hestia, Vesta
**Roman goddess of hope** Spes
**Roman goddess of horses** Epona
**Roman goddess of love** Venus
**Roman goddess of moon** Dian(a), Luna, Phoebe
**Roman goddess of night** Nox, Nyx
**Roman goddess of peace** Pax
**Roman goddess of plenty** Ops
**Roman goddess of prosperity** Salus
**Roman goddess of underworld** Proserpina
**Roman goddess of vengeance** Nemesis
**Roman goddess of war** Bellona
**Roman goddess of wisdom** Minerva
**Roman god of boundaries** Termirius
**Roman god of dead** Orcus
**Roman god of death** Mors
**Roman god of doors and gates** Janus
**Roman god of eloquence** Mercury
**Roman god of fertility** Priapus
**Roman god of fire** Vulcan
**Roman god of forests** Silvanus
**Roman god of healing** Aesculapius
**Roman god of household** lar, Penates
**Roman god of love** Amor, Cupid
**Roman god of marriage** Hymen
**Roman god of medicine** Aesculapius
**Roman god of metalworking** Vulcan(us)
**Roman god of nature and fertlity** Faunus
**Roman god of pastoral** Faunus
**Roman god of revelry** Comus
**Roman god of sea** Neptune
**Roman god of sleep** Morpheus, Somnus
**Roman god of sowing** Satum
**Roman god of underworld** Dis, Orcus, Pluto
**Roman god of war** Mars
**Roman god of wine** Bacchus
**Roman god of woods** Pan
**Roman hall** atrium
**Roman hatchet** dolabra
**Roman herald** Fetial
**Roman household god** lar
**Romanian circle dance** hora
**Romanian money** leu
**Romanian plain** banat
**Roman killers** crucifiers
**Roman language** Latin
**Roman magistrate** (a)edile, archon, praetor, tribune
**Roman market-place** forum
**Roman music-hall** odeum
**Roman name for Ireland** Hibernia

**Roman officer in command of a century** centurion
**Roman official** (a)edile, prefect, tribune
**Roman official in Judea** Pilate
**Roman official responsible for public works** (a)edile
**Roman orator** Cicero
**Roman poet** Catullus, Cicero, Horace, Martial, Ovid, Virgil
**Roman pound** as, libra
**Roman public baths** thermae
**Roman raiment** toga
**Roman relish** garum
**Roman road** fossway, iter, via
**Roman robe** toga
**Roman rural deity** Faun
**Roman sea-god** Neptune
**Roman soldier belonging to a legion** legionary
**Roman statesman** Cato
**Roman supreme god** Jove, Jupiter
**Roman supreme goddess** Juno
**Roman temple** pantheon
**romantic** extravagant, fabulous, fanciful, fantastic, fictitious, glamorous, imaginary, imaginative, picturesque, unpractical, unreal
**romantic intrigue** affair
**romantic man** Romeo
**romantic missive** love letter
**romantic popular song** torch
**romantic song** serenade, ballad
**romantic way to dance** cheek-to-cheek
**Roman tunic** toga
**Roman tutelary god** lar
**Roman two-handled flask** ampulla
**Roman tyrant** Nero
**Roman weight** as, bes, libra, solidus
**Roman wine festival** vinalia
**Roman world of the dead** Orcus
**Roman writer** Catullus, Cicero, Horace, Martial, Ovid, Virgil
**Romany** gipsy, gypsy
**Rome river** Tiber
**romp** bounce, caper, carouse, cavort, celebrate, frisk, frolic, jollification, orgy, play, rollick, scamper, spree, spring, vault
**romping girl** stag, tomboy
**Romulus's twin** Remus
**Röntgen's discovery** X-rays
**rood** crucifix
**roof** awning, canopy, ceiling, cover(ing), eaves, housetop, shanty, shelter, tarpaulin, top, wigwam
**roof angle** hip
**roof beam** rafter
**roof channel** gutter
**roof cover** slater
**roof covering** shingle, slate, thatch, tile
**roofed colonnade** stoa
**roof edge** eaves

**roofed portico behind an open arcade**
loggia
**roofed shelter** shed
**roof gutter** rone
**roofing material** shingle, slate, thatch, tile
**roofing metal** zinc
**roofing of straw** thatch
**roof in the form of a dome** cupola
**roof of the mouth** palate
**roof overhang** eaves
**roof room** attic, loft
**roof specialist** tiler
**roof supported by a series of arches** arcade
**roof timber** joist
**roof trough** gutter
**roof window** dormer, skylight
**rook** beguile, bilk, castle, cheat, crow, delude, diddle, dupe, embezzle, fleece, outwit, pilfer, rob, swindle, trick
**rookie** apprentice, beginner, cadet, colt, freshman, newcomer, novice, novitiate, recruit, roofie, tiro, tyro
**rook's cry** caw
**room** area, bunk, capacity, chamber, leeway, live, lodge, lodging, margin, quarters, reside, sala (Sp), scope, space, territory
**room below ground level of house** cellar
**room below stage** mezzanine
**room between kitchen and dining room** servery
**room designer** decorator
**room divider** partition
**roomer** tenant
**room for broadcasting programmes** studio
**room for children** nursery
**room for distilling** still-room
**room for keeping food** larder, pantry
**room for meals** refectory
**room for paintings** gallery
**room for storing food** larder, pantry
**room for table linen** ewery
**room for taking hot baths** caldarium
**room for wine** cellar
**room from which a broadcast is made** studio
**room from which meals are served** servery
**room in church** vestry
**rooming house** tenement
**room in harem** oda
**room in prison** cell
**room in roof of a house** attic, garret, loft
**room in tower** belfry
**room in which wine is stored** cellar

**room leading to a more important one** anteroom
**room on ship** berth, cabin
**room over church porch** parvis
**room's general aspect** décor
**room side** wall
**room's inner upper surface** ceiling
**room under building** cellar
**room where goods are displayed** showroom
**roomy** ample, capacious, commodious, generous, large, sizable, spacious, wide
**roost** alight, bar, domicile, house, lodging, perch, rest, rod, rookery, seat, settle, sit, sojourn, tree
**rooster** cock(erel)
**root** base, basis, beginning, cause, cheer, commencement, encourage, establish, exterminate, implant, origin, radix, reason, set, source, start, stem, support
**root after cropping** ratoon
**rootcrop** beetroot, carrot, leek, onion, parsnip, potato, radish, swede, turnip
**rootless** drifting, itinerant, nomadic, pleurodont, rambling, roving, strolling, travelling, vagabond, vagrant, wandering
**rootlike subdivision of nerve or vein** radicle
**root of all evil** money
**root of ginger** race
**root of South American plant, used as emetic** ipecacuanha
**root out** abolish, annihilate, destroy, discover, eliminate, eradicate, erase, exterminate, extirpate, produce, remove, uncover, unearth, uproot, weed
**root plant used in salads** beet(root), carrot, radish
**roots** background, beginning(s), birthplace, family, heritage, home, origin
**root used in poi** taro
**root vegetable** beet, carrot, leek, onion, parsnip, potato, radish, swede, turnip
**rope** bind, cable, cord, fasten, hawser, lash, lasso, leash, line, moor, pinion, strand, tether, tie
**ropeable** angry, furious, intractable, irascible, irate, ropable, wild
**rope coil** loop
**rope-dance** acrobat, equilibrist
**rope fastened in the corner of sail** sheet
**rope fastening upper corner of sail to yard** earing
**rope fibre** coir, hemp, sisal
**rope fibre plant** agave

**rope for catching cattle** lasso
**rope for confining an animal** tether
**rope for leading an animal** halter, leash
**rope for lowering or raising round objects** parbuckle
**rope for raising or lowering sail** halyard
**rope for tethering horses** lariat, lasso, reata
**rope in** engage, enlist, involve, lure, persuade
**rope in sailing** mainsheet
**rope join** knot
**rope-knotting art** macrame
**ropemaker** ratliner
**rope-making plant** hemp
**rope on a yacht** sheet
**ropes** cables, cordage, cords, hawsers, strands
**rope-soled shoe with canvas upper** espadrille
**rope supporting a mast** stay
**rope used for life-saving** lifeline
**rope used for tethering** lariat
**rope used on towing** warp
**rope used to break in horse** hackamore
**rope used to lower sail** halyard
**rope-walker** equilibrist, funambulist
**rope with running noose** lasso
**rosaceous tree** apple
**rosary** beads, chaplet, garland, prayer, rose-garden, string
**rosary component** bead
**rosebay** oleander
**rose-breasted cockatoo** galah
**rose-coloured** roseate
**rose cultivator** rosarian
**rose essence** attar, otto
**rose garden** rosery
**rose leaf** petal
**rose of Sharon** althea
**rose-petal oil** attar, otto
**rose prickle** thorn
**rose-red dye** eosin
**rose-scented snuff** maccabaw, maccaboy, maccoboy
**rose-shaped ribbon** rosette
**rosette** bond, bow, braid, cockade, connection, joint, knot, ligature, loop, tie
**rosin** colophony, resin, rub, seal, smear
**rosta** podia
**roster** agenda, beadroll, calendar, directory, docket, inventory, list, record, register, roll, rota, schedule, slate
**rostrum** ambo, beak, bow, dais, desk, lectern, platform, podium, pulpit, ram, stage, stand, stem

**rosy** bright, cheerful, flushed, healthy, optimistic, pink, promising, reddish
**rosy-cheeked** ruddy
**rosy shade** pink
**rosy tint** blush
**rot** banter, blight, corrode, corrupt(ion), decay, decompose, decomposition, decompound, degenerate, dilapidation, disconcert, drat, mould(er), nonsense, perish, putrefaction, putrify, rottenness, rubbish, spoil
**rota** agenda, catalogue, list, register, roll, roster, scroll, table
**rotary** gyrating, revolving, rotating, spinning, turning, whirling
**rotary engine** turbine
**rotary force** torque
**rotary machine part** cam
**rotary tool** borer
**rotate** alternate, gyrate, pivot, reel, replace, revolt, revolve, roll, spin, switch, swivel, turn, twiddle, twirl, twist
**rotate mast** slew
**rotate numbers on telephones** dial
**rotating blade** rotor
**rotating drum** cylinder
**rotating part** roller, rotor
**rotating shaft in machine** arbor
**rotating source of power** windmill
**rotating toy** top
**rotation** cycle, gyration, orbit, reel, revolution, sequence, spin(ning), succession, switching, turn(ing), wheel
**rote** groove, habit, repetition, ritual, routine, rut
**rotgut** plonk
**rotisserie rod** spit
**rotten** addled, bad, contemptible, corrupt, decayed, deceitful, decomposed, defective, disgusting, dishonest, f(o)etid, foul, off, offensive, putrefied, putrescent, putrid, soft, tainted, unsound, yielding
**rotten state** decay
**rotter** blackguard, blighter, cad, cur, good-for-nothing, louse, rat, stinker, swine, toad
**rotting dead flesh** carrion
**rotund** bulbous, corpulent, obese, orbical, plump, podgy, stout, tubby
**roturier** plebeian
**roucou** annatto
**roué** debauchee, lecher, rake
**rough** agitated, boisterous, coarse, craggy, crude, dishonest, disorderly, disturbed, grating, harsh, imperfect, inclement, incomplete, inconvenient, inharmonious, irregular, jarring, noisy, riotous, rude, rugged, scabrous, severe, sharp, stormy, tempestuous, turbulent, uncivil, uncomfortable, uncouth, uncultured, uncut, undressed, uneven, unfinished, unpolished, unprepared, unrefined, violent, wild
**roughage** fibre
**roughage cereal** bran
**rough and blowy** stormy
**rough-and-ready** adequate, approximate, crude, makeshift, primitive, provisional, sketchy, stop-gap, unpolished, unrefined
**rough and scaly** scabrous
**rough-and-tumble** disorderly, fight, horseplay, melee, mêlée, rough, rowdy, scrambling, scrimmage, scuffle
**rough and unkempt** shaggy
**rough boyish girl** tomboy
**rough calculation** approximation, estimate
**rough country region** backveld, boondock, bundu, gramadoelas
**rough draft** outline
**rough drawing** sketch
**rough dry taste** yarrish
**rough edge** burr, jagged
**roughen** abrade, coarsen, graze, harshen, rough, scuff
**rough exterior bark** ross
**rough fellow** bear
**rough, grainy leather** shagreen
**rough heavy boot** stogie, stogy
**rough idea** approximation
**rough lawless fellow** ruffian, skollie, tsotsi
**rough lump of native gold** nugget
**roughly** grosso mode, approximately
**roughly-built hut** shack
**roughly-cut portion** wedge
**rough-mannered person** lout
**rough metal edge** burr
**rough mineral** ore
**roughness** asperity, austerity, coarseness, crinkledness, fury, hairiness, imperfectness, jaggedness, nodosity, pertness, rage, rudeness, ruggedness, stoniness, tactlessness, uncourtliness
**roughness of surface** asperity
**roughness of temper** asperity
**rough out** adumbrate, delineate, demarcate, outline, sketch
**rough plaster** parget
**rough quarrel** scrap
**rough shoe of untanned leather** brogue, vel(d)skoen
**rough silk fabric** honan
**rough similarity** assonance
**rough-skinned apple** russet
**rough steep rock** crag, krans
**rough stone** rubble
**rough track** trail
**rough uncultured person** backvelder, barbarian
**rough untanned leather** shagreen
**rough up** beat, manhandle, pummel, thrash
**rough water** riptide, tide-rip
**rouncy** riding horse
**round** annular, arched, candid, circle, circular, complete, curve(d), cycle, cylinder, cylindrical, entire, full, globular, honest, orbed, period, plain, positive, quick, revolution, rotund, rung, sonorous, spherical, unmodified, upright, whole
**roundabout** circuitous, devious, erratic, indirect, meandering, oblique, rambling, random, sinuous, winding, zigzag
**roundabout method** circumbendibus
**roundabout tour** detour
**round and plump** chubby
**round angle** perigon
**round before a semifinal** quarterfinal
**round boiled sweet on small stick** lollipop
**round building** rotunda
**round cap with a flap at the back** montero
**round cask** barrel
**round container** basin, dish
**round domed building** rotunda
**round Dutch cheese** Edam
**rounded** bulbous, rotund
**rounded oblong** ellipse
**rounded part of a church** apse
**rounded seed vessel** boll
**rounded stone** cobble, pebble
**rounded summit of hill** dome
**rounded tile** crease
**rounded valley** cwym
**round embroidery frame** hoop, tabo(u)ret
**round flat cloth cap** beret
**round flat loaf** bannock
**round glass ball** marble
**round hall** rotunda
**round handle** knob
**round-headed loaf** cob
**round hide boat** coracle
**round hillock** knob, knoll, koppie, morro
**round hollow** cirque
**round of applause** cheers, éclat, hand, plaudit, salvo
**round off** cap, close, complete, conclude, crown, end, finish, perfect, settle
**round on** abuse, attack, retaliate
**round outline** rondure

**round pillar** column
**round plate** disc
**round roll** bun
**round roof** dome
**round Scottish cap** tam-o'-shanter
**round sports equipment** ball
**round stiff hat** bowler
**round stone tower built in Scotland** broch
**round the bend** screwy, weird
**round the twist** crazy, insane, mad
**round-town road** bypass
**round up** assemble, collect, drive, gather, group, herd, marshal, rally
**round-up of cattle** rodeo
**round vessel** pot, bowl
**round window** oculus, oxeye, roundel
**roundworm** nematode
**roundworm disease** ascariasis
**rouse** agitate, anger, animate, awake, bestir, call, disturb, excite, incense, incite, inflame, instigate, move, provoke, rise, startle, stimulate, stir, wake
**rouseabout** handyman
**rouse from sleep** awake(n), wake
**rouse to lively action** bestir
**rouse up** excite, spur, stimulate
**rousing** brisk, electrifying, inspiring, lively, stirring, vigorous
**rousing effect** stimulus
**rout** beat, brawl, canaille, chase, conquer, conquest, debacle, defeat, destroy, discomfit, drubbing, examine, fracas, fuss, herd, hunt, mob, overwhelm, rabble, repulse, riffraff, ruin, rummage, scatter, search, stampede, subjugate, subjugation, thrashing, vanquish
**route** ambit, chart, circle, circuit, course, (free)way, highway, itinerary, journey, lane, map, path, road(way), speedway, track
**route deviation** detour
**route used by aircraft** skyway
**routine** boring, conventional, custom(ary), drill, dull, everyday, familiar, formula, groove, habitual, humdrum, method, normal, order, ordinary, pattern, practice, predictable, procedure, programme, regular, schedule, standard, system, tedious, tiresome, typical, usage, usual, way
**routinely** regularly
**routine of duty** rota
**routine task** chore
**rove** gallivant, meander, prowl, ramble, range, roam, traipse, wander
**rove around** prowl
**rove in search of pleasure** gad

**rover** corsair, drifter, freebooter, globetrotter, gypsy, hiker, itinerant, marauder, migrant, nomad, pirate, raider, rambler, ranger, roamer, stroller, tinker, transient, traveller, vagabond, vagrant, voyager, walker, wanderer, wayfarer
**rover's seat** thwart
**roving musician** minstrel, troubadour
**row** alteration, argue, argument, bank, brawl, column, debate, din, disagree(ment), dispute, disturbance, fight, file, fracas, fray, fuss, line, noise, oar, paddle, procession, progression, pull, punt, quarrel, queue, racket, range, rank, retinue, rumpus, scold, sequence, series, skull, spar, squabble, string, tier, tiff, train, trouble, tumult, tussle, uproar, wrangle
**rowan tree** mountain ash
**rowdy** atrocious, boisterous, brute, brutish, bully, demoniacal, devilish, disorderly, evil, gangster, hoodlum, hooligan, lawless, loud, lout, mugger, noisy, roguish, rough, rowdyish, ruffian, savage, sinister, skollie, tough, tsotsi, unruly, uproarious, wild, yahoo
**rowdy behaviour** randan, spree
**rowdy celebration** rag
**rowdy child** hellion
**rowdy gang** tribulation
**rowdy party** jol, orgy, riot, rort(y)
**rowdy spree** razzle-dazzle
**rowdy youngster** larrikin
**rowen** aftermath
**rower** oar(sman), paddler
**rower of gondola** gondolier
**rower's aid** oar
**rower sitting nearest the stern** stroke
**rowing blade** oar
**rowing boat** gig, skiff
**rowing crew** eight
**rowing eight** oarsmen
**rowing need** oar
**rowing pivot** oarlock
**rowing spar** oar
**rowing team** crew
**rowing tool** oar
**rowing vessel** boat, canoe
**row of arches on pillars** arcade
**row of columns** colonnade
**row of linked houses** terrace
**row of links** chain
**row of persons** file, line, queue
**row of pillars** colonnade
**row of semi-detached houses** terrace
**row of series** string
**row of short pillars** balustrade
**row of shrubs** hedge
**row of uniform houses** terrace

**rows of soldiers** ranks
**row with it** oar
**royal** august, grand, imperial, impressive, kinglike, kingly, magnificent, majestic, monarchical, princely, queenlike, queenly, regal, sovereign, splendid, stately, superb, superior
**royal attendant** lady-in-waiting, yeoman
**royal authority** reign
**royal colour** purple
**royal crown** diadem
**royal daughter** princess
**royal Di's maiden name** Spencer
**royal dog** borzoi, corgi
**royal flush card** ace
**royal fur** ermine
**royal guard** yeoman
**royal headwear** crown
**royal home** palace
**Royal Horse Guard** Blues
**royal house** palace
**royal household** court
**royal house of Britain** Plantagenet, Stuart, Tudor, Windsor, York
**royal insignia** regalia
**royal mace** sceptre
**royal male** prince
**royal mansion** palace, palais (F)
**royal persons** royalty
**royal residence** palace
**royal Scottish house** Stuart
**royal seat** throne
**royal son** prince
**royal staff** sceptre
**royalty** autocracy, dynasty, grandeur, kingship, nobility, prestige, queenship, regality, regally, stateliness, supremacy
**Royal Worcester** chinaware
**rub** abrade, buff, chafe, friction, irritate, massage, obstacle, polish, problem, scour, scrub, smear, smooth, stroke, wipe
**rub as to clean or dry** wipe
**rub away by friction** abrade
**rubber** caoutchouc, caucho, condom, ebonite, elastic, eraser, gum, latex, masseur
**rubber band** elastic
**rubber boot** gumboot
**rubber boot reaching knee** wellington
**rubber cheque** bouncer
**rubber disc used in ice hockey** puck
**rubber-edged implement for cleaning windows** squeegee
**rubber fluid** latex
**rubber on rim** tyre
**rubber overshoe** galosh
**rubber plant sap** latex
**rubber ring** tyre

**rubber shoe** gumboot, gumshoe
**rubber-soled canvas sport shoe** plimsoll
**rubber stamp** dater
**rubber tree** ule, syringa
**rubber tree sap** latex
**rubber wheel** tyre
**rubbing and kneading of the muscles** massage
**rubbing away** attrition
**rubbing out** erasure
**rubbish** castaways, cul(t)ch, debris, detritus, discards, dregs, dross, eyewash, garbage, junk, leavings, litter, malark(e)y, nonsense, offal, orts, poppycock, refuse, rejects, remains, rot, rubble, scrap, scum, sweepings, swill, tosh, trash, tripe, waste, wreckage
**rubbish container** (litter-)bin
**rubbish from a mine** mullock
**rubbish on tip** refuse
**rubbish pile** scrap heap
**rubbish tip** dump
**rubbishy** cheap, dirty, gaudy, inferior, obscene, scrubby, shabby, shoddy, trashy, wretched
**rubble** bits, debris, dross, fragments, hulk, litter, pieces, remains, rubbish, ruins, waste, wrack, wreck(age)
**rub down** groom, manipulate, massage
**rub elbows with** associate, fraternise, socialise
**rubeola** measle, morbilli
**rub gently** stroke
**rub gently with the nose** nuzzle
**rubicund** rosy, ruddy
**rub in ointment** inunction
**rub lightly** wipe
**rub off** abrade
**rub out** cancel, delete, destroy, efface, erase, execute, expunge, exterminate, kill, murder, obliterate, remove, slaughter
**rub over with oil** anoint
**rub shiny** polish
**rub up** burnish
**rub with grease** smear
**rub with harsh noise** scrape
**rub with oil** anoint
**rub with something sharp** scrape
**ruby glass** schmelze
**ruched strip of cloth** frill
**rucksack** knapsack
**ruckus** disturbance, riot, ruction, uproar
**ruction** brawl, commotion, disturbance, row, tumult
**rudder** helm
**rudder control** tiller
**ruddy** blushing, florid, flushed, reddish, roseate, rosy, rubicund, sanguine

**rude** amorphous, artless, boorish, brusque, brutal, caustic, coarse, cruel, curt, discourteous, fierce, fresh, ignorant, ill-mannered, impertinent, impolite, impudent, inartistic, inelegant, insolent, insulting, pert, raw, rough, saucy, simple, sturdy, tempestuous, uncivil, uncouth, uncultured, undecorated, uneducated, ungallant, unlearned, unmannerly, unrefined, untaught, untrained, untutored
**rude act** incivility
**rude child** brat
**rude dwelling** cabin
**rude fellow** cad
**rudely** artlessly, boorishly, brutishly, churlishly, coarsely, crudely, curtly, discourteously, gracelessly, grossly, harshly, impertinently, impolitely, impudently, inartistically, inelegantly, insolently, insultingly, lowly, oafishly, obscenely, primitively, rawly, roughly, savagely, sharply, shortly, suddenly, uncouthly, violently, vulgarly
**rudely abrupt** curt
**rudely assertive** bumptious
**rudeness** acerbity, arrogance, austerity, barbarity, boorishness, brashness, brutality, causticity, cheek(iness), churlishness, coarseness, crudeness, crudity, cruelty, curtness, derision, discourteousness, disrespect, effrontery, ferocity, flippancy, frenzy, fury, gaucherie, gracelessness, hoydenism, ignorance, illiteracy, impertinence, impoliteness, impudence, impudentness, incivility, indecorum, insolence, lowness, oafishness, obscenity, pertness, petulance, presumption, rage, ribaldry, roughness, rusticity, sarcasm, savagery, shortness, simplicity, tactlessness, turbulence, ungraciousness, vehemence, vigour, violence, virulence, vulgarity, vulgarness
**rude person** boor, oaf
**rudimentary** basic, elemental, elementary, embryonic, formative, fundamental, imperfect, initial, initiatory, introductory, original, premature, primary, primitive, undeveloped, unfledged, unripe
**rudimentary stem** caulicle
**rudiments** basics, beginning, commencement, elements, foundation, mainspring, nucleus, root
**Rudolph Hess's prison** Spandau

**rue** bemoan, deplore, lament, miss, mourn, regret, repent
**rueful** contrite, doleful, grievous, melancholy, mournful, repentant, sad, sorry, woeful
**ruff** buoyancy, elation, glee, joy
**ruffed monkey** saki
**ruffian** brute, bully, cutthroat, gangster, hooligan, knave, lout, rogue, roughneck, rowdy, scoundrel, thug, villain
**ruffle** agitate, annoy, bustle, commotion, confusion, damage, disarrange, disorder, disturb, frill, irritate, rearrange, ruff, rumple, tousle, trouble, tumult, upset, wrinkle
**ruffling of water's surface** ripple
**rug** blanket, carpet, cover(let)
**rugby back** centre
**rugby formation** scrum
**rugby team** fifteen
**rugby touch-down** try
**rugged** broken, cacophonous, craggy, crude, difficult, grating, hard, harsh, hilly, irregular, rough, rude, severe, stormy, tempestuous, trying, ugly, unpolished, unrefined
**rugged crest** arête
**rugged peak** crag, krans
**Ruhr city** Essen
**ruin** bane, damage, decay, defeat, destroy, destruction, devastation, dish, doom, downfall, fall, havoc, injure, mar, perdition, ravage, spoil, wreck
**ruin completely** destroy
**ruined** destroyed, devastated, impoverished, overthrew, overturned, overwhelmed, rased, razed, shattered, smashed, wrecked
**ruinous** antagonistic, corrupted, decayed, defaced, degraded, demolished, devastated, devastating, dilapidated, disastrous, distracting, dreadful, ravaged, rusty, seedy, time-worn
**ruins in Egypt** Abydos, Memphis, pyramids, Thebes
**ruins in El Salvador** Tazumal
**ruins in Greece** Acropolis, Corinth, Delos, Elevsis, Pellas, Samos
**rule** administer, administration, authority, canon, command, conduct, control, convention, decide, decree, direction, dominate, domination, dominion, establish, govern(ment), guide, judge, law, manage, mastery, order, precept, principle, regulation, reign, settle, standard
**rule badly** misgovern
**rule cruelly** tyrannise

**ruled by voting** democracy
**ruled mark** line
**ruled out** ineligible, unacceptable, unfit
**rule for conduct** precept
**rule of action** law
**rule of conduct** law, maxim
**rule of despot** depotism
**rule of evidence** estoppel
**rule out** ban, bar, disallow, dismiss, eliminate, exclude, forbid, ignore, overlook, preclude, prevent, prohibit, reject
**ruler** commander, controller, dynast, edge, emperor, empress, governor, king, measure, monarch, potentate, queen, regent, sovereign, straight-edge, sultan, yardstick
**ruler in Italy** duce
**ruler of Algeria** bey, dey
**ruler of duchy** duke
**ruler of Ethiopia** negus
**ruler of Muslim state** caliph, sultan
**ruler of Russia** czar, tsar
**ruler of Sikkim's title** Chogyal
**ruler of small state** toparch
**ruler of Venice** doge
**ruler of Yemen** ima(u)m
**ruler's decree** edict
**ruler with great power** potentate
**rules of correct behaviour** etiquette
**rules of diet** dietetics
**rules of speech** grammar
**rule with an iron hand** oppress
**rule with authority** govern
**ruling** adjudication, call, commanding, current, decision, dominant, governing, hegemonic, holding, judg(e)ment, managing, opinion, outcome, penalty, regent, resolution, sentence, verdict
**ruling class of rich people** plutocracy
**ruling period** reign
**ruling principal** regent
**rum** odd, peculiar, queer, ron (Sp), strange
**rum and water** grog
**rumble** barrage, drumming, echo, growl, resonance, resound, reverberate, roar, thunder
**rumbling in stomach** collywobbles
**rumbling sound** curmurring
**rumbustious** boisterous, bouncy, clamorous, impetuous, loud, noisy, riotous, rollicking, rowdy, unrestrained, unruly, uproarious, vociferous, wild
**rumbustious** loudness, noisiness, riotousness, rowdiness, unruliness, uproariousness, vociferousness, wildness
**rum distilled from molasses** tafia

**ruminant** antelope, camel, cattle, cow, deer, goat, llama, sheep
**ruminant's stomach** manyplies, omasum, rumen, tripe
**ruminant with a heavy coat of wool** sheep
**ruminate** chew, cud, meditate, muse, ponder, reflect, think
**ruminated food** cud
**rummage** clutter, comb, debris, disarrange, discover, examine, explore, ferret, find, forage, grub, hunt, inquest, inquiry, junk, litter, oddments, probe, quest, rake, ransack, refuse, scour, screen, search, sweep, trash, uncover, unearth, waste
**rummage through** ransack
**rumour** assertion, bruit, canard, chatter, fable, gossip, grapevine, hearsay, hoax, information, innuendo, insinuation, intimate, report, reveal, say, scandal, skinder, story, suggest, tale, talk, tattle, tell, whisper
**rump** balance, breech, buttocks, crust, end, excess, heel, hindquarters, loins, others, posterior, remainder, remnants, residue, rest, stub, stump
**rump bone** aitchbone
**rumple** break, bruise, crease, crinkle, crumble, crumple, crush, derange, discompose, disorder, fold, furrow, mash, mess, muss, pucker, pulverise, ruffle, smash, tousle, wrinkle
**rumps** buttocks
**rumpus** ado, argument, bedlam, brawl, broil, commotion, confusion, dispute, disturbance, fight, fracas, hassle, melee, mêlée, quarrel, row, squabble, storm, tumult, uproar, words
**run** average, canter, challenge, channel, chase, company, compete, conduct, contend, continue, creep, drive, extend, ferry, flock, flood, flow, fuse, go, hasten, hie, hunt, hurry, ladder, liquefy, manage, melt, move, operate, ordinary, overflow, pack, pour, pride, proceed, progress, pursue, race, reach, scud, smelt, speed, spread, sprint, stab, standard, stream, stretch, thrust, track, transport, trot
**run about briskly** scamper
**run across** encounter, meet
**run after** chase, follow, pursue, pursue, stalk, tail
**run aground** strand
**run amuck** rampage
**run a paper** edit

**run around in a murderous frenzy** amok, amuck
**run a short distance at great speed** sprint
**run at the nose** snivel
**run away** abduct, abscond, bolt, decamp, elope, escape, flee, skedaddle
**runaway** absconder, deserter, escaped, escapee, escaper, fleeing, fugitive, refugee, truant
**runaway bride** eloper
**run away from** flee
**runaway lovers** elopers
**run away secretly** abscond
**run away to marry** elope
**run away with** abduce, abduct, kidnap
**run before the wind** scud
**run company** administrate, manage
**run down** belittle, criticise, curtail, cut, decrease, decrepit, defame, denigrate, depreciate, disparage, drop, exhaust, hit, reduce, seedy, strike, tire, trim, weaken(ed)
**rundown** briefing, cut, decline, decrease, lessening, outline, précis, recap, reduction, résumé, review, run-through, sketch, summary, synopsis
**run-down** broken-down, decrepit, dilapidated, dingy, drained, exhausted, fatigued, ramshackle, seedy, shabby, tumble-down, unhealthy, weak, weary, worn-out
**run-down area** slum
**run-down car** jalopy
**rune having the sound of modern English** wen
**run excitedly** scamper
**run fast** hare
**run for it** abscond, flee, fly, skedaddle
**run for one's money** race
**run getter** scorer
**rung of a ladder** spoke
**run hastily** scamper, scurry
**runic alphabet** futhork
**runic symbol** edh, eth
**run in** arrest, bust, pinch
**run in panic, as cattle** stampede
**run in stockings** ladder, tear
**run into** encounter, hit, meet, ram, smash, strike
**run its course** fly
**run like mad** race, scramble
**run naked** streak
**runnel** brook, gutter, rill
**runner** athlete, competitor, courier, jogger, messenger, miler, participant, shoot, sprinter, sprout, stem
**runner for instance** athlete
**runner or string** bean

**runner-up** second
**running** administration, charge, competing, competition, conduct(ing), consecutive, constant, contention, contest, continuous, control(ling), current, departing, directing, direction, escaping, featuring, fleeing, functioning, galloping, going, leading, leaking, managing, operating, performance, proceeding, spilling, streaming, supervising, supervision, together, unbroken, unceasing, uninterrupted
**running away** bolt, fleeing
**running bird** courser
**running chore** errand
**running company badly** mismanaging
**running down** denigrating
**running lengthwise** longitudinal
**running loop on rope** noose
**running naked** streaking
**running quickly over** cursory
**running stream** current
**running track** stadium
**running water** stream
**run not credited to a batsman** extra
**runny** adulterated, diluted, flowing, fluid, insipid, liquefied, liquid, melted, molten, tasteless, thawed, thin, washy, watery, weak, wet
**run off** abscond, bolt, decamp, duplicate, elope, escape, flee, print, produce, scarper, tap
**run off hastily** scoot, skedaddle
**run off with** abduce, abduct, kidnap, seduce
**run off with lover** elope
**run-of-the-mill** average, common(place), everyday, fair, mediocre, middling, ordinary, routine, tolerable, undistinguished, unexceptional, unexciting, unimpressive, unremarkable
**run one's eye over** read, scan, study
**run out** cease, close, conclude, end, expire, fail, finish, terminate
**run out of** consume, deplete, exhaust, expend, finish
**run out on** abandon, desert, forsake
**run over** brim, duplicate, echo, exceed, hit, iterate, overflow, overgo, rehearse, reiterate, review, spill, strike, survey, trample, transcend
**run quickly** scud, sprint
**run riot** rampage, wanton
**run short distance** sprint
**run slowly** idle, jog
**run swiftly** race
**runt** chit, dwarf, elf, fingerling, gnome, lilliputian, littlest, manikin, midget, pipsqueak, pygmy, Thumbelina, urchin, weakling

**run the eye over** peruse, scrutinise
**run the show** command, dominate, manage, oversee, regulate, supervise
**run through** eviscerate, exhaust, gut, impale, pierce, squander, stab, waste
**run up** ascend, escalate
**run up an account** owe
**runway surface** tarmac
**run wild** amok, ramble, rampage, straggle, stray
**run with** abduct, abscond, elope
**run with easy strides** lope, trot
**run with long bounding strides** lope
**rupture** breach, break(ing), burst(ing), cleavage, cleave, cleft, contention, crack, disrupt(ing), disruption, divide, end, fault, feud, fissure, flaw, fracture, gap, hernia, hostility, quarrel, rent, rift, schism, scissure, separate, sever(ance), slice, space, split, tear
**rural** agrarian, agrestic, agricultural, agronomical, Arcadian, boorish, bucolic, country, crude, georgic, inurban, pastoral, provincial, regional, rough, rugged, rustic, sylvan, unsophisticated, up-country
**rural deity** Faun
**rural districts** country(side), (platte)land
**rural festival** fête champetre (F)
**rural house** cottage, farmhouse
**rurality** rusticity
**rural labourer** peasant
**rural poetry** georgic
**rural scene** paysage
**rural South Africa** platteland
**ruse** artifice, deception, device, dodge, feint, hoax, imposture, manoeuvre, ploy, pretence, stratagem, subterfuge, trick, wile
**rush** accelerate, advance, assault, attack, bulrush, career, cattail, dart, dash, drag, expedite, force, haste, hurry, hurtle, hustle, impel, move, onslaught, overcome, pass, plant, race, reed(s), roll, run, scramble, scurry, speed, spurt, stem, sudden, surge, swarm, urgency
**rush about** dart
**rush about wildly** rampage
**rush abroad** flush
**rush against** charge
**rush away** bolt, flee, scuttle
**rush down** trace
**rush for weaving** frail
**rush hastily** dash
**rush headlong** boil, career, ruin, spurn, stampede
**rushing** furious, huddling, hurl, impetuous, scud

**rushing attack** charge
**rushing of wind** gust
**rushing sound as of wind in trees** sough
**rushing stream** torrent
**rush-like plant** sedge
**rush off** skedaddle
**rush of liquid** fluid, head
**rush of water** cataract, fresh, shoot, spout, swash
**rush of water in a mine** swellet
**rush of wind** gust
**rush of words** spate
**rush out suddenly** sally
**rush to conclusion** misjudge
**rush with a weapon** lunge
**russet-yellow** filemot
**Russian** Muscovite
**Russian alcoholic drink** vodka
**Russian Arctic native** Siberian
**Russian aristocrat** boyar(d)
**Russian artificial earth satellite** sputnik
**Russian astronaut** cosmonaut
**Russian author** Dostoevsky, Solzhenitsyn, Tolstoy
**Russian beetroot soup** borscht
**Russian carriage** dros(h)ky, troika
**Russian cavalryman** cossack
**Russian central government** Kremlin
**Russian Christian** uniat
**Russian coin** copeck, kopeck, r(o)uble
**Russian commune** mir
**Russian communist** Bolshevik
**Russian composer** Arenski, Tchaikovsky
**Russian concierge** dvornik
**Russian council of state** duma
**Russian country-dance** ziganka
**Russian country house** dacha
**Russian court favourite** Rasputin
**Russian dance** kazatzka, ziganka
**Russian decree** ukase
**Russian desert** tundra
**Russian drink** vodka
**Russian earth satellite** Sputnik
**Russian emperor** czar, tsar
**Russian empress** czarina, tsarina
**Russian-English war** Crimea
**Russian fighter plane** MiG
**Russian fur** sable
**Russian gala-dress** sarafan
**Russian glass** chark
**Russian goddess of night** Nox
**Russian government** Kremlin
**Russian guitar** balalaika
**Russian guitar-like instrument** domra
**Russian horseman** Cossack
**Russian illicitly distilled vodka** samogen
**Russian king** czar, tsar
**Russian leather** bulgar, juchten, yuft

**Russian length** verst
**Russian liquor** vodka
**Russian local assembly** zemstvo
**Russian log hut** isba
**Russian measure** arshin, verst
**Russian monarch** czar, tsar
**Russian monetary unit** r(o)uble
**Russian monk** Rasputin
**Russian mountain** Al(t)ai, Pamirs, Stanovoi, Ural
**Russian mountain range** Ural
**Russian museum** Hermitage
**Russian name** Igor
**Russian news agency** Novosti, Tass
**Russian official** beriya
**Russian peasant** kulak, moujik, muzhik
**Russian peninsula** Kanin, Kola, Taimyr
**Russian pianist and composer** Rachmaninov
**Russian plain** steppe
**Russian policy** perestroika
**Russian revolutionary** Lenin, Stalin, Trotsky
**Russian ruler** czar, tsar
**Russian ruler's daughter** czarevna, tsarevna
**Russian rye-beer** kvass
**Russian satellite** Sputnik
**Russian sea** Aral
**Russian spirit** vodka
**Russian state-owned farm** sovkhoz
**Russian tea urn** samovar
**Russian tent** yurt
**Russian tribesman** Tartar
**Russian tyrant** czar, tsar
**Russian vehicle** dros(h)ky, troika
**Russian village** mir
**Russian wagon** telega
**Russian whip** knout
**Russian wolfhound** borzoi
**Russia's first cosmonaut into space** Gagarin
**rust** corrode, corrosion, decay, decline, degenerate, deteriorate, oxidation, oxidise, rot, stain, tarnish
**rust-coloured** ferruginous
**rustic** Arcadian, artless, awkward, bucolic, clownish, coarse, homely, pastoral, peasant, plain, rude, rural, simple, sylvan, uncouth, unpolished, unsophisticated
**rustic byway** lane
**rusticity** agrarianism, artlessness, crudeness, gracelessness, homeliness, informality, modesty, naïveté, normality, openness, pastorality, plainness, rudeness, ruralism, rurality, simplicity, unaffect
**rustic labourer** peasant
**rustic person** backvelder, countryman, farmer, hick, peasant
**rustic poem** idyll
**rustic scene** idyll
**rustic worker** peasant
**rust in plants** uredo
**rustle** abduct, agitate, flap, kidnap, move, plash, purloin, steal, stir, susurrate, whisper
**rustle up** assemble, find, forage, get, hunt
**rustling of dress** frou-frou
**rusty** corroded, faded, feeble, impaired, oxidised, patinated, poorly, reddish, rusted, shabby, stained, tarnished, worn
**rusty sound** squeak
**rusty sword** shabble
**rut** depression, ditch, donga, furrow, grind, groove, hollow, indentation, routine, score, track, trench, trough
**rutabaga** swede
**ruthless** adamant, barbarous, brutal, callous, cruel, ferocious, fierce, hard(-hearted), harsh, heartless, implacable, inexorable, inhuman, merciless, pitiless, relentless, savage, severe, stern, unfeeling, unmerciful, unpitying, unrelenting
**Ruth's mother-in-law** Naomi
**rye** ergot, grain
**rye disease** ergot

# S

**sabaism** star-worship
**Sabbath** Sunday
**SABC award** Artes
**sable or seal** fur
**sabot** clog
**sabotage** damage, destroy, destruction, disable, disrupt(ion), hindrance, ruination, subvert, subversion, treachery, treason, undermine, vandalise, wreck(ing)
**sabotaging sprite** gremlin
**saboteur** underminer
**Sabra** Israeli
**sabre** (fencing) sword, yataghan
**sabre-ratting** intimidation
**sac** bag, bursa, cyst, follicle, pouch, tumour
**saccharine** delicious, mawkish, nauseating, nectared, oversweet, sugary, sweet(ened)
**sac containing morbid matter** cyst
**sacerdotal** apostolic, churchly, clerical, consecrated, divine, ecclesiastical, episcopal, hierarchic, hieratical, ministerial, papal, pontifical, priestly, sacred, vicarly
**sachet** bag, cushion, pouch, scent
**sack** bag, destroy, destruction, devastate, devastation, dismiss, fire, loot(ing), pillage, pillaging, plunder(ing), pouch, ravage, rob, ruin, spoil, valise
**sackcloth and ashes** grief, lamentation, mortification, penitence, remorse, repentence
**sacking** burlap, demolishing, destroying, discharging, dismissing, hessian, jinny, jute, looting, marauding, pillaging, plundering, raiding, robbing, ruining, stripping, textile
**sacking of priest** unfrocking
**sack of equine refreshment** nosebag
**sac-like cavity** bursa
**sacrament** act, assurance, ceremonial, ceremony, covenant, custom, eucharist, form, liturgy, mystery, oath, obligation, observance, pledge, practice, procedure, rite, ritual, service, sign, solemnity, symbol, usage, vow
**sacramental** devotional, priestly
**sacramental host holder** pyx
**sacramental wine** tent
**sacrament of the Lord's Supper** Eucharist
**Sacramento tribe** Yana
**sacranium** church, sanctuary, shrine, temple
**sacred** blessed, celestial, clean, consecrated, dedicated, deiform, devoted, devotional, divine, exalted, hallowed, holy, immune, inviolable,

inviolate, protected, purified, religious, revered, sacrosanct, sainted, sanctified, unspotted
**sacred asp emblem** uraeus
**sacred banner of St Denis** oriflamme
**sacred bean** lotus
**sacred beetle of ancient Egypt** scarab
**sacred bird of Egypt** ibis
**sacred book of Buddhists** Dhammapada
**sacred book of Hindus** shaster, s(h)astra
**sacred book of Islam** Koran, Quran
**sacred book of Parsis** Zend-Avesta
**sacred book of Judaism** Bible
**sacred books of Japan** Kojiki, Nihongi
**sacred Buddhist language** Pali
**sacred building at Mecca containing the sacred black stone** Caaba, Kaaba
**sacred bull** apis, hapi, zebu
**sacred bull of Egypt** Apis
**sacred chalice** (Holy) Grail, Sangraal
**sacred chest** arca
**sacred choral composition** cantata
**sacred College member** cardinal
**sacred composition** motet
**sacred destination** Mecca
**sacred Egyptian beetle** scarab
**sacred Egyptian stork** ibis
**sacred fish** kannune
**sacred goblet** chalice
**sacred Hindu word** Om
**sacred hymn** psalm
**sacred image** icon, idol
**sacred Indian fig-tree** bo tree, peepul, pipal
**sacred Indian monkey** entellus
**Sacred Isle** Ireland
**sacred lily** lotus
**sacred literature** Veda
**sacred Mecca shrine** Caaba, Kaaba
**sacred music** anthem
**sacred musical work** oratorio
**sacred picture** icon
**sacred place** sanctuary, shrine, temple
**sacred river** Alph, Ganges
**sacred song** anthem, chant, hymn, motet, psalm
**sacred statue** icon, idol
**sacred tower** pagoda, tope
**sacred tree of Buddha** bo, peepul, pipal
**sacred vessel** ark
**sacred vow** oath
**sacred well at Mecca** zemzem
**sacred word** Logos
**sacred writings** Scripture
**sacred writings included in the Bible** canon

**sacrifice** concession, forego, forfeit, immolate, loss, oblation, offer(ing), relinquish, renunciation, surrender
**sacrificed soldier** perdu(e)
**sacrificial offering** oblation
**sacrificial surface** altar
**sacristy table** altar
**sacrosanct** celestial, consecrated, divine, hallowed, heavenly, holy, impregnable, inviolable, purified, religious, sacred, sanctified, untouchable, venerated
**sacrosanctity** inviolableness
**sad** blue, cheerless, crestfallen, dejected, depressed, despondent, disastrous, disconsolate, dismal, downcast, downhearted, dull, gloomy, glum, grave, grief-stricken, grievous, hurt, lamentable, low-spirited, melancholy, miserable, mournful, pitiable, poignant, rueful, somber, sorrowful, sorry, tearful, tragic, unhappy, upsetting, woeful
**sad and abandoned** forlorn
**sadden** dash, deject, depress, desolate, dishearten, grieve
**saddle attachment** stirrup
**saddlebag made of leather or canvas** alforja
**saddle boot** gambado
**saddle cantle** hindbow
**saddle cinch** girth
**saddle cloth** manta, tilpah
**saddle footrest** stirrup
**saddle girth** cinch
**saddle horse** mount, pad, palfrey
**saddle horse originating in New South Wales** Waler
**saddle knob** pommel
**saddle loop** stirrup
**saddle pommel** crutch, saddlebow, tore
**saddle's rear** cantle
**saddler's trade** saddlery
**saddle stirrup** gambado
**saddle strap** crupper, girth, latigo
**sad film** tear-jerker
**sadist** algolagnist, barbarian, beast, brute, devil, fiend, monster, ogre
**sadistic** barbarous, brutal, cruel, perverse, perverted, ruthless, vicious
**sadly** alas, badly, calamitously, con dolore (I), darkly, deplorably, disconsolately, dismally, dolefully, gloomily, glumly, grievously, lamentably, lugubriously, miserably, mournfully, pathetically, pensively, pitiably, pitifully, poignantly, regrettably, seriously, shabbily, sombrely, sorrily, tearfully, tragically, unfortunately, unhappily, wistfully, wretchedly

**sadness** agony, bleakness, cheerlessness, dejection, despair, despondency, discouragement, dolefulness, grief, grievousness, melancholia, miserableness, misery, unhappiness, woe(fulness)
**sadness and depression** melancholy
**sad poem** elegy
**sad song** dirge, lament
**sad sound** sigh
**sad to say** alas
**safe** bombproof, cautious, chest, crypt, defended, depository, disabled, guaranteed, guarded, hale, harmless, hors de combat (F), immune, impotent, intact, locker, moneybox, non-poisonous, protected, reliable, repository, satisfactory, scrupulous, secure, sheltered, sound, strongbox, sure, treasury, true, trunk, trustworthy, unassailable, unhurt, unscathed
**safeguard** aegis, armour, bulwark, convoy, defence, defend, escort, preserve, protect, screen, security, shelter, shield, surety
**safekeeping** storage
**safely** cautiously, conservatively, dependably, discreetly, guardedly, harmlessly, prudently, purely, realistically, reliably, securely, surely, tamely, trustworthily, wholesomely
**safe port** haven
**safe to fly** airworthy
**safety** care, caution, dependability, protection, prudence, reliability, safeness, sanctuary, security, shelter
**safety barrier** rail
**safety catch** clevis
**safety device** lock
**safety margin** leeway
**safety measure** precaution
**safety razor inventor** Gilette
**safety zone** island
**sag** bag, bend, decline, dip, drift, droop, drop, dwindle, fail, fall, give, hang, settle, sink, slide, slip, slump, weaken, wilt
**saga** account, adventure, allegory, anecdote, annals, chronicle, epic, fable, fiction, legend, memoirs, myth, narration, narrative, novel, parable, recital, record, relation, report, romance, story, tale, tradition, yarn
**sagacious** acute, adroit, artful, astute, bright, calculating, canny, clever, crafty, cunning, discerning, intelligent, judicious, keen, knowing, perceptive, perspicacious, sage, sapient, sharp, shrewd, sly, wise
**sagacity** acumen, acuteness, astuteness, balance, discretion,

discrimination, foresight,
forethought, ingenuity, intelligence,
judg(e)ment, judiciousness,
penetration, perception, perspicacity,
prudence, sagaciousness, sanity,
sapience, sense, sharpness,
shrewdness, understanding, wisdom
**sage** adviser, advisor, astute, discreet,
genius, guide, guru, intellectual,
intelligent, magus, mentor, nestor,
oracle, philosopher, prophet,
prudent, pundit, sagacious, savant,
sensible, shrewd, sorcerer,
statesman, wise, wizard
**sagging** abating, baggy, bending,
billowing, bulging, declining, dilating,
distending, drooping, droopy,
dropping, dying, ebbing, enlarging,
expanding, fading, failing, fainting,
falling, flagging, floppy, ill-fitting,
languishing, loose, oversize, pining,
projecting, protruding, roomy,
seated, sinking, slack, slumping,
succumbing, waning, weakening,
wearying, wilting
**Sagittarius** Archer
**sago** cycad, palm, starch
**sago palm** cycad, ejoo, sahuaro
**saguaro** cactus
**Sahara shifting sand dune** erg
**Sahara wind** gibleh, harmattan,
khamsin, leste, sirocco
**said after mistake** oops
**said audibly** aloud
**said by Spanish bullfighter** olé
**said in pain** ow
**said of numb limb** asleep
**said on leaving** bye
**said to be** reputed
**said to startle child** boo
**sail** accost, canvas, captain, cruise,
drift, embark, float, foresail, gale,
glide, jib, lateen, lug, mainsail,
navigate, ringsail, soar, steer,
stunsail, voyage
**sail above royal** skysail
**sail along the coast** accost
**sail around** double, turn
**sail away** depart
**sail back and forth** ply
**sail before the wind** spoon
**sailboat** cat, frigate, galleon, ketch,
lugger, schooner, sloop, yacht, yawl
**sail briskly** spank
**sail by the wind** stretch
**sail close to wind** conform, pinch
**sail completely around** circumnavigate
**sail down** avale, awale
**sail extended by spar** spritsail
**sail fastener** clew, foot
**sailing** captaining, cruising, drifting,
embarking, floating, flying, gliding,
navigating, scudding, shooting,
skimming, skippering, soaring,
steering, sweeping, voyaging,
winging
**sailing boat** brig, clipper, ketch,
pinnace, schooner, ship, skiff, sloop,
yacht, yawl
**sailing enthusiast** yachtie, yachtsman
**sailing jacket** reefer
**sailing nausea** sea-sickness
**sailing race** regatta
**sailing ship** bark, barque, brig,
catamaran, clipper, corvette, cutter,
dhow, felucca, gallivat, junk, lugger,
pinnace, sampan, schooner, skiff,
sloop, xebec, yacht, yawl
**sailing warship** frigate
**sail in specified direction** stand
**sailmaker's awl** stabber
**sail nearer the wind** luff
**sail of windmill** arm, awe, eie, eighe,
fan, flyer, swift, van
**sail on course** haul, work
**sailor** Ab, mariner, matelot, matlo(w),
navigator, rating, salt, seafarer,
seaman, tar, yachtsman
**sailor's biscuit** hardtack
**sailor's blouse** middy
**sailor's bunk** berth
**sailor's call** ahoy, avast
**sailor's carving** scrimshaw
**sailor's church** Bethel
**sailor's dance** hornpipe, jig
**sailor's dish** lobscouse
**sailor's drink** grog, rum
**sailor's furlough** leave
**sailors lively dance** hornpipe
**sailor's loose jacket** jumper
**sailor's officer** boatswain, bosun
**sailor's oilskin hat** tarpaulin
**sailors' saint** Elmo
**sailor's short double-breasted
overcoat** pea-jacket
**sailor's song** chanty, shant(e)y
**sailor's stew** lobscouse
**sailor's storage-chest** sea-chest
**sailor's story** yarn
**sailor's tarred or oilskin hat** tarpaulin
**sailor's yes** aye
**sailor who finds the way** navigator
**sail pole** mast
**sail quietly** ghost
**sail rapidly** scur, skirr
**sail rope** halliard, halyard
**sail's edge** leach, leech
**sail's lower corner** clew
**sail supporter** mast
**sail swiftly** ramp
**sail to windward** thrash
**sail upward** soar
**sail with wind abeam** lask
**sail yard** rae (Sc)
**saint** angel, benefactor, guardian,
martyr, promoter, sponsor, supporter
**Saint Anthony's fire** ergotism,
erysipelas
**Saint George's sword** Ascalon,
Askelon
**Saint John's bread** algarroba, carob
**saintly** angelic, believing, celestial,
devout, ethereal, godly, good, holy,
immaculate, innocent, moral,
religious, reverent, saintlike, virtuous
**saint's relic box** chasse
**saint's tomb** shrine
**Saint Vitus's dance** (Sydenham's)
chorea
**saint who protects seamen** Elmo
**sake** account, advantage, aim, behalf,
cause, end, object, purpose, regard,
respect
**Saki** Munro
**salacious** beastly, bestial, debauched,
dirty, hot-blooded, lecherous,
libertine, libidinous, lubricious,
lustful, offfensive, passionate, ribald
**salad bar** buffet
**salad berry** tomato
**salad choice** endive
**salad days** heyday
**salad dressing item** mayonnaise, oil,
vinegar
**salad fruit** tomato
**salad garnish** cress, dressing
**salad leaf** lettuce
**salad plant** borage, celery, cress,
cucumber, endive, lettuce, tomato
**salad relish plant** radish
**salad stick** celery
**salad vegetable** borage, cabbage,
celery, cress, cucumber, endive,
leek, lettuce, onion, radish, spinach,
tomato
**salamander** eft, evet, newt, olm,
urodele
**salaried class** salariat
**salary** earnings, emolument, income,
pay, remuneration, stipend, wages
**salary increase** raise
**salary of clergyman** stipend
**salary-payer** employer
**salary upgrade** raise
**sale** auction, bargain, discount,
offering, reduction, transaction
**sale announcement** ad(vertisement),
notice
**sale of articles by lottery** raffle
**sale of goods by large quantities**
wholesale
**sale of thing bought** resale
**saleratus** baking-soda
**saleratus weed** glasswort
**sales docket** receipt

**salesman** agent, dealer, hawker, monger, pedlar, rep(resentative), rouper, seller, smous, tradesman, vendor, wholesaler
**salesman's spiel** patter
**salesman who carries his own goods** pedlar, smous
**sales talk** approach, pitch, spiel
**saleswoman** shopgirl, vendeuse
**sale to consumer** retail
**salicaceous tree** poplar, willow
**salient** arched, arrant, chief, conspicuous, convex, important, imposing, jutting, obvious, projecting, prominent, protruding, remarkable, striking, superior
**salient angle** ar(r)is, cant, piend
**salient point** detail, feature, trait
**saline** salt
**saline astringent** alum
**saline basin** saltpan
**saline solution** brine
**saliva** drool, froth, salivation, slobber, spit(tle), sputum
**salivary gland** parotid
**salivate** discharge, drool, secrete
**sallow** anaemic, ashen, ashy, colourless, drained, livid, pale, pallid, wan, willow-tree, yellow(ish)
**sally** erupt, escapade, issue, jaunt, outburst, raid, rush, sortie, surge, thrust, trip, witticism
**Sally Lunn** teacake
**salmon** bluecap, chinook, dog, haddo, kahawai, keta, kipper, laspring, laurel, parr, pink, samlet, sawmont, silver, springer
**salmon after spawning** baggit, kelt, shedder
**salmon before spawning** girling, gilling
**salmon enclosure** yair
**salmon in second year** gilling, hepper, smolt, sprod
**salmon in third year** mort, pug
**salmon on first return from sea** grilse
**salon** assembly, boutique, gallery, hall, lounge, meeting, parlour, reception room, saloon, shop
**saloon** bar(room), cabin, cafe, gallery, hall, lounge, pub(lic-house), sedan, shebeen, tavern
**saloon car** sedan
**saloon counter** bar
**salpetre** nitre
**salt** condiment, enliven, flavour, humour, preserve, pungency, sailor, sal (L), saline, season, seasoning, sel (F), taste, wit
**saltation** dancing, jumping, leaping
**saltatorial insect** flea

**salt away** accumulate, amass, bank, cache, collect, hide, hoard, save, stash, stockpile, store
**salted and smoked fish** kipper
**salted, crisp biscuit** pretzel
**salted fish** cor
**salted sturgeon roe** caviar(e)
**salted water** brine, sea-water
**salt factory** saltern
**salt lake** salina
**salt lake in South Australia** Torrens
**salt lake in Tibet** Tengri Nor
**salt lake in Turkey** Van
**saltless** insipid
**salt of acetic acid** acetate
**salt of hydriodic acid** iodide
**salt of iodic acid** iodate
**salt of nitric acid** nitrate
**salt of nitrous acid** nitrite
**salt of pectic acid** pectate
**salt of silicic acid** silicate
**salt of the earth** elect, elite, wealthy
**salt or acid relish** achar, atjar
**salt, pepper set** cruet
**saltpetre** nitre
**salt pillar's spouse** Lot
**salt rock** halite
**salt solution** brine, pickle, saline
**salt water** brine, ocean, sea
**salt water lake** lagoon
**salty** bawdy, briny, earthy, indecent, piquant, racy, risque, rude, saline, salt, spicy, witty
**salty biscuit** pretzel
**salty water** brine
**salubrious** healthful, healthy, hygienic, invigorating, nourishing, nutritious, refreshing, salutary, stimulating, stimulative, tonic, wholesome
**salutary** beneficial, health-giving, healthful, healthy, salubrious, wholesome
**salutation** address, aloha, ave, curts(e)y, embrace, greeting, hail, hallo, hello, homage, kiss, obeisance, respects, salaam, salute, welcome
**salute** acclaim, acknowledge, address, aloha, eulogise, greet(ing), hail, hallo, hello, honour, laud, ovation, receive, recognise, recognition, salaam, salutation, testimonialise, toast, welcome
**salute by firing rifles on a ceremonial occasion** feu de joie (F)
**salvage** junk, leftovers, ransom, reclamation, recover(y), remains, rescue, restoration, restore, retrieval, retrieve, salvation, save, saving, scrap
**salvation** deliverance, escape, exemption, immunity, liberation, preservation, protection, rebirth, recovery, redemption, release, rescue, retrieval, saving
**Salvation Army meeting-hall** citadel
**Salvation Army's founder** Booth
**salve** appease, balm, balsam, cerate, comfort, cream, cure, ease, embrocation, liniment, ointment, relieve, remedy, restorative, sooth
**salver** bowl, dish, plate, platter, tray
**salvo** applause, barrage, blast, blow-up, bombardment, burst, cannonade, cheering, crash, discharge, éclat, explosion, firing, fusillade, gunfire, hail, outburst, outcry, salute, shelling, shots, sniping, volley, whistling
**Samaria native** Samaritan
**Samar native** Bikol
**Sambal language** Tino
**sambur** elk, sambar
**same** agreeing, alike, ditto, equal, exact, idem (L), identic(al), iso-, like(wise), similar, unchanging, unvarying, very
**same age** coeval
**same in appearance** alike
**same in number** equal
**same mind** consensus
**sameness** identicalness, identity, likeness, monotony, oneness, repetition, resemblance, similarity, tedium, uniformity
**same thing** ditto
**Samnite** Oscan
**Samoa cloth** tapa
**Samoa loincloth** lava-lava
**Samoan** Polynesian
**samovar** urn
**samp** hominy
**sampan** boat, skiff
**sample** blueprint, design, display, dummy, example, exemplar, exhibit, experiment, guide, illustration, model, original, paradigm, part, partake, pattern, piece, plan, prototype, specimen, taste, test, try
**sample food** taste
**Samson's mistress** Delilah
**Samuel's teacher** Eli
**Samurai code of ethics** Bushido
**sanatorium** asylum, haven, hospice, hospital, hôtel-Dieu (F), infirmary, refuge, resort, retreat, sanctuary, sanitarium
**Sancho Panza's mount** ass
**sanctification** consecration, purification
**sanctify** anoint, beautify, bless, cleanse, confirm, consecrate, dedicate, enshrine, exalt, hallow, honour, justify, purify, sanction

**sanctimonious** canting, hypocritical, pharisaical, pious, self-satisfied, smug
**sanctimony** affectation, duplicity, feigning, hallowness, hypocrisy, pietism, sanctimoniousness
**sanction** advocacy, allow(ance), approval, approve, authority, authorise, countenance, endorse, liberty, permission, ratification, support, validation
**sanctity** chastity, devotion, godliness, grace, holiness, piety, purity, religiousness, sacredness, saintliness, sanctitude, solemnity, spirituality, virtue
**sanctuary** adytum, altar, asylum, church, haven, oratory, refuge, reliquary, sanctum, shrine, synagogue, tabernacle, temple
**sanctum** adytum, chamber, cloister, cubbyhole, den, haven, island, oasis, refuge, retreat, sanctuary, snuggery, study
**sand** burnish, debris, emery, file, grain, granule, gravel, grit, pumice, sandpaper, scour, smooth
**sandalwood** algum, incense
**sandalwood tree** maire, santal
**sand and small stones** gravel
**sandarac** realgar, sandarach
**sandarac wood** alerce, arar, citron wood, thyine
**sandbank** atoll, bar, drift, ford, hurst, island, reef, ridge, shallow, shoal
**sand bar** shoal
**sand-blind** bleary, purblind
**sand hill** dene, dune
**sand-laden wind** samiel, simoom, simoon
**sand-like particles** grit
**sand mound** dune
**sand particle** grain
**sandpiper** dunlin, knot, ree(ve), ruff, stint, terek
**sand region** desert, erg
**sand ridge** dune
**sandshoes** sneakers, tackies
**sandstone** arenite
**sandstone boulder** sarsen
**sandwich spread** paste
**sandy** arenaceous, gravelly, gritty, hazardous, saffron, unsafe, unstable, unsteady
**sandy hollow as obstacle in golf-course** bunker
**sandy material** grit
**sandy point projecting into the sea** spit
**sandy shore** beach
**sandy tract** dene, dean
**sandy waste** desert, dune

**sane** balanced, coherent, compos mentis (L), intelligent, logical, lucid, normal, rational, reasonable, sensible, sober, sound, wise
**sang-froid** aplomb, balance, calmness, composure, cool(ness), countenance, dispassion, nerve, poise, self-restraint, steadiness
**sanguinary** barbarous, bloodthirsty, bloody, brutal, cruel, fatal, gory, homicidal, internecine, lethal, murderous, savage, slaughterous
**sanguine** animated, ardent, blithe, bloody, buoyant, cheerful, confident, elated, enthusiastic, expectant, feverish, gory, happy, hopeful, inflamed, light-hearted, lively, optimistic, (re)assured, red, ruddy, rusty, spirited, sunburned, zestful
**sanitary** clean, germ-free, healthy, hygienic, salutary, unpolluted
**sanitary principles** hygiene
**sanity** acuity, astuteness, clear-headedness, cogency, discretion, intelligence, judg(e)ment, lucidity, normality, pragmatism, rationality, reason, saneness, sense, thoughtfulness, wisdom, wits
**sank** collapsed, decayed, declined, diminished, dipped, drooped, dropped, ebbed, faded, lessened, merged, plunged, sagged, sloped, submerged, subsided
**sank on her maiden voyage** Titanic
**San Marino mountain** Titano
**Santa Barbara island** Anacapa
**Santa Catalina resort** Avalon
**Santa Cruz island** Ndeni
**Santa Domingo** Hispaniola
**Santa's draught animals** reindeer
**Santa's reindeer** Blitzen, Comet, Cupid, Dancer, Dasher, Donner, Prancer, Rudolph, Vixen
**Sao Paulo plain** Ypiranga
**sap** demolish, destroy, drain, enervate, erode, essence, exhaust, fool, idiot, juice, latex, lifeblood, noddy, remove, rob, simpleton, trench, undermine, weaken
**sapid** tasty
**sapience** acuity, cunning, deepness, discretion, insight, intelligence, prudence, reason, sagacity, shrewdness, smartness, soundness, wisdom
**sapient** apt, astute, aware, brainy, bright, clever, discerning, enlightened, erudite, informed, intelligent, judicious, keen, oracular, percipient, prudent, quickwitted, reasonable, sagacious, sensible, shrewd, sound, wise

**sapindaceous tree** a(c)kee
**sapodilla** naseberry, sapota, sapote, tree
**sapper** engineer, impairer, underminer
**sap system** stele
**sapwood** alburnum
**Saracen** Arab, Moor
**sarcasm** bitterness, derision, gibe, irony, ridicule, taunt
**sarcastic** abrupt, acrid, arrogant, biting, bitter, brutal, cruel, curt, cynical, derisive, incisive, insulting, ironic(al), mocking, mordant, nipping, sardonic, satiric(al), scornful, sneering, taunting
**sarcastically perverse** ironic
**sarcastic jest** quip
**sarcastic remark** gird, hit, quip, slant
**sardine-like Alpine fish** agon
**sardonic** astringent, biting, bitter, cynical, derisive, dry, heartless, ironic(al), jeering, malicious, malignant, mocking, sarcastic, saturnine, scornful, sharp, sneering, wry
**sark** chemise, shirt
**sarsaparilla plant** smilax
**sartor** tailor
**sartorial splendour** finery
**sash** belt, girdle, obi, scarf, tobe
**sasin** blackbuck
**sass** cheek, impudence
**sassaby** basterhartbees
**sassy** cheeky, pert, saucy
**Satan** Apollyon, Beelzebub, Belial, Clootie, devil, Diabolus, Lucifer, Moloch, Shaitan
**satanic** accursed, atrocious, demoniac(al), demonic, devilish, diabolic(al), evil, fiendish, ghoulish, godless, hellish, immoral, infernal, inhuman, unholy, vile, wicked
**satanical** devilish
**satchel** (school)bag
**sate** accloy, allay, content, fill, glut, gorge, gratify, overabundance, overfeed, quench, satiate, satisfy, saturate, slake, stuff, suffice, surfeit
**sated** appeased, bored, brimful, complete, contended, crammed, dulled, entire, filled, full, glutted, gorged, indulged, intact, jaded, loaded, pacified, packed, quenched, replenished, replete, satiated, satisfied, saturated, stocked, stuffed, surfeited, swelled
**satellite** acolyte, advisor, assistant, attendant, barnacle, companion, courtier, dependant, follower, hanger-on, lackey, minion, moon, orbiter, parasite, puppet, retainer,

sectarian, spacecraft, sputnik, toady, tributary, vassal
**satellite course** orbit
**satellite of Jupiter** Callisto, Europa, Ganymede, Io
**satellite of Neptune** Nereid
**satellite of Saturn** Iapetus
**satellite of the earth** moon
**satellite's trajectory** orbit
**satiate** cloy, (en)glut, exhaust, fill, gag, gorge, indulge, inundate, jade, nauseate, overdo, overfeed, overfill, pall, sate, satisfy, saturate, sicken, slake, stall, stuff, surfeit, weary
**satiety** abundance, excess, ful(l)ness, gratification, inundation, nausea, overabundance, overful(l)ness, plethora, repletion, saturation, satiation, sufficiency, superfluity, surfeit
**satin striped silk** tabaret
**satire** acrimony, aspersion, burlesque, caricature, cartoon, irony, lampoon, mockery, parody, pasquinade, ridicule, sarcasm, skit, taunting, travesty
**satiric** biting, caustic, cynical, ironical, mocking, sarcastic, satirical
**satirical drawing** cartoon
**satirical likeness** caricature
**satirical play** revue
**satirical remark** jest, skit
**satirical sketch** skit
**satirise** abuse, attack, burlesque, criticise, denounce, deride, expose, lampoon, lash, mimic, mock, parody, pasquinade, ridicule, squib, travesty
**satisfaction** atonement, comfort, compensation, contentment, ease, enjoyment, gratification, payment, pleasure, recompense, repayment, requital, restitution
**satisfactory** acceptable, adequate, competent, OK, okay, passable, sufficient, suitable
**satisfied** answered, appeased, assuaged, complacent, content, convinced, filled, happy, indulged, pacified, pleased, positive, qualified, quenched, sated, smug, sufficed, sure, surfeited
**satisfy** answer, appease, assuage, assure, compensate, content, convince, delight, equal, fulfil, gladden, gratify, indemnify, indulge, meet, pacify, persuade, placate, please, qualify, quench, reassure, remunerate, repay, resolve, sate, satiate, suffice, surfeit
**satisfy to the full** sate, satiate
**saturate** deluge, drench, drown, fill, flood, glut, imbue, immerse,

impregnate, ingrain, instill, inundate, penetrate, permeate, pervade, ret, rinse, sate, satiate, soak, sop, souse, steep, submerge, suffuse, swamp, waterlog, wet, whelm
**Saturday and Sunday** weekend
**saturnalia** bacchanal(ia), carnival, carouse, carousal, debauch, feast, festival, festivity, frolic, orgy, party(ing), revelry
**SATV award** Artes
**satyr** adulterer, Casanova, corrupter, debauchee, gigolo, lady-killer, lecher, letch, pervert, philanderer, rapist, roué, seducer, womaniser
**sauce** audacity, condiment, dressing, flavouring, gravy, impertinence, impudence, insolence, rudeness, seasoning
**sauce base** roux
**sauce container on table** gravy-boat
**sauce for fried fish** tartar
**sauce for roast beef** horseradish
**sauce for roast lamb** mint
**sauce made from fermented beans** soy(a)
**saucer-shaped bell** gong
**saucer-shaped cup on stand** tazza
**saucy** audacious, bold, brash, brazen, cheeky, cocky, fresh, gaudy, impertinent, impolite, impudent, insolent, jaunty, ostentatious, presumptuous, pert, rude, sassy, shameless
**saucy girl** hussy, minx, quean, snip
**Saudi Arabian region** Asir
**Saudi language** Arabic
**Saudi native** Arab(ian)
**Saul of Tarsis** Paul
**Saul's army leader** Abner
**Saul's successor** David
**sault** jump, leap
**sauna item** steam
**saunter** amble, dawdle, delay, idle, lag, loiter, meander, mosey, promenade, ramble, range, roam, rove, sidle, stroll, traipse, walk
**saurian** lizard
**sausage** banger, bologna, frank(furter), salame, salami, wors, wurst
**sauté** fry
**sautéd chopped vegetables** mirepoix
**savage** angry, barbaric, barbarous, beastly, cruel, feral, ferocious, fierce, merciless, ravenous, rough, rude, rugged, ruthless, sylvan, truculent, uncivilised, uncultivated, unpolished, wild
**savage cruelty** barbarity
**savagely cruel** brutal
**savagely fierce** ferocious
**savage nature** beast

**savage remark** snarl
**savagery** barbarity, bestiality, cruelty, ferocity, inhumanity, sadism, viciousness
**save** but, collect, conserve, deliver, economise, except, hoard, liberate, preserve, recover, redeem, rescue, reserve, safeguard, salvage, shield, spare
**saved from hanging** gallows-free
**save from danger** rescue
**save from loss at sea** salve
**save from wreck** salvage
**saving** cache, conservative, economy, freeing, frugality, maintaining, management, preserving, price-cut, protective, prudence, reduction, releasing, rescuing, reserve, safeguarding, sustaining, thrift
**saving economically** sparing
**saving of the soul** salvation
**savings** assets, bargains, capital, discounts, finances, funds, means, reductions, reserves, resources
**Saviour** Messiah
**saviour** champion, defender, deliverer, emancipator, freer, guardian, liberator, lifesaver, manumitter, preserver, protector, redeemer, rescuer, salvation
**savoir-faire** ability, adroitness, culture, diplomacy, finesse, gentility, graciousness, perceptiveness, refinement, suavity, skill, sophistication, style, tact, urbanity
**savour** appetise, appreciate, aroma, enjoy, flavour, hint, partake, relish, scent, smack, smell, suggest, taste, tinge
**savoury** agreeable, appetising, decent, delectable, meaty, palatable, spicy, tangy, tasty, wholesome
**savoury jelly** aspic
**savoury of oysters wrapped in bacon and served on toast** angels-on-horseback
**savoury on toast** canapé
**savoury paste** paté
**savoury sauce** gravy
**savoury sausage** boerewors, russian, salami
**savoury smell** aroma, odour
**savoury snack** canapé
**savvy** comprehension, understand
**saw** adage, aphorism, axiom, beheld, byword, descried, dictum, discerned, distinguished, espied, glimpsed, heeded, identified, looked, marked, maxim, noted, noticed, observed, perceived, proverb, recognised, regarded, saying, sighted, spotted, viewed, witnessed

**saw-billed duck** smew
**sawder** flattery
**sawlike organ** serra
**sawn-off branch** log
**sawn pine** deal
**saxatile** rock-dwelling
**say** affirm, allege, declare, express, maintain, pronounce, recite, remark, speak, state, tell, utter
**say again** iterate, repeat
**say cheese** smile
**say further** add
**say grace** pray
**say gratingly** rasp
**say hello** greet
**say 'here's to you'** cheers, toast
**say in answer** reply, respond
**saying** adage, adding, affirming, alleging, announcing, aphorism, asserting, axiom, byword, claiming, declaring, dictum, divulging, gnome, maintaining, maxim, mentioning, pronouncing, proverb, replying, reporting, responding, saw, speaking, stating, telling, uttering, voicing
**saying adopted as a rule of conduct** motto
**sayings of Jesus not recorded in the canonical Gospels** agrapha
**say no** refuse
**say no to** dissent, oppose, remonstrate
**say one is sorry** apologise, pardon
**say on leaving** bye
**say over again** reiterate, repeat
**say repeatedly** reiterate
**say sorry** apologise
**say the same** echo
**say yes** assent
**say yes or no** answer
**scab** blackleg, crust
**scabbard** case, casing, covering, encasement, envelope, sheath(ing), wrapper
**scabbard holder** frog
**scaffold** drop, gallows, gibbet, guillotine
**scaffold support** trestle
**scalar** ladderlike
**scalare** angelfish
**scald** bard, blanch, burn, cleanse, heat, injury, wound
**scale** ascend, balance, climb, coating, crust, flake, gamut, lamina, mount, pan, peel, plate, progress, rate, series, steelyard, steps, weigh(bridge)
**scale down** lessen, reduce, trim
**scale duck** merganser, sheldrake
**scale fish** clean, scrape
**scale insect** cochineal
**scalelike structure** squama
**scale model** replica

**scale on plant** bract, palea
**scale replica** model
**scale's first note** doh
**scaling of wall with ladder** escalade
**scaling tool** ladder
**scallion** leek, shallot
**scallywag** rascal, scamp
**scaly ant-eater** pangolin
**scam** con, swindle
**scamp** cad, devil, imp, knave, monkey, pug, rascal, rogue, scapegrace, scaramouche, scoundrel, skollie, troublemaker, tyke, villain
**scamper** canter, caper, dart, dash, hasten, hurry, jump, lope, romp, run, scoot, scour, scramble, scud, scurry, scuttle, sprint
**scan** examine, glance, inspect, peruse, probe, research, review, scrutinise, skim, study, survey
**scandal** aspersion, damage, defamation, detraction, discredit, disgrace, dishonour, obloquy, offence, outrage, shame, slander
**scandalmonger** babbler, blether, busybody, chatterer, gossip, skinderbek, tattler, telltale
**Scandinavian** Dane, Finn, Lapp, Nordic, Norse, Swede, Viking
**Scandinavian chieftain or noble** jarl
**Scandinavian coin** krona, krone, öre
**Scandinavian country** Denmark, Finland, Iceland, Norway, Sweden
**Scandinavian dwarf** troll
**Scandinavian goblin** nis
**Scandinavian god of the dead** Odin
**Scandinavian god of war** Odin, Tyr
**Scandinavian god of wisdom and war** Odin, Wotan
**Scandinavian imp** troll
**Scandinavian kingdom** Norway
**Scandinavian parliament** Thing
**Scandinavian runic alphabet** futharc, futhark, futhorc, futhork
**Scandinavian sea** Baltic
**Scandinavian sea-warrior** Viking
**Scandinavian settlers** Ostmen
**Scandinavian supernatural being** troll
**Scandinavian toast** skoal, skol
**scanning device** radar
**scant** bare, deficient, exiguous, inadequate, insufficient, limited, little, meagre, minimal, scrimpy, skimpy, sparse
**scantiness** bareness, inadequateness, meagreness, narrowness, poorness, shortness, skimpiness, slenderness, sparingness, sparseness, thinness
**scanty** deficient, exiguous, gaunt, inadequate, insufficient, meagre, narrow, paltry, poor, scant, short, skimpily, slender, sparse, thin

**scanty allowance** pittance
**scanty supply** dearth, paucity
**scapegoat** butt, casualty, fatality, martyr, quarry, sacrifice, sufferer, target, victim
**scapula** shoulder-blade
**scar** blemish, bruise, cicatrice, cicatrix, damage, disfigure, gash, impair, injury, mark, scaur, seam, wound
**scarab** beetle
**scarce** deficient, exiguous, inadequate, infrequent, insufficient, meagre, notable, occasional, rare, scant(y), singular, skimpy, uncommon, unique, unplentiful, unusual
**scarcely** barely, dimly, faintly, hardly, just, scantly, slightly
**scarcely any** few, handful
**scarce thing** rarity
**scarcity** dearth, deficiency, deprivation, destitution, drought, famine, inadequacy, infrequency, insufficiency, lack, meagreness, need, paucity, poorness, poverty, rareness, rarity, shortage, sparseness, uncommonness, want
**scare** afraid, alarm, alert, dismay, fright(en), horrify, intimidate, panic, shock, start, startle, terrify, terror
**scaremonger** alarmist
**scare to death** appall, horrify, terrify
**scare word** boo
**scarf** bandanna, barb, boa, chadri, cravat, cummerband, doily, fichu, kaffiyeh, mantilla, muffetee, muffler, neckpiece, necktie, nubia, purda(h), rebozo, runner, sash, shawl, stole, tallith, tippet, yashmac, yashmak
**scarf round the hat to keep off the sun's rays** pugaree, puggree
**scar left by a healed wound** cicatrice
**scarlet** cardinalate, carmine, fever, heinous, immoral, lewd, red, sinful
**scarlet fever** scarlatina
**scarlet runner** bean
**Scarlett O'Hara's home** Tara
**scar-like vestment** orale, fanon
**scar on tree bark** cicatrice, cicatrix
**scar tissue** adhesion, keloid
**scary** appalling, crawly, creepy, dismaying, disturbing, frightening, goosepimply, hair-raising, horrifying, intimating, menacing, shocking, terrifying, threatening
**scary word** boo
**scathe** destroy, harm, hurt, injury
**scatter** diffuse, disband, dispel, disperse, disseminate, dissipate, distribute, fling, litter, scurry, separate, shower, sow, spread, sprinkle, strew
**scatter about** disseminate

**scatter abroad** spread
**scatter among** intersperse
**scatter-brain** feather-brain, madcap
**scatter-brained** absent-minded, bird-brained, feather-brained, flighty, giddy, reckless, scatty, silly, stupid, wild
**scattered** bestrewn, intermittent, irregular, occasional, sporadic
**scattered remains** disjecta membra (L)
**scattered rubbish** debris, litter
**scatter finely** sprinkle
**scatter in between** intersperse
**scattering** diffusing, disbanding, dispelling, dispersal, dispersing, disseminating, dissipating, few, flinging, handful, littering, scatter, showering, smatter(ing), sowing, spreading, sprinkling, strewing
**scattering of light** diffusion
**scatter in small drops** sprinkle
**scatter over a surface** strew
**scatter seed** sow
**scatter small drops on** sprinkle
**scatter water** splash
**scaup** seaduck
**scavenger** forager, hunter, rummager, scrounge(r), searcher, seeker, sweeper
**scenario** screenplay
**scene** affair, arena, episode, eruption, focus, landscape, locality, locate, milieu, outlook, panorama, place, setting, situation, sphere, view, vista
**scene of action** arena, locale, stage, theatre, venue
**scene of battle** battlefield
**scene of confusion** babel, bedlam, madhouse
**scene of contest** arena
**scene of event** venue
**scene of first flight** Kitty Hawk
**scene of horror** inferno
**scene of intense activity** arena
**scene of Persian defeat** Issus
**scenery** landscape, panorama, scene, seascape, skyscape, sweep, view, vista, waterscape
**scenery and stage embellishments** décor
**scenery chewer** ham
**scene within a narrative** episode
**scenic** breathtaking, bucolic, grand, impressive, panoramic, pastoral, picturesque, rustic, unmarred, unspoiled
**scenic exhibition** stagery
**scenic painting** scape
**scenic public tract** park
**scenic view** panorama, scape
**scent** aroma, attar, condiment, cosmetic, fragrance, incense, lavender, musk, odour, pastille, perfume, pomade, sachet, sandalwood, smell, spicery, spoor, thyme, track, trail, vanilla
**scented** aromatic, fragrant, perfumed, sweet-smelling
**scented bulbous plant** narcissus
**scented bush** frangipani
**scented herb** lavender
**scented ointment** pomade
**scented resin** storax
**scented shrub** lilac
**scented wood** sandalwood
**scent from Cyprus** chypre (F)
**scent maker** perfumer
**sceptic** agnostic, cynic, disbeliever, doubter, scoffer, unbeliever
**sceptre of Poseidon** trident
**schedule** agenda, allot, appoint, arrange, assign, budget, calendar, catalogue, inventory, itinerary, plan, program(me), register, roll, slate, syllabus, timetable
**schedule anew** replan
**scheduled** anticipated, awaited, billed, booked, due, expected, slated
**scheduled to arrive** due
**schedule for action** slate
**schedule for meeting** agenda
**schedule of events** timetable
**schema** diagram, outline, plan, scheme, synopsis
**scheme** arrangement, blueprint, cabal, chart, conspiracy, contrivance, contrive, design, device, diagram, disposition, draft, idea, intrigue, layout, machination, manoeuvre, outline, pattern, plan, plot, ploy, program(me), project, proposal, schema, stratagem, strategy, system, tactics, theory
**scheme of life annuity** tontine
**schemer** conniver, conspirator, deceiver, intriguer, machinator, mastermind, plotter, politician, wheeler-dealer, wire-puller
**scheme together** conspire
**schism** breach, break, contingent, cult, detachment, disconnection, discord, disjuncture, disunion, divergence, division, estrangement, faction, faith, group, party, persuasion, quarrel, rift, rupture, scission, sect, separation, severance, side, splintering, split
**scholar** academic, disciple, pupil, sage, savant, student
**scholarly** academic, erudite, learned
**scholarly people** literati
**scholar of Islamic holy law** mollah, mulla(h)

**scholarship** education, erudition, intellectual, knowledge, learning, research, wisdom
**scholastic** academic
**school** academy, belief, college, educate, faction, institute, instruct, teach, tutor
**school adage** motto
**schoolbag** satchel
**schoolbook** primer, speller
**schoolboy's headgear** cap
**schoolchild with position of authority** prefect
**school class** lesson
**school composition** essay
**school dance** hop, prom
**school defaulter** truant
**school disciplinarian** prefect
**school dress** gymslip, tunic
**school dullard** dunce
**schooled** educated
**school form** class
**school for priests** seminary
**school for teaching young children** crèche, kindergarten, preprimary
**school grades** marks
**school group** class
**schooling for both sexes** co-education
**school mark** grade
**schoolmaster** coach, dominie (Sc), don, educator, governor, guide, instructor, lecturer, mentor, pedagogue, professor, teacher, trainer, tutor
**school-masterly** pedantic
**school mistress** dame, ma'am
**school monitor** prefect
**school of Buddhism** Zen
**school of fish** shoal
**school of music** conservatoire
**school of opinion** sect
**school of trout** hover
**school of whales** gam, herd, pod
**school outfit** uniform
**school period** term
**school preparation** homework
**school principal** head
**school quitter** drop-out
**schoolroom furniture** desk
**school session** quarter, semester, term
**school sport** athletics, chess, cricket, hockey, netball, rugby, soccer
**schoolteacher** educator, master, pedagogue
**school test** exam(ination)
**school theme** essay
**school tyrant** bully
**school uniform** blazer, tunic
**school vehicle** bus
**schoolwork** lessons
**school year division** quarter, semester, term

schooner spar mast
sciatic pain coxalgia
science art, discipline, field, knowledge, physics, proficiency, scientia, skill, specialisation, technique
science and practice of gunnery artillery
science branch chemistry, physics
science fiction novelist Verne, Wells
science of action of drugs on the body pharmacology
science of agriculture agronomy
science of algae algology
science of ancestry genealogy
science of animal behaviour ethology
science of animal structure zoology
science of antiquities archaeology, palaeology
science of aquatic mammals cetology
science of aqueous vapour atmology
science of articulations of the body synosteology
science of atmosphere and its phenomena meteorology
science of atmospheric conditions aerography, climatology, meteorology
science of atoms atomics
science of bacteria bacteriology
science of beauty kalology
science of being ontology
science of bell ringing campanology
science of biological statistics biometry
science of birds ornithology
science of blazoning coats of arms heraldry
science of blindness typhlology
science of blood and lymph vessels angiology
science of bodily disease pathology
science of bodily structure anatomy
science of body tissue histology
science of bones osteography
science of bones osteology
science of books bibliology
science of breeding genetics
science of breeding domestic animals and plants thremmatology
science of causes of disease (a)etiology
science of caves speleology
science of cells cytology
science of character-forming ethology
science of children paedology
science of classification of diseases nosology
science of climate aerography, climatology, meteorology
science of coins and medals numismatics, numismatology

science of commercial activities economics
science of composition and structure of rocks lithology, petrology
science of computing dates chronology
science of correct reasoning logic
science of correcting ocular deviation orthoptics
science of crime criminology
science of crystal structure crystallography
science of cultivating ground agriculture
science of customs ethology
science of deciphering ancient inscriptions palaeography
science of designing and constructing buildings architecture
science of development and variation of character characterology
science of diet dietetics, sit(i)ology
science of disease pathology
science of diseased origins etiology
science of doses dosology, posology
science of drugs pharmacology
science of duty deontology
science of ear otology
science of ear diseases otology
science of earth geology
science of earth's formation geogony
science of earth's surface physiography
science of earthquakes seismology
science of education propaedeutics
science of elections psephology
science of elementary vocal sounds phonology
science of embryo embryology
science of environment ecology
science of epidemics epidemiology
science of eye and its diseases ophthalmology
science of fermentation zymology
science of ferns pteridology
science of flight aeronautics
science of flight of projectiles ballistics
science of flow and deformation of matter rheology
science of flying aircraft aviation
science of foreign exchange cambistry
science of forests forestry
science of forms of speech grammar
science of fossil animals and plants palaeontology
science of fruit-growing pomology
science of fruits and seeds carpology
science of functioning of organisms physiology
science of funds management finance

science of fungi mycology
science of future futurology
science of gems gemmary, gemology
science of glands endocrinology
science of God divinity
science of good eating and drinking gastronomy
science of government archology, politics
science of hair trichology
science of health maintenance hygiene
science of hearing audiology
science of heart cardiology
science of heat pyrology, thermotics
science of heavenly bodies astronomy
science of heraldry armory
science of history of earth geology
science of human antiquities archaeology
science of human body anatomy
science of human body disease pathology
science of human mind psychology
science of human races and their relations to one another ethnology
science of human remains archaeology
science of human settlements ekistics
science of hypnosis hypnotism
science of ideas ideology
science of industrial arts technology
science of insects entomology
science of intellect noology
science of interacting surfaces in relative motion tribology
science of land culture and crops agronomy
science of land management agronomics
science of languages linguistics, philology
science of larval forms silphology
science of law jurisprudence, nomology
science of life biology
science of life influences eugenics
science of life of trees silvics
science of light optics, photology
science of mammals mammology, therology
science of man in the widest sense anthropology
science of map-making cartography
science of measuring altitudes altimetry
science of measuring the earth's surface geodesy
science of measuring time horology
science of medieval chemistry alchemy

science of mental disorders psychopathology
science of method methodology
science of midwifery obstetrics, tokology
science of military movements logistics
science of mind psychology
science of minerals mineralogy
science of mites and ticks acarology
science of molluscs malacology
science of moon selenology
science of moral duty ethics
science of morals in human conduct ethics
science of mosses bryology
science of mountains orology
science of muscles myology
science of museum organisation museology
science of names onomatology
science of natural soils pedology
science of navigation in space astronautics
science of nerve systems neurology
science of normal function of living things physiology
science of nose and its disease rhinology
science of noses rhinology
science of number combinations algebra
science of numbers arithmetic
science of ocean oceanography
science of old age and its diseases geriatrics
science of old age and process of ageing gerontology
science of organic tissues histology
science of origin and evolution of language semantics
science of origin and history of words etymology
science of origin of man anthrogenesis, anthropogeny
science of origin of tissues histogenesis
science of origins epistemology, etiology
science of perimetrical figures isoperimetry
science of persuading a god theurgy
science of pests pestology
science of phenomena phenomenology
science of phenomena of sleep hypnology
science of physical characteristics of earth geophysics
science of physical life in all its phases biology

science of physiological functions and diseases of women gynaecology
science of place-names toponymy
science of plants botany
science of poisons toxicology
science of prison management penology
science of production and distribution of wealth economics
science of projectiles and firearms ballistics
science of proper use of terms terminology
science of properties and relations of magnitudes in space geometry
science of properties of light and vision optics
science of properties of water hydrology
science of propositions rhematic
science of pure motion kinematics
science of quantity of drugs posology
science of races ethnography, ethnology
science of racial improvement eugenics
science of reality ontology
science of reasoning logic
science of recording genealogies heraldry
science of rectum proctology
science of reflexes reflexology
science of refrigeration cryology
science of relation between mind and body psychophysics
science of relation of environment to man euthenics
science of religious or of sacred literature hierology
science of remedies acology
science of revenue finance
science of rocks petrology
science of seas, lakes, rivers hydrography
science of sera and their effects serology
science of shapes and surfaces topology
science of signs sem(e)iology, sem(e)iotics
science of skin dermatology
science of skulls craniology
science of smells osmics
science of soil management and crop production agronomy
science of soils pedology
science of sound and its phenomena acoustics, phonics
science of space and number mathematics
science of spatial magnitudes geometry

science of species speciology
science of spleen splenology
science of structure of animals anatomy
science of structures morphology
science of surface of the earth geography
science of teaching pedagogy
science of technological application of electricity electrotechnology
science of teeth odontology
science of the atmosphere aerology
science of the physical organs of sensation aestho-physiology
science of tides tidology
science of touch data haptics
science of treating diseases by bathing and medicinal springs balneology
science of tumours oncology
science of universe cosmology
science of upper atmosphere aeronautics, aeronomy
science of values axiology
science of varieties of the human race ethnology
science of versification prosody
science of virtue aretaics
science of viruses virology
science of vocal sounds phonology
science of volcanoes volcanology, vulcanology
science of wars polemology
science of water hydrology
science of weather aerography, climatology, meteorology
science of weight or gravity barology
science of weights and measures metrology
science of winds anemology
science of wines o(e)nology
science of word pronunciation orthoepy
science of X-rays radiology
science principle logic
science room laboratory
science study physics
scientific academic, controlled, natural, orderly, physical, punditic, regular, scholarly, scientistic, technical
scientific enquiry research
scientific farming agronomy
scientific measurement of the human body anthropometry
scientific research dissection vivisection
scientist boffin, researcher, savant
scientist skilled in chemistry chemist
scintilla hint, particle, trace
scintillating animated, blazing, bright, brilliant, dazzling, ebullient, exciting,

**scion** flickering, glittering, lively, lustrous, radiant, shimmering, sparkling, stimulating, vivacious, vivid, witty
**scion** branch, cion, descendant, heir, imp, offshoot, root, shoot, sprig, sprout
**scission** division, rift, split
**scissor** clipper, secateur, shear
**sclerosis** scleroma
**sclerous** bony, indurated
**scoff** aspersion, banter, chaff, contempt, deride, detract, disdain, fleer, food, gibe, humiliate, jeer, jest, jibe, laugh, meal, mock(ery), quip, rail, ridicule, scorn, sneer, snigger, taunt
**scoff at** belittle, deride, flout, jeer, ridicule
**scoff at derisively** mock
**scoffer** abderite, fool, mocker, simpleton
**scold** abuse, admonish, berate, bicker, blame, castigate, censure, chide, exprobate, jaw, nag, rant, rate, rebuke, reprimand, reproach, reprove, revile, shrew, slate, strafe, termagant, upbraid, virago, Xantippe
**scold angrily** rate
**scold constantly** nag
**scold harshly** berate
**scolding** accusation, admonishment, berating, blame, blaming, castigating, censuring, chastisement, chiding, condemnation, contumely, derogation, disapproval, indictment, lecture, lecturing, objection, obloquy, rebuke, reprimanding, reproval, row, stricture, tirade, vituperating
**scolding slander** abuse
**scold severely** rate
**scold vehemently** rant
**scold violently** slang
**sconce** cranium
**scoop** bale, beat, burrow, dipper, excavate, hollow, ladle, shovel, spoon
**scoop off** remove, skim
**scoop out** burrow, gouge
**scoop up with tongue** lap
**scoop water out** bail, bale
**scoot** dart, run, skedaddle
**scooter** cycle
**scope** ambit, area, end, extent, facilities, field, function, latitude, liberty, margin, meaning, opportunity, outlet, outlook, play, purview, range, room, rope, sweep
**scorch** bake, blacken, brown, burn, char, condemn, criticise, heat, parch, roast, scald, sear, sere, shrivel, singe, sunburn, tan, toast, torrefy, wither

**scorched earth** desert, desolation, havoc
**scorching** baking, boiling, burning, fiery, roasting, searing, sweltering, torrid, tropical
**score** account, amount, basis, bill, calculation, cause, charge, computation, consideration, count, cut, debt, grade, grievance, ground(s), grudge, injury, injustice, line, mark, motive, notch, outcome, points, purpose, reason, reckon(ing), record, result, scratch, stroke, sum, tally, total, twenty, wrong
**score a victory** win
**score in cricket** run
**score in soccer** goal
**scorekeeper** tallyman
**score off** humiliate, win
**score of nothing by batsman** duck
**score on a serve** ace
**score up** calculate, compute, count, reckon, tally
**scoring** achieving, adapting, counting, cutting, gaining, indenting, marking, notching, recording, scraping, setting, tallying, triumphing, winning
**scoring unit** point
**scorn** abstain, contemn, contempt, contumely, deride, derision, despise, despite, disregard, disdain(fulness), disparage, disrespect, ignore, insolence, jeering, loftiness, mockery, opprobrium, reject, reproach, revile, ridicule, scoff, scornfulness, scout, sneer, snob, snort, snub, spurn
**scornful** defiant, derisive, derisory, disdainful, insolent, jeering, mocking, scathing, sneering, withering
**scornful anger at supposed injustice** indignation
**scornful insult** contumely
**scornful look** sneer
**scorning** contemning, deriding, disdaining, flouting, rejecting, slighting, spurning
**scorpion's claw** chela
**scot** tax
**Scot** Caledonian, Gael, Glaswegian, Highlander
**Scotch** whisky
**Scotch elm** witch-elm, wych-elm
**Scotch whisky liqueur** Drambuie
**scot-free** clear, safe, undamaged, unharmed, unhurt, uninjured, unpunished, unscathed
**Scot Joplin music** rag
**scotodinia** dizziness, giddiness
**Scot or Irishman** Gael
**Scots John** Ian
**Scottish bagpipe dirge** pibroch

**Scottish borough** burgh
**Scottish boy** lad(die)
**Scottish breed of black hornless cattle** Aberdeen, Angus
**Scottish cap** tam(-o'-shanter)
**Scottish Celt** Gael
**Scottish cheese** dunlop
**Scottish chequered design** tartan
**Scottish chieftain** thane
**Scottish child** bairn, whean
**Scottish church** kirk
**Scottish church officer** beadle
**Scottish country dance** petronella
**Scottish cultural festival** mod
**Scottish dagger** dirk
**Scottish dance** fling, reel, strathspey
**Scottish dish** haggis
**Scottish draughtboard** damboard
**Scottish ejaculation** och
**Scottish emblem** thistle
**Scottish fabric** tweed
**Scottish family group** clan
**Scottish Gaelic** Erse
**Scottish girl** lass(ie)
**Scottish golf course** Gleneagles
**Scottish halfpenny** bawbee
**Scottish Highlander's cap** glengarry
**Scottish Highlander's cloth** tartan
**Scottish Highlander's dagger** skean
**Scottish Highlander's kilt** filibeg
**Scottish Highlander's skirt** kilt
**Scottish Highland war-cry** slogan
**Scottish hillside** brae
**Scottish inlet** firth, frith
**Scottish-Irish** Erse
**Scottish island** Iona, Skye
**Scottish islands** Hebrides, Shetland
**Scottish lake** loch, Lomond, Ness
**Scottish landowner** laird, thane
**Scottish loch** Ness
**Scottish lowland dialect** Lallan(s)
**Scottish malicious water sprite** kelpie
**Scottish minister's house** manse
**Scottish missionary** David Livingstone
**Scottish mountain valley** glen
**Scottish musician** piper
**Scottish name prefix** Mac-
**Scottish national emblem** thistle
**Scottish New Year's Eve** Hogmanay
**Scottish nickname** Jock
**Scottish oatcake** farl(e)
**Scottish plaid** tartan
**Scottish poet** Burns
**Scottish port** Ayr, Oban
**Scottish pouch** sporran
**Scottish schoolmaster** dominie
**Scottish serving dish** ashet
**Scottish sheepdog** collie
**Scottish shoes** chillies
**Scottish social gathering** ceilidh
**Scottish soup of chicken and leek** cock-a-leekie, cock(e)leekie

**Scottish tax** cess
**Scottish town or borough** burgh
**Scottish tribe** clan
**Scottish two-edged broadsword** claymore
**Scottish valley** glen
**Scottish war song** pibroch
**Scottish waterfall** Glomach
**Scottish water spirit** kelpie
**Scottish woman's cap** mutch
**Scottish woollen cap** glengarry
**Scottish yes** aye
**Scott novel** *Ivanhoe*
**scoundrel** cad, knave, miscreant, mountebank, poltroon, rapscallion, rascal, rogue, scamp, trickster, villain
**scour** abrade, afflict, beat, burnish, chastise, clean, comb, harass, oppress, polish, range, ransack, rove, rub, scrub, search
**scourer** abrasive
**scourge** afflict(ion), bane, correct, flogging, harass, lash, nuisance, pest, plague, punish(ment), strap, torment, visitation, whip
**scouring whip** knout
**scour with a brush** scrub
**scout** Boy Scout, contemn, decry, deprecate, deride, despise, disdain, emissary, explore, guide, inspect, jeer, leader, loathe, mock, observe, recce, reconnoitre, ridicule, scoff, spy, study, survey
**scouting party** patrol
**Scout rally** jamboree
**Scout unit** troop
**scowl** frown, glare, gloom, glower, grimace, gruffness, look, lour, lower, menace, sullenness, threaten
**scram** shoo, vamoose, voetsek
**scramble** challenge, compete, contend, disarrange, disarray, disorganise, fuddle, hurry, hustle, intermingle, intermix, jumble, merge, mix, obscure, oppose, rush, scamper, scurry, scuttle, struggle, vie, whisk
**scrambled word** anagram
**scrap** argument, bit, chip, crumb, discard, fight, fragment, iota, leftover, morsel, ort, particle, piece, remnant, segment, shred, trifle, tussle
**scrapbook** album
**scrape** abrade, bark, burnish, conserve, decorticate, economise, excoriate, file, grate, gride, grind, husk, mar, peel, polish, pumice, rasp, scar, scour, shave, skin, stridulate, strip
**scrape away** abrade
**scraped area** abrasion

**scrape leaves** rake
**scrape together** amass, glean
**scrape up** amass, assemble, compile, garner, gather, glean, obtain
**scraping implement** leveler
**scrap of cloth** rag
**scrap of food** ort
**scrapper** brawler, breaker, breker, fighter
**scrappy** bitty, disjointed, perfunctory, quarrelsome, sketchy
**scraps** clues, discards, leavings, leftovers, remainders, residue, semblances, shards, throwaways, vestiges
**scraps of food** leavings, leftovers, refuse, remains, residue
**scratch** abrade, annul, bark, blemish, cancel, chafe, claw, cut, damage, delete, eliminate, erase, etch, expunge, gash, grate, graze, grind, impromptu, incise, laceration, mark, obliterate, rake, rasp, rough, rub, score, scrape, scuff, skin, withdraw, wound
**scrawny** attenuated, bony, emaciated, lanky, lean, meagre, scraggy, sinewy, skinny, stunted, thin
**scream** caterwaul, clown, comedian, cry, howl, joker, roar, screak, screech, shout, shout, shriek, squall, squeal, stridulate, wail, yell, yelp, yowl
**scree** slope, talus
**screech** bawl, bellow, call, clamour, complaint, creak, cry, exclaim, grate, grind, groan, hail, howl, noise, outburst, outcry, protest, rasp, roar, scrape, scratch, scream, shout, shriek, squeak, squeal, uproar, whoop, yell
**screed** address, diatribe, exhortation, harangue, lecture, oration, speech, tirade
**screen** awning, barrier, buffer, camouflage, canopy, cloak, conceal, cover, defend, disguise, divider, fence, hedge, lattice, mantle, mask, netting, parasol, partition, protect(ion), reredos, riddle, (safe)guard, shade, shelter, shield, shroud, sieve, sift, umbrella, veil
**screen across room** divider
**screen again** recheck
**screen behind altar** reredos
**screen dog** Lassie
**screen from view** seclude
**screen of cloth concealing the stage** curtain
**screenplay** scenario
**screen show** film
**screen test** audition

**screen to protect the eyes** sun-visor
**screw** contort, extort, extract, oppress, tighten, turn, twist, wring, wrinkle
**screwed bolt end** nut
**screwy** batty, bedonderd, crackers, crazy, dotty, eccentric, mad, nutty, odd, queer, weird
**scribble** cacography, doodle, scrabble, scratch, scrawl, scribbling
**scribbling on wall** graffiti
**scribe** amanuensis, author, calligrapher, carve, chirographer, clerk, copier, copyist, critic, dramatist, editorialist, engrave, essayist, etch, groove, incise, inscriber, mark, newswriter, novelist, penman, scratch, scrivener, secretary, transcriber, writer
**scrimmage** scrum, struggle
**scrimp** barely, narrow, niggardly, scanty, scarcely, skimp
**script** book, copy, dialogue, handwriting, lettres, libretto, lines, notation, text, words, writing
**script for opera** libretto
**scriptural** authentic, biblical, canonical, divine, evangelic, inspired, prophetic, prophetical
**Scriptures** Bible
**scrivener** copyist, notary
**scrofula** tuberculosis
**Scrooge** meanie, miser, moneygrubber, niggard, penny-pincher, skinflint, tightwad
**scrounge** beg, borrow, cadge, forage, mooch, poach, shnorre (Y), sponge
**scrounger** beggar, borrower, cadger, moocher, scambler
**scrub** abandon, cancel, cleanse, delete, rub, scour
**scrubbing broom** hog
**scrub fowl** megapode
**scruff** nape, scum
**scruffy person** ragamuffin
**scruffy TV detective** Columbo
**scrum** struggle
**scrummage** scrimmage, scrum
**scrumptious** delectable, delicious, delightful, mouth-watering
**scrunch up** nestle
**scruple** conscience, disbelief, distrust, doubt, hesitation, misbelief, mistrust, qualm, quantity, reluctance, reservation, restraint, unit, weight
**scrutineer** censor, checker, critic, custodian, examiner, inspector, investigator, monitor, overseer, protector, supervisor, watchdog
**scrutinise** analyse, dissect, examine, explore, inspect, investigate, observe, peruse, probe, scan, search, sift, study, survey, vet

**scrutiny** analysis, canvass, examination, exploration, inquiry, inspection, investigation, observance, observation, overview, perusal, probe, research, search, sifting, study, surveillance, survey
**scryer** seer
**scuba** aqualung
**scuba swimmer** (skin) diver
**scud** fly, gust, run, slap, spank
**scuffle** clash, fight, jostle, mêlée, scrap, struggle, tussle
**scull** oar, paddle, propel, pull, row, sweep
**scullery** kitchen
**scullery worker** maid
**sculling boat** skiff
**sculpt** carve, chisel, cut, sculp, shape
**sculpted figure** statue
**sculptor's chisel** gradine
**sculptor's framework** armature
**sculptor's material** alabaster
**sculptor's studio** atelier
**sculptor's tool** chisel
**sculptor's workbench** banker
**sculpture** carve, carving, cast, chisel, cut, figure(head), form, hew, marble, model, mould, sculp(t), shape, statuary, statue(tte), tool, xylography
**sculptured basket** corbeil
**sculptured female figure used as a supporting pillar** carytid
**sculptured figure** statue
**sculpture in low relief** bas-relief
**sculpture of Virgin Mary holding dead body of Christ on her lap** pietà
**sculpt with knife** whittle
**scum** algae, canaille, crust, dregs, dross, film, froth, hovel, impurities, rabble, rubbish, scruff, trash
**scum of the earth** dregs, rabble, riffraff, underworld, vermin
**scurf** dandruff, mob, riffraff, scum, trash
**scurrilous piece of satire** lampoon
**scurry** dart, dash, fly, hurry, race, scamper, scatter, scoot, scud, scuttle, sprint, whirl
**scurry off** scoot
**scurvy** base, contemptible, despicable, low, mean, worthless
**scut** tail
**scuttle** bolt, dash, fly, haste(n), hod, hurry, race, run, rush, scamper, scoot, scud(dle), scurry, speed, sprint, spurt
**scythe** crop, cut, mow, shear, sickle, sye, trim
**scythe handle** snath
**sea** Aegean, Arabian, Banda, Black, briny, Caspian, cean, Celebes, Celtic, Coral, East China, Ioanian, Mediterranean, mer (F), North, ocean, Red, Sea of Japan, South China, Tasman, Timor, Weddell, Yellow
**sea acorn** barnacle
**sea air** ozone
**sea anchor** drogue
**sea anemone** actina
**sea-angel** angel-fish
**sea animal** coral, dugong, manatee, seal, walrus, whale
**sea beach** plage
**sea-bed wreckage** lagan
**sea-bird** albatross, auk, cormorant, eider, ern(e), fulmar, gannet, gull, osprey, penguin, petrel, puffin, skua, tern
**sea-bird droppings** guano
**sea-bird such as puffin** auk
**sea blubber** jellyfish
**seaboard** seashore
**sea-bottom plant** alga, enalid
**sea butterfly** pteropod
**sea captain** skipper
**sea channel** strait
**seacoast** seaboard, (sea)shore
**sea cow** dugong, manatee, sirenian, walrus
**sea creature** dolphin, octopus, whale
**sea cucumber** bêche-de-mer, trepang
**sea deity** Neptune, Poseidon
**sea dog** pirate, sailor, seal, tar
**sea duck** eider, merganser, scoter
**sea eagle** ern(e), tern
**sea ear** abalone, ormer, perlemoen
**sea explorer** navigator
**seafaring man** sailor
**sea fennel** samphire
**sea flow** tide
**sea foam** meerschaum (G)
**seafood** clan, crab, oyster, scampi, shellfish
**sea force under one command** fleet
**seafowl** penguin, sea-bird
**seafront walkway** esplanade
**sea froth** spume
**sea full of small islands** archipelago
**sea gem** pearl
**sea god** Neptune, Proteus, Triton
**seagoing troop** marine
**seagoing vessel** ship
**sea goose** solan
**sea gooseberry** ctenophore
**sea grape** glasswort, sargasso
**seagreen** celadon
**seagull** gull, mew, sniper, tern
**sea-hawk** osprey, skua
**sea hedgehog** sea-urchin
**sea hog** porpoise
**sea horse** walrus
**sea in Europe** Baltic
**sea inlet** bay, estuary, ria
**sea in USSR** Aral
**sea journey** voyage
**sea kale beet** chard
**seal** assurance, assure, attest, clinch, close, conclude, confirm, consummate, cork, enclose, establish, fasten, finalise, imprimatur, insignia, notification, plug, ratify, secure, settle, shut, stamp, stop(per), validate, waterproof
**sea life** halobiont
**sea line** horizon
**sealing cement for window glass** putty
**seal off** isolate, quarantine, segregate
**seal ring** signet
**sealskin coat** netcha
**sea mammal** dolphin, porpoise, seal, whale
**seaman** Ab, bluejacket, mariner, sailor, salt, seafarer, tar
**seaman's church** bethel
**seaman's jacket** reefer
**seaman's jersey** vareuse
**sea mile** knot
**sea mollusc with eight suckered tentacles** octopus
**sea monster** kraken, leviathan, orc
**seamstress** sewer
**seamy** abhorrent, bad, detestable, disagreeable, disgusting, foul, low, mean, nauseous, obnoxious, odious, scandalous, shameful, sordid, unpleasant, vile, vitiated
**sea near Italy** Adriatic
**sea nymph** nereid
**sea open to navigation by shipping of all nations** mare liberum (L)
**sea perch** bass
**sea peril** undertow
**sea plunderer** pirate(er)
**seaport in Africa** Accra, Alexandria, Cairo, Cape Town, Casablanca, Dakar, Dar es Salaam, Durban, Freetown, Mombasa, Port Elizabeth, Walvis Bay
**seaport in Alaska** Juneau
**seaport in Albania** Durazzo, Valona
**seaport in Algeria** Algiers, Bejaia, Oran
**seaport in Angola** Luanda
**seaport in Arabia** Aden
**seaport in Argentina** Buenos Aires, La Plata
**seaport in Australia** Brisbane, Fremantle, Sydney
**seaport in Barbados** Bridgetown
**seaport in Belgium** Antwerp, Ostend, Zeebrugge
**seaport in Cameroon** D(o)uala, Kribi
**seaport in Corsica** Ajaccio, Bastia
**seaport in Cuba** Cienfuegos, Havana
**seaport in Cyprus** Larnaca

**seaport in Denmark** A(a)lborg, Copenhagen, Helsingor, Odense
**seaport in Egypt** Alexandria, Suez
**seaport in Equador** Guayaquil
**seaport in France** Bayonne, Bordeaux, Boulogne, Calais, Dunkirk, Lorient, Marseilles, Nantes, Quimper, Toulon
**seaport in French Guiana** Cayenne
**seaport in Germany** Bremerhaven, Kiel, Lubeck, Schleswig, Stralsund, Wismar
**seaport in Ghana** Takoradi
**seaport in Granada** St Georges
**seaport in Greece** Lepanto, Navarino, Patras, Piraeus, Salonika
**seaport in Guinea** Conakry
**seaport in Guyana** Georgetown
**seaport in Hawaii** Honolulu
**seaport in Hong Kong** Victoria
**seaport in India** Bombay, Calcutta, Cochin, Daman, Madras
**seaport in Ireland** Belfast, Cobh, Dundalk, Waterford
**seaport in Israel** Ashdod, Eilat, Elath, Tel Aviv
**seaport in Lebanon** Beirut, Saida, Sidon, Tyr(e)
**seaport in Libya** Bengasi, Derna, Homs, Sidri, Tobruk
**seaport in Malaysia** Penang
**seaport in Mexico** Acapulco, Mazatlan, Tampico, Veracruz
**seaport in Netherlands** Amsterdam, Flushing, Rotterdam
**seaport in Philippines** Aparri, Batangas, Dakao, Zamboanga
**seaport in Portugal** Lisbon
**seaport in Samoa** Apia
**seaport in Sardinia** Cagliari
**seaport in Scotland** Aberdeen, Alloa, Dundee, Glasgow, Leith, Oban
**seaport in Senegal** Dakar
**seaport in Sicily** Aci, Catania, Marsala, Messina, Palermo, Trapani
**seaport in Sierra Leone** Bonthe, Hepel, sulima
**seaport in South Africa** Cape Town, Durban, East London, Port Elizabeth
**seaport in South Korea** Inchon, Mokpu, Pusan
**seaport in Spain** Algeciras, Badalona, Barcelona, Castellon, Palos, Valencia, Vigo
**seaport in Sri Lanka** Colombo, Galle, Jaffna
**seaport in Tasmania** Hobart
**seaport in Tunisia** Bizerte, Sousse
**seaport in Turkey** Enos, Istanbul, Izmir, Mersin, Samsun, Trabzon
**seaport in Uganda** Mombasa
**seaport in Ukraine** Odessa

**seaport in Wales** Llanelly, Swansea
**seaport in Yemen** Aden, Mocha, Mokha
**seaport in Yugoslavia** Dubrovnik, Pula, Split, Zadar
**sea promenade** pier
**sear** blacken, blister, brand, burn, cauterise, char, dehydrate, desiccate, drain, evaporate, harden, parch, roast, scorch, sere, shrivel, singe, wither
**search** analysis, chase, comb, delve, examination, examine, exploration, explore, frisk, hunt, inquest, inspect(ion), investigate, penetrate, peruse, probe, pursuit, query, quest(ioning), research, rummage, scan, scour, scrutinise, scrutiny, seek, winnow
**search about** scrounge
**search among refuse** scavenge
**search and rob** ransack, rifle
**search blindly** grope
**search by touch** feel
**search drawers** rummage
**searcher** hunter, prospector, questor, seeker
**search for** hunt, seek
**search for food** forage
**search for fugitive** manhunt
**search industriously** mouser
**searching** close, combing, intent, piercing, probing, severe
**searching for** seeking
**searching look** scrutiny
**search party** posse
**search thoroughly** comb, ransack
**search through** rifle, rummage
**search uncertainly** grope
**search untidily** rummage
**search with grapnel** drag
**sea reptile** turtle
**sea robber** pirate, rover
**seashore** beach, coast, seaboard
**seashore bindweed** sea-bells
**seasickness** mal de mer (F), nausea
**seaside** coastal
**seaside air** ozone
**seaside dune** dene
**seaside golf course** links
**seaside grass** marram
**seaside haunt** resort
**seaside structure** pier
**seaside walk** esplanade
**sea slug** trepang
**sea snail** nerita
**sea snake** eel
**season** accent, age, autumn, enliven, interval, mature, period, ripen, salt, spice, spring, summer, temper, time, winter

**seasonable good intention** New Year's resolution
**seasonal weather** snow
**seasonal wind in South Asia** monsoon
**seasoned mixture** stuffing
**seasoned roll of pounded fish** quenelle
**seasoned smoked sausage** frankfurter
**seasoned soldier** vet(eran)
**seasoner** ager
**seasoning** allspice, basil, caper, capsicum, caraway, caviar, cayenne, chilli, chutney, cinnamon, clove, condiment, curry, dressing, flavouring, nutmeg, onion, oregano, paprika, pepper(corn), pickles, relish, rosemary, saffron, sage, salt, spice, thyme, turmeric
**seasoning for food** condiment
**seasoning substance** spice
**season of the year** autumn, spring, summer, winter
**season ticket-holder** commuter
**sea speed** knot
**sea spray** spume
**sea studded with islands** archipelago
**sea swallow** tern
**sea swell** surf
**seat** armchair, bench, buttocks, chair, chesterfield, couch, cushion, divan, equilibrium, fundament, locale, locality, location, ottoman, pew, pouffe, saddle, settee, site, sofa, stall, stool, throne
**seat belt** safety belt
**seat for riders** saddle
**seat in church** pew
**seat in pub** bar-stool
**seat of activity** focus
**seat of affections** breast, heart
**seat of authority** chair
**seat of bishop** apse, see
**seat of emotion** liver, spleen
**seat of intellect** brain
**seat of Irish kings** Tara
**seat of one's affections** breast, hearth
**seat of power** throne
**seat on elephant** howdah
**seat on horse** saddle
**seat oneself** sit
**seat on the beach** deck-chair
**sea trip** cruise, sail, voyage
**sea trunk** chest
**sea turtle** chelonid
**seat with canopy for riding an elephant** houdah, howdah
**seat without arms or back** tabouret
**sea unicorn** narwal, narwhal(e)
**sea vessel** boat, liner, ship
**sea wall** breakwater, dyke, groyne
**sea warning device** fog-bell, foghorn
**seawater taste** salt

**seaweed** agar, alga(e), dulse, kelp, laver, limu, nori, ore, sargasso, sion, tang, tangle, varec, vraic, wrack
**seaweed ashes** kelp
**seaweed cast ashore** wrack
**seaweed culture** agar
**seaweed fertiliser** varec, vraic
**seaweed killer** algicide
**sea with many islands** archipelago
**sea worm** annelid, lurg, nereis, sao
**seaworthy** navigable, seafaring, stanch
**sebaceous** fatty, oily
**sebaceous cyst** wen
**sec** dry
**secede** abdicate, disaffiliate, leave, quit, resign, retire, separate, withdraw
**seclude** confine, exclude, exile, hide, imprison, isolate, retire(ment), segregate, separate, sequestrate
**secluded dwelling** hermitage
**secluded hollow** glen
**secluded road** byway
**secluded spot** nook
**secluded valley** dell, glen, hollow
**seclude from outside world** enclose
**seclusion** asylum, avoidance, concealment, detention, exclusion, hermitage, hiding, isolation, loneliness, monasticism, privacy, remoteness, retreat, secrecy, segregation, shelter, solitude, tranquillity
**second** additional, alternative, approve, duplicate, flash, inferior, instant, lesser, moment, secondary, succeeding
**secondary feature** adjunct
**secondary residence** pied-à-terre
**secondary road** bystreet
**secondary source of income** sideline
**second athlete** runner-up
**second childhood** dotage, folly, senility
**second crop** after-crop, aftermath, fog, rowen
**second endorsement** countersignature
**second Gospel** Mark
**second growth** aftermath, rowen
**secondhand** imitative, indirectly, used, worn
**secondhand information** gossip, hearsay
**second hearing** retrial
**second in command** depute, deputy, vice
**second in line** next
**second largest bird** emu
**second largest ocean** Atlantic
**second largest planet** Saturn
**second last** penultimate
**second last colour of the rainbow** indigo

**second longest river in US** Mississippi
**second man** Cain
**second marriage** digamy
**second marriage while first is still valid** bigamy
**second most holy city of Islam** Medina
**second mowing of grass** aftermath
**second nature** habit
**second of two** latter, other
**second person pronoun** you
**second-rate** cheap, inferior, low-grade, mediocre, poor, shoddy
**second-rate actor** cabotin
**second self** alter ego
**second showing** rerun
**second sight** clairvoyance
**second Sunday before Lent** Sexagesima
**second to none** nulli secundus (L), peerless, unequalled, unexcelled, unique, unrivalled, unsurpassed
**second troth** re-engagement
**second wife in polygamous societies** concubine
**second-year salmon** smolt, sprod
**second-year student** sophomore
**secrecy** burial, concealment, confidentiality, covertness, coverture, evasion, furtiveness, isolation, muteness, mystery, privacy, quietness, reticence, seclusion, secretness, silence, slyness, sneakiness, solitude, stealthiness, subterfuge, taciturnity
**secret** abstruse, arcane, clandestine, confidential, covert, cryptic, esoteric, hidden, hush-hush, mysterious, mystery, obscure, private, privy, retired, unknown, unrevealed
**secret agent** spy
**secret agent infiltrating a group** agent provocateur (F)
**secretaire** bureau, desk, escritoire
**secret amour** intrigue
**secretary** amanuensis, assistant, correspondent, desk, stenographer, typist
**secretary bird** slangvreter
**secret assembly** conclave
**secret behaviour** stealth
**secret code** cypher
**secret criminal society** mafia
**secret dungeon with trapdoor entrance** oubliette
**secrete** bury, cache, camouflage, cloak, closet, conceal, cover, discharge, disguise, dissemble, dribble, emanate, emit, ensconce, enshroud, entomb, excrete, expel, extrude, exude, filter, hide, leak, ooze, perspire, salivate, seclude,

seep, sequester, shroud, stash, transude, veil, withdraw
**secreted by liver** bile, gall
**secrete milk** lactate
**secreting internally** endocrine
**secreting sweat** perspire, sudoriferous
**secret intrigue** cabal, conspiracy, plot
**secretion caused by excitement** adrenaline
**secretive** cag(e)y, close, cryptic, enigmatic, reticent, sly, tight-lipped, withdrawn
**secret love affair** amour
**secretly** clandestinely, confidentially, covertly, furtively, privately, quietly, stealthily, unobserved
**secret marrier** eloper
**secret matter** mystery
**secret meeting** tryst
**secret message** scytale (Gr)
**secret organisation** Maf(f)ia
**secret place** hide-out, hideaway, hiding-place, recess, sanctum, shelter
**secret plan** cabal, intrigue, plot, scheme
**secret procedure** stealth
**secret remedy** arcanum
**secret retreat** hideaway
**Secret Service** Intelligence
**Secret Service spy** agent provocateur (F)
**secret stockpile** hoard
**secret store** cache
**secret supply** stash
**secret term** codeword
**secret that only the select know** esoteric
**secret vote** ballot
**secret watcher** spy
**secret word** password
**sect** achar(a), branch, brotherhood, cabal, coterie, cult, denomination, division, faction, group, offshoot, order, section, sisterhood
**section** area, chapter, clause, compartment, detachment, divide, division, element, extract, factor, fraction, group, item, parcel, part, piece, portion, sample, sector, segment, slice, subdivision, unit, wedge
**section of book** chapter
**section of bowls match** end
**section of cavalry** troop
**section of chapter** paragraph
**section of door** panel
**section of letter** paragraph
**section of long poem** canto
**section of orchestra** strings
**section of play** act
**section of play in bowls** end

**section of poem** verse
**section of solid** frustum
**section of story** passus
**section of window glass** pane
**section of zodiac** trigon
**section of play** act
**sector** area, category, district, division, part, quarter, region, stratum, subdivision, zone
**section of wall between two openings** trumeau
**secular** civil, communicant, earthly, laic(al), lay(man), laypreacher, laywoman, material, mundane, nonreligious, nonspiritual, parishioner, profane, state, temporal, worldly
**secularity** worldliness
**secular people** laity
**secure** batten, catch, certain, close, confident, confine, enclose, ensure, fasten(ed), firm, fixed, gain, get, guarantee, guard, lock, moor, nail, obtain, pin, protect(ed), reliable, safe(guard), sketch, stable, sure, tie, untroubled
**secure again** repin
**secure and free from danger** safe and sound
**secure by force** extort
**secure by scheming** wangle
**secure cabinet** locker
**secured by religious sanction** sacrosanct
**secured payment** bonded
**secure hold** cinch
**secure papers** staple
**secure refuge** stronghold
**secure retreat** strength
**secure ship** anchor, moor
**secure with brads** nail
**secure with rope** lash
**securing rope and anchor** mooring
**security** collateral, defence, guarantee, pledge, protection, safeguards, safety, stock
**security after dark** night watch
**security against damage or loss** indemnity
**security agreement** lien, mortgage
**security body** NATO, UN
**security device** alarm, lock
**security money of prisoner** bail
**sedan** auto(mobile), car, carrying-chair, limousine, litter, motorcar
**sedate** calm, collected, composed, contemplative, decorous, demure, dignified, grave, placid, quiet, serene, serious, sober, staid, tranquil(lise), unexcited, unperturbed, unruffled

**sedateness** calmness, collectedness, coolness, deliberateness, earnestness, graveness, placidness, properness, quietness, seemliness, sereneness, seriousness, soberness, solemnness, staidness, tranquilness
**sedative** analgesic, anodyne, assuasive, balsamic, calmative, calming, depressant, drug, hypnotic, narcotic, numbing, opiate, painkilling, palliative, relaxing, soothing, soporific, tranquilliser
**sedative drug** bromide, heroin, morphine, opium, veronal
**sedentary** calm, dormant, fixed, immobile, inactive, peaceful, quiet, relaxed, reposeful, routine, seated, serene, sitting, stagnant, static, stationary, tranquil, unchanging, undisturbed, unmoving, unruffled, vegetative
**sediment** deposit(ion), dirt, draff, dregs, dross, grounds, leavings, lees, marsh, precipitate, remains, residue, residuum, scum, silt, sullage
**sedimentary rock** limestone
**sedition** insurrection, mutiny, riot, treason, uprising
**seditious** anarchic, defiant, disaffected, disloyal, disobedient, disorderly, faithless, false, insubordinate, insurgent, lawless, mutinous, perfidious, rebellious, recalcitrant, riotous, seditious, subversive, traitorous, treacherous, treasonable, turbulent, two-faced, undisciplined, unfaithful, unpatriotic, unruly, untrustworthy, wild
**seduce** allure, attract, beguile, bewitch, cajole, captivate, corrupt, debauch, decoy, dishonour, enrapture, entice, induce, inveigle, lure, outrage, persuade, ruin, tempt, violate
**seducer** betrayer, cad, charmer, chaser, debaucher, enticer, flirt, heartbreaker, philanderer, playboy
**seductive** alluring, attractive, bewitching, captivating, enticing, flirtatious, inviting, irresistible, provocative, ravishing, specious, tempting
**seductively attractive woman** femme fatale (F)
**seductress** charmer, Circe, enchantress, Lorelei, siren, temptress, vamp, witch
**sedulity** perseverance
**sedulous** assiduous, busy, diligent, intent, untiring
**sedulously** assiduously, diligently

**see** behold, comprehend, compromise, consider, diocese, discern, distinguish, entertain, escort, espy, eye, lo, look, notice, observe, parish, penetrate, perceive, realise, regard, think, undergo, understand, vide, visit, watch, witness
**see about** consider, investigate, mind
**see above** vide supra
**see as above** vide ut supra
**see below** vide infra
**seed** beginning, children, egg, embryo, germ, grain, heirs, kernel, nucleus, pip, progeny, sesame, source
**seed coat** aril, testa
**seed container** pod, seed-lop
**seeder** sower
**seed fertiliser** pollen
**seed holder** pod
**seed in fruit** pip
**seedleaf** cotyledon
**seedless plant** fern, fungus
**seedless raisin** sultana
**seedlike gourd that rattles when shaken** maraca
**seed of cereal** grain, oats
**seed of flax** linseed
**seed of large tree** acorn
**seed protector** nutshell, pod
**seeds of corn** grain
**seeds to burst open** dehisce, gape
**seeds used in curry** cumin
**seeds used to flavour bread and cakes** caraway
**seed vessel** capsule, pod
**seedy** decaying, dilapidated, faded, grubby, mangy, old, run-down, shabby, sleazy, slovenly, squalid, tattered, unwell, worn
**seedy fruit** fig, pomegranate
**seedy London district** Soho
**see eye to eye** accord, agree, coincide, concur, harmonise
**seeing dimly** bleary
**seeing organ** eye
**seeing that** as
**seeing the whole at one view** panoptic
**seeing universals as mental concepts** conceptualistics
**seek** aim, ask, aspire, attempt, beg, beseech, endeavour, entreat, essay, explore, follow, hunt, inquire, inspect, investigate, invite, petition, pursue, quest, ransack, request, research, rummage, scour, scrutinise, search, solicit, strive, try
**seek advice from** consult
**seek after** hunt, strive
**seek blindly** grope
**seek charity** beg
**seek damage at law** sue

**seeker** hunter, inquirer, inquisitor, questor, searcher
**seeker of pleasure** hedonist
**seek information** enquire
**seek information from** consult
**seeking for better things** aspiration
**seeking knowledge** inquisitive
**seeking seat** stand for parliament
**seeking to avoid the issue** evasive
**seeking woman's hand in marriage** suit
**seek justice from** sue
**seek knowledge** study
**seek out** search, scrounge
**seek the opinion of** consult
**seek to attain** aspire
**seek to marry** woo
**seek to master** attempt
**seek water** dowse
**seem** appear, assume, evidence, exhibit, look, manifest, pretend, sound
**seeming** alleged, apparent, appearance, appearing, assuming, external, feigned, looking, ostensible, outward, presumable, presumed, pretence, pretending, probable, semblance
**seeming as if trouble is at hand** ominous
**seemingly endless** eternal
**seemingly true** plausible
**seem likely** promise, suggest, tend
**seemliness** decorum
**seemly** appropriate, apropos, apt, becoming, comely, decent, decorous, dignified, elegant, fit(ting), judicious, meet, politic, pretty, suitable, tasteful
**seen at zoos** animals
**see over** examine, inspect
**seep** dribble, drip, leak, ooze, osmose, trickle
**seepage** discharge, effluence, effusion, exudate, filtration, leakage, ooze, percolation, secretion, seep
**seep mud** mire
**seep out** ooze
**seer** augur, clairvoyant, conjurer, eyewitness, forecaster, foreseer, foreteller, guru, medium, observer, onlooker, oracle, philosopher, predictor, prophet, pundit, pythoness, sage, sangoma, scryer, sibyl, Solomon, soothsayer, sorcerer, spiritualist, theorist, thinker, venerable, witness
**see red** burst, explode, madden, rile
**seesaw** alternate, oscillate, pitch, swing, teeter, totter
**seethe** boil, braise, bubble, drench, ferment, flame, foam, froth, fume, imbue, immerse, inundate, marinate, parboil, plunge, roll, saturate, simmer, smoke, smoulder, soak, sodden, souse, steam, steep, stew, surge, swelter
**seethed** boiled, bubbled, churned, fermented, foamed, fumed, raged, simmered, stormed, swarmed, teemed
**seether** fumer
**seethe with anger** fume
**seething** boiling, bubbling, churning, fermenting, fizzing, foaming, fuming, raging, simmering, swarming, teeming
**see-through** clear, diaphanous, filmy, flimsy, gauzy, sheer, translucent, transparent
**see through** assist, detect, fathom, penetrate, persist, tide over
**see to medically** treat
**segment** bit, division, part, portion, section, sector, slice, wedge
**segmented sense-organ at mouth of insect** palpus
**segregate** dissociate, divide, expatriate, isolate, quarantine, separate
**seine** (fishing-)net, trap
**seismic vibrations** earthquake
**seize** apprehend, arrest, attach, capture, catch, clutch, comprehend, confiscate, fasten, grab, grasp, grip, hold, impound, lash, nab, nap, possess, snatch, steal, take, trap, usurp, wrest
**seize again** recapture
**seized with fascination** smitten
**seize en route** intercept
**seize the present opportunity** carpe diem (L)
**seize with the teeth** bite
**seize wrongfully** usurp
**seizure** abduction, annexation, apoplexy, arrest, attack, bite, capture, commandeering, confiscation, convulsion, extent, fit, grabbing, grasping, grip, gripe, hijacking, ictus, interception, kidnapping, looting, paroxysm, piracy, pit, robbery, skyjacking, snatching, spasm, stroke, taking, theft
**seizure of property by force** pillage, rapine, robbery
**selachian** elasmobranch
**seldom** hardly, infrequently, occasionally, rarely, scarcely
**select** choice, choose, cull, differentiate, distinguish, elect, elite, excellent, exclusive, fastidious, favour, pick, prefer(red), screen, selected, selective, sort, special, unique, valuable
**select carefully** pick
**select circle in society** coterie
**selected for grafting** scion
**selected list of candidates** leet
**select freely** choose
**select group** élite
**selecting for testing** sampling
**selection** assortment, choice, medley, mixture, option, pick, potpourri, preference, range, variety
**selection by vote** appointment, co-optation, election, nomination
**selection of book** chapter
**selection of songs** medley
**selective** careful, cautious, choosing, choosy, discriminating, finicky, particular
**selector** culler
**self** auto-, ego, sel (Sc)
**self-acting machine** automaton
**self-analysis** introspection
**self-asserting talk** bluster
**self-assertively** aggressively
**self-assurance** assertiveness, confidence, positiveness, self-confidence
**self-centred** egocentric, egoist(ic), narcissistic, self-absorbed, self-seeking, selfish
**self-centred person** ego(t)ist
**self-concern** egoism
**self-confidence** aplomb, confidence, nerve, poise, self-respect
**self-confident** assured, fearless, poised, secure
**self-conscious** shy
**self-contained flat** unit
**self-contained underwater breathing apparatus** scuba
**self-contradictory person** paradox
**self-control** refrain, restraint
**self-defence art** karate
**self-destruction** suicide
**self-discipline** ascesis
**self-disciplined** austere
**self-effacing** modest
**self-esteem** amour propre (F), confidence, ego(ism), independence, pride, self-assurance, self-regard, self-reliance, self-respect, vanity
**self-evident truth** axiom, truism
**self-fertilisation in flowering plants** autogamy
**self-governing** democratic
**self-government** independence
**self-image** ego
**self-importance** ego
**self-important petty official** jack-in-office

**self-inflicted disaster** suicide
**self-interest** egoism
**self-interested hanger-on** parasite
**selfish** acquisitive, autistic, avaricious, covetous, dissocial, egocentric, egoistic, egotistic(al), greedy, illiberal, mean, miserly, monopolistic, mundane, narcissistic, niggardly, parsimonious, penurious, personal, piggish, possessive, self-indulgent, self-regarding, self-seeking, stingy, tightfisted, uncharitable, ungenerous, vain
**selfishly** inconsiderately
**selfish motorist** roadhog
**selfish person** egoist
**self-love** egotism
**self-murderer** felo-de-se, felodese, suicide
**self-possessed** calm, composed, controlled
**self-possession** aplomb, assurance, calm(ness), collectedness, composure, confidence, coolness, courage, dignity, dispassion, equanimity, impassivity, nerve, poise, sang-froid, sedateness, self-assurance, self-command, self-confidence, serenity, tranquillity
**self-pride** ego
**self-protection** defence
**self-punishment** penance
**self-recording barometer** barograph
**self-respect** amour-propre (F), confidence, dignity, pride, self-esteem
**self-restrained** temperate
**self-satisfied** boastful, bragging, complacent, content, inflated, pleased, serene, smug, tranquil, triumphant
**self-seeker** egoist
**self-service** buffet
**self-service restaurant** cafeteria
**self-styled** pretended, so-called, soi-disant (F)
**self-styled law enforcer** vigilante
**self-taught person** autodidact
**self-willed** ba(u)lky, contrary, determined, difficult, disobedient, dogged, firm, headstrong, heedless, impulsive, inflexible, intractable, mulish, obdurate, obstinate, opinionated, persistent, perverse, pig-headed, querulous, rash, recalcitrant, restive, steadfast, stubborn, stupid, tenacious, troublesome, unco-operative, unruly, unshakable, wild, wilful
**self-willed and obstinate** headstrong
**sell** advertise, auction, betray, dispose, flog, hawk, market, merchandise, peddle, promote, retail, tout, trade, vend, wholesale
**sell after buying** resell
**sell betting info** tout
**sell by lottery** raffle
**seller** agent, dealer, hawker, merchant, retailer, salesman, shopkeeper, smous, tradesman, vendor
**seller of arrows** fletcher
**seller of men's clothes** clothier
**seller of outfits** outfitter
**seller of rare books** bibliopole, bibliopolist
**seller of ship's supplies** chandler
**seller of wares** salesperson
**seller of writing materials** stationer
**seller's demand** asking price
**seller's display** demo
**sell from door to door** hawk, peddle, trade, vend
**sell in a store** retail
**selling** bartering, exchanging, handling, marketing, peddling, plying, retailing, stocking, trading, vending
**selling aid** promo
**selling place** market
**sell on commission** peddle
**sell short** beggar, belittle, derogate, detract, extenuate, underestimate, underrate
**sell to consumers** retail
**selsyn** synchro
**semantics** semasiology
**semaphore** signal
**semasiology** semantics
**semblance** air, appearance, aspect, bearing, form, guise, image, likeness, mien, show, similarity
**semester** half, session, term
**semibreve** note
**semicircular church recess** apse
**semicircular pie** pasty
**semicircular window** fanlight
**semiconductor** diode
**semidarkness** twilight
**semidigested food** chyme
**semidivine maiden** nymph
**semidramatic composition of sacred music** oratorio
**semi-independent country in the Pyrenees** Andorra
**semiliquid food** slop, soup, yoghurt
**semiliquid fruit** pap, pulp
**seminar talk** lecture
**semiology** semeiology, sem(e)iotics, symptomatology
**semipellucid mineral** agate
**semiprecious stone** agate, amethyst, cairngorm, garnet, jade, moonstone, onyx, opal, sard, tiger's eye
**semisolid dispersion** gel
**semisolid lubrication** grease
**semisolid lump** dollop
**semisweet wine** Sauternes, stein
**Semite** Arab, Hebrew
**Semitic deity** Baal
**semitranslucent porcelain** bone china
**semitransparent** translucent
**sempiternal** eternal, everlasting, immortal, infinite, undying
**senate house of Rome** curia
**send** broadcast, communicate, consign, convey, delight, deliver, despatch, direct, discharge, dispatch, drive, electrify, emit, enthral, excite, fling, forward, guide, hurl, mail, move, post, project, propel, rail, remit, stir, thrill, transmit
**send abroad** export
**send after** chase, pursue
**send away** dismiss
**send back** remand, remit
**send back to country of birth** repatriate
**send by post** mail
**send by printer** telex
**send by telegraph** wire
**send by train** rail
**send for** command, order, request, summon
**send forth** blossom, emanate, emit, generate, issue, launch, produce, propagate, shed, yield
**send forth light** emit
**send goods by railway** freight
**send goods out of the country** export
**send into exile** ban, deport, seclude
**send message** fax, telex
**send money** remit
**send off** begin, commence, launch
**send-off** departure, farewell, going-away, leave-taking, start
**send on** forward, redirect, transmit
**send out** emit, issue, radiate
**send out of the country** export
**send packing** banish, discharge, dismiss, expel, oust
**send payment** remit
**send people away from place of danger** evacuate
**send to prison** lag
**send to sleep** bore, lull
**send to the chair** electrocute
**send to the gallows** hang
**send up** imitate, mimic, mock, parody, ridicule, satirise
**send-up** imitation, mockery, parody, satire, skit, spoof, take-off
**send with speed** express
**Senegal antelope** nagor, reedbuck
**senile** anile, confused, daft, decrepit, doting, failing, feeble-minded,

foolish, forgetful, gaga, imbecile, infirm, senescent, simple, waning
**senility** caducity, childishness, decrepitude, dotage, foolishness
**senior** advanced, elder, higher, major, older, superior, veteran
**senior Brownie** Guide
**senior citizen** oldster, pensioner
**senior city councillor** alderman
**senior civil servant in imperial China** mandarin
**senior diplomat** ambassador, envoy
**senior female member** doyenne
**seniority** age, eldership, priority, rank, superiority
**senior journalist** editor
**senior maintaining discipline** prefect
**senior member** doyen
**senior member of the corps de ballet** coryphée
**senior member of town council** alderman
**senior nurse** matron, sister
**senior of company** nestor
**senior officer's mess on warship** wardroom
**senior of two** elder
**senior pupil** monitor, prefect
**senior scout** rover
**senior teaching position at university** professor
**sennight** week
**sensation** animation, commotion, excitement, feeling, sense, stimulation
**sensational** amazing, astounding, dramatic, electrifying, exciting, lurid, marvellous, melodramatic, outstanding, revealing, shocking, spectacular, staggering, startling, stimulating, thrilling
**sensationally horrifying** lurid
**sensational novel** shocker
**sensation of taste** sapor
**sense** apprehension, awareness, consciousness, denotation, discern, estimation, feel(ing), hearing, import, impression, interpretation, meaning, nous, perceive, perception, realisation, sensation, sight, significance, smell, taste, touch, understanding, wit
**senseless** crazy, daft, inane, insensate, insensible, numb, nutty, silly, unconscious, unimaginative, useless
**senseless chatter** nonsense, poppycock
**senseless damage to property** vandalism
**senseless person** idiot

**senseless talk** balderdash, boloney, drivel
**senseless writing** balderdash
**sense of community with other people** closeness, togetherness, ubuntu, unity
**sense of feeling** touch
**sense of hearing** audition, ear
**sense of injury** umbrage
**sense of obligation** gratefulness, gratitude, thankfulness
**sense of proportion** perspective
**sense of sight** eye, optic
**sense of smell** nose, olfaction, smelling
**sense of taste** palate
**sense of touch** feeling, taction
**sense of values** perspective, posture, stance
**sense of wrong** guilt
**sense organ** ear, eye, nose, skin, tongue
**sensible** appreciable, canny, cognizant, conscious, considerable, discreet, far-sighted, intelligent, judicious, perceptible, practical, prudent, rational, realistic, reasonable, sage, sane, shrewd, sober, sound, understanding, wise
**sensitive** acute, conscious, delicate, generous, impressionable, keen, kind, perceptive, petulant, reactive, responsive, sentient, sore, susceptive, sympathetic, testy, tetchy, touchy
**sensitive back of eye** retina
**sensitive feelings of a person** susceptibility
**sensitive plant** mimosa
**sensitive to all colours** panchromatic
**sensitive to cold** chilly, nesh
**sensitive wound** sore
**sensitivity** acuteness, admiration, appreciation, awareness, cognizance, compassion, concern, delicacy, esteem, finesse, hypersensitivity, kindliness, knowledge, perception, purity, receptivity, refinement, regard, respect, sensitiveness, sympathy, tact, taste, tenderness, touchiness, valuation, warmth
**sensitivity to beauty** aestheticism
**sensitivity to certain foods** allergy
**sensory** afferent, sensual
**sensory appendage** palp(us)
**sensory fibre** nerve
**sensory nerve** afferent
**sensory nerve ending** receptor
**sensual** animal, beastly, bestial, bodily, brutal, brutish, carnal, earthy, erotic, fleshly, licentious, lustful, luxurious, originating, pampered, riotous,

sensuous, sexy, unchaste, voluptuous, wallowing
**sensual desire** lust
**sensual man** animal, hunk
**sentence** condemn(ation), decision, decree, doom, judg(e)ment, penalise, punishment, ruling, verdict
**sentence in heraldic crest** motto
**sentence seeking answer** question
**sententious** bombastic, capsule, compendious, concise, condensed, didactic, epigrammatic, grandiose, laconic, lofty, magisterial, orotund, pithy, pompous, succinct, terse, turgid
**sententiously brief** laconic
**sententiousness** pompousness
**sentiment** attitude, disposition, emotion, feeling, judg(e)ment, sensitiveness, tenderness
**sentimental** affectionate, compassionate, emotional, feeling, impressible, loving, maudlin, mawkish, nostalgic, receptive, responsive, romantic, soft, swayed, sympathetic, tender, warm(-hearted)
**sentimental in feeble way** mawkish
**sentimental item** keepsake
**sentimentality** corniness, gush, mush, nostalgia, pathos, romanticism, slosh, tenderness
**sentimental singer** crooner
**sentimental yearning for the past** nostalgia
**sentinel** guard, lookout, patrol, picket, sentry, watch(man)
**sentinel's appointed course** beat
**sentry** custodian, defender, guard, lookout, patrol, picket, scout, sentinel, spotter, warder, watch(man)
**Seoul** Keijo (J), Kyongsong
**separate** alone, apart, cleave, detach, disarticulate, disconnect, discrete, disengage, disentangle, disjoin, dissociate, distinct, disunite, divide, divorce, independent, individual, intersect, interspace, part, segregate, sever, sort, space, uncouple, unyoke, withdraw
**separate addition to newspaper** supplement
**separate article** item
**separate chaff by wind** winnow
**separate clause** article
**separate completely** divorce
**separated** alone, apart, divided, divorced
**separated husks of corn** chaff
**separate existence** individuality
**separate in identity** other
**separately** abide, alone, apart, detachedly, discretely, disjointly,

distinctly, exclusively, independently, individually, particularly, personally, respectively, severally, singly
**separate part** piece
**separate portion of anything written** article
**separation into parties** split
**separatism** secessionism
**seppuku** hara-kiri
**septate** partioned
**septet** heptad
**septic** festering, infected, poisoned, pussy, putrefactive, putrefying, putrid, toxic
**septicaemia** blood-poisoning
**septic condition** sepsis
**septuple** sevenfold
**sepulchral monument** tomb
**sepulchre** bury, entomb, grave, ossuary, tomb, vault
**sequel** conclusion, consequence, continuation, encore, follow-up, issue, outcome, result, upshot
**sequence** arrangement, following, order, outcome, result, series, succession
**sequence of people** queue
**sequence of six balls in cricket** over
**sequence of three cards in the same suit** t(i)erce
**sequential set** series
**sequester** detach, disconnect, divorce, insulate, isolate, quarantine, seclude, segregrate, separate
**sequestrator** liquidator
**sequin** paillette, spangle
**ser** weight
**sera** antitoxins
**seraglio** harem, palace, serai(l), zenana
**seraglio site** Constantinople
**serai** inn, caravanserai
**seraph** angel
**seraphic** angelic, beatific, blissful, celestial, divine, heavenly, holy, pure
**seraphim** angels
**Serbian** Yugoslav
**Serbian nationalist guerilla** Chetnik
**Serbian town** Nis(h)
**sere** arid, burnt, dehydrated, dessicated, dry, parched, scorch(ed), sear, shrivelled, withered
**serene** bright, calm, clear, composed, cool, imperturbable, peaceful, placid, sedate, tranquil, undisturbed, unperturbed, unruffled, untroubled
**serenity** aplomb, brightness, calm(ness), collectedness, composure, cool, dignity, ease, equability, fairness, hush, peace(fulness), placidity, poise,

quiet(ness), repose, sedateness, smoothness, stillness, tranquillity
**sere that originates in dry surroundings** xerosere
**serf** bondman, bondwoman, cotter, helot, peasant, peon, servant, slave, thrall, vassal, villain, villein
**Seric** Chinese
**series** arrangement, chain, course, cycle, line, order, progression, run, sequence, set, string, succession, train
**series gathered together** sorites
**series of abstracts** syllabus
**series of arches** arcade
**series of ballet turns** chaine
**series of battles** war
**series of boat races** regatta
**series of cells** filament
**series of characters** cline
**series of chess moves** cook
**series of chirps** chirrup
**series of degrees** scale
**series of descriptive comments** commentary
**series of eight notes** octachord
**series of even stages** gradation
**series of events** action, epos
**series of games** rubber
**series of high sea-waves** tsunami
**series of images** dream
**series of legends** saga
**series of links** chain
**series of loud sounds** noise
**series of meetings** session
**series of military operations** campaign
**series of movements** dance
**series of musical notes** scale
**series of nine** ennead
**series of operations** campaign
**series of ornamental grooves** fluting
**series of reasons** argument
**series of repeated attacks** harassment
**series of stairs** flight
**series of stamps** set
**series of steps** stair, terrace
**series of three books in literature** trilogy
**series of tones** scale
**series of verses** antiphon
**series of vertebrae extending from skull** backbone, spine
**serious** bad, cheerless, critical, dangerous, dejected, demure, earnest, glum, grave, grim, humourless, important, melancholic, momentous, saturnine, sedate, sober, solemn, staid, sullen, thoughtful, unsmiling
**serious affliction** scourge
**serious and solemn** grave
**serious attention** application, care

**serious crime** felony
**serious love affair** grande passion (F)
**seriously** au sérieux (F)
**sermon** address, diatribe, discourse, exhortation, harangue, homily, lecture, monologue, preaching, rebuke, speech, talk, tirade, valedictory
**sermon attender** churchgoer
**sermonise** admonish, advocate, censure, declaim, decry, denounce, discourse, exhort, expound, harangue, homilise, inculcate, indoctrinate, lecture, moralise, orate, preach, predicate, prelect, propagate, pulpit, speak, talk, urge
**sermon subject** text
**serous fluid** serum
**serous membrane** serosa
**serpent** asp, snake
**serpent slain by Apollo** Python
**serpent slain by Hercules** Hydra
**serpent's venom-tooth** fang
**serpent worship** ophiolatry, ophism
**serrated organ** serra
**serrated-proboscis fish** sawfish
**serrated tool** saw
**serum** antidote
**serum for inoculation** vaccine
**servant** attendant, batman, bonne (F), char(woman), domestic, employee, flunk(e)y, footman, handmaiden, help(er), maid(servant), retainer, servitor, skivvy, slave, valet, vassal, waiter
**servant for drudgery** scullion
**servant managing his master's affairs** factotum
**servant of ship** steward
**servant's boss** master
**servant's uniform** livery
**serve** assist, attend, cater, forward, function, help, promote, purvey, succour, suffice, tend
**serve as justification for** legitimise
**serve at table** wait
**served in flaming brandy** flambé(e)
**served on toast** anchovette, poached eggs
**served with jam and cream** scone
**serve food** cater
**serve in an army** soldier
**serve the purpose** do
**service** agency, aid, assistance, availability, benefit, ceremony, effort, help, maintain, office, repair, system, treatment
**serviceable** adaptable, aiding, applicable, capable, commodious, convenient, effective, expedient, functional, good, helpful,

multi-purpose, practical, pragmatic, sensible, usable, useful
**service charge** admission, fee, minimum
**service charge included in the price** service compris (F)
**service club member** Rotarian
**serviceman killed in action** casualty
**serviceman's distinctive garb** uniform
**serviceman's time off** leave
**service of the Eucharist** Mass
**service station** garage
**serviette** bib, napkin
**servile** abject, base, creepy, cringing, despicable, dishonourable, fawning, grovelling, ignominious, low, mean, menial, obsequious, oily, slavish, slimy, submissive, sycophantic, unctuous, vile, worthless
**servile agent** minion, slave
**servile dependant** minion
**servile flatterer** sycophant, toady
**servile flattery** adulation
**servile follower** lackey, myrmidon
**servile person** flunk(e)y
**servility** acquiescence, baseness, blandishment, cajolery, compliance, crawling, crouching, diffidence, docility, fawning, flattery, humbleness, humility, lowliness, meanness, meekness, modesty, obeisance, obsequiousness, slavishness, squirming, submissiveness, subservience, sycophancy, toadyism, unassertiveness, whining
**serving as an example** typical
**serving as a rule** precedent
**serving as sample** token
**serving as the means** instrumental
**serving as warning** exemplary
**serving bottle for alcoholic drink** decanter
**serving dish** platter, tray
**serving many purposes** multipurpose
**serving no purpose** functionless, otiose, useless
**serving platter** tray
**serving several purposes at once** omnibus
**serving spoon** ladle
**serving temporarily** acting
**serving to build** constructive
**serving to discover** heuristic
**serving to distinguish** typical
**serving to expel** expulsive
**serving to express** expressive
**serving to improve** promotional
**serving to prepare** preparatory
**serving to prevent** preventive
**serving to purify** laxative, purgative

**servitude** bondage, bonds, obedience, slavery, subjugation, vassalage
**sesame plant** benne, gingih, til
**sesame sweet** halavah, halva(h)
**sessile-flowered species of oak** durmast
**session** assembly, episode, gathering, meeting, period, seance, sitting, term
**session of a society** seance
**session of considerable spending** spree
**set** appoint, attune, cabal, circle, clique, congeal, coterie, determined, establish, evaluate, gel, harden, kit, locate, ordain, place, pose, position, post, price, put, rate, rigid, rote, serie, solidify, station, stiff, stubborn, unmoving, value
**seta** bristle
**set ablaze** fire, torch
**set about** assail, assault, attack, begin, lambast(e), launch, pioneer, start, tackle, undertake
**set afire** ignite, lit
**set afloat** launch
**set against** alienate, balance, compare, contrast, disunite, divide, juxtapose, oppose, weigh
**set age** era
**set alight** ignite, inflame, kindle, torched
**set a lure** bait
**set apart** accumulate, alone, amass, assign, choose, distinguish, earmark, elect, isolate, reserve, separate, sequester
**set apart as holy** sanctify
**set apart from others** segregate
**set a price or value on** appraise
**set aside** abrogate, allocate, annul, cancel, discard, dismiss, earmark, eliminate, keep, overrule, overturn, reject, repudiate, reserve, reverse, save, select, separate, store, supercede, waive, withdraw
**set aside decision of** overrule
**set at an angle** cant
**set at liberty** free
**set at naught** belittle, cut, disavow, disregard, rebuff, slight, snub
**set back** delay, frustrate, hamper, hinder, hindrance, impede, inhibit, interrupt, obstruct, retard, slow
**set ceremony** ritual
**set copy ready for printing** typescript, typeset
**set down** codify, embarrass, enrol, list, record, register, tabulate
**set down a foot** tread
**set down heavily** dump
**set down in words** write
**set eyes on** glimpse, spy
**set fire to** ignite, inflame, kindle

**set firmly** plant
**set forth** allege, enunciate, posit, postulate, pronounce, submit, utter
**set forth in detail** expound
**set forth in words** describe
**set free** absolve, acquit, emancipate, enfranchise, extricate, liberate, manumit, release, unchain, unlease
**set free from danger** rescue
**set going** begin, initiate, launch
**Seth's father** Adam
**set in** arise, arrive, begin, dawn
**set in good order** trim
**set in line** array
**set in motion** activate, excite, inaugurate, initiate, stir
**set in one's ways** hidebound
**set in order** address, arrange, array
**set in place** put
**set in row** align, aline
**set in soil** plant
**set in to and fro motion** rock
**set of actors** cast
**set of artificial teeth** denture
**set of beliefs** creed
**set of bells** carillon, chimes
**set of books** plenary
**set of cards** pack
**set of chimes** doorbell
**set of clothes** costume, outfit, suit
**set of documents** dossier
**set of drums** timpani, tympani
**set of eating utensils** canteen
**set of eggs for hatching** clutch
**set of eight** octet, ogdoad
**set of electric cells** battery
**set of equipment** outfit
**set off** begin, contrast(ed), depart, detonate, display, embark, enhance, explode, ignite, inflame, leave, light, present, shatter, trigger
**set off bomb** detonate
**set of four** quaternion, tetrad, warp
**set of furniture** suite
**set of garments** suit
**set of horses kept for breeding** stud
**set of ideas** system
**set of kettledrums** timpani, tympani
**set of laws** code
**set of leaves** corolla
**set of letters used in language** alphabet
**set of links** chain
**set of loaves** batch
**set of moral principles** ethic
**set of nine** annead
**set of numbers to be added** addend
**set of opinions** credo, creed
**set of organ pipes** stop
**set of outer clothes** suit
**set of persons in attendance** suit, train
**set of persons working together** team

**set of players** team
**set of playing cards** pack
**set of prayers** liturgy
**set of questions** questionnaire
**set of rooms** story, suite
**set of rules** code, equity, law
**set of rural parishes** deanery
**set of scales** balance
**set of seven** septet
**set of shelves** buffet, dresser, whatnot
**set of shoes** pair
**set of stables** mews
**set of steps** ladder, stair
**set of steps over fence** stile
**set of supplies** kit
**set of symbols** formula
**set of teeth** denture, ratchet
**set of ten** decade
**set of ten things of same kind** decuplet
**set of three** bale, leash, tern, trey, trio, triplet
**set of three related works by the same author** trilogy
**set of tools** kit
**set of tuned metal bars struck with a small hammer** glockenspiel
**set of twelve** dozen
**set of twenty** score
**set of two** pair
**set of vats** solera
**set of verses** stave
**set on** aggress, assail, assault, attack, incite, urge
**set once more** reset
**set oneself against** oppose, resist
**set one's sights on** aim
**set on fire** burn, (en)kindle, ignite
**set on foot** begin
**set on operation** drive
**set out** arrange, begin, define, describe, detail, display, dispose, elaborate, elucidate, exhibit, explain, present, recite, relate, report, sally
**set piece in rugby** scrum
**set piece of work** task
**set price for any of a variety of set meals** prix fixe
**set right** adjust, disabuse
**set sail** embark
**set solidly** embed
**set, stick together** gel
**set store by** appreciate, esteem, prize, value
**set straight again** redress
**settee** davenport, sofa
**set the table** lay
**set the timing in rowing** stroke
**setting** aiming, allocating, applying, arena, arranging, assigning, backdrop, background, concluding, context, decade, directing,
environment, fastening, fixing, laying, locale, locating, location, lodging, milieu, mounting, naming, parking, period, perspective, placing, planting, regulating, resolving, scenario, scene(ry), scheduling, seating, set(-up), site, situation, stage, stationing, surroundings, turning
**setting apart from others** segregating
**setting fires** arson
**setting fire to** igniting
**setting of the William Tell legend** Altdorf
**setting up a golf ball** teeing
**settle** adjust, agree, allay, calm, colonise, compose, confirm, decide, discharge, establish, fix, inhabit, liquidate, pacify, quiet, reconcile, rectify, (re)pay, resolve, rest, set, subside, upon
**settle a score** repay, retaliate
**settle bill in advance** prepay
**settle by combat** fight
**settle comfortably** nestle
**settle conclusively** clinch
**settled** stable
**settled debt** (re)paid
**settled existence** groove
**settled habit of living** rut
**settled in advance** predesigned, predetermined, preplanned
**settle down cosily** nestle
**settled way of behaving** habit
**settle finally** conclude
**settle firmly** ensconce
**settle in a camp** encamp
**settle in another country** emigrate
**settlement** accord, adjustment, agreement, amount, colony, payment, reconciliation, resolution
**settlement by agreement** mise
**settlement in Israel** kibbutz
**settlement of debt** acquittance
**settlement of dispute by mutual concession** compromise
**settle on fixed body** perch
**settle oneself comfortably** nestle
**settler** colonist, immigrant, pioneer, planter
**settler of Algeria** Colon, Piednor
**settle safely** ensconce
**settles disputes** arbitrator, ombudsman
**settle up** pay
**settle upon** choose, prefer, select
**settling** colonising
**settling in** adjustment
**set-to** altercation, argument, brush, conflict, contest, disagreement, dust-up, exchange, fight, fracas, quarrel, row, scrap, scuffle, spat, squabble, wrangle
**set to explode** armed
**set to rights** tidy
**set up** arrange, assemble, back, begin, boost, build, compose, construct, create, design, elevate, erect, established, form, found, gratify, inaugurate, initiate, install, institute, introduce, organise, pitch, prepare, prime, promote, raise, start, strengthen
**set-up** arrangement, business, circumstances, conditions, organisation, régime, structure, system
**set upon** ambush, assail, assault, attack
**set upright** rear
**set up tents** camp
**seven-branched candelabrum used in Jewish worship** menorah
**seven day period** week
**seven dwarfs** Bashful, Doc, Dopey, Grumpy, Happy, Sleepy, Sneezy
**sevenfold** septuple
**seven gods of luck in Japan** Benten, Bishamonten, Daikotu, Ebisu, Fukurokuju, Hotei, Jurojin
**seven-hilled city** Rome
**seven hills of Rome** Aventine, Caelian, Capitoline, Esquiline, Palatine, Quirinal, Viminal
**seven-lobed ornamental figure** septfoil
**seven mortal sins** avarice, envy, gluttony, lust, pride, sloth, wrath
**seven musicians** septet
**seven sages of Greece** Bias, Chilon, Cleobulus, Periander, Pittacus, Solon, Thales
**seven seas** Antarctic, Arctic, Indian, north Atlantic, south Atlantic, north Pacific, south Pacific
**seven-sided figure** heptagon
**seven stars in Ursa Major** triones
**seven-stringed musical instrument** heptacord
**seventh day after a festival** octave
**seventh heaven** elevation, euphoria, nirvana, Utopia
**seventh Jewish month** Nisan
**seventh planet from sun** Uranus
**seventh satellite of Saturn** Hyperian
**seven times as much** septuple, sevenfold
**seven virtues** charity, faith, fortitude, hope, justice, prudence, temperance
**seven wonders of the ancient world** Colossus of Rhodes, Egyptian pyramids, hanging gardens of Babylon, Mausoleum, Pharos at Alexandria, statue of Zeus at Olympia, temple of Artemis

**sever** alienate, bisect, bob, break, classify, cleave, cut, detach, disconnect, disencumber, disjoin(t), dissect, dissociate, dissolve, disunite, divide, divorce, estrange, part, release, remove, rend, rive, separate, slash, slit, split, take, terminate, uncouple, wrench
**several** assorted, certain, different, disparate, distinct, diverse, individual, many, particular, respective, single, some, specific, sundry, umpteen, various
**severally** differently, disparately, distinctly, diversely, individually, particularly, respectively, variously
**several verses** poem
**severe** abrupt, accurate, acerbic, astringent, austere, biting, burdensome, chaste, critical, cut(ting), dangerous, drastic, exigent, extreme, grave, grievous, grim, hard, harsh, keen, mordacious, mordant, onerous, peremptory, plain, rigid, rigorous, satirical, serious, short, stern, strict, stringent, systematic, unrelenting
**severe abdominal pain** colic
**severe abscess in the skin** carbuncle
**severe affliction** scourge, tribulation
**severe anger** rage
**severe blow** klap, oner
**severe cephalalgia** splitting headache
**severe criticism** stricture
**severe defeat** whipping
**severe headache** migraine
**severe home sickness** nostalgia
**severe itching of the skin** pruritus
**severe look** frown
**severely** strictly
**severely abstinent** ascetic
**severely critical** censorius
**severely scornful** abusive, opprobrious
**severely simple** austere
**severe malnutrition of infants and young children** kwashiorkor
**severe mental deficiency** amentia
**severe mental disorder** psychosis
**severe mental illness** lunacy
**severe mental suffering** torment
**severe pain in the intestines** colic
**severe physical pain** anguish
**severe pressure of pain** distress
**severe privation** hardship
**severe rebuke** scolding
**severe shortage of food** famine
**severe skin disease** rupia
**severe snowstorm** blizzard
**severe suffering** hardship
**severe trial** ordeal
**severe weather** inclement

**severity** acerbity, acrimony, asperity, astringency, austereness, cruelty, exactness, extremity, harshness, implacability, inhumanity, meticulousness, persistence, pitilessness, rigidness, rigour, roughness, savagery, seriousness, simplicity, solemnity, straitness, strictness, stringency, unremittance, unyieldingness
**sever limbs** dismember
**seville and jaffa** orange
**sew** alter, attach, baste, fasten, fix, gather, hem, join, mend, pleat, repair, seam, secure, smock, stitch, tie, tuck
**sewage** contamination, defilement, dirt, drainage, dung, effluent, effluvium, excrement, excreta, faeces, filth(iness), foulness, garbage, grime, muck, nastiness, ordure, pollutant, pollution, refuse, slime, sludge, squalor, uncleanness, waste
**sewage dumping vessel** sludger
**sewer** drain
**sewer's finger protection** thimble
**sewing** needlework, stitching
**sewing aid** needle, thimble
**sewing case** etui
**sewing instrument** needle, sewing-machine
**sewing machine inventor** Singer
**sewing thread** cotton
**sewing tool** awl, bobbin, needle, pin
**sew together** seam, stitch
**sew together loosely** baste, tack
**sew up a torn item** mend
**sew up the eyelids of a hawk** seel
**sex** gender, libido, lust
**sexangular** hexagonal
**sex appeal** beauty, charm, it, lovableness, oomph, personality, SA
**sexiness** libido
**sex party** orgy
**sexton** grave-digger
**sexton of parish church** sacrist(an)
**sextuple** sixfold
**sexual** coital, conjugal, erotic, genital, intimate, sensual
**sexual assault** rape
**sexual desire** erot(ic)ism
**sexual heat of animals** oestrum, oestrus
**sexual literature** erotica
**sexual love** Eros
**sexual love directed towards children** paedophilia
**sexually alluring** voluptuous
**sexually immoral person** pimp, prostitute, rentboy, whore
**sexual maturity** puberty
**sexual maturity in larval form** neoteny

**sexual offender** nonce
**sexual torture** sadism
**Seychelles island** Mahe
**shabbily dressed** seedy
**shabbiness** cheapness, despicableness, fadedness, ignobleness, meanness, poorness, raggedness, scuffiness, seediness, shamefulness, tattiness, unworthiness
**shabby** beggarly, condemned, contemptible, decrepit, dilapidated, dingy, dirty, dishonourable, disreputable, drab, frayed, impoverished, mean, paltry, ragged, ramshackle, rotten, ruinous, scruffy, seedy, slummy, tacky, tattered, tatty, worn
**shabby artistic type** bohemian
**shabby from wear** old
**shabby odds and ends** tat
**Shache** Soche, Yarkand
**shack** cabin, dump, hovel, hut, pondok, shanty, shiel
**shackle** bandage, belt, block, bond, chain, confine, congest, cord, coupling, enchain, encumbrance, enslave, fetter, hamper, handcuff, hobble, impede, impediment, iron, manacle, obstacle, obstruction, restrain, strap, stultify, tether, tie, trammel, union
**shackle for feet** fetter
**shadbird** sandpiper, snipe
**shade** amount, awning, blind, canopy, cloud, colour, conceal, cover, curtain, darken, darkness, degree, dim(ness), dusk, ghost, gloom(iness), hair, hide, hue, mute, nuance, obfuscate, obscure, obscurity, phantom, protect, screen, shadow, shelter, shield, spectre, spirit, stain, suggestion, tinge, tint, tone, variation, veil
**shaded walk** arbour, mall
**shade of blue** navy, saxe
**shade of brown** sepia, tan
**shade of crimson** magenta
**shade of colour** hue
**shade of green** olive
**shade of meaning** nuance
**shade provider** tree
**shade tree** alder, elm, sycamore
**shading into white** albescent
**shading lines** hachure
**shadow** adumbration, cast, darken, dimness, follow, foreshadow, hint, image, omen, phantom, protection, screen, shade, shelter, silhouette, suggestion, tail, trace, track, trail, type, umbra, vestige
**shadow-boxing** sparring

**shadow-clock** sundial
**shadow drawing** silhouette
**shadowy** dark, dim, dusky, gloomy, indistinct, murky, obscure, shady, vague
**shady** cool, dim, disreputable, dubious, leafy, shadowy, suspicious, umbrageous, unethical
**shady dell** dingle
**shady gum tree** coolabah
**shady retreat** alcove, bower
**shaft** arrow, axle, beam, dart, duct, excavation, flagpole, flue, handle, passage, pillar, pipe, pit, pole, ray, rod, stem, stick, streak, support, thrust, tunnel, well
**shaft in mine** pit
**shaft of column** scape
**shaft of light** beam
**shaft of oar** loom
**shaft of spear** truncheon
**shaft of sword** hilt
**shaft of vehicle** thill
**shaft on which something turns** pivot
**shaft on which wheels rotate** axle(tree)
**shaft used by painters to support the right hand** maulstick
**shag** cormorant
**shaggy** bristly, brushy, crinite, dishevelled, entangled, hairy, harsh, hirsute, hispid, matted, messy, piliferous, rough, shagrag, snarled, swag, tangled, tatty, untidy, villous
**shaggy dog** collie
**shag tobacco** caporal
**Shaka's people** Zulus
**shake** disturb, flourish, intimidate, move, oscillate, quake, quiver, rattle, shiver, shock, sway, totter, tremble, tremor, unsettle, vibrate, waver, weaken, wobble
**shake a leg** dance, haste, hurry, rush
**shake confidence** unnerve
**shake down** condition
**shake head** nod
**shake in wind** flap
**shake noisily** judder, rattle
**shake off** banish, dislodge, elude, extricate, free, liberate, loose(n), outdistance, outstrip
**shake one's faith** discredit, disprove, invalidate
**Shakespeare** dramatist, poet
**Shakespearean character** Brutus, Caesar, Cassius, Coriolanus, Desdemona, Falstaff, Hamlet, Iago, Macbeth, Ophelia, Portia, Prospero, Romeo, Shylock, Timon
**Shakespearean forest** Arden
**Shakespearean home** Avon

**Shakespearean king** Claudius, Duncan, Henry, John, Lear, Macbeth, Oberon, Richard
**Shakespearean play** Julius Caesar, Hamlet, King Lear, Macbeth, Othello, Tempest, Twelfth Night
**Shakespearean spirit** Ariel
**Shakespeare's river** Avon
**Shakespeare's violent storm** Tempest
**shake to and fro** oscillate, wag
**shake up** agitate, churn, disturb, overturn, shock, unsettle, upset
**shake-up** disturbance, rearrangement, reorganisation, reshuffle, upheaval
**shake with cold** shiver
**shake with fear** tremble
**shake with jerk** jolt
**shake with tremulous motion** quiver
**shaking** bumping, discomposing, distressing, frightening, intimidating, jarring, moving, quaking, rocking, shivering, shocking, shuddering, swaying, tottering, trembling, tremorous, unnerving, upsetting, vibrating, wavering, waving
**shaking paralysis** palsy
**shaky** insecure, quivery, rickety, rocky, suspect, trembling, uncertain, unstable, unsteady, weak, wobbly
**shall** will
**shallot** bulb, eschalot, onion, scallion
**shallow** empty, foolish, meaningless, shoal, superficial, surface, trivial
**shallow basket for fish** caul, creel
**shallow body of water** lagoon
**shallow cavity** fossa
**shallow circular vessel** plate
**shallow cup mounted on a foot** tazza
**shallow dish** basin, coupe, plate
**shallow garden basket** trug
**shallow lake** lagoon, lagune
**shallow recess** alcove, niche
**shallow round dish** plate
**shallow rowing boat** wherry
**shallow trough below eaves** gutter
**shallow vessel** basin
**shalom** farewell, greeting, hello, peace
**sham** artificial, bogus, concealment, counterfeit, deceive, deception, disguise, duplicity, fake, false, farce, feign, forgery, fraud, humbug, imitation, mockery, pretence, pretend(ed), pseudo, simulate, spurious, trick, unreal
**sham attack** feint
**shamble** shuffle
**shambles** anarchy, confusion, debacle, disarray, disorder, havoc, mess, muddle
**shambling walk** slouch
**shame** abasement, abash(ment), chagrin, contempt, derision, disgrace, dishonour, humble, humiliation, ignominy, infamy, obloquy, opprobrium, reproach, scandalise, shend
**shameful** base, degrading, disgraceful, humiliating, ignominious, indecent, infamous, low, mean, scandalous, shaming, unbecoming, vile, wicked
**shameful act** ignominy
**shameful depravity** turpitude
**shamefully humiliated** mortified
**shameless** adamant, audacious, bare-faced, brazen, depraved, dissolute, hardened, immodest, impudent, indecent, indelicate, insolent, reprobate, unabashed, unashamed, unblushing
**shameless audacity** chutzpah
**shameless insolence** effrontery
**shamelessly immoral** profligate
**shamelessness** immodesty, impudence
**shameless untruths** barefaced lies
**shameless woman** hussy, Jezebel
**sham medicine** placebo
**shamming** copying, duplicating, faking
**shammy** chamois
**sham story** flam
**Shangaan** Tsonga
**shank** stem
**shanty** cabin, cottage, house, hovel, hut, pondok, shack
**shanty-town built of drums, etc.** bidonville
**shape** adjust, arrangement, aspect, build, cast, condition, configuration, contours, create, cut, disguise, fashion, fettle, figure, form, frame, guise, health, kilter, likeness, lines, make, model, mould, order, outline, pattern, profile, regulate, semblance, silhouette, situation, state, term, trim, word
**shaped for piston** cylindrical
**shaped like arrowhead** sagittate, sagittiform
**shaped like bean** fabiform
**shaped like bell** campanulate
**shaped like berry** bacciform
**shaped like boat** navicular(e), scaphoid
**shaped like body of fiddle** pandurate, panduriform
**shaped like bow** arcuate
**shaped like bunch of grapes** aciniform, botryoidal
**shaped like circle** circular
**shaped like club** clavate, claviform
**shaped like coil** circinate
**shaped like coin** nummular
**shaped like comb** pectinate(d)
**shaped like cone** coniform, conoid, fastigiate

**shaped like crescent** lunate
**shaped like cross** cruciate, cruciform
**shaped like cup** cotyloid, cupulate, scyphiform
**shaped like dome** domal
**shaped like eagle's beak** aquiline
**shaped like ear** auriculate, auriform
**shaped like eel** anguilliform
**shaped like egg** oval, ovate, ovoid
**shaped like feather** pinnate
**shaped like foot** pediform
**shaped like funnel** infundibuliform
**shaped like globe** globate
**shaped like hand** palmate
**shaped like head** capitate, cephaloid
**shaped like head of arrow** sagittate
**shaped like heart** cordate, cordiform
**shaped like hood** cucullate
**shaped like horn** corniform, cornual
**shaped like keel** carinate
**shaped like kidney** reniform
**shaped like knife blade** cultrate
**shaped like leaf** foliate
**shaped like letter S** sigmoidal, sigmois
**shaped like needle** acerose, acerous
**shaped like patella** patellate, patelliform
**shaped like pear** pyriform
**shaped like pine cone** pineal, strobilaceous
**shaped like pouch or sac** bursiform, saccate
**shaped like ring** annular, toroid
**shaped like rod** vigate
**shaped like sausage** allantoid
**shaped like scimitar** acinaciform
**shaped like shield** clypeate, peltate, sculate, scutellate
**shaped like shoe or slipper** calceiform, calceolate
**shaped like short rod** bacillary, bacilliform, virgate, virgulate
**shaped like sickle** falcate, falciform
**shaped like small sac** sacculiform
**shaped like snail's shell** cochleate
**shaped like snake** anguiform, anguine
**shaped like spearhead** hastate, lanceolate
**shaped like spiral** helical, turbinal, turbinate
**shaped like star** astroid, stellate
**shaped like string of beads** moniliform
**shaped like sword** ensiform, gladiate, xiphoid
**shaped like tongue** linguiform, lingulate, lingulated
**shaped like tooth** dentiform
**shaped like tortoise** testudinal, testudinary
**shaped like tree** dendriform, dendroid
**shaped like triangle** deltoid
**shaped like turnip** napiform

**shaped like urn** urceolate
**shaped like wedge** cuneal, cuneate, sphenic
**shaped like wheel** trochal
**shaped like wing** alar, aliform, wing-like
**shaped stone for tool-sharpening** whetstone
**shaped with axe** hewn
**shape generally** outline
**shapeless** amorphous, basic, crude, deformed, distorted, embryonic, formless, imperfect, incomplete, misshapen, nebulous, raw, rough, rudimentary, structureless, uncarved, unformed, unshaped, vague
**shapeless lump of food** dollop
**shapeless mass** chaos, lump, mammock
**shapely** comely, curvaceous, elegant, neat, trim, well-formed
**shapely fruit** pear
**shape on a mould** model
**shape to hold shoe** (shoe)tree
**shape up** crystallise, improve, progress
**shape with knife** whittle
**shaping dish** mould
**shaping machine** lathe
**shaping tool** chisel, gouge, swage
**shard** beetle, elytron, fragment, (pot)sherd, shell
**share** allotment, apportion, contribution, divide, dole, lot, part, partake, participate, ploughshare, (pro)portion, quota
**share allotted to one** allotment
**share certificate** scrip
**shared** between, communal, joint
**shared activity** community
**share dealing** stockbroking
**share equally** halve
**shareholder** associate, contributor, member, party, stockholder
**share in common** joint, participate
**share of profit** lay
**share out** allocate, allot, apportion, assign, deal, distribute, divide, mete
**share secrets** confide
**share the same view** agree
**share with** partake, partner
**sharing digs** rooming
**sharing of emotion** sympathy
**sharing of opinion** agreement
**sharing out** allotting
**shark** charlatan, cheat(er), criminal, crook, deceiver, dodger, double-crosser, fraud, imposter, mountebank, porbeagle, rascal, robber, rogue, sharper, swindler, thief, trickster, villain
**shark parasite** remora

**sharkskin** shagreen
**sharp** abrupt, acerb, acrid, active, acute, alert, biting, brisk, burning, caustic, clever, cold, distinct, eager, fierce, high, hot, intense, keen(-edge), marked, painful, peaked, penetrating, piquant, pointed, quick, severe, shrill, spicy, sudden, tart, trenchant, vigilant
**sharp answer** retort
**sharp bark** yap, yelp
**sharp bend** kink
**sharp billiards stroke** masse
**sharp blow** punch, rap, slap, swat
**sharp coldness of weather** nip
**sharp-cornered** angular
**sharp crest** arête, ridge
**sharp cry** ouch, yell, yelp
**sharp device fixed to heel of rider's boot** spur
**sharp division** dichotomy
**sharp duelling-sword** épée
**sharp edged** cultrate
**sharpen** acuminate, edge, file, grind, hone, point, strop, taper, tip, whet
**sharpen by rubbing** whet
**sharp end** point
**sharpening** edging, grinding, honing, stropping, whetting
**sharpening machine** grinder
**sharpening stone** hone, whet
**sharp-eyed** attentive, vigilant
**sharp-eyed cat** lynx
**sharp flavour** bite, tang, tartness
**sharp growth** thorn
**sharp high-heels** stilettos
**sharp in speech** acrid
**sharp intake of breath** gasp
**sharp in taste** piquant, tart
**sharp intermittent pain along the course of a nerve** neuralgia
**sharp jerking movement** yank
**sharp knock** rap
**sharply** tartly
**sharply directional aerial** ari-al, Yagi
**sharp metal object** spike
**sharp momentary local pain** twinge
**sharp mountain ridge** arête
**sharpness** abruptness, acerbity, acidity, acrimony, acrity, acuity, acumen, acuteness, alertness, aptness, brightness, distinctness, edge, edginess, extremeness, jaggedness, keenness, markedness, perceptiveness, pluck, pungency, quickness, subtleness, suddenness, whet, wit
**sharp of breath** gasp
**sharp or sour** acid
**sharp pain** pang, sting, twinge
**sharp pain in chest** angina pectoris
**sharp pain in side** stitch

**sharp peak of rock** aiguille
**sharp point** barb, cusp, spike
**sharp pointed stick for urging on cattle** goad
**sharp-pointed sword** épée
**sharp-pointed war instrument** assegai, spear
**sharp point of anything** neb
**sharp practice** deceit, deception, fake, fiddle, fraud, swindle
**sharp practise** trickery
**sharp process on plant** thorn
**sharp prod** jab
**sharp projection** barb, jag
**sharp pull** yank
**sharp reply** retort, riposte
**sharp ridge of mountain** arête
**sharpshooter** jaeler, jäger, sniper
**sharp side** edge
**sharp slap** smack, thwack
**sharp smelling** acrid
**sharp sound** clap, pop, snap
**sharp strike** rap
**sharp struggle** tussle
**sharp, sudden pull** jerk
**sharp-tailed duck** pintail
**sharp-tasting** acid, bitter, tangy, tart
**sharp-tasting acid** citric
**sharp-tasting sauce** worcester
**sharp-tempered** edgy, acid
**sharp, tinkling sound** clink
**sharp-toned growl** snarl
**sharp-tongued** sarcastic
**sharp tooth** fang, incisor
**sharp toothlike projection** jag
**sharp top of mountain** peak, spits(kop)
**sharp twinge** ache, pain
**sharp twist or bend in wire** kink
**sharp weapon** assegai, spear
**sharp-witted** alert, attentive, keen, vigilant, watchful
**shatter** break, burst, crack, crush, dash, demolish, destroy, devastate, exhaust, explode, implode, overturn, ruin, shiver, smash, split
**shattering** crushing, smashing
**shave** barber, brush, clip, crop, curtail, cut, dock, graze, lop, nick, notch, pare, prune, shear, slice, snip, tidy, trim
**shaved** clipped, cropped, curtailed, cut, docked, lopped, nicked, notched, pared, pruned, sheared, shorn, snipped, tidied, trimmed
**shaven crown** tonsure
**shaver** razor, youngster
**shave the head** tonsure
**shaving cut** nick
**shaving foam** lather
**shaving instrument** razor
**shawl** (shoulder-)wrap, stole
**she** ella (Sp), elle (F)

**shear** clip, scissors
**shearer** clipper
**shear off** deprive, divest, remove, strip
**shear wool** clip
**she-ass** jenny
**sheath** case, casing, coat(ing), cover(ing), envelope, folder, hull, husk, jacket, ocrea, peel, rind, scabbard, shell, skin, sleeve, wrapper, wrapping
**sheathed** absorbed, blanketed, bound, cloaked, concealed, covered, embraced, encased, enclosed, enfolded, engulfed, enveloped, folded, muffled, obscured, ocreate, retracted, shrouded, surrounded, swathed, veiled, wound, wrapped
**sheath for sword** scabbard
**sheath of collective tissue** epimysium
**she casts spells** witch
**shed** abandon, abri, addition, annex, barn, booth, cabin, cast, cote, decrease, disaccustom, discard, discharge, dispel, doff, drop, emit, exude, exuviate, flake, hovel, hut, lean-to, moult, outhouse, peel, pen, pondok, radiate, release, repulse, resist, scatter, shack, shanty, shelter, slough, spill, spilt, spread, stall, storage, strew, structure, sty
**shed blood** broach
**shed copiously** rain
**shed dead tissue** slough
**shedding leaves** deciduous
**shedding light** luminous
**shedding of hair** psilosis
**shedding of skin** ecdysis
**shed drops** drizzle
**shed feathers** mew, moult
**shed for livestock** shippen
**shed for sheep** cote, shealing
**shed from a surface** scale
**shed hair** moult
**she displays clothes** mannequin, model
**shed light on** clarify, elucidate, explain, illuminate, lighten, simplify
**shed over mineshaft** coe
**shed skin** moult
**shed tears** cry, give, weep
**shed to house aircraft** hangar
**shed to protect soldiers** testudo
**sheen** beautiful, brightness, brilliance, burnish, glint, gloss, glow, lustre, opalescence, patina, polish, radiance, rare, shine, sparkle, splendour, twinkle
**sheep** ewe, jumbuck, ram, teg, wether
**sheep breed** cheviot, merino
**sheep clipper** shearer
**sheep disease** coe, gid, tagsore
**sheepdog** collie, kelpie, shepherd

**sheep enclosure** fold
**sheep farmer** pastoralist
**sheep group** flock
**sheep hair** wool
**sheep in its second year** teg(g)
**sheepish** bashful, blushing, constrained, coy, diffident, discomfited, distressed, doubtful, embarrassed, guilty, hesitant, humiliated, insecure, mortified, nervous, prudish, reluctant, remorseful, reserved, shamefaced, shy, timid, unsure, withdrawn
**sheep-killing parrot** kea
**sheeplike** ovine
**sheeplike state** trance
**sheep of the Himalayas** urial
**sheep oil** lanolin
**sheep pelt** fleece, wool
**sheep's cry** baa, bleat
**sheep's flesh** mutton
**sheep shelter** cote
**sheep shorn once** shearling
**sheepskin** ovine
**sheepskin binding** roan
**sheepskin cap** calpac(k)
**sheepskin leather** bock, buck, mocha, roan, skiver
**sheep's nape of neck** scrag
**sheep's noise** baa
**sheep's shed** cote
**sheep's wool** fleece
**sheep tender** shepherd
**sheep that leads the herd** bellwether
**sheep walk** slait
**sheep yielding fine wool** merino
**sheer** abrupt, absolute, arrant, complete, downright, fine, gauzy, mere, perpendicular, pure, simple, steep, swerve, transparent, unassisted, uncompounded, undiluted, unmitigated, unqualified, utter
**sheer material** voile
**sheer off** avoid, deviate, recede, swerve
**sheer rock** cliff
**sheer stocking** nylon
**sheet for corpse** shroud
**sheet metal** stabile
**sheet of advertising matter** leaflet
**sheet of frozen water** (ice-)floe
**sheet of glass** pane
**sheet of stationery** paper
**sheet of window glass** pane
**sheets** linen
**sheets of paper fastened together in a block** pad
**she-fox** vixen
**she-goat** nanny
**sheik's women** harem

**shelf** bench, bracket, ledge, lodge, mantel(piece), overhang, projection, protrusion, reef, ridge, sandbank
**shell** bomb, canister, cartouche, cartridge, case, cassette, conch, cowrie, crust, framework, husk, pod, shot, structure, test, triton, tunicate
**shellac** resin, varnish
**shellac varnish for furniture** French polish
**shell carving** cameo
**shell-firing gun** cannon
**shellfish** abalone, clam, crab, crayfish, kreef, lobster, mussel, oyster, perlemoen, prawn, shrimp
**shellfish gem** pearl
**shell fragments** shrapnel
**shellhole** crater
**shell of tortoise** carapace
**shell out** contribute, disburse, dissipate, donate, expend, give, outlay, spend, squander, subscribe, waste
**shell-shaped ovenproof dish** coquille
**shells of grain** husks
**shell that fails to explode** dud
**shell used as money** cowrie
**she lost her sheep** Bo Peep
**shelter** abri, asylum, cover(ing), defence, defend, guard, harbour, haven, hide, lee, protect(ion), refuge, retreat, roof, safeguard, safety, sanctuary, screen, security, shield, umbrella
**sheltered** (a)lee
**sheltered abode** shade
**sheltered bay** cove
**sheltered corner** nook
**sheltered from wind** (a)lee
**sheltered inlet** cove
**sheltered recess** cove
**sheltered side** lee(ward)
**sheltered walk as promenade** mall
**shelter for cows** byre
**shelter for sheep** sheepcote
**shelter for tropical plants** hothouse
**shelter from sun** shade
**shelterwards** alee
**shelve** defer, dismiss, freeze, mothball, pigeonhole, postpone, retire, waive
**shemozzle** brawl, muddle, rumpus
**shenanigan** deception, mischief, nonsense, roguishness, trickery
**shepherd's hut** shieling (Sc)
**shepherd's staff** crook
**sherbet glass** supreme
**she reaches low notes** contralto
**sheriff's band** posse
**sheriff's officer** bailiff
**Sherlock Holmes's author** Doyle
**Sherlock Holmes's friend** Watson
**Sherlock Holmes's hat** deerstalker

**Sherlock Holmes's necessity** clue
**Sherpaland** Nepal
**sherry** jerez (Sp)
**sherry glass** copita
**sherry or port** wine
**she sank on her maiden voyage** *Titanic*
**she's in charge of a hospital** matron
**Shetland fjord** Geo
**she was a gift from France to America** Statue of Liberty
**she was first** Eve
**she went to Wonderland** Alice
**shield** aegis, buckler, conceal, cover, defend, defence, aegis, ensconce, escutcheon, guard(ian), pavis(e), pelta, protect(ion), protector, sentinel, sentry, shelter, targe, watchdog, watchman
**shield against danger** screen
**shield bearing coat of arms** escutcheon
**shield border** orle
**shield from** deflect, divert, parry
**shield-like** elytral
**shield of Zeus** aegis
**shield or sponsor** aegis
**shield-shaped** thyroid
**shield with coat-of-arms** escutcheon
**shift** alter, budge, change, dislodge, move, pass, substitute, swerve, switch, transfer, variation
**shifting round** veer
**shifting sands** erg
**shiftless** idle
**shiftless person** drifter
**shift of men** gang
**shifty** deceitful, evasive, sly
**Shiite leader** ayatolla(h)
**shilling** bob
**shilpit** puny, thin, weak-looking
**shimmer** beam, brighten, brilliance, flame, gleam, glimmer, glint, glisten, glitter, glow, illuminate, luminosity, luster, quivering, radiate, ray, shine, spark, streak, twinkling
**shinbone** tibia
**shindy** brawl, disturbance, noise, row
**shine** beam, gleam, glimmer, glisten, gloss, glow, lustre, polish, radiance, radiate, sparkle
**shine like thing intensely heated** glow
**shine of varnish** gorm
**shine oppressively** glare
**shiner** mackerel
**shine radiantly** glow
**shine softly** glow
**shine unsteadily** blink, flicker
**shine upon** irradiate
**shine up to** kowtow
**shine with tremulous light** glitter, shimmer

**shingle** beach, coast, cover, cut, gravel, pebble, sands, (sea)shore, seaside, sign, strand, tile
**shingles** herpes, zoster
**shining** aglow, bright, brilliant, conspicuous, eminent, gleaming, glistening, glorious, illuminated, lucent, outstanding, radiant, shimmering, sparkling, sunny
**shining surface** lustre
**shining through** translucent
**shining with good health** aglow, radiant
**shin of veal cooked with wine and tomatoes** osso bucco
**Shinto deity** Kami
**Shinto place of worship** shrine
**shiny** agleam, bright, burnished, gleaming, glistening, glossy, lustrous, polished, satiny, sheeny
**shiny black colour** raven
**shiny fabric** satin
**shiny paint** enamel, gloss
**ship** boat, craft, deliver, dispatch, embark, forward, galleon, keel, liner, mail, route, schooner, send, steamer, tanker, transport, vessel, xebec
**shipbuilders' prop** thwart
**ship carrying cargo** merchantman
**ship carrying oil** tanker
**ship channel** gat
**ship crew's tour of duty** watch
**ship fever** typhus
**ship fitted as church** bethel
**ship in liquor trade** coper
**shipload** cargo, lading
**shipman** sailor, skipper
**shipmaster** captain, skipper
**shipment** cargo, freight, load
**ship of Columbus** *Nina, Pinta, Santa Maria*
**ship of the desert** camel, dromedary, oont
**shipping box** carton, crate
**shipping collectively** marine
**shipping container** crate
**shipping document** waybill
**shipping hazard** iceberg, reef
**shipping route** sea-lane
**ship powered by engine** collier, freighter, liner, tanker, trawler, tug, whaleback
**ship powered by oars** bireme, Bucentaur, galley, galliot, longship, trireme
**ship powered by sail** argosy, barque, bilander, brig, brigantine, caravel, clipper, cutter, dandy, dromond, galleon, ketch, schooner, sloop, tartan, xebec, yawl
**ship repair stage** dry-dock

**ship sailing with another** consort
**ship's anchorage** berth, mooring
**ship's anchor chain** cable
**ship's armour** plating
**ship's beak** bow, prow, ram
**ship's beam** ke(e)lson
**ship's biscuit** hardtack
**ship's boat** cutter, gig
**ship's body** hull
**ship's boom** spar
**ship's bottom** bilge
**ship's bow** prow
**ship's breadth** beam
**ship's bunk** berth
**ship's cannon** carronade
**ship's canvas** (top)sail
**ship's capacity** tonnage, tunnage
**ship's captain** master, skipper
**ship's cargo** freight
**ship's carpenter** shipwright
**ship's chimney** stack
**ship's coastal sighting** landfall
**ships collectively** sail
**ship's company** crew
**ship's compartment** cabin, fore-castle, hold, stateroom
**ship's compass stand** binnacle
**ship's complement** crew
**ship's crane** davit
**ship's crew member** hand, mate, steward, stoker, yeoman
**ship's deck** orlop, poop
**ship's deck drain** scupper
**ship's deck opening** hatch
**ship's diary** log
**ship's dock** basin, slip
**ship's flag** ensign
**ship's floor** deck
**ship's framework** hull
**ship's front** bow, prow, stem
**shipshape** accurate, arranged, businesslike, clean, dainty, methodical, neat, nice, ordered, orderly, organised, regular, smart, spruce, straight, systematic, tidy, trim, well-ordered
**ship-shaped clock** nef
**ship's hauling device** capstan
**ship's hold** hole, holl
**ship's hospital** bay
**ship's jail** brig
**ship's journal** log
**ship's keel extension** skeg
**ship's kitchen** galley
**ship's load or freight** cargo
**ship's long timber** keel
**ship's lookout** crow's-nest
**ship's lowest deck** orlop
**ship's main cabin** saloon
**ship's mast** spar
**ship's master** captain
**ship's mate** officer

**ship's measure** last
**ship's midsection** waist
**ships moor alongside it** wharf
**ship's navigation aid** compass, radar, sonar, star
**ship's officer** captain, mate, purser
**ship's officers' deck** bridge
**ship's part** deck, hull, keel, mast, rib, rudder
**ship's personnel** crew
**ship's place at wharf** berth
**ship's plank's curve** sny
**ship's prison** brig
**ship's propeller** screw
**ship's radio distress call** mayday
**ship's rear** aft, stern
**ship's record** log
**ship's retaining chain** anchor
**ship's rigging** cordage
**ship's room** cabin
**ship's rope** guy, shroud, tye
**ship's sail** canvas
**ship's servant** steward
**ship's side** beam
**ship's small boat** lifeboat, pinnace
**ship's staff** crew
**ship's stairs** companionway
**ship's station** anchorage, berth, mooring
**ship's steadying device** stabiliser
**ship's steering vane** rudder
**ship's stem** prow
**ship's stern** afterpart, poop
**ship's superstructure** island
**ship's telegrapher** coder
**ship's tiller** helm
**ship's timber** mast, spar
**ship's track** furrow, wake
**ship's underside** keel
**ship's waiter** steward
**ship's window** porthole
**ship that travels along coast** coaster
**ship torpedoed May 1915** Lusitania
**ship used as prison** hulk
**ship used in certain trading** slaver
**ship used to clear away mines** mine-sweeper
**ship with an admiral on board** flagship
**ship with decks reduced** razee
**ship with one mast** sloop
**ship with three masts** bark
**ship with two masts** brig, snow
**shipworm** borer, broma, cobra, lug, teredo
**shipwreck** disaster, ruin
**shipwrecked goods** flotsam
**shipwrecked sailor** castaway, Crusoe
**shiralee** swag
**shire** county, district, province, subdivision

**shirk** avoid, dodge, duck, elude, evade, ignore, malinger, shun, sidestep, skip
**shirk duty** skulk
**shirker** absentee, deserter, dodger, evader, fainéant, idler, loafer, malingerer, procastinator, quitter, slacker, sponger, truant
**shirk work** malinger
**shirt** blouse, chemise, sark
**shirt-collar apparel** necktie
**shirt neck** collar
**shirtwaist** blouse
**shiver** flicker, flutter, quake, quaver, quiver, shake, shimmy, shudder, sputter, tremble, twitter
**shiver fearfully** tremble
**shivering fit** ague, rigor
**shivering tree** aspen
**shivery fever** ague, malaria
**shoal** reef, sandbank, shallow, shelf
**shoal of whales** pod
**shock** agitation, appal, astound, blow, clash, collision, commotion, concussion, disgust, dismay, disturbance, dum(b)found, encounter, impact, numb, offend, paralyse, stagger, startle, stun, stupefy, surprise, trauma
**shock absorber** snubber
**shocked sound** gasp
**shocking** awful, detestable, disgraceful, dreadful, egregious, hideous, horrible, monstrous, odious, scandalising, tragic
**shockingly sensational** lurid
**shock of sheaves** stook
**shock with alarm** astound
**shoddy** careless, contemptible, inconsiderate, inferior, nasty, poor, reprehensible, shabby, sloppy
**shoe** boot, brodekin, brogan, buskin, clog, klomp, loafer, pump, sabot(ine), sandle, sandshoe, scrae, slipper, slipslop, sneaker, tackie, vel(d)skoen
**shoeblack** bootblack
**shoe bottom** sole
**shoe cord** lace
**shoe fastener** lace, latchet
**shoe flap** tongue
**shoe for grinding** muller
**shoe for mule** planche
**shoe front** vamp
**shoeing smith** farrier
**shoe in truss or frame** skewback
**shoelace** lac(h)et
**shoelace tag** a(i)glet
**shoe leather strip** rand, welt
**shoeless** barefoot
**shoe made of a single block of wood** sabot

**shoe made of deerskin or sheepskin**
buckskin
**shoemaker** archer, cobbler,
cordwainer, corviser, cozier, crispen,
farrier, foxer, fudger, shoeman,
soutar, souter
**shoemaker's form** last, tree
**shoe-maker's nail** brade, sparable,
(tin)tack
**shoemaker's patron** Crispin
**shoemaker's thread** lingel, lingle
**shoe-maker's tool** last, awl
**shoemaking** snobbing
**shoe-mender** cobbler
**shoe not fastened on** pump
**shoe of comic actor** baxa
**shoe of ox** cue
**shoe of sledge** hob
**shoe of subway car** pan
**shoe part** heel, insole, last, rand, sole, upper, vamp, welt
**shoe part to urge horses on** spur
**shoe plate** cleat
**shoe-repairer** cobbler, jackman
**shoes and stockings** feet
**shoe-scraping requisite** doormat
**shoe spike** cleat
**shoe stretcher** tree
**shoestring** (shoe)lace
**shoe tip** toe
**shoe to check wheel** drag, skid
**shoe upper** vamp
**shoe used as brake** skate
**shoe with fringed laces** ghillie
**shoe with the toe cut away** peeptoe
**shoe with thick wooden sole** clog
**shoe worn on either foot** straight
**shogun** tycoon
**shoo** beat it, begone, dismiss, scat, scram, voetsek
**shook noisily** rattled
**shoot** bine, bolt, bombard, bud, dart, discharge, eject, emit, fire, hunt, hurl, kill, pepper, pot, practise, propel, ratoon, scion, snipe, spray, sprig, sprout, stolo(n), tendril, throw, volley, wound
**shoot a marble** knuckle, lag, taw
**shoot aside from mark** drib
**shoot at** essay, undertake
**shoot at long range** snipe
**shoot a whale** strike
**shoot down** splash
**shoot ducks** skag
**shooter** blaster, gunman, gunster, pluffer, shotman, skeeter, tirailleur
**shooter marble** taw
**shooter's lure** decoy
**shoot forth** gleam, jet, spire
**shoot from cover** ambush, snipe
**shoot from deer's antler** speller
**shoot gun** fire

**shoot indiscriminately** brown
**shooting** cocking, gunning, gunplay, hunting, potting
**shooting contest** tir (F)
**shooting from ambush** sniping
**shooting iron** pistol, revolver, sixgun
**shooting marble** agate, taw
**shooting match** tir
**shooting objective** target
**shooting pain** pang
**shooting star** cowslip, fireball, leonid, meteor, perseid, primwort, shooter
**shoot moose or deer** yard
**shoot off** tiebreaker
**shoot of plant** bine, gemma, scion, sprig, sprit, sprout, stolon
**shoot of tree** branch, lance, stow, whip
**shoot out** burgeon, chit, dart, eradiate, jut, sprout
**shoot out lava** erupt
**shoot seal** swatch
**shoots used as fodder** browse
**shoot up** spire, spurt
**shop** atelier, boutique, browse, business, buy, department, emporium, factory, market, mart, office, patronise, plant, store, studio, winkel, workshop
**shop clearance** sale
**shop display space** window
**shop in barracks** canteen
**shopkeeper** haberdasher, retailer, storekeeper, trader
**shop messenger** errand boy
**shopper's memo** list
**shopping binge** spree
**shopping centre** mall, plaza
**shopping holdall** bag
**shopping mall** arcade
**shopping mission** errand
**shopping place** arcade, boutique, fleamarket, mall, mart, store
**shopping square** plaza
**shopping wagon** cart, trolley
**shop selling wine** bodega
**shop's nameplate** facia
**shop's supplies** stock
**shop-window awning** blind
**shopworn** used
**shore** bank, beach, buttress, coast, margin, ora (L), rivage, riverbank, seashore, stay, strand, support, waterfront
**shore bird** avocet, wader
**shore grass** marram
**shoreline** coast
**shoreline timber** driftwood
**shore of the sea** beach
**shore recess** inlet
**shore up** bolster
**short** aback, abrupt(ly), blunt, brief, brittle, close, concise, condensed, crumbly, curt, deficient, dwarfish, inferior, laconic, less, low, near, poor, scant(y), scarce, sharp, skimpy, small, stumpy, succinct, suddenly, terse, unacceptable, uncivil, ungracious

**shortage** absence, dearth, deficiency, deficit, inadequacy, incomplete, insufficiency, lack, loss, missing, omission, scarcity, shortcoming, shortfall, want
**short allowance** ration
**short and dumpy** squat
**short and fat** chubby, dumpy, fleshy, plump, podgy, stout, tubby
**short and flat** camus
**short and pithy** sententious
**short and simple sonata** sonatina
**short and strongly built** stocky
**short and sweet** appropriate, apt, brief, concise, direct, pertinent, straightforward, succinct
**short and the long** essence, pith
**short and thick** chunky, dumpy, squat, stocky, stubby, stumpy, trunch(ed)
**short and thickset** nuggety
**short and to the point** curt, terse
**short aria** arietta
**short arm of river** creek
**short article** paragraph
**short article in newspaper** item
**short artillery piece** mortar
**short as of wool** fribby
**short ballet skirt** tutu
**short bark** yap
**short beard** imperial
**short-billed rail** crake, sora
**short blast of breath** puff
**short bolt** stud
**short bombardment** rafale
**short book on a single subject** monograph
**short bout** setto
**short branch** spur
**short break in musical programme** interlude
**short-breathed** winded, pursy
**short broad-bladed oar** paddle
**short broadsword** backsword, cutlass
**short bushman** pygmy
**short catchy phrase** slogan
**short cavalry sword** estoc (F)
**shortchange** swindle
**short chubby person** podge
**shortcircuit** bypass, mar, spoil
**short cloak** cape, talma
**short cloth gaiter** spat
**short club** billy, knobkierie
**short coat** jacket, jerkin, topper, waistcoat
**short comic play** skit
**short comic verse** clerihew

**shortcoming** blemish, defect, deficiency, failure, foible, inadequacy, insufficiency, shortage, sin, want
**short communication** note
**short composition** essay, etude
**short concluding stanza of a poem** envoy
**short conversation** word
**short-coupled** chuffie, chuffy
**short crowbar** jemmy
**short curtain** valance, valence
**short curved sword** scimitar
**short cut** beeline, byway
**shortcut** cutoff
**short delivery trip** errand
**short distance** span, step
**short-distance runner** sprinter
**short division of a Bible chapter** verse
**short doze** catnap
**short drapery** valance
**short dress** mini
**short drive** run
**short-eared owl** momo
**short, elaborately ornamented piece of music** arabesque
**shorten** abbreviate, abridge, abstract, alter, brief, clip, condense, contract, curtail, cut, decrease, digest, diminish, dock, lessen, limit, narrow, prune, reduce, restrict, retrench, shear, trim, truncate
**shortened form** abbreviation
**shortened version of a written work** abridgement
**shortening** butter, fat, lard, suet
**shorten sail** reef
**shorter than the average** shorty
**shortest or longest day** solstice
**shortest route** beeline
**short fall of rain** shower
**short, fast race** sprint
**short fat person** squab
**short fibres** noil
**short film account of recent news** newsreel
**short first sura of Koran** Fatiha(h)
**short flap** tab
**short flight** hop
**short focus** wideangle
**short for ammunition** ammo
**short for nitwit** nit
**short gaiter** spat
**short grass** turf, sward
**short gust of smoke** puff
**short haircut** bob, trim
**shorthand** stenography
**short handbill** flyer
**shorthand system** Gregg, Pitman
**shorthand typist** stenographer
**shorthand writing** stenography
**short heavy stick** bludgeon

**short high-pitched cry** squeak
**short hit** bunt
**shorthorn** newcomer
**short informal letter** chit, note
**short informal speech** talk
**short instrumental refrain** ritornello
**short intensive course of study** seminar
**short intermission** recess
**short jacket** bolero, eton, jerkin
**short jerky movement** bob
**short journey** errand, trip
**short jump** hop
**short-legged dog** basset, corgi, dachshund
**short-legged horse** cob
**short-legged stocking** sock
**short leisurely walk** stroll
**short letter** billet, chit, letteret, line, memo, note
**short light automatic rifle** carbine
**short light sleep** nap, doze
**short line under staff** ledger
**short list** chosen, final, picked, selected, selection
**short literary composition** morceau
**short-lived** brief, decaying, ephemeral, fleeting, flying, fragile, fugitive, hasty, momentary, passing, perishable, quick, short, swift, temporary, transient, transitory, unstable
**short-living animal** ephemera
**short look** glance, glimpse
**short love poem or song** madrigal
**shortly** abruptly, anon, briefly, concisely, curtly, directly, mañana (Sp), presently, quickly, rudely, soon, tersely
**short measure** inch
**short metal pin** rivet
**short missile** dart, javelin
**short musical play** operetta
**short music piece** étude
**short nap** catnap
**short-nap fabric** ras
**short narrative** anecdote, conte, novella, story
**short negligee** camisole
**shortness** brevity, curtness, unlength
**shortness of breath** short-windedness, wheeziness
**short news piece** item
**short note** billet, line
**short notice** haste
**short novel** novelette, novella
**short of** besides, disregarding, except, excluding, inferior, lacking, missing, poor, wanting
**short of breath** panting
**short of cash** moneyless, needy, penniless
**short of full standard** small

**short open spout** lip
**short opera** operetta
**short or simple symphony** sinfonietta
**short passage** pericope
**short pastoral poem** eclogue
**short pause in line of verse** caesura
**short pencil** stub
**short period** spell
**short period of calm** lull
**short period of light sleep** nap
**short period of time** second
**short person** punch
**short piece of drapery** lambrequin
**short pillar** baluster
**short pithy saying** proverb
**short plant stalk** stipe
**short play** skit
**short pleasurable excursion** jaunt, outing
**short poem** eclogue
**short poem set to music** lyric, song
**short poem with witty or satirical ending** epigram
**short pointed beard** goatee
**short pointed stabbing-weapon** dagger, stiletto
**short popular saying** proverb
**short post on traffic island** bollard
**short prayer** benediction, collect, grace
**short projection** stub
**short prose composition on a subject** essay
**short race** dash, sprint
**short raid** foray
**short range** tactical
**short ride** spin
**short rifle used by cavalry** carbine
**short rope ladder** etrier
**shorts** drawers, trunks
**short satirical composition** squib
**short shot in golf** chip
**short shower of driving rain** scud
**short shrift** haste, pause, pitilessness
**short side-whiskers** sideburns
**short-sighted** careless, deficient, hasty, ill-advised, ill-considered, impolite, impractical, improvident, imprudent, injudicious, lacking, myop(t)ic, near-sighted, purblind, sanded, unimaginative
**short-sightedness** myopia, near-sightedness
**short-sighted person** myope
**short, simple instrumental piece** cavatina
**short simple song** ballad, ditty
**short skirt** mini
**short skirt worn by native men** moocha, mutya
**short sleep** (cat)nap, doze, siesta, snooze
**short-sleeved body-garment** tunic

**short-sleeved Indian blouse** choli
**short slender rod** wand
**short snooze** nap
**short sock** anklet
**short sonata** sonatina
**short song** ditty, lay
**short speech at end of play** epilogue
**short spell of pain** spasm
**short spoken** abrupt, curt, terse
**short stabbing weapon** dagger
**short stalk** stipe
**short stem** tigella
**short-stemmed rice** aus
**short stockings** socks
**short stop** break, pause
**short story** anecdote, conte, fable, parable, tale
**short sudden effort** spurt
**short surplice** cotta
**short swim** dip
**short sword** creese, cutlass, dagger, dirk, estoc, kukri, whinger, whinyard
**short syllable** mora
**short tail** bobtail, bun, scut
**short-tailed African eagle** bateleur
**short-tailed bird** breve
**short tail of deer and rabbit** scut
**short-tempered** crusty, fiery, irascible, irritable, snippy, snuffy, touchy
**short-term** floating
**short thick-bladed dagger** stiletto
**short thick club** baton, cudgel, truncheon
**short thick lump of wood** chump
**short time** jiff(y), second, spell, tick, trice
**short trip** excursion, outing
**short trip in an aeroplane** flip, hop
**short twist in rope** kink
**short underground stem** tuber
**short, unpretentious composition** bagatelle
**short version** brief
**short visit** call, chat, coze
**short vowel mark** breve
**short walk** step
**short weapon** dagger, stiletto
**short-winded** asthmatic, pursive, pursy, wheezy
**short-winged hawk** goshawk
**short wool-combings** noil
**short woollen jacket** spencer
**short written note** chit
**Shoshonean Indian** Ute
**shot and shell** ammunition
**shot ball** pellet
**shot from ambush** snipe
**shot from bow** arrow
**shot in billiards** carom, in-off
**shot in the arm** encouragement, excitement, impetus, incentive, motive, provocative, stimulus

**shot in the dark** guess, random
**shots from each side** crossfire
**should** ought, if
**shoulder armour** pauldron
**shoulder bag** haversack, rucksack
**shoulder belt** baldric, bandolier
**shoulder blade** omoplate, scapula
**shoulder loop** epaulet
**shoulder movement** shrug
**shoulder of road** berm
**shoulder one's way** thrust
**shoulder ornament** bars, epaulette, loop
**shoulder to shoulder** abreast, co-operatively, jointly, together, united
**shoulder wrap** cape, manta, shawl, stole
**should the need arise** if necessary
**shout** bay, bellow, bray, burst, call, cheer, clamour, clap, cri (F), cry, ejaculation, holler, howl, outcry, racket, roar, scream, yap, yell, yelp
**shout at bullring** olé
**shout down** drown, heckle, overwhelm, silence
**shout encouragement** cheer
**shouting** bellowing, booing, yelling
**shout loudly** bellow, yell
**shout of applause** acclaim, cheer
**shout of approval** cheer
**shout of derision** hiss, hoot
**shout of disapproval** boo
**shout of encouragement** cheer
**shout of joy** ho, hurrah
**shout of pain** ouch
**shout out** yell
**shout used at sea** ahoy
**shout with pain** bellow
**shove** bump, elbow, force, impel, jostle, nudge, prod, propel, push, shoulder, thrust
**shovel** convey, dig, dredge, excavate, gouge, groove, ladle, load, scoop, spade, spoon, spud, toss, trench, trowel
**shove rudely** elbow
**shove up** brace
**show** accompany, allege, appear, array, assert, conduct, confer, demonstrate, disclose, display, divulge, dramatise, evince, exhibit(ion), feature, guide, indicate, interpret, lead, look, model, pageant, parade, plead, prove, reveal, seem, stage, teach, usher
**show a bold front** oppose, resist, withstand
**show age of** date
**show a lively interest** enthuse
**show amount owed** debit
**show amusement** laugh

**show anger** fume
**show appreciation** applaud, cheer, clap, honour, recognise, reward
**show approval** applaud, clap, nod, smile
**show as evidence** exhibit
**show as false** belie
**show buoyancy** resile
**show-business celebrity** star
**show clearly** evince, prove
**show concern for** care
**show contempt** scoff, sneer
**show contrary to be true** disprove
**show cynical contempt** sneer
**show deference to** respect
**show disagreement** boo, frown, hiss
**show discontent** grouch
**show disdain** sneer
**show disparity** contrast
**show displeasure** pout
**show dogs** bench
**showdown** battle, clash, climax, conflict, confrontation, contest, crisis, culmination, disclosure, discovery, encounter, exposure, publication, revelation, settlement, truth
**show effect** react
**show enthusiasm** drool
**shower** deluge, drizzle, flurry, inundate, mist, rain(fall), spatter, spray, sprinkle, sprinkling, torrent, volley, wet
**shower of ice** sleet
**shower-proof garment** raincoat
**shower with missiles** pelt
**showery weather** raininess
**show evidence of** demonstrate
**show fear** funk, quail
**show feeling** emote
**show fight** defend, defy, retaliate
**show fondness** dote, hug, pet
**show for royalty** command performance
**show forth** blaze, cipher
**show friendliness** greet, smile, welcome
**show gratitude** thank
**show great fondness** dote
**showily** brassily, brightly, brilliantly, cheaply, complexly, complicatedly, elaborately, flamboyantly, flashily, flauntingly, fussily, garishly, gaudily, glaringly, glitteringly, loudly, meretriciously, ornately, ostentatiously, raffishly, richly, tastelessly, tawdrily, theatrically, vulgarly
**showily but falsely attractive** meretricious
**show impatience** champ
**show in** usher, welcome

**showiness** brassiness, cheapness, complexness, elaborateness, flamboyant, flashiness, fussiness, garishness, gaudiness, loudness, ornateness, ostentation, ostentatiousness, raffishness, tawdriness
**showing a desire to possess** possessive
**showing anger** angry
**showing a predilection** preferring
**showing care and effort** diligent
**showing caution** cautious
**showing contempt** sneering
**showing contempt for morality** cynical
**showing continuing allegiance** loyal
**showing deference** respectful
**showing dependence** reliant
**showing directly** ostensive
**showing early development** precocious
**showing enclosure at cattle market** arena
**showing enthusiasm for visionary ideals** quixotic
**showing exuberant energy** energetic
**showing faith** faithful
**showing foresight** provident
**showing friendliness** kind
**showing friendly feeling** amicable
**showing good taste** elegant
**showing gratitude** grateful
**showing great caution** gingerly
**showing great knowledge** profound
**showing great learning** erudite
**showing grief** mournful
**showing joy** happy, pleased
**showing judgement** sage, wise
**showing lack of judgement** injudicious
**showing lack of patience** impatient
**showing moral rectitude** virtuous
**showing no mercy** pitiless, merciless
**showing off** ostentation, swagger
**showing optimism** optimistic
**showing outline only** silhouette
**showing peevish annoyance** petulant
**showing poor taste or style** tacky
**showing practical sense** realistic
**showing rainbow colours** iridescent
**showing signs of effort** laboured
**showing signs of stress and worry** careworn
**showing sorrow** sad
**showing the way** directing
**showing the weakness of old age** senile
**showing to seat** ushering
**showing understanding** sympathetic
**showing unfriendly temper** surly
**showing warmth and friendliness** affable
**showing wisdom** sapiential

**show in public celebration** pageant
**show itself** appear
**show-jumping competition, involving large obstacles** puissance
**showman** actor, busker, clown, compère, conjurer, demonstrator, entertainer, juggler, performer
**show mercy** forgive, pardon, pity, relent, spare
**show much pleasure** drool
**show of boldness** bravado
**show of cowboy skills** rodeo
**show-off** boaster, brag, brandish, egotist, exhibitionist, flash, flaunt, parade, peacock, pose(ur), posture, prank, self-advertiser, sport, swagger(er), swank(er)
**show off** advertise, boast, brag, brandish, demonstrate, display, enhance, exhibit, flaunt, grandstand, parade, strut, swagger, swank
**show of learning** sciolism
**show of light** blink
**show of reason** colour
**show of respect** homage
**show of stockmen's skills** rodeo
**show of vanity** air
**show of water** aquacade
**show oneself** attend, be
**show one's face** approach, come
**show one's teeth** bridle, growl, snap, snarl, spit
**show one's wares** hawk, peddle
**show openly** display, evince, expose
**showpiece** chef-d'oeuvre (F), magnum opus, pièce de résistance (F)
**show pigeon** fantail
**showplace** museum, theatre
**show pleasure** smile
**show position of** meith
**show preference** opt
**show promise** frame, shape
**show publicly** exhibit
**show reluctance** demur
**show resistance to** oppose
**show respect for** regard
**show reverse trend** react
**shows broken bones** X-ray
**show scorn** sneer
**shows good will** kindly, disposed
**show signs of giving way** waver
**show signs of illness** grudge
**show someone the door** eject, oust
**show someone the way** direct
**show sudden reluctance** shy
**show sum owing** debit
**show the bottom** keel
**show the sights** lionise
**show the teeth** grin
**show the way** conduct, direct, guide, lead
**show to another chair** reseat

**show to be false** belie, disprove
**show to be true** prove
**show to seat** usher
**show unkindness** wait
**show up** appear, arrive, come, disclose, disgrace, dwarf, eclipse, embarrass, expose, highlight, humiliate, mortify, pinpoint, reveal, shame, show, unmask
**show without substance** form
**showy** airy, brilliant, colourful, dramatic, dressy, flamboyant, flashy, florid, garish, gaudy, gay, gorgeous, larney, loud, luxurious, magnificent, ornamental, ostentatious, pompous, sensational, spectacular, stagy, striking, superb, tawdry, theatrical, vain, vulgar
**showy attitude** arabesque, pose
**showy but worthless** gaudy, tawdry, trumpery
**showy clothing** finery
**showy daisy** aster
**showy display** éclat, fanfare
**showy dress** finery
**showy exhibition** splurge
**showy flower** anemone, aster, azalea, calla, canna, chrysanthemum, godetia, ixia, lily, orchid, peony, rose, tulip
**showy in appearance** flamboyant
**showy man** spark
**showy march** parade
**showy ornament** gaud, sequin, spangle
**showy shrub** oleander, pincushion, poinsettia
**showy sight** spectacle
**showy talk** bombast, claptrap
**showy trappings** regalia
**showy without taste** tawdry
**shred** atom, bit, fragment, fritter, grain, grate, iota, jot, lacerate, mammock, mite, particle, piece, rag, ribbon, scrap, slice, slither, snippet, strip, tatter, trace, whit, wisp
**shred cheese** grate
**shrew** harpy, harridan, nag, (shrew-)mouse, virago, Xant(h)ippe
**shrewd** acute, astute, cag(e)y, canny, crafty, cunning, cute, discerning, discriminating, ingenious, intelligent, keen, knowing, perceptive, sagacious, sage, sensible, severe, sharp, shrewish, sly, smart, spiteful, troublesome, vixenish, wicked
**shrewd and cautious** canny
**shrewdly** astutely
**shrewdly knowing** cagey
**shriek** cry, howl, scream, screech, shout, shrill, squall, squawk, squeal, stridor, whoop, yell, yelp

**shrill** acute, ear-piercing, forceful, harsh, high(-pitched), intense, keen, loud, penetrating, piercing, reedy, screech(ing), sharp, stridulous, strong
**shrill bark** yap, yelp
**shrill cry** screech, shriek, squeak, squeal
**shrill cry of pain** yelp
**shrill insect** cicada
**shrill of bagpiper** skirl
**shrill pipe** whistle
**shrill scream** shriek
**shrill sound** squeak
**shrill trumpet** clarion
**shrill voice** falsetto
**shrill yelp** squeal
**shrine** aedicule, altar, cairn, cenotaph, chapel, church, gravestone, mausoleum, memorial, monument, obelisk, pillar, reliquary, sanctuary, sanctum, sepulchre, statue, stupa, tabernacle, temple, tomb(stone), tope
**shrine city** Lourdes
**shrine erected in honour of martyr** martyry
**shrine for saint's relics** feretory
**shrine in Texas** Alamo
**shrink** contract, decrease, diminish, dwindle, recoil, retreat, shrivel, withdraw, wither
**shrinkage** constriction, contraction, cutback, decline, decrease, depreciation, diminution, dwindling, ebb, lessening, loss, narrowing, outage, reduction, shortening, shrink, subsidence, waste
**shrink and wrinkle** shrivel
**shrink back** cringe, recoil, resile, withdrew
**shrink with horror** abhor
**shrivel** contort, contract, decay, decline, decompose, decrease, dehydrate, desiccate, deteriorate, fade, perish, pucker, rot, shrink, wilt, wither, wizen, wrinkle
**shrivel up** buckle, pucker, wither, wrinkle
**shroud** conceal, cover(ing), garment, hide, screen, winding-sheet
**shrub** croton, erica, frutex, hebe, oleander, privet, senna
**shrubby border** hedge
**shrub that doesn't lose its leaves** evergreen
**shrug off** disregard, ignore, overlook
**shudder** agitation, convulse, palpitate, pulsate, quake, quiver, rattle, shake, shiver, spasm, splutter, throb, tremble, tremor, twitch, twitter
**shudder with cold** shiver

**shuffle** confuse, disorder, drag, intermix, jumble, rearrange, scrape, scuffle, shamble
**shuffleboard weight** ship
**shuffle off** discard
**shun** abstain, avoid, boycott, bypass, dislike, disregard, dodge, elude, eschew, evade, forbear, forgo, ignore, neglect, ostracise, recoil, refrain, refuse, reject, shelve, shirk, shy, sidestep, snub, spurn
**shun socially** ostracise
**shut** bar, close(d), exclude, fastened, prohibit, sealed, slam
**shut down** cease, close, discontinue, drop, halt, inactivate, stop, strike, suspend, terminate
**shut forcefully** slam
**shut in** barricade, confine, constrain, corral, enclose, fence, imprison, isolate, penned, pent, restrain
**shut inside** enclosed
**shut noisily** slam
**shut off** cut, estrange, isolate, remove, seclude, segregate, separate, sequester
**shut off from sacraments of church** excommunicate
**shut oneself up** seclude
**shut out** banish, bar, conceal, cover, debar, exclude, hide, mask, omit, ostracise, preclude, prevent, prohibit, reject, relegate, repudiate, screen, spurn, veil
**shut the door on** debar, exclude
**shutting** closing
**shutting down** closure
**shuttle** carry, convey, ferry, ship, transport
**shuttlecock racket** battledore
**shut up** cage, confine, coop, gag, hush, immure, impound, imprison, incarcerate, intern, jail, pent, seclude, silenced
**shut with a bang** slam
**shy** afraid, averse, bashful, cant, careful, cast, chary, coy, dart, diffident, fearful, fling, jerk, nervous, reluctant, reserved, retiring, scared, short, throw, timid, timorous, unconfident, wary
**shy flower** violet
**shy look** leer
**shyly** coyly, timidly
**shyness** bashfulness, constraint, coyness, diffidence, discomfort, hesitation, modesty, nervousness, reserve, reticence, self-consciousness, timidity, timidness
**Siamese** T(h)ai
**Siamese coin** att

**Siamese tribe** T(h)ai
**sib** kin, relative
**Siberian antelope** saiga
**Siberian fur** calabar, calaber
**Siberian ibex** tek
**Siberian lake** Baikal
**Siberian language** Enisei, Yenisei
**Siberian mink** kolinsky
**Siberian mongoloid** ta(r)tar
**Siberian mountains** Anadyr
**Siberian peninsula** Taimyr
**Siberian plain** steppe
**Siberian plant** badan
**Siberian river** Lena
**Siberian sledge-dog** samoyed
**Siberian squill** scilla
**Siberian squirrel** miniver
**Siberian swamp** Urman
**Siberian tent** yurt(a)
**Siberian wasteland** steppe
**Siberian windstorm** buran
**sibilant** hissing, sibilatory, sibilous, wheezy, whispery, whistling
**sibilant sound** hiss
**sibilate** hiss, lisp, rasp, wheeze, whisper, whistle
**sibling** brother, sib, sister
**sibling's child** niece
**sibyl** augur, clairvoyant, crystal-gazer, diviner, forecaster, medium, oracle, palmist, predictor, prophet, pythoness, sangoma, seer, soothsayer, sorceress, witch
**sic** thus, so
**Sicilian feud** vendetta
**Sicilian volcano** Etna
**Sicilian wine** marsala
**sick** ailing, airsick, bedridden, carsick, confined, deranged, disabled, disturbed, ill, impaired, indisposed, infirm, nauseated, nauseous, pale, queasy, seasick, unhealthy, unsound, unwell
**sick at heart** heart-broken, inconsolable
**sick bay** infirmary
**sicken** ail, contract, disgust, nauseate, repel, revolt
**sickle** scythe
**sickly** ailing, bilious, decrepit, delicate, faint, feeble, hypochondriac, ill, infirm, invalid, languid, mawkish, nauseous, pale, peaky, peelie-wally (Sc), puny, undernourished, unhealthy, unwell, weak(ly)
**sickly and pallid** anaemic, asthenic
**sickly sentimental** maudlin
**sickly yellow** sallow
**sick people are carried on this** stretcher
**side** angle, aspect, bank, border, boundary, brim, brink, camp, edge, face(t), faction, flank(ing), fringe,

**side away from wind**
gang, hand, incidental, indirect, irrelevant, lateral, lesser, limit, margin(al), minor, oblique, part(y), perimeter, periphery, quarter, region, rim, sector, slant, stand(point), team, verge, view(point)
**side away from wind** lee
**side below waist** hip
**sideboard** buffet, credenza, dresser
**side-boundary in football** touchline
**side by side** abreast, alongside, co-operatively, collateral, conjointly, flanked, jointly, parallel
**side casing of fireplace** hob
**side channel of river** bayou, snye
**side conduit** lateral
**side face** profile
**sideline** activity, diversion, hobby, pastime, periphery, relaxation
**sidelong** indirect, oblique
**sidelong look** leer
**side of building** flank
**side of doorframe** jamb
**side of gem** facet
**side of pork salted and cured** flitch
**side of the head** temple
**side of triangle** hypotenuse
**side-on view** profile
**side petal of blossom** ala
**siderite** chalybite
**sideshow attraction** freak
**sideslip** skid
**sidestep** bypass, circumvent, dodge, duck, elude, evade, skip
**side towards the wind** windward
**sideview** contour, outline, profile, silhouette
**sidewalk** alley, avenue, footpath, lane, path(way), pavement, promenade, trail, walk
**side way entrance** postern
**sideways** askance, askant, askew, asquint, awry, crabwise, edgeways, edgewise, indirect(ly), lateral(ly), oblique(ly), sidelong, sidewise, slanted
**sideways somersault** cart-wheel
**side with** back, befriend, favour, join, support
**sidle** cower, edge, lurk, pad, skulk, slink, slip, smuggle, sneak, steal
**siege** attack, besieging, blockade, closure, encircle, hindrance, impediment, invest, obstacle, obstruction, restriction, stoppage, surround
**Sierra Nevada lake** Tahoe
**Sierra Nevada pass** Donner
**siesta** (cat)nap, rest, sleep, snooze
**sieve** colander, filter, remove, riddle, screen, separate, sift(er), strain(er)
**sieve for clay** laun

**sievelike** ethmoid
**sift** analyse, examine, fathom, filter, investigate, probe, riddle, scatter, screen, scrutinise, search, separate, sieve, spread, strain, winnow
**sifted gravel** hoggin
**sifted husks of corn** bran
**sifter** colander, filter, investigator, sieve, sorter
**sifting implement** sieve
**sigh** aspirate, breathe, complain, exhale, gasp, grieve, moan, sob, sorrow, sough, wail, whine
**sigh for** desire, languish, long, mourn, yearn
**sigh like the wind** moan, sob, sough
**sight** aim, aperçu (F), appearance, aspect, behold, coup d'oeil (F), curiosity, discern, display, distinguish, exhibition, eye(sight), feeling, gaze, glance, glimpse, glisk (Sc), image, inspection, judg(e)ment, ken, look, miracle, observation, observe, opinion, pageant, perceive, perception, ray, scene, scrutiny, see(ing), show, spectacle, spot, view(ing), vision, vista, wonder
**sighting** beholding, discerning, distinguishing, eyeing, observing, perceiving, seeing, spotting
**sighting of shore** landfall
**sightless** amaurotic, blind, eyeless, imperceivable, invisible, unseeable, unseeing, unseen, unsighted, visionless
**sight organ** eye
**sightseeing** touring
**sightseeing trip** tour
**sightseer** globe-trotter, inquisitor, spectator, tourist, traveller, visitor
**sight unseen** blind
**sign** badge, betoken, emblem, endorse, hint, indicate, indication, mark, notice, omen, portent, shingle, signal, signify, symbol, token, trace, vestige
**signal** beacon, command, cue, direction, gesture, guiding, important, indicate, indication, motion, reckon, semaphore, show, sign, warning
**signal agreement by moving head** nod
**signal by bell** toll
**signal code** morse
**signal fire** flare
**signal fire on hill** beacon
**signal for help** SOS
**signal light** beacon
**signal light used at sea** flare
**signalling code** morse
**signalling lamp** Aldis

**signalling light** beacon
**signal on stage** cue
**signal reflected by radar target** echo
**signal station** beacon
**signal success** éclat
**signal system** code
**signal to retire** taps
**signatory** endorser
**signature on cheque** endorsement
**sign away** abandon, forgo, release, remit, sacrifice, waive
**sign cheque on the back** endorse, indorse
**sign gas** neon
**signed document acknowledging debt** IOU
**significance** consideration, force, import, meaning, message, point, purport, sense, weight
**significant** consequential, critical, eloquent, expressive, important, indicative, knowing, material, meaning(ful), momentous, noteworthy, serious, suggestive, vital, weighty
**significant discovery** breakthrough
**significant event in life** milestone
**significantly** critically, eloquently, expressively, importantly, knowingly, materially, notedly, seriously, suggestively, vitally, weightily
**signify** betoken, communicate, connote, convey, denote, evidence, exhibit, express, imply, indicate, intimate, matter, mean, portend, proclaim, represent, show, signal, suggest, symbolise
**signify assent** nod
**signify by some sign** betoken
**sign indicating direction** arrow
**sign indicating phonetic value** diacritic(al)
**sign light** neon
**sign of assent** nod
**sign of authenticity** cachet
**sign of boredom** yawn
**sign of chafing** redness
**sign of cold** sneeze
**sign of disease** symptom
**sign of displeasure** pout
**sign of existence of something** symptom
**sign of fire** smoke
**sign of future event** omen
**sign of something to come** omen, portent
**sign of sorrow** tear
**sign of Zodiac** Aquarius, Aries, Cancer, Capricon, Gemini, Leo, Libra, Pisces, Sagittarius, Scorpio, Taurus, Virgo
**sign on** enlist, enrol, join, register

**sign over** consign, deliver, entrust, negotiate, surrender, transfer, vend
**sign over theatre door** exit
**signpost at cross-roads** fingerpost
**signs of course pursued** spoor, trace
**signs of rain** drops
**sign the back of cheque** endorse, indorse
**sign the first letters of one's name** initial
**sign to convey an order** signal
**sign up** appoint, contract, employ, engage, enlist, enrol, hire, recruit, register, volunteer
**Sikh** akali, mazhabi, singh, sirdar, udasi
**Sikh's headwear** turban
**Sikh title of respect** bhai
**silence** calm, gag, hush, languor, muteness, noiseless, peace, quiescence, quiet(ness), soundlessness, speechlessness, stillness
**silencer** muffler
**silent** catlike, dormant, dumb, frictionless, hushed, mum, mute, noiseless, quiet, soundless, speechless, still, tacit(urn), voiceless
**silent acting** mime
**silent actor** mummer
**silent letter** mute
**silently** dumbly, implicitly, mutely, noiselessly, quietly, soundlessly, speechlessly, stilly, tacitly, taciturnly, voicelessly, wordlessly
**silent monk** Trappist
**silhouette** circumference, contour, delineation, figure, outline, portrait, profile, shadow(graph), skiagraph
**silica gem** opal
**silica mineral** quartz
**silicate of zinc** smithsonite
**siliceous rock used for millstones** burr
**silicic acid in a state of purity** silica
**silicon dioxide** silica
**silicon rich rocks** sial, sima
**silicon steel** stalloy
**silk apron put on bishop's lap at Mass** gremial
**silk cotton** kapok
**silken** delicate, elegant, fragile, luxurious, sericeous, silklike, silky, sleek, smooth
**silken band** sash
**silken fabric** gros
**silken waistband** sash
**silk fabric** alamode, armure, brocade, caffa, gros, honan, moff, ninon, pekin, pongee, samite, sarcenet, satin, sendal, shantung, surah, tulle, velvet
**silk hat** tile

**silk lace of delicate pattern** Chantilly
**silk net** tulle
**silk or wool fabric** armure
**silk stuff wrought with figures** brocade
**silk tape** ferret
**silk thread** floss, tram
**silk veil** orale
**silk veiling** tulle
**silk voile** ninon
**silk weight** denier
**silkworm** bombyx, caterpillar, eri(a)
**silkworm-breeding** sericulture
**silkworm covering** cocoon
**silk worn around the waist** obi (J), sash
**silky** sericeous, silken, sleek, smooth, soft, velvety
**silk yarn maker** throwster
**silky fabric** floss, satin, taffeta
**silky gloss** sheen
**silky-haired hound** Afghan
**silky-haired rabbit** angora
**sill** ledge
**sillier** absurder, dafter, foolhardier, giddier
**silliness** absurdity, absurdness, brainlessness, childishness, daftness, dazedness, fatuousness, folly, foolhardiness, foolishness, frivolousness, giddiness, idleness, immatureness, inanity, meaninglessness, nonsense, pointlessness, ridiculousness, simplicity, stupidness
**silly** absurd, anserine, apish, asinine, childish, daft, dazed, dopy, dull-witted, foolish, frivolous, giddy, idiotic, imbecile, inane, inept, preposterous, ridiculous, senseless, stupid
**silly act** antic
**silly behaviour** antic
**silly bird** goose
**silly blunder** boner, goof
**silly fool** alec(k)
**silly girl** skit
**silly mistake** boob
**silly nonsense** drivel, twaddle
**silly person** ass, dolt, domkop, flibbertigibbet, fool, stupid
**silly sentiment** slush
**silly talk** blah, drivel
**silly, weak-minded person** twerp, twirp
**silt deposit** lo(e)ss
**silver** argent, crumb, luna, slice
**silver coin** asper, drachma, ducat, ecu, florin, obol, real, shekel, thaler, tickey
**silver coin of ancient Greece** drachma, obol
**silver coin of ancient Persia** siglos

**silver coin of ancient Rome** sesterce, sestertius
**silver coin of France** ecu
**silver coin of Germany** thaler
**silver coin of Spain** ducat
**silver orfe** ide
**silver salmon** coho
**silver tray** salver
**silver-white element** calcium
**silvery** argent(ine)
**silvery grey colour** ash
**silvery metallic element** yttrium
**silvery semi-metallic element** arsenic
**silvery-white mineral** talc
**simian** ape, baboon, monkey
**similar** affinity, akin, alike, analogic, analogous, as, assonant, close, comparable, equal, kindred, like, matching, near, quasi, resemblance, resembling, seeming, such, twin, uniform
**similar grain to rosewood** gumwood
**similar in character** kindred
**similar in function** analogue
**similar in some respects** analogous
**similarity** agreement, analogousness, analogy, approximation, coincidence, comparability, concordance, consistency, homogeneity, kinship, likeness, parallelism, resemblance, sameness, semblance, similitude, uniformity
**similarity in structure** affinity
**similarity of colours** match
**similarly** likewise
**similar occurrence** coincidence
**similar things** suchlike
**similar to** like
**similar to a snake** anguine
**similar to whole-wheat flour** graham flour
**similitude** agreement, comparison, counterpart, image, likeness, metaphor, portrayal, reflection, replica, reproduction, resemblance, similarity, simile, simulacrum
**simmer** boil, bubble, burble, foam, gurgle, seethe, stew
**simmer eggs slowly** coddle
**simmer slowly** stew
**simpatico** compatible, congenial, likeable
**simple** artless, basic, clear, common, easy, elemental, elementary, foolish, imbecile, innocent, lucid, manageable, mere, naïve, natural, ordinary, plain, sincere, soft, straight-forward, stupid, unadorned, uncomplicated, uninvolved, unlearned
**simple and basic fashion** classic

**simple and effective** elegant
**simple and elegant** neat
**simple and harmonious in style** classical
**simple as ABC** elementary
**simple boardgame** ludo
**simple country fellow** plaasjapie, yokel
**simple eyes of insects** ocelli
**simple grammar book** primer
**simple in style** chaste
**simple melody** air
**simple narrative** idyll
**simpler** easier
**simple seat** stool
**simple song** ballad, ditty
**simplest** easiest, plainest
**simplest chemical compound** molecule
**simple substance** element
**simpleton** abderite, ass, blockhead, boob, coot, daw, dolt, dunce, fool, gaby, gawk, goose, idiot, muggins, nincompoop, ninny, noddy, oaf, saphead, scoffer, stupid
**simple tune** air
**simple verse** rhyme
**simple vowel** monophtong
**simplicity** candour, clarity, ease, elementariness, modesty, naïveté, naivety, plainness
**simplicity of style** chastity
**simplified form of a language** pidgin
**simply** absolutely, barely, clearly, completely, directly, easily, intelligibly, just, literally, merely, modestly, naturally, obviously, only, plainly, purely, quite, really, sincerely, solely, straightforwardly, totally, undeniably, uneffectively, unpretentiously, unquestionably, utterly, wholly
**simulate** acquire, act, adopt, affect, ape, appropriate, assume, borrow, contrive, copy, duplicate, feign, imitate, impersonate, malinger, mimic, mock, obtain, pilfer, posture, pretend, reflect, sham, steal, take, travesty, use, usurp
**simulation of virtue** hypocrisy
**simultaneous firing of weapons** salvo
**simultaneous occurrence of events** concurrence
**simultaneous sounds of different pitch** chord
**sin** blasphemy, debase, err, evil, fault, godlessness, heinousness, hurt, impiety, injure, lapse, malign, misbehave, misdeed, offence, offend, profanation, profane(ness), sacrilege, transgress(ion), trespass, vice, viciousness, violation, wrong(doing)

**Sinbad's bird** roc
**since** ago, as, because, seeing, subsequently, syne (Sc)
**since Christ was born** AD
**sincere** artless, candid, earnest, frank, genuine, guileless, heartfelt, honest, natural, open, plain, real, serious, true, unaffected, unfeigned
**sincerely** earnestly, genuinely, honestly, really, seriously, truly, wholeheartedly
**sincerity** alertness, candour, earnestness, frankness, genuineness, guilelessness, honesty, probity, seriousness, straightforwardness, truth, wholeheartedness
**sine anno** undated
**sinew** backbone, courage, firmness, flesh, fortitude, health, ligament(um), might, muscle, nerve, physique, robustness, stamina, stoutness, strength, sturdiness, tendon, thew, toughness
**sinewy** adamantine, corded, elastic, fibroid, fibrous, muscular, powerful, robust, ropy, springy, stalwart, steely, stringy, strong, tough, virile, wiry
**sinful** bad, base, blameworthy, corrupt, criminal, culpable, depraved, disgraceful, erring, evil, fallen, falling, guilty, heinous, ignoble, immoral, impenitent, impious, iniquitous, irreligious, obdurate, obnoxious, odious, peccable, shameful, ungodly, unholy, unrighteous, vicious, vile, villainous, wicked, wrong(ful)
**sinfulness** badness, corruptness, iniquitousness, ungodliness, wickedness
**sing** carol, chant, chirp, croon, lilt, lullaby, melodise, serenade, trill, vocalise, warble, whine, yodel
**singe** burn, cauterise, char, grill, scorch, sear, shrivel, sunburn, tan, toast, torrefy
**singed bread** toast
**singer** alto, bass, cantor, diva, soprano, tenor, vocalist
**singer of ballads** balladeer
**sing in Alpine style** yodel
**singing bird** blackbird, canary, lark, nightingale, oriole, pipit, redstart, robin, warbler, wren
**singing girl** alma, almeh
**singing group** choir, chorus, quartet, sextet, trio
**singing of hymns** hymnody
**singing syllable** la, tra
**singing twosome** duo

**singing voice** alto, baritone, bass(o), contralto, mezzo, soprano, tenor
**sing in tune** harmonise
**single** ace, alone, bachelor, celibacy, celibate, distinct, divorced, exclusive, free, husbandless, individual, indivisible, isolated, lone(ly), mateless, monastic, monkish, mono, one, only, particular, personal, rare, real, separate, simple, singular, sole, solitary, solo, spinster, spouseless, unaccompanied, unaided, uncommon, unique, unit, unmarried, unmixed, unwed, wifeless, yae (Sc)
**single action** oner
**single-coloured** monochromatic
**single combat** duel
**single-decker bus** coach
**single element** unit
**single entity** one, unit
**single eye-glass** monocle
**single fact** datum
**single-handed** alone, solo, unaided
**single individual** one
**single item** one
**single man** bachelor
**single-masted vessel** sloop, smack, tartan
**single missile** shot
**singleness** oneness
**single note** monotone
**single number** one
**single oar** scull
**single occurrence** event
**single offspring** only child
**single one** unit
**single out** choose, cull, distinguish, elect, (hand-)pick, isolate, pinpoint, prefer, select, separate, set apart, winnow
**single out beforehand** spot
**single part in contract** clause
**single person or thing** unit
**single piece of information** datum
**single precious stone set by itself** solitaire
**single quantity** unit
**single room in house** apartment
**single run** one
**single run in race** heat
**single step in series** stair
**single step in walking** pace
**single stone used as upright in circles or avenues** monolith
**single-storey house** bungalow, mansion
**single symbol used in speaking** word
**singlet** vest
**single thickness** ply
**single thing** unit
**single time** once
**singleton** one

**single tone** note
**single-track rail** monorail
**single uncomplicated speech sound** phone
**single unit** one
**sing like the Swiss** yodel
**sing lullaby** croon
**singly** alone, apart, distinctly, exclusively, once, purely, separately, solo, specially, unaided
**sing out** bawl, bellow, call, cry, halloo, holler, shout, yell
**sing out in carefree jovial manner** troll
**sing rhythmically** lilt
**sing softly and gently** croon
**singsong intonation in speech** chant
**sing the praises of** applaud, congratulate
**sing to** serenade
**singular** atypical, bizarre, conspicuous, curious, eccentric, eminent, exceptional, extraordinary, individual, odd, oner, outstanding, peculiar, prodigious, queer, rare, remarkable, single, sole, strange, uncommon, unique, unparalleled, unusual
**singular of opus** opera
**singular person** one
**sing unto the Lord** cantate Domino (L)
**sing with lips closed** hum
**sing with quavers** warble
**sinister** adverse, bad, base, corrupt, depraved, disastrous, dishonest, evil, frightening, harmful, left, macabre, malignant, ominous, portending, presageful, threatening, unfavourable, unfortunate, villainous, wicked
**sinister activity** skulduggery
**sinister and evil** dark
**sink** basin, collapse, decline, decrease, degenerate, descend, droop, drop, ebb, engulf, fall, flag, immerse, lapse, merge, plummet, plunge, recede, sag, scuttle, slump, submerge, subside, wilt
**sink a ship** scuttle
**sinkhole** drain
**sinking ship deserter** rat
**sink in mud** mire
**sink in the middle** sag
**sink outlet** drainpipe
**sink through fear** cower
**sink under pressure** sag
**sinless** blameless, clear, exquisite, faultless, flawless, guiltless, immaculate, impeccable, incorrupt, innocent, perfect, precise, pure, saintly, spotless, unblemished, undefiled, unimpeachable, unmarred, unsullied, untainted, virtuous
**sinner** evil-doer, miscreant, offender, transgressor, trespasser
**sinuous** ambiguous, anfractuous, arched, bent, bowed, circuitous, convoluted, crooked, curved, curving, devious, flexuous, humped, indirect, meandering, oblique, roundabout, rounded, serpentine, slinky, snaky, spiral, sweeping, tortuous, turned, turning, twisted, undulating, winding
**sinuous fold of brain surface** convolution, gyrus
**Sioux tent** tepee
**sip** absorb, drink, drop, extract, sample, savour, sup, swallow, taste, thimbleful
**sip continuously alcohol** tipple
**siphon** canal, conduit, pump
**sipper** straw
**sir** guvnor, title
**sire** beget(ter), father, get, guardian, mother, parent, pater, patriarch, procreate
**sired** begat, begot, fathered, got, procreated
**siren** alarm, charmer, enchanting, fascinating, seductive, seductress, sirenic, temptress, vamp
**sirenian** manatee, sea-cow
**sir in Malaysia** tuan
**sissy** cowardly, effeminate, milksop, weak
**sister** abbess, clergywoman, kinswoman, nun, nurse, prioress, relative, sibling, sis(i), soeur (F)
**sister-in-law of Orpah** Ruth
**sister of Aaron** Miriam
**sister of Absalom** Tamar
**sister of Agave** Autonoe, Ino, Semele
**sister of Ahaziah** Jehosheba
**sister of Apollo** Artemis, Diana
**sister of Ares** Eris
**sister of Cordelia** Goneril, Regan
**sister of Iscah** Milcah
**sister of Kohath** Jochebed
**sister of Laban** Rebekah
**sister of Lazarus** Martha, Mary
**sister of Leah** Rachel
**sister of Moses** Miriam
**sister of Nahson** Elisheba
**sister of one's father or mother** aunt
**sister of Osiris** Isis
**sister of Rachel** Leah
**sister of Zeus** Hera, Hestia
**sister's daughter** niece
**sister's son** nephew
**sit** abide, assemble, convene, deliberate, dwell, lie, meet, officiate, perch, pose, preside, repose, rest, settle, stay
**sit as hen on eggs** brood
**sit as judge** adjudicate
**sit as model** pose
**sit at head of table** preside
**sit down together** consult, convene, meet, parley
**site** install, locale, locality, locate, location, place, position, setting, spot, whereabouts
**site for event** venue
**site for large poster** bill-board
**site of Acropolis** Athens
**site of Alhambra** Granada
**site of Blue Grotto** Capri
**site of Disneyland** Anaheim
**site of event** venue
**site of Everest** Nepal
**site of extensive neolithic stone circle** Avebury
**site of final effort** last ditch
**site of Statue of Liberty** Liberty Island
**site of Taj Mahal** Agra
**sit for picture** pose
**sit in judgement** adjudicate, arbitrate, preside
**sitiology** dietetics, sitology
**sit lazily** laze, loll, recline
**sit on** perch, rest
**sit on haunches** squat
**sit on the throne** prevail
**Sitsang person** Tibetan
**sitter** baby-sitter, minder, model, poser, testee
**sitting** assembling, congress, consultation, convening, deliberating, hearing, meeting, officiating, perching, period, posing, presiding, resting, seance, seated, sedent(ary), session, settling
**sitting accommodation** seating
**sitting part of human body** bottom
**sitting-room** boudoir, lounge, parlour
**situate** locate
**situated at foot of mountain** submontane
**situated at front of neck** adam's apple
**situated behind** back
**situated below** nether
**situated below earth's surface** subterranean
**situated beneath** nether
**situated beyond** meta-, trans-, ulterior
**situated in** at
**situated in city** urban
**situated in front** fore
**situated inside a house** indoor
**situated in the middle** medial, median, mesial
**situated near by** neighbouring
**situated on bank of river** riparian

**situated on both sides of spine** loin
**situated on outside** external
**situated on upper part of the side** supralateral
**situated towards centre of body** proximal
**situated within** inward
**situated within walls** intramural
**situation** condition, locale, location, place, plight, position, post, predicament, state
**situation comedy** sitcom
**situation in which no progress can be made** deadlock
**situation of a building** site
**sit up for** await
**six deliveries in cricket** over
**sixfold** sextuple
**six-leafed plant** sexfoil
**six-line stanza** sestet
**six million** trillion
**six-month term** semester
**six on some clocks** VI
**six-shooter item** bullet
**six-sided** hexagonal, sexangular
**six-sided figure** hexagon
**sixteen ounces** pound
**sixteenth century playwright** Marlowe
**sixteenth century Scottish theologian** Knox
**sixteenth century song** madrigal
**sixteenth of pound** ounce
**sixth brightest star in constellation** Zeta
**sixth of florin** fourpence
**sixth satellite of Jupiter** Himalia
**sixth sense** intuition
**sixtieth part of degree** minute
**sixtieth part of hour** minute
**sixtieth part of minute** second
**six times as much** sixfold
**sixty** threescore
**sixty-fourth of semibreve** hemidemisemiquaver
**sixty grains** dram
**sixty minutes** hour
**sixty seconds** minute
**six wives of Henry VIII** Anne Boleyn, Anne of Cleves, Catherine Howard, Catherine of Aragon, Catherine Parr, Jane Seymour
**size** bigness, bulk, catalogue, dimensions, extent, magnitude, measure, proportions, range, volume
**size of bullet** calibre
**size of dose** dosage
**size of type** pica
**sizing material** sealer
**skater's jump** axel
**skating arena** rink
**skating figure** figure-of-eight

**skating game** ice-hockey
**skating surface** ice
**skating venue** rink
**skedaddle** scoot
**skein of yarn** hank
**skeletal disorder** achondroplasia
**skeleton** anatomy, backbone, bones, chassis, diagram, draft, framework, layout, outline, platform, sketch, spine, structure, support, vertebra
**skeleton part** bone, skull
**sketch** act, blueprint, delineate, delineation, demarcate, depict, design, diagram, draft, draw(ing), extracts, illustration, limns, outline, play, representation, scenario, stint, study, trace
**sketched** adumbrated, draw, outlined
**sketch plan** design
**sketchy** bitty, crude, inadequate, incomplete, outline, rough, scrappy, skimpy, unfinished, vague
**skew** biased, distort(ed), slanting, wry
**skewer** brochette, spit
**skewered meat** kebab
**skey** yoke-bar
**skid** arrest, check, coast, deviate, glide, glissade, move, retard, runner, sideslip, skate, skim, slide, slip, swerve, veer
**skier's desire** snow
**skier's obstacle race** slalom
**skier's surface** slope
**skiing behind a towing horse or vehicle** skijoring
**skiing diagonally** traversing
**skiing race** slalom
**skiing slope** piste
**skilful** able, accomplished, adept, adroit, apt, capable, clever, competent, d(a)edal, deft, dext(e)rous, efficient, experienced, expert, facile, gifted, habile, handy, inventive, masterly, nimble-fingered, practised, professional, proficient, qualified, quick, ready, skilled, tactical, talented, trained
**skilful deed** feat
**skilful in hunting** agreutic
**skilfully** ably, adeptly, adroitly, aptly, cleverly, expertly, handily, professionally
**skilfully done** artistic
**skilfully showy** arty
**skilful speaker** orator
**skill** ability, adroitness, apt(itude), art, cleverness, craft, cunning, dexterity, expertise, expertness, facility, finesse, flair, gift, knack, mastership, mastery, proficiency, prowess, style, talent, versatility, workmanship
**skill applied to task** technique

**skilled** able, accomplished, adept, astute, competent, educated, expert, practised, skilful, wise
**skilled at deceiving people** cunning
**skilled craftsman** artificer, artisan, Daedalus
**skilled dock-worker who loads and unloads ships** stevedore
**skilled in horse-riding** equestrian
**skilled in music** musical
**skilled joiner** cabinet-maker
**skilled marksman** sharpshooter, William Tell
**skilled painter** artist, master
**skilled performer of conjuring tricks** conjurer, conjuror
**skilled person** expert
**skilled shot** marksman
**skilled stone worker** mason
**skilled trade** craft
**skilled workman** artisan, carpenter, craftsperson, mason, mechanic, technician
**skillet** (fry)pan
**skill in evasion** lubricity
**skill in handling things** dexterity
**skill in law** jurisprudent
**skill in navigating** seamanship
**skill in needlework** needlecraft
**skill in rowing** oarsmanship
**skill in selling** salesmanship
**skill in wit** repartee
**skill of workman** workmanship
**skim** coast, cream, despumate, fly, glide, remove, scan, skate, skip, spot-check
**skim along** scud
**ski manoeuvre** stem
**skimming milk** creaming
**skimp** pinch, scamp, scant, scrimp, stint, withhold
**skimpy** chary, cheap, economical, incomplete, insufficient, meagre, mean, mere, minute, miserly, niggardly, prudent, scant(y), short, shy, small
**skimpy bodice tied behind the neck** halter
**skin** covering, crust, cutis, (epi)dermis, excoriate, flay, fur, hide, integument, outside, pare, peel, pelt, shell, strip
**skin ailment** acne
**skin alive** chide, scold, upbraid
**skin and bone** scraggy, skeletal, skinny, twiggy
**skin and hair of top of head** scalp
**skin application** poultice
**skin at base of finger-nail or toe-nail** cuticle
**skin blemish** blister, comedo, mole, naevus, papule, rash, wart, wen
**skin brush** loofah

**skin bubble** blister
**skin complaint** acne, eczema
**skin cream** lotion
**skin curing site** tannery
**skin decoration** tattoo
**skin-deep** exterior, inconsiderable, shallow, superficial
**skin disease** acne, dermatitis, eczema, elephantiasis, eruption, erysipelas, herpes zoster, hives, hydrosis, icthyosis, impetigo, leprosy, lichen, lupus, mange, myxoedema, nettlerash, pimple, pityriasis, psoriasis, rash, ringworm, rosacea, scab(ies), seborrhea, shingles, St Anthony's fire, tinea, urticaria, xanthoma
**skin-diver's aid** fins, scuba, snorkel
**skin doctor** dermatologist
**skin eruption** acne, hives, impetigo, rash
**skinflint** churl, harpy, hoarder, lickpenny, miser, moneygrubber, niggard, screw, scrimp, scrooge, tightwad, usurer
**skin from prematurely born calf** hair calf, slink
**skin growth** wart
**skin infection** leprosy
**skin irritation** itch, scabies
**skin jacket with hood** parka
**skin layer** corium, cutis, derm(a), dermis, enderon, epiderm(is)
**skinless anatomical figure** ecorche
**skin medication** liniment
**skinny** attenuate, dermatoid, dermoid, emaciated, epidermal, epidermic, gaunt, lank(y), lean, scraggy, skeletal, skinlike, slender, thin, twiggy, underfed, undernourished, wasted, withered
**skinny person** ectomorph
**skin of drum** drumhead
**skin of fruit** rind
**skin of young beast** kip
**skin oil** sebum
**skin on head** scalp
**skin opening** pore
**skin pigment** melanin
**skin prepared for writing** parchment
**skin problem** acne
**skin rash or eruption** efflorescence
**skins dealer** furrier, tanner
**skin sensitivity** allergy
**skin shed by snake** slough
**skin's outer layer** epidermis
**skin specialist** dermatologist
**skin spot** freckle
**skintight garment** leotard
**skin tincture** iodine
**skin tissue** membrane
**skin trouble** eczema

**skin tuberculosis** lupus
**skin ulcer** boil, rupia
**skin vesicle** blister
**skin with hair** fell
**skin with hair covering the top of head** scalp
**skip** bob, bolt, bounce, busket, caper, dance, disregard, eschew, flit, frisk, gambol, hop(per), jump, miss, omit, prance, rebound, ricochet, run, scamper, spring, trip
**skip around** prowl, range, rove, straggle
**skip like goat** caper, capriole
**skip over** omit
**skip over water** skitter
**skipper** boss, captain, chief, commander, cruise, head, leader, master, navigate, officer, pilot, sail, steer, voyage
**skirmish** affair, affray, battle, brawl, clash, collide, combat, comment, consent, fight, fracas, grapple, incident, mêlée, scrap, scrum, spar, struggle, tussle
**skirt** border, dirndl, edge, flank, kilt, lava-lava, maxiskirt, midiskirt, miniskirt, pareu
**skirt border** hem
**skirt fold** pleat
**skirting board** dado
**skirt-like Malay garment** sarong
**skirt-like Maori garment** puipui
**skirt panel** gore
**skirt's edge** hem
**ski run** piste, schuss
**ski surface** snow
**skit** burlesque, caricature, crowd, imitation, jig, lampoon, number, parody, playlet, satire, sketch, squib
**skite** braggart
**ski trail** piste
**skittish** arch, backward, bashful, coy, demure, excitable, fickle, fidgety, frivolous, jumpy, lively, modest, nervous, playful, prudish, reserved, restive, shy, timid
**skittles** ninepins
**skittles player** keglar
**skiver** truant
**skivvy** dogsbody, drudge, serf, servant, slave, vassal, villein
**skulk** creep, loiter, lurk, malinger, pad, prowl, shirk, slink, sneak
**skull** cranium, head, oar, pate
**skull bone** vomer
**skullcap** beanie, calotte, chechia, kippa, koefiah, yarmulke, zucchetto
**skull cavity** sinus, fossa
**skull point** tylion
**skull skin** scalp
**skunk** polecat, zoril(lo)

**sky** air, atmosphere, azure, cerulean, ciel (F), empyrean, ether, firmament, heaven(s), welkin
**sky blue** azure, c(a)erulean, celeste
**sky-blue dye used in pottery** zaphara
**sky-blue mineral** kyanite
**sky controlled by a country** airspace
**skydiver** parachutist
**skylight** abat-jour, star
**skyline** horizon
**sky regarded as a vault** firmament
**sky twinkler** star
**skyward** above, overhead, up(ward)
**slab at side of pavement** kerbstone
**slab inscribed with laws** Table
**slab of wood or stone at bottom of a door** sill, threshold
**slack** abate, decrease, dilatory, dull, idle, inactive, lax, laziness, lazy, loose(ning), mitigate, moderate, neglect, negligent, quiet, reduce, relax(ed), remiss, shirk, slow(ing), sluggish, weak
**slacken** abate, arrest, check, curb, decrease, ease, limit, relax, release, relent, retard, slack, slow
**slackening** abating, decreasing, diminishing, lessening, loosening, moderating, reducing, relaxing, releasing, relenting
**slacken off** abate, decrease, diminish, fail, flag, lessen, loosen, moderate, reduce, relax, release, tire
**slacken speed** slow
**slack in trigger** creep
**slack off** abate, decelerate, fade, loosen, relax, slacken
**slack of rope** slatch
**slacks** jeans, pants, trousers
**slacks with bib** dungaree
**slag** clinker
**slag ember** cinder
**slag of metals** scoria
**slake** abate, allay, appease, assuage, calm, chill, cool, curb, dampen, decrease, extinguish, fill, gratify, indulge, pacify, please, quench, quiet, reduce, refresh, relieve, salve, sate, satiate, satisfy, stem, still, stimulate, subdue, surfeit, tame, temper
**slalom entrant** skier
**slalom passage** gate
**slam** bang, bump, crash, hit, slap, smash
**slander** abuse, aspersion, berate, calumniate, calumny, censure, curse, decry, defamation, defame, denigrate, denigration, detract, disgrace, falsehood, impugn, invective, libel, lie, malign, obloquy,

**slanderous statement** calumny
scandal, smear, traduce, untruth, vilify
**slang** abuse, argot, cant, dialect, jargon, malign, revile, vituperate
**slangy negative** nope
**slant** angle, bend, bent, bevel, bias, cant, deviate, dip, diverge(nce), grade, imbalance, inclination, incline, keel, lean(ing), oblique, obliquity, pitch, point, position, prejudice, ramp, sheer, skew, slope, sloping, sway, tilt, tip, twist, veer
**slanted** angled, bent, bevelled, biased, canted, coloured, distorted, inclined, leaned, listed, shelved, sloped, tilted, twisted, weighted
**slanting** angled, canted, oblique, sideways, skew, sloping, tilted
**slanting across** aslant, athwart
**slanting bank** berm
**slanting line used to mark division of words** solidus, virgule
**slanting obliquely** bias
**slanting position** cant
**slanting print** italic
**slanting surface** bevel, splay
**slantwise** aslant
**slap** bang, chastise, clout, hit, klap, scud (Sc), smack, spank, wallop
**slapdash** careless, casual, directly, disorderly, haphazard, hasty, hurried, lax, messy, negligent, perfunctory, rash, right, slack, slipshod, sloppy, smack, speedy, thoughtless, unmindful, untidy
**slap down** rebuke, reprimand, restrain, squash
**slap gently** pat
**slap in the face** affront, blow, humiliation, insult, rebuke, rejection
**slap lightly** pat
**slap on buttocks** spank
**slap-up** elaborate, excellent, first-class, first-rate, lavish, luxurious, magnificent, splendid, sumptuous, superb
**slap with hand on ear** box
**slap with the hand** spank
**slash** alter, cut, gash, hack, oblique, reduce, slice, slit, stroke, virgule, wound
**slash open** rip
**slate** berate, blame, censure, criticise, frame, pan, rag, roofing, scold, slat, tablet, thatch, tile
**slate-coloured** blae (Sc)
**slate cutter's hammer** sax
**slate pencil material** tuesite
**slatted window** louvre
**slattern** sloven

**slatternly** bad, careless, dishevelled, disorderly, dissolute, dowdy, frumpish, immoral, loose, messy, promiscuous, shabby, sloppy, slovenly, sluttish, trollopy, untidy, wanton
**slaughter** battle, bloodbath, bloodshed, butcher(y), carnage, decimate, destroy, destruction, execution, exterminate, fusillade, genocide, holocaust, homicide, kill(ing), massacre, murder, noyade, pogrom, purge, scupper, slay, slaying
**slaughter according to Muslim law** hal(l)al
**slaughterhouse** abattoir
**slave** addict, alcoholic, bond(sman), drudge, enslave, enthrall, fag, grind, hack, helot, indentured, labour(er), moil, odalisque, serf, servant, struggle, subjugate, sweat, thrall, toil(er), vassal, workhorse
**slave-driver** oppressor
**slaver** dribble, drivel, drool, saliva, slabber, slobber, spit(tle), toadeat
**slavery** bondage, captivity, enthralment, serfdom, servitude, subjection, toil, vassalage
**slave wages** modicum
**slavishly imitative** apish
**slay** assassinate, butcher, demolish, destroy, eradicate, execute, extinguish, extirpate, kill, murder, obliterate, ruin, slaughter, wreck
**slayer** assassin, butcher, destroyer, executioner, exterminator, gunman, killer, murderer, slaughterer
**slayer of Abner** Joab
**slayer of Absalom** Joab
**slayer of Acastus** Peleus
**slayer of Achilles** Paris
**slayer of Acis** Polyphemus
**slayer of Acrisius** Perseus
**slayer of Adonijah** Benaiah
**slayer of Adonis** Area, boar
**slayer of Debir** Joshua
**slayer of Elkana** Zichri
**slayer of Jezebel** Jehu
**slayer of Minos** Cocalus
**slayer of Ulysses** Telegonus
**sleazy** cheap, decayed, decaying, dilapidated, dirty, faded, flimsy, foul, grubby, loose, low, mangy, nasty, old, repulsive, run-down, seedy, shabby, shoddy, slatternly, slovenly, slummy, sordid, squalid, tawdry, unclean, unkempt, worn
**sled** sledge, sleigh, tode
**sledge** dan, dray, gurry, kibitka, komatik, luge, paddock, pulka, sleigh, slide, toboggan, trolley
**sledge-dog** husky

**sledge for criminals** hurdle
**sledgehammer** smasher
**sled owner's delight** snow
**sleek** burnished, combed, glossy, lustrous, polished, satiny, shiny, silky, smooth, spruce, streamlined, suave, unctuous, varnished, waxed, well-fed, well-groomed
**sleep** catnap, doss, doze, drowse, estivate, hibernate, inactivity, kip, nap, nod, repose, rest, retire, siesta, slumber, snooze, vegetate
**sleep artificially produced** hypnosis
**sleep beyond intended time of waking** oversleep
**sleep briefly** nap
**sleeper's vision** dream
**sleep inducer** opiate, soporic
**sleep inducing** narcotic, opiate, sedative, soporific
**sleep-inducing drug** barbiturate, narcotic
**sleepiness** comatoseness, dormancy, drowsiness, lassitude, latency, lethargy, oscitance, quiescence, slumberousness, somnolence, torpidness, torpor
**sleeping** asleep, calm, catnapping, daydreaming, dormant, dozing, drowsing, heedless, hibernating, idle, inactive, inattentive, musing, napping, quiescent, repose, reposing, resting, slumber(ing), snoozing, snoring, unaware
**sleeping berth** bunk
**sleeping car** pullman, wagon-lit
**sleeping chamber** bedroom
**sleeping noisily** snoring
**sleeping place** bed(room), berth, bunk, cot, crib, futon, hammock
**sleeping place on ship** berth
**sleeping position** prone, supine
**sleeping room** dormitory
**sleeping sickness** encephalitis
**sleeping-sickness fly** tsetse
**sleeping suit** pyjamas
**sleepless** insomnious
**sleeplessness** alertness, insomnia, insomnolence, restlessness, vigil(ance), vigilantness, wakefulness, watchfulness
**sleep lightly** doze
**sleeplike state** trance
**sleep noisily** snore
**sleep on it** meditate, think
**sleep producing** soporific
**sleep quietly** slumber
**sleep through summer** aestivate
**sleep through winter** hibernate
**sleep vision** dream
**sleepwalker** noctambulist, somnambulist

**sleepwalking** noctambulation, noctambulism, somnambulation, somnambulism
**sleepwear** nightie, pyjamas
**sleepy** asleep, dormant, drowsy, dull, fatigued, heavy, hypnotic, inactive, latent, lazy, lethargic, mesmeric, narcotic, nodding, opiate, quiet, slow, sluggish, slumb(e)rous, slumbery, somnolent, soporific, tired, torpid, yawning
**sleepy and inattentive** oscitant
**sleepy reflex** yawn
**sleet** hail, ice, snow
**sleeve card** ace
**sleeved glove** gauntlet
**sleeve edge** cuff
**sleeveless cloak** cape
**sleeveless garment** aba, cape, cowl, dolman, mantle, poncho, vest
**sleeveless jacket** jerkin, vest
**sleeve without shoulder seam** raglan
**sleigh** dray, jumper, sled(ge), toboggan
**sleight** artifice, cunning, dexterity, illusion, magic, skill, sorcery
**sleight of hand** cheating, chicane, conjuration, deceit, deception, feint, fraud(ulence), hocus-pocus, juggling, legerdemain, magic, manipulation, prestidigitation, thaumaturgy, trickery
**sleight of hand artist** juggler, legerdemainist, magician
**slender** attenuate, breakable, feeble, fine, flimsy, fragile, gracile, inadequate, insufficient, lank(y), lean, lissome, meagre, narrow, reedy, scanty, shapely, sleek, slight, slim, slivery, small, spare, skinny, stalky, svelte, sylphic, tenuous, thin, trim, trivial, twiggy, weak, willowy, wispy
**slender and straight** virgate
**slender bar** rod
**slender bristle** awn
**slender candle** taper
**slender cord** line
**slender curl of hair** tendril
**slender decorative candlestand** torchère
**slender fish** eel, gar, pipefish
**slender lemur** loris
**slender mark** line
**slender metal bar** rod
**slender metal piece** needle, pin
**slender missile** arrow, dart
**slender mountain peak** pinnacle
**slender nail** brad
**slender plant organ** roothair, stolon, tendril
**slender pointed instrument** stiletto, stylet

**slender spar** yard
**slender spine** seta
**slender stick** rod, wand
**slender support of leaf** stalk
**slender sword** rapier
**slender thread** filament, film
**slender turret** minaret
**slender unsegmented worm** nematode
**slender woman** sylph
**slept for twenty years** Rip van Winkle
**sleuth** detective, dick, PI, (private) investigator, sleuth-hound
**slew** swerve, veer
**slice** carve, chunk, cleave, cut, divide, fragment, hunk, knife, pare, part, piece, portion, section, segment, separate, sever, share, slab, sliver, split, whittle
**slice meat** carve
**slice of bacon** rasher
**slice off pieces** whittle
**slice of fruit coated in batter** fritter
**slice of meat** collop, escalope
**slice of meat for grilling** steak
**slice or joint of meat rolled up** roulade
**slice up** carve
**slick** adroit, clever, cunning, deft, dext(e)rous, glib, neat, plausible, polished, quick, sharp, skilful, sleek, smooth, specious
**slicker** mackintosh, raincoat
**slide** coast, decline, deviate, fall, glide, glissade, lapse, plane, progress, skate, ski(d), slew, (slide)slip, slither, slue, transparency, tumble, veer
**slide backwards** regress
**slide rule** gauge
**sliding ballet step** glisse
**sliding bar** bolt
**sliding barrier** door
**sliding brass instrument** trombone
**sliding compartment** drawer
**sliding machine part** piston
**sliding mass of snow** avalanche
**sliding receptacle** drawer
**sliding thread holder** shuttle
**sliding window frame** sash
**slier** craftier
**slight** affront, confuse, delicate, disdain, disregard, distract, feeble, flimsy, fragile, frail, ignore, insignificant, insult, light, little, microscopic, miniature, minikin, minute, neglect, paltry, remote, ruffle, slender, slim, slur, small, snub, subtle, superficial, thin, tiny, trifling, trivial, upset, weak
**slight amount** grain, sign, trace, vestige
**slight aversion** distaste
**slight blow** dab, rap

**slight cold** chill
**slight colour** tinge
**slight craziness** dottiness
**slight decline** dip
**slight depression** dent, dint, hollow
**slight earthquake** tremor
**slight error** lapse, slip
**slightest amount** vestige
**slight haze** film
**slight illness** ailment, complaint, disorder, indisposition, pain
**slight incline** glacis, slope
**slight knowledge** inkling, smattering
**slightly cold** cool
**slightly crazy** daffy, daft, dotty, gaga, goofy, wacky
**slightly damp** moist
**slightly depressed spot** areola
**slightly drunk** jolly, squiffy, tiddly, tipsy
**slightly hungry** peckish
**slightly ill** indisposed
**slightly indecent** racy, risqué (F)
**slightly intoxicated** tipsy
**slightly leavened bread, in a large flat leaf shape** naan, nan bread
**slightly mad** batty
**slightly open** ajar
**slightly sour** acescent, acidulous
**slightly sparkling wine** perlé
**slightly sticky** tacky
**slightly tipsy** merry
**slightly unwell** indisposed
**slightly warm** tepid
**slightly wet** damp, moist
**slightly windy** breezy
**slight mental disorder** psychoneurosis
**slight mist** haze
**slight mistake** lapse, slip
**slight movement of head** nod
**slight offence** fault, peccadillo
**slight quarrel** spat, tiff
**slight regret** compunction
**slight ridge on surface** stria
**slight shake** joggle
**slight slip** lapse
**slight sourness** acescence
**slight splash** spatter
**slight suggestion** inkling
**slight taste** sip
**slight tint** tinge
**slight trace** soupçon
**slight twist** kink
**slim** crafty, diet, lean, meagre, narrow, paltry, scanty, shapely, slender, slight, small, svelte, thin, trifling
**slim and sinuous** slinky
**slim cigar** cheroot
**slime** defilement, dirt, dust, filth, gleet, grime, impurity, marsh, mess, mire, muck, mud, mush, ooze, slop, sludge, slush, smudge, squalor, squash, swill

**slimmed down** condensed, summarised
**slimmer's regimen** diet
**slimy** clammy, glutinous, miry, oozy, servile, unctuous, viscous
**sling** cast, catapult, chuck, dangle, fling, hang, heave, hurl, lob, pitch, suspend, swing, throw, toss
**slingshot** catapult
**slink** couch, creep, lurk, prowl, pussyfoot, sidle, skulk, slip, sneak, steal
**slip** bloomer, blunder, boob, certificate, coupon, creep, cutting, disappear, elude, err(or), escape, failure, fault, faux pas, glide, hide, indiscretion, lapse, misadventure, mistake, omission, oversight, petticoat, piece, skate, skid, slide, slink, slip-up, strip
**slip attached to object** label
**slip away** elapse, evade
**slip away from** dodge, elude, escape
**slip back** lapse
**slip backwards** regress, relapse
**slip by** elapse
**slipknot** noose
**slip of memory** lapse
**slip of the memory** lapsus calami (L)
**slip of the tongue** blunder, faux pas, indiscretion, lapse, lapsus linguae, slip, stupidity, tactlessness
**slip out of course** swerve
**slipper** pantoffle
**slippery** crafty, dangerous, deceitful, dishonest, disloyal, elusive, fragile, glossy, greasy, lubricated, oily, perilous, skiddy, sleek, slick, smooth, snaky, soapy, synovial, treacherous, unsafe, unsteady, untrustworthy, waxed
**slippery fellow** eel
**slippery with cold** icy
**slip placed on a stringed instrument to soften the tone** mute
**slip sideways** skid
**slip smoothly along** slide
**slip through one's fingers** escape
**slip up** blunder, err(or)
**slit** cut, gash, incision, knife, lance, opening, pierce, rent, rip, slash, split, tear
**slither** glide, shuffle, skid, slide, slink, slip, snake
**sliver** atom, bit, chip, cut, fraction, fragment, grain, helping, mite, morsel, part(icle), piece, portion, remnant, scrap, segment, share, shiver, shred, slice, splinter
**slobber** drool, slabber, slaver, splutter, sputter
**sloe** blackthorn

**slog** effort, exertion, hit, plod, slave, slug, toil, wallop
**slogan** byword, catchword, logo, motto, phrase, saying, shibboleth, watchword
**slogan of the cautious** safety first
**sloop-like vessel** dandy
**slop** dabble, hogwash, mire, muck, orts, overflow, paddle, plash, rubbish, scraps, shower, slosh, spatter, spill, splash, spray, spread, sprinkle, squirt, strew, swill, wade, waste, wet
**slope** acclivity, bank, brae (Sc), cant, descent, fall, glacis, glissade, gradient, incline, lean, pitch, ramp, rise, scarp, slant, tilt, upgrade, uprise
**slope backwards** recede
**slope downwards** decline, dip
**sloped walkway** ramp
**slope from one level to another** ramp
**slope gradually** shelve
**slope of roof** curb
**slope on which ships are built** slip
**slope upwards** ascend, batter, climb
**sloping** aslant, bevelled, cant, falling, inclined, inclining, leaning, oblique, pitching, rising, slanting, tilting
**sloping board along a gable roof** barge-board
**sloping channel** chute
**sloping ground** declivity
**sloping letters** italics
**sloping mass of débris at the base of a cliff** scree
**sloping path** ramp
**sloping position** cant
**sloping road** grade
**sloping roadway** ramp
**sloping sharply** steep
**sloping side of hill** hillside
**sloping side of square sail** leech
**sloping surface** ascent, bevel, incline, ramp, slope
**sloping type of print** italic
**sloping walkway** ramp
**sloppy** careless, clumsy, inattentive, messy, slipshod, slovenly, sludgy, slushy, splashy, unkempt, untidy, watery, weak, wet
**sloppy person** slob, sloven
**slosh** beat, blow, slush, thrash
**slot** aperture, channel, groove, hole, latch, notch, opening, position, receptacle, rut, slit, space, trail
**sloth** acedia, ai, edentate, faineance, idleness, inaction, inactivity, indolence, inertia, laxity, laziness, lethargy, listlessness, negligence, otiosity, phlegm, slackness, sluggishness, stagnation, supineness, torpor, unambitiousness

**slothful** apathetic, comatose, drowsy, dull, fainéant, idle, inactive, indolent, inert, languid, lazy, lethargic, listless, shiftless, skiving, slack, sleepy, slow, sluggish, somnolent, torpid, work-shy
**slothfully** lazily
**slouch about** lop
**slouch hat** stetson
**slough** bog, exuviate, fen, marsh, mire, morass, quagmire, quicksand, slue, swamp, vlei
**sloven** slattern, slob
**slovenliness** carelessness, disorderliness, looseness, slackness, untidiness
**slovenly** careless, disorderly, frowzy, heedless, loose, messy, negligent, raunchy, slack, slapdash, slipshod, sloppy, unkempt, untidy
**slovenly person** slattern, slob, slut
**slow** adagio, deliberate, dragging, dull, gradual, hinder, impede, indolent, laggard, late, lazy, leisurely, lento, moderate, overdue, poky, retard, sluggish, snail-like, tardy, tarrying, tedious, unhurried
**slow, affected diction** drawl
**slow at learning** dunce
**slow at understanding** obtuse, stupid
**slow capsule** spansule
**slowcoach** slowpoke, snail
**slow creature** snail, tortoise
**slow dance** pavan(e)
**slow disintegration** erosion, rust
**slow down** brake, decelerate, retard
**slow down from tiredness** flag
**slow drip** leak
**slow easy gallop** canter
**slower than sound** subsonic
**slow flow** ooze, trickle
**slow gait** saunter
**slow gallop** canter
**slow gastropod** slug, snail
**slowing device** brake
**slow in music** adagio
**slow in progress** tardy
**slowish run** trot
**slow learner** moron
**slow Lutheran hymn** chorale
**slowly** adagio, backwardly, conservatively, dawdlingly, dully, easily, gradually, inactively, largo, lately, lazily, leisurely, lentamente, lento, lingeringly, ploddingly, ponderously, slackly, sleepily, tediously, unhurriedly
**slowly running** trotting
**slow mollusc** snail
**slow mournful song** dirge
**slow-moving** creepy
**slow-moving boat** tub

**slow-moving creature** slug, snail, tortoise
**slowness** backwardness, conservativeness, deadness, deliberateness, denseness, dilatoriness, dimness, dullness, easiness, gradualness, lateness, laziness, leadenness, leisureliness, obtuseness, ponderousness, protractedness, quietness, slackness, sleepiness, sluggishness, stupidness, tameness, tardiness, tediousness, thickness
**slow of perception** obtuse
**slow on the uptake** dim-witted, oafish, stupid
**slow person** slowcoach
**slow regular trot** jogtrot
**slow reptile** tortoise
**slow Scottish dance** strathspey
**slow ship** bucket
**slow South American ballroom dance** tango
**slow Spanish dance** saraband
**slow speech** drawl
**slow stately dance** minuet
**slow tempo** largo
**slow to act** tardy
**slow to understand** obtuse
**slow train** local
**slow traveller** snail, tortoise
**slow trot** jog
**slow up** lag, retard
**slow-witted** dense, stupid
**sludge** clay, contamination, defilement, dire, dirt, dung, excrement, excreta, faeces, filth(iness), foulness, garbage, grime, muck, mud, nastiness, ooze, ordure, pollution, refuse, sewage, silt, slime, squalor, uncleanness
**sluggard** drone
**sluggish** apathetic, crawling, dopey, inactive, indifferent, inert, languid, languorous, latent, lazy, lethargic, lifeless, logy, lumpish, pap, slack, slow, stagnant, supine, torpid, unstirred, wan
**sluggish flow** ooze
**sluggishness** acedia, apathy, drowsiness, dullness, heaviness, inactivity, indolence, inertia, languidness, languor, laziness, lethargy, otiosity, sloth, somnolence, torpor, worthlessness
**sluggish state** torpor
**sluggish waterway** bayou
**sluice** channel, clough, clow, conduit, ditch, drain, duct, flume, gool, gutter, launder, penstock, pipe, sloot, slush, spillway, trench, trough, tube, waste, weir

**sluice gate in a dyke** aboideau, aboiteau
**slum** dump, ghetto, hovel, mess, pigsty, shack, shanty(town), warren
**slum area** ghetto
**slumber** abeyance, catnap, dormancy, doze, drowse, hibernate, kip, nap, repose, siesta, sleep, snooze, suspense
**slumbering** asleep, dozing, drowsing, reposing, resting, sleeping
**slum building** tenement
**slum dweller** guttersnipe
**slum dwelling** hovel
**slump** collapse, crash, decline, depression, deteriorate, downturn, failure, fall, plunge, recession, sag, sink, trough
**slur** affront, asperse, aspersion, blot, calumniate, calumny, discredit, disgrace, disparage, ignore, insult, lisp, mark, overlook, reproach, slander, slight, smear, stain, stigma
**slur over** elide
**slush** mess, muck, slime, slop, slosh, soppiness, squash
**slush fund** bribe
**slut** baggage, broad, drab, hag, harlot, hussy, jezebel, mantrap, minx, piece, slattern, sloven, strumpet, tart, temptress, trollop, wanton, whore
**sluttish** disreputable, drabby, frowzy, mangy, ragged, run-down, scruffy, seedy, shabby, slatternly, slovenly, slutty, sordid, squalid, tattered, untidy
**sly** arch, artful, clandestine, crafty, cunning, deceitful, devious, foxy, insidious, leery, roguish, secret(ive), shrewd, sleekit (Sc), stealthy, wily
**sly and spiteful** cattish
**sly animal** fox
**sly girl** minx
**sly glance** leer
**sly grin** smirk
**sly look** leer, ogle, peek
**slyly derogatory** snide
**slyness** artfulness, astuteness, cleverness, craftiness, cunningness, deviousness, furtiveness, guile(fulness), shiftiness, stealthiness, subtleness, wiliness
**sly peep** peek
**Sly role** Rambo, Rocky
**smack** chastise, clap, clout, flavour, hit, klap, slap, spank, tap
**smack in the eye** blow, rebuff, repulse, setback
**smack one's lips** anticipate, covet, devour, enjoy
**small** abbreviated, ashamed, bantam, brief, dainty, delicate, diminutive, exiguous, feeble, few, humble, lepto-, little, low, meagre, mean, meek, micro, mini, minor, minute, modest, narrow, paltry, petit (F), petty, pigmy, puny, scant(y), secondary, selfish, skimpy, slender, slight, soft, stingy, teeny, thin, tight, tiny, trifling, trivial, ungenerous, unimportant, weak, wee (Sc)

**small abode** hut
**small abscess on gum** gumboil
**small advertisement** ad
**small African antelope** duiker, oribi
**small African bushman** pigmy, pygmy
**small African desert rodent** jerboa
**small African monkey** grivet
**smallage** celery
**small air bubble** bleb
**small air pocket** bubble
**small airport** aerodrome
**small American Indian pony used by cowboys** cayuse
**small American leopard** ocelot
**small American pike-perch** sauger
**small American rattlesnake** massasauga
**small amount** bit, crumb, dab, driblet, few, iota, jot, little, minim, mite, modicum, pennyworth, pittance, rap, scanty, smattering, smidgen, snatch, trifle, whit
**small amount of liquid imbibed** sip
**small amount of money** doit, sou, tickey
**small amphibious creature** newt
**small anchor** grapnel, kedge, killick, killock
**small anchovy** anchoveta
**small and cramped** poky
**small and dainty** petite
**small and delicate** mignon
**small and elegant** bijou
**small and feeble** puny
**small and numerous** miliary
**small and spruce** dapper
**small and sturdy** chunky
**small and thick** dump(t)y
**small and weak** puny
**small animal** runt, shrew
**small animal popular as pet** hamster
**small antelope** duiker, duyker, gazelle, klipspringer, oribi, suni
**small antlike insect** termite
**small appliance** gadget
**small aquatic edible decapod crustacean** shrimp
**small arachnid** mite
**small arch** archlet
**small arctic animal** sable
**small arctic rodent** lemming
**small area** areola, plot, quadrate
**small area of still water** pond
**small armadillo** peba, peva

small arm of the sea  inlet
small arms workman  gunsmith
small article  item, paragraph
small article of virtue  bibelot
small artistic object  objet d'art (F)
small Asian deer  muntjac
small Asian rutaceous tree  citron
small auditory organ  ear
small Australian short-tailed wallaby
 quokka
small Australian tree  quandong,
 quantong
small aviary  birdcage
small bag  pouch, purse, sachet,
 satchel, wallet
small ball  bead, pellet, pill
small band  trangle
small banner  banderole, banneret,
 pennant
small bar  bistro
small barn  shed
small bar of metal  billet
small barracuda  sennet, spet
small barrel  keg
small basin for porridge  porringer
small basket  punnet
small bay  cove, creek, inlet, voe
small beads made of shells  wampum
small beam  scantling
small bear  cub
small beard  goatee
small bed  bassinet, cot, crib, pallet,
 truckle
small beer  trash, trivia
small beetle  curculio, ladybird, weevil
small bell  tinkler
small binoculars for use at opera or
 theatre  opera glasses
small bird  daw, finch, junco, linnet,
 manakin, mossie, pewee, pipit, quail,
 robin, sparrow, starling, tit, tody,
 tomtit, weaver, wheatear, white-eye,
 wren
small bit  piece, smidgen
small bite  nibble, nip
small biting insect  flea, gnat, midge
small bit of bread  crumb, morsel
small black and white songbird
 stonechat
small black tailless breed of dog
 schipperke
small bladder  cyst, vesicle
small blister  bleb, vesicle
small block of wood  nog
small blunder  slip
small blunt rounded snout whale
 porpoise
small board used in spiritualistic
 experiments  planchette
small boat  canoe, cog, coracle, cot,
 dinghy, dory, nacelle, sampan,
 shallop

small bodkin  eyeleteer
small body of soldiers  picket, platoon
small body of water  mere, pond, pool
small body travelling through space
 meteor
small bomb  grenade, petard
small bone  ossicle
small bone of the fingers or toes
 phalanx
small book  booklet, pamphlet
small book for memoranda  notebook
small booth  kiosk
small bottle  phial, vial
small bouquet  nosegay, spray
small box  pyxis
small box for holding tea  caddy
small boy  lad, nipper, pik(kie), tad
small branch  shoot, sprig, twig
small bread  bun, croute, roll
small breed of dog  chihuahua, corgi,
 dachshund, (maltese) poodle, peke,
 pom, terrier
small breed of fowl  bantam
small breed of pony  Shetland
small British coin  penny
small brook  rill(et), run
small brown bird  wren
small brushlike tuft of hairs especially
 on bee's leg  scopa
small bubble in glass  boil, seed
small bud  pip
small buffalo  anoa
small building apart from house
 outhouse
small building for Christian worship
 chapel
small bunch  wisp
small bunch of flowers  nosegay, posy
small bundle  fascicle, wad
small bundle of straw  wisp
small buoy used as marker in
 deep-sea fishing  dan
small burrowing animal  mole
small bus  minibus
small bush  shrub
small bush fruit  berry
small bushy aromatic herb  hyssop
small but assertive person  bantam
small but elegant and tasteful  bijou
small but fatal weakness  Achilles heel
small but tangible  certain
small cable  hawser
small café bar  bistro
small cage  hutch
small cake  baba, biscuit, bun, cookie,
 madeline, muffin, tart
small candle  taper
small canine  lapdog
small cape on dress  bertha
small carnivorous mammal
 mongoose, shrew
small carpet  rug

small carriage  cabriolet, fiacre
small carriage for a child
 perambulator
small carved shell  cameo
small case  etui, valise
small cask  firkin, keg, tub
small catarrhine monkey  rhesus
small cat-like carnivore  civet
small cave  grotto
small cavity  alveolus, locule, loculus,
 pore
small cavity in rock  vugh, vug(g)
small cell  cellule, utricle
small Channel Isle  Sark
small chapel for private worship
 oratory
small chicken  bantam, pullet
small child  baby, bairn, infant, lightie,
 mite, moppet, nipper, piccanin,
 pik(kie), toddler, tot, tyke,
 whipper-snapper
small chimney  flue
small chip or plastic basket  punnet
small chubby naked boy representing
 cupid  amoretto
small chunk  gob
small church  chapel
small circle  circlet
small circle of light around moon
 corona
small circular cut of meat  medallion
small citrus fruit  mandarin, na(a)rtjie,
 tangerine
small civet  rasse
small cloth inset  gusset
small coal  slack
small codfish  codling
small coffee-cup  demitasse
small coin  at, cent, mite, obolus,
 penny, rap, soldo, sou
small common flower  daisy
small community  town, village
small compartment  cubicle
small container  caddy, canister
small container for liquid  cruet
small cord  string
small cormorant  shag
small country house  cottage
small country villa in Russia  dacha
small crab  fiddler
small crawling animal with many legs
 centipede, millepede, songololo
small crease  wrinkle
small creature  mite, scallywag
small crevice  chink
small crow  daw
small crown  coronet
small crucifix  pax
small crustacean  shrimp
small cube used in games  die
small cucumber  gherkin
small cup  tassie

small cupboard  closet
small cuplike body  calicle
small cut  (s)nick
small daffodil  jonquil
small dagger  poniard, stiletto
small dam  weir
small dark-furred Arctic mammal  sable
small dark growth on the skin  mole
small dark-purple plum  damson
small decorative object  objet d'art (F)
small deer  roe
small deerlike animal  chevrotain
small deer male  roebuck
small defended place  fort
small delicate fish  vendace
small demon  devilet, imp
small demonstration  demo
small dent in chin  dimple
small depression  dent, dimple, dint
small desk at which the litany is read  faldstool
small destroyer  frigate
small detached piece  rag, scrap
small devil  imp
small diagram within a larger one  inset
small dining-room  diner
small dipterous fly  drosophila
small disc  roundel
small distance  centimetre, inch, millimetre
small district  canton
small dipteran  gnat, muggie
small diving bird  murrelet
small division of a country  canton
small dog  feist, peke, pekinese, pom, pug, pup(py), spaniel, terrier, toy, wappet
small dome on roof  cupola
small domestic wooden objects  treen
small donkey  burro
small draught  tass
small draught of alcoholic drink  dram, tiff
small dried grape  currant, raisin
small drink  dram, nip, noggin, peg, sip, snort, tass, tot
small drinking vessel  pannikin
small drop  blob, guttule
small drop of liquid  nip
small drought-resistant tree  wilga
small drum  bongo, tabor(et), tabret, tambourine
small dry carpel  ach(a)ene
small duck  teal
small ductless gland at base of brain  pituitary
small dumplings served with a sauce  gnocchi (I)
small dynamo  magneto
small earthenware jar  pipkin

small earthquake  tremor
small economical car  runabout
small edible freshwater fish  loach
small edible nut of tropical tree  cashew
small edible sea snail  whelk, winkle
small eel  grig
small Egyptian snake  asp
small electric generator  magneto
small electric kitchen appliance  kettle, toaster
small elevation  hill, mound
small enclosed field  croft
small enclosure  coop, fold, paddock, pen
small engine  mule
small entertainment  peepshow
small entrance hall  vestibule
smaller  constricted, contracted, less, minor, punier, shrunk, unimportant
smaller area of ocean  sea
smaller in size  less
smaller of two groups  minority
smaller part of brain  cerebellum
smaller party  minority
small error  slip
smaller than an atom  subatomic
smaller than a small farm  smallholding
smaller than a town  village
smaller version  miniature
smallest  least, tiniest
smallest piglet  tantony, runt
smallest planet  Mercury
smallest possible amount  ace, iota
smallest species of wild goose  brent
smallest state in USA  Rhode Island
smallest tidal rise  neap
smallest unit in computer's memory  bit
smallest whole number  one
small European barracuda  spet
small European country  Andorra, Luxembourg, Monte Carlo
small European legless lizard  slow-worm
small European tree  holly, mastic, medlar
small evergreen tree in New Zealand  ngaio
small evil-smelling animal of weasel family  polecat
small exclusive group of people  clique
small explosive shell  grenade
small explosive sound  pop
small extinct volcanic cone  puy
small fairy  elf
small falcon  kestrel, merlin
small farm  croft
small farmer  bywoner, crofter, peasant
small fast sailing ship  cutter
small fat person  dumpling

small fat river-fish  chub
small feather  tectrix
small fertile area  oasis
small fibre  fibril
small field  paddock
small fillet of beef in strip of suet  tournedos
small fillet steak  filet mignon (F)
small finch  linnet, serin, sparrow
small firearm  culverin, pistol
small firework  squib
small fish  anchovy, dace, darter, fingerling, fry, ide, harder, maasbanker, minnow, orfe, sand-eel, sardine, shiner, smeelin, smelt, sprat
small fishing-boat  yawl, smack
small fish with rich flavour  anchovy
small flag  banneret, pennant
small flake of soot  smut
small flap  tab
small flat  flatlet
small flat bread  chapat(t)i, chupatty
small flat container for face-powder  compact
small flat island in river  ait
small flat loose-skinned deep-coloured orange  mandarin
small flat metal disk  washer
small flat moulding  fillet
small flat scale  flake
small flattish dough cake  scone
small fleet  flotilla
small floor covering  mat
small flower  erica, floret, spiraea
small flute  fife, piccolo
small fly  gnat, midge, muggie, noseeum
small folded card for informal letter  brieflet, notelet
small food fish  pilchard, sardine
small format newspaper  tabloid
small fort  redoubt, sconce
small four-stringed guitar of Hawaiian origin  ukelele
small four-wheeled cab  fiacre
small fowl  bantam
small fox  fennec
small fraenum  fr(a)enulum
small fragment  crumb, shiver, sliver, splinter
small fragments  smithereens
small French river  Selle
small freshwater duck  teal
small freshwater fish  ablet, minnow
small frog  tadpole
small fruit  achene, achenium, akene, berry, cherry, grape, olive, sultana
small fruit basket  pottle
small fry  kids, lighties, minnow, nobodies
small furrow for seeds  drill

small furrow in the skin wrinkle
small furry rodent kept as pet hamster, mouse
small gallery kitchenette
small game bird partridge
small gannet booby
small garden bird mossie, robin, sparrow
small garden tool trowel
small garment apron
small gate wicket
small gear cog
small gibbon hoolock
small girl's companion doll
small glass bottle cruet, phial, vial
small glass vessel ampule
small glazed earthenware pot gallipot
small globe globule
small glowing particle spark
small gnat midge, muggie
small goat kid
small goby mapo
small goose brent
small graceful antelope gazelle
small grain granule
small green vegetable pea
small green vegetable marrow courgette (F)
small grey goose brent
small greyhound whippet
small groove stria
small group of animals pod
small group of people covey
small group of soldiers commando, platoon
small group of whales pod
small grove shaw
small growth at back of nose adenoids
small growth of mucous membrane polyp
small guitar banjo, ukelele
small hall lobby
small hammer gavel
small hand-drum ghomma
small hand-grip tab
small hand-mill for pepper quern
small hand-saw tenon
small hand-tool gimlet
small harbour cove, creek
small hard bed pallet
small hard inflamed spot on skin pimple
small hard mass forming in gall bladder gallstones
small hard particles grains
small hard seed grain, pip
small, hardy variety of horse galloway
small harmless lizard gecko
small harmonium melodeon
small harpsichord spinet

small harpsichord-like instrument virginal
small hat cap, tam, toque
small hawk hobby, kestrel, kite, merlin
small-headed nail brad
small herbivorous rodent vole
small heron aigrette, bittern
small herring alewife, brisling, sild, sprat
small herring-like marine fish sardine
small hill butte, hillock, knoll, koppie, monticule, mound, tump
small, hinged case holding a picture or keepsake locket
small hole eyelet, pore
small hollow areola, dent, fossette
small horned ruminant goat
small horse cob, genet, jennet, pony, tit
small horse-drawn carriage gharri), gharry
small horse for riding nag
small hotel inn
small hound beagle
small hours morning
small house box, cabin, chalet, cottage, flat, hut(ch), lodge, maisonette, pondok, rondavel, shack
small house lizard gecko
small imaginary being fairy
small in breadth narrow
small Indian monkey rhesus
small inlet cove, ria
small in number few
small insect ant, aphid, flea, midge, mite, muggie
small insects infesting vines vine fretter
small insect with pinchers at the tail earwig
small interstice areola, areole
small in worth poor
small island ait, cay, eyot, isle(t)
small island near Italy Elba
small isolated land isle
small item of bric-à-brac curio
small jumping insect flea
small kangaroo joey, wallaby
small kiang onager
small kind of cuttlefish squid
small kind of slate scantle
small kitchen kitchenette
small knob knobble, nub
small knotty tumour ganglion, node, nodule
small lace loop picot
small lake mere, pond, pool
small landowner yeoman
small Laotian coin at
small large-bore pistol derringer
small larklike bird pipit
small lead pellet shot
small leaf of paper leaflet

small ligament checking motion of organ fr(a)enum
small light anchor kedge
small light fast ship caravel
small light rowboat skiff
small light thin piece flake
small lilac flower lavender
small limbless creeping creature worm
small liquid measure dram
small live coal ember
small lizard anole, eft, eit, gecko
small loaf bap, bun, roll
small lobe lobule
small lockable cupboard locker
small locomotive dolly
small long-handled pot skillet
small long-handled spade paddle
small loop eyelet
small loop of thread picot
small loose stones scree
small lorry bakkie, van
small lory lorikeet
small low island cay, key
small lump node, nodule, nub
small machine part cog, gear, pin
small mallet gavel
small mammal mole, mouse, rabbit, shrew
small map inset
small marine animal coral, salp(a), salpid
small mark dot, iota, spot, tittle
small marking fleck, speckle
small marrow courgette
small mask domino
small mass lump, wad
small mass surrounded by sea isle
small mat for drinking glass coaster
small matter minor
small meal snack
small measure centimetre, gill, inch, millimetre, noggin, tot
small mechanical tool gadget
small medicine ball pill
small Mediterranean coasting vessel felucca
small merganser smeath, smee, smew
small metal bar billet
small metal drinking-cup pannikin
small metal spike nail
small metal vessel can
small middle Eastern coin piastre
small migratory bird quail, swallow
small military assignment detail
small military formation commando, squad
small-minded bigoted, envious, hidebound, insular, intolerant, mean, narrow(-minded), petty, rigid, ungenerous, verkramp

**small-minded person** meanie, meany, verkrampte
**small mischievous sprite in Irish folklore** leprechaun
**small misdemeanour** peccadillo
**small miserable dwelling** hovel
**small missile** arrow, dart
**small monkey** marmoset, titi, vervet
**small mosaic tile** tessera
**small motorcycle** moped, scooter
**small mound of earth** noggin
**small mound thrown up by mole in burrowing** molehill
**small mountain** hill
**small mountain lake** tarn
**small mouthful of liquid** sip
**small mouthlike opening of lower animals** stoma
**small muddy pool** puddle
**small mug** cup, noggin
**small musical instrument** harmonica, ocarina, piccolo
**small musical sound** tinkle
**small nail** brad, sprig, tintack
**small napkin** doily
**small narrow spade for weeding** spud
**small narrow strait** gut
**small needle case** etui
**smallness of quantity** paucity
**small newspaper** tabloid
**small New Zealand tree** ngaio
**small node in plant** nodule
**small noise** pop, tap
**small notch** nick
**small note** billet, memo
**small notebook** jotter
**small novel** novelette
**small number** few, handful, paucity
**small number of soldiers** commando, squad
**small object** mite, trifle, trinket
**small ocean** sea
**small of the back** loins
**small oily fruit** olive
**small one-horse vehicle** ekka
**small one-seeded fruit** achene
**small opening** cranny, gap, pore, slot
**small open pavilion** kiosk
**small operation** op
**small orange-like fruit** na(a)rtjie, tangerine
**small ornament** bead, charm, knick-knack, trinket
**small ornamental case** locket
**small oval drupe** olive
**small ovenproof dish** cocotte
**small owl** owlet
**small ox of Celebus** anoa
**small package** packet, parcel
**small packet** sachet
**small pad of fibrous material** wad
**small pair of pincers** tweezers

**small pale yellow grape** sultana
**small pancake** crêpe, crumpet, fritter, pikelet
**small parakeet** budgerigar
**small parasite** aphid, aphis, flea
**small parcel** packet
**small parrot** parakeet, paroquet
**small part** atom, bit, detail, fraction, piece, snippet
**small particle** atom, fleck, granule, mite, mote, speck
**small particle in plant cytoplasm** lipoplast
**small particles** dust, powder, sand
**small part in play** bit
**small part of** detail
**small party** squad
**small patrol vessel** vedette, vidette
**small pearl** pearlet
**small pedal-operated pleasure boat** pedalo
**small peg** spigot, spill
**small perforation** pinhole
**small pericarp** achene
**small permanent dark spot on human skin** mole
**small person** child, dwarf, fry, infant, midge, piccanin, pik(kie), poppet, runt
**small Peruvian dog** alco
**small pest** bug, gnat, muggie
**small pet dog** lapdog
**small pheasant** bobwhite, chukar, francolin
**small photo in large one** inset
**small piano** spinet
**small pickle** gherkin
**small pie** patty, tart
**small piece** bit, chip, collop, fragment, morsel, particle, patch, scrap, snip(pet), strip, swatch
**small piece of bread or toast with a savoury topping** canapé
**small piece of butter** pat
**small piece of cloth** rag, strip, swatch
**small piece of earth** hill(ock), koppie
**small piece of food** morsel
**small piece of fried bread served with soup** croûton
**small piece of land** plot
**small piece of lava thrown from volcano** lapillus
**small piece of live coal** ember
**small piece of meat** cutlet
**small piece of metal used in enamelling for decoration** paillette
**small piece of practical information** hint
**small piece of rock** stone
**small pieces of wood** kindling
**small pier** jetty
**small pig** piggy, pigling, runt
**small pill** globule, pil(l)ule

**small pin** lill
**small pincer-like instrument** tweezers
**small pincers** pliers
**small pipe in body** tubule
**small pistol** derringer
**small pit on the belly** navel
**small plane surface** facet
**small planet** asteroid
**small plant growing in masses on a surface** moss
**small platform** podium
**small pleasure-boat** dinghy
**small plot of land** patch, plat
**small plug** pledget, spile
**small plum** damson
**small pocket for watch** fob
**small point** dot, iota, jot, tittle
**small pointed instrument** awl, needle, pin, sprig
**small pointed missile** dart
**small pointed wheel on a horseman's spur** rowel
**small poisonous snake** adder, krait, massasauga, viper
**small pond** pool
**small pony** nag
**small pool** pond
**small portion** bit, dram, drop, fragment, modicum, morsel, remnant, scantlet, sip, soupçon, taste
**small portion of liquor** dollop, heeltap
**small portmanteau** valise
**small portrait** miniature
**small portrait-case** locket
**small pot** nog
**small pouch** saccule
**small powerful boat** tugboat
**smallpox** variola
**small prawn** shrimp
**small predator** shrew, weasel
**small private chapel** oratory
**small private room** boudoir, closet
**small projectile** bullet
**small projecting ridge** knurl
**small projection** tab
**small prominence at entrance of external ear** tragus
**small protuberance** wart
**small pruning-shears** secateurs
**small puff-pastry case** bouchée
**small puncture** pinprick
**small quail** bobwhite
**small quake** tremor
**small quantity** bit(e), dram, dreg, driblet, drop(let), handful, iota, lick, little, modicum, morsel, ounce, scanty, sip, smidgen, spot, sprinkle, taste, thimbleful, wheen
**small quantity of spirits** nip
**small quarrel** jar, runin, spat
**small racer** kart
**small racket** battledore

small radio portable
small rag lapje, lappie
small ragged child urchin
small rascal elf
small rat-like rodent hamster, vole
small receptacle inro
small recess bole, niche
small red or purple spot on the skin petechia
small religious group sect
small remaining quantity remnant
small rented farm croft
small report pop
small restaurant bistro, café, coffeeshop, tearoom
small ribbed melon cantaloup(e), spanspek
small rich cake eclair, madeline, torte
small riding horse nag, pony
small ring annulet, ringlet
small river brook, creek, runnel, stream
small riverfish dace, trout
small river isle ait, eyot
small road avenue, lane
small rock stone
small rocky island Skerry
small rodent mouse, squirrel, vole
small rod for plucking strings of lyre plectrum
small roll bun
small room cabin, cell, closet, den, stall
small room leading to main one anteroom
small room used as kitchen kitchenette
small root radicle
small rorqual sei
small rough Canadian horse Canuck
small rough dwelling hut, pondok, shack
small round boat coracle
small round bread muffin, roosterkoek
small round cake scone
small rounded hill knoll, mamelon
small rounded lump nodule
small rounded pebbles shingle
small roundish boat coracle
small roundish stone pebble
small round mark dot
small round pastry cake filled with cream choux
small round piece of meat noisette
small round skullcap worn by certain ecclesiastics zucchetto
small round tower roundel
small rowboat cog
small ruffle frislet
small rug mat
small rural house cottage
small sac follicle, saccule
small sack rucksack, satchel
small saddle horse palfrey

small sail jigger, royal
small sailing vessel smack
small salmon peal, skirling
small salmon-like fish smelt
small salty fish anchovy
small sandpiper duntin, stint
small saw tenon
small scale model miniature
small scented lozenge cachou
small scrap shred, snippet
small scythe sickle
small seafish harder, gosnick, maasbanker, pilchard, sardine, sprat
small seal signet
small sealed jar ampoule
small seed ovule
small seedless raisin currant
small segmented animal with many legs centipede, millipede, songololo
small segment of compound bulb clove
small separate sleeping compartment cubicle
small sesamoid bone in mammals fabella
small shabby bistro estaminet
small shallow boat cockle
small shallow vessel cupel
small share moiety
small shark dogfish, tope
small sharp broad-headed nail tack
small shellfish cockle, shrimp, whelk
small shelter cabin, shack
small shelter for dog kennel
small shield buckler, ecu
small Shiite sect Ismaili
small shining particle spark
small ship boat, felucca, lugger, sloop
small shoot sprig, twig
small shop selling clothes and items of fashion boutique
small short-handled axe hatchet
small shot pellet
small shot of whisky dram
small shovel scoop
small shrill flute fife
small shrimp-like creature krill
small shrubby plant erica, heath
small side road bylane
small singing bird whinchat
small slab tablet
small sledge luge
small slender fish minnow
small smooth area facet
small snacks of raw fish and cold rice sushi (J)
small snail brad
small snub-nosed dog peke, pug
small snug compartment cubby-hole
small social insect ant, bee
small sofa settee
small soft bread loaf bap (Sc)

small soft round stone fruit cherry
small song bird chiff-chaff, tit, wren
small soup basin porringer
small South African antelope klipspringer, oribi, steenbok
small South American rodent chinchilla
small South American squirrel monkey tamarin
small South American tiger cat margay
small spade spaddle, spittle
small spade-like instrument for weeding spud
small Spanish horse jennet
small spar sprit
small sparkling object spangle
small sparrow-like songbird accentor
small species of kangaroo wallaby
small species of merganser smew
small species of shark tope
small speck dot, fleck, nit, speckle, stain
small sphere drop, spherule
small spicy sausage chipolata
small spike nail
small spine spinule
small spiny fish stickleback
small spirit stove etna
small spit or skewer brochette
small sponge cake with jam or coconut filling madeleine
small spore sporule
small spot dot, freckle, speck(le)
small spot of colour fleck
small spot on radar screen blip
small spotted cat ocelot
small squares of pasta ravioli
small squirrel monkey tamarin
small stain blot, spot
small stalk pedicel, stemlet
small stand tabo(u)ret
small star starlet
small statue figurine, statuette
small steps on toe points (pas de) bourrée
small stick of cosmetic for colouring lips lipstick
small sticks for lightning fire kindling
small stipule stipel
small stirrup-shaped bone in ear of mammal stapes
small stoatlike animal mink
small stone pebble
small stone arch squinch
small stoneless fruit berry
small store shoppe
small stove etna
small streak of smoke wisp
small stream beck, bourn, brook, burn, creek, rill(et), rivulet, runnel, spruit, streamlet

**small strip of fish deep-fried** goujon (F)
**small strip of paper** slip
**small sturdy motor vehicle** buggy, Jeep
**small sturgeon** sterlet
**small suitcase** valise
**small sum** mite
**small sum of money** cent, dime, farthing, pence
**small support for golf ball** tee
**small surface** facet
**small surgical knife** scalpel
**small surgical pincers** forceps
**small swallow-tailed flag** pennon
**small sweet or savoury snacks** antipasto, dim sum, mezze
**small swine** piggy
**small swivelled wheel** caster
**small symphony-orchestra** sinfonietta
**small table** stand
**small table brazier** tessie
**small table mat** doily
**small tablet** pellet
**small-tailed amphibian** newt
**small tailless breed of dog** schipperke
**small tailless nocturnal lemur** loris
**small talk** (chit-)chat, chitter-chatter, gossip, natter, poppycock, prattle
**small tarred line** marline
**small tart** tartlet
**small task** errand
**small taste** sip
**small tavern** cabaret
**small telescope** spyglass
**small tender horny place on toe** corn
**small thin bone separating nostrils** vomer
**small thing** snippet
**small thin person** wisp
**small thorn** prickle
**small three-legged tea table** teapoy
**small three-masted Mediterranean vessel** xebec
**small tile** tilette
**small tilthammer** oliver
**small timber** scantling
**small-time** inconsequential, insignificant, minor, petty, unimportant
**small tin cup** pannikin
**small tinkling bell** tintinnabulum
**small tin vessel** canteen
**small tip, gift or reward** bonsella
**small tipple** dram
**small toe** minimus
**small tool for plucking strings of stringed musical instruments** plectrum, quill
**small tooth** denticle
**small tower** turret
**small town** burg, dorp, hamlet

**small tray** coaster
**small tree** bonsai, seedling
**small tree branch** twig
**small triangular bone at base of spinal column** coccyx
**small tropical fruit** lime
**small truck** bakkie, ute
**small tub** gawn
**small tube** tubule
**small tube to transfer fluid from one vessel to another** pipette
**small tuft of hair** scopula, tate
**small tumour** nodule, pimple, polyp, pustule, wen
**small tumour of dentine** odontoma
**small tumour of the skin** pimple
**small twig** sprig
**small two-winged biting insect** gnat
**small type of onion** shallot
**small type of rusk** zwieback (G)
**small unglazed window** bole
**small untanned hide** kip
**small vacation house** cottage
**small valley** combe, coomb, dale, dell, dene, glen, vale
**small variety of palm** palmetto
**small variety of pear** seckel
**small vase** patella
**small vein** venule
**small venomous snake** adder, asp
**small verse** versicle
**small very dark sour cherry** morello
**small vesicle** follicle
**small vessel with handle** skillet
**small vial** ampoule
**small village** dorp, hamlet
**small villa in a park** villino
**small violin** kit
**small viper** asp
**small wading bird** knot, phalarope
**small wager** flutter
**small waggon** cart
**small wallaby** quokka
**small wallet** satchel, scrip
**small warship** gunboat, monitor, sloop
**small water-bird** moorhen
**small watercourse** spruit
**small waterfall** cascade
**small wave** ripple, wavelet
**small weakness in person's character** foible
**small weight** carat, dram, gerah, gram, mite, ounce, rider, scruple
**small wheel** caster, castor
**small wheeled cart** trolley
**small wheeled handcart** barrow
**small whirlpool** eddy
**small width of** narrow
**small wild ox of Celebes** anoa
**small wild plant** celandine
**small wind instrument** flageolet, harmonica, ocarina

**small window** dormer
**small window as for tickets** guichet (F)
**small windowed room** oriel
**small window over door** fanlight
**small wingless jumping insect** flea
**small wood** bosk, copse, grove, holt, spinney
**small wooded area** grove
**small wooded hollow** dell
**small wooden cask used for butter** firkin
**small wooden domestic object** treen
**small wooden house** hut
**small wooden peg** pin, spile
**small wooden tub** kid
**small woodpecker** piculet
**small worker insect** ant
**small writing desk** davenport
**small young pig** piglet
**small youth** lad, piccanin, pik(kie)
**small zoo** menagerie
**smalto** tessera
**smarmy** fulsome, ingratiating, oily
**smart** adept, adroit, affront, agile, alert, bright, brisk, chic, clever, elegant, fashionable, hurt, insult, intelligent, nifty, pain(ful), poignant, posh, prompt, quick, severe, sharp, shrewd, spruce, sting, stylish, swish, voguish, wound
**smart and fashionable** snappy
**smart blow** biff, rap
**smarten** adorn, beautify, groom, plume, polish, preen, prettify, titivate, trim
**smarten up** groom, neaten, spruce (up), tidy, tit(t)ivate
**smarting pain** sting
**smartly** acutely, adeptly, agilely, aptly, astutely, brightly, briskly, cannily, chicly, cleverly, effectively, elegantly, finely, impertinently, ingeniously, intelligently, keenly, modishly, neatly, nimbly, quickly, readily, saucily, sharply, shrewdly, snappily, sprucely, stylishly, trimly, wittily
**smartly groomed** chic, elegant, fashionable, modish, stylish
**smartness** alacrity, intelligence, style
**smart painful blow** stinger
**smart remark** wisecrack
**smart saying** quip
**smart slight blow** rap
**smart stamp of the foot** appel
**smash** bash, batter, blow, break, catastrophe, collision, crash, crumble, crunch, crush, dash, defeat, demolition, destroy, destruction, failure, impact, jolt, overthrow, ruin, shatter(ing), slap, smack, smashing, splinter, wreck

smash in  bash
smashing a skull  braining
smash into  bump
smear  asperse, bedaub, bedim,
    blacken, blot(ch), blur, calumniate,
    calumny, coat, cover, daub, dirty,
    libel, patch, plaster, slander,
    smudge, soil, splotch, stain, streak,
    sully, tarnish, traduce, vilification,
    vilify
smear with oil or unguent  anoint
smell  aroma, bouquet, breath, detect,
    discern, feel, flavour, fragrance,
    fume, hint, inhale, mephitis, nose,
    odour, olfaction, perceive, perfume,
    redolence, reek, scent, sense, sniff,
    stench, stink, trace, trail, whiff
smell a rat  suspect
smelling  f(o)etid
smelling like musk  musky
smelling of beer  beery
smelling of damp  fusty
smelling of goat  capric
smelling salts  sal volatile
smell unpleasantly  reek
smelly  airless, dank, decayed, frowsty,
    fusty, mildewed, mouldy, musty,
    odorous, old, olid, stale, stuffy
smelly creature  skunk
smelting oven  furnace
smile  beam, benediction, countenance,
    favour, fleer, grimace, grin, laugh,
    simper, smirk, snicker, support
smile affectedly  simper, smirk
smile broadly  beam, grin
smile coyly  simper
smile derisively  sneer
smile in a silly way  simper
smile playfully  chuckle
smile scornfully  smirk, sneer
smile toothily  grin
smile widely  beam
smiling  cheerful, riant
smirch  blacken, calumniate, decry,
    defame, defile, denigrate, dishonour,
    malign, slander, smear, soil, stain,
    sully, taint, tarnish, traduce, vilify
smirk  appearance, aspect, expression,
    frown, giggle, grimace, grin, leer,
    look, pout, scowl, simper, smile,
    sneer, snicker
smite  affect, afflict, assail, assault,
    attack, batter, beat, besiege, blast,
    box, chastise, crash, demolish,
    desolate, devastate, gut, hammer,
    haunt, hit, knock, lash, pelt, pound,
    prostrate, punish, shatter, slap,
    smack, smash, storm, strike, thrash,
    thwack, wreck
smith's iron block  anvil
smith who shoes horses  farrier
smith who works in iron  blacksmith

smoke  blaze, burn, flame, flare, flash,
    flicker, fume, glow, mist, pollution,
    reek, smog, vapour
smoke and fog  smog
smoke and haze  smaze
smoked beef  pastrami
smoked fish  fumado
smoked glass  shade
smoked herring  kipper
smoked salmon  lox
smoked sausage  frankfurter, vienna
smoke duct  flue(way)
smoke executed in the sky by an
    aeroplane  skywriting
smokeless explosive  cordite
smoker's accessory  cheroot,
    cigar(ette), lighter, match, pipe,
    tobacco
smoker's requisite  ashtray
smoker's shop  tobacconist
smoke stack  funnel
smoke vent  chimney
smokily gloomy  murky
smoky fog  smog
smooch  lallygag, lollygag, neck, pet,
    vry
smooth  agreeable, better, bland, calm,
    courteous, courtly, easy, elegant,
    equable, even, flashy, flat, flowing,
    glabrous, glib, level, peaceful,
    polished, regular, silken, sleek, slick,
    soft(en), soothe, suave, tonsured,
    undisturbed, unruffled
smooth and concise  terse
smooth and rounded  terete
smooth and shiny  sleek
smooth-barked tree  beech
smooth briskly  rub
smooth compact type of kaolin
    lithomarge
smooth fabric  ciré
smooth flattering speech  blarney
smooth golf club  iron
smooth hard coating  enamel
smooth hard-wearing linen fabric
    holland
smoothie  spieler
smoothing tool  file, plane
smooth in manner  bland
smoothly  blandly, calmly, equably,
    evenly, faxilely, flatly, fluently,
    glassily, glibly, glossily, horizontally,
    legato, levelly, mildly, peacefully,
    persuasively, plainly, pleasantly,
    regularly, serenely, slickly, softly,
    soothingly, steadily, suavely,
    tranquilly, unbanely
smoothly and evenly  legato
smoothly polite  suave, urbane
smooth paint  enamel
smooth piece of grass  lawn
smooth surface  plane

smooth the way  pave
smooth thread  lisle
smooth-tongued  glib
smooth white sauce made with stock
    velouté (F)
smother  asphyxiate, blanket, choke,
    conceal, envelop, garotte, hide,
    mask, muffle, quiet, shroud, soften,
    squash, stifle, strangle, suffocate,
    suppress, veil
smothering  choking, concealing,
    hiding, muffling, repressing, snuffing,
    stifling, strangling, suffocation,
    suppressing
smouldering ash  ember
smoulder with rage  fume
smudge  begrime, blemish, blot, blur,
    daub, dirty, mar, smear, smirch,
    smut(ch), soil, stain, streak, sully
smudgy  smeary
smug  cocksure, complacent,
    conceited, content, glossy, neat,
    overconfident, overproud, priggish,
    proud, self-opinionated,
    self-satisfied, smart, smooth, spruce,
    superior, vain
smuggled goods  contraband
smuggled letter  kite
smugness  complacency
smug smile  smirk
smut  bawdiness, coarseness,
    corruption, crudity, depravity, dirt,
    filth, foulness, grime, immodestly,
    impurity, indecency, indecorum,
    indelicacy, lechery, lewdness,
    obscenity, pornography, profligacy,
    ribaldry, roughness, soot,
    uncouthness, unevenness, vileness,
    vulgarity
smutty chimney deposit  soot
snack  bite, break, nibble, refreshment,
    sandwich, titbit
snack bar  buffet, cafe
snack booth  kiosk
snacks  bites, breaks, nibbles, titbits
snag  bit, block(ade), breakdown, catch,
    complication, damage, delay,
    difficulty, drag, drawback, embargo,
    hindrance, hitch, impediment,
    inconvenience, knot, objection,
    obstacle, obstruction, problem,
    projection, prominence, setback,
    stoppage, stump, tangle, tear
snail  escargot, slowcoach
snail-like  slow
snake  adder, anaconda, asp, boa,
    boomslang, coil, crawl, cribo, curl,
    entwine, (king) cobra, krait, loop,
    mamba, meander, python, ramble,
    rinkhals, serpent, spiral, stray, stroll,
    taipan, traitor, twist, viper, wind,
    worm, wreathe, wriggle, zigzag

**snake charmer's clarinet** been, pungi
**snake-killing mammal** mongoose
**snake-like** colubrine, sinuous
**snake-like fish** eel
**snake or lizard** reptile
**snake poison** venom
**snake's cast skin** slough
**snake's sound** hiss
**snake's tooth** fang
**snaky** angry, anguine, bad-tempered, disloyal, eely, faithless, insidious, malicious, noxious, sinuous, subtle, toxic, treacherous, underhanded, venomous, virulent
**snall opening** foramen
**snap** break, catch, cinch, clasp, click, crack, fasten, nip, photo(graph), pop, spell
**snapdragon** antirrhinum
**snap of the fingers** fillip
**snap one's fingers at** defy, flout, scorn
**snap out of it** recover
**snapper** food fish, jocu
**snapping beetle** skipjack
**snappish dog** cur
**snappy** brisk, cross, hasty, irritable, modish, natty, smart, snappish, testy
**snappy comeback** repartee, retort, return, riposte
**snapshot** photo
**snapshot book** album
**snapshot taker** camera
**snap up** grab, grasp, nab, seize
**snare** ambush, bait, (booby) trap, catch, deadfall, diversion, drum, enigma, entangle, entrap, gin, hook, lure, mine, net, noose, pitfall, plant, springe, waylay, web
**snare user** trap
**snarky** irritable, short-tempered
**snarl** complain, complicate, confuse, confusion, entangle, growl, grumble, involve(ment), knot, tangle
**snarl-up** confusion, jumble, mess, mix-up, muddle, tangle, traffic jam
**snatch** catch, clench, confiscate, grab, grasp, grip(e), impound, jerk, nab, nip, part, piece, pluck, pull, rescue, seize, snag, wrest, yank
**snatcher** grabber
**snatch suddenly** grab
**sneak** ambush, conspire, coward, creep, disappear, evade, loiter, lurk(er), poach, prowl, shun, skulk, slink, sneaker, snoop, steal, telltale, tiptoe, vanish
**sneak away** abscond
**sneakers** sandshoes, tackies
**sneaky** clandestine, cloaked covert, crafty, deceitful, devious, dishonest, fraudulent, furtive, hidden, secret(ive), skulking, slinking, sly,
sneaking, snoopy, stealthy, surreptitious, treacherous, underhand
**sneck** catch, latch
**sneer** criticise, deride, derision, disdain, gibe, jeer, leer, ridicule, scoff, scorn, smirk, snigger
**sneer at** belittle, flout
**sneering** cynical, deriding, disdaining, gibing, jeering, laughing, mocking, ridiculing, scoffing, scorning, snide, sniggering
**sneeze** sniff(le), snuffle, sternutation, wheeze
**snick the cricket ball** edge
**snide** base, bogus, counterfeit, cynical, derogatory, dishonest, disparaging, ill-natured, insinuating, malicious, mean, nasty, sarcastic, scornful, sneering, spiteful, unkind
**snide remark** innuendo
**sniff** breathe, inhale, smell, sniffle, snivel, snuff(le), trace, track, trail, whiff
**sniff and cry** snivel
**sniff at** contemn, ignore, nose, reject, scorn, spout, spurn
**sniffing tobacco** snuff
**sniffling** smelling
**sniff out** smell
**sniff sadly** snivel
**snigger** chortle, chuckle, guffaw, laugh, sneer, snicker, snort, titter
**snip** bargain, clip, crop, cut, fragment, nick, piece, scrap, shave, snippet, trim
**sniper** marksman, sharpshooter
**snippet** cutting, fragment, part, piece, scrap, shred
**snivel** cry, mewl, moan, sniffle, weep, whin(g)e
**snob** boaster, braggart, cobbler, ego(t)ist, snoot, stiff-neck, toffee-nose
**snobbish** arrogant, cocky, complacent, conceited, condescending, contemptuous, disdainful, egocentric, ego(t)istic, hoity-toity, lofty, patronising, pompous, pretentious, proud, pry, scornful, self-admiring, self-loving, sneak, sniffish, snobby, snooty, snotty, spy, stuck-up, superior, uppish, vainglorious
**snog** kiss, (kiss and) cuddle, vry
**snooker aid** rest
**snooker article** cue
**snookered** baffled, beaten, confused, defeated, lost, thwarted
**snooker game** frame
**snooker stick** cue
**snooker-type game** billiards

**snoop** brevit, crouch, eavesdrop, ferret, gaze, gumshoe, hide, inspect, interfere, lurk, peek, peep, peer, piroot, prowl, pry, rummage, scan, skulk, slink, sneak, spy
**snooper** agent, impimpi, informer, investigator, prier, spy
**snoot** nose
**snooty** aloof, arrogant, audacious, bumptious, conceited, haughty, insolent, stuck-up, supercilious, vain
**snooty person** snob
**snooze** (cat)nap, doze, siesta, snap
**snore like a barn owl** curr
**snotty** conceited, contemptible, nasty, snobbish
**snout** muzzle, nose, nozzle, proboscis, projection, structure
**snow** sna (Sc)
**snow and rain together** sleet
**snow cart** sled
**snow colour** white
**snow eater** chinook
**snow goose** wav(e)y
**snow house** igloo, iglu
**snow leopard** ounce
**snow lily** violet
**snowman** Yeti
**snow mixed with rain** sleet
**snow mouse** vole
**snow on glacier** névé
**snow remover** scraper
**snow runner** ski, sled
**snow shelter** igloo
**snow slippage** avalanche
**snow storm** bura(n)
**snow traveller** skier
**snow under** engulf, inundate, submerge, swamp
**snow vehicle** sled(ge), sleigh, toboggan
**snowy rain** sleet
**snub** affront, contemn, disdain, humble, humiliate, insult, mortify, rebuff, rebuke, reprove, slight
**snug** close, comfortable, comfy, compact, cosy, homely, intimate, sheltered, tight, warm
**snuggle** bundle, caress, cling, cuddle, embrace, fawn, fondle, hug, neck, nestle, nuzzle, press, snug, vry
**snugly** comfortably, cosily, intimately, warmly
**snug retreat** nest, den
**so** accordingly, as, consequently, ergo, hence, ita (L), sae (Sc), therefore, thus
**soak** absorb, bathe, charge, damp, drench, imb(r)ue, immerse, infuse, marinate, moisten, penetrate, permeate, ret, saturate, sop, steep, wet

**soaked through** sodden
**soaked with liquid** soggy, soppy
**soak flax** ret
**soak in hot liquid** seethe
**soak in liquid** steep
**soak in salt water** brine
**soak thoroughly** saturate
**soak through** dampen, drip, infiltrate, leak, saturate, seep
**soak to separate fibres** ret
**soak totally** saturate
**soak up** absorb, blot
**soapbox orator** firebrand
**soap froth** lather, suds
**soap-making frame** sess
**soap plant** amole
**soapstone** talc
**soapy** sudsy
**soapy water** suds
**soar** ascend, fly, mount, rise, tower
**soaring** rising
**so as to disgust or nauseate** ad nauseam
**so as to prevent** lest
**sob** bawl, cry, howl, snivel, weep
**so be it** amen
**sober** abstemious, abstinent, calm, cold, collected, composed, controlled, cool, dark, dispassionate, drab, dull, grave, joyless, lucid, moderate, peaceful, plain, practical, quiet, rational, realistic, reasonable, sane, sedate, serene, serious, severe, solemn, sombre, sound, staid, steady, subdued, temperate, unexcited, unruffled, untoxicated
**sobriety** abstinence, calmness, coolness, gravity, moderation, solemnity
**sobriquet** agnomen, (by)name, denomination, designation, diminutive, epithet, label, (nick)name, pseudonym, term, title
**sob without restraint** blubber
**so-called** alleged, nominal, ostensible, pretended, professed, self-styled, supposed
**soccer** football
**soccer arbitrator** ref(eree)
**sociable** affable, extroverted, gracious, gregarious, outgoing, social
**sociable person** extrovert
**social** affable, amiable, familiar, friendly, gentle, sociable
**social assembly for dancing** ball
**social blunder** faux pas, gaffe
**social class** background, breeding, caste
**social climber** parvenu, snob
**social club for university women** sorority
**social compact** contrat social (F)

**social conduct** manners
**social custom** dharma
**social disorder** anarchy
**social distinction** éclat
**social division** caste
**social engagement** date
**social entertainment** party
**social equal** peer
**social evening** soirée
**social event** party, soirée
**social exclusion** ostracism
**social function** party
**social gathering** ceilidh, party, sociality, tea(party)
**social get-together** reunion
**social group** clan, class, society
**social insect** ant, bee, wasp
**socialise** chat, gab, gossip, mingle, mix, talk
**Socialist** Red
**Socialist revolutionary** Bolshevik
**social level** stratum
**socially awkward** gauche
**socially superior group** élite
**social mood of life** society
**social occasion** function
**social oddball** misfit
**social outcast** leper, pariah
**social parasite** toady
**social position** estate, status
**social relationship** footing
**social rules** etiquette
**social science** sociology
**social science dealing with health and welfare of old people** geriatric
**social standing** prestige, stature, status
**social status** estate, position
**social surroundings** milieu
**social system** caste, regime
**society** association, brotherhood, circle, civilisation, club, élite, fellowship, fraternity, gentry, group, humanity, organisation, public
**society bud** deb, débutante
**Society of Friends member** Quaker
**society of scholars** academy, college
**society to advance arts** academy
**socket of the hip-joint** acetabulum
**socket of tooth** alveolus
**sockeye salmon** nerka
**socks** hose, stockings
**socle** plinth
**sod** clay, clod, dirt, divot, dust, earth, field, grass, green, ground, land, loam, mould, soil, sward, swarth, terrain, topsoil, turf
**soda maker** siphon
**sodden** flooded, inundated, marinated, marshy, muggy, soaked, soggy, sopping, steeped, waterlogged, wet
**sodium bicarbonate** saleratus

**sodium chloride** salt, soda
**sodium compound** soda
**sodium hydroxide** lye
**sodium nitrate** nitre
**sodium tetraborate** borax
**sodium thiosulphate** hypo
**sodomy with a boy** pederasty
**sofa** couch, divan, dos-à-dos, lounge, ottoman, settee, siamoise, three-seater
**so far** yet
**soft** affected, balmy, bland, comfortable, compassionate, cushiony, delicate, doughy, downy, easy, fleecy, flexible, floppy, flowing, gentle, impressible, irresolute, lenient, low, malleable, mellow, mild, mollifying, plastic, pleasant, pleasing, plushy, pulpy, silky, smooth, soothing, squashy, subdued, sweet, tender, undecided, unstarched, velvety, weak, yielding
**soft and lustrous fabric** velvet
**soft and pale** pastel
**soft and pulpy** mushy, pappy
**soft antifriction alloy** babbit
**soft-bodied and hard-shelled animal** mollusc
**soft breeze** zephyr
**soft cake** bun
**soft candy** cream, fudge, marshmallow
**soft cap** beret
**soft chalky rock** malm
**soft cheese** brie, camembert, ricotta
**soft copal** animé
**soft-cover** paperback
**soft crumbly earth** marl
**soft down** flue, fluff
**soft drink** Coke, cola, lemonade, pop, rootbeer, soda, squash
**soft earth** mud
**soften** abate, allay, alleviate, assuage, calm, drench, ease, mellow, melt, mitigate, moderate, modify, mollify, palliate, pulp, qualify, quiet, relent, soothe, still, subdue, tame, temper, tenderise, thaw, unbend
**soften by soaking** ret
**soften by steeping** macerate
**softened by age** mellow
**softened grain** malt
**soften flax by soaking** ret
**soften grain** gree
**softening of bone by loss of mineral substance** osteomalacia
**soften in temper** relent
**soften up** conciliate, disarm, melt, persuade, soft-soap, weaken
**soft explosion** pop
**soft feathers** down, eider
**soft felt hat** fedora, trilby
**soft flat bread roll** bap

**soft fleshy part of fruit** pulp
**soft flexible leather from sheepskin** roan
**soft food** jelly, mash, mush, pap, porridge
**soft fruit** bilberry, blueberry, boysenberry, cranberry, gooseberry, loganberry, mulberry, strawberry, whortleberry
**soft fuel** peat
**soft gentle wind** zephyr
**soft glove leather with suede finish** mocha
**soft hair of sheep** wool
**soft hairs** down
**soft hat** beret
**soft-hearted** kind, sympathetic, tender
**soft ice from floes** lolly
**soft in quality** tender
**soft in shade** pastel
**soft in temper** flexible, easy
**soft internal tissue of plants** medulla
**soft in texture** supple
**soft in tint** pastel
**soft in tone** low
**soft kid leather** suede
**soft kind of toffee** nougat
**soft leather** chamois, kid, nap(p)a, roan, suede
**soft leather shoe** moccasin
**soft light dress-material** challis
**soft light fabric** leno
**soft light silk** alamode
**soft limestone** chalk, malm
**soft lining metal** babbitt
**soft lump** wad
**soft lustrous fibre** silk
**softly** balmily, blandly, caressingly, delicately, diffusely, dimly, elastically, flexibly, flowingly, fluidly, kindly, leise (G), lightly, lowly, mildly, palely, piano, pleasingly, pliably, quietly, restfully, sensitively, silkily, singly, smoothly, supplely, sweetly, sympathetically, tenderly
**softly radiant** lambent
**soft mass** pulp, wad
**soft material for dressing wounds** lint
**soft metal** lead, tin
**soft mild gentle wind** zephyr
**soft mixture** amalgam, mash
**soft moist part of fruit** pulp
**soft murmuring tone** coo
**soft muslin** mull
**soft ointment** salve
**soft palate** vela, velum
**soft palate lobe** uvula
**soft part** pulp
**soft part of nut** kernel
**soft-piled fabric** velvet
**soft place in moor** hag
**soft pulp** mush

**soft rich cheese** cream cheese
**soft rock** soapstone
**soft rock that splits easily** shale
**soft roll** bap, croissant
**soft round many-seeded fruit** fig
**soft shade** pastel, tint
**soft sheepskin with a suede finish, used for gloves** mocha
**soft shoe leather with a glossy finish** glacé kid
**soft shoes** slippers
**soft silk** floss
**soft silk fabric** surah
**soft soap** flatter(y)
**soft-soled shoe** creeper, sneaker, tackie
**soft sound on the flute** tootle
**soft-spoken** bland, courteous, mealy, suave
**soft spongy tumour occurring in horses and oxen** ambury, anbury
**soft spot on bill** cere
**soft sticky mud** slime, muck
**soft striped woollen cloth** algerine
**soft stuffed couch** pouffe
**soft substance between skin and bones** flesh
**soft sweet** fondant
**soft thin leather from hair side of sheepskin** skiver
**soft toffee** fudge
**soft undressed Chinese silk** shantung
**soft velvet** panne
**soft viscous mass** blob
**soft wart on a horse's neck** ambury, anbury
**soft watery mud** mire, sludge
**soft white limestone** chalk
**soft white mineral** talc
**soft wool** botany, merino
**soft woollen fabric** flannel, tweed
**soft yellow fruit** peach
**soggy** clammy, damp, dank, dewy, dripping, drizzly, fluid, humid, liquid, marshy, misty, moist, muggy, saturated, soaking, sodden, sopping, squelchy, vaporous, waterlogged, watery, wet
**soil** befoul, begrime, besmirch, clay, defile, dirt(y), earth, foul, ground, land, loam, muddy, pollute, region, smear, spatter, stain, sully, tarnish
**soil beneath the surface soil** subsoil
**soil loss** erosion
**soil tiller** farmer
**soirée** gathering, party, rout
**sol** sun
**solace** alleviate, comfort, consolation, mitigate, relief, soothe
**solan goose** gannet
**solar body** asteroid, comet, moon, planet, satellite, star, sun

**solar disk god** Aten, Aton
**solar illumination** sunlight
**solar ray** sunbeam
**solar source** sun
**soldering alloy** spelter
**soldier** brave, cavalier, centurion, champion, fighter, GI, grenadier, hero, infantry, knight, lancer, NSM, poilu, private, rifleman, sapper, serviceman, sowar, squaddy, tommy, trooper, warrior
**soldier armed with carbine or short rifle** carabineer
**soldier armed with fusil or light musket** fusilier
**soldier armed with grenades** grenadier
**soldier for hire** mercenary
**soldier liable only for home defence** fence
**soldier of cavalry regiment** lancer
**soldier of fortune** adventurer
**soldier of French Foreign Legion** legionnaire
**soldier of light cavalry regiment** hussar
**soldier on guard** sentry
**soldiers** troops
**soldier's coat** capote
**soldier's equipment** accoutrement
**soldiers fighting on foot** infantry
**soldier's metal meal-tray** varkpan
**soldier's non-military duty** fatigue
**soldier's ration bag** haversack
**soldier's shelter** tent
**soldier's shoulder belt** bandolier
**soldier's thick outer garment** greatcoat
**soldier's wakening call** reveille
**soldier's water flask** canteen
**soldier who threw grenades** grenadier
**sole** alone, bottom, exclusive, (flat)fish, foundation, individual, lone, mere, one, only, single, solitary, tread, undersurface, unique, unmarried, vola (pedis)
**solely** alone, entirely, exclusive, merely, only, single, singly
**solemn** awe-inspiring, awesome, awful, ceremonious, dignified, earnest, formal, grand, grave, great, hallowed, imposing, impressive, long-faced, mirthless, po-faced, reverential, ritual, sacred, serious, sober, sombre, staid, unsmiling, venerable
**solemn affirmation** protestation
**solemn and dull** owlish
**solemn appeal** conjuration
**solemn assent** amen
**solemn assertion** oath, vow
**solemn bell sound** knell

**solemn customary act** ritual
**solemn declaration** oath, vow
**solemn ecclesiastical curse** anathema
**solemn looking** owlish
**solemnly declare** asseverate
**solemn offer** pledge
**solemn promise** oath, pledge, vow
**solemn religious ceremony** sacrament
**solemn supplication** litany
**solemn vow** oath
**solemn wonder** awe
**sole of foot** vola (pedis)
**sole of plough** slade
**sole possession of anything** monopoly
**sole ruler with absolute power** autocrat
**so let it be** amen
**solicit** accost, activate, ask, awaken, beg, beseech, canvass, crave, entreat, excite, impel, implore, importune, influence, petition, pray, proposition, request, seek, supplicate
**solicit charity** beg
**solicit custom** tout
**solicitor** advocate, aide, asker, attorney, authority, barrister, canvasser, coach, confidant, consultant, counsel(lor), guide, helper, lawyer, mentor, petitionary, requester, suitor, suppliant, tutor
**solicitude** anxiety, ardour, care, concern, consideration, desire, desirousness, eagerness, earnestness, fear(fulness), gush, intensity, regard, thought, zeal
**solicit votes** canvass
**solid** compact, complete, concrete, cubic, dense, entire, firm, genuine, hard, heavy, honest, real, reliable, solvent, sound, stout, strong, sturdy, successful, thick, thorough, unbroken, undivided, wealthy, whole
**solid alcohol** sterol
**solid blow** wham
**solid figure contained by many faces** polyhedron
**solid figure having eight plane faces** octahedron
**solid figure having four plane faces** tetrahedron
**solid figure having nine plane faces** enneahedron
**solid figure having ten plane faces** decahedron
**solid figure having twelve plane faces** dodecahedron
**solid food** meat, vegetables
**solid fuel** coal, coke
**solid horned ungulate** deer
**solidify** ally, cake, clot, coagulate, cohere, combine, compress, concrete, congeal, fuse, gel, harden, jell(ify), join, merge, set, thicken, unite
**solidify by cooling** congeal, freeze
**solidify like jelly** set
**solidity** constancy, density, firmness, fixedness, gel, hardness, inelasticity, inflexibility, resistance, rigidity, set, stability, stiffness, strength
**solidly built** permanent, pukka
**solid silver** sterling
**solid six-sided square** cube
**solid sound** klop, thump
**solid square** cube
**solids suspended in water** slurry
**solid substance left after heating coal** coke
**solidus** slash, virgule
**solitary** alone, anchorite, cloistered, companionless, deserted, eremite, hermit, hidden, isolated, lone(ly), one, only, private, recluse, remote, secluded, single, sole, stylite, unaided, unattended
**solitary abode** hermitage
**solitary confinement** isolation
**solitary person** loner
**solitude** aloneness, desert, desolation, emptiness, hermitry, isolation, loneliness, privacy, reclusion, reclusiveness, remoteness, retirement, seclusion, separation, solitariness, wilderness
**solo** alone, aria, lone, single, sole, unaided, unit
**solo composition** etude
**solo dance in ballet** pas de seul (F)
**solo musical performance** recital
**solo number** one
**solo song** aria, cavatina
**solo voice** soprano, tenor
**solubility gauge** lysimeter
**solution** answer, blend, key, liquid, resolution, solving
**solution of problem** answer
**solve** answer, decipher, explain, resolve, unravel
**solvent** acetone, afloat, creditworthy, debt-free, liquefaction, liquid, reliable, responsible, solid, sound
**solver of riddles** Oedipus
**soma** body
**Somali model** Iman
**Somali port** Merca
**somatic** bodily
**sombre** cloudy, dark, depressive, dim, dismal, doleful, drab, dull, dusky, gloomy, grave, grim, joyless, lifeless, melancholy, morbid, mournful, obscure, sad, sedate, sepulchral, serious, shadowy, shady, sober, solemn, staid

**sombre colour** black
**some** about, any, approximately, certain, few, many, part, several, specific
**someone made to take the blame** scapegoat
**someone stationed to keep guard** sentry
**someone who refuses to support a strike** scab
**someone who's not present** absentee
**some other place** elsewhere
**somersault** handspring
**some shoes have them** laces
**something accomplished** achievement
**something added** addendum, annexe, appendix
**something added on** accretion
**something added to fill up a deficiency** supplement
**something additional** accessory
**something composed of number of parts** compound
**something considered perfection** ideal
**something curved in shape** arc(h)
**something deleted** erasure
**something delicious** ambrosia
**something done incorrectly** mistake
**something easily achieved** pushover
**something entrusted to be done** commission
**something extra inserted** inset
**something extraordinary** phenomenon
**something false** fraud
**something fitting into and filling a hole** plug
**something flowing out invisibly** effluvium
**something handed down by a predecessor** legacy
**something happening by chance** accident
**something hastily improvised** autoschediasm
**something indispensable** sine qua non (L)
**something intended to tempt** bait
**something investigated by police** case
**something left in a will** bequest
**something left out** omission
**something left over** oddment
**something left over from the past** relic
**something made only once** one-off
**something not in earnest** joke
**something of interest** concern
**something of no concern** inessential, insignificancy, trifle
**something of value** asset
**something reasonable** plausible

**something reputed to cure all ailments** cure-all, elixir, panacea
**something ruined** wreck
**something said to gain admission** password
**something set up to be aimed at** mark
**something short-lived** ephemera
**something showing irregularity** anomalous
**something small and valuable** nugget
**something spoken** utterance
**something spoken in defence** apology
**something startling** eye-opener
**something subordinate** bye
**something that confines** restriction
**something that has been left out** omission
**something that has survived from the past** relic
**something that hurts one's dignity** humiliation
**something that induces relaxation** opiate, relaxant, sedative, tranquilliser
**something that is certain** certainty
**something that is easily done** pushover
**something that resembles an earlier or more primitive type** throwback
**something that rouses to activity** stimulus
**something to be added** addendum
**something to be learned** lesson
**something told confidentially** confidence
**something undertaken to boost one's image** ego trip
**something used to cover the eyes** blindfold
**something very small** pinhead
**something vile** carrion
**something well worth having** asset
**something which involves war** casus belli (L)
**something which serves to keep in memory** memorial
**something with objective reality** entity
**something won** conquest
**something worn as a charm** amulet
**sometime back** once
**somewhat** adequately, fairly, fractionally, gently, halfway, moderately, partially, partly, passably, piecemeal, quite, rather, reasonably, relatively, slightly, tolerably
**somewhat acid** acidulous
**somewhat cold** chilly
**somewhat obscured** dimmish
**somewhat pale** palish, palely
**somewhat random** long
**somewhat rough** choppy

**somewhat sharp** tartish
**somewhat sour** acescent
**somewhat thick** thickish
**somewhere near** about
**some while ago** erst
**somite** metamere
**somnambulist** nightwalker, noctambulant, noctambulist, sleepwalker, somnambulator, somnambule
**somnolence** doziness, drowsiness, grogginess, sleepiness, slumb(e)rousness
**somnolent** drowsy, narcotic, noddy, oscitant, sleepiness, sleepy, slumb(e)rous, somniferous, soporific
**so much** such
**so much as it may be worth** quantum valea (L)
**so much the better** tant mieux (F)
**so much the worse** tant pis (F)
**sonar** asdic
**song** aria, ballad, carol, ditty, glee, hymn, lay, lied (G), lyric, melody, number, tune, verse
**song and dance** ado, commotion, to-do
**songbird** canary, chat, lark, linnet, nightingale, oriole, pipit, robin, siskin, tit(mouse), vireo, wagtail, warbler, wren
**song for one** solo
**song for one voice** aria, monody
**song for two** duet
**song from opera** aria
**songlike poem** lyric, ode
**song of dawn** aubade
**song of gladness** anthem
**song of gondolier** barcarole
**song of joy or praise** carol
**song of lamentation** elegy, threnody
**song of loyalty** anthem
**song of mourning** dirge
**song of praise** anthem, chant, hymn, magnificat, paean, psalm
**song organ of birds** syrinx
**song refrain** chorus
**songster** warbler
**song thrush** blackbird, mavis, throstle
**song used in advertising** jingle
**song written to celebrate a marriage** epithalamium, epithalmion
**son-in-law of Augustus** Agrippa
**son-in-law of Caesar** Pompey
**son-in-law of Jethro** Moses
**son of Aaron** Abihu, Eleazar, Ithamar, Nadab
**son of Abi** Hezekiah
**son of Abigail** Amasa, Chileab, Daniel
**son of Abihail** Zuriel
**son of Abijah** Asa, Hezekiah
**son of Abinoah** Barak
**son of Abishua** Bukki

**son of Abner** Jaasiel
**son of Abraham** Isaac, Ishbak, Ishmael, Jockshan, Jocshon, Medan, Midian, Shuah, Zimion, Zimram
**son of Abraham and Hagar** Ishmael
**son of Acacallis** Amphithemis, Garamas
**son of Achim** Eliud
**son of Adam** Abel, Cain, Seth
**son of Aeacus** Peleus, Phocus, Telamon
**son of Aegeus** Theseus
**son of Agamemnon** Orestes
**son of Agave** Pentheus
**son of Agee** Shammah
**son of Agenor** Cadmus, Cilix, Phoenix
**son of Agrippina** Nero
**son of a gun** rascal, rogue
**son of Ahaz** Hezekiah
**son of Ahimelech** Abiathar
**son of Aphrodite** Eros
**son of Ali** Ahmed
**son of Aloeus** Ephialtes, Otus
**son of Amon** Josiah
**son of Amoz** Isaiah
**son of Amphitrite** Triton
**son of Amram** Aaron, Moses
**son of Anne of Austria** Louis XIV
**son of Aphrodite** Aeneas, Cupid, Eros
**son of Apollo** Asclepius, Iamus, Ion
**son of Asenath** Ephraim, Manasseh
**son of Azriel** Seraiah
**son of Azubah** Jehoshaphat
**son of Barachel** Elihu
**son of Bathsheba** Nathan, Shimea, Shobab, Solomon
**son of Bela** Ard
**son of Belial** Rebel, Rioter
**son of Benjamin** Ard, Ashbel, Becher, Bela, Cera, Ehi, Hupham, Huppim, Muppim, Naaman, Rosa
**son of Boas** Obed
**son of Buzi** Ezekiel
**son of Caesar** Caesarion
**son of Cain** Enoch
**son of Caleb** Hur
**son of Chaos** Erebus
**son of Columbus** Diego
**son of Daedalus** Icarus
**son of David** Absalom, Amnon, Eliphalet, Solomon
**son of Dodo** Eleazar, Elhanan
**son of Ebed** Gaal
**son of Elah** Hoshea
**son of Eli** Hophni, Phinefas
**son of Eliab** Abiram, Dathan
**son of Elimelech** Chilion, Mahlon
**son of Eliphaz** Teman
**son of Elisabeth** John
**son of Elishama** Nethaniah
**son of Elkanah** Samuel

**son of Enoch** Methuselah
**son of Enos** Cainan
**son of Ephah** Haran
**son of Ephod** Hanniel
**son of Ephraim** Ezer
**son of Ephratah** Hur
**son of Er** Elmodam
**son of Esau** Edom, Eliphaz, Jaalam, Jeush, Korah, Reuel
**son of Eve** Abel, Cain, Seth
**son of Ezer** Hushah
**son of Frigga** Balder
**son of Gad** Eri
**son of Gilead** Jephthah
**son of god of sleep** Morpheus
**son of Gordius** Midas
**son of Hagar** Ishmael
**son of Haggith** Adonijah
**son of Ham** Canaan, Cush, Mizraim, Phut
**son of Hammedatha** Haman
**son of Hamutal** Jehoahaz, Zedekia
**son of Hanani** Jehu
**son of Hannah** Samuel
**son of Hareph** Bethgader
**son of Hilkia** Eliakim, Gemariah, Jeremiah
**son of Hur** Rephaiah
**son of Huri** Abihail
**son of Iddo** Ahinadab
**son of Irad** Mehujael
**son of Isaac** Esau, Israel, Jacob
**son of Ishmael** Noah
**son of Isis** Horus
**son of Ithra** Amasa
**son of Jacob** Asher, Benjamin, Dan, Gad, Issachar, Joseph, Judah, Levi, Naphtali, Reuben, Simeon, Zebulun
**son of Jacosta** Oedipus
**son of Jair** Elhanan, Mordecai
**son of Janna** Melchi
**son of Japhet** Gomer, Javan, Madai, Magog, Tubal
**son of Jedidah** Josiah
**son of Jehiel** Gibeon, Obadiah
**son of Jephunnen** Caleb
**son of Jered** Enoch
**son of Jeremiah** Jazaniah
**son of Jeroham** Elkanah
**son of Jesse** David
**son of Jocasta** Oedipus
**son of Jochebed** Aaron, Moses
**son of Joktan** Jerah, Ophir, Uzal
**son of Jona** Peter
**son of Jonathan** Mephibosheth
**son of Joseph** Ephraim, Igal, Manasseh
**son of Josiah** Jehoahaz
**son of Judah** Onan
**son of king or queen** prince
**son of Kish** Saul
**son of Kohath** Amram

**son of Kolilaiah** Ahab
**son of Laertes** Ulysses
**son of Laius** Oedipus
**son of Lamech** Jabal, Jubal, Noah, Tubalcain
**son of Leah** Issachar, Judah, Levi, Reuben, Simeon, Zebulun
**son of Levi** Gershon, Kohath, Merari
**son of Maacah** Absalom
**son of Mahlon** Elimelech
**son of Manoah** Samson
**son of Mars** Remus, Romulus
**son of Mephibosheth** Micha
**son of Micah** Abdon
**son of Micha** Mattaniah
**son of Michaiah** Abijah
**son of Minos** Androgeos, Deucalion
**son of Naamah** Rehoboam
**son of Nahor** Huz, Terah
**son of Nahson** Salmon
**son of Naomi** Chilion
**son of Nebuchadnezzar** Belshazzar
**son of Neleus** Alastor, Nestor
**son of Ner** Abner
**son of Nethaniah** Ishmael, Jehudi
**son of Noah** Ham, Japheth, Shem
**son of Nothan** Jehiel
**son of Nun** Joshua
**son of Obadiah** Ishmaiah
**son of Obed** Azariah, Jesse
**son of Odin** Balder, Bragi, Thor, Tyr, Vale
**son of Odysseus** Telegonus, Telemachus
**son of Omri** Ahab
**son of Osiris** Anubis, Horus
**son of Pallu** Eliab
**son of Paruah** Jehoshaphat
**son of Peleth** On
**son of Peleus** Achilles, Pelides
**son of Pelops** Thyestes
**son of Persues** Alcaeus
**son of Petheul** Joel
**son of Polonius** Laertes
**son of Poseidon** Antaeus, Triton
**son of Priam and Hecuba** Paris
**son of Rachel** Benjamin, Joseph
**son of Rebecca** Esau, Jacob
**son of Reuben** Carni, Pallu
**son of Reuel** Eliasaph
**son of Rhea** Neptune, Pluto
**son of Rizpah** Armoni, Mephibosheth
**son of Ruth** Jesse, Obed
**son of Salmon** Boaz
**son of Sarah** Isaac
**son of Saul** Ishbosheth, Jonathan
**son of Seb** Osiris, Set
**son of Seth** Enos
**son of Shakespeare** Hamnet
**son of Shammua** Abda
**son of Shaphat** Elisha
**son of Shem** Elam

**son of Simeon** Jachin, Shaul
**son of Simon** Judas
**son of Tantalus** Pelops
**son of the soil** peasant
**son of Thetis** Achilles
**son of Tobit** Tobias
**son of tsar** tsarevitch
**son of Ulysses** Telemachus
**son of Ur** Eliphal
**son of Uranus** Cydops, Kronos, Themis
**son of Venus** Cupid
**son of Zachariah** John
**son of Zebedee** James, John
**son of Zebulun** Elon
**son of Zechariah** Iddo
**son of Zeruah** Jeroboam
**son of Zeus** Aeacus, Amphion, Apollo, Arcas, Ares, Argus, Dionysus, Heracles, Hercules, Hermes, Minos, Tantalus
**son of Zibeon** Anah
**son of Zilpah** Asher, Gad
**son of Zipporah** Eliezer
**son of Zippor** Balak
**sonorous** full-sounding, resonant
**soon** anon, apace, betimes, directly, early, erelong, eventually, freely, gladly, immediately, instantaneously, presently, promptly, quickly, readily, shortly, speedily, straightaway, willingly
**soon after** anon
**soon afterwards** eftsoons
**sooner** earlier
**sooner or later** automatically, eventually, finally, ultimately
**sooner than** before, ere
**so or thus** sic
**soot** ash, black, smudge, smut
**soothe** allay, alleviate, appease, assuage, calm, comfort, compose, deaden, dulcify, dull, ease, heal, hush, lull, mitigate, mollify, pacify, palliate, quiet, reassure, relieve, salve, settle, sober, soften, solace, still, tranquillise
**soothing** allaying, alleviating, appeasing, assuaging, balsamic, calming, composing, demulcent, easeful, easing, emollient, lulling, mitigating, nervine, pacifying, palliative, relaxing, relieving, restful
**soothing balm** balsam
**soothing drug** sedative
**soothing influence** opiate
**soothing medicine** paregoric
**soothing ointment** balm, salve
**soothing song to send child to sleep** lullaby
**soothing throat medicine** linctus

**soothsayer** augur, diviner, foreteller, oracle, prophet, pythoness, sangoma, seer, sibyl
**sooty** black(ened), dark, dirty, fuliginous, grimy, inky, jet, miry, opaque, raven, smeared, smirched, smutchy, soiled, swarthy
**sooty stain** smut
**sop** bribe, concession, gasp
**sophist** arguer, casuist, deceiver, doubletalker, equivocator, evader, expert, fudger, hedger, highbrow, intellectual, Jesuit, liar, paralogist, pedant, philosopher, pundit, quack, quibbler, savant, scholar, tergiversator, vacillator, weasel
**sophisticated** advanced, deceptive, educated, elegant, excellent, fancy, faulty, gourmet, intellectual, inured, jaded, knowledg(e)able, realistic, refined, seasoned, suave, unimpressed, unsound, urbane, worldly
**soporific** anaesthetic, hypnotic, opiate, sedative, sleepy, somnolent, tranquilliser, tranquillising
**soporific song** lullaby
**sorbets** ices
**sorcerer** conjurer, demonologist, diabolist, enchanter, magician, magus, necromancer, seer, shaman, soothsayer, thaumaturgist, theurgist, warlock, witch, wizard
**sorceress** witch
**sorcery** conjuration, coven, diablerie, diabolism, divination, enchantment, exorcism, gramarye, hoodoo, illusionism, magic, necromancy, obeah, obi(ism), occultness, rite, spell, spiritualism, superstition, voodoo, witchcraft, witchery, wizardry
**sorcery akin to obeah** myalism
**sordid** base, close, degraded, dirty, foul, ignoble, mean, mercenary, miserly, niggardly, seamy, squalid, stingy
**sordid gain** lucre
**sore** acute, afflicted, afflictive, aggrieved, angry, burning, cancer, chafed, depressed, desperate, distressed, grieved, grievous, hurt, infection, irritated, painful, raw, reddened, sair (Scot.), sensitive, severe, sorrowful, tender, troublesome, ulcer, wound
**sore after riding a horse** saddle-sore
**sore at root of fingernail** agnail
**sorely** badly, extremely, greatly, grievously, painfully, pressingly, severely
**sore made by chafing** gall
**sore matter** pus

**sore on eyelid** stye
**sore protector** scab
**sorrow** adversity, bemoan, distress, dolour, grief, grieve, misery, misfortune, mourn, regret, sadness, woe, wretchedness
**sorrowful** depressed, heartbroken, lamentable, miserable, sad, tearful, unhappy, woeful
**sorrowful gulping sound** sob
**sorrowful song or poem** elegy
**sorry** abject, contrite, deplorable, grievous, melancholy, miserable, pitiable, regretful, remorseful, repentant, rueful, sad, sorrowing, sympathetic, unhappy
**sorry plight** pickle
**sort** arrange, assort, character, class(ify), description, divide, example, fashion, grade, group, ilk, kind, manner, means, method, mode, nature, order, quality, race, rank, select, separate, type, variety
**sortie** assault, attack, charge, flight, foray, incursion, inroad, invasion, onset, raid, rush, sally, seizure
**sorting process** triage
**sort of** moderately, rather, reasonably, somewhat
**sort of grape** malmsey
**sort of sack** gunny
**sort of tide** neap
**sort out** clarify, divide, organise, resolve, segregate, select, separate, sift
**sort through** sift
**sosatie** kebab
**so-so** average, middling, tolerable
**so soon** already
**sot** alcoholic, alkie, alky, bibber, bibbler, boozer, dipsomaniac, dipsomaniac, drinker, dronkie, dronklap, drunk(ard), guzzler, inebriate, lush, soak, souse, sponge, swiller, tippler, toper, tosspot, winebibber, wino
**Sotho dialect** Pedi
**sotto voce remark** aside
**soufflé ingredient** egg
**sough** groan, moan, rustle, sigh
**sought** hunted, wanted
**sought by the police** wanted
**soul** animation, being, body, creature, essence, individual, inspiration, intellect, life, mind, mortal, person(ification), psyche, quintessence, reason, soul, spirit, type, vitality, (wo)man
**soul mate** friend
**sound** audio, complete, correct, cry, deep, determine, din, dive, drift, echo, enduring, entire, established,

examine, express, fair, fathom, firm, fit, hale, healthy, honest, inspect, intact, just, logical, noise, perfect, plumb, plunge, probe, profound, pronounce, proper, proven, rational, reliable, report, reputable, reverberation, right, robust, sane, secure, sensible, solid, solvent, sonance, sough, sturdy, tone, true, trustworthy, truthful, unbroken, unharmed, unhurt, uninjured, utter, valid, valid, vigorous, voice, whole, wise
**sound a bell** ring
**sound-absorbing panel** gobo
**sound accompanying breathing** rale
**sound channel** track
**sound coming from throat** guttural
**sounded with a hiss** sibilant
**sound effect** stereo
**sound equipment** hi-fi
**sound expressing agony** groan
**sound from angry dog** growl
**sound harshly** rasp
**sound horn** hoot
**sound imitation** echoism, onomatopoeia
**sound in body** healthy
**sounding device** sonde
**sounding very foreign** outlandish
**sound in mind** sane, compos mentis
**sound judgement** rationality, wisdom
**soundless** anacoustic, asonant, calm, deathlike, dumb, echoless, frictionless, hushed, inarticulate, inaudible, low, muffled, mute(d), noiseless, peaceful, quiescent, quiet, silent, soft, soundproof, still, unspoken, unuttered, voiceless
**soundlessness** calm, silence, speechlessness, stillness
**sound like a bee** buzz, hum
**sound like a dog** bark, growl
**sound like a donkey** bray
**sound like a frog** croak
**sound like a rook** caw
**sound like a sheep** bleat
**sound loudly** blare, blast
**sound made by hesitant person** um
**sound made by men to show admiration for women** wolf-whistle
**sound measure** decibel, phon
**sound mind in a sound body** mens sana incorpore sano (L)
**sound modulation** tone
**soundness** completeness, correctness, entireness, firmness, intactness, justness, reasonableness, safeness, sanity, sensibleness, solidity, solidness, stableness, strength, sturdiness, validness, wholeness

**soundness of body** health
**soundness of mind** sanity
**soundness of moral principle** integrity
**sound of automobile horn** beep, honk
**sound of baby feet** patter
**sound of bees** buzz, drone, hum
**sound of bell** chime, ding, knell, peal, toll
**sound of bullet** ping
**sound of cock crowing** cock-a-doodle doo
**sound of contempt** hiss, whistle
**sound of death bell** knell
**sound of derision** raspberry
**sound of disapproval** boo, hiss
**sound of disdain** snort
**sound of disgust** ugh
**sound of distress** moan
**sound of dove** coo
**sound of dry leaves** rustle
**sound of explosion** pow
**sound off** speak, tirade
**sound of footstep** footfall
**sound of funeral bell** knell
**sound of hard blow** wham
**sound of hesitation** er, um
**sound of horn** hoot, toot
**sound of knocking on a door** ratatat(-tat)
**sound of laughter** peal
**sound of lion** roar
**sound of loose piston** slap
**sound of lung abnormality** rale
**sound of mind** compos mentis (L)
**sound of mule** bray
**sound of pain** groan, moan, ouch, ow
**sound of plucked string** twang
**sound of rain** patter
**sound of relief** sigh
**sound of silk** rustle
**sound of small bell** ting, tinkle
**sound of step** footfall
**sound of surf** rote
**sound of thunder** clap
**sound of time passing** tick
**sound of trumpet** blare, blast, taratantara
**sound of turkey cock** gobble
**sound of wind** sough, whistle
**sound ominously** knell
**sound out** approach, blare, canvass, examine, probe
**sound perception organ** ear
**sound quality** tone
**sound reflection** echo
**sound repetition** alliteration, assonance, echo
**sound resemblance** assonance, assonant
**sound resonantly** ring
**sound smoothly** purr
**sound state** weal

**sound system** stereo(phonic)
**sound thought** logic
**sound to attract attention** pst
**sound to frighten** boo
**sound unit** decibel, phon
**soup** bisk, bisque, bouillon, broth, consommé, julienne, mulligatawny, pot(t)age, purée, stock
**soup basis** barley, beans, chicken, fish, lentils, meat(-bone), mushroom, rice, stock, vegetables
**soup bean** lentil
**soup bowl** tureen
**soupçon** atom, bit(e), breath, crumb, dash, dram, drop, fraction, fragment, grain, hint, jot, mite, morsel, nip, particle, piece, pinch, portion, scrap, segment, shade, shred, sip, slice, snippet, taste, trace
**soup container** stockpot
**soup dish** tureen
**soupfin shark** tope
**soup garnish of fried bread** crouton
**soup spoon** ladle
**soup thickened with okra** gumbo
**soup utensil** spoon
**soup vessel** tureen
**soup with curry** mulligatawny
**sour** acerb(ic), acetic, acetose, acid, acrid, austere, bitter, cantankerous, churlish, cross, crude, curdled, cynical, discontented, distasteful, embittered, grudging, ill-natured, morose, off, peevish, petulant, pungent, rancid, rude, severe, sharp, snappish, spoil, stale, tart, testy, touchy, ungenerous, unpleasant, waspish
**sour ale** alegar
**sour aspect** dour
**sour beer** faro
**source** adviser, ancestry, author, basis, beginning, birth, cause, dawn, derivation, egg, element, father, first, fountainhead, genesis, germ, informant, natal, nativity, notifier, origin(al), parentage, protoplasm, root, seed, start, wellspring
**source and origin** fons et origo (L)
**source of aluminium** bauxite
**source of amusement** fun
**source of aniseed** anise
**source of annoyance** irritant, nuisance
**source of arrowroot** pia
**source of a stream** headspring
**source of caviar** beluga
**source of cocaine** coca
**source of danger** threat
**source of disease** bacillus, bacterium, germ, virus
**source of distress** torment
**source of fuel** oil well

**source of glaciers** firn
**source of heat** coal, electricity, etna, fire, fuel, gas, steam, sun
**source of help** aid, backup, recourse, resource
**source of iodine** kelp
**source of irritation** nuisance
**source of light** candle, gas, lamp, sun
**source of linen** flax
**source of milk products** dairy
**source of motivation** drive
**source of nuclear energy** uranium
**source of oil** olive, sunflower
**source of opium** poppy
**source of ore** mine
**source of origin** root
**source of perfume** musk
**source of potassium salts** salin
**source of power** engine, steam
**source of pride** honour
**source of relief** solace
**source of ruin** bane
**source of security** anchor
**source of strength and sweetness** oenomel
**source of sugar** beet, cane
**source of thorium** thorite
**source of valuable material** Klondike, reef
**source of vexation** torment
**source of vitamin A** carrot
**source of vitamin D** sun
**source of water** fountain, rain, spring, well
**source of zest** spice
**sour cherry** amarelle, morello
**sour condiment** vinegar
**soured wine** vinegar
**sour fruit** lemon, lime
**sour grapes** jealousy
**sour grass** oxalis, sorrel
**sour gum tree** tupelo
**sour in aspect** dour
**sourish** acescent
**sourish fruit** quince
**sour milk drink** (a)maas, amasi, laban, leben, yogurt
**sourness** acerbity, acidity
**sour substance** acid
**sour-tasting** acerb, acidic, acrid, tart
**sour-tempered** cross, morose
**sour wine** plum
**souse** drench, dunk, immerse, marinate, pickle, soak, steep
**south** sud (F)
**South African kingdom** Lesotho
**South African mining magnate** Barnato, Beit, Oppenheimer, Rhodes
**South African province** Eastern Cape, Eastern Transvaal, Kwazulu/Natal, Northern Cape, Northern Transvaal,

North West, Free State, PWV, Western Cape
**South African satirist** Pieter Dirk Uys
**South African traditional dish** afval, bobotie, braaivleis, bredie, geelrys, putu, rosyntjierys, skaapboud
**South American alligator** cayman
**South American animal** alpaca, llama, tapir
**South American aquatic rodent** coypu
**South American armadillo** tatouay, tatu
**South American arrow poison** curare
**South American bean** tonka
**South American beast of burden** llama
**South American bird** ara, coin, condor, curassow, rhea
**South American camel** llama
**South American cape** Horn
**South American cat** eyra, jaguarondi, kodkod, ocelot, puma
**South American coin** peso
**South American country** Argentina, Bolivia, Brazil, Chile, Colombia, Ecuador, Paraguay, Peru, Uruguay, Venezuela
**South American cowboy** gaucho
**South American crested bird of prey** harpy
**South American cud-chewing mammal** llama
**South American dance** conga, r(h)umba, samba, tango
**South American duck** pato
**South American fish** acara, arapaima, dorado, ispe
**South American flightless bird** rhea, emu
**South American fox-wolf** zorro
**South American guinea pig** agouti, cavy
**South American hare** tapeti
**South American hawk** caracara
**South American horseman** gaucho, llanero
**South American humming bird** sylph
**South American Indian** Carib, Ge, Inca, Mayan, Ona
**South American Indian hut** toldo
**South American labourer** peon
**South American land** Argentina, Bolivia, Brazil, Chile, Colombia, Ecuador, Paraguay, Peru, Uruguay, Venezuela
**South American liberator** Bolivar
**South American liquor** chicha
**South American lungfish** lepidosiren
**South American mammal** alpaca, capybara, coati, coati-mondi, coati-mundi, llama

**South American mammal-like llama** vicuna
**South American monkey** capuchin, marmoset, titi
**South American mountain range** Andes
**South American narcotic shrub** cocaa, cula
**South American ocelot** kuichua
**South American opossum** gamba, quica, saigue
**South American ostrich** rhea
**South American owl** utum
**South American palm** plassaba, piassava
**South American parrot** macaw
**South American pig** peccary
**South American plain** llano, pampas
**South American plain wind** pampero
**South American ranch** estancia
**South American ruminant** alpaca, guanaco, llama, vicuna
**South American shawl** serape
**South American shoe dance** zapateado (Sp)
**South American shrub** ipecac, jaborandi
**South American skunk** zorra
**South American slow-moving mammal** sloth
**South American spider monkey** sapajou
**South American steppe** llano
**South American strait** Megellan
**South American three-toed ostrich** rhea
**South American throwing weapon** bola(s)
**South American tree** balsa, carob, mora, vera
**South American treeless plain** llano, pampas
**South American tree whose milky sap yields rubber** hevea
**South American tuber** oca
**South American vulture** condor, urubu
**South American water opossum** yapok
**South American wildcat** eyra, yaguarunki
**South American wind** pampero
**South Asian rainy season** monsoon
**South East Asian elk** sambar, sambur
**South East Asian nut** betel
**South East Asia peninsula** Malay
**South England chalk uplands** Downs
**southern** austral
**southern constellation** Ara, Argo, Crux, Dorado, Eridanus, Vela
**Southern Cross** Crux
**southern French coast** Riviera
**southern Italian peninsula** Calabria

**southern Nigerian** Ibo
**southern part of Great Britain** England
**southern part of Israel** Negev
**southern region in South America** Patagonia
**southern tip of Africa** Cape Agulhas
**southern tropic** Capricorn
**southern US states** Dixieland
**South of France** Midi
**South Pacific boat** proa
**South Pacific island** Bali, Bikini, Guadalcanal, Pitcairn, Tahiti
**South Pole** Antarctica
**South Sea island** Tahiti
**South Seas island group** Samoa
**South West Africa** Namibia
**South Yemen port** Aden
**souvenir** album, autograph, keepsake, memento, memorial, record, relic, remembrance, reminder, scrapbook, snapshot, token, trophy, vestige
**sovereign** chief, effective, emperor, empress, extreme, greatest, king(ly), majestic, monarch, paramount, potentate, predominant, prince, principal, regal, royal, rule(r), senate, supreme
**sovereign authority** seignory
**sovereign higher than a king** emperor
**sovereign of an empire** emperor
**sovereign of Iran** shah
**sovereign power** majesty
**sovereign remedy** elixir, panacea
**sovereign ruler** king, prince, queen
**sovereign's headdress** crown
**sovereign's residence** palace
**sovereignty** raj, rule
**Soviet** Red, Russian, Siberian
**Soviet bureau** agitprop
**Soviet cosmonaut** Yuri Gagarin
**Soviet government offices** Kremlin
**Soviet grassland** steppe
**Soviet headquarters** Kremlin
**Soviet lake** Aral
**Soviet mountain** Ural
**Soviet news agency** Tass
**Soviet official** commissar
**Soviet prison camp** Gulag
**Soviet region** Siberia
**Soviet republic** Estonia, Georgia, Latvia, Lithuania, Moldavia, Uzbeck
**Soviet sea** Aral, Caspian
**Soviet's spy** Burgess, Maclean, Philby
**sow** broadcast, inseminate, lodge, plant, scatter, seed
**sower** seeder
**sowing** broadcasting, disseminating, implanting, lodging, planting, scattering, seeding,
**sowing machine** seeder
**sowing of seed** semination
**sow's home** sty

**sozzled** drunk, inebriated
**spa** bath, hydro, resort, spring
**space** area, arrange, cosmos, distance, distribute, expanse, expansion, extend, extension, gap, immensity, infinity, interval, margin, order, organise, period, place, region, room, span, spread, universe, vastness, void, volume
**space above stage** flies
**space agency** NASA
**space behind** rear
**space between eyes** lore
**space between the meeting of two lines** angle
**space between things** distance, gap
**space between two columns** bay
**space between veins** areola, areole
**space between windows or pillars** bay
**space body** NASA
**spacecraft** Apollo, Challenger, Gemini, Mariner, Sputnik
**spacecraft's circular trip** orbit
**spacecraft to moon** Apollo
**spacecraft unit** module
**space devoid of air** vacuum
**space dog** Streika
**space enclosed by printed lines** box
**space exhausted of air** vacuum
**space exploration series** Apollo
**space for goods** storage
**space from place to place** distance
**space from thumb to little finger as measure** span
**space in an amphitheatre** arena
**space interval** distance
**space monkey** Enos
**space of eight notes** octave
**space of time** day, hour, month, term, while
**space on reverse of coin** exergue
**space pilot** astronaut, cosmonaut
**space project** probe
**space round** ambit
**space surrounding a home** garden, lawn, yard
**space traveller** astronaut, cosmonaut
**space visitor** alien, ET, Martian
**spacing block** quad
**spacious** airy, ample, baggy, boundless, broad, capacious, commodious, enormous, expansive, extended, extensive, global, great, immense, infinite, large, roomy, sizable, vast, voluminous, wide(spread)
**spade** shovel
**spade-depth of earth** spit
**spade-shaped** palaceous
**spae** foretell, prophesy
**spaghetti or noodles** pasta

**Spain** España, Hesperia, Iberia
**Spain and Portugal** Iberia
**spa in England** Bath, Harrogate
**spa in France** Vichy
**spa in Germany** Baden, Ems
**spa in South Africa** Caledon, Goudini, Montagu, Warmbaths
**span** amount, arch, bestride, bridge, cover, cross(ing), distance, duration, extension, extent, length, link, measure, period, piece, reach, spell, spread, stretch, team, term, traverse, vault
**spangle** paillette, sequin
**Spaniard** señor
**Spanish** Iberian
**Spanish abbey** abadia
**Spanish affirmative** si
**Spanish afternoon** tarde
**Spanish American cattle farm** estancia, hacienda, rancho
**Spanish American labourer** peon
**Spanish article** el, la, las, un, una, uno
**Spanish artist** Picasso
**Spanish author** Alarcon
**Spanish baby** nena, nina
**Spanish bar** cantina
**Spanish bay** Aludia, Bahia, Biscay
**Spanish bayonet** yucca
**Spanish beard** moss
**Spanish being** ente
**Spanish blanket** manta, poncho, serape
**Spanish boy** niño
**Spanish bravo** olé
**Spanish cape** Nao, Trafalgar
**Spanish capital punishment by strangulation** garote, gar(r)otte
**Spanish card game** pedro, ombre
**Spanish castanet dance** saraband(e)
**Spanish castle** Alcazar
**Spanish cathedral city** Seville
**Spanish chaperone** duen(n)a
**Spanish cheer** olé
**Spanish cherry** oloroso
**Spanish chief** cid, jefe
**Spanish child** niño
**Spanish clay building** adobe, tapia
**Spanish cloak** capa, poncho
**Spanish clothes** ropa
**Spanish coarse grass** esparto
**Spanish coin** centavo, escudo, maravedi, peseta, peso, real
**Spanish cold vegetable soup** gazpacho
**Spanish cooking pot** olla
**Spanish council** junta
**Spanish courtyard** patio
**Spanish cowboy** gaucho, llanero
**Spanish cry of approval** olé
**Spanish cup** taza
**Spanish currency** peseta

**Spanish dance** baile, bolero, cachucha, fandango, flamenco, guaracha, jota, malaguena, pavan(e), seguidilla, tango, zapateado
**Spanish day** dia
**Spanish dialect** Ladino
**Spanish dictator** Franco
**Spanish dish** bacalao, olla, paella
**Spanish drink** sangria
**Spanish dry sherry** manzanilla
**Spanish estate with a dwelling house** hacienda
**Spanish exclamation** olé
**Spanish farewell** adios
**Spanish farm** granja, hacienda, ranco
**Spanish festival** fiesta
**Spanish fleet** armada
**Spanish fortress** Alcazar
**Spanish friend** amigo
**Spanish game** pelota
**Spanish gentleman** caballero, don, hidalgo, señor
**Spanish girl** chica, nina, señorita
**Spanish gold coin** doblón, doubloon, pistole
**Spanish governess** duenna
**Spanish grass** esparto
**Spanish guitarist** Segovia
**Spanish gypsy** gitano, zincalo
**Spanish gypsy music** flamenco
**Spanish hat** sombrero
**Spanish head covering** mantilla
**Spanish herb** yerba
**Spanish hero** El Cid
**Spanish holiday** fiesta
**Spanish house** casa, hacienda
**Spanish islands** Balearics, Canaries
**Spanish judge** alca(l)de, juez
**Spanish kind of operetta** zarzuela
**Spanish king's palace** Escirial, Escorial
**Spanish knife** machet(t)e
**Spanish lace headscarf** mantilla
**Spanish lady** dama, dona, señora
**Spanish lively dance** guaracha
**Spanish man** don, señor
**spanish meadow** vega
**Spanish means of execution** gar(r)otte
**Spanish measure** vara
**Spanish military dictator** caudillo
**Spanish miss** señorita
**Spanish mister** señor
**Spanish money** peseta, peso
**Spanish mother** madre
**Spanish motorway** autopista
**Spanish mountains** Pyrenees
**Spanish musical instrument** castanet, guitar, tambourine
**Spanish name for Japurá** Yapurá
**Spanish nanny** duenna
**Spanish national museum** Prado

**Spanish nobleman** don, grandee, hidalgo
**Spanish novelist** Aleman, Baroja, Ibáñez
**Spanish painter** Dali, El Greco, Goya, Miro, Murillo, Ribera, Velázquez, Zurbaran
**Spanish palace** Alhambra, Escorial, Escurial
**Spanish parliament** Cortes
**Spanish pear** avocado
**Spanish peninsula** Iberia
**Spanish pepper** chili, pimento
**Spanish plain** Urgel
**Spanish plantation** hacienda
**Spanish police** rurales
**Spanish port** Abdera, Adra, Alicante, Almeria, Barcelona, Cadiz, Corunna, Gades, Gadir, Gijon, Malaga, Noya, Palos, Vigo
**Spanish priest** padre
**Spanish princess** infanta
**Spanish province** Avila, Granada
**Spanish provinces** Canary Islands
**Spanish queen** Isabella
**Spanish range** Pyrenees, Sierra Nevada
**Spanish red pepper** pimiento
**Spanish region** Aragon, Castile, Catalonia, Galicia, Leon
**Spanish relative** tio
**Spanish resort** Malaga
**Spanish rice dish** paella
**Spanish sailing vessel** galleon
**Spanish saint** Dominic, Ignatius, Teresa
**Spanish sergeant** alguazil
**Spanish shawl** mantilla, serape
**Spanish sheepskin jacket** zamarra
**Spanish sherry** amontillado, jerez
**Spanish solo dance** cachucha
**Spanish soup** gazpacho
**Spanish stock farm** rancho
**Spanish strait** Gibraltar
**Spanish sword** bilbo, espadon, toledo
**Spanish sword city** Toledo
**Spanish title of address** don, señor, señora, señorita
**Spanish treasure ship** galleon
**Spanish unit of length** vara
**Spanish unit of weight** arroba
**Spanish vehicle** volante
**Spanish waiter** mozo
**Spanish war hero** Hobson
**Spanish warship** galleon
**Spanish water pot** olla
**Spanish weapon** bolas
**Spanish wine** malaga, manzanilla, navarra, riojas, sherry
**Spanish woman's head covering** mantilla
**Spanish yes** si

**Spanish young lady** señorita
**spank** beat, belt, clout, klap, larrup, paddle, punish, skelp, slap, smack, strap, tan, trounce, wallop, welt, whack, whip
**spanning** astraddle, astride, straggling
**span of oxen** team
**span of years** age
**spar** argue, bicker, box, dispute, mast, rafter, scrap, skirmish, squabble, wrangle, wrestle
**spare** careful, economical, emaciated, extra, forbear, frugal, gaunt, lean, meagre, omit, pardon, reserve, restricted, save, scanty, slender, slight, surplus, thin, withhold
**spare piece** remnant
**spare wheel** stepney
**sparing** careful, cost-conscious, economical, frugal, thrifty
**sparing of words** taciturn
**spark** amourist, atom, beau, belle, bit, coxcomb, dab, dandy, dash, flame, flare, flash, fleck, flicker, fop, gleam, glimmer, glint, hint, ignite, iota, jot, mite, scintilla(te), scrap, sparkle, speck, spirit, suitor, swell, tinge, touch, trace, vestige, vigour, vim, vivacity, warmth, wooer, zest
**sparkle** beam, brilliance, bubble, coruscate, dance, dash, dazzle, effervesce, élan, fizz(le), flame, flash, flicker, gaiety, gleam, glint, glisten, glister, glitter, glow, life, light, lustre, quiver, radiance, scintillate, shimmer, shine, spark, spirit, twinkle, twinkling, vitality, vivacity, wink
**sparkling wine** asti, champagne
**spar projection from bow of ship** browsprit
**sparring partner** boxer
**sparse** meagre, scant(y), scattered, spare, thin
**Sparta** Lacedaemon, Laconia
**spartan** abstemious, abstinent, ascetic, austere, bleak, bold, brave, controlled, demanding, difficult, disciplined, doric, extreme, fearless, forbiddng, frugal, grim, hard, harsh, heroic, intrepid, plain, rigid, rigorous, severe, stern, strict, sturdy, valiant
**Spartan dog** bloodhound
**Spartan queen** Leda
**Spartan serf** helot
**spasm** ague, chorea, contraction, convulsion, cramp, eclampsia, epilepsy, eruption, explosion, fit, frenzy, jerk, orgasm, paroxysm, rage, rigour, seizure, spell, tarantism, tetanus, throb, throe, tic, twitch

**spasmodic** broken, convulsive, desultory, disconnected, discontinuous, disturbed, erratic, fitful, fluctuating, fragmentary, haphazard, impulsive, incomplete, intermittent, interrupted, irregular, jerky, sporadic, variable
**spasmodic breathing** gasping
**spasmodic contraction** tic
**spasmodic swallowing of air** aerophagia
**spasm of the chest** angina pectoris
**spat** ejected, expectorated, gaiter, spit, spluttered, tiff
**spate** cascade, cataclysm, deluge, downpour, flood, flow, gush, hail, inundation, outbreak, outpouring, overflow(ing), plague, rain, rush, shower, stream, tide, torrent, wave
**spatter** splash
**spawn** beget, dam, eggs, generate, issue, multiply, ova, propagate, reproduce, roe, seed, sire, spore, spread
**spawning** creative, fertile, productive, prolific, teeming
**spawning place** redd
**spawn of shellfish** spat
**spay** castrate, geld, neuter
**spayed animal** neuter
**speak** address, argue, articulate, comment, communicate, converse, declaim, declare, disclose, express, lecture, mention, orate, plead, pronounce, say, state, talk, tell, utter, voice
**speak angrily** snap, snarl
**speak at great length** expatiate
**speak at length** descant, discourse, dissert, enlarge, expatiate, perorate
**speak at top of voice** bawl
**speak badly of** backbite
**speak boastfully** bluster
**speak cynically** snarl
**speak derisively** scoff
**speak didactically** preach
**speaker** elocutionist, me, orator, sayer
**speaker of a convocation** prolocutor
**speaker's platform** dais, podium, rostrum
**speaker's platform in assembly in ancient Athens** bema, bima(h)
**speak evil of** traduce, vilify
**speak falsely** lie
**speak falsely of** belie
**speak first** accost, greet
**speak foolishly** blather (Sc), blether, prate
**speak for** advocate, recommend, represent, support, uphold
**speak from memory** recite

**speak haltingly** lisp, stammer, stumble, stutter
**speak hoarsely** croak
**speak ill of** defame, malign, slander, traduce
**speak imperfectly** lisp, stammer, stutter
**speak impromptu** ad lib
**speak in a piercing voice** shrill
**speak in a soft murmur** coo
**speak inaudibly** mutter
**speak in barely audible manner** mutter
**speak incoherently** rave
**speak in court** plead
**speak indistinctly** burr, mumble, mutter, slur
**speaking art** rhetoric
**speaking for** advocating
**speaking in several languages** polyglot
**speaking loftily** magniloquent
**speaking many languages** multilingual, polyglot
**speaking only one language** monolingual
**speaking skill** oratory
**speaking spitefully** catty
**speaking three languages** trilingual
**speaking to job applicants** interviewing
**speaking with a burr** rolling one's r's
**speak in hushed tone** whisper
**speak in low tones** murmur, whisper
**speak in public** orate
**speak insincerely** cant
**speak irreverently** blaspheme
**speak irritably to** snap
**speak lazily** drawl
**speak like a baby** babble
**speak misleadingly** prevaricate
**speak mockingly** scoff
**speak nasally** snuffle
**speak of** mention
**speak off the cuff** ad lib
**speak on behalf of** defend, plead
**speak out** affirm, announce, avouch, declare, proclaim, protest
**speak out for** announce, testify
**speak out loud** utter
**speak pompously** pontificate
**speak publicly** orate
**speak quietly** murmur, whisper
**speak scornfully** sneer
**speak sharply** snap
**speak sibilantly** hiss, whisper
**speak slightingly of** disparage
**speak slowly** drawl
**speak softly** whisper
**speak to** accost, address, reprimand, scold
**speak together** chat, converse

**speak under breath** mutter
**speak unthinkingly** blurt
**speak very distinctly** articulate
**speak violently** inveigh, rage, rave
**speak well of** commend, promote
**speak with contempt** sneer
**speak with difficulty** stutter
**speak with emphasis** accent, stress
**speak with fervour** enthuse
**speak without preparation** extemporise
**speak with repetitions of syllables** stammer
**speak with the mouth nearly closed** mutter
**spear** assagai, assegai, cut, dart, dig, gore, halberd, harpoon, impale, injure, insert, jab, javelin, knife, lance, leister, penetrate, pierce, pike, poke, prod, puncture, spike, stab, thrust, trident, wound
**spear a fish** gaff, gig
**spearfish** marlin
**spear-like missile** harpoon
**spear point** pike
**spear-shaped** hastate
**special** diffident, distinct, distinguished, especial, extraordinary, particular, peculiar, plain, single, uncommon, unusual
**special ability** talent, skill
**special ability to do something** power
**special advantage** privilege
**special anniversary** jubilee
**special aptitude** talent
**special capacity** knack
**special clothes for a job** uniform
**special corps** élite
**special countenance** patronage
**special disposal of stock at low prices** sale
**special edition** extra
**special effort** stunt
**special emphasis** stress
**special event** occasion
**special feat** stunt
**special feature** speciality
**special flavour** tang
**special food shop** delicatessen
**special gift or skill** talent
**special group** élite, quorum
**specialised skill** expertise, know-how
**specialist in cultivation of trees** arborist
**specialist in ear diseases** aurist
**specialist in internal disease** internist
**specialist in medical diagnosis and treatment** physician
**specialist in mental diseases** alienist, psychiatrist, psychotherapist
**specialist in obstetrics** obstetrician

**specialist in treatment of eye diseases and defects** oculist, ophthalmologist
**specialist who operates** surgeon
**specially chosen** select
**specially designed garment** creation
**specially efficacious for something** specific
**specially fast** express
**specially skilled opinion** advice
**specially trained animal** guide-dog, police-dog
**special messenger** courier
**special outfit** costume
**special personal quality** charisma
**special pleasure** treat
**special product** speciality
**special skill** talent
**special study group** seminar
**special support** patronage
**special time** holiday, season, vacation
**species** branch, brand, breed, category, class, description, division, genre, group(ing), kind, manner genus, section, set, sort, style, subdivision, type, variety
**species of cabbage** broccoli
**species of clover** alsike
**species of goat** gnu
**species of hawk** gavilan
**species of parakeet** lovebird
**species of pepper** betel
**species of reed** papyrus
**species of small toad** natterjack
**species of swallow** martin
**species of violet** pansy
**species of wild ass** dzigettai
**species of willow** osier
**specific** characteristic, conditional, defined, definite, definitive, detailed, diagnostic, especial, exact, explicit, express, indicative, limited, obvious, particular, peculiar, pointed, precise, regarding, special, specified, symptomatic, unequivocal
**specification** agreement, average, canon, circumstance, clause, condition, contract, criterion, detail, engagement, example, fact, feature, grade, guide, item, measure, model, norm, particular, pattern, principle, provision, qualification, requirement, restriction, rule, sample, settlement, standard, stipulation, term, type
**specific engagement** date
**specific variety** kind
**specified person** one
**specify** assign, choose, cite, clarify, define, delineate, demarcate, design(ate), distinguish, enumerate, establish, exemplify, explain, express, identify, indicate, itemise,

mention, name, nominate, prescribe, select, state, stipulate
**specimen** copy, example, exemplification, exhibit, individual, model, part, pattern, proof, prototype, sample, swatch, type
**specious** absurd, appearing, artificial, avowed, bogus, counterfeit, deceitful, deceptive, dissembling, ersatz, fake, fallacious, false, faulty, fraudulent, hypocritical, illogical, imitation, incorrect, insincere, misleading, mock, nominal, paralogical, plausible, presumed, probable, reputed, simulated, supposed, two-faced, unsound, untrue
**specious argument** sophism, sophistry
**specious show** gloze
**speck** atom, blemish, blot, defect, dot, fault, fleck, iota, mark, mite, mote, particle, tittle
**speckle** besmirch, blot, dirty, dot, fleck, mark, soil, spatter, splodge, spot, stain, sully, taint, tarnish
**speckled** dappled, dotted, flecked, mottled, spotted, sprinkled
**speckled bird** guinea-fowl, starling
**speckled horse** roan
**speck of dirt** smut
**speck of dust** mote
**spectacle** curiosity, display, event, exhibition, extravaganza, marvel, pageant, parade, performance, scene, show, sight, wonder
**spectacles** bifocal, (eye)glasses, goggles, lorgnette, monocle, specs, sunglasses
**spectacular act** stunt
**spectacular display** pageantry
**spectacular display of swimming and diving** aquacade
**spectacular freestyle skiing** hotdogging
**spectacular procession** pageant
**spectator** bystander, eyewitness, observer, onlooker, viewer, watcher, witness
**spectator at a card game** kibitzer
**spectators watching a tennis match** dedans
**spectral** ashen, awesome, deathlike, dim, dreamlike, eerie, faint, fearful, frightening, frightful, ghastly, ghostlike, ghostly, grim, grisly, gruesome, illusory, imaginary, livid, mysterious, mystic, nebulous, obscure, occult, pale, pallid, paranormal, phantom, shocking, strange, terrible, uncanny, vague, wan, weird

**spectre** apparition, bog(e)y, bogle, chimera, demon, eidolon, elf, fetch, ghost, illusion, image, imp, phantasm, phantom, poltergeist, presence, revenant, shade, shadow, shape, sight, soul, spirit, spook, sprite, vision, wraith
**specular** mirror-like
**speculate** cogitate, conjecture, consider, contemplate, deliberate, gamble, guess, hazard, hypothesise, imagine, invest, meditate, muse, ponder, risk, scheme, suppose, surmise, theorise, think, venture, wonder
**speculated about** theorised
**speculate for a fall** bear
**speculate for a rise** bull
**speculate whimsically** fantasise
**speculation** conjecture, gambling, hypothesis, investing, supposition, surmise, theory
**speculative** theoretical
**speculative believer** gnostic
**speculum** mirror
**speech** address, assertion, asseveration, comment, communication, conversation, declaration, dialect, discourse, language, oration, parlance, remark, talk, tongue, utterance, words
**speech art** elocution
**speech centre** cortex
**speech defect** aphasia, lalia, lallation, lisp, stammer, stutter
**speech disorder** impediment
**speech expert** phonetist
**speech form** idiom
**speech hesitation** er, um
**speechify** address, argue, declaim, descant, discourse, harangue, lecture, orate, perorate, plead, preach, rail, rant, speak, spout
**speech in praise of person** eulogy
**speech interrupter** heckler
**speechless** dumb(founded), dumbstruck, mute, shocked, silent, stunned
**speech loss** aphasia
**speech of censure** tirade
**speech of district** dialect
**speech of praise** eulogy, panegyric
**speech sound with hissing effect** sibilant
**speech to an assembly** harangue
**speech with an accent** dialect
**speed** alacrity, celerity, direct, dispatch, expedite, expedition, gallop, guide, haste, hurry, pace, quickness, race, rapidity, rate, run, rush, swiftness, tempo, velocity
**speed car** racer

**speed-checking device** radar
**speed contest** race, sprint
**speed contestant** racer
**speed control** timing
**speedily** apace, rapidly
**speed indicator** tachymeter
**speeding** advancing, aiding, assisting, boosting, careering, dispatching, expediting, facilitating, flashing, galloping, hastening, helping, hurrying, impelling, promoting, quickening, racing, rushing, sprinting, tearing, urging, zooming
**speed off** run
**speed of music** tempo
**speed of sound** Mach (one)
**speed of stepping** pace
**speed on foot** run
**speed record** time
**speed regulator** brake, gearbox
**speed trap** camera, radar
**speed up** accelerate, hasten, increase, precipitate, quicken, urge
**speed up motor** race, rev
**speedway** racetrack
**speed writing** shorthand
**speedy** express, fast, fleet, hasty, immediate, quick, rapid, winged
**speedy horse** Arab, racehorse
**speedy postal message** telegram
**speedy warship** cruiser
**spell** abracadabra, bout, charm, exorcism, hex, interval, magic, period, stretch, term, trance
**spellbind** bewitch, charm, enchant, enrapture, ensnare, enthrall, entrance, entrap, hook, hypnotise, mesmerise, overpower
**spellbound** agape, astonished, bewitched, enchanted, enraptured, enthralled, hypnotised, rapt, speechless
**spell of bowling** over
**spell of drinking** bout, fuddle
**spell of lawbreaking** crime wave
**spell of teaching** lesson
**spell of work** stint
**spell out** clarify, discern, elucidate, explicit, specify
**spend** apply, consume, deplete, disburse, dissipate, employ, exhaust, expend, impoverish, lavish, outlay, splurge, squander, use, waste
**spend badly** misspend
**spend extravagantly** splurge
**spend futilely** waste
**spending binge** spree
**spending excessively** extravagant
**spend lavishly** pour, squander
**spend needlessly** waste
**spend period in prison** do time, serve time

**spendthrift** prodigal, spender, squanderer, wasteful, waster, wastrel
**spend time doing nothing** laze
**spend time frivolously** gallivant
**spend time idly** loaf, loiter
**spend time in idleness** dally
**spend time on petty details** niggle, nitpick
**spend wastefully** squander
**spend winter in dormant state** hibernate
**spent salmon** judy, ligger, runfish, slat
**sperm whale** cachalot
**spew forth** belch
**sphere** ball, circle, coterie, district, domain, environment, field, globe, globule, luminary, moon, orb(it), oval, planet, precinct, quarter, range, rank, round, shell, situation, spheroid, spherule, star, stratum
**sphere of activity** arena, fief, scene
**sphere of combat** arena
**sphere of contest** court, field, oval, ring, rink
**sphere of existence** world
**sphere of observation** scope
**spherical** bulbous, egg-shaped, global, globate, globe-shaped, globular, orbicular, oval, ovate, ovoid, pyriform, rotund, round, spheroid, sphery
**spherical body** ball, globe, orb
**spherical cheese** Edam
**spherical microbe found in chain-like groups** streptococcus
**spheroidal** globate
**spice** amaracus, aniseed, cardamom, cassia, cayenne, chervil, chil(l)i, chive, cinnamon, clove, coriander, dill, dittany, endive, fennel, fenugreek, garlic, gentian, ginger, horseradish, mace, marjoram, mint, mustard, nutmeg, oregano, orpine, paprika, parsley, pepper, peppermint, rape, rosemary, rue, saffron, sage, season(ing), tarragon, thyme, turmeric, verbena, watercress, yerba
**spiced balls of meat** koftas
**spiced bread roll** bun, mosbolletjie
**spiced gingery cake** parkin
**spiced liquid** marinade
**spiced port drink** negus
**spiced sausage** salami
**spiced wine** mead
**spice holder** cruet
**Spice Islands** Moluccas
**spice mixture** curry
**spick and span** brand-new, clean, fresh, immaculate, neat, polished, scrubbed, spotless, spruce, tidy, trim, well-kept

**spicy** acid, acrid, aromatic, balmy, biting, colourful, hot, interesting, juicy, pefumed, peppery, piquant, pungent, racy, risqué, savoury, seasoned, sensational, sharp, sour, suggestive, tart
**spicy fragrance** aroma
**spicy hot dish** chil(l)i
**spicy sausage** salami
**spicy stew** goulash, olla, ragout
**spider** arachnid, skillet, tarantula, trivet, weaver
**spider's home** web
**spider's nest** (cob)web, nidus
**spider's trap** (cob)web, trapdoor
**spider's web** net
**spidery mesh** web
**spiel** orate, patter, speech, story, talk
**spieler** smoothie, smoothy
**spignel** baldmoney, meu
**spigot** cock, faucet, peg, plug, spile, spill, stopcock, stopper, stopple, tap, valve, wad, wedge
**spike** annul, barb, bolt, check, discard, dowel, drop, eliminate, gad, impale, lose, nail, peg, penetrate, pierce, pike, pin, point, pricker, projection, prong, rivet, skewer, spear, spica, spine, spit, spur, stake, stick, thorn, toggle, trenail, void
**spike a cannon** cloy
**spiked** spicate, tined
**spiked club** mace
**spiked helmet of German army** pickelhaube
**spiked stick for urging cattle** goad
**spikelet** alicole, chat, locusta, spicule
**spikelet in barley** awn
**spike-like** spinate
**spikenard** nard
**spike-nosed fish** gar
**spike of antler** tine
**spike of corn** cob, ear
**spike of flowers** ament
**spike of fork** prong, tine
**spike of ice** icicle
**spike of maize** corn-cob, mealie
**spike of wheat** ear
**spike on golf shoe** cleat
**spike on rose** thorn
**spiketail** pintail
**spikewood** trenail
**spill** confess, disclose, divulge, dribble, drop, fall, leak, mess, overflow, pour, reveal, slop, slosh, splash, taper, upset
**spill clumsily** slop
**spillikin** jackstraw
**spill the beans** blab, confess, inform, tattle
**spilt beer** ullage
**spilt liquid** mess(ed)

**spilt milk** loss
**spin** birl (Sc), coil, extend, fabricate, flip, gyrate, gyration, lengthen, narrate, pirouette, prolong, protract, reel, relate, revolution, revolve, roll, rotate, run, swim, toss, turn, twirl, twist, wheel, whirl
**spin a floating log with the feet** birl
**spinal bone** vertebra
**spinal column** axis, axon, backbone, spine
**spinal curvature** lordosis, scoliosis
**spinal injury** slipped disc
**spinal marrow** medulla, pith
**spinal membrane** dura
**spinal segment** vertebra
**spin coin** flip
**spindle** axis, axle, mandrel, mandril, pin, pivot, rod, shaft, swivel
**spindle-shaped body of an aeroplane** fuselage
**spine** acicula, backbone, barb, bristle, hair, needle, point, prickle, prong, quill, ray, spike, spinal column, spur, stubble, thorn, vertebrae, whisker
**spine and joint doctor** orthopaedic surgeon
**spinel** balas, gahnite, gem, inkle, picotite, ruby
**spineless** afraid, cowardly, fearful, feeble, flaccid, indecisive, infirm, invertebrate, irresolute, lax, limp, rubbery, slack, thewless, timid, undetermined, weak
**spine of a porcupine** quill
**spinet** espinet, giraffe, harpsichord, octavina, sourdine, virginal
**spinner of yarns** raconteur, storyteller
**spinney** copse, thicket
**spinning round on the toe** pirouette
**spinning top** peerie (Sc)
**spinning toy** top, yo-yo
**spinning wheel** chark(h)a, turn
**spin of engine** rev
**spin-off** consequence, derivative, effect, fruit, issue, legacy, offshoot, outcome, product, result, returns, upshot, yield
**spin on axis** gyrate, rotate
**spin out** amplify, delay, prolong, protract
**spin round** twirl
**spinster** miss, old maid
**spiny** acanthoid, aciculate, barbed, briery, bristly, difficult, echinate, prickly, spiculate, spiniferous, spinous, thistly, thorny, troublesome
**spiny anteater** echidna
**spiny-finned food fish** mackerel, pompano
**spiny fish** goby, perch, porcupine fish
**spiny plant** cactus

**spiny rodent** hedgehog, porcupine
**spiny sea-creature** urchin
**spiny shrub** gorse, mesquite
**spiral** cochleate, coil(ed), corkscrew, curl(icue), gyre, gyroidal, helical, helicine, helix, ringlet, sinuate, spin, spire, spiroid, strophe, twirly, volute, whorl(ed), wreathe
**spiral cavity of internal ear** cochlea
**spiral channel on record** groove
**spiral nail** screw
**spiral of wire** coil
**spiral opener** corkscrew
**spiral part of screw** worm
**spiral shell** conch
**spiral spring** coil
**spiral staircase** caracol(e), dressage
**spire** apex, belfry, crest, minaret, obelisk, peak, pinnacle, shaft, steeple, summit, tip, tower, turret, vertex
**spirit** angel, animate, animation, apparition, ardour, attitude, atua (M), consciousness, elf, embodiment, energy, fairy, fire, geist (G), genie, ghost, gin, gist, grit, (hob)goblin, inspirit, instil, life, liquor, liveliness, mettle, mind, morale, sense, soul, spectre, tenor, tone, vitality, vivacity, zealousness
**spirit away** abduct, kidnap, seduce
**spirit distilled from malted barley** whisky
**spirit distilled from sugar cane** rum
**spirit distilled from wine** brandy
**spirited** alive, animated, ardent, brilliant, courageous, eager, energetic, excitable, gusty, impetuous, lively, mettlesome, plucky, resolute, tenacious, valiant, vehement
**spirited animation** sparkle
**spirited girl** filly
**spirited horse** arab, courser, steed, warhorse
**spirited song** lilt
**spiritless** apathetic, dull, mopy, vapid
**spirit measure** dra(ch)m
**spirit meeting** seance
**spirit of air** sylph
**spirit of community** ethos
**spirit of enmity** animosity
**spirit of evil** demon, devil
**spirit of hostility** animosity
**spirit of man** soul
**spirit of the age** zeitgeist (G)
**spirit of the place** genius loci (L)
**spirits and water** grog
**spirit session** seance
**spirit stove** etna
**spiritual being** angel, cherub, ens, essence, seraph

**spiritual enlightenment** rebirth
**spiritual gift** charism(a)
**spiritual glow** aura
**spiritualism board** ouija
**spiritualist** medium, occultist
**spiritualistic session** seance
**spiritual knowledge** gnosis
**spiritual leader** shepherd
**spiritual life** sanctity
**spiritually emotional** soulful
**spiritually moving** uplifting
**spiritual meeting** seance
**spiritual mentor** guru
**spiritual part of human being** soul
**spiritual ruin** damnation, perdition, reprobacy
**spiritual sloth** accidie, acedia
**spiritual teacher** guru, (maha)rishi, swami
**spit** drool, saliva, spew, spittle, sputum
**spit and image** clone, copy, counterpart, ditto, duplicate, twin
**spite** annoy, hate, hurt, injure, malevolence, malice, malignity, rancour, spleen, thwart, venom
**spiteful** acerb, avenging, barbed, bitter, catty, cruel, demoniac, evil-minded, harsh, hateful, ill-disposed, ill-natured, malevolent, malicious, mean, merciless, nasty, pitiless, rancorous, retaliative, retributive, revengeful, sardonic, unforgiving, unkindly, vengeful, venomous, vicious, vindictive, wanton
**spiteful fierce-tempered woman** hellcat
**spiteful in talk** catty
**spiteful old woman** grimalkin
**spiteful woman** vixen
**spit out** eject, splutter, vomit
**spitting of blood from the lower air passage** haemoptysis
**spitting snake** cobra, rinkhals
**spittle** drool, saliva, spit, sputum
**spittlebug** froghopper
**spittoon** cuspidor
**splash** advertise, bedew, bespatter, break, dampen, dash, daub, display, impact, lap, moisten, paddle, slop, slosh, spatter, spill, splodge, spray, sprinkle, squirt, wade
**splash about** dabble
**splash against** lap
**splash around** swim, wallow
**splashing** bathing, battering, breaking, buffeting, dabbling, dashing, plunging, showering, slopping, spattering, spraying, spreading, sprinkling, squirting, striking, surging, wading, wallowing, wetting
**splashing about** sossing
**splash out** spend, splurge

**splash with mud** splatter
**splay** bevel, clumsy, expand, slope, spread
**spleen** acrimony, anger, annoyance, asperity, bitterness, displeasure, exasperation, fury, indignation, ire, irritability, irritation, mordancy, outrage, passion, peevishness, pique, rage, rancour, resentment, sarcasm, tartness, temper, vexation, virulence, wrath
**spleen of mammals** milt
**splendid** admirable, beautiful, brilliant, costly, dazzling, elegant, eminent, glorious, gorgeous, grand, great, heroic, imposing, impressive, lustrous, luxurious, magnificent, rare, rich, striking, sumptuous, superb
**splendid array** panoply
**splendid display** pomp
**splendidly generous** munificent
**splendidly lavish** magnificent
**splendid raiment** sheen
**splendour** brightness, brilliance, distinction, éclat, esteem, glory, grandeur, grandiosity, honour, importance, lambency, luminosity, lustre, magnificence, nobleness, pomp, prestige, radiance, renown, repute, richness, sheen, spectacle, stateliness, superbness, weight
**splenetic** abrupt, argumentative, bad-tempered, bearish, cross, disagreeable, fractious, grumpy, ill-natured, ill-tempered, irascible, irritable, peevish, rude, snappish, snarling, splenetical, surly, terse, testy, uncivil, unfriendly
**splenic fever** anthrax
**splinter** chip, flake, fracture, fragment, insertion, part, piece, segment, separate, shiver, sliver, spall, split, stinger
**splintered pottery fragment** ostracon, (pot)sherd, shard
**splinter group** schism, sect
**splinter of stone** gallet
**splinter of wood** spell, spillikin
**splinter party** schism
**split** apportion, break, cleave, cleft, crack, disagree(ment), diverge, divide, divided, rend, rent, rift, rive, schism, separate, sever, shake, tear, undecided
**split asunder** rive
**split down the middle** bisect
**split fish** scrod
**split from** secede, withdraw
**split grain** dal
**split hairs** cavil, nitpick, pettifog, quibble
**split into opposing groups** polarise

**split in two** rend
**split leather into thin layers** skive
**split pen-point** nib
**split personality** schizophrenia
**split second** instant
**splitting device** wedge
**splitting knife** flammer
**split up** disband, dissolve, divide, divorce, part, separate
**spoil** corrupt, damage, demolish, destroy, disfigure, harm, impair, injure, mar, ravage, rob, ruin, sour, vitiate, waste
**spoil appearance of** deface
**spoil by disgrace** stain
**spoiled** gâté (F)
**spoiled child** brat
**spoil or favour** indulge
**spoilsport** damper, killjoy, meddler, misery, nark, wet blanket, wowser
**spoilt children** enfant gâté (F)
**spoil the beauty of** blemish
**spoil with luxury** pamper
**spoked disc** wheel
**spoken** expressed, oral, phonetic, uttered, verbal, voiced
**spoken exam** oral
**spoken in England** English
**spoken in Germany** German
**spoken in Holland** Dutch
**spoken in Ireland** Irish
**spoken in Italy** Italian
**spoken in Milan** Italian
**spoken in Paris** French
**spoken in Portugal** Portuguese
**spoken in Scotland** Scottish
**spoken in Spain** Spanish
**spoken in Sri Lanka** Tamil
**spoken in Wales** Welsh
**spoken word** agraph
**spoliate** demolish, desolate, despoil, destroy, devastate, extirpate, foray, loot, maraud, obliterate, pillage, plunder, raid, reive (Sc), rob, ruin, strip
**spondulics** money, notes
**sponge** clean, loofah, mooch, mop, porifer, scrounge, swab, wipe
**sponge-cake dessert** trifle
**sponge fisher** hooker
**sponge lightly** dab
**sponge out** cancel, delete, efface, erase, expunge, obliterate
**sponger** appendage, beggar, bootlicker, borrower, cadger, courtier, flatterer, flunk(e)y, follower, freeloader, hanger-on, lackey, leech, mendicant, minion, parasite, scrounger, supplicant, tramp, vagrant
**sponge up** absorb
**sponging** bathing, cadging, clean(s)ing, disinfecting, laundering,
purging, purifying, rinsing, scrounging, scrubbing, soaking, soaping, swabbing, washing
**spongy sweetmeat** marshmallow
**sponsor** advocate, back(er), finance, godparent, patron, support
**sponsorship** aegis
**spontaneous** automatic, dense, effortless, extempore, free, gratuitous, impetuous, impulsive, instinctive, intuitive, irresistible, lush, luxuriant, native, natural, offhand, open, rank, rash, self-acting, snap, unbidden, uncaused, unconscious, unconstrained, uncontrollable, unforced, unpremeditated, unprompted, unrequested, unrestrained, unwitting, voluntary, wild, willing
**spontaneous abortion** miscarriage
**spontaneous activity** play
**spontaneous applause** ovation
**spontaneously** proprio motu (L)
**spoof** hoax, humbug, lampoon, parody, skit, swindle
**spook** ghost, ghoul, spectre
**spooky** eerie, ghostly, weird
**spool** bobbin, cop, mandrel, reel
**spoon** ladle
**spoonful of butter** dob, pat
**sporadic** different, dispersed, erratic, few, fitful, infrequent, intermittent, irregular, isolated, occasional, periodic, rare, scarce, solitary, unassociated, uncustomary, unusual
**spore bearer** sorus
**spore producer on fungus** uredinium, uredium, uredosorus
**sport** amusement, athletics, baseball, cricket, derision, diversion, entertainment, frolic, fun, gambol, game, jesting, jukskei, mockery, netball, pastime, play(thing), recreation, ridicule, rugby, soccer, tennis, toy, trifle
**sport arena** stadium
**sport for riders** polo(crosse)
**sporting attacker** forward
**sporting competition** tournament
**sporting dog** pointer, retriever, setter, spaniel
**sporting jacket** blazer
**sporting side** team
**sportive** amusing, carnival, cheery, comical, festal, festive, frisky, frolicsome, gala, gamesome, happy, humorous, impish, jocular, jolly, jovial, joyful, jubilant, lively, merry, mischievous, playful, rascally, roguish, sprightly
**sportman's timepiece** stop-watch
**sport of hunting** venery
**sport on the river** angling
**sport participant** player
**sport played on horseback** polo(crosse)
**sports arena** field, oval, rink, stadium
**sports broadcaster** commentator
**sports champion** victor ludorum (L)
**sports competition anyone may enter** open
**sports enclosure** arena
**sports fixture** game
**sports gear** kit
**sports ground** pitch
**sports group** team
**sports hall** gym(nasium)
**sportsman** competitor, contender, contestant, runner
**sportsman's attendant** gillie
**sports match** game
**sports meeting** tournament
**sports official** referee, umpire
**sportsperson** athlete
**sports ring** arena
**sports shoe** sneaker
**sports side** team
**sports theatre** arena
**sports trainer** coach
**sportswoman** competitor, contender, contestant, runner
**sport venue** arena, field, oval, rink, stadium
**sport viewer** spectator
**sporty** athletic, gay, loud, stylish
**spot** blemish, blot, dot, eye, flaw, fleck, locale, locality, mark, pimple, place, site, situation, soil, speckle, stain, stigma, taint, tarnish
**spotless** blameless, chaste, clean, faultless, flawless, immaculate, impeccable, perfect, pure, scrubbed, speckless, stainless, unblemished, unsoiled, unspoiled, unspotted, unsullied, untarnished
**spotlessly** flawlessly, immaculately
**spot of bother** brush
**spot on decayed fruit** blet
**spot on dice** pip
**spot on peacock's tail** eye
**spotted and streaked** brindled
**spotted beetle** ladybird
**spotted cat** cheetah, leopard, ocelot
**spotted catlike mammal** genet
**spotted deer** chital
**spotted dog** Dalmatian
**spotted garden dweller** ladybird
**spotted horse** piebald
**spotted pelt** leopardskin
**spotted sandpiper** peetweet
**spotted shark** dogfish
**spotted wildcat** ocelot
**spotty** bitty, blotchy, dotted, erratic, fitful, irregular, patchy, pimpled,

random, sketchy, speckled, spotted, uneven
**spotty skin** acne
**spouse** companion, consort, husband, mate, partner, wife
**spouse's boy** stepson
**spout** jet, nozzle, pipe, pour, spurt, squirt, stream
**spout to disperse rainwater** gargoyle
**sprag** chock
**sprain** injure, overstrain, stave (Sc), strain, twist, wrench
**sprawl** branch, extend, languid, loll, lounge, meander, recline, slouch, slump, spread, straggle
**spray** aerosol, atomiser, bough, bouquet, branch, burst, corsage, diffuse, disperse, drizzle, greenery, scatter, shoot, shower, splash, sprig, sprinkle(r)
**spray blown along surface of sea** spindrift
**spray can** aerosol
**spray of flowers worn in buttonhole** bouttonnière
**spray of gemstones** aigrette
**spraypainting** airbrushing
**spread** circulate, cloth, cover, deploy, diffuse, dilate, disperse, display, dispose, disseminate, distribute, expand, extend, feast, open, overlay, preserve, proliferate, promulgate, reach, scatter, shed, splay, sprawl, stretch, tablecloth, unfold, unroll
**spread about** strew
**spread for drying** ted
**spreading legs** straddling
**spreading of disease** contagion, infection
**spreading out from a point** divergent
**spread on** anoint, rub
**spread out** deploy, diffuse, expand, flat, radiate, splay
**spread over** overlay
**spread rumours** gossip(y), skinder(y)
**spread seed by bursting** dehisce
**spread throughout** pervade
**spree** amusement, beano, binge, caper, carouse, carousal, debauch, escapade, festivity, fling, frolic, jag, jol, orgy, randan, revel, rollick, romp, skylarking, splurge
**sprig** twig
**sprightly** active, agile, alert, brisk, gay, jaunty, joyous, lively, pert, spry, vivacious
**spring** arise, beginning, bend, bounce, bound, buck, buoyancy, cause, come, crack, dart, derive, descend, develop, elasticity, emanate, emerge, explode, flexibility, flow, fly,
geyser, grow, hop, issue, jump, leap, origin(ate), pounce, proceed, rebound, recoil, resilience, rise, root, shoot, source, spa, split, springtime, start, stem, vault, warp, well
**spring as from fountain** well
**spring back** rebound, recoil, resile
**spring bulb** daffodil, freesia, sparaxis, tulip
**spring crop** rabi
**spring festival in northern hemisphere** Easter
**spring flower** anemone, crocus, daffodil, freesia, sparaxis, tulip, violet
**spring from** emanate, result, source
**springing up anew** renascent
**springlike** vernal
**spring on foot** hop, jump
**spring or autumn** season
**spring rice** boro
**spring up** accrue, arise
**spring upon suddenly** pounce
**springy** bouncy, buoyant, elastic, extensible, flexible, stretchable, stretchy, youthful
**springy leap** bound
**springy substance from jaw of some whales** whalebone
**springy toy** jack-in-the-box, pogo stick
**sprinkle** bespatter, diversity, fling, rain, scatter, spray, spread, strew, water
**sprinkle with flour** dredge
**sprinkle with liquid** spatter
**sprint** dart, dash, race, run, scamper, shoot, tear
**sprinter** runner
**sprinting** running
**sprite** ariel, dryad, elf, fairy, fay, genie, gnome, goblin, gremlin, hop, imp, jinn(ee), kelpie, kobold, leprechaun, naiad, nix(ie), nymph, peri, pixie, pixy, pug, sylph, tokoloshe, troll
**sprocket part** tooth
**sprout** blossom, bud, burgeon, develop, flourish, flower, germinate, grow, increase, luxuriate, multiply, offshoot, push, shoot, sprig, spring
**sprouted grain** malt
**spruce** chic, dainty, dapper, elegant, natty, neat, nifty, orderly, smart, stylish, trim, well-groomed
**spruce up** groom, neaten, preen, primp, smarten (up), tidy, tit(t)ivate
**spry** active, agile, alert, brisk, energetic, lively, nimble, ready, sprightly
**spud** potato, tater
**spud bud** eye
**spume** foam, froth, surf
**spun by arachnid** cobweb
**spun from wool** worsted
**spun silk** schappe
**spun thread** yarn
**spur** animate, drive, goad, impel, impetus, impulse, incentive, incite(ment), induce(ment), instigate, instigation, motive, press, prick, prod, prompt, provocation, provoke, stimulant, stimulate, stimulus, urge
**spur disc** rowel
**spurious** adulterine, bogus, counterfeit, deceitful, false, fictitious, illegitimate, pretend, sham
**spurious literary work** pseudograph
**spuriously aesthetic** arty
**spurious writings** pseudepigrapha
**spurn** condemn, contempt, contumely, decline, despise, disapprove, disavow, disdain, dissent, eliminate, exempt, expel, jilt, refuse, reject(ion), repel, return, scorn, snob
**spur of mountain** rib
**spur on to break the law** suborn
**spurt** flow, gush, issue, outburst, rush, spout, spring, stream
**spur wheel** rowel
**sputter in frying** frizz
**spy** agent, descry, detect(ive), determine, discern, discover, eavesdrop, espy, explore, gossip, identify, impimpi, informant, informer, investigator, mole, nark, observe, operative, pry, scan, scout, secret, see, snoop(er), survey, tout, view, watch
**spy glass** telescope
**spying** descrying, espionage, espying, glimpsing, noticing, observing, spotting
**spying aperture** peephole
**spy's alias** codename, codeword
**squabble** altercate, altercation, argue, argument, bicker, brawl, clash, cohort, conflict, contest, debate, differ, disagree(ment), dispute, fight, jangle, quarrel, row, spar, tiff, wrangle
**squad** band, brigade, cadre, cohort, commando, company, corps, crew, detachment, detail, force, gang, group, outfit, party, platoon, section, squadron, team, troop, unit
**squalid** decayed, dirty, filthy, nasty, repulsive, seedy, slummy, sordid, unclean, unkempt
**squalid area** slum
**squalid house** hovel
**squalid place** slum
**squall of wind** flaw, gust
**squander** abuse, blow, deplete, dissipate, drain, exhaust, fritter, gamble, impoverish, lavish, lose, misspend, misuse, overspend, slather, spend, splurge, void, waste

**squanderer** wastrel
**square** agree, align, boring, conservative, conventional, dullard, even, hick, honest, plaza, quadrate, reconcile, rectangle, settle
**square block** cube
**square block used in mosaic** tessera
**square bone at root of nose** ethmoid bone
**square cap of various colours** biretta
**square dance** hoe-dance, quadrille
**square dance figure** allemande
**square edge of sail** leech
**square garment** kaross
**square off** challenge, collide, conflict, confront, disagree
**square of material for wiping nose** handkerchief, hanky
**square or diamond shape** quarry
**square or smooth** even
**square peg in round hole** misfit
**square sail** lug
**squares on map** grid
**square stiff-sided cap** biretta
**square tile** quadral, quarrel
**square timber** ba(u)lk
**squash** butternut, calabaza, courgette, gem, Hubbard, pattypan, zucchini
**squash court quarter-circle** arc
**squat** bend, bow, crouch, descend, duck, dumpy, dwarfish, fubsy, hunch, incline, kneel, lean, little, low, miniature, petite, pygmy, short, sit, small, stoop, stunted, tiny
**squat beer bottle** dumpie, stubby
**squat on** claim, pre-empt
**squatter** dweller, intruder, nester, resident, settler, trespasser, usurper
**squatting** bending, bowing, crouching, descending, ducking, hunching, inclining, kneeling, leaning, stooping
**squaw's baby** papoose
**squeal** creak, scrape, scream, screech, shout, shriek, squeak, wail, yell, yelp, yowl
**squealer** complainer
**squeamish** fastidious, finical, prudish, queasy
**squeeze** clasp, clutch, compress, crush, embrace, extract, grip, hug, jam, pinch, press, stuff
**squeeze against wall** mure
**squeeze and twist** wring
**squeeze-box** concertina
**squeeze money from** extort
**squeeze sharply** nip
**squeeze skin** pinch
**squeeze through** thrust, wedge
**squeeze together** compress, nestle
**squeeze water out** wring
**squid** calamari, chokka, cuttlefish, tjokka

**squiggle** curlicue, curly
**squint** askew, asymmetric, awry, crooked, glance, gley, look, lopsided, off-centre, peek, peep, slanted, tilting, unbalanced, uneven, view
**squint at** peek, peep, peer
**squire** accompany, attend(ant), companion, conduct, convoy, courtier, escort, follower, footboy, gentleman, guard, guide, lead, page(boy), partner, protect, servant, train-bearer, usher
**squire of Quixote** Sancho Panza
**squire's property** estate
**squirm** bustle, chafe, contort, crawl, creep, distort, fidget, insinuate, jerk, slither, turn, twist, wag, wiggle, worm, worry, wriggle, writhe
**squirrel** xerus
**squirrel away** store
**squirrel-like tree-climbing lemur** aye-aye
**squirrel monkey** saimiri
**squirrel's food** acorn
**squirrel's nest** dray, drey
**Sri Lankan language** Tamil
**s-shaped fluting** strigil
**s-shaped line** ess, ogee, ogive
**s-shaped moulding** ogee
**s-shaped worm** ess
**stab** gore, knife, penetrate, pierce, plunge, spear, thrust, wound
**stabber** knifer
**stabbing weapon** dagger, knife, poniard, stiletto, sword
**stabbing weapon fixed to a rifle** bayonet
**stabilise** steady
**stabiliser** anchor, balance, ballast, equilibrium, sandbag, weight
**stabilising fin** anal
**stability** constancy, firmness, permanence, solidity, soundness, steadfastness, steadiness, strength
**stab in the back** betray(al), deceive, duplicity
**stable** abiding, barn, constant, enduring, eternal, firm, lasting, mew, permanent, reliable, rigid, secure, settled, solid, staunch, steadfast, steady, strong, sturdy, unvarying, unwavering
**stable attendant** groom, (h)ostler, syce
**stableboy** jackboy, lad, mafoo, mafu
**stable compartment** stall
**stable keeper** liveryman
**stableman at inn** (h)ostler
**stable-rack** hay-rack
**stables cleaned by Hercules** Augean
**stable yard converted into dwellings** mews

**stab with dagger** poniard
**stab with needle** jab
**stack** accumulate, accumulation, amass, assemble, bank, bunch, chimney, clamp, cock, drift, file, funnel, haycock, hayrick, heap, hill, hoard, load, mass, mound, mountain, pile, pyramid, rick, smokestack, stalk, steeple
**stadium** amphitheatre, arena, bowl, circus, coliseum, colosseum, field, ground, hippodrome, oval, park, pitch, ring
**stadium centre** arena
**stadium entrance** gate
**staff** baton, cane, employees, group, manage, personnel, rod, stick, work(ers)
**staff of authority** baton, mace, sceptre, truncheon
**staff of bishop** crosier
**staff officer** aide
**staff of life** bread
**staff on plane** aircrew
**staff's nucleus** cadre
**staff wreathed with ivy** thyrsus
**stage** arena, bandstand, contrive, deck, drama, engineer, floor, juncture, level, manage, manipulate, perform, period, phase, platform, present, produce, rostrum, scaffold, show, state, step, story, theatre, tier
**stage direction** enter
**stage drama** play
**stage for drying fish** flake
**stage in development** phase
**stage in natural descent** generation
**stage in sequence of events** phase
**stage lover** jeune premier (F)
**stage name** alias
**stage of ancient theatre** proscenium
**stage of clergyman** altar, pulpit
**stage of development** phase
**stage of insect's life between grub and fly** chrysalis
**stage of journey** leg
**stage of theatre** scene
**stage part** role
**stage performer** actor, actress
**stage play** drama
**stage point** etape
**stage remark** aside
**stage scenery** décor
**stage scenery item** prop
**stage set** scene
**stage setting** décor, scenery
**stage twosome** duo
**stage whisper** aside
**stagger** alternate, astonish, astound, dum(b)found, falter, hesitate, lurch, nonplus, reel, shock, teeter, totter(ing), vacillate, waver

**staggering** alternating, amazing, astonishing, faltering, hesitating, lurching, overwhelming, reeling, shaking, stunning, swaying, unsteady, vacillating, wavering
**stagily** affectedly, artificially, ceremoniously, exaggeratedly, falsely, forcedly, insincerely, (melo)dramatically, pompously, showily, stiffly, stiltedly, studiedly, theatrically, unnaturally
**staging again** re-enacting
**stagnant** brackish, idle, inactive, polluted, quiet, sluggish, stale, standing, static, still, torpid
**stagnant region** eddy
**stagnate** cease, decay, decompose, degenerate, desist, deteriorate, halt, idle, putrefy, rest, rot, slumber, spoil, stop, suppurate, vegetate
**stagnation** boredom, depression, doldrums, dullness, ennui, gloom, heaviness, inactivity, indolence, inertia, lassitude, listlessness, lowness, malaise, recession, sloth, slump, stasis, tedium, torpidity, torpor, vegetation
**stag's horn** antler
**stag's mate** doe
**stagy plot** hokum
**staid** composed, decorous, proper, sedate, serious, settled, sober, solemn, steady
**stain** blemish, blot, debase, defile, dirty, discolour, dishonour, dye, mark, reagent, slur, smudge, soil, speckle, spot, stigma, streak, sully, taint, tarnish, tint
**stained glass** vitrail
**stained with ink** inky
**stain on character** slur
**stain on one's good name** stigma
**stain with blood** ensanguine
**stain with ink** blot
**stair** ascent, degree, step(s), stile
**stair part** riser, tread
**stair post** newel
**stair rail** ban(n)ister
**stairway** flight
**stairway part** riser
**stairway post** newel
**stake** ante, bet, chance, claim, concern, gamble, hazard, imperil, interest, investment, jackpot, jeopardy, palisade, peril, picket, pike, pledge, post, pot, purse, risk, share, spike, stick, venture, wager, winnings
**stake a claim** occupy, pre-empt
**stake at poker** ante
**stake of gambler** pool, pot
**stake out** define, delimit, demarcate, outline, reverse, survey, watch

**stakes ratio** odds
**stale** banal, commonplace, conventional, dry, flat, hackneyed, hard, hardened, inane, insipid, mif, mouldy, musty, off, rancid, sour, stereotyped, tasteless, trite, unfresh, uninspired, uninteresting, useless, vapid, vigourless, weary, wilted, withered, worn-out
**stale joke** chestnut
**stalemate** bewilder, blockage, cease, check(mate), collapse, confuse, corner, deadlock, defeat, dilemma, halt, hinder, impede, intercept, obstruct, standstill, stop, tie, undermine
**staleness of smell** mustiness
**stale-smelling** fusty
**stalk** axle, cane, caulis, chase, culm, filament, foliage, follow, gait, ha(u)lm, hunt, pace, prance, pursue, scape, shaft, shank, stem, stride, strut, support, swagger, trunk, walk
**stalk of flower** stem
**stalk of plant** pedicel, peduncle
**stalks used as stewed fruit** rhubarb
**stalk vegetable** celery
**stall** adjourn, avoid, bench, block, bookstall, booth, box, cage, cavity, cease, cell, chair, chamber, clog, compartment, conclude, congest, corral, counter, crib, cubicle, dally, dawdle, defer, delay, desist, discontinue, dodge, dungeon, enclosure, end, equivocate, evade, fail, fake, falsify, finish, fudge, halt, hedge, jam, kiosk, kraal, linger, loge, loiter, manger, misrepresent, newsstand, obstruct, pause, pen, pew, postpone, procrastinate, prolong, protract, quit, refrain, retard, seat, settle, shelve, shuffle, slant, stable, stand, stop
**stall at a fair** booth
**stall in mud** mire, stog
**stallion** horse, stud
**stalwart** bold, brave, daring, fearless, firm, formidable, muscular, resolute, robust, strapping, strong, sturdy, valiant, vigorous
**stalwart person** Trojan
**stamina** backbone, courage, doggedness, endurance, energy, grit, patience, perseverance, power, resistance, staunchness, steadfastness, strength, tone, vigour
**staminate plant** husband
**stammer** falter, hesitate, mumble, pause, splutter, sputter, stumble, stutter
**stamp** abolish, beat, block, brand, character(ise), crush, cut, design, die, distinguish, eliminate, eradicate, hallmark, impress(ion), imprint, iron, kind, mark, mould, pound, seal, sigil, sort, squash, strike, style, trample, type
**stamp after assay** touch
**stamp book cover** blind
**stamp charge** postage
**stamp collecting** philately, timbrology
**stamp-collecting book** album
**stamp collector** philatelist
**stamp cost** postage
**stampede** flight, frighten, panic, rush
**stamp fencing** appel
**stamp for cutting dough** docker
**stamping** beating, crushing, engraving, fixing, franking, impressing, imprinting, inscribing, marking, moulding, printing, trampling
**stamping device** dater, die
**stamping ground** hangout, haunt, home
**stamping machine** dater, press
**stamp of approval** acceptance, OK, seal
**stamp of good taste** cachet
**stamp on silverware** EPNS
**stamp out** crush, destroy, eliminate, end, eradicate, expunge, extinguish, kill, quell, scotch, subdue, suppress
**stamp pad** inker
**stamp sheet section** pane
**stamp upon** trample, tread
**stance** attitude, bearing, carriage, pose, posture, stand, viewpoint
**stand** abide, admit, allow, attitude, base, bear, continue, copse, encounter, endure, erf, fix, halt, lot, meet, oppose, pause, pedestal, persist, place, platform, position, put, rank, remain, resist, rest, set, stall, station, stay, stop, suffer, sustain, table, tolerate
**stand about idly** linger, loiter
**stand a drink** treat
**stand against** resist
**standard** average, banner, basic, criterion, emblem, ensign, example, flag, gauge, grade, guide, ideal, measure, model, norm(al), orthodox, par, pattern, rule, sample, support, test, typical, upright
**standard-bred** pacer
**standard computer language** BASIC
**standard embroidery needle** crewel
**standard habit** uniform
**standardise** equalise, homogenise, normalise, regulate, stabilise, systemise
**standardised concept** stereotype
**standard of comparison** yardstick
**standard of excellence** ideal

**standard of pattern** norm
**standard of perfection** ideal
**standard of reckoning** rate
**standard pattern** norm
**standard quantity** unit
**standard score for hole in golf** par
**standard spirit strength** proof
**stand astride** straddle
**stand astride of** bestride
**stand at fête** stall
**stand at the ready** wait
**stand behind** testify
**stand by** adhere, affirm, back, befriend, champion, defend, help, reiterate, repeat, reserve, support, uphold
**stand down** abdicate, quit, resign, withdraw
**stand firm** persevere, resist, withstand
**stand for** advocate, bear, countenance, denote, endure, exemplify, illustrate, indicate, mean, personify, promote, represent, signify, suffer, support, symbolise, tolerate, typify
**stand for displaying ornaments** étagère (F)
**stand idly** loiter
**stand in** proxy, replacement
**stand-in-doctor** locum
**stand in for** deputise, proxy, replace, represent, substitute for, understudy
**standing** circumstance, condition, continuing, credit, durable, duration, echelon, effective, endurance, erect, established, estate, existence, fixed, grade, idle, immobile, level, longevity, membership, operative, order, permanence, perpendicular, position, rampant, rank, reputability, reputation, stagnant, state, stationary, status, still, unmoving, unused, upright, vertical
**standing applause** ovation
**standing inoperative** idle
**standing on end** erect
**standing upright** perpendicular
**standing wooden support** easel
**stand in lazy attitude** loll
**stand in line** queue
**stand-in monarch** regent
**stand in queue** wait one's turn
**stand in the way** bar, exclude, prevent
**standoffish** aloof
**stand on end** bristle
**stand one's ground** insist
**stand on hind legs** rear up
**stand out** bulge, distinct, excurve, extend, jut, obtrude, overhang, project
**stand out, academically** shine

**stand over with legs apart** astride, bestride
**stand pat** cling
**standpoint** angle, position, post, stance
**stand proud** bulge
**standstill** stoppage
**stand up** arise, last, stand, survive, wear
**stand up for** assert, champion, defend, support, uphold
**stand up to** brave, challenge, confront, defy, endure, face, front, oppose, oppugn, question, resist, withstand
**stand with hands on hips** akimbo
**stand with legs close to body** crouch
**stanza** verse
**stanza of eight lines** octave, octet
**stanza of four lines** quatrain
**stanza of six lines** sestet, sextain, sextet
**staple** chief, main, marketable, principal, settled
**staple food** maize, rice
**star** actor, actress, asterisk, asteroid, brilliant, celebrated, celebrity, chief, comet, destiny, diva, excel, fate, idol, kismet, lead, lot, luck, luminary, main, major, meteor, name, nova, orb, planet, principal, prominant, shine, showcase, stern (G), sun, top
**star award** Artes, Oscar
**starboard** dextrality, right
**starch** amylum, polysaccharide
**starch from dried tubers of orchidaceous plants** salep
**starch gum** dextrin
**starch obtained from the pith of palms** sago
**starch source** arum, cassava, taro
**starch sugar** maltose
**starchy** formal, hard, rigid, stiff, unbending
**starchy dessert** tapioca
**starch-yielding plant** pia, taro
**starchy pudding** sago
**starchy root** taro, yam
**starchy substance used for puddings** sago, semolina, tapioca
**star customer** reader
**stardom** fame
**stare** dare, eye(ball), gape, gawk, gawp, gaze, glare, glore, goggle, look, ogle, scrutinise
**stare angrily** glower
**stare at** eye, ogle
**stare fiercely** glare
**stare fixedly** gaze
**stare hard and angrily** glower
**stare idly** go(a)ve
**stare lewdly** leer
**stare open-mouthed** gape
**stare vacantly** gawk

**stare with open mouth** gape
**starfish** asteroid(al)
**star forecaster** astrologer, magus
**star fruit** carambola
**star group** Orion
**star in Cygnus** Deneb
**staring** agog, astare, goggle, googly, haggard, steep
**staring at** eyeing, ogling
**stark** absolute, blunt, completely, desolate, downright, drear(y), entire, harsh, mere, sheer, simple, stiff, utter(ly)
**stark mad** raving
**stark modern style, without decorations** Brutalism
**stark raving mad** demented
**starling** blackbord, huia, myna(h)
**star-of-Bethlehem** starflower
**star on army officer's shoulder** pip
**star or planet too close to the sun to be visible** combust
**starry** alight, asteroidal, astral, empyreal, empyrean, glittering, heavenly, shining, sidereal, star-shaped, starlike, star-spangled, star-studded, stellar, stellate, twinkling, uranic
**star's adoring letters** fan mail
**star sapphire** asteria
**star-shaped** stellate
**star-shaped sign** asterisk
**star sign** Aquarius, Aries, Cancer, Capricorn, Gemini, Leo, Libra, Pisces, Sagittarius, Scorpio, Taurus, Virgo
**star system** galaxy
**start** activate, appear, arise, begin(ning), chance, come, commence, create, depart, embark, enter, establish, flinch, found, impulse, inaugurate, inception, initiate, initiation, instigate, institute, introduce, issue, jerk, jump, launch, leave, onset, open, origin(ate), outset, pioneer, recoil, rise, spasm, twitch, undertake
**start a business** open
**start again** reopen
**start aside** shy
**starter** antipasto, appetizer, entrée, hors-d'œuvre, novice, tyro
**starting again** de nova (L), resuming
**starting point** beginning, genesis, origin
**starting to grow** nascent
**start in motion** transit
**startle** agitate, alarm, amaze, astonish, disturb, scare, shock, surprise
**startling** agitating, alarming, amazing, dynamic, frightening, scaring, shocking, surprising

**start of era** epoch
**start of illness** onset
**start of river** source
**start of show in theatre** curtain-up
**start of spore** archesporium
**start playing golf** tee off
**start shooting** open fire
**start the bidding** open
**start the day** arise
**start to grow** bud
**star used as guide in navigation** lodestar, polestar
**star used to measure distances** cepheid
**starvation** depletion, emptiness, exhaustion, famine, hunger, inanition, lack, need, want
**starve** crave, deny, deprive, famish, hunger, want
**starving** emaciated, famished, hungry, illfed, meagre, ravenous, scraggy, starveling, undernourished, withered
**star who is revered** idol
**star-worship** Sabaism
**star worshipped by fans** idol
**stash** cache, hoard, store
**stash away** hoard, secrete
**state** affirm, articulate, assert, aver, avow, case, circumstance, commonwealth, community, condition, country, declare, determine, dignified, dilemma, display, environment, etat (F), explain, express, federation, fix, government, kingdom, land, nation, pass, plight, position, predicament, present, rank, report, republic, say, settle, situation, specify, stately, status, surroundings, territory, utter, voice
**state affirmatively** affirm
**state an opposite view** contradict
**state a price for** quote
**state as fact** affirm
**state categorically** assert
**state clearly** enunciate
**stated in detail** explicit
**stated value** par
**state firmly** assert, aver
**state governed by priests** theocracy
**state governed by small group of people** oligarchy
**state in America** Alabama, Alaska, Arizona, Arkansas, California, Colorado, Connecticut, Delaware, Florida, Georgia, Hawaii, Idaho, Illinois, Indiana, Iowa, Kansas, Kentucky, Louisiana, Maine, Maryland, Massachusetts, Michigan, Minnesota, Mississippi, Missouri, Montana, Nebraska, Nevada, New Hampshire, New Jersey, New Mexico, New York, North Carolina, North Dakota, Ohio, Oklahoma, Oregon, Pennsylvania, Rhode Island, South Carolina, South Dakota, Tennessee, Texas, Utah, Vermont, Virginia, Washington, Wisconsin, Wyoming
**state in definite terms** enunciate
**state inhabitant** citizen
**state in Mexico** Yucatan
**state in opposition** object
**state in Pacific** Fiji
**state in West Indies** Haiti
**stateless person** refugee
**stately** dignified, elegant, grand, imposing, magnificent, majestic, noble, regal
**stately and dignified** majestic
**stately building** dome
**stately building as a tomb** mausoleum
**stately dance** minuet
**stately old Spanish dance** saraband
**stately residence** chateau, mansion, palace, palazzo
**stately Spanish dance** saraband(e)
**stately tree** elm, oak, yellow wood
**statement** account, announcement, assertion, averment, avowal, communication, communiqué, declaration, explanation, presentment, proclamation, recital, relation, report, utterance
**statement exaggerated for special effect** hyperbole
**statement given with authority** command
**statement in honour of somebody** tribute
**statement of belief** credo, creed
**statement of fact** truth
**statement of money owing** account
**statement of praise** tribute
**statement of prisoner** plea
**statement of reasons** rationale
**statement of regret** apology
**statement that seems absurd but may be true** paradox
**statement that things are not true** denial
**state of affairs** conjuncture, position, situation
**state of agitation** flap, snit
**state of a hobo** vagrantness
**state of alarm** fantod, fear
**state of annoyance** tracasserie
**state of balance** equilibrium
**state of banishment** exile
**state of becoming dated** obsolescence
**state of being** existence
**state of being allied** alliance
**state of being a man** manhood
**state of being away** absence
**state of being balanced** libration
**state of being base** ignobility
**state of being concerned** anxiety
**state of being dulcet** sweetness
**state of being faithful** loyalty
**state of being forgotten** oblivion
**state of being gawky** ungainliness
**state of being inferior** inferiority
**state of being kept hidden** secrecy
**state of being like cleric** priestliness
**state of being male or female** gender
**state of being obscure** mystery
**state of being of the same opinion** agreement, concord, harmony
**state of being only partly dressed** deshabille, dishabille
**state of being on the lookout** watch
**state of being perpendicular** aplomb
**state of being pure** purity
**state of being svelte** slenderness
**state of being typical** normality
**state of being unforthcoming** reticence
**state of being unusual** strangeness
**state of being valuable** preciousness
**state of being very bad** egregiousness
**state of bliss** nirvana, paradise
**state of burning** combustion, fire, flame
**state of concentration induced by meditation** samadhi
**state of conflict** strife
**state of confusion** chaos, mess, muss, untidiness
**state of deep unconsciousness** coma
**state of disgusting dirt and filth** squalor
**state of disorder** derangement
**state of disrepair** dilapidation
**state of distress** affliction
**state of ease and contentment** comfort
**state of estrangement from the real world** alienation
**state of excitement** stew
**state of fear** trepidation
**state of freezing** frost
**state of grace** blessedness
**state of hostility** war
**state of insensibility** anaesthesia, narcosis
**state of intoxication** swacked
**state of mental confusion** delirium
**state of mental deterioration** dementia
**state of mental discomfort** dysphoria
**state of murderous frenzy** amok
**state of nervous agitation** tizzy
**state of nervousness, fear or depression** funk
**state of oblivion** limbo
**state of pain or distress** purgatory
**state of peacefulness** quiet

**state of perplexity** deadlock, nonplus, quandary, standstill
**state of rapture** ecstasy
**state of rest** inertia
**state of restful tranquility** repose
**state of restlessness or unease** fantod
**state of stopped flow** stagnation, stasis
**state of supreme happiness** Eden, nirvana
**state of temporary unconsciousness** blackout
**state of thriving** prosperity
**state of total disorder** shambles
**state of uncertainty** suspense
**state of unconsciousness** coma
**state of unease** dysphoria
**state of untidy confusion** mess
**state of uproar** bedlam
**state of violent emotion** nympholepsy
**state of war** campaigning, conflict, fighting, hostilities, warfare
**state of worry** fantod
**state one's attitude reluctantly** confess
**state politics** haute politique (F)
**state positively** assert, aver
**state prison** penitentiary
**state repeatedly** iterate
**state ruled by a prince** principality, principate
**state secrets** arcana imperii (L)
**state solemnly** asseverate
**state something on oath** swear
**state too strongly** overstate
**state treasury** fisc
**state under oath** testify
**state-wide** national
**state without proof** allege
**static** changeless, constant, inert, motionless, stagnant, stationary, still, unvarying
**static situation** stasis
**stating maiden name** née
**station** appointment, assign, business, calling, depot, dignity, establish, locate, location, occupation, office, place, position, post, rank, situation, standing
**stationary** anchored, changeless, fixed, immobile, immovable, inert, invariable, moored, motionless, parked, reliable, rooted, sedentary, set, stable, standing, static, statuelike, steady, (stock-)still, unmoving
**station at end of bus route** terminus
**stationed** based
**stationed troops** garrison
**stationery** bond, letterhead, paper, writing-materials
**station or grade** rank

**station person as spy** plant
**station porter** redcap
**statistical calendar** almanac
**statistical study of elections and voting** psephology
**statistics** data, facts, figures, information, numbers
**statue** icon, image, likeness, monument
**statue at Rhodes** Colossus
**statue base** pedestal, plinth
**Statue of Liberty poetess** Lazarus
**statue of the Virgin Mary** madonna
**statues overlaid with gold and ivory** chryselephantine
**statuesque** beautiful, tall
**statue supporting masonry** telamon
**statuette** figuline, figurine
**stature** ability, altitude, calibre, capacity, caste, credit, elevation, endowment, esteem, faculty, fame, force, gifts, height, highness, honour, importance, loftiness, merit, name, opinion, position, prestige, quality, reputation, scope, status, talent, worth
**status** class, condition, footing, position, rank, standing, state
**statuses** conditions, consequences, degrees, distinctions, grades, positions, ranks, standings
**status of belonging to particular nation** nationality
**status of younger branch of family** cadency
**status seeker** snob
**statute** act, canon, decree, law, legislation, ordinance
**staunch** able-bodied, adamant, ardent, athletic, attached, bold, caring, committed, concerned, constant, dedicated, definite, dependable, determined, devoted, devout, dutiful, faithful, fervent, firm, fit, fixed, fond, hale, hardy, healthy, hearty, inflexible, intense, intent, loving, loyal, lusty, manly, muscular, obdurate, obstinate, persevering, persistent, powerful, reliable, resolute, resolved, robust, rude, rugged, severe, solid, sound, stable, stalwart, steadfast, steady, stem, stop, stout, strong, sturdy, substantial, trusty, watertight
**staunch colleague** trouper
**staunchness** allegiance, constancy, devotion, faithfulness, fidelity, firmness, fitness, inflexibility, integrity, loyalty, obduracy, patriotism, powerfulness, resolution, resolve, robustness, stoutness, strictness, trustiness, trustworthiness, vigorousness

**staunch trust** faith
**stave** bar, baton, beat, board, break, cane, crush, cudgel, pommel, rod, shiver, slat, smash, stay, wand, whack
**stave off** avert, avoid, deflect, dodge, evade, fence, halt, obstruct, parry, preclude, rebuff, repel, stop
**stay** abide, adjourn, arrest, await, bide, bolster, check, continue, delay, detain, dwell, halt, hinder, last, linger, lodge, obstruct, pause, prevent, remain, reside, rest, restrain, sojourn, stop, support, sustain, tarry, wait
**stay away from** avoid
**stay clear of** parry, shun, sidestep
**stay here** hotel, house, inn, motel
**stay in bed until late** lie in
**staying alive** survival
**staying power** endurance, stamina, strength, toughness
**stay longer than** outstay
**stay on** linger
**stay over** sojourn
**stays** corset, girdle
**stay with** remain
**stead** accommodation, aid, lieu, place, room, space, utility
**steadfast** constant, dependable, established, firm, fixed, loyal, reliable, resolute, stable, staunch, strong, sure
**steadfast desire** aspiration
**steadfast in allegiance** loyal
**steadfast persistence** perseverance
**steadily** calmly, ceaselessly, consistently, constantly, continuously, dependably, equably, evenly, faithfully, firmly, fixedly, habitually, imperturbably, incessantly, level-headedly, persistently, regularly, reliably, rhythmically, safely, sensibly, serenely, soberly, stably, staidly, steadfastly, substantially, uniformly, uninterruptedly
**steadiness** stability
**steady** constant, dependable, even, firm, fixed, habitual, invariable, regular, reliable, stabilise, stable, staid, unchangeable, unchanging, undeviating, uniform, unremitting, unwavering
**steady brisk pace** trot
**steady footing** stability
**steady hand** cool, unshakableness
**steak** meat, porterhouse
**steak cut** fillet, rump, T-bone, topside
**steak cut from halibut** flitch
**steak order** medium, rare, well-done

**steal** annex, appropriate, bone, burgle, creep, embezzle, filch, fleece, lift, lurk, nick, pilfer, pinch, plagiarise, plunder, poach, purloin, remove, rip off, rob, rustle, shoplift, slink, slip, snatch, sneak, swindle, swipe, take, thieve, tiptoe
**steal about suspiciously** lurch
**steal a look** peep
**steal cattle** duff, rustle
**steal from** rob, thieve
**steal from home** burgle
**steal game** poach
**stealing compulsion** kleptomania
**stealing from** robbing
**steal in small quantities** pilfer
**steal retail goods** shoplift
**stealth** furtiveness, secrecy, slyness, sneakiness
**steal the show** upstage
**stealthy** clandestine, covert, furtive, insidious, secret, shifty, sly, sneaky, surreptitious, treacherous, undercover, underhand
**stealthy intrusion** encroachment
**stealthy sportsman** stalker
**steal unobserved** sneak
**steal up to game** stalk
**steam** energy, power, speed, vapour
**steam bath** sauna
**steam bath taken to induce sweating** sudatorium
**steam burn** scald
**steamed coffee** espresso, expresso
**steam locomotive** steam billy
**steam organ** calliope
**steamship** liner
**steed** horse, charger
**steed of Nereid** seahorse
**steel beam** girder
**steel joist** I-beam
**steel pipe** rod
**steel plating on ships** armour
**steel shoe** solleret
**steel supporting-beam** girder
**steel wedge** froe
**steep** abrupt, hilly, immerse, precipitous, saturate, sheer, soak
**steep bank** bluff, brae, hillside
**steep bank under a rampart** escarp
**steep barley** malt
**steep cliff** precipice
**steep craggy outcrop of mountain** sca(u)r
**steep downward plunge of aeroplane** (nose)dive
**steeped beverage** tea
**steeped grain** malt
**steep face of cliff** precipice
**steep face on side of hill** scarp
**steep flax** ret
**steep hill** brae, scarp, spitskop

**steep in liquid** ret
**steep in liquor** infuse
**steep in marinade** marinate
**steep in water** immerse, infuse
**steeple** belfry, belltower, campanile, minaret, spire, tower, turret
**steep promontary bank** bluff
**steep rock** crag, craig (Sc), krans
**steep rock-face** cliff, krans
**steep rugged rock** crag
**steep-sided flat-floored valley** strath (Sc)
**steep-sided flat-topped hill** butte
**steep slope** scarp
**steep slope at edge of a plateau** escarpment
**steer** bull(ock), con(duct), control, direct, drive, fly, guide, handle, lead, manage, navigate, operate, ox, pilot, run, work
**steer a ship** con
**steer clear of** avoid, beware, circumvent, eschew, evade, shun
**steering apparatus** helm
**steering by the stars** astronavigating
**steering device** rudder, wheel
**steering gear** helm
**steering vane** rudder
**steersman** helmsman, pilot
**steer violently** swerve
**steer wild** yaw
**stellar** astral, bright, brilliant, chief, dazzling, first-rate, foremost, outstanding, primary, principal, sidereal, starlike, starry, twinkling
**stellar rays** starlight
**stellate** starshaped
**stem** ancestry, arise, arrest, axis, bine, breast, check, corm, dam, descent, family, foliage, ha(u)lm, hinder, lineage, mainstay, obstruct, oppose, originate, pedicel, pedigree, peduncle, petiole, plug, prow, quote, restrain, rise, runner, scape, (s)cion, shank, stalk, sta(u)nch, stay, stock, stop, support, tendril, trunk, withstand
**stem covering** ocrea
**stem decoration on goblet** knop
**stem formation** thallus
**stem from** derive, descend
**stem fungus** stipe
**stemless** sessile
**stem of arrow** shaft
**stem of bananas** count
**stem of bean plant** beanstalk
**stem of climbing plant** bine
**stem of flower** pedicel
**stem of glass** baluster
**stem of grapes** rape
**stem of grass** culm
**stem of hookah** snake
**stem of hop** bane, bine

**stem of leaf** petiole
**stem of match** shaft
**stem of mushroom** stipe
**stem of musical note** filum, tail, virgula
**stem of palm** rattan
**stem of pipe** stapple
**stem of plant** axis, caulus, culm, runt, stalk
**stem of rattan** cane
**stem of ship** prow, stempost
**stem of tree** bole, caudex, trunk
**stem the flow of liquid** sta(u)nch
**stem underground** tuber
**stem used for flogging** birch
**stench** exhaust, f(o)etor, foulness, fumes, gas, (mal)odour, mephitis, miasma, noisomeness, pollution, putridness, rancidity, rancidness, rankness, reek, smell, smog, smoke, stink, taint, vapour
**stencil** design, diagram, guide, instructions, original, pattern, plan, template
**stenographer** typist
**step** footfall, level, pace, pas (F), phase, procedure, rung, stage, stair, stride, tread, walk
**step by step** gradual
**step down** abdicate, leave, quit, resign, retire, withdraw
**stepfather of Salome** Herod
**step forward** breakthrough
**step in** intercede, interpose, intervene
**step in ballet** pas
**steplike excavation in a mine** stope
**stepmotherly** novercal
**step off** alight
**step of ladder** rung
**step on** kick, press, trample, tread(le)
**step on it** hasten
**step on the gas** hustle
**step or walk** tread
**step out of** deplane, detrain, disembark
**step over** bestride
**stepped** moved, paced, trod(den), walked
**stepped like a ladder** scalary
**stepped mine** stope
**stepping stone** aid, assist(ance), bridge, foothold, help, opening, push, support
**steps** course, journey, ladder, passage, path, stair(case), stairway, trip
**steps over fence** stile
**step through water** wade
**step up** accelerate, augment, boost, escalate, increase, intensify, raise
**step up a motor** rev
**stereo** hi-fi, stereophonic, stereoscopic
**stereo disc** record
**stereo sound unit** speaker

**stereotype** printing-plate
**stereotyped** boring, commonplace, conventional, dull, hackneyed, insipid, ordinary, settled, trite, uninteresting
**stereotyped phrase** cliché
**sterile** antiseptic, aseptic, barren, dry, fruitless, germ-free, uncontaminated, uncorrupted
**sterilise** addle, castrate, cleanse, disinfect, fumigate, geld, neuter, purify, sanitate, spay
**sterilise by heating** pasteurise
**sterilised** aseptic
**sterilise female animal by removing ovaries** spay
**sterling** actual, admirable, authentic, brilliant, clear, commendable, correct, estimable, excellent, exemplary, fine, genuine, glorious, good, grand, honest, ideal, laudable, legitimate, meritorious, model, natural, original, outstanding, praiseworthy, pure, rare, real, refined, solid, sound, true, unalloyed, unpolluted, veritable
**sterling metal** silver
**sterling unit** pound
**stern** adamant, aft, ascetic, austere, blunt, cold, cruel, dour, firm, flinty, forbidding, formidable, grim, gaunt, hard, harsh, inexorable, inflexible, irksome, obdurate, pitiless, rear, resolute, rigid, rigorous, severe, sober, stark, steadfast, strict, stringent, stubborn, taciturn, uncompromising, unfeeling, unkind, unsympathetic, wilful
**stern and incorruptible judge** Rhadamanthus
**stern in manner** austere
**stern of ship** poop
**sternutation** sneeze, sneezing
**sternwards** aft
**steroid alcohol** sterol
**stet** retain
**stevedore** docker
**stew** boil, bother, braise, bredie, chowder, fluster, fret, fricassee, fuss, hash, hotchpotch, hotpot, mash, olio, ragout, salmi, seethe, simmer, steep, worry
**steward** aide, assistant, attendant, auxiliary, butler, caretaker, companion, curator, custodian, defender, escort, fiduciary, flunk(e)y, follower, foreman, gaoler, guard(ian), governor, guide, helper, jailer, janitor, keeper, overseer, preserver, servant, server, trustee, usher, waiter, warden, warder, watchman

**stewardess** hostess
**steward of medieval great house** seneschal
**stewed chicken dish** fricassee
**stewed fish** matelote
**stew made from left-over meat** scouse
**stew of beef and onions cooked in beer** carbonade
**stew of meat and vegetables** daube, ragout
**stew of meat or poultry, with haricot beans** cassoulet
**stew of sailor** lobscouse
**stew to be thrown away** waste
**stick** abide, adhere, attach, baton, branch, cement, cleave, cling, cohere, delay, glue, hiatus, impale, interruption, paste, pause, penetrate, persist, pierce, pin, puncture, remain, rod, shoot, spear, stab, standstill, stay, stoppage, switch, thrust, transfix
**stick around** linger
**stick at** continue, demur, doubt, falter, hesitate, persist, waver
**stick down** seal
**stick down again** reseal
**stick for beating drum** drumstick
**stick for cleaning gun barrel** ramrod
**stick for drawing lines** ruler
**sticking** adherent
**sticking out** prominent
**sticking together** cohesion, cohesive
**stick in one's throat** acerbate, embitter, envenom, rankle
**stick it out** bear, endure
**stickler** despot, disciplinarian, formalist, martinet, pedant, purist, taskmaster, tyrant
**stickler for customs** tradition(al)ist
**stick of chalk** crayon
**stick of herdsman** goad
**stick of wax with a wick** candle
**stick one's nose into** interfere, meddle, obtrude
**stick out** bulge, distend, extend, jut, obtrude, protect, protrude, protuberate, swell
**stick to** adhere, honour, keep, persevere in
**stick together** affix, agglutinate, cohere, glue
**stick up for** champion, defend, protect, safeguard, support, sustain, uphold
**stick used in two-up** kip
**stick with iron hook for landing large fish** gaff
**sticky** adhesive, awkward, clinging, delicate, difficult, embarrassing, gluey, glutinous, gooey, gummy, nasty, painful, syrupy, tacky, tenacious, thorny, tricky, unpleasant, viscid, viscous
**sticky black substance** tar
**sticky mud** slime
**sticky substance** glue, goo, gum, paste, resin
**sticky sweet** toffee
**sticky wound cover** plaster
**stiff** austere, awkward, compact, crude, dogmatic, firm, formal, great, harsh, inflexible, obstinate, pompous, powerful, prim, resolved, rigid, severe, solid, starchy, steady, stilted, strict, strong, tense, unbending, unyielding, violent
**stiff bristle at top of grain-sheath** awn
**stiff broom** besom
**stiff classical style of riding** haute école
**stiff cotton cloth** buckram, organdie
**stiffen** brace, clot, coagulate, congeal, crystallise, harden, jell, reinforce, rigidify, set, solidify, starch, strengthen, tauten, tense, thicken, toughen
**stiff hair** bristle, seta
**stiff hat** boater, bowler, derby, kelly
**stiff in manner** stilted
**stiff light transparent muslin** organdie
**stiffly** rigidly
**stiffly formal** prim, stilted
**stiff paper** card
**stiff ribbed cotton fabric** piqué
**stiff silk fabric** taffeta
**stiff tenacious earth** clay
**stiff thin fabric** organza
**stifle** check, crush, destroy, prevent, repress, smother, stop, suffocate, suppress
**stigma** blemish, blot, blur, brand, defamation, disgrace, dishonour, disparagement, disrepute, label, mark, reproach, shame, slur, smear, smirch, smudge, spot, stain, taint, tarnish
**stiletto** dagger, stylet
**still** appease, but, calm, compose, even, fixed, however, idle, immobile, immovable, inactive, inert, mild, motionless, mute, nevertheless, noiseless, pacific, pacify, passive, peaceable, peaceful, placid, quiet, sedate, serene, silence, silent, smooth, smother, soothe, soundless, speechless, stable, stagnant, static, stationary, stifle, subdued, tranquil, unmoving, unstirring, yet
**still and all** anyway, nevertheless, nonetheless
**still existing** extant
**still owed** unpaid
**still sealed** unopened

**still to be dealt with** outstanding
**still to be tested** untried
**still to come** yet
**still unpaid** owing
**stilted** artificial, bombastic, constrained, forced, pedantic, pompous, pretentious, stiff, unnatural
**stimulant** abetment, anti-depressant, bracer, coffee, fillip, goad, incentive, inebriant, intoxicant, provocative, stimulus, temptation, urge
**stimulant drug** amphetamine, upper
**stimulant found in tea and coffee** caffeine
**stimulate** activate, animate, arouse, encourage, excite, fan, fire, goad, impel, incite, inflame, instigate, invigorate, prick, prompt, provoke, quicken, rouse, spur, stir, urge
**stimulate interest of** motivate
**stimulating drink** bracer
**stimulating flavour** zest
**stimulus** booster, encouragement, enticement, excitant, fillip, goad, impetus, impulse, incentive, inducement, lash, motive, persuasion, provocative, spur, taunt, temptation
**stimulus receiver** sensor
**sting** ache, barb, bite, burn, irritate, irritation, needle, nettle, nip, prick, prompt, provoke, smart, spur, trouble, vex
**stinger** bee, nettle, wasp
**stinginess** cheapness, niggardliness, parsimony, tight-fistedness, tightness
**stinging ant** kelep
**stinging arachnid** scorpion
**stinging fish** ray
**stinging insect** bee, hornet, wasp
**stinging plant** nettle
**sting of wit** barb
**stingy** avaricious, close, giftless, greedy, grudging, illiberal, mean, mingy, miserly, niggardly, parsimonious, penurious, pinching, possessive, scraping, selfish, sparing, tight, venal
**stingy person** miser, niggard, scrooge
**stink** aroma, f(o)etor, halitosis, mephitis, miasma, odour, rancidity, reek, smell, stench
**stinker** polecat
**stinking** f(o)etid, old
**stinking badger of Java** teledu
**stinking iris** gladdon
**stinking person** stinkard, stinker
**stinkwood** Ocotea bullata
**stint** allotment, care, charge, chore, circumscribe, conserve, constraint, dose, duty, economise, limit, lot, measure, pinch, portion, restraint, restrict(ion), scrimp, share, skimp, straiten
**stipend** allocation, allowance, amount, benefit, compensation, earnings, emolument, fee, gain, grant, income, lot, measure, pay(ment), pension, portion, proceeds, profits, quota, ration, receipts, recompense, remuneration, return, reward, salary, share, stint, subsidy, takings, wages
**stipulation** agreement, arrangement, clause, condition, contingency, demand, don(n)ée (F), essential, obligation, promise, proviso, requirement, specification, term
**stir** ado, aggravate, agitate, arouse, brew, bustle, churn, commotion, disturb(ance), electrify, excite, ferment, furore, inspire, irritate, mingle, mix, move, prison, quiver, rouse, rustle, shiver, startle, stimulate, to-do, tumult, turmoil, twitch
**stir into activity** arouse
**stirrer** agitator
**stirring** animating, arousing, dramatic, impassioned, lively, moving, rousing, spirited, thrilling
**stirring eggs in a pan** scramble
**stirring language** sensationalism
**stirring utensil** spoon
**stirrup** étrier (F)
**stirrup-shaped bone in the middle ear** stapes
**stir suddenly** rouse
**stir together** mix
**stir up** agitate, animate, arouse, awake(n), excite, foment, incite, inflame, instigate, kindle, mix, prompt, provoke, quicken, raise, roust, spur, stimulate, urge
**stir up a fire** stoke
**stir up into action** incite
**stir up sediment** rile, roil
**stitch** baste, connect, darn, embroider, fix, gather, join, knit, pain, pang, pleat, purl, repair, secure, sew, smock, suture, tack, tuck, twinge, twitch
**stitch again** resew
**stitched fold** tuck
**stitched to inside of garment** lining
**stitch loosely together** baste, tack
**stitch together** sew
**St John's bread** carob
**stoa** portico
**stoat** ermine
**stoat-like animal** weasel
**stoat's winter coat** ermine
**stock** ancestry, cattle, descent, family, goods, hoard, house, inventory, keep, line, livestock, ordinary, parentage, pedigree, provision, race, reserve, store, supplies, tribe, usual
**stockbroker** sharebroker
**stock classification** ordinary, preference, preferred
**stocked up** provided
**stock exchange in Paris** Bourse
**stock-farm** ranch
**stock for the future** hoard, store
**stockholder** shareholder
**stocking fabric** lisle
**stocking ladder** run
**stocking material** nylon
**stocking run** ladder
**stockings** hose, nylons
**stockings and socks** hosiery
**stocking support** garter
**stocking thread** lisle
**stocking yarn** nylon
**stock-jobbing** agiotage
**stock keeper** storeman
**stock market crash** panic
**stock market optimist** bull
**stock market pessimist** bear
**stock of clothes** wardrobe
**stock of drugs** pharmacopoeia
**stock often used in fish dishes** court bouillon
**stock of wines** cellar
**stock or clear broth** bouillon
**stockpile** accumulate, hoard, store
**stocks and shares** investments
**stock up** accumulate, amass, equip, fill, furnish, gather, hoard, provision, replenish, save, store, supply
**stocky** burly, chunky, dumpy, solid, stubby, thickset
**stodgy** drab, dull, filling, heavy, indigestible
**stogy** cigar, stogey
**stoical** apathetic, calm, cold, composed, cool, dull, easygoing, emotionless, frigid, heavy, impassive, insensible, listless, long-suffering, passive, patient, philosophic(al), phlegmatic, quiet, resigned, serene, stoic, submissive, tolerant, torpid, uncomplaining, unconcerned, undemonstrative, unemotional, unfeeling, uninterested, unmoved, unresponsive
**stoical indifference** ataraxia, ataraxy
**stoicism** acceptance, calmness, dispassion, fatalism, forbearance, fortitude, impassivity, indifference, long-suffering, patience, resignation, stolidity
**stoker** fireman
**stoker's spade** shovel
**stole** shawl, shoulder-covering, wrap
**stolen goods** loot, swag

**stolid** apathetic, bovine, dense, doltish, dull, impassive, indifferent, lumpish, obtuse, stoical, stupid, unemotional, wooden
**stoma** opening, orifice, ostiole, pore
**stomach** abdomen, appetite, belly, boep, brook, craw, croa, digest, endure, gizzard, guts, hunger, maw, paunch, stand, tolerate, yen
**stomach-ache** bellyache, colic, fantad, gastralgia, gullion
**stomach acidity** acor
**stomach lesion** ulcer
**stomach-lining of cattle** tripe
**stomach neutraliser** antacid
**stomach of animal** craw, maw
**stomach of bird** craw, croa, gizzard, maw
**stomach of ox** tripe
**stomach of pig** jaudie
**stomach of ruminant** omasum, rumen, tripe
**stomach opening** pylorus
**stomach pain** colic
**stomach sore** ulcer
**stomata** ora
**stomatitis** noma
**stone** boulder, eolith, gem, marble, pebble, pelt, pip, pit, rock, stean (Sc), steen (Sc), throw, yonnie
**stone age tool** eolith
**stone artisan** mason
**stone block for paving** sett
**stone brake** fern
**stone brick** ashlar
**stone broke** penniless
**stone carving implement** chisel
**stone coal** anthracite
**stone coffin** sarcophagus
**stone cut in relief** cameo
**stone cutter** lapicide, mason
**stonecutter's tool** chisel, drove
**stoned because he would not cede his vineyard** Naboth
**stone doorway** trilith
**stone dressing with chisel** tooling
**stone edging to pavement** kerb
**stone excavation** quarry
**stone formed in the body** calculus
**stone for sharpening tools** whetstone
**stone fragments ejected from volcanoes** lapilli
**stone fruit** apricot, cherry, drupe, olive, peach, plum
**stone garden** rockery
**stone hammer** kevel, knapper, mash
**stone implement** celt, (n)eolith
**stone lily** crinoid, fossil
**stone lining of well** steening
**stone mound marker** cairn
**stone needle** obelisk
**stone of fruit** pip, pit

**stone of silica** quartz
**stone of two layers cut in ornamental relief** cameo
**stone over doorway** lintel
**stone-parapeted walk** rampart
**stone particles** grit
**stone pier** mole
**stone pillar** herm, stela, stele
**stone pillar as monument** obelisk
**stone sling** onager, trebuchet
**stone tablet** slate
**stone to death** kill, lapidate
**stone tool** celt, (n)eolith, scraper
**stone urn** steen
**stone vessel for holy water** stoup
**stone wall to break the force of the sea** pier
**stoneware** gres (F)
**stonework** masonry
**stoneworker** mason
**stony** adamant, gritty, hard, motionless, obdurate, rigid, rocky, stiff, unbending, unfeeling
**stony meteorite** aerolite
**stony ridge** rand
**stooge** butt, confederate, decoy, subordinate
**stool** bench, chair, pew, seat, settle, stall, tabo(u)ret
**stool pigeon** nark, pig
**stoop** bend, bow, concede, condescend, condescension, couch, crouch, deign, descend, dip, duck, hunch, incline, indignity, kneel, lean, pounce, squat, vouchsafe
**stoop over** bend
**stoop up** condescend, deign, resort, sink, vouchsafe
**stop** arrest, avast, bar, block, cease, check, control, depot, desist, end, halt, hinder, hindrance, impede, interrupt, obstruct, pause, preclude, prevent, repress, station, stopover, suppress, withhold
**stop beforehand** forestall
**stop briefly** cease, delay, pause
**stop by** lodge, remain, sojourn, visit
**stop command** whoa
**stop flowing** stagnate
**stop from happening** prevent
**stop from suckling** wean
**stop in one's tracks** freeze, immobilise, petrify, transfix
**stop making a noise** pipe down
**stoppage** arrest, blockage, discontinuance, discontinuation, halt, hindrance, interruption, obstruction, occlusion, standstill, stopping
**stoppage of circulation** stasis
**stoppage of flow of blood** haemostasis

**stopper** block, bung, choke, close, cork, cover, enclose, fasten, fid, fill, gag, pack, peg, pledget, plug, seal(ant), secure, shut, spigot, spike, spill, stop(cock), stopple, stuff, tap, wad, waterproof, wedge
**stopping** arresting, barring, blocking, breaking, ceasing, cessation, checking, closing, concluding, desisting, discontinuing, ending, finishing, frustrating, halting, hindering, impeding, intercepting, interrupting, lodging, obstructing, pausing, plugging, preventing, quitting, refraining, repressing, resting, restraining, sealing, silencing, sojourning, stalling, staunching, staying, stemming, suspending, tarry, terminating
**stopping before fruition** aborting
**stopping bleeding** styptic
**stopping device** brake
**stopping of hostilities** armistice
**stopping of progress** arrestation
**stopping place for railway trains** station
**stopping place in car race** pit
**stop progress of** intercept
**stop short** ba(u)lk
**stop temporarily** pause
**stop up** block, fill, obstruct, occlude, seal, tamp, wad
**stopwatch** timer
**stop work as a protest** strike
**stop working** leave, resign
**storage** closet, memory, protection, reserve, safekeeping, safety, salvation, security, stockpile, support, warehousing
**storage battery** accumulator
**storage box** bin
**storage building** barn, depot, shed, silo, warehouse
**storage container** canister
**storage crib** bin
**storage dam** reservoir
**storage in freezer** deepfreeze
**storage in silo** silage
**storage place** chest
**storage pond** tank
**storage register in computer** accumulator, memory
**storage tower** silo
**storage unit** buffer
**store** abundance, accumulate, accumulation, cache, confidence, cupboard, deposit(ory), fund, grocery, hoard, keep(ing), lot, market, mart, mine, outlet, plenty, profusion, provision, quantity, repository, reserve, reservoir, save, shop, stash, stock(pile), storehouse,

storeroom, stow, supermarket, supply, treasure, value, warehouse, wealth
**store away** hoard, stash, stow
**store cargo** steeve
**store-cupboard** larder
**store-cupboard for junk** glory hole
**store fodder in a silo** ensile
**store for weapons** arsenal, gunroom
**storehouse** depot, etape (F)
**storehouse for threshed grain** granary
**store in silo** ensile
**storekeeper** merchant, trader
**store of weapons** arsenal
**storeplace for wool** lanary
**storeroom** a(u)mbry, attic, cellar, closet, gola, larder, pantry
**stores ashes** urn
**store secretly** stash
**storeship** flute
**store supervisor** floorwalker
**store up** accumulate, amass, hive, hoard, save, stash
**storey** floor
**storey below ground level** basement
**storing building** shed
**storing of fodder in a silo** ensilage
**storm** assault, attack, blizzard, blow, commotion, cyclone, fume, gale, hurricane, northeaster, orage (F), outbreak, outburst, rage, rain, rave, rush, sirocco, squall, strife, tempest, tornado, typhoon, violence
**storm angrily** rage
**storm door** dingle
**storm in a tea cup** overestimation, overreaction
**storm's centre** eye
**storm sound** thunder
**storm with violent wind** hurricane
**stormy** boisterous, dirty, foul, gusty, squally, tempestuous, turbulent, windy
**stormy bird** petrel
**stormy conversation** scene
**story** account, allegation, anecdote, chronicle, description, drama, episode, fable, history, myth, narration, narrative, novel, play, plot, recital, report, romance, script, tale, theme, yarn
**story about a family** saga
**storybook** novel
**storybook bear** Baloo(h), Bruin, Rupert, Winnie the Pooh
**storybook writer** fictionist
**story in episodes** serial
**story not based on fact** fable
**story of a person's life** biography
**story of one's own life** autobiography
**story outline** plot
**story's good guy** hero

**storyteller** author, bard, chronicler, commentator, narrator, raconteur, reporter
**story that teaches** apologue, fable, parable
**story told in instalments** serial
**story to music** opera
**story with a moral** allegory, fable, parable
**stout** able-bodied, bold, brave, brawny, bulky, corpulent, doughty, fat, fearless, firm, fleshy, heavy, indomitable, intrepid, plump, resolute, stalwart, strong, stubborn, sturdy, thick(-set), vigorous
**stout and short** bunty, chuffy, pluggy, thickset
**stout cord** rope
**stout cotton** ferret
**stout glove with long loose wrist** gauntlet
**stout-hearted** valiant
**stoutness** bigness, boldness, brawniness, bulkiness, burliness, courageousness, embonpoint (F), fatness, gallantness, heaviness, lustiness, manliness, plumpness, portliness, resoluteness, robustness, sturdiness, substantialness, toughness, tubbiness, valiantness
**stout pole** spar
**stout shoe with a low heel** oxford
**stout tree** oak
**stout twist of fibre** rope
**stout unglazed cotton cloth** cretonne
**stout walking shoe** brogue
**stove** cooker, kiln, oast, range
**stovepipe residue** soot
**stow** deposit, load, pack, secrete, tuck
**stow away** pack, stash
**stowing gear on ship** steeve
**St Peter's wort** samphire
**strabismus** squint(ing)
**straddle the fence** equivocate, shuffle, tergiversate, waffle
**straddling** astride
**Stradivarius** violin(-maker)
**straggle** amble, detour, deviate, digress, drift, flit, gad, jaunt, lag, meander, peregrinate, prowl, ramble, range, rove, stray, wander
**straggler** idler, laggard, loafer, loiterer, nomad, roamer, rover, stroller, tramp, vagabond, wanderer
**straight** candid, correct, direct, equitable, frank, honest, honourable, just, linear, right, upright
**straightaway** immediately
**straight ditch** trench
**straight edge** ruler
**straighten** adjust, align, aline, clean, correct, disentangle, expand, flatten,

groom, neaten, open, order, readjust, rectify, right, square, tidy, unbend, uncurl, undo, unfold, unfurl, unravel, unsnarl, untangle, unwrap
**straightening muscle** extensor
**straighten out** correct, disentangle, rectify, reform, regularise, resolve, revise, settle, sort out, unsnarl
**straighten up** arrange, order, tidy
**straightforward** candid, direct, easy, frank, genuine, honest, simple, truthful, undemanding
**straightforward action** plainsailing
**straight from the shoulder** bluntly, candidly, directly, explicitly, frankly, outright, plainly, tactlessly, unambiguous
**straight line joining two points on a curve** chord
**straight long incision** slit
**straight rod** shaft
**straight to the point** direct
**strain** ancestry, character, clasp, descent, effort, embrace, exert, family, filter, force, hug, impair, injure, percolate, pressure, purify, seep, sift, sprain, stock, streak, stress, stretch, tauten, tear, tension, tighten, trace, trait, twist, weaken, wrench
**strained** agonistic, artificial, awkward, embarrassed, laboured, stiff, tense, uneasy, unrelaxed
**strained food** purée
**strained to stiffness** tense
**strainer** colander, filter, riddle, screen, sieve, sifter, tammy
**straining at the leash** impatient
**strain in the character** streak
**strait** canal, catastrophe, channel, crisis, difficult(y), dilemma, disaster, duct, embarrassment, emergency, extremity, furrow, groove, gutter, main, mess, narrow, need, passage, perplexity, pinch, predicament, problem, quandary, trouble
**strait between Australia and Tasmania** Bass
**strait between Australia and New Guinea** Torres
**strait between Belgium and south-east England** Dover
**strait between Borneo and Indonesia** Macassar, Makas(s)ar
**strait between Corsica and Sardinia** Bonifacio
**strait between East and South China seas** Formosa
**strait between Greenland and Iceland** Denmark
**strait between Greenland and Baffin Island** Davis

**strait between India and Sri Lanka** Palk
**strait between Iran and United Arab Emirates** Hormuz
**strait between Italy and Albania** Otranto
**strait between Italy and Sicily** Messina
**strait between New Zealand and Stewart Island** Foveaux
**strait between North and South Islands** Cook
**strait between South Atlantic and South Pacific** Magellan
**strait between Sumatra and Indonesia** Sunda
**straitjacket** camisole, compressor, fetter, straightjacket
**straitlaced** moralistic, narrow(-minded), prim, proper, puritanic(al), strict, stuffy, verkramp
**strait off Cape York, Queensland** Torres
**strait of Singapore** Johore, Sembilan
**strait with strong current** Euripus
**strand** beach, braid, catgut, coast, cordage, curl, fibre, leave, ligament, line, maroon, plait, quit, rope, seacoast, (sea)shore, seaside, (ship)wreck, string, thread, tress, twine, twirl, twist, waterfront, waterside, yarn
**strand on desolate island** maroon
**strange** abnormal, alien, bizzare, curious, eccentric, eerie, exotic, extraordinary, foreign, irregular, new, novel, odd, peculiar, queer, rare, rum, singular, unaccustomed, unacquainted, unconventional, unexplained, unfamiliar, unused, unusual, weird
**strange appearance** apparition
**strange event** oddity
**strange folk** odd-balls
**strangely** abnormally, bizarrely, curiously, exceptionally, exotically, fantastically, funnily, mystifyingly, newly, oddly, peculiarly, queerly, rarely, remotely, strangely, uncannily, weirdly
**strangely beautiful** exotic
**strange old man** codger
**strange person** oddity
**stranger** alien, Ausländer (G), foreigner, funnier, guest, incomer, newcomer, newer, outlander, outsider, queerer, rarer, uitlander, visitor, weirder
**stranger to the truth** liar
**strangle** asphyxiate, burke, check, choke, gag, gar(r)otte, inhibit, obstruct, repress, restrain, smother, squeeze, stifle, strangulate, subdue, suffocate, suppress, throttle
**strangler** killer, murderer, throttler
**strangle with wire** gar(r)otte
**strap** belt, buckle, fasten, leash, rein, scourge, secure, thong, tie, truss, whip
**strap for bit** rein
**strap round middle of horse** girth
**straps to support trousers from shoulders** brace
**strap to control horse** rein
**stratagem** artifice, conspiracy, deception, device, dodge, feint, gambit, intrigue, manoeuvre, plan, plot, ploy, ruse, scheme, snare, subterfuge, tactic, trick(ery), wile
**strategic** critical, crucial, deliberate, diplomatic, politic, tactical, vital
**strategic advantage** leverage
**strategic board-game** chess
**strategic point** position
**strategic weapon** missile
**strategy** design, management, planning, policy, skilful, tactics
**Stratford river** Avon
**stratified** bedded, layered, tiered, varved
**stratified metamorphic rock** schist
**stratify** arrange, plan, plot
**stratigraphic level** horizon
**stratum** band, bed, class, coat, degree, deposit, gradation, grade, lamina, layer, level, lode, rock, seam, sheet, stage, status, streak, tier, tissue, vein
**straw** hay, sipper
**straw bed** pallet, palliasse, shakedown
**straw beehive** skep, skip
**straw broom** besom
**straw for plants** mulch
**straw hat** boater, panama
**straw man** scarecrow
**straw mattress** pallet, palliasse
**straw roof** thatch
**stray** amble, derelict, deviate, digress, divagate, diverge, drift, err, homeless, lost, maverick, meander, nomad, ramble, roam, rove, saunter, scatter(ed), separate, sin, straggle(r), stroll, swerve, transgress, veer, waif, wander(er)
**stray calf** maverick
**stray child** waif
**stray domestic animal** astray, estray
**stray from subject** digress, diverge
**stray from the main body** straggle
**straying** deviating, diverging, drifting, errant, erring, meandering, rambling, ranging, roaming, roving, straggling, wandering
**straying from moral standard** aberrant, aberration
**stray off the subject** digress
**stray thing** waif
**streak** band, dart, dash, element, fly, hurtle, line, slash, speed, sprint, strain, strip(e), stroke, tear, touch, trace, vein, zoom
**streaked agate** onyx
**stream** afflux, arroyo, beck, bourn, brook, burn (Sc), cascade, channel, course, creek, current, ebb, emanate, flow, freshet, inflow, issue, outflow, pour, rill, riptide, river, rivulet, run, rush, slide, sluice, streamlet, tide, torrent, watercourse
**streamer** badge, banner, burgee, colours, ensign, flag, jack, pennant, pennon, standard
**stream falling over precipice** waterfall
**stream flowing from larger stream** effluent
**stream joining another** confluent
**streamlet** rill, rivulet, runnel
**streamlined** abridged, aerodynamic, disentangled, elegant, facilitated, fit, shapely, simplified, sleek, slender, slim, speedy, trim(med), willowy
**streamliner on motorcycle** fairing
**stream of abuse** diatribe, invective, jeremiad, philippic, screed, tirade
**stream of fresh water flowing into sea** freshet
**stream out** shed
**stream that feeds another larger one** tributary
**street** alley, avenue, boulevard, highway, path, road, rue (F), thoroughfare, way
**streetcar** tram, trolley
**street carnival** parade
**street entertainer** busker, minstrel, troubadour
**street in Paris** rue
**street island for pedestrians** refuge
**street light support** lamppost
**street location** address
**street march** parade
**street musician** busker
**street of London** Bond, Downing, Fleet, Haymarket, Regent, Saville
**street railway** tramway
**street refuse** fullage, scavage
**streets ahead** far superior
**street show** pageant, parade, raree
**street ticket seller** tout
**street uprising** riot
**street urchin** gamin, guttersnipe, stroller
**street vendor** hawker, huckster, peddler, pedlar
**street water outlet** hydrant

**strength of an alcoholic liquor**
alcoholicity
**strength** capacity, courage, effectiveness, energy, firmness, force, intensity, loudness, potency, power, prop, resolution, stay, support, tenacity, validity, vividness
**strengthen** brace, enhance, fortify, harden, intensify, invigorate, prop, reinforce, support, toughen
**strengthened cement** reinforced cement
**strengthening drug** roborant
**strengthening iron bracket** gusset
**strength gained from drink** Dutch courage
**strength-giving medicine** tonic
**strength of character** backbone
**strength of will** indomitableness, inflexibility
**strenuous** active, acute, aggressive, ardent, arduous, burdensome, determined, difficult, eager, energetic, forced, laborious, resolute, spirited, tenacious, toilsome, vibrant, vigorous
**strenuous effort** exertion
**stress** accent(uate), anxiety, difficulty, distortion, emphasis(e), exertion, hardship, ictus, importance, pressure, pronunciation, prosody, strain, tension, weight
**stress hormone** adrenaline
**stress of the voice** accent
**stress on words** emphasis
**stretch** dilate, distance, eke, elongate, enlarge, exaggerate, expanse, extend, length(en), reach, spread, strain, tauten, widen
**stretched out** craned, prolate, sprawled
**stretched skin** membrane
**stretched tight** tense
**stretcher** litter
**stretch forth** extend
**stretching** elasticated
**stretch neck** crane
**stretch of broken water** rip
**stretch of hills** fell
**stretch of ice** rink
**stretch of land** tract
**stretch of littoral sand** beach
**stretch of moorland** fell
**stretch of turf** sward
**stretch one's legs** exercise, promenade, stroll, walk
**stretch out** eke, elongate, extend, lie, reach, relax, spread
**stretch tightly** strain
**stretchy** elastic, pliable, soft, wieldy
**strew** bestrew, broadcast, diffuse, disperse, disseminate, distribute, overspread, promulgate, propagate, publish, scatter, sow, spread, sprinkle
**strewn with boulders** rocky
**strew seeds** sow
**stria** groove, striation
**strict** absolute, accurate, austere, careful, close, critical, demanding, exact(ing), harsh, illiberal, inflexible, minute, precise, religious, rigid, rigorous, severe, stern, stringent, unbending, uncompromising
**strict conformity to truth** fidelity
**strict disciplinarian** martinet
**strict hermit** ascetic
**strictly** stringently
**strictly accurate** exact
**strictly confidential** private, privy, top-secret
**strict observer of Sunday** Sabbatarian
**strict person** martinet
**strict usage of language** purism
**strict vegetarian** vegan
**stride** advance, bearing, file, footstep, gait, go, hike, impression, march, measure, pace, parade, patrol, pound, print, saunter, stalk, step, straddle, stroll, strut, trace, track, tramp, tread, walk
**strident** acute, blatant, coarse, crude, deafening, discordant, dissonant, glaring, guttural, harsh, high, jarring, loud, noisy, penetrating, piercing, rasping, raucous, resounding, sharp, shrill, sonorous, stentorian, thundering, treble, turbulent, uproarious, vociferous
**strident creak** screech
**striding** pacing
**strife** conflict, difference, disagreement, discord, opposition, quarrel, struggle, war
**strike** achieve, arrange, assail, batter, beat, belt, cancel, chime, cuff, effect, hit, klap, knock, punch, rap, reach, ring, serif, slap, slug, smite, streak, tap, thrash, wallop, whack, whip
**strike a fly** swat
**strike back** retaliate
**strike ball** hit
**strikebreaker** scab
**strike continuously** batter
**strike down** afflict, assassinate, destroy, kill, murder, ruin, smite
**strike down by blow** fell
**strike dumb** silence
**strike forcefully** ram
**strike gentle blow** tap
**strike gently** pat
**strike heavily** slog, thump, whack, wham, whang
**strike lightly** tap
**strike notes of stringed instrument unskilfully** strum
**strike out** cancel, dele(te), erase, expunge, remove
**striker** assistant, batsman, hitter, player, revolter
**strike repeatedly** batter, beat, drum, pummel
**strike sharply** rap, swat
**strike terror into** frighten
**strike the first blow** initiate, instigate, start
**strike violently** whale
**strike with beak** peck
**strike with cutting blows** hew
**strike with fist** bop, box, hit, pummel, punch
**strike with hand** cuff, klap, slap, smack
**strike with missile** hit
**strike with sudden terror** scare
**strike with terror** petrify
**strike with wonder** amaze, stun
**striking** arresting, attractive, bashing, beautiful, brilliant, charming, clear, comely, conspicuous, distinct, effective, explicit, flagrant, grand, impressive, magnificent, majestic, miraculous, obtrusive, obvious, overt, plain, prominent, salient, splendid, stupendous, unusual, well-groomed, wonderful
**striking effect** éclat
**striking likeness** resemblance
**strikingly attractive** stunning
**strikingly beautiful** gorgeous
**strikingly fortunate** providential
**string** cable, catgut, chain, c(h)ord, cortege, extend, fiber, gut, lace, ligament, line, range, ribbon, rope, sequence, series, strand, stretch, thread, twine, wire, yarn
**string along** bamboozle, bluff, deceive, dupe, fool, trick
**stringed instrument** balalaika, banjo, bouzouki, cello, dulcimer, guitar, harp, koto, lute, lyre, mandolin(e), piano(forte), psaltery, ramkietjie, sitar, viola, violin, zither
**stringed spinning toy** yo-yo
**stringent** adamant, binding, compelling, convincing, effective, firm, fixed, immovable, immutable, implacable, incontrovertible, inflexible, intractable, invariable, narrow, obdurate, powerful, relentless, rigid, rigorous, set, severe, strict, stubborn, unalterable, unbending, unyielding, urgent
**stringently** strictly
**string of beads** necklace
**string of coral islands** atoll
**string of pearls** strand

**string out** continue, elongate, outreach, prolong, protract, stretch
**string puppet** marionette
**string shoe** espadrille
**string together** bead
**string up** gibbet, hang, lynch, noose
**stringy** rop(e)y, viscid
**stringy pasta** spaghetti
**strip** band, decorticate, denude, deprive, derive, desolate, despoil, devastate, dismantle, dispossess, peel, plunder, remove, shred, spoil, strap, tape, uncover, undress
**strip away** peel
**strip bare** denude
**stripe** band, bar, beating, cast, ilk, lash, layer, line, marble, race, ridge, score, seam, streak, striate, striation, strip, stroke, style, thrashing, vein, whack
**striped animal** bongo, koedoe, kudu, okapi, quagga, tiger, zebra
**striped fabric** seersucker
**striped feline** tiger, tigress
**striped stinging insect** wasp
**strip for measuring** ruler
**strip light gas** neon
**strip of carpet** runner
**strip of cloth** tape
**strip of cloth used for binding up wounds** bandage
**strip of dried meat** biltong
**strip off** divest, peel, scale, skin
**strip of garden** border
**strip of land** belt, doab, isthmus, neck
**strip of land left unploughed** ba(u)lk
**strip of leather** strap
**strip of material** ribbon
**strip of meat** fillet
**strip of paper** streamer
**strip of pasta** noodle
**strip of rind** peel
**strip of wood** lath, slat
**strip of wood used for measuring** ruler
**strip on which to hang pictures** rail
**stripper** ecdysiast
**strip skin from** flay
**strip skin from whale** flense
**strips of dough** noodles
**strips of foil** tinsel
**stripteaser** ecdysiast, stripper
**strip the feathers from** pluck
**strip used to bind** band
**strip worn around waist** belt
**strive** aim, aspire, attempt, compete, contend, endeavour, essay, exert, labour, strain, struggle, toil, try, undertake, venture, vie
**strive for** aspire
**strive for superiority** vie
**strive hard** struggle

**striver** aspirant
**strive to equal** emulate
**strive towards goal** aspire
**striving** agonising, attempting, competing, contending, effort, endeavouring, fighting, labouring, straining, struggling, toiling, trying
**striving for effect** agonistic, strained
**stroke** accomplishment, achievement, apoplexy, attack, beat, blow, caress, clap, collapse, feat, fit, flourish, fondle, heartbeat, hitting, knock, massage, move(ment), paralysis, pat, pet, pulsation, rub, seizure, shock, striking, sweep, throb
**stroke given with whip** lash
**stroke in billiards made with cue held vertical** massé
**stroke in golf** approach
**stroke in tennis** backhand, forehand
**stroke lightly** pat
**stroke lovingly** caress, fondle
**stroke of bell** knell
**stroke of fortune** godsend, luck, windfall
**stroke of luck** break, fluke, scoop
**stroke of policy** coup d'état (F)
**stroll** airing, amble, excursion, hike, jaunt, journey, meander, perambulate, promenade, ramble, range, roam, rove, saunter, stray, tour, travel, tread, turn, walk, wander
**stroller** ambler, drifter, gypsy, itinerant, nomad, rambler, ranger, rover, street child, traveller, vagabond, voyager, wanderer
**strong** able, aromatic, athletic, bold, brave, brawny, cogent, compact, courageous, distinct, eager, energetic, firm, forceful, forcible, hale, hearty, Herculean, intense, mighty, muscular, potent, powerful, pungent, robust, smelly, stalwart, stiff, stout, sturdy, tough, vigorous, vivid
**strong affection** love
**strong alcoholic spirit** aqua vitae (L)
**strong ale** porter
**strong and active** robust, vigorous
**strong and glaring in colour** lurid
**strong and healthy** hale
**strong and sturdy** robust
**strong and sweet wine** jerepigo, malmsey
**strong and swift horse** percheron
**strong aversion** antipathy, disgust, repugnance
**strong beer** nog
**strong belief** faith
**strong bitter leaves** sage
**strongbox** chest, coffer, lockbox, safe, till, treasury, vault

**strong breeze** blow
**strong brown colour** rust
**strong cart for heavy goods** dray
**strong cart horse** percheron
**strong-clawed crustacean** crab, lobster
**strong coarse calico** dowlas
**strong coarse cloth** canvas, dungaree
**strong coarse dark tobacco** caporal
**strong coarse material used for straps** webbing
**strong coffee** espresso
**strong condemnation** reprobation
**strong cord** cable, rope, twine
**strong cotton fabric** denim, drill, lisle
**strong cotton trousers** denim, jeans
**strong curse** anathema, imprecation
**strong dark beer with roasted malt** stout
**strong desire** craving, greed, hankering, hunger, longing, lust, yearning
**strong desire for success** ambition
**strong dislike** animosity, aversion, hate, scunner
**strong drink** rum
**strong ebb** riptide
**strong effect** impact
**strong emotion** passion
**strong enough to resist an attack** impregnable
**stronger** braver, brawnier, burlier, deeper, fiercer, firmer, greater, hardier, healthier, mightier, pluckier, severer, stauncher, sturdier, tougher, weightier
**strong fabric** canvas, denim, hessian, sackcloth, sisal, webbing
**strong fabric coated to resemble leather** leathercloth
**strong feeling** emotion, passion
**strong fibre** bast
**strong fibre of coconut husk** coir
**strong flavour** tang
**strong force** posse
**strong forward rush** surge
**strong fume** reek
**strong giant** Titan
**strong grasp** grip
**strong gust of wind** blast
**stronghold** bastion, bulwark, castle, château, citadel, donjon, fort(ification), fortress, haven, headquarters, hotbed, rampart, redoubt, refuge, stockade, tower
**strong impulse** urge
**strong inclination** penchant
**strong light synthetic polymer** nylon
**strong low cart** dray
**strongly attractive** charismatic, magnetic
**strongly audible** loudly

**strongly built** athletic, stalwart, sturdy
**strongly desirous** ambitious
**strongly expressive** eloquent
**strongly-flavoured leaves** rosemary
**strongly laxative** purgative
**strongly marked** pronounced
**strongly poisonous** virulent
**strongly worded** hard-hitting
**strong material** denim
**strong person** Titan
**strong pliant cane** supplejack
**strong point** bastion, forte, fortress
**strong praise** accolade
**strong protest** outcry
**strong red wine** port
**strong resentment** ire
**strong rope** cable
**strong rush** surge
**strong-scented** gamy, olid, rank, redolent
**strong-scented flower** phlox
**strong shoe** brogan, brogue
**strong-smelling gum resin** ammoniac
**strong-smelling herb** rue, yarrow
**strong-smelling shrub** saltwort
**strong sodium hydroxide** lye
**strong spirit** firewater, mampoer, moonshine, rakee, raki, skokiaan, witblits
**strong steel wire** cable
**strong string** twine
**strong sudden pull** yank
**strong sweet wine** jerepigo, malmsey
**strong taste** tang
**strong thick cord** cable, rope
**strong thread** twine
**strong twill cloth** lasting
**strong twilled fabric** galatea, serge
**strong twine** cord
**strong unbleached cloth** canvas
**strong vehicle for heavy goods** lorry, truck
**strong verbal attack** abuse, broadside, diatribe, invective, tirade
**strong wind** cyclone, gale, gust, hurricane, northeaster, puna, southeaster, storm, tempest, tornado, typhoon
**strong wire rope** cable
**strong woman** Amazon
**stroppy** angry, awkward, bad-tempered, obstreperous
**struck** collided, connected, hit, smitten, smote
**struck by the sun's rays** heatstroke, sunburnt, sunstroke
**struck out** deleted
**struck with amazement** aghast
**struck with fear** afraid
**struck with sudden fear** scare
**struck with terror** aghast
**struck with the knee** kneed

**struck with wonder** agape, (over)awed
**structural defect in eye or lens** astigmatism
**structural geology** tectonics
**structurally safe** firm, solid, sound
**structure** architecture, anatomy, arrangement, brickwork, bridge, building, complex, composition, construction, edifice, erection, form, frame(work), make, mould, organisation, shape, skeleton, stonework, system, woodwork
**structure along base of ship** keel
**structure containing germ cell in female plant** ovule
**structure enclosing a fireplace** mantel
**structure formed of piles** piling
**structure for spectators** stand
**structure for the hanging of criminals** gallows
**structure in Pisa** tower
**structure marking path for aircraft** pylon
**structure of cross laths** lattice
**structure of two upright stones supporting a lintel stone** trilithon
**structure of wire** stabile
**structure running into the sea as a landing stage** pier
**structures in the inner ear of mammals** corti
**structure supporting aircraft engine** pylon
**structure supporting a wall** buttress
**structure surrounding stems** oc(h)rea
**struggle** battle, brush, clash, conflict, contend, contest, encounter, endeavour, fight, flounder, scuffle, skirmish, strife, strive, tussle, wrestle
**struggle for control** strive
**struggle for promotion** rat race
**struggle hard** toil
**struggle helplessly** flounder
**struggle with** antagonise
**struggle with others for** scramble
**strum** thrum
**struma** goitre, scrofula
**strum a guitar** play
**strung up** tense
**strut** brace, flaunt, flourish, parade, prance, promenade, prop, stretcher, support, swagger
**strut about** stalk, swagger
**strutting gait** swagger
**stub** butt, end, remnant, stompie, stump, tail
**stubborn** adamant, contrary, contumacious, difficult, dogged, fixed, fractious, hard, headstrong, immovable, incorrigible, inexorable, intractable, mulish, obdurate, obstinate, persevering, persistent, perverse, pigheaded, recalcitrant, resolute, rigid, stiff, tenacious, unbending, uncompromising, unpliable, unruly, unyielding, wilful
**stubborn creature** mule
**stubbornly persistent** indomitable
**stubbornly resolute** adamant
**stubbornness** application, determination, diligence, doggedness, firmness, intransigence, obstinacy, persistence, resolution, resolve, tenacity
**stubborn refusal to obey** contumacy
**stub holder** ashtray
**stub of cigar** stump
**stucco** overlay, (wall)plaster
**stuck** adhered, affixed, attached, baffled, bonded, cemented, cleaved, fast(ened), firm, fixed, fused, glued, inserted, jabbed, joined, nonplussed, pasted, penetrated, pierced, pinned, prodded, stabbed, welded
**stuck in role** typecast
**stuck on** crazy about
**stuck-up** aloof, arrogant, big-headed, conceited, condescending, exclusive, haughty, proud, snobbish, snooty, toffee-nosed, uppity
**stuck-up person** snob
**stud** bejewel, boss, bulk, bump, fastener, knob, knot, lump, nub(ble), ornament, point, projection, protuberance, rivet, snag, spangle, speckle, spot, swelling, tip, tumour
**studded** nailed
**student** learner, matriculant, observer, pupil, scholar
**student of ancient times** antiquary
**student of archery** toxophilite
**student of birds** ornithologist
**student of Cape Town university** Ikey
**student of divinity** theologian
**student of drugs** pharmacologist
**student of English language or literature** Anglist
**student of fishes** ichthyologist
**student of fossils** palaeontologist
**student of fungi** mycologist
**student of human behaviour** psychologist
**student of humankind** anthropologist
**student of insects** entomologist
**student of law** templar
**student of law-making** nomologist
**student of mosses** bryologist
**student of precious stones** gemmologist
**student of reason** logician
**student of Stellenbosch university** Matie

**student of the Middle Ages** medi(a)evalist
**student of the past** historian
**student of wine** oenologist
**student of words** etymologist
**student without financial support from college** commoner
**studio** atelier, loft, school, workroom, (work)shop
**studious** academic, assiduous, attentive, careful, diligent, eager, earnest, hardworking, industrious, intellectual, reflective, scholarly, serious, thoughtful
**stud on a boot** hobnail
**stud sheep** ram
**study** area, assiduity, attention, cogitation, con(sideration), contemplate, den, endeavour, etude, examine, field, inquiry, investigate, investigation, learn, meditation, ponder, pore, practise, read, reflect(ion), research, reverie, scrutinise, sedulousness, subject, swot, think, thought, weigh
**study all at once** cram
**study closely** examine
**study concerning icons** iconology
**study for examination** cram, revise, stew, swot
**study in silence** muse
**study of ageing** gerontology, nostology
**study of agricultural pests** pestology
**study of airborne micro-organisms** aerobiology
**study of algae** algology
**study of ancient inscriptions** epigraphy
**study of ancient papyri** papyrology
**study of ancient writing and inscriptions** palaeography
**study of animal behaviour** ethology
**study of animal cells** cytology
**study of animals** ethology, zoology
**study of ants** myrmecology
**study of arachnids** arachnology
**study of archaeological strata** stratigraphy
**study of atmosphere away from ground** aerology
**study of beards** pogonology
**study of beliefs about demons** demonology
**study of bells** campanology
**study of biological cells** cytology
**study of birds** ornithology
**study of bird's eggs** oology
**study of bodies of fresh water** limnology
**study of causes of diseases** aetiology
**study of cell nuclea** karyology
**study of cells** cytology

**study of children** paedology
**study of children's diseases** paediatrics
**study of Chinese language, history and customs** Sinology
**study of Christian religion** theology
**study of church festivals** heortology
**study of church unity** irenics
**study of cleanliness** hygiene
**study of clouds** nephology
**study of codes and ciphers** cryptology
**study of coins** numismatics
**study of coprolites** scatology
**study of diseases of ancient man** palaeopathology
**study of diseases of the nervous system** neuropathology
**study of doctrines relating to the devil** satanology
**study of dreams** oneirology
**study of drugs** pharmacology
**study of dust in the air and its effects** coniology, koniology
**study of earth's shape** geodesy, geodetics
**study of economy as a whole** macroeconomics
**study of eggs** oology
**study of Egyptian antiquities** Egyptology
**study of elderly** gerontology
**study of electricity in motion** electrodynamics
**study of external conformation of a person's cranium** phrenology
**study of ferns** pteridology
**study of final causes** teleology
**study of fishes** ichthyology
**study of flags** vexillology
**study of flight** aeronautics
**study of flowers** anthoecology
**study of forms of organisms** morphology
**study of forms of words** morphology
**study of fossil animals** palaeontology, palaeozoology
**study of fossil animals and plants** palaeoecology
**study of fossil excretion** scatology
**study of fossil footprints** ichnology
**study of fossils** palaeontology
**study of fresh waters and their organic life** limnology
**study of fruits and seeds** carpology
**study of fruit trees** pomology
**study of functions of the nervous system** neurophysiololgy
**study of fungi** mycology
**study of geographical distribution of animals and plants** chorology
**study of gliders** aerodonetics

**study of God, religion and revelation** theology
**study of grasses** agrostology
**study of hair** trichology
**study of handwriting** chirography, graphology
**study of heart functions and diseases** cardiology
**study of heavenly bodies** astrology, astronomy
**study of history of language** glottochronology
**study of human antiquities** archaeology
**study of humankind** anthropology
**study of human settlements** ekistics
**study of hymn composition** hymnody, hymnology
**study of hypnosis** hipnotism
**study of icons** iconology
**study of Indian history** Indology
**study of inscriptions** epigraphy
**study of insects** entomology
**study of lakes** limnology
**study of land** geography
**study of language** philology
**study of languages and their structure** linguistics
**study of life in geological past** palaeontology
**study of literary and external history of Bible** isagogics
**study of liturgies** liturgiology, liturgis
**study of make-up** cosmetology
**study of mammals** therology
**study of manuscripts** codicology
**study of mapmaking** cartography
**study of mapping of regions** chorography
**study of mapping of the moon** selenography
**study of meanings** semantics, semasiology
**study of measuring time** horology
**study of mechanical arts and applied sciences** technology
**study of mechanics of body movements** kinesiology
**study of mental disease** psychiatry
**study of metal** metallography
**study of micro-organisms** microbiology
**study of missiles** missil(e)ry
**study of mites and ticks** acarology
**study of molluscs** malacology
**study of mollusc shells** conchology
**study of monsters** teratology
**study of moon** selenography
**study of mosses** bryology
**study of mountains** orology
**study of mouth disorders** stomatology
**study of music** musicology

**study of myths** mythology
**study of nasal disease** rhinology
**study of nature** science
**study of nature and origin of knowledge** epistemology
**study of nature of being or existence** ontology
**study of numbers** numerology
**study of obscene language and literature** scatology
**study of occult meaning of numbers** numerology
**study of oceans** oceanography
**study of old people** gerontology
**study of old things** archaeology
**study of organisms not yet extinct** neonatology
**study of origin of people** anthropogenesis, anthropogeny
**study of origins of words** etymology
**study of parasitic worms** helminthology
**study of pedigrees** genealogy
**study of physical phenomena of lakes** limnology
**study of physiology of blood** haematology
**study of place names of a region** toponymy
**study of plant diseases** phytopathology
**study of plant nutrition** agrobiology
**study of plants** phytology, botany
**study of pollen in connection with plant geography** palynology
**study of population** larithmics
**study of population statistics** demography
**study of portraits** iconography
**study of postage stamps** philately
**study of prehistoric man** palaeoethnology
**study of prisons and treatment of criminals** penology
**study of quantities in which drugs should be administered** posology
**study of religious belief** theology
**study of reptiles and amphibians** herpetology
**study of resistance to infection in people and animals** immunology
**study of rights and duties of citizenship** civics
**study of rivers** potamology
**study of rocks** geology, lithology, petrology
**study of rule of arts** aesthetics
**study of seals** sigillography
**study of seismic phenomena** seismography, seismology
**study of settlements and their development** ekistics

**study of sexual life** sexology
**study of sexual love** erotology
**study of shape and area of the earth** geodesy, geodetics
**study of shape of the skull** phrenology
**study of shells and shellfish** conchology
**study of skin and its diseases** dermatology
**study of sleep and hypnosis** hypnology
**study of snakes** ophiology
**study of society and social problems** sociology
**study of soils and their potential productivity** agrology
**study of sound and sound waves** acoustics
**study of sounds in a language** phonology
**study of sound travelling through water** hydrocoustics
**study of speech-rhythms** prosody
**study of speech sounds** phonemics, phonetics
**study of spelling** orthography
**study of stars** astronomy
**study of steady state magnetic fields** magnetostatics
**study of stellar physics** astrophysics
**study of structure of fruit and seeds** carpology
**study of structure of nervous system** neuroanatomy
**study of structure of tissues** histology
**study of structure, physiology and ecology of lichens** lichenology
**study of structures surrounding teeth** periodontics, periodontology
**study of technique of using language effectively** rhetoric
**study of the atmosphere** aerology
**study of chemical composition of the crust of the earth** geochemistry
**study of Christian church** ecclesiology
**study of the heart** cardiology
**study of the mind** psychology
**study of the skull** craniology, phrenology
**study of timepieces** horology
**study of trees** dendrology
**study of trends in elections and voting** psephology
**study of tumours** oncology
**study of types** typology
**study of underlying principles and ultimate reality** metaphysics
**study of units of measurement** metrology
**study of universe** cosmology
**study of urinary tract** urology

**study of venereal diseases** venereology
**study of versification** prosody
**study of viruses** virology
**study of vocabulary** lexicology
**study of vocal sounds** phonetics
**study of whales** cetology
**study of winds** anemology
**study of wines** oenology
**study of writings of the Fathers of the Church** patrology
**study of word meanings** lexicology
**study of words** etymology
**study room** den
**study table** desk
**study with care** peruse
**stuff** belongings, brocade, capabilities, character, cram, crowd, effects, equipment, fabric, fill, force, gear, gorge, guzzle, impedimenta, inanity, jam, junk, kit, load, luggage, material, matter, nonsense, objects, obstruct, overindulge, pack, pad, plug, press, push, qualities, ram, sate, shove, squeeze, stow, substance, tackle, textile, things, trappings, trash, wedge
**stuff and nonsense** bunk
**stuffed, rolled meat slice** roulade
**stuffed shirt** snob
**stuffing** cramming, crowding, filler, filling, forcing, gorging, jamming, loading, overindulging, packing, padding, pushing, ramming, sating, shoving, squeezing, stowing, wadding, wedging
**stuffing seasoning** sage
**stuff into** ram
**stuff with food** gorge
**stuffy** airless, deadly, muggy, musty, oppressive, staid, stale, straitlaced, unventilated
**stumble** blunder, discover, falter, lurch, misstep, stagger, trip
**stumble upon** discover, encounter, find, meet
**stumbling block** bar(rier), blockade, drawback, hindrance, impediment, obstacle, obstruction, snag
**stump** baffle, bewilder, confuse, mystify, outwit, puzzle, stop, stub
**stump of a tree** stub
**stumps of cut grain** stubble
**stump up** contribute, donate, pay, shell out
**stun** astound, daze, dum(b)found, flabbergast, overwhelm, shock, stupefy
**stunned** aghast, astonished, astounded, bewildered, confounded, confused, overcome, overpowered, shocked, staggered, stupefied

**stunned state** daze
**stunning** breathtaking, brilliant, dazzling, impressive, remarkable, smashing, spectacular
**stunning weapon** cosh
**stunt** act, deed, exploit, feat(ure), trick
**stunted animal** runt
**stunted forest growth** scrub
**stunted person** dwarf
**stunt flying** aerobatics
**stunt man** adventurer, daredevil, desperado, madcap, show-off
**stupe** flannel, fomentation, fool
**stupefy** amaze, astound, bemuse, benumb, bewilder, daze, drug, dum(b)found, shock, stagger, startle, stun
**stupefy person with drugs** hocus
**stupefy with drink** besot
**stupendous** amazing, astonishing, astounding, breathtaking, colossal, enormous, gigantic, huge, marvellous, overwhelming, phenomenal, prodigious, staggering, superb, surprising, vast, wonderful
**stupid** anserine, asinine, boring, brainless, crass, dazed, dim(-witted), dom, dopey, dozy, dull, dumb, feeble-minded, foolish, glaikit (Sc), groggy, half-witted, headless, idiotic, ill-advised, imbecilic, inane, indiscreet, insipid, irrelevant, irresponsible, ludicrous, meaningless, mindless, moronic, naïve, nonsensical, obtuse, pointless, puerile, semiconscious, senseless, short-sighted, simple(-minded), slow, sluggish, stunned, stupefied, tedious, thick, uninteresting, witless
**stupid deed** mindless act
**stupid error** faux pas
**stupid horse** ass
**stupidity** absurdity, asininity, banality, bêtise, blankness, brainlessness, denseness, density, dimness, dull-wittedness, dullness, fatuity, folly, idiocy, imbecility, immaturity, inanely, inanity, ineptitude, insipidity, insipidness, lunacy, madness, naïveté, obstinacy, obtuseness, puerility, silliness, simplicity, slowness, supineness, thickness, triviality, unintelligence, voidness
**stupidly** asininely, brainlessly, crassly, dazedly, deficiently, densely, dimly, dully, foolishly, futilely, groggily, gullibly, idiotically, inanely, indiscreetly, insensately, ludicrously, mindlessly, naïvely, obtusely, pointlessly, rashly, senselessly, slowly, sluggishly, stolidly, thickly

**stupid mistake** boner
**stupid or spiritless fellow** dowf
**stupid person** alec(k), ass, block, booby, clot, cuddy, dolt, domkop, drip, drongo, duffer, dunce, dunderhead, fathead, goof, goon, halfwit, imbecile, jackass, lout, lubber, lummox, moegoe, mompara, moron, mule, mutt, nerd, ninny, nit(wit), num(b)skull, nurd, oaf, simpleton, slop, sop, twerp, wally
**stupor** amazement, anaesthesia, catalepsy, coma, daze, helplessness, hypnosis, insensibility, lethargy, narcosis, numbness, paralysis, sopor, state, torpidity, torpor, trance, unconsciousness
**sturdy** hardy, hefty, lusty, muscular, robust, sinewy, solid, stalwart, stout, strapping, strong, unbeatable, unconquerable, vigorous, well-built
**sturdy dog breed** boxer, bulldog, bull terrier, Rottweiler
**sturdy material** khaki
**sturdy shoe** brogue
**sturdy shortlegged horse for riding** cob
**sturdy tree** oak
**sturgeon eggs** roe
**stutter** defect, falter, hesitate, pause, quake, splutter, stammer, stumble
**sty** coop, fold, hovel, hutch, (pig)pen
**Stygian** dark, gloomy, hellish, morose, murky, saturnine
**style** appearance, approach, character, chic, craze, culture, cut, design(ate), dignity, dressiness, éclat, élan, elegance, fashion, gnostic, grace, kind, line, manner, method, mode, neatness, pattern, smartness, sort, system, trend, trimness, type, vogue
**style and vigour** élan
**style of action painting** tachisme
**style of architecture** Baroque, Bauhaus, Corinthian, Doric, Ionic, Palladianism, Rococo, Romanesque, Tudor
**style of art or literature** genre
**style of bowing in string playing** marellando, martellato
**style of coiffure** bun
**style of cooking** cuisine
**style of furniture** Sheraton
**style of hairdressing** bob, coiffure, eton, pompadour, punk
**style of interior decoration** decor
**style of movement** action
**style of painting with vivid use of colour** fauvism
**style of printer's typeface** Aldine, bold (face), italic, roman, san(s-)serif, serif
**style of publication** format

**style of speaking** elocution
**style of speech** language
**stylet** awl, perforator, probe, stiletto, trocar
**stylish** á la mode, chic, classy, dressy, elegant, fashionable, flashy, luxurious, mod(ern), modish, natty, nifty, polished, popular, smart, snazzy, sophisticated, suave, trim, urbane, voguish
**stylish building** edifice
**stylishly elegant** chic
**stylishness** elegance
**stylish shop** salon
**stylist** artist, author, couturière, craftsperson, decorator, designer, orator
**stylus** gad, greffe, needle, pointel, pyropen, style, tracer
**stymie** hinder, stymy, thwart
**styptic** alum, astringent, contraction
**styptic substance** alum
**styrene-filled bag** beanbag
**sty resident** pig, swine
**sty sound** grunt, oink
**Styx ferryman** Charon
**suable** actionable
**suave** affable, agreeable, bland, charming, civil(ised), courteous, debonair, diplomatic, elegant, graceful, gracious, nonchalant, pleasant, pleasing, polite, refined, smooth, sophisticated, svelte, tactful, urbane, worldly
**suave person** smoothie
**suavity** blandness, debonairness, glibness, oiliness, smoothness, urbanity
**subarctic antlered animal** reindeer
**subconscious** deep-rooted, hidden, inmost, inner(most), latent, repressed, suppressed, unconscious
**subdivision** arm, branch, clause, department, division, edition, genus, paragraph, part, phrase, portion, region, sector, (sub)category, (sub)section, (sub)segment
**subdivision of a country** canton, province
**subdivision of a fibre** fibril
**subdivision of an infantry company** platoon
**subdivision of a play** scene
**subdue** beat, break, capture, chasten, conquer, control, crush, defeat, discipline, dominate, dull, foil, force, intimidate, lower, master, mellow, melt, moderate, mollify, muffle, mute, oppress, overcome, overpower, overrun, overthrow, overwhelm, prevail, quell, quiet, reduce, restrict, rout, silence, soften, subjugate,

**subdue by force** overpower
**subdue by self-denial** mortify
**subdued** ashamed, broken, calm, chaste(ned), collected, composed, conquered, controlled, docile, dull, gentle, hushed, mak, mute(d), passive, quiet, reserved, resigned, restrained, sedate, sober, soft, solemn, sombre, spiritless, tame, tranquil, unagitated, unimpassioned, unresponsive
**subdued colour** undertone
**subdued grumbling** mutter
**subdued shade** pastel
**subdued sparkle** shimmer
**subduer** tamer
**subdue the pride of** chasten
**subjacent** underlying
**subject** conception, control, dependent, dominate, ground, inferior, influence, liable, matter, motive, obedient, object, reason, subject, theme, thesis, topic
**subject for discussion** theme
**subject matter** text
**subject to** provided
**subject to a contingency** conditional
**subject to conversation** topic
**subject to custom charges** dutiable
**subject to death** mortal
**subject to decay** perishable
**subject to defects** imperfect
**subject to extreme pain** torture
**subject to morals** censor
**subject to objection** exceptionable
**subject to one's will** control, dominate, subdue
**subject to severe questioning** grill
**subject to speedy decay** perishable
**subjugate** capture, conquer, defeat, dominate, domineer, enslave, enthrall, master, oppress, overcome, overmaster, overpower, quash, quell, reduce, repress, subdue, subject, suppress, vanquish
**subjugate by force** oppress
**subjugation** constraint, control, despotism, domination, enslavement, repression, restraint, suppression, tyranny
**sublease** relet
**sublime** exalted, lofty, majestic, splendid, superb, transcendent
**sub-machine-gun** AK47, sten, Uzi
**submarine** U-boat
**submarine detecting device** sonar
**submarine missile** torpedo
**submarine telegraph line** cable
**submerge** bathe, deluge, descend, dip, dive, douse, drench, drown, duck, engulf, flood, founder, immerse, inundate, overflow, overwhelm, plunge, rise, saturate, sink, souse, submerse, swamp, wet
**submerge and bear down** overwhelm
**submerged** drowned, enigmatic, hidden, immersed, impenetrable, inundated, obscured, puzzling, shrouded, submarine, submersed, sunk(en), swamped, undersea, underwater, unseen
**submerged enigma** lost city of Atlantis
**submerged reef** bombora
**submerged rock in the sea** scar
**submersible vessel** submarine
**submission** acquiescence, argument, assent, capitulation, compliance, contention, deference, docility, entry, meekness, obedience, passivity, presentation, proposal, resignation, suggestion, surrender, tendering, yielding
**submission to fate** fatalism
**submissive** accommodating, amenable, compliant, deferential, docile, dutiful, humble, ingratiating, long-suffering, meek, obedient, passive, patient, resigned, subdued, subservient, tame, tractable, uncomplaining, unresisting, yielding
**submissive in opinion** deferent
**submissively** abjectly, basely, compliantly, controllably, deferentially, despicably, docilely, dutifully, easily, fawningly, humbly, ignominiously, meanly, meekly, mildly, modestly, obediently, patiently, peacefully, pliantly, respectfully, softly, tractably, vilely
**submit** accept, acquiesce, advance, appeal, apply, bow, capitulate, comply, concur, defer, fall, grant, introduce, lose, obey, observe, present, propose, propound, render, represent, resign, succumb, suggest, surrender, volunteer, yield
**submit a dispute to an umpire** arbitrate
**submit for consideration** exhibit
**submit for decision** refer
**submit to** bow, yield
**subordinate** ancillary, below, dependent, inferior, junior, lesser, lower, reduce, secondary, subservient, under(ling)
**subordinate official** satrap
**subordinate parts of an undertaking** infrastructure
**subordinate side of coin** reverse
**subscribe** accept, aid, assume, endorse, guarantee, help, recommend, remit, sign, underwrite
**subscription** abonnement (F), alimony, amendment, contract, cost, endowment, grant, money, obligation, payment, pension, price, signature, signing, underwriting
**subscription extension** renewal
**subscript letter** subfix
**subsequent** after, coming, consecutive, consequent, designate, ensuing, following, future, junior, later, next, posterior, sequacious, sequent, succeeding, successive, youngest
**subsequently** after(wards), anon, consequently, later, since, successively
**subside** (a)bate, decline, decrease, descend, die, diminish, dip, droop, drop, dwindle, ebb, intermit, lapse, lessen, mitigate, moderate, obsolesce, precipitate, recede, retire, sag, settle, sink, slacken, slump, wane
**subsidiary** accessory, affiliate, ancillary, assistant, auxiliary, branch, contributory, division, helpful, lesser, offshoot, secondary, section, subordinate, subservient, supplementary, tributary, useful
**subsidiary consequence** ramification
**subsidiary interest giving income** sideline
**subsidy** aid, fellowship, grant, scholarship, subvention, support
**subsist** be, continue, endure, exist, live, remain, survive
**subsisting by catching living prey** rapacious
**substance** body, core, element, essence, hypostasis, marrow, material, matter, solidity, wealth
**substance able to destroy bacteria** antibiotic, bactericide
**substance causing irritation of nose** sternutation
**substance for destroying pests** pesticide
**substance for killing germs** germicide, penicillin
**substance for killing insects** insecticide
**substance formed in carrots** carotene
**substance from pine trees** resin
**substance maintaining life indefinitely** elixir
**substance of trees** wood
**substance of which a thing is made up** matter
**substance poisonous to cells** cytotoxin
**substance prepared from seaweed** agar-agar

**substance that can be spun** fibre
**substance that can kill** poison
**substance that causes sneezing** sternutatory
**substance that destroys germs** germicide
**substance that is chewed** gum
**substance that kills algae** algicide
**substance that prevents acidity** antacid
**substance that produces cancer** carcinogen
**substance to destroy fungus** fungicide
**substance used for cleaning things** cleaner
**substance used for stiffening linen** starch
**substance used in candies** tallow
**substance used in curative treatment** medicament
**substance which neutralises an acid** antacid
**substandard** inferior
**substantial** actual, ample, big, bulky, considerable, durable, enduring, firm, full-bodied, generous, hefty, important, influential, large, makulu, massive, material, positive, resolute, significant, sizable, solid, sound, stable, stout, strong, sturdy, valuable, wealthy, well-built, worthwhile, worthy
**substantial amount** chunk
**substantially** en effet (F)
**substantial rather than imaginary** tangible
**substitute** alternate, copy, delegate, deputy, ersatz (G), exchange, imitation, interchange, locum, proxy, relief, relieve, replace(ment), ringer, secondary, sub, supersede, surrogate, switch, understudy
**substitute for** supply
**substitute in an emergency** stopgap
**substitute player** reserve
**substitute sound** dub
**substitute tooth** crown
**subterfuge** ambages, artifice, blow, complot, conspiracy, contrivance, coup, deception, device, dodge, evasion, excuse, expedient, feint, fetch, manoeuvre, ploy, pretence, quibble, ruse, scheme, shift, sleight, stall, stratagem, strategy, trick(ery)
**subterranean cemetery** catacomb
**subterranean passage** tunnel
**subterranean spirit in folklore** gnome
**subtle** acute, adroit, artful, astute, clever, crafty, deep, delicate, expert, faint, fine, ingenious, intricate, mysterious, sheer, skilful, strategic, thin, transparent

**subtle distinction** nuance
**subtle emanation from any body** aura
**subtle extra quality** overtone
**subtle management** finesse
**subtle pervasive quality** aroma
**subtle point of delicacy** nicety
**subtle shade** nuance
**subtly** carefully, critically, deftly, delicately, elegantly, exactly, exquisitely, fastidiously, finely, gracefully, lightly, meticulously, nicely, precisely, rigorously, scrupulously, sensitively, skilfully, softly, strictly, tactfully
**subtract** deduct, detract, diminish, lessen, withdraw
**subtract from salary for taxes** deduct
**suburban avenue tree** acacia, jacaranda, oak
**suburban house** villa
**subversive agent** spy
**subvert** confound, conquer, corrupt, demean, demolish, deprave, destroy, invert, overthrow, overturn, overwhelm, pervert, sabotage, topple, undermine, unseat, upheave, vitiate, weaken, wreck
**subway** el, metro, tube, tunnel, underground
**subway inspection access** manhole
**succeed** accomplish, achieve, advance, attain, complete, conquer, do, ensue, flourish, follow, inherit, manage, prevail, progress, prosper, realise, replace, result, success, supervene, thrive, triumph, win, work
**succeed in doing** accomplish, manage
**succeed in examination** pass
**succeed to** accede, inherit, replace, supercede
**success** accomplishment, attainment, issue, outcome, prosperity, triumph, victory, wealth
**successful** acknowledged, effective, fruitful, prosperous, proven, useful, victorious, wealthy
**successful combatant** champion
**successfully completed** accomplished, accomplishment
**successfully prevent** thwart
**successful move** score
**successful publication** best seller
**successful stroke** coup
**successful thing** winner
**successive** consecutive, following, ordered, sequential, succeeding
**successor** heir
**successor of Nero** Galba
**succinct** abrupt, brief, brusque, clipped, compact, concise, condensed, cryptic, curtailed, epigrammatic, neat, short, summary, synoptic, terse, tight, tucked
**succose** juicy, sappy
**succour** aid, assist(ance), help, nurse, relief, rescue
**succulent** doughy, healthful, healthy, juicy, luscious, lush, mellow, moist, mushy, nourishing, nutritious, pappy, rich, salubrious, sappy, soft, spongy
**succulent leaf vegetable** spinach
**succulent plant** aloe, cactus, gasteria, haworthia, herb, houseleek
**succumb** capitulate, cease, die, fall, resist, submit, surrender, yield
**succumb anew** relapse
**succumbing to temptation** fall
**such** akin, as, corresponding, kindred, representing, similar, so, (such)like, tal (Sp)
**such and no more** mere
**such as** like
**sucker** catspaw, chub, chupon, dupe, foil, gonotyl, lollipop, moegoe, mullet, pushover, ratoon, sobole, surculus, tiller
**suck in** deceive, defraud, hoodwink, misinform, mislead
**sucking device** teat
**sucking fish** remora
**sucking tubes of insects** proboscis
**suckle** (breast-)feed, foster, nourish, nurse, nurture, parent, raise, rear, sustain, tend
**suck up** absorb
**sucrose** sugar
**Sudan grass** garawi
**sudate** sweat
**sudden whim** fancy
**sudden** abrupt, quick, unanticipated, unexpected, unforeseen, unpredicted
**sudden advance** dash
**sudden alarm** panic
**sudden attack** alert, assault, coup de main (F), foray, raid, sally
**sudden attack of apoplexy** seizure
**sudden attack of illness** seizure
**sudden blast of wind** gust
**sudden boost** surge
**sudden breaking off in speech** aposiopesis
**sudden bright idea** brainwave, inspiration
**sudden burst of activity** spasm, flurry
**sudden burst of emotion or violence** flare-up
**sudden burst of light** flash
**sudden change in a situation** coup de théâtre (F)
**sudden check given to horse** saccade
**sudden chill with shivering** rigor
**sudden collapse** debacle
**sudden commercial activity** boom

**sudden convulsion** cramp, fit, spasm
**sudden dash** break
**sudden descent from the exalted to the ridiculous** bathos
**sudden desire** yen, impulse
**sudden difficulty** facer
**sudden disaster** catastrophe
**sudden disastrous collapse** debacle
**sudden downward swoop** souse
**sudden enlightment** satori (J)
**sudden escape** lam
**sudden event needing prompt action** emergency
**sudden fall in prices** slump
**sudden fall of rain** onding
**sudden fancy** whim
**sudden fear** fright, panic
**sudden feeling of sickness** qualm
**sudden flight** lam, stampede
**sudden flood** spate
**sudden forceful stream** spurt
**sudden forward motion** lunge
**sudden fright** alarm, panic
**sudden fright and scattering of animals** stampede
**sudden great disaster** catastrophe
**sudden gush** spurt
**sudden gust of wind** flaw, scud, squall
**sudden heavy rush** surge
**sudden impulsive change of opinion** caprice
**sudden inclination to act** impulse
**sudden influx** inrush
**sudden inspiration** brainstorm
**sudden intake of breath** gasp
**sudden intensive attack** blitz
**sudden intense pain in the chest** angina pectoris
**sudden involuntary muscular contraction** spasm
**sudden jolt** lurch
**sudden leap** volt
**sudden light** flash
**sudden loud noise** bang
**sudden loud voice** boom
**suddenly** abruptly, immediately, instantly, presto, promptly, straightaway, unawares subito (I), unexpectedly
**suddenly excited** electric
**suddenly jump** start
**suddenly lose consciousness** faint
**suddenly narrowing stretch of road** bottleneck
**suddenly see** espy, notice
**suddenly surprised** startled
**suddenly sway to one side** lurch
**suddenly veer** swerve
**suddenly without warning** all at once
**sudden misfortune** disaster
**sudden move** gambade
**sudden movement** jerk, start

**sudden muscular contraction** spasm
**sudden onrush** avalanche
**sudden outbreak** eruption, mêlée, riot
**sudden outburst** ebullition, spate, spurt
**sudden outburst of emotion** ebullition, temper
**sudden outburst of flame** flare
**sudden overthrow of government** coup d'état (F)
**sudden overwhelming terror** panic
**sudden pain** pang, twinge
**sudden painful stiffness in the neck** crick
**sudden paralysis** apoplexy
**sudden plunge** nosedive
**sudden pull** jerk
**sudden raid** interruption
**sudden rebound** snapback
**sudden recoil in machinery** backlash
**sudden reverse in drama** peripeteia
**sudden rush** dash, sally, stampede
**sudden rush forward** surge
**sudden rush of current in a circuit** surge
**sudden rush of mob** stampede
**sudden rush of smoke** gust
**sudden seizure of epilepsy** fit
**sudden sharp pain** pang
**sudden start into activity** outburst, sally
**sudden stream** gush
**sudden stroke** apoplexy
**sudden strong rush for increase** surge
**sudden strong wind** gust, squall
**sudden surge of sales** boom
**sudden surprise attack** raid
**sudden tendency to act** impulse
**sudden terror** affright, panic
**sudden thrust** dab, jab, lunge
**sudden transition** saltation
**sudden unexpected difficulty** facer
**sudden vigorous attack** coup de main (F)
**sudden violent attack of pain** paroxysm
**sudden violent rainstorm** cloudburst
**sudden violent upset** upheaval
**sudden whim** impulse
**sudden wind** gust
**sudden yen** urge
**suds** bubbles, foam, froth, head, lather, soap(suds), spray, spume
**sudsy** soapy
**sudsy brew** ale
**sudsy** soapy
**sue** accuse, adjure, arraign, charge, entreat, importune, imprecate, indict, litigate, petition, prosecute, solicit, summon, supplicate, try
**suede** leather
**suede ankle boot** chukka

**suer** accuser, complainant, litigant, plaintiff, prosecutor
**suet pudding** roly-poly
**suffer** ache, agonise, ail, allow, bear, deteriorate, endure, experience, feel, grieve, hurt, permit, stand, support, sustain, tolerate, undergo
**suffer acutely** agonise
**suffer defeat** lose
**sufferer for a cause** martyr
**sufferer from haemophelia** haemopheliac
**sufferer from sleeplessness** insomniac
**suffer from hunger** starve
**suffer from the heat** swelter
**suffering** ache, affliction, agony, anguish, blow, convulsion, cramp, discomfort, distress, martyrdom, misery, ordeal, pain, pang, pinch, shock, soreness, sorrow, spasm, torture, trial, tribulation, woe
**suffering caused by lack of drink** thirst
**suffering caused by pain** distress
**suffering from alopecia** baldness
**suffering from concussion as the result of repeated blows** punch-drunk
**suffering from disorder of the liver** jaundiced, liverish
**suffering from ennui** bored
**suffering from extreme poverty** poverty-stricken
**suffering from high temperature** feverish
**suffering from ill health** ailing, diseased, disordered, feeble, indisposed, poorly, sick, unwell, weak
**suffering from inflamed joints** arthritic
**suffering from mental derangement** psychopath
**suffering from mental disease** mad, insane
**suffering from muscular rigidity** catatonic
**suffering from thirst** thirsty
**suffering insomnia** sleepless
**suffering preceding death** agony
**suffering reaction from overexcitement** overwrought
**suffering submitted to as an expression of penitence** penance
**suffer in the heat** swelter
**suffer loss** lose
**suffer mental anguish** ache, pain
**suffer mental pain** agonise
**suffer pain** ache, travail
**suffer the consequences** pay
**suffer the pains of childbirth** travail
**suffer under oppressive heat** swelter

**suffice** abound, adequate, answer, content, do, enough, sate, satiate, satisfy, serve
**sufficience** enough
**sufficiency** adequacy, competence, enough, fairness, fund, mass, mine, mountain(s), plenty, plethora, quantity, satisfactoriness, store, tolerability
**sufficient** abundant, adequate, admissible, ample, competent, complete, contenting, enough, plenteous, plentiful, plenty, presentable, satisfactory, sufficing, tolerable
**sufficient amount of** sufficiency
**sufficient and more** abundance, ample
**sufficient in quantity** adequate
**sufficient scope to function** elbow-room
**sufficient to cause death** lethal
**suffix** -ancy, -ase, -eme, -ent, -ese, -ess, -ey, -ial, -ian, -ier, -ine, -ing, -ise, -ite, -oidea, -ol, -ose, -ous, -ty, -ure, -yl, -yne
**suffix denoting disease** -itis
**suffix forming adjectives** -ate, -atory, -ean, -ern, -ey, -fic, -ial, -ine, -ish, -ose, -otic, -ous
**suffix forming adverbs** -fically, -ly
**suffix forming diminutives** -cle, -kin
**suffix forming female nouns** -ess
**suffix forming nouns** -ade, -ard, -ase, -ator, -eme, -ent, -er, -ian, -ier, -ile, -ine, -ing, -ist, -ite, -ol, -ty, -ule, -ure, -yne
**suffix forming plural nouns** -inae
**suffix forming verbs** -ing, -ise, -le
**suffix for name** -onym
**suffix indicating process** -osis
**suffix of nouns** -et
**suffix of numerals** -ty
**suffocate** asphyxiate, burke, choke, extinguish, gar(r)otte, smother, stifle, strangle, strangulate, subdue, suppress, throttle
**suffocate in water** drown
**suffocating atmosphere** fug
**suffocation** asphyxia(tion), burking, choking, dampening, extinguishment, gar(r)otting, smothering, stifling, strangulation, suppression, throttling, thuggee
**suffrage** approval, ballot, choice, consent, determination, franchise, option, petition, prayer, say, voice, vote
**suffuse** imbue, infuse, overspread, permeate, pervade, steep, transfuse
**sugar** fructose, glucose, lactose, sucrose, sweetener
**sugar and water** eau sucrée (F)

**sugar cane shoot** glucose, lalo, sucrose
**sugar cane spirit** rum
**sugar-coated nut** comfit
**sugar coating on cake** icing
**sugar daddy** fondler
**sugared almond** praline
**sugar factory** refinery
**sugar found in fruit juice** fructose, glucose
**sugar found in honey** fructose
**sugar found in milk** lactose
**sugar found in sugar cane** sucrose
**sugar icing for cakes** frosting
**sugar in roots** inulin
**sugar lump** cube
**sugar measure** saccharometer
**sugar paste candy** nougat
**sugar pea** mangetout
**sugar pinchers** tongs
**sugar plant** cane
**sugar plantation** trapiche
**sugar root** beet
**sugar source** beet, cane
**sugar tree** maple
**sugary** candied, flattering, honeyed, honied, nectareous, pleasant, savoury, sentimental, suave, sugared, sweet(ened), syrupy, unctuous
**sugary sentimentality** schmaltz
**suggest** advance, advise, connote, evoke, hint, imply, indicate, insinuate, intimate, introduce, mention, moot, move, propose, propound, recommend
**suggestion** advice, breath, counsel, dash, hint, idea, implication, indication, innuendo, instance, intimation, motion, opinion, plan, proposal, proposition, recommendation, suspicion, thought, tinge, touch, trace, whisper
**suggestion arising from oneself** autosuggestion
**suggestion of terms** proposition
**suggestive** allusive, dirty, evocative, evoking, expressive, indecent, lewd, obscene, provocative, racy, reminiscent, risqué, rude, vulgar
**suggestive look** leer
**suggestive of evil** sinister
**suggest obliquely** hint
**suicidal** anxious, brokenhearted, dangerous, deadly, death-defying, dejected, depressed, despairing, desperate, despondent, disconsolate, downcast, frantic, griefstricken, hopeless, impetuous, inconsolable, lethal, melancholy, miserable, perilous, rash, reckless, self-destructive, unsafe, wretched

**suicidal air attack by Japanese pilot** kamikaze
**suicidal animal** lemming
**suicide** felo de se (L), hara-kiri, self-immolation, self-murder, seppuku (J), suttee
**suicide pilot** kamikaze
**suicide place of Juda** Aceldama
**suicide spot** lovers' leap
**sui generis** peculiar, unique
**suit** accord, adapt, agree, answer, befit, cause, correspond, dress, fit, harmonise, match, modify, request, tally
**suitability** appropriateness, aptitude, aptness, capability, competence, decorum, expediency, fitness, gift, justness, leaning, opportuneness, proclivity, relevance, rightness, talent, timeliness
**suitable** acceptable, accordant, adaptable, adjusted, agreeable, applicable, apply, apposite, appropriate, apt(ly), becoming, congenial, decent, due, eligible, felicitous, fit, good, meet, opportune, pat, pertinent, proper, relevant, right, satisfactory, suited
**suitable for drinking** potable
**suitable for housing** residential
**suitable for living in** habitable
**suitable for male and female** unisex
**suitable for ploughing** arable
**suitable for private houses** residential
**suitable for producing strength and grace** callisthenic
**suitable for raising crops** arable
**suitable for singing** melic
**suitable for stage performance** acting
**suitable for treatment by surgical operation** operable
**suitable for warfare** martial
**suitableness** aptitude, aptness, honesty, propriety
**suitable only for children** puerile
**suitable place in life** niche
**suitable time** season
**suitable to the circumstances** expedient
**suitable to the season** seasonable
**suitably** apropos, aptly, fitly, gradely, meetly, timely
**suit at law** case, litigation
**suitcase** bag, cap(case), dorlach, keester, valise
**suitcase and bags** luggage
**suitcase-bill bird** pelican
**suit component** vest
**suite** apartment, cycle, ensemble, equipage, partita, retinue, series, set, suit, tail

**suited** accommodated, adapt(ed), adjusted, agreed, answered, apt, assorted, became, befitted, congenial, fit(ted), gratified, harmonised, matched, satisfied, seemly
**suited for the occasion** befitting
**suite for persons in attendance** retinue
**suite in music** partita
**suite of mouldings** ledgement
**suite of rooms** chamber, flat
**suiting** cheviot, covert, serge, sharkskin, tweed
**suitmaker** tailor
**suit of armour** panoply
**suit of cards** clubs, diamonds, hearts, spades
**suit of mail** armour
**suitor** admirer, applicant, beau, beloved, boyfriend, candidate, darling, date, dear, escort, follower, gallant, girlfriend, lover, man, mistress, paramour, petitioner, servant, suppli(c)ant, swain, sweetheart, wooer
**sulcate** chanelled, fluted, grooved
**sulcus** depression, furrow, groove
**sulfide mixture** matte
**sulk** brood, grumpiness, mope, pique, pout, snit
**sulker** pouter
**sulkiness** dourness
**sulky** aloof, churlish, cross, ill-humoured, moody, morose, perverse, petulant, querulous, resentful, sullen, vexed
**sullage** filth, refuse, sewage, silt, waste
**sullen** acerb, acrimonious, brooding, cheerless, clouded, cross, crusty, dismal, dour, dull, embittered, gloomy, glum, heavy, irascible, irritable, moody, morose, mournful, obstinate, peeved, reserved, scowling, silent, slow, sombre, sour, splenetic, stagnant, sulky, surly, taciturn, tetchy, unsociable
**sullen and grim** dour
**sullenly** broodingly, cheerlessly, crossly, dismally, dully, gloomily, grumpily, heavily, moodily, morosely, obstinately, silently, sombrely, sourly, surlily
**sullenly rude** surly
**sullenness** dourness, glumness, heaviness, moodiness, moroseness, sulks
**Sullivan's partner** Gilbert
**sully** bedraggle, begrime, blemish, contaminate, corrupt, defame, defile, dirty, disgrace, maculate, mar, pollute, scandalise, smear, smirch, smudge, soil, spoil, spot, stain, taint, tarnish, vilify
**sulphate used in sizing paper** alum
**sulphur** brimstone
**sulphuric acid** vitriol
**sultan** fowl, Saladin, selim, sovereign
**sultanate** authority, Oman, rank, saladin
**sultan's decree** irade
**sultan's entourage** harem
**sultan's wife** sultana
**sultan's wives** harem
**sultry** close, fainty, feverish, hot, humid, muggy, oppressive, overheated, scorching, stuffy, suffocating, sweltering, sweltry, torrid, tropical, warm
**sultry wind** berg wind, chinook, sirocco
**sum** aggregate, amount, quantity, score, tally, total, whole
**sum charged for loan** interest
**sum deducted from account** debit
**Sumerian city** Ur
**Sumerian deity** Abu
**Sumerian sky god** An
**sum fixed as a penalty** fine
**sum for ex-spouse** alimony
**summarise** abbreviate, abridge, abstract, brief, compact, compress, concentrate, condense, contract, digest, epitomise, recap(itulate), reduce, rehash, review, shorten, synopsise
**summary** abridg(e)ment, brief, compact, compendium, concise, digest, essence, extract, laconic, outline, peremptory, pithy, précis, résumé, short, succinct, synopsis
**summary of a play** scenario
**summary of belief** credo, creed
**summary of essential points** précis
**summer** ete (F)
**summer annoyance** heat, rash, sunburn, sweat
**summer colouring** suntan
**summer complaint** diarrhoea, heat rash, sunburn, sunstroke
**summer dish** salad
**summer drink** juice, (lemon)ade
**summer fabric** cotton, linen, seersucker
**summer footwear** sandals, slip slops, thongs
**summer fruit** apple, apricot, peach, pear
**summer hat** panama, straw
**summerhouse** belvedere, gazebo, pergola
**summer retreat** beach, camp, resort
**summer shoe** sandal
**summer sport** cricket, tennis

**summit** acme, apex, (a)top, climax, conference, crest, crown, culmination, extreme, head, heaven, height, highest, maximum, meridian, objective, peak, pinnacle, pitch, point, pole, roof, sky, spire, supremacy, tip(top), top, utmost, vertex, zenith
**summon** activate, adjure, approach, arouse, ask, assemble, bid, call, cite, clepe, command, convene, convoke, demand, evoke, incite, invite, litigate, muster, order, page, request, require, rouse, signal, subpoena, tell
**summon for compulsory military service** conscript
**summon publicly** page
**summons** writ
**summons for military service** call up
**summon to appear in court** cite
**summon to assemble** convoke
**summon to phone** page
**summon to return** recall
**summon up** arouse
**sum of money handed over** payment
**sum of money paid as penalty** fine
**sum owed** debt
**sum paid by tenant** rental
**sum paid every year** annuity
**sum paid for insurance** premium
**sum paid to persuade someone** bribe
**sumptuous** costly, dazzling, dear, elevated, exorbitant, expensive, extravagant, gorgeous, grand, high-priced, imposing, inestimable, lavish, lofty, luxurious, majestic, opulent, plush, pre-eminent, precious, priceless, remarkable, rich, splendid, stately, superb, supreme, valuable
**sumptuous meal** feast
**sum total** aggregate, amount
**sum up** add, close, conclude, recap(itulate), review, summarise, total
**sun** daystar, Helios, sol (L), tan
**sunbathe** bask, tan
**sunbeam** ray
**sunbonnet** poke
**sun-bronzed colour** tan
**sunburned** blistery, bronzed, brown, burned, chapped, inflamed, peeling, red(dened), ruddy, scarlet, tan(ned)
**sunburnt** adust
**Sunday entrée** roast
**sunder** apart, cleave, cut, divide, part, rend, rive, sever, tear
**sundial pointer** gnomon
**sundown** dark, dusk, eve(ning), eventide, gloaming, half-light, nightfall, sunset, twilight

**sundowner** cocktail, drink, hobo, swagman, tramp, tussocker, whaler
**sun-dried brick** adobe, dobi
**sundry** assorted, chowchow, different, divers, miscellaneous, several, some, varied, various
**sunflower state** Kansas
**sung by choir** choral
**sung in church** hymn, psalm, song
**sunglasses** shades
**sun god** Amen, Apollo, Frey, Ra, Sol
**sun goddess** Amaterasu
**sung poem** ode
**sunhat** sombrero
**sun helmet** topee, topi
**sunken fence** ha(w)-ha(w)
**sunken liner 1912** Titanic
**sunken panel in ceiling or vault** coffer(ing)
**sunken place** pit
**sunken ship** wreck
**sunken wreckage** lagan
**sunk in oblivion** bygone, fallen
**sunless spot** shade
**sunlit hours** day
**sunny side** yellow
**sunny-side up** fried
**sun parlour** solarium
**sun peak** visor
**sun personified** Sol
**sun porch** solarium
**sunrise** cockcrow, dawn, daybreak, daylight, east, orient
**sunrise direction** east, orient
**sun room** solarium
**sunset** dusk, eventide, gloaming, nightfall, sundown
**sunset to sunrise** night
**sunshade** parasol, roundel, sombrero, tiresol, umbrella
**sun shelter** awning, blind, parasol, visor
**sun shield** cloud, visor
**sun specs** dark glasses
**sunstroke** coup de soleil (F)
**sun umbrella** parasol
**super** admirable, delicious, exceeding, excellent, fabulous, fine, glorious, good, grand, great, heavenly, hyper, magnificent, marvellous, outstanding, perfect, pleasurable, scrumptious, smashing, splendid, stunning, superb, superfine, superior, swell, terrific, wizard, wonderful
**superable** surmountable
**superb** ace, admirable, excellent, exquisite, grand, magnificent, majestic, rich, splendid, stately
**supercharge** boost
**supercharger** booster

**supercilious** arrogant, cavalier, conceited, contemptuous, contumelious, despising, dictatorial, disdainful, domineering, haughty, imperious, insolent, lofty, lordly, overbearing, pompous, pretentious, prideful, proud, scornful, snide, sniffish, snobbish, snooty, superior
**superficial** airy, cursory, external, flippant, outward, perfunctory, shallow, skin-deep
**superficial additions** trappings
**superficial burn** singe
**superficial extent** area
**superficial furrow** stria
**superficial inflammation of the skin in patches** erythema
**superficial knowledge** sciolism, smattering
**superficial lustre** gloss
**superficially polite** suave
**superficial person** snob
**superficial pretender to knowledge** sciolist
**superficial pretensions to knowledge** sciolism
**superficial show** gloss, veneer
**superficial skin** cuticle
**superfluity** dispensability, excess(iveness), exorbitance, exuberance, immoderacy, needlessness, overliberality, profuseness, spare, spillover, surplus, uselessness
**superfluous** copious, de trop, excess(ive), expendable, extra(vagant), extreme, needless, otiose, overabundant, overgenerous, redundant, spare, superabundant, unnecessary, unneeded, unrequired, unwanted, valueless
**superfluous amount** superfluity
**superhuman** Titan
**superimpose** add, coat, face, overlay, pave, plate, superinduce, supplement, veneer
**superimposed photograph** inset
**superintend** administer, control, direct, inspect, manage, oversee, preside, supervise
**superintendence** administration, care, conduct, control, direction, execution, government, guidance, management, overseeing, oversight, performance, provision, supervision
**superintendent** administrator, boss, chief, conductor, director, inspector, manager, overseer, provost, supervisor, warden
**superior** better, boss, choice, class(y), excellent, exceptional, fine(r), greater, haughty, high, incomparable, outstanding, pre-eminent, pretentious, prime, sanctimonious, select, senior, superlative, supervisor, supreme, unrivalled, upper

**superior ability** prowess
**superior black tea** pekoe
**superior force** vis major
**superior in** above
**superior in quality** superb
**superior in rank** senior
**superiority in office** seniority
**superior leather** buff
**superior manner** style
**superior of monastery** abbot, father
**superior person** oner
**superior power** force majeure
**superior Turkish tobacco** Latakia
**superior skill** prowess
**superlative ending** -est
**supermarket vehicle** cart, trolley
**supernatural** abnormal, anomalous, arcane, astral, bewitched, cabalistic, celestial, dark, divine, exceptional, extraordinary, fabulous, fey, ghostly, godly, hidden, hypernormal, magical, miraculous, mysterious, mystic, occult, omnipotent, paranormal, phantom, preternatural, psychic, spectral, sublime, superhuman, superphysical, supranatural, thaumaturgic, uncanny, unearthly, unnatural, wondrous
**supernatural being** elf, spirit, tokoloshe, troll, witch
**supernatural event** miracle
**supernatural power** whammy
**supernatural sense** ESP
**supernatural spirit** genie
**supersede** annul, displace, overrule, replace, rescind, revoke, succeed
**supersede arrogantly** override
**supervene** arise, attend, befall, chance, derive, ensue, follow, happen, issue, proceed, result, stem, succeed
**supervise** administer, conduct, control, direct, handle, lead, manage, oversee, regulate
**supervise examinees** invigilate
**supervisor** administrator, advisor, bureaucrat, captain, chief, commander, director, executive, foreman, guide, head, inspector, manager, marshall, official, overlooker, overseer, principal, skipper, steward
**supervisor in large shop** shopwalker
**supervisor of morals** censor
**supine** careless, indolent, listless, negligent, reclining, recumbent

**supplant** depose, dismiss, displace, eject, exchange, expel, interchange, oust, relieve, remove, replace, substitute, succeed, supersede, swap, unseat, usurp
**supplanter** replacer, usurper
**supple** agreeable, cringing, elastic, flexible, grovelling, limber, lissom(e), lithe, obsequious, plastic, pliable, pliant, servile, whippy, yielding
**supplement** accessory, addendum, addition, adjunct, amendment, ancilla, appendage, appendix, attachment, complement, complete, eke, enlarge, epilogue, extension, insert, lift, raise, reinforcement, suffix, support
**supplemental** accessory, added, additional, additory, adscititious, appended, auxiliary, extra, fresh, further, more, new, other, supplementary
**supplementary** accessory, added, addition(al), additory, adjunct, aide, ancillary, annexed, appended, attendant, auxiliary, coadjutor, codicillary, complementary, extension, extra, extraneous, helper, incidental, reserved, ripieno, secondary, subordinate, supplement(al), upgrading
**supplementary addition** codicil
**supplementary building** annexe
**supplementary part** accessory
**supplementary player** ripieno
**supplementary thing** addition
**supplement to a will** codicil
**suppliant** appellant, applicant, aspirant, beggar, begging, petitioner, petitioning, petitionist, pleader, praying, solicitant, solicitor, solicitous, supplicant
**supplicate** adjure, appeal, apply, ask, beg, beseech, call, claim, crave, demand, desire, entreat, implore, importune, petition, plead, pray, refer, request, seek, solicit, sue, supplicate
**supplication** appeal, entreaty, invocation, petition, plea, prayer, request, suit
**supplier of equipment** outfitter
**supplier of meals** caterer
**supply** cater, deliver, endue, equip, extend, feed, fill, fulfil, fund, furnish, give, inventory, issuance, issue, maintain, occupy, offer, provide, quantity, replenish, satisfy, service, stock, store
**supply again** refuel, replace, replenish
**supply channel** pipeline
**supply food** cater, purvey

**supply hidden for future use** hoard
**supply in abundance** replenish
**supply in niggardly amount** stint
**supply meagrely** skimp
**supply money** fund
**supply of food** provision
**supply of money** fund
**supply party food** cater
**supply ship** co(o)per
**supply weapons to** arm
**supply with a crew** man
**supply with air** aerate
**supply with food** feed, nourish
**supply with oxygen** aerate
**supply with what is needed** equip
**support** abet, advocate, assistance, back(ing), base, bear, bolster, brace, buttress, confirm, corroborate, countenance, endorse, espousal, espouse, forward, further, help, living, maintain, nourish, nurture, prop, relieve, second, stand, stay, stomach, subsistence, succour, suffer, sustain, sustenance, truss, undergo, uphold, upkeep
**support at sea** raft
**support beneath a chair** leg
**support built against wall** buttress
**supporter** ally, champion, co-worker, defender, friend, helper, partisan, patron, sponsor, stayer
**supporter in a struggle** ally
**supporter of bellicose policy** jingo
**supporter of monarchy** monarchist, royalist
**supporter of the government** ministerialist
**support for artist's canvas** easel
**support for bathroom basin** pedestal
**support for blackboard** easel
**support for broken bone** sling, splint
**support for building** pillar
**support for climbing plants** trellis
**support for cornice** ancon
**support for golf ball** tee
**support for injured arm** sling
**support for lame person** crutch
**support for power cables** pylon
**support for sails** mast
**support for statue** pedestal
**support for table** trestle
**support for washing line** prop
**support from beneath** underpin
**support garment** bra(ssière), truss
**support idea** espouse
**supporting bar** rail
**supporting beam** girder, template, templet
**supporting central post of winding stairs** newel
**supporting column in form of female figure** caryatid

**supporting framework** trestle
**supporting opinion** suffrage
**supporting part** base
**supporting rib between main ribs in Gothic vault** lierne
**supporting strap** suspender
**supporting structure for table** trestle
**supporting timber** beam
**support of column** base, pedestal, plinth
**support prop in coal mine** sprag
**supports plant** stem
**support with timbers** shore
**suppose** assume, believe, conceive, expect, guess, imagine, opine, presume, suspect, think
**supposed communication with the dead** necromancy
**supposed inhabitant of Mars** Martian
**supposed to bring luck** mascot
**suppose to be true** presume
**supposing that** if
**supposition** assumption, attitude, belief, conclusion, conjecture, conviction, doubt, guess, hypothesis, idea, if, notion, opinion, posit, position, premise, presumption, speculation, surmise, suspicion, theory, view
**suppress** block, censor, check, conceal, conquer, contain, counteract, crush, curb, deter, elide, eliminate, eradicate, extinguish, gag, hamper, hide, inhibit, muffle, muzzle, obliterate, obviate, oppress, overpower, overthrow, quash, quell, quench, repress, restrain, silence, smother, squash, stifle, stop, strangle, subdue, subvert, suffocate, vanquish, withdraw, withhold
**suppressed laugh** chuckle
**suppurate** discharge, drain, excrete, fester, matter, maturate, rankle, ripen, weep
**suppurative tonsilitis** quinsy
**supreme** cardinal, chief, extreme, final, foremost, greatest, head, paramount, peerless, prime, ultimate, utmost
**supreme being** Brahma, God
**supreme commander** generalissimo
**supreme deity** Hansa, Hanse
**supreme dominion** empire
**supreme Germanic god** Woden, Wotan
**supreme in authority** imperial
**supreme in excellence** transcendent
**supremely evil** satanic
**supremely excellent** ideal
**supremely excellent person** paragon
**supreme Norse god** Odin
**supreme power** authority, supremacy

**supreme remedy** elixir, panacea
**supreme ruler** sovereign
**sure** certain, confident, convinced, destined, honest, indubitable, inevitable, infallible, positive, precise, solid, stable, trusty, undoubted, unerring, yes
**sure enough** undeniably
**sure in one's own mind** presumptuous
**surely** absolutely, assuredly, certainly, clearly, confidently, definitely, doggedly, doubtless(ly), firmly, indubitably, inevitably, positively, securely, solidly, undoubtedly
**surely not** never
**sure of oneself** assured, poised, pragmatic, self-reliant
**sure sign** hallmark
**sure thing** certificate
**sure to produce a desired result** efficacious
**surety** aegis, armour, assurance, bail, bond, bulwark, captive, certainty, collateral, contract, convoy, covenant, defence, deposit, earnest, escort, gage, guarantee, guarantor, guaranty, hostage, indemnity, indisputibility, insurance, mortgagor, pawn, pledge, positiveness, prisoner, promise, safeguard, safety, security, shield, sponsor, trustee, undertaking, warranty, warrentor, word
**surface** appearance, emerge, exterior, outside, pave, rise, shell, top
**surface appearance** patina
**surface a road** pave, tar
**surface bubbles** foam
**surface coating** veneer
**surface hollow** dent
**surface injury** abrasion
**surface on ship** deck
**surface road again** retar
**surface rock** outcrop
**surface slant** bevel
**surf duck** coot, scoter, skunkhead
**surfeit** abundance, cloy, cram, excess, glut, gorge, indulge, lavishness, nauseate, overabundance, overeat, overfull, overload, oversupply, plethora, sate, satiate, satiety, surplus, waste
**surf-riding** aquatics
**surge** ascend, billow, bulge, climb, efflux, escalation, flood, growth, gush, increase, inflation, mount, outpouring, pour, rise, rush, stream, swell, upcurve, uprush, upsurge, wave
**surgeon** operator
**surgeon's attendant** loblolly
**surgeon's cylindrical saw** trepan

**surgeon's instrument** spatula
**surgeon's instrument for scraping bones** xyster
**surgeon's knife** scalpel
**surgeon's mate** loblolly
**surgeon's overall** gown
**surgeon's saw** trepan
**surgeon's scalpel** bistoury
**surgeon's small scraping instrument** curette
**surge out** shed
**surgery** care, cure, healing, medicine, operation, remedy, treatment
**surgery dealing with fractures** agmatology
**surgery performed on the nervous system** neurosurgery
**surgical appliance** splint
**surgical boring tool** trepan
**surgical cutting device** ecraseur
**surgical cutting of a nerve** neurotomy
**surgical dressing material** lint
**surgical hook or forceps** tenaculum
**surgical incision of abdominal wall** laparomoty
**surgical incision of kidney** nephrotomy
**surgical incision of iris** iridotomy
**surgical incision of intestine** enterectomy
**surgical incision of loin** laparomoty
**surgical incision of rib** costotomy
**surgical incision of spleen** splenotomy
**surgical incision of tendon** tenotomy
**surgical incision of trachea** tracheotomy
**surgical incision of uterus** hysterotomy
**surgical instrument** ablator, forceps, lancet, probe, scalpel, trepan, trocar, tweezers
**surgical knife** scalpel
**surgical loop** curet(te)
**surgically sterile** aseptic
**surgical opening of the chest cavity** thoractomy
**surgical pincher** forcep
**surgical puncture of the heart** cardiocentesis
**surgical removal** -ectomy
**surgical removal of adenoids** adenoidectomy
**surgical removal of appendix** append(ic)ectomy
**surgical removal of bladder** cystectomy
**surgical removal of bone or piece of bone** ostectomy
**surgical removal of breast** mastectomy
**surgical removal of calculus in urinary bladder** lithotomy

**surgical removal of dead tissue** necrotomy
**surgical removal of gall bladder** cholecystectomy
**surgical removal of gallstones** cholelithotomy
**surgical removal of gland** adenectomy
**surgical removal of kidney** nephrectomy
**surgical removal of kidney stone** lithonephrotomy
**surgical removal of larynx** laryngectomy
**surgical removal of liver** hepatectomy
**surgical removal of lung** pneumonectomy
**surgical removal of nerve segment** neurectomy
**surgical removal of part of eye** iridectomy
**surgical removal of part of root of tooth** apisectomy
**surgical removal of part of skull** craniotomy
**surgical removal of ovary** oophorectomy, ovariectomy
**surgical removal of sympathetic ganglion** sympathectomy
**surgical removal of testicle** orchidectomy
**surgical removal of tongue** glossectomy
**surgical removal of tonsil** tonsillectomy
**surgical removal of tumour in breast** lumpectomy
**surgical removal of thymus** thymectomy
**surgical removal of uterus** hysterectomy
**surgical removal of womb** hysterectomy
**surgical removal or severing of a Fallopian tube** salpingectomy
**surgical scraper** curet(te)
**surgical sewing** suture
**surgical stitch material** catgut
**surgical support** truss
**surgical thread** seton, suture
**surgical treatment** operation
**suricate** meerkat
**surly** biting, brusque, churlish, crabbed, cranky, cross, crotchety, crusty, curt, cynical, gruff, grumpy, ill-natured, irascible, irritable, morose, peppery, perverse, quarrelsome, rough, sarcastic, sharp, sulky, sullen, testy, tetchy, thorny, touchy, uncivil, ungracious
**surly child** brat
**surly individual** cynic

**surly person** churl, crab, curmudgeon, grouch, grump, sorehead
**surly youth** yob
**surmise** conclude, conclusion, conjecture, consider, deduce, deduction, fancy, guess, idea, imagine, infer(ence), notion, opine, possibility, presume, speculate, speculation, suppose, supposition, suspect, suspicion, think
**surmising** concluding, conjecturing, considering, deducing, deeming, fancying, guessing, imagining, inferring, presuming, speculating, supposing, suspecting
**surmount** ascend, clear, climb, command, conquer, dominate, scale, survive, vault
**surmountable** superable
**surpass** above, beat, better, cap, eclipse, exceed, excel, outdo, outrival, outstrip, override, overshadow, pass, top, transcend, trump
**surpass in cunning** outfox
**surpass in growth** outgrow
**surpass in quality** outclass
**surplus** excess, extra, flood, glut, odd, over(age), overflow, oversupply, plethora, redundant, remainder, remaining, remnants, residual, residue, spare, superabundance, superfluity, superfluous, surfeit, surviving, unused
**surplus requirements** redundant
**surprise** amaze(ment), ambush, astonish(ment), astound, discover, dum(b)found, revelation, shock, stagger, startle, stun, wonder
**surprise attack** ambush
**surprise attempt to overthrow the existing power** coup, putsch
**surprise greatly** amaze, astonish, astound
**surprise sound** eh
**surprising circumstances** eye-opener
**surprising trick** feat
**surrealist** Dali
**surrender** abandon, abdicate, capitulate, cede, cession, forfeit, forgo, leave, obedience, passiveness, quit, relinquish, resign(ation), servitude, slavishness, submit, vacate, waive, yield
**surrender offender to foreign country** extradite
**surrender on terms** capitulate
**surrender right** release
**surrender territory** cede
**surreptitious substitute** changeling
**surround** begird, beset, besiege, blockade, bound, circumvent, encase, encircle, enclose, encompass, enfold, entrap, envelop, environ, enwrap, enwreathe, gird(le), hem, inundate, overflow, ring, throng, wrap
**surround closely** clip
**surrounded by** amid, among(st), with
**surrounded by barrier** fenced
**surrounded by foreign territory** enclave
**surrounded by water** enisled
**surround for painting** picture frame
**surrounding** ambient, belt, border, boundary, circle, coat, context, covering, enclosure, fence, nearby, neighbouring, perimeter
**surrounding atmosphere** ambience, aura
**surrounding circumstances** context, milieu
**surrounding district** vicinage, vicinity
**surrounding embankment of fort** rampart
**surrounding parts** neighbourhood
**surrounding region** periphery
**surroundings** ambit, atmosphere, background, confines, environment, habitat, milieu, precincts, scene, setting
**surroundings of an event** mise en scène (F)
**surround with a halo** enhalo
**surround with water** enisle
**survey** appraise, assess, contemplate, estimate, examination, examine, eye, inquiry, inspect(ion), measure, observe, overview, perusal, plan, plot, poll, prospect, research, review, scan, scrutinise, scrutiny, study, triangulate, view, watch
**surveying instrument** theodolite
**surveying method** stadia
**survey instrument** level
**survey of the past** retrospect
**surveyor's marking flag** fanion
**surving female spouse** widow
**survive** continue, endure, exist, (out)last, (out)live, outwear, persist, remain, subsist, succeed
**survive longer than** outlast
**surviving husband** widower
**surviving object** relic
**surviving trace** fossil, remnant
**surviving wife** widow
**susceptible** liable, responsive, sensitive, subject, thin-skinned, vulnerable
**suspect** believe, conjecture, consider, distrust, imagine, misdoubt, mistrust, suppose
**suspend** adjourn, append, cease, debar, defer, delay, dismiss, eject, eliminate, end, hang, intermit, interrupt, postpone, quit, reject, retard, swing, withhold
**suspend a meeting** adjourn
**suspended** delayed, depending, inactive, pending, postponed, shelved, unresolved, unsettled, withheld
**suspended ornament** pendant
**suspending hook** hanger
**suspense** doubt, hesitation, incertitude, interruption, irresolution, pause, quiescence, remission, respite, scruple, stay, surcease, suspension, uncertainty, wavering
**suspense story** thriller
**suspension of commerce** embargo
**suspension of criminal sentence** reprieve
**suspension of hostilities** armistice, truce
**suspicion** distrust, doubt, guess, idea, inkling, mistrust, notion, suggestion, trace
**suspicion of the existence of something** surmise
**suspicious** chary, debatable, distrustful, doubtful, dubious, irregular, jealous, leery, odd, peculiar, queer, questionable, sceptical, shady, shaky, strange, suspect, uneasy, unsure, untrustworthy, wary
**suspiciously obscure** murky
**sustain** aid, approve, bear, corroborate, endure, establish, furnish, help, nourish, nurture, prop, purvey, subsist, support, undergo, uphold
**sustain in fluid** suspend
**sustain with food** nourish
**sustenance** aliment, foodstuffs, groceries, livelihood, maintenance, menu, nourishment, nutriment, nutrition, provision, snack, support, sustainment, viands
**suture** stitch
**svelte** delicate, elegant, fine, graceful, lanky, lean, lissom(e), lithe, slender, slim, sophisticated, supple, sylphlike, urbane
**swab** clean, cloth, mop, rub, scour, scrub, sponge, swob, wash
**swag** bluey, goods, loot, shiralee, valuables
**swagger** affectation, arrogance, blow, boast(ing), brag, bravado, fashionable, flourish, gait, gasconade, insolence, manner, march, parade, pomp, prance, smart, strut, swank, swash, vaunt, walk

**swagman** sundowner, tramp
**swagman's bundle** shiralee
**Swahili title** bwana
**swain** admirer, adorer, beau, boyfriend, clown, countryman, date, fiancé, flame, follower, gallant, inamorato, lover, man, rustic, shepherd, steady, suitor, wooer, yokel
**swallow** absorb, assimilate, consume, devour, draught, drink, eat, engulf, gorge, gulp, imbibe, ingest, mouthful, receive, swill
**swallow a little at a time** sip, sup
**swallow greedily** engorge, gulp
**swallow hastily** bolt, gulp
**swallow one's words** withdraw
**swallow up** absorb, engulf
**swamp** besiege, bog, drench, drown, engulf, everglade, fen, flood, flush, immerse, inundate, marsh, mire, morass, moss, overload, overwhelm, quag(mire), saturate, sludge, stream, submerge, vlei, wetland
**swamp craft** airboat
**swamp fever** equine infectious anaemia
**swamp grass** reed, sedge
**swamp reptile** alligator
**swampy** boggy, fenny, marish, marshy, miry, quaggy, wet
**swampy ground** bog, mire, mud
**swan** cygnet, pen, whooper
**swank** active, agile, bluff, ostentation, pliant, swagger
***Swan Lake* dancer** ballerina, Pavlova
**swap** bandy, barter, commute, exchange, interchange, invert, permute, substitute, switch, swop, trade, traffic, transpose
**sward** clod, common, divot, grass(plot), green, lawn, sod, swarth, turf
**swarm** abound, bevy, flock, herd, horde, mass, multitude, shoal, teem, throng
**swarming insect** bee
**swarm into** invade
**swarm of bees** hive
**swarm of insects** flight
**swarm over** infest
**swarm with** abound, bristle, crawl, exuberate, hotch, pack, pullulate, stuff, team
**swastika** fylfot, hakenkreuz (G)
**swat** biff, clout, crush, cuff, hit, slap, squash, strike, swipe
**swathe** apparel, attire, bandage, cloak, clothe, conceal, cover, deck, drape, dress, embrace, enclose, enfold, enwrap, garb, hide, invest, obscure, outfit, rig, robe, sheathe, shroud, veil, wrap

**swathe in bandages** swaddle
**sway** agitate, authority, bend, bias, brandish, control, convince, deviate, dominate, equivocate, fluctuate, impel, impress, incline, influence, mastery, oscillate, persuade, reign, rock, rule, stimulate, stray, swerve, swing, teeter, tilt, touch, undulate, vacillate, veer, vibrate, wave(r), wobble
**sway from side to side** swag, wobble
**swaying impulse** bias
**sway to and fro** rock
**Swaziland's head of state** King Mswati
**swear** acknowledge, admit, affirm, assert, attest, aver, avow, blaspheme, confess, curse, declare, pledge, profess, promise, state, testify, vow
**swear at** abuse
**swear by** admire, believe, confirm, demonstrate, document, substantiate, trust, venerate, warrant
**swear word** blasphemy, curse, execration, expletive, impiety, imprecation, impropriety, indecency, indelicacy, malediction, oath, obscenity, profanity, sacrilege, swearing, vulgarism
**sweat** agitation, agonise, anxiety, chafe, chore, distress, drudgery, effort, execrate, exertion, exudation, exude, glow, labour, panic, perspiration, perspire, strain, sudate, sudor, suffer, swelter, toil, transude, worry
**sweater** jumper, pullover, turtleneck, woolly
**sweat it out** endure
**sweat profusely** swelter
**swede** rutabaga
**Swede's Sweden** Sverige
**Swedish measure** ref
**Swedish money** krona, krone, kronor
**Swedish operatic soprano** Nilsson
**Swedish parliament** Riksdag
**Swedish prize** Nobel
**sweep** blow, brush, curve, encircle, extend, glance, reach, scour, scrub, vacuum, whisk
**sweep along** haste, hurry, run, rush, scamper, scurry
**sweep along easily and swiftly** scud
**sweep away** brush, clean, dust, mop, scrub, vacuum, whisk, wipe
**sweeping implement** broom
**sweepstake** draw, lottery, raffle
**sweet** agreeable, ambrosial, attractive, balmy, beloved, bonbon, candy, charming, clean, dear, dessert, dulcet, enjoyable, gracious, harmonious, honeyed, kind, lolly, lovable, manageable, mellow, melodious, mild, musical, nectar, new, nougat, perfumed, pleasant, pleasing, pleasurable, pure, soft, sugary, toffee, treacle, tuneful
**sweet ale** bragget
**sweet and charming** winsome
**sweet as honey** mellifluous
**sweet bag** sachet
**sweet bay** laurel, magnolia
**sweetbread** burr, pancreas, ris, thymus
**sweetbread of deer** inchpin
**sweetbrier** bedeguar, eglantine
**sweet cake** bun, cruller, tart
**sweet calabash** kuruba
**sweet cassava** aipi(m)
**sweet cherry** mazzard
**sweet cicely** chervil, myrrh
**sweet clover** lotus, melilot
**sweet corn** goldenbantam
**sweet course of meal** dessert
**sweet crystalline vegetable substance** sugar
**sweet cumin** anise
**sweet dish** dessert, mousse, pie, pudding
**sweet drink** ade, julep, nectar, pop
**sweetened brandy with mint** julep
**sweetened drink of spirits** sling
**sweetened milk set with rennet** junket
**sweetened wine drink** negus
**sweetener** saccharin(e), suganon, sugar
**sweet fern** polypody
**sweetfish** ayu
**sweet flag** beewort, calamus, sedge
**sweet fluid** honey, mel, molasses, nectar, syrup
**sweet fruit-flavoured lozenge** jujube
**sweet gale** gagel
**sweet grape** hanepoot
**sweet grass** mannagrass, reed
**sweetgum** liquidambar, storax
**sweetheart** amoret, darling, fiancé(e), jo (Sc), lover, skat, truelove, valentine
**sweet Hungarian wine** Tokay
**sweet idleness** dolce far niente (I)
**sweet in a great degree** luscious
**sweet liqueur** anisette, creme, kümmel, maraschino, ratafia
**sweet liquid** syrup
**sweetly** cutely
**sweet maker** confectioner
**sweetmeat** candy, confection, dragee, fondant, liquorice, lollipop, mebos, nougat
**sweet milk dish** flummery
**sweet music** melody, tunefulness
**sweet oatcake** flapjack
**sweet on a stick** lollipop
**sweet or pleasant smell** aroma
**sweet or unpleasant smell** odour

**sweet pepper** pimiento
**sweet potato** batata, camote (Sp), kumara, yam
**sweet powder** sherbet
**sweet red wine** alicante, jerepigo
**sweet roll** bun, danish
**sweets** dessert
**sweet sauce** custard
**sweet scent** fragrance
**sweet secretion of plants** nectar
**sweet singer of Israel** David
**sweet singer of myth** siren
**sweet smell** aroma, perfume
**sweet-smelling** aromatic, fragrant, (red)olent, scented
**sweet-smelling bush** lavender
**sweet-smelling plant** camomile
**sweet sound** melody, music
**sweet-sounding** dulcet, melodic
**sweet spiced bread toasted** Zwieback (G)
**sweet spice used by Jews in making incense** stacte
**sweet substance** honey, jam, molasses, sugar, syrup, treacle
**sweet substance from coal tar** saccharine
**sweet temper** amiability
**sweet tone** dulcet
**sweet to the ear** dulcet
**sweet viscid material** honey
**sweet white wine** falerne, late harvest, malaga, Sauternes, stein
**sweet wild cherry** mazzard
**sweet wine** angelica, hanepoot, jerepigo, malaga, muscatel, port
**swell** arise, billow, bloat, bulge, dandy, dilate, distend, distension, elegant, enlarge, expand, fop, glow, grand, grow, increase, inflate, inflation, protrude, puff, sea, strut, surge, wave, wax
**swelling** aggravating, augmenting, ballooning, bellying, billowing, bloating, bruise, bubo, bulge, bulging, bump, dilating, dilation, distending, enhancing, enlargement, enlarging, expanding, extending, growing, heightening, increasing, inflammation, intensifying, lump, mounting, node, oedema, protruding, proturberance, rising, surging, tumefying, tumour, turgescent
**swelling due to air in body tissue** emphysema
**swelling in hollow of horse's hock** thoroughpin
**swelling intumescence** oncosis
**swelling of the big toe** bunion
**swelling out of part of artery** aneurism, aneurysm

**swelling over** beetle
**swelling reducer** ice pack
**swelling wave** roller
**swell of sea foam** surf
**swell out** bag
**swell outwards** bulge
**swell up** inflate
**swept off one's feet** infatuated, smitten
**swerve** bend, deflect, depart, deviate, digress, diverge, incline, sheer, shift, slew, stray, swing, turn, veer, wander, wind
**swift** agile, arrowy, dashing, eager, electric, fast, fleet, hasty, immediate, instantaneous, lively, lizard, nimble, prompt, quick, rapid, smart, snappy, speedy, winged, zealous, zippy
**swift downward plunge by aircraft** nosedive
**swift downward sweep** swoop
**swift-flowing river section** rapids
**swift horse** courser, steed
**swiftly** apace, fast, hotfoot, quickly, rapidly, speedily
**swiftness** alacrity, briskness, bustle, celerity, dispatch, expedition, fleetness, haste, hurry, hustle, nimbleness, quickness, scramble, scurry, speed, sprint, velocity
**swift rodent** hare
**swift-running flightless bird** ostrich
**swift rush** race
**swill** consume, drench, flush, guzzle, rinse, sluice, swallow, waste
**swim** bathe, compete, crawl, dog paddle, float, glide, natate, paddle, progress, reel, scull, skim, skinny-dip, traverse, undulate, whirl
**swimming** floating, natant
**swimming aid** waterwings
**swimming bird** duck, swan
**swimming contest** gala
**swimming costume** bather, cossie
**swimming event** gala
**swimming hole** pool
**swimming organ** fin
**swimming pool** bath, lido, natatorium, natatory
**swimming sea-bird with flippers and unable to fly** penguin
**swimming stroke** breaststroke, butterfly, crawl, freestyle, overarm, trudgen
**swimming tank** pool
**swindle** cheat, chicane, con(fidence), deceive, deception, defraud, dupe, fleece, fraud, game, gip, gull, gyp, imposture, job, knavery, overcharge, rig, ruse, scam, stratagem, trick(ery), verneuk, victimise
**swindler** bilk, charlatan, cheat(er), chiseller, criminal, crook, defrauder, diddler, duper, fraud, hawk, highbinder, hoaxer, hustler, impostor, lawbreaker, mountebank, racketeer, rascal, robber, rogue, rook, shark, thief, trickster, twister
**swindler's confederate** decoy
**swine** animal, boar, hog, oinker, peccary, pig(let), porker, sow
**swineherd of Ulysses** Eumaeus
**swine pen** sty
**swing** curve, jazz, librate, lurch, pendulate, rock, scope, steer, turn, twist, vacillate, veer, warp, waver, yaw, zigzag
**swing around** swerve, veer
**swinging arm** pendulum
**swinging bed** hammock
**swinging crossbar** trapeze
**swing leg** malinger
**swing on one foot** pivot
**swing rapidly round** whirl
**swings cradle** rocks, mother
**swing to and fro** oscillate, sway
**swing to music** dance
**swing to other side** gybe
**swing turn in skiing** telemark
**swing unsteadily** sway
**swirl** agitate, boil, churn, eddy, scud, spin, surge, swish, swoosh, twirl, twist, wheel, whirl, whorl
**swish** agitate, flourish, hiss, hum, murmur, ritzy, rustle, sigh, wave, whir, whish, whisk
**Swiss** Helvetian, Helvetic(a)
**Swiss call** yodel
**Swiss canton** Aargua, Basel, Bern, Fribourg, Genève, Glarus, Grisons, Jura, Luzern, Neuchâtel, Obwalden, Schwyz, Thurgau, Ticino, Uri, Valais, Vaud, Zug, Zurich
**Swiss cheese** emment(h)al, emmenthaler, gruyère, sapsago
**Swiss cottage** chalet
**Swiss dialect** Ladin
**Swiss division** canton
**Swiss house** chalet
**Swiss lake** Constance, Lucerne
**Swiss language** French, German, Italian
**Swiss mathematician** Euler, Lambert
**Swiss money** franc
**Swiss mountain** Alps, Eiger, Matterhorn
**Swiss mountaineer's song** yodel
**Swiss mountain hut** chalet
**Swiss mountains** Alps
**Swiss Protestant reformer** Zwingli
**Swiss tourist resort** Gstaad, St Moritz
**Swiss warble** yodel
**switch** alteration, button, (ex)change, lever, shift, stick, swap, swing, trade, transfer, whip

**switchboard operator** telephonist
**switch off** deactivate, inactivate, turn off
**switch on** activate
**swivel** axis, axle, bobbin, circle, fulcrum, gimbals, gun, hinge, pin(tle), pirouette, pivot, reel, revolve, rotate, spin(dle), spool, thole, turn, twist
**swollen** aggravated, augmented, ballooned, bellied, billowed, bloated, bulged, dilated, distended, enhanced, enlarged, expanded, extended, grown, heightened, increased, inflamed, intensified, mounted, protruded, puffy, risen, surged, tumefied, tumid, turgid
**swollen eyelid** stye
**swollen gums** uloncus
**swollen-headed** conceited
**swollen state of tissue in the body** oedema
**swollen thyroid gland** goitre
**swollen tissue** tumour
**swollen veins at or near the anus** haemorrhoids
**swoon** blackout, collapse, crumple, drop, faint, limpen, succumb, unconsciousness
**swoop** attack, descend, dip, drop, lunge, (nose) dive, plunge, pounce, rush, seize, snatch, stoop, sweep
**swoop suddenly downwards** souse
**swoop upon something** pounce
**sword** bilbo, blade, brand, broadsword, claymore, cutlass, épée, foil, katana, lance, pata, rapier, sabre, scimitar, tachi, toledo, tuck, weapon
**swordbearer** portglave, selictar, verger
**sword belt** baldric(k), bawdric
**sword case** sheath
**sword city** Toledo
**sword contest** duel
**sword dancer** matachin
**swordfight** duel
**swordfish** espada, scombroid
**sword for fencing** épeé, foil, saber, sabre
**sword handle** haft, hilt
**sword holder** scabbard
**sword lily** gladiolus
**sword of Arthur** Excalibur
**sword of India** pata
**sword of Lancelot** Arondight
**sword of matador** estoque
**sword of Roland** Durandal
**swordplay** fencing, spadroon
**sword-shaped** ensate, ensiform, gladiate, xiphoid
**sword-shaped plant** iris
**swordsman** blader, combatant, duellist, fencer, foilsman, sabreur

(F), slasher, swashbuckler, swordplayer, thruster
**swordtail** helleri
**sword thrust** lunge
**sword used by sailors** cutlass
**sword without a point, symbolic of mercy** curtana
**sworn statement** affidavit, deposition, oath, pledge, vow, witness, word
**sworn vassal** liegeman
**swot** cram, study
**sybaritic** debauched, dissipated, epicurean, grand, gratifying, hedonistic, lush, luxurious, pleasure-seeking, refined, rich, sensual, sensuous, sumptuous, voluptuous
**sybaritism** luxury
**sycophant** bootlicker, cringer, fawner, flatterer, jackal, lackey, parasite, puppet, slave, stooge, toady, truckler, yes man
**Sydenham's chorea** St Vitus's dance
**sye** scythe
**syllabic script used in Sanskrit texts** Devanagari
**syllabic writing system** cree
**syllabus** abstract, analects, analysis, aperçu, compendium, compilation, contents, curriculum, epitome, extracts, headnote, list, outline, prospectus, reduction, résumé, statement, subjects, summary, synopsis, table
**sylvan deity** Satyr, wood-god
**symbiosis** co-operation, lichenism, life, mutualism, nutricism
**symbol** amulet, archetype, badge, brand, ceremony, code, crest, cross, eagle, emblem, epaulet, example, fish, flag, icon, ideogram, idol, image, insignia, key, logo(gram), mandala, mark, model, neum(e), phraseogram, representative, ring, seal, sign, standard, token, trademark, type
**symbol as road sign** glyph
**symbol denoting a number** numeral
**symbol for insertion** caret
**symbol for long distance** DX
**symbol for wavelength** lambda
**symbolic** allegoric, ceremonial, ceremony, emblematic, formality, representing, ritual
**symbolic action** charade
**symbolic acts** tokenism
**symbolic brooch** badge
**symbolic diagram** graph
**symbolic eye** uta
**symbolic female figure** orant
**symbolic pole** totem
**symbol indicating direction** arrow

**symbol in Morse code** dash, dot
**symbolism** iconology
**symbol of authority** fasces, mace, trident
**symbol of bad luck** hex
**symbol of crusader** cross
**symbol of death** cypress
**symbol of dependence** apron string
**symbol of France** lily
**symbol of grief** rue
**symbol of Holy Spirit** dove
**symbol of immortality** phoenix
**symbol of life** ankh
**symbol of marriage** ring
**symbol of monk** cowl
**symbol of mourning** armband, crepe, sackcloth
**symbol of Nazis** swastika
**symbol of peace** calumet, dove
**symbol of penitence** sackcloth
**symbol of physician** caduceus
**symbol of pilgrimage** scallop
**symbol of power** trident
**symbol of purity** lily
**symbol of railroad** herald
**symbol of something** token
**symbol of strength** atlas, horn, sinew
**symbol of sun** disc, disk
**symbol of unchangeableness** leopard
**symbol of universe** mandala
**symbol of victory** palm, vee
**symbol of wedding** ring
**symbol of wisdom** owl
**symbology** cipher, code, dectylogy, secrecy
**symbol standing for musical sound** note
**symbol used on manufacturer's goods** trademark
**symmetry** balance, congruity, equilibrium, parity, regularity, uniformity
**symmetry of balance** proportion
**sympathetic** affectionate, agreeing, attached, compassionate, congenial, humane, kind, piteous, tender
**sympathetic reaction** empathy
**sympathetic response** echo
**sympathetic vibration** resonance
**sympathise** applaud, assuage, comfort, commiserate, console, favour, like, pity, solace
**sympathiser** commiserator
**sympathy** accord, agreement, compassion, empathy, pity, sensitivity, understanding
**symphony composer** Beethoven, Haydn, Mozart, Schubert
**symphony players** orchestra
**symposiarch** toastmaster
**symposium** assembly, colloquy, conference, congress, debate,

pourparler (F), seminar, survey, synod, synopsis, treatise
**symptom** change, characteristic, concomitant, cue, evidence, existence, feature, feeling, indication, mark, notice, peculiarity, portent, red light, representation, sign(al), specific, token, warning
**symptomatic** denotative, indicative, prognostic
**symptomatology** semiology
**synagogue singer** cantor
**synchro** selsyn
**synchronisation** timing
**synchronise** time
**synchronously** concurrently, contemporaneously, together
**syncopated jazz music** ragtime
**synonym** euphonym, polyonym
**synopsis** abridg(e)ment, abstract, brief, condensation, epitome, précis, summary
**syntactic relation** function
**synthetic** acrylic, artificial, ersatz, fake, man-made, mock, plastic, pretended, sham, spurious, ungenuine, unnatural
**synthetic blood plasma** dextran
**synthetic fibre** acrylic, nylon, polyester, rayon
**synthetic hormone** cortisone
**synthetic material** nylon, rayon, terylene, vinyl
**synthetic moulded material** plastic
**synthetic resin** bakelite, polyester, silicone
**synthetic rubber** neoprene
**synthetic silk** nylon
**synthetic stretch fabric** spandex
**synthetic yarn** nylon
**Syria** Aram
**Syrian bishop** abba
**Syrian camel hair cloth** aba
**Syrian coin** Syrian pound
**Syrian garment** aba(ya)
**Syrian language** Arabic
**syringa** lilac
**syrup drained from raw sugar** molasses, treacle
**syrup flavoured with orange-flower water** capillaire

**syrup-soaked yeast cake** savarin
**syrupy sentimentality** schmaltz(y)
**system** arrangement, assemblage, classification, combination, concord, course, formula, habit, harmony, method, order, organisation, plan, procedure, routine, rule, scheme, setup, standard, uniformity, universe, way, world
**systematic** arranged, businesslike, conducted, efficient, methodical, orderly, organised, philosophic, precise, rational, regular, taxonomic, well-ordered
**systematically arranged collection of dried plants** herbarium
**systematic arrangement of literary work** ordonnance
**systematic attack** siege
**systematic description of diseases** nosography
**systematic forecasting of the future** futurology
**systematic instruction** education, practice
**systematic knowledge** science
**systematic list** catalogue, table
**systematic regulation** code
**systematic selfishness** egoism
**systematic study of subject** science
**systematise** arrange, organise
**systematised way of life** regimen
**system for mutual understanding** lingua franca
**system for strengthening memory** mnemonic
**system of belief** creed
**system of beliefs** credo
**system of betting** pari mutuel (F)
**system of chronology** era
**system of communications using gestures** sign language
**system of credit transfer** giro
**system of deities** pantheism
**system of doubling stakes at gambling** martingale
**system of drains** drainage
**system of exercise** aerobics
**system of existence** nature
**system of faith** creed
**system of government** regime

**system of Hindu philosophy** yoga
**system of illegal trade** black market
**system of inducing a hypnotic state** mesmerism
**system of joints** cleat
**system of laws** code, lex
**system of lines** network
**system of lines in eyepiece** retic(u)le
**system of logic** ramism
**system of management** regime
**system of marine markers** buoyage
**system of measures** metric, troy
**system of morality** ethos
**system of names** nomenclature, terminology
**system of naming notes** solmisation
**system of numerals** algorism, algorithm
**system of philosophy** hobbism, humanism, stoicism
**system of principles** code
**system of religious belief** creed
**system of religious philosophy** gnosticism
**system of religious worship** cult
**system of roads** network
**system of rule** regime
**system of rules** art, code
**system of rules for conduct** discipline
**system of rules to aid the memory** mnemonics
**system of symbols** code
**system of telephones** telephony
**system of tens** decimal
**system of traffic by aircraft** airline
**system of values** ethos
**system of weights** troy
**system of worship** cult(us), denomination, religion
**system of writing** alphabet, braille, kanji (J)
**system of writing in which each character represents a word** lexigraphy
**system to aid the memory** mnemonics
**systole** contraction
**syzygy** dipody
**szopelka** oboe

# T

**tabby** cat
**table** board, chart, postpone, record, schedule, stand, syllabus, tabulation
**tableau** pageant, picture, scene, spectacle
**table bird** capon, fowl
**table condiment** pepper, salt
**table dish** platter
**table game** billiards, snooker
**tableland** bench, berm(e), mesa, plain, plateau, steppe, upland
**table light** lamp
**table linen** damask, napery
**table mat** doily, doyley
**table napkin** serviette
**table of contents** index
**table of fixed charges** tariff
**table protector** mat
**table scrap** leaving, left-over, ort
**table seasoning** pepper, salt, vinegar
**table-shaped hill** mesa
**table support** leg, trestle
**tablet** capsule, drug, gravestone, lozenge, memorial, pad, pill, plank, plaque, slab, slate, tabloid, tombstone, troche
**table tennis** ping-pong
**tabloid** daily, gazette, journal, magazine, monthly, newspaper, paper, periodical, record, register, review, sheet, weekly
**taboo** ban(ned), bar, disapproved, exclude, exclusion, forbid(den), interdicted, interdiction, ostracise, prohibited, prohibition, proscribe, sacred, tabu, unmentionable, vetoed
**tabouret** stool
**tabular statement of assets and liabilities** balance sheet
**tabulated figures** tables
**tabulated list** index
**tabulated statement** schedule
**tabulation of the year** calender
**tachymeter** speed-indicator, speedometer
**tacit** implicit, implied, inferred, mum, mute, quiet, silent, speechless, undeclared, understood, unexpressed, unsaid, unspoken, unvoiced, voiceless
**tacit consent** sufferance
**tacitly conveyed but not expressed** implicit
**tacit reservation** salvo
**taciturn** aloof, cold, distant, mum, mute, quiet, reserved, reticent, saturnine, secretive, shy, silent, sluggish, stern, sullen, tacit, uncommunicative, unconversible, unforthcoming, unsociable, voiceless
**taciturnity** distantness, dourness, gloom, muteness, reticence, saturnity, shyness, silence, silentness, sluggishness, sternness, tacitness, unsociableness
**tack** affix, approach, attach, baste, bearing, course, direction, fasten, fix, heading, line, nail, path, pin, staple, stitch, way
**tacking course** zigzag
**tackle** accoutrements, apparatus, equipment, gear, implements, outfit, rig(ging), tools
**tack on** append
**tacky** adhesive, clinging, gluey, glutinous, gummy, holding, seedy, sneaker, sticking, sticky, syrupy, tackie, tatty, tenacious, viscous
**tact** consideration, delicacy, diplomacy, discretion, finesse, perception, savoir-faire, skill, understanding
**tactful** adroit, clever, diplomatic, perceptive, polite, sensitive, skilful, understanding
**tactful person** diplomat
**tactic** adept, adroit, artful, course, manoeuvre, method, plan, ploy, policy, scheme, skilful, stratagem, strategy, tactical, trick
**tactical** adroit, cunning, shrewd, skilful, smart, strategic
**tactical stroke** coup
**tactical trap** ambush
**tactician** ambassador, conspirator, co-ordinator, diplomat, intriguer, manager, mastermind, overseer, planner, politician, schemer, strategist, supervisor
**tactics** arrangement, direction, generalship, logistics, manoeuvres, manoeuvring, procedure, program(me), strategems, strategics, strategy, supervision
**tactless** abrupt, brash, brusque, careless, clumsy, disagreeable, discourteous, disrespectful, gauche, harsh, impertinent, impolite, impolitic, improper, inconsiderate, indiscreet, inept, injudicious, insensitive, maladroit, rash, rough, rude, sharp, thoughtless, unadvisable, uncouth, undiplomatic, unfeeling, ungentlemanly, unkind, unladylike, unpleasant, unseemly, unsuitable, unwise
**tactless mistake** faux pas
**taenia** headband
**tag** addendum, append, brand, butt, cliché, docket, earmark, end, flap, game, label, lap, loop, mark, name, particle, sticker, stigma, stub, supplement, tab, tail, ticket
**tag along** accompany, attend, follow, shadow, tail, trail
**tag-like ornament on uniform** a(i)glet, aiguilette
**tag on** append
**tag player** it
**tail** conclusion, end, extremity, file, follow, hindmost, line, queue, shadow, stalk, track, trail, train
**tailcoat** tails
**tailed amphibian** eft, newt, salamander
**tail-end** rump
**tail-end defenders** rearguard
**tail lamp** rear-light
**tailless** acaudal, acaudate, anurous, ecaudate
**tailless amphibian** frog, toad
**tailless cat** manx
**tailless monkey** ape
**tailless rodent** paca
**tail-like appendage** cercus
**tail motion** wag
**tail off** decrease, dwindle, fade, fail, wane
**tailor** bushelman, clothier, costumer, costumier, couturier, cutter, dressmaker, fitter, modiste, outfitter, sartor(ial), seamstress, sewer, stitcher, suitmaker
**tailor's iron** goose
**tailor's machine** presser
**tailor's need** pin
**tailor's smoothing-iron** gooses
**tails** conclusions, dresscoat, extremities, files, follows, queues, shadows, tailcoat, tracks, trails, verso
**tain** tinfoil
**taint** blemish, blot, contaminate, contamination, corrupt(ion), defilement, discredit, disgrace, fault, infect, pollute, stain, sully, tarnish
**taint with malice** envenom
**taint with mildew** blight
**Taiwan seaport** Chilung
**Taj Mahal country** India
**Taj Mahal site** Agra
**take** accept, acquire, assume, attract, bear, captivate, capture, carry,

catch, charm, cheat, conduct, consider, deceive, deduct, defraud, demand, do, employ, endure, engage, escort, exact, execute, get, grasp, obtain, perform, pick, procure, receive, regard, remove, require, secure, seize, suppose, tolerate
**take aback** astonish, astound, bewilder, disconcert, dismay, dum(b)found, flabbergast, shock, stagger, startle, stun, surprise, upset
**take a break** pause, rest
**take academic degree** graduate
**take account of** appreciate, consider
**take a chair** sit
**take a chance** hazard, imperil, risk
**take action** move, steps
**take a dim view** disapprove, reject, suspect
**take a dip** bathe
**take advantage of** abuse, avail, (mis)use
**take a flyer** guess(ing)
**take after** copy, favour, image, reflect, resemble
**take a header** fall
**take a meal** eat
**take and return** borrow
**take an oath** vow
**take apart** analyse, disassemble, dismantle, resolve, sunder
**take a part** act
**take a pew** sit
**take a price for** sell
**take a recess** rest
**take a risk** adventure
**take as an affront** resent
**take a seat** sit
**take a shine to** fancy
**take a short breath** gasp
**take a short sleep** nap, snooze
**take as one's own** adopt
**take a stand against** oppose
**take a turn for the better** convalesce, improve
**take a turn for the worse** backslide, degenerate, weaken, worsen
**take away** abstract, adeem, deduct, detract, diminish, reduce, remove, subtract, toll, weaken, withdraw
**take away from** deprive, detract
**take back** deny, disavow, exchange, forgive, recant, reclaim, renounce, repossess, repudiate, retake, retract, withdraw
**take back to the community** resettle
**take back usually after nonpayment** repossess
**take beforehand** pre-empt
**take by force** abduct, kidnap, rape, ravish, reave, rob, seize, wreck, wrest

**take by open force** plunder
**take by sips** sup
**take by surprise** startle
**take by theft** rob, steal
**take captive** arrest, catch, entrap, snare
**take care** beware, gardez (F), mind, tend
**take care of** attend, handle, mind, nourish, nurse, nurture, sustain, tend
**take care of horse** groom
**take chance** gamble, risk
**take charge** boss
**take charge of** manage, undertake
**take cognizance of** notice
**take cover** hide, shelter
**take dimensions of** measure
**take dinner** dine
**take down** deflate, demolish, depress, disassemble, dismantle, humble, humiliate, level, lower, minute, mortify, note, raze, record, reduce, remove, transcribe, write
**take down a peg** declass, disrate, downgrade, humble
**take drugs orally** pop
**take eagerly** embrace
**take easy strides** trot
**take effect** begin, inure, work
**take exception** cavil, challenge, demur, disagree, dissent, object, oppugn, quibble
**take exception to** cavil, challenge, demur, dissent, oppose, question
**take feloniously** steal
**take first prize** win
**take first step** toddle
**take flight** abscond, bolt, decamp, run
**take food** eat
**take food orders** waiter
**take for gospel** profess
**take for granted** assume, postulate, presume, (pre)suppose
**take for oneself** adopt, undertake
**take fright** boggle
**take from reputation** detract
**take general view of** survey
**take great pleasure in** delight, revel
**take great risks with** dice
**take greedily** grab, snatch
**take hastily** grab, snatch
**take heart** revive
**take heed** beware
**take hold of** apprehend, seize
**take home amount** net
**take ill again** relapse
**take illegally** steal
**take illicitly** scrounge
**take in** absorb, accommodate, admit, annex, appreciate, assimilate, bamboozle, board, cheat, comprehend, comprise, con,

contain, cover, deceive, digest, do, dupe, embrace, enclose, encompass, fool, grasp, hoodwink, imagine, imbibe, include, incorporate, kid, lodge, mislead, realise, receive, shelter, swindle, trick, understand
**take in alcohol** imbibe
**take in as a member** enrol
**take in food** eat, ingest
**take in for grazing payment** agist
**take in gradually** digest
**take in liquid** drink
**take in livestock to feed** agist
**take in marriage** espouse
**take in one's arms** embrace, hug
**take in sustenance** eat
**take in the slack** tighten
**take into account** consider, include, regard
**take into consideration** weigh
**take into custody** apprehend, arrest
**take into mouth** eat
**take in too much** overeat
**take into relationship** adopt
**take into service again** rehire
**take in with eye** embrace
**take issue** challenge, disagree, dispute, oppose
**take it easy** relax, rest
**take it on the lam** escape, flee
**take it out of** drain, enervate, exhaust, fatigue, weary
**take it too far** overdo
**take keen delight in** revel
**take legal action** sue
**take legal possession of** impound
**take liberties** presume
**take liking to** fancy
**take little bites** nibble
**take longer strides than** outstep
**take long steps** stride
**taken aback** amazed, astonished, bewildered, discomposed, disconcerted, dum(b)founded, flabbergasted, perplexed, startled, surprised
**taken as a whole** overall
**taken as one's own** adopted
**taken before dinner** anteprandial
**taken for granted** implicit, understood, unspoken
**taken in** included
**take no care of** neglect
**taken off guard** surprised, unprepared, unready
**take no notice of** ignore, neglect, overlook, waive
**take note of** heed
**take notes for the future** record
**take notice of** heed, observe
**take nourishment** eat

**taken out of context** per se
**taken over by terrorists** hijacked
**taken secretly** stolen
**take oath** swear
**take off** ascent, caricature, decamp, depart(ure), disappear, discard, divest, doff, drop, expand, flourish, flying, go, imitate, imitation, lampoon, launch, leave, mimic, mock, mounting, parody, remove, rising, satir(is)e, shed, soar, strip
**take off after** chase, follow, pursue, stalk, track
**take off bottle** wean
**take offence** grudge, resent
**take off field** sideline
**take office** accede
**take off milk** wean
**take off one's clothes** undress
**take off strip** runway
**take off the cream** skim
**take off weight** reduce
**take on** accept, acquire, adopt, assume, complain, employ, engage, enlist, enrol, face, fire, hire, lament, oppose, retain, tackle, undertake
**take on cargo** load
**take one's breath away** amaze, astonish, astound, boggle, excite, startle
**take one's leave** depart, exit
**take one's part** side
**take one's time** dally, dawdle, linger, loiter, tarry
**take on loan** borrow
**take out** cancel, delete, extract, remove
**take out a bank loan** borrow
**take out book again** renew
**take out cover** insure
**take out of the owner's hands** expropriate
**take over** adopt, annex, hijack, pre-empt
**takeover** amalgamation, coalition, combination, coup, incorporation, merger
**take over duties from** relieve
**take over from** succeed
**takeover occupant** squatter
**take pains to investigate** study
**take paper off a gift** unwrap
**take part** associate, compete, contribute, join, partake, participate, vote
**take part in competition** enter
**take part in contest** compete
**take part in football match** play
**take part in game** play, sport
**take part in race** run
**take part in the slalom** ski
**take part in tournament** joust
**take part on stage** act

**take pity** rue
**take pity on** forgive, melt, misery, pardon, reprieve
**take place** arrive, befall, chance, happen, intervene, occur, supervene
**take place of** replace
**take pleasure** bask
**take pleasure in** admire, enjoy, indulge
**take possession** seize
**take possession of** annex, appropriate, occupy
**take possession of unjustly** usurp
**take prisoner** apprehend
**taker** grasper
**take reprisals** avenge
**take responsibility for** assume
**take rest** sleep
**take revenge** avenge, retaliate
**take risk** gamble
**take root** develop, germinate, spread, sprout, thrive
**take satisfaction for** avenge
**takes blame for others** scapegoat
**take scum from surface of liquid** skim
**takes cynical views** sceptic
**take seat** sit
**take secretly** rob, steal, thieve
**take sips** sup
**take skin off** scrape
**take small bites** nibble
**take steps** act, intervene, prepare
**take stock** appraise, estimate
**take supper** sup
**take that offered** accept
**take the bit between one's teeth** defy, rebel, resist, revolt
**take the covering off** strip
**take the edge off** blunt, mitigate
**take the heart out of** oppress
**take the helm** steer
**take the leading role** star
**take the offer** accept
**take the part of** support
**take the place of** substitute, supersede, supplant
**take the road** peregrinate
**take the top off** uncap
**take the wheel** drive, steer
**take threatening posture** ramp
**take to be true** assume
**take to court** litigate, sue
**take to flight** abscond, decamp, flee, retreat, withdraw
**take to heart** heed
**take to oneself** appropriate
**take to one's heels** escape, flee, skedaddle
**take to pieces** dismantle, strip
**take to task** blame, contemn, decry, denounce, impute, incrimate, indict, recriminate, reproach, reprove
**take to the air** fly

**take turns** alternate, interchange, reciprocate, rotate, switch
**take unaware** surprise
**take unlawfully** rob, steal, thieve
**take up** absorb, accept, adopt, arrest, assume, begin, burrow, consume, continue, cover, effect, engross, fasten, fill, interrupt, lift, monopolise, occupy, overspread, proceed, raise, recommence, (re)start, resume, secure
**take up again** resume
**take up liquid** lap
**take up position** manoeuvre
**take up residence** locate
**take vengeance** avenge
**take wing** fly
**take wing and fly away** flush
**take without right** steal
**taking a break** rest
**taking a flier** guessing
**taking an oath** swearing
**taking apart** dismantling
**taking away** removal
**taking care not to hurt others** considerate
**taking everything into account** circumspect
**taking food** eating
**taking for granted** presumption
**taking heed** careful
**taking in everything** omnivorous
**taking in excess** greedy
**taking liberties** presumptuous
**taking many forms** protean
**taking neither side in a war** neutral
**taking no part** neutral
**taking on** acceptance
**taking on cargo** loading
**taking one's ease** resting
**taking over** accession
**taking part in race** running
**taking part in slalom** skiing
**taking place** on
**taking place outside the court** extrajudicial
**taking random sample** sampling
**taking what is offered** accepting
**tale** account, alibi, allegory, anecdote, apologue, description, epic, episode, excuse, fable, falsehood, fib, fiction, gossip, legend, lie, myth, narration, narrative, novel, numeration, parable, recital, report, romance, saga, script, story, untruth, yarn
**talent** ability, aptitude, capacity, endowment, faculty, flair, forte, genius, gift, knack, nous
**talented** able, artistic, brilliant, gifted, well-endowed
**talented group with seven members** pleiad

**tale of heroism** saga
**talipes** club foot
**talisman** amulet, charm, fetish, mascot, periapt
**talk** chat, colloquy, communicate, communication, confer, consult, conversation, converse, dialect, dialogue, discourse, discuss, gab, gossip, parley, prate, prattle, report, rumour, skinder(y), speak, speech(ify)
**talk about oneself** egotise
**talk around** argue
**talkative** chatty, garrulous, long-drawn, loquacious, prolix, verbose, wordy
**talkative person** chatterbox, gasbag, skinderbek
**talk at length** orate
**talk babyishly** lisp
**talk back to** lip, sass
**talk big** boast, brag, exaggerate, rodomontade, swagger, vaunt
**talk boastfully** brag, swagger
**talk bombastically** rant
**talk childishly** prattle
**talk deliriously** rave
**talk dogmatically** lecture
**talk down** deprecate, disparage, outdo, outtalk
**talk dreamily** maunder
**talk drunkenly** slur
**talk easily** chat, voluble
**talk enthusiastically** rave
**talker** blabber, boaster, causeur (F), chatterbox, commentator, communicator, conversationalist, gossipmonger, haranguer, informer, jabberer, lecturer, orator, prater, speaker, speechmaker, vaunter
**talk excitedly** rant
**talk foolishly** haver, prate
**talk glibly** spiel
**talk idly** babble, chatter, gab, gas, prate
**talk imperfectly** lisp, mumble, stammer, stutter
**talk impiously** blaspheme
**talk incessantly** chatter
**talk in childish fashion** prattle
**talk in confused manner** moither
**talk indiscreetly** blab
**talk indistinctly** slur
**talk in familiar way** chat
**talk informally** chat, hobnob
**talking bird** myna(h), parrot
**talking senselessly** blithering
**talking to** earbashing
**talking to oneself** soliloquy
**talk into** coax, convince, encourage, induce, overrule, persuade, sway
**talk irrelevantly** prate
**talk lightly** jest
**talk loudly and foolishly** quack

**talk monotonously** drone
**talk noisily** rant
**talk nonsensically** waffle
**talk of the town** hearsay
**talk out of** caution, deter, discourage, dissuade, protest
**talk over** discuss, parley
**talk petulantly** carp
**talk pointlessly** gas
**talk pompously** speechify
**talk profanely** blaspheme
**talk profusely** palaver
**talk rapidly** chatter, patter
**talk softly** murmer, murmur
**talk tediously** prose
**talk to** address
**talk to a waiter** order
**talk to God** pray
**talk too fast** gabble
**talk too much** prate
**talk to oneself** soliloquise
**talk trash** dote
**talk unwisely** blab
**talk up** advertise, promote, publicise
**talk wildly** babble, rant, rave
**tall** elevated, gangling, high, lofty, soaring, towering
**tall and slim** rangy
**tall and thin** lank(y), lean, spindly
**tall Australian grass** paspalum
**tall building** edifice, skyscraper, tower
**tall chest of drawers** tallboy
**tall chimney** stack
**tall China cup** tyg
**tall Cuban hand drum** conga
**tall drinking glass** schooner
**tallest living animal** giraffe
**tall fan palm** talipot
**tall flower** hollyhock
**tall fur cap of hussars and guardsmen** bearskin, busby
**tall glass** rummer, schooner
**tall grass** bamboo, reed
**tall herbaceous plant** lupin
**tall hound** Saluki, wolfhound
**tall marsh plant** reed
**tall masculine woman** Amazon
**tall narrow coal scuttle** hod
**tallness** bigness, hardness, height, highness, lankiness, loftiness
**tall ornamental vessel** vase
**tallow** candle grease
**tallow light** candle
**tallow product** candle, soap
**tallow refuse** greaves
**tall story** fable, lie, yarn
**tall structure** tower
**tall swamp-plant** reed
**tall tale** yarn
**tall thin person** beanpole, beanstalk
**tall timber tree** rewa-rewa, tawa
**tall tower** steeple

**tall tower by a mosque** minaret
**tall tropical plant** coco
**tall wading bird** flamingo, ibis, stork
**tall water-grass** reed
**tally** accord, agree, calculate, coincide, correspond, count, enumerate, harmonise, invoice, label, list, match, notch, post, reckon(ing), record, register, roll, score, slash, square, sticker, stroke, tab(ulate), tell, total
**tally again** rescore
**tallyman** scorekeeper
**talon** claw, nail, nipper, ogee, pincer, pounce, tentacle
**talus** anklebone, (astra)galus, debris, scree, slope, wall
**tambour** drum
**tambourine** timbrel
**tame** calm, cowardly, crushed, docile, domesticate(d), dull, fearless, flat, gentle, insipid, meek, mild, prosaic, soften, spiritless, subdue(d), subjugate, submissive, suppressed, tractable, unanimated, uninspiring, uninteresting, vapid
**tame animal** pet
**tamp** charge, compact, compress, cram, fill, jam, mob, pack, press, ram, stuff, throng, wedge
**tamper** adulterate, corrupt, debate, juggle, manoeuvre, meddle, pollute
**tamper with racehorse** nobble
**tan** bronze, brown, khaki, roan, sandy, sorrel, sunbathe, sunburn, tawny
**tan-coloured horse** palomino
**tan fabric** pongee
**tang** acidity, bite, flavour, piquancy, poignancy, pungency, seaweed, sharpness, smack, snappiness, spiciness, suggestion, taste, zest
**tangerine** mandarin, na(a)rtjie
**tangible** certain, corporeal, definite, discernible, evident, genuine, material, materiate, open, palpable, perceivable, sensible, specific, substantial, tactile, touchable
**tangle** chaos, coil, complexity, complicate, complication, confusion, disorder, (en)mesh, entanglement, entwine, jumble, knot, labyrinth, mass, mat, ravelment, scramble, skein, snarl, turmoil, twist
**tangled lock of hair** elflock
**tangled mass** shac, tat
**tangled thread** sleave
**tangle hair** mat
**tangy** biting, piquant, pungent, sour, tart
**Tanis** Zoan
**tank** cistern, container, vat
**tankard** cup, facer, hanap, mug, pewter, pot, stein, vessel
**tanker** oiler

**tank for keeping fish** aquarium
**tank-insulation** lagging
**tank wheel** bog(e)y, bogie
**tanned hide** leather
**tanning agent** tannin
**tanning material** sumac
**tantalise** allure, baffle, bait, disappoint, enchant, entice, excite, frustrate, irk, irritate, motivate, plague, provoke, seduce, stimulate, taunt, tease, tempt, torment, torture, vex
**tantalising question** teaser
**Tantalus's daughter** Niobe
**tantamount** equal, equivalent, synonymous
**Tanzanian island** Mafia, Pemba, Zanzibar
**tap** beat, bleed, broach, bung, dance, drain, drum, exploit, faucet, knock, milk, mine, open, pat, pierce, rap, spigot, spout, stopcock, stopper, strike, touch, (un)plug, use, utilise, valve
**tape** band, record, ribbon, strip, video
**tape cartridge** cassette
**taped film** video
**tape from television** video
**taper** candle, narrow, spill
**tapered block** wedge
**tapered coat extension** coattail
**tapered fruit** pear
**tapered part of bottle** neck
**tapered slip of wood** shim
**tapering body** spire
**tapering gradually** attenuate
**tapering ice-formation** icicle
**tapering off** abatement
**tapering shaft of stone** obelisk
**tapering structure** spike
**tapering tube** funnel
**tapestry** arras
**tapeworm** cestode, cestoid, taenia
**tapeworm remedy** embelia
**tap for barrel** faucet
**tapioca-like pod** sago
**tapioca** cassava
**tap lightly** pat
**tap seal** washer
**tapster** barman, bartender
**tap with the hand** pat
**tar** asphalt, bitumen, gob, pitch, sailor, seaman, (tar)macadam
**tarantula** spider
**tardily** backwardly, belatedly, carelessly, dilatorily, forgetfully, heedlessly, inactively, inattentively, lately, laxly, lazily, neglectfully, negligently, overdue, permissively, remissly, slackly, slowly, thoughtlessly
**tardiness** backwardness, belatedness, carelessness, dilatoriness,

heedlessness, idleness, inactivity, inattentiveness, indolence, lateness, laxness, laziness, neglectfulness, overdue, remissness, slackness, sloth, slowness, thoughtlessness, unpunctuality
**tardy** backward, behind, belated, careless, creeping, delayed, dilatory, forgetful, heedless, idle, inactive, inattentive, lame, late, lax, lazy, leisurely, neglected, negligent, overdue, owing, permissive, reluctant, remiss, slack, slow, sluggish, thoughtless, unmindful, unpunctual, unpunctual
**tardy arrival** latecomer
**tare** fodder, weed
**target** aim, ambition, end, goal, mark, object(ive), patsy, pigeon, plan, prey, victim
**target mark** tee
**target of ridicule** butt
**target ring** inner, outer
**tariff** assessment, charges, contribution, custom, duty, exaction, excise, fee, impost, levy, menu, payment, rate, schedule, surcharge, tax, tenth, tithe, toll
**tariff charge** rate
**tarnish** blemish, blot, damage, dirty, discolour, discredit, disgrace, dishonour, dull, fade, rust, shame, smudge, soil, spoil, spot, stain, stigma, sully, taint
**taro** dasheen, eddo, elephant's-ear, root
**taro-based dish** poi
**tarpaulin material** canvas
**tar product** creosol
**tarragon** estragon
**tarry** abide, anchor, (a)wait, bide, continue, dally, dawdle, delay, dwell, expect, flag, halt, hesitate, lag, linger, loiter, pause, remain, reside, rest, saunter, sojourn, stay, stop
**tarry suspiciously** loiter
**tarsia** intarsia
**tart** acid, astringent, biting, caustic, cutting, pastry, pie, piquant, sharp(-tasting), sour
**tartan** chequer, highlander, plaid
**tartan cloth** plaid
**tartan skirt** kilt
**tartan trousers** trews
**tartar on teeth** scale
**tartly** bitterly, sharply
**Tarzan's habitat** jungle
**Tarzan's mate** Jane
**task** assignment, burden, chore, devoir, difficulty, drudgery, duty, encumber, errand, exercise, homework, job, labour, lesson,

mission, onus, oppress, overload, passion, strain, sweat, toil, trail, work
**task assigned** stint
**task for after school** homework
**task force** mission
**task performed** opus operatum (L)
**task set for training** exercise
**task to be performed** mission
**Tasmanian devil** dasyure
**tassel-shaped curl** bob
**taste** character, degustation, discernment, disposition, experience, flavour, gustation, libation, liking, manner, morsel, palate, perception, predilection, preference, relish, sample, savour, sensation, sense, sip, smack, style, try, undergo
**taste for fine art** vertu, virtu
**tasteful** aesthetically, artistic, cultivated, cultured, delicate, elegant, exquisite, graceful, handsome, harmonious, polished, refined, smart, stylish
**tasteful style** elegance
**taste in dress** style
**tasteless** coarse, crude, flavourless, garish, gaudy, gawdy, inelegant, insipid, jejune, shoddy, stale, tactless, tawdry, unappetising, unflavoured, uninteresting, unsavoury, vapid, vulgar, watery, weak, wearisome
**tasteless action** vulgarity
**tasteless from age** stale
**tastelessly showy** gaudy
**tasteless with age** stale
**taste of lemon** sour
**taste of of one's own medicine** retaliation
**taste of quinine** bitter
**taster** sipper
**tasting** assaying, assessment, differentiating, discerning, nibbling, perceiving, relishing, sampling, savouring, sipping, testing, trial, trying
**tasting like nuts** nutty
**tasting like quinine** bitter
**tasting like sugar** sweet
**tasty** ambrosial, appetising, crotchety, decorous, delectable, delicious, gourmet, gustable, juicy, luscious, nice, palatable, piquant, pungent, refined, relishable, sapid, savoury, spicy, succulent, tasteful, toothsome
**tasty dish** morsel
**tat** crochet, rag
**tatter** bit, piece, rag, scrap, shred
**tatters** cast-offs, patches, rags, scraps
**tattle** abuse, aspersion, blether, chat(ter), dirt, gabble, gossip,

**tattoo** hearsay, patter, prate, prattle, rumours, scandal, skinder(y), talk
**tattoo** beat, call, drum(ming), patter, pulsate, rap, ratatat, reverberate, rhythm, summons, tap, throb(bing)
**tatty** inferior, ragged, shabby, tawdry, unkempt, untidy, worn-out
**taunt** censure, deride, derision, gibe, guy, harass, insult, jeer, jive, mock, provoke, rag, reproach, ridicule, sarcasm, scoff, scorn, tease, torment, twit, upbraid
**taunting** deriding, flouting, gibing, insulting, jeering, mocking, reviling, ridiculing, teasing, tormenting, upbraiding
**taurine** bovine, bull-like
**Taurus sign** bull
**taut** contracted, drawn, flexed, neat, orderly, rigid, smart, spruce, strained, stressed, stretched, tense, tidy, tight, unrelaxed
**tautness** rigidity, strainedness, tenseness, tension, tensity, tightness
**tautology** battology, pleonasm, prolixity, redundancy, repetition, verbosity
**tavern** alehouse, bar(room), bistro, brasserie, cabaret, café, caravanserai, grill, honky-tonk, hostel(ry), hotel, inn, motel, nightclub, pub(lic house), roadhouse, shebeen
**tavern counter** bar
**tavern in a barracks** canteen
**tawdry** cheap, flashy, gaudy, gimcrack, meretricious, ostentatious, plastic, raffish, showy, sleazy, tasteless, tinsel, vulgar
**tawny** yellowish-brown
**tawny carnivore** lion
**tawny hue** tan
**tawpie** foolish, silly, tawpy, thoughtless
**tax** assess(ment), burden, capitation, censure, cess, charge, customs, demand, duty, excise, exhaust, impeach, impost, levy, onus, overburden, overload, payment, rate, scot, strain, surtax, toll, VAT, weight
**taxation income** revenue
**taxation officer** assessor
**taxi** cab, convey, fiacre, hirecar, move, ricksaw, run, start, taxicab
**taxi charge** fare
**taxi driver** cabby
**taxing** accusing, arraigning, assessing, blaming, burdening, burdensome, charging, costing, demanding, draining, enervating, exacting, grueling, heavy, impeaching, incriminating, loading, onerous, pushing, rating, severe, straining, strenuous, tiring, tough, trying, weakening, wearing, wearying
**taxi passenger** fare
**tax levied on salary** PAYE
**tax of one-tenth** tithe
**tax one's powers** test
**tax on goods** octroi
**tax per head** capitation
**tax too highly** overtax
**tea break** smoke
**teacake** scone
**tea canister** caddy
**teach** annotate, clarify, demonstrate, drill, edify, educate, enlighten, explain, guide, indicate, indoctrinate, inform, instruct, interpret, preach, propagate, publish, train, tutor
**teach as a professor** profess
**teacher** advisor, apostle, coach, don, educationist, educator, guru, instructor, lecturer, lehrer (G), maestro (I), magister (L), maitre (F), master, mentor, minister, mulla(h), pedagogue, pedant, preacher, preceptor, priest, professor, rabbi, schoolmaster, schoolmistress, schoolteacher, sensei (J), trainer, tutor
**teacher of Achilles** Ch(e)iron
**teacher of alphabet** abecedarian
**teacher of ethics** moralist
**teacher of highest rank** professor
**teacher of Leonardo** Verrocchio
**teacher of morals** moralist
**teacher of mystical doctrines** mystagogue
**teacher of rhetoric** rhetor
**teacher of Samuel** Eli
**teacher of young children** pedagogue
**teaching** advising, coaching, directing, drilling, educating, enlightening, guiding, imparting, implanting, inculcating, informing, instilling, instructing, schooling, showing, training, tutoring
**teaching perfectionist** pedant
**teaching session** lecture, lesson, tutorial
**teaching specialist** educationalist
**tea container** caddy
**tea gown** loose dress
**team** band, club, collaborate, co-operate, crew, faction, gang, group, join, side, squad
**team contest** relay race
**team game** football, (ice) hockey, lacrosse, rugby
**team in quiz** panel
**team of horses** span
**team of judges in contest** panel
**team of oxen** span
**team parlour game** charade
**team race** relay
**team spirit** esprit de corps
**team up** co-operate, combine, couple, join, link, match, unite
**team with rain** pelt
**tea of superior quality** pekoe
**teapot cover** cosy
**tear** affliction, belt, bolt, career, charge, chase, cleave, cut, dart, dash, distress, divide, fly, gash, grab, grief, hurry, injure, lacerate, mangle, mutilate, passion, pull, race, rage, regret, rend, rent, rip, run, rupture, rush, scratch, seize, sever, shatter, shoot, shred, snatch, sorrow, speed, split, sprint, sunder, teardrop, wound, wrest, yank
**tear apart** rend, rip, rive, split
**tear away** rend
**tear down** rase, raze
**tearer** ripper
**tearful** crying, lachrymose, lamentable, sad, sobbing, tantalise, weeping, weepy, whimpering, worry
**tearfully sentimental** maudlin
**tearful vegetable** onion
**tear gas** lachrimator
**tear into strips** shred
**tear jaggedly** lacerate
**tear-jerking** maudlin, sad
**tearless** dry-eyed
**tearoom** café
**tear open** rip
**tear roughly** lacerate
**tear to bits** shred
**tear up by roots** eradicate
**tease** aggravate, annoy, bait, bother, chaff, cod, disturb, dress, harry, hector, irritate, kid, needle, plague, provoke, rag, rib, separate, shred, tantalise, taunt, torment, trouble, vex, worry
**tease by repeated acts** annoy
**teaser** pester, tantaliser
**teashop** café, tearoom
**teat** nipple
**tea tester** taster
**tea urn** samovar
**technical** arcane, expert, obscure, professional, scientific, specialised
**technical facts** data
**technical name for brain** encaphalon
**technical name for language** lingua
**technical phraseology** jargon, lingo
**technical word for the buttocks** nates
**technical word for the tongue** glossa
**technique of measuring wind speed and direction** anemometry
**technique of recording wind measurements** anemography

**technique of using small arms** musketry
**technique used in cartoons** animation
**tedious** boring, draggy, dreary, exhausting, fatiguing, irksome, laboured, long, tiresome, tiring, wearing, wearisome
**tedious discourse** prose
**tedious journey on foot** traipse
**tediously lengthy** long-winded
**tediously long** interminable
**tediously long time** eternity
**tedious moralising discourse** homily
**tedious person** bore
**tedious stretch of time** longueur
**tedious task** chore
**tedious work** drudgery
**tedium** banality, boredom, deadness, drabness, dullness, monotony, tediousness
**teem** abound, bear, brim, bristle, egest, overflow, pour, produce, swarm, throng, void
**teeming with ideas** pregnant
**teen** grief, minor, misfortune, pain, sorrow, teenage, young
**teenage** adolescent, immature, juvenile, minor, pubescent, teen, young, youthful
**teenager** adolescent, boy, girl, juvenile, minor, youth
**teeny** small, tiny, wee
**tee off** drive
**teeter** jerk, jiggle, librate, lurch, oscillate, reel, rock, seesaw, stagger, sway, totter, waver, wobble
**teeterboard** seesaw
**teeth** bite, denture, fangs, grinders, molars
**teeth decay** caries
**teeth sockets** alveoli
**teetotaller** nondrinker
**Teflon** polytetrafluoroethylene
**teg** sheep
**Teheran is there** Iran
**teind** tenth, tithe
**Telamon** Atlas
**Tel Aviv native** Israeli
**telegram** cable, message, wire
**telegram in ordinary language** en clair (F)
**telegram sent abroad** cable
**telegraph code** Morse
**telegraphed message** telex
**telegraph inventor** Morse
**telegraph message sent by undersea cable** cablegram
**teleost** apoda, eel, saury
**telephone** blower, call, dial, line, phone
**telephone book** directory
**telephone box** booth, cubicle, kiosk
**telephone operator** central

**telephone support** cradle
**telephonic signal** beep
**teleprinter** telex
**telescope** abbreviate, abridge, abstract, binoculars, compact, compress, condense, crush, curtail, cut, glass, (peri)scope, reduce, shorten, spyglass, squash, trim, truncate
**telescope inventor** Galileo
**television advertisement** commercial
**television award** Artes, Emmy
**television compere** presenter
**television entertainment** series
**television film** video
**television fund raiser** Telethon
**television picture tube** screen
**television play in instalments** serial
**television recorder** video
**television sound** audio
**television satellite** Telstar
**television system** scophony
**tell** acknowledge, admit, announce, apprise, bid, calculate, cast, command, communicate, compute, confess, count, depict, describe, direct, discern, disclose, discover, divulge, enjoin, enumerate, espy, estimate, explain, express, identify, impart, inform, instruct, mention, mouth, narrate, notify, number, order, own, portray, proclaim, publicise, publish, reckon, recount, rehearse, relate, report, require, reveal, say, speak, state, summon, tally, teach, urge, utter
**tell a lie** fib, perjure, prevaricate
**tell a story** narrate, relate
**tell confidentially** confide
**teller** cashier, narrator, relater
**teller of anecdotes** raconteur
**teller of fables** Aesop
**tell falsehood** lie
**tell in detail** recount
**telling of fortunes with playing cards** cartomancy
**telling untruth** lying
**tell it** tale
**tell off** berate, censure, chide, lecture, rebuke, reprimand, reproach, reprove, scold, upbraid
**tell on** blab, tattle
**tell positively** assure
**tell secretly** whisper
**tell secrets** tattle
**tells lies** liar
**tell story** narrate
**telltale** babbler, blether, busybody, chatterer, gossip, informer, scandalmonger, skinderbek, sneak, tattler
**tell tales** blab, lie, sneak, tattle

**telltale sign** hallmark
**tell the story** narrate
**tell to go** send
**tell untruths** deceive, lie
**temerity** audacity, boldness, bravery, cheek, courage, daring, fearlessness, grit, guts, immodesty, impudence, nerve, pluck, rashness, shamelessness, spirit
**temper** abate, adapt, admix, allay, anger, anneal, annoyance, assuage, attitude, blend, calm(ness), composure, disposition, equanimity, fit, fury, hardness, heat, humour, irritability, irritation, make-up, mind, mitigate, mix, moderate, moderation, modify, mollify, mood, nature, paddy, passion, peevishness, petulance, rage, resentment, restrain, soften, soothe, surliness, tantrum, temperament, tranquillity, vein, work
**tempera** distemper
**temperament** appetite, bent, character, complexion, constitution, direction, disposition, grain, humour, idiosyncrasy, liability, make-up, mettle, mood, nature, outlook, personality, proclivity, quality, soul, spirit, temper, tendency, weakness
**temperamental** capricious, curt, distinctive, eccentric, emotional, erratic, excitable, fiery, high-strung, impatient, inconsistent, irritable, moody, nervous, passionate, peculiar, peevish, sensitive, singular, snappish, snappy, special, touchy, unique, unreliable, volatile
**temperance** forbearance, moderation
**temperance advocate** blue ribboner, prohibitionist
**temperate** abstemious, abstinent, calm, continent, detached, mild, moderate, self-restrained, sober, warm
**temperature regulator** thermostat
**temperature scale** Celsius, Fahrenheit
**temperature unit** kelvin
**temper by heat** anneal
**temper fit** tantrum
**tempest** commotion, cyclone, disturbance, ferment, gale, hurricane, storm, tornado, tumult, typhoon, uproar
**tempestuous** agitated, blustery, breezy, fiery, furious, gusty, raging, stormy, turbulent, violent
**template** design, diagram, guide, instructions, matrix, original, pattern(-guide), plan, stencil
**temple** basilica, chapel, church, duomo (I), mosque, pagoda, sanctuary, shrine, synagogue, tabernacle

**temple gateway** pylon, torii
**temple in Kampuchea** Angkorwat
**temple of all the gods** pantheon
**temple of Athena** Parthenon
**temple of Jupiter in Rome** Capitoline
**tempo** beat, cadence, career, gait, intermittence, measure, metre, motion, movement, pace, periodicity, pulse, rate, rhythm, speed, throb, time, timing, velocity
**temporal** carnal, civil, earthly, ephemeral, fleshly, human, laic, lay, material, mortal, mundane, physical, profane, secular, state, terrestrial, transient, worldly
**temporal possession** world
**temporary** brief, ephemeral, evanescent, fleeting, fugitive, interim, momentary, transient, transitory
**temporary cessation** lull, pause
**temporary cessation of hostilities** truce
**temporary cessation of work** recess
**temporary decline** recession
**temporary delay** respite
**temporary employee** temp
**temporary encampment without tents** bivouac
**temporary fortification** sandbag
**temporary framework** scaffolding
**temporary grant** loan
**temporary insanity** frenzy
**temporary lodging** pied-à-terre
**temporary loss of memory** aberration
**temporary platform for workers** scaffold
**temporary possession** lend
**temporary power cut** black out
**temporary relief** reprieve, respite
**temporary residence** pied-à-terre, stay
**temporary resting place of troops** bivouac
**temporary retirement** retreat
**temporary right on debtor's property** lien
**temporary shelter** booth, tent
**temporary stay** sojourn
**temporary stop** delay, pause
**temporary substitute** makeshift, stopgab
**temporary suspension** abeyance
**temporary suspension of hostility** armistice
**temporary tenure** leasehold
**temporary time in between** interim
**temporary tint** rinse
**temporise** delay, hedge
**tempt** allure, attract, bait, decoy, entice, induce, inveigle, invite, lure, provoke, seduce, tantalise

**temptation** allurement, attraction, bait, charm, incentive, invitation, lure, seduction, spell, stimulus
**temptation of Eve** apple
**tempting** alluring, attractive, inducing, inviting, seductive
**temptress** Circe, siren
**ten** deca-, decade, denary
**tenable** arguable, believable, defensible, justifiable, rationable, sound, viable
**tenacious** adhesive, clinging, cohesive, dogged, obstinate, persistent, pertinacious, positive, sticky, stubborn, viscous
**tenaciously** adamantly, determinedly, doggedly, firmly, forcefully, inflexibly, obstinately, persistently, resolutely, staunchly, strongly, stubbornly, surely, tightly
**tenacious substance** glue
**tenacity** adhesiveness, diligence, doggedness, firmness, forcefulness, persistence, resolve, retention, stickiness, strength, toughness
**tenancy agreement** lease
**tenant** holder, inhabitant, leaseholder, lessee, occupier, rent-payer, resident, roomer
**tenanted** developed, held, inhabited, let, occupied, populated, settled
**tenant farmer who pays part of crop as rent** bywoner, share-cropper
**tenant's contract** lease
**tenant's fee** rent
**tenant's position** tenancy
**tenant under lease** lessee
**ten-armed marine cephalopod** squid
**ten cent US coin** dime
**Ten Commandments** Decalogue
**tend** aid, aim, assist, attend, bend, care, conduce, doctor, foster, groom, guard, help, incline, lean, manage, nurse, nurture, protect, relieve, serve, set, succour, trend, verge, watch
**tend a horse** groom
**ten decibels** bel
**tendency** direction, disposition, drift, inclination, leaning, prejudice, proclivity, proneness, propensity, trend
**tendency to be emotionally attached to animals** zoophilism
**tendency to be untruthful** mendacity
**tendency to bleed severely from even a slight injury** haemophilia
**tendency to blindness** cecutiency
**tendency to good or evil** propensity
**tendency to see the worst side of things** pessimism
**tendency to unite** cohesion

**tender** affectionate, amatory, boat, breakable, compassionate, delicate, dinghy, frangible, friable, gentle, immature, kind, lenient, loving, merciful, offer, overture, pitiful, presentation, presentment, proffer, proposal, sensitive, sentimental, skiff, soft, sore, sympathetic, ticklish, weak, young, youthful
**tender feelings** bowels, pithy
**tender look** languish
**tenderly** affectionately, affettuoso, amorously, compassionately, delicately, fondly, fragilely, gently, immaturely, kindly, lovingly, newly, painfully, pitifully, rawly, sensitively, softly, touchily, vulnerable, warmly, weakly
**tender of the sick** nurse
**tender shoot** flush
**tender slice of meat** fillet, rump, steak
**tender spot** sore
**tend furnace** stoke
**tending garden** digging, hoeing, weeding
**tending to become glass** vitrescent
**tending to become liqud** liquescent
**tending to brag** boastful
**tending to calm** sedative
**tending to cause itchiness** scratchy
**tending to compel** compulsive
**tending to debase a race** dysgenic
**tending to dissuade** averse
**tending to fatness** stout
**tending to increase** augmentative
**tending to indecency** indelicate
**tending to peace** pacific
**tending to produce sleep** soporific
**tending to secure** fixative
**tending to seek revenge** vindictive
**tending to show off** boastful
**tending to sit** sedentary
**tending to split** fissile
**tending to stir up strife** incendiary
**tending to tremble** doddery
**tending to turn into glass** vitrescent
**ten-dollar gold piece** eagle
**tendon** ligament, sinew, thew
**tendon-cutting** tenotomy
**tend the garden** weed
**tend the sick** nurse
**tend to prove guilt of** incriminate
**tenebrous** dark, dim, gloomy, obscure
**tenement** apartment, domicile, duplex, dwelling(-house), flat, habitation, home, lodge, lodgings, penthouse, residence, warren
**tenet** -ism, belief, credo, doctrine, dogma, opinion, principle, rule, thesis, view
**ten events athletic contest** decathlon
**tenfold** decuple, denary

**ten-footed crustacean** crab, decapod
**ten-gallon hat** sombrero, stetson
**ten litres** decalitre
**ten million** crore
**tennis ball wrongly served** fault
**tennis bat** racket, racquet
**tennis court divider** net
**tennis cup** Davis, Wimbledon
**tennis delivery** service
**tennis division** set
**tennis for two** singles
**tennis foursome** doubles
**tennis gear** racket
**tennis ground** court
**tennis match** doubles, singles
**tennis need** ball, court, racket
**tennis point** ace
**tennis return** boast, get
**tennis score** advantage, deuce, love, match, set
**tennis serve** ace, fault
**tennis set decider** tiebreaker
**tennis shoe** sandshoe, tackie
**tennis stroke** ace, backhand, chop, cut, drop shot, forehand, lob, volley
**tennis surface** grass court, hard court
**tennis term** ace, deuce, set, volley
**tenon** cog, tooth, tusk
**tenor** aim, approach, burden, course, custom, drift, effect, genre, gist, habit, humour, intent, line, manner, meaning, method, mode, mood, point, practice, process, purport, purpose, routine, sense, singer, spirit, style, substance, tendency, theme, trend, usage, vein, way, wont
**tenor tuba** euphonium
**ten percent paid to church** tithe
**tense** anxious, apprehensive, edgy, exciting, fidgety, jittery, jumpy, moving, nervous, nervy, neurotic, overwrought, restless, rigid, strained, stressful, taut(en), uneasy, (up)tight, worrying
**tense and nervously excitable** highly strung
**tensed** braced, closed, congealed, cramped, fastened, fixed, hardened, jelled, narrowed, reinforced, screwed, secured, set, solidified, starched, stretched, tautened, thickened
**tensely** edgily, excitingly, jumpily, nervily, nervously, restlessly, rigidly, tautly, tightly, worryingly
**ten-sided figure** decagon
**tension** anxiety, chagrin, discontent, displeasure, excitement, extension, force, hostility, pain, pressure, rigidity, rigour, strain, stress, stretch, tautness, tightness, unrest, worry

**tent** booth, canopy, canvas, marquee, sukkah (H), tepee, wigwam
**tentacle** arm, feeler
**tentacle of nautilus** sail
**tentative** cautious, conjectural, diffident, doubtful, experimental, faltering, hesitant, indefinite, probationary, provisional, speculative, timid, trial, uncertain, unconfirmed, unsettled, unsure
**tentative proposal** feeler
**tent dweller** Arab, camper, nomad
**tented area** camp
**tent fastener** peg
**tent flap** door, fly
**tenth** tithe, decimal
**tenth and smallest letter of Hebrew alphabet** yod
**tenth cranial nerve** vagus
**tenth muse** Sappho
**tenth of a metre** decimetre
**ten thousand** myriad
**ten thousand square metres** hectare
**ten thousand things** myriad
**tenth part** deci, tithe
**tenth part of a Roman legion** cohort
**tenth sign of the zodiac** Capricorn, Goat
**tent material** canvas
**tent pitching area** campsite
**tent rope** guy
**tents collectively** tentage
**tent show** carnival, circus
**tents of an army** camp
**tent town** camp
**tenuous** fragile, insignificant, rare(fied), slender, small, thin, trivial, unsubstantial
**tenure** condition, duration, estate, holding, possession, residence, right, stay, tenancy, term, visit
**tenure of authority** command
**tenure of land** holding
**ten years** decade
**tepee** teepee, tent, tipi, wigwam
**tepid** apathetic, cool, lukewarm, unenthusiastic, warm(ish)
**tepidity** apathy
**teratism** monster
**tercet** triplet
**terebra** ovipositor
**tergiversate** apostatise, equivocate, prevaricate
**term** age, call, characterise, condition, designation, duration, epoch, era, expression, limit, name, period, phrase, provision, semester, stipulation, tenure, time, usance, word
**termagant** chider, crone, faultfinder, fury, grouch, grumbler, hag, harpy, harridan, henpecker, nag, rebuker,

shrew, spitfire, virago, vixen, witch, Xanthippe
**terminal** border, boundary, closing, concluding, deadly, definite, determinate, end, extremity, fatal, lethal, mortal, polar, terminus, ultimate
**terminal air sac of lung** alveolus
**terminal point** end, limit, terminus
**terminal section of bird's wing** pinion
**terminate** abort, achieve, cease, close, complete, conclude, decide, determinate, determine, end, eventuate, expire, expressible, finish, finite, issue, lapse, limit, prove, settle, stop
**terminated** over
**terminate pregnancy** abort
**terminate prematurely** abort
**terminating in sharp point** acute
**termination** achievement, cessation, close, closure, consummation, denouncement, end(ing), epilogue, expiry, finish, limit, peroration
**terminology** argot, cant, description, language, nomenclature, phraseology, terms
**term in prison** sentence
**term in school** semester
**terminus** boundary, close, depot, end, extremity, goal, limit, station, stop, target, terminal, termination
**termite** ant, woodlouse
**term of address** madam, miss, miss(is), missus, mister, ms, sir
**term of address for a king** sire
**term of address for a knight** sir
**term of bill of exchange** usance
**term of endearment** cupcake, darling, dear, honey, liefie, skat, sweetheart
**term of office** administration, tenure
**terms** articles, charges, clauses, conditions, demands, fee, footing, language, particulars, payment, phraseology, points, price, provisions, provisos, qualifications, rates, relations, specifications, stipulations, terminology
**terms of reference** function
**term used wrongly** misnomer
**ternary** third, triple
**terra** earth, land
**terrace** avenue, balcony, lane, road(way), row, street, veranda
**terrain** area, district, ground, milieu, region, scenery, territory, topography, tract, zone
**terrene** earth(l)y, mundane, region, terrain, terrestrial
**terrestrial** earthbound, earthly, global, ground, land, mundane, temporal, worldly

**terrestrial American cuckoo** roadrunner
**terrible** appalling, awful, bad, beastly, dangerous, dire, distressing, dreadful, excessive, extreme, frightful, gruesome, horrendous, horrible, horrid, horrifying, serious, severe, terrific, tremendous
**terrible fate** doom
**terrible happening** disaster
**terrible Russian** Ivan
**terrier-like dog** griffon
**terrific** enormous, extraordinary, extreme, fabulous, great, superb, terrifying, tremendous, wonderful
**terrified** afraid, aghast, awe-struck, frozen, horrified, petrified, scared, stupefied, undone, unnerved
**terrify** alarm, awe, frighten, horrify, intimidate, paralyse, petrify, stun, terrorise
**terrifying dream** nightmare
**terrifying person** ogre
**terrine** paté
**territorial division** canton
**territorial unit** kingdom, state
**territory** area, bailiwick, department, district, domain, land, region, terrain
**territory in Algeria** Ainsefra, Ghardala, Touggourt
**territory in Canada** Yukon
**territory in India** Goa
**territory ruled by sultan** sultanate
**terror** alarm, dismay, fear, fright, horror, panic
**terrorise** coerce, dominate, frighten, intimidate, panic, scare
**terrorist** anarchist, arsonist, bandolero (Sp), criminal, desperado, destroyer, felon, gangster, hoodlum, insurgent, intimidator, marauder, nihilist, outlaw, pirate, rapparee, rebel, revolutionary, ruffian, thug, villain
**terry** towelling
**terse** abbreviated, abrupt, brief, compact, compressed, concise, condensed, crisp, curt, direct, elliptical, emphatic, epigrammatic, exact, gnomic, incisive, laconic, mordant, neat, pithy, pointed, short, succinct
**tersely cogent** pithy
**terse saying** adage, aphorism, apophthegm, idiom, motto, saw
**tertiary epoch** Eocene
**tervalent** trivalent
**tessellated floor** parquet
**tessellating** tiling
**tessera** smalto, tile
**test** analyse, assay, check, covering, essay, exam(ination), examine, experiment, oral, ordeal, proof, prove, quiz, research, sample, taste, tempt, trial, try
**test accuracy of** prove
**testament** bequest, codicil, covenant, will
**tester** examiner
**test for beginners** pons asinorum (L)
**test grades** marks
**testical sac in mammals** scrotum
**testify** admit, affirm, allege, assert, attest, certify, confirm, declare, evidence, manifest, plead, proclaim, promise, protest, prove, swear, vow, witness
**testify to** assert
**testimonial** approval, certificate, citation, credential, endorsement, letter, medal, memorial, (re)commendation, reference, referral, tribute, trophy, voucher
**testimony** affidavit, attestation, avowal, corroboration, deposition, evidence, profession, statement, submission, witness
**testing of metal** assay
**test of horse's power to jump high obstacles** puissance
**test of knowledge** exam(ination), quiz
**test person's religious beliefs** act of faith
**test print** proof
**test qualities of** prove
**test quality of metals** assay
**test the flavour** taste
**test the knowledge of** examine
**test word** shibboleth
**testy** acrimonious, angry, annoyed, astringent, bad-tempered, bitter, brusque, cantankerous, captious, caustic, censorious, choleric, churlish, contrary, crabby, cross, crotchety, crusty, cutting, difficult, disagreeable, fractious, fretful, grouchy, gruff, grumpy, ill-humoured, ill-tempered, impatient, irascible, irritable, mordant, peevish, perverse, pettish, petulant, pungent, quarrelsome, querulous, rancorous, sarcastic, severe, sharp, snappish, spiteful, surly, tart, touchy, trenchant
**tetanus** lockjaw
**tetchy** cantankerous, fretful, irritable, peevish, techy, touchy
**tête-à-tête** chat, confabulation, parley, talk
**tether** bind, chain, connection, cord, enslave, fasten, fetter, halter, handcuff, hitch, lash, lead, leash, line, link, manacle, picket, rein, restrain, restrict, rope, secure, shackle, stake, thong, tie
**tethering rope** lariat, reata
**Teuton** German
**Texan's hat** stetson
**Texas cold wind** norther
**Texas longhorn** steer
**Texas product** oil
**text** book, content, script, subject, words, writing
**text book** manual, publication, reader, roll, tome, tract, volume, work
**text division** paragraph
**textile dealer** draper, mercer
**textile fabric** acrylic, cotton, crêpe, dacron, dynel, linen, nylon, orlon, polyester, rayon, rep, silk, terylene, twill, wool
**textile fabric made from woven glass fibre** fibreglass
**textile operator** spinner
**textile wall-hanging** tapestry
**text of broadcaster's announcement** script
**text of play** script
**text of vocal music** libretto
**text passage** excerpt
**Thai** Siamese, Tai
**Thai feline** Siamese cat
**Thailand demon** nat
**Thailand island** Ko-Chang, Ko-Kut, Ko-tao, Phuket
**Thai monetary unit** baht
**Thai temple** vat, wat
**thalassian** sea turtle
**thallophyte** algae, fungi, lichens
**thank** acknowledge, bless
**thankful** appreciative, beholden, grateful, indebted, obliged, pleased
**thankfully** gratefully
**thankfulness** appreciation, credit, gratefulness, gratitude, indebtedness, obligedness, recognition, thanks, wishes
**thankless person** ingrate
**thanks** appreciation, blessing, credit, da, grace, gratefulness, gratitude, recognition, ta, thanksgiving
**thanks be to God** Deo gratias (L), grâce à Dieu (F)
**thanksgiving prayer** grace
**thanks to** because
**thank you** ta, merci (F)
**that** as, because, ce (F), it, so, what, which, who, yon
**that always will exist** eternal
**that belonging to me** mine
**that boy** he
**that can be defended** justifiable
**that can be heard** audible
**that can be managed** manageable
**that can be overcome** superable
**that can be perceived by the senses** sensible

that can be understood comprehensible
that cannot be appeased implacable, inexorable
that cannot be believed incredible
that cannot be destroyed indestructable
that cannot be disputed incontestable
that cannot be doubted indubitable
that cannot be endured intolerable
that cannot be escaped inescapable
that cannot be imagined inconceivable
that cannot be justified indefensible
that cannot be loosened inextricable
that cannot be rubbed out indelible
that cannot be tired out indefatigable, unremitting, unwearing
that causes vomiting emetic
thatch nipa, roofing, sirky, slate, thrum
that checks bleeding styptic
thatching grass reeds
that fellow him
that for which a thing is bought or sold price
that for which one is liable debts, liability
that girl her, she
that goes without saying cela va sans dire (F)
that has died out extinct
that has fallen in social class declassé
that is a matter of course ça va sans dire (F)
that is in the middle mid
that is open to to argument moot
that is to be expected prospect
that is to say namely
that man he, him
that may be exacted exigible
that may be readily moved portable
that may be repeated iterant
that may be touched palpable
that must be done compulsory, necessary
that must not be uttered ineffable
that object it
that once was quondam
that one it
that on which anything is supported mount
that or those which whichever
that's c'est (F)
that's good à la bonne heure (F)
that's life! c'est la vie (F)
that thing it
that was once former, quondam
that which attracts magnet
that which binds bond
that which can be ploughed arable
that which can be used usable
that which cannot be read illegible

that which completes something complement
that which exists being
that which follows sequel
that which is agreed on pact
that which is heard sound
that which is known knowledge
that which is left remainder, remnant, residue
that which is owned property
that which is taught doctrine
that which is yielded produce
that which may be thrown to do damage missile
that which one thinks opinion
that which will always exist eternal
that which will counteract antidote
that will go ça ira (F)
that will happen under certain conditions eventual
that woman her, she
thaumaturgy miracle
thaw clarify, defrost, dissolve, heat, liquefy, melt, puddle, relax, soften, unclot, unfreeze, warm
thawing snow slosh, slush
the das (G), der (G), die (G), el (Sp), il (I), la (F), la (I), la (Sp), las (Sp), le (F), le (I), les (F), lo (I), los (Sp), per, ye
the ability to return to life after apparent death anabiosis
the abominable snowman Yeti
the above ditto
the absent are always wrong absents ont toujours tort (F)
the act of choosing option
the act of cutting off abscission
the act of rolling volutation
the act of worshipping adoration
the act of yawning oscitance, oscitancy
the aftermost mast of a three-masted ship miz(z)enmast
the age of youth adolescence
the Almighty God
the ampersand and
the 'and' sign ampersand
the Archer Sagittarius
the art of bluffing kidology
the art of dancing choreography
the art of fishing halieutics
the art of making maps or charts cartography
the art of reading character from features of the face physiognomy
the art of war strategy
the art of writing chirography
the art or process of compiling lexicons lexicography
theatre amphitheatre, arena, cinema, coliseum, hall, lyceum, odeum, orpheum, pantheon, playhouse, stage

theatre attendant usher
theatre box loge
theatre employee scene-shifter
theatre lobby foyer
theatre part stage
theatre patrons audience
theatre performance matinée
theatre play drama
theatre production play
theatre seat loge, stall
theatre stall resembling armchair fauteuil
theatrical dramatic
theatrical dance ballet
theatrical drapery curtain
theatrical effect coup de théâtre (F)
theatrical entertainment revue
theatrical hangings and background scenery
theatrical part role
theatrical pose attitude
theatrical show revue
theatrical sketch skit
theatrical star hero(ine)
the awning of a tent tentory
the baby in Popeye cartoons Sweetpea
the balsam poplar tacamahac, tacmahack
Theban king Laius
the bay of a stag bell
the Bear Ursa
the beard of corn and grasses awn
the beginning alpha
the beginning of a period epoch
the belladonna lily amaryllis
the belly boep, kite (Sc), kyte, paunch
the best cream, élite, prime
the best policy honesty
the bewitching of something witchery
the bitter end limit, ultimate, utmost
the Blessed Virgin Beata Maria, Virgo (L)
the book of psalms psalter
the botany of seaweeds or algae phycology
the box TV, television
the boy he
the boy's his
the briny sea
the Bull Taurus
the burden of proving onus probandi
the business of changing currencies agiotage
the call to a horse to turn to the left hie
the case being such so
the casting of the skin ecdysis
the chocolate tree cacao
the choicest part pick

the chosen few  élite
the Christmas festival  Yule
the close of day  evening
the collection of postage stamps  philately
the coming of Christ  Advent
the coming of darkness at the end of day  nightfall
the common people  commonalty, Demos, hoi polloi, populace, vulgus (L)
the complete  all
the condition of being sexually attracted to children  paedophilia
the conscious subject  ego
the correct part of religion  Al Sirat (Islam)
the cougar  puma
the course taken  direction
the cream  élite, best
the cream of the cream  crème de la crème (F)
the creed  credo
the Cross of Christ  Rood
the crowd  masses, people, proletarian, public, rabble, riffraff
the cultivating of citrus fruit  citriculture
the cup that cheers  alcohol
the curative art  therapy
the cutwater  prow
the dark  night
the day before  eve, yesterday
the Day of Judgement  Dies Irae (L)
the dead body of an animal  carcass
the death struggle  agony
the denial of purpose in life  dysteleology
the depths of despond  nadir
the description of human races  ethnography
the Desert Rat  Rommel
the destruction of a foetus  aborticide
the Devil  Apollyon, archfiend, Beelzebub, Lucifer, Nick, Satan, Tempter
the devil's advocate  advocatus diaboli (L)
the die is cast  jacta alea est (L)
the difference in value between paper and metallic money  agio
the dissection of the head  cephalotomy
the doctrine of causation  aetiology
the doctrine of elements  stoichiology
the doctrine of final causes  teleology
the doctrine of the final issue of things  eschatology
the doctrine that matter has no objective assistance  immaterialism
the dried gum of the bully-tree  balata

the dry lees of wine  addle
thee  you
the earlier-born  elder
the eating of raw meat  omophagia, omophagy
the edge of the sea  shore
the electorate  voters
the electrode by which current enters a device  anode
the end  finis, insufferable, intolerable, omega, unendurable
the end crowns the work  finis coronat opus (L)
the end of a musical phrase  cadence
the end of the day  bedtime
the entire range  gamut
the entrails of deer  grallock
the essence of a thing  quiddity
the Eternal City  Rome
the exactly appropriate expression  mot juste (F)
the excision of a tumour  oncotomy
the extent of musical voice  range
the eyes of beans  hila
the fact that  although
the faithful  adherents, believers, brethren, followers
the father of a family  pater familias
the father of this country  pater patriae (L)
the fight game  boxing
the figurative use of words  tropology
the first five books of the Old Testament  Pentateuch
the first satellite of Jupiter  Io
the five lines on which music is written  staff
the five on dice  cinq(ue)
the flat country around Rome  Campagna
the flat of the hand  palm
the fluid we breathe  air
the following day  morrow
the Forbidden City  Lhasa
the forty days of fast preceding Easter  Lent, Quadragesima
the fox  Reynard
the frame of a saddle  saddletree
the French capital  Paris
theft  assumption, bootlegging, burglary, capture, copying, dispossession, fraud, hijacking, kidnapping, larceny, pilfering, plunder, robbery, smuggling, stealing, swindle, swindling, thievery
the fundamental principles of a science  philosophy
the Galilean  Christ, Jesus
the Garden of Eden  Paradise
the general effect  le tout ensemble (F)
the gentleman  he
the girl  she

the girl's  her
the glory has departed  Ichabod
the gods have decided otherwise  dis aliter visum (L)
the golden mean  juste milieu (F)
the good life  dolce vita
the good old days  history
the great beyond  afterworld, destination, destiny, future, hereafter
the great claw of a lobster  nipper
the great toe  hallux
the Green Isle  Eire, Erin, Ireland
the grounds of a university  campus
the habit of eating earth  geophagy
the heavenly regions  sky
the heavens  ether, firmament, sky
the highest amount possible  maximum
the highest mountain in the Alps  Mont Blanc
the highest point  brink
the highest string of a musical instrument  chanterelle
the holiest city of Islam  Mecca
the holly genus  ilex
the homeless  bergies, hobos, squatters, strollers, vagrants
the hour  time
the hours of light  daytime
the human foot  pes
the humanities  Humaniora (L)
the human mind  psyche
the human race  man, (hu)mankind
the human soul  psyche
the Hun  Attila
the husk of nutmeg  mace
the hymn of the Virgin Mary used as a canticle  Magnificat
the ideal  perfection
the identical words  ipsissima verba (L)
the indefinite future  mañana (Sp)
theine  caffeine
the insignia of royalty  regalia
the insult to beauty scorned  spretae injuria formae (L)
the intellectual faculties  mind
the interior  inside
the introductory part  preamble
the Iranian language of the Pathans  Pashto
the Irish Free State  Eire
the itch  scabies
the item here  this
the jerks  convulsions, palsy, spasms, trembling, tremors
the jitters  nerves
the judges collectively  legislature
the judgement of God  judicium Dei (L)
the jurisdiction of this court  leet
the Kontiki  raft
the lad  he
the lady  she, her

the lady's  hers
the Lady with the Lamp  Florence Nightingale
the largest ape  gorilla
the largest atoll in the world  Kiritimati
the Last Judgement  doom
the last of three  third
the last straw  limit
the last word  best, cream, dernier cri (F), finis, summation, ultimate, ultimatum
the law  Decalogue, Ten Commandments
the law of nations  jus genitium
the law of nature  jus naturae (L)
the law of retaliation  lex talionis
the leading bass in a choir  succentor
the least bit  rap
the Left  Communists, liberals, radicals, socialists
the leopard  pard
the light and shade in a picture  chiaroscuro
the lightest element  hydrogen
the light of the world  lux mundi (L)
the limit  enough, ne plus ultra (L)
the long and the short of  core, kernel, nucleus, pith
the Lord  Adonai (Heb)
the Lord be with you  Dominus vobiscum (L)
the Lord is my light  Dominus illuminatio mea (L)
the lot  all, et al (L), everything
the love of country is sweet  dulcis amor patriae (L)
the lower jaw  chap
the lowest point  nadir
the lowest throw at dice  ambsace, amesace
them  'em, les (F), los (Sp), those
the man  he, him
the management of land  agronomy
the man in the White House  president
the man's  his
the manufacture of lead oxide by melting and oxidising lead  cupellation
the many  crowd, majority, masses, multitude
the marriage tie  ring
the married state  wedlock
the masses  commonalty, crowd, humanity, multitude, peasants, proletariat
theme  argument, composition, idea, keynote, leitmotiv, matter, motif, point, subject, text, thesis, thread, topic
the measurement of the strength and permanence of odours  odorimetry
theme of discussion  topic

the merry man  l'allegro (I)
the Messiah  Christ, Jesus
the Middle Ages  moyen âge (F)
the middle part  midst
the military  army
the mob that rules  mobocracy
the mock orange  syringa
the moment a plane lands  touchdown
the mopes  blues, low spirits
the more difficult feats of dressage  haute école (F)
the most excellent  best
the most sacred Muslim shrine in Mecca  Caaba, Kaaba
the motto of Oxford University  Dominus illuminatio mea (L)
then  accordingly, before, consequently, earlier, ergo, formerly, once, previously, so, therefore, thus, whence
then again  anon
the name of thirteen popes  Leo
the name signifying rank  title
the natural history of animals  zoology
the Nazarene  Christ, Jesus
the near future  tomorrow
the Netherlands  Holland
the next day  tomorrow
the night before  eve
the number four  tetrad
the number one  monad, unit
the number that must be present  quorum
the number two  dyad
the object  it
the object of a hunt  quarry
theocritean poem  idyll
the old  aged, elderly, pensioners, retired
the old nobility  ancienne noblesse
the old order  ancien régime (F)
theological school  seminary, theologate
theological virtues  charity, faith, hope, love
theomachy  strife
the one in front  leader
the one over here  this
the ones here  these
the ones there  those
the one there  that
the open air  outdoors, plein-air
the order of priests or holy men  hagiarchy
the ordinary people  Demos, rank and file
theorem  argumentation, axiom, rule, symbol, topic
theoretical  abstract, academic, conjectural, doctrinaire, impractical, notional, platonic, presumptive, pure,

putative, speculative, suppositive, theoric, unapplied
the origin of the universe  cosmogony
theorise  speculate
theory  conception, conjecture, explanation, formulation, hypothesis, idea, -ism, notion, observation, plan, scheme, speculation, statement, supposition, system, view(point)
theory based on chance  tychism
theory of art  aesthetics
theory of being and knowing  metaphysics
theory of dramatics  dramaturgy
theory of Einstein  relativity
theory of knowledge  epistemology, gnosiology
theory of Newton  gravity
theory of the formation of the earth  geogony
theory of the universe and its creation  cosmogony
theory of value  axiology
theory that everything turns to evil  pessimism
the outer boundary of a plane figure  perimeter
the outer side  contra
the outer skin  epidermis
the outside ear  auricle
the outside of a material body  surface
the owner of adjoining property  abutter
the papal office  tiara
the papal system  papacy
the paper reed  papyrus
the past  antiquity, bygone days, history, yesteryear
the past twenty-four hours  yesterday
the peace of the world  pax orbis terratum (L)
the people's  their
the period preceding the First World War  belle époque (F)
the person next door  neighbour
the philosophy of taste  aesthetics
the pick of  élite
the place of the seal  locus sigilli
the plant Veronica  Hebe
the point towards which one looks  direction
the power of inertness  vis inertiae (L)
the practice of magic  witchcraft
the precise words  ipsissima verba (L)
the present  now, today
the present position  status quo
the press  columnists, correspondents, journalism, journalists, media, newsmen, newspapers, reporters
the prestige of being a celebrity  stardom
the price asked for goods  charge

**the pricking of conscience** compunction
**the process of freeing from living germs** sterilisation
**the process of growing old** ag(e)ing
**the proprieties** ceremony, courtliness, formalities, formalness, tradition
**the provinces** backveld, frontier, hinterlands, wilderness
**the pulpit** clericals, episcopacy, parsons, pastorate, prelacy, priesthood, priests
**the push** discharge, dismissal
**the queen of fairies** Titania
**the rabble** commonalty, commoners, outcasts, proletariat, riffraff, trash, vermin
**the Ram** Aries
**therapeutic** beneficial, corrective, curative, good, healing, remedial, restorative, sanative, therapy, treatment
**therapy** cure, healing, regimen, remedy, treatment
**there** at, viola (F)
**there and then** immediately
**the reason for a thing's existence** raison d'être (F)
**the red cap of liberty** chapeau rouge (F)
**the red planet** Mars
**therefore** accordingly, consequently, ergo, hence, so, then, thus, wherefore
**therefore, let us rejoice** gaudeamus igitur (L)
**the refrain of a song** chorus
**the refuse products in sugar-making** bagasse
**there is a possibility** perhaps
**there is no place like this** home
**the relationship of husband and wife** connubial
**thereon** upon
**the rest** others
**the rest is wanting** cetera desunt (L)
**the results of a disaster** aftermath
**theretofore** ere
**thereupon** after, immediately, so, soon, when, whereat
**the ridge between a horse's shoulder blades** withers
**the right of a husband to the property of his wife** jus mariti (L)
**the right of choosing** choice
**the right of the widow** jus relictae (L)
**the right of voting** franchise
**the right to hold a local court** soke
**the ring for a Scout's neckerchief** woggle
**the rise and fall of the voice in speaking** cadence

**thermal** calorific, heated, sudorific, thermic, updraught, warm
**thermal unit** calorie, joule, therm
**thermionic valve with three electrodes** triode
**thermometer metal** mercury
**thermometer scale** Celsius, Fahrenheit
**thermos** flask
**therology** mammalogy
**the rook in chess** castle
**the rope** halter, hanging, lynching, noose
**the Royal Military Acadamy** Sandhurst
**the rule** norm
**the same** alike, ditto, do, equal, idem (L), identical
**the same state as before** status quo ante (L)
**the same to all men** omnibus idem (L)
**thesaurus** dictionary, (en)cyclopaedia, lexicon, synonymy
**the scene of an action** venue
**the science of** -ology
**the score for instrumentalists** music
**these** ces (F)
**the sea** briny
**the self** ego
**the sense of taste** palate
**the seven seas** Antarctic, Arctic, Indian, North Atlantic, North Pacific, South Atlantic, South Pacific
**the silky sheath round a chrysalis** cocoon
**the simplest microscopic animal** amoeba
**thesis** argument, assumption, composition, discourse, dissertation, essay, exposition, guess, hypothesis, idea, issue, keynote, matter, monograph, opinion, pamphlet, point, postulate, premise, proposal, proposition, speculation, study, subject, surmise, text, theme, theory, topic, tract, treatise, work
**thesis writer** dissertationist
**the six on dice** sice
**the sixteenth century** cinquecento
**the skull** cranium
**the sky** empyrean, heavens
**the smallest infinite cardinal number** aleph-null, aleph-zero
**the so-called Tasmanian wolf** thylacine
**the source and origin of our miseries** fons et origo malorum (L)
**the south wind** Auster
**the species** flesh, humanity, (hu)mankind
**the speed of piece of music** tempo
**thespian** actor, actress, player, trouper
**the sport of princes** polo
**the stage of the theatre** scene

**the Stagirite** Aristotle
**the stars** horoscope
**the state of being ancient** antiquity
**the state of being forgotten** oblivion
**the state of being motionless** inertia
**the state of perfect bliss** nirvana
**the stoic way** stoicism
**the story relates to you** de te fabula narratur (L)
**the study of new growths** oncology
**the study of the distribution of plant and animal life** biogeography
**the substance of the offence** corpus delicti (L)
**the sum of** all
**the sun** Sol
**the systematic culture of trees and shrubs** arboriculture
**the talipot palm** fan palm
**the tallest mammal** giraffe
**the technique of recording wind instruments** anemography
**the Ten Commandments** Decalogue
**the Terrible Tsar** Ivan
**the territory of a nation** country
**the theatre** art, drama(turgy)
**the theory of fermentation** zymology
**the theory of the formation of the earth** geogony
**the thing** it, res (L)
**the thing here** this
**the thing mentioned** that
**the things here** these
**the things there** those
**the thing there** that
**the Three Furies** Alecto, Magaera, Tisiphone
**the three in cards** trey
**the time being** nonce
**the time of the Last Judgement** Doomsday
**the time something lasts** duration
**the top** summit
**the top of the head** cranium, crown, pate
**the tops** best
**the total amount** all
**the treatment of diseases** therapy
**the tree of knowledge** clever oak
**the turf** racecourse, racing, track
**the two** both
**the two on dice** deuce
**the two together** both
**the ultimate basis of reality** Absolute
**the Underworld** Hades
**the United States** America
**the universe** cosmos, world
**the unwritten law** lex non scripta
**the upper middle class** haute bourgeoisie (F)
**the use of spies** espionage
**the use of words** diction

**the very best** élite
**the very limit** utmost
**the very same** identical
**the visible horizon** skyline
**the vocal art** singing
**the voice of the people** vox populi
**the voice of the stars** vox stellarum (L)
**the way out** egress, exit
**the West** Occident
**the West Wind** zephyr
**the whole amount** all
**the whole lot** caboodle, shebang
**the whole of** all, everything
**the whole world** universe
**the will** volition
**the windpipe** trachea
**the Wise Men from the East** Magi
**the woman** her
**the Word** Bible, Gospel, Scriptures
**the Word of God** Logos
**the words of a song** lyrics
**the works** all
**the world** earth
**the worldly rich** Mammon
**the world of fashion** le beau monde (F)
**the world of man** microcosm
**the world's largest monolith** Ayers Rock
**the written word remains** litera scripta manet (L)
**they are inherited** genes
**they can cause disease** bacteria
**they cause reactions** chemicals
**they do as they are told** obeyers
**they get answers** questions
**they group in gaggles** geese
**they hold up socks** elastic, garters
**they keep law and order** police
**they keep the hands warm** gloves
**they link towns** roads
**they look after passengers on plane** cabin crew
**they never die** old soldiers
**the young of a bird of prey** aerie, eyrie
**they pry** snoopers
**thiamine** aneurin
**thiamine deficiency disease** beri-beri
**thick** abundant, broad, bulky, chunky, deep, dense, dumb, fat, intimate, strong, viscous
**thick and fleshy** juicy, succulent
**thick black liquid** pitch, tar
**thick blanket** mackinaw
**thick blunt needle** bodkin
**thick-bodied river fish** chub
**thick bone between knee and hip** femur
**thick broad piece** slab
**thick cloth placed under saddle** numdah, numnah

**thick-coated breed of dog** chow, St Bernard
**thick cord** rope
**thick corded silk ribbon** petersham
**thick cord to pull car** towrope
**thick creamy sauce** hollandaise, mayonnaise
**thick dark inflammable liquid** pitch, tar
**thick darkness** murk
**thicken and get sour** curdle
**thickening mixture** roux
**thicket** boscage, boskage, bracken, brushwood, bushveld, coppice, copse, covert, forest, grove, hedges, jungle, scrub, shrubs, spinney, timber, undergrowth, wood
**thick finger on hand** thumb
**thick firm cushion for kneeling** hassock
**thick flat slice** slab
**thick foliage** boscage, boskage
**thick French shellfish soup** bisque
**thick French soup of vegetables and meat** pot-au-feu
**thick greasy mud** sludge
**thick growth** thicket
**thick leather** butt
**thickly packed** dense
**thickly wooded** arboreous
**thick mass of hair** mop
**thick milk** curd
**thick mist** fog, smog
**thickness** calibre, closeness, denseness, density, diameter, gauge, layer, ply, radius, sheet, size, stratum, viscosity, weight, width
**thick paint** impasto
**thick piece** chunk
**thick piece of firewood** billet
**thick piece of something** chunk
**thick pile carpet** moquette
**thick-piled fabric** velvet
**thick quilted woollen stuff** ratteen
**thick rope of fibre** cable
**thick round root** tuber
**thick round steak cut from a fillet of beef** tournedos
**thick sauce for dessert** custard, sabayon
**thickset** burly, close(-packed), compact, compressed, condensed, consolidated, crowded, dense, gross, heavy, impassable, impenetrable, impermeable, opaque, serried, solid, substantial, thick, tight
**thickset horse** cob
**thick-skinned** insensitive
**thick-skinned animal** pachyderm
**thick slice** chunk, slab
**thick slice of meat** steak
**thick slippery mud** slime
**thick soft cotton yarn** candlewick

**thick-soled boot** buskin
**thick solution of sugar and water** syrup
**thick soup** bisk, bisque, chowder, minestrone, pot(t)age, purée, vichyssoise
**thick sticky fluid lubricating body joints** sinovia
**thick stiff paper** board
**thick string** cord
**thick sweet liqueur of egg yolks and brandy** advokaat
**thick sweet liquid** syrup
**thick twilled cotton cloth** fustian
**thick vapour** fog, smog
**thick wedge** slab
**thick woollen cloth** tweed
**thick woollen overcoat** pea coat, petersham
**thick woollen wrap** rug
**thief** bandit, burglar, cheat, cracksman, embezzler, filcher, housebreaker, larcenist, mugger, pickpocket, pilferer, plunderer, reiver, robber, shoplifter, stealer, swindler
**thief's assistance** stall
**thieve** appropriate, arrogate, burgle, cheat, defraud, embezzle, filch(er), finger, heist, hijack, lift, loot, misappropriate, mooch, peculate, pilfer, pillage, pinch, pirate, plunder, poach, purloin, ransack, rob, rook, scrounge, shoplift, smuggle, steal, swindle, swipe
**thieves' slang** argot, cant
**thieving** larcenous
**thievish bird** (jack)daw
**thigh armour** cuisse, taslet, tasse(t)
**thighbone** femur
**thigh of hog** ham
**thin** attenuated, bony, deficient, delicate, dilute, feeble, filmy, fine, flimsy, gaunt, gossamer, inadequate, lame, lank(y), lean, light, mawger, meagre, narrow, poor, rare(fied), reedy, runny, scant(y), scarce, scattered, scrawny, shallow, sheer, skimpy, skinny, slender, slight, slim, spare, sparse, superficial, threadlike, transparent, unsubstantial, watery, weak, wispy
**thin and angular** spidery
**thin and bony** gaunt, scraggy
**thin and underdone** rare
**thin animal tissue** membrane
**thin as a rail** attenuate, lank(y), lean, reedy, skinny, slender, stalky, thin, twiggy
**thin atmospheric vapour** haze
**thin band** wisp
**thin batter cake** pancake
**thin biscuit** wafer

**thin board** slat
**thin boards for lining** sarking (Sc)
**thin cake made of oatmeal** oatcake
**thin cake of batter fried in pan** pancake
**thin cake of flour, water and ghee** paratha
**thin candle** taper
**thin candle lighter** spill
**thin clear soup** bouillon, broth, consommé
**thin coating** film, lacker, lacquer, veneer
**thin cotton** voile
**thin crisp biscuit** cracker, wafer
**thin crisp cake** wafer
**thin crisp sweet cake** jumbal, jumble
**thin crisp toast** melba
**thin cushion** pad
**thin dagger** stiletto
**thin fabric** leno, organza, silesia, taffeta, toile, tulle, voile
**thin fish** racer, sole
**thin flat cake of unleavened wholemeal bread** chapatti
**thin flat circular object** disc, disk
**thin flat piece cut off** slice
**thin fluid mortar** grout
**thin fog** mist
**thing** article, being, entity, event, it(em), matter, object, occurrence, res (L)
**thing accomplished** acta, deed
**thing achieved** accomplishment
**thing added** accession, addendum, appendix, insertion, inset
**thing aimed at** objective, target
**thing annexed to a house** fixture
**thin garment** gossamer
**thing causing happiness** felicity
**thing chosen** option
**thing conceived** conception, idea
**thing consciously done** deed
**thing constructed** structure
**thing done** act(a), actus, deed, fact
**thing existing only in the imagination** figment
**thing feigned** fiction
**thing fixed in position** fixture
**thing following** sequel
**thing found** trove
**thing given as compensation** pro quo (L), quid, solatium
**thing given over as security** pledge
**thing hard to get rid of** hydra
**thing having real existence** entity
**thing hidden** stash
**thing illustrating a general rule** example
**thing incorrectly done** mistake
**thing in itself** noumenon
**thing in law** chose, les, re(s)

**thing in the way** barrier, hindrance, obstacle, obstruction
**thing joined to another** adjunct
**thing kept in memory of its giver** keepsake
**thing known to be true** fact
**thin glass** mousseline
**thing left out** omission
**thin glossy silk stuff** taffeta
**thing obstructing progress** obstacle
**thing offered to divine being** oblation
**thing of little value** bauble, gewgaw, stiver, trifle, trinket, trivia
**thing of no importance** nonentity
**thing of remembrance** memento, souvenir, token
**thing of small value** trifle
**thing of the past** archaism, history
**thing of value** asset
**thing omitted** omission
**thing representing something** symbol
**thing said incidentally** obiter dictum
**thing said to excite laughter** joke
**thing sensed** phenomenon
**thing serving to remind** memento
**thing's existence** entity
**things indicated** these
**things let out** emission
**things lying about untidily** clutter
**things needed** want
**things of short-lived use** ephemera
**things owned** belongings, personals, property
**things past** bygones
**thing's position** locality
**things produced** production
**things that exist** reality
**things there** those
**things to be corrected** corrigenda
**things to be done** agenda
**things to eat** comestibles
**thing subordinate to** adjunct, ancillary
**thing supposed to bring good luck** mascot, talisman
**thing that gives great pleasure** treat
**thing that has survived from the past** relic
**thing that happens by chance** happenstance
**thing that helps** adminicle
**thing that is known to be true** fact
**thing that is no good** dud
**thing that obstructs progress** obstacle
**thing to be added** addendum
**thing to be corrected** corrigendum
**thing to be done** agenda
**thing to be learned** lesson
**thing to be regretted** damage
**thing to exhibit** bravery
**thing to sleep on** bed
**thing which appertains to** appurtenance

**thing worn about the person as charm** amulet, periapt
**thing written in cipher** cryptogram
**thing wrongly done** fault
**thing wrongly placed** anachronism
**thin high-necked long-sleeved garment** skivvy
**think** account, anticipate, believe, cerebrate, cogitate, conceive, consider, contemplate, design, imagine, intend, judge, mean, meditate, opine, picture, ponder, recall, recollect, reflect, remember, ruminate, suppose
**thinkable** conceivable, possible
**think about** consider, meditate
**think back** remember
**think better of** re-examine, recheck, reconsider, review, tergiversate
**think deeply** cogitate, concentrate, meditate
**thinker** intellectual, logician, metaphysician, philosopher, sage, theorist
**think favourably of** esteem
**think highly of** admire, approve, esteem
**thinking too much of oneself** overweening
**think logically** reason
**think moodily** brood
**think much of** admire, esteem, respect
**think of as a material thing** reify
**think out** devise, excogitate, plan, scheme
**think over** brood, consider, contemplate, deliberate, digest, meditate, mull, muse, ponder, reflect, ruminate
**think through** analyse
**think together** associate
**think up** conceive, concoct, construct, contrive, create, design, draft, frame, imagine, improvise, invent, mint, visualise
**think upon** brood
**think well of** admire, approve
**thin layer** flake, lamina, veneer
**thin linen** cambric
**thin line or groove** stria
**thin loosely-woven cotton fabric** cheesecloth
**thinly scattered** sparse
**thinly shrill** reedy
**thin material** georgette, leno, organza, silesia, taffeta, toile, tulle, voile
**thin membrane that forms a sheath around nerve fibres** neurolemma
**thin metal disk** paten
**thin metal sheet** foil
**thin nail** brad
**thin narrow strip of wood** lath

**thin on the ground**  few, rare, sparse, uncommon, unusual
**thin opening**  slit
**thin out**  rarefy
**thin outer coating**  lacker, lacquer, veneer
**thin outer covering**  skin
**thin out the herd**  cull
**thin packing strip**  shim
**thin pancake**  crêpe
**thin paper**  flimsy, tissue
**thin pencil mark**  line
**thin piece of**  slice
**thin plate**  lamina
**thin porridge**  gruel
**thin rich silk material**  sendal
**thin rod**  spindle
**thin rope**  cord
**thin round crisp Indian bread**  poppadom, poppadum
**thin satin**  satinet
**thin savoury biscuit**  cracker
**thin sheet iron**  taggers
**thin-shelled nut**  pecan
**thin silk or cotton**  organza
**thin slice**  sliver
**thin slice of bacon**  rasher
**thin slices of meat, fried with vegetables and seasoning**  stir fry, sukiyaki (J)
**thin slip of wood**  lath
**thin soft fabric**  foulard
**thin soup**  bouillon, broth, consommé
**thin stiff open muslin**  tarlatan
**thin stream**  trickle
**thin string**  ribbon
**thin strip of cloth**  tape
**thin strip of leather**  thong
**thin strip of wood**  lath, slat, spill, splint
**thin tissue of fine silk**  sarcenet, sarsenet
**thin twilled cotton**  silesia
**thin varnish**  shellac
**thin waterproof jacket with a hood**  cagoule
**thin waxed spill**  taper
**thin worsted yarn for tapestry**  crewel
**third**  tierce, treble
**third actor in Greek play**  tritagonist
**third canonical hour**  terce
**third-class**  inferior, poor
**third day**  tertian
**Third Empire**  Germany
**third from last**  antepenultimate
**third in degree**  tertiary
**third in line**  thirdly
**third king of Juda**  Asa
**third note of diatonic scale**  mediant
**third part**  thirding
**third part of insect's leg**  femur
**third part of small intestines**  ileum
**third power**  cube

**third queen of Palmyra**  Zenobia
**third-rate**  inferior, poor
**third son of Adam**  Seth
**third son of Noah**  Japhet
**third stomach of ruminant**  omasum, psalterium
**third Sunday before Lent**  Septuagesima
**Third World**  Africa, Asia, Latin America, underdeveloped countries
**third-year salmon**  mort
**thirl**  hole, opening
**thirst**  crave, craving, desire, eagerness, hankering, hunger, sed (Sp), yearning
**thirst for**  covet
**thirsty**  arid, dehydrated, desirous, dry, eager, greedy, itching, lusting, parched
**thirteenth century assize**  oyer
**this**  esta, este (Sp), hoc (L)
**this and this**  these
**this calls doctor to telephone**  bleeper
**this day**  today
**this describes genial cheerful disposition**  sunny
**this describes hot and humid weather**  tropical
**this describes new snow**  powdery
**this dog is ownerless**  pi(e), pye
**this grows on rocks**  moss
**this illuminates star on stage**  spotlight
**this is the cause of the trouble**  hinc illae lacrimae (L)
**this minute**  immediately, now, pronto
**this month**  instant
**this one, for instance**  clue
**this place**  here
**this planet**  earth, terra
**this provides a flickering light**  candle
**this time**  now
**thistle-like Eurasian plant**  artichoke
**this tree is the carob tree**  locust
**this twenty-four hours**  today
**this way**  thus, so
**this will attract metal objects**  magnet
**this will speed delivery of letter**  post(al) code
**thither**  there, yon(der)
**thitherto**  ere
**thong**  belt, cord, rope, strap, strip, tether, whip(lash)
**thong for holding dog**  leash
**thoracic**  chesty
**thorax**  chest
**thorax in crustacea**  pereoin
**thorn**  affliction, bane, barb, curse, prickle, scourge, spike, spur, torment, torture, trouble, woe
**thorn-bush enclosure**  boma

**thorn in one's flesh**  annoyance, curse, irritation, nuisance, plague, torment, trouble
**thorny plant**  briar, brier, chanar, hawthorn, thistle
**thorough**  complete, detailed, done, entire, finished, rigorous, total, unqualified
**thoroughbred**  à la mode (F), aristocratic, blue-blooded, charming, courageous, courteous, courtly, cultivated, daring, debonair, delicate, elegant, fearless, fiery, full-blooded, genteel, gentle, gracious, graceful, high-spirited, high-strung, high-bred, mannerly, mettlesome, modish, noble, passionate, pedigreed, plucky, polished, proud, pur sang (F), pure(bred), refined, stylish, untainted, urbane, valiant, well-bred, well-mannered, wilful
**thoroughbred horse**  racer
**thorough check with repairs if necessary**  overhaul
**thoroughfare**  avenue, path, road, street
**thoroughgoing**  absolute, arrant, assiduous, careful, complete, conscientious, downright, efficient, entire, exhaustive, extreme, full, intensive, out-and-out, painstaking, perfect, pure, scrupulous, sheer, sweeping, total, uncompromising, unqualified, utter
**thoroughly**  à fond (F)
**thoroughly efficient**  adept, expert
**thoroughly proficient**  adept
**thoroughly soak**  drench
**thoroughly tenacious**  pertinaceous
**those**  them
**those canonised**  saints
**those in favour**  ayes
**those in hospital**  inpatients
**those in the know**  cognoscenti
**those invited**  guests
**those manning airplanes**  aircrews
**those near and dear**  ménage
**those of high birth**  noblesse
**those people**  them, they
**those who are not present**  absentees
**those who are older first**  seniores priores (L)
**those who speed**  racers
**thou**  du (G), tu (F)
**though**  albeit, allowing, granted, notwithstanding, while
**thought**  belief, cogitation, concept, consideration, contemplation, conviction, expectation, idea, intention, judg(e)ment, musing, notion, opinion, reflection, speculation, tenet, thinking, view

**thoughtful** attentive, benevolent, careful, compassionate, considerate, contemplative, discreet, kind(hearted), meditative, mindful, musing, pensive, pondering, profound, prudent, reflective, regardful, respectful, reverent, serious, tender
**thoughtless** careless, disregardful, foolhardy, foolish, forgetful, impolite, imprudent, inattentive, incogitant, inconsiderate, indiscreet, insensible, insensitive, mindless, neglectful, negligent, precipitate, rash, reckless, regardless, remiss, rude, silly, stupid, tactless, uncaring, unkind, unmindful, unsolicitous, unthinking, unwise
**thoughtless act** folly
**thoughtless girl** tawpie, tawpy
**thoughtlessly cruel** wanton
**thought transference** telepathy
**thousand-armed giant** Bana
**thousand ergs** kilerg
**thousand million kilograms** megaton
**thousand millions** milliard
**thousand square metres** decare
**thousandth of millimetre** micron
**thousand thousands** million
**thousand years anniversary** millennium
**thpeakth thith way** lisps
**thrash** beat, belabour, belt, cane, cream, defeat, donder, drub, flog, lam(baste), lash, maul, nonsense, punish, rubbish, scourge, sjambok, spank, strap, trounce, wallop, whip(lash)
**thrashing stick** cane
**thrash out** debate, discuss, review, settle, solve
**thread** cotton, direction, fibre, meander, motif, plot, strain, strand, string, wind
**threadbare** antiquated, banal, common, damaged, destitute, dingy, everyday, frayed, hackneyed, insipid, insubstantial, jejune, lean, meagre, moth-eaten, napless, ordinary, outdated, outworn, overworked, pathetic, penniless, platitudinous, poor, ragged, scanty, shabby, slight, stale, stereotyped, stock, tattered, timeworn, tired, trite, untidy, vapid, worn(-out)
**thread cutter** die
**thread-cutting machine** lathe
**threaded nail** screw
**thread feeding flame of candle** wick
**thread for weft** woof
**thread holder** spool
**threadlike body** filament

**threadlike element** fibre
**threadlike extension of a nerve cell** axon
**thread of screw** worm
**thread of shoemaker** lingel, lingle
**threads that cross the warp in weaving** weft, woof
**threat** commination, danger, hazard, menace, omen, peril, remark, risk, warning
**threaten** endanger, forebode, impend, menace, portend, prognosticate
**threatening** foreboding, imminent, intimidating, menacing, ominous, sinister, terrorising, warning
**threatening look** glare, glower, scowl
**threatening with divine wrath** commination
**three** drei (G), tre (I), tri (G), tri-, trois (F)
**three-armed tool** tribrachial
**three asterisks arranged in a triangle** asterism
**three at dice** trey
**three babies born at once** triplets
**three-cornered hat** tricorn(e)
**three-cornered sail** jib, lateen, sailage, trinket
**three dimensional** cubic
**three Fates** Atropos, Clotho, Lachesis
**three feet** yard
**threefold** threeway, treble, triple, triplicate
**three Furies** Alecto, Megaera, Tisiphone
**three given to congratulate** cheers
**three Graces** Aglaia, Euphrosyne, Thalia
**three-handed card game** skat
**three-headed** tricephalous
**three-headed watchdog of Hades** Cerberus
**three-horse carriage** troika
**three-horse team** randem
**three-hundred year anniversary** tercentenary, tricentennial
**three in cards** trey
**three in dice** trey
**three in music** ter
**three in one** triune
**three joints** trinodal
**three-leafed** ternate
**three-leafed pasture flower** clover
**three-legged chair** stool
**three-legged pot** trivet
**three-legged stand** teapoy, tripod, trivet
**three-masted ship** bark, frigate, tern, xebec
**three-monthly journal** quarterly
**three-monthly payment** quarterage
**three-oar boat** randan
**three of a kind** triplet

**three-pronged** tridental
**three-pronged spear** trident
**threescore** sixty
**three sheets in the wind** groggy, jolly, oiled, screwed
**three-sided** triangular
**three-sided polygon** triangle
**threesome** triad, trio, triple(t)
**three-spotted domino** trey
**three-stringed musical instrument** balalaika, rebec, samisen (J)
**three times** thrice
**three times a week** tri-weekly
**three-toed bird** stilt
**three-toed ostrich** rhea
**three-toed sloth** ai
**three under par** albatross
**three-wheeled vehicle** tricycle, trishaw
**three wise men** Balthazar, Gaspar, Magi, Melchior
**three-year anniversary** triennial
**thresh** agitate, beat, cane, curry, flail, flap, flog, flutter, lash, seed, shake, spank, swing, swish, thrash, vibrate, wag, wave, whip
**thresher shark** sea fox
**threshing instrument** flail
**threshold** brink, commencement, doorsill, doorstep, doorway, edge, entrance, groundsel, inception, limen, portal, prelude, start, verge
**thresh out** debate, discuss, review, settle, solve
**thrice-married** trigamous
**thrift** carefulness, economy, frugality, parsimony, prudence, reasonableness, saving, sea-pink
**thrifty** abstemious, accurate, careful, cautious, conscientious, discreet, economical, fastidious, frugal, growing, meagre, painstaking, parsimonious, precise, prosperous, provident, prudent, saving, scrimping, sparing, thoughtful, thriving
**thrill** adventure, arouse, charge, elate, electrify, enrapture, enthral, excite, exhilarate, flush, impress, inspirit, pleasure, pulsation, quiver, sensation, sensitise, shudder, stimulate, throb, tingle, titillate, tremble, vibrate, vibration
**thrilling** dynamic, electrifying, exciting, rousing, stirring, vibrating
**thrill of emotion** pulse
**thrive** advance, bloom, blossom, boom, burgeon, develop, flourish, gain, grow, increase, luxuriate, profit, progress, prosper, score, sprout, succeed, wax
**thrive at another's expense** batten
**throat appendage** tonsil

**throat clearing** ahem
**throat disease** croup, quinsy, tonsillitis
**throat glands** adenoids
**throat wrap** boa, scarf
**throaty** guttural, hoarse
**throaty cry of hen** cluck
**throaty in sound** guttural
**throb** ache, beat, belk, drum, flack, flichter, leap, palpitate, pant, pitapat, pound(ing), pulsate, pulse, quop, stang, stound, thrill, thump(ing), vibrate, vibration, wallop
**throbbing of the arteries** pulse
**throb in pain** shoot
**throb painfully** ache
**throe** convulsion, fit, pain, pang, paroxysm, seizure, spasm, stroke
**throes** agony, anguish, cataclysm, chaos, confusion, convulsions, disorder, disruption, distress, excruciation, ordeal, pandemonium, pangs, paroxysms, spasms, storm, suffering, torture, tumult, turbulence, turmoil, upheaval
**throng** assemblage, assemble, bunch, converge, cram, crowd, crush, fill, flock, herd, horde, host, jam, jostle, mass, mob, multitude, pack, press, swarm, teem, troop
**thronged** bunched, converged, crammed, crowded, filled, flocked, herded, jammed, packed, pressed
**throttle** accelerator, asphyxiate, choke, congest, gag, gar(r)otte, gibbet, gullet, impede, obstruct, smother, strangle, strangulate, suffocate, throat, throttler, windpipe
**throttler** killer, murderer, strangler
**through** à travers (F), between, by, completed, completely, di(a)-, done, during, ended, entirely, finished, fully, in, past, per, thro', throughout, using, via, wholly
**through all the ages** eternally
**through and through** altogether, completely, entirely, fully, thoroughly, totally, unreservedly, utterly, wholly
**throughout** di(a)-, through
**throughout the world** everywhere
**through right or wrong** per fas aut nefas (L)
**through the mouth** peroral
**through the nose** nasally
**through which** whereby
**throw** blanket, cast, dash, drive, evict, fling, force, hurl, launch, lob, pelt, pitch, project, propel, scarf, send, shy, sling, stab, toss, venture
**throw a baseball pitch** hang
**throw about** bounce
**throw a fit** rage, storm
**throw a monkey wrench** mar, scotch

**throw a party** host
**throw aside** divest, discard, fling, toss
**throw away** bandy, blow, dice, discard, dispose, ditch, doff, dump, jettison, lose, project, reject, scrap, squander, waive, waste
**throwback** atavism, reversion
**throw back** repel, retort, revert
**throw backwards** retroject
**throw ball slowly in high arc** lob
**throw carelessly** chuck, cob
**throw coin** toss
**throw cold water on** chill, dampen
**throw dice** jeff
**throw down** demolish, deturb, even, fell, flatten, fling, flump, lodge, pile, raze, wreck
**throw down flat** prostrate
**throw dust in the eyes of** confuse, deceive, fool, mislead
**throw fishing line** cast
**throw fishing line again** recast
**throw forward** launch
**throw hard** hurl
**throw heedlessly** slight
**throw here and there** scatter
**throw hurriedly** fling
**throw in an arc** lob
**throwing dice** diceing
**throwing stones at** pelting
**throwing weapon** assegai, javelin, spear
**throw in one's lot with** join, support
**throw in the towel** give-up, quit, surrender, yield
**throw into confusion** derange, disrupt, disturb, pie
**throw into disorder** confuse, derange, disarray, disrupt, embroil, jumble, mess, muss, pi(e), untidiness
**throw into perplexity** flummox
**throw into the shade** eclipse
**throw into turmoil** disrupt
**throw in with** join
**throw lightly** flip, lob
**throw light on** clarify, elucidate, explain, illume, illuminate, simplify
**thrown into ecstasy** enrapt
**throw of dice** main
**throw off** abandon, abort, beguile, cant, cast, confuse, deceive, delude, deport, discard, disconcert, dismiss, disturb, doff, drop, eject, elude, emit, evict, expel, misguide, mislead, outrun, reject, relegate, renounce, repudiate, shed, slough, throw, unburden, unsaddle, unseat, unsettle, upset
**throw off balance** ba(u)lk, foil, frustrate, intervene
**throw off course** derail
**throw of six at dice** sise

**throw of two** ambsace, amesace
**throw one's lot in with** affiliate, bind, league, marry, wed
**throw or cast** toss
**throw or toss a ball** lob
**throw out** banish, boot, bounce, confuse, discard, disconcert, dismiss, disturb, dumped, eject, emit, evict, exile, expel, jettison, ostracise, prohibit, radiate, reject, rid, rubbish, scrap, unhouse, unsettle, upset, utter
**throw out from within** eject
**throw out of school** expel
**throw over** abandon, desert, discard, jilt, overturn
**throw overboard** disuse, jettison, lighten
**throw quickly** lash
**throw sidewise** shy
**throw smartly** slat
**throw sticks** squail
**throw stones** lapidate, pelt
**throw the body about** flounce
**throw together** huddle, mingle, mix, skimp
**throw up** abandon, abdicate, abjure, chuck, crustate, desert, disgorge, excrete, heave, leave, nag, produce, quit, regorge, regurgitate, relinquish, renounce, resign, retch, reveal, spew, void, vomit
**throw up in air** toss
**throw violently** ding, hurtle, pash, precipitate, smash, whop
**throw water on** douse, wet
**throw with a jerk** cant
**throw with force** hurl
**thrum** buzz, drone, hum, mumble, murmur, purr, sing, strum, throb, vibrate, whir
**thrush** aphtha, fieldfare
**thrust** actuate, boost, chuck, cram, force, forward, impel, jab, jostle, lunge, pierce, prod, propel, push, stab, stick, toss, wedge
**thrust aside** elbow(ed)
**thrust back** repel
**thrust forward** assert, protrude
**thrust forward unduly** obtrude
**thrust in** encroach, infringe, interlope, interpose, intervene, intrude, invade, irrupt, obtrude
**thrusting forward** protrusive
**thrusting weapon** assegai, épée, estoc, rapier, spear, stock
**thrust out** exert, extend, extrude, outstretch, reach
**thrust out with foot** kick
**thrust upon** coerce, constrain, enforce, impose, necessitate
**thrust violently into a hole** ram

**thrust with a finger** poke
**thrust with knife** stab
**thrust with sword** lunge
**thug** assassin, bandit, bruiser, bully, cutthroat, gangster, hood, hooligan, killer, lout, mugger, murderer, robber, ruffian, skollie, tough, tsotsi
**thuggery** gangsterism
**thumb** ovolo, pollex
**thumb a lift** hitchhike
**thumb one's nose at** deride, flout, mock, ridicule
**thumbs down** disapproval, negation, no, prohibition, refusal, rejection, veto
**thunder** crash, denounce, detonate, explode, menace, resound, reverberate, roar, roll, rumble, rumbling
**Thursday is named after him** Thor
**thus** accordingly, consequently, der (G), hence, ita (L), sic (L), so, therefore
**thus far** hitherto, yet
**thus in many places** sic passim (L)
**thus in the original** sic in originali (L)
**thus the law stands written** ita lex scripta (L)
**thus used** sic
**thwart** across, adverse, avoid, baffle, check, contravene, counter, cross(-grained), crosswise, encounter, foil, frustrate, hinder, interrupt, oblique, obstruct, oppose, prevent, seat, stall, stymie, transverse
**thyme is one** herb
**thyroid** shield-shaped
**thyroid projection** Adam's apple
**tiara** coronet, crown, diadem, headdress, headgear, mitre, regalia
**Tibet** Lamaland
**Tibetan antelope** goa, sus
**Tibetan breed of cattle** dzo, z(h)o
**Tibetan Buddhist monk** lama
**Tibetan capital** Lhasa
**Tibetan cattle** yak
**Tibetan dialect** dzongkha
**Tibetan gazelle** goa
**Tibetan horned ruminant** takin
**Tibetan ox** yak
**Tibetan priest** lama
**Tibetan wild sheep** sha
**tibia** shinbone
**tic** blink, flutter, jerk, pull, spasm, twinge, twitch(ing)
**tick** acarid, check, credit, ked, mattress, mite, moment
**ticket scalper** tout
**ticket window** grille, guichet
**ticking over** idle, idling

**tickle** amuse, divert, enchant, fascinate, gladden, prick, rejoice, sting, tingle, twitch
**tickled pink** amused
**tickling the ivories** playing
**ticklish** awkward, critical, delicate, risky, thorny, touchy, tricky, uncertain, unsteady
**tick off** berate, chide, rebuke, reprimand, scold
**tick over** idle
**tidal bore** eagre
**tidal current** rip
**tidal mouth of large river** estuary
**tidal phase** neap
**tidal wave** bore, eagre, flood, spate
**tiddly** small, tiny, tipsy
**tiddlywinks** ludo
**tide** befall, course, current, drift, ebb, flood, flow, movement, neap, rip, season, surf, surge, time, trend
**tide over** aid, assist, endure, help, weather
**tide reflux** ebb
**tidily** cleanly, methodically, neatly, sprucely, trimly
**tidiness** neatness, order(liness), spruceness, symmetry, systematicness, trim(ness)
**tidings** advice, greeting, information, news, notification, rumour, whisper, word
**tidy** arranged, attentive, careful, clean, exact, fastidious, immaculate, methodical, meticulous, neat, orderly, particular, prim, schematic, shipshape, spruce, systematic, thorough, trim
**tidy arrangement** order
**tidy feathers** preen
**tie** affiliation, allegiance, anchor, attach(ment), band, bind, bond, commitment, confine, connect(ion), contest, cord, cravat, deadlock, deuce, draw, duty, equal, fasten(ing), fixture, game, gird, hamper, hinder, hindrance, hold, join(t), knot, lace, lash, liaison, ligament, limit(ation), link, lock, match, moor, neckwear, obligate, obligation, oblige, relationship, restrain(t), restrict(ion), rope, secure, stalemate, strap, string, tether, unite
**tie a boat** moor
**tie again** retie
**tie a score** even
**tie down** secure
**tied shoe** laced
**tied up** bound
**tie fast** bind
**tie in** connect
**tie in tennis** deuce

**tie of cord** knot
**tie on shoe** lace
**tier** bank, echelon, file, hierarchy, layer, level, line, order, range, rank, row, series, stratum
**tiered garden** terrace
**ties of blood** kin(ship), relation
**tie together** bundle
**tie up** attach, bind, bundle, conclude, end, engage, engross, fasten, lash, ligate, moor, occupy, pinion, restrain, rope, secure, settle, terminate, tether, truss, unite
**tie-up** bottleneck, clog, congestion, connection, delay, entanglement, retardation, slowdown, stoppage
**tie up boat** moor
**tie up with** implicate
**tie with rope** bind
**tiff** affray, argument, brawl, breach, clash, conflict, contention, contretemps, controversy, debate, difference, disagreement, discord(ance), dispute, dram, feud, fight, fracas, fray, imbroglio, noise, quarrel, row, rumpus, scrap, spat, squabble, strife, tumult, uproar, vendetta, wrangle
**tiger's warning** roar
**tight** close, compact, constricted, crowded, difficult, firmly, rigid, scarce, snug, stingy, strict, taut(ly), tense(ly)
**tight Chinese dress with high collar and slit skirt** cheongsam
**tighten spring in clock** wind
**tighten spring in clock again** rewind
**tight-fisted** close, mean, mingy, miserly, near, niggardly, parsimonious, stingy, ungenerous
**tight-fitting garment** hose, leotard, tricot
**tight loop** kink(le)
**tightly closed hand** fist
**tightly drawn** taut
**tightly moored** girt
**tight-rope walker** aerialist, funambulist
**tight tartan trousers** trews
**tightwad** churl, harpy, hoarder, hunks, miser, niggard, scrooge, skinflint
**Tigris ferry boat** gufa
**tile** carreau, imbrex, lump, maintile, pament, pantile, quarry, slat, slate(r), tessera
**tiled part of house** roof
**tiler** hel(li)er
**tile used in mosaic** abaculus, tessera
**tiling** tessellating
**till** cash register, cultivate, dig, money-drawer, plough, until

**tillable** arable, cultiva(ta)ble, farmable, fecund, fertile, fruitful, ploughable, productive, prolific, workable
**tillage** agriculture, cultivation, culture, farming, husbandry
**till doomsday** eternally
**tiller** agriculturist, agronomist, cultivator, farmer, gardener, helm, husbandman, plower, plowman, sapling, seedling, shoot, sprout, sucker
**till now** hitherto
**till operator** cashier
**till shortage** deficit
**till the cows come home** forever
**till the end of time** perpetually
**till the land** farm
**till we meet again** au revoir (F), auf Wiedersehen (G), goodbye
**tilt** angle, attack, battle, cant, clash, contend, contest, duel, encounter, fence, fight, incline, joust, lean, list, oppose, pitch, skirmish, slant, slope, spar, tip, upend
**tilted and nearly falling** atilt
**tilted position** cant
**tilted window** dowager
**tilth** cultivation, tillage, tilling
**tilt of road** camber
**tilt over to one side** careen
**timbal** kettledrum
**timber** beams, boards, copse, forest, logs, lumber, (red)wood, thicket, trees
**timber bend** camber, sny
**timber disease** dry rot
**timber for flooring** batten
**timber machine** sawmill
**timber measure** stere
**timber-processing plant** sawmill
**timber recess** rabber
**timber resembling mahogany** sapele
**timber source** tree
**timber support for rails** sleeper
**timber thickness** ply
**timber tool** adze
**timber to support a vessel while being launched** poppet
**timber tree** ash, cedar, imbuia, maple, teak, tombotie, yellow wood
**timber wolf** lobo
**timbrel** tambourine
**timbrology** philately, stamp collecting
**time** age, attention, chance, duration, era, experience, gauge, instant, interval, lifetime, measure, moment, months, opportunity, period, regulate, rhythm, season, tempo, tide, years
**time after time** recurrently, repeatedly
**time after which one must stay indoors** curfew

**time and again** frequently, often, repeatedly
**time at one's disposal** leisure
**time at which the proceeds of a policy are due to be paid** maturity
**time before Noah's flood** antediluvian
**time between lunch and the evening** afternoon
**timed** clocked
**time due to arrive** ETA
**time flies** tempus fugit (L)
**time for chocolate eggs** Easter
**time free from work** leisure
**time gone by** ago, past
**time immediately before rocket launch** countdown
**time immemorial** antiquity
**time in class** schooldays
**time indicator** clock, sundial, watch
**time in office** term
**time intervening** interim
**time in which an army keeps the field** campaign
**time in which one is away** absence
**time just before** eve
**timekeeper** chronometer
**timeless** ageless, amaranthine, dateless, endless, eternal, everlasting, immortal, perpetual, undying
**time limit** deadline
**time long ago** yore
**timely** cogent, convenient, due, duly, favourable, fortunate, happy, judicious, lucky, opportune, pat, prompt, punctual, seasonable, suitable, timeful, towardly, well-timed
**time-measuring instrument** chronometer, sun-dial
**time of darkness** night
**time off** furlough, leave, vacation
**time of fasting** Lent, Ramad(h)an, Yom Kippur
**time off for a funeral** compassionate leave
**time off for illness** sick leave
**time of flowering** florescence
**time off sentence** remission
**time off when ill** sick leave
**time of gathering grapes** vintage
**time of greatest prosperity** heyday
**time of life** age
**time of rejoicing** jubilee
**time on one's hands** idleness
**timeous state** earliness
**time past** ago
**time period** aeon, age, day, epoch, era, hour, moment, month, series, span, week, year
**timepiece** clock, dial, horologe, watch
**timepiece pointer** hand
**time-related decree** nisi

**time required to retrieve piece of stored information** access time
**time signals** pips
**time to be off the streets** curfew
**time to come** future
**time unit** hour, minute, month, second, year
**time when a thing happens** occasion
**time without end** eternity, perpetually
**time worked in addition to regular hours** overtime
**time zone symbol** EST
**timid** bashful, cowardly, diffident, faint-hearted, fearful, humble, meek, pavid, pusillanimous, sheepish, shrinking, shy, spineless, timorous, unassuming, weak-kneed
**timidity** bashfulness, cowardice, diffidence, fearfulness, humility, modesty, shyness, timidness, trepidation
**timidly** meekly, shyly
**timid or cowardly** nesh
**timid rodent** mouse
**timing device** stopwatch
**timing piece** cam
**timorous** afraid, alarmed, anxious, apprehensive, backward, bashful, constrained, cowardly, coy, craven, dastardly, diffident, doubtful, fearful, frightened, insecure, intimidated, meek, nervous, reluctant, reserved, scared, self-conscious, shy, soft, suspicious, timid, unsure, weak
**timothy** fodder grass
**tin** can(ister)
**tincal** borax
**tincture** aroma, colour, complexion, concentrate, distillate, dye(stuff), essence, extract, flavour, hint, hue, infusion, paint, pigment, scent, shade, smell, stain, tinge, tint, tone, trace
**tincture of opium** laudanum, paregoric
**tincture of some evil quality** taint
**tincture used in treating bruises** arnica
**tin cup** pannikin
**tinder** kindling
**tinder from fungi** amadou
**tine** fork, prong, snag, tooth
**tinea** ringworm
**tinfoil** tain
**tinge** cast, colour, dye, flavour, hue, imbue, instil, nuance, season, shade, smack, soupçon, stain, taste, tincture, tint, tone, touch, trace
**tinge with gold** gild
**tingle** adventure, arouse, bite, blush, burn, colour, consciousness, crawl, electrify, excite, feeling, fill, flush, glow, hurt, impression, irritate, itch,

move, pain, perception, pleasure, prickle, radiate, sensation, sense, smart, stimulate, sting, stir, thrill, throb, tickle, titillation, wound
**tinker** putter, botch
**tinkle** chime, clank, clink, ding, jangle, jingle, knell, peal, ring, ting, toll
**tinkling of bells** tintinnabulation
**tin lizzie** jalopy, tjorrie
**tin mine** stannary
**tinny** metallic
**tin or iron** metal
**tint** colour, dye, hue, rinse, stain, tincture, tinge
**tinted glasses** shades
**tintinnabulation** bell, chime, clang, ding, gong, jingle, peal, resounding, rhyme, ring, tinkle
**tintinnabulum** bell
**tiny** animalcular, bantam, delicate, diminutive, dwarfish, itsy-bitsy, lilliputian, little, microscopic, midget, mini(ature), minuscule, minute, peewee, pygmy, small, teeny, wee
**tiny amount** iota, trace
**tiny aperture** pinhole
**tiny arachnid** mite
**tiny bird** mossie, wren
**tiny bottle** phial
**tiny child** piccanin, pik(kie), tot
**tiny farm** smallholding
**tiny fragments** smithereens
**tiny insect** ant, flea, gnat, midge, mite, mosquito, muggie
**tiny instrument with sharp point** pin
**tiny invertebrate animal** insect
**tiny loop** eyelet
**tiny mammal** bat, mouse, shrew
**tiny measure** micron
**tiny organism** microbe
**tiny parasite** gnat
**tiny particle** atom, electron
**tiny people in** *Gulliver's Travels* Lilliputians
**tiny piece** little, minim, particle, portion, scanty, whit
**tiny republic** San Marino
**tiny sphere** spherule
**tiny sum of money** mite
**tiny tree** bonsai
**tiny water plant** alga
**tip** advice, apex, capsize, clue, crown, dump, end, extra, extremity, gratuity, hint, incline, list, peak, pinnacle, pitch, point(er), pourboire (F), prong, reward, slant, tap, tilt, top(ple), tumble, upturn, warning
**tip of boot** toe cap
**tip of cone** apex
**tip-off** clue, hint, warning
**tip of tail** tag
**tip of triangle** apex

**tip one's hat** doff
**tip over** cant, overturn, upend, upset
**tippler** alestake, boozer, drinker, dronkie, dronklap, drunk, imbiber, maltworm, soak, sot, souse, winer
**tipster's choice** nap
**tipsy** dronk, drunk, happy, loaded, merry, pickled, soused, stewed, stoned, tiddly, tight
**tiptoe** caution, cautious, creep, eager, sneak, stealth
**tip to one side** careen, heel, tilt
**tirade** diatribe, harangue, outburst
**tirailleur** gunman, rifleman, shooter, skirmisher, sniper
**tire** exasperate, exhaust, fatigue, jade, weary
**tired** drowsy, exhausted, fatigue(d), sleepy, weary
**tired and sluggish** lethargic
**tiredness** drowsiness, fatigue, lethargy, sleepiness, weariness
**tired out** exhausted, jaded, spent, whacked, worn
**tire out** exhaust
**tiresome** annoying, dull, fatiguing, tedious, vexatious, wearisome
**tiresome person** bore
**tiring** annoying, arduous, boring, draining, drooping, exacting, exhausting, failing, fatiguing, flagging, harassing, irking, irritating, laborious, onerous, sinking, strenuous, tedious, tough, wearisome, wear(y)ing
**tiring walk** slog
**tiro** learner, tyro
**tisane** ptisan
**tissue** accumulation, agglomeration, brawn, chain, character, coating, collection, combination, concatenation, conglomeration, consistency, fabric, fabrication, film, flesh, gauze, grain, interweaving, layer, mass, meat, membrane, mesh, network, pack, paper, pile, quality, scum, series, structure, stuff, texture, tissue-paper, weave, web, weight
**tissue analysis** biopsy
**tissue around the embryo in seeds** endosperm
**tissue attached to muscle** tendon
**tissue binding bones** ligament
**tissue decay** gangrene
**tissue examination** biopsy
**tissue hardening** sclerosis
**tissue in bone cavity** marrow
**tissue lining** membrane
**Titan** giant

**titanic** colossal, gigantic, herculean, huge, immense, mighty, monstrous, stout, vast
**titanium oxide** rutile
**titanium principal ore** ilmenite
**Titan who shouldered the heavens** Atlas
**titbit** bite, dainty, dash, delicacy, luxury, morsel, mouthful, nibble, nip, relish, sample, savoury, snack, touch
**tit for tat** reprisal, retaliation
**tithe** teind (Sc), tenth
**Titian red** auburn
**titivate** adorn, preen, primp, smarten
**title** appellation, championship, claim, denominate, denomination, designation, entitle, esquire, graf (G), name, right, sir
**title assumed by Mussolini** duce
**title before a man's name** mister, mr
**titled class** aristocracy
**titled classes** peerage
**titled ecclesiastic** prelate
**titled man** baron, count, knight, sir
**titled woman** dame, lady
**titleholder** champ(ion), exceller, incumbent, owner, titlist, victor, winner
**title of ancient kings of Peru** Inca
**title of baronet** sir
**title of canonised person** saint
**title of cardinal** Eminence
**title of clergyman** Reverend
**title of distinction** honourable
**title of eminent Frenchman** monseigneur
**title of emperor of Japan** mikado
**title of former ruler of Persia** shah
**title of Frenchman** Monsieur
**title of Gandhi** Mahatma
**title of German man** herr
**title of German married woman** frau
**title of governor in India** nawab
**title of honour** baronet, earl, lord, sir
**title of Italian man** signor
**title of Italian unmarried woman** signorina
**title of Italian woman** signora
**title of knight** sir
**title of monk** fra
**title of nobility** lord
**title of prelate** monsignor
**title of property** deed
**title of rank** baron(ess), lady, lordship, sir(e)
**title of royalty** highness
**title of some Indian princes** maharaja
**title of unmarried woman** miss, ms
**title of various Muslim rulers** amir
**title of woman of rank** lady
**title on cross** INRI
**titmouse** tomtit

**titter** chortle, chuckle, giggle, smirk, snicker, snigger
**tittle-tattle** bavardage (F), blab, chatter, dob, gabble, gossip, hearsay, murmur, ouï-dire (F), palaver, prattle, report, rumour, skinder
**titular** appellative, designatory, epithetic, eponym, formal, honorary, named, naming, nominal, official, ostensible, powerless, pretended, professed, puppet, putative, self-styled, supposed, tagged, theoretical, token
**titular head of university** chancellor
**TNT** trinitrotoluene, trotyl
**to** against, at, tae (Sc), towards, until, unto
**to a certain extent** somewhat
**to act or speak evasively** prevaricate
**toad** amphibian, frog
**toadeater** parasite, sycophant
**toadfish** puffer, sapo
**toadflax** linaria, ransted
**to a disgusting extent** ad nauseam
**toadstool** canker, fungus, grisette
**toady** crawl(er), creep, cringe, fawn(er), flatter(er), grovel, hanger-on, jackal, kowtow, lackey, parasite, stooge, sycophant
**to a fault** excessively, immoderately, ridiculously, unduly
**to a great extent** chiefly, largely, mainly, widely
**to a higher position** up
**to all intentions and purposes** practically, virtually
**to a man** everyone, unanimously
**to an appreciable extent** considerably
**to and fro** around
**to and upon** onto
**to angle** fish
**to a nicety** exactly, meticulously, precisely
**to an increasing extent** increasingly
**to a noticeable degree** fairly
**to any point** anywhere
**to a position within** into
**to appropriate money in trust** embezzle
**to ascribe** credit
**toast** darling, drink, favourite, grill, health, pledge, roast, saluation, salute, tribute
**toasted cheese** rarebit
**toastmaster** symposiarch
**toast oneself** bask
**toast when drinking** cheers, l' chaim, nazdarovya, prosit, salud, skoal, yasas
**to attract or please the rabble** ad captandum vulgus (L)

**to a turn** correctly, exactly, perfectly, precisely
**to a vessel's stem** aft
**tobacco alkaloid** nicotine
**tobacco bag** pouch
**tobacco box** humidor
**tobacco chewing** cud, plug, quid
**tobacco disease** calico, mosaic
**tobacco juice** ambeer, praiss
**tobacco kiln** oast
**tobacco left in pipe** dottel, dottle
**tobacco narcotic** nicotine
**tobacco pipe** meerschaum
**tobacco powder** snuff
**tobacco pressed hard** plug
**tobacco product** cheroot, cigar(ette)
**tobacco shreds** shag
**to ban** forbid
**to bare** uncover
**to bargain** haggle
**to be** esse (L), exist, ser (Sp)
**to be added** plus
**to be astonished at nothing** nil admirari (L)
**to beat noisily** bang, whang
**to be contiguous** abut
**to be effusive** gush
**to be found** occur
**to begin with** first
**to be in agony** throe
**to be in debt** owe
**to be kept private** secret
**to be overcome with anger** fume
**to be paid** owing
**to be reckoned with** consequential, important, influential, powerful, strong, weighty
**to be rendered stupid** hebetate
**to be sure** bien entendu (F), indeed
**to be unwilling to prosecute** nolle prosequi
**toboggan** car(r)iole, coast, drop, sled(ge)
**to border upon** abut
**to break** infract
**to bridge** span
**to bring up** nurture, raise
**to build a nest** nidificate, nidify
**toby** jug, mug
**to change into stone** lapidify
**tocher** dowry, lobola
**to choose** elect, opt
**to cite as an example or proof** adduce
**to clear** rid
**to clear from blame** exonerate
**tocology** midwifery, obstetrics, tokology
**to come** future, impending, later
**to come back** return
**to complete** finalise
**to confirm** endorse
**to congeal** set

**to conquer or die** aut vincere aut mori (L)
**tocopherol** vitamin E
**to couple** twin
**to court a woman** woo
**to crow** exult
**to cut into pieces** cantle
**tod** bush, fox
**to date** now
**today** nowadays
**toddle** amble, stroll, totter
**toddler** baby, brat, child, descendant, infant, issue, juvenile, kid, lightie, minor, offspring, piccanin, pik(kie), progeny, suckling, tot, youngster
**to destroy the validity of** annul
**to die by submersion** drown
**to dip in liquid** sop
**to dirty** smirch
**to divine** scry
**to-do** ado, commotion, fuss, quarrel, rumpus
**to do a favour for** oblige
**to do this is human** err
**to dress up** tog
**to drive back** repel
**toe** tae (Sc)
**to each his own** suum cuique (L)
**to each one** apiece
**to eat dinner** dine
**toe bursa** bunion
**to elbow** nudge
**to engraft** implant
**to enliven** animate
**to entertain** divert
**to entrance** enthrall
**to erase** raze
**to err is human** errare est humanum (L)
**toe-stubbing obstacle** stone
**toe the line** acquiesce, conform, obey
**to exclude from a place** debar
**to exercise the mind** think
**to exploit** use
**to extremities** à outrance (F)
**to eye** ogle
**to feast and give pleasure to** regale
**toffee** sweet
**toffee-nosed person** pretentious, snob, superciliou s
**to fill with fear** alarm
**to flag** droop
**to flatter servilely** adulate
**to free** rid
**to frequent** haunt
**toft** hillock, homestead
**toga** robe
**to get** obtain
**together** along, closely, co-, coincidentally, collectively, concurrently, conjointly, contemporaneously, en block, en

masse, en même temps (F), mutually, reciprocally, simultaneously, successively, syn-, synchronously, united
**together again** reunited
**together with** along, and, including
**to give a name to** entitle
**to give out** emit
**to gloss over** varnish
**to go among people** mingle
**to go before** precede
**to go on plundering raid** maraud
**to harness** inspan
**to her** lui (F)
**to hit ball** bunt, lob, swat
**to humble** abase, humiliate
**toil** drudge, effort, exert(ion), grub, labour, moil, slavery, strain, strive, task, travail, work
**toilet** ablutions, bathing, bathroom, closet, convenience, dressing, grooming, latrine, lavatory, loo, outhouse, privy, toilette, urinal, washroom, WC
**toilet powder** talc
**toiletries** cosmetics
**toilet tank** cistern
**toilet water** cologne, perfume
**toilsome** laborious
**toil tediously** droil
**toil wearily** moil
**to infinity** ad infinitum
**to inform against** peach
**to inject drugs** shoot
**token** badge, emblem, memento, minimal, portent, sign, superficial, symbol(ic), ticket
**token given as present** gift voucher
**token of affection** embrace, kiss
**to kindle** ignite
**tokology** midwifery, obstetrics, tocology
**Tokyo drama** no(h)
**Tokyo of old** Edo
**Tokyo street** Ginza
**to labour** toil
**to lance** spear
**told in verse** poetical
**to leave by will or testament** bequeath
**to leeward** alee
**tolerable** abidable, acceptable, adequate, allowance, average, bearable, endurable, fair, indifferent, mediocre, ordinary, passable, permissible
**tolerance** endurance, lenience, lenity, mercifulness, patience, stamina, sympathy, variation
**tolerant** abiding, accepting, clement, complaisant, considerate, easy(-going), gentle, indulgent, lax, lenient, liberal, merciful, patient, soft,

understanding, undogmatic, unprejudiced
**tolerant towards people** understanding
**tolerate** abide, accord, admit, allow, approve, bear, countenance, endure, favour, gratify, indulge, oblige, permit, recognise, sanction, suffer, take, vouchsafe, warrant, withstand
**toleration** allowance, condonation, consideration, endurance, forbearance, franchise, generosity, humanity, indulgence, laissez faire, latitude, lenity, liberality, liberty, license, mercy, play, range, sufferance
**to let** offering, rentable
**to level with the ground** rase, raze
**to live** exist
**toll** assessment, charge, dues, duty, fee, impost, knell, levy, payment, peal, ring, strike, tariff, tax
**toll gate** turnpike
**tolling** calling, chiming, clanging, pealing, ringing, signalling, sounding, striking, warning
**toll of bell** knell
**tolu** balsam
**tomahawk** hatchet
**to make a cat's howling cry** caterwaul
**to make a garment** sew
**to make an escape** get away
**to make legal** legalise
**to make tea** brew
**tomato** fruit, love-apple, vegetable
**tomato-coloured** red
**tomato sauce** ketchup
**to mature** age, mellow, ripen
**tomb** burial, catacomb, cerotaph, chamber, cromlech, crypt, dolmen, excavation, grave, mastaba, mausoleum, memorial, monument, pyramid, reliquary, sarcophagus, sepulchre, shrine, tabut, vault
**tomb in church** sacellum
**tomb inscription** epitaph
**tomb-like monument to persons buried elsewhere** cenotaph
**tomb marker** gravestone
**tomb of a saint** shrine
**tomboy** coquette, flirt, gamine, hemp, hoyden, hussy, imp, jade, madcap, minx, ramp, romp, tomrig, urchin, wanton, whippersnapper
**tomb site of Tutankhamen** Karnak
**tombstone inscription** epitaph
**tomcat** gib
**to mint** coin
**to mirror** reflect
**to mistake the meaning of** misconstrue
**tomorrow** mañana (Sp)

**to move swiftly like clouds** scud
**Tom's cartoon partner** Jerry
**to muse or think about deeply** meditate
**tonal difference** schisma
**to name** dub, nominate
**tone** attitude, firm, hue, moderate, pitch, quality, sound, temper, tenor
**tone down** alleviate, assuage, bleach, dampen, dim, etiolate, fade, mitigate, moderate, modify, modulate, muffle, mute, pale, quiet, reduce, restrain, silence, soft-pedal, soften, subdue, temper, whiten
**tone in with** harmonise
**toneless** boring, colourless, deep, droning, dull, flat, hollow, humdrum, low, monotonous, muffled, muted, plodding, repetitive, repetitious, rumbling, soporific, tedious, tiresome, unchanging, unvaried
**tone up** freshen, retouch, spruce
**tongue** dialect, language, lingua(l), patois, vernacular
**tongue in cheek** facetiously, insincerely, jestingly, jokingly, mockingly, sarcastically
**tongue-lashing** earful
**tongue of bell** clapper
**tongue of fire** flame
**tongue-tied** aphasic, astounded, bashful, dumb(stricken), dumbstruck, inarticulate, mum, mute, quiet, shocked, silent, soundless, speechless, taciturn, untalkative, voiceless, wordless
**tonic** boost, cordial, fillip, keynote, medicine, pickup, refresher, roborant, stimulant
**to no degree** not
**to no purpose** futilely, uselessly
**tonsil** adenoid, amygdala
**tonsor** barber
**too** also, besides, excessively, exorbitantly, extremely, further, inordinately, likewise, moreover, over(ly), ridiculous, tae (Sc), unduly, unreasonable, very
**too delicately wrought** finical, finicking, finicky
**too difficult** insoluble
**too distant** overfar
**too dry for vegetables** arid
**too fancifully** overimaginatively
**too fussy** finical, finicky, finicking
**too great for description in words** ineffable
**too hasty** premature
**too heavy** corpulent, obesity, overheavy, overponderous, overweight
**too high an opinion of oneself** pride

**too highly strung** overstrung
**too highly valued** overrated
**too insignificant for serious consideration** derisory
**took a second job** moonlighted
**tool** agency, agent, aid, apparatus, appliance, auger, awl, axe, brush, chisel, contraption, contrivance, device, dupe, gadget, hacksaw, handle, hireling, implement, instrument, intermediary, lathe, lever, machine, means, medium, minion, pawn, plane, puppet, rasp, reamer, saw, spanner, stooge, trigger, trowel, utensil, vehicle, weapon
**tool for boring** drill
**tool for chopping** axe
**tool for cutting grass** sickle
**tool for digging** spade
**tool for engraving** burin
**tool for gripping** pincers
**tool for gripping nut of a screw** spanner, wrench
**tool for hollowing out** scoop
**tool for lath splitting** frow
**tool for making holes** awl
**tool for perforating** punch
**tool for pruning** bill
**tool for removing weeds** weeder
**tool for shaping wood** spokeshave
**tool for tuning a harp** wrest
**tool for twisting** wrench
**tool handle** helve
**too light** underweight
**too long delayed** late, tardy
**tool to pierce holes** (brad)awl
**tool to shave hides** skiver, slater
**tool to surface wood** plane
**tool used by cobbler** awl
**too many to be counted** innumerable
**too much** excess(ive), over
**too much pride in oneself** conceit
**to one's face** directly, openly, straight
**to one side** agee, ajee, apart, aside, askew, away, awry
**to one's liking** agreeable
**to one's taste** ad gustum (L), agreeable
**too old** overage
**too pat** glib
**too proper** prim
**too quickly** hastily
**too ready to believe** credulous
**too sacred to be uttered** ineffable
**too small to be considered** negligible
**too small to be noticed** imperceptible
**too small to be perceived** insensible
**too soon** early, premature
**too strong a response** overreaction
**too sure of oneself** smug

**tooth** biter, canine, cog, fang, grinder, incisor, laniary, milktooth, molar, point, premolar, projection, tine, tusk
**toothache** dentalgia, odontalgia
**tooth and nail** fiercely, frantically, furiously, madly, savagely, wildly
**toothbed** gum
**tooth coating** enamel
**tooth decay** caries, cavity
**tooth distress** ache
**tooth doctor** dentist
**tooth drill** burr
**toothed bar** ratchet
**toothed instrument** comb, rasp, rowel, saw
**toothed irregularly** erose
**toothed metal fastener** zip
**toothed rack** ratchet
**toothed wheel** cog, gear, pinion, ratchet, roulette, rowel, sprocket
**tooth filing** amalgam, inlay
**tooth for tooth** reprisal
**tooth gear** cog
**tooth gnashing** bruxism
**toothless** edental, edentate, edentulous, gummy
**toothlike** odontoid
**toothlike projection** dentil
**tooth of comb** dent
**tooth of snake** fang
**tooth of wheel** cog
**toothpaste flavour** mint
**tooth problem** ache
**tooth projection** cusp
**tooth puller** dentist, forceps
**tooth socket** alveolus
**toothsome** palatable, tasty
**tooth specialist** dentist
**tooth substitute** denture
**tooth support** gum
**tooth trouble** ache
**toothy smile** grin
**too unusual to be described** indescribable
**to outdo** cap
**too young** underage
**top** acme, apex, best, brow, cap, ceiling, chief, crop, culmination, excel, greatest, head, lid, outdo, peak, principal, summit, surpass, uppermost, upside, vertex
**top actor** star
**to pale** blanch
**topaz hummingbird** ava
**top banana** boss
**top can do it** spin
**top card** ace
**top competitor** champion
**top course of masonry in wall** coping
**tope** booze, carouse, revel, tipple
**to peel off** flake

**toper** alcoholic, alkie, boozer, dipsomaniac, drinker, dronkie, dronklap, drunk(ard), inebriate, soak, sot, sponge, tippler, wino
**top fighter pilot** ace
**top for pan** lid
**top hat** beaver, headgear, topper
**top high school qualification** matriculation
**topi** sun-helmet, topee
**topic** affair, agenda, argument, axiom, case, chapter, class, concept, concern, declaration, idea, interest, issue, keynote, matter, notion, opinion, point, policy, section, subject, text, theme, theorem, theory, thesis
**topical** circulated, current, district, familiar, local, parochial, popular, regional, territorial, thematic(al)
**topical comedy show** revue
**topic of discourse** subject, theme
**to pieces** apart
**to pierce with horn or tusk** gore
**top in priority** uppermost
**to pity** ad misericordiam (L)
**topknot** crest, tuft
**top level** ceiling, high
**topmast crossbar** fid
**topmost** highest
**top of altar** mensa
**top of anything** apex
**top of bottle** neck
**top of doorway** lintel
**top of dress** yoke
**top of foot** instep
**top of head** cranium, crown, pate, scalp, sconce
**top of hill** crest
**top of its suit** ace
**top of leg** thigh
**top of milk** cream
**top of mine shaft** pithead
**top of nose** nasion
**top of pollen-bearing stamen in a flower** anther
**top of room** ceiling
**top of volcano** crater
**top of wall** coping
**top of wave** crest
**topographer** mapmaker
**topographical name** toponym
**toponym** place name
**top or bottom post of stair rail** newel
**top order batsman** opener
**top part of shoe** upper
**top performer** star, ace
**top playing card** ace
**topple** capsize, collapse, drop, fall, fell, lurch, overbalance, overthrow, overturn, pitch, subvert, tip, unseat, upset

**toppled** defeated, overthrown
**toppling** cascading, collapsing, crashing, dashing, descending, diving, falling, hurtling, lurching, pitching, plunging, tipping
**top point** tip
**top pupil** dux
**to preserve from decay** embalm
**to profane** desecrate
**top room** attic
**top secret** hush-hush
**topsoil** surface
**top spun with fingers** teetotum
**to pull** lug
**top up** fill, replenish
**to put off project until later date** mothball
**to put to practical use** apply
**toque** cap, hat, turban
**tor** hill, koppie
**Torah** Pentateuch
**to raise** uplift
**torch** (fire)brand, flashlight, link
**torch music** blues
**toreador** bullfighter, torero
**to rear of ship** astern
**to reason** argue
**to relax government restrictions** unfreeze
**to represent on the stage** perform
**torero** bullfighter, toreador
**to resist to the uttermost** ditch
**to rights** arranged, straight, tidy
**to risk one's money** bet
**torment** afflict, agonise, agony, anguish, annoy, bait, bedevil, distress, excruciate, fret, harass, irritate, needle, pain, plague, rack, rag, tantalise, taunt, tease, torture, trouble, vex
**torment acutely** excruciate
**tormentor** torturer
**torment with disappointment** tantalise
**torn** cut, divided, irresolute, jagged, lacerated, ragged, reft, rent, ripped, riven, slit, uncertain, unsure, wavering
**tornado** cyclone, gale, hurricane, squall, storm, tempest, twister, typhoon, whirlwind
**torn cloth** rag
**torn clothes** rags
**torn piece** shred
**torn shred** tatter
**torn skin at root of fingernail** agnail
**torn strip** fragment, shred
**torn violently** riven
**toro** bull
**torpid** anergic, apathetic, benumbed, comatose, dead, dormant, dull, heavy, inactive, indolent, inert, insensible, languid, latent, lax,
lethargic, lifeless, numb, passive, slow, sluggish, spiritless, stagnant
**torpidity** apathy, inaction, inertia, languor, lassitude, lethargy, listlessness, sloth, stagnation, stupor, torpor
**torpidness** apathetic, coolness, drowsiness, dullness, heaviness, idleness, inactivity, indolence, inertness, laziness, lifelessness, listlessness, numbness, passiveness, slackness, slowness, sluggishness, stillness, stupidity, stupidness, unfeelingness
**torpor** anergy, apathy, coma, coolness, deadness, dormancy, drowsiness, dullness, heaviness, idleness, immobility, impassivity, inaction, inactivity, indifference, inertia, insensibility, languor, lassitude, lethargy, listlessness, numbness, passiveness, passivity, rest, sleep, sloth, sluggishness, stoicism, stupor, torpidity, unconcern, unfeelingness, unresponsiveness
**torque** collar, force, necklace
**torrent** cascade, deluge, downpour, flow, outburst, stream
**torrid** ardent, arid, blazing, blistering, erotic, fervent, fiery, hot, humid, inflamed, lustful, muggy, parching, passionate, roasting, scorching, steamy, sultry, sweltering, sweltry, tropical
**torrid zone** tropics
**torso** trunk
**torticollis** wryneck
**tortilla with a meat or cheese filling** taco (Sp)
**tortilla with meat and chili sauce** enchilada
**tortoise** emyd, galapago, reptile, slowcoach, terrapin, turtle
**tortuosity** coil, turn, twist
**tortuous** bent, crooked, curved, evasive, indirect, roundabout, sinuate, twisted, twisting, winding
**tortuous of mind** devious
**torture** afflict, agony, anguish, curse, distress, disturb, grieve, hurt, inflict(ion), lacerate, martyr, misery, mistreat, oppress, pain, persecution, pervert, plague, punishment, rack, strain, suffering, torment, woe, wrench
**torturer** tormenter
**to run** trot
**Tory** conservative
**to scare** frighten
**to sea** asea
**to see and to be seen** visum visu (L)
**to seek out** hunt
**to set** gel
**to set on its side** upend
**tosh** bosh, rubbish
**to shock** appal
**to show clearly** evince
**to sin** err
**to skip** hop
**to slander** calumniate, malign
**to sleep on** bed
**to slope or incline** shelve
**to slow down vehicle** brake
**to soak in marinade** marinate
**to some extent** partially, partly, somewhat
**to sound a bell** ring
**to spectator's left** dexter
**toss** fling, flip, heave, hurl, lob, pitch, throw
**tossed by Highlanders** caber (Sc)
**tossed greens** salad
**tossing** agitating, casting, disturbing, flinging, hurling, jolting, launching, pitching, projecting, propelling, rocking, rolling, shaking, shying, slinging, thrashing, throwing, tumbling
**tossing and turning** insomnia, sleeplessness, wakefulness
**to start with** first
**to stop a vehicle** brake
**to stop up** occlude
**to such an extent** insofar, insomuch, so
**tot** add, babe, baby, calculate, child, dram, infant, lightie, measure, nip, piccanin, pik(kie), reckon, shot, tally, toddler, total
**to take back** withdraw
**total** add, aggregate, all, amount, collection, collective, combined, complete, entire(ty), extensive, final, finished, full, integral, lump, mass, net, outright, sum(ma), totality, universal, utter, whole, widespread
**total abstainer** non-drinker, teetotaller
**total abstinence from intoxicants** teetotalism
**total amount** entire, sum
**total blindness** amaurosis
**total break up** debacle
**total confusion** bedlam
**totality** aggregate, all(ness), completeness, entireness, entirety, fullness, universality, wholeness
**totality of members** union
**totalizator** tote
**total loss of speech** aphasia
**total loss of strength** exhaustion
**totally** absolutely, altogether, completely, entirely, fully, quite,

thoroughly, unconditionally, utterly, wholly
**totally wiped out** annihilated
**total number of employees** workforce
**total number of ens** ennage
**total of anything** amount
**total of opposite sides of dice** seven
**total points** score
**total possession** estate
**total property of deceased** estate
**total stock of words in language** lexis
**total up** add
**tote** carry, convey, drag, lug, totalizator
**to that extent** pro tanto (L), so
**to that place** there, thither
**to that time** till, until
**to the appointed day** ad diem (L)
**to the bad** astray
**to the bitter end** à outrance (F)
**to the bottom** à fond (F)
**to the centre** into
**to the death** à outrance (F)
**to the end** à outrance (F), ad finem (L)
**to the end of time** eternally
**to the extent that** inasmuch
**to the extreme** ad extremum (L)
**to the fore** ahead, available, forthcoming, ready
**to the full** entirely, fully, thoroughly, up
**to the good** up
**to the greater glory of God** ad majorem Dei gloriam (L)
**to the highest degree** par excellence (F)
**to the highest point** ad summum (L)
**to the hilt** completely, entirely, totally, wholly
**to the interior of** into
**to the left** aport, haw
**to the letter** accurately, canonicle, conforming, exactly, literally, orthodox, precisely, scriptural, verbatim
**to the man** ad hominem (L)
**to the memory of** in memoriam
**to the midpoint** halfway
**to the Orient** eastwards
**to the original tempo** atempo
**to the other side** over
**to the point** à propos (F), ad rem (L), applicable, apposite, appropriate, apt, brief, concise, direct, laconic, pertinent
**to the point of disgust** ad nauseam
**to the power of three** cube
**to the purpose** applicable, apposite, apropos, apt
**to the rear** aft, astern, back, behind
**to the rear of** abaft
**to the rear of a ship** aft
**to the same extent** as, even, so, such
**to the sheltered side** alee

**to the side of** by
**to the skies** excessively, extravagantly, highly, profusely
**to the stars** ad astra (L)
**to the teeth** completely, entirely, fully
**to the third power** cubed
**to the top** up
**to the utmost** à outrance (F)
**to the well-deserving** bene merenti (L)
**to the wide** completely
**to the word** ad verbum (L)
**to this** here(un)to
**to this degree** thus
**to this extent** quoad hoc (L), thus
**to this matter** hereto
**to this place** hither
**to throw missiles** pelt
**to tie up with rope** tether
**tot of liquor** dram
**to trade** swap
**tot's constant query** why
**totter** dodder, falter, reel, shake, stagger, teeter, toddle, tremble, waver
**tottery and weak** feeble
**tot up** add
**touch** abut, affect, attain, blow, contact, feel, handle, hint, impress, improve, meet, melt, modify, move, pat, reach, regard, stir, strike, tap, trace, trait, treat
**touch down** alight, arrive, land, stop
**touch gently** dab, tap
**touch given with lips** kiss
**touchiness** captiousness, crossness, crustiness, fretfulness, grumpiness, hypersensitivity, irascibility, irritability, jealousy, peevishness, petulance, sensitiveness, sensitivity, tetchiness
**touching** abutting, affecting, against, bordering, brushing, contacting, converging, disturbing, equalling, fondling, handling, impressing, marking, melting, moving, patting, piteous, pitiful, poignant, sad, stirring, striking, tapping, tender
**touching without intersecting** tangent
**touch judge** linesman
**touch lightly** dab, pat, tap
**touch lightly in passing** graze
**touch lovingly** caress, fondle
**touch made with sword at conferring of knighthood** accolade
**touch of bitterness** amari aliquid (L)
**touch off** actuate, arouse, begin, cause, fire, ignite, inflame, initiate, invoke, light, provoke
**touch of frost** nip
**touch on** broach, cite, cover, mention, quote, review, treat
**touch on the shoulder** tap

**touch the edge** lip
**touch up** improve, mend, perfect, renovate, titivate, upgrade
**touch with lips** kiss
**touch with the elbow** nudge
**touchy** cantankerous, captious, crabbed, cross, grouchy, grumpy, irritable, peevish, testy, tetchy, ticklish
**tough** brawny, callous, difficult, durable, firm, fit, hard(ened), hardy, irksome, knotty, leathery, merciless, obstinate, regrettable, resilient, resistant, resolute, rigid, rigorous, rough, ruffianly, rugged, ruthless, seasoned, severe, solid, stalwart, stern, stiff, stout, strenuous, strict, strong, sturdy, thorny, thug, troublesome, unbending, uphill, vicious, vigorous, violent, wiry
**toughen** anneal, buttress, fortify, harden, reinforce, rigidify, strengthen, temper, tighten
**toughen metal by heating and slow cooling** anneal
**tough fabric** denim
**tough fibrous body tissue** ligament
**tough flexible tissue** cartilage, gristle
**tough flexible twig** withe, withy
**tough light plastic** polythene
**tough light transparent plastic** perspex
**tough steel** armour plate
**tough synthetic rubber-like substance** neoprene
**tough thermoplastic** perspex
**tough white flexible tissue** cartilage
**tough wood** ash
**toupee** hairpiece, (peri)wig, peruke, rug, tuft
**tour** cruise, excursion, expedition, explore, jaunt, journey, outing, peregrinate, pilgrimage, safari, sail, sightsee, travel, trek, trip, visit, voyage
**tour guide** cicerone
**touring** sightseeing
**touring guide** map
**tourist** holiday-maker, rubberneck, sightseer, traveller, tripper, voyager
**tourist highlight** sight
**tour leader** cicerone, dragoman, guide
**tour of a number of inns** pub-crawl
**tour of duty** spell
**to use cigarettes** smoke
**to use up or reduce** deplete
**tousle** derange, disarrange, discompose, muss, ruffle, rumple, tangle, untidy, wrinkle
**tousled** disordered, messy, mussed, tangled, uncombed, untidy

**tout** advertise, advise, announce, broadcast, display, flaunt, headline, notify, plaster, praise, proclaim, promote, publicise, publish, splash, tipster, trumpet
**tout at auction** barker
**tout one's goods** peddle
**to veil** disguise
**tow** drag, haul, lift, pull
**to walk unsteadily** diddle, falter, stagger, totter
**toward** at, to(wards), unto
**towards** about, ad-, almost, approaching, approximately, apt, at, close, concerning, facing, favourable, for, imminent, near(ly), opportune, perfectly, practically, regarding, roughly, timely, to
**towards centre of a vessel** amidships
**towards earth** earthward
**towards front** forward, onward
**towards ground** down
**towards home** homeward
**towards interior** into, inwards
**towards land** landward, onshore
**towards left side of ship** aport
**towards lower part of** adown
**towards middle** into
**towards outside of ship** outboard
**towards setting sun** westward
**towards sheltered side** alee, leewards
**towards side** lateral(ly)
**towards sky** skyward(s)
**towards stern** astern
**towards sunrise** eastern
**towards sunset** west
**towards top** up
**to waste time** diddle
**to weary** tire
**towed vehicle** caravan, trailer
**to weed** hoe
**to welcome** greet
**towelling** terry
**towel pronoun** hers, his
**tower** ascend, barbican, bastille, bastion, belfry, belltower, campanile, castle, citadel, column, dome, dominate, exceed, fort(ification), fortress, keep, loom, minaret, mount, obelisk, overlook, overshadow, pagoda, pillar, rear, rise, skyscraper, soar, spire, steeple, stronghold, surpass, top, transcend, turret
**Tower Bridge city** London
**tower erected as landmark for aircraft** pylon
**tower for storing fodder or grain** silo
**tower for suspension of electric cables** pylon
**Tower of London guard** Beefeater
**tower of strength** comforter
**tower supporting cables** pylon

**to what place** whither
**to whom a debt is owing** creditor
**to wind into loops** coil
**towing rope** cable, hawser
**towing vessel** tug(boat)
**to wit** namely
**town** borough, burg, city, community, dorp, hamlet, machi (J), metropolis, township, village
**town-crier's call** oyez
**townee** townsman
**town expansion** urbanisation
**town house** maisonette
**town road** street
**town with a corporation** borough
**town with harbour** seaport
**town with local self-government** municipality
**to write on** paper
**to wrong** disserve
**toxic** deadly, harmful, lethal, noxious, pernicious, poisonous, septic, unhealthy
**toxic shrub** oleander
**toxic substance** poison
**toxin** poison, venom, virus
**toxin in tobacco** nicotine
**toxophilist loves it** archery
**toxophilite** archer
**toy** ball, dally, doll, gadget, golliwog, miniature, plaything, rattle, small, teddy(bear), trifle, trinket, yo-yo
**toy baby** doll
**toy bear** teddy
**toy catapult** slingshot
**toy on a string** yo-yo
**toy on string** kite
**toy spaniel** papillon
**tracasserie** ado, fuss, turmoil
**trace** copy, dab, delineate, diagram, discover, draw, evidence, footprint, hint, mark, record, sign, suggestion, taste, tinge, touch, trail, vestige
**trace back** refer
**trace of some colour** tinge
**trace out** spell
**tracer** bullet, inquirer, tracker
**trace symbols** write
**trace to** attribute
**trachea** airpipe, airway, duct, gullet, vessel, windpipe
**tracheocele** goitre, tumour
**tracing family descent** genealogical
**track** course, dog, follow, footprints, path, pursue, spoor, trail
**track along canal** towpath
**track and field events** athletics
**track by smell** scent
**track competitor** athlete
**track distance** lap

**track down** apprehend, capture, catch, detect, discover, expose, find, scrounge, trace, unearth
**tracked vehicle for use on snow** weasel
**tracker** pursuer
**track event** race
**track for horse riders** bridle-way
**track for jockeys** racecourse
**track for recreation** park, playground
**track for rolling stock** railway
**tracking device** radar, sonar
**tracking dog** bloodhound
**track left by ship** wake
**track of animal** spoor
**track of deer** slot
**track of hunted animal** foil
**track of satellite** orbit
**track or field competitor** athlete
**track or lane** path
**track punter** racegoer
**tract** area, dissertation, district, essay, leaflet, lot, pamphlet, plot, sermon, space, stretch, territory, treatise
**tractable** amendable, docile, ductile, flexible, governable, malleable, manageable, pliable, pliant, soft, tame, wieldy, willing, yielding
**tract between rivers** doab
**tract of cultivated land** farm
**tract of grassland** lea, prairie, veld
**tract of land** area, field, region, terrain
**tract of land with growing trees** wood
**tract of level country** plain, veld
**tract of level highland** plateau
**tract of marshy land** fen
**tract of open ground** lea
**tract of public land** park
**tract of treeless land** prairie
**tract of wasteland** moor
**tract on border of forest** purlieu
**tractor used for agricultural purposes** agrimotor
**tradable** exchangeable, merchantable
**trade** avocation, bargain, barter, business, commerce, craft, deal, employment, exchange, interchange, living, occupation, sale, traffic, vocation
**trade acceptance** draft
**trade agreement** cartel
**trade allowance** tret
**trade association** union
**trade ban** embargo
**trade body** union
**trade centre** mart
**trade discount** tret
**trade for money** sell
**trade goods** barter
**trade language** pidgin
**trademark** badge, brand, company, crest, hallmark, identification,

**trademark design**  insignia, label, logo(type), mark, marque de fabrique (F), motto, name, sign, slogan, stamp, symbol, tab, tag
**trademark design**  logo
**trademark for an organ formerly widely used in cinemas**  Wurlitzer
**trade name**  brand, kind, type
**trade name for amphetamine**  Benzedrine
**trade or exchange**  swap
**trade organisation**  union
**trade prohibition**  embargo
**trader**  broker, business(wo)man, businessperson, buyer, colporteur, dealer, hawker, merchant, retailer, salesman, salesperson, seller, shopkeeper, storekeeper, vendor
**trade rebate**  tret
**trade recession**  slump
**trader's bazaar stand**  stall
**trader to the army**  sutler
**tradesperson**  business(wo)man, businessperson, chandler, colporteur, craftsman, dealer, hawker, merchant, salesman, salesperson, seller, shopkeeper, storekeeper, vendor, workman
**trade with**  deal
**trading**  dealing
**trading authority**  franchise
**trading centre**  emporium, mart
**trading pact**  cartel
**tradition**  belief, convention, custom, folklore, legend, lore, rite
**traditional**  ancestral, conventional, customary, established, historic, typical, usual
**traditional beliefs**  folklore
**traditional Easter fruit cake**  simnel
**traditional fiction**  (folk)lore, legend, myth
**traditional Indian dress**  sari
**traditional in style**  classical
**traditional Irish belt**  crios
**traditional Italian dance**  saltarello
**traditional Japanese drama**  no(h)
**traditional Japanese inn**  ryokan
**traditional jazz**  trad
**traditional Jewish school**  yeshiva
**traditional knowledge**  lore
**traditional maxim**  adage, saw
**traditional narrative**  myth
**traditional pantomime character**  harlequin, pierrot
**traditional South African dish made of offal**  afval
**traditional story**  (folk)lore, legend, myth
**traditional tale**  legend
**traditional tales**  folklore
**traditional wisdom**  lore

**traduce**  abuse, blacken, calumniate, curse, decry, defame, denigrate, dishonour, disparage, insult, libel, malign, misrepresent, revile, slander, smear, smirch, stain, sully, taint, upbraid, vilify
**traffic**  business, dealings, intercourse, proceedings, transactions, vehicles
**traffic board**  stop-sign
**traffic congestion**  jam
**trafficker**  dealer
**traffic light**  robot
**traffic-light colour**  amber, green, red
**traffic roundabout**  circle, island
**traffic standstill**  jam, tie-up
**traffic ticket**  speeding fine
**traffic track**  autobahn (G), avenue, freeway, highway, lane, street
**tragedy**  adversity, affliction, calamity, disaster, grief, heartbreak, misery, misfortune
**tragic**  calamitous, disastrous, drama, fatal, melancholy, mournful, sad, shocking, sorrowful
**tragic actor**  thespian
**tragic situation**  drama
**trail**  appendage, course, drag, draw, follow, hunt, lag, lug, ordeal, path, pursue, queue, scent, shadow, spoor, stalk, straggle, test, trace, track, train, trawl, way
**trailing plant**  arbutus, climber, creeper, ivy, periwinkle, vine
**trail off**  disappear, fade
**trail of wild animals**  spoor
**trail shot**  sighter
**train**  aim, appendage, caravan, chain, coach, column, convoy, course, court, direct, drill, educate, entourage, exercise, file, focus, followers, guide, instruct, level, order, point, practise, prepare, procession, railroad, rear, retinue, school, sequence, series, set, spar, staff, string, suite, tail, teach, trail, tutor
**train diner**  buffet car
**trained by practice**  expert
**trained craftsperson**  artisan
**trained fighter in ancient Roman shows**  gladiator
**trained hospital social worker**  almoner
**trained skill**  craft, science
**trainee**  amateur, apprentice, beginner, cadet, convert, cub, disciple, fledg(e)ling, greenhorn, initiate, learner, neophyte, novice, novitiate, pupil, recruit, roofie, rookie, scholar, starter, student, tenderfoot, tyro
**trainee officer**  cadet

**trainee on sheep or cattle station**  jackaroo, jackeroo
**train engine**  loco(motive)
**trainer**  breeder, coach, disciplinarian, instructor, teacher, tutor
**trainer of hawks**  falconer
**train halt**  station
**training**  drilling, education, guidance, instruction, lessons, practice, teaching
**training college for priests**  seminary
**training horses in obedience**  dressage
**training in military exercise**  drill
**training nucleus**  cadre
**training riders and horses in dressage techniques**  manège
**train mentally and morally**  educate
**train of attendance**  retinue
**train of thought**  reasoning
**train operator**  driver, engineer
**train system**  railway
**train track**  rail(way)
**train tracks**  rails
**train troops**  drill
**train undercarriage**  bogie
**trait**  attribute, characteristic, feature, habit, idiosyncrasy, lineament, mannerism, peculiarity, quality, quirk
**traitor**  back-stabber, betrayer, Brutus, collaborator, deceiver, defector, deserter, dissenter, double-crosser, double-dealer, dropout, forsaker, impimpi, informer, Judas, mutineer, quisling, quitter, rat, rebel, renegade, revolter, revolutionary, seceder, seditionist, turncoat
**tram**  streetcar
**trammel**  burden, clog, cramp, embarrass, encumber, hamper, handicap, hinder, impede, inconvenience, obstruct, oppress, overload, retard, saddle
**tramp**  bergie, crush, drab, hike, hobo, journey, march, meander, mush, pace, plod, plow, ramble, range, roam, rove, saunter, shuffle, slog, stamp, stride, stroller, toil, traipse, trample, travel, tread, trek, trudge, vagabond, vagrant, walk, wander, yomp
**tramp along on foot**  pad
**trample**  crush, hoof, hurt, infringe, march, much, pace, plod, plow, shuffle, squash, stamp, step, stride, stump, tramp, tread, trudge, violate, walk
**trampled underfoot**  downtrodden, oppressed
**trample out**  conquer, extinguish, overpower, vanquish
**trample upon**  bully, mishandle, mistreat

**trampoline** springboard
**trampolinist** jumper
**tramp on** crush, squash, stamp, trample
**tramp wearily** traipse
**trance** abstraction, catalepsy, coma, daze, drowsiness, ecstasy, lethargy, rapture, semi-conscious, slumber, spell, stupor, torpor
**tranquil** becalmed, calm, composed, cool, inexcitable, pacific, palmy, peaceful, placid, quiescent, quiet, relaxed, reposeful, restful, secluded, sedate, serene, soothe, still, undisturbed, unexcited, unruffled, untroubled, unworried, windless
**tranquil demeanour** composure
**tranquil happiness** contentment
**tranquillise** calm, compose, lull, pacify, quell, relax, sedate, soothe
**tranquilliser** barbiturate, bromide, opiate, sedative
**tranquillity** ataraxia, calm(ness), hush, peace(fulness), placidity, placidness, poise, quietness, quietude, repose, rest, sedateness, sereneness, serenity, stillness
**tranquillity system** meditation, yoga
**transact** conduct, enact, manage, negotiate, perform
**transact business with** bank
**transaction** act(ion), affair, bargain, business, commission, concern, coup, deal(ings), deed, doings, enactment, enterprise, interest, involvement, matters, passage, perpetration, procedure, proceeding, sale, undertaking
**transept** cross-aisle
**transfer** assign, bring, carrying, cede, change, consignment, convey, decal, deeding, deliver(y), move, relegation, relocate, send, shift, shipment, transmit, transporting
**transferable to another owner** alienable
**transfer legally** cede
**transfer of estate by will** demise
**transfer ownership of** alienate
**transfer plant** repot
**transfix** astound, attach, captivate, enchant, fascinate, fasten, fix, halt, impale, mesmerise, nail, pierce, pin, possess, puncture, rivet, skewer, spear, stab, stick, stun, tack, transpierce
**transform** alter, change, convert, metamorphose, transfigure, transmute
**transgress** breach, break, contravene, disobey, disregard, encroach, err, exceed, infract, infringe, invade, offend, overstep, scorn, sin, trespass, violate
**transgression** abuse, breach, crime, delinquency, dereliction, enormity, error, fault, felony, grievance, illegality, immorality, impropriety, infraction, infringement, iniquity, injury, injustice, lapse, malpractice, misbehaviour, misconduct, misdeed, misdemeanour, naughtiness, offence, outrage, overstepping, peccadillo, scrape, sin(fulness), trespass, vice, wrong
**transgressor** criminal, culprit, delinquent, evildoer, felon, offender, sinner, trespasser
**transient** brief, ephemeral, fleeting, flying, fugitive, momentary, passing, short, temporary, transitory
**transient craze** fad
**transient light** gleam
**transistor** semiconductor
**transistor radio** portable
**transitorily** ephemerally
**transitory** ephemeral, fleeting, impermanent, short-lived, temporary, transient
**translate** clarify, construe, convey, decode, define, ecclesiasticise, elucidate, explain, expound, illustrate, interpret, render, rephrase, retransmit, reword, simplify, transcribe, transfer, transliterate, turn, unfold
**translating** altering, carrying, changing, converting, conveying, decoding, elucidating, explaining, interpreting, (re)moving, rendering, sending, simplifying, transcribing, transferring, transforming, transporting, turning
**translation** conversion, interpretation, paraphrase, rendering, treatment, version
**translator** exegete, interpolator, interpreter, linguist, metaphrast, paraphrast, polygot
**translators are traitors** traduttori traditori (I)
**translucent** pellucid, semi-opaque, semitransparent, translucid, transparent
**transmission density** absorbance
**transmission shift** gear lever
**transmit** broadcast, call, carry, cart, communicate, converse, convey, deliver, describe, dispatch, fax, forward, mail, narrate, notify, post, relay, remit, send, telecast, telegram, telegraph, telephone, transfer, transport, wire
**transmitter of heredity** gene

**transom** lintel, traverse
**transparency** clarity, clearness, diaphanousness, directness, frankness, honesty, limpidity, lucidity, obviousness, openness, pellucidity, pellucidness, photograph, sheerness, simplicity, slide, translucency
**transparent** apparent, candid, clear, diaphanous, direct, distinct, easy, evident, explicit, filmy, forthright, frank, limpid, lucent, lucid, manifest, obvious, open, patent, pellucid, plain, straight, translucent, visible
**transparent jelly-like tissue filling the eyeball** vitreous
**transparent membrane covering iris and pupil of eyeball** cornea
**transparent quartz** crystal
**transplanted tissue** graft
**transplant operation** graft
**transport** car(ry), convey(ance), ecstasy, exile, happiness, (mini)bus, omnibus, rapture, transportation, trolley-bus, troopship
**transportation by ferry** ferriage
**transport by road** haul
**transported by wind** wind-borne
**transport of goods** haulage
**transports the sick** ambulance
**transport up mountain** cable-car
**transpose** alter, commute, (ex)change, interchange, invert, move, rearrange, relocate, reorder, reverse, shift, substitute, swap, switch, trade, transfer
**Transvaal flag** Vierkleur
**Transvaal goldfields** Rand
**Transvaal raider** Jameson
**transverse** cater-cornered, cross(piece), crossways, diagonal, oblique, thwart, traverse
**transversely** aslant, crossly, obliquely, tangentially
**transversely corded fabric** rep
**transvestism** eonism
**trap** ambush, bait, buggy, cage, carriage, catch, decoy, diversion, enigma, enmesh, (en)snare, entrap, gin, lure, net, noose, pitfall, receptacle, stratagem, surprise, tree, weir
**trap device** radar
**trapdoor** hatch
**trap door** pit(fall)
**trapeze artist** aerialist
**trap for catching animals** snare
**trapper** hunter
**trapping** ambushing, catching, cornering, deceiving, duping, enmeshing, (en)snaring, inveigling, taking, tricking

**trapping device** snare
**trappings** accoutrements, adornments, apparatus, apparel, dress, equipment, finery, fittings, fixtures, gear, livery, panoply, raiment, vestment, wear
**trash** bunkum, debris, dirt, dregs, drivel, garbage, junk, lam, leftovers, litter, nonsense, offal, rabble, rascal, refuse, remains, riff-raff, rogue, rubbish, scraps, scum, sweepings, swill, vagrant, waste
**trash can** (dust)bin
**trauma** anxiety, bombshell, burden, collapse, distress, injury, pressure, shock, strain, stress, stupor, tension, upset, worry, wound
**travail** childbirth, contractions, delivery, drudgery, effort, exertion, industry, labour, pains, parturition, slog, sweat, throes, toil
**travel** cross, drive, go, itinerate, journey, move, peregrinate, proceed, progress, ramble, ride, roam, rove, tour(ism), traverse, visit, voyage, walk, wander, wend
**travel bag** valise
**travel by air** fly
**travel by bike** ride
**travel by boat** sail
**travel by car** drive, ride
**travel by foot** walk
**travel by seeking free rides in passing vehicles** hitch-hike
**travel by water** sail
**travel cost** fare
**travel document** passport, visa
**travel from place to place** itinerate, peregrinate, wander
**travel in circles** orbit
**travel industry** tourism
**travel into new territory** explore
**travelled over water** boated
**traveller** adventurer, explorer, hiker, itinerant, mariner, nomad, pilgrim, pioneer, rep(resentative), roamer, rover, sailor, sight-seer, tourist, tripper, voyager
**traveller by sea** sailor, seafarer
**traveller from space** ET
**traveller in space** astronaut
**traveller on bus** passenger
**traveller on foot** wayfarer
**traveller on public transport** passenger
**traveller's accommodation** camp, hotel, inn, motel
**traveller's belongings** luggage
**traveller's tale** yarn
**travelling** crossing, going, itinerant, journeying, migrant, mobile, moving, proceeding, rambling, roaming, roving, touring, traversing, unsettled, voyaging, wandering, wayfaring
**travelling allowance** mileage, per diem
**travelling bag** kitbag, luggage, portmanteau, (suit)case, valise
**travelling from place to place** itinerant
**travelling house** caravan
**travelling salesperson** drummer, peddler, rep(resentative), seller, smous
**travelling show** carnival, circus
**travelling tinker** caird (Sc)
**travelling vendor of small wares** pedlar
**travel malady** airsickness, carsickness, seasickness
**travel on foot** pad
**travel on horse** ride
**travel on ice** skate
**travel on water** sail
**travel over snow** ski
**travel over the legal limit** speed
**travel permit** passport, visa
**travel receipt** ticket
**travel regularly to work** commute
**travel safety action** belt up
**travel tax** airport tax, toll
**travel too fast** speed
**travel with** associate, consort, know, mingle, socialise
**traverse** bar(rier), bridge, contradict, cross(bar), crosspiece, deny, frustrate, lattice, obstruct, transom
**traverse in all directions** range
**travesty** caricature, disgrace, farce, lampoon, mockery, parody, perversion, sham, spoof
**trawl** troll
**trawling equipment** (trail-)net
**tray** ashtray, board, coaster, compartment, dish, plate, platter, receptacle, salver, server, waiter
**tray for outgoing documents** out tray
**tray on wheels** trolley
**treacherous** deceitful, disloyal, faithless, insecure, insidious, perfidious, recreant, snaky, stealthy, traitorous, treasonable, treasonous, unstable
**treacherous area** quicksand
**treacherous disciple** Judas
**treacherous killer** assassin
**treacherously** mala fide
**treacherously deceived** betrayed
**treacherous part of beach** quicksand
**treacherous person** breach, defection, desertion, impimpi, infidelity, quisling, snake, sneak, treason
**treachery** betrayal, breach, defection, desertion, disloyalty, duplicity, infidelity, perfidy, treason
**treacle** molasses, syrup
**tread** hike, march, quell, squash, stamp, step, stride, subdue, suppress, trample, trudge, walk
**tread down** crush, destroy, oppress
**treadle** foot-pedal
**tread on someone's toes** affront, annoy, disgruntle, displease, incense, infringe, injure, insult, irk, offend, vex
**tread roughly under foot** trample
**treason** betrayal, disaffection, disloyalty, lese-majesty, sedition, treachery
**treasonable** disloyal, faithless, lawless, mutinous, perfidious, rebellious, seditionary, seditious, traitorous, treacherous, treasonous, turncoat, unfaithful, untrue
**treasure** accumulate, assets, cache, cherish, esteem, gem, hoard, husband, jewel, money, pride, prize, revere, riches, save, skat, stock, store, trove, valuables, value, wealth
**treasure box** chest, coffer
**treasure ship** galleon
**treasury** anthology, bank, coffer, collection, compendium, exchequer, fiscus (L), repository, storehouse, strongbox, thesaurus, vault
**treat** banquet, consider, contain, delight, discuss, doctor, enjoyment, entertain, entertainment, feast, fun, gift, give, handle, joy, luxury, manage, nurse, party, pleasure, provide, regale, regard, satisfaction, settle, surprise, thrill, use
**treatable** curable
**treat animal hide** tan
**treat as celebrity** lionise
**treat as equal** equate
**treat as invalid** coddle
**treat badly** abuse
**treat carefully** nurse
**treated animal hide** leather
**treated like dirt** henpecked
**treated sheepskin** parchment
**treating of moral questions** ethic
**treating serious matters lightly** flippant
**treatise** brochure, composition, discourse, disquisition, dissertation, essay, homily, investigation, leaflet, monograph, pamphlet, paper, publication, screed, study, thesis, tract, work, writing
**treat lavishly** regale
**treat leather** tan
**treat like a child** patronise
**treat maliciously** spite
**treatment** care, conduct, management, medication, medicine, reception, remedy, surgery, therapy

**treatment by hypnotism** hypnotherapy
**treatment by operation** surgery
**treatment for anxiety** valarian
**treatment for babies' colic** gripe water
**treatment for diabetes** insulin
**treatment for malaria** quinine
**treatment for shock** noradrenalin(e)
**treatment of aged** geriatrics
**treatment of damaged trees by filling cavities** tree surgery
**treatment of disease** therapy
**treatment of disease by bathing** balneotherapy
**treatment of disease by light** actinotherapy
**treatment of disease by mental influence** psychotherapy
**treatment of disease by medicinal drugs** chemotherapy
**treatment of disease by radiation** radiotherapy
**treatment of disease by usual means** allopathy
**treatment of feet** chiropody, pedicure
**treatment of fingernails and hands** manicure
**treatment of injury by massage** physiotherapy
**treatment of light and shade in painting** chiaroscuro
**treatment of mental diseases** psychiatry
**treatment with impregnated mud** mudpack
**treat roughly** manhandle, tousle
**treats muscles and joints** masseur, masseuse
**treat unfairly** aggrieve
**treat with affection** caress
**treat with air** aerate
**treat with consideration** respect
**treat with contempt** deride, spurn
**treat with diabolic violence** bedevil
**treat with great respect** revere
**treat with iodine** iodise
**treat with partiality** favour
**treat with scorn** deride
**treat with vaccine** inoculate
**treat wound by searing** cauterise
**treaty** agreement, alliance, bargain, bond, compact, concordat, contract, convention, covenant, entente, pact
**treaty clause** provision
**treaty of peace** pacification
**treble** soprano, threefold, triple
**trebly** thrice
**tree** acacia, alder, antiar, arbor, ash, aspen, balsa, beech, birch, carob, cedar, conifer, cork, elder, elm, evergreen, fir, jacaranda, kiaat, kiepersol, kola, larch, lime, maple, mimosa, oak, palm, plant, poplar, sapele, shoot, shrub, sycamore, tambuti, timber, twig, upas, willow, yellow wood, yew
**tree and nut** almond, beech, hickory, pecan, walnut
**tree branch** limb
**treed road** avenue
**tree dwelling** arboreal
**tree frog** hyla
**tree gum** resin
**tree home** nest
**treeless Arctic region** tundra
**treeless grassland in North America** prairie
**treeless grassland in South America** llano
**treeless moor** wold
**treeless plain** savanna
**treeless plains in South America** llanos, pampas
**treeless region** highmoor
**treelike** aboreal
**tree limb** bough
**tree-lined road** boulevard
**tree-lined street** avenue
**tree-lined walk** alameda
**tree marsupial** koala
**tree nymph** (hama)dryad
**tree of heaven** ailanthus
**tree of peace** olive
**tree of willow family** poplar
**tree part** branch, leaf, stem, twig
**tree-planting** forestating
**tree runner** sitella
**tree sacred to Venus** myrtle
**tree's anchor** root
**trees growing in a particular region** silva, sylva
**tree-shaped** dendroid
**tree skin** bark
**tree's shoot** sprig
**tree trunk** bole, log
**tree with edible pods** carob
**tree with edible roots** ti
**tree with poisonous seeds** laburnum
**tree with serrated leaves** elm
**tree yielding furniture wood** walnut
**tree yielding gum arabic** acasia
**tree yielding milky sap** upas
**tree yielding strychnine** nux vomica
**tree yielding turpentine** terebinth
**trefoil** clover
**treillage** latticework, trellis
**trek** expedition, hike, journey, march, odyssey, plod, roam, tramp, travel, trip, wander, yomp
**trellis** arbour, espalier, lattice, pergola, treillage
**trellis-covered verandah** pergola, stoep
**trellised window** lattice

**tremble** dither, dodder, oscillate, quake, quaver, quiver, rock, shake, shiver, shudder, teeter, totter, tremor, vibrate, vibration
**tremble from age** dodder
**tremble from cold** shiver
**tremble in speech** quaver
**tremble violently** shudder
**tremble with fear** palpitate
**trembling** shaky
**trembling poplar tree** aspen
**tremendous** awful, colossal, gigantic, horrendous, horrifying, huge, leviathan, mammoth, terrible, titanic
**tremor** agitation, (earth)quake, quaking, shaking, shudder, temblor (Sp), vibration
**tremor of emotion** thrill
**tremorous** quaking
**tremulous** aspen, quaking, quivering, trembling
**tremulous agitation** trepidation
**tremulous poplar tree** aspen
**tremulous warble** trill
**trench** adit, canal, channel, dike, ditch, excavation, furrow, moat, sewer, trough, watercourse
**trenchant wit** satire
**trench made by plough** furrow
**trench warfare protection** sandbag
**trend** course, drift, extend, fashion, incline, stretch, style, tendency
**trend of opinion** tide
**trendy** chic, fashionable, in, latest, modish, smart, stylish
**trepan** entice, lure, snare, trap
**trepang** sea slug
**trepid** agitated, shaking
**trepidation** alarm, angst, anxiety, consternation, dread, fear, malaise, nervousness, panic, perturbation, qualm, quivering, shivers, shudder, spasm, trembling, twitter, unease, unrest
**trespass** advance, crime, encroach(ment), enter, entrench, err(or), impose, infiltrate, infringe(ment), intrude, intrusion, invade, invasion, misdeed, misdemeanour, mistake, obtrude, offence, offend, penetrate, sin, transgress, violate, wrong
**trespasser** encroacher
**tress** braid, curl, lock, plait, ringlet, strand
**tresses** hair
**triad** threesome, trio, triple(t), triumvirate, troika
**trial** adversity, affliction, assay, attempt, audition, check, contest, criterion, distress, effort, enquiry, examination, experience,

**trial impression** experiment(al), grief, hardship, hearing, litigation, misery, misfortune, nuisance, ordeal, pain, proof, standard, struggle, suffering, test(ing), tribulation, tribunal, trouble, unhappiness, vexation
**trial impression** proof
**trial of strength** bout
**trial performance** rehearsal
**trial run** pretest
**triangle** polygon
**triangle point** vertex
**triangle-shaped** deltoid, scalene
**triangle with two equal sides** isosceles
**triangle with unequal sides** scalene
**triangular** arrow-headed, cuneiform, deltoid, three-cornered, threesome, tricornered, trigonous, trilateral, wedge-shaped
**triangular file** sawfile
**triangular flat end of anchor arm** fluke
**triangular harp** trigon(on)
**triangular inset** gore, gusset
**triangular part of wall or roof** gable
**triangular piece of material inserted in a dress** godet, gore, gusset
**triangular river mouth** delta
**triangular sail** jib, lateen, raffle
**triangular solid** pyramid
**triangular space over Greek portico** pediment
**triangular topsail** raffe
**Triassic period rock system** Rh(a)etic
**tribal Arab** Bedouin
**tribal area in ancient Greece** Deme
**tribal chief** sagamore
**tribal communal dwelling** longhouse
**tribal discussion** palaver
**tribal priest** shaman
**tribal senior** elder
**tribal symbol** totem
**tribal unit** township
**tribe** blood, breed, caste, clan, class, community, division, genus, group, lot, people, race, sect, seed, stock
**tribe of Afghanistan** Baloch, Baluch, Hazara, Pathan, Safi, Tajik, Ulus, Uzbek
**tribe of Albania** Cham, Geg, Gheg, Tosk
**tribe of Israel** Asher, Dan, Gad, Issachar, Joseph, Juda, Levi, Naphtali, Reuben, Simeon, Zebulon
**tribulation** adversity, affliction, burden, curse, distress, grief, hardship, heartache, misery, misfortune, ordeal, reverse
**tribunal** Areopagites, bar, bench, board, chancery, commission, court, dais, forum, hearing, judicature,
judiciary, platform, rostrum, seat, session, trial
**tributary stream** affluent
**tribute** bribe, compliment, eulogy, gratitude, homage, honour, levy, memorial, ransom, recognition, respect, tax, toll
**trice** haul, instant, jiffy, moment, tie
**trichoid** hairlike
**trick** appearance, beguile, cheat(ing), cozen, deceit, deceive, deception, defraud, delude, device, dodge, dupe, duplicity, expedient, fool, fraud, hoax, hoodwink, illude, jig, jugglery, legerdemain, prank, rig, ruse, shift, stratagem, subterfuge, swindle, trickery, wile
**trickery** betrayal, charlatanry, cheating, chicanery, deceit, deception, dishonesty, disloyalty, fraud, guile, hypocrisy, imposition, imposture, shrewdness, skul(l)duggery, slyness, subterfuge, swindling, treachery
**trick into awkward situation** shanghai
**trickle** crawl, creep, dribble, drip, drizzle, drop, exude, ooze, percolate, plash, run, seep(age), sprinkle, stream, trill
**trick of fate** quirk
**trick of style** mannerism
**trick of the imagination** delusion, illusion, phantasm
**trick played on someone** joke, prank
**tricksy** capricious, mischievous, sportive, tricky
**tricky** complicated, crafty, delicate, devious, difficult, dodgy, foxy, problematic, risky, sticky, thorny, ticklish
**tricky dick** deceiver
**tricky problem** poser, puzzle
**trifle** bagatelle, bauble, bit, dabble, dally, doit, fico, fidget, gewgaw, idle, inessential, jot, little, minutiae, mite, palter, plaything, scrap, secondary, small, tinge, touch, toy, trinket, trivia(lity), unimportant
**trifle in love** flirt
**trifle with** dally, fiddle, flirt, handle, philander, play, toy
**trifling** frivolous, immaterial, insignificant, mere, negligible, paltry, petty, piffling, shallow, tiny, trivial, trying, unimportant, worthless
**trifling details** minutiae
**trifling fault** peccadillo
**trifling ornament** (k)nick-(k)nack
**trifling portion** snack
**trifling talk** tattle
**trifoliate plant** clover, shamrock
**trigeminal** threefold
**trigeminal neuralgia** tic
**trigonometrical function** (co)secant, (co)sine, (co)tangent
**trill** quaver, sing, warble
**trilling** warbling
**trill in singing** quaver
**trill of cricket** chirr
**trim** adjust, adorn, arrange, array, case, chic, clip, compact, curtail, cut, deck, decorate, dress, edging, embellish, garnish, lop, modify, neat, order, pare, plight, preen, prepare, prune, reduce, shape, shave, shear, situation, smart, tidy
**trim at the barber** haircut, shave
**trim feathers** preen
**trim from** pare
**trim hair** clip, cut
**trimmed grass** lawn
**trimmer** neater
**trimming tool** clippers, scissors, shears
**trim off** pare
**trim up** preen, primp, smarten
**trinity** threesome, triad, triangle, triarchy, trine, trion, triple(t), triplex, troika
**trinket** bagatelle, bauble, bijou, bric-à-brac, gewgaw, (k)nick-(k)nack, ornament, toy, trifle
**trinket worn on bracelet** charm
**trio** three, threesome, triad, triple(t), triumvirate, troika
**triolein** olein
**trio number** three
**trip** err(atum), error, excursion, hop, jaunt, journey, junket, misstep, mistake, overlook, oversight, pilgrimage, skip, slip, stumble, tour, travel, voyage
**tripe** bunkum, claptrap, drivel, garbage, nonsense, rubbish, trash, twaddle
**triple** thee-branched, three-ply, three-way, threefold, threesome, treble, triad, trine, trinity, trio, triplet, triplicate, triumvirate, troika
**triple crown** tiara
**triple rhyme** tiercet
**triplet** threesome, triad, trio, triple
**triplicate** threefold
**trip made by theatre company** tour
**tripod** easel
**tripoli** diatomite
**Tripoli currency** piaster
**Tripoli native** Libyan
**trip over** fall, stumble
**trip to Mecca** hadj, hajj, pilgrimage
**triptych** threesome, triad, trinity, trio, triplet, triune, triumvirate
**trismus** lockjaw
**trist** dismal, sad, sorrowful, triste, tristful
**trite** banal, common(place), hackneyed, ordinary, stale,

stereotyped, trivial, well-trodden,
worn-out
**trite remark** banality, cliché, platitude
**trite thing** banality
**Triton's shell-trumpet** conch
**triumph** accomplish, celebrate,
celebration, conquer, conquest,
coup, exult(ation), feat, gloat, glory,
jubilance, jubilate, jubilation,
overwhelm, prevail, rejoice, rejoicing,
succeed, success, swagger, victory,
win
**triumphant** celebrative, elated,
exultant, gleeful, happy, jubilant,
leading, pleased, succeeding,
successful, victorious, winning
**triumphed** celebrated, exulted,
gloated, gloried, rejoiced, revelled
**triumphing** winning
**triumph over** overpower, subdue,
surmount
**triumvirate** troika
**trivalent** tervalent
**trivia** details, inconsequentia, minutiae,
trifles, trivialities
**trivial** flimsy, frivolous, immaterial,
inessential, insignificant, light, little,
mere, minor, paltry, petty, slight,
trifling, unimportant
**trivial detail** fike
**triviality** cheapness, childishness,
emptiness, facetiousness,
flightiness, flippancy, folly, frivolity,
fun, gaiety, giddiness, hollowness,
idleness, inconsequence,
insignificance, insincerity,
irrelevance, jest, levity, lightness,
nonsense, paltriness, pettiness,
puerility, shallowness, silliness,
superficiality, trifling, unimportance,
worthlessness
**trivial lie** fib
**trivial matters** fiddle-faddle
**trivial point of criticism** quibble
**trivial remark** fadaise (F)
**trivial verse** doggerel
**trodden way** path
**troglodyte** cave-dweller, caveman,
hermit
**troglodyte's abode** cave
**troika** triumvirate
**Trojan hero** Aeneas
**Trojan hero in Homer's** *Iliad* Hector
**Trojan prince** Aeneas
**Trojan war cause** Helen
**Trojan war poem** *Iliad*
**troll** demon, dwarf, gnome, trawl
**trolley** cart
**trolley car** tram
**trolleyman** conductor
**troll for fish** harl
**trombone** brass

**trombone mouthpiece** bocal
**troop** assemblage, assemble,
associate, band, body, collect,
company, consort, convene, crowd,
gather, group, party, throng, unit
**troopie** soldier
**troop leader** scoutmaster
**troop of Tartars** horde
**troops** armies, bands, bodies,
companies, contingents, crowds,
droves, flocks, gangs, gatherings,
groups, herds, hordes, marches,
multitudes, parades, soldiers,
squads, streams, swarms, teams,
units
**troops detached to protect back**
rearguard
**troops' eating place** mess
**troops trained to descend by**
**parachute** paratroops
**troops who fight on foot** infantry
**troops who fight on horseback**
cavalry
**troop under a captain** company
**trophy** award, cup, laurels, medal,
memento, pot, prize, remembrance,
souvenir, token
**tropical** hot
**tropical African hardwood** iroko
**tropical American lizard** iguana
**tropical American smilax** sarsaparilla
**tropical animal** tapir
**tropical aroid plant** taro
**tropical Atlantic shark** gata
**tropical bird** ani, ara, macaw, oriole,
parrot, toucan, trogon
**tropical blackbird** ani
**tropical climbing plant** liana
**tropical cyclone** typhoon
**tropical disease** beri-beri, malaria,
sprue, tinea
**tropical fish** big-eye, gourami, robalo,
salema, sargo, tetra
**tropical fruit** avocado, banana,
coconut, date, guava, mango,
papaya, pa(w)paw
**tropical giant grass** bamboo
**tropical house-lizard** gecko
**tropical hurricane** typhoon
**tropical lizard** iguana, monitor
**tropical palm** areca
**tropical plant** cycad, hibiscus,
ipomoea, okra, taro
**tropical root vegetable** taro
**tropical shrub** henna, hibiscus
**tropical skin disease** yaws
**tropical songbird** oriole
**tropical spider** tarantula
**tropical storm** tornado, typhoon
**tropical sweet potato** yam
**tropical tree** acacia, a(c)kee, calabash,
palm

**tropical vine** liana
**trot** bustle, canter, jog(-trot), lope,
pace, run, scamper, scurry, scuttle
**troth** certie, certy, confidence, faith,
fidelity, plight, truth
**trot out** exhibit, recite, rehearse,
reiterate, relate, repeat
**trotting gig** sulky
**trot very slowly, in dressage** piaffe
**trotyl** TNT, trinitrotoluene
**troubadour** balladeer, minstrel, singer
**trouble** agitate, ail(ment), annoy(ance),
bother, complaint, concern, confuse,
derange, disarrange, discommode,
discontent, disorder, distress,
disturb, failure, grief, ill,
inconvenience, irritate, misfortune,
plague, torment, tribulation, upset,
woe, worry
**troubled** afflicted, agitated, annoyed,
bothered, burdened, concerned,
disconcerted, disquieted, distressed,
disturbed, fretted, grieved, harassed,
incommoded, pained, perplexed,
perturbed, pestered, plagued,
saddened, tormented, upset, vexed,
worried
**trouble persistently** pester
**troublesome** annoying, arduous,
bothersome, burdensome, difficult,
disorderly, harassing, hard,
insubordinate, irritating, laborious,
oppressive, perplexing, pesky,
recalcitrant, rowdy, taxing, tiresome,
trying, turbulent, unco-operative,
undisciplined, unruly, upsetting,
vexatious, violent, wearisome
**troublesome child** pickle
**troublesome contagious skin disease**
scabies
**troublesome ghost** poltergeist
**troublesome person** handicap,
liability, pest
**troublesome plant** weed
**trough** basin, bowl, cave, cavity,
channel, conduit, cup, dent,
depression, ditch, donga, drain,
duct, failure, gutter, hole, hollow,
indentation, pipe, pit, sloot, sluice,
trench, tube
**trough for horses or cattle to eat from**
manger
**trounce** beat, castigate, crush,
discipline, drub, lambast(e),
overwhelm, pound, pummel, punish,
rout, thrash, vanquish
**troupe of minstrels** minstrelsy
**trouper** actor, actress, artist, master,
performer, play-actor, player, starlet,
Thespian, tragedian, veteran
**trouser leg** slop

**trousers** briefs, jeans, knickers, pants, slacks, trews
**trousers made of chino** chinos
**trousers made of tartan cloth** trews
**trouser straps** braces
**trout** steelhead
**trouvaille** windfall
**truancy** absence, malingering
**truant** absentee, defaulter, derelict, deserter, dodger, evader, fainéant, idle, lazy, lull, neglectful, otiose, pact, remiss, respite, rest, shiftless, shirk(er), skiver, treaty
**truce** armistice, ceasefire, lull, pact, peace, treaty
**truck** bargain, barter, business, commerce, commodities, convey, deal, exchange, goods, lorry, merchandise, stock, stuff, swap, swop, trade, traffic, transfer, transport, van, wares
**truck for moving** van
**truck fuel** diesel
**truck part** cab
**truculence** hostility
**truculent** aggressive, bellicose, brutal, combative, contentious, cross, defiant, ferocious, fierce, hostile, obstreperous, overbearing, pugnacious, savage, sullen, threatening, violent
**trudge** crawl, creep, haul, hike, hobble, limp, lumber, march, mush, plod, shuffle, slog, stump, traipse, tramp, trog, walk, yomp
**true** accurate(ly), agreeing, authentic, constant, equitable, exact(ly), factual, fair, faithful, genuine, honest(ly), just, legitimate, loyal, precise, proper, real, reliable, right(ful), shape, sincere, staunch, steady, truly, trustworthy, truthful, unerring, unfailing, veracious
**true art is to conceal art** ars est celare artem (L)
**true cause** causa vera (L)
**true copy** estreat
**true gentleman** sahib
**truelove** lover, sweetheart
**true olive** olea
**true saying** axiom, postulate
**true skin** cutis, derma, dermis, enderon
**true statement** verity
**true subject** liege
**true-to-life style of writing** naturalism
**true to one purpose** single-minded
**true to type** genuine, typical, usual
**truism** axiom, platitude
**truly** absolutely, assuredly, certainly, definitely, indeed, indubitably, positively, really, surely, unequivocally, verily, yea

**trump** outdo
**trumpery amount** bagatelle
**trumpet** buccina, bugle, clarion, horn
**trumpet call** clarion
**trumpet fanfare** tantara
**trumpet flourish** fanfare
**trumpeting sound** blare
**trumpet-like instrument** bugle
**trumpet's cousin** cornet
**trumpet sound** blare, fanfare
**trump up** conceive, concoct, contrive, create, devise, fabricate, invent
**truncate** abbreviate, abridge, clip, condense, crop, curtail, cut, digest, lop, pare, prune, retrench, shorten, trim
**truncheon** bat(on), bludgeon, club, cosh, cudgel, mace, rod, staff, stick, wand
**trundle** caster, clump, elapse, flow, gyrate, lumber, pass, pivot, plod, push, reel, revolve, roll(er), rotate, stump, swivel, trudge, turn, twirl, wheel, whirl
**trunk** body, bole, case, chest, coffer, crate, kist, portmanteau, proboscis, snout, stem, stock, torso
**trunk and head connector** neck
**trunk covering** bark
**trunk of arterial system** aorta
**trunk of human body** torso
**trunk of tree** bole
**trust** assurance, belief, believe, cartel, charge, commitment, confidence, credence, credit, custody, dependence, faith, hope, reliance, rely, responsibility, security
**trusted adviser** advisor, mentor
**trusted friend** alter ego
**trustful** artless, candid, childlike, confiding, credulous, frank, guileless, gullible, honest, ingenuous, innocent, naïve, open, simple, unfeigned, unreserved, unsuspicious, unwary
**trusting** reliant
**trustworthy** allegiant, believable, credible, dependable, dutiful, earnest, faithful, honest, honourable, just, loyal, reliable, reputable, respectable, responsible, staunch, steady, straightforward, sure, true, trusted, trusty, valid
**trustworthy but uncouth** rough diamond
**trusty** faithful, firm, honest, reliable, responsible, staunch, steady, strong, true, trustworthy
**trusty supporter** henchman
**truth** accuracy, actuality, candour, fact, fidelity, genuineness, honesty, ingenuousness, integrity, precision, probity, reality, validity, veracity, verity, virtue
**truth conquers all things** veritas omnia vincit (L)
**truthful** accurate, artless, candid, correct, factual, honest, open, reliable, sincere, straightforward, true, veracious
**truthfulness** accurateness, candidness, correctness, exactness, faithfulness, honestness, honesty, literalness, preciseness, reliableness, sincereness, veracity
**truth is great and all-powerful** magna est veritas et praevalet (L)
**try** aim, assay, assess, attempt, consider, effort, endeavour, essay, evaluate, examine, experiment, extract, inspect, opportunity, prove, push, render, sample, seek, strive, struggle, test(ing), trial, undertake, venture
**try again** reattempt, rehear, retry
**try flavour of** taste
**try for** aspire
**try hard** strive, struggle
**trying** attempting, testing, wearisome
**trying experience** ordeal, tribulation
**trying food** tasting
**trying out** testing
**try judicially** hear
**try on clothes** fit
**try one's hand at** attempt, essay
**try out** appraise, evaluate, inspect, sample, taste, test
**try out a car** roadtest, test-drive
**try resolution** tempt
**try severely** test
**tryst** appointment, arrangement, assignation, consultation, date, engagement, interview, meeting, rendezvous, session
**try to avoid** shirk
**try to bite** snap
**try to clear from blame** excuse
**try to do something** endeavour
**try to equal** emulate
**try to find** hunt
**try to forget** unlearn
**try to get a tan** sunbathe
**try to move away by pressure** push
**try to reach** aspire
**try to reach an agreement** negotiate
**try to win** enter
**try to win favour** court
**tsarina** empress
**tsar's daughter** tsarevna
**tsar's edict** ukase
**T-shaped aerial** dipole
**Tsonga** Shangaan
**tuan** brush-tailed phalanger, wambenger

**tub** barrel, basin, bath(tub), bucket, cask, keg, receptacle, vat, vessel
**tube** duct, pipe, valve
**tube cover** tyre
**tubed pasta** cannelloni, macaroni, penne
**tube for measuring liquid in drops** stactometer
**tube for sucking** straw
**tube leading from kidney** ureter
**tube of meat** sausage
**tube of metal** pipe
**tuber** potato, rhizome, root, stem, yam
**tuberculosis** phthisis, scrofula
**tuberculosis of skin** lupus
**tuberlike plant part** bulb
**tuberous flower** dahlia
**tuberous herb** ginger, una
**tube-shaped Australian instrument** didgeridoo
**tube with small bowl at end** pipe
**tube with very small bore** capillary
**tubular** cannular, cylindric, pipy, quilled, tubate
**tubular pasta** cannelloni, macaroni, penne
**tucker** food
**tuck in** enfold, swaddle
**tuck up** hem, shorten
**tuft** crest, plume, topknot, tussock
**tufted marsh plant** sedge
**tufted plant** dryas
**tuft of air** topknot
**tuft of feathers** aigret(te), crest
**tuft of hair** fetlock, floccus
**tuft of hair on bee** scopa
**tuft of hair on spider** scopula
**tuft of ribbon** pompon
**tuft of weeds** dollop
**tuft of wool** flock
**tuft on cap** tassel
**tug** drag, haul, jerk, pull, tow, wrench, yank
**tug at** pull
**tugboat** tow
**tug-of-war** rivalry
**tulip-shaped sherry glass** copita
**tumble** chaos, collapse, confusion, decline, downfall, fail, fall, heave, mess, overturn, pitch, reel, roll, skid, slip, slump, somersault, sprawl, stagger, stumble, topple, totter, trip
**tumble about** flop
**tumble down** topple
**tumble gems** rumble
**tumbler** acrobat, glass
**tumbling head over heels** somersault
**tumefy** balloon, belly, billow, bulge, dilate, distend, enlarge, expand, extend, increase, inflate, protrude, swell

**tumid** bombastic, bulging, distended, enlarged, pompous, swollen, turgid
**tummy-button** belly-button, navel
**tumour** blight, boss, bulk, bump, cancer, canker, carcinoma, corruption, evil, knob, malignancy, melanoma, neoplasm, polyp, protrusion, sarcoma, snag, stud, swelling
**tumour composed of fatty tissue** lipoma
**tumour composed of nerve tissue** neuroma
**tumour consisting of mass of blood vessels** angioma
**tumour in thymus** thymoma
**tumour of bone marrow** myeloma
**tumour of fibrous tissue** fibroma
**tumour of mucus tissue** myxoma
**tumour on horse's leg** spavin
**tumours of veins of rectum** haemorrhoids, piles
**tumult** ado, agitation, chaos, commotion, confusion, discomposure, disorder, disquiet, disturbance, excitement, ferment, fray, frenzy, fury, hysteria, mêlée, mutiny, noise, outbreak, perturbation, rabblement, rampage, revolt, revolution, riot, turbulence, turmoil, upheaval, uproar
**tumultuous** agitated, boisterous, clamorous, confused, disorderly, excited, fierce, hectic, raging, violent
**tumulus** barrow
**tuna** tunny
**tune** accord, adapt, adjust, air, aria, chant, concert, dirge, harmony, hymn, melody, music, pitch, song, strain, unison
**tuned set of bells** chime
**tuneful** agreeable, dulcet, euphonic, harmonious, lyrical, mellifluous, melodic, melodious, pleasant
**tunefully** agreeably, compatibly, concordantly, congruously, euphoniously, fully, harmoniously, lyrically, mellow, melodiously, musically, richly, sweetly
**tuneful show** musical
**tune in** listen
**tune played on bells** carillon
**tungsten** wolfram
**tunic** coat, jacket, robe, sheath, toga
**tunic worn by schoolgirls** gymslip
**tuning fork** diapason
**Tunisian port** Bizerte
**tunnel** burrow, channel, dig, excavate, mine, passageway, penetrate, shaft, subway
**tunnel-shaped hut** Nissen
**tunny fish** albacore, bonito, tuna

**tup** ram
**turbine wheel** rotor
**turbulent** agitated, anarchic, blustery, disordered, disturbed, foaming, furious, insubordinate, raging, rebellious, riotous, seditious, stormy, tempestuous, tumultuous, unruly, unstable, violent, wild
**turbulent air** cyclone, hurricane, typhoon, whirlwind
**turbulent river current** rapid
**turbulent woman** harpy, harridan, virago, Xant(h)ippe
**turf** grass, green, peat, sod, sward
**turf adviser** tipster
**turf out** dismiss, eject
**turf piece** sod
**turgescent** swelling
**turgid** bombastic, distended, pompous, pretentious, swollen, tumid
**turgid speech or writing** fustian
**Turk** Ottoman
**turkey-cock** bubbly-jock, gobbler, stag
**Turkish army corps** ordu
**Turkish bath** hammam
**Turkish bath feature** steam
**Turkish caliph** Ali
**Turkish cap** fez
**Turkish capital** Ankara
**Turkish carpet** smyrna
**Turkish cavalryman** spahee, spahi
**Turkish commander** aga, ameer, amir
**Turkish constable** kavass
**Turkish cymbal** crotalo
**Turkish decree** irade
**Turkish empire** Othman, Ottoman
**Turkish flag** alem
**Turkish frigate** caravel
**Turkish government** Porte
**Turkish governor** bey, pasha
**Turkish guard house** derbend
**Turkish hat** fez
**Turkish hill** dagh
**Turkish hospice for pilgrims** imaret
**Turkish inn** caravansary, imaret, serai
**Turkish judge** aga, cadi, kadi, mulla(h)
**Turkish knife** ataghan, yatag(h)an
**Turkish lake** Tuz, Van
**Turkish language** Osmanli
**Turkish leader** aga
**Turkish manna** trehala
**Turkish military title** aga
**Turkish minister** vizier
**Turkish mosque attendant** softa
**Turkish name for Scanderbeg** Iskender Bey
**Turkish nobleman** aga
**Turkish palace** seraglio, serail
**Turkish policeman** Zabtieh, Zaptia
**Turkish port** Samsun
**Turkish prayer rug** melas
**Turkish province** Beylie, Vilayet

**Turkish regiment** alai
**Turkish robe** dolman
**Turkish ruler** caliph, khan, sultan
**Turkish sabre** yataghan
**Turkish sea** Aegean, Marmara
**Turkish seaport** Enos, Istanbul, Izmir, Mersin, Samsun, Trabzon
**Turkish soldier** janizary, nizam
**Turkish soldier of elite guard** janissary, janizary
**Turkish strait** Bosporus, Dardanelles
**Turkish sultan** osman
**Turkish sword** (y)ataghan
**Turkish title** aga, bey, cadi, dey, effendi, emir, pasha
**Turkish title of respect** aga
**Turkish tobacco** Latakia
**Turkish tribe** Kurd
**Turkish warrior of high rank** ghazi
**Turkish weight** oka, oke
**turmoil** ado, agitation, bedlam, bustle, chaos, commotion, confusion, disorder, disquiet, disturbance, flurry, noise, row, stir, strife, tracasserie, trouble, tumult, uproar, violence
**turn** alter, bend, cast, change, convert, deflect, derange, deviation, direction, distract, disturb, divert, exigency, infatuate, need, reverse, revolution, revolve, roll, rotate, sour, spin, swerve, tendency, transfer, transform, transmute, turning, twist, veer
**turn a blind eye** disregard, ignore
**turn about** swing, wheel, yaw
**turn a deaf ear to** disregard, ignore
**turn against** disagree, disobey, dissent, mutiny, oppose, protest, rebel, revolt, spurn
**turn and turnabout** alternation, exchange, retaliation, retribution, rotation
**turn and twist** twizzle
**turn an organ or part inside out** evaginate
**turn around** revolve, rotate, twirl
**turn aside** avert, deflect, deter, divert, forfend, parry, shunt, swerve, veer
**turn attention to** advert
**turn away** alienate, avert, deflect, depart, discharge, dismiss, reject, withdraw
**turn away from** avert, avoid, eschew
**turn back** rebuff, repel, repulse, resist, retrace, return, revert
**turn back the clock** rejuvenate
**turncoat** apostate, betrayer, deserter, forsaker, impimpi, quisling, renegade, traitor
**turn down** decline, decrease, diminish, disallow, disapprove, hush, lessen, lower, muffle, mute, quiet(en), rebuff, reduce, refuse, reject, repudiate, resist, soften, spurn, waive
**turned backwards** retroverted
**turned down collar** rabat
**turned edge of jacket** lapel
**turned edge of skirt** hem
**turned inwards** introrse
**turned to one side** distorted, skew, wry
**turned up** attended, retroussé
**turned up nose** retroussé, snob
**turned upside down** topsyturvy
**turner's machine** lathe
**turn from one railway line to another** switch
**turn in** deliver, enter, register, retire, return, submit, surrender, tender
**turn in baseball** inning
**turn informer** grass, snitch
**turning** rolling, rotating, swerving
**turning aside** averting
**turning away** alienation
**turning away from the sun** apheliotropic
**turning in certain direction at night** nyctitropic
**turning machine** lathe
**turning part** rotor
**turning point** change, climacteric, climax, conjuncture, crisis, crossroads
**turning power** torque
**turning round** revolve, volte-face
**turning sour** acescent
**turning spit** rotisserie
**turning up** appearance
**turning upside down** inversion
**turn inside out** evert, forage, hunt, invert, rummage, search
**turn into bone** ossify
**turn into steel** acierate
**turn into stone** petrify
**turn into vapour** evaporate
**turn into verse** versify
**turnip** neep, vegetable
**turnip cabbage** kohlrabi
**turnkey** gaoler, guard, jailer, jailkeeper, locksman, screw, warden, warder
**turn key to make secure** lock
**turn land into forest** afforest
**turn like a wheel** rotate
**turn oar** feather
**turn off** alienate, bore, deviate, discourage, disenchant, disgust, displease, divert, irritate, leave, nauseate, offend, quit, repel, sicken, stop
**turn of mind** bent, inclination, wish
**turn of phrase** idiom
**turn of spirals** whorl
**turn of year** solstice
**turn on** activate, arouse, assail, attack, energise, excite, ignite, impel, initiate, open, please, start, stimulate, thrill, unseal
**turn on again** restart
**turn on a lamp** light
**turn on a pivot** swivel
**turn one's attention** advert
**turn one's back on** abandon, disregard, ignore, neglect, reject, repudiate, tergiversate
**turn out** afford, appear, arise, assemble, banish, become, clear, clothe, deport, develop, discharge, dismiss, dress, emerge, empty, ensue, eventuate, evict, expel, fabricate, happen, make, manufacture, oust, present, produce, result, sack, terminate, transpire, unplug, withdraw, yield
**turnout** assembly, attendance, audience, costume, crowd, output, production, throng, turnover
**turn out to be** end up
**turn outward** evert
**turn over** capsize, consider, consign, contemplate, deliberate, deliver, entrust, examine, flip, fold, give, inverse, keel, mull, overset, overthrow, overturn, ponder, relegate, sell, spill, subvert, transfer, upend, upset, upturn
**turnover** business, change, flow, income, movement, output, production, productivity, profits, replacement, volume, yield
**turn over and over** roll
**turn over a new leaf** advance, alter, amend, change, convert, improve, metamorphose, reform, regenerate
**turn over quickly** flip
**turn over to dry** ted
**turn pale** blanch
**turn pancake** toss
**turnpike bar** tollgate
**turn quickly** spin
**turn rapidly** whirl
**turn red** blush, flush
**turn ship on side for cleaning** careen
**turn solid by cold** freeze
**turn tail** back, escape, flee, recoil, retreat
**turn the mind to** attend
**turn the other way** reverse
**turn the soil** till
**turn the tables** requite, reverse
**turn the tide** alter, change, reverse
**turn thumbs down** deny, nay, prohibit, reject, veto
**turn to** become, dedicate, devote, resort
**turn to advantage** exploit
**turn to bone** ossify
**turn to ice** freeze

**turn to solid**  freeze, gel, set
**turn to upright position**  upend
**turn to use**  utilise
**turn to wrong use**  pervert
**turn up**  appear, arrive, cultivate, discover, expose, increase, intensify, plow, unearth
**turn upside down**  invert, forage, disarrange
**turn up with spade**  dig
**turn white**  pale
**turpitude**  atrocity, baseness, depravity, disgrace, evilness, outrageousness, viciousness, villainy, wickedness
**turret**  column, cupola, spire, steeple, tourelle (F), tower
**tursio**  dolphin
**turtle**  thalassian
**turtle-back**  carapace
**turtle enclosure**  crawl
**turtle flesh**  calipee
**turtleneck**  sweater
**Tuscany city**  Florence, Pisa, Siena
**Tuscany island**  Elba
**tusk**  canine, ivory, tooth, tush
**tusked sea creature**  narwhal, walrus
**tusk material**  ivory
**tussle**  conflict, fight, fracas, scrap, scuffle, struggle, wrestle
**tussock**  lock, tuft
**tutelary deity**  genius, numen
**tutelary Roman god**  lar
**tutor**  coach, educator, governor, instructor, lecturer, master, mentor, professor, teacher
**tutorial**  class, coaching, didactic, guiding, instructional, lesson, seminar, teaching
**twaddle**  balderdash, blather, bunkum, claptrap, gab(ble), garbage, gossip, guff, hogwash, nonsense, piffle, prattle, rigmarole, rot, rubbish, tattle
**Twain character**  Huckleberry Finn, Tom Sawyer
**twang**  cacophony, clink, ding, jingle, pluck, resonance, resound, reverberate, shrillness, strum, tinkle, vibration
**twangy**  nasal
**twee**  quaint, sweet
**tweet**  chirp
**twelfth month of Jewish year**  Adar
***Twelfth Night* clown**  Feste
**twelfth part of a foot**  inch
**twelfth satellite of Jupiter**  Ananka
**twelve**  dozen
**twelve a.m.**  midday, noon
**twelve dozen**  gross
**twelve inch unit**  foot
**twelve months**  year
**twelve o'clock**  midday, midnight, noon
**twelve p.m.**  midnight

**twelve points**  em
**twelve point type**  pica
**twelve-sided solid figure**  dodecahedron
**twelve to the inch**  elite
**twelve tribes of Israel**  Asher, Benjamin, Dan, Gad, Issachar, Joseph, Judah, Levi, Naphtali, Reuben, Simeon, Zebulun
**twenty**  score
**twenty-four grains**  pennyweight
**twenty-four hour period**  day
**twenty-four hours ago**  yesterday
**twenty-four hours' time**  tomorrow
**twenty-four sheets of paper**  quire
**twenty-one shillings**  guinea
**twenty quires**  ream
**twenty-two over seven**  pi
**twenty years**  vicennial
**twerp**  drongo, nerd, ninny
**twice**  bi-, bis (L), di-, double
**twice a month**  bimonthly
**twice as fast as normal**  alla breve (I)
**twice size of jeroboam**  rehoboam
**twice yearly**  biannually, half-yearly
**twig**  baton, birch, branch, bud, cane, limb, offshoot, petiole, pole, rod, runner, scion, shoot, slip, spray, sprig, sprout, spur, staff, stake, stem, stick, switch, tendril, wand, withe, withy
**twigs for sweeping**  besom
**twilight**  decline, dimness, dusk, ebb, eve(ntide), gloaming, nightfall, sundown, sunset
**twilight sleep**  narcosis
**twilled cloth**  cord, denim, pique, rep, serge, surah
**twilled woollen cloth**  kerseymere, plaid, serge
**twin**  alter ego, analogous, companion, complement, counterpart, double, dual, duplicate, equal, equivalent, identical, kindred, likeness, match, paired, same, similar, two(fold)
**twin brother of Castor**  Pollux
**twin chromosomes**  diploid
**twine**  binding, cable, clasp, coil, cord, embrace, enlace, entwine, interlace, knot, roll, rope, rotate, spire, string, tie, twist, wind, wreathe, yarn
**twinge**  bite, cramp, crick, gripe, pain, pang, prick, smart, spasm, stab, stitch, suffering, thrill, throb, tic, tingle, twitch
**twinhulled vessel**  catamaran
**twining plant**  bindweed, climber, creeper, scammony, smilax, winder
**twining shoot**  tendril
**twining stem**  bine
**twining tropical plant**  ipomoea, liana

**twinkle**  beam, blaze, blink, brilliance, burst, coruscate, dazzle, flare, flash, flicker, glare, gleam, glimmer, glint, glisten, glitter, glow, light, radiance, radiate, ray, reflection, scintillate, shaft, shimmer, shine, spark(le), streak, twinkle, twinkling, wink
**twinkling of star**  scintillation
**twin of Agni**  Indra
**twin of Romulus**  Remus
**twin-track recording**  stereo
**twirl**  birl, coil, gyrate, helix, pirouette, pivot, revolve, rotate, spin, spiral, twiddle, twine, volute, wheel, whirl
**twist**  alter, bend, braid, change, coil, combine, contort, curl, curve, distort, gnarl, intertwine, kink, pervert, revolve, roll, screw, slew, spin, spiral, sprain, turn, tweak, twine, twirl, warp, wind, wrench, wriggle
**twist about**  writhe
**twist and turn**  meander, squirm, wiggle, wriggle, writhe
**twist around**  slew
**twist around one's little finger**  control, manipulate, (mis)use
**twisted**  altered, changed, coiled, contorted, distorted, entwined, misquoted, ricked, screwed, sprained, tortuous, warped, wound, wreathed, wrenched, wry
**twisted away from midline of body**  valgus
**twisted cord**  twine
**twisted cotton thread**  lisle
**twisted lock of hair**  curl
**twisted roll of wool**  slub
**twisted scroll**  torsade
**twisted sideways**  slew
**twisted spirally**  torse
**twisted state**  contortion
**twisting**  altering, changing, coiling, contorting, curling, distorting, entwining, misquoting, spinning, spraining, turning, warping, weaving, wrapping, wrenching, wringing
**twisting force**  torque, torsion
**twisting movement**  circumvolution
**twisting together**  convolution, entwining
**twist into confused mess**  entangle
**twist into ringlets**  curl
**twist into thread**  spin
**twist in wire**  kink
**twist of hair**  wisp
**twist one's body about**  writhe
**twist out of shape**  contort, distort, warp
**twist sharply**  tweak
**twist sideways**  slew
**twist someone's arm**  bully, coerce, force, persuade
**twist to and fro**  wrench, wriggle, wring

**twist violently** wrest
**twist violently round** wrench
**twit** berate, clown, fool, halfwit, hiss, hoot, idiot, lampoon, mock, moegoe, nitwit, pluck, rally, rebuke, revile, ridicule, scorn, simpleton, skit, sneer, taunt, upbraid
**twitch** contraction, convulse, jerk, move(ment), noose, pang, pull, pulse, seizure, spasm, throb, tic, tweak
**twitch suddenly** start
**two** bi-, couple, di-, dos (Sp), dyad, pair, twa (Sc)
**two colours** dichromic
**two-door car** coupé
**two dozen** thrave
**two-edged sword** claymore, pata, rapier
**two ens** em
**two-faced** hypocritical, insincere
**two-faced Roman god** Janus
**two family homes** duplex
**twofold** binary, double, doubly, dual, duple
**two-footed animal** biped
**two halves** one
**two-handed** ambidextrous, bimanual
**two-handled vessel** amphora, crater, diota, krater
**two-headed muscle** biceps
**two-horsed Roman chariot** biga
**two-hulled boat** catamaram
**two-humped camel** bactrian
**two hundred milligrams** carat
**two hundredth anniversary** bicentenary
**two leaves or folds** diptych
**two-legged creature** biped
**two lines** couple
**two lines of verse** couplet
**two make an em** ens
**two-masted sailboat** piragua, yawl
**two-masted ship** brig(antine), scow
**two matching things** pair
**two month period** bimester
**two notes** duplet
**two oar banks galley** bireme
**two of same kind** couple, pair
**two of similar tastes** Arcades ambo (L)
**two or more letters interwoven** monogram
**two pairs of wheels** cut(t)s
**two-person contest** duel
**two-piece swimsuit** bikini
**two pints** quart
**two pipper** lieutenant
**two points of earth's axis** poles
**two prefix** bi-
**two-quart** flagon
**two-quart wine bottle** magnum
**two rhyming lines** couplet

**two-seater motor car** coupé
**two-sided** bifacial, bihedral, bilateral, dihedral
**two-sided contest** dual
**twosome** duet, duo, pair
**two-spot card** deuce
**two-strand cord** marline
**two strokes under par at golf** eagle
**two successive lines of verse** couplet
**two-syllable foot** iamb(us), pyrrhic, spondee, trochee
**two thousand pounds** ton
**two times** twice
**two weeks** fortnight
**two-wheeled vehicle** bicycle, bike, calash, cart, chariot, croydon, curricle, landau, tilbury, trap, tumbrel, tumbril
**two-wheeler** bicycle
**two-winged** dipteral
**two-winged biting fly** gnat
**two-winged insect** diptera, fly
**two-yearly** biennial
**two-year-old deer** brock(et)
**two-year-old salmon** smolt
**two-year-old sheep** bident, hogg, teg(g)
**tycoon** autocrat, boss, despot, dictator, director, entrepreneur, enterpriser, financier, magnate, manager, mogul, nabob, shogun, tyrant
**tying up** mooring
**tympanic membrane** eardrum
**tympanum** ear(drum)
**type** category, character, clan, class(ification), creed, example, family, form, gender, group, ilk, kin(d), model, nature, order, pattern, print, prototype, race, sample, sort, species, strain, tribe, typeface, variety
**typeface** Aldine, (bold-)face, italic, roman, sans serif, (san)serif
**type measure** em, en, pica
**type of acid** itaconic
**type of aerial** dipole
**type of aircraft** jet
**type of ale** bitter
**type of alga** nostoc
**type of amine** ptomaine
**type of amphibian** toad
**type of anaesthetic** ether
**type of ancient gallery** trireme
**type of aneroid barometer** orometer
**type of animal** breed
**type of anorak** cagoule
**type of arch** horseshoe, keel, lancet, ogee, parabolic, round, segmented, shouldered, stilted, trefoil, tudor
**type of architecture** ionic
**type of athletic contest** biathlon
**type of atom** isotope

**type of automobile** sedan
**type of bacon** streaky
**type of ball game** handball
**type of barometer** aneroid
**type of battery** dry cell
**type of beam** laser
**type of bean** butter, green, haricot, kidney, lima, mung, snap, soy(a), stringless
**type of bear** American, Andean, Asiatic, bhalu, black, brown, grizzly, Himalayan, Japanese, Malay, Mongolian, panda, polar, sloth, spectacled, Tibetan
**type of beer** sorghum
**type of beet** sugar
**type of beetle** trimera
**type of bend** S
**type of bingo** lotto, tombola
**type of biscuit** cream cracker
**type of bomb** atomic, neutron, nuclear
**type of book** omnibus
**type of boomerang** kylie
**type of brake** servo
**type of bread** rye, whole wheat
**type of breed of terrier** Skye
**type of brooch** cameo
**type of butterfly** brushfooted, milkweed, monarch, red admiral, skipper, swift
**type of button** toggle
**type of cabbage** chou, kale, savoy
**type of candy** floss
**type of car** sedan
**type of carp** ide
**type of carpet** Axminster, Persian
**type of cat** Siamese
**type of cauliflower** broccoli
**type of caviar** beluga
**type of cedar** deodar
**type of cell involved in forming dental enamel** ameloblast
**type of cement** mastic
**type of cemetery** urnfield
**type of chair** easy
**type of cheese** blue, Brie, Caerphilly, Camembert, Cheddar, cream, edam, gouda, gruyere, mysost, romano, stilton, Swiss
**type of cigar** cheroot, panatella
**type of clock** cuckoo
**type of cloth made of camel hair** aba
**type of coati** civet, racoon
**type of cocktail** highball, martini
**type of coffee** espresso
**type of colonnade** systyle
**type of column** ionic
**type of comedy** burlesque, slapstick
**type of compass** gyro
**type of computer** digital
**type of concrete** precast
**type of constrictor** boa

type of contract for renting property   leasehold
type of cookout   barbecue, braai
type of corrosive   peracid
type of cotton fabric   galatea
type of crab   hermit, limulus, mangrove, mantis, mud, sand, spider, squilla
type of cravat   ascot
type of cricket bowler   seamer, spinner
type of crow   magpie
type of crumpet   pikelet
type of cured meat   salt-pork
type of curve   trochoid
type of dance   ballroom, bebop, rumba(h), tango, waltz
type of deer   musk
type of defence used by accused   alibi
type of denim jeans reinforced with rivets   Levis
type of desert   junket
type of disinfectant   lysol
type of dog   hound
type of doll   kewpie
type of dormer window   lucarne
type of drum   ngoma
type of duck   eider, muscovy
type of dulcimer   cimbalom
type of dwelling   tenement
type of earth   sienna
type of earthenware   terracotta
type of edible mushroom   cep
type of eel   conger
type of engine   diesel, oil-cooled, petrol
type of entertainment   cabaret
type of envelope   manila
type of ermine   stoat
type of excavation in mining   slope
type of fabric   rep, tapa
type of fencing   barbed wire
type of fern   nardoo
type of film   western
type of finch   linnet
type of firework   squib
type of fish   sardelle, tetra
type of fishing net   flue
type of flamenco dance   farruca
type of flat   duplex
type of fountain pen   stylograph
type of fuel   ethane, gas, peat
type of fungus   agaric
type of fur   mink, vair
type of gas   neon
type of grapnel   creeper
type of grass   buffalo, couch, esparto, kikuyu
type of growth   cyst
type of gun   sten
type of gypsum   alabaster
type of hairclip with spring   kirbygrip
type of hammer   claw
type of handgun   pistol

type of haricot bean   French-bean
type of hat   fedora, toque
type of hawk   harrier
type of health bread   rye
type of heather   erica
type of hedge   myrtle
type of hickory   pecan
type of horse race   steeplechase
type of icing   glace
type of igneous rock   felsite
type of Indian cooking   tandoori
type of insect   beetle
type of Italian pottery   majolica
type of jacket   double-breasted, eton
type of jazz   trad
type of jug   ewer
type of junction   T
type of knot   granny, reef
type of ladies' stocking   lisle
type of large pick   mattock
type of lathe   facer
type of lawn grass   fescue
type of leather   suede
type of lettuce   cos, savoy
type of light   neon
type of light anti-aircraft gun   Bofors
type of lily   arum, crinum, lotus, scilla
type of limestone   marble
type of loaf   coburg
type of lock   mortise, Yale
type of lumber jacket   windjammer
type of lute   mandolin
type of mackerel   atka
type of mahogany   acajou
type of menu   á la carte
type of mint herb   thyme
type of moulding   ogee
type of music   kwela, soul
type of musical chord   arpeggio
type of musket   matchlock
type of neuralgia   sciatica
type of nut   almond, cashew, hazel, hickory, peanut, pecan, pistachio, walnut
type of nylon   bri, enkalon
type of onion   shallot
type of orange   mandarin, navel, osage, seville, tangerine, valencia
type of orchid   musk
type of oven   microwave
type of owl   tawny
type of paint   duco
type of painting   genre
type of palm   nipa
type of palm tree   areca
type of paper   manila
type of pasta   cannelloni, macaroni, noodles, vermicelli
type of pea   mangetout
type of peach   nectarine
type of pear   avocado, bartlett

type of pedestrian crossing   pelican, zebra
type of pendant   locket
type of petal   galea
type of pickle   dill, gherkin
type of pie   apple
type of pigeon   fantail
type of pike   gar
type of plant   fern
type of plaster   stucco
type of play   satire
type of poem   ode, sonnet
type of poison   veratrin
type of polygon   triangle
type of poplar   aspen
type of potherb   savory
type of primitive man   Neanderthal
type of print   Aldin, bold, italic, roman, sanserif
type of prophet   geomancer
type of protein   actin
type of pudding   bread, sago
type of pump   suction
type of puppet that covers the hand   glove
type of racer   dragster
type of rectangular temple tower   ziggurat, zik(k)urat
type of reef   coral
type of resin   anime, lac
type of rigging   balloon sail, lateen
type of rock   basalt, greisen, shale
type of rodent   agouti
type of rose   rambler
type of rot   dry
type of rummy   gin
type of sail   lateen, spencer, studdingsail
type of sailing ship   barque
type of sausage   liverwurst, vienna
type of saw   tenon
type of sea bird   tern
type of sea shell   conch
type of seaweed   nullipore
type of serious actress   tragedienne
type of sheep   merino
type of sherry   olorosa
type of shoe heel   cuban
type of show   revue
type of shrub   gorse
type of silk   tram
type of sleeping sickness   narcolepsy
type of small shrill flute   fife
type of smooth silk or rayon fabric   peau de soie (F)
type of sofa   divan
type of soil   loam
type of soprano   mezzo
type of spinner   leg break, off break
type of squash   gem
type of stencil   template
type of stew and setter   Irish

**type of stocking** nylon
**type of stork** marabou
**type of straw hat** leghorn
**type of sugar** glucose, heptose
**type of swallow** martin
**type of sweet** chocolate, marshmallow, mint, nougat, peppermint
**type of sweet dish** pavlova
**type of terrier** cairn
**type of textile fibre** rayon
**type of thief** kleptomaniac
**type of tide** neap
**type of tie** bow
**type of tonic** myrica
**type of trade discount** tret
**type of tree** adler, ash
**type of triangle** isosceles
**type of trousers** hipsters
**type of turtle** snapper
**type of tweed** harris
**type of type** italic, roman
**type of tyre** radial
**type of ulcer** duodenal
**type of vase** urn
**type of verb** stative
**type of vermouth** martini
**type of verse** iambic
**type of vine** cissus
**type of violin** cello, cremona, stradivarius, viola

**type of wall painting** secco
**type of weave** leno, weft
**type of West Indian popular music** reggae
**type of whisky** bourbon, rye
**type of willow** osier
**type of window** oriel
**type of window blind** venetian
**type of wolf** aardwolf
**type of wrestling** tag
**type of year** calendar, fiscal, leap, lunar, solar
**typesetter** printer
**type specimen** holotype
**type square** em
**type style** Aldine, bold, italic, roman, (san)serif
**type term** em, en
**typewriter lever** key
**typewriter roller** platen
**typhlosis** blindness
**typhoid fever** enteric
**typhus carrier** lice
**typical** average, characteristic, conventional, normal, regular, representative, usual
**typical example** archetype, norm, paradigm
**typing space mark** tab
**typist** stenographer

**typographical error** erratum, misprint
**Tyr** Jupiter, Tiu, Zeus
**tyrannical** arbitrary, autocratic, brutal, cruel, despotic, dictatorial, domineering, hard, harsh, imperious, inhuman, iron-handed, oppressive, sadistic, savage, severe, strict, tyrannous, unyielding
**tyrannical government** despotism
**tyrant** absolutist, autarch, autocrat, bully, despot, dictator, martinet, monarch, monocrat, Nero, ogre, oppressor, slave-driver
**tyre** radial
**tyre face** tread
**tyre fill** air
**tyre pattern** tread
**tyre support** rim
**tyro** abecedarian, apprentice, beginner, catechumen, entrant, initiate, learner, neophyte, newcomer, novice, plebe, probationer, protégé, pupil, recruit, roofie, rookie, starter, student, tiro, trainee
**Tyrolean dress** dirndl
**Tyrolean singer** yodeler
**Tyrolean singing** yodel
**tzigane** gypsy

# U

**ubiety** presence
**ubiquitous** all-over, everpresent, everywhere, omnipresent, pervasive, universal
**ubiquitous beverage** tea
**ubiquitousness** omnipresence, pervasiveness
**ubiquity** diffusion, diffusiveness, dispersal, omnipresence, pervasion, universality
**udder** breast, dug, pap, tit
**udder part** nipple, teat
**udder product** milk
**ugly** amoral, awful, base, corrupt, disagreeable, displeasing, hideous, homely, ill-favoured, nasty, offensive, plain, quarrelsome, repulsive, revolting, spiteful, surly, terrible, unattractive, unlovely, unpleasant, unsightly, vile
**ugly demon** goblin
**ugly lovable visitor** ET
**ugly old woman** crone, hag, harpy

**ugly sight** eyesore
**ugly symbol** toad
**ugly-tempered** snarlish
**ugly woman** beldam, hag
**uintathere** dinoceras
**ukase** decree, edict, ordinance
**Ukrainian assembly** rada
**Ukrainian currency** grivna, shagiv
**Ukrainian dance** gopak
**Ukrainian native** Cossack
**Ukrainian port** Odessa
**ulcer** abscess, bane, blain, blight, blister, boil, cancer, canker, carbuncle, corruption, cyst, fester, furuncle, gumboil, infection, lesion, pimple, pustule, rot, sore, swelling, ulceration
**ulcerous disease of animals** canker, lupus
**ulcerous skin** lupus
**ulcerous sore** canker
**ulmaceous tree** elm
**ulster** overcoat

**Ulster capital** Belfast
**ulterior** concealed, covert, hidden, undisclosed, unexpressed
**ulterior motive** arrière-pensée (F)
**ultimate** conclusive, decisive, end, eventual, extreme, farthest, final, furthest, greatest, highest, last, paramount, superlative, supreme, topmost, utmost
**ultimate aim** intention
**ultimate reach** pitch
**ultimo** past
**ultra** downright, exceptional, excessive, exorbitant, extraordinary, extravagant, extreme, immoderate, inordinate, notable, outrageous, outstanding, radical, sheer, thorough, uncompromising, unmitigated
**ultramarine** azure, blue, cobalt, navy, pigment, sapphire
**ultra modern** advanced, avant-garde (F), forward-looking, futuristic,

**ululate** modernistic, new, progressive, way-out
**ululate** hoot, howl, wail
**ululating** howling, wailing
**Ulysses' friend** Mentor
**umbilicus** navel
**umbra** cloudiness, dimness, duskiness, gloom, murk(iness), obscureness, semi-darkness, shade, shadiness, shadow(iness), sombreness, spectre, twilight
**umbrage** anger, displeasure, grudge, huff, indignation, offence, offense, pique, resentment
**umbrella** brolly, cover, gamp, parasol, protection, sunshade
**umbrella-like flower** umbel
**umbrella-like thing** canopy
**umbrella part** cover, rib
**umbrella rod** stretcher
**umbrella's end-piece** ferrule
**Umbria river** Tevere
**Umbria town** Assisi
**umiak** oomiac, oomiak
**umlaut** dieresis, metaphony, mutation
**umpire** adjudicate, adjudicator, arbiter, arbitrate, arbitrator, decide(r), determine, judge, linesman, moderator, negotiator, peacemaker, reconciler, ref(eree), sentencer
**umpteen** several
**un** one
**un-** de-
**unabashed** blatant, bold(-faced), unawed, unconcerned
**unable** cannot, forceless, impotent, impuissant, incapable, incompetent, ineffective, ineffectual, powerless, unfit(ted), unproficient, unqualified, useless
**unable to bear young** barren
**unable to be heard** inaudible
**unable to be read** illegible
**unable to be set on fire** non-inflammable
**unable to concentrate** scatterbrained
**unable to express oneself clearly** inarticulate
**unable to fly** flightless
**unable to follow** lost
**unable to hear** deaf
**unable to move or feel** torpid
**unable to pay debts** insolvent
**unable to perform a task** incompetent, inefficient
**unable to produce vegetation** barren
**unable to read and write** illiterate
**unable to see** blind
**unable to see far** nearsighted
**unable to sleep** sleepless, wakeful
**unable to speak** dumb
**unable to walk normally** lame

**unabridged** complete, full-length, uncondensed, uncut, unshortened, whole
**unaccented** atonic, unaccentuated, unemphasised, unstressed, weak
**unacceptable** alien, bad, distasteful, improper, ineligible, intolerable, objectionable, unallowable, unsatisfactory, unseemly, unsuitable, unwelcome, wrong
**unaccepted offer** pollicitation
**unaccompanied** alone, apart, companionless, lone(ly), separate, single, sole, solitary, solo, unattended, unescorted
**unaccompanied man** stag
**unaccompanied performer** soloist
**unaccompanied song** aria
**unadulterated** fit, pure, sheer, unmixed, unspoilt
**unaffected** frank, genuine, honest, ingenuous, naïve, natural, simple, sincere, unbothered, undisturbed, unstirred, untouched, wholesome
**unaffected by** impervious
**unaffected in manner** natural
**unailowable** immaterial, inadmissible, inappropriate, incompetent, irrelevant, unacceptable, unqualified
**unalloyed joy** bliss
**unalterably obligatory** irremissible
**unambiguous** apparent, audible, blunt, clear, coherent, definite, distinct, evident, explicit, express, lucid, obvious, palpable, plain, precise, recognisable, specific, unequivocal
**unanimity** accord, agreement, concert, harmony, unison, unity
**unapparent** invisible, undisclosed, unnoticeable
**unappreciated woman** femme incomprise (F)
**unappreciative person** ingrate
**unapt** inapplicable, inappropriate, indisposed, irrelevant, slow, unfit(ted), unlikely, unsuitable, unsuited
**unarmed** weaponless
**unarmed self defence** karate
**unashamed** brazen
**unasked for** spontaneous, unsolicited
**unaspirated consonant** lene
**unassailable** impregnable, invincible, irrefutable, secure
**unassembled** centrifugal
**unassuming** difficult, humble, meek, modest, quiet, reserved, simple, unobtrusive, unpretentious
**unattached** alloidal, apart, available, datable, divorced, free, heretic, independent, lonely, loose, separate,

single, unassociated, unconnected, unescorted, untied, unwed
**unattached journalist** free-lance
**unattended** abandoned, alone, companionless, forgotten, lone(some), neglected, solo, unappreciated, unescorted, unwatched
**unattractive** cheerless, disliked, homely, ugly, undesired, unpleasant, unpleasing, unwanted
**unattractive girl** frump
**unattractively dull** dowdy
**unauthorised patrolman** vigilante
**unauthorised visitor** trespasser
**unavailing** abortive, fruitless, futile, idle, ineffective, pointless, unproductive, useless, vain
**unavoidable** assured, certain, clear, compulsory, evident, fated, imperative, indefeasible, inescapable, inevasible, inevitable, necessary, obligatory, ordained, plain, predestined, predetermined, required, secured, unquestionable
**unaware** apathetic, asleep, backward, blind, clueless, dull, heedless, ignorant, inattentive, insensate, insensible, misinformed, misled, oblivious, simple, stupid, unacquainted, unadvised, unconscious, unenlightened, unfeeling, unknowing, unmindful, unprepared, unwarned, unwary, witless
**unaware of** blind
**unaware of something** oblivious
**unbearable** insufferable, insupportable, intolerable, unendurable, unlivable
**unbearableness** insufferableness, intolerableness
**unbearably conceited** insufferable
**unbelievable** astonishing, impossible, inconceivable, incredible, staggering, unthinkable
**unbeliever** agnostic, atheist, disbeliever, doubter, gentile, heathen, heretic, infidel, minimifidian, nihilist, nullifidian, pagan, sceptic
**unbelieving** cynical, derisive, disloyal, doubtful, doubting, dubious, faithless, false, fickle, inconstant, incredulous, ironic, jealous, misanthropical, mocking, perfidious, pessimistic, sarcastic, sardonic, sceptical, scornful, sneering, suspicious, traitorous, treacherous, unfaithful, unreliable, untrue, untrustworthy, untruthful, wary
**unbelieving Thomas** doubter

**unbend** relax, slacken, uncoil, uncurl, unwind
**unbending** firm, formal, inflexible, obstinate, rigid, starchy, stiff, strict, stubborn, tough, uncompromising
**unbiased** detached, disinterested, equitable, impartial, independent, neutral, tolerant, unprejudiced
**unbleached cotton** calico
**unbleached linen** ecru
**unbleached silk** pongee
**unblock** clear, crack, open, unbar, unclose, uncork, uncover, undo, unfasten, unlock, unseal, untie, unwrap
**unborn offspring** embryo, foetus
**unbounded** autocratic, boundless, ceaseless, constant, continual, despotic, dictatorial, endless, enormous, eternal, everlasting, full, immense, immortal, incessant, inestimable, infinite, interminable, limitless, loose, measureless, perpetual, sovereign, stupendous, supreme, unbroken, unconditional, unlimited, unqualified, unquestionable, unrestricted, vast, wide
**unbranded calf or yearling** maverick
**unbreakable plastic** perspex
**unbridled** extravagant, immoderate, loose, prodigal, rampant, unchecked, unconstrained, uncontrolled, uncurbed, unreined, unrestrained, wild
**unbroken** complete, deep, entire, intact, solid, total, undisturbed, unimpaired, uninterrupted, whole
**unbroken horse** bronco, brumby
**unbroken view of surrounding region** panorama
**unburden** confess, confide, discharge, disclose, empty, lighten, relieve, reveal, rid, unload
**unburnt sun-dried brick** adobe
**unburnt tobacco left in pipe** dottle
**uncalled for** needless, unnecessary
**uncanny** creepy, eerie, extraordinary, fantastic, mysterious, preternatural, remarkable, strange, supernatural, unearthly, unnatural, weird
**uncare for** neglect
**uncastrated male horse** stallion
**uncaused** natural, spontaneous
**unceremonious attire** negligé, negligee
**unceremonious dismissal** congé
**unceremonious haste** abruptness
**uncertain** changeable, doubtful, dubious, fitful, improbable, indefinite, indeterminate, indistinct, insecure, irregular, perilous, precarious, unassured, undecided, undetermined, unfixed, unpredictable, unreliable, unsafe, unstable, unsure, vague, variable
**uncertain estimate** guess
**uncertain in movement** erratic
**uncertain state** limbo
**uncertainty** ambiguity, confusion, doubt, hesitancy, hesitation, indecision, perplexity, quandary, scepticism, suspense, unpredictability, vagueness
**unchain** acquit, clear, deliver, discharge, disenthrall, disimprison, dismiss, drop, emancipate, extricate, free, liberate, manumit, redeem, release, rescue, unbind, unbridle, uncage, undo, unfasten, unfetter, unhook, unleash, (un)loose, unpen, unshackle, untie
**unchangeable** balanced, changeless, constant, enduring, finer, immoral, immutable, invariable, lasting, perpetual, reliable, solid, sound, stable, steadfast
**unchanging** boring, changeless, colourless, consistent, constant, continual, dependable, dull, endless, enduring, equable, eternal, even, everlasting, fixed, flat, humdrum, immortal, immutable, inflexible, invariable, lifelong, monotonous, perennial, permanent, perpetual, persistent, regular, rigid, smooth, soporific, stable, steady, tedious, temperate, toneless, tranquil, undeviating, unfailing, uniform, unvarying
**uncharitable** abusive, austere, brutal, cruel, despotic, merciless, pitiless, remorseless, selfish, stern, stringent, unchristian, unconcerned, unfriendly, ungenerous, unkind
**unchaste** abandoned, bad, corrupt, debauched, dissolute, immodest, immoral, impure, indecent, lascivious, libertine, loose, obscene, unclean, wanton
**unchaste man** lecher, pervert, satyr
**unchaste woman** whore
**unchecked** abandoned, excessive, free, furious, inordinate, intemperate, licentious, natural, rampant, riotous, unbounded, unbridled, uncontrolled, undisciplined, uninhibited, unrestrained, unruly, violent, wanton
**uncial** letter, script, strokes, symbols
**uncivil** boorish, discourteous, impolite, rude, uncivilised, uncouth, unmannerly
**uncivilised** antisocial, barbarian, barbaric, boorish, gross, illbred, illiterate, primitive, savage, uncouth, uncultured, uneducated, untamed, vulgar, wild
**uncivilised person** savage
**unclad** nude, naked
**unclaimed goods** bona vacantia
**unclassified** crude
**uncle** eme (Sc), oom, tio (Sp)
**unclean** base, contaminated, corrupt, defiled, dirty, dusty, evil, filthy, foul, grubby, impure, lewd, nasty, soiled, stained, unchaste, unhygienic
**unclean atmosphere** miasma
**unclear** ambiguous, bleary, blurred, confused, dim, doubtful, dubious, faint, hazy, indefinite, indeterminate, indistinct, muddled, nebulous, obscure, shadowy, uncertain, vague
**unclear to the mind** intangible
**uncle of Bethuel** Abraham
**uncle of Esther** Mordecai
**uncle of Joab** David
**uncle of Jonadab** David
**uncle of Mahalah** Gilead
**uncle of Saul** Ner
**uncle's son** nephew
**uncle's wife** aunt
**unclosed** open
**unclothe** denude, disrobe, divest, strip, uncloak, uncover, undrape, undress, unrobe, unscreen
**unclothed** bare, buff, naked
**unco** news, notable, remarkably, strange(r), unusual, very
**uncoil** slacken, undo, unreel, unroll, untwine, untwist, unwind
**uncomely** improper, unseemly
**uncomfortable** anxious, apprehensive, concerned, discomforting, disquieting, distressed, disturbed, fearful, miserable, nervous, perturbed, squirming, strained, stressful, tense, troubled, uneasy, unhappy, unpleasant, worried, writhing
**uncommitted** available, floating, free, independent, neutral, unattached, unbound, undecided, unengaged, uninvolved, unpledged, unpromised
**uncommon** abnormal, curious, distinctive, exceptional, exotic, few, freakish, freaky, infrequent, new, noteworthy, novel, occasional, odd, outstanding, peculiar, queer, rare, remarkable, scarce, singular, special, strange, unfamiliar, unique, unusual, unwonted, weird
**uncommon thing** rarity
**uncommunicative** cag(e)y, dumb, reserved, reticent, secretive, silent, speechless, taciturn, unsociable

**uncomplicated** adept, adroit, clear, easy, effortless, elementary, facile, fluent, intelligible, light, lucid, painless, plain, quick, rudimentary, simple, skilful, smooth, straightforward, undemanding, uninvolved, unrefined

**uncompromising** firm, inexorable, inflexible, intransigent, strict, stubborn, unbending

**unconcealed** apparent, manifest, obvious, open, overt, plain, uncovered, unveiled

**unconcerned with morality** amoral, nonmoral

**unconnected** detached, disconnected, disjointed, illogical, incoherent, independent, irrelevant, meaningless, separate, unrelated

**unconditional** absolute, categorical, complete, unqualified, unreserved, unrestricted

**unconditional authorisation** carte blanche

**unconditionally** absolutely, altogether, completely, entirely, fully, positively, totally, unreservedly

**unconfirmed report** rumour

**unconscious** accidental, heedless, ignorant, inherent, innate, insensible, numb, oblivious, out, reflex, repressed, senseless, stunned, unaware, unintentional, unknowing, unwitting

**unconscious condition** faint

**unconsciously artless** naïve

**unconsciousness** heedlessness, numbness, obliviousness, senselessness, unawareness

**unconscious state** coma

**unconstitutional** banned, black-market, bootleg, criminal, felonious, forbidden, illegal, illegitimate, illicit, improper, lawless, outlawed, prohibited, proscribed, unauthorised, unlawful, unlicensed, unofficial, wrongful

**uncontrollable** frantic, furious, helpless, irrepressible, mad, strong, unmanageable, unruly, violent, wild

**uncontrollable impulse to start fires** pyromania

**uncontrollable temper** rampage

**uncontrollably emotional** hysterical

**uncontrolled anger** rage

**uncontrolled excitement** hysteria

**unconventional** bizarre, bohemian, eccentric, individual, informal, odd, offbeat, unorthodox, unusual

**unconventional person** bohemian, bolshy, freak

**uncooked** au naturel (F), fresh, natural, raw, undressed, unprepared

**uncooked porridge** oatmeal

**uncooked rice** bigas

**uncooked vegetables served with a dressing** salad

**uncouple** detach, disconnect, disengage, disentangle, disjoin, disunite, divide, free, isolate, loosen, part, remove, separate, sever, split, sunder, unfasten

**uncouth** awkward, boorish, clumsy, coarse, crude, discourteous, disrespectful, gauche, graceless, ill-bred, ill-mannered, impolite, indecorous, peculiar, raffish, rough, rude, uncivil(ised), uncultivated, unknown, unrefined, unseemly, unusual, vulgar

**uncouth person** ape, codger, hairyback, peasant, sakai, yahoo, yokel

**uncover** bare, discase, disclose, discover, divest, divulge, expose, impart, open, reveal, strip, unearth, unmask, unveil, unwrap

**uncovered enclosure connected with house** patio

**uncovering** disclosure, exposure, revelation, unmasking, unveiling

**uncrystallised syrup drained from raw sugar** molasses

**unction holder** chrismatory

**unctuous** ardent, fervid, greasy, insincere, lubricated, lubricous, oily, oleaginous, pious, saponaceous, slippery, slithery, smooth, soapy, sycophantic, urbane, waxy

**uncultivated land** fallow

**uncultured** barbaric, discourteous, ignoble, impolite, inelegant, rough, rude, unladylike, unmannerly, unrefined

**uncured kipper** herring

**uncut** unabridged

**uncut movie** uncensored

**undaunted** audacious, bold, brave, fearless, firm, intrepid, manful, persistent, resolute, steadfast, unalarmed, undiscouraged, unfazed, unperturbed, valiant

**undecided** contestable, doubtful, hesitating, irresolute, pending, uncertain, undetermined, unset, unsettled, unsure

**undefeated** triumphant, unbeaten, victorious

**undefiled** abstinent, chaste, clean, fair, good, graceful, honest, honourable, innocent, intact, moral, pure, refined, sinless, spotless, stainless,

unaffected, unmixed, unsoiled, virtuous

**undeniable** certain, clear, evident, incontestable, indisputable, indubitable, irrefutable, obvious, unimpeachable

**undeniable truth** hard fact

**under** below, beneath, downward, immersed, inferior, less, lower, sub-; submerged, underneath

**under a cloud** distrusted, suspect(ed)

**under a curse** accursed, accurst

**under age** minor

**under an assumed name** alias, incognito, unknown

**under an obligation** grateful, indebted, obligated, thankful

**under an unusual nervous strain** overwrought

**under arms** armed

**under a roof** indoors

**under a spell** bewitched, mesmerised, spellbound

**underbodice** camisole

**under care of bishop** diocese

**under consideration** pending, sub judice

**under-cooked meat** rare

**undercover** clandestinely, covertly, stealthily

**undercover agent** mole, sleeper, spy

**undercover work** espionage, spying

**underdone** incomplete, insufficient, partial, rare, raw, undone

**underfed** diminutive, dwarfish, feeble, frail, little, malnourished, puny, sickly, stunted, tiny, weak(ly)

**under feudal tenure** liege

**underfoot** afoot, begun, going

**under foreign allegiance** alien

**undergarment** bra(ssière), briefs, chemise, corset, girdle, knickers, lingerie, petticoat, slip, underclothes, underpants, underwear, undies, vest

**undergo** abide, allow, bear, encounter, endure, experience, permit, suffer, sustain, tolerate

**undergo decomposition** decay, rot

**undergo oxidation** rust

**undergo pain** suffer

**underground** buried, clandestine, covertly, furtively, hidden, privately, secret(ly), sneakingly, stealthily, subterraneanly, tunnel, under-the-table, undercover, underhandedly, underworld

**underground cave** catacomb, cavern, cove, grotto, subterranean, subterraneous

**underground cell** crypt, dungeon, vault

**underground cemetery** catacomb

**underground chamber** cave, hypogeum, vault
**underground channel** culvert
**underground drain** sewer
**underground fighter** Maquis, Partisan, terrorist
**underground hollow** cavern
**underground part of a plant** root
**underground passage** conduit, subway, tunnel
**underground pool** artesian well
**underground railway** metro, subway, tube
**underground reservoir** cistern
**underground river** Phlegethon, Styx
**underground room** cellar
**underground stem** corm, rhizome, root, tuber
**underground tomb** catacomb
**underground train** metro, subway, tube
**underhand** clandestine, crooked, devious, dishonourable, dubious, fraudulent, illegal, illicit, immoral, insincere, misdealing, occult, secret, shady, sly, sneaky, stealthy, surreptitious, suspicious, treacherous, unethical, wrong
**underhand dealings** skulduggery
**underhanded** corrupt, covert, criminal, crooked, deceitful, dirty, dishonourable, illicit, immoral, left-handed, perfidious, sinful, sly, sneaky, understaffed, unfair, wrong
**underhand malpractices** sculduggery, skulduggery
**underhand plan** scheme
**underhand plotting** intrigue
**underhand scheming** jiggery-pokery
**underlying** basic, fundamental, hidden, latent, low, subjacent, supporting, undermost
**undermine** burrow, debilitate, erode, excavate, impair, mine, sabotage, sap, subvert, threaten, tunnel, undercut, weaken, wreck
**undermine credibility** discredit, disprove, invalidate, refute
**underminer** saboteur
**undermining of the state** sedition
**underneath** below, beneath, bottom, down, inferior, junior, lesser, lower, menial, minor, secondary, sole, subordinate, subsidiary, unbefitting, under(side)
**under no circumstances** never
**under obligation** beholden
**under one's breath** sotto voce (I)
**under one's own power** independently, personally
**under one's wing** cloistered, protected, sheltered

**underpants** briefs
**underpart of shoe** sole
**undersea** subaqueous, submarine, submerged, sunken, underwater
**undersea boat** submarine, U-boat
**undersea dweller** fish, mermaid
**undersea sound** sonar
**undersea wreckage** lagan
**under sentence** doomed
**undershirt** camisa, semmit (Sc), shirt, singlet, vest, wrapper
**underside** bottom
**undersized** atrophied, bony, dwarfish, emaciated, puny, skinny, squat, stubby, underdeveloped, underfed, underweight
**undersized animal** runt, scal(l)awag, scallywag
**undersized person** runt
**understand** accept, appreciate, apprehend, assume, believe, commiserate, comprehend, conceive, conclude, discern, fathom, follow, gather, get, grasp, hear, know, learn, penetrate, perceive, presume, realise, recognise, savvy, see, seize, suppose, sympathise, think
**understandable by the few** esoteric
**understandable by the many** exoteric
**understand fully** realise
**understanding** accord, agreement, appreciation, arrangement, awareness, belief, compassion(ate), comprehension, conclusion, considerate, discerning, discernment, entente, forgiving, grasp, idea, insight, judg(e)ment, kind, knowledge, notion, opinion, pact, patient, perception, perceptive, rapport, reception, sense, sensitive, sympathetic, sympathy, tactful, tolerant, view
**understatement** litotes
**understood** accepted, appreciated, apprehended, assumed, believed, conceived, concluded, discerned, followed, got, heard, implicit, inferred, penetrated, perceived, presumed, tacit, thought, unspoken, unstated
**understood by few** arcane
**understood without words** tacit
**under strain** tense
**under stress** harassed, worried
**under strict control** regimented
**undersurface of foot** sole
**undersurface of hand** palm
**under suspicion** implicated, involved, suspected
**undertake a journey** travel
**undertake a voyage** sail

**undertaker** embalmer, entrepreneur, mortician
**undertaker's vehicle** hearse
**undertaking** adventure, assurance, campaign, commission, commitment, effort, engagement, enterprise, guarantee, oath, operation, pledge, project, promise, quest, task, testimony, venture, vow, word
**undertaking of long duration** marathon
**undertaking of risk** venture
**undertaking to do or not to do something** promise
**under the best of circumstances** ideally
**under the blankets** abed
**under the counter** illegal, unlawful, wrongful
**under the influence** drunk, inebriated, intoxicated
**under the name** as
**under the protection of the law** in gremio legis (L)
**under the skin** subcutaneous
**under the tongue** hypoglossal
**under the weather** crapulent, drunk, ill, indisposed
**under the window** sill
**undervest** singlet
**under water** flooded, inundated
**underwater boat** submarine
**underwater detector** sonar
**underwater expert** Cousteau
**underwater gear** scuba
**underwater missile** torpedo
**underwater radar** sonar
**underwater ridge** reef
**underwater swimmer** diver, frogman
**underwater swimmer's flipper** fin
**underwater vessel** submarine
**underwater weapon** torpedo
**underwater worker** diver, frogman
**under way** afoot, begun, forward, going, launched, moving, started
**underwear** bra(ssière), briefs, camisole, corset, dainties, drawers, (half)slip, lingerie, panties, petticoat, teddies, underclothes, underdress, undergarments, underpants, undershorts, (under)vest, undies
**underworld** Avernus, Dis, Hades, Orcus, Sheol
**underworld for heroes** Valhalla
**underworld river** Acheron, Lethe, Phlegethon, Styx
**underworld watchdog** Cerberus
**underwriter** backer
**undesirable material** smut
**undetermined** hesitating, irresolute, undecided

**undeveloped** adolescent, crude, dormant, embryo(nic), green, immature, juvenile, latent, premature, underlying, ungrown, unmanifested, unripe, untrained, young
**undeveloped area** wild
**undeveloped germ** embryo
**undiagnosed disease** itis
**undignified behaviour** levity
**undiluted** clear, neat, pure, straight, unmingled, unmixed, untinged
**undim** clear
**undiplomatic** tactless
**undisturbed** calm, collected, composed, equable, even, impassive, quiet, serene, uninterrupted, untouched
**undivided** combined, complete, comprehensive, entire, exclusive, full, indivisible, intact, one, perfect, solid, thorough, total, unbroken, uncut, unimpaired, whole
**undivided unit** whole
**undo** annul, cancel, disjoin, loosen, open, unfasten, unravel, untie
**undo door** unbolt
**undo metal fasteners** unzip
**undo sewing** unpick
**undoubted** certain, definite, evident, obvious, sure
**undoubted fact** certainty
**undoubtedly** absolutely, assuredly, certainly, clearly, definitely, doubtless, easily, indubitably, positively, surely, undeniably, unmistakably, unquestionably
**undress** change, denude, disrobe, expose, shed, strip, unclothe, undrape, unrobe, unveil, unwrap
**undressed hide** pelt
**undressed kid** suede
**undress oneself** strip
**undue** de trop (F), excessive, extravagant, extreme, gratuitous, improper, intemperate, needless, overmuch, unapt, unearned, unjustified, unmerited, unseemly, unwarranted
**undue economy** parsimony
**undue favour in appointing one's relatives to office** nepotism
**undue politeness** genteelness
**undue slowness to act** sloth
**undue speed** haste
**undulating** rolling
**unduly anxious about one's health** valetudinarian
**unduly confident** presumptuous
**unduly curious** inquisitive
**unduly defensive batting** stonewalling
**unduly fearful** paranoid

**unduly high** steep
**unduly inquiring** inquisitive
**unduly long harangue** screed
**unduly quick** hasty, precipitate, rash
**unduly scrupulous** squeamish
**undyed cloth** greige
**undying** abiding, ageless, ceaseless, classic, constant, continual, deathless, endless, enduring, eternal, everlasting, immortal, incessant, indefatigable, ineradicable, infinite, interminable, invariable, lasting, permanent, perpetual, persistent, sempiternal, unbounded, unbroken, unceasing, unending, unlimited, untiring, unwearied
**unearthly** eerie, ghostly, haunted, outrageous, spine-chilling, strange, supernatural, ungodly, unreasonable, weird
**uneasiness** anxiety, disquiet(ude), fretfulness, inquietude, restlessness
**uneasiness caused by want of drink** thirst
**uneasy** agitated, alarmed, anxious, awkward, disturbed, edgy, fidgety, jittery, nervous, queasy, rattled, restive, restless, ruffled, stiff, tense, troubled, uncomfortable, upset, worried
**uneasy feeling** malaise
**uneasy in mind** anxious, apprehensive
**uneatability** inedibility
**uneatable** inedible
**uneducated** crude, ignorant, illiterate, innocent, rude, unaware, undisciplined, unenlightened, uninformed, uninitiated, uninstructed, unlettered, unrefined, untaught, untutored, unwitting
**unelevated** low, base
**unemotional** apathetic, callous, calm, cold, cool, hardened, impassive, languid, listless, neutral, sedate, stoical, unexcitable, unimpressible, unmoved, untouched
**unemotional person** stoic
**unemployed** idle, inactive, inoperative, jobless, latent, leisured, redundant, unapplied, unbusied, unexercised, unoccupied, untapped, unused, workless
**unemployment relief** dole, social security, UIF
**unencumbered** clear
**unending** ceaseless, constant, endless, eternal, everlasting, perpetual, unremitting
**unenlightened person** heathen

**unequal** different, dissimilar, incompatible, inharmonious, uneven, unidentical, unlike, variable, varying
**unequally balanced** one-sided
**unequal to** deficient, equitable, insufficient, lacking, lopsided, one-sided, overbalanced, partial, unbalanced, uneven, unfair, unjust, wanting
**unerring** certain, correct, exact, infallible, precise, true, unfailing
**unescapable** ineluctable
**unescorted** alone, fellowless, friendless, lone, solitary, unaccompanied, unpaired, unpartnered
**unethical lawyer** shyster
**uneven** angled, askew, awry, broken, bumpy, coarse, craggy, crooked, curved, defective, disproportioned, distorted, erose, faulty, flawed, furrowed, incomplete, infrequent, irregular, jagged, jerky, knobby, lumpy, nodular, odd, rough, rutty, slanted, tilted, unbalanced, unequal, wavering
**uneven condition** asperity
**uneven in colour** streaky
**uneven in quality** patchy
**unevenly** awry
**unevenly shaped** erose, scalene
**unevenness of surface** inequality
**unevenness of the teeth** odontotoxia
**uneven shingles** shims
**uneventful** boring, dull, humdrum, monotonous, ordinary, unexciting
**unexampled** atypical, distinctive, first, incomparable, individual, original, rare, special, unconventional, unequalled, unique, unorthodox, unprecedented, unusual
**unexpected** abrupt, accidental, astonishing, startling, sudden, surprising, unanticipated, unforeseen, unpredicted, untimely, unusual
**unexpected benefit** manna
**unexpected change** switch
**unexpected drawback** snag
**unexpected gift** surprise
**unexpected good fortune** windfall
**unexpected job hold-up** snag
**unexpected mishap** contretemps
**unexpected pleasure** treat
**unexpected reward** jackpot
**unexpected thing** godsend
**unexplained death of baby** cot death, SIDS
**unexplained thing** secret
**unexplored region** terra incognita (L)
**unfailing** bottomless, ceaseless, certain, constant, continuous,

**unfair** biased, deceitful, dishonest, excessive, inequitable, interested, jaundiced, partial, prejudiced, underhand, undue, unequal, unethical, uneven, unjust, unreasonable, unscrupulous, unsporting, unwarranted, warped, wrongful — endless, loyal, persistent, reliable, staunch, sure, true, unlimited

**unfair electoral practice** gerrymandering

**unfairly** bigotedly, dishonestly, one-sidedly, partially, unethically, unevenly, unjustly, unscrupulously, unsportingly, wrongly

**unfairly preferential treatment** favouritism, nepotism

**unfair money lender** usurer

**unfair player** unsportsmanlike

**unfaithful** apostate, disloyal, false, incorrect, inexact, insidious, recreant, traitorous, treacherous, uncandid, unsteady

**unfaithfulness** deceitfulness, faithlessness, falseness, fickleness, infidelity, perfidiousness, treacherousness

**unfaithfulness to the marriage-bed** adultery

**unfaltering** assiduous, constant, determined, obstinate, persistent, pertinaceous, resolved, sedulous, tenacious, tireless, unfailing, untiring, unyielding

**unfamiliar** alien, curious, new, novel, strange, unaccustomed, uncommon, unknown, unusual

**unfashionable** antiquated, dowdy, obsolete, old, outmoded, passé, unpopular

**unfashionably dressed** dowdy

**unfasten** detach, disconnect, loose(n), open, release, rip, separate, uncouple, undo, unlace, unlock, untie

**unfavourable** adverse, bad, contradictory, contrary, dark, detrimental, gloomy, hostile, ill, inapt, inconvenient, inopportune, noxious, ominous, poor, regrettable, sinister, undesirable, unfortunate, unhappy, unlucky, unsuited, untimely, untoward, unwise

**unfavourable to comfort** inconvenient

**unfavourable to health** insalubrious

**unfavourable to one's interests** adverse

**unfavourably** adversely, badly, hostilely, inauspiciously, lowly, negatively, poorly, threateningly, unfortunately, unluckily

**unfavoured opponent** underdog

**unfeeling** callous, cold-hearted, cruel, drugged, feelingless, hard-hearted, hardened, insensate, insensible, merciless, numb, sedated, senseless, stony, uncaring, unemotional, unimpressive, unsympathetic

**unfeigned** absolute, actual, ardent, artless, authentic, certain, childlike, cordial, credulous, deep, devout, earnest, factual, fervent, genuine, guileless, heartfelt, honest, ingenuous, innocent, intrinsic, naïve, positive, profound, real, right(ful), simple, sincere, true, trustful, trusting, valid, veritable, warm

**unfermented wine** must

**unfertilised ovum** ovule

**unfilled** available, bare, blank, clean, clear, drained, empty, free, hollow, idle, plain, spotless, unemployed, unoccupied, untenanted, vacant, void

**unfilled space** blank, gap, hiatus, lacuna, void

**unfinished timber** log

**unfinished work** backlog

**unfit** inadequate, incapable, incompetent, inefficient, inept, unhealthy, unsuited, useless

**unfit for further use** worn-out

**unfit for solitary life** social

**unfit to continue a contest** hors de combat (F)

**unfit to eat** rotted, rotten, stale

**unflappable** easy-going, even-tempered, imperturbable, inexcitable

**unfledged youngster** nestling

**unflurried** calm

**unfold** clarify, deploy, describe, disclose, disentangle, divulge, expand, explain, flatten, illustrate, open, present, reveal, show, straighten, unbidden, uncover, undo, unfurl, unravel

**unfold gradually** develop, grow

**unfolding of life** evolutionary

**unforced** natural

**unforged metal** pig

**unfortunate** adverse, bad, calamitous, cursed, disastrous, doomed, hapless, hopeless, ill-fated, inopportune, luckless, poor, regrettable, ruinous, unhappy, unlucky, unsuccessful, untoward

**unfortunate accident** mishap

**unfortunate chance** pity

**unfortunately** adversely, alas, cursedly, disastrously, haplessly, ill-advisedly, infelicitously, lamentably, poorly, regrettably, ruinously, sadly, unbecomingly, unfavourably, unhappily, unluckily, unsuccessfully, unsuitably, wretchedly

**unfortunate occurrence** contretemps

**unfounded** baseless, fabricated, false, groundless, idle, spurious, unproven, untrue

**unfounded belief** fancy

**unfounded rumour** canard

**unfree person** serf

**unfree Spartan** helot

**unfreeze** defrost, liquefy, melt, soften, thaw

**unfreeze frozen food** defrost

**unfriendly** aloof, antagonistic, distant, estranged, hostile, inimical, sour, surly, unkind(ly)

**unfriendly in manner** frosty

**unfruitful** barren, fruitless, sterile, unproductive, unprofitable, useless

**ungainly** awkward(ly), bovine, clumsy, gauche, gawky, gawkish, inelegant(ly), inept, inexpert, lubberly, slapdash, slovenly, ungraceful, unhandy, unskilful, unwieldy

**ungentlemanly** abrupt, bad-mannered, boorish, brusque, caddish, churlish, coarse, crass, curt, despicable, discourteous, ill-bred, ill-mannered, impolite, indecorous, indelicate, insolent, loutish, low, offhand, rough, rude, uncivil, uncouth, ungallant, ungracious, unladylike, unmannerly, unrefined, vulgar

**unglazed pottery** biscuit, bisque

**unglazed white porcelain** bisque

**ungodliness** corruptness, depravedness, godlessness, impiety, impiousness, profaneness, sinfulness, vileness, wickedness

**ungodly** depraved, impious, irreligious, polluted, profane, vile, wicked

**ungraceful** artless, awkward, blundering, bungling, clownish, clumsy, coarse, crude, gauche, gawky, graceless, ham-fisted, indecorous, inelegant, inept, inexpert, jerky, lumbering, maladroit, oafish, rude, stiff, uncoordinated, uncouth, ungainly, unpolished, unrefined, unskilful, unskilled, unsupple

**ungracefully lean and long** lanky

**ungratefulness** ingratitude, nonacknowledg(e)ment, nonrecognition, thanklessness, unthankfulness

**ungrateful person** ingrate

**unguarded** defenceless, imprudent, incautious, naked, undefended, unprotected

**unguent** balm, embrocation, liniment, lotion, lubrication, nard, ointment, salve
**unguis** claw, nail
**ungula** claw, hoof, talon
**ungulate** hooved
**ungulate animal** daman, hyrax, tapir
**unhappily** sadly
**unhappiness** awkwardness, blueness, clumsiness, cursedness, dispiritedness, gaucheness, gloominess, haplessness, ineptness, miserableness, misery, sadness, sorrowfulness, tactlessness, unsuitableness,
**unhappy** afflicted, awkward, blue, clumsy, cursed, dejected, depressed, disconsolate, discontented, dispirited, distressed, down, gauche, gloomy, hapless, ill-fated, inept, infelicitous, malapropos, miserable, mournful, sad, sorrowful, tactless, unapt, unfavourable, unfortunate, unpropitious, wretched
**unharmed** intact, safe, sound, undamaged, unhurt, unscathed, untouched, whole
**unharness** unyoke
**unhealthily fat** obese
**unhealthy** afflicted, delicate, diseased, enfeebled, feeble, frail, sickly, unsanitary, unwholesome, weak
**unhealthy condition of body or mind** cachexia
**unhealthy sounding breathing** râle
**unhewn timber** log
**unholy** awful, corrupt, evil, heinous, impious, irreligious, profane, sinful, unearthly, unreasonable, vile, wicked
**unholy din** racket
**unhorse** unsaddle, unseat
**unhouse** dislodge, eject, evict
**unhurried** calm, deliberate, easy(-going), laid-back, leisurely, sedate, slow
**unhurt** complete, entire, firm, fit, guarded, hale, healthy, intact, perfect, protected, robust, safe, secure, solid, sound, sturdy, substantial, together, unbroken, undamaged, unharmed, unhurt, uninjured, unscathed, untouched, unviolated, vigorous, virgin, whole
**unicorn's adversary** lion
**unidentified plant** hordock
**uniform** agreeing, alike, consistent, constant, equable, equal, even, identical, invariable, plain, regular, solid, unchanged, unvaried, unvarying

**uniform change of sea level world wide** eustasy
**uniformed doorman** commissionaire
**uniform in quality** even
**uniform in quantity** even
**uniform jacket** tunic
**unify** blend, combine, consolidate, fuse, merge, unite
**unilateral** one-sided
**unimaginative** barren, dry, dull, inane, lifeless, ordinary, prosaic, senseless, unromantic, usual
**unimaginative person** stodge
**unimpaired** entire, intact, integral, unbroken, unhurt, whole
**unimportant** commonplace, expendable, foolish, forgivable, immaterial, inconsequent, inessential, inferior, insignificant, irrelevant, minor, negligible, nominal, paltry, petty, powerless, puny, secondary, slight, tawdry, trivial, unnecessary, venial, worthless
**unimportant details** minutiae
**unimportant thing** bagatelle, trifle
**unimportant to be considered** negligible
**unimpregnated roe of lobster** coral
**uninclined to exert oneself** languid
**uninhibited** abandoned, earthy, free, inordinate, intemperate, natural, unbounded, unchecked, uncontrolled, unrestrained
**uninspiring** characterless, dull, indeterminate, insipid, mousy, nondescript, ordinary, prosaic, stale, stock, tame, undistinguished, uninteresting, unremarkable, vague
**uninstructive** unedifying, uneducational, uninformative, unmoralistic
**unintelligent** brainless, deficient, dense, dim-witted, dull(-witted), dumb, foolish, ignorant, inane, mindless, obtuse, slow, stupid, subnormal, thick, unaware, uninformed, witless
**unintelligible speech** gibberish
**unintentional** accidental, automatic, fortuitous, inadvertent, indeliberate, involuntary, reflex, spontaneous, unconscious, unexpected, unforeseen, unintended, unplanned, unwitting
**unintentional act** accident
**unintentional loss** leak
**uninterested** apathetic, blasé, bored, distant, impassive, listless, unconcerned, uninvolved
**uninteresting** bland, boring, drab, dreary, dry, dull, flat, humdrum, stodgy, tiresome, vapid, wearisome

**unintoxicated** sober
**uninvited guest** (gate)crasher, intruder
**uninvited guest brought by invited one** umbra
**union** alignment, alliance, association, bond, combination, confederacy, confluence, conjunction, junction, marriage, merge, society, unity
**union by marriage** alliance
**Union Castle vessel** mailboat
**union of Greece and Cyprus** enosis
**union of manufacturers to control prices** cartel
**union of states** confederacy
**union of two** duad
**union walkout** strike
**unique** absolute, alone, different, distinctive, exceptional, incomparable, infrequent, lone, matchless, nonpareil, odd, one, only, peculiar, rare, single, singular, sole, solitary, strange, sui generis (L), uncommon, unequalled, unexampled, unexcelled, unmatched, unparalleled, unrepeated, unrivalled, unusual
**unique person** oner
**unique thing** oner, unicum
**unisex** epicene, sexless
**unisex handbag** pochette
**unison** agreement, concord
**unit** ace, assembly, cell, component, division, element, entity, formation, group, integer, item, member, module, monad, one, part, piece, quantity, section, system, thing, undivided, whole
**unit of current** amp(ere)
**unite** ally, amalgamate, associate, band, bind, blend, bond, chain, coalesce, cohere, combine, conglomerate, connect, consolidate, couple, fasten, federate, fuse, glue, join, link, marry, mate, merge, mingle, mix, solidify, team, tie, unify, weld, zygo-
**unite by heat** fuse
**unite by treaty** ally
**unite closely** wed
**united** allied, joined, one, together
**united group** crew, team
**united in opinion** consentient, unanimous
**United Kingdom boys' school** Eton
**United Kingdom currency unit** pound
**United Kingdom driving licence demerit** endorsement
**United Kingdom driving side** left
**United Kingdom flag** Union Jack
**United Kingdom government headquarters** Westminister
**United Kingdom port** Dover

**United Kingdom racecourse** Ascot, Epsom
**United Kingdom royal family** Windsor
**United Kingdom royal racecourse** Ascot
**united state** solidarity
**United States burrowing rodent** gopher
**United States coin** cent, dime
**United States Congress building** Capitol
**United States emblem** eagle
**United States female student** co-ed
**United States five cents** nickel
**United States football field** gridiron
**United States gambling city** Las Vegas, Reno
**United States holly shrub** yaupon
**United States Indian** redskin
**United States infantryman of the First World War** doughboy
**United States inventor** Edison
**United States Jupiter space probe** Voyager
**United States military headquarters** Pentagon
**United States monetary unit** dollar
**United States money** dollar
**United States Mormon state** Utah
**United States mountain range** Wasatch
**United States national park in East California** Yosemite
**United States oil state** Texas
**United States Pacific base** Guam
**United States piebald horse** pinto
**United States potato state** Idaho
**United States president's wife** First Lady
**United States prison** Alcatraz, Sing Sing
**United States road on which toll is collected at gates** turnpike
**United States sailor** gob
**United States satellite** Explorer
**United States second-year university student** sophomore
**United States Senate procedure** cloture
**United States soldier** GI
**United States space agency** NASA
**United States space programme** Apollo
**United States spies** CIA
**United States uncle** Sam
**United States university** Harvard, Princeton, UCLA, Yale
**United States urban motorway** expressway
**United States wheat state** Kansas
**United States's windy city** Chicago
**unite edges** butt, rabbet

**unite firmly** knit, solder, wed
**unite in league** amalgamate, federate
**unite in matrimony** wed
**unite two companies** amalgamate
**unite with** attach
**unite with glue** agglutinate
**unit for measuring a quantity of heat** calorie, joule
**unit for measuring electric current** amp(ere)
**unit for measuring fineness of silk** denier
**unit for measuring lengths of yarn** lea
**unit for measuring power of engine** horsepower
**unit for measuring energy value of food** calorie, kilojoule
**unit for measuring volumetric rate of flow** cusec
**unit in apiary** beehive
**unit in collection** item
**unit in counting fish** mease
**unit in earthwork** float, floor
**uniting force** bond
**uniting substance** glue
**unit in list** item
**unit measuring horse's height** hand
**unit of acceleration** (milli)gal, newton
**unit of acoustics** bel
**unit of action** episode
**unit of area** acre, hectare
**unit of army** platoon, squad
**unit of binary digits** byte
**unit of brightness** lambert, stilb
**unit of capacitance** farad
**unit of capacity** amphora, gallon, litre, pint, quart
**unit of capacity used in measuring fresh herring** cran
**unit of colour saturation** satron
**unit of conductance** mho, siemens
**unit of counting** point
**unit of current** amp(ere)
**unit of data transmission speed** baud
**unit of design** larme
**unit of discourse** phoneme, word
**unit of distance** furlong, kilometre, league, mile
**unit of dry measure** bushel, peck
**unit of elastance** daraf
**unit of electrical capacity** farad
**unit of electrical force** (kilo)volt
**unit of electrical intensity** amp(ere), oersted
**unit of electrical power** kilowatt, megawatt
**unit of electrical reluctance** kilohm, megohm, ohm, rel, statohm
**unit of electrical resistance** (ab)ohm, rel
**unit of electric charge** coulomb
**unit of electric current** amp(ere)

**unit of electric intensity** ampere, oersted
**unit of electricity** amp(ere), coulomb, es, (kilo)watt, volt
**unit of electric light** lumen, pyr, watt
**unit of electrolics** ion
**unit of electrolysis** faraday, ion
**unit of electromotive force** volt
**unit of electrons** ion
**unit of electrostatic force** volt
**unit of energy** (atom)erg, ergon, joule, quantum, rad
**unit of energy obtained from foods** calorie, calory, kilojoule
**unit of explosive force** kiloton, megaton
**unit of fineness** carat, karat
**unit of flow** cusec
**unit of fluidity** rhe
**unit of flux density** gauss
**unit of force** dene, dyne, newton, poundal, stapp, sthene
**unit of frequency** (kilo)hertz, megahertz
**unit of gem weight** carat
**unit of gravity** gal
**unit of heat** calorie, calory, joule, therm
**unit of heredity** gene
**unit of hundred men** century
**unit of illumination** phot
**unit of infantry** battalion
**unit of information** hartley
**unit of instruction** lesson
**unit of interstellar distance** parsec
**unit of land in feudal period** manor
**unit of land measurement** morgen, hectare
**unit of language** syllable
**unit of length** angstrom, inch, metre, mile, parsec, yard
**unit of lens power** dioptre
**unit of light** lumen
**unit of light energy** rad
**unit of linear measure** (kilo)metre, mile, yard
**unit of liquid measure** gallon, litre, pint, quart
**unit of loudness** phon, sone
**unit of luminous intensity** candela, candlepower
**unit of magnetic field strength** oersted
**unit of magnetic flux** maxwell, weber
**unit of magnetic intensity** oersted
**unit of mass** slug
**unit of measurement** em, tog
**unit of medicine** dosage, dose, dram, pill, tablet
**unit of memory** bit, mnemon
**unit of metric system** gram, metre, stere
**unit of money** dollar, pound, rand
**unit of noise** decibel

**unit of nylon fineness** denier
**unit of optical frequency** fresnel
**unit of pain intensity** dol
**unit of perceived noisiness** noy
**unit of persons** group
**unit of power** dyne, (kilo)watt
**unit of power in ratio** decibel
**unit of pressure** bar(ad), centibar, gwely, megabar, millibar, pascal, torr
**unit of quantity of heat** calorie, calory, joule
**unit of radiation dose** rad
**unit of radioactivity** curie
**unit of resistance** ohm
**unit of score at bridge** trick
**unit of sound** decible, sone
**unit of sound intensity** (deci)bel
**unit of speech** word
**unit of speed** baud, knot
**unit of square measure** a(c)re, rod
**unit of stellar distance** parsec
**unit of three** trinity
**unit of time** century, day, decade, era, hour, minute, month, second, week, year
**unit of trading** contract
**unit of type-size** pica
**unit of velocity** velo
**unit of viscosity** poise, seconds, stoke
**unit of wavelength measurement** angström
**unit of weight** carat, denier, grain, gram, kantar, kilo, liang, libra, ounce, pound, quintal, se(e)r, tod, ton(ne), wey
**unit of width** em, en
**unit of wire measure** mil
**unit of work** crop, dinamode, erg(on), hour, joule, kilerg
**unit of yarn** lea
**unit used to measure volume of stacked timber** stere
**unity** agreement, concert, concord, harmony, individuality, oneness, union, unison
**univalvular shellfish** nautilus
**universal** common, cosmic, entire, general, total, unlimited, whole, widespread, worldwide
**universal cure** panacea
**universal joint** cardan
**universal knowledge** pantology
**universal language** Udo, Volapuk
**universal remedy** azoth, catholicon, cure-all, elixir, panacea
**universe** area, cosmos, creation, firmament, heavens, macrocosm, milieu, nature, orbit, plenum, sky, space, sphere, world
**university** academy, college, foundation, hospital, institute, institution, school, seminary, society, varsity
**university degree** BA, diploma, Honours, MA, PhD
**university degree of bachelor** baccalaureate
**university fellow** don
**university grounds** campus
**university in California** Berkley, UCLA
**university in England** Cambridge, London, Oxford
**university in Florida** Stenton
**university in Germany** Freiburg, Heidelberg
**university in Portugal** Coimbra
**university in Scotland** Glasgow, Aberdeen
**university in South Africa** Fort Hare, RAU, Rhodes, UCT, UWC
**university official** proctor, rector
**university one attended** Alma Mater
**university pass** degree
**university quitter** dropout
**university sportsman** blue
**university teacher** don, lecturer, magister, professor, tutor
**unjust** biased, inequitable, partial, prejudiced, undeserved, undue, unfair, unjustified, unmerited, wrong(ful)
**unjust act** injustice
**unjustified belief** intuition
**unjustly take advantage of someone** exploit
**unjust practice** abuse
**unkeeled bird** ratite
**unkempt** boorish, coarse, crude, disarranged, disarrayed, dishevelled, disordered, messy, rough, rumpled, rustic, scruffy, shaggy, sloppy, slovenly, squalid, tousled, uncombed, uncouth, ungainly, ungroomed, untidy
**unkempt or shaggy mass of hair** shock
**unkind** cruel, harsh, hurtful, inconsiderate, thoughtless, uncharitable, unmerciful
**unknown author** anon(ymous)
**unknown land** terra incognita (L)
**unknown person** alien, foreigner, stranger
**unknown to fame** obscure
**unladen vehicle weight** tare
**unlash** unfasten, untie
**unlatch** open, unbar, unfasten
**unlawful** actionable, banned, bastard, criminal, forbidden, illegal, illegitimate, illicit, natural, outlawed, prohibited, spurious, unlicensed
**unlawful act** crime
**unlawful action** misdeed
**unlawful and deliberate killing of human being** murder
**unlawful killing of human being** manslaughter
**unlawful lover** leman
**unlawful outbreak** mêlée, riot
**unlawful plot** conspiracy
**unlawful to import** smuggle
**unleash** loose
**unleavened bread** matzo, tortilla
**unleavened flaky Indian bread** puree, puri
**unless** except, lest, nisi (L)
**unless previously** nisi
**unlicensed bar** shebeen
**unlike** contrasted, different, dissimilar, divergent, diverse, incompatible, opposite, unequal
**unlikelihood** doubtfulness, implausibility, improbability, inconceivability, incredibility, incredibleness, unlikeliness
**unlikely** doomed, doubtful, dubious, faint, improbable, incredible, ominous, questionable, remote, slight, unbelievable, uncertain, unconvincing, unpromising, unsure
**unlikely to marry** bachelor, spinster
**unlimited** boundless, countless, extensive, great, infinite, limitless, total, unbounded, unconditional, unconstrained, universal, unrestrained, unrestricted
**unlit** blurred, cloudy, dark, dim, dusky, ebony, indistinct, inky, jet, murky, obscure, overcast, pitch-black, shadowy, shady, sombre, sunless, tenebrous, veiled
**unload** alleviate, disburden, discard, discharge, disencumber, disengage, divide, dump, ease, empty, jettison, relieve, separate, transfer, unbar, unbolt, unburden, unlade, unpack, unship, uplift
**unlock** free, open, release, unbar, unbolt, undo, unlatch
**unlocks lock** key
**unlovely** ugly
**unlucky** cursed, doomed, fortuneless, hapless, ill-fated, ill-omened, infelicitous, luckless, menacing, miserable, ominous, star-crossed, unblessed, unfortunate, unhappy, unpromising, unprosperous, unsuccessful, wretched
**unlucky accident** mishap
**unlucky days** dies nefasti (L)
**unlucky event** misadventure, mishap
**unmanageable person** tartar
**unmannered person** cad, ruffian
**unmannerly** disrespectful, ill-bred, impolite, rude, uncivil, uncouth

**unmannerly act** solecism
**unmarked ski run** off-piste
**unmarried** bachelor, celibate, maiden, single, unwedded, virgin
**unmarried man** bachelor, celibate, single
**unmarried woman** mademoiselle, maiden, miss, ms, signorina (I), spinster, towdie
**unmask** bare, decry, detect, disclose, discover, exhume, expose, reveal, uncloak, uncover, unearth, unveil
**unmasking** exposure
**unmatched** inimitable, matchless, unexampled, unique, unrivalled
**unmerciful** cruel, merciless, pitiless, relentless, unpitying, unsparing
**unmethodical** desultory
**unmindful** careless, heedless, inattentive, neglectful, negligent, regardless
**unmistakable** apparent, certain, clear, decided, distinct, en évidence (F), evident, exact, indisputable, manifest, obvious, palpable, patent, plain, positive, precise, self-evident, strict, sure, unequivocal, vivid
**unmitigated** complete, grim, harsh, perfect, sheer
**unmixed** pure, unadulterated, unalloyed, unmingled
**unmoved** aloof, cool, dry-eyed, fast, firm, soulless, unaffected, unimpressed, untouched
**unmoving** changeless, fixed, grounded, immobile, motionless, rooted, secure, stationary, stock-still, unchangeable
**unmusical sound** cacophony, noise
**unnamed** anonymous, nameless
**unnatural** abnormal, affected, anomalous, evil, hard-hearted, heartless, inhuman, irregular, strained, unusual
**unnatural birth** abortion, caesarean, miscarriage
**unnaturally high-pitched voice** falsetto
**unnatural narrowing of a body channel** atresia
**unnatural sexual intercourse** sodomy
**unnatural unconsciousness** coma
**unnecessarily bossy** officious
**unnecessary** de trop (F), dispensable, expendable, needless, redundant, superfluous, unessential, unneeded
**unnerve** alarm, confound, daunt, disarm, disconcert, discourage, dismay, dispirit, enervate, fluster, frighten, intimidate, shake, upset

**unobstructed** clear, empty, free, open, smooth, unhampered, unhindered, unimpeded, unlimited
**unobtrusive** inconspicuous, unremarkable, unspectacular
**unobtrusive presence** low profile
**unoccupied** abandoned, bare, derelict, desert, devoid, disengage, empty, idle, inactive, tenantless, unemployed, uninhabitable, uninhabited, unpeopled, untaken, untenanted, unwanted, vacant, vacuous
**unoccupied post** vacancy
**unofficial union** common-law marriage
**unopened flower** bud
**unorthodox** abnormal, deviant, heretic(al), heterodox, irregular, nonobservant, uncommon, unobservant, unofficial, unscriptural, unusual, unwanted
**unorthodox believer** heretic
**unorthodox person** maverick
**unpaid** amateur, due, honorary, outstanding, overdue, owing, payable, unpaid, unsettled, voluntary
**unpaid bill** debt
**unpaid due** arrear
**unpaid part of loan** residue
**unpaid player** amateur
**unpaid worker** volunteer
**unparalleled** best, champion, eminent, excellent, exceptional, greatest, highest, matchless, noteworthy, outstanding, peerless, prodigious, rare, remarkable, sans pareil (F), singular, special, superlative, supreme, transcendent, uncommon, unequalled, unique, unmatched, unrivalled, unsurpassed
**unpigmented person** albino
**unplayed golf hole** bye
**unpleasant** bad, disagreeable, draggy, horrid, irksome, nasty, noisome, obnoxious, offensive, repulsive, unappetising, unattractive, unlikeable, unpalatable
**unpleasant and harmful** noxious
**unpleasant coldness** chill
**unpleasantly accurate** brutal
**unpleasantly cold** chilly
**unpleasantly damp** clammy, dank
**unpleasantly noticeable** obtrusive
**unpleasantly prominent** stark
**unpleasantly slippery** slimy
**unpleasantly sticky** clammy
**unpleasantly suave** smarmy
**unpleasantly wet** dank
**unpleasant person** creep, crud, sod
**unpleasant shock** jar
**unpleasant situation** galère (F), predicament

**unpleasant smelling breath** halitosis
**unpleasant smell of decaying matter** effluvium
**unpleasant to look at** ugly
**unploughed strip** lynchet
**unplowed edge of field** rand
**unpolluted** pure
**unpowered aircraft** glider
**unpredictable** chance, doubtful, erratic, fickle, inconstant, irregular, random, unreliable, variable
**unpredictable in behaviour** erratic
**unprejudiced** balanced, fair, impartial, just, objective, open-minded, unbiased, unbigoted, uninfluenced
**unpremeditated** automatic, extempore, impetuous, impromptu, impulsive, involuntary, offhand, spontaneous, unintended, unintentional, unplanned, unprepared, unschemed
**unprepared** abashed, casual, confused, inexperienced, random, unqualified, unready, unskilled, untrained
**unprepared for attack** off-guard
**unpretentiously lowly** humble
**unprincipled** abandoned, amoral, corrupt, debased, deceitful, dishonest, disloyal, false, immoral, perverted, reprobate, underhand, unloyal, unscrupulous, untrustworthy, wicked
**unprincipled person** knave, rogue, rotter
**unprocessed mineral** ore
**unproductive** barren, fruitless, futile, sterile, useless, worthless
**unprofessional** amateur, inefficient, inexpert, negligent, unseemly, untrained, unworthy
**unprofessional person** laity
**unprofitable** abortive, bare, barren, dry, failing, forlorn, fruitless, futile, ineffectual, losing, nugatory, pointless, profitless, senseless, unavailing, uneconomic, unimportant, unproductive, unsuccessful, useless, vain, valueless, worthless
**unprompted** impulsive, instinctive, natural, snap, spontaneous, unasked, uncoerced, unconscious, uninvited, unsolicited, unthinking, voluntary, volunteer
**unprotected** defenceless, exposed, helpless, naked, open, unarmed, undefended, unguarded, unshielded
**unproved statement** allegation
**unprovoked attack** aggression
**unprovoked attacker** aggressor

**unpunctual** behind, belated, delayed, eccentric, erratic, fitful, fluctuating, haphazard, intermittent, irregular, late, occasional, overdue, patchy, slow, spasmodic, sporadic, tardy, unsteady, variable

**unqualified** absolute, complete, downright, ill-equipped, incapable, incompetent, ineligible, outright, thorough, total, unfit, unmitigated, unprepared, unreserved, utter

**unqualified practitioner of medicine** quack

**unquestionable** absolute, certain, clear, definite, faultless, flawless, incontestable, indisputable, indubitable, irrefutable, patent, perfect, sure, undeniable

**unravel** disentangle, extricate, free, separate, undo, unknot, untangle, unwind

**unravelling of plot** denouement

**unread** ignorant, illiterate, uneducated, unexampled

**unready** inexperienced, undeveloped, unfinished, unprepared, unskilled

**unreal** fake, fanciful, illusory, imaginary, insincere, mock, mythical, pretended, sham

**unrealistic** credulous, foolish, hypothetical, illogical, imaginary, impractical, misguided, misjudging, muddled, subjective, unlikely, unnatural, unreal, unreasonable, wrong

**unreasonable contempt for danger** temerity

**unreasonable dislike** blind hate

**unreasonable fear of the unknown** superstition

**unreasonably obstinate** stubborn

**unreasonably persistent idea in the mind** obsession

**unreasoning terror** panic, scare

**unrefined** coarse, crude, earthy, inelegant, raw, rough, rude, uncultured, unfinished, unpolished, unpurified, unsophisticated, untreated, vulgar

**unrefined mineral** ore

**unrehearsed** extempore, impromptu, impulsive, precipitant, spontaneous, unorganised, unprepared, untrained, unwarned

**unrehearsed quip** ad-lib

**unrelenting** constant, continual, hard, harsh, implacable, incessant, inexorable, merciless, persevering, persistent, pitiless, relentless, remorseless, ruthless, unabating, unremitting

**unreliable** contestable, dicey, doubtful, erratic, fickle, frivolous, impulsive, inconstant, indecisive, irresolute, refutable, risky, undependable, untenable, untrustworthy, untrusty, volatile

**unremarkable** inconspicuous, unobtrusive, unspectacular

**unremitting** relentless

**unrented** unlet

**unrepentant** impenitent, remorseless, uncontrite

**unrequited love ballad** torch song

**unreserved** candid, complete, entire, frank, full, open, undesigning, unlimited

**unresisting** nonresisting, passive, submissive, unopposing

**unrest** animosity, anxiety, concern, discord, disquiet, dissatisfaction, dissent, dread, fear, hostility, nervousness, rebellion, restlessness, riot, unease, unquietness, worry

**unrestrained** abandoned, free, independent, masterless, natural, permitted, rampant, random, unbridled, unchecked, unconditional, unfettered, unhindered, unimpeded, unobstructed, unshackled

**unrestrained extravagance** splurge

**unrestrained utterance** effusion

**unrestraint** abandon, agitation, dash, excitement, frenzy, furore, intoxication, madness, recklessness, riot, uproar, wantonness, wildness

**unrestricted** absolute, allodial, arbitrary, free(hand), freehold, independent, loose, masterless, open, unbounded, uncommitted, unconditional, unlimited, unregulated

**unreticent** bold, candid, free(-speaking), outspoken, unchecked, unconstrained, uninhibited, unreserved

**unreturnable tennis serve** ace

**unrevealed fact** secret

**unripe** green, immature

**unroll** open

**unruffled** calm, cool, impassive, ironed, sedate, serene, solemn, staid, steady, tranquil, unagitated, uncreased, unexcitable, unflustered, unmussed, unstirred

**unruliness** fractiousness, lawlessness, mutinousness, rebelliousness, riotousness, rowdiness, rumbustiousness, waywardness, wildness, wilfulness

**unruly** disorderly, insubordinate, obstreperous, refractory, rumbustious, turbulent, uncontrollable, uncontrolled, ungovernable, unmanageable

**unruly child** brat

**unruly crowd** mob, rabble

**unruly outbreak** mêlée, riot

**unruly outburst** disturbance

**unruly person** rebel

**unsaddle** unhorse

**unsafe** chancy, dangerous, decrepit, exposed, hazardous, insecure, jeopardous, ominous, perilous, precarious, risky, threatening, uncertain, unguarded, unprotected, unstable, wobbly

**unsafe building** fire-trap

**unsaid** assumed, implicit, implied, meant, suggested, tacit, undeclared, unexpressed, unmentioned, unspoken, untold, unuttered

**unsatisfactory** deficient, disappointing, inadequate, inadmissible, inept, unacceptable

**unsatisfied longing** desire

**unsatisfying to the mind** jejune

**unsavoury** distasteful, nasty, nauseating, obnoxious, offensive, repellent, repulsive, revolting, unappetising, unpleasant

**unsay** retract, withdraw

**unscheduled news item** flash

**unscrupulous** amoral, conscienceless, corrupt, devious, dishonest, dishonourable, immoral, roguish, ruthless, unconscionable, unrestrained, unrestricted

**unscrupulous behaviour** sculduggery, skul(l)duggery

**unscrupulous flirt** vamp

**unscrupulous lawyer** shyster

**unscrupulous person** rogue, scoundrel, villain

**unseal** open

**unseasonably** malapropos

**unseat** depose, discharge, dislodge, dismiss, displace, impeach, oust, (over)throw, remove, topple, unsaddle

**unseated** abolished, beaten, defeated, deleted, deposed, detached, dethroned, discharged, displaced, doffed, ejected, erased, evicted, expelled, mastered, ousted, overt, purged, relegated, removed, supplanted, toppled, undermined, unhorsed

**unsecured bond** debenture

**unseeingly** blindly

**unseemly** improper, inappropriate, indecent, indecorous, unbecoming, unbefitting

**unseen** concealed, hidden, invisible, obscure, unobtrusive, veiled

**unselfish** altruistic, broad, fair, free, generous, great-hearted, humanitarian, impartial, just, liberal, magnanimous, noble, open-handed, selfless, ungrudging, unprejudiced, unsparing
**unselfishness** altruism
**unsettle** agitate, bother, confuse, disconcert, disorder, disturb, fluster, perturb, ruffle, trouble, unbalance, upset
**unsettled** agitated, anxious, bothered, changing, confused, disconcerted, disorderly, disrupted, doubtful, due, flustered, inconstant, indefinite, moot, open, outstanding, owing, payable, perturbed, restive, restless, shaky, tense, troubled, uncertain, undetermined, unsettled, unstable, variable
**unshakable** absolute, adamant, constant, determined, firm, fixed, resolute, stable, staunch, steadfast, sure, unassailable, unwavering
**unshapely mass** lump
**unsightliness** ugliness
**unsightly** disagreeable, distasteful, hideous, homely, horrible, horrid, inelegant, odious, offensive, repellent, repulsive, revolting, sickening, ugly, unattractive, uncomely, unkempt, unlovely, unpleasant, untidy
**unsightly suburbs** subtopia
**unsightly urban area** blight
**unskilful** amateurish, artless, awkward, clumsy, coarse, doltish, gauche, gawky, incapable, incompetent, inelegant, inept, inexperienced, inexpert, inhabile (F), insufficient, loutish, lumbering, maladroit, oafish, rude, uncoordinated, uncouth, ungraceful, unhandy, unrefined, untrained, useless
**unskilful acting** bungling
**unskilful in execution** amateur
**unskilfully** artlessly, awkwardly, bunglingly, clownishly, clumsily, coarsely, gauchely, gawkily, gracelessly, incompetently, inelegantly, ineptly, inexpertly, insufficiently, lumberingly, maladroitly, oafishly, rudely, stiffly, uncouthly, unprofessionally
**unskilled** amateurish, inept, inexperienced, uneducated, unprofessional, unqualified, untalented, untrained
**unskilled actor** ham
**unskilled labourer** bohunk, navvy
**unskilled practitioner of medicine** quack

**unskilled worker** labourer
**unslaked lime** quicklime
**unsociable** aloof, chilly, cold, distant, hostile, introverted, reclusive, reserved, retiring, taciturn, uncongenial, unfriendly, unneighbourly, unsocial, withdrawn
**unsociable from resentment** sulky
**unsoiled** clean
**unsophisticated** authentic, childlike, genuine, innocent, inurbane, naïve, real, solid, true, unadulterated, uncouth, undeveloped, ungraceful, unguarded, unmixed, unwary, unworldly
**unsorted Indian flour** at(t)a
**unsound** decayed, defective, erroneous, fallacious, faulty, fragile, impaired, infirm, invalid, rotten, sick(ly), unfounded, unhealthy, unreliable
**unspeakable** awful, bad, dreadful, evil, frightful, indescribable, ineffable, inexpressible, odious, unimaginable, unutterable, wonderful
**unspecified person** someone
**unspecified quantity** some
**unspecified system** -ism
**unspecified way** somehow
**unspectacular** inconspicuous, unobtrusive, unremarkable
**unspoiled** intact, unaffected, unchanged, undamaged, unspoilt, unstudied, untouched
**unspoilt state** pristine
**unspoken** assumed, dum(b)founded, implicit, mute, silent, tacit, undeclared, understood, unexpressed, unstated, voiceless, wordless
**unstable** astatic, desultory, eccentric, inconstant, indefinite, insecure, irregular, jerky, mutable, perilous, precarious, queer, risky, rocky, shaky, spastic, stumbling, undecided, unreliable, unsettled, unsteadfast, unsteady, vacillating, variable, wavering, wavy, wobbly
**unstable form of oxygen** ozone
**unstated** implicit, implied, inferred, silent, tacit, undeclared, understood, unexpressed, unspoken
**unsteady** erratic, infirm, insecure, reeling, rocky, shaky, uncertain, unsafe, unsettled, unstable, volatile, wobbly
**unsteady light** flare
**unsteady walk** toddle
**unsuccessful** abortive, fortuneless, frustrated, futile, ill-fated, poor, unavailing, unfortunate, unlucky,

unproductive, useless, vain, worthless
**unsuccessful business** wash-out
**unsuccessful person** also-ran, failure, loser
**unsuitability** impropriety, indecency, indecorum, vulgarity
**unsuitable** impolite, improper, inappropriate, inapt, incongruous, inconvenient, indiscreet, ineligible, inept, inexpedient, infelicitous, tactless, unacceptable, unbecoming, unbefitting, uncongenial, unfitting, unseemly, unsuited, untimely, useless
**unsuitable marriage** misalliance
**unsure** ambivalent, bashful, constrained, demure, distrustful, doubtful, dubious, hesitant, insecure, mistrustful, reserved, sceptical, self-conscious, shy, skeptical, suspicious, timid, unassured, uncertain, unconfident, unconvinced, undecided
**unsurpassed** ascendant, best, chief, choicest, consummate, distinguished, dominant, excellent, finest, first, foremost, highest, inimitable, leading, outstanding, peerless, perfect, pre-eminent, primary, prime, superlative, supreme, top(most), unexcelled, uppermost
**unsuspected difficulty** pitfall
**unsweetened wine** brut, sack, sec
**untainted** pristine, pure, virginal
**untamed** barbarous, feral, fierce, savage, unbroken, uncontrollable, wild
**untamed horse** warrigal
**untanned leather** rawhide
**untanned skin** pelt
**untarnished** blameless, clear, excellent, faultless, flawless, guiltless, ideal, immaculate, impeccable, incorrupt, innocent, perfect, pure, sinless, splendid, spotless, sublime, taintless, unimpeachable, unmarred, unpolluted, virtuous
**untaught** amateur, green, ignorant, illiterate, inexperienced, naïve, natural, raw, spontaneous, unaware, uneducated, unlettered, unqualified, unread, unskilled, untrained, untutored
**untenable** defenceless, exposed, helpless, indefensible, unprotected, unsafe, untenable, vulnerable, weak
**untenanted** available, empty, free, idle, unemployed, unfilled, vacant, void

**unthinkable** inconceivable, unimaginable, unjustifiable, unwarranted
**untidiness** mess
**untidy** chaotic, cluttered, confused, disarranged, disarrayed, disordered, disorderly, disorganised, entangled, littered, messy, rumpled, slatternly, slipshod, sloppy, slovenly, tousle, turbid, unkempt
**untidy collection of things** clutter
**untidy muddle** mess
**untidy person** pig, scruff, slob, sloven
**untidy pile** heap
**untidy place** (pig)sty
**untidy state of things** mess
**untidy woman** slattern, slut, trollop
**untidy writing** scrawl
**untie** disconnect, disentangle, disjoin, disunite, loose(n), penetrate, release, resolve, unbind, undo, unfasten, unknot, unlace, unlash, unlock, unravel, unsnarl, unstring, untwine
**until** before, meanwhile, pending, till, (un)to, up-to
**until now** heretofore, hitherto
**until this time** hitherto
**until we see each other again** auf Wiedersehn (G), au revoir (F), goodbye
**untimely** awkward, early, ill-timed, inappropriate, inconvenient, inopportune, mistimed, premature, unexpected, unfortunate, unpropitious, unseasonable
**unto** toward
**untouched** clean, dry-eyed, flawless, indifferent, intact, perfect, pristine, pure, spotless, unaffected, unconcerned, undamaged, uneaten, unexplored, unhandled, unhurt, unimpressed, unmarked, unmoved, unused
**untrained** amateur, green, inexperienced, raw, uneducated, unschooled, unskilled, untutored
**untried** alien, artless, callow, creative, exotic, fertile, foreign, fresh, green, inexperienced, ingenious, inventive, maiden, natural, new, novel, original, raw, remote, resourceful, strange, unfamiliar, unknown, untapped, untested, untrained, unused, unusual, youthful
**untroubled sailing on a clear course** plainsailing
**untrue** bogus, confuted, deceiving, deceptive, disproved, erroneous, fake, fallacious, false, faulty, feigned, fictitious, hypocritical, imaginary, incorrect, insincere, lying, mendacious, phon(e)y, sham, spurious, unfactual, unfounded, unreal, untruthful
**untrue recital** tale
**untrue statement** falsehood, lie
**untrue story** fiction
**untrustworthy** deceitful, dishonest, disreputable, questionable, treacherous, undependable, untrusty
**untrustworthy person** heel
**untruth** fable, fabrication, falsehood, fib, fiction, lie, mendacity
**untruthful** deceitful, dishonest, false, fibbing, lying, mendacious
**untruthful person** liar
**untwisted silk** sleave
**unused** fresh, idle, leftover, mint, new, remanent, reserve, saved, spare, surplus, unconsumed, unemployed, unexercised, unhandled, unspent, untouched
**unused audio cassette** blank cartridge
**unusual** abnormal, astonishing, bizarre, curious, especial, exceptional, exotic, extraordinary, freakish, funny, miraculous, mysterious, notable, odd, offbeat, outre, peculiar, queer, rare, remarkable, single, singular, special, strange, supernatural, unco (Sc), uncommon, unconventional, uncustomary, unique, unknown, weird, wonderful
**unusual act** stunt
**unusual collector's item** curio
**unusual excellence** rarity
**unusual item** oddity
**unusually** oddly
**unusually large** bumper, outsize
**unusually supple** double-jointed
**unusual object** curio
**unusual person** corker, oner
**unusual thing** freak, oddity, oner, rarity
**unvarying** constant, immutable, same, unchanging, uniform
**unveil** bare, disclose, divulge, expose, open, reveal, uncover, unwrap
**unvulcanised rubber** caoutchouc
**unwanted** de trop (F), estranged, outcast, rejected, unasked, uncalled for, undesired, uninvited, unneeded, unsolicited, unsought, unwelcome, useless
**unwanted plant** weed
**unwanted sediment** dreg
**unwanted third person** gooseberry
**unwarranted** gratuitous, groundless, undue, unjust(ified), unprovoked, unreasonable
**unwavering** assiduous, constant, determined, enduring, firm, indefatigable, inexorable, patient, persistent, resolute, resolved, steadfast, steady, stubborn, sure, tenacious, tireless, unbeaten, undeviating, unfailing, unfaltering, untiring, unyielding
**unweaned child** suckling
**unwed** single
**unwed man** bachelor, celibate, monk
**unwed woman** nun, spinster
**unwelcome person** persona non grata (L)
**unwelcome task** fag
**unwelcome to mind** bitter
**unwell** ailing, anaemic, colour, delicate, feeble, frail, ill, indisposed, invalid, off, pale, pallid, poorly, run down, sallow, seedy, sick(ly), unhealthy, wan, weak
**unwholesome** bad, conscienceless, degrading, demoralising, destructive, evil, injurious, noxious, pale, pallid, septic, sinful, unhealthful, unhealthy, unhygienic, wicked
**unwholesome air** miasma
**unwholesomely damp** dank
**unwieldy** awkward, bulky, clumsy, cumbersome, cumbrous, heavy, hefty, huge, inconvenient, large, massive, ponderous, substantial, unhandy, unmanageable
**unwilling** against, averse, demurring, disinclined, grudging, indisposed, indocile, involuntary, laggard, lo(a)th, obstinate, obstreperous, opposed, perverse, recalcitrant, reluctant, resistant, unenthusiastic
**unwillingness** averseness, reluctance, stubbornness
**unwillingness to communicate** reticence
**unwilling to believe** incredulous
**unwilling to work** lazy
**unwind** dekink, disentangle, evolve, neaten, rectify, relax, slacken, straighten, uncoil, unfurl, unravel, unreel, unroll, untangle, untwine, untwist, unweave
**unwise** foolish, ill-advised, ill-judged, impolite, imprudent, indiscreet, injudicious, rash, reckless, senseless, silly, stupid
**unwithered** fresh
**unworn** brand-new
**unworthy** base, inadequate, indign, unacceptable, unbefitting, undeserving, worthless
**unworthy of** beneath
**unwrap** open, undo
**unwrap flag** unfurl
**unwritten** oral, parol
**unwrought metal** ore

**unyielding** adamant, firm, hard(line), indomitable, inexorable, inflexible, intransigent, ironbound, obdurate, obstinate, relentless, resolute, rigid, steadfast, stern, stiff, stubborn, tough, unbending, uncompromising
**unyoke** unharness
**up** above, active, add, ahead, alert, aloft, amiss, ana-, awake, boom, compute, concluded, ended, high(er), informed, over, ready, reckon, toward, upright, wrong
**up above** aloft, atop
**up against** into
**up and about** astir, conscious, wakeful, watchful
**up-and-coming** ambitious, eager, enterprising, go-getting, promising, pushing
**up-and-down** undulatory, vertical, wavy
**up-and-down movement** seesaw
**Upanishads** Vedanta
**upas** antiar
**update** reconstruct, redo, renew, reshape
**upend** capsize, demolish, destroy, invert, level, overbalance, overturn, raze, reverse, ruin, spill, subvert, tilt, topple, transpose, tumble, upset, upturn
**up for grabs** accessible, attainable, available, obtainable
**upgrade** advance, better, elevate, enhance, exalt, improve, promote, raise
**upheaval** agitation, blowup, breakdown, cataclysm, chaos, clamour, collapse, commotion, confusion, convulsion, debacle, disorder, disquiet, disruption, disturbance, (earth)quake, eruption, explosion, ferment, outbreak, outburst, outcry, overthrow, revolution, shake-up, tumult, turmoil, unrest, upset, volcano
**uphill** accending
**uphold** countenance, elevate, maintain, raise, support, sustain
**upholder of gospel beliefs** evangelical
**upholstered seat** armchair, fauteuil, sofa
**upholstery fabric** moquette, tabaret
**up in arms** angry, excited, incensed, indignant, roused, wrathful
**up in the air** indefinite, pending, perturbed, unsettled, vexed
**upkeep** expenses, keep, maintenance, outlay, repair, support, sustenance
**uplift** advance, beatify, civilise, cultivate, deify, dignify, edify, elevate, enhance, erect, exalt, heave, hoist, improve, inspire, lift, meliorate, raise, rear, upgrade, upheave, upraise
**uplifting** elevating, inspiring
**uplift spirit** edify
**upon** at, atop, epi-, on(to), sur (F), thereon
**upon that** thereon
**upon which** whereon
**upper** elevated, greater, higher, superior, top
**upper air** ether, welkin
**upper angle between branch and trunk** axil
**upper arm bone** humerus
**upper arm muscle** triceps
**upper atmosphere** stratosphere
**upper body-shell of tortoise** carapace
**upper cavities of the heart** auricle
**upper chamber of parliament** Senate
**upper circle** balcony
**upper-class** aristocracy, élite, posh
**upper-class gentleman** nob
**upper class man** senior
**upper council of university** senate
**uppercut** blow
**upper edge** (b)rim
**upper front of body** breast
**upper front part of shoe** vamp
**upper front surface of the body** chest
**upper half of skull** sinciput
**upper hand** advantage, ascendancy, authority, control, domination, dominion, edge, influence, mastery, power, predominance, superiority, supremacy, sway
**upper heart chamber** atrium
**upper house** senate
**upper house member** senator
**upper jawbone** maxilla
**upper layer of water in lake** epilimnion
**upper leg** thigh
**upper limb** arm
**upper limit** ceiling
**upper lip of insect** labrum
**uppermost** highest, loftiest, predominant, supreme, topmost
**uppermost part** top
**upper outer ear** pinna
**upper part** top(side)
**upper part in piano duet** primo
**upper part of apron** bib
**upper part of atmosphere** stratosphere
**upper part of dungaree** bib
**upper part of loin of beef** sirloin
**upper part of transom** taffrail
**upper regions** ether
**upper rim** brim
**upper room** attic, loft
**upper shell of crustacean** carapace
**upper shell of tortoise** carapace
**upper shell of turtle** calipash
**upper side** top
**upper space** ether
**upper surface** upside
**upper surface of room** ceiling
**upper tone of tetrachord** nete
**uppity person** snob
**upright** conscientious, erect, honest, honourable, just, perpendicular, prop, righteous, straightforward, support, vertical, virtuous
**upright dividing bar in a window** mullion
**upright person** Daniel
**upright pole** post
**upright post** newel
**upright slab** monolith, stela, stele
**upright stair part** riser
**upright support** column, stanchion, standard
**uprising** disturbance, mutiny, outbreak, rebellion, revolt, riot, rising, upheaval
**uproar** agitation, ballyhoo, bedlam, brawl, brouhaha, chaos, clamour, clatter, commotion, confusion, din, disorder, disturbance, farrago, ferment, fight, fracas, frenzy, furore, hubbub, loudness, madhouse, mayhem, mêlée, noise, noisiness, outcry, pandemonium, racket, riot, row(diness), ruction, rumpus, shambles, stramash (Sc), tumult, turmoil
**uproarious** clamorous, confused, hilarious, loud, noisy, riotous, rowdy, turbulent
**uprush** surge
**upset** agitate, annoy, capsize, confuse, defeat, depose, disarrange, disconcert, displace, disquiet, distract, distress, disturb, flurry, fluster, frighten, invert, overset, overthrow, overturn, perturb, precipitate, reverse, rile, scatter, spill, spoil, topple, trouble, tumble, unnerve, upend, worried
**upset badly** distress
**upset greatly** distressed
**upset stomach** dyspepsia
**upsetting** distressful
**upshot** by-product, conclusion, consequence, crop, crux, effect, end, essence, eventuation, finale, focus, fruit, issue, marrow, offshoot, outcome, principle, result, yield
**upside down** chaotic, confused, deranged, disarranged, disordered, disorderly, higgledy-piggledy, inverted, jumbled, messy, muddled, overturned, topsy-turvy, untidy, upset, upturned
**upstairs room** attic
**upstart** arriviste, imposter, intruder, nobody, parvenu, pretender, snob

**up the creek** perplexed
**up to** until
**up to a certain point** partly
**up-to-date** à la mode, à la page (F), au courant (F), au fait (F), contemporary, current, fashionable, modern, newest, trendy
**up to grade** acceptable, adequate, satisfactory, sufficient, suitable
**up to now** hitherto
**up to one's elbows** absorbed, busy, engaged, immersed, occupied
**up to one's eyes** busy, engaged, inundated, overwhelmed
**up to par** acceptable, adequate, admissible, passable, respectable, satisfactory, sufficient
**up to scratch** able, acceptable, adequate, capable, competent, satisfactory
**up to the mark** au fait (F), expert
**up to the minute** fashionable, in, latest, modern, newest, smart, stylish, trendy
**up to the time** until
**up to this time** yet
**uptown** suburbs
**upturned Jack in cribbage** nob
**up until now** yet
**upward bend in stair rail** ramp
**upward climb** ascent
**upward mobility** advancing, betterment, progress, promotion, success, upgrading
**upward movement** ascent
**upward projection on front of saddle** pommel
**upwards** above, acclivitous, ana-, ascendent, ascending, aspiring, climbing, increasing, mounting, rising, skywards, upgoing, uphill, uplong, upriver, upstream
**upwards jump in dressage** capriole
**upward slope** acclivity
**upward thrust** boost
**upward turn** hoik
**Ural-Altaic family of languages** Turanian
**urban** burghal, citified, city, civic, cosmopolitan, metropolitan, municipal, oppidan, town
**urban air problem** smog
**urban area** city
**urban centre** CBD, downtown
**urbane** amiable, civic, civil(ised), complaisant, cosmopolitan, courteous, dignified, elegant, gallant, genteel, gracious, honourable, mannerly, noble, polished, polite, refined, respectful, smooth(-mannered), sophisticated, suave, wellbred

**urbanisation** citification
**urbanise** citify
**urbanity** accomplishment, affability, agreeability, blandly, breeding, charm, chic, civility, conduct, courtesy, cultivation, culture, education, elegance, erudition, finesse, flair, gallantry, gentility, grace, graciously, graciousness, manners, panache, polish, politeness, properness, refinement, smartness, smoothly, sophistication, style, suavely, suaveness, suavity, tact, taste
**urban motorway** expressway, highway
**urban road** street
**urban robber** burglar
**urban train** el
**urchin** brat, child, gamin, imp, lightie, piccanin, pik(kie), youngster
**urea** carbamide
**uredosorus** ured(in)ium
**urge** activate, constrain, declare, drive, egg, encourage, entreat, exhort, force, goad, hasten, impel, importune, impulse, incite, induce, influence, instigate, itch, motivate, move, persuade, press, prompting, push, recommend, solicit, spur, stimulate
**urge by moral action** impel
**urge earnestly** exhort
**urge for travel** wanderlust
**urge forward** impel
**urgency** crisis, emergency, exigency, extremity, gravity, hurry, imperativeness, importance, importunity, insistence, instancy, necessity, need, press(ure), stress
**urgency of movement** haste
**urgent** clamorous, compelling, compulsory, critical, crucial, earnest, emergency, essential, exigent, immediate, imperative, important, importunate, indispensable, insistent, instant, intense, necessary, obligatory, peremptory, persistent, persuasive, pressing, primary, serious, vital
**urgent appeal for help** SOS
**urgent entreaty** plea
**urgently needed** essential, imperative
**urgent need** dire, exigency
**urge on** actuate, egg, impel, incite
**urge on by shouts** cheer
**urge on to inadvisable action** instigate
**urge or irritation** itch
**urge to an action** impel
**urging strongly** pressing
**uric acid disorder** gout
**uric acid salt** urate
**urinary duct** urethra

**urine duct** ureter
**urine of horses and cattle** stale
**urn** amphora, bowl, capanna, crock, cruse, ewer, jar, pot, samovar, vase, vessel
**urn for bones** ossuary
**urning** gay, homosexual
**urodele amphibian** newt, salamander
**urogenital** genitourinary
**urogenital tract study** urology
**urogram** X-ray
**Ursa Major** Great Bear
**Ursa Minor** Little Bear
**ursine animal** bear
**ursine pelt** bearskin
**urticaria** nettle rash, urtication
**us** we
**usable property** asset
**usage** control, custom, employment, habit, management, method, mode, operation, use
**usance** term
**use** accustom, advantage, applicable, application, apply, appropriate, avail, benefit, bring, cause, consume, custom, employ(ment), end, enjoy, exercise, exhaust, expend, exploit, fitness, good, habit(uate), handle, handling, help, manipulate, mileage, necessity, need, object, occasion, operate, operation, point, practice, profit, purpose, reason, service, spend, treat(ment), usage, usefulness, utilisation, utilise, utility, value, waste, way, wield, work, worth
**use ambiguous words to conceal the truth** equivocate, prevaricate
**use another's work as your own** plagiarise
**use artful flattery** cajole
**use asphalt** pave
**use bad language** curse, swear
**use badly** illtreat
**use beak** peck
**use bombastic language** rant
**use broom** sweep
**use car** drive
**use computer** compute
**use couch** sit
**use coupon** redeem
**use crystal in crystal-gazing** scry
**used** cast-off, old, second-hand, shopsoiled, (shop)worn
**used around waist** cummerbund, girdle, obi (J), sash
**used as an anaesthetic** ether
**used as basis of perfumes** musk
**used as fuel** peat
**used as roofing material** slate
**used at sea** marine
**used by an ear doctor** otoscope
**used by boatman** oars

**used by golfer** niblick
**used by smokers** ashtray
**used by voter** ballot paper
**used car deal** resale
**used for binding wounds** bandage
**used for brewing** malt
**used for butts** ashtray
**used for counting** abacus, soroban
**used for floor cleaning** mop, swab
**used for measuring** ruler
**used for rubbish** bin
**used for smelling** nose
**used for sucking** teat
**used for thatching** straw
**used for toilet powder** talc
**used for underwater swimming** snorkel
**used in billiard game** cue, balls
**used in circus** trapeze
**used in couples** pair
**used in courts of law** forensic
**used in East to darken eyelids** kohl
**used in gardens** hoe
**used in home** appliance
**used in Italian cooking** pasta
**used in legal proceedings** forensic
**used in medicine** iodine
**used in negative sense** non
**used in radiotherapy** cobalt
**used in scents** myrrh
**used in sewing** thimble
**used to** accustomed
**used to be** was, were
**used to be Siamese** Thai
**used to catch butterflies** net
**used to catch fish** net
**used to control horse** harness, rein
**used to flavour liqueurs** aniseed, cherry, na(a)rtjie, orange
**used to make holes in leather** awl
**used to moisten food** gravy
**used to moor ship** anchor
**used to own** had
**used to propel boat** oar
**used to stop horse** whoa
**used to tie things together** rope
**used to tie up parcels** string
**used to turn coals** poker
**used to wash the hair** shampoo
**used until damaged** worn
**use economically** husband
**use efforts** exert
**use extravagantly** waste
**use for baking** kiln, oven
**use for clothing** wear
**use for cutting corn** sickle
**use for horse threats** duress
**useful** advantageous, beneficial, effective, efficient, fruitful, handy, helpful, practical, profitable, salutary, serviceable, useable, utile, valuable, worthwhile
**useful hint** tip
**useful mechanical device** gadget
**usefulness** adaptability, applicability, serviceability, usability, use, utility
**useful plant** herb
**useful quality** asset
**useful thing** convenience
**useful vessel** utensil
**use garden tool** hoe
**use handle** lever
**use key** open, unlock
**use ladle** dip
**useless** abortive, barren, dud, frivolous, fruitless, futile, hopeless, idle, impracticable, inadequate, inane, ineffective, ineffectual, inoperative, inutile, kaput (G), otiose, profitless, purposeless, superfluous, trivial, unavailing, unserviceable, vain, valueless, worthless
**useless household articles** lumber
**useless information** trivia
**useless plant** weed
**useless remains of rags** tatters
**useless remnant** fag
**useless structure** folly
**useless stuff** lumber
**use money** spend
**use natatorium** swim
**use needle** sew
**use needles and yarn** knit
**use oars** row
**use of arches in buildings** arcuation
**use of bow and arrows** archery
**use of cloth** wipe
**use office machine** type
**use of force or threats** duress
**use of light in the treatment of disease** phototherapy
**use of magic** witchcraft
**use of microscope** microscopic
**use of new words** neologism, neology
**use of ridicule** lampooning, satire
**use of the eyes** seeing
**use of wrong name** misnomer
**use phone** call
**use piggy bank** save
**user** addict, consumer, employer, junkie, junky
**use razor** shave
**user of bow and arrow** archer
**user of magic arts** sorcerer, witch, wizard
**user of quantitative data** statistician
**use rudder** steer
**use sabre** fence
**use scissors** snip
**use shovel** dig, spade
**use sieve** sift
**use spade** dig
**use sparingly** economise, husband, ration, scrimp
**use spoon** stir
**use stencil** trace
**use stethoscope** ausculate
**use stopwatch** time
**use straw** sip
**use swords** fence
**use syllogisms** ratiocinate
**use teeth** bite
**use temporarily** borrow
**use the service of** employ
**use tobacco** smoke
**use to get contents out of can** opener
**use to one's advantage** avail
**use to reach high places** ladder
**use up** absorb, apply, consume, deplete, devour, drain, exhaust, expend, finish, fritter, sap, spend, squander, swallow, waste
**use vehicle** ride
**use violent language** rant
**use waste material** recycle
**use when colouring in** crayons
**use whip on** flagellate, scourge
**use with skill** wield
**use wrong name or term** misnomer
**usher** announce, assistant, attendant, conduct, director, doorkeeper, escort, gatekeeper, guide, herald, initiate, leader, official, page, porter, precede, servant, show in, teacher, usherette
**usher in** admit, announce, herald, inaugurate, initiate, introduce, launch, precede, present
**usher or maid** attendant
**using** exploiting, utilising
**using a lure** decoying
**using an assumed name** pseudonymous
**using few words** laconic
**using insulting language** abusive, reviling
**using no fluid** aneroid
**using offensive language** abusive
**using of new words** neologism, neology
**using only one colour** monochrome
**using razor** shaving
**using selection** selective
**using unnecessary force** violent
**using violence on robbery** predatory
**using yarn** darning, mending
**USSR money** kope(c)k
**USSR port** Vladivostok
**USSR sea** Aral
**usual** accustomed, average, common(ly), customary, expected, familiar, fixed, frequent, general(ly), habitual, norm, normal(ly), ordinary,

usual action  practice
usually  chronically, commonly, constantly, conventionally, customarily, expectedly, familiarly, fixedly, frequently, generally, habitually, mainly, mostly, normally, often, ordinarily, persistently, predominantly, regularly, repeatedly, routinely, typically, predictable, prevalent, regular, routinely, typical
usually blue  Monday
usually eaten raw  oyster
usually follow downs  ups
usually served with custard  jelly, pudding
usual practice  custom, habit
usual procedure  routine
usual standard  norm
usual time of eating  mealtime
usurp  arrogate, assume, commandeer, dispossess, encroach, expropriate, grab, infringe, overthrow, pirate, pre-empt, seize, steal, supercede, upstage
usurper  invader
Utah Indian  Yute
Utah mountains  Uinta
utensil  apparatus, appliance, container, contraption, contrivance, device, gadget, gimmick, implement, instrument, invention, machine, mechanism, pan, pot, receptacle, tool, vessel
uterus  matrix, womb
utile  usable, useful
utilisation  using
utilise  apply, employ, exercise, exploit, operate, practise, use, wield
utilise to excess  overuse
utilising  employing, exercising, using
utility  adaptability, advantage, advantageousness, avail, benefit, convenience, efficacy, fitness, handy, helpfulness, point, practicality, profit, reserve, service, usability, use(fulness), value
utmost  cardinal, extreme, foremost, furthest, greatest, highest, limit, major, principal, supreme, uttermost
utmost degree  limit
Utopia  bliss, Cockaigne, Eden, heaven, limbo, nirvana, paradise
Utopian  airy, dream(er), fantasy, ideal, idealist(ic), illusory, perfect, romantic, visionary
utter  absolute, announce, circulate, comment, complete, declare, divulge, downright, enunciate, express, extreme, pronounce, publish, remark, reveal, say, sheer, speak, state, unqualified, vocalise, voice
utter a long audible breath of relief  sigh
utterance expressing affection  endearment
utterance of blessing  benediction
utterance of grievance  complaint
utter an oath  swear
utter a sharp cry  bark
utter childishly  prattle
utter collapse  debacle
utter confusion  chaos, pandemonium
utter curses upon  execrate
utter damnation against  curse
utter defeat  débâcle, rout
utter discordantly  bray
utter distinctly  articulate
uttered in the throat  guttural, throaty
utter failure  débâcle
utter falsehood  lie
utter fool  idiot
utter foolishness  idiocy
utter forcibly  belch
utter formally  pronounce
utter happiness  bliss
utter horror  sheer terror
utter in a low voice  murmur
utter incoherently with spitting sounds  splutter
uttering of curse  malediction
utter in harsh tone  grate
utter loud laughter  roar
utter loudly  bellow, cry
utterly  absolutely, completely, entirely, extremely, fully, perfectly, sheerly, starkly, thoroughly, totally
utterly absurd  preposterous
utterly confused  chaotic
utterly destroy  exterminate, shatter
utterly foolish  idiotic
utterly odious  heinous
utterly penitent  contrite
utterly reckless  desperate
utterly villainous  flagitious
utter melodious sounds  sing, warble
uttermost  extreme, furthest
utter musical sound  sing
utter noisily  vociferate
utter nonsense  tomfoolery, tommyrot
utter piercing cry  scream
utter predictions  prophesy
utter profanity about  blaspheme, revile
utter rubbish  tommyrot, twaddle
utter shrill cry  screech, squeal
utter sounds of pain  groan
utter suddenly  ejaculate
utter surprise  astonishment
utter while sobbing  blubber
utter wildly  rave
utter with spitting sounds  splutter
utter with the speaking voice  say
utter witty remarks  epigrammatise
utter words  speak
U-turn  about-turn, backtrack, reversal, volte-face

# V

vacant  blank, empty, free, thoughtless, unemployed, unoccupied, untenanted, unthinking, vacuous, void, wanting
vacantly silly  fatuous
vacant smile  grin
vacation  break, breather, cruise, excursion, furlough, holiday, intermission, leave, pause, recess, rest, travel, trip, voyage
vacation place  resort
vaccinate  inoculate
vacillate  change, deviate, dither, fluctuate, flutter, hesitate, hover, oscillate, pause, reel, seesaw, stagger, sway, swing, tremble, vibrate, waver, wobble
vacuous  absent, blank, brainless, dense, dull, empty(-headed), exhausted, expressionless, fatuous, frivolous, futile, hollow, idiotic, inane, mindless, puerile, senseless, silly, trifling, unemployed, unintelligent, vacant, vain, vapid, void, worthless
vacuum  clean, emptiness, gap, space, sweep, void
vacuum flask  thermos
vade-mecum  enchiridion, guide, handbook, manual, primer, textbook

**vagabond** beggar, bum, derelict, drifter, hobo, homeless, idler, loafer, migrant, nomad(ic), outcast, rover, scamp, stroller, tramp, truant, vagrant, wandering, worthless
**vagary** caprice, fancy, megrim, notion, whim(sy)
**vagrant** beachcomber, bedouin, beggar, bergie, bohemian, bum, castaway, derelict, drifter, gipsy, gypsy, hobo, idler, itinerant, loafer, migrator, nomadic, pariah, rascal, rover, runagate, straggler, strayer, stroller, tramp, unsettled, vagabond, wanderer
**vagrant mongrel** pi-dog, pye-dog
**vagrant worker** swagman
**vague** abstract, abstruse, baffling, confused, cryptic, dim, doubtful, enigmatic, hazy, hesitant, ill-defined, imprecise, indefinite, indistinct, inexact, lax, loose, mysterious, nebulous, nondescript, nonspecific, obscure, puzzling, shadowy, sketchy, uncertain, unclear, undecided, undetermined, unknown, unspecific, unspecified, wavering, woolly
**vague expectation** presentiment
**vagueness of meaning** ambiguity
**vague notion** glimpse, idea
**vague opinion** notion
**vague report** breeze
**vail** doff, gratuity, tip, yield
**vain** arrogant, conceited, egotistic(al), futile, hollow, inflated, nugatory, proud, trivial, unavailing, unimportant, useless, vapid, worthless
**vain boaster** braggart
**vain empty-headed young man** puppy
**vain person** egotist
**valance** canopy, curtain, drapery, edging, frontlet, palmette, pand, pelmet
**vale** combe, coomb, dale, dell, dene, dingle, farewell, glen, hollow, kloof, strath, valley
**valet** butler, de chambre (F), footservant, lackey, (man)servant, steward, valet
**valetudinarian** hypochondriac, invalid, valetudinary
**valiant** audacious, aweless, bold, brave, chivalrous, courageous, dauntless, decent, deserving, doughty, dreadless, due, equitable, excellent, firm, gallant, good, gritty, heroic, honest, intrepid, invincible, lion-hearted, manly, meritorious, plucky, reputable, resolute, righteous, stout(-hearted), sturdy, unhesitating, valorous, virile, worthy
**valiant enthusiast** crusader
**valid** binding, cogent, effective, efficient, just, lawful, legal, logical, sound, weighty
**validate** allow, authenticate, circumstantiate, codify, confirm, enable, entitle, invest, permit, ratify, sanction, seal, substantiate, support, verify, warrant
**validity** acceptability, authenticity, fact, legality, logic, potency, power, soundness, truthfulness
**valise** case, luggage, portmanteau, suitcase
**valley** barranca, barranco, basin, canyon, combe, coomb, cove, dale, dell, dene, depression, dingle, dip, gap, glen (Sc), gorge, gully, hollow, ravine, ria, strath, trough, vail, vale, wadi
**valley on side of hill** combe, coomb
**valley on the moon** rille
**valour** ability, audacity, boldness, bravery, capability, courage, daring, efficacy, energy, fearlessness, firmness, force, fortitude, gallantry, grit, guts, hardiness, heroism, intrepidity, manhood, manliness, masculinity, maturity, mettle, might, nerve, pluck(iness), potency, power, prowess, resolution, spirit, strength, sway, valiance, vigour, virility
**valuable** cherished, costly, dear, expensive, helpful, important, precious, serviceable, useful, worthy
**valuable card** ace
**valuable discovery** find
**valuable fur** chinchilla, ermine, mink, sable, seal
**valuable hint** tip, wrinkle
**valuable metal** gold, platinum, silver
**valuable possessions** riches
**valuable property** asset
**valuables** acquisitions, gems, gold, heirlooms, jewel(le)ry, jewels, treasures
**valuable violin** Amati, Stradivarius
**valuate** appraise, estimate
**value** account, advantage, appraise, appreciate, assess, benefit, cherish, cost, desirability, esteem, estimate, estimation, ethics, evaluation, force, help, importance, merit, price, principles, profit, rate, regard, respect, standards, survey, treasure, use, utility, worth
**value greatly** treasure
**valueless thing** trifle
**value received** consideration
**value too high** overestimate
**valve** inlet, mitral
**valve closing mouth of shell** operculum
**valve that controls a sluice** draw-gate
**valve that controls water supply** stopcock
**vamoose** scamper, scoot, scram, voetsak, voetsek
**vamp** Circe, enchantress, femme fatale (F), seductress, siren, vampire
**van** bakkie, bus, camper, car, dray, lorry, trailer, truck, vehicle, wagon
**vandal** barbarian, deliquent, despoiler, hoodlum, hooligan, Hun, looter, marauder, mutilator, plunderer, raider, ransacker, robber, rowdy, tsotsi, tough
**vane** weathercock
**vaned wheel** flier, flyer
**vane of a feather** vexillum
**vane of helicopter** rotor
**vanguard** avante-garde, forefront, innovators, leaders, pacemakers, pacesetters, pioneers, trendsetters, van
**vanish** cease, dematerialise, depart, disappear, disperse, dissipate, ebb, end, evanesce, evaporate, fade, flee, recede, retire, retreat, retrocede
**vanity** airs, amour-propre (F), arrogance, conceit, egotism, emptiness, ostentation, pride, self-esteem, sham
**vanity box** etui
**vanity case for face-powder** flapjack
**vanquish** attack, beat, capture, conquer, crush, defeat, foil, overcome, overmaster, overpower, overthrow, predominate, prevail, quell, reduce, rout, storm, subdue, subjucate, take, win
**vantage point** perspective, standpoint, view
**vapid** boring, dull, empty, flat, inane, insipid, jejune, lifeless, meaningless, mundane, prosaic, stale, tasteless, tedious, thin, tired, trite, watery, wishy-washy
**vapour** breath, brume, dampness, dew, fog, gas, haze, miasma, mist, smaze, smog, steam
**vapour floating in the air** cloud
**vapour remover** demister
**variable** changeable, changeful, fluctuating, inconstant, uneven, unsteady, vacillating, wavering
**variable according to price** elastic
**variable colour** coral
**variable resistance instrument** rheostat
**variable star** nova, pulsar

**variance** cross-purpose, difference, disagreement, discord, discrepancy, dissension, divergence, inconsistency, strife, variation
**variant** nonstandard, state, version
**variant of same colour** shade
**variation** alteration, change, deviation, difference, modification, mutation
**varicella** chickenpox
**varied in content** heterogeneous
**variegate** alter, checker, colour, diversify, modify, stain, streak, stripe
**variegated** brilliant, flecked, multicoloured, opaline, pied, prismatic, speckled, streaked
**varieties of gold and silver lace** orris
**variety** array, assortment, brand, breed, category, change, class, collection, difference, divergence, diversity, group, kind, make, medley, mixture, order, range, sort, species, strain, type, variation
**variety act** turn
**variety entertainment** vaudeville
**variety of apple** pearmain
**variety of beryl** emerald
**variety of billiards** pool
**variety of cabbage** broccoli, Brussels sprout, cauliflower, kail, kale
**variety of chalcedony** sard
**variety of cheese** Wensleydale
**variety of cocktail** sidecar
**variety of fir** spruce
**variety of golf** skins
**variety of graphite** kish
**variety of grass** fescue
**variety of gypsum** selenite
**variety of ju-jitsu** judo
**variety of leopard** panther
**variety of lettuce** cos
**variety of lizard** salamander
**variety of musk melon** cantaloup(e), spanspek
**variety of olivine** chrysolite
**variety of onion** shallot
**variety of pea** marrowfat
**variety of pear** bartlett
**variety of pet dog** poodle
**variety of pickle** piccalilli
**variety of polecat** fetter
**variety of porcelain** Chantilly, Coalport, Dresden, Limoges, Meissen
**variety of quartz** onyx
**variety of rum** tafia
**variety of sausage** salami
**variety of sheep** merino
**variety of sheepskin** roan
**variety of smooth-skinned peach** nectarine
**variety of sprouting broccoli** calabrese

**variety of tetanus** lockjaw, trismus
**variety of turnip** swede
**variety of wheat** einkorn, spelt
**variety of wine** riesling
**variety of zircon** malacon
**variety show** musical, revue
**variola** smallpox
**various** assorted, different, differing, disparate, distinct, divers(e), heterogeneous, many, several, sundry, varied, variegated
**various ancient sacred writings of Hinduism** Vedas
**various colours** particoloured, pied
**various countries under one rule** empire
**various exotic plants with showy flowers** orchid
**varlet** rascal
**varnish** lacquer, shellac, veneer
**varnished leather** patent
**varnish ingredient** lac, resin
**varnish resin** anime, elemi
**vary** alter, assort, change, differ, diversify, fluctuate, modify, transform
**vary between limits** range
**vary erratically** fluctuate
**vary from a direct course** digress, wind
**varying** unequal
**varying products to spread risk** diversification
**varying the voice's pitch** intonating
**vary in tone** modulate
**vary irregularly** fluctuate
**vascular cryptogamous plant** fern
**vase** amphora, bottle, canister, carafe, container, cruse, decanter, ewer, jar, jug, receptacle, urn, vessel
**vase-shaped** vasiform
**vasiform** duct-shaped, vase-shaped
**vassal** bondman, dependant, feudatory, liege, liegeman, serf, slave, subject, wretch
**vast** boundless, colossal, enormous, extensive, giant, huge, immense, leviathan, mammoth, massive, stupendous, titanic, tremendous, unlimited, untold, voluminous
**vast age** aeon, eternity
**vast amount** host
**vast area** expanse
**vast continent** Asia
**vast crowd** horde, swarm
**vast domain** empire
**vast expanse of water** ocean, sea
**vast treeless Arctic region** tundra
**vastness** immenseness, immensity, magnitude, massiveness, spaciousness
**vat** bac, barrel, bucket, cask, cauldron, container, keeve, keg, pail,

puncheon, receptacle, tank, tub, vessel
**vat for bleaching** keir, kier
**Vatical chapel** Sistine
**vaticinate** foretell, prophesy
**vat of blended wine of uniform quality** cuvée
**vaudeville act** skit
**vault** arch, bend, bound, bow, ceiling, cellar, clear, crypt, curve, depository, hurdle, jump, leap, roof, safe, span, spring, strongroom, tomb
**vaulter's aid** pole
**vault for disposal of dead bodies** tomb
**vault of heaven** firmament, sky
**vault under church** crypt
**vaunt** brag, flaunt, parade
**veal braised or roasted with vegetables** fricandeau, fricando
**veal cutlet** schnitzel
**veal or hare stewed with shallots and spices** stifado (Gr)
**Vedanta** Upanishads
**Vedic god of fire** Agni
**veer** bend, change, curve, deviate, diverge, dodge, drift, jibe, sheer, shift, shy, sidestep, swerve, swing, tack, turn, twist, warp, wheel, yaw
**veer off** sheer, swerve
**vegan** vegetarian
**vegetable** artichoke, asparagus, aubergine, bean, beet(root), brinjal, broccoli, Brussels sprout, butternut, cabbage, calabrese, carrot, cauliflower, celery, chive, cucumber, endive, kale, leek, legume, lettuce, marrow, onion, parsnip, pea, potato, pumpkin, radish, rhubarb, sauerkraut, shallot, spinach, sprouts, swede, tomato, turnip
**vegetable anatomy** phytotomy
**vegetable caterpillar** aweto
**vegetable cutter** dicer
**vegetable dealer** greengrocer
**vegetable dish** salad
**vegetable fuel** coal, peat
**vegetable leaves** greens
**vegetable oil source** olive, peanut
**vegetable peeler** parer
**vegetable pulp** puree
**vegetable retailer** greengrocer
**vegetable root** rhizome
**vegetable seed** bean, pea
**vegetable skinner** peeler
**vegetable soup** minestrone
**vegetable stem** asparagus
**vegetable substance** resin
**vegetarian** vegan
**vegetative part of fungus** mycelium
**vehemence** eagerness, emphasis, energy, enthusiasm, fervour, fire,

**vehement** force(fulness), heat, intensity, keenness, passion, vigour, warmth, zeal

**vehement** ardent, assertive, burning, eager, earnest, emphatic, fervent, forcible, impassioned, impetuous, passionate, violent

**vehement desire for drink** thirst

**vehemently aggressive** fierce

**vehement speech** tirade

**vehicle** agent, automobile, bakkie, car, conveyance, gig, instrument, means, (mini)bus, tool, transportation, truck, van, wag(g)on

**vehicle beyond repair** write off

**vehicle carrying a display** float

**vehicle for conveying coffin at funeral** hearse

**vehicle for couple** two-seater

**vehicle for travelling in outer space** spacecraft

**vehicle on runners for sliding on snow** sledge, sleigh, toboggan

**vehicle overhaul** service

**vehicle propulsion** traction

**vehicle spoiler** air dam

**vehicles using highway** traffic

**vehicle that carries injured people** ambulance

**vehicle that runs on rails** tram

**vehicle transporting bulk liquid** tanker

**vehicle weight** tare

**veil** blanket, blind, camouflage, canopy, chadri, cloak, cloud, conceal(ment), cover(ing), curtain, dim, disguise, façade, face, falsify, film, fog, guise, haze, headdress, hide, mantilla, mantle, mask, masquerade, obscure, orale, pretence, purdah, scarf, screen, shade, shadow, shield, shroud, yas(h)mak

**veiling fabric** tulle

**veiling-like material** voile

**vein** aorta, artery, blood vessel, channel, course, dash, furrow, groove, hint, lode, mine, ridge, seam, sloot, stratum, stripe, style, tenor, trait, vena, watercourse

**veined leaves** nervate

**vein of coal** streak

**vein of leaf** rib

**vein of ore** lode, reef

**velar** guttural, palatal

**veld succulent** aloe

**vellum** kidskin

**velocity** action, alacrity, briskness, celerity, fastness, fleetness, hurry, liveliness, pace, precipitation, promptness, quickness, rapidity, rate, speed, swiftness, tempo, timing

**velocity guage** speedometer

**velutinous** velvety

**velvety** downy, feathery, fleecy, glossy, polished, rounded, shiny, silken, silky, sleek, smooth, soft, velutinous

**velvety fabric** panne, plush, velour

**velvety flower** pansy

**velvety growth on rocks** moss

**velvety leather** suede

**vena** aorta, artery, vein

**venal** bent, bribable, buyable, corrupt(ible), covetous, grafting, greedy, mercenary, purchasable, rapacious, selfish

**vend** auction, barter, handle, hawk, huckster, market, peddle, print, publish, retail, sell, stock, trade

**vendetta** acrimony, argument, avengement, bitterness, brawl, clash, conflict, contention, controversy, feud, quarrel, revenge, rivalry, scrimmage, squabble, war(fare)

**vendible** saleable, venal

**vendor** agent, broker, colporteur, dealer, distributor, entrepreneur, merchant, monger, peddler, purveyor, rep(resentative), retailer, salesman, seller, shopkeeper, trader, tradesman, wholesaler

**vendor of antiques** antiquary

**vendue** auction, outcry, sale

**venerable** adorable, aged, ancient, archaic, august, eminent, esteemed, gray, grey, hallowed, hoary, honoured, illustrious, respected, revered, venerated

**venerable old man** patriarch

**venerate** admire, adore, dread, esteem, hallow, honour, idolise, revere(nce), worship

**veneration** admiration, adoration, awe, deference, devotion, dread, fear, homage, respect

**veneration of evil** devil worship

**veneration of saints** hagiolatry

**venereal disease** AIDS, gonorrhea, lues, syphilis

**Venetian beach** Lido

**venetian blind section** slat

**Venetian boat** bucentaur, gondola

**Venetian boatman** gondolier

**Venetian boat song** barcarole

**Venetian bridge** Rialto

**Venetian magistrate** doge, podesta

**Venetian mosaic** terrazo

**Venetian nobleman** doge

**Venetian oarsman** gondolier

**Venetian red** sienna

**Venetian resort** Lido

**Venetian steamboat** vaporetto

**Venetian traveller** Marco Polo

**Venetian white glass** vitro-di-trina

**Venezuelan dance** joropo

**Venezuelan state** Lara

**Venezuelan tree snake** lora

**vengeance** avengement, counterstroke, malevolence, reprisal, requital, retaliation, retribution, revenge, ruthlessness

**vengeful** vindictive

**venial** allowable, excusable, forgivable, minor, pardonable, trivial

**venial sin** peccadillo

**Venice district** Rialto

**Venice is there** Italy

**venom** acerbity, acrimony, malevolence, malice, malignity, (snake) poison, spite(fulness), virulence, virus

**venomous fish** stonefish

**venomous satire on individual** lampoon

**venomous snake** adder, asp, boomslang, cobra, krait, mamba, rattler, rinkhals, taipan, viper

**venomous spider** black widow, button, katipo, redback, tarantula

**venom tooth** fang

**vent** air, aperture, blowhole, discharge, duct, emit, empty, express, hole, opening, orifice, outlet, release, split, utter, voice

**ventilate** aerate, aerify, air, circulate, divulge, fan, refresh, report, vent, voice, winnow

**ventilating airway** upcast

**ventilating machine** fan

**ventilation** aeration, air(ing), circulation, display, drying, exposure, expression, freshening, publicity, utterance, vent

**ventilation shaft in a mine** intake, upcast

**vent in earth's crust** volcano

**vent peg** spigot

**ventriloquist's partner** dummy

**venture** adventure, aim, assay, dare, endanger, endeavour, enterprise, hazard, intend, jeopardise, peril, presume, risk, speculate, speculation, task, try, undertaking

**venturesome** adventurous, brave, daring, hazardous, intrepid

**venue** area, arena, bearings, locale, location, locus, place, point, position, site, situation, spot, station, whreabouts

**Venus** Hesperus

**Venus' love** Adonis

**veracious** accurate, actual, careful, conscionable, credible, definite, earnest, ethical, exact, factual, faithful, faultless, genuine, honest, honourable, identical, just, methodical, moral, noble, orderly, particular, precise, real(istic), reliable, right, scrupulous, sincere, true, trustworthy, trusty, truthful, unerring, valid

**veracity** axiom, bluntness, candour, certainty, correctness, earnestness, fact, frankness, genuineness, honesty, precision, probity, sincerity, straightforwardness, theorem, truth(fulness)

**veranda** balcony, lanai, outside gallery, lobby, loggia, piazza (I), porch, portico, stoep, terrace, verandah

**verbal** fluent, grammatical, lexical, literal, nominal, nuncupative, oral, said, spoken, titular, unwritten, verbatim, vocabular, vocal, voiced, word-of-mouth, worded

**verbal engagement** argument, debate, dispute, polemic

**verbal examination** oral

**verbal expression of feeling** sentiment

**verbal instruction** dictation

**verbally** ad verbum (L), literally, orally, wordily

**verbal narrative** account

**verbal onslaught** diatribe, invective, jeremiad, philippic, screed, tirade

**verbal SOS** Mayday

**verbal suffix** -ise

**verbal trickery** chicanery

**verbatim** accurate(ly), clear, exact(ly), explicit, faithfully, honestly, literal(ly), literatim, precise(ly), strict(ly)

**verb ending** -ing

**verb form** active, gerund, participle, passive

**verb modifier** adverb

**verbose** diffuse, pleonastic, prolix, windy, wordy

**verb prefex** de-

**verdant** flourishing, fresh, grassy, green(-coloured), ignorant, immature, inexperienced, inexpert, ingenuous, innocent, sea green, unsophisticated, verdurous

**Verdi character** Aïda, Ammeris, Azucena, Radames

**verdict** consensus, decision, determination, diagnosis, evaluation, judg(e)ment, ruling

**verdict of not guilty** acquittal

**verdigris** aerugo

**Verdi heroine** Aïda

**Verdi opera** Aïda, Don Carlos, Falstaff, Il Trovatore, La Traviata, Macbeth, Nabucco, Otello, Rigoletto

**Verdi production** opera

**verdure** foliage, grass(land), greenery, greenness, greens, herbage, leafage, lushness, luxuriance, meadow, turf, vegetation, verdancy, vigour

**verge** area, belt, border, brim, brink, edge, flange, incline, limit, lip, margin, rim, side, strip, tend, wand

**verge on** abut, approach, near

**verging on** approximate

**veridity** genuineness

**verifiable piece of information** fact

**verified copy of will** probate

**verifier** attester

**verify** ascertain, attest, authenticate, certify, check, confirm, convince, corroborate, ensure, establish, guarantee, prove, recheck, sample, substantiate, support, test, try, validate, vindicate

**verily** really, tru(e)ly, yea

**verisimilitude** accuracy, apparently, credibility, genuineness, lifelikeness, plausibility, probability, realism, realness, truth

**verity** actuality, actualness, certainty, fact(uality), gospel, law, principle, realism, reality, realness, rule, soundness, theorem, truth, validity, validness

**vermiform** wormlike, worm-shaped

**vermillion** cinnabar, red

**vermin** lice, pests, rabble, rats, reptile, scoundrel, scum, snake

**vermin destroyer** rat-catcher

**Vermont hero** Allen, Warner

**vermouth** chambery, cinzano, it, wine

**vermouth cocktail** martini

**vernal season** spring

**vernier rocket** thruster

**versatile** accomplished, adaptable, many-sided, multifaceted, resourceful, useful

**verse** ballad, canto, composition, couplet, extract, limerick, line, lyric, meter, numbers, ode, paragraph, passage, piece, poem, poesy, poetry, quotation, rhyme, rune, section, sentence, song, sonnet, stanza, stave, stitch, strophe, text, versification

**verse analysis** scansion

**verse couplet** distich

**versed** accomplished, conversant, experienced, familiar, proficient, skilled

**versed in legal principles** jurisprudent

**versed in literature** well-read

**versed in many languages** polyglot

**verse form** ballad, ode, poem, rondel, rondo, sonnet, tercet, triolet

**verse of eight measures** octameter, octonarius

**verse of five measures** pentameter

**verse of four measures** tetrameter

**verse of seven feet** septinarius

**verse of seven measures** heptameter

**verse of six feet** senarius

**verse of six iambic measures** alexandrine

**verse of six measures** hexameter

**verse of three feet** tripody

**verse of three measures** trimeter

**verse of two measures** dimeter, dipody

**verse rhythm** metre

**verse set to music** lyric(s)

**verse stress** ictus

**verse writer** bard, poet

**versifier** bard, lyricist, meterer, poet, rhymer, verser

**version** account, adaptation, construe, copy, depiction, exegesis, exercise, form, impression, interlinear, interpretation, lection, metaphrase, portrayal, reading, rendering, rendition, rewording, side, story, translation, variant, variation

**version of the Scripture** Vulgate

**versus** against

**vertex** acme, aerie, apex, apice, apogee, cap, crest, crown, head, height, hill, loft, meridian, mountain, peak, pinnacle, pitch, point, spire, summit, tip(top), top, zenith

**vertical** abrupt, apeak, bold, craggy, erect, high, perpendicular, plumb, precipitous, right-angular, sharp, sheer, standing, steep, straight, up(right), zenithal

**vertical bar dividing lights in window** mullion

**vertical bolt used as pivot** kingpin

**vertical cliff** precipice

**vertical flaw in stocking** ladder

**vertical joint** build

**vertical part of stair** riser

**vertical passage for lift** shaft

**vertical pipe** riser

**vertical pole** mast

**vertical pole used as a support** stanchion

**vertical stairway piece** riser

**vertical structure with flue to expel smoke** chimney

**vertical strut** stanchion

**vertical support** pillar

**vertical window in roof** dormer

**vertigo** dizziness, fainting, giddiness, light-headedness, reeling, unsteadiness

**verve** animation, ardour, dash, drive, dynamism, élan, energy, enthusiasm, fire, force, intensity, liveliness, panache, passion, pep, punch, spirit, vigorousness, vigour, vim, vitality, vivacity, zest

**very** absolute, actual, appropriate, complete, correct, deeply, desired, especially, essential, exactly, extremely, greatly, highly, identical, mere, most, muy (Sp), necessary, obvious, perfect, positively, precise, quite, really, same, total(ly), tres (F), unco (Sc), uncommonly, unduly, unusually, utter(ly), whole
**very abundant** luxuriant
**very active** hectic
**very alluring** irresistible
**very angry** fume, furious, irate, livid, raging, savage
**very attractive** dishy, lovely
**very bad** atrocious, awful, dreadful, egregious, evil, shocking, terrible
**very bad smell** malodorous, stench
**very big** astronomical, enormous, huge, large, tremendous
**very big person** giant
**very bitter attack** vitriolic
**very black** inky
**very brave** heroic
**very brief portion of time** fraction, moment
**very brief time** flash
**very bright** vivid
**very busy** hectic
**very careful** scrupulous
**very careful and precise** meticulous
**very careful in matters of choice** fastidious
**very charitable** saintly
**very cheap** dirt-cheap, low-cost
**very childish** infantile
**very clever** brainy, brilliant
**very close and intimate friend** alter ego
**very cold** freezing, gelid, icily, icy, snowy, wintry
**very convincing** cogent
**very cruel** Draconian, Draconic, sadistic
**very dear** beloved
**very deep gulf** abyss
**very deep sleep** coma
**very delicate** ethereal
**very distressing** nerve-(w)racking
**very drunk** besotted, blotto, inebriated, legless, sozzled, stoned
**very dry** arid, parched
**very dry champagne** brut
**very dry sherry** fino, Manzanilla
**very dry white wine** Chablis, grand cru
**very eager** avid
**very early sailor** Noah
**very edge** brink
**very enjoyable** ripping
**very enthusiastic** lyrical
**very essence** epitome
**very evident** obvious

**very excited** agog
**very fast** prestissimo, presto, rapid
**very fast vehicle** flier
**very fat** obese
**very fierce** ferocious, truculent
**very fine corduroy fabric** needlecord
**very fine rain** drizzle
**very flimsy paper** tissue
**very foolish** idiotic, insane
**very funny** hilarious
**very generous** bountiful, munificent
**very good** excellent, exemplary, vintage
**very great** abysmal, enormous, immense, infinite, stupendous, vast
**very great amount** oodles
**very great in very small matters** maximus in minimus (L)
**very greedy** insatiable
**very greedy person** glutton
**very handsome youth** Adonis
**very hard** adamantine
**very hard mineral** corundum, emery
**very hard paving brick** clinker, klinker
**very hard stone** adamant, diamond
**very heavy** leaden
**very heavy weight** ton
**very high in position** lofty
**very highly esteemed** precious
**very high quality** superb
**very high waterproof boot** wade
**very holy** saintly
**very hot** boiling, piping, roasting, sizzling, torrid, tropical
**very hot day** scorcher
**very hungry** ravenous, voracious
**very important people** bigwig, celebrity, élite, star, VIP
**very indirect** remote
**very intelligent person** genius
**very keen** anxious, avid, eager, enthusiastic
**very knowledgeable** learned
**very large** bulky, collosal, decuman, enorm(ous)
**very large fish** marlin, tunny
**very large hound** mastiff
**very large number** astronomical figure
**very large self-service store** hypermarket
**very learned** erudite, profound
**very learned man** pundit
**very light boxing weight** bantam
**very light brown** beige
**very light muffin** popover
**very light untarnishable metal** aluminium
**very light wood** balsa
**very little** atom, stim
**very little bit** jot, whit
**very loathsome** abominable
**very long** lengthy

**very long television programme** telethon
**very long time** aeon, ages, eternity
**very loud** deafening, fortissimo, thunderous
**very loud voice** stentorian, stentorious
**very lovely** beautiful
**very loyal** devoted
**very many** umpteen, zillions
**very much** excessive
**very near** adjacent
**very nearly** almost
**very numerous** multitudinous
**very obvious** blatant
**very old** age-long, age-old, aged, ancient, antique
**very old person** Methuselah
**very painful** grievous, excruciating
**very painful swelling on fingernail** whitlow
**very pale** ashen
**very pale blue** ice blue
**very pleased** chuffed, delighted
**very pleasing person** smasher
**very plump** fat
**very poor** needy, penniless
**very poor person** pauper
**very positive** cocksure
**very powerful** prepotent
**very quickly** apace
**very rapidly** presto
**very recent or topical** red-hot
**very religious character** Tobit
**very remarkable** wonderful
**very remote place** Timbuctoo, Timbuktu
**very restrained** prim
**very rich man** Croesus, millionaire, nabob, nawab
**very rich source of wealth** Klondike, Klondyke
**very sad** tragic, unhappy
**very salt water** brine
**very same** identical, selfsame
**very select** élite
**very serious sin** grievous
**very short jacket with wide lapels** Eton jacket
**very short margin** hair's breadth
**very short space of time** moment
**very short story** anecdote
**very short time** jiffy
**very skilful** adept, masterly
**very skinny** bony
**very sleepy** drowsy
**very slow** snail-like
**very slowly** largo, lentissimo
**very small** diminutive, dwarf(ish), fine, infinitesimal, least, little, micro-, microscopic, miniature, minikin, minimal, minuscule, minute, petit,

petty, pigmy, pygmy, teeny, tiny,
titchy, trivial, wee
**very small acaridan arachnid**  mite
**very small adult**  midget
**very small allowance**  pittance
**very small amount**  iota, jot, mite,
scruple, smidgen
**very small amount of money**  cent,
doit, mite, sou (F)
**very small bit**  particle
**very small cavity**  vacuole
**very small contribution**  mite
**very small creature**  midget, mite
**very small delicately worked flint**
microlith
**very small dog**  chihuahua
**very small drinking glass**  pony
**very small dwelling**  hut, pondok
**very small fish**  fry, tiddler
**very small in amount**  negligible
**very small insect**  mite
**very small horse**  Shetland pony
**very small mark**  speck
**very small monkey**  marmoset
**very small person**  dwarf, midget,
pik(kie), pygmy, tich
**very small portion**  atom
**very small quantity**  dash, scruple,
soupçon
**very small remuneration**  pittance
**very small room**  cubbyhole
**very small songbird**  wren
**very small sphere**  spherule
**very small sum**  sou
**very small wave**  ripplet
**very smart**  snazzy
**very soft**  squashy
**very steep**  precipitous, sheer, slant
**very steep cliff**  precipice
**very strict**  severe
**very striking**  spectacular
**very strong**  intense
**very strong man**  Hercules, Milo,
Samson
**very strong person**  titan
**very strong wind**  gale
**very stupid**  idiotic
**very stupid person**  cretin, moron
**very surprised**  agape
**very sweet substance used as**
**substitute for sugar**  saccharin
**very tall**  towering
**very tall building**  skyscraper
**very tall tree**  sequoia
**very thin**  emaciated
**very thin and bony**  scrawny
**very thin layer**  film
**very thin metal**  foil
**very tidy**  faultless, immaculate,
impeccable, perfect, spotless
**very tiny**  minute
**very ugly**  hideous, revolting

**very uncommon**  odd, peculiar, rare,
unique, unusual
**very unfortunate person**  wretch
**very unhappy**  miserable
**very unpleasant**  dreadful, hellish,
objectionable, obnoxious, putrid
**very unusual**  extraordinary, rare
**very upset**  sad
**very warm**  hot
**very weak**  feeble
**very well**  certainly
**very wicked person**  fiend
**very wide**  broad
**very wise man**  sage
**very wise person**  Solomon
**very young child**  baby
**very young plant**  seedling
**vesica**  bladder, vessel
**vesicle**  bead, blister, bubble, cell, cyst,
drop(let), globule
**vesper**  evensong
**vessel**  ark, barrel, boat, boiler, bottle,
bucket, canister, carafe, cask,
clipper, collier, corvette, craft,
decanter, flagship, galleon, keg,
ketch, kettle, liner, pail, pot,
receptacle, schooner, ship, tankard,
tanker, tern, tub, urn, vat, xebec, yawl
**vessel carrying blood from the heart**
artery
**vessel for ashes of dead**  urn
**vessel for baptismal water**  font
**vessel for burning incense**  censer
**vessel for drinking**  cup, mug
**vessel for flowers**  vase
**vessel for holding liquids**  bottle
**vessel for infusion**  teapot
**vessel for keeping consecrated bread**
pyx
**vessel for liquors**  decanter, flagon,
flask
**vessel for making butter**  churn
**vessel for mixing pottery ingredients**
blunger
**vessel for sacred uses**  ampulla
**vessel for storing ashes**  urn
**vessel for storing liquids**  tank
**vessel for vinegar**  cruet
**vessel for washing**  basin
**vessel for water**  bucket, pail
**vessel like catamaran**  trimaran
**vessel made of plaited twigs**  basket
**vessels of baked clay**  earthenware
**vessel to spit into**  spittoon
**vessel with perforated lid**  dredge
**vessel with tap**  urn
**vessel with three hulls**  trimaran
**vest**  attire, bestow, bodice, bodywear,
doublet, endow, garment, give,
grant, invest, jerkin, jersey, jumper,
pullover, singlet, spencer, sweater,

undergarment, undershirt, waistcoat,
zephyr
**vestal**  chaste, fresh, girl, immaculate,
maidenly, modest, new, pure,
undefiled, untouched, unused, virgin
**vestibule**  antechamber, anteroom,
entrance, entry, foyer, hall, lobby,
locutorium, loggia, lounge, parlour,
porch, portico
**vestige**  evidence, footstep, hint,
indication, mark, memento, relic,
remainder, remains, remnant,
residue, scrap, shadow, sign, spoor,
suspicion, token, trace, track, whiff
**vestment**  alb, attire, bestowment,
cassock, cloack, clothes, clothing,
cover, cowl, drape, empowerment,
endowment, garments, habiliments,
hood, placement, robes, settlement,
shield, shroud, veil
**vestment of bishop**  alb, chimer
**vestment worn at mass**  amice,
chasuble
**vesture**  attire, clothes, clothing,
costume, dress, ensemble, garb,
garments, gear, habits, outfit,
raiment, togs, vestments, wardrobe,
wear
**vesuvianite**  idocrase, mineral, vesuvian
**vet**  appraise, check, examine,
investigate, review, scan, screen,
scrutinise, veterinarian
**vetch seed**  tare
**veteran**  campaigner, ex-serviceman,
ex-soldier, expert, master, old-timer,
trouper, warhorse, warrior
**veterinary's cautery**  giring-iron
**veterinary surgeon**  veterinarian
**veterinary surgery**  farriery
**veto**  ban, disallow, embargo, forbid,
interdict, negative, oppose, prohibit,
reject
**vetoer**  prohibitor
**vex**  acerbate, afflict, aggravate,
agitate, anger, annoy, bother,
distress, disturb, fret, gall, grieve,
harass, irk, irritate, molest, needle,
nettle, offend, persecute, pester,
plague, prickle, provoke, rile, tease,
torment, torture, trouble, try, upset,
worry
**vexation**  aggravation, anger,
annoyance, bustle, chagrin, difficulty,
displeasure, disturbance,
exasperation, fury, fuss, harassment,
indignation, ire, irritability, irritation,
nuisance, outrage, passion, pique,
provocation, rage, strain, temper,
trouble, upset, worry, wrath
**vexatious**  annoying, bothersome,
chaotic, confused, dogging, hateful,
hounding, incensing, irksome,

irritating, litigating, pesky, pestering, plaguy, provoking, tormenting, unbearable, untoward
**vexed question** quaestic vexata (L)
**vexing** afflicting, agitating, annoying, bothering, bothersome, displeasing, distressing, disturbing, exasperating, harassing, irritating, molesting, offending, perplexing, pestering, plaguing, provoking, riling, teasing, tormenting, troubling, upsetting, worrisome, worrying
**vexing puzzle** teaser
**vex playfully** tease
**via** along, beside, by, near, over, past, per, through, using
**viable** attainable, economic, effective, feasible, functional, going, likely, operational, possible, practicable, practical, productive, profit-making, profitable, ready, reasonable, remunerative, solvent, usable, useful, workable, working
**vial** ampoule, cruet, phial
**vials of wrath** anger
**viand** cates, diet, dish, edibles, fare, food, meats, nourishment, provision, viands, victual(s)
**vibrant speech sounds** phonate
**vibrate** echo, judder, oscillate, pendulate, pulse, quake, quiver, resound, shake, tremble, tremble
**vibration** oscillation, pulse, quiver, shaking, throb, trembling, tremor
**vibrato** tremolo, trill
**vibratory motion** tremor
**vibratory shock** percussion
**vibratory sign** whir
**vicar** parson, rector
**vicaress** abbess, amma
**vicar's assistant** curate
**vice** assistant, blemish, clamp, corruption, crime, defect, demerit, depravity, deputy, error, evil, failing, fault, grip, guilt, illegality, imperfection, iniquity, nippers, sin, taint, tool, weakness, wickedness
**viceroy in Egypt during Ottoman control** khedive
**vice versa** conversely, inversely, reversely
**vicinity** adjacency, area, environs, nearness, neighbourhood, precinct, proximity, scene, suburbs
**vicious** abandoned, bad, blameworthy, brutal, censurable, defective, depraved, immoral, improper, iniquitous, malevolent, profligate, sinful, spiteful, wrong
**vicious criminal** thug, tsotsi
**vicious elephant** rogue
**vicious growl** snarl

**viciousness** brutality
**vicious old woman** harridan
**vicious person** brute
**vicious rodent** rat
**victim** casualty, dupe, gull, martyr, moegoe, pawn, prey, quarry, scapegoat, sufferer, target
**victimise** afflict, blame, cheat, deceive, domineer, dupe, exploit, injure, intimidate, mislead, outwit, persecute, prey, pursue, sacrifice, stalk, swindle, terrorise, torment, torture
**victim of Achilles** Hector
**victim of David** Goliath, Uriah
**victim of deception** dupe
**victim of Jezebel** Naboth
**victim of Joab** Abner
**victim of Samuel** Agag
**victor** champion, conqueror, hero, master, subjugator, vindicator, winner
**Victorian father** papa
**Victoria's consort** Albert
**victorious** conquering, exultant, jubilant, successful, truimphant, winning
**victory** ascendancy, conquest, success, supremacy, triumph, win
**victory letter** vee
**victory of Alexander** Arbela, Issus
**victory wreath** laurel
**victuals** bread, eatables, edibles, meal, rations, repast
**video recorder format** Beta, VHS
**viduage** widowhood, widows
**vie** compete, contend, contest, rival, strive, struggle
**Vienna's royal family** Habsburg
**Vienna's white horses** lipizzaner
**Viennese dance** waltz
**Viennese musician** Mozart, Strauss
**Vietnamese capital** Hanoi
**vieux jeu** hackneyed, old-fashioned
**view** account, appearance, aspect, assessment, behold, belief, conception, contemplate, contemplation, description, examine, idea, impression, inspect, intent(ion), judg(e)ment, look, notion, opinion, outlook, panorama, prospect, reason, regard, scene(ry), see, sight, survey, theory, thought, vision, vista, watch
**viewed speculatively** eyed
**view expressed by voting** suffrage
**view held as probable** opinion
**view in a certain direction** aspect
**viewing speculatively** ey(e)ing
**vie with** rival
**view mentally** contemplate
**view of the sea** seascape
**view of the sky** skyscape

**view overall** survey
**viewpoint** angle, aspect, attitude, opinion, outlook, perspective, posture, sentiment, slant, stance, standpoint, vantage
**view speculatively** eye
**view through an avenue** vista
**vigil** insomnia, sleeplessness, wakefulness
**vigilance** caution, circumspection, guard, keenness, observation, precaution, surveillance, wakefulness, watchfulness
**vigilant** alert, attendant, awake, careful, cautious, circumspect, conscientious, expectant, mindful, observant, on-guard, prepared, ready, regardful, tutelary, wakeful, wary, watchful
**vigorous** active, brisk, energetic, forcible, hale, hearty, lively, lusty, robust, strong, sturdy
**vigorous campaign** crusade
**vigorous campaigner** crusader
**vigorous exercise** aerobics
**vigorously** actively, briskly, con brio, effectively, energetically, flourishingly, forcefully, hardily, healthily, intensely, lustily, powerfully, robustly, soundly, spiritedly, strongly, vigoroso, vitally
**vigorously hearty** backslapping
**vigorous physical labour** elbow grease
**vigour** activity, animation, ardour, brio, dash, dynamism, élan, energy, enthusiasm, fervour, fire, force, gusto, health, intensity, life, liveliness, lustiness, might, pep, potency, power, punch, soundness, spirit, stamina, strength, verve, vim, virility, vitality, vivacity, zest, zip
**vigour of speech** emphasis, expression
**Viking** Dane, Norse(man)
**viking poet** scald, skald
**vile** atrocious, bad, base, depraved, disgusting, evil, foul, low, nasty, nauseating, obnoxious, obscene, offensive, paltry, poor, repellent, repulsive, revolting, ugly, valueless, vicious, vulgar, wretched
**vile wretch** miscreant
**vilify** abuse, defame, depreciate, malign, revile, slander, slur, traduce
**village** community, dorp, hamlet, kraal, municipality, thorp(e), town, whistle-stop
**village fair** walk
**village moneylender** gombeeman
**villain** baddy, blackguard, bounder, churl, criminal, crook, devil, evildoer,

**villainous** felon, fiend, imposter, knave, miscreant, offender, profligate, rascal, renegade, reprobate, rogue, ruffian, scamp, scoundrel, serf, skollie, stinker, tsotsi, twister, villein, wretch

**villainous** bad, base, criminal, cruel, debased, evil, fiendish, hateful, infamous, mean, ruffianly, sinful, thievish, vicious, vile, wicked

**villain's greeting** hiss

**villainy** corruption, crime, degradation, dishonesty, flagitiousness, flagrancy, foulness, heinousness, immorality, meanness, reprobacy, roguery, sin, vice, vileness

**vim** briskness, dash, eagerness, ebullience, élan, energy, enthusiasm, force, liveliness, pep, power, spirit, strenght, vigour(ness), vitality, zeal, zest, zip

**vindicate** absolve, clear, defend, exonerate, justify, maintain, support

**vindictive** antagonistic, grudge-bearing, hostile, ill-disposed, malevolent, malicious, malignant, rancorous, resentful, retaliatory, retributive, revengeful, spiteful, unforgiving, unreconciling, vengeful, venomous

**vindictive retaliation** revenge

**vine** climber, creeper, rambler, runner

**vine drink** wine

**vine fruit** grape

**vinegar** acetum, alegar

**vinegar acid** acetic

**vinegar ale** alegar

**vinegar bottle** cruet

**vinegar flavouring plant** tarragon

**vinegary** acetic

**vine-grower** vigneron

**vine insect** phylloxera

**vine offshoot** tendril

**vine on college walls** ivy

**vine support** trellis

**vine variety** cultivar

**vine vegetable** pumpkin

**vineyard** cru, vina, winery

**viniculture** viticulture, winegrowing

**vinification** winemaking

**vino** wine

**vinous** winy

**vintage** age, best, choice, classic, collection, crop, dated, epoch, era, fine, generation, harvest, mature, maturity, old(-fashioned), origin, period, prime, rare, ripe, select, superior, venerable, veteran, year

**vintage motor cycle** BSA

**vinyl flooring** lino

**viola flower** pansy

**violate** abuse, assault, attack, break, debauch, defoul, desecrate, disobey, disturb, encroach, force, hurt, infract, infringe, injure, intrude, outrage, rape, ravish, ruin, transgress, trespass, wreak

**violate a law** infringe

**violating decorum** outré

**violation** abuse, assault, breach, corruption, defilement, desecration, destruction, disturbing, illegality, infraction, infringement, offense, outrage, ravishment, ruination, sacrilege, transgression, trespass

**violation of decency** outrage

**violation of others' rights** outrage

**violation of what is sacred** sacrilege

**violator** invader

**violator of the marriage-bed** adulterer

**violence** assault, commotion, destruction, destructiveness, force, impetuosity, inhumanity, misuse, rage, severity, turbulence, vehemence

**violence of storm** fury

**violent** brutal, explosive, ferocious, fierce, forceful, furious, intense, rabid, raging, savage, strong, tumultuous, vehement

**violent action** affray, mayhem

**violent altercation** quarrel

**violent anger** rage, wrath

**violent attack** onset, onslaught

**violent attack in words** invective

**violent behaviour** rampage

**violent change** cataclysm

**violent collision** crash

**violent confusion** mayhem

**violent criminal** gangster, ruffian, tsotsi

**violent cyclonic storm** typhoon

**violent disagreement** quarrel

**violent disaster** cataclysm

**violent downpour** torrent

**violent dread** horror

**violent effort** strain, struggle

**violent entry** irruption

**violent flow** onrush

**violent gale** storm

**violent gush** spirt, spurt

**violent hit at ball** slog

**violent hooligan** thug

**violent hurricane** cyclone, typhoon

**violent influx** inrush

**violently agitated** seethe

**violently furious** rabid

**violently hot** torrid

**violent mêlée** riot

**violent outburst** explosion

**violent pangs** throe

**violent reckless criminal** desperado

**violent revolt** uprising

**violent robbery** plunder

**violent speech** tirade

**violent storm** cyclone, tempest, tornado

**violent stream of water** torrent

**violent street ruffian** apache, tsotsi

**violent tactics** terrorism

**violent tempered woman** nag, shrew

**violent theft** robbery

**violent tumult** tempest

**violent twist** wrench

**violent upheaval** cataclysm

**violent uprising** putsch

**violent verbal attack** invective

**violent weather** storm

**violent wind** storm, tempest, tornado

**violent woman** virago

**violet blue dye** indigo

**violet colour** amethyst, aubergine, heliotrope

**violet plant** pansy

**violin** fiddle

**violinist** fiddler

**violin made by Antonio Stradivari** Stradivarius

**violin's kin** cello, viola

**violin's partner** bow

**viol player** gambist

**VIP** celebrity, notable, star

**viper** adder, asp, collaborator, conspirator, impimpi, informer, pharisee, quisling, renegade, reptile, rogue, rotter, scoundrel, scum, serpent, snake, spy, swindler, traitor, villain, wretch

**virago** Amazon, beldam(e), fury, hag, harpy, harridan, hellcat, nag, scold, shrew, tartar, termagant, Xant(h)ippe

**viral cold sores** herpes

**viral disease** dengue

**viral infection** cold

**virgin** chaste, fresh, maiden, new, pristine, pure, unadulterated, undefiled, unpolluted, unsullied, untouched, untried, vestal

**virginal** celibate, chaste, immaculate, impeccable, incorrupt, innocent, pristine, pure, righteous, sinless, spotless, stainless, upright, virtuous

**Virginia county** Arlington

**Virgin Mary** Madonna

**virgule** solidus

**viridity** greenness, verdancy

**virile** athletic, bold, brave, brawny, burly, capable, courageous, daring, fearless, forceful, gallant, hale, hardy, healthy, hearty, herioc, macho, male, manlike, manly, masculine, noble, powerful, resolute, robust, stalwart, stout, strapping, strong, sturdy, valiant, valorous, vigorous

**virility** audacity, brawn, courage, doughtiness, machismo, manhood, masculinity, pluck, stamina, toughness, vigour, vitality
**virtually nothing** nominal
**virtue** chastity, effectiveness, excellence, faith, goodness, hope, integrity, justice, merit, morality, probity, prudence, purity, rectitude, uprightness, virginity
**virtuous** angelic, blameless, chaste, correct, ethical, fair, good, honest, honourable, impeccable, just, loyal, modest, moral, noble, pure, right(eous), upstanding, veracious, worthy
**virulent** acrimonious, deadly, hostile, malignant, poisonous, venomous
**virulent epidemic** pest
**virus** bug
**virus disease causing blisters on the skin** herpes
**virus disease in rabbits** myxomatosis
**virus disease of sheep** scrapie
**virus student** virologist
**virus which destroys bacteria** bacteriophage
**visage** aspect, countenance, face, look, physiognomy, semblance
**viscera** bowels, brain, colons, guts, heart, internals, intestines, liver, vitals
**visceral** abdominal, bodily, crude, emotional, immediate, instinctive, intestinal, physical, splanchnic, spontaneous
**viscid** gelatinous, gluey, glutinous, gummy, jelly-like, mucilaginous, semifluid, sticky, viscous
**viscid substance formed by mucus membrane** phlegm
**viscose** rayon
**viscount** baron, count, duke, earl, lord, marquess, noble, nobleman, peer
**viscous** adhesive, clammy, clinging, gelatinous, gluey, glutinous, gummy, jelly-like, miry, mucilaginous, muddy, ropy, slimy, sticky, syrupy, tacky, thick, viscid
**viscous and sweet** treacly
**viscous globule** blob
**viscous substance** gel, glue, grease, tar
**viscous substance extracted from plants** mucilage
**Vishnu consort** Sri
**Vishnu in his eighth avatar** Juggernaut
**visible** apparent, clear, conspicuous, discernible, evident, manifest, obvious, open, overt, perceptible
**visible combustion** flame
**visible depression** dent

**visible to the naked eye** macroscopic
**vision** anticipation, apparition, conception, discernment, dream, eyesight, idea, image, insight, penetration, perception, perspicacity, seeing, sight, spectre, view
**visionary** delusory, dreamer, enthusiast, fancied, fanciful, fey, ideal, idealist(ic), ideologue, illusory, imaginary, impracticable, impractical, phantasmal, romantic, speculative, theoretical, theorist, unfeasible, unreal(istic), zealot
**visionary speculation** ideology
**visionary unsubstantial** dreamlike, fata morgana (l), illusion, mirage
**vision cleanser** eyewash
**vision of an absent person** phantasm
**vision of light** photism
**visit** afflict, call, converse, excursion, see, sojourn, stay, stop(over), talk, tarriance, trip, visitation
**visit casually** run in
**visit frequently** haunt
**visit in order to ask for votes** canvass
**visitor** caller, company, guest, tourist, traveller, visitant
**visit or telephone** call
**visor** eyeshade, mask, peak
**visorless cap** beret
**visor of a helmet** beaver
**vista** horizon, landscape, lookout, outlook, panorama, perspective, prospect, scene(ry), sight, view
**visual** discernible, observable, ocular, optic(al), perceivable, perceptible, seeable, seeing, visible
**visual aids** specs, spectacles
**visualise** behold, contemplate, daydream, envisage, envision, fancy, idealise, imagine, picture, project, see
**visually unattractive** ugly
**visual orb** eye
**vital** alive, animated, axial, basic, cardinal, critical, crucial, deadly, decisive, dynamic, eager, energetic, enthusiastic, essential, fatal, forceful, important, indispensable, key, lethal, life-giving, live(ly), necessary, needful, requisite, significant, spirited, urgent, vigorous, vivacious, zestful
**vital body part** organ
**vital circulating juice** sap
**vital fluid** blood
**vital ingredient of plastic** resin
**vitality** animation, endurance, energy, essentiality, exuberance, go, hardiness, intensity, life, liveliness, pep, power, sparkle, spirit, stamina,

strength, sturdiness, vigour, vim, vivacity, zeal
**vitally important** essential
**vital organ** heart, liver, lungs, pancreas, spleen
**vital organs** viscera
**vital plant juice** sap
**vital power** vitality
**vital thing** necessity
**vitamin A** dehydroretinol
**vitamin B$_1$** thiamin(e)
**vitamin B$_2$** riboflavine
**vitamin B$_6$** pyridoxine
**vitamin B$_{12}$** cyanocobalamin
**vitamin C** ascorbic acid
**vitamin C source** guava, orange, tomato
**vitamin D$_2$** calciferol
**vitamin D$_3$** cholecalciferol
**vitamin deficiency disease** beri-beri, kwashiorkor, pellagra, rachitis, rickets, scurvy
**vitamin E** tocopheral
**vitamin K$_1$** phylloquinone
**vitamin K$_2$** menaquinone
**vitamin P** citrin
**vitiate** abuse, blemish, blight, contaminate, corrupt, damage, debase, debauch, deface, defile, deprave, desecrate, harm, hurt, impair, injure, maltreat, mar, misuse, pervert, pollute, ruin, scar, seduce, spoil, stain, taint, tarnish, weaken, wrong
**vitiation** abasement, abolition, abrogation, annulment, cancellation, contamination, corruption, decadence, defilement, degradation, depreciation, desecration, destruction, detriment, dilution, erasure, fall, impairment, infection, obliteration, poisoning, pollution, reduction, undoing, voidance, withdrawal
**viticulture** viniculture, winegrowing
**viticulturist** winegrower
**vitrified cinders** slag
**vituperate** abuse, berate, censure, reproach, revile, upbraid
**vivacious** animated, cheerful, ebullient, frolicsome, gay, high-spirited, jolly, light-hearted, lively, merry, pert, spirited, sportive, sprightly, vital
**vivaciousness** alive, animation, blithe, bright, buoyant, frisky, jaunty, spirited, sportive, vivid
**vivacity** animation, ardour, cheerfulness, cheeriness, dash, drive, élan, energy, exhilaration, fire, force(fulness), gaiety, life, liveliness, optimism, power, punch, quickness,

raciness, sparkle, spirit, verve, vigour, vitality, warmth
**vivacity and dash** élan
**viverrine** civet
**vivid** animated, apparent, bright, brilliant, clear, distinct, eidetic, energetic, evident, glittering, glowing, graphic, intense, lifelike, lively, lucid, lurid, memorable, nitid, picturesque, powerful, radiant, realistic, resplendent, rich, seeable, sharp, spirited, stirring, striking, strong, telling, vigorous, visible, visual
**vivid emotion of pleasure** joy
**vivid in shocking detail** lurid
**vivid language** imagery
**vividly striking** dramatic
**vivid red** carmine
**vivid yellow spice** saffron, turmeric
**vixen** she-fox
**vocabulary** argot, dialect, diction(ary), glossary, idiom, jargon, language, lexicon, patois, style, thesaurus, tone, wordbook, words
**vocal** articulated, choral, expressed, loud, noisy, oral, phonetic, spoken, uttered, vociferous, voiced
**vocal chords** larynx
**vocal composition** oration, song, speech
**vocal expression** tone
**vocalise** croon, sing, solfeggio, warb
**vocalise written words** read
**vocalist** cantor, caroller, chanter, chorister, crooner, diva, hymner, jongleur, melodist, minstrel, precentor, singer, soloist, songster, troubadour, warbler
**vocal music** song
**vocal organ of a bird** syrinx
**vocal solo** aria, arioso, song, tune
**vocal sound** phonic, tone, voice
**vocation** business, calling, employment, métier, occupation, profession
**vociferous** boisterous, clamorous, loud, noisy, obstreperous, shrill
**vodka base** wheat
**voetsek** shoo, vamoose
**vogue** acceptance, craze, design, esteem, fad, fashion, favour, in, mode, popularity, prevalence, rage, style, stylishness, trend(y), voguish
**voice** air, declare, express, pronounce, role, say, sing, sound, speech, state, voce (I), vox (L)
**voice and nothing more** vox et praeterea nihil (L)
**voice between soprano and contralto** mezzo-soprano
**voice box** larynx

**voice inflection** tone
**voice in music** alto, baritone, bass, contralto, soprano, tenor
**voiceless** dumb, mute, speechless
**voiceless consonant** surd
**voiceless sound** cedilla
**voice management** elocution
**voice of young boy before puberty** soprano
**voice quality** timbre
**void** abrogate, annul, bare, blank, cancel, clear, dead, devoid, discharge, drain(ed), egest, eject, eliminate, emptied, empty, evacuate, excrete, expel, free, hole, inane, ineffective, ineffectual, inoperative, invalid(ate), lacking, negate, null(ify), quash, revoke, space, unfilled, unreal, useless, vacant, vacuum, vain, vent, worthless
**void of anxiety** carefree
**void of suspicion** naïve, trustful, trusting
**volatile** brief, changeful, erratic, eruptive, explodable, explosive, fiery, flighty, giddy, heated, impulsive, inconstant, inflammatory, mercurial, tense, undependable, unsteady, variable, volcanic
**volatile gas** ether
**volatile liquid** alcohol, ether
**volatile perfume** essence
**volcanic ashes** scoriae
**volcanic convulsion of surface of earth** earthquake
**volcanic crater** maar
**volcanic discharge** lava
**volcanic explosion** eruption
**volcanic formation** puy
**volcanic glass** obsidian, perlite, pumice
**volcanic island** Ischia, Iwo, Krakatoa, Lipari, Sicily
**volcanic matter** lava
**volcanic orifice** blower
**volcanic outburst** eruption
**volcanic residue** fiorite
**volcanic rock** lava, obsidian
**volcano** Ararat, Erebus, Etna, Fuji, Hekla, Mauna Loa, Pico, de Teide, Popocatepetl, Stromboli, Vesuvius
**volcano ash** tuff
**volcano hole** crater, mouth, pit
**volcano in Alaska** Douglas, Griggs, Iliamna, Katmai, Kukak, Mageik, Martin, Redoubt, Torbert, Trident, Wrangell
**volcano in California** Lassen Peak
**volcano in Canary Island** Teneguia
**volcano in Colombia** Purace
**volcano in Comoros** Karthala
**volcano in Costa Rica** Irazu, Poas
**volcano in Ecuador** Antisana, Cotopaxi

**volcano in El Salvador** Izalco
**volcano in Guatemala** Agua, Atitlan, Pacaya, Tacana
**volcano in Hawaii** Hualalai, Kilauea, Maunakea, Maunaloa
**volcano in Iceland** Askja, Eldfell, Hekla, Laki
**volcano in Indonesia** Agung, Gede, Marapi, Sinila, Slamet, Tambora
**volcano in Italy** Etna, Somma, Stromboli, Vesuvius
**volcano in Japan** Asama, Aso, Asosan, Fuji, Fujiyama, Hakusan, Usu
**volcano in Mexico** Colima, Jorullo, Paricutin, Toluca
**volcano in New Zealand** Ngauruhoe, Ruapehu, Tongariro
**volcano in Peru** Misti, Yucamani
**volcano in Philippines** Apo, Bulosan, Canlaon, Mayon, Taal
**volcano in Russia** Alaid, Shiveluch, Tolbachik
**volcano in Sicily** Etna
**volcano in Tanzania** Kibo, Kilimanjaro
**volcano in West Indies** Soupriere
**volcano lava** slag
**volcano opening** crater
**volition** choice, discretion, option, preference, will
**volleyball stroke** spike
**volley of shots** salvo
**volley of sound** peal
**voluble** fluent, glib, loquacious, talkative, talky, verbal
**voluble talk** yammer
**voluble talker** windbag
**volume** abundance, amount, amplification, bigness, book, bulk, capacity, dimensions, entirety, loudness, magnitude, manuscript, measure(ment), output, plenty, profusion, publication, quantity, size, softness, sound, sum, tome, total, vastness, work
**volume containing several works** omnibus
**volume of maps** atlas
**voluntarily** freely, gratuitously, intentionally, optionally, spontaneously, willingly
**voluntary** considered, deliberate, designed, elective, free(ly), gratis, gratuitous, honorary, intended, intentional, optional, (pre)planned, purposeful, spontaneous, unasked, uncompelled, unconstrained, unforced, unobliged, unpaid, unrequested, unrequired, volitional, volitive, wilful, willing
**voluntary decision not to act** abstention

**voluntary fee** honorarium
**voluntary separation of a part of the body** autotomy
**volunteer** advance, bestow, communicate, enlist, extend, grant, offer, present, propose, suggest, tender, undertake
**voluptuous** ample, buxom, dissolute, enticing, epicurean, erotic, hedonistic, indulgent, licentious, luscious, luxurious, provocative, seductive, sensual, sensuous, shapely, sybaritic, wanton
**vomit** disgorge, eject, emit, heave, puke, regorge, regurgitate, retch
**vomit-inducing drug** emetic
**vomiting of blood** haematemesis
**voracious** ambitious, anxious, avaricious, avid, devoted, eager, edacious, gluttonous, greedy, gross, impatient, insatiable, keen, mad, rabid, ravenous, zealous
**voracious sea bird** cormorant
**voracious eel** moray
**voracious fish** perai, pike, piranha, piraya, shark
**voracious insect** locust
**voracity** appetite, ardour, desire, eagerness, edacity, emptiness, famine, gluttony, greed(iness), hunger, impatience, itch, keenness, longing, lust, mania, rapacity, ravenousness, starvation, thirst, voraciousness, yearning, zeal
**vortex** countercurrent, cyclone, eddy, gurge, maelstrom, storm, swirl, tempest, tornado, typhoon, undercurrent, whirl(pool)
**vote** ballot, choose, decision, elect, poll, referendum, select(ion)
**vote against** blackball, blacklist, veto

**vote counter** teller
**vote for** elect
**vote for prohibition** veto
**vote into office** elect
**vote of dissent** nay, no
**vote on behalf of someone else** proxy
**voter** ballot caster, balloter, constituent, elector, poller, suffragist, taxpayer
**voter or native** citizen
**vote successfully** elect
**voting** ballot(ing), electing, election, opting, poling, returning
**voting paper** ballot
**voting place** poll
**voting public** electorate
**voting qualification** franchise
**votive light** candle
**vouch** affirm, assert, back, certify, confirm, guarantee, support, uphold
**voucher** acknowledg(e)ment, agreement, bail, card, certificate, chit, collateral, contract, coupon, credentials, deed, deposit, diploma, docket, earnest, ensurer, guarantee, licence, missive, mortgage, note, oath, obligation, pact, pass, patron, pawn, pledge, receipt, slip, stub, surety, testimonial, ticket, token, treaty, underwriter, warrant
**vouch for** accredit, affirm, assert, assure, authorise, back, certify, confirm, endorse, guarantee, sponsor, support, testify, uphold
**vow** declare, oath, pledge, plight, promise, swear, troth
**vowel** vocable
**vowel accent** acute, breve
**vowel gradation** ablaut
**vowel sound or system** vocalism
**vow publicly** nuncupate

**voyage** cruise, excursion, flight, journey, peregrination, safari, sail, sojourn, travel, trip
**voyage record** log
**voyageur** boatman, explorer, guide, trapper, woodsman
**vraic** kelp, seaweed
**V-shaped** cuneate
**V-shaped chock** wedge
**V-shaped mark** notch
**V-shaped nick** notch
**vulcanite** ebonite
**vulgar** artless, brutish, coarse, colloquial, common, crude, depraved, gauche, ignorant, immoral, indecent, indelicate, inelegant, lewd, libertine, loutish, obscene, outré, perverted, pleb, raffish, rakish, rank, raunchy, ribald, risqué, rough, rude, sensual, sexy, unacceptable, uncouth, uncultured, uneducated, unrefined, untaught, vernacular
**vulgar art** kitsch
**vulgarian** backvelder, barbarian, bounder, brute, cad, churl, clown, illiterate, knave, lout, mompara, parvenu, rustic, snob, swine, upstart, yokel
**vulgarity** coarseness, crudeness, dirt, filth, ignorance, indecorum, indelicacy, inferiority, naïveté, obscenity, pornography, rawness, ribaldry, roughness, rudeness, smut, tawdriness, unawareness, uncivility, uncouthness
**vulgar phrase** oath
**vulgar publicity** ballyhoo
**vulnerability to being tricked** gullibility
**vulnerable part of Achilles** heel
**vulture** condor

# W

**wabble** totter, wobble
**wacky** crazy, eccentric, fey, mad, odd, screwy, wild
**wad** ball, bankroll, block, bundle, chunk, compress, cram, hunk, lump, mass, pad, pencil, plug, press, roll, stopper, stuff
**wadding material** cotton, hemp, kapok
**waddle** bob, (duck)walk, paddle, sway, swing, toddle, wag(gle), wamble (Sc), wiggle, wobble

**waddy** bludgeon, cane, club, cowboy, heat, kill, stick, strike, warclub
**wade** cross, ford, paddle, splash, walk
**wade across** ford
**wade in mud** slush
**wade into** attack, tackle
**wader** bird, boot
**wade through** drudge, grind, peruse, plod, plow, read, study, toil
**wading bird** avocet, boatbill, crane, curlew, egret, flamingo, heron, ibis,

jabiru, jacana, knot, phalarope, plover, rail, redshank, sandpiper, shoebill, snipe, sora, spoonbill, stilt, stork, umber
**wad of bills** bankroll
**wafer** abret, biscuit, cake, cracker, disc, disk, pastry, snap
**wafer container** pix, pyx
**wafer holder** ciborium
**waffle** batter cake, cereal, dodge, duck, equivocate, prevaricate,

waffle dough / walk doggedly

rubbish, shuffle, tergiversate, twaddle, weasel
**waffle dough** batter
**waffle iron** griddle
**waft** bear, carry, convey, current, drift, float, glide, gust, puff, ride, sail, transport, wave, whiff, whisk
**wag** beat, bobble, buffoon, comic, dance, droll, flap, flip, flit, fluctuate, flutter, harlequin, humorist, jerk, nod, pendulate, punner, rock, sway, switch, turn, twitch, undulate, waggle, wave(r), wiggle, wisecracker, wit, wobble, writhe
**wage** allowance, carry on, compensation, continue, earnings, emolument, fee, hire, incur, levy, pay(ment), remuneration, requital, reward, salary, stipend
**wager** ante, bet(ting), chance, flutter, gage, gamble, gambling, guaranty, hazard, parlay, pledge, punt, risk, security, speculation, stake, venture, wit
**wagering** betting, chancing, gambling, laying, pledging, punting, risking, staking
**wages** allowance, compensation, earnings, emolument, fee, gain, honorarium, pay(ment), recompense, remuneration, requital, returns, reward, salary, stipend
**waggery** sarcasm, wit
**waggish** clever, comical, elfish, impish, jesting, joking, jolly, jovial, merry, mischievous, naughty, puckish, ridiculous, riotous, roguish, sportive, unserious
**waggish person** card
**waggle** wabble, waddle
**waggly** rocky, shaky, unsteady
**waging war** belligerent
**wagon** buggy, caravan, carriage, cart, dray, truck, vehicle, waggon, wain
**wagon body** bed
**wagon builder** wainwright
**wagonload** fother, freight
**wagon pin** clevis
**wagon pole** tongue
**wagon shaft** thill
**wagon side** rave
**wagon tongue** neap, pole, shaft, thill
**wagon track** rut
**wagon train** caravan
**wagtail** bird, lark, pipit
**wag the tongue** chatter, gab, skinder, talk
**waif** arab, castaway, child, derelict, foundling, gamin, itinerant, mudlark, nomad, orphan, outcast, pariah, stray, stroller, tramp, vagabond, vagrant, wanderer, wastrel
**wail** bemoan, bewail, complain(t), cry, deplore, grief, grieve, groan, howl, keen, lament(ation), moan, requiem, sob, ululate, weep(ing), whine
**wailing** bemoaning, crying, deploring, grieving, howling, lamenting, mourning, sobbing, sorrowing, weeping
**wailing device** siren
**wailing spirit** banshee
**Wailing Wall city** Jerusalem
**Wailing Wall task** lamenting, prayer
**wail over the dead** keen
**wain** wagon
**wainscot** lining, panel
**waist** bodice, camise, middle, taille, undergarment
**waistband** band, belt, cummerbund, fillet, girdle, sash
**waistbelt attachment for sword** frog
**waist circler** belt
**waistcloth** loincloth
**waistcoat** benjy, bolero, gilet, jerkin, vest
**waistcoat pocket** fob
**waister** novice
**waistline** girth, midriff
**waist of dress** traille
**waist ribbon** sash
**waist sash** cummerbund, obi (J)
**waist strap** belt
**wait** (a)bide, ambush, anticipate, await, defer, delay, expect, halt, hesitate, hover, linger(ing), pause, postpone, remain, rest, stay, stop, tarry
**waited on chair** sat
**waiter** attendant, garçon, server, steward
**waiter in charge of wines** sommelier
**waiter's assistant** busboy
**waiter's bonus** tip
**wait for** await, expect
**wait for opportune moment** bide one's time
**wait in ambush** lurk, waylay
**wait in expectation** bide
**waiting for something** anticipate, expect(ant)
**waiting line** cue, queue
**waiting room** antechamber, foyer, hallway, lobby, lounge, parlour, vestibule
**waiting to be used** ready
**wait on** attend, cater, provide, serve, supply, tend
**wait up** delay, halt, stop
**wait upon** (at)tend
**waive** abandon, abstain, avoid, decline, defer, delay, disclaim, dismiss, disregard, eliminate, eschew, forego, overlook, postpone, refrain, refuse, relinquish, remit, renounce, surrender
**waiver** abdication, abrogation, annulment, forfeiture, relinquishment
**wake** activate, animate, arise, arouse, awake(n), backwash, bestir, deathwatch, enliven, excite, fire, kindle, lament, motivate, path, provoke, quicken, raise, revive, rouse, stimulate, stir, trace, track, trail, vigil, wauk (Sc)
**wakeful** alert, astir, awake, chary, insomniac, insomnious, insomnolent, observant, prudent, restless, sleepless, vigilant, watchful
**wakefulness** ahypnia, alertness, aliveness, attentiveness, consciousness, heedfulness, insomnia, restlessness, sleeplessness, slumberlessness, vigilantness, wariness, watchfulness
**wakeless** dead, unbroken, unconscious
**waker** alarm, guard, sentinel, watch
**wakes memories of** reminder
**wakes you up** alarm
**wake up** arise, arouse, awake
**wake up clock** alarm
**wake up late** oversleep
**wale** belt, bruise, timber, weal, welt, whip
**Wales** Cambria, Cymru, Cymry
**Wales county** Breconshire, Flintshire, Radnorshire
**Wales emblem** dragon, leek
**Wales island** Bardsey, Caldy, Holyhead, Ramsey, Skomer
**Wales lake** Bala
**Wales musical instrument** pibcorn
**Wales poetic name** Cambria
**walk** alley, ambulate, area, avenue, beat, carriage, conduct, constitutional, course, field, footpath, gad, gait, hike, lane, march, move, pace, path, perambulate, plod, promenade, saunter, sphere, stalk, step, stride, stroll, tramp, tread, trod
**walk a beat** patrol
**walk about** pace, (per)ambulate
**walk about aimlessly** traipse
**walk affectedly** mince, strut
**walk all over** tyrannise
**walk around** circle, examine
**walk arrogantly** swagger
**walk at slow easy pace** amble
**walk back and forth** pace
**walk barefoot in shallow water** paddle
**walk between seats in church** aisle
**walk bordered with trees** avenue
**walk clumsily** lollop
**walk doggedly** plod, slog

**walker** ambulator, footman, hiker, hobo, hoofer, itinerant, marcher, nomad, pacer, pedestrian, peregrinator, rambler, tinker, tramper, vagabond, wayfarer
**walk feebly** dodder, totter
**walk for pleasure** ramble, stroll
**walk haltingly** limp
**walk heavily** lumber, plod, plop, slog, tramp, tread
**walkie-talkie** receiver, sender, telecommunication, transmitter, walky-talky
**walk in** enter
**walk in affected manner** mince
**walk in brook** wade
**walk in ostentatious way** sashay
**walking about** ambulate
**walking aid for disabled** crutch, zimmer
**walking encyclopaedia** bookworm, pundit
**walking limb** leg
**walking manner** gait
**walking meter** pedometer
**walking mode** gait, pace
**walking on air** happy
**walking on outer side of the foot** taligrade
**walking pole** stilt
**walking step** pace
**walking stick** cane, crook, crosier, phasmid, pogo, rattan, rod, staff, stilt
**walking style** gait, pace, stride
**walking track** pathway
**walking trip** hike
**walk in leisurely manner** amble, mosey, saunter, stroll
**walk in stately manner** stalk
**walk in step** march
**walk in the streets** prowl
**walk in water** wade
**walk laboriously** hike
**walk lamely** hitch, hobble, limp
**walk leisurely** loiter, stroll
**walk like a crab** crawl, sidle
**walk like a duck** waddle
**walk noisily** stump
**walk obliquely** sidle
**walk off with** steal, win
**walk of life** activity, area, arena, calling, career, conduct, course, field, line, métier, occupation, profession, pursuit, sphere, trade, vocation
**walk on** tramp, tread
**walk on air** exult, frisk
**walk on foot** pad
**walk on rope** funambulate
**walk out** leave, protest, rebellion, revolt, stoppage, strike

**walk out on** abandon, desert, forsake, jilt, leave
**walk out with** court
**walkover** cinch, doddle, pushover
**walk pompously** stalk, strut, swagger
**walk proudly** prance
**walk round about** circumambulate
**walk shakily** totter
**walk silently** tiptoe
**walk slowly** amble, dawdle, mooch, saunter
**walk softly** pad
**walk stealthily** tiptoe
**walk stiffly** stalk
**walk the beat** patrol
**walk through** perambulate, read, rehearse
**walk through water** wade
**walk tiredly** traipse, trapes
**walk unsteadily** paddle, stagger, stumble, teeter, toddle, totter
**walk-up** apartment
**walk up and down** pace
**walk very quietly** tiptoe
**walk warily** tiptoe
**walkway** aisle, alley, esplanade, footpath, lane, path(way), pavement, promenade, sidewalk
**walk wearily** plod, trail, trudge
**walk with awkward gait** shamble
**walk with bounds** prance
**walk with firm heavy tread** tramp
**walk with high steps** prance
**walk with long steps** stride
**walk with measured steps** pace
**walk with military step** march
**walk with muffled step** pad
**walk with short steps** waddle
**walk with shuffling gait** shamble
**wall** barricade, barrier, battlement, block, bulwark, divide(r), embankment, enclose, enclosure, fence, fortification, hedge, impediment, mur (F), obstacle, obstruction, panel, parapet, partition, protect, rampart, screen, separation, structure, supporter
**wallaroo** euro, kangaroo
**wall around fortress** rampart
**wall band** cordon
**wall base** skirting
**wall beam support** template
**wall border** dado, ogee
**wall bracket** sconce
**wall chart** graph
**wall column** pilaster
**wall covering** arras, paint, panelling, paper, plaster, stucco, wallpaper
**wall decoration** mural
**walled city** Canterbury, Chester, Kano, Kuh, Scanno, York

**walled in** cloistered, impounded, imprisoned, interned, pent
**walled water** dam
**wallet** billfold, (note)case, pocketbook, porte-monnaie (F), pouch, purse
**walleye** exotropia
**wall-eyed fish** dore, dory, pike
**wall fern** polypody
**wallflower** cheir, heart's-ease, keiri, rebuff, rejection
**wall graph** chart
**wall hanging** tapestry
**wall hangings** tenture
**wall hole for cannon** embrasure
**wall in** coop, immure
**wall lizard** gecko
**wall material** bricks, cement, lime, marble, panels, stones, timber
**wall of coral** reef
**wall of defence** parapet
**wall of scantling and bricks** nogging
**wallop** backhander, belt, blow, boil, clobber, clout, defeat, hammer, hit, lam, larrup, paddle, pound, pummel, slap, slog, spank, strap, strike, swat, swipe, thrash, thump, thwack, trounce, welt, whack
**wall opening** bay, scuttle, window
**walloper** policeman
**wallow** appreciate, billow, delight, enjoy, falter, fancy, float, flounder, love, lurch, puff, relish, revel, roll, stagger, surge, swell, swim, tumble, waddle, waft, waver, welter, writhe
**wallow in** enjoy, superabound
**wallowish** flat, insipid, stale
**wall painting** fresco, mural
**wall painting done on dry plaster** secco
**wall panelling** wainscot
**wallpaper adhesive** paste
**wallpaper measure** bolt
**wall piece** template, templet
**wall pier** anta
**wall plaster** stucco
**wall projecting into sea** mole, pier
**wall recess** alcove, niche
**wall section** dado, panel
**wall space** crevice, niche
**wall support** buttress
**wall tapestry** arras
**walnut** (ban)nut, fruit
**walnut skin** zest
**walrus** amphibian, carnivore, mammal, morse, moustache, rosmarine, sea cow, seal, tusker
**walrus herd** pod
**walrus tusk** ivory
**waltz** dance, spin, valse, whirl
**waltz king** Strauss
**waltz or jig** dance

**wambenger** brush-tailed phalanger, tuan
**wame** belly
**wampum** beads, coinage, ornament, peag(e), seawan, shells
**wampum snake** hoop snake
**wamus** cardigan, doublet, jacket
**wan** achromatic, albino, anaemic, ashen, ashy, bleached, cadaverous, colourless, dim, dismal, faded, faint, feeble, gloomy, haggard, livid, lustreless, miserable, pale, pallid, sallow, sickly, weak, white
**wan appearance** paleness, pallidness, pallor
**wand** baton, branch, mace, osier, pole, reed, rod, sceptre, shoot, sprig, sprout, staff, stick, tendril, twig
**wander** ambulate, bum, deviate, digress, divert, drift, err, gallivant, itinerate, meander, migrate, move, nomadise, pass, ramble, rave, roam, rove, saunter, stray, stroll, swerve, travel, traverse, walk
**wander aimlessly** drift, flounder, meander, traipse
**wander aimlessly about** moon
**wander around** ambulate, meander, prowl, ramble, roam, rove, straggle
**wander at random** meander
**wanderer** adventurer, bedouin, drifter, explorer, gypsy, hiker, hobo, itinerant, landloper, migrant, nomad, rambler, roamer, rover, straggler, strayer, stroller, tourist, tramp, traveller, vag(abond), vagrant, voyager, wayfarer
**wander idly** bum, drift, gad
**wandering** aberrant, astray, cruising, digressing, drifting, errant, erratic, erring, homeless, itinerant, lapsing, meandering, migratory, nomadic, odyssey, perambulation, rambling, roaming, rootless, roving, straggling, strolling, travelling, tripping, vagabond, vagrant
**wandering animal** (e)stray, maverick
**wandering by night** noctivagant, noctivagous
**wandering cell** phagocyte
**wandering from duty** truant
**wandering in mind** delirious, delirium, senile, senility
**wandering in search of adventure** errant
**wandering minstrel** bard
**wandering musician** busker, troubadour
**wandering of the mind** delirium
**wandering person** bedouin, gipsy, gypsy, nomad
**wandering race** gypsy

**wandering with loss of memory** fugue
**wanderlust** restlessness, unsettled
**wander off** stray
**wander over** meander, rove, traverse
**wander restlessly** gad
**wander unrestrained** expatiate
**wandflower** galax
**wand of Bacchus** thyrse, thyrsus
**wane** abate, decay, decline, decrease, decrescence, defect, deliquesce, dim(inish), diminution, droop, dwindle, dying, ebb, exhaustion, fail(ing), failure, lessen, obsolesce, recession, shrivel, sinking, slump, subside(nce)
**wangle** arrange, fix, manage, manipulate, manoeuvre, work, wriggle
**wanhap** misfortune, mishap
**waning** abating, declining, decreasing, decrescent, dimming, dropping, dwindling, ebbing, fading, failing, lessening, sinking, subsiding, weakening, withering
**wanion** curse, plague
**wanly** pallidly
**want** absence, appetite, covet, crave, craving, dearth, default, deficiency, demand, desire, destitution, famine, fancy, hankering, hunger, inadequacy, indigence, lack, longing, meagreness, miss, need, paucity, penury, poverty, privation, require(ment), scantiness, scarceness, scarcity, shortage, thirst, wish
**wanted** desired, sought-after, sought-for
**wanted man** desperado, escapee, outlaw
**want greatly** crave
**wanting** bereft, defective, deficient, faulty, imperfect, incomplete, lacking, less, limited, minus, missing, needing, partial, poor, short, shy, sketchy, sorry, unsound, without
**wanting brilliance** dull, gray
**wanting confidence** bashful
**wanting courage** timid
**wanting good sight** purblind
**wanting in effect** feeble
**wanting knowledge** ignorant, stupid
**wanting moisture** arid, dry
**wanting power** ambitious
**want of appetite** anorexia, asitia, dysorexia
**want of comforts** privation
**want of energy** atony
**want of feelings** apathy
**want of interest in things** boredom, ennui, listlessness
**want of proportion** asymmetry

**want of sight** ablepsy
**want of sleep** insomnia, sleeplessness, wakefulness
**want of success** failure
**want of tone** atony
**want of wellbeing** dysphoria
**wanton** calculated, careless, deliberate, dissolute, groundless, heedless, inconsiderate, lawless, loose, luxurious, magnificent, malicious, reckless, unbridled, unjustifiable, unruly, wild, wilful
**wanton destroyer** vandal
**wanton destruction** sabotage
**wanton girl** fillock, gig
**wanton glance** eyeliad
**wanton look** leer
**want to scratch** itch
**wanty** girth, rope, tie
**wapiti** deer, elk, stag
**war** attack, battle, blitzkrieg, bloodshed, clash, combat, conflict, contend, contest, crusade, dissession, enmity, fight(ing), hostilities, jehad, jihad, quarrel, strife, struggle, warfare
**war axe** tomahawk
**warble** carol, chirp, sing, trill, yodel
**warbler** yellowthroat
**warbling note** chirl
**war booty** loot
**war cart** chariot
**war club** mace, pogamoggan, waddy
**warcraft** strategy
**war cry** catchword, rallying-cry, slogan, watchword
**ward** area, avert, care, charge, custody, defend, dependant, detention, district, division, fend, hospital, keeping, minor, precinct, protection, protégé, pupil, quarter, sickbay, stave, watch, zone
**war decoration** medal
**warden** caretaker, concierge, curator, custodian, defender, guard(ian), janitor, keeper, preserver, ranger, steward, superintendent, warder, watchdog, watchman
**warder** custodian, gaoler, guard, jailer, keeper, official, sentinel, turnkey, warden, watchdog, watchman
**warder of Tower of London** Beefeater
**ward off** avert, avoid, deflect, (for)fend, parry, prevent, rebuff, repel, repulse, stave
**ward off an attack** defend
**ward off blow** parry
**ward off the protective plate** shield
**ward of Mordecai** Esther
**war dog** hawk, militant
**wardrobe** apparel, attire, chest, closet, clothes, outfit, press

**wardship** guardianship
**warehouse** depository, depot, loft, silo, stockroom, storage, store(house)
**warehouse platform** pallet
**warehouse room** loft
**warehousing space** storage
**wares** commodities, merchandise, staples, stock, supplies
**warfare** action, arms, battle, blows, bout, brawl, clash, combat, conflict, contest, discord, encounter, fighting, hostilities, resistance, scuffle, skirmish, strategy, strife, struggle, war
**war god** Ares, Mars
**war group** army
**war hawk** chauvinist, jingo
**warhorse** charger, steed
**warlike** aggressive, bellicose, belligerent, choleric, combative, cruel, hawkish, hostile, hot-tempered, inimical, irascible, irritable, jingoistic, martial, militaristic, military, operational, petulant, pugnacious, quarrelsome, soldierly, strategical, tactical, unfriendly
**warlike dance-drama with song** corroboree
**warlike quality** belligerence
**warlock** conjurer, enchanter, fortune-teller, magician, sorcerer, witch, wizard
**warm** ami(c)able, amorous, angry, animate, ardent, attached, balmy, brisk, close, cordial, eager, enthusiastic, excited, fervent, fervid, fiery, friendly, furious, genial, glowing, hearty, intimate, kind, loving, lukewarm, passionate, rouse, strong, sympathetic, tepid, tropical, vehement, vexed, vigorous, waken, zealous
**warm and balmy** summery, sunny
**warm and bright** sunny
**warm and cosy** snug
**warm and damp** humid
**warm and humid** muggy
**warm and snug** cosy
**warm-blooded** ardent, fiery, passionate, temperamental
**warm by rubbing** chafe
**warm compress** stupe
**warm covering** blanket, duvet
**warm drink** caudle, coffee, tea
**warm dry wind** chinook
**warmed** defrosted, heated, melted, softened, thawed
**warmed-up dish** réchauffé
**war memorial** cenotaph
**warm fibre** wool

**warm-hearted** affable, affectionate, agreeable, attached, caring, cheerful, cordial, devoted, doting, fond, friendly, generous, genial, hearty, intimate, kind, loving, sociable, sympathetic, tender, warm
**warm jacket** anorak, windcheater
**warm oneself** bask
**warmonger** belligerent, hawk, jingo, militarist
**warm oven in advance** preheat
**warm over** reheat
**warm region** tropics
**warm room in baths** tepidarium
**warm room in monastery** calefactory
**warm season** summer
**warms you in winter** fire, heater
**warmth** affability, affection, amorousness, ardour, cordiality, earnestness, enthusiasm, glow, heat, hotness, intensity, kindliness, tenderness, violence, warmness, zeal
**warm the heart** gladden
**warmth of anger** heat
**warmth of feeling** ardour, passion
**warm to** befriend
**warm up** deepen, practice, prepare, (re)heat, worsen
**warm-up exercise** loosener
**warn** admonish, alert, apprise, caution, exhort, expostulate, forewarn, inform, notify, precaution, signal, tell, urge
**warner** flagman
**warning** admonishing, admonition, advice, advising, alarm, alert(ing), augury, caution(ing), caveat, foreboding, forewarning, hint, indication, informing, menace, notice, notification, notifying, omen, ominous, premonition, proviso, sign(al), summoning, threat, tip, token, ultimatum
**warning bell** alarm
**warning call** alert
**warning colour** red
**warning cry** fore
**warning device** alarm, klaxon, siren
**warning given by watchers** alert
**warning gong** tocsin
**warning horn** siren
**warning light** amber, flare
**warning of danger** alarm, alerting
**warning of death** knell
**warning or alarm** signal
**warning or hint** tip-off
**warning signal** alarm, siren, tocsin
**warning sound** alarm, fire alarm, signal, siren
**warning system** dew
**warning traffic light** amber

**warning whistle** siren
**warn off** debar, inhibit, prohibit, threaten
**war of extermination** bellum internecinum (L)
**war of words** argument, logomachy, polemic
**warp** bend, bias, contort, curve, deform, deviate, distort, misshape, oddity, peculiarity, pervert, prejudice, propensity, slew, slue, sway, swerve, turn, twist, veer, wrench
**warp and woof** basis, fabric
**warp beam** loom, roller
**warped** wry
**warplane** bomber
**war prize** medal, scalp
**warp thread** abb, lease, stamen
**war push** offensive
**warrant** allowance, approval, approve, assurance, authorisation, authority, basis, cause, certificate, commission, credential, deserve, document, entitlement, evidence, grounds, guarantee, justification, licence, merit, permission, permit, pledge, promise, reason, secure, security, statement
**warrant committing person to prison** mittimus
**warranty** assurance, authority, bail, bond, certainty, contract, covenant, cover, deposit, guarantee, guaranty, indemnity, instalment, insurance, justification, pledge, promise, protection, retainer, safeguard, security, stake, surety, undertaking, word
**warrigal** dingo
**warrior** ace, battler, cavalier, champion, cohort, combatant, die-hard, fighter, infantryman, knight, mercenary, soldier, stalwart, struggler, trouper, valiant
**warrior slain by Achilles** Hector
**warship** aircraft carrier, battleship, corvette, cruiser, destroyer, frigate, ironclad minelayer, minesweeper, submarine, U-boat
**warship plating** armour
**warship prison** brig
**warship's small boat** pinnace
**warship tower** turret
**wart** growth, tumour, verruca, wen
**wartime allowance** ration
**wartime civilian prison** concentration camp
**wartime ditch** trench
**wartime friend** ally
**wartime Nazi leader** Hess, Hitler
**wartorn** devastated
**war trumpet** clarion

**warty** humpy, noded
**warty creature** toad
**war vessel** bomber, carrier, cruiser, destroyer, torpedo, warship
**wary** alert, cag(e)y, canny, careful, cautious, chary, circumspect, conservative, discreet, distrustful, experimental, gingerly, guarded, hedging, heedful, leery, prepared, prudential, safe, scrupulous, secretive, shy, tentative, vigilant, watchful, wise
**was** existed, were
**was able to** could
**was Abyssinia** Ethiopia
**was Basutoland** Lesotho
**was borne along** rode
**was carried** borne
**was carried along** rode
**was Ceylon** Sri Lanka
**was concerned** cared
**was Dutch Guiana** Surinam
**wase** bundle, pad, wisp
**wash** ablution, bath(e), bog, brush, chasten, clean(ing), cleanse, cleansing, dampen, drench, flush, launder(ing), lavage, lave, moisten, mop, morass, purify, rinse, rub, saturate, scour, scrub, shampoo, shower, sponge, swab, swamp, washing, wet
**wash away** erode, move, purge
**wash away germs** disinfect
**wash basin** font, laver, piscina, tub
**wash clothes** launder
**washed out** blanched, bleached, colourless, drained, etiolated, exhausted, faded, mat, pale, tired
**washed up** finished
**washer** shim
**washerman** dhobi, launderer
**wash for gold** pan
**wash house** laundry
**wash in clean water** rinse
**washing** bathing, clean(s)ing, damping, laundering, laundry, moistening, soaking, watering, wetting
**washing bar** soap
**washing compound** soda
**washing out of an organ** lavage
**washing place** ablution
**washing solution** lye
**Washington fort** Lewis
**washing up room** scullery
**washing vessel** basin
**wash leather** chamois, losh
**wash lightly** rinse
**wash oneself** ablute
**wash one's hands of** abandon
**wash out** bleach, elute, purge, rinse

**washout** chasm, failure, fizzle, flop, gully, stumor
**wash out suds** rinse
**wash pan** basin
**wash the linen** launder
**wash up** end, finish, terminate
**wash vigorously** scrub
**was incorrect** erred, error
**was indignant** resented
**was informed** heard
**was in session** sat
**was insubordinate** defied
**was overfond** doted
**was part of Yugoslavia** Croatia
**was Persia** Iran
**waspish** caustic, cross, dangerous, fierce, fiery, prickly, sensitive, spiteful, touchy
**wasp's home** nest
**wasp's nest** vespiary
**wassail** carouse, drink
**was Siamese** Thai
**was sorry** apologetic, regretted, repented, rued
**waste** atrophy, consume, corrode, crumble, desolate, despoil, destroy, devastate, diminish, dissipate, dross, emaciate, enfeeble, erode, expend, extra, lavish, misspend, misuse, ort, pillage, plunder, rape, ravage, reduce, refuse, rubbish, ruin, sack, spend, spoil, squander, unused, useless
**waste allowance** tare, tret
**waste away** atrophy, crumble, decay, decline, decompose, deteriorate, diffuse, dim, disappear, disintegrate, disperse, dissipate, dissolve, droop, dwindle, ebb, emaciate, evaporate, fade, fail, fall, gnaw, languish, perish, (re)pine, rot, shrink, shrivel, vanish
**waste away by fasting** macerate
**waste bin** garbage can, trash can
**waste cloth** rag
**wasted beer** ullage
**wasted effort** futility
**wasted time** dallied
**waste fibre** noil
**wasteful** extravagant, lavish, loafer, prodigal, profuse, ruinous, shiftless, spender, spendthrift, thriftless, uneconomical, westrel
**wastefulness** dissipation, extravagance, lavishness, overspending, profusion, waste
**wasteland** bog, desert, emptiness, heath, marsh, moor, morass, scrub, wilderness
**waste material** refuse, rubbish, scrap
**waste matter** dreg, dross, sewage
**waste metal** dross, gate, slag

**waste organ** kidney
**waste paper** broke
**waste pipe** drain, sewer
**waste place in colliery** goaf
**waster** good-for-nothing, idler, layabout, prodigal, profligate, scapegrace, spender, wastrel
**waste silk** frison, knub, noil
**waste silk fibres** floss
**waste stuff** offal
**waste time** dally, dawdle, idle, loaf
**waste water pipe** drain
**waste weir** spillway
**wasteyard** dump
**was there** been
**wasting away** atrophy, pining, tabes
**wasting disease of the lungs** consumption, phthisis
**wasting of bodily tissue** dystrophy
**wastrel** idler, loafer, loser, malingerer, prodigal, spender, spendthrift, squanderer, vagabond, waster
**was United Arab Republic** Egypt
**was victorious** won
**watch** await, clock, contemplate, expect, eye, guard, inspection, invigilate, look(out), mark, note, observe, patrol, period, protect, regard, safeguard, see, sentry, spy, timekeeper, timepiece, view, vigil, watchman
**watch accessory** chain, strap
**watch and pray** vigilate et orate (L)
**watch by a dead body** wake
**watch carefully** observe
**watch chain** albert, fob
**watch closely** eye, guard, spy
**watch dial** face
**watchdog** mastiff, ombudsman
**watch duty** patrol
**watcher** bystander, spectator, witness
**watch face** dial
**watch for** anticipate, await, expect
**watchful** alert, careful, cautious, circumspect, heedful, observant, regardant, vigilant, wary
**watchful guardian** Argus, Cerberus, Heimdall
**watchmaker** horologist
**watchman** caretaker, custodian, guard(er), guardian, jailer, keeper, protector, scout, sentinel, sentry, warden, warder, watch(dog)
**watch one's step** beware, care, mind
**watch one's weight** diet
**watch out** beware, heed, notice
**watch over** chaperon, defend, guard, mind, nurse, preserve, protect, safeguard, shelter, shield, tend, treasure
**watch part** bezel, crown, escapement, jewel, stud

watch pocket　fob
watch secretly　snoop, spy
watch sharply　eye
watch suspiciously　eye, spy
watchtower　bantayan, beacon, garret, martello, mirador, signal tower
watch used for timing sporting events　stopwatch
watch with satisfaction　gloat
watchword　byword, catchword, keyword, mot de passe (F), motto, passe-parole (F), password, sign(al), slogan
water　adulterate, agua (Sp), a(c)qua (I), dampen, dilute, drench, eau (F), flood, hose, hydro-, irrigate, moisten, soak, souse, spray, sprinkle, thin, wasser (G), weaken
water animal　aquatic, aquatile, seal
water antelope　kob
water appearance on silk　moire
water around castle　moat
water arum　calla
water at the mouth　dribble, drivel
water barrier　dam, mole, weir
water bear　tardigate
water bird　avocet, coot, crane, duck, egret, ern, goose, grebe, gull, heron, ibis, pelican, rail, stilt, swan, tern
water boiler　kettle
water bottle　carafe, decanter, flagon, skin
waterbrash　heartburn, pyrosis
water buffalo　caraboa
water butt　barrel
water by canals　irrigate
water carrier in former times　bhishti
water channel　flume, gat, gully, gutter, penstock, sloot, sluice, tail-race
water clock　clepsydra
water closet　lavatory, privy, WC
water cock　tap
water conveyor　cutter, pipe
water-cooled furnace nozzle　tuyere
watercourse　arroyo (Sp), bed, brook, canal, channel, creek, ria, river, stream
water-covered　awash
water craft　ark, barge, boat, canoe, dinghy, liner, ship, vessel, yacht
watercress　brooklime, erker, mustard, potherb
water crytogram　alga
water cure　hydropathy
water demon　nicker, nixy
water device　sprinkler
water diviner　dowser
water down　adulterate, blunt, dilute, mix, qualify, soften, thin, water, weaken
water duct　flume, gutter, race
water duct from eaves　leader

watered appearance on silk　moire
watered fabric　moire, tabby
watered fabric of silk and wool　tabinet
water elf　nix
water-encircled land　island
water excursion　cruise, sail
waterfall　Angel, cascade, catadupe, cataract, Churchill, chute, falls, Giessbach, Hamilton, Iguaçú, Krimmler, linn (Sc), Niagara, rapids, Ribbon, sault, Stanley, Sutherland, Victoria, weir, Yosemite
waterfall in Africa　Augrabies, Fincha, Howick, Kalambo, Ruacana, Tessisat, Tugela, Victoria
waterfall in America　Akaka, Bridalveil, Feather, Narada, Palouse, Passaic, Ribbon, Twin, Yellowstone, Yosemite
waterfall in Brazil　Glass
waterfall in Ecuador　Agoyan
waterfall in Ethiopia　Dalverme, Fincha, Tesissat
waterfall in France　Gavernie
waterfall in Guyana　Kaieteur, Marina
waterfall in India　Cauvery, Gokak, Jog
waterfall in Italy　Frua, Toce
waterfall in Laos　Mekong
waterfall in Lesotho　Maletsunyane
waterfall in New Zealand　Bowen, Helena, Stirling, Sutherland
waterfall in Norway　Skykje, Vetti, Voring
waterfall in Scotland　Glomach
waterfall in South Africa　Augrabies, Howick, Mac-Mac, Tugela
waterfall in South America　Iguassu
waterfall in Sweden　Handol, Tannforsen
waterfall in Tanzania　Kalambo
waterfall in Uganda　Kabalega
waterfall in Venezuela　Angel, Cuquenan
waterfall in Wales　Cain, Rhaiadr
waterfall in Zambia　Victoria
waterfall in Zimbabwe　Victoria
water-filled hollow　vlei
water flask　canteen
water flower　lily
water flying in small drops　spray
water fowl　brant, brent, egret
waterfront　beach, coast, shore
water gap　gorge, poort, ravine
water gate　sluice
water gauge　nilometer
water glass　tumbler
water grass　reeds
water heater　boiler, geyser
water hole　billabong, oasis, pond, pool, spring, well
water ice　sorbet
water in fine drops　mist
water in frozen state　ice

watering can　sprinkler
watering the lawn　hosing
water in pharmacy　aqua
water in soil　chresard
water in solid state　ice
water in the hold of ship　bilge
water inundation　flood
water jar　ewer, hydria, lota(h), olla
water jug　ewer, olla
water kudu　nakong
waterless　anhydrous, arid, barren, dehydrated, desert, dry, parched, sapless, scorched, sterile, thirsty, torrid, withered
water lifting device　noria, taboot, tabut
water lily　lotus, nenuphar, wocas
water lily leaf　pad
water lily tree　magnolia
waterline　tidemark
waterlogged　dank, drenched, dripping, flooded, imbued, inundated, saturated, soaked, soaking, sodden, soggy, sopping, soused, steeped, streaming, submerged, suffused, swamped, wet
Waterloo victor　Wellington
water made alkaline with wood ashes　lye
water mammal　dolphin, dugong, manatee, otter, porpoise, seacow, seal, whale
water mattress　lilo
water monster　nicker, nixy
water music writer　Handel
water nymph　mermaid, naiad, nereid, sea-maid, siren, undine
water obstruction　dam, plug, weir
water of the sea　brine
water on the brain　hydrocephalus
water passage　canal, channel, poort, sloot, sluice, sound, strait
water pitcher　ewer
water plant　alisma, aquatile, flag, lily, limu, lotus, reed, seaweed, starfruit
waterproof　(en)close, fasten, impervious, mac(kintosh), overcoat, plug, raincoat, seal, secure, shut, slicker, sound, stop(per), watertight
waterproof canopy　awning
waterproof cloth　canvas, gossamer, tarp(aulin)
waterproof coat　mac(kintosh), raincoat, slicker
waterproof garment　gossamer
waterproof hat with broad flap at back　sou'wester
waterproof jacket　anorak
waterproof overshoe　galosh
waterproof raincoat　mac(kintosh), slicker
water rat　muskam, vole
water receptacle in church　font

**water reptile** turtle
**water resort** lido, spa
**water-ringed tract** island
**water safety ring** lifebelt
**water saturated with salt** brine, seawater
**water scorpion** nepa
**water's edge** beach, shore
**water show** aquacade
**waters of the earth's surface** hydrosphere
**water sound** drip, lap, plash, purl, splash
**water source** well
**water spirit** ariel, sprite, undine
**water sport** diving, parasailing, polo, skiing, swimming
**water sport venue** lido
**waterspout** funnel, geyser, spate
**water sprite** kelpie, nicker, nix(y)
**water stalactite** icicle
**water storage** cistern, dam, reservoir, tank
**water stream obstruction** dam, weir
**water surface** ryme
**water sweetened with sugar** eau sucrée (F)
**watertank** cistern, container, receptacle, reservoir, sink, tub, vessel
**water the garden** hose
**watertight** airtight, dropdry, firm, flawless, foolproof, impregnable, leakproof, sound, unassailable
**water tortoise** terrapin, turtle
**water trench round castle** moat
**water vapour** fog, mist, steam
**water vessel** boat, canoe, ferry, liner, lota(h), sail, ship, yacht
**waterway** aqueduct, bayou, brook, canal, channel, gutter, rill, river, runnel, sloot, spring, streamer, streamlet
**water wheel** danaide, noria, sakia, saki(y)eh, turbine, tympanum
**water without flow** stagnant
**waterworn ravine** donga, gully
**watery** adulterated, aquatic, aqueous, damp, diluted, fluid, hydrated, insipid, marshy, moist, runny, serous, soggy, squelchy, tasteless, tearful, thin, vapid, washy, weak, wet
**watery broth or soup** skilly
**watery discharge** rheum, serum
**watery liquid** serum
**watery mixture** slurry
**watery mud** slosh, slush
**watery part of blood** serum
**watery part of milk** whey
**wattle** acacia
**wattlebird** honeybird
**wattle honey-eater** lao, manuao

**wattle tree** acacia, boree, mulga, myall
**wave** agitate, backwash, brandish, breaker, convolution, float, flourish, fluctuate, flutter, ola (Sp), onde (F), oscillate, ridge, ripple, roller, sway, swell, undulate, undulation, waft, wag
**wave at** beckon
**wave down** hail
**waveless** calm, smooth, tranquil
**wavelet** ripple
**wave of surf** breaker, comber
**waver** change, dither, falter, flicker, float, fluctuate, hesitate, indecision, oscillate, quiver, reel, rock, saw, see, shake, stagger, submit, sway, teeter, totter, tremble, vacillate, vary, veer, waffle, wave, wobble, yield
**wave recorder** ondograph
**waverer** ditherer
**wavering** dithering, faltering, fickle, flickering, fluctuating, hesitating, quivering, reeling, seesawing, shaking, swaying, undecided, undulating, unsettled, vacillating, variable, varying, waving, weaving, wobbling
**wavering sound** tremolo
**waver in opinion** doubt
**waver up and down** seesaw
**wave to and fro** flap, wag
**wave top** crest, whitecap
**wavy** curly, furrowed, grooved, ridged, snaky, twisting, undulating, winding, wrinkled
**wavy fabric** taffeta
**wavy moulding** cyma
**wavy ski-descent technique** godille
**wax** accelerate, amplify, become, broaden, cera (Sp), develop, dilate, enlarge, expand, extend, grow, increase, inflate, lengthen, magnify, spread, swell, widen
**wax and wane** fluctuate, pulsate
**wax artist** Tussaud
**wax bean** butterbean
**waxbill** cedarbird
**wax candle** bougie, cierge, taper
**waxcloth** oilcloth
**waxed spill** taper
**waxen** grey, pale, pallid, whitish
**waxing** developing, dilating, enlarging, expanding, growing, increasing, magnifying, mounting, recording, rising, swelling
**waxing moon** crescent
**waxlike membrane at base of some birds' beaks** cere
**wax match** vesta
**wax myrtle** candleberry
**wax ointment** cerate
**wax pencil** crayon
**wax plant** carnauba, indianpipe

**wax red** copper
**waxy** angry, ceral, cerate, temperamental
**waxy flower** begonia
**waxy ointment** cerate
**waxy part of beak** ceres
**waxy secretion of whale** ambergris
**way** access, avenue, channel, course, custom, detour, direction, distance, entrance, fashion, habit, highway, itinerary, lane, manner, means, mode, particular, passage, path, plan, practice, procedure, progress, respect, road, route, scheme, space, style, technique, track, via
**way a thing is done** manner
**way a thing operates** modus operandi
**way a thing works** operation
**way back** yore
**way between rows of seats** aisle, gangway
**wayfarer** drifter, gadabout, gallivanter, globetrotter, hiker, itinerant, meanderer, nomad, pilgrim, roamer, rover, sightseer, stroller, tourist, tramp, traveller, voyager, walker, wanderer
**wayfarer's stop** inn
**way hair is arranged** coiffure
**way in** access, adit, door(way), entrance, entry, gate, inlet, opening, passageway, portal
**way in which a word is pronounced** pronunciation
**way in which thing is done** mode
**waylay** accost, ambush, attack, bait, bore, catch, decoy, ensnare, grab, intercept, inveigle, lure, lurk, skulk, surprise, tempt, trick
**way of acting** manner
**way of doing something** method
**way of living** modus vivendi
**way of looking at things** aspect, perspective
**way of making a living** career
**way of putting it** presentation
**way of speaking** parlance
**way of swimming** breast(stroke), butterfly, crawl, freestyle, overarm
**way of swindling** rig
**way of thinking** sentiments
**way of travel** route
**way of walking** gait, pace
**way out** door, egress, escape, exit, exodus, gate, outlet, precautionary measure, vent, withdrawal
**way over a fence** stile
**way round** circuit
**ways and means** fashion, manner, means, methods, mode, procedure, style
**wayside** roadside

**wayside haven** caravanserai, hotel, inn, motel, tavern
**wayside tavern** inn
**way taken** route
**way through** opening, passage
**way to increase** add
**way up or down** staircase, stairway
**wayward** capricious, changeable, contrary, cross-grained, disobedient, erratic, fickle, forward, headstrong, incorrigible, insubordinate, mulish, obdurate, obstinate, perverse, rebellious, self-willed, stubborn, undependable, unpredictable, unruly, wilful
**waywardly** capriciously, contrarily, disobediently, erratically, flightily, mulishly, obdurately, obstinately, perversely, stubbornly, unpredictably, wilfully
**wayworn** fatigued, tired, weary
**WC tank** cistern
**we** nos (L), ourselves, us
**we admire one** hero
**weak** anile, breakable, debile, delicate, effete, faint, feckless, feeble, foolish, fragile, frail, frangible, impotent, ineffective, ineffectual, inefficient, infirm, invalid, lame, old, puny, sickly, silly, simple, stupid, unhealthy, unintelligent, unsteady, unwell, vague, weakly
**weak cider** ciderkin, perkin
**weaken** abate, attenuate, cut, debase, debilitate, deplete, depress, devitalise, dilute, diminish, droop, dwindle, enervate, enfeeble, exhaust, fade, fail, fatigue, flag, impair, impoverish, incapacitate, invalidate, lessen, lower, minimise, moderate, reduce, sap, strain, temper, thin, tire, undermine, unnerve, wane
**weaken a drink** mix, thin, water
**weakened** chronic, failure, flagging
**weakened by age** decrepit
**weakened condition** hyposthenia
**weakened solution** dilution
**weaken gradually** peter, sap, undermine
**weakening agent** diluent, solvent
**weaken in strength** impair
**weaken physically** enervate
**weaken with water** dilute
**weaker** attenuated
**weak-eyed** purblind
**weakhearted** afraid, cowardly
**weak indecisive person** jellyfish
**weak in intellect** silly
**weak-kneed** cowardly, unsteady

**weakling** coward, drip, milksop, mollycoddle, mouse, reckling, runt, sissy, slink, softling, softy, wimp, wrig
**weakly** ailing, decrepitly, deficiently, delicately, distantly, effetely, faintly, feeble, feebly, fragilely, frailly, impotently, indecisively, irresolutely, poorly, quietly, shakily, softly, spinelessly, tenderly, unsoundly, unsteadily
**weakly sentimental** maudlin, namby-pamby
**weakly sentimental utterance** slop
**weak-minded** daft, dotty, dull, foolish, slow, stupid, unsound
**weakness** asthenia, atony, craze, debility, defect, defenceless, delicacy, failing, fault, feebleness, fetish, flaw, foible, fondness, foolishness, fragility, frailty, infirmity, liability, liking, tendency, tenderness, unsoundness, vulnerability
**weakness of character** foible
**weakness of muscles** myasthenia
**weakness of Samson** hair
**weakness of will** akrasia
**weak point** blemish, defect, drawback, failing, fault, flaw, foible, imperfection, lack, shortcoming, snag, taint, weakness
**weak rum** grog
**weak shrill cry of young bird** cheep
**weak spot** blemish, defect, failing, fault, flaw, gall, imperfection, speck, weakness
**weak-stemmed** leggy
**weak with old age** infirm
**weal** blemish, choice, good, profit, prosperity, ridge, utility, wale, wealth, welfare, welt, wheal
**wealth** abundance, affluence, assets, bounty, capital, cash, estate, fortune, fullness, funds, goods, lucre, means, money, opulence, pelf, plenty, possessions, profusion, property, resources, riches, richness, substance, treasure
**wealth and resources of a community** economy
**wealth regarded as evil influence** mammon
**wealth stored up** treasure
**wealthy** abounding, abundant, affluent, ample, bien (Sc), comfortable, elegant, flush, glittering, lavish, loaded, moneyed, monied, opulent, profuse, prosperous, replete, rich, rife, sumptuous, well-off
**wealthy and influential person** magnate
**wealthy businessman** tycoon
**wealthy class** plutocracy

**wealthy fashionable young people** jeunesse dorée (F)
**wealthy person** Croesus, magnate, Midas, nabob, plutocrat
**wealthy trader** tycoon
**wealthy widow** dowager
**wean** alienate, child
**wean from the breast** ablacate
**weapon** arm(ament), arme (F), arms, arrow, bomb, bow, club, defence, gun, halberd, lance, mace, missile, projectile, protection, rifle, rocket, spear, sword
**weapon emplacement** nest
**weapon for shooting arrows** bow
**weaponless** unarmed
**weapon of gaucho** bolas
**weapon store** armoury, arsenal, cache
**weapon supplier** armer
**weapon to expel stones** slingshot
**weapon with blade** assegai, axe, dagger, knife, panga, spear, sword
**wear** abrade, abrasion, affect, annoy, apparel, attire, attrition, bear, carry, clothes, clothing, damage, depreciation, deteriorate, deterioration, display, don, endure, erode, erosion, exhibit, fray, friction, garb, garments, gear, grind, habit, impair, irk, last, rub, service, show, sport, use, utility, waste
**wear and tear** atrophy, corrosion, depreciation, deterioration, dilapidation, erosion, ravages
**wear at the edges** fray
**wear away** abrade, consume, corrode, eat, erode, fray, fret, rot, rub, rust
**wear by friction** abrade, erase, rub
**wear down** abrade, consume, corrode, diminish, erode, lessen, oppress, overcome, reduce, undermine
**wearer of red suspenders** firefighter, fireman
**wearily indifferent** listless
**weariness** boredom, debility, drowsiness, enervation, ennui, exhaustion, fatigue, heaviness, languor, lassitude, lethargy, listlessness, prostration, sleepiness, sluggishness, tedium, tiredness
**weariness after exertion** fatigue
**weariness of life** taedium vitae
**wearing a light crown** tiaraed
**wearing away** ablation, abrasion, atrophy, attrition, eroding, erosive, rusty
**wearing away process** abrasion, erosion
**wearing chain mail** armoured
**wearing down** attrition
**wearing Highland attire** kilted

**wearing low-necked garment**
   décolleté
**wearing mittens** gloved
**wearing shoes** shod
**wear into shreds** fray
**wearisome** annoying, boring,
   bothersome, burdensome, dree (Sc),
   dull, exhausting, fatiguing, humdrum,
   irksome, monotonous, oppressive,
   plaguy, prolix, prosaic, prosy,
   tedious, tiresome, toilsome,
   troublesome, trying, vexatious,
   wearing, weary
**wearisome person** bore, drip, pest,
   square
**wearisome routine** chore, treadmill
**wearisome talker** bore
**wearisome task** fag
**wearisome through sameness**
   monotonous
**wear off** abate, abrade, decrease,
   diminish, disappear, dwindle, ebb,
   efface, fade, lessen, pass, subside,
   vanish, wane, weaken
**wear out** consume, deteriorate,
   enervate, erode, exhaust, fag,
   fatigue, fray, impair, sap, tire, weary
**wear seat belt** belt up
**wear sullen look** scowl
**wear the crown** prevail
**wear the pants** control, decide,
   determine, dispose, dominate, rule
**wear through by rubbing** fray
**wear too much** overdress
**weary** arduous, bore, dissatisfied,
   drained, droop, drowsy, enervate,
   exhausted, fade, fag, fail, fatigue,
   flagging, harass, harry, irk(some),
   jaded, laborious, sap, sleepy, spent,
   tedious, tire(d), tiresome, wearied,
   worn
**weary Willie** hobo, tramp
**weasand** gullet, oesophagus, throat,
   windpipe
**weasel** cane, ermine, ferret, marten,
   otter, sable, stoat, vermin
**weasel-like** musterline
**weasel-like animal yielding valuable
   fur** marten
**weather** climate, clime, confront,
   disintegrate, dry, endure, gale,
   hurricane, season, (snow)storm,
   temperature, thunderstorm, wear,
   windstorm
**weather-beaten** exhausted, tanned,
   tired, wearied, worn
**weathercoat** mac(kintosh), raincoat
**weathercock** girouette, vane
**weather conditions of area** climate
**weather curve** isobar
**weathered** aged, hardened, seasoned,
   worn, wrinkled

**weather forecaster** barometer,
   meteorologist
**weatherglass** barometer
**weather house** hygroscope
**weather indicator** anemometer,
   barometer, vane
**weathering the storm** coping with a
   crisis
**weatherman** meteorologist
**weather map line** isobar
**weather meter** rain gauge
**weather satellite** nimbus, Tiros
**weather shed** dingle
**weather side** windward
**weather vane** cock, indication,
   indicator, omen, pointer, sign,
   weathercock
**weather word** clear, cloudy, cold, dry,
   fair, fog, frost, hail, humid, icy,
   overcast, rain, snow, sunshine,
   warm, wet
**weatherworn stone** boulder
**weave** blend, braid, build, construct,
   contrive, create, entwine, fabricate,
   fuse, insert, interlace, intermingle,
   intertwine, introduce, knit, make,
   merge, plait, spin, twist, unite, wind
**weave a rope** reeve
**weave in textiles** leno
**weaverbird** baya, maya, taha, whidah
**weaver's reed** sley
**weaver's reel** pirn
**weave together** braid, knit, raddle
**weave with needles** knit
**weave wool** knit
**weaving apparatus** loom
**weaving harness** heald
**weaving material** fiber, reed, wicker,
   yarn
**weaving reel** pirn
**weaving term** lisse
**weaving tool** batten, evener, shuttle
**web** cobweb, coil, confusion, fabric,
   girder, knot, lattice, membrane,
   mesh, net, network, ply, screen,
   snare, stratagem, tangle, tela,
   texture, tissue, trap
**webbing on duck's feet** palama
**web-footed bird** avocet, cormorant,
   duck, gannet, goose, loon, pelican,
   penguin, swan
**web-footed mammal** muskrat, otter
**weblike membrane** tela
**web maker** spider, weaver
**web of paper** roll
**we breathe it** air
**web spinner** arachnid, spider
**web spinning** retiary, telarian, telary
**webwork** mesh, net, rete
**webworm** caterpillar
**we cannot all do everything** non
   omnia possumus omnes (L)

**wed** ally, attach, betroth, bond,
   coalesce, cohere, connect, couple,
   elope, espouse, join, marry, match,
   mate, merge, partner, seal, unite,
   wive, yoke
**wed again** remarry
**wedding** alliance, bridal, ceremony,
   espousing, join(t)ing, liaison,
   marriage, marrying, matrimony,
   melding, mixing, nuptials, spousal,
   unification, union, uniting, wedlock
**wedding anniversary** bronze, china,
   copper, coral, cotton, crystal,
   diamond, emerald, fine china, fruit,
   gold, iron, ivory, lace, leather, paper,
   pearl, ruby, sapphire, silk, silver,
   steel, tin, wood
**wedding attendant** best man,
   bride(smaid), flower girl,
   groomsman, pageboy
**wedding band** ring
**wedding gift** dowry
**wedding gown fabric** lace, satin, silk
**wedding missiles** confetti, petals, rice,
   streamers
**wedding proclamation** banns
**wedding reception** infare
**wedding shower dots** confetti
**wedding song** hymeneal
**wedding trip** honeymoon
**wedge** cam, chunk, cleat, coign, froe,
   gib, glut, gore, interjection, key, peg,
   quoin, stopper, vee
**wedged** blocked, crammed, forced,
   jammed, keyed, lodged, packed,
   split, squeezed, stuffed, thrusted
**wedge in** jam
**wedge of cloth** gore
**wedge-shaped** cuneal, cuneated,
   cuneiformed, shim, sphenoid
**wedge-shaped dessert** pie
**wedge-shaped piece** gib, shim, vee
**wedge-shaped piece in garment** gore
**wedge-shaped support** cleat
**wedge-tailed eagle** eaglehawk
**wedge under vehicle wheel** chock
**wedlock** marriage, match, matrimony,
   nuptials, union, wedding
**wed secretly** elope
**wee** baby, bantam, diminutive, dwarf,
   elfin, immature, infinitesimal,
   insignificant, little, midget,
   mini(ature), minute, negligible, petit,
   puny, pygmy, short, slender, slight,
   small, teeny, tiny, trifling, undersized
**weed** band, bush, cull, extract, gather,
   hoe, pick, pull, remove, shrub, tare,
   thistle, tobacco, uproot
**weeder** culler
**weeding tool** hoe
**weedkiller** paraquat

**weed out** eject, eliminate, eradicate, purge, remove, uproot, winnow
**weed tool** hoe, spud
**weedy** overgrown
**weedy plant** blackjack, chickweed, coltsfoot, dock, khakibos, knawel, lalanc
**week** cycle, hebdomad, period, sennet, sennight
**week day** feria
**week division** day
**weekend day** Saturday, Sunday
**weekly** aweek, hebdomadal, hebdomadary, journal, magazine, periodical, publication
**weel** basket, cave, creel, pit
**ween** conjecture, fancy, think
**weep** bawl, bemoan, bewail, blubber, boohoo, complain, complain, cry, effuse, exude, greet (Sc), grieve, groan, howl, lament, moan, mourn, orp (Sc), snivel, sob, ululate, wail, whimper, whine, whinge
**weep audibly** sob
**weep for** bemoan, bewail
**weeping** bemoaning, bewailing, complaining, crying, lamenting, moaning, mourning, sad, snivelling, sobbing, tearful, ululating, whimpering
**weeping monkey** capuchin, sai
**weeping stone** Niobe
**weeping willow** tree
**weep loudly** bawl
**weep over** bewail
**weep with sniffling** snivel
**weepy** blubbering, crying, lachrymose, melting, snivelling, sobbing, tearful, teary, weeping
**weevil** beetle, borer, insect, turk, vermin
**weevil wing cover** shard
**we fight them** enemies
**we have two of these organs** ears, eyes, kidneys, lungs
**weigh** balance, burden, consider, contemplate, count, estimate, evaluate, examine, heft, impress, influence, measure, oppress, ponder, prey, raise, study, tell
**weigh anchor** embark, sail
**weighbridge** scale
**weigh carefully** consider, ponder
**weigh down** afflict, burden, depress, hamper, handicap, load, oppress, overburden, overload, tax, torment, trouble, worry
**weigh heavily upon** oppress
**weigh in** enter, report
**weighing device** balance, beam, scale, steelyard, trone (Sc)
**weigh in with** introduce, present
**weigh merits of** consider

**weigh more** preponderate
**weigh one's words** deliberate
**weight** abbas, atom, avoirdupois, bob, carat, consequence, dram, dumbell, es, grain, gram, gravity, heaviness, heft, import, influence, iron, load, mass, mite, moment, obol, onus, ounce, poundage, power, ser, significance, standard, stone, ton, value
**weight after tare deduction** suttle
**weight allowance** tare, tret
**weight balance** rider
**weight carried by horse in handicap** impost
**weight cloth** flock
**weighted** adjusted, bias, loaded
**weighted hook used in trolling** drail
**weighter** fuller
**weight for hurling** hammer
**weight for jewels** carat
**weight for lead** fother, fotmal
**weight for wool** clove, sappler, tod
**weight in dream** incubus, succuba, succubus
**weightiness** force, heaviness
**weighting** compensation
**weight in pile driver** ram
**weightless** feathery
**weightlifting machine** crane
**weightlifting rod** barbell
**weight machine** balance, scale, trones
**weight measure of precious stones** carat
**weight of Afghanistan** karwar, khurds, pau, paw, ser, sir
**weight of Algeria** rotl
**weight of ancient Rome** as, bes
**weight of ancient times** mina, talent
**weight of apothecary** dram, grain, scruple
**weight of Arabia** dirhem, kella
**weight of Asia** can, hubba, ta, tael
**weight of boxer** bantamweight, featherweight, heavyweight, middleweight
**weight of broadside** gunpowder
**weight of Burma** kyat
**weight of China** catty, hao, kin, li, liang, picul, tael, tan
**weight of coal** keel
**weight of coffee** mat
**weight of Denmark** es, lod, ort
**weight of Egypt** deben, kat
**weight of England** stone
**weight of five unciae** quincunx
**weight of forty bushels** wey
**weight of France** livre, once
**weight of Greece** drachme, mina
**weight of Holland** esterlin, wichtse
**weight of hundred pounds** cental, centena, centner

**weight of hydrogen** crith
**weight of India** pollam, seer, ser, tola
**weight of Italy** libra
**weight of Japan** fun, mo, rin
**weight of Libya** kele
**weight of metal** journey
**weight of Mongolia** lan
**weight of one hundredth tael** fen
**weight of one tenth tael** mace
**weight of pendulum** bob
**weight of Persia** abbas, sir
**weight of pile driver** tup
**weight of raw silk** pari
**weight of responsibility** onus
**weight of Russia** dola, lot
**weight of silk or rayon** drammage
**weight of Spain** arroba
**weight of Sweden** lod, ort
**weight of Syria** cola
**weight of Thailand** coyan, hap, pai
**weight of thousand livres** millier
**weight of Turkey** dirhem, oka
**weight of unladen vehicle** tare
**weight on fishline** sinker
**weight on mine sweeper** kite
**weight on sashcord** mouse
**weight on steel yard** pea
**weight on watch chain** fob
**weight pile driver** ram
**weight-producing** gravific
**weight science** metrology
**weight system** avoirdupois, troy
**weight to bend hot metal** dumper
**weight to detect false coins** passir
**weight to hinder motion** clog
**weight unit** ounce, pound, ton
**weight watcher** dieter
**weight which vessel can carry** tonnage
**weighty** ample, awkward, backbreaking, bulky, burdensome, colossal, cumbersome, dense, earnest, enormous, forceful, forcible, gigantic, grave, heavy, hefty, immense, important, influential, leading, massy, onerous, ponderous, portentous, serious, significant, solid, substantial, titanic, valid
**weighty book** tome
**weigh up** assess, balance, consider, contemplate, deliberate, discuss, examine, ponder
**weigh upon** bear
**weigh with** equal
**Weil's disease** jaundice
**we inhale it** air
**weir** bank, barrage, barrier, dam, enclosure, fence, garth, levee, net, trap, waterfall
**weird** bewildering, bizarre, creepy, eccentric, eerie, eldritch, enigmatic,

fantastic, freakish, ghostly, grotesque, mysterious, mystic, nightmarish, occult, odd, perdu, puzzling, spooky, strange, unaccountable, uncanny, unearthly, unnatural, unusual, wizardly

**weirdly** eerily

**weirdness** bizarreness, eeriness, freakishness, grotesqueness, mysteriousness, oddness, queerness, strangeness, uncanniness, unnaturalness

**welcome** accepted, address, admit, ave, ben venuto (I), grateful, greet(ing), haeremai (M), hail, happy, hello, hospitality, hullo, invited, meet, pleasing, pleasure, receive, salaam, salutations, salute, willkommen (G)

**welcome enthusiastically** acclaim

**welcome visitor** guest

**weld** adhere, affix, agglutinate, attach, bind, bond, cleave, fasten, fix, fuse, glue, gum, join, seal, solder, stick, unite

**welding mixture** thermit

**welfare** advantage, benefit, good, happiness, health, interest, profit, prosperity, success, wellbeing

**welfare relief** dole

**welkin** air, ether, firmament, heaven, sky

**well** able, abyss, adequately, attentively, aweel (Sc), bene (L), beneficially, bien (F), bore, certainly, closely, commendably, concavity, crater, crevice, fit, fortunately, fountain, fully, greatly, gush, happily, headspring, nicely, personally, pit, pool, properly, prosperously, satisfactorily, shaft, smoothly, soundly, spring, stream, water hole

**well-acquainted** conversant

**well-acquainted with** au fait (F), familiar

**well-adapted for** fit

**welladay** alas

**well-advised** prudent

**well-aged** mature, ripe

**well and good** à la bonne heure (F), fine, okay

**well-arranged** orderly

**well-assured** confident

**well-balanced** matched, sane, sober, sound

**well-behaved** controlled, decorous, disciplined, dutiful, good, law-abiding, mannerly, nice, obedient, orderly, polite, proper, quiet, seemly

**wellbeing** bene esse (L), euphoria, fit, happy, health, hearty, prosperity, prosperous, welfare

**well-beloved** bien aimé (F)

**well bored for water which rises by itself** artesian

**well-boring device** derrick, jar, rig

**well-bred** courteous, cultivated, delicate, exquisite, gallant, genteel, gracious, mannerly, pedigreed, polite, refined, suave

**well-bred fellow** gent(leman)

**well-bred woman** lady

**well-built** athletic, beefy, big, brawny, bulky, burly, determined, durable, firm, flourishing, hard-wearing, hardy, hearty, heavy-duty, hefty, muscular, powerful, reinforced, resolute, robust, secure, solid, staunch, steadfast, stocky, stout, strapping, strong, sturdy, substantial, vigorous, well-made

**well-chosen phrase** felicity

**well-combed** kempt

**well done** bravo, bully, euge (L)

**well-dressed** chic, elegant, fashionable, smart

**well-dressed person** toff

**well-educated** learned, lettered

**well-enough** rather, somewhat

**well-established** entrenched, established, fixed, habitual, immovable, irrevocable, reliable, rooted, settled, sound, stable, unchangeable, venerable

**well-expressed** apposite

**well-favoured** attractive, comely, shapely

**well-fed** fat

**well-feeling** euphoria

**well-fitted for the purpose** suitable

**well-fortified** strong

**well-groomed** chic, clean(-cut), coiffured, elegant, manicured, meticulous, natty, smart, soigné, soignée (F), spruce, well-dressed

**well-grounded** informal, solid, valid

**well-heeled** prosperous, rich, wealthy, well-off

**well-informed** knowing, knowledgeable

**well-invented** ben trovato (I)

**well-judged** prudent, sensible, wise

**well-known** common, eminent, everyday, fabled, familiar, famous, great, historical, immortal, notable, noted, notorious, prominent, stock

**well-known canal** Panama, Suez

**well-known German prison** Spandau

**well-known person** celebrity

**well-known singing cage bird** canary

**well-known storyteller** Aesop

**well-known street in London** Regent

**well-liked** popular

**well lining** steen(ing)

**well-marked** defined, distinguished

**well-matured** mellow

**well-nigh** nearly, scarcely, virtually

**well-off** affluent, comfortable, loaded, moneyed, prosperous, rich, wealthy, well-to-do

**well over** brim

**well-preserved corpse** mummy

**well-read** erudite, lettered, literate, skill, versed

**well-schooled** educated

**well-skilled** adept

**well-stocked** replete

**well-suited** fit

**well-thought-of** admired, distinguished, esteemed, exalted, honoured, respected, valuable, venerable

**well-thought-out** sensible

**well-timed** opportune

**well up and spread over** suffuse

**well-ventilated** airy

**well-versed** erudite, expert, fluent, proficient, skilled

**well-wishing** felicitation

**well-worn** aged, dilapidated, hackneyed, overused, trite

**well worth doing** rewarding

**we look up to see it** sky

**Welsh** Cambrian, Celt(ic), Cymric

**Welsh bardic assembly** Gorsedd

**Welsh boat** coracle

**Welsh coal-tip disaster village** Aberfan

**Welsh dish** rarebit

**Welsh dog** corgi

**Welsh emblem** leek

**Welsh festival** eisteddfod

**Welsh fiddler** crowder

**Welsh fishing boat** coracle

**Welsh giant** Idris

**Welsh god of sea** Dylan

**Welsh language** Celtic, Keltic

**Welshman** Cambrian, Celt

**Welshman's nickname** Taffy

**Welsh onion** cibol

**Welsh pit** coal mine

**Welsh port** Llanelli, Swansea

**Welsh rabbit** rarebit

**Welsh saint** Asaph

**Welsh terrier** sealyham

**Welsh town** Llandudno, Llanelli

**Welsh trout** gwyniad, powan

**welt** beat, border, broil, flog, flounder, lash, punch, ribbing, ridge, spank, strip, turmoil, wale, wallow, weal

**wench** girl, hag, woman

**wend** travel

**went by air** flew

**went by car** motored

**went hastily** ran
**went in** entered
**went missing** was inadvertently mislaid
**went to pieces** fragmented
**went with speed** haste, ran
**went wrong** erred
**were there** attended
**werewolf** lycanthrope
**we should fight our own** battles
**Wesleyan** Methodist
**West African baboon** mandril
**West African charm** juju
**West African fox** zamouse
**West African lemur** kinkajou, potto
**West African mango** dika
**West African monkey** mangabey, patas
**West African republic** Burkina Faso, Cameroon, Gambia, Ghana, Guinea, Ivory Coast, Liberia, Mauritania, Nigeria, Senegal, Togo
**West African seaport** Accra, Dakar, Lagos
**West African tongue** Gur
**West African tree** akee, cola, iroko, odoom, odum, sapele
**West African tribe** I(g)bo
**West Asian republic** Syria
**West Australian eucalypt** jarrah, karri
**West England county** Somerset
**western** occidental
**Western alliance** NATO
**western Aramaic** Syriac
**western Australian gulf** Admiralty, Exmouth
**western Australian wallaby** quokka
**western gambling city** Las Vegas, Reno
**western hemisphere** Occident
**western Hispaniola** Haiti
**western American Indian** Ute
**westernise** occidentalise
**Western Isles** Hebrides
**Western Province rugby emblem** disa
**western roundup** rodeo
**western Soviet port** Riga
**western Thrace** Greece
**West European** German
**West European range** Pyrenees
**West Indian ballad** calypso
**West Indian bird** courlan, limpkin, tody
**West Indian citrus fruit** ugli
**West Indian dance** cha-cha, limbo
**West Indian drink** rum
**West Indian drum** bongo
**West Indian fish** boga, cero, pega, pelon, testar
**West Indian folk song** calypso
**West Indian fruit** genipap, ugli
**West Indian fruit tree** akee
**West Indian hut** ajoupa

**West Indian island** Antilles, Aruba, Bahamas, Cuba, Haiti, Martinique, Nevis, Tobago
**West Indian knife** machete, matchet
**West Indian liquor** rum, tafia
**West Indian lizard** arbalo
**West Indian magic** obeah, obi(a)
**West Indian music** calypso, reggae
**West Indian plant** anil, arrowroot
**West Indian rodent** hutia
**West Indian ruler** cacique
**West Indian shark** gata
**West Indian shrub** anil, milkwood, ratwood
**West Indian snake** fer de lance
**West Indian song** calypso
**West Indian sorcery** obeah, obi
**West Indian spirit** rum
**West Indian thunderstorm** houvari
**West Indian timber tree** sabicu
**West Indian tree** aralie, bonace, calaba, genip, mabi, yagua
**West Indian vegetable** yautia
**West Indian vessel** droger
**West Indian witchcraft** obi, obeah
**West Indies** Antilles, Caribbees
**West Indies islands** Antilles, Leeward
**West Indies state** Bahamas
**Westminster clock** Big Ben
**Westminister landmark** Abbey
**West Pointer** cadet
**West Point freshman** plebe
**west wind** afer, zephyr
**wet** clamminess, damp(ness), drenched, innocent, liquid, moist(ened), naïve, rainy, saturated, soggy, wat (Sc), waterlogged
**wet-and-dry thermometer** psychrometer
**wet and muddy** splashy
**wet and soft earth** mud
**wet, as the weather** rainy
**wet behind the ears** immature, inexperienced, innocent, naive
**wet blanket** killjoy, misery, spoil-sport, wowser
**wet boggy ground** fen, marsh, quagmire, slough, vlei, wetland
**wet clay** loam
**wet intermittently** dabble
**wet mud** ooze
**wet nurse** amah, coddle, foster, provider
**wet or dry gully** donga
**wet plaster painting** fresco
**we try to shed unwanted ones** kilos
**wet slightly** dampen, moisten
**wet soil** mud
**wet spongy earth** bog, mire
**wet thoroughly** drench, soak, souse
**wet through** inundated, saturated, sodden, soggy, waterlogged

**wet weather** rain
**wet weather footwear** galosh, gumshoe
**wet weather garment** mac(kintosh), raincoat
**wet with condensed moisture** dew
**wet with rain** sloppy
**we work for this** profit
**whale** beat, beluga, cachalot, ceta(cean), finback, giant, grampus, humpback, leviathan, mammal, narwhal, orc, orca (L), right, sperm, thrash, whip
**whalebird** petrel
**whalebone** baleen, supporter, whalefin
**whalebone whale** rorqual
**whale carcass** krank, kreng
**whale diet** brit
**whale fat** blubber
**whale food** krill, plankton
**whale genus** Orca
**whale hunter** Ahab
**whale oil** sperm oil
**whale oil cask** cardel, rier
**whale oil derivative** spermaceti
**whaler's spear** harpoon, lance
**whale school** gam
**whale's forelimb** paddle
**whale shark** mhor
**whale skin** rind
**whale's waxy secretion** ambergris
**whale tail part** fluke
**whale with dorsal fin** rorqual
**whaling barb** harpoon
**whaling greenhorn** waister
**whaling toggle iron** towiron
**whaling weapon** harpoon, lance
**whangdoodle** nonsense
**wharf** dock, jetty, pier, quay
**wharfage** jettage, quayage
**wharf labourer** stevedore
**wharf landing** staith
**wharf owner** wharfinger
**wharf rat** loader, loafer, thief
**wharf worker** stevedore
**what** eh, how, pronoun, whatever, when, where, who
**what audiences do** hear
**what donkeys do** bray
**what-d'you-call-it** thing(am)y, thingum(a)bob, thingumajig, thingummy
**whatever** any, which
**whatever circumstances** always
**whatever the consequences may be** quand même (F)
**whatever you like** anything
**what follows** sequel
**what greedy people want** all
**what he touched turned to gold** Midas
**what is bad** evil
**what is bought** purchase

**what is carried** load
**what is destined to happen** fate
**what is just** right
**what is left over** residue
**what is meant** meaning
**what is mined** ore
**what is owed** debt
**what is put in** input
**what is spent on something** outlay
**what is spilt** spilth
**what is taught** doctrine
**what is told** information
**what magicians do** tricks
**what means** how
**what NB stands for** nota bene
**whatnot** bookcase, cabinet, credence, etagere, knick-knack, trivia
**what one believes** credo
**what one expects** expectation
**what one hears** gossip, hearsay
**what one is to expect** prospect
**what one knows** knowledge
**what one owes** due
**what one thinks about something** opinion
**what oologists study** eggs
**what other people say** gossip, hearsay, skinder(y)
**what person** who
**what place** where
**what provides an effect** cause
**what reason** why
**what remains** residuum
**what remains over** surplus
**what's-his-name** thing(am)y, thingum(a)bob, thingumajig, thingummy
**what's more** additionally, besides, moreover
**whatsoever** whatever
**what takes unawares** surprise
**what will be, will be** che sarà sarà (I)
**what will happen** future
**what you are called by** name
**what you do on stage** act
**wheal** postule, swelling, welt
**wheat** cereal, durum, einkorn, grain, spelt, suji
**wheat beard** awn
**wheat disease** bunt, smut
**wheat ear** spica, spike
**wheat grinder** mill
**wheat grower** farmer
**wheat head** ear, spike
**wheat kernel** grain
**wheat meal** flour
**wheat middlings** semolina
**wheat storage place** elevator, silo
**wheat with hard seeds** durum
**wheedle** cajole, charm, coax, court, draw, entice, flatter, persuade
**wheedling** cajolery

**wheel** bike, caster, castor, circle, cylinder, disc, disk, drum, gyrate, hoop, pivot, pulley, reel, ring, rotate, rotator, round, trolley
**wheel about** spin, turn
**wheel and block** sheave
**wheel bar** arbour, axle, spindle
**wheelbarrow** handcart
**wheel belt** strake
**wheel casing** tyre
**wheel centre** hob, hub, nave
**wheel charged with diamond dust** slitter
**wheel controlling rudder** helm
**wheel covering** tyre
**wheeled box for coal** tub
**wheeled home** caravan, trailer
**wheeled stretcher** trolley
**wheeled vehicle** car(riage), cart, trolley, wagon
**wheel for executions** rat
**wheel furrow** rut
**wheel guard** fender
**wheel holder** axle
**wheelhouse** pilothouse
**wheel hub** hob, nave
**wheel in knitting machine** bur(r)
**wheel in timepiece** balance
**wheel lock** rewet
**wheelman** helmsman
**wheelman in roulette** tourneur
**wheel mark** rut
**wheel mounting** axle
**wheel nave** hob
**wheel of life** zoetrope
**wheel on spur** rowel
**wheel part** cam, cog, felly, hob, hub, rim, spoke, tyre
**wheel projection** cam, cog
**wheel radius** spoke
**wheel rim band** tyre
**wheel rod** axle
**wheel rubber** tyre
**wheel shaft** axle
**wheel-shaped** rotate, trochal
**wheel spindle** arbor, axis, axle
**wheel spoke** radius, rung
**wheel tooth** cock, cog
**wheel track** rut
**wheel with teeth** gear
**wheezy** asthmatic, short-winded
**whelk** acne, mollusc, pimple, snail
**whelp** cub, pup(py)
**when** as
**when all is said and done** finally
**when and where** address, date, situation, time
**whence** how, origin, source
**when main part has been cut away** stump
**when the hands are together** noon, prayer

**when wages are received** payday
**where** ubi (L)
**where animals are viewed** game reserve, zoo
**where ark landed** Ararat
**whereas** forasmuch, inasmuch, seeing, since, while
**where beer is produced** brewery
**where bird rests** nest
**whereby** how
**where children like to climb** tree
**where dead bodies are kept** morgue
**where flat dwellers can grow flowers** window box
**wherefore** why
**wherefrom** origin, source, whence
**where General Smuts lived** Irene
**where Jesus grew up** Nazareth
**where Las Palmas is** Canary Island
**where Napoleon was finally defeated** Waterloo
**where one can go wrong** pitfall
**where the Dutch come from** Holland, Low Countries, Netherlands
**where the elated walk** on air
**where the Magna Charta was signed** Runnymede
**where the sun comes up** east
**where to buy a best seller** bookshop
**where to buy a puppy** pet shop
**where to buy snacks at school** tuckshop
**where trains are seen** station
**where vegetables are sold** greengrocer, market
**wherewithal** ability, capital, cash, essentials, finance, funds, means, money, ready, remedy, reserves, resources, supplies, technique, way, wherewith
**where yachts are made** boatyard
**whet** awaken, edge, grind, hone, incite, increase, rouse, sharpen, stir
**whether** if
**whether by right or not** de facto
**whether one likes it or not** willy-nilly
**whetstone** burr
**whetstone for sharpening tools** hone
**whey of milk** sera, serum
**which** whatever
**which can be overlooked** negligible
**whichever** any, either, whichsoever
**whichever is chosen** any
**which is to be especially noted** quod bene notandum (L)
**which person** who
**which thing** what
**which was to be done** quod erat faciendum (L)
**which was to be proved** QED, quod erat demonstrandum (L)
**which way** how

**whidah** widow bird
**while** albeit, although, as, besides, duration, interval, meantime, notwithstanding, occupy, period, season, space, span, stretch, term, though, time, when, whereas, whilst, yet
**while awaiting** pending
**while away** beguile
**while in action** during
**whim** caprice, conceit, craze, fad, fancy, freak, humour, impulse, kink, notion, quirk, sudden, thought, toy, vagary, whims(e)y, whimwham
**whimper** blubber, cry, groan, keen, mewl, moan, pule, sniffle, snivel, sob, wail, weep, whine
**whimsical** abnormal, amusing, arbitrary, bizarre, capricious, comic(al), crotchety, curious, deviant, different, diverting, dreamy, droll, eccentric, entertaining, erratic, exotic, extraordinary, fanciful, fantastic, farcical, freak(ish), funny, grotesque, high-flown, humorous, idealistic, imaginative, inconsistent, irregular, jocular, ludicrous, odd, old-fashioned, optional, peculiar, personal, quaint, queer, quixotic, random, rare, remarkable, ridiculous, risible, rococo, romantic, singular, strange, subjective, uncommon, unreal, unreasonable, unusual, utopian, visionary, weird, witty
**whimsical concept** fancy
**whimsical person** eccentric
**whin** gorse
**whine** blubber, complain, cry, grizzle, grouse, grudge, grumble, henpeck, keen, lamentation, moan, mumble, nag, object, pule, sniffle, snivel, wail, whimper, whinge, yammer
**whinge** bawl, (be)wail, blubber, complain, cry, gripe, lament, snivel, sob, weep, whimper, whine
**whining** carping, complaining, crying, grousing, grumbling, moaning, peevish, querulous, sobbing, wailing
**whinny** neigh
**whip** agitate, beat, cane, crop, dart, drive, flagellate, flail, flay, flog, hem, knout, lambast(e), lash, leather, scourge, sew, sjambok, spank, strike, tackle, thong, thrash, urge, whale
**whip around into** bustle, fly, hie, rampage, scoot, scramble, scuttle, speed, sprint, wisk
**whipcord** catgut
**whip handle** crop
**whip in** gather, herd
**whiplash** thong, thrash

**whip leather** rawhide
**whip mark** wale, w(h)eal
**whip off** divert
**whipped cream** chantilly
**whippet** greyhound
**whipping boy** scapegoat
**whippy** flexible, springy, supple
**whip severely** lambast(e)
**whip stock** crop
**whip up** arouse
**whirl** carousel, chain, cycle, daze, eddy, elevation, festivity, gurge, gyrate, gyroscope, pirouette, pivot, reel, revolve, roll, rotate, rotation, round, skit, somersault, spin, swing, swirl, swivel, turn, twirl, twister, typhoon, vortex, wheel
**whirl about** reel, scurry
**whirl around** spin
**whirlbone** kneepan, patella
**whirling** eddying
**whirling liquid** vortex
**whirling motion** swirl
**whirling sensation** dizzy
**whirling warrior** dervish
**whirling wind** cyclone, tornado, twister
**whirlpool** countercurrent, counterflow, eddy, gurge, maelstrom, swirl, undercurrent, undertow, vortex, weel (Sc), whirl, wiel (Sc)
**whirlwind** cyclone, gale, hasty, headlong, lightning, maelstrom, quick, rapid, rash, short, speedy, swift, tornado, twister, vortex, waterspout
**whirlybird** helicopter
**whirr** burr, hiss, rasp, shrill, sibilate, wheeze, whir(r), whistle, whiz
**whirring sound** burr
**whisk** abduct, abstract, agitate, beat, bolt, charge, convey, dart, dash, eggbeater, flash, hurtle, jerk, panicle, produce, purloin, race, remove, seize, shoot, speed, steal, sweep, whip
**whisk broom** wisp
**whisker** antenna, barb, beard, bristle, brush, feeler, hair(line), moustache, prickle, sideburns, spine, stubble, tentacle, thorn, vibrissa, weeper
**whisky** bourbon, moonshine, poteen, Scotch
**whisky and ginger wine** mac
**whisky and hot water** toddy
**whisky from illicit still** moonshine, poteen
**whisky measure** dram
**whisky mixer** soda
**whisky, soda and ice in a tall glass** highball
**whisper** breath(e), fraction, gossip, hint, hiss, innuendo, insinuate,

insinuation, intimate, lisp, murmur, report, rumour, rustle, shadow, sigh, suggestion, suspicion, tinge, trace, undertone, whiff
**whispered in the ear** auricular
**whispered report** buzz
**whispered rumour** breeze
**whispering sound** susurrus
**whist hand** tenace
**whistle** blow, call, cheep, dart, fife, hiss, horn, megaphone, peep, pipe, play, rasp, shrill, sibilate, sing, siren, sound, streak, toot(er), ululate, warble, wheeze, whirr, whiz, wonder
**whistle at** jeer, mock
**whistle-duck** goldeneye
**whistler** bird, canary, marmot
**whistle sound** toot
**whistling swan** olor
**whist sweep** slam
**whit** atom, bit, doit, dot, iota, jot, little
**white** ashy, hoar, pale, snowy
**white Alpine flower** edelweiss
**white animal** albino
**white ant** termite
**white as a sheet** panic-stricken, shaken
**white bear** polar
**white beet** chard
**whitebill** coot
**white bird** egret, gull, heron, stork, swan
**white, black and cayenne** pepper
**white blood-corpuscle which devours germs** phagocyte
**white bony substance** ivory
**white brain matter** alba
**white Burgundy wine** Chablis
**white cedar** arborvitae
**white cinnamon** canella
**white clerical vestment** alb
**White Cliffs site** Dover
**white cockatoo** corella
**white-collar bandit** fleecer
**white-collar job** clerk, officework
**white corpuscle** leucocyte
**white crow** vulture
**white crystalline compound** borax
**white element** iridium, silver
**white elephant land** Thailand
**whiteface** Hereford
**white-faced** ashen, pale
**white feather** cowardice
**white fibre** sisal
**whitefish** cisco, lavaret
**white flag** surrender
**white-flecked horse** roan
**white-flowered tree** elder
**white frost** hoarfrost, rime
**white fur** ermine, miniver
**white grape** hanepoot, malaga, riesling
**white-handed gibbon** lar
**white hawk** celander

**whitehead** milium
**white heron** egret
**white horselike animal with a long single horn** unicorn
**white horses of Vienna** Lippizaner
**white lie** deceit, falsehood, fib, untruth
**white lightning** alcohol
**white limestone** chalk
**white liquid** milk
**white marble** carrara
**white mark on horse's forehead** blaze
**white matter of brain** alba
**white meat** chicken, fish, pork, poultry, veal
**white metal** zinc
**white metallic transuranic element** americium
**whiten** achromatise, blanch, bleach, blench, decolour, dim, droop, etiolate, fade, gray, pale, sag
**whiteness** pallor, purity
**white oak** overcup, roble
**white of egg** albumen, glair(e)
**white of eye** sclerotic
**white opacity of cornea** leucoma
**white or grey metallic mineral** arsenopyrite, mispickel
**white or snow** niveous
**white pigment** anatase, ceruse, lithopone
**white playing marble** alley
**white poplar** abele, aspen
**white precious metal** silver
**white robes worn by Muslim pilgrims to Mecca** ihram
**white scurf** dandruff
**white silk veil** orale
**white space** blanks, margin
**white sparkling wine** champagne
**white sturgeon** beluga
**white substance forming sheath of nerve fibre** myelin
**white substance made from opium** codeine
**white substance of nervous system** alba
**white vegetable** turnip
**white vestment** alb, amice
**white wader** egret
**white weasel** ermine
**white whale** beluga, huse, huso
**white wine** chardonnay, colombard, gewürztraminer, hock, malaga, moselle, riesling, sack, sauterne, sherry, steen, stein
**white wispy cloud** cirrus
**white with age** hoary
**white yam** ube
**whither goes thou?** quo vadis
**whiting** hake
**whitish** light, pale
**whitish gem** moonstone, onyx, opal

**whitlow** felon
**Whit Sunday** Pentecost
**whittle** carve, consume, cut, destroy, erode, hew, pare, reduce, shape, shave, trim
**who** oms (F)
**whodunit** novel, thriller
**whodunit link** clue
**whoever** anyone
**who goes there?** challenge, qui vive, qui-va-la
**whole** all, collectively, complete, entire(ly), flawless, gross, holo-, inclusive, intact, integral, lot, one, perfect, seamless, sound, sum, total, unbroken, undamaged, undivided, unharmed, unhurt, unimpaired, unit, well
**whole amount** all, gross, sum, total
**whole body of peers** aristocracy, peerage
**whole bunch** all, everything
**whole-hearted** committed, dedicated, determined, devoted, earnest, enthusiastic, fervent, genuine, real, resolute, sincere, true, unreserved, unstinting, warm, zealous
**whole jury** panel
**wholemeal rye bread** pumpernickel
**whole number** integer
**whole of** all
**whole or complete** entire
**whole range of anything** gamut
**wholesaler** merchant, middleman
**wholesaler who delivers goods** distributor
**whole series** gamut
**wholesome** beneficial, clean, hale, healing, healthful, moral, nutritious, refreshing, remedial, restorative, robust, salubrious, salutary, stimulating, strong, tonic, well
**whole sum** all
**whole sweep of scythe** swat
**whole total** sum
**wholly engrossed** entranced, rapt, spellbound
**wholly occupied** rapt
**who must be obeyed** God, She
**whooper** swan
**whooping cough** pertussis
**whoop it up** celebrate, raise, revel
**whop** beat, cane, clout, hit, klap, paddle, spank, thrash, thump, whack
**whopper** lie
**why** wherefore
**whydah** widow bird
**wicked** abandoned, abominable, amoral, arch, atrocious, bad, corrupt, debased, devilish, difficult, dissolute, egregious, evil, fiendish, flagitious, foul, galling, guilty, heinous, immoral, impish, iniquitous, irreligious, mischievous, naughty, nefarious, playful, rascally, scandalous, shameful, sinful, spiteful, troublesome, unpleasant, unrighteous, vicious, vile, villainous, wicked, worthless

**wicked act** atrocity
**wicked action** iniquity
**wicked child** brat
**wicked city** Gomorrah, Sodom
**wicked deed** atrocity
**wicked doing** evil
**wicked monster** ogre
**wickedness** atrociousness, badness, corruptness, depravity, dissoluteness, evil(ness), fiendishness, foulness, guiltiness, heinousness, nefariousness, shamefulness, sin, sinfulness, unrighteousness, viciousness, worthlessness
**wicked person** caitiff, felon, fiend, rogue, scoundrel, swindler
**wicked Thebes queen** Circe
**wicker** osier, twig, withe
**wicker basket** cesta, kipsy, pannier
**wicker container** basket
**wicker-covered bottle** fiasco
**wicker cradle** bassinet
**wicker hamper** creel, crate
**wicker hut** jacal
**wickerwork** basket, network, plaiting, rattan, weaving
**wickerwork basket** hamper
**wickerwork material** rattan
**wicket crosspiece** bail
**wicket down** dismissal
**wicket in cricket** pitch, stumps
**wicket in croquet** hoop
**wide** ample, astray, away, baggy, broad, cavalier, commodious, completely, comprehensive, dilated, distant, distended, encyclopaedic, expanded, expansive, extemporaneous, extempore, full(y), general, immense, inclusive, informal, large, loose, off, out(spread), outstretched, remote, roomy, spacious, sweeping, unpremeditated, vast
**wide area of land** expanse
**wide-awake** alert, keen, knowing, live, wary
**wide boy** trickster
**wide-brimmed felt hat** terai
**wide-brimmed Mexican hat** sombrero
**wide camera sweep** pan
**wide extent** latitude
**wide inlet of the sea** bay
**widely** baggily, broadly, comprehensively, distantly,

expansively, extensively, fully, generally, immensely, inclusively, largely, remotely, spaciously, sweepingly, vastly
**widely known** celebrated, common, famed
**widely liked** popular
**widely used language** English
**wide-mouthed jar** ewer, ol(l)a
**widen** broaden, dilate, enlarge, expand, extend, ream, spread, stretch
**wide neck scarf** ascot
**wideness** ampleness, breadth, broadness, distantness, distendedness, expansiveness, fullness, immenseness, largeness, looseness, remoteness, roominess, scope, spaciousness, sweepingness, vastness, width
**widen in area** extend
**widening channel of river** estuary
**wide off the mark** (a)miss, astray, defective, errant, erroneous, fallacious, faulty, imprecise, inaccurate, inexact, off-target, pointless
**wide open** agape, defenceless, exposed, uncovered, untrammelled
**wide open dish** basin
**wide pedal** treadle
**wide pleated waist sash worn with formal suit** cummerbund
**wide screen** cinemascope
**wide smile** grin
**widespread** broad, common, diffuse, epidemic, extensive, general, pandemic, popular, prevalent, prolate, rife, sweeping, universal, wholesale
**widespread destruction** havoc
**widespread disease** epidemic, pandemic
**widespread dislike** odium
**widespread dominion** empire
**widespread fear** panic
**widespread language** English
**widespread principle** generality
**widespread reputation** renown
**widespread tumult** riot, emeute (F)
**widest part of barrel** bilge
**wide street** avenue, boulevard
**wide tidal mouth of river** estuary
**wide view** panorama, survey, vista
**widgeon** smee
**widow** bereave, dowager, relict, survivor
**widow bird** whydah
**widowed** husbandless, vidual, wifeless
**widowhood** viduage
**widow in cards** skat
**widow's coin** mite

**widow's dower** terce
**widow's income** dower
**widow's mite** bit
**widow's mourning garments** weeds
**widow's right** dower, scot, terce
**widow's tears** spiderwort
**width** breadth, broadness, capacity, diameter, extent, gauge, radius, scope, section, spaciousness, span, stretch, vastness, wideness, wingspread
**width measure** em, en
**width of sympathy** liberality
**wield** control, employ, exercise, exert, flourish, handle, lift, manage, manipulate, ply, raise, shake, sway, swing, use, utilise, wave
**wield diligently** ply
**wield the sceptre** command, govern, prevail
**wield vigorously** ply
**wieldy** compliant, controllable, docile, easy, handy, manageable, submissive, tractable
**wife** bride, consort, femme, helpmate, matron, partner, rib, spouse
**wife bound** henpecked
**wife killing** uxoricide
**wife loving** uxorious
**wifely** conjugal, connubial, marital, married, matrimonial, nuptial
**wife of Aaron** Elisheba
**wife of Abner** Rizpah
**wife of Abraham** Hagar, Keturah, Sarah
**wife of Acastus** Hippolyte
**wife of Acrisius** Aganippe, Eurydice
**wife of Aeacus** Endeis
**wife of Aegaeon** Aemilia
**wife of Aeneas** Creusa, Lavinia
**wife of Agamemnon** Clytemnestra
**wife of Agenor** Telephassa
**wife of Ahab** Jezebel
**wife of Ahasuerus** Esther, Vashti
**wife of Ahaz** Abi
**wife of Aleous** Iphimedia
**wife of Alexander** Roxana
**wife of Ali** Fatima
**wife of Amon** Jedidah
**wife of Amram** Jochebed
**wife of Ananias** Sapphira
**wife of baronet** dame
**wife of Bath** Alice
**wife of Boaz** Ruth
**wife of brother** sister-in-law
**wife of Caesar** Calpurnia, Pompeia
**wife of Caleb** Azubah, Jerioth
**wife of Ceyx** Alcyone
**wife of David** Abigail, Ahinoam, Bathsheba, Macaah, Michal
**wife of David Copperfield** Dora
**wife of Edward VII** Alexandra

**wife of Elimelech** Naomi
**wife of Elkana** Hannah
**wife of Esau** Adah, Bashemath, Judith
**wife of Florestan** Leonora
**wife of Geraint** Enid
**wife of Germanicus** Agrippina
**wife of Heber** Jael
**wife of Hector** Andromache
**wife of Hercules** Deianira, Hebe, Mecara
**wife of Herod** Herodias
**wife of Herzon** Abia
**wife of Indian prince** maharani
**wife of Isaac** Rebecca, Rebekah
**wife of Italian marquis** marchesa
**wife of Ithra** Abigail
**wife of Jacob** Leah, Rachel
**wife of Joseph** Asenath, Mary
**wife of Josiah** Hamutal
**wife of Jupiter** Juno
**wife of king** queen
**wife of King Priam of Troy** Hecuba
**wife of Lamech** Adah, Zillah
**wife of Lapidoth** Deborah
**wife of Louis XIII** Anne of Austria
**wife of maharaja** maharanee, maharani
**wife of Mark Antony** Octavia
**wife of marquis** marchioness
**wife of Minos** Pasiphae
**wife of Moses** Zip(p)orah
**wife of Nabal** Abigail
**wife of Nahor** Milcah
**wife of Napoleon** Josephine
**wife of nobleman** peeress
**wife of Oberon** Titania
**wife of Oceanus** Tethys
**wife of Odin** Frigg
**wife of Odysseus** Penelope
**wife of one's uncle** aunt
**wife of Osiris** Isis
**wife of Othello** Desdemona
**wife of Othni** Achsah
**wife of Peleus** Antigone, Thetis
**wife of Perseus** Andromeda
**wife of Pluto** Proserpine
**wife of Poseidon** Amphitrite
**wife of prince** princess
**wife of rajah** ranee, rani
**wife of Saturn** Ops
**wife of Shakespeare** Anne
**wife of Socrates** Xanthippe
**wife of Solomon** Naamah
**wife of sultan** sultana
**wife of Tantalus** Clytia, Dione, Taygete
**wife of tsar** tsarevna, tsarina
**wife of Tyndareus** Leda
**wife of Ulysses** Penelope
**wife of uncle** aunt
**wife of Uriah** Bathsheba
**wife of Wagner** Cosina

**wife of William Shakespeare**  Anne Hathaway
**wife of Zacharias**  Elisabeth
**wife of Zebedee**  Salome
**wife of Zeus**  Hera, Juno, Metis
**wife's allowance**  alimony, maintenance, pin money
**wife's partner**  husband
**wife's property**  dos, dowry
**wife's self-immolation**  suttee
**wig**  hairpiece, merkin, periwig, peruke, switch, toupee
**wig repair**  careen
**wigwam**  te(e)pee, tent, tipi
**wild**  barbaric, capricious, deserted, desolate, feral, fierce, frantic, savage, uncivilised, untamed, wayward
**wild Aboriginal**  warrigal
**wild adventurous prank**  escapade
**wild alder**  goutweed
**wild allspice**  spicebush
**wild and woolly**  careless, reckless, unkempt, unruly
**wild and reckless**  harum-scarum
**wild anger**  fury
**wild animal**  brute, buck, cheetah, impala, leopard, lion, tiger
**wild animal collection**  menagerie, zoo
**wild animal related to dog**  hyaena, jackal, wolf
**wild animal's den**  lair
**wild animal's trail**  slot, spoor, spur, track
**wild antelope**  chamois
**wild apple**  creeper
**wild ass**  kulan(n), onager, quagga
**wild Australian dog**  dingo
**wild Australian horse**  warrigal
**wild banana**  fei
**wild beast's lair**  den
**wild beet**  pifweed
**wild birds**  gallinae
**wild bullock**  scrabdangler
**wild canary**  serin
**wild card**  joker
**wild cat**  eyra, genet, lynx, ocelot, panther
**wild cattle**  gaurs
**wild celery**  smallage
**wild cherry**  gean
**wild cinnamon**  bayberry
**wild confusion**  mayhem, pandemonium
**wild cranberry**  pembina
**wild cut**  slash
**wild disorderly person**  maniac
**wild dog**  dhole, dingo, tanate
**wild donkey**  onager
**wild drake**  duck, mallard
**wild duck**  mallard, scaup, teal, wi(d)geon

**wildebeest**  gnu
**wild enthusiasm**  furore
**wilderness**  chaos, confusion, desert, desolation, jungle, waste, wild
**wilderness expedition**  safari
**wild excitement**  frenzy
**wild-eyed**  frenzied, haggard
**wild feline**  leopard, lion, ocelot, tiger
**wild female buffalo of India**  arnee
**wild flax**  toadflax
**wild flight**  rout, stampede
**wild flower**  bugle, buttercup, campion, cosmos, cowslip, daisy, dandelion, erica, gentian, harebell, primrose, protea, speedwell, violet
**wild folly**  frenzy
**wild fright**  panic, terror
**wild game hunt**  safari
**wild garlic**  moly
**wild ginger**  asarum
**wild girl**  blowze
**wild goat**  ibex, tahr, thar, tur
**wild goose**  barnacle, brant, graylag, greylag, jacobite
**wild-goose chase**  futility
**wild goose's cry**  honk
**wild growing plant**  agrestal
**wild guess**  shot, speculation, stab
**wild Himalayan goat**  bharal, markhor
**wild hog**  bene, boar
**wild honeybee**  dingar
**wild horse**  bronco, brumby, mustang, russar, tarpan, warrigal
**wild hyacinth**  bluebell
**wild Indian dog**  dhole
**wild Indian ox**  gaur
**wild indulgence**  orgy
**wildlife official**  game warden
**wildlife preservation**  nature conservation
**wildlife preserve**  sanctuary
**wildlife ranger**  game ranger
**wildlife sanctuary**  Kruger National Park
**wild lime**  colima
**wildly**  ferociously, fiercely, frantically, freely, natively, naturally, savagely
**wildly cruel**  ferocious
**wildly excited**  frantic
**wildly extravagant**  profligate
**wildly fanciful**  chimerical
**wildly foolish**  lunatic, mad, senseless
**wildly funny**  hysterical
**wildly happy**  ecstatic
**wildly impulsive person**  madcap
**wildly inappropriate**  absurd
**wildly moved**  frantic
**wild male buffalo of India**  arna
**wild marjoram**  oregano, origan
**wild mountain goat**  ibex
**wild mountain sheep**  aoudad, Barbary sheep, moufflon

**wild mustang**  bronco
**wild mustard**  charlock
**wild olive**  oleaster
**wild orchid**  orchis
**wild ox**  anoa, aurochs, banteng, bison, buf(f), gaur, reem, sapi-utan, unicorn, urus, yak
**wild pansy**  heart's-ease, johnny-jump-up
**wild parsley**  keck, lovage
**wild party**  knees-up, orgy, revel
**wild person**  sakai
**wild pig**  boar, peccary
**wild pigeon**  dove
**wild plant**  fern, moss, tare, weed
**wild plum**  islay, sloe
**wild pony**  bronco
**wild prairie horse**  mustang
**wild rage**  fury
**wild region**  desert, heath, waste, wilderness
**wild revelry**  orgy, riot, spree
**wild rice**  zizania
**wild rose bush**  briar, brier
**wild sheep**  aoudad, argali, bighorn, sha, urial
**wild shrub**  gorse
**wild South American feline**  ocelot
**wild swan**  whooper
**wild swine**  boar
**wild thyme**  hillwort
**wild tract of land**  heath
**wild turnip**  navew, swede
**wild uncontrollable emotion**  hysteria
**wild unwanted plant**  weed
**wild vanilla**  liatris
**Wild West bar**  saloon
**Wild West country**  prairie
**Wild West hero**  Butch Cassidy, Wyatt Earp
**Wild West horseman**  cowboy
**Wild West show**  rodeo
**wild yam**  colicroot
**wild yeast**  anamite
**wile**  artifice, craftiness, cunning, device, lure, ploy, slyness
**wilful**  arbitrary, conscious, deliberate, determined, disobedient, dogged, headstrong, inflexible, intentional, irascible, obdurate, obstinate, persistent, perverse, purposeful, restive, self-willed, stubborn, unruly, unyielding, voluntary, willed
**wilful falsehood**  perjury
**wilful fire-starting**  arson
**wilfully**  consciously, deliberately, determinedly, doggedly, inflexibly, intentionally, obstinately, persistently, perversely, purposefully, purposely, stubbornly, voluntarily
**wilfully damage**  vandalise

**wilfully disregard** ignore
**wilful utterance of false statement while on oath** perjury
**will** backbone, behest, bequeath, choice, choose, consent, decision, decree, demise, desire, determination, direct, elect, faculty, fancy, inclination, intention, option, prerogative, shall, testament, wish
**will be** future
**willing** agreeable, amenable, desirous, eager, favourable, game, pleased, prepared, ready
**willing and able** ready, volens et valens (L)
**willing horse** trier, volunteer
**willingly** agreeably, amenably, cheerfully, choice, consentingly, contently, desirously, eagerly, enthusiastically, favourably, freely, gamely, gladly, happily, heartily, readily, voluntarily, willingly
**willingness** agreeableness, agreement, amenableness, assent, consent, desire, desirousness, eagerness, enthusiasm, favour, gameness, happiness, inclination, readiness, volition
**willingness to deceive** deceit(fulness)
**willing to agree** agreeable
**willing to do what pleases others** complaisant
**willing to help** accommodating
**willing to obey** obedient
**willing to overlook faults** indulgent
**willing to submit** meek, submissive, unresisting
**willing to take risks** (ad)venturous, venturesome
**will inheritor** devisee
**will maker** devisor, testator
**will not** won't
**will-o'-the-wisp** corposant, firedrake, foxfire, glow-worm, (ignis) fatuus, wildfire
**willow** osier, salix, sallow, tree
**willow basket** prickle
**willow extract** salicin
**willow green** reseda
**willow plantation** holt, salicetum
**willow rod** osier
**willow shoot** osier, sallow
**willow twig** osier, wicker, withe, withy
**willowy** fit, flexible, lean, narrow, shapely, sleek, slender, slight, slim, streamlined, trim
**willpower** control, firmness, resolution, strength
**will supplement** codicil
**wilt** abate, decay, decline, dim, disappear, disperse, dissolve, droop, dwindle, ebb, end, fade, fail, faint, fall, languish, lapse, pass, perish, pine, sag, shrivel, sink, slump, succumb, vanish, wane, weaken, weary, wither
**wilting** decaying, declining, decreasing, dimming, disappearing, dissolving, drying, dwindling, dying, ebbing, ending, fading, failing, flagging, lapsing, passing, sinking, tiring, vanishing, waning, withering
**wily** adroit, age, ancient, antediluvian, artful, astute, cag(e)y, crafty, crooked, cunning, decayed, deceitful, deceptive, dilapidated, dishonest, elderly, expected, false, familiar, fly, former, foxy, guileful, intelligent, intriguing, knowing, olden, passé, past, perfidious, primitive, scheming, sensible, shifty, shrewd, slippery, sly, smooth, subtle, thoughtful, treacherous, tricky, two-faced, underhand(ed)
**wily stratagem** ploy
**Wimbledon game** tennis
**wimple** fold, gorget, headdress, headgear, plait, ripple, veil
**win** accomplish, achieve, acquire, attain, catch, collect, conquer, conquest, earn, entice, gain, get, net, obtain, overcome, prevail, procure, profit, receive, secure, succeed, success, triumph, victorious, victory
**win advantage over** best
**win all the tricks from** capot
**win at chess** checkmate
**win back** recoup, recover
**wince** blench, cower, cringe, flinch, quail, recoil, shrink, start
**wind** breeze, curve, easterly, loop, meander, northerly, snake, southerly, twine, twist, westerly
**wind about** meander
**wind and weather permitting** perhaps, possibly
**wind around** roll, twine, twist
**wind bandage round** swaddle
**wind blast** flaw, gust
**windblown spray** fume, scud
**wind-borne** aeolian
**windcheater** anorak, jacket, windjammer
**wind colic** bloat
**wind-deposited earth** loess
**wind down** decline, diminish, dwindle, lessen, reduce, relax, slacken, subside, unwind
**wind-driven clouds** scud
**wind-driven ship** sail-borne
**win decisively** trounce
**windfall** acquisition, blessing, bonanza, boon, find, gain, gift, godsend, hit, inheritance, jackpot, legacy, receiving, strike, treasure-trove, trouvaille (F), winning
**windflower** anemone
**wind gauge** anemograph, anemometer, vane, ventometer
**wind gust** flurry, flaw
**wind indicator** anemometer, cone, sleeve, sock, stocking, vane
**windiness** breeziness, flatulence, gustiness, storminess, verbosity
**winding** anfractuous, bent, bending, circuitous, coiling, convoluted, convolution, crooked, curling, curve, curving, flexuous, furling, indirect, looping, meander(ing), reeling, rolling, roundabout, serpentine, sinuous, spiral(ling), spooling, tortuous, turn(ing), twining, twist(ing), undulation, wreathing
**winding river** Ess
**winding sheet** shroud
**winding staircase** caracol(e)
**winding stair pillar** newel
**wind in rings** coil
**wind instrument** accordion, alp(en)horn, althorn, aulos, bagpipe, bassoon, bugle, clarin(et), clarion, cornet, flageolet, flute, horn, musette, oboe, ocarina, organ, panpipe, pennywhistle, recorder, reed, saxhorn, saxophone, syrinx, trombone, trumpet, tuba, woodwind
**wind into a ball** clew
**wind into a hank** skein
**wind into a spiral** coil
**windjammer** (sailing) ship, schooner, windcheater
**windlass** artifice, capstan, crab, drawbeam, fearn, hoist, manoeuvre, tackle, winch, windas, windle
**windless** balmy, calm, mild, pacific, peaceful, placid, quiet, restful, serene, smooth, still, tranquil
**windless ship** becalmed
**wind measure** anemometer, ventometer
**windmill arm** vane
**windmill part** arm
**wind of Australia** buster
**wind off** unwind
**wind of France** bise
**wind of Spanish coast** solano
**window** aperture, camouflage, dormer, eye, fanlight, loop, opening, oriel, peeper, porthole, skylight, ventilator
**window above a door** transom
**window box** planter
**window box flower** geranium
**window built out** bay window
**window casing** frame
**window cement** putty

**window compartment** pane
**window cover** blind, screen, shutter, stormsash
**window decorator** trimmer
**window divider** mullion
**window drape fastener** tieback
**window drapery** curtain
**window dressing** facade, falsefront, trim
**window frame** casement, casing, reveal, sash
**window glass** light, pane, sheet
**window groove to hold glass** fillister
**window in roof** dormer, skylight
**window in ship's cabin** porthole
**window lead** came
**window ledge** cill, sill
**window lowering device** sash cord
**window of two lights** couplet
**window over a door** transom
**window oyster** copis
**window pane** glass, light, sheet
**window panel** pane
**window part** pane, sash, sill
**window plant** mesembryanthemum
**window-setter** glazier
**window shelf** sill
**window strip** came
**window that opens on hinges** casement
**window weight** mouse
**windpipe** airpipe, airway, gullet, trachea, weasand
**wind player** piper
**windrose** poppy
**wind sail** badgir
**wind science** anemology
**windscreen cleaner** squeegee, wiper
**wind sock** cone, sleeve
**wind sound** moan, sigh, sob, sough, whisper, whistle
**wind speed meter** anemometer
**wind-speed unit** knot
**wind spirally** coil
**wind squall** gust
**wind storm** gale, hurricane, tempest
**wind thread on bobbin** quill
**wind together** coil, plait, twist
**wind toy** kite
**wind up** close, conclude, end, excite, finalise, finish, furl, liquidate, outcome, result, settle, terminate
**wind vane** pointer, weathercock
**wind vibrator** reed
**windward** alee, exposed
**Windward Island** Dominica, Grenada, Martinique
**windy** apprehensive, attendant, blowing, blowy, blustery, boastful, boisterous, bragging, diffuse, drafty, empty, everywhere, flatulent, frightened, gusty, inflated, nervous, present, scared, timid, ubiquitous, verbose, windswept, wordy
**Windy City** Chicago
**wine** asti, canary, cardinal, carmine, catawba, champagne, cherry, chianti, claret, coral, crimson, hock, madeira, muscat, oeno-, port, rosé, ruby, scarlet, sherry, tokay, vermilion, vin (F), vino (I)
**wine and honey drink** mulse, oenomel
**wine and spice drink** glühwein (G), negus, sangaree, sangria (Sp)
**wine barrel** vat
**wine bottle** carafe, decanter, flask, jeroboam, magnum
**wine-bottle size** baby, balthasar, jeroboam, magnum, Methuselah, nebuchadnezzar, nip, rehoboam, Salmanazar
**wine cabinet** cellaret
**wine cask** pipe, vat
**wine cellar** buttery
**wine connoisseur** oenophile
**wine connoisseur's pride** cellar
**wine container** barrel, carafe, cask, decanter, flask
**wine cup** amula, chalice, goblet
**wine dealer** vintner
**wine district in California** Napa
**wine district in France** Alsace, Bordeaux, Burgundy, Champagne, Médoc
**wine district in South Africa** Constantia, Franschhoek, Paarl, Robertson, Stellenbosch
**wine dregs** vinasse
**wine fermentation** cuvage
**wine-flask** carafe
**wine flavour** mull, seve
**wine flavoured with aromatic herbs** vermouth
**wine fruit** grape
**wine funnel** tundish
**wine glass** flute, rummer, tulip
**wine grape refuse** marc
**wine grower** viniculturist, viticulturist
**wine growing** viniculture, viticulture
**wine house** bar, tavern
**wine jug** carafe
**wine-making** vinification
**wine-making fruit** grape
**wine measure** aam, bottle, orna, orne, pipe
**wine merchant** vintner
**wine of a given year** vintage
**wine room** cellar
**wine sediment** lees
**wine seller** vintner
**wine-serving bottle** decanter
**wine store** bodega (Sp), cellar
**wine storeroom** buttery, cellar
**wine study** oenology
**wine town in Italy** Asti
**wine used locally** vin de pays
**wine valley** Barossa, Hex River, Napa, Sonoma
**wine vessel** cask, chalice, cuve, flask, flute, magnum, olpe, tun, vat
**wine waiter** sommelier
**wing** adjunct, aile (F), ala, alula, annex, arm, branch, circle, clip, clique, el, extension, fleet, fly, glide, hasten, limb, penna, pennon, pinion, pinna, plumage, section, set, soar, wound
**winged** alar, alate(d), elevated, exalted, expeditious, flew, hurried, inspired, noble, pennate, pterygoid, quick, sublime, swift, wing-like
**winged dragon of European mythology** wivern, wyvern
**winged figure** (e)idolon
**winged fruit** samara
**winged goddess of the dawn** Eos
**winged hat of Mercury** petasus
**winged horse** Pegasus
**winged insect** bee, cicada, fly, gnat, mosquito, moth, wasp
**winged monster of Greek myth** Harpy
**winged sandals** talaria
**winged seed of the horseradish tree** ben
**winged serpent** dragon
**winged shoes of Hermes** talaria
**winged steed** Pegasus
**wing feather** pinion, tertial
**wing flap** aileron
**wing footed animal** aliped
**wing it** extemporise, improvise
**wingless** apteral, apterous, dealated
**wingless bird** apteryx, kiwi, moa
**wingless insect** apterous, louse
**wingless jumping insect** flea
**winglike** alar(y), alate, pteric, pteroid
**winglike organ** ptere
**winglike part** ala
**wing membrane of bat** patagium
**wing movement** beat, flap, flutter
**wing nut** thumbnut
**wing of beetle** tegman, tegmina
**wing of building** annex, el(l)
**wing of car** fender
**wing of church** aisle, transept
**wing of triptych** volet
**wing-shaped** alar(y), alate, aliform
**wingspread** width
**wing tuft** alula
**win in competition** gain
**wink** bat, bit, blink, close, flash, flutter, fulgurate, gleam, glimmer(ing), glint, glisten, glitter, hint, instant, jot, moment, nictitate, particle, scintillate, second, shine, sign(al), sparkle, twinkle, whit

**wink at** allow, condone, disregard, ignore, overlook, tolerate, turnaway
**wink eyes rapidly** flutter
**winkle out** dislodge, extract, extricate
**winless racehorse** maiden
**winner** ace, champ(ion), conqueror, first, hero, master, victor
**winning** achieving, acquiring, alluring, amiable, bewitching, captivating, charming, conquering, delightful, disarming, earning, endearing, engaging, fetching, lovely, overcoming, pleasing, prevailing, procuring, receiving, succeeding, sweet, triumphing, victorious
**winning card** trump
**winning numbers** tern
**winning of all tricks at cards** vole
**winning position** first
**winning shot** ace
**winning ways** cajolery, caressiveness
**winnow** bolt, choose, divide, filter, part, pick, riddle, select, separate, sieve, sift, straun
**winnowing machine** fan
**win of all tricks in bridge** slam
**win of all tricks in piquet** capot
**win out** prevail, succeed
**win over** allure, attract, carry, charm, convert, convince, defeat, disarm, incline, influence, lead, persuade, predispose, sway
**win over from hostility** conciliate, reconcile
**win over with a gift** bribe
**winsome** affable, agreeable, amiable, appealing, attractive, benign, bewitching, bonny, captivating, charming, cheerful, cute, delightful, elegant, engaging, enjoyable, exquisite, fair, fetching, friendly, genial, graceful, handsome, kind(ly), likable, lovable, lovely, nice, obliging, pleasant, pleasing, pretty, refined, seductive, sociable, sweet, sympathetic, winning
**winter cabbage** savoy
**winter cap** tuque
**winter coaster** sled
**winter deluge** snow(storm)
**winter driving hazard** ice, snow
**winter fodder** hay
**winter ground cover** snow
**winter jacket with hood** anorak
**winter precipitation** snow
**winter road hazard** ice
**winter sight** icicle
**winter sleep** hibernation
**winter sport** rugby, skating, skiing, soccer
**winter sports person** skier
**winter toy** sled

**winter vehicle** sled(ge), sleigh, snowplow, toboggan
**winter wind in Europe** mistral
**win the goodwill of** conciliate
**win through** accomplish, achieve, gain, triumph
**win through effort** deserve, earn
**wintry** bleak, boreal, brumal, brumous, cheerless, chilly, cold, desolate, dismal, dreary, foggy, freezing, harsh, hiemal, hyemal, icy, snowy, winterbound
**wintry flakes** snow
**wintry weather** sleet
**win without playing** bye
**winy** vinous
**wipe** clean(se), dry, dust, mop, rub, scour, scrub, smooth, stroke, swab, swipe
**wipe out** abolish, annihilate, delete, demolish, destroy, efface, eliminate, eradicate, erase, expunge, exterminate, extinguish, massacre, obliterate, raze, vanquish
**wiping out** abolition, extirpation
**wire** bind, cable, circuit, filament, inform, install, message, metal, send, telegram, telegraph
**wire coil** spring
**wire cutting tool** pliers
**wire device for straightening teeth** brace
**wire enclosure** cage, camp
**wire for holding papers in order** file
**wire-haired dog** terrier
**wire in electric fire** element
**wire in light bulb** filament
**wireless** radio
**wireless antenna** aerial
**wireless inventor** Marconi
**wireless message** aerogram
**wireless receiving set** radio
**wireless telegram** marconigram
**wire loop for removing tumours and polyps** snare
**wire measure** gauge, mil, stone
**wire of electrical cord** flex
**wire pen** cage
**wire rope** cable
**wire spiral** spring
**wire-toothed brush** card
**wirewalker** funambulist
**wiry** bristly, hardened, lank, powerful, prickly, rigid, spare, stiff, strong, stubby, thorny, tough
**wiry grass** bent
**wisdom** acumen, astuteness, attainment, brains, education, erudition, experience, foresight, gnosis, intelligence, knowledge, learning, lore, perspicuity, piety, rationality, sagacity, sageness,

sagesse (F), sapience, scholarship, sense, shrewdness, soundness, understanding, wit
**wisdom after the event** hindsight
**wisdom book** Proverbs
**wisdom personified** Solomon
**wisdom tooth** molar
**wise** balanced, capable, competent, educated, erudite, intelligent, judicious, knowledgeable, learned, penetrating, sagacious, sage, sapient, sensible, shrewd, smart
**wiseacre** gotham, know-all, sage, solonist, wisehead, wiseling
**wise advisor** mentor
**wise and good judgement** wisdom
**wise answer** oracle, prophecy
**wise bird** owl
**wise counsellor** mentor, Nestor
**wisecrack** barb, gag, jest, jibe, joke, pun, quip, remark, wit(ticism)
**wise female advisor** Ageria
**wise guy** know-all, smarty, wiseacre, witling
**wise king of Israel** Solomon
**wise king of Pylos** Nestor
**wisely** cleverly, discerningly, eruditely, informedly, intelligently, judiciously, knowingly, perceptively, reasonably, sagaciously, sagely, sapiently, sensibly, soundly
**wise man** adviser, advisor, genius, master, mentor, Nestor, philosopher, sage, seer, Solomon, thinker
**wise man's gift** frankincense, gold, myrrh
**wise men** magi, sages
**wise mysterious utterance** oracle
**wisent** aurocks, bison
**wise old bird** owl
**wise old man** Nestor
**wise ruler** Solomon
**wise saying** adage, oracle
**wise scholar** savant
**wish** aspire, command, covet, crave, desiderate, desire, hanker, hope, longing, request, want, yearning
**wishbone** furculum
**wish evil upon** curse
**wish for** bid, covet, crave, desire, fancy, long, relish, want, yearn
**wish for wrongly** covet
**wishful** ambitious, anticipative, aspiring, covetous, desirous, dissatisfied, eager, expectant, hopeful, illogical, liking, longing, optimistic, unsatisfied, yearning
**wish fulfilment** dream, fantasy, gratification
**wishful thinking** belief, credulity, desire
**wish happiness** bless
**wishing** hoping

**wishing ill to others** malevolent
**wish joy to** felicitate
**wish otherwise** regret
**wish someone a pleasant journey** bon voyage (F)
**wisp** flock, shred
**wisp of hair** tate (Sc)
**wisp of smoke** floc
**wispy** deficient, meagre, scanty, scarce, scattered, skimpy, sparse, thin
**wispy cloud** cirrus
**wistful** dreaming, forlorn, longing, mournful, musing, nostalgic, pensive, sad, yearning
**wistful sound** sigh
**wit** acuity, aptness, banter, brains, caricature, cleverness, comic, esprit, facetiousness, fun(niness), humour, ingenuity, insight, intellect, intelligence, irony, jocularity, levity, mind, parody, piquancy, sagacity, sarcasm, satire, savvy, saying, sense, shrewdness, understanding, wag(gery), wisdom, wisecrack, witticism, wordplay
**witch** battle-ax, beldam(e), crone, enchantress, fishwife, fortune teller, hag, hellcat, hex, lamia, magician, medium, nag, occultist, ogress, seer, sibyl, sorceress, vixen
**witchcraft** allure, conjuration, deviltry, diabolism, gramarye, incantation, magic, magnetism, necromancy, obeah, occultism, pishogue, psychomancy, Satanism, sorcery, sortilage, spellbinding, theurgy, voodoo, witchery, wizardry
**witchcraft charm** obeah, obi
**witchcraft connected with devils** diablerie
**witch doctor** bocor, bokor, goofer, guffer, medicine man, sangoma, shaman, witchman, wizard
**witches' broom** hexenbesen, stagheap
**witches' familiar** cat, toad
**witches' group** coven
**witch-hunt** bewitch, inquisition
**witch-hunt victim** dissenter
**witching time** midnight
**witch's bane plant** haemony
**witch's brew** concoction, potion
**witch's pot** cauldron
**witch's stick** broom, wand
**witch's transport** broom
**with** along, co-, cum (L), de (Sp), mit (G), near, nearness, per (L), syn-, wi (Sc)
**with a chip on one's shoulder** bitter, resentful
**with addition of** plus
**with a different pitch** enharmonically

**with advancing motion** onward
**with affection** con amore (I)
**with a grain of salt** cum grano salis (L)
**with a heavy hand** awkwardly, severely, tyrannically
**with a high hand** arrogantly, dictatorially, domineeringly, presumptuously
**withal** also, likewise
**with a leg on either side** astride
**with a lot of din** noisily
**with an advancing motion** onward
**with an hourglass figure** slender, snake-hipped
**with animation** con spirito (I)
**with a pinch of salt** cynically, disbelievingly, doubtfully, sceptically
**with a plump innocent face** cherubic
**with a side glance** askance, askant
**with a vengeance** fiercely, forcefully, furiously, vehemently, violently, wildly
**with avoidance or detachment** aloof
**with bated breath** breathless
**with blind sac** caecum
**with both feet on the ground** sensibly
**with broad level surface** flat
**with certainty** surely
**with clean habits** cleanly
**with clean hands** honestly
**with compassion** tenderly
**with consummate ease** facilely
**with daring** audaciously
**with dash of spirit added** laced
**with dexterity** adroitly
**with difficulty** edgewise, hardly
**with disordered mind** mad
**withdraw** abdicate, abduce, abjure, abolish, annul, detract, disclaim, disengage, ebb, extract, nullify, recall, recant, recede, recoil, remove, reneg(u)e, resign, retire, retract, retreat, retrocede, reverse, revoke, secede, seclude, subtract, void, yield
**withdrawal** abdication, congé, departure, embarkation, escape, evacuation, exit, exodus, extraction, leave, recall, recession, removal, retirement, retreat, separation, yielding
**withdrawal from** abandonment, evacuation
**withdrawal of labour** strike
**withdrawal's priority** deposit
**withdraw formally** recede
**withdraw from** abandon, evacuate, quit
**withdraw from contest** scratch
**withdraw from work** resign, retire
**withdraw into solitude** seclude
**withdrawn** abstracted, aloof, apart, departed, detached, disavowed, disclaimed, disengaged, distant, extracted, gone, introverted, left, morose, quiet, recalled, removed, reserved, retired, retiring, seceded, secluded, shy, silent, taciturn, unsaid
**withdrawn in thought** abstracted
**withdraw statement** retract
**withdrew formally from union** seceded
**with due alteration of details** mutatis mutandis (L)
**with each other** together
**wither** atrophy, contract, decay, desiccate, die, droop, dry, dwindle, fade, fail, perish, pucker, sag, sear, sere, shrink, shrivel, wane, wilt, wrinkle
**wither away** decrease, die, disappear, dwindle, shrink, shrivel, wilt
**withered** abashed, blasted, blighted, decayed, declined, disintegrated, dried, drooped, faded, languished, mortified, perished, sere, shamed, shrank, shrunk, snubbed, waned, wasted, wilted
**withered old woman** crone
**withering** contemptuous, deadly, death-dealing, destructive, devastating, humiliating, mortifying, scathing, scornful, searing, snubbing, wilting, wounding
**withershins** anticlockwise, counterclockwise, widdershins
**with everything included** altogether
**with everything included in the price** all-in
**with eyes bandaged** blindfolded
**with feeling** affettuoso
**with fervour** zeloso (I)
**with force** amain
**with full authority** pleno jure (L)
**with full force** amain, eagerly
**with full hips** haunchy
**with full powers** plenipotentiary
**with God** Deo (L)
**with good will** de bonne grâce (F)
**with grace** adagio
**with gradual decrease in loudness** diminuendo
**with gradual increase in loudness** crescendo
**with great ability** ably
**with great strength** amain
**with grief** con dolore (It)
**with guns** armed
**with gusto** energetically
**with hands on hips** akimbo
**withhold** abnegate, arrest, bury, contain, control, deny, detain, forbid, interdict, keep, repress, restrain, screen, secrete, shroud, suppress, veil
**withhold business from** boycott

**withhold consent** decline, refuse
**withhold food from** starve
**within** behind, enclosed, ento-, in(doors), inner, inside, interior(ly), internally, into, intra, inwardly, scope
**within a building** indoors
**within a muscle** intramuscular
**within a short distance** near
**within close range** near
**with increasing slowness** allargando
**within doors** at home, in
**within earshot** audible
**within given area** locally
**within one nation** intranational
**within one's grasp** achievable
**within one's reach** available, handy
**within reach** attainable
**within reason** acceptable, justifiable, proper, rational, reasonable, sensible
**within restrictions** limited
**with integrity** honestly
**within the bounds of possibility** imaginable
**within the eyeball** intraocular
**within the law** legal
**within the moon's orbit** sublunary
**within the powers** intra vires (L)
**within these four walls** confidentially, privately
**within the walls** intramural, intra muros (L)
**within the womb** intrauterine
**within walking distance** close(by), locally, nearby
**within which** wherein
**with labour and honour** labore et honore (L)
**with legal force** validly
**with legs apart** astride
**with light quick steps** pit-a-pat
**with little margin** narrow, near
**with little noise** quiet
**with loud voice** aloud
**with love** con amore (I)
**with many curves** sinuous
**with maturity** ripely
**with might** amain
**with might and main** energetically, forcefully, intensely, mightily, powerfully, robustly, staunchly, vigorously
**with milk** au lait
**with mind fixed** intent
**with mixed feelings** ambivalent
**with no appointed date** sine die (L)
**with nobody disagreeing** nemine contradicente (L), unanimously
**with no one to turn to** friendless
**with one end raised** atilt
**with one's back to the wall** hard-pressed
**with one's family** en famille (F)

**with one's heart in one's mouth** apprehensively, fearfully
**with one's mental faculties awake** conscious
**with one's own hand** manu propria (L)
**with open arms** cordially, friendly, graciously, warmly
**without** away, beyond, excluding, in-, lacking, less, minus, ohne (G), outside, past, requiring, sans (F), sine
**without a backbone** invertebrate
**without a break** incessantly, nonstop, persistently
**without accent** atonic
**without a cent** destitute, distressed, impecunious, indigent, moneyless, needy, penniless, poverty-stricken, sans sou (F)
**without a centre** acentric
**without a dad** fatherless
**without a doubt** absolutely, naturally, really
**without affectation** natural
**without a friend in the world** friendless
**without a heart** acardiac
**without aim or purpose** random
**without a leg to stand on** helpless, powerless
**without a name** anonymous
**without an equal** incomparable
**without an ounce of fat** wiry
**without anxiety** careless
**without any money** broke
**without anyone else** independently, personally
**without any other** alone
**without ardour** cold
**without artfulness** ingenuous, unsophisticated
**without a saddle** bareback
**without a sense of reason** insensate
**without a sound** silent
**without assistance** single-handed, unaided
**without audience** unheard
**without beginning or end** eternal
**without being put into words** tacitly
**without bend** straight
**without bodily sensation** insensate, numbness
**without bracts** ebracteate
**without centre** acentric
**without ceremony** informal
**without change of pitch** monotone
**without character** null
**without charge** complimentary, free, gratis
**without circumlocution** sans phrase (F)
**without clothes** naked, nude
**without colour** achromatic, white

**without columns** astylar
**without companions** lone, solitary
**without company** alone, lonely
**without compassion** heartless, remorseless, ruthless
**without complaints** content, happy, snug
**without concealment** frankly, openly, publicly
**without consideration** regardless
**without cost** free, gratis
**without cover** bare, open
**without culture** illiberal
**without current** stagnant
**without decorum** undignified
**without deduction** clear
**without defect** correct
**without delay** directly, forthwith, immediate(ly), instant, now
**without depth** facile, superficial
**without difficulty** easily, readily
**without digression** ad rem (L)
**without discomfort** painless
**without dissent** unanimous
**without doubt** certainly, sine dubio (L), yes
**without duties or office** sine cura (L)
**without ease or grace** gauche
**without effort** easily
**without elevation** flat
**without emotion** impassive
**without end** ad infinitum, bottomless, ceaseless, endless(ly), eternal, ever, infinite
**without energy** atony, listless, weak
**without equal** matchless, peerless, unequalled, unexcelled, unique
**without error** accurate, correct, precise
**without exception** always, strict
**without external excitement** spontaneous, voluntary
**without fail** à coup sûr (F), conscientiously, constantly, punctually, religiously
**without family** lorn
**without fat** lean
**without faults** good
**without fear** brave, fearless
**without fear and without blame** sans peur et sans reproche (F)
**without fear or favour** impartial
**without feeling** callous, insensitive, numb
**without feet** apod
**without fever** afebrile, apyretic
**without fingers or toes** adactylous
**without flavour** insipid, tasteless
**without fluctuating** consistent
**without foliage** leafless
**without foresight** blind
**without foundation** baseless
**without friends** lorn

**without funds** moneyless, penniless, penurious
**without gender** asexual, it
**without guile** above board, artless
**without guilt** innocent
**without hair** bald
**without harm or loss** scot-free
**without haste** easily, leisurely, slowly, unhurriedly
**without help** single-handed, unassisted
**without hesitation** readily
**without humour** mirthless
**without hurry** leisurely
**without hurt** painless
**without identity** faceless
**without independence** servile, slavish
**without inherent power of action** inert
**without injury** scatheless
**without interruption** endless
**without interval** continuous
**without joint** acondylose
**without large plants** treeless
**without life** amort, dead
**without light** black, dark
**without limit** ad infinitum (L)
**without limitations** wholly
**without limits of duration** ageless
**without lips** achilous
**without lustre** dull, matt
**without luxury** austere
**without marked qualities** neutral
**without marks** blank, clear
**without mate** odd
**without material existence** incorporeal
**without meaning** purposeless
**without means of communication** incommunicado (Sp)
**without merit** worthless
**without moisture** dry
**without moral stain** sinless
**without motive** groundless, wanton
**without necessities** needy
**without noise** calm, quiet, still
**without number** incalculable, infinite, innumerable, many, myriad, untold
**without object** aimless
**without offence to modesty** salvo pudore (L)
**without offspring** sine prole (L)
**without omission** inclusive
**without parents** orphan
**without pattern** plain
**without pause** immediately
**without pigment** achronic, albino
**without pity** ruthless
**without power** powerless
**without precedent** unheard of
**without prejudice** salvo jure (L), sine praejudicio (L)
**without preparation** ad lib, extempore, impromptu, offhand, spontaneously
**without preparation** impulsive, offhand, unprepared
**without previous thought** offhand
**without price** cherished, precious, prized, treasured
**without prior warning** unawares
**without punishment** scot-free
**without purpose** adrift, aimless, idle, idly
**without rays** abactinal
**without real worth** vain
**without reason** insensate, motiveless
**without refinement** coarse
**without religious faith** faithless
**without reservation** implicitly, outright, unconditionally, unreservedly
**without reserve** brusquely, candidly, directly, explicitly, frankly, freely, outspokenly, plainly, tactlessly
**without resistance** inert
**without resources** destitute
**without restraint** ad lib, freely
**without restriction** unreservedly
**without result** blank
**without rhyme** blank, erratically, fancifully
**without sensation** numb
**without sense** pointless
**without sensibility** insensate
**without sepals** asepalous
**without settled home** vagabond, vagrant
**without sex** asexual
**without shelf** ledgeless
**without shelter** homeless
**without shoes** barefooted
**without showing reluctance** readily, willingly
**without sight** blind
**without skin** apellous
**without small leaves below calyx** bractless
**without sound** asonant, dumb, mute, noiseless, silent, toneless
**without speech** aphasic, dumb, mute, silent
**without stress** atonic
**without striking a blow** easily, effortlessly
**without strings** unconditional
**without surface movement** still
**without teeth** edentate, edentulous, gummy, toothless
**without thinking** impetuously
**without thought** mechanical
**without ties** friendless
**without title** nameless
**without veins** avenous
**without warmth** tepid
**without warning** sudden, unexpected
**without weapons** unarmed
**without will or energy** limp
**without work** idle
**without yeast** unleavened
**with passion** appassionato
**with pleasure** gladly, happily
**with praise** cum laude
**with privilege** cum privilegio (L)
**with projecting jaws** prognathous
**with reason** accordingly, justifiably, logically, properly, rightly
**with reference** about, re
**with reference to** apropos, concerning, re(garding)
**with regard to** re
**with reservation** cum grano salis (L)
**with reservations** limited, provisional
**with rigour** arduously
**with same heat** isotherm
**with some allowance** cum grano salis (L)
**with spirit** con spirito (I)
**withstand** bar, bear, brave, check, combat, confront, contest, continue, defy, dispute, endure, experience, face, fight, hinder, impede, last, obstruct, offer, oppose, persevere, persist, prevent, repel, resist, stand, strive, struggle, suffer, support, survive, sustain, thwart, tolerate, undergo
**withstand use** wear
**with stiff joints** arthritic
**with stronger reason** a fortiori
**with the** au (F)
**with the addition** plus
**with the consent of** pace (L)
**with the deduction of** less, minus
**with the desired outcome** successfully
**with the exception of** but
**with the eyes covered** blindfold
**with the favour of God** Deo favente (L)
**with the margin notched** emarginate
**with the mouth wide open** agape
**with the order of terms changed** vice versa
**with the stern first** astern
**with this** herewith
**with three axes** triaxon
**with three electrodes** triode
**with three leaves** trifoliate
**with three ribs** tricostate
**with toes** toed
**with toothed edge** serrated
**with toothlike notches** dentate
**with two foci** bifocal
**with two meanings** ambiguous
**with two poles** dipolar
**with two sides** bilateral
**with understanding** emphatically, insight
**with vigour** actively, dynamically, energetically
**with water all round** enisled

**with weak vision** dim-eyed
**with what** wherewith
**with yet stronger reason** a fortiori
**witless** absurd, brainless, crazy, dense, doltish, dull, fatuous, foolish, idiotic, imbecilic, inane, inept, ludicrous, mindless, senseless, silly, stupid, thoughtless, unintelligent
**witless chatter** blether, gab, gabble, prattle, twaddle
**witness** assertion, attest(ant), beholder, bystander, certify, data, depose, endorse, evidence, eyewitness, facts, observe(r), onlooker, passer-by, see, spectator, statement, swear, testifier, testify, testimony, view(er), vouch, warrant, watch(er)
**witnessing clause of a writ** teste
**witness place in court** stand
**wits** acumen, astuteness, banters, brains, cleverness, comprehensions, cunning, esprit, faculties, humours, ingenuity, intellect, intelligence, judg(e)ment, minds, nous, reason, sense(s), understanding
**witticism** badinage, banter, barb, epigram, frolic, fun, gibe, hoax, jab, jape, jest, joke, josh, lark, mot, play, pleasantry, poke, prank, pun, quip, quirk, repartee, retort, sally, sport, (wise)crack, yarn
**wittiness** cleverness, drollness, facetiousness, fancifulness, funniness, gayness, humorousness, ingeniousness, liveliness, piquantness, waggishness, whimsicalness
**wittingly** deliberately, intending, intentionally, knowingly, purposely
**witty** amusing, bright, clever, comic, epigrammatic, facetious, farcical, funny, gay, humorous, ingenious, jocular, jolly, mirthful, original, piquant, punster, quick, salty, scintillating, sharp, smart, wag(gish), whimsical
**witty comment** jeu d'esprit (F)
**witty exchange** repartee
**witty person** comic, wag, wit
**witty poem** epigram
**witty remark** crack, epigram, jest, mot, one-liner, quip, sally, witticism
**witty remarks** facetiae, pleasantries, witticisms
**witty reply** mot, quip, repartee, retort
**witty retort** knack, quip, repartee, zinger
**witty saying** mot
**wizard** augur, charmer, clairvoyant, conjurer, diabolist, dowser, enchanter, genius, geomancer, mage, magician, magus, necromancer, occultist, oracle, pundit, seer, soothsayer, sorcerer, theurgist, voodoo(ist), warlock, witch
**wizardly** magical
**wizened** dehydrated, desiccated, dry, faded, sere, shriveled, shrunken, wilted, withered, wrinkled
**wobble** bounce, caper, falter, flicker, fluctuate, hesitate, lurch, prance, quake, quiver, reel, seesaw, shake, skip, stagger, sway, teeter, totter, tremble, twitch, undulate, vacillate, vary, vibrate, wave(r), weave
**wobbly** hesitantly, shaky, teetering, trembling, unstable, unsteady, unsure, wavering
**wobbly dessert** jelly
**wobbly walker** waddler
**woe** adversity, affliction, agony, alas, anguish, anxiety, bane, burden, calamities, cares, concern, curse, depression, despair, disaster, distress, dole, gloom, grief, hardship, ill, melancholy, misery, pain, problems, remorse, sadness, sorrow, suffering, trials, tribulation, troubles, unhappiness, vexation, worry, wretchedness
**woebegone** afflicted, cheerless, dejected, desolate, despairing, discouraged, dismal, doleful, down, forlorn, joyless, low-spirited, mean, melancholic, miserable, sad, woeful, worried, wretched
**woeful** awful, catastrophic, cruel, disastrous, disgraceful, distressing, lamentable, piteous, pitiful, rueful, sad, sorrowful, tragic, wretched
**woe is me** alas
**woken** activated, animated, arisen, aroused, astir, awakened, bestirred, enlivened, excited, fired, galvanised, kindled, provoked, quickened, roused, stimulated, stirred
**wolf** bolt, bolt, consume, coyote, cram, devour, dog, eat, feed, glut, gobble, gorge, gulp, guzzle, lupus, overeat, philanderer, quaff, rake, stuff, swallow
**wolf at the door** poverty
**wolffish** barbel, catfish
**wolf in sheep's clothing** deceiver, hypocrite, pharisee, pretender
**wolfish** lupine
**wolflike dog** Alsatian
**wolfram** tungsten
**wolf's-bane** aconite, monkshood
**wolf's home** lair
**wolf spider** lycosid, tarantula
**woman** dame, female, femme (F), gyne, lady, ma'am, madam, Miss, Mrs, Ms, she, spouse, wench
**woman adviser** Egeria
**woman capable of using black magic** witch
**woman comedian** comedienne
**woman emperor** empress
**woman employed to clean a house** charwoman
**woman employed to manage household** housekeeper
**woman employed to sell goods** saleswoman
**woman engaged to be married** fiancée
**woman family ruler** matriarch
**woman from rib** Eve
**woman getting married** bride
**woman hater** misanthrope, misogyne, misogynist
**woman homosexual** dike, dyke, lesbian, tribade
**womanhood** feminity, feminineness, femininity, muliebrity, wifehood, wifeliness, womankind, womanliness
**woman in charge of nurses in hospital** matron
**woman in white** nurse
**woman is changeable** donna è mobile (I)
**womanise** philander
**womaniser** debauchee, lecher, letch, libertine, philanderer, rake, reprobate, roué, satyr, seducer
**womanish** delicate, effeminate, effete, emasculate, feministic, feminine, ladylike, motherly, mulebral, refined, unmanly, unvirile, womanly
**woman keeper of a brothel** bawd
**woman killing** femicide
**woman lawyer** Portia
**womanly** delicate, feminine, gentle, graceful, ladylike, modest, soft, tender
**woman married to a man** wife
**woman of courage** heroine
**woman of good social standing** lady
**woman of ill repute** slut
**woman of rank** dame, lady
**woman of stately bearing and regal beauty** Juno
**woman of the hour** heroine
**woman of violent temper** shrew
**woman on her wedding day** bride
**woman party giver** hostess
**woman possessing the gift of prophecy** sibyl
**woman practising sorcery** enchantress, sorceress, witch
**woman ruler** maharani, princess, queen
**woman's brimless hat** toque (F)
**woman's cape** pelerine
**woman's cloak** dolman
**woman's close fitting hat** cloche

**woman's cloth hat** bonnet
**woman's collar of lace** collarette
**woman's coronet** tiara
**woman's dancing shoe** slipper
**woman's disorder** amenorrhea, eclampsia, endometriosis, mastitis, puerperal fever
**woman's divided skirt** culotte
**woman's dowry** dot
**woman's drawers** knickers
**woman's dress and coat** ensemble
**woman's dress with tight waistband and full skirt** dirndl
**woman servant in house** housemaid
**woman's feathery scarf** boa
**woman's foundation garment** corset
**woman's fur throat-wrap** boa
**woman's garment** apron, blouson, bodice, burka, costume, dress, jupon, mantua, overall, simar, skirt veil
**woman's headdress** cap, hat, tiara, veil
**woman's headgear with strings** bonnet
**woman's indoor cap** mobcap
**woman's light flimsy dressing-gown** négligé, negligee, pegnoir
**woman's light triangular scarf** fichu
**woman's long coat** redingote
**woman's long fur or feather throat-wrap** boa
**woman's long loose dress** caftan
**woman's long loose outer garment** stole
**woman's long thin scarf** boa
**woman's matching outfit** ensemble
**woman's measurements** vital statistics
**woman's nightclothes** lingerie
**woman's outer petticoat** kirtle
**woman's partner in marriage** hubby, husband
**woman's private room** boudoir
**woman's purse** reticule
**woman's riding costume** habit, joseph
**woman's saddle horse** palfrey
**woman's scarf** boa
**woman's shoe with narrow, tapering high heel** stiletto
**woman's short bodice** camisole
**woman's short cape** pelerine
**woman's short coat** topper
**woman's short fur-trimmed jacket** cymar
**woman's short open jacket** bolero
**woman's shoulder cape** bertha
**woman's singing voice** alto, soprano
**woman's skirt** dirndl
**woman's sleeveless jacket** bolero
**woman's small triangular shawl** fichu
**woman's stocking support** garter, suspender
**woman's title** Miss, Mrs, Ms

**woman's triangular shawl** fichu
**woman's trousers cut to resemble a skirt** culottes
**woman's undergarment** bra(ssière), chemise, petticoat, slip
**woman's underskirt** petticoat
**woman's underwear** lingerie
**woman's waistcoat** gilet
**woman's work** distaff
**woman's work basket** cabas
**woman's wrap** stole
**woman teacher** mistress
**woman tending the sick** nurse
**woman trained to assist women in childbirth** midwife
**woman turned to stone** Niobe
**woman under religious vows** nun
**woman warrior** Amazon
**woman who affects great modesty** prude
**woman who employs other persons** mistress
**woman who has borne only one child** (primi)para
**woman who has lost her husband** widow
**woman who is dowdy** frump
**woman who is head of family** matriarch
**woman who is pregnant for the first time** primigravida
**woman who is unattractive** frump
**woman who leaves a will** testatrix
**woman who make corsets** corsetière
**woman who massages** masseuse
**woman who moves in fashionable society** mondaine
**woman who owns a boarding house** landlady
**woman who sews** seamstress
**woman who will receive legacy** heiress
**woman with bad temper** fury, shrew, virago, vixen
**woman with dark brown hair** brunette
**womb** cavity, matrix, uterus
**wombat** badger, beaverlike, koala, marsupial
**women of Royal Navy Service** Wren
**women's libber** feminist
**women's quarters** harem, seraglio, thalamus, zenana
**wonder** admiration, amazement, astonishment, awe, bewilderment, boggle, conjecture, curiosity, fascination, gape, gawk, marvel, meditate, miracle, ponder, portent, prodigy, query, question, rarity, sight, spectacle, speculate, stare, surprise, think
**wonder and fear** awe
**wonder at** admire

**wonderful** admirable, amazing, appropriate, astounding, brilliant, convenient, excellent, extraordinary, favourable, felicitous, fit(ted), great, inspiring, magnificent, marvellous, miraculous, odd, outstanding, peculiar, propitious, remarkable, sensational, staggering, startling, suitable, superb, tremendous, well-timed, wondrous
**wonderful thing** marvel
**wonderful to relate** mirabile dictu (L)
**wonderful to see** mirabile visu (L)
**Wonderland girl** Alice
**wonderment** amazement, astonishment, awe, stupefaction, surprise, wonder
**wonder mingled with delight** admiration, esteem
**wont** convention, custom, habit, observance, practice, routine, tradition, usage, use, way
**won through effort** earned
**woo** address, chase, court, date, entreat, implore, incur, invite, press, pursue, serenade, solicit, urge
**wood** aloe, beams, beech, boards, bois (F), bush, cedar, coppice, ebony, elm, fir, forest, grove, jungle, logs, maple, oak, pine, planks, softwood, teak, thicket, timber, trees, trunk, woodland, xylem
**wood alcohol** methanol
**wood ash substance** potash
**wood beetle** sawyer
**woodbine** creeper, honeysuckle, ivy
**wood coal** charcoal, lignite
**woodcut** xylography
**woodcutter** feller, forester, lumberjack, lumberman, sawyer, woodchopper
**woodcutter's cleaver** froe
**woodcutters's tool** axe
**wood-eating insect** termite
**wooded** arboured, bosky, forested, hylean, nemorous, sylvan, treey
**wooded area** forest
**wooded countryside** boscage
**wooded hill** holt, hurst
**wooded hollow** dell, gully
**wooded place** forest
**wooded plateau in south-eastern Belgium** Ardennes
**wooded region** forest
**wooded scenery** boscage, boskage
**wooded valley** dell
**wooden** awkward, blank, clumsy, dense, dim(-witted), doltish, dull, empty, gauche, impassive, inexpressive, lifeless, ligneous, ligniform, oafish, obtuse, rigid, slow-witted, spiritless, stiff, stodgy,

stuffy, ungainly, vacant, witless, wood(y), xyloid
**wooden ball** bowl
**wooden barrel** cask
**wooden basket** trug
**wooden blind strip** slat
**wooden bowl** cog, sebilla
**wooden box** crate
**wooden bucket** soe
**wooden container** barrel, box, case, crate
**wooden cup** noggin
**wooden drinking-bowl** cap
**wooden frame for drying cheese** hake
**wooden framework** lattice
**wooden golf club** brassie, driver, spoon
**wooden hammer** mallet, maul
**woodenhead** blockhead, dunce
**woodenheaded** stupid
**wooden image supposed to have fallen from heaven** xoanon
**wooden joint** tenon
**wooden lining of walls of room** wainscot
**wooden match** vesta
**wooden nail** peg, trannel, trenail
**wooden object** treen
**wooden packing case** crate
**wooden peg** dowel, knag, nog
**wooden pin** coag, dowel, fid, nog, peg, spile, thole, trenail
**wooden plant** tree
**wooden platform** deck
**wooden platter for serving food** trencher
**wooden pole** rod, staff
**wooden post** stake
**wooden rod** dowel
**wooden shoe** clog, klomp, patten, racket, racquet, sabot
**wooden slat** strip
**wooden-soled shoe** clog
**wooden strip** batten, lath
**wooden sword** strickle, waster
**wooden tap** spigot
**wooden tile** shingle
**wooden tower** brattice
**wooden tub** soe
**wooden vessel** bucket, cask
**wooden vessel for butter** firkin
**wooden villa** chalet, dacha
**wooden wedding** fifth
**wooden wedge** brob
**wooden wheel rim** felloe, felly
**wood fastener** fid, nail, nog, peg, pin
**wood file** rasp
**wood for bow** yew
**wood for fire** logs
**wood fragment** chip
**wood groove** chamfer
**wood gum** xylan

**wood ibis** tantalus
**wood joint** mitre, mortise, tenon
**wood knot** knar, knur(r)
**woodland** forest
**woodland avenue** glade
**woodland bird** tanager
**woodland clear space** glade
**woodland deity** faun, Pan, satyr
**woodland path** trail
**woodland plant** mandrake
**wood lath** slat
**wood-like** xyloid
**wood louse** pillbug, slater, sowbug
**wood measure** cord, foot, metre
**wood mosaic** (in)tarsia
**wood nymph** dryas, (hama)dryad, moth, napea, satyr, sprite
**wood of East Indian tree** eng
**wood of sandarac tree** alerce
**wood pigeon** cushat (Sc)
**wood pore** lenticel
**wood preservative** creosote
**wood prop** sprag
**wood pulp fabric** xylolin
**wood pussy** skunk
**wood resembling mahogany** acajou, sapele
**woods** bosk, bosque, bush, copse, forest, grove, nemo, silvi, sylvi, timbers, trees, woodland
**wood shack** shed
**woodshaping tool** adze, chisel, plane
**wood shaver** plane
**woodsman** forester
**wood sorrel** oca
**wood strip** lath
**wood-turning machine** lathe
**wood used in furniture** oak, stinkwood, walnut, yellowwood
**wood used to cane scholars** ferule
**woodwind instrument** bassoon, clarinet, clarion(et), flute, oboe
**woodwork** carpentry
**woodworker** carpenter, joiner
**woodwork fastener** dowel, fid, nail, nog, peg, screw
**woodworking tool** adze
**woodworm** borer, termite, weevil
**woody area** forest
**woody climbing or trailing plant** ivy
**woody corn spike** cob
**woody grass** cane
**woody grass stem** bamboo, reed
**woody plant** shrub, tree
**woody tissue of plant** xylem
**woody twig** rod
**wooer** admirer, beau, boyfriend, escort, fiancé, gallant, lover, paramour, suitor, sweetheart
**wooer's song** serenade
**woofer** loudspeaker
**woof in weaving** weft

**wooing** chasing, courting, courtship, pursuing, romancing
**wool** fleece, hair, lana (Sp), yarn
**wool-bearing** laniferous, lanigerous
**wool bundle** bale, skein
**wool cap** tuque
**wool combings** noils
**wool crop** clip
**wool dryer** fugal
**wool fabric** armure, moreen, worsted
**wool fibre** noil, pile, sliver
**wool for knitting stockings** fingering
**wool grease** lanolin(e), yok
**wool knot** burl, nep, noil
**woollen** fleecy
**woollen blanket material** yerga
**woollen cap** balaclava
**woollen cloth** tweed, wadmoll
**woollen cluster** nep
**woollen covering for bed** blanket
**woollen fabric** beige, challis, delaine, flannel, moreen, ratine, serge, tamine, tamis, tweed
**woollen helmet** balaclava
**woollen jacket** reefer
**woollen jumper** sweater
**woollen refuse** fud, mungo
**woollen shawl** paisley
**woollen stuff** sagathy
**woollen surface of cloth** nap
**woollen tuft** tassel
**woollen yarn** sayette, worsted
**woolly animal** sheep
**woolly bear** caterpillar
**woolly camel** alpaca, llama, vicuna
**woolly clouds** cumulus
**woolly coat of sheep** fleece
**woolly fur** astrakhan
**woolly hair** shag
**woolly surface of cloth** nap
**woolly toy bear** teddy
**wool measure** heer, tod
**wool package** bale, fadge
**woolsack** tribunal
**woolshed worker** shearer
**wool sheep** merino
**woolsorter's disease** anthrax
**wool surface** nap, nep, pile
**wool variety** alpaca, angora, challis, merino
**wool wave** crimp
**wool weight** cloce, nail, sappler, tod
**wool yarn** worsted
**word** assurance, command, etymon, ideogram, injunction, mandate, message, mot (F), name, oath, order, parole, pledge, promise, representation, sign, symbol, term, tidings, ultimatum, warrant
**word account** description, narrative
**word added to noun** adjective
**word added to verb** adverb

word background  context
word battle  logomachy
word blind  dyslectic
word blindness  alexia, dyslexia
wordbook  dictionary, glossary, lexicon, thesaurus
word by word  verbatim
word deafness  aphasia
word denoting opposition  adversative
word expressing obligation  should
word formed from another  derivative
word for word  accurate, clear, exact, explicit, literal(ly), mot à mot (F), strict, verbatim
word for word and letter for letter  verbatim et literatum (L)
word game  crambo, scrabble
word governing noun or pronoun  preposition
word hard to pronounce  jawbreaker
word having the same meaning as another  synonym
word imitating a sound  onomatope
word indicating action  verb
word indicating choice  or
word in the ear  hint, whisper
wordless acting  charade, dumbshow, mime
wordless singing  hum
word letter  epistolo, logogram
word of agreement  ay(e), yea, yes
word of assent  yes
word of choice  or
word of commiseration  alas
word of consent  amen, yes
word of contrary meaning to another  antonym
word of denial  no(t)
word of dissent  no
word of excuse  sorry
word of God  Bible, Scripture
word of greeting  hello
word of honour  assurance, oath, parole d'honneur (F), parol(e), pledge, promise, surety
word of inquiry  what
word of lamentation  alas
word of misuse  malapropism
word of mouth  hearsay
word of negation  no(t)
word of opposed meaning  antonym
word of pity  alas
word of promise  parole, pledge
word of recognition  password, shibboleth
word of refusal  no
word of regret  alas
word of similar meaning  synonym
word of similar sound  homomorph
word of similar spelling  heteronym
word often used in Psalms  selah
word on Pentagon documents  secret

word opposed in meaning to another  antonym
word play  badinage, banter, chaff, drollery, equivoque, mockery, persiflage, pleasantry, pun, quip, raillery, repartee, riposte, sally, teasing, waggery, wit(ticism)
word puzzle  acrostic, anagram, charade, crambo, crossword, logograph, rebus
word removed from text  deletion
word repetition  ploce
word representing noun  pronoun
words  argument, babble, bavardage (F), chatter, debate, discussion, patter, squabble, talk
words below illustration  caption
words of consolation  better luck next time
words of encouragement  assurance
word so formed  parasyntheton
words of play  lines
words of song  lyric(s)
words on tomb  epitaph, inscription
words opposite in meaning  antonyms
word source study  etymology
word square  palindrome
words set to music  song
words used as charm  spell
word that is a name  noun
word that reads alike backward and forward  palindrome
word to describe a verb  adverb
word to the wise  clue, hint, tip
word used as name  noun
word which modifies a verb  adverb
word with air or cake  hot
word with opposite meaning  antonym
word with same meaning  synonym
wordy  diffuse, garrulous, prolix, rambling, verbose, windy
work  calling, duty, effort, exertion, job, labour, operate, opus, profession, sweat, toil, travail
workable  able, achievable, actable, attainable, controllable, cultivatable, directable, fit, functional, manageable, manipulatable, operable, pliable, possible, practicable, tillable, useful, wieldable
workaday  ordinary
work against  antagonise, counteract, hinder, oppose
work aimlessly  putter
work appearing in successive parts  serial
work at  do, operate, ply, practise
work at loom  weave
work at steadily  ply
work bag  cabas, toolbag, (tool)kit
work basket  caba

work by author of the highest excellence  classic
work crew  gang
work diligently  ply
work dodging  skiving
work dough  knead
worked by rope  funicular
worked by water  hydraulic
worked out in detail  elaborated
worked out mine  goaf, gob
worked toward  strive
worker  ant, artisan, bee, craftsman, employee, farmer, hand, labourer, toiler, tradesman
worker bee  drone
worker hired on a daily wage  journeyman
worker in alloys  pewtere
worker in metal  (black)smith
worker in plant nursery  nurseryman
worker in rattan  caner
worker in stone  mason
worker in stucco  plasterer
worker in timber  carpenter
worker on the land  peasant
worker's assistant  mate
workers' organisation  union
worker's outer wear  overall
worker's policy of going slowly  cacanny
worker's union  artel
work feebly  totter
work flour into dough  knead
work for  assist, earn
workforce  labour
work for several solo singers and a choir  cantata
work gang  crew
work group  gang
work hard  drudge, labour, ply, slave, slog, sweat, tew (Sc), toil
work hard to attain  strive
work horse  drudge
work in  implant, inject, insert, interject, introduce
work in another's style and manner  pastiche
working  acting, action, active, diggings, effective, employed, excavations, functioning, going, labouring, manner, method, mine, on stream, operation(al), operative, pit, practical, quarry, routine, running, shaft, slaving, sweating, toiling, useful, viable
working agreement  code, contract
working at secondary job  moonlighting
working automaton  robot
working class  proletariat
working easily  facile
working horse  percheron

**working in either of two media**
　ambidextrous
**working merely for money**　mercenary
**working party**　squad
**working relation**　gear
**working room of painter**　atelier, studio
**working table**　bench
**work in partnership**　collaborate
**work in superficial manner**　dibble
**work in terms of heat**　ergon
**work is prayer**　laborates est orare (L)
**work laboriously**　plod, toil
**work like a Trojan**　toil
**workman**　labourer
**workmanship**　art(istry), craftsmanship, execution, expertise, skill, technique
**workman's overall**　dungaree
**workman's pay**　earnings, emolument, remuneration, salary, wage
**workman who saws timber**　sawyer
**work of art**　etching, masterpiece, oeuvre (F), painting
**work off**　exercise, lose, undo
**work of fiction**　novel
**work of genius**　masterpiece
**work of low quality**　slopwork
**work of music**　opus
**work of no set form, often based on folk tunes**　rhapsody
**work of religious art**　pietà
**work on**　cajole, coax, importune, influence, nag, press, pursuade, push, soft-soap, sweet-talk, wheedle
**work on copy**　edit
**work on the lives of saints**　hagiology
**work out**　accomplish, achieve, arrange, attain, calculate, construct, contrive, crack, decipher, develop, devise, elaborate, evolve, formulate, happen, invent, plan, produce, reckon, (re)solve, result, understand, unlock, unravel
**work out in advance**　plan, plot, premeditate, scheme
**work out in detail**　elaborate
**work over again**　rehash, revamp
**work overmuch**　slave
**work over to new form**　recast
**work place**　premises
**work produced**　output
**workroom of artist**　studio
**workshop**　atelier, class, factory, garage, lab(oratory), loft, shop, studio
**work shy**　idle, lazy
**works of an author, painter or composer**　oeuvre
**work's restaurant**　canteen
**work steadily**　plod, ply
**work supervisor**　boss, overseer
**work table**　desk
**work the land**　farm, till
**work together**　collaborate, liaise, team

**work too hard**　overdo, overwork
**work trainee**　apprentice
**work under another**　serve
**work unit**　erg
**work up**　agitate, animate, arouse, elaborate, excite, expand, foment, generate, incite, increase, inflame, instigate, move, prompt, rouse, spur, whet
**work upon**　affect, motivate, persuade, pressure
**work very hard**　toil
**work wearisomely**　moil
**work with**　assist
**work with difficulty**　struggle
**work with loom**　weave
**work with spade**　dig
**work with wool**　knit
**world**　atlas, cosmos, creation, earth, globe, planet, realm, sphere, universe
**world beyond**　hereafter
**world body**　UNO
**world fair**　expo(sition)
**world in miniature**　microcosm
**world language**　Esperanto
**worldly**　avaricious, blasé, carnal, civil, covetous, earthly, experienced, fleshly, grasping, human, knowing, laic, lay, materialistic, mundane, physical, politic, profane, secular, selfish, sophisticated, temporal, terrene, terrestrial, urbane
**worldly-wise**　sophisticated
**world's highest mountain**　Everest
**world's largest monolith**　Ayers Rock
**world's only Hindu kingdom**　Nepal
**World War II hero**　Bader
**World War II battle**　El Alamein
**World War II weapon**　bren
**world-weary**　blasé
**worldwide**　ecumenical, extensive, far-reaching, general, global, international, pandemic, spacious, ubiquitous, universal, widespread
**worldwide company**　multinational
**world without end**　eternally, forever, persistently
**worm**　annelid, blight, crawl, eis, eria, ess, ipo, larva, leech, loa, nematode, nemertean, parasite, platyhelminth, polyclad, squirm, tinea
**worm-eaten**　decayed, impaired, maggoty, pitted, vermiculate, vermoulu, wermethe
**worm-eating mammal**　tenrec
**wormer**　angler
**worm feeler**　palp(us)
**wormhole**　piqure
**wormil**　botfly, maggot
**worm in hawks**　filander
**worm into**　crawl, enter, wriggle

**worm larva**　loa
**wormlike**　crawling, crouching, sinuous, slavish, slithering, sneaking, squirming, subservient, vermian, vermicular, vermiform, winding
**wormlike form of insect**　larva
**worm out**　draw, extract, pump
**wormseed**　ambrosia
**worm-shaped**　vermiform
**worm used for bait**　tagtail
**wormwood**　absinth(e), composit, cudweed, herb, mingwort, moxa, mugwort, sagebrush, santonica, unsavouriness, vermifuge
**wormy**　earthy
**worn**　bushed, crumbled, decayed, decomposed, decrepit, exhausted, fagged, fatigued, mouldy, tired, weary
**worn around waist**　cummerbund, girdle, obi (J), sash
**worn by acrobat**　leotard
**worn by kings**　crown, ermine, purple
**worn clothes**　rags
**worn-down pencil**　stub
**worn garment**　dud
**worn into shreds**　frayed, tattered, torn
**worn-looking**　haggard, pale, pallid, run down, tired, weary
**worn on the head**　beret, cap, hat
**worn-out**　abandoned, antiquated, antique, banal, battered, crumbling, dated, decadent, decayed, decrepit, deteriorated, dilapidated, dissipated, dissolute, dog-tired, effete, exhausted, frayed, hackneyed, jaded, knackered, moth-eaten, neglected, obsolete, old, overworked, passé, ragged, ramshackle, rejected, rickety, shabby, spent, stale, stereotyped, tattered, tatty, threadbare, tired, trite, unorginal, used, useless, valueness, weary
**worn-out horse**　hack, jade, knacker, nag, plug, rip, Rosinante (Sp), screw
**worn-out state**　triteness
**worn with blouses**　skirt
**worn with shirt**　tie
**worried and edgy**　fretful
**worried woman**　fretter
**worrisome**　vexing
**worry**　adversity, agitate, agitation, annoy, anxiety, bother, burden, care, chafe, concern, discomfort, dismay, distress, fret, harass, harry, headache, irk, nag, nervousness, problem, rattle, solicitude, trouble, uneasiness, vex, weary
**worrying**　agonising, annoying, bothering, brooding, disquieting, distressing, disturbing, fretting,

harassing, harrying, importuning, irritating, perturbing, pestering, plaguing, tantalising, teasing, tormenting, troubling, unsettling, upsetting, vexing

**worry too much** fuss

**worsen** aggravate, crumble, decay, decline, decompose, degenerate, deteriorate, exacerbate, increase, retrograde, retrogress, weaken

**worship** admiration, admire, adoration, adore, adulate, cherish, deify, devotion, esteem, eulogise, exalt, extol, glorification, homage, honour, idolise, laud(ation), love, praise, prayer, respect, revere(nce), treasure, venerate

**worship as god** deify

**worshipful** awed, ceremonious, respectful, reverent, solemn

**worship of all gods** pantheism

**worship of idols** idolism, idolatry

**worship of images** iconolatry, idolatry

**worship of more than one god** polytheism

**worship of one God** monolatry

**worship of saints** hagiolatry

**worship of self** autolatry

**worship of Shakespeare** bardolatry

**worship of stars** astrolatry, sabaism

**worship of the dead** necrolatry

**worship of wealth** plutolatry

**worship paid to God** adoration

**worshipped animal** totem

**worshipper** adherent, admirer, adorer, apostle, believer, devotee, disciple, doter, enthusiast, fan, follower, habitué, hajji, idolator, partisan, pupil, ritualist, supporter, votary

**worshipper of Bacchus** bacchanal

**worshipper of false gods** idolator

**worsted cloth** serge

**worsted cuff worn on wrist** muffetee

**worsted fabric** serge

**worsted trench coat** Burberry

**worsted yarn** caddis, genappe

**worth** aid, assessment, avail, benefit, cost, deserving, estimation, evaluation, excellence, merit, perfection, price, profit, quality, superiority, use(fulness), utility, valuation, value, virtue

**worth a lot** costly, expensive, high-priced, valuable

**worth a packet** valuable

**worth as fad** novelty value

**worth having** desirable

**worthiness** commendableness, creditableness, decentness, desert, estimableness, goodness, honestness, laudableness, merit, reliableness, reputableness, respectableness, righteousness, uprightness, valuableness, worship

**worthless** bad, barren, empty, flimsy, futile, idle, impotent, impracticable, inadequate, inane, ineffective, no-good, nugatory, petty, profitless, rascally, trashy, trivial, unimported, vain, valueless, vicious, vile

**worthless animal** carrion

**worthless article** dud

**worthless dog** brak, cur, mongrel, mutt

**worthless fellow** bum, cad, cuss, loser, mauvais sujet (F), scal(l)awag, scallywag, scoundrel, spalpeen

**worthless girl** hussy

**worthless hand at cards** bust

**worthless horse** jade, nag, rip

**worthless leaving** ort

**worthless matter** corpus vile, dregs, rubbish

**worthlessness** baseness, futileness, ineffectualness, meaninglessness, nugacity, nullity, paltriness, pointlessness, poorness, trashiness, trivialness, uselessness, vileness

**worthless object** punk

**worthless part** chaff, dregs, husk

**worthless people** trash

**worthless person** loser, punk, scum

**worthless scrap** ort

**worthless shell** husk

**worthless stuff** punk, rubbish, trash, tripe

**worthless trifle** fico

**worthless woman** baggage, hussy

**worth more than it cost** cheap

**worth one's time and effort** moneymaking

**worth repeating** quotable

**worthwhile** advantageous, beneficial, constructive, expedient, gainful, good, helpful, important, justifiable, lucrative, moneymaking, productive, profitable, rewarding, substantial, useful, valuable, worthy

**worthy** apposite, blameless, commendable, deserving, dignitary, distinguished, eminence, eminent, estimable, excellent, famous, fit, laudable, meritorious, moral, noble, notable, personage, proper, reliable, reputable, trustworthy, valuable

**worthy of palm of victory** palmary

**worthy of attention** noteworthy

**worthy of being chosen** eligible

**worthy of being remembered** memorable

**worthy of belief** credible

**worthy of esteem** estimable

**worthy of mention** deserving

**worthy of note** notable, remarkable

**worthy of notice** eminent, notable, noteworthy, remarkable

**worthy of praise** commendable

**worthy of recommendation** advisable

**worthy of respect** estimable, reverend, venerable

**worthy of reverence** venerable

**worthy of utmost respect and love** adorable

**worthy of worship** adorable

**worthy to be chosen** eligible

**wound** anguish, annoy, confusion, cut, damage, distress, gash, gore, grief, harm, heartbreak, hurt, injure, injury, insult, irritate, lacerate, laceration, lesion, methodical, offend, pain, pang, pierce, regular, scar, shock, slash, sore, stab, sting, systematic, tied, torment, trauma, trim, well-regulated, wrapped

**wound binding strip** bandage

**wound caused by insect** sting

**wound covering** bandage, dressing, scab, scar, tape

**wounded** annoyed, cut, damaged, distressed, gashed, grieved, harmed, hurt, injured, lacerated, offended, pained, pierced, shocked

**wounded pride** pique

**wounded with dagger** stabbed

**wounding organ of bees** sting

**wounding remark** barb, sarcasm

**wound mark** cut, scab, scar

**wound's crust** scab

**wound slightly** graze

**wounds with a sword** fleshes

**wound the pride of** pique

**wound with horn** gore

**wound with knife** stab

**wound with maxilla** bite

**wound with tusks** bore

**woven** crossed, grained, ribbed, textile, textural, twilled

**woven artwork** tapestry

**woven cloth** fabric, mesh

**woven fabric** arras, blanket, cloth, galloon, linen, serge, textile, texture, tissue, web

**woven figurative design** faconne, façonné (F)

**woven flax ball** poi

**woven in mesh** net

**woven material** cloth, textile

**woven threads** woof

**woven with an open mesh** cellular

**woven woollen stuff** flannel

**wow** admirable, astonishing, impressive, sensational, wonderful

**wowser** fanatic, killjoy, prude, puritan, spoilsport, teetotaller

**wrack and ruins** smithereens

**wraith** apparition, ghost, phantom, spectre
**wrangle** argue, argument, bicker, brawl, clash, contend, disagreement, dispute, fight, fisticuffs, haggle, hassle, jar, quarrel, row, scrap, spar, squabble
**wrangler** arguer, disputer, squabbler
**wrangler's rope** lariat, lasso
**wrangling** arguing
**wrap** absorb, bind, boa, cape, cere, cloak, conceal, cover, encase, enclose, enfold, (en)swathe, envelop, fold, mantle, muffle, obscure, pack, roll, scarf, shawl, sheathe, shroud, stole, surround, tie, wind
**wrap corpse** cere
**wrap in mystery** envelop
**wrapper** bandage, case, cover, dressing, envelope, gown, housecoat, jacket, paper, robe, shawl, sheath, shroud
**wrapping** envelope, garments, paper, pliofilm, sheath, wraps
**wrapping for a corpse** shroud
**wrap round and round** roll
**wrap up** complete, conclude, enclose, end, enfold, envelop, enwrap, pack(age), parcel, terminate
**wrath** anger, avengement, bitterness, displeasure, exacerbation, ferocity, fury, indignation, ire, passion, punishment, rage, resentment, revenge, temper, vengeance, violence
**wrathful** affronted, angry, belligerent, bilious, cross, enraged, fiery, fuming, furious, hysterical, impassionate, impassioned, irate, ireful, irritable, overwrought, peeved, peppery, quarrelsome, ranting, raving, touchy, upset, vexed, volatile
**wrathful state** rage
**wreak** avenge, exact, execute, fury, gratify, inflict, resentment, revenge, vengeance
**wreak havoc upon** devastate, spoliate
**wreak vengeance** retaliate
**wreath** anadem, circle(t), coil, coronal, coronet, curl, diadem, festoon, garland, green, lei, loop, ring, spiral
**wreathe** adorn, coil, decorate, embrace, envelop, festoon, garland, laurel, spiral, twine, twist, weave, wrap
**wreathed with laurel as honour** laureate
**wreath for head** chaplet
**wreath of flowers** garland
**wreath of olive** irsine

**wreck** accident, collide, collision, crash, crush, debris, demolish, desolate, destroy, devastate, explode, havoc, hulk, mar, mess, quash, ravage, ruin, smash
**wreckage** debris, flotsam, fragments, jetsam, remains, rubble, shambles, wrack
**wreckage found floating** flotsam
**wreckage lying on bed of sea** lagan
**wrecked ship** hulk
**wrecked state** smash
**wrecking company** salvagers
**wrench** bend, distort, force, injure, jerk, pull, shock, spanner, sprain, strain, stretch, tool, twist, wrest, wring
**wrench ankle** sprain
**wrench away** wrest
**wrench out of shape** distort
**wrench tool** spanner
**wrest** elicit, garble, rend, snatch, turn, twist, wrench, wring
**wrest illegally** extort
**wrestle** battle, clinch, combat, fight, grab, grapple, joust, labour, persevere, persist, scuffle, strive, struggle, tackle, throw, travail, tussle
**wrestler's rug** mat
**wrestling as combat** judo, jujitsu
**wrestling hold** chancery, crotch, headlock, keylock, nelson, scissors, sidehold, wristlock
**wrestling in Japan** sumo
**wrestling or boxing trial** bout
**wrestling pad** mat
**wrestling throw** hipe, hype, thraw
**wretched** afflicted, careworn, crushed, disconsolate, dismal, forlorn, gloomy, heartbroken, ill, inferior, miserable, piteous, pitiable, poor, sad, sorry, unhappy, unimportant, vile, woeful
**wretched hut** hovel, pondok
**wretchedly bad** vile
**wretchedness** abjectness, calamitous, cheerlessness, comfortlessness, dejectedness, deplorableness, forlornness, gloominess, haplessness, hopelessness, miserableness, misery, paltriness, pitifulness, poorness, sorriness, unhappiness, woefulness
**wriggle** crawl, dodge, jerk, slink, snake, sneak, squirm, turn, twist, wag, wangle, wiggle, worm, writhe, zigzag
**wriggly** eely, evasive, slippery, squirming, wiggly, wriggling, writhing
**wright** craftsman, maker, workman
**wring** agonise, clasp, distort, extort, extract, force, harass, pierce,

squeeze, stab, torment, torsion, torture, twist, wound, wrench, wrest
**wring money by blackmail** extort
**wring out** dry, extort
**wrinkle** corrugate, crease, crinkle, crow's-foot, crumple, fold, furrow, gather, line, pucker, ruck, rumple, scheme, stunt, trick, wheeze
**wrinkled** corrugated, creased, crêpey, crinkled, crumpled, folded, furrowed, gathered, lined, puckered, rucked, rugate, rugose, rugous, wrinkly
**wrinkle the brow** frown
**wrist** carpus
**wristband** bracelet, cuff
**wrist bone** scaphoid
**wrist bones** carpi
**wrist guard** brace
**wrist ornament** bangle, bracelet, watch
**writ** capias, decree, document, subpoena, summons
**write** communicate, compose, copy, correspond, draft, indite, inscribe, lucubrate, pen, scrawl, scribble, (tran)scribe
**write above** superscribe
**write a poem** indite
**write a speech** indite
**write back** answer, reply
**write briefly** jot
**write by machine** type
**write by way of introduction** premise
**write carelessly** scrawl, scribble
**write directions on envelope** address
**write down** catalogue, jot, note, record, register, transcribe
**write down brief points** jot
**write down in columns** tabulate
**write hastily** scrawl
**write home about** describe, mention, note, remark, state, tell
**write in different alphabet** transliterate
**write in different key** transpose
**write in symbols** notate
**write letters without joining** print
**write marginal notes** gloss, postil
**write music** compose, notate
**write name** sign
**write name on list** enrol
**write off** amortise, annul, cancel, crash, delete, destroy, disregard, eradicate, erase, expunge, scrub, wreck
**write one's name** sign
**write out in large letters** engross
**write poorly** scrawl, scribble
**writer** author, composer, contributor, copyist, copywriter, dissertator, dramaturgist, essayist, ironist, journalist, librettist, novelist, penman, playwright, poet, prosaist, recorder,

**writer about love** reporter, satirist, scrawler, scribe, scribler, scriptwriter, scrivener
**writer about love** amorist
**writer noted for humour** humorist
**writer of book** author
**writer of essays** essayist
**writer of fables** Aesop
**writer of glosses** glossator
**writer of history** historian
**writer of literary works** literateur
**writer of novels** novelist
**writer of pamphlets** pamphleteer
**writer of prose** prosaist
**writer of Proverbs** Solomon
**writer of Psalms** David
**writer of tragedies** tragedian
**writer of verse** poet
**writer on public concerns** publicist
**writer's assumed name** nom de plume
**writer's cramp** graphospasm
**writes shorthand** stenographer
**write tentatively** pencil
**write untidily** scrawl, scribble
**write up** account, cover, describe, detail, investigate, narrate, recount, relate, ticket
**write with strong hostility** inveigh
**write wrongly** misspell
**writhe** contort, deform, distort, flail, jerk, misshape, pervert, squirm, struggle, thrash, thresh, toss, twist, warp, welter, w(r)iggle
**writ including delay** nisi
**writing** book, cacography, calligraphy, chirography, composing, composition, creating, document, drafting, epistle, handwriting, inscription, letter, opus, penmanship, penning, print, publication, recording, scrabble, scrawl, scribble, script, stylography, tome, transcribing, volume
**writing art** calligraphy, penmanship, rhetoric
**writing character** letter, uncial, wedge
**writing desk** bureau, escritoire, secretaire
**writing fluid** ink
**writing fluid well** inkpot
**writing for the blind** Braille
**writing gear** stationery
**writing implement** ballpoint, chalk, pen(cil), stylus
**writing in praise of** eulogy
**writing machine** typewriter
**writing material** (note)paper
**writing materials** stationery
**writing of history** historiography
**writing of saints' lives** hagiography
**writing of shorthand** stenography
**writing on the wall** indication, omen, portent, warning
**writing on wax** cerograph
**writing or speech in praise of a person** eulogy
**writing paper package** ream
**writings** literature
**writings not considered genuine** apocrypha
**writing stone** slate
**writing system** orthography
**writing table** bureau, desk, escritoire, secretaire
**writing tablet** pad, slate, tabula
**writing tool** pen(cil)
**writing with bold curves** roundhand
**writ of execution** elegit
**writ requiring attendance at a court** subpoena
**written** documented, noted, recorded
**written acceptance of debt** debenture
**written account** annal, chronicle, memoirs
**written agreement** cartel, contract, pact, treaty
**written attestation** testimonial
**written backward name** ananym
**written below the line** subscript
**written by hand** manuscript
**written communication** letter, memo(randum), note
**written composition** essay, theme
**written copy** transcript
**written declaration upon oath** affidavit
**written decree of Sultan of Turkey** irade
**written defamation** libel
**written discourse** essay, treatise
**written document serving as proof** voucher
**written edict of Muslim ruler** irade
**written exposition** treatise
**written information from computer** printout
**written in seven languages** heptaglot
**written laughter** ha ha, ho ho
**written law** statute
**written message** letter
**written mistake** erratum
**written order from law-court** writ
**written permission** permit
**written promise to pay** bond, IOU
**written record** log, register
**written reminder** memo(randum)
**written statement confirmed by oath** affidavit
**written test** exam(ination)
**written under a false name** pseudonymous
**written with a running hand** cursive
**written works** literature
**writ to arrest** capias
**wrong** abuse, amiss, astray, bad, crime, dishonour, err(oneous), evil, false, faulty, harass, illegal, illicit, immoral, improper, inaccurate, incorrect, injure, lawbreaking, misdoing, misfortune, mistake(n), oddness, queerness, sin, transgression, unfair, unjust, unlawful, unsuitable, untrue, violate, wicked
**wrong act** derelict(um), misdeed, tort
**wrong designation** misnomer
**wrongdoer** criminal, culprit, delinquent, evildoer, felon, killer, lawbreaker, lout, miscreant, murderer, offender, sinner, skollie, terrorist, thief, transgressor, trespasser, tsotsi, vandal, villain
**wrongdoing** badness, baseness, blame, corruption, crime, delinquency, disgrace, evil, felony, guilt, immorality, iniquity, malpractice, misconduct, misdeed, offence, offending, scandal, sin(fulness), sinning, transgressing, transgression, trespassing, vice, villainy, wickedness, wrong
**wrongful** blameworthy, criminal, dishonest, dishonourable, evil, illegal, illegitimate, illicit, immoral, improper, reprehensible, unethical, unfair, unjust, unlawful, wicked, wrong
**wrongful act** tort
**wrongful disposition** ouster
**wrongfully assume power** usurp
**wrong-headed** contrary, dogged, headstrong, intractable, obdurate, obstinate, perverse, wilful
**wrong idea** misconception
**wrong in opinion** mistaken
**wrong instruction** misinterpretation
**wrong interpretation** misconception
**wrongly** amiss, badly, criminally, crookedly, defectively, dishonestly, erroneously, evilly, fallaciously, falsely, faultily, illegally, illicitly, immorally, improperly, inaccurately, inaptly, incorrectly, mistakenly, sinfully, unfairly, unjustly, unlawfully, unsoundly, wickedly, wrongfully
**wrongly conceived** mistaken
**wrongly overthrow** usurp
**wrong move** misstep
**wrong name** misnomer
**wrong opinion** error
**wrong time** intempestivity
**wroth** angry, distraught, enraged, fuming, heated, incensed, irate, irrational, raving, violent, wrathful, wroth
**wrought** acted, controlled, directed, drudged, handled, laboured,

managed, manipulated, moved, operated, slaved, toiled
**wrought iron process** puddling
**wrought up** agitated, angry, annoyed, aroused, delirious, edgy, excited, fervid, fiery, flushed, frantic, fuming, furious, irritated, mad, nervous, raging, ruffled, stimulated, tense, uneasy, upset, vexed, zealous
**wry** askew, aslant, awry, bent, contorted, contrary, crooked, deformed, deviate, distort(ed), inclined, ironic, lopsided, misread, oblique, perverted, quizzical, sardonic, tilted, turn(ed), twisted, warped, wrest, writhe
**wry face** grimace
**wryneck** torticollis
**Wyatt** Earp
**Wycliffe follower** Lollard

# X

**xanthic** yellow(ish)
**Xanthippe** crone, fishwife, fury, hag, harpy, harridan, nag, she-wolf, shrew, virago, witch, Xantippe
**Xanthippe's spouse** Socrates
**xanthous** golden, honey, saffron, topaz, yellowish
**xebec** boat, ship, vessel
**xenagogue** guide
**xenium** dainty, delicacy, gift, present
**xenodochy** hospitality
**xenogamy** (cross-)fertilisation
**xenogenesis** abiogenesis
**xenophobe** enemy, foe, phobia
**xenophobic** anti-semitic, chauvinistic, confined, distant, fearful, jingoistic, limited, nationalist, parochial, provincial, racist, regional, shy, small-minded, unassertive
**xeres** jerez, sherry
**xeric** dry
**xeroderma** ichthyosis, xerodermia
**xerography** photography, printing
**xerophilous animal** camel
**xerophilous plant** cactus, xerophyte
**xerus** squirrel
**xiphoid** ensiform, sword-shaped
**Xmas** Christmas, Noel, Yule(tide)
**Xmas cravat** Yule tie
**Xmas farce** pantomime
**Xmas glitter** tinsel
**Xmas month** December
**Xmas season** yule(tide)
**Xmas song** carol
**Xmas sprig** holly
**X-ray** radiograph, roentgenogram, skiagraph, urogram
**X-ray discoverer** Roentgen, Röntgen
**X-ray photograph of the brain** encephalogram
**X-ray radiography** sciagraphy, skiagraphy
**X-shape** cross
**X-shaped** crossed, cruciate, decussate, ex
**Xtian standard** labarum
**xylem** wood
**xylograph** engraving, impression, print, woodcut
**xyloid** ligneous, woody
**xylonite** celluloid
**xylophone** gigelira, marimba, regal, saron, sticcado, vibraharp
**xylophone-like instrument with tuned stones** lithophone
**xyrid** iris
**xyst** portico, stoa, terrace
**xyster** bone-scraper
**xystus** portico, stoa, terrace, walk, xyst

# Y

**yacht** motorboat, racer, sail(boat), speedboat, travel, voyage
**yacht basin** marina
**yachting** cruising, maritime, nautical, naval, sailing, seafaring
**yacht pole** spar
**yacht race** regatta
**yacht racing** sonderclass
**yak** babble, bovine, buffalo, chatter, gab, gyag, jabber, ox, sarlak, talk, zobo
**yak country** Tibet
**yale** latch
**yam** root, shrub, sweet potato, tuber
**yammer** bawl, complain, groan, grouse, growl, grumble, henpeck, howl, mewl, moan, mumble, murmur, mutter, nag, pule, roar, utter, whimper, whine
**Yank** American, Yankee
**yank** hitch, jerk, jog, pluck, pull, snatch, tug, twitch, wrench
**Yankee** American, New Englander
**yap** blab, blather, chatter, converse, gabble, gossip, gush, jabber, lecture, palaver, prattle, rave, scold, skinder, talk, tattle, yawp, yelp, yip
**yard** area, backyard, dockyard, enclosure, farmground, shipyard, space, store, verge, workshop
**yardstick** benchmark, criterion, gauge, guideline, ideal, measure, model, norm, paradigm, paragon, pattern, regulation, ruler, scale, standard, touchstone
**yardstick division** foot
**Yarkand** Shache
**yarmulke** skullcap
**yarn** anecdote, clew, crewel, fable, fabrication, falsehood, fibre, fiction, invention, story, strand, tale, thread, wool
**yarn ball** clew
**yarn bundle** skein
**yarn fibre** strand
**yarn fluff** lint
**yarn for the warp** abb
**yarn quantity** ball, hank, reel, skein

**yarn reel** pirn
**yarn worker** spinner
**yarrow** herb, milfoil
**yashmak** cloak, cover, veil
**yaw** zig-zag
**yawn** gape
**yawn inducer** bore
**yawning** agape, cavernous, chasmal, drowsy, gaping, sleepy, tired, vast, weary, wide
**yawning hollow** chasm
**yawn open** gape
**yclept** named
**yean** lamb
**year** age, annum, date, make, model, period, session, space, span, spell, stretch, term, time, vintage
**year after year** annually
**yearbook** almanac, annals, annual, calendar, registry
**year division** season
**year in and year out** everlasting, interminably, regularly, unchangingly
**yearly** annual(ly), endlessly, regularly, unfailingly
**yearly amount** annuity
**yearly book** annual
**yearly calendar** almanac
**yearly celebration** anniversary, birthday, Christmas, Easter, Lent
**yearly payment** annuity
**yearly records of events** annals
**yearly return of a date** anniversary
**yearn** ache, aspire, chase, covet, crave, desire, hanker, hope, hunger, itch, languish, long, lust, miss, need, pant, pine, pray, prefer, require, sigh, want, welcome, wish
**yearn for** covet, crave, desire, pine, want
**yearning for the past** nostalgia
**yearning sound** sigh
**yearning with little hope** wistful
**year of wonders** annus mirabilis (L)
**year-old bird** annotine
**years ago** once
**years between forty and sixty** middle age
**year's crops** annona
**years from thirteen to nineteen** teens
**years of one's life** age
**year's record** annal
**yeast** agitation, bubbles, confusion, ferment, foam, hubbub, lather, leaven, mould, rise, spume(scence), zyme
**yeast on brewing liquor** barm
**yebo** yes
**yell** bark, bawl, bellow, boo, call, cheer, clamour, cry, ejaculate, holler, howl, roar, scream, screech, shout, shriek, squall, squeal, ululate, utter, yelp, yowl
**yell for one's team** root
**yell guide** cheerleader
**yelling** screaming, shouting
**yellow** amber, jaundiced, sallow, xanthic
**yellow alloy of copper** brass
**yellow and orange gem** amber, chrysoberyl, citrine, topaz
**yellow bark** calisaya
**yellow bird** canary
**yellow brown** fawn-coloured, sorrel
**yellow brown gem** tiger's-eye
**yellow brown horse** chestnut
**yellow bugle** iva
**yellow cornelian** sard
**yellow cotton cloth** nankeen
**yellow dye** tartrazine, uranin, weld, wold
**yellow fever** jaundice
**yellow fever mosquito** aedes
**yellow flag** infectious, quarantine
**yellow-fleshed turnip** swede
**yellow flower** alyssum, daffodil, primrose
**yellow fossil resin** amber
**yellow fruit** banana
**yellow gem** topaz
**yellow gray colour** drab
**yellow green colour** olive
**yellow green mineral** epidote
**yellowing of the skin** jaundice
**yellow internal part of egg** yolk
**yellowish** xanthic
**yellowish brown colour** khaki, tan, tawny
**yellowish brown variety of sapphire** oriental topaz
**yellowish edible fungus** chanterelle
**yellowish gem** topaz
**yellowish green** chartreuse, lime, reseda
**yellowish green gem** chrysoberyl
**yellowish green mineral** olivine
**yellowish green variety of andradite garnet** topazolite
**yellowish pigment** ochre
**yellowish red** maroon
**yellowish red dye** isatin(e)
**yellowish viscous matter** pus
**yellowish white wall paint** ochre
**yellow jacket** eucalypt, hornet, wasp
**yellow light** amber
**yellow like gold** gilt
**yellow liquid enjoyed with pudding** custard
**yellow ocker** etiolin, sil
**yellow of egg** yoke
**yellow paint pigment** cadmium sulphide
**yellow pigment** carotene, flavin, gamboge, massicot, ochre, puccoon
**yellow pond lily** nuphar
**yellow red** coral
**yellow resin** amber
**yellow rice** geelrys
**Yellow Sea** Hwanghai
**yellow shade** amber
**yellow singing-bird** canary
**yellow skin disease** jaundice
**yellow-skinned fruit** banana
**yellow songbird** canary
**yellow spring flower** daffodil
**yellow stone** citrine, topaz
**yellow stoneware** caneware
**yellow streak** cowardice
**yellowthroat** warbler
**yellow tincture** arnica
**yellow toadflax** ranstead
**yellow traffic light** amber
**yellow tropical fruit** banana, pineapple
**yellow variety of quartz** topaz
**yellow weed** dandelion
**yellowwood** avidire, geelhout
**yelp** bark, cry, yap, yip
**yelping dog** wappet
**Yemen goverment seat** Taiz
**Yemen port** Aden, Mocha, Mukha
**Yemen ruler** imam
**Yemen sect** Zaidi
**yen** ambition, craving, desire, hankering, itch, longing, money, yearn(ing)
**yeoman** assistant, cavalry, clerk, countryman, freeholder, landowner, retainer, rustic, servant, warder
**yeomanly** allegiant, dedicated, devoted, faithful, firm, loyal, patriotic, stable, staunch, true
**Yeoman of the Guard** Beefeater
**yeomanry** army, cavalry, volunteer
**yes** affirmative, ay(e), da (R), ja, OK, oui (F), si (I), si (Sp), yah, yea, yebo
**yes man** flatterer, bootlicker, minion, sponger, sycophant, toady
**yesterday** hier (F)
**yes to invitation** acceptance
**yes vote** aye
**yet** besides, but, further, however, nonetheless, still, though, while
**yet to be paid** owing
**yet to come** future, tomorrow, unborn
**Yiddish** Jewish, language
**Yiddish bless** bensh
**Yiddish synagogue** shul
**yield** accede, acquiesce, afford, bear, bow, (con)cede, confess, consent, crop, defer, give, net, obey, produce, profit, relax, relent, relinquish, repent, return, submit, succumb, supply, surrender, waive

**yielding** accommodating, acquiescent, agreeable, amenable, capitulating, ceding, compliant, consenting, docile, easy, elastic, flexible, generating, gentle, meek, obedient, pliable, pliant, producing, providing, quaggy, resilient, soft, spongy, submissive, subservient, timid, tractable, tractile, unresistant, unresisting
**yielding an acid in water solution** acidic
**yielding considerable profits** lucrative
**yielding copper** cupriferous
**yielding gold** auriferous
**yielding iron** ferriferous
**yielding oil** oleiferous
**yielding profit** profitable
**yielding silver** argentiferous
**yielding to pressure** soft
**yield precious metals** pan
**yields bitter juice** aloe
**yields copra** coconut
**yield the means** afford
**yield to pressure** buckle, crack, fold, give
**yield under pressure** break, give, relent
**yield without restraint** abandon
**yobbo** lout
**yodel** warble
**yoga** bhakti, concentration, jnana, meditation
**yoga posture** asana
**yogi** ascetic, devotee, fakir, swami, yogin
**yoke** attachment, bond, buckle, burden, chain, collar, connective, couple, frame, harness, join, knot, link, servitude, team, tie
**yoke bar** skey
**yoked beast** ox
**yoked beasts** oxen
**yokel** boor, bucolic, backvelder, bumpkin, clodhopper, hick, peasant, rube
**yoke of beasts** span
**yoking** bout, bracketing, connecting, contest, coupling, harnessing, hitching, joining, linking, tying, uniting
**yolk of egg** vitellus
**yolky** eggy, yellowish
**Yom Kippur** Holy Day
**yon** distant, remote, that, yonder
**yonder** afar, faraway, farther, further, inaccessible, remote, there, tramontane, unapproachable, yon
**Yorkshire man** tyke
**you** du (G), te (Sp), thee, thon (Sc), thou, tu (L), ye
**you also** tu quoque (L)
**you and I** we

**you and me** us, we
**you bet your life** absolutely
**you blow it up** balloon
**you change it** gear
**you hit it** ball
**young** adolescent, ageless, boyish, callow, childish, cub, girlish, immature, inexperienced, infant, jejune, junior, juvenile, kitten, litter, minor, new, puerile, raw, teenage, tender, underage, vigorous, whelp, youth(ful)
**young aches** growing pains
**young actress** starlet
**young African boy** kwedin(i), umfaan
**young amphibian** tadpole
**young and inexperienced person** beginner, fledg(e)ling, novice, tyro
**young animal** calf, cub, kid, pup
**young animal's earliest stage** embryo
**young antelope** kid
**young aspiring professional** yuppie
**young badger** cub
**young barracuda** spet
**young bear** cub
**young bird** chick, eya, flapper, fledg(e)ling, nestling, owlet, piper
**young bird of prey** eaglet
**young birds from one hatching** brood
**young bird's home** nest
**young blossom** bud
**young bluefish** snapper
**young boar** calf, piglet, squeaker
**young boy** lad, lightie, piccanin
**young branch** shoot, sucker
**young bull** bullock, stirk
**young canine** pup(py), whelp
**young cat** kit(ten)
**young chap** boy, lad
**young chicken** chick, fryer, pullet
**young chicken bred for eating** poussin
**young child** bambino, changeling, chit, lightie, nipper, nursling, papoose, piccanin, pik(kie), tad, toddler, tot
**young child's sweet** jelly baby
**young coalfish** grayfish, podler, podley
**young cock** cockerel
**young cod** scrod, sprag
**young cow** calf, heifer
**young dandy** fopling
**young deer** calf, fawn, kid, spitter
**young devil** imp
**young doctor working in hospital** intern
**young doe** tag, teg
**young dog** pup(py), whelp
**young domestic cock** cockerel
**young domestic fowl** poult, pullet
**young dove** dovelet
**young duck** duckling
**young eagle** eaglet

**young eel** elver
**young elephant** calf
**young elk** deacon
**younger** junior
**younger son** cadet
**youngest son of Jesse** David
**young falcon** eyas
**young fallow deer** fawn
**young farm animal** bullock, calf, cockerel, colt, eanling, filly, foal, heifer, kitten, lamb, piglet, pullet, pup(py), shoat, steer, stirk, stot, teg, whelp, (y)eanling, yearling
**young fatted animal** fatling
**young feline** kitten
**young fellow** boy, lad
**young female** girl, miss
**young female donkey** filly
**young female hog** gilt
**young female horse** filly
**young fish** alevin, fingerling, fry, minnow, parr
**young fishes fresh from the spawn** fry
**young foreigner** au pair (F)
**young fowl** bird, poult
**young fox** cub, kit
**young frog** tadpole
**young game bird** poult
**young girl** bud, chit, flapper, lass, maid(en), rosebud, titty
**young Girl Scout** Brownie
**young goat** kid, yearling
**young goose** gosling
**young greyhound** sapling
**young guillemot** willock
**young guinea-fowl** keet
**young gull** scaurie (Sc)
**young haddock** scrod
**young hare** leveret
**young hawk** bowess, bowet, brancher, eyas, kite, nias
**young heir** scion
**young hen** chicken, pullet
**young herring** brit, sardine, sild, sprat, sprot
**young hog** shoat, shote
**young hooligan** larrikin
**young hooting bird** owlet
**young horse** colt, filly, foal, yearling
**young insect** nit
**young kangaroo** joey
**young knight** bachelor
**young lad** gossoon
**young lady** belle, damsel, fraulein (G), girl, juvenile, lass, maiden, miss, teenager, youngster
**young lamb** (y)eanling
**young leaf** leaflet
**young leopard** cub, whelp
**young lion** cub, lionet
**young mackerel** spike
**young male** boy, lad

**young male bovine** steer
**young male donkey** colt, foal
**young male horse** colt
**young male ox** steer
**young mammal** cub
**young man** boy, chiel (Sc), jawan, lad
**young man in love** Romeo
**young man paid by older woman for his attention** gigolo
**young mare** filly
**young member of a family** scion
**young menhaden** sardine
**young miss** girl, lass
**young night bird** owlet
**young nymph** nymphet
**young of animals** brood
**young onion** scallion
**young otter** cub
**young owl** owlet
**young ox** steer, stot
**young oyster** spat
**young partridge** flapper
**young peafowl** peachick
**young person** child, juvenile, lightie, nipper, piccanin, pik(kie), youngster
**young personal attendant** page
**young pet** kitten, puppy
**young pig** piglet, pigling, shoat, shote
**young pigeon** squab
**young pike** pickerel
**young pilchard** sardine
**young plant** phytum, seedling, set, springer
**young polecat** kit
**young prince** princeling
**young rabbit** bunny, leveret, nestling
**young racehorse** yearling
**young rhinoceros** calf

**young river salmon** smolt
**young roguish child** imp, rogue, urchin
**young rowdy** hoodlum
**young ruffian** hooligan, punk
**young rustic** swain
**young salmon** alevin, essling, fog, grilse, jerkin, minnow, parr, pinks, samlet, skeggar, smolt
**young screen star** starlet
**young seal** cub, pup, whelp
**young sheep** hog, lamb, teg
**young shellfish** spat
**young shoot** cyme
**young society woman** débutante
**young sow** gilt
**young sponge** ascon
**young steer** stot
**youngster** adolescent, baby, boy, child, girl, juvenile, kid, lad, lightie, nipper, offspring, piccanin, pik(kie), progeny, shaver, tad, teenager, tot, youth
**young street rowdy** hooligan, larrikin
**young swan** cygnet
**young swine** pig
**young thug** hoodlum, skollie
**young tiger** cub
**young tree** sapling
**young tree frog** peeper
**young trout** alevin
**young turkey** po(u)lt
**young unmarried woman** damsel, maiden
**young walrus** calf
**young weaned pig** shoat
**young whale** calf
**young wild-duck** flapper

**young woman** damsel, filly, girl, lass, maid(en), sheila, wench
**young woman in charge of a child** nursemaid
**young woman making social début** débutante
**young zebra** colt, filly, foal
**younker** knight, nobleman, stripling
**you pray on them** knees
**your** votre (F)
**your equal** peer
**your majesty** sire
**yours and mine** ours
**yourself** ti (Sp)
**you take one to move** step
**youth** adolescence, adolescent, boy(hood), childhood, girl(hood), immaturity, infancy, juvenescence, kid, lad, neophyte, stripling, teenager, youngster
**youthful** juvenile, young
**youthful years** teens
**youth loved by Venus** Adonis
**youth not fully grown** stripling
**youth shelter** hostel
**Ypres** leper (Flemish)
**Yugoslav** Croat, Serb(ian), Slovene
**Yugoslavian money** dinar, para
**Yugoslavian province** Banat
**Yugoslav leader** Tito
**Yugoslav region** Bosnia
**Yugoslav terrorists** Ustashi
**Yukon mountain peak** Logan
**Yule** Christmas
**Yumen Indian** Mohave
**yummy** delicious, tasty, toothsome

# Z

**zacatilla** cochineal
**zany** clownish, foolish, madcap
**zeal** alacrity, ardour, bounce, compliance, determination, devotedness, devotion, eagerness, ecstasy, élan, elation, enthusiasm, fervency, fervour, gusto, interest, keenness, passion, spirit, vigour, vitality, willingness, zest
**zealot** bigot, devotee, enthusiast, extremist, fanatic, maniac, militant, partisan, promotor, radical, supporter
**zealotry** bias, bigotry, dogmatism, fanaticism, insanity, intolerance,
monomania, narrow-mindedness, obsession, passion, prejudice
**zealous** ardent, devoted, eager, earnest, energetic, enthusiastic, fanatical, fervent, fervid, fierce, pious, rabid, raging, raving, religious, tenacious, vehement, vigorous
**zealous about beauty** aesthetic
**zealously** fast, heartily, innerly
**zealously loyal** devoted
**zebrawood** araroba, zingana
**zeitgeist** conatus, direction, drift, inclination, liking, nisus, penchant, spirit, tempo, tendency, tenor, time spirit, trend

**zenana** harem, seralgio
**zenana resident** concubine, odalisk, odalisque
**zenith** acme, apex, climax, crown, culmination, extreme, height, meridian, peak, perfection, pinnacle, spire, summit, supremacy, tip, top, vertex
**Zeno's followers** Stoics
**zephyr** air, breeze, wind
**zeppelin** airship, balloon, blimp
**zero** love, nil, nobody, nonentity, nothing, nought, nullity, zilch
**zero handicap** scratch
**zero hour** crisis

**zero in tennis** love
**zero number** nothing
**zest** appetite, dash, drive, dynamism, edge, élan, energy, enthusiasm, fire, flavour, gust(o), intensity, interest, joy, keenness, liveliness, lustiness, piquancy, pleasure, relish, smack, spice, spurt, taste, verve, vigour
**zestful** animated, brisk, curried, energetic, hearty, hot, lively, peppery, piquant, pungent, savoury, spicy, vivacious, vivid
**zestful enjoyment** gusto
**zibet** cat, civet
**zigzag** yaw
**zigzag embroidery stitch** featherstitch
**zigzag ski race** slalom
**zilch** nothing
**Zimbabwe's former name** Rhodesia
**zinc alloy** bidri, oriode
**zinc and copper alloy** pinchbeck
**zinc carbonate** calamine
**zinc ore** blende
**zinc oxide** tutty
**zing** energy, pep, spirit, vigour, vim, vitality, zest

**Zion location** Jerusalem
**zip** animation, buzz, dash, drive, energy, force, gusto, hiss, impact, intensity, life, liveliness, pep, punch, spirit, strength, verve, vigour, vim, vivacity, whine, whistle, zest
**zipping up** fastening
**zircon** azorite, gem, jacinth, jargon
**zither harp** koto
**Zoan** Tanis
**zobo** ox, yak, zebu
**zodiac** bawdrick, girdle, signifier
**zodiacal study** astrology
**zodiac bull** Taurus
**zodiac lion** Leo
**zodiac prediction** horoscope
**zodiac ram** Aries
**zodiac sign** Aquarius, Aries, Cancer, Capricorn, Gemini, Leo, Libra, Pisces, Sagittarius, Scorpio, Taurus, Virgo
**zodiac twins** Gemini
**zona** zoster
**zonal** regional
**zone** area, belt, district, division, domain, expanse, hemisphere, locale, locality, location, orbit, province, quarter, region, section, sector, sphere, territory
**zone of ecologic struggle** ecotone, region
**zoo** menagerie
**zoo animal** ape, buck, camel, elephant, giraffe, leopard, lion, panda, tiger
**zoological warder** keeper
**zoophilia** bestiality
**zoophyte** coral, hydroid, sponge
**zoo ship** ark
**zoril** polecat
**Zoroastrian sacred writings** Avesta
**zoster** zona
**zucchini** courgette
**Zulu medicine** muti
**Zulu spear** assegai
**Zulu warriors** impi
**zygal** H-shaped
**zyme** enzyme, ferment, yeast
**zymosis** fermentation

# Abbreviations

## A

abbess abb
abbreviation abbr
ablative abl
about c, ca (circa)
above sup (supra)
abridge abr
abridgement abr
absent without official leave AWOL
absolute abs
absolute temperature T
academy Acad
acceptance acc
according to the value ad val (ad valorem)
account acct, a/c
account of a/o
Account Sales A/S
accused acc
acre A
acting actg, ad int (ad interim)
Active Citizen Force ACF
address addr
adjective a, adj
Adjutant Adj
Administration Adm
Administrator General AG
Admiral Adm
adverb adv
adverbial adv
advertisement advt
Advocate Adv
African National Congress ANC
African National Congress Youth League ANCYL
Afrikaans Afr
Afrikaanse Handelsinstituut AHI
Afrikaanse Studentebond ASB
Afrikaanse Taal- en Kultuurvereniging ATKV
Afrikaner Weerstandsbeweging AWB
after date a/d
after sight a/s
against all risks AAR
agriculture agr(ic)
aide-de-camp ADC
air-to-air missile AAM
air-to-surface missile ASM
Air Traffic Control ATC
Alcoholics Anonymous AA
algebra alg
algebraic alg
alphabet ABC
alternate alt
alternating current AC
altitude alt
America Am
American Broadcasting Company ABC
amount amt
ampere(s) amp
amplitude modulation AM
analysis anal
and elsewhere et al (et alibi)
and others cs (cum suis), et al (et alii)
and so forth etc (et cetera)
and the following et seq (et sequens)
Anglo-Saxon AS
annual general meeting AGM
answer ans
anti-ballistic missile ABM
Apostolic Faith Mission AFM
appellant app
appendage app
Arabian Arab
Arabic Arab
archaeology archaeol
archaic arch
Archbishop Abp
architecture arch
argon A
arithmetic(al) arith
arranged by arr
arrival arr
article art
artificial insemination AI
artificial insemination by husband AIH
artillery art
as above us (ut supra)
as below ui (ut infra)
as loud as possible fff (fortissimo)
as much as suffices qs (quantum sufficit)
assistant asst
Associated Press AP
associate in arts AA
Associate of the Royal Academy ARA
Associate of the Royal College of Music ARCM
Associate of the South African Library Association ASALA
Association Assoc, Ass(n)
Association of Chambers of Commerce of South Africa ASSOCOM
as softly as possible ppp (pianisissimo)
assorted ass
astrology astrol
Astronomical Society of Southern Africa ASSA
astronomy astr
Atlantic Standard Time AST
atmosphere atm
at pleasure ad lib (ad libitum)
at the age of aet, aetat (aetatis)
attorney atty
Attorney-General AG
attribute attrib
Audit Bureau of Circulation ABC
author auth
Automobile Association AA
auxiliary verb aux v
Avenue Av(e)
average av
Azanian People's Liberation Army APLA
Azanian People's Organisation AZAPO

## B

Bachelor of Agricultural Science BSc Agric
Bachelor of Architecture BArch
Bachelor of Arts BA
Bachelor of Arts (Social Sciences) BA(Soc Sc)
Bachelor of Civil Law BCL
Bachelor of Commerce BCom(m)
Bachelor of Dental Surgery BChD
Bachelor of Divinity BD
Bachelor of Economics BEcon
Bachelor of Education BEd
Bachelor of Engineering BEng
Bachelor of Laws LLB
Bachelor of Letters BLit(t)
Bachelor of Medicine BM
Bachelor of Military Science BMil
Bachelor of Music BMus
Bachelor of Philosophy BPhil
Bachelor of Physical Education BEdPh
Bachelor of Science BSc
Bachelor of Surgery BCh
Bachelor of Veterinary Science BVSc
balance bal
balance sheet bs
barometer bar
Baronet Bart, Bt
barrel bl
battalion Bn, Batn
battery batty, batt
bed and breakfast b&b
before Christ BC
before noon am (ante meridiem)
before the day ad (ante diem)
Belgium Belg
below inf (infra)
Bible Bib
Bible Society of South Africa BSSA

bilingual dictionary BD
bills payable B/P
bills receivable B/R
biology biol
Black Consciousness Movement BCM
book bk
bookkeeping bkk, bookk
Bophuthatswana Bop
born n (natus)
born, née b, n (natus)
botany bot
Botswana Bot
Boys' High School BHS
brake horsepower bhp
breadth b
Brigadier Brig
Britain Br, Brit
British Br, Brit
British and Foreign Bible Society BFBS
British Broadcasting Corporation BBC
British Empire Service League BESL
brother b, bro
Brothers Bros
brought forward B/F
building bldg
Building Society Institute BSI
built-in-cupboards bic
by the grace of God DG (Dei Gratia)

## C

calorie cal
candela cd
candidate officer co
candlepower cp
Cape Colony CC
Cape Peninsula Local Authorities CPLA
Cape Performing Arts Board CAPAB
Cape Province Agricultural Union CPAU
Cape Teachers' Professional Association CTPA
capital cap
Captain Capt
carat car, ct
care of c/o
carriage paid carr pd
case c
cash-book C/B
cash on delivery COD
cash with order CWO
catalogue cat
caught c
caught and bowled c and b
cent c
centiare(s) ca
Centigrade C, Cels

centigram cg
centilitre cl
centimetre cm
central business district CBD
Central Intelligence Agency CIA
Central Organisation of Technical Training COTT
certificate cert
chairman ch, C
Chamber of Commerce C of C
chapter ch(ap), c
chartered accountant CA
Chartered Institute of Secretaries CIS
chemical chem
chemistry chem
Christ Chr
Christian Chr
Christian National Education CNE
classics class
close corporation CC
collectively coll
College Coll
Colonel Col
Commandant Comdt
Commander Cdr, Comd(r)
Commander-in-Chief C-in-C
Commanding Officer CO
commerce comm
commission comm
commissioner comm
committee com
Commodore Cdre, Comm
Communications Satellite COMSAT
Communist Information Bureau Cominform
Communist International Comintern
Company Co, Coy
comparative comp
compare cp, cf
compound comp
conductor cond
Congress of Industrial Organisations CIO
Congress of South African Trade Unions COSATU
conjugation conj
conjunction conj
conjunctive conj
Conservative Cons
Conservative Party CP
consignment cons
consonant cons
Constable Const
co-operative co-op
corner cor
Corporal Cpl, Corp
Corporation Corp
correspondence corr
correspondent corr
cosecant cosec
cosine cos
cost, insurance, freight cif

cotangent cot
Councillor Cllr, Cr
Council of Education Research CER
Council of Scientific and Industrial Research CSIR
credit Cr
credit balance CB
cubic cu(b)
cubic centimetre cc
cubic feet per second cusec
cum dividend cd, cum div (cum dividendo)
currency cur

## D

data processing DP
data transmission DT
dative dat, d
debit note D/N
debtor Dr
decagram Dg
decalitre Dl
decametre Dm
decibel dB
Deciduous Fruit Board DFB
decigram dg
decilitre dl
decimetre dm
declension decl
declination dec
Decoration for Meritorious Service DMS
defective mental development DMD
Defence Headquarters DHQ
Defence Rifle Association DRA
defendant def
definition def
degree deg
delete dele (deleatur)
delirium tremens DT
delivery order D/O
Democrat Dem
Democratic Dem
Democratic Party DP
Democratic Turnhalle Alliance DTA
demonstrative dem
dentist dent
dentistry dent
deoxyribonucleic acid DNA
Department Dept
departure dep
deputy dep
derivation der
Deutsche Mark DM
dialect dial
dichlorodiphenyltrichloroethane DDT
dictionary dict
died d
difference diff
different diff

diminutive dim
Diploma Dip
Diploma in Public Health DPH
Diploma in Veterinary Public Health DVPH
Diplomatic Corps CD (Corps Diplomatique)
direct current DC
Director Dir
Director-General DG
Director of Education DE
disc jockey DJ
discount dis(c)
displaced person DP
distant early warning DEW
Distinguished Conduct Medal DCM
Distinguished Service Order DSO
district dist
ditto do
dividend div
division div
Doctor Dr
doctorand(us) Drs
Doctor of Civil Law DCL
Doctor of Divinity DD
Doctor of Economics DEcon
Doctor of Education DEd
Doctor of Engineering DEng
Doctor of Laws LLD
Doctor of Literature DLit(t)
Doctor of Literature and Philosophy DLit(t) et Phil
Doctor of Medicine DM, Dr Med
Doctor of Music MusD(oc)
Doctor of Philosophy DPhil, Dr Phil
Doctor of Science DSc
Doctor of Theology Dr Th
Doctor of Veterinary Science DMedVet, DVSc
Doctors Drs
document against acceptance D/A
document against payment D/P
do-it-yourself DIY
double garage dgar
dozen doz
drachm dr
drew it del (delineavit)
duplicate dup
Durban Dbn
Dutch East India Company DEIC
Dutch Reformed DR
Dutch Reformed Church DRC

## E

East E
Eastern Province EP
Eastern Standard Time EST
East Germanic EGer
East London EL
east longitude Elong
east-north-east ENE
east-south-east ESE
Ecclesiastes Eccles
Ecclesiasticus Ecclus
Economic Commission for Europe ECE
Economic Commission for Africa ECA
economics econ
edition ed
editor Ed
electricity elec
Electricity Supply Commission Escom, Eskom
electrocardiogram ECG
electroconvulsive therapy ECT
electroencephalogram EEG
electromotive force EMF
Eminence Em
enclosed encl
enclosure encl
engineer eng
England Eng
errors and omissions excepted E and OE
especially esp
Esquire Esq
estimated time of arrival ETA
ethnology ethnol
etymology etym
Europe Eur
European Eur
European Atomic Energy Commission Euratom
European Common Market ECM
European Development Fund EDF
European Economic Community EEC
European Union EU
example ex
Excellency Exc
Executive Committee Exco
Executive Council Ex Council
exercise ex
extension ext
extrasensory perception ESP

## F

Fahrenheit F
faithfully yours tt (totus tuus)
family fam
farad F
Father Fr
Federal Bureau of Investigation FBI
Federal Chambers of Industries FCI
Fellow of the College of Physicians (SA) FCP (SA)
Fellow of the Institute of Actuaries FIA
Fellow of the Royal Academy of Music FRAM
Fellow of the Royal College of Music FRCM
feminine f, fem
Field Cornet FC
Field Marshal FM
figurative fig
figure fig
first in first out FIFO
Fishing Industry Research Institute FIRI
Flanders Fl
Flemish Fl
floor fl
florin fl
folio fol
following fol, seq (sequens)
Food and Agriculture Organisation FAO
foot f, ft
Football Association of South Africa FASA
Football Club FC
for example eg (exempli gratia)
for instance fi
for the greater glory of God AMDG (ad majorem Dei gloriam)
franc fr, F
France Fr
free alongside ship fas
free on board fob
free on quay foq
free on rail for
French Fr
frequency modulation FM
Friday F, Fri
from fr
from date ad (a dato)
from the beginning DC (da capo)
Fuel Research Institute FRI
full container load fcl
furlong fur
future fut

## G

Gaelic Gael
Gallic Gall
gallon gal
garage gar
General Gen
General Headquarters GHQ
General Officer Commanding GOC
General Post Office GPO
general practitioner GP
General Sales Tax GST
General Staff GS
genitive gen
geodesy geod
geography geog
geology geol
geometrica geom

geometry	geom
George Cross	GC
German	Ger
German Democratic Republic	GDR
German Federal Republic	GFR
Germanism	Ger
German Standard	DIN (Deutsche Industrie-Norm)
Germany	Ger
Girls' High School	GHS
glossary	gloss
God willing	DV (Deo volente)
Gothic	Goth
Government	Govt
Government Garage	GG
Government Gazette	GG
Government Gazette Extraordinary	GGE
government issue	GI
Government Notice	GN
Governor	Gov
grain	gr
gram	g
grammar	gram
Great Britain	GB
greatest common divisor	GCD
Greece	Gr
Greek	Gr
Greenwich Mean Time	GMT
Griqualand West	GW
gross	gr(o)
gross national product	GNP
gross vehicle mass	GVM
growing in force	cresc (crescendo)
guinea	g
Gunner	Gnr
gymnasium	gym

## H

hail to the reader	LS (lectori salutem)
headquarters	HQ
hectare	ha
hectogram	hg
hectolitre	hl
hectometre	hm
height	h
henry	H
heraldry	her
Her Excellency	HE
Her Highness	HH
Her Majesty	HM
Her Royal Highness	HRH
hertz	Hz
he, she carved it	sc, sculp (sculpsit)
he, she wrote it	scr (scripsit)
Higher Education Diploma	HED
Higher Secondary Education Diploma	HSED
highest common factor	HCF
High German	HG
high pressure	hp
hire-purchase	hp
His Eminence	HEm
His Excellency	HE
His Highness	HH
His Imperial Highness	HIH
His Majesty	HM
His Royal Highness	HRH
history	hist
Holy Roman Empire	HRE
honorary	hc (honoris causa)
Honorary Secretary	Hon Sec
Honourable	Hon
horsepower	hp
Hottentot	Hott
hour	h (hora)
Human Sciences Research Council	HSRC
hundredweight	cwt

## I

if you please	svp (s'il vous plaît)
illicit diamond buying	IDB
illustrated	illus
imperative	imp
imperfect	imp, imperf
Imperial Light Horse	ILH
impersonal	impers
impudent lass	minx
inch	in
including	incl
indefinite	indef
indefinitely	sd (sine die)
independent television	ITV
index	ind
India	Ind
indicative	ind, indic
Indo-European	IE
Indo-Germanic	IG
Indonesia	Indon
infantry	inf
infinitive	inf
in his capacity	qq (qualitate qua)
initial teaching alphabet	ita, ITA
in its place	in loc (in loco)
in memory	In Mem (in memoriam)
inorganic	inorg
inspection	insp
inspector	insp
instead of a seal	LS (loco sigilli)
institute	inst
Institute for Medical Research	IMR
Institute of Race Relations	IRR
instruction	instr
instrumental	instr
insurance	ins
intelligence quotient	IQ
interest	int
intermediate-range ballistic missile	IRBM
International Aeronautical Federation	FAI
International Amateur Athletic Federation	IAAF
International Amateur Swimming Federation	FINA
International Atomic Energy Agency	IAEA
International Bureau of Weights and Measures	BIPM
International Chamber of Commerce	ICC
International Chess Federation	FIDE
International Civil Aviation Organisation	ICAO
International Finance Corporation	IFC
International Monetary Fund	IMF
International Olympic Committee	IOC
International Press Institute	IPI
International Rugby Board	IRB
International Telecommunication Union	ITU
International Tennis Federation	ITF
International Wool Secretariat	IWS
in the afternoon	pm (post meridiem)
in the name of God	IND (in nomine Dei)
in the place cited	ad loc (ad locum), lc
in the same place	ib, ibid (ibidem)
in this case	ic (in casu)
intransitive	intr
introduction	intro
introductory	introd
invoice	inv
Irish Republican Army	IRA
Iron and Steel Corporation	Iscor
Island	I, Is
Israel	Isr
italic	ital
Italy	It
it is not permitted	nl (non lice)

## J

Japan	Jap
Japanese	Jap
Javanese	Jav
Jesus Christ	JC
Johannesburg	Jhb
Johannesburg Stock Exchange	JSE
joule	J
July	Jul
Junction	Junc
June	Jun
Junior	Jr, Jnr, Jun(r)
Junior Certificate	JC
jurisprudence	jurisp
Justice of the Peace	JP

## K

kelvin K
Kenya African National Union KANU
kilogram kg
kilogram-metre kgm
kilohertz kHz
kilojoule kJ
kilolitre kl
kilometre km
kilometres per hour km/h
kilopascal kPa
kilosecond ks
kilovolt kV
kilovolt-ampere kVA
kilowatt kW
kilowatt-hour kWh
King's Counsel KC
kitchen, pantry, bathroom kpb
Knight Bachelor KB
Knight of the Garter KG
knock-out KO
knot kn
Koöperatiewe Wijnbouwers-Vereniging KWV
krone kr

## L

Ladies Golf Union LGU
Lake L
Lance-Corporal L/Cpl
last ult (ultimo)
last in first out LIFO
last signal for help SOS
late d
Latin Lat
latitude lat
Lawn Tennis Association LTA
Lawyers for Human Rights LHR
least common multiple LCM
left l
left-hand drive lhd
left to right l to r
legal leg
leg before wicket lbw
Legislative Council legco
length l
less loud dim (diminuendo)
let it be printed imp (imprimatur)
letter of credit L/C
Licenciate L
Licenciate in Dental Surgery LDS
Licenciate of the London College of Music LLCM
Lieutenant Lieut, Lt
Lieutenant-Colonel Lt-Col
Lieutenant-Commander Lt-Com
Lieutenant-General Lt-Gen
light-emitting diode LED
limited Ltd
line l
lira l
literary lit
literature lit
litre l
little p (poco)
logarithm log
London Missionary Society LMS
London School of Economics LSE
longitude long
long-playing record LP
loud f (forte)
Louw Wepener Decoration LWD
lower case lc
low frequency LF
low pressure lp
lumen lm
Lutheran Luth

## M

Madame Mme
Mademoiselle Mlle
Major Maj
Major General Maj Gen
Malayan Mal
Managing Director MD
manuscript MS
manuscripts MSS
March Mar
mark well NB (nota bene)
Marylebone Cricket Club MCC
masculine m, masc
Master of Agricultural Science MScAgric
Master of Arts MA
Master of Business Association MBA
master of ceremonies MC
Master of Commerce MCom(m)
Master of Economics MEcon
Master of Education MEd
Master of Engineering MEng
Master of Laws LLM
Master of Medicine MMed
Master of Science MSc
Master of Surgery ChM
Master of Theology MTh
mathematics math
maximum max
medical med
Medical Association of South Africa MASA
Medical Officer of Health MOH
Medical Research Council MRC
medicine med
medium frequency MF
meeting mtg
megahertz MHz
megajoule MJ
megavolt MV
megawatt MW
Member of Parliament MP
Member of the Executive Council MEC
Member of the Legislative Assembly MLA
Member of the Legislative Council MLC
Member of the Provincial Council MPC
Member of the Royal College of Physicians MRCP
Memorable Order of Tin Hats MOTH
Mesdames Mmes
Messieurs Messrs
Metal Workers' Union of South Africa MEWUSA
metaphor metaph
metaphysics metaph
meteorology met(eor)
metonymy meton
metre m
Middle Dutch MDu
Middle English ME
Middle High German MHG
mile m, ml
miles per gallon mpg
miles per hour mph
military mil
Military Cross MC
Military Medal MM
Military Police MP
military science mil sc
milliampere mA
millibar mbar
milligram mg
millilitre ml
millimetre mm
mineralogy min(eral)
Mineworkers' Union MWU
minimum min
mining min
Minister Min
minute m, min
Mister Mr
Mistress Mrs
modern conveniences mod cons
Monday M, Mon
money order MO
Monsignor Mgr
month m, mo
months after date m/d
Moral Rearmament MRA
motor ship MS
motor vessel MV
Mrs/Miss Ms
music mus

## N

namely sc, scll (scilicet), viz (videlicet)
Natal Agriculture Union NAU
Natal Performing Arts Council NAPAC

Natal Teachers' Association  NTA
National  Nat
National Aeronautics and Space Administration  NASA
National Association for Democratic Lawyers  NADEL
National Building Research Institute  NBRI
National Congress of Trade Unions  NACTU
National Council for Social Research  NCSR
National Council of Women  NCW
National Monument Council  NMC
National Party  NP
National Road Safety Council  NRSC
National Theatre Organisation  NTO
National Union of Metalworkers of South Africa  NUMSA
National Union of Mineworkers  NUM
National Union of South African Students  NUSAS
Natural Resources Development Council  NRDC
nautical mile  naut mi
Navy, Army and Air Force Institutes  NAAFI
Netherlands  Neth
neuter  n, neut
New Dutch  ND
new line  nl
New South Wales  NSW
Newspaper Press Union  NPU
New Style  NS
New Testament  NT
newton  N
no date  nd
Non-aligned Movement  NAM
non-commissioned officer  NCO
North  N
north-east  NE
north-north-east  NNE
north-north-west  NNW
not applicable  na
note  n
not out  no
noun  n
November  Nov
number  No (numero)
numbers  Nos
numeral  num

## O

Officer Commanding  OC
officially  eo (ex officio)
of the Christian period  AD (Anno Domini)
of the next month  prox (proximo)
Old Norse  ON
Old Saxon  OS
Old Style  OS
Old Testament  OT
on account  on a/c
Orange Free State  OFS
Order of Merit  OM
ordinance  Ord
Organisation of Petroleum Exporting Countries  OPEC
Organisation for African Unity  OAU
original  orig
or nearest offer  ono
other things being equal  cet par (ceteris paribus)
otherwise  al (alias)
ounce  oz

## P

page  p
pages  pp
paginas  pp
paid  pd
Palestine Liberation Organisation  PLO
Pan Africanist Congress  PAC
Paper, Printing and Allied Workers' Union  PPAWU
paragraph  par
Parent-Teachers' Association  PTA
Parliament  Parl
part  pt
participle  part
pascal  Pa
pay-as-you-earn  PAYE
penny  d (denarius)
pennyweight  dwt
per  p
per day  pd (per diem)
per foot  pft
Performing Arts Council of the OFS  PACOFS
Performing Arts Council of Transvaal  PACT
per hour  ph
Peri-urban Areas Health Board  PAHB
Permanent Force  PF
per minute  pm
per month  pm (per mensem)
Persian  Pers
person  pers
per week  pw
per yard  pyd
philosophy  phil
Phosphate Development Corporation  Foskor
physical education  PE
physics  phys
physiology  physiol
pint  pt
please turn over  PTO
plural  pl
point  pt
police constable  PC
politics  pol
population  pop
Port Elizabeth  PE
Portugal  Port
possessive  poss
possible  poss
postal order  PO
Postmaster  PM
Postmaster-General  PMG
Post Office  PO
Post and Telecommunication Workers' Association  POTWA
postscript  PS (post scriptum)
Potchefstroom University  PU
pound  pd, lb (libra)
pounds, shillings, pennies  Lsd (librae, solidi, denarii)
praise be to God  LD (Laus Deo)
preacher of the word of God  VDM (Verbi Dei [Divini] Minister)
prefix  pref
preposition  prep
present  pres
President  Pres
Pretoria  Pta
primarius  prim
Primary Education  Prim Ed
Prime Minister  PM
prisoner of war  POW
Private  Pte
pro  p
probable  prob
Professional Golfers' Association  PGA
Professor  Prof
Progressive  Prog
Progressive Party  PP
promissory note  pn
pronoun  pron
Proprietary  Pty
Protestant  Prot
Province  Prov
Provincial Council  PC
Provincial Notice  PN
Psalm  Ps
pseudonym  ps
public  pub
Public Relations Institute of South Africa  PRISA
public relations officer  PRO
Public Servants' Association  PSA
Public Works  PW
Public Works Department  PWD

## Q

quality  qlty
quantity  qt, qty
quarter  qr
Queen's Council  QC

# R

**radius** R
**railway** rly, ry
**rand** R
**Rand Afrikaans University** RAU
**rather loud** mf (mezzo-forte)
**rather soft** mp (mezzo-piano)
**read** r, l (lege)
**received** recd
**reduplication** redup
**reference** ref
**refer to drawer** R/D
**Reformed Ecumenical Synod** RES
**Regiment** Regt
**Regimental Sergeant-Major** RSM
**registered** regd
**relative** rel
**remark** rem
**reply paid** RP
**Republic** Rep
**Republic of South Africa** RSA
**Resident Magistrate** RM
**respectively** resp
**respondent** resp
**rest in peace** RIP (requiescat in pace)
**retired** ret
**Reverend** Rev(d)
**revolution per minute** rpm
**Rhodes University** RU
**right** r
**Right Honourable** Rt Hon
**right to left** r to l
**Road Motor Service** RMS
**Roman Catholic** RC
**room** rm
**Royal** R
**Royal Dutch Airlines** KLM
**Rugby Football Club** RFC

# S

**Saint** St
**Sanskrit** Skr
**Saturday** S, Sa(t)
**Scandinavia** Scand
**Scripture** Script
**secant** sec
**second** s, sec
**Secondary Education** SE
**Secondary Education Diploma** SED
**secretary** sec, secy
**section** sect
**see** v, vid (vide, videatur)
**Senate** Sen
**Senator** Sen
**Senior** Snr, Sr, Sen(r)
**senior advocate** SA
**Senior Council** SC (Senior Consultus)
**September** Sep(t)
**Sergeant** Sergt, Sgt
**Sergeant-Major** Sgt-Maj
**servant** serv
**servant's room** sr
**shilling** s (solidus)
**siemens** S
**signed** sgd
**sine** sin
**singular** s, sing
**slower** rit (ritardando)
**Small Business Development Corporation** SBDC
**Socialist** Soc
**Society** Soc
**Society for the Prevention of Cruelty to Animals** SPCA
**softly** p (piano)
**son** sn
**Sons of England** SOE
**South** S
**South Africa** SA
**South African Agricultural Union** SAAU
**South African Air Force** SAAF
**South African Airways** SAA
**South African Amateur Athletic Union** SAAAU
**South African Association of Arts** SAAA
**South African Association of Municipal Employees** SAAME
**South African Broadcasting Corporation** SABC
**South African Bureau for Racial Affairs** SABRA
**South African Bureau of Standards** SABS
**South African Clothing and Textile Workers' Union** SACTWU
**South African Coal, Oil and Gas Corporation** Sasol
**South African College School** SACS
**South African Congress of Trade Unions** SACTU
**South African Council of Churches** SACC
**South African Cricket Board of Control** SACBOC
**South African Cricket Union** SACU
**South African Democratic Teachers' Union** SADTU
**South African National Defence Force** SANDF
**South African Fundamental Atomic Research Installation** Safari
**South African Golf Union** SAGU
**South African Institute for Medical Research** SAIMR
**South African Institute of Building** SAIB
**South African Institute of Race Relations** SAIRR
**South African Institute of Translators and Interpreters** SAITINT
**South African Library Association** SALA
**South African Maize Producers' Institute** SAMPI
**South African Medical and Dental Council** SAMDC
**South African Miners' Union** SAMU
**South African Municipal Workers' Union** SAMWU
**South African National Council on Alcoholism** SANCA
**South African National Council for the Blind** SANCB
**South African National Council for the Care of the Aged** SANCCA
**South African National Council for Child Welfare** SANCCW
**South African National Council for the Deaf** SANCD
**South African Nursing Association** SANA
**South African Permanent Force** SAPF
**South African Police Services** SAPS
**South African Press Association** SAPA
**South African Police Union** SAPU
**South African Railways and Harbours** SAR & H
**South African Railway and Harbour Workers' Union** SARHWU
**South African Republic** SAR
**South African Rugby Union** SARU
**South African Ship** SAS
**South African Teachers' Association** SATA
**South African Tennis Union** SATU
**South African Tourist Corporation** Satour
**South African Transport Services** SATS
**South African Union of Journalists** SAUJ
**South African Women's Agricultural Union** SAWAU
**South African Women's Federation** SAWF
**South America** SA, SAm
**south-east** SE
**Southern Cross Medal** SM
**Southern Oil Exploration Corporation** Soecor, Soekor
**south-south-east** SSE
**south-south-west** SSW
**Spain** Sp
**special** spec
**specific gravity** sp, sg
**Squadron** Sqn
**square** sq
**Standard** Std
**Star of South Africa** SSA
**State President** SP
**Station** Sta

Station-Master SM
steamship SS
sterling stg
street st
student stud
Student Christian Movement SCM
Students' Christian Association SCA
Students' Representative Council SRC
stumped st
subject subj
Suid-Afrikaanse Nasionale Lewenassuransiemaatskappy Sanlam
Suid-Afrikaanse Nasionale Trust- en Assuransiemaatskappy Santam
Suid-Afrikaanse Onderwysersunie SAOU
Sunday S, Sun
Superintendent Supt
supplement suppl
surface-to-air missile SAM
SWA People's Organisation SWAPO

## T

table tab
tangent tan
Teachers' Educational and Professional Association TEPA
technical tech
technical knock-out TKO
telegram tel, telegr
telegraphic address tel add
telephone tel, teleph
temperature temp
tempo t
thanks be to God DG (Deo gratias)
that is ie (id est)
the Honourable the Hon
Their Excellencies TE
theology theol
the order being reversed vv (vice versa)
the Reverend the Rev(d)
the Right Honourable the Rt Hon
the same do, id (idem)
the speaker sp
Thursday Th, Thur(s)
to God alone the honour SDG (soli Deo gloria)
ton t
to take leave ppc (pour prendre congé)
to the end ad fin (ad finem)
to which I witness qa (quad attestor)
Trade Union Council of South Africa TUCSA
translation trans(l)
transpose trs
Transvaal Agricultural Union TAU
Transvaal Education Department TED
Transvaal Municipal Association TMA
Transvaal Provincial Administration TPA
Transvaal Teachers' Association TTA
Treasurer Treas
trinitrotoluene TNT
tuberculosis TB
Tuesday Tu(es)

## U

ultra-high frequency UHF
Umkhonto weSizwe MK
under a specified word sv (sub verbo, sub voce)
under direction of udo
unidentified flying object UFO
Union of Socialist Soviet Republics USSR
United Arab Republic UAR
United Kingdom UK
United Municipal Executive UME
United Nations UN
United Press UP
University Univ
University Education Diploma UED
University of Cape Town UCT
University of Natal UN
University of Port Elizabeth UPE
University of Pretoria UP
University of South Africa UNISA
University of Stellenbosch US
University of the Orange Free State UOFS
University of the Western Cape UWC
University of the Witwatersrand UW, Wits
upper case uc
usually usu

## V

value-added tax VAT
venereal disease VD
verb v, vb
verse v
versus v, vs
very high frequency VHF
very important person VIP
very loudly ff (fortissimo)
very softly pp (pianissimo)
Vice-Chairperson VC
Vice-Chancellor VC
Vice-President VP
Victoria Cross VC
village management board VMB
vocative voc
volt V
volt-ampere VA
volt-coulomb VC
volume vol
Voluntary Aid Department VAD
Vrouesendingbond VSB
vulgar vulg
Vulgate Vulg

## W

Warrant Officer WO
water-closet WC
watt W
watt-hour Wh(r)
weber Wb
Wednesday W, Wed
week w
weight wt
West W
Western European Union WEU
West Indies WI
west-north-west WNW
which is qe (quod est)
which see qqv (quae vide)
which was to be demonstrated QED (quod erat demonstrandum)
which was to be done QEF (quod erat faciendum)
with decreasing pace rall (rallentando)
with effect from wef
without date sa (sine anno)
without dividend ex div (extra dividendum)
with sudden emphasis sfz (sforzando, sforzato)
with the necessary changes mm (mutatis mutandis)
Women's Agricultural Union WAU
Women's Royal Naval Service WRNS
word wd
words per minute wpm
World Boxing Association WBA
World Boxing Council WBC
World Council of Churches WCC
World Health Organisation WHO

## Y

yard yd
year a, yr
yearly pa (per annum)
Young Men's Christian Association YMCA
Young Women's Christian Association YWCA
Your Honour Yr Hon
yours yrs

## Z

Zimbabwe Zim
Zimbabwe African National Union ZANU
Zimbabwe African People's Union ZAPU
zoology zool

# Car registration numbers*

## A

Aberdeen  CAB
Adelaide  CFJ
Albertinia  CES
Alexandria  CAD
Alfred  NA
Alice  CFD, GCA
Aliwal North  CAE
Aranos  N...A

## B

Babanango  NBA
Bafokeng  YBD
Barkly East  CAF
Barkly West  CAG
Barrydale  CCK
Bathurst  CAH
Beaufort West  CZ
Bedford  CAJ
Bellville  CY
Bergville  NB
Bethanie  N...B
Bethlehem  OA
Bethulie  OC
Bizana  XAF
Bloemfontein  OB
Bochum  LEB 11
Bolobedu  LEB 7
Bonnievale  CER
Boshoff  OD
Bothaville  OMB
Botswana  RB
Brackenfell  CFR
Brandfort  OBB
Brandvlei  CAN
Bredasdorp  CS
Britstown  CAL
Bultfontein  OKB
Bulwer  NIP
Burgersdorp  CAC
Butha Buthe  B
Butterworth  XB

## C

Cacadu  XR
Cala  XS
Caledon  CAM
Calitzdorp  CO
Calvinia  CAN
Camperdown  NC
Cape Town  CA
Caprivi  ECZ
Carnarvon  CAO
Cathcart  CAP
Centani  XY
Ceres  CT
Ciskei Prisons  GC 2-
Clanwilliam  CAR
Clocolan  OND
Cofimvaba  XD
Colenso  NCO
Colesberg  CAS
Cradock  CAT

## D

Damaraland  N...FA
Daniëlskuil  CEV
Dannhauser  NDH
Darling  CK
De Aar  CM
Dealesville  ODD
De Doorns  CW
Defence Force Botswana  BDF
Despatch  CCN
Dewetsdorp  OBD
Diplomatic Missions and Personnel
    Botswana  CD, CDA, CDM
Ditsobotla  YBE
Dordrecht  CCU
Douglas  CBC
Dundee  NDE
Durban  ND
Durban City Council  NDC
Durbanville  CY
Dzanani  VV

## E

East London  CE
Edenburg  OE
Edenville  OMG
Elliot  CDA
Elliotdale  XAD
Empangeni  NUF
Engcobo  XE
Eshowe  NES
Estcourt  NE
Excelsior  OXG

## F

Fauresmith  OF
Ficksburg  OG
Fish Hoek  CA
Flagstaff  XAH
Fort Beaufort  CAU
Fouriesburg  OGB
Francistown  BA, BA 1 A
Frankfort  OH
Franschhoek  CJ
Fraserburg  CAV

## G

Gaborone  BD 1 A, BD 1 B, BZ
Gans Bay  CEM
Ganyesa  YBM
Garies  CEC
Gatyana  XAG
Gcuwa  XB
George  CAW
Ghanzi  BI
Gibeon  N....N
Giyani  GY
Glencoe  NGL
Gobabis  N....X
Gonubie  CE
Goodwood  CY
Gordon's Bay  CEY
Graaff-Reinet  CAZ
Grabouw  CEO
Grahamstown  CF
Greytown  NUM
Griquatown  CBB
Groblershoop  CFS
Grootfontein  N...F

## H

Hankey  CED
Hanover  CBA
Harding  NA
Harrismith  OHS
Hartenbos  CBS
Hartswater  CEU
Heidelberg  CEG
Heilbron  OJ
Henneman  OXH
Hereroland East  N...EA
Hereroland West  N...EB
Hermanus  CEM
Herschel  XT
Hertzogville  ODB
Hewu  GCB
Hhohho District  H
Himeville  NUD
Hlabisa  NHL
Hobhouse  ONB
Hofmeyr  CBO
Hoopstad  OK
Hopefield  CR

---

*  subject to change

Hopetown CBE
Howick NR
Humansdorp CBF

# I

Idutywa XN
Impendle NIM
Inanda NJ
Indwe CEN
Ingwavuma NIN
international, Albania AL
international, Alderney GBA
international, Algeria DZ
international, Andorra AND
international, Angola P
international, Argentine Republic RA
international, Australia AUS
international, Austria A
international, Bahamas BS
international, Bahrain BRN
international, Barbados BDS
international, Belgium B
international, Botswana RB
international, Brazil BR
international, British Honduras BH
international, Bulgaria BG
international, Burma BUR
international, Burundi RU
international, Canada CDN
international, Central Africa RCA
international, Ceylon CL
international, China RC, RCH
international, Colombia CO
international, Congo RCB
international, Cuba C
international, Cyprus CY
international, Czechoslovakia CZ
international, Denmark DK
international, Dominica WD
international, East Africa Uganda EAU
international, Ecuador EC
international, Finland SF
international, France F
international, Germany D
international, Ghana GH
international, Gibraltar GBZ
international, Great Britain GB
international, Grenada WG
international, Guatemala GCA
international, Guernsey GBG
international, Guyana BRG
international, Haiti RH
international, Iceland IS
international, Indonesia RI
international, Iran IR
international, Iraq IRQ
international, Ireland IRL
international, Isle of Man GBM
international, Israel IL
international, Ivory Coast CI
international, Jamaica JA
international, Japan J
international, Jersey GBJ
international, Jordan HKJ
international, Kenya EAK
international, Korea ROK
international, Kuwait KWT
international, Laos LAO
international, Lebanon RL
international, Lesotho LS
international, Liberia LB
international, Luxembourg L
international, Malawi MW
international, Malaysia MAL
international, Mali RMM
international, Malta M
international, Mauritania RIM
international, Mexico MEX
international, Monaco MC
international, Morocco MA
international, Mozambique P
international, Namibia N
international, Netherlands NL
international, Netherlands Antilles NA
international, New Zealand NZ
international, Niger NIG
international, Norway N
international, Pakistan PAK
international, Panama PA
international, Paraguay PY
international, Peru PE
international, Philippines RI
international, Poland PL
international, Portugal P
international, Rwanda RWA
international, San Marino RSM
international, Senegal SN
international, Seychelles SY
international, Singapore SGP
international, South Africa ZA
international, Soviet Union SU
international, Spain E
international, St Lucia WL
international, St Vincent WV
international, Surinam SME
international, Swaziland SD
international, Sweden S
international, Switzerland CH
international, Syria SYR
international, Tanzania EAT
international, Thailand T
international, Togo TG
international, Tunisia TN
international, Turkey TR
international, United States of America USA
international, Uruguay U
international, USSR SU
international, Vatican City V
international, Venezuela YV
international, Vietnam VN
international, Western Samoa WS
international, Yugoslavia YU
international, Zaïre ZRE
international, Zambia Z
international, Zimbabwe ZW
Ixopo NIX

# J

Jacobsdal OL
Jagersfontein OFB
Jamestown CEH
Jan Kempdorp CEU
Jansenville CBG
Jeffreys Bay CBF
Joubertina CET

# K

Kakamas CFH
Kanye BG
Kaokoland N...DA
Karasburg N...A
Karibib N...P
Kasane BK
Kavango N...CA
Keetmanshoop N...K
Keimoes CFO
Keiskammahoek CFK, GCC
Kenhardt CBH
Kentani XY
Kestell OAF
Kimberley CC
King William's Town CD
Kirkwood CEB
Klawer CCP
Kleinmond CAM
Klip River NKR
Knysna CX
Koffiefontein OFD
Kokstad NCW
Komga CBJ
Koppies OVE
Kraaifontein CY
Kranskop NKK
Kroonstad OM
Kuils River CFR
Kuruman CBK
Kwabhaca XK

# L

Ladismith CBL
Ladybrand ON
Lady Frere XR
Lady Grey CEJ
Ladysmith NKR
Laingsburg CBM
Lambert's Bay CAR
Langebaan CR
Lehurutshe YBG
Leribe C
Letlhakane BO

Libode XU
Lindley OO
Lions River NR
Lobatse BF
Loeriesfontein CAN
Louwsburg NS
Lower Tugela NT
Lower Umfolosi NUF
Lower Umzimkulu NPS
Loxton CCR
Lubombo District L
Luckhoff OF
Lüderitz N...L
Lusikisiki XC

## M

Mabopane YBX
Machaneng BC
Maclear CDL
Madikwe YBJ
Mafeteng E
Mafikeng CBN, YBA
Magudu NMG
Mahalapye BM
Mahlabatini NMA
Malamulele GM
Malmesbury CK
Maltahöhe N...M
Maluti XL
Mankwe YBL
Manzini District M
Mapulaneng LEB 5
Mapumulo NM
Mariental N...N
Marquard ORD
Maseru A
Matatiele XL, NCX
Maun BJ
Maxesibeni XJ
Mcgregor CCD
Mdantsane GCE
Melmoth NO
Memel OUB
Mhala GH
Middelburg CBP
Middledrift GCD
Middledrift CDX
Milnerton CA
Mochudi BL
Mohale's Hoek F
Mokerong LEB 3
Mokhotlong J
Molepolole BE
Molopo YBA
Molteno CFB
Montagu CBR
Mooi River NMR
Moorreesburg CEA
Moretele YBC
Mossel Bay CBS
Mount Ayliff XJ

Mount Fletcher XW
Mount Frere XK
Mpofu GCH
Mqanduli XAE
Msinga NF
Mtonjaneni NO
Mtubatuba NHL
Mtunzini NZ
Murraysburg CBT
Mutale VV

## N

Namakgale LEB 13
Naphuno LEB 8
Napier CS
Ndwedwe NDW
Nebo LEB 6
Newcastle NN
New Hanover NH
Ngotshe NS
Ngqeleni XZ
Nieu-Bethesda CAS
Nkandla NKA
Nongoma NND
Noupoort CEL
Nqamakwe XAA
Nqutu NTU

## O

Odendaalsrus OKC
Odi YBB
Okahandja N...H
Olifantshoek CEW
Omaruru N...Y
Onrus River CEM
Oranjemund N...C
Otavi N...E
Otjiwarongo N...O
Oudtshoorn CG
Outjo N...J
Owambo N...BA

## P

Paarl CJ
Palapye BP
Parow CY
Parys OV
Paterson CAD
Paulpietersburg NPP
Paul Roux ORE
Pearston CBV
Peddie CBW, GCF
Petrusburg OFH
Petrus Steyn OOE
Petrusville CBX
Philippolis OP
Philipstown CBX
Phuthaditjhaba OBW
Pietermaritzburg NP

Pietermaritzburg City Council NPC
Piketberg CBY
Pinelands CA
Pinetown NPN
Pinetown City Council NPNC
Plettenberg Bay CX
Pofadder CEK
Polela NIP
Port Alfred CAH
Port Elizabeth CB
Porterville CEX
Port Nolloth CU
Port Shepstone NPS
Port St Johns XF
Postmasburg CEV
Praktiseer LEB 12-
Prieska CBZ
Prince Albert CCA

## Q

Qacha's Neck H
Queenstown CH
Qumbu XV
Quthing G

## R

Ramotswa BR
Reddersburg OBG
Rehoboth N...R
Reitz OAB
Reivilo CCS
Richmond CCB
Richmond NK
Ritavi GR
Riversdale CCC
Robertson CCD
Rouxville ORX

## S

Sasolburg OIL
Scottburgh NX
Sedgefield CX
Sekgosese LEB 10
Sekhukhune LEB 2
Selebi-Phikwe BS
Senekal OR
Serowe BB
Seshego LEB 4
Seymour CCH
Shiselweni District S
Sibasa VV
Simon's Town CA
Siphaqeni XAH
Sishen CEW
Smithfield OS
Somerset East CCE
Somerset West CFM
Springbok CBU
Springfontein OCC

Stanford CEM
Stanger NT
Stellenbosch CL
Sterkspruit XT
Sterkstroom CEP
Steynsburg CCF
Steynsrus OOD
Steytlerville CCG
St Helena Bay CFG
Stilbaai CCC
Strand CEY
Strydenburg CBE
Stutterheim CFC
Sutherland CCJ
Swakopmund N...S
Swaziland royal vehicles S
Swellendam CCK

## T

Tabankulu XAB
Tanzania EAT
Tarkastad CCL
Taung CFN, YBN
Teya-Teyaneng D
Thabamoopo LEB 1
Thaba Nchu YBK
Thaba-Tseka K
Theunissen OXD
Tlhabane YBD
Tlhaping-Tlharo YBH
Tlokweng BR
Touwsrivier CW
Trompsburg OEB
Tshabong BH
Tsolo XO
Tsomo XAC

Tsumeb N...T
Tugela Ferry NF
Tulbagh CCM
Tuli Block BC
Tutume BT

## U

Ubombo NUB
Uitenhage CCN
Umbumbulu NUL
Umlazi NUZ
Umtata XA
Umzimkhulu XH
Umzimvubu XF
Umzinto NX
Underberg NUD
Uniondale CCO
Upington CAY
Usakos N...U
Utrecht NUT

## V

Vanderkloof CBX
Vanrhynsdorp CCP
Velddrif CFP
Venda VV
Ventersburg OXF
Venterstad CDZ
Verulam NJ
Victoria West CCR
Viljoenskroon OMF
Villiers OHB
Virginia OXV
Vosburg CCR
Vrede OU

Vredefort OVB
Vredenburg CFG
Vredendal CV
Vryburg CCS
Vryheid NV
Vuwani VV

## W

Walvis Bay CWB
Warden OIC
Warrenton CEE
Weenen NW
Welkom OKE
Wellington CN
Wepener OW
Wesselsbron OKD
Whittlesea CEF
Williston CEZ
Willowmore CCT
Willowvale XAG
Winburg OX
Windhoek N...W
Witsieshoek OBW
Wolseley CFA
Worcester CW

## X

Xalanga XS
Xhora XAD

## Z

Zastron OZ
Zwelitsha GCJ

# Elements

## A
**Actinium** Ac
**Aluminium** Al
**Americium** Am
**Antimony** Sb
**Argon** Ar
**Arsenic** As
**Astatine** At
**Aurum/Gold** Au

## B
**Barium** Ba
**Berkelium** Bk
**Beryllium** Be
**Bismuth** Bi
**Boron** B
**Bromine** Br

## C
**Cadmium** Cd
**Caesium** Cs
**Calcium** Ca
**Californium** Cf
**Carbon** C
**Cerium** Ce
**Chlorine** Cl
**Chromium** Cr
**Cobalt** Co
**Copper** Cu
**Curium** Cm

## D
**Dysprosium** Dy

## E
**Einsteinium** Es
**Erbium** Er
**Europium** Eu

## F
**Fermium** Fm
**Ferrum/Iron** Fe
**Fluorine** F
**Francium** Fr

## G
**Gadolinium** Gd
**Gallium** Ga
**Germanium** Ge
**Gold/Aurum** Au

## H
**Hafnium** Hf
**Helium** He
**Holmium** Ho
**Hydrogen** H

## I
**Indium** In
**Iodine** I
**Iridium** Ir
**Iron/Ferrum** Fe

## K
**Krypton** Kr

## L
**Lanthanum** La
**Lawrencium** Lr/Lw
**Lead** Pb
**Lithium** Li
**Lutetium** Lu

## M
**Magnesium** Mg
**Manganese** Mn
**Mendelevium** Md
**Mercury** Hg
**Molybdenum** Mo

## N
**Neodymium** Nd
**Neon** Ne
**Neptunium** Np
**Nickel** Ni
**Niobium** Nb
**Nitrogen** N
**Nobelium** No

## O
**Osmium** Os
**Oxygen** O

## P
**Palladium** Pd
**Phosphorus** P
**Platinum** Pt
**Plutonium** Pu
**Polonium** Po
**Potassium** K
**Praseodymium** Pr
**Promethium** Pm
**Protactinium** Pa

## R
**Radium** Ra
**Radon** Rn
**Rhenium** Re
**Rhodium** Rh
**Rubidium** Rb
**Ruthenium** Ru

## S
**Samarium** Sm
**Scandium** Sc
**Selenium** Se
**Silicon** Si
**Silver** Ag
**Sodium** Na
**Strontium** Sr
**Sulphur** S

## T
**Tantalum** Ta
**Technetium** Tc
**Tellurium** Te
**Terbium** Tb
**Thallium** Tl
**Thorium** Th
**Thulium** Tm
**Tin** Sn
**Titanium** Ti
**Tungsten** W

## U
**Uranium** U

## V
**Vanadium** V

## X
**Xenon** Xe

## Y
**Ytterbium** Yb
**Yttrium** Y

## Z
**Zinc** Zn
**Zirconium** Zr

## Greek alphabet

alpha
beta
gamma
delta
epsilon
zeta
eta
theta
iota
koppa
lambda
mu
nu
xi
omicron
pi
rho
sigma
tau
upsilon
phi
chi
psi
omega

## Hebrew alphabet

aleph
beth
gimel
daleth/daled
he
vav/waw
zayin
heth/cheth
teth/teh
yod/yodh
kaph
lamedh
mem
nun
samekh
ayin
pe
sadhe/sade/tsade
qoph/koph
resh
sin
shin
taw/tav

## Roman numerals

| | | | | | |
|---|---|---|---|---|---|
| 1 | I | 60 | LX | 400 | CD |
| 2 | II | 70 | LXX | 419 | CDXIX |
| 3 | III | 80 | LXXX | 420 | CDXX |
| 4 | IV | 88 | LXXXVIII | 499 | CDXCIX |
| 5 | V | 90 | XC | 500 | D |
| 6 | VI | 99 | XCIX | 519 | DXIX |
| 7 | VII | 100 | C | 520 | DXX |
| 8 | VIII | 101 | CI | 550 | DL |
| 9 | IX | 119 | CXIX | 599 | DXCIX |
| 10 | X | 120 | CXX | 600 | DC |
| 11 | XI | 130 | CXXX | 700 | DCC |
| 12 | XII | 140 | CXL | 800 | DCCC |
| 13 | XIII | 150 | CLY | 888 | DCCCLXXXVIII |
| 14 | XIV | 160 | CLX | 900 | CM |
| 15 | XV | 170 | CLXX | 1000 | M |
| 16 | XVI | 180 | CLXXX | 1500 | MD |
| 17 | XVII | 190 | CXC | 1800 | MDCCC |
| 18 | XVIII | 199 | CXCIX | 1994 | MCMXCIV |
| 19 | XIX | 200 | CC | 2000 | MM |
| 20 | XX | 219 | CCXIX | 5000 | V |
| 30 | XXX | 220 | CCXX | 10000 | X |
| 40 | XL | 300 | CCC | 490000 | XD |
| 50 | L | 319 | CCCXIX | 500000 | D |
| 55 | LV | 320 | CCCXX | | |